The Most Complete

Ethiopian
Bible

157-Book Collection in English

Majestic Edition Including Lost Apocrypha and
Rarely Seen Sacred Texts

Sheba's Wisdom Press

This page intentionally left blank

3

Unlock Exclusive Perks Inside the Book

Go to page 468 of the Bible, and scan the QR

Disclaimer

This volume, published by Sheba's Wisdom Press, represents the culmination of extensive research and careful curation of texts from a wide range of sources, including ancient manuscripts, monastic libraries, and scholarly commentaries. Every effort has been made to ensure the accuracy and authenticity of the content presented herein. The texts included have been reworked and elaborated with great care, to provide an accessible and comprehensive resource for understanding the Ethiopian Christian tradition.

It should be noted that many of the texts within this collection are considered apocryphal or gnostic and may not be recognized as canonical by all Christian denominations. The views and interpretations contained within these texts do not necessarily reflect those of Sheba's Wisdom Press, but are presented here for their historical, cultural, and theological value. This compilation is intended for educational and informational purposes, and readers are encouraged to approach these works with an open and critical mind.

Copyright

Introduction

Exploring the Richness of Ethiopian Scriptural Heritage: Canonical, Deuterocanonical, and Gnostic Texts

The creation of this comprehensive volume represents an extensive and dedicated effort to collect, curate, and organize one of the most diverse and significant collections of sacred texts in history. This compilation aims to provide readers with an in-depth, authentic representation of the Ethiopian Orthodox Biblical Canon, while also presenting an expansive selection of deuterocanonical, apocryphal, and gnostic texts that reflect the spiritual richness of Ethiopia. The journey to compile this collection has been an arduous and rewarding endeavor, driven by a desire to preserve, share, and make accessible the profound spiritual, cultural, and historical knowledge embedded within these works, ensuring they remain a living testament to the resilience and depth of Ethiopian Christianity.

The Ethiopian Bible stands apart from other biblical traditions, with its canon incorporating a multitude of texts that are not found in other Christian Bibles. This uniqueness reflects the deep cultural, historical, and spiritual heritage of Ethiopia—a heritage that has been preserved and passed down through centuries of devotion, resilience, and faith. Assembling this compilation required meticulous research across a wide array of sources, including ancient manuscripts, historical texts, and oral traditions, as well as extensive collaboration with specialists in theology, biblical history, and Ethiopian studies. The process involved cross-referencing translations, consulting academic commentaries, and utilizing the most reputable collections of biblical and apocryphal manuscripts available, ensuring accuracy and authenticity. Furthermore, the project required engagement with local scholars and monastic communities, whose intimate knowledge of these texts has been invaluable. The result is a volume that is not only comprehensive in its scope but also accessible and enriching for readers of all backgrounds—whether they are seasoned scholars or individuals newly exploring these sacred traditions. The Ethiopian Bible, with its unique and expanded canon, offers a window into a deeply spiritual world, preserving insights and perspectives that have shaped the faith and identity of Ethiopian Christianity for millennia.

This collection is divided into three key sections to guide the reader through the rich and intricate tapestry of Ethiopian scriptural traditions. The first section includes the Old and New Testaments, which encompass the traditional canonical texts shared by many branches of Christianity. However, these Ethiopian versions contain notable differences in content, structure, and order, reflecting the distinct Ethiopian Christian perspective and its theological priorities. Unlike other Christian Bibles, these texts have been preserved in the Ge'ez language, the ancient and sacred liturgical language of Ethiopia, which adds a unique cultural and spiritual dimension to this compilation. Ge'ez, as a language of worship and scholarship, imbues these texts with a deep sense of heritage and continuity, connecting modern readers to the practices and beliefs of early Ethiopian Christians. The Ethiopian versions of these books often contain unique variations, additional passages, and expanded narratives that are not found in other biblical traditions, thereby offering a richer and more nuanced understanding of the scriptures. These distinctive features provide readers with new insights into well-known biblical stories, highlighting aspects of the faith that are emphasized within the Ethiopian tradition, such as the enduring struggle between good and evil, the emphasis on divine wisdom, and the importance of communal faith practices.

The second section presents the Deuterocanonical and Apocryphal Books that are accepted in the Ethiopian Orthodox canon but are often omitted in other Christian traditions. These include works like The Wisdom of Solomon, 1, 2, and 3 Meqabyan (which are distinct from the Books of Maccabees in other Christian Bibles), and the Book of Enoch, a foundational text that holds special significance within Ethiopian Christianity. The inclusion of these texts provides insight into the broader theological and spiritual framework of the Ethiopian Church, emphasizing themes such as divine wisdom, righteousness, the battle between light and darkness, and the ongoing struggle between good and evil. The Book of Enoch, in particular, is a cornerstone of Ethiopian Christian thought, offering detailed visions of heaven, the fall of the angels, and the end times. This remarkable text is divided into several sections, including the Book of the Watchers, which describes the descent of rebellious angels to earth; the Similitudes of Enoch, which contain visions of judgment; and the Astronomical Book, which provides insights into the workings of the heavens. Its influence extends far beyond Ethiopia, having played a significant role in shaping early Christian theology and apocalyptic literature before it was excluded from most Western canons. The preservation of these texts within the Ethiopian tradition offers readers an opportunity to explore dimensions of early Christian spirituality that have been largely lost to Western readers, highlighting the richness and depth of Ethiopian biblical heritage.

The third section of the volume features a broad selection of Gnostic and other Supplementary Texts. These works, while not officially part of the Ethiopian canon, provide crucial insight into early Christian thought, gnostic philosophy, and the diversity of beliefs that flourished during the early centuries of Christianity. Texts such as The Gospel of Thomas, The Apocalypse of Peter, and The Acts of John are included to offer readers a deeper understanding of the theological debates and spiritual reflections that shaped the Christian world beyond the boundaries of established orthodoxy. The Gnostic Gospels present an alternative perspective on the teachings of Jesus, focusing on inner knowledge and the mystical aspects of faith, which contrasts with the more institutionalized doctrines of mainstream Christianity. By including these texts, this volume invites readers to explore the rich diversity of early Christian spirituality and to appreciate the varied ways in which different communities understood the message of Jesus.

The process of assembling this compilation has been both exhaustive and enlightening. Researchers and scholars involved in this project have painstakingly gathered texts from a wide range of sources, including ancient manuscripts, monastic libraries, and private collections. Many of these texts have been preserved in the monasteries of Ethiopia, which have acted as guardians of Christian heritage for centuries. The monastic tradition in Ethiopia is deeply intertwined with the preservation of scripture, and the dedication of Ethiopian monks to copying and safeguarding these texts has been instrumental in ensuring their survival to the present day. This compilation is, therefore, not only a scholarly endeavor but also a tribute to the enduring legacy of Ethiopian monasticism and its role in the preservation of Christian wisdom.

By presenting these different categories of texts within a single volume, this compilation not only provides an unparalleled resource for understanding the Ethiopian Christian tradition but also serves as a testament to the diversity of early Christian literature. Each book in this collection is accompanied by a brief introduction, offering context and historical background to help the reader understand its place within the broader framework of biblical literature. The division into canonical, deuterocanonical, and supplementary gnostic/apocryphal texts allows readers to navigate the collection with ease, gaining insights into the profound spiritual traditions that have shaped the Ethiopian Orthodox Church. The introductions also highlight the historical and cultural significance of each text, providing readers with a deeper appreciation of the unique theological perspectives that have emerged within Ethiopian Christianity.

The Ethiopian Orthodox Church, one of the oldest Christian communities in the world, has a rich tradition that is reflected in its unique biblical canon. The inclusion of texts like Jubilees, 1 Enoch, and the Meqabyan books speaks to the church's emphasis on the continuity of divine revelation from the creation of the world to the present day. This continuity is a key theme in Ethiopian Christianity, which views the Bible not just as a historical document but as a living testament to God's ongoing relationship with humanity. The Meqabyan books, for instance, offer stories of faith, resistance, and divine justice that resonate deeply with the Ethiopian experience of maintaining their Christian faith through centuries of external pressures and challenges.

It is our hope that this volume serves as both a scholarly resource and an inspiring spiritual journey, offering readers an opportunity to delve into the profound depths of Ethiopian Christianity. The labor of assembling these texts, from canonical scriptures to lesser-known apocrypha and gnostic writings, reflects a deep dedication to honoring the vast spiritual heritage of Ethiopia and making these sacred writings accessible to all who wish to explore their richness and depth. This endeavor has been guided by a commitment to preserving the voices, traditions, and teachings that have shaped Ethiopian spirituality for nearly two millennia.

By exploring these texts, readers are invited to embark on a journey through the spiritual landscape of Ethiopia—one that reveals the profound wisdom, resilience, and unwavering faith that have defined the Ethiopian Orthodox Church through centuries of change and challenge. The Ethiopian tradition is characterized by a deep sense of continuity, viewing the scriptures not merely as historical documents but as a living testament to God's enduring relationship with humanity. This volume offers readers a chance to witness firsthand the theological diversity and spiritual insight that make Ethiopian Christianity unique.

Whether approached from a scholarly, spiritual, or cultural perspective, this compilation serves as a window into the heart of one of the world's most enduring Christian traditions. It provides a deeper understanding of the texts that have shaped the beliefs, rituals, and practices of millions of Ethiopian Christians, illuminating the continuity of faith, the richness of cultural heritage, and the profound spiritual insights that have withstood the test of time. May this work inspire, educate, and guide those who seek to uncover the treasures of Ethiopian scriptural tradition and find new meaning in the timeless wisdom it has to offer.

The Canonization of Ethiopian Scripture and the Broader Biblical Tradition

The Ethiopian Orthodox Tewahedo Church is home to one of the most extensive biblical canons in Christianity. Unlike the Western and Eastern branches of the Christian Church, which adhere to a smaller collection of canonical books, the Ethiopian Orthodox Church incorporates a wide range of texts, including many that are considered deuterocanonical, apocryphal, or gnostic in other Christian traditions. The canonization process of the Ethiopian Bible reflects the unique cultural, historical, and theological context of Ethiopia and its deep connection to early Christianity. The Ethiopian canon serves not only as a testament to the breadth of the church's theological heritage but also as a reflection of the enduring values and spiritual concerns of Ethiopian Christianity.

The canon of the Ethiopian Orthodox Church includes 81 books, comprising both the Old and New Testaments, along with numerous additional texts that are not part of the canons of other Christian denominations. Among these are the books of Enoch, Jubilees, and the three books of Meqabyan, which are distinct from the Maccabees found in the Roman Catholic and Eastern Orthodox traditions. The inclusion of these texts offers a broader and more nuanced perspective on the biblical narrative, emphasizing themes such as divine justice, cosmic struggle, and the intimate relationship between God and humanity. The canonization of these books was not merely an ecclesiastical decision but a reflection of the lived religious experience of Ethiopian Christians, who saw these texts as central to their understanding of the divine.

The process of canonization in Ethiopia was influenced by several factors, including the church's historical isolation, its connection to Jewish traditions, and the theological priorities of the Ethiopian Christian community. Unlike the more centralized and structured canonization processes that took place in the Roman Catholic and Eastern Orthodox Churches, the Ethiopian canon evolved organically over time, shaped by the spiritual needs of the community and the influence of monastic leaders. The Ethiopian Church's unique position, situated at the crossroads of African, Middle Eastern, and Mediterranean cultures, also played a role in the formation of its canon, allowing for the incorporation of a diverse range of texts that reflect the rich tapestry of influences that have shaped Ethiopian Christianity.

One of the most distinctive features of the Ethiopian biblical canon is the inclusion of the Book of Enoch. This text, which was excluded from the canonical scriptures of most other Christian traditions, holds a special place in Ethiopian Christianity. The Book of Enoch provides a detailed account of the fall of the angels, the nature of heaven, and the end times, themes that resonate deeply with the Ethiopian Christian worldview. The inclusion of Enoch in the Ethiopian canon highlights the church's emphasis on the cosmic dimensions of the struggle between good and evil and the belief in the ultimate triumph of divine justice. The text's vivid descriptions of heavenly visions and the fate of the wicked serve as a powerful reminder of the importance of righteousness and the consequences of sin, themes that are central to Ethiopian Christian theology.

Another significant text in the Ethiopian canon is the Book of Jubilees, also known as the Lesser Genesis. This text offers a retelling of the events of Genesis, with additional details and emphasis on the observance of the Sabbath and the importance of ritual purity. The Book of Jubilees reflects the close connection between Ethiopian Christianity and Jewish traditions, emphasizing the continuity of God's covenant with humanity from the time of creation to the present. The inclusion of Jubilees in the Ethiopian canon underscores the church's belief in the enduring relevance of the Old Testament and the continuity of divine revelation throughout history. The text's focus on the observance of sacred times and the importance of maintaining purity in worship resonates with the liturgical practices of the Ethiopian Orthodox Church, which places a strong emphasis on ritual and the sanctity of the divine order.

The three books of Meqabyan, which are unique to the Ethiopian canon, provide another example of the distinctiveness of Ethiopian scripture. These texts, which are unrelated to the Maccabees found in other Christian traditions, tell stories of faith, resistance, and divine justice. The Meqabyan books emphasize the theme of steadfastness in the face of persecution and the belief in God's ultimate justice, themes that have resonated deeply with the Ethiopian Christian community throughout its history. The inclusion of these texts in the canon reflects the historical experiences of the Ethiopian Church, which has faced periods of persecution and struggle, and the belief in the importance of remaining faithful to God even in the face of adversity.

The broader Ethiopian biblical tradition also includes a wealth of apocryphal and gnostic texts that, while not officially part of the canon, have played an important role in shaping the theological and spiritual landscape of Ethiopian Christianity. Texts such as the Gospel of Thomas, the Apocalypse of Peter, and the Acts of John offer alternative perspectives on the teachings of Jesus and the early Christian community, emphasizing the importance of inner knowledge and the mystical dimensions of faith. These texts, which were often marginalized or suppressed in other Christian traditions, have found a place within the Ethiopian spiritual heritage, reflecting the church's openness to diverse expressions of Christian thought and its commitment to preserving the full breadth of early Christian literature.

The inclusion of these diverse texts in the Ethiopian canon and broader biblical tradition highlights the unique theological perspective of the Ethiopian Orthodox Church. Unlike other Christian traditions that have sought to establish a fixed and uniform canon, the Ethiopian Church has embraced a more expansive and inclusive approach, recognizing the value of a wide range of texts in conveying the richness of the Christian message. This inclusivity is reflected not only in the content of the canon but also in the church's liturgical practices, which incorporate readings from both canonical and non-canonical texts, allowing the faithful to engage with the full spectrum of the Christian tradition.

The process of canonization in Ethiopia was not without its challenges. The diversity of texts and the lack of a centralized ecclesiastical authority meant that the formation of the canon was a gradual and sometimes contested process. Different monastic communities and theological schools had their own preferences and priorities, leading to variations in the selection of texts and the order in which they were arranged. Despite these challenges, the Ethiopian Orthodox Church ultimately arrived at a canon that reflects the spiritual needs and theological priorities of its community—a canon that is both rooted in the ancient traditions of the church and open to the diverse influences that have shaped Ethiopian Christianity over the centuries.

The Ethiopian biblical canon, with its inclusion of deuterocanonical, apocryphal, and gnostic texts, offers a unique window into the theological and spiritual world of Ethiopian Christianity. It reflects a tradition that is deeply rooted in the past yet open to the diversity of Christian thought, a tradition that values both the continuity of divine revelation and the richness of human spiritual experience. The canonization of these texts is a testament to the enduring faith of the Ethiopian Christian community and its commitment to preserving the full breadth of its spiritual heritage.

In conclusion, the canonization of Ethiopian scripture is a reflection of the unique historical, cultural, and theological context of the Ethiopian Orthodox Church. The inclusion of a wide range of texts, from the canonical books of the Old and New Testaments to the apocryphal and gnostic writings, highlights the church's commitment to preserving the richness of the Christian tradition in all its diversity. The Ethiopian canon serves as a testament to the resilience and depth of Ethiopian Christianity, offering a comprehensive and nuanced understanding of the biblical narrative that is both distinct from and complementary to other Christian traditions. Through its expansive and inclusive approach to scripture, the Ethiopian Orthodox Church invites believers to engage with the full spectrum of the Christian tradition, exploring the profound mysteries of faith and the enduring truths of God's revelation.

Overview of the Collected Works in This Volume

The comprehensive collection presented in this volume includes an array of texts that span canonical, deuterocanonical, apocryphal, and gnostic works, each of which contributes uniquely to the rich tapestry of Ethiopian Christian scripture. These texts represent not only the theological and spiritual heritage of the Ethiopian Orthodox Tewahedo Church but also the cultural and historical narratives that have shaped Ethiopian Christianity over the centuries. The inclusion of a wide range of books, from those commonly found in Western Christian Bibles to those unique to the Ethiopian tradition, offers readers an unparalleled opportunity to explore the full breadth of early Christian literature and its diverse expressions.

The volume begins with the Old and New Testaments, which are foundational to the Christian faith. These books are presented with particular emphasis on the unique variations found in the Ethiopian tradition. The Ethiopian Orthodox Church's approach to scripture incorporates both the familiar and the distinctive, ensuring that readers gain insights not only into the shared heritage of Christianity but also into the particular theological perspectives that are integral to Ethiopian belief. The Ethiopian versions of these canonical books often contain additional passages and unique emphases, reflecting the distinct cultural and spiritual context in which they have been preserved. This volume, therefore, allows readers to engage with the biblical narrative in a way that is both familiar and enriched by the nuances of Ethiopian tradition.

In addition to the canonical books, this collection includes a range of deuterocanonical texts that hold significant importance in the Ethiopian Orthodox Church but are often absent from other Christian traditions. Among these are the books of Enoch, Jubilees, and the three books of Meqabyan. The Book of Enoch, for instance, is a seminal text that provides detailed visions of the heavenly realms, the fall of the angels, and eschatological prophecies that have profoundly influenced Ethiopian Christian thought. The inclusion of these deuterocanonical books highlights the Ethiopian Church's broader theological framework, one that emphasizes the cosmic struggle between good and evil, divine justice, and the ongoing relationship between God and humanity. By exploring these texts, readers can gain a deeper appreciation for the theological richness that characterizes Ethiopian Christianity.

The apocryphal and gnostic texts included in this volume further expand the scope of the collection, offering insights into the diverse beliefs and theological debates that shaped early Christianity. These texts, such as the Gospel of Thomas, the Apocalypse of Peter, and the Acts of John, present alternative perspectives on the teachings of Jesus and the nature of early Christian communities. The inclusion of these works underscores the Ethiopian Orthodox Church's openness to a wide range of spiritual writings, recognizing their value in conveying different aspects of Christian thought and spirituality. These texts provide readers with a glimpse into the mystical and esoteric dimensions of early Christianity, emphasizing the importance of inner knowledge, divine revelation, and the pursuit of spiritual wisdom.

The Ethiopian Orthodox Church's canonization process has always been influenced by its historical context, geographical location, and the cultural interactions that have shaped Ethiopia as a unique center of Christianity. Unlike other Christian traditions that established a fixed canon through centralized ecclesiastical councils, the Ethiopian canon evolved organically, reflecting the lived spiritual experience of its community. This inclusive approach to scripture is evident in the breadth of texts contained within this volume, which not only convey theological truths but also capture the cultural and historical narratives that have defined Ethiopian Christianity for millennia. Each book in this collection has been carefully selected to reflect its significance within the Ethiopian tradition, providing readers with a holistic view of the Ethiopian biblical canon.

The structure of this volume is intended to guide readers through the different categories of texts, beginning with the canonical books of the Old and New Testaments, followed by the deuterocanonical texts, and concluding with the apocryphal and gnostic writings. Each section is accompanied by introductory commentary that provides historical context, theological insights, and an explanation of the significance of the texts within the Ethiopian Orthodox tradition. This organization allows readers to navigate the collection with ease while gaining a deeper understanding of the unique theological perspectives that have emerged from Ethiopian Christianity.

In presenting this collection, it is our hope that readers will not only gain a greater understanding of the Ethiopian Orthodox biblical canon but also appreciate the profound spiritual heritage that it represents. The inclusion of 157 books in this volume reflects the Ethiopian Orthodox Church's commitment to preserving the fullest possible expression of Christian scripture. This comprehensive collection includes canonical books, deuterocanonical works, apocryphal texts, and gnostic writings, each carefully selected for its theological and historical significance. The decision to include 157 books allows for a richer, more expansive view of early Christianity and highlights the unique theological, cultural, and historical context of Ethiopian scripture. The Ethiopian Orthodox Church, as one of the oldest Christian communities in the world, has preserved a tradition that is both deeply rooted in the early church and enriched by its own unique cultural and spiritual insights. The texts in this volume reflect that heritage, offering readers an opportunity to engage with the scriptures in a way that is both intellectually rigorous and spiritually enriching. Whether approached from a scholarly perspective or as a source of personal inspiration, the collection provides a window into the heart of Ethiopian Christianity and its enduring commitment to preserving the sacred word of God in all its fullness.

The Old Testament

Book 1. Genesis

The Creation of the World

1:1 In the beginning[1] God[2] created[3] the heavens and the earth.[4]

1:2 Now[5] the earth[6] was without shape and empty, and darkness was over the surface of the watery deep, but the Spirit of God was moving over the surface of the water. **1:3** God said, "Let there be light." And there was light! **1:4** God saw that the light was good, so God separated the light from the darkness. **1:5** God called the light "day" and the darkness "night." There was evening, and there was morning, marking the first day.

1:6 God said, "Let there be an expanse in the midst of the waters and let it separate water from water. **1:7** So God made the expanse and separated the water under the expanse from the water above it. It was so. **1:8** God called the expanse "sky." There was evening, and there was morning, a second day.

1:9 God said, "Let the water under the sky be gathered to one place and let dry ground appear." It was so. **1:10** God called the dry ground "land" and the gathered waters he called "seas." God saw that it was good.

1:11 God said, "Let the land produce vegetation: plants yielding seeds according to their kinds, and trees bearing fruit with seed in it according to their kinds." It was so. **1:12** The land produced vegetation – plants yielding seeds according to their kinds, and trees bearing fruit with seed in it according to their kinds. God saw that it was good. **1:13** There was evening, and there was morning, a third day.

1:14 God said, "Let there be lights in the expanse of the sky to separate the day from the night, and let them be signs to indicate seasons and days and years, **1:15** and let them serve as lights in the expanse of the sky to give light on the earth." It was so. **1:16** God made two great lights – the greater light to rule over the day and the lesser light to rule over the night. He made the stars also. **1:17** God placed the lights in the expanse of the sky to shine on the earth, **1:18** to preside over the day and the night, and to separate the light from the darkness. God saw that it was good. **1:19** There was evening, and there was morning, a fourth day.

1:20 God said, "Let the water swarm with swarms of living creatures and let birds fly above the earth across the expanse of the sky." **1:21** God created the great sea creatures and every living and moving thing with which the water swarmed, according to their kinds, and every winged bird according to its kind. God saw that it was good. **1:22** God blessed them and said, "Be fruitful and multiply and fill the water in the seas, and let the birds multiply on the earth." **1:23** There was evening, and there was morning, a fifth day.

1:24 God said, "Let the land produce living creatures according to their kinds: cattle, creeping things, and wild animals, each according to its kind." It was so. **1:25** God made the wild animals according to their kinds, the cattle according to their kinds, and all the creatures that creep along the ground according to their kinds. God saw that it was good.

1:26 Then God said, "Let us make
humankind in our image, after our likeness, so they may rule over the fish of the sea and the birds of the air, over the cattle, and over all the earth, and over all the creatures that move on the earth."

1:27 God created humankind in his own image,
in the image of God he created them,
male and female he created them.

1:28 God blessed them and said to them, "Be fruitful and multiply! Fill the earth and subdue it! Rule over the fish of the sea and the birds of the air and every creature that moves on the ground." **1:29** Then God said, "I now give you every seed-bearing plant on the face of the entire earth and every tree that has fruit with seed in it. They will be yours for food. **1:30** And to all the animals of the earth, and to every bird of the air, and to all the creatures that move on the ground – everything that has the breath of life in it – I give every green plant for food." It was so.

1:31 God saw all that he had made – and it was very good! There was evening, and there was morning, the sixth day.

2:1 The heavens and the earth were completed with everything that was in them. **2:2** By the seventh day God finished the work that he had been doing, and he ceased on the seventh day all the work that he had been doing. **2:3** God blessed the seventh day and made it holy because on it he ceased all the work that he had been doing in creation.

The Creation of Man and Woman

2:4 This is the account of the heavens and
the earth when they were created – when the Lord God made the earth and heavens.

2:5 Now no shrub of the field had yet grown on the earth, and no plant of the field had yet sprouted, for the Lord God had not caused it to rain on the earth, and there was no man to cultivate the ground. **2:6** Springs would well up from the earth and water the whole surface of the ground. **2:7** The Lord God formed the man from the soil of the ground and breathed into his nostrils the breath of life, and the man became a living being.

2:8 The Lord God planted an orchard in the east, in Eden; and there he placed the man he had formed. **2:9** The Lord God made all kinds of trees grow from the soil, every tree that was pleasing to look at and good for food. (Now the tree of life and the tree of the knowledge of good and evil were in the middle of the orchard.)

2:10 Now a river flows from Eden to
water the orchard, and from there it divides into four headstreams. **2:11** The name of the first is Pishon; it runs through the entire land of Havilah, where there is gold. **2:12** (The gold of that land is pure; pearls and lapis lazuli are also there). **2:13** The name of the second river is Gihon; it runs through the entire land of Cush. **2:14** The name of the third river is Tigris; it runs along the east side of Assyria. The fourth river is the Euphrates.

2:15 The Lord God took the man and placed him in the orchard in Eden to care for it and to maintain it. **2:16** Then the Lord God commanded the man, "You may freely eat fruit from every tree of the orchard, **2:17** but you must not eat from the tree of the knowledge of good and evil, for when you eat from it you will surely die."

2:18 The Lord God said, "It is not good for the man to be alone. I will make a companion for him who corresponds to him." **2:19** The Lord God formed out of the ground every living animal of the field and every bird of the air. He brought them to the man to see what he would name them, and whatever the man called each living creature, that was its name. **2:20** So the man named all the animals, the birds of the air, and the living creatures of the field, but for Adam no companion who corresponded to him was found. **2:21** So the Lord God caused the man to fall into a deep sleep, and while he was asleep, he took part of the man's side and closed up the place with flesh. **2:22** Then the Lord God made a

---

[1] **tn** The translation assumes that the form translated "beginning" is in the absolute state rather than the construct ("in the beginning of," or "when God created"). In other words, the clause in v. 1 is a main clause, v. 2 has three clauses that are descriptive and supply background information, and v. 3 begins the narrative sequence proper. The referent of the word "beginning" has to be defined from the context since there is no beginning or ending with God.

sn *In the beginning.* The verse refers to the beginning of the world as we know it; it affirms that it is entirely the product of the creation of God. But there are two ways that this verse can be interpreted: (1) It may be taken to refer to the original act of creation with the rest of the events on the days of creation completing it. This would mean that the disjunctive clauses of v. 2 break the sequence of the creative work of the first day. (2) It may be taken as a summary statement of what the chapter will record, that is, vv. 3-31 are about God's creating the world as we know it. If the first view is adopted, then we have a reference here to original creation; if the second view is taken, then Genesis itself does not account for the original creation of matter. To follow this view does not deny that the Bible teaches that God created everything out of nothing (cf. John 1:3) – it simply says that Genesis is not making that affirmation. This second view presupposes the existence of pre-existent matter, when God said, "Let there be light." The first view includes the description of the primordial state as part of the events of day one. The following narrative strongly favors the second view, for the "heavens/sky" did not exist prior to the second day of creation (see v. 8) and "earth/dry land" did not exist, at least as we know it, prior to the third day of creation (see v. 10).

[2] **sn** *God.* This frequently used Hebrew name for God (אֱלֹהִים, 'elohim) is a plural form. When it refers to the one true God, the singular verb is normally used, as here. The plural form indicates majesty; the name stresses God's sovereignty and incomparability – he is the "God of gods."

[3] **tn** The English verb "create" captures well the meaning of the Hebrew term in this context. The verb בָּרָא (bara') always describes the divine activity of fashioning something new, fresh, and perfect. The verb does not necessarily describe creation out of nothing (see, for example, v. 27, where it refers to the creation of man); it often stresses forming anew, reforming, renewing (see Ps 51:10; Isa 43:15, 65:17).

[4] **tn** Or "the entire universe"; or "the sky and the dry land." This phrase is often interpreted as a merism, referring to the entire ordered universe, including the heavens and the earth and everything in them. The "heavens and the earth" were completed in seven days (see Gen 2:1) and are characterized by fixed laws (see Jer 33:25). "Heavens" refers specifically to the sky, created on the second day (see v. 8), while "earth" refers specifically to the dry land, created on the third day (see v. 10). Both are distinct from the sea/seas (see v. 10 and Exod 20:11).

[5] **tn** The disjunctive clause (conjunction + subject + verb) at the beginning of v. 2 gives background information for the following narrative, explaining the state of things when "God said..." (v. 3). Verse one is a title to the chapter, v. 2 provides information about the state of things when God spoke, and v. 3 begins the narrative per se with the typical narrative construction (vav [ı] consecutive followed by the prefixed verbal form). (This literary structure is paralleled in the second portion of the book: Gen 2:4 provides the title or summary of what follows, 2:5-6 use disjunctive clause structures to give background information for the following narrative, and 2:7 begins the narrative with the vav consecutive attached to a prefixed verbal form.) Some translate 1:2a "and the earth became," arguing that v. 1 describes the original creation of the earth, while v. 2 refers to a judgment that reduced it to a chaotic condition. Verses 3ff. then describe the re-creation of the earth. However, the disjunctive clause at the beginning of v. 2 cannot be translated as if it were relating the next event in a sequence. If v. 2 were sequential to v. 1, the author would have used the vav consecutive followed by a prefixed verbal form and the subject.

[6] **tn** That is, what we now call "the earth." The creation of the earth as we know it is described in vv. 9-10. Prior to this the substance which became the earth (= dry land) lay dormant under the water.

woman from the part he had taken out of the man, and he brought her to the man. **2:23** Then the man said,

"This one at last is bone of my bones
and flesh of my flesh;
this one will be called 'woman,'
for she was taken out of man."

2:24 That is why a man leaves his father and mother and unites with his wife, and they become a new family. **2:25** The man and his wife were both naked, but they were not ashamed.

The Temptation and the Fall

3:1 Now the serpent was more shrewd than any of the wild animals that the LORD God had made. He said to the woman, "Is it really true that God said, 'You must not eat from any tree of the orchard'?" **3:2** The woman said to the serpent, "We may eat of the fruit from the trees of the orchard; **3:3** but concerning the fruit of the tree that is in the middle of the orchard God said, 'You must not eat from it, and you must not touch it, or else you will die.'" **3:4** The serpent said to the woman, "Surely you will not die, **3:5** for God knows that when you eat from it your eyes will open and you will be like divine beings who know good and evil."

3:6 When the woman saw that the tree produced fruit that was good for food, was attractive to the eye, and was desirable for making one wise, she took some of its fruit and ate it. She also gave some of it to her husband who was with her, and he ate it. **3:7** Then the eyes of both of them opened, and they knew they were naked; so they sewed fig leaves together and made coverings for themselves.

The Judgment Oracles of God at the Fall

3:8 Then the man and his wife heard the sound of the LORD God moving about in the orchard at the breezy time of the day, and they hid from the LORD God among the trees of the orchard. **3:9** But the LORD God called to the man and said to him, "Where are you?" **3:10** The man replied, "I heard you moving about in the orchard, and I was afraid because I was naked, so I hid." **3:11** And the LORD God said, "Who told you that you were naked? Did you eat from the tree that I commanded you not to eat from?" **3:12** The man said, "The woman whom you gave me, she gave me some fruit from the tree and I ate it." **3:13** So the LORD God said to the woman, "What is this you have done?" And the woman replied, "The serpent tricked me, and I ate."

3:14 The LORD God said to the serpent,

"Because you have done this,
cursed are you above all the wild beasts
and all the living creatures of the field!
On your belly you will crawl
and dust you will eat all the days of your life.
3:15 And I will put hostility between you and the woman
and between your offspring and her offspring;
her offspring will attack your head,
and you will attack her offspring's heel."

3:16 To the woman he said,

"I will greatly increase your labor pains;
with pain you will give birth to children.
You will want to control your husband,
but he will dominate you."

3:17 But to Adam he said,

"Because you obeyed your wife
and ate from the tree about which I commanded you,
'You must not eat from it,'
cursed is the ground thanks to you;
in painful toil you will eat of it all the days of your life.
3:18 It will produce thorns and thistles for you,
but you will eat the grain of the field.
3:19 By the sweat of your brow you will eat food
until you return to the ground,
for out of it you were taken;
for you are dust, and to dust you will return."

3:20 The man named his wife Eve, because she was the mother of all the living. **3:21** The LORD God made garments from skin for Adam and his wife, and clothed them. **3:22** And the LORD God said, "Now that the man has become like one of us, knowing good and evil, he must not be allowed to stretch out his hand and take also from the tree of life and eat, and live forever." **3:23** So the LORD God expelled him from the orchard in Eden to cultivate the ground from which he had been taken. **3:24** When he drove the man out, he placed on the eastern side of the orchard in Eden angelic

sentries who used the flame of a whirling sword to guard the way to the tree of life.

The Story of Cain and Abel

4:1 Now the man had marital relations with his wife Eve, and she became pregnant and gave birth to Cain. Then she said, "I have created a man just as the LORD did!" **4:2** Then she gave birth to his brother Abel. Abel took care of the flocks, while Cain cultivated the ground.

4:3 At the designated time Cain brought some of the fruit of the ground for an offering to the LORD. **4:4** But Abel brought some of the firstborn of his flock – even the fattest of them. And the LORD was pleased with Abel and his offering, **4:5** but with Cain and his offering he was not pleased. So Cain became very angry, and his expression was downcast.

4:6 Then the LORD said to Cain, "Why are you angry, and why is your expression downcast? **4:7** Is it not true that if you do what is right, you will be fine? But if you do not do what is right, sin is crouching at the door. It desires to dominate you, but you must subdue it."

4:8 Cain said to his brother Abel, "Let's go out to the field." While they were in the field, Cain attacked his brother Abel and killed him.

4:9 Then the LORD said to Cain, "Where is your brother Abel?" And he replied, "I don't know! Am I my brother's guardian?" **4:10** But the LORD said, "What have you done? The voice of your brother's blood is crying out to me from the ground! **4:11** So now, you are banished from the ground, which has opened its mouth to receive your brother's blood from your hand. **4:12** When you try to cultivate the

ground it will no longer yield its best for you. You will be a homeless wanderer on the earth." **4:13** Then Cain said to the LORD, "My punishment is too great to endure! **4:14** Look! You are driving me off the land today, and I must hide from your presence. I will be a homeless wanderer on the earth; whoever finds me will kill me." **4:15** But the LORD said to him, "All right then, if anyone kills Cain, Cain will be avenged seven times as much." Then the LORD put a special mark on Cain so that no one who found him would strike him down. **4:16** So Cain went out from the presence of the LORD and lived in the land of Nod, east of Eden.

The Beginning of Civilization

4:17 Cain had marital relations with his wife, and she became pregnant and gave birth to Enoch. Cain was building a city, and he named the city after his son Enoch. **4:18** To Enoch was born Irad, and Irad was the father of Mehujael. Mehujael was the father of Methushael, and Methushael was the father of Lamech.

4:19 Lamech took two wives for himself; the name of the first was Adah, and the name of the second was Zillah. **4:20** Adah gave birth to Jabal; he was the first of those who live in tents and keep livestock. **4:21** The name of his brother was Jubal; he was the first of all who play the harp and the flute. **4:22** Now Zillah also gave birth to Tubal-Cain, who heated metal and shaped all kinds of tools made of bronze and iron. The sister of Tubal-Cain was Naamah.

4:23 Lamech said to his wives,

"Adah and Zillah! Listen to me!
You wives of Lamech, hear my words!
I have killed a man for wounding me,
a young man for hurting me.
4:24 If Cain is to be avenged seven times as much,
then Lamech seventy-seven times!"

4:25 And Adam had marital relations with his wife again, and she gave birth to a son. She named him Seth, saying, "God has given me another child in place of Abel because Cain killed him." **4:26** And a son was also born to Seth, whom he named Enosh. At that time people began to worship the LORD.

From Adam to Noah

5:1 This is the record of the family line of Adam.

When God created humankind, he made them in the likeness of God. **5:2** He created them male and female; when they were created, he blessed them and named them "humankind."

5:3 When Adam had lived 130 years he fathered a son in his own likeness, according to his image, and he named him Seth. **5:4** The length of time Adam lived after he became the father of Seth was 800 years; during this time he had other sons and daughters. **5:5** The entire lifetime of Adam was 930 years, and then he died.

5:6 When Seth had lived 105 years, he became the father of Enosh. **5:7** Seth lived 807 years after he became the father of Enosh, and he had other sons and daughters. **5:8** The entire lifetime of Seth was 912 years, and then he died.

5:9 When Enosh had lived 90 years, he became the father of Kenan. **5:10** Enosh lived 815 years after he became the father of Kenan, and he had other sons and daughters. **5:11** The entire lifetime of Enosh was 905 years, and then he died.

5:12 When Kenan had lived 70 years, he became the father of Mahalalel. **5:13** Kenan lived 840 years after he became the father of Mahalalel, and he had other sons and daughters. **5:14** The entire lifetime of Kenan was 910 years, and then he died.

5:15 When Mahalalel had lived 65 years, he became the father of Jared. **5:16** Mahalalel lived 830 years after he became the father of Jared, and he had other sons and daughters. **5:17** The entire lifetime of Mahalalel was 895 years, and then he died.

5:18 When Jared had lived 162 years, he became the father of Enoch. **5:19** Jared lived 800 years after he became the father of Enoch, and he had other sons and daughters. **5:20** The entire lifetime of Jared was 962 years, and then he died.

5:21 When Enoch had lived 65 years, he became the father of Methuselah. **5:22** After he became the father of Methuselah, Enoch walked with God for 300 years, and he had other sons and daughters. **5:23** The entire lifetime of Enoch was 365 years. **5:24** Enoch walked with God, and then he disappeared because God took him away.

5:25 When Methuselah had lived 187 years, he became the father of Lamech. **5:26** Methuselah lived 782 years after he became the father of Lamech, and he had other sons and daughters. **5:27** The entire lifetime of Methuselah was 969 years, and then he died.

5:28 When Lamech had lived 182 years, he had a son. **5:29** He named him Noah, saying, "This one will bring us comfort from our labor and from the painful toil of our hands because of the ground that the LORD has cursed." **5:30** Lamech lived 595 years after he became the father of Noah, and he had other sons and daughters. **5:31** The entire lifetime of Lamech was 777 years, and then he died.

5:32 After Noah was 500 years old, he became the father of Shem, Ham, and Japheth.

God's Grief over Humankind's Wickedness

6:1 When humankind began to multiply on the face of the earth, and daughters were born to them, **6:2** the sons of God saw that the daughters of humankind were beautiful. Thus they took wives for themselves from any they chose. **6:3** So the LORD said, "My spirit will not remain in humankind indefinitely, since they are mortal. They will remain for 120 more years."

6:4 The Nephilim were on the earth in those days (and also after this) when the sons of God were having sexual relations with the daughters of humankind, who gave birth to their children. They were the mighty heroes of old, the famous men.

6:5 But the LORD saw that the wickedness of humankind had become great on the earth. Every inclination of the thoughts of their minds was only evil all the time. **6:6** The LORD regretted that he had made humankind on the earth, and he was highly offended. **6:7** So the LORD said, "I will wipe humankind, whom I have created, from the face of the earth – everything from humankind to animals, including creatures that move on the ground and birds of the air, for I regret that I have made them."

6:8 But Noah found favor in the sight of the LORD.

The Judgment of the Flood

6:9 This is the account of Noah.

Noah was a godly man; he was blameless

among his contemporaries. He walked with God. **6:10** Noah had three sons: Shem, Ham, and Japheth.

6:11 The earth was ruined in the sight of God; the earth was filled with violence. **6:12** God saw the earth, and indeed it was ruined, for all living creatures on the earth were sinful. **6:13** So God said to Noah, "I have decided that all living creatures must die, for the earth is filled with violence because of them. Now I am about to destroy them and the earth. **6:14** Make for yourself an ark of cypress wood. Make rooms in the ark, and cover it with pitch inside and out. **6:15** This is how you should make it: The ark is to be 450 feet long, 75 feet wide, and 45 feet high. **6:16** Make a roof for the ark and finish it, leaving 18 inches from the top. Put a door in the side of the ark, and make lower, middle, and upper decks. **6:17** I am about to bring floodwaters on the earth to destroy from under the sky all the living creatures that have the breath of life in them. Everything that is on the earth will die, **6:18** but I will confirm my covenant with you. You will enter the ark – you, your sons, your wife, and your sons' wives with you. **6:19** You must bring into the ark two of every kind of living creature from all flesh, male and female, to keep them alive with you. **6:20** Of the birds after their kinds, and of the cattle after their kinds, and of every creeping thing of the ground after its kind, two of every kind will come to you so you can keep them alive. **6:21** And you must take for yourself every kind of food that is eaten, and gather it together. It will be food for you and for them."

6:22 And Noah did all that God commanded him – he did indeed.

7:1 The LORD said to Noah, "Come into the ark, you and all your household, for I consider you godly among this generation. **7:2** You must take with you seven of every kind of clean animal, the male and its mate, two of every kind of unclean animal, the male and its mate, **7:3** and also seven of every kind of bird in the sky, male and female, to preserve their offspring on the face of the earth. **7:4** For in seven days I will cause it to rain on the earth for forty days and forty nights, and I will wipe from the face of the ground every living thing that I have made."

7:5 And Noah did all that the LORD commanded him.

7:6 Noah was 600 years old when the floodwaters engulfed the earth. **7:7** Noah entered the ark along with his sons, his wife, and his sons' wives because of the floodwaters. **7:8** Pairs of clean animals, of unclean animals, of birds, and of everything that creeps along the ground, **7:9** male and female, came into the ark to Noah, just as God had commanded him. **7:10** And after seven days the floodwaters engulfed the earth.

7:11 In the six hundredth year of Noah's life, in the second month, on the seventeenth day of the month – on that day all the fountains of the great deep burst open and the floodgates of the heavens were opened. **7:12** And the rain fell on the earth forty days and forty nights.

7:13 On that very day Noah entered the ark, accompanied by his sons Shem, Ham, and Japheth, along with his wife and his sons' three wives. **7:14** They entered, along with every living creature after its kind, every animal after its kind, every creeping thing that creeps on the earth after its kind, and every bird after its kind, everything with wings. **7:15** Pairs of all creatures that have the breath of life came into the ark to Noah. **7:16** Those that entered were male and female, just as God commanded him. Then the LORD shut him in.

7:17 The flood engulfed the earth for forty days. As the waters increased, they lifted the ark and raised it above the earth. **7:18** The waters completely overwhelmed the earth, and the ark floated on the surface of the waters. **7:19** The waters completely inundated the earth so that even all the high mountains under the entire sky were covered. **7:20** The waters rose more than twenty feet above the mountains. **7:21** And all living things that moved on the earth died, including the birds, domestic animals, wild animals, all the creatures that swarm over the earth, and all humankind. **7:22** Everything on dry land that had the breath of life in its nostrils died. **7:23** So the LORD destroyed every living thing that was on the surface of the ground, including people, animals, creatures that creep along the ground, and birds of the sky. They were wiped off the earth. Only Noah and those who were with him in the ark survived. **7:24** The waters prevailed over the earth for 150 days.

8:1 But God remembered Noah and all the wild animals and domestic animals that were with him in the ark. God caused a wind to blow over the earth and the waters receded. **8:2** The fountains of the deep and the floodgates of heaven were closed, and the rain stopped falling from the sky. **8:3** The waters kept receding steadily from the earth, so that they had gone down by the end of the 150 days. **8:4** On the seventeenth day of the seventh month, the ark came to rest on one of the mountains of Ararat. **8:5** The waters kept on receding until the tenth month. On the first day of the tenth month, the tops of the mountains became visible.

8:6 At the end of forty days, Noah opened the window he had made in the ark **8:7** and sent out a raven; it kept flying back and forth until the waters had dried up on the earth.

8:8 Then Noah sent out a dove to see if the waters had receded from the surface of the ground. **8:9** The dove could not find a resting place for its feet because water still covered the surface of the entire earth, and so it returned to Noah in the ark. He stretched out his hand, took the dove, and brought it back into the ark. **8:10** He waited seven more days and then sent out the dove again from the ark. **8:11** When the dove returned to him in the evening, there was a freshly plucked olive leaf in its beak! Noah knew that the waters had receded from the earth. **8:12** He waited another seven days and sent the dove out again, but it did not return to him this time.

8:13 In Noah's six hundred and first year, in the first day of the first month, the waters had dried up from the earth, and Noah removed the covering from the ark and saw that the surface of the ground was dry. **8:14** And by the twenty-seventh day of the second month the earth was dry.

8:15 Then God spoke to Noah and said, **8:16** "Come out of the ark, you, your wife, your sons, and your sons' wives with you. **8:17** Bring out with you all the living creatures that are with you. Bring out every living thing, including the birds, animals, and every creeping thing that creeps on the earth. Let them increase and be fruitful and multiply on the earth!"

8:18 Noah went out along with his sons, his wife, and his sons' wives. **8:19** Every living creature, every creeping thing, every bird, and everything that moves on the earth went out of the ark in their groups.

8:20 Noah built an altar to the LORD. He then took some of every kind of clean animal and clean bird and offered burnt offerings on the altar. **8:21** And the LORD smelled the soothing aroma and said to himself, "I will never again curse the ground because of humankind, even though the inclination of their minds is evil from childhood on. I will never again destroy everything that lives, as I have just done.

8:22 "While the earth continues to exist,
planting time and harvest,
cold and heat,
summer and winter,
and day and night will not cease."

God's Covenant with Humankind through Noah

9:1 Then God blessed Noah and his sons and said to them, "Be fruitful and multiply and fill the earth. **9:2** Every living creature of the earth and every bird of the sky will be terrified of you. Everything that creeps on the ground and all the fish of the sea are under your authority. **9:3** You may eat any moving thing that lives. As I gave you the green plants, I now give you everything.

9:4 But you must not eat meat with its life (that is, its blood) in it. **9:5** For your lifeblood I will surely exact punishment, from every living creature I will exact punishment. From each person I will exact punishment for the life of the individual since the man was his relative.

9:6 "Whoever sheds human blood,
by other humans
must his blood be shed;
for in God's image
God has made humankind."

9:7 But as for you, be fruitful and multiply; increase abundantly on the earth and multiply on it."

9:8 God said to Noah and his sons, **9:9** "Look! I now confirm my covenant with you and your descendants after you **9:10** and with every living creature that is with you, including the birds, the domestic animals, and every living creature of the earth with you, all those that came out of the ark with you – every living creature of the earth. **9:11** I confirm my covenant with you: Never again will all living things be wiped out by the waters of a flood; never again will a flood destroy the earth."

9:12 And God said, "This is the guarantee of the covenant I am making with you and every living creature with you, a covenant for all subsequent generations: **9:13** I will place my rainbow in the clouds, and it will become a guarantee of the covenant between me and the earth. **9:14** Whenever I bring clouds over the earth and the rainbow appears in the clouds, **9:15** then I will remember my covenant with you and with all living creatures of all kinds. Never again will the waters become a flood and destroy all living things. **9:16** When the rainbow is in the clouds, I will notice it and remember the perpetual covenant between God and all living creatures of all kinds that are on the earth."

9:17 So God said to Noah, "This is the guarantee of the covenant that I am confirming between me and all living things that are on the earth."

The Curse of Canaan

9:18 The sons of Noah who came out of the ark were Shem, Ham, and Japheth. (Now Ham was the father of Canaan.) **9:19** These were the sons of Noah, and from them the whole earth was populated.

9:20 Noah, a man of the soil, began to plant a vineyard. **9:21** When he drank some of the wine, he got drunk and uncovered himself inside his tent. **9:22** Ham, the father of Canaan, saw his father's nakedness and told his two brothers who were outside. **9:23** Shem and Japheth took the garment and placed it on their shoulders. Then they walked in backwards and covered up their father's nakedness. Their faces were turned the other way so they did not see their father's nakedness.

9:24 When Noah awoke from his drunken stupor he learned what his youngest son had done to him. **9:25** So he said,

"Cursed be Canaan!
The lowest of slaves
he will be to his brothers."

9:26 He also said,

"Worthy of praise is the LORD, the God of Shem!
May Canaan be the slave of Shem!
9:27 May God enlarge Japheth's territory and numbers!
May he live in the tents of Shem
and may Canaan be his slave!"

9:28 After the flood Noah lived 350 years. **9:29** The entire lifetime of Noah was 950 years, and then he died.

The Table of Nations

10:1 This is the account of Noah's sons Shem, Ham, and Japheth. Sons were born to them after the flood.

10:2 The sons of Japheth were Gomer, Magog, Madai, Javan, Tubal, Meshech, and Tiras. **10:3** The sons of Gomer were Askenaz, Riphath, and Togarmah. **10:4** The sons of Javan were Elishah, Tarshish, the Kittim, and the Dodanim. **10:5** From these the coastlands of the nations were separated into their lands, every one according to its language, according to their families, by their nations.

10:6 The sons of Ham were Cush, Mizraim, Put, and Canaan. **10:7** The sons of Cush were Seba, Havilah, Sabtah, Raamah, and Sabteca. The sons of Raamah were Sheba and Dedan.

10:8 Cush was the father of Nimrod; he began to be a valiant warrior on the earth. **10:9** He was a mighty hunter before the LORD. (That is why it is said, "Like Nimrod, a mighty hunter before the LORD.") **10:10** The primary regions of his kingdom were Babel, Erech, Akkad, and Calneh in the land of Shinar. **10:11** From that land he went to Assyria, where he built Nineveh, Rehoboth-Ir, Calah, **10:12** and Resen, which is between Nineveh and the great city Calah.

10:13 Mizraim was the father of the Ludites, Anamites, Lehabites, Naphtuhites, **10:14** Pathrusites, Casluhites (from whom the Philistines came), and Caphtorites.

10:15 Canaan was the father of Sidon his firstborn, Heth, **10:16** the Jebusites, Amorites, Girgashites, **10:17** Hivites, Arkites, Sinites, **10:18** Arvadites, Zemarites, and Hamathites. Eventually the families of the Canaanites were scattered **10:19** and the borders of Canaan extended from Sidon all the way to Gerar as far as Gaza, and all the way to Sodom, Gomorrah, Admah, and Zeboiim, as far as Lasha. **10:20** These are the sons of Ham, according to their families, according to their languages, by their lands, and by their nations.

10:21 And sons were also born to Shem (the older brother of Japheth), the father of all the sons of Eber.

10:22 The sons of Shem were Elam, Asshur, Arphaxad, Lud, and Aram. **10:23** The sons of Aram were Uz, Hul, Gether, and Mash. **10:24** Arphaxad was the father of Shelah, and Shelah was the father of Eber. **10:25** Two sons were born to Eber: One was named Peleg because in his days the earth was divided, and his brother's name was Joktan. **10:26** Joktan was the father of Almodad, Sheleph, Hazarmaveth, Jerah, **10:27** Hadoram, Uzal, Diklah, **10:28** Obal, Abimael, Sheba, **10:29** Ophir, Havilah, and Jobab. All these were sons of Joktan. **10:30** Their dwelling place was from Mesha all the way to Sephar in the eastern hills. **10:31** These are the sons of Shem according to their families, according to their languages, by their lands, and according to their nations.

10:32 These are the families of the sons of Noah, according to their genealogies, by their nations, and from these these nations spread over the earth after the flood.

The Dispersion of the Nations at Babel

11:1 The whole earth had a common language and a common vocabulary. **11:2** When the people moved eastward, they found a plain in Shinar and settled there. **11:3** Then they said to one another, "Come, let's make bricks and bake them thoroughly." (They had brick instead of stone and tar instead of mortar.) **11:4** Then they said, "Come, let's build ourselves a city and a tower with its top in the heavens so that we may make a name for ourselves. Otherwise we will be scattered across the face of the entire earth."

11:5 But the LORD came down to see the city and the tower that the people had started building. **11:6** And the LORD said, "If as one people all sharing a common language they have begun to do this, then nothing they plan to do will be beyond them. **11:7** Come, let's go down and confuse their language so they won't be able to understand each other."

11:8 So the LORD scattered them from there across the face of the entire earth, and they stopped building the city. **11:9** That is why its name was called Babel – because there the LORD confused the language of the entire world, and from there the LORD scattered them across the face of the entire earth.

The Genealogy of Shem

11:10 This is the account of Shem.
Shem was 100 old when he became the father of Arphaxad, two years after the flood. **11:11** And after becoming the father of Arphaxad, Shem lived 500 years and had other sons and daughters.

11:12 When Arphaxad had lived 35 years, he became the father of Shelah. **11:13** And after he became the father of Shelah, Arphaxad lived 403 years and had other sons and daughters.

11:14 When Shelah had lived 30 years, he became the father of Eber. **11:15** And after he became the father of Eber, Shelah lived 403 years and had other sons and daughters.

11:16 When Eber had lived 34 years, he became the father of Peleg. **11:17** And after he became the father of Peleg, Eber lived 430 years and had other sons and daughters.

11:18 When Peleg had lived 30 years, he became the father of Reu. **11:19** And after he became the father of Reu, Peleg lived 209 years and had other sons and daughters.

11:20 When Reu had lived 32 years, he became the father of Serug. **11:21** And after he became the father of Serug, Reu lived 207 years and had other sons and daughters.

11:22 When Serug had lived 30 years, he became the father of Nahor. **11:23** And after he became the father of Nahor, Serug lived 200 years and had other sons and daughters.

11:24 When Nahor had lived 29 years, he became the father of Terah. **11:25** And after he became the father of Terah, Nahor lived 119 years and had other sons and daughters.

11:26 When Terah had lived 70 years, he became the father of Abram, Nahor, and Haran.

The Record of Terah

11:27 This is the account of Terah.
Terah became the father of Abram, Nahor, and Haran. And Haran became the father of Lot. **11:28** Haran died in the land of his birth, in Ur of the Chaldeans, while his father Terah was still alive. **11:29** And Abram and Nahor took wives for themselves. The name of Abram's wife was Sarai, and the name of Nahor's wife was Milcah; she was the daughter of Haran, the father of both Milcah and Iscah. **11:30** But Sarai was barren; she had no children.

11:31 Terah took his son Abram, his grandson Lot (the son of Haran), and his daughter-in-law Sarai, his son Abram's wife, and with them he set out from Ur of the Chaldeans to go to Canaan. When they came to Haran, they settled there. **11:32** The lifetime of Terah was 205 years, and he died in Haran.

The Obedience of Abram

12:1 Now the LORD said to Abram,
"Go out from your country, your relatives, and your father's household
to the land that I will show you.
12:2 Then I will make you into a great nation, and I will bless you,
and I will make your name great,
so that you will exemplify divine blessing.
12:3 I will bless those who bless you,
but the one who treats you lightly I must curse,
and all the families of the earth will bless one another by your name."

12:4 So Abram left, just as the LORD had told him to do, and Lot went with him. (Now Abram was 75 years old when he departed from Haran.) **12:5** And Abram took his wife Sarai, his nephew Lot, and all the possessions they had accumulated and the people they had acquired in Haran, and they left for the land of Canaan. They entered the land of Canaan.

12:6 Abram traveled through the land as far as the oak tree of Moreh at Shechem. (At that time the Canaanites were in the land.) **12:7** The LORD appeared to Abram and said, "To your descendants I will give this land." So Abram built an altar there to the LORD, who had appeared to him. **12:8** Then he moved from there to the hill country east of Bethel and pitched his tent, with Bethel on the west and Ai on the east. There he built an altar to the LORD and worshiped the LORD. **12:9** Abram continually journeyed by stages down to the Negev.

The Promised Blessing Jeopardized

12:10 There was a famine in the land, so Abram went down to Egypt to stay for a while because the famine was severe. **12:11** As he approached Egypt, he said to his wife Sarai, "Look, I know that you are a beautiful woman. **12:12** When the Egyptians see you they will say, 'This is his wife.' Then they will kill me but will keep you alive. **12:13** So tell them you are my sister so that it may go

well for me because of you and my life will be spared on account of you."

12:14 When Abram entered Egypt, the Egyptians saw that the woman was very beautiful. **12:15** When Pharaoh's officials saw her, they praised her to Pharaoh. So Abram's wife was taken into the household of Pharaoh, **12:16** and he did treat Abram well on account of her. Abram received sheep and cattle, male donkeys, male servants, female servants, female donkeys, and camels.

12:17 But the LORD struck Pharaoh and his household with severe diseases because of Sarai, Abram's wife. **12:18** So Pharaoh summoned Abram and said, "What is this you have done to me? Why didn't you tell me that she was your wife? **12:19** Why did you say, 'She is my sister,' so that I took her to be my wife? Here is your wife! Take her and go!" **12:20** Pharaoh gave his men orders about Abram, and so they expelled him, along with his wife and all his possessions.

Abram's Solution to the Strife

13:1 So Abram went up from Egypt into the Negev. He took his wife and all his possessions with him, as well as Lot. **13:2** (Now Abram was very wealthy in livestock, silver, and gold.)

13:3 And he journeyed from place to place from the Negev as far as Bethel. He returned to the place where he had pitched his tent at the beginning, between Bethel and Ai. **13:4** This was the place where he had first built the altar, and there Abram worshiped the LORD.

13:5 Now Lot, who was traveling with Abram, also had flocks, herds, and tents. **13:6** But the land could not support them while they were living side by side. Because their possessions were so great, they were not able to live alongside one another. **13:7** So there were quarrels between Abram's herdsmen and Lot's herdsmen. (Now the Canaanites and the Perizzites were living in the land at that time.)

13:8 Abram said to Lot, "Let there be no quarreling between me and you, and between my herdsmen and your herdsmen, for we are close relatives. **13:9** Is not the whole land before you? Separate yourself now from me. If you go to the left, then I'll go to the right, but if you go to the right, then I'll go to the left."

13:10 Lot looked up and saw the whole region of the Jordan. He noticed that all of it was well-watered (before the LORD obliterated Sodom and Gomorrah) like the garden of the LORD, like the land of Egypt, all the way to Zoar. **13:11** Lot chose for himself the whole region of the Jordan and traveled toward the east.

So the relatives separated from each other. **13:12** Abram settled in the land of Canaan, but Lot settled among the cities of the Jordan plain and pitched his tents next to Sodom. **13:13** (Now the people of Sodom were extremely wicked rebels against the LORD.)

13:14 After Lot had departed, the LORD said to Abram, "Look from the place where you stand to the north, south, east, and west. **13:15** I will give all the land that you see to you and your descendants forever. **13:16** And I will make your descendants like the dust of the earth, so that if anyone is able to count the dust of the earth, then your descendants also can be counted. **13:17** Get up and walk throughout the land, for I will give it to you."

13:18 So Abram moved his tents and went to live by the oaks of Mamre in Hebron, and he built an altar to the LORD there.

The Blessing of Victory for God's People

14:1 At that time Amraphel king of Shinar, Arioch king of Ellasar, Kedorlaomer king of Elam, and Tidal king of nations **14:2** went to war against Bera king of Sodom, Birsha king of Gomorrah, Shinab king of Admah, Shemeber king of Zeboiim, and the king of Bela (that is, Zoar). **14:3** These last five kings joined forces in the Valley of Siddim (that is, the Salt Sea). **14:4** For twelve years they had served Kedorlaomer, but in the thirteenth year they rebelled. **14:5** In the fourteenth year, Kedorlaomer and the kings who were his allies came and defeated the Rephaites in Ashteroth Karnaim, the Zuzites in Ham, the Emites in Shaveh Kiriathaim, **14:6** and the Horites in their hill country of Seir, as far as El Paran, which is near the desert. **14:7** Then they attacked En Mishpat (that is, Kadesh) again, and they conquered all the territory of the Amalekites, as well as the Amorites who were living in Hazazon Tamar.

14:8 Then the king of Sodom, the king of Gomorrah, the king of Admah, the king of Zeboiim, and the king of Bela (that is, Zoar) went out and

prepared for battle. In the Valley of Siddim they met **14:9** Kedorlaomer king of Elam, Tidal king of nations, Amraphel king of Shinar, and Arioch king of Ellasar. Four kings fought against five. **14:10** Now the Valley of Siddim was full of tar pits. When the kings of Sodom and Gomorrah fled, they fell into them, but some survivors fled to the hills. **14:11** The four victorious kings took all the possessions and food of Sodom and Gomorrah and left. **14:12** They also took Abram's nephew Lot and his possessions when they left, for Lot was living in Sodom.

14:13 A fugitive came and told Abram the Hebrew. Now Abram was living by the oaks of Mamre the Amorite, the brother of Eshcol and Aner. (All these were allied by treaty with Abram.) **14:14** When Abram heard that his nephew had been taken captive, he mobilized his 318 trained men who had been born in his household, and he pursued the invaders as far as Dan. **14:15** Then, during the night, Abram divided his forces against them and defeated them. He chased them as far as Hobah, which is north of Damascus. **14:16** He retrieved all the stolen property. He also brought back his nephew Lot and his possessions, as well as the women and the rest of the people.

14:17 After Abram returned from defeating Kedorlaomer and the kings who were with him, the king of Sodom went out to meet Abram in the Valley of Shaveh (known as the King's Valley). **14:18** Melchizedek king of Salem brought out bread and wine. (Now he was the priest of the Most High God.) **14:19** He blessed Abram, saying,

"Blessed be Abram by the Most High God,
Creator of heaven and earth.

14:20 Worthy of praise is the Most High God,
who delivered your enemies into your hand."

Abram gave Melchizedek a tenth of everything.

14:21 Then the king of Sodom said to Abram, "Give me the people and take the possessions for yourself." **14:22** But Abram replied to the king of Sodom, "I raise my hand to the LORD, the Most High God, Creator of heaven and earth, and vow **14:23** that I will take nothing belonging to you, not even a thread or the strap of a sandal. That way you can never say, 'It is I who made Abram rich.' **14:24** I will take nothing except compensation for what the young men have eaten. As for the share of the men who went with me – Aner, Eshcol, and Mamre – let them take their share."

The Cutting of the Covenant

15:1 After these things the word of the LORD came to Abram in a vision: "Fear not, Abram! I am your shield and the one who will reward you in great abundance."

15:2 But Abram said, "O sovereign LORD, what will you give me since I continue to be childless, and my heir is Eliezer of Damascus?" **15:3** Abram added, "Since you have not given me a descendant, then look, one born in my house will be my heir!"

15:4 But look, the word of the LORD came to him: "This man will not be your heir, but instead a son who comes from your own body will be your heir." **15:5** The LORD took him outside and said, "Gaze into the sky and count the stars – if you are able to count them!" Then he said to him, "So will your descendants be."

15:6 Abram believed the LORD, and the LORD considered his response of faith as proof of genuine loyalty.

15:7 The LORD said to him, "I am the LORD who brought you out from Ur of the Chaldeans to give you this land to possess." **15:8** But Abram said, "O sovereign LORD, by what can I know that I am to possess it?"

15:9 The LORD said to him, "Take for me a heifer, a goat, and a ram, each three years old, along with a dove and a young pigeon." **15:10** So Abram took all these for him and then cut them in two and placed each half opposite the other, but he did not cut the birds in half. **15:11** When birds of prey came down on the carcasses, Abram drove them away.

15:12 When the sun went down, Abram fell sound asleep, and great terror overwhelmed him. **15:13** Then the LORD said to Abram, "Know for certain that your descendants will be strangers in a foreign country. They will be enslaved and oppressed for four hundred years. **15:14** But I will execute judgment on the nation that they will serve. Afterward they will come out with many possessions. **15:15** But as for you, you will go to your ancestors in peace and be buried at a good old age. **15:16** In the fourth generation your descendants will return here, for the sin of the Amorites has not yet reached its limit."

15:17 When the sun had gone down and it was dark, a smoking firepot with a flaming torch passed between the animal parts. **15:18** That day the LORD made a covenant with Abram: "To your descendants I give this land, from the river of Egypt to the great river, the Euphrates River – **15:19** the land of the Kenites, Kenizzites, Kadmonites, **15:20** Hittites, Perizzites, Rephaites, **15:21** Amorites, Canaanites, Girgashites, and Jebusites."

The Birth of Ishmael

16:1 Now Sarai, Abram's wife, had not given birth to any children, but she had an Egyptian servant named Hagar. **16:2** So Sarai said to Abram, "Since the LORD has prevented me from having children, have sexual relations with my servant. Perhaps I can have a family by her." Abram did what Sarai told him.

16:3 So after Abram had lived in Canaan for ten years, Sarai, Abram's wife, gave Hagar, her Egyptian servant, to her husband to be his wife. **16:4** He had sexual relations with Hagar, and she became pregnant. Once Hagar realized she was pregnant, she despised Sarai. **16:5** Then Sarai said to Abram, "You have brought this wrong on me! I allowed my servant to have sexual relations with you, but when she realized that she was pregnant, she despised me. May the LORD judge between you and me!"

16:6 Abram said to Sarai, "Since your servant is under your authority, do to her whatever you think best." Then Sarai treated Hagar harshly, so she ran away from Sarai.

16:7 The LORD's angel found Hagar near a spring of water in the desert – the spring that is along the road to Shur. **16:8** He said, "Hagar, servant of Sarai, where have you come from, and where are you going?" She replied, "I'm running away from my mistress, Sarai."

16:9 Then the LORD's angel said to her, "Return to your mistress and submit to her authority. **16:10** I will greatly multiply your descendants," the LORD's angel added, "so that they will be too numerous to count." **16:11** Then the LORD's angel said to her,

"You are now pregnant
and are about to give birth to a son.
You are to name him Ishmael,
for the LORD has heard your painful groans.
16:12 He will be a wild donkey of a man.
He will be hostile to everyone,
and everyone will be hostile to him.
He will live away from his brothers."

16:13 So Hagar named the LORD who spoke to her, "You are the God who sees me," for she said, "Here I have seen one who sees me!" **16:14** That is why the well was called Beer Lahai Roi. (It is located between Kadesh and Bered.)

16:15 So Hagar gave birth to Abram's son, whom Abram named Ishmael. **16:16** (Now Abram was 86 years old when Hagar gave birth to Ishmael.)

The Sign of the Covenant

17:1 When Abram was 99 years old, the LORD appeared to him and said, "I am the sovereign God. Walk before me and be blameless. **17:2** Then I will confirm my covenant between me and you, and I will give you a multitude of descendants."

17:3 Abram bowed down with his face to the ground, and God said to him, **17:4** "As for me, this is my covenant with you: You will be the father of a multitude of nations. **17:5** No longer will your name be Abram. Instead, your name will be Abraham because I will make you the father of a multitude of nations. **17:6** I will make you extremely fruitful. I will make nations of you, and kings will descend from you. **17:7** I will confirm my covenant as a perpetual covenant between me and you. It will extend to your descendants after you throughout their generations. I will be your God and the God of your descendants after you. **17:8** I will give the whole land of Canaan – the land where you are now residing – to you and your descendants after you as a permanent possession. I will be their God."

17:9 Then God said to Abraham, "As for you, you must keep the covenantal requirement I am imposing on you and your descendants after you throughout their generations. **17:10** This is my requirement that you and your descendants after you must keep: Every male among you must be circumcised. **17:11** You must circumcise the flesh of your foreskins. This will be a reminder of the covenant between me and you. **17:12** Throughout your generations every male among you who is eight days old must be circumcised, whether born in your house or bought with money from any foreigner who is not one of your descendants. **17:13** They must indeed be circumcised, whether born in your house or bought with money. The sign of my covenant will be visible in your flesh as a permanent reminder. **17:14** Any uncircumcised male who has not been circumcised in the flesh of his foreskin will be cut off from his people – he has failed to carry out my requirement."

17:15 Then God said to Abraham, "As for your wife, you must no longer call her Sarai; Sarah will be her name. **17:16** I will bless her and will give you a son through her. I will bless her and she will become a mother of nations. Kings of countries will come from her!"

17:17 Then Abraham bowed down with his face to the ground and laughed as he said to himself, "Can a son be born to a man who is a hundred years old? Can Sarah bear a child at the age of ninety?" **17:18** Abraham said to God, "O that Ishmael might live before you!"

17:19 God said, "No, Sarah your wife is going to bear you a son, and you will name him Isaac. I will confirm my covenant with him as a perpetual covenant for his descendants after him. **17:20** As for Ishmael, I have heard you. I will indeed bless him, make him fruitful, and give him a multitude of descendants. He will become the father of twelve princes; I will make him into a great nation. **17:21** But I will establish my covenant with Isaac, whom Sarah will bear to you at this set time next year." **17:22** When he finished speaking with Abraham, God went up from him.

17:23 Abraham took his son Ishmael and every male in his household (whether born in his house or bought with money) and circumcised them on that very same day, just as God had told him to do. **17:24** Now Abraham was 99 years old when he was circumcised; **17:25** his son Ishmael was thirteen years old when he was circumcised. **17:26** Abraham and his son Ishmael were circumcised on the very same day. **17:27** All the men of his household, whether born in his household or bought with money from a foreigner, were circumcised with him.

Three Special Visitors

18:1 The LORD appeared to Abraham by the oaks of Mamre while he was sitting at the entrance to his tent during the hottest time of the day. **18:2** Abraham looked up and saw three men standing across from him. When he saw them he ran from the entrance of the tent to meet them and bowed low to the ground.

18:3 He said, "My lord, if I have found favor in your sight, do not pass by and leave your servant. **18:4** Let a little water be brought so that you may all wash your feet and rest under the tree. **18:5** And let me get a bit of food so that you may refresh yourselves since you have passed by your servant's home. After that you may be on your way." "All right," they replied, "you may do as you say."

18:6 So Abraham hurried into the tent and said to Sarah, "Quick! Take three measures of fine flour, knead it, and make bread." **18:7** Then Abraham ran to the herd and chose a fine, tender calf, and gave it to a servant, who quickly prepared it. **18:8** Abraham then took some curds and milk, along with the calf that had been prepared, and placed the food before them. They ate while he was standing near them under a tree.

18:9 Then they asked him, "Where is Sarah your wife?" He replied, "There, in the tent." **18:10** One of them said, "I will surely return to you when the season comes round again, and your wife Sarah will have a son!" (Now Sarah was listening at the entrance to the tent, not far behind him. **18:11** Abraham and Sarah were old and advancing in years; Sarah had long since passed menopause.) **18:12** So Sarah laughed to herself, thinking, "After I am worn out will I have pleasure, especially when my husband is old too?"

18:13 The LORD said to Abraham, "Why did Sarah laugh and say, 'Will I really have a child when I am old?' **18:14** Is anything impossible for the LORD? I will return to you when the season comes round again and Sarah will have a son." **18:15** Then Sarah lied, saying, "I did not laugh," because she was afraid. But the LORD said, "No! You did laugh."

Abraham Pleads for Sodom

18:16 When the men got up to leave, they looked out over Sodom. (Now Abraham was walking with them to see them on their way.) **18:17** Then the LORD said, "Should I hide from Abraham what I am about to do? **18:18** After all, Abraham will surely become a great and powerful nation, and all the nations on the earth will pronounce blessings on one another using his name. **18:19** I have chosen him so that he may command his children and his household after him to keep the way of the LORD by doing what is right and just. Then the LORD will give to Abraham what he promised him."

18:20 So the LORD said, "The outcry against Sodom and Gomorrah is so great and their sin so blatant **18:21** that I must go down and see if they are as wicked as the outcry suggests. If not, I want to know."

18:22 The two men turned and headed toward Sodom, but Abraham was still standing before the LORD. **18:23** Abraham approached and said, "Will you sweep away the godly along with the wicked? **18:24** What if there are fifty godly people in the city? Will you really wipe it out and not spare the place for the sake of the fifty godly people who are in it? **18:25** Far be it from you to do such a thing – to kill the godly with the wicked, treating the godly and the wicked alike! Far be it from you! Will not the judge of the whole earth do what is right?"

18:26 So the LORD replied, "If I find in the city of Sodom fifty godly people, I will spare the whole place for their sake."

18:27 Then Abraham asked, "Since I have undertaken to speak to the Lord (although I am but dust and ashes), **18:28** what if there are five less than the fifty godly people? Will you destroy the whole city because five are lacking?" He replied, "I will not destroy it if I find forty-five there."

18:29 Abraham spoke to him again, "What if forty are found there?" He replied, "I will not do it for the sake of the forty."

18:30 Then Abraham said, "May the Lord not be angry so that I may speak! What if thirty are found there?" He replied, "I will not do it if I find thirty there."

18:31 Abraham said, "Since I have undertaken to speak to the Lord, what if only twenty are found there?" He replied, "I will not destroy it for the sake of the twenty."

18:32 Finally Abraham said, "May the Lord not be angry so that I may speak just once more. What if ten are found there?" He replied, "I will not destroy it for the sake of the ten."

18:33 The LORD went on his way when he had finished speaking to Abraham. Then Abraham returned home.

The Destruction of Sodom and Gomorrah

19:1 The two angels came to Sodom in the evening while Lot was sitting in the city's gateway. When Lot saw them, he got up to meet them and bowed down with his face toward the ground.

19:2 He said, "Here, my lords, please turn aside to your servant's house. Stay the night and wash your feet. Then you can be on your way early in the morning." "No," they replied, "we'll spend the night in the town square."

19:3 But he urged them persistently, so they turned aside with him and entered his house. He prepared a feast for them, including bread baked without yeast, and they ate. **19:4** Before they could lie down to sleep, all the men – both young and old, from every part of the city of Sodom – surrounded the house. **19:5** They shouted to Lot, "Where are the men who came to you tonight? Bring them out to us so we can have sex with them!"

19:6 Lot went outside to them, shutting the door behind him. **19:7** He said, "No, my brothers! Don't act so wickedly! **19:8** Look, I have two daughters who have never had sexual relations with a man. Let me bring them out to you, and you can do to them whatever you please. Only don't do anything to these men, for they have come under the protection of my roof."

19:9 "Out of our way!" they cried, and "This man came to live here as a foreigner, and now he dares to judge us! We'll do more harm to you than to them!" They kept pressing in on Lot until they were close enough to break down the door.

19:10 So the men inside reached out and pulled Lot back into the house as they shut the door. **19:11** Then they struck the men who were at the door of the house, from the youngest to the oldest, with blindness. The men outside wore themselves out trying to find the door. **19:12** Then the two visitors said to Lot, "Who else do you have here? Do you have any sons-in-law, sons, daughters, or other relatives in the city? Get them out of this place **19:13** because we are about to destroy it. The outcry against this place is so great before the LORD that he has sent us to destroy it."

19:14 Then Lot went out and spoke to his sons-in-law who were going to marry his daughters. He said, "Quick, get out of this place because the LORD is about to destroy the city!" But his sons-in-law thought he was ridiculing them.

19:15 At dawn the angels hurried Lot along, saying, "Get going! Take your wife and your two daughters who are here, or else you will be destroyed when the city is judged!" **19:16** When Lot hesitated, the men grabbed his hand and the hands of his wife and two daughters because the LORD had compassion on them. They led them away and placed them outside the city. **19:17** When they had brought them outside, they said, "Run for your lives! Don't look behind you or stop anywhere in the valley! Escape to the mountains or you will be destroyed!"

19:18 But Lot said to them, "No, please, Lord! **19:19** Your servant has found favor with you, and you have shown me great kindness by sparing my life. But I am not able to escape to the mountains because this disaster will overtake me and I'll die. **19:20** Look, this town over here is close enough to escape to, and it's just a little one. Let me go there. It's just a little place, isn't it? Then I'll survive."

19:21 "Very well," he replied, "I will grant this request too and will not overthrow the town you mentioned. **19:22** Run there quickly, for I cannot do anything until you arrive there." (This incident explains why the town was called Zoar.)

19:23 The sun had just risen over the land as Lot reached Zoar. **19:24** Then the LORD rained down sulfur and fire on Sodom and Gomorrah. It was sent down from the sky by the LORD. **19:25** So he overthrew those cities and all that region, including all the inhabitants of the cities and the vegetation that grew from the ground. **19:26** But Lot's wife looked back longingly and was turned into a pillar of salt.

19:27 Abraham got up early in the morning and went to the place where he had stood before the LORD. **19:28** He looked out toward Sodom and Gomorrah and all the land of that region. As he did so, he saw the smoke rising up from the land like smoke from a furnace.

19:29 So when God destroyed the cities of the region, God honored Abraham's request. He removed Lot from the midst of the destruction when he destroyed the cities Lot had lived in.

19:30 Lot went up from Zoar with his two daughters and settled in the mountains because he was afraid to live in Zoar. So he lived in a cave with his two daughters. **19:31** Later the older daughter said to the younger, "Our father is old, and there is no man anywhere nearby to have sexual relations with us, according to the way of all the world. **19:32** Come, let's make our father drunk with wine so we can have sexual relations with him and preserve our family line through our father."

19:33 So that night they made their father drunk with wine, and the older daughter came and had sexual relations with her father. But he was not aware that she had sexual relations with him and then got up. **19:34** So in the morning the older daughter said to the younger, "Since I had sexual relations with my father last night, let's make him drunk again tonight. Then you go and have sexual relations with him so we can preserve our family line through our father." **19:35** So they made their father drunk that night as well, and the younger one came and had sexual relations with him. But he was not aware that she had sexual relations with him and then got up.

19:36 In this way both of Lot's daughters became pregnant by their father. **19:37** The older daughter gave birth to a son and named him Moab. He is the ancestor of the Moabites of today. **19:38** The younger daughter also gave birth to a son and named him Ben-Ammi. He is the ancestor of the Ammonites of today.

Abraham and Abimelech

20:1 Abraham journeyed from there to the Negev region and settled between Kadesh and Shur. While he lived as a temporary resident in Gerar, **20:2** Abraham said about his wife Sarah, "She is my sister." So Abimelech, king of Gerar, sent for Sarah and took her.

20:3 But God appeared to Abimelech in a dream at night and said to him, "You are as good as dead because of the woman you have taken, for she is someone else's wife."

20:4 Now Abimelech had not gone near her. He said, "Lord, would you really slaughter an innocent nation? **20:5** Did Abraham not say to me, 'She is my sister'? And she herself said, 'He is my brother.' I have done this with a clear conscience and with innocent hands!"

20:6 Then in the dream God replied to him, "Yes, I know that you have done this with a clear conscience. That is why I have kept you from sinning against me and why I did not allow you to touch her. **20:7** But now give back the man's wife. Indeed he is a prophet and he will pray for you; thus you will live. But if you don't give her back, know that you will surely die along with all who belong to you."

20:8 Early in the morning Abimelech summoned all his servants. When he told them about all these things, they were terrified. **20:9** Abimelech summoned Abraham and said to him, "What have you done to us? What sin did I commit against you that would cause you to bring such great guilt on me and my kingdom? You have done things to me that should not be done!" **20:10** Then Abimelech asked Abraham, "What prompted you to do this thing?"

20:11 Abraham replied, "Because I thought, 'Surely no one fears God in this place. They will kill me because of my wife.' **20:12** What's more, she is indeed my sister, my

father's daughter, but not my mother's daughter. She became my wife. **20:13** When God made me wander from my father's house, I told her, 'This is what you can do to show your loyalty to me: Every place we go, say about me, "He is my brother."'"

20:14 So Abimelech gave sheep, cattle, and male and female servants to Abraham. He also gave his wife Sarah back to him. **20:15** Then Abimelech said, "Look, my land is before you; live wherever you please."

20:16 To Sarah he said, "Look, I have given a thousand pieces of silver to your 'brother.' This is compensation for you so that you will stand vindicated before all who are with you."

20:17 Abraham prayed to God, and God healed Abimelech, as well as his wife and female slaves so that they were able to have children. **20:18** For the LORD had caused infertility to strike every woman in the household of Abimelech because he took Sarah, Abraham's wife.

The Birth of Isaac

21:1 The LORD visited Sarah just as he had said he would and did for Sarah what he had promised. **21:2** So Sarah became pregnant and bore Abraham a son in his old age at the appointed time that God had told him. **21:3** Abraham named his son – whom Sarah bore to him – Isaac. **21:4** When his son Isaac was eight days old, Abraham circumcised him just as God had commanded him to do. **21:5** (Now Abraham was a hundred years old when his son Isaac was born to him.)

21:6 Sarah said, "God has made me laugh. Everyone who hears about this will laugh with me." **21:7** She went on to say, "Who would have said to Abraham that Sarah would nurse children? Yet I have given birth to a son for him in his old age!"

21:8 The child grew and was weaned. Abraham prepared a great feast on the day that Isaac was weaned. **21:9** But Sarah noticed the son of Hagar the Egyptian – the son whom Hagar had borne to Abraham – mocking. **21:10** So she said to Abraham, "Banish that slave woman and her son, for the son of that slave woman will not be an heir along with my son Isaac!" **21:11** Sarah's demand displeased Abraham greatly because Ishmael was his son. **21:12** But God said to Abraham, "Do not be upset about the boy or your slave wife. Do all that Sarah is telling you because through Isaac your descendants will be counted. **21:13** But I will also make the son of the slave wife into a great nation, for he is your descendant too."

21:14 Early in the morning Abraham took some food and a skin of water and gave them to Hagar. He put them on her shoulders, gave her the child, and sent her away. So she went wandering aimlessly through the wilderness of Beer Sheba. **21:15** When the water in the skin was gone, she shoved the child under one of the shrubs. **21:16** Then she went and sat down by herself across from him at quite a distance, about a bowshot away; for she thought, "I refuse to watch the child die." So she sat across from him and wept uncontrollably.

21:17 But God heard the boy's voice. The angel of God called to Hagar from heaven and asked her, "What is the matter, Hagar? Don't be afraid, for God has heard the boy's voice right where he is crying. **21:18** Get up! Help the boy up and hold him by the hand, for I will make him into a great nation." **21:19** Then God enabled Hagar to see a well of water. She went over and filled the skin with water, and then gave the boy a drink.

21:20 God was with the boy as he grew. He lived in the wilderness and became an archer. **21:21** He lived in the wilderness of Paran. His mother found a wife for him from the land of Egypt.

21:22 At that time Abimelech and Phicol, the commander of his army, said to Abraham, "God is with you in all that you do. **21:23** Now swear to me right here in God's name that you will not deceive me, my children, or my descendants. Show me, and the land where you are staying, the same loyalty that I have shown you."

21:24 Abraham said, "I swear to do this." **21:25** But Abraham lodged a complaint against Abimelech concerning a well that Abimelech's servants had seized. **21:26** "I do not know who has done this thing," Abimelech replied. "Moreover, you did not tell me. I did not hear about it until today."

21:27 Abraham took some sheep and cattle and gave them to Abimelech. The two of them made a treaty. **21:28** Then Abraham set seven ewe lambs apart from the flock by themselves. **21:29** Abimelech asked Abraham, "What is the meaning of these seven ewe lambs that you have set apart?" **21:30** He replied, "You must take these seven ewe lambs from my hand as legal proof that I dug this well." **21:31** That is why he named that place Beer Sheba, because the two of them swore an oath there.

21:32 So they made a treaty at Beer Sheba. Then Abimelech and Phicol, the commander of his army, returned to the land of the Philistines. **21:33** Abraham planted a tamarisk tree in Beer Sheba. There he worshiped the LORD, the eternal God. **21:34** So Abraham stayed in the land of the Philistines for quite some time.

The Sacrifice of Isaac

22:1 Some time after these things God tested Abraham. He said to him, "Abraham!" "Here I am!" Abraham replied. **22:2** God said, "Take your son – your only son, whom you love, Isaac – and go to the land of Moriah! Offer him up there as a burnt offering on one of the mountains which I will indicate to you."

22:3 Early in the morning Abraham got up and saddled his donkey. He took two of his young servants with him, along with his son Isaac. When he had cut the wood for the burnt offering, he started out for the place God had spoken to him about. **22:4** On the third day Abraham caught sight of the place in the distance. **22:5** So he said to his servants, "You two stay here with the donkey while the boy and I go up there. We will worship and then return to you."

22:6 Abraham took the wood for the burnt offering and put it on his son Isaac. Then he took the fire and the knife in his hand, and the two of them walked on together. **22:7** Isaac said to his father Abraham, "My father?" "What is it, my son?" he replied. "Here is the fire and the wood," Isaac said, "but where is the lamb for the burnt offering?" **22:8** "God will provide for himself the lamb for the burnt offering, my son," Abraham replied. The two of them continued on together.

22:9 When they came to the place God had told him about, Abraham built the altar there and arranged the wood on it. Next he tied up his son Isaac and placed him on the altar on top of the wood. **22:10** Then Abraham reached out his hand, took the knife, and prepared to slaughter his son. **22:11** But the LORD's angel called to him from heaven, "Abraham! Abraham!" "Here I am!" he answered. **22:12** "Do not harm the boy!" the angel said. "Do not do anything to him, for now I know that you fear God because you did not withhold your son, your only son, from me."

22:13 Abraham looked up and saw behind him a ram caught in the bushes by its horns. So he went over and got the ram and offered it up as a burnt offering instead of his son. **22:14** And Abraham called the name of that place "The LORD provides." It is said to this day, "In the mountain of the LORD provision will be made."

22:15 The LORD's angel called to Abraham a second time from heaven **22:16** and said, "'I solemnly swear by my own name,' decrees the LORD, 'that because you have done this and have not withheld your son, your only son, **22:17** I will indeed bless you, and I will greatly multiply your descendants so that they will be as countless as the stars in the sky or the grains of sand on the seashore. Your descendants will take possession of the strongholds of their enemies. **22:18** Because you have obeyed me, all the nations of the earth will pronounce blessings on one another using the name of your descendants.'"

22:19 Then Abraham returned to his servants, and they set out together for Beer Sheba where Abraham stayed.

22:20 After these things Abraham was told, "Milcah also has borne children to your brother Nahor – **22:21** Uz the firstborn, his brother Buz, Kemuel (the father of Aram), **22:22** Kesed, Hazo, Pildash, Jidlaph, and Bethuel." **22:23** (Now Bethuel became the father of Rebekah.) These were the eight sons Milcah bore to Abraham's brother Nahor. **22:24** His concubine, whose name was Reumah, also bore him children – Tebah, Gaham, Tahash, and Maacah.

The Death of Sarah

23:1 Sarah lived 127 years. **23:2** Then she died in Kiriath Arba (that is, Hebron) in the land of Canaan. Abraham went to mourn for Sarah and to weep for her.

23:3 Then Abraham got up from mourning his dead wife and said to the sons of Heth, **23:4** "I am a temporary settler among you. Grant me ownership of a burial site among you so that I may bury my dead."

23:5 The sons of Heth answered Abraham, **23:6** "Listen, sir, you are a mighty prince among us! You may bury your dead in the choicest of our tombs. None of us will refuse you his tomb to prevent you from burying your dead."

23:7 Abraham got up and bowed down to the local people, the sons of Heth. **23:8** Then he said to them, "If you agree that I may bury my dead, then hear me out. Ask Ephron the son of Zohar **23:9** if he will sell me the cave of Machpelah that belongs to him; it is at the end of his field. Let him sell it to me publicly for the full price, so that I may own it as a burial site."

23:10 (Now Ephron was sitting among the sons of Heth.) Ephron the Hethite replied to Abraham in the hearing of the sons of Heth – before all who entered the gate of his city – **23:11** "No, my lord! Hear me out. I sell you both the field and the cave that is in it. In the presence of my people I sell it to you. Bury your dead."

23:12 Abraham bowed before the local people **23:13** and said to Ephron in their hearing, "Hear me, if you will. I pay to you the price of the field. Take it from me so that I may bury my dead there."

23:14 Ephron answered Abraham, saying to him, **23:15** "Hear me, my lord. The land is worth 400 pieces of silver, but what is that between me and you? So bury your dead."

23:16 So Abraham agreed to Ephron's price and weighed out for him the price that Ephron had quoted in the hearing of the sons of Heth – 400 pieces of silver, according to the standard measurement at the time.

23:17 So Abraham secured Ephron's field in Machpelah, next to Mamre, including the field, the cave that was in it, and all the trees that were in the field and all around its border, **23:18** as his property in the presence of the sons of Heth before all who entered the gate of Ephron's city.

23:19 After this Abraham buried his wife Sarah in the cave in the field of Machpelah next to Mamre (that is, Hebron) in the land of Canaan. **23:20** So Abraham secured the field and the cave that was in it as a burial site from the sons of Heth.

The Wife for Isaac

24:1 Now Abraham was old, well advanced in years, and the LORD had blessed him in everything. **24:2** Abraham said to his servant, the senior one in his household who was in charge of everything he had, "Put your hand under my thigh **24:3** so that I may make you solemnly promise by the LORD, the God of heaven and the God of the earth: You must not acquire a wife for my son from the daughters of the Canaanites, among whom I am living. **24:4** You must go instead to my country and to my relatives to find a wife for my son Isaac."

24:5 The servant asked him, "What if the woman is not willing to come back with me to this land? Must I then take your son back to the land from which you came?"

24:6 "Be careful never to take my son back there!" Abraham told him. **24:7** "The LORD, the God of heaven, who took me from my father's house and the land of my relatives, promised me with a solemn oath, 'To your descendants I will give this land.' He will send his angel before you so that you may find a wife for my son from there. **24:8** But if the woman is not willing to come back with you, you will be free from this oath of mine. But you must not take my son back there!" **24:9** So the servant placed his hand under the thigh of his master Abraham and gave his solemn promise he would carry out his wishes.

24:10 Then the servant took ten of his master's camels and departed with all kinds of gifts from his master at his disposal. He journeyed to the region of Aram Naharaim and the city of Nahor. **24:11** He made the camels kneel down by the well outside the city. It was evening, the time when the women would go out to draw water. **24:12** He prayed, "O LORD, God of my master Abraham, guide me today. Be faithful to my master Abraham. **24:13** Here I am, standing by the spring, and the daughters of the people who live in the town are coming out to draw water. **24:14** I will say to a young woman, 'Please lower your jar so I may drink.' May the one you have chosen for your servant Isaac reply, 'Drink, and I'll give your camels water too.' In this way I will know that you have been faithful to my master."

24:15 Before he had finished praying, there came Rebekah with her water jug on her shoulder. She was the daughter of Bethuel son of Milcah (Milcah was the wife of Abraham's brother Nahor). **24:16** Now the young woman was very beautiful. She was a virgin; no man had ever had sexual relations with her. She went down to the spring, filled her jug, and came back up. **24:17** Abraham's servant ran to meet her and said, "Please give me a sip of water from your jug." **24:18** "Drink, my lord," she replied, and quickly lowering her jug to her hands, she gave him a drink. **24:19** When she had done so, she said, "I'll draw water for your camels too, until they have drunk as much as they want." **24:20** She quickly emptied her jug into the watering trough and ran back to the well to draw more water until she had drawn enough for all his camels. **24:21** Silently the man watched her with interest to determine if the LORD had made his journey successful or not.

24:22 After the camels had finished drinking, the man took out a gold nose ring weighing a beka and two gold bracelets weighing ten shekels and gave them to her. **24:23** "Whose daughter are you?" he asked. "Tell me, is there room in your father's house for us to spend the night?"

24:24 She said to him, "I am the daughter of Bethuel the son of Milcah, whom Milcah bore to Nahor. **24:25** We have plenty of straw and feed," she added, "and room for you to spend the night."

24:26 The man bowed his head and worshiped the LORD, **24:27** saying "Praised be the LORD, the God of my master Abraham, who has not abandoned his faithful love for my master! The LORD has led me to the house of my master's relatives!"

24:28 The young woman ran and told her mother's household all about these things. **24:29** (Now Rebekah had a brother named Laban.) Laban rushed out to meet the man at the spring. **24:30** When he saw the bracelets on his sister's wrists and the nose ring and heard his sister Rebekah say, "This is what the man said to me," he went out to meet the man. There he was, standing by the camels near the spring. **24:31** Laban said to him, "Come, you who are blessed by the LORD! Why are you standing out here when I have prepared the house and a place for the camels?"

24:32 So Abraham's servant went to the house and unloaded the camels. Straw and feed were given to the camels, and water was provided so that he and the men who were with him could wash their feet. **24:33** When food was served, he said, "I will not eat until I have said what I want to say." "Tell us," Laban said.

24:34 "I am the servant of Abraham," he began. **24:35** "The LORD has richly blessed my master and he has become very wealthy. The LORD has given him sheep and cattle, silver and gold, male and female servants, and camels and donkeys. **24:36** My master's wife Sarah bore a son to him when she was old, and my master has given him everything he owns. **24:37** My master made me swear an oath. He said, 'You must not acquire a wife for my son from the daughters of the Canaanites, among whom I am living, **24:38** but you must go to the family of my father and to my relatives to find a wife for my son.' **24:39** But I said to my master, 'What if the woman does not want to go with me?' **24:40** He answered, 'The LORD, before whom I have walked, will send his angel with you. He will make your journey a success and you will find a wife for my son from among my relatives, from my father's family. **24:41** You will be free from your oath if you go to my relatives and they will not give her to you. Then you will be free from your oath.' **24:42** When I came to the spring today, I prayed, 'O LORD, God of my master Abraham, if you have decided to make my journey successful, may events unfold as follows: **24:43** Here I am, standing by the spring. When the young woman goes out to draw water, I'll say, "Give me a little water to drink from your jug." **24:44** Then she will reply to me, "Drink, and I'll draw water for your camels too." May that woman be the one whom the LORD has chosen for my master's son.'

24:45 "Before I finished praying in my heart, along came Rebekah with her water jug on her shoulder! She went down to the spring and drew water. So I said to her, 'Please give me a drink.' **24:46** She quickly lowered her jug from her shoulder and said, 'Drink, and I'll give your camels water too.' So I drank, and she also gave the camels water. **24:47** Then I asked her, 'Whose daughter are you?' She replied, 'The daughter of Bethuel the son of Nahor, whom Milcah bore to Nahor.' I put the ring in her nose and the bracelets on her wrists. **24:48** Then I bowed down and worshiped the LORD. I praised the LORD, the God of my master Abraham, who had led me on the right path to find the granddaughter of my master's brother for his son. **24:49** Now, if you will show faithful love to my master, tell me. But if not, tell me as well, so that I may go on my way."

24:50 Then Laban and Bethuel replied, "This is the LORD's doing. Our wishes are of no concern. **24:51** Rebekah stands here before you. Take her and go so that she may become the wife of your master's son, just as the LORD has decided."

24:52 When Abraham's servant heard their words, he bowed down to the ground before the LORD. **24:53** Then he brought out gold, silver jewelry, and clothing and gave them to Rebekah. He also gave valuable gifts to her brother and to her mother. **24:54** After this, he and the men who were with him ate a meal and stayed there overnight.

When they got up in the morning, he said, "Let me leave now so I can return to my master." **24:55** But Rebekah's brother and her mother replied, "Let the girl stay with us a few more days, perhaps ten. Then she can go." **24:56** But he said to them, "Don't detain me – the LORD has granted me success on my journey. Let me leave now so I may return to my master." **24:57** Then they said, "We'll call the girl and find out what she wants to do." **24:58** So they called Rebekah and asked her, "Do you want to go with this man?" She replied, "I want to go."

24:59 So they sent their sister Rebekah on her way, accompanied by her female attendant, with Abraham's servant and his men. **24:60** They blessed Rebekah with these words:

"Our sister, may you become the mother of thousands of ten thousands! May your descendants possess the strongholds of their enemies."

24:61 Then Rebekah and her female servants mounted the camels and rode away with the man. So Abraham's servant took Rebekah and left.

24:62 Now Isaac came from Beer Lahai Roi, for he was living in the Negev. **24:63** He went out to relax in the field in the early evening. Then he looked up and saw that there were camels approaching. **24:64** Rebekah looked up and saw Isaac. She got down from her camel **24:65** and asked Abraham's servant, "Who is that man walking in the field toward us?" "That is my master," the servant replied. So she took her veil and covered herself.

24:66 The servant told Isaac everything that had happened. **24:67** Then Isaac brought Rebekah into his mother Sarah's tent. He took her as his wife and loved her. So Isaac was comforted after his mother's death.

The Death of Abraham

25:1 Abraham had taken another wife, named Keturah. **25:2** She bore him Zimran, Jokshan, Medan, Midian, Ishbak, and Shuah. **25:3** Jokshan became the father of Sheba and Dedan. The descendants of Dedan were the Asshurites, Letushites, and Leummites. **25:4** The sons of Midian were Ephah, Epher, Hanoch, Abida, and Eldaah. All these were descendants of Keturah.

25:5 Everything he owned Abraham left to his son Isaac. **25:6** But while he was still alive, Abraham gave gifts to the sons of his concubines and sent them off to the east, away from his son Isaac.

25:7 Abraham lived a total of 175 years. **25:8** Then Abraham breathed his last and died at a good old age, an old man who had lived a full life. He joined his ancestors. **25:9** His sons Isaac and Ishmael buried him in the cave of Machpelah near Mamre, in the field of Ephron the son of Zohar, the Hethite. **25:10** This was the field Abraham had purchased from the sons of Heth. There Abraham was buried with his wife Sarah. **25:11** After Abraham's death, God blessed his son Isaac. Isaac lived near Beer Lahai Roi.

The Sons of Ishmael

25:12 This is the account of Abraham's son Ishmael, whom Hagar the Egyptian, Sarah's servant, bore to Abraham.

25:13 These are the names of Ishmael's sons, by their names according to their records: Nebaioth (Ishmael's firstborn), Kedar, Adbeel, Mibsam, **25:14** Mishma, Dumah, Massa, **25:15** Hadad, Tema, Jetur, Naphish, and Kedemah. **25:16** These are the sons of Ishmael, and these are their names by their settlements and their camps – twelve princes according to their clans.

25:17 Ishmael lived a total of 137 years. He breathed his last and died; then he joined his ancestors. **25:18** His descendants settled from Havilah to Shur, which runs next to Egypt all the way to Asshur. They settled away from all their relatives.

Jacob and Esau

25:19 This is the account of Isaac, the son of Abraham.

Abraham became the father of Isaac. **25:20** When Isaac was forty years old, he married Rebekah, the daughter of Bethuel the Aramean from Paddan Aram and sister of Laban the Aramean.

25:21 Isaac prayed to the LORD on behalf of his wife because she was childless. The LORD answered his prayer, and his wife Rebekah became pregnant. **25:22** But the children struggled inside her, and she said, "If it is going to be like this, I'm not so sure I want to be pregnant!" So she asked the LORD, **25:23** and the LORD said to her,

"Two nations are in your womb,
and two peoples will be separated from within you.
One people will be stronger than the other,
and the older will serve the younger."

25:24 When the time came for Rebekah to give birth, there were twins in her womb. **25:25** The first came out reddish all over, like a hairy garment, so they named him Esau. **25:26** When his brother came out with his hand clutching Esau's heel, they named him Jacob. Isaac was sixty years old when they were born.

25:27 When the boys grew up, Esau became a skilled hunter, a man of the open fields, but Jacob was an even-tempered man, living in tents. **25:28** Isaac loved Esau because he had a taste for fresh game, but Rebekah loved Jacob.

25:29 Now Jacob cooked some stew, and when Esau came in from the open fields, he was famished. **25:30** So Esau said to Jacob, "Feed me some of the red stuff – yes, this red stuff – because I'm starving!" (That is why he was also called Edom.)

25:31 But Jacob replied, "First sell me your birthright." **25:32** "Look," said Esau, "I'm about to die! What use is the birthright to me?" **25:33** But Jacob said, "Swear an oath to me now." So Esau swore an oath to him and sold his birthright to Jacob.

25:34 Then Jacob gave Esau some bread and lentil stew; Esau ate and drank, then got up and went out. So Esau despised his birthright.

Isaac and Abimelech

26:1 There was a famine in the land, subsequent to the earlier famine that occurred in the days of Abraham. Isaac went to Abimelech king of the Philistines at Gerar. **26:2** The LORD appeared to Isaac and said, "Do not go down to Egypt; settle down in the land that I will point out to you. **26:3** Stay in this land. Then I will be with you and will bless you, for I will give all these lands to you and to your descendants, and I will fulfill the solemn promise I made to your father Abraham. **26:4** I will multiply your descendants so they will be as numerous as the stars in the sky, and I will give them all these lands. All the nations of the earth will pronounce blessings on one another using the name of your descendants. **26:5** All this will come to pass because Abraham obeyed me and kept my charge, my commandments, my statutes, and my laws." **26:6** So Isaac settled in Gerar.

26:7 When the men of that place asked him about his wife, he replied, "She is my sister." He was afraid to say, "She is my wife," for he thought to himself, "The men of this place will kill me to get Rebekah because she is very beautiful."

26:8 After Isaac had been there a long time, Abimelech king of the Philistines happened to look out a window and observed Isaac caressing his wife Rebekah. **26:9** So Abimelech summoned Isaac and said, "She is really your wife! Why did you say, 'She is my sister'?" Isaac replied, "Because I thought someone might kill me to get her."

26:10 Then Abimelech exclaimed, "What in the world have you done to us? One of the men might easily have had sexual relations with your wife, and you would have brought guilt on us!" **26:11** So Abimelech commanded all the people, "Whoever touches this man or his wife will surely be put to death."

26:12 When Isaac planted in that land, he reaped in the same year a hundred times what he had sown, because the LORD blessed him. **26:13** The man became wealthy. His influence continued to grow until he became very prominent. **26:14** He had so many sheep and cattle and such a great household of servants that the Philistines became jealous of him. **26:15** So the Philistines took dirt and filled up all the wells that his father's servants had dug back in the days of his father Abraham.

26:16 Then Abimelech said to Isaac, "Leave us and go elsewhere, for you have become much more powerful than we are." **26:17** So Isaac left there and settled in the Gerar Valley. **26:18** Isaac reopened the wells that had been dug back in the days of his father Abraham, for the Philistines had stopped them up after Abraham died. Isaac gave these wells the same names his father had given them.

26:19 When Isaac's servants dug in the valley and discovered a well with fresh flowing water there, **26:20** the herdsmen of Gerar quarreled with Isaac's herdsmen, saying, "The water belongs to us!" So Isaac named the well Esek because they argued with him about it. **26:21** His servants dug another well, but they quarreled over it too, so Isaac named it Sitnah. **26:22** Then he moved away from there and dug another well. They did not quarrel over it, so Isaac named it Rehoboth, saying, "For now the LORD has made room for us, and we will prosper in the land."

26:23 From there Isaac went up to Beer Sheba. **26:24** The LORD appeared to him that night and said, "I am the God of your father Abraham. Do not be afraid, for I am with you. I will bless you and multiply your descendants for the sake of my servant Abraham." **26:25** Then Isaac built an altar there and worshiped the LORD. He pitched his tent there, and his servants dug a well.

26:26 Now Abimelech had come to him from Gerar along with Ahuzzah his friend and Phicol the commander of his army. **26:27** Isaac asked them, "Why have you come to me? You hate me and sent me away from you." **26:28** They replied, "We could plainly see that the LORD is with you. So we decided there should be a pact between us – between us and you. Allow us to make a treaty with you **26:29** so that you will not do us any harm, just as we have not harmed you, but have always treated you well before sending you away in peace. Now you are blessed by the LORD."

26:30 So Isaac held a feast for them and they celebrated. **26:31** Early in the morning the men made a treaty with each other. Isaac sent them off; they separated on good terms.

26:32 That day Isaac's servants came and told him about the well they had dug. "We've found water," they reported. **26:33** So he named it Shibah; that is why the name of the city has been Beer Sheba to this day.

26:34 When Esau was forty years old, he married Judith the daughter of Beeri the Hittite, as well as Basemath the daughter of Elon the Hittite. **26:35** They caused Isaac and Rebekah great anxiety.

Jacob Cheats Esau out of the Blessing

27:1 When Isaac was old and his eyes were so weak that he was almost blind, he called his older son Esau and said to him, "My son!" "Here I am!" Esau replied. **27:2** Isaac said, "Since I am so old, I could die at any time. **27:3** Therefore, take your weapons – your quiver and your bow – and go out into the open fields and hunt down some wild game for me. **27:4** Then prepare for me some tasty food, the kind I love, and bring it to me. Then I will eat it so that I may bless you before I die."

27:5 Now Rebekah had been listening while Isaac spoke to his son Esau. When Esau went out to the open fields to hunt down some wild game and bring it back, **27:6** Rebekah said to her son Jacob, "Look, I overheard your father tell your brother Esau, **27:7** 'Bring me some wild game and prepare for me some tasty food. Then I will eat it and bless you in the presence of the LORD before I die.' **27:8** Now then, my son, do exactly what I tell you! **27:9** Go to the flock and get me two of the best young goats. I'll prepare them in a tasty way for your father, just the way he loves them. **27:10** Then you will take it to your father. Thus he will eat it and bless you before he dies."

27:11 "But Esau my brother is a hairy man," Jacob protested to his mother Rebekah, "and I have smooth skin! **27:12** My father may touch me! Then he'll think I'm mocking him and I'll bring a curse on myself instead of a blessing." **27:13** So his mother told him, "Any curse against you will fall on me, my son! Just obey me! Go and get them for me!"

27:14 So he went and got the goats and brought them to his mother. She prepared some tasty food, just the way his father loved it. **27:15** Then Rebekah took her older son Esau's best clothes, which she had with her in the house, and put them on her younger son Jacob. **27:16** She put the skins of the young goats on his hands and the smooth part of his neck. **27:17** Then she handed the tasty food and the bread she had made to her son Jacob.

27:18 He went to his father and said, "My father!" Isaac replied, "Here I am. Which are you, my son?" **27:19** Jacob said to his father, "I am Esau, your firstborn. I've done as you told me. Now sit up and eat some of my wild game so that you can bless me." **27:20** But Isaac asked his son, "How in the world did you find it so quickly, my son?" "Because the LORD your God brought it to me," he replied. **27:21** Then Isaac said to Jacob, "Come closer so I can touch you, my son, and know for certain if you really are my son Esau." **27:22** So Jacob went over to his father Isaac, who felt him and said, "The voice is Jacob's, but the hands are Esau's." **27:23** He did not recognize him because his hands were hairy, like his brother Esau's hands. So Isaac blessed Jacob. **27:24** Then he asked, "Are you really my son Esau?" "I am," Jacob replied. **27:25** Isaac said, "Bring some of the wild game for me to eat, my son. Then I will bless you." So Jacob brought it to him, and he ate it. He also brought him wine, and Isaac drank. **27:26** Then his father Isaac said to him, "Come here and kiss me, my son." **27:27** So Jacob went over and kissed him. When Isaac caught the scent of his clothing, he blessed him, saying,

"Yes, my son smells
like the scent of an open field
which the LORD has blessed.
27:28 May God give you
the dew of the sky
and the richness of the earth,
and plenty of grain and new wine.
27:29 May peoples serve you
and nations bow down to you.
You will be lord over your brothers,
and the sons of your mother will bow down to you.
May those who curse you be cursed,
and those who bless you be blessed."

27:30 Isaac had just finished blessing Jacob, and Jacob had scarcely left his father's presence, when his brother Esau returned from the hunt. **27:31** He also prepared some tasty food and brought it to his father. Esau said to him, "My father, get up and eat some of your son's wild game. Then you can bless me." **27:32** His father Isaac asked, "Who are you?" "I am your firstborn son," he replied, "Esau!" **27:33** Isaac began to shake violently and asked, "Then who else hunted game and brought it to me? I ate all of it just before you arrived, and I blessed him. He will indeed be blessed!"

27:34 When Esau heard his father's words, he wailed loudly and bitterly. He said to his father, "Bless me too, my father!" **27:35** But Isaac replied, "Your brother came in here deceitfully and took away your blessing." **27:36** Esau exclaimed, "'Jacob' is the right name for him! He has tripped me up two times! He took away my birthright, and now, look, he has taken away my blessing!" Then he asked, "Have you not kept back a blessing for me?"

27:37 Isaac replied to Esau, "Look! I have made him lord over you. I have made all his relatives his servants and provided him with grain and new wine. What is left that I can do for you, my son?" **27:38** Esau said to his father, "Do you have only that one blessing, my father? Bless me too!" Then Esau wept loudly.

27:39 So his father Isaac said to him,

"Indeed, your home will be
away from the richness of the earth,
and away from the dew of the sky above.
27:40 You will live by your sword
but you will serve your brother.
When you grow restless,
you will tear off his yoke
from your neck."

27:41 So Esau hated Jacob because of the blessing his father had given to his brother. Esau said privately, "The time of mourning for my father is near; then I will kill my brother Jacob!"

27:42 When Rebekah heard what her older son Esau had said, she quickly summoned her younger son Jacob and told him, "Look, your brother Esau is planning to get revenge by killing you. **27:43** Now then, my son, do what I say. Run away immediately to my brother Laban in Haran. **27:44** Live with him for a little while until your brother's rage subsides. **27:45** Stay there until your brother's anger against you subsides and he forgets what you did to him. Then I'll send someone to bring you back from there. Why should I lose both of you in one day?"

27:46 Then Rebekah said to Isaac, "I am deeply depressed because of these daughters of Heth. If Jacob were to marry one of these daughters of Heth who live in this land, I would want to die!"

28:1 So Isaac called for Jacob and blessed him. Then he commanded him, "You must not marry a Canaanite woman! **28:2** Leave immediately for

Paddan Aram! Go to the house of Bethuel, your mother's father, and find yourself a wife there, among the daughters of Laban, your mother's brother. **28:3** May the sovereign God bless you! May he make you fruitful and give you a multitude of descendants! Then you will become a large nation. **28:4** May he give you and your descendants the blessing he gave to Abraham so that you may possess the land God gave to Abraham, the land where you have been living as a temporary resident." **28:5** So Isaac sent Jacob on his way, and he went to Paddan Aram, to Laban son of Bethuel the Aramean and brother of Rebekah, the mother of Jacob and Esau.

28:6 Esau saw that Isaac had blessed Jacob and sent him off to Paddan Aram to find a wife there. As he blessed him, Isaac commanded him, "You must not marry a Canaanite woman." **28:7** Jacob obeyed his father and mother and left for Paddan Aram. **28:8** Then Esau realized that the Canaanite women were displeasing to his father Isaac. **28:9** So Esau went to Ishmael and married Mahalath, the sister of Nebaioth and daughter of Abraham's son Ishmael, along with the wives he already had.

Jacob's Dream at Bethel

28:10 Meanwhile Jacob left Beer Sheba and set out for Haran. **28:11** He reached a certain place where he decided to camp because the sun had gone down. He took one of the stones and placed it near his head. Then he fell asleep in that place **28:12** and had a dream. He saw a stairway erected on the earth with its top reaching to the heavens. The angels of God were going up and coming down it **28:13** and the LORD stood at its top. He said, "I am the LORD, the God of your grandfather Abraham and the God of your father Isaac. I will give you and your descendants the ground you are lying on. **28:14** Your descendants will be like the dust of the earth, and you will spread out to the west, east, north, and south. All the families of the earth will pronounce blessings on one another using your name and that of your descendants. **28:15** I am with you! I will protect you wherever you go and will bring you back to this land. I will not leave you until I have done what I promised you!"

28:16 Then Jacob woke up and thought, "Surely the LORD is in this place, but I did not realize it!" **28:17** He was afraid and said, "What an awesome place this is! This is nothing else than the house of God! This is the gate of heaven!"

28:18 Early in the morning Jacob took the stone he had placed near his head and set it up as a sacred stone. Then he poured oil on top of it. **28:19** He called that place Bethel, although the former name of the town was Luz. **28:20** Then Jacob made a vow, saying, "If God is with me and protects me on this journey I am taking and gives me food to eat and clothing to wear, **28:21** and I return safely to my father's home, then the LORD will become my God. **28:22** Then this stone that I have set up as a sacred stone will be the house of God, and I will surely give you back a tenth of everything you give me."

The Marriages of Jacob

29:1 So Jacob moved on and came to the land of the eastern people. **29:2** He saw in the field a well with three flocks of sheep lying beside it, because the flocks were watered from that well. Now a large stone covered the mouth of the well. **29:3** When all the flocks were gathered there, the shepherds would roll the stone off the mouth of the well and water the sheep. Then they would put the stone back in its place over the well's mouth.

29:4 Jacob asked them, "My brothers, where are you from?" They replied, "We're from Haran." **29:5** So he said to them, "Do you know Laban, the grandson of Nahor?" "We know him," they said. **29:6** "Is he well?" Jacob asked. They replied, "He is well. Now look, here comes his daughter Rachel with the sheep." **29:7** Then Jacob said, "Since it is still the middle of the day, it is not time for the flocks to be gathered. You should water the sheep and then go and let them graze some more." **29:8** "We can't," they said, "until all the flocks are gathered and the stone is rolled off the mouth of the well. Then we water the sheep."

29:9 While he was still speaking with them, Rachel arrived with her father's sheep, for she was tending them. **29:10** When Jacob saw Rachel, the daughter of his uncle Laban, and the sheep of his uncle Laban, he went over and rolled the stone off the mouth of the well and watered the sheep of his uncle Laban. **29:11** Then Jacob kissed Rachel and began to weep loudly. **29:12** When Jacob explained to Rachel that he was a relative of her father and the son of Rebekah, she ran and told her father. **29:13** When Laban heard this news about Jacob, his sister's son, he rushed out to meet him. He embraced him and kissed him and brought him to his house. Jacob told Laban how he was related to him. **29:14** Then Laban said to him, "You are indeed my own flesh and blood." So Jacob stayed with him for a month.

29:15 Then Laban said to Jacob, "Should you work for me for nothing because you are my relative? Tell me what your wages should be." **29:16** (Now Laban had two daughters; the older one was named Leah, and the younger one Rachel. **29:17** Leah's eyes were tender, but Rachel had a lovely figure and beautiful appearance.) **29:18** Since Jacob had fallen in love with Rachel, he said, "I'll serve you seven years in exchange for your younger daughter Rachel." **29:19** Laban replied, "I'd rather give her to you than to another man. Stay with me." **29:20** So Jacob worked for

seven years to acquire Rachel. But they seemed like only a few days to him because his love for her was so great.

29:21 Finally Jacob said to Laban, "Give me my wife, for my time of service is up. I want to have marital relations with her." **29:22** So Laban invited all the people of that place and prepared a feast. **29:23** In the evening he brought his daughter Leah to Jacob, and Jacob had marital relations with her. **29:24** (Laban gave his female servant Zilpah to his daughter Leah to be her servant.)

29:25 In the morning Jacob discovered it was Leah! So Jacob said to Laban, "What in the world have you done to me! Didn't I work for you in exchange for Rachel? Why have you tricked me?" **29:26** "It is not our custom here," Laban replied, "to give the younger daughter in marriage before the firstborn. **29:27** Complete my older daughter's bridal week. Then we will give you the younger one too, in exchange for seven more years of work."

29:28 Jacob did as Laban said. When Jacob completed Leah's bridal week, Laban gave him his daughter Rachel to be his wife. **29:29** (Laban gave his female servant Bilhah to

his daughter Rachel to be her servant.) **29:30** Jacob had marital relations with Rachel as well. He loved Rachel more than Leah, so he worked for Laban for seven more years.

The Family of Jacob

29:31 When the LORD saw that Leah was unloved, he enabled her to become pregnant while Rachel remained childless. **29:32** So Leah became pregnant and gave birth to a son. She named him Reuben, for she said, "The LORD has looked with pity on my oppressed condition. Surely my husband will love me now."

29:33 She became pregnant again and had another son. She said, "Because the LORD heard that I was unloved, he gave me this one too." So she named him Simeon.

29:34 She became pregnant again and had another son. She said, "Now this time my husband will show me affection, because I have given birth to three sons for him." That is why he was named Levi.

29:35 She became pregnant again and had another son. She said, "This time I will praise the LORD." That is why she named him Judah. Then she stopped having children.

30:1 When Rachel saw that she could not give Jacob children, she became jealous of her sister. She said to Jacob, "Give me children or I'll die!" **30:2** Jacob became furious with Rachel and exclaimed, "Am I in the place of God, who has kept you from having children?" **30:3** She replied, "Here is my servant Bilhah! Have sexual relations with her so that she can bear children for me and I can have a family through her."

30:4 So Rachel gave him her servant Bilhah as a wife, and Jacob had marital relations with her. **30:5** Bilhah became pregnant and gave Jacob a son. **30:6** Then Rachel said, "God has vindicated me. He has responded to my prayer and given me a son." That is why she named him Dan.

30:7 Bilhah, Rachel's servant, became pregnant again and gave Jacob another son. **30:8** Then Rachel said, "I have fought a desperate struggle with my sister, but I have won." So she named him Naphtali.

30:9 When Leah saw that she had stopped having children, she gave her servant Zilpah to Jacob as a wife. **30:10** Soon Leah's servant Zilpah gave Jacob a son. **30:11** Leah said, "How fortunate!" So she named him Gad.

30:12 Then Leah's servant Zilpah gave Jacob another son. **30:13** Leah said, "How happy I am, for women will call me happy!" So she named him Asher.

30:14 At the time of the wheat harvest Reuben went out and found some mandrake plants in a field and brought them to his mother Leah. Rachel said to Leah, "Give me some of your son's mandrakes." **30:15** But Leah replied, "Wasn't it enough that you've taken away my husband? Would you take away my son's mandrakes too?" "All right," Rachel said, "he may sleep with you tonight in exchange for your son's mandrakes." **30:16** When Jacob came in from the fields that evening, Leah went out to meet him and said, "You must sleep with me because I have paid for your services with my son's mandrakes." So he had marital relations with her that night. **30:17** God paid attention to Leah; she became pregnant and gave Jacob a son for the fifth time. **30:18** Then Leah said, "God has granted me a reward because I gave my servant to my husband as a wife." So she named him Issachar.

30:19 Leah became pregnant again and gave Jacob a son for the sixth time. **30:20** Then Leah said, "God has given me a good gift. Now my husband will honor me because I have given him six sons." So she named him Zebulun.

30:21 After that she gave birth to a daughter and named her Dinah.

30:22 Then God took note of Rachel. He paid attention to her and enabled her to become pregnant. **30:23** She became pregnant and gave birth to a son. Then she said, "God has taken away my shame." **30:24** She named him Joseph, saying, "May the LORD give me yet another son."

The Flocks of Jacob

30:25 After Rachel had given birth to Joseph, Jacob said to Laban, "Send me on my way so that I can go home to my own country. **30:26** Let me take my wives and my children whom I have acquired by working for you. Then I'll depart, because you know how hard I've worked for you."

30:27 But Laban said to him, "If I have found favor in your sight, please stay here, for I have learned by divination that the LORD has blessed me on account of you." **30:28** He added, "Just name your wages – I'll pay whatever you want."

30:29 "You know how I have worked for you," Jacob replied, "and how well your livestock have fared under my care. **30:30** Indeed, you had little before I arrived, but now your possessions have increased many times over. The LORD has blessed you wherever I worked. But now, how long must it be before I do something for my own family too?"

30:31 So Laban asked, "What should I give you?" "You don't need to give me a thing," Jacob replied, "but if you agree to this one condition, I will continue to care for your flocks and protect them: **30:32** Let me walk among all your flocks today and remove from them every speckled or spotted sheep, every dark-colored lamb, and the spotted or speckled goats. These animals will be my wages. **30:33** My integrity will testify for me later on. When you come to verify that I've taken only the wages we agreed on, if I have in my possession any goat that is not speckled or spotted or any sheep that is not dark-colored, it will be considered stolen." **30:34** "Agreed!" said Laban, "It will be as you say."

30:35 So that day Laban removed the male goats that were streaked or spotted, all the female goats that were speckled or spotted (all that had any white on them), and all the dark-colored lambs, and put them in the care of his sons. **30:36** Then he separated them from Jacob by a three-day journey, while Jacob was taking care of the rest of Laban's flocks.

30:37 But Jacob took fresh-cut branches from poplar, almond, and plane trees. He made white streaks by peeling them, making the white inner wood in the branches visible. **30:38** Then he set up the peeled branches in all the watering troughs where the flocks came to drink. He set up the branches in front of the flocks when they were in heat and came to drink. **30:39** When the sheep mated in front of the branches, they gave birth to young that were streaked or speckled or spotted. **30:40** Jacob removed these lambs, but he made the rest of the flock face the streaked and completely dark-colored animals in Laban's flock. So he made separate flocks for himself and did not mix them with Laban's flocks. **30:41** When the stronger females were in heat, Jacob would set up the branches in the troughs in front of the flock, so they would mate near the branches. **30:42** But if the animals were weaker, he did not set the branches there. So the weaker animals ended up belonging to Laban and the stronger animals to Jacob. **30:43** In this way Jacob became extremely prosperous. He owned large flocks, male and female servants, camels, and donkeys.

Jacob's Flight from Laban

31:1 Jacob heard that Laban's sons were complaining, "Jacob has taken everything that belonged to our father! He has gotten rich at our father's expense!" **31:2** When Jacob saw the look on Laban's face, he could tell his attitude toward him had changed.

31:3 The LORD said to Jacob, "Return to the land of your fathers and to your relatives. I will be with you." **31:4** So Jacob sent a message for Rachel and Leah to come to the field where his flocks were. **31:5** There he said to them, "I can tell that your father's attitude toward me has changed, but the God of my father has been with me. **31:6** You know that I've worked for your father as hard as I could, **31:7** but your father has humiliated me and changed my wages ten times. But God has not permitted him to do me any harm. **31:8** If he said, 'The speckled animals will be your wage,' then the entire flock gave birth to speckled offspring. But if he said, 'The streaked animals will be your wage,' then the entire flock gave birth to streaked offspring. **31:9** In this way God has snatched away your father's livestock and given them to me.

31:10 "Once during breeding season I saw in a dream that the male goats mating with the flock were streaked, speckled, and spotted. **31:11** In the dream the angel of God said to me, 'Jacob!' 'Here I am!' I replied. **31:12** Then he said, 'Observe that all the male goats mating with the flock are streaked, speckled, or spotted, for I have observed all that Laban has done to you. **31:13** I am the God of Bethel, where you anointed the sacred stone and made a vow to me. Now leave this land immediately and return to your native land.'"

31:14 Then Rachel and Leah replied to him, "Do we still have any portion or inheritance in our father's house? **31:15** Hasn't he treated us like foreigners? He not only sold us, but completely wasted the money paid for us! **31:16** Surely all the wealth that God snatched away from our father belongs to us and to our children. So now do everything God has told you."

31:17 So Jacob immediately put his children and his wives on the camels. **31:18** He took away all the livestock he had acquired in Paddan Aram and all his moveable property that he had accumulated. Then he set out toward the land of Canaan to return to his father Isaac. **31:19** While Laban had gone to shear his sheep, Rachel stole the household idols that belonged to her father. **31:20** Jacob also deceived Laban the Aramean by not telling him that he was leaving. **31:21** He left with all he owned. He quickly crossed the Euphrates River and headed for the hill country of Gilead.

31:22 Three days later Laban discovered Jacob had left. **31:23** So he took his relatives with him and pursued Jacob for seven days. He caught up with him in the hill country of Gilead. **31:24** But God came to Laban the Aramean in a dream at night and warned him, "Be careful that you neither bless nor curse Jacob."

31:25 Laban overtook Jacob, and when Jacob pitched his tent in the hill country of Gilead, Laban and his relatives set up camp there too. **31:26** "What have you done?" Laban demanded of Jacob. "You've deceived me and carried away my daughters as if they were captives of war! **31:27** Why did you run away secretly and deceive me? Why didn't you tell me so I could send you off with a celebration complete with singing, tambourines, and harps? **31:28** You didn't even allow me to kiss my daughters and my grandchildren good-bye. You have acted foolishly! **31:29** I have the power to do you harm, but the God of your father told me last night, 'Be careful that you neither bless nor curse Jacob.' **31:30** Now I understand that you have gone away because you longed desperately for your father's house. Yet why did you steal my gods?"

31:31 "I left secretly because I was afraid!" Jacob replied to Laban. "I thought you might take your daughters away from me by force. **31:32** Whoever has taken your gods will be put to death! In the presence of our relatives identify whatever is yours and take it." (Now Jacob did not know that Rachel had stolen them.)

31:33 So Laban entered Jacob's tent, and Leah's tent, and the tent of the two female servants, but he did not find the idols. Then he left Leah's tent and entered Rachel's. **31:34** (Now Rachel had taken the idols and put them inside her camel's saddle and sat on them.) Laban searched the whole tent, but did not find them. **31:35** Rachel said to her father, "Don't be angry, my lord. I cannot stand up in your presence because I am having my period." So he searched thoroughly, but did not find the idols.

31:36 Jacob became angry and argued with Laban. "What did I do wrong?" he demanded of Laban. "What sin of mine prompted you to chase after me in hot pursuit? **31:37** When you searched through all my goods, did you find anything that belonged to you? Set it here before my relatives and yours, and let them settle the dispute between the two of us! **31:38** "I have been with you for the past twenty years. Your ewes and female goats have not miscarried, nor have I eaten rams from your flocks. **31:39** Animals torn by wild beasts I never brought to you; I always absorbed the loss myself. You always made me pay for every missing animal, whether it was taken by day or at night. **31:40** I was consumed by scorching heat during the day and by piercing cold at night, and I went without sleep. **31:41** This was my lot for twenty years in your house: I worked like a slave for you – fourteen years for your two daughters and six years for your flocks, but you changed my wages ten times! **31:42** If the God of my father – the God of Abraham, the one whom Isaac fears – had not been with me, you would certainly have sent me away empty-handed! But God saw how I was oppressed and how hard I worked, and he rebuked you last night."

31:43 Laban replied to Jacob, "These women are my daughters, these children are my grandchildren, and these flocks are my flocks. All that you see belongs to me. But how can I harm these daughters of mine today or the children to whom they have given birth? **31:44** So now, come, let's make a formal agreement, you and I, and it will be proof that we have made peace."

31:45 So Jacob took a stone and set it up as a memorial pillar. **31:46** Then he said to his relatives, "Gather stones." So they brought stones and put them in a pile. They ate there by the pile of stones. **31:47** Laban called it Jegar Sahadutha, but Jacob called it Galeed.

31:48 Laban said, "This pile of stones is a witness of our agreement today." That is why it was called Galeed. **31:49** It was also called Mizpah because he said, "May the LORD watch between us when we are out of sight of one another. **31:50** If you mistreat my daughters or if you take wives besides my daughters, although no one else is with us, realize that God is witness to your actions."

31:51 "Here is this pile of stones and this pillar I have set up between me and you," Laban said to Jacob. **31:52** "This pile of stones and the pillar are reminders that I will not pass beyond this pile to come to harm you and that you will not pass beyond this pile and this pillar to come to harm me. **31:53** May the God of Abraham and the god of Nahor, the gods of their father, judge between us." Jacob took an oath by the God whom his father Isaac feared. **31:54** Then Jacob offered a sacrifice on the mountain and invited his relatives to eat the meal. They ate the meal and spent the night on the mountain.

31:55 (32:1) Early in the morning Laban kissed his grandchildren and his daughters goodbye and blessed them. Then Laban left and returned home.

Jacob Wrestles at Peniel

32:1 So Jacob went on his way and the angels of God met him. **32:2** When Jacob saw them, he exclaimed, "This is the camp of God!" So he named that place Mahanaim.

32:3 Jacob sent messengers on ahead to his brother Esau in the land of Seir, the region of Edom. **32:4** He commanded them, "This is what you must say to my lord Esau: 'This is what your servant Jacob says: I have been staying with Laban until now. **32:5** I have oxen, donkeys, sheep, and male and female servants. I have sent this message to inform my lord, so that I may find favor in your sight.'"

32:6 The messengers returned to Jacob and said, "We went to your brother Esau. He is coming to meet you and has four hundred men with him." **32:7** Jacob was very afraid and upset. So he divided the people who were with him into two camps, as well as the flocks, herds, and camels. **32:8** "If Esau attacks one camp," he thought, "then the other camp will be able to escape."

32:9 Then Jacob prayed, "O God of my father Abraham, God of my father Isaac, O LORD, you said to me, 'Return to your land and to your relatives and I will make you prosper.' **32:10** I am not worthy of all the faithful love you have shown your servant. With only my walking stick I crossed the Jordan, but now I have become two camps. **32:11** Rescue me, I pray, from the hand of my brother Esau, for I am afraid he will come and attack me, as well as the mothers with their children. **32:12** But you said, 'I will certainly make you prosper and will make your descendants like the sand on the seashore, too numerous to count.'"

32:13 Jacob stayed there that night. Then he sent as a gift to his brother Esau **32:14** two hundred female goats and twenty male goats, two hundred ewes and twenty rams, **32:15** thirty female camels with their young, forty cows and ten bulls, and twenty female donkeys and ten male donkeys. **32:16** He entrusted them to his servants, who divided them into herds. He told his servants, "Pass over before me, and keep some distance between one herd and the next." **32:17** He instructed the servant leading the first herd, "When my brother Esau meets you and asks, 'To whom do you belong? Where are you going? Whose herds are you driving?' **32:18** then you must say, 'They belong to your servant Jacob. They have been sent as a gift to my lord Esau. In fact Jacob himself is behind us.'"

32:19 He also gave these instructions to the second and third servants, as well as all those who were following the herds, saying, "You must say the same thing to Esau when you meet him. **32:20** You must also say, 'In fact your servant Jacob is behind us.'" Jacob thought, "I will first appease him by sending a gift ahead of me. After that I will meet him. Perhaps he will accept me." **32:21** So the gifts were sent on ahead of him while he spent that night in the camp.

32:22 During the night Jacob quickly took his two wives, his two female servants, and his eleven sons and crossed the ford of the Jabbok. **32:23** He took them and sent them across the stream along with all his possessions. **32:24** So Jacob was left alone. Then a man wrestled with him until daybreak. **32:25** When the man saw that he could not defeat Jacob, he struck the socket of his hip so the socket of Jacob's hip was dislocated while he wrestled with him.

32:26 Then the man said, "Let me go, for the dawn is breaking." "I will not let you go," Jacob replied, "unless you bless me." **32:27** The man asked him, "What is your name?" He answered, "Jacob." **32:28** "No longer will your name be Jacob," the man told him, "but Israel, because you have fought with God and with men and have prevailed."

32:29 Then Jacob asked, "Please tell me your name." "Why do you ask my name?" the man replied. Then he blessed Jacob there. **32:30** So Jacob named the place Peniel, explaining, "Certainly I have seen God face to face and have survived."

32:31 The sun rose over him as he crossed over Penuel, but he was limping because of his hip. **32:32** That is why to this day the Israelites do not eat the sinew which is attached to the socket of the hip, because he struck the socket of Jacob's hip near the attached sinew.

Jacob Meets Esau

33:1 Jacob looked up and saw that Esau was coming along with four hundred men. So he divided the children among Leah, Rachel, and the two female servants. **33:2** He put the servants and their children in front, with Leah and her children behind them, and Rachel and Joseph behind them. **33:3** But Jacob himself went on ahead of them, and he bowed toward the ground seven times as he approached his brother. **33:4** But Esau ran to meet him, embraced him, hugged his neck, and kissed him. Then they both wept. **33:5** When Esau looked up and saw the women and the children, he asked, "Who are these people with you?" Jacob replied, "The children whom God has graciously given your servant." **33:6** The female servants came forward with their children and bowed down. **33:7** Then Leah came forward with her children and they bowed down. Finally Joseph and Rachel came forward and bowed down.

33:8 Esau then asked, "What did you intend by sending all these herds to meet me?" Jacob replied, "To find favor in your sight, my lord." **33:9** But Esau said, "I have plenty, my brother. Keep what belongs to you." **33:10** "No, please take them," Jacob said. "If I have found favor in your sight, accept my gift from my hand. Now that I have seen your face and you have accepted me, it is as if I have seen the face of God. **33:11** Please take my present that was brought to you, for God has been generous to me and I have all I need." When Jacob urged him, he took it.

33:12 Then Esau said, "Let's be on our way! I will go in front of you." **33:13** But Jacob said to him, "My lord knows that the children are young, and that I have to look after the sheep and cattle that are nursing their young. If they are driven too hard for even a single day, all the animals will die. **33:14** Let my lord go on ahead of his servant. I will travel more slowly, at the pace of the herds and the children, until I come to my lord at Seir."

33:15 So Esau said, "Let me leave some of my men with you." "Why do that?" Jacob replied. "My lord has already been kind enough to me." **33:16** So that same day Esau made his way back to Seir. **33:17** But Jacob traveled to Succoth where he built himself a house and made shelters for his livestock. That is why the place was called Succoth.

33:18 After they left Paddan Aram, Jacob came safely to the city of Shechem in the land of Canaan, and he camped near the city. **33:19** Then he purchased the portion of the field where he had pitched his tent; he bought it from the sons of Hamor, Shechem's father, for a hundred pieces of money. **33:20** There he set up an altar and called it "The God of Israel is God."

Dinah and the Shechemites

34:1 Now Dinah, Leah's daughter whom she bore to Jacob, went to meet the young women of the land. **34:2** When Shechem son of Hamor the Hivite, who ruled that area, saw her, he grabbed her, forced himself on her, and sexually assaulted her. **34:3** Then he became very attached to Dinah, Jacob's daughter. He fell in love with the young woman and spoke romantically to her. **34:4** Shechem said to his father Hamor, "Acquire this young girl as my wife." **34:5** When Jacob heard that Shechem had violated his daughter Dinah, his sons were with the livestock in the field. So Jacob remained silent until they came in.

34:6 Then Shechem's father Hamor went to speak with Jacob about Dinah. **34:7** Now Jacob's sons had come in from the field when they heard the news. They were offended and very angry because Shechem had disgraced Israel by sexually assaulting Jacob's daughter, a crime that should not be committed.

34:8 But Hamor made this appeal to them: "My son Shechem is in love with your daughter. Please give her to him as his wife. **34:9** Intermarry with us. Let us marry your daughters, and take our daughters as wives for yourselves. **34:10** You may live among us, and the land will be open to you. Live in it, travel freely in it, and acquire property in it." **34:11** Then Shechem said to Dinah's father and brothers, "Let me find favor in your sight, and whatever you require of me I'll give. **34:12** You can make the bride price and the gift I must bring very expensive, and I'll give whatever you ask of me. Just give me the young woman as my wife!"

34:13 Jacob's sons answered Shechem and his father Hamor deceitfully when they spoke because Shechem had violated their sister Dinah. **34:14** They said to them, "We cannot give our sister to a man who is not circumcised, for it would be a disgrace to us. **34:15** We will give you our consent on this one condition: You must become like us by circumcising all your males. **34:16** Then we will give you our daughters to marry, and we will take your daughters as wives for ourselves, and we will live among you and become one people. **34:17** But if you do not agree to our terms by being circumcised, then we will take our sister and depart."

34:18 Their offer pleased Hamor and his son Shechem. **34:19** The young man did not delay in doing what they asked because he wanted Jacob's daughter Dinah badly. (Now he was more important than anyone in his father's household.) **34:20** So Hamor and his son Shechem went to the gate of their city and spoke to the men of their city, **34:21** "These men are at peace with us. So let them live in the land and travel freely in it, for the land is wide enough for them. We will take their daughters for wives, and we will give them our daughters to marry. **34:22** Only on this one condition will these men consent to live with us and become one people: They demand that every male among us be circumcised just as they are circumcised. **34:23** If we do so, won't their livestock, their property, and all their animals become ours? So let's consent to their demand, so they will live among us."

34:24 All the men who assembled at the city gate agreed with Hamor and his son Shechem. Every male who assembled at the city gate was circumcised. **34:25** In three days, when they were still in pain, two of Jacob's sons, Simeon and Levi, Dinah's brothers, each took his sword and went to the unsuspecting city and slaughtered every male. **34:26** They killed Hamor and his son Shechem with the sword, took Dinah from Shechem's house, and left. **34:27** Jacob's sons killed them and looted the city because their sister had been violated. **34:28** They took their flocks, herds, and donkeys, as well as everything in the city and in the surrounding fields. **34:29** They captured as plunder all their wealth, all their little ones, and their wives, including everything in the houses.

34:30 Then Jacob said to Simeon and Levi, "You have brought ruin on me by making me a foul odor among the inhabitants of the land – among the Canaanites and the Perizzites. I am few in number; they will join forces against me and attack me, and both I and my family will be destroyed!" **34:31** But Simeon and Levi replied, "Should he treat our sister like a common prostitute?"

The Return to Bethel

35:1 Then God said to Jacob, "Go up at once to Bethel and live there. Make an altar there to God, who appeared to you when you fled from your brother Esau." **35:2** So Jacob told his household and all who were with him, "Get rid of the foreign gods you have among you. Purify yourselves and change your clothes. **35:3** Let us go up at once to Bethel. Then I will make an altar there to God, who responded to me in my time of distress and has been with me wherever I went."

35:4 So they gave Jacob all the foreign gods that were in their possession and the rings that were in their ears. Jacob buried them under the oak near Shechem **35:5** and they started on their journey. The surrounding cities were afraid of God, and they did not pursue the sons of Jacob.

35:6 Jacob and all those who were with him arrived at Luz (that is, Bethel) in the land of Canaan. **35:7** He built an altar there and named the place El Bethel because there God had revealed himself to him when he was fleeing from his brother. **35:8** (Deborah, Rebekah's nurse, died and was buried under the oak below Bethel; thus it was named Oak of Weeping.) **35:9** God appeared to Jacob again after he returned from Paddan Aram and blessed him. **35:10** God said to him, "Your name is Jacob, but your name will no longer be called Jacob; Israel will be your name." So God named him Israel. **35:11** Then God said to him, "I am the sovereign God. Be fruitful and multiply! A nation – even a company of nations – will descend from you; kings will be among your descendants! **35:12** The land I gave to Abraham and Isaac I will give to you. To your descendants I will also give this land." **35:13** Then God went up from the place where he spoke with him. **35:14** So Jacob set up a sacred stone pillar in the place where God spoke with him. He poured out a drink offering on it, and then he poured oil on it. **35:15** Jacob named the place where God spoke with him Bethel.

35:16 They traveled on from Bethel, and when Ephrath was still some distance away, Rachel went into labor – and her labor was hard. **35:17** When her labor was at its hardest, the midwife said to her, "Don't be afraid, for you are having another son." **35:18** With her dying breath, she named him Ben-Oni. But his father called him Benjamin instead. **35:19** So Rachel died and was buried on the way to Ephrath (that is, Bethlehem). **35:20** Jacob set up a marker over her grave; it is the Marker of Rachel's Grave to this day.

35:21 Then Israel traveled on and pitched his tent beyond Migdal Eder. **35:22** While Israel was living in that land, Reuben had sexual relations with Bilhah, his father's concubine, and Israel heard about it.

Jacob had twelve sons:

35:23 The sons of Leah were Reuben, Jacob's firstborn, as well as Simeon, Levi, Judah, Issachar, and Zebulun.

35:24 The sons of Rachel were Joseph and Benjamin.

35:25 The sons of Bilhah, Rachel's servant, were Dan and Naphtali.

35:26 The sons of Zilpah, Leah's servant, were Gad and Asher.

These were the sons of Jacob who were born to him in Paddan Aram.

35:27 So Jacob came back to his father Isaac in Mamre, to Kiriath Arba (that is, Hebron), where Abraham and Isaac had stayed. **35:28** Isaac lived to be 180 years old. **35:29** Then Isaac breathed his last and joined his ancestors. He died an old man who had lived a full life. His sons Esau and Jacob buried him.

The Descendants of Esau

36:1 What follows is the account of Esau (also known as Edom).

36:2 Esau took his wives from the Canaanites: Adah the daughter of Elon the Hittite, and Oholibamah the daughter of Anah and granddaughter of Zibeon the Hivite, **36:3** in addition to Basemath the daughter of Ishmael and sister of Nebaioth.

36:4 Adah bore Eliphaz to Esau, Basemath bore Reuel, **36:5** and Oholibamah bore Jeush, Jalam, and Korah. These were the sons of Esau who were born to him in the land of Canaan.

36:6 Esau took his wives, his sons, his daughters, all the people in his household, his livestock, his animals, and all his possessions which he had acquired in the land of Canaan and went to a land some distance away from Jacob his brother **36:7** because they had too many possessions to be able to stay together and the land where they had settled was not able to support them because of their livestock. **36:8** So Esau (also known as Edom) lived in the hill country of Seir.

36:9 This is the account of Esau, the father of the Edomites, in the hill country of Seir.

36:10 These were the names of Esau's sons:

Eliphaz, the son of Esau's wife Adah, and Reuel, the son of Esau's wife Basemath.

36:11 The sons of Eliphaz were:

Teman, Omar, Zepho, Gatam, and Kenaz.

36:12 Timna, a concubine of Esau's son Eliphaz, bore Amalek to Eliphaz. These were the sons of Esau's wife Adah.

36:13 These were the sons of Reuel: Nahath, Zerah, Shammah, and Mizzah. These were the sons of Esau's wife Basemath.

36:14 These were the sons of Esau's wife Oholibamah the daughter of Anah and granddaughter of Zibeon: She bore Jeush, Jalam, and Korah to Esau.

36:15 These were the chiefs among the descendants of Esau, the sons of Eliphaz, Esau's firstborn: chief Teman, chief Omar, chief Zepho, chief Kenaz, **36:16** chief Korah, chief Gatam, chief Amalek. These were the chiefs descended from Eliphaz in the land of Edom; these were the sons of Adah.

36:17 These were the sons of Esau's son Reuel: chief Nahath, chief Zerah, chief Shammah, chief Mizzah. These were the chiefs descended from Reuel in the land of Edom; these were the sons of Esau's wife Basemath.

36:18 These were the sons of Esau's wife Oholibamah: chief Jeush, chief Jalam, chief Korah. These were the chiefs descended from Esau's wife Oholibamah, the daughter of Anah.

36:19 These were the sons of Esau (also known as Edom), and these were their chiefs.

36:20 These were the sons of Seir the Horite, who were living in the land: Lotan, Shobal, Zibeon, Anah, **36:21** Dishon, Ezer, and Dishan. These were the chiefs of the Horites, the descendants of Seir in the land of Edom.

36:22 The sons of Lotan were Hori and Homam; Lotan's sister was Timna.

36:23 These were the sons of Shobal: Alvan, Manahath, Ebal, Shepho, and Onam.

36:24 These were the sons of Zibeon: Aiah and Anah (who discovered the hot springs in the wilderness as he pastured the donkeys of his father Zibeon).

36:25 These were the children of Anah: Dishon and Oholibamah, the daughter of Anah.

36:26 These were the sons of Dishon: Hemdan, Eshban, Ithran, and Keran.

36:27 These were the sons of Ezer: Bilhan, Zaavan, and Akan.

36:28 These were the sons of Dishan: Uz and Aran.

36:29 These were the chiefs of the Horites: chief Lotan, chief Shobal, chief Zibeon, chief Anah, **36:30** chief Dishon, chief Ezer, chief Dishan. These were the chiefs of the Horites, according to their chief lists in the land of Seir.

36:31 These were the kings who reigned in the land of Edom before any king ruled over the Israelites:

36:32 Bela the son of Beor reigned in Edom; the name of his city was Dinhabah.

36:33 When Bela died, Jobab the son of Zerah from Bozrah reigned in his place.

36:34 When Jobab died, Husham from the land of the Temanites reigned in his place.

36:35 When Husham died, Hadad the son of Bedad, who defeated the Midianites in the land of Moab, reigned in his place; the name of his city was Avith.

36:36 When Hadad died, Samlah from Masrekah reigned in his place.

36:37 When Samlah died, Shaul from Rehoboth by the River reigned in his place.

36:38 When Shaul died, Baal-Hanan the son of Achbor reigned in his place.

36:39 When Baal-Hanan the son of Achbor died, Hadad reigned in his place; the name of his city was Pau. His wife's name was Mehetabel, the daughter of Matred, the daughter of Me-Zahab.

36:40 These were the names of the chiefs of Esau, according to their families, according to their places, by their names: chief Timna, chief Alvah, chief Jetheth, **36:41** chief Oholibamah, chief Elah, chief Pinon, **36:42** chief Kenaz, chief Teman, chief Mibzar, **36:43** chief Magdiel, chief Iram. These were the chiefs of Edom, according to their settlements in the land they possessed. This was Esau, the father of the Edomites.

Joseph's Dreams

37:1 But Jacob lived in the land where his father had stayed, in the land of Canaan.

37:2 This is the account of Jacob.

Joseph, his seventeen-year-old son, was taking care of the flocks with his brothers. Now he was a youngster working with the sons of Bilhah and Zilpah, his father's wives. Joseph brought back a bad report about them to their father.

37:3 Now Israel loved Joseph more than all his sons because he was a son born to him late in life, and he made a special tunic for him. **37:4** When Joseph's brothers saw that their father loved him more than any of them, they hated Joseph and were not able to speak to him kindly.

37:5 Joseph had a dream, and when he told his brothers about it, they hated him even more. **37:6** He said to them, "Listen to this dream I had: **37:7** There we were, binding sheaves of grain in the middle of the field. Suddenly my sheaf rose up and stood upright and your sheaves surrounded my sheaf and bowed down to it!" **37:8** Then his brothers asked him, "Do you really think you will rule over us or have dominion over us?" They hated him even more because of his dream and because of what he said.

37:9 Then he had another dream, and told it to his brothers. "Look," he said. "I had another dream. The sun, the moon, and eleven stars were bowing down to me." **37:10** When he told his father and his brothers, his father rebuked him, saying, "What is this dream that you had? Will I, your mother, and your brothers really come and bow down to you?" **37:11** His brothers were jealous of him, but his father kept in mind what Joseph said.

37:12 When his brothers had gone to graze their father's flocks near Shechem, **37:13** Israel said to Joseph, "Your brothers are grazing the flocks near Shechem. Come, I will send you to them." "I'm ready," Joseph replied. **37:14** So Jacob said to him, "Go now and check on the welfare of your brothers and of the flocks, and bring me word." So Jacob sent him from the valley of Hebron.

37:15 When Joseph reached Shechem, a man found him wandering in the field, so the man asked him, "What are you looking for?" **37:16** He replied, "I'm looking for my brothers. Please tell me where they are grazing their flocks." **37:17** The man said, "They left this area, for I heard them say, 'Let's go to Dothan.'" So Joseph went after his brothers and found them at Dothan.

37:18 Now Joseph's brothers saw him from a distance, and before he reached them, they plotted to kill him. **37:19** They said to one another, "Here comes this master of dreams! **37:20** Come now, let's kill him, throw him into one of the cisterns, and then say that a wild animal ate him. Then we'll see how his dreams turn out!"

37:21 When Reuben heard this, he rescued Joseph from their hands, saying, "Let's not take his life!" **37:22** Reuben continued, "Don't shed blood! Throw him into this cistern that is here in the wilderness, but don't lay a hand on him." (Reuben said this so he could rescue Joseph from them and take him back to his father.)

37:23 When Joseph reached his brothers, they stripped him of his tunic, the special tunic that he wore. **37:24** Then they took him and threw him into the cistern. (Now the cistern was empty; there was no water in it.)

37:25 When they sat down to eat their food, they looked up and saw a caravan of Ishmaelites coming from Gilead. Their camels were carrying spices, balm, and myrrh down to Egypt. **37:26** Then Judah said to his brothers, "What profit is there if we kill our brother and cover up his blood? **37:27** Come, let's sell him to the Ishmaelites, but let's not lay a hand on him, for after all, he is our brother, our own flesh." His brothers agreed. **37:28** So when the Midianite merchants passed by, Joseph's brothers pulled him out of the cistern and sold him to the Ishmaelites for twenty pieces of silver. The Ishmaelites then took Joseph to Egypt.

37:29 Later Reuben returned to the cistern to find that Joseph was not in it! He tore his clothes, **37:30** returned to his brothers, and said, "The boy isn't there! And I, where can I go?" **37:31** So they took Joseph's tunic, killed a young goat, and dipped the tunic in the blood. **37:32** Then they brought the special tunic to their father and said, "We found this. Determine now whether it is your son's tunic or not."

37:33 He recognized it and exclaimed, "It is my son's tunic! A wild animal has eaten him! Joseph has surely been torn to pieces!" **37:34** Then Jacob tore his clothes, put on sackcloth, and mourned for his son many days. **37:35** All his sons and daughters stood by him to console him, but he refused to be consoled. "No," he said, "I will go to the grave mourning my son." So Joseph's father wept for him.

37:36 Now in Egypt the Midianites sold Joseph to Potiphar, one of Pharaoh's officials, the captain of the guard.

Judah and Tamar

38:1 At that time Judah left his brothers and stayed with an Adullamite man named Hirah.

38:2 There Judah saw the daughter of a Canaanite man named Shua. Judah acquired her as a wife and had marital relations with her. **38:3** She became pregnant and had a son. Judah named him Er. **38:4** She became pregnant again and had another son, whom she named Onan. **38:5** Then she had yet another son, whom she named Shelah. She gave birth to him in Kezib.

38:6 Judah acquired a wife for Er his firstborn; her name was Tamar. **38:7** But Er, Judah's firstborn, was evil in the LORD's sight, so the LORD killed him.

38:8 Then Judah said to Onan, "Have sexual relations with your brother's wife and fulfill the duty of a brother-in-law to her so that you may raise up a descendant for your brother." **38:9** But Onan knew that the child would not be considered his. So whenever he had sexual relations with his brother's wife, he withdrew prematurely so as not to give his brother a descendant. **38:10** What he did was evil in the LORD's sight, so the LORD killed him too.

38:11 Then Judah said to his daughter-in-law Tamar, "Live as a widow in your father's house until Shelah my son grows up." For he thought, "I don't want him to die like his brothers." So Tamar went and lived in her father's house.

38:12 After some time Judah's wife, the daughter of Shua, died. After Judah was consoled, he left for Timnah to visit his sheepshearers, along with his friend Hirah the Adullamite. **38:13** Tamar was told, "Look, your father-in-law is going up to Timnah to shear his sheep." **38:14** So she removed her widow's clothes and covered herself with a veil. She wrapped herself and sat at the entrance to Enaim which is on the way to Timnah. (She did this because she saw that she had not been given to Shelah as a wife, even though he had now grown up.)

38:15 When Judah saw her, he thought she was a prostitute because she had covered her face. **38:16** He turned aside to her along the road and said, "Come on! I want to have sex with you." (He did not realize it was his daughter-in-law.) She asked, "What will you give me in exchange for having sex with you?" **38:17** He replied, "I'll send you a young goat from the flock." She asked, "Will you give me a pledge until you send it?" **38:18** He said, "What pledge should I give you?" She replied, "Your seal,

your cord, and the staff that's in your hand." So he gave them to her and had sex with her. She became pregnant by him. **38:19** She left immediately, removed her veil, and put on her widow's clothes.

38:20 Then Judah had his friend Hirah the Adullamite take a young goat to get back from the woman the items he had given in pledge, but Hirah could not find her. **38:21** He asked the men who were there, "Where is the cult prostitute who was at Enaim by the road?" But they replied, "There has been no cult prostitute here." **38:22** So he returned to Judah and said, "I couldn't find her. Moreover, the men of the place said, 'There has been no cult prostitute here.'" **38:23** Judah said, "Let her keep the things for herself. Otherwise we will appear to be dishonest. I did indeed send this young goat, but you couldn't find her."

38:24 After three months Judah was told, "Your daughter-in-law Tamar has turned to prostitution, and as a result she has become pregnant." Judah said, "Bring her out and let her be burned!" **38:25** While they were bringing her out, she sent word to her father-in-law: "I am pregnant by the man to whom these belong." Then she said, "Identify the one to whom the seal, cord, and staff belong." **38:26** Judah recognized them and said, "She is more upright than I am, because I wouldn't give her to Shelah my son." He did not have sexual relations with her again.

38:27 When it was time for her to give birth, there were twins in her womb. **38:28** While she was giving birth, one child put out his hand, and the midwife took a scarlet thread and tied it on his hand, saying, "This one came out first." **38:29** But then he drew back his hand, and his brother came out before him. She said, "How you have broken out of the womb!" So he was named Perez. **38:30** Afterward his brother came out – the one who had the scarlet thread on his hand – and he was named Zerah.

Joseph and Potiphar's Wife

39:1 Now Joseph had been brought down to Egypt. An Egyptian named Potiphar, an official of Pharaoh and the captain of the guard, purchased him from the Ishmaelites who had brought him there. **39:2** The LORD was with Joseph. He was successful and lived in the household of his Egyptian master. **39:3** His master observed that the LORD was with him and that the LORD made everything he was doing successful. **39:4** So Joseph found favor in his sight and became his personal attendant. Potiphar appointed Joseph overseer of his household and put him in charge of everything he owned. **39:5** From the time Potiphar appointed him over his household and over all that he owned, the LORD blessed the Egyptian's household for Joseph's sake. The blessing of the LORD was on everything that he had, both in his house and in his fields. **39:6** So Potiphar left everything he had in Joseph's care; he gave no thought to anything except the food he ate.

Now Joseph was well built and good-looking. **39:7** Soon after these things, his master's wife took notice of Joseph and said, "Have sex with me." **39:8** But he refused, saying to his master's wife, "Look, my master does not give any thought to his household with me here, and everything that he owns he has put into my care. **39:9** There is no one greater in this household than I am. He has withheld nothing from me except you because you are his wife. So how could I do such a great evil and sin against God?" **39:10** Even though she continued to speak to Joseph day after day, he did not respond to her invitation to have sex with her.

39:11 One day he went into the house to do his work when none of the household servants were there in the house. **39:12** She grabbed him by his outer garment, saying, "Have sex with me!" But he left his outer garment in her hand and ran outside. **39:13** When she saw that he had left his outer garment in her hand and had run outside, **39:14** she called for her household servants and said to them, "See, my husband brought in a Hebrew man to us to humiliate us. He tried to have sex with me, but I screamed loudly. **39:15** When he heard me raise my voice and scream, he left his outer garment beside me and ran outside."

39:16 So she laid his outer garment beside her until his master came home. **39:17** This is what she said to him: "That Hebrew slave you brought to us tried to humiliate me, **39:18** but when I raised my voice and screamed, he left his outer garment and ran outside."

39:19 When his master heard his wife say, "This is the way your slave treated me," he became furious. **39:20** Joseph's master took him and threw him into the prison, the place where the king's prisoners were confined. So he was there in the prison.

39:21 But the LORD was with Joseph and showed him kindness. He granted him favor in the sight of the prison warden. **39:22** The warden put all the prisoners under Joseph's care. He was in charge of whatever they were doing. **39:23** The warden did not concern himself with anything that was in Joseph's care because the LORD was with him and whatever he was doing the LORD was making successful.

The Cupbearer and the Baker

40:1 After these things happened, the cupbearer to the king of Egypt and the royal baker offended their master, the king of Egypt. **40:2** Pharaoh was enraged with his two officials, the cupbearer and the baker, **40:3** so he imprisoned them in the house of the captain of the guard in the same facility where Joseph was confined. **40:4** The captain of the guard appointed Joseph to be their attendant, and he served them.

They spent some time in custody. **40:5** Both of them, the cupbearer and the baker of the king of Egypt, who were confined in the prison, had a dream the same night. Each man's dream had its own meaning. **40:6** When Joseph came to them in the morning, he saw that they were looking depressed. **40:7** So he asked Pharaoh's officials, who were with him in custody in his master's house, "Why do you look so sad today?" **40:8** They told him, "We both had dreams, but there is no one to interpret them." Joseph responded, "Don't interpretations belong to God? Tell them to me."

40:9 So the chief cupbearer told his dream to Joseph: "In my dream, there was a vine in front of me. **40:10** On the vine there were three branches. As it budded, its blossoms opened and its clusters ripened into grapes. **40:11** Now Pharaoh's cup was in my hand, so I took the grapes, squeezed them into his cup, and put the cup in Pharaoh's hand."

40:12 "This is its meaning," Joseph said to him. "The three branches represent three days. **40:13** In three more days Pharaoh will reinstate you and restore you to your office. You will put Pharaoh's cup in his hand, just as you did before when you were cupbearer. **40:14** But remember me when it goes well for you, and show me kindness. Make mention of me to Pharaoh and bring me out of this prison, **40:15** for I really was kidnapped from the land of the Hebrews and I have done nothing wrong here for which they should put me in a dungeon."

40:16 When the chief baker saw that the interpretation of the first dream was favorable, he said to Joseph, "I also appeared in my dream and there were three baskets of white bread on my head. **40:17** In the top basket there were baked goods of every kind for Pharaoh, but the birds were eating them from the basket that was on my head."

40:18 Joseph replied, "This is its meaning: The three baskets represent three days. **40:19** In three more days Pharaoh will decapitate you and impale you on a pole. Then the birds will eat your flesh from you."

40:20 On the third day it was Pharaoh's birthday, so he gave a feast for all his servants.

He "lifted up" the head of the chief cupbearer and the head of the chief baker in the midst of his servants. **40:21** He restored the chief cupbearer to his former position so that he placed the cup in Pharaoh's hand, **40:22** but the chief baker he impaled, just as Joseph had predicted. **40:23** But the chief cupbearer did not remember Joseph – he forgot him.

Joseph's Rise to Power

41:1 At the end of two full years Pharaoh had a dream. As he was standing by the Nile, **41:2** seven fine-looking, fat cows were coming up out of the Nile, and they grazed in the reeds. **41:3** Then seven bad-looking, thin cows were coming up after them from the Nile, and they stood beside the other cows at the edge of the river. **41:4** The bad-looking, thin cows ate the seven fine-looking, fat cows. Then Pharaoh woke up.

41:5 Then he fell asleep again and had a second dream: There were seven heads of grain growing on one stalk, healthy and good. **41:6** Then seven heads of grain, thin and burned by the east wind, were sprouting up after them. **41:7** The thin heads swallowed up the seven healthy and full heads. Then Pharaoh woke up and realized it was a dream.

41:8 In the morning he was troubled, so he called for all the diviner-priests of Egypt and all its wise men. Pharaoh told them his dreams, but no one could interpret them for him. **41:9** Then the chief cupbearer said to Pharaoh, "Today I recall my failures. **41:10** Pharaoh was enraged with his servants, and he put me in prison in the house of the captain of the guards – me and the chief baker. **41:11** We each had a dream one night; each of us had a dream with its own meaning. **41:12** Now a young man, a Hebrew, a servant of the captain of the guards, was with us there. We told him our dreams, and he interpreted the meaning of each of our respective dreams for us. **41:13** It happened just as he had said to us – Pharaoh restored me to my office, but he impaled the baker."

41:14 Then Pharaoh summoned Joseph. So they brought him quickly out of the dungeon; he shaved himself, changed his clothes, and came before Pharaoh. **41:15** Pharaoh said to Joseph, "I had a dream, and there is no one who can interpret it. But I have heard about you, that you can interpret dreams." **41:16** Joseph replied to Pharaoh, "It is not within my power, but God will speak concerning the welfare of Pharaoh."

41:17 Then Pharaoh said to Joseph, "In my dream I was standing by the edge of the Nile. **41:18** Then seven fat and fine-looking cows were coming up out of the Nile, and they grazed in the reeds. **41:19** Then seven other cows came up after them; they were scrawny, very bad-looking, and lean. I had never seen such bad-looking cows as these in all the land of Egypt! **41:20** The lean, bad-looking cows ate up the seven fat cows. **41:21** When they had eaten them, no one would have known that they had done so, for they were just as bad-looking as before. Then I woke up. **41:22** I also saw in my dream seven heads of grain growing on one stalk, full and good. **41:23** Then seven heads of grain, withered and thin and burned with the east wind, were sprouting up after them. **41:24** The thin heads of grain swallowed up the seven good heads of grain. So I told all this to the diviner-priests, but no one could tell me its meaning."

41:25 Then Joseph said to Pharaoh, "Both dreams of Pharaoh have the same meaning. God has revealed to Pharaoh what he is about to do. **41:26** The seven good cows represent seven years, and the seven good heads of grain represent seven years. Both dreams have the same meaning. **41:27** The seven lean, bad-looking cows that came up after them represent seven years, as do the seven empty heads of grain burned with the east wind. They represent seven years of famine. **41:28** This is just what I told Pharaoh: God has shown Pharaoh what he is about to do. **41:29** Seven years of great abundance are coming throughout the whole land of Egypt. **41:30** But seven years of famine will occur after them, and all the abundance will be forgotten in the land of Egypt. The famine will devastate the land. **41:31** The previous abundance of the land will not be remembered because of the famine that follows, for the famine will be very severe. **41:32** The dream was repeated to Pharaoh because the matter has been decreed by God, and God will make it happen soon.

41:33 "So now Pharaoh should look for a wise and discerning man and give him authority over all the land of Egypt. **41:34** Pharaoh should do this – he should appoint officials throughout the land to collect one-fifth of the produce of the land of Egypt during the seven years of abundance. **41:35** They should gather all the excess food during these good years that are coming. By Pharaoh's authority they should store up grain so the cities will have food, and they should preserve it. **41:36** This food should be held in storage for the land in preparation for the seven years of famine that will occur throughout the land of Egypt. In this way the land will survive the famine."

41:37 This advice made sense to Pharaoh and all his officials. **41:38** So Pharaoh asked his officials, "Can we find a man like Joseph, one in whom the Spirit of God is present?" **41:39** So Pharaoh said to Joseph, "Because God has enabled you to know all this, there is no one as wise and discerning as you are! **41:40** You will oversee my household, and all my people will submit to your commands. Only I, the king, will be greater than you.

41:41 "See here," Pharaoh said to Joseph, "I place you in authority over all the land of Egypt." **41:42** Then Pharaoh took his signet ring from his own hand and put it on Joseph's. He clothed him with fine linen clothes and put a gold chain around his neck. **41:43** Pharaoh had him ride in the chariot used by his second-in-command, and they cried out before him, "Kneel down!" So he placed him over all the land of Egypt. **41:44** Pharaoh also said to Joseph, "I am Pharaoh, but without your permission no one will move his hand or his foot in all the land of Egypt." **41:45** Pharaoh gave Joseph the name Zaphenath-Paneah. He also gave him Asenath daughter of Potiphera, priest of On, to be his wife. So Joseph took charge of all the land of Egypt.

41:46 Now Joseph was 30 years old when he began serving Pharaoh king of Egypt. Joseph was commissioned by Pharaoh and was in charge of all the land of Egypt. **41:47** During the seven years of abundance the land produced large, bountiful harvests. **41:48** Joseph collected all the excess food in the land of Egypt during the seven years and stored it in the cities. In every city he put the food gathered from the fields around it. **41:49** Joseph stored up a vast amount of grain, like the sand of the sea, until he stopped measuring it because it was impossible to measure.

41:50 Two sons were born to Joseph before the famine came. Asenath daughter of Potiphera, priest of On, was their mother. **41:51** Joseph named the firstborn Manasseh, saying, "Certainly God has made me forget all my trouble and all my father's house." **41:52** He named the second child Ephraim, saying, "Certainly God has made me fruitful in the land of my suffering."

41:53 The seven years of abundance in the land of Egypt came to an end. **41:54** Then the seven years of famine began, just as Joseph had predicted. There was famine in all the other lands, but throughout the land of Egypt there was food. **41:55** When all the land of Egypt experienced the famine, the people cried out to Pharaoh for food. Pharaoh said to all the people of Egypt, "Go to Joseph and do whatever he tells you."

41:56 While the famine was over all the earth, Joseph opened the storehouses and sold grain to the Egyptians. The famine was severe throughout the land of Egypt. **41:57** People from every country came to Joseph in Egypt to buy grain because the famine was severe throughout the earth.

Joseph's Brothers in Egypt

42:1 When Jacob heard there was grain in Egypt, he said to his sons, "Why are you looking at each other?" **42:2** He then said, "Look, I hear that there is grain in Egypt. Go down there and buy grain for us so that we may live and not die."

42:3 So ten of Joseph's brothers went down to buy grain from Egypt. **42:4** But Jacob did not send Joseph's brother Benjamin with his brothers, for he said, "What if some accident happens to him?" **42:5** So Israel's sons came to buy grain among the other travelers, for the famine was severe in the land of Canaan.

42:6 Now Joseph was the ruler of the country, the one who sold grain to all the people of the country. Joseph's brothers came and bowed down before him with their faces to the ground. **42:7** When Joseph saw his brothers, he recognized them, but he pretended to be a stranger to them and spoke to them harshly. He asked, "Where do you come from?" They answered, "From the land of Canaan, to buy grain for food."

42:8 Joseph recognized his brothers, but they did not recognize him. **42:9** Then Joseph remembered the dreams he had dreamed about them, and he said to them, "You are spies; you have come to see if our land is vulnerable!"

42:10 But they exclaimed, "No, my lord! Your servants have come to buy grain for food! **42:11** We are all the sons of one man; we are honest men! Your servants are not spies."

42:12 "No," he insisted, "but you have come to see if our land is vulnerable." **42:13** They replied, "Your servants are from a family of twelve brothers. We are the sons of one man in the land of Canaan. The youngest is with our father at this time, and one is no longer alive."

42:14 But Joseph told them, "It is just as I said to you: You are spies! **42:15** You will be tested in this way: As surely as Pharaoh lives, you will not depart from this place unless your youngest brother comes here. **42:16** One of you must go and get your brother, while the rest of you remain in prison. In this way your words may be tested to see if you are telling the truth. If not, then, as surely as Pharaoh lives, you are spies!" **42:17** He imprisoned them all for three days. **42:18** On the third day Joseph said to them, "Do as I say and you will live, for I fear God. **42:19** If you are honest men, leave one of your brothers confined here in prison while the rest of you go and take grain back for your hungry families. **42:20** But you must bring your youngest brother to me. Then your words will be verified and you will not die." They did as he said.

42:21 They said to one other, "Surely we're being punished because of our brother, because we saw how distressed he was when he cried to us for mercy, but we refused to listen. That is why this distress has come on us!" **42:22** Reuben said to them, "Didn't I say to you, 'Don't sin against the boy,' but you wouldn't listen? So now we must pay for shedding his blood!" **42:23** (Now they did not know that Joseph could understand them, for he was speaking through an interpreter.) **42:24** He turned away from them and wept. When he turned around and spoke to them again, he had Simeon taken from them and tied up before their eyes.

42:25 Then Joseph gave orders to fill their bags with grain, to return each man's money to his sack, and to give them provisions for the journey. His orders were carried out. **42:26** So they loaded their grain on their donkeys and left.

42:27 When one of them opened his sack to get feed for his donkey at their resting place, he saw his money in the mouth of his sack. **42:28** He said to his brothers, "My money was returned! Here it is in my sack!" They were dismayed; they turned trembling one to another and said, "What in the world has God done to us?"

42:29 They returned to their father Jacob in the land of Canaan and told him all the things that had happened to them, saying, **42:30** "The man, the lord of the land, spoke harshly to us and treated us as if we were spying on the land. **42:31** But we said to him, 'We are honest men; we are not spies! **42:32** We are from a family of twelve brothers; we are the sons of one father. One is no longer alive, and the youngest is with our father at this time in the land of Canaan.'

42:33 "Then the man, the lord of the land, said to us, 'This is how I will find out if you are honest men. Leave one of your brothers with me, and take grain for your hungry households and go. **42:34** But bring your youngest brother back to me so I will know that you are honest men and not spies. Then I will give your brother back to you and you may move about freely in the land.'"

42:35 When they were emptying their sacks, there was each man's bag of money in his sack! When they and their father saw the bags of money, they were afraid. **42:36** Their father Jacob said to them, "You are making me childless! Joseph is gone. Simeon is gone. And now you want to take Benjamin! Everything is against me."

42:37 Then Reuben said to his father, "You may put my two sons to death if I do not bring him back to you. Put him in my care and I will bring him back to you." **42:38** But Jacob replied, "My son will not go down there with you, for his brother is dead and he alone is left. If an accident happens to him on the journey you have to make, then you will bring down my gray hair in sorrow to the grave."

The Second Journey to Egypt

43:1 Now the famine was severe in the land. **43:2** When they finished eating the grain they had brought from Egypt, their father said to them, "Return, buy us a little more food."

43:3 But Judah said to him, "The man solemnly warned us, 'You will not see my face unless your brother is with you.' **43:4** If you send our brother with us, we'll go down and buy food for you. **43:5** But if you will not send him, we won't go down there because the man said to us, 'You will not see my face unless your brother is with you.'"

43:6 Israel said, "Why did you bring this trouble on me by telling the man you had one more brother?"

43:7 They replied, "The man questioned us thoroughly about ourselves and our family, saying, 'Is your father still alive? Do you have another brother?' So we answered him in this way. How could we possibly know that he would say, 'Bring your brother down'?"

43:8 Then Judah said to his father Israel, "Send the boy with me and we will go immediately. Then we will live and not die – we and you and our little ones. **43:9** I myself pledge security for him; you may hold me liable. If I do not bring him back to you and place him here before you, I will bear the blame before you all my life. **43:10** But if we had not delayed, we could have traveled there and back twice by now!"

43:11 Then their father Israel said to them, "If it must be so, then do this: Take some of the best products of the land in your bags, and take a gift down to the man – a little balm and a little honey, spices and myrrh, pistachios and almonds. **43:12** Take double the money with you; you must take back the money that was returned in the mouths of your sacks – perhaps it was an oversight. **43:13** Take your brother too, and go right away to the man. **43:14** May the sovereign God grant you mercy before the man so that he may release your other brother and Benjamin! As for me, if I lose my children I lose them."

43:15 So the men took these gifts, and they took double the money with them, along with Benjamin. Then they hurried down to Egypt and stood before Joseph. **43:16** When Joseph saw Benjamin with them, he said to the servant who was over his household, "Bring the men to the house. Slaughter an animal and prepare it, for the men will eat with me at noon." **43:17** The man did just as Joseph said; he brought the men into Joseph's house.

43:18 But the men were afraid when they were brought to Joseph's house. They said, "We are being brought in because of the money that was returned in our sacks last time. He wants to capture us, make us slaves, and take our donkeys!" **43:19** So they approached the man who was in charge of Joseph's household and spoke to him at the entrance to the house. **43:20** They said, "My lord, we did indeed come down the first time to buy food. **43:21** But when we came to the place where we spent the night, we opened our sacks and each of us found his money – the full amount – in the mouth of his sack. So we have returned it. **43:22** We have brought additional money with us to buy food. We do not know who put the money in our sacks!"

43:23 "Everything is fine," the man in charge of Joseph's household told them. "Don't be afraid. Your God and the God of your father has given you treasure in your sacks. I had your money." Then he brought Simeon out to them.

43:24 The servant in charge brought the men into Joseph's house. He gave them water, and they washed their feet. Then he gave food to their donkeys. **43:25** They got their gifts ready for Joseph's arrival at noon, for they had heard that they were to have a meal there.

43:26 When Joseph came home, they presented him with the gifts they had brought inside, and they bowed down to the ground before him. **43:27** He asked them how they were doing. Then he said, "Is your aging father well, the one you spoke about? Is he still alive?" **43:28** "Your servant our father is well," they replied. "He is still alive." They bowed down in humility.

43:29 When Joseph looked up and saw his brother Benjamin, his mother's son, he said, "Is this your youngest brother, whom you told me about?" Then he said, "May God be gracious to you, my son." **43:30** Joseph hurried out, for he was overcome by affection for his brother and was at the point of tears. So he went to his room and wept there.

43:31 Then he washed his face and came out. With composure he said, "Set out the food." **43:32** They set a place for him, a separate place for his brothers, and another for the Egyptians who were eating with him. (The Egyptians are not able to eat with Hebrews, for the Egyptians think it is disgusting to do so.) **43:33** They sat before him, arranged by order of birth, beginning with the firstborn and ending with the youngest. The men looked at each other in astonishment. **43:34** He gave them portions of the food set before him, but the portion for Benjamin was five times greater than the portions for any of the others. They drank with Joseph until they all became drunk.

The Final Test

44:1 He instructed the servant who was over his household, "Fill the sacks of the men with as much food as they can carry and put each man's money in the mouth of his sack. **44:2** Then put my cup – the silver cup – in the mouth of the youngest one's sack, along with the money for his grain." He did as Joseph instructed.

44:3 When morning came, the men and their donkeys were sent off. **44:4** They had not gone very far from the city when Joseph said to the servant who was over his household, "Pursue the men at once! When you overtake them, say to them, 'Why have you repaid good with evil? **44:5** Doesn't my master drink from this cup and use it for divination? You have done wrong!'"

44:6 When the man overtook them, he spoke these words to them. **44:7** They answered him, "Why does my lord say such things? Far be it from your servants to do such a thing! **44:8** Look, the money that we found in the mouths of our sacks we brought back to you from the land of Canaan. Why then would we steal silver or gold from your master's house? **44:9** If one of us has it, he will die, and the rest of us will become my lord's slaves!"

44:10 He replied, "You have suggested your own punishment! The one who has it will become my slave, but the rest of you will go free." **44:11** So each man quickly lowered his sack to the ground and opened it. **44:12** Then the man searched. He began with the oldest and finished with the youngest. The cup was found in Benjamin's sack! **44:13** They all tore their clothes! Then each man loaded his donkey, and they returned to the city.

44:14 So Judah and his brothers came back to Joseph's house. He was still there, and they threw themselves to the ground before him. **44:15** Joseph said to them, "What did you think you were doing? Don't you know that a man like me can find out things like this by divination?"

44:16 Judah replied, "What can we say to my lord? What can we speak? How can we clear ourselves? God has exposed the sin of your servants! We are now my lord's slaves, we and the one in whose possession the cup was found."

44:17 But Joseph said, "Far be it from me to do this! The man in whose hand the cup was found will become my slave, but the rest of you may go back to your father in peace."

44:18 Then Judah approached him and said, "My lord, please allow your servant to speak a word with you. Please do not get angry with your servant, for you are just like Pharaoh. **44:19** My lord asked his servants, 'Do you have a father or a brother?' **44:20** We said to my lord, 'We have an aged father, and there is a young boy who was born when our father was old. The boy's brother is dead. He is the only one of his mother's sons left, and his father loves him.'

44:21 "Then you told your servants, 'Bring him down to me so I can see him.' **44:22** We said to my lord, 'The boy cannot leave his father. If he leaves his father, his father will die.' **44:23** But you said to your servants, 'If your youngest brother does not come down with you, you will not see my face again.' **44:24** When we returned to your servant my father, we told him the words of my lord.

44:25 "Then our father said, 'Go back and buy us a little food.' **44:26** But we replied, 'We cannot go down there. If our youngest brother is with us, then we will go, for we won't be permitted to see the man's face if our youngest brother is not with us.'

44:27 "Then your servant my father said to us, 'You know that my wife gave me two sons. **44:28** The first disappeared and I said, "He has surely been torn to pieces." I have not seen him since. **44:29** If you take this one from me too and an accident happens to him, then you will bring down my gray hair in tragedy to the grave.'

44:30 "So now, when I return to your servant my father, and the boy is not with us – his very life is bound up in his son's life. **44:31** When he sees the boy is not with us, he will die, and your servants will bring down the gray hair of your servant our father in sorrow to the grave. **44:32** Indeed, your servant pledged security for the boy with my father, saying, 'If I do not bring him back to you, then I will bear the blame before my father all my life.'

44:33 "So now, please let your servant remain as my lord's slave instead of the boy. As for the boy, let him go back with his brothers. **44:34** For how can I go back to my father if the boy is not with me? I couldn't bear to see my father's pain."

The Reconciliation of the Brothers

45:1 Joseph was no longer able to control himself before all his attendants, so he cried out, "Make everyone go out from my presence!" No one remained with Joseph when he made himself known to his brothers. **45:2** He wept loudly; the Egyptians heard it and Pharaoh's household heard about it.

45:3 Joseph said to his brothers, "I am Joseph! Is my father still alive?" His brothers could not answer him because they were dumbfounded before him. **45:4** Joseph said to his brothers, "Come closer to me," so they came near. Then he said, "I am Joseph your brother, whom you sold into Egypt. **45:5** Now, do not be upset and do not be angry with yourselves because you sold me here, for God sent me ahead of you to preserve life! **45:6** For these past two years there has been famine in the land and for five more years there will be neither plowing nor harvesting. **45:7** God sent me ahead of you to preserve you on the earth and to save your lives by a great deliverance. **45:8** So now, it is not you who sent me here, but God. He has made me an adviser to Pharaoh, lord over all his household, and ruler over all the land of Egypt. **45:9** Now go up to my father quickly and tell him, 'This is what your son Joseph says: "God has made me lord of all Egypt. Come down to me; do not delay! **45:10** You will live in the land of Goshen, and you will be near me – you, your children, your grandchildren, your flocks, your herds, and everything you have. **45:11** I will provide you with food there because there will be five more years of famine. Otherwise you would become poor – you, your household, and everyone who belongs to you."' **45:12** You and my brother Benjamin can certainly see with your own eyes that I really am the one who speaks to you. **45:13** So tell my father about all my honor in Egypt and about everything you have seen. But bring my father down here quickly!"

45:14 Then he threw himself on the neck of his brother Benjamin and wept, and Benjamin wept on his neck. **45:15** He kissed all his brothers and wept over them. After this his brothers talked with him.

45:16 Now it was reported in the household of Pharaoh, "Joseph's brothers have arrived." It pleased Pharaoh and his servants. **45:17** Pharaoh said to Joseph, "Say to your brothers, 'Do this: Load your animals and go to the land of Canaan! **45:18** Get your father and your households and come to me! Then I will give you the best land in Egypt and you will eat the best of the land.' **45:19** You are also commanded to say, 'Do this: Take for yourselves wagons from the land of Egypt for your little ones and for your wives. Bring your father and come. **45:20** Don't worry about your belongings, for the best of all the land of Egypt will be yours.'"

45:21 So the sons of Israel did as he said. Joseph gave them wagons as Pharaoh had instructed, and he gave them provisions for the journey. **45:22** He gave sets of clothes to each one of them, but to Benjamin he gave three hundred pieces of silver and five sets of clothes. **45:23** To his father he sent the following: ten donkeys loaded with the best products of Egypt and ten female donkeys loaded with grain, food, and provisions for his father's journey. **45:24** Then he sent his brothers on their way and they left. He said to them, "As you travel don't be overcome with fear."

45:25 So they went up from Egypt and came to their father Jacob in the land of Canaan. **45:26** They told him, "Joseph is still alive and he is ruler over all the land of Egypt!" Jacob was stunned, for he did not believe them. **45:27** But when they related to him everything Joseph had said to them, and when he saw the wagons that Joseph had sent to transport him, their father Jacob's spirit revived. **45:28** Then Israel said, "Enough! My son Joseph is still alive! I will go and see him before I die."

The Family of Jacob goes to Egypt

46:1 So Israel began his journey, taking with him all that he had. When he came to Beer Sheba he offered sacrifices to the God of his father Isaac. **46:2** God spoke to Israel in a vision during the night and said, "Jacob, Jacob!" He replied, "Here I am!" **46:3** He said, "I am God, the God of your father. Do not be afraid to go down to Egypt, for I will make you into a great nation there. **46:4** I will go down with you to Egypt and I myself will certainly bring you back from there. Joseph will close your eyes."

46:5 Then Jacob started out from Beer Sheba, and the sons of Israel carried their father Jacob, their little children, and their wives in the wagons that Pharaoh had sent along to transport him. **46:6** Jacob and all his descendants took their livestock and the possessions they had acquired in the land of Canaan, and they went to Egypt. **46:7** He brought with him to Egypt his sons and grandsons, his daughters and granddaughters – all his descendants.

46:8 These are the names of the sons of Israel who went to Egypt – Jacob and his sons:

Reuben, the firstborn of Jacob.

46:9 The sons of Reuben:

Hanoch, Pallu, Hezron, and Carmi.

46:10 The sons of Simeon:

Jemuel, Jamin, Ohad, Jakin, Zohar,

and Shaul (the son of a Canaanite woman).

46:11 The sons of Levi:

Gershon, Kohath, and Merari.

46:12 The sons of Judah:

Er, Onan, Shelah, Perez, and Zerah

(but Er and Onan died in the land of Canaan).

The sons of Perez were Hezron and Hamul.

46:13 The sons of Issachar:

Tola, Puah, Jashub, and Shimron.

46:14 The sons of Zebulun:

Sered, Elon, and Jahleel.

46:15 These were the sons of Leah, whom she bore to Jacob in Paddan Aram, along with Dinah his daughter. His sons and daughters numbered thirty-three in all.

46:16 The sons of Gad:

Zephon, Haggi, Shuni, Ezbon, Eri, Arodi, and Areli.

46:17 The sons of Asher:

Imnah, Ishvah, Ishvi, Beriah, and Serah their sister.

The sons of Beriah were Heber and Malkiel.

46:18 These were the sons of Zilpah, whom Laban gave to Leah his daughter. She bore these to Jacob, sixteen in all.

46:19 The sons of Rachel the wife of Jacob:

Joseph and Benjamin.

46:20 Manasseh and Ephraim were born to Joseph in the land of Egypt. Asenath daughter of Potiphera, priest of On, bore them to him.

46:21 The sons of Benjamin:

Bela, Beker, Ashbel, Gera, Naaman, Ehi, Rosh, Muppim, Huppim and Ard.

46:22 These were the sons of Rachel who were born to Jacob, fourteen in all.

46:23 The son of Dan: Hushim.

46:24 The sons of Naphtali:

Jahziel, Guni, Jezer, and Shillem.

46:25 These were the sons of Bilhah, whom Laban gave to Rachel his daughter. She bore these to Jacob, seven in all.

46:26 All the direct descendants of Jacob who went to Egypt with him were sixty-six in number. (This number does not include the wives of Jacob's sons.) **46:27** Counting the two sons of Joseph who were born to him in Egypt, all the people of the household of Jacob who were in Egypt numbered seventy.

46:28 Jacob sent Judah before him to Joseph to accompany him to Goshen. So they came to the land of Goshen. **46:29** Joseph harnessed his chariot and went up to meet his father Israel in Goshen. When he met him, he hugged his neck and wept on his neck for quite some time. **46:30** Israel said to Joseph, "Now let me die since I have seen your face and know that you are still alive." **46:31** Then Joseph said to his brothers and his father's household, "I will go up and tell Pharaoh, 'My brothers and my father's household who were in the land of Canaan have come to me. **46:32** The men are shepherds; they take care of livestock. They have brought their flocks and their herds and all that they have.' **46:33** Pharaoh will summon you and say, 'What is your occupation?' **46:34** Tell him, 'Your servants have taken care of cattle from our youth until now, both we and our fathers,' so that you may live in the land of Goshen, for everyone who takes care of sheep is disgusting to the Egyptians."

Joseph's Wise Administration

47:1 Joseph went and told Pharaoh, "My father, my brothers, their flocks and herds, and all that they own have arrived from the land of Canaan. They are now in the land of Goshen." **47:2** He took five of his brothers and introduced them to Pharaoh.

47:3 Pharaoh said to Joseph's brothers, "What is your occupation?" They said to Pharaoh, "Your servants take care of flocks, just as our ancestors did." **47:4** Then they said to Pharaoh, "We have come to live as temporary residents in the land. There is no pasture for your servants' flocks because the famine is severe in the land of Canaan. So now, please let your servants live in the land of Goshen."

47:5 Pharaoh said to Joseph, "Your father and your brothers have come to you. **47:6** The land of Egypt is before you; settle your father and your brothers in the best region of the land. They may live in the land of Goshen. If you know of any highly capable men among them, put them in charge of my livestock."

47:7 Then Joseph brought in his father Jacob and presented him before Pharaoh. Jacob blessed Pharaoh. **47:8** Pharaoh said to Jacob, "How long have you lived?" **47:9** Jacob said to Pharaoh, "All the years of my travels are 130. All the years of my life have been few and painful; the years of my travels are not as long as those of my ancestors." **47:10** Then Jacob blessed Pharaoh and went out from his presence.

47:11 So Joseph settled his father and his brothers. He gave them territory in the land of Egypt, in the best region of the land, the land of Rameses, just as Pharaoh had commanded. **47:12** Joseph also provided food for his father, his brothers, and all his father's household, according to the number of their little children.

47:13 But there was no food in all the land because the famine was very severe; the land of Egypt and the land of Canaan wasted away because of the famine. **47:14** Joseph collected all the money that could be found in the land of Egypt and in the land of Canaan as payment for the grain they were buying. Then Joseph brought the money into Pharaoh's palace. **47:15** When the money from the lands of Egypt and Canaan was used up, all the Egyptians came to Joseph and said, "Give us food! Why should we die before your very eyes because our money has run out?"

47:16 Then Joseph said, "If your money is gone, bring your livestock, and I will give you food in exchange for your livestock." **47:17** So they brought their livestock to Joseph, and Joseph gave them food in exchange for their horses, the livestock of their flocks and herds, and their donkeys. He got them through that year by giving them food in exchange for livestock.

47:18 When that year was over, they came to him the next year and said to him, "We cannot hide from our lord that the money is used up and the livestock and the animals belong to our lord. Nothing remains before our lord except our bodies and our land. **47:19** Why should we die before your very eyes, both we and our land? Buy us and our land in exchange for food, and we, with our land, will become Pharaoh's slaves. Give us seed that we may live and not die. Then the land will not become desolate."

47:20 So Joseph bought all the land of Egypt for Pharaoh. Each of the Egyptians sold his field, for the famine was severe. So the land became Pharaoh's. **47:21** Joseph made all the people slaves from one end of Egypt's border to the other end of it. **47:22** But he did not purchase the land of the priests because the priests had an allotment from Pharaoh and they ate from their allotment that Pharaoh gave them. That is why they did not sell their land.

47:23 Joseph said to the people, "Since I have bought you and your land today for Pharaoh, here is seed for you. Cultivate the land. **47:24** When you gather in the crop, give one-fifth of it to Pharaoh, and the rest will be yours for seed for the fields and for you to eat, including those in your households and your little children." **47:25** They replied, "You have saved our lives! You are showing us favor, and we will be Pharaoh's slaves."

47:26 So Joseph made it a statute, which is in effect to this day throughout the land of Egypt: One-fifth belongs to Pharaoh. Only the land of the priests did not become Pharaoh's.

47:27 Israel settled in the land of Egypt, in the land of Goshen, and they owned land there. They were fruitful and increased rapidly in number.

47:28 Jacob lived in the land of Egypt seventeen years; the years of Jacob's life were 147 in all. **47:29** The time for Israel to die approached, so he called for his son Joseph and said to him, "If now I have found favor in your sight, put your hand under my thigh and show me kindness and faithfulness. Do not bury me in Egypt, **47:30** but when I rest with my fathers, carry me out of Egypt and bury me in their burial place." Joseph said, "I will do as you say."

47:31 Jacob said, "Swear to me that you will do so." So Joseph gave him his word. Then Israel bowed down at the head of his bed.

Manasseh and Ephraim

48:1 After these things Joseph was told, "Your father is weakening." So he took his two sons Manasseh and Ephraim with him. **48:2** When Jacob was told, "Your son Joseph has just come to you," Israel regained strength and sat up on his bed. **48:3** Jacob said to Joseph, "The sovereign God appeared to me at Luz in the land of Canaan and blessed me. **48:4** He said to me, 'I am going to make you fruitful and will multiply you. I will make you into a group of nations, and I will give this land to your descendants as an everlasting possession.'

48:5 "Now, as for your two sons, who were born to you in the land of Egypt before I came to you in Egypt, they will be mine. Ephraim and Manasseh will be mine just as Reuben and Simeon are. **48:6** Any children that you father after them will be yours; they will be listed under the names of their brothers in their inheritance. **48:7** But as for me, when I was returning from Paddan, Rachel died – to my sorrow – in the land of Canaan. It happened along the way, some distance from Ephrath. So I buried her there on the way to Ephrath" (that is, Bethlehem).

48:8 When Israel saw Joseph's sons, he asked, "Who are these?" **48:9** Joseph said to his father, "They are the sons God has given me in this place." His father said, "Bring them to me so I may bless them." **48:10** Now Israel's eyes were failing because of his age; he was not able to see well. So Joseph brought his sons near to him, and his father kissed them and embraced them. **48:11** Israel said to Joseph, "I never expected to see you again, but now God has allowed me to see your children too."

48:12 So Joseph moved them from Israel's knees and bowed down with his face to the ground. **48:13** Joseph positioned them; he put Ephraim on his right hand across from Israel's left hand, and Manasseh on his left hand across from Israel's right hand. Then Joseph brought them closer to his father. **48:14** Israel stretched out his right hand and placed it on Ephraim's head, although he was the younger. Crossing his hands, he put his left hand on Manasseh's head, for Manasseh was the firstborn.

48:15 Then he blessed Joseph and said,

"May the God before whom my fathers
Abraham and Isaac walked –
the God who has been my shepherd
all my life long to this day,
48:16 the Angel who has protected me
from all harm –
bless these boys.
May my name be named in them,
and the name of my fathers Abraham and Isaac.
May they grow into a multitude on the earth."

48:17 When Joseph saw that his father placed his right hand on Ephraim's head, it displeased him. So he took his father's hand to move it from Ephraim's head to Manasseh's head. **48:18** Joseph said to his father, "Not so, my father, for this is the firstborn. Put your right hand on his head."

48:19 But his father refused and said, "I know, my son, I know. He too will become a nation and he too will become great. In spite of this, his younger brother will be even greater and his descendants will become a multitude of nations." **48:20** So he blessed them that day, saying,

"By you will Israel bless, saying,
'May God make you like Ephraim and Manasseh.'"

So he put Ephraim before Manasseh.

48:21 Then Israel said to Joseph, "I am about to die, but God will be with you and will bring you back to the land of your fathers. **48:22** As one who is above your brothers, I give to you the mountain slope, which I took from the Amorites with my sword and my bow."

The Blessing of Jacob

49:1 Jacob called for his sons and said, "Gather together so I can tell you what will happen to you in the future.

49:2 "Assemble and listen, you sons of Jacob;
listen to Israel, your father.
49:3 Reuben, you are my firstborn,
my might and the beginning of my strength,
outstanding in dignity, outstanding in power.
49:4 You are destructive like water and will not excel,
for you got on your father's bed,
then you defiled it – he got on my couch!
49:5 Simeon and Levi are brothers,
weapons of violence are their knives!
49:6 O my soul, do not come into their council,
do not be united to their assembly, my heart,
for in their anger they have killed men,
and for pleasure they have hamstrung oxen.
49:7 Cursed be their anger, for it was fierce,
and their fury, for it was cruel.
I will divide them in Jacob,

and scatter them in Israel!

49:8 Judah, your brothers will praise you.
Your hand will be on the neck of your enemies,
your father's sons will bow down before you.
49:9 You are a lion's cub, Judah,
from the prey, my son, you have gone up.
He crouches and lies down like a lion;
like a lioness – who will rouse him?
49:10 The scepter will not depart from Judah,
nor the ruler's staff from between his feet,
until he comes to whom it belongs;
the nations will obey him.
49:11 Binding his foal to the vine,
and his colt to the choicest vine,
he will wash his garments in wine,
his robes in the blood of grapes.
49:12 His eyes will be dark from wine,
and his teeth white from milk.
49:13 Zebulun will live by the haven of the sea
and become a haven for ships;
his border will extend to Sidon.
49:14 Issachar is a strong-boned donkey
lying down between two saddlebags.
49:15 When he sees a good resting place,
and the pleasant land,
he will bend his shoulder to the burden
and become a slave laborer.
49:16 Dan will judge his people
as one of the tribes of Israel.
49:17 May Dan be a snake beside the road,
a viper by the path,
that bites the heels of the horse
so that its rider falls backward.
49:18 I wait for your deliverance, O LORD.
49:19 Gad will be raided by marauding bands,
but he will attack them at their heels.
49:20 Asher's food will be rich,
and he will provide delicacies to royalty.
49:21 Naphtali is a free running doe,
he speaks delightful words.
49:22 Joseph is a fruitful bough,
a fruitful bough near a spring
whose branches climb over the wall.
49:23 The archers will attack him,
they will shoot at him and oppose him.
49:24 But his bow will remain steady,
and his hands will be skillful;
because of the hands of the Mighty One of Jacob,
because of the Shepherd, the Rock of Israel,
49:25 because of the God of your father,
who will help you,
because of the sovereign God,
who will bless you
with blessings from the sky above,
blessings from the deep that lies below,
and blessings of the breasts and womb.
49:26 The blessings of your father are greater
than the blessings of the eternal mountains
or the desirable things of the age-old hills.
They will be on the head of Joseph
and on the brow of the prince of his brothers.
49:27 Benjamin is a ravenous wolf;
in the morning devouring the prey,
and in the evening dividing the plunder."

49:28 These are the twelve tribes of Israel. This is what their father said to them when he blessed them. He gave each of them an appropriate blessing.
49:29 Then he instructed them, "I am about to go to my people. Bury me with my fathers in the cave in the field of Ephron the Hittite. **49:30** It is the cave in the field of Machpelah, near Mamre in the land of Canaan, which Abraham bought for a burial plot from Ephron the Hittite. **49:31** There they buried Abraham and his wife Sarah; there they buried Isaac and his wife Rebekah; and there I buried Leah. **49:32** The field and the cave in it were acquired from the sons of Heth."
49:33 When Jacob finished giving these instructions to his sons, he pulled his feet up onto the bed, breathed his last breath, and went to his people.

The Burials of Jacob and Joseph
50:1 Then Joseph hugged his father's face. He wept over him and kissed him. **50:2** Joseph instructed the physicians in his service to embalm his father, so the physicians embalmed Israel. **50:3** They took forty days, for that is the full time needed for embalming. The Egyptians mourned for him seventy days.

50:4 When the days of mourning had passed, Joseph said to Pharaoh's royal court, "If I have found favor in your sight, please say to Pharaoh, **50:5** 'My father made me swear an oath. He said, "I am about to die. Bury me in my tomb that I dug for myself there in the land of Canaan." Now let me go and bury my father; then I will return.'" **50:6** So Pharaoh said, "Go and bury your father, just as he made you swear to do."
50:7 So Joseph went up to bury his father; all Pharaoh's officials went with him – the senior courtiers of his household, all the senior officials of the land of Egypt, **50:8** all Joseph's household, his brothers, and his father's household. But they left their little children and their flocks and herds in the land of Goshen. **50:9** Chariots and horsemen also went up with him, so it was a very large entourage.
50:10 When they came to the threshing floor of Atad on the other side of the Jordan, they mourned there with very great and bitter sorrow. There Joseph observed a seven day period of mourning for his father. **50:11** When the Canaanites who lived in the land saw them mourning at the threshing floor of Atad, they said, "This is a very sad occasion for the Egyptians." That is why its name was called Abel Mizraim, which is beyond the Jordan.
50:12 So the sons of Jacob did for him just as he had instructed them. **50:13** His sons carried him to the land of Canaan and buried him in the cave of the field of Machpelah, near Mamre. This is the field Abraham purchased as a burial plot from Ephron the Hittite. **50:14** After he buried his father, Joseph returned to Egypt, along with his brothers and all who had accompanied him to bury his father.
50:15 When Joseph's brothers saw that their father was dead, they said, "What if Joseph bears a grudge and wants to repay us in full for all the harm we did to him?" **50:16** So they sent word to Joseph, saying, "Your father gave these instructions before he died: **50:17** 'Tell Joseph this: Please forgive the sin of your brothers and the wrong they did when they treated you so badly.' Now please forgive the sin of the servants of the God of your father." When this message was reported to him, Joseph wept. **50:18** Then his brothers also came and threw themselves down before him; they said, "Here we are; we are your slaves." **50:19** But Joseph answered them, "Don't be afraid. Am I in the place of God? **50:20** As for you, you meant to harm me, but God intended it for a good purpose, so he could preserve the lives of many people, as you can see this day. **50:21** So now, don't be afraid. I will provide for you and your little children." Then he consoled them and spoke kindly to them.
50:22 Joseph lived in Egypt, along with his father's family. Joseph lived 110 years. **50:23** Joseph saw the descendants of Ephraim to the third generation. He also saw the children of Makir the son of Manasseh; they were given special inheritance rights by Joseph.
50:24 Then Joseph said to his brothers, "I am about to die. But God will surely come to you and lead you up from this land to the land he swore on oath to give to Abraham, Isaac, and Jacob." **50:25** Joseph made the sons of Israel swear an oath. He said, "God will surely come to you. Then you must carry my bones up from this place." **50:26** So Joseph died at the age of 110. After they embalmed him, his body was placed in a coffin in Egypt.

Book 2. Exodus

Blessing during Bondage in Egypt
1:1 These are the names of the sons of Israel who entered Egypt – each man with his household entered with Jacob: **1:2** Reuben, Simeon, Levi, and Judah, **1:3** Issachar, Zebulun, and Benjamin, **1:4** Dan and Naphtali, Gad and Asher. **1:5** All the people who were directly descended from Jacob numbered seventy. But Joseph was already in Egypt, **1:6** and in time Joseph and his brothers and all that generation died. **1:7** The Israelites, however, were fruitful, increased greatly, multiplied, and became extremely strong, so that the land was filled with them.
1:8 Then a new king, who did not know about Joseph, came to power over Egypt. **1:9** He said to his people, "Look at the Israelite people, more numerous and stronger than we are! **1:10** Come, let's deal wisely with them. Otherwise they will continue to multiply, and if a war breaks out, they will ally themselves with our enemies and fight against us and leave the country."
1:11 So they put foremen over the Israelites to oppress them with hard labor. As a result they built Pithom and Rameses as store cities for Pharaoh. **1:12** But the more the Egyptians oppressed them, the more they multiplied and spread. As a result the Egyptians loathed the Israelites, **1:13** and they made the Israelites serve rigorously. **1:14** They made their lives bitter by hard service with mortar and bricks and by all kinds of service in the fields. Every kind of service the Israelites were required to give was rigorous.
1:15 The king of Egypt said to the Hebrew midwives, one of whom was named Shiphrah and the other Puah, **1:16** "When you assist the Hebrew women in childbirth, observe at the delivery: If it is a son, kill him, but if it is a daughter, she may live." **1:17** But the midwives feared God and did not do what the king of Egypt had told them; they let the boys live.

1:18 Then the king of Egypt summoned the midwives and said to them, "Why have you done this and let the boys live?" **1:19** The midwives said to Pharaoh, "Because the Hebrew women are not like the Egyptian women – for the Hebrew women are vigorous; they give birth before the midwife gets to them!" **1:20** So God treated the midwives well, and the people multiplied and became very strong. **1:21** And because the midwives feared God, he made households for them.

1:22 Then Pharaoh commanded all his people, "All sons that are born you must throw into the river, but all daughters you may let live."

The Birth of the Deliverer

2:1 A man from the household of Levi married a woman who was a descendant of Levi. **2:2** The woman became pregnant and gave birth to a son. When she saw that he was a healthy child, she hid him for three months. **2:3** But when she was no longer able to hide him, she took a papyrus basket for him and sealed it with bitumen and pitch. She put the child in it and set it among the reeds along the edge of the Nile. **2:4** His sister stationed herself at a distance to find out what would happen to him.

2:5 Then the daughter of Pharaoh came down to wash herself by the Nile, while her attendants were walking alongside the river, and she saw the basket among the reeds. She sent one of her attendants, took it, **2:6** opened it, and saw the child – a boy, crying! – and she felt compassion for him and said, "This is one of the Hebrews' children."

2:7 Then his sister said to Pharaoh's daughter, "Shall I go and get a nursing woman for you from the Hebrews, so that she may nurse the child for you?" **2:8** Pharaoh's daughter said to her, "Yes, do so." So the young girl went and got the child's mother. **2:9** Pharaoh's daughter said to her, "Take this child and nurse him for me, and I will pay your wages." So the woman took the child and nursed him.

2:10 When the child grew older she brought him to Pharaoh's daughter, and he became her son. She named him Moses, saying, "Because I drew him from the water."

The Presumption of the Deliverer

2:11 In those days, when Moses had grown up, he went out to his people and observed their hard labor, and he saw an Egyptian man attacking a Hebrew man, one of his own people. **2:12** He looked this way and that and saw that no one was there, and then he attacked the Egyptian and concealed the body in the sand. **2:13** When he went out the next day, there were two Hebrew men fighting. So he said to the one who was in the wrong, "Why are you attacking your fellow Hebrew?"

2:14 The man replied, "Who made you a ruler and a judge over us? Are you planning to kill me like you killed that Egyptian?" Then Moses was afraid, thinking, "Surely what I did has become known." **2:15** When Pharaoh heard about this event, he sought to kill Moses. So Moses fled from Pharaoh and

settled in the land of Midian, and he settled by a certain well.

2:16 Now a priest of Midian had seven daughters, and they came and began to draw water and fill the troughs in order to water their father's flock. **2:17** When some shepherds came and drove them away, Moses came up and defended them and then watered their flock. **2:18** So when they came home to their father Reuel, he asked, "Why have you come home so early today?" **2:19** They said, "An Egyptian man rescued us from the shepherds, and he actually drew water for us and watered the flock!" **2:20** He said to his daughters, "So where is he? Why in the world did you leave the man? Call him, so that he may eat a meal with us."

2:21 Moses agreed to stay with the man, and he gave his daughter Zipporah to Moses in marriage. **2:22** When she bore a son, Moses named him Gershom, for he said, "I have become a resident foreigner in a foreign land."

The Call of the Deliverer

2:23 During that long period of time the king of Egypt died, and the Israelites groaned because of the slave labor. They cried out, and their desperate cry because of their slave labor went up to God. **2:24** God heard their groaning, God remembered his covenant with Abraham, with Isaac, and with Jacob, **2:25** God saw the Israelites, and God understood….

3:1 Now Moses was shepherding the flock of his father-in-law Jethro, the priest of Midian, and he led the flock to the far side of the desert and came to the mountain of God, to Horeb. **3:2** The angel of the LORD appeared to him in a flame of fire from within a bush. He looked – and the bush was ablaze with fire, but it was not being consumed! **3:3** So Moses thought, "I will turn aside to see this amazing sight. Why does the bush not burn up?" **3:4** When the LORD saw that he had turned aside to look, God called to him from within the bush and said, "Moses, Moses!" And Moses said, "Here I am." **3:5** God said, "Do not approach any closer! Take your sandals off your feet, for the place where you are standing is holy ground." **3:6** He added, "I am the God of your father, the God of Abraham, the God of Isaac, and the God of Jacob." Then Moses hid his face, because he was afraid to look at God.

3:7 The LORD said, "I have surely seen the affliction of my people who are in Egypt. I have heard their cry because of their taskmasters, for I know their sorrows. **3:8** I have come down to deliver them from the hand of the Egyptians and to bring them up from that land to a land that is both good and spacious, to a land flowing with milk and honey, to the region

of the Canaanites, Hittites, Amorites, Perizzites, Hivites, and Jebusites. **3:9** And now indeed the cry of the Israelites has come to me, and I have also seen how severely the Egyptians oppress them. **3:10** So now go, and I will send you to Pharaoh to bring my people, the Israelites, out of Egypt."

3:11 Moses said to God, "Who am I, that I should go to Pharaoh, or that I should bring the Israelites out of Egypt?" **3:12** He replied, "Surely I will be with you, and this will be the sign to you that I have sent you: When you bring the people out of Egypt, you and they will serve God on this mountain."

3:13 Moses said to God, "If I go to the Israelites and tell them, 'The God of your fathers has sent me to you,' and they ask me, 'What is his name?' – what should I say to them?"

3:14 God said to Moses, "I AM that I AM." And he said, "You must say this to the Israelites, 'I AM has sent me to you.'" **3:15** God also said to Moses, "You must say this to the Israelites, 'The LORD – the God of your fathers, the God of Abraham, the God of Isaac, and the God of Jacob – has sent me to you. This is my name forever, and this is my memorial from generation to generation.'

3:16 "Go and bring together the elders of Israel and tell them, 'The LORD, the God of your fathers, appeared to me – the God of Abraham, Isaac, and Jacob – saying, "I have attended carefully to you and to what has been done to you in Egypt, **3:17** and I have promised that I will bring you up out of the affliction of Egypt to the land of the Canaanites, Hittites, Amorites, Perizzites, Hivites, and Jebusites, to a land flowing with milk and honey."'

3:18 "The elders will listen to you, and then you and the elders of Israel must go to the king of Egypt and tell him, 'The LORD, the God of the Hebrews, has met with us. So now, let us go three days' journey into the wilderness, so that we may sacrifice to the LORD our God.' **3:19** But I know that the king of Egypt will not let you go, not even under force. **3:20** So I will extend my hand and strike Egypt with all my wonders that I will do among them, and after that he will release you.

3:21 "I will grant this people favor with the Egyptians, so that when you depart you will not leave empty-handed. **3:22** Every woman will ask her neighbor and the one who happens to be staying in her house for items of silver and gold and for clothing. You will put these articles on your sons and daughters – thus you will plunder Egypt!"

The Source of Sufficiency

4:1 Moses answered again, "And if they do not believe me or pay attention to me, but say, 'The LORD has not appeared to you'?" **4:2** The LORD said to him, "What is that in your hand?" He said, "A staff." **4:3** The LORD said, "Throw it to the ground." So he threw it to the ground, and it became a snake, and Moses ran from it. **4:4** But the LORD said to Moses, "Put out your hand and grab it by the tail" – so he put out his hand and caught it, and it became a staff in his hand – **4:5** "that they may believe that the LORD, the God of their fathers, the God of Abraham, the God of Isaac, and the God of Jacob, has appeared to you."

4:6 The LORD also said to him, "Put your hand into your robe." So he put his hand into his robe, and when he brought it out – there was his hand, leprous like snow! **4:7** He said, "Put your hand back into your robe." So he put his hand back into his robe, and when he brought it out from his robe – there it was, restored like the rest of his skin! **4:8** "If they do not believe you or pay attention to the former sign, then they may believe the latter sign. **4:9** And if they do not believe even these two signs or listen to you, then take some water from the Nile and pour it out on the dry ground. The water you take out of the Nile will become blood on the dry ground."

4:10 Then Moses said to the LORD, "O my Lord, I am not an eloquent man, neither in the past nor since you have spoken to your servant, for I am slow of speech and slow of tongue."

4:11 The LORD said to him, "Who gave a mouth to man, or who makes a person mute or deaf or seeing or blind? Is it not I, the LORD? **4:12** So now go, and I will be with your mouth and will teach you what you must say."

4:13 But Moses said, "O my Lord, please send anyone else whom you wish to send!"

4:14 Then the LORD became angry with Moses, and he said, "What about your brother Aaron the Levite? I know that he can speak very well. Moreover, he is coming to meet you, and when he sees you he will be glad in his heart.

4:15 "So you are to speak to him and put the words in his mouth. And as for me, I will be with your mouth and with his mouth, and I will teach you both what you must do. **4:16** He will speak for you to the people, and it will be as if he were your mouth and as if you were his God. **4:17** You will also take in your hand this staff, with which you will do the signs."

The Return of Moses

4:18 So Moses went back to his father-in-law Jethro and said to him, "Let me go, so that I may return to my relatives in Egypt and see if they are still alive." Jethro said to Moses, "Go in peace." **4:19** The LORD said to Moses in Midian, "Go back to Egypt, because all the men who were seeking your life are dead." **4:20** Then Moses took his wife and sons and put them on a donkey and headed back to the land of Egypt, and Moses took the staff of God in his hand. **4:21** The LORD said to Moses, "When you go back to Egypt, see that you do before Pharaoh all the wonders I have put under your control. But I will harden his heart and he will not let the people go. **4:22** You must say to Pharaoh, 'Thus says the LORD, "Israel is my son, my firstborn, **4:23** and I said to you, 'Let my son go that he may serve me,' but since you have refused to let him go, I will surely kill your son, your firstborn!"'"

4:24 Now on the way, at a place where they stopped for the night, the LORD met Moses and sought to kill him. **4:25** But Zipporah took a flint knife, cut off the foreskin of her son and touched it to Moses' feet, and said, "Surely you are a bridegroom of blood to me." **4:26** So the LORD let him alone. (At that time she said, "A bridegroom of blood," referring to the circumcision.)

4:27 The LORD said to Aaron, "Go to the wilderness to meet Moses. So he went and met him at the mountain of God and greeted him with a kiss. **4:28** Moses told Aaron all the words of the LORD who had sent him and all the signs that he had commanded him. **4:29** Then Moses and Aaron went and brought together all the Israelite elders. **4:30** Aaron spoke all the words that the LORD had spoken to Moses and did the signs in the sight of the people, **4:31** and the people believed. When they heard that the LORD had attended to the Israelites and that he had seen their affliction, they bowed down close to the ground.

Opposition to the Plan of God

5:1 Afterward Moses and Aaron went to Pharaoh and said, "Thus says the LORD, the God of Israel, 'Release my people so that they may hold a pilgrim feast to me in the desert.'" **5:2** But Pharaoh said, "Who is the LORD that I should obey him by releasing Israel? I do not know the LORD, and I will not release Israel!" **5:3** And they said, "The God of the Hebrews has met with us. Let us go a three-day journey into the desert so that we may sacrifice to the LORD our God, so that he does not strike us with plague or the sword." **5:4** The king of Egypt said to them, "Moses and Aaron, why do you cause the people to refrain from their work? Return to your labor!" **5:5** Pharaoh was thinking, "The people of the land are now many, and you are giving them rest from their labor."

5:6 That same day Pharaoh commanded the slave masters and foremen who were over the people: **5:7** "You must no longer give straw to the people for making bricks as before. Let them go and collect straw for themselves. **5:8** But you must require of them the same quota of bricks that they were making before. Do not reduce it, for they are slackers. That is why they are crying, 'Let us go sacrifice to our God.' **5:9** Make the work harder for the men so they will keep at it and pay no attention to lying words!"

5:10 So the slave masters of the people and their foremen went to the Israelites and said, "Thus says Pharaoh: 'I am not giving you straw. **5:11** You go get straw for yourselves wherever you can find it, because there will be no reduction at all in your workload.'" **5:12** So the people spread out through all the land of Egypt to collect stubble for straw. **5:13** The slave masters were pressuring them, saying, "Complete your work for each day, just like when there was straw!" **5:14** The Israelite foremen whom Pharaoh's slave masters had set over them were beaten and were asked, "Why did you not complete your requirement for brickmaking as in the past – both yesterday and today?"

5:15 The Israelite foremen went and cried out to Pharaoh, "Why are you treating your servants this way? **5:16** No straw is given to your servants, but we are told, 'Make bricks!' Your servants are even being beaten, but the fault is with your people."

5:17 But Pharaoh replied, "You are slackers! Slackers! That is why you are saying, 'Let us go sacrifice to the LORD.' **5:18** So now, get back to work! You will not be given straw, but you must still produce your quota of bricks!" **5:19** The Israelite foremen saw that they were in trouble when they were told, "You must not reduce the daily quota of your bricks."

5:20 When they went out from Pharaoh, they encountered Moses and Aaron standing there to meet them, **5:21** and they said to them, "May the LORD look on you and judge, because you have made us stink in the opinion of Pharaoh

and his servants, so that you have given them an excuse to kill us!"

The Assurance of Deliverance

5:22 Moses returned to the LORD, and said, "Lord, why have you caused trouble for this people? Why did you ever send me? **5:23** From the time I went to speak to Pharaoh in your name, he has caused trouble for this people, and you have certainly not rescued them!"

6:1 Then the LORD said to Moses, "Now you will see what I will do to Pharaoh, for compelled by my strong hand he will release them, and by my strong hand he will drive them out of his land."

6:2 God spoke to Moses and said to him, "I am the LORD. **6:3** I appeared to Abraham, to Isaac, and to Jacob as God Almighty, but by my name 'the LORD' I was not known to them. **6:4** I also established my covenant with them to give them the land of Canaan, where they were living as resident foreigners. **6:5** I have also heard the groaning of the Israelites, whom the Egyptians are enslaving, and I have remembered my covenant. **6:6** Therefore, tell the Israelites, 'I am the LORD. I will bring you out from your enslavement to the Egyptians, I will rescue you from the hard labor they impose, and I will redeem you with an outstretched arm and with great judgments. **6:7** I

will take you to myself for a people, and I will be your God. Then you will know that I am the LORD your God, who brought you out from your enslavement to the Egyptians. **6:8** I will bring you to the land I swore to give to Abraham, to Isaac, and to Jacob – and I will give it to you as a possession. I am the LORD!'"

6:9 Moses told this to the Israelites, but they did not listen to him because of their discouragement and hard labor. **6:10** Then the LORD said to Moses, **6:11** "Go, tell Pharaoh king of Egypt that he must release the Israelites from his land." **6:12** But Moses replied to the LORD, "If the Israelites did not listen to me, then how will Pharaoh listen to me, since I speak with difficulty?"

6:13 The LORD spoke to Moses and Aaron and gave them a charge for the Israelites and Pharaoh king of Egypt to bring the Israelites out of the land of Egypt.

The Ancestry of the Deliverer

6:14 These are the heads of their fathers' households:

The sons of Reuben, the firstborn son of Israel, were Hanoch and Pallu, Hezron and Carmi. These were the clans of Reuben.

6:15 The sons of Simeon were Jemuel, Jamin, Ohad, Jakin, Zohar, and Shaul, the son of a Canaanite woman. These were the clans of Simeon.

6:16 Now these are the names of the sons of Levi, according to their records: Gershon, Kohath, and Merari. (The length of Levi's life was 137 years.)

6:17 The sons of Gershon, by their families, were Libni and Shimei.

6:18 The sons of Kohath were Amram, Izhar, Hebron, and Uzziel. (The length of Kohath's life was 133 years.)

6:19 The sons of Merari were Mahli and Mushi. These were the clans of Levi, according to their records.

6:20 Amram married his father's sister Jochebed, and she bore him Aaron and Moses. (The length of Amram's life was 137 years.)

6:21 The sons of Izhar were Korah, Nepheg, and Zikri.

6:22 The sons of Uzziel were Mishael, Elzaphan, and Sithri.

6:23 Aaron married Elisheba, the daughter of Amminadab and sister of Nahshon, and she bore him Nadab and Abihu, Eleazar and Ithamar.

6:24 The sons of Korah were Assir, Elkanah, and Abiasaph. These were the Korahite clans.

6:25 Now Eleazar son of Aaron married one of the daughters of Putiel and she bore him Phinehas.

These are the heads of the fathers' households of Levi according to their clans.

6:26 It was the same Aaron and Moses to whom the LORD said, "Bring the Israelites out of the land of Egypt by their regiments." **6:27** They were the men who were speaking to Pharaoh king of Egypt, in order to bring the Israelites out of Egypt. It was the same Moses and Aaron.

The Authentication of the Word

6:28 When the LORD spoke to Moses in the land of Egypt, **6:29** he said to him, "I am the LORD. Tell Pharaoh king of Egypt all that I am telling you." **6:30** But Moses said before the LORD, "Since I speak with difficulty, why should Pharaoh listen to me?"

7:1 So the LORD said to Moses, "See, I have made you like God to Pharaoh, and your brother Aaron will be your prophet. **7:2** You are to speak everything I command you, and your brother Aaron is to tell Pharaoh that he must release the Israelites from his land. **7:3** But I will harden Pharaoh's heart, and although I will multiply my signs and my wonders in the land of Egypt, **7:4** Pharaoh will not listen to you. I will reach into Egypt and bring out my regiments, my people the Israelites, from the land of Egypt with great acts of judgment. **7:5** Then the Egyptians will know that I am the LORD, when I extend my hand over Egypt and bring the Israelites out from among them.

7:6 And Moses and Aaron did so; they did just as the LORD commanded them. **7:7** Now Moses was eighty years old and Aaron was eighty-three years old when they spoke to Pharaoh.

7:8 The LORD said to Moses and Aaron, **7:9** "When Pharaoh says to you, 'Do a miracle,' and you say to Aaron, 'Take your staff and throw it down before Pharaoh,' it will become a snake." **7:10** When Moses and Aaron went to Pharaoh, they did so, just as the LORD had commanded them – Aaron threw down his staff before Pharaoh and his servants and it became a snake. **7:11** Then Pharaoh also summoned wise men and sorcerers, and the magicians of Egypt by their secret arts did the same thing. **7:12** Each man threw down his staff, and the staffs became snakes. But Aaron's staff swallowed up their staffs. **7:13** Yet Pharaoh's heart became hard, and he did not listen to them, just as the LORD had predicted.

The First Blow: Water to Blood

7:14 The LORD said to Moses, "Pharaoh's heart is hard; he refuses to release the people. **7:15** Go to Pharaoh in the morning when he goes out to the water. Position yourself to meet him by the edge of the Nile, and take in your hand the staff that was turned into a snake. **7:16** Tell him, 'The LORD, the God of the Hebrews, has sent me to you to say, "Release my people, that they may serve me in the desert!" But until now you have not listened. **7:17** Thus says the LORD: "By this you will know that I am the LORD: I am going to strike the water of the Nile with the staff that is in my hand, and it will be turned into blood. **7:18** Fish in the Nile will die, the Nile will stink, and the Egyptians will be unable to drink water from the Nile."'" **7:19** Then the LORD said to Moses, "Tell Aaron, 'Take your staff and stretch out your hand over Egypt's waters – over their rivers, over their canals, over their ponds, and over all their reservoirs – so that it becomes blood.' There will be blood everywhere in the land of Egypt, even in wooden and stone containers." **7:20** Moses and Aaron did so, just as the LORD had commanded. Moses raised the staff and struck the water that was in the Nile right before the eyes of Pharaoh and his servants, and all the water that was in the Nile was turned to

blood. **7:21** When the fish that were in the Nile died, the Nile began to stink, so that the Egyptians could not drink water from the Nile. There was blood everywhere in the land of Egypt! **7:22** But the magicians of Egypt did the same by their secret arts, and so Pharaoh's heart remained hard, and he refused to listen to Moses and Aaron – just as the LORD had predicted. **7:23** And Pharaoh turned and went into his house. He did not pay any attention to this. **7:24** All the Egyptians dug around the Nile for water to drink, because they could not drink the water of the Nile.

The Second Blow: Frogs

7:25 Seven full days passed after the LORD struck the Nile. **8:1** (7:26) Then the LORD said to Moses, "Go to Pharaoh and tell him, 'Thus says the LORD: "Release my people in order that they may serve me! **8:2** But if you refuse to release them, then I am going to plague all your territory with frogs. **8:3** The Nile will swarm with frogs, and they will come up and go into your house, in your bedroom, and on your bed, and into the houses of your servants and your people, and into your ovens and your kneading troughs. **8:4** Frogs will come up against you, your people, and all your servants."'"

8:5 The LORD spoke to Moses, "Tell Aaron, 'Extend your hand with your staff over the rivers, over the canals, and over the ponds, and bring the frogs up over the land of Egypt.'" **8:6** So Aaron extended his hand over the waters of Egypt, and frogs came up and covered the land of Egypt.

8:7 The magicians did the same with their secret arts and brought up frogs on the land of Egypt too.

8:8 Then Pharaoh summoned Moses and Aaron and said, "Pray to the LORD that he may take the frogs away from me and my people, and I will release the people that they may sacrifice to the LORD." **8:9** Moses said to Pharaoh, "You may have the honor over me – when shall I pray for you, your servants, and your people, for the frogs to be removed from you and your houses, so that they will be left only in the Nile?" **8:10** He said, "Tomorrow." And Moses said, "It will be as you say, so that you may know that there is no one like the LORD our God. **8:11** The frogs will depart from you, your houses, your servants, and your people; they will be left only in the Nile."

8:12 Then Moses and Aaron went out from Pharaoh, and Moses cried to the LORD because of the frogs that he had brought on Pharaoh. **8:13** The LORD did as Moses asked – the frogs died out of the houses, the villages, and the fields. **8:14** The Egyptians piled them in countless heaps, and the land stank. **8:15** But when

Pharaoh saw that there was relief, he hardened his heart and did not listen to them, just as the LORD had predicted.

The Third Blow: Gnats

8:16 The LORD said to Moses, "Tell Aaron, 'Extend your staff and strike the dust of the ground, and it will become gnats throughout all the land of Egypt.'" **8:17** They did so; Aaron extended his hand with his staff, he struck the dust of the ground, and it became gnats on people and on animals. All the dust of the ground became gnats throughout all the land of Egypt. **8:18** When the magicians attempted to bring forth gnats by their secret arts, they could not. So there were gnats on people and on animals. **8:19** The magicians said to Pharaoh, "It is the finger of God!" But Pharaoh's heart remained hard, and he did not listen to them, just as the LORD had predicted.

The Fourth Blow: Flies

8:20 The LORD said to Moses, "Get up early in the morning and position yourself before Pharaoh as he goes out to the water, and tell him, 'Thus says the LORD, "Release my people that they may serve me! **8:21** If you do not release my people, then I am going to send swarms of flies on you and on your servants and on your people and in your houses. The houses of the Egyptians will be full of flies, and even the ground they stand on. **8:22** But on that day I will mark off the land of Goshen, where my people are staying, so that no swarms of flies will be there, that you may know that I am the LORD in the midst of this land. **8:23** I will put a division between my people and your people. This sign will take place tomorrow."'" **8:24** The LORD did so; a thick swarm of flies came into Pharaoh's house and into the houses of his servants, and throughout the whole land of Egypt the land was ruined because of the swarms of flies.

8:25 Then Pharaoh summoned Moses and Aaron and said, "Go, sacrifice to your God within the land." **8:26** But Moses said, "That would not be the right thing to do, for the sacrifices we make to the LORD our God would be an abomination to the Egyptians. If we make sacrifices that are an abomination to the Egyptians right before their eyes, will they not stone us? **8:27** We must go on a three-day journey into the desert and sacrifice to the LORD our God, just as he is telling us."

8:28 Pharaoh said, "I will release you so that you may sacrifice to the LORD your God in the desert. Only you must not go very far. Do pray for me."

8:29 Moses said, "I am going to go out from you and pray to the LORD, and the swarms of flies will go away from Pharaoh, from his servants, and from his people tomorrow. Only do not let Pharaoh deal falsely again by not releasing the people to sacrifice to the LORD." **8:30** So Moses went out from Pharaoh and prayed to the LORD, **8:31** and the LORD did as Moses asked – he removed the swarms of flies from Pharaoh, from his servants, and from his people. Not one remained! **8:32** But Pharaoh hardened his heart this time also and did not release the people.

The Fifth Blow: Disease

9:1 Then the LORD said to Moses, "Go to Pharaoh and tell him, 'Thus says the LORD, the God of the Hebrews, "Release my people that they may serve me! **9:2** For if you refuse to release them and continue holding them, **9:3** then the hand of the LORD will surely bring a very terrible plague on your livestock in the field, on the horses, the donkeys, the camels, the herds, and the flocks. **9:4** But the Lord will distinguish between the livestock of Israel and the livestock of Egypt, and nothing will die of all that the Israelites have."'"

9:5 The LORD set an appointed time, saying, "Tomorrow the LORD will do this in the land." **9:6** And the LORD did this on the next day; all the livestock of the Egyptians died, but of the Israelites' livestock not one died. **9:7** Pharaoh sent representatives to investigate, and indeed, not even one of the livestock of Israel had died. But Pharaoh's heart remained hard, and he did not release the people.

The Sixth Blow: Boils

9:8 Then the LORD said to Moses and Aaron, "Take handfuls of soot from a furnace, and have Moses throw it into the air while Pharaoh is watching. **9:9** It will become fine dust over the whole land of Egypt and will cause boils to break out and fester on both people and animals in all the land of Egypt." **9:10** So they took soot from a furnace and stood before Pharaoh, Moses threw it into the air, and it caused festering boils to break out on both people and animals.

9:11 The magicians could not stand before Moses because of the boils, for boils were on the magicians and on all the Egyptians. **9:12** But the LORD hardened Pharaoh's heart, and he did not listen to them, just as the LORD had predicted to Moses.

The Seventh Blow: Hail

9:13 The LORD said to Moses, "Get up early in the morning, stand before Pharaoh, and tell him, 'Thus says the LORD, the God of the Hebrews: "Release my people so that they may serve me! **9:14** For this time I will send all my plagues on your very self and on your servants and your people, so that you may know that there is no one like me in all the earth. **9:15** For by now I could have stretched out my hand and struck you and your people with plague, and you would have been destroyed from the earth. **9:16** But for this purpose I have caused you to stand: to show you my strength, and so that my name may be declared in all the earth. **9:17** You are still exalting yourself against my people by not releasing them. **9:18** I am going to cause very severe hail to rain down about this time tomorrow, such hail as has never occurred in Egypt from the day it was founded until now. **9:19** So now, send instructions to gather your livestock and all your possessions in the fields to a safe place. Every person or animal caught in the field and not brought into the house – the hail will come down on them, and they will die!"'"

9:20 Those of Pharaoh's servants who feared the word of the LORD hurried to bring their servants and livestock into the houses, **9:21** but those who did not take the word of the LORD seriously left their servants and their cattle in the field.

9:22 Then the LORD said to Moses, "Extend your hand toward the sky that there may be hail in all the land of Egypt, on people and on animals, and on everything that grows in the field in the land of Egypt." **9:23** When Moses extended his staff toward the sky, the LORD sent thunder and hail, and fire fell to the earth; so the LORD caused hail to rain down on the land of Egypt. **9:24** Hail fell and fire mingled with the hail; the hail was so severe that there had not been any like it in all the land of Egypt since it had become a nation. **9:25** The hail struck everything in the open fields, both people and animals, throughout all the land of Egypt. The hail struck everything that grows in the field, and it broke all the trees of the field to pieces. **9:26** Only in the land of Goshen, where the Israelites lived, was there no hail.

9:27 So Pharaoh sent and summoned Moses and Aaron and said to them, "I have sinned this time! The LORD is righteous, and I and my people are guilty. **9:28** Pray to the LORD, for the mighty thunderings and hail are too much! I will release you and you will stay no longer." **9:29** Moses said to him, "When I leave the city I will spread my hands to the LORD, the thunder will cease, and there will be no more hail, so that you may know that the earth belongs to the LORD. **9:30** But as for you and your servants, I know that you do not yet fear the LORD God." **9:31** (Now the flax and the barley were struck by the hail, for the barley had ripened and the flax was in bud. **9:32** But the wheat and the spelt were not struck, for they are later crops.)

9:33 So Moses left Pharaoh, went out of the city, and spread out his hands to the LORD, and the thunder and the hail ceased, and the rain stopped pouring on the earth. **9:34** When Pharaoh saw that the rain and hail and thunder ceased, he sinned again: both he and his servants hardened their hearts. **9:35** So Pharaoh's heart remained hard, and he did not release the Israelites, as the LORD had predicted through Moses.

The Eighth Blow: Locusts

10:1 The LORD said to Moses, "Go to Pharaoh, for I have hardened his heart and the heart of his servants, in order to display these signs of mine before him, **10:2** and in order that in the hearing of your son and your grandson you may tell how I made fools of the Egyptians and about my signs that I displayed among them, so that you may know that I am the LORD."

10:3 So Moses and Aaron came to Pharaoh and told him, "Thus says the LORD, the God of the Hebrews: 'How long do you refuse to humble yourself before me? Release my people so that they may serve me! **10:4** But if you refuse to release my people, I am going to bring locusts into your territory tomorrow. **10:5** They will cover the surface of the earth, so that you will be unable to see the ground. They will eat the remainder of what escaped – what is left over for you – from the hail, and they will eat every tree that grows for you from the field. **10:6** They will fill your houses, the houses of your servants, and all the houses of Egypt, such as neither your fathers nor your grandfathers have seen since they have been in the land until this day!'" Then Moses turned and went out from Pharaoh.

10:7 Pharaoh's servants said to him, "How long will this man be a menace to us? Release the people so that they may serve the LORD their God. Do you not know that Egypt is destroyed?"

10:8 So Moses and Aaron were brought back to Pharaoh, and he said to them, "Go, serve the LORD your God. Exactly who is going with you?" **10:9** Moses said, "We will go with our young and our old, with our sons and our daughters, and with our sheep and our cattle we will go, because we are to hold a pilgrim feast for the LORD."

10:10 He said to them, "The LORD will need to be with you if I release you and your dependents! Watch out! Trouble is right in front of you! **10:11** No! Go, you men only, and serve the LORD, for that is what you want." Then Moses and Aaron were driven out of Pharaoh's presence.

10:12 The LORD said to Moses, "Extend your hand over the land of Egypt for the locusts, that they may come up over the land of Egypt and eat everything that grows in the ground, everything that the hail has left." **10:13** So Moses extended his staff over the land of Egypt, and then the LORD brought an east wind on the land all that day and all night. The morning came, and the east wind had brought up the locusts! **10:14** The locusts went up over all the land of Egypt and settled down in all the territory of Egypt. It was very severe; there had been no locusts like them before, nor will there be such ever again. **10:15** They covered the surface of all the ground, so that the ground became dark with them, and they ate all the vegetation of the ground and all the fruit of the trees that the hail had left. Nothing green remained on the trees or on anything that grew in the fields throughout the whole land of Egypt.

10:16 Then Pharaoh quickly summoned Moses and Aaron and said, "I have sinned against the LORD your God and against you! **10:17** So now, forgive my sin this time only, and pray to the LORD your God that he would only take this death away from me." **10:18** Moses went out from Pharaoh and prayed to the LORD, **10:19** and the LORD turned a very strong west wind, and it picked up the locusts and blew them into the Red Sea. Not one locust remained in all the territory of Egypt. **10:20** But the LORD hardened Pharaoh's heart, and he did not release the Israelites.

The Ninth Blow: Darkness

10:21 The LORD said to Moses, "Extend your hand toward heaven so that there may be darkness over the land of Egypt, a darkness so thick it can be felt." **10:22** So Moses extended his hand toward heaven, and there was absolute darkness throughout the land of Egypt for three days. **10:23** No one could see another person, and no one could rise from his place for three days. But the Israelites had light in the places where they lived.

10:24 Then Pharaoh summoned Moses and said, "Go, serve the LORD – only your flocks and herds will be detained. Even your families may go with you."

10:25 But Moses said, "Will you also provide us with sacrifices and burnt offerings that we may present them to the LORD our God? **10:26** Our livestock must also go with us! Not a hoof is to be left behind! For we must take these animals to serve the LORD our God. Until we arrive there, we do not know what use to serve the LORD."

10:27 But the LORD hardened Pharaoh's heart, and he was not willing to release them. **10:28** Pharaoh said to him, "Go from me! Watch out for yourself! Do not appear before me again, for when you see my face you will die!" **10:29** Moses said, "As you wish! I will not see your face again."

The Tenth Blow: Death

11:1 The LORD said to Moses, "I will bring one more plague on Pharaoh and on Egypt; after that he will release you from this place. When he releases you, he will drive you out completely from this place. **11:2** In-struct the people that each man and each woman is to request from his or her neighbor items of silver and gold."

11:3 (Now the LORD granted the people favor with the Egyptians. Moreover, the man Moses was very great in the land of Egypt, respected by Pharaoh's servants and by the Egyptian people.)

11:4 Moses said, "Thus says the LORD: 'About midnight I will go throughout Egypt, **11:5** and all the firstborn in the land of Egypt will die, from the firstborn son of Pharaoh who sits on his throne, to the firstborn son of the slave girl who is at her hand mill, and all the firstborn of the cattle. **11:6** There will be a great cry throughout the whole land of Egypt, such as there has never been, nor ever will be again. **11:7** But against any of the Israelites not even a dog will bark against either people or animals, so that you may know that the LORD distinguishes between Egypt and Israel.' **11:8** All these your servants will come down to me and bow down to me, saying, 'Go, you and all the people who follow you,' and after that I will go out." Then Moses went out from Pharaoh in great anger.

11:9 The LORD said to Moses, "Pharaoh will not listen to you, so that my wonders may be multiplied in the land of Egypt."

11:10 So Moses and Aaron did all these wonders before Pharaoh, but the LORD hardened Pharaoh's heart, and he did not release the Israelites from his land.

The Institution of the Passover

12:1 The LORD said to Moses and Aaron in the land of Egypt, **12:2** "This month is to be your beginning of months; it will be your first month of the year. **12:3** Tell the whole community of Israel, 'In the tenth day of this month they each must take a lamb for themselves according to their families – a lamb for each household. **12:4** If any household is too small for a lamb, the man and his next-door neighbor are to take a lamb according to the number of people – you will make your count for the lamb according to how much each one can eat. **12:5** Your lamb must be perfect, a male, one year old; you may take it from the sheep or from the goats. **12:6** You must care for it until the fourteenth day of this month, and then the whole community of Israel will kill it around sundown. **12:7** They will take some of the blood and put it on the two side posts and top of the doorframe of the houses where they will eat it. **12:8** They will eat the meat the same night; they will eat it roasted over the fire with bread made without yeast and with bitter herbs. **12:9** Do not eat it raw or boiled in water, but roast it over the fire with its head, its legs, and its entrails. **12:10** You must leave nothing until morning, but you must burn with fire whatever remains of it until morning. **12:11** This is how you are to eat it – dressed to travel, your sandals on your feet, and your staff in your hand. You are to eat it in haste. It is the LORD's Passover.

12:12 I will pass through the land of Egypt in the same night, and I will attack all the firstborn in the land of Egypt, both of humans and of animals, and on all the gods of Egypt I will execute judgment. I am the LORD. **12:13** The blood will be a sign for you on the houses where you are, so that when I see the blood I will pass over you, and this plague will not fall on you to destroy you when I attack the land of Egypt.

12:14 This day will become a memorial for you, and you will celebrate it as a festival to the LORD – you will celebrate it perpetually as a lasting ordinance. **12:15** For seven days you must eat bread made without yeast. Surely on the first day you must put away yeast from your houses because anyone who eats bread made with yeast from the first day to the seventh day will be cut off from Israel.

12:16 On the first day there will be a holy convocation, and on the seventh day there will be a holy convocation for you. You must do no work of any kind on them, only what every person will eat – that alone may be prepared for you. **12:17** So you will keep the Feast of Unleavened Bread, because on this very day I brought your regiments out from the land of Egypt, and so you must keep this day perpetually as a lasting ordinance. **12:18** In the first month, from the fourteenth day of the month, in the evening, you will eat bread made without yeast until the twenty-first day of the month in the evening. **12:19** For seven days yeast must not be found in your houses, for whoever eats what is made with yeast – that person will be cut off from the community of Israel, whether a foreigner or one born in the land. **12:20** You will not eat anything made with yeast; in all the places where you live you must eat bread made without yeast.'"

12:21 Then Moses summoned all the elders of Israel, and told them, "Go and select for yourselves a lamb or young goat for your families, and kill the Passover animals. **12:22** Take a branch of hyssop, dip it in the blood that is in the basin, and apply to the top of the doorframe and the two side posts some of the blood that is in the basin. Not one of you is to go out the door of his house until morning. **12:23** For the LORD will pass through to strike Egypt, and when he sees the blood on the top of the doorframe and the two side posts, then the LORD will pass over the door, and he will not permit the destroyer to enter your houses to strike you. **12:24** You must observe this event as an ordinance for you and for your children forever. **12:25** When you enter the land that the LORD will give to you, just as he said, you must observe this ceremony. **12:26** When your children ask you, 'What does this ceremony mean to you?' – **12:27** then you will say, 'It is the sacrifice of the LORD's Passover, when he passed over the houses of the Israelites in Egypt, when he struck Egypt and delivered our households.'" The people bowed down low to the ground,

12:28 and the Israelites went away and did exactly as the LORD had commanded Moses and Aaron.

The Deliverance from Egypt

12:29 It happened at midnight – the LORD attacked all the firstborn in the land of Egypt, from the firstborn of Pharaoh who sat on his throne to the firstborn of the captive who was in the prison, and all the firstborn of the cattle. **12:30** Pharaoh got up in the night, along with all his servants and all Egypt, and there was a great cry in Egypt, for there was no house in which there was not someone dead. **12:31** Pharaoh summoned Moses and Aaron in the night and said, "Get up, get out from among my people, both you and the Israelites! Go, serve the LORD as you have requested! **12:32** Also, take your flocks and your herds, just as you have requested, and leave. But bless me also."

12:33 The Egyptians were urging the people on, in order to send them out of the land quickly, for they were saying, "We are all dead!" **12:34** So the people took their dough before the yeast was added, with their kneading troughs bound up in their clothing on their shoulders. **12:35** Now the Israelites had done as Moses told them – they had requested from the Egyptians silver and gold items and clothing. **12:36** The LORD gave the people favor in the sight of the Egyptians, and they gave them whatever they wanted, and so they plundered Egypt. **12:37** The Israelites journeyed from Rameses to Sukkoth. There were about 600,000 men on foot, plus their dependants. **12:38** A mixed multitude also went up with them, and flocks and herds – a very large number of cattle. **12:39** They baked cakes of bread without yeast using the dough they had brought from Egypt, for it was made without yeast – because they were thrust out of Egypt and were not able to delay, they could not prepare food for themselves either. **12:40** Now the length of time the Israelites lived in Egypt was 430 years. **12:41** At the end of the 430 years, on the very day, all the regiments of the LORD went out of the land of Egypt. **12:42** It was a night of vigil for the LORD to bring them out from the land of Egypt, and so on this night all Israel is to keep the vigil to the LORD for generations to come.

Participation in the Passover

12:43 The LORD said to Moses and Aaron, "This is the ordinance of the Passover. No
foreigner may share in eating it. **12:44** But everyone's servant who is bought for money, after you have circumcised him, may eat it. **12:45** A foreigner and a hired worker must not eat it. **12:46** It must be eaten in one house; you must not bring any of the meat outside the house, and you must not break a bone of it. **12:47** The whole community of Israel must observe it.

12:48 "When a foreigner lives with you and wants to observe the Passover to the LORD, all his males must be circumcised, and then he may approach and observe it, and he will be like one who is born in the land – but no uncircumcised person may eat of it. **12:49** The same law will apply to the person who is native-born and to the foreigner who lives among you."

12:50 So all the Israelites did exactly as the LORD commanded Moses and Aaron. **12:51** And on this very day the LORD brought the Israelites out of the land of Egypt by their regiments.

The Law of the Firstborn

13:1 The LORD spoke to Moses: **13:2** "Set apart to me every firstborn male – the first offspring of every womb among the Israelites, whether human or animal; it is mine."

13:3 Moses said to the people, "Remember this day on which you came out from Egypt, from the place where you were enslaved, for the LORD brought you out of there with a mighty hand – and no bread made with yeast may be eaten. **13:4** On this day, in the month of Abib, you are going out.

13:5 When the LORD brings you to the land of the Canaanites, Hittites, Amorites, Hivites, and Jebusites, which he swore to your fathers to give you, a land flowing with milk and honey, then you will keep this ceremony in this month. **13:6** For seven days you must eat bread made without yeast, and on the seventh day there is to be a festival to the LORD. **13:7** Bread made without yeast must be eaten for seven days; no bread made with yeast shall be seen among you, and you must have no yeast among you within any of your borders.

13:8 You are to tell your son on that day, 'It is because of what the LORD did for me when I came out of Egypt.' **13:9** It will be a sign for you on your hand and a memorial on your forehead, so that the law of the LORD may be in your mouth, for with a mighty hand the LORD brought you out of Egypt. **13:10** So you must keep this ordinance at its appointed time from year to year.

13:11 When the LORD brings you into the land of the Canaanites, as he swore to you and to your fathers, and gives it to you, **13:12** then you must give over to the LORD the first offspring of every womb. Every firstling of a beast that you have – the males will be the LORD's. **13:13** Every firstling of a donkey you must redeem with a lamb, and if you do not redeem it, then you must break its neck.

Every firstborn of your sons you must redeem.

13:14 In the future, when your son asks you 'What is this?' you are to tell him, 'With a mighty hand the LORD brought us out from Egypt, from the land of slavery. **13:15** When Pharaoh stubbornly refused to release us, the LORD killed all the firstborn in the land of Egypt, from the firstborn of people to the firstborn of animals. That is why I am sacrificing to the LORD the first male offspring of every womb, but all my firstborn sons I redeem.' **13:16** It will be for a sign on your hand and for frontlets on your forehead, for with a mighty hand the LORD brought us out of Egypt."

The Leading of God

13:17 When Pharaoh released the people, God did not lead them by the way to the land of the Philistines, although that was nearby, for God said, "Lest the people change their minds and return to Egypt when they experience war." **13:18** So God brought the people around by the way of the desert to the Red Sea, and the Israelites went up from the land of Egypt prepared for battle.

13:19 Moses took the bones of Joseph with him, for Joseph had made the Israelites solemnly swear, "God will surely attend to you, and you will carry my bones up from this place with you."

13:20 They journeyed from Sukkoth and camped in Etham, on the edge of the desert. **13:21** Now the LORD was going before them by day in a pillar of cloud to lead them in the way, and by night in a pillar of fire to give them light, so that they could travel day or night. **13:22** He did not remove the pillar of cloud by
day nor the pillar of fire by night from before the people.

The Victory at the Red Sea

14:1 The LORD spoke to Moses: **14:2** "Tell the Israelites that they must turn and camp before Pi-hahiroth, between Migdol and the sea; you are to camp by the sea before Baal Zephon opposite it. **14:3** Pharaoh will think regarding the Israelites, 'They are wandering around confused in the land – the desert has closed in on them.' **14:4** I will harden Pharaoh's heart, and he will chase after them. I will gain honor because of Pharaoh and because of all his army, and the Egyptians will know that I am the LORD." So this is what they did.

14:5 When it was reported to the king of Egypt that the people had fled, the heart of Pharaoh and his servants was turned against the people, and the king and his servants said, "What in the world have we done? For we have released the people of Israel from serving us!" **14:6** Then he prepared his chariots and took his army with him. **14:7** He took six hundred select chariots, and all the rest of the chariots of Egypt, and officers on all of them.

14:8 But the LORD hardened the heart of Pharaoh king of Egypt, and he chased after the Israelites. Now the Israelites were going out defiantly. **14:9** The Egyptians chased after them, and all the horses and chariots of Pharaoh and his horsemen and his army overtook them camping by the sea, beside Pi-hahiroth, before Baal-Zephon. **14:10** When Pharaoh got closer, the Israelites looked up, and there were the Egyptians marching after them, and they were terrified. The Israelites cried out to the LORD, **14:11** and they said to Moses, "Is it because there are no graves in Egypt that you have taken us away to die in the desert? What in the world have you done to us by bringing us out of Egypt? **14:12** Isn't this what we told you in Egypt, 'Leave us alone so that we can serve the Egyptians, because it is better for us to serve the Egyptians than to die in the desert!'"

14:13 Moses said to the people, "Do not fear! Stand firm and see the salvation of the LORD that he will provide for you today; for the Egyptians that you see today you will
never, ever see again. **14:14** The LORD will fight for you, and you can be still."

14:15 The LORD said to Moses, "Why do you cry out to me? Tell the Israelites to move on. **14:16** And as for you, lift up your staff and extend your hand toward the sea and divide it, so that the Israelites may go through the middle of the sea on dry ground. **14:17** And as for me, I am going to harden the hearts of the Egyptians so that they will come after them, that I may be honored because of Pharaoh and his army and his chariots and his horsemen. **14:18** And the Egyptians will know that I am the LORD when I have gained my honor because of Pharaoh, his chariots, and his horsemen."

14:19 The angel of God, who was going before the camp of Israel, moved and went behind them, and the pillar of cloud moved from before them and stood behind them. **14:20** It came between the Egyptian camp and the Israelite camp; it was a dark cloud and it lit up the night so that one camp did not come near the other the whole night. **14:21** Moses stretched out his hand toward the sea, and the LORD drove the sea apart by a strong east wind all that night, and he made the sea into dry land, and the water was divided. **14:22** So the Israelites went through the middle of the sea on dry ground, the water forming a wall for them on their right and on their left.

14:23 The Egyptians chased them and followed them into the middle of the sea – all the horses of Pharaoh, his chariots, and his
horsemen. **14:24** In the morning watch the LORD looked down on the Egyptian army through the pillar of fire and cloud, and he threw the Egyptian army into a panic. **14:25** He jammed the wheels of their chariots so that they had difficulty driving, and the Egyptians said, "Let's flee from Israel, for the LORD fights for them against Egypt!"

14:26 The LORD said to Moses, "Extend your hand toward the sea, so that the waters may flow back on the Egyptians, on their chariots, and on their horsemen!" **14:27** So Moses extended his hand toward the sea, and the sea returned to its normal state when the sun began to rise. Now the Egyptians were fleeing before it, but the LORD overthrew the Egyptians in the middle of the sea. **14:28** The water returned and covered the chariots and the horsemen and all the army of Pharaoh that was coming after the Israelites into the sea – not so much as one of them survived! **14:29** But the Israelites walked on dry ground in the middle of the sea, the water forming a wall for them on their right and on their left. **14:30** So the LORD saved Israel on that day from the power of the Egyptians, and Israel saw the Egyptians dead on the shore of the sea. **14:31** When Israel saw the great power that the LORD had exercised over the Egyptians, they feared the LORD, and they believed in the LORD and in his servant Moses.

The Song of Triumph

15:1 Then Moses and the Israelites sang this song to the LORD. They said,
"I will sing to the LORD, for he has triumphed gloriously,
the horse and its rider he has thrown into the sea.
15:2 The LORD is my strength and my song,
and he has become my salvation.
This is my God, and I will praise him,
my father's God, and I will exalt him.
15:3 The LORD is a warrior,
the LORD is his name.
15:4 The chariots of Pharaoh and his army he has thrown into the sea,
and his chosen officers were drowned in the Red Sea.
15:5 The depths have covered them,
they went down to the bottom like a stone.
15:6 Your right hand, O LORD, was majestic in power,
your right hand, O LORD, shattered the enemy.
15:7 In the abundance of your majesty you have overthrown
those who rise up against you.
You sent forth your wrath;
it consumed them like stubble.
15:8 By the blast of your nostrils the waters were piled up,
the flowing water stood upright like a heap,
and the deep waters were solidified in the heart of the sea.
15:9 The enemy said, 'I will chase, I will overtake,
I will divide the spoil;
my desire will be satisfied on them.
I will draw my sword, my hand will destroy them.'
15:10 But you blew with your breath, and the sea covered them.
They sank like lead in the mighty waters.
15:11 Who is like you, O LORD, among the gods?
Who is like you? – majestic in holiness, fearful in praises, working wonders?
15:12 You stretched out your right hand,
the earth swallowed them.
15:13 By your loyal love you will lead the people whom you have redeemed;
you will guide them by your strength to your holy dwelling place.
15:14 The nations will hear and tremble;
anguish will seize the inhabitants of Philistia.
15:15 Then the chiefs of Edom will be terrified,
trembling will seize the leaders of Moab,
and the inhabitants of Canaan will shake.
15:16 Fear and dread will fall on them;
by the greatness of your arm they will be as still as stone
until your people pass by, O LORD,
until the people whom you have bought pass by.
15:17 You will bring them in and plant them in the mountain of your inheritance,
in the place you made for your residence, O LORD,
the sanctuary, O LORD, that your hands have established.
15:18 The LORD will reign forever and ever!
15:19 For the horses of Pharaoh came with his chariots and his footmen into the sea,
and the LORD brought back the waters of the sea on them,
but the Israelites walked on dry land in the middle of the sea."
15:20 Miriam the prophetess, the sister of Aaron, took a hand-drum in her hand, and all the women went out after her with hand-drums and with dances. **15:21** Miriam sang in response to them, "Sing to the LORD, for he has triumphed gloriously; the horse and its rider he has thrown into the sea."

The Bitter Water

15:22 Then Moses led Israel to journey away from the Red Sea. They went out to the Desert of Shur, walked for three days into the desert, and found no water. **15:23** Then they came to Marah, but they were not able to drink the waters of Marah, because they were bitter. (That is why its name was Marah.) **15:24** So the people murmured against Moses, saying, "What can we drink?" **15:25** He cried out to the LORD, and the LORD showed him a tree. When Moses threw it into the water, the water became safe to drink. There the LORD made for them a binding ordinance, and there he tested them. **15:26** He said, "If you will diligently obey the LORD your God, and do what is right in his sight, and pay attention to his commandments, and keep all his statutes, then all the diseases that I brought on the Egyptians I will not bring on you, for I, the LORD, am your healer."

15:27 Then they came to Elim, where there were twelve wells of water and seventy palm trees, and they camped there by the water.

The Provision of Manna

16:1 When they journeyed from Elim, the entire company of Israelites came to the Desert of Sin, which is between Elim and Sinai, on the fifteenth day of the second month after their exodus from the land of Egypt. **16:2** The entire company of Israelites murmured against Moses and Aaron in the desert. **16:3** The Israelites said to them, "If only we had died by the hand of the LORD in the land of Egypt, when we sat by the pots of meat, when we ate bread to the full, for you have brought us out into this desert to kill this whole assembly with hunger!"

16:4 Then the LORD said to Moses, "I am going to rain bread from heaven for you, and the people will go out and gather the amount for each day, so that I may test them. Will they will walk in my law or not? **16:5** On the sixth day they will prepare what they bring in, and it will be twice as much as they gather every other day."

16:6 Moses and Aaron said to all the Israelites, "In the evening you will know that the LORD has brought you out of the land of Egypt, **16:7** and in the morning you will see the glory of the LORD, because he has heard your murmurings against the LORD. As for us, what are we, that you should murmur against us?" **16:8** Moses said, "You will know this when the LORD gives you meat to eat in the evening and bread in the morning to satisfy you, because the LORD has heard your murmurings that you are murmuring against him. As for us, what are we? Your murmurings are not against us, but against the LORD."

16:9 Then Moses said to Aaron, "Tell the whole community of the Israelites, 'Come before the LORD, because he has heard your murmurings.'" **16:10** As Aaron spoke to the whole community of the Israelites and they looked toward the desert, there the glory of the LORD appeared in the cloud, **16:11** and the LORD spoke to Moses: **16:12** "I have heard the murmurings of the Israelites. Tell them, 'During the evening you will eat meat, and in the morning you will be satisfied with bread, so that you may know that I am the LORD your God.'"

16:13 In the evening the quail came up and covered the camp, and in the morning a layer of dew was all around the camp. **16:14** When the layer of dew had evaporated, there on the surface of the desert was a thin flaky substance, thin like frost on the earth. **16:15** When the Israelites saw it, they said to one another, "What is it?" because they did not know what it was. Moses said to them, "It is the bread that the LORD has given you for food. **16:16** "This is what the LORD has commanded: 'Each person is to gather from it what he can eat, an omer per person according to the number of your people; each one will pick it up for whoever lives in his tent.'" **16:17** The Israelites did so, and they gathered – some more, some less. **16:18** When they measured with an omer, the one who gathered much had nothing left over, and the one who gathered little lacked nothing; each one had gathered what he could eat.

16:19 Moses said to them, "No one is to keep any of it until morning." **16:20** But they did not listen to Moses; some kept part of it until morning, and it was full of worms and began to stink, and Moses was angry with them. **16:21** So they gathered it each morning, each person according to what he could eat, and when the sun got hot, it would melt. **16:22** And on the sixth day they gathered twice as much food, two omers per person; and all the leaders of the community came and told Moses. **16:23** He said to them, "This is what the LORD has said: 'Tomorrow is a time of cessation from work, a holy Sabbath to the LORD. Whatever you want to bake, bake today; whatever you want to boil, boil today; whatever is left put aside for yourselves to be kept until morning.'"

16:24 So they put it aside until the morning, just as Moses had commanded, and it did not stink, nor were there any worms in it. **16:25** Moses said, "Eat it today, for today is a Sabbath to the LORD; today you will not find it in the area. **16:26** Six days you will gather it, but on the seventh day, the Sabbath, there will not be any."

16:27 On the seventh day some of the people went out to gather it, but they found nothing. **16:28** So the LORD said to Moses, "How long do you refuse to obey my commandments and my instructions? **16:29** See, because the LORD has given you the Sabbath, that is why he is giving you food for two days on the sixth day. Each of you stay where you are; let no one go out of his place on the seventh day." **16:30** So the people rested on the seventh day.

16:31 The house of Israel called its name "manna." It was like coriander seed and was white, and it tasted like wafers with honey.

16:32 Moses said, "This is what the LORD has commanded: 'Fill an omer with it to be kept for generations to come, so that they may see the food I fed you in the desert when I brought you out from the land of Egypt.'" **16:33** Moses said to Aaron, "Take a jar and put in it an omer full of manna, and place it before the LORD to be kept for generations to come." **16:34** Just as the LORD commanded Moses, so Aaron placed it before the Testimony for safekeeping.

16:35 Now the Israelites ate manna forty years, until they came to a land that was inhabited; they ate manna until they came to the border of the land of Canaan. **16:36** (Now an omer is one tenth of an ephah.)
Water at Massa and Meribah
17:1 The whole community of the Israelites traveled on their journey from the Desert of Sin according to the LORD's instruction, and they pitched camp in Rephidim. Now there was no water for the people to drink. **17:2** So the people contended with Moses, and they said, "Give us water to drink!" Moses said to them, "Why do you contend with me? Why do you test the LORD?" **17:3** But the people were very thirsty there for water, and they murmured against Moses and said, "Why in the world did you bring us up out of Egypt – to kill us and our children and our cattle with thirst?"
17:4 Then Moses cried out to the LORD, "What will I do with this people? – a little more and they will stone me!" **17:5** The LORD said to Moses, "Go over before the people; take with you some of the elders of Israel and take in your hand your staff with which you struck the Nile and go. **17:6** I will be standing before you there on the rock in Horeb, and you will strike the rock, and water will come out of it so that the people may drink." And Moses did so in plain view of the elders of Israel.
17:7 He called the name of the place Massah and Meribah, because of the contending of the Israelites and because of their testing the LORD, saying, "Is the LORD among us or not?"
Victory over the Amalekites
17:8 Amalek came and attacked Israel in Rephidim. **17:9** So Moses said to Joshua, "Choose some of our men and go out, fight against Amalek. Tomorrow I will stand on top of the hill with the staff of God in my hand."
17:10 So Joshua fought against Amalek just as Moses had instructed him;and Moses and Aaron and Hur went up to the top of the hill. **17:11** Whenever Moses would raise his hands, then Israel prevailed, but whenever he would rest his hands, then Amalek prevailed. **17:12** When the hands of Moses became heavy, they took a stone and put it under him, and Aaron and Hur held up his hands, one on one side and one on the other, and so his hands were steady until the sun went down. **17:13** So Joshua destroyed Amalek and his army with the sword.
17:14 The LORD said to Moses, "Write this as a memorial in the book, and rehearse it in Joshua's hearing; for I will surely wipe out the remembrance of Amalek from under heaven. **17:15** Moses built an altar, and he called it "The LORD is my Banner," **17:16** for he said, "For a hand was lifted up to the throne of the LORD – that the LORD will have war with Amalek from generation to generation."
The Advice of Jethro
18:1 Jethro, the priest of Midian, Moses' father-in-law, heard about all that God had done for Moses and for his people Israel, that the LORD had brought Israel out of Egypt.
18:2 Jethro, Moses' father-in-law, took Moses' wife Zipporah after he had sent her back, **18:3** and her two sons, one of whom was named Gershom (for Moses had said, "I have been a foreigner in a foreign land"), **18:4** and the other Eliezer (for Moses had said, "The God of my father has been my help and delivered me from the sword of Pharaoh").
18:5 Jethro, Moses' father-in-law, together with Moses' sons and his wife, came to Moses in the desert where he was camping by the mountain of God. **18:6** He said to Moses, "I, your father-in-law Jethro, am coming to you, along with your wife and her two sons with her." **18:7** Moses went out to meet his father-in-law and bowed down and kissed him; they each asked about the other's welfare, and then they went into the tent. **18:8** Moses told his father-in-law all that the LORD had done to Pharaoh and to Egypt for Israel's sake, and all the hardship that had come on them along the way, and how the LORD had delivered them.
18:9 Jethro rejoiced because of all the good that the LORD had done for Israel, whom he had delivered from the hand of Egypt. **18:10** Jethro said, "Blessed be the LORD who has delivered you from the hand of Egypt, and from the hand of Pharaoh, who has delivered the people from the Egyptians' control! **18:11** Now I know that the LORD is greater than all the gods, for in the thing in which they dealt proudly against them he has destroyed them." **18:12** Then Jethro, Moses' father-in-law, brought a burnt offering and sacrifices for God, and Aaron and all the elders of Israel came to eat food with the father-in-law of Moses before God.
18:13 On the next day Moses sat to judge the people, and the people stood around Moses from morning until evening. **18:14** When Moses' father-in-law saw all that he was doing for the people, he said, "What is this that you are doing for the people? Why are you sitting by yourself, and all the people stand around you from morning until evening?"
18:15 Moses said to his father-in-law, "Because the people come to me to inquire of God. **18:16** When they have a dispute, it comes to me and I decide between a man and his neighbor, and I make known the decrees of God and his laws."
18:17 Moses' father-in-law said to him, "What you are doing is not good! **18:18** You will surely wear out, both you and these people who are with you, for this is too heavy a burden for you; you are not able to do it by yourself. **18:19** Now listen to me, I will give you advice, and may God be with you: You be a representative for the people to God, and you bring

their disputes to God; **18:20** warn them of the statutes and the laws, and make known to them the way in which they must walk and the work they must do. **18:21** But you choose from the people capable men, God-fearing, men of truth, those who hate bribes, and put them over the people as rulers of thousands, rulers of hundreds, rulers of fifties, and rulers of tens. **18:22** They will judge the people under normal circumstances, and every difficult case they will bring to you, but every small case they themselves will judge, so that you may make it easier for yourself, and they will bear the burden with you. **18:23** If you do this thing, and God so commands you, then you will be able to endure, and all these people will be able to go home satisfied."
18:24 Moses listened to his father-in-law and did everything he had said. **18:25** Moses chose capable men from all Israel, and he made them heads over the people, rulers of thousands, rulers of hundreds, rulers of fifties, and rulers of tens. **18:26** They judged the people under normal circumstances; the difficult cases they would bring to Moses, but every small case they would judge themselves.
18:27 Then Moses sent his father-in-law on his way, and so Jethro went to his own land.
Israel at Sinai
19:1 In the third month after the Israelites went out from the land of Egypt, on the very day, they came to the Desert of Sinai. **19:2** After they journeyed from Rephidim, they came to the Desert of Sinai, and they camped in the desert; Israel camped there in front of the mountain.
19:3 Moses went up to God, and the LORD called to him from the mountain, "Thus you will tell the house of Jacob, and declare to the people of Israel: **19:4** 'You yourselves have seen what I did to Egypt and how I lifted you on eagles' wings and brought you to myself. **19:5** And now, if you will diligently listen to me and keep my covenant, then you will be my special possession out of all the nations, for all the earth is mine, **19:6** and you will be to me a kingdom of priests and a holy nation.' These are the words that you will speak to the Israelites."
19:7 So Moses came and summoned the elders of Israel. He set before them all these words that the LORD had commanded him, **19:8** and all the people answered together, "All that the LORD has commanded we will do!" So Moses brought the words of the people back to the LORD.
19:9 The LORD said to Moses, "I am going to come to you in a dense cloud, so that the people may hear when I speak with you and so that they will always believe in you." And Moses told the words of the people to the LORD.
19:10 The LORD said to Moses, "Go to the people and sanctify them today and tomorrow, and make them wash their clothes **19:11** and be ready for the third day, for on the third day the LORD will come down on Mount Sinai in the sight of all the people. **19:12** You must set boundaries for the people all around, saying, 'Take heed to yourselves not to go up on the mountain nor touch its edge. Whoever touches the mountain will surely be put to death! **19:13** No hand will touch him – but he will surely be stoned or shot through, whether a beast or a human being; he must not live.' When the ram's horn sounds a long blast they may go up on the mountain."
19:14 Then Moses went down from the mountain to the people and sanctified the people, and they washed their clothes. **19:15** He said to the people, "Be ready for the third day. Do not go near your wives."
19:16 On the third day in the morning there was thunder and lightning and a dense cloud on the mountain, and the sound of a very loud horn; all the people who were in the camp trembled. **19:17** Moses brought the people out of the camp to meet God, and they took their place at the foot of the mountain. **19:18** Now Mount Sinai was completely covered with smoke because the LORD had descended on it in fire, and its smoke went up like the smoke of a great furnace, and the whole mountain shook violently. **19:19** When the sound of the horn grew louder and louder, Moses was speaking and God was answering him with a voice.
19:20 The LORD came down on Mount Sinai, on the top of the mountain, and the LORD summoned Moses to the top of the mountain, and Moses went up. **19:21** The LORD said to Moses, "Go down and solemnly warn the people, lest they force their way through to the LORD to look, and many of them perish. **19:22** Let the priests also, who approach the LORD, sanctify themselves, lest the LORD break through against them."
19:23 Moses said to the LORD, "The people are not able to come up to Mount Sinai, because you solemnly warned us, 'Set boundaries for the mountain and set it apart.'" **19:24** The LORD said to him, "Go, get down, and come up, and Aaron with you, but do not let the priests and the people force their way through to come up to the LORD, lest he break through against them." **19:25** So Moses went down to the people and spoke to them.
The Decalogue
20:1 God spoke all these words:
20:2 "I, the LORD, am your God, who brought you from the land of Egypt, from the house of slavery.
20:3 "You shall have no other gods before me.
20:4 "You shall not make for yourself a carved image or any likeness of anything that is in heaven above or that is on the earth beneath or that is in the water below. **20:5** You shall not bow down to them or serve them,

for I, the LORD, your God, am a jealous God, responding to the transgression of fathers by dealing with children to the third and fourth generations of those who reject me, **20:6** and showing covenant faithfulness to a thousand generations of those who love me and keep my commandments.

20:7 "You shall not take the name of the LORD your God in vain, for the LORD will not hold guiltless anyone who takes his name in vain.

20:8 "Remember the Sabbath day to set it apart as holy. **20:9** For six days you may labor and do all your work, **20:10** but the seventh day is a Sabbath to the LORD your God; on it you shall not do any work, you, or your son, or your daughter, or your male servant, or your female servant, or your cattle, or the resident foreigner who is in your gates. **20:11** For in six days the LORD made the heavens and the earth and the sea and all that is in them, and he rested on the seventh day; therefore the LORD blessed the Sabbath day and set it apart as holy.

20:12 "Honor your father and your mother, that you may live a long time in the land the LORD your God is giving to you.

20:13 "You shall not murder.

20:14 "You shall not commit adultery.

20:15 "You shall not steal.

20:16 "You shall not give false testimony against your neighbor.

20:17 "You shall not covet your neighbor's house. You shall not covet your neighbor's wife, nor his male servant, nor his female servant, nor his ox, nor his donkey, nor anything that belongs to your neighbor."

20:18 All the people were seeing the thundering and the lightning, and heard the sound of the horn, and saw the mountain smoking – and when the people saw it they trembled with fear and kept their distance. **20:19** They said to Moses, "You speak to us and we will listen, but do not let God speak with us, lest we die." **20:20** Moses said to the people, "Do not fear, for God has come to test you, that the fear of him may be before you so that you do not sin." **20:21** The people kept their distance, but Moses drew near the thick darkness where God was.

The Altar

20:22 The LORD said to Moses: "Thus you will tell the Israelites: 'You yourselves have seen that I have spoken with you from heaven. **20:23** You must not make gods of silver alongside me, nor make gods of gold for yourselves.

20:24 'You must make for me an altar made of earth, and you will sacrifice on it your burnt offerings and your peace offerings, your sheep and your cattle. In every place where I cause my name to be honored I will come to you and I will bless you. **20:25** If you make me an altar of stone, you must not build it of stones shaped with tools, for if you use your tool on it you have defiled it. **20:26** And you must not go up by steps to my altar, so that your nakedness is not exposed.'

The Decisions

21:1 "These are the decisions that you will set before them:

Hebrew Servants

21:2 "If you buy a Hebrew servant, he is to serve you for six years, but in the seventh year he will go out free without paying anything. **21:3** If he came in by himself he will go out by himself; if he had a wife when he came in, then his wife will go out with him. **21:4** If his master gave him a wife, and she bore sons or daughters, the wife and the children will belong to her master, and he will go out by himself. **21:5** But if the servant should declare, 'I love my master, my wife, and my children; I will not go out free,' **21:6** then his master must bring him to the judges, and he will bring him to the door or the doorposts, and his master will pierce his ear with an awl, and he shall serve him forever.

21:7 "If a man sells his daughter as a female servant, she will not go out as the male servants do. **21:8** If she does not please her master, who has designated her for himself, then he must let her be redeemed. He has no right to sell her to a foreign nation, because he has dealt deceitfully with her. **21:9** If he designated her for his son, then he will deal with her according to the customary rights of daughters. **21:10** If he takes another wife, he must not diminish the first one's food, her clothing, or her marital rights. **21:11** If he does not provide her with these three things, then she will go out free, without paying money.

Personal Injuries

21:12 "Whoever strikes someone so that he dies must surely be put to death. **21:13** But if he does not do it with premeditation, but it happens by accident, then I will appoint for you a place where he may flee. **21:14** But if a man willfully attacks his neighbor to kill him cunningly, you will take him even from my altar that he may die.

21:15 "Whoever strikes his father or his mother must surely be put to death.

21:16 "Whoever kidnaps someone and sells him, or is caught still holding him, must surely be put to death.

21:17 "Whoever treats his father or his mother disgracefully must surely be put to death.

21:18 "If men fight, and one strikes his neighbor with a stone or with his fist and he does not die, but must remain in bed, **21:19** and then if he gets up and walks about outside on his staff, then the one who struck him is innocent, except he must pay for the injured person's loss of time and see to it that he is fully healed.

21:20 "If a man strikes his male servant or his female servant with a staff so that he or she dies as a result of the blow, he will surely be punished. **21:21** However, if the injured servant survives one or two days, the owner will not be punished, for he has suffered the loss.

21:22 "If men fight and hit a pregnant woman and her child is born prematurely, but there is no serious injury, he will surely be punished in accordance with what the woman's husband demands of him, and he will pay what the court decides. **21:23** But if there is serious injury, then you will give a life for a life, **21:24** eye for eye, tooth for tooth, hand for hand, foot for foot, **21:25** burn for burn, wound for wound, bruise for bruise.

21:26 "If a man strikes the eye of his male servant or his female servant so that he destroys it, he will let the servant go free as compensation for the eye. **21:27** If he knocks out the tooth of his male servant or his female servant, he will let the servant go free as compensation for the tooth.

Laws about Animals

21:28 "If an ox gores a man or a woman so that either dies, then the ox must surely be stoned and its flesh must not be eaten, but the owner of the ox will be acquitted. **21:29** But if the ox had the habit of goring, and its owner was warned, and he did not take the necessary precautions, and then it killed a man or a woman, the ox must be stoned and the man must be put to death. **21:30** If a ransom is set for him, then he must pay the redemption for his life according to whatever amount was set for him. **21:31** If the ox gores a son or a daughter, the owner will be dealt with according to this rule. **21:32** If the ox gores a male servant or a female servant, the owner must pay thirty shekels of silver, and the ox must be stoned.

21:33 "If a man opens a pit or if a man digs a pit and does not cover it, and an ox or a donkey falls into it, **21:34** the owner of the pit must repay the loss. He must give money to its owner, and the dead animal will become his. **21:35** If the ox of one man injures the ox of his neighbor so that it dies, then they will sell the live ox and divide its proceeds, and they will also divide the dead ox. **21:36** Or if it is known that the ox had the habit of goring, and its owner did not take the necessary precautions, he must surely pay ox for ox, and the dead animal will become his.

Laws about Property

22:1 (21:37) "If a man steals an ox or a sheep and kills it or sells it, he must pay back five head of cattle for the ox, and four sheep for the one sheep.

22:2 "If a thief is caught breaking in and is struck so that he dies, there will be no blood guilt for him. **22:3** If the sun has risen on him, then there is blood guilt for him. A thief must surely make full restitution; if he has nothing, then he will be sold for his theft. **22:4** If the stolen item should in fact be found alive in his possession, whether it be an ox or a donkey or a sheep, he must pay back double.

22:5 "If a man grazes his livestock in a field or a vineyard, and he lets the livestock loose and they graze in the field of another man, he must make restitution from the best of his own field and the best of his own vineyard.

22:6 "If a fire breaks out and spreads to thorn bushes, so that stacked grain or standing grain or the whole field is consumed, the one who started the fire must surely make restitution.

22:7 "If a man gives his neighbor money or articles for safekeeping, and it is stolen from the man's house, if the thief is caught, he must repay double. **22:8** If the thief is not caught, then the owner of the house will be brought before the judges to see whether he has laid his hand on his neighbor's goods. **22:9** In all cases of illegal possessions, whether for an ox, a donkey, a sheep, a garment, or any kind of lost item, about which someone says 'This belongs to me,' the matter of the two of them will come before the judges, and the one whom the judges declare guilty must repay double to his neighbor. **22:10** If a man gives his neighbor a donkey or an ox or a sheep or any beast to keep, and it dies or is hurt or is carried away without anyone seeing it, **22:11** then there will be an oath to the LORD between the two of them, that he has not laid his hand on his neighbor's goods, and its owner will accept this, and he will not have to pay. **22:12** But if it was stolen from him, he will pay its owner. **22:13** If it is torn in pieces, then he will bring it for evidence, and he will not have to pay for what was torn.

22:14 "If a man borrows an animal from his neighbor, and it is hurt or dies when its owner was not with it, the man who borrowed it will surely pay. **22:15** If its owner was with it, he will not have to pay; if it was hired, what was paid for the hire covers it.

Moral and Ceremonial Laws

22:16 "If a man seduces a virgin who is not engaged and has sexual relations with her, he must surely endow her to be his wife. **22:17** If her father refuses to give her to him, he must pay money for the bride price of virgins.

22:18 "You must not allow a sorceress to live.

22:19 "Whoever has sexual relations with a beast must surely be put to death.

22:20 "Whoever sacrifices to a god other than the LORD alone must be utterly destroyed.

22:21 "You must not wrong a foreigner nor oppress him, for you were foreigners in the land of Egypt.

22:22 "You must not afflict any widow or orphan. **22:23** If you afflict them in any way and they cry to me, I will surely hear their cry, **22:24** and my anger will burn and I will kill you with the sword, and your wives will be widows and your children will be fatherless.

22:25 "If you lend money to any of my people who are needy among you, do not be like a moneylender to him; do not charge him interest. **22:26** If you do take the garment of your neighbor in pledge, you must return it to him by the time the sun goes down, **22:27** for it is his only covering – it is his garment for his body. What else can he sleep in? And when he cries out to me, I will hear, for I am gracious.

22:28 "You must not blaspheme God or curse the ruler of your people.

22:29 "Do not hold back offerings from your granaries or your vats. You must give me the firstborn of your sons. **22:30** You must also do this for your oxen and for your sheep; seven days they may remain with their mothers, but give them to me on the eighth day.

22:31 "You will be holy people to me; you must not eat any meat torn by animals in the field. You must throw it to the dogs.

Justice

23:1 "You must not give a false report. Do not make common cause with the wicked to be a malicious witness.

23:2   "You must not follow a crowd in doing evil things; in a lawsuit you must not offer testimony that agrees with a crowd so as to pervert justice, **23:3** and you must not show partiality to a poor man in his lawsuit.

23:4 "If you encounter your enemy's ox or donkey wandering off, you must by all means return it to him. **23:5** If you see the donkey of someone who hates you fallen under its load, you must not ignore him, but be sure to help him with it.

23:6 "You must not turn away justice for your poor people in their lawsuits. **23:7** Keep your distance from a false charge – do not kill the innocent and the righteous, for I will not justify the wicked.

23:8 "You must not accept a bribe, for a bribe blinds those who see and subverts the words of the righteous.

23:9 "You must not oppress a foreigner, since you know the life of a foreigner, for you were foreigners in the land of Egypt.

Sabbaths and Feasts

23:10 "For six years you are to sow your land and gather in its produce. **23:11** But in the seventh year you must let it lie fallow and leave it alone so that the poor of your people may eat, and what they leave any animal in the field may eat; you must do likewise with your vineyard and your olive grove. **23:12** For six days you are to do your work, but on the seventh day you must cease, in order that your ox and your donkey may rest and that your female servant's son and any hired help may refresh themselves.

23:13 "Pay attention to do everything I have told you, and do not even mention the names of other gods – do not let them be heard on your lips.

23:14 "Three times in the year you must make a pilgrim feast to me.

23:15 You are to observe the Feast of Unleavened Bread; seven days you must eat bread made without yeast, as I commanded you, at the appointed time of the month of Abib, for at that time you came out of Egypt. No one may appear before me empty-handed.

23:16 "You are also to observe the Feast of Harvest, the firstfruits of your labors that you have sown in the field, and the Feast of Ingathering at the end of the year when you have gathered in your harvest out of the field. **23:17** At three times in the year all your males will appear before the Lord GOD.

23:18 "You must not offer the blood of my sacrifice with bread containing yeast; the fat of my festal sacrifice must not remain until morning. **23:19** The first of the firstfruits of your soil you must bring to the house of the LORD your God.

"You must not cook a young goat in its mother's milk.

The Angel of the Presence

23:20 "I am going to send an angel before you to protect you as you journey and to bring you into the place that I have prepared. **23:21** Take heed because of him, and obey his voice; do not rebel against him, for he will not pardon your transgressions, for my name is in him. **23:22** But if you diligently obey him and do all that I command, then I will be an enemy to your enemies, and I will be an adversary to your adversaries. **23:23** For my angel will go before you and bring you to the Amorites, the Hittites, the Perizzites, the Canaanites, the Hivites, and the Jebusites, and I will destroy them completely.

23:24 "You must not bow down to their gods; you must not serve them or do according to their practices. Instead you must completely overthrow them and smash their standing stones to pieces. **23:25** You must serve the LORD your God, and he will bless your bread and your water, and I will remove sickness from your midst. **23:26** No woman will miscarry her young or be barren in your land. I will fulfill the number of your days.

23:27 "I will send my terror before you, and I will destroy all the people whom you encounter; I will make all your enemies turn their backs to you. **23:28** I will send hornets before you that will drive out the Hivite, the Canaanite, and the Hittite before you. **23:29** I will not drive them out before you in one year, lest the land become desolate and the wild animals multiply against you. **23:30** Little by little I will drive them out

before you, until you become fruitful and inherit the land. **23:31** I will set your boundaries from the Red Sea to the sea of the Philistines, and from the desert to the River, for I will deliver the inhabitants of the land into your hand, and you will drive them out before you.

23:32 "You must make no covenant with them or with their gods. **23:33** They must not live in your land, lest they make you sin against me, for if you serve their gods, it will surely be a snare to you."

The Lord Ratifies the Covenant

24:1 But to Moses the LORD said, "Come up to the LORD, you and Aaron, Nadab and Abihu, and seventy of the elders of Israel, and worship from a distance. **24:2** Moses alone may come near the LORD, but the others must not come near, nor may the people go up with him."

24:3 Moses came and told the people all the LORD's words and all the decisions. All the people answered together, "We are willing to do all the words that the LORD has said," **24:4** and Moses wrote down all the words of the LORD. Early in the morning he built an altar at the foot of the mountain and arranged twelve standing stones – according to the twelve tribes of Israel. **24:5** He sent young Israelite men, and they offered burnt offerings and sacrificed young bulls for peace offerings to the LORD. **24:6** Moses took half of the blood and put it in bowls, and half of the blood he splashed on the altar. **24:7** He took the Book of the Covenant and read it aloud to the people, and they said, "We are willing to do and obey all that the LORD has spoken." **24:8** So Moses took the blood and splashed it on the people and said, "This is the blood of the covenant that the LORD has made with you in accordance with all these words."

24:9 Moses and Aaron, Nadab and Abihu, and the seventy elders of Israel went up, **24:10** and they saw the God of Israel. Under his feet there was something like a pavement made of sapphire, clear like the sky itself. **24:11** But he did not lay a hand on the leaders of the Israelites, so they saw God, and they ate and they drank.

24:12 The LORD said to Moses, "Come up to me to the mountain and remain there, and I will give you the stone tablets with the law and the commandments that I have written, so that you may teach them." **24:13** So Moses set out with Joshua his attendant, and Moses went up the mountain of God. **24:14** He told the elders, "Wait for us in this place until we return to you. Here are Aaron and Hur with you. Whoever has any matters of dispute can approach them."

24:15 Moses went up the mountain, and the cloud covered the mountain. **24:16** The glory of the LORD resided on Mount Sinai, and the cloud covered it for six days. On the seventh day he called to Moses from within the cloud. **24:17** Now the appearance of the glory of the LORD was like a devouring fire on the top of the mountain in plain view of the people. **24:18** Moses went into the cloud when he went up the mountain, and Moses was on the mountain forty days and forty nights.

The Materials for the Sanctuary

25:1 The LORD spoke to Moses: **25:2** "Tell the Israelites to take an offering for me; from every person motivated by a willing heart you are to receive my offering. **25:3** This is the offering you are to accept from them: gold, silver, bronze, **25:4** blue, purple, scarlet, fine linen, goat's hair, **25:5** ram skins dyed red, fine leather, acacia wood, **25:6** oil for the light, spices for the anointing oil and for fragrant incense, **25:7** onyx stones, and other gems to be set in the ephod and in the breastpiece. **25:8** Let

them make for me a sanctuary, so that I may live among them. **25:9** According to all that I am showing you – the pattern of the tabernacle and the pattern of all its furnishings – you must make it exactly so.

The Ark of the Covenant

25:10 "They are to make an ark of acacia wood – its length is to be three feet nine inches, its width two feet three inches, and its height two feet three inches. **25:11** You are to overlay it with pure gold – both inside and outside you must overlay it, and you are to make a surrounding border of gold over it. **25:12** You are to cast four gold rings for it and put them on its four feet, with two rings on one side and two rings on the other side. **25:13** You are to make poles of acacia wood, overlay them with gold, **25:14** and put the poles into the rings at the sides of the ark in order to carry the ark with them. **25:15** The poles must remain in the rings of the ark; they must not be removed from it. **25:16** You are to put into the ark the testimony that I will give to you.

25:17 "You are to make an atonement lid of pure gold; its length is to be three feet nine inches, and its width is to be two feet three inches. **25:18** You are to make two cherubim of gold; you are to make them of hammered metal on the two ends of the atonement lid. **25:19** Make one cherub on one end and one cherub on the other end; from the atonement lid you are to make the cherubim on the two ends. **25:20** The cherubim are to be spreading their wings upward, overshadowing the atonement lid with their wings, and the cherubim are to face each other, looking toward the atonement lid. **25:21** You are to put the atonement lid on top of the ark, and in the ark you are to put the testimony I am giving you. **25:22** I will meet with you

there, and from above the atonement lid, from between the two cherubim that are over the ark of the testimony, I will speak with you about all that I will command you for the Israelites.

The Table for the Bread of the Presence

25:23 "You are to make a table of acacia wood; its length is to be three feet, its width one foot six inches, and its height two feet three inches. **25:24** You are to overlay it with pure gold, and you are to make a surrounding border of gold for it. **25:25** You are to make a surrounding frame for it about three inches broad, and you are to make a surrounding border of gold for its frame. **25:26** You are to make four rings of gold for it and attach the rings at the four corners where its four legs are. **25:27** The rings are to be close to the frame to provide places for the poles to carry the table. **25:28** You are to make the poles of acacia wood and overlay them with gold, so that the table may be carried with them. **25:29** You are to make its plates, its ladles, its pitchers, and its bowls, to be used in pouring out offerings; you are to make them of pure gold. **25:30** You are to set the Bread of the Presence on the table before me continually.

The Lampstand

25:31 "You are to make a lampstand of pure gold. The lampstand is to be made of hammered metal; its base and its shaft, its cups, its buds, and its blossoms are to be from the same piece. **25:32** Six branches are to extend from the sides of the lampstand, three branches of the lampstand from one side of it and three branches of the lampstand from the other side of it. **25:33** Three cups shaped like almond flowers with buds and blossoms are to be on one branch, and three cups shaped like almond flowers with buds and blossoms are to be on the next branch, and the same for the six branches extending from the lampstand. **25:34** On the lampstand there are to be four cups shaped like almond flowers with buds and blossoms, **25:35** with a bud under the first two branches from it, and a bud under the next two branches from it, and a bud under the third two branches from it, according to the six branches that extend from the lampstand. **25:36** Their buds and their branches will be one piece, all of it one hammered piece of pure gold.

25:37 "You are to make its seven lamps, and then set its lamps up on it, so that it will give light to the area in front of it. **25:38** Its trimmers and its trays are to be of pure gold. **25:39** About seventy-five pounds of pure gold is to be used for it and for all these utensils. **25:40** Now be sure to make them according to the pattern you were shown on the mountain.

The Tabernacle

26:1 "The tabernacle itself you are to make with ten curtains of fine twisted linen and blue and purple and scarlet; you are to make them with cherubim that are the work of an artistic designer. **26:2** The length of each curtain is to be forty-two feet, and the width of each curtain is to be six feet – the same size for each of the curtains. **26:3** Five curtains are to be joined, one to another, and the other five curtains are to be joined, one to another. **26:4** You are to make loops of blue material along the edge of the end curtain in one set, and in the same way you are to make loops in the outer edge of the end curtain in the second set. **26:5** You are to make fifty loops on the one curtain, and you are to make fifty loops on the end curtain which is on the second set, so that the loops are opposite one to another. **26:6** You are to make fifty gold clasps and join the curtains together with the clasps, so that the tabernacle is a unit.

26:7 "You are to make curtains of goats' hair for a tent over the tabernacle; you are to make eleven curtains. **26:8** The length of each curtain is to be forty-five feet, and the width of each curtain is to be six feet – the same size for the eleven curtains. **26:9** You are to join five curtains by themselves and six curtains by themselves. You are to double over the sixth curtain at the front of the tent. **26:10** You are to make fifty loops along the edge of the end curtain in one set and fifty loops along the edge of the curtain that joins the second set. **26:11** You are to make fifty bronze clasps and put the clasps into the loops and join the tent together so that it is a unit. **26:12** Now the part that remains of the curtains of the tent – the half curtain that remains will hang over at the back of the tabernacle. **26:13** The foot and a half on the one side and the foot and a half on the other side of what remains in the length of the curtains of the tent will hang over the sides of the tabernacle, on one side and the other side, to cover it.

26:14 "You are to make a covering for the tent out of ram skins dyed red and over that a covering of fine leather.

26:15 "You are to make the frames for the tabernacle out of acacia wood as uprights. **26:16** Each frame is to be fifteen feet long, and each frame is to be two feet three inches wide, **26:17** with two projections per frame parallel one to another. You are to make all the frames of the tabernacle in this way. **26:18** So you are to make the frames for the tabernacle: twenty frames for the south side, **26:19** and you are to make forty silver bases to go under the twenty frames – two bases under the first frame for its two projections, and likewise two bases under the next frame for its two projections; **26:20** and for the second side of the tabernacle, the north side, twenty frames, **26:21** and their forty silver bases, two bases under the first frame, and two bases under the next frame. **26:22** And for the back of the tabernacle on the west side you will make six frames. **26:23** You are to make two frames for the corners of the tabernacle on the back. **26:24** At the two corners they must be doubled at the lower end and finished together at the top in one ring. So it will be for both. **26:25** So there are to be eight frames and their silver bases, sixteen bases, two bases under the first frame, and two bases under the next frame.

26:26 "You are to make bars of acacia wood, five for the frames on one side of the tabernacle, **26:27** and five bars for the frames on the second side of the tabernacle, and five bars for the frames on the back of the tabernacle on the west. **26:28** The middle bar in the center of the frames will reach from end to end. **26:29** You are to overlay the frames with gold and make their rings of gold to provide places for the bars, and you are to overlay the bars with gold. **26:30** You are to set up the tabernacle according to the plan that you were shown on the mountain.

26:31 "You are to make a special curtain of blue, purple, and scarlet yarn and fine twisted linen; it is to be made with cherubim, the work of an artistic designer. **26:32** You are to hang it with gold hooks on four posts of acacia wood overlaid with gold, set in four silver bases. **26:33** You are to hang this curtain under the clasps and bring the ark of the testimony in there behind the curtain. The curtain will make a division for you between the Holy Place and the Most Holy Place. **26:34** You are to put the atonement lid on the ark of the testimony in the Most Holy Place. **26:35** You are to put the table outside the curtain and the lampstand on the south side of the tabernacle, opposite the table, and you are to place the table on the north side.

26:36 "You are to make a hanging for the entrance of the tent of blue, purple, and scarlet yarn and fine twined linen, the work of an embroiderer. **26:37** You are to make for the hanging five posts of acacia wood and overlay them with gold, and their hooks will be gold, and you are to cast five bronze bases for them.

The Altar

27:1 "You are to make the altar of acacia wood, seven feet six inches long, and seven feet six inches wide; the altar is to be square, and its height is to be four feet six inches. **27:2** You are to make its four horns on its four corners; its horns will be part of it, and you are to overlay it with bronze. **27:3** You are to make its pots for the ashes, its shovels, its tossing bowls, its meat hooks, and its fire pans – you are to make all its utensils of bronze. **27:4** You are to make a grating for it, a network of bronze, and you are to make on the network four bronze rings on its four corners. **27:5** You are to put it under the ledge of the altar below, so that the network will come halfway up the altar. **27:6** You are to make poles for the altar, poles of acacia wood, and you are to overlay them with bronze. **27:7** The poles are to be put into the rings so that the poles will be on two sides of the altar when carrying it. **27:8** You are to make the altar hollow, out of boards. Just as it was shown you on the mountain, so they must make it.

The Courtyard

27:9 "You are to make the courtyard of the tabernacle. For the south side there are to be hangings for the courtyard of fine twisted linen, one hundred fifty feet long for one side, **27:10** with twenty posts and their twenty bronze bases, with the hooks of the posts and their bands of silver. **27:11** Likewise for its length on the north side, there are to be hangings for one hundred fifty feet, with twenty posts and their twenty bronze bases, with silver hooks and bands on the posts. **27:12** The width of the court on the west side is to be seventy-five feet with hangings, with their ten posts and their ten bases. **27:13** The width of the court on the east side, toward the sunrise, is to be seventy-five feet. **27:14** The hangings on one side of the gate are to be twenty-two and a half feet long, with their three posts and their three bases. **27:15** On the second side there are to be hangings twenty-two and a half feet long, with their three posts and their three bases. **27:16** For the gate of the courtyard there is to be a curtain of thirty feet, of blue, purple, and scarlet yarn and fine twined linen, the work of an embroiderer, with four posts and their four bases. **27:17** All the posts around the courtyard are to have silver bands; their hooks are to be silver, and their bases bronze. **27:18** The length of the courtyard is to be one hundred fifty feet and the width seventy-five feet, and the height of the fine twisted linen hangings is to be seven and a half feet, with their bronze bases. **27:19** All the utensils of the tabernacle used in all its service, all its tent pegs, and all the tent pegs of the courtyard are to be made of bronze.

Offering the Oil

27:20 "You are to command the Israelites that they bring to you pure oil of pressed olives for the light, so that the lamps will burn regularly. **27:21** In the tent of meeting outside the curtain that is before the testimony, Aaron and his sons are to arrange it from evening to morning before the LORD. This is to be a lasting ordinance among the Israelites for generations to come.

The Clothing of the Priests

28:1 "And you, bring near to you your brother Aaron and his sons with him from among the Israelites, so that they may minister as my priests – Aaron, Nadab and Abihu, Eleazar and Ithamar, Aaron's sons. **28:2** You must make holy garments for your brother Aaron, for glory and for beauty. **28:3** You are to speak to all who are specially skilled, whom I have filled with the spirit of wisdom, so that they may make Aaron's garments to set him apart to minister as my priest. **28:4** Now these are the garments that they are to make: a breastpiece, an ephod, a robe, a fitted tunic, a turban, and a sash. They are to make holy garments for your brother Aaron and for his sons, that they may minister as my priests. **28:5** The artisans are to use the gold, blue, purple, scarlet, and fine linen.

28:6 "They are to make the ephod of gold, blue, purple, scarlet, and fine twisted linen, the work of an artistic designer. **28:7** It is to have two shoulder pieces attached to two of its corners, so it can be joined together. **28:8** The artistically woven waistband of the ephod that is on it is to be like it, of one piece with the ephod, of gold, blue, purple, scarlet, and fine twisted linen.

28:9 "You are to take two onyx stones and engrave on them the names of the sons of Israel, **28:10** six of their names on one stone, and the six remaining names on the second stone, according to the order of their birth. **28:11** You are to engrave the two stones with the names of the sons of Israel with the work of an engraver in stone, like the engravings of a seal; you are to have them set in gold filigree settings. **28:12** You are to put the two stones on the shoulders of the ephod, stones of memorial for the sons of Israel, and Aaron will bear their names before the LORD on his two shoulders for

a memorial. **28:13** You are to make filigree settings of gold **28:14** and two braided chains of pure gold, like a cord, and attach the chains to the settings.

28:15 "You are to make a breastpiece for use in making decisions, the work of an artistic designer; you are to make it in the same fashion as the ephod; you are to make it of gold, blue, purple, scarlet, and fine twisted linen. **28:16** It is to be square when doubled, nine inches long and nine inches wide. **28:17** You are to set in it a setting for stones, four rows of stones, a row with a ruby, a topaz, and a beryl – the first row; **28:18** and the second row, a turquoise, a sapphire, and an emerald; **28:19** the third row, a jacinth, an agate, and an amethyst; **28:20** and the fourth row, a chrysolite, an onyx, and a jasper. They are to be enclosed in gold in their filigree settings. **28:21** The stones are to be for the names of the sons of Israel, twelve, according to the number of their names. Each name according to the twelve tribes is to be like the engravings of a seal.

28:22 "You are to make for the breastpiece braided chains like cords of pure gold, **28:23** and you are to make for the breastpiece two gold rings and attach the two rings to the upper two ends of the breastpiece. **28:24** You are to attach the two gold chains to the two rings at the ends of the breastpiece; **28:25** the other two ends of the two chains you will attach to the two settings and then attach them to the shoulder pieces of the ephod at the front of it. **28:26** You are to make two rings of gold and put them on the other two ends of the breastpiece, on its edge

that is on the inner side of the ephod. **28:27** You are to make two more gold rings and attach them to the bottom of the two shoulder pieces on the front of the ephod, close to the juncture above the waistband of the ephod. **28:28** They are to tie the breastpiece by its rings to the rings of the ephod by blue cord, so that it may be above the waistband of the ephod, and so that the breastpiece will not be loose from the ephod. **28:29** Aaron will bear the names of the sons of Israel in the breastpiece of decision over his heart when he goes into the holy place, for a memorial before the LORD continually.

28:30 "You are to put the Urim and the Thummim into the breastpiece of decision; and they are to be over Aaron's heart when he goes in before the LORD. Aaron is to bear the decisions of the Israelites over his heart before the LORD continually.

28:31 "You are to make the robe of the ephod completely blue. **28:32** There is to be an opening in its top in the center of it, with an edge all around the opening, the work of a weaver, like the opening of a collar, so that it cannot be torn. **28:33** You are to make pomegranates of blue, purple, and scarlet all around its hem and bells of gold between them all around. **28:34** The pattern is to be a gold bell and a pomegranate, a gold bell and a pomegranate, all around the hem of the robe. **28:35** The robe is to be on Aaron as he ministers, and his sound will be heard when he enters the Holy Place before the LORD and when he leaves, so that he does not die.

28:36 "You are to make a plate of pure gold and engrave on it the way a seal is engraved: "Holiness to the LORD." **28:37** You are to attach to it a blue cord so that it will be on the turban; it is to be on the front of the turban, **28:38** It will be on Aaron's forehead, and Aaron will bear the iniquity of the holy things, which the Israelites to sanctify by all their holy gifts; it will always be on his forehead, for their acceptance before the LORD. **28:39** You are to weave the tunic of fine linen and make the turban of fine linen, and make the sash the work of an embroiderer.

28:40 "For Aaron's sons you are to make tunics, sashes, and headbands for glory and for beauty.

28:41 "You are to clothe them – your brother Aaron and his sons with him – and anoint them and ordain them and set them apart as holy, so that they may minister as my priests. **28:42** Make for them linen undergarments to cover their naked bodies; they must cover from the waist to the thighs. **28:43** These must be on Aaron and his sons when they enter to the tent of meeting, or when they approach the altar to minister in the Holy Place, so that they bear no iniquity and die. It is to be a perpetual ordinance for him and for his descendants after him.

The Consecration of Aaron and His Sons

29:1 "Now this is what you are to do for them to consecrate them so that they may minister as my priests. Take a young bull and two rams without blemish; **29:2** and bread made without yeast, and perforated cakes without yeast mixed with oil, and wafers without yeast spread with oil – you are to make them using fine wheat flour. **29:3** You are to put them in one basket and present them in the basket, along with the bull and the two rams.

29:4 "You are to present Aaron and his sons at the entrance of the tent of meeting. You are to wash them with water **29:5** and take the garments and clothe Aaron with the tunic, the robe of the ephod, the ephod, and the breastpiece; you are to fasten the ephod on him by using the skillfully woven waistband. **29:6** You are to put the turban on his head and put the holy diadem on the turban. **29:7** You are to take the anointing oil and pour it on his head and anoint him. **29:8** You are to present his sons and clothe them with tunics **29:9** and wrap the sashes around Aaron and his sons and put headbands on them, and so the ministry of priesthood will belong to them by a perpetual ordinance. Thus you are to consecrate Aaron and his sons.

29:10 "You are to present the bull at the front of the tent of meeting, and Aaron and his sons are to put their hands on the head of the bull. **29:11** You are to kill the bull before the LORD at the entrance to the tent of meeting **29:12** and take some of the blood of the bull and put it on the horns of the altar with your finger; all the rest of the blood you are to pour out at the base of the altar. **29:13** You are to take all the fat that covers the entrails, and the lobe that is above the liver, and the two kidneys and the fat that is on them, and burn them on the altar. **29:14** But the meat of the bull, its skin, and its dung you are to burn up outside the camp. It is the purification offering.

29:15 "You are to take one ram, and Aaron and his sons are to lay their hands on the ram's head, **29:16** and you are to kill the ram and take its blood and splash it all around on the altar. **29:17** Then you are to cut the ram into pieces and wash the entrails and its legs and put them on its pieces and on its head **29:18** and burn the whole ram on the altar. It is a burnt offering to the LORD, a soothing aroma; it is an offering made by fire to the LORD.

29:19 "You are to take the second ram, and Aaron and his sons are to lay their hands on the ram's head, **29:20** and you are to kill the ram and take some of its blood and put it on the tip of the right ear of Aaron, on the tip of the right ear of his sons, on the thumb of their right hand, and on the big toe of their right foot, and then splash the blood all around on the altar. **29:21** You are to take some of the blood that is on the altar and some of the anointing oil and sprinkle it on Aaron, on his garments, on his sons, and on his sons' garments with him, so that he may be holy, he and his garments along with his sons and his sons' garments.

29:22 "You are to take from the ram the fat, the fat tail, the fat that covers the entrails, the lobe of the liver, the two kidneys and the fat that is on them, and the right thigh – for it is the ram for consecration – **29:23** and one round flat cake of bread, one perforated cake of oiled bread, and one wafer from the basket of bread made without yeast that is before the LORD. **29:24** You are to put all these in Aaron's hands and in his sons' hands, and you are to wave them as a wave offering before the LORD. **29:25** Then you are to take them from their hands and burn them on the altar for a burnt offering, for a soothing aroma before the LORD. It is an offering made by fire to the LORD. **29:26** You are to take the breast of the ram of Aaron's consecration; you are to wave it as a wave offering before the LORD, and it is to be your share. **29:27** You are to sanctify the breast of the wave offering and the thigh of the contribution, which were waved and lifted up as a contribution from the ram of consecration, from what belongs to Aaron and to his sons. **29:28** It is to belong to Aaron and to his sons from the Israelites, by a perpetual ordinance, for it is a contribution. It is to be a contribution from the Israelites from their peace offerings, their contribution to the LORD.

29:29 "The holy garments that belong to Aaron are to belong to his sons after him, so that they may be anointed in them and consecrated in them. **29:30** The priest who succeeds him from his sons, when he first comes to the tent of meeting to minister in the Holy Place, is to wear them for seven days.

29:31 "You are to take the ram of the consecration and cook its meat in a holy place. **29:32** Aaron and his sons are to eat the meat of the ram and the bread that was in the basket at the entrance of the tent of meeting. **29:33** They are to eat those things by which atonement was made to consecrate and to set them apart, but no one else may eat them, for they are holy. **29:34** If any of the meat from the consecration offerings or any of the bread is left over until morning, then you are to burn up what is left over. It must not be eaten, because it is holy.

29:35 "Thus you are to do for Aaron and for his sons, according to all that I have commanded you; you are to consecrate them for seven days. **29:36** Every day you are to prepare a bull for a purification offering for atonement. You are to purge the altar by making atonement for it, and you are to anoint it to set it apart as holy. **29:37** For seven days you are to make atonement for the altar and set it apart as holy. Then the altar will be most holy. Anything that touches the altar will be holy.

29:38 "Now this is what you are to prepare on the altar every day continually: two lambs a year old. **29:39** The first lamb you are to prepare in the morning, and the second lamb you are to prepare around sundown. **29:40** With the first lamb offer a tenth of an ephah of fine flour mixed with a fourth of a hin of oil from pressed olives, and a fourth of a hin of wine as a drink offering. **29:41** The second lamb you are to offer around sundown; you are to prepare for it the same meal offering as for the morning and the same drink offering, for a soothing aroma, an offering made by fire to the LORD.

29:42 "This will be a regular burnt offering throughout your generations at the entrance of the tent of meeting before the LORD, where I will meet with you to speak to you there. **29:43** There I will meet with the Israelites, and it will be set apart as holy by my glory.

29:44 "So I will set apart as holy the tent of meeting and the altar, and I will set apart as holy Aaron and his sons, that they may minister as priests to me. **29:45** I will reside among the Israelites, and I will be their God, **29:46** and they will know that I am the LORD their God, who brought them out from the land of Egypt, so that I may reside among them. I am the LORD their God.

The Altar of Incense

30:1 "You are to make an altar for burning incense; you are to make it of acacia wood. **30:2** Its length is to be a foot and a half and its width a foot and a half; it will be square. Its height is to be three feet, with its horns of one piece with it. **30:3** You are to overlay it with pure gold – its top, its four walls, and its horns – and make a surrounding border of gold for it. **30:4** You are to make two gold rings for it under its border, on its two flanks; you are to make them on its two sides. The rings will be places for poles to carry it with. **30:5** You are to make the poles of acacia wood and overlay them with gold.

30:6 "You are to put it in front of the curtain that is before the ark of the testimony (before the atonement lid that is over the testimony), where I will meet you. **30:7** Aaron is to burn sweet incense on it morning by morning; when he attends to the lamps he is to burn incense. **30:8** When Aaron sets up the lamps around sundown he is to burn incense on it; it is to be a regular incense offering before the LORD throughout your generations. **30:9** You must not offer strange incense on it, nor burnt offering, nor meal offering, and you must not pour out a drink offering on it. **30:10** Aaron is to make atonement on its horns once in the year with some of the blood of the sin offering for atonement; once in the year he is to make atonement on it throughout your generations. It is most holy to the LORD."

The Ransom Money

30:11 The LORD spoke to Moses: **30:12** "When you take a census of the Israelites according to their number, then each man is to pay a ransom for his life to the LORD when you number them, so that there will be no plague among them when you number them. **30:13** Everyone who crosses over to those who are numbered is to pay this: a half shekel according to the shekel of the sanctuary (a shekel weighs twenty gerahs). The half shekel is to be an offering to the LORD. **30:14** Everyone who crosses over to those numbered, from twenty years old and up, is to pay an offering to the LORD. **30:15** The rich are not to increase it, and the poor are not to pay less than the half shekel when giving the offering of the LORD, to make atonement for your lives. **30:16** You are to receive the atonement money from the Israelites and give it for the service of the tent of meeting. It will be a memorial for the Israelites before the LORD, to make atonement for your lives."

The Bronze Laver

30:17 The LORD spoke to Moses: **30:18** "You are also to make a large bronze basin with a bronze stand for washing. You are to put it between the tent of meeting and the altar and put water in it, **30:19** and Aaron and his sons must wash their hands and their feet from it. **30:20** When they enter the tent of meeting, they must wash with water so that they do not die. Also, when they approach the altar to minister by burning incense as an offering made by fire to the LORD, **30:21** they must wash their hands and their feet so that they do not die. And this will be a perpetual ordinance for them and for their descendants throughout their generations."

Oil and Incense

30:22 The LORD spoke to Moses: **30:23** "Take choice spices: twelve and a half pounds of free-flowing myrrh, half that – about six and a quarter pounds – of sweet-smelling cinnamon, six and a quarter pounds of sweet-smelling cane, **30:24** and twelve and a half pounds of cassia, all weighed according to the sanctuary shekel, and four quarts of olive oil. **30:25** You are to make this into a sacred anointing oil, a perfumed compound, the work of a perfumer. It will be sacred anointing oil.

30:26 "With it you are to anoint the tent of meeting, the ark of the testimony, **30:27** the table and all its utensils, the lampstand and its utensils, the altar of incense, **30:28** the altar for the burnt offering and all its utensils, and the laver and its base. **30:29** So you are to sanctify them, and they will be most holy; anything that touches them will be holy.

30:30 "You are to anoint Aaron and his sons and sanctify them, so that they may minister as my priests. **30:31** And you are to tell the Israelites: 'This is to be my sacred anointing oil throughout your generations. **30:32** It must not be applied to people's bodies, and you must not make any like it with the same recipe. It is holy, and it must be holy to you. **30:33** Whoever makes perfume like it and whoever puts any of it on someone not a priest will be cut off from his people.'"

30:34 The LORD said to Moses: "Take spices, gum resin, onycha, galbanum, and pure frankincense of equal amounts **30:35** and make it into an incense, a perfume, the work of a perfumer. It is to be finely ground, and

pure and sacred. **30:36** You are to beat some of it very fine and put some of it before the ark of the testimony in the tent of meeting where I will meet with you; it is to be most holy to you. **30:37** And the incense that you are to make, you must not make for yourselves using the same recipe; it is to be most holy to you, belonging to the LORD. **30:38** Whoever makes anything like it, to use as perfume, will be cut off from his people."

Willing Artisans

31:1 The LORD spoke to Moses: **31:2** "See, I have chosen Bezalel son of Uri, the son of Hur, of the tribe of Judah, **31:3** and I have filled him with the Spirit of God in skill, in understanding, in knowledge, and in all kinds of craftsmanship, **31:4** to make artistic designs for work with gold, with silver, and with bronze, **31:5** and with cutting and setting stone, and with cutting wood, to work in all kinds of craftsmanship. **31:6** Moreover, I have also given him Oholiab son of Ahisamach, of the tribe of Dan, and I have given ability to all the specially skilled, that they may make everything I have commanded you: **31:7** the tent of meeting, the ark of the testimony, the atonement lid that is on it, all the furnishings of the tent, **31:8** the table with its utensils, the pure lampstand with all its utensils, the altar of incense, **31:9** the altar for the burnt offering with all its utensils, the large basin with its base, **31:10** the woven garments, the holy garments for Aaron the priest and the garments for his sons, to minister as priests, **31:11** the anointing oil, and sweet incense for the Holy Place. They will make all these things just as I have commanded you."

Sabbath Observance

31:12 The LORD said to Moses, **31:13** "Tell the Israelites, 'Surely you must keep my Sabbaths, for it is a sign between me and you throughout your generations, that you may know that I am the LORD who sanctifies you. **31:14** So you must keep the Sabbath, for it is holy for you. Everyone who defiles it must surely be put to death; indeed, if anyone does any work on it, then that person will be cut off from among his people. **31:15** Six days work may be done, but on the seventh day is a Sabbath of complete rest, holy to the LORD; anyone who does work on the Sabbath day must surely be put to death. **31:16** The Israelites must keep the Sabbath by observing the Sabbath throughout their generations as a perpetual covenant. **31:17** It is a sign between me and the Israelites forever; for in six days the LORD made the heavens and the earth, and on the seventh day he rested and was refreshed.'"

31:18 He gave Moses two tablets of testimony when he had finished speaking with him on Mount Sinai, tablets of stone written by the finger of God.

The Sin of the Golden Calf

32:1 When the people saw that Moses delayed in coming down from the mountain, they gathered around Aaron and said to him, "Get up, make us gods that will go before us. As for this fellow Moses, the man who brought us up from the land of Egypt, we do not know what has become of him!"

32:2 So Aaron said to them, "Break off the gold earrings that are on the ears of your wives, your sons, and your daughters, and bring them to me." **32:3** So all the people broke off the gold earrings that were on their ears and brought them to Aaron. **32:4** He accepted the gold from them, fashioned it with an engraving tool, and made a molten calf. Then they said, "These are your gods, O Israel, who brought you up out of Egypt."

32:5 When Aaron saw this, he built an altar before it, and Aaron made a proclamation and said, "Tomorrow will be a feast to the LORD." **32:6** So they got up early on the next day and offered up burnt offerings and brought peace offerings, and the people sat down to eat and drink, and they rose up to play.

32:7 The LORD spoke to Moses: "Go quickly, descend, because your people, whom you brought up from the land of Egypt, have acted corruptly. **32:8** They have quickly turned aside from the way that I commanded them – they have made for themselves a molten calf and have bowed down to it and sacrificed to it and said, 'These are your gods, O Israel, which brought you up from the land of Egypt.'"

32:9 Then the LORD said to Moses: "I have seen this people. Look what a stiff-necked people they are! **32:10** So now, leave me alone so that my anger can burn against them and I can destroy them, and I will make from you a great nation."

32:11 But Moses sought the favor of the LORD his God and said, "O LORD, why does your anger burn against your people, whom you have brought out from the land of Egypt with great power and with a mighty hand? **32:12** Why should the Egyptians say, 'For evil he led them out to kill them in the mountains and to destroy them from the face of the earth'? Turn from your burning anger, and relent of this evil against your people. **32:13** Remember Abraham, Isaac, and Israel your servants, to whom you swore by yourself and told them, 'I will multiply your descendants like the stars of heaven, and all this land that I have spoken about I will give to your descendants, and they will inherit it forever.'"

32:14 Then the LORD relented over the evil that he had said he would do to his people.

32:15 Moses turned and went down from the mountain with the two tablets of the testimony in his hands. The tablets were written on both sides – they were written on the front and on the back. **32:16** Now the tablets were the work of God, and the writing was the writing of God, engraved on the tablets. **32:17** When Joshua heard the noise of the people as they shouted, he said to Moses, "It is the sound of war in the camp!" **32:18** Moses said, "It is not the sound of those who shout for victory, nor is it the sound of those who cry because they are overcome, but the sound of singing I hear."

32:19 When he approached the camp and saw the calf and the dancing, Moses became extremely angry. He threw the tablets from his hands and broke them to pieces at the bottom of the mountain. **32:20** He took the calf they had made and burned it in the fire, ground it to powder, poured it out on the water, and made the Israelites drink it.

32:21 Moses said to Aaron, "What did this people do to you, that you have brought on them so great a sin?" **32:22** Aaron said, "Do not let your anger burn hot, my lord; you know these people, that they tend to evil. **32:23** They said to me, 'Make us gods that will go before us, for as for this fellow Moses, the man who brought us up out of the land of Egypt, we do not know what has happened to him.' **32:24** So I said to them, 'Whoever has gold, break it off.' So they gave it to me, and I threw it into the fire, and this calf came out."

32:25 Moses saw that the people were running wild, for Aaron had let them get completely out of control, causing derision from their enemies. **32:26** So Moses stood at the entrance of the camp and said, "Whoever is for the LORD, come to me." All the Levites gathered around him, **32:27** and he said to them, "Thus says the LORD, the God of Israel, 'Each man fasten his sword on his side, and go back and forth from entrance to entrance throughout the camp, and each one kill his brother, his friend, and his neighbor.'" **32:28** The Levites did what Moses ordered, and that day about three thousand men of the people died. **32:29** Moses said, "You have been consecrated today for the LORD, for each of you was against his son or against his brother, so he has given a blessing to you today."

32:30 The next day Moses said to the people, "You have committed a very serious sin, but now I will go up to the LORD – perhaps I can make atonement on behalf of your sin." **32:31** So Moses returned to the LORD and said, "Alas, this people has committed a very serious sin, and they have made for themselves gods of gold. **32:32** But now, if you will forgive their sin…, but if not, wipe me out from your book that you have written." **32:33** The LORD said to Moses, "Whoever has sinned against me – that person I will wipe out of my book. **32:34** So now go, lead the people to the place I have spoken to you about. See, my angel will go before you. But on the day that I punish, I will indeed punish them for their sin."

32:35 And the LORD sent a plague on the people because they had made the calf – the one Aaron made.

33:1 The LORD said to Moses, "Go up from here, you and the people whom you brought up out of the land of Egypt, to the land I promised on oath to Abraham, to Isaac, and to Jacob, saying, 'I will give it to your descendants.' **33:2** I will send an angel before you, and I will drive out the Canaanite, the Amorite, the Hittite, the Perizzite, the Hivite, and the Jebusite. **33:3** Go up to a land flowing with milk and honey. But I will not go up among you, for you are a stiff-necked people, and I might destroy you on the way."

33:4 When the people heard this troubling word they mourned; no one put on his ornaments. **33:5** For the LORD had said to Moses, "Tell the Israelites, 'You are a stiff-necked people. If I went up among you for a moment, I might destroy you. Now take off your ornaments, that I may know what I should do to you.'" **33:6** So the Israelites stripped off their ornaments by Mount Horeb.

The Presence of the Lord

33:7 Moses took the tent and pitched it outside the camp, at a good distance from the camp, and he called it the tent of meeting. Anyone seeking the LORD would go out to the tent of meeting that was outside the camp. **33:8** And when Moses went out to the tent, all the people would get up and stand at the entrance to their tents and watch Moses until he entered the tent. **33:9** And whenever Moses entered the tent, the pillar of cloud would descend and stand at the entrance of the tent, and the LORD would speak with Moses. **33:10** When all the people would see the pillar of cloud standing at the entrance of the tent, all the people, each one at the entrance of his own tent, would rise and worship. **33:11** The LORD would speak to Moses face to face, the way a person speaks to a friend. Then Moses would return to the camp, but his servant, Joshua son of Nun, a young man, did not leave the tent.

33:12 Moses said to the LORD, "See, you have been saying to me, 'Bring this people up,' but you have not let me know whom you will send with me. But you said, 'I know you by name, and also you have found favor in my sight.' **33:13** Now if I have found favor in your sight, show me your way, that I may know you, that I may continue to find favor in your sight. And see that this nation is your people."

33:14 And the LORD said, "My presence will go with you, and I will give you rest."

33:15 And Moses said to him, "If your presence does not go with us, do not take us up from here. **33:16** For how will it be known then that I have found favor in your sight, I and your people? Is it not by your going with us, so that we will be distinguished, I and your people, from all the people who are on the face of the earth?"

33:17 The LORD said to Moses, "I will do this thing also that you have requested, for you have found favor in my sight, and I know you by name."

33:18 And Moses said, "Show me your glory."

33:19 And the LORD said, "I will make all my goodness pass before your face, and I will proclaim the LORD by name before you; I will be gracious to whom I will be gracious, I will show mercy to whom I will show mercy." **33:20** But he added, "You cannot see my face, for no one can see me and live." **33:21** The LORD said, "Here is a place by me; you will station yourself on a rock. **33:22** When my glory passes by, I will put you in a cleft in the rock and will cover you with my hand while I pass by. **33:23** Then I will take away my hand, and you will see my back, but my face must not be seen."

The New Tablets of the Covenant

34:1 The LORD said to Moses, "Cut out two tablets of stone like the first, and I will write on the tablets the words that were on the first tablets, which you smashed. **34:2** Be prepared in the morning, and go up in the morning to Mount Sinai, and station yourself for me there on the top of the mountain. **34:3** No one is to come up with you; do not let anyone be seen anywhere on the mountain; not even the flocks or the herds may graze in front of that mountain." **34:4** So Moses cut out two tablets of stone like the first; early in the morning he went up to Mount Sinai, just as the LORD had commanded him, and he took in his hand the two tablets of stone.

34:5 The LORD descended in the cloud and stood with him there and proclaimed the LORD by name. **34:6** The LORD passed by before him and proclaimed: "The LORD, the LORD, the compassionate and gracious God, slow to anger, and abounding in loyal love and faithfulness, **34:7** keeping loyal love for thousands, forgiving iniquity and transgression and sin. But he by no means leaves the guilty unpunished, responding to the transgression of fathers by dealing with children and children's children, to the third and fourth generation."

34:8 Moses quickly bowed to the ground and worshiped **34:9** and said, "If now I have found favor in your sight, O Lord, let my Lord go among us, for we are a stiff-necked people; pardon our iniquity and our sin, and take us for your inheritance."

34:10 He said, "See, I am going to make a covenant before all your people. I will do wonders such as have not been done in all the earth, nor in any nation. All the people among whom you live will see the work of the LORD, for it is a fearful thing that I am doing with you.

34:11 "Obey what I am commanding you this day. I am going to drive out before you the Amorite, the Canaanite, the Hittite, the Perizzite, the Hivite, and the Jebusite. **34:12** Be careful not to make a covenant with the inhabitants of the land where you are going, lest it become a snare among you. **34:13** Rather you must destroy their altars, smash their images, and cut down their Asherah poles. **34:14** For you must not worship any other god, for the LORD, whose name is Jealous, is a jealous God. **34:15** Be careful not to make a covenant with the inhabitants of the land, for when they prostitute themselves to their gods and sacrifice to their gods, and someone invites you, you will eat from his sacrifice; **34:16** and you then take his daughters for your sons, and when his daughters prostitute themselves to their gods, they will make your sons prostitute themselves to their gods as well. **34:17** You must not make yourselves molten gods.

34:18 "You must keep the Feast of Unleavened Bread. For seven days you must eat bread made without yeast, as I commanded you; do this at the appointed time of the month Abib, for in the month Abib you came out of Egypt.

34:19 "Every firstborn of the womb belongs to me, even every firstborn of your cattle that is a male, whether ox or sheep. **34:20** Now the firstling of a donkey you may redeem with a lamb, but if you do not redeem it, then break its neck. You must redeem all the firstborn of your sons.

"No one will appear before me empty-handed.

34:21 "On six days you may labor, but on the seventh day you must rest; even at the time of plowing and of harvest you are to rest.

34:22 "You must observe the Feast of Weeks – the firstfruits of the harvest of wheat – and the Feast of Ingathering at the end of the year. **34:23** At three times in the year all your men must appear before the Lord GOD, the God of Israel. **34:24** For I will drive out the nations before you and enlarge your borders; no one will covet your land when you go up to appear before the LORD your God three times in the year.

34:25 "You must not offer the blood of my sacrifice with yeast; the sacrifice from the feast of Passover must not remain until the following morning.

34:26 "The first of the firstfruits of your soil you must bring to the house of the LORD your God.

You must not cook a young goat in its mother's milk."

34:27 The LORD said to Moses, "Write down these words, for in accordance with these words I have made a covenant with you and with Israel." **34:28** So he was there with the LORD forty days and forty nights; he did not eat bread, and he did not drink water. He wrote on the tablets the words of the covenant, the ten commandments.

The Radiant Face of Moses

34:29 Now when Moses came down from Mount Sinai with the two tablets of the testimony in his hand – when he came down from the mountain, Moses did not know that the skin of his face shone while he talked with him. **34:30** When Aaron and all the Israelites saw Moses, the skin of his face shone; and they were afraid to approach him. **34:31** But Moses called to them, so Aaron and all the leaders of the community came back to him, and Moses spoke to them. **34:32** After this all the Israelites approached, and he commanded them all that the LORD had spoken to him on Mount Sinai. **34:33** When Moses finished speaking with them, he would put a veil on his face. **34:34** But when Moses went in before the LORD to speak with him, he would remove the veil until he came out. Then he would come out and tell the Israelites what he had been commanded. **34:35** When the Israelites would see the face of Moses, that the skin of Moses' face shone, Moses would put the veil on his face again, until he went in to speak with the LORD.

Sabbath Regulations

35:1 Moses assembled the whole community of the Israelites and said to them, "These are the things that the LORD has commanded you to do. **35:2** In six days work may be done, but on the seventh day there must be a holy day for you, a Sabbath of complete rest to the LORD. Anyone who does work on it will be put to death. **35:3** You must not kindle a fire in any of your homes on the Sabbath day."

Willing Workers

35:4 Moses spoke to the whole community of the Israelites, "This is the word that the LORD has commanded: **35:5** 'Take an offering for the LORD. Let everyone who has a willing heart bring an offering to the LORD: gold, silver, bronze, **35:6** blue, purple, and scarlet yarn, fine linen, goat's hair, **35:7** ram skins dyed red, fine leather, acacia wood, **35:8** olive oil for the light, spices for the anointing oil and for the fragrant incense, **35:9** onyx stones, and other gems for mounting on the ephod and the breastpiece. **35:10** Every skilled person among you is to come and make all that the LORD has commanded: **35:11** the tabernacle with its tent, its covering, its clasps, its frames, its crossbars, its posts, and its bases; **35:12** the ark, with its poles, the atonement lid, and the special curtain that conceals it; **35:13** the table with its poles and all its vessels, and the Bread of the Presence; **35:14** the lampstand for the light and its accessories, its lamps, and oil for the light; **35:15** and the altar of incense with its poles, the anointing oil, and the fragrant incense; the hanging for the door at the entrance of the tabernacle; **35:16** the altar for the burnt offering with its bronze grating that is on it, its poles, and all its utensils; the large basin and its pedestal; **35:17** the hangings of the courtyard, its posts and its bases, and the curtain for the gateway to the courtyard; **35:18** tent pegs for the tabernacle and tent pegs for the courtyard and their ropes; **35:19** the woven garments for serving in the holy place, the holy garments for Aaron the priest, and the garments for his sons to minister as priests."

35:20 So the whole community of the Israelites went out from the presence of Moses. **35:21** Everyone whose heart stirred him to action and everyone whose spirit was willing came and brought the offering for the LORD for the work of the tent of meeting, for all its service, and for the holy garments. **35:22** They came, men and women alike, all who had willing hearts. They brought brooches, earrings, rings and ornaments, all kinds of gold jewelry, and everyone came who waved a wave offering of gold to the LORD.

35:23 Everyone who had blue, purple, or scarlet yarn, fine linen, goats' hair, ram skins dyed red, or fine leather brought them. **35:24** Everyone making an offering of silver or bronze brought it as an offering to the LORD, and everyone who had acacia wood for any work of the service brought it. **35:25** Every woman who was skilled spun with her hands and brought what she had spun, blue, purple, or scarlet yarn, or fine linen, **35:26** and all the women whose heart stirred them to action and who were skilled spun goats' hair.

35:27 The leaders brought onyx stones and other gems to be mounted for the ephod and the breastpiece, **35:28** and spices and olive oil for the light, for the anointing oil, and for the fragrant incense.

35:29 The Israelites brought a freewill offering to the LORD, every man and woman whose heart was willing to bring materials for all the work that the LORD through Moses had commanded them to do.

35:30 Moses said to the Israelites, "See, the LORD has chosen Bezalel son of Uri, the son of Hur, of the tribe of Judah. **35:31** He has filled him with the Spirit of God – with skill, with understanding, with knowledge, and in all kinds of work, **35:32** to design artistic designs, to work in gold, in silver, and in bronze, **35:33** and in cutting stones for their setting, and in cutting wood, to do work in every artistic craft. **35:34** And he has put it in his heart to teach, he and Oholiab son of Ahisamach, of the tribe of Dan. **35:35** He has filled them with skill to do all kinds of work as craftsmen, as designers, as embroiderers in blue, purple, and scarlet yarn and in fine linen, and as weavers. They are craftsmen in all the work and artistic designers. **36:1** So Bezalel and Oholiab and every skilled person in whom the LORD has put skill and ability to know how to do all the work for the

service of the sanctuary are to do the work according to all that the LORD has commanded."

36:2 Moses summoned Bezalel and Oholiab and every skilled person in whom the LORD had put skill – everyone whose heart stirred him to volunteer to do the work, **36:3** and they received from Moses all the offerings the Israelites had brought to do the work for the service of the sanctuary, and they still continued to bring him a freewill offering each morning. **36:4** So all the skilled people who were doing all the work on the sanctuary came from the work they were doing **36:5** and told Moses, "The people are bringing much more than is needed for the completion of the work which the LORD commanded us to do!"

36:6 Moses instructed them to take his message throughout the camp, saying, "Let no man or woman do any more work for the offering for the sanctuary." So the people were restrained from bringing any more. **36:7** Now the materials were more than enough for them to do all the work.

The Building of the Tabernacle

36:8 All the skilled among those who were doing the work made the tabernacle with ten curtains of fine twisted linen and blue and purple and scarlet; they were made with cherubim that were the work of an artistic designer. **36:9** The length of one curtain was forty-two feet, and the width of one curtain was six feet – the same size for each of the curtains. **36:10** He joined five of the curtains to one another, and the other five curtains he joined to one another. **36:11** He made loops of blue material along the edge of the end curtain in the first set; he did the same along the edge of the end curtain in the second set. **36:12** He made fifty loops on the first curtain, and he made fifty loops on the end curtain that was in the second set, with the loops opposite one another. **36:13** He made fifty gold clasps and joined the curtains together to one another with the clasps, so that the tabernacle was a unit.

36:14 He made curtains of goats' hair for a tent over the tabernacle; he made eleven curtains. **36:15** The length of one curtain was forty-five feet, and the width of one curtain was six feet – one size for all eleven curtains. **36:16** He joined five curtains by themselves and six curtains by themselves. **36:17** He made fifty loops along the edge of the end curtain in the first set and fifty loops along the edge of the curtain that joined the second set. **36:18** He made fifty bronze clasps to join the tent together so that it might be a unit. **36:19** He made a covering for the tent out of ram skins dyed red and over that a covering of fine leather.

36:20 He made the frames for the tabernacle of acacia wood as uprights. **36:21** The length of each frame was fifteen feet, the width of each frame was two and a quarter feet, **36:22** with two projections per frame parallel one to another. He made all the frames of the tabernacle in this way. **36:23** So he made frames for the tabernacle: twenty frames for the south side. **36:24** He made forty silver bases under the twenty frames – two bases under the first frame for its two projections, and likewise two bases under the next frame for its two projections, **36:25** and for the second side of the tabernacle, the north side, he made twenty frames **36:26** and their forty silver bases, two bases under the first frame and two bases under the next frame. **36:27** And for the back of the tabernacle on the west he made six frames. **36:28** He made two frames for the corners of the tabernacle on the back. **36:29** At the two corners they were doubled at the lower end and finished together at the top in one ring. So he did for both. **36:30** So there were eight frames and their silver bases, sixteen bases, two bases under each frame.

36:31 He made bars of acacia wood, five for the frames on one side of the tabernacle **36:32** and five bars for the frames on the second side of the tabernacle, and five bars for the frames of the tabernacle for the back side on the west. **36:33** He made the middle bar to reach from end to end in the center of the frames. **36:34** He overlaid the frames with gold and made their rings of gold to provide places for the bars, and he overlaid the bars with gold.

36:35 He made the special curtain of blue, purple, and scarlet yarn and fine twisted linen; he made it with cherubim, the work of an artistic designer. **36:36** He made for it four posts of acacia wood and overlaid them with gold, with gold hooks, and he cast for them four silver bases.

36:37 He made a hanging for the entrance of the tent of blue, purple, and scarlet yarn and fine twisted linen, the work of an embroiderer, **36:38** and its five posts and their hooks. He overlaid their tops and their bands with gold, but their five bases were bronze.

The Making of the Ark

37:1 Bezalel made the ark of acacia wood; its length was three feet nine inches, its width two feet three inches, and its height two feet three inches. **37:2** He overlaid it with pure gold, inside and out, and he made a surrounding border of gold for it. **37:3** He cast four gold rings for it that he put on its four feet, with two rings on one side and two rings on the other side. **37:4** He made poles of acacia wood, overlaid them with gold, **37:5** and put the poles into the rings on the sides of the ark in order to carry the ark.

37:6 He made an atonement lid of pure gold; its length was three feet nine inches, and its width was two feet three inches. **37:7** He made two cherubim of gold; he made them of hammered metal on the two ends of the atonement lid, **37:8** one cherub on one end and one cherub on the other end. He made the cherubim from the atonement lid on its two ends.

37:9 The cherubim were spreading their wings upward, overshadowing the atonement lid with their wings. The cherubim faced each other, looking toward the atonement lid.

The Making of the Table

37:10 He made the table of acacia wood; its length was three feet, its width one foot six inches, and its height two feet three inches. **37:11** He overlaid it with pure gold, and he made a surrounding border of gold for it. **37:12** He made a surrounding frame for it about three inches wide, and he made a surrounding border of gold for its frame. **37:13** He cast four gold rings for it and attached the rings at the four corners where its four legs were. **37:14** The rings were close to the frame to provide places for the poles to carry the table. **37:15** He made the poles of acacia wood and overlaid them with gold, to carry the table. **37:16** He made the vessels which were on the table out of pure gold, its plates, its ladles, its pitchers, and its bowls, to be used in pouring out offerings.

The Making of the Lampstand

37:17 He made the lampstand of pure gold. He made the lampstand of hammered metal; its base and its shaft, its cups, its buds, and its blossoms were from the same piece. **37:18** Six branches were extending from its sides, three branches of the lampstand from one side of it, and three branches of the lampstand from the other side of it. **37:19** Three cups shaped like almond flowers with buds and blossoms were on the first branch, and three cups shaped like almond flowers with buds and blossoms were on the next branch, and the same for the six branches that were extending from the lampstand. **37:20** On the lampstand there were four cups shaped like almond flowers with buds and blossoms, **37:21** with a bud under the first two branches from it, and a bud under the next two branches from it, and a bud under the third two branches from it; according to the six branches that extended from it. **37:22** Their buds and their branches were of one piece; all of it was one hammered piece of pure gold. **37:23** He made its seven lamps, its trimmers, and its trays of pure gold. **37:24** He made the lampstand and all its accessories with seventy-five pounds of pure gold.

The Making of the Altar of Incense

37:25 He made the incense altar of acacia wood. Its length was a foot and a half and its width a foot and a half – a square – and its height was three feet. Its horns were of one piece with it. **37:26** He overlaid it with pure gold – its top, its four walls, and its horns – and he made a surrounding border of gold for it. **37:27** He also made two gold rings for it under its border, on its two sides, on opposite sides, as places for poles to carry it with. **37:28** He made the poles of acacia wood and overlaid them with gold.

37:29 He made the sacred anointing oil and the pure fragrant incense, the work of a perfumer.

The Making of the Altar for the Burnt Offering

38:1 He made the altar for the burnt offering of acacia wood seven feet six inches long and seven feet six inches wide – it was square – and its height was four feet six inches. **38:2** He made its horns on its four corners; its horns were part of it, and he overlaid it with bronze. **38:3** He made all the utensils of the altar – the pots, the shovels, the tossing bowls, the meat hooks, and the fire pans – he made all its utensils of bronze. **38:4** He made a grating for the altar, a network of bronze under its ledge, halfway up from the bottom. **38:5** He cast four rings for the four corners of the bronze grating, to provide places for the poles. **38:6** He made the poles of acacia wood and overlaid them with bronze. **38:7** He put the poles into the rings on the sides of the altar, with which to carry it. He made the altar hollow, out of boards.

38:8 He made the large basin of bronze and its pedestal of bronze from the mirrors of the women who served at the entrance of the tent of meeting.

The Construction of the Courtyard

38:9 He made the courtyard. For the south side the hangings of the courtyard were of fine twisted linen, one hundred fifty feet long, **38:10** with their twenty posts and their twenty bronze bases, with the hooks of the posts and their bands of silver. **38:11** For the north side the hangings were one hundred fifty feet, with their twenty posts and their twenty bronze bases, with the hooks of the posts and their bands of silver. **38:12** For the west side there were hangings seventy-five feet long, with their ten posts and their ten bases, with the hooks of the posts and their bands of silver. **38:13** For the east side, toward the sunrise, it was seventy-five feet wide, **38:14** with hangings on one side of the gate that were twenty-two and a half feet long, with their three posts and their three bases, **38:15** and for the second side of the gate of the courtyard, just like the other, the hangings were twenty-two and a half feet long, with their three posts and their three bases. **38:16** All the hangings around the courtyard were of fine twisted linen. **38:17** The bases for the posts were bronze. The hooks of the posts and their bands were silver, their tops were overlaid with silver, and all the posts of the courtyard had silver bands. **38:18** The curtain for the gate of the courtyard was of blue, purple, and scarlet yarn and fine twisted linen, the work of an embroiderer. It was thirty feet long, and like the hangings in the courtyard, it was seven and a half feet high, **38:19** with four posts and their four bronze bases. Their hooks and their bands

were silver, and their tops were overlaid with silver. **38:20** All the tent pegs of the tabernacle and of the courtyard all around were bronze.

The Materials of the Construction

38:21 This is the inventory of the tabernacle, the tabernacle of the testimony, which was counted by the order of Moses, being the work of the Levites under the direction of Ithamar, son of Aaron the priest. **38:22** Now Bezalel son of Uri, the son of Hur, of the tribe of Judah, made everything that the LORD had commanded Moses; **38:23** and with him was Oholiab son of Ahisamach, of the tribe of Dan, an artisan, a designer, and an embroiderer in blue, purple, and scarlet yarn and fine linen.

38:24 All the gold that was used for the work, in all the work of the sanctuary (namely, the gold of the wave offering) was twenty-nine talents and 730 shekels, according to the sanctuary shekel.

38:25 The silver of those who were numbered of the community was one hundred talents and 1,775 shekels, according to the sanctuary shekel, **38:26** one beka per person, that is, a half shekel, according to the sanctuary shekel, for everyone who crossed over to those numbered, from twenty years old or older, 603,550 in all. **38:27** The one hundred talents of silver were used for casting the bases of the sanctuary and the bases of the special curtain – one hundred bases for one hundred talents, one talent per base. **38:28** From the remaining 1,775 shekels he made hooks for the posts, overlaid their tops, and made bands for them.

38:29 The bronze of the wave offering was seventy talents and 2,400 shekels. **38:30** With it he made the bases for the door of the tent of meeting, the bronze altar, the bronze grating for it, and all the utensils of the altar, **38:31** the bases for the courtyard all around, the bases for the gate of the courtyard, all the tent pegs of the tabernacle, and all the tent pegs of the courtyard all around.

The Making of the Priestly Garments

39:1 From the blue, purple, and scarlet yarn they made woven garments for serving in the sanctuary; they made holy garments that were for Aaron, just as the LORD had commanded Moses.

The Ephod

39:2 He made the ephod of gold, blue, purple, scarlet, and fine twisted linen. **39:3** They hammered the gold into thin sheets and cut it into narrow strips to weave them into the blue, purple, and scarlet yarn, and into the fine linen, the work of an artistic designer. **39:4** They made shoulder pieces for it, attached to two of its corners, so it could be joined together. **39:5** The artistically woven waistband of the ephod that was on it was like it, of one piece with it, of gold, blue, purple, and scarlet yarn and fine twisted linen, just as the LORD had commanded Moses.

39:6 They set the onyx stones in gold filigree settings, engraved as with the engravings of a seal with the names of the sons of Israel. **39:7** He put them on the shoulder pieces of the ephod as stones of memorial for the Israelites, just as the LORD had commanded Moses.

The Breastpiece of Decision

39:8 He made the breastpiece, the work of an artistic designer, in the same fashion as the ephod, of gold, blue, purple, and scarlet, and fine twisted linen. **39:9** It was square – they made the breastpiece doubled, nine inches long and nine inches wide when doubled. **39:10** They set on it four rows of stones: a row with a ruby, a topaz, and a beryl – the first row; **39:11** and the second row, a turquoise, a sapphire, and an emerald; **39:12** and the third row, a jacinth, an agate, and an amethyst; **39:13** and the fourth row, a chrysolite, an onyx, and a jasper. They were enclosed in gold filigree settings. **39:14** The stones were for the names of the sons of Israel, twelve, corresponding to the number of their names. Each name corresponding to one of the twelve tribes was like the engravings of a seal.

39:15 They made for the breastpiece braided chains like cords of pure gold, **39:16** and they made two gold filigree settings and two gold rings, and they attached the two rings to the upper two ends of the breastpiece. **39:17** They attached the two gold chains to the two rings at the ends of the breastpiece; **39:18** the other two ends of the two chains they attached to the two settings, and they attached them to the shoulder pieces of the ephod at the front of it. **39:19** They made two rings of gold and put them on the other two ends of the breastpiece on its edge, which is on the inner side of the ephod. **39:20** They made two more gold rings and attached them to the bottom of the two shoulder pieces on the front of the ephod, close to the juncture above the waistband of the ephod. **39:21** They tied the breastpiece by its rings to the rings of the ephod by blue cord, so that it was above the waistband of the ephod, so that the breastpiece would not be loose from the ephod, just as the LORD had commanded Moses.

The Other Garments

39:22 He made the robe of the ephod completely blue, the work of a weaver. **39:23** There was an opening in the center of the robe, like the opening of a collar, with an edge all around the opening so that it could not be torn. **39:24** They made pomegranates of blue, purple, and scarlet yarn and twisted linen around the hem of the robe. **39:25** They made bells of pure gold and attached the bells between the pomegranates around the hem of the robe between the pomegranates. **39:26** There was a bell and a pomegranate, a bell and a pomegranate, all around the hem of the robe, to be used in ministering, just as the LORD had commanded Moses.

39:27 They made tunics of fine linen – the work of a weaver, for Aaron and for his sons – **39:28** and the turban of fine linen, the headbands of fine linen, and the undergarments of fine twisted linen. **39:29** The sash was of fine twisted linen and blue, purple, and scarlet yarn, the work of an embroiderer, just as the LORD had commanded Moses. **39:30** They made a plate, the holy diadem, of pure gold and wrote on it an inscription, as on the engravings of a seal, "Holiness to the LORD." **39:31** They attached to it a blue cord, to attach it to the turban above, just as the LORD had commanded Moses.

Moses Inspects the Sanctuary

39:32 So all the work of the tabernacle, the tent of meeting, was completed, and the Israelites did according to all that the LORD had commanded Moses – they did it exactly so. **39:33** They brought the tabernacle to Moses, the tent and all its furnishings, clasps, frames, bars, posts, and bases; **39:34** and the coverings of ram skins dyed red, the covering of fine leather, and the protecting curtain; **39:35** the ark of the testimony and its poles, and the atonement lid; **39:36** the table, all its utensils, and the Bread of the Presence; **39:37** the pure lampstand, its lamps, with the lamps set in order, and all its accessories, and oil for the light; **39:38** and the gold altar, and the anointing oil, and the fragrant incense; and the curtain for the entrance to the tent; **39:39** the bronze altar and its bronze grating, its poles, and all its utensils; the large basin with its pedestal; **39:40** the hangings of the courtyard, its posts and its bases, and the curtain for the gateway of the courtyard, its ropes and its tent pegs, and all the furnishings for the service of the tabernacle, for the tent of meeting; **39:41** the woven garments for serving in the sanctuary, the holy garments for Aaron the priest, and the garments for his sons to minister as priests. **39:42** The Israelites did all the work according to all that the LORD had commanded Moses. **39:43** Moses inspected all the work – and they had done it just as the LORD had commanded – they had done it exactly – and Moses blessed them.

Setting Up the Sanctuary

40:1 Then the LORD spoke to Moses: **40:2** "On the first day of the first month you are to set up the tabernacle, the tent of meeting. **40:3** You are to place the ark of the testimony in it and shield the ark with the special curtain. **40:4** You are to bring in the table and set out the things that belong on it; then you are to bring in the lampstand and set up its lamps. **40:5** You are to put the gold altar for incense in front of the ark of the testimony and put the curtain at the entrance to the tabernacle. **40:6** You are to put the altar for the burnt offering in front of the entrance to the tabernacle, the tent of meeting. **40:7** You are to put the large basin between the tent of meeting and the altar and put water in it. **40:8** You are to set up the courtyard around it and put the curtain at the gate of the courtyard. **40:9** And take the anointing oil, and anoint the tabernacle and all that is in it, and sanctify it and all its furnishings, and it will be holy. **40:10** Then you are to anoint the altar for the burnt offering with all its utensils; you are to sanctify the altar, and it will be the most holy altar. **40:11** You must also anoint the large basin and its pedestal, and you are to sanctify it.

40:12 "You are to bring Aaron and his sons to the entrance of the tent of meeting and wash them with water. **40:13** Then you are to clothe Aaron with the holy garments and anoint him and sanctify him so that he may minister as my priest. **40:14** You are to bring his sons and clothe them with tunics **40:15** and anoint them just as you anointed their father, so that they may minister as my priests; their anointing will make them a priesthood that will continue throughout their generations." **40:16** This is what Moses did, according to all the LORD had commanded him – so he did.

40:17 So the tabernacle was set up on the first day of the first month, in the second year. **40:18** When Moses set up the tabernacle and put its bases in place, he set up its frames, attached its bars, and set up its posts. **40:19** Then he spread the tent over the tabernacle and put the covering of the tent over it, as the LORD had commanded Moses. **40:20** He took the testimony and put it in the ark, attached the poles to the ark, and then put the atonement lid on the ark. **40:21** And he brought the ark into the tabernacle, hung the protecting curtain, and shielded the ark of the testimony from view, just as the LORD had commanded Moses.

40:22 And he put the table in the tent of meeting, on the north side of the tabernacle, outside the curtain. **40:23** And he set the bread in order on it before the LORD, just as the LORD had commanded Moses.

40:24 And he put the lampstand in the tent of meeting opposite the table, on the south side of the tabernacle. **40:25** Then he set up the lamps before the LORD, just as the LORD had commanded Moses.

40:26 And he put the gold altar in the tent of meeting in front of the curtain, **40:27** and he burned fragrant incense on it, just as the LORD had commanded Moses.

40:28 Then he put the curtain at the entrance to the tabernacle. **40:29** He also put the altar for the burnt offering by the entrance to the tabernacle, the tent of meeting, and offered on it the burnt offering and the meal offering, just as the LORD had commanded Moses.

40:30 Then he put the large basin between the tent of meeting and the altar and put water in it for washing. **40:31** Moses and Aaron and his sons would wash their hands and their feet from it. **40:32** Whenever they entered the tent of meeting, and whenever they approached the altar, they would wash, just as the LORD had commanded Moses.

40:33 And he set up the courtyard around the tabernacle and the altar, and put the curtain at the gate of the courtyard. So Moses finished the work.

40:34 Then the cloud covered the tent of meeting, and the glory of the LORD filled the tabernacle. **40:35** Moses was not able to enter the tent of meeting because the cloud settled on it and the glory of the LORD filled the tabernacle. **40:36** But when the cloud was lifted up from the tabernacle, the Israelites would set out on all their journeys; **40:37** but if the cloud was not lifted up, then they would not journey further until the day it was lifted up. **40:38** For the cloud of the LORD was on the tabernacle by day, but fire would be on it at night, in plain view of all the house of Israel, throughout all their journeys.

Book 3. Leviticus

Introduction to the Sacrificial Regulations

1:1 Then the LORD called to Moses and spoke to him from the Meeting Tent: **1:2** "Speak to the Israelites and tell them, 'When someone among you presents an offering to the LORD, you must present your offering from the domesticated animals, either from the herd or from the flock.

Burnt Offering Regulations: Animal from the Herd

1:3 "'If his offering is a burnt offering from the herd he must present it as a flawless male; he must present it at the entrance of the Meeting Tent for its acceptance before the LORD. **1:4** He must lay his hand on the head of the burnt offering, and it will be accepted for him to make atonement on his behalf. **1:5** Then the one presenting the offering must slaughter the bull before the LORD, and the sons of Aaron, the priests, must present the blood and splash the blood against the sides of the altar which is at the entrance of the Meeting Tent. **1:6** Next, the one presenting the offering must skin the burnt offering and cut it into parts, **1:7** and the sons of Aaron, the priest, must put fire on the altar and arrange wood on the fire. **1:8** Then the sons of Aaron, the priests, must arrange the parts with the head and the suet on the wood that is in the fire on the altar. **1:9** Finally, the one presenting the offering must wash its entrails and its legs in water and the priest must offer all of it up in smoke on the altar – it is a burnt offering, a gift of a soothing aroma to the LORD.

Animal from the Flock

1:10 "'If his offering is from the flock for a burnt offering – from the sheep or the goats – he must present a flawless male, **1:11** and must slaughter it on the north side of the altar before the LORD, and the sons of Aaron, the priests, will splash its blood against the altar's sides. **1:12** Next, the one presenting the offering must cut it into parts, with its head and its suet, and the priest must arrange them on the wood which is in the fire, on the altar. **1:13** Then the one presenting the offering must wash the entrails and the legs in water, and the priest must present all of it and offer it up in smoke on the altar – it is a burnt offering, a gift of a soothing aroma to the LORD.

From the Birds

1:14 "'If his offering to the LORD is a burnt offering from the birds, he must present his offering from the turtledoves or from the young pigeons. **1:15** The priest must present it at the altar, pinch off its head and offer the head up in smoke on the altar, and its blood must be drained out against the side of the altar. **1:16** Then the priest must remove its entrails by cutting off its tail feathers, and throw them to the east side of the altar into the place of fatty ashes, **1:17** and tear it open by its wings without dividing it into two parts. Finally, the priest must offer it up in smoke on the altar on the wood which is in the fire – it is a burnt offering, a gift of a soothing aroma to the LORD.

Grain Offering Regulations: Offering of Raw Flour

2:1 "'When a person presents a grain offering to the LORD, his offering must consist of choice wheat flour, and he must pour olive oil on it and put frankincense on it. **2:2** Then he must bring it to the sons of Aaron, the priests, and the priest must scoop out from there a handful of its choice wheat flour and some of its olive oil in addition to all of its frankincense, and the priest must offer its memorial portion up in smoke on the altar – it is a gift of a soothing aroma to the LORD. **2:3** The remainder of the grain offering belongs to Aaron and to his sons – it is most holy from the gifts of the LORD.

Processed Grain Offerings

2:4 "'When you present an offering of grain baked in an oven, it must be made of choice wheat flour baked into unleavened loaves mixed with olive oil or unleavened wafers smeared with olive oil. **2:5** If your offering is a grain offering made on the griddle, it must be choice wheat flour mixed with olive oil, unleavened. **2:6** Crumble it in pieces and pour olive oil on it – it is a grain offering. **2:7** If your offering is a grain offering made in a pan, it must be made of choice wheat flour deep fried in olive oil.

2:8 "'You must bring the grain offering that must be made from these to the LORD. Present it to the priest, and he will bring it to the altar. **2:9** Then the priest must take up from the grain offering its memorial portion and offer it up in smoke on the altar – it is a gift of a soothing aroma to the LORD. **2:10** The remainder of the grain offering belongs to Aaron and to his sons – it is most holy from the gifts of the LORD.

Additional Grain Offering Regulations

2:11 "'No grain offering which you present to the LORD can be made with yeast, for you must not offer up in smoke any yeast or honey as a gift to the LORD. **2:12** You can present them to the LORD as an offering of first fruit, but they must not go up to the altar for a soothing aroma. **2:13** Moreover, you must season every one of your grain offerings with salt; you must not allow the salt of the covenant of your God to be missing from your grain offering – on every one of your grain offerings you must present salt.

2:14 "'If you present a grain offering of first ripe grain to the LORD, you must present your grain offering of first ripe grain as soft kernels roasted in fire – crushed bits of fresh grain. **2:15** And you must put olive oil on it and set frankincense on it – it is a grain offering. **2:16** Then the priest must offer its memorial portion up in smoke – some of its crushed bits, some of its olive oil, in addition to all of its frankincense – it is a gift to the LORD.

Peace Offering Regulations: Animal from the Herd

3:1 "'Now if his offering is a peace offering sacrifice, if he presents an offering from the herd, he must present before the LORD a flawless male or a female. **3:2** He must lay his hand on the head of his offering and slaughter it at the entrance of the Meeting Tent, and the sons of Aaron, the priests, must splash the blood against the altar's sides. **3:3** Then the one presenting the offering must present a gift to the LORD from the peace offering sacrifice: He must remove the fat that covers the entrails and all the fat that surrounds the entrails, **3:4** the two kidneys with the fat on their sinews, and the protruding lobe on the liver (which he is to remove along with the kidneys). **3:5** Then the sons of Aaron must offer it up in smoke on the altar atop the burnt offering that is on the wood in the fire as a gift of a soothing aroma to the LORD.

Animal from the Flock

3:6 "'If his offering for a peace offering sacrifice to the LORD is from the flock, he must present a flawless male or female. **3:7** If he presents a sheep as his offering, he must present it before the LORD. **3:8** He must lay his hand on the head of his offering and slaughter it before the Meeting Tent, and the sons of Aaron must splash its blood against the altar's sides. **3:9** Then he must present a gift to the LORD from the peace offering sacrifice: He must remove all the fatty tail up to the end of the spine, the fat covering the entrails, and all the fat on the entrails, **3:10** the two kidneys with the fat on their sinews, and the protruding lobe on the liver (which he is to remove along with the kidneys). **3:11** Then the priest must offer it up in smoke on the altar as a food gift to the LORD.

3:12 "'If his offering is a goat he must present it before the LORD, **3:13** lay his hand on its head, and slaughter it before the Meeting Tent, and the sons of Aaron must splash its blood against the altar's sides. **3:14** Then he must present from it his offering as a gift to the LORD: the fat which covers the entrails and all the fat on the entrails, **3:15** the two kidneys with the fat on their sinews, and the protruding lobe on the liver (which he is to remove along with the kidneys). **3:16** Then the priest must offer them up in smoke on the altar as a food gift for a soothing aroma – all the fat belongs to the LORD. **3:17** This is a perpetual statute throughout your generations in all the places where you live: You must never eat any fat or any blood.'"

Sin Offering Regulations

4:1 Then the LORD spoke to Moses: **4:2** "Tell the Israelites, 'When a person sins by straying unintentionally from any of the LORD's commandments which must not be violated, and violates any one of them –

For the Priest

4:3 "'If the high priest sins so that the people are guilty, on account of the sin he has committed he must present a flawless young bull to the LORD for a sin offering. **4:4** He must bring the bull to the entrance of the Meeting Tent before the LORD, lay his hand on the head of the bull, and slaughter the bull before the LORD. **4:5** Then that high priest must take some of the blood of the bull and bring it to the Meeting Tent. **4:6** The priest must dip his finger in the blood and sprinkle some of it seven times before the LORD toward the front of the veil-canopy of the sanctuary. **4:7** The priest must put some of the blood on the horns of the altar of fragrant incense that is before the LORD in the Meeting Tent, and all the rest of the bull's blood he must pour out at the base of the altar of burnt offering that is at the entrance of the Meeting Tent.

4:8 "'Then he must take up all the fat from the sin offering bull: the fat covering the entrails and all the fat surrounding the entrails, **4:9** the two kidneys with the fat on their sinews, and the protruding lobe on the liver (which he is to remove along with the kidneys) **4:10** – just as it is taken from the ox of the peace offering sacrifice – and the priest must offer them up in smoke on the altar of burnt offering. **4:11** But the hide of the bull, all its flesh along with its head and its legs, its entrails, and its dung – **4:12** all the rest of the bull – he must bring outside the camp to a ceremonially clean place, to the fatty ash pile, and he must burn it on a wood fire; it must be burned on the fatty ash pile.

For the Whole Congregation

4:13 "'If the whole congregation of Israel strays unintentionally and the matter is not noticed by the assembly, and they violate one of the LORD's commandments, which must not be violated, so they become guilty, **4:14** the assembly must present a young bull for a sin offering when the sin they have committed becomes known. They must bring it before the Meeting Tent, **4:15** the elders of the congregation must lay their hands on the head of the bull before the LORD, and someone must slaughter the bull before the LORD. **4:16** Then the high priest must bring some of the blood of the bull to the Meeting Tent, **4:17** and that priest must dip his finger in the blood and sprinkle some of the blood seven times before the LORD toward the front of the veil-canopy. **4:18** He must put some of the blood on the horns of the altar which is before the LORD in the Meeting Tent, and all the rest of the blood he must pour out at the base of the altar of burnt offering that is at the entrance of the Meeting Tent.

4:19 "'Then the priest must take all its fat and offer the fat up in smoke on the altar. **4:20** He must do with the rest of the bull just as he did with the bull of the sin offering; this is what he must do with it. So the priest will make atonement on their behalf and they will be forgiven. **4:21** He must bring the rest of the bull outside the camp and burn it just as he burned the first bull – it is the sin offering of the assembly.

For the Leader

4:22 "'Whenever a leader, by straying unintentionally, sins and violates one of the commandments of the LORD his God which must not be violated, and he pleads guilty, **4:23** or his sin that he committed is made known to him, he must bring a flawless male goat as his offering. **4:24** He must lay his hand on the head of the male goat and slaughter it in the place where the burnt offering is slaughtered before the LORD – it is a sin offering. **4:25** Then the priest must take some of the blood of the sin offering with his finger and put it on the horns of the altar of burnt offering, and he must pour out the rest of its blood at the base of the altar of burnt offering. **4:26** Then the priest must offer all of its fat up in smoke on the altar like the fat of the peace offering sacrifice. So the priest will make atonement on his behalf for his sin and he will be forgiven.

For the Common Person

4:27 "'If an ordinary individual sins by straying unintentionally when he violates one of the LORD's commandments which must not be violated, and he pleads guilty **4:28** or his sin that he committed is made known to him, he must bring a flawless female goat as his offering for the sin that he committed. **4:29** He must lay his hand on the head of the sin offering and slaughter the sin offering in the place where the burnt offering is slaughtered. **4:30** Then the priest must take some of its blood with his finger and put it on the horns of the altar of burnt offering, and he must pour out all the rest of its blood at the base of the altar. **4:31** Then he must remove all of its fat (just as fat was removed from the peace offering sacrifice) and the priest must offer it up in smoke on the altar for a soothing aroma to the LORD. So the priest will make atonement on his behalf and he will be forgiven.

4:32 "'But if he brings a sheep as his offering, for a sin offering, he must bring a flawless female. **4:33** He must lay his hand on the head of the sin offering and slaughter it for a sin offering in the place where the burnt offering is slaughtered. **4:34** Then the priest must take some of the blood of the sin offering with his finger and put it on the horns of the altar of burnt offering, and he must pour out all the rest of its blood at the base of the altar. **4:35** Then the one who brought the offering must remove all its fat (just as the fat of the sheep is removed from the peace offering sacrifice) and the priest must offer them up in smoke on the altar on top of the other gifts of the LORD. So the priest will make atonement on his behalf for his sin which he has committed and he will be forgiven.

Additional Sin Offering Regulations

5:1 "'When a person sins in that he hears a public curse against one who fails to testify and he is a witness (he either saw or knew what had happened) and he does not make it known, then he will bear his punishment for iniquity. **5:2** Or when there is a person who touches anything ceremonially unclean, whether the carcass of an unclean wild animal, or the carcass of an unclean domesticated animal, or the carcass of an unclean creeping thing, even if he did not realize it, but he himself has become unclean and is guilty; **5:3** or when he touches human uncleanness with regard to anything by which he can become unclean, even if he did not realize it, but he himself has later come to know it and is guilty; **5:4** or when a person swears an oath, speaking thoughtlessly with his lips, whether to do evil or to do good, with regard to anything which the individual might speak thoughtlessly in an oath, even if he did not realize it, but he himself has later come to know it and is guilty with regard to one of these oaths – **5:5** when an individual becomes guilty with regard to one of these things he must confess how he has sinned, **5:6** and he must bring his penalty for guilt to the LORD for his sin that he has committed, a female from the flock, whether a female sheep or a female goat, for a sin offering. So the priest will make atonement on his behalf for his sin.

5:7 "'If he cannot afford an animal from the flock, he must bring his penalty for guilt for his sin that he has committed, two turtledoves or two young pigeons, to the LORD, one for a sin offering and one for a burnt offering. **5:8** He must bring them to the priest and present first the one that is for a sin offering. The priest must pinch its head at the nape of its neck, but must not sever the head from the body. **5:9** Then he must sprinkle some of the blood of the sin offering on the wall of the altar, and the remainder of the blood must be squeezed out at the base of the altar – it is a sin offering. **5:10** The second bird he must make a burnt offering according to the standard regulation. So the priest will make atonement on behalf of this person for his sin which he has committed, and he will be forgiven.

5:11 "'If he cannot afford two turtledoves or two young pigeons, he must bring as his offering for his sin which he has committed a tenth of an ephah of choice wheat flour for a sin offering. He must not place olive oil on it and he must not put frankincense on it, because it is a sin offering. **5:12** He must bring it to the priest and the priest must scoop out from it a handful as its memorial portion and offer it up in smoke on the altar on top of the other gifts of the LORD – it is a sin offering. **5:13** So the priest will make atonement on his behalf for his sin which he has committed by doing one of these things, and he will be forgiven. The remainder of the offering will belong to the priest like the grain offering.'"

Guilt Offering Regulations: Known Trespass

5:14 Then the LORD spoke to Moses: **5:15** "When a person commits a trespass and sins by straying unintentionally from the regulations about the LORD's holy things, then he must bring his penalty for guilt to the LORD, a flawless ram from the flock, convertible into silver shekels according to the standard of the sanctuary shekel, for a guilt offering. **5:16** And whatever holy thing he violated he must restore and must add one fifth to it and give it to the priest. So the priest will make atonement on his behalf with the guilt offering ram and he will be forgiven."

Unknown trespass

5:17 "If a person sins and violates any of the LORD's commandments which must not be violated (although he did not know it at the time, but later realizes he is guilty), then he will bear his punishment for iniquity **5:18** and must bring a flawless ram from the flock, convertible into silver shekels, for a guilt offering to the priest. So the priest will make atonement on his behalf for his error which he committed (although he himself had not known it) and he will be forgiven. **5:19** It is a guilt offering; he was surely guilty before the LORD."

Trespass by Deception and False Oath

6:1 (5:20) Then the LORD spoke to Moses: **6:2** "When a person sins and commits a trespass against the LORD by deceiving his fellow citizen in regard to something held in trust, or a pledge, or something stolen, or by extorting something from his fellow citizen, **6:3** or has found something lost and denies it and swears falsely concerning any one of the things that someone might do to sin – **6:4** when it happens that he sins and he is found guilty, then he must return whatever he had stolen, or whatever he had extorted, or the thing that he had held in trust, or the lost thing that he had found, **6:5** or anything about which he swears falsely. He must restore it in full and add one fifth to it; he must give it to its owner when he is found guilty. **6:6** Then he must bring his guilt offering to the LORD, a flawless ram from the flock, convertible into silver shekels, for a guilt offering to the priest. **6:7** So the priest will make atonement on his behalf before the LORD and he will be forgiven for whatever he has done to become guilty."

Sacrificial Instructions for the Priests: The Burnt Offering

6:8 (6:1) Then the LORD spoke to Moses: **6:9** "Command Aaron and his sons, 'This is the law of the burnt offering. The burnt offering is to remain on the hearth on the altar all night until morning, and the fire of the altar must be kept burning on it. **6:10** Then the priest must put on his linen robe and must put linen leggings over his bare flesh, and he must take up the fatty ashes of the burnt offering that the fire consumed on the altar, and he must place them beside the altar. **6:11** Then he must take off his clothes and put on other clothes, and he must bring the fatty ashes outside the camp to a ceremonially clean place, **6:12** but the fire which is on the altar must be kept burning on it. It must not be extinguished. So the priest must kindle wood on it morning by morning, and he must arrange the burnt offering on it and offer the fat of the peace offering up in smoke on it. **6:13** A continual fire must be kept burning on the altar. It must not be extinguished.

The Grain Offering of the Common Person

6:14 "'This is the law of the grain offering. The sons of Aaron are to present it before the LORD in front of the altar, **6:15** and the priest must take up with his hand some of the choice wheat flour of the grain offering and some of its olive oil, and all of the frankincense that is on the grain offering, and he must offer its memorial portion up in smoke on the altar as a soothing aroma to the LORD. **6:16** Aaron and his sons are to eat what is left over from it. It must be eaten unleavened in a holy place; they are to eat it in the courtyard of the Meeting Tent. **6:17** It must not be baked with yeast. I have given it as their portion from my gifts. It is most holy, like the sin offering and the guilt offering. **6:18** Every male among the sons of Aaron may eat it. It is a perpetual allotted portion throughout your generations from the gifts of the LORD. Anyone who touches these gifts must be holy.'"

The Grain Offering of the Priests

6:19 Then the LORD spoke to Moses: **6:20** "This is the offering of Aaron and his sons which they must present to the LORD on the day when he is anointed: a tenth of an ephah of choice wheat flour as a continual grain offering, half of it in the morning and half of it in the evening. **6:21** It must be made with olive oil on a griddle and you must bring it well soaked, so you must present a grain offering of broken pieces as a soothing aroma to the LORD. **6:22** The high priest who succeeds him from among his sons must do it. It is a perpetual statute; it must be offered up in smoke as a whole offering to the LORD. **6:23** Every grain offering of a priest must be a whole offering; it must not be eaten."

The Sin Offering

6:24 Then the LORD spoke to Moses: **6:25** "Tell Aaron and his sons, 'This is the law of the sin offering. In the place where the burnt offering is slaughtered the sin offering must be slaughtered before the LORD. It is most holy. **6:26** The priest who offers it for sin is to eat it. It must be eaten in a holy place, in the court of the Meeting Tent. **6:27** Anyone who touches its meat must be holy, and whoever spatters some of its blood on a garment, you must wash whatever he spatters it on in a holy place. **6:28** Any clay vessel it is boiled in must be broken, and if it was boiled in a bronze vessel, then that vessel must be rubbed out and rinsed in water. **6:29** Any male among the priests may eat it. It is most holy. **6:30** But any sin offering from which some of its blood is brought into the Meeting Tent to make atonement in the sanctuary must not be eaten. It must be burned up in the fire.

The Guilt Offering

7:1 "'This is the law of the guilt offering. It is most holy. **7:2** In the place where they slaughter the burnt offering they must slaughter the guilt offering, and the officiating priest must splash the blood against the altar's sides. **7:3** Then the one making the offering must present all its fat: the fatty tail, the fat covering the entrails, **7:4** the two kidneys and the fat on their sinews, and the protruding lobe on the liver (which he must remove along with the kidneys). **7:5** Then the priest must offer them up in smoke on the altar as a gift to the LORD. It is a guilt offering. **7:6** Any male among the priests may eat it. It must be eaten in a holy place. It is most holy. **7:7** The law is the same for the sin offering and the guilt offering; it belongs to the priest who makes atonement with it.

Priestly Portions of Burnt and Grain Offerings

7:8 "'As for the priest who presents someone's burnt offering, the hide of that burnt offering which he presented belongs to him. **7:9** Every grain offering which is baked in the oven or made in the pan or on the griddle belongs to the priest who presented it. **7:10** Every grain offering, whether mixed with olive oil or dry, belongs to all the sons of Aaron, each one alike.

The Peace Offering

7:11 "'This is the law of the peace offering sacrifice which he is to present to the LORD. **7:12** If he presents it on account of thanksgiving, along with the thank offering sacrifice he must present unleavened loaves mixed with olive oil, unleavened wafers smeared with olive oil, and well soaked ring-shaped loaves made of choice wheat flour mixed with olive oil. **7:13** He must present this grain offering in addition to ring-shaped loaves of leavened bread which regularly accompany the sacrifice of his thanksgiving peace offering. **7:14** He must present one of each kind of grain offering as a contribution offering to the LORD; it belongs to the priest who splashes the blood of the peace offering. **7:15** The meat of his thanksgiving peace offering must be eaten on the day of his offering; he must not set any of it aside until morning.

7:16 "If his offering is a votive or freewill sacrifice, it may be eaten on the day he presents his sacrifice, and also the leftovers from it may be eaten on the next day, **7:17** but the leftovers from the meat of the sacrifice must be burned up in the fire on the third day. **7:18** If some of the meat of his peace offering sacrifice is ever eaten on the third day it will not be accepted; it will not be accounted to the one who presented it, since it is spoiled, and the person who eats from it will bear his punishment for iniquity. **7:19** The meat which touches anything ceremonially unclean must not be eaten; it must be burned up in the fire. As for ceremonially clean meat, everyone who is ceremonially clean may eat the meat. **7:20** The person who eats meat from the peace offering sacrifice which belongs to the LORD while his uncleanness persists will be cut off from his people. **7:21** When a person touches anything unclean (whether human uncleanness, or an unclean animal, or an unclean detestable creature) and eats some of the meat of the peace offering sacrifice which belongs to the LORD, that person will be cut off from his people.'"

Sacrificial Instructions for the Common People: Fat and Blood

7:22 Then the LORD spoke to Moses: **7:23** "Tell the Israelites, 'You must not eat any fat of an ox, sheep, or goat. **7:24** Moreover, the fat of an animal that has died of natural causes and the fat of an animal torn by beasts may be used for any other purpose, but you must certainly never eat it. **7:25** If anyone eats fat from the animal from which he presents a gift to the LORD, that person will be cut off from his people. **7:26** And you must not eat any blood of the birds or the domesticated land animals in any of the places where you live. **7:27** Any person who eats any blood – that person will be cut off from his people.'"

Priestly Portions of Peace Offerings

7:28 Then the LORD spoke to Moses: **7:29** "Tell the Israelites, 'The one who presents his peace offering sacrifice to the LORD must bring his offering to the LORD from his peace offering sacrifice. **7:30** With his own hands he must bring the LORD's gifts. He must bring the fat with the breast to wave the breast as a wave offering before the LORD, **7:31** and the priest must offer the fat up in smoke on the altar, but the breast will belong to Aaron and his sons. **7:32** The right thigh you must give as a contribution offering to the priest from your peace offering sacrifices. **7:33** The one from Aaron's sons who presents the blood of the peace offering and fat will have the right thigh as his share, **7:34** for the breast of the wave offering and the thigh of the contribution offering I have taken from the Israelites out of their peace offering sacrifices and have given them to Aaron the priest and to his sons from the people of Israel as a perpetual allotted portion.'"

7:35 This is the allotment of Aaron and the allotment of his sons from the LORD's gifts on the day Moses presented them to serve as priests to the LORD. **7:36** This is what the LORD commanded to give to them from the Israelites on the day Moses anointed them – a perpetual allotted portion throughout their generations.

Summary of Sacrificial Regulations in Leviticus 6:8-7:36

7:37 This is the law for the burnt offering, the grain offering, the sin offering, the guilt offering, the ordination offering, and the peace offering sacrifice, **7:38** which the LORD commanded Moses on Mount Sinai on the day he commanded the Israelites to present their offerings to the LORD in the wilderness of Sinai.

Ordination of the Priests

8:1 Then the LORD spoke to Moses: **8:2** "Take Aaron and his sons with him, and the garments, the anointing oil, the sin offering bull, the two rams, and the basket of unleavened bread, **8:3** and assemble the whole congregation at the entrance of the Meeting Tent." **8:4** So Moses did just as the LORD commanded him, and the congregation assembled at the entrance of the Meeting Tent. **8:5** Then Moses said to the congregation: "This is what the LORD has commanded to be done."

Clothing Aaron

8:6 So Moses brought Aaron and his sons forward and washed them with water. **8:7** Then he put the tunic on Aaron, wrapped the sash around him, and clothed him with the robe. Next he put the ephod on him and placed on him the decorated band of the ephod, and fastened the ephod closely to him with the band. **8:8** He then set the breastpiece on him and put the Urim and Thummim into the breastpiece. **8:9** Finally, he set the turban on his head and attached the gold plate, the holy diadem, to the front of the turban just as the LORD had commanded Moses.

Anointing the Tabernacle and Aaron, and Clothing Aaron's Sons

8:10 Then Moses took the anointing oil and anointed the tabernacle and everything in it, and so consecrated them. **8:11** Next he sprinkled some of it on the altar seven times and so anointed the altar, all its vessels, and the wash basin and its stand to consecrate them. **8:12** He then poured some of the anointing oil on the head of Aaron and anointed him to consecrate him. **8:13** Moses also brought forward Aaron's sons, clothed them with tunics, wrapped sashes around them, and wrapped headbands on them just as the LORD had commanded Moses.

Consecration Offerings

8:14 Then he brought near the sin offering bull and Aaron and his sons laid their hands on the head of the sin offering bull, **8:15** and he slaughtered it. Moses then took the blood and put it all around on the horns of the altar with his finger and decontaminated the altar, and he poured out the rest of the blood at the base of the altar and so consecrated it to make atonement on it. **8:16** Then he took all the fat on the entrails, the protruding lobe of the liver, and the two kidneys and their fat, and Moses offered it all up in smoke on the altar, **8:17** but the rest of the bull – its hide, its flesh, and its dung – he completely burned up outside the camp just as the LORD had commanded Moses.

8:18 Then he presented the burnt offering ram and Aaron and his sons laid their hands on the head of the ram, **8:19** and he slaughtered it. Moses then splashed the blood against the altar's sides. **8:20** Then he cut the ram into parts, and Moses offered the head, the parts, and the suet up in smoke, **8:21** but the entrails and the legs he washed with water, and Moses offered the whole ram up in smoke on the altar – it was a burnt offering for a soothing aroma, a gift to the LORD, just as the LORD had commanded Moses.

8:22 Then he presented the second ram, the ram of ordination, and Aaron and his sons laid their hands on the head of the ram **8:23** and he slaughtered it. Moses then took some of its blood and put it on Aaron's right earlobe, on the thumb of his right hand, and on the big toe of his right foot. **8:24** Next he brought Aaron's sons forward, and Moses put some of the blood on their right earlobes, on their right thumbs, and on the big toes of their right feet, and Moses splashed the rest of the blood against the altar's sides.

8:25 Then he took the fat (the fatty tail, all the fat on the entrails, the protruding lobe of the liver, and the two kidneys and their fat) and the right thigh, **8:26** and from the basket of unleavened bread that was before the LORD he took one unleavened loaf, one loaf of bread mixed with olive oil, and one wafer, and placed them on the fat parts and on the right thigh. **8:27** He then put all of them on the palms of Aaron and his sons, who waved them as a wave offering before the LORD. **8:28** Moses then

took them from their palms and offered them up in smoke on the altar on top of the burnt offering – they were an ordination offering for a soothing aroma; it was a gift to the LORD. **8:29** Finally, Moses took the breast and waved it as a wave offering before the LORD from the ram of ordination. It was Moses' share just as the LORD had commanded Moses.

Anointing Aaron, his Sons, and their Garments

8:30 Then Moses took some of the anointing oil and some of the blood which was on the altar and sprinkled it on Aaron and his garments, and on his sons and his sons' garments with him. So he consecrated Aaron, his garments, and his sons and his sons' garments with him. **8:31** Then Moses said to Aaron and his sons, "Boil the meat at the entrance of the Meeting Tent, and there you are to eat it and the bread which is in the ordination offering basket, just as I have commanded, saying, 'Aaron and his sons are to eat it,' **8:32** but the remainder of the meat and the bread you must burn with fire. **8:33** And you must not go out from the entrance of the Meeting Tent for seven days, until the day when your days of ordination are completed, because you must be ordained over a seven-day period. **8:34** What has been done on this day the LORD has commanded to be done to make atonement for you. **8:35** You must reside at the entrance of the Meeting Tent day and night for seven days and keep the charge of the LORD so that you will not die, for this is what I have been commanded." **8:36** So Aaron and his sons did all the things the LORD had commanded through Moses.

Inauguration of Tabernacle Worship

9:1 On the eighth day Moses summoned Aaron and his sons and the elders of Israel, **9:2** and said to Aaron, "Take for yourself a bull calf for a sin offering and a ram for a burnt offering, both flawless, and present them before the LORD. **9:3** Then tell the Israelites: 'Take a male goat for a sin offering and a calf and lamb, both a year old and flawless, for a burnt offering, **9:4** and an ox and a ram for peace offerings to sacrifice before the LORD, and a grain offering mixed with olive oil, for today the LORD is going to appear to you.'" **9:5** So they took what Moses had commanded to the front of the Meeting Tent and the whole congregation presented them and stood before the LORD. **9:6** Then Moses said, "This is what the LORD has commanded you to do so that the glory of the LORD may appear to you." **9:7** Moses then said to Aaron, "Approach the altar and make your sin offering and your burnt offering, and make atonement on behalf of yourself and on behalf of the people; and also make the people's offering and make atonement on behalf of them just as the LORD has commanded."

The Sin Offering for the Priests

9:8 So Aaron approached the altar and slaughtered the sin offering calf which was for himself. **9:9** Then Aaron's sons presented the blood to him and he dipped his finger in the blood and put it on the horns of the altar, and the rest of the blood he poured out at the base of the altar. **9:10** The fat and the kidneys and the protruding lobe of the liver from the sin offering he offered up in smoke on the altar just as the LORD had commanded Moses, **9:11** but the flesh and the hide he completely burned up outside the camp.

The Burnt Offering for the Priests

9:12 He then slaughtered the burnt offering, and his sons handed the blood to him and he splashed it against the altar's sides. **9:13** The burnt offering itself they handed to him by its parts, including the head, and he offered them up in smoke on the altar, **9:14** and he washed the entrails and the legs and offered them up in smoke on top of the burnt offering on the altar.

The Offerings for the People

9:15 Then he presented the people's offering. He took the sin offering male goat which was for the people, slaughtered it, and performed a decontamination rite with it like the first one. **9:16** He then presented the burnt offering, and did it according to the standard regulation. **9:17** Next he presented the grain offering, filled his hand with some of it, and offered it up in smoke on the altar in addition to the morning burnt offering. **9:18** Then he slaughtered the ox and the ram – the peace offering sacrifices which were for the people – and Aaron's sons handed the blood to him and he splashed it against the altar's sides. **9:19** As for the fat parts from the ox and from the ram (the fatty tail, the fat covering the entrails, the kidneys, and the protruding lobe of the liver), **9:20** they set those on the breasts and he offered the fat parts up in smoke on the altar. **9:21** Finally Aaron waved the breasts and the right thigh as a wave offering before the LORD just as Moses had commanded.

9:22 Then Aaron lifted up his hands toward the people and blessed them and descended from making the sin offering, the burnt offering, and the peace offering. **9:23** Moses and Aaron then entered into the Meeting Tent. When they came out, they blessed the people, and the glory of the LORD appeared to all the people. **9:24** Then fire went out from the presence of the LORD and consumed the burnt offering and the fat parts on the altar, and all the people saw it, so they shouted loudly and fell down with their faces to the ground.

Nadab and Abihu

10:1 Then Aaron's sons, Nadab and Abihu, each took his fire pan and put fire in it, set incense on it, and presented strange fire before the LORD, which he had not commanded them to do. **10:2** So fire went out from the presence of the LORD and consumed them so that they died before the LORD. **10:3** Moses then said to Aaron, "This is what the LORD spoke: 'Among the ones close to me I will show myself holy, and in the presence of all the people I will be honored.'" So Aaron kept silent. **10:4** Moses then called to Mishael and Elzaphan, the sons of Uzziel, Aaron's uncle, and said to them, "Come near, carry your brothers away from the front of the sanctuary to a place outside the camp." **10:5** So they came near and carried them away in their tunics to a place outside the camp just as Moses had spoken. **10:6** Then Moses said to Aaron and to Eleazar and Ithamar his other two sons, "Do not dishevel the hair of your heads and do not tear your garments, so that you do not die and so that wrath does not come on the whole congregation. Your brothers, all the house of Israel, are to mourn the burning which the LORD has caused, **10:7** but you must not go out from the entrance of the Meeting Tent lest you die, for the LORD's anointing oil is on you." So they acted according to the word of Moses.

Perpetual Statutes the Lord Spoke to Aaron

10:8 Then the LORD spoke to Aaron, **10:9** "Do not drink wine or strong drink, you and your sons with you, when you enter into the Meeting Tent, so that you do not die, which is a perpetual statute throughout your generations, **10:10** as well as to distinguish between the holy and the common, and between the unclean and the clean, **10:11** and to teach the Israelites all the statutes that the LORD has spoken to them through Moses."

Perpetual Statutes Moses spoke to Aaron

10:12 Then Moses spoke to Aaron and to Eleazar and Ithamar, his remaining sons, "Take the grain offering which remains from the gifts of the LORD and eat it unleavened beside the altar, for it is most holy. **10:13** You must eat it in a holy place because it is your allotted portion and the allotted portion of your sons from the gifts of the LORD, for this is what I have been commanded. **10:14** Also, the breast of the wave offering and the thigh of the contribution offering you must eat in a ceremonially clean place, you and your sons and daughters with you, for they have been given as your allotted portion and the allotted portion of your sons from the peace offering sacrifices of the Israelites. **10:15** The thigh of the contribution offering and the breast of the wave offering they must bring in addition to the gifts of the fat parts to wave them as a wave offering before the LORD, and it will belong to you and your sons with you for a perpetual statute just as the LORD has commanded."

The Problem with the Inaugural Sin Offering

10:16 Later Moses sought diligently for the sin offering male goat, but it had actually been burnt. So he became angry at Eleazar and Ithamar, Aaron's remaining sons, saying, **10:17** "Why did you not eat the sin offering in the sanctuary? For it is most holy and he gave it to you to bear the iniquity of the congregation, to make atonement on their behalf before the LORD. **10:18** See here! Its blood was not brought into the holy place within! You should certainly have eaten it in the sanctuary just as I commanded!" **10:19** But Aaron spoke to Moses, "See here! Just today they presented their sin offering and their burnt offering before the LORD and such things as these have happened to me! If I had eaten a sin offering today would the LORD have been pleased?" **10:20** When Moses heard this explanation, he was satisfied.

Clean and Unclean Land Creatures

11:1 The LORD spoke to Moses and Aaron, saying to them, **11:2** "Tell the Israelites: 'This is the kind of creature you may eat from among all the animals that are on the land. **11:3** You may eat any among the animals that has a divided hoof (the hooves are completely split in two) and that also chews the cud. **11:4** However, you must not eat these from among those that chew the cud and have divided hooves: The camel is unclean to you because it chews the cud even though its hoof is not divided. **11:5** The rock badger is unclean to you because it chews the cud even though its hoof is not divided. **11:6** The hare is unclean to you because it chews the cud even though its hoof is not divided. **11:7** The pig is unclean to you because its

hoof is divided (the hoof is completely split in two), even though it does not chew the cud. **11:8** You must not eat from their meat and you must not touch their carcasses; they are unclean to you.

Clean and Unclean Water Creatures

11:9 "'These you can eat from all creatures that are in the water: Any creatures in the water that have both fins and scales, whether in the seas or in the streams, you may eat. **11:10** But any creatures that do not have both fins and scales, whether in the seas or in the streams, from all the swarming things of the water and from all the living creatures that are in the water, are detestable to you. **11:11** Since they are detestable to you, you must not eat their meat and their carcass you must detest. **11:12** Any creature in the water that does not have both fins and scales is detestable to you.

Clean and Unclean Birds

11:13 "'These you are to detest from among the birds – they must not be eaten, because they are detestable: the griffon vulture, the bearded vulture, the black vulture, **11:14** the kite, the buzzard of any kind, **11:15** every kind of crow, **11:16** the eagle owl, the short-eared owl, the long-eared owl, the hawk of any kind, **11:17** the little owl, the cormorant, the

screech owl, **11:18** the white owl, the scops owl, the osprey, **11:19** the stork, the heron of any kind, the hoopoe, and the bat.

Clean and Unclean Insects

11:20 "'Every winged swarming thing that walks on all fours is detestable to you. **11:21** However, this you may eat from all the winged swarming things that walk on all fours, which have jointed legs to hop with on the land. **11:22** These you may eat from them: the locust of any kind, the bald locust of any kind, the cricket of any kind, the grasshopper of any kind. **11:23** But any other winged swarming thing that has four legs is detestable to you.

Carcass Uncleanness

11:24 "'By these you defile yourselves; anyone who touches their carcass will be unclean until the evening, **11:25** and anyone who carries their carcass must wash his clothes and will be unclean until the evening.

Inedible Land Quadrupeds

11:26 "'All animals that divide the hoof but it is not completely split in two and do not chew the cud are unclean to you; anyone who touches them becomes unclean. **11:27** All that walk on their paws among all the creatures that walk on all fours are unclean to you. Anyone who touches their carcass will be unclean until the evening, **11:28** and the one who carries their carcass must wash his clothes and be unclean until the evening; they are unclean to you.

Creatures that Swarm on the Land

11:29 "'Now this is what is unclean to you among the swarming things that swarm on the land: the rat, the mouse, the large lizard of any kind, **11:30** the Mediterranean gecko, the spotted lizard, the wall gecko, the skink, and the chameleon. **11:31** These are the ones that are unclean to you among all the swarming things. Anyone who touches them when they die will be unclean until evening. **11:32** Also, anything they fall on when they die will become unclean – any wood vessel or garment or article of leather or sackcloth. Any such vessel with which work is done must be immersed in water and will be unclean until the evening. Then it will become clean. **11:33** As for any clay vessel they fall into, everything in it will become unclean and you must break it. **11:34** Any food that may be eaten which becomes soaked with water will become unclean. Anything drinkable in any such vessel will become unclean. **11:35** Anything their carcass may fall on will become unclean. An oven or small stove must be smashed to pieces; they are unclean, and they will stay unclean to you. **11:36** However, a spring or a cistern which collects water will be clean, but one who touches their carcass will be unclean. **11:37** Now, if such a carcass falls on any sowing seed which is to be sown, it is clean, **11:38** but if water is put on the seed and such a carcass falls on it, it is unclean to you.

Edible Land Quadrupeds

11:39 "'Now if an animal that you may eat dies, whoever touches its carcass will be unclean until the evening. **11:40** One who eats from its carcass must wash his clothes and be unclean until the evening, and whoever carries its carcass must wash his clothes and be unclean until the evening. **11:41** Every swarming thing that swarms on the land is detestable; it must not be eaten. **11:42** You must not eat anything that crawls on its belly or anything that walks on all fours or on any number of legs of all the swarming things that swarm on the land, because they are detestable. **11:43** Do not make yourselves detestable by any of the swarming things. You must not defile yourselves by them and become unclean by them, **11:44** for I am the LORD your God and you are to sanctify yourselves and be holy because I am holy. You must not defile yourselves by any of the swarming things that creep on the ground, **11:45** for I am the LORD who brought you up from the land of Egypt to be your God, and you are to be holy because I am holy. **11:46** This is the law of the land animals, the birds, all the living creatures that move in the water, and all the creatures that swarm on the land, **11:47** to distinguish between the unclean and the clean, between the living creatures that may be eaten and the living creatures that must not be eaten.'"

Purification of a Woman after Childbirth

12:1 The LORD spoke to Moses: **12:2** "Tell the Israelites, 'When a woman produces offspring and bears a male child, she will be unclean seven days, as she is unclean during the days of her menstruation. **12:3** On the eighth day the flesh of his foreskin must be circumcised. **12:4** Then she will remain thirty-three days in blood purity. She must not touch anything holy and she must not enter the sanctuary until the days of her purification are fulfilled. **12:5** If she bears a female child, she will be impure fourteen days as during her menstrual flow, and she will remain sixty-six days in blood purity.

12:6 "'When the days of her purification are completed for a son or for a daughter, she must bring a one year old lamb for a burnt offering and a young pigeon or turtledove for a sin offering to the entrance of the Meeting Tent, to the priest. **12:7** The priest is to present it before the LORD and make atonement on her behalf, and she will be clean from her flow of blood. This is the law of the one who bears a child, for the male or the female child. **12:8** If she cannot afford a sheep, then she must take two turtledoves or two young pigeons, one for a burnt offering and one for a sin offering, and the priest is to make atonement on her behalf, and she will be clean.'"

Infections on the Skin

13:1 The Lord spoke to Moses and Aaron: **13:2** "When someone has a swelling or a scab or a bright spot on the skin of his body that may become a diseased infection, he must be brought to Aaron the priest or one of his sons, the priests. **13:3** The priest must then examine the infection on the skin of the body, and if the hair in the infection has turned white and the infection appears to be deeper than the skin of the body, then it is a diseased infection, so when the priest examines it he must pronounce the person unclean.

A Bright Spot on the Skin

13:4 "If it is a white bright spot on the skin of his body, but it does not appear to be deeper than the skin, and the hair has not turned white, then the priest is to quarantine the person with the infection for seven days. **13:5** The priest must then examine it on the seventh day, and if, as far as he can see, the infection has stayed the same and has not spread on the skin, then the priest is to quarantine the person for another seven days. **13:6** The priest must then examine it again on the seventh day, and if the infection has faded and has not spread on the skin, then the priest is to pronounce the person clean. It is a scab, so he must wash his clothes and be clean. **13:7** If, however, the scab is spreading further on the skin after he has shown himself to the priest for his purification, then he must show himself to the priest a second time. **13:8** The priest must then examine it, and if the scab has spread on the skin, then the priest is to pronounce the person unclean. It is a disease.

A Swelling on the Skin

13:9 "When someone has a diseased infection, he must be brought to the priest. **13:10** The priest will then examine it, and if a white swelling is on the skin, it has turned the hair white, and there is raw flesh in the swelling, **13:11** it is a chronic disease on the skin of his body, so the priest is to pronounce him unclean. The priest must not merely quarantine him, for he is unclean. **13:12** If, however, the disease breaks out on the skin so that the disease covers all the skin of the person with the infection from his head to his feet, as far as the priest can see, **13:13** the priest must then examine it, and if the disease covers his whole body, he is to pronounce the person with the infection clean. He has turned all white, so he is clean. **13:14** But whenever raw flesh appears in it he will be unclean, **13:15** so the priest is to examine the raw flesh and pronounce him unclean – it is diseased. **13:16** If, however, the raw flesh once again turns white, then he must come to the priest. **13:17** The priest will then examine it, and if the infection has turned white, the priest is to pronounce the person with the infection clean – he is clean.

A Boil on the Skin

13:18 "When someone's body has a boil on its skin and it heals, **13:19** and in the place of the boil there is a white swelling or a reddish white bright spot, he must show himself to the priest. **13:20** The priest will then examine it, and if it appears to be deeper than the skin and its hair has turned white, then the priest is to pronounce the person unclean. It is a diseased infection that has broken out in the boil. **13:21** If, however, the priest examines it, and there is no white hair in it, it is not deeper than the skin, and it has faded, then the priest is to quarantine him for seven days. **13:22** If it is spreading further on the skin, then the priest is to pronounce him unclean. It is an infection. **13:23** But if the bright spot stays in its place and has not spread, it is the scar of the boil, so the priest is to pronounce him clean.

A Burn on the Skin

13:24 "When a body has a burn on its skin and the raw area of the burn becomes a reddish white or white bright spot, **13:25** the priest must examine it, and if the hair has turned white in the bright spot and it appears to be deeper than the skin, it is a disease that has broken out in the burn. The priest is to pronounce the person unclean. It is a diseased infection. **13:26** If, however, the priest examines it and there is no white hair in the bright spot, it is not deeper than the skin, and it has faded, then the priest is to quarantine him for seven days. **13:27** The priest must then examine it on the seventh day, and if it is spreading further on the skin, then the priest is to pronounce him unclean. It is a diseased infection. **13:28** But if the bright spot stays in its place, has not spread on the skin, and it has faded, then it is the swelling of the burn, so the priest is to pronounce him clean, because it is the scar of the burn.

Scall on the Head or in the Beard

13:29 "When a man or a woman has an infection on the head or in the beard, **13:30** the priest is to examine the infection, and if it appears to be deeper than the skin and the hair in it is reddish yellow and thin, then the priest is to pronounce the person unclean. It is scall, a disease of the head or the beard. **13:31** But if the priest examines the scall infection and it does not appear to be deeper than the skin, and there is no black hair in it, then the priest is to quarantine the person with the scall infection for seven days. **13:32** The priest must then examine the infection on the seventh day, and if the scall has not spread, there is no reddish yellow hair in it, and the scall does not appear to be deeper than the skin, **13:33** then the individual is to shave himself, but he must not shave the area affected by the scall, and the priest is to quarantine the person with the scall for another seven days. **13:34** The priest must then examine the scall on the seventh day, and if the scall has not spread on the skin and it does

not appear to be deeper than the skin, then the priest is to pronounce him clean. So he is to wash his clothes and be clean. **13:35** If, however, the scall spreads further on the skin after his purification, **13:36** then the priest is to examine it, and if the scall has spread on the skin the priest is not to search further for reddish yellow hair. The person is unclean. **13:37** If, as far as the priest can see, the scall has stayed the same and black hair has sprouted in it, the scall has been healed; the person is clean. So the priest is to pronounce him clean.

Bright White Spots on the Skin

13:38 "When a man or a woman has bright spots – white bright spots – on the skin of their body, **13:39** the priest is to examine them, and if the bright spots on the skin of their body are faded white, it is a harmless rash that has broken out on the skin. The person is clean.

Baldness on the Head

13:40 "When a man's head is bare so that he is balding in back, he is clean. **13:41** If his head is bare on the forehead so that he is balding in front, he is clean. **13:42** But if there is a reddish white infection in the back or front bald area, it is a disease breaking out in his back or front bald area. **13:43** The priest is to examine it, and if the swelling of the infection is reddish white in the back or front bald area like the appearance of a disease on the skin of the body, **13:44** he is a diseased man. He is unclean. The priest must surely pronounce him unclean because of his infection on his head.

The Life of the Person with Skin Disease

13:45 "As for the diseased person who has the infection, his clothes must be torn, the hair of his head must be unbound, he must cover his mustache, and he must call out 'Unclean! Unclean!' **13:46** The whole time he has the infection he will be continually unclean. He must live in isolation, and his place of residence must be outside the camp.

Infections in Garments, Cloth, or Leather

13:47 "When a garment has a diseased infection in it, whether a wool or linen garment, **13:48** or in the warp or woof of the linen or the wool, or in leather or anything made of leather, **13:49** if the infection in the garment or leather or warp or woof or any article of leather is yellowish green or reddish, it is a diseased infection and it must be shown to the priest. **13:50** The priest is to examine and then quarantine the article with the infection for seven days. **13:51** He must then examine the infection on the seventh day. If the infection has spread in the garment, or in the warp, or in the woof, or in the leather – whatever the article into which the leather was made – the infection is a malignant disease. It is unclean. **13:52** He must burn the garment or the warp or the woof, whether wool or linen, or any article of leather which has the infection in it. Because it is a malignant disease it must be burned up in the fire. **13:53** But if the priest examines it and the infection has not spread in the garment or in the warp or in the woof or in any article of leather, **13:54** the priest is to command that they wash whatever has the infection and quarantine it for another seven days. **13:55** The priest must then examine it after the infection has been washed out, and if the infection has not changed its appearance even though the infection has not spread, it is unclean. You must burn it up in the fire. It is a fungus, whether on the back side or front side of the article. **13:56** But if the priest has examined it and the infection has faded after it has been washed, he is to tear it out of the garment or the leather or the warp or the woof. **13:57** Then if it still appears again in the garment or the warp or the woof, or in any article of leather, it is an outbreak. Whatever has the infection in it you must burn up in the fire. **13:58** But the garment or the warp or the woof or any article of leather which you wash and infection disappears from it is to be washed a second time and it will be clean."

Summary of Infection Regulations

13:59 This is the law of the diseased infection in the garment of wool or linen, or the warp or woof, or any article of leather, for pronouncing it clean or unclean.

Purification of Diseased Skin Infections

14:1 The Lord spoke to Moses: **14:2** "This is the law of the diseased person on the day of his purification, when he is brought to the priest. **14:3** The priest is to go outside the camp and examine the infection. If the infection of the diseased person has been healed, **14:4** then the priest will command that two live clean birds, a piece of cedar wood, a scrap of crimson fabric, and some twigs of hyssop be taken up for the one being cleansed. **14:5** The priest will then command that one bird be slaughtered into a clay vessel over fresh water. **14:6** Then he is to take the live bird along with the piece of cedar wood, the scrap of crimson fabric, and the twigs of hyssop, and he is to dip them and the live bird in the blood of the bird slaughtered over the fresh water, **14:7** and sprinkle it seven times on the one being cleansed from the disease, pronounce him clean, and send the live bird away over the open countryside.

The Seven Days of Purification

14:8 "The one being cleansed must then wash his clothes, shave off all his hair, and bathe in water, and so be clean. Then afterward he may enter the camp, but he must live outside his tent seven days. **14:9** When the seventh day comes he must shave all his hair – his head, his beard, his eyebrows, all his hair – and he must wash his clothes, bathe his body in water, and so be clean.

The Eighth Day Atonement Rituals

14:10 "On the eighth day he must take two flawless male lambs, one flawless yearling female lamb, three-tenths of an ephah of choice wheat flour as a grain offering mixed with olive oil, and one log of olive oil, **14:11** and the priest who pronounces him clean will have the man who is being cleansed stand along with these offerings before the LORD at the entrance of the Meeting Tent.

14:12 "The priest is to take one male lamb and present it for a guilt offering along with the log of olive oil and present them as a wave offering before the LORD. **14:13** He must then slaughter the male lamb in the place where the sin offering and the burnt offering are slaughtered, in the sanctuary, because, like the sin offering, the guilt offering belongs to the priest; it is most holy. **14:14** Then the priest is to take some of the blood of the guilt offering and put it on the right earlobe of the one being cleansed, on the thumb of his right hand, and on the big toe of his right foot. **14:15** The priest will then take some of the log of olive oil and pour it into his own left hand. **14:16** Then the priest is to dip his right forefinger into the olive oil that is in his left hand, and sprinkle some of the olive oil with his finger seven times before the LORD. **14:17** The priest will then put some of the rest of the olive oil that is in his hand on the right earlobe of the one being cleansed, on the thumb of his right hand, and on the big toe of his right foot, on the blood of the guilt offering, **14:18** and the remainder of the olive oil that is in his hand the priest is to put on the head of the one being cleansed. So the priest is to make atonement for him before the LORD.

14:19 "The priest must then perform the sin offering and make atonement for the one being cleansed from his impurity. After that he is to slaughter the burnt offering, **14:20** and the priest is to offer the burnt offering and the grain offering on the altar. So the priest is to make atonement for him and he will be clean.

The Eighth Day Atonement Rituals for the Poor Person

14:21 "If the person is poor and does not have sufficient means, he must take one male lamb as a guilt offering for a wave offering to make atonement for himself, one-tenth of an ephah of choice wheat flour mixed with olive oil for a grain offering, a log of olive oil, **14:22** and two turtledoves or two young pigeons, which are within his means. One will be a sin offering and the other a burnt offering.

14:23 "On the eighth day he must bring them for his purification to the priest at the entrance of the Meeting Tent before the LORD, **14:24** and the priest is to take the male lamb of the guilt offering and the log of olive oil and wave them as a wave offering before the LORD. **14:25** Then he is to slaughter the male lamb of the guilt offering, and the priest is to take some of the blood of the guilt offering and put it on the right earlobe of the one being cleansed, on the thumb of his right hand, and on the big toe of his right foot. **14:26** The priest will then pour some of the olive oil into his own left hand, **14:27** and sprinkle some of the olive oil that is in his left hand with his right forefinger seven times before the LORD. **14:28** Then the priest is to put some of the olive oil that is in his hand on the right earlobe of the one being cleansed, on the thumb of his right hand, and on the big toe of his right foot, on the place of the blood of the guilt offering, **14:29** and the remainder of the olive oil that is in the hand of the priest he is to put on the head of the one being cleansed to make atonement for him before the LORD.

14:30 "He will then make one of the turtledoves or young pigeons, which are within his means, **14:31** a sin offering and the other a burnt offering along with the grain offering. So the priest is to make atonement for the one being cleansed before the LORD. **14:32** This is the law of the one in whom there is a diseased infection, who does not have sufficient means for his purification."

Purification of Disease-Infected Houses

14:33 The LORD spoke to Moses and Aaron: **14:34** "When you enter the land of Canaan which I am about to give to you for a possession, and I put a diseased infection in a house in the land you are to possess, **14:35** then whoever owns the house must come and declare to the priest, 'Something like an infection is visible to me in the house.' **14:36** Then the priest will command that the house be cleared before the priest enters to examine the infection so that everything in the house does not become unclean, and afterward the priest will enter to examine the house. **14:37** He is to examine the infection, and if the infection in the walls of the house consists of yellowish green or reddish eruptions, and it appears to be deeper than the surface of the wall, **14:38** then the priest is to go out of the house to the doorway of the house and quarantine the house for seven days. **14:39** The priest must return on the seventh day and examine it, and if the infection has spread in the walls of the house, **14:40** then the priest is to command that the stones that had the infection in them be pulled and thrown outside the city into an unclean place. **14:41** Then he is to have the house scraped all around on the inside, and the plaster which is scraped off must be dumped outside the city into an unclean place. **14:42** They are then to take other stones and replace those stones, and he is to take other plaster and replaster the house.

14:43 "If the infection returns and breaks out in the house after he has pulled out the stones, scraped the house, and it is replastered, **14:44** the priest is to come and examine it, and if the infection has spread in the

house, it is a malignant disease in the house. It is unclean. **14:45** He must tear down the house, its stones, its wood, and all the plaster of the house, and bring all of it outside the city to an unclean place. **14:46** Anyone who enters the house all the days the priest has quarantined it will be unclean until evening. **14:47** Anyone who lies down in the house must wash his clothes. Anyone who eats in the house must wash his clothes.

14:48 "If, however, the priest enters and examines it, and the infection has not spread in the house after the house has been replastered, then the priest is to pronounce the house clean because the infection has been healed. **14:49** Then he is to take two birds, a piece of cedar wood, a scrap of crimson fabric, and some twigs of hyssop to decontaminate the house, **14:50** and he is to slaughter one bird into a clay vessel over fresh water. **14:51** He must then take the piece of cedar wood, the twigs of hyssop, the scrap of crimson fabric, and the live bird, and dip them in the blood of the slaughtered bird and in the fresh water, and sprinkle the house seven times. **14:52** So he is to decontaminate the house with the blood of the bird, the fresh water, the live bird, the piece of cedar wood, the twigs of hyssop, and the scrap of crimson fabric, **14:53** and he is to send the live bird away outside the city into the open countryside. So he is to make atonement for the house and it will be clean.

Summary of Purification Regulations for Infections

14:54 "This is the law for all diseased infections, for scall, **14:55** for the diseased garment, for the house, **14:56** for the swelling, for the scab, and for the bright spot, **14:57** to teach when something is unclean and when it is clean. This is the law for dealing with infectious disease."

Male Bodily Discharges

15:1 The LORD spoke to Moses and Aaron: **15:2** "Speak to the Israelites and tell them, 'When any man has a discharge from his body, his discharge is unclean. **15:3** Now this is his uncleanness in regard to his discharge – whether his body secretes his discharge or blocks his discharge, he is unclean. All the days that his body has a discharge or his body blocks his discharge, this is his uncleanness.

15:4 "'Any bed the man with a discharge lies on will be unclean, and any furniture he sits on will be unclean. **15:5** Anyone who touches his bed must wash his clothes, bathe in water, and be unclean until evening. **15:6** The one who sits on the furniture the man with a discharge sits on must wash his clothes, bathe in water, and be unclean until evening. **15:7** The one who touches the body of the man with a discharge must wash his clothes, bathe in water, and be unclean until evening. **15:8** If the man with a discharge spits on a person who is ceremonially clean, that person must wash his clothes, bathe in water, and be unclean until evening. **15:9** Any means of riding the man with a discharge rides on will be unclean. **15:10** Anyone who touches anything that was under him will be unclean until evening, and the one who carries those items must wash his clothes, bathe in water, and be unclean until evening. **15:11** Anyone whom the man with the discharge touches without having rinsed his hands in water must wash his clothes, bathe in water, and be unclean until evening. **15:12** A clay vessel which the man with the discharge touches must be broken, and any wooden utensil must be rinsed in water.

Purity Regulations for Male Bodily Discharges

15:13 "'When the man with the discharge becomes clean from his discharge he is to count off for himself seven days for his purification, and he must wash his clothes, bathe in fresh water, and be clean. **15:14** Then on the eighth day he is to take for himself two turtledoves or two young pigeons, and he is to present himself before the LORD at the entrance of the Meeting Tent and give them to the priest, **15:15** and the priest is to make one of them a sin offering and the other a burnt offering. So the priest is to make atonement for him before the LORD for his discharge.

15:16 "'When a man has a seminal emission, he must bathe his whole body in water and be unclean until evening, **15:17** and he must wash in water any clothing or leather that has semen on it, and it will be unclean until evening. **15:18** When a man has sexual intercourse with a woman and there is a seminal emission, they must bathe in water and be unclean until evening.

Female Bodily Discharges

15:19 "'When a woman has a discharge and her discharge is blood from her body, she is to be in her menstruation seven days, and anyone who touches her will be unclean until evening. **15:20** Anything she lies on during her menstruation will be unclean, and anything she sits on will be unclean. **15:21** Anyone who touches her bed must wash his clothes, bathe in water, and be unclean until evening. **15:22** Anyone who touches any furniture she sits on must wash his clothes, bathe in water, and be unclean until evening. **15:23** If there is something on the bed or on the furniture she sits on, when he touches it he will be unclean until evening, **15:24** and if a man actually has sexual intercourse with her so that her menstrual impurity touches him, then he will be unclean seven days and any bed he lies on will be unclean.

15:25 "'When a woman's discharge of blood flows many days not at the time of her menstruation, or if it flows beyond the time of her menstruation, all the days of her discharge of impurity will be like the days of her menstruation – she is unclean. **15:26** Any bed she lies on all the days of her discharge will be to her like the bed of her menstruation, any furniture she sits on will be unclean like the impurity of her menstruation, **15:27**

and anyone who touches them will be unclean, and he must wash his clothes, bathe in water, and be unclean until evening.

Purity Regulations from Female Bodily Discharges

15:28 "'If she becomes clean from her discharge, then she is to count off for herself seven days, and afterward she will be clean. **15:29** Then on the eighth day she must take for herself two turtledoves or two young pigeons and she must bring them to the priest at the entrance of the Meeting Tent, **15:30** and the priest is to make one a sin offering and the other a burnt offering. So the priest is to make atonement for her before the LORD from her discharge of impurity.

Summary of Purification Regulations for Bodily Discharges

15:31 "'Thus you are to set the Israelites apart from their impurity so that they do not die in their impurity by defiling my tabernacle which is in their midst. **15:32** This is the law of the one with a discharge: the one who has a seminal emission and becomes unclean by it, **15:33** the one who is sick in her menstruation, the one with a discharge, whether male or female, and a man who has sexual intercourse with an unclean woman.'"

The Day of Atonement

16:1 The LORD spoke to Moses after the death of Aaron's two sons when they approached the presence of the LORD and died, **16:2** and the LORD said to Moses: "Tell Aaron your brother that he must not enter at any time into the holy place inside the veil-canopy in front of the atonement plate that is on the ark so that he may not die, for I will appear in the cloud over the atonement plate.

Day of Atonement Offerings

16:3 "In this way Aaron is to enter into the sanctuary – with a young bull for a sin offering and a ram for a burnt offering. **16:4** He must put on a holy linen tunic, linen leggings are to cover his body, and he is to wrap himself with a linen sash and wrap his head with a linen turban. They are holy garments, so he must bathe his body in water and put them on. **16:5** He must also take two male goats from the congregation of the Israelites for a sin offering and one ram for a burnt offering. **16:6** Then Aaron is to present the sin offering bull which is for himself and is to make atonement on behalf of himself and his household. **16:7** He must then take the two goats and stand them before the LORD at the entrance of the Meeting Tent, **16:8** and Aaron is to cast lots over the two goats, one lot for the LORD and one lot for Azazel. **16:9** Aaron must then present the goat which has been designated by lot for the LORD, and he is to make it a sin offering, **16:10** but the goat which has been designated by lot for Azazel is to be stood alive before the LORD to make atonement on it by sending it away to Azazel into the wilderness.

The Sin Offering Sacrificial Procedures

16:11 "Aaron is to present the sin offering bull which is for himself, and he is to make atonement on behalf of himself and his household. He is to slaughter the sin offering bull which is for himself, **16:12** and take a censer full of coals of fire from the altar before the LORD and a full double handful of finely ground fragrant incense, and bring them inside the veil-canopy. **16:13** He must then put the incense on the fire before the LORD, and the cloud of incense will cover the atonement plate which is above the ark of the testimony, so that he will not die. **16:14** Then he is to take some of the blood of the bull and sprinkle it with his finger on the eastern face of the atonement plate, and in front of the atonement plate he is to sprinkle some of the blood seven times with his finger.

16:15 "He must then slaughter the sin offering goat which is for the people. He is to bring its blood inside the veil-canopy, and he is to do with its blood just as he did to the blood of the bull: He is to sprinkle it on the atonement plate and in front of the atonement plate. **16:16** So he is to make atonement for the holy place from the impurities of the Israelites and from their transgressions with regard to all their sins, and thus he is to do for the Meeting Tent which resides with them in the midst of their impurities. **16:17** Nobody is to be in the Meeting Tent when he enters to make atonement in the holy place until he goes out, and he has made atonement on his behalf, on behalf of his household, and on behalf of the whole assembly of Israel.

16:18 "Then he is to go out to the altar which is before the LORD and make atonement for it. He is to take some of the blood of the bull and some of the blood of the goat, and put it all around on the horns of the altar. **16:19** Then he is to sprinkle on it some of the blood with his finger seven times, and cleanse and consecrate it from the impurities of the Israelites.

The Live Goat Ritual Procedures

16:20 "When he has finished purifying the holy place, the Meeting Tent, and the altar, he is to present the live goat. **16:21** Aaron is to lay his two hands on the head of the live goat and confess over it all the iniquities of the Israelites and all their transgressions in regard to all their sins, and thus he is to put them on the head of the goat and send it away into the wilderness by the hand of a man standing ready. **16:22** The goat is to bear on itself all their iniquities into an inaccessible land, so he is to send the goat away in the wilderness.

The Concluding Rituals

16:23 "Aaron must then enter the Meeting Tent and take off the linen garments which he had put on when he entered the sanctuary, and leave them there. **16:24** Then he must bathe his body in water in a holy place, put on his clothes, and go out and make his burnt offering and the people's burnt offering. So he is to make atonement on behalf of himself and the people.

16:25 "Then he is to offer up the fat of the sin offering in smoke on the altar, **16:26** and the one who sent the goat away to Azazel must wash his clothes, bathe his body in water, and afterward he may reenter the camp. **16:27** The bull of the sin offering and the goat of the sin offering, whose blood was brought to make atonement in the holy place, must be brought outside the camp and their hide, their flesh, and their dung must be burned up, **16:28** and the one who burns them must wash his clothes and bathe his body in water, and afterward he may reenter the camp.

Review of the Day of Atonement

16:29 "This is to be a perpetual statute for you. In the seventh month, on the tenth day of the month, you must humble yourselves and do no work of any kind, both the native citizen and the foreigner who resides in your midst, **16:30** for on this day atonement is to be made for you to cleanse you from all your sins; you must be clean before the LORD. **16:31** It is to be a Sabbath of complete rest for you, and you must humble yourselves. It is a perpetual statute.

16:32 "The priest who is anointed and ordained to act as high priest in place of his father is to make atonement. He is to put on the linen garments, the holy garments, **16:33** and he is to purify the Most Holy Place, he is to purify the Meeting Tent and the altar, and he is to make atonement for the priests and for all the people of the assembly. **16:34** This is to be a perpetual statute for you to make atonement for the Israelites for all their sins once a year." So he did just as the LORD had commanded Moses.

The Slaughter of Animals

17:1 The LORD spoke to Moses: **17:2** "Speak to Aaron, his sons, and all the Israelites, and tell them: 'This is the word that the LORD has commanded: **17:3** "Blood guilt will be accounted to any man from the house of Israel who slaughters an ox or a lamb or a goat inside the camp or outside the camp, **17:4** but has not brought it to the entrance of the Meeting Tent to present it as an offering to the LORD before the tabernacle of the LORD. He has shed blood, so that man will be cut off from the midst of his people. **17:5** This is so that the Israelites will bring their sacrifices that they are sacrificing in the open field to the LORD at the entrance of the Meeting Tent to the priest and sacrifice them there as peace offering sacrifices to the LORD. **17:6** The priest is to splash the blood on the altar of the LORD at the entrance of the Meeting Tent, and offer the fat up in smoke for a soothing aroma to the LORD. **17:7** So they must no longer offer their sacrifices to the goat demons, acting like prostitutes by going after them. This is to be a perpetual statute for them throughout their generations.

17:8 "You are to say to them: 'Any man from the house of Israel or from the foreigners who reside in their midst, who offers a burnt offering or a sacrifice **17:9** but does not bring it to the entrance of the Meeting Tent to offer it to the LORD – that person will be cut off from his people.

Prohibition against Eating Blood

17:10 "'Any man from the house of Israel or from the foreigners who reside in their midst who eats any blood, I will set my face against that person who eats the blood, and I will cut him off from the midst of his people, **17:11** for the life of every living thing is in the blood. So I myself have assigned it to you on the altar to make atonement for your lives, for the blood makes atonement by means of the life. **17:12** Therefore, I have said to the Israelites: No person among you is to eat blood, and no resident foreigner who lives among you is to eat blood.

17:13 "'Any man from the Israelites or from the foreigners who reside in their midst who hunts a wild animal or a bird that may be eaten must pour out its blood and cover it with soil, **17:14** for the life of all flesh is its blood. So I have said to the Israelites: You must not eat the blood of any living thing because the life of every living thing is its blood – all who eat it will be cut off.

Regulations for Eating Carcasses

17:15 "'Any person who eats an animal that has died of natural causes or an animal torn by beasts, whether a native citizen or a foreigner, must wash his clothes, bathe in water, and be unclean until evening; then he becomes clean. **17:16** But if he does not wash his clothes and does not bathe his body, he will bear his punishment for iniquity.'"

Exhortation to Obedience and Life

18:1 The LORD spoke to Moses: **18:2** "Speak to the Israelites and tell them, 'I am the LORD your God! **18:3** You must not do as they do in the land of Egypt where you have been living, and you must not do as they do in the land of Canaan into which I am about to bring you; you must not walk in their statutes. **18:4** You must observe my regulations and you must be sure to walk in my statutes. I am the LORD your God. **18:5** So you must keep my statutes and my regulations; anyone who does so will live by keeping them. I am the LORD.

Laws of Sexual Relations

18:6 "'No man is to approach any close relative to have sexual intercourse with her. I am the LORD. **18:7** You must not expose your father's nakedness by having sexual intercourse with your mother. She is your mother; you must not have intercourse with her. **18:8** You must not have sexual intercourse with your father's wife; she is your father's nakedness. **18:9** You must not have sexual intercourse with your sister, whether she is your father's daughter or your mother's daughter, whether she is born in the same household or born outside it; you must not have sexual intercourse with either of them. **18:10** You must not expose the nakedness of your son's daughter or your daughter's daughter by having sexual intercourse with them, because they are your own nakedness. **18:11** You must not have sexual intercourse with the daughter of your father's wife born of your father; she is your sister. You must not have intercourse with her. **18:12** You must not have sexual intercourse with your father's sister; she is your father's flesh. **18:13** You must not have sexual intercourse with your mother's sister, because she is your mother's flesh. **18:14** You must not expose the nakedness of your father's brother; you must not approach his wife to have sexual intercourse with her. She is your aunt. **18:15** You must not have sexual intercourse with your daughter-in-law; she is your son's wife. You must not have intercourse with her. **18:16** You must not have sexual intercourse with your brother's wife; she is your brother's nakedness. **18:17** You must not have sexual intercourse with both a woman and her daughter; you must not take as wife either her son's daughter or her daughter's daughter to have intercourse with them. They are closely related to her – it is lewdness. **18:18** You must not take a woman in marriage and then marry her sister as a rival wife while she is still alive, to have sexual intercourse with her.

18:19 "'You must not approach a woman in her menstrual impurity to have sexual intercourse with her. **18:20** You must not have sexual intercourse with the wife of your fellow citizen to become unclean with her. **18:21** You must not give any of your children as an offering to Molech, so that you do not profane the name of your God. I am the Lord! **18:22** You must not have sexual intercourse with a male as one has sexual intercourse with a woman; it is a detestable act. **18:23** You must not have sexual intercourse with any animal to become defiled with it, and a woman must not stand before an animal to have sexual intercourse with it; it is a perversion.

Warning against the Abominations of the Nations

18:24 "'Do not defile yourselves with any of these things, for the nations which I am about to drive out before you have been defiled with all these things. **18:25** Therefore the land has become unclean and I have brought the punishment for its iniquity upon it, so that the land has vomited out its inhabitants. **18:26** You yourselves must obey my statutes and my regulations and must not do any of these abominations, both the native citizen and the resident foreigner in your midst, **18:27** for the people who were in the land before you have done all these abominations, and the land has become unclean. **18:28** So do not make the land vomit you out because you defile it just as it has vomited out the nations that were before you. **18:29** For if anyone does any of these abominations, the persons who do them will be cut off from the midst of their people. **18:30** You must obey my charge to not practice any of the abominable statutes that have been done before you, so that you do not defile yourselves by them. I am the Lord your God.'"

Religious and Social Regulations

19:1 The Lord spoke to Moses: **19:2** "Speak to the whole congregation of the Israelites and tell them, 'You must be holy because I, the Lord your God, am holy. **19:3** Each of you must respect his mother and his father, and you must keep my Sabbaths. I am the Lord your God. **19:4** Do not turn to idols, and you must not make for yourselves gods of cast metal. I am the Lord your God.

Eating the Peace Offering

19:5 "'When you sacrifice a peace offering sacrifice to the Lord, you must sacrifice it so that it is accepted for you. **19:6** It must be eaten on the day of your sacrifice and on the following day, but what is left over until the third day must be burned up. **19:7** If, however, it is eaten on the third day, it is spoiled, it will not be accepted, **19:8** and the one who eats it will bear his punishment for iniquity because he has profaned what is holy to the Lord. That person will be cut off from his people.

Leaving the Gleanings

19:9 "'When you gather in the harvest of your land, you must not completely harvest the corner of your field, and you must not gather up the gleanings of your harvest. **19:10** You must not pick your vineyard bare, and you must not gather up the fallen grapes of your vineyard. You must leave them for the poor and the foreigner. I am the Lord your God.

Dealing Honestly

19:11 "'You must not steal, you must not tell lies, and you must not deal falsely with your fellow citizen. **19:12** You must not swear falsely in my name, so that you do not profane the name of your God. I am the Lord. **19:13** You must not oppress your neighbor or commit robbery against him. You must not withhold the wages of the hired laborer overnight until morning. **19:14** You must not curse a deaf person or put a stumbling block in front of a blind person. You must fear your God; I am the Lord.

Justice, Love, and Propriety

19:15 "'You must not deal unjustly in judgment: you must neither show partiality to the poor nor honor the rich. You must judge your fellow citizen fairly. **19:16** You must not go about as a slanderer among your people. You must not stand idly by when your neighbor's life is at stake.

I am the Lord. **19:17** You must not hate your brother in your heart. You must surely reprove your fellow citizen so that you do not incur sin on account of him. **19:18** You must not take vengeance or bear a grudge against the children of your people, but you must love your neighbor as yourself. I am the Lord. **19:19** You must keep my statutes. You must not allow two different kinds of your animals to breed, you must not sow your field with two different kinds of seed, and you must not wear a garment made of two different kinds of fabric.

Lying with a Slave Woman

19:20 "'When a man has sexual intercourse with a woman, although she is a slave woman designated for another man and she has not yet been ransomed, or freedom has not been granted to her, there will be an obligation to pay compensation. They must not be put to death, because she was not free. **19:21** He must bring his guilt offering to the Lord at the entrance of the Meeting Tent, a guilt offering ram, **19:22** and the priest is to make atonement for him with the ram of the guilt offering before the Lord for his sin that he has committed, and he will be forgiven of his sin that he has committed.

The Produce of Fruit Trees

19:23 "'When you enter the land and plant any fruit tree, you must consider its fruit to be forbidden. Three years it will be forbidden to you; it must not be eaten. **19:24** In the fourth year all its fruit will be holy, praise offerings to the Lord. **19:25** Then in the fifth year you may eat its fruit to add its produce to your harvest. I am the Lord your God.

Blood, Hair, and Body

19:26 "'You must not eat anything with the blood still in it. You must not practice either divination or soothsaying. **19:27** You must not round off the corners of the hair on your head or ruin the corners of your beard. **19:28** You must not slash your body for a dead person or incise a tattoo on yourself. I am the Lord. **19:29** Do not profane your daughter by making her a prostitute, so that the land does not practice prostitution and become full of lewdness.

Purity, Honor, Respect, and Honesty

19:30 "'You must keep my Sabbaths and fear my sanctuary. I am the Lord. **19:31** Do not turn to the spirits of the dead and do not seek familiar spirits to become unclean by them. I am the Lord your God. **19:32** You must stand up in the presence of the aged, honor the presence of an elder, and fear your God. I am the Lord. **19:33** When a foreigner resides with you in your land, you must not oppress him. **19:34** The foreigner who resides with you must be to you like a native citizen among you; so you must love him as yourself, because you were foreigners in the land of Egypt. I am the Lord your God. **19:35** You must not do injustice in the regulation of measures, whether of length, weight, or volume. **19:36** You must have honest balances, honest weights, an honest ephah, and an honest hin. I am the Lord your God who brought you out from the land of Egypt. **19:37** You must be sure to obey all my statutes and regulations. I am the Lord.'"

Prohibitions against Illegitimate Family Worship

20:1 The Lord spoke to Moses: **20:2** "You are to say to the Israelites, 'Any man from the Israelites or from the foreigners who reside in Israel who gives any of his children to Molech must be put to death; the people of the land must pelt him with stones. **20:3** I myself will set my face against that man and cut him off from the midst of his people, because he has given some of his children to Molech and thereby defiled my sanctuary and profaned my holy name. **20:4** If, however, the people of the land shut their eyes to that man when he gives some of his children to Molech so that they do not put him to death, **20:5** I myself will set my face against that man and his clan. I will cut off from the midst of their people both him

and all who follow after him in spiritual prostitution, to commit prostitution by worshiping Molech.

Prohibition against Spiritists and Mediums

20:6 "'The person who turns to the spirits of the dead and familiar spirits to commit prostitution by going after them, I will set my face against that person and cut him off from the midst of his people.

Exhortation to Holiness and Obedience

20:7 "'You must sanctify yourselves and be holy, because I am the Lord your God. **20:8** You must be sure to obey my statutes. I am the Lord who sanctifies you.

Family Life and Sexual Prohibitions

20:9 "'If anyone curses his father and mother he must be put to death. He has cursed his father and mother; his blood guilt is on himself. **20:10** If a man commits adultery with his neighbor's wife, both the adulterer and the adulteress must be put to death. **20:11** If a man has sexual intercourse with his father's wife, he has exposed his father's nakedness. Both of them must be put to death; their blood guilt is on themselves. **20:12** If a man has sexual intercourse with his daughter-in-law, both of them must be put to death. They have committed perversion; their blood guilt is on themselves. **20:13** If a man has sexual intercourse with a male as one has sexual intercourse with a woman, the two of them have committed an abomination. They must be put to death; their blood guilt is on themselves. **20:14** If a man has sexual intercourse with both a woman and her mother, it is lewdness. Both he and they must be burned to death, so there is no lewdness in your midst. **20:15** If a man has sexual intercourse with any animal, he must be put to death, and you must kill the animal. **20:16** If a woman approaches any animal to have sexual intercourse with it, you must kill the woman, and the animal must be put to death; their blood guilt is on themselves.

20:17 "'If a man has sexual intercourse with his sister, whether the daughter of his father or his mother, so that he sees her nakedness and she sees his nakedness, it is a disgrace. They must be cut off in the sight of the children of their people. He has exposed his sister's nakedness; he will bear his punishment for iniquity. **20:18** If a man has sexual intercourse with a menstruating woman and uncovers her nakedness, he has laid bare her fountain of blood and she has exposed the fountain of her blood, so both of them must be cut off from the midst of their people. **20:19** You must not expose the nakedness of your mother's sister and your father's sister, for such a person has laid bare his own close relative. They must bear their punishment for iniquity. **20:20** If a man has sexual intercourse with his aunt, he has exposed his uncle's nakedness; they must bear responsibility for their sin, they will die childless. **20:21** If a man has sexual intercourse with his brother's wife, it is indecency. He has exposed his brother's nakedness; they will be childless.

Exhortation to Holiness and Obedience

20:22 "'You must be sure to obey all my statutes and regulations, so that the land to which I am about to bring you to take up residence there does not vomit you out. **20:23** You must not walk in the statutes of the nation which I am about to drive out before you, because they have done all these things and I am filled with disgust against them. **20:24** So I have said to you: You yourselves will possess their land and I myself will give it to you for a possession, a land flowing with milk and honey. I am the LORD your God who has set you apart from the other peoples. **20:25** Therefore you must distinguish between the clean animal and the unclean, and between the unclean bird and the clean, and you must not make yourselves detestable by means of an animal or bird or anything that creeps on the ground – creatures I have distinguished for you as unclean. **20:26** You must be holy to me because I, the LORD, am holy, and I have set you apart from the other peoples to be mine.

Prohibition against Spiritists and Mediums

20:27 "'A man or woman who has in them a spirit of the dead or a familiar spirit must be put to death. They must pelt them with stones; their blood guilt is on themselves.'"

Rules for the Priests

21:1 The LORD said to Moses: "Say to the priests, the sons of Aaron – say to them, 'For a dead person no priest is to defile himself among his people, **21:2** except for his close relative who is near to him: his mother, his father, his son, his daughter, his brother, **21:3** and his virgin sister who is near to him, who has no husband; he may defile himself for her. **21:4** He must not defile himself as a husband among his people so as to profane himself. **21:5** Priests must not have a bald spot shaved on their head, they must not shave the corner of their beard, and they must not cut slashes in their body.

21:6 "'They must be holy to their God, and they must not profane the name of their God, because they are the ones who present the LORD's gifts, the food of their God. Therefore they must be holy. **21:7** They must not take a wife defiled by prostitution, nor are they to take a wife divorced from her husband, for the priest is holy to his God. **21:8** You must sanctify him because he presents the food of your God. He must be holy to you because I, the LORD who sanctifies you all, am holy. **21:9** If a daughter of a priest profanes herself by engaging in prostitution, she is profaning her father. She must be burned to death.

Rules for the High Priest

21:10 "'The high priest – who is greater than his brothers, on whose head the anointing oil is poured, who has been ordained to wear the priestly garments – must neither dishevel the hair of his head nor tear his garments. **21:11** He must not go where there is any dead person; he must not defile himself even for his father and his mother. **21:12** He must not go out from the sanctuary and must not profane the sanctuary of his God, because the dedication of the anointing oil of his God is on him. I am the LORD. **21:13** He must take a wife who is a virgin. **21:14** He must not marry a widow, a divorced woman, or one profaned by prostitution; he may only take a virgin from his people as a wife. **21:15** He must not profane his children among his people, for I am the LORD who sanctifies him.'"

Rules for the Priesthood

21:16 The LORD spoke to Moses: **21:17** "Tell Aaron, 'No man from your descendants throughout their generations who has a physical flaw is to approach to present the food of his God. **21:18** Certainly no man who has a physical flaw is to approach: a blind man, or one who is lame, or one with a slit nose, or a limb too long, **21:19** or a man who has had a broken leg or arm, **21:20** or a hunchback, or a dwarf, or one with a spot in his eye, or a festering eruption, or a feverish rash, or a crushed testicle. **21:21** No man from the descendants of Aaron the priest who has a physical flaw may step forward to present the LORD's gifts; he has a physical flaw, so he must not step forward to present the food of his God. **21:22** He may eat both the most holy and the holy food of his God, **21:23** but he must

not go into the veil-canopy or step forward to the altar because he has a physical flaw. Thus he must not profane my holy places, for I am the LORD who sanctifies them.'"

21:24 So Moses spoke these things to Aaron, his sons, and all the Israelites.

Regulations for the Eating of Priestly Stipends

22:1 The LORD spoke to Moses: **22:2** "Tell Aaron and his sons that they must deal respectfully with the holy offerings of the Israelites, which they consecrate to me, so that they do not profane my holy name. I am the LORD. **22:3** Say to them, 'Throughout your generations, if any man from all your descendants approaches the holy offerings which the Israelites consecrate to the LORD while he is impure, that person must be cut off from before me. I am the LORD. **22:4** No man from the descendants of Aaron who is diseased or has a discharge may eat the holy offerings until he becomes clean. The one who touches anything made unclean by contact with a dead person, or a man who has a seminal emission, **22:5** or a man who touches a swarming thing by which he becomes unclean, or touches a person by which he becomes unclean, whatever that person's impurity – **22:6** the person who touches any of these will be unclean until evening and must not eat from the holy offerings unless he has bathed his body in water. **22:7** When the sun goes down he will be clean, and afterward he may eat from the holy offerings, because they are his food. **22:8** He must not eat an animal that has died of natural causes or an animal torn by beasts and thus become unclean by it. I am the LORD. **22:9** They must keep my charge so that they do not incur sin on account of it and therefore die because they profane it. I am the LORD who sanctifies them. **22:10** "'No lay person may eat anything holy. Neither a priest's lodger nor a hired laborer may eat anything holy, **22:11** but if a priest buys a person with his own money, that person may eat the holy offerings, and those born in the priest's own house may eat his food. **22:12** If a priest's daughter marries a lay person, she may not eat the holy contribution offerings, **22:13** but if a priest's daughter is a widow or divorced, and she has no children so that she returns to live in her father's house as in her youth, she may eat from her father's food, but no lay person may eat it. **22:14** "'If a man eats a holy offering by mistake, he must add one fifth to it and give the holy offering to the priest. **22:15** They must not profane the holy offerings which the Israelites contribute to the LORD, **22:16** and so cause them to incur a penalty for guilt when they eat their holy offerings, for I am the LORD who sanctifies them.'"

Regulations for Offering Votive and Freewill Offerings

22:17 The LORD spoke to Moses: **22:18** "Speak to Aaron, his sons, and all the Israelites and tell them, 'When any man from the house of Israel or from the foreigners in Israel presents his offering for any of the votive or freewill offerings which they present to the LORD as a burnt offering, **22:19** if it is to be acceptable for your benefit it must be a flawless male from the cattle, sheep, or goats. **22:20** You must not present anything that has a flaw, because it will not be acceptable for your benefit. **22:21** If a man presents a peace offering sacrifice to the LORD for a special votive offering or for a freewill offering from the herd or the flock, it must be flawless to be acceptable; it must have no flaw.

22:22 "'You must not present to the LORD something blind, or with a broken bone, or mutilated, or with a running sore, or with a festering eruption, or with a feverish rash. You must not give any of these as a gift on the altar to the LORD. **22:23** As for an ox or a sheep with a limb too long or stunted, you may present it as a freewill offering, but it will not be acceptable for a votive offering. **22:24** You must not present to the LORD something with testicles that are bruised, crushed, torn, or cut off; you must not do this in your land. **22:25** Even from a foreigner you must not present the food of your God from such animals as these, for they are ruined and flawed; they will not be acceptable for your benefit.'"

22:26 The LORD spoke to Moses: **22:27** "When an ox, lamb, or goat is born, it must be under the care of its mother seven days, but from the eighth day onward it will be acceptable as an offering gift to the LORD. **22:28** You must not slaughter an ox or a sheep and its young on the same day. **22:29** When you sacrifice a thanksgiving offering to the LORD, you must sacrifice it so that it is acceptable for your benefit. **22:30** On that very day it must be eaten; you must not leave any part of it over until morning. I am the LORD.

22:31 "You must be sure to do my commandments. I am the LORD. **22:32** You must not profane my holy name, and I will be sanctified in the midst of the Israelites. I am the LORD who sanctifies you, **22:33** the one who brought you out from the land of Egypt to be your God. I am the LORD."

Regulations for Israel's Appointed Times

23:1 The LORD spoke to Moses: **23:2** "Speak to the Israelites and tell them, 'These are the LORD's appointed times which you must proclaim as holy assemblies – my appointed times:

The Weekly Sabbath

23:3 "'Six days work may be done, but on the seventh day there must be a Sabbath of complete rest, a holy assembly. You must not do any work; it is a Sabbath to the LORD in all the places where you live.

The Festival of Passover and Unleavened Bread

23:4 "'These are the LORD's appointed times, holy assemblies, which you must proclaim at their appointed time. **23:5** In the first month, on the fourteenth day of the month, at twilight, is a Passover offering to the LORD. **23:6** Then on the fifteenth day of the same month will be the festival of unleavened bread to the LORD; seven days you must eat unleavened bread. **23:7** On the first day there will be a holy assembly for you; you must not do any regular work. **23:8** You must present a gift to the LORD for seven days, and the seventh day is a holy assembly; you must not do any regular work.'"

The Presentation of First Fruits

23:9 The LORD spoke to Moses: **23:10** "Speak to the Israelites and tell them, 'When you enter the land that I am about to give to you and you gather in its harvest, then you must bring the sheaf of the first portion of your harvest to the priest, **23:11** and he must wave the sheaf before the LORD to be accepted for your benefit – on the day after the Sabbath the priest is to wave it. **23:12** On the day you wave the sheaf you must also offer a flawless yearling lamb for a burnt offering to the LORD,
23:13 along with its grain offering, two tenths of an ephah of choice wheat flour mixed with olive oil, as a gift to the LORD, a soothing aroma, and its drink offering, one fourth of a hin of wine. **23:14** You must not eat bread, roasted grain, or fresh grain until this very day, until you bring the offering of your God. This is a perpetual statute throughout your generations in all the places where you live.

The Festival of Weeks

23:15 "'You must count for yourselves seven weeks from the day after the Sabbath, from the day you bring the wave offering sheaf; they must be complete weeks. **23:16** You must count fifty days – until the day after the seventh Sabbath – and then you must present a new grain offering to the LORD. **23:17** From the places where you live you must bring two loaves of bread for a wave offering; they must be made from two tenths of an ephah of fine wheat flour, baked with yeast, as first fruits to the LORD. **23:18** Along with the loaves of bread, you must also present seven flawless yearling lambs, one young bull, and two rams. They are to be a burnt offering to the LORD along with their grain offering and drink offerings, a gift of a soothing aroma to the LORD. **23:19** You must also offer one male goat for a sin offering and two yearling lambs for a peace offering sacrifice, **23:20** and the priest is to wave them – the two lambs – along with the bread of the first fruits, as a wave offering before the LORD; they will be holy to the LORD for the priest.
23:21 "'On this very day you must proclaim an assembly; it is to be a holy assembly for you. You must not do any regular work. This is a perpetual statute in all the places where you live throughout your generations. **23:22** When you gather in the harvest of your land, you must not completely harvest the corner of your field, and you must not gather up the gleanings of your harvest. You must leave them for the poor and the foreigner. I am the LORD your God.'"

The Festival of Horn Blasts

23:23 The LORD spoke to Moses: **23:24** "Tell the Israelites, 'In the seventh month, on the first day of the month, you must have a complete rest, a memorial announced by loud horn blasts, a holy assembly. **23:25** You must not do any regular work, but you must present a gift to the LORD.'"

The Day of Atonement

23:26 The LORD spoke to Moses: **23:27** "The tenth day of this seventh month is the Day of Atonement. It is to be a holy assembly for you, and you must humble yourselves and present a gift to the LORD. **23:28** You must not do any work on this particular day, because it is a day of atonement to make atonement for yourselves before the LORD your God. **23:29** Indeed, any person who does not behave with humility on this particular day will be cut off from his people. **23:30** As for any person who does any work on this particular day, I will exterminate that person from the midst of his people! **23:31** You must not do any work. This is a perpetual statute throughout your generations in all the places where you live. **23:32** It is a Sabbath of complete rest for you, and you must humble yourselves on the ninth day of the month in the evening, from evening until evening you must observe your Sabbath."

The Festival of Booths

23:33 The LORD spoke to Moses: **23:34** "Tell the Israelites, 'On the fifteenth day of this seventh month is the Festival of Temporary Shelters for seven days to the LORD. **23:35** On the first day is a holy assembly; you must do no regular work. **23:36** For seven days you must present a gift to the LORD. On the eighth day there is to be a holy assembly for you, and you must present a gift to the LORD. It is a solemn assembly day; you must not do any regular work.
23:37 "'These are the appointed times of the LORD that you must proclaim as holy assemblies to present a gift to the LORD – burnt offering, grain offering, sacrifice, and drink offerings, each day according to its regulation, **23:38** besides the Sabbaths of the LORD and all your gifts, votive offerings, and freewill offerings which you must give to the LORD.
23:39 "'On the fifteenth day of the seventh month, when you gather in the produce of the land, you must celebrate a pilgrim festival of the LORD for seven days. On the first day is a complete rest and on the eighth day is complete rest. **23:40** On the first day you must take for yourselves branches from majestic trees – palm branches, branches of leafy trees, and willows of the brook – and you must rejoice before the LORD your God for seven days. **23:41** You must celebrate it as a pilgrim festival to

the LORD for seven days in the year. This is a perpetual statute throughout your generations; you must celebrate it in the seventh month. **23:42** You must live in temporary shelters for seven days; every native citizen in Israel must live in temporary shelters, **23:43** so that your future generations may know that I made the Israelites live in temporary shelters when I brought them out from the land of Egypt. I am the LORD your God.'"
23:44 So Moses spoke to the Israelites about the appointed times of the LORD.

Regulations for the Lampstand and Table of Bread

24:1 The LORD spoke to Moses: **24:2** "Command the Israelites to bring to you pure oil of beaten olives for the light, to make a lamp burn continually. **24:3** Outside the veil-canopy of the congregation in the Meeting Tent Aaron must arrange it from evening until morning before the LORD continually. This is a perpetual statute throughout your generations. **24:4** On the ceremonially pure lampstand he must arrange the lamps before the LORD continually.
24:5 "You must take choice wheat flour and bake twelve loaves; there must be two tenths of an ephah of flour in each loaf, **24:6** and you must set them in two rows, six in a row, on the ceremonially pure table before the LORD. **24:7** You must put pure frankincense on each row, and it will become a memorial portion for the
bread, a gift to the LORD. **24:8** Each Sabbath day Aaron must arrange it before the LORD continually; this portion is from the Israelites as a perpetual covenant. **24:9** It will belong to Aaron and his sons, and they must eat it in a holy place because it is most holy to him, a perpetual allotted portion from the gifts of the LORD."

A Case of Blaspheming the Name

24:10 Now an Israelite woman's son whose father was an Egyptian went out among the Israelites, and the Israelite woman's son and an Israelite man had a fight in the camp. **24:11** The Israelite woman's son misused the Name and cursed, so they brought him to Moses. (Now his mother's name was Shelomith daughter of Dibri, of the tribe of Dan.) **24:12** So they placed him in custody until they were able to make a clear legal decision for themselves based on words from the mouth of the LORD.
24:13 Then the LORD spoke to Moses: **24:14** "Bring the one who cursed outside the camp, and all who heard him are to lay their hands on his head, and the whole congregation is to stone him to death. **24:15** Moreover, you are to tell the Israelites, 'If any man curses his God he will bear responsibility for his sin, **24:16** and one who misuses the name of the LORD must surely be put to death. The whole congregation must surely stone him, whether he is a foreigner or a native citizen; when he misuses the Name he must be put to death.
24:17 "'If a man beats any person to death, he must be put to death. **24:18** One who beats an animal to death must make restitution for it, life for life. **24:19** If a man inflicts an injury on his fellow citizen, just as he has done it must be done to him – **24:20** fracture for fracture, eye for eye, tooth for tooth – just as he inflicts an injury on another person that same injury must be inflicted on him. **24:21** One who beats an animal to death must make restitution for it, but one who beats a person to death must be put to death. **24:22** There will be one regulation for you, whether a foreigner or a native citizen, for I am the LORD your God.'"
24:23 Then Moses spoke to the Israelites and they brought the one who cursed outside the camp and stoned him with stones. So the Israelites did just as the LORD had commanded Moses.

Regulations for the Sabbatical Year

25:1 The LORD spoke to Moses at Mount Sinai: **25:2** "Speak to the Israelites and tell them, 'When you enter the land that I am giving you, the land must observe a Sabbath to the LORD. **25:3** Six years you may sow your field, and six years you may prune your vineyard and gather the produce, **25:4** but in the seventh year the land must have a Sabbath of complete rest – a Sabbath to the LORD. You must not sow your field or prune your vineyard. **25:5** You must not gather in the aftergrowth of your harvest and you must not pick the grapes of your unpruned vines; the land must have a year of complete rest. **25:6** You may have the Sabbath produce of the land to eat – you, your male servant, your female servant, your hired worker, the resident foreigner who stays with you, **25:7** your cattle, and the wild animals that are in your land – all its produce will be for you to eat.

Regulations for the Jubilee Year of Release

25:8 "'You must count off seven weeks of years, seven times seven years, and the days of the seven weeks of years will amount to forty-nine years. **25:9** You must sound loud horn blasts – in the seventh month, on the tenth day of the month, on the Day of Atonement – you must sound the horn in your entire land. **25:10** So you must consecrate the fiftieth year, and you must proclaim a release in the land for all its inhabitants. That year will be your jubilee; each one of you must return to his property and each one of you must return to his clan. **25:11** That fiftieth year will be your jubilee; you must not sow the land, harvest its aftergrowth, or pick the grapes of its unpruned vines. **25:12** Because that year is a jubilee, it will be holy to you – you may eat its produce from the field.

Release of Landed Property

25:13 "'In this year of jubilee you must each return to your property. **25:14** If you make a sale to your fellow citizen or buy from your fellow citizen, no one is to wrong his brother. **25:15** You may buy it from your fellow citizen according to the number of years since the last jubilee; he may sell it to you according to the years of produce that are left. **25:16** The more years there are, the more you may make its purchase price, and the fewer years there are, the less you must make its purchase price, because he is only selling to you a number of years of produce. **25:17** No one is to oppress his fellow citizen, but you must fear your God, because I am the LORD your God. **25:18** You must obey my statutes and my regulations; you must be sure to keep them so that you may live securely in the land.

25:19 ‘‘The land will give its fruit and you may eat until you are satisfied, and you may live securely in the land. **25:20** If you say, ‘What will we eat in the seventh year if we do not sow and gather our produce?’ **25:21** I will command my blessing for you in the sixth year so that it may yield the produce for three years, **25:22** and you may sow the eighth year and eat from that sixth year’s produce – old produce. Until you bring in the ninth year’s produce, you may eat old produce. **25:23** The land must not be sold without reclaim because the land belongs to me, for you are foreigners and residents with me. **25:24** In all your landed property you must provide for the right of redemption of the land.

25:25 ‘‘If your brother becomes impoverished and sells some of his property, his near redeemer is to come to you and redeem what his brother sold. **25:26** If a man has no redeemer, but he prospers and gains enough for its redemption, **25:27** he is to calculate the value of the years it was sold, refund the balance to the man to whom he had sold it, and return to his property. **25:28** If he has not prospered enough to refund a balance to him, then what he sold will belong to the one who bought it until the jubilee year, but it must revert in the jubilee and the original owner may return to his property.

Release of Houses

25:29 ‘‘If a man sells a residential house in a walled city, its right of redemption must extend until one full year from its sale; its right of redemption must extend to a full calendar year. **25:30** If it is not redeemed before the full calendar year is ended, the house in the walled city will belong without reclaim to the one who bought it throughout his generations; it will not revert in the jubilee. **25:31** The houses of villages, however, which have no wall surrounding them must be considered as the field of the land; they will have the right of redemption and must revert in the jubilee. **25:32** As for the cities of the Levites, the houses in the cities which they possess, the Levites must have a perpetual right of redemption. **25:33** Whatever someone among the Levites might redeem – the sale of a house which is his property in a city – must revert in the jubilee, because the houses of the cities of the Levites are their property in the midst of the Israelites. **25:34** Moreover, the open field areas of their cities must not be sold, because that is their perpetual possession.

Debt and Slave Regulations

25:35 ‘‘If your brother becomes impoverished and is indebted to you, you must support him; he must live with you like a foreign resident. **25:36** Do not take interest or profit from him, but you must fear your God and your brother must live with you. **25:37** You must not lend him your money at interest and you must not sell him food for profit. **25:38** I am the LORD your God who brought you out from the land of Egypt to give you the land of Canaan – to be your God.

25:39 ‘‘If your brother becomes impoverished with regard to you so that he sells himself to you, you must not subject him to slave service. **25:40** He must be with you as a hired worker, as a resident foreigner; he must serve with you until the year of jubilee, **25:41** but then he may go free, he and his children with him, and may return to his family and to the property of his ancestors. **25:42** Since they are my servants whom I brought out from the land of Egypt, they must not be sold in a slave sale. **25:43** You must not rule over him harshly, but you must fear your God.

25:44 ‘‘As for your male and female slaves who may belong to you – you may buy male and female slaves from the nations all around you. **25:45** Also you may buy slaves from the children of the foreigners who reside with you, and from their families that are with you, whom they have fathered in your land, they may become your property. **25:46** You may give them as inheritance to your children after you to possess as property. You may enslave them perpetually. However, as for your brothers the Israelites, no man may rule over his brother harshly.

25:47 ‘‘If a resident foreigner who is with you prospers and your brother becomes impoverished with regard to him so that he sells himself to a resident foreigner who is with you or to a member of a foreigner’s family, **25:48** after he has sold himself he retains a right of redemption. One of his brothers may redeem him, **25:49** or his uncle or his cousin may redeem him, or anyone of the rest of his blood relatives – his family – may redeem him, or if he prospers he may redeem himself. **25:50** He must calculate with the one who bought him the number of years from the year he sold himself to him until the jubilee year, and the cost of his sale must correspond to the number of years, according to the rate of wages a hired worker would have earned while with him. **25:51** If there are still many years, in keeping with them he must refund most of the cost of his purchase for his redemption, **25:52** but if only a few years remain until the jubilee, he must calculate for himself in keeping with the remaining years

and refund it for his redemption. **25:53** He must be with the one who bought him like a yearly hired worker. The one who bought him must not rule over him harshly in your sight. **25:54** If, however, he is not redeemed in these ways, he must go free in the jubilee year, he and his children with him, **25:55** because the Israelites are my own servants; they are my servants whom I brought out from the land of Egypt. I am the LORD your God.

Exhortation to Obedience

26:1 ‘‘You must not make for yourselves idols, so you must not set up for yourselves a carved image or a pillar, and you must not place a sculpted stone in your land to bow down before it, for I am the LORD your God. **26:2** You must keep my Sabbaths and reverence my sanctuary. I am the LORD.

The Benefits of Obedience

26:3 ‘‘If you walk in my statutes and are sure to obey my commandments, **26:4** I will give you your rains in their time so that the land will give its yield and the trees of the field will produce their fruit. **26:5** Threshing season will extend for you until the season for harvesting grapes, and the season for harvesting grapes will extend until sowing season, so you will eat your bread until you are satisfied, and you will live securely in your land. **26:6** I will grant peace in the land so that you will lie down to sleep without anyone terrifying you. I will remove harmful animals from the land, and no sword of war will pass through your land. **26:7** You will pursue your enemies and they will fall before you by the sword. **26:8** Five of you will pursue a hundred, and a hundred of you will pursue ten thousand, and your enemies will fall before you by the sword. **26:9** I will turn to you, make you fruitful, multiply you, and maintain my covenant with you. **26:10** You will still be eating stored produce from the previous year and will have to clean out what is stored from the previous year to make room for new.

26:11 ‘‘I will put my tabernacle in your midst and I will not abhor you. **26:12** I will walk among you, and I will be your God and you will be my people. **26:13** I am the LORD your God who brought you out from the land of Egypt, from being their slaves, and I broke the bars of your yoke and caused you to walk upright.

The Consequences of Disobedience

26:14 ‘‘If, however, you do not obey me and keep all these commandments – **26:15** if you reject my statutes and abhor my regulations so that you do not keep all my commandments and you break my covenant – **26:16** I for my part will do this to you: I will inflict horror on you, consumption and fever, which diminish eyesight and drain away the vitality of life. You will sow your seed in vain because your enemies will eat it. **26:17** I will set my face against you. You will be struck down before your enemies, those who hate you will rule over you, and you will flee when there is no one pursuing you.

26:18 ‘‘If, in spite of all these things, you do not obey me, I will discipline you seven times more on account of your sins. **26:19** I will break your strong pride and make your sky like iron and your land like bronze. **26:20** Your strength will be used up in vain, your land will not give its yield, and the trees of the land will not produce their fruit.

26:21 ‘‘If you walk in hostility against me and are not willing to obey me, I will increase your affliction seven times according to your sins. **26:22** I will send the wild animals against you and they will bereave you of your children, annihilate your cattle, and diminish your population so that your roads will become deserted.

26:23 ‘‘If in spite of these things you do not allow yourselves to be disciplined and you walk in hostility against me, **26:24** I myself will also walk in hostility against you and strike you seven times on account of your sins. **26:25** I will bring on you an avenging sword, a covenant vengeance. Although you will gather together into your cities, I will send pestilence among you and you will be given into enemy hands. **26:26** When I break off your supply of bread, ten women will bake your bread in one oven; they will ration your bread by weight, and you will eat and not be satisfied.

26:27 ‘‘If in spite of this you do not obey me but walk in hostility against me, **26:28** I will walk in hostile rage against you and I myself will also discipline you seven times on account of your sins. **26:29** You will eat the flesh of your sons and the flesh of your daughters. **26:30** I will destroy your high places and cut down your incense altars, and I will stack your dead bodies on top of the lifeless bodies of your idols. I will abhor you. **26:31** I will lay your cities waste and make your sanctuaries desolate, and I will refuse to smell your soothing aromas. **26:32** I myself will make the land desolate and your enemies who live in it will be appalled. **26:33** I will scatter you among the nations and unsheathe the sword after you, so your land will become desolate and your cities will become a waste.

26:34 ‘‘Then the land will make up for its Sabbaths all the days it lies desolate while you are in the land of your enemies; then the land will rest and make up its Sabbaths. **26:35** All the days of the desolation it will have the rest it did not have on your Sabbaths when you lived on it.

26:36 ‘‘As for the ones who remain among you, I will bring despair into their hearts in the lands of their enemies. The sound of a blowing leaf will pursue them, and they will flee as one who flees the sword and fall down even though there is no pursuer. **26:37** They will stumble over each other as those who flee before a sword, though there is no pursuer, and there will be no one to take a stand for you before your enemies. **26:38** You will perish among the nations; the land of your enemies will consume you.

Restoration through Confession and Repentance

26:39 "'As for the ones who remain among you, they will rot away because of their iniquity in the lands of your enemies, and they will also rot away because of their ancestors' iniquities which are with them. **26:40** However, when they confess their iniquity and their ancestors' iniquity which they committed by trespassing against me, by which they also walked in hostility against me **26:41** (and I myself will walk in hostility against them and bring them into the land of their enemies), and then their uncircumcised hearts become humbled and they make up for their iniquity, **26:42** I will remember my covenant with Jacob and also my covenant with Isaac and also my covenant with Abraham, and I will remember the land. **26:43** The land will be abandoned by them in order that it may make up for its Sabbaths while it is made desolate without them, and they will make up for their iniquity because they have rejected my regulations and have abhorred my statutes. **26:44** In spite of this, however, when they are in the land of their enemies I will not reject them and abhor them to make a complete end of them, to break my covenant with them, for I am the LORD their God. **26:45** I will remember for them the covenant with their ancestors whom I brought out from the land of Egypt in the sight of the nations to be their God. I am the LORD.'"

Summary Colophon

26:46 These are the statutes, regulations, and instructions which the LORD established between himself and the Israelites at Mount Sinai through Moses.

Redemption of Vowed People

27:1 The LORD spoke to Moses: **27:2** "Speak to the Israelites and tell them, 'When a man makes a special votive offering based on the conversion value of persons to the LORD, **27:3** the conversion value of the male from twenty years old up to sixty years old is fifty shekels by the standard of the sanctuary shekel. **27:4** If the person is a female, the conversion value is thirty shekels. **27:5** If the person is from five years old up to twenty years old, the conversion value of the male is twenty shekels, and for the female ten shekels. **27:6** If the person is one month old up to five years old, the conversion value of the male is five shekels of silver, and for the female the conversion value is three shekels of silver. **27:7** If the person is from sixty years old and older, if he is a male the conversion value is fifteen shekels, and for the female ten shekels. **27:8** If he is too poor to pay the conversion value, he must stand the person before the priest and the priest will establish his conversion value; according to what the man who made the vow can afford, the priest will establish his conversion value.

Redemption of Vowed Animals

27:9 "'If what is vowed is a kind of animal from which an offering may be presented to the LORD, anything which he gives to the LORD from this kind of animal will be holy. **27:10** He must not replace or exchange it, good for bad or bad for good, and if he does indeed exchange one animal for another animal, then both the original animal and its substitute will be holy. **27:11** If what is vowed is an unclean animal from which an offering must not be presented to the LORD, then he must stand the animal before the priest, **27:12** and the priest will establish its conversion value, whether good or bad. According to the assessed conversion value of the priest, thus it will be. **27:13** If, however, the person who made the vow redeems the animal, he must add one fifth to its conversion value.

Redemption of Vowed Houses

27:14 "'If a man consecrates his house as holy to the LORD, the priest will establish its conversion value, whether good or bad. Just as the priest establishes its conversion value, thus it will stand. **27:15** If the one who consecrates it redeems his house, he must add to it one fifth of its conversion value in silver, and it will belong to him.

Redemption of Vowed Fields

27:16 "'If a man consecrates to the LORD some of his own landed property, the conversion value must be calculated in accordance with the amount of seed needed to sow it, a homer of barley seed being priced at fifty shekels of silver. **27:17** If he consecrates his field in the jubilee year, the conversion value will stand, **27:18** but if he consecrates his field after the jubilee, the priest will calculate the price for him according to the years that are left until the next jubilee year, and it will be deducted from the conversion value. **27:19** If, however, the one who consecrated the field redeems it, he must add to it one fifth of the conversion price and it will belong to him. **27:20** If he does not redeem the field, but sells the field to someone else, he may never redeem it. **27:21** When it reverts in the jubilee, the field will be holy to the LORD like a permanently dedicated field; it will become the priest's property. **27:22** "'If he consecrates to the LORD a field he has purchased, which is not part of his own landed property, **27:23** the priest will calculate for him the amount of its conversion value until the jubilee year, and he must pay the conversion value on that jubilee day as something that is holy to the LORD. **27:24** In the jubilee year the field will return to the one from whom he bought it, the one to whom it belongs as landed property. **27:25**

Every conversion value must be calculated by the standard of the sanctuary shekel; twenty gerahs to the shekel.

Redemption of the Firstborn

27:26 "'Surely no man may consecrate a firstborn that already belongs to the LORD as a firstborn among the animals; whether it is an ox or a sheep, it belongs to the LORD. **27:27** If, however, it is among the unclean animals, he may ransom it according to its conversion value and must add one fifth to it, but if it is not redeemed it must be sold according to its conversion value.

Things Permanently Dedicated to the Lord

27:28 "'Surely anything which a man permanently dedicates to the LORD from all that belongs to him, whether from people, animals, or his landed property, must be neither sold nor redeemed; anything permanently dedicated is most holy to the LORD. **27:29** Any human being who is permanently dedicated must not be ransomed; such a person must be put to death.

Redemption of the Tithe

27:30 "'Any tithe of the land, from the grain of the land or from the fruit of the trees, belongs to the LORD; it is holy to the LORD. **27:31** If a man redeems part of his tithe, however, he must add one fifth to it. **27:32** All the tithe of herd or flock, everything which passes under the rod, the tenth one will be holy to the LORD. **27:33** The owner must not examine the animals to distinguish between good and bad, and he must not exchange it. If, however, he

does exchange it, both the original animal and its substitute will be holy. It must not be redeemed.'"

Final Colophon

27:34 These are the commandments which the LORD commanded Moses to tell the Israelites at Mount Sinai.

Book 4. Numbers

Organizing the Census of the Israelites

1:1 Now the LORD[2] spoke[3] to Moses in the tent of meeting in the wilderness of Sinai on the first day of the second month of the second year after the Israelites departed from the land of Egypt. He said: **1:2** "Take a census of the entire Israelite community by their clans and families, counting the name of every individual male. **1:3** You and Aaron are to number all in Israel who can serve in the army, those who are twenty years old or older, by their divisions. **1:4** And to help you there is to be a man from each tribe, each man the head of his family. **1:5** Now these are the names of the men who are to help you:

from Reuben, Elizur son of Shedeur;

1:6 from Simeon, Shelumiel son of Zurishaddai;

1:7 from Judah, Nahshon son of Amminadab;

1:8 from Issachar, Nethanel son of Zuar;

1:9 from Zebulun, Eliab son of Helon;

1:10 from the sons of Joseph:

from Ephraim, Elishama son of Ammihud;

from Manasseh, Gamaliel son of Pedahzur;

1:11 from Benjamin, Abidan son of Gideoni;

1:12 from Dan, Ahiezer son of Ammishaddai;

1:13 from Asher, Pagiel son of Ocran;

1:14 from Gad, Eliasaph son of Deuel;

1:15 from Naphtali, Ahira son of Enan."

The Census of the Tribes

1:16 These were the ones chosen from the community, leaders of their ancestral tribes. They were the heads of the thousands of Israel.

1:17 So Moses and Aaron took these men who had been mentioned specifically by name, **1:18** and they assembled the entire community together on the first day of the second month. Then the people recorded their ancestry by their clans and families, and the men who were twenty years old or older were listed by name individually, **1:19** just as the LORD had commanded Moses. And so he numbered them in the wilderness of Sinai.

1:20 And they were as follows:

The descendants of Reuben, the firstborn son of Israel: According to the records of their clans and families, all the males twenty years old or older who could serve in the army were listed by name individually. **1:21** Those of them who were numbered from the tribe of Reuben were 46,500.

1:22 From the descendants of Simeon: According to the records of their clans and families, all the males numbered of them twenty years old or older who could serve in the army were listed by name individually. **1:23** Those of them who were numbered from the tribe of Simeon were 59,300.

1:24 From the descendants of Gad: According to the records of their clans and families, all the males twenty years old or older who could serve in the army were listed by name. **1:25** Those of them who were numbered from the tribe of Gad were 45,650.

1:26 From the descendants of Judah: According to the records of their clans and families, all the males twenty years old or older who could serve in the army were listed by name. **1:27** Those of them who were numbered from the tribe of Judah were 74,600.

1:28 From the descendants of Issachar: According to the records of their clans and families, all the males twenty years old or older who could serve in the army were listed by name. **1:29** Those of them who were numbered from the tribe of Issachar were 54,400.

1:30 From the descendants of Zebulun: According to the records of their clans and families, all the males twenty years old or older who could serve in the army were listed by name. **1:31** Those of them who were numbered from the tribe of Zebulun were 57,400.

1:32 From the sons of Joseph:

From the descendants of Ephraim: According to the records of their clans and families, all the males twenty years old or older who could serve in the army were listed by name. **1:33** Those of them who were numbered from the tribe of Ephraim were 40,500. **1:34** From the descendants of Manasseh: According to the records of their clans and families, all the males twenty years old or older who could serve in the army were listed by name. **1:35** Those of them who were numbered from the tribe of Manasseh were 32,200.

1:36 From the descendants of Benjamin: According to the records of their clans and families, all the males twenty years old or older who could serve in the army were listed by name. **1:37** Those of them who were numbered from the tribe of Benjamin were 35,400.

1:38 From the descendants of Dan: According to the records of their clans and families, all the males twenty years old or older who could serve in the army were listed by name. **1:39** Those of them who were numbered from the tribe of Dan were 62,700.

1:40 From the descendants of Asher: According to the records of their clans and families, all the males twenty years old or older who could serve in the army were listed by name. **1:41** Those of them who were numbered from the tribe of Asher were 41,500.

1:42 From the descendants of Naphtali: According to the records of their clans and families, all the males twenty years old or older who could serve in the army were listed by name. **1:43** Those of them who were numbered from the tribe of Naphtali were 53,400.

1:44 These were the men whom Moses and Aaron numbered along with the twelve leaders of Israel, each of whom was from his own family. **1:45** All the Israelites who were twenty years old or older, who could serve in Israel's army, were numbered according to their families. **1:46** And all those numbered totaled 603,550.

The Exemption of the Levites

1:47 But the Levites, according to the tribe of their fathers, were not numbered among them. **1:48** The LORD had said to Moses, **1:49** "Only the tribe of Levi you must not number or count with the other Israelites. **1:50** But appoint the Levites over the tabernacle of the testimony, over all its furnishings and over everything in it. They must carry the tabernacle and all its furnishings; and they must attend to it and camp around it. **1:51** Whenever the tabernacle is to move, the Levites must take it down, and whenever the tabernacle is to be reassembled, the Levites must set it up. Any unauthorized person who approaches it must be killed.

1:52 "The Israelites will camp according to their divisions, each man in his camp, and each man by his standard. **1:53** But the Levites must camp around the tabernacle of the testimony, so that the LORD's anger will not fall on the Israelite community. The Levites are responsible for the care of the tabernacle of the testimony."

1:54 The Israelites did according to all that the LORD commanded Moses – that is what they did.

The Arrangement of the Tribes

2:1 The LORD spoke to Moses and to Aaron: **2:2** "Every one of the Israelites must camp under his standard with the emblems of his family; they must camp at some distance around the tent of meeting.

The Tribes on the East

2:3 "Now those who will be camping on the east, toward the sunrise, are the divisions of the camp of Judah under their standard. The leader of the people of Judah is Nahshon son of Amminadab. **2:4** Those numbered in his division are 74,600. **2:5** Those who will be camping next to them are the tribe of Issachar. The leader of the people of Issachar is Nethanel son of Zuar. **2:6** Those numbered in his division are 54,400. **2:7** Next will be the tribe of Zebulun. The leader of the people of Zebulun is Eliab son of Helon. **2:8** Those numbered in his division are 57,400. **2:9** All those numbered of the camp of Judah, according to their divisions, are 186,400. They will travel at the front.

The Tribes on the South

2:10 "On the south will be the divisions of the camp of Reuben under their standard. The leader of the people of Reuben is Elizur son of Shedeur. **2:11** Those numbered in his division are 46,500. **2:12** Those who will be camping next to them are the tribe of Simeon. The leader of the people of Simeon is Shelumiel son of Zurishaddai. **2:13** Those numbered in his division are 59,300. **2:14** Next will be the tribe of Gad. The leader of the people of Gad is Eliasaph son of Deuel. **2:15** Those numbered in his division are 45,650. **2:16** All those numbered of the camp of Reuben, according to their divisions, are 151,450. They will travel second.

The Tribe in the Center

2:17 "Then the tent of meeting with the camp of the Levites will travel in the middle of the camps. They will travel in the same order as they camped, each in his own place under his standard.

The Tribes on the West

2:18 "On the west will be the divisions of the camp of Ephraim under their standard. The leader of the people of Ephraim is Elishama son of Amihud. **2:19** Those numbered in his division are 40,500. **2:20** Next to them will be the tribe of Manasseh. The leader of the people of Manasseh is Gamaliel son of Pedahzur. **2:21** Those numbered in his division are 32,200. **2:22** Next will be the tribe of Benjamin. The leader of the people of Benjamin is Abidan son of Gideoni. **2:23** Those numbered in his division are 35,400. **2:24** All those numbered of the camp of Ephraim, according to their divisions, are 108,100. They will travel third.

The Tribes on the North

2:25 "On the north will be the divisions of the camp of Dan, under their standards. The leader of the people of Dan is Ahiezer son of Ammishaddai. **2:26** Those numbered in his division are 62,700. **2:27** Those who will be camping next to them are the tribe of Asher. The leader of the people of Asher is Pagiel son of Ocran. **2:28** Those numbered in his division are 41,500. **2:29** Next will be the tribe of Naphtali. The leader of the people of Naphtali is Ahira son of Enan. **2:30** Those numbered in his division are 53,400. **2:31** All those numbered of the camp of Dan are 157,600. They will travel last, under their standards."

Summary

2:32 These are the Israelites, numbered according to their families. All those numbered in the camps, by their divisions, are 603,550. **2:33** But the Levites were not numbered among the other Israelites, as the LORD commanded Moses.

2:34 So the Israelites did according to all that the LORD commanded Moses; that is the way they camped under their standards, and that is the way they traveled, each with his clan and family.

The Sons of Aaron

3:1 Now these are the records of Aaron and Moses when the LORD spoke with Moses on Mount Sinai. **3:2** These are the names of the sons of Aaron: Nadab, the firstborn, and Abihu, Eleazar, and Ithamar. **3:3** These are the names of the sons of Aaron, the anointed priests, whom he consecrated to minister as priests.

3:4 Nadab and Abihu died before the LORD when they offered strange fire before the LORD in the wilderness of Sinai, and they had no children. So Eleazar and Ithamar ministered as priests in the presence of Aaron their father.

The Assignment of the Levites

3:5 The LORD spoke to Moses: **3:6** "Bring the tribe of Levi near, and present them before Aaron the priest, that they may serve him. **3:7** They are responsible for his needs and the needs of the whole community before the tent of meeting, by attending to the service of the tabernacle. **3:8** And they are responsible for all the furnishings of the tent of meeting, and for the needs of the Israelites, as they serve in the tabernacle. **3:9** You are to assign the Levites to Aaron and his sons; they will be assigned exclusively to him out of all the Israelites. **3:10** So you are to appoint Aaron and his sons, and they will be responsible for their priesthood; but the unauthorized person who comes near must be put to death."

3:11 Then the LORD spoke to Moses: **3:12** "Look, I myself have taken the Levites from among the Israelites instead of every firstborn who opens the womb among the Israelites. So the Levites belong to me, **3:13** because all the firstborn are mine. When I destroyed all the firstborn in the land of Egypt, I set apart for myself all the firstborn in Israel, both man and beast. They belong to me. I am the LORD."

The Numbering of the Levites

3:14 Then the LORD spoke to Moses in the wilderness of Sinai: **3:15** "Number the Levites by their clans and their families; every male from a month old and upward you are to number." **3:16** So Moses numbered them according to the word of the LORD, just as he had been commanded.

The Summary of Families

3:17 These were the sons of Levi by their names: Gershon, Kohath, and Merari.

3:18 These are the names of the sons of Gershon by their families: Libni and Shimei. **3:19** The sons of Kohath by their families were: Amram, Izhar, Hebron, and Uzziel. **3:20** The sons of Merari by their families were Mahli and Mushi. These are the families of the Levites by their clans.

The Numbering of the Gershonites

3:21 From Gershon came the family of the Libnites and the family of the Shimeites; these were the families of the Gershonites. **3:22** Those of them who were numbered, counting every male from a month old and upward, were 7,500. **3:23** The families of the Gershonites were to camp behind the tabernacle toward the west. **3:24** Now the leader of the clan of the Gershonites was Eliasaph son of Lael.

3:25 And the responsibilities of the Gershonites in the tent of meeting included the tabernacle, the tent with its covering, the curtain at the entrance of the tent of meeting, **3:26** the hangings of the courtyard, the curtain at the entrance to the courtyard that surrounded the tabernacle and the altar, and their ropes, plus all the service connected with these things.

The Numbering of the Kohathites

3:27 From Kohath came the family of the Amramites, the family of the Izharites, the family of the Hebronites, and the family of the Uzzielites; these were the families of the Kohathites. **3:28** Counting every male from a month old and upward, there were 8,600. They were responsible for the care of the sanctuary. **3:29** The families of the Kohathites were to camp on the south side of the tabernacle. **3:30** Now the leader of the clan of the families of the Kohathites was Elizaphan son of Uzziel.

3:31 Their responsibilities included the ark, the table, the lampstand, the altars, and the utensils of the sanctuary with which they ministered, the curtain, and all their service. **3:32** Now the head of all the Levitical leaders was Eleazar son of Aaron the priest. He was appointed over those who were responsible for the sanctuary.

The Numbering of Merari

3:33 From Merari came the family of the Mahlites and the family of the Mushites; these were the families of Merari. **3:34** Those of them who were numbered, counting every male from a month old and upward, were 6,200. **3:35** Now the leader of the clan of the families of Merari was Zuriel son of Abihail. These were to camp on the north side of the tabernacle.

3:36 The appointed responsibilities of the Merarites included the frames of the tabernacle, its crossbars, its posts, its sockets, its utensils, plus all the service connected with these things, **3:37** and the pillars of the courtyard all around, with their sockets, their pegs, and their ropes.

3:38 But those who were to camp in front of the tabernacle on the east, in front of the tent of meeting, were Moses, Aaron, and his sons. They were responsible for the needs of the sanctuary and for the needs of the Israelites, but the unauthorized person who approached was to be put to death. **3:39** All who were numbered of the Levites, whom Moses and Aaron numbered by the word of the LORD, according to their families, every male from a month old and upward, were 22,000.

The Substitution for the Firstborn

3:40 Then the LORD said to Moses, "Number all the firstborn males of the Israelites from a month old and upward, and take the number of their names. **3:41** And take the Levites for me – I am the LORD – instead of all the firstborn males among the Israelites, and the livestock of the Levites instead of all the firstborn of the livestock of the Israelites." **3:42** So Moses numbered all the firstborn males among the Israelites, as the LORD had commanded him. **3:43** And all the firstborn males, by the number of the names from a month old and upward, totaled 22,273.

3:44 Then the LORD spoke to Moses: **3:45** "Take the Levites instead of all the firstborn males among the Israelites, and the livestock of the Levites instead of their livestock. And the Levites will be mine. I am the LORD. **3:46** And for the redemption of the 273 firstborn males of the Israelites who exceed the number of the Levites, **3:47** collect five shekels for each one individually; you are to collect this amount in the currency of the sanctuary shekel (this shekel is twenty gerahs). **3:48** And give the money for the redemption of the excess number of them to Aaron and his sons."

3:49 So Moses took the redemption money from those who were in excess of those redeemed by the Levites. **3:50** From the firstborn males of the Israelites he collected the money, 1,365 shekels, according to the sanctuary shekel. **3:51** Moses gave the redemption money to Aaron and his sons, according to the word of the LORD, as the LORD had commanded Moses.

The Service of the Kohathites

4:1 Then the LORD spoke to Moses and Aaron: **4:2** "Take a census of the Kohathites from among the Levites, by their families and by their clans, **4:3** from thirty years old and upward to fifty years old, all who enter the company to do the work in the tent of meeting. **4:4** This is the service of the Kohathites in the tent of meeting, relating to the most holy things. **4:5** When it is time for the camp to journey, Aaron and his sons must come and take down the screening curtain and cover the ark of the testimony with it. **4:6** Then they must put over it a covering of fine leather and spread over that a cloth entirely of blue, and then they must insert its poles.

4:7 "On the table of the presence they must spread a blue cloth, and put on it the dishes, the pans, the bowls, and the pitchers for pouring, and the Bread of the Presence must be on it continually. **4:8** They must spread over them a scarlet cloth, and cover the same with a covering of fine leather; and they must insert its poles. **4:9** "They must take a blue cloth and cover the lampstand of the light, with its lamps, its wick-trimmers, its trays, and all its oil vessels, with which they service it. **4:10** Then they must put it with all its utensils in a covering of fine leather, and put it on a carrying beam.

4:11 "They must spread a blue cloth on the gold altar, and cover it with a covering of fine leather; and they must insert its poles. **4:12** Then they must take all the utensils of the service, with which they serve in the sanctuary, put them in a blue cloth, cover them with a covering of fine leather, and put them on a carrying beam. **4:13** Also, they must take away the ashes from the altar and spread a purple cloth over it. **4:14** Then they must place on it all its implements with which they serve there – the trays, the meat forks, the shovels, the basins, and all the utensils of the altar – and they must spread on it a covering of fine leather, and then insert its poles.

4:15 "When Aaron and his sons have finished covering the sanctuary and all the furnishings of the sanctuary, when the camp is ready to journey, then the Kohathites will come to carry them; but they must not touch any holy thing, or they will die. These are the responsibilities of the Kohathites with the tent of meeting.

4:16 "The appointed responsibility of Eleazar son of Aaron the priest is for the oil for the light, and the spiced incense, and the daily grain offering, and the anointing oil; he also has the appointed responsibility over all the tabernacle with all that is in it, over the sanctuary and over all its furnishings."

4:17 Then the LORD spoke to Moses and Aaron: **4:18** "Do not allow the tribe of the families of the Kohathites to be cut off from among the Levites; **4:19** but in order that they will live and not die when they approach the most holy things, do this for them: Aaron and his sons will go in and appoint each man to his service and his responsibility. **4:20** But the Kohathites are not to go in to watch while the holy things are being covered, or they will die."

The Service of the Gershonites

4:21 Then the LORD spoke to Moses: **4:22** "Also take a census of the Gershonites, by their clans and by their families. **4:23** You must number them from thirty years old and upward to fifty years old, all who enter the company to do the work of the tent of meeting. **4:24** This is the service of the families of Gershonites, as they serve and carry it. **4:25** They must carry the curtains for the tabernacle and the tent of meeting with its covering, the covering of fine leather that is over it, the curtains for the entrance of the tent of meeting, **4:26** the hangings for the courtyard, the curtain for the entrance of the gate of the court, which is around the tabernacle and the altar, and their ropes, along with all the furnishings for their service and everything that is made for them. So they are to serve.

4:27 "All the service of the Gershonites, whether carrying loads or for any of their work, will be at the direction of Aaron and his sons. You will assign them all their tasks as their responsibility. **4:28** This is the service of the families of the Gershonites concerning the tent of meeting. Their responsibilities will be under the authority of Ithamar son of Aaron the priest.

The Service of the Merarites

4:29 "As for the sons of Merari, you are to number them by their families and by their clans. **4:30** You must number them from thirty years old and upward to fifty years old, all who enter the company to do the work of the tent of meeting. **4:31** This is what they are responsible to carry as their entire service in the tent of meeting: the frames of the tabernacle, its crossbars, its posts, its sockets, **4:32** and the posts of the surrounding courtyard with their sockets, tent pegs, and ropes, along with all their furnishings and everything for their service. You are to assign by names the items that each man is responsible to carry. **4:33** This is the service of the families of the Merarites, their entire service concerning the tent of meeting, under the authority of Ithamar son of Aaron the priest."

Summary

4:34 So Moses and Aaron and the leaders of the community numbered the Kohathites by their families and by clans, **4:35** from thirty years old and upward to fifty years old, everyone who entered the company for the work in the tent of meeting; **4:36** and those of them numbered by their families were 2,750. **4:37** These were those numbered from the families of the Kohathites, everyone who served in the tent of meeting, whom Moses and Aaron numbered according to the word of the LORD by the authority of Moses.

4:38 Those numbered from the Gershonites, by their families and by their clans, **4:39** from thirty years old and upward to fifty years old, everyone who entered the company for the work in the tent of meeting – **4:40** those of them numbered by their families, by their clans, were 2,630. **4:41** These were those numbered from the families of the Gershonites, everyone who served in the tent of meeting, whom Moses and Aaron numbered according to the word of the LORD.

4:42 Those numbered from the families of the Merarites, by their families, by their clans, **4:43** from thirty years old and upward to fifty years old, everyone who entered the company for the work in the tent of meeting – **4:44** those of them numbered by their families were 3,200. **4:45** These are those numbered from the families of the Merarites, whom Moses and Aaron numbered according to the word of the LORD by the authority of Moses.

4:46 All who were numbered of the Levites, whom Moses, Aaron, and the leaders of Israel numbered by their families and by their clans, **4:47** from thirty years old and upward to fifty years old, everyone who entered to do the work of service and the work of carrying relating to the tent of meeting – **4:48** those of them numbered were 8,580. **4:49** According to the word of the LORD they were numbered, by the authority of Moses, each according to his service and according to what he was to carry. Thus were they numbered by him, as the LORD had commanded Moses.

Separation of the Unclean

5:1 Then the LORD spoke to Moses: **5:2** "Command the Israelites to expel from the camp every leper, everyone who has a discharge, and whoever becomes defiled by a corpse. **5:3** You must expel both men and women; you must put them outside the camp, so that they will not defile their camps, among which I live." **5:4** So the Israelites did so, and expelled them outside the camp. As the LORD had spoken to Moses, so the Israelites did.

Restitution for Sin

5:5 Then the LORD spoke to Moses: **5:6** "Tell the Israelites, 'When a man or a woman commits any sin that people commit, thereby breaking faith with the LORD, and that person is found guilty, **5:7** then he must confess his sin that he has committed and must make full reparation, add one fifth to it, and give it to whomever he wronged. **5:8** But if the individual has no close relative to whom reparation can be made for the wrong, the reparation for the wrong must be paid to the LORD for the priest, in addition to the ram of atonement by which atonement is made for him. **5:9** Every offering of all the Israelites' holy things that they bring to the priest will be his. **5:10** Every man's holy things will be his; whatever any man gives the priest will be his.'"

The Jealousy Ordeal

5:11 The LORD spoke to Moses: **5:12** "Speak to the Israelites and tell them, 'If any man's wife goes astray and behaves unfaithfully toward him, **5:13** and a man has sexual relations with her without her husband knowing it, and it is hidden that she has defiled herself, since there was no witness against her, nor was she caught – **5:14** and if jealous feelings come over him and he becomes suspicious of his wife, when she is defiled; or if jealous feelings come over him and he becomes suspicious of his wife, when she is not defiled – **5:15** then the man must bring his wife to the priest, and he must bring the offering required for her, one tenth of an ephah of barley meal; he must not pour olive oil on it or put frankincense on it, because it is a grain offering of suspicion, a grain offering for remembering, for bringing iniquity to remembrance.

5:16 "'Then the priest will bring her near and have her stand before the LORD. **5:17** The priest will then take holy water in a pottery jar, and take some of the dust that is on the floor of the tabernacle, and put it into the water. **5:18** Then the priest will have the woman stand before the LORD, uncover the woman's head, and put the grain offering for remembering in her hands, which is the grain offering of suspicion. The priest will hold in his hand the bitter water that brings a curse. **5:19** Then the priest will put the woman under oath and say to the her, "If no other man has had sexual relations with you, and if you have not gone astray and become defiled while under your husband's authority, may you be free from this bitter water that brings a curse. **5:20** But if you have gone astray while under your husband's authority, and if you have defiled yourself and some man other than your husband has had sexual relations with you...." **5:21** Then the priest will put the woman under the oath of the curse and will say to the her, "The LORD make you an attested curse among your people, if the LORD makes your thigh fall away and your abdomen swell; **5:22** and this water that causes the curse will go into your stomach, and make your abdomen swell and your thigh rot." Then the woman must say, "Amen, amen."

5:23 "'Then the priest will write these curses on a scroll and then scrape them off into the bitter water. **5:24** He will make the woman drink the bitter water that brings a curse, and the water that brings a curse will enter her to produce bitterness. **5:25** The priest will take the grain offering of suspicion from the woman's hand, wave the grain offering before the LORD, and bring it to the altar. **5:26** Then the priest will take a handful of the grain offering as its memorial portion, burn it on the altar, and afterward make the woman drink the water. **5:27** When he has made her drink the water, then, if she has defiled herself and behaved unfaithfully toward her husband, the water that brings a curse will enter her to produce bitterness – her abdomen will swell, her thigh will fall away, and the woman will become a curse among her people. **5:28** But if the woman has not defiled herself, and is clean, then she will be free of ill effects and will be able to bear children.

5:29 "'This is the law for cases of jealousy, when a wife, while under her husband's authority, goes astray and defiles herself, **5:30** or when jealous feelings come over a man and he becomes suspicious of his wife; then he must have the woman stand before the LORD, and the priest will carry out all this law upon her. **5:31** Then the man will be free from iniquity, but that woman will bear the consequences of her iniquity.'"

The Nazirite Vow

6:1 Then the LORD spoke to Moses: **6:2** "Speak to the Israelites, and tell them, 'When either a man or a woman takes a special vow, to take a vow as a Nazirite, to separate himself to the LORD, **6:3** he must separate himself from wine and strong drink, he must drink neither vinegar made from wine nor vinegar made from strong drink, nor may he drink any juice of grapes, nor eat fresh grapes or raisins. **6:4** All the days of his separation he must not eat anything that is produced by the grapevine, from seed to skin.

6:5 "'All the days of the vow of his separation no razor may be used on his head until the time is fulfilled for which he separated himself to the LORD. He will be holy, and he must let the locks of hair on his head grow long.

6:6 "'All the days that he separates himself to the LORD he must not contact a dead body. **6:7** He must not defile himself even for his father or his mother or his brother or his sister if they die, because the separation

for his God is on his head. **6:8** All the days of his separation he must be holy to the LORD.

Contingencies for Defilement

6:9 "'If anyone dies very suddenly beside him and he defiles his consecrated head, then he must shave his head on the day of his purification – on the seventh day he must shave it. **6:10** On the eighth day he is to bring two turtledoves or two young pigeons to the priest, to the entrance to the tent of meeting. **6:11** Then the priest will offer one for a purification offering and the other as a burnt offering, and make atonement for him, because of his transgression in regard to the corpse. So he must reconsecrate his head on that day. **6:12** He must rededicate to the LORD the days of his separation and bring a male lamb in its first year as a reparation offering, but the former days will not be counted because his separation was defiled.

Fulfilling the Vows

6:13 "'Now this is the law of the Nazirite: When the days of his separation are fulfilled, he must be brought to the entrance of the tent of meeting, **6:14** and he must present his offering to the LORD: one male lamb in its first year without blemish for a burnt offering, one ewe lamb in its first year without blemish for a purification offering, one ram without blemish for a peace offering, **6:15** and a basket of bread made without yeast, cakes of fine flour mixed with olive oil, wafers made without yeast and smeared with olive oil, and their grain offering and their drink offerings.

6:16 "'Then the priest must present all these before the LORD and offer his purification offering and his burnt offering. **6:17** Then he must offer the ram as a peace offering to the LORD, with the basket of bread made without yeast; the priest must also offer his grain offering and his drink offering.

6:18 "'Then the Nazirite must shave his consecrated head at the entrance to the tent of meeting and must take the hair from his consecrated head and put it on the fire where the peace offering is burning. **6:19** And the priest must take the boiled shoulder of the ram, one cake made without yeast from the basket, and one wafer made without yeast, and put them on the hands of the Nazirite after he has shaved his consecrated head; **6:20** then the priest must wave them as a wave offering before the LORD; it is a holy portion for the priest, together with the breast of the wave offering and the thigh of the raised offering. After this the Nazirite may drink wine.'

6:21 "This is the law of the Nazirite who vows to the LORD his offering according to his separation, as well as whatever else he can provide. Thus he must fulfill his vow that he makes, according to the law of his separation."

The Priestly Benediction

6:22 The LORD spoke to Moses: **6:23** "Tell Aaron and his sons, 'This is the way you are to bless the Israelites. Say to them:

6:24 "The LORD bless you and protect you;

6:25 The LORD make his face to shine upon you,
and be gracious to you;

6:26 The LORD lift up his countenance upon you
and give you peace."'

6:27 So they will put my name on the Israelites, and I will bless them."

The Leader's Offerings

7:1 When Moses had completed setting up the tabernacle, he anointed it and consecrated it and all its furnishings, and he anointed and consecrated the altar and all its utensils. **7:2** Then the leaders of Israel, the heads of their clans, made an offering. They were the leaders of the tribes; they were the ones who had been supervising the numbering. **7:3** They brought their offering before the LORD, six covered carts and twelve oxen – one cart for every two of the leaders, and an ox for each one; and they presented them in front of the tabernacle.

The Distribution of the Gifts

7:4 Then the LORD spoke to Moses: **7:5** "Receive these gifts from them, that they may be used in doing the work of the tent of meeting; and you must give them to the Levites, to every man as his service requires."

7:6 So Moses accepted the carts and the oxen and gave them to the Levites. **7:7** He gave two carts and four oxen to the Gershonites, as their service required; **7:8** and he gave four carts and eight oxen to the Merarites, as their service required, under the authority of Ithamar son of Aaron the priest. **7:9** But to the Kohathites he gave none, because the service of the holy things, which they carried on their shoulders, was their responsibility.

The Time of Presentation

7:10 The leaders offered gifts for the dedication of the altar when it was anointed. And the leaders presented their offering before the altar. **7:11** For the LORD said to Moses, "They must present their offering, one leader for each day, for the dedication of the altar."

The Tribal Offerings

7:12 The one who presented his offering on the first day was Nahshon son of Amminadab, from the tribe of Judah. **7:13** His offering was one silver platter weighing 130 shekels, and one silver sprinkling bowl weighing 70 shekels, both according to the sanctuary shekel, each of them full of fine flour mixed with olive oil as a grain offering; **7:14** one gold pan weighing 10 shekels, full of incense; **7:15** one young bull, one

ram, and one male lamb in its first year, for a burnt offering; **7:16** one male goat for a purification offering; **7:17** and for the sacrifice of peace offerings: two bulls, five rams, five male goats, and five male lambs in their first year. This was the offering of Nahshon son of Amminadab.
7:18 On the second day Nethanel son of Zuar, leader of Issachar, presented an offering. **7:19** He offered for his offering one silver platter weighing 130 shekels and one silver sprinkling bowl weighing 70, both according to the sanctuary shekel, each of them full of fine flour mixed with olive oil as a grain offering; **7:20** one gold pan weighing 10 shekels, full of incense; **7:21** one young bull, one ram, and one male lamb in its first year, for a burnt offering; **7:22** one male goat for a purification offering; **7:23** and for the sacrifice of peace offerings: two bulls, five rams, five male goats, and five male lambs in their first year. This was the offering of Nethanel son of Zuar.
7:24 On the third day Eliab son of Helon, leader of the Zebulunites, presented an offering. **7:25** His offering was one silver platter weighing 130 shekels and one silver sprinkling bowl weighing 70 shekels, both according to the sanctuary shekel, each of them full of fine flour mixed with olive oil as a grain offering; **7:26** one gold pan weighing 10 shekels, full of incense; **7:27** one young bull, one ram, and one male lamb in its first year, for a burnt offering; **7:28** one male goat for a purification offering; **7:29** and for the sacrifice of peace offerings: two bulls, five rams, five male goats, and five male lambs in their first year. This was the offering of Eliab son of Helon.
7:30 On the fourth day Elizur son of Shedeur, leader of the Reubenites, presented an offering. **7:31** His offering was one silver platter weighing 130 shekels and one silver sprinkling bowl weighing 70 shekels, both according to the sanctuary shekel, each of them full of fine flour mixed with olive oil as a grain offering; **7:32** one gold pan weighing 10 shekels, full of incense; **7:33** one young bull, one ram, and one male lamb in its first year, for a burnt offering; **7:34** one male goat for a purification offering; **7:35** and for the sacrifice of peace offerings: two bulls, five rams, five male goats, and five lambs in their first year. This was the offering of Elizur son of Shedeur.
7:36 On the fifth day Shelumiel son of Zurishaddai, leader of the Simeonites, presented an offering. **7:37** His offering was one silver platter weighing 130 shekels and one silver sprinkling bowl weighing 70 shekels, both according to the sanctuary shekel, each of them full of fine flour mixed with olive oil as a grain offering; **7:38** one gold pan weighing 10 shekels; **7:39** one young bull, one ram, and one male lamb in its first year, for a burnt offering; **7:40** one male goat for a purification offering; **7:41** and for the sacrifice of peace offerings: two bulls, five rams, five male goats, and five lambs in their first year. This was the offering of Sheloumiel son of Zurishaddai.
7:42 On the sixth day Eliasaph son of Deuel, leader of the Gadites, presented an offering. **7:43** His offering was one silver platter weighing 130 shekels and one silver sprinkling bowl weighing 70 shekels, both according to the sanctuary shekel, each of them full of fine flour mixed with olive oil as a grain offering; **7:44** one gold pan weighing 10 shekels; **7:45** one young bull, one ram, and one male lamb in its first year, for a burnt offering; **7:46** one male goat for a purification offering; **7:47** and for the sacrifice of peace offerings: two bulls, five rams, five male goats, and five lambs in their first year. This was the offering of Eliasaph son of Deuel.
7:48 On the seventh day Elishama son of Ammihud, leader of the Ephraimites, presented an offering. **7:49** His offering was one silver platter weighing 130 shekels and one silver sprinkling bowl weighing 70 shekels, both according to the sanctuary shekel, each of them full of fine flour mixed with olive oil as a grain offering; **7:50** one gold pan weighing 10 shekels, full of incense; **7:51** one young bull, one ram, and one male lamb in its first year, for a burnt offering; **7:52** one male goat for a purification offering; **7:53** and for the sacrifice of peace offerings: two bulls, five rams, five male goats, and five lambs in their first year. This was the offering of Elishama son of Ammihud.
7:54 On the eighth day Gamaliel son of Pedahzur, leader of the Manassehites, presented an offering. **7:55** His offering was one silver platter weighing 130 shekels and one silver sprinkling bowl weighing 70 shekels, both according to the sanctuary shekel, each of them full of fine flour mixed with olive oil as a grain offering; **7:56** one gold pan weighing 10 shekels, full of incense; **7:57** one young bull, one ram, and one male lamb in its first year, for a burnt offering; **7:58** one male goat for a purification offering; **7:59** and for the sacrifice of peace offerings: two bulls, five rams, five male goats, and five lambs in their first year. This was the offering of Gamaliel son of Pedahzur.
7:60 On the ninth day Abidan son of Gideoni, leader of the Benjaminites, presented an offering. **7:61** His offering was one silver platter weighing 130 shekels and one silver sprinkling bowl weighing 70 shekels, both according to the sanctuary shekel, each of them full of fine flour mixed with olive oil as a grain offering; **7:62** one gold pan weighing 10 shekels, full of incense; **7:63** one young bull, one ram, and one male lamb in its first year, for a burnt offering; **7:64** one male goat for a purification offering; **7:65** and for the sacrifice of peace offerings: two bulls, five rams,

five male goats, and five lambs in their first year. This was the offering of Abidan son of Gideoni.
7:66 On the tenth day Ahiezer son of Amishaddai, leader of the Danites, presented an offering. **7:67** His offering was one silver platter weighing 130 shekels and one silver sprinkling bowl weighing 70 shekels, both according to the sanctuary shekel, each of them full of fine flour mixed with olive oil as a grain offering; **7:68** one gold pan weighing 10 shekels, full of incense; **7:69** one young bull, one ram, and one male lamb in its first year, for a burnt offering; **7:70** one male goat for a purification offering; **7:71** and for the sacrifice of peace offerings: two bulls, five rams, five male goats, and five lambs in their first year. This was the offering of Ahiezer son of Amishaddai.
7:72 On the eleventh day Pagiel son of Ocran, leader of the Asherites, presented an offering. **7:73** His offering was one silver platter weighing 130 shekels and one silver sprinkling bowl weighing 70 shekels, both according to the sanctuary shekel, each of them full of fine flour mixed with olive oil as a grain offering; **7:74** one gold pan weighing 10 shekels, full of incense; **7:75** one young bull, one ram, and one male lamb in its first year, for a burnt offering; **7:76** one male goat for a purification offering; **7:77** and for the sacrifice of peace offerings: two bulls, five rams, five male goats, and five lambs in their first year. This was the offering of Pagiel son of Ocran.
7:78 On the twelfth day Ahira son of Enan, leader of the Naphtalites, presented an offering. **7:79** His offering was one silver platter weighing 130 shekels and one silver sprinkling bowl weighing 70 shekels, both according to the sanctuary shekel, each of them full of fine flour mixed with olive oil as a grain offering; **7:80** one gold pan weighing 10 shekels; **7:81** one young bull, one ram, and one male lamb in its first year, for a burnt offering; **7:82** one male goat for a purification offering; **7:83** and for the sacrifice of peace offerings: two bulls, five rams, five male goats, and five lambs in their first year. This was the offering of Ahira son of Enan.

Summary
7:84 This was the dedication for the altar from the leaders of Israel, when it was anointed: twelve silver platters, twelve silver sprinkling bowls, and twelve gold pans. **7:85** Each silver platter weighed 130 shekels, and each silver sprinkling bowl weighed 70 shekels. All the silver of the vessels weighed 2,400 shekels, according to the sanctuary shekel. **7:86** The twelve gold pans full of incense weighed 10 shekels each, according to the sanctuary shekel; all the gold of the pans weighed 120 shekels. **7:87** All the animals for the burnt offering were 12 young bulls, 12 rams, 12 male lambs in their first year, with their grain offering, and 12 male goats for a purification offering. **7:88** All the animals for the sacrifice for the peace offering were 24 young bulls, 60 rams, 60 male goats, and 60 lambs in their first year. These were the dedication offerings for the altar after it was anointed.
7:89 Now when Moses went into the tent of meeting to speak with the LORD, he heard the voice speaking to him from above the atonement lid that was on the ark of the testimony, from between the two cherubim. Thus he spoke to him.

Lighting the Lamps
8:1 The LORD spoke to Moses: **8:2** "Speak to Aaron and tell him, 'When you set up the lamps, the seven lamps are to give light in front of the lampstand.'"
8:3 And Aaron did so; he set up the lamps to face toward the front of the lampstand, as the LORD commanded Moses. **8:4** This is how the lampstand was made: It was beaten work in gold; from its shaft to its flowers it was beaten work. According to the pattern which the LORD had shown Moses, so he made the lampstand.

The Separation of the Levites
8:5 Then the LORD spoke to Moses: **8:6** "Take the Levites from among the Israelites and purify them. **8:7** And do this to them to purify them: Sprinkle water of purification on them; then have them shave all their body and wash their clothes, and so purify themselves. **8:8** Then they are to take a young bull with its grain offering of fine flour mixed with olive oil; and you are to take a second young bull for a purification offering. **8:9** You are to bring the Levites before the tent of meeting and assemble the entire community of the Israelites. **8:10** Then you are to bring the Levites before the LORD, and the Israelites are to lay their hands on the Levites; **8:11** and Aaron is to offer the Levites before the LORD as a wave offering from the Israelites, that they may do the work of the LORD. **8:12** When the Levites lay their hands on the heads of the bulls, offer the one for a purification offering and the other for a whole burnt offering to the LORD, to make atonement for the Levites. **8:13** You are to have the Levites stand before Aaron and his sons, and then offer them as a wave offering to the LORD. **8:14** And so you are to separate the Levites from among the Israelites, and the Levites will be mine.
8:15 "After this, the Levites will go in to do the work of the tent of meeting. So you must cleanse them and offer them like a wave offering. **8:16** For they are entirely given to me from among the Israelites. I have taken them for myself instead of all who open the womb, the firstborn sons of all the Israelites. **8:17** For all the firstborn males among the Israelites are mine, both humans and animals; when I destroyed all the firstborn in the land of Egypt I set them apart for myself. **8:18** So I have taken the Le-

vites instead of all the firstborn sons among the Israelites. **8:19** I have given the Levites as a gift to Aaron and his sons from among the Israelites, to do the work for the Israelites in the tent of meeting, and to make atonement for the Israelites, so there will be no plague among the Israelites when the Israelites come near the sanctuary."

8:20 So Moses and Aaron and the entire community of the Israelites did this with the Levites. According to all that the LORD commanded Moses concerning the Levites, this is what the Israelites did with them. **8:21** The Levites purified themselves and washed their clothing; then Aaron presented them like a wave offering before the LORD, and Aaron made atonement for them to purify them. **8:22** After this, the Levites went in to do their work in the tent of meeting before Aaron and before his sons. As the LORD had commanded Moses concerning the Levites, so they did.

The Work of the Levites

8:23 Then the LORD spoke to Moses: **8:24** "This is what pertains to the Levites: At the age of twenty-five years and upward one may begin to join the company in the work of the tent of meeting, **8:25** and at the age of fifty years they must retire from performing the work and may no longer work. **8:26** They may assist their colleagues in the tent of meeting, to attend to needs, but they must do no work. This is the way you must establish the Levites regarding their duties."

Passover Regulations

9:1 The LORD spoke to Moses in the wilderness of Sinai, in the first month of the second year after they had come out of the land of Egypt: **9:2** "The Israelites are to observe the Passover at its appointed time. **9:3** In the fourteenth day of this month, at twilight, you are to observe it at its appointed time; you must keep it in accordance with all its statutes and all its customs." **9:4** So Moses instructed the Israelites to observe the Passover. **9:5** And they observed the Passover on the fourteenth day of the first month at twilight in the wilderness of Sinai; in accordance with all that the LORD had commanded Moses, so the Israelites did.

9:6 It happened that some men who were ceremonially defiled by the dead body of a man could not keep the Passover on that day, so they came before Moses and before Aaron on that day. **9:7** And those men said to him, "We are ceremonially defiled by the dead body of a man; why are we kept back from the LORD's offering at its appointed time among the Israelites?" **9:8** So Moses said to them, "Remain here and I will hear what the LORD will command concerning you."

9:9 The LORD spoke to Moses: **9:10** "Tell the Israelites, 'If any of you or of your posterity become ceremonially defiled by touching a dead body, or are on a journey far away, then he may observe the Passover to the LORD. **9:11** They may observe it on the fourteenth day of the second month at twilight; they are to eat it with bread made without yeast and with bitter herbs. **9:12** They must not leave any of it until morning, nor break any of its bones; they must observe it in accordance with every statute of the Passover.

9:13 But the man who is ceremonially clean, and was not on a journey, and fails to keep the Passover, that person must be cut off from his people. Because he did not bring the LORD's offering at its appointed time, that man must bear his sin. **9:14** If a resident foreigner lives among you and wants to keep the Passover to the LORD, he must do so according to the statute of the Passover, and according to its custom. You must have the same statute for the resident foreigner and for the one who was born in the land.'"

The Leading of the Lord

9:15 On the day that the tabernacle was set up, the cloud covered the tabernacle – the tent of the testimony – and from evening until morning there was a fiery appearance over the tabernacle. **9:16** This is the way it used to be continually: The cloud would cover it by day, and there was a fiery appearance by night. **9:17** Whenever the cloud was taken up from the tabernacle, then after that the Israelites would begin their journey; and in whatever place the cloud settled, there the Israelites would make camp. **9:18** At the commandment of the LORD the Israelites would begin their journey, and at the commandment of the LORD they would make camp; as long as the cloud remained settled over the tabernacle they would camp. **9:19** When the cloud remained over the tabernacle many days, then the Israelites obeyed the instructions of the LORD and did not journey.

9:20 When the cloud remained over the tabernacle a number of days, they remained camped according to the LORD's commandment, and according to the LORD's commandment they would journey. **9:21** And when the cloud remained only from evening until morning, when the cloud was taken up the following morning, then they traveled on. Whether by day or by night, when the cloud was taken up they traveled. **9:22** Whether it was for two days, or a month, or a year, that the cloud prolonged its stay over the tabernacle, the Israelites remained camped without traveling; but when it was taken up, they traveled on. **9:23** At the commandment of the LORD they camped, and at the commandment of the LORD they traveled on; they kept the instructions of the LORD according to the commandment of the LORD, by the authority of Moses.

The Blowing of Trumpets

10:1 The LORD spoke to Moses: **10:2** "Make two trumpets of silver; you are to make them from a single hammered piece. You will use them for assembling the community and for directing the traveling of the camps.

10:3 When they blow them both, all the community must come to you to the entrance of the tent of meeting.

10:4 "But if they blow with one trumpet, then the leaders, the heads of the thousands of Israel, must come to you. **10:5** When you blow an alarm, then the camps that are located on the east side must begin to travel. **10:6** And when you blow an alarm the second time, then the camps that are located on the south side must begin to travel. An alarm must be sounded for their journeys. **10:7** But when you assemble the community, you must blow, but you must not sound an alarm. **10:8** The sons of Aaron, the priests, must blow the trumpets; and they will be to you for an eternal ordinance throughout your generations. **10:9** If you go to war in your land against an adversary who opposes you, then you must sound an alarm with the trumpets, and you will be remembered before the LORD your God, and you will be saved from your enemies.

10:10 "Also in the time when you rejoice, such as on your appointed festivals or at the beginnings of your months, you must blow with your trumpets over your burnt offerings and over the sacrifices of your peace offerings, so that they may become a memorial for you before your God: I am the LORD your God."

The Journey From Sinai to Kadesh

10:11 On the twentieth day of the second month, in the second year, the cloud was taken up from the tabernacle of the testimony. **10:12** So the Israelites set out on their journeys from the wilderness of Sinai; and the cloud settled in the wilderness of Paran.

Judah Begins the Journey

10:13 This was the first time they set out on their journey according to the commandment of the LORD, by the authority of Moses.

10:14 The standard of the camp of the Judahites set out first according to their companies, and over his company was Nahshon son of Amminadab. **10:15** Over the company of the tribe of Issacharites was Nathanel son of Zuar, **10:16** and over the company of the tribe of the Zebulunites was Elion son of Helon. **10:17** Then the tabernacle was dismantled, and the sons of Gershon and the sons of Merari set out, carrying the tabernacle.

Journey Arrangements for the Tribes

10:18 The standard of the camp of Reuben set out according to their companies; over his company was Elizur son of Shedeur. **10:19** Over the company of the tribe of the Simeonites was Shelumiel son of Zurishaddai, **10:20** and over the company of the tribe of the Gadites was Eliasaph son of Deuel. **10:21** And the Kohathites set out, carrying the articles for the sanctuary; the tabernacle was to be set up before they arrived. **10:22** And the standard of the camp of the Ephraimites set out according to their companies; over his company was Elishama son of Ammihud. **10:23** Over the company of the tribe of the Manassehites was Gamaliel son of Pedahzur, **10:24** and over the company of the tribe of Benjaminites was Abidan son of Gideoni.

10:25 The standard of the camp of the Danites set out, which was the rear guard of all the camps by their companies; over his company was Ahiezer son of Ammishaddai. **10:26** Over the company of the tribe of the Asherites was Pagiel son of Ocran, **10:27** and over the company of the tribe of the Naphtalites was Ahira son of Enan. **10:28** These were the traveling arrangements of the Israelites according to their companies when they traveled.

The Appeal to Hobab

10:29 Moses said to Hobab son of Reuel, the Midianite, Moses' father-in-law, "We are journeying to the place about which the LORD said, 'I will give it to you.' Come with us and we will treat you well, for the LORD has promised good things for Israel." **10:30** But Hobab said to him, "I will not go, but I will go instead to my own land and to my kindred." **10:31** Moses said, "Do not leave us, because you know places for us to camp in the wilderness, and you could be our guide. **10:32** And if you come with us, it is certain that whatever good things the LORD will favor us with, we will share with you as well."

10:33 So they traveled from the mountain of the LORD three days' journey; and the ark of the covenant of the LORD was traveling before them during the three days' journey, to find a resting place for them. **10:34** And the cloud of the LORD was over them by day, when they traveled from the camp. **10:35** And when the ark traveled, Moses would say, "Rise up, O LORD! May your enemies be scattered, and may those who hate you flee before you!" **10:36** And when it came to rest he would say, "Return, O LORD, to the many thousands of Israel!"

The Israelites Complain

11:1 When the people complained, it displeased the LORD. When the LORD heard it, his anger burned, and so the fire of the LORD burned among them and consumed some of the outer parts of the camp. **11:2** When the people cried to Moses, he prayed to the LORD, and the fire died out. **11:3** So he called the name of that place Taberah because the fire of the LORD burned among them.

Complaints about Food

11:4 Now the mixed multitude who were among them craved more desirable foods, and so the Israelites wept again and said, "If only we had meat to eat! **11:5** We remember the fish we used to eat freely in Egypt, the cucumbers, the melons, the leeks, the onions, and the garlic. **11:6** But now we are dried up, and there is nothing at all before us except this manna!" **11:7** (Now the manna was like coriander seed, and its color like the color of bdellium. **11:8** And the people went about and gathered it, and ground it with mills or pounded it in mortars; they baked it in pans and made cakes of it. It tasted like fresh olive oil. **11:9** And when the dew came down on the camp in the night, the manna fell with it.)

Moses' Complaint to the Lord

11:10 Moses heard the people weeping throughout their families, everyone at the door of his tent; and when the anger of the LORD was kindled greatly, Moses was also displeased. **11:11** And Moses said to the LORD, "Why have you afflicted your servant? Why have I not found favor in your sight, that you lay the burden of this entire people on me? **11:12** Did I conceive this entire people? Did I give birth to them, that you should say to me, 'Carry them in your arms, as a foster father bears a nursing child,' to the land which you swore to their fathers? **11:13** From where shall I get meat to give to this entire people, for they cry to me, 'Give us meat, that we may eat!' **11:14** I am not able to bear this entire people alone, because it is too heavy for me! **11:15** But if you are going to deal with me like this, then kill me immediately. If I have found favor in your sight then do not let me see my trouble."

The Response of God

11:16 The LORD said to Moses, "Gather to me seventy men of the elders of Israel, whom you know are elders of the people and officials over them, and bring them to the tent of meeting; let them take their position there with you. **11:17** Then I will come down and speak with you there, and I will take part of the spirit that is on you, and will put it on them, and they will bear some of the burden of the people with you, so that you do not bear it all by yourself.

11:18 "And say to the people, 'Sanctify yourselves for tomorrow, and you will eat meat, for you have wept in the hearing of the LORD, saying, "Who will give us meat to eat, for life was good for us in Egypt?" Therefore the LORD will give you meat, and you will eat. **11:19** You will eat, not just one day, nor two days, nor five days, nor ten days, nor twenty days, **11:20** but a whole month, until it comes out your nostrils and makes you sick, because you have despised the LORD who is among you and have wept before him, saying, "Why did we ever come out of Egypt?"'"

11:21 Moses said, "The people around me are 600,000 on foot; but you say, 'I will give them meat, that they may eat for a whole month.' **11:22** Would they have enough if the flocks and herds were slaughtered for them? If all the fish of the sea were caught for them, would they have enough?" **11:23** And the LORD said to Moses, "Is the LORD's hand shortened? Now you will see whether my word to you will come true or not!"

11:24 So Moses went out and told the people the words of the LORD. He then gathered seventy men of the elders of the people and had them stand around the tabernacle. **11:25** And the LORD came down in the cloud and spoke to them, and he took some of the Spirit that was on Moses and put it on the seventy elders. When the Spirit rested on them, they prophesied, but did not do so again.

Eldad and Medad

11:26 But two men remained in the camp; one's name was Eldad, and the other's name was Medad. And the spirit rested on them. (Now they were among those in the registration, but had not gone to the tabernacle.) So they prophesied in the camp. **11:27** And a young man ran and told Moses, "Eldad and Medad are prophesying in the camp!" **11:28** Joshua son of Nun, the servant of Moses, one of his choice young men, said, "My lord Moses, stop them!" **11:29** Moses said to him, "Are you jealous for me? I wish that all the LORD's people were prophets, that the LORD would put his Spirit on them!" **11:30** Then Moses returned to the camp along with the elders of Israel.

Provision of Quail

11:31 Now a wind went out from the LORD and brought quail from the sea, and let them fall near the camp, about a day's journey on this side, and about a day's journey on the other side, all around the camp, and about three feet high on the surface of the ground. **11:32** And the people stayed up all that day, all that night, and all the next day, and gathered the quail. The one who gathered the least gathered ten homers, and they spread them out for themselves all around the camp. **11:33** But while the meat was still between their teeth, before they chewed it, the anger of the LORD burned against the people, and the LORD struck the people with a very great plague.

11:34 So the name of that place was called Kibroth Hattaavah, because there they buried the people that craved different food. **11:35** The people traveled from Kibroth Hattaavah to Hazeroth, and they stayed at Hazeroth.

Miriam and Aaron Oppose Moses

12:1 Then Miriam and Aaron spoke against Moses because of the Cushite woman he had married (for he had married an Ethiopian woman). **12:2** They said, "Has the LORD only spoken through Moses? Has he not also spoken through us?" And the LORD heard it.

12:3 (Now the man Moses was very humble, more so than any man on the face of the earth.)

The Response of the Lord

12:4 The LORD spoke immediately to Moses, Aaron, and Miriam: "The three of you come to the tent of meeting." So the three of them went. **12:5**

And the LORD came down in a pillar of cloud and stood at the entrance of the tent; he then called Aaron and Miriam, and they both came forward. **12:6** The LORD said, "Hear now my words: If there is a prophet among you, I the LORD will make myself known to him in a vision; I will speak with him in a dream. **12:7** My servant Moses is not like this; he is faithful in all my house. **12:8** With him I will speak face to face, openly, and not in riddles; and he will see the form of the LORD. Why then were you not afraid to speak against my servant Moses?" **12:9** The anger of the LORD burned against them, and he departed. **12:10** When the cloud departed from above the tent, Miriam became leprous as snow. Then Aaron looked at Miriam, and she was leprous!

The Intercession of Moses

12:11 So Aaron said to Moses, "O my lord, please do not hold this sin against us, in which we have acted foolishly and have sinned! **12:12** Do not let her be like a baby born dead, whose flesh is half-consumed when it comes out of its mother's womb!"

12:13 Then Moses cried to the LORD, "Heal her now, O God." **12:14** The LORD said to Moses, "If her father had only spit in her face, would she not have been disgraced for seven days? Shut her out from the camp seven days, and afterward she can be brought back in again."

12:15 So Miriam was shut outside of the camp for seven days, and the people did not journey on until Miriam was brought back in. **12:16** After that the people moved from Hazeroth and camped in the wilderness of Paran.

Spies Sent Out

13:1 The LORD spoke to Moses:

13:2 "Send out men to investigate the land of Canaan, which I am giving to the Israelites. You are to send one man from each ancestral tribe, each one a leader among them." **13:3** So Moses sent them from the wilderness of Paran at the command of the LORD. All of them were leaders of the Israelites.

13:4 Now these were their names: from the tribe of Reuben, Shammua son of Zaccur; **13:5** from the tribe of Simeon, Shaphat son of Hori; **13:6** from the tribe of Judah, Caleb son of Jephunneh; **13:7** from the tribe of Issachar, Igal son of Joseph; **13:8** from the tribe of Ephraim, Hoshea son of Nun; **13:9** from the tribe of Benjamin, Palti son of Raphu; **13:10** from the tribe of Zebulun, Gaddiel son of Sodi; **13:11** from the tribe of Joseph, namely, the tribe of Manasseh, Gaddi son of Susi; **13:12** from the tribe of Dan, Ammiel son of Gemalli; **13:13** from the tribe of Asher, Sethur son of Michael; **13:14** from the tribe of Naphtali, Nahbi son of Vophsi; **13:15** from the tribe of Gad, Geuel son of Maki. **13:16** These are the names of the men whom Moses sent to investigate the land. And Moses gave Hoshea son of Nun the name Joshua.

The Spies' Instructions

13:17 When Moses sent them to investigate the land of Canaan, he told them, "Go up through the Negev, and then go up into the hill country **13:18** and see what the land is like, and whether the people who live in it are strong or weak, few or many, **13:19** and whether the land they live in is good or bad, and whether the cities they inhabit are like camps or fortified cities, **13:20** and whether the land is rich or poor, and whether or not there are forests in it. And be brave, and bring back some of the fruit of the land." Now it was the time of year for the first ripe grapes.

The Spies' Activities

13:21 So they went up and investigated the land from the wilderness of Zin to Rehob, at the entrance of Hamath. **13:22** When they went up through the Negev, they came to Hebron where Ahiman, Sheshai, and Talmai, descendants of Anak, were living. (Now Hebron had been built seven years before Zoan in Egypt.) **13:23** When they came to the valley of Eshcol, they cut down from there a branch with one cluster of grapes, and they carried it on a staff between two men, as well as some of the pomegranates and the figs. **13:24** That place was called the Eshcol Valley, because of the cluster of grapes that the Israelites cut from there. **13:25** They returned from investigating the land after forty days.

The Spies' Reports

13:26 They came back to Moses and Aaron and to the whole community of the Israelites in the wilderness of Paran at Kadesh. They reported to the whole community and showed the fruit of the land. **13:27** They told Moses, "We went to the land where you sent us. It is indeed flowing with milk and honey, and this is its fruit. **13:28** But the inhabitants are strong, and the cities are fortified and very large. Moreover we saw the descendants of Anak there. **13:29** The Amalekites live in the land of the Negev; the Hittites, Jebusites, and Amorites live in the hill country; and the Canaanites live by the sea and along the banks of the Jordan."

13:30 Then Caleb silenced the people before Moses, saying, "Let us go up and occupy it, for we are well able to conquer it." **13:31** But the men who had gone up with him said, "We are not able to go up against these people, because they are stronger than we are!" **13:32** Then they presented the Israelites with a discouraging report of the land they had investigated, saying, "The land that we passed through to investigate is a land that devours its inhabitants. All the people we saw there are of great stature. **13:33** We even saw the Nephilim there (the descendants of Anak came from the Nephilim), and we seemed liked grasshoppers both to ourselves and to them."

The Israelites Respond in Unbelief

14:1 Then all the community raised a loud cry, and the people wept that night. **14:2** And all the Israelites murmured against Moses and Aaron, and the whole congregation said to them, "If only we had died in the land of Egypt, or if only we had perished in this wilderness! **14:3** Why has the LORD brought us into this land only to be killed by the sword, that our wives and our children should become plunder? Wouldn't it be better for us to return to Egypt?" **14:4** So they said to one another, "Let's appoint a leader and return to Egypt."

14:5 Then Moses and Aaron fell down with their faces to the ground before the whole assembled community of the Israelites. **14:6** And Joshua son of Nun and Caleb son of Jephunneh, two of those who had investigated the land, tore their garments. **14:7** They said to the whole community of the Israelites, "The land we passed through to investigate is an exceedingly good land. **14:8** If the LORD delights in us, then he will bring us into this land and give it to us – a land that is flowing with milk and honey. **14:9** Only do not rebel against the LORD, and do not fear the people of the land, for they are bread for us. Their protection has turned aside from them, but the LORD is with us. Do not fear them!"

14:10 However, the whole community threatened to stone them. But the glory of the LORD appeared to all the Israelites at the tent of meeting.

The Punishment from God

14:11 The LORD said to Moses, "How long will this people despise me, and how long will they not believe in me, in spite of the signs that I have done among them? **14:12** I will strike them with the pestilence, and I will disinherit them; I will make you into a nation that is greater and mightier than they!"

14:13 Moses said to the LORD, "When the Egyptians hear it – for you brought up this people by your power from among them – **14:14** then they will tell it to the inhabitants of this land. They have heard that you, LORD, are among this people, that you, LORD, are seen face to face, that your cloud stands over them, and that you go before them by day in a pillar of cloud and in a pillar of fire by night. **14:15** If you kill this entire people at once, then the nations that have heard of your fame will say, **14:16** 'Because the LORD was not able to bring this people into the land that he swore to them, he killed them in the wilderness.' **14:17** So now, let the power of my Lord be great, just as you have said, **14:18** 'The LORD is slow to anger and abounding in loyal love, forgiving iniquity and transgression, but by no means clearing the guilty, visiting the iniquity of the fathers on the children until the third and fourth generations.' **14:19** Please forgive the iniquity of this people according to your great loyal love, just as you have forgiven this people from Egypt even until now."

14:20 Then the LORD said, "I have forgiven them as you asked. **14:21** But truly, as I live, all the earth will be filled with the glory of the LORD. **14:22** For all the people have seen my glory and my signs that I did in Egypt and in the wilderness, and yet have tempted me now these ten times, and have not obeyed me, **14:23** they will by no means see the land that I swore to their fathers, nor will any of them who despised me see it. **14:24** Only my servant Caleb, because he had a different spirit and has followed me fully – I will bring him into the land where he had gone, and his descendants will possess it. **14:25** (Now the Amalekites and the Canaanites were living in the valleys.) Tomorrow, turn and journey into the wilderness by the way of the Red Sea."

14:26 The LORD spoke to Moses and Aaron: **14:27** "How long must I bear with this evil congregation that murmurs against me? I have heard the complaints of the Israelites that they murmured against me. **14:28** Say to them, 'As I live, says the LORD, I will surely do to you just what you have spoken in my hearing. **14:29** Your dead bodies will fall in this wilderness – all those of you who were numbered, according to your full number, from twenty years old and upward, who have murmured against me. **14:30** You will by no means enter into the land where I swore to settle you. The only exceptions are Caleb son of Jephunneh and Joshua son of Nun. **14:31** But I will bring in your little ones, whom you said would become victims of war, and they will enjoy the land that you have despised. **14:32** But as for you, your dead bodies will fall in this wilderness, **14:33** and your children will wander in the wilderness forty years and suffer for your unfaithfulness, until your dead bodies lie finished in the wilderness. **14:34** According to the number of the days you have investigated this land, forty days – one day for a year – you will suffer for your iniquities, forty years, and you will know what it means to thwart me. **14:35** I, the LORD, have said, "I will surely do so to all this evil congregation that has gathered together against me. In this wilderness they will be finished, and there they will die!"'"

14:36 The men whom Moses sent to investigate the land, who returned and made the whole community murmur against him by producing an evil report about the land, **14:37** those men who produced the evil report about the land, died by the plague before the LORD. **14:38** But Joshua son of Nun and Caleb son of Jephunneh, who were among the men who went to investigate the land, lived. **14:39** When Moses told these things to all the Israelites, the people mourned greatly.

14:40 And early in the morning they went up to the crest of the hill country, saying, "Here we are, and we will go up to the place that the LORD commanded, for we have sinned." **14:41** But Moses said, "Why are you now transgressing the commandment of the LORD? It will not succeed! **14:42** Do not go up, for the LORD is not among you, and you will be defeated before your enemies. **14:43** For the Amalekites and the Canaanites are there before you, and you will fall by the sword. Because you have turned away from the LORD, the LORD will not be with you."

14:44 But they dared to go up to the crest of the hill, although neither the ark of the covenant of the LORD nor Moses departed from the camp. **14:45** So the Amalekites and the Canaanites who lived in that hill country swooped down and attacked them as far as Hormah.

Sacrificial Rulings

15:1 The LORD spoke to Moses: **15:2** "Speak to the Israelites and tell them, 'When you enter the land where you are to live, which I am giving you, **15:3** and you make an offering by fire to the LORD from the herd or from the flock (whether a burnt offering or a sacrifice for discharging a vow or as a freewill offering or in your solemn feasts) to create a pleasing aroma to the LORD, **15:4** then the one who presents his offering to the LORD must bring a grain offering of one-tenth of an ephah of finely ground flour mixed with one fourth of a hin of olive oil. **15:5** You must also prepare one-fourth of a hin of wine for a drink offering with the burnt offering or the sacrifice for each lamb. **15:6** Or for a ram, you must prepare as a grain offering two-tenths of an ephah of finely ground flour mixed with one-third of a hin of olive oil, **15:7** and for a drink offering you must offer one-third of a hin of wine as a pleasing aroma to the LORD. **15:8** And when you prepare a young bull as a burnt offering or a sacrifice for discharging a vow or as a peace offering to the LORD, **15:9** then a grain offering of three-tenths of an ephah of finely ground flour mixed with half a hin of olive oil must be presented with the young bull, **15:10** and you must present as the drink offering half a hin of wine with the fire offering as a pleasing aroma to the LORD. **15:11** This is what is to be done for each ox, or each ram, or each of the male lambs or the goats. **15:12** You must do so for each one according to the number that you prepare.

15:13 "'Every native-born person must do these things in this way to present an offering made by fire as a pleasing aroma to the LORD. **15:14** If a resident foreigner is living with you – or whoever is among you in future generations – and prepares an offering made by fire as a pleasing aroma to the LORD, he must do it the same way you are to do it. **15:15** One statute must apply to you who belong to the congregation and to the resident foreigner who is living among you, as a permanent statute for your future generations. You and the resident foreigner will be alike before the LORD. **15:16** One law and one custom must apply to you and to the resident foreigner who lives alongside you.'"

Rules for First Fruits

15:17 The LORD spoke to Moses: **15:18** "Speak to the Israelites and tell them, 'When you enter the land to which I am bringing you **15:19** and you eat some of the food of the land, you must offer up a raised offering to the LORD. **15:20** You must offer up a cake of the first of your finely ground flour as a raised offering; as you offer the raised offering of the threshing floor, so you must offer it up. **15:21** You must give to the LORD some of the first of your finely ground flour as a raised offering in your future generations.

Rules for Unintentional Offenses

15:22 "'If you sin unintentionally and do not observe all these commandments that the LORD has spoken to Moses – **15:23** all that the LORD has commanded you by the authority of Moses, from the day that the LORD commanded Moses and continuing through your future generations – **15:24** then if anything is done unintentionally without the knowledge of the community, the whole community must prepare one young bull for a burnt offering – for a pleasing aroma to the LORD – along with its grain offering and its customary drink offering, and one male goat for a purification offering. **15:25** And the priest is to make atonement for the whole community of the Israelites, and they will be forgiven, because it was unintentional and they have brought their offering, an offering made by fire to the LORD, and their purification offering before the LORD, for their unintentional offense. **15:26** And the whole community of the Israelites and the resident foreigner who lives among them will be forgiven, since all the people were involved in the unintentional offense.

15:27 "'If any person sins unintentionally, then he must bring a yearling female goat for a purification offering. **15:28** And the priest must make atonement for the person who sins unintentionally – when he sins unintentionally before the LORD – to make atonement for him, and he will be forgiven. **15:29** You must have one law for the person who sins unintentionally, both for the native-born among the Israelites and for the resident foreigner who lives among them.

Deliberate Sin

15:30 "'But the person who acts defiantly, whether native-born or a resident foreigner, insults the LORD. That person must be cut off from among his people. **15:31** Because he has despised the word of the LORD and has broken his commandment, that person must be completely cut off. His iniquity will be on him.'"

15:32 When the Israelites were in the wilderness they found a man gathering wood on the Sabbath day. **15:33** Those who found him gathering wood brought him to Moses and Aaron and to the whole community.

15:34 They put him in custody, because there was no clear instruction about what should be done to him. **15:35** Then the LORD said to Moses, "The man must surely be put to death; the whole community must stone him with stones outside the camp." **15:36** So the whole community took him outside the camp and stoned him to death, just as the LORD commanded Moses.

Rules for Tassels

15:37 The LORD spoke to Moses: **15:38** "Speak to the Israelites and tell them to make tassels for themselves on the corners of their garments throughout their generations, and put a blue thread on the tassel of the corners. **15:39** You must have this tassel so that you may look at it and remember all the commandments of the LORD and obey them and so that you do not follow after your own heart and your own eyes that lead you to unfaithfulness. **15:40** Thus you will remember and obey all my commandments and be holy to your God. **15:41** I am the LORD your God, who brought you out of the land of Egypt to be your God. I am the LORD your God."

The Rebellion of Korah

16:1 Now Korah son of Izhar, the son of Kohath, the son of Levi, and Dathan and Abiram, the sons of Eliab, and On son of Peleth, who were Reubenites, took men **16:2** and rebelled against Moses, along with some of the Israelites, 250 leaders of the community, chosen from the assembly, famous men. **16:3** And they assembled against Moses and Aaron, saying to them, "You take too much upon yourselves, seeing that the whole community is holy, every one of them, and the LORD is among them. Why then do you exalt yourselves above the community of the LORD?" **16:4** When Moses heard it he fell down with his face to the ground. **16:5** Then he said to Korah and to all his company, "In the morning the LORD will make known who are his, and who is holy. He will cause that person to approach him; the person he has chosen he will cause to approach him. **16:6** Do this, Korah, you and all your company: Take censers, **16:7** put fire in them, and set incense on them before the LORD tomorrow, and the man whom the LORD chooses will be holy. You take too much upon yourselves, you sons of Levi!" **16:8** Moses said to Korah, "Listen now, you sons of Levi! **16:9** Does it seem too small a thing to you that the God of Israel has separated you from the community of Israel to bring you near to himself, to perform the service of the tabernacle of the LORD, and to stand before the community to minister to them? **16:10** He has brought you near and all your brothers, the sons of Levi, with you. Do you now seek the priesthood also? **16:11** Therefore you and all your company have assembled together against the LORD! And Aaron – what is he that you murmur against him?" **16:12** Then Moses summoned Dathan and Abiram, the sons of Eliab, but they said, "We will not come up. **16:13** Is it a small thing that you have brought us up out of the land that flows with milk and honey, to kill us in the wilderness? Now do you want to make yourself a prince over us? **16:14** Moreover, you have not brought us into a land that flows with milk and honey, nor given us an inheritance of fields and vineyards. Do you think you can blind these men? We will not come up."

16:15 Moses was very angry, and he said to the LORD, "Have no respect for their offering! I have not taken so much as one donkey from them, nor have I harmed any one of them!"

16:16 Then Moses said to Korah, "You and all your company present yourselves before the LORD – you and they, and Aaron – tomorrow. **16:17** And each of you take his censer, put incense in it, and then each of you present his censer before the LORD: 250 censers, along with you, and Aaron – each of you with his censer." **16:18** So everyone took his censer, put fire in it, and set incense on it, and stood at the entrance of the tent of meeting, with Moses and Aaron. **16:19** When Korah assembled the whole community against them at the entrance of the tent of meeting, then the glory of the LORD appeared to the whole community.

The Judgment on the Rebels

16:20 The LORD spoke to Moses and Aaron: **16:21** "Separate yourselves from among this community, that I may consume them in an instant." **16:22** Then they threw themselves down with their faces to the ground and said, "O God, the God of the spirits of all people, will you be angry with the whole community when only one man sins?"

16:23 So the LORD spoke to Moses: **16:24** "Tell the community: 'Get away from around the homes of Korah, Dathan, and Abiram.'" **16:25** Then Moses got up and went to Dathan and Abiram; and the elders of Israel went after him. **16:26** And he said to the community, "Move away from the tents of these wicked men, and do not touch anything they have, lest you be destroyed because of all their sins." **16:27** So they got away from the homes of Korah, Dathan, and Abiram on every side, and Dathan and Abiram came out and stationed themselves in the entrances of their tents with their wives, their children, and their toddlers. **16:28** Then Moses said, "This is how you will know that the LORD has sent me to do all these works, for I have not done them of my own will. **16:29** If these men die a natural death, or if they share the fate of all men, then the LORD has not sent me. **16:30** But if the LORD does something entirely new, and the earth opens its mouth and swallows them up along with all that they have,

and they go down alive to the grave, then you will know that these men have despised the LORD!"

16:31 When he had finished speaking all these words, the ground that was under them split open, **16:32** and the earth opened its mouth and swallowed them, along with their households, and all Korah's men, and all their goods. **16:33** They and all that they had went down alive into the pit, and the earth closed over them. So they perished from among the community. **16:34** All the Israelites who were around them fled at their cry, for they said, "What if the earth swallows us too?" **16:35** Then a fire went out from the LORD and devoured the 250 men who offered incense.

The Atonement for the Rebellion

16:36 (17:1) The LORD spoke to Moses: **16:37** "Tell Eleazar son of Aaron the priest to pick up the censers out of the flame, for they are holy, and then scatter the coals of fire at a distance. **16:38** As for the censers of these men who sinned at the cost of their lives, they must be made into hammered sheets for covering the altar, because they presented them before the LORD and sanctified them. They will become a sign to the Israelites." **16:39** So Eleazar the priest took the bronze censers presented by those who had been burned up, and they were hammered out as a covering for the altar. **16:40** It was a memorial for the Israelites, that no outsider who is not a descendant of Aaron should approach to burn incense before the LORD, that he might not become like Korah and his company – just as the LORD had spoken by the authority of Moses. **16:41** But on the next day the whole community of Israelites murmured against Moses and Aaron, saying, "You have killed the LORD's people!" **16:42** When the community assembled against Moses and Aaron, they turned toward the tent of meeting – and the cloud covered it, and the glory of the LORD appeared. **16:43** Then Moses and Aaron stood before the tent of meeting.

16:44 The LORD spoke to Moses: **16:45** "Get away from this community, so that I can consume them in an instant!" But they threw themselves down with their faces to the ground. **16:46** Then Moses said to Aaron, "Take the censer, put burning coals from the altar in it, place incense on it, and go quickly into the assembly and make atonement for them, for wrath has gone out from the LORD – the plague has begun!" **16:47** So Aaron did as Moses commanded and ran into the middle of the assembly, where the plague was just beginning among the people. So he placed incense on the coals and made atonement for the people. **16:48** He stood between the dead and the living, and the plague was stopped. **16:49** Now 14,700 people died in the plague, in addition to those who died in the event with Korah. **16:50** Then Aaron returned to Moses at the entrance of the tent of meeting, and the plague was stopped.

The Budding of Aaron's Staff

17:1 The LORD spoke to Moses: **17:2** "Speak to the Israelites, and receive from them a staff from each tribe, one from every tribal leader, twelve staffs; you must write each man's name on his staff. **17:3** You must write Aaron's name on the staff of Levi; for one staff is for the head of every tribe. **17:4** You must place them in the tent of meeting before the ark of the covenant where I meet with you. **17:5** And the staff of the man whom I choose will blossom; so I will rid myself of the complaints of the Israelites, which they murmur against you."

17:6 So Moses spoke to the Israelites, and each of their leaders gave him a staff, one for each leader, according to their tribes – twelve staffs; the staff of Aaron was among their staffs. **17:7** Then Moses placed the staffs before the LORD in the tent of the testimony.

17:8 On the next day Moses went into the tent of the testimony – and the staff of Aaron for the house of Levi had sprouted, and brought forth buds, and produced blossoms, and yielded almonds! **17:9** So Moses brought out all the staffs from before the LORD to all the Israelites. They looked at them, and each man took his staff.

The Memorial

17:10 The LORD said to Moses, "Bring Aaron's staff back before the testimony to be preserved for a sign to the rebels, so that you may bring their murmurings to an end before me, that they will not die." **17:11** So Moses did as the LORD commanded him – this is what he did.

17:12 The Israelites said to Moses, "We are bound to die! We perish, we all perish! **17:13 (17:28)** Anyone who even comes close to the tabernacle of the LORD will die! Are we all to die?"

Responsibilities of the Priests

18:1 The LORD said to Aaron, "You and your sons and your tribe with you must bear the iniquity of the sanctuary, and you and your sons with you must bear the iniquity of your priesthood.

18:2 "Bring with you your brothers, the tribe of Levi, the tribe of your father, so that they may join with you and minister to you while you and your sons with you are before the tent of the testimony. **18:3** They must be responsible to care for you and to care for the entire tabernacle. However, they must not come near the furnishings of the sanctuary and the altar, or both they and you will die. **18:4** They must join with you, and they will be responsible for the care of the tent of meeting, for all the service of the tent, but no unauthorized person may approach you. **18:5** You will be responsible for the care of the sanctuary and the care of the altar, so that there will be no more wrath on the Israelites. **18:6** I myself have chosen your brothers the Levites from among the Israelites. They are given to you as a gift from the LORD, to perform the duties of the tent of meeting. **18:7** But you and your sons with you are responsible for your priestly duties, for everything at the altar and within the curtain. And you must serve. I give you the priesthood as a gift for service; but the unauthorized person who approaches must be put to death."

The Portion of the Priests

18:8 The LORD spoke to Aaron, "See, I have given you the responsibility for my raised offerings; I have given all the holy things of the Israelites to you as your priestly portion and to your sons as a perpetual ordinance. **18:9** Of all the most holy offerings reserved from the fire this will be yours: Every offering of theirs, whether from every grain offering or from every purification offering or from every reparation offering which they bring to me, will be most holy for you and for your sons. **18:10** You are to eat it as a most holy offering; every male may eat it. It will be holy to you.

18:11 "And this is yours: the raised offering of their gift, along with all the wave offerings of the Israelites. I have given them to you and to your sons and daughters with you as a perpetual ordinance. Everyone who is ceremonially clean in your household may eat of it.

18:12 "All the best of the olive oil and all the best of the wine and of the wheat, the first fruits of these things that they give to the LORD, I have given to you. **18:13** And whatever first ripe fruit in their land they bring to the LORD will be yours; everyone who is ceremonially clean in your household may eat of it.

18:14 "Everything devoted in Israel will be yours. **18:15** The firstborn of every womb which they present to the LORD, whether human or animal, will be yours. Nevertheless, the firstborn sons you must redeem, and the firstborn males of unclean animals you must redeem. **18:16** And those that must be redeemed you are to redeem when they are a month old, according to your estimation, for five shekels of silver according to the sanctuary shekel (which is twenty gerahs). **18:17** But you must not redeem the firstborn of a cow or a sheep or a goat; they are holy. You must splash their blood on the altar and burn their fat for an offering made by fire for a pleasing aroma to the LORD. **18:18** And their meat will be yours, just as the breast and the right hip of the raised offering is yours. **18:19** All the raised offerings of the holy things that the Israelites offer to the LORD, I have given to you, and to your sons and daughters with you, as a perpetual ordinance. It is a covenant of salt forever before the LORD for you and for your descendants with you."

Duties of the Levites

18:20 The LORD spoke to Aaron, "You will have no inheritance in their land, nor will you have any portion of property among them – I am your portion and your inheritance among the Israelites. **18:21** See, I have given the Levites all the tithes in Israel for an inheritance, for their service which they perform – the service of the tent of meeting. **18:22** No longer may the Israelites approach the tent of meeting, or else they will bear their sin and die. **18:23** But the Levites must perform the service of the tent of meeting, and they must bear their iniquity. It will be a perpetual ordinance throughout your generations that among the Israelites the Levites have no inheritance. **18:24** But I have given to the Levites for an inheritance the tithes of the Israelites that are offered to the LORD as a raised offering. That is why I said to them that among the Israelites they are to have no inheritance."

Instructions for the Levites

18:25 The LORD spoke to Moses: **18:26** "You are to speak to the Levites, and you must tell them, 'When you receive from the Israelites the tithe that I have given you from them as your inheritance, then you are to offer up from it as a raised offering to the LORD a tenth of the tithe. **18:27** And your raised offering will be credited to you as though it were grain from the threshing floor or as new wine from the winepress. **18:28** Thus you are to offer up a raised offering to the LORD of all your tithes which you receive from the Israelites; and you must give the LORD's raised offering from it to Aaron the priest. **18:29** From all your gifts you must offer up every raised offering due the LORD, from all the best of it, and the holiest part of it.'

18:30 "Therefore you will say to them, 'When you offer up the best of it, then it will be credited to the Levites as the product of the threshing floor and as the product of the winepress. **18:31** And you may eat it in any place, you and your household, because it is your wages for your service in the tent of meeting. **18:32** And you will bear no sin concerning it when you offer up the best of it. And you must not profane the holy things of the Israelites, or else you will die.'"

The Red Heifer Ritual

19:1 The LORD spoke to Moses and Aaron: **19:2** "This is the ordinance of the law which the LORD has commanded: 'Instruct the Israelites to bring you a red heifer without blemish, which has no defect and has never carried a yoke. **19:3** You must give it to Eleazar the priest so that he can take it outside the camp, and it must be slaughtered before him. **19:4** Eleazar the priest is to take some of its blood with his finger, and sprinkle some of its blood seven times directly in front of the tent of meeting. **19:5** Then the heifer must be burned in his sight – its skin, its flesh, its blood, and its offal is to be burned. **19:6** And the priest must take cedar wood, hyssop, and scarlet wool and throw them into the midst of the fire where the heifer is burning. **19:7** Then the priest must wash his clothes and bathe himself in water, and afterward he may come into the camp, but the priest will be ceremonially unclean until evening. **19:8** The one who burns it must wash his clothes in water and bathe himself in water. He will be ceremonially unclean until evening.

19:9 "'Then a man who is ceremonially clean must gather up the ashes of the red heifer and put them in a ceremonially clean place outside the camp. They must be kept for the community of the Israelites for use in the water of purification – it is a purification for sin. **19:10** The one who gathers the ashes of the heifer must wash his clothes and be ceremonially unclean until evening. This will be a permanent ordinance both for the Israelites and the resident foreigner who lives among them.

Purification from Uncleanness

19:11 "'Whoever touches the corpse of any person will be ceremonially unclean seven days. **19:12** He must purify himself with water on the third day and on the seventh day, and so will be clean. But if he does not purify himself on the third day and the seventh day, then he will not be clean. **19:13** Anyone who touches the corpse of any dead person and does not purify himself defiles the tabernacle of the LORD. And that person must be cut off from Israel, because the water of purification was not sprinkled on him. He will be unclean; his uncleanness remains on him.

19:14 "'This is the law: When a man dies in a tent, anyone who comes into the tent and all who are in the tent will be ceremonially unclean seven days. **19:15** And every open container that has no covering fastened on it is unclean. **19:16** And whoever touches the body of someone killed with a sword in the open fields, or the body of someone who died of natural causes, or a human bone, or a grave, will be unclean seven days.

19:17 "'For a ceremonially unclean person you must take some of the ashes of the heifer burnt for purification from sin and pour fresh running water over them in a vessel. **19:18** Then a ceremonially clean person must take hyssop, dip it in the water, and sprinkle it on the tent, on all its furnishings, and on the people who were there, or on the one who touched a bone, or one killed, or one who died, or a grave. **19:19** And the clean person must sprinkle the unclean on the third day and on the seventh day; and on the seventh day he must purify him, and then he must wash his clothes, and bathe in water, and he will be clean in the evening. **19:20** But the man who is unclean and does not purify himself, that person must be cut off from among the community, because he has polluted the sanctuary of the LORD; the water of purification was not sprinkled on him, so he is unclean.

19:21 "'So this will be a perpetual ordinance for them: The one who sprinkles the water of purification must wash his clothes, and the one who touches the water of purification will be unclean until evening. **19:22** And whatever the unclean person touches will be unclean, and the person who touches it will be unclean until evening.'"

The Israelites Complain Again

20:1 Then the entire community of Israel entered the wilderness of Zin in the first month, and the people stayed in Kadesh. Miriam died and was buried there.

20:2 And there was no water for the community, and so they gathered themselves together against Moses and Aaron. **20:3** The people contended with Moses, saying, "If only we had died when our brothers died before the LORD! **20:4** Why have you brought up the LORD's community into this wilderness? So that we and our cattle should die here? **20:5** Why have you brought us up from Egypt only to bring us to this dreadful place? It is no place for grain, or figs, or vines, or pomegranates; nor is there any water to drink!"

Moses Responds

20:6 So Moses and Aaron went from the presence of the assembly to the entrance to the tent of meeting. They then threw themselves down with their faces to the ground, and the glory of the LORD appeared to them. **20:7** Then the LORD spoke to Moses: **20:8** "Take the staff and assemble the community, you and Aaron your brother, and then speak to the rock before their eyes. It will pour forth its water, and you will bring water out of the rock for them, and so you will give the community and their beasts water to drink."

20:9 So Moses took the staff from before the LORD, just as he commanded him. **20:10** Then Moses and Aaron gathered the community together in front of the rock, and he said to them, "Listen, you rebels, must we bring water out of this rock for you?" **20:11** Then Moses raised his hand, and struck the rock twice with his staff. And water came out abundantly. So the community drank, and their beasts drank too.

The Lord's Judgment

20:12 Then the LORD spoke to Moses and Aaron, "Because you did not trust me enough to show me as holy before the Israelites, therefore you will not bring this community into the land I have given them."

20:13 These are the waters of Meribah, because the Israelites contended with the LORD, and his holiness was maintained among them.

Rejection by the Edomites

20:14 Moses sent messengers from Kadesh to the king of Edom: "Thus says your brother Israel: 'You know all the hardships we have experienced, **20:15** how our ancestors went down into Egypt, and we lived in Egypt a long time, and the Egyptians treated us and our ancestors badly.

20:16 So when we cried to the LORD, he heard our voice and sent a messenger, and has brought us up out of Egypt. Now we are here in Kadesh, a town on the edge of your country. **20:17** Please let us pass through your country. We will not pass through the fields or through the vineyards, nor will we drink water from any well. We will go by the King's Highway; we will not turn to the right or the left until we have passed through your region.'"

20:18 But Edom said to him, "You will not pass through me, or I will come out against you with the sword." **20:19** Then the Israelites said to him, "We will go along the highway, and if we or our cattle drink any of your water, we will pay for it. We will only pass through on our feet, without doing anything else."

20:20 But he said, "You may not pass through." Then Edom came out against them with a large and powerful force. **20:21** So Edom refused to give Israel passage through his border; therefore Israel turned away from him.

Aaron's Death

20:22 So the entire company of Israelites traveled from Kadesh and came to Mount Hor. **20:23** And the LORD spoke to Moses and Aaron in Mount Hor, by the border of the land of Edom. He said: **20:24** "Aaron will be gathered to his ancestors, for he will not enter into the land I have given to the Israelites because both of you rebelled against my word at the waters of Meribah. **20:25** Take Aaron and Eleazar his son, and bring them up on Mount Hor. **20:26** Remove Aaron's priestly garments and put them on Eleazar his son, and Aaron will be gathered to his ancestors and will die there."

20:27 So Moses did as the LORD commanded; and they went up Mount Hor in the sight of the whole community. **20:28** And Moses removed Aaron's garments and put them on his son Eleazar. So Aaron died there on the top of the mountain. And Moses and Eleazar came down from the mountain. **20:29** When all the community saw that Aaron was dead, the whole house of Israel mourned for Aaron thirty days.

Victory at Hormah

21:1 When the Canaanite king of Arad who lived in the Negev heard that Israel was approaching along the road to Atharim, he fought against Israel and took some of them prisoner. **21:2** So Israel made a vow to the LORD and said, "If you will indeed deliver this people into our hand, then we will utterly destroy their cities." **21:3** The LORD listened to the voice of Israel and delivered up the Canaanites, and they utterly destroyed them and their cities. So the name of the place was called Hormah.

Fiery Serpents

21:4 Then they traveled from Mount Hor by the road to the Red Sea, to go around the land of Edom, but the people became impatient along the way. **21:5** And the people spoke against God and against Moses, "Why have you brought us up out of Egypt to die in the wilderness, for there is no bread or water, and we detest this worthless food."

21:6 So the LORD sent poisonous snakes among the people, and they bit the people; many people of Israel died. **21:7** Then the people came to Moses and said, "We have sinned, for we have spoken against the LORD and against you. Pray to the LORD that he would take away the snakes from us." So Moses prayed for the people. **21:8** The LORD said to Moses, "Make a poisonous snake and set it on a pole. When anyone who is bitten looks at it, he will live." **21:9** So Moses made a bronze snake and put it on a pole, so that if a snake had bitten someone, when he looked at the bronze snake he lived.

The Approach to Moab

21:10 The Israelites traveled on and camped in Oboth. **21:11** Then they traveled on from Oboth and camped at Iye Abarim, in the wilderness that is before Moab, on the eastern side. **21:12** From there they moved on and camped in the valley of Zered. **21:13** From there they moved on and camped on the other side of the Arnon, in the wilderness that extends from the regions of the Amorites, for Arnon is the border of Moab, between Moab and the Amorites. **21:14** This is why it is said in the Book of the Wars of the LORD,

"Waheb in Suphah and the wadis,
the Arnon **21:15** and the slope of the valleys
that extends to the dwelling of Ar,
and falls off at the border of Moab."

21:16 And from there they traveled to Beer; that is the well where the LORD spoke to Moses, "Gather the people and I will give them water." **21:17** Then Israel sang this song:

"Spring up, O well, sing to it!
21:18 The well which the princes dug,
which the leaders of the people opened
with their scepters and their staffs."

And from the wilderness they traveled to Mattanah; **21:19** and from Mattanah to Nahaliel; and from Nahaliel to Bamoth; **21:20** and from Bamoth to the valley that is in the country of Moab, near the top of Pisgah, which overlooks the wilderness.

The Victory over Sihon and Og

21:21 Then Israel sent messengers to King Sihon of the Amorites, saying,

21:22 "Let us pass through your land; we will not turn aside into the fields or into the vineyards, nor will we drink water from any well, but we will go along the King's Highway until we pass your borders." **21:23** But Sihon did not permit Israel to pass through his border; he gathered all his forces together and went out against Israel into the wilderness. When he came to Jahaz, he fought against Israel. **21:24** But the Israelites defeated him in battle and took possession of his land from the Arnon to the Jabbok, as far as the Ammonites, for the border of the Ammonites was strongly defended. **21:25** So Israel took all these cities; and Israel settled in all the cities of the Amorites, in Heshbon, and in all its villages. **21:26** For Heshbon was the city of King Sihon of the Amorites. Now he had fought against the former king of Moab and had taken all of his land from his control, as far as the Arnon. **21:27** That is why those who speak in proverbs say,

"Come to Heshbon, let it be built.
Let the city of Sihon be established!
21:28 For fire went out from Heshbon,
a flame from the city of Sihon.
It has consumed Ar of Moab
and the lords of the high places of Arnon.
21:29 Woe to you, Moab.
You are ruined, O people of Chemosh!
He has made his sons fugitives,
and his daughters the prisoners of King Sihon of the Amorites.
21:30 We have overpowered them;
Heshbon has perished as far as Dibon.
We have shattered them as far as Nophah,
which reaches to Medeba."

21:31 So the Israelites lived in the land of the Amorites. **21:32** Moses sent spies to reconnoiter Jaazer, and they captured its villages and dispossessed the Amorites who were there.

21:33 Then they turned and went up by the road to Bashan. And King Og of Bashan and all his forces marched out against them to do battle at Edrei. **21:34** And the LORD said to Moses, "Do not fear him, for I have delivered him and all his people and his land into your hand. You will do to him what you did to King Sihon of the Amorites, who lived in Heshbon. **21:35** So they defeated Og, his sons, and all his people, until there were no survivors, and they possessed his land.

Balaam Refuses to Curse Israel

22:1 The Israelites traveled on and camped in the plains of Moab on the side of the Jordan River across from Jericho. **22:2** Balak son of Zippor saw all that the Israelites had done to the Amorites. **22:3** And the Moabites were greatly afraid of the people, because they were so numerous. The Moabites were sick with fear because of the Israelites.

22:4 So the Moabites said to the elders of Midian, "Now this mass of people will lick up everything around us, as the bull devours the grass of the field. Now Balak son of Zippor was king of the Moabites at this time. **22:5** And he sent messengers to Balaam son of Beor at Pethor, which is by the Euphrates River in the land of Amaw, to summon him, saying, "Look, a nation has come out of Egypt. They cover the face of the earth, and they are settling next to me. **22:6** So now, please come and curse this nation for me, for they are too powerful for me. Perhaps I will prevail so that we may conquer them and drive them out of the land. For I know that whoever you bless is blessed, and whoever you curse is cursed."

22:7 So the elders of Moab and the elders of Midian departed with the fee for divination in their hand. They came to Balaam and reported to him the words of Balak. **22:8** He replied to them, "Stay here tonight, and I will bring back to you whatever word the LORD may speak to me." So the princes of Moab stayed with Balaam. **22:9** And God came to Balaam and said, "Who are these men with you?" **22:10** Balak said to God, "Balak son of Zippor, king of Moab, has sent a message to me, saying, **22:11** "Look, a nation has come out of Egypt, and it covers the face of the earth. Come now and put a curse on them for me; perhaps I will be able to defeat them and drive them out." **22:12** But God said to Balaam, "You must not go with them; you must not curse the people, for they are blessed."

22:13 So Balaam got up in the morning, and said to the princes of Balak, "Go to your land, for the LORD has refused to permit me to go with you." **22:14** So the princes of Moab departed and went back to Balak and said, "Balaam refused to come with us."

Balaam Accompanies the Moabite Princes

22:15 Balak again sent princes, more numerous and more distinguished than the first. **22:16** And they came to Balaam and said to him, "Thus says Balak son of Zippor: 'Please do not let anything hinder you from coming to me. **22:17** For I will honor you greatly, and whatever you tell me I will do. So come, put a curse on this nation for me.'"

22:18 Balaam replied to the servants of Balak, "Even if Balak would give me his palace full of silver and gold, I could not transgress the commandment of the LORD my God to do less or more. **22:19** Now therefore, please stay the night here also, that I may know what more the LORD might say to me." **22:20** God came to Balaam that night, and said to him, "If the men have come to call you, get up and go with them; but the word that I will say to you, that you must do." **22:21** So Balaam got up in the morning, saddled his donkey, and went with the princes of Moab.

God Opposes Balaam

22:22 Then God's anger was kindled because he went, and the angel of the LORD stood in the road to oppose him. Now he was riding on his donkey and his two servants were with him. **22:23** And the donkey saw the angel of the LORD standing in the road with his sword drawn in his hand, so the donkey turned aside from the road and went into the field. But Balaam beat the donkey, to make her turn back to the road.

22:24 Then the angel of the LORD stood in a path among the vineyards, where there was a wall on either side. **22:25** And when the donkey saw the angel of the LORD, she pressed herself into the wall, and crushed Balaam's foot against the wall. So he beat her again.

22:26 Then the angel of the LORD went farther, and stood in a narrow place, where there was no way to turn either to the right or to the left. **22:27** When the donkey saw the angel of the LORD, she crouched down under Balaam. Then Balaam was angry, and he beat his donkey with a staff.

22:28 Then the LORD opened the mouth of the donkey, and she said to Balaam, "What have I done to you that you have beaten me these three times?" **22:29** And Balaam said to the donkey, "You have made me look stupid; I wish there were a sword in my hand, for I would kill you right now." **22:30** The donkey said to Balaam, "Am not I your donkey that you have ridden ever since I was yours until this day? Have I ever attempted to treat you this way?" And he said, "No." **22:31** Then the LORD opened Balaam's eyes, and he saw the angel of the LORD standing in the way with his sword drawn in his hand; so he bowed his head and threw himself down with his face to the ground. **22:32** The angel of the LORD said to him, "Why have you beaten your donkey these three times? Look, I came out to oppose you because what you are doing is perverse before me. **22:33** The donkey saw me and turned from me these three times. If she had not turned from me, I would have killed you but saved her alive." **22:34** Balaam said to the angel of the LORD, "I have sinned, for I did not know that you stood against me in the road. So now, if it is evil in your sight, I will go back home." **22:35** But the angel of the LORD said to Balaam, "Go with the men, but you may only speak the word that I will speak to you." So Balaam went with the princes of Balak.

Balaam Meets Balak

22:36 When Balak heard that Balaam was coming, he went out to meet him at a city of Moab which was on the border of the Arnon at the boundary of his territory. **22:37** Balak said to Balaam, "Did I not send again and again to you to summon you? Why did you not come to me? Am I not able to honor you?" **22:38** Balaam said to Balak, "Look, I have come to you. Now, am I able to speak just anything? I must speak only the word that God puts in my mouth." **22:39** So Balaam went with Balak, and they came to Kiriath-huzoth. **22:40** And Balak sacrificed bulls and sheep, and sent some to Balaam, and to the princes who were with him. **22:41** Then on the next morning Balak took Balaam, and brought him up to Bamoth Baal. From there he saw the extent of the nation.

Balaam Blesses Israel

23:1 Balaam said to Balak, "Build me seven altars here, and prepare for me here seven bulls and seven rams." **23:2** So Balak did just as Balaam had said. Balak and Balaam then offered on each altar a bull and a ram. **23:3** Balaam said to Balak, "Station yourself by your burnt offering, and I will go off; perhaps the LORD will come to meet me, and whatever he reveals to me I will tell you." Then he went to a deserted height. **23:4** Then God met Balaam, who said to him, "I have prepared seven altars, and I have offered on each altar a bull and a ram." **23:5** Then the LORD put a message in Balaam's mouth and said, "Return to Balak, and speak what I tell you."

23:6 So he returned to him, and he was still standing by his burnt offering, he and all the princes of Moab. **23:7** Then Balaam uttered his oracle, saying,

"Balak, the king of Moab, brought me from Aram,
out of the mountains of the east, saying,
'Come, pronounce a curse on Jacob for me;
come, denounce Israel.'
23:8 How can I curse one whom God has not cursed,
or how can I denounce one whom the LORD has not denounced?
23:9 For from the top of the rocks I see them;
from the hills I watch them.
Indeed, a nation that lives alone,
and it will not be reckoned among the nations.
23:10 Who can count the dust of Jacob,
Or number the fourth part of Israel?
Let me die the death of the upright,
and let the end of my life be like theirs."

Balaam Relocates

23:11 Then Balak said to Balaam, "What have you done to me? I brought you to curse my enemies, but on the contrary you have only blessed them!" **23:12** Balaam replied, "Must I not be careful to speak what the LORD has put in my mouth?" **23:13** Balak said to him, "Please come with me to another place from which you can observe them. You will see only a part of them, but you will not see all of them. Curse them for me from there."

23:14 So Balak brought Balaam to the field of Zophim, to the top of Pisgah, where he built seven altars and offered a bull and a ram on each altar. **23:15** And Balaam said to Balak, "Station yourself here by your burnt offering, while I meet the LORD there. **23:16** Then the LORD met Balaam and put a message in his mouth and said, "Return to Balak, and speak what I tell you." **23:17** When Balaam came to him, he was still standing by his burnt offering, along with the princes of Moab. And Balak said to him, "What has the LORD spoken?"

Balaam Prophesies Again

23:18 Balaam uttered his oracle, and said,

"Rise up, Balak, and hear;
Listen to me, son of Zippor:
23:19 God is not a man, that he should lie,
nor a human being, that he should change his mind.
Has he said, and will he not do it?
Or has he spoken, and will he not make it happen?
23:20 Indeed, I have received a command to bless;
he has blessed, and I cannot reverse it.
23:21 He has not looked on iniquity in Jacob,
nor has he seen trouble in Israel.
The LORD their God is with them;
his acclamation as king is among them.
23:22 God brought them out of Egypt.
They have, as it were, the strength of a wild bull.
23:23 For there is no spell against Jacob,
nor is there any divination against Israel.
At this time it must be said of Jacob
and of Israel, 'Look at what God has done!'
23:24 Indeed, the people will rise up like a lioness,
and like a lion raises himself up;
they will not lie down until they eat their prey,
and drink the blood of the slain."

Balaam Relocates Yet Again

23:25 Balak said to Balaam, "Neither curse them at all nor bless them at all!" **23:26** But Balaam replied to Balak, "Did I not tell you, 'All that the LORD speaks, I must do'?" **23:27** Balak said to Balaam, "Come, please; I will take you to another place. Perhaps it will please God to let you curse them for me from there." **23:28** So Balak took Balaam to the top of Peor, that looks toward the wilderness. **23:29** Then Balaam said to Balak, "Build seven altars here for me, and prepare seven bulls and seven rams." **23:30** So Balak did as Balaam had said, and offered a bull and a ram on each altar.

Balaam Prophesies Yet Again

24:1 When Balaam saw that it pleased the LORD to bless Israel, he did not go as at the other times to seek for omens, but he set his face toward the wilderness. **24:2** When Balaam lifted up his eyes, he saw Israel camped tribe by tribe; and the Spirit of God came upon him. **24:3** Then he uttered this oracle:

"The oracle of Balaam son of Beor;
the oracle of the man whose eyes are open;
24:4 the oracle of the one who hears the words of God,
who sees a vision from the Almighty,
although falling flat on the ground with eyes open:
24:5 'How beautiful are your tents, O Jacob,
and your dwelling places, O Israel!
24:6 They are like valleys stretched forth,
like gardens by the river's side,
like aloes that the LORD has planted,
and like cedar trees beside the waters.
24:7 He will pour the water out of his buckets,
and their descendants will be like abundant water;
their king will be greater than Agag,
and their kingdom will be exalted.
24:8 God brought them out of Egypt.
They have, as it were, the strength of a young bull;
they will devour hostile people
and will break their bones
and will pierce them through with arrows.
24:9 They crouch and lie down like a lion,
and as a lioness, who can stir him?
Blessed is the one who blesses you,
and cursed is the one who curses you!'"

24:10 Then Balak became very angry at Balaam, and he struck his hands together. Balak said to Balaam, "I called you to curse my enemies, and look, you have done nothing but bless them these three times! **24:11** So now, go back where you came from! I said that I would greatly honor you; but now the LORD has stood in the way of your honor." **24:12** Balaam said to Balak, "Did I not also tell your messengers whom you sent to me, **24:13** 'If Balak would give me his palace full of silver and gold, I cannot go beyond the commandment of the LORD to do either good or evil of my own will, but whatever the LORD tells me I must speak'? **24:14** And now, I am about to go back to my own people. Come now, and I will advise you as to what this people will do to your people in the future."

Balaam Prophesies a Fourth Time

24:15 Then he uttered this oracle:
"The oracle of Balaam son of Beor;
the oracle of the man whose eyes are open;
24:16 the oracle of the one who hears the words of God,
and who knows the knowledge of the Most High,
who sees a vision from the Almighty,
although falling flat on the ground with eyes open:
24:17 'I see him, but not now;
I behold him, but not close at hand.
A star will march forth out of Jacob,
and a scepter will rise out of Israel.
He will crush the skulls of Moab,
and the heads of all the sons of Sheth.
24:18 Edom will be a possession,
Seir, his enemies, will also be a possession;
but Israel will act valiantly.
24:19 A ruler will be established from Jacob;
he will destroy the remains of the city.'"

Balaam's Final Prophecies

24:20 Then Balaam looked on Amalek and delivered this oracle:
"Amalek was the first of the nations,
but his end will be that he will perish."
24:21 Then he looked on the Kenites and uttered this oracle:
"Your dwelling place seems strong,
and your nest is set on a rocky cliff.
24:22 Nevertheless the Kenite will be consumed.
How long will Asshur take you away captive?"
24:23 Then he uttered this oracle:
"O, who will survive when God does this!
24:24 Ships will come from the coast of Kittim,
and will afflict Asshur, and will afflict Eber,
and he will also perish forever."
24:25 Balaam got up and departed and returned to his home, and Balak also went his way.

Israel's Sin with the Moabite Women

25:1 When Israel lived in Shittim, the people began to commit sexual immorality with the daughters of Moab. **25:2** These women invited the people to the sacrifices of their gods; then the people ate and bowed down to their gods. **25:3** When Israel joined themselves to Baal-peor, the anger of the LORD flared up against Israel.

God's Punishment

25:4 The LORD said to Moses, "Arrest all the leaders of the people, and hang them up before the LORD in broad daylight, so that the fierce anger of the LORD may be turned away from Israel." **25:5** So Moses said to the judges of Israel, "Each of you must execute those of his men who were joined to Baal-peor."

25:6 Just then one of the Israelites came and brought to his brothers a Midianite woman in the plain view of Moses and of the whole community of the Israelites, while they were weeping at the entrance of the tent of meeting. **25:7** When Phinehas son of Eleazar, the son of Aaron the priest, saw it, he got up from among the assembly, took a javelin in his hand, **25:8** and went after the Israelite man into the tent and thrust through the Israelite man and into the woman's abdomen. So the plague was stopped from the Israelites. **25:9** Those that died in the plague were 24,000.

The Aftermath

25:10 The LORD spoke to Moses: **25:11** "Phinehas son of Eleazar, the son of Aaron the priest, has turned my anger away from the Israelites, when he manifested such zeal for my sake among them, so that I did not consume the Israelites in my zeal. **25:12** Therefore, announce: 'I am going to give to him my covenant of peace. **25:13** So it will be to him and his descendants after him a covenant of a permanent priesthood, because he has been zealous for his God, and has made atonement for the Israelites.'"

25:14 Now the name of the Israelite who was stabbed – the one who was stabbed with the Midianite woman – was Zimri son of Salu, a leader of a clan of the Simeonites. **25:15** The name of the Midianite woman who was killed was Cozbi daughter of Zur. He was a leader over the people of a clan of Midian. **25:16** Then the LORD spoke to Moses: **25:17** "Bring trouble to the Midianites, and destroy them, **25:18** because they bring trouble to you by their treachery with which they have deceived you in the matter of Peor, and in the matter of Cozbi, the daughter of a prince of Midian, their sister, who was killed on the day of the plague that happened as a result of Peor."

A Second Census Required

26:1 After the plague the LORD said to Moses and to Eleazar son of Aaron the priest, **26:2** "Take a census of the whole community of Israelites, from twenty years old and upward, by their clans, everyone who can serve in the army of Israel." **26:3** So Moses and Eleazar the priest spoke with them in the plains of Moab, by the Jordan River across from Jericho. They said, **26:4** "Number the people from twenty years old and upward, just as the LORD commanded Moses and the Israelites who went out from the land of Egypt."

Reuben

26:5 Reuben was the firstborn of Israel. The Reubenites: from Hanoch, the family of the Hanochites; from Pallu, the family of the Palluites; **26:6** from Hezron, the family of the Hezronites; from Carmi, the family of the Carmites. **26:7** These were the families of the Reubenites; and those numbered of them were 43,730. **26:8** Pallu's descendant was Eliab. **26:9** Eliab's descendants were Nemuel, Dathan, and Abiram. It was Dathan and Abiram who as leaders of the community rebelled against Moses and Aaron with the followers of Korah when they rebelled against the LORD. **26:10** The earth opened its mouth and swallowed them and Korah at the time that company died, when the fire consumed 250 men. So they became a warning. **26:11** But the descendants of Korah did not die.

Simeon

26:12 The Simeonites by their families: from Nemuel, the family of the Nemuelites; from Jamin, the family of the Jaminites; from Jakin, the family of the Jakinites; **26:13** from Zerah, the family of the Zerahites; and from Shaul, the family of the Shaulites. **26:14** These were the families of the Simeonites, 22,200.

Gad

26:15 The Gadites by their families: from Zephon, the family of the Zephonites; from Haggi, the family of the Haggites; from Shuni, the family of the Shunites; **26:16** from Ozni, the family of the Oznites; from Eri, the family of the Erites; **26:17** from Arod, the family of the Arodites, and from Areli, the family of the Arelites. **26:18** These were the families of the Gadites according to those numbered of them, 40,500.

Judah

26:19 The descendants of Judah were Er and Onan, but Er and Onan died in the land of Canaan. **26:20** And the Judahites by their families were: from Shelah, the family of the Shelahites; from Perez, the family of the Perezites; and from Zerah, the family of the Zerahites. **26:21** And the Perezites were: from Hezron, the family of the Hezronites; from Hamul, the family of the Hamulites. **26:22** These were the families of Judah according to those numbered of them, 76,500.

Issachar

26:23 The Issacharites by their families: from Tola, the family of the Tolaites; from Puah, the family of the Puites; **26:24** from Jashub, the family of the Jashubites; and from Shimron, the family of the Shimronites. **26:25** These were the families of Issachar, according to those numbered of them, 64,300.

Zebulun

26:26 The Zebulunites by their families: from Sered, the family of the Sardites; from Elon, the family of the Elonites; from Jahleel, the family of the Jahleelites. **26:27** These were the families of the Zebulunites, according to those numbered of them, 60,500.

Manasseh

26:28 The descendants of Joseph by their families: Manasseh and Ephraim. **26:29** The Manassehites: from Machir, the family of the Machirites (now Machir became the father of Gilead); from Gilead, the family of the Gileadites. **26:30** These were the Gileadites: from Iezer, the family of the Iezerites; from Helek, the family of the Helekites; **26:31** from Asriel, the family of the Asrielites; from Shechem, the family of the Shechemites; **26:32** from Shemida, the family of the Shemidaites; from Hepher, the family of the Hepherites. **26:33** Now Zelophehad son of Hepher had no sons, but only daughters; and the names of the daughters of Zelophehad were Mahlah, Noah, Hoglah, Milcah, and Tirzah. **26:34** These were the families of Manasseh; those numbered of them were 52,700.

Ephraim

26:35 These are the Ephraimites by their families: from Shuthelah, the family of the Shuthelahites; from Beker, the family of the Bekerites; from Tahan, the family of the Tahanites. **26:36** Now these were the Shuthelahites: from Eran, the family of the Eranites. **26:37** These were the families of the Ephraimites, according to those numbered of them, 32,500. These were the descendants of Joseph by their families.

Benjamin

26:38 The Benjaminites by their families: from Bela, the family of the Belaites; from Ashbel, the family of the Ashbelites; from Ahiram, the family of the Ahiramites; **26:39** from Shupham, the family of the Shuphamites; from Hupham, the family of the Huphamites. **26:40** The descendants of Bela were Ard and Naaman. From Ard, the family of the Ardites; from Naaman, the family of the Naamanites. **26:41** These are the Benjaminites, according to their families, and according to those numbered of them, 45,600.

Dan

26:42 These are the Danites by their families: from Shuham, the family of the Shuhamites. These were the families of Dan, according to their families. **26:43** All the families of the Shuhahites according to those numbered of them were 64,400.

Asher

26:44 The Asherites by their families: from Imnah, the family of the Imnahites; from Ishvi, the family of the Ishvites; from Beriah, the family of the Beriahites. **26:45** From the Beriahites: from Heber, the family of the Heberites; from Malkiel, the family of the Malkielites. **26:46** Now the name of the daughter of Asher was Serah. **26:47** These are the families of the Asherites, according to those numbered of them, 53,400.

Naphtali

26:48 The Naphtalites by their families: from Jahzeel, the family of the Jahzeelites; from Guni, the family of the Gunites; **26:49** from Jezer, the family of the Jezerites; from Shillem, the family of the Shillemites. **26:50** These were the families of Naphtali according to their families; and those numbered of them were 45,400.

Total Number and Division of the Land

26:51 These were those numbered of the Israelites, 601,730.

26:52 Then the LORD spoke to Moses: **26:53** "To these the land must be divided as an inheritance according to the number of the names. **26:54** To a larger group you will give a larger inheritance, and to a smaller group you will give a smaller inheritance. To each one its inheritance must be given according to the number of people in it. **26:55** The land must be divided by lot; and they will inherit in accordance with the names of their ancestral tribes. **26:56** Their inheritance must be apportioned by lot among the larger and smaller groups.

26:57 And these are the Levites who were numbered according to their families: from Gershon, the family of the Gershonites; of Kohath, the family of the Kohathites; from Merari, the family of the Merarites. **26:58** These are the families of the Levites: the family of the Libnites, the family of the Hebronites, the family of the Mahlites, the family of the Mushites, the family of the Korahites. Kohath became the father of Amram. **26:59** Now the name of Amram's wife was Jochebed, daughter of Levi, who was born to Levi in Egypt. And to Amram she bore Aaron, Moses, and Miriam their sister. **26:60** And to Aaron were born Nadab and Abihu, Eleazar and Ithamar. **26:61** But Nadab and Abihu died when they offered strange fire before the LORD. **26:62** Those of them who were numbered were 23,000, all males from a month old and upward, for they were not numbered among the Israelites; no inheritance was given to them among the Israelites.

26:63 These are those who were numbered by Moses and Eleazar the priest, who numbered the Israelites in the plains of Moab along the Jordan River opposite Jericho. **26:64** But there was not a man among these who had been among those numbered by Moses and Aaron the priest when they numbered the Israelites in the wilderness of Sinai. **26:65** For the LORD had said of them, "They will surely die in the wilderness." And there was not left a single man of them, except Caleb son of Jephunneh and Joshua son of Nun.

Special Inheritance Laws

27:1 Then the daughters of Zelophehad son of Hepher, the son of Gilead, the son of Machir, the son of Manasseh of the families of Manasseh, the son Joseph came forward. Now these are the names of his daughters: Mahlah, Noah, Hoglah, Milcah, and Tirzah. **27:2** And they stood before Moses and Eleazar the priest and the leaders of the whole assembly at the entrance to the tent of meeting and said, **27:3** "Our father died in the wilderness, although he was not part of the company of those that gathered themselves together against the LORD in the company of Korah; but he died for his own sin, and he had no sons. **27:4** Why should the name of our father be lost from among his family because he had no son? Give us a possession among the relatives of our father."

27:5 So Moses brought their case before the LORD. **27:6** The LORD said to Moses: **27:7** "The daughters of Zelophehad have a valid claim. You must indeed give them possession of an inheritance among their father's relatives, and you must transfer the inheritance of their father to them. **27:8** And you must tell the Israelites, 'If a man dies and has no son, then you must transfer his inheritance to his daughter; **27:9** and if he has no daughter, then you are to give his inheritance to his brothers; **27:10** and if he has no brothers, then you are to give his inheritance to his father's brothers; **27:11** and if his father has no brothers, then you are to give his inheritance to his relative nearest to him from his family, and he will possess it. This will be for the Israelites a legal requirement, as the LORD commanded Moses.'"

Leadership Change

27:12 Then the LORD said to Moses, "Go up this mountain of the Abarim range, and see the land I have given to the Israelites. **27:13** When you have seen it, you will be gathered to your ancestors, as Aaron your brother was gathered to his ancestors. **27:14** For in the wilderness of Zin when the community rebelled against me, you rebelled against my command to show me as holy before their eyes over the water – the water of Meribah in Kadesh in the wilderness of Zin."

27:15 Then Moses spoke to the LORD: **27:16** "Let the LORD, the God of the spirits of all humankind, appoint a man over the community, **27:17** who will go out before them, and who will come in before them, and who will lead them out, and who will bring them in, so that the community of the LORD may not be like sheep that have no shepherd."

27:18 The LORD replied to Moses, "Take Joshua son of Nun, a man in whom is such a spirit, and lay your hand on him; **27:19** set him before Eleazar the priest and before the whole community, and commission him publicly. **27:20** Then you must delegate some of your authority to him, so that the whole community of the Israelites will be obedient. **27:21** And he will stand before Eleazar the priest, who will seek counsel for him before the LORD by the decision of the Urim. At his command they will go out, and at his command they will come in, he and all the Israelites with him, the whole community."

27:22 So Moses did as the LORD commanded him; he took Joshua and set him before Eleazar the priest and before the whole community. **27:23** He laid his hands on him and commissioned him, just as the LORD commanded, by the authority of Moses.

Daily Offerings

28:1 The LORD spoke to Moses: **28:2** "Command the Israelites: 'With regard to my offering, be sure to offer my food for my offering made by fire, as a pleasing aroma to me at its appointed time.' **28:3** You will say to them, 'This is the offering made by fire which you must offer to the LORD: two unblemished lambs one year old each day for a continual burnt offering. **28:4** The first lamb you must offer in the morning, and the second lamb you must offer in the late afternoon, **28:5** with one-tenth of an ephah of finely ground flour as a grain offering mixed with one quarter of a hin of pressed olive oil. **28:6** It is a continual burnt offering that was instituted on Mount Sinai as a pleasing aroma, an offering made by fire to the LORD.

28:7 "'And its drink offering must be one quarter of a hin for each lamb. You must pour out the strong drink as a drink offering to the LORD in the holy place. **28:8** And the second lamb you must offer in the late afternoon; just as you offered the grain offering and drink offering in the morning, you must offer it as an offering made by fire, as a pleasing aroma to the LORD.

Weekly Offerings

28:9 "'On the Sabbath day, you must offer two unblemished lambs a year old, and two-tenths of an ephah of finely ground flour as a grain offering, mixed with olive oil, along with its drink offering. **28:10** This is the burnt offering for every Sabbath, besides the continual burnt offering and its drink offering.

Monthly Offerings

28:11 "'On the first day of each month you must offer as a burnt offering to the LORD two young bulls, one ram, and seven unblemished lambs a year old, **28:12** with three-tenths of an ephah of finely ground flour mixed with olive oil as a grain offering for each bull, and two-tenths of an ephah of finely ground flour mixed with olive oil as a grain offering for the ram, **28:13** and one-tenth of an ephah of finely ground flour mixed with olive oil as a grain offering for each lamb, as a burnt offering for a pleasing aroma, an offering made by fire to the LORD. **28:14** For their drink offerings, include half a hin of wine with each bull, one-third of a hin for the ram, and one-fourth of a hin for each lamb. This is the burnt offering for each month throughout the months of the year. **28:15** And one male goat must be offered to the LORD as a purification offering, in addition to the continual burnt offering and its drink offering.

Passover and Unleavened Bread

28:16 "'On the fourteenth day of the first month is the LORD's Passover. **28:17** And on the fifteenth day of this month is the festival. For seven days bread made without yeast must be eaten. **28:18** And on the first day there is to be a holy assembly; you must do no ordinary work on it. **28:19** "'But you must offer to the LORD an offering made by fire, a burnt offering of two young bulls, one ram, and seven lambs one year old; they must all be unblemished. **28:20** And their grain offering is to be of finely ground flour mixed with olive oil. For each bull you must offer three-tenths of an ephah, and two-tenths for the ram. **28:21** For each of the seven lambs you are to offer one-tenth of an ephah, **28:22** as well as one goat for a purification offering, to make atonement for you. **28:23** You must offer these in addition to the burnt offering in the morning which is for a continual burnt offering. **28:24** In this manner you must offer daily throughout the seven days the food of the sacrifice made by fire as a sweet aroma to the LORD. It is to be offered in addition to the continual burnt offering and its drink offering. **28:25** On the seventh day you are to have a holy assembly, you must do no regular work.

Firstfruits

28:26 "'Also, on the day of the first fruits, when you bring a new grain offering to the LORD during your Feast of Weeks, you are to have a holy assembly. You must do no ordinary work. **28:27** But you must offer as the burnt offering, as a sweet aroma to the LORD, two young bulls, one ram, seven lambs one year old, **28:28** with their grain offering of finely ground flour mixed with olive oil: three-tenths of an ephah for each bull, two-tenths for the one ram, **28:29** with one-tenth for each of the seven lambs, **28:30** as well as one male goat to make an atonement for you. **28:31** You are to offer them with their drink offerings in addition to the continual burnt offering and its grain offering – they must be unblemished.

Blowing Trumpets

29:1 "'On the first day of the seventh month you are to hold a holy assembly. You must not do your ordinary work, for it is a day of blowing trumpets for you. **29:2** You must offer a burnt offering as a sweet aroma to the LORD: one young bull, one ram, and seven lambs one year old without blemish.

29:3 "'Their grain offering is to be of finely ground flour mixed with olive oil, three-tenths of an ephah for the bull, two-tenths of an ephah for the ram, **29:4** and one-tenth for each of the seven lambs, **29:5** with one male goat for a purification offering to make an atonement for you; **29:6** this is in addition to the monthly burnt offering and its grain offering, and the daily burnt offering with its grain offering and their drink offerings as prescribed, as a sweet aroma, a sacrifice made by fire to the LORD.

The Day of Atonement

29:7 "'On the tenth day of this seventh month you are to have a holy assembly. You must humble yourselves; you must not do any work on it. **29:8** But you must offer a burnt offering as a pleasing aroma to the LORD, one young bull, one ram, and seven lambs one year old, all of them without blemish. **29:9** Their grain offering must be of finely ground flour mixed with olive oil, three-tenths of an ephah for the bull, two-tenths for the ram, **29:10** and one-tenth for each of the seven lambs, **29:11** along with one male goat for a purification offering, in addition to the purification offering for atonement and the continual burnt offering with its grain offering and their drink offerings.

The Feast of Temporary Shelters

29:12 "'On the fifteenth day of the seventh month you are to have a holy assembly; you must do no ordinary work, and you must keep a festival to the LORD for seven days. **29:13** You must offer a burnt offering, an offering made by fire as a pleasing aroma to the LORD: thirteen young bulls, two rams, and fourteen lambs each one year old, all of them without blemish. **29:14** Their grain offering must be of finely ground flour mixed with olive oil, three-tenths of an ephah for each of the thirteen bulls, two-tenths of an ephah for each of the two rams, **29:15** and one-tenth for each of the fourteen lambs, **29:16** along with one male goat for a purification offering, in addition to the continual burnt offering with its grain offering and its drink offering.

29:17 "'On the second day you must offer twelve young bulls, two rams, fourteen lambs one year old, all without blemish, **29:18** and their grain offering and their drink offerings for the bulls, for the rams, and for the lambs, according to their number as prescribed, **29:19** along with one male goat for a purification offering, in addition to the continual burnt offering with its grain offering and their drink offerings.

29:20 "'On the third day you must offer eleven bulls, two rams, fourteen lambs one year old, all without blemish, **29:21** and their grain offering and their drink offerings for the bulls, for the rams, and for the lambs, according to their number as prescribed, **29:22** along with one male goat for a purification offering, in addition to the continual burnt offering with its grain offering and its drink offering.

29:23 "'On the fourth day you must offer ten bulls, two rams, and fourteen lambs one year old, all without blemish, **29:24** and their grain offering and their drink offerings for the bulls, for the rams, and for the lambs, according to their number as prescribed, **29:25** along with one male goat for a purification offering, in addition to the continual burnt offering with its grain offering and its drink offering.

29:26 "'On the fifth day you must offer nine bulls, two rams, and fourteen lambs one year old, all without blemish, **29:27** and their grain offering and their drink offerings for the bulls, for the rams, and for the lambs, according to their number as prescribed, **29:28** along with one male goat for a purification offering, in addition to the continual burnt offering with its grain offering and its drink offering.

29:29 "'On the sixth day you must offer eight bulls, two rams, and fourteen lambs one year old, all without blemish, **29:30** and their grain offering and their drink offerings for the bulls, for the rams, and for the lambs, according to their number as prescribed, **29:31** along with one male goat for a purification offering, in addition to the continual burnt offering with its grain offering and its drink offering.

29:32 "'On the seventh day you must offer seven bulls, two rams, and fourteen lambs one year old, all without blemish, **29:33** and their grain offering and their drink offerings for the bulls, for the rams, and for the lambs, according to their number as prescribed, **29:34** along with one male goat for a purification offering, in addition to the continual burnt offering with its grain offering and its drink offering.

29:35 "'On the eighth day you are to have a holy assembly; you must do no ordinary work on it. **29:36** But you must offer a burnt offering, an offering made by fire, as a pleasing aroma to the LORD, one bull, one ram, seven lambs one year old, all of them without blemish, **29:37** and with their grain offering and their drink offerings for the bull, for the ram, and for the lambs, according to their number as prescribed, **29:38** along with one male goat for a purification offering, in addition to the continual burnt offering with its grain offering and its drink offering.

29:39 "'These things you must present to the LORD at your appointed times, in addition to your vows and your freewill offerings, as your burnt offerings, your grain offerings, your drink offerings, and your peace offerings.'" **29:40** (30:1) So Moses told the Israelites everything, just as the LORD had commanded him.

Vows Made by Men

30:1 Moses told the leaders of the tribes concerning the Israelites, "This is what the LORD has commanded: **30:2** If a man makes a vow to the LORD or takes an oath of binding obligation on himself, he must not break his word, but must do whatever he has promised.

Vows Made by Single Women

30:3 "If a young woman who is still living in her father's house makes a vow to the LORD or places herself under an obligation, **30:4** and her father hears of her vow or the obligation to which she has pledged herself, and her father remains silent about her, then all her vows will stand, and every obligation to which she has pledged herself will stand. **30:5** But if her father overrules her when he hears about it, then none of her vows or her obligations which she has pledged for herself will stand. And the LORD will release her from it, because her father overruled her.

Vows Made by Married Women

30:6 "And if she marries a husband while under a vow, or she uttered anything impulsively by which she has pledged herself, **30:7** and her husband hears about it, but remains silent about her when he hears about it, then her vows will stand and her obligations which she has pledged for herself will stand. **30:8** But if when her husband hears it he overrules her, then

he will nullify the vow she has taken, and whatever she uttered impulsively which she has pledged for herself. And the LORD will release her from it.

Vows Made by Widows

30:9 "But every vow of a widow or of a divorced woman which she has pledged for herself will remain intact. **30:10** If she made the vow in her husband's house or put herself under obligation with an oath, **30:11** and her husband heard about it, but remained silent about her, and did not overrule her, then all her vows will stand, and every obligation which she pledged for herself will stand. **30:12** But if her husband clearly nullifies them when he hears them, then whatever she says by way of vows or obligations will not stand. Her husband has made them void, and the LORD will release her from them.

30:13 "Any vow or sworn obligation that would bring affliction to her, her husband can confirm or nullify. **30:14** But if her husband remains completely silent about her from day to day, he thus confirms all her vows or all her obligations which she is under; he confirms them because he remained silent about when he heard them. **30:15** But if he should nullify them after he has heard them, then he will bear her iniquity."

30:16 These are the statutes that the LORD commanded Moses, relating to a man and his wife, and a father and his young daughter who is still living in her father's house.

The Midianite War

31:1 The LORD spoke to Moses: **31:2** "Exact vengeance for the Israelites on the Midianites – after that you will be gathered to your people."

31:3 So Moses spoke to the people: "Arm men from among you for the war, to attack the Midianites and to execute the LORD's vengeance on Midian. **31:4** You must send to the battle a thousand men from every tribe throughout all the tribes of Israel." **31:5** So a thousand from every tribe, twelve thousand armed for battle in all, were provided out of the thousands of Israel.

Campaign Against the Midianites

31:6 So Moses sent them to the war, one thousand from every tribe, with Phinehas son of Eleazar the priest, who was in charge of the holy articles and the signal trumpets. **31:7** They fought against the Midianites, as the LORD commanded Moses, and they killed every male. **31:8** They killed the kings of Midian in addition to those slain – Evi, Rekem, Zur, Hur, and Reba – five Midianite kings. They also killed Balaam son of Beor with the sword.

31:9 The Israelites took the women of Midian captives along with their little ones, and took all their herds, all their flocks, and all their goods as plunder. **31:10** They burned all their towns where they lived and all their encampments. **31:11** They took all the plunder and all the spoils, both people and animals. **31:12** They brought the captives and the spoils and the plunder to Moses, to Eleazar the priest, and to the Israelite community, to the camp on the plains of Moab, along the Jordan River across from Jericho. **31:13** Moses, Eleazar the priest, and all the leaders of the community went out to meet them outside the camp.

The Death of the Midianite Women

31:14 But Moses was furious with the officers of the army, the commanders over thousands and commanders over hundreds, who had come from service in the war. **31:15** Moses said to them, "Have you allowed all the women to live? **31:16** Look, these people through the counsel of Balaam caused the Israelites to act treacherously against the LORD in the matter of Peor – which resulted in the plague among the community of the LORD! **31:17** Now therefore kill every boy, and kill every woman who has had sexual intercourse with a man. **31:18** But all the young women who have not had sexual intercourse with a man will be yours.

Purification After Battle

31:19 "Any of you who has killed anyone or touched any of the dead, remain outside the camp for seven days; purify yourselves and your captives on the third day, and on the seventh day. **31:20** You must purify each garment and everything that is made of skin, everything made of goat's hair, and everything made of wood."

31:21 Then Eleazar the priest said to the men of war who had gone into the battle, "This is the ordinance of the law that the LORD commanded Moses: **31:22** 'Only the gold, the silver, the bronze, the iron, the tin, and the lead, **31:23** everything that may stand the fire, you are to pass through the fire, and it will be ceremonially clean, but it must still be purified with the water of purification. Anything that cannot withstand the fire you must pass through the water. **31:24** You must wash your clothes on the seventh day, and you will be ceremonially clean, and afterward you may enter the camp.'"

The Distribution of Spoils

31:25 Then the LORD spoke to Moses: **31:26** "You and Eleazar the priest, and all the family leaders of the community, take the sum of the plunder that was captured, both people and animals. **31:27** Divide the plunder into two parts, one for those who took part in the war – who went out to battle – and the other for all the community.

31:28 "You must exact a tribute for the LORD from the fighting men who went out to battle: one life out of five hundred, from the people, the cattle, and from the donkeys and the sheep. **31:29** You are to take it from their half-share and give it to Eleazar the priest for a raised offering to the LORD. **31:30** From the Israelites' half-share you are to take one portion out of fifty of the people, the cattle, the donkeys, and the sheep – from every kind of animal – and you are to give them to the Levites, who are responsible for the care of the LORD's tabernacle."

31:31 So Moses and Eleazar the priest did as the LORD commanded Moses. **31:32** The spoil that remained of the plunder which the fighting men had gathered was 675,000 sheep, **31:33** 72,000 cattle, **31:34** 61,000 donkeys, **31:35** and 32,000 young women who had never had sexual intercourse with a man.

31:36 The half-portion of those who went to war numbered 337,500 sheep; **31:37** the LORD's tribute from the sheep was 675. **31:38** The cattle numbered 36,000; the LORD's tribute was 72. **31:39** The donkeys were 30,500, of which the LORD's tribute was 61. **31:40** The people were 16,000, of which the LORD's tribute was 32 people.

31:41 So Moses gave the tribute, which was the LORD's raised offering, to Eleazar the priest, as the LORD commanded Moses.

31:42 From the Israelites' half-share that Moses had separated from the fighting men, **31:43** there were 337,500 sheep from the portion belonging to the community, **31:44** 36,000 cattle, **31:45** 30,500 donkeys, **31:46** and 16,000 people.

31:47 From the Israelites' share Moses took one of every fifty people and animals and gave them to the Levites who were responsible for the care of the LORD's tabernacle, just as the LORD commanded Moses.

31:48 Then the officers who were over the thousands of the army, the commanders over thousands and the commanders over hundreds, approached Moses **31:49** and said to him, "Your servants have taken a count of the men who were in the battle, who were under our authority, and not one is missing. **31:50** So we have brought as an offering for the LORD what each man found: gold ornaments, armlets, bracelets, signet rings, earrings, and necklaces, to make atonement for ourselves before the LORD." **31:51** Moses and Eleazar the priest took the gold from them, all of it in the form of ornaments. **31:52** All the gold of the offering they offered up to the LORD from the commanders of thousands and the commanders of hundreds weighed 16,750 shekels. **31:53** Each soldier had taken plunder for himself. **31:54** So Moses and Eleazar the priest received the gold from the commanders of thousands and commanders of hundreds and brought it into the tent of meeting as a memorial for the Israelites before the LORD.

The Petition of the Reubenites and Gadites

32:1 Now the Reubenites and the Gadites possessed a very large number of cattle. When they saw that the lands of Jazer and Gilead were ideal for cattle, **32:2** the Gadites and the Reubenites came and addressed Moses, Eleazar the priest, and the leaders of the community. They said, **32:3** "Ataroth, Dibon, Jazer, Nimrah, Heshbon, Elealeh, Sebam, Nebo, and Beon, **32:4** the land that the LORD subdued before the community of Israel, is ideal for cattle, and your servants have cattle." **32:5** So they said, "If we have found favor in your sight, let this land be given to your servants for our inheritance. Do not have us cross the Jordan River."

Moses' Response

32:6 Moses said to the Gadites and the Reubenites, "Must your brothers go to war while you remain here? **32:7** Why do you frustrate the intent of the Israelites to cross over into the land which the LORD has given them? **32:8** Your fathers did the same thing when I sent them from Kadesh Barnea to see the land. **32:9** When they went up to the Eshcol Valley and saw the land, they frustrated the intent of the Israelites so that they did not enter the land that the LORD had given them. **32:10** So the anger of the LORD was kindled that day, and he swore, **32:11** 'Because they have not followed me wholeheartedly, not one of the men twenty years old and upward who came from Egypt will see the land that I swore to give to Abraham, Isaac, and Jacob, **32:12** except Caleb son of Jephunneh the Kenizzite, and Joshua son of Nun, for they followed the LORD wholeheartedly.' **32:13** So the LORD's anger was kindled against the Israelites,

and he made them wander in the wilderness for forty years, until all that generation that had done wickedly before the LORD was finished. **32:14** Now look, you are standing in your fathers' place, a brood of sinners, to increase still further the fierce wrath of the LORD against the Israelites. **32:15** For if you turn away from following him, he will once again abandon them in the wilderness, and you will be the reason for their destruction."

The Offer of the Reubenites and Gadites

32:16 Then they came very close to him and said, "We will build sheep folds here for our flocks and cities for our families, **32:17** but we will maintain ourselves in armed readiness and go before the Israelites until whenever we have brought them to their place. Our descendants will be living in fortified towns as a protection against the inhabitants of the land. **32:18** We will not return to our homes until every Israelite has his inheritance. **32:19** For we will not accept any inheritance on the other side of the Jordan River and beyond, because our inheritance has come to us on this eastern side of the Jordan."

32:20 Then Moses replied, "If you will do this thing, and if you will arm yourselves for battle before the LORD, **32:21** and if all your armed men cross the Jordan before the LORD until he drives out his enemies from his presence **32:22** and the land is subdued before the LORD, then afterward you may return and be free of your obligation to the LORD and to Israel. This land will then be your possession in the LORD's sight.

32:23 "But if you do not do this, then look, you will have sinned against the LORD. And know that your sin will find you out. **32:24** So build cities for your descendants and pens for your sheep, but do what you have said you would do."

32:25 So the Gadites and the Reubenites replied to Moses, "Your servants will do as my lord commands. **32:26** Our children, our wives, our flocks, and all our livestock will be there in the cities of Gilead, **32:27** but your servants will cross over, every man armed for war, to do battle in the LORD's presence, just as my lord says."

32:28 So Moses gave orders about them to Eleazar the priest, to Joshua son of Nun, and to the heads of the families of the Israelite tribes. **32:29** Moses said to them: "If the Gadites and the Reubenites cross the Jordan with you, each one equipped for battle in the LORD's presence, and you conquer the land, then you must allot them the territory of Gilead as their possession. **32:30** But if they do not cross over with you armed, they must receive possessions among you in Canaan." **32:31** Then the Gadites and the Reubenites answered, "Your servants will do what the LORD has spoken. **32:32** We will cross armed in the LORD's presence into the land of Canaan, and then the possession of our inheritance that we inherit will be ours on this side of the Jordan River."

Land Assignment

32:33 So Moses gave to the Gadites, the Reubenites, and to half the tribe of Manasseh son of Joseph the realm of King Sihon of the Amorites, and the realm of King Og of Bashan, the entire land with its cities and the territory surrounding them. **32:34** The Gadites rebuilt Dibon, Ataroth, Aroer, **32:35** Atroth Shophan, Jazer, Jogbehah, **32:36** Beth Nimrah, and Beth Haran as fortified cities, and constructed pens for their flocks. **32:37** The Reubenites rebuilt Heshbon, Elealeh, Kiriathaim, **32:38** Nebo, Baal Meon (with a change of name), and Sibmah. They renamed the cities they built.

32:39 The descendants of Machir son of Manasseh went to Gilead, took it, and dispossessed the Amorites who were in it. **32:40** So Moses gave Gilead to Machir, son of Manasseh, and he lived there. **32:41** Now Jair son of Manasseh went and captured their small towns and named them Havvoth Jair. **32:42** Then Nobah went and captured Kenath and its villages and called it Nobah after his own name.

Wanderings from Egypt to Sinai

33:1 These are the journeys of the Israelites, who went out of the land of Egypt by their divisions under the authority of Moses and Aaron. **33:2** Moses recorded their departures according to their journeys, by the commandment of the LORD; now these are their journeys according to their departures. **33:3** They departed from Rameses in the first month, on the fifteenth day of the first month; on the day after the Passover the Israelites went out defiantly in plain sight of all the Egyptians. **33:4** Now the Egyptians were burying all their firstborn, whom the LORD had killed among them; the LORD also executed judgments on their gods.

33:5 The Israelites traveled from Rameses and camped in Succoth. **33:6** They traveled from Succoth, and camped in Etham, which is on the edge of the wilderness. **33:7** They traveled from Etham, and turned again to Pi-hahiroth, which is before Baal-Zephon; and they camped before Migdal. **33:8** They traveled from Pi-hahiroth, and passed through the middle of the sea into the wilderness, and went three days' journey in the wilderness of Etham, and camped in Marah. **33:9** They traveled from Marah and came to Elim; in Elim there are twelve fountains of water and seventy palm trees, so they camped there.

33:10 They traveled from Elim, and camped by the Red Sea. **33:11** They traveled from the Red Sea and camped in the wilderness of Zin. **33:12** They traveled from the wilderness of Zin and camped in Dophkah. **33:13** And they traveled from Dophkah, and camped in Alush.

33:14 They traveled from Alush and camped at Rephidim, where there was no water for the people to drink. **33:15** They traveled from Rephidim and camped in the wilderness of Sinai.

Wanderings in the Wilderness

33:16 They traveled from the desert of Sinai and camped at Kibroth Hattaavah. **33:17** They traveled from Kibroth Hattaavah and camped at Hazeroth. **33:18** They traveled from Hazeroth and camped in Rithmah. **33:19** They traveled from Rithmah and camped at Rimmon-perez. **33:20** They traveled from Rimmon-perez and camped in Libnah. **33:21** They traveled from Libnah and camped at Rissah. **33:22** They traveled from Rissah and camped in Kehelathah. **33:23** They traveled from Kehelathah and camped at Mount Shepher. **33:24** They traveled from Mount Shepher and camped in Haradah. **33:25** They traveled from Haradah and camped in Makheloth. **33:26** They traveled from Makheloth and camped at Tahath. **33:27** They traveled from Tahath and camped at Terah. **33:28** They traveled from Terah and camped in Mithcah. **33:29** They traveled from Mithcah and camped in Hashmonah. **33:30** They traveled from Hashmonah and camped in Moseroth. **33:31** They traveled from Moseroth and camped in Bene-jaakan. **33:32** They traveled from Bene-jaakan and camped at Hor-haggidgad. **33:33** They traveled from Hor-haggidgad and camped in Jotbathah. **33:34** They traveled from Jotbathah and camped in Abronah. **33:35** They traveled from Abronah and camped at Ezion-geber. **33:36** They traveled from Ezion-geber and camped in the wilderness of Zin, which is Kadesh.

Wanderings from Kadesh to Moab

33:37 They traveled from Kadesh and camped in Mount Hor at the edge of the land of Edom. **33:38** Aaron the priest ascended Mount Hor at the command of the LORD, and he died there in the fortieth year after the Israelites had come out of the land of Egypt on the first day of the fifth month. **33:39** Now Aaron was 123 years old when he died in Mount Hor. **33:40** The king of Arad, the Canaanite king who lived in the south of the land of Canaan, heard about the approach of the Israelites. **33:41** They traveled from Mount Hor and camped in Zalmonah. **33:42** They traveled from Zalmonah and camped in Punon. **33:43** They traveled from Punon and camped in Oboth. **33:44** They traveled from Oboth and camped in Iye-abarim, on the border of Moab. **33:45** They traveled from Iim and camped in Dibon-gad. **33:46** They traveled from Dibon-gad and camped in Almon-diblathaim. **33:47** They traveled from Almon-diblathaim and camped in the mountains of Abarim before Nebo. **33:48** They traveled from the mountains of Abarim and camped in the plains of Moab by the Jordan River across from Jericho. **33:49** They camped by the Jordan, from Beth-jeshimoth as far as Abel-shittim in the plains of Moab.

At the Border of Canaan

33:50 The LORD spoke to Moses in the plains of Moab by the Jordan, across from Jericho. He said: **33:51** "Speak to the Israelites and tell them, 'When you have crossed the Jordan into the land of Canaan, **33:52** you must drive out all the inhabitants of the land before you. Destroy all their carved images, all their molten images, and demolish their high places. **33:53** You must dispossess the inhabitants of the land and live in it, for I have given you the land to possess it. **33:54** You must divide the land by lot for an inheritance among your families. To a larger group you must give a larger inheritance, and to a smaller group you must give a smaller inheritance. Everyone's inheritance must be in the place where his lot falls. You must inherit according to your ancestral tribes. **33:55** But if you do not drive out the inhabitants of the land before you, then those whom you allow to remain will be irritants in your eyes and thorns in your side, and will cause you trouble in the land where you will be living. **33:56** And what I intended to do to them I will do to you."

The Southern Border of the Land

34:1 Then the LORD spoke to Moses: **34:2** "Give these instructions to the Israelites, and tell them: 'When you enter Canaan, the land that has been assigned to you as an inheritance, the land of Canaan with its borders, **34:3** your southern border will extend from the wilderness of Zin along the Edomite border, and your southern border will run eastward to the extremity of the Salt Sea, **34:4** and then the border will turn from the south to the Scorpion Ascent, continue to Zin, and then its direction will be from the south to Kadesh Barnea. Then it will go to Hazar Addar and pass over to Azmon. **34:5** There the border will turn from Azmon to the Brook of Egypt, and then its direction is to the sea.

The Western Border of the Land

34:6 "'And for a western border you will have the Great Sea. This will be your western border.

The Northern Border of the Land

34:7 "'And this will be your northern border: From the Great Sea you will draw a line to Mount Hor; **34:8** from Mount Hor you will draw a line to Lebo Hamath, and the direction of the border will be to Zedad. **34:9** The border will continue to Ziphron, and its direction will be to Hazar Enan. This will be your northern border.

The Eastern Border of the Land

34:10 "'For your eastern border you will draw a line from Hazar Enan to Shepham. **34:11** The border will run down from Shepham to Riblah, on the east side of Ain, and the border will descend and reach the eastern side of the Sea of Chinnereth. **34:12** Then the border will continue down the Jordan River and its direction will be to the Salt Sea. This will be your land by its borders that surround it.'"

34:13 Then Moses commanded the Israelites: "This is the land which you will inherit by lot, which the LORD has commanded to be given to the nine and a half tribes, **34:14** because the tribe of the Reubenites by their families, the tribe of the Gadites by their families, and half of the tribe of Manasseh have received their inheritance. **34:15** The two and a half tribes have received their inheritance on this side of the Jordan, east of Jericho, toward the sunrise."

Appointed Officials

34:16 The LORD said to Moses: **34:17** "These are the names of the men who are to allocate the land to you as an inheritance: Eleazar the priest and Joshua son of Nun. **34:18** You must take one leader from every tribe to assist in allocating the land as an inheritance. **34:19** These are the names of the men: from the tribe of Judah, Caleb son of Jephunneh; **34:20** from the tribe of the Simeonites, Shemuel son of Ammihud; **34:21** from the tribe of Benjamin, Elidad son of Kislon; **34:22** and from the tribe of the Danites, a leader, Bukki son of Jogli. **34:23** From the Josephites, Hanniel son of Ephod, a leader from the tribe of Manasseh; **34:24** from the tribe of the Ephraimites, a leader, Kemuel son of Shiphtan; **34:25** from the tribe of the Zebulunites, a leader, Elizaphan son of Parnach; **34:26** from the tribe of the Issacharites, a leader, Paltiel son of Azzan; **34:27** from the tribe of the Asherites, a leader, Ahihud son of Shelomi; **34:28** and from the tribe of the Naphtalites, a leader, Pedahel son of Ammihud." **34:29** These are the ones whom the LORD commanded to divide up the inheritance among the Israelites in the land of Canaan.

The Levitical Cities

35:1 Then the LORD spoke to Moses in the Moabite plains by the Jordan near Jericho. He said: **35:2** "Instruct the Israelites to give the Levites towns to live in from the inheritance the Israelites will possess. You must also give the Levites grazing land around the towns. **35:3** Thus they will have towns in which to live, and their grazing lands will be for their cattle, for their possessions, and for all their animals. **35:4** The grazing lands around the towns that you will give to the Levites must extend to a distance of 500 yards from the town wall. **35:5** "You must measure from outside the wall of the town on the east 1,000 yards, and on the south side 1,000 yards, and on the west side 1,000 yards, and on the north side 1,000 yards, with the town in the middle. This territory must belong to them as grazing land for the towns. **35:6** Now from these towns that you will give to the Levites you must select six towns of refuge to which a person who has killed someone may flee. And you must give them forty-two other towns. **35:7** "So the total of the towns you will give the Levites is forty-eight. You must give these together with their grazing lands. **35:8** The towns you will give must be from the possession of the Israelites. From the larger tribes you must give more; and from the smaller tribes fewer. Each must contribute some of its own towns to the Levites in proportion to the inheritance allocated to each.

The Cities of Refuge

35:9 Then the LORD spoke to Moses: **35:10** "Speak to the Israelites and tell them, 'When you cross over the Jordan River into the land of Canaan, **35:11** you must then designate some towns as towns of refuge for you, to which a person who has killed someone unintentionally may flee. **35:12** And they must stand as your towns of refuge from the avenger in order that the killer may not die until he has stood trial before the community. **35:13** These towns that you must give shall be your six towns for refuge. **35:14** "You must give three towns on this side of the Jordan, and you must give three towns in the land of Canaan; they must be towns of refuge. **35:15** These six towns will be places of refuge for the Israelites, and for the foreigner, and for the settler among them, so that anyone who kills any person accidentally may flee there.

35:16 "But if he hits someone with an iron tool so that he dies, he is a murderer. The murderer must surely be put to death. **35:17** If he strikes him by throwing a stone large enough that he could die, and he dies, he is a murderer. The murderer must surely be put to death. **35:18** Or if he strikes him with a wooden hand weapon so that he could die, and he dies, he is a murderer. The murderer must surely be put to death. **35:19** The avenger of blood himself must kill the murderer; when he meets him, he must kill him.

35:20 "But if he strikes him out of hatred or throws something at him intentionally so that he dies, **35:21** or with enmity he strikes him with his hand and he dies, the one who struck him must surely be put to death, for he is a murderer. The avenger of blood must kill the murderer when he meets him.

35:22 "But if he strikes him suddenly, without enmity, or throws anything at him unintentionally, **35:23** or with any stone large enough that a man could die, without seeing him, and throws it at him, and he dies, even though he was not his enemy nor sought his harm, **35:24** then the community must judge between the slayer and the avenger of blood according to these decisions. **35:25** The community must deliver the slayer out of the hand of the avenger of blood, and the community must restore him to the town of refuge to which he fled, and he must live there until the death of the high priest, who was anointed with the consecrated oil. **35:26** But if the slayer at any time goes outside the boundary of the town to which he had fled, **35:27** and the avenger of blood finds him outside the borders of the town of refuge, and the avenger of blood kills the slayer, he will not be guilty of blood, **35:28** because the slayer should have stayed in his town of refuge until the death of the high priest. But after the death of the high priest, the slayer may return to the land of his possessions. **35:29** So these things must be a statutory ordinance for you throughout your generations, in all the places where you live.

35:30 "Whoever kills any person, the murderer must be put to death by the testimony of witnesses; but one witness cannot testify against any person to cause him to be put to death. **35:31** Moreover, you must not accept a ransom for the life of a murderer who is guilty of death; he must surely be put to death. **35:32** And you must not accept a ransom for anyone who has fled to a town of refuge, to allow him to return home and live on his own land before the death of the high priest.

35:33 "You must not pollute the land where you live, for blood defiles the land, and the land cannot be cleansed of the blood that is shed there, except by the blood of the person who shed it. **35:34** Therefore do not defile the land that you will inhabit, in which I live, for I the LORD live among the Israelites."

Women and Land Inheritance

36:1 Then the heads of the family groups of the Gileadites, the descendant of Machir, the descendant of Manasseh, who were from the Josephite families, approached and spoke before Moses and the leaders who were the heads of
the Israelite families. **36:2** They said, "The LORD commanded my lord to give the land as an inheritance by lot to the Israelites; and my lord was commanded by the LORD to give the inheritance of our brother Zelophehad to his daughters. **36:3** Now if they should be married to one of the men from another Israelite tribe, their inheritance would be taken from the inheritance of our fathers and added to the inheritance of the tribe into which they marry. As a result, it will be taken from the lot of our inheritance. **36:4** And when the Jubilee of the Israelites is to take place, their inheritance will be added to the inheritance of the tribe into which they marry. So their inheritance will be taken away from the inheritance of our ancestral tribe."

Moses' Decision

36:5 Then Moses gave a ruling to the Israelites by the word of the LORD: "What the tribe of the Josephites is saying is right. **36:6** This is what the LORD has commanded for Zelophehad's daughters: 'Let them marry whomever they think best, only they must marry within the family of their father's tribe. **36:7** In this way the inheritance of the Israelites will not be transferred from tribe to tribe. But every one of the Israelites must retain the ancestral heritage. **36:8** And every daughter who possesses an inheritance from any of the tribes of the Israelites must become the wife of a man from any family in her father's tribe, so that every Israelite may retain the inheritance of his fathers. **36:9** No inheritance may pass from tribe to tribe. But every one of the tribes of the Israelites must retain its inheritance."

36:10 As the LORD had commanded Moses, so the daughters of Zelophehad did. **36:11** For the daughters of Zelophehad – Mahlah, Tirzah, Hoglah, Milcah, and Noah – were married to the sons of their uncles. **36:12** They were married into the families of the Manassehites, the descendants of Joseph, and their inheritance remained in the tribe of their father's family.

36:13 These are the commandments and the decisions that the LORD commanded the Israelites through the authority of Moses, on the plains of Moab by the Jordan River opposite Jericho.

Book 5. Deuteronomy

The Covenant Setting

1:1 This is what Moses said to the assembly of Israel in the Transjordanian wastelands, the arid country opposite Suph, between Paran and Tophel, Laban, Hazeroth, and Di Zahab **1:2** Now it is ordinarily an eleven-day journey from Horeb to Kadesh Barnea by way of Mount Seir. **1:3** However, it was not until the first day of the eleventh month of the fortieth year that Moses addressed the Israelites just as the LORD had instructed him to do. **1:4** This took place after the defeat of King Sihon of the Amorites, whose capital was in Heshbon, and King Og of Bashan, whose capital was in Ashtaroth, specifically in Edrei. **1:5** So it was in the Transjordan, in Moab, that Moses began to deliver these words:

Events at Horeb

1:6 The LORD our God spoke to us at Horeb and said, "You have stayed in the area of this mountain long enough. **1:7** Get up now, resume your journey, heading for the Amorite hill country, to all its areas including the arid country, the highlands, the Shephelah, the Negev, and the coastal plain – all of Canaan and Lebanon as far as the Great River, that is, the Euphrates. **1:8** Look! I have already given the land to you. Go, occupy the territory that I, the LORD, promised to give to your ancestors Abraham, Isaac, and Jacob, and to their descendants." **1:9** I also said to you at that time, "I am no longer able to sustain you by myself. **1:10** The LORD

your God has increased your population to the point that you are now as numerous as the very stars of the sky. **1:11** Indeed, may the LORD, the God of your ancestors, make you a thousand times more numerous than you are now, blessing you just as he said he would! **1:12** But how can I alone bear up under the burden of your hardship and strife? **1:13** Select wise and practical men, those known among your tribes, whom I may appoint as your leaders." **1:14** You replied to me that what I had said to you was good. **1:15** So I chose as your tribal leaders wise and well-known men, placing them over you as administrators of groups of thousands, hundreds, fifties, and tens, and also as other tribal officials. **1:16** I furthermore admonished your judges at that time that they should pay attention to issues among your fellow citizens and judge fairly, whether between one citizen and another or a citizen and a resident foreigner. **1:17** They must not discriminate in judgment, but hear the lowly and the great alike. Nor should they be intimidated by human beings, for judgment belongs to God. If the matter being adjudicated is too difficult for them, they should bring it before me for a hearing.

Instructions at Kadesh Barnea

1:18 So I instructed you at that time regarding everything you should do. **1:19** Then we left Horeb and passed through all that immense, forbidding wilderness that you saw on the way to the Amorite hill country as the LORD our God had commanded us to do, finally arriving at Kadesh Barnea. **1:20** Then I said to you, "You have come to the Amorite hill country which the
LORD our God is about to give us. **1:21** Look, he has placed the land in front of you! Go up, take possession of it, just as the LORD, the God of your ancestors, said to do. Do not be afraid or discouraged!" **1:22** So all of you approached me and said, "Let's send some men ahead of us to scout out the land and bring us back word as to how we should attack it and what the cities are like there." **1:23** I thought this was a good idea, so I sent twelve men from among you, one from each tribe. **1:24** They left and went up to the hill country, coming to the Eshcol Valley, which they scouted out. **1:25** Then they took some of the produce of the land and carried it back down to us. They also brought a report to us, saying, "The land that the LORD our God is about to give us is good."

Disobedience at Kadesh Barnea

1:26 You were not willing to go up, however, but instead rebelled against the LORD your God. **1:27** You complained among yourselves privately and said, "Because the LORD hates us he brought us from Egypt to deliver us over to the Amorites so they could destroy us! **1:28** What is going to happen to us? Our brothers have drained away our courage by describing people who are more numerous and taller than we are, and great cities whose defenses appear to be as high as heaven itself! Moreover, they said they saw Anakites there." **1:29** So I responded to you, "Do not be terrified of them! **1:30** The LORD your God is about to go ahead of you; he will fight for you, just as you saw him do in Egypt **1:31** and in the desert, where you saw him carrying you along like a man carries his son. This he did everywhere you went until you came to this very place." **1:32** However, through all this you did not have confidence in the LORD your God, **1:33** the one who was constantly going before you to find places for you to set up camp. He appeared by fire at night and cloud by day, to show you the way you ought to go.

Judgment at Kadesh Barnea

1:34 When the LORD heard you, he became angry and made this vow: **1:35** "Not a single person of this evil generation will see the good land that I promised to give to your ancestors! **1:36** The exception is Caleb son of Jephunneh; he will see it and I will give him and his descendants the territory on which he has walked, because he has wholeheartedly followed me." **1:37** As for me, the LORD was also angry with me on your account. He said, "You also will not be able to go there. **1:38** However, Joshua son of Nun, your assistant, will go. Encourage him, because he will enable Israel to inherit the land. **1:39** Also, your infants, who you thought would die on the way, and your children, who as yet do not know good from bad, will go there; I will give them the land and they will possess it. **1:40** But as for you, turn back and head for the desert by the way to the Red Sea."

Unsuccessful Conquest of Canaan

1:41 Then you responded to me and admitted, "We have sinned against the LORD. We will now go up and fight as the LORD our God has told us to do." So you each put on your battle gear and prepared to go up to the hill country. **1:42** But the LORD told me: "Tell them this: 'Do not go up and fight, because I will not be with you and you will be defeated by your enemies.'" **1:43** I spoke to you, but you did not listen. Instead you rebelled against the LORD and recklessly went up to the hill country. **1:44** The Amorite inhabitants of that area confronted you and chased you like a swarm of bees, striking you down from Seir as far as Hormah. **1:45** Then you came back and wept before the LORD, but he paid no attention to you whatsoever. **1:46** Therefore, you remained at Kadesh for a long time – indeed, for the full time.

The Journey from Kadesh Barnea to Moab

2:1 Then we turned and set out toward the desert land on the way to the Red Sea just as the LORD told me to do, detouring around Mount Seir for a long time. **2:2** At this point the LORD said to me, **2:3** "You have circled around this mountain long enough; now turn north. **2:4** Instruct these people as follows: 'You are about to cross the border of your relatives the descendants of Esau, who inhabit Seir. They will be afraid of you, so watch yourselves carefully. **2:5** Do not be hostile toward them, because I am not giving you any of their land, not even a footprint, for I have given Mount Seir as an inheritance for Esau. **2:6** You may purchase food to eat and water to drink from them. **2:7** All along the way I, the LORD your God, have blessed your every effort. I have been attentive to your travels through this great wasteland. These forty years I have been with you; you have lacked for nothing.'"

2:8 So we turned away from our relatives the descendants of Esau, the inhabitants of Seir, turning from the desert route, from Elat and Ezion Geber, and traveling the way of the Moab wastelands. **2:9** Then the LORD said to me, "Do not harass Moab and provoke them to war, for I will not give you any of their land as your territory. This is because I have given Ar to the descendants of Lot as their possession. **2:10** (The Emites used to live there, a people as powerful, numerous, and tall as the Anakites. **2:11** These people, as well as the Anakites, are also considered Rephaites; the Moabites call them Emites. **2:12** Previously the Horites lived in Seir but the descendants of Esau dispossessed and destroyed them and settled in their place, just as Israel did to the land it came to possess, the land the LORD gave them.) **2:13** Now, get up and cross the Wadi Zered." So we did so. **2:14** Now the length of time it took for us to go from Kadesh Barnea to the crossing of Wadi Zered was thirty-eight years, time for all the military men of that generation to die, just as the LORD had vowed to them. **2:15** Indeed, it was the very hand of the LORD that eliminated them from within the camp until they were all gone.

Instructions Concerning Ammon

2:16 So it was that after all the military men had been eliminated from the community, **2:17** the LORD said to me, **2:18** "Today you are going to cross the border of Moab, that is, of Ar. **2:19** But when you come close to the Ammonites, do not harass or provoke them because I am not giving you any of the Ammonites' land as your possession; I have already given it to Lot's descendants as their possession.

2:20 (That also is considered to be a land of the Rephaites. The Rephaites lived there originally; the Ammonites call them Zamzummites. **2:21** They are a people as powerful, numerous, and tall as the Anakites. But the LORD destroyed the Rephaites in advance of the Ammonites, so they dispossessed them and settled down in their place. **2:22** This is exactly what he did for the descendants of Esau who lived in Seir when he destroyed the Horites before them so that they could dispossess them and settle in their area to this very day. **2:23** As for the Avvites who lived in settlements as far west as Gaza, Caphtorites who came from Crete destroyed them and settled down in their place.)

2:24 Get up, make your way across Wadi Arnon. Look! I have already delivered over to you Sihon the Amorite, king of Heshbon, and his land. Go ahead! Take it! Engage him in war! **2:25** This very day I will begin to fill all the people of the earth with dread and to terrify them when they hear about you. They will shiver and shake in anticipation of your approach."

Defeat of Sihon, King of Heshbon

2:26 Then I sent messengers from the Kedemoth Desert to King Sihon of Heshbon with an offer of peace: **2:27** "Let me pass through your land; I will keep strictly to the roadway. I will not turn aside to the right or the left. **2:28** Sell me food for cash so that I can eat and sell me water to drink. Just allow me to go through on foot, **2:29** just as the descendants of Esau who live at Seir and the Moabites who live in Ar did for me, until I cross the Jordan to the land the LORD our God is giving us." **2:30** But King Sihon of Heshbon was unwilling to allow us to pass near him because the LORD our God had made him obstinate and stubborn so that he might deliver him over to you this very day. **2:31** The LORD said to me, "Look! I have already begun to give over Sihon and his land to you. Start right now to take his land as your possession." **2:32** When Sihon and all his troops emerged to encounter us in battle at Jahaz, **2:33** the LORD our God delivered him over to us and we struck him down, along with his sons and everyone else. **2:34** At that time we seized all his cities and put every one of them under divine judgment, including even the women and children; we left no survivors. **2:35** We kept only the livestock and plunder from the cities for ourselves. **2:36** From Aroer, which is at the edge of Wadi Arnon (it is the city in the wadi), all the way to Gilead there was not a town able to resist us – the LORD our God gave them all to us. **2:37** However, you did not approach the land of the Ammonites, the Wadi Jabbok, the cities of the hill country, or any place else forbidden by the LORD our God.

Defeat of King Og of Bashan

3:1 Next we set out on the route to Bashan, but King Og of Bashan and his whole army came out to meet us in battle at Edrei. **3:2** The LORD, however, said to me, "Don't be afraid of him because I have already given him, his whole army, and his land to you. You will do to him exactly what you did to King Sihon of the Amorites who lived in Heshbon." **3:3** So the LORD our God did indeed give over to us King Og of Bashan and his whole army and we struck them down until not a single survivor was left. **3:4** We captured all his cities at that time – there was not a town

we did not take from them – sixty cities, all the region of Argob, the dominion of Og in Bashan. **3:5** All of these cities were fortified by high walls, gates, and locking bars; in addition there were a great many open villages. **3:6** We put all of these under divine judgment just as we had done to King Sihon of Heshbon – every occupied city, including women and children. **3:7** But all the livestock and plunder from the cities we kept for ourselves. **3:8** So at that time we took the land of the two Amorite kings in the Transjordan from Wadi Arnon to Mount Hermon **3:9** (the Sidonians call Hermon Sirion and the Amorites call it Senir), **3:10** all the cities of the plateau, all of Gilead and Bashan as far as Salecah and Edrei, cities of the kingdom of Og in Bashan. **3:11** Only King Og of Bashan was left of the remaining Rephaites. (It is noteworthy that his sarcophagus was made of iron. Does it not, indeed, still remain in Rabbath of the Ammonites? It is thirteen and a half feet long and six feet wide according to standard measure.)

Distribution of the Transjordanian Allotments

3:12 This is the land we brought under our control at that time: The territory extending from Aroer by the Wadi Arnon and half the Gilead hill country with its cities I gave to the Reubenites and Gadites. **3:13** The rest of Gilead and all of Bashan, the kingdom of Og, I gave to half the tribe of Manasseh. (All the region of Argob, that is, all Bashan, is called the land of Rephaim. **3:14** Jair, son of Manasseh, took all the Argob region as far as the border with the Geshurites and Maacathites (namely Bashan) and called it by his name, Havvoth-Jair, which it retains to this very day.) **3:15** I gave Gilead to Machir. **3:16** To the Reubenites and Gadites I allocated the territory extending from Gilead as far as Wadi Arnon (the exact middle of the wadi was a boundary) all the way to the Wadi Jabbok, the Ammonite border. **3:17** The Arabah and the Jordan River were also a border, from the sea of Chinnereth to the sea of the Arabah (that is, the Salt Sea), beneath the watershed of Pisgah to the east.

Instructions to the Transjordanian Tribes

3:18 At that time I instructed you as follows: "The LORD your God has given you this land for your possession. You warriors are to cross over before your fellow Israelites equipped for battle. **3:19** But your wives, children, and livestock (of which I know you have many) may remain in the cities I have given you. **3:20** You must fight until the LORD gives your countrymen victory as he did you and they take possession of the land that the LORD your God is giving them on the other side of the Jordan River. Then each of you may return to his own territory that I have given you." **3:21** I also commanded Joshua at the same time, "You have seen everything the LORD your God did to these two kings; he will do the same to all the kingdoms where you are going. **3:22** Do not be afraid of them, for the LORD your God will personally fight for you."

Denial to Moses of the Promised Land

3:23 Moreover, at that time I pleaded with the LORD, **3:24** "O, Lord GOD, you have begun to show me your greatness and strength. (What god in heaven or earth can rival your works and mighty deeds?) **3:25** Let me please cross over to see the good land on the other side of the Jordan River – this good hill country and the Lebanon!" **3:26** But the LORD was angry at me because of you and would not listen to me. Instead, he said to me, "Enough of that! Do not speak to me anymore about this matter. **3:27** Go up to the top of Pisgah and take a good look to the west, north, south, and east, for you will not be allowed to cross the Jordan. **3:28** Commission Joshua, and encourage and strengthen him, because he will lead these people over and will enable them to inherit the land you will see." **3:29** So we settled down in the valley opposite Beth Peor.

The Privileges of the Covenant

4:1 Now, Israel, pay attention to the statutes and ordinances I am about to teach you, so that you might live and go on to enter and take possession of the land that the LORD, the God of your ancestors, is giving you. **4:2** Do not add a thing to what I command you nor subtract from it, so that you may keep the commandments of the LORD your God that I am delivering to you. **4:3** You have witnessed what the LORD did at Baal Peor, how he eradicated from your midst everyone who followed Baal Peor. **4:4** But you who remained faithful to the LORD your God are still alive to this very day, every one of you. **4:5** Look! I have taught you statutes and ordinances just as the LORD my God told me to do, so that you might carry them out in the land you are about to enter and possess. **4:6** So be sure to do them, because this will testify of your wise understanding to the people who will learn of all these statutes and say, "Indeed, this great nation is a very wise people." **4:7** In fact, what other great nation has a god so near to them like the LORD our God whenever we call on him? **4:8** And what other great nation has statutes and ordinances as just as this whole law that I am about to share with you today?

Reminder of the Horeb Covenant

4:9 Again, however, pay very careful attention, lest you forget the things you have seen and disregard them for the rest of your life; instead teach them to your children and grandchildren. **4:10** You stood before the LORD your God at Horeb and he said to me, "Assemble the people before me so that I can tell them my commands. Then they will learn to revere me all the days they live in the land, and they will instruct their children." **4:11** You approached and stood at the foot of the mountain, a mountain ablaze to the sky above it and yet dark with a thick cloud. **4:12** Then the LORD spoke to you from the middle of the fire; you heard speech but you could not see anything – only a voice was heard. **4:13** And he revealed to you the covenant he has commanded you to keep, the ten commandments, writing them on two stone tablets. **4:14** Moreover, at that same time the LORD commanded me to teach you statutes and ordinances for you to keep in the land which you are about to enter and possess.

The Nature of Israel's God

4:15 Be very careful, then, because you saw no form at the time the LORD spoke to you at Horeb from the middle of the fire. **4:16** I say this so you will not corrupt yourselves by making an image in the form of any kind of figure. This includes the likeness of a human male or female, **4:17** any kind of land animal, any bird that flies in the sky, **4:18** anything that crawls on the ground, or any fish in the deep waters of the earth. **4:19** When you look up to the sky and see the sun, moon, and stars – the whole heavenly creation – you must not be seduced to worship and serve them, for the LORD your God has assigned them to all the people of the world. **4:20** You, however, the LORD has selected and brought from Egypt, that iron-smelting furnace, to be his special people as you are today. **4:21** But the LORD became angry with me because of you and vowed that I would never cross the Jordan nor enter the good land that he is about to give you. **4:22** So I must die here in this land; I will not cross the Jordan. But you are going over and will possess that good land. **4:23** Be on guard so that you do not forget the covenant of the LORD your God that he has made with you, and that you do not make an image of any kind, just as he has forbidden you. **4:24** For the LORD your God is a consuming fire; he is a jealous God.

Threat and Blessing following Covenant Disobedience

4:25 After you have produced children and grandchildren and have been in the land a long time, if you become corrupt and make an image of any kind and do other evil things before the LORD your God that enrage him, **4:26** I invoke heaven and earth as witnesses against you today that you will surely and swiftly be removed from the very land you are about to cross the Jordan to possess. You will not last long there because you will surely be annihilated. **4:27** Then the LORD will scatter you among the peoples and there will be very few of you among the nations where the LORD will drive you. **4:28** There you will worship gods made by human hands – wood and stone that can neither see, hear, eat, nor smell. **4:29** But if you seek the LORD your God from there, you will find him, if, indeed, you seek him with all your heart and soul. **4:30** In your distress when all these things happen to you in the latter days, if you return to the LORD your God and obey him **4:31** (for he is a merciful God), he will not let you down or destroy you, for he cannot forget the covenant with your ancestors that he confirmed by oath to them.

The Uniqueness of Israel's God

4:32 Indeed, ask about the distant past, starting from the day God created humankind on the earth, and ask from one end of heaven to the other, whether there has ever been such a great thing as this, or even a rumor of it. **4:33** Have a people ever heard the voice of God speaking from the middle of fire, as you yourselves have, and lived to tell about it? **4:34** Or has God ever before tried to deliver a nation from the middle of another nation, accompanied by judgments, signs, wonders, war, strength, power, and other very terrifying things like the LORD your God did for you in Egypt before your very eyes? **4:35** You have been taught that the LORD alone is God – there is no other besides him. **4:36** From heaven he spoke to you in order to teach you, and on earth he showed you his great fire from which you also heard his words. **4:37** Moreover, because he loved your ancestors, he chose their descendants who followed them and personally brought you out of Egypt with his great power **4:38** to dispossess nations greater and stronger than you and brought you here this day to give you their land as your property. **4:39** Today realize and carefully consider that the LORD is God in heaven above and on earth below – there is no other! **4:40** Keep his statutes and commandments that I am setting forth today so that it may go well with you and your descendants and that you may enjoy longevity in the land that the LORD your God is about to give you as a permanent possession.

The Narrative Concerning Cities of Refuge

4:41 Then Moses selected three cities in the Transjordan, toward the east. **4:42** Anyone who accidentally killed someone without hating him at the time of the accident could flee to one of those cities and be safe. **4:43** These cities are Bezer, in the desert plateau, for the Reubenites; Ramoth in Gilead for the Gadites; and Golan in Bashan for the Manassehites.

The Setting and Introduction of the Covenant

4:44 This is the law that Moses set before the Israelites. **4:45** These are the stipulations, statutes, and ordinances that Moses spoke to the Israelites after he had brought them out of Egypt, **4:46** in the Transjordan, in the valley opposite Beth Peor, in the land of King Sihon of the Amorites, who lived in Heshbon. (It is he whom Moses and the Israelites attacked after they came out of Egypt. **4:47** They possessed his land and that of King Og of Bashan – both of whom were Amorite kings in the Transjordan, to the east. **4:48** Their territory extended from Aroer at the edge of the Arnon valley as far as Mount Siyon – that is, Hermon – **4:49** including all the Arabah of the Transjordan in the east to the sea of the Arabah, beneath the watershed of Pisgah.)

The Opening Exhortation

5:1 Then Moses called all the people of Israel together and said to them: "Listen, Israel, to the statutes and ordinances that I am about to deliver to you today; learn them and be careful to keep them! **5:2** The LORD our God made a covenant with us at Horeb. **5:3** He did not make this covenant with our ancestors but with us, we who are here today, all of us living now. **5:4** The LORD spoke face to face with you at the mountain, from the middle of the fire. **5:5** (I was standing between the LORD and you at that time to reveal to you the message of the LORD, because you were afraid of the fire and would not go up the mountain.) He said:

The Ten Commandments

5:6 "I am the LORD your God, he who brought you from the land of Egypt, from the place of slavery. **5:7** You must not have any other gods besides me. **5:8** You must not

make for yourself an image of anything in heaven above, on earth below, or in the waters beneath. **5:9** You must not worship or serve them, for I, the LORD your God, am a jealous God. I punish the sons, grandsons, and great-grandsons for the sin of the fathers who reject me, **5:10** but I show covenant faithfulness to the thousands who choose me and keep my commandments. **5:11** You must not make use of the name of the LORD your God for worthless purposes, for the LORD will not exonerate anyone who abuses his name that way. **5:12** Be careful to observe the Sabbath day just as the LORD your God has commanded you. **5:13** You are to work and do all your tasks in six days, **5:14** but the seventh day is the Sabbath of the LORD your God. On that day you must not do any work, you, your son, your daughter, your male slave, your female slave, your ox, your donkey, any other animal, or the foreigner who lives with you, so that your male and female slaves, like yourself, may have rest. **5:15** Recall that you were slaves in the land of Egypt and that the LORD your God brought you out of there by strength and power. That is why the LORD your God has commanded you to observe the Sabbath day. **5:16** Honor your father and your mother just as the LORD your God has commanded you to do, so that your days may be extended and that it may go well with you in the land that he is about to give you. **5:17** You must not murder. **5:18** You must not commit adultery. **5:19** You must not steal. **5:20** You must not offer false testimony against another. **5:21** You must not desire another man's wife, nor should you crave his house, his field, his male and female servants, his ox, his donkey, or anything else he owns."

The Narrative of the Sinai Revelation and Israel's Response

5:22 The LORD said these things to your entire assembly at the mountain from the middle of the fire, the cloud, and the darkness with a loud voice, and that was all he said. Then he inscribed the words on two stone tablets and gave them to me. **5:23** Then, when you heard the voice from the midst of the darkness while the mountain was ablaze, all your tribal leaders and elders approached me. **5:24** You said, "The LORD our God has shown us his great glory and we have heard him speak from the middle of the fire. It is now clear to us that God can speak to human beings and they can keep on living. **5:25** But now, why should we die, because this intense fire will consume us! If we keep hearing the voice of the LORD our God we will die! **5:26** Who is there from the entire human race who has heard the voice of the living God speaking from the middle of the fire as we have, and has lived? **5:27** You go near so that you can hear everything the LORD our God is saying and then you can tell us whatever he says to you; then we will pay attention and do it." **5:28** When the LORD heard you speaking to me, he said to me, "I have heard what these people have said to you – they have spoken well. **5:29** If only it would really be their desire to fear me and obey all my commandments in the future, so that it may go well with them and their descendants forever. **5:30** Go and tell them, 'Return to your tents!' **5:31** But as for you, remain here with me so I can declare to you all the commandments, statutes, and ordinances that you are to teach them, so that they can carry them out in the land I am

about to give them." **5:32** Be careful, therefore, to do exactly what the LORD your God has commanded you; do not turn right or left! **5:33** Walk just as he has commanded you so that you may live, that it may go well with you, and that you may live long in the land you are going to possess.

Exhortation to Keep the Covenant Principles

6:1 Now these are the commandments, statutes, and ordinances that the LORD your God instructed me to teach you so that you may carry them out in the land where you are headed **6:2** and that you may so revere the LORD your God that you will keep all his statutes and commandments that I am giving you – you, your children, and your grandchildren – all your lives, to prolong your days. **6:3** Pay attention, Israel, and be careful to do this so that it may go well with you and that you may increase greatly in number – as the LORD, God of your ancestors, said to you, you will have a land flowing with milk and honey.

The Essence of the Covenant Principles

6:4 Listen, Israel: The LORD is our God, the LORD is one! **6:5** You must love the LORD your God with your whole mind, your whole being, and all your strength.

Exhortation to Teach the Covenant Principles

6:6 These words I am commanding you today must be kept in mind, **6:7** and you must teach them to your children and speak of them as you sit in your house, as you walk along the road, as you lie down, and as you get up. **6:8** You should tie them as a reminder on your forearm and fasten them as symbols on your forehead. **6:9** Inscribe them on the doorframes of your houses and gates.

Exhortation to Worship the LORD Exclusively

6:10 Then when the LORD your God brings you to the land he promised your ancestors Abraham, Isaac, and Jacob to give you – a land with large, fine cities you did not build, **6:11** houses filled with choice things you did not accumulate, hewn out cisterns you did not dig, and vineyards and olive groves you did not plant – and you eat your fill, **6:12** be careful not to forget the LORD who brought you out of Egypt, that place of slavery. **6:13** You must revere the LORD your God, serve him, and take oaths using only his name. **6:14** You must not go after other gods, those of the surrounding peoples, **6:15** for the LORD your God, who is present among you, is a jealous God and his anger will erupt against you and remove you from the land.

Exhortation to Obey the LORD Exclusively

6:16 You must not put the LORD your God to the test as you did at Massah. **6:17** Keep his commandments very carefully, as well as the stipulations and statutes he commanded you to observe. **6:18** Do whatever is proper and good before the LORD so that it may go well with you and that you may enter and occupy the good land that he promised your ancestors, **6:19** and that you may drive out all your enemies just as the LORD said.

Exhortation to Remember the Past

6:20 When your children ask you later on, "What are the stipulations, statutes, and ordinances that the LORD our God commanded you?" **6:21** you must say to them, "We were Pharaoh's slaves in Egypt, but the LORD brought us out of Egypt in a powerful way. **6:22** And he brought signs and great, devastating wonders on Egypt, on Pharaoh, and on his whole family before our very eyes. **6:23** He delivered us from there so that he could give us the land he had promised our ancestors. **6:24** The LORD commanded us to obey all these statutes and to revere him so that it may always go well for us and he may preserve us, as he has to this day. **6:25** We will be innocent if we carefully keep all these commandments before the LORD our God, just as he demands."

The Dispossession of Nonvassals

7:1 When the LORD your God brings you to the land that you are going to occupy and forces out many nations before you – Hittites, Girgashites, Amorites, Canaanites, Perizzites, Hivites, and Jebusites, seven nations more numerous and powerful than you – **7:2** and he delivers them over to you and you attack them, you must utterly annihilate them. Make no treaty with them and show them no mercy! **7:3** You must not intermarry with them. Do not give your daughters to their sons or take their daughters for your sons, **7:4** for they will turn your sons away from me to worship other gods. Then the anger of the LORD will erupt against you and he will quickly destroy you. **7:5** Instead, this is what you must do to them: You must tear down their altars, shatter their sacred pillars, cut down their sacred Asherah poles, and burn up their idols. **7:6** For you are a people holy to the LORD your God. He has chosen you to be his people, prized above all others on the face of the earth.

The Basis of Israel's Election

7:7 It is not because you were more numerous than all the other peoples that the LORD favored and chose you – for in fact you were the least numerous of all peoples. **7:8** Rather it is because of his love for you and his faithfulness to the promise he solemnly vowed to your ancestors that the LORD brought you out with great power, redeeming you from the place of slavery, from the power of Pharaoh king of Egypt. **7:9** So realize that the LORD your God is the true God, the faithful God who keeps covenant faithfully with those who love him and keep his commandments, to a thousand generations, **7:10** but who pays back those who hate him as they deserve and destroys them. He will not ignore those who hate him but will repay them as they deserve! **7:11** So keep the commandments, statutes, and ordinances that I today am commanding you to do.

Promises of Good for Covenant Obedience

7:12 If you obey these ordinances and are careful to do them, the LORD your God will faithfully keep covenant with you as he promised your ancestors. **7:13** He will love and bless you, and make you numerous. He will bless you with many children, with the produce of your soil, your grain, your new wine, your oil, the offspring of your oxen, and the young of your flocks in the land which he promised your ancestors to give you. **7:14** You will be blessed beyond all peoples; there will be no barrenness among you or your livestock. **7:15** The LORD will protect you from all sickness, and you will not experience any of the terrible diseases that you knew in Egypt; instead he will inflict them on all those who hate you.

Exhortation to Destroy Canaanite Paganism

7:16 You must destroy all the people whom the LORD your God is about to deliver over to you; you must not pity them or worship their gods, for that will be a snare to you. **7:17** If you think, "These nations are more numerous than I – how can I dispossess them?" **7:18** you must not fear them. You must carefully recall what the LORD your God did to Pharaoh and all Egypt, **7:19** the great judgments you saw, the signs and wonders,

the strength and power by which he brought you out – thus the LORD your God will do to all the people you fear. **7:20** Furthermore, the LORD your God will release hornets among them until the very last ones who hide from you perish. **7:21** You must not tremble in their presence, for the LORD your God, who is present among you, is a great and awesome God. **7:22** He, the God who leads you, will expel the nations little by little. You will not be allowed to destroy them all at once lest the wild animals overrun you. **7:23** The LORD your God will give them over to you; he will throw them into a great panic until they are destroyed. **7:24** He will hand over their kings to you and you will erase their very names from memory. Nobody will be able to resist you until you destroy them. **7:25** You must burn the images of their gods, but do not covet the silver and gold that covers them so much that you take it for yourself and thus become ensnared by it; for it is abhorrent to the LORD your God. **7:26** You must not bring any abhorrent thing into your house and thereby become an object of divine wrath along with it. You must absolutely detest and abhor it, for it is an object of divine wrath.

The LORD's Provision in the Desert

8:1 You must keep carefully all these commandments I am giving you today so that you may live, increase in number, and go in and occupy the land that the LORD promised to your ancestors. **8:2** Remember the whole way by which he has brought you these forty years through the desert so that he might, by humbling you, test you to see if you have it within you to keep his commandments or not. **8:3** So he humbled you by making you hungry and then feeding you with unfamiliar manna. He did this to teach you that humankind cannot live by bread alone, but also by everything that comes from the LORD's mouth. **8:4** Your clothing did not wear out nor did your feet swell all these forty years. **8:5** Be keenly aware that just as a parent disciplines his child, the LORD your God disciplines you. **8:6** So you must keep his commandments, live according to his standards, and revere him. **8:7** For the LORD your God is bringing you to a good land, a land of brooks, springs, and fountains flowing forth in valleys and hills, **8:8** a land of wheat, barley, vines, fig trees, and pomegranates, of olive trees and honey, **8:9** a land where you may eat food in plenty and find no lack of anything, a land whose stones are iron and from whose hills you can mine copper. **8:10** You will eat your fill and then praise the LORD your God because of the good land he has given you.

Exhortation to Remember That Blessing Comes from God

8:11 Be sure you do not forget the LORD your God by not keeping his commandments, ordinances, and statutes that I am giving you today. **8:12** When you eat your fill, when you build and occupy good houses, **8:13** when your cattle and flocks increase, when you have plenty of silver and gold, and when you have abundance of everything, **8:14** be sure you do not feel self-important and forget the LORD your God who brought you from the land of Egypt, the place of slavery, **8:15** and who brought you through the great, fearful desert of venomous serpents and scorpions, an arid place with no water. He made water flow from a flint rock and **8:16** fed you in the desert with manna (which your ancestors had never before known) so that he might by humbling you test you and eventually bring good to you. **8:17** Be careful not to say, "My own ability and skill have gotten me this wealth." **8:18** You must remember the LORD your God, for he is the one who gives ability to get wealth; if you do this he will confirm his covenant that he made by oath to your ancestors, even as he has to this day. **8:19** Now if you forget the LORD your God at all and follow other gods, worshiping and prostrating yourselves before them, I testify to you today that you will surely be annihilated. **8:20** Just like the nations the LORD is about to destroy from your sight, so he will do to you because you would not obey him.

Theological Justification of the Conquest

9:1 Listen, Israel: Today you are about to cross the Jordan so you can dispossess the nations there, people greater and stronger than you who live in large cities with extremely high fortifications. **9:2** They include the Anakites, a numerous and tall people whom you know about and of whom it is said, "Who is able to resist the Anakites?" **9:3** Understand today that the LORD your God who goes before you is a devouring fire; he will defeat and subdue them before you. You will dispossess and destroy them quickly just as he has told you. **9:4** Do not think to yourself after the LORD your God has driven them out before you, "Because of my own righteousness the LORD has brought me here to possess this land." It is because of the wickedness of these nations that the LORD is driving them out ahead of you. **9:5** It is not because of your righteousness, or even your inner uprightness, that you have come here to possess their land. Instead, because of the wickedness of these nations the LORD your God is driving them out ahead of you in order to confirm the promise he made on oath to your ancestors, to Abraham, Isaac, and Jacob. **9:6** Understand, therefore, that it is not because of your righteousness that the LORD your God is about to give you this good land as a possession, for you are a stubborn people!

The History of Israel's Stubbornness

9:7 Remember – don't ever forget – how you provoked the LORD your God in the desert; from the time you left the land of Egypt until you came to this place you were constantly rebelling against him. **9:8** At Horeb you provoked him and he was angry enough with you to destroy you. **9:9**

When I went up the mountain to receive the stone tablets, the tablets of the covenant that the LORD made with you, I remained there forty days and nights, eating and drinking nothing. **9:10** The LORD gave me the two stone tablets, written by the very finger of God, and on them was everything he said to you at the mountain from the midst of the fire at the time of that assembly. **9:11** Now at the end of the forty days and nights the LORD presented me with the two stone tablets, the tablets of the covenant. **9:12** And he said to me, "Get up, go down at once from here because your people whom you brought out of Egypt have sinned! They have quickly turned from the way I commanded them and have made for themselves a cast metal image." **9:13** Moreover, he said to me, "I have taken note of these people; they are a stubborn lot! **9:14** Stand aside and I will destroy them, obliterating their very name from memory, and I will make you into a stronger and more numerous nation than they are."

9:15 So I turned and went down the mountain while it was blazing with fire; the two tablets of the covenant were in my hands. **9:16** When I looked, you had indeed sinned against the LORD your God and had cast for yourselves a metal calf; you had quickly turned aside from the way he had commanded you! **9:17** I grabbed the two tablets, threw them down, and shattered them before your very eyes. **9:18** Then I again fell down before the LORD for forty days and nights; I ate and drank nothing because of all the sin you had committed, doing such evil before the LORD as to enrage him. **9:19** For I was terrified at the LORD's intense anger that threatened to destroy you. But he listened to me this time as well. **9:20** The LORD was also angry enough at Aaron to kill him, but at that time I prayed for him too. **9:21** As for your sinful thing that you had made, the calf, I took it, melted it down, ground it up until it was as fine as dust, and tossed the dust into the stream that flows down the mountain. **9:22** Moreover, you continued to provoke the LORD at Taberah, Massah, and Kibroth-Hattaavah. **9:23** And when he sent you from Kadesh-Barnea and told you, "Go up and possess the land I have given you," you rebelled against the LORD your God and would neither believe nor obey him. **9:24** You have been rebelling against him from the very first day I knew you!

Moses' Plea on Behalf of the LORD's Reputation

9:25 I lay flat on the ground before the LORD for forty days and nights, for he had said he would destroy you. **9:26** I prayed to him: O, Lord GOD, do not destroy your people, your valued property that you have powerfully redeemed, whom you brought out of Egypt by your strength. **9:27** Remember your servants Abraham, Isaac, and Jacob; ignore the stubbornness, wickedness, and sin of these people. **9:28** Otherwise the people of the land from which you brought us will say, "The LORD was unable to bring them to the land he promised them, and because of his hatred for them he has brought them out to kill them in the desert." **9:29** They are your people, your valued property, whom you brought out with great strength and power.

The Opportunity to Begin Again

10:1 At that same time the LORD said to me, "Carve out for yourself two stone tablets like the first ones and come up the mountain to me; also make for yourself a wooden ark. **10:2** I will write on the tablets the same words that were on the first tablets you broke, and you must put them into the ark." **10:3** So I made an ark of acacia wood and carved out two stone tablets just like the first ones. Then I went up the mountain with the two tablets in my hands. **10:4** The LORD then wrote on the tablets the same words, the ten commandments, which he had spoken to you at the mountain from the middle of the fire at the time of that assembly, and he gave them to me. **10:5** Then I turned, went down the mountain, and placed the tablets into the ark I had made – they are still there, just as the LORD commanded me.

Conclusion of the Historical Resume

10:6 "During those days the Israelites traveled from Beeroth Bene-Yaaqan to Moserah. There Aaron died and was buried, and his son Eleazar became priest in his place. **10:7** From there they traveled to Gudgodah, and from Gudgodah to Jotbathah, a place of flowing streams. **10:8** At that time the LORD set apart the tribe of Levi to carry the ark of the LORD's covenant, to stand before the LORD to serve him, and to formulate blessings in his name, as they do to this very day. **10:9** Therefore Levi has no allotment or inheritance among his brothers; the LORD is his inheritance just as the LORD your God told him. **10:10** As for me, I stayed at the mountain as I did the first time, forty days and nights. The LORD listened to me that time as well and decided not to destroy you. **10:11** Then he said to me, "Get up, set out leading the people so they may go and possess the land I promised to give to their ancestors."

An Exhortation to Love Both God and People

10:12 Now, Israel, what does the LORD your God require of you except to revere him, to obey all his commandments, to love him, to serve him with all your mind and being, **10:13** and to keep the LORD's commandments and statutes that I am giving you today for your own good? **10:14** The heavens – indeed the highest heavens – belong to the LORD your God, as does the earth and everything in it. **10:15** However, only to your ancestors did he show his loving favor, and he chose you, their descendants, from all peoples – as is apparent today. **10:16** Therefore, cleanse your heart and stop being so stubborn! **10:17** For the LORD your God is God of gods and Lord of lords, the great, mighty, and awesome God who is unbiased and takes no bribe, **10:18** who justly treats the orphan and widow, and who loves resident foreigners, giving them food and clothing. **10:19** So you must love the resident foreigner because you were foreigners in the land of Egypt. **10:20** Revere the LORD your God, serve him, be loyal to him and take oaths only in his name. **10:21** He is the one you should praise; he is your God, the one who has done these great and awesome things for you that you have seen. **10:22** When your ancestors went down to Egypt, they numbered only seventy, but now the LORD your God has made you as numerous as the stars of the sky.

Reiteration of the Call to Obedience

11:1 You must love the LORD your God and do what he requires; keep his statutes, ordinances, and commandments at all times. **11:2** Bear in mind today that I am not speaking to your children who have not personally experienced the judgments of the LORD your God, which revealed his greatness, strength, and power. **11:3** They did not see the awesome deeds he performed in the midst of Egypt against Pharaoh king of Egypt and his whole land, **11:4** or what he did to the army of Egypt, including their horses and chariots, when he made the waters of the Red Sea overwhelm them while they were pursuing you and he annihilated them. **11:5** They did not see what he did to you in the desert before you reached this place, **11:6** or what he did to Dathan and Abiram, sons of Eliab the Reubenite, when the earth opened its mouth in the middle of the Israelite camp and swallowed them, their families, their tents, and all the property they brought with them. **11:7** I am speaking to you because you are the ones who saw all the great deeds of the LORD!

The Abundance of the Land of Promise

11:8 Now pay attention to all the commandments I am giving you today, so that you may be strong enough to enter and possess the land where you are headed, **11:9** and that you may enjoy long life in the land the LORD promised to give to your ancestors and their descendants, a land flowing with milk and honey. **11:10** For the land where you are headed is not like the land of Egypt from which you came, a land where you planted seed and which you irrigated by hand like a vegetable garden. **11:11** Instead, the land you are crossing the Jordan to occupy is one of hills and valleys, a land that drinks in water from the rains, **11:12** a land the LORD your God looks after. He is constantly attentive to it from the beginning to the end of the year. **11:13** Now, if you pay close attention to my commandments that I am giving you today and love the LORD your God and serve him with all your mind and being, **11:14** then he promises, "I will send rain for your land in its season, the autumn and the spring rains, so that you may gather in your grain, new wine, and olive oil. **11:15** I will provide pasture for your livestock and you will eat your fill."

Exhortation to Instruction and Obedience

11:16 Make sure you do not turn away to serve and worship other gods! **11:17** Then the anger of the LORD will erupt against you and he will close up the sky so that it does not rain. The land will not yield its produce, and you will soon be removed from the good land that the LORD is about to give you. **11:18** Fix these words of mine into your mind and being, and tie them as a reminder on your hands and let them be symbols on your forehead. **11:19** Teach them to your children and speak of them as you sit in your house, as you walk along the road, as you lie down, and as you get up. **11:20** Inscribe them on the doorframes of your houses and on your gates **11:21** so that your days and those of your descendants may be extended in the land which the LORD promised to give to your ancestors, like the days of heaven itself. **11:22** For if you carefully observe all of these commandments I am giving you and love the LORD your God, live according to his standards, and remain loyal to him, **11:23** then he will drive out all these nations ahead of you, and you will dispossess nations greater and stronger than you. **11:24** Every place you set your foot will be yours; your border will extend from the desert to Lebanon and from the River (that is, the Euphrates) as far as the Mediterranean Sea. **11:25** Nobody will be able to resist you; the LORD your God will spread the fear and terror of you over the whole land on which you walk, just as he promised you.

Anticipation of a Blessing and Cursing Ceremony

11:26 Take note – I am setting before you today a blessing and a curse: **11:27** the blessing if you take to heart the commandments of the LORD your God that I am giving you today, **11:28** and the curse if you pay no attention to his commandments and turn from the way I am setting before you today to pursue other gods you have not known. **11:29** When the LORD your God brings you into the land you are to possess, you must pronounce the blessing on Mount Gerizim and the curse on Mount Ebal. **11:30** Are they not across the Jordan River, toward the west, in the land of the Canaanites who live in the Arabah opposite Gilgal near the oak of Moreh? **11:31** For you are about to cross the Jordan to possess the land the LORD your God is giving you, and you will possess and inhabit it. **11:32** Be certain to keep all the statutes and ordinances that I am presenting to you today.

The Central Sanctuary

12:1 These are the statutes and ordinances you must be careful to obey as long as you live in the land the LORD, the God of your ancestors, has given you to possess. **12:2** You must by all means destroy all the places where the nations you are about to dispossess worship their gods – on the high mountains and hills and under every leafy tree. **12:3** You must tear down their altars, shatter their sacred pillars, burn up their sacred Asherah poles, and cut down the images of their gods; you must eliminate their very memory from that place. **12:4** You must not worship the LORD your God the way they worship. **12:5** But you must seek only the place he chooses from all your tribes to establish his name as his place of residence, and you must go there. **12:6** And there you must take your burnt offerings, your sacrifices, your tithes, the personal offerings you have prepared, your votive offerings, your freewill offerings, and the firstborn of your herds and flocks. **12:7** Both you and your families must feast there before the LORD your God and rejoice in all the output of your labor with which he has blessed you. **12:8** You must not do like we are doing here today, with everyone doing what seems best to him, **12:9** for you have not yet come to the final stop and inheritance the LORD your God is giving you. **12:10** When you do go across the Jordan River and settle in the land he is granting you as an inheritance and you find relief from all the enemies who surround you, you will live in safety. **12:11** Then you must come to the place the LORD your God chooses for his name to reside, bringing everything I am commanding you – your burnt offerings, sacrifices, tithes, the personal offerings you have prepared, and all your choice votive offerings which you devote to him. **12:12** You shall rejoice in the presence of the LORD your God, along with your sons, daughters, male and female servants, and the Levites in your villages (since they have no allotment or inheritance with you). **12:13** Make sure you do not offer burnt offerings in any place you wish, **12:14** for you may do so only in the place the LORD chooses in one of your tribal areas – there you may do everything I am commanding you.

Regulations for Profane Slaughter

12:15 On the other hand, you may slaughter and eat meat as you please when the LORD your God blesses you in all your villages. Both the ritually pure and impure may eat it, whether it is a gazelle or an ibex. **12:16** However, you must not eat blood – pour it out on the ground like water. **12:17** You will not be allowed to eat in your villages your tithe of grain, new wine, olive oil, the firstborn of your herd and flock, any votive offerings you have vowed, or your freewill and personal offerings. **12:18** Only in the presence of the LORD your God may you eat these, in the place he chooses. This applies to you, your son, your daughter, your male and female servants, and the Levites in your villages. In that place you will rejoice before the LORD your God in all the output of your labor. **12:19** Be careful not to overlook the Levites as long as you live in the land.

The Sanctity of Blood

12:20 When the LORD your God extends your borders as he said he would do and you say, "I want to eat meat just as I please," you may do so as you wish. **12:21** If the place he chooses to locate his name is too far for you, you may slaughter any of your herd and flock he has given you just as I have stipulated; you may eat them in your villages just as you wish. **12:22** Like you eat the gazelle or ibex, so you may eat these; the ritually impure and pure alike may eat them. **12:23** However, by no means eat the blood, for the blood is life itself – you must not eat the life with the meat! **12:24** You must not eat it! You must pour it out on the ground like water. **12:25** You must not eat it so that it may go well with you and your children after you; you will be doing what is right in the LORD's sight. **12:26** Only the holy things and votive offerings that belong to you, you must pick up and take to the place the LORD will choose. **12:27** You must offer your burnt offerings, both meat and blood, on the altar of the LORD your God; the blood of your other sacrifices you must pour out on his altar while you eat the meat. **12:28** Pay careful attention to all these things I am commanding you so that it may always go well with you and your children after you when you do what is good and right in the sight of the LORD your God.

The Abomination of Pagan Gods

12:29 When the LORD your God eliminates the nations from the place where you are headed and you dispossess them, you will settle down in their land. **12:30** After they have been destroyed from your presence, be careful not to be ensnared like they are; do not pursue their gods and say, "How do these nations serve their gods? I will do the same." **12:31** You must not worship the LORD your God the way they do! For everything that is abhorrent to him, everything he hates, they have done when worshiping their gods. They even burn up their sons and daughters before their gods!

Idolatry and False Prophets

12:32 (13:1) You must be careful to do everything I am commanding you. Do not add to it or subtract from it! **13:1** Suppose a prophet or one who foretells by dreams should appear among you and show you a sign or wonder, **13:2** and the sign or wonder should come to pass concerning what he said to you, namely, "Let us follow other gods" – gods whom you have not previously known – "and let us serve them." **13:3** You must not listen to the words of that prophet or dreamer, for the LORD your God will be testing you to see if you love him with all your mind and being. **13:4** You must follow the LORD your God and revere only him; and you must observe his commandments, obey him, serve him, and remain loyal to him. **13:5** As for that prophet or dreamer, he must be executed because he encouraged rebellion against the LORD your God who brought you

from the land of Egypt, redeeming you from that place of slavery, and because he has tried to entice you from the way the LORD your God has commanded you to go. In this way you must purge out evil from within.

False Prophets in the Family

13:6 Suppose your own full brother, your son, your daughter, your beloved wife, or your closest friend should seduce you secretly and encourage you to go and serve other gods that neither you nor your ancestors have previously known, **13:7** the gods of the surrounding people (whether near you or far from you, from one end of the earth to the other). **13:8** You must not give in to him or even listen to him; do not feel sympathy for him or spare him or cover up for him. **13:9** Instead, you must kill him without fail! Your own hand must be the first to strike him, and then the hands of the whole community. **13:10** You must stone him to death because he tried to entice you away from the LORD your God, who delivered you from the land of Egypt, that place of slavery. **13:11** Thus all Israel will hear and be afraid; no longer will they continue to do evil like this among you.

Punishment of Community Idolatry

13:12 Suppose you should hear in one of your cities, which the LORD your God is giving you as a place to live, that **13:13** some evil people have departed from among you to entice the inhabitants of their cities, saying, "Let's go and serve other gods" (whom you have not known before). **13:14** You must investigate thoroughly and inquire carefully. If it is indeed true that such a disgraceful thing is being done among you, **13:15** you must by all means slaughter the inhabitants of that city with the sword; annihilate with the sword everyone in it, as well as the livestock. **13:16** You must gather all of its plunder into the middle of the plaza and burn the city and all its plunder as a whole burnt offering to the LORD your God. It will be an abandoned ruin forever – it must never be rebuilt again. **13:17** You must not take for yourself anything that has been placed under judgment. Then the LORD will relent from his intense anger, show you compassion, have mercy on you, and multiply you as he promised your ancestors. **13:18** Thus you must obey the LORD your God, keeping all his commandments that I am giving you today and doing what is right before him.

The Holy and the Profane

14:1 You are children of the LORD your God. Do not cut yourselves or shave your forehead bald for the sake of the dead. **14:2** For you are a people holy to the LORD your God. He has chosen you to be his people, prized above all others on the face of the earth. **14:3** You must not eat any forbidden thing. **14:4** These are the animals you may eat: the ox, the sheep, the goat, **14:5** the ibex, the gazelle, the deer, the wild goat, the antelope, the wild oryx, and the mountain sheep. **14:6** You may eat any animal that has hooves divided into two parts and that chews the cud. **14:7** However, you may not eat the following animals among those that chew the cud or those that have divided hooves: the camel, the hare, and the rock badger. (Although they chew the cud, they do not have divided hooves and are therefore ritually impure to you). **14:8** Also the pig is ritually impure to you; though it has divided hooves, it does not chew the cud. You may not eat their meat or even touch their remains. **14:9** These you may eat from among water creatures: anything with fins and scales you may eat, **14:10** but whatever does not have fins and scales you may not eat; it is ritually impure to you. **14:11** All ritually clean birds you may eat. **14:12** These are the ones you may not eat: the eagle, the vulture, the black vulture, **14:13** the kite, the black kite, the dayyah after its species, **14:14** every raven after its species, **14:15** the ostrich, the owl, the seagull, the falcon after its species, **14:16** the little owl, the long-eared owl, the white owl, **14:17** the jackdaw, the carrion vulture, the cormorant, **14:18** the stork, the heron after its species, the hoopoe, the bat, **14:19** and any winged thing on the ground are impure to you – they may not be eaten. **14:20** You may eat any clean bird. **14:21** You may not eat any corpse, though you may give it to the resident foreigner who is living in your villages and he may eat it, or you may sell it to a foreigner. You are a people holy to the LORD your God. Do not boil a young goat in its mother's milk.

The Offering of Tribute

14:22 You must be certain to tithe all the produce of your seed that comes from the field year after year. **14:23** In the presence of the LORD your God you must eat from the tithe of your grain, your new wine, your olive oil, and the firstborn of your herds and flocks in the place he chooses to locate his name, so that you may learn to revere the LORD your God always. **14:24** When he blesses you, if the place where he chooses to locate his name is distant, **14:25** you may convert the tithe into money, secure the money, and travel to the place the LORD your God chooses for himself. **14:26** Then you may spend the money however you wish for cattle, sheep, wine, beer, or whatever you desire. You and your household may eat there in the presence of the LORD your God and enjoy it. **14:27** As for the Levites in your villages, you must not ignore them, for they have no allotment or inheritance along with you. **14:28** At the end of every three years you must bring all the tithe of your produce, in that very year, and you must store it up in your villages. **14:29** Then the Levites (because they have no allotment or inheritance with you), the resident foreigners, the orphans, and the widows of your villages may come and eat their fill so that the LORD your God may bless you in all the work you do.

Release for Debt Slaves

15:1 At the end of every seven years you must declare a cancellation of debts. **15:2** This is the nature of the cancellation: Every creditor must remit what he has loaned to another person; he must not force payment from his fellow Israelite, for it is to be recognized as "the LORD's cancellation of debts." **15:3** You may exact payment from a foreigner, but whatever your fellow Israelite owes you, you must remit. **15:4** However, there should not be any poor among you, for the LORD will surely bless you in the land that he is giving you as an inheritance, **15:5** if you carefully obey him by keeping all these commandments that I am giving you today. **15:6** For the LORD your God will bless you just as he has promised; you will lend to many nations but will not borrow from any, and you will rule over many nations but they will not rule over you.

The Spirit of Liberality

15:7 If a fellow Israelite from one of your villages in the land that the LORD your God is giving you should be poor, you must not harden your heart or be insensitive to his impoverished condition. **15:8** Instead, you must be sure to open your hand to him and generously lend him whatever he needs. **15:9** Be careful lest you entertain the wicked thought that the seventh year, the year of cancellation of debts, has almost arrived, and your attitude be wrong toward your impoverished fellow Israelite and you do not lend him anything; he will cry out to the LORD against you and you will be regarded as having sinned. **15:10** You must by all means lend to him and not be upset by doing it, for because of this the LORD your God will bless you in all your work and in everything you attempt. **15:11** There will never cease to be some poor people in the land; therefore, I am commanding you to make sure you open your hand to your fellow Israelites who are needy and poor in your land.

Release of Debt Slaves

15:12 If your fellow Hebrew – whether male or female – is sold to you and serves you for six years, then in the seventh year you must let that servant go free. **15:13** If you set them free, you must not send them away empty-handed. **15:14** You must supply them generously from your flock, your threshing floor, and your winepress – as the LORD your God has blessed you, you must give to them. **15:15** Remember that you were a slave in the land of Egypt and the LORD your God redeemed you; therefore, I am commanding you to do this thing today. **15:16** However, if the servant says to you, "I do not want to leave you," because he loves you and your household, since he is well off with you, **15:17** you shall take an awl and pierce a hole through his ear to the door. Then he will become your servant permanently (this applies to your female servant as well). **15:18** You should not consider it difficult to let him go free, for he will have served you for six years, twice the time of a hired worker; the LORD your God will bless you in everything you do.

Giving God the Best

15:19 You must set apart for the LORD your God every firstborn male born to your herds and flocks. You must not work the firstborn of your bulls or shear the firstborn of your flocks. **15:20** You and your household must eat them annually before the LORD your God in the place he chooses. **15:21** If they have any kind of blemish – lameness, blindness, or anything else – you may not offer them as a sacrifice to the LORD your God. **15:22** You may eat it in your villages, whether you are ritually impure or clean, just as you would eat a gazelle or an ibex. **15:23** However, you must not eat its blood; you must pour it out on the ground like water.

The Passover-Unleavened Bread Festival

16:1 Observe the month Abib and keep the Passover to the LORD your God, for in that month he brought you out of Egypt by night. **16:2** You must sacrifice the Passover animal (from the flock or the herd) to the LORD your God in the place where he chooses to locate his name. **16:3** You must not eat any yeast with it; for seven days you must eat bread made without yeast, symbolic of affliction, for you came out of Egypt hurriedly. You must do this so you will remember for the rest of your life the day you came out of the land of Egypt. **16:4** There must not be a scrap of yeast within your land for seven days, nor can any of the meat you sacrifice on the evening of the first day remain until the next morning. **16:5** You may not sacrifice the Passover in just any of your villages that the LORD your God is giving you, **16:6** but you must sacrifice it in the evening in the place where he chooses to locate his name, at sunset, the time of day you came out of Egypt. **16:7** You must cook and eat it in the place the LORD your God chooses; you may return the next morning to your tents. **16:8** You must eat bread made without yeast for six days. The seventh day you are to hold an assembly for the LORD your God; you must not do any work on that day.

The Festival of Weeks

16:9 You must count seven weeks; you must begin to count them from the time you begin to harvest the standing grain. **16:10** Then you are to celebrate the Festival of Weeks before the LORD your God with the voluntary offering that you will bring, in proportion to how he has blessed you. **16:11** You shall rejoice before him – you, your son, your daughter, your male and female slaves, the Levites in your villages, the resident foreigners, the orphans, and the widows among you – in the place where

the LORD chooses to locate his name. **16:12** Furthermore, remember that you were a slave in Egypt, and so be careful to observe these statutes.

The Festival of Temporary Shelters

16:13 You must celebrate the Festival of Temporary Shelters for seven days, at the time of the grain and grape harvest. **16:14** You are to rejoice in your festival, you, your son, your daughter, your male and female slaves, the Levites, the resident foreigners, the orphans, and the widows who are in your villages. **16:15** You are to celebrate the festival seven days before the LORD your God in the place he chooses, for he will bless you in all your productivity and in whatever you do; so you will indeed rejoice! **16:16** Three times a year all your males must appear before the LORD your God in the place he chooses for the Festival of Unleavened Bread, the Festival of Weeks, and the Festival of Temporary Shelters; and they must not appear before him empty-handed. **16:17** Every one of you must give as you are able, according to the blessing of the LORD your God that he has given you.

Provision for Justice

16:18 You must appoint judges and civil servants for each tribe in all your villages that the LORD your God is giving you, and they must judge the people fairly. **16:19** You must not pervert justice or show favor. Do not take a bribe, for bribes blind the eyes of the wise and distort the words of the righteous. **16:20** You must pursue justice alone so that you may live and inherit the land the LORD your God is giving you.

Examples of Legal Cases

16:21 You must not plant any kind of tree as a sacred Asherah pole near the altar of the LORD your God which you build for yourself. **16:22** You must not erect a sacred pillar, a thing the LORD your God detests. **17:1** You must not sacrifice to him a bull or sheep that has a blemish or any other defect, because that is considered offensive to the LORD your God. **17:2** Suppose a man or woman is discovered among you – in one of your villages that the LORD your God is giving you – who sins before the LORD your God and breaks his covenant **17:3** by serving other gods and worshiping them – the sun, moon, or any other heavenly bodies which I have not permitted you to worship. **17:4** When it is reported to you and you hear about it, you must investigate carefully. If it is indeed true that such a disgraceful thing is being done in Israel, **17:5** you must bring to your city gates that man or woman who has done this wicked thing – that very man or woman – and you must stone that person to death. **17:6** At the testimony of two or three witnesses they must be executed. They cannot be put to death on the testimony of only one witness. **17:7** The witnesses must be first to begin the execution, and then all the people are to join in afterward. In this way you will purge evil from among you.

Appeal to a Higher Court

17:8 If a matter is too difficult for you to judge – bloodshed, legal claim, or assault – matters of controversy in your villages – you must leave there and go up to the place the LORD your God chooses. **17:9** You will go to the Levitical priests and the judge in office in those days and seek a solution; they will render a verdict. **17:10** You must then do as they have determined at that place the LORD chooses. Be careful to do just as you are taught. **17:11** You must do what you are instructed, and the verdict they pronounce to you, without fail. Do not deviate right or left from what they tell you. **17:12** The person who pays no attention to the priest currently serving the LORD your God there, or to the verdict – that person must die, so that you may purge evil from Israel. **17:13** Then all the people will hear and be afraid, and not be so presumptuous again.

Provision for Kingship

17:14 When you come to the land the LORD your God is giving you and take it over and live in it and then say, "I will select a king like all the nations surrounding me," **17:15** you must select without fail a king whom the LORD your God chooses. From among your fellow citizens you must appoint a king – you may not designate a foreigner who is not one of your fellow Israelites. **17:16** Moreover, he must not accumulate horses for himself or allow the people to return to Egypt to do so, for the LORD has said you must never again return that way. **17:17** Furthermore, he must not marry many wives lest his affections turn aside, and he must not accumulate much silver and gold. **17:18** When he sits on his royal throne he must make a copy of this

law on a scroll given to him by the Levitical priests. **17:19** It must be with him constantly and he must read it as long as he lives, so that he may learn to revere the LORD his God and observe all the words of this law and these statutes and carry them out. **17:20** Then he will not exalt himself above his fellow citizens or turn from the commandments to the right or left, and he and his descendants will enjoy many years ruling over his kingdom in Israel.

Provision for Priests and Levites

18:1 The Levitical priests – indeed, the entire tribe of Levi – will have no allotment or inheritance with Israel; they may eat the burnt offerings of the LORD and of his inheritance. **18:2** They will have no inheritance in the midst of their fellow Israelites; the LORD alone is their inheritance, just as he had told them. **18:3** This shall be the priests' fair allotment from the people who offer sacrifices, whether bull or sheep – they must give to the priest the shoulder, the jowls, and the stomach. **18:4** You must give them the best of your grain, new wine, and olive oil, as well as the best of your wool when you shear your flocks. **18:5** For the LORD your God has chosen them and their sons from all your tribes to stand and serve in his name permanently. **18:6** Suppose a Levite comes by his own free will from one of your villages, from any part of Israel where he is living, to the place the LORD chooses **18:7** and serves in the name of the LORD his God like his fellow Levites who stand there before the LORD. **18:8** He must eat the same share they do, despite any profits he may gain from the sale of his family's inheritance.

Provision for Prophetism

18:9 When you enter the land the LORD your God is giving you, you must not learn the abhorrent practices of those nations. **18:10** There must never be found among you anyone who sacrifices his son or daughter in the fire, anyone who practices divination, an omen reader, a soothsayer, a sorcerer, **18:11** one who casts spells, one who conjures up spirits, a practitioner of the occult, or a necromancer. **18:12** Whoever does these things is abhorrent to the LORD and because of these detestable things the LORD your God is about to drive them out from before you. **18:13** You must be blameless before the LORD your God. **18:14** Those nations that you are about to dispossess listen to omen readers and diviners, but the LORD your God has not given you permission to do such things.

18:15 The LORD your God will raise up for you a prophet like me from among you – from your fellow Israelites; you must listen to him. **18:16** This accords with what happened at Horeb in the day of the assembly. You asked the LORD your God: "Please do not make us hear the voice of the LORD our God any more or see this great fire any more lest we die." **18:17** The LORD then said to me, "What they have said is good. **18:18** I will raise up a prophet like you for them from among their fellow Israelites. I will put my words in his mouth and he will speak to them whatever I command. **18:19** I will personally hold responsible anyone who then pays no attention to the words that prophet speaks in my name.

18:20 "But if any prophet presumes to speak anything in my name that I have not authorized him to speak, or speaks in the name of other gods, that prophet must die. **18:21** Now if you say to yourselves, 'How can we tell that a message is not from the LORD?' – **18:22** whenever a prophet speaks in my name and the prediction is not fulfilled, then I have not spoken it; the prophet has presumed to speak it, so you need not fear him."

Laws Concerning Manslaughter

19:1 When the LORD your God destroys the nations whose land he is about to give you and you dispossess them and settle in their cities and houses, **19:2** you must set apart for yourselves three cities in the middle of your land that the LORD your God is giving you as a possession. **19:3** You shall build a roadway and divide into thirds the whole extent of your land that the LORD your God is providing as your inheritance; anyone who kills another person should flee to the closest of these cities. **19:4** Now this is the law pertaining to one who flees there in order to live, if he has accidentally killed another without hating him at the time of the accident. **19:5** Suppose he goes with someone else to the forest to cut wood and when he raises the ax to cut the tree, the ax head flies loose from the handle and strikes his fellow worker so hard that he dies. The person responsible may then flee to one of these cities to save himself. **19:6** Otherwise the blood avenger will chase after the killer in the heat of his anger, eventually overtake him, and kill him, though this is not a capital case since he did not hate him at the time of the accident. **19:7** Therefore, I am commanding you to set apart for yourselves three cities. **19:8** If the LORD your God enlarges your borders as he promised your ancestors and gives you all the land he pledged to them, **19:9** and then you are careful to observe all these commandments I am giving you today (namely, to love the LORD your God and to always walk in his ways), then you must add three more cities to these three. **19:10** You must not shed innocent blood in your land that the LORD your God is giving you as an inheritance, for that would make you guilty. **19:11** However, suppose a person hates someone else and stalks him, attacks him, kills him, and then flees to one of these cities. **19:12** The elders of his own city must send for him and remove him from there to deliver him over to the blood avenger to die. **19:13** You must not pity him, but purge out the blood of the innocent from Israel, so that it may go well with you.

Laws Concerning Witnesses

19:14 You must not encroach on your neighbor's property, which will have been defined in the inheritance you will obtain in the land the LORD your God is giving you.

19:15 A single witness may not testify against another person for any trespass or sin that he commits. A matter may be legally established only on the testimony of two or three witnesses. **19:16** If a false witness testifies against another person and accuses him of a crime, **19:17** then both parties to the controversy must stand before the LORD, that is, before the priests and judges who will be in office in those days. **19:18** The judges will thoroughly investigate the matter, and if the witness should prove to be false and to have given false testimony against the accused, **19:19** you must do to him what he had intended to do to the accused. In this way you will purge evil from among you. **19:20** The rest of the people will hear and become afraid to keep doing such evil among you. **19:21** You

must not show pity; the principle will be a life for a life, an eye for an eye, a tooth for a tooth, a hand for a hand, and a foot for a foot.

Laws Concerning War with Distant Enemies

20:1 When you go to war against your enemies and see chariotry and troops who outnumber you, do not be afraid of them, for the LORD your God, who brought you up out of the land of Egypt, is with you. **20:2** As you move forward for battle, the priest will approach and say to the soldiers, **20:3** "Listen, Israel! Today you are moving forward to do battle with your enemies. Do not be fainthearted. Do not fear and tremble or be terrified because of them, **20:4** for the LORD your God goes with you to fight on your behalf against your enemies to give you victory." **20:5** Moreover, the officers are to say to the troops, "Who among you has built a new house and not dedicated it? He may go home, lest he die in battle and someone else dedicate it. **20:6** Or who among you has planted a vineyard and not benefited from it? He may go home, lest he die in battle and someone else benefit from it. **20:7** Or who among you has become engaged to a woman but has not married her? He may go home, lest he die in battle and someone else marry her." **20:8** In addition, the officers are to say to the troops, "Who among you is afraid and fainthearted? He may go home so that he will not make his fellow soldier's heart as fearful as his own." **20:9** Then, when the officers have finished speaking, they must appoint unit commanders to lead the troops.

20:10 When you approach a city to wage war against it, offer it terms of peace. **20:11** If it accepts your terms and submits to you, all the people found in it will become your slaves. **20:12** If it does not accept terms of peace but makes war with you, then you are to lay siege to it. **20:13** The LORD your God will deliver it over to you and you must kill every single male by the sword. **20:14** However, the women, little children, cattle, and anything else in the city – all its plunder – you may take for yourselves as spoil. You may take from your enemies the plunder that the LORD your God has given you. **20:15** This is how you are to deal with all those cities located far from you, those that do not belong to these nearby nations.

Laws Concerning War with Canaanite Nations

20:16 As for the cities of these peoples that the LORD your God is going to give you as an inheritance, you must not allow a single living thing to survive. **20:17** Instead you must utterly annihilate them – the Hittites, Amorites, Canaanites, Perizzites, Hivites, and Jebusites – just as the LORD your God has commanded you, **20:18** so that they cannot teach you all the abhorrent ways they worship their gods, causing you to sin against the LORD your God. **20:19** If you besiege a city for a long time while attempting to capture it, you must not chop down its trees, for you may eat fruit from them and should not cut them down. A tree in the field is not human that you should besiege it! **20:20** However, you may chop down any tree you know is not suitable for food, and you may use it to build siege works against the city that is making war with you until that city falls.

Laws Concerning Unsolved Murder

21:1 If a homicide victim should be found lying in a field in the land the LORD your God is giving you, and no one knows who killed him, **21:2** your elders and judges must go out and measure how far it is to the cities in the vicinity of the corpse. **21:3** Then the elders of the city nearest to the corpse must take from the herd a heifer that has not been worked – that has never pulled with the yoke – **21:4** and bring the heifer down to a wadi with flowing water, to a valley that is neither plowed nor sown. There at the wadi they are to break the heifer's neck. **21:5** Then the Levitical priests will approach (for the LORD your God has chosen them to serve him and to pronounce blessings in his name, and to decide every judicial verdict) **21:6** and all the elders of that city nearest the corpse must wash their hands over the heifer whose neck was broken in the valley. **21:7** Then they must proclaim, "Our hands have not spilled this blood, nor have we witnessed the crime. **21:8** Do not blame your people Israel whom you redeemed, O LORD, and do not hold them accountable for the bloodshed of an innocent person." Then atonement will be made for the bloodshed. **21:9** In this manner you will purge out the guilt of innocent blood from among you, for you must do what is right before the LORD.

Laws Concerning Wives

21:10 When you go out to do battle with your enemies and the LORD your God allows you to prevail and you take prisoners, **21:11** if you should see among them an attractive woman whom you wish to take as a wife, **21:12** you may bring her back to your house. She must shave her head, trim her nails, **21:13** discard the clothing she was wearing when captured, and stay in your house, lamenting for her father and mother for a full month. After that you may have sexual relations with her and become her husband and she your wife. **21:14** If you are not pleased with her, then you must let her go where she pleases. You cannot in any case sell her; you must not take advantage of her, since you have already humiliated her.

Laws Concerning Children

21:15 Suppose a man has two wives, one whom he loves more than the other, and they both bear him sons, with the firstborn being the child of the less loved wife. **21:16** In the day he divides his inheritance he must not appoint as firstborn the son of the favorite wife in place of the other wife's son who is actually the firstborn. **21:17** Rather, he must acknowledge the son of the less loved wife as firstborn and give him the double portion of all he has, for that son is the beginning of his father's procreative power – to him should go the right of the firstborn. **21:18** If a person has a stubborn, rebellious son who pays no attention to his father or mother, and they discipline him to no avail, **21:19** his father and mother must seize him and bring him to the elders at the gate of his city. **21:20** They must declare to the elders of his city, "Our son is stubborn and rebellious and pays no attention to what we say – he is a glutton and drunkard." **21:21** Then all the men of his city must stone him to death. In this way you will purge out wickedness from among you, and all Israel will hear about it and be afraid.

Disposition of a Criminal's Remains

21:22 If a person commits a sin punishable by death and is executed, and you hang the corpse on a tree, **21:23** his body must not remain all night on the tree; instead you must make certain you bury him that same day, for the one who is left exposed on a tree is cursed by God. You must not defile your land which the LORD your God is giving you as an inheritance.

Laws Concerning Preservation of Life

22:1 When you see your neighbor's ox or sheep going astray, do not ignore it; you must return it without fail to your neighbor. **22:2** If the owner does not live near you or you do not know who the owner is, then you must corral the animal at your house and let it stay with you until the owner looks for it; then you must return it to him. **22:3** You shall do the same to his donkey, his clothes, or anything else your neighbor has lost and you have found; you must not refuse to get involved. **22:4** When you see your neighbor's donkey or ox fallen along the road, do not ignore it; instead, you must be sure to help him get the animal on its feet again.

22:5 A woman must not wear men's clothing, nor should a man dress up in women's clothing, for anyone who does this is offensive to the LORD your God.

22:6 If you happen to notice a bird's nest along the road, whether in a tree or on the ground, and there are chicks or eggs with the mother bird sitting on them, you must not take the mother from the young. **22:7** You must be sure to let the mother go, but you may take the young for yourself. Do this so that it may go well with you and you may have a long life.

22:8 If you build a new house, you must construct a guard rail around your roof to avoid being culpable in the event someone should fall from it.

Illustrations of the Principle of Purity

22:9 You must not plant your vineyard with two kinds of seed; otherwise the entire yield, both of the seed you plant and the produce of the vineyard, will be defiled. **22:10** You must not plow with an ox and a donkey harnessed together. **22:11** You must not wear clothing made with wool and linen meshed together. **22:12** You shall make yourselves tassels for the four corners of the clothing you wear.

Purity in the Marriage Relationship

22:13 Suppose a man marries a woman, has sexual relations with her, and then rejects her, **22:14** accusing her of impropriety and defaming her reputation by saying, "I married this woman but when I had sexual relations with her I discovered she was not a virgin!" **22:15** Then the father and mother of the young woman must produce the evidence of virginity for the elders of the city at the gate. **22:16** The young woman's father must say to the elders, "I gave my daughter to this man and he has rejected her. **22:17** Moreover, he has raised accusations of impropriety by saying, 'I discovered your daughter was not a virgin,' but this is the evidence of my daughter's virginity!" The cloth must then be spread out before the city's elders. **22:18** The elders of that city must then seize the man and punish him. **22:19** They will fine him one hundred shekels of silver and give them to the young woman's father, for the man who made the accusation ruined the reputation of an Israelite virgin. She will then become his wife and he may never divorce her as long as he lives.

22:20 But if the accusation is true and the young woman was not a virgin, **22:21** the men of her city must bring the young woman to the door of her father's house and stone her to death, for she has done a disgraceful thing in Israel by behaving like a prostitute while living in her father's house. In this way you will purge evil from among you.

22:22 If a man is caught having sexual relations with a married woman both the man who had relations with the woman and the woman herself must die; in this way you will purge evil from Israel.

22:23 If a virgin is engaged to a man and another man meets her in the city and has sexual relations with her, **22:24** you must bring the two of them to the gate of that city and stone them to death, the young woman because she did not cry out though in the city and the man because he violated his neighbor's fiancée; in this way you will purge evil from among you. **22:25** But if the man came across the engaged woman in the field and overpowered her and raped her, then only the rapist must die. **22:26** You must not do anything to the young woman – she has done nothing deserving of death. This case is the same as when someone attacks another person and murders him, **22:27** for the man met her in the field and the engaged woman cried out, but there was no one to rescue her.

22:28 Suppose a man comes across a virgin who is not engaged and overpowers and rapes her and they are discovered. **22:29** The man who has raped her must pay her father fifty shekels of silver and she must become his wife because he has violated her; he may never divorce her as long as he lives.

22:30 (23:1) A man may not marry his father's former wife and in this way dishonor his father.

Purity in Public Worship

23:1 A man with crushed or severed genitals may not enter the assembly of the LORD. **23:2** A person of illegitimate birth may not enter the assembly of the LORD; to the tenth generation no one related to him may do so. **23:3** An Ammonite or Moabite may not enter the assembly of the LORD; to the tenth generation none of their descendants shall ever do so, **23:4** for they did not meet you with food and water on the way as you came from Egypt, and furthermore, they hired Balaam son of Beor of Pethor in Aram Naharaim to curse you. **23:5** But the LORD your God refused to listen to Balaam and changed the curse to a blessing, for the LORD your God loves you. **23:6** You must not seek peace and prosperity for them through all the ages to come. **23:7** You must not hate an Edomite, for he is your relative; you must not hate an Egyptian, for you lived as a foreigner in his land. **23:8** Children of the third generation born to them may enter the assembly of the LORD.

Purity in Personal Hygiene

23:9 When you go out as an army against your enemies, guard yourselves against anything impure. **23:10** If there is someone among you who is impure because of some nocturnal emission, he must leave the camp; he may not reenter it immediately. **23:11** When evening arrives he must wash himself with water and then at sunset he may reenter the camp.

23:12 You are to have a place outside the camp to serve as a latrine. **23:13** You must have a spade among your other equipment and when you relieve yourself outside you must dig a hole with the spade and then turn and cover your excrement. **23:14** For the LORD your God walks about in the middle of your camp to deliver you and defeat your enemies for you. Therefore your camp should be holy, so that he does not see anything indecent among you and turn away from you.

Purity in the Treatment of the Nonprivileged

23:15 You must not return an escaped slave to his master when he has run away to you. **23:16** Indeed, he may live among you in any place he chooses, in whichever of your villages he prefers; you must not oppress him.

Purity in Cultic Personnel

23:17 There must never be a sacred prostitute among the young women of Israel nor a sacred male prostitute among the young men of Israel. **23:18** You must never bring the pay of a female prostitute or the wage of a male prostitute into the temple of the LORD your God in fulfillment of any vow, for both of these are abhorrent to the LORD your God.

Respect for Others' Property

23:19 You must not charge interest on a loan to your fellow Israelite, whether on money, food, or anything else that has been loaned with interest. **23:20** You may lend with interest to a foreigner, but not to your fellow Israelite; if you keep this command the LORD your God will bless you in all you undertake in the land you are about to enter to possess. **23:21** When you make a vow to the LORD your God you must not delay in fulfilling it, for otherwise he will surely hold you accountable as a sinner. **23:22** If you refrain from making a vow, it will not be sinful. **23:23** Whatever you vow, you must be careful to do what you have promised, such as what you have vowed to the LORD your God as a freewill offering. **23:24** When you enter the vineyard of your neighbor you may eat as many grapes as you please, but you must not take away any in a container. **23:25** When you go into the ripe grain fields of your neighbor you may pluck off the kernels with your hand, but you must not use a sickle on your neighbor's ripe grain.

24:1 If a man marries a woman and she does not please him because he has found something offensive in her, then he may draw up a divorce document, give it to her, and evict her from his house. **24:2** When she has left him she may go and become someone else's wife. **24:3** If the second husband rejects her and then divorces her, gives her the papers, and evicts her from his house, or if the second husband who married her dies, **24:4** her first husband who divorced her is not permitted to remarry her after she has become ritually impure, for that is offensive to the LORD. You must not bring guilt on the land which the LORD your God is giving you as an inheritance.

24:5 When a man is newly married, he need not go into the army nor be obligated in any way; he must be free to stay at home for a full year and bring joy to the wife he has married.

24:6 One must not take either lower or upper millstones as security on a loan, for that is like taking a life itself as security.

24:7 If a man is found kidnapping a person from among his fellow Israelites, and regards him as mere property and sells him, that kidnapper must die. In this way you will purge evil from among you.

Respect for Human Dignity

24:8 Be careful during an outbreak of leprosy to follow precisely all that the Levitical priests instruct you; as I have commanded them, so you should do. **24:9** Remember what the LORD your God did to Miriam along the way after you left Egypt.

24:10 When you make any kind of loan to your neighbor, you may not go into his house to claim what he is offering as security. 24:11 You must stand outside and the person to whom you are making the loan will bring out to you what he is offering as security. 24:12 If the person is poor you may not use what he gives you as security for a covering. 24:13 You must by all means return to him at sunset the item he gave you as security so that he may sleep in his outer garment and bless you for it; it will be considered a just deed by the LORD your God.

24:14 You must not oppress a lowly and poor servant, whether one from among your fellow Israelites or from the resident foreigners who are living in your land and villages. 24:15 You must pay his wage that very day before the sun sets, for he is poor and his life depends on it. Otherwise he will cry out to the LORD against you, and you will be guilty of sin.

24:16 Fathers must not be put to death for what their children do, nor children for what their fathers do; each must be put to death for his own sin.

24:17 You must not pervert justice due a resident foreigner or an orphan, or take a widow's garment as security for a loan. 24:18 Remember that you were slaves in Egypt and that the LORD your God redeemed you from there; therefore I am commanding you to do all this. 24:19 Whenever you reap your harvest in your field and leave some unraked grain there, you must not return to get it; it should go to the resident foreigner, orphan, and widow so that the LORD your God may bless all the work you do. 24:20 When you beat your olive tree you must not repeat the procedure; the remaining olives belong to the resident foreigner, orphan, and widow. 24:21 When you gather the grapes of your vineyard you must not do so a second time; they should go to the resident foreigner, orphan, and widow. 24:22 Remember that you were slaves in the land of Egypt; therefore, I am commanding you to do all this.

25:1 If controversy arises between people, they should go to court for judgment. When the judges hear the case, they shall exonerate the innocent but condemn the guilty. 25:2 Then, if the guilty person is sentenced to a beating, the judge shall force him to lie down and be beaten in his presence with the number of blows his wicked behavior deserves. 25:3 The judge may sentence him to forty blows, but no more. If he is struck with more than these, you might view your fellow Israelite with contempt.

25:4 You must not muzzle your ox when it is treading grain.

Respect for the Sanctity of Others

25:5 If brothers live together and one of them dies without having a son, the dead man's wife must not remarry someone outside the family. Instead, her late husband's brother must go to her, marry her, and perform the duty of a brother-in-law. 25:6 Then the first son she bears will continue the name of the dead brother, thus preventing his name from being blotted out of Israel. 25:7 But if the man does not want to marry his brother's widow, then she must go to the elders at the town gate and say, "My husband's brother refuses to preserve his brother's name in Israel; he is unwilling to perform the duty of a brother-in-law to me!" 25:8 Then the elders of his city must summon him and speak to him. If he persists, saying, "I don't want to marry her," 25:9 then his sister-in-law must approach him in view of the elders, remove his sandal from his foot, and spit in his face. She will then respond, "Thus may it be done to any man who does not maintain his brother's family line!" 25:10 His family name will be referred to in Israel as "the family of the one whose sandal was removed."

25:11 If two men get into a hand-to-hand fight, and the wife of one of them gets involved to help her husband against his attacker, and she reaches out her hand and grabs his genitals, 25:12 then you must cut off her hand – do not pity her.

25:13 You must not have in your bag different stone weights, a heavy and a light one. 25:14 You must not have in your house different measuring containers, a large and a small one. 25:15 You must have an accurate and correct stone weight and an accurate and correct measuring container, so that your life may be extended in the land the LORD your God is about to give you. 25:16 For anyone who acts dishonestly in these ways is abhorrent to the LORD your God.

Treatment of the Amalekites

25:17 Remember what the Amalekites did to you on your way from Egypt, 25:18 how they met you along the way and cut off all your stragglers in the rear of the march when you were exhausted and tired; they were unafraid of God. 25:19 So when the LORD your God gives you relief from all the enemies who surround you in the land he is giving you as an inheritance, you must wipe out the memory of the Amalekites from under heaven – do not forget!

Presentation of the First Fruits

26:1 When you enter the land that the LORD your God is giving you as an inheritance, and you occupy it and live in it, 26:2 you must take the first of all the ground's produce you harvest from the land the LORD your God is giving you, place it in a basket, and go to the place where he chooses to locate his name. 26:3 You must go to the priest in office at that time and say to him, "I declare today to the LORD your God that I have come into the land that the LORD promised to our ancestors to give us." 26:4 The

priest will then take the basket from you and set it before the altar of the LORD your God. 26:5 Then you must affirm before the LORD your God, "A wandering Aramean was my ancestor, and he went down to Egypt and lived there as a foreigner with a household few in number, but there he became a great, powerful, and numerous people. 26:6 But the Egyptians mistreated and oppressed us, forcing us to do burdensome labor. 26:7 So we cried out to the LORD, the God of our ancestors, and he heard us and saw our humiliation, toil, and oppression. 26:8 Therefore the LORD brought us out of Egypt with tremendous strength and power, as well as with great awe-inspiring signs and wonders. 26:9 Then he brought us to this place and gave us this land, a land flowing with milk and honey. 26:10 So now, look! I have brought the first of the ground's produce that you, LORD, have given me." Then you must set it down before the LORD your God and worship before him. 26:11 You will celebrate all the good things that the LORD your God has given you and your family, along with the Levites and the resident foreigners among you.

Presentation of the Third-year Tithe

26:12 When you finish tithing all your income in the third year (the year of tithing), you must give it to the Levites, the resident foreigners, the orphans, and the widows so that they may eat in your settlement in your villages. 26:13 Then you shall say before the LORD your God, "I have removed the sacred offering from my house and given it to the Levites, the resident foreigners, the orphans, and the widows just as you have commanded me. I have not violated or forgotten your commandments. 26:14 I have not eaten anything when I was in mourning, or removed any of it while ceremonially unclean, or offered any of it to the dead; I have obeyed you and have done everything you have commanded me. 26:15 Look down from your holy dwelling place in heaven and bless your people Israel and the land you have given us, just as you promised our ancestors – a land flowing with milk and honey."

Narrative Interlude

26:16 Today the LORD your God is commanding you to keep these statutes and ordinances, something you must do with all your heart and soul. 26:17 Today you have declared the LORD to be your God, and that you will walk in his ways, keep his statutes, commandments, and ordinances, and obey him. 26:18 And today the LORD has declared you to be his special people (as he already promised you) so you may keep all his commandments. 26:19 Then he will elevate you above all the nations he has made and you will receive praise, fame, and honor. You will be a people holy to the LORD your God, as he has said.

The Assembly at Shechem

27:1 Then Moses and the elders of Israel commanded the people: "Pay attention to all the commandments I am giving you today. 27:2 When you cross the Jordan River to the land the LORD your God is giving you, you must erect great stones and cover them with plaster. 27:3 Then you must inscribe on them all the words of this law when you cross over, so that you may enter the land the LORD your God is giving you, a land flowing with milk and honey just as the LORD, the God of your ancestors, said to you. 27:4 So when you cross the Jordan you must erect on Mount Ebal these stones about which I am commanding you today, and you must cover them with plaster. 27:5 Then you must build an altar there to the LORD your God, an altar of stones – do not use an iron tool on them. 27:6 You must build the altar of the LORD your God with whole stones and offer burnt offerings on it to the LORD your God. 27:7 Also you must offer fellowship offerings and eat them there, rejoicing before the LORD your God. 27:8 You must inscribe on the stones all the words of this law, making them clear."

27:9 Then Moses and the Levitical priests spoke to all Israel: "Be quiet and pay attention, Israel. Today you have become the people of the LORD your God. 27:10 You must obey him and keep his commandments and statutes that I am giving you today." 27:11 Moreover, Moses commanded the people that day: 27:12 "The following tribes must stand to bless the people on Mount Gerizim when you cross the Jordan: Simeon, Levi, Judah, Issachar, Joseph, and Benjamin. 27:13 And these other tribes must stand for the curse on Mount Ebal: Reuben, Gad, Asher, Zebulun, Dan, and Naphtali.

The Covenant Curses

27:14 "The Levites will call out to every Israelite with a loud voice: 27:15 'Cursed is the one who makes a carved or metal image – something abhorrent to the LORD, the work of the craftsman – and sets it up in a secret place.' Then all the people will say, 'Amen!' 27:16 'Cursed is the one who disrespects his father and mother.' Then all the people will say, 'Amen!' 27:17 'Cursed is the one who moves his neighbor's boundary marker.' Then all the people will say, 'Amen!' 27:18 'Cursed is the one who misleads a blind person on the road.' Then all the people will say, 'Amen!' 27:19 'Cursed is the one who perverts justice for the resident foreigner, the orphan, and the widow.' Then all the people will say, 'Amen!' 27:20 'Cursed is the one who has sexual relations with his father's former wife, for he dishonors his father.' Then all the people will say, 'Amen!' 27:21 'Cursed is the one who commits bestiality.' Then all the people will say, 'Amen!' 27:22 'Cursed is the one who has sexual relations with his sister, the daughter of either his father or mother.' Then all the people will say, 'Amen!' 27:23 'Cursed is the one who has sexual relations with his mother-in-law.' Then all the people will say, 'Amen!' **27:24** 'Cursed is the one who kills his neighbor in private.' Then all the people will say, 'Amen!' **27:25** 'Cursed is the one who takes a bribe to kill an innocent person.' Then all the people will say, 'Amen!' **27:26** 'Cursed is the one who refuses to keep the words of this law.' Then all the people will say, 'Amen!'

The Covenant Blessings

28:1 "If you indeed obey the LORD your God and are careful to observe all his commandments I am giving you today, the LORD your God will elevate you above all the nations of the earth. **28:2** All these blessings will come to you in abundance if you obey the LORD your God: **28:3** You will be blessed in the city and blessed in the field. **28:4** Your children will be blessed, as well as the produce of your soil, the offspring of your livestock, the calves of your herds, and the lambs of your flocks. **28:5** Your basket and your mixing bowl will be blessed. **28:6** You will be blessed when you come in and blessed when you go out. **28:7** The LORD will cause your enemies who attack you to be struck down before you; they will attack you from one direction but flee from you in seven different directions. **28:8** The LORD will decree blessing for you with respect to your barns and in everything you do – yes, he will bless you in the land he is giving you. **28:9** The LORD will designate you as his holy people just as he promised you, if you keep his commandments and obey him. **28:10** Then all the peoples of the earth will see that you belong to the LORD, and they will respect you. **28:11** The LORD will greatly multiply your children, the offspring of your livestock, and the produce of your soil in the land which he promised your ancestors he would give you. **28:12** The LORD will open for you his good treasure house, the heavens, to give you rain for the land in its season and to bless all you do; you will lend to many nations but you will not borrow from any. **28:13** The LORD will make you the head and not the tail, and you will always end up at the top and not at the bottom, if you obey his commandments which I am urging you today to be careful to do. **28:14** But you must not turn away from all the commandments I am giving you today, to either the right or left, nor pursue other gods and worship them.

Curses as Reversal of Blessings

28:15 "But if you ignore the LORD your God and are not careful to keep all his commandments and statutes I am giving you today, then all these curses will come upon you in full force: **28:16** You will be cursed in the city and cursed in the field. **28:17** Your basket and your mixing bowl will be cursed. **28:18** Your children will be cursed, as well as the produce of your soil, the calves of your herds, and the lambs of your flocks. **28:19** You will be cursed when you come in and cursed when you go out.

Curses by Disease and Drought

28:20 "The LORD will send on you a curse, confusing you and opposing you in everything you undertake until you are destroyed and quickly perish because of the evil of your deeds, in that you have forsaken me. **28:21** The LORD will plague you with deadly diseases until he has completely removed you from the land you are about to possess. **28:22** He will afflict you with weakness, fever, inflammation, infection, sword, blight, and mildew; these will attack you until you perish. **28:23** The sky above your heads will be bronze and the earth beneath you iron. **28:24** The LORD will make the rain of your land powder and dust; it will come down on you from the sky until you are destroyed.

Curses by Defeat and Deportation

28:25 "The LORD will allow you to be struck down before your enemies; you will attack them from one direction but flee from them in seven directions and will become an object of terror to all the kingdoms of the earth. **28:26** Your carcasses will be food for every bird of the sky and wild animal of the earth, and there will be no one to chase them off. **28:27** The LORD will afflict you with the boils of Egypt and with tumors, eczema, and scabies, all of which cannot be healed. **28:28** The LORD will also subject you to madness, blindness, and confusion of mind. **28:29** You will feel your way along at noon like the blind person does in darkness and you will not succeed in anything you do; you will be constantly oppressed and continually robbed, with no one to save you. **28:30** You will be engaged to a woman and another man will rape her. You will build a house but not live in it. You will plant a vineyard but not even begin to use it. **28:31** Your ox will be slaughtered before your very eyes but you will not eat of it. Your donkey will be stolen from you as you watch and will not be returned to you. Your flock of sheep will be given to your enemies and there will be no one to save you. **28:32** Your sons and daughters will be given to another people while you look on in vain all day, and you will be powerless to do anything about it. **28:33** As for the produce of your land and all your labor, a people you do not know will consume it, and you will be nothing but oppressed and crushed for the rest of your lives. **28:34** You will go insane from seeing all this. **28:35** The LORD will afflict you in your knees and on your legs with painful, incurable boils – from the soles of your feet to the top of your head. **28:36** The LORD will force you and your king whom you will appoint over you to go away to a people whom you and your ancestors have not known, and you will serve other gods of wood and stone there. **28:37** You will become an occasion of horror, a proverb, and an object of ridicule to all the peoples to whom the LORD will drive you.

The Curse of Reversed Status

28:38 "You will take much seed to the field but gather little harvest, because locusts will consume it. **28:39** You will plant vineyards and cultivate them, but you will not drink wine or gather in grapes, because worms will eat them. **28:40** You will have olive trees throughout your territory but you will not anoint yourself with olive oil, because the olives will drop off the trees while still unripe. **28:41** You will bear sons and daughters but not keep them, because they will be taken into captivity. **28:42** Whirring locusts will take over every tree and all the produce of your soil. **28:43** The foreigners who reside among you will become higher and higher over you and you will become lower and lower. **28:44** They will lend to you but you will not lend to them; they will become the head and you will become the tail!

28:45 All these curses will fall on you, pursuing and overtaking you until you are destroyed, because you would not obey the LORD your God by keeping his commandments and statutes that he has given you. **28:46** These curses will be a perpetual sign and wonder with reference to you and your descendants.

The Curse of Military Siege

28:47 "Because you have not served the LORD your God joyfully and wholeheartedly with the abundance of everything you have, **28:48** instead in hunger, thirst, nakedness, and poverty you will serve your enemies whom the LORD will send against you. They will place an iron yoke on your neck until they have destroyed you. **28:49** The LORD will raise up a distant nation against you, one from the other side of the earth as the eagle flies, a nation whose language you will not understand, **28:50** a nation of stern appearance that will have no regard for the elderly or pity for the young. **28:51** They will devour the offspring of your livestock and the produce of your soil until you are destroyed. They will not leave you with any grain, new wine, olive oil, calves of your herds, or lambs of your flocks until they have destroyed you. **28:52** They will besiege all of your villages until all of your high and fortified walls collapse – those in which you put your confidence throughout the land. They will besiege all your villages throughout the land the LORD your God has given you. **28:53** You will then eat your own offspring, the flesh of the sons and daughters the LORD your God has given you, because of the severity of the siege by which your enemies will constrict you. **28:54** The man among you who is by nature tender and sensitive will turn against his brother, his beloved wife, and his remaining children. **28:55** He will withhold from all of them his children's flesh that he is eating (since there is nothing else left), because of the severity of the siege by which your enemy will constrict you in your villages. **28:56** Likewise, the most tender and delicate of your women, who would never think of putting even the sole of her foot on the ground because of her daintiness, will turn against her beloved husband, her sons and daughters, **28:57** and will secretly eat her afterbirth and her newborn children (since she has nothing else), because of the severity of the siege by which your enemy will constrict you in your villages.

The Curse of Covenant Termination

28:58 "If you refuse to obey all the words of this law, the things written in this scroll, and refuse to fear this glorious and awesome name, the LORD your God, **28:59** then the LORD will increase your punishments and those of your descendants – great and long-lasting afflictions and severe, enduring illnesses. **28:60** He will infect you with all the diseases of Egypt that you dreaded, and they will persistently afflict you. **28:61** Moreover, the LORD will bring upon you every kind of sickness and plague not mentioned in this scroll of commandments, until you have perished. **28:62** There will be very few of you left, though at one time you were as numerous as the stars in the sky, because you will have disobeyed the LORD your God. **28:63** This is what will happen: Just as the LORD delighted to do good for you and make you numerous, he will take delight in destroying and decimating you. You will be uprooted from the land you are about to possess. **28:64** The LORD will scatter you among all nations, from one end of the earth to the other. There you will worship other gods that neither you nor your ancestors have known, gods of wood and stone. **28:65** Among those nations you will have no rest nor will there be a place of peaceful rest for the soles of your feet, for there the LORD will give you an anxious heart, failing eyesight, and a spirit of despair. **28:66** Your life will hang in doubt before you; you will be terrified by night and day and will have no certainty of surviving from one day to the next. **28:67** In the morning you will say, 'If only it were evening!' And in the evening you will say, 'I wish it were morning!' because of the things you will fear and the things you will see. **28:68** Then the LORD will make you return to Egypt by ship, over a route I said to you that you would never see again. There you will sell yourselves to your enemies as male and female slaves, but no one will buy you."

Narrative Interlude

29:1 (28:69) These are the words of the covenant that the LORD commanded Moses to make with the people of Israel in the land of Moab, in addition to the covenant he had made with them at Horeb.

The Exodus, Wandering, and Conquest Reviewed

29:2 Moses proclaimed to all Israel as follows: "You have seen all that the LORD did in the land of Egypt to Pharaoh, all his servants, and his land. **29:3** Your eyes have seen the great judgments, those signs and mighty wonders. **29:4** But to this very day the LORD has not given you an understanding mind, perceptive eyes, or discerning ears! **29:5** I have led you through the desert for forty years. Your clothing has not worn out nor have your sandals deteriorated. **29:6** You have eaten no bread and drunk no wine or beer – all so that you might know that I am the LORD your God! **29:7** When you came to this place King Sihon of Heshbon and King Og of Bashan came out to make war and we defeated them. **29:8** Then we took their land and gave it as an inheritance to Reuben, Gad, and half the tribe of Manasseh.

The Present Covenant Setting

29:9 "Therefore, keep the terms of this covenant and obey them so that you may be successful in everything you do. **29:10** You are standing today, all of you, before the LORD your God – the heads of your tribes, your elders, your officials, every Israelite man, **29:11** your infants, your wives, and the foreigners living in your encampment, those who chop wood and those who carry water – **29:12** so that you may enter by oath into the covenant the LORD your God is making with you today. **29:13** Today he will affirm that you are his people and that he is your God, just as he promised you and as he swore by oath to your ancestors Abraham, Isaac, and Jacob. **29:14** It is not with you alone that I am making this covenant by oath, **29:15** but with whoever stands with us here today before the LORD our God as well as those not with us here today.

The Results of Disobedience

29:16 "(For you know how we lived in the land of Egypt and how we crossed through the nations as we traveled. **29:17** You have seen their detestable things and idols of wood, stone, silver, and gold.) **29:18** Beware that the heart of no man, woman, clan, or tribe among you turns away from the LORD our God today to pursue and serve the gods of those nations; beware that there is among you no root producing poisonous and bitter fruit. **29:19** When such a person hears the words of this oath he secretly blesses himself and says, "I will have peace though I continue to walk with a stubborn spirit." This will destroy the watered ground with the parched. **29:20** The LORD will be unwilling to forgive him, and his intense anger will rage against that man; all the curses written in this scroll will fall upon him and the LORD will obliterate his name from memory. **29:21** The LORD will single him out for judgment from all the tribes of Israel according to all the curses of the covenant written in this scroll of the law. **29:22** The generation to come – your descendants who will rise up after you, as well as the foreigner who will come from distant places – will see the afflictions of that land and the illnesses that the LORD has brought on it. **29:23** The whole land will be covered with brimstone, salt, and burning debris; it will not be planted nor will it sprout or produce grass. It will resemble the destruction of Sodom and Gomorrah, Admah and Zeboiim, which the LORD destroyed in his intense anger. **29:24** Then all the nations will ask, "Why has the LORD done all this to this land? What is this fierce, heated display of anger all about?" **29:25** Then people will say, "Because they abandoned the covenant of the LORD, the God of their ancestors, which he made with them when he brought them out of the land of Egypt. **29:26** They went and served other gods and worshiped them, gods they did not know and that he did not permit them to worship. **29:27** That is why the LORD's anger erupted against this land, bringing on it all the curses written in this scroll. **29:28** So the LORD has uprooted them from their land in anger, wrath, and great rage and has deported them to another land, as is clear today." **29:29** Secret things belong to the LORD our God, but those that are revealed belong to us and our descendants forever, so that we might obey all the words of this law.

The Results of Covenant Reaffirmation

30:1 "When you have experienced all these things, both the blessings and the curses I have set before you, you will reflect upon them in all the nations where the LORD your God has banished you. **30:2** Then if you and your descendants turn to the LORD your God and obey him with your whole mind and being just as I am commanding you today, **30:3** the LORD your God will reverse your captivity and have pity on you. He will turn and gather you from all the peoples among whom he has scattered you. **30:4** Even if your exiles are in the most distant land, from there the LORD your God will gather you and bring you back. **30:5** Then he will bring you to the land your ancestors possessed and you also will possess it; he will do better for you and multiply you more than he did your ancestors. **30:6** The LORD your God will also cleanse your heart and the hearts of your descendants so that you may love him with all your mind and being and so that you may live. **30:7** Then the LORD your God will put all these curses on your enemies, on those who hate you and persecute you. **30:8** You will return and obey the LORD, keeping all his commandments I am giving you today. **30:9** The LORD your God will make the labor of your hands abundantly successful and multiply your children, the offspring of your cattle, and the produce of your soil. For the LORD your God will once more rejoice over you to make you prosperous just as he rejoiced over your ancestors, **30:10** if you obey the LORD your God and keep his commandments and statutes that are written in this scroll of the law. But you must turn to him with your whole mind and being.

Exhortation to Covenant Obedience

30:11 "This commandment I am giving you today is not too difficult for you, nor is it too remote. **30:12** It is not in heaven, as though one must say, "Who will go up to heaven to get it for us and proclaim it to us so we may obey it?" **30:13** And it is not across the sea, as though one must say, "Who will cross over to the other side of the sea and get it for us and proclaim it to us so we may obey it?" **30:14** For the thing is very near you – it is in your mouth and in your mind so that you can do it.

30:15 "Look! I have set before you today life and prosperity on the one hand, and death and disaster on the other. **30:16** What I am commanding you today is to love the LORD your God, to walk in his ways, and to obey his commandments, his statutes, and his ordinances. Then you will live and become numerous and the LORD your God will bless you in the land which you are about to possess. **30:17** However, if you turn aside and do not obey, but are lured away to worship and serve other gods, **30:18** I declare to you this very day that you will certainly perish! You will not extend your time in the land you are crossing the Jordan to possess. **30:19** Today I invoke heaven and earth as a witness against you that I have set life and death, blessing and curse, before you. Therefore choose life so that you and your descendants may live! **30:20** I also call on you to love the LORD your God, to obey him and be loyal to him, for he gives you life and enables you to live continually in the land the LORD promised to give to your ancestors Abraham, Isaac, and Jacob."

Succession of Moses by Joshua

31:1 Then Moses went and spoke these words to all Israel. **31:2** He said to them, "Today I am a hundred and twenty years old. I am no longer able to get about, and the LORD has said to me, 'You will not cross the Jordan.' **31:3** As for the LORD your God, he is about to cross over before you; he will destroy these nations before you and dispossess them. As for Joshua, he is about to cross before you just as the LORD has said. **31:4** The LORD will do to them just what he did to Sihon and Og, the Amorite kings, and to their land, which he destroyed. **31:5** The LORD will deliver them over to you and you will do to them according to the whole commandment I have given you. **31:6** Be strong and courageous! Do not fear or tremble before them, for the LORD your God is the one who is going with you. He will not fail you or abandon you!" **31:7** Then Moses called out to Joshua in the presence of all Israel, "Be strong and courageous, for you will accompany these people to the land that the LORD promised to give their ancestors, and you will enable them to inherit it. **31:8** The LORD is indeed going before you – he will be with you; he will not fail you or abandon you. Do not be afraid or discouraged!"

The Deposit of the Covenant Text

31:9 Then Moses wrote down this law and gave it to the Levitical priests, who carry the ark of the LORD's covenant, and to all Israel's elders. **31:10** He commanded them: "At the end of seven years, at the appointed time of the cancellation of debts, at the Feast of Temporary Shelters, **31:11** when all Israel comes to appear before the LORD your God in the place he chooses, you must read this law before them within their hearing. **31:12** Gather the people – men, women, and children, as well as the resident foreigners in your villages – so they may hear and thus learn about and fear the LORD your God and carefully obey all the words of this law. **31:13** Then their children, who have not known this law, will also hear about and learn to fear the LORD your God for as long as you live in the land you are crossing the Jordan to possess."

The Commissioning of Joshua

31:14 Then the LORD said to Moses, "The day of your death is near. Summon Joshua and present yourselves in the tent of meeting so that I can commission him." So Moses and Joshua presented themselves in the tent of meeting. **31:15** The LORD appeared in the tent in a pillar of cloud that stood above the door of the tent. **31:16** Then the LORD said to Moses, "You are about to die, and then these people will begin to prostitute themselves with the foreign gods of the land into which they are going. They will reject me and break my covenant that I have made with them. **31:17** At that time my anger will erupt against them and I will abandon them and hide my face from them until they are devoured. Many disasters and distresses will overcome them so that they will say at that time, 'Have not these disasters overcome us because our God is not among us?' **31:18** But I will certainly hide myself at that time because of all the wickedness they will have done by turning to other gods. **31:19** Now write down for yourselves the following song and teach it to the Israelites. Put it into their very mouths so that this song may serve as my witness against the Israelites! **31:20** For after I have brought them to the land I promised to their ancestors – one flowing with milk and honey – and they eat their fill and become fat, then they will turn to other gods and worship them; they will reject me and break my covenant. **31:21** Then when many disasters and distresses overcome them this song will testify against them, for their descendants will not forget it. I know the intentions they have in mind today, even before I bring them to the land I have promised." **31:22** So on that day Moses wrote down this song and taught it to the Israelites, **31:23** and the LORD commissioned Joshua son of Nun, "Be strong and courageous, for you will take the Israelites to the land I have promised them, and I will be with you."

Anticipation of Disobedience

31:24 When Moses finished writing on a scroll the words of this law in their entirety, **31:25** he commanded the Levites who carried the ark of the LORD's covenant, **31:26** "Take this scroll of the law and place it beside the ark of the covenant of the LORD your God. It will remain there as a witness against you, **31:27** for I know about your rebellion and stubbornness. Indeed, even while I have been living among you to this very day, you have rebelled against the LORD; you will be even more rebellious after my death! **31:28** Gather to me all your tribal elders and officials so I can speak to them directly about these things and call the heavens and the earth to witness against them. **31:29** For I know that after I die you will totally corrupt yourselves and turn away from the path I have commanded you to walk. Disaster will confront you in the days to come because you will act wickedly before the LORD, inciting him to anger because of your actions." **31:30** Then Moses recited the words of this song from start to finish in the hearing of the whole assembly of Israel.

Invocation of Witnesses

32:1 Listen, O heavens, and I will speak;
hear, O earth, the words of my mouth.
32:2 My teaching will drop like the rain,
my sayings will drip like the dew,
as rain drops upon the grass,
and showers upon new growth.
32:3 For I will proclaim the name of the LORD;
you must acknowledge the greatness of our God.
32:4 As for the Rock, his work is perfect,
for all his ways are just.
He is a reliable God who is never unjust,
he is fair and upright.
32:5 His people have been unfaithful to him;
they have not acted like his children – this is their sin.
They are a perverse and deceitful generation.
32:6 Is this how you repay the LORD,
you foolish, unwise people?
Is he not your father, your creator?
He has made you and established you.
32:7 Remember the ancient days;
bear in mind the years of past generations.
Ask your father and he will inform you,
your elders, and they will tell you.
32:8 When the Most High gave the nations their inheritance,
when he divided up humankind,
he set the boundaries of the peoples,
according to the number of the heavenly assembly.
32:9 For the LORD's allotment is his people,
Jacob is his special possession.
32:10 The LORD found him in a desolate land,
in an empty wasteland where animals howl.
He continually guarded him and taught him;
he continually protected him like the pupil of his eye.
32:11 Like an eagle that stirs up its nest,
that hovers over its young,
so the LORD spread out his wings and took him,
he lifted him up on his pinions.
32:12 The LORD alone was guiding him,
no foreign god was with him.
32:13 He enabled him to travel over the high terrain of the land,
and he ate of the produce of the fields.
He provided honey for him from the cliffs,
and olive oil from the hardest of rocks,
32:14 butter from the herd
and milk from the flock,
along with the fat of lambs,
rams and goats of Bashan,
along with the best of the kernels of wheat;
and from the juice of grapes you drank wine.

Israel's Rebellion

32:15 But Jeshurun became fat and kicked,
you got fat, thick, and stuffed!
Then he deserted the God who made him,
and treated the Rock who saved him with contempt.
32:16 They made him jealous with other gods,
they enraged him with abhorrent idols.
32:17 They sacrificed to demons, not God,
to gods they had not known;
to new gods who had recently come along,
gods your ancestors had not known about.
32:18 You have forgotten the Rock who fathered you,
and put out of mind the God who gave you birth.

A Word of Judgment

32:19 But the LORD took note and despised them
because his sons and daughters enraged him.
32:20 He said, "I will reject them,
I will see what will happen to them;
for they are a perverse generation,
children who show no loyalty.
32:21 They have made me jealous with false gods,
enraging me with their worthless gods;
so I will make them jealous with a people they do not recognize,
with a nation slow to learn I will enrage them.
32:22 For a fire has been kindled by my anger,
and it burns to lowest Sheol;
it consumes the earth and its produce,
and ignites the foundations of the mountains.
32:23 I will increase their disasters,
I will use up my arrows on them.
32:24 They will be starved by famine,
eaten by plague, and bitterly stung;
I will send the teeth of wild animals against them,
along with the poison of creatures that crawl in the dust.
32:25 The sword will make people childless outside,
and terror will do so inside;
they will destroy both the young man and the virgin,
the infant and the gray-haired man.

The Weakness of Other Gods

32:26 "I said, 'I want to cut them in pieces.
I want to make people forget they ever existed.
32:27 But I fear the reaction of their enemies,
for their adversaries would misunderstand
and say, "Our power is great,
and the LORD has not done all this!"'
32:28 They are a nation devoid of wisdom,
and there is no understanding among them.
32:29 I wish that they were wise and could understand this,
and that they could comprehend what will happen to them."

32:30 How can one man chase a thousand of them,
and two pursue ten thousand;
unless their Rock had delivered them up,
and the LORD had handed them over?
32:31 For our enemies' rock is not like our Rock,
as even our enemies concede.
32:32 For their vine is from the stock of Sodom,
and from the fields of Gomorrah.
Their grapes contain venom,
their clusters of grapes are bitter.
32:33 Their wine is snakes' poison,
the deadly venom of cobras.
32:34 "Is this not stored up with me?" says the LORD,
"Is it not sealed up in my storehouses?
32:35 I will get revenge and pay them back
at the time their foot slips;
for the day of their disaster is near,
and the impending judgment is rushing upon them!"
32:36 The LORD will judge his people,
and will change his plans concerning his servants;
when he sees that their power has disappeared,
and that no one is left, whether confined or set free.
32:37 He will say, "Where are their gods,
the rock in whom they sought security,
32:38 who ate the best of their sacrifices,
and drank the wine of their drink offerings?
Let them rise and help you;
let them be your refuge!

The Vindication of the LORD

32:39 "See now that I, indeed I, am he!" says the LORD,
"and there is no other god besides me.
I kill and give life,
I smash and I heal,
and none can resist my power.
32:40 For I raise up my hand to heaven,
and say, 'As surely as I live forever,
32:41 I will sharpen my lightning-like sword,
and my hand will grasp hold of the weapon of judgment;
I will execute vengeance on my foes,
and repay those who hate me!
32:42 I will make my arrows drunk with blood,
and my sword will devour flesh –
the blood of the slaughtered and captured,
the chief of the enemy's leaders!'"
32:43 Cry out, O nations, with his people,
for he will avenge his servants' blood;
he will take vengeance against his enemies,
and make atonement for his land and people.

Narrative Interlude

32:44 Then Moses went with Joshua son of Nun and recited all the words of this song to the people. **32:45** When Moses finished reciting all these words to all Israel **32:46** he said to them, "Keep in mind all the words I am solemnly proclaiming to you today; you must command your children to observe carefully all the words of this law. **32:47** For this is no idle word for you – it is your life! By this word you will live a long time in the land you are about to cross the Jordan to possess."

Instructions about Moses' Death

32:48 Then the LORD said to Moses that same day, **32:49** "Go up to this Abarim hill country, to Mount Nebo (which is in the land of Moab opposite Jericho) and look at the land of Canaan that I am giving to the Israelites as a possession. **32:50** You will die on the mountain that you ascend and join your deceased ancestors, just as Aaron your brother died on Mount Hor and joined his deceased ancestors, **32:51** for both of you rebelled against me among the Israelites at the waters of Meribah Kadesh in the desert of Zin when you did not show me proper respect among the Israelites. **32:52** You will see the land before you, but you will not enter the land that I am giving to the Israelites."

Introduction to the Blessing of Moses

33:1 This is the blessing Moses the man of God pronounced upon the Israelites before his death. **33:2** He said:

A Historical Review

The LORD came from Sinai
and revealed himself to Israel from Seir.
He appeared in splendor from Mount Paran,
and came forth with ten thousand holy ones.
With his right hand he gave a fiery law to them.
33:3 Surely he loves the people;
all your holy ones are in your power.
And they sit at your feet,
each receiving your words.
33:4 Moses delivered to us a law,
an inheritance for the assembly of Jacob.
33:5 The LORD was king over Jeshurun,
when the leaders of the people assembled,
the tribes of Israel together.

Blessing on Reuben

33:6 May Reuben live and not die,
and may his people multiply.

Blessing on Judah

33:7 And this is the blessing to Judah. He said,
Listen, O LORD, to Judah's voice,
and bring him to his people.
May his power be great,
and may you help him against his foes.

Blessing on Levi

33:8 Of Levi he said:
Your Thummim and Urim belong to your godly one,
whose authority you challenged at Massah,
and with whom you argued at the waters of Meribah.
33:9 He said to his father and mother, "I have not seen him,"
and he did not acknowledge his own brothers
or know his own children,
for they kept your word,
and guarded your covenant.
33:10 They will teach Jacob your ordinances
and Israel your law;
they will offer incense as a pleasant odor,
and a whole offering on your altar.
33:11 Bless, O LORD, his goods,
and be pleased with his efforts;
undercut the legs of any who attack him,
and of those who hate him, so that they cannot stand.

Blessing on Benjamin

33:12 Of Benjamin he said:
The beloved of the LORD will live safely by him;
he protects him all the time,
and the LORD places him on his chest.

Blessing on Joseph

33:13 Of Joseph he said:
May the LORD bless his land
with the harvest produced by the sky, by the dew,
and by the depths crouching beneath;
33:14 with the harvest produced by the daylight
and by the moonlight;
33:15 with the best of the ancient mountains
and the harvest produced by the age-old hills;
33:16 with the harvest of the earth and its fullness
and the pleasure of him who resided in the burning bush.
May blessing rest on Joseph's head,
and on the top of the head of the one set apart from his brothers.
33:17 May the firstborn of his bull bring him honor,
and may his horns be those of a wild ox;

with them may he gore all peoples,
all the far reaches of the earth.
They are the ten thousands of Ephraim,
and they are the thousands of Manasseh.

Blessing on Zebulun and Issachar

33:18 Of Zebulun he said:
Rejoice, Zebulun, when you go outside,
and Issachar, when you are in your tents.
33:19 They will summon peoples to the mountain,
there they will sacrifice proper sacrifices;
for they will enjoy the abundance of the seas,
and the hidden treasures of the shores.

Blessing on Gad

33:20 Of Gad he said:
Blessed be the one who enlarges Gad.
Like a lioness he will dwell;
he will tear at an arm – indeed, a scalp.
33:21 He has selected the best part for himself,
for the portion of the ruler is set aside there;
he came with the leaders of the people,
he obeyed the righteous laws of the LORD
and his ordinances with Israel.

Blessing on Dan

33:22 Of Dan he said:
Dan is a lion's cub;
he will leap forth from Bashan.

Blessing on Naphtali

33:23 Of Naphtali he said:
O Naphtali, overflowing with favor,
and full of the LORD's blessing,
possess the west and south.

Blessing on Asher

33:24 Of Asher he said:
Asher is blessed with children,
may he be favored by his brothers
and may he dip his foot in olive oil.
33:25 The bars of your gates will be made of iron and bronze,
and may you have lifelong strength.

General Praise and Blessing

33:26 There is no one like God, O Jeshurun,
who rides through the sky to help you,
on the clouds in majesty.
33:27 The everlasting God is a refuge,
and underneath you are his eternal arms;
he has driven out enemies before you,
and has said, "Destroy!"
33:28 Israel lives in safety,
the fountain of Jacob is quite secure,
in a land of grain and new wine;
indeed, its heavens rain down dew.
33:29 You have joy, Israel! Who is like you?
You are a people delivered by the LORD,
your protective shield
and your exalted sword.
May your enemies cringe before you;
may you trample on their backs.

The Death of Moses

34:1 Then Moses ascended from the deserts of Moab to Mount Nebo, to the summit of Pisgah, which is opposite Jericho. The LORD showed him the whole land – Gilead to Dan, **34:2** and all of Naphtali, the land of Ephraim and Manasseh, all the land of Judah as far as the distant sea, **34:3** the Negev, and the plain of the valley of Jericho, the city of the date palm trees, as far as Zoar. **34:4** Then the LORD said to him, "This is the land I promised to Abraham, Isaac, and Jacob when I said, 'I will give it to your descendants.' I have let you see it, but you will not cross over there."

34:5 So Moses, the servant of the LORD, died there in the land of Moab as the LORD had said. **34:6** He buried him in the land of Moab near Beth Peor, but no one knows his exact burial place to this very day. **34:7** Moses was 120 years old when he died, but his eye was not dull nor had his vitality departed. **34:8** The Israelites mourned for Moses in the deserts of Moab for thirty days; then the days of mourning for Moses ended.

The Epitaph of Moses

34:9 Now Joshua son of Nun was full of the spirit of wisdom, for Moses had placed his hands on him; and the Israelites listened to him and did just what the LORD had commanded Moses. **34:10** No prophet ever again arose in Israel like Moses, who knew the LORD face to face. **34:11** He did all the signs and wonders the LORD had sent him to do in the land of Egypt, to Pharaoh, all his servants, and the whole land, **34:12** and he displayed great power and awesome might in view of all Israel.

Book 6. Joshua

The LORD Commissions Joshua

1:1 After Moses the LORD's servant died, the LORD said to Joshua son of Nun, Moses' assistant: **1:2** "Moses my servant is dead. Get ready! Cross the Jordan River! Lead these people into the land which I am ready to hand over to them. **1:3** I am handing over to you every place you set foot, as I promised Moses. **1:4** Your territory will extend from the wilderness in the south to Lebanon in the north. It will extend all the way to the great River Euphrates in the east (including all of Syria) and all the way to the Mediterranean Sea in the west. **1:5** No one will be able to resist you all the days of your life. As I was with Moses, so I will be with you. I will not abandon you or leave you alone. **1:6** Be strong and brave! You must lead these people in the conquest of this land that I solemnly promised their ancestors I would hand over to them. **1:7** Make sure you are very strong and brave! Carefully obey all the law my servant Moses charged you to keep! Do not swerve from it to the right or to the left, so that you may be successful in all you do. **1:8** This law scroll must not leave your lips! You must memorize it day and night so you can carefully obey all that is written in it. Then you will prosper and be successful. **1:9** I repeat, be strong and brave! Don't be afraid and don't panic, for I, the LORD your God, am with you in all you do."

Joshua Prepares for the Invasion

1:10 Joshua instructed the leaders of the people: **1:11** "Go through the camp and command the people, 'Prepare your supplies, for within three days you will cross the Jordan River and begin the conquest of the land the LORD your God is ready to hand over to you.'"

1:12 Joshua told the Reubenites, Gadites, and the half tribe of Manasseh: **1:13** "Remember what Moses the LORD's servant commanded you. The LORD your God is giving you a place to settle and is handing this land over to you. **1:14** Your wives, children and cattle may stay in the land that Moses assigned to you east of the Jordan River. But all you warriors must cross over armed for battle ahead of your brothers. You must help them **1:15** until the LORD gives your brothers a place like yours to settle and they conquer the land the LORD your God is ready to hand over to them. Then you may go back to your allotted land and occupy the land Moses the LORD's servant assigned you east of the Jordan."

1:16 They told Joshua, "We will do everything you say. We will go wherever you send us. **1:17** Just as we obeyed Moses, so we will obey you. But may the LORD your God be with you as he was with Moses! **1:18** Any man who rebels against what you say and does not obey all your commands will be executed. But be strong and brave!"

Joshua Sends Spies into the Land

2:1 Joshua son of Nun sent two spies out from Shittim secretly and instructed them: "Find out what you can about the land, especially Jericho." They stopped at the house of a prostitute named Rahab and spent the night there. **2:2** The king of Jericho received this report: "Note well! Israelite men have come here tonight to spy on the land." **2:3** So the king of Jericho sent this order to Rahab: "Turn over the men who came to you – the ones who came to your house – for they have come to spy on the whole land!" **2:4** But the woman hid the two men and replied, "Yes, these men were clients of mine, but I didn't know where they came from. **2:5** When it was time to shut the city gate for the night, the men left. I don't know where they were heading. Chase after them quickly, for you have time to catch them!" **2:6** (Now she had taken them up to the roof and had hidden them in the stalks of flax she had spread out on the roof.) **2:7** Meanwhile the king's men tried to find them on the road to the Jordan River near the fords. The city gate was shut as soon as they set out in pursuit of them.

2:8 Now before the spies went to sleep, Rahab went up to the roof. **2:9** She said to the men, "I know the LORD is handing this land over to you. We are absolutely terrified of you, and all who live in the land are cringing before you. **2:10** For we heard how the LORD dried up the water of the Red Sea before you when you left Egypt and how you annihilated the two Amorite kings, Sihon and Og, on the other side of the Jordan. **2:11** When we heard the news we lost our courage and no one could even breathe for fear of you. For the LORD your God is God in heaven above and on earth below! **2:12** So now, promise me this with an oath sworn in the LORD's name. Because I have shown allegiance to you, show allegiance to my family. Give me a solemn pledge **2:13** that you will spare the lives of my father, mother, brothers, sisters, and all who belong to them, and rescue us from death." **2:14** The men said to her, "If you die, may we die too! If you do not report what we've been up to, then, when the LORD hands the land over to us, we will show unswerving allegiance to you."

2:15 Then Rahab let them down by a rope through the window. (Her house was built as part of the city wall; she lived in the wall.) **2:16** She told them, "Head to the hill country, so the ones chasing you don't find you. Hide from them there for three days, long enough for those chasing you to return. Then you can be on your way." **2:17** The men said to her, "We are not bound by this oath you made us swear unless the following conditions are met: **2:18** When we invade the land, tie this red rope in the window through which you let us down, and gather together in your

house your father, mother, brothers, and all who live in your father's house. **2:19** Anyone who leaves your house will be responsible for his own death – we are innocent in that case! But if anyone with you in the house is harmed, we will be responsible. **2:20** If you should report what we've been up to, we are not bound by this oath you made us swear." **2:21** She said, "I agree to these conditions." She sent them on their way and then tied the red rope in the window. **2:22** They went to the hill country and stayed there for three days, long enough for those chasing them to return. Their pursuers looked all along the way but did not find them. **2:23** Then the two men returned – they came down from the hills, crossed the river, came to Joshua son of Nun, and reported to him all they had discovered. **2:24** They told Joshua, "Surely the LORD is handing over all the land to us! All who live in the land are cringing before us!"

Israel Crosses the Jordan

3:1 Bright and early the next morning Joshua and the Israelites left Shittim and came to the Jordan. They camped there before crossing the river. **3:2** After three days the leaders went through the camp **3:3** and commanded the people: "When you see the ark of the covenant of the LORD your God being carried by the Levitical priests, you must leave here and walk behind it. **3:4** But stay about three thousand feet behind it. Keep your distance so you can see which way you should go, for you have not traveled this way before."

3:5 Joshua told the people, "Ritually consecrate yourselves, for tomorrow the LORD will perform miraculous deeds among you." **3:6** Joshua told the priests, "Pick up the ark of the covenant and pass on ahead of the people." So they picked up the ark of the covenant and went ahead of the people.

3:7 The LORD told Joshua, "This very day I will begin to honor you before all Israel so they will know that I am with you just as I was with Moses. **3:8** Instruct the priests carrying the ark of the covenant, 'When you reach the bank of the Jordan River, wade into the water.'"

3:9 Joshua told the Israelites, "Come here and listen to the words of the LORD your God!" **3:10** Joshua continued, "This is how you will know the living God is among you and that he will truly drive out before you the Canaanites, Hittites, Hivites, Perizzites, Girgashites, Amorites, and Jebusites. **3:11** Look! The ark of the covenant of the Ruler of the whole earth is ready to enter the Jordan ahead of you. **3:12** Now select for yourselves twelve men from the tribes of Israel, one per tribe. **3:13** When the feet of the priests carrying the ark of the LORD, the Ruler of the whole earth, touch the water of the Jordan, the water coming downstream toward you will stop flowing and pile up."

3:14 So when the people left their tents to cross the Jordan, the priests carrying the ark of the covenant went ahead of them. **3:15** When the ones carrying the ark reached the Jordan and the feet of the priests carrying the ark touched the surface of the water – (the Jordan is at flood stage all during harvest time) – **3:16** the water coming downstream toward them stopped flowing. It piled up far upstream at Adam (the city near Zarethan); there was no water at all flowing to the sea of the Arabah (the Salt Sea). The people crossed the river opposite Jericho. **3:17** The priests carrying the ark of the covenant of the LORD stood firmly on dry ground in the middle of the Jordan. All Israel crossed over on dry ground until the entire nation was on the other side.

Israel Commemorates the Crossing

4:1 When the entire nation was on the other side, the LORD told Joshua, **4:2** "Select for yourselves twelve men from the people, one per tribe. **4:3** Instruct them, 'Pick up twelve stones from the middle of the Jordan, from the very place where the priests stand firmly, and carry them over with you and put them in the place where you camp tonight.'"

4:4 Joshua summoned the twelve men he had appointed from the Israelites, one per tribe. **4:5** Joshua told them, "Go in front of the ark of the LORD your God to the middle of the Jordan. Each of you is to put a stone on his shoulder, according to the number of the Israelite tribes. **4:6** The stones will be a reminder to you. When your children ask someday, 'Why are these stones important to you?' **4:7** tell them how the water of the Jordan stopped flowing before the ark of the covenant of the LORD. When it crossed the Jordan, the water of the Jordan stopped flowing. These stones will be a lasting memorial for the Israelites."

4:8 The Israelites did just as Joshua commanded. They picked up twelve stones, according to the number of the Israelite tribes, from the middle of the Jordan as the LORD had instructed Joshua. They carried them over with them to the camp and put them there. **4:9** Joshua also set up twelve stones in the middle of the Jordan in the very place where the priests carrying the ark of the covenant stood. They remain there to this very day.

4:10 Now the priests carrying the ark of the covenant were standing in the middle of the Jordan until everything the LORD had commanded Joshua to tell the people was accomplished, in accordance with all that Moses had commanded Joshua. The people went across quickly, **4:11** and when all the people had finished crossing, the ark of the LORD and the priests crossed as the people looked on. **4:12** The Reubenites, Gadites, and the half-tribe of Manasseh crossed over armed for battle ahead of the Israelites, just as Moses had instructed them. **4:13** About forty thousand battle-ready troops marched past the LORD to fight on the plains of Jericho. **4:14**

That day the LORD brought honor to Joshua before all Israel. They respected him all his life, just as they had respected Moses.

4:15 The LORD told Joshua, **4:16** "Instruct the priests carrying the ark of the covenantal laws to come up from the Jordan." **4:17** So Joshua instructed the priests, "Come up from the Jordan!" **4:18** The priests carrying the ark of the covenant of the LORD came up from the middle of the Jordan, and as soon as they set foot on dry land, the water of the Jordan flowed again and returned to flood stage.

4:19 The people went up from the Jordan on the tenth day of the first month and camped in Gilgal on the eastern border of Jericho. **4:20** Now Joshua set up in Gilgal the twelve stones they had taken from the Jordan. **4:21** He told the Israelites, "When your children someday ask their fathers, 'What do these stones represent?' **4:22** explain to your children, 'Israel crossed the Jordan River on dry ground.' **4:23** For the LORD your God dried up the water of the Jordan before you while you crossed over. It was just like when the LORD your God dried up the Red Sea before us while we crossed it. **4:24** He has done this so all the nations of the earth might recognize the LORD's power and so you might always obey the LORD your God."

5:1 When all the Amorite kings on the west side of the Jordan and all the Canaanite kings along the seacoast heard how the LORD had dried up the water of the Jordan before the Israelites while they crossed, they lost their courage and could not even breathe for fear of the Israelites.

A New Generation is Circumcised

5:2 At that time the LORD told Joshua, "Make flint knives and circumcise the Israelites once again." **5:3** So Joshua made flint knives and circumcised the Israelites on the Hill of the Foreskins. **5:4** This is why Joshua had to circumcise them: All the men old enough to fight when they left Egypt died on the journey through the desert after they left Egypt. **5:5** Now all the men who left were circumcised, but all the sons born on the journey through the desert after they left Egypt were uncircumcised. **5:6** Indeed, for forty years the Israelites traveled through the desert until all the men old enough to fight when they left Egypt, the ones who had disobeyed the LORD, died off. For the LORD had sworn a solemn oath to them that he would not let them see the land he had sworn on oath to give them, a land rich in milk and honey. **5:7** He replaced them with their sons, whom Joshua circumcised. They were uncircumcised; their fathers had not circumcised them along the way. **5:8** When all the men had been circumcised, they stayed there in the camp until they had healed. **5:9** The LORD said to Joshua, "Today I have taken away the disgrace of Egypt from you." So that place is called Gilgal even to this day.

5:10 So the Israelites camped in Gilgal and celebrated the Passover in the evening of the fourteenth day of the month on the plains of Jericho. **5:11** They ate some of the produce of the land the day after the Passover, including unleavened bread and roasted grain. **5:12** The manna stopped appearing the day they ate some of the produce of the land; the Israelites never ate manna again.

Israel Conquers Jericho

5:13 When Joshua was near Jericho, he looked up and saw a man standing in front of him holding a drawn sword. Joshua approached him and asked him, "Are you on our side or allied with our enemies?" **5:14** He answered, "Truly I am the commander of the LORD's army. Now I have arrived!" Joshua bowed down with his face to the ground and asked, "What does my master want to say to his servant?" **5:15** The commander of the LORD's army answered Joshua, "Remove your sandals from your feet, because the place where you stand is holy." Joshua did so.

6:1 Now Jericho was shut tightly because of the Israelites. No one was allowed to leave or enter. **6:2** The LORD told Joshua, "See, I am about to defeat Jericho for you, along with its king and its warriors. **6:3** Have all the warriors march around the city one time; do this for six days. **6:4** Have seven priests carry seven rams' horns in front of the ark. On the seventh day march around the city seven times, while the priests blow the horns. **6:5** When you hear the signal from the ram's horn, have the whole army give a loud battle cry. Then the city wall will collapse and the warriors should charge straight ahead."

6:6 So Joshua son of Nun summoned the priests and instructed them, "Pick up the ark of the covenant, and seven priests must carry seven rams' horns in front of the ark of the LORD." **6:7** And he told the army, "Move ahead and march around the city, with armed troops going ahead of the ark of the LORD."

6:8 When Joshua gave the army its orders, the seven priests carrying the seven rams' horns before the LORD moved ahead and blew the horns as the ark of the covenant of the LORD followed behind. **6:9** Armed troops marched ahead of the priests blowing the horns, while the rear guard followed along behind the ark blowing rams' horns. **6:10** Now Joshua had instructed the army, "Do not give a battle cry or raise your voices; say nothing until the day I tell you, 'Give the battle cry.' Then give the battle cry!" **6:11** So Joshua made sure they marched the ark of the LORD around the city one time. Then they went back to the camp and spent the night there.

6:12 Bright and early the next morning Joshua had the priests pick up the ark of the LORD. **6:13** The seven priests carrying the seven rams' horns before the ark of the LORD marched along blowing their horns. Armed troops marched ahead of them, while the rear guard followed along behind the ark of the LORD blowing rams' horns. **6:14** They marched around the city one time on the second day, then returned to the camp. They did this six days in all.

6:15 On the seventh day they were up at the crack of dawn and marched around the city as before – only this time they marched around it seven times. **6:16** The seventh time around, the priests blew the rams' horns and Joshua told the army, "Give the battle cry, for the LORD is handing the city over to you! **6:17** The city and all that is in it must be set apart for the LORD, except for Rahab the prostitute and all who are with her in her house, because she hid the spies we sent. **6:18** But be careful when you are setting apart the riches for the LORD. If you take any of it, you will make the Israelite camp subject to annihilation and cause a disaster. **6:19** All the silver and gold, as well as bronze and iron items, belong to the LORD. They must go into the LORD's treasury."

6:20 The rams' horns sounded and when the army heard the signal, they gave a loud battle cry. The wall collapsed and the warriors charged straight ahead into the city and captured it. **6:21** They annihilated with the sword everything that breathed in the city, including men and women, young and old, as well as cattle, sheep, and donkeys. **6:22** Joshua told the two men who had spied on the land, "Enter the prostitute's house and bring out the woman and all who belong to her as you promised her." **6:23** So the young spies went and brought out Rahab, her father, mother, brothers, and all who belonged to her. They brought out her whole family and took them to a place outside the Israelite camp. **6:24** But they burned the city and all that was in it, except for the silver, gold, and bronze and iron items they put in the treasury of the LORD's house. **6:25** Yet Joshua spared Rahab the prostitute, her father's family, and all who belonged to her. She lives in Israel to this very day because she hid the messengers Joshua sent to spy on Jericho. **6:26** At that time Joshua made this solemn declaration: "The man who attempts to rebuild this city of Jericho will stand condemned before the LORD. He will lose his firstborn son when he lays its foundations and his youngest son when he erects its gates!" **6:27** The LORD was with Joshua and he became famous throughout the land.

Achan Sins and is Punished

7:1 But the Israelites disobeyed the command about the city's riches. Achan son of Carmi, son of Zabdi, son of Zerah, from the tribe of Judah, stole some of the riches. The LORD was furious with the Israelites.

7:2 Joshua sent men from Jericho to Ai (which is located near Beth Aven, east of Bethel) and instructed them, "Go up and spy on the land." So the men went up and spied on Ai. **7:3** They returned and reported to Joshua, "Don't send the whole army. About two or three thousand men are adequate to defeat Ai. Don't tire out the whole army, for Ai is small." **7:4** So about three thousand men went up, but they fled from the men of Ai. **7:5** The men of Ai killed about thirty-six of them and chased them from in front of the city gate all the way to the fissures and defeated them on the steep slope. The people's courage melted away like water.

7:6 Joshua tore his clothes; he and the leaders of Israel lay face down on the ground before the ark of the LORD until evening and threw dirt on their heads. **7:7** Joshua prayed, "O, Master, LORD! Why did you bring these people across the Jordan to hand us over to the Amorites so they could destroy us? **7:8** If only we had been satisfied to live on the other side of the Jordan! O Lord, what can I say now that Israel has retreated before its enemies? **7:9** When the Canaanites and all who live in the land hear about this, they will turn against us and destroy the very memory of us from the earth. What will you do to protect your great reputation?"

7:10 The LORD responded to Joshua, "Get up! Why are you lying there face down? **7:11** Israel has sinned; they have violated my covenantal commandment! They have taken some of the riches; they have stolen them and deceitfully put them among their own possessions. **7:12** The Israelites are unable to stand before their enemies; they retreat because they have become subject to annihilation. I will no longer be with you, unless you destroy what has contaminated you. **7:13** Get up! Ritually consecrate the people and tell them this: 'Ritually consecrate yourselves for tomorrow, because the LORD God of Israel says, "You are contaminated, O Israel! You will not be able to stand before your enemies until you remove what is contaminating you." **7:14** In the morning you must approach in tribal order. The tribe the LORD selects must approach by clans. The clan the LORD selects must approach by families. The family the LORD selects must approach man by man. **7:15** The one caught with the riches must be burned up along with all who belong to him, because he violated the LORD's covenant and did such a disgraceful thing in Israel.'"

7:16 Bright and early the next morning Joshua made Israel approach in tribal order and the tribe of Judah was selected. **7:17** He then made the clans of Judah approach and the clan of the Zerahites was selected. He made the clan of the Zerahites approach and Zabdi was selected. **7:18** He then made Zabdi's family approach man by man and Achan son of Carmi, son of Zabdi, son of Zerah, from the tribe of Judah, was selected. **7:19** So Joshua said to Achan, "My son, honor the LORD God of Israel and give him praise! Tell me what you did; don't hide anything from me!" **7:20** Achan told Joshua, "It is true. I have sinned against the LORD God of Israel in this way: **7:21** I saw among the goods we seized a nice robe from Babylon, two hundred silver pieces, and a bar of gold weighing fifty shekels. I wanted them, so I took them. They are hidden in the ground right in the middle of my tent with the silver underneath." **7:22** Joshua sent messengers who ran to the tent. The things were hidden right in his tent, with the silver underneath. **7:23** They took it all from the middle of the tent, brought it to Joshua and all the Israelites, and placed it before the LORD. **7:24** Then Joshua and all Israel took Achan, son of Zerah, along with the silver, the robe, the bar of gold, his sons, daughters, ox, donkey, sheep, tent, and all that belonged to him and brought them up to the Valley of Disaster. **7:25** Joshua said, "Why have you brought disaster on us? The LORD will bring disaster on you today!" All Israel stoned him to death. (They also stoned and burned the others.) **7:26** Then they erected over him a large pile of stones (it remains to this very day) and the LORD's anger subsided. So that place is called the Valley of Disaster to this very day.

Israel Conquers Ai

8:1 The LORD told Joshua, "Don't be afraid and don't panic! Take the whole army with you and march against Ai! See, I am handing over to you the king of Ai, along with his people, city, and land. **8:2** Do to Ai and its king what you did to Jericho and its king, except you may plunder its goods and cattle. Set an ambush behind the city!"

8:3 Joshua and the whole army marched against Ai. Joshua selected thirty thousand brave warriors and sent them out at night. **8:4** He told them, "Look, set an ambush behind the city. Don't go very far from the city; all of you be ready! **8:5** I and all the troops who are with me will approach the city. When they come out to fight us like before, we will retreat from them. **8:6** They will attack us until we have lured them from the city, for they will say, 'They are retreating from us like before.' We will retreat from them. **8:7** Then you rise up from your hiding place and seize the city. The LORD your God will hand it over to you. **8:8** When you capture the city, set it on fire. Do as the LORD says! See, I have given you my orders." **8:9** Joshua sent them away and they went to their hiding place west of Ai, between Bethel and Ai. Joshua spent that night with the army.

8:10 Bright and early the next morning Joshua gathered the army, and he and the leaders of Israel marched at the head of it to Ai. **8:11** All the troops that were with him marched up and drew near the city. They camped north of Ai on the other side of the valley. **8:12** He took five thousand men and set an ambush west of the city between Bethel and Ai. **8:13** The army was in position – the main army north of the city and the rear guard west of the city. That night Joshua went into the middle of the valley.

8:14 When the king of Ai saw Israel, he and his whole army quickly got up the next day and went out to fight Israel at the meeting place near the Arabah. But he did not realize men were hiding behind the city. **8:15** Joshua and all Israel pretended to be defeated by them and they retreated along the way to the desert. **8:16** All the reinforcements in Ai were ordered to chase them; they chased Joshua and were lured away from the city. **8:17** No men were left in Ai or Bethel; they all went out after Israel. They left the city wide open and chased Israel.

8:18 The LORD told Joshua, "Hold out toward Ai the curved sword in your hand, for I am handing the city over to you." So Joshua held out toward Ai the curved sword in his hand. **8:19** When he held out his hand, the men waiting in ambush rose up quickly from their place and attacked. They entered the city, captured it, and immediately set it on fire. **8:20** When the men of Ai turned around, they saw the smoke from the city ascending into the sky and were so shocked they were unable to flee in any direction. In the meantime the men who were retreating to the desert turned against their pursuers. **8:21** When Joshua and all Israel saw that the men in ambush had captured the city and that the city was going up in smoke, they turned around and struck down the men of Ai. **8:22** At the same time the men who had taken the city came out to fight, and the men of Ai were trapped in the middle. The Israelites struck them down, leaving no survivors or refugees. **8:23** But they captured the king of Ai alive and brought him to Joshua.

8:24 When Israel had finished killing all the men of Ai who had chased them toward the desert (they all fell by the sword), all Israel returned to Ai and put the sword to it. **8:25** Twelve thousand men and women died that day, including all the men of Ai. **8:26** Joshua kept holding out his curved sword until Israel had annihilated all who lived in Ai. **8:27** But Israel did plunder the cattle and the goods of the city, in accordance with the LORD's orders to Joshua. **8:28** Joshua burned Ai and made it a permanently uninhabited mound (it remains that way to this very day). **8:29** He hung the king of Ai on a tree, leaving him exposed until evening. At sunset Joshua ordered that his corpse be taken down from the tree. They threw it down at the entrance of the city gate and erected over it a large pile of stones (it remains to this very day).

Covenant Renewal

8:30 Then Joshua built an altar for the LORD God of Israel on Mount Ebal, **8:31** just as Moses the LORD's servant had commanded the Israelites. As described in the law scroll of Moses, it was made with uncut stones untouched by an iron tool. They offered burnt sacrifices on it and sacrificed tokens of peace. **8:32** There, in the presence of the Israelites, Joshua inscribed on the stones a duplicate of the law written by Moses.

8:33 All the people, rulers, leaders, and judges were standing on either side of the ark, in front of the Levitical priests who carried the ark of the covenant of the LORD. Both resident foreigners and native Israelites were there. Half the people stood in front of Mount Gerizim and the other half in front of Mount Ebal, as Moses the LORD's servant had previously instructed to them to do for the formal blessing ceremony. **8:34** Then Joshua read aloud all the words of the law, including the blessings and the curses, just as they are written in the law scroll. **8:35** Joshua read aloud every commandment Moses had given before the whole assembly of Israel, including the women, children, and resident foreigners who lived among them.

The Gibeonites Deceive Israel

9:1 When the news reached all the kings on the west side of the Jordan – in the hill country, the lowlands, and all along the Mediterranean coast as far as Lebanon (including the Hittites, Amorites, Canaanites, Perizzites, Hivites, and Jebusites) – **9:2** they formed an alliance to fight against Joshua and Israel.

9:3 When the residents of Gibeon heard what Joshua did to Jericho and Ai, **9:4** they did something clever. They collected some provisions and put worn-out sacks on their donkeys, along with worn-out wineskins that were ripped and patched. **9:5** They had worn-out, patched sandals on their feet and dressed in worn-out clothes. All their bread was dry and hard. **9:6** They came to Joshua at the camp in Gilgal and said to him and the men of Israel, "We have come from a distant land. Make a treaty with us." **9:7** The men of Israel said to the Hivites, "Perhaps you live near us. So how can we make a treaty with you?" **9:8** But they said to Joshua, "We are willing to be your subjects." So Joshua said to them, "Who are you and where do you come from?" **9:9** They told him, "Your subjects have come from a very distant land because of the reputation of the LORD your God, for we have heard the news about all he did in Egypt **9:10** and all he did to the two Amorite kings on the other side of the Jordan – King Sihon of Heshbon and King Og of Bashan in Ashtaroth. **9:11** Our leaders and all who live in our land told us, 'Take provisions for your journey and go meet them. Tell them, "We are willing to be your subjects. Make a treaty with us."' **9:12** This bread of ours was warm when we packed it in our homes the day we started out to meet you, but now it is dry and hard. **9:13** These wineskins we filled were brand new, but look how they have ripped. Our clothes and sandals have worn out because it has been a very long journey." **9:14** The men examined some of their provisions, but they failed to ask the LORD's advice. **9:15** Joshua made a peace treaty with them and agreed to let them live. The leaders of the community sealed it with an oath.

9:16 Three days after they made the treaty with them, the Israelites found out they were from the local area and lived nearby. **9:17** So the Israelites set out and on the third day arrived at their cities – Gibeon, Kephirah, Beeroth, and Kiriath Jearim. **9:18** The Israelites did not attack them because the leaders of the community had sworn an oath to them in the name of the LORD God of Israel. The whole community criticized the leaders, **9:19** but all the leaders told the whole community, "We swore an oath to them in the name of the LORD God of Israel. So now we can't hurt them! **9:20** We must let them live so we can escape the curse attached to the oath we swore to them." **9:21** The leaders then added, "Let them live." So they became woodcutters and water carriers for the whole community, as the leaders had decided.

9:22 Joshua summoned the Gibeonites and said to them, "Why did you trick us by saying, 'We live far away from you,' when you really live nearby? **9:23** Now you are condemned to perpetual servitude as woodcutters and water carriers for the house of my God." **9:24** They said to Joshua, "It was carefully reported to your subjects how the LORD your God commanded Moses his servant to assign you the whole land and to destroy all who live in the land from before you. Because of you we were terrified we would lose our lives, so we did this thing. **9:25** So now we are in your power. Do to us what you think is good and appropriate. **9:26** Joshua did as they said; he kept the Israelites from killing them **9:27** and that day made them woodcutters and water carriers for the community and for the altar of the LORD at the divinely chosen site. (They continue in that capacity to this very day.)

Israel Defeats an Amorite Coalition

10:1 Adoni-Zedek, king of Jerusalem, heard how Joshua captured Ai and annihilated it and its king as he did Jericho and its king. He also heard how the people of Gibeon made peace with Israel and lived among them. **10:2** All Jerusalem was terrified because Gibeon was a large city, like one of the royal cities. It was larger than Ai and all its men were warriors. **10:3** So King Adoni-Zedek of Jerusalem sent this message to King Hoham of Hebron, King Piram of Jarmuth, King Japhia of Lachish, and King Debir of Eglon: **10:4** "Come to my aid so we can attack Gibeon, for it has made peace with Joshua and the Israelites." **10:5** So the five Amorite kings (the kings of Jerusalem, Hebron, Jarmuth, Lachish, and Eglon) and all their troops gathered together and advanced. They deployed their troops and fought against Gibeon.

10:6 The men of Gibeon sent this message to Joshua at the camp in Gilgal, "Do not abandon your subjects! Rescue us! Help us! For all the Amorite kings living in the hill country are attacking us." **10:7** So Joshua and his whole army, including the bravest warriors, marched up from Gilgal. **10:8** The LORD told Joshua, "Don't be afraid of them, for I am handing them over to you. Not one of them can resist you." **10:9** Joshua attacked them by surprise after marching all night from Gilgal. **10:10** The LORD routed them before Israel. Israel thoroughly defeated them at Gibeon. They chased them up the road to the pass of Beth Horon and struck them down all the way to Azekah and Makkedah. **10:11** As they fled from Israel on the slope leading down from Beth Horon, the LORD threw down on them large hailstones from the sky, all the way to Azekah. They died – in fact, more died from the hailstones than the Israelites killed with the sword.

10:12 The day the LORD delivered the Amorites over to the Israelites, Joshua prayed to the LORD before Israel:

"O sun, stand still over Gibeon!

O moon, over the Valley of Aijalon!"

10:13 The sun stood still and the moon stood motionless while the nation took vengeance on its enemies. The event is recorded in the Scroll of the Upright One. The sun stood motionless in the middle of the sky and did not set for about a full day. **10:14** There has not been a day like it before or since. The LORD obeyed a man, for the LORD fought for Israel! **10:15** Then Joshua and all Israel returned to the camp at Gilgal.

10:16 The five Amorite kings ran away and hid in the cave at Makkedah. **10:17** Joshua was told, "The five kings have been found hiding in the cave at Makkedah." **10:18** Joshua said, "Roll large stones over the mouth of the cave and post guards in front of it. **10:19** But don't you delay! Chase your enemies and catch them! Don't allow them to retreat to their cities, for the LORD your God is handing them over to you." **10:20** Joshua and the Israelites almost totally wiped them out, but some survivors did escape to the fortified cities. **10:21** Then the whole army safely returned to Joshua at the camp in Makkedah. No one dared threaten the Israelites. **10:22** Joshua said, "Open the cave's mouth and bring the five kings out of the cave to me." **10:23** They did as ordered; they brought the five kings out of the cave to him – the kings of Jerusalem, Hebron, Jarmuth, Lachish, and Eglon. **10:24** When they brought the kings out to Joshua, he summoned all the men of Israel and said to the commanders of the troops who accompanied him, "Come here and put your feet on the necks of these kings." So they came up and put their feet on their necks. **10:25** Then Joshua said to them, "Don't be afraid and don't panic! Be strong and brave, for the LORD will do the same thing to all your enemies you fight. **10:26** Then Joshua executed them and hung them on five trees. They were left hanging on the trees until evening. **10:27** At sunset Joshua ordered his men to take them down from the trees. They threw them into the cave where they had hidden and piled large stones over the mouth of the cave. (They remain to this very day.)

Joshua Launches a Southern Campaign

10:28 That day Joshua captured Makkedah and put the sword to it and its king. He annihilated everyone who lived in it; he left no survivors. He did to its king what he had done to the king of Jericho.

10:29 Joshua and all Israel marched from Makkedah to Libnah and fought against it. **10:30** The LORD handed it and its king over to Israel, and Israel put the sword to all who lived there; they left no survivors. They did to its king what they had done to the king of Jericho.

10:31 Joshua and all Israel marched from Libnah to Lachish. He deployed his troops and fought against it. **10:32** The LORD handed Lachish over to Israel and they captured it on the second day. They put the sword to all who lived there, just as they had done to Libnah. **10:33** Then King Horam of Gezer came up to help Lachish, but Joshua struck down him and his army until no survivors remained.

10:34 Joshua and all Israel marched from Lachish to Eglon. They deployed troops and fought against it. **10:35** That day they captured it and put the sword to all who lived there. That day they annihilated it just as they had done to Lachish.

10:36 Joshua and all Israel marched up from Eglon to Hebron and fought against it. **10:37** They captured it and put the sword to its king, all its surrounding cities, and all who lived in it; they left no survivors. As they had done at Eglon, they annihilated it and all who lived there.

10:38 Joshua and all Israel turned to Debir and fought against it. **10:39** They captured it, its king, and all its surrounding cities and put the sword to them. They annihilated everyone who lived there; they left no survivors. They did to Debir and its king what they had done to Libnah and its king and to Hebron.

10:40 Joshua defeated the whole land, including the hill country, the Negev, the lowlands, the slopes, and all their kings. He left no survivors. He annihilated everything that breathed, just as the LORD God of Israel had commanded. **10:41** Joshua conquered the area between Kadesh Barnea and Gaza and the whole region of Goshen, all the way to Gibeon. **10:42** Joshua captured in one campaign all these kings and their lands, for the LORD God of Israel fought for Israel. **10:43** Then Joshua and all Israel returned to the camp at Gilgal.

Israel Defeats a Northern Coalition

11:1 When King Jabin of Hazor heard the news, he organized a coalition, including King Jobab of Madon, the king of Shimron, the king of Acshaph, **11:2** and the northern kings who ruled in the hill country, the

Arabah south of Kinnereth, the lowlands, and the heights of Dor to the west. **11:3** Canaanites came from the east and west; Amorites, Hittites, Perizzites, and Jebusites from the hill country; and Hivites from below Hermon in the area of Mizpah. **11:4** These kings came out with their armies; they were as numerous as the sand on the seashore and had a large number of horses and chariots. **11:5** All these kings gathered and joined forces at the Waters of Merom to fight Israel.

11:6 The LORD told Joshua, "Don't be afraid of them, for about this time tomorrow I will cause all of them to lie dead before Israel. You must hamstring their horses and burn their chariots." **11:7** Joshua and his whole army caught them by surprise at the Waters of Merom and attacked them. **11:8** The LORD handed them over to Israel and they struck them down and chased them all the way to Greater Sidon, Misrephoth Maim, and the Mizpah Valley to the east. They struck them down until no survivors remained. **11:9** Joshua did to them as the LORD had commanded him; he hamstrung their horses and burned their chariots.

11:10 At that time Joshua turned, captured Hazor, and struck down its king with the sword, for Hazor was at that time the leader of all these kingdoms. **11:11** They annihilated everyone who lived there with the sword – no one who breathed remained – and burned Hazor.

11:12 Joshua captured all these royal cities and all their kings and annihilated them with the sword, as Moses the LORD's servant had commanded. **11:13** But Israel did not burn any of the cities located on mounds, except for Hazor; it was the only one Joshua burned. **11:14** The Israelites plundered all the goods of these cities and the cattle, but they totally destroyed all the people and allowed no one who breathed to live. **11:15** Moses the LORD's servant passed on the LORD's commands to Joshua, and Joshua did as he was told. He did not ignore any of the commands the LORD had given Moses.

A Summary of Israel's Victories

11:16 Joshua conquered the whole land, including the hill country, all the Negev, all the land of Goshen, the lowlands, the Arabah, the hill country of Israel and its lowlands, **11:17** from Mount Halak on up to Seir, as far as Baal Gad in the Lebanon Valley below Mount Hermon. He captured all their kings and executed them. **11:18** Joshua campaigned against these kings for quite some time. **11:19** No city made peace with the Israelites (except the Hivites living in Gibeon); they had to conquer all of them, **11:20** for the LORD determined to make them obstinate so they would attack Israel. He wanted Israel to annihilate them without mercy, as he had instructed Moses.

11:21 At that time Joshua attacked and eliminated the Anakites from the hill country – from Hebron, Debir, Anab, and all the hill country of Judah and Israel. Joshua annihilated them and their cities. **11:22** No Anakites were left in Israelite territory, though some remained in Gaza, Gath, and Ashdod. **11:23** Joshua conquered the whole land, just as the LORD had promised Moses, and he assigned Israel their tribal portions. Then the land was free of war.

12:1 Now these are the kings of the land whom the Israelites defeated and drove from their land on the east side of the Jordan, from the Arnon Valley to Mount Hermon, including all the eastern Arabah:

12:2 King Sihon of the Amorites who lived in Heshbon and ruled from Aroer (on the edge of the Arnon Valley) – including the city in the middle of the valley and half of Gilead – all the way to the Jabbok Valley bordering Ammonite territory. **12:3** His kingdom included the eastern Arabah from the Sea of Kinnereth to the Sea of the Arabah (the Salt Sea), including the route to Beth Jeshimoth and the area southward below the slopes of Pisgah.

12:4 The territory of King Og of Bashan, one of the few remaining Rephaites, who lived in Ashtaroth and Edrei **12:5** and ruled over Mount Hermon, Salecah, all of Bashan to the border of the Geshurites and Maacathites, and half of Gilead as far as the border of King Sihon of Heshbon.

12:6 Moses the LORD's servant and the Israelites defeated them and Moses the LORD's servant assigned their land to Reuben, Gad, and the half tribe of Manasseh.

12:7 These are the kings of the land whom Joshua and the Israelites defeated on the west side of the Jordan, from Baal Gad in the Lebanon Valley to Mount Halak on up to Seir. Joshua assigned this territory to the Israelite tribes, **12:8** including the hill country, the lowlands, the Arabah, the slopes, the wilderness, and the Negev – the land of the Hittites, Amorites, Canaanites, Perizzites, Hivites, and Jebusites:

12:9 the king of Jericho (one),

the king of Ai – located near Bethel – (one),

12:10 the king of Jerusalem (one),

the king of Hebron (one),

12:11 the king of Jarmuth (one),

the king of Lachish (one),

12:12 the king of Eglon (one),

the king of Gezer (one),

12:13 the king of Debir (one),

the king of Geder (one),

12:14 the king of Hormah (one),

the king of Arad (one),

12:15 the king of Libnah (one),
the king of Adullam (one),
12:16 the king of Makkedah (one),
the king of Bethel (one),
12:17 the king of Tappuah (one),
the king of Hepher (one),
12:18 the king of Aphek (one),
the king of Lasharon (one),
12:19 the king of Madon (one),
the king of Hazor (one),
12:20 the king of Shimron Meron (one),
the king of Acshaph (one),
12:21 the king of Taanach (one),
the king of Megiddo (one),
12:22 the king of Kedesh (one),
the king of Jokneam near Carmel (one),
12:23 the king of Dor – near Naphath Dor – (one),
the king of Goyim – near Gilgal – (one),
12:24 the king of Tirzah (one),
a total of thirty-one kings.

The Lord Speaks to Joshua

13:1 When Joshua was very old, the LORD told him, "You are very old, and a great deal of land remains to be conquered. **13:2** This is the land that remains: all the territory of the Philistines and all the Geshurites, **13:3** from the Shihor River east of Egypt northward to the territory of Ekron (it is regarded as Canaanite territory), including the area belonging to the five Philistine lords who ruled in Gaza, Ashdod, Ashkelon, Gath, and Ekron, as well as Avvite land **13:4** to the south; all the Canaanite territory, from Arah in the region of Sidon to Aphek, as far as Amorite territory; **13:5** the territory of Byblos and all Lebanon to the east, from Baal Gad below Mount Hermon to Lebo Hamath. **13:6** I will drive out before the Israelites all who live in the hill country from Lebanon to Misrephoth Maim, all the Sidonians; you be sure to parcel it out to Israel as I instructed you." **13:7** Now, divide up this land among the nine tribes and the half-tribe of Manasseh."

Tribal Lands East of the Jordan

13:8 The other half of Manasseh, Reuben, and Gad received their allotted tribal lands beyond the Jordan, just as Moses, the LORD's servant, had assigned them. **13:9** Their territory started from Aroer (on the edge of the Arnon Valley), included the city in the middle of the valley, the whole plain of Medeba as far as Dibon, **13:10** and all the cities of King Sihon of the Amorites who ruled in Heshbon, and ended at the Ammonite border. **13:11** Their territory also included Gilead, Geshurite and Maacathite territory, all Mount Hermon, and all Bashan to Salecah – **13:12** the whole kingdom of Og in Bashan, who ruled in Ashtaroth and Edrei. (He was one of the few remaining Rephaites.) Moses defeated them and took their lands. **13:13** But the Israelites did not conquer the Geshurites and Maacathites; Geshur and Maacah live among Israel to this very day. **13:14** However, Moses did not assign land as an inheritance to the Levites; their inheritance is the sacrificial offerings made to the LORD God of Israel, as he instructed them.

13:15 Moses assigned land to the tribe of Reuben by its clans. **13:16** Their territory started at Aroer (on the edge of the Arnon Valley) and included the city in the middle of the valley, the whole plain of Medeba, **13:17** Heshbon and all its surrounding cities on the plain, including Dibon, Bamoth Baal, Beth Baal Meon, **13:18** Jahaz, Kedemoth, Mephaath, **13:19** Kiriathaim, Sibmah, Zereth Shahar on the hill in the valley, **13:20** Beth Peor, the slopes of Pisgah, and Beth Jeshimoth. **13:21** It encompassed all the cities of the plain and the whole realm of King Sihon of the Amorites who ruled in Heshbon. Moses defeated him and the Midianite leaders Evi, Rekem, Zur, Hur, and Reba (they were subjects of Sihon and lived in his territory). **13:22** The Israelites killed Balaam son of Beor, the omen reader, along with the others. **13:23** The border of the tribe of Reuben was the Jordan. The land allotted to the tribe of Reuben by its clans included these cities and their towns.

13:24 Moses assigned land to the tribe of Gad by its clans. **13:25** Their territory included Jazer, all the cities of Gilead, and half of Ammonite territory as far as Aroer near Rabbah. **13:26** Their territory ran from Heshbon to Ramath Mizpah and Betonim, and from Mahanaim to the territory of Debir. **13:27** It included the valley of Beth Haram, Beth Nimrah, Succoth, and Zaphon, and the rest of the realm of King Sihon of Heshbon, the area east of the Jordan to the end of the Sea of Kinnereth. **13:28** The land allotted to the tribe of Gad by its clans included these cities and their towns.

13:29 Moses assigned land to the half-tribe of Manasseh by its clans. **13:30** Their territory started at Mahanaim and encompassed all Bashan, the whole realm of King Og of Bashan, including all sixty cities in Havvoth Jair in Bashan. **13:31** Half of Gilead, Ashtaroth, and Edrei, cities in the kingdom of Og in Bashan, were assigned to the descendants of Makir son of Manasseh, to half the descendants of Makir by their clans.

13:32 These are the land assignments made by Moses on the plains of Moab east of the Jordan River opposite Jericho. **13:33** However, Moses did not assign land as an inheritance to the Levites; their inheritance is the LORD God of Israel, as he instructed them.

Judah's Tribal Lands

14:1 The following is a record of the territory assigned to the Israelites in the land of Canaan by Eleazar the priest, Joshua son of Nun, and the Israelite tribal leaders. **14:2** The land assignments to the nine-and-a-half tribes were made by drawing lots, as the LORD had instructed Moses. **14:3** Now Moses had assigned land to the two-and-a-half tribes east of the Jordan, but he assigned no land to the Levites. **14:4** The descendants of Joseph were considered as two tribes, Manasseh and Ephraim. The Levites were allotted no territory, though they were assigned cities in which to live, along with the grazing areas for their cattle and possessions. **14:5** The Israelites followed the LORD's instructions to Moses and divided up the land.

14:6 The men of Judah approached Joshua in Gilgal, and Caleb son of Jephunneh the Kenizzite said to him, "You know what the LORD said about you and me to Moses, the man of God, at Kadesh Barnea. **14:7** I was forty years old when Moses, the LORD's servant, sent me from Kadesh Barnea to spy on the land and I brought back to him an honest report. **14:8** My countrymen who accompanied me frightened the people, but I remained loyal to the LORD my God. **14:9** That day Moses made this solemn promise: 'Surely the land on which you walked will belong to you and your descendants permanently, for you remained loyal to the LORD your God.' **14:10** So now, look, the LORD has preserved my life, just as he promised, these past forty-five years since the LORD spoke these words to Moses, during which Israel traveled through the wilderness. Now look, I am today eighty-five years old. **14:11** Today I am still as strong as when Moses sent me out. I can fight and go about my daily activities with the same energy I had then. **14:12** Now, assign me this hill country which the LORD promised me at that time! No doubt you heard at that time that the Anakites live there in large, fortified cities. But, assuming the LORD is with me, I will conquer them, as the LORD promised." **14:13** Joshua asked God to empower Caleb son of Jephunneh and assigned him Hebron. **14:14** So Hebron remains the assigned land of Caleb son of Jephunneh the Kenizzite to this very day because he remained loyal to the LORD God of Israel. **14:15** (Hebron used to be called Kiriath Arba. Arba was a famous Anakite.) Then the land was free of war.

15:1 The land allotted to the tribe of Judah by its clans reached to the border of Edom, to the Wilderness of Zin in the Negev far to the south. **15:2** Their southern border started at the southern tip of the Salt Sea, **15:3** extended south of the Scorpion Ascent, crossed to Zin, went up from the south to Kadesh Barnea, crossed to Hezron, went up to Addar, and turned toward Karka. **15:4** It then crossed to Azmon, extended to the Stream of Egypt, and ended at the sea. This was their southern border.

15:5 The eastern border was the Salt Sea to the mouth of the Jordan River.

The northern border started north of the Salt Sea at the mouth of the Jordan, **15:6** went up to Beth Hoglah, crossed north of Beth Arabah, and went up to the Stone of Bohan son of Reuben. **15:7** It then went up to Debir from the Valley of Achor, turning northward to Gilgal (which is opposite the Pass of Adummim south of the valley), crossed to the waters of En Shemesh and extended to En Rogel. **15:8** It then went up the Valley of Ben Hinnom to the slope of the Jebusites on the south (that is, Jerusalem), going up to the top of the hill opposite the Valley of Ben Hinnom to the west, which is at the end of the Valley of the Rephaites to the north. **15:9** It then went from the top of the hill to the spring of the waters of Nephtoah, extended to the cities of Mount Ephron, and went to Baalah (that is, Kiriath Jearim). **15:10** It then turned from Baalah westward to Mount Seir, crossed to the slope of Mount Jearim on the north (that is Kesalon), descended to Beth Shemesh, and crossed to Timnah. **15:11** It then extended to the slope of Ekron to the north, went toward Shikkeron, crossed to Mount Baalah, extended to Jabneel, and ended at the sea.

15:12 The western border was the Mediterranean Sea. These were the borders of the tribe of Judah and its clans.

15:13 Caleb son of Jephunneh was assigned Kiriath Arba (that is Hebron) within the tribe of Judah, according to the LORD's instructions to Joshua. (Arba was the father of Anak.) **15:14** Caleb drove out from there three Anakites – Sheshai, Ahiman, and Talmai, descendants of Anak. **15:15** From there he attacked the people of Debir. (Debir used to be called Kiriath Sepher.) **15:16** Caleb said, "To the man who attacks and captures Kiriath Sepher I will give my daughter Acsah as a wife." **15:17** When Othniel son of Kenaz, Caleb's brother, captured it, Caleb gave Acsah his daughter to him as a wife.

15:18 One time Acsah came and charmed her father so that she could ask him for some land. When she got down from her donkey, Caleb said to her, "What would you like?" **15:19** She answered, "Please give me a special present. Since you have given me land in the Negev, now give me springs of water. So he gave her both upper and lower springs.

15:20 This is the land assigned to the tribe of Judah by its clans: **15:21** These cities were located at the southern extremity of Judah's tribal land near the border of Edom: Kabzeel, Eder, Jagur, **15:22** Kinah, Dimonah, Adadah, **15:23** Kedesh, Hazor, Ithnan, **15:24** Ziph, Telem, Bealoth, **15:25** Hazor Hadattah, Kerioth Hezron (that is, Hazor), **15:26** Amam, Shema,

Moladah, **15:27** Hazar Gaddah, Heshbon, Beth Pelet, **15:28** Hazar Shual, Beer Sheba, Biziothiah, **15:29** Baalah, Iim, Ezem, **15:30** Eltolad, Kesil, Hormah, **15:31** Ziklag, Madmannah, Sansannah, **15:32** Lebaoth, Shilhim, Ain, and Rimmon – a total of twenty-nine cities and their towns.

15:33 These cities were in the lowlands: Eshtaol, Zorah, Ashnah, **15:34** Zanoah, En Gannim, Tappuah, Enam, **15:35** Jarmuth, Adullam, Socoh, Azekah, **15:36** Shaaraim, Adithaim, and Gederah (or Gederothaim) – a total of fourteen cities and their towns.

15:37 Zenan, Hadashah, Migdal Gad, **15:38** Dilean, Mizpah, Joktheel, **15:39** Lachish, Bozkath, Eglon, **15:40** Cabbon, Lahmas, Kitlish, **15:41** Gederoth, Beth Dagon, Naamah, and Makkedah – a total of sixteen cities and their towns.

15:42 Libnah, Ether, Ashan, **15:43** Iphtah, Ashnah, Nezib, **15:44** Keilah, Aczib, and Mareshah – a total of nine cities and their towns.

15:45 Ekron and its surrounding towns and settlements; **15:46** from Ekron westward, all those in the vicinity of Ashdod and their towns; **15:47** Ashdod with its surrounding towns and settlements, and Gaza with its surrounding towns and settlements, as far as the Stream of Egypt and the border at the Mediterranean Sea.

15:48 These cities were in the hill country: Shamir, Jattir, Socoh, **15:49** Dannah, Kiriath Sannah (that is, Debir), **15:50** Anab, Eshtemoh, Anim, **15:51** Goshen, Holon, and Giloh – a total of eleven cities and their towns.

15:52 Arab, Dumah, Eshan, **15:53** Janim, Beth Tappuah, Aphekah, **15:54** Humtah, Kiriath Arba (that is, Hebron), and Zior – a total of nine cities and their towns.

15:55 Maon, Carmel, Ziph, Juttah, **15:56** Jezreel, Jokdeam, Zanoah, **15:57** Kain, Gibeah, and Timnah – a total of ten cities and their towns.

15:58 Halhul, Beth Zur, Gedor, **15:59** Maarath, Beth Anoth, and Eltekon – a total of six cities and their towns.

15:60 Kiriath Baal (that is, Kiriath Jearim) and Rabbah – a total of two cities and their towns.

15:61 These cities were in the desert: Beth Arabah, Middin, Secacah, **15:62** Nibshan, the city of Salt, and En Gedi – a total of six cities and their towns.

15:63 The men of Judah were unable to conquer the Jebusites living in Jerusalem. The Jebusites live with the people of Judah in Jerusalem to this very day.

Joseph's Tribal Lands

16:1 The land allotted to Joseph's descendants extended from the Jordan at Jericho to the waters of Jericho to the east, through the desert and on up from Jericho into the hill country of Bethel. **16:2** The southern border extended from Bethel to Luz, and crossed to Arkite territory at Ataroth. **16:3** It then descended westward to Japhletite territory, as far as the territory of lower Beth Horon and Gezer, and ended at the sea. **16:4** Joseph's descendants, Manasseh and Ephraim, were assigned their land. **16:5** The territory of the tribe of Ephraim by its clans included the following: The border of their assigned land to the east was Ataroth Addar as far as upper Beth Horon. **16:6** It then extended on to the sea, with Micmethath on the north. It turned eastward to Taanath Shiloh and crossed it on the east to Janoah. **16:7** It then descended from Janoah to Ataroth and Naarah, touched Jericho, and extended to the Jordan River. **16:8** From Tappuah it went westward to the Valley of Kanah and ended at the sea. This is the land assigned to the tribe of Ephraim by its clans. **16:9** Also included were the cities set apart for the tribe of Ephraim within Manasseh's territory, along with their towns. **16:10** The Ephraimites did not conquer the Canaanites living in Gezer. The Canaanites live among the Ephraimites to this very day and do hard labor as their servants.

17:1 The tribe of Manasseh, Joseph's firstborn son, was also allotted land. The descendants of Makir, Manasseh's firstborn and the father of Gilead, received land, for they were warriors. They were assigned Gilead and Bashan. **17:2** The rest of Manasseh's descendants were also assigned land by their clans, including the descendants of Abiezer, Helek, Asriel, Shechem, Hepher, and Shemida. These are the male descendants of Manasseh son of Joseph by their clans. **17:3** Now Zelophehad son of Hepher, son of Gilead, son of Makir, son of Manasseh, had no sons, only daughters. These are the names of his daughters: Mahlah, Noah, Hoglah, Milcah, and Tirzah. **17:4** They went before Eleazar the priest, Joshua son of Nun, and the leaders and said, "The LORD told Moses to assign us land among our relatives." So Joshua assigned them land among their uncles, as the LORD had commanded. **17:5** Manasseh was allotted ten shares of land, in addition to the land of Gilead and Bashan east of the Jordan, **17:6** for the daughters of Manasseh were assigned land among his sons. The land of Gilead belonged to the rest of the descendants of Manasseh. **17:7** The border of Manasseh went from Asher to Micmethath which is near Shechem. It then went south toward those who live in Tappuah. **17:8** (The land of Tappuah belonged to Manasseh, but Tappuah, located on the border of Manasseh, belonged to the tribe of Ephraim.) **17:9** The border then descended southward to the Valley of Kanah. Ephraim was assigned cities there among the cities of Manasseh, but the border of Manasseh was north of the valley and ended at the sea. **17:10** Ephraim's territory was to the south, and Manasseh's to the north. The sea was Manasseh's

western border and their territory touched Asher on the north and Issachar on the east. **17:11** Within Issachar's and Asher's territory Manasseh was assigned Beth Shean, Ibleam, the residents of Dor, En Dor, the residents of Taanach, the residents of Megiddo, the three of Napheth, and the towns surrounding all these cities. **17:12** But the men of Manasseh were unable to conquer these cities; the Canaanites managed to remain in those areas. **17:13** Whenever the Israelites were strong militarily, they forced the Canaanites to do hard labor, but they never totally conquered them.

17:14 The descendants of Joseph said to Joshua, "Why have you assigned us only one tribal allotment? After all, we have many people, for until now the LORD has enabled us to increase in number." **17:15** Joshua replied to them, "Since you have so many people, go up into the forest and clear out a place to live in the land of the Perizzites and Rephaites, for the hill country of Ephraim is too small for you." **17:16** The descendants of Joseph said, "The whole hill country is inadequate for us, and the Canaanites living down in the valley in Beth Shean and its surrounding towns and in the Valley of Jezreel have chariots with iron-rimmed wheels." **17:17** Joshua said to the family of Joseph – to both Ephraim and Manasseh: "You have many people and great military strength. You will not have just one tribal allotment. **17:18** The whole hill country will be yours; though it is a forest, you can clear it and it will be entirely yours. You can conquer the Canaanites, though they have chariots with iron-rimmed wheels and are strong."

The Tribes Meet at Shiloh

18:1 The entire Israelite community assembled at Shiloh and there they set up the tent of meeting. Though they had subdued the land, **18:2** seven Israelite tribes had not been assigned their allotted land. **18:3** So Joshua said to the Israelites: "How long do you intend to put off occupying the land the LORD God of your ancestors has given you? **18:4** Pick three men from each tribe. I will send them out to walk through the land and make a map of it for me. **18:5** Divide it into seven regions. Judah will stay in its territory in the south, and the family of Joseph in its territory in the north. **18:6** But as for you, map out the land into seven regions and bring it to me. I will draw lots for you here before the LORD our God. **18:7** But the Levites will not have an allotted portion among you, for their inheritance is to serve the LORD. Gad, Reuben, and the half-tribe of Manasseh have already received their allotted land east of the Jordan which Moses the LORD's servant assigned them."

18:8 When the men started out, Joshua told those going to map out the land, "Go, walk through the land, map it out, and return to me. Then I will draw lots for you before the LORD here in Shiloh." **18:9** The men journeyed through the land and mapped it and its cities out into seven regions on a scroll. Then they came to Joshua at the camp in Shiloh. **18:10** Joshua drew lots for them in Shiloh before the LORD and divided the land among the Israelites according to their allotted portions.

Benjamin's Tribal Lands

18:11 The first lot belonged to the tribe of Benjamin by its clans. Their allotted territory was between Judah and Joseph. **18:12** Their northern border started at the Jordan, went up to the slope of Jericho on the north, ascended westward to the hill country, and extended to the desert of Beth Aven. **18:13** It then crossed from there to Luz, to the slope of Luz to the south (that is, Bethel), and descended to Ataroth Addar located on the hill that is south of lower Beth Horon. **18:14** It then turned on the west side southward from the hill near Beth Horon on the south and extended to Kiriath Baal (that is, Kiriath Jearim), a city belonging to the tribe of Judah. This is the western border. **18:15** The southern side started on the edge of Kiriath Jearim and extended westward to the spring of the waters of Nephtoah. **18:16** The border then descended to the edge of the hill country near the Valley of Ben Hinnom located in the Valley of the Rephaites to the north. It descended through the Valley of Hinnom to the slope of the Jebusites to the south and then down to En Rogel. **18:17** It went northward, extending to En Shemesh and Geliloth opposite the Pass of Adummim, and descended to the Stone of Bohan son of Reuben. **18:18** It crossed to the slope in front of the Arabah to the north and descended into the Arabah. **18:19** It then crossed to the slope of Beth Hoglah to the north and ended at the northern tip of the Salt Sea at the mouth of the Jordan River. This was the southern border. **18:20** The Jordan River borders it on the east. These were the borders of the land assigned to the tribe of Benjamin by its clans.

18:21 These cities belonged to the tribe of Benjamin by its clans: Jericho, Beth Hoglah, Emek Keziz, **18:22** Beth Arabah, Zemaraim, Bethel, **18:23** Avvim, Parah, Ophrah, **18:24** Kephar Ammoni, Ophni, and Geba – a total of twelve cities and their towns.

18:25 Gibeon, Ramah, Beeroth, **18:26** Mizpah, Kephirah, Mozah, **18:27** Rekem, Irpeel, Taralah, **18:28** Zelah, Haeleph, the Jebusite city (that is, Jerusalem), Gibeah, and Kiriath – a total of fourteen cities and their towns. This was the land assigned to the tribe of Benjamin by its clans.

Simeon's Tribal Lands

19:1 The second lot belonged to the tribe of Simeon by its clans. **19:2** Their assigned land included Beer Sheba, Moladah, **19:3** Hazar Shual, Balah, Ezem, **19:4** Eltolad, Bethul, Hormah, **19:5** Ziklag, Beth Marcaboth, Hazar Susah, **19:6** Beth Lebaoth, and Sharuhen – a total of thirteen cities and their towns, **19:7** Ain, Rimmon, Ether, and Ashan – a total of four cities and their towns, **19:8** as well as all the towns around these cities as far as Baalath Beer (Ramah of the Negev). This was the land assigned to the tribe of Simeon by its clans. **19:9** Simeon's assigned land was taken from Judah's allotted portion, for Judah's territory was too large for them; so Simeon was assigned land within Judah.

Zebulun's Tribal Lands

19:10 The third lot belonged to the tribe of Zebulun by its clans. The border of their territory extended to Sarid. **19:11** Their border went up westward to Maralah and touched Dabbesheth and the valley near Jokneam. **19:12** From Sarid it turned eastward to the territory of Kisloth Tabor, extended to Daberath, and went up to Japhia. **19:13** From there it crossed eastward to Gath Hepher and Eth Kazin and extended to Rimmon, turning toward Neah. **19:14** It then turned on the north to Hannathon and ended at the Valley of Iphtah El. **19:15** Their territory included Kattah, Nahalal, Shimron, Idalah, and Bethlehem; in all they had twelve cities and their towns. **19:16** This was the land assigned to the tribe of Zebulun by its clans, including these cities and their towns.

Issachar's Tribal Lands

19:17 The fourth lot belonged to the tribe of Issachar by its clans. **19:18** Their assigned land included Jezreel, Kesulloth, Shunem, **19:19** Hapharaim, Shion, Anaharath, **19:20** Rabbith, Kishion, Ebez, **19:21** Remeth, En Gannim, En Haddah and Beth Pazzez. **19:22** Their border touched Tabor, Shahazumah, and Beth Shemesh, and ended at the Jordan. They had sixteen cities and their towns. **19:23** This was the land assigned to the tribe of Issachar by its clans, including the cities and their towns.

Asher's Tribal Lands

19:24 The fifth lot belonged to the tribe of Asher by its clans. **19:25** Their territory included Helkath, Hali, Beten, Acshaph, **19:26** Alammelech, Amad, and Mishal. Their border touched Carmel to the west and Shihor Libnath. **19:27** It turned eastward toward Beth Dagon, touched Zebulun and the Valley of Iphtah El to the north, as well as the Valley of Emek and Neiel, and extended to Cabul on the north **19:28** and on to Ebron, Rehob, Hammon, and Kanah, as far as Greater Sidon. **19:29** It then turned toward Ramah as far as the fortified city of Tyre, turned to Hosah, and ended at the sea near Hebel, Aczib, **19:30** Umah, Aphek, and Rehob. In all they had twenty-two cities and their towns. **19:31** This was the land assigned to the tribe of Asher by its clans, including these cities and their towns.

Naphtali's Tribal Lands

19:32 The sixth lot belonged to the tribe of Naphtali by its clans. **19:33** Their border started at Heleph and the oak of Zaanannim, went to Adami Nekeb, Jabneel and on to Lakkum, and ended at the Jordan River. **19:34** It turned westward to Aznoth Tabor, extended from there to Hukok, touched Zebulun on the south, Asher on the west, and the Jordan on the east. **19:35** The fortified cities included Ziddim, Zer, Hammath, Rakkath, Kinnereth, **19:36** Adamah, Ramah, Hazor, **19:37** Kedesh, Edrei, En Hazor, **19:38** Yiron, Migdal El, Horem, Beth Anath, and Beth Shemesh. In all they had nineteen cities and their towns. **19:39** This was the land assigned to the tribe of Naphtali by its clans, including the cities and their towns.

Dan's Tribal Lands

19:40 The seventh lot belonged to the tribe of Dan by its clans. **19:41** Their assigned land included Zorah, Eshtaol, Ir Shemesh, **19:42** Shaalabbin, Aijalon, Ithlah, **19:43** Elon, Timnah, Ekron, **19:44** Eltekeh, Gibbethon, Baalath, **19:45** Jehud, Bene Berak, Gath Rimmon, **19:46** the waters of Jarkon, and Rakkon, including the territory in front of Joppa. **19:47** (The Danites failed to conquer their territory, so they went up and fought with Leshem and captured it. They put the sword to it, took possession of it, and lived in it. They renamed it Dan after their ancestor.) **19:48** This was the land assigned to the tribe of Dan by its clans, including these cities and their towns.

Joshua Receives Land

19:49 When they finished dividing the land into its regions, the Israelites gave Joshua son of Nun some land. **19:50** As the LORD had instructed, they gave him the city he requested – Timnath Serah in the Ephraimite hill country. He built up the city and lived in it.

19:51 These are the land assignments which Eleazar the priest, Joshua son of Nun, and the Israelite tribal leaders made by drawing lots in Shiloh before the LORD at the entrance of the tent of meeting. So they finished dividing the land.

Israel Designates Cities of Refuge

20:1 The LORD instructed Joshua: **20:2** "Have the Israelites select the cities of refuge that I told you about through Moses. **20:3** Anyone who accidentally kills someone can escape there; these cities will be a place of asylum from the avenger of blood. **20:4** The one who committed manslaughter should escape to one of these cities, stand at the entrance of the city gate, and present his case to the leaders of that city. They should then bring him into the city, give him a place to stay, and let him live there. **20:5** When the avenger of blood comes after him, they must not hand over to him the one who committed manslaughter, for he accidentally killed his fellow man without premeditation. **20:6** He must remain in that city until his case is decided by the assembly and the high priest dies.

Then the one who committed manslaughter may return home to the city from which he escaped."

20:7 So they selected Kedesh in Galilee in the hill country of Naphtali, Shechem in the hill country of Ephraim, and Kiriath Arba (that is, Hebron) in the hill country of Judah. **20:8** Beyond the Jordan east of Jericho they selected Bezer in the desert on the plain belonging to the tribe of Reuben, Ramoth in Gilead belonging to the tribe of Gad, and Golan in Bashan belonging to the tribe of Manasseh. **20:9** These were the cities of refuge appointed for all the Israelites and for resident foreigners living among them. Anyone who accidentally killed someone could escape there and not be executed by the avenger of blood, at least until his case was reviewed by the assembly.

Levitical Cities

21:1 The tribal leaders of the Levites went before Eleazar the priest and Joshua son of Nun and the Israelite tribal leaders **21:2** in Shiloh in the land of Canaan and said, "The LORD told Moses to assign us cities in which to live along with the grazing areas for our cattle." **21:3** So the Israelites assigned these cities and their grazing areas to the Levites from their own holdings, as the LORD had instructed.

21:4 The first lot belonged to the Kohathite clans. The Levites who were descendants of Aaron the priest were allotted thirteen cities from the tribes of Judah, Simeon, and Benjamin. **21:5** The rest of Kohath's descendants were allotted ten cities from the clans of the tribe of Ephraim, and from the tribe of Dan and the half-tribe of Manasseh. **21:6** Gershon's descendants were allotted thirteen cities from the clans of the tribe of Issachar, and from the tribes of Asher and Naphtali and the half-tribe of Manasseh in Bashan. **21:7** Merari's descendants by their clans were allotted twelve cities from the tribes of Reuben, Gad, and Zebulun. **21:8** So the Israelites assigned to the Levites by lot these cities and their grazing areas, as the LORD had instructed Moses.

21:9 They assigned from the tribes of Judah and Simeon the cities listed below. **21:10** They were assigned to the Kohathite clans of the Levites who were descendants of Aaron, for the first lot belonged to them. **21:11** They assigned them Kiriath Arba (Arba was the father of Anak), that is, Hebron, in the hill country of Judah, along with its surrounding grazing areas. **21:12** (Now the city's fields and surrounding towns they had assigned to Caleb son of Jephunneh as his property.) **21:13** So to the descendants of Aaron the priest they assigned Hebron (a city of refuge for one who committed manslaughter), Libnah, **21:14** Jattir, Eshtemoa, **21:15** Holon, Debir, **21:16** Ain, Juttah, and Beth Shemesh, along with the grazing areas of each – a total of nine cities taken from these two tribes. **21:17** From the tribe of Benjamin they assigned Gibeon, Geba, **21:18** Anathoth, and Almon, along with the grazing areas of each – a total of four cities. **21:19** The priests descended from Aaron received thirteen cities and their grazing areas.

21:20 The rest of the Kohathite clans of the Levites were allotted cities from the tribe of Ephraim. **21:21** They assigned them Shechem (a city of refuge for one who committed manslaughter) in the hill country of Ephraim, Gezer, **21:22** Kibzaim, and Beth Horon, along with the grazing areas of each – a total of four cities. **21:23** From the tribe of Dan they assigned Eltekeh, Gibbethon, **21:24** Aijalon, and Gath Rimmon, along with the grazing areas of each – a total of four cities. **21:25** From the half-tribe of Manasseh they assigned Taanach and Gath Rimmon, along with the grazing areas of each – a total of two cities. **21:26** The rest of the Kohathite clans received ten cities and their grazing areas.

21:27 They assigned to the Gershonite clans of the Levites the following cities: from the half-tribe of Manasseh: Golan in Bashan (a city of refuge for one who committed manslaughter) and Beeshtarah, along with the grazing areas of each – a total of two cities; **21:28** from the tribe of Issachar: Kishon, Daberath, **21:29** Jarmuth, and En Gannim, along with the grazing areas of each – a total of four cities; **21:30** from the tribe of Asher: Mishal, Abdon, **21:31** Helkath, and Rehob, along with the grazing areas of each – a total of four cities; **21:32** from the tribe of Naphtali: Kedesh in Galilee (a city of refuge for one who committed manslaughter), Hammoth Dor, and Kartan, along with the grazing areas of each – a total of three cities. **21:33** The Gershonite clans received thirteen cities and their grazing areas.

21:34 They assigned to the Merarite clans (the remaining Levites) the following cities: from the tribe of Zebulun: Jokneam, Kartah, **21:35** Dimnah, and Nahalal, along with the grazing areas of each – a total of four cities; **21:36** from the tribe of Reuben: Bezer, Jahaz, **21:37** Kedemoth, and Mephaath, along with the grazing areas of each – a total of four cities; **21:38** from the tribe of Gad: Ramoth in Gilead (a city of refuge for one who committed manslaughter), Mahanaim, **21:39** Heshbon, and Jazer, along with the grazing areas of each – a total of four cities. **21:40** The Merarite clans (the remaining Levites) were allotted twelve cities.

21:41 The Levites received within the land owned by the Israelites forty-eight cities in all and their grazing areas. **21:42** Each of these cities had grazing areas around it; they were alike in this regard.

21:43 So the LORD gave Israel all the land he had solemnly promised to their ancestors, and they conquered it and lived in it. **21:44** The LORD made them secure, in fulfillment of all he had solemnly promised their ancestors. None of their enemies could resist them. **21:45** Not one of the

LORD's faithful promises to the family of Israel was left unfulfilled; every one was realized.

Joshua Sends Home the Eastern Tribes

22:1 Then Joshua summoned the Reubenites, Gadites, and the half-tribe of Manasseh **22:2** and told them: "You have carried out all the instructions of Moses the LORD's servant, and you have obeyed all I have told you. **22:3** You have not abandoned your fellow Israelites this entire time, right up to this very day. You have completed the task given you by the LORD your God. **22:4** Now the LORD your God has made your fellow Israelites secure, just as he promised them. So now you may turn around and go to your homes in your own land which Moses the LORD's servant assigned to you east of the Jordan. **22:5** But carefully obey the commands and instructions Moses the LORD's servant gave you. Love the LORD your God, follow all his instructions, obey his commands, be loyal to him, and serve him with all your heart and being!"

22:6 Joshua rewarded them and sent them on their way; they returned to their homes. **22:7** (Now to one half-tribe of Manasseh, Moses had assigned land in Bashan; and to the other half Joshua had assigned land on the west side of the Jordan with their fellow Israelites.) When Joshua sent them home, he rewarded them, **22:8** saying, "Take home great wealth, a lot of cattle, silver, gold, bronze, iron, and a lot of clothing. Divide up the goods captured from your enemies with your brothers." **22:9** So the Reubenites, Gadites, and half-tribe of Manasseh left the Israelites in Shiloh in the land of Canaan and headed home to their own land in Gilead, which they acquired by the LORD's command through Moses.

Civil War is Averted

22:10 The Reubenites, Gadites, and half-tribe of Manasseh came to Geliloth near the Jordan in the land of Canaan and built there, near the Jordan, an impressive altar. **22:11** The Israelites received this report: "Look, the Reubenites, Gadites, and half-tribe of Manasseh have built an altar at the entrance to the land of Canaan, at Geliloth near the Jordan on the Israelite side." **22:12** When the Israelites heard this, the entire Israelite community assembled at Shiloh to launch an attack against them.

22:13 The Israelites sent Phinehas, son of Eleazar, the priest, to the land of Gilead to the Reubenites, Gadites, and the half-tribe of Manasseh. **22:14** He was accompanied by ten leaders, one from each of the Israelite tribes, each one a family leader among the Israelite clans. **22:15** They went to the land of Gilead to the Reubenites, Gadites, and the half-tribe of Manasseh, and said to them: **22:16** "The entire community of the LORD says, 'Why have you disobeyed the God of Israel by turning back today from following the LORD? You built an altar for yourselves and have rebelled today against the LORD. **22:17** The sin we committed at Peor was bad enough. To this very day we have not purified ourselves; it even brought a plague on the community of the LORD. **22:18** Now today you dare to turn back from following the LORD! You are rebelling today against the LORD; tomorrow he may break out in anger against the entire community of Israel. **22:19** But if your own land is impure, cross over to the LORD's own land, where the LORD himself lives, and settle down among us. But don't rebel against the LORD or us by building for yourselves an altar aside from the altar of the LORD our God. **22:20** When Achan son of Zerah disobeyed the command about the city's riches, the entire Israelite community was judged, though only one man had sinned. He most certainly died for his sin!'"

22:21 The Reubenites, Gadites, and the half-tribe of Manasseh answered the leaders of the Israelite clans: **22:22** "El, God, the LORD! El, God, the LORD! He knows the truth! Israel must also know! If we have rebelled or disobeyed the LORD, don't spare us today! **22:23** If we have built an altar for ourselves to turn back from following the LORD by making burnt sacrifices and grain offerings on it, or by offering tokens of peace on it, the LORD himself will punish us. **22:24** We swear we have done this because we were worried that in the future your descendants would say to our descendants, 'What relationship do you have with the LORD God of Israel? **22:25** The LORD made the Jordan a boundary between us and you Reubenites and Gadites. You have no right to worship the LORD.' In this way your descendants might cause our descendants to stop obeying the LORD. **22:26** So we decided to build this altar, not for burnt offerings and sacrifices, **22:27** but as a reminder to us and you, and to our descendants who follow us, that we will honor the LORD in his very presence with burnt offerings, sacrifices, and tokens of peace. Then in the future your descendants will not be able to say to our descendants, 'You have no right to worship the LORD.' **22:28** We said, 'If in the future they say such a thing to us or to our descendants, we will reply, "See the model of the LORD's altar that our ancestors made, not for burnt offerings or sacrifices, but as a reminder to us and you."' **22:29** Far be it from us to rebel against the LORD by turning back today from following after the LORD by building an altar for burnt offerings, sacrifices, and tokens of peace aside from the altar of the LORD our God located in front of his dwelling place!"

22:30 When Phinehas the priest and the community leaders and clan leaders who accompanied him heard the defense of the Reubenites, Gadites, and the Manassehites, they were satisfied. **22:31** Phinehas, son of Eleazar, the priest, said to the Reubenites, Gadites, and the Manassehites, "Today we know that the LORD is among us, because you have

not disobeyed the LORD in this. Now you have rescued the Israelites from the LORD's judgment."

22:32 Phinehas, son of Eleazar, the priest, and the leaders left the Reubenites and Gadites in the land of Gilead and reported back to the Israelites in the land of Canaan. **22:33** The Israelites were satisfied with their report and gave thanks to God. They said nothing more about launching an attack to destroy the land in which the Reubenites and Gadites lived. **22:34** The Reubenites and Gadites named the altar, "Surely it is a Reminder to us that the LORD is God."

Joshua Challenges Israel to be Faithful

23:1 A long time passed after the LORD made Israel secure from all their enemies, and Joshua was very old. **23:2** So Joshua summoned all Israel, including the elders, rulers, judges, and leaders, and told them: "I am very old. **23:3** You saw everything the LORD your God did to all these nations on your behalf, for the LORD your God fights for you. **23:4** See, I have parceled out to your tribes these remaining nations, from the Jordan to the Mediterranean Sea in the west, including all the nations I defeated. **23:5** The LORD your God will drive them out from before you and remove them, so you can occupy their land as the LORD your God promised you. **23:6** Be very strong! Carefully obey all that is written in the law scroll of Moses so you won't swerve from it to the right or the left, **23:7** or associate with these nations that remain near you. You must not invoke or make solemn declarations by the names of their gods! You must not worship or bow down to them! **23:8** But you must be loyal to the LORD your God, as you have been to this very day.

23:9 "The LORD drove out from before you great and mighty nations; no one has been able to resist you to this very day. **23:10** One of you makes a thousand run away, for the LORD your God fights for you as he promised you he would. **23:11** Watch yourselves carefully! Love the LORD your God! **23:12** But if you ever turn away and make alliances with these nations that remain near you, and intermarry with them and establish friendly relations with them, **23:13** know for certain that the LORD our God will no longer drive out these nations from before you. They will trap and ensnare you; they will be a whip that tears your sides and thorns that blind your eyes until you disappear from this good land the LORD your God gave you.

23:14 "Look, today I am about to die. You know with all your heart and being that not even one of all the faithful promises the LORD your God made to you is left unfulfilled; every one was realized – not one promise is unfulfilled! **23:15** But in the same way every faithful promise the LORD your God made to you has been realized, it is just as certain, if you disobey, that the LORD will bring on you every judgment until he destroys you from this good land which the LORD your God gave you. **23:16** If you violate the covenantal laws of the LORD your God which he commanded you to keep, and follow, worship, and bow down to other gods, the LORD will be very angry with you and you will disappear quickly from the good land which he gave to you."

Israel Renews its Commitment to the Lord

24:1 Joshua assembled all the Israelite tribes at Shechem. He summoned Israel's elders, rulers, judges, and leaders, and they appeared before God. **24:2** Joshua told all the people, "Here is what the LORD God of Israel says: 'In the distant past your ancestors lived beyond the Euphrates River, including Terah the father of Abraham and Nahor. They worshiped other gods, **24:3** but I took your father Abraham from beyond the Euphrates and brought him into the entire land of Canaan. I made his descendants numerous; I gave him Isaac, **24:4** and to Isaac I gave Jacob and Esau. To Esau I assigned Mount Seir, while Jacob and his sons went down to Egypt. **24:5** I sent Moses and Aaron, and I struck Egypt down when I intervened in their land. Then I brought you out. **24:6** When I brought your fathers out of Egypt, you arrived at the sea. The Egyptians chased your fathers with chariots and horsemen to the Red Sea. **24:7** Your fathers cried out for help to the LORD; he made the area between you and the Egyptians dark, and then drowned them in the sea. You witnessed with your very own eyes what I did in Egypt. You lived in the wilderness for a long time. **24:8** Then I brought you to the land of the Amorites who lived east of the Jordan. They fought with you, but I handed them over to you; you conquered their land and I destroyed them from before you. **24:9** Balak son of Zippor, king of Moab, launched an attack against Israel. He summoned Balaam son of Beor to call down judgment on you. **24:10** I refused to respond to Balaam; he kept prophesying good things about you, and I rescued you from his power. **24:11** You crossed the Jordan and came to Jericho. The leaders of Jericho, as well as the Amorites, Perizzites, Canaanites, Hittites, Girgashites, Hivites, and Jebusites, fought with you, but I handed them over to you. **24:12** I sent terror ahead of you to drive out before you the two Amorite kings. I gave you the victory; it was not by your swords or bows. **24:13** I gave you a land in which you had not worked hard; you took up residence in cities you did not build and you are eating the produce of vineyards and olive groves you did not plant.'

24:14 Now obey the LORD and worship him with integrity and loyalty. Put aside the gods your ancestors worshiped beyond the Euphrates and in Egypt and worship the LORD. **24:15** If you have no desire to worship the LORD, choose today whom you will worship, whether it be the gods whom your ancestors worshiped beyond the Euphrates, or the gods of the Amorites in whose land you are living. But I and my family will worship the LORD!"

24:16 The people responded, "Far be it from us to abandon the LORD so we can worship other gods! **24:17** For the LORD our God took us and our fathers out of slavery in the land of Egypt and performed these awesome miracles before our very eyes. He continually protected us as we traveled and when we passed through nations. **24:18** The LORD drove out from before us all the nations, including the Amorites who lived in the land. So we too will worship the LORD, for he is our God!"

24:19 Joshua warned the people, "You will not keep worshiping the LORD, for he is a holy God. He is a jealous God who will not forgive your rebellion or your sins. **24:20** If you abandon the LORD and worship foreign gods, he will turn against you; he will bring disaster on you and destroy you, though he once treated you well."

24:21 The people said to Joshua, "No! We really will worship the LORD!" **24:22** Joshua said to the people, "Do you agree to be witnesses against yourselves that you have chosen to worship the LORD?" They replied, "We are witnesses!" **24:23** Joshua said, "Now put aside the foreign gods that are among you and submit to the LORD God of Israel."

24:24 The people said to Joshua, "We will worship the LORD our God and obey him."

24:25 That day Joshua drew up an agreement for the people, and he established rules and regulations for them in Shechem. **24:26** Joshua wrote these words in the Law Scroll of God. He then took a large stone and set it up there under the oak tree near the LORD's shrine. **24:27** Joshua said to all the people, "Look, this stone will be a witness against you, for it has heard everything the LORD said to us. It will be a witness against you if you deny your God." **24:28** When Joshua dismissed the people, they went to their allotted portions of land.

An Era Ends

24:29 After all this Joshua son of Nun, the LORD's servant, died at the age of one hundred ten. **24:30** They buried him in his allotted territory in Timnath Serah in the hill country of Ephraim, north of Mount Gaash. **24:31** Israel worshiped the LORD throughout Joshua's lifetime and as long as the elderly men who outlived him remained alive. These men had experienced firsthand everything the LORD had done for Israel.

24:32 The bones of Joseph, which the Israelites had brought up from Egypt, were buried at Shechem in the part of the field that Jacob bought from the sons of Hamor, the father of Shechem, for one hundred pieces of money. So it became the inheritance of the tribe of Joseph.

24:33 Eleazar son of Aaron died, and they buried him in Gibeah in the hill country of Ephraim, where his son Phinehas had been assigned land.

Book 7. Judges

Judah Takes the Lead

1:1 After Joshua died, the Israelites asked the LORD, "Who should lead the invasion against the Canaanites and launch the attack?" **1:2** The LORD said, "The men of Judah should take the lead. Be sure of this! I am handing the land over to them." **1:3** The men of Judah said to their relatives, the men of Simeon, "Invade our allotted land with us and help us attack the Canaanites. Then we will go with you into your allotted land." So the men of Simeon went with them.

1:4 The men of Judah attacked, and the LORD handed the Canaanites and Perizzites over to them. They killed ten thousand men at Bezek. **1:5** They met Adoni-Bezek at Bezek and fought him. They defeated the Canaanites and Perizzites. **1:6** When Adoni-Bezek ran away, they chased him and captured him. Then they cut off his thumbs and big toes. **1:7** Adoni-Bezek said, "Seventy kings, with thumbs and big toes cut off, used to lick up food scraps under my table. God has repaid me for what I did to them." They brought him to Jerusalem, where he died. **1:8** The men of Judah attacked Jerusalem and captured it. They put the sword to it and set the city on fire.

1:9 Later the men of Judah went down to attack the Canaanites living in the hill country, the Negev, and the lowlands. **1:10** The men of Judah attacked the Canaanites living in Hebron. (Hebron used to be called Kiriath Arba.) They killed Sheshai, Ahiman, and Talmai. **1:11** From there they attacked the people of Debir. (Debir used to be called Kiriath Sepher.) **1:12** Caleb said, "To the man who attacks and captures Kiriath Sepher I will give my daughter Acsah as a wife." **1:13** When Othniel son of Kenaz, Caleb's younger brother, captured it, Caleb gave him his daughter Acsah as a wife.

1:14 One time Acsah came and charmed her father so she could ask him for some land. When she got down from her donkey, Caleb said to her, "What would you like?" **1:15** She answered, "Please give me a special present. Since you have given me land in the Negev, now give me springs of water." So Caleb gave her both the upper and lower springs.

1:16 Now the descendants of the Kenite, Moses' father-in-law, went up with the people of Judah from the City of Date Palm Trees to Arad in the desert of Judah, located in the Negev. They went and lived with the people of Judah.

1:17 The men of Judah went with their brothers the men of Simeon and defeated the Canaanites living in Zephath. They wiped out Zephath. So people now call the city Hormah. **1:18** The men of Judah captured Gaza, Ashkelon, Ekron, and the territory surrounding each of these cities.

1:19 The LORD was with the men of Judah. They conquered the hill country, but they could not conquer the people living in the coastal plain, because they had chariots with iron-rimmed wheels. **1:20** Caleb received Hebron, just as Moses had promised. He drove out the three Anakites.

1:21 The men of Benjamin, however, did not conquer the Jebusites living in Jerusalem. The Jebusites live with the people of Benjamin in Jerusalem to this very day.

Partial Success

1:22 When the men of Joseph attacked Bethel, the LORD was with them. **1:23** When the men of Joseph spied out Bethel (it used to be called Luz), **1:24** the spies spotted a man leaving the city. They said to him, "If you show us a secret entrance into the city, we will reward you." **1:25** He showed them a secret entrance into the city, and they put the city to the sword. But they let the man and his extended family leave safely. **1:26** He moved to Hittite country and built a city. He named it Luz, and it has kept that name to this very day.

1:27 The men of Manasseh did not conquer Beth Shan, Taanach, or their surrounding towns. Nor did they conquer the people living in Dor, Ibleam, Megiddo or their surrounding towns. The Canaanites managed to remain in those areas. **1:28** Whenever Israel was strong militarily, they forced the Canaanites to do hard labor, but they never totally conquered them.

1:29 The men of Ephraim did not conquer the Canaanites living in Gezer. The Canaanites lived among them in Gezer.

1:30 The men of Zebulun did not conquer the people living in Kitron and Nahalol. The Canaanites lived among them and were forced to do hard labor.

1:31 The men of Asher did not conquer the people living in Acco or Sidon, nor did they conquer Ahlab, Aczib, Helbah, Aphek, or Rehob. **1:32** The people of Asher live among the Canaanites residing in the land because they did not conquer them.

1:33 The men of Naphtali did not conquer the people living in Beth Shemesh or Beth Anath. They live among the Canaanites residing in the land. The Canaanites living in Beth Shemesh and Beth Anath were forced to do hard labor for them.

1:34 The Amorites forced the people of Dan to live in the hill country. They did not allow them to live in the coastal plain. **1:35** The Amorites managed to remain in Har Heres, Aijalon, and Shaalbim. Whenever the tribe of Joseph was strong militarily, the Amorites were forced to do hard labor. **1:36** The border of Amorite territory ran from the Scorpion Ascent to Sela and on up.

Confrontation and Repentance at Bokim

2:1 The LORD's angelic messenger went up from Gilgal to Bokim. He said, "I brought you up from Egypt and led you into the land I had solemnly promised to give to your ancestors. I said, 'I will never break my agreement with you, **2:2** but you must not make an agreement with the people who live in this land. You should tear down the altars where they worship.' But you have disobeyed me. Why would you do such a thing? **2:3** At that time I also warned you, 'If you disobey, I will not drive out the Canaanites before you. They will ensnare you and their gods will lure you away.'"

2:4 When the LORD's messenger finished speaking these words to all the Israelites, the people wept loudly. **2:5** They named that place Bokim and offered sacrifices to the LORD there.

The End of an Era

2:6 When Joshua dismissed the people, the Israelites went to their allotted portions of territory, intending to take possession of the land. **2:7** The people worshiped the LORD throughout Joshua's lifetime and as long as the elderly men who outlived him remained alive. These men had witnessed all the great things the LORD had done for Israel. **2:8** Joshua son of Nun, the LORD's servant, died at the age of one hundred ten. **2:9** The people buried him in his allotted land in Timnath Heres in the hill country of Ephraim, north of Mount Gaash. **2:10** That entire generation passed away; a new generation grew up that had not personally experienced the LORD's presence or seen what he had done for Israel.

A Monotonous Cycle

2:11 The Israelites did evil before the LORD by worshiping the Baals. **2:12** They abandoned the LORD God of their ancestors who brought them out of the land of Egypt. They followed other gods – the gods of the nations who lived around them. They worshiped them and made the LORD angry. **2:13** They abandoned the LORD and worshiped Baal and the Ashtars.

2:14 The LORD was furious with Israel and handed them over to robbers who plundered them. He turned them over to their enemies who lived around them. They could not withstand their enemies' attacks. **2:15** Whenever they went out to fight, the LORD did them harm, just as he had warned and solemnly vowed he would do. They suffered greatly.

2:16 The LORD raised up leaders who delivered them from these robbers. **2:17** But they did not obey their leaders. Instead they prostituted themselves to other gods and worshiped them. They quickly turned aside from the path their ancestors had walked. Their ancestors had obeyed the LORD's commands, but they did not. **2:18** When the LORD raised up leaders for them, the LORD was with each leader and delivered the people from their enemies while the leader remained alive. The LORD felt sorry for them when they cried out in agony because of what their harsh oppressors did to them. **2:19** When a leader died, the next generation would again act more wickedly than the previous one. They would follow after other gods, worshiping them and bowing down to them. They did not give up their practices or their stubborn ways.

A Divine Decision

2:20 The LORD was furious with Israel. He said, "This nation has violated the terms of the agreement I made with their ancestors by disobeying me. **2:21** So I will no longer remove before them any of the nations that Joshua left unconquered when he died. **2:22** Joshua left those nations to test Israel. I wanted to see whether or not the people would carefully walk in the path marked out by the LORD, as their ancestors were careful to do." **2:23** This is why the LORD permitted these nations to remain and did not conquer them immediately; he did not hand them over to Joshua.

3:1 These were the nations the LORD permitted to remain so he could use them to test Israel – he wanted to test all those who had not experienced battle against the Canaanites. **3:2** He left those nations simply because he wanted to teach the subsequent generations of Israelites, who had not experienced the earlier battles, how to conduct holy war. **3:3** These were the nations: the five lords of the Philistines, all the Canaanites, the Sidonians, and the Hivites living in Mount Lebanon, from Mount Baal Hermon to Lebo-Hamath. **3:4** They were left to test Israel, so the LORD would know if his people would obey the commands he gave their ancestors through Moses.

3:5 The Israelites lived among the Canaanites, Hittites, Amorites, Perizzites, Hivites, and Jebusites. **3:6** They took the Canaanites' daughters as wives and gave their daughters to the Canaanites; they worshiped their gods as well.

Othniel: A Model Leader

3:7 The Israelites did evil in the LORD's sight. They forgot the LORD their God and worshiped the Baals and the Asherahs. **3:8** The LORD was furious with Israel and turned them over to King Cushan-Rishathaim of Aram-Naharaim. They were Cushan-Rishathaim's subjects for eight years. **3:9** When the Israelites cried out for help to the LORD, he raised up a deliverer for the Israelites who rescued them. His name was Othniel son of Kenaz, Caleb's younger brother. **3:10** The LORD's spirit empowered him and he led Israel. When he went to do battle, the LORD handed over to him King Cushan-Rishathaim of Aram and he overpowered him. **3:11** The land had rest for forty years; then Othniel son of Kenaz died.

Deceit, Assassination, and Deliverance

3:12 The Israelites again did evil in the LORD's sight. The LORD gave King Eglon of Moab control over Israel because they had done evil in the LORD's sight. **3:13** Eglon formed alliances with the Ammonites and Amalekites. He came and defeated Israel, and they seized the City of Date Palm Trees. **3:14** The Israelites were subject to King Eglon of Moab for eighteen years.

3:15 When the Israelites cried out for help to the LORD, he raised up a deliverer for them. His name was Ehud son of Gera the Benjaminite, a left-handed man. The Israelites sent him to King Eglon of Moab with their tribute payment. **3:16** Ehud made himself a sword – it had two edges and was eighteen inches long. He strapped it under his coat on his right thigh. **3:17** He brought the tribute payment to King Eglon of Moab. (Now Eglon was a very fat man.)

3:18 After Ehud brought the tribute payment, he dismissed the people who had carried it. **3:19** But he went back once he reached the carved images at Gilgal. He said to Eglon, "I have a secret message for you, O king." Eglon said, "Be quiet!" All his attendants left. **3:20** When Ehud approached him, he was sitting in his well-ventilated upper room all by himself. Ehud said, "I have a message from God for you." When Eglon rose up from his seat, **3:21** Ehud reached with his left hand, pulled the sword from his right thigh, and drove it into Eglon's belly. **3:22** The handle went in after the blade, and the fat closed around the blade, for Ehud did not pull the sword out of his belly. **3:23** As Ehud went out into the vestibule, he closed the doors of the upper room behind him and locked them.

3:24 When Ehud had left, Eglon's servants came and saw the locked doors of the upper room. They said, "He must be relieving himself in the well-ventilated inner room." **3:25** They waited so long they were embarrassed, but he still did not open the doors of the upper room. Finally they took the key and opened the doors. Right before their eyes was their master, sprawled out dead on the floor! **3:26** Now Ehud had escaped while they were delaying. When he passed the carved images, he escaped to Seirah.

3:27 When he reached Seirah, he blew a trumpet in the Ephraimite hill country. The Israelites went down with him from the hill country, with Ehud in the lead. **3:28** He said to them, "Follow me, for the LORD is about to defeat your enemies, the Moabites!" They followed him, captured the fords of the Jordan River opposite Moab, and did not let anyone

cross. **3:29** That day they killed about ten thousand Moabites – all strong, capable warriors; not one escaped. **3:30** Israel humiliated Moab that day, and the land had rest for eighty years.

3:31 After Ehud came Shamgar son of Anath; he killed six hundred Philistines with an oxgoad and, like Ehud, delivered Israel.

Deborah Summons Barak

4:1 The Israelites again did evil in the LORD's sight after Ehud's death. **4:2** The LORD turned them over to King Jabin of Canaan, who ruled in Hazor. The general of his army was Sisera, who lived in Harosheth Haggoyim. **4:3** The Israelites cried out for help to the LORD, because Sisera had nine hundred chariots with iron-rimmed wheels, and he cruelly oppressed the Israelites for twenty years.

4:4 Now Deborah, a prophetess, wife of Lappidoth, was leading Israel at that time. **4:5** She would sit under the Date Palm Tree of Deborah between Ramah and Bethel in the Ephraimite hill country. The Israelites would come up to her to have their disputes settled.

4:6 She summoned Barak son of Abinoam from Kedesh in Naphtali. She said to him, "Is it not true that the LORD God of Israel is commanding you? Go, march to Mount Tabor! Take with you ten thousand men from Naphtali and Zebulun. **4:7** I will bring Sisera, the general of Jabin's army, to you at the Kishon River, along with his chariots and huge army. I will hand him over to you." **4:8** Barak said to her, "If you go with me, I will go. But if you do not go with me, I will not go." **4:9** She said, "I will indeed go with you. But you will not gain fame on the expedition you are undertaking, for the LORD will turn Sisera over to a woman." Deborah got up and went with Barak to Kedesh. **4:10** Barak summoned men from Zebulun and Naphtali to Kedesh. Ten thousand men followed him; Deborah went up with him as well. **4:11** Now Heber the Kenite had moved away from the Kenites, the descendants of Hobab, Moses' father-in-law. He lived near the great tree in Zaanannim near Kedesh.

4:12 When Sisera heard that Barak son of Abinoam had gone up to Mount Tabor, **4:13** he ordered all his chariotry – nine hundred chariots with iron-rimmed wheels – and all the troops he had with him to go from Harosheth-Haggoyim to the River Kishon. **4:14** Deborah said to Barak, "Spring into action, for this is the day the LORD is handing Sisera over to you! Has the LORD not taken the lead?" Barak quickly went down from Mount Tabor with ten thousand men following him. **4:15** The LORD routed Sisera, all his chariotry, and all his army with the edge of the sword. Sisera jumped out of his chariot and ran away on foot. **4:16** Now Barak chased the chariots and the army all the way to Harosheth Haggoyim. Sisera's whole army died by the edge of the sword; not even one survived!

4:17 Now Sisera ran away on foot to the tent of Jael, wife of Heber the Kenite, for King Jabin of Hazor and the family of Heber the Kenite had made a peace treaty. **4:18** Jael came out to welcome Sisera. She said to him, "Stop and rest, my lord. Stop and rest with me. Don't be afraid." So Sisera stopped to rest in her tent, and she put a blanket over him. **4:19** He said to her, "Give me a little water to drink, because I'm thirsty." She opened a goatskin container of milk and gave him some milk to drink. Then she covered him up again. **4:20** He said to her, "Stand watch at the entrance to the tent. If anyone comes along and asks you, 'Is there a man here?' say 'No.'" **4:21** Then Jael wife of Heber took a tent peg in one hand and a hammer in the other. She crept up on him, drove the tent peg through his temple into the ground while he was asleep from exhaustion, and he died. **4:22** Now Barak was chasing Sisera. Jael went out to welcome him. She said to him, "Come here and I will show you the man you are searching for." He went with her into the tent, and there he saw Sisera sprawled out dead with the tent peg in his temple.

4:23 That day God humiliated King Jabin of Canaan before the Israelites. **4:24** Israel's power continued to overwhelm King Jabin of Canaan until they did away with him.

Celebrating the Victory in Song

5:1 On that day Deborah and Barak son of Abinoam sang this victory song:

5:2 "When the leaders took the lead in Israel,
When the people answered the call to war –
Praise the LORD!
5:3 Hear, O kings!
Pay attention, O rulers!
I will sing to the LORD!
I will sing to the LORD God of Israel!
5:4 O LORD, when you departed from Seir,
when you marched from Edom's plains,
the earth shook, the heavens poured down,
the clouds poured down rain.
5:5 The mountains trembled before the LORD, the God of Sinai;
before the LORD God of Israel.
5:6 In the days of Shamgar son of Anath,
in the days of Jael caravans disappeared;
travelers had to go on winding side roads.
5:7 Warriors were scarce,
they were scarce in Israel,
until you arose, Deborah,

until you arose as a motherly protector in Israel.
5:8 God chose new leaders,
then fighters appeared in the city gates;
but, I swear, not a shield or spear could be found,
among forty military units in Israel.
5:9 My heart went out to Israel's leaders,
to the people who answered the call to war.
Praise the LORD!
5:10 You who ride on light-colored female donkeys,
who sit on saddle blankets,
you who walk on the road, pay attention!
5:11 Hear the sound of those who divide the sheep among the watering places;
there they tell of the Lord's victorious deeds,
the victorious deeds of his warriors in Israel.
Then the LORD's people went down to the city gates –
5:12 Wake up, wake up, Deborah!
Wake up, wake up, sing a song!
Get up, Barak!
Capture your prisoners of war, son of Abinoam!
5:13 Then the survivors came down to the mighty ones;
the LORD's people came down to me as warriors.
5:14 They came from Ephraim, who uprooted Amalek,
they follow after you, Benjamin, with your soldiers.
From Makir leaders came down,
from Zebulun came the ones who march carrying an officer's staff.
5:15 Issachar's leaders were with Deborah,
the men of Issachar supported Barak;
into the valley they were sent under Barak's command.
Among the clans of Reuben there was intense heart searching.
5:16 Why do you remain among the sheepfolds,
listening to the shepherds playing their pipes for their flocks?
As for the clans of Reuben – there was intense searching of heart.
5:17 Gilead stayed put beyond the Jordan River.
As for Dan – why did he seek temporary employment in the shipyards?
Asher remained on the seacoast,
he stayed by his harbors.
5:18 The men of Zebulun were not concerned about their lives;
Naphtali charged on to the battlefields.
5:19 Kings came, they fought;
the kings of Canaan fought,
at Taanach by the waters of Megiddo,
but they took no silver as plunder.
5:20 From the sky the stars fought,
from their paths in the heavens they fought against Sisera.
5:21 The Kishon River carried them off;
the river confronted them – the Kishon River.
Step on the necks of the strong!
5:22 The horses' hooves pounded the ground;
the stallions galloped madly.
5:23 'Call judgment down on Meroz,' says the LORD's angelic messenger;
'Be sure to call judgment down on those who live there,
because they did not come to help in the LORD's battle,
to help in the LORD's battle against the warriors.'
5:24 The most rewarded of women should be Jael,
the wife of Heber the Kenite!
She should be the most rewarded of women who live in tents.
5:25 He asked for water,
and she gave him milk;
in a bowl fit for a king,
she served him curds.
5:26 Her left hand reached for the tent peg,
her right hand for the workmen's hammer.
She "hammered" Sisera,
she shattered his skull,
she smashed his head,
she drove the tent peg through his temple.
5:27 Between her feet he collapsed,
he fell limp and was lifeless;
between her feet he collapsed and fell limp,
in the spot where he collapsed,
there he fell limp – violently murdered!
5:28 Through the window she looked;
Sisera's mother cried out through the lattice:
'Why is his chariot so slow to return?
Why are the hoofbeats of his chariot-horses delayed?'
5:29 The wisest of her ladies answer;
indeed she even thinks to herself,
5:30 'No doubt they are gathering and dividing the plunder –
a girl or two for each man to rape!
Sisera is grabbing up colorful cloth,
he is grabbing up colorful embroidered cloth,
two pieces of colorful embroidered cloth,
for the neck of the plunderer!'
5:31 May all your enemies perish like this, O LORD!
But may those who love you shine
like the rising sun at its brightest!"
And the land had rest for forty years.

Oppression and Confrontation

6:1 The Israelites did evil in the LORD's sight, so the LORD turned them over to Midian for seven years. **6:2** The Midianites overwhelmed Israel. Because of Midian the Israelites made shelters for themselves in the hills, as well as caves and strongholds. **6:3** Whenever the Israelites planted their crops, the Midianites, Amalekites, and the people from the east would attack them. **6:4** They invaded the land and devoured its crops all the way to Gaza. They left nothing for the Israelites to eat, and they took away the sheep, oxen, and donkeys. **6:5** When they invaded with their cattle and tents, they were as thick as locusts. Neither they nor their camels could be counted. They came to devour the land. **6:6** Israel was so severely weakened by Midian that the Israelites cried out to the LORD for help.

6:7 When the Israelites cried out to the LORD for help because of Midian, **6:8** he sent a prophet to the Israelites. He said to them, "This is what the LORD God of Israel says: 'I brought you up from Egypt and took you out of that place of slavery. **6:9** I rescued you from Egypt's power and from the power of all who oppressed you. I drove them out before you and gave their land to you. **6:10** I said to you, "I am the LORD your God! Do not worship the gods of the Amorites, in whose land you are now living!" But you have disobeyed me.'"

Gideon Meets Some Visitors

6:11 The LORD's angelic messenger came and sat down under the oak tree in Ophrah owned by Joash the Abiezrite. He arrived while Joash's son Gideon was threshing wheat in a winepress so he could hide it from the Midianites. **6:12** The LORD's messenger appeared and said to him, "The LORD is with you, courageous warrior!" **6:13** Gideon said to him, "Pardon me, but if the LORD is with us, why has such disaster overtaken us? Where are all his miraculous deeds our ancestors told us about? They said, 'Did the LORD not bring us up from Egypt?' But now the LORD has abandoned us and handed us over to Midian." **6:14** Then the LORD himself turned to him and said, "You have the strength. Deliver Israel from the power of the Midianites! Have I not sent you?" **6:15** Gideon said to him, "But Lord, how can I deliver Israel? Just look! My clan is the weakest in Manasseh, and I am the youngest in my family." **6:16** The LORD said to him, "Ah, but I will be with you! You will strike down the whole Midianite army." **6:17** Gideon said to him, "If you really are pleased with me, then give me a sign as proof that it is really you speaking with me. **6:18** Do not leave this place until I come back with a gift and present it to you." The LORD said, "I will stay here until you come back."

6:19 Gideon went and prepared a young goat, along with unleavened bread made from an ephah of flour. He put the meat in a basket and the broth in a pot. He brought the food to him under the oak tree and presented it to him. **6:20** God's messenger said to him, "Put the meat and unleavened bread on this rock, and pour out the broth." Gideon did as instructed. **6:21** The LORD's messenger touched the meat and the unleavened bread with the tip of his staff. Fire flared up from the rock and consumed the meat and unleavened bread. The LORD's messenger then disappeared.

6:22 When Gideon realized that it was the LORD's messenger, he said, "Oh no! Master, LORD! I have seen the LORD's messenger face to face!" **6:23** The LORD said to him, "You are safe! Do not be afraid! You are not going to die!" **6:24** Gideon built an altar for the LORD there, and named it "The LORD is on friendly terms with me." To this day it is still there in Ophrah of the Abiezrites.

Gideon Destroys the Altar

6:25 That night the LORD said to him, "Take the bull from your father's herd, as well as a second bull, one that is seven years old. Pull down your father's Baal altar and cut down the nearby Asherah pole. **6:26** Then build an altar for the LORD your God on the top of this stronghold according to the proper pattern. Take the second bull and offer it as a burnt sacrifice on the wood from the Asherah pole that you cut down." **6:27** So Gideon took ten of his servants and did just as the LORD had told him. He was too afraid of his father's family and the men of the city to do it in broad daylight, so he waited until nighttime.

6:28 When the men of the city got up the next morning, they saw the Baal altar pulled down, the nearby Asherah pole cut down, and the second bull sacrificed on the newly built altar. **6:29** They said to one another, "Who did this?" They investigated the matter thoroughly and concluded that Gideon son of Joash had done it. **6:30** The men of the city said to Joash, "Bring out your son, so we can execute him! He pulled down the Baal altar and cut down the nearby Asherah pole." **6:31** But Joash said to all those who confronted him, "Must you fight Baal's battles? Must you rescue him? Whoever takes up his cause will die by morning! If he really is a god, let him fight his own battles! After all, it was his altar that was pulled down." **6:32** That very day Gideon's father named him Jerub-Baal, because he had said, "Let Baal fight with him, for it was his altar that was pulled down."

Gideon Summons an Army and Seeks Confirmation

6:33 All the Midianites, Amalekites, and the people from the east assembled. They crossed the Jordan River and camped in the Jezreel Valley. **6:34** The LORD's spirit took control of Gideon. He blew a trumpet, summoning the Abiezrites to follow him. **6:35** He sent messengers throughout Manasseh and summoned them to follow him as well. He also sent messengers throughout Asher, Zebulun, and Naphtali, and they came up to meet him. **6:36** Gideon said to God, "If you really intend to use me to deliver Israel, as you promised, then give me a sign as proof. **6:37** Look, I am putting a wool fleece on the threshing floor. If there is dew only on the fleece, and the ground around it is dry, then I will be sure that you will use me to deliver Israel, as you promised." **6:38** The LORD did as he asked. When he got up the next morning, he squeezed the fleece, and enough dew dripped from it to fill a bowl. **6:39** Gideon said to God, "Please do not get angry at me, when I ask for just one more sign. Please allow me one more test with the fleece. This time make only the fleece dry, while the ground around it is covered with dew." **6:40** That night God did as he asked. Only the fleece was dry and the ground around it was covered with dew.

Gideon Reduces the Ranks

7:1 Jerub-Baal (that is, Gideon) and his men got up the next morning and camped near the spring of Harod. The Midianites were camped north of them near the hill of Moreh in the valley. **7:2** The LORD said to Gideon, "You have too many men for me to hand Midian over to you. Israel might brag, 'Our own strength has delivered us.' **7:3** Now, announce to the men, 'Whoever is shaking with fear may turn around and leave Mount Gilead.'" Twenty-two thousand men went home; ten thousand remained. **7:4** The LORD spoke to Gideon again, "There are still too many men. Bring them down to the water and I will thin the ranks some more. When I say, 'This one should go with you,' pick him to go; when I say, 'This one should not go with you,' do not take him." **7:5** So he brought the men down to the water. Then the LORD said to Gideon, "Separate those who lap the water as a dog laps from those who kneel to drink." **7:6** Three hundred men lapped; the rest of the men kneeled to drink water. **7:7** The LORD said to Gideon, "With the three hundred men who lapped I will deliver the whole army and I will hand Midian over to you. The rest of the men should go home." **7:8** The men who were chosen took supplies and their trumpets. Gideon sent all the men of Israel back to their homes; he kept only three hundred men. Now the Midianites were camped down below in the valley.

Gideon Reassured of Victory

7:9 That night the LORD said to Gideon, "Get up! Attack the camp, for I am handing it over to you. **7:10** But if you are afraid to attack, go down to the camp with Purah your servant **7:11** and listen to what they are saying. Then you will be brave and attack the camp." So he went down with Purah his servant to where the sentries were guarding the camp. **7:12** Now the Midianites, Amalekites, and the people from the east covered the valley like a swarm of locusts. Their camels could not be counted; they were as innumerable as the sand on the seashore. **7:13** When Gideon arrived, he heard a man telling another man about a dream he had. The man said, "Look! I had a dream. I saw a stale cake of barley bread rolling into the Midianite camp. It hit a tent so hard it knocked it over and turned it upside down. The tent just collapsed." **7:14** The other man said, "Without a doubt this symbolizes the sword of Gideon son of Joash, the Israelite. God is handing Midian and all the army over to him."

Gideon Routs the Enemy

7:15 When Gideon heard the report of the dream and its interpretation, he praised God. Then he went back to the Israelite camp and said, "Get up, for the LORD is handing the Midianite army over to you!" **7:16** He divided the three hundred men into three units. He gave them all trumpets and empty jars with torches inside them. **7:17** He said to them, "Watch me and do as I do. Watch closely! I am going to the edge of the camp. Do as I do! **7:18** When I and all who are with me blow our trumpets, you also blow your trumpets all around the camp. Then say, 'For the LORD and for Gideon!'"

7:19 Gideon took a hundred men to the edge of the camp at the beginning of the middle watch, just after they had changed the guards. They blew their trumpets and broke the jars they were carrying. **7:20** All three units blew their trumpets and broke their jars. They held the torches in their left hand and the trumpets in their right. Then they yelled, "A sword for the LORD and for Gideon!" **7:21** They stood in order all around the camp. The whole army ran away; they shouted as they scrambled away. **7:22** When the three hundred men blew their trumpets, the LORD caused the Midianites to attack one another with their swords throughout the camp. The army fled to Beth Shittah on the way to Zererah. They went to the border of Abel Meholah near Tabbath. **7:23** Israelites from Naphtali, Asher, and Manasseh answered the call and chased the Midianites.

Gideon Appeases the Ephraimites

7:24 Now Gideon sent messengers throughout the Ephraimite hill country who announced, "Go down and head off the Midianites. Take control of the fords of the streams all the way to Beth Barah and the Jordan River."

When all the Ephraimites had assembled, they took control of the fords all the way to Beth Barah and the Jordan River. **7:25** They captured the two Midianite generals, Oreb and Zeeb. They executed Oreb on the rock of Oreb and Zeeb in the winepress of Zeeb. They chased the Midianites and brought the heads of Oreb and Zeeb to Gideon, who was now on the other side of the Jordan River.

8:1 The Ephraimites said to him, "Why have you done such a thing to us? You did not summon us when you went to fight the Midianites!" They argued vehemently with him. **8:2** He said to them, "Now what have I accomplished compared to you? Even Ephraim's leftover grapes are better quality than Abiezer's harvest! **8:3** It was to you that God handed over the Midianite generals, Oreb and Zeeb! What did I accomplish to rival that?" When he said this, they calmed down.

Gideon Tracks Down the Midianite Kings

8:4 Now Gideon and his three hundred men had crossed over the Jordan River, and even though they were exhausted, they were still chasing the Midianites. **8:5** He said to the men of Succoth, "Give some loaves of bread to the men who are following me, because they are exhausted. I am chasing Zebah and Zalmunna, the kings of Midian." **8:6** The officials of Succoth said, "You have not yet overpowered Zebah and Zalmunna. So why should we give bread to your army?" **8:7** Gideon said, "Since you will not help, after the LORD hands Zebah and Zalmunna over to me, I will thresh your skin with desert thorns and briers." **8:8** He went up from there to Penuel and made the same request. The men of Penuel responded the same way the men of Succoth had. **8:9** He also threatened the men of Penuel, warning, "When I return victoriously, I will tear down this tower."

8:10 Now Zebah and Zalmunna were in Karkor with their armies. There were about fifteen thousand survivors from the army of the eastern peoples; a hundred and twenty thousand sword-wielding soldiers had been killed. **8:11** Gideon went up the road of the nomads east of Nobah and Jogbehah and ambushed the surprised army. **8:12** When Zebah and Zalmunna ran away, Gideon chased them and captured the two Midianite kings, Zebah and Zalmunna. He had surprised their entire army.

8:13 Gideon son of Joash returned from the battle by the pass of Heres. **8:14** He captured a young man from Succoth and interrogated him. The young man wrote down for him the names of Succoth's officials and city leaders – seventy-seven men in all. **8:15** He approached the men of Succoth and said, "Look what I have! Zebah and Zalmunna! You insulted me, saying, 'You have not yet overpowered Zebah and Zalmunna. So why should we give bread to your exhausted men?'" **8:16** He seized the leaders of the city, along with some desert thorns and briers; he then "threshed" the men of Succoth with them. **8:17** He also tore down the tower of Penuel and executed the city's men.

8:18 He said to Zebah and Zalmunna, "Describe for me the men you killed at Tabor." They said, "They were like you. Each one looked like a king's son." **8:19** He said, "They were my brothers, the sons of my mother. I swear, as surely as the LORD is alive, if you had let them live, I would not kill you." **8:20** He ordered Jether his firstborn son, "Come on! Kill them!" But Jether was too afraid to draw his sword, because he was still young. **8:21** Zebah and Zalmunna said to Gideon, "Come on, you strike us, for a man is judged by his strength." So Gideon killed Zebah and Zalmunna, and he took the crescent-shaped ornaments which were on the necks of their camels.

Gideon Rejects a Crown but Makes an Ephod

8:22 The men of Israel said to Gideon, "Rule over us – you, your son, and your grandson. For you have delivered us from Midian's power." **8:23** Gideon said to them, "I will not rule over you, nor will my son rule over you. The LORD will rule over you." **8:24** Gideon continued, "I would like to make one request. Each of you give me an earring from the plunder you have taken." (The Midianites had gold earrings because they were Ishmaelites.) **8:25** They said, "We are happy to give you earrings." So they spread out a garment, and each one threw an earring from his plunder onto it. **8:26** The total weight of the gold earrings he requested came to seventeen hundred gold shekels. This was in addition to the crescent-shaped ornaments, jewelry, purple clothing worn by the Midianite kings, and the necklaces on the camels. **8:27** Gideon used all this to make an ephod, which he put in his hometown of Ophrah. All the Israelites prostituted themselves to it by worshiping it there. It became a snare to Gideon and his family.

Gideon's Story Ends

8:28 The Israelites humiliated Midian; the Midianites' fighting spirit was broken. The land had rest for forty years during Gideon's time. **8:29** Then Jerub-Baal son of Joash went home and settled down. **8:30** Gideon fathered seventy sons through his many wives. **8:31** His concubine, who lived in Shechem, also gave him a son, whom he named Abimelech. **8:32** Gideon son of Joash died at a very old age and was buried in the tomb of his father Joash located in Ophrah of the Abiezrites.

Israel Returns to Baal-Worship

8:33 After Gideon died, the Israelites again prostituted themselves to the Baals. They made Baal-Berith their god. **8:34** The Israelites did not remain true to the LORD their God, who had delivered them from all the enemies who lived around them. **8:35** They did not treat the family of

Jerub-Baal (that is, Gideon) fairly in return for all the good he had done for Israel.

Abimelech Murders His Brothers

9:1 Now Abimelech son of Jerub-Baal went to Shechem to see his mother's relatives. He said to them and to his mother's entire extended family, **9:2** "Tell all the leaders of Shechem this: 'Why would you want to have seventy men, all Jerub-Baal's sons, ruling over you, when you can have just one ruler? Recall that I am your own flesh and blood.'" **9:3** His mother's relatives spoke on his behalf to all the leaders of Shechem and reported his proposal. The leaders were drawn to Abimelech; they said, "He is our close relative." **9:4** They paid him seventy silver shekels out of the temple of Baal-Berith. Abimelech then used the silver to hire some lawless, dangerous men as his followers. **9:5** He went to his father's home in Ophrah and murdered his half-brothers, the seventy legitimate sons of Jerub-Baal, on one stone. Only Jotham, Jerub-Baal's youngest son, escaped, because he hid. **9:6** All the leaders of Shechem and Beth Millo assembled and then went and made Abimelech king by the oak near the pillar in Shechem.

Jotham's Parable

9:7 When Jotham heard the news, he went and stood on the top of Mount Gerizim. He spoke loudly to the people below, "Listen to me, leaders of Shechem, so that God may listen to you!

9:8 "The trees were determined to go out and choose a king for themselves. They said to the olive tree, 'Be our king!' **9:9** But the olive tree said to them, 'I am not going to stop producing my oil, which is used to honor gods and men, just to sway above the other trees!'

9:10 "So the trees said to the fig tree, 'You come and be our king!' **9:11** But the fig tree said to them, 'I am not going to stop producing my sweet figs, my excellent fruit, just to sway above the other trees!'

9:12 "So the trees said to the grapevine, 'You come and be our king!' **9:13** But the grapevine said to them, 'I am not going to stop producing my wine, which makes gods and men so happy, just to sway above the other trees!'

9:14 "So all the trees said to the thornbush, 'You come and be our king!' **9:15** The thornbush said to the trees, 'If you really want to choose me as your king, then come along, find safety under my branches! Otherwise may fire blaze from the thornbush and consume the cedars of Lebanon!'

9:16 "Now, if you have shown loyalty and integrity when you made Abimelech king, if you have done right to Jerub-Baal and his family, if you have properly repaid him – **9:17** my father fought for you; he risked his life and delivered you from Midian's power. **9:18** But you have attacked my father's family today. You murdered his seventy legitimate sons on one stone and made Abimelech, the son of his female slave, king over the leaders of Shechem, just because he is your close relative. **9:19** So if you have shown loyalty and integrity to Jerub-Baal and his family today, then may Abimelech bring you happiness and may you bring him happiness! **9:20** But if not, may fire blaze from Abimelech and consume the leaders of Shechem and Beth Millo! May fire also blaze from the leaders of Shechem and Beth Millo and consume Abimelech!" **9:21** Then Jotham ran away to Beer and lived there to escape from Abimelech his half-brother.

God Fulfills Jotham's Curse

9:22 Abimelech commanded Israel for three years. **9:23** God sent a spirit to stir up hostility between Abimelech and the leaders of Shechem. He made the leaders of Shechem disloyal to Abimelech. **9:24** He did this so the violent deaths of Jerub-Baal's seventy sons might be avenged and Abimelech, their half-brother who murdered them, might have to pay for their spilled blood, along with the leaders of Shechem who helped him murder them. **9:25** The leaders of Shechem rebelled against Abimelech by putting bandits in the hills, who robbed everyone who traveled by on the road. But Abimelech found out about it.

9:26 Gaal son of Ebed came through Shechem with his brothers. The leaders of Shechem transferred their loyalty to him. **9:27** They went out to the field, harvested their grapes, squeezed out the juice, and celebrated. They came to the temple of their god and ate, drank, and cursed Abimelech. **9:28** Gaal son of Ebed said, "Who is Abimelech and who is Shechem, that we should serve him? Is he not the son of Jerub-Baal, and is not Zebul the deputy he appointed? Serve the sons of Hamor, the father of Shechem! But why should we serve Abimelech? **9:29** If only these men were under my command, I would get rid of Abimelech!" He challenged Abimelech, "Muster your army and come out for battle!"

9:30 When Zebul, the city commissioner, heard the words of Gaal son of Ebed, he was furious. **9:31** He sent messengers to Abimelech, who was in Arumah, reporting, "Beware! Gaal son of Ebed and his brothers are coming to Shechem and inciting the city to rebel against you. **9:32** Now, come up at night with your men and set an ambush in the field outside the city. **9:33** In the morning at sunrise quickly attack the city. When he and his men come out to fight you, do what you can to him."

9:34 So Abimelech and all his men came up at night and set an ambush outside Shechem – they divided into four units. **9:35** When Gaal son of Ebed came out and stood at the entrance to the city's gate, Abimelech and his men got up from their hiding places. **9:36** Gaal saw the men and said to Zebul, "Look, men are coming down from the tops of the hills." But

Zebul said to him, "You are seeing the shadows on the hills – it just looks like men." **9:37** Gaal again said, "Look, men are coming down from the very center of the land. A unit is coming by way of the Oak Tree of the Diviners." **9:38** Zebul said to him, "Where now are your bragging words, 'Who is Abimelech that we should serve him?' Are these not the men you insulted? Go out now and fight them!" **9:39** So Gaal led the leaders of Shechem and fought Abimelech. **9:40** Abimelech chased him, and Gaal ran from him. Many Shechemites fell wounded at the entrance of the gate. **9:41** Abimelech went back to Arumah; Zebul drove Gaal and his brothers out of Shechem.

9:42 The next day the Shechemites came out to the field. When Abimelech heard about it, **9:43** he took his men and divided them into three units and set an ambush in the field. When he saw the people coming out of the city, he attacked and struck them down. **9:44** Abimelech and his units attacked and blocked the entrance to the city's gate. Two units then attacked all the people in the field and struck them down. **9:45** Abimelech fought against the city all that day. He captured the city and killed all the people in it. Then he leveled the city and spread salt over it.

9:46 When all the leaders of the Tower of Shechem heard the news, they went to the stronghold of the temple of El-Berith. **9:47** Abimelech heard that all the leaders of the Tower of Shechem were in one place. **9:48** He and all his men went up on Mount Zalmon. He took an ax in his hand and cut off a tree branch. He put it on his shoulder and said to his men, "Quickly, do what you have just seen me do!" **9:49** So each of his men also cut off a branch and followed Abimelech. They put the branches against the stronghold and set fire to it. All the people of the Tower of Shechem died – about a thousand men and women.

9:50 Abimelech moved on to Thebez; he besieged and captured it. **9:51** There was a fortified tower in the center of the city, so all the men and women, as well as the city's leaders, ran into it and locked the entrance. Then they went up to the roof of the tower. **9:52** Abimelech came and attacked the tower. When he approached the entrance of the tower to set it on fire, **9:53** a woman threw an upper millstone down on his head and shattered his skull. **9:54** He quickly called to the young man who carried his weapons, "Draw your sword and kill me, so they will not say, 'A woman killed him.'" So the young man stabbed him and he died. **9:55** When the Israelites saw that Abimelech was dead, they went home.

9:56 God repaid Abimelech for the evil he did to his father by murdering his seventy half-brothers. **9:57** God also repaid the men of Shechem for their evil deeds. The curse spoken by Jotham son of Jerub-Baal fell on them.

Stability Restored

10:1 After Abimelech's death, Tola son of Puah, grandson of Dodo, from the tribe of Issachar, rose up to deliver Israel. He lived in Shamir in the Ephraimite hill country. **10:2** He led Israel for twenty-three years, then died and was buried in Shamir.

10:3 Jair the Gileadite rose up after him; he led Israel for twenty-two years. **10:4** He had thirty sons who rode on thirty donkeys and possessed thirty cities. To this day these towns are called Havvoth Jair – they are in the land of Gilead. **10:5** Jair died and was buried in Kamon.

The Lord's Patience Runs Short

10:6 The Israelites again did evil in the LORD's sight. They worshiped the Baals and the Ashtars, as well as the gods of Syria, Sidon, Moab, the Ammonites, and the Philistines. They abandoned the LORD and did not worship him. **10:7** The LORD was furious with Israel and turned them over to the Philistines and Ammonites. **10:8** They ruthlessly oppressed the Israelites that eighteenth year – that is, all the Israelites living east of the Jordan in Amorite country in Gilead. **10:9** The Ammonites crossed the Jordan to fight with Judah, Benjamin, and Ephraim. Israel suffered greatly.

10:10 The Israelites cried out for help to the LORD: "We have sinned against you. We abandoned our God and worshiped the Baals." **10:11** The LORD said to the Israelites, "Did I not deliver you from Egypt, the Amorites, the Ammonites, the Philistines, **10:12** the Sidonians, Amalek, and Midian when they oppressed you? You cried out for help to me, and I delivered you from their power. **10:13** But since you abandoned me and worshiped other gods, I will not deliver you again. **10:14** Go and cry for help to the gods you have chosen! Let them deliver you from trouble!" **10:15** But the Israelites said to the LORD, "We have sinned. You do to us as you see fit, but deliver us today!" **10:16** They threw away the foreign gods they owned and worshiped the LORD. Finally the LORD grew tired of seeing Israel suffer so much.

An Outcast Becomes a General

10:17 The Ammonites assembled and camped in Gilead; the Israelites gathered together and camped in Mizpah. **10:18** The leaders of Gilead said to one another, "Who is willing to lead the charge against the Ammonites? He will become the leader of all who live in Gilead!"

11:1 Now Jephthah the Gileadite was a brave warrior. His mother was a prostitute, but Gilead was his father. **11:2** Gilead's wife also gave him sons. When his wife's sons grew up, they made Jephthah leave and said to him, "You are not going to inherit any of our father's wealth, because you are another woman's son." **11:3** So Jephthah left his half-brothers

and lived in the land of Tob. Lawless men joined Jephthah's gang and traveled with him.
11:4 It was some time after this when the Ammonites fought with Israel. **11:5** When the Ammonites attacked, the leaders of Gilead asked Jephthah to come back from the land of Tob. **11:6** They said, "Come, be our commander, so we can fight with the Ammonites." **11:7** Jephthah said to the leaders of Gilead, "But you hated me and made me leave my father's house. Why do you come to me now, when you are in trouble?" **11:8** The leaders of Gilead said to Jephthah, "That may be true, but now we pledge to you our loyalty. Come with us and fight with the Ammonites. Then you will become the leader of all who live in Gilead." **11:9** Jephthah said to the leaders of Gilead, "All right! If you take me back to fight with the Ammonites and the LORD gives them to me, I will be your leader." **11:10** The leaders of Gilead said to Jephthah, "The LORD will judge any grievance you have against us, if we do not do as you say." **11:11** So Jephthah went with the leaders of Gilead. The people made him their leader and commander. Jephthah repeated the terms of the agreement before the LORD in Mizpah.

Jephthah Gives a History Lesson
11:12 Jephthah sent messengers to the Ammonite king, saying, "Why have you come against me to attack my land?" **11:13** The Ammonite king said to Jephthah's messengers, "Because Israel stole my land when they came up from Egypt – from the Arnon River in the south to the Jabbok River in the north, and as far west as the Jordan. Now return it peaceably!"
11:14 Jephthah sent messengers back to the Ammonite king **11:15** and said to him, "This is what Jephthah says, 'Israel did not steal the land of Moab and the land of the Ammonites. **11:16** When they left Egypt, Israel traveled through the desert as far as the Red Sea and then came to Kadesh. **11:17** Israel sent messengers to the king of Edom, saying, "Please allow us to pass through your land." But the king of Edom rejected the request. Israel sent the same request to the king of Moab, but he was unwilling to cooperate. So Israel stayed at Kadesh. **11:18** Then Israel went through the desert and bypassed the land of Edom and the land of Moab. They traveled east of the land of Moab and camped on the other side of the Arnon River; they did not go through Moabite territory (the Arnon was Moab's border). **11:19** Israel sent messengers to King Sihon, the Amorite king who ruled in Heshbon, and said to him, "Please allow us to pass through your land to our land." **11:20** But Sihon did not trust Israel to pass through his territory. He assembled his whole army, camped in Jahaz, and fought with Israel. **11:21** The LORD God of Israel handed Sihon and his whole army over to Israel and they defeated them. Israel took all the land of the Amorites who lived in that land. **11:22** They took all the Amorite territory from the Arnon River on the south to the Jabbok River on the north, from the desert in the east to the Jordan in the west. **11:23** Since the LORD God of Israel has driven out the Amorites before his people Israel, do you think you can just take it from them? **11:24** You have the right to take what Chemosh your god gives you, but we will take the land of all whom the LORD our God has driven out before us. **11:25** Are you really better than Balak son of Zippor, king of Moab? Did he dare to quarrel with Israel? Did he dare to fight with them? **11:26** Israel has been living in Heshbon and its nearby towns, in Aroer and its nearby towns, and in all the cities along the Arnon for three hundred years! Why did you not reclaim them during that time? **11:27** I have not done you wrong, but you are doing wrong by attacking me. May the LORD, the Judge, judge this day between the Israelites and the Ammonites!'" **11:28** But the Ammonite king disregarded the message sent by Jephthah.

A Foolish Vow Spells Death for a Daughter
11:29 The LORD's spirit empowered Jephthah. He passed through Gilead and Manasseh and went to Mizpah in Gilead. From there he approached the Ammonites. **11:30** Jephthah made a vow to the LORD, saying, "If you really do hand the Ammonites over to me, **11:31** then whoever is the first to come through the doors of my house to meet me when I return safely from fighting the Ammonites – he will belong to the LORD and I will offer him up as a burnt sacrifice." **11:32** Jephthah approached the Ammonites to fight with them, and the LORD handed them over to him. **11:33** He defeated them from Aroer all the way to Minnith – twenty cities in all, even as far as Abel Keramim! He wiped them out! The Israelites humiliated the Ammonites.
11:34 When Jephthah came home to Mizpah, there was his daughter hurrying out to meet him, dancing to the rhythm of tambourines. She was his only child; except for her he had no son or daughter. **11:35** When he saw her, he ripped his clothes and said, "Oh no! My daughter! You have completely ruined me! You have brought me disaster! I made an oath to the LORD, and I cannot break it." **11:36** She said to him, "My father, since you made an oath to the LORD, do to me as you promised. After all, the LORD vindicated you before your enemies, the Ammonites." **11:37** She then said to her father, "Please grant me this one wish. For two months allow me to walk through the hills with my friends and mourn my virginity." **11:38** He said, "You may go." He permitted her to leave for two months. She went with her friends and mourned her virginity as she walked through the hills. **11:39** After two months she returned to her father, and he did to her as he had vowed. She died a virgin. Her tragic death gave rise to a custom in Israel. **11:40** Every year Israelite women commemorate the daughter of Jephthah the Gileadite for four days.

Civil Strife Mars the Victory
12:1 The Ephraimites assembled and crossed over to Zaphon. They said to Jephthah, "Why did you go and fight with the Ammonites without asking us to go with you? We will burn your house down right over you!" **12:2** Jephthah said to them, "My people and I were entangled in controversy with the Ammonites. I asked for your help, but you did not deliver me from their power. **12:3** When I saw that you were not going to help, I risked my life and advanced against the Ammonites, and the LORD handed them over to me. Why have you come up to fight with me today?" **12:4** Jephthah assembled all the men of Gilead and they fought with Ephraim. The men of Gilead defeated Ephraim, because the Ephraimites insulted them, saying, "You Gileadites are refugees in Ephraim, living within Ephraim's and Manasseh's territory." **12:5** The Gileadites captured the fords of the Jordan River opposite Ephraim. Whenever an Ephraimite fugitive said, "Let me cross over," the men of Gilead asked him, "Are you an Ephraimite?" If he said, "No," **12:6** then they said to him, "Say 'Shibboleth!'" If he said, "Sibboleth" (and could not pronounce the word correctly), they grabbed him and executed him right there at the fords of the Jordan. On that day forty-two thousand Ephraimites fell dead. **12:7** Jephthah led Israel for six years; then he died and was buried in his city in Gilead.

Order Restored
12:8 After him Ibzan of Bethlehem led Israel. **12:9** He had thirty sons. He arranged for thirty of his daughters to be married outside his extended family, and he arranged for thirty young women to be brought from outside as wives for his sons. Ibzan led Israel for seven years; **12:10** then he died and was buried in Bethlehem.
12:11 After him Elon the Zebulunite led Israel for ten years. **12:12** Then Elon the Zebulunite died and was buried in Aijalon in the land of Zebulun.
12:13 After him Abdon son of Hillel the Pirathonite led Israel. **12:14** He had forty sons and thirty grandsons who rode on seventy donkeys. He led Israel for eight years. **12:15** Then Abdon son of Hillel the Pirathonite died and was buried in Pirathon in the land of Ephraim, in the hill country of the Amalekites.

Samson's Birth
13:1 The Israelites again did evil in the LORD's sight, so the LORD handed them over to the Philistines for forty years.
13:2 There was a man named Manoah from Zorah, from the Danite tribe. His wife was infertile and childless. **13:3** The LORD's angelic messenger appeared to the woman and said to her, "You are infertile and childless, but you will conceive and have a son. **13:4** Now be careful! Do not drink wine or beer, and do not eat any food that will make you ritually unclean. **13:5** Look, you will conceive and have a son. You must never cut his hair, for the child will be dedicated to God from birth. He will begin to deliver Israel from the power of the Philistines."
13:6 The woman went and said to her husband, "A man sent from God came to me! He looked like God's angelic messenger – he was very awesome. I did not ask him where he came from, and he did not tell me his name. **13:7** He said to me, 'Look, you will conceive and have a son. So now, do not drink wine or beer and do not eat any food that will make you ritually unclean. For the child will be dedicated to God from birth till the day he dies.'"
13:8 Manoah prayed to the LORD, "Please, Lord, allow the man sent from God to visit us again, so he can teach us how we should raise the child who will be born." **13:9** God answered Manoah's prayer. God's angelic messenger visited the woman again while she was sitting in the field. But her husband Manoah was not with her. **13:10** The woman ran at once and told her husband, "Come quickly, the man who visited me the other day has appeared to me!" **13:11** So Manoah got up and followed his wife. When he met the man, he said to him, "Are you the man who spoke to my wife?" He said, "Yes." **13:12** Manoah said, "Now, when your announcement comes true, how should the child be raised and what should he do?" **13:13** The LORD's messenger told Manoah, "Your wife should pay attention to everything I told her. **13:14** She should not drink anything that the grapevine produces. She must not drink wine or beer, and she must not eat any food that will make her ritually unclean. She should obey everything I commanded her to do." **13:15** Manoah said to the LORD's messenger, "Please stay here awhile, so we can prepare a young goat for you to eat." **13:16** The LORD's messenger said to Manoah, "If I stay, I will not eat your food. But if you want to make a burnt sacrifice to the LORD, you should offer it." (He said this because Manoah did not know that he was the LORD's messenger.) **13:17** Manoah said to the LORD's messenger, "Tell us your name, so we can honor you when your announcement comes true." **13:18** The LORD's messenger said to him, "You should not ask me my name, because you cannot comprehend it." **13:19** Manoah took a young goat and a grain offering and offered them on a rock to the LORD. The LORD's messenger did an amazing thing as Manoah and his wife watched. **13:20** As the flame went up from the altar

toward the sky, the LORD's messenger went up in it while Manoah and his wife watched. They fell facedown to the ground. **13:21** The LORD's messenger did not appear again to Manoah and his wife. After all this happened Manoah realized that the visitor had been the LORD's messenger. **13:22** Manoah said to his wife, "We will certainly die, because we have seen a supernatural being!" **13:23** But his wife said to him, "If the LORD wanted to kill us, he would not have accepted the burnt offering and the grain offering from us. He would not have shown us all these things, or have spoken to us like this just now."
13:24 Manoah's wife gave birth to a son and named him Samson. The child grew and the LORD empowered him. **13:25** The LORD's spirit began to control him in Mahaneh Dan between Zorah and Eshtaol.

Samson's Unconsummated Marriage

14:1 Samson went down to Timnah, where a Philistine girl caught his eye. **14:2** When he got home, he told his father and mother, "A Philistine girl in Timnah has caught my eye. Now get her for my wife." **14:3** But his father and mother said to him, "Certainly you can find a wife among your relatives or among all our people! You should not have to go and get a wife from the uncircumcised Philistines." But Samson said to his father, "Get her for me, because she is the right one for me." **14:4** Now his father and mother did not realize this was the LORD's doing, because he was looking for an opportunity to stir up trouble with the Philistines (for at that time the Philistines were ruling Israel).

14:5 Samson went down to Timnah. When he approached the vineyards of Timnah, he saw a roaring young lion attacking him. **14:6** The LORD's spirit empowered him and he tore the lion in two with his bare hands as easily as one would tear a young goat. But he did not tell his father or mother what he had done.

14:7 Samson continued on down to Timnah and spoke to the girl. In his opinion, she was just the right one. **14:8** Some time later, when he went back to marry her, he turned aside to see the lion's remains. He saw a swarm of bees in the lion's carcass, as well as some honey. **14:9** He scooped it up with his hands and ate it as he walked along. When he returned to his father and mother, he offered them some and they ate it. But he did not tell them he had scooped the honey out of the lion's carcass.

14:10 Then Samson's father accompanied him to Timnah for the marriage. Samson hosted a party there, for this was customary for bridegrooms to do. **14:11** When the Philistines saw he had no attendants, they gave him thirty groomsmen who kept him company. **14:12** Samson said to them, "I will give you a riddle. If you really can solve it during the seven days the party lasts, I will give you thirty linen robes and thirty sets of clothes. **14:13** But if you cannot solve it, you will give me thirty linen robes and thirty sets of clothes." They said to him, "Let us hear your riddle." **14:14** He said to them,
"Out of the one who eats came something to eat;
out of the strong one came something sweet."
They could not solve the riddle for three days.

14:15 On the fourth day they said to Samson's bride, "Trick your husband into giving the solution to the riddle. If you refuse, we will burn up you and your father's family. Did you invite us here to make us poor?" **14:16** So Samson's bride cried on his shoulder and said, "You must hate me; you do not love me! You told the young men a riddle, but you have not told me the solution." He said to her, "Look, I have not even told my father or mother. Do you really expect me to tell you?" **14:17** She cried on his shoulder until the party was almost over. Finally, on the seventh day, he told her because she had nagged him so much. Then she told the young men the solution to the riddle. **14:18** On the seventh day, before the sun set, the men of the city said to him,
"What is sweeter than honey?
What is stronger than a lion?"
He said to them,
"If you had not plowed with my heifer,
you would not have solved my riddle!"
14:19 The LORD's spirit empowered him. He went down to Ashkelon and murdered thirty men. He took their clothes and gave them to the men who had solved the riddle. He was furious as he went back home. **14:20** Samson's bride was then given to his best man.

Samson Versus the Philistines

15:1 Sometime later, during the wheat harvest, Samson took a young goat as a gift and went to visit his bride. He said to her father, "I want to have sex with my bride in her bedroom!" But her father would not let him enter. **15:2** Her father said, "I really thought you absolutely despised her, so I gave her to your best man. Her younger sister is more attractive than she is. Take her instead!" **15:3** Samson said to them, "This time I am justified in doing the Philistines harm!" **15:4** Samson went and captured three hundred jackals and got some torches. He tied the jackals in pairs by their tails and then tied a torch to each pair. **15:5** He lit the torches and set the jackals loose in the Philistines' standing grain. He burned up the grain heaps and the standing grain, as well as the vineyards and olive groves. **15:6** The Philistines asked, "Who did this?" They were told, "Samson, the Timnite's son-in-law, because the Timnite took Samson's bride and gave her to his best man." So the Philistines went up and

burned her and her father. **15:7** Samson said to them, "Because you did this, I will get revenge against you before I quit fighting." **15:8** He struck them down and defeated them. Then he went down and lived for a time in the cave in the cliff of Etam.

15:9 The Philistines went up and invaded Judah. They arrayed themselves for battle in Lehi. **15:10** The men of Judah said, "Why are you attacking us?" The Philistines said, "We have come up to take Samson prisoner so we can do to him what he has done to us." **15:11** Three thousand men of Judah went down to the cave in the cliff of Etam and said to Samson, "Do you not know that the Philistines rule over us? Why have you done this to us?" He said to them, "I have only done to them what they have done to me." **15:12** They said to him, "We have come down to take you prisoner so we can hand you over to the Philistines." Samson said to them, "Promise me you will not kill me." **15:13** They said to him, "We promise! We will only take you prisoner and hand you over to them. We promise not to kill you." They tied him up with two brand new ropes and led him up from the cliff. **15:14** When he arrived in Lehi, the Philistines shouted as they approached him. But the LORD's spirit empowered him. The ropes around his arms were like flax dissolving in fire, and they melted away from his hands. **15:15** He happened to see a solid jawbone of a donkey. He grabbed it and struck down a thousand men. **15:16** Samson then said,
"With the jawbone of a donkey
I have left them in heaps;
with the jawbone of a donkey
I have struck down a thousand men!"
15:17 When he finished speaking, he threw the jawbone down and named that place Ramath Lehi.

15:18 He was very thirsty, so he cried out to the LORD and said, "You have given your servant this great victory. But now must I die of thirst and fall into hands of the Philistines?" **15:19** So God split open the basin at Lehi and water flowed out from it. When he took a drink, his strength was restored and he revived. For this reason he named the spring En Hakkore. It remains in Lehi to this very day. **15:20** Samson led Israel for twenty years during the days of Philistine prominence.

Samson's Downfall

16:1 Samson went to Gaza. There he saw a prostitute and went in to have sex with her. **16:2** The Gazites were told, "Samson has come here!" So they surrounded the town and hid all night at the city gate, waiting for him to leave. They relaxed all night, thinking, "He will not leave until morning comes; then we will kill him!" **16:3** Samson spent half the night with the prostitute; then he got up in the middle of the night and left. He grabbed the doors of the city gate, as well as the two posts, and pulled them right off, bar and all. He put them on his shoulders and carried them up to the top of a hill east of Hebron.

16:4 After this Samson fell in love with a woman named Delilah, who lived in the Sorek Valley. **16:5** The rulers of the Philistines went up to visit her and said to her, "Trick him! Find out what makes him so strong and how we can subdue him and humiliate him. Each one of us will give you eleven hundred silver pieces."

16:6 So Delilah said to Samson, "Tell me what makes you so strong and how you can be subdued and humiliated." **16:7** Samson said to her, "If they tie me up with seven fresh bowstrings that have not been dried, I will become weak and be just like any other man." **16:8** So the rulers of the Philistines brought her seven fresh bowstrings which had not been dried and they tied him up with them. **16:9** They hid in the bedroom and then she said to him, "The Philistines are here, Samson!" He snapped the bowstrings as easily as a thread of yarn snaps when it is put close to fire. The secret of his strength was not discovered.

16:10 Delilah said to Samson, "Look, you deceived me and told me lies! Now tell me how you can be subdued." **16:11** He said to her, "If they tie me tightly with brand new ropes that have never been used, I will become weak and be just like any other man." **16:12** So Delilah took new ropes and tied him with them and said to him, "The Philistines are here, Samson!" (The Philistines were hiding in the bedroom.) But he tore the ropes from his arms as if they were a piece of thread.

16:13 Delilah said to Samson, "Up to now you have deceived me and told me lies. Tell me how you can be subdued." He said to her, "If you weave the seven braids of my hair into the fabric on the loom and secure it with the pin, I will become weak and be like any other man." **16:14** So she made him go to sleep, wove the seven braids of his hair into the fabric on the loom, fastened it with the pin, and said to him, "The Philistines are here, Samson!" He woke up and tore away the pin of the loom and the fabric.

16:15 She said to him, "How can you say, 'I love you,' when you will not share your secret with me? Three times you have deceived me and have not told me what makes you so strong." **16:16** She nagged him every day and pressured him until he was sick to death of it. **16:17** Finally he told her his secret. He said to her, "My hair has never been cut, for I have been dedicated to God from the time I was conceived. If my head were shaved, my strength would leave me; I would become weak, and be just like all other men." **16:18** When Delilah saw that he had told her his secret, she sent for the rulers of the Philistines, saying, "Come up here again, for he has told me his secret." So the rulers of the Philistines went up to visit her, bringing the silver in their hands. **16:19** She made him go to sleep on her lap and then called a man in to shave off the seven braids of his hair. She made him vulnerable and his strength left him. **16:20** She said, "The Philistines are here, Samson!" He woke up and thought, "I will do as I did before and shake myself free." But he did not realize that the LORD had left him. **16:21** The Philistines captured him and gouged out his eyes. They brought him down to Gaza and bound him in bronze chains. He became a grinder in the prison. **16:22** His hair began to grow back after it had been shaved off.

Samson's Death and Burial

16:23 The rulers of the Philistines gathered to offer a great sacrifice to Dagon their god and to celebrate. They said, "Our god has handed Samson, our enemy, over to us." **16:24** When the people saw him, they praised their god, saying, "Our god has handed our enemy over to us, the one who ruined our land and killed so many of us!"

16:25 When they really started celebrating, they said, "Call for Samson so he can entertain us!" So they summoned Samson from the prison and he entertained them. They made him stand between two pillars. **16:26** Samson said to the young man who held his hand, "Position me so I can touch the pillars that support the temple. Then I can lean on them." **16:27** Now the temple was filled with men and women, and all the rulers of the Philistines were there. There were three thousand men and women on the roof watching Samson entertain. **16:28** Samson called to the LORD, "O Master, LORD, remember me! Strengthen me just one more time, O God, so I can get swift revenge against the Philistines for my two eyes!" **16:29** Samson took hold of the two middle pillars that supported the temple and he leaned against them, with his right hand on one and his left hand on the other. **16:30** Samson said, "Let me die with the Philistines!" He pushed hard and the temple collapsed on the rulers and all the people in it. He killed many more people in his death than he had killed during his life. **16:31** His brothers and all his family went down and brought him back. They buried him between Zorah and Eshtaol in the tomb of Manoah his father. He had led Israel for twenty years.

Micah Makes His Own Religion

17:1 There was a man named Micah from the Ephraimite hill country. **17:2** He said to his mother, "You know the eleven hundred pieces of silver which were stolen from you, about which I heard you pronounce a curse? Look here, I have the silver. I stole it, but now I am giving it back to you." His mother said, "May the LORD reward you, my son!" **17:3** When he gave back to his mother the eleven hundred pieces of silver, his mother said, "I solemnly dedicate this silver to the LORD. It will be for my son's benefit. We will use it to make a carved image and a metal image." **17:4** When he gave the silver back to his mother, she took two hundred pieces of silver to a silversmith, who made them into a carved image and a metal image. She then put them in Micah's house. **17:5** Now this man Micah owned a shrine. He made an ephod and some personal idols and hired one of his sons to serve as a priest. **17:6** In those days Israel had no king. Each man did what he considered to be right.

Micah Hires a Professional

17:7 There was a young man from Bethlehem in Judah. He was a Levite who had been temporarily residing among the tribe of Judah. **17:8** This man left the town of Bethlehem in Judah to find another place to live. He came to the Ephraimite hill country and made his way to Micah's house. **17:9** Micah said to him, "Where do you come from?" He replied, "I am a Levite from Bethlehem in Judah. I am looking for a new place to live." **17:10** Micah said to him, "Stay with me. Become my adviser and priest. I will give you ten pieces of silver per year, plus clothes and food." **17:11** So the Levite agreed to stay with the man; the young man was like a son to Micah. **17:12** Micah paid the Levite; the young man became his priest and lived in Micah's house. **17:13** Micah said, "Now I know God will make me rich, because I have this Levite as my priest."

The Tribe of Dan Finds an Inheritance

18:1 In those days Israel had no king. And in those days the Danite tribe was looking for a place to settle, because at that time they did not yet have a place to call their own among the tribes of Israel. **18:2** The Danites sent out from their whole tribe five representatives, capable men from Zorah and Eshtaol, to spy out the land and explore it. They said to them, "Go, explore the land." They came to the Ephraimite hill country and spent the night at Micah's house. **18:3** As they approached Micah's house, they recognized the accent of the young Levite. So they stopped there and said to him, "Who brought you here? What are you doing in this place? What is your business here?" **18:4** He told them what Micah had done for him, saying, "He hired me and I became his priest." **18:5** They said to him, "Seek a divine oracle for us, so we can know if we will be successful on our mission." **18:6** The priest said to them, "Go with confidence. The LORD will be with you on your mission."

18:7 So the five men journeyed on and arrived in Laish. They noticed that the people there were living securely, like the Sidonians do, undisturbed and unsuspecting. No conqueror was troubling them in any way. They lived far from the Sidonians and had no dealings with anyone. **18:8** When the Danites returned to their tribe in Zorah and Eshtaol, their kinsmen asked them, "How did it go?" **18:9** They said, "Come on, let's attack them, for we saw their land and it is very good. You seem lethargic, but don't hesitate to invade and conquer the land. **18:10** When you invade, you will encounter unsuspecting people. The land is wide! God is handing it over to you – a place that lacks nothing on earth!"

18:11 So six hundred Danites, fully armed, set out from Zorah and Eshtaol. **18:12** They went up and camped in Kiriath Jearim in Judah. (To this day that place is called Camp of Dan. It is west of Kiriath Jearim.) **18:13** From there they traveled through the Ephraimite hill country and arrived at Micah's house. **18:14** The five men who had gone to spy out the land of Laish said to their kinsmen, "Do you realize that inside these houses are an ephod, some personal idols, a carved image, and a metal image? Decide now what you want to do." **18:15** They stopped there, went inside the young Levite's house (which belonged to Micah), and asked him how he was doing. **18:16** Meanwhile the six hundred Danites, fully armed, stood at the entrance to the gate. **18:17** The five men who had gone to spy out the land broke in and stole the carved image, the ephod, the personal idols, and the metal image, while the priest was standing at the entrance to the gate with the six hundred fully armed men. **18:18** When these men broke into Micah's house and stole the carved image, the ephod, the personal idols, and the metal image, the priest said to them, "What are you doing?" **18:19** They said to him, "Shut up! Put your hand over your mouth and come with us! You can be our adviser and priest. Wouldn't it be better to be a priest for a whole Israelite tribe than for just one man's family?" **18:20** The priest was happy. He took the ephod, the personal idols, and the carved image and joined the group.

18:21 They turned and went on their way, but they walked behind the children, the cattle, and their possessions. **18:22** After they had gone a good distance from Micah's house, Micah's neighbors gathered together and caught up with the Danites. **18:23** When they called out to the Danites, the Danites turned around and said to Micah, "Why have you gathered together?" **18:24** He said, "You stole my gods that I made, as well as this priest, and then went away. What do I have left? How can you have the audacity to say to me, 'What do you want?'" **18:25** The Danites said to him, "Don't say another word to us, or some very angry men will attack you, and you and your family will die." **18:26** The Danites went on their way; when Micah realized they were too strong to resist, he turned around and went home.

18:27 Now the Danites took what Micah had made, as well as his priest, and came to Laish, where the people were undisturbed and unsuspecting. They struck them down with the sword and burned the city. **18:28** No one came to the rescue because the city was far from Sidon and they had no dealings with anyone. The city was in a valley near Beth Rehob. The Danites rebuilt the city and occupied it. **18:29** They named it Dan after their ancestor, who was one of Israel's sons. But the city's name used to be Laish. **18:30** The Danites worshiped the carved image. Jonathan, descendant of Gershom, son of Moses, and his descendants served as priests for the tribe of Dan until the time of the exile. **18:31** They worshiped Micah's carved image the whole time God's authorized shrine was in Shiloh.

Sodom and Gomorrah Revisited

19:1 In those days Israel had no king. There was a Levite living temporarily in the remote region of the Ephraimite hill country. He acquired a concubine from Bethlehem in Judah. **19:2** However, she got angry at him and went home to her father's house in Bethlehem in Judah. When she had been there four months, **19:3** her husband came after her, hoping he could convince her to return. He brought with him his servant and a pair of donkeys. When she brought him into her father's house and the girl's father saw him, he greeted him warmly. **19:4** His father-in-law, the girl's father, persuaded him to stay with him for three days, and they ate and drank together, and spent the night there. **19:5** On the fourth day they woke up early and the Levite got ready to leave. But the girl's father said to his son-in-law, "Have a bite to eat for some energy, then you can go." **19:6** So the two of them sat down and had a meal together. Then the girl's father said to the man, "Why not stay another night and have a good time!" **19:7** When the man got ready to leave, his father-in-law convinced him to stay another night. **19:8** He woke up early in the morning on the fifth day so he could leave, but the girl's father said, "Get some energy. Wait until later in the day to leave!" So they ate a meal together. **19:9** When the man got ready to leave with his concubine and his servant, his father-in-law, the girl's father, said to him, "Look! The day is almost over! Stay another night! Since the day is over, stay another night here and have a good time. You can get up early tomorrow and start your trip home." **19:10** But the man did not want to stay another night. He left and traveled as far as Jebus (that is, Jerusalem). He had with him a pair of saddled donkeys and his concubine.

19:11 When they got near Jebus, it was getting quite late and the servant said to his master, "Come on, let's stop at this Jebusite city and spend the night in it." **19:12** But his master said to him, "We should not stop at a foreign city where non-Israelites live. We will travel on to Gibeah." **19:13** He said to his servant, "Come on, we will go into one of the other towns and spend the night in Gibeah or Ramah." **19:14** So they traveled on, and the sun went down when they were near Gibeah in the territory of Benjamin. **19:15** They stopped there and decided to spend the night in Gibeah. They came into the city and sat down in the town square, but no one invited them to spend the night.

19:16 But then an old man passed by, returning at the end of the day from his work in the field. The man was from the Ephraimite hill country; he was living temporarily in Gibeah. (The residents of the town were Benjaminites.) **19:17** When he looked up and saw the traveler in the town square, the old man said, "Where are you heading? Where do you come from?" **19:18** The Levite said to him, "We are traveling from Bethlehem in Judah to the remote region of the Ephraimite hill country. That's where I'm from. I had business in Bethlehem in Judah, but now I'm heading home. But no one has invited me into their home. **19:19** We have enough straw and grain for our donkeys, and there is enough food and wine for me, your female servant, and the young man who is with your servants. We lack nothing." **19:20** The old man said, "Everything is just fine! I will take care of all your needs. But don't spend the night in the town square." **19:21** So he brought him to his house and fed the donkeys. They washed their feet and had a meal.

19:22 They were having a good time, when suddenly some men of the city, some good-for-nothings, surrounded the house and kept beating on the door. They said to the old man who owned the house, "Send out the man who came to visit you so we can have sex with him." **19:23** The man who owned the house went outside and said to them, "No, my brothers! Don't do this wicked thing! After all, this man is a guest in my house. Don't do such a disgraceful thing! **19:24** Here are my virgin daughter and my guest's concubine. I will send them out and you can abuse them and do to them whatever you like. But don't do such a disgraceful thing to this man!" **19:25** The men refused to listen to him, so the Levite grabbed his concubine and made her go outside. They raped her and abused her all night long until morning. They let her go at dawn. **19:26** The woman arrived back at daybreak and was sprawled out on the doorstep of the house where her master was staying until it became light. **19:27** When her master got up in the morning, opened the doors of the house, and went outside to start on his journey, there was the woman, his concubine, sprawled out on the doorstep of the house with her hands on the threshold. **19:28** He said to her, "Get up, let's leave!" But there was no response. He put her on the donkey and went home. **19:29** When he got home, he took a knife, grabbed his concubine, and carved her up into twelve pieces. Then he sent the pieces throughout Israel. **19:30** Everyone who saw the sight said, "Nothing like this has happened or been witnessed during the entire time since the Israelites left the land of Egypt! Take careful note of it! Discuss it and speak!"

Civil War Breaks Out

20:1 All the Israelites from Dan to Beer Sheba and from the land of Gilead left their homes and assembled together before the LORD at Mizpah. **20:2** The leaders of all the people from all the tribes of Israel took their places in the assembly of God's people, which numbered four hundred thousand sword-wielding foot soldiers. **20:3** The Benjaminites heard that the Israelites had gone up to Mizpah. Then the Israelites said, "Explain how this wicked thing happened!" **20:4** The Levite, the husband of the murdered woman, spoke up, "I and my concubine stopped in Gibeah in the territory of Benjamin to spend the night. **20:5** The leaders of Gibeah attacked me and at night surrounded the house where I was staying. They wanted to kill me; instead they abused my concubine so badly that she died. **20:6** I grabbed hold of my concubine and carved her up and sent the pieces throughout the territory occupied by Israel, because they committed such an unthinkable atrocity in Israel. **20:7** All you Israelites, make a decision here!"

20:8 All Israel rose up in unison and said, "Not one of us will go home! Not one of us will return to his house! **20:9** Now this is what we will do to Gibeah: We will attack the city as the lot dictates. **20:10** We will take ten of every group of a hundred men from all the tribes of Israel (and a hundred of every group of a thousand, and a thousand of every group of ten thousand) to get supplies for the army. When they arrive in Gibeah of Benjamin they will punish them for the atrocity which they committed in Israel." **20:11** So all the men of Israel gathered together at the city as allies.

20:12 The tribes of Israel sent men throughout the tribe of Benjamin, saying, "How could such a wicked thing take place? **20:13** Now, hand over the good-for-nothings in Gibeah so we can execute them and purge Israel of wickedness." But the Benjaminites refused to listen to their Israelite brothers. **20:14** The Benjaminites came from their cities and assembled at Gibeah to make war against the Israelites. **20:15** That day the Benjaminites mustered from their cities twenty-six thousand sword-wielding soldiers, besides seven hundred well-trained soldiers from Gibeah. **20:16** Among this army were seven hundred specially-trained left-handed soldiers. Each one could sling a stone and hit even the smallest target. **20:17** The men of Israel (not counting Benjamin) had mustered four hundred thousand sword-wielding soldiers, every one an experienced warrior.

20:18 The Israelites went up to Bethel and asked God, "Who should lead the charge against the Benjaminites?" The LORD said, "Judah should lead." **20:19** The Israelites got up the next morning and moved against Gibeah. **20:20** The men of Israel marched out to fight Benjamin; they arranged their battle lines against Gibeah. **20:21** The Benjaminites attacked from Gibeah and struck down twenty-two thousand Israelites that day.

20:22 The Israelite army took heart and once more arranged their battle lines, in the same place where they had taken their positions the day before. **20:23** The Israelites went up and wept before the LORD until evening. They asked the LORD, "Should we again march out to fight the Benjaminites, our brothers?" The LORD said, "Attack them!" **20:24** So the Israelites marched toward the Benjaminites the next day. **20:25** The Benjaminites again attacked them from Gibeah and struck down eighteen thousand sword-wielding Israelite soldiers.

20:26 So all the Israelites, the whole army, went up to Bethel. They wept and sat there before the LORD; they did not eat anything that day until evening. They offered up burnt sacrifices and tokens of peace to the LORD. **20:27** The Israelites asked the LORD (for the ark of God's covenant was there in those days; **20:28** Phinehas son of Eleazar, son of Aaron, was serving the LORD in those days), "Should we once more march out to fight the Benjaminites our brothers, or should we quit?" The LORD said, "Attack, for tomorrow I will hand them over to you."

20:29 So Israel hid men in ambush outside Gibeah. **20:30** The Israelites attacked the Benjaminites the next day; they took their positions against Gibeah just as they had done before. **20:31** The Benjaminites attacked the army, leaving the city unguarded. They began to strike down their enemy just as they had done before. On the main roads (one leads to Bethel, the other to Gibeah) and in the field, they struck down about thirty Israelites. **20:32** Then the Benjaminites said, "They are defeated just as before." But the Israelites said, "Let's retreat and lure them away from the city into the main roads." **20:33** All the men of Israel got up from their places and took their positions at Baal Tamar, while the Israelites hiding in ambush jumped out of their places west of Gibeah. **20:34** Ten thousand men, well-trained soldiers from all Israel, then made a frontal assault against Gibeah – the battle was fierce. But the Benjaminites did not realize that disaster was at their doorstep. **20:35** The LORD annihilated Benjamin before Israel; the Israelites struck down that day 25,100 sword-wielding Benjaminites. **20:36** Then the Benjaminites saw they were defeated.

The Israelites retreated before Benjamin, because they had confidence in the men they had hid in ambush outside Gibeah. **20:37** The men hiding in ambush made a mad dash to Gibeah. They attacked and put the sword to the entire city. **20:38** The Israelites and the men hiding in ambush had arranged a signal. When the men hiding in ambush sent up a smoke signal from the city, **20:39** the Israelites counterattacked. Benjamin had begun to strike down the Israelites; they struck down about thirty men. They said, "There's no doubt about it! They are totally defeated as in the earlier battle." **20:40** But when the signal, a pillar of smoke, began to rise up from the city, the Benjaminites turned around and saw the whole city going up in a cloud of smoke that rose high into the sky. **20:41** When the Israelites turned around, the Benjaminites panicked because they could see that disaster was on their doorstep. **20:42** They retreated before the Israelites, taking the road to the wilderness. But the battle overtook them as men from the surrounding cities struck them down. **20:43** They surrounded the Benjaminites, chased them from Nohah, and annihilated them all the way to a spot east of Geba. **20:44** Eighteen thousand Benjaminites, all of them capable warriors, fell dead. **20:45** The rest turned and ran toward the wilderness, heading toward the cliff of Rimmon. But the Israelites caught five thousand of them on the main roads. They stayed right on their heels all the way to Gidom and struck down two thousand more. **20:46** That day twenty-five thousand sword-wielding Benjaminites fell in battle, all of them capable warriors. **20:47** Six hundred survivors turned and ran away to the wilderness, to the cliff of Rimmon. They stayed there four months. **20:48** The Israelites returned to the Benjaminite towns and put the sword to them. They wiped out the cities, the animals, and everything they could find. They set fire to every city in their path.

600 Brides for 600 Brothers

21:1 The Israelites had taken an oath in Mizpah, saying, "Not one of us will allow his daughter to marry a Benjaminite." **21:2** So the people came to Bethel and sat there before God until evening, weeping loudly and uncontrollably. **21:3** They said, "Why, O LORD God of Israel, has this happened in Israel?" An entire tribe has disappeared from Israel today!"

21:4 The next morning the people got up early and built an altar there. They offered up burnt sacrifices and token of peace. **21:5** The Israelites asked, "Who from all the Israelite tribes has not assembled before the LORD?" They had made a solemn oath that whoever did not assemble before the LORD at Mizpah must certainly be executed. **21:6** The Israelites regretted what had happened to their brother Benjamin. They said, "Today we cut off an entire tribe from Israel! **21:7** How can we find wives for those who are left? After all, we took an oath in the LORD's name not to give them our daughters as wives." **21:8** So they asked, "Who from all the Israelite tribes did not assemble before the LORD at Mizpah?" Now it just so happened no one from Jabesh Gilead had come to the gathering. **21:9** When they took roll call, they noticed none of the inhabitants of Jabesh Gilead were there. **21:10** So the assembly sent 12,000 capable warriors against Jabesh Gilead. They commanded them, "Go and kill with your swords the inhabitants of Jabesh Gilead, including the women and little children. **21:11** Do this: exterminate every male, as well as every woman who has had sexual relations with a male. But spare the lives of any virgins." So they did as instructed. **21:12** They found among the inhabitants of Jabesh Gilead four hundred young girls who were virgins – they had never had sexual relations with a male. They brought them back to the camp at Shiloh in the land of Canaan.

21:13 The entire assembly sent messengers to the Benjaminites at the cliff of Rimmon and assured them they would not be harmed. **21:14** The Benjaminites returned at that time, and the Israelites gave to them the women they had spared from Jabesh Gilead. But there were not enough to go around.

21:15 The people regretted what had happened to Benjamin because the LORD had weakened the Israelite tribes. **21:16** The leaders of the assembly said, "How can we find wives for those who are left? After all, the Benjaminite women have been wiped out. **21:17** The remnant of Benjamin must be preserved. An entire Israelite tribe should not be wiped out. **21:18** But we can't allow our daughters to marry them, for the Israelites took an oath, saying, 'Whoever gives a woman to a Benjaminite will be destroyed!' **21:19** However, there is an annual festival to the LORD in Shiloh, which is north of Bethel (east of the main road that goes up from Bethel to Shechem) and south of Lebonah." **21:20** So they commanded the Benjaminites, "Go hide in the vineyards, **21:21** and keep your eyes open. When you see the daughters of Shiloh coming out to dance in the celebration, jump out from the vineyards. Each one of you, catch yourself a wife from among the daughters of Shiloh and then go home to the land of Benjamin. **21:22** When their fathers or brothers come and protest to us, we'll say to them, "Do us a favor and let them be, for we could not get each one a wife through battle. Don't worry about breaking your oath! You would only be guilty if you had voluntarily given them wives.'"

21:23 The Benjaminites did as instructed. They abducted two hundred of the dancing girls to be their wives. They went home to their own territory, rebuilt their cities, and settled down. **21:24** Then the Israelites dispersed from there to their respective tribal and clan territories. Each went from there to his own property. **21:25** In those days Israel had no king. Each man did what he considered to be right.

Book 8. Ruth

A Family Tragedy: Famine and Death

1:1 During the time of the judges there was a famine in the land of Judah. So a man from Bethlehem in Judah went to live as a resident foreigner in the region of Moab, along with his wife and two sons. **1:2** (Now the man's name was Elimelech, his wife was Naomi, and his two sons were Mahlon and Kilion. They were of the clan of Ephrath from Bethlehem in Judah.) They entered the region of Moab and settled there. **1:3** Sometime later Naomi's husband Elimelech died, so she and her two sons were left alone. **1:4** So her sons married Moabite women. (One was named Orpah and the other Ruth.) And they continued to live there about ten years. **1:5** Then Naomi's two sons, Mahlon and Kilion, also died. So the woman was left all alone – bereaved of her two children as well as her husband! **1:6** So she decided to return home from the region of Moab, accompanied by her daughters-in-law, because while she was living in Moab she had heard that the LORD had shown concern for his people, reversing the famine by providing abundant crops.

Ruth Returns with Naomi

1:7 Now as she and her two daughters-in-law began to leave the place where she had been living to return to the land of Judah, **1:8** Naomi said to her two daughters-in-law, "Listen to me! Each of you should return to your mother's home! May the LORD show you the same kind of devotion that you have shown to your deceased husbands and to me! **1:9** May the LORD enable each of you to find security in the home of a new husband!" Then she kissed them goodbye and they wept loudly. **1:10** But they said to her, "No! We will return with you to your people."

1:11 But Naomi replied, "Go back home, my daughters! There is no reason for you to return to Judah with me! I am no longer capable of giving birth to sons who might become your husbands! **1:12** Go back home, my daughters! For I am too old to get married again. Even if I thought that there was hope that I could get married tonight and conceive sons, **1:13** surely you would not want to wait until they were old enough to marry! Surely you would not remain unmarried all that time! No, my daughters, you must not return with me. For my intense suffering is too much for you to bear. For the LORD is afflicting me!"

1:14 Again they wept loudly. Then Orpah kissed her mother-in-law goodbye, but Ruth clung tightly to her. **1:15** So Naomi said, "Look, your sister-in-law is returning to her people and to her god. Follow your sister-in-law back home!" **1:16** But Ruth replied,

"Stop urging me to abandon you!
For wherever you go, I will go.
Wherever you live, I will live.
Your people will become my people,
and your God will become my God.
1:17 Wherever you die, I will die – and there I will be buried.

May the LORD punish me severely if I do not keep my promise! Only death will be able to separate me from you!"

1:18 When Naomi realized that Ruth was determined to go with her, she stopped trying to dissuade her. **1:19** So the two of them journeyed together until they arrived in Bethlehem.

Naomi and Ruth Arrive in Bethlehem

When they entered Bethlehem, the whole village was excited about their arrival. The women of the village said, "Can this be Naomi?" **1:20** But she replied to them, "Don't call me 'Naomi'! Call me 'Mara' because the Sovereign One has treated me very harshly. **1:21** I left here full, but the LORD has caused me to return empty-handed. Why do you call me 'Naomi,' seeing that the LORD has opposed me, and the Sovereign One has caused me to suffer?" **1:22** So Naomi returned, accompanied by her Moabite daughter-in-law Ruth, who came back with her from the region of Moab. (Now they arrived in Bethlehem at the beginning of the barley harvest.)

Ruth Works in the Field of Boaz

2:1 Now Naomi had a relative on her husband's side of the family named Boaz. He was a wealthy, prominent man from the clan of Elimelech. **2:2** One day Ruth the Moabite said to Naomi, "Let me go to the fields so I can gather grain behind whoever permits me to do so." Naomi replied, "You may go, my daughter." **2:3** So Ruth went and gathered grain in the fields behind the harvesters. Now she just happened to end up in the portion of the field belonging to Boaz, who was from the clan of Elimelech.

Boaz and Ruth Meet

2:4 Now at that very moment, Boaz arrived from Bethlehem and greeted the harvesters, "May the LORD be with you!" They replied, "May the LORD bless you!" **2:5** Boaz asked his servant in charge of the harvesters, "To whom does this young woman belong?" **2:6** The servant in charge of the harvesters replied, "She's the young Moabite woman who came back with Naomi from the region of Moab. **2:7** She asked, 'May I follow the harvesters and gather grain among the bundles?' Since she arrived she has been working hard from this morning until now – except for sitting in the resting hut a short time."

2:8 So Boaz said to Ruth, "Listen carefully, my dear! Do not leave to gather grain in another field. You need not go beyond the limits of this field. You may go along beside my female workers. **2:9** Take note of the field where the men are harvesting and follow behind with the female workers. I will tell the men to leave you alone. When you are thirsty, you may go to the water jars and drink some of the water the servants draw."

2:10 Ruth knelt before him with her forehead to the ground and said to him, "Why are you so kind and so attentive to me, even though I am a foreigner?" **2:11** Boaz replied to her, "I have been given a full report of all that you have done for your mother-in-law following the death of your husband – how you left your father and your mother, as well as your homeland, and came to live among people you did not know previously. **2:12** May the LORD reward your efforts! May your acts of kindness be repaid fully by the LORD God of Israel, from whom you have sought protection!" **2:13** She said, "You really are being kind to me, sir, for you have reassured and encouraged me, your servant, even though I am not one of your servants!"

2:14 Later during the mealtime Boaz said to her, "Come here and have some food! Dip your bread in the vinegar!" So she sat down beside the harvesters. Then he handed her some roasted grain. She ate until she was full and saved the rest. **2:15** When she got up to gather grain, Boaz told his male servants, "Let her gather grain even among the bundles! Don't chase her off! **2:16** Make sure you pull out ears of grain for her and drop them so she can gather them up. Don't tell her not to!" **2:17** So she gathered grain in the field until evening. When she threshed what she had gathered, it came to about thirty pounds of barley!

Ruth Returns to Naomi

2:18 She carried it back to town, and her mother-in-law saw how much grain she had gathered. Then Ruth gave her the roasted grain she had saved from mealtime. **2:19** Her mother-in-law asked her, "Where did you gather grain today? Where did you work? May the one who took notice of you be rewarded!" So Ruth told her mother-in-law with whom she had worked. She said, "The name of the man with whom I worked today is Boaz." **2:20** Naomi said to her daughter-in-law, "May he be rewarded by the LORD because he has shown loyalty to the living on behalf of the dead!" Then Naomi said to her, "This man is a close relative of ours; he is our guardian." **2:21** Ruth the Moabite replied, "He even told me, 'You may go along beside my servants until they have finished gathering all my harvest!'" **2:22** Naomi then said to her daughter-in-law Ruth, "It is good, my daughter, that you should go out to work with his female servants. That way you will not be harmed, which could happen in another field." **2:23** So Ruth worked beside Boaz's female servants, gathering grain until the end of the barley harvest as well as the wheat harvest. After that she stayed home with her mother-in-law.

Naomi Instructs Ruth

3:1 At that time, Naomi, her mother-in-law, said to her, "My daughter, I must find a home for you so you will be secure. **3:2** Now Boaz, with whose female servants you worked, is our close relative. Look, tonight he is winnowing barley at the threshing floor. **3:3** So bathe yourself, rub on some perfumed oil, and get dressed up. Then go down to the threshing floor. But don't let the man know you're there until he finishes his meal. **3:4** When he gets ready to go to sleep, take careful notice of the place where he lies down. Then go, uncover his legs, and lie down beside him. He will tell you what you should do." **3:5** Ruth replied to Naomi, "I will do everything you have told me to do."

Ruth Visits Boaz

3:6 So she went down to the threshing floor and did everything her mother-in-law had instructed her to do. **3:7** When Boaz had finished his meal and was feeling satisfied, he lay down to sleep at the far end of the grain heap. Then Ruth crept up quietly, uncovered his legs, and lay down beside him. **3:8** In the middle of the night he was startled and turned over. Now he saw a woman lying beside him! **3:9** He said, "Who are you?" She replied, "I am Ruth, your servant. Marry your servant, for you are a guardian of the family interests." **3:10** He said, "May you be rewarded by the LORD, my dear! This act of devotion is greater than what you did before. For you have not sought to marry one of the young men, whether rich or poor. **3:11** Now, my dear, don't worry! I intend to do for you everything you propose, for everyone in the village knows that you are a worthy woman. **3:12** Now yes, it is true that I am a guardian, but there is another guardian who is a closer relative than I am. **3:13** Remain here tonight. Then in the morning, if he agrees to marry you, fine, let him do so. But if he does not want to do so, I promise, as surely as the LORD lives, to marry you. Sleep here until morning." **3:14** So she slept beside him until morning. She woke up while it was still dark. Boaz thought, "No one must know that a woman visited the threshing floor." **3:15** Then he said, "Hold out the shawl you are wearing and grip it tightly." As she held it tightly, he measured out about sixty pounds of barley into the shawl and put it on her shoulders. Then he went into town, **3:16** and she returned to her mother-in-law.

Ruth Returns to Naomi

When Ruth returned to her mother-in-law, Naomi asked, "How did things turn out for you, my daughter?" Ruth told her about all the man had done for her. **3:17** She said, "He gave me these sixty pounds of barley, for he said to me, 'Do not go to your mother-in-law empty-handed.'" **3:18** Then Naomi said, "Stay put, my daughter, until you know how the matter turns out. For the man will not rest until he has taken care of the matter today."

Boaz Settles the Matter

4:1 Now Boaz went up to the village gate and sat there. Then along came the guardian whom Boaz had mentioned to Ruth! Boaz said, "Come here and sit down, 'John Doe'!" So he came and sat down. **4:2** Boaz chose ten of the village leaders and said, "Sit down here!" So they sat down. **4:3** Then Boaz said to the guardian, "Naomi, who has returned from the region of Moab, is selling the portion of land that belongs to our relative Elimelech. **4:4** So I am legally informing you: Acquire it before those sitting here and before the leaders of my people! If you want to exercise your right to redeem it, then do so. But if not, then tell me so I will know. For you possess the first option to redeem it; I am next in line after you." He replied, "I will redeem it." **4:5** Then Boaz said, "When you acquire the field from Naomi, you must also acquire Ruth the Moabite, the wife of our deceased relative, in order to preserve his family name by raising up a descendant who will inherit his property." **4:6** The guardian said, "Then I am unable to redeem it, for I would ruin my own inheritance in that case. You may exercise my redemption option, for I am unable to redeem it." **4:7** (Now this used to be the customary way to finalize a transaction involving redemption in Israel: A man would remove his sandal and give it to the other party. This was a legally binding act in Israel.) **4:8** So the guardian said to Boaz, "You may acquire it," and he removed his sandal. **4:9** Then Boaz said to the leaders and all the people, "You are witnesses today that I have acquired from Naomi all that belonged to Elimelech, Kilion, and Mahlon. **4:10** I have also acquired Ruth the Moabite, the wife of Mahlon, as my wife to raise up a descendant who will inherit his property so the name of the deceased might not disappear from among his relatives and from his village. You are witnesses today." **4:11** All the people who were at the gate and the elders replied, "We are witnesses. May the LORD make the woman who is entering your home like Rachel and Leah, both of whom built up the house of Israel! May you prosper in Ephrathah and become famous in Bethlehem. **4:12** May your family become like the family of Perez – whom Tamar bore to Judah – through the descendants the LORD gives you by this young woman."

A Grandson is Born to Naomi

4:13 So Boaz married Ruth and had sexual relations with her. The LORD enabled her to conceive and she gave birth to a son. **4:14** The village women said to Naomi, "May the LORD be praised because he has not left you without a guardian today! May he become famous in Israel! **4:15** He will encourage you and provide for you when you are old, for your daughter-in-law, who loves you, has given you birth. She is better to you than seven sons!" **4:16** Naomi took the child and placed him on her lap; she became his caregiver. **4:17** The neighbor women named him, saying, "A son has been born to Naomi." They named him Obed. Now he became the father of Jesse – David's father!

Epilogue: Obed in the Genealogy of David

4:18 These are the descendants of Perez: Perez was the father of Hezron, **4:19** Hezron was the father of Ram, Ram was the father of Amminadab, **4:20** Amminadab was the father of Nachshon, Nachshon was the father of Salmah, **4:21** Salmon was the father of Boaz, Boaz was the father of Obed, **4:22** Obed was the father of Jesse, and Jesse was the father of David.

Book 9. 1 Samuel

Hannah Gives Birth to Samuel

1:1 There was a man from Ramathaim Zophim, from the hill country of Ephraim, whose name was Elkanah. He was the son of Jeroham, the son of Elihu, the son of Tohu, the son of Zuph, an Ephraimite. **1:2** He had two wives; the name of the first was Hannah and the name of the second was Peninnah. Now Peninnah had children, but Hannah was childless.

1:3 Year after year this man would go up from his city to worship and to sacrifice to the LORD of hosts at Shiloh. It was there that the two sons of Eli, Hophni and Phineas, served as the LORD's priests. **1:4** Whenever the day came for Elkanah to sacrifice, he used to give meat portions to his wife Peninnah and to all her sons and daughters. **1:5** But he would give a double portion to Hannah, because he especially loved her. Now the LORD had not enabled her to have children. **1:6** Her rival wife used to upset her and make her worry, for the LORD had not enabled her to have children. **1:7** Peninnah would behave this way year after year. Whenever Hannah went up to the LORD's house, Peninnah would upset her so that she would weep and refuse to eat. **1:8** Finally her husband Elkanah said to her, "Hannah, why do you weep and not eat? Why are you so sad? Am I not better to you than ten sons?"

1:9 On one occasion in Shiloh, after they had finished eating and drinking, Hannah got up. (Now at the time Eli the priest was sitting in his chair by the doorpost of the LORD's temple.) **1:10** She was very upset as she prayed to the LORD, and she was weeping uncontrollably. **1:11** She made a vow saying, "O LORD of hosts, if you will look with compassion on the suffering of your female servant, remembering me and not forgetting your servant, and give a male child to your servant, then I will dedicate him to the LORD all the days of his life. His hair will never be cut."

1:12 As she continued praying to the LORD, Eli was watching her mouth. **1:13** Now Hannah was speaking from her heart. Although her lips were moving, her voice was inaudible. Eli therefore thought she was drunk. **1:14** So he said to her, "How often do you intend to get drunk? Put away your wine!"

1:15 But Hannah replied, "That's not the way it is, my lord! I am under a great deal of stress. I have drunk neither wine nor beer. Rather, I have poured out my soul to the LORD. **1:16** Don't consider your servant a wicked woman, for until now I have spoken from my deep pain and anguish."

1:17 Eli replied, "Go in peace, and may the God of Israel grant the request that you have asked of him." **1:18** She said, "May I, your servant, find favor in your sight." So the woman went her way and got something to eat. Her face no longer looked sad.

1:19 They got up early the next morning and after worshiping the LORD, they returned to their home at Ramah. Elkanah had marital relations with his wife Hannah, and the LORD remembered her. **1:20** After some time Hannah became pregnant and gave birth to a son. She named him Samuel, thinking, "I asked the LORD for him.

Hannah Dedicates Samuel to the Lord

1:21 This man Elkanah went up with all his family to make the yearly sacrifice to the LORD and to keep his vow, **1:22** but Hannah did not go up with them. Instead she told her husband, "Once the boy is weaned, I will bring him and appear before the LORD, and he will remain there from then on."

1:23 So her husband Elkanah said to her, "Do what you think best. Stay until you have weaned him. May the LORD fulfill his promise."

So the woman stayed and nursed her son until she had weaned him. **1:24** Once she had weaned him, she took him up with her, along with three bulls, an ephah of flour, and a container of wine. She brought him to the LORD's house at Shiloh, even though he was young. **1:25** Once the bull had been slaughtered, they brought the boy to Eli. **1:26** She said, "Just as surely as you are alive, my lord, I am the woman who previously stood here with you in order to pray to the LORD. **1:27** I prayed for this boy, and the LORD has given me the request that I asked of him. **1:28** Now I dedicate him to the LORD. From this time on he is dedicated to the LORD." Then they worshiped the LORD there.

Hannah Exalts the Lord in Prayer

2:1 Hannah prayed,

"My heart rejoices in the LORD;
my horn is exalted high because of the LORD.
I loudly denounce my enemies,
for I am happy that you delivered me.
2:2 No one is holy like the LORD!
There is no one other than you!
There is no rock like our God!

2:3 Don't keep speaking so arrogantly,
letting proud talk come out of your mouth!
For the LORD is a God who knows;
he evaluates what people do.
2:4 The bows of warriors are shattered,
but those who stumble find their strength reinforced.
2:5 Those who are well-fed hire themselves out to earn food,
but the hungry no longer lack.
Even the barren woman gives birth to seven,
but the one with many children withers away.
2:6 The LORD both kills and gives life;
he brings down to the grave and raises up.
2:7 The LORD impoverishes and makes wealthy;
he humbles and he exalts.
2:8 He lifts the weak from the dust;
he raises the poor from the ash heap
to seat them with princes
and to bestow on them an honored position.
The foundations of the earth belong to the LORD,
and he has placed the world on them.
2:9 He watches over his holy ones,
but the wicked are made speechless in the darkness,
for it is not by one's own strength that one prevails.
2:10 The LORD shatters his adversaries;
he thunders against them from the heavens.
The LORD executes judgment to the ends of the earth.
He will strengthen his king
and exalt the power of his anointed one."

2:11 Then Elkanah went back home to Ramah. But the boy was serving the LORD under the supervision of Eli the priest.

Eli's Sons Misuse Their Sacred Office

2:12 The sons of Eli were wicked men. They did not recognize the LORD's authority. **2:13** Now the priests would always treat the people in the following way: Whenever anyone was making a sacrifice, while the meat was boiling, the priest's attendant would come with a three-pronged fork in his hand. **2:14** He would jab it into the basin, kettle, caldron, or pot, and everything that the fork brought up the priest would take for himself. This is what they used to do to all the Israelites when they came there to Shiloh.
2:15 Even before they burned the fat, the priest's attendant would come and say to the person who was making the sacrifice, "Hand over some meat for the priest to roast! He won't take boiled meat from you, but only raw." **2:16** If the individual said to him, "First let the fat be burned away, and then take for yourself whatever you wish," he would say, "No! Hand it over right now! If you don't, I will take it forcibly!"
2:17 The sin of these young men was very great in the LORD's sight, for they treated the LORD's offering with contempt.
2:18 Now Samuel was ministering before the LORD. The boy was dressed in a linen ephod. **2:19** His mother used to make him a small robe and bring it up to him at regular intervals when she would go up with her husband to make the annual sacrifice. **2:20** Eli would bless Elkanah and his wife saying, "May the LORD raise up for you descendants from this woman to replace the one that she dedicated to the LORD." Then they would go to their home. **2:21** So the LORD graciously attended to Hannah, and she was able to conceive and gave birth to three sons and two daughters. The boy Samuel grew up at the LORD's sanctuary.
2:22 Now Eli was very old when he heard about everything that his sons used to do to all the people of Israel and how they used to have sex with the women who were stationed at the entrance to the tent of meeting. **2:23** He said to them, "Why do you behave in this way? For I hear about these evil things from all these people. **2:24** This ought not to be, my sons! For the report that I hear circulating among the LORD's people is not good. **2:25** If a man sins against a man, one may appeal to God on his behalf. But if a man sins against the LORD, who then will intercede for him?" But Eli's sons would not listen to their father, for the LORD had decided to kill them.
2:26 Now the boy Samuel was growing up and finding favor both with the LORD and with people.

The Lord Judges the House of Eli

2:27 A man of God came to Eli and said to him, "This is what the LORD says: 'Did I not plainly reveal myself to your ancestor's house when they were in Egypt in the house of Pharaoh? **2:28** I chose your ancestor from all the tribes of Israel to be my priest, to offer sacrifice on my altar, to burn incense, and to bear the ephod before me. I gave to your ancestor's house all the fire offerings made by the Israelites. **2:29** Why are you scorning my sacrifice and my offering that I commanded for my dwelling place? You have honored your sons more than you have me by having made yourselves fat from the best parts of all the offerings of my people Israel.'
2:30 Therefore the LORD, the God of Israel, says, 'I really did say that your house and your ancestor's house would serve me forever.' But now the LORD says, 'May it never be! For I will honor those who honor me, but those who despise me will be cursed! **2:31** In fact, days are coming when I will remove your strength and the strength of your father's house. There will not be an old man in your house! **2:32** You will see trouble in my dwelling place! Israel will experience blessings, but there will not be an old man in your house for all time. **2:33** Any one of you that I do not cut off from my altar, I will cause your eyes to fail and will cause you grief. All of those born to your family will die in the prime of life. **2:34** This will be a confirming sign for you that will be fulfilled through your two sons, Hophni and Phinehas: in a single day they both will die! **2:35** Then I will raise up for myself a faithful priest. He will do what is in my heart and soul. I will build for him a secure dynasty and he will serve my chosen one for all time. **2:36** Everyone who remains in your house will come to bow before him for a little money and for a scrap of bread. Each will say, 'Assign me to a priestly task so I can eat a scrap of bread.'"

The Call of Samuel

3:1 Now the boy Samuel continued serving the LORD under Eli's supervision. Word from the LORD was rare in those days; revelatory visions were infrequent.
3:2 Eli's eyes had begun to fail, so that he was unable to see well. At that time he was lying down in his place, **3:3** and the lamp of God had not yet been extinguished. Samuel was lying down in the temple of the LORD as well; the ark of God was also there. **3:4** The LORD called to Samuel, and he replied, "Here I am!" **3:5** Then he ran to Eli and said, "Here I am, for you called me." But Eli said, "I didn't call you. Go back and lie down." So he went back and lay down. **3:6** The LORD again called, "Samuel!" So Samuel got up and went to Eli and said, "Here I am, for you called me." But Eli said, "I didn't call you, my son. Go back and lie down."
3:7 Now Samuel did not yet know the LORD; the word of the LORD had not yet been revealed to him. **3:8** Then the LORD called Samuel a third time. So he got up and went to Eli and said, "Here I am, for you called me!" Eli then realized that it was the LORD who was calling the boy. **3:9** So Eli said to Samuel, "Go back and lie down. When he calls you, say, "Speak, LORD, for your servant is listening." So Samuel went back and lay down in his place.
3:10 Then the LORD came and stood nearby, calling as he had previously done, "Samuel! Samuel!" Samuel replied, "Speak, for your servant is listening!" **3:11** The LORD said to Samuel, "Look! I am about to do something in Israel; when anyone hears about it, both of his ears will tingle. **3:12** On that day I will carry out against Eli everything that I spoke about his house – from start to finish! **3:13** You should tell him that I am about to judge his house forever because of the sin that he knew about. For his sons were cursing God, and he did not rebuke them. **3:14** Therefore I swore an oath to the house of Eli, 'The sin of the house of Eli can never be forgiven by sacrifice or by grain offering.'"
3:15 So Samuel lay down until morning. Then he opened the doors of the LORD's house. But Samuel was afraid to tell Eli about the vision. **3:16** However, Eli called Samuel and said, "Samuel, my son!" He replied, "Here I am." **3:17** Eli said, "What message did he speak to you? Don't conceal it from me. God will judge you severely if you conceal from me anything that he said to you!"
3:18 So Samuel told him everything. He did not hold back anything from him. Eli said, "The LORD will do what he pleases." **3:19** Samuel continued to grow, and the LORD was with him. None of his prophecies fell to the ground unfulfilled. **3:20** All Israel from Dan to Beer Sheba realized that Samuel was confirmed as a prophet of the LORD. **3:21** Then the LORD again appeared in Shiloh, for it was in Shiloh that the LORD had revealed himself to Samuel through the word of the LORD. **4:1** Samuel revealed the word of the LORD to all Israel.

The Ark of the Covenant is Lost to the Philistines

Then the Israelites went out to fight the Philistines. They camped at Ebenezer, and the Philistines camped at Aphek. **4:2** The Philistines arranged their forces to fight Israel. As the battle spread out, Israel was defeated by the Philistines, who killed about four thousand men in the battle line in the field.
4:3 When the army came back to the camp, the elders of Israel said, "Why did the LORD let us be defeated today by the Philistines? Let's take with us the ark of the covenant of the LORD from Shiloh. When it is with us, it will save us from the hand of our enemies.
4:4 So the army sent to Shiloh, and they took from there the ark of the covenant of the LORD of hosts who sits between the cherubim. Now the two sons of Eli, Hophni and Phineas, were there with the ark of the covenant of God. **4:5** When the ark of the covenant of the LORD arrived at the camp, all Israel shouted so loudly that the ground shook.
4:6 When the Philistines heard the sound of the shout, they said, "What is this loud shout in the camp of the Hebrews?" Then they realized that the ark of the LORD had arrived at the camp. **4:7** The Philistines were scared because they thought that gods had come to the camp. They said, "Too bad for us! We've never seen anything like this! **4:8** Too bad for us! Who can deliver us from the hand of these mighty gods? These are the gods who struck the Egyptians with all sorts of plagues in the desert! **4:9** Be strong and act like men, you Philistines, or else you will wind up serving the Hebrews the way they have served you! Act like men and fight!"

4:10 So the Philistines fought. Israel was defeated; they all ran home. The slaughter was very great; thirty thousand foot soldiers fell in battle. **4:11** The ark of God was taken, and the two sons of Eli, Hophni and Phineas, were killed.

Eli Dies

4:12 On that day a Benjaminite ran from the battle lines and came to Shiloh. His clothes were torn and dirt was on his head. **4:13** When he arrived in Shiloh, Eli was sitting in his chair watching by the side of the road, for he was very worried about the ark of God. As the man entered the city to give his report, the whole city cried out.

4:14 When Eli heard the outcry, he said, "What is this commotion?" The man quickly came and told Eli. **4:15** Now Eli was ninety-eight years old and his eyes looked straight ahead; he was unable to see.

4:16 The man said to Eli, "I am the one who came from the battle lines! Just today I fled from the battle lines!" Eli asked, "How did things go, my son?" **4:17** The messenger replied, "Israel has fled from the Philistines! The army has suffered a great defeat! Your two sons, Hophni and Phineas, are dead! The ark of God has been captured!"

4:18 When he mentioned the ark of God, Eli fell backward from his chair beside the gate. He broke his neck and died, for he was old and heavy. He had judged Israel for forty years.

4:19 His daughter-in-law, the wife of Phineas, was pregnant and close to giving birth. When she heard that the ark of God was captured and that her father-in-law and her husband were dead, she doubled over and gave birth. But her labor pains were too much for her. **4:20** As she was dying, the women who were there with her said, "Don't be afraid! You have given birth to a son!" But she did not reply or pay any attention.

4:21 She named the boy Ichabod, saying, "The glory has departed from Israel," referring to the capture of the ark of God and the deaths of her father-in-law and her husband. **4:22** She said, "The glory has departed from Israel, because the ark of God has been captured."

The Ark Causes Trouble for the Philistines

5:1 Now the Philistines had captured the ark of God and brought it from Ebenezer to Ashdod. **5:2** The Philistines took the ark of God and brought it into the temple of Dagon, where they positioned it beside Dagon. **5:3** When the residents of Ashdod got up early the next day, Dagon was lying on the ground before the ark of the LORD. So they took Dagon and set him back in his place. **5:4** But when they got up early the following day, Dagon was again lying on the ground before the ark of the LORD. The head of Dagon and his two hands were sheared off and were lying at the threshold. Only Dagon's body was left intact. **5:5** (For this reason, to this very day, neither Dagon's priests nor anyone else who enters Dagon's temple step on Dagon's threshold in Ashdod.)

5:6 The LORD attacked the residents of Ashdod severely, bringing devastation on them. He struck the people of both Ashdod and the surrounding area with sores. **5:7** When the people of Ashdod saw what was happening, they said, "The ark of the God of Israel should not remain with us, for he has attacked both us and our god Dagon!"

5:8 So they assembled all the leaders of the Philistines and asked, "What should we do with the ark of the God of Israel?" They replied, "The ark of the God of Israel should be moved to Gath." So they moved the ark of the God of Israel.

5:9 But after it had been moved the LORD attacked that city as well, causing a great deal of panic. He struck all the people of that city with sores. **5:10** So they sent the ark of God to Ekron.

But when the ark of God arrived at Ekron, the residents of Ekron cried out saying, "They have brought the ark of the God of Israel here to kill our people!" **5:11** So they assembled all the leaders of the Philistines and said, "Get the ark of the God of Israel out of here! Let it go back to its own place so that it won't kill us and our people!" The terror of death was throughout the entire city; God was attacking them very severely there. **5:12** The people who did not die were struck with sores; the city's cry for help went all the way up to heaven.

The Philistines Return the Ark

6:1 When the ark of the LORD had been in the land of the Philistines for seven months, **6:2** the Philistines called the priests and the omen readers, saying, "What should we do with the ark of the LORD? Advise us as to how we should send it back to its place."

6:3 They replied, "If you are going to send the ark of the God of Israel back, don't send it away empty. Be sure to return it with a guilt offering. Then you will be healed, and you will understand why his hand is not removed from you." **6:4** They inquired, "What is the guilt offering that we should send to him?"

They replied, "The Philistine leaders number five. So send five gold sores and five gold mice, for it is the same plague that has afflicted both you and your leaders. **6:5** You should make images of the sores and images of the mice that are destroying the land. You should honor the God of Israel. Perhaps he will release his grip on you, your gods, and your land. **6:6** Why harden your hearts like the Egyptians and Pharaoh did? When God treated them harshly, didn't the Egyptians send the Israelites on their way? **6:7** So now go and make a new cart. Get two cows that have calves and that have never had a yoke placed on them. Harness the cows to the cart and take their calves from them back to their stalls. **6:8** Then take the

ark of the LORD and place it on the cart, and put in a chest beside it the gold objects you are sending to him as a guilt offering. You should then send it on its way. **6:9** But keep an eye on it. If it should go up by the way of its own border to Beth Shemesh, then he has brought this great calamity on us. But if that is not the case, then we will know that it was not his hand that struck us; rather, it just happened to us by accident."

6:10 So the men did as instructed. They took two cows that had calves and harnessed them to a cart; they also removed their calves to their stalls. **6:11** They put the ark of the LORD on the cart, along with the chest, the gold mice, and the images of the sores. **6:12** Then the cows went directly on the road to Beth Shemesh. They went along, mooing as they went; they turned neither to the right nor to the left. The leaders of the Philistines were walking along behind them all the way to the border of Beth Shemesh.

6:13 Now the residents of Beth Shemesh were harvesting wheat in the valley. When they looked up and saw the ark, they were pleased at the sight. **6:14** The cart was coming to the field of Joshua, who was from Beth Shemesh. It paused there near a big stone. Then they cut up the wood of the cart and offered the cows as a burnt offering to the LORD. **6:15** The Levites took down the ark of the LORD and the chest that was with it, which contained the gold objects. They placed them near the big stone. At that time the people of Beth Shemesh offered burnt offerings and made sacrifices to the LORD. **6:16** The five leaders of the Philistines watched what was happening and then returned to Ekron on the same day.

6:17 These are the gold sores that the Philistines brought as a guilt offering to the LORD – one for each of the following cities: Ashdod, Gaza, Ashkelon, Gath, and Ekron. **6:18** The gold mice corresponded in number to all the Philistine cities of the five leaders, from the fortified cities to hamlet villages, to greater Abel, where they positioned the ark of the LORD until this very day in the field of Joshua who was from Beth Shemesh.

6:19 But the LORD struck down some of the people of Beth Shemesh because they had looked into the ark of the LORD; he struck down 50,070 of the men. The people grieved because the LORD had struck the people with a hard blow. **6:20** The residents of Beth Shemesh asked, "Who is able to stand before the LORD, this holy God? To whom will the ark go up from here?"

6:21 So they sent messengers to the residents of Kiriath Jearim, saying, "The Philistines have returned the ark of the LORD. Come down here and take it back home with you."

7:1 Then the people of Kiriath Jearim came and took the ark of the LORD; they brought it to the house of Abinadab located on the hill. They consecrated Eleazar his son to guard the ark of the LORD.

Further Conflict with the Philistines

7:2 It was quite a long time – some twenty years in all – that the ark stayed at Kiriath Jearim. All the people of Israel longed for the LORD. **7:3** Samuel said to all the people of Israel, "If you are really turning to the LORD with all your hearts, remove from among you the foreign gods and the images of Ashtoreth. Give your hearts to the LORD and serve only him. Then he will deliver you from the hand of the Philistines." **7:4** So the Israelites removed the Baals and images of Ashtoreth. They served only the LORD.

7:5 Then Samuel said, "Gather all Israel to Mizpah, and I will pray to the LORD on your behalf." **7:6** After they had assembled at Mizpah, they drew water and poured it out before the LORD. They fasted on that day, and they confessed there, "We have sinned against the LORD." So Samuel led the people of Israel at Mizpah.

7:7 When the Philistines heard that the Israelites had gathered at Mizpah, the leaders of the Philistines went up against Israel. When the Israelites heard about this, they were afraid of the Philistines. **7:8** The Israelites said to Samuel, "Keep crying out to the LORD our God so that he may save us from the hand of the Philistines!" **7:9** So Samuel took a nursing lamb and offered it as a whole burnt offering to the LORD. Samuel cried out to the LORD on Israel's behalf, and the LORD answered him.

7:10 As Samuel was offering burnt offerings, the Philistines approached to do battle with Israel. But on that day the LORD thundered loudly against the Philistines. He caused them to panic, and they were defeated by Israel. **7:11** Then the men of Israel left Mizpah and chased the Philistines, striking them down all the way to an area below Beth Car.

7:12 Samuel took a stone and placed it between Mizpah and Shen. He named it Ebenezer, saying, "Up to here the LORD has helped us." **7:13** So the Philistines were defeated; they did not invade Israel again. The hand of the LORD was against the Philistines all the days of Samuel.

7:14 The cities that the Philistines had captured from Israel were returned to Israel, from Ekron to Gath. Israel also delivered their territory from the control of the Philistines. There was peace between Israel and the Amorites. **7:15** So Samuel led Israel all the days of his life. **7:16** Year after year he used to travel the circuit of Bethel, Gilgal, and Mizpah; he used to judge Israel in all of these places. **7:17** Then he would return to Ramah, because his home was there. He also judged Israel there and built an altar to the LORD there.

Israel Seeks a King

8:1 In his old age Samuel appointed his sons as judges over Israel. **8:2** The name of his firstborn son was Joel, and the name of his second son was Abijah. They were judges in Beer Sheba. **8:3** But his sons did not follow his ways. Instead, they made money dishonestly, accepted bribes, and perverted justice.

8:4 So all the elders of Israel gathered together and approached Samuel at Ramah. **8:5** They said to him, "Look, you are old, and your sons don't follow your ways. So now appoint over us a king to lead us, just like all the other nations have."

8:6 But this request displeased Samuel, for they said, "Give us a king to lead us." So Samuel prayed to the LORD. **8:7** The LORD said to Samuel, "Do everything the people request of you. For it is not you that they have rejected, but it is me that they have rejected as their king. **8:8** Just as they have done from the day that I brought them up from Egypt until this very day, they have rejected me and have served other gods. This is what they are also doing to you. **8:9** So now do as they say. But seriously warn them and make them aware of the policies of the king who will rule over them."

8:10 So Samuel spoke all the words of the LORD to the people who were asking him for a king. **8:11** He said, "Here are the policies of the king who will rule over you: He will conscript your sons and put them in his chariot forces and in his cavalry; they will run in front of his chariot. **8:12** He will appoint for himself leaders of thousands and leaders of fifties, as well as those who plow his ground, reap his harvest, and make his weapons of war and his chariot equipment. **8:13** He will take your daughters to be ointment makers, cooks, and bakers. **8:14** He will take your best fields and vineyards and give them to his own servants. **8:15** He will demand a tenth of your seed and of the produce of your vineyards and give it to his administrators and his servants. **8:16** He will take your male and female servants, as well as your best cattle and your donkeys, and assign them for his own use. **8:17** He will demand a tenth of your flocks, and you yourselves will be his servants. **8:18** In that day you will cry out because of your king whom you have chosen for yourselves, but the LORD won't answer you in that day."

8:19 But the people refused to heed Samuel's warning. Instead they said, "No! There will be a king over us! **8:20** We will be like all the other nations. Our king will judge us and lead us and fight our battles."

8:21 So Samuel listened to everything the people said and then reported it to the LORD. **8:22** The LORD said to Samuel, "Do as they say and install a king over them." Then Samuel said to the men of Israel, "Each of you go back to his own city."

Samuel Meets with Saul

9:1 There was a Benjaminite man named Kish son of Abiel, the son of Zeror, the son of Becorath, the son of Aphiah of Benjamin. He was a prominent person. **9:2** He had a son named Saul, a handsome young man. There was no one among the Israelites more handsome than he was; he stood head and shoulders above all the people.

9:3 The donkeys of Saul's father Kish wandered off, so Kish said to his son Saul, "Take one of the servants with you and go look for the donkeys." **9:4** So Saul crossed through the hill country of Ephraim, passing through the land of Shalisha, but they did not find them. So they crossed through the land of Shaalim, but they were not there. Then he crossed through the land of Benjamin, and still they did not find them.

9:5 When they came to the land of Zuph, Saul said to his servant who was with him, "Come on, let's head back before my father quits worrying about the donkeys and becomes anxious about us!" **9:6** But the servant said to him, "Look, there is a man of God in this town. He is highly respected. Everything that he says really happens. Now let's go there. Perhaps he will tell us where we should go from here." **9:7** So Saul said to his servant, "All right, we can go. But what can we bring the man, since the food in our bags is used up? We have no gift to take to the man of God. What do we have?" **9:8** The servant went on to answer Saul, "Look, I happen to have in my hand a quarter shekel of silver. I will give it to the man of God and he will tell us where we should go." **9:9** (Now it used to be in Israel that whenever someone went to inquire of God he would say, "Come on, let's go to the seer." For today's prophet used to be called a seer.) **9:10** So Saul said to his servant, "That's a good idea! Come on. Let's go." So they went to the town where the man of God was.

9:11 As they were going up the ascent to the town, they met some girls coming out to draw water. They said to them, "Is this where the seer is?" **9:12** They replied, "Yes, straight ahead! But hurry now, for he came to the town today, and the people are making a sacrifice at the high place. **9:13** When you enter the town, you can find him before he goes up to the high place to eat. The people won't eat until he arrives, for he must bless the sacrifice. Once that happens, those who have been invited will eat. Now go on up, for this is the time when you can find him!"

9:14 So they went up to the town. As they were heading for the middle of the town, Samuel was coming in their direction to go up to the high place. **9:15** Now the day before Saul arrived, the LORD had told Samuel: **9:16** "At this time tomorrow I will send to you a man from the land of Benjamin. You must consecrate him as a leader over my people Israel. He will save my people from the hand of the Philistines. For I have looked with favor on my people. Their cry has reached me!"

9:17 When Samuel saw Saul, the LORD said, "Here is the man that I told you about! He will rule over my people." **9:18** As Saul approached Samuel in the middle of the gate, he said, "Please tell me where the seer's house is."

9:19 Samuel replied to Saul, "I am the seer! Go up in front of me to the high place! Today you will eat with me and in the morning I will send you away. I will tell you everything that you are thinking. **9:20** Don't be concerned about the donkeys that you lost three days ago, for they have been found. Whom does all Israel desire? Is it not you, and all your father's family?"

9:21 Saul replied, "Am I not a Benjaminite, from the smallest of Israel's tribes, and is not my family clan the smallest of all the tribes of Benjamin? Why do you speak to me in this way?"

9:22 Then Samuel brought Saul and his servant into the room and gave them a place at the head of those who had been invited. There were about thirty people present. **9:23** Samuel said to the cook, "Give me the portion of meat that I gave to you – the one I asked you to keep with you."

9:24 So the cook picked up the leg and brought it and set it in front of Saul. Samuel said, "What was kept is now set before you! Eat, for it has been kept for you for this meeting time, from the time I said, 'I have invited the people.'" So Saul ate with Samuel that day.

9:25 When they came down from the high place to the town, Samuel spoke with Saul on the roof. **9:26** They got up at dawn and Samuel called to Saul on the roof, "Get up, so I can send you on your way." So Saul got up and the two of them – he and Samuel – went outside. **9:27** While they were going down to the edge of town, Samuel said to Saul, "Tell the servant to go on ahead of us." So he did. Samuel then said, "You remain here awhile, so I can inform you of God's message."

Samuel Anoints Saul

10:1 Then Samuel took a small container of olive oil and poured it on Saul's head. Samuel kissed him and said, "The LORD has chosen you to lead his people Israel! You will rule over the LORD's people and you will deliver them from the power of the enemies who surround them. This will be your sign that the LORD has chosen you as leader over his inheritance. **10:2** When you leave me today, you will find two men near Rachel's tomb at Zelzah on Benjamin's border. They will say to you, 'The donkeys you have gone looking for have been found. Your father is no longer concerned about the donkeys but has become anxious about you two! He is asking, "What should I do about my son?"'

10:3 "As you continue on from there, you will come to the tall tree of Tabor. At that point three men who are going up to God at Bethel will meet you. One of them will be carrying three young goats, one of them will be carrying three round loaves of bread, and one of them will be carrying a container of wine. **10:4** They will ask you how you're doing and will give you two loaves of bread. You will accept them. **10:5** Afterward you will go to Gibeah of God, where there are Philistine officials. When you enter the town, you will meet a company of prophets coming down from the high place. They will have harps, tambourines, flutes, and lyres, and they will be prophesying. **10:6** Then the spirit of the LORD will rush upon you and you will prophesy with them. You will be changed into a different person.

10:7 "When these signs have taken place, do whatever your hand finds to do, for God will be with you. **10:8** You will go down to Gilgal before me. I am going to join you there to offer burnt offerings and to make peace offerings. You should wait for seven days, until I arrive and tell you what to do."

Saul Becomes King

10:9 As Saul turned to leave Samuel, God changed his inmost person. All these signs happened on that very day. **10:10** When Saul and his servant arrived at Gibeah, a company of prophets was coming out to meet him. Then the spirit of God rushed upon Saul and he prophesied among them. **10:11** When everyone who had known him previously saw him prophesying with the prophets, the people all asked one another, "What on earth has happened to the son of Kish? Does even Saul belong with the prophets?"

10:12 A man who was from there then replied, "And who is their father?" Therefore this became a proverb: "Is even Saul among the prophets?" **10:13** When Saul had finished prophesying, he went to the high place.

10:14 Saul's uncle asked him and his servant, "Where did you go?" Saul replied, "To look for the donkeys. But when we realized they were lost, we went to Samuel." **10:15** Saul's uncle said, "Tell me what Samuel said to you." **10:16** Saul said to his uncle, "He assured us that the donkeys had been found." But Saul did not tell him what Samuel had said about the matter of kingship.

10:17 Then Samuel called the people together before the LORD at Mizpah. **10:18** He said to the Israelites, "This is what the LORD God of Israel says, 'I brought Israel up from Egypt and I delivered you from the power of the Egyptians and from the power of all the kingdoms that oppressed you. **10:19** But today you have rejected your God who saves you from all your trouble and distress. You have said, "No! Appoint a king over us." Now take your positions before the LORD by your tribes and by your clans.'"

10:20 Then Samuel brought all the tribes of Israel near, and the tribe of Benjamin was chosen by lot. **10:21** Then he brought the tribe of Benjamin near by its families, and the family of Matri was chosen by lot. At last Saul son of Kish was chosen by lot. But when they looked for him, he was nowhere to be found. **10:22** So they inquired again of the LORD, "Has the man arrived here yet?" The LORD said, "He has hidden himself among the equipment."

10:23 So they ran and brought him from there. When he took his position among the people, he stood head and shoulders above them all. **10:24** Then Samuel said to all the people, "Do you see the one whom the LORD has chosen? Indeed, there is no one like him among all the people!" All the people shouted out, "Long live the king!"

10:25 Then Samuel talked to the people about how the kingship would work. He wrote it all down on a scroll and set it before the LORD. Then Samuel sent all the people away to their homes. **10:26** Even Saul went to his home in Gibeah. With him went some brave men whose hearts God had touched. **10:27** But some wicked men said, "How can this man save us?" They despised him and did not even bring him a gift. But Saul said nothing about it.

Saul Comes to the Aid of Jabesh

11:1 Nahash the Ammonite marched against Jabesh Gilead. All the men of Jabesh Gilead said to Nahash, "Make a treaty with us and we will serve you."

11:2 But Nahash the Ammonite said to them, "The only way I will make a treaty with you is if you let me gouge out the right eye of every one of you and in so doing humiliate all Israel!"

11:3 The elders of Jabesh said to him, "Leave us alone for seven days so that we can send messengers throughout the territory of Israel. If there is no one who can deliver us, we will come out voluntarily to you."

11:4 When the messengers went to Gibeah (where Saul lived) and informed the people of these matters, all the people wept loudly. **11:5** Now Saul was walking behind the oxen as he came from the field. Saul asked, "What has happened to the people? Why are they weeping?" So they told him about the men of Jabesh.

11:6 The Spirit of God rushed upon Saul when he heard these words, and he became very angry. **11:7** He took a pair of oxen and cut them up. Then he sent the pieces throughout the territory of Israel by the hand of messengers, who said, "Whoever does not go out after Saul and after Samuel should expect this to be done to his oxen!" Then the terror of the LORD fell on the people, and they went out as one army. **11:8** When Saul counted them at Bezek, the Israelites were 300,000 strong and the men of Judah numbered 30,000.

11:9 They said to the messengers who had come, "Here's what you should say to the men of Jabesh Gilead: 'Tomorrow deliverance will come to you when the sun is fully up.'" When the messengers went and told the men of Jabesh Gilead, they were happy. **11:10** The men of Jabesh said, "Tomorrow we will come out to you and you can do with us whatever you wish."

11:11 The next day Saul placed the people in three groups. They went to the Ammonite camp during the morning watch and struck them down until the hottest part of the day. The survivors scattered; no two of them remained together.

Saul Is Established as King

11:12 Then the people said to Samuel, "Who were the ones asking, 'Will Saul reign over us?' Hand over those men so we may execute them!"

11:13 But Saul said, "No one will be killed on this day. For today the LORD has given Israel a victory!" **11:14** Samuel said to the people, "Come on! Let's go to Gilgal and renew the kingship there." **11:15** So all the people went to Gilgal, where they established Saul as king in the LORD's presence. They offered up peace offerings there in the LORD's presence. Saul and all the Israelites were very happy.

12:1 Samuel said to all Israel, "I have done everything you requested. I have given you a king. **12:2** Now look! This king walks before you. As for me, I am old and gray, though my sons are here with you. I have walked before you from the time of my youth till the present day. **12:3** Here I am. Bring a charge against me before the LORD and before his chosen king. Whose ox have I taken? Whose donkey have I taken? Whom have I wronged? Whom have I oppressed? From whose hand have I taken a bribe so that I would overlook something? Tell me, and I will return it to you!"

12:4 They replied, "You have not wronged us or oppressed us. You have not taken anything from the hand of anyone." **12:5** He said to them, "The LORD is witness against you, and his chosen king is witness this day, that you have not found any reason to accuse me." They said, "He is witness!"

12:6 Samuel said to the people, "The LORD is the one who chose Moses and Aaron and who brought your ancestors up from the land of Egypt. **12:7** Now take your positions, so I may confront you before the LORD regarding all the LORD's just actions toward you and your ancestors. **12:8** When Jacob entered Egypt, your ancestors cried out to the LORD. The LORD sent Moses and Aaron, and they led your ancestors out of Egypt and settled them in this place.

12:9 "But they forgot the LORD their God, so he gave them into the hand of Sisera, the general in command of Hazor's army, and into the hand of the Philistines and into the hand of the king of Moab, and they fought against them. **12:10** Then they cried out to the LORD and admitted, 'We have sinned, for we have forsaken the LORD and have served the Baals and the images of Ashtoreth. Now deliver us from the hand of our enemies so that we may serve you.' **12:11** So the LORD sent Jerub-Baal, Barak, Jephthah, and Samuel, and he delivered you from the hand of the enemies all around you, and you were able to live securely.

12:12 "When you saw that King Nahash of the Ammonites was advancing against you, you said to me, 'No! A king will rule over us' – even though the LORD your God is your king! **12:13** Now look! Here is the king you have chosen – the one that you asked for! Look, the LORD has given you a king! **12:14** If you fear the LORD, serving him and obeying him and not rebelling against what he says, and if both you and the king who rules over you follow the LORD your God, all will be well. **12:15** But if you don't obey the LORD and rebel against what the LORD says, the hand of the LORD will be against both you and your king.

12:16 "So now, take your positions and watch this great thing that the LORD is about to do in your sight. **12:17** Is this not the time of the wheat harvest? I will call on the LORD so that he makes it thunder and rain. Realize and see what a great sin you have committed before the LORD by asking for a king for yourselves."

12:18 So Samuel called to the LORD, and the LORD made it thunder and rain that day. All the people were very afraid of both the LORD and Samuel. **12:19** All the people said to Samuel, "Pray to the LORD your God on behalf of us – your servants – so we won't die, for we have added to all our sins by asking for a king."

12:20 Then Samuel said to the people, "Don't be afraid. You have indeed sinned. However, don't turn aside from the LORD. Serve the LORD with all your heart. **12:21** You should not turn aside after empty things that can't profit and can't deliver, since they are empty. **12:22** The LORD will not abandon his people because he wants to uphold his great reputation. The LORD was pleased to make you his own people. **12:23** As far as I am concerned, far be it from me to sin against the LORD by ceasing to pray for you! I will instruct you in the way that is good and upright. **12:24** However, fear the LORD and serve him faithfully with all your heart. Just look at the great things he has done for you! **12:25** But if you continue to do evil, both you and your king will be swept away."

Saul Fails the Lord

13:1 Saul was [thirty] years old when he began to reign; he ruled over Israel for [forty] years. **13:2** Saul selected for himself three thousand men from Israel. Two thousand of these were with Saul at Micmash and in the hill country of Bethel; the remaining thousand were with Jonathan at Gibeah in the territory of Benjamin. He sent all the rest of the people back home.

13:3 Jonathan attacked the Philistine outpost that was at Geba and the Philistines heard about it. Then Saul alerted all the land saying, "Let the Hebrews pay attention!" **13:4** All Israel heard this message, "Saul has attacked the Philistine outpost, and now Israel is repulsive to the Philistines!" So the people were summoned to join Saul at Gilgal.

13:5 For the battle with Israel the Philistines had amassed 3,000 chariots, 6,000 horsemen, and an army as numerous as the sand on the seashore. They went up and camped at Micmash, east of Beth Aven. **13:6** The men of Israel realized they had a problem because their army was hard pressed. So the army hid in caves, thickets, cliffs, strongholds, and cisterns. **13:7** Some of the Hebrews crossed over the Jordan River to the land of Gad and Gilead. But Saul stayed at Gilgal; the entire army that was with him was terrified. **13:8** He waited for seven days, the time period indicated by Samuel. But Samuel did not come to Gilgal, and the army began to abandon Saul.

13:9 So Saul said, "Bring me the burnt offering and the peace offerings." Then he offered a burnt offering. **13:10** Just when he had finished offering the burnt offering, Samuel appeared on the scene. Saul went out to meet him and to greet him.

13:11 But Samuel said, "What have you done?" Saul replied, "When I saw that the army had started to abandon me and that you didn't come at the appointed time and that the Philistines had assembled at Micmash, **13:12** I thought, 'Now the Philistines will come down on me at Gilgal and I have not sought the LORD's favor.' So I felt obligated to offer the burnt offering."

13:13 Then Samuel said to Saul, "You have made a foolish choice! You have not obeyed the commandment that the LORD your God gave you. Had you done that, the LORD would have established your kingdom over Israel forever! **13:14** But now your kingdom will not continue! The LORD has sought out for himself a man who is loyal to him and the LORD has appointed him to be leader over his people, for you have not obeyed what the LORD commanded you."

13:15 Then Samuel set out and went up from Gilgal to Gibeah in the territory of Benjamin. Saul mustered the army that remained with him; there were about six hundred men. **13:16** Saul, his son Jonathan, and the army that remained with them stayed in Gibeah in the territory of Benjamin, while the Philistines camped in Micmash. **13:17** Raiding bands went out from the camp of the Philistines in three groups. One band turned toward the road leading to Ophrah by the land of Shual; **13:18** another band turned toward the road leading to Beth Horon; and yet another band turned toward the road leading to the border that overlooks the valley of Zeboim in the direction of the desert.

13:19 A blacksmith could not be found in all the land of Israel, for the Philistines had said, "This will prevent the Hebrews from making swords and spears." **13:20** So all Israel had to go down to the Philistines in order to get their plowshares, cutting instruments, axes, and sickles sharpened. **13:21** They charged two-thirds of a shekel to sharpen plowshares and cutting instruments, and a third of a shekel to sharpen picks and axes, and to set ox goads. **13:22** So on the day of the battle no sword or spear was to be found in the hand of anyone in the army that was with Saul and Jonathan. No one but Saul and his son Jonathan had them.

Jonathan Ignites a Battle

13:23 A garrison of the Philistines had gone out to the pass at Micmash. **14:1** Then one day Jonathan son of Saul said to his armor bearer, "Come on, let's go over to the Philistine garrison that is opposite us." But he did not let his father know.

14:2 Now Saul was sitting under a pomegranate tree in Migron, on the outskirts of Gibeah. The army that was with him numbered about six hundred men. **14:3** Now Ahijah was carrying an ephod. He was the son of Ahitub, who was the brother of Ichabod and a son of Phineas, son of Eli, the priest of the LORD in Shiloh. The army was unaware that Jonathan had left.

14:4 Now there was a steep cliff on each side of the pass through which Jonathan intended to go to reach the Philistine garrison. One cliff was named Bozez, the other Seneh. **14:5** The cliff to the north was closer to Micmash, the one to the south closer to Geba.

14:6 Jonathan said to his armor bearer, "Come on, let's go over to the garrison of these uncircumcised men. Perhaps the LORD will intervene for us. Nothing can prevent the LORD from delivering, whether by many or by a few." **14:7** His armor bearer said to him, "Do everything that is on your mind. Do as you're inclined. I'm with you all the way!"

14:8 Jonathan replied, "All right! We'll go over to these men and fight them. **14:9** If they say to us, 'Stay put until we approach you,' we will stay right there and not go up to them. **14:10** But if they say, 'Come up against us,' we will go up. For in that case the LORD has given them into our hand – it will be a sign to us."

14:11 When they made themselves known to the Philistine garrison, the Philistines said, "Look! The Hebrews are coming out of the holes in which they hid themselves." **14:12** Then the men of the garrison said to Jonathan and his armor bearer, "Come on up to us so we can teach you a thing or two!" Then Jonathan said to his armor bearer, "Come up behind me, for the LORD has given them into the hand of Israel!"

14:13 Jonathan crawled up on his hands and feet, with his armor bearer following behind him. Jonathan struck down the Philistines, while his armor bearer came along behind him and killed them. **14:14** In this initial skirmish Jonathan and his armor bearer struck down about twenty men in an area that measured half an acre.

14:15 Then fear overwhelmed those who were in the camp, those who were in the field, all the army in the garrison, and the raiding bands. They trembled and the ground shook. This fear was caused by God.

14:16 Saul's watchmen at Gibeah in the territory of Benjamin looked on as the crowd of soldiers seemed to melt away first in one direction and then in another. **14:17** So Saul said to the army that was with him, "Muster the troops and see who is no longer with us." When they mustered the troops, Jonathan and his armor bearer were not there. **14:18** So Saul said to Ahijah, "Bring near the ephod," for he was at that time wearing the ephod. **14:19** While Saul spoke to the priest, the panic in the Philistines' camp was becoming greater and greater. So Saul said to the priest, "Withdraw your hand!"

14:20 Saul and all the army that was with him assembled and marched into battle, where they found the Philistines in total panic killing one another with their swords. **14:21** The Hebrews who had earlier gone over to the Philistine side joined the Israelites who were with Saul and Jonathan. **14:22** When all the Israelites who had hidden themselves in the hill country of Ephraim heard that the Philistines had fled, they too pursued them in battle. **14:23** So the LORD delivered Israel that day, and the battle shifted over to Beth Aven.

Jonathan Violates Saul's Oath

14:24 Now the men of Israel were hard pressed that day, for Saul had made the army agree to this oath: "Cursed be the man who eats food before evening! I will get my vengeance on my enemies!" So no one in the army ate anything.

14:25 Now the whole army entered the forest and there was honey on the ground. **14:26** When the army entered the forest, they saw the honey flowing, but no one ate any of it, for the army was afraid of the oath. **14:27** But Jonathan had not heard about the oath his father had made the army take. He extended the end of his staff that was in his hand and dipped it in the honeycomb. When he ate it, his eyes gleamed. **14:28** Then someone from the army informed him, "Your father put the army under a strict oath saying, 'Cursed be the man who eats food today!' That is why

the army is tired." **14:29** Then Jonathan said, "My father has caused trouble for the land. See how my eyes gleamed when I tasted just a little of this honey. **14:30** Certainly if the army had eaten some of the enemies' provisions that they came across today, would not the slaughter of the Philistines have been even greater?"

14:31 On that day the army struck down the Philistines from Micmash to Aijalon, and they became very tired. **14:32** So the army rushed greedily on the plunder, confiscating sheep, cattle, and calves. They slaughtered them right on the ground, and the army ate them blood and all.

14:33 Now it was reported to Saul, "Look, the army is sinning against the LORD by eating even the blood." He said, "All of you have broken the covenant! Roll a large stone over here to me." **14:34** Then Saul said, "Scatter out among the army and say to them, 'Each of you bring to me your ox and sheep and slaughter them in this spot and eat. But don't sin against the LORD by eating the blood." So that night each one brought his ox and slaughtered it there. **14:35** Then Saul built an altar for the LORD; it was the first time he had built an altar for the LORD.

14:36 Saul said, "Let's go down after the Philistines at night; we will rout them until the break of day. We won't leave any of them alive!" They replied, "Do whatever seems best to you." But the priest said, "Let's approach God here." **14:37** So Saul asked God, "Should I go down after the Philistines? Will you deliver them into the hand of Israel?" But he did not answer him that day.

14:38 Then Saul said, "All you leaders of the army come here. Find out how this sin occurred today. **14:39** For as surely as the LORD, the deliverer of Israel, lives, even if it turns out to be my own son Jonathan, he will certainly die!" But no one from the army said anything.

14:40 Then he said to all Israel, "You will be on one side, and I and my son Jonathan will be on the other side." The army replied to Saul, "Do whatever you think is best."

14:41 Then Saul said, "O LORD God of Israel! If this sin has been committed by me or by my son Jonathan, then, O LORD God of Israel, respond with Urim. But if this sin has been committed by your people Israel, respond with Thummim." Then Jonathan and Saul were indicated by lot, while the army was exonerated. **14:42** Then Saul said, "Cast the lot between me and my son Jonathan!" Jonathan was indicated by lot.

14:43 So Saul said to Jonathan, "Tell me what you have done." Jonathan told him, "I used the end of the staff that was in my hand to taste a little honey. I must die!" **14:44** Saul said, "God will punish me severely if Jonathan doesn't die!"

14:45 But the army said to Saul, "Should Jonathan, who won this great victory in Israel, die? May it never be! As surely as the LORD lives, not a single hair of his head will fall to the ground! For it is with the help of God that he has acted today." So the army rescued Jonathan from death.

14:46 Then Saul stopped chasing the Philistines, and the Philistines went back home. **14:47** After Saul had secured his royal position over Israel, he fought against all their enemies on all sides – the Moabites, Ammonites, Edomites, the kings of Zobah, and the Philistines. In every direction that he turned he was victorious. **14:48** He fought bravely, striking down the Amalekites and delivering Israel from the hand of its enemies.

Members of Saul's Family

14:49 The sons of Saul were Jonathan, Ishvi, and Malki-Shua. He had two daughters; the older one was named Merab and the younger Michal. **14:50** The name of Saul's wife was Ahinoam, the daughter of Ahimaaz. The name of the general in command of his army was Abner son of Ner, Saul's uncle. **14:51** Kish was the father of Saul, and Ner the father of Abner was the son of Abiel.

14:52 There was fierce war with the Philistines all the days of Saul. So whenever Saul saw anyone who was a warrior or a brave individual, he would conscript him.

Saul Is Rejected as King

15:1 Then Samuel said to Saul, "I was the one the LORD sent to anoint you as king over his people Israel. Now listen to what the LORD says. **15:2** Here is what the LORD of hosts says: 'I carefully observed how the Amalekites opposed Israel along the way when Israel came up from Egypt. **15:3** So go now and strike down the Amalekites. Destroy everything that they have. Don't spare them. Put them to death – man, woman, child, infant, ox, sheep, camel, and donkey alike.'"

15:4 So Saul assembled the army and mustered them at Telaim. There were 200,000 foot soldiers and 10,000 men of Judah. **15:5** Saul proceeded to the city of Amalek, where he set an ambush in the wadi. **15:6** Saul said to the Kenites, "Go on and leave! Go down from among the Amalekites! Otherwise I will sweep you away with them! After all, you were kind to all the Israelites when they came up from Egypt." So the Kenites withdrew from among the Amalekites.

15:7 Then Saul struck down the Amalekites all the way from Havilah to Shur, which is next to Egypt. **15:8** He captured King Agag of the Amalekites alive, but he executed all Agag's people with the sword. **15:9** However, Saul and the army spared Agag, along with the best of the flock, the cattle, the fatlings, and the lambs, as well as everything else that was of value. They were not willing to slaughter them. But they did slaughter everything that was despised and worthless.

15:10 Then the word of the LORD came to Samuel: **15:11** "I regret that I have made Saul king, for he has turned away from me and has not done what I told him to do." Samuel became angry and he cried out to the LORD all that night.
15:12 Then Samuel got up early to meet Saul the next morning. But Samuel was informed, "Saul has gone to Carmel where he is setting up a monument for himself. Then Samuel left and went down to Gilgal."
15:13 When Samuel came to him, Saul said to him, "May the LORD bless you! I have done what the LORD said."
15:14 Samuel replied, "If that is the case, then what is this sound of sheep in my ears and the sound of cattle that I hear?" **15:15** Saul said, "They were brought from the Amalekites; the army spared the best of the flocks and cattle to sacrifice to the LORD our God. But everything else we slaughtered."
15:16 Then Samuel said to Saul, "Wait a minute! Let me tell you what the LORD said to me last night." Saul said to him, "Tell me." **15:17** Samuel said, "Is it not true that when you were insignificant in your own eyes, you became head of the tribes of Israel? The LORD chose you as king over Israel. **15:18** The LORD sent you on a campaign saying, 'Go and exterminate those sinful Amalekites! Fight against them until you have destroyed them.' **15:19** Why haven't you obeyed the LORD? Instead you have greedily rushed upon the plunder! You have done what is wrong in the LORD's estimation."
15:20 Then Saul said to Samuel, "But I have obeyed the LORD! I went on the campaign the LORD sent me on. I brought back King Agag of the Amalekites after exterminating the Amalekites. **15:21** But the army took from the plunder some of the sheep and cattle – the best of what was to be slaughtered – to sacrifice to the LORD your God in Gilgal."
15:22 Then Samuel said,
"Does the LORD take pleasure in burnt offerings and sacrifices
as much as he does in obedience?
Certainly, obedience is better than sacrifice;
paying attention is better than the fat of rams.
15:23 For rebellion is like the sin of divination,
and presumption is like the evil of idolatry.
Because you have rejected the word of the LORD,
he has rejected you as king."
15:24 Then Saul said to Samuel, "I have sinned, for I have disobeyed what the LORD commanded and what you said as well. For I was afraid of the army, and I followed their wishes. **15:25** Now please forgive my sin! Go back with me so I can worship the LORD."
15:26 Samuel said to Saul, "I will not go back with you, for you have rejected the word of the LORD, and the LORD has rejected you from being king over Israel!"
15:27 When Samuel turned to leave, Saul grabbed the edge of his robe and it tore. **15:28** Samuel said to him, "The LORD has torn the kingdom of Israel from you this day and has given it to one of your colleagues who is better than you! **15:29** The Preeminent One of Israel does not go back on his word or change his mind, for he is not a human being who changes his mind." **15:30** Saul again replied, "I have sinned. But please honor me before the elders of my people and before Israel. Go back with me so I may worship the LORD your God." **15:31** So Samuel followed Saul back, and Saul worshiped the LORD.

Samuel Puts Agag to Death

15:32 Then Samuel said, "Bring me King Agag of the Amalekites." So Agag came to him trembling, thinking to himself, "Surely death is bitter!" **15:33** Samuel said, "Just as your sword left women childless, so your mother will be the most bereaved among women!" Then Samuel hacked Agag to pieces there in Gilgal before the LORD.
15:34 Then Samuel went to Ramah, while Saul went up to his home in Gibeah of Saul. **15:35** Until the day he died Samuel did not see Saul again. Samuel did, however, mourn for Saul, but the LORD regretted that he had made Saul king over Israel.

Samuel Anoints David as King

16:1 The LORD said to Samuel, "How long do you intend to mourn for Saul? I have rejected him as king over Israel. Fill your horn with olive oil and go! I am sending you to Jesse in Bethlehem, for I have selected a king for myself from among his sons."
16:2 Samuel replied, "How can I go? Saul will hear about it and kill me!" But the LORD said, "Take a heifer with you and say, 'I have come to sacrifice to the LORD.' **16:3** Then invite Jesse to the sacrifice, and I will show you what you should do. You will anoint for me the one I point out to you."
16:4 Samuel did what the LORD told him. When he arrived in Bethlehem, the elders of the city were afraid to meet him. They said, "Do you come in peace?" **16:5** He replied, "Yes, in peace. I have come to sacrifice to the LORD. Consecrate yourselves and come with me to the sacrifice." So he consecrated Jesse and his sons and invited them to the sacrifice.
16:6 When they arrived, Samuel noticed Eliab and said to himself, "Surely, here before the LORD stands his chosen king!" **16:7** But the LORD said to Samuel, "Don't be impressed by his appearance or his height, for I have rejected him. God does not view things the way men do. People look on the outward appearance, but the LORD looks at the heart."

16:8 Then Jesse called Abinadab and presented him to Samuel. But Samuel said, "The LORD has not chosen this one, either." **16:9** Then Jesse presented Shammah. But Samuel said, "The LORD has not chosen this one either." **16:10** Jesse presented seven of his sons to Samuel. But Samuel said to Jesse, "The LORD has not chosen any of these." **16:11** Then Samuel said to Jesse, "Is that all of the young men?" Jesse replied, "There is still the youngest one, but he's taking care of the flock." Samuel said to Jesse, "Send and get him, for we cannot turn our attention to other things until he comes here."
16:12 So Jesse had him brought in. Now he was ruddy, with attractive eyes and a handsome appearance. The LORD said, "Go and anoint him. This is the one!" **16:13** So Samuel took the horn full of olive oil and anointed him in the presence of his brothers. The Spirit of the LORD rushed upon David from that day onward. Then Samuel got up and went to Ramah.

David Appears before Saul

16:14 Now the Spirit of the LORD had turned away from Saul, and an evil spirit from the LORD tormented him. **16:15** Then Saul's servants said to him, "Look, an evil spirit from God is tormenting you!" **16:16** Let our lord instruct his servants who are here before you to look for a man who knows how to play the lyre. Then whenever the evil spirit from God comes upon you, he can play the lyre and you will feel better." **16:17** So Saul said to his servants, "Find me a man who plays well and bring him to me." **16:18** One of his attendants replied, "I have seen a son of Jesse in Bethlehem who knows how to play the lyre. He is a brave warrior and is articulate and handsome, for the LORD is with him."
16:19 So Saul sent messengers to Jesse and said, "Send me your son David, who is out with the sheep. **16:20** So Jesse took a donkey loaded with bread, a container of wine, and a young goat and sent them to Saul with his son David. **16:21** David came to Saul and stood before him. Saul liked him a great deal, and he became his armor bearer. **16:22** Then Saul sent word to Jesse saying, "Let David be my servant, for I really like him."
16:23 So whenever the spirit from God would come upon Saul, David would take his lyre and play it. This would bring relief to Saul and make him feel better. Then the evil spirit would leave him alone.

David Kills Goliath

17:1 The Philistines gathered their troops for battle. They assembled at Socoh in Judah. They camped in Ephes Dammim, between Socoh and Azekah. **17:2** Saul and the Israelite army assembled and camped in the valley of Elah, where they arranged their battle lines to fight against the Philistines. **17:3** The Philistines were standing on one hill, and the Israelites on another hill, with the valley between them.
17:4 Then a champion came out from the camp of the Philistines. His name was Goliath; he was from Gath. He was close to seven feet tall. **17:5** He had a bronze helmet on his head and was wearing scale body armor. The weight of his bronze body armor was five thousand shekels. **17:6** He had bronze shin guards on his legs, and a bronze javelin was slung over his shoulders. **17:7** The shaft of his spear was like a weaver's beam, and the iron point of his spear weighed six hundred shekels. His shield bearer was walking before him.
17:8 Goliath stood and called to Israel's troops, "Why do you come out to prepare for battle? Am I not the Philistine, and are you not the servants of Saul? Choose for yourselves a man so he may come down to me! **17:9** If he is able to fight with me and strike me down, we will become your servants. But if I prevail against him and strike him down, you will become our servants and will serve us." **17:10** Then the Philistine said, "I defy Israel's troops this day! Give me a man so we can fight each other!" **17:11** When Saul and all the Israelites heard these words of the Philistine, they were upset and very afraid.
17:12 Now David was the son of this Ephrathite named Jesse from Bethlehem in Judah. He had eight sons, and in Saul's days he was old and well advanced in years. **17:13** Jesse's three oldest sons had followed Saul to war. The names of the three sons who went to war were Eliab, his firstborn, Abinadab, the second oldest, and Shammah, the third oldest. **17:14** Now David was the youngest. While the three oldest sons followed Saul, **17:15** David was going back and forth from Saul in order to care for his father's sheep in Bethlehem.
17:16 Meanwhile for forty days the Philistine approached every morning and evening and took his position. **17:17** Jesse said to his son David, "Take your brothers this ephah of roasted grain and these ten loaves of bread; go quickly to the camp to your brothers. **17:18** Also take these ten portions of cheese to their commanding officer. Find out how your brothers are doing and bring back their pledge that they received the goods. **17:19** They are with Saul and the whole Israelite army in the valley of Elah, fighting with the Philistines."
17:20 So David got up early in the morning and entrusted the flock to someone else who would watch over it. After loading up, he went just as Jesse had instructed him. He arrived at the camp as the army was going out to the battle lines shouting its battle cry. **17:21** Israel and the Philistines drew up their battle lines opposite one another. **17:22** After David had entrusted his cargo to the care of the supply officer, he ran to the battlefront. When he arrived, he asked his brothers how they were doing.

17:23 As he was speaking with them, the champion named Goliath, the Philistine from Gath, was coming up from the battle lines of the Philistines. He spoke the way he usually did, and David heard it. **17:24** When all the men of Israel saw this man, they retreated from his presence and were very afraid.

17:25 The men of Israel said, "Have you seen this man who is coming up? He does so to defy Israel. But the king will make the man who can strike him down very wealthy! He will give him his daughter in marriage, and he will make his father's house exempt from tax obligations in Israel."

17:26 David asked the men who were standing near him, "What will be done for the man who strikes down this Philistine and frees Israel from this humiliation? For who is this uncircumcised Philistine, that he defies the armies of the living God?" **17:27** The soldiers told him what had been promised, saying, "This is what will be done for the man who can strike him down."

17:28 When David's oldest brother Eliab heard him speaking to the men, he became angry with David and said, "Why have you come down here? To whom did you entrust those few sheep in the desert? I am familiar with your pride and deceit! You have come down here to watch the battle!"

17:29 David replied, "What have I done now? Can't I say anything?" **17:30** Then he turned from those who were nearby to someone else and asked the same question, but they gave him the same answer as before. **17:31** When David's words were overheard and reported to Saul, he called for him.

17:32 David said to Saul, "Don't let anyone be discouraged. Your servant will go and fight this Philistine!" **17:33** But Saul replied to David, "You aren't able to go against this Philistine and fight him! You're just a boy! He has been a warrior from his youth!"

17:34 David replied to Saul, "Your servant has been a shepherd for his father's flock. Whenever a lion or bear would come and carry off a sheep from the flock, **17:35** I would go out after it, strike it down, and rescue the sheep from its mouth. If it rose up against me, I would grab it by its jaw, strike it, and kill it. **17:36** Your servant has struck down both the lion and the bear. This uncircumcised Philistine will be just like one of them. For he has defied the armies of the living God!" **17:37** David went on to say, "The LORD who delivered me from the lion and the bear will also deliver me from the hand of this Philistine!" Then Saul said to David, "Go! The LORD will be with you."

17:38 Then Saul clothed David with his own fighting attire and put a bronze helmet on his head. He also put body armor on him. **17:39** David strapped on his sword over his fighting attire and tried to walk around, but he was not used to them. David said to Saul, "I can't walk in these things, for I'm not used to them." So David removed them. **17:40** He took his staff in his hand, picked out five smooth stones from the stream, placed them in the pouch of his shepherd's bag, took his sling in hand, and approached the Philistine.

17:41 The Philistine kept coming closer to David, with his shield bearer walking in front of him. **17:42** When the Philistine looked carefully at David, he despised him, for he was only a ruddy and handsome boy. **17:43** The Philistine said to David, "Am I a dog, that you are coming after me with sticks?" Then the Philistine cursed David by his gods. **17:44** The Philistine said to David, "Come here to me, so I can give your flesh to the birds of the sky and the wild animals of the field!"

17:45 But David replied to the Philistine, "You are coming against me with sword and spear and javelin. But I am coming against you in the name of the LORD of hosts, the God of Israel's armies, whom you have defied! **17:46** This very day the LORD will deliver you into my hand! I will strike you down and cut off your head. This day I will give the corpses of the Philistine army to the birds of the sky and the wild animals of the land. Then all the land will realize that Israel has a God **17:47** and all this assembly will know that it is not by sword or spear that the LORD saves! For the battle is the LORD's, and he will deliver you into our hand."

17:48 The Philistine drew steadily closer to David to attack him, while David quickly ran toward the battle line to attack the Philistine. **17:49** David reached his hand into the bag and took out a stone. He slung it, striking the Philistine on the forehead. The stone sank deeply into his forehead, and he fell down with his face to the ground.

17:50 David prevailed over the Philistine with just the sling and the stone. He struck down the Philistine and killed him. David did not even have a sword in his hand. **17:51** David ran and stood over the Philistine. He grabbed Goliath's sword, drew it from its sheath, killed him, and cut off his head with it. When the Philistines saw their champion was dead, they ran away.

17:52 Then the men of Israel and Judah charged forward, shouting a battle cry. They chased the Philistines to the valley and to the very gates of Ekron. The Philistine corpses lay fallen along the Shaaraim road to Gath and Ekron. **17:53** When the Israelites returned from their hot pursuit of the Philistines, they looted their camp. **17:54** David took the head of the Philistine and brought it to Jerusalem, and he put Goliath's weapons in his tent.

17:55 Now as Saul watched David going out to fight the Philistine, he asked Abner, the general in command of the army, "Whose son is this young man, Abner?" Abner replied, "As surely as you live, O king, I don't know." **17:56** The king said, "Find out whose son this boy is!"

17:57 So when David returned from striking down the Philistine, Abner took him and brought him before Saul. He still had the head of the Philistine in his hand. **17:58** Saul said to him, "Whose son are you, young man?" David replied, "I am the son of your servant Jesse in Bethlehem."

Saul Comes to Fear David

18:1 When David had finished talking with Saul, Jonathan and David became bound together in close friendship. Jonathan loved David as much as he did his own life. **18:2** Saul retained David on that day and did not allow him to return to his father's house. **18:3** Jonathan made a covenant with David, for he loved him as much as he did his own life. **18:4** Jonathan took off the robe he was wearing and gave it to David, along with the rest of his gear, including his sword, his bow, and even his belt.

18:5 On every mission on which Saul sent him, David achieved success. So Saul appointed him over the men of war. This pleased not only all the army, but also Saul's servants.

18:6 When the men arrived after David returned from striking down the Philistine, the women from all the cities of Israel came out singing and dancing to meet King Saul. They were happy as they played their tambourines and three-stringed instruments. **18:7** The women who were playing the music sang,

"Saul has struck down his thousands,
but David his tens of thousands!"

18:8 This made Saul very angry. The statement displeased him and he thought, "They have attributed to David tens of thousands, but to me they have attributed only thousands. What does he lack, except the kingdom?" **18:9** So Saul was keeping an eye on David from that day onward.

18:10 The next day an evil spirit from God rushed upon Saul and he prophesied within his house. Now David was playing the lyre that day. There was a spear in Saul's hand, **18:11** and Saul threw the spear, thinking, "I'll nail David to the wall!" But David escaped from him on two different occasions.

18:12 So Saul feared David, because the LORD was with him but had departed from Saul. **18:13** Saul removed David from his presence and made him a commanding officer. David led the army out to battle and back. **18:14** Now David achieved success in all he did, for the LORD was with him. **18:15** When Saul saw how very successful he was, he was afraid of him. **18:16** But all Israel and Judah loved David, for he was the one leading them out to battle and back.

18:17 Then Saul said to David, "Here's my oldest daughter, Merab. I want to give her to you in marriage. Only be a brave warrior for me and fight the battles of the LORD." For Saul thought, "There's no need for me to raise my hand against him. Let it be the hand of the Philistines!" **18:18** David said to Saul, "Who am I? Who are my relatives or the clan of my father in Israel that I should become the king's son-in-law?" **18:19** When the time came for Merab, Saul's daughter, to be given to David, she instead was given in marriage to Adriel, who was from Meholah.

18:20 Now Michal, Saul's daughter, loved David. When they told Saul about this, it pleased him. **18:21** Saul said, "I will give her to him so that she may become a snare to him and the hand of the Philistines may be against him." So Saul said to David, "Today is the second time for you to become my son-in-law."

18:22 Then Saul instructed his servants, "Tell David secretly, 'The king is pleased with you, and all his servants like you. So now become the king's son-in-law.'" **18:23** So Saul's servants spoke these words privately to David. David replied, "Is becoming the king's son-in-law something insignificant to you? I'm just a poor and lightly-esteemed man!"

18:24 When Saul's servants reported what David had said, **18:25** Saul replied, "Here is what you should say to David: 'There is nothing that the king wants as a price for the bride except a hundred Philistine foreskins, so that he can be avenged of his enemies.'" (Now Saul was thinking that he could kill David by the hand of the Philistines.)

18:26 So his servants told David these things and David agreed to become the king's son-in-law. Now the specified time had not yet expired **18:27** when David, along with his men, went out and struck down two hundred Philistine men. David brought their foreskins and presented all of them to the king so he could become the king's son-in-law. Saul then gave him his daughter Michal in marriage.

18:28 When Saul realized that the LORD was with David and that his daughter Michal loved David, **18:29** Saul became even more afraid of him. Saul continued to be at odds with David from then on. **18:30** Then the leaders of the Philistines would march out, and as often as they did so, David achieved more success than all of Saul's servants. His name was held in high esteem.

Saul Repeatedly Attempts to Take David's Life

19:1 Then Saul told his son Jonathan and all his servants to kill David. But Saul's son Jonathan liked David very much. **19:2** So Jonathan told David, "My father Saul is trying to kill you. So be careful tomorrow morning. Find a hiding place and stay in seclusion. **19:3** I will go out and stand beside my father in the field where you are. I will speak about you to my father. When I find out what the problem is, I will let you know." **19:4** So Jonathan spoke on David's behalf to his father Saul. He said to him, "The king should not sin against his servant David, for he has not sinned against you. On the contrary, his actions have been very beneficial for you. **19:5** He risked his life when he struck down the Philistine and the LORD gave all Israel a great victory. When you saw it, you were happy. So why would you sin against innocent blood by putting David to death for no reason?"

19:6 Saul accepted Jonathan's advice and took an oath, "As surely as the LORD lives, he will not be put to death." **19:7** Then Jonathan called David and told him all these things. Jonathan brought David to Saul, and he served him as he had done formerly.

19:8 Now once again there was war. So David went out to fight the Philistines. He defeated them thoroughly and they ran away from him. **19:9** Then an evil spirit from the LORD came upon Saul. He was sitting in his house with his spear in his hand, while David was playing the lyre. **19:10** Saul tried to nail David to the wall with the spear, but he escaped from Saul's presence and the spear drove into the wall. David escaped quickly that night.

19:11 Saul sent messengers to David's house to guard it and to kill him in the morning. Then David's wife Michal told him, "If you do not save yourself tonight, tomorrow you will be dead!" **19:12** So Michal lowered David through the window, and he ran away and escaped.

19:13 Then Michal took a household idol and put it on the bed. She put a quilt made of goat's hair over its head and then covered the idol with a garment. **19:14** When Saul sent messengers to arrest David, she said, "He's sick."

19:15 Then Saul sent the messengers back to see David, saying, "Bring him up to me on his bed so I can kill him." **19:16** When the messengers came, they found only the idol on the bed and the quilt made of goat's hair at its head.

19:17 Saul said to Michal, "Why have you deceived me this way by sending my enemy away? Now he has escaped!" Michal replied to Saul, "He said to me, 'Help me get away or else I will kill you!'"

19:18 Now David had run away and escaped. He went to Samuel in Ramah and told him everything that Saul had done to him. Then he and Samuel went and stayed at Naioth. **19:19** It was reported to Saul saying, "David is at Naioth in Ramah." **19:20** So Saul sent messengers to capture David. When they saw a company of prophets prophesying with Samuel standing there as their leader, the spirit of God came upon Saul's messengers, and they also prophesied. **19:21** When it was reported to Saul, he sent more messengers, but they prophesied too. So Saul sent messengers a third time, but they also prophesied. **19:22** Finally Saul himself went to Ramah. When he arrived at the large cistern that is in Secu, he asked, "Where are Samuel and David?" They said, "At Naioth in Ramah."

19:23 So Saul went to Naioth in Ramah. The Spirit of God came upon him as well, and he walked along prophesying until he came to Naioth in Ramah. **19:24** He even stripped off his clothes and prophesied before Samuel. He lay there naked all that day and night. (For that reason it is asked, "Is Saul also among the prophets?")

Jonathan Seeks to Protect David

20:1 David fled from Naioth in Ramah. He came to Jonathan and asked, "What have I done? What is my offense? How have I sinned before your father? For he is seeking my life!"

20:2 Jonathan said to him, "By no means are you going to die! My father does nothing large or small without making me aware of it. Why would my father hide this matter from me? It just won't happen!"

20:3 Taking an oath, David again said, "Your father is very much aware of the fact that I have found favor with you, and he has thought, 'Don't let Jonathan know about this, or he will be upset.' But as surely as the LORD lives and you live, there is about one step between me and death!"

20:4 Jonathan replied to David, "Tell me what I can do for you."

20:5 David said to Jonathan, "Tomorrow is the new moon, and I am certainly expected to join the king for a meal. You must send me away so I can hide in the field until the third evening from now. **20:6** If your father happens to miss me, you should say, 'David urgently requested me to let him go to his city Bethlehem, for there is an annual sacrifice there for his entire family.' **20:7** If he should then say, 'That's fine,' then your servant is safe. But if he becomes very angry, be assured that he has decided to harm me. **20:8** You must be loyal to your servant, for you have made a covenant with your servant in the LORD's name. If I am guilty, you yourself kill me! Why bother taking me to your father?"

20:9 Jonathan said, "Far be it from you to suggest this! If I were at all aware that my father had decided to harm you, wouldn't I tell you about it?" **20:10** David said to Jonathan, "Who will tell me if your father answers you harshly?" **20:11** Jonathan said to David, "Come on. Let's go out to the field."

When the two of them had gone out into the field, **20:12** Jonathan said to David, "The LORD God of Israel is my witness. I will feel out my father about this time the day after tomorrow. If he is favorably inclined toward David, will I not then send word to you and let you know? **20:13** But if my father intends to do you harm, may the LORD do all this and more to

Jonathan, if I don't let you know and send word to you so you can go safely on your way. May the LORD be with you, as he was with my father. **20:14** While I am still alive, extend to me the loyalty of the LORD, or else I will die! **20:15** Don't ever cut off your loyalty to my family, not even when the LORD has cut off every one of David's enemies from the face of the earth **20:16** and called David's enemies to account." So Jonathan made a covenant with the house of David. **20:17** Jonathan once again took an oath with David, because he loved him. In fact Jonathan loved him as much as he did his own life. **20:18** Jonathan said to him, "Tomorrow is the new moon, and you will be missed, for your seat will be empty. **20:19** On the third day you should go down quickly and come to the place where you hid yourself the day this all started. Stay near the stone Ezel. **20:20** I will shoot three arrows near it, as though I were shooting at a target. **20:21** When I send a boy after them, I will say, "Go and find the arrows." If I say to the boy, 'Look, the arrows are on this side of you; get them,' then come back. For as surely as the LORD lives, you will be safe and there will no problem. **20:22** But if I say to the boy, "Look, the arrows are on the other side of you,' get away. For in that case the LORD has sent you away. **20:23** With regard to the matter that you and I discussed, the LORD is the witness between us forever!"

20:24 So David hid in the field. When the new moon came, the king sat down to eat his meal. **20:25** The king sat down in his usual place by the wall, with Jonathan opposite him and Abner at his side. But David's place was vacant. **20:26** However, Saul said nothing about it that day, for he thought, "Something has happened to make him ceremonially unclean. Yes, he must be unclean." **20:27** But the next morning, the second day of the new moon, David's place was still vacant. So Saul said to his son Jonathan, "Why has Jesse's son not come to the meal yesterday or today?"

20:28 Jonathan replied to Saul, "David urgently requested that he be allowed to go to Bethlehem. **20:29** He said, 'Permit me to go, for we are having a family sacrifice in the city, and my brother urged me to be there. So now, if I have found favor with you, let me go to see my brothers.' For that reason he has not come to the king's table."

20:30 Saul became angry with Jonathan and said to him, "You stupid traitor! Don't I realize that to your own disgrace and to the disgrace of your mother's nakedness you have chosen this son of Jesse? **20:31** For as long as this son of Jesse is alive on the earth, you and your kingdom will not be established. Now, send some men and bring him to me. For he is as good as dead!"

20:32 Jonathan responded to his father Saul, "Why should he be put to death? What has he done?" **20:33** Then Saul threw his spear at Jonathan in order to strike him down. So Jonathan was convinced that his father had decided to kill David. **20:34** Jonathan got up from the table enraged. He did not eat any food on that second day of the new moon, for he was upset that his father had humiliated David.

20:35 The next morning Jonathan, along with a young servant, went out to the field to meet David. **20:36** He said to his servant, "Run, find the arrows that I am about to shoot." As the servant ran, Jonathan shot the arrow beyond him. **20:37** When the servant came to the place where Jonathan had shot the arrow, Jonathan called out to the servant, "Isn't the arrow further beyond you?" **20:38** Jonathan called out to the servant, "Hurry! Go faster! Don't delay!" Jonathan's servant retrieved the arrow and came back to his master. **20:39** (Now the servant did not understand any of this. Only Jonathan and David knew what was going on.) **20:40** Then Jonathan gave his equipment to the servant who was with him. He said to him, "Go, take these things back to the city."

20:41 When the servant had left, David got up from beside the mound, knelt with his face to the ground, and bowed three times. Then they kissed each other and they both wept, especially David. **20:42** Jonathan said to David, "Go in peace, for the two of us have sworn together in the name of the LORD saying, 'The LORD will be between me and you and between my descendants and your descendants forever.'"

David Goes to Nob

(21:1) Then David got up and left, while Jonathan went back to the city. **21:1** (21:2) David went to Ahimelech the priest in Nob. Ahimelech was shaking with fear when he met David, and said to him, "Why are you by yourself with no one accompanying you?" **21:2** David replied to Ahimelech the priest, "The king instructed me to do something, but he said to me, 'Don't let anyone know the reason I am sending you or the instructions I have given you.' I have told my soldiers to wait at a certain place. **21:3** Now what do you have at your disposal? Give me five loaves of bread, or whatever can be found."

21:4 The priest replied to David, "I don't have any ordinary bread at my disposal. Only holy bread is available, and then only if your soldiers have abstained from sexual relations with women." **21:5** David said to the priest, "Certainly women have been kept away from us, just as on previous occasions when I have set out. The soldiers' equipment is holy, even on an ordinary journey. How much more so will they be holy today, along with their equipment!"

21:6 So the priest gave him holy bread, for there was no bread there other than the bread of the Presence. It had been removed from before the LORD in order to replace it with hot bread on the day it had been taken away. **21:7** (One of Saul's servants was there that day, detained before the Lord. His name was Doeg the Edomite, who was in charge of Saul's shepherds.) **21:8** David said to Ahimelech, "Is there no sword or spear here at your disposal? I don't have my own sword or equipment in hand due to the urgency of the king's instructions."

David Goes to Gath

21:9 The priest replied, "The sword of Goliath the Philistine, whom you struck down in the valley of Elah, is wrapped in a garment behind the ephod. If you wish, take it for yourself. Other than that, there's nothing here." David said, "There's nothing like it! Give it to me!" **21:10** So on that day David arose and fled from Saul. He went to King Achish of Gath. **21:11** The servants of Achish said to him, "Isn't this David, the king of the land? Isn't he the one that they sing about when they dance, saying,

'Saul struck down his thousands,
But David his tens of thousands'?"

21:12 David thought about what they said and was very afraid of King Achish of Gath. **21:13** He altered his behavior in their presence. Since he was in their power, he pretended to be insane, making marks on the doors of the gate and letting his saliva run down his beard. **21:14** Achish said to his servants, "Look at this madman! Why did you bring him to me? **21:15** Do I have a shortage of fools, that you have brought me this man to display his insanity in front of me? Should this man enter my house?"

David Goes to Adullam and Mizpah

22:1 So David left there and escaped to the cave of Adullam. When his brothers and the rest of his father's family learned about it, they went down there to him. **22:2** All those who were in trouble or owed someone money or were discontented gathered around him, and he became their leader. He had about four hundred men with him. **22:3** Then David went from there to Mizpah in Moab, where he said to the king of Moab, "Please let my father and mother stay with you until I know what God is going to do for me." **22:4** So he had them stay with the king of Moab; they stayed with him the whole time that David was in the stronghold. **22:5** Then Gad the prophet said to David, "Don't stay in the stronghold. Go to the land of Judah." So David left and went to the forest of Hereth.

Saul Executes the Priests

22:6 But Saul found out the whereabouts of David and the men who were with him. Now Saul was sitting at Gibeah under the tamarisk tree at an elevated location with his spear in hand and all his servants stationed around him. **22:7** Saul said to his servants who were stationed around him, "Listen up, you Benjaminites! Is Jesse's son giving fields and vineyards to all of you? Or is he making all of you commanders and officers? **22:8** For all of you have conspired against me! No one informs me when my own son makes an agreement with this son of Jesse! Not one of you feels sorry for me or informs me that my own son has commissioned my own servant to hide in ambush against me, as is the case today!"

22:9 But Doeg the Edomite, who had stationed himself with the servants of Saul, replied, "I saw this son of Jesse come to Ahimelech son of Ahitub at Nob. **22:10** He inquired of the Lord for him and gave him provisions. He also gave him the sword of Goliath the Philistine."

22:11 Then the king arranged for a meeting with the priest Ahimelech son of Ahitub and all the priests of his father's house who were at Nob. They all came to the king. **22:12** Then Saul said, "Listen, son of Ahitub." He replied, "Here I am, my lord." **22:13** Saul said to him, "Why have you conspired against me, you and this son of Jesse? You gave him bread and a sword and inquired of God on his behalf, so that he opposes me and waits in ambush, as is the case today!"

22:14 Ahimelech replied to the king, "Who among all your servants is faithful like David? He is the king's son-in-law, the leader of your bodyguard, and honored in your house! **22:15** Was it just today that I began to inquire of God on his behalf? Far be it from me! The king should not accuse his servant or any of my father's house. For your servant is not aware of all this – not in whole or in part!"

22:16 But the king said, "You will surely die, Ahimelech, you and all your father's house! **22:17** Then the king said to the messengers who were stationed beside him, "Turn and kill the priests of the Lord, for they too have sided with David! They knew he was fleeing, but they did not inform me." But the king's servants refused to harm the priests of the Lord.

22:18 Then the king said to Doeg, "You turn and strike down the priests!" So Doeg the Edomite turned and struck down the priests. He killed on that day eighty-five men who wore the linen ephod. **22:19** As for Nob, the city of the priests, he struck down with the sword men and women, children and infants, oxen, donkeys, and sheep – all with the sword.

22:20 But one of the sons of Ahimelech son of Ahitub escaped and fled to David. His name was Abiathar. **22:21** Abiathar told David that Saul had killed the priests of the Lord. **22:22** Then David said to Abiathar, "I knew that day when Doeg the Edomite was there that he would certainly tell Saul! I am guilty of all the deaths in your father's house! **22:23** Stay with me. Don't be afraid! Whoever seeks my life is seeking your life as well. You are secure with me."

David Delivers the City of Keilah

23:1 They told David, "The Philistines are fighting in Keilah and are looting the threshing floors." **23:2** So David asked the Lord, "Should I go and strike down these Philistines?" The Lord said to David, "Go, strike down the Philistines and deliver Keilah."

23:3 But David's men said to him, "We are afraid while we are still here in Judah! What will it be like if we go to Keilah against the armies of the Philistines?" **23:4** So David asked the Lord once again. But again the Lord replied, "Arise, go down to Keilah, for I will give the Philistines into your hand."

23:5 So David and his men went to Keilah and fought the Philistines. He took away their cattle and thoroughly defeated them. David delivered the inhabitants of Keilah.

David Eludes Saul Again

23:6 Now when Abiathar son of Ahimelech had fled to David at Keilah, he had brought with him an ephod. **23:7** When Saul was told that David had come to Keilah, Saul said, "God has delivered him into my hand, for he has boxed himself into a corner by entering a city with two barred gates." **23:8** So Saul mustered all his army to go down to Keilah and besiege David and his men.

23:9 When David realized that Saul was planning to harm him, he told Abiathar the priest, "Bring the ephod!" **23:10** Then David said, "O Lord God of Israel, your servant has clearly heard that Saul is planning to come to Keilah to destroy the city because of me. **23:11** Will the leaders of Keilah deliver me into his hand? Will Saul come down as your servant has heard? O Lord God of Israel, please inform your servant!"

Then the Lord said, "He will come down." **23:12** David asked, "Will the leaders of Keilah deliver me and my men into Saul's hand?" The Lord said, "They will deliver you over."

23:13 So David and his men, who numbered about six hundred, set out and left Keilah; they moved around from one place to another. When told that David had escaped from Keilah, Saul called a halt to his expedition. **23:14** David stayed in the strongholds that were in the desert and in the hill country of the desert of Ziph. Saul looked for him all the time, but God did not deliver David into his hand. **23:15** David realized that Saul had come out to seek his life; at that time David was in Horesh in the desert of Ziph.

23:16 Then Jonathan son of Saul left and went to David at Horesh. He encouraged him through God. **23:17** He said to him, "Don't be afraid! For the hand of my father Saul cannot find you. You will rule over Israel, and I will be your second in command. Even my father Saul realizes this." **23:18** When the two of them had made a covenant before the Lord, David stayed on at Horesh, but Jonathan went to his house.

23:19 Then the Ziphites went up to Saul at Gibeah and said, "Isn't David hiding among us in the strongholds at Horesh on the hill of Hakilah, south of Jeshimon? **23:20** Now at your own discretion, O king, come down. Delivering him into the king's hand will be our responsibility."

23:21 Saul replied, "May you be blessed by the Lord, for you have had compassion on me. **23:22** Go and make further arrangements. Determine precisely where he is and who has seen him there, for I am told that he is extremely cunning. **23:23** Locate precisely all the places where he hides and return to me with dependable information. Then I will go with you. If he is in the land, I will find him among all the thousands of Judah."

23:24 So they left and went to Ziph ahead of Saul. Now David and his men were in the desert of Maon, in the Arabah to the south of Jeshimon. **23:25** Saul and his men went to look for him. But David was informed and went down to the rock and stayed in the desert of Maon. When Saul heard about it, he pursued David in the desert of Maon. **23:26** Saul went on one side of the mountain, while David and his men went on the other side of the mountain. David was hurrying to get away from Saul, but Saul and his men were surrounding David and his men so they could capture them. **23:27** But a messenger came to Saul saying, "Come quickly, for the Philistines have raided the land!"

23:28 So Saul stopped pursuing David and went to confront the Philistines. Therefore that place is called Sela Hammahlekoth. **23:29** (24:1) Then David went up from there and stayed in the strongholds of En Gedi.

David Spares Saul's Life

24:1 (24:2) When Saul returned from pursuing the Philistines, they told him, "Look, David is in the desert of En Gedi." **24:2** So Saul took three thousand select men from all Israel and went to find David and his men in the region of the rocks of the mountain goats. **24:3** He came to the sheepfolds by the road, where there was a cave. Saul went into it to relieve himself.

Now David and his men were sitting in the recesses of the cave. **24:4** David's men said to him, "This is the day about which the Lord said to you, 'I will give your enemy into your hand, and you can do to him whatever seems appropriate to you.'" So David got up and quietly cut off an edge of Saul's robe. **24:5** Afterward David's conscience bothered him because he had cut off an edge of Saul's robe. **24:6** He said to his men, "May the Lord keep me far away from doing such a thing to my lord, who is the Lord's chosen one, by extending my hand against him. After all, he is the Lord's chosen one." **24:7** David restrained his men with these words and did not allow them to rise up against Saul. Then Saul left the cave and started down the road.

24:8 Afterward David got up and went out of the cave. He called out after Saul, "My lord, O king!" When Saul looked behind him, David kneeled down and bowed with his face to the ground. **24:9** David said to Saul, "Why do you pay attention when men say, 'David is seeking to do you harm'? **24:10** Today your own eyes see how the LORD delivered you – this very day – into my hands in the cave. Some told me to kill you, but I had pity on you and said, 'I will not extend my hand against my lord, for he is the LORD's chosen one.' **24:11** Look, my father, and see the edge of your robe in my hand! When I cut off the edge of your robe, I didn't kill you. So realize and understand that I am not planning evil or rebellion. Even though I have not sinned against you, you are waiting in ambush to take my life. **24:12** May the LORD judge between the two of us, and may the LORD vindicate me over you, but my hand will not be against you. **24:13** It's like the old proverb says: 'From evil people evil proceeds.' But my hand will not be against you. **24:14** Who has the king of Israel come out after? Who is it that you are pursuing? A dead dog? A single flea? **24:15** May the LORD be our judge and arbiter. May he see and arbitrate my case and deliver me from your hands!"

24:16 When David finished speaking these words to Saul, Saul said, "Is that your voice, my son David?" Then Saul wept loudly. **24:17** He said to David, "You are more innocent than I, for you have treated me well, even though I have tried to harm you! **24:18** You have explained today how you have treated me well. The LORD delivered me into your hand, but you did not kill me. **24:19** Now if a man finds his enemy, does he send him on his way in good shape? May the LORD repay you with good this day for what you have done to me. **24:20** Now look, I realize that you will in fact be king and that the kingdom of Israel will be established in your hand. **24:21** So now swear to me in the LORD's name that you will not kill my descendants after me or destroy my name from the house of my father."

24:22 David promised Saul this on oath. Then Saul went to his house, and David and his men went up to the stronghold.

The Death of Samuel

25:1 Samuel died, and all Israel assembled and mourned him. They buried him at his home in Ramah. Then David left and went down to the desert of Paran.

David Marries Abigail the Widow of Nabal

25:2 There was a man in Maon whose business was in Carmel. This man was very wealthy; he owned three thousand sheep and a thousand goats. At that time he was shearing his sheep in Carmel. **25:3** The man's name was Nabal, and his wife's name was Abigail. She was both wise and beautiful, but the man was harsh and his deeds were evil. He was a Calebite.

25:4 When David heard in the desert that Nabal was shearing his sheep, **25:5** he sent ten servants, saying to them, "Go up to Carmel to see Nabal and give him greetings in my name. **25:6** Then you will say to my brother, "Peace to you and your house! Peace to all that is yours! **25:7** Now I hear that they are shearing sheep for you. When your shepherds were with us, we neither insulted them nor harmed them the whole time they were in Carmel. **25:8** Ask your own servants; they can tell you! May my servants find favor in your sight, for we have come at the time of a holiday. Please provide us – your servants and your son David – with whatever you can spare."

25:9 So David's servants went and spoke all these words to Nabal in David's name. Then they paused. **25:10** But Nabal responded to David's servants, "Who is David, and who is this son of Jesse? This is a time when many servants are breaking away from their masters! **25:11** Should I take my bread and my water and my meat that I have slaughtered for my shearers and give them to these men? I don't even know where they came from!"

25:12 So David's servants went on their way. When they had returned, they came and told David all these things. **25:13** Then David instructed his men, "Each of you strap on your sword!" So each one strapped on his sword, and David also strapped on his sword. About four hundred men followed David up, while two hundred stayed behind with the equipment.

25:14 But one of the servants told Nabal's wife Abigail, "David sent messengers from the desert to greet our lord, but he screamed at them. **25:15** These men were very good to us. They did not insult us, nor did we sustain any loss during the entire time we were together in the field. **25:16** Both night and day they were a protective wall for us the entire time we were with them, while we were tending our flocks. **25:17** Now be aware of this, and see what you can do. For disaster has been planned for our lord and his entire household. He is such a wicked person that no one tells him anything!"

25:18 So Abigail quickly took two hundred loaves of bread, two containers of wine, five prepared sheep, five seahs of roasted grain, a hundred bunches of raisins, and two hundred lumps of pressed figs. She loaded them on donkeys **25:19** and said to her servants, "Go on ahead of me. I will come after you." But she did not tell her husband Nabal.

25:20 Riding on her donkey, she went down under cover of the mountain. David and his men were coming down to meet her, and she encountered them. **25:21** Now David had been thinking, "In vain I guarded everything that belonged to this man in the desert. I didn't take anything from him. But he has repaid my good with evil. **25:22** God will severely punish David, if I leave alive until morning even one male from all those who belong to him!"

25:23 When Abigail saw David, she got down quickly from the donkey, threw herself down before David, and bowed to the ground. **25:24** Falling at his feet, she said, "My lord, I accept all the guilt! But please let your female servant speak with my lord! Please listen to the words of your servant! **25:25** My lord should not pay attention to this wicked man Nabal. He simply lives up to his name! His name means 'fool,' and he is indeed foolish! But I, your servant, did not see the servants my lord sent. **25:26** "Now, my lord, as surely as the LORD lives and as surely as you live, it is the LORD who has kept you from shedding blood and taking matters into your own hands. Now may your enemies and those who seek to harm my lord be like Nabal. **25:27** Now let this present that your servant has brought to my lord be given to the servants who follow my lord. **25:28** Please forgive the sin of your servant, for the LORD will certainly establish the house of my lord, because my lord fights the battles of the LORD. May no evil be found in you all your days! **25:29** When someone sets out to chase you and to take your life, the life of my lord will be wrapped securely in the bag of the living by the LORD your God. But he will sling away the lives of your enemies from the sling's pocket! **25:30** The LORD will do for my lord everything that he promised you, and he will make you a leader over Israel. **25:31** Your conscience will not be overwhelmed with guilt for having poured out innocent blood and for having taken matters into your own hands. When the LORD has granted my lord success, please remember your servant."

25:32 Then David said to Abigail, "Praised be the LORD, the God of Israel, who has sent you this day to meet me! **25:33** Praised be your good judgment! May you yourself be rewarded for having prevented me this day from shedding blood and taking matters into my own hands! **25:34** Otherwise, as surely as the LORD, the God of Israel, lives – he who has prevented me from harming you – if you had not come so quickly to meet me, by morning's light not even one male belonging to Nabal would have remained alive!" **25:35** Then David took from her hand what she had brought to him. He said to her, "Go back to your home in peace. Be assured that I have listened to you and responded favorably."

25:36 When Abigail went back to Nabal, he was holding a banquet in his house like that of the king. Nabal was having a good time and was very intoxicated. She told him absolutely nothing until morning's light. **25:37** In the morning, when Nabal was sober, his wife told him about these matters. He had a stroke and was paralyzed. **25:38** After about ten days the LORD struck Nabal down and he died.

25:39 When David heard that Nabal had died, he said, "Praised be the LORD who has vindicated me and avenged the insult that I suffered from Nabal! The LORD has kept his servant from doing evil, and he has repaid Nabal for his evil deeds." Then David sent word to Abigail and asked her to become his wife.

25:40 So the servants of David went to Abigail at Carmel and said to her, "David has sent us to you to bring you back to be his wife." **25:41** She arose, bowed her face toward the ground, and said, "Your female servant, like a lowly servant, will wash the feet of the servants of my lord." **25:42** Then Abigail quickly went and mounted her donkey, with five of her female servants accompanying her. She followed David's messengers and became his wife.

25:43 David had also married Ahinoam from Jezreel; the two of them became his wives. **25:44** (Now Saul had given his daughter Michal, David's wife, to Paltiel son of Laish, who was from Gallim.)

David Spares Saul's Life Again

26:1 The Ziphites came to Saul at Gibeah and said, "Isn't David hiding on the hill of Hakilah near Jeshimon?" **26:2** So Saul arose and went down to the desert of Ziph, accompanied by three thousand select men of Israel, to look for David in the desert of Ziph. **26:3** Saul camped by the road on the hill of Hakilah near Jeshimon, but David was staying in the desert. When he realized that Saul had come to the desert to find him, **26:4** David sent scouts and verified that Saul had indeed arrived.

26:5 So David set out and went to the place where Saul was camped. David saw the place where Saul and Abner son of Ner, the general in command of his army, were sleeping. Now Saul was lying in the entrenchment, and the army was camped all around him. **26:6** David said to Ahimelech the Hittite and Abishai son of Zeruiah, Joab's brother, "Who will go down with me to Saul in the camp?" Abishai replied, "I will go down with you."

26:7 So David and Abishai approached the army at night and found Saul lying asleep in the entrenchment with his spear stuck in the ground by his head. Abner and the army were lying all around him. **26:8** Abishai said to David, "Today God has delivered your enemy into your hands. Now let me drive the spear right through him into the ground with one swift jab! A second jab won't be necessary!"

26:9 But David said to Abishai, "Don't kill him! Who can extend his hand against the LORD's chosen one and remain guiltless?" **26:10** David went on to say, "As the LORD lives, the LORD himself will strike him down. Either his day will come and he will die, or he will go down into battle and be swept away. **26:11** But may the LORD prevent me from extending my hand against the LORD's chosen one! Now take the spear by Saul's head and the jug of water, and let's get out of here!" **26:12** So David took the spear and the jug of water by Saul's head, and they got out of there. No one saw them or was aware of their presence or woke up. All of them were asleep, for the LORD had caused a deep sleep to fall on them.

26:13 Then David crossed to the other side and stood on the top of the hill some distance away; there was a considerable distance between them. **26:14** David called to the army and to Abner son of Ner, "Won't you answer, Abner?" Abner replied, "Who are you, that you have called to the king?" **26:15** David said to Abner, "Aren't you a man? After all, who is like you in Israel? Why then haven't you protected your lord the king? One of the soldiers came to kill your lord the king. **26:16** This failure on your part isn't good! As surely as the LORD lives, you people who have not protected your lord, the LORD's chosen one, are as good as dead! Now look where the king's spear and the jug of water that was by his head are!"

26:17 When Saul recognized David's voice, he said, "Is that your voice, my son David?" David replied, "Yes, it's my voice, my lord the king." **26:18** He went on to say, "Why is my lord chasing his servant? What have I done? What wrong have I done? **26:19** So let my lord the king now listen to the words of his servant. If the LORD has incited you against me, may he take delight in an offering. But if men have instigated this, may they be cursed before the LORD! For they have driven me away this day from being united with the LORD's inheritance, saying, 'Go on, serve other gods!' **26:20** Now don't let my blood fall to the ground away from the LORD's presence, for the king of Israel has gone out to look for a flea the way one looks for a partridge in the hill country."

26:21 Saul replied, "I have sinned. Come back, my son David. I won't harm you, for you treated my life with value this day. I have behaved foolishly and have made a very terrible mistake!" **26:22** David replied, "Here is the king's spear. Let one of your servants cross over and get it. **26:23** The LORD rewards each man for his integrity and loyalty. Even though today the LORD delivered you into my hand, I was not willing to extend my hand against the LORD's chosen one. **26:24** In the same way that I valued your life this day, may the LORD value my life and deliver me from all danger." **26:25** Saul replied to David, "May you be rewarded, my son David! You will without question be successful!" So David went on his way, and Saul returned to his place.

David Aligns Himself with the Philistines

27:1 David thought to himself, "One of these days I'm going to be swept away by the hand of Saul! There is nothing better for me than to escape to the land of the Philistines. Then Saul will despair of searching for me through all the territory of Israel and I will escape from his hand."

27:2 So David left and crossed over to King Achish son of Maoch of Gath accompanied by his six hundred men. **27:3** David settled with Achish in Gath, along with his men and their families. David had with him his two wives, Ahinoam the Jezreelite and Abigail the Carmelite, Nabal's widow. **27:4** When Saul learned that David had fled to Gath, he did not mount a new search for him.

27:5 David said to Achish, "If I have found favor with you, let me be given a place in one of the country towns so that I can live there. Why should your servant settle in the royal city with you?" **27:6** So Achish gave him Ziklag on that day. (For that reason Ziklag has belonged to the kings of Judah until this very day.) **27:7** The length of time that David lived in the Philistine countryside was a year and four months.

27:8 Then David and his men went up and raided the Geshurites, the Girzites, and the Amalekites. (They had been living in that land for a long time, from the approach to Shur as far as the land of Egypt.) **27:9** When David would attack a district, he would leave neither man nor woman alive. He would take sheep, cattle, donkeys, camels, and clothing and would then go back to Achish. **27:10** When Achish would ask, "Where did you raid today?" David would say, "The Negev of Judah" or "The Negev of Jerahmeel" or "The Negev of the Kenites." **27:11** Neither man nor woman would David leave alive so as to bring them back to Gath. He was thinking, "This way they can't tell on us, saying, 'This is what David did.'" Such was his practice the entire time that he lived in the country of the Philistines. **27:12** So Achish trusted David, thinking to himself, "He is really hated among his own people in Israel! From now on he will be my servant."

The Witch of Endor

28:1 In those days the Philistines gathered their troops for war in order to fight Israel. Achish said to David, "You should fully understand that you and your men must go with me into the battle." **28:2** David replied to Achish, "That being the case, you will come to know what your servant can do!" Achish said to David, "Then I will make you my bodyguard from now on."

28:3 Now Samuel had died, and all Israel had lamented over him and had buried him in Ramah, his hometown. In the meantime Saul had removed the mediums and magicians from the land. **28:4** The Philistines assembled; they came and camped at Shunem. Saul mustered all Israel and camped at Gilboa. **28:5** When Saul saw the camp of the Philistines, he was absolutely terrified. **28:6** So Saul inquired of the LORD, but the LORD did not answer him – not by dreams nor by Urim nor by the prophets. **28:7** So Saul instructed his servants, "Find me a woman who is a medium, so that I may go to her and inquire of her." His servants replied to him, "There is a woman who is a medium in Endor."

28:8 So Saul disguised himself and put on other clothing and left, accompanied by two of his men. They came to the woman at night and said, "Use your ritual pit to conjure up for me the one I tell you."

28:9 But the woman said to him, "Look, you are aware of what Saul has done; he has removed the mediums and magicians from the land! Why are you trapping me so you can put me to death?" **28:10** But Saul swore an oath to her by the LORD, "As surely as the LORD lives, you will not incur guilt in this matter!" **28:11** The woman replied, "Who is it that I should bring up for you?" He said, "Bring up for me Samuel."

28:12 When the woman saw Samuel, she cried out loudly. The woman said to Saul, "Why have you deceived me? You are Saul!" **28:13** The king said to her, "Don't be afraid! What have you seen?" The woman replied to Saul, "I have seen one like a god coming up from the ground!" **28:14** He said to her, "What about his appearance?" She said, "An old man is coming up! He is wrapped in a robe!"

Then Saul realized it was Samuel, and he bowed his face toward the ground and kneeled down. **28:15** Samuel said to Saul, "Why have you disturbed me by bringing me up?" Saul replied, "I am terribly troubled! The Philistines are fighting against me and God has turned away from me. He does not answer me – not by the prophets nor by dreams. So I have called on you to tell me what I should do."

28:16 Samuel said, "Why are you asking me, now that the LORD has turned away from you and has become your enemy? **28:17** The LORD has done exactly as I prophesied! The LORD has torn the kingdom from your hand and has given it to your neighbor David! **28:18** Since you did not obey the LORD and did not carry out his fierce anger against the Amalekites, the LORD has done this thing to you today. **28:19** The LORD will hand you and Israel over to the Philistines! Tomorrow both you and your sons will be with me. The LORD will also hand the army of Israel over to the Philistines!"

28:20 Saul quickly fell full length on the ground and was very afraid because of Samuel's words. He was completely drained of energy, not having eaten anything all that day and night. **28:21** When the woman came to Saul and saw how terrified he was, she said to him, "Your servant has done what you asked. I took my life in my own hands and did what you told me. **28:22** Now it's your turn to listen to your servant! Let me set before you a bit of bread so that you can eat. When you regain your strength, you can go on your way."

28:23 But he refused, saying, "I won't eat!" Both his servants and the woman urged him to eat, so he gave in. He got up from the ground and sat down on the bed. **28:24** Now the woman had a well-fed calf at her home that she quickly slaughtered. Taking some flour, she kneaded bread and baked it without leaven. **28:25** She brought it to Saul and his servants, and they ate. Then they arose and left that same night.

David Is Rejected by the Philistine Leaders

29:1 The Philistines assembled all their troops at Aphek, while Israel camped at the spring that is in Jezreel. **29:2** When the leaders of the Philistines were passing in review at the head of their units of hundreds and thousands, David and his men were passing in review in the rear with Achish.

29:3 The leaders of the Philistines asked, "What about these Hebrews?" Achish said to the leaders of the Philistines, "Isn't this David, the servant of King Saul of Israel, who has been with me for quite some time? I have found no fault with him from the day of his defection until the present time!"

29:4 But the leaders of the Philistines became angry with him and said to him, "Send the man back! Let him return to the place that you assigned him! Don't let him go down with us into the battle, for he might become our adversary in the battle. What better way to please his lord than with the heads of these men? **29:5** Isn't this David, of whom they sang as they danced,

'Saul has struck down his thousands,
but David his tens of thousands'?"

29:6 So Achish summoned David and said to him, "As surely as the LORD lives, you are an honest man, and I am glad to have you serving with me in the army. I have found no fault with you from the day that you first came to me until the present time. But in the opinion of the leaders, you are not reliable. **29:7** So turn and leave in peace. You must not do anything that the leaders of the Philistines consider improper!"

29:8 But David said to Achish, "What have I done? What have you found in your servant from the day that I first came into your presence until the present time, that I shouldn't go and fight the enemies of my lord the king?" **29:9** Achish replied to David, "I am convinced that you are as reliable as the angel of God! However, the leaders of the Philistines have said, 'He must not go up with us in the battle.' **29:10** So get up early in the morning along with the servants of your lord who have come with you. When you get up early in the morning, as soon as it is light enough to see, leave."

29:11 So David and his men got up early in the morning to return to the land of the Philistines, but the Philistines went up to Jezreel.

David Defeats the Amalekites

30:1 On the third day David and his men came to Ziklag. Now the Amalekites had raided the Negev and Ziklag. They attacked Ziklag and burned it. **30:2** They took captive the women who were in it, from the youngest to the oldest, but they did not kill anyone. They simply carried them off and went on their way.

30:3 When David and his men came to the city, they found it burned. Their wives, sons, and daughters had been taken captive. **30:4** Then David and the men who were with him wept loudly until they could weep no more. **30:5** David's two wives had been taken captive – Ahinoam the Jezreelite and Abigail the Carmelite, Nabal's widow. **30:6** David was very upset, for the men were thinking of stoning him; each man grieved bitterly over his sons and daughters. But David drew strength from the LORD his God.

30:7 Then David said to the priest Abiathar son of Ahimelech, "Bring me the ephod." So Abiathar brought the ephod to David. **30:8** David inquired of the LORD, saying, "Should I pursue this raiding band? Will I overtake them?" He said to him, "Pursue, for you will certainly overtake them and carry out a rescue!"

30:9 So David went, accompanied by his six hundred men. When he came to the Wadi Besor, those who were in the rear stayed there. **30:10** David and four hundred men continued the pursuit, but two hundred men who were too exhausted to cross the Wadi Besor stayed there.

30:11 Then they found an Egyptian in the field and brought him to David. They gave him bread to eat and water to drink. **30:12** They gave him a slice of pressed figs and two bunches of raisins to eat. This greatly refreshed him, for he had not eaten food or drunk water for three days and three nights. **30:13** David said to him, "To whom do you belong, and where are you from?" The young man said, "I am an Egyptian, the servant of an Amalekite man. My master abandoned me when I was ill for three days. **30:14** We conducted a raid on the Negev of the Kerethites, on the area of Judah, and on the Negev of Caleb. We burned Ziklag." **30:15** David said to him, "Can you take us down to this raiding party?" He said, "Swear to me by God that you will not kill me or hand me over to my master, and I will take you down to this raiding party."

30:16 So he took David down, and they found them spread out over the land. They were eating and drinking and enjoying themselves because of all the loot they had taken from the land of the Philistines and from the land of Judah. **30:17** But David struck them down from twilight until the following evening. None of them escaped, with the exception of four hundred young men who got away on camels. **30:18** David retrieved everything the Amalekites had taken; he also rescued his two wives. **30:19** There was nothing missing, whether small or great. He retrieved sons and daughters, the plunder, and everything else they had taken. David brought everything back. **30:20** David took all the flocks and herds and drove them in front of the rest of the animals. People were saying, "This is David's plunder!"

30:21 Then David approached the two hundred men who had been too exhausted to go with him, those whom they had left at the Wadi Besor. They went out to meet David and the people who were with him. When David approached the people, he asked how they were doing. **30:22** But all the evil and worthless men among those who had gone with David said, "Since they didn't go with us, we won't give them any of the loot we retrieved! They may take only their wives and children. Let them lead them away and be gone!"

30:23 But David said, "No! You shouldn't do this, my brothers. Look at what the LORD has given us! He has protected us and has delivered into our hands the raiding party that came against us. **30:24** Who will listen to you in this matter? The portion of the one who went down into the battle will be the same as the portion of the one who remained with the equipment! Let their portions be the same!"

30:25 From that time onward it was a binding ordinance for Israel, right up to the present time.

30:26 When David came to Ziklag, he sent some of the plunder to the elders of Judah who were his friends, saying, "Here's a gift for you from the looting of the LORD's enemies!" **30:27** The gift was for those in the following locations: for those in Bethel, Ramoth Negev, and Jattir; **30:28** for those in Aroer, Siphmoth, Eshtemoa, **30:29** and Racal; for those in the cities of the Jerahmeelites and Kenites; **30:30** for those in Hormah, Bor Ashan, Athach, **30:31** and Hebron; and for those in whatever other places David and his men had traveled.

The Death of Saul

31:1 Now the Philistines were fighting against Israel. The men of Israel fled from the Philistines and many of them fell dead on Mount Gilboa. **31:2** The Philistines stayed right on the heels of Saul and his sons. They struck down Saul's sons Jonathan, Abinadab, and Malki-Shua. **31:3** Saul himself was in the thick of the battle; the archers spotted him and wounded him severely.

31:4 Saul said to his armor bearer, "Draw your sword and stab me with it! Otherwise these uncircumcised people will come, stab me, and torture me." But his armor bearer refused to do it, because he was very afraid. So Saul took his sword and fell on it. **31:5** When his armor bearer saw that Saul was dead, he also fell on his own sword and died with him. **31:6** So Saul, his three sons, his armor bearer, and all his men died together that day.

31:7 When the men of Israel who were in the valley and across the Jordan saw that the men of Israel had fled and that Saul and his sons were dead, they abandoned the cities and fled. The Philistines came and occupied them.

31:8 The next day, when the Philistines came to strip loot from the corpses, they discovered Saul and his three sons lying dead on Mount Gilboa. **31:9** They cut off Saul's head and stripped him of his armor. They sent messengers to announce the news in the temple of their idols and among their people throughout the surrounding land of the Philistines. **31:10** They placed Saul's armor in the temple of the Ashtoreths and hung his corpse on the city wall of Beth Shan.

31:11 When the residents of Jabesh Gilead heard what the Philistines had done to Saul, **31:12** all their warriors set out and traveled throughout the night. They took Saul's corpse and the corpses of his sons from the city wall of Beth Shan and went to Jabesh, where they burned them. **31:13** They took the bones and buried them under the tamarisk tree at Jabesh; then they fasted for seven days.

Book 10. 2 Samuel

David Learns of the Deaths of Saul and Jonathan

1:1 After the death of Saul, when David had returned from defeating the Amalekites, he stayed at Ziklag for two days. **1:2** On the third day a man arrived from the camp of Saul with his clothes torn and dirt on his head. When he approached David, the man threw himself to the ground.

1:3 David asked him, "Where are you coming from?" He replied, "I have escaped from the camp of Israel." **1:4** David inquired, "How were things going? Tell me!" He replied, "The people fled from the battle and many of them fell dead. Even Saul and his son Jonathan are dead!" **1:5** David said to the young man who was telling him this, "How do you know that Saul and his son Jonathan are dead?" **1:6** The young man who was telling him this said, "I just happened to be on Mount Gilboa and came across Saul leaning on his spear for support. The chariots and leaders of the horsemen were in hot pursuit of him. **1:7** When he turned around and saw me, he called out to me. I answered, 'Here I am!' **1:8** He asked me, 'Who are you?' I told him, 'I'm an Amalekite.' **1:9** He said to me, 'Stand over me and finish me off! I'm very dizzy, even though I'm still alive.' **1:10** So I stood over him and put him to death, since I knew that he couldn't live in such a condition. Then I took the crown which was on his head and the bracelet which was on his arm. I have brought them here to my lord."

1:11 David then grabbed his own clothes and tore them, as did all the men who were with him. **1:12** They lamented and wept and fasted until evening because of Saul, his son Jonathan, the LORD's people, and the house of Israel had fallen by the sword.

1:13 David said to the young man who told this to him, "Where are you from?" He replied, "I am an Amalekite, the son of a resident foreigner." **1:14** David replied to him, "How is it that you were not afraid to reach out your hand to destroy the LORD's anointed?" **1:15** Then David called one of the soldiers and said, "Come here and strike him down!" So he struck him down, and he died. **1:16** David said to him, "Your blood be on your own head! Your own mouth has testified against you, saying 'I have put the LORD's anointed to death.'"

David's Tribute to Saul and Jonathan

1:17 Then David chanted this lament over Saul and his son Jonathan. **1:18** (He gave instructions that the people of Judah should be taught "The Bow." Indeed, it is written down in the Book of Yashar.)

1:19 The beauty of Israel lies slain on your high places!
How the mighty have fallen!

1:20 Don't report it in Gath,
don't spread the news in the streets of Ashkelon,
or the daughters of the Philistines will rejoice,
the daughters of the uncircumcised will celebrate!

1:21 O mountains of Gilboa,
may there be no dew or rain on you, nor fields of grain offerings!
For it was there that the shield of warriors was defiled;
the shield of Saul lies neglected without oil.

1:22 From the blood of the slain, from the fat of warriors,
the bow of Jonathan was not turned away.
The sword of Saul never returned empty.

1:23 Saul and Jonathan were greatly loved during their lives,
and not even in their deaths were they separated.
They were swifter than eagles, stronger than lions.

1:24 O daughters of Israel, weep over Saul,
who clothed you in scarlet as well as jewelry,
who put gold jewelry on your clothes.

1:25 How the warriors have fallen
in the midst of battle!
Jonathan lies slain on your high places!
1:26 I grieve over you, my brother Jonathan!
You were very dear to me.
Your love was more special to me than the love of women.
1:27 How the warriors have fallen!
The weapons of war are destroyed!

David is Anointed King

2:1 Afterward David inquired of the LORD, "Should I go up to one of the cities of Judah?" The LORD told him, "Go up." David asked, "Where should I go?" The LORD replied, "To Hebron." **2:2** So David went up, along with his two wives, Ahinoam the Jezreelite and Abigail, formerly the wife of Nabal the Carmelite. **2:3** David also brought along the men who were with him, each with his family. They settled in the cities of Hebron. **2:4** The men of Judah came and there they anointed David as king over the people of Judah.

David was told, "The people of Jabesh Gilead are the ones who buried Saul." **2:5** So David sent messengers to the people of Jabesh Gilead and told them, "May you be blessed by the LORD because you have shown this kindness to your lord Saul by burying him. **2:6** Now may the LORD show you true kindness! I also will reward you, because you have done this deed. **2:7** Now be courageous and prove to be valiant warriors, for your lord Saul is dead. The people of Judah have anointed me as king over them."

David's Army Clashes with the Army of Saul

2:8 Now Abner son of Ner, the general in command of Saul's army, had taken Saul's son Ish-bosheth and had brought him to Mahanaim. **2:9** He appointed him king over Gilead, the Geshurites, Jezreel, Ephraim, Benjamin, and all Israel. **2:10** Ish-bosheth son of Saul was forty years old when he began to rule over Israel. He ruled two years. However, the people of Judah followed David. **2:11** David was king in Hebron over the people of Judah for seven and a half years.

2:12 Then Abner son of Ner and the servants of Ish-bosheth son of Saul went out from Mahanaim to Gibeon. **2:13** Joab son of Zeruiah and the servants of David also went out and confronted them at the pool of Gibeon. One group stationed themselves on one side of the pool, and the other group on the other side of the pool. **2:14** Abner said to Joab, "Let the soldiers get up and fight before us." Joab said, "So be it!"

2:15 So they got up and crossed over by number: twelve belonging to Benjamin and to Ish-bosheth son of Saul, and twelve from the servants of David. **2:16** As they grappled with one another, each one stabbed his opponent with his sword and they fell dead together. So that place is called the Field of Flints; it is in Gibeon. **2:17** Now the battle was very severe that day; Abner and the men of Israel were overcome by David's soldiers. **2:18** The three sons of Zeruiah were there – Joab, Abishai, and Asahel. (Now Asahel was as quick on his feet as one of the gazelles in the field.) **2:19** Asahel chased Abner, without turning to the right or to the left as he followed Abner. **2:20** Then Abner turned and asked, "Is that you, Asahel?" He replied, "Yes it is!" **2:21** Abner said to him, "Turn aside to your right or to your left. Capture one of the soldiers and take his equipment for yourself!" But Asahel was not willing to turn aside from following him. **2:22** So Abner spoke again to Asahel, "Turn aside from following me! I do not want to strike you to the ground. How then could I show my face in the presence of Joab your brother?" **2:23** But Asahel refused to turn aside. So Abner struck him in the abdomen with the back end of his spear. The spear came out his back; Asahel collapsed on the spot and died there right before Abner. Everyone who now comes to the place where Asahel fell dead pauses in respect. **2:24** So Joab and Abishai chased Abner. At sunset they came to the hill of Ammah near Giah on the way to the wilderness of Gibeon. **2:25** The Benjaminites formed their ranks behind Abner and were like a single army, standing at the top of a certain hill. **2:26** Then Abner called out to Joab, "Must the sword devour forever? Don't you realize that this will turn bitter in the end? When will you tell the people to turn aside from pursuing their brothers?" **2:27** Joab replied, "As surely as God lives, if you had not said this, it would have been morning before the people would have abandoned pursuit of their brothers!" **2:28** Then Joab blew the ram's horn and all the people stopped in their tracks. They stopped chasing Israel and ceased fighting. **2:29** Abner and his men went through the Arabah all that night. They crossed the Jordan River and went through the whole region of Bitron and came to Mahanaim.

2:30 Now Joab returned from chasing Abner and assembled all the people. Nineteen of David's soldiers were missing, in addition to Asahel. **2:31** But David's soldiers had slaughtered the Benjaminites and Abner's men – in all, 360 men had died! **2:32** They took Asahel's body and buried him in his father's tomb at Bethlehem. Joab and his men then traveled all that night and reached Hebron by dawn. **3:1** However, the war was prolonged between the house of Saul and the house of David. David was becoming steadily stronger, while the house of Saul was becoming increasingly weaker.

3:2 Now sons were born to David in Hebron. His firstborn was Amnon, born to Ahinoam the Jezreelite. **3:3** His second son was Kileab, born to Abigail the widow of Nabal the Carmelite. His third son was Absalom, the son of Maacah daughter of King Talmai of Geshur. **3:4** His fourth son was Adonijah, the son of Haggith. His fifth son was Shephatiah, the son of Abitail. **3:5** His sixth son was Ithream, born to David's wife Eglah. These sons were all born to David in Hebron.

Abner Defects to David's Camp

3:6 As the war continued between the house of Saul and the house of David, Abner was becoming more influential in the house of Saul. **3:7** Now Saul had a concubine named Rizpah daughter of Aiah. Ish-bosheth said to Abner, "Why did you have sexual relations with my father's concubine?"

3:8 These words of Ish-bosheth really angered Abner and he said, "Am I the head of a dog that belongs to Judah? This very day I am demonstrating loyalty to the house of Saul your father and to his relatives and his friends! I have not betrayed you into the hand of David. Yet you have accused me of sinning with this woman today! **3:9** God will severely judge Abner if I do not do for David exactly what the LORD has promised him, **3:10** namely, to transfer the kingdom from the house of Saul and to establish the throne of David over Israel and over Judah all the way from Dan to Beer Sheba!" **3:11** Ish-bosheth was unable to answer Abner with even a single word because he was afraid of him.

3:12 Then Abner sent messengers to David saying, "To whom does the land belong? Make an agreement with me, and I will do whatever I can to cause all Israel to turn to you." **3:13** So David said, "Good! I will make an agreement with you. I ask only one thing from you. You will not see my face unless you bring Saul's daughter Michal when you come to visit me."

3:14 David sent messengers to Ish-bosheth son of Saul with this demand: "Give me my wife Michal whom I acquired for a hundred Philistine foreskins." **3:15** So Ish-bosheth took her from her husband Paltiel son of Laish. **3:16** Her husband went along behind her, weeping all the way to Bahurim. Finally Abner said to him, "Go back!" So he returned home.

3:17 Abner advised the elders of Israel, "Previously you were wanting David to be your king. **3:18** Act now! For the LORD has said to David, 'By the hand of my servant David I will save my people Israel from the Philistines and from all their enemies.'"

3:19 Then Abner spoke privately with the Benjaminites. Abner also went to Hebron to inform David privately of all that Israel and the entire house of Benjamin had agreed to. **3:20** When Abner, accompanied by twenty men, came to David in Hebron, David prepared a banquet for Abner and the men who were with him. **3:21** Abner said to David, "Let me leave so that I may go and gather all Israel to my lord the king so that they may make an agreement with you. Then you will rule over all that you desire." So David sent Abner away, and he left in peace.

Abner Is Killed

3:22 Now David's soldiers and Joab were coming back from a raid, bringing a great deal of plunder with them. Abner was no longer with David in Hebron, for David had sent him away and he had left in peace. **3:23** When Joab and all the army that was with him arrived, Joab was told: "Abner the son of Ner came to the king; he sent him away, and he left in peace!"

3:24 So Joab went to the king and said, "What have you done? Abner has come to you! Why would you send him away? Now he's gone on his way! **3:25** You know Abner the son of Ner! Surely he came here to spy on you and to determine when you leave and when you return and to discover everything that you are doing!"

3:26 Then Joab left David and sent messengers after Abner. They brought him back from the well of Sirah. (But David was not aware of it.) **3:27** When Abner returned to Hebron, Joab took him aside at the gate as if to speak privately with him. Joab then stabbed him in the abdomen and killed him, avenging the shed blood of his brother Asahel.

3:28 When David later heard about this, he said, "I and my kingdom are forever innocent before the LORD of the shed blood of Abner son of Ner! **3:29** May his blood whirl over the head of Joab and the entire house of his father! May the males of Joab's house never cease to have someone with a running sore or a skin disease or one who works at the spindle or one who falls by the sword or one who lacks food!"

3:30 So Joab and his brother Abishai killed Abner, because he had killed their brother Asahel in Gibeon during the battle.

3:31 David instructed Joab and all the people who were with him, "Tear your clothes! Put on sackcloth! Lament before Abner!" Now King David followed behind the funeral bier. **3:32** So they buried Abner in Hebron. The king cried loudly over Abner's grave and all the people wept too. **3:33** The king chanted the following lament for Abner:

"Should Abner have died like a fool?
3:34 Your hands were not bound,
and your feet were not put into irons.
You fell the way one falls before criminals."

All the people wept over him again. **3:35** Then all the people came and encouraged David to eat food while it was still day. But David took an oath saying, "God will punish me severely if I taste bread or anything whatsoever before the sun sets!"

3:36 All the people noticed this and it pleased them. In fact, everything the king did pleased all the people. **3:37** All the people and all Israel realized on that day that the killing of Abner son of Ner was not done at the king's instigation.

3:38 Then the king said to his servants, "Do you not realize that a great leader has fallen this day in Israel? **3:39** Today I am weak, even though I am anointed as king. These men, the sons of Zeruiah, are too much for me to bear! May the LORD punish appropriately the one who has done this evil thing!"

Ish-bosheth is killed

4:1 When Ish-bosheth the son of Saul heard that Abner had died in Hebron, he was very disheartened, and all Israel was afraid. **4:2** Now Saul's son had two men who were in charge of raiding units; one was named Baanah and the other Recab. They were sons of Rimmon the Beerothite, who was a Benjaminite. (Beeroth is regarded as belonging to Benjamin, **4:3** for the Beerothites fled to Gittaim and have remained there as resident foreigners until the present time.)

4:4 Now Saul's son Jonathan had a son who was crippled in both feet. He was five years old when the news about Saul and Jonathan arrived from Jezreel. His nurse picked him up and fled, but in her haste to get away, he fell and was injured. Mephibosheth was his name.

4:5 Now the sons of Rimmon the Beerothite – Recab and Baanah – went at the hottest part of the day to the home of Ish-bosheth, as he was enjoying his midday rest. **4:6** They entered the house under the pretense of getting wheat and mortally wounded him in the stomach. Then Recab and his brother Baanah escaped.

4:7 They had entered the house while Ish-bosheth was resting on his bed in his bedroom. They mortally wounded him and then cut off his head. Taking his head, they traveled on the way of the Arabah all that night. **4:8** They brought the head of Ish-bosheth to David in Hebron, saying to the king, "Look! The head of Ish-bosheth son of Saul, your enemy who sought your life! The LORD has granted vengeance to my lord the king this day against Saul and his descendants!"

4:9 David replied to Recab and his brother Baanah, the sons of Rimmon the Beerothite, "As surely as the LORD lives, who has delivered my life from all adversity, **4:10** when someone told me that Saul was dead – even though he thought he was bringing good news – I seized him and killed him in Ziklag. That was the good news I gave to him! **4:11** Surely when wicked men have killed an innocent man as he slept in his own house, should I not now require his blood from your hands and remove you from the earth?"

4:12 So David issued orders to the soldiers and they put them to death. Then they cut off their hands and feet and hung them near the pool in Hebron. But they took the head of Ish-bosheth and buried it in the tomb of Abner in Hebron.

David Is Anointed King Over Israel

5:1 All the tribes of Israel came to David at Hebron saying, "Look, we are your very flesh and blood! **5:2** In the past, when Saul was our king, you were the real leader in Israel. The LORD said to you, 'You will shepherd my people Israel; you will rule over Israel.'"

5:3 When all the leaders of Israel came to the king at Hebron, King David made an agreement with them in Hebron before the LORD. They designated David as king over Israel. **5:4** David was thirty years old when he began to reign and he reigned for forty years. **5:5** In Hebron he reigned over Judah for seven years and six months, and in Jerusalem he reigned for thirty-three years over all Israel and Judah.

David Occupies Jerusalem

5:6 Then the king and his men advanced to Jerusalem against the Jebusites who lived in the land. The Jebusites said to David, "You cannot invade this place! Even the blind and the lame will turn you back, saying, 'David cannot invade this place!'"

5:7 But David captured the fortress of Zion (that is, the city of David). **5:8** David said on that day, "Whoever attacks the Jebusites must approach the 'lame' and the 'blind' who are David's enemies by going through the water tunnel." For this reason it is said, "The blind and the lame cannot enter the palace."

5:9 So David lived in the fortress and called it the City of David. David built all around it, from the terrace inwards. **5:10** David's power grew steadily, for the LORD God who commands armies was with him.

5:11 King Hiram of Tyre sent messengers to David, along with cedar logs, carpenters, and stonemasons. They built a palace for David. **5:12** David realized that the LORD had established him as king over Israel and that he had elevated his kingdom for the sake of his people Israel. **5:13** David married more concubines and wives from Jerusalem after he arrived from Hebron. Even more sons and daughters were born to David.

5:14 These are the names of children born to him in Jerusalem: Shammua, Shobab, Nathan, Solomon, **5:15** Ibhar, Elishua, Nepheg, Japhia, **5:16** Elishama, Eliada, and Eliphelet.

Conflict with the Philistines

5:17 When the Philistines heard that David had been designated king over Israel, they all went up to search for David. When David heard about it, he went down to the fortress. **5:18** Now the Philistines had arrived and spread out in the valley of Rephaim. **5:19** So David asked the LORD, "Should I march up against the Philistines? Will you hand them over to me?" The LORD said to David, "March up, for I will indeed hand the Philistines over to you."

5:20 So David marched against Baal Perazim and defeated them there. Then he said, "The LORD has burst out against my enemies like water bursts out." So he called the name of that place Baal Perazim. **5:21** The Philistines abandoned their idols there, and David and his men picked them up.

5:22 The Philistines again came up and spread out in the valley of Rephaim. **5:23** So David asked the LORD what he should do. This time the LORD said to him, "Don't march straight up. Instead, circle around behind them and come against them opposite the trees. **5:24** When you hear the sound of marching in the tops of the trees, act decisively. For at that moment the LORD is going before you to strike down the army of the Philistines." **5:25** David did just as the LORD commanded him, and he struck down the Philistines from Gibeon all the way to Gezer.

David Brings the Ark to Jerusalem

6:1 David again assembled all the best men in Israel, thirty thousand in number. **6:2** David and all the men who were with him traveled to Baalah in Judah to bring up from there the ark of God which is called by the name of the LORD of hosts, who sits enthroned between the cherubim that are on it. **6:3** They loaded the ark of God on a new cart and carried it from the house of Abinadab, which was on the hill. Uzzah and Ahio, the sons of Abinadab, were guiding the new cart. **6:4** They brought it with the ark of God up from the house of Abinadab on the hill. Ahio was walking in front of the ark, **6:5** while David and all Israel were energetically celebrating before the LORD, singing and playing various stringed instruments, tambourines, rattles, and cymbals.

6:6 When they arrived at the threshing floor of Nacon, Uzzah reached out and grabbed hold of the ark of God, because the oxen stumbled. **6:7** The LORD was so furious with Uzzah, he killed him on the spot for his negligence. He died right there beside the ark of God.

6:8 David was angry because the LORD attacked Uzzah; so he called that place Perez Uzzah, which remains its name to this very day. **6:9** David was afraid of the LORD that day and said, "How will the ark of the LORD ever come to me?" **6:10** So David was no longer willing to bring the ark of the LORD to be with him in the City of David. David left it in the house of Obed-Edom the Gittite. **6:11** The ark of the LORD remained in the house of Obed-Edom the Gittite for three months. The LORD blessed Obed-Edom and all his family. **6:12** David was told, "The LORD has blessed the family of Obed-Edom and everything he owns because of the ark of God." So David went and joyfully brought the ark of God from the house of Obed-Edom to the City of David. **6:13** Those who carried the ark of the LORD took six steps and then David sacrificed an ox and a fatling calf. **6:14** Now David, wearing a linen ephod, was dancing with all his strength before the LORD. **6:15** David and all Israel were bringing up the ark of the LORD, shouting and blowing trumpets.

6:16 As the ark of the LORD entered the City of David, Saul's daughter Michal looked out the window. When she saw King David leaping and dancing before the LORD, she despised him. **6:17** They brought the ark of the LORD and put it in its place in the middle of the tent that David had pitched for it. Then David offered burnt sacrifices and peace offerings before the LORD. **6:18** When David finished offering the burnt sacrifices and peace offerings, he pronounced a blessing over the people in the name of the LORD of hosts. **6:19** He then handed out to each member of the entire assembly of Israel, both men and women, a portion of bread, a date cake, and a raisin cake. Then all the people went home. **6:20** When David went home to pronounce a blessing on his own house, Michal, Saul's daughter, came out to meet him. She said, "How the king of Israel has distinguished himself this day! He has exposed himself today before his servants' slave girls the way a vulgar fool might do!"

6:21 David replied to Michal, "It was before the LORD! I was celebrating before the LORD, who chose me over your father and his entire family and appointed me as leader over the LORD's people Israel. **6:22** I am willing to shame and humiliate myself even more than this! But with the slave girls whom you mentioned let me be distinguished!" **6:23** Now Michal, Saul's daughter, had no children to the day of her death.

The Lord Establishes a Covenant with David

7:1 The king settled into his palace, for the LORD gave him relief from all his enemies on all sides. **7:2** The king said to Nathan the prophet, "Look! I am living in a palace made from cedar, while the ark of God sits in the middle of a tent." **7:3** Nathan replied to the king, "You should go and do whatever you have in mind, for the LORD is with you." **7:4** That night the LORD told Nathan, **7:5** "Go, tell my servant David: 'This is what the LORD says: Do you really intend to build a house for me to live in? **7:6** I have not lived in a house from the time I brought the Israelites up from Egypt to the present day. Instead, I was traveling with them and living in a tent. **7:7** Wherever I moved among all the Israelites, I did not say to any of the leaders whom I appointed to care for my people Israel, "Why have you not built me a house made from cedar?"'

7:8 "So now, say this to my servant David: 'This is what the LORD of hosts says: I took you from the pasture and from your work as a shepherd to make you leader of my people Israel. **7:9** I was with you wherever you went, and I defeated all your enemies before you. Now I will make you as famous as the great men of the earth. **7:10** I will establish a place for my people Israel and settle them there; they will live there and not be disturbed any more. Violent men will not oppress them again, as they did in the beginning **7:11** and during the time when I appointed judges to lead my people Israel. Instead, I will give you relief from all your enemies. The LORD declares to you that he himself will build a dynastic house for you. **7:12** When the time comes for you to die, I will raise up your descendant, one of your own sons, to succeed you, and I will establish his kingdom. **7:13** He will build a house for my name, and I will make his dynasty permanent. **7:14** I will become his father and he will become my son. When he sins, I will correct him with the rod of men and with wounds inflicted by human beings. **7:15** But my loyal love will not be removed from him as I removed it from Saul, whom I removed from before you. **7:16** Your house and your kingdom will stand before me permanently; your dynasty will be permanent.'" **7:17** Nathan told David all these words that were revealed to him.

David Offers a Prayer to God

7:18 King David went in, sat before the LORD, and said, "Who am I, O LORD God, and what is my family, that you should have brought me to this point? **7:19** And you didn't stop there, O LORD God! You have also spoken about the future of your servant's family. Is this your usual way of dealing with men, O LORD God? **7:20** What more can David say to you? You have given your servant special recognition, O LORD God! **7:21** For the sake of your promise and according to your purpose you have done this great thing in order to reveal it to your servant. **7:22** Therefore you are great, O LORD God, for there is none like you! There is no God besides you! What we have heard is true! **7:23** Who is like your people, Israel, a unique nation on the earth? Their God went to claim a nation for himself and to make a name for himself! You did great and awesome acts for your land, before your people whom you delivered for yourself from the Egyptian empire and its gods. **7:24** You made Israel your very own people for all time. You, O LORD, became their God. **7:25** So now, O LORD God, make this promise you have made about your servant and his family a permanent reality. Do as you promised, **7:26** so you may gain lasting fame, as people say, 'The LORD of hosts is God over Israel!' The dynasty of your servant David will be established before you, **7:27** for you, O LORD of hosts, the God of Israel, have told your servant, 'I will build you a dynastic house.' That is why your servant has had the courage to pray this prayer to you. **7:28** Now, O sovereign LORD, you are the true God! May your words prove to be true! You have made this good promise to your servant! **7:29** Now be willing to bless your servant's dynasty so that it may stand permanently before you, for you, O sovereign LORD, have spoken. By your blessing may your servant's dynasty be blessed on into the future!"

David Subjugates Nearby Nations

8:1 Later David defeated the Philistines and subdued them. David took Metheg Ammah from the Philistines. **8:2** He defeated the Moabites. He made them lie on the ground and then used a rope to measure them off. He put two-thirds of them to death and spared the other third. The Moabites became David's subjects and brought tribute. **8:3** David defeated King Hadadezer son of Rehob of Zobah when he came to reestablish his authority over the Euphrates River. **8:4** David seized from him 1,700 charioteers and 20,000 infantrymen. David cut the hamstrings of all but a hundred of the chariot horses. **8:5** The Arameans of Damascus came to help King Hadadezer of Zobah, but David killed 22,000 of the Arameans. **8:6** David placed garrisons in the territory of the Arameans of Damascus; the Arameans became David's subjects and brought tribute. The LORD protected David wherever he campaigned. **8:7** David took the golden shields that belonged to Hadadezer's servants and brought them to Jerusalem. **8:8** From Tebah and Berothai, Hadadezer's cities, King David took a great deal of bronze.

8:9 When King Toi of Hamath heard that David had defeated the entire army of Hadadezer, **8:10** he sent his son Joram to King David to extend his best wishes and to pronounce a blessing on him for his victory over Hadadezer, for Toi had been at war with Hadadezer. He brought with him various items made of silver, gold, and bronze. **8:11** King David dedicated these things to the LORD, along with the dedicated silver and gold that he had taken from all the nations that he had subdued, **8:12** including Aram, Moab, the Ammonites, the Philistines, and Amelek. This also included some of the plunder taken from King Hadadezer son of Rehob of Zobah.

8:13 David became famous when he returned from defeating the Arameans in the Valley of Salt, he defeated 18,000 in all. **8:14** He placed garrisons throughout Edom, and all the Edomites became David's subjects. The LORD protected David wherever he campaigned. **8:15** David reigned over all Israel; he guaranteed justice for all his people.

David's Cabinet

8:16 Joab son of Zeruiah was general in command of the army; Jehoshaphat son of Ahilud was secretary; **8:17** Zadok son of Ahitub and Ahimelech son of Abiathar were priests; Seraiah was scribe; **8:18** Benaiah son of Jehoida supervised the Kerithites and Pelethites; and David's sons were priests.

David Finds Mephibosheth

9:1 Then David asked, "Is anyone still left from the family of Saul, so that I may extend kindness to him for the sake of Jonathan?" **9:2** Now there was a servant from Saul's house named Ziba, so he was summoned to David. The king asked him, "Are you Ziba?" He replied, "At your service." **9:3** The king asked, "Is there not someone left from Saul's family, that I may extend God's kindness to him?" Ziba said to the king, "One of Jonathan's sons is left; both of his feet are crippled." **9:4** The king asked him, "Where is he?" Ziba told the king, "He is at the house of Makir son of Ammiel in Lo Debar."

9:5 So King David had him brought from the house of Makir son of Ammiel in Lo Debar. **9:6** When Mephibosheth son of Jonathan, the son of Saul, came to David, he bowed low with his face toward the ground. David said, "Mephibosheth?" He replied, "Yes, at your service."

9:7 David said to him, "Don't be afraid, because I will certainly extend kindness to you for the sake of Jonathan your father. You will be a regular guest at my table." **9:8** Then Mephibosheth bowed and said, "Of what importance am I, your servant, that you show regard for a dead dog like me?"

9:9 Then the king summoned Ziba, Saul's attendant, and said to him, "Everything that belonged to Saul and to his entire house I hereby give to your master's grandson. **9:10** You will cultivate the land for him – you and your sons and your servants. You will bring its produce and it will be food for your master's grandson to eat. But Mephibosheth, your master's grandson, will be a regular guest at my table." (Now Ziba had fifteen sons and twenty servants.)

9:11 Ziba said to the king, "Your servant will do everything that my lord the king has instructed his servant to do." So Mephibosheth was a regular guest at David's table, just as though he were one of the king's sons.

9:12 Now Mephibosheth had a young son whose name was Mica. All the members of Ziba's household were Mephibosheth's servants. **9:13** Mephibosheth was living in Jerusalem, for he was a regular guest at the king's table. But both his feet were crippled.

David and the Ammonites

10:1 Later the king of the Ammonites died and his son Hanun succeeded him. **10:2** David said, "I will express my loyalty to Hanun son of Nahash just as his father was loyal to me." So David sent his servants with a message expressing sympathy over his father's death. When David's servants entered the land of the Ammonites, **10:3** the Ammonite officials said to their lord Hanun, "Do you really think David is trying to honor your father by sending these messengers to express his sympathy? No, David has sent his servants to you to get information about the city and spy on it so they can overthrow it!"

10:4 So Hanun seized David's servants and shaved off half of each one's beard. He cut the lower part of their robes off so that their buttocks were exposed, and then sent them away. **10:5** Messengers told David what had happened, so he summoned them, for the men were thoroughly humiliated. The king said, "Stay in Jericho until your beards have grown again; then you may come back."

10:6 When the Ammonites realized that David was disgusted with them, they sent and hired 20,000 foot soldiers from Aram Beth Rehob and Aram Zobah, in addition to 1,000 men from the king of Maacah and 12,000 men from Ish-tob.

10:7 When David heard the news, he sent Joab and the entire army to meet them. **10:8** The Ammonites marched out and were deployed for battle at the entrance of the city gate, while the men from Aram Zobah, Rehob, Ish-tob, and Maacah were by themselves in the field.

10:9 When Joab saw that the battle would be fought on two fronts, he chose some of Israel's best men and deployed them against the Arameans. **10:10** He put his brother Abishai in charge of the rest of the army and they were deployed against the Ammonites. **10:11** Joab said, "If the Arameans start to overpower me, you come to my rescue. If the Ammonites start to overpower you, I will come to your rescue. **10:12** Be strong! Let's fight bravely for the sake of our people and the cities of our God! The LORD will do what he decides is best!"

10:13 So Joab and his men marched out to do battle with the Arameans, and they fled before him. **10:14** When the Ammonites saw the Arameans flee, they fled before his brother Abishai and went into the city. Joab withdrew from fighting the Ammonites and returned to Jerusalem.

10:15 When the Arameans realized that they had been defeated by Israel, they consolidated their forces. **10:16** Then Hadadezer sent for Arameans from beyond the Euphrates River, and they came to Helam. Shobach, the general in command of Hadadezer's army, led them.

10:17 When David was informed, he gathered all Israel, crossed the Jordan River, and came to Helam. The Arameans deployed their forces against David and fought with him. **10:18** The Arameans fled before Israel. David killed 700 Aramean charioteers and 40,000 foot soldiers. He also struck down Shobach, the general in command of the army, who died there. **10:19** When all the kings who were subject to Hadadezer saw they were defeated by Israel, they made peace with Israel and became subjects of Israel. The Arameans were no longer willing to help the Ammonites.

David Commits Adultery with Bathsheba

11:1 In the spring of the year, at the time when kings normally conduct wars, David sent out Joab with his officers and the entire Israelite army. They defeated the Ammonites and besieged Rabbah. But David stayed behind in Jerusalem. **11:2** One evening David got up from his bed and walked around on the roof of his palace. From the roof he saw a woman bathing. Now this woman was very attractive. **11:3** So David sent someone to inquire about the woman. The messenger said, "Isn't this Bathsheba, the daughter of Eliam, the wife of Uriah the Hittite?"

11:4 David sent some messengers to get her. She came to him and he had sexual relations with her. (Now at that time she was in the process of purifying herself from her menstrual uncleanness.) Then she returned to her home. **11:5** The woman conceived and then sent word to David saying, "I'm pregnant."

11:6 So David sent a message to Joab that said, "Send me Uriah the Hittite." So Joab sent Uriah to David. **11:7** When Uriah came to him, David asked about how Joab and the army were doing and how the campaign was going. **11:8** Then David said to Uriah, "Go down to your home and relax." When Uriah left the palace, the king sent a gift to him. **11:9** But Uriah stayed at the door of the palace with all the servants of his lord. He did not go down to his house.

11:10 So they informed David, "Uriah has not gone down to his house." So David said to Uriah, "Haven't you just arrived from a journey? Why haven't you gone down to your house?" **11:11** Uriah replied to David, "The ark and Israel and Judah reside in temporary shelters, and my lord Joab and my lord's soldiers are camping in the open field. Should I go to my house to eat and drink and have marital relations with my wife? As surely as you are alive, I will not do this thing!" **11:12** So David said to Uriah, "Stay here another day. Tomorrow I will send you back." So Uriah stayed in Jerusalem both that day and the following one. **11:13** Then David summoned him. He ate and drank with him, and got him drunk. But in the evening he went out to sleep on his bed with the servants of his lord; he did not go down to his own house.

11:14 In the morning David wrote a letter to Joab and sent it with Uriah. **11:15** In the letter he wrote: "Station Uriah in the thick of the battle and then withdraw from him so he will be cut down and killed."

11:16 So as Joab kept watch on the city, he stationed Uriah at the place where he knew the best enemy soldiers were. **11:17** When the men of the city came out and fought with Joab, some of David's soldiers fell in battle. Uriah the Hittite also died.

11:18 Then Joab sent a full battle report to David. **11:19** He instructed the messenger as follows: "When you finish giving the battle report to the king, **11:20** if the king becomes angry and asks you, 'Why did you go so close to the city to fight? Didn't you realize they would shoot from the wall? **11:21** Who struck down Abimelech the son of Jerub-Besheth? Didn't a woman throw an upper millstone down on him from the wall so that he died in Thebez? Why did you go so close to the wall?' just say to him, 'Your servant Uriah the Hittite is also dead.'"

11:22 So the messenger departed. When he arrived, he informed David of all the news that Joab had sent with him. **11:23** The messenger said to David, "The men overpowered us and attacked us in the field. But we forced them to retreat all the way to the door of the city gate. **11:24** Then the archers shot at your servants from the wall and some of the king's soldiers died. Your servant Uriah the Hittite is also dead." **11:25** David said to the messenger, "Tell Joab, 'Don't let this thing upset you. There is no way to anticipate whom the sword will cut down. Press the battle against the city and conquer it.' Encourage him with these words."

11:26 When Uriah's wife heard that her husband Uriah was dead, she mourned for him. **11:27** When the time of mourning passed, David had her brought to his palace. She became his wife and she bore him a son. But what David had done upset the LORD.

Nathan the Prophet Confronts David

12:1 So the LORD sent Nathan to David. When he came to David, Nathan said, "There were two men in a certain city, one rich and the other poor. **12:2** The rich man had a great many flocks and herds. **12:3** But the poor man had nothing except for a little lamb he had acquired. He raised it, and it grew up alongside him and his children. It used to eat his food, drink from his cup, and sleep in his arms. It was just like a daughter to him.

12:4 "When a traveler arrived at the rich man's home, he did not want to use one of his own sheep or cattle to feed the traveler who had come to visit him. Instead, he took the poor man's lamb and cooked it for the man who had come to visit him."

12:5 Then David became very angry at this man. He said to Nathan, "As surely as the LORD lives, the man who did this deserves to die! **12:6** Because he committed this cold-hearted crime, he must pay for the lamb four times over!"

12:7 Nathan said to David, "You are that man! This is what the LORD God of Israel says: 'I chose you to be king over Israel and I rescued you

from the hand of Saul. **12:8** I gave you your master's house, and put your master's wives into your arms. I also gave you the house of Israel and Judah. And if all that somehow seems insignificant, I would have given you so much more as well! **12:9** Why have you shown contempt for the word of the LORD by doing evil in my sight? You have struck down Uriah the Hittite with the sword and you have taken his wife as your own! You have killed him with the sword of the Ammonites. **12:10** So now the sword will never depart from your house. For you have despised me by taking the wife of Uriah the Hittite as your own!' **12:11** This is what the LORD says: 'I am about to bring disaster on you from inside your own household! Right before your eyes I will take your wives and hand them over to your companion. He will have sexual relations with your wives in broad daylight! **12:12** Although you have acted in secret, I will do this thing before all Israel, and in broad daylight.'"

12:13 Then David exclaimed to Nathan, "I have sinned against the LORD!" Nathan replied to David, "Yes, and the LORD has forgiven your sin. You are not going to die. **12:14** Nonetheless, because you have treated the LORD with such contempt in this matter, the son who has been born to you will certainly die."

12:15 Then Nathan went to his home. The LORD struck the child that Uriah's wife had borne to David, and the child became very ill. **12:16** Then David prayed to God for the child and fasted. He would even go and spend the night lying on the ground. **12:17** The elders of his house stood over him and tried to lift him from the ground, but he was unwilling, and refused to eat food with them.

12:18 On the seventh day the child died. But the servants of David were afraid to inform him that the child had died, for they said, "While the child was still alive he would not listen to us when we spoke to him. How can we tell him that the child is dead? He will do himself harm!"

12:19 When David saw that his servants were whispering to one another, he realized that the child was dead. So David asked his servants, "Is the child dead?" They replied, "Yes, he's dead." **12:20** So David got up from the ground, bathed, put on oil, and changed his clothes. He went to the house of the LORD and worshiped. Then, when he entered his palace, he requested that food be brought to him, and he ate.

12:21 His servants said to him, "What is this that you have done? While the child was still alive, you fasted and wept. Once the child was dead you got up and ate food!" **12:22** He replied, "While the child was still alive, I fasted and wept because I thought, 'Perhaps the LORD will show pity and the child will live. **12:23** But now he is dead. Why should I fast? Am I able to bring him back? I will go to him, but he cannot return to me!'"

12:24 So David comforted his wife Bathsheba. He went to her and had marital relations with her. She gave birth to a son, and David named him Solomon. Now the LORD loved the child **12:25** and sent word through Nathan the prophet that he should be named Jedidiah for the LORD's sake.

David's Forces Defeat the Ammonites

12:26 So Joab fought against Rabbah of the Ammonites and captured the royal city. **12:27** Joab then sent messengers to David, saying, "I have fought against Rabbah and have captured the water supply of the city. **12:28** So now assemble the rest of the army and besiege the city and capture it. Otherwise I will capture the city and it will be named for me." **12:29** So David assembled all the army and went to Rabbah and fought against it and

captured it. **12:30** He took the crown of their king from his head – it was gold, weighed about seventy-five pounds, and held a precious stone – and it was placed on David's head. He also took from the city a great deal of plunder. **12:31** He removed the people who were in it and made them do hard labor with saws, iron picks, and iron axes, putting them to work at the brick kiln. This was his policy with all the Ammonite cities. Then David and all the army returned to Jerusalem.

The Rape of Tamar

13:1 Now David's son Absalom had a beautiful sister named Tamar. In the course of time David's son Amnon fell madly in love with her. **13:2** But Amnon became frustrated because he was so lovesick over his sister Tamar. For she was a virgin, and to Amnon it seemed out of the question to do anything to her.

13:3 Now Amnon had a friend named Jonadab, the son of David's brother Shimeah. Jonadab was a very crafty man. **13:4** He asked Amnon, "Why are you, the king's son, so depressed every morning? Can't you tell me?" So Amnon said to him, "I'm in love with Tamar the sister of my brother Absalom." **13:5** Jonadab replied to him, "Lie down on your bed and pretend to be sick. When your father comes in to see you, say to him, 'Please let my sister Tamar come in so she can fix some food for me. Let her prepare the food in my sight so I can watch. Then I will eat from her hand.'"

13:6 So Amnon lay down and pretended to be sick. When the king came in to see him, Amnon said to the king, "Please let my sister Tamar come in so she can make a couple of cakes in my sight. Then I will eat from her hand."

13:7 So David sent Tamar to the house saying, "Please go to the house of Amnon your brother and prepare some food for him." **13:8** So Tamar

went to the house of Amnon her brother, who was lying down. She took the dough, kneaded it, made some cakes while he watched, and baked them. **13:9** But when she took the pan and set it before him, he refused to eat. Instead Amnon said, "Get everyone out of here!" So everyone left.
13:10 Then Amnon said to Tamar, "Bring the cakes into the bedroom; then I will eat from your hand." So Tamar took the cakes that she had prepared and brought them to her brother Amnon in the bedroom. **13:11** As she brought them to him to eat, he grabbed her and said to her, "Come on! Get in bed with me, my sister!"
13:12 But she said to him, "No, my brother! Don't humiliate me! This just isn't done in Israel! Don't do this foolish thing! **13:13** How could I ever be rid of my humiliation? And you would be considered one of the fools in Israel! Just speak to the king, for he will not withhold me from you." **13:14** But he refused to listen to her. He overpowered her and humiliated her by raping her. **13:15** Then Amnon greatly despised her. His disdain toward her surpassed the love he had previously felt toward her. Amnon said to her, "Get up and leave!"
13:16 But she said to him, "No I won't, for sending me away now would be worse than what you did to me earlier!" But he refused to listen to her. **13:17** He called his personal attendant and said to him, "Take this woman out of my sight and lock the door behind her!" **13:18** (Now she was wearing a long robe, for this is what the king's virgin daughters used to wear.) So Amnon's attendant removed her and bolted the door behind her. **13:19** Then Tamar put ashes on her head and tore the long robe she was wearing. She put her hands on her head and went on her way, wailing as she went.
13:20 Her brother Absalom said to her, "Was Amnon your brother with you? Now be quiet, my sister. He is your brother. Don't take it so seriously!" Tamar, devastated, lived in the house of her brother Absalom.
13:21 Now King David heard about all these things and was very angry. **13:22** But Absalom said nothing to Amnon, either bad or good, yet Absalom hated Amnon because he had humiliated his sister Tamar.
Absalom Has Amnon Put to Death
13:23 Two years later Absalom's sheepshearers were in Baal Hazor, near Ephraim. Absalom invited all the king's sons. **13:24** Then Absalom went to the king and said, "My shearers have begun their work. Let the king and his servants go with me."
13:25 But the king said to Absalom, "No, my son. We shouldn't all go. We shouldn't burden you in that way." Though Absalom pressed him, the king was not willing to go. Instead, David blessed him.
13:26 Then Absalom said, "If you will not go, then let my brother Amnon go with us." The king replied to him, "Why should he go with you?" **13:27** But when Absalom pressed him, he sent Amnon and all the king's sons along with him.
13:28 Absalom instructed his servants, "Look! When Amnon is drunk and I say to you, 'Strike Amnon down,' kill him then and there. Don't fear! Is it not I who have given you these instructions? Be strong and courageous!" **13:29** So Absalom's servants did to Amnon exactly what Absalom had instructed. Then all the king's sons got up; each one rode away on his mule and fled.
13:30 While they were still on their way, the following report reached David: "Absalom has killed all the king's sons; not one of them is left!" **13:31** Then the king stood up and tore his garments and lay down on the ground. All his servants were standing there with torn garments as well.
13:32 Jonadab, the son of David's brother Shimeah, said, "My lord should not say, 'They have killed all the young men who are the king's sons.' For only Amnon is dead. This is what Absalom has talked about from the day that Amnon humiliated his sister Tamar. **13:33** Now don't let my lord the king be concerned about the report that has come saying, 'All the king's sons are dead.' It is only Amnon who is dead."
13:34 In the meantime Absalom fled. When the servant who was the watchman looked up, he saw many people coming from the west on a road beside the hill. **13:35** Jonadab said to the king, "Look! The king's sons have come! It's just as I said!"
13:36 Just as he finished speaking, the king's sons arrived, wailing and weeping. The king and all his servants wept loudly as well. **13:37** But Absalom fled and went to King Talmai son of Ammihud of Geshur. And David grieved over his son every day.
13:38 After Absalom fled and went to Geshur, he remained there for three years. **13:39** The king longed to go to Absalom, for he had since been consoled over the death of Amnon.

David Permits Absalom to Return to Jerusalem
14:1 Now Joab son of Zeruiah realized that the king longed to see Absalom. **14:2** So Joab sent to Tekoa and brought from there a wise woman. He told her, "Pretend to be in mourning and put on garments for mourning. Don't anoint yourself with oil. Instead, act like a woman who has been mourning for the dead for some time. **14:3** Go to the king and speak to him in the following fashion." Then Joab told her what to say.
14:4 So the Tekoan woman went to the king. She bowed down with her face to the ground in deference to him and said, "Please help me, O king!" **14:5** The king replied to her, "What do you want?" She answered, "I am a widow; my husband is dead. **14:6** Your servant has two sons.

When the two of them got into a fight in the field, there was no one present who could intervene. One of them struck the other and killed him. **14:7** Now the entire family has risen up against your servant, saying, 'Turn over the one who struck down his brother, so that we can execute him and avenge the death of his brother whom he killed. In so doing we will also destroy the heir.' They want to extinguish my remaining coal, leaving no one on the face of the earth to carry on the name of my husband."
14:8 Then the king told the woman, "Go to your home. I will give instructions concerning your situation." **14:9** The Tekoan woman said to the king, "My lord the king, let any blame fall on me and on the house of my father. But let the king and his throne be innocent!"
14:10 The king said, "Bring to me whoever speaks to you, and he won't bother you again!" **14:11** She replied, "In that case, let the king invoke the name of the LORD your God so that the avenger of blood may not kill! Then they will not destroy my son!" He replied, "As surely as the LORD lives, not a single hair of your son's head will fall to the ground."
14:12 Then the woman said, "Please permit your servant to speak to my lord the king about another matter." He replied, "Tell me." **14:13** The woman said, "Why have you devised something like this against God's people? When the king speaks in this fashion, he makes himself guilty, for the king has not brought back the one he has banished. **14:14** Certainly we must die, and are like water spilled on the ground that cannot be gathered up again. But God does not take away life; instead he devises ways for the banished to be restored. **14:15** I have now come to speak with my lord the king about this matter, because the people have made me fearful. But your servant said, 'I will speak to the king! Perhaps the king will do what his female servant asks. **14:16** Yes! The king may listen and deliver his female servant from the hand of the man who seeks to remove both me and my son from the inheritance God has given us!' **14:17** So your servant said, 'May the word of my lord the king be my security, for my lord the king is like the angel of God when it comes to deciding between right and wrong! May the LORD your God be with you!'"
14:18 Then the king replied to the woman, "Don't hide any information from me when I question you." The woman said, "Let my lord the king speak!" **14:19** The king said, "Did Joab put you up to all of this?" The woman answered, "As surely as you live, my lord the king, there is no deviation to the right or to the left from all that my lord the king has said. For your servant Joab gave me instructions. He has put all these words in your servant's mouth. **14:20** Your servant Joab did this so as to change this situation. But my lord has wisdom like that of the angel of God, and knows everything that is happening in the land."
14:21 Then the king said to Joab, "All right! I will do this thing! Go and bring back the young man Absalom! **14:22** Then Joab bowed down with his face toward the ground and thanked the king. Joab said, "Today your servant knows that I have found favor in your sight, my lord the king, because the king has granted the request of your servant!"
14:23 So Joab got up and went to Geshur and brought Absalom back to Jerusalem. **14:24** But the king said, "Let him go over to his own house. He may not see my face." So Absalom went over to his own house; he did not see the king's face.
14:25 Now in all Israel everyone acknowledged that there was no man as handsome as Absalom. From the sole of his feet to the top of his head he was perfect in appearance. **14:26** When he would shave his head – at the end of every year he used to shave his head, for it grew too long and he would shave it – he used to weigh the hair of his head at three pounds according to the king's weight. **14:27** Absalom had three sons and one daughter, whose name was Tamar. She was a very attractive woman.
14:28 Absalom lived in Jerusalem for two years without seeing the king's face. **14:29** Then Absalom sent a message to Joab asking him to send him to the king, but Joab was not willing to come to him. So he sent a second message to him, but he still was not willing to come. **14:30** So he said to his servants, "Look, Joab has a portion of field adjacent to mine and he has some barley there. Go and set it on fire." So Absalom's servants set Joab's portion of the field on fire.
14:31 Then Joab got up and came to Absalom's house. He said to him, "Why did your servants set my portion of field on fire?" **14:32** Absalom said to Joab, "Look, I sent a message to you saying, 'Come here so that I can send you to the king with this message: "Why have I come from Geshur? It would be better for me if I were still there."' Let me now see the face of the king. If I am at fault, let him put me to death!"
14:33 So Joab went to the king and informed him. The king summoned Absalom, and he came to the king. Absalom bowed down before the king with his face toward the ground and the king kissed him.
Absalom Leads an Insurrection against David
15:1 Some time later Absalom managed to acquire a chariot and horses, as well as fifty men to serve as his royal guard. **15:2** Now Absalom used to get up early and stand beside the road that led to the city gate. Whenever anyone came by who had a complaint to bring to the king for arbitration, Absalom would call out to him, "What city are you from?" The person would answer, "I, your servant, am from one of the tribes of Israel." **15:3** Absalom would then say to him, "Look, your claims are legiti-

mate and appropriate. But there is no representative of the king who will listen to you." **15:4** Absalom would then say, "If only they would make me a judge in the land! Then everyone who had a judicial complaint could come to me and I would make sure he receives a just settlement."
15:5 When someone approached to bow before him, Absalom would extend his hand and embrace him and kiss him. **15:6** Absalom acted this way toward everyone in Israel who came to the king for justice. In this way Absalom won the loyalty of the citizens of Israel.
15:7 After four years Absalom said to the king, "Let me go and repay my vow that I made to the LORD while I was in Hebron. **15:8** For I made this vow when I was living in Geshur in Aram: 'If the LORD really does allow me to return to Jerusalem, I will serve the LORD.'" **15:9** The king replied to him, "Go in peace." So Absalom got up and went to Hebron.
15:10 Then Absalom sent spies through all the tribes of Israel who said, "When you hear the sound of the horn, you may assume that Absalom rules in Hebron." **15:11** Now two hundred men had gone with Absalom from Jerusalem. Since they were invited, they went naively and were unaware of what Absalom was planning. **15:12** While he was offering sacrifices, Absalom sent for Ahithophel the Gilonite, David's adviser, to come from his city, Giloh. The conspiracy was gaining momentum, and the people were starting to side with Absalom.

David Flees from Jerusalem
15:13 Then a messenger came to David and reported, "The men of Israel are loyal to Absalom!" **15:14** So David said to all his servants who were with him in Jerusalem, "Come on! Let's escape! Otherwise no one will be delivered from Absalom! Go immediately, or else he will quickly overtake us and bring disaster on us and kill the city's residents with the sword." **15:15** The king's servants replied to the king, "We will do whatever our lord the king decides."
15:16 So the king and all the members of his royal court set out on foot, though the king left behind ten concubines to attend to the palace. **15:17** The king and all the people set out on foot, pausing at a spot some distance away. **15:18** All his servants were leaving with him, along with all the Kerethites, all the Pelethites, and all the Gittites – some six hundred men who had come on foot from Gath. They were leaving with the king.
15:19 Then the king said to Ittai the Gittite, "Why should you come with us? Go back and stay with the new king, for you are a foreigner and an exile from your own country. **15:20** It seems like you arrived just yesterday. Today should I make you wander around by going with us? I go where I must go. But as for you, go back and take your men with you. May genuine loyal love protect you!"
15:21 But Ittai replied to the king, "As surely as the LORD lives and as my lord the king lives, wherever my lord the king is, whether dead or alive, there I will be as well!" **15:22** So David said to Ittai, "Come along then." So Ittai the Gittite went along, accompanied by all his men and all the dependents who were with him.
15:23 All the land was weeping loudly as all these people were leaving. As the king was crossing over the Kidron Valley, all the people were leaving on the road that leads to the desert. **15:24** Zadok and all the Levites who were with him were carrying the ark of the covenant of God. When they positioned the ark of God, Abiathar offered sacrifices until all the people had finished leaving the city.
15:25 Then the king said to Zadok, "Take the ark of God back to the city. If I find favor in the LORD's sight he will bring me back and enable me to see both it and his dwelling place again. **15:26** However, if he should say, 'I do not take pleasure in you,' then he will deal with me in a way that he considers appropriate."
15:27 The king said to Zadok the priest, "Are you a seer? Go back to the city in peace! Your son Ahimaaz and Abiathar's son Jonathan may go with you and Abiathar. **15:28** Look, I will be waiting at the fords of the desert until word from you reaches me." **15:29** So Zadok and Abiathar took the ark of God back to Jerusalem and remained there.
15:30 As David was going up the Mount of Olives, he was weeping as he went; his head was covered and his feet were bare. All the people who were with him also had their heads covered and were weeping as they went up. **15:31** Now David had been told, "Ahithophel has sided with the conspirators who are with Absalom. So David prayed, "Make the advice of Ahithophel foolish, O LORD!"
15:32 When David reached the summit, where he used to worship God, Hushai the Arkite met him with his clothes torn and dirt on his head. **15:33** David said to him, "If you leave with me you will be a burden to me. **15:34** But you will be able to counter the advice of Ahithophel if you go back to the city and say to Absalom, 'I will be your servant, O king! Previously I was your father's servant, and now I will be your servant.' **15:35** Zadok and Abiathar the priests will be there with you. Everything you hear in the king's palace you must tell Zadok and Abiathar the priests. **15:36** Furthermore, their two sons are there with them, Zadok's son Ahimaaz and Abiathar's son Jonathan. You must send them to me with any information you hear."
15:37 So David's friend Hushai arrived in the city, just as Absalom was entering Jerusalem.

David Receives Gifts from Ziba
16:1 When David had gone a short way beyond the summit, Ziba the servant of Mephibosheth was there to meet him. He had a couple of donkeys that were saddled, and on them were two hundred loaves of bread, a hundred raisin cakes, a hundred baskets of summer fruit, and a container of wine.
16:2 The king asked Ziba, "Why did you bring these things?" Ziba replied, "The donkeys are for the king's family to ride on, the loaves of bread and the summer fruit are for the attendants to eat, and the wine is for those who get exhausted in the desert." **16:3** The king asked, "Where is your master's grandson?" Ziba replied to the king, "He remains in Jerusalem, for he said, 'Today the house of Israel will give back to me my grandfather's kingdom.'" **16:4** The king said to Ziba, "Everything that was Mephibosheth's now belongs to you." Ziba replied, "I bow before you. May I find favor in your sight, my lord the king."

Shimei Curses David and His Men
16:5 Then King David reached Bahurim. There a man from Saul's extended family named Shimei son of Gera came out, yelling curses as he approached. **16:6** He threw stones at David and all of King David's servants, as well as all the people and the soldiers who were on his right and on his left. **16:7** As he yelled curses, Shimei said, "Leave! Leave! You man of bloodshed, you wicked man! **16:8** The LORD has punished you for all the spilled blood of the house of Saul, in whose place you rule. Now the LORD has given the kingdom into the hand of your son Absalom. Disaster has overtaken you, for you are a man of bloodshed!"
16:9 Then Abishai son of Zeruiah said to the king, "Why should this dead dog curse my lord the king? Let me go over and cut off his head!" **16:10** But the king said, "What do we have in common, you sons of Zeruiah? If he curses because the LORD has said to him, 'Curse David!', who can say to him, 'Why have you done this?'" **16:11** Then David said to Abishai and to all his servants, "My own son, my very own flesh and blood, is trying to take my life. So also now this Benjaminite! Leave him alone so that he can curse, for the LORD has spoken to him. **16:12** Perhaps the LORD will notice my affliction and this day grant me good in place of his curse."
16:13 So David and his men went on their way. But Shimei kept going along the side of the hill opposite him, yelling curses as he threw stones and dirt at them. **16:14** The king and all the people who were with him arrived exhausted at their destination, where David refreshed himself.

The Advice of Ahithophel
16:15 Now when Absalom and all the men of Israel arrived in Jerusalem, Ahithophel was with him. **16:16** When David's friend Hushai the Arkite came to Absalom, Hushai said to him, "Long live the king! Long live the king!"
16:17 Absalom said to Hushai, "Do you call this loyalty to your friend? Why didn't you go with your friend?" **16:18** Hushai replied to Absalom, "No, I will be loyal to the one whom the LORD, these people, and all the men of Israel have chosen. **16:19** Moreover, whom should I serve? Should it not be his son? Just as I served your father, so I will serve you."
16:20 Then Absalom said to Ahithophel, "Give us your advice. What should we do?" **16:21** Ahithophel replied to Absalom, "Have sex with your father's concubines whom he left to care for the palace. All Israel will hear that you have made yourself repulsive to your father. Then your followers will be motivated to support you." **16:22** So they pitched a tent for Absalom on the roof, and Absalom had sex with his father's concubines in the sight of all Israel.
16:23 In those days Ahithophel's advice was considered as valuable as a prophetic revelation. Both David and Absalom highly regarded the advice of Ahithophel.

The Death of Ahithophel
17:1 Ahithophel said to Absalom, "Let me pick out twelve thousand men. Then I will go and pursue David this very night. **17:2** When I catch up with him he will be exhausted and worn out. I will rout him, and the entire army that is with him will flee. I will kill only the king **17:3** and will bring the entire army back to you. In exchange for the life of the man you are seeking, you will get back everyone. The entire army will return unharmed."
17:4 This seemed like a good idea to Absalom and to all the leaders of Israel. **17:5** But Absalom said, "Call for Hushai the Arkite, and let's hear what he has to say." **17:6** So Hushai came to Absalom. Absalom said to him, "Here is what Ahithophel has advised. Should we follow his advice? If not, what would you recommend?"
17:7 Hushai replied to Absalom, "Ahithophel's advice is not sound this time." **17:8** Hushai went on to say, "You know your father and his men – they are soldiers and are as dangerous as a bear out in the wild that has been robbed of her cubs. Your father is an experienced soldier; he will not stay overnight with the army. **17:9** At this very moment he is hiding out in one of the caves or in some other similar place. If it should turn out that he attacks our troops first, whoever hears about it will say, 'Absalom's army has been slaughtered!' **17:10** If that happens even the bravest soldier – one who is lion-hearted – will virtually melt away. For all Israel knows that your father is a warrior and that those who are with him are brave. **17:11** My advice therefore is this: Let all Israel from Dan to Beer Sheba – in number like the sand by the sea! – be mustered to you, and

you lead them personally into battle. **17:12** We will come against him wherever he happens to be found. We will descend on him like the dew falls on the ground. Neither he nor any of the men who are with him will be spared alive – not one of them! **17:13** If he regroups in a city, all Israel will take up ropes to that city and drag it down to the valley, so that not a single pebble will be left there!"

17:14 Then Absalom and all the men of Israel said, "The advice of Hushai the Arkite sounds better than the advice of Ahithophel." Now the LORD had decided to frustrate the sound advice of Ahithophel, so that the LORD could bring disaster on Absalom.

17:15 Then Hushai reported to Zadok and Abiathar the priests, "Here is what Ahithophel has advised Absalom and the leaders of Israel to do, and here is what I have advised. **17:16** Now send word quickly to David and warn him, "Don't spend the night at the fords of the desert tonight. Instead, be sure you cross over, or else the king and everyone who is with him may be overwhelmed."

17:17 Now Jonathan and Ahimaaz were staying in En Rogel. A female servant would go and inform them, and they would then go and inform King David. It was not advisable for them to be seen going into the city. **17:18** But a young man saw them on one occasion and informed Absalom. So the two of them quickly departed and went to the house of a man in Bahurim. There was a well in his courtyard, and they got down in it. **17:19** His wife then took the covering and spread it over the top of the well and scattered some grain over it. No one was aware of what she had done.

17:20 When the servants of Absalom approached the woman at her home, they asked, "Where are Ahimaaz and Jonathan?" The woman replied to them, "They crossed over the stream." Absalom's men searched but did not find them, so they returned to Jerusalem.

17:21 After the men had left, Ahimaaz and Jonathan climbed out of the well. Then they left and informed King David. They advised David, "Get up and cross the stream quickly, for Ahithophel has devised a plan to catch you." **17:22** So David and all the people who were with him got up and crossed the Jordan River. By dawn there was not one person left who had not crossed the Jordan.

17:23 When Ahithophel realized that his advice had not been followed, he saddled his donkey and returned to his house in his hometown. After setting his household in order, he hanged himself. So he died and was buried in the grave of his father.

17:24 Meanwhile David had gone to Mahanaim, while Absalom and all the men of Israel had crossed the Jordan River. **17:25** Absalom had made Amasa general in command of the army in place of Joab. (Now Amasa was the son of an Israelite man named Jether, who had married Abigail the daughter of Nahash and sister of Zeruiah, Joab's mother.) **17:26** The army of Israel and Absalom camped in the land of Gilead.

17:27 When David came to Mahanaim, Shobi the son of Nahash from Rabbah of the Ammonites, Makir the son of Ammiel from Lo Debar, and Barzillai the Gileadite from Rogelim **17:28** brought bedding, basins, and pottery utensils. They also brought food for David and all who were with him, including wheat, barley, flour, roasted grain, beans, lentils, **17:29** honey, curds, flocks, and cheese. For they said, "The people are no doubt hungry, tired, and thirsty there in the desert."

The Death of Absalom

18:1 David assembled the army that was with him. He appointed leaders of thousands and leaders of hundreds. **18:2** David then sent out the army – a third under the leadership of Joab, a third under the leadership of Joab's brother Abishai son of Zeruiah, and a third under the leadership of Ittai the Gittite. The king said to the troops, "I too will indeed march out with you."

18:3 But the soldiers replied, "You should not do this! For if we should have to make a rapid retreat, they won't be too concerned about us. Even if half of us should die, they won't be too concerned about us. But you are like ten thousand of us! So it is better if you remain in the city for support." **18:4** Then the king said to them, "I will do whatever seems best to you."

So the king stayed beside the city gate, while all the army marched out by hundreds and by thousands. **18:5** The king gave this order to Joab, Abishai, and Ittai: "For my sake deal gently with the young man Absalom." Now the entire army was listening when the king gave all the leaders this order concerning Absalom.

18:6 Then the army marched out to the field to fight against Israel. The battle took place in the forest of Ephraim. **18:7** The army of Israel was defeated there by David's men. The slaughter there was great that day – 20,000 soldiers were killed. **18:8** The battle there was spread out over the whole area, and the forest consumed more soldiers than the sword devoured that day.

18:9 Then Absalom happened to come across David's men. Now as Absalom was riding on his mule, it went under the branches of a large oak tree. His head got caught in the oak and he was suspended in midair, while the mule he had been riding kept going. **18:10** When one of the men saw this, he reported it to Joab saying, "I saw Absalom hanging in an oak tree. **18:11** Joab replied to the man who was telling him this, "What! You saw this? Why didn't you strike him down

right on the spot? I would have given you ten pieces of silver and a commemorative belt!"

18:12 The man replied to Joab, "Even if I were receiving a thousand pieces of silver, I would not strike the king's son! In our very presence the king gave this order to you and Abishai and Ittai, 'Protect the young man Absalom for my sake.' **18:13** If I had acted at risk of my own life – and nothing is hidden from the king! – you would have abandoned me."

18:14 Joab replied, "I will not wait around like this for you!" He took three spears in his hand and thrust them into the middle of Absalom while he was still alive in the middle of the oak tree. **18:15** Then ten soldiers who were Joab's armor bearers struck Absalom and finished him off.

18:16 Then Joab blew the trumpet and the army turned back from chasing Israel, for Joab had called for the army to halt. **18:17** They took Absalom, threw him into a large pit in the forest, and stacked a huge pile of stones over him. In the meantime all the Israelite soldiers fled to their homes. **18:18** Prior to this Absalom had set up a monument and dedicated it to himself in the King's Valley, reasoning "I have no son who will carry on my name." He named the monument after himself, and to this day it is known as Absalom's Memorial.

David Learns of Absalom's Death

18:19 Then Ahimaaz the son of Zadok said, "Let me run and give the king the good news that the LORD has vindicated him before his enemies." **18:20** But Joab said to him, "You will not be a bearer of good news today. You will bear good news some other day, but not today, for the king's son is dead."

18:21 Then Joab said to the Cushite, "Go and tell the king what you have seen." After bowing to Joab, the Cushite ran off. **18:22** Ahimaaz the son of Zadok again spoke to Joab, "Whatever happens, let me go after the Cushite." But Joab said, "Why is it that you want to go, my son? You have no good news that will bring you a reward." **18:23** But he said, "Whatever happens, I want to go!" So Joab said to him, "Then go!" So Ahimaaz ran by the way of the Jordan plain, and he passed the Cushite.

18:24 Now David was sitting between the inner and outer gates, and the watchman went up to the roof over the gate at the wall. When he looked, he saw a man running by himself. **18:25** So the watchman called out and informed the king. The king said, "If he is by himself, he brings good news." The runner came ever closer.

18:26 Then the watchman saw another man running. The watchman called out to the gatekeeper, "There is another man running by himself." The king said, "This one also is bringing good news." **18:27** The watchman said, "It appears to me that the first runner is Ahimaaz son of Zadok." The king said, "He is a good man, and he comes with good news."

18:28 Then Ahimaaz called out and said to the king, "Greetings!" He bowed down before the king with his face toward the ground and said, "May the LORD your God be praised because he has defeated the men who opposed my lord the king!"

18:29 The king replied, "How is the young man Absalom?" Ahimaaz replied, "I saw a great deal of confusion when Joab was sending the king's servant and me, your servant, but I don't know what it was all about." **18:30** The king said, "Turn aside and take your place here." So he turned aside and waited.

18:31 Then the Cushite arrived and said, "May my lord the king now receive the good news! The LORD has vindicated you today and delivered you from the hand of all who have rebelled against you!" **18:32** The king asked the Cushite, "How is the young man Absalom?" The Cushite replied, "May the enemies of my lord the king and all who have plotted against you be like that young man!"

18:33 (19:1) The king then became very upset. He went up to the upper room over the gate and wept. As he went he said, "My son, Absalom! My son, my son, Absalom! If only I could have died in your place! Absalom, my son, my son!"

19:1 (19:2) Joab was told, "The king is weeping and mourning over Absalom." **19:2** So the victory of that day was turned to mourning as far as all the people were concerned. For the people heard on that day, "The king is grieved over his son." **19:3** That day the people stole away to go to the city the way people who are embarrassed steal away in fleeing from battle. **19:4** The king covered his face and cried out loudly, "My son, Absalom! Absalom, my son, my son!"

19:5 So Joab visited the king at his home. He said, "Today you have embarrassed all your servants who have saved your life this day, as well as the lives of your sons, your daughters, your wives, and your concubines. **19:6** You seem to love your enemies and hate your friends! For you have as much as declared today that leaders and servants don't matter to you. I realize now that if Absalom were alive and all of us were dead today, it would be all right with you. **19:7** So get up now and go out and give some encouragement to your servants. For I swear by the LORD that if you don't go out there, not a single man will stay here with you tonight! This disaster will be worse for you than any disaster that has overtaken you from your youth right to the present time!"

19:8 So the king got up and sat at the city gate. When all the people were informed that the king was sitting at the city gate, they all came before him.

David Goes Back to Jerusalem

But the Israelite soldiers had all fled to their own homes. **19:9** All the people throughout all the tribes of Israel were arguing among themselves saying, "The king delivered us from the hand of our enemies. He rescued us from the hand of the Philistines, but now he has fled from the land because of Absalom. **19:10** But Absalom, whom we anointed as our king, has died in battle. So now why do you hesitate to bring the king back?"

19:11 Then King David sent a message to Zadok and Abiathar the priests saying, "Tell the elders of Judah, 'Why should you delay any further in bringing the king back to his palace, when everything Israel is saying has come to the king's attention. **19:12** You are my brothers – my very own flesh and blood! Why should you delay any further in bringing the king back?' **19:13** Say to Amasa, 'Are you not my flesh and blood? God will punish me severely, if from this time on you are not the commander of my army in place of Joab!'"

19:14 He won over the hearts of all the men of Judah as though they were one man. Then they sent word to the king saying, "Return, you and all your servants as well." **19:15** So the king returned and came to the Jordan River.

Now the people of Judah had come to Gilgal to meet the king and to help him cross the Jordan. **19:16** Shimei son of Gera the Benjaminite from Bahurim came down quickly with the men of Judah to meet King David. **19:17** There were a thousand men from Benjamin with him, along with Ziba the servant of Saul's household, and with him his fifteen sons and twenty servants. They hurriedly crossed the Jordan within sight of the king. **19:18** They crossed at the ford in order to help the king's household cross and to do whatever he thought appropriate.

Now after he had crossed the Jordan, Shimei son of Gera threw himself down before the king. **19:19** He said to the king, "Don't think badly of me, my lord, and don't recall the sin of your servant on the day when you, my lord the king, left Jerusalem! Please don't call it to mind! **19:20** For I, your servant, know that I sinned, and I have come today as the first of all the house of Joseph to come down to meet my lord the king."

19:21 Abishai son of Zeruiah replied, "For this should not Shimei be put to death? After all, he cursed the LORD's anointed!" **19:22** But David said, "What do we have in common, you sons of Zeruiah? You are like my enemy today! Should anyone be put to death in Israel today? Don't you realize that today I am king over Israel?" **19:23** The king said to Shimei, "You won't die." The king vowed an oath concerning this.

19:24 Now Mephibosheth, Saul's grandson, came down to meet the king. From the day the king had left until the day he safely returned, Mephibosheth had not cared for his feet nor trimmed his mustache nor washed his clothes. **19:25** When he came from Jerusalem to meet the king, the king asked him, "Why didn't you go with me, Mephibosheth?" **19:26** He replied, "My lord the king, my servant deceived me! I said, 'Let me get my donkey saddled so that I can ride on it and go with the king,' for I am lame. **19:27** But my servant has slandered me to my lord the king. But my lord the king is like an angel of God. Do whatever seems appropriate to you. **19:28** After all, there was no one in the entire house of my grandfather who did not deserve death from my lord the king. But instead you allowed me to eat at your own table! What further claim do I have to ask the king for anything?"

19:29 Then the king replied to him, "Why should you continue speaking like this? You and Ziba will inherit the field together." **19:30** Mephibosheth said to the king, "Let him have the whole thing! My lord the king has returned safely to his house!"

19:31 Now when Barzillai the Gileadite had come down from Rogelim, he crossed the Jordan with the king so he could send him on his way from there. **19:32** But Barzillai was very old – eighty years old, in fact – and he had taken care of the king when he stayed in Mahanaim, for he was a very rich man. **19:33** So the king said to Barzillai, "Cross over with me, and I will take care of you while you are with me in Jerusalem."

19:34 Barzillai replied to the king, "How many days do I have left to my life, that I should go up with the king to Jerusalem? **19:35** I am presently eighty years old. Am I able to discern good and bad? Can I taste what I eat and drink? Am I still able to hear the voices of male and female singers? Why should I continue to be a burden to my lord the king? **19:36** I will cross the Jordan with the king and go a short distance. Why should the king reward me in this way? **19:37** Let me return so that I may die in my own city near the grave of my father and my mother. But look, here is your servant Kimham. Let him cross over with my lord the king. Do for him whatever seems appropriate to you."

19:38 The king replied, "Kimham will cross over with me, and I will do for him whatever I deem appropriate. And whatever you choose, I will do for you."

19:39 So all the people crossed the Jordan, as did the king. After the king had kissed him and blessed him, Barzillai returned to his home. **19:40** When the king crossed over to Gilgal, Kimham crossed over with him. Now all the soldiers of Judah along with half of the soldiers of Israel had helped the king cross over.

19:41 Then all the men of Israel began coming to the king. They asked the king, "Why did our brothers, the men of Judah, sneak the king away and help the king and his household cross the Jordan – and not only him but all of David's men as well?"

19:42 All the men of Judah replied to the men of Israel, "Because the king is our close relative! Why are you so upset about this? Have we eaten at the king's expense? Or have we misappropriated anything for our own use?" **19:43** The men of Israel replied to the men of Judah, "We have ten shares in the king, and we have a greater claim on David than you do! Why do you want to curse us? Weren't we the first to suggest bringing back our king?" But the comments of the men of Judah were more severe than those of the men of Israel.

Sheba's Rebellion

20:1 Now a wicked man named Sheba son of Bicri, a Benjaminite, happened to be there. He blew the trumpet and said,

"We have no share in David;
we have no inheritance in this son of Jesse!
Every man go home, O Israel!"

20:2 So all the men of Israel deserted David and followed Sheba son of Bicri. But the men of Judah stuck by their king all the way from the Jordan River to Jerusalem.

20:3 Then David went to his palace in Jerusalem. The king took the ten concubines he had left to care for the palace and placed them under confinement. Though he provided for their needs, he did not have sexual relations with them. They remained in confinement until the day they died, living out the rest of their lives as widows.

20:4 Then the king said to Amasa, "Call the men of Judah together for me in three days, and you be present here with them too." **20:5** So Amasa went out to call Judah together. But in doing so he took longer than the time that the king had allotted him.

20:6 Then David said to Abishai, "Now Sheba son of Bicri will cause greater disaster for us than Absalom did! Take your lord's servants and pursue him. Otherwise he will secure fortified cities for himself and get away from us." **20:7** So Joab's men, accompanied by the Kerethites, the Pelethites, and all the warriors, left Jerusalem to pursue Sheba son of Bicri.

20:8 When they were near the big rock that is in Gibeon, Amasa came to them. Now Joab was dressed in military attire and had a dagger in its sheath belted to his waist. When he advanced, it fell out. **20:9** Joab said to Amasa, "How are you, my brother?" With his right hand Joab took hold of Amasa's beard as if to greet him with a kiss. **20:10** Amasa did not protect himself from the knife in Joab's other hand, and Joab stabbed him in the abdomen, causing Amasa's intestines to spill out on the ground. There was no need to stab him again; the first blow was fatal. Then Joab and his brother Abishai pursued Sheba son of Bicri. **20:11** One of Joab's soldiers who stood over Amasa said, "Whoever is for Joab and whoever is for David, follow Joab!" **20:12** Amasa was squirming in his own blood in the middle of the path, and this man had noticed that all the soldiers stopped. Having noticed that everyone who came across Amasa stopped, the man pulled him away from the path and into the field and threw a garment over him. **20:13** Once he had removed Amasa from the path, everyone followed Joab to pursue Sheba son of Bicri.

20:14 Sheba traveled through all the tribes of Israel to Abel of Beth Maacah and all the Berite region. When they had assembled, they too joined him. **20:15** So Joab's men came and laid siege against him in Abel of Beth Maacah. They prepared a siege ramp outside the city which stood against its outer rampart. As all of Joab's soldiers were trying to break through the wall so that it would collapse, **20:16** a wise woman called out from the city, "Listen up! Listen up! Tell Joab, 'Come near so that I may speak to you.'"

20:17 When he approached her, the woman asked, "Are you Joab?" He replied, "I am." She said to him, "Listen to the words of your servant." He said, "Go ahead. I'm listening." **20:18** She said, "In the past they would always say, 'Let them inquire in Abel,' and that is how they settled things. **20:19** I represent the peaceful and the faithful in Israel. You are attempting to destroy an important city in Israel. Why should you swallow up the LORD's inheritance?"

20:20 Joab answered, "Get serious! I don't want to swallow up or destroy anything! **20:21** That's not the way things are. There is a man from the hill country of Ephraim named Sheba son of Bicri. He has rebelled against King David. Give me just this one man, and I will leave the city." The woman said to Joab, "This very minute his head will be thrown over the wall to you!"

20:22 Then the woman went to all the people with her wise advice and they cut off Sheba's head and threw it out to Joab. Joab blew the trumpet, and his men dispersed from the city, each going to his own home. Joab returned to the king in Jerusalem.

20:23 Now Joab was the general in command of all the army of Israel. Benaiah the son of Jehoida was over the Kerethites and the Perethites. **20:24** Adoniram was supervisor of the work crews. Jehoshaphat son of Ahilud was the secretary. **20:25** Sheva was the scribe, and Zadok and Abiathar were the priests. **20:26** Ira the Jairite was David's personal priest.

The Gibeonites Demand Revenge

21:1 During David's reign there was a famine for three consecutive years. So David inquired of the LORD. The LORD said, "It is because of Saul and his bloodstained family, because he murdered the Gibeonites." **21:2** So the king summoned the Gibeonites and spoke with them. (Now the Gibeonites were not descendants of Israel; they were a remnant of the Amorites. The Israelites had made a promise to them, but Saul tried to kill them because of his zeal for the people of Israel and Judah.) **21:3** David said to the Gibeonites, "What can I do for you, and how can I make amends so that you will bless the LORD's inheritance?"

21:4 The Gibeonites said to him, "We have no claim to silver or gold from Saul or from his family, nor would we be justified in putting to death anyone in Israel." David asked, "What then are you asking me to do for you?" **21:5** They replied to the king, "As for this man who exterminated us and who schemed against us so that we were destroyed and left without status throughout all the borders of Israel – **21:6** let seven of his male descendants be turned over to us, and we will execute them before the LORD in Gibeah of Saul, who was the LORD's chosen one." The king replied, "I will turn them over."

21:7 The king had mercy on Mephibosheth son of Jonathan, the son of Saul, in light of the LORD's oath that had been taken between David and Jonathan son of Saul. **21:8** So the king took Armoni and Mephibosheth, the two sons of Aiah's daughter Rizpah whom she had born to Saul, and the five sons of Saul's daughter Merab whom she had born to Adriel the son of Barzillai the Meholathite. **21:9** He turned them over to the Gibeonites, and they executed them on a hill before the LORD. The seven of them died together; they were put to death during harvest time – during the first days of the beginning of the barley harvest.

21:10 Rizpah the daughter of Aiah took sackcloth and spread it out for herself on a rock. From the beginning of the harvest until the rain fell on them, she did not allow the birds of the air to feed on them by day, nor the wild animals by night. **21:11** When David was told what Rizpah daughter of Aiah, Saul's concubine, had done, **21:12** he went and took the bones of Saul and of his son Jonathan from the leaders of Jabesh Gilead. (They had secretly taken them from the plaza at Beth Shan. It was there that Philistines publicly exposed their corpses after they had killed Saul at Gilboa.) **21:13** David brought the bones of Saul and of Jonathan his son from there; they also gathered up the bones of those who had been executed.

21:14 They buried the bones of Saul and his son Jonathan in the land of Benjamin at Zela in the grave of his father Kish. After they had done everything that the king had commanded, God responded to their prayers for the land.

Israel Engages in Various Battles with the Philistines

21:15 Another battle was fought between the Philistines and Israel. So David went down with his soldiers and fought the Philistines. David became exhausted. **21:16** Now Ishbi-Benob, one of the descendants of Rapha, had a spear that weighed three hundred bronze shekels, and he was armed with a new weapon. He had said that he would kill David. **21:17** But Abishai the son of Zeruiah came to David's aid, striking the Philistine down and killing him. Then David's men took an oath saying, "You will not go out to battle with us again! You must not extinguish the lamp of Israel!"

21:18 Later there was another battle with the Philistines, this time in Gob. On that occasion Sibbekai the Hushathite killed Saph, who was one of the descendants of Rapha. **21:19** Yet another battle occurred with the Philistines in Gob. On that occasion Elhanan the son of Jair the Bethlehemite killed the brother of Goliath the Gittite, the shaft of whose spear was like a weaver's beam. **21:20** Yet another battle occurred in Gath. On that occasion there was a large man who had six fingers on each hand and six toes on each foot, twenty-four in all! He too was a descendant of Rapha. **21:21** When he taunted Israel, Jonathan, the son of David's brother Shimeah, killed him. **21:22** These four were the descendants of Rapha who lived in Gath; they were killed by David and his soldiers.

David Sings to the Lord

22:1 David sang to the LORD the words of this song when the LORD rescued him from the power of all his enemies, including Saul. **22:2** He said:

"The LORD is my high ridge, my stronghold, my deliverer.
22:3 My God is my rocky summit where I take shelter,
my shield, the horn that saves me, my stronghold,
my refuge, my savior. You save me from violence!
22:4 I called to the LORD, who is worthy of praise,
and I was delivered from my enemies.
22:5 The waves of death engulfed me;
the currents of chaos overwhelmed me.
22:6 The ropes of Sheol tightened around me;
the snares of death trapped me.
22:7 In my distress I called to the LORD;
I called to my God.
From his heavenly temple he heard my voice;
he listened to my cry for help.
22:8 The earth heaved and shook;

the foundations of the sky trembled.
They heaved because he was angry.
22:9 Smoke ascended from his nose;
fire devoured as it came from his mouth;
he hurled down fiery coals.
22:10 He made the sky sink as he descended;
a thick cloud was under his feet.
22:11 He mounted a winged angel and flew;
he glided on the wings of the wind.
22:12 He shrouded himself in darkness,
in thick rain clouds.
22:13 From the brightness in front of him
came coals of fire.
22:14 The LORD thundered from the sky;
the sovereign One shouted loudly.
22:15 He shot arrows and scattered them,
lightning and routed them.
22:16 The depths of the sea were exposed;
the inner regions of the world were uncovered
by the LORD's battle cry,
by the powerful breath from his nose.
22:17 He reached down from above and grabbed me;
he pulled me from the surging water.
22:18 He rescued me from my strong enemy,
from those who hate me,
for they were too strong for me.
22:19 They confronted me in my day of calamity,
but the LORD helped me.
22:20 He brought me out into a wide open place;
he delivered me because he was pleased with me.
22:21 The LORD repaid me for my godly deeds;
he rewarded my blameless behavior.
22:22 For I have obeyed the LORD's commands;
I have not rebelled against my God.
22:23 For I am aware of all his regulations,
and I do not reject his rules.
22:24 I was blameless before him;
I kept myself from sinning.
22:25 The LORD rewarded me for my godly deeds;
he took notice of my blameless behavior.
22:26 You prove to be loyal to one who is faithful;
you prove to be trustworthy to one who is innocent.
22:27 You prove to be reliable to one who is blameless,
but you prove to be deceptive to one who is perverse.
22:28 You deliver oppressed people,
but you watch the proud and bring them down.
22:29 Indeed, you are my lamp, LORD.
The LORD illumines the darkness around me.
22:30 Indeed, with your help I can charge against an army;
by my God's power I can jump over a wall.
22:31 The one true God acts in a faithful manner;
the LORD's promise is reliable;
he is a shield to all who take shelter in him.
22:32 Indeed, who is God besides the LORD?
Who is a protector besides our God?
22:33 The one true God is my mighty refuge;
he removes the obstacles in my way.
22:34 He gives me the agility of a deer;
he enables me to negotiate the rugged terrain.
22:35 He trains my hands for battle;
my arms can bend even the strongest bow.
22:36 You give me your protective shield;
your willingness to help enables me to prevail.
22:37 You widen my path;
my feet do not slip.
22:38 I chase my enemies and destroy them;
I do not turn back until I wipe them out.
22:39 I wipe them out and beat them to death;
they cannot get up;
they fall at my feet.
22:40 You give me strength for battle;
you make my foes kneel before me.
22:41 You make my enemies retreat;
I destroy those who hate me.
22:42 They cry out, but there is no one to help them;
they cry out to the LORD, but he does not answer them.
22:43 I grind them as fine as the dust of the ground;
I crush them and stomp on them like clay in the streets.
22:44 You rescue me from a hostile army;
you preserve me as a leader of nations;
people over whom I had no authority are now my subjects.
22:45 Foreigners are powerless before me;
when they hear of my exploits, they submit to me.

22:46 Foreigners lose their courage;
they shake with fear as they leave their strongholds.
22:47 The LORD is alive!
My protector is praiseworthy!
The God who delivers me is exalted as king!
22:48 The one true God completely vindicates me;
he makes nations submit to me.
22:49 He delivers me from my enemies;
you snatch me away from those who attack me;
you rescue me from violent men.
22:50 So I will give you thanks, O LORD, before the nations!
I will sing praises to you.
22:51 He gives his chosen king magnificent victories;
he is faithful to his chosen ruler,
to David and to his descendants forever!"

David's Final Words

23:1 These are the final words of David:

"The oracle of David son of Jesse,
the oracle of the man raised up as
the ruler chosen by the God of Jacob,
Israel's beloved singer of songs:
23:2 The LORD's spirit spoke through me;
his word was on my tongue.
23:3 The God of Israel spoke,
the protector of Israel spoke to me.
The one who rules fairly among men,
the one who rules in the fear of God,
23:4 is like the light of morning when the sun comes up,
a morning in which there are no clouds.
He is like the brightness after rain
that produces grass from the earth.
23:5 My dynasty is approved by God,
for he has made a perpetual covenant with me,
arranged in all its particulars and secured.
He always delivers me,
and brings all I desire to fruition.
23:6 But evil people are like thorns –
all of them are tossed away,
for they cannot be held in the hand.
23:7 The one who touches them
must use an iron instrument
or the wooden shaft of a spear.
They are completely burned up right where they lie!"

David's Warriors

23:8 These are the names of David's warriors:
Josheb-Basshebeth, a Tahkemonite, was head of the officers. He killed eight hundred men with his spear in one battle. **23:9** Next in command was Eleazar son of Dodo, the son of Ahohi. He was one of the three warriors who were with David when they defied the Philistines who were assembled there for battle. When the men of Israel retreated, **23:10** he stood his ground and fought the Philistines until his hand grew so tired that it seemed stuck to his sword. The LORD gave a great victory on that day. When the army returned to him, the only thing left to do was to plunder the corpses.
23:11 Next in command was Shammah son of Agee the Hararite. When the Philistines assembled at Lehi, where there happened to be an area of a field that was full of lentils, the army retreated before the Philistines. **23:12** But he made a stand in the middle of that area. He defended it and defeated the Philistines; the LORD gave them a great victory.
23:13 At the time of the harvest three of the thirty leaders went down to David at the cave of Adullam. A band of Philistines was camped in the valley of Rephaim. **23:14** David was in the stronghold at the time, while a Philistine garrison was in Bethlehem. **23:15** David was thirsty and said, "How I wish someone would give me some water to drink from the cistern in Bethlehem near the gate!" **23:16** So the three elite warriors broke through the Philistine forces and drew some water from the cistern in Bethlehem near the gate. They carried it back to David, but he refused to drink it. He poured it out as a drink offering to the LORD **23:17** and said, "O LORD, I will not do this! It is equivalent to the blood of the men who risked their lives by going." So he refused to drink it. Such were the exploits of the three elite warriors.
23:18 Abishai son of Zeruiah, the brother of Joab, was head of the three. He killed three hundred men with his spear and gained fame among the three. **23:19** From the three he was given honor and he became their officer, even though he was not one of the three.
23:20 Benaiah son of Jehoida was a brave warrior from Kabzeel who performed great exploits. He struck down the two sons of Ariel of Moab. He also went down and killed a lion in a cistern on a snowy day. **23:21** He also killed an impressive-looking Egyptian. The Egyptian wielded a spear, while Benaiah attacked him with a club. He grabbed the spear out of the Egyptian's hand and killed him with his own spear. **23:22** Such were the exploits of Benaiah son of Jehoida, who gained fame among the

three elite warriors. **23:23** He received honor from the thirty warriors, though he was not one of the three elite warriors. David put him in charge of his bodyguard.
23:24 Included with the thirty were the following: Asahel the brother of Joab, Elhanan son of Dodo from Bethlehem, **23:25** Shammah the Harodite, Elika the Harodite, **23:26** Helez the Paltite, Ira son of Ikkesh from Tekoa, **23:27** Abiezer the Anathothite, Mebunnai the Hushathite, **23:28** Zalmon the Ahohite, Maharai the Netophathite, **23:29** Heled son of Baanah the Netophathite, Ittai son of Ribai from Gibeah in Benjamin, **23:30** Benaiah the Pirathonite, Hiddai from the wadis of Gaash, **23:31** Abi-Albon the Arbathite, Azmaveth the Barhumite, **23:32** Eliahba the Shaalbonite, the sons of Jashen, Jonathan **23:33** son of Shammah the Hararite, Ahiam son of Sharar the Hararite, **23:34** Eliphelet son of Ahasbai the Maacathite, Eliam son of Ahithophel the Gilonite, **23:35** Hezrai the Carmelite, Paarai the Arbite, **23:36** Igal son of Nathan from Zobah, Bani the Gadite, **23:37** Zelek the Ammonite, Naharai the Beerothite (the armor-bearer of Joab son of Zeruiah), **23:38** Ira the Ithrite, Gareb the Ithrite **23:39** and Uriah the Hittite. Altogether there were thirty-seven.

David Displeases the Lord by Taking a Census

24:1 The LORD's anger again raged against Israel, and he incited David against them, saying, "Go count Israel and Judah." **24:2** The king told Joab, the general in command of his army, "Go through all the tribes of Israel from Dan to Beer Sheba and muster the army, so I may know the size of the army."
24:3 Joab replied to the king, "May the LORD your God make the army a hundred times larger right before the eyes of my lord the king! But why does my master the king want to do this?"
24:4 But the king's edict stood, despite the objections of Joab and the leaders of the army. So Joab and the leaders of the army left the king's presence in order to muster the Israelite army.
24:5 They crossed the Jordan and camped at Aroer, on the south side of the city, at the wadi of Gad, near Jazer. **24:6** Then they went on to Gilead and to the region of Tahtim Hodshi, coming to Dan Jaan and on around to Sidon. **24:7** Then they went to the fortress of Tyre and all the cities of the Hivites and the Canaanites. Then they went on to the Negev of Judah, to Beer Sheba. **24:8** They went through all the land and after nine months and twenty days came back to Jerusalem.
24:9 Joab reported the number of warriors to the king. In Israel there were 800,000 sword-wielding warriors, and in Judah there were 500,000 soldiers.
24:10 David felt guilty after he had numbered the army. David said to the LORD, "I have sinned greatly by doing this! Now, O LORD, please remove the guilt of your servant, for I have acted very foolishly."
24:11 When David got up the next morning, the LORD had already spoken to Gad the prophet, David's seer: **24:12** "Go, tell David, 'This is what the LORD says: I am offering you three forms of judgment. Pick one of them and I will carry it out against you.'"
24:13 Gad went to David and told him, "Shall seven years of famine come upon your land? Or shall you flee for three months from your enemy with him in hot pursuit? Or shall there be three days of plague in your land? Now decide what I should tell the one who sent me." **24:14** David said to Gad, "I am very upset! I prefer that we be attacked by the LORD, for his mercy is great; I do not want to be attacked by men!"
24:15 So the LORD sent a plague through Israel from the morning until the completion of the appointed time. Seventy thousand men died from Dan to Beer Sheba. **24:16** When the angel extended his hand to destroy Jerusalem, the LORD relented from his judgment. He told the angel who was killing the people, "That's enough! Stop now!" (Now the LORD's angel was near the threshing floor of Araunah the Jebusite.)
24:17 When he saw the angel who was destroying the people, David said to the LORD, "Look, it is I who have sinned and done this evil thing! As for these sheep – what have they done? Attack me and my family."

David Acquires a Threshing Floor and Constructs an Altar There

24:18 So Gad went to David that day and told him, "Go up and build an altar for the LORD on the threshing floor of Araunah the Jebusite." **24:19** So David went up as Gad instructed him to do, according to the LORD's instructions.
24:20 When Araunah looked out and saw the king and his servants approaching him, he went out and bowed to the king with his face to the ground. **24:21** Araunah said, "Why has my lord the king come to his servant?" David replied, "To buy from you the threshing floor so I can build an altar for the LORD, so that the plague may be removed from the people." **24:22** Araunah told David, "My lord the king may take whatever he wishes and offer it. Look! Here are oxen for burnt offerings, and threshing sledges and harnesses for wood. **24:23** I, the servant of my lord the king, give it all to the king!" Araunah also told the king, "May the LORD your God show you favor!" **24:24** But the king said to Araunah, "No, I insist on buying it from you! I will not offer to the LORD my God burnt sacrifices that cost me nothing."
So David bought the threshing floor and the oxen for fifty pieces of silver. **24:25** Then David built an altar for the LORD there and offered burnt sacrifices and peace offerings. And the LORD accepted prayers for the land, and the plague was removed from Israel.

Book 11. 1 Kings

Adonijah Tries to Seize the Throne

1:1 King David was very old; even when they covered him with blankets, he could not get warm. **1:2** His servants advised him, "A young virgin must be found for our master, the king, to take care of the king's needs and serve as his nurse. She can also sleep with you and keep our master, the king, warm." **1:3** So they looked through all Israel for a beautiful young woman and found Abishag, a Shunammite, and brought her to the king. **1:4** The young woman was very beautiful; she became the king's nurse and served him, but the king did not have sexual relations with her. **1:5** Now Adonijah, son of David and Haggith, was promoting himself, boasting, "I will be king!" He managed to acquire chariots and horsemen, as well as fifty men to serve as his royal guard. **1:6** (Now his father had never corrected him by saying, "Why do you do such things?" He was also very handsome and had been born right after Absalom.) **1:7** He collaborated with Joab son of Zeruiah and with Abiathar the priest, and they supported him. **1:8** But Zadok the priest, Benaiah son of Jehoiada, Nathan the prophet, Shimei, Rei, and David's elite warriors did not ally themselves with Adonijah. **1:9** Adonijah sacrificed sheep, cattle, and fattened steers at the Stone of Zoheleth near En Rogel. He invited all his brothers, the king's sons, as well as all the men of Judah, the king's servants. **1:10** But he did not invite Nathan the prophet, Benaiah, the elite warriors, or his brother Solomon.

1:11 Nathan said to Bathsheba, Solomon's mother, "Has it been reported to you that Haggith's son Adonijah has become king behind our master David's back? **1:12** Now let me give you some advice as to how you can save your life and your son Solomon's life. **1:13** Visit King David and say to him, 'My master, O king, did you not solemnly promise your servant, "Surely your son Solomon will be king after me; he will sit on my throne"? So why has Adonijah become king?' **1:14** While you are still there speaking to the king, I will arrive and verify your report."

1:15 So Bathsheba visited the king in his private quarters. (The king was very old, and Abishag the Shunammite was serving the king.) **1:16** Bathsheba bowed down on the floor before the king. The king said, "What do you want?" **1:17** She replied to him, "My master, you swore an oath to your servant by the LORD your God, 'Solomon your son will be king after me and he will sit on my throne.' **1:18** But now, look, Adonijah has become king! But you, my master the king, are not even aware of it! **1:19** He has sacrificed many cattle, steers, and sheep and has invited all the king's sons, Abiathar the priest, and Joab, the commander of the army, but he has not invited your servant Solomon. **1:20** Now, my master, O king, all Israel is watching anxiously to see who is named to succeed my master the king on the throne. **1:21** If a decision is not made, when my master the king is buried with his ancestors, my son Solomon and I will be considered state criminals."

1:22 Just then, while she was still speaking to the king, Nathan the prophet arrived. **1:23** The king was told, "Nathan the prophet is here." Nathan entered and bowed before the king with his face to the floor. **1:24** Nathan said, "My master, O king, did you announce, 'Adonijah will be king after me; he will sit on my throne'? **1:25** For today he has gone down and sacrificed many cattle, steers, and sheep and has invited all the king's sons, the army commanders, and Abiathar the priest. At this moment they are having a feast in his presence, and they have declared, 'Long live King Adonijah!' **1:26** But he did not invite me – your servant – or Zadok the priest, or Benaiah son of Jehoiada, or your servant Solomon. **1:27** Has my master the king authorized this without informing your servants who should succeed my master the king on his throne?"

David Picks Solomon as His Successor

1:28 King David responded, "Summon Bathsheba!" She came and stood before the king. **1:29** The king swore an oath: "As certainly as the LORD lives (he who has rescued me from every danger), **1:30** I will keep today the oath I swore to you by the LORD God of Israel: 'Surely Solomon your son will be king after me; he will sit in my place on my throne.'" **1:31** Bathsheba bowed down to the king with her face to the floor and said, "May my master, King David, live forever!"

1:32 King David said, "Summon Zadok the priest, Nathan the prophet, and Benaiah son of Jehoiada." They came before the king, **1:33** and he told them, "Take your master's servants with you, put my son Solomon on my mule, and lead him down to Gihon. **1:34** There Zadok the priest and Nathan the prophet will anoint him king over Israel; then blow the trumpet and declare, 'Long live King Solomon!' **1:35** Then follow him up as he comes and sits on my throne. He will be king in my place; I have decreed that he will be ruler over Israel and Judah." **1:36** Benaiah son of Jehoiada responded to the king: "So be it! May the LORD God of my master the king confirm it! **1:37** As the LORD is with my master the king, so may he be with Solomon, and may he make him an even greater king than my master King David!"

1:38 So Zadok the priest, Nathan the prophet, Benaiah son of Jehoiada, the Kerethites, and the Pelethites went down, put Solomon on King David's mule, and led him to Gihon. **1:39** Zadok the priest took a horn filled with olive oil from the tent and poured it on Solomon; the trumpet was blown and all the people declared, "Long live King Solomon!" **1:40** All the people followed him up, playing flutes and celebrating so loudly they made the ground shake.

1:41 Now Adonijah and all his guests heard the commotion just as they had finished eating. When Joab heard the sound of the trumpet, he asked, "Why is there such a noisy commotion in the city?" **1:42** As he was still speaking, Jonathan son of Abiathar the priest arrived. Adonijah said, "Come in, for an important man like you must be bringing good news." **1:43** Jonathan replied to Adonijah: "No! Our master King David has made Solomon king. **1:44** The king sent with him Zadok the priest, Nathan the prophet, Benaiah son of Jehoiada, the Kerethites, and the Pelethites and they put him on the king's mule. **1:45** Then Zadok the priest and Nathan the prophet anointed him king in Gihon. They went up from there rejoicing, and the city is in an uproar. That is the sound you hear. **1:46** Furthermore, Solomon has assumed the royal throne. **1:47** The king's servants have even come to congratulate our master King David, saying, 'May your God make Solomon more famous than you and make him an even greater king than you!' Then the king leaned on the bed **1:48** and said this: 'The LORD God of Israel is worthy of praise because today he has placed a successor on my throne and allowed me to see it.'"

1:49 All of Adonijah's guests panicked; they jumped up and rushed off their separate ways. **1:50** Adonijah feared Solomon, so he got up and went and grabbed hold of the horns of the altar. **1:51** Solomon was told, "Look, Adonijah fears you; see, he has taken hold of the horns of the altar, saying, 'May King Solomon solemnly promise me today that he will not kill his servant with the sword.'" **1:52** Solomon said, "If he is a loyal subject, not a hair of his head will be harmed, but if he is found to be a traitor, he will die." **1:53** King Solomon sent men to bring him down from the altar. He came and bowed down to King Solomon, and Solomon told him, "Go home."

David's Final Words to Solomon

2:1 When David was close to death, he told Solomon his son: **2:2** "I am about to die. Be strong and become a man! **2:3** Do the job the LORD your God has assigned you by following his instructions and obeying his rules, commandments, regulations, and laws as written in the law of Moses. Then you will succeed in all you do and seek to accomplish, **2:4** and the LORD will fulfill his promise to me, 'If your descendants watch their step and live faithfully in my presence with all their heart and being, then,' he promised, 'you will not fail to have a successor on the throne of Israel.'

2:5 "You know what Joab son of Zeruiah did to me – how he murdered two commanders of the Israelite armies, Abner son of Ner and Amasa son of Jether. During peacetime he struck them down like he would in battle; when he shed their blood as if in battle, he stained his own belt and the sandals on his feet. **2:6** Do to him what you think is appropriate, but don't let him live long and die a peaceful death.

2:7 "Treat fairly the sons of Barzillai of Gilead and provide for their needs, because they helped me when I had to flee from your brother Absalom.

2:8 "Note well, you still have to contend with Shimei son of Gera, the Benjaminite from Bahurim, who tried to call down upon me a horrible judgment when I went to Mahanaim. He came down and met me at the Jordan, and I solemnly promised him by the LORD, 'I will not strike you down with the sword.' **2:9** But now don't treat him as if he were innocent. You are a wise man and you know how to handle him; make sure he has a bloody death."

2:10 Then David passed away and was buried in the city of David. **2:11** David reigned over Israel forty years; he reigned in Hebron seven years, and in Jerusalem thirty-three years.

Solomon Secures the Throne

2:12 Solomon sat on his father David's throne, and his royal authority was firmly solidified.

2:13 Haggith's son Adonijah visited Bathsheba, Solomon's mother. She asked, "Do you come in peace?" He answered, "Yes." **2:14** He added, "I have something to say to you." She replied, "Speak." **2:15** He said, "You know that the kingdom was mine and all Israel considered me king. But then the kingdom was given to my brother, for the LORD decided it should be his. **2:16** Now I'd like to ask you for just one thing. Please don't refuse me." She said, "Go ahead and ask." **2:17** He said, "Please ask King Solomon if he would give me Abishag the Shunammite as a wife, for he won't refuse you." **2:18** Bathsheba replied, "That's fine, I'll speak to the king on your behalf."

2:19 So Bathsheba visited King Solomon to speak to him on Adonijah's behalf. The king got up to greet her, bowed to her, and then sat on his throne. He ordered a throne to be brought for the king's mother, and she sat at his right hand. **2:20** She said, "I would like to ask you for just one small favor. Please don't refuse me." He said, "Go ahead and ask, my mother, for I would not refuse you." **2:21** She said, "Allow Abishag the Shunammite to be given to your brother Adonijah as a wife." **2:22** King Solomon answered his mother, "Why just request Abishag the Shunammite for him? Since he is my older brother, you should also request the kingdom for him, for Abiathar the priest, and for Joab son of Zeruiah!"

2:23 King Solomon then swore an oath by the LORD, "May God judge me severely, if Adonijah does not pay for this request with his life! **2:24** Now, as certainly as the LORD lives (he who made me secure, allowed me to sit on my father David's throne, and established a dynasty for me as he promised), Adonijah will be executed today!" **2:25** King Solomon then sent Benaiah son of Jehoiada, and he killed Adonijah.

2:26 The king then told Abiathar the priest, "Go back to your property in Anathoth. You deserve to die, but today I will not kill you because you did carry the ark of the sovereign LORD before my father David and you suffered with my father through all his difficult times." **2:27** Solomon dismissed Abiathar from his position as priest of the LORD, fulfilling the decree of judgment the LORD made in Shiloh against the family of Eli.

2:28 When the news reached Joab (for Joab had supported Adonijah, although he had not supported Absalom), he ran to the tent of the LORD and grabbed hold of the horns of the altar. **2:29** When King Solomon heard that Joab had run to the tent of the LORD and was right there beside the altar, he ordered Benaiah son of Jehoiada, "Go, strike him down." **2:30** When Benaiah arrived at the tent of the LORD, he said to him, "The king says, 'Come out!'" But he replied, "No, I will die here!" So Benaiah sent word to the king and reported Joab's reply. **2:31** The king told him, "Do as he said! Strike him down and bury him. Take away from me and from my father's family the guilt of Joab's murderous, bloody deeds. **2:32** May the LORD punish him for the blood he shed; behind my father David's back he struck down and murdered with the sword two men who were more innocent and morally upright than he – Abner son of Ner, commander of Israel's army, and Amasa son of Jether, commander of Judah's army. **2:33** May Joab and his descendants be perpetually guilty of their shed blood, but may the LORD give perpetual peace to David, his descendants, his family, and his dynasty." **2:34** So Benaiah son of Jehoiada went up and executed Joab; he was buried at his home in the wilderness. **2:35** The king appointed Benaiah son of Jehoiada to take his place at the head of the army, and the king appointed Zadok the priest to take Abiathar's place.

2:36 Next the king summoned Shimei and told him, "Build yourself a house in Jerusalem and live there – but you may not leave there to go anywhere! **2:37** If you ever do leave and cross the Kidron Valley, know for sure that you will certainly die! You will be responsible for your own death." **2:38** Shimei said to the king, "My master the king's proposal is acceptable. Your servant will do as you say." So Shimei lived in Jerusalem for a long time.

2:39 Three years later two of Shimei's servants ran away to King Achish son of Maacah of Gath. Shimei was told, "Look, your servants are in Gath." **2:40** So Shimei got up, saddled his donkey, and went to Achish at Gath to find his servants; Shimei went and brought back his servants from Gath. **2:41** When Solomon was told that Shimei had gone from Jerusalem to Gath and had then returned, **2:42** the king summoned Shimei and said to him, "You will recall that I made you take an oath by the LORD, and I solemnly warned you, 'If you ever leave and go anywhere, know for sure that you will certainly die.' You said to me, 'The proposal is acceptable; I agree to it.' **2:43** Why then have you broken the oath you made before the LORD and disobeyed the order I gave you?" **2:44** Then the king said to Shimei, "You are well aware of the way you mistreated my father David. The LORD will punish you for what you did. **2:45** But King Solomon will be empowered and David's dynasty will endure permanently before the LORD." **2:46** The king then gave the order to Benaiah son of Jehoiada who went and executed Shimei.

So Solomon took firm control of the kingdom.

The Lord Gives Solomon Wisdom

3:1 Solomon made an alliance by marriage with Pharaoh, king of Egypt; he married Pharaoh's daughter. He brought her to the City of David until he could finish building his residence and the temple of the LORD and the wall around Jerusalem. **3:2** Now the people were offering sacrifices at the high places, because in those days a temple had not yet been built to honor the LORD. **3:3** Solomon demonstrated his loyalty to the LORD by following the practices of his father David, except that he offered sacrifices and burned incense on the high places.

3:4 The king went to Gibeon to offer sacrifices, for it had the most prominent of the high places. Solomon would offer up a thousand burnt sacrifices on the altar there. **3:5** One night in Gibeon the LORD appeared to Solomon in a dream. God said, "Tell me what I should give you." **3:6** Solomon replied, "You demonstrated great loyalty to your servant, my father David, as he served you faithfully, properly, and sincerely. You have maintained this great loyalty to this day by allowing his son to sit on his throne. **3:7** Now, O LORD my God, you have made your servant king in my father David's place, even though I am only a young man and am inexperienced. **3:8** Your servant stands among your chosen people; they are a great nation that is too numerous to count or number. **3:9** So give your servant a discerning mind so he can make judicial decisions for your people and distinguish right from wrong. Otherwise no one is able to make judicial decisions for this great nation of yours." **3:10** The Lord was pleased that Solomon made this request. **3:11** God said to him, "Because you asked for the ability to make wise judicial decisions, and not for long life, or riches, or vengeance on your enemies, **3:12** I grant your request,

and give you a wise and discerning mind superior to that of anyone who has preceded or will succeed you. **3:13** Furthermore, I am giving you what you did not request – riches and honor so that you will be the greatest king of your generation. **3:14** If you follow my instructions by obeying my rules and regulations, just as your father David did, then I will grant you long life." **3:15** Solomon then woke up and realized it was a dream. He went to Jerusalem, stood before the ark of the Lord's covenant, offered up burnt sacrifices, presented peace offerings, and held a feast for all his servants.

Solomon Demonstrates His Wisdom

3:16 Then two prostitutes came to the king and stood before him. **3:17** One of the women said, "My master, this woman and I live in the same house. I had a baby while she was with me in the house. **3:18** Then three days after I had my baby, this woman also had a baby. We were alone; there was no one else in the house except the two of us. **3:19** This woman's child suffocated during the night when he rolled on top of him. **3:20** She got up in the middle of the night and took my son from my side, while your servant was sleeping. She put him in her arms, and put her dead son in my arms. **3:21** I got up in the morning to nurse my son, and there he was, dead! But when I examined him carefully in the morning, I realized it was not my baby." **3:22** The other woman said, "No! My son is alive; your son is dead!" But the first woman replied, "No, your son is dead; my son is alive." Each presented her case before the king.

3:23 The king said, "One says, 'My son is alive; your son is dead,' while the other says, 'No, your son is dead; my son is alive.'" **3:24** The king ordered, "Get me a sword!" So they placed a sword before the king. **3:25** The king then said, "Cut the living child in two, and give half to one and half to the other!" **3:26** The real mother spoke up to the king, for her motherly instincts were aroused. She said, "My master, give her the living child! Whatever you do, don't kill him!" But the other woman said, "Neither one of us will have him! Let them cut him in two!" **3:27** The king responded, "Give the first woman the living child; don't kill him. She is the mother." **3:28** When all Israel heard about the judicial decision which the king had rendered, they respected the king, for they realized that he possessed supernatural wisdom to make judicial decisions.

Solomon's Royal Court and Administrators

4:1 King Solomon ruled over all Israel. **4:2** These were his officials: Azariah son of Zadok was the priest.

4:3 Elihoreph and Ahijah, the sons of Shisha, wrote down what happened.

Jehoshaphat son of Ahilud was in charge of the records.

4:4 Benaiah son of Jehoiada was commander of the army.

Zadok and Abiathar were priests.

4:5 Azariah son of Nathan was supervisor of the district governors.

Zabud son of Nathan was a priest and adviser to the king.

4:6 Ahishar was supervisor of the palace.

Adoniram son of Abda was supervisor of the work crews.

4:7 Solomon had twelve district governors appointed throughout Israel who acquired supplies for the king and his palace. Each was responsible for one month in the year. **4:8** These were their names:

Ben-Hur was in charge of the hill country of Ephraim.

4:9 Ben-Deker was in charge of Makaz, Shaalbim, Beth Shemesh, and Elon Beth Hanan.

4:10 Ben-Hesed was in charge of Arubboth; he controlled Socoh and all the territory of Hepher.

4:11 Ben-Abinadab was in charge of Naphath Dor. (He was married to Solomon's daughter Taphath.)

4:12 Baana son of Ahilud was in charge of Taanach and Megiddo, as well as all of Beth Shan next to Zarethan below Jezreel, from Beth Shan to Abel Meholah and on past Jokmeam.

4:13 Ben-Geber was in charge of Ramoth Gilead, he controlled the tent villages of Jair son of Manasseh in Gilead, as well as the region of Argob in Bashan, including sixty large walled cities with bronze bars locking their gates.

4:14 Ahinadab son of Iddo was in charge of Mahanaim.

4:15 Ahimaaz was in charge of Naphtali. (He married Solomon's daughter Basemath.)

4:16 Baana son of Hushai was in charge of Asher and Aloth.

4:17 Jehoshaphat son of Paruah was in charge of Issachar.

4:18 Shimei son of Ela was in charge of Benjamin.

4:19 Geber son of Uri was in charge of the land of Gilead (the territory which had once belonged to King Sihon of the Amorites and to King Og of Bashan). He was sole governor of the area.

Solomon's Wealth and Fame

4:20 The people of Judah and Israel were as innumerable as the sand on the seashore; they had plenty to eat and drink and were happy. **4:21** (5:1) Solomon ruled all the kingdoms from the Euphrates River to the land of the Philistines, as far as the border of Egypt. These kingdoms paid tribute as Solomon's subjects throughout his lifetime. **4:22** Each day Solomon's royal court consumed thirty cors of finely milled flour, sixty cors of cereal, **4:23** ten calves fattened in the stall, twenty calves from the pasture, and a hundred sheep, not to mention rams, gazelles, deer, and well-fed birds. **4:24** His royal court was so large because he ruled over all the kingdoms west of the Euphrates River from Tiphsah to Gaza; he was at peace with all his neighbors. **4:25** All the people of Judah and Israel had security; everyone from Dan to Beer Sheba enjoyed the produce of their vines and fig trees throughout Solomon's lifetime. **4:26** Solomon had 4,000 stalls for his chariot horses and 12,000 horses. **4:27** The district governors acquired supplies for King Solomon and all who ate in his royal palace. Each was responsible for one month in the year; they made sure nothing was lacking. **4:28** Each one also brought to the assigned location his quota of barley and straw for the various horses.

4:29 God gave Solomon wisdom and very great discernment; the breadth of his understanding was as infinite as the sand on the seashore. **4:30** Solomon was wiser than all the men of the east and all the sages of Egypt. **4:31** He was wiser than any man, including Ethan the Ezrahite or Heman, Calcol, and Darda, the sons of Mahol. He was famous in all the neighboring nations. **4:32** He composed 3,000 proverbs and 1,005 songs. **4:33** He produced manuals on botany, describing every kind of plant, from the cedars of Lebanon to the hyssop that grows on walls. He also produced manuals on biology, describing animals, birds, insects, and fish. **4:34** People from all nations came to hear Solomon's display of wisdom; they came from all the kings of the earth who heard about his wisdom.

Solomon Gathers Building Materials for the Temple

5:1 (5:15) King Hiram of Tyre sent messengers to Solomon when he heard that he had been anointed king in his father's place. (Hiram had always been an ally of David.) **5:2** Solomon then sent this message to Hiram: **5:3** "You know that my father David was unable to build a temple to honor the LORD his God, for he was busy fighting battles on all fronts while the LORD subdued his enemies. **5:4** But now the LORD my God has made me secure on all fronts; there is no adversary or dangerous threat. **5:5** So I have decided to build a temple to honor the LORD my God, as the LORD instructed my father David, 'Your son, whom I will put on your throne in your place, is the one who will build a temple to honor me.' **5:6** So now order some cedars of Lebanon to be cut for me. My servants will work with your servants. I will pay your servants whatever you say is appropriate, for you know that we have no one among us who knows how to cut down trees like the Sidonians."

5:7 When Hiram heard Solomon's message, he was very happy. He said, "The LORD is worthy of praise today because he has given David a wise son to rule over this great nation." **5:8** Hiram then sent this message to Solomon: "I received the message you sent to me. I will give you all the cedars and evergreens you need. **5:9** My servants will bring the timber down from Lebanon to the sea. I will send it by sea in raft-like bundles to the place you designate. There I will separate the logs and you can carry them away. In exchange you will supply the food I need for my royal court."

5:10 So Hiram supplied the cedars and evergreens Solomon needed, **5:11** and Solomon supplied Hiram annually with 20,000 cors of wheat as provision for his royal court, as well as 20,000 baths of pure olive oil. **5:12** So the LORD gave Solomon wisdom, as he had promised him. And Hiram and Solomon were at peace and made a treaty.

5:13 King Solomon conscripted work crews from throughout Israel, 30,000 men in all. **5:14** He sent them to Lebanon in shifts of 10,000 men per month. They worked in Lebanon for one month, and then spent two months at home. Adoniram was supervisor of the work crews. **5:15** Solomon also had 70,000 common laborers and 80,000 stonecutters in the hills, **5:16** besides 3,300 officials who supervised the workers. **5:17** By royal order they supplied large valuable stones in order to build the temple's foundation with chiseled stone. **5:18** Solomon's and Hiram's construction workers, along with men from Byblos, did the chiseling and prepared the wood and stones for the building of the temple.

The Building of the Temple

6:1 In the four hundred and eightieth year after the Israelites left Egypt, in the fourth year of Solomon's reign over Israel, during the month Ziv (the second month), he began building the LORD's temple. **6:2** The temple King Solomon built for the LORD was 90 feet long, 30 feet wide, and 45 feet high. **6:3** The porch in front of the main hall of the temple was 30 feet long, corresponding to the width of the temple. It was 15 feet wide, extending out from the front of the temple. **6:4** He made framed windows for the temple. **6:5** He built an extension all around the walls of the temple's main hall and holy place and constructed side rooms in it. **6:6** The bottom floor of the extension was seven and a half feet wide, the middle floor nine feet wide, and the third floor ten and a half feet wide. He made ledges on the temple's outer walls so the beams would not have to be inserted into the walls. **6:7** As the temple was being built, only stones shaped at the quarry were used; the sound of hammers, pickaxes, or any other iron tool was not heard at the temple while it was being built. **6:8** The entrance to the bottom level of side rooms was on the south side of the temple; stairs went up to the middle floor and then on up to the third floor. **6:9** He finished building the temple and covered it with rafters and boards made of cedar. **6:10** He built an extension all around the temple; it was seven and a half feet high and it was attached to the temple by cedar beams.

6:11 The LORD said to Solomon: **6:12** "As for this temple you are building, if you follow my rules, observe my regulations, and obey all my commandments, I will fulfill through you the promise I made to your father David. **6:13** I will live among the Israelites and will not abandon my people Israel."

6:14 So Solomon finished building the temple. **6:15** He constructed the walls inside the temple with cedar planks; he paneled the inside with wood from the floor of the temple to the rafters of the ceiling. He covered the temple floor with boards made from the wood of evergreens. **6:16** He built a wall 30 feet in from the rear of the temple as a partition for an inner sanctuary that would be the most holy place. He paneled the wall with cedar planks from the floor to the rafters. **6:17** The main hall in front of the inner sanctuary was 60 feet long. **6:18** The inside of the temple was all cedar and was adorned with carvings of round ornaments and of flowers in bloom. Everything was cedar; no stones were visible.

6:19 He prepared the inner sanctuary inside the temple so that the ark of the covenant of the LORD could be placed there. **6:20** The inner sanctuary was 30 feet long, 30 feet wide, and 30 feet high. He plated it with gold, as well as the cedar altar. **6:21** Solomon plated the inside of the temple with gold. He hung golden chains in front of the inner sanctuary and plated the inner sanctuary with gold. **6:22** He plated the entire inside of the temple with gold, as well as the altar inside the inner sanctuary.

6:23 In the inner sanctuary he made two cherubs of olive wood; each stood 15 feet high. **6:24** Each of the first cherub's wings was seven and a half feet long; its entire wingspan was 15 feet. **6:25** The second cherub also had a wingspan of 15 feet; it was identical to the first in measurements and shape. **6:26** Each cherub stood 15 feet high. **6:27** He put the cherubs in the inner sanctuary of the temple. Their wings were spread out. One of the first cherub's wings touched one wall and one of the other cherub's wings touched the opposite wall. The first cherub's other wing touched the second cherub's other wing in the middle of the room. **6:28** He plated the cherubs with gold.

6:29 On all the walls around the temple, inside and out, he carved cherubs, palm trees, and flowers in bloom. **6:30** He plated the floor of the temple with gold, inside and out. **6:31** He made doors of olive wood at the entrance to the inner sanctuary; the pillar on each doorpost was five-sided. **6:32** On the two doors made of olive wood he carved cherubs, palm trees, and flowers in bloom, and he plated them with gold. He plated the cherubs and the palm trees with hammered gold. **6:33** In the same way he made doorposts of olive wood for the entrance to the main hall, only with four-sided pillars. **6:34** He also made two doors out of wood from evergreens; each door had two folding leaves. **6:35** He carved cherubs, palm trees, and flowers in bloom and plated them with gold, leveled out over the carvings. **6:36** He built the inner courtyard with three rows of chiseled stones and a row of cedar beams.

6:37 In the month Ziv of the fourth year of Solomon's reign the foundation was laid for the LORD's temple. **6:38** In the eleventh year, in the month Bul (the eighth month) the temple was completed in accordance with all its specifications and blueprints. It took seven years to build.

The Building of the Royal Palace

7:1 Solomon took thirteen years to build his palace. **7:2** He named it "The Palace of the Lebanon Forest"; it was 150 feet long, 75 feet wide, and 45 feet high. It had four rows of cedar pillars and cedar beams above the pillars. **7:3** The roof above the beams supported by the pillars was also made of cedar; there were forty-five beams, fifteen per row. **7:4** There were three rows of windows arranged in sets of three. **7:5** All of the entrances were rectangular in shape and they were arranged in sets of three. **7:6** He made a colonnade 75 feet long and 45 feet wide. There was a porch in front of this and pillars and a roof in front of the porch. **7:7** He also made a throne room, called "The Hall of Judgment," where he made judicial decisions. It was paneled with cedar from the floor to the rafters. **7:8** The palace where he lived was constructed in a similar way. He also constructed a palace like this hall for Pharaoh's daughter, whom he had married. **7:9** All of these were built with the best stones, chiseled to the right size and cut with a saw on all sides, from the foundation to the edge of the roof and from the outside to the great courtyard. **7:10** The foundation was made of large valuable stones, measuring either 15 feet or 12 feet. **7:11** Above the foundation the best stones, chiseled to the right size, were used along with cedar. **7:12** Around the great courtyard were three rows of chiseled stones and one row of cedar beams, like the inner courtyard of the LORD's temple and the hall of the palace.

Solomon Commissions Hiram to Supply the Temple

7:13 King Solomon sent for Hiram of Tyre. **7:14** He was the son of a widow from the tribe of Naphtali, and his father was a craftsman in bronze from Tyre. He had the skill and knowledge to make all kinds of works of bronze. He reported to King Solomon and did all the work he was assigned.

7:15 He fashioned two bronze pillars; each pillar was 27 feet high and 18 feet in circumference. **7:16** He made two bronze tops for the pillars; each was seven-and-a-half feet high. **7:17** The latticework on the tops of the pillars was adorned with ornamental wreaths and chains; the top of each pillar had seven groupings of ornaments. **7:18** When he made the pillars, there were two rows of pomegranate-shaped ornaments around the latticework covering the top of each pillar. **7:19** The tops of the two pillars in the porch were shaped like lilies and were six feet high. **7:20** On the top of each pillar, right above the bulge beside the latticework, there were two hundred pomegranate-shaped ornaments arranged in rows all the way around. **7:21** He set up the pillars on the porch in front of the main hall. He erected one pillar on the right side and called it Jakin; he erected the other pillar on the left side and called it Boaz. **7:22** The tops of the pillars were shaped like lilies. So the construction of the pillars was completed. **7:23** He also made the large bronze basin called "The Sea." It measured 15 feet from rim to rim, was circular in shape, and stood seven-and-a-half feet high. Its circumference was 45 feet. **7:24** Under the rim all the way around it were round ornaments arranged in settings 15 feet long. The ornaments were in two rows and had been cast with "The Sea." **7:25** "The Sea" stood on top of twelve bulls. Three faced northward, three westward, three southward, and three eastward. "The Sea" was placed on top of them, and they all faced outward. **7:26** It was four fingers thick and its rim was like that of a cup shaped like a lily blossom. It could hold about 12,000 gallons.

7:27 He also made ten bronze movable stands. Each stand was six feet long, six feet wide, and four-and-a-half feet high. **7:28** The stands were constructed with frames between the joints. **7:29** On these frames and joints were ornamental lions, bulls, and cherubs. Under the lions and bulls were decorative wreaths. **7:30** Each stand had four bronze wheels with bronze axles and four supports. Under the basin the supports were fashioned on each side with wreaths. **7:31** Inside the stand was a round opening that was a foot-and-a-half deep; it had a support that was two and one-quarter feet long. On the edge of the opening were carvings in square frames. **7:32** The four wheels were under the frames and the crossbars of the axles were connected to the stand. Each wheel was two and one-quarter feet high. **7:33** The wheels were constructed like chariot wheels; their crossbars, rims, spokes, and hubs were made of cast metal. **7:34** Each stand had four supports, one per side projecting out from the stand. **7:35** On top of each stand was a round opening three-quarters of a foot deep; there were also supports and frames on top of the stands. **7:36** He engraved ornamental cherubs, lions, and palm trees on the plates of the supports and frames wherever there was room, with wreaths all around. **7:37** He made the ten stands in this way. All of them were cast in one mold and were identical in measurements and shape.

7:38 He also made ten bronze basins, each of which could hold about 240 gallons. Each basin was six feet in diameter; there was one basin for each stand. **7:39** He put five basins on the south side of the temple and five on the north side. He put "The Sea" on the south side, in the southeast corner.

7:40 Hiram also made basins, shovels, and bowls. He finished all the work on the LORD's temple he had been assigned by King Solomon. **7:41** He made the two pillars, the two bowl-shaped tops of the pillars, the latticework for the bowl-shaped tops of the two pillars, **7:42** the four hundred pomegranate-shaped ornaments for the latticework of the two pillars (each latticework had two rows of these ornaments at the bowl-shaped top of the pillar), **7:43** the ten movable stands with their ten basins, **7:44** the big bronze basin called "The Sea" with its twelve bulls underneath, **7:45** and the pots, shovels, and bowls. All these items King Solomon assigned Hiram to make for the LORD's temple were made from polished bronze. **7:46** The king had them cast in earth foundries in the region of the Jordan between Succoth and Zarethan. **7:47** Solomon left all these items unweighed; there were so many of them they did not weigh the bronze.

7:48 Solomon also made all these items for the LORD's temple: the gold altar, the gold table on which was kept the Bread of the Presence, **7:49** the pure gold lampstands at the entrance to the inner sanctuary (five on the right and five on the left), the gold flower-shaped ornaments, lamps, and tongs, **7:50** the pure gold bowls, trimming shears, basins, pans, and censers, and the gold door sockets for the inner sanctuary (the most holy place) and for the doors of the main hall of the temple. **7:51** When King Solomon finished constructing the LORD's temple, he put the holy items that belonged to his father David (the silver, gold, and other articles) in the treasuries of the LORD's temple.

Solomon Moves the Ark into the Temple

8:1 Then Solomon convened in Jerusalem Israel's elders, all the leaders of the Israelite tribes and families, so they could witness the transferal of the ark of the LORD's covenant from the city of David (that is, Zion). **8:2** All the men of Israel assembled before King Solomon during the festival in the month Ethanim (the seventh month). **8:3** When all Israel's elders had arrived, the priests lifted the ark. **8:4** The priests and Levites carried the ark of the LORD, the tent of meeting, and all the holy items in the tent. **8:5** Now King Solomon and all the Israelites who had assembled with him went on ahead of the ark and sacrificed more sheep and cattle than could be counted or numbered.

8:6 The priests brought the ark of the LORD's covenant to its assigned place in the inner sanctuary of the temple, in the most holy place, under the wings of the cherubs. **8:7** The cherubs' wings extended over the place where the ark sat; the cherubs overshadowed the ark and its poles. **8:8** The poles were so long their ends were visible from the holy place in front of the inner sanctuary, but they could not be seen from beyond that point. They have remained there to this very day. **8:9** There was nothing

in the ark except the two stone tablets Moses had placed there in Horeb. It was there that the LORD made an agreement with the Israelites after he brought them out of the land of Egypt. **8:10** Once the priests left the holy place, a cloud filled the LORD's temple. **8:11** The priests could not carry out their duties because of the cloud; the LORD's glory filled his temple. **8:12** Then Solomon said, "The LORD has said that he lives in thick darkness. **8:13** O LORD, truly I have built a lofty temple for you, a place where you can live permanently." **8:14** Then the king turned around and pronounced a blessing over the whole Israelite assembly as they stood there. **8:15** He said, "The LORD God of Israel is worthy of praise because he has fulfilled what he promised my father David. **8:16** He told David, 'Since the day I brought my people Israel out of Egypt, I have not chosen a city from all the tribes of Israel to build a temple in which to live. But I have chosen David to lead my people Israel.' **8:17** Now my father David had a strong desire to build a temple to honor the LORD God of Israel. **8:18** The LORD told my father David, 'It is right for you to have a strong desire to build a temple to honor me. **8:19** But you will not build the temple; your very own son will build the temple for my honor.' **8:20** The LORD has kept the promise he made. I have taken my father David's place and have occupied the throne of Israel, as the LORD promised. I have built this temple for the honor of the LORD God of Israel **8:21** and set up in it a place for the ark containing the covenant the LORD made with our ancestors when he brought them out of the land of Egypt."

Solomon Prays for Israel

8:22 Solomon stood before the altar of the LORD in front of the entire assembly of Israel and spread out his hands toward the sky. **8:23** He prayed: "O LORD, God of Israel, there is no god like you in heaven above or on earth below! You maintain covenantal loyalty to your servants who obey you with sincerity. **8:24** You have kept your word to your servant, my father David; this very day you have fulfilled what you promised. **8:25** Now, O LORD, God of Israel, keep the promise you made to your servant, my father David, when you said, 'You will never fail to have a successor ruling before me on the throne of Israel, provided that your descendants watch their step and serve me as you have done.' **8:26** Now, O God of Israel, may the promise you made to your servant, my father David, be realized.

8:27 "God does not really live on the earth! Look, if the sky and the highest heaven cannot contain you, how much less this temple I have built! **8:28** But respond favorably to your servant's prayer and his request for help, O LORD my God. Answer the desperate prayer your servant is presenting to you today. **8:29** Night and day may you watch over this temple, the place where you promised you would live. May you answer your servant's prayer for this place. **8:30** Respond to the request of your servant and your people Israel for this place. Hear from inside your heavenly dwelling place and respond favorably.

8:31 "When someone is accused of sinning against his neighbor and the latter pronounces a curse on the alleged offender before your altar in this temple, be willing to forgive the accused if the accusation is false. **8:32** Listen from heaven and make a just decision about your servants' claims. Condemn the guilty party, declare the other innocent, and give both of them what they deserve.

8:33 "The time will come when your people Israel are defeated by an enemy because they sinned against you. If they come back to you, renew their allegiance to you, and pray for your help in this temple, **8:34** then listen from heaven, forgive the sin of your people Israel, and bring back to the land you gave to their ancestors.

8:35 "The time will come when the skies are shut up tightly and no rain falls because your people sinned against you. When they direct their prayers toward this place, renew their allegiance to you, and turn away from their sin because you punish them, **8:36** then listen from heaven and forgive the sin of your servants, your people Israel. Certainly you will then teach them the right way to live and send rain on your land that you have given your people to possess.

8:37 "The time will come when the land suffers from a famine, a plague, blight and disease, or a locust invasion, or when their enemy lays siege to the cities of the land, or when some other type of plague or epidemic occurs. **8:38** When all your people Israel pray and ask for help, as they acknowledge their pain and spread out their hands toward this temple, **8:39** then listen from your heavenly dwelling place, forgive their sin, and act favorably toward each one based on your evaluation of his motives. (Indeed you are the only one who can correctly evaluate the motives of all people.) **8:40** Then they will obey you throughout their lifetimes as they live on the land you gave to our ancestors.

8:41 "Foreigners, who do not belong to your people Israel, will come from a distant land because of your reputation. **8:42** When they hear about your great reputation and your ability to accomplish mighty deeds, they will come and direct their prayers toward this temple. **8:43** Then listen from your heavenly dwelling place and answer all the prayers of the foreigners. Then all the nations of the earth will acknowledge your reputation, obey you like your people Israel do, and recognize that this temple I built belongs to you.

8:44 "When you direct your people to march out and fight their enemies, and they direct their prayers to the LORD toward his chosen city and this temple I built for your honor, **8:45** then listen from heaven to their prayers for help and vindicate them.

8:46 "The time will come when your people will sin against you (for there is no one who is sinless!) and you will be angry with them and deliver them over to their enemies, who will take them as prisoners to their own land, whether far away or close by. **8:47** When your people come to their senses in the land where they are held prisoner, they will repent and beg for your mercy in the land of their imprisonment, admitting, 'We have sinned and gone astray; we have done evil.' **8:48** When they return to you with all their heart and being in the land where they are held prisoner, and direct their prayers to you toward the land you gave to their ancestors, your chosen city, and the temple I built for your honor, **8:49** then listen from your heavenly dwelling place to their prayers for help and vindicate them. **8:50** Forgive all the rebellious acts of your sinful people and cause their captors to have mercy on them. **8:51** After all, they are your people and your special possession whom you brought out of Egypt, from the middle of the iron-smelting furnace.

8:52 "May you be attentive to your servant's and your people Israel's requests for help and may you respond to all their prayers to you. **8:53** After all, you picked them out of all the nations of the earth to be your special possession, just as you, O sovereign LORD, announced through your servant Moses when you brought our ancestors out of Egypt."

8:54 When Solomon finished presenting all these prayers and requests to the LORD, he got up from before the altar of the LORD where he had kneeled and spread out his hands toward the sky. **8:55** When he stood up, he pronounced a blessing over the entire assembly of Israel, saying in a loud voice: **8:56** "The LORD is worthy of praise because he has made Israel his people secure just as he promised! Not one of all the faithful promises he made through his servant Moses is left unfulfilled! **8:57** May the LORD our God be with us, as he was with our ancestors. May he not abandon us or leave us. **8:58** May he make us submissive, so we can follow all his instructions and obey the commandments, rules, and regulations he commanded our ancestors. **8:59** May the LORD our God be constantly aware of these requests of mine I have presented to him, so that he might vindicate his servant and his people Israel as the need arises. **8:60** Then all the nations of the earth will recognize that the LORD is the only genuine God. **8:61** May you demonstrate wholehearted devotion to the LORD our God by following his rules and obeying his commandments, as you are presently doing."

Solomon Dedicates the Temple

8:62 The king and all Israel with him were presenting sacrifices to the LORD. **8:63** Solomon offered as peace offerings to the LORD 22,000 cattle and 120,000 sheep. Then the king and all the Israelites dedicated the LORD's temple. **8:64** That day the king consecrated the middle of the courtyard that is in front of the LORD's temple. He offered there burnt sacrifices, grain offerings, and the fat from the peace offerings, because the bronze altar that stood before the LORD was too small to hold all these offerings. **8:65** At that time Solomon and all Israel with him celebrated a festival before the LORD our God for two entire weeks. This great assembly included people from all over the land, from Lebo Hamath in the north to the Brook of Egypt in the south. **8:66** On the fifteenth day after the festival started, he dismissed the people. They asked God to empower the king and then went to their homes, happy and content because of all the good the LORD had done for his servant David and his people Israel.

The Lord Gives Solomon a Promise and a Warning

9:1 After Solomon finished building the LORD's temple, the royal palace, and all the other construction projects he had planned, **9:2** the LORD appeared to Solomon a second time, in the same way he had appeared to him at Gibeon. **9:3** The LORD said to him, "I have answered your prayer and your request for help that you made to me. I have consecrated this temple you built by making it my permanent home; I will be constantly present there. **9:4** You must serve me with integrity and sincerity, just as your father David did. Do everything I commanded and obey my rules and regulations. **9:5** Then I will allow your dynasty to rule over Israel permanently, just as I promised your father David, 'You will not fail to have a successor on the throne of Israel.'

9:6 "But if you or your sons ever turn away from me, fail to obey the regulations and rules I instructed you to keep, and decide to serve and worship other gods, **9:7** then I will remove Israel from the land I have given them, I will abandon this temple I have consecrated with my presence, and Israel will be mocked and ridiculed among all the nations. **9:8** This temple will become a heap of ruins; everyone who passes by it will be shocked and will hiss out their scorn, saying, 'Why did the LORD do this to this land and this temple?' **9:9** Others will then answer, 'Because they abandoned the LORD their God, who led their ancestors out of Egypt. They embraced other gods whom they worshiped and served. That is why the LORD has brought all this disaster down on them.'"

Foreign Affairs and Building Projects

9:10 After twenty years, during which Solomon built the LORD's temple and the royal palace, **9:11** King Solomon gave King Hiram of Tyre twenty cities in the region of Galilee, because Hiram had supplied Solomon with cedars, evergreens, and all the gold he wanted. **9:12** When Hiram went out from Tyre to inspect the cities Solomon had given him, he was not pleased with them. **9:13** Hiram asked, "Why did you give me these cities, my friend?" He called that area the region of Cabul, a name which it has retained to this day. **9:14** Hiram had sent to the king one hundred twenty talents of gold.

9:15 Here are the details concerning the work crews King Solomon conscripted to build the LORD's temple, his palace, the terrace, the wall of Jerusalem, and the cities of Hazor, Megiddo, and Gezer. **9:16** (Pharaoh, king of Egypt, had attacked and captured Gezer. He burned it and killed the Canaanites who lived in the city. He gave it as a wedding present to his daughter, who had married Solomon.) **9:17** Solomon built up Gezer, lower Beth Horon, **9:18** Baalath, Tadmor in the wilderness, **9:19** all the storage cities that belonged to him, and the cities where chariots and horses were kept. He built whatever he wanted in Jerusalem, Lebanon, and throughout his entire kingdom. **9:20** Now several non-Israelite peoples were left in the land after the conquest of Joshua, including the Amorites, Hittites, Perizzites, Hivites, and Jebusites. **9:21** Their descendants remained in the land (the Israelites were unable to wipe them out completely). Solomon conscripted them for his work crews, and they continue in that role to this very day. **9:22** Solomon did not assign Israelites to these work crews; the Israelites served as his soldiers, attendants, officers, charioteers, and commanders of his chariot forces. **9:23** These men were also in charge of Solomon's work projects; there were a total of 550 men who supervised the workers. **9:24** Solomon built the terrace as soon as Pharaoh's daughter moved up from the city of David to the palace Solomon built for her.

9:25 Three times a year Solomon offered burnt offerings and peace offerings on the altar he had built for the LORD, burning incense along with them before the LORD. He made the temple his official worship place.

9:26 King Solomon also built ships in Ezion Geber, which is located near Elat in the land of Edom, on the shore of the Red Sea. **9:27** Hiram sent his fleet and some of his sailors, who were well acquainted with the sea, to serve with Solomon's men. **9:28** They sailed to Ophir, took from there four hundred twenty talents of gold, and then brought them to King Solomon.

Solomon Entertains a Queen

10:1 When the queen of Sheba heard about Solomon, she came to challenge him with difficult questions. **10:2** She arrived in Jerusalem with a great display of pomp, bringing with her camels carrying spices, a very large quantity of gold, and precious gems. She visited Solomon and discussed with him everything that was on her mind. **10:3** Solomon answered all her questions; there was no question too complex for the king. **10:4** When the queen of Sheba saw for herself Solomon's extensive wisdom, the palace he had built, **10:5** the food in his banquet hall, his servants and attendants, their robes, his cupbearers, and his burnt offerings which he presented in the LORD's temple, she was amazed. **10:6** She said to the king, "The report I heard in my own country about your wise sayings and insight was true! **10:7** I did not believe these things until I came and saw them with my own eyes. Indeed, I didn't hear even half the story! Your wisdom and wealth surpass what was reported to me. **10:8** Your attendants, who stand before you at all times and hear your wise sayings, are truly happy! **10:9** May the LORD your God be praised because he favored you by placing you on the throne of Israel! Because of the LORD's eternal love for Israel, he made you king so you could make just and right decisions." **10:10** She gave the king 120 talents of gold, a very large quantity of spices, and precious gems. The quantity of spices the queen of Sheba gave King Solomon has never been matched. **10:11** (Hiram's fleet, which carried gold from Ophir, also brought from Ophir a very large quantity of fine timber and precious gems. **10:12** With the timber the king made supports for the LORD's temple and for the royal palace and stringed instruments for the musicians. No one has seen so much of this fine timber to this very day.) **10:13** King Solomon gave the queen of Sheba everything she requested, besides what he had freely offered her. Then she left and returned to her homeland with her attendants.

Solomon's Wealth

10:14 Solomon received 666 talents of gold per year, **10:15** besides what he collected from the merchants, traders, Arabian kings, and governors of the land. **10:16** King Solomon made two hundred large shields of hammered gold; 600 measures of gold were used for each shield. **10:17** He also made three hundred small shields of hammered gold; three minas of gold were used for each of these shields. The king placed them in the Palace of the Lebanon Forest.

10:18 The king made a large throne decorated with ivory and overlaid it with pure gold. **10:19** There were six steps leading up to the throne, and the back of it was rounded on top. The throne had two armrests with a statue of a lion standing on each side. **10:20** There were twelve statues of lions on the six steps, one lion at each end of each step. There was nothing like it in any other kingdom.

10:21 All of King Solomon's cups were made of gold, and all the household items in the Palace of the Lebanon Forest were made of pure gold. There were no silver items, for silver was not considered very valuable in Solomon's time. **10:22** Along with Hiram's fleet, the king had a fleet of

large merchant ships that sailed the sea. Once every three years the fleet came into port with cargoes of gold, silver, ivory, apes, and peacocks. **10:23** King Solomon was wealthier and wiser than any of the kings of the earth. **10:24** Everyone in the world wanted to visit Solomon to see him display his God-given wisdom. **10:25** Year after year visitors brought their gifts, which included items of silver, items of gold, clothes, perfume, spices, horses, and mules.
10:26 Solomon accumulated chariots and horses. He had 1,400 chariots and 12,000 horses. He kept them in assigned cities and in Jerusalem. **10:27** The king made silver as plentiful in Jerusalem as stones; cedar was as plentiful as sycamore fig trees are in the lowlands. **10:28** Solomon acquired his horses from Egypt and from Que; the king's traders purchased them from Que. **10:29** They paid 600 silver pieces for each chariot from Egypt and 150 silver pieces for each horse. They also sold chariots and horses to all the kings of the Hittites and to the kings of Syria.

The Lord Punishes Solomon for Idolatry

11:1 King Solomon fell in love with many foreign women (besides Pharaoh's daughter), including Moabites, Ammonites, Edomites, Sidonians, and Hittites. **11:2** They came from nations about which the LORD had warned the Israelites, "You must not establish friendly relations with them! If you do, they will surely shift your allegiance to their gods." But Solomon was irresistibly attracted to them.
11:3 He had 700 royal wives and 300 concubines; his wives had a powerful influence over him. **11:4** When Solomon became old, his wives shifted his allegiance to other gods; he was not wholeheartedly devoted to the LORD his God, as his father David had been. **11:5** Solomon worshiped the Sidonian goddess Astarte and the detestable Ammonite god Milcom. **11:6** Solomon did evil in the LORD's sight; he did not remain loyal to the LORD, like his father David had. **11:7** Furthermore, on the hill east of Jerusalem Solomon built a high place for the detestable Moabite god Chemosh and for the detestable Ammonite god Milcom. **11:8** He built high places for all his foreign wives so they could burn incense and make sacrifices to their gods.
11:9 The LORD was angry with Solomon because he had shifted his allegiance away from the LORD, the God of Israel, who had appeared to him on two occasions **11:10** and had warned him about this very thing, so that he would not follow other gods. But he did not obey the LORD's command. **11:11** So the LORD said to Solomon, "Because you insist on doing these things and have not kept the covenantal rules I gave you, I will surely tear the kingdom away from you and give it to your servant. **11:12** However, for your father David's sake I will not do this while you are alive. I will tear it away from your son's hand instead. **11:13** But I will not tear away the entire kingdom; I will leave your son one tribe for my servant David's sake and for the sake of my chosen city Jerusalem."
11:14 The LORD brought against Solomon an enemy, Hadad the Edomite, a descendant of the Edomite king. **11:15** During David's campaign against Edom, Joab, the commander of the army, while on a mission to bury the dead, killed every male in Edom. **11:16** For six months Joab and the entire Israelite army stayed there until they had exterminated every male in Edom. **11:17** Hadad, who was only a small boy at the time, escaped with some of his father's Edomite servants and headed for Egypt. **11:18** They went from Midian to Paran; they took some men from Paran and went to Egypt. Pharaoh, king of Egypt, supplied him with a house and food and even assigned him some land. **11:19** Pharaoh liked Hadad so well he gave him his sister-in-law (Queen Tahpenes' sister) as a wife. **11:20** Tahpenes' sister gave birth to his son, named Genubath. Tahpenes raised him in Pharaoh's palace; Genubath grew up in Pharaoh's palace among Pharaoh's sons. **11:21** While in Egypt Hadad heard that David had passed away and that Joab, the commander of the army, was dead. So Hadad asked Pharaoh, "Give me permission to leave so I can return to my homeland." **11:22** Pharaoh said to him, "What do you lack here that makes you want to go to your homeland?" Hadad replied, "Nothing, but please give me permission to leave."
11:23 God also brought against Solomon another enemy, Rezon son of Eliada who had run away from his master, King Hadadezer of Zobah. **11:24** He gathered some men and organized a raiding band. When David tried to kill them, they went to Damascus, where they settled down and gained control of the city. **11:25** He was Israel's enemy throughout Solomon's reign and, like Hadad, caused trouble. He loathed Israel and ruled over Syria.
11:26 Jeroboam son of Nebat, one of Solomon's servants, rebelled against the king. He was an Ephraimite from Zeredah whose mother was a widow named Zeruah. **11:27** This is what prompted him to rebel against the king: Solomon built a terrace and he closed up a gap in the wall of the city of his father David. **11:28** Jeroboam was a talented man; when Solomon saw that the young man was an accomplished worker, he made him the leader of the work crew from the tribe of Joseph. **11:29** At that time, when Jeroboam had left Jerusalem, the prophet Ahijah the Shilonite met him on the road; the two of them were alone in the open country. Ahijah was wearing a brand new robe, **11:30** and he grabbed the robe and tore it into twelve pieces. **11:31** Then he told Jeroboam, "Take ten pieces, for this is what the LORD God of Israel says: 'Look, I am about to tear the kingdom from Solomon's hand and I will give ten tribes to you. **11:32** He

will retain one tribe, for my servant David's sake and for the sake of Jerusalem, the city I have chosen out of all the tribes of Israel. **11:33** I am taking the kingdom from him because they have abandoned me and worshiped the Sidonian goddess Astarte, the Moabite god Chemosh, and the Ammonite god Milcom. They have not followed my instructions by doing what I approve and obeying my rules and regulations, like Solomon's father David did. **11:34** I will not take the whole kingdom from his hand. I will allow him to be ruler for the rest of his life for the sake of my chosen servant David who kept my commandments and rules. **11:35** I will take the kingdom from the hand of his son and give ten tribes to you. **11:36** I will leave his son one tribe so my servant David's dynasty may continue to serve me in Jerusalem, the city I have chosen as my home. **11:37** I will select you; you will rule over all you desire to have and you will be king over Israel. **11:38** You must obey all I command you to do, follow my instructions, do what I approve, and keep my rules and commandments, like my servant David did. Then I will be with you and establish for you a lasting dynasty, as I did for David; I will give you Israel. **11:39** I will humiliate David's descendants because of this, but not forever." **11:40** Solomon tried to kill Jeroboam, but Jeroboam escaped to Egypt and found refuge with King Shishak of Egypt. He stayed in Egypt until Solomon died.

Solomon's Reign Ends

11:41 The rest of the events of Solomon's reign, including all his accomplishments and his wise decisions, are recorded in the scroll called the Annals of Solomon. **11:42** Solomon ruled over all Israel from Jerusalem for forty years. **11:43** Then Solomon passed away and was buried in the city of his father David. His son Rehoboam replaced him as king.

Rehoboam Loses His Kingdom

12:1 Rehoboam traveled to Shechem, for all Israel had gathered in Shechem to make Rehoboam king. **12:2** When Jeroboam son of Nebat heard the news, he was still in Egypt, where he had fled from King Solomon and had been living ever since. **12:3** They sent for him, and Jeroboam and the whole Israelite assembly came and spoke to Rehoboam, saying, **12:4** "Your father made us work too hard. Now if you lighten the demands he made and don't make us work as hard, we will serve you." **12:5** He said to them, "Go away for three days, then return to me." So the people went away.
12:6 King Rehoboam consulted with the older advisers who had served his father Solomon when he had been alive. He asked them, "How do you advise me to answer these people?" **12:7** They said to him, "Today if you show a willingness to help these people and grant their request, they will be your servants from this time forward." **12:8** But Rehoboam rejected their advice and consulted the young advisers who served him, with whom he had grown up. **12:9** He asked them, "How do you advise me to respond to these people who said to me, 'Lessen the demands your father placed on us'?" **12:10** The young advisers with whom Rehoboam had grown up said to him, "Say this to these people who have said to you, 'Your father made us work hard, but now lighten our burden.' Say this to them: 'I am a lot harsher than my father! **12:11** My father imposed heavy demands on you; I will make them even heavier. My father punished you with ordinary whips; I will punish you with whips that really sting your flesh.'"
12:12 Jeroboam and all the people reported to Rehoboam on the third day, just as the king had ordered when he said, "Return to me on the third day." **12:13** The king responded to the people harshly. He rejected the advice of the older men **12:14** and followed the advice of the younger ones. He said, "My father imposed heavy demands on you; I will make them even heavier. My father punished you with ordinary whips; I will punish you with whips that really sting your flesh." **12:15** The king refused to listen to the people, because the LORD was instigating this turn of events so that he might bring to pass the prophetic announcement he had made through Ahijah the Shilonite to Jeroboam son of Nebat.
12:16 When all Israel saw that the king refused to listen to them, the people answered the king, "We have no portion in David, no share in the son of Jesse! Return to your homes, O Israel! Now, look after your own dynasty, O David!" So Israel returned to their homes. **12:17** (Rehoboam continued to rule over the Israelites who lived in the cities of Judah.) **12:18** King Rehoboam sent Adoniram, the supervisor of the work crews, out after them, but all Israel stoned him to death. King Rehoboam managed to jump into his chariot and escape to Jerusalem. **12:19** So Israel has been in rebellion against the Davidic dynasty to this very day. **12:20** When all Israel heard that Jeroboam had returned, they summoned him to the assembly and made him king over all Israel. No one except the tribe of Judah remained loyal to the Davidic dynasty.
12:21 When Rehoboam arrived in Jerusalem, he summoned 180,000 skilled warriors from all of Judah and the tribe of Benjamin to attack Israel and restore the kingdom to Rehoboam son of Solomon. **12:22** But God told Shemaiah the prophet, **12:23** "Say this to King Rehoboam son of Solomon of Judah, and to all Judah and Benjamin, as well as the rest of the people, **12:24** 'The LORD says this: "Do not attack and make war with your brothers, the Israelites. Each of you go home, for I have caused this to happen."'" They obeyed the LORD and went home as the LORD had ordered them to do.

Jeroboam Makes Golden Calves

12:25 Jeroboam built up Shechem in the Ephraimite hill country and lived there. From there he went out and built up Penuel. **12:26** Jeroboam then thought to himself: "Now the Davidic dynasty could regain the kingdom. **12:27** If these people go up to offer sacrifices in the LORD's temple in Jerusalem, their loyalty could shift to their former master, King Rehoboam of Judah. They might kill me and return to King Rehoboam of Judah." **12:28** After the king had consulted with his advisers, he made two golden calves. Then he said to the people, "It is too much trouble for you to go up to Jerusalem. Look, Israel, here are your gods who brought you up from the land of Egypt." **12:29** He put one in Bethel and the other in Dan. **12:30** This caused Israel to sin; the people went to Bethel and Dan to worship the calves.

12:31 He built temples on the high places and appointed as priests people who were not Levites. **12:32** Jeroboam inaugurated a festival on the fifteenth day of the eighth month, like the festival celebrated in Judah. On the altar in Bethel he offered sacrifices to the calves he had made. In Bethel he also appointed priests for the high places he had made.

A Prophet from Judah Visits Bethel

12:33 On the fifteenth day of the eighth month (a date he had arbitrarily chosen) Jeroboam offered sacrifices on the altar he had made in Bethel. He inaugurated a festival for the Israelites and went up to the altar to offer sacrifices. **13:1** Just then a prophet from Judah, sent by the LORD, arrived in Bethel, as Jeroboam was standing near the altar ready to offer a sacrifice. **13:2** With the authority of the LORD he cried out against the altar, "O altar, altar! This is what the LORD says, 'Look, a son named Josiah will be born to the Davidic dynasty. He will sacrifice on you the priests of the high places who offer sacrifices on you. Human bones will be burned on you.'" **13:3** That day he also announced a sign, "This is the sign the LORD has predetermined: The altar will be split open and the ashes on it will fall to the ground." **13:4** When the king heard what the prophet cried out against the altar in Bethel, Jeroboam, standing at the altar, extended his hand and ordered, "Seize him!" The hand he had extended shriveled up and he could not pull it back. **13:5** The altar split open and the ashes fell from the altar to the ground, in fulfillment of the sign the prophet had announced with the LORD's authority. **13:6** The king pled with the prophet, "Seek the favor of the LORD your God and pray for me, so that my hand may be restored." So the prophet sought the LORD's favor and the king's hand was restored to its former condition. **13:7** The king then said to the prophet, "Come home with me and have something to eat. I'd like to give a present." **13:8** But the prophet said to the king, "Even if you were to give me half your possessions, I could not go with you and eat and drink in this place. **13:9** For the LORD gave me strict orders, 'Do not eat or drink there and do not go home the way you came.'" **13:10** So he started back on another road; he did not travel back on the same road he had taken to Bethel.

13:11 Now there was an old prophet living in Bethel. When his sons came home, they told their father everything the prophet had done in Bethel that day and all the words he had spoken to the king. **13:12** Their father asked them, "Which road did he take?" His sons showed him the road the prophet from Judah had taken. **13:13** He then told his sons, "Saddle the donkey for me." When they had saddled the donkey for him, he mounted it **13:14** and took off after the prophet, whom he found sitting under an oak tree. He asked him, "Are you the prophet from Judah?" He answered, "Yes, I am." **13:15** He then said to him, "Come home with me and eat something." **13:16** But he replied, "I can't go back with you or eat and drink with you in this place. **13:17** For the LORD gave me strict orders, 'Do not eat or drink there; do not go back the way you came.'" **13:18** The old prophet then said, "I too am a prophet like you. An angel told me with the LORD's authority, 'Bring him back with you to your house so he can eat and drink.'" But he was lying to him. **13:19** So the prophet went back with him and ate and drank in his house.

13:20 While they were sitting at the table, the LORD spoke through the old prophet **13:21** and he cried out to the prophet from Judah, "This is what the LORD says, 'You have rebelled against the LORD and have not obeyed the command the LORD your God gave you. **13:22** You went back and ate and drank in this place, even though he said to you, "Do not eat or drink there." Therefore your corpse will not be buried in your ancestral tomb.'"

13:23 When the prophet from Judah finished his meal, the old prophet saddled his visitor's donkey for him. **13:24** As the prophet from Judah was traveling, a lion attacked him on the road and killed him. His corpse was lying on the road, and the donkey and the lion just stood there beside it. **13:25** Some men came by and saw the corpse lying in the road with the lion standing beside it. They went and reported what they had seen in the city where the old prophet lived. **13:26** When the old prophet who had invited him to his house heard the news, he said, "It is the prophet who rebelled against the LORD. The LORD delivered him over to the lion and it ripped him up and killed him, just as the LORD warned him." **13:27** He told his sons, "Saddle my donkey," and they did so. **13:28** He went and found the corpse lying in the road with the donkey and the lion standing beside it; the lion had neither eaten the corpse nor attacked the donkey. **13:29** The old prophet picked up the corpse of the prophet, put it on the donkey, and brought it back. The old prophet then entered the city to mourn him and to bury him. **13:30** He put the corpse into his own tomb, and they mourned over him, saying, "Ah, my brother!" **13:31** After he buried him, he said to his sons, "When I die, bury me in the tomb where the prophet is buried; put my bones right beside his bones, **13:32** for the prophecy he announced with the LORD's authority against the altar in Bethel and against all the temples on the high places in the cities of the north will certainly be fulfilled."

A Prophet Announces the End of Jeroboam's Dynasty

13:33 After this happened, Jeroboam still did not change his evil ways; he continued to appoint common people as priests at the high places. Anyone who wanted the job he consecrated as a priest. **13:34** This sin caused Jeroboam's dynasty to come to an end and to be destroyed from the face of the earth.

14:1 At that time Jeroboam's son Abijah became sick. **14:2** Jeroboam told his wife, "Disguise yourself so that people cannot recognize you are Jeroboam's wife. Then go to Shiloh; Ahijah the prophet, who told me I would rule over this nation, lives there. **14:3** Take ten loaves of bread, some small cakes, and a container of honey and visit him. He will tell you what will happen to the boy."

14:4 Jeroboam's wife did as she was told. She went to Shiloh and visited Ahijah. Now Ahijah could not see; he had lost his eyesight in his old age. **14:5** But the LORD had told Ahijah, "Look, Jeroboam's wife is coming to find out from you what will happen to her son, for he is sick. Tell her so-and-so. When she comes, she will be in a disguise." **14:6** When Ahijah heard the sound of her footsteps as she came through the door, he said, "Come on in, wife of Jeroboam! Why are you pretending to be someone else? I have been commissioned to give you bad news. **14:7** Go, tell Jeroboam, 'This is what the LORD God of Israel says: "I raised you up from among the people and made you ruler over my people Israel. **14:8** I tore the kingdom away from the Davidic dynasty and gave it to you. But you are not like my servant David, who kept my commandments and followed me wholeheartedly by doing only what I approve. **14:9** You have sinned more than all who came before you. You went and angered me by making other gods, formed out of metal; you have completely disregarded me. **14:10** So I am ready to bring disaster on the dynasty of Jeroboam. I will cut off every last male belonging to Jeroboam in Israel, including even the weak and incapacitated. I will burn up the dynasty of Jeroboam, just as one burns manure until it is completely consumed. **14:11** Dogs will eat the members of your family who die in the city, and the birds of the sky will eat the ones who die in the country."' Indeed, the LORD has announced it!

14:12 "As for you, get up and go home. When you set foot in the city, the boy will die. **14:13** All Israel will mourn him and bury him. He is the only one in Jeroboam's family who will receive a decent burial, for he is the only one in whom the LORD God of Israel found anything good. **14:14** The LORD will raise up a king over Israel who will cut off Jeroboam's dynasty. It is ready to happen! **14:15** The LORD will attack Israel, making it like a reed that sways in the water. He will remove Israel from this good land he gave to their ancestors and scatter them beyond the Euphrates River, because they angered the LORD by making Asherah poles. **14:16** He will hand Israel over to their enemies because of the sins which Jeroboam committed and which he made Israel commit."

14:17 So Jeroboam's wife got up and went back to Tirzah. As she crossed the threshold of the house, the boy died. **14:18** All Israel buried him and mourned for him, just as the LORD had predicted through his servant the prophet Ahijah.

Jeroboam's Reign Ends

14:19 The rest of the events of Jeroboam's reign, including the details of his battles and rule, are recorded in the scroll called the Annals of the Kings of Israel. **14:20** Jeroboam ruled for twenty-two years; then he passed away. His son Nadab replaced him as king.

Rehoboam's Reign over Judah

14:21 Now Rehoboam son of Solomon ruled in Judah. He was forty-one years old when he became king and he ruled for seventeen years in Jerusalem, the city the LORD chose from all the tribes of Israel to be his home. His mother was an Ammonite woman named Naamah.

14:22 Judah did evil in the sight of the LORD. They made him more jealous by their sins than their ancestors had done. **14:23** They even built for themselves high places, sacred pillars, and Asherah poles on every high hill and under every green tree. **14:24** There were also male cultic prostitutes in the land. They committed the same horrible sins as the nations that the LORD had driven out from before the Israelites.

14:25 In King Rehoboam's fifth year, King Shishak of Egypt attacked Jerusalem. **14:26** He took away the treasures of the LORD's temple and of the royal palace; he took everything, including all the golden shields that Solomon had made. **14:27** King Rehoboam made bronze shields to replace them and assigned them to the officers of the royal guard who protected the entrance to the royal palace. **14:28** Whenever the king visited the LORD's temple, the royal guard carried them and then brought them back to the guardroom.

14:29 The rest of the events of Rehoboam's reign, including his accomplishments, are recorded in the scroll called the Annals of the

Kings of Judah. **14:30** Rehoboam and Jeroboam were continually at war with each other. **14:31** Rehoboam passed away and was buried with his ancestors in the city of David. His mother was an Ammonite named Naamah. His son Abijah replaced him as king.

Abijah's Reign over Judah

15:1 In the eighteenth year of the reign of Jeroboam son of Nebat, Abijah became king over Judah. **15:2** He ruled for three years in Jerusalem. His mother was Maacah, the daughter of Abishalom. **15:3** He followed all the sinful practices of his father before him. He was not wholeheartedly devoted to the LORD his God, as his ancestor David had been. **15:4** Nevertheless for David's sake the LORD his God maintained his dynasty in Jerusalem by giving him a son to succeed him and by protecting Jerusalem. **15:5** He did this because David had done what he approved and had not disregarded any of his commandments his entire lifetime, except for the incident involving Uriah the Hittite. **15:6** Rehoboam and Jeroboam were continually at war with each other throughout Abijah's lifetime. **15:7** The rest of the events of Abijah's reign, including all his accomplishments, are recorded in the scroll called the Annals of the Kings of Judah. Abijah and Jeroboam had been at war with each other. **15:8** Abijah passed away and was buried in the city of David. His son Asa replaced him as king.

Asa's Reign over Judah

15:9 In the twentieth year of Jeroboam's reign over Israel, Asa became the king of Judah. **15:10** He ruled for forty-one years in Jerusalem. His grandmother was Maacah daughter of Abishalom. **15:11** Asa did what the LORD approved like his ancestor David had done. **15:12** He removed the male cultic prostitutes from the land and got rid of all the disgusting idols his ancestors had made. **15:13** He also removed Maacah his grandmother from her position as queen because she had made a loathsome Asherah pole. Asa cut down her Asherah pole and burned it in the Kidron Valley. **15:14** The high places were not eliminated, yet Asa was wholeheartedly devoted to the LORD throughout his lifetime. **15:15** He brought the holy items that he and his father had made into the LORD's temple, including the silver, gold, and other articles.

15:16 Now Asa and King Baasha of Israel were continually at war with each other. **15:17** King Baasha of Israel attacked Judah and established Ramah as a military outpost to prevent anyone from leaving or entering the land of King Asa of Judah. **15:18** Asa took all the silver and gold that was left in the treasuries of the LORD's temple and of the royal palace and handed it to his servants. He then told them to deliver it to Ben Hadad son of Tabrimmon, the son of Hezion, king of Syria, ruler in Damascus, along with this message: **15:19** "I want to make a treaty with you, like the one our fathers made. See, I have sent you silver and gold as a present. Break your treaty with King Baasha of Israel, so he will retreat from my land." **15:20** Ben Hadad accepted King Asa's offer and ordered his army commanders to attack the cities of Israel. They conquered Ijon, Dan, Abel Beth Maacah, and all the territory of Naphtali, including the region of Kinnereth. **15:21** When Baasha heard the news, he stopped fortifying Ramah and settled down in Tirzah. **15:22** King Asa ordered all the men of Judah (no exemptions were granted) to carry away the stones and wood that Baasha had used to build Ramah. King Asa used the materials to build up Geba (in Benjamin) and Mizpah.

15:23 The rest of the events of Asa's reign, including all his successes and accomplishments, as well as a record of the cities he built, are recorded in the scroll called the Annals of the Kings of Judah. Yet when he was very old he developed a foot disease. **15:24** Asa passed away and was buried with his ancestors in the city of his ancestor David. His son Jehoshaphat replaced him as king.

Nadab's Reign over Israel

15:25 In the second year of Asa's reign over Judah, Jeroboam's son Nadab became the king of Israel; he ruled Israel for two years. **15:26** He did evil in the sight of the LORD. He followed in his father's footsteps and encouraged Israel to sin.

15:27 Baasha son of Ahijah, from the tribe of Issachar, conspired against Nadab and assassinated him in Gibbethon, which was in Philistine territory. This happened while Nadab and all the Israelite army were besieging Gibbethon. **15:28** Baasha killed him in the third year of Asa's reign over Judah and replaced him as king. **15:29** When he became king, he executed Jeroboam's entire family. He wiped out everyone who breathed, just as the LORD had predicted through his servant Ahijah the Shilonite. **15:30** This happened because of the sins which Jeroboam committed and which he made Israel commit. These sins angered the LORD God of Israel.

15:31 The rest of the events of Nadab's reign, including all his accomplishments, are recorded in the scroll called the Annals of the Kings of Israel. **15:32** Asa and King Nadab of Israel were continually at war with each other.

Baasha's Reign over Israel

15:33 In the third year of Asa's reign over Judah, Baasha son of Ahijah became king over all Israel in Tirzah; he ruled for twenty-four years. **15:34** He did evil in the sight of the LORD; he followed in Jeroboam's footsteps and encouraged Israel to sin.

16:1 Jehu son of Hanani received from the LORD this message predicting Baasha's downfall: **16:2** "I raised you up from the dust and made you ruler over my people Israel. Yet you followed in Jeroboam's footsteps and encouraged my people Israel to sin; their sins have made me angry. **16:3** So I am ready to burn up Baasha and his family, and make your family like the family of Jeroboam son of Nebat. **16:4** Dogs will eat the members of Baasha's family who die in the city, and the birds of the sky will eat the ones who die in the country."

16:5 The rest of the events of Baasha's reign, including his accomplishments and successes, are recorded in the scroll called the Annals of the Kings of Israel. **16:6** Baasha passed away and was buried in Tirzah. His son Elah replaced him as king. **16:7** The prophet Jehu son of Hanani received from the LORD the message predicting the downfall of Baasha and his family because of all the evil Baasha had done in the sight of the LORD. His actions angered the LORD (including the way he had destroyed Jeroboam's dynasty), so that his family ended up like Jeroboam's.

Elah's Reign over Israel

16:8 In the twenty-sixth year of King Asa's reign over Judah, Baasha's son Elah became king over Israel; he ruled in Tirzah for two years. **16:9** His servant Zimri, a commander of half of his chariot force, conspired against him. While Elah was drinking heavily at the house of Arza, who supervised the palace in Tirzah, **16:10** Zimri came in and struck him dead. (This happened in the twenty-seventh year of Asa's reign over Judah.) Zimri replaced Elah as king. **16:11** When he became king and occupied the throne, he killed Baasha's entire family. He did not spare any male belonging to him; he killed his relatives and his friends. **16:12** Zimri destroyed Baasha's entire family, just as the LORD had predicted to Baasha through Jehu the prophet. **16:13** This happened because of all the sins which Baasha and his son Elah committed and which they made Israel commit. They angered the LORD God of Israel with their worthless idols.

16:14 The rest of the events of Elah's reign, including all his accomplishments, are recorded in the scroll called the Annals of the Kings of Israel.

Zimri's Reign over Israel

16:15 In the twenty-seventh year of Asa's reign over Judah, Zimri became king over Israel; he ruled for seven days in Tirzah. Zimri's revolt took place while the army was deployed in Gibbethon, which was in Philistine territory. **16:16** While deployed there, the army received this report: "Zimri has conspired against the king and assassinated him." So all Israel made Omri, the commander of the army, king over Israel that very day in the camp. **16:17** Omri and all Israel went up from Gibbethon and besieged Tirzah. **16:18** When Zimri saw that the city was captured, he went into the fortified area of the royal palace. He set the palace on fire and died in the flames. **16:19** This happened because of the sins he committed. He did evil in the sight of the LORD and followed in Jeroboam's footsteps and encouraged Israel to continue sinning.

16:20 The rest of the events of Zimri's reign, including the details of his revolt, are recorded in the scroll called the Annals of the Kings of Israel.

Omri's Reign over Israel

16:21 At that time the people of Israel were divided in their loyalties. Half the people supported Tibni son of Ginath and wanted to make him king; the other half supported Omri. **16:22** Omri's supporters were stronger than those who supported Tibni son of Ginath. Tibni died; Omri became king.

16:23 In the thirty-first year of Asa's reign over Judah, Omri became king over Israel. He ruled for twelve years, six of them in Tirzah. **16:24** He purchased the hill of Samaria from Shemer for two talents of silver. He launched a construction project there and named the city he built after Shemer, the former owner of the hill of Samaria. **16:25** Omri did more evil in the sight of the LORD than all who were before him. **16:26** He followed in the footsteps of Jeroboam son of Nebat and encouraged Israel to sin; they angered the LORD God of Israel with their worthless idols.

16:27 The rest of the events of Omri's reign, including his accomplishments and successes, are recorded in the scroll called the Annals of the Kings of Israel. **16:28** Omri passed away and was buried in Samaria. His son Ahab replaced him as king.

Ahab Promotes Idolatry

16:29 In the thirty-eighth year of Asa's reign over Judah, Omri's son Ahab became king over Israel. Ahab son of Omri ruled over Israel for twenty-two years in Samaria. **16:30** Ahab son of Omri did more evil in the sight of the LORD than all who were before him. **16:31** As if following in the sinful footsteps of Jeroboam son of Nebat were not bad enough, he married Jezebel the daughter of King Ethbaal of the Sidonians. Then he worshiped and bowed to Baal. **16:32** He set up an altar for Baal in the temple of Baal he had built in Samaria. **16:33** Ahab also made an Asherah pole; he did more to anger the LORD God of Israel than all the kings of Israel who were before him.

16:34 During Ahab's reign, Hiel the Bethelite rebuilt Jericho. Abiram, his firstborn son, died when he laid the foundation; Segub, his youngest son, died when he erected its gates, just as the LORD had warned through Joshua son of Nun.

Elijah Visits a Widow in Sidonian Territory

17:1 Elijah the Tishbite, from Tishbe in Gilead, said to Ahab, "As certainly as the LORD God of Israel lives (whom I serve), there will be no dew or rain in the years ahead unless I give the command." **17:2** The LORD told him: **17:3** "Leave here and travel eastward. Hide out in the Kerith Valley near the Jordan. **17:4** Drink from the stream; I have already told the ravens to bring you food there." **17:5** So he did as the LORD told him; he went and lived in the Kerith Valley near the Jordan. **17:6** The ravens would bring him bread and meat each morning and evening, and he would drink from the stream.

17:7 After a while, the stream dried up because there had been no rain in the land. **17:8** The LORD told him, **17:9** "Get up, go to Zarephath in Sidonian territory, and live there. I have already told a widow who lives there to provide for you." **17:10** So he got up and went to Zarephath. When he went through the city gate, there was a widow gathering wood. He called out to her, "Please give me a cup of water, so I can take a drink." **17:11** As she went to get it, he called out to her, "Please bring me a piece of bread." **17:12** She said, "As certainly as the LORD your God lives, I have no food, except for a handful of flour in a jar and a little olive oil in a jug. Right now I am gathering a couple of sticks for a fire. Then I'm going home to make one final meal for my son and myself. After we have eaten that, we will die of starvation." **17:13** Elijah said to her, "Don't be afraid. Go and do as you planned. But first make a small cake for me and bring it to me; then make something for yourself and your son. **17:14** For this is what the LORD God of Israel says, 'The jar of flour will not be empty and the jug of oil will not run out until the day the LORD makes it rain on the surface of the ground.'" **17:15** She went and did as Elijah told her; there was always enough food for Elijah and for her and her family. **17:16** The jar of flour was never empty and the jug of oil never ran out, just as the LORD had promised through Elijah.

17:17 After this the son of the woman who owned the house got sick. His illness was so severe he could no longer breathe. **17:18** She asked Elijah, "Why, prophet, have you come to me to confront me with my sin and kill my son?" **17:19** He said to her, "Hand me your son." He took him from her arms, carried him to the upper room where he was staying, and laid him down on his bed. **17:20** Then he called out to the LORD, "O LORD, my God, are you also bringing disaster on this widow I am staying with by killing her son?" **17:21** He stretched out over the boy three times and called out to the LORD, "O LORD, my God, please let this boy's breath return to him." **17:22** The LORD answered Elijah's prayer; the boy's breath returned to him and he lived. **17:23** Elijah took the boy, brought him down from the upper room to the house, and handed him to his mother. Elijah then said, "See, your son is alive!" **17:24** The woman said to Elijah, "Now I know that you are a prophet and that the LORD really does speak through you."

Elijah Meets the King's Servant

18:1 Some time later, in the third year of the famine, the LORD told Elijah, "Go, make an appearance before Ahab, so I may send rain on the surface of the ground." **18:2** So Elijah went to make an appearance before Ahab.

Now the famine was severe in Samaria. **18:3** So Ahab summoned Obadiah, who supervised the palace. (Now Obadiah was a very loyal follower of the LORD. **18:4** When Jezebel was killing the LORD's prophets, Obadiah took one hundred prophets and hid them in two caves in two groups of fifty. He also brought them food and water.) **18:5** Ahab told Obadiah, "Go through the land to all the springs and valleys. Maybe we can find some grazing areas so we can keep the horses and mules alive and not have to kill some of the animals." **18:6** They divided up the land between them; Ahab went one way and Obadiah went the other.

18:7 As Obadiah was traveling along, Elijah met him. When he recognized him, he fell facedown to the ground and said, "Is it really you, my master, Elijah?" **18:8** He replied, "Yes, go and say to your master, 'Elijah is back.'" **18:9** Obadiah said, "What sin have I committed that you are ready to hand your servant over to Ahab for execution? **18:10** As certainly as the LORD your God lives, my master has sent to every nation and kingdom in an effort to find you. When they say, 'He's not here,' he makes them swear an oath that they could not find you. **18:11** Now you say, 'Go and say to your master, "Elijah is back."' **18:12** But when I leave you, the LORD's spirit will carry you away so I can't find you. If I go tell Ahab I've seen you, he won't be able to find you and he will kill me. That would not be fair, because your servant has been a loyal follower of the LORD from my youth. **18:13** Certainly my master is aware of what I did when Jezebel was killing the LORD's prophets. I hid one hundred of the LORD's prophets in two caves in two groups of fifty and I brought them food and water. **18:14** Now you say, 'Go and say to your master, "Elijah is back,"' but he will kill me." **18:15** But Elijah said, "As certainly as the LORD who rules over all lives (whom I serve), I will make an appearance before him today."

Elijah Confronts Baal's Prophets

18:16 When Obadiah went and informed Ahab, the king went to meet Elijah. **18:17** When Ahab saw Elijah, he said to him, "Is it really you, the one who brings disaster on Israel?" **18:18** Elijah replied, "I have not brought disaster on Israel. But you and your father's dynasty have, by abandoning the LORD's commandments and following the Baals. **18:19** Now send out messengers and assemble all Israel before me at Mount Carmel, as well as the 450 prophets of Baal and 400 prophets of Asherah whom Jezebel supports.

18:20 Ahab sent messengers to all the Israelites and had the prophets assemble at Mount Carmel. **18:21** Elijah approached all the people and said, "How long are you going to be paralyzed by indecision? If the LORD is the true God, then follow him, but if Baal is, follow him!" But the people did not say a word. **18:22** Elijah said to them: "I am the only prophet of the LORD who is left, but there are 450 prophets of Baal. **18:23** Let them bring us two bulls. Let them choose one of the bulls for themselves, cut it up into pieces, and place it on the wood. But they must not set it on fire. I will do the same to the other bull and place it on the wood. But I will not set it on fire. **18:24** Then you will invoke the name of your god, and I will invoke the name of the LORD. The god who responds with fire will demonstrate that he is the true God." All the people responded, "This will be a fair test."

18:25 Elijah told the prophets of Baal, "Choose one of the bulls for yourselves and go first, for you are the majority. Invoke the name of your god, but do not light a fire." **18:26** So they took a bull, as he had suggested, and prepared it. They invoked the name of Baal from morning until noon, saying, "Baal, answer us." But there was no sound and no answer. They jumped around on the altar they had made. **18:27** At noon Elijah mocked them, "Yell louder! After all, he is a god; he may be deep in thought, or perhaps he stepped out for a moment or has taken a trip. Perhaps he is sleeping and needs to be awakened." **18:28** So they yelled louder and, in accordance with their prescribed ritual, mutilated themselves with swords and spears until their bodies were covered with blood. **18:29** Throughout the afternoon they were in an ecstatic frenzy, but there was no sound, no answer, and no response.

18:30 Elijah then told all the people, "Approach me." So all the people approached him. He repaired the altar of the LORD that had been torn down. **18:31** Then Elijah took twelve stones, corresponding to the number of tribes that descended from Jacob, to whom the LORD had said, "Israel will be your new name." **18:32** With the stones he constructed an altar for the LORD. Around the altar he made a trench large enough to contain two seahs of seed. **18:33** He arranged the wood, cut up the bull, and placed it on the wood. **18:34** Then he said, "Fill four water jars and pour the water on the offering and the wood." When they had done so, he said, "Do it again." So they did it again. Then he said, "Do it a third time." So they did it a third time. **18:35** The water flowed down all sides of the altar and filled the trench. **18:36** When it was time for the evening offering, Elijah the prophet approached the altar and prayed: "O LORD God of Abraham, Isaac, and Israel, prove today that you are God in Israel and that I am your servant and have done all these things at your command. **18:37** Answer me, O LORD, answer me, so these people will know that you, O LORD, are the true God and that you are winning back their allegiance." **18:38** Then fire from the LORD fell from the sky. It consumed the offering, the wood, the stones, and the dirt, and licked up the water in the trench. **18:39** When all the people saw this, they threw themselves down with their faces to the ground and said, "The LORD is the true God! The LORD is the true God!" **18:40** Elijah told them, "Seize the prophets of Baal! Don't let even one of them escape!" So they seized them, and Elijah led them down to the Kishon Valley and executed them there.

18:41 Then Elijah told Ahab, "Go on up and eat and drink, for the sound of a heavy rainstorm can be heard." **18:42** So Ahab went on up to eat and drink, while Elijah climbed to the top of Carmel. He bent down toward the ground and put his face between his knees. **18:43** He told his servant, "Go on up and look in the direction of the sea." So he went on up, looked, and reported, "There is nothing." Seven times Elijah sent him to look. **18:44** The seventh time the servant said, "Look, a small cloud, the size of the palm of a man's hand, is rising up from the sea." Elijah then said, "Go and tell Ahab, 'Hitch up the chariots and go down, so that the rain won't overtake you.'" **18:45** Meanwhile the sky was covered with dark clouds, the wind blew, and there was a heavy rainstorm. Ahab rode toward Jezreel. **18:46** Now the LORD energized Elijah with power; he tucked his robe into his belt and ran ahead of Ahab all the way to Jezreel.

Elijah Runs for His Life

19:1 Ahab told Jezebel all that Elijah had done, including a detailed account of how he killed all the prophets with the sword. **19:2** Jezebel sent a messenger to Elijah with this warning, "May the gods judge me severely if by this time tomorrow I do not take your life as you did theirs!"

19:3 Elijah was afraid, so he got up and fled for his life to Beer Sheba in Judah. He left his servant there, **19:4** while he went a day's journey into the desert. He went and sat down under a shrub and asked the LORD to take his life: "I've had enough! Now, O LORD, take my life. After all, I'm no better than my ancestors." **19:5** He stretched out and fell asleep under the shrub. All of a sudden an angelic messenger touched him and said, "Get up and eat." **19:6** He looked and right there by his head was a cake baking on hot coals and a jug of water. He ate and drank and then slept some more. **19:7** The LORD's angelic messenger came back again, touched him, and said, "Get up and eat, for otherwise you won't be able to make the journey." **19:8** So he got up and ate and drank. That meal gave him the strength to travel forty days and forty nights until he reached Horeb, the mountain of God.

19:9 He went into a cave there and spent the night. All of a sudden the LORD spoke to him, "Why are you here, Elijah?" **19:10** He answered, "I have been absolutely loyal to the LORD, the sovereign God, even though the Israelites have abandoned the agreement they made with you, torn down your altars, and killed your prophets with the sword. I alone am left and now they want to take my life." **19:11** The LORD said, "Go out and stand on the mountain before the LORD. Look, the LORD is ready to pass by."

A very powerful wind went before the LORD, digging into the mountain and causing landslides, but the LORD was not in the wind. After the windstorm there was an earthquake, but the LORD was not in the earthquake. **19:12** After the earthquake, there was a fire, but the LORD was not in the fire. After the fire, there was a soft whisper. **19:13** When Elijah heard it, he covered his face with his robe and went out and stood at the entrance to the cave. All of a sudden a voice asked him, "Why are you here, Elijah?" **19:14** He answered, "I have been absolutely loyal to the LORD, the sovereign God, even though the Israelites have abandoned the agreement they made with you, torn down your altars, and killed your prophets with the sword. I alone am left and now they want to take my life." **19:15** The LORD said to him, "Go back the way you came and then head for the Desert of Damascus. Go and anoint Hazael king over Syria. **19:16** You must anoint Jehu son of Nimshi king over Israel, and Elisha son of Shaphat from Abel Meholah to take your place as prophet. **19:17** Jehu will kill anyone who escapes Hazael's sword, and Elisha will kill anyone who escapes Jehu's sword. **19:18** I still have left in Israel seven thousand followers who have not bowed their knees to Baal or kissed the images of him."

19:19 Elijah went from there and found Elisha son of Shaphat. He was plowing with twelve pairs of oxen; he was near the twelfth pair. Elijah passed by him and threw his robe over him. **19:20** He left the oxen, ran after Elijah, and said, "Please let me kiss my father and mother goodbye, then I will follow you." Elijah said to him, "Go back! Indeed, what have I done to you?" **19:21** Elisha went back and took his pair of oxen and slaughtered them. He cooked the meat over a fire that he made by burning the harness and yoke. He gave the people meat and they ate. Then he got up and followed Elijah and became his assistant.

Ben Hadad Invades Israel

20:1 Now King Ben Hadad of Syria assembled all his army, along with thirty-two other kings with their horses and chariots. He marched against Samaria and besieged and attacked it. **20:2** He sent messengers to King Ahab of Israel, who was in the city. **20:3** He said to him, "This is what Ben Hadad says, 'Your silver and your gold are mine, as well as the best of your wives and sons.'" **20:4** The king of Israel replied, "It is just as you say, my master, O king. I and all I own belong to you."

20:5 The messengers came again and said, "This is what Ben Hadad says, 'I sent this message to you, "You must give me your silver, gold, wives, and sons." **20:6** But now at this time tomorrow I will send my servants to you and they will search through your palace and your servants' houses. They will carry away all your valuables.'" **20:7** The king of Israel summoned all the leaders of the land and said, "Notice how this man is looking for trouble. Indeed, he demanded my wives, sons, silver, and gold, and I did not resist him." **20:8** All the leaders and people said to him, "Do not give in or agree to his demands." **20:9** So he said to the messengers of Ben Hadad, "Say this to my master, the king, 'I will give you everything you demanded at first from your servant, but I am unable to agree to this latest demand.'" So the messengers went back and gave their report.

20:10 Ben Hadad sent another message to him, "May the gods judge me severely if there is enough dirt left in Samaria for my soldiers to scoop up in their hands." **20:11** The king of Israel replied, "Tell him the one who puts on his battle gear should not boast like one who is taking it off." **20:12** When Ben Hadad received this reply, he and the other kings were drinking in their quarters. He ordered his servants, "Get ready to attack!" So they got ready to attack the city.

The Lord Delivers Israel

20:13 Now a prophet visited King Ahab of Israel and said, "This is what the LORD says, 'Do you see this huge army? Look, I am going to hand it over to you this very day. Then you will know that I am the LORD.'" **20:14** Ahab asked, "By whom will this be accomplished?" He answered, "This is what the LORD says, 'By the servants of the district governors.'" Ahab asked, "Who will launch the attack?" He answered, "You will." **20:15** So Ahab assembled the 232 servants of the district governors. After that he assembled all the Israelite army, numbering 7,000. **20:16** They marched out at noon, while Ben Hadad and the thirty-two kings allied with him were drinking heavily in their quarters. **20:17** The servants of the district governors led the march. When Ben Hadad sent messengers, they reported back to him, "Men are marching out of Samaria." **20:18** He ordered, "Whether they come in peace or to do battle, take them alive." **20:19** They marched out of the city with the servants of the district governors in the lead and the army behind them. **20:20** Each one struck down an enemy soldier; the Syrians fled and Israel chased them. King Ben Hadad of Syria escaped on horseback with some horsemen. **20:21** Then the king of Israel marched out and struck down the horses and chariots; he thoroughly defeated Syria.

The Lord Gives Israel Another Victory

20:22 The prophet visited the king of Israel and instructed him, "Go, fortify your defenses. Determine what you must do, for in the spring the king of Syria will attack you." **20:23** Now the advisers of the king of Syria said to him: "Their God is a god of the mountains. That's why they overpowered us. But if we fight them in the plains, we will certainly overpower them. **20:24** So do this: Dismiss the kings from their command, and replace them with military commanders. **20:25** Muster an army like the one you lost, with the same number of horses and chariots. Then we will fight them in the plains; we will certainly overpower them." He approved their plan and did as they advised.

20:26 In the spring Ben Hadad mustered the Syrian army and marched to Aphek to fight Israel. **20:27** When the Israelites had mustered and had received their supplies, they marched out to face them in battle. When the Israelites deployed opposite them, they were like two small flocks of goats, but the Syrians filled the land. **20:28** The prophet visited the king of Israel and said, "This is what the LORD says: 'Because the Syrians said, "The LORD is a god of the mountains and not a god of the valleys," I will hand over to you this entire huge army. Then you will know that I am the LORD.'"

20:29 The armies were deployed opposite each other for seven days. On the seventh day the battle began, and the Israelites killed 100,000 Syrian foot soldiers in one day. **20:30** The remaining 27,000 ran to Aphek and went into the city, but the wall fell on them. Now Ben Hadad ran into the city and hid in an inner room. **20:31** His advisers said to him, "Look, we have heard that the kings of the Israelite dynasty are kind. Allow us to put sackcloth around our waists and ropes on our heads and surrender to the king of Israel. Maybe he will spare our lives." **20:32** So they put sackcloth around their waists and ropes on their heads and went to the king of Israel. They said, "Your servant Ben Hadad says, 'Please let me live!'" Ahab replied, "Is he still alive? He is my brother." **20:33** The men took this as a good omen and quickly accepted his offer, saying, "Ben Hadad is your brother." Ahab then said, "Go, get him." So Ben Hadad came out to him, and Ahab pulled him up into his chariot. **20:34** Ben Hadad said, "I will return the cities my father took from your father. You may set up markets in Damascus, just as my father did in Samaria." Ahab then said, "I want to make a treaty with you before I dismiss you." So he made a treaty with him and then dismissed him.

A Prophet Denounces Ahab's Actions

20:35 One of the members of the prophetic guild, speaking with divine authority, ordered his companion, "Wound me!" But the man refused to wound him. **20:36** So the prophet said to him, "Because you have disobeyed the LORD, as soon as you leave me a lion will kill you." When he left him, a lion attacked and killed him. **20:37** He found another man and said, "Wound me!" So the man wounded him severely. **20:38** The prophet then went and stood by the road, waiting for the king. He also disguised himself by putting a bandage down over his eyes. **20:39** When the king passed by, he called out to the king, "Your servant went out into the heat of the battle, and then a man turned aside and brought me a prisoner. He told me, 'Guard this prisoner. If he ends up missing for any reason, you will pay with your life or with a talent of silver.' **20:40** Well, it just so happened that while your servant was doing this and that, he disappeared." The king of Israel said to him, "Your punishment is already determined by your own testimony." **20:41** The prophet quickly removed the bandage from his eyes and the king of Israel recognized he was one of the prophets. **20:42** The prophet then said to him, "This is what the LORD says, 'Because you released a man I had determined should die, you will pay with your life and your people will suffer instead of his people.'" **20:43** The king of Israel went home to Samaria bitter and angry.

Ahab Murders Naboth

21:1 After this the following episode took place. Naboth the Jezreelite owned a vineyard in Jezreel adjacent to the palace of King Ahab of Samaria. **21:2** Ahab said to Naboth, "Give me your vineyard so I can make a vegetable garden out of it, for it is adjacent to my palace. I will give you an even better vineyard in its place, or if you prefer, I will pay you silver for it." **21:3** But Naboth replied to Ahab, "The LORD forbid that I should sell you my ancestral inheritance."

21:4 So Ahab went into his palace, bitter and angry that Naboth the Jezreelite had said, "I will not sell to you my ancestral inheritance." He lay down on his bed, pouted, and would not eat. **21:5** Then his wife Jezebel came in and said to him, "Why do you have a bitter attitude and refuse to eat?" **21:6** He answered her, "While I was talking to Naboth the Jezreelite, I said to him, 'Sell me your vineyard for silver, or if you prefer, I will give you another vineyard in its place.' But he said, 'I will not sell you my vineyard.'" **21:7** His wife Jezebel said to him, "You are the king of Israel! Get up, eat some food, and have a good time. I will get the vineyard of Naboth the Jezreelite for you."

21:8 She wrote out orders, signed Ahab's name to them, and sealed them with his seal. She then sent the orders to the leaders and to the nobles who lived in Naboth's city. **21:9** This is what she wrote: "Observe a time of fasting and seat Naboth in front of the people. **21:10** Also seat two villains opposite him and have them testify, 'You cursed God and the king.' Then take him out and stone him to death."

21:11 The men of the city, the leaders and the nobles who lived there, followed the written orders Jezebel had sent them. 21:12 They observed a time of fasting and put Naboth in front of the people. 21:13 The two villains arrived and sat opposite him. Then the villains testified against Naboth right before the people, saying, "Naboth cursed God and the king." So they dragged him outside the city and stoned him to death. 21:14 Then they reported to Jezebel, "Naboth has been stoned to death."
21:15 When Jezebel heard that Naboth had been stoned to death, she said to Ahab, "Get up, take possession of the vineyard Naboth the Jezreelite refused to sell you for silver, for Naboth is no longer alive; he's dead." 21:16 When Ahab heard that Naboth was dead, he got up and went down to take possession of the vineyard of Naboth the Jezreelite.
21:17 The LORD told Elijah the Tishbite: 21:18 "Get up, go down and meet King Ahab of Israel who lives in Samaria. He is at the vineyard of Naboth; he has gone down there to take possession of it. 21:19 Say to him, 'This is what the LORD says: "Haven't you committed murder and taken possession of the property of the deceased?"' Then say to him, 'This is what the LORD says: "In the spot where dogs licked up Naboth's blood they will also lick up your blood – yes, yours!"'"
21:20 When Elijah arrived, Ahab said to him, "So, you have found me, my enemy!" Elijah replied, "I have found you, because you are committed to doing evil in the sight of the LORD. 21:21 The LORD says, 'Look, I am ready to bring disaster on you. I will destroy you and cut off every last male belonging to Ahab in Israel, including even the weak and incapacitated. 21:22 I will make your dynasty like those of Jeroboam son of Nebat and Baasha son of Ahijah because you angered me and made Israel sin.' 21:23 The LORD says this about Jezebel, 'Dogs will devour Jezebel by the outer wall of Jezreel.' 21:24 As for Ahab's family, dogs will eat the ones who die in the city, and the birds of the sky will eat the ones who die in the country." 21:25 (There had never been anyone like Ahab, who was firmly committed to doing evil in the sight of the LORD, urged on by his wife Jezebel. 21:26 He was so wicked he worshiped the disgusting idols, just like the Amorites whom the LORD had driven out from before the Israelites.)
21:27 When Ahab heard these words, he tore his clothes, put on sackcloth, and fasted. He slept in sackcloth and walked around dejected. 21:28 The LORD said to Elijah the Tishbite, 21:29 "Have you noticed how Ahab shows remorse before me? Because he shows remorse before me, I will not bring disaster on his dynasty during his lifetime, but during the reign of his son."

Ahab Dies in Battle

22:1 There was no war between Syria and Israel for three years. 22:2 In the third year King Jehoshaphat of Judah came down to visit the king of Israel. 22:3 The king of Israel said to his servants, "Surely you recognize that Ramoth Gilead belongs to us, though we are hesitant to reclaim it from the king of Syria." 22:4 Then he said to Jehoshaphat, "Will you go with me to attack Ramoth Gilead?" Jehoshaphat replied to the king of Israel, "I will support you; my army and horses are at your disposal." 22:5 Then Jehoshaphat added, "First seek an oracle from the LORD." 22:6 So the king of Israel assembled about four hundred prophets and asked them, "Should I attack Ramoth Gilead or not?" They said, "Attack! The sovereign one will hand it over to the king." 22:7 But Jehoshaphat asked, "Is there not a prophet of the LORD still here, that we may ask him?" 22:8 The king of Israel answered Jehoshaphat, "There is still one man through whom we can seek the LORD's will. But I despise him because he does not prophesy prosperity for me, but disaster. His name is Micaiah son of Imlah. Jehoshaphat said, "The king should not say such things." 22:9 The king of Israel summoned an official and said, "Quickly bring Micaiah son of Imlah."
22:10 Now the king of Israel and King Jehoshaphat of Judah were sitting on their respective thrones, dressed in their robes, at the threshing floor at the entrance of the gate of Samaria. All the prophets were prophesying before them. 22:11 Zedekiah son of Kenaanah made iron horns and said, "This is what the LORD says, 'With these you will gore Syria until they are destroyed.'" 22:12 All the prophets were prophesying the same, saying, "Attack Ramoth Gilead! You will succeed; the LORD will hand it over to the king." 22:13 Now the messenger who went to summon Micaiah said to him, "Look, the prophets are in complete agreement that the king will succeed. Your words must agree with theirs; you must predict success." 22:14 But Micaiah said, "As certainly as the LORD lives, I will say what the LORD tells me to say."
22:15 When he came before the king, the king asked him, "Micaiah, should we attack Ramoth Gilead or not?" He answered, "Attack! You will succeed; the LORD will hand it over to the king." 22:16 The king said to him, "How many times must I make you solemnly promise in the name of the LORD to tell me only the truth?" 22:17 Micaiah said, "I saw all Israel scattered on the mountains like sheep that have no shepherd. Then the LORD said, 'They have no master. They should go home in peace.'" 22:18 The king of Israel said to Jehoshaphat, "Didn't I tell you he does not prophesy prosperity for me, but disaster?" 22:19 Micaiah said, "That being the case, hear the word of the LORD. I saw the LORD sitting on his throne, with all the heavenly assembly standing on his right and on his left. 22:20 The LORD said, 'Who will deceive Ahab, so he will

attack Ramoth Gilead and die there?' One said this and another that. 22:21 Then a spirit stepped forward and stood before the LORD. He said, 'I will deceive him.' The LORD asked him, 'How?' 22:22 He replied, 'I will go out and be a lying spirit in the mouths of all his prophets.' The LORD said, 'Deceive and overpower him. Go out and do as you have proposed.' 22:23 So now, look, the LORD has placed a lying spirit in the mouths of all these prophets of yours; but the LORD has decreed disaster for you." 22:24 Zedekiah son of Kenaanah approached, hit Micaiah on the jaw, and said, "Which way did the LORD's spirit go when he went from me to speak to you?" 22:25 Micaiah replied, "Look, you will see in the day when you go into an inner room to hide." 22:26 Then the king of Israel said, "Take Micaiah and return him to Amon the city official and Joash the king's son. 22:27 Say, 'This is what the king says, "Put this man in prison. Give him only a little bread and water until I safely return."'" 22:28 Micaiah said, "If you really do safely return, then the LORD has not spoken through me." Then he added, "Take note, all you people."
22:29 The king of Israel and King Jehoshaphat of Judah attacked Ramoth Gilead. 22:30 The king of Israel said to Jehoshaphat, "I will disguise myself and then enter into the battle; but you wear your royal robes." So the king of Israel disguised himself and then entered into the battle. 22:31 Now the king of Syria had ordered his thirty-two chariot commanders, "Do not fight common soldiers or high-ranking officers; fight only the king of Israel." 22:32 When the chariot commanders saw Jehoshaphat, they said, "He must be the king of Israel." So they turned and attacked him, but Jehoshaphat cried out. 22:33 When the chariot commanders realized he was not the king of Israel, they turned away from him. 22:34 Now an archer shot an arrow at random, and it struck the king of Israel between the plates of his armor. The king ordered his charioteer, "Turn around and take me from the battle line, because I'm wounded." 22:35 While the battle raged throughout the day, the king stood propped up in his chariot opposite the Syrians. He died in the evening; the blood from the wound ran down into the bottom of the chariot. 22:36 As the sun was setting, a cry went through the camp, "Each one should return to his city and to his homeland." 22:37 So the king died and was taken to Samaria, where they buried him. 22:38 They washed off the chariot at the pool of Samaria (this was where the prostitutes bathed); dogs licked his blood, just as the LORD had said would happen.
22:39 The rest of the events of Ahab's reign, including a record of his accomplishments and how he built a luxurious palace and various cities, are recorded in the scroll called the Annals of the Kings of Israel. 22:40 Ahab passed away. His son Ahaziah replaced him as king.

Jehoshaphat's Reign over Judah

22:41 In the fourth year of King Ahab's reign over Israel, Asa's son Jehoshaphat became king over Judah. 22:42 Jehoshaphat was thirty-five years old when he became king and he reigned for twenty-five years in Jerusalem. His mother was Azubah, the daughter of Shilhi. 22:43 He followed in his father Asa's footsteps and was careful to do what the LORD approved. (22:44) However, the high places were not eliminated; the people continued to offer sacrifices and burn incense on the high places. 22:44 (22:45) Jehoshaphat was also at peace with the king of Israel.
22:45 The rest of the events of Jehoshaphat's reign, including his successes and military exploits, are recorded in the scroll called the Annals of the Kings of Judah. 22:46 He removed from the land any male cultic prostitutes who had managed to survive the reign of his father Asa. 22:47 There was no king in Edom at this time; a governor ruled. 22:48 Jehoshaphat built a fleet of large merchant ships to travel to Ophir for gold, but they never made the voyage because they were shipwrecked in Ezion Geber. 22:49 Then Ahaziah son of Ahab said to Jehoshaphat, "Let my sailors join yours in the fleet," but Jehoshaphat refused.
22:50 Jehoshaphat passed away and was buried with his ancestors in the city of his ancestor David. His son Jehoram replaced him as king.

Ahaziah's Reign over Israel

22:51 In the seventeenth year of King Jehoshaphat's reign over Judah, Ahab's son Ahaziah became king over Israel in Samaria. He ruled for two years over Israel. 22:52 He did evil in the sight of the LORD and followed in the footsteps of his father and mother; like Jeroboam son of Nebat, he encouraged Israel to sin. 22:53 He worshiped and bowed down to Baal, angering the LORD God of Israel just as his father had done.

Book 12. 2 Kings

Elijah Confronts the King and His Commanders

1:1 After Ahab died, Moab rebelled against Israel. 1:2 Ahaziah fell through a window lattice in his upper chamber in Samaria and was injured. He sent messengers with these orders, "Go, ask Baal Zebub, the god of Ekron, if I will survive this injury."
1:3 But the LORD's angelic messenger told Elijah the Tishbite, "Get up, go to meet the messengers from the king of Samaria. Say this to them: 'You must think there is no God in Israel! That explains why you are on your way to seek an oracle from Baal Zebub the god of Ekron. 1:4 Therefore this is what the LORD says, "You will not leave the bed you lie on, for you will certainly die!"'" So Elijah went on his way.

1:5 When the messengers returned to the king, he asked them, "Why have you returned?" **1:6** They replied, "A man came up to meet us. He told us, "Go back to the king who sent you and tell him, 'This is what the LORD says: "You must think there is no God in Israel! That explains why you are sending for an oracle from Baal Zebub, the god of Ekron. Therefore you will not leave the bed you lie on, for you will certainly die."'" **1:7** The king asked them, "Describe the appearance of this man who came up to meet you and told you these things." **1:8** They replied, "He was a hairy man and had a leather belt tied around his waist." The king said, "He is Elijah the Tishbite."

1:9 The king sent a captain and his fifty soldiers to retrieve Elijah. The captain went up to him, while he was sitting on the top of a hill. He told him, "Prophet, the king says, 'Come down!'" **1:10** Elijah replied to the captain, "If I am indeed a prophet, may fire come down from the sky and consume you and your fifty soldiers!" Fire then came down from the sky and consumed him and his fifty soldiers.

1:11 The king sent another captain and his fifty soldiers to retrieve Elijah. He went up and told him, "Prophet, this is what the king says, 'Come down at once!'" **1:12** Elijah replied to them, "If I am indeed a prophet, may fire come down from the sky and consume you and your fifty soldiers!" Fire from God came down from the sky and consumed him and his fifty soldiers.

1:13 The king sent a third captain and his fifty soldiers. This third captain went up and fell on his knees before Elijah. He begged for mercy, "Prophet, please have respect for my life and for the lives of these fifty servants of yours. **1:14** Indeed, fire came down from the sky and consumed the two captains who came before me, along with their men. So now, please have respect for my life." **1:15** The LORD's angelic messenger said to Elijah, "Go down with him. Don't be afraid of him." So he got up and went down with him to the king.

1:16 Elijah said to the king, "This is what the LORD says, 'You sent messengers to seek an oracle from Baal Zebub, the god of Ekron. You must think there is no God in Israel from whom you can seek an oracle! Therefore you will not leave the bed you lie on, for you will certainly die.'"

1:17 He died just as the LORD had prophesied through Elijah. In the second year of the reign of King Jehoram son of Jehoshaphat over Judah, Ahaziah's brother Jehoram replaced him as king of Israel, because he had no son. **1:18** The rest of the events of Ahaziah's reign, including his accomplishments, are recorded in the scroll called the Annals of the Kings of Israel.

Elijah Makes a Swift Departure

2:1 Just before the LORD took Elijah up to heaven in a windstorm, Elijah and Elisha were traveling from Gilgal. **2:2** Elijah told Elisha, "Stay here, for the LORD has sent me to Bethel." But Elisha said, "As certainly as the LORD lives and as you live, I will not leave you." So they went down to Bethel. **2:3** Some members of the prophetic guild in Bethel came out to Elisha and said, "Do you know that today the LORD is going to take your master from you?" He answered, "Yes, I know. Be quiet."

2:4 Elijah said to him, "Elisha, stay here, for the LORD has sent me to Jericho." But he replied, "As certainly as the LORD lives and as you live, I will not leave you." So they went to Jericho. **2:5** Some members of the prophetic guild in Jericho approached Elisha and said, "Do you know that today the LORD is going to take your master from you?" He answered, "Yes, I know. Be quiet."

2:6 Elijah said to him, "Stay here, for the LORD has sent me to the Jordan." But he replied, "As certainly as the LORD lives and as you live, I will not leave you." So they traveled on together. **2:7** The fifty members of the prophetic guild went and stood opposite them at a distance, while Elijah and Elisha stood by the Jordan. **2:8** Elijah took his cloak, folded it up, and hit the water with it. The water divided, and the two of them crossed over on dry ground.

2:9 When they had crossed over, Elijah said to Elisha, "What can I do for you, before I am taken away from you?" Elisha answered, "May I receive a double portion of the prophetic spirit that energizes you." **2:10** Elijah replied, "That's a difficult request! If you see me taken from you, may it be so, but if you don't, it will not happen."

2:11 As they were walking along and talking, suddenly a fiery chariot pulled by fiery horses appeared. They went between Elijah and Elisha, and Elijah went up to heaven in a windstorm. **2:12** While Elisha was watching, he was crying out, "My father, my father! The chariot and horsemen of Israel!" Then he could no longer see him. He grabbed his clothes and tore them in two. **2:13** He picked up Elijah's cloak, which had fallen off him, and went back and stood on the shore of the Jordan. **2:14** He took the cloak that had fallen off Elijah, hit the water with it, and said, "Where is the LORD, the God of Elijah?" When he hit the water, it divided and Elisha crossed over.

2:15 When the members of the prophetic guild in Jericho, who were standing at a distance, saw him do this, they said, "The spirit that energized Elijah rests upon Elisha." They went to meet him and bowed down to the ground before him. **2:16** They said to him, "Look, there are fifty capable men with your servants. Let them go and look for your master, for the wind sent from the LORD may have carried him away and dropped him on one of the hills or in one of the valleys." But Elisha replied,

"Don't send them out." **2:17** But they were so insistent, he became embarrassed. So he said, "Send them out." They sent the fifty men out and they looked for three days, but could not find Elijah. **2:18** When they came back, Elisha was staying in Jericho. He said to them, "Didn't I tell you, 'Don't go'?"

Elisha Demonstrates His Authority

2:19 The men of the city said to Elisha, "Look, the city has a good location, as our master can see. But the water is bad and the land doesn't produce crops." **2:20** Elisha said, "Get me a new jar and put some salt in it." So they got it. **2:21** He went out to the spring and threw the salt in. Then he said, "This is what the LORD says, 'I have purified this water. It will no longer cause death or fail to produce crops.'" **2:22** The water has been pure to this very day, just as Elisha prophesied.

2:23 He went up from there to Bethel. As he was traveling up the road, some young boys came out of the city and made fun of him, saying, "Go on up, baldy! Go on up, baldy!" **2:24** When he turned around and saw them, he called God's judgment down on them. Two female bears came out of the woods and ripped forty-two of the boys to pieces. **2:25** From there he traveled to Mount Carmel and then back to Samaria.

Moab Fights with Israel

3:1 In the eighteenth year of King Jehoshaphat's reign over Judah, Ahab's son Jehoram became king over Israel in Samaria; he ruled for twelve years. **3:2** He did evil in the sight of the LORD, but not to the same degree as his father and mother. He did remove the sacred pillar of Baal that his father had made. **3:3** Yet he persisted in the sins of Jeroboam son of Nebat, who encouraged Israel to sin; he did not turn from them.

3:4 Now King Mesha of Moab was a sheep breeder. He would send as tribute to the king of Israel 100,000 male lambs and the wool of 100,000 rams. **3:5** When Ahab died, the king of Moab rebelled against the king of Israel. **3:6** At that time King Jehoram left Samaria and assembled all Israel for war. **3:7** He sent this message to King Jehoshaphat of Judah: "The king of Moab has rebelled against me. Will you fight with me against Moab?" Jehoshaphat replied, "I will join you in the campaign; my army and horses are at your disposal." **3:8** He then asked, "Which invasion route are we going to take?" Jehoram answered, "By the road through the Desert of Edom." **3:9** So the kings of Israel, Judah, and Edom set out together. They wandered around on the road for seven days and finally ran out of water for the men and animals they had with them. **3:10** The king of Israel said, "Oh no! Certainly the LORD has summoned these three kings so that he can hand them over to the king of Moab!" **3:11** Jehoshaphat asked, "Is there no prophet of the LORD here that we might seek the LORD's direction?" One of the servants of the king of Israel answered, "Elisha son of Shapat is here; he used to be Elijah's servant." **3:12** Jehoshaphat said, "The LORD speaks through him." So the king of Israel and Jehoshaphat and the king of Edom went down to visit him.

3:13 Elisha said to the king of Israel, "Why are you here? Go to your father's prophets or your mother's prophets!" The king of Israel replied to him, "No, for the LORD is the one who summoned these three kings so that he can hand them over to Moab." **3:14** Elisha said, "As certainly as the LORD who rules over all lives (whom I serve), if I did not respect King Jehoshaphat of Judah, I would not pay attention to you or acknowledge you. **3:15** But now, get me a musician." When the musician played, the LORD energized him, **3:16** and he said, "This is what the LORD says, 'Make many cisterns in this valley,' **3:17** for this is what the LORD says, 'You will not feel any wind or see any rain, but this valley will be full of water and you and your cattle and animals will drink.' **3:18** This is an easy task for the LORD; he will also hand Moab over to you. **3:19** You will defeat every fortified city and every important city. You must chop down every productive tree, stop up all the springs, and cover all the cultivated land with stones."

3:20 Sure enough, the next morning, at the time of the morning sacrifice, water came flowing down from Edom and filled the land. **3:21** Now all Moab had heard that the kings were attacking, so everyone old enough to fight was mustered and placed at the border. **3:22** When they got up early the next morning, the sun was shining on the water. To the Moabites, who were some distance away, the water looked red like blood. **3:23** The Moabites said, "It's blood! The kings are totally destroyed! They have struck one another down! Now, Moab, seize the plunder!" **3:24** When they approached the Israelite camp, the Israelites rose up and struck down the Moabites, who then ran from them. The Israelites thoroughly defeated Moab. **3:25** They tore down the cities and each man threw a stone into every cultivated field until they were covered. They stopped up every spring and chopped down every productive tree.

Only Kir Hareseth was left intact, but the slingers surrounded it and attacked it. **3:26** When the king of Moab realized he was losing the battle, he and 700 swordsmen tried to break through and attack the king of Edom, but they failed. **3:27** So he took his firstborn son, who was to succeed him as king, and offered him up as a burnt sacrifice on the wall. There was an outburst of divine anger against Israel, so they broke off the attack and returned to their homeland.

Elisha Helps a Widow and Her Sons

4:1 Now a wife of one of the prophets appealed to Elisha for help, saying, "Your servant, my husband is dead. You know that your servant was a loyal follower of the LORD. Now the creditor is coming to take away my two boys to be his servants." **4:2** Elisha said to her, "What can I do for you? Tell me, what do you have in the house?" She answered, "Your servant has nothing in the house except a small jar of olive oil." **4:3** He said, "Go and ask all your neighbors for empty containers. Get as many as you can. **4:4** Go and close the door behind you and your sons. Pour the olive oil into all the containers; set aside each one when you have filled it." **4:5** So she left him and closed the door behind her and her sons. As they were bringing the containers to her, she was pouring the olive oil. **4:6** When the containers were full, she said to one of her sons, "Bring me another container." But he answered her, "There are no more." Then the olive oil stopped flowing. **4:7** She went and told the prophet. He said, "Go, sell the olive oil. Repay your creditor, and then you and your sons can live off the rest of the profit."

Elisha Gives Life to a Boy

4:8 One day Elisha traveled to Shunem, where a prominent woman lived. She insisted that he stop for a meal. So whenever he was passing through, he would stop in there for a meal. **4:9** She said to her husband, "Look, I'm sure that the man who regularly passes through here is a very special prophet. **4:10** Let's make a small private upper room and furnish it with a bed, table, chair, and lamp. When he visits us, he can stay there."

4:11 One day Elisha came for a visit; he went into the upper room and rested. **4:12** He told his servant Gehazi, "Ask the Shunammite woman to come here." So he did so and she came to him. **4:13** Elisha said to Gehazi, "Tell her, 'Look, you have treated us with such great respect. What can I do for you? Can I put in a good word for you with the king or the commander of the army?'" She replied, "I'm quite secure." **4:14** So he asked Gehazi, "What can I do for her?" Gehazi replied, "She has no son, and her husband is old." **4:15** Elisha told him, "Ask her to come here." So he did so and she came and stood in the doorway. **4:16** He said, "About this time next year you will be holding a son." She said, "No, my master! O prophet, do not lie to your servant!" **4:17** The woman did conceive, and at the specified time the next year she gave birth to a son, just as Elisha had told her.

4:18 The boy grew and one day he went out to see his father who was with the harvest workers. **4:19** He said to his father, "My head! My head!" His father told a servant, "Carry him to his mother." **4:20** So he picked him up and took him to his mother. He sat on her lap until noon and then died. **4:21** She went up and laid him down on the prophet's bed. She shut the door behind her and left. **4:22** She called to her husband, "Send me one of the servants and one of the donkeys, so I can go see the prophet quickly and then return." **4:23** He said, "Why do you want to go see him today? It is not the new moon or the Sabbath." She said, "Everything's fine." **4:24** She saddled the donkey and told her servant, "Lead on. Do not stop unless I say so."

4:25 So she went to visit the prophet at Mount Carmel. When he saw her at a distance, he said to his servant Gehazi, "Look, it's the Shunammite woman. **4:26** Now, run to meet her and ask her, 'Are you well? Are your husband and the boy well?'" She told Gehazi, "Everything's fine." **4:27** But when she reached the prophet on the mountain, she grabbed hold of his feet. Gehazi came near to push her away, but the prophet said, "Leave her alone, for she is very upset. The LORD has kept the matter hidden from me; he didn't tell me about it." **4:28** She said, "Did I ask my master for a son? Didn't I say, 'Don't mislead me?'" **4:29** Elisha told Gehazi, "Tuck your robes into your belt, take my staff, and go! Don't stop to exchange greetings with anyone! Place my staff on the child's face." **4:30** The mother of the child said, "As certainly as the LORD lives and as you live, I will not leave you." So Elisha got up and followed her back.

4:31 Now Gehazi went on ahead of them. He placed the staff on the child's face, but there was no sound or response. When he came back to Elisha he told him, "The child did not wake up." **4:32** When Elisha arrived at the house, there was the child lying dead on his bed. **4:33** He went in by himself and closed the door. Then he prayed to the LORD. **4:34** He got up on the bed and spread his body out over the boy; he put his mouth on the boy's mouth, his eyes over the boy's eyes, and the palms of his hands against the boy's palms. He bent down over him, and the boy's skin grew warm. **4:35** Elisha went back and walked around in the house. Then he got up on the bed again and bent down over him. The child sneezed seven times and opened his eyes. **4:36** Elisha called to Gehazi and said, "Get the Shunammite woman." So he did so and she came to him. He said to her, "Take your son." **4:37** She came in, fell at his feet, and bowed down. Then she picked up her son and left.

Elisha Makes a Meal Edible

4:38 Now Elisha went back to Gilgal, while there was famine in the land. Some of the prophets were visiting him and he told his servant, "Put the big pot on the fire and boil some stew for the prophets." **4:39** Someone went out to the field to gather some herbs and found a wild vine. He picked some of its fruit, enough to fill up the fold of his robe. He came back, cut it up, and threw the slices into the stew pot, not knowing they were harmful. **4:40** The stew was poured out for the men to eat. When they ate some of the stew, they cried out, "Death is in the pot, O prophet!" They could not eat it. **4:41** He said, "Get some flour." Then he threw

it into the pot and said, "Now pour some out for the men so they may eat." There was no longer anything harmful in the pot.

Elisha Miraculously Feeds a Hundred People

4:42 Now a man from Baal Shalisha brought some food for the prophet – twenty loaves of bread made from the firstfruits of the barley harvest, as well as fresh ears of grain. Elisha said, "Set it before the people so they may eat." **4:43** But his attendant said, "How can I feed a hundred men with this?" He replied, "Set it before the people so they may eat, for this is what the LORD says, 'They will eat and have some left over.'" **4:44** So he set it before them; they ate and had some left over, just as the LORD predicted.

Elisha Heals a Syrian General

5:1 Now Naaman, the commander of the king of Syria's army, was esteemed and respected by his master, for through him the LORD had given Syria military victories. But this great warrior had a skin disease. **5:2** Raiding parties went out from Syria and took captive from the land of Israel a young girl, who became a servant to Naaman's wife. **5:3** She told her mistress, "If only my master were in the presence of the prophet who is in Samaria! Then he would cure him of his skin disease."

5:4 Naaman went and told his master what the girl from the land of Israel had said. **5:5** The king of Syria said, "Go! I will send a letter to the king of Israel." So Naaman went, taking with him ten talents of silver, six thousand shekels of gold, and ten suits of clothes. **5:6** He brought the letter to king of Israel. It read: "This is a letter of introduction for my servant Naaman, whom I have sent to be cured of his skin disease." **5:7** When the king of Israel read the letter, he tore his clothes and said, "Am I God? Can I kill or restore life? Why does he ask me to cure a man of his skin disease? Certainly you must see that he is looking for an excuse to fight me!"

5:8 When Elisha the prophet heard that the king had torn his clothes, he sent this message to the king, "Why did you tear your clothes? Send him to me so he may know there is a prophet in Israel." **5:9** So Naaman came with his horses and chariots and stood in the doorway of Elisha's house. **5:10** Elisha sent out a messenger who told him, "Go and wash seven times in the Jordan; your skin will be restored and you will be healed." **5:11** Naaman went away angry. He said, "Look, I thought for sure he would come out, stand there, invoke the name of the LORD his God, wave his hand over the area, and cure the skin disease. **5:12** The rivers of Damascus, the Abana and Pharpar, are better than any of the waters of Israel! Could I not wash in them and be healed?" So he turned around and went away angry. **5:13** His servants approached and said to him, "O master, if the prophet had told you to do some difficult task, you would have been willing to do it. It seems you should be happy that he simply said, 'Wash and you will be healed.'" **5:14** So he went down and dipped in the Jordan seven times, as the prophet had instructed. His skin became as smooth as a young child's and he was healed.

5:15 He and his entire entourage returned to the prophet. Naaman came and stood before him. He said, "For sure I know that there is no God in all the earth except in Israel! Now, please accept a gift from your servant." **5:16** But Elisha replied, "As certainly as the LORD lives (whom I serve), I will take nothing from you." Naaman insisted that he take it, but he refused. **5:17** Naaman said, "If not, then please give your servant a load of dirt, enough for a pair of mules to carry, for your servant will never again offer a burnt offering or sacrifice to a god other than the LORD. **5:18** May the LORD forgive your servant for this one thing: When my master enters the temple of Rimmon to worship, and he leans on my arm and I bow down in the temple of Rimmon, may the LORD forgive your servant for this." **5:19** Elisha said to him, "Go in peace."

When he had gone a short distance, **5:20** Gehazi, the prophet Elisha's servant, thought, "Look, my master did not accept what this Syrian Naaman offered him. As certainly as the LORD lives, I will run after him and accept something from him." **5:21** So Gehazi ran after Naaman. When Naaman saw someone running after him, he got down from his chariot to meet him and asked, "Is everything all right?" **5:22** He answered, "Everything is fine. My master sent me with this message, 'Look, two servants of the prophets just arrived from the Ephraimite hill country. Please give them a talent of silver and two suits of clothes.'" **5:23** Naaman said, "Please accept two talents of silver." He insisted, and tied up two talents of silver in two bags, along with two suits of clothes. He gave them to two of his servants and they carried them for Gehazi. **5:24** When he arrived at the hill, he took them from the servants and put them in the house. Then he sent the men on their way.

5:25 When he came and stood before his master, Elisha asked him, "Where have you been, Gehazi?" He answered, "Your servant hasn't been anywhere." **5:26** Elisha replied, "I was there in spirit when a man turned and got down from his chariot to meet you. This is not the proper time to accept silver or to accept clothes, olive groves, vineyards, sheep, cattle, and male and female servants. **5:27** Therefore Naaman's skin disease will afflict you and your descendants forever!" When Gehazi went out from his presence, his skin was as white as snow.

Elisha Makes an Ax Head Float

6:1 Some of the prophets said to Elisha, "Look, the place where we meet with you is too cramped for us. **6:2** Let's go to the Jordan. Each of us will get a log from there and we will build a meeting place for ourselves there." He said, "Go." **6:3** One of them said, "Please come along with your servants." He replied, "All right, I'll come." **6:4** So he went with them. When they arrived at the Jordan, they started cutting down trees. **6:5** As one of them was felling a log, the ax head dropped into the water. He shouted, "Oh no, my master! It was borrowed!" **6:6** The prophet asked, "Where did it drop in?" When he showed him the spot, Elisha cut off a branch, threw it in at that spot, and made the ax head float. **6:7** He said, "Lift it out." So he reached out his hand and grabbed it.

Elisha Defeats an Army

6:8 Now the king of Syria was at war with Israel. He consulted his advisers, who said, "Invade at such and such a place." **6:9** But the prophet sent this message to the king of Israel, "Make sure you don't pass through this place because Syria is invading there." **6:10** So the king of Israel sent a message to the place the prophet had pointed out, warning it to be on its guard. This happened on several occasions. **6:11** This made the king of Syria upset. So he summoned his advisers and said to them, "One of us must be helping the king of Israel." **6:12** One of his advisers said, "No, my master, O king. The prophet Elisha who lives in Israel keeps telling the king of Israel the things you say in your bedroom." **6:13** The king ordered, "Go, find out where he is, so I can send some men to capture him." The king was told, "He is in Dothan." **6:14** So he sent horses and chariots there, along with a good-sized army. They arrived during the night and surrounded the city.

6:15 The prophet's attendant got up early in the morning. When he went outside there was an army surrounding the city, along with horses and chariots. He said to Elisha, "Oh no, my master! What will we do?" **6:16** He replied, "Don't be afraid, for our side outnumbers them." **6:17** Then Elisha prayed, "O LORD, open his eyes so he can see." The LORD opened the servant's eyes and he saw that the hill was full of horses and chariots of fire all around Elisha. **6:18** As they approached him, Elisha prayed to the LORD, "Strike these people with blindness." The LORD struck them with blindness as Elisha requested. **6:19** Then Elisha said to them, "This is not the right road or city. Follow me, and I will lead you to the man you're looking for." He led them to Samaria.

6:20 When they had entered Samaria, Elisha said, "O LORD, open their eyes, so they can see." The LORD opened their eyes and they saw that they were in the middle of Samaria. **6:21** When the king of Israel saw them, he asked Elisha, "Should I strike them down, my master?" **6:22** He replied, "Do not strike them down! You did not capture them with your sword or bow, so what gives you the right to strike them down? Give them some food and water, so they can eat and drink and then go back to their master." **6:23** So he threw a big banquet for them and they ate and drank. Then he sent them back to their master. After that no Syrian raiding parties again invaded the land of Israel.

The Lord Saves Samaria

6:24 Later King Ben Hadad of Syria assembled his entire army and attacked and besieged Samaria. **6:25** Samaria's food supply ran out. They laid siege to it so long that a donkey's head was selling for eighty shekels of silver and a quarter of a kab of dove's droppings for five shekels of silver.

6:26 While the king of Israel was passing by on the city wall, a woman shouted to him, "Help us, my master, O king!" **6:27** He replied, "No, let the LORD help you. How can I help you? The threshing floor and winepress are empty." **6:28** Then the king asked her, "What's your problem?" She answered, "This woman said to me, 'Hand over your son; we'll eat him today and then eat my son tomorrow.' **6:29** So we boiled my son and ate him. Then I said to her the next day, 'Hand over your son and we'll eat him.' But she hid her son!" **6:30** When the king heard what the woman said, he tore his clothes. As he was passing by on the wall, the people could see he was wearing sackcloth under his clothes. **6:31** Then he said, "May God judge me severely if Elisha son of Shaphat still has his head by the end of the day!"

6:32 Now Elisha was sitting in his house with the community leaders. The king sent a messenger on ahead, but before he arrived, Elisha said to the leaders, "Do you realize this assassin intends to cut off my head?" Look, when the messenger arrives, shut the door and lean against it. His master will certainly be right behind him." **6:33** He was still talking to them when the messenger approached and said, "Look, the LORD is responsible for this disaster! Why should I continue to wait for the LORD to help?" **7:1** Elisha replied, "Hear the word of the LORD! This is what the LORD says, 'About this time tomorrow a seah of finely milled flour will sell for a shekel and two seahs of barley for a shekel at the gate of Samaria.'" **7:2** An officer who was the king's right-hand man responded to the prophet, "Look, even if the LORD made it rain by opening holes in the sky, could this happen so soon?" Elisha said, "Look, you will see it happen with your own eyes, but you will not eat any of the food!"

7:3 Now four men with a skin disease were sitting at the entrance of the city gate. They said to one another, "Why are we just sitting here waiting to die? **7:4** If we go into the city, we'll die of starvation, and if we stay here we'll die! So come on, let's defect to the Syrian camp! If they spare us, we'll live; if they kill us – well, we were going to die anyway." **7:5** So they started toward the Syrian camp at dusk. When they reached the edge

of the Syrian camp, there was no one there. **7:6** The LORD had caused the Syrian camp to hear the sound of chariots and horses and a large army. Then they said to one another, "Look, the king of Israel has paid the kings of the Hittites and Egypt to attack us!" **7:7** So they got up and fled at dusk, leaving behind their tents, horses, and donkeys. They left the camp as it was and ran for their lives. **7:8** When the men with a skin disease reached the edge of the camp, they entered a tent and had a meal. They also took some silver, gold, and clothes and went and hid it all. Then they went back and entered another tent. They looted it and went and hid what they had taken. **7:9** Then they said to one another, "It's not right what we're doing! This is a day to celebrate, but we haven't told anyone. If we wait until dawn, we'll be punished. So come on, let's go and inform the royal palace." **7:10** So they went and called out to the gatekeepers of the city. They told them, "We entered the Syrian camp and there was no one there. We didn't even hear a man's voice. But the horses and donkeys are still tied up, and the tents remain up." **7:11** The gatekeepers relayed the news to the royal palace.

7:12 The king got up in the night and said to his advisers, "I will tell you what the Syrians have done to us. They know we are starving, so they left the camp and hid in the field, thinking, 'When they come out of the city, we will capture them alive and enter the city.'" **7:13** One of his advisers replied, "Pick some men and have them take five of the horses that are left in the city. (Even if they are killed, their fate will be no different than that of all the Israelite people – we're all going to die!) Let's send them out so we can know for sure what's going on." **7:14** So they picked two horsemen and the king sent them out to track the Syrian army. He ordered them, "Go and find out what's going on." **7:15** So they tracked them as far as the Jordan. The road was filled with clothes and equipment that the Syrians had discarded in their haste. The scouts went back and told the king. **7:16** Then the people went out and looted the Syrian camp. A seah of finely milled flour sold for a shekel, and two seahs of barley for a shekel, just as the LORD had said they would.

7:17 Now the king had placed the officer who was his right-hand man at the city gate. When the people rushed out, they trampled him to death in the gate. This fulfilled the prophet's word which he had spoken when the king tried to arrest him. **7:18** The prophet told the king, "Two seahs of barley will sell for a shekel, and a seah of finely milled flour for a shekel; this will happen about this time tomorrow in the gate of Samaria." **7:19** But the officer replied to the prophet, "Look, even if the LORD made it rain by opening holes in the sky, could this happen so soon?" Elisha said, "Look, you will see it happen with your own eyes, but you will not eat any of the food!" **7:20** This is exactly what happened to him. The people trampled him to death in the city gate.

Elisha Again Helps the Shunammite Woman

8:1 Now Elisha advised the woman whose son he had brought back to life, "You and your family should go and live somewhere else for a while, for the LORD has decreed that a famine will overtake the land for seven years." **8:2** So the woman did as the prophet said. She and her family went and lived in the land of the Philistines for seven years. **8:3** After seven years the woman returned from the land of the Philistines and went to ask the king to give her back her house and field. **8:4** Now the king was talking to Gehazi, the prophet's servant, and said, "Tell me all the great things which Elisha has done." **8:5** While Gehazi was telling the king how Elisha had brought the dead back to life, the woman whose son he had brought back to life came to ask the king for her house and field. Gehazi said, "My master, O king, this is the very woman and this is her son whom Elisha brought back to life!" **8:6** The king asked the woman about it, and she gave him the details. The king assigned a eunuch to take care of her request and ordered him, "Give her back everything she owns, as well as the amount of crops her field produced from the day she left the land until now."

Elisha Meets with Hazael

8:7 Elisha traveled to Damascus while King Ben Hadad of Syria was sick. The king was told, "The prophet has come here." **8:8** So the king told Hazael, "Take a gift and go visit the prophet. Request from him an oracle from the LORD. Ask him, 'Will I recover from this sickness?'" **8:9** So Hazael went to visit Elisha. He took along a gift, as well as forty camel loads of all the fine things of Damascus. When he arrived, he stood before him and said, "Your son, King Ben Hadad of Syria, has sent me to you with this question, 'Will I recover from this sickness?'" **8:10** Elisha said to him, "Go and tell him, 'You will surely recover,' but the LORD has revealed to me that he will surely die." **8:11** Elisha just stared at him until Hazael became uncomfortable. Then the prophet started crying. **8:12** Hazael asked, "Why are you crying, my master?" He replied, "Because I know the trouble you will cause the Israelites. You will set fire to their fortresses, kill their young men with the sword, smash their children to bits, and rip open their pregnant women." **8:13** Hazael said, "How could your servant, who is as insignificant as a dog, accomplish this great military victory?" Elisha answered, "The LORD has revealed to me that you will be the king of Syria." **8:14** He left Elisha and went to his master. Ben Hadad asked him, "What did Elisha tell you?" Hazael replied, "He told me you would surely recover." **8:15** The next day Hazael took a piece of cloth, dipped it in water, and spread it over Ben Hadad's face until he died. Then Hazael replaced him as king.

Jehoram's Reign over Judah

8:16 In the fifth year of the reign of Israel's King Joram, son of Ahab, Jehoshaphat's son Jehoram became king over Judah. **8:17** He was thirty-two years old when he became king and he reigned for eight years in Jerusalem. **8:18** He followed in the footsteps of the kings of Israel, just as Ahab's dynasty had done, for he married Ahab's daughter. He did evil in the sight of the LORD. **8:19** But the LORD was unwilling to destroy Judah. He preserved Judah for the sake of his servant David to whom he had promised a perpetual dynasty.

8:20 During his reign Edom freed themselves from Judah's control and set up their own king. **8:21** Joram crossed over to Zair with all his chariots. The Edomites, who had surrounded him, attacked at night and defeated him and his chariot officers. The Israelite army retreated to their homeland. **8:22** So Edom has remained free from Judah's control to this very day. At that same time Libnah also rebelled.

8:23 The rest of the events of Joram's reign, including a record of his accomplishments, are recorded in the scroll called the Annals of the Kings of Judah. **8:24** Joram passed away and was buried with his ancestors in the city of David. His son Ahaziah replaced him as king.

Ahaziah Takes the Throne of Judah

8:25 In the twelfth year of the reign of Israel's King Joram, son of Ahab, Jehoram's son Ahaziah became king over Judah. **8:26** Ahaziah was twenty-two years old when he became king and he reigned for one year in Jerusalem. His mother was Athaliah, the granddaughter of King Omri of Israel. **8:27** He followed in the footsteps of Ahab's dynasty and did evil in the sight of the LORD, like Ahab's dynasty, for he was related to Ahab's family.

8:28 He joined Ahab's son Joram in a battle against King Hazael of Syria at Ramoth Gilead in which the Syrians defeated Joram. **8:29** King Joram returned to Jezreel to recover from the wounds he received from the Syrians in Ramah when he fought against King Hazael of Syria. King Ahaziah son of Jehoram of Judah went down to visit Joram son of Ahab in Jezreel, for he was ill.

Jehu Becomes King

9:1 Now Elisha the prophet summoned a member of the prophetic guild and told him, "Tuck your robes into your belt, take this container of olive oil in your hand, and go to Ramoth Gilead. **9:2** When you arrive there, look for Jehu son of Jehoshaphat son of Nimshi and take him aside into an inner room. **9:3** Take the container of olive oil, pour it over his head, and say, 'This is what the LORD says, "I have designated you as king over Israel."' Then open the door and run away quickly!"

9:4 So the young prophet went to Ramoth Gilead. **9:5** When he arrived, the officers of the army were sitting there. So he said, "I have a message for you, O officer." Jehu asked, "For which one of us?" He replied, "For you, O officer." **9:6** So Jehu got up and went inside. Then the prophet poured the olive oil on his head and said to him, "This is what the LORD God of Israel says, 'I have designated you as king over the LORD's people Israel. **9:7** You will destroy the family of your master Ahab. I will get revenge against Jezebel for the shed blood of my servants the prophets and for the shed blood of all the LORD's servants. **9:8** Ahab's entire family will die. I will cut off every last male belonging to Ahab in Israel, including even the weak and incapacitated. **9:9** I will make Ahab's dynasty like those of Jeroboam son of Nebat and Baasha son of Ahijah. **9:10** Dogs will devour Jezebel on the plot of ground in Jezreel; she will not be buried.'" Then he opened the door and ran away.

9:11 When Jehu rejoined his master's servants, they asked him, "Is everything all right? Why did this madman visit you?" He replied, "Ah, it's not important. You know what kind of man he is and the kinds of things he says." **9:12** But they said, "You're lying! Tell us what he said." So he told them what he had said. He also related how he had said, "This is what the LORD says, 'I have designated you as king over Israel.'" **9:13** Each of them quickly took off his cloak and they spread them out at Jehu's feet on the steps. The trumpet was blown and they shouted, "Jehu is king!" **9:14** Then Jehu son of Jehoshaphat son of Nimshi conspired against Joram.

Jehu the Assassin

Now Joram had been in Ramoth Gilead with the whole Israelite army, guarding against an invasion by King Hazael of Syria. **9:15** But King Joram had returned to Jezreel to recover from the wounds he received from the Syrians when he fought against King Hazael of Syria. Jehu told his supporters, "If you really want me to be king, then don't let anyone escape from the city to go and warn Jezreel." **9:16** Jehu drove his chariot to Jezreel, for Joram was recuperating there. (Now King Ahaziah of Judah had come down to visit Joram.)

9:17 Now the watchman was standing on the tower in Jezreel and saw Jehu's troops approaching. He said, "I see troops!" Jehoram ordered, "Send a rider out to meet them and have him ask, 'Is everything all right?'" **9:18** So the horseman went to meet him and said, "This is what the king says, 'Is everything all right?'" Jehu replied, "None of your business! Follow me." The watchman reported, "The messenger reached them, but hasn't started back." **9:19** So he sent a second horseman out to them and he said, "This is what the king says, 'Is everything all right?'"

Jehu replied, "None of your business! Follow me." **9:20** The watchman reported, "He reached them, but hasn't started back. The one who drives the lead chariot drives like Jehu son of Nimshi; he drives recklessly." **9:21** Jehoram ordered, "Hitch up my chariot." When his chariot had been hitched up, King Jehoram of Israel and King Ahaziah of Judah went out in their respective chariots to meet Jehu. They met up with him in the plot of land that had once belonged to Naboth of Jezreel.

9:22 When Jehoram saw Jehu, he asked, "Is everything all right, Jehu?" He replied, "How can everything be all right as long as your mother Jezebel promotes idolatry and pagan practices?" **9:23** Jehoram turned his chariot around and took off. He said to Ahaziah, "It's a trap, Ahaziah!" **9:24** Jehu aimed his bow and shot an arrow right between Jehoram's shoulders. The arrow went through his heart and he fell to his knees in his chariot. **9:25** Jehu ordered his officer Bidkar, "Pick him up and throw him into the part of the field that once belonged to Naboth of Jezreel. Remember, you and I were riding together behind his father Ahab, when the LORD pronounced this judgment on him, **9:26** 'Know for sure that I saw the shed blood of Naboth and his sons yesterday,' says the LORD, "and that I will give you what you deserve right here in this plot of land," says the LORD.' So now pick him up and throw him into this plot of land, just as the LORD said."

9:27 When King Ahaziah of Judah saw what happened, he took off up the road to Beth Haggan. Jehu chased him and ordered, "Shoot him too." They shot him while he was driving his chariot up the ascent of Gur near Ibleam. He fled to Megiddo and died there. **9:28** His servants took his body back to Jerusalem and buried him in his tomb with his ancestors in the city of David. **9:29** Ahaziah had become king over Judah in the eleventh year of Joram son of Ahab.

9:30 Jehu approached Jezreel. When Jezebel heard the news, she put on some eye liner, fixed up her hair, and leaned out the window. **9:31** When Jehu came through the gate, she said, "Is everything all right, Zimri, murderer of his master?" **9:32** He looked up at the window and said, "Who is on my side? Who?" Two or three eunuchs looked down at him. **9:33** He said, "Throw her down!" So they threw her down, and when she hit the ground, her blood splattered against the wall and the horses, and Jehu drove his chariot over her. **9:34** He went inside and had a meal. Then he said, "Dispose of this accursed woman's corpse. Bury her, for after all, she was a king's daughter." **9:35** But when they went to bury her, they found nothing left but the skull, feet, and palms of the hands. **9:36** When they went back and told him, he said, "The LORD's word through his servant, Elijah the Tishbite, has come to pass. He warned, 'In the plot of land at Jezreel, dogs will devour Jezebel's flesh. **9:37** Jezebel's corpse will be like manure on the surface of the ground in the plot of land at Jezreel. People will not be able to even recognize her.'"

Jehu Wipes Out Ahab's Family

10:1 Ahab had seventy sons living in Samaria. So Jehu wrote letters and sent them to Samaria to the leading officials of Jezreel and to the guardians of Ahab's dynasty. This is what the letters said, **10:2** "You have with you the sons of your master, chariots and horses, a fortified city, and weapons. So when this letter arrives, **10:3** pick the best and most capable of your master's sons, place him on his father's throne, and defend your master's dynasty."

10:4 They were absolutely terrified and said, "Look, two kings could not stop him! How can we?" **10:5** So the palace supervisor, the city commissioner, the leaders, and the guardians sent this message to Jehu, "We are your subjects! Whatever you say, we will do. We will not make anyone king. Do what you consider proper."

10:6 He wrote them a second letter, saying, "If you are really on my side and are willing to obey me, then take the heads of your master's sons and come to me in Jezreel at this time tomorrow." Now the king had seventy sons, and the prominent men of the city were raising them. **10:7** When they received the letter, they seized the king's sons and executed all seventy of them. They put their heads in baskets and sent them to him in Jezreel. **10:8** The messenger came and told Jehu, "They have brought the heads of the king's sons." Jehu said, "Stack them in two piles at the entrance of the city gate until morning." **10:9** In the morning he went out and stood there. Then he said to all the people, "You are innocent. I conspired against my master and killed him. But who struck down all of these men? **10:10** Therefore take note that not one of the judgments the LORD announced against Ahab's dynasty has failed to materialize. The LORD had done what he announced through his servant Elijah." **10:11** Then Jehu killed all who were left of Ahab's family in Jezreel, and all his nobles, close friends, and priests. He left no survivors.

10:12 Jehu then left there and set out for Samaria. While he was traveling through Beth Eked of the Shepherds, **10:13** Jehu encountered the relatives of King Ahaziah of Judah. He asked, "Who are you?" They replied, "We are Ahaziah's relatives. We have come down to see how the king's sons and the queen mother's sons are doing." **10:14** He said, "Capture them alive!" So they captured them alive and then executed all forty-two of them in the cistern at Beth Eked. He left no survivors.

10:15 When he left there, he met Jehonadab, son of Rekab, who had been looking for him. Jehu greeted him and asked, "Are you as committed to me as I am to you?" Jehonadab answered, "I am!" Jehu replied, "If so, give me your hand." So he offered his hand and Jehu pulled him up into the chariot. **10:16** Jehu said, "Come with me and see how zealous I am for the LORD's cause." So he took him along in his chariot. **10:17** He went to Samaria and exterminated all the members of Ahab's family who were still alive in Samaria, just as the LORD had announced to Elijah.

Jehu Executes the Prophets and Priests of Baal

10:18 Jehu assembled all the people and said to them, "Ahab worshiped Baal a little; Jehu will worship him with great devotion. **10:19** So now, bring to me all the prophets of Baal, as well as all his servants and priests. None of them must be absent, for I am offering a great sacrifice to Baal. Any of them who fail to appear will lose their lives." But Jehu was tricking them so he could destroy the servants of Baal. **10:20** Then Jehu ordered, "Make arrangements for a celebration for Baal." So they announced it. **10:21** Jehu sent invitations throughout Israel, and all the servants of Baal came; not one was absent. They arrived at the temple of Baal and filled it up from end to end. **10:22** Jehu ordered the one who was in charge of the wardrobe, "Bring out robes for all the servants of Baal." So he brought out robes for them. **10:23** Then Jehu and Jehonadab son of Rekab went to the temple of Baal. Jehu said to the servants of Baal, "Make sure there are no servants of the LORD here with you; there must be only servants of Baal." **10:24** They went inside to offer sacrifices and burnt offerings. Now Jehu had stationed eighty men outside. He had told them, "If any of the men inside get away, you will pay with your lives!" **10:25** When he finished offering the burnt sacrifice, Jehu ordered the royal guard and officers, "Come in and strike them down! Don't let any escape!" So the royal guard and officers struck them down with the sword and left their bodies lying there. Then they entered the inner sanctuary of the temple of Baal. **10:26** They hauled out the sacred pillar of the temple of Baal and burned it. **10:27** They demolished the sacred pillar of Baal and the temple of Baal; it is used as a latrine to this very day. **10:28** So Jehu eradicated Baal worship from Israel.

A Summary of Jehu's Reign

10:29 However, Jehu did not repudiate the sins which Jeroboam son of Nebat had encouraged Israel to commit; the golden calves remained in Bethel and Dan. **10:30** The LORD said to Jehu, "You have done well. You have accomplished my will and carried out my wishes with regard to Ahab's dynasty. Therefore four generations of your descendants will rule over Israel." **10:31** But Jehu did not carefully and wholeheartedly obey the law of the LORD God of Israel. He did not repudiate the sins which Jeroboam had encouraged Israel to commit.

10:32 In those days the LORD began to reduce the size of Israel's territory. Hazael attacked their eastern border. **10:33** He conquered all the land of Gilead, including the territory of Gad, Reuben, and Manasseh, extending all the way from the Aroer in the Arnon Valley through Gilead to Bashan.

10:34 The rest of the events of Jehu's reign, including all his accomplishments and successes, are recorded in the scroll called the Annals of the Kings of Israel. **10:35** Jehu passed away and was buried in Samaria. His son Jehoahaz replaced him as king. **10:36** Jehu reigned over Israel for twenty-eight years in Samaria.

Athaliah is Eliminated

11:1 When Athaliah the mother of Ahaziah saw that her son was dead, she was determined to destroy the entire royal line. **11:2** So Jehosheba, the daughter of King Joram and sister of Ahaziah, took Ahaziah's son Joash and sneaked him away from the rest of the royal descendants who were to be executed. She hid him and his nurse in the room where the bed covers were stored. So he was hidden from Athaliah and escaped execution. **11:3** He hid out with his nurse in the LORD's temple for six years, while Athaliah was ruling over the land.

11:4 In the seventh year Jehoiada summoned the officers of the units of hundreds of the Carians and the royal bodyguard. He met with them in the LORD's temple. He made an agreement with them and made them swear an oath of allegiance in the LORD's temple. Then he showed them the king's son. **11:5** He ordered them, "This is what you must do. One third of the unit that is on duty during the Sabbath will guard the royal palace. **11:6** Another third of you will be stationed at the Foundation Gate. Still another third of you will be stationed at the gate behind the royal guard. You will take turns guarding the palace. **11:7** The two units who are off duty on the Sabbath will guard the LORD's temple and protect the king. **11:8** You must surround the king. Each of you must hold his weapon in his hand. Whoever approaches your ranks must be killed. You must accompany the king wherever he goes."

11:9 The officers of the units of hundreds did just as Jehoiada the priest ordered. Each of them took his men, those who were on duty during the Sabbath as well as those who were off duty on the Sabbath, and reported to Jehoiada the priest. **11:10** The priest gave to the officers of the units of hundreds King David's spears and the shields that were kept in the LORD's temple. **11:11** The royal bodyguard took their stations, each holding his weapon in his hand. They lined up from the south side of the temple to the north side and stood near the altar and the temple, surrounding the king. **11:12** Jehoiada led out the king's son and placed on him the crown and the royal insignia. They proclaimed him king and poured olive

oil on his head. They clapped their hands and cried out, "Long live the king!"

11:13 When Athaliah heard the royal guard shout, she joined the crowd at the LORD's temple. **11:14** Then she saw the king standing by the pillar, according to custom. The officers stood beside the king with their trumpets and all the people of the land were celebrating and blowing trumpets. Athaliah tore her clothes and screamed, "Treason, treason!" **11:15** Jehoiada the priest ordered the officers of the units of hundreds, who were in charge of the army, "Bring her outside the temple to the guards. Put the sword to anyone who follows her." The priest gave this order because he had decided she should not be executed in the LORD's temple. **11:16** They seized her and took her into the precincts of the royal palace through the horses' entrance. There she was executed.

11:17 Jehoiada then drew up a covenant between the LORD and the king and people, stipulating that they should be loyal to the LORD. **11:18** All the people of the land went and demolished the temple of Baal. They smashed its altars and idols to bits. They killed Mattan the priest of Baal in front of the altar. Jehoiada the priest then placed guards at the LORD's temple. **11:19** He took the officers of the units of hundreds, the Carians, the royal bodyguard, and all the people of land, and together they led the king down from the LORD's temple. They entered the royal palace through the Gate of the Royal Bodyguard, and the king sat down on the royal throne. **11:20** All the people of the land celebrated, for the city had rest now that they had killed Athaliah with the sword in the royal palace.

Joash's Reign over Judah

11:21 (12:1) Jehoash was seven years old when he began to reign. **12:1** (12:2) In Jehu's seventh year Jehoash became king; he reigned for forty years in Jerusalem. His mother was Zibiah, who was from Beer Sheba. **12:2** Throughout his lifetime Jehoash did what the LORD approved, just as Jehoiada the priest taught him. **12:3** But the high places were not eliminated; the people continued to offer sacrifices and burn incense on the high places.

12:4 Jehoash said to the priests, "I place at your disposal all the consecrated silver that has been brought to the LORD's temple, including the silver collected from the census tax, the silver received from those who have made vows, and all the silver that people have voluntarily contributed to the LORD's temple. **12:5** The priests should receive the silver they need from the treasurers and repair any damage to the temple they discover."

12:6 By the twenty-third year of King Jehoash's reign the priests had still not repaired the damage to the temple. **12:7** So King Jehoash summoned Jehoiada the priest along with the other priests, and said to them, "Why have you not repaired the damage to the temple? Now, take no more silver from your treasurers unless you intend to use it to repair the damage." **12:8** The priests agreed not to collect silver from the people and relieved themselves of personal responsibility for the temple repairs.

12:9 Jehoiada the priest took a chest and drilled a hole in its lid. He placed it on the right side of the altar near the entrance of the LORD's temple. The priests who guarded the entrance would put into it all the silver brought to the LORD's temple. **12:10** When they saw the chest was full of silver, the royal secretary and the high priest counted the silver that had been brought to the LORD's temple and bagged it up. **12:11** They would then hand over the silver that had been weighed to the construction foremen assigned to the LORD's temple. They hired carpenters and builders to work on the LORD's temple, **12:12** as well as masons and stonecutters. They bought wood and chiseled stone to repair the damage to the LORD's temple and also paid for all the other expenses. **12:13** The silver brought to the LORD's temple was not used for silver bowls, trimming shears, basins, trumpets, or any kind of gold or silver implements. **12:14** It was handed over to the foremen who used it to repair the LORD's temple. **12:15** They did not audit the treasurers who disbursed the funds to the foremen, for they were honest. **12:16** (The silver collected in conjunction with reparation offerings and sin offerings was not brought to the LORD's temple; it belonged to the priests.)

12:17 At that time King Hazael of Syria attacked Gath and captured it. Hazael then decided to attack Jerusalem. **12:18** King Jehoash of Judah collected all the sacred items that his ancestors Jehoshaphat, Jehoram, and Ahaziah, kings of Judah, had consecrated, as well as his own sacred items and all the gold that could be found in the treasuries of the LORD's temple and the royal palace. He sent it all to King Hazael of Syria, who then withdrew from Jerusalem.

12:19 The rest of the events of Joash's reign, including all his accomplishments, are recorded in the scroll called the Annals of the Kings of Judah. **12:20** His servants conspired against him and murdered Joash at Beth-Millo, on the road that goes down to Silla. **12:21** His servants Jozabad son of Shimeath and Jehozabad son of Shomer murdered him. He was buried with his ancestors in the city of David. His son Amaziah replaced him as king.

Jehoahaz's Reign over Israel

13:1 In the twenty-third year of the reign of Judah's King Joash son of Ahaziah, Jehu's son Jehoahaz became king over Israel. He reigned in Samaria for seventeen years. **13:2** He did evil in the sight of the LORD. He continued in the sinful ways of Jeroboam son of Nebat who had encouraged Israel to sin; he did not repudiate those sins. **13:3** The LORD was furious with Israel and handed them over to King Hazael of Syria and to Hazael's son Ben Hadad for many years.

13:4 Jehoahaz asked for the LORD's mercy and the LORD responded favorably, for he saw that Israel was oppressed by the king of Syria. **13:5** The LORD provided a deliverer for Israel and they were freed from Syria's power. The Israelites once more lived in security. **13:6** But they did not repudiate the sinful ways of the family of Jeroboam, who encouraged Israel to sin; they continued in those sins. There was even an Asherah pole standing in Samaria. **13:7** Jehoahaz had no army left except for fifty horsemen, ten chariots, and 10,000 foot soldiers. The king of Syria had destroyed his troops and trampled on them like dust.

13:8 The rest of the events of Jehoahaz's reign, including all his accomplishments and successes, are recorded in the scroll called the Annals of the Kings of Israel. **13:9** Jehoahaz passed away and was buried in Samaria. His son Joash replaced him as king.

Jehoash's Reign over Israel

13:10 In the thirty-seventh year of King Joash's reign over Judah, Jehoahaz's son Jehoash became king over Israel. He reigned in Samaria for sixteen years. **13:11** He did evil in the sight of the LORD. He did not repudiate the sinful ways of Jeroboam son of Nebat who encouraged Israel to sin; he continued in those sins. **13:12** The rest of the events of Joash's reign, including all his accomplishments and his successful war with King Amaziah of Judah, are recorded in the scroll called the Annals of the Kings of Israel. **13:13** Joash passed away and Jeroboam succeeded him on the throne. Joash was buried in Samaria with the kings of Israel.

Elisha Makes One Final Prophecy

13:14 Now Elisha had a terminal illness. King Joash of Israel went down to visit him. He wept before him and said, "My father, my father! The chariot and horsemen of Israel!" **13:15** Elisha told him, "Take a bow and some arrows," and he did so. **13:16** Then Elisha told the king of Israel, "Aim the bow." He did so, and Elisha placed his hands on the king's hands. **13:17** Elisha said, "Open the east window," and he did so. Elisha said, "Shoot!" and

he did so. Elisha said, "This arrow symbolizes the victory the LORD will give you over Syria. You will annihilate Syria in Aphek!" **13:18** Then Elisha said, "Take the arrows," and he did so. He told the king of Israel, "Strike the ground!" He struck the ground three times and stopped. **13:19** The prophet got angry at him and said, "If you had struck the ground five or six times, you would have annihilated Syria! But now, you will defeat Syria only three times."

13:20 Elisha died and was buried. Moabite raiding parties invaded the land at the beginning of the year. **13:21** One day some men were burying a man when they spotted a raiding party. So they threw the dead man into Elisha's tomb. When the body touched Elisha's bones, the dead man came to life and stood on his feet.

13:22 Now King Hazael of Syria oppressed Israel throughout Jehoahaz's reign. **13:23** But the LORD had mercy on them and felt pity for them. He extended his favor to them because of the promise he had made to Abraham, Isaac, and Jacob. He has been unwilling to destroy them or remove them from his presence to this very day. **13:24** When King Hazael of Syria died, his son Ben Hadad replaced him as king. **13:25** Jehoahaz's son Jehoash took back from Ben Hadad son of Hazael the cities that he had taken from his father Jehoahaz in war. Joash defeated him three times and recovered the Israelite cities.

Amaziah's Reign over Judah

14:1 In the second year of the reign of Israel's King Joash son of Joahaz, Joash's son Amaziah became king over Judah. **14:2** He was twenty-five years old when he began to reign, and he reigned for twenty-nine years in Jerusalem. His mother was Jehoaddan, who was from Jerusalem. **14:3** He did what the LORD approved, but not like David his father. He followed the example of his father Joash. **14:4** But the high places were not eliminated; the people continued to offer sacrifices and burn incense on the high places.

14:5 When he had secured control of the kingdom, he executed the servants who had assassinated his father. **14:6** But he did not execute the sons of the assassins. He obeyed the LORD's commandment as recorded in the law scroll of Moses, "Fathers must not be put to death for what their sons do, and sons must not be put to death for what their fathers do. A man must be put to death only for his own sin."

14:7 He defeated 10,000 Edomites in the Salt Valley; he captured Sela in battle and renamed it Joktheel, a name it has retained to this very day. **14:8** Then Amaziah sent messengers to Jehoash son of Jehu, king of Israel. He said, "Come, let's meet face to face." **14:9** King Jehoash of Israel sent this message back to King Amaziah of Judah, "A thornbush in Lebanon sent this message to a cedar in Lebanon, 'Give your daughter to my son as a wife.' Then a wild animal of Lebanon came by and trampled down the thorn. **14:10** You thoroughly defeated Edom and it has gone to your

head! Gloat over your success, but stay in your palace. Why bring calamity on yourself? Why bring down yourself and Judah along with you?" **14:11** But Amaziah would not heed the warning, so King Jehoash of Israel attacked. He and King Amaziah of Judah met face to face in

Beth Shemesh of Judah. **14:12** Judah was defeated by Israel, and each man ran back home. **14:13** King Jehoash of Israel captured King Amaziah of Judah, son of Jehoash son of Ahaziah, in Beth Shemesh. He attacked Jerusalem and broke down the wall of Jerusalem from the Gate of Ephraim to the Corner Gate – a distance of about six hundred feet. **14:14** He took away all the gold and silver, all the items found in the LORD's temple and in the treasuries of the royal palace, and some hostages. Then he went back to Samaria.

(**14:15** The rest of the events of Jehoash's reign, including all his accomplishments and his successful war with King Amaziah of Judah, are recorded in the scroll called the Annals of the Kings of Israel. **14:16** Jehoash passed away and was buried in Samaria with the kings of Israel. His son Jeroboam replaced him as king.)

14:17 King Amaziah son of Joash of Judah lived for fifteen years after the death of King Jehoash son of Jehoahaz of Israel. **14:18** The rest of the events of Amaziah's reign are recorded in the scroll called the Annals of the Kings of Judah. **14:19** Conspirators plotted against him in Jerusalem, so he fled to Lachish. But they sent assassins after him and they killed him there. **14:20** His body was carried back by horses and he was buried in Jerusalem with his ancestors in the city of David. **14:21** All the people of Judah took Azariah, who was sixteen years old, and made him king in his father Amaziah's place. **14:22** Azariah built up Elat and restored it to Judah after the king had passed away.

Jeroboam II's Reign over Israel

14:23 In the fifteenth year of the reign of Judah's King Amaziah, son of Joash, Jeroboam son of Joash became king over Israel. He reigned for forty-one years in Samaria. **14:24** He did evil in the sight of the LORD; he did not repudiate the sinful ways of Jeroboam son of Nebat who encouraged Israel to sin. **14:25** He restored the border of Israel from Lebo Hamath in the north to the sea of the Arabah in the south, in accordance with the word of the LORD God of Israel announced through his servant Jonah son of Amittai, the prophet from Gath Hepher. **14:26** The LORD saw Israel's intense suffering; everyone was weak and incapacitated and Israel had no deliverer. **14:27** The LORD had not decreed that he would blot out Israel's memory from under heaven, so he delivered them through Jeroboam son of Joash.

14:28 The rest of the events of Jeroboam's reign, including all his accomplishments, his military success in restoring Israelite control over Damascus and Hamath, are recorded in the scroll called the Annals of the Kings of Israel. **14:29** Jeroboam passed away and was buried in Samaria with the kings of Israel. His son Zechariah replaced him as king.

Azariah's Reign over Judah

15:1 In the twenty-seventh year of King Jeroboam's reign over Israel, Amaziah's son Azariah became king over Judah. **15:2** He was sixteen years old when he began to reign, and he reigned for fifty-two years in Jerusalem. His mother's name was Jecholiah, who was from Jerusalem. **15:3** He did what the LORD approved, just as his father Amaziah had done. **15:4** But the high places were not eliminated; the people continued to offer sacrifices and burn incense on the high places. **15:5** The LORD afflicted the king with an illness; he suffered from a skin disease until the day he died. He lived in separate quarters, while his son Jotham was in charge of the palace and ruled over the people of the land.

15:6 The rest of the events of Azariah's reign, including all his accomplishments, are recorded in the scroll called the Annals of the Kings of Judah. **15:7** Azariah passed away and was buried with his ancestors in the city of David. His son Jotham replaced him as king.

Zechariah's Reign over Israel

15:8 In the thirty-eighth year of King Azariah's reign over Judah, Jeroboam's son Zechariah became king over Israel. He reigned in Samaria for six months. **15:9** He did evil in the sight of the LORD, as his ancestors had done. He did not repudiate the sinful ways of Jeroboam son of Nebat who encouraged Israel to sin. **15:10** Shallum son of Jabesh conspired against him; he assassinated him in Ibleam and took his place as king. **15:11** The rest of the events of Zechariah's reign are recorded in the scroll called the Annals of the Kings of Israel. **15:12** His assassination brought to fulfillment the LORD's word to Jehu, "Four generations of your descendants will rule over Israel." That is exactly what happened.

15:13 Shallum son of Jabesh became king in the thirty-ninth year of King Uzziah's reign over Judah. He reigned for one month in Samaria. **15:14** Menahem son of Gadi went up from Tirzah to Samaria and attacked Shallum son of Jabesh. He killed him and took his place as king. **15:15** The rest of the events of Shallum's reign, including the conspiracy he organized, are recorded in the scroll called the Annals of the Kings of Israel. **15:16** At that time Menahem came from Tirzah and attacked Tiphsah. He struck down all who lived in the city and the surrounding territory, because they would not surrender. He even ripped open the pregnant women.

Menahem's Reign over Israel

15:17 In the thirty-ninth year of King Azariah's reign over Judah, Menahem son of Gadi became king over Israel. He reigned for twelve years in Samaria. **15:18** He did evil in

the sight of the LORD; he did not repudiate the sinful ways of Jeroboam son of Nebat who encouraged Israel to sin.

During his reign, **15:19** Pul king of Assyria invaded the land, and Menahem paid him a thousand talents of silver to gain his support and to solidify his control of the kingdom. **15:20** Menahem got this silver by taxing all the wealthy men in Israel; he took fifty shekels of silver from each one of them and paid it to the king of Assyria. Then the king of Assyria left; he did not stay there in the land.

15:21 The rest of the events of Menahem's reign, including all his accomplishments, are recorded in the scroll called the Annals of the Kings of Israel. **15:22** Menahem passed away and his son Pekahiah replaced him as king.

Pekahiah's Reign over Israel

15:23 In the fiftieth year of King Azariah's reign over Judah, Menahem's son Pekahiah became king over Israel. He reigned in Samaria for two years. **15:24** He did evil in the sight of the LORD; he did not repudiate the sinful ways of Jeroboam son of Nebat who encouraged Israel to sin. **15:25** His officer Pekah son of Remaliah conspired against him. He and fifty Gileadites assassinated Pekahiah, as well as Argob and Arieh, in Samaria in the fortress of the royal palace. Pekah then took his place as king.

15:26 The rest of the events of Pekahiah's reign, including all his accomplishments, are recorded in the scroll called the Annals of the Kings of Israel.

Pekah's Reign over Israel

15:27 In the fifty-second year of King Azariah's reign over Judah, Pekah son of Remaliah became king over Israel. He reigned in Samaria for twenty years. **15:28** He did evil in the sight of the LORD; he did not repudiate the sinful ways of Jeroboam son of Nebat who encouraged Israel to sin. **15:29** During Pekah's reign over Israel, King Tiglath-pileser of Assyria came and captured Ijon, Abel Beth Maacah, Janoah, Kedesh, Hazor, Gilead, and Galilee, including all the territory of Naphtali. He deported the people to Assyria. **15:30** Hoshea son of Elah conspired against Pekah son of Remaliah. He assassinated him and took his place as king, in the twentieth year of the reign of Jotham son of Uzziah.

15:31 The rest of the events of Pekah's reign, including all his accomplishments, are recorded in the scroll called the Annals of the Kings of Israel.

Jotham's Reign over Judah

15:32 In the second year of the reign of Israel's King Pekah son of Remaliah, Uzziah's son Jotham became king over Judah. **15:33** He was twenty-five years old when he began to reign, and he reigned for sixteen years in Jerusalem. His mother was Jerusha the daughter of Zadok. **15:34** He did what the LORD approved, just as his father Uzziah had done. **15:35** But the high places were not eliminated; the people continued to offer sacrifices and burn incense on the high places. He built the Upper Gate to the LORD's temple.

15:36 The rest of the events of Jotham's reign, including his accomplishments, are recorded in the scroll called the Annals of the Kings of Judah. **15:37** In those days the LORD prompted King Rezin of Syria and Pekah son of Remaliah to attack Judah. **15:38** Jotham passed away and was buried with his ancestors in the city of his ancestor David. His son Ahaz replaced him as king.

Ahaz's Reign over Judah

16:1 In the seventeenth year of the reign of Pekah son of Remaliah, Jotham's son Ahaz became king over Judah. **16:2** Ahaz was twenty years old when he began to reign, and he reigned for sixteen years in Jerusalem. He did not do what pleased the LORD his God, in contrast to his ancestor David. **16:3** He followed in the footsteps of the kings of Israel. He passed his son through the fire, a horrible sin practiced by the nations whom the LORD drove out from before the Israelites. **16:4** He offered sacrifices and burned incense on the high places, on the hills, and under every green tree.

16:5 At that time King Rezin of Syria and King Pekah son of Remaliah of Israel attacked Jerusalem. They besieged Ahaz, but were unable to conquer him. **16:6** (At that time King Rezin of Syria recovered Elat for Syria; he drove the Judahites from there. Syrians arrived in Elat and live there to this very day.) **16:7** Ahaz sent messengers to King Tiglath-pileser of Assyria, saying, "I am your servant and your dependent. March up and rescue me from the power of the king of Syria and the king of Israel, who have attacked me." **16:8** Then Ahaz took the silver and gold that were in the LORD's temple and in the treasuries of the royal palace and sent it as tribute to the king of Assyria. **16:9** The king of Assyria responded favorably to his request; he attacked Damascus and captured it. He deported the people to Kir and executed Rezin.

16:10 When King Ahaz went to meet with King Tiglath-pileser of Assyria in Damascus, he saw the altar there. King Ahaz sent to Uriah the priest a drawing of the altar and a blueprint for its design. **16:11** Uriah the priest built an altar in conformity with the plans King Ahaz had sent from Damascus. Uriah the priest finished it before King Ahaz arrived back from Damascus. **16:12** When the king arrived back from Damascus and saw the altar, he approached it and offered a sacrifice on it. **16:13** He offered his burnt sacrifice and his grain offering. He poured out his libation and sprinkled the blood from his peace offerings on the altar. **16:14** He moved the bronze altar that stood in the LORD's presence from the front of the

temple (between the altar and the LORD's temple) and put it on the north side of the new altar. **16:15** King Ahaz ordered Uriah the priest, "On the large altar offer the morning burnt sacrifice, the evening grain offering, the royal burnt sacrifices and grain offering, the burnt sacrifice for all the people of Israel, their grain offering, and their libations. Sprinkle all the blood of the burnt sacrifice and other sacrifices on it. The bronze altar will be for my personal use." **16:16** So Uriah the priest did exactly as King Ahaz ordered.

16:17 King Ahaz took off the frames of the movable stands, and removed the basins from them. He took "The Sea" down from the bronze bulls that supported it and put it on the pavement. **16:18** He also removed the Sabbath awning that had been built in the temple and the king's outer entranceway, on account of the king of Assyria.

16:19 The rest of the events of Ahaz's reign, including his accomplishments, are recorded in the scroll called the Annals of the Kings of Judah. **16:20** Ahaz passed away and was buried with his ancestors in the city of David. His son Hezekiah replaced him as king.

Hoshea's Reign over Israel

17:1 In the twelfth year of King Ahaz's reign over Judah, Hoshea son of Elah became king over Israel. He reigned in Samaria for nine years. **17:2** He did evil in the sight of the LORD, but not to the same degree as the Israelite kings who preceded him. **17:3** King Shalmaneser of Assyria threatened him; Hoshea became his subject and paid him tribute. **17:4** The king of Assyria discovered that Hoshea was planning a revolt. Hoshea had sent messengers to King So of Egypt and had not sent his annual tribute to the king of Assyria. So the king of Assyria arrested him and imprisoned him. **17:5** The king of Assyria marched through the whole land. He attacked Samaria and besieged it for three years. **17:6** In the ninth year of Hoshea's reign, the king of Assyria captured Samaria and deported the people of Israel to Assyria. He settled them in Halah, along the Habor (the river of Gozan), and in the cities of the Medes.

A Summary of Israel's Sinful History

17:7 This happened because the Israelites sinned against the LORD their God, who brought them up from the land of Egypt and freed them from the power of Pharaoh king of Egypt. They worshiped other gods; **17:8** they observed the practices of the nations whom the LORD had driven out from before Israel, and followed the example of the kings of Israel. **17:9** The Israelites said things about the LORD their God that were not right. They built high places in all their cities, from the watchtower to the fortress. **17:10** They set up sacred pillars and Asherah poles on every high hill and under every green tree. **17:11** They burned incense on all the high places just like the nations whom the LORD had driven away from before them. Their evil practices made the LORD angry. **17:12** They worshiped the disgusting idols in blatant disregard of the LORD's command. **17:13** The LORD solemnly warned Israel and Judah through all his prophets and all the seers, "Turn back from your evil ways; obey my commandments and rules that are recorded in the law. I ordered your ancestors to keep this law and sent my servants the prophets to remind you of its demands." **17:14** But they did not pay attention and were as stubborn as their ancestors, who had not trusted the LORD their God. **17:15** They rejected his rules, the covenant he had made with their ancestors, and the laws he had commanded them to obey. They paid allegiance to worthless idols, and so became worthless to the LORD. They copied the practices of the surrounding nations in blatant disregard of the LORD's command. **17:16** They abandoned all the commandments of the LORD their God; they made two metal calves and an Asherah pole, bowed down to all the stars in the sky, and worshiped Baal. **17:17** They passed their sons and daughters through the fire, and practiced divination and omen reading. They committed themselves to doing evil in the sight of the LORD and made him angry.

17:18 So the LORD was furious with Israel and rejected them; only the tribe of Judah was left. **17:19** Judah also failed to keep the commandments of the LORD their God; they followed Israel's example. **17:20** So the LORD rejected all of Israel's descendants; he humiliated them and handed them over to robbers, until he had thrown them from his presence. **17:21** He tore Israel away from David's dynasty, and Jeroboam son of Nebat became their king. Jeroboam drove Israel away from the LORD and encouraged them to commit a serious sin. **17:22** The Israelites followed in the sinful ways of Jeroboam son of Nebat and did not repudiate them. **17:23** Finally the LORD rejected Israel just as he had warned he would do through all his servants the prophets. Israel was deported from its land to Assyria and remains there to this very day.

The King of Assyria Populates Israel with Foreigners

17:24 The king of Assyria brought foreigners from Babylon, Cuthah, Avva, Hamath, and Sepharvaim and settled them in the cities of Samaria in place of the Israelites. They took possession of Samaria and lived in its cities. **17:25** When they first moved in, they did not worship the LORD. So the LORD sent lions among them and the lions were killing them. **17:26** The king of Assyria was told, "The nations whom you deported and settled in the cities of Samaria do not know the requirements of the God of the land, so he has sent lions among them. They are killing the people because they do not know the requirements of the God of the land." **17:27** So the king of Assyria ordered, "Take back one of the priests whom you deported from there. He must settle there and teach them the requirements of the God of the land." 17:28 So one of the priests whom they had deported from Samaria went back and settled in Bethel. He taught them how to worship the LORD.

17:29 But each of these nations made its own gods and put them in the shrines on the high places that the people of Samaria had made. Each nation did this in the cities where they lived. 17:30 The people from Babylon made Succoth Benoth, the people from Cuth made Nergal, the people from Hamath made Ashima, 17:31 the Avvites made Nibhaz and Tartak, and the Sepharvites burned their sons in the fire as an offering to Adrammelech and Anammelech, the gods of Sepharvaim. 17:32 At the same time they worshiped the LORD. They appointed some of their own people to serve as priests in the shrines on the high places. 17:33 They were worshiping the LORD and at the same time serving their own gods in accordance with the practices of the nations from which they had been deported.

17:34 To this very day they observe their earlier practices. They do not worship the LORD; they do not obey the rules, regulations, law, and commandments that the LORD gave the descendants of Jacob, whom he renamed Israel. 17:35 The LORD made an agreement with them and instructed them, "You must not worship other gods. Do not bow down to them, serve them, or offer sacrifices to them. 17:36 Instead you must worship the LORD, who brought you up from the land of Egypt by his great power and military ability; bow down to him and offer sacrifices to him. 17:37 You must carefully obey at all times the rules, regulations, law, and commandments he wrote down for you. You must not worship other gods. 17:38 You must never forget the agreement I made with you, and you must not worship other gods. 17:39 Instead you must worship the LORD your God; then he will rescue you from the power of all your enemies." 17:40 But they pay no attention; instead they observe their earlier practices. 17:41 These nations are worshiping the LORD and at the same time serving their idols; their sons and grandsons do just as their fathers have done, to this very day.

Hezekiah Becomes King of Judah

18:1 In the third year of the reign of Israel's King Hoshea son of Elah, Ahaz's son Hezekiah became king over Judah. 18:2 He was twenty-five years old when he began to reign, and he reigned twenty-nine years in Jerusalem. His mother was Abi, the daughter of Zechariah. 18:3 He did what the LORD approved, just as his ancestor David had done. 18:4 He eliminated the high places, smashed the sacred pillars to bits, and cut down the Asherah pole. He also demolished the bronze serpent that Moses had made, for up to that time the Israelites had been offering incense to it; it was called Nehushtan. 18:5 He trusted in the LORD God of Israel; in this regard there was none like him among the kings of Judah either before or after. 18:6 He was loyal to the LORD and did not abandon him. He obeyed the commandments which the LORD had given to Moses. 18:7 The LORD was with him; he succeeded in all his endeavors. He rebelled against the king of Assyria and refused to submit to him. 18:8 He defeated the Philistines as far as Gaza and its territory, from the watchtower to the city fortress.

18:9 In the fourth year of King Hezekiah's reign (it was the seventh year of the reign of Israel's King Hoshea, son of Elah), King Shalmaneser of Assyria marched up against Samaria and besieged it. 18:10 After three years he captured it (in the sixth year of Hezekiah's reign); in the ninth year of King Hoshea's reign over Israel Samaria was captured. 18:11 The king of Assyria deported the people of Israel to Assyria. He settled them in Halah, along the Habor (the river of Gozan), and in the cities of the Medes. 18:12 This happened because they did not obey the LORD their God and broke his agreement with them. They did not pay attention to and obey all that Moses, the LORD's servant, had commanded.

Sennacherib Invades Judah

18:13 In the fourteenth year of King Hezekiah's reign, King Sennacherib of Assyria marched up against all the fortified cities of Judah and captured them. 18:14 King Hezekiah of Judah sent this message to the king of Assyria, who was at Lachish, "I have violated our treaty. If you leave, I will do whatever you demand." So the king of Assyria demanded that King Hezekiah of Judah pay three hundred talents of silver and thirty talents of gold. 18:15 Hezekiah gave him all the silver in the LORD's temple and in the treasuries of the royal palace. 18:16 At that time King Hezekiah of Judah stripped the metal overlays from the doors of the LORD's temple and from the posts which he had plated and gave them to the king of Assyria.

18:17 The king of Assyria sent his commanding general, the chief eunuch, and the chief adviser from Lachish to King Hezekiah in Jerusalem, along with a large army. They went up and arrived at Jerusalem. They went and stood at the conduit of the upper pool which is located on the road to the field where they wash and dry cloth. 18:18 They summoned the king, so Eliakim son of Hilkiah, the palace supervisor, accompanied by Shebna the scribe and Joah son of Asaph, the secretary, went out to meet them.

18:19 The chief adviser said to them, "Tell Hezekiah: 'This is what the great king, the king of Assyria, says: "What is your source of confidence? 18:20 Your claim to have a strategy and military strength is just empty talk. In whom are you trusting that you would dare to rebel against me? 18:21 Now look, you must be trusting in Egypt, that splintered reed staff. If a man leans for support on it, it punctures his hand and wounds him. That is what Pharaoh king of Egypt does to all who trust in him. 18:22 Perhaps you will tell me, 'We are trusting in the LORD our God.' But Hezekiah is the one who eliminated his high places and altars and then told the people of Judah and Jerusalem, 'You must worship at this altar in Jerusalem.' 18:23 Now make a deal with my master the king of Assyria, and I will give you two thousand horses, provided you can find enough riders for them. 18:24 Certainly you will not refuse one of my master's minor officials and trust in Egypt for chariots and horsemen. 18:25 Furthermore it was by the command of the LORD that I marched up against this place to destroy it. The LORD told me, 'March up against this land and destroy it.'"'"

18:26 Eliakim son of Hilkiah, Shebna, and Joah said to the chief adviser, "Speak to your servants in Aramaic, for we understand it. Don't speak with us in the Judahite dialect in the hearing of the people who are on the wall." 18:27 But the chief adviser said to them, "My master did not send me to speak these words only to your master and to you. His message is also for the men who sit on the wall, for they will eat their own excrement and drink their own urine along with you."

18:28 The chief adviser then stood there and called out loudly in the Judahite dialect, "Listen to the message of the great king, the king of Assyria. 18:29 This is what the king says: 'Don't let Hezekiah mislead you, for he is not able to rescue you from my hand! 18:30 Don't let Hezekiah talk you into trusting in the LORD when he says, "The LORD will certainly rescue us; this city will not be handed over to the king of Assyria." 18:31 Don't listen to Hezekiah!' For this is what the king of Assyria says, 'Send me a token of your submission and surrender to me. Then each of you may eat from his own vine and fig tree and drink water from his own cistern, 18:32 until I come and take you to a land just like your own – a land of grain and new wine, a land of bread and vineyards, a land of olive trees and honey. Then you will live and not die. Don't listen to Hezekiah, for he is misleading you when he says, "The LORD will rescue us." 18:33 Have any of the gods of the nations actually rescued his land from the power of the king of Assyria? 18:34 Where are the gods of Hamath and Arpad? Where are the gods of Sepharvaim, Hena, and Ivvah? Indeed, did any gods rescue Samaria from my power? 18:35 Who among all the gods of the lands has rescued their lands from my power? So how can the LORD rescue Jerusalem from my power?'" 18:36 The people were silent and did not respond, for the king had ordered, "Don't respond to him."

18:37 Eliakim son of Hilkiah, the palace supervisor, accompanied by Shebna the scribe and Joah son of Asaph, the secretary, went to Hezekiah with their clothes torn and reported to him what the chief adviser had said. 19:1 When King Hezekiah heard this, he tore his clothes, put on sackcloth, and went to the LORD's temple. 19:2 He sent Eliakim the palace supervisor, Shebna the scribe, and the leading priests, clothed in sackcloth, with this message to the prophet Isaiah son of Amoz: 19:3 "This is what Hezekiah says: 'This is a day of distress, insults, and humiliation, as when a baby is ready to leave the birth canal, but the mother lacks the strength to push it through. 19:4 Perhaps the LORD your God will hear all these things the chief adviser has spoken on behalf of his master, the king of Assyria, who sent him to taunt the living God. When the LORD your God hears, perhaps he will punish him for the things he has said. So pray for this remnant that remains.'"

19:5 When King Hezekiah's servants came to Isaiah, 19:6 Isaiah said to them, "Tell your master this: 'This is what the LORD says: "Don't be afraid because of the things you have heard – these insults the king of Assyria's servants have hurled against me. 19:7 Look, I will take control of his mind; he will receive a report and return to his own land. I will cut him down with a sword in his own land."'"

19:8 When the chief adviser heard the king of Assyria had departed from Lachish, he left and went to Libnah, where the king was campaigning. 19:9 The king heard that King Tirhakah of Ethiopia was marching out to fight him. He again sent messengers to Hezekiah, ordering them: 19:10 "Tell King Hezekiah of Judah this: 'Don't let your God in whom you trust mislead you when he says, "Jerusalem will not be handed over to the king of Assyria." 19:11 Certainly you have heard how the kings of Assyria have annihilated all lands. Do you really think you will be rescued? 19:12 Were the nations whom my ancestors destroyed – the nations of Gozan, Haran, Rezeph, and the people of Eden in Telassar – rescued by their gods? 19:13 Where are the king of Hamath, the king of Arpad, and the king of Lair, Sepharvaim, Hena, and Ivvah?'"

19:14 Hezekiah took the letter from the messengers and read it. Then Hezekiah went up to the LORD's temple and spread it out before the LORD. 19:15 Hezekiah prayed before the LORD: "LORD God of Israel, who is enthroned on the cherubs! You alone are God over all the kingdoms of the earth. You made the sky and the earth. 19:16 Pay attention, LORD, and hear! Open your eyes, LORD, and observe! Listen to the message Sennacherib sent and how he taunts the living God! 19:17 It is true, LORD, that the kings of Assyria have destroyed the nations and their lands. 19:18 They have burned the gods of the nations, for they are not really gods, but only the product of human hands manufactured from wood and stone. That is why the Assyrians could destroy them. **19:19** Now, O LORD our God, rescue us from his power, so that all the kingdoms of the earth will know that you, LORD, are the only God." **19:20** Isaiah son of Amoz sent this message to Hezekiah: "This is what the LORD God of Israel says: 'I have heard your prayer concerning King Sennacherib of Assyria. **19:21** This is what the LORD says about him:

"The virgin daughter Zion
despises you, she makes fun of you;
Daughter Jerusalem
shakes her head after you.
19:22 Whom have you taunted and hurled insults at?
At whom have you shouted,
and looked so arrogantly?
At the Holy One of Israel!
19:23 Through your messengers you taunted the sovereign master,
'With my many chariots
I climbed up the high mountains,
the slopes of Lebanon.
I cut down its tall cedars,
and its best evergreens.
I invaded its most remote regions,
its thickest woods.
19:24 I dug wells and drank
water in foreign lands.
With the soles of my feet I dried up
all the rivers of Egypt.'
19:25 Certainly you must have heard!
Long ago I worked it out,
In ancient times I planned it;
and now I am bringing it to pass.
The plan is this:
Fortified cities will crash
into heaps of ruins.
19:26 Their residents are powerless,
they are terrified and ashamed.
They are as short-lived as plants in the field,
or green vegetation.
They are as short-lived as grass on the rooftops
when it is scorched by the east wind.
19:27 I know where you live,
and everything you do.
19:28 Because you rage against me,
and the uproar you create has reached my ears;
I will put my hook in your nose,
and my bridle between your lips,
and I will lead you back the way
you came."

19:29 This will be your confirmation that I have spoken the truth: This year you will eat what grows wild, and next year what grows on its own from that. But in the third year you will plant seed and harvest crops; you will plant vines and consume their produce. **19:30** Those who remain in Judah will take root in the ground and bear fruit. **19:31** For a remnant will leave Jerusalem; survivors will come out of Mount Zion. The intense devotion of the sovereign LORD to his people will accomplish this. **19:32** So this is what the LORD says about the king of Assyria:

"He will not enter this city,
nor will he shoot an arrow here.
He will not attack it with his shield-carrying warriors,
nor will he build siege works against it.
19:33 He will go back the way he came.
He will not enter this city," says the LORD.
19:34 I will shield this city and rescue it for the sake of my reputation and because of my promise to David my servant.'"

19:35 That very night the LORD's messenger went out and killed 185,000 men in the Assyrian camp. When they got up early the next morning, there were all the corpses. **19:36** So King Sennacherib of Assyria broke camp and went on his way. He went home and stayed in Nineveh. **19:37** One day, as he was worshiping in the temple of his god Nisroch, his sons Adrammelech and Sharezer struck him down with the sword. They escaped to the land of Ararat; his son Esarhaddon replaced him as king.

Hezekiah is Healed

20:1 In those days Hezekiah was stricken with a terminal illness. The prophet Isaiah son of Amoz visited him and told him, "This is what the LORD says, 'Give your household instructions, for you are about to die; you will not get well.'" **20:2** He turned his face to the wall and prayed to the LORD, **20:3** "Please, LORD. Remember how I have served you faithfully and with wholehearted devotion, and how I have carried out your will." Then Hezekiah wept bitterly.

20:4 Isaiah was still in the middle courtyard when the LORD told him, **20:5** "Go back and tell Hezekiah, the leader of my people: 'This is what the LORD God of your ancestor David says: "I have heard your prayer; I have seen your tears. Look, I will heal you. The day after tomorrow you will go up to the LORD's temple. **20:6** I will add fifteen years to your life and rescue you and this city from the king of Assyria. I will shield this city for the sake of my reputation and because of my promise to David my servant."'" **20:7** Isaiah ordered, "Get a fig cake." So they did as he ordered and placed it on the ulcerated sore, and he recovered.

20:8 Hezekiah had said to Isaiah, "What is the confirming sign that the LORD will heal me and that I will go up to the LORD's temple the day after tomorrow?" **20:9** Isaiah replied, "This is your sign from the LORD confirming that the LORD will do what he has said. Do you want the shadow to move ahead ten steps or to go back ten steps?" **20:10** Hezekiah answered, "It is easy for the shadow to lengthen ten steps, but not for it to go back ten steps." **20:11** Isaiah the prophet called out to the LORD, and the LORD made the shadow go back ten steps on the stairs of Ahaz.

Messengers from Babylon Visit Hezekiah

20:12 At that time Merodach-Baladan son of Baladan, king of Babylon, sent letters and a gift to Hezekiah, for he had heard that Hezekiah was ill. **20:13** Hezekiah welcomed them and showed them his whole storehouse, with its silver, gold, spices, and high quality olive oil, as well as his armory and everything in his treasuries. Hezekiah showed them everything in his palace and in his whole kingdom. **20:14** Isaiah the prophet visited King Hezekiah and asked him, "What did these men say? Where do they come from?" Hezekiah replied, "They come from the distant land of Babylon." **20:15** Isaiah asked, "What have they seen in your palace?" Hezekiah replied, "They have seen everything in my palace. I showed them everything in my treasuries." **20:16** Isaiah said to Hezekiah, "Listen to the word of the LORD, **20:17** 'Look, a time is coming when everything in your palace and the things your ancestors have accumulated to this day will be carried away to Babylon; nothing will be left,' says the LORD. **20:18** 'Some of your very own descendants whom you father will be taken away and will be made eunuchs in the palace of the king of Babylon.'" **20:19** Hezekiah said to Isaiah, "The LORD's word which you have announced is appropriate." Then he added, "At least there will be peace and stability during my lifetime."

20:20 The rest of the events of Hezekiah's reign and all his accomplishments, including how he built a pool and conduit to bring water into the city, are recorded in the scroll called the Annals of the Kings of Judah. **20:21** Hezekiah passed away and his son Manasseh replaced him as king.

Manasseh's Reign over Judah

21:1 Manasseh was twelve years old when he became king, and he reigned for fifty-five years in Jerusalem. His mother was Hephzibah. **21:2** He did evil in the sight of the LORD and committed the same horrible sins practiced by the nations whom the LORD drove out from before the Israelites. **21:3** He rebuilt the high places that his father Hezekiah had destroyed; he set up altars for Baal and made an Asherah pole just like King Ahab of Israel had done. He bowed down to all the stars in the sky and worshiped them. **21:4** He built altars in the LORD's temple, about which the LORD had said, "Jerusalem will be my home." **21:5** In the two courtyards of the LORD's temple he built altars for all the stars in the sky. **21:6** He passed his son through the fire and practiced divination and omen reading. He set up a ritual pit to conjure up underworld spirits, and appointed magicians to supervise it. He did a great amount of evil in the sight of the LORD, provoking him to anger. **21:7** He put an idol of Asherah he had made in the temple, about which the LORD had said to David and to his son Solomon, "This temple in Jerusalem, which I have chosen out of all the tribes of Israel, will be my permanent home. **21:8** I will not make Israel again leave the land I gave to their ancestors, provided that they carefully obey all I commanded them, the whole law my servant Moses ordered them to obey." **21:9** But they did not obey, and Manasseh misled them so that they sinned more than the nations whom the LORD had destroyed from before the Israelites.

21:10 So the LORD announced through his servants the prophets: **21:11** "King Manasseh of Judah has committed horrible sins. He has sinned more than the Amorites before him and has encouraged Judah to sin by worshiping his disgusting idols. **21:12** So this is what the LORD God of Israel says, 'I am about to bring disaster on Jerusalem and Judah. The news will reverberate in the ears of those who hear about it. **21:13** I will destroy Jerusalem the same way I did Samaria and the dynasty of Ahab. I will wipe Jerusalem clean, just as one wipes a plate on both sides. **21:14** I will abandon this last remaining tribe among my people and hand them over to their enemies; they will be plundered and robbed by all their enemies, **21:15** because they have done evil in my sight and have angered me from the time their ancestors left Egypt right up to this very day!'"

21:16 Furthermore Manasseh killed so many innocent people, he stained Jerusalem with their blood from end to end, in addition to encouraging Judah to sin by doing evil in the sight of the LORD.

21:17 The rest of the events of Manasseh's reign and all his accomplishments, as well as the sinful acts he committed, are recorded in the scroll called the Annals of the Kings of Judah. **21:18** Manasseh passed away and was buried in his palace garden, the garden of Uzzah, and his son Amon replaced him as king.

Amon's Reign over Judah

21:19 Amon was twenty-two years old when he became king, and he reigned for two years in Jerusalem. His mother was Meshullemeth, the daughter of Haruz, from Jotbah. **21:20** He did evil in the sight of the LORD, just like his father Manasseh had done. **21:21** He followed in the footsteps of his father and worshiped and bowed down to the disgusting idols which his father had worshiped. **21:22** He abandoned the LORD God of his ancestors and did not follow the LORD's instructions. **21:23** Amon's servants conspired against him and killed the king in his palace. **21:24** The people of the land executed all those who had conspired against King Amon, and they made his son Josiah king in his place. **21:25** The rest of Amon's accomplishments are recorded in the scroll called the Annals of
the Kings of Judah. **21:26** He was buried in his tomb in the garden of Uzzah, and his son Josiah replaced him as king.

Josiah Repents

22:1 Josiah was eight years old when he became king, and he reigned for thirty-one years in Jerusalem. His mother was Jedidah, daughter of Adaiah, from Bozkath. **22:2** He did what the LORD approved and followed in his ancestor David's footsteps; he did not deviate to the right or the left.

22:3 In the eighteenth year of King Josiah's reign, the king sent the scribe Shaphan son of Azaliah, son of Meshullam, to the LORD's temple with these orders: **22:4** "Go up to Hilkiah the high priest and have him melt down the silver that has been brought by the people to the LORD's temple and has been collected by the guards at the door. **22:5** Have them hand it over to the construction foremen assigned to the LORD's temple. They in turn should pay the temple workers to repair it, **22:6** including craftsmen, builders, and masons, and should buy wood and chiseled stone for the repair work. **22:7** Do not audit the foremen who disburse the silver, for they are honest."

22:8 Hilkiah the high priest informed Shaphan the scribe, "I found the law scroll in the LORD's temple." Hilkiah gave the scroll to Shaphan and he read it. **22:9** Shaphan the scribe went to the king and reported, "Your servants melted down the silver in the temple and handed it over to the construction foremen assigned to the LORD's temple." **22:10** Then Shaphan the scribe told the king, "Hilkiah the priest has given me a scroll." Shaphan read it out loud before the king. **22:11** When the king heard the words of the law scroll, he tore his clothes. **22:12** The king ordered Hilkiah the priest, Ahikam son of Shaphan, Acbor son of Micaiah, Shaphan the scribe, and Asaiah the king's servant, **22:13** "Go, seek an oracle from the LORD for me and the people – for all Judah. Find out about the words of this scroll that has been discovered. For the LORD's fury has been ignited against us, because our ancestors have not obeyed the words of this scroll by doing all that it instructs us to do."

22:14 So Hilkiah the priest, Ahikam, Acbor, Shaphan, and Asaiah went to Huldah the prophetess, the wife of Shallum son of Tikvah, the son of Harhas, the supervisor of the wardrobe. (She lived in Jerusalem in the Mishneh district.) They stated their business, **22:15** and she said to them: "This is what the LORD God of Israel says: 'Say this to the man who sent you to me: **22:16** "This is what the LORD says: 'I am about to bring disaster on this place and its residents, the details of which are recorded in the scroll which the king of Judah has read. **22:17** This will happen because they have abandoned me and offered sacrifices to other gods, angering me with all the idols they have made. My anger will ignite against this place and will not be extinguished!'" **22:18** Say this to the king of Judah, who sent you to seek an oracle from the LORD: "This is what the LORD God of Israel says concerning the words you have heard: **22:19** 'You displayed a sensitive spirit and humbled yourself before the LORD when you heard how I intended to make this place and its residents into an appalling example of an accursed people. You tore your clothes and wept before me, and I have heard you,' says the LORD. **22:20** 'Therefore I will allow you to die and be buried in peace. You will not have to witness all the disaster I will bring on this place.'"'" Then they reported back to the king.

The King Institutes Religious Reform

23:1 The king summoned all the leaders of Judah and Jerusalem. **23:2** The king went up to the LORD's temple, accompanied by all the people of Judah, all the residents of Jerusalem, the priests, and the prophets. All the people were there, from the youngest to the oldest. He read aloud all the words of the scroll of the covenant that had been discovered in the LORD's temple. **23:3** The king stood by the pillar and renewed the covenant before the LORD, agreeing to follow the LORD and to obey his commandments, laws, and rules with all his heart and being, by carrying out the terms of this covenant recorded on this scroll. All the people agreed to keep the covenant.

23:4 The king ordered Hilkiah the high priest, the high-ranking priests, and the guards to bring out of the LORD's temple all the items that were used in the worship of Baal, Asherah, and all the stars of the sky. The king burned them outside of Jerusalem in the terraces of Kidron, and carried their ashes to Bethel. **23:5** He eliminated the pagan priests whom the kings of Judah had appointed to offer sacrifices on the high places in the cities of Judah and in the area right around Jerusalem. (They offered sacrifices to Baal, the sun god, the moon god, the constellations, and all the stars in the sky.) **23:6** He removed the Asherah pole from the LORD's

temple and took it outside Jerusalem to the Kidron Valley, where he burned it. He smashed it to dust and then threw the dust in the public graveyard. **23:7** He tore down the quarters of the male cultic prostitutes in the LORD's temple, where women were weaving shrines for Asherah.

23:8 He brought all the priests from the cities of Judah and ruined the high places where the priests had offered sacrifices, from Geba to Beer Sheba. He tore down the high place of the goat idols situated at the entrance of the gate of Joshua, the city official, on the left side of the city gate. **23:9** (Now the priests of the high places did not go up to the altar of the LORD in Jerusalem, but they did eat unleavened cakes among their fellow priests.) **23:10** The king ruined Topheth in the Valley of Ben Hinnom so that no one could pass his son or his daughter through the fire to Molech. **23:11** He removed from the entrance to the LORD's temple the statues of horses that the kings of Judah had placed there in honor of the sun god. (They were kept near the room of Nathan Melech the eunuch, which was situated among the courtyards.) He burned up the chariots devoted to the sun god. **23:12** The king tore down the altars the kings of Judah had set up on the roof of Ahaz's upper room, as well as the altars Manasseh had set up in the two courtyards of the LORD's temple. He crushed them up and threw the dust in the Kidron Valley. **23:13** The king ruined the high places east of Jerusalem, south of the Mount of Destruction, that King Solomon of Israel had built for the detestable Sidonian goddess Astarte, the detestable Moabite god Chemosh, and the horrible Ammonite god Milcom. **23:14** He smashed the sacred pillars to bits, cut down the Asherah pole, and filled those shrines with human bones.

23:15 He also tore down the altar in Bethel at the high place made by Jeroboam son of Nebat, who encouraged Israel to sin. He burned all the combustible items at that high place and crushed them to dust; including the Asherah pole. **23:16** When Josiah turned around, he saw the tombs there on the hill. So he ordered the bones from the tombs to be brought; he burned them on the altar and defiled it. This fulfilled the LORD's announcement made by the prophet while Jeroboam stood by the altar during a festival. King Josiah turned and saw the grave of the prophet who had foretold this. **23:17** He asked, "What is this grave marker I see?" The men from the city replied, "It's the grave of the prophet who came from Judah and foretold these very things you have done to the altar of Bethel." **23:18** The king said, "Leave it alone! No one must touch his bones." So they left his bones undisturbed, as well as the bones of the Israelite prophet buried beside him.

23:19 Josiah also removed all the shrines on the high places in the cities of Samaria. The kings of Israel had made them and angered the LORD. He did to them what he had done to the high place in Bethel. **23:20** He sacrificed all the priests of the high places on the altars located there, and burned human bones on them. Then he returned to Jerusalem.

23:21 The king ordered all the people, "Observe the Passover of the LORD your God, as prescribed in this scroll of the covenant." **23:22** He issued this edict because a Passover like this had not been observed since the days of the judges; it was neglected for the entire period of the kings of Israel and Judah. **23:23** But in the eighteenth year of King Josiah's reign, such a Passover of the LORD was observed in Jerusalem.

23:24 Josiah also got rid of the ritual pits used to conjure up spirits, the magicians, per-
sonal idols, disgusting images, and all the detestable idols that had appeared in the land of Judah and in Jerusalem. In this way he carried out the terms of the law recorded on the scroll that Hilkiah the priest had discovered in the LORD's temple. **23:25** No king before or after repented before the LORD as he did, with his whole heart, soul, and being in accordance with the whole law of Moses.

23:26 Yet the LORD's great anger against Judah did not subside; he was still infuriated by all the things Manasseh had done. **23:27** The LORD announced, "I will also spurn Judah, just as I spurned Israel. I will reject this city that I chose – both Jerusalem and the temple, about which I said, "I will live there."

23:28 The rest of the events of Josiah's reign and all his accomplishments are recorded in the scroll called the Annals of the Kings of Judah. **23:29** During Josiah's reign Pharaoh Necho king of Egypt marched toward the Euphrates River to help the king of Assyria. King Josiah marched out to fight him, but Necho killed him at Megiddo when he saw him. **23:30** His servants transported his dead body from Megiddo in a chariot and brought it to Jerusalem, where they buried him in his tomb. The people of the land took Josiah's son Jehoahaz, poured olive oil on his head, and made him king in his father's place.

Jehoahaz's Reign over Judah

23:31 Jehoahaz was twenty-three years old when he became king, and he reigned three months in Jerusalem. His mother was Hamutal the daughter of Jeremiah, from Libnah. **23:32** He did evil in the sight of the LORD as his ancestors had done. **23:33** Pharaoh Necho imprisoned him in Riblah in the land of Hamath and prevented him from ruling in Jerusalem. He imposed on the land a special tax of one hundred talents of silver and a talent of gold. **23:34** Pharaoh Necho made Josiah's son Eliakim king in Josiah's place, and changed his name to Jehoiakim. He took Jehoahaz to Egypt, where he died. **23:35** Jehoiakim paid Pharaoh the required amount of silver and gold, but to meet Pharaoh's demands Jehoiakim had to tax the land. He collected an assessed amount from each man among the people of the land in order to pay Pharaoh Necho.

Jehoiakim's Reign over Judah

23:36 Jehoiakim was twenty-five years old when he became king, and he reigned for eleven years in Jerusalem. His mother was Zebidah the daughter of Pedaiah, from Rumah. **23:37** He did evil in the sight of the LORD as his ancestors had done.

24:1 During Jehoiakim's reign, King Nebuchadnezzar of Babylon attacked. Jehoiakim was his subject for three years, but then he rebelled against him. **24:2** The LORD sent against him Babylonian, Syrian, Moabite, and Ammonite raiding bands; he sent them to destroy Judah, as he had warned he would do through his

servants the prophets. **24:3** Just as the LORD had announced, he rejected Judah because of all the sins which Manasseh had committed. **24:4** Because he killed innocent people and stained Jerusalem with their blood, the LORD was unwilling to forgive them.

24:5 The rest of the events of Jehoiakim's reign and all his accomplishments, are recorded in the scroll called the Annals of the Kings of Judah. **24:6** He passed away and his son Jehoiachin replaced him as king. **24:7** The king of Egypt did not march out from his land again, for the king of Babylon conquered all the territory that the king of Egypt had formerly controlled between the Brook of Egypt and the Euphrates River.

Jehoiachin's Reign over Judah

24:8 Jehoiachin was eighteen years old when he became king, and he reigned three months in Jerusalem. His mother was Nehushta the daughter of Elnathan, from Jerusalem. **24:9** He did evil in the sight of the LORD as his ancestors had done.

24:10 At that time the generals of King Nebuchadnezzar of Babylon marched to Jerusalem and besieged the city. **24:11** King Nebuchadnezzar of Babylon came to the city while his generals were besieging it. **24:12** King Jehoiachin of Judah, along with his mother, his servants, his officials, and his eunuchs surrendered to the king of Babylon. The king of Babylon, in the eighth year of his reign, took Jehoiachin prisoner. **24:13** Nebuchadnezzar took from there all the riches in the treasuries of the LORD's temple and of the royal palace. He removed all the gold items which King Solomon of Israel had made for the LORD's temple, just as the LORD had warned. **24:14** He deported all the residents of Jerusalem, including all the officials and all the soldiers (10,000 people in all). This included all the craftsmen and those who worked with metal. No one was left except for the poorest among the people of the land. **24:15** He deported Jehoiachin from Jerusalem to Babylon, along with the king's mother and wives, his eunuchs, and the high-ranking officials of the land. **24:16** The king of Babylon deported to Babylon all the soldiers (there were 7,000), as well as 1,000 craftsmen and metal workers. This included all the best warriors. **24:17** The king of Babylon made Mattaniah, Jehoiachin's uncle, king in Jehoiachin's place. He renamed him Zedekiah.

Zedekiah's Reign over Judah

24:18 Zedekiah was twenty-one years old when he became king, and he ruled for eleven years in Jerusalem. His mother was Hamutal, the daughter of Jeremiah, from Libnah. **24:19** He did evil in the sight of the LORD, as Jehoiakim had done.

24:20 What follows is a record of what happened to Jerusalem and Judah because of the LORD's anger; he finally threw them out of his presence. Zedekiah rebelled against the king of Babylon. **25:1** So King Nebuchadnezzar of Babylon came against Jerusalem with his whole army and set up camp outside it. They built siege ramps all around it. He arrived on the tenth day of the tenth month in the ninth year of Zedekiah's reign. **25:2** The city remained under siege until King Zedekiah's eleventh year. **25:3** By the ninth day of the fourth month the famine in the city was so severe the residents had

no food. **25:4** The enemy broke through the city walls, and all the soldiers tried to escape. They left the city during the night. They went through the gate between the two walls that is near the king's garden. (The Babylonians were all around the city.) Then they headed for the Jordan Valley. **25:5** But the Babylonian army chased after the king. They caught up with him in the plains of Jericho, and his entire army deserted him. **25:6** They captured the king and brought him up to the king of Babylon at Riblah, where he passed sentence on him. **25:7** Zedekiah's sons were executed while Zedekiah was forced to watch. The king of Babylon then had Zedekiah's eyes put out, bound him in bronze chains, and carried him off to Babylon.

Nebuchadnezzar Destroys Jerusalem

25:8 On the seventh day of the fifth month, in the nineteenth year of King Nebuchadnezzar of Babylon, Nebuzaradan, the captain of the royal guard who served the king of Babylon, arrived in Jerusalem. **25:9** He burned down the LORD's temple, the royal palace, and all the houses in Jerusalem, including every large house. **25:10** The whole Babylonian army that came with the captain of the royal guard tore down the walls that surrounded Jerusalem. **25:11** Nebuzaradan, the captain of the royal guard, deported the rest of the people who were left in the city, those who had deserted to the king of Babylon, and the rest of the craftsmen. **25:12** But he left behind some of the poor of the land and gave them fields and vineyards.

25:13 The Babylonians broke the two bronze pillars in the LORD's temple, as well as the movable stands and the big bronze basin called the "The Sea." They took the bronze to Babylon. **25:14** They also took the pots, shovels, trimming shears, pans, and all the bronze utensils used by the priests. **25:15** The captain of the royal guard took the golden and silver censers and basins. **25:16** The bronze of the items that King Solomon made for the LORD's temple – including the two pillars, the big bronze basin called "The Sea," the twelve bronze bulls under "The Sea," and the movable stands – was too heavy to be weighed. **25:17** Each of the pillars was about twenty-seven feet high. The bronze top of one pillar was about four and a half feet high and had bronze latticework and pomegranate shaped ornaments all around it. The second pillar with its latticework was like it.

25:18 The captain of the royal guard took Seraiah the chief priest and Zephaniah, the priest who was second in rank, and the three doorkeepers. **25:19** From the city he took a eunuch who was in charge of the soldiers, five of the king's advisers who were discovered in the city, an official army secretary who drafted citizens for military service, and sixty citizens from the people of the land who were discovered in the city. **25:20** Nebuzaradan, captain of the royal guard, took them and brought them to the king of Babylon at Riblah. **25:21** The king of Babylon ordered them to be executed at Riblah in the territory of Hamath. So Judah was deported from its land.

Gedaliah Appointed Governor

25:22 Now King Nebuchadnezzar of Babylon appointed Gedaliah son of Ahikam, son of Shaphan, as governor over the people whom he allowed to remain in the land of Judah. **25:23** All of the officers of the Judahite army and their troops heard that the king of Babylon had appointed Gedaliah to govern. So they came to Gedaliah at Mizpah. The officers who came were Ishmael son of Nethaniah, Johanan son of Kareah, Seraiah son of Tanhumeth the Netophathite, and Jaazaniah son of the Maacathite. **25:24** Gedaliah took an oath so as to give them and their troops some assurance of safety. He said, "You don't need to be afraid to submit to the Babylonian officials. Settle down in the land and submit to the king of Babylon. Then things will go well for you." **25:25** But in the seventh month Ishmael son of Nethaniah, son of Elishama, who was a member of the royal family, came with ten of his men and murdered Gedaliah, as well as the Judeans and Babylonians who were with him at Mizpah. **25:26** Then all the people, from the youngest to the oldest, as well as the army officers, left for Egypt, because they were afraid of what the Babylonians might do.

Jehoiachin in Babylon

25:27 In the thirty-seventh year of the exile of King Jehoiachin of Judah, on the twenty-seventh day of the twelfth month, King Evil-Merodach of Babylon, in the first year of his reign, pardoned King Jehoiachin of Judah and released him from prison. **25:28** He spoke kindly to him and gave him a more prestigious position than the other kings who were with him in Babylon. **25:29** Jehoiachin took off his prison clothes and ate daily in the king's presence for the rest of his life. **25:30** He was given daily provisions by the king for the rest of his life until the day he died.

Book 13. 1 Chronicles

Adam's Descendants

1:1 Adam, Seth, Enosh, **1:2** Kenan, Mahalalel, Jered, **1:3** Enoch, Methuselah, Lamech, **1:4** Noah, Shem, Ham, and Japheth.

Japheth's Descendants

1:5 The sons of Japheth:
Gomer, Magog, Madai, Javan, Tubal, Meshech, and Tiras.

1:6 The sons of Gomer:
Ashkenaz, Riphath, and Togarmah.

1:7 The sons of Javan:
Elishah, Tarshish, the Kittites, and the Rodanites.

Ham's Descendants

1:8 The sons of Ham:
Cush, Mizraim, Put, and Canaan.

1:9 The sons of Cush:
Seba, Havilah, Sabta, Raamah, and Sabteca.

The sons of Raamah:
Sheba and Dedan.

1:10 Cush was the father of Nimrod, who established himself as a mighty warrior on earth.

1:11 Mizraim was the father of the Ludites, Anamites, Lehabites, Naphtuhites, **1:12** Pathrusites, Casluhites (from whom the Philistines descended), and the Caphtorites.

1:13 Canaan was the father of Sidon – his firstborn – and Heth, **1:14** as well as the Jebusites, Amorites, Girgashites, **1:15** Hivites, Arkites, Sinites, **1:16** Arvadites, Zemarites, and Hamathites.

Shem's Descendants

1:17 The sons of Shem:
Elam, Asshur, Arphaxad, Lud, and Aram.

The sons of Aram:
Uz, Hul, Gether, and Meshech.

1:18 Arphaxad was the father of Shelah, and Shelah was the father of Eber. **1:19** Two sons were born to Eber: the first was named Peleg, for during his lifetime the earth was divided; his brother's name was Joktan. **1:20** Joktan was the father of Almodad, Sheleph, Hazarmaveth, Jerah, **1:21** Hadoram, Uzal, Diklah, **1:22** Ebal, Abimael, Sheba, **1:23** Ophir, Havilah, and Jobab. All these were the sons of Joktan.

1:24 Shem, Arphaxad, Shelah, **1:25** Eber, Peleg, Reu, **1:26** Serug, Nahor, Terah, **1:27** Abram (that is, Abraham).

1:28 The sons of Abraham:

Isaac and Ishmael.

1:29 These were their descendants:

Ishmael's Descendants

Ishmael's firstborn son was Nebaioth; the others were Kedar, Adbeel, Mibsam, **1:30** Mishma, Dumah, Massa, Hadad, Tema, **1:31** Jetur, Naphish, and Kedemah. These were the sons of Ishmael.

Keturah's Descendants

1:32 The sons to whom Keturah, Abraham's concubine, gave birth:

Zimran, Jokshan, Medan, Midian, Ishbak, Shuah.

The sons of Jokshan:

Sheba and Dedan.

1:33 The sons of Midian:

Ephah, Epher, Hanoch, Abida, and Eldaah. All these were the sons of Keturah.

Isaac's Descendants

1:34 Abraham was the father of Isaac. The sons of Isaac:

Esau and Israel.

Esau's Descendants

1:35 The sons of Esau:

Eliphaz, Reuel, Jeush, Jalam, and Korah.

1:36 The sons of Eliphaz:

Teman, Omar, Zephi, Gatam, Kenaz, and (by Timna) Amalek.

1:37 The sons of Reuel:

Nahath, Zerah, Shammah, and Mizzah.

The Descendants of Seir

1:38 The sons of Seir:

Lotan, Shobal, Zibeon, Anah, Dishon, Ezer, and Dishan.

1:39 The sons of Lotan:

Hori and Homam. (Timna was Lotan's sister.)

1:40 The sons of Shobal:

Alyan, Manahath, Ebal, Shephi, and Onam.

The sons of Zibeon:

Aiah and Anah.

1:41 The son of Anah:

Dishon.

The sons of Dishon:

Hamran, Eshban, Ithran, and Keran.

1:42 The sons of Ezer:

Bilhan, Zaavan, Jaakan.

The sons of Dishan:

Uz and Aran.

Kings of Edom

1:43 These were the kings who reigned in the land of Edom before any king ruled over the Israelites:

Bela son of Beor; the name of his city was Dinhabah.

1:44 When Bela died, Jobab son of Zerah from Bozrah succeeded him.

1:45 When Jobab died, Husham from the land of the Temanites succeeded him.

1:46 When Husham died, Hadad son of Bedad succeeded him. He struck down the Midianites in the plains of Moab; the name of his city was Avith.

1:47 When Hadad died, Samlah from Masrekah succeeded him.

1:48 When Samlah died, Shaul from Rehoboth on the river succeeded him.

1:49 When Shaul died, Baal-Hanan son of Achbor succeeded him.

1:50 When Baal-Hanan died, Hadad succeeded him; the name of his city was Pai. His wife was Mehetabel, daughter of Matred, daughter of Me-Zahab.

1:51 Hadad died.

Tribal Chiefs of Edom

The tribal chiefs of Edom were:

Timna, Alvah, Jetheth, **1:52** Oholibamah, Elah, Pinon, **1:53** Kenaz, Teman, Mibzar, **1:54** Magdiel, Iram. These were the tribal chiefs of Edom.

Israel's Descendants

2:1 These were the sons of Israel:

Reuben, Simeon, Levi, and Judah;

Issachar and Zebulun;

2:2 Dan, Joseph, and Benjamin;

Naphtali, Gad, and Asher.

Judah's Descendants

2:3 The sons of Judah:

Er, Onan, and Shelah. These three were born to him by Bathshua, a Canaanite woman. Er, Judah's firstborn, displeased the LORD, so the LORD killed him.

2:4 Tamar, Judah's daughter-in-law, bore to him Perez and Zerah. Judah had five sons in all.

2:5 The sons of Perez:

Hezron and Hamul.

2:6 The sons of Zerah:

Zimri, Ethan, Heman, Kalkol, Dara – five in all.

2:7 The son of Carmi:

Achan, who brought the disaster on Israel when he stole what was devoted to God.

2:8 The son of Ethan:

Azariah.

2:9 The sons born to Hezron:

Jerahmeel, Ram, and Caleb.

Ram's Descendants

2:10 Ram was the father of Amminadab, and Amminadab was the father of Nahshon, the tribal chief of Judah. **2:11** Nahshon was the father of Salma, and Salma was the father of Boaz. **2:12** Boaz was the father of Obed, and Obed was the father of Jesse.

2:13 Jesse was the father of Eliab, his firstborn; Abinadab was born second, Shimea third, **2:14** Nethanel fourth, Raddai fifth, **2:15** Ozem sixth, David seventh. **2:16** Their sisters were Zeruiah and Abigail. Zeruiah's three sons were Abshai, Joab, and Asahel. **2:17** Abigail bore Amasa, whose father was Jether the Ishmaelite.

Caleb's Descendants

2:18 Caleb son of Hezron fathered sons by his wife Azubah (also known as Jerioth). Her sons were Jesher, Shobab, and Ardon. **2:19** When Azubah died, Caleb married Ephrath, who bore him Hur. **2:20** Hur was the father of Uri, and Uri was the father of Bezalel.

2:21 Later Hezron had sexual relations with the daughter of Makir, the father of Gilead. (He had married her when he was sixty years old.) She bore him Segub. **2:22** Segub was the father of Jair, who owned twenty-three cities in the land of Gilead. **2:23** (Geshur and Aram captured the towns of Jair, along with Kenath and its sixty surrounding towns.) All these were descendants of Makir, the father of Gilead.

2:24 After Hezron's death, Caleb had sexual relations with Ephrath, his father Hezron's widow, and she bore to him Ashhur the father of Tekoa.

Jerahmeel's Descendants

2:25 The sons of Jerahmeel, Hezron's firstborn, were Ram, the firstborn, Bunah, Oren, Ozem, and Ahijah. **2:26** Jerahmeel had another wife named Atarah; she was Onam's mother.

2:27 The sons of Ram, Jerahmeel's firstborn, were Maaz, Jamin, and Eker.

2:28 The sons of Onam were Shammai and Jada.

The sons of Shammai:

Nadab and Abishur.

2:29 Abishur's wife was Abihail, who bore him Ahban and Molid.

2:30 The sons of Nadab:

Seled and Appaim. (Seled died without having sons.)

2:31 The son of Appaim:

Ishi.

The son of Ishi:

Sheshan.

The son of Sheshan:

Ahlai.

2:32 The sons of Jada, Shammai's brother:

Jether and Jonathan. (Jether died without having sons.)

2:33 The sons of Jonathan:

Peleth and Zaza.

These were the descendants of Jerahmeel.

2:34 Sheshan had no sons, only daughters. Sheshan had an Egyptian servant named Jarha. **2:35** Sheshan gave his daughter to his servant Jarha as a wife; she bore him Attai.

2:36 Attai was the father of Nathan, and Nathan was the father of Zabad. **2:37** Zabad was the father of Ephlal, and Ephlal was the father of Obed. **2:38** Obed was the father of Jehu, and Jehu was the father of Azariah. **2:39** Azariah was the father of Helez, and Helez was the father of Eleasah. **2:40** Eleasah was the father of Sismai, and Sismai was the father of Shallum. **2:41** Shallum was the father of Jekamiah, and Jekamiah was the father of Elishama.

More of Caleb's Descendants

2:42 The sons of Caleb, Jerahmeel's brother:

His firstborn Mesha, the father of Ziph, and his second son Mareshah, the father of Hebron.

2:43 The sons of Hebron:

Korah, Tappuah, Rekem, and Shema.

2:44 Shema was the father of Raham, the father of Jorkeam. Rekem was the father of Shammai. **2:45** Shammai's son was Maon, who was the father of Beth-Zur.

2:46 Caleb's concubine Ephah bore Haran, Moza, and Gazez. Haran was the father of Gazez.

2:47 The sons of Jahdai:

Regem, Jotham, Geshan, Pelet, Ephah, and Shaaph.

2:48 Caleb's concubine Maacah bore Sheber and Tirhanah. **2:49** She also bore Shaaph the father of Madmannah and Sheva the father of Machbenah and Gibea. Caleb's daughter was Achsah.

2:50 These were the descendants of Caleb.

The sons of Hur, the firstborn of Ephrath:

Shobal, the father of Kiriath Jearim, **2:51** Salma, the father of Bethlehem, Hareph, the father of Beth-Gader.

2:52 The sons of Shobal, the father of Kiriath Jearim, were Haroeh, half of the Manahathites, **2:53** the clans of Kiriath Jearim – the Ithrites, Puthites, Shumathites, and Mishraites. (The Zorathites and Eshtaolites descended from these groups.)

2:54 The sons of Salma:

Bethlehem, the Netophathites, Atroth Beth-Joab, half the Manahathites, the Zorites, **2:55** and the clans of the scribes who lived in Jabez: the Tirathites, Shimeathites, and Sucathites. These are the Kenites who descended from Hammath, the father of Beth-Rechab.

David's Descendants

3:1 These were the sons of David who were born to him in Hebron:

The firstborn was Amnon, whose mother was Ahinoam from Jezreel;

the second was Daniel, whose mother was Abigail from Carmel;

3:2 the third was Absalom whose mother was Maacah, daughter of King Talmai of Geshur;

the fourth was Adonijah, whose mother was Haggith;

3:3 the fifth was Shephatiah, whose mother was Abital;

the sixth was Ithream, whose mother was Eglah.

3:4 These six were born to David in Hebron, where he ruled for seven years and six months.

He ruled thirty-three years in Jerusalem. **3:5** These were the sons born to him in Jerusalem:

Shimea, Shobab, Nathan, and Solomon – the mother of these four was Bathsheba the daughter of Ammiel.

3:6 The other nine were Ibhar, Elishua, Elpelet, **3:7** Nogah, Nepheg, Japhia, **3:8** Elishama, Eliada, and Eliphelet.

3:9 These were all the sons of David, not counting the sons of his concubines. Tamar was their sister.

Solomon's Descendants

3:10 Solomon's son was Rehoboam,

followed by Abijah his son,

Asa his son,

Jehoshaphat his son,

3:11 Joram his son,

Ahaziah his son,

Joash his son,

3:12 Amaziah his son,

Azariah his son,

Jotham his son,

3:13 Ahaz his son,

Hezekiah his son,

Manasseh his son,

3:14 Amon his son,

Josiah his son.

3:15 The sons of Josiah:

Johanan was the firstborn; Jehoiakim was born second; Zedekiah third; and Shallum fourth.

3:16 The sons of Jehoiakim:

his son Jehoiachin and his son Zedekiah.

3:17 The sons of Jehoiachin the exile:

Shealtiel his son, **3:18** Malkiram, Pedaiah, Shenazzar, Jekamiah, Hoshama, and Nedabiah.

3:19 The sons of Pedaiah:

Zerubbabel and Shimei.

The sons of Zerubbabel:

Meshullam and Hananiah. Shelomith was their sister.

3:20 The five others were Hashubah, Ohel, Berechiah, Hasadiah, and Jushab-Hesed.

3:21 The descendants of Hananiah:

Pelatiah, Jeshaiah, the sons of Rephaiah, of Arnan, of Obadiah, and of Shecaniah.

3:22 The descendants of Shecaniah:

Shemaiah and his sons: Hattush, Igal, Bariah, Neariah, and Shaphat – six in all.

3:23 The sons of Neariah:

Elioenai, Hizkiah, and Azrikam – three in all.

3:24 The sons of Elioenai:

Hodaviah, Eliashib, Pelaiah, Akkub, Johanan, Delaiah, and Anani – seven in all.

Judah's Descendants

4:1 The descendants of Judah:

Perez, Hezron, Carmi, Hur, and Shobal.

4:2 Reaiah the son of Shobal was the father of Jahath, and Jahath was the father of Ahumai and Lahad. These were the clans of the Zorathites.

4:3 These were the sons of Etam:

Jezreel, Ishma, and Idbash. Their sister was Hazzelelponi.

4:4 Penuel was the father of Gedor, and Ezer was the father of Hushah. These were the descendants of Hur, the firstborn of Ephrathah and the father of Bethlehem.

4:5 Ashhur the father of Tekoa had two wives, Helah and Naarah. **4:6** Naarah bore him Ahuzzam, Hepher, Temeni, and Haahashtari. These were the sons of Naarah. **4:7** The sons of Helah: Zereth, Zohar, Ethnan, **4:8** and Koz, who was the father of Anub, Hazzobebah, and the clans of Aharhel the son of Harum.

4:9 Jabez was more respected than his brothers. His mother had named him Jabez, for she said, "I experienced pain when I gave birth to him." **4:10** Jabez called out to the God of Israel, "If only you would greatly bless me and expand my territory! May your hand be with me! Keep me from harm so I might not endure pain!" God answered his prayer.

4:11 Kelub, the brother of Shuhah, was the father of Mehir, who was the father of Eshton. **4:12** Eshton was the father of Beth-Rapha, Paseah, and Tehinnah, the father of Ir Nahash. These were the men of Recah.

4:13 The sons of Kenaz:

Othniel and Seraiah.

The sons of Othniel:

Hathath and Meonothai. **4:14** Meonothai was the father of Ophrah. Seraiah was the father of Joab, the father of those who live in Ge Harashim, who were craftsmen.

4:15 The sons of Caleb son of Jephunneh:

Iru, Elah, and Naam.

The son of Elah:

Kenaz.

4:16 The sons of Jehallelel:

Ziph, Ziphah, Tiria, and Asarel.

4:17 The sons of Ezrah:

Jether, Mered, Epher, and Jalon.

Mered's wife Bithiah gave birth to Miriam, Shammai, and Ishbah, the father of Eshtemoa. **4:18** (His Judahite wife gave birth to Jered the father of Gedor, Heber the father of Soco, and Jekuthiel the father of Zanoah.) These were the sons of Pharaoh's daughter Bithiah, whom Mered married.

4:19 The sons of Hodiah's wife, the sister of Naham:

the father of Keilah the Garmite, and Eshtemoa the Maacathite.

4:20 The sons of Shimon:

Amnon, Rinnah, Ben-Hanan, and Tilon.

The descendants of Ishi:

Zoheth and Ben Zoheth.

4:21 The sons of Shelah son of Judah:

Er the father of Lecah, Laadah the father of Mareshah, the clans of the linen workers at Beth-Ashbea, **4:22** Jokim, the men of Cozeba, and Joash and Saraph, both of whom ruled in Moab and Jashubi Lehem. (This information is from ancient records.) **4:23** They were the potters who lived in Netaim and Gederah; they lived there and worked for the king.

Simeon's Descendants

4:24 The descendants of Simeon:

Nemuel, Jamin, Jarib, Zerah, Shaul, **4:25** his son Shallum, his son Mibsam, and his son Mishma.

4:26 The descendants of Mishma:

His son Hammuel, his son Zaccur, and his son Shimei.

4:27 Shimei had sixteen sons and six daughters. But his brothers did not have many sons, so their whole clan was not as numerous as the sons of Judah. **4:28** They lived in Beer Sheba, Moladah, Hazar Shual, **4:29** Bilhah, Ezem, Tolad, **4:30** Bethuel, Hormah, Ziklag, **4:31** Beth Marcaboth, Hazar Susim, Beth Biri, and Shaaraim. These were their towns until the reign of David. **4:32** Their settlements also included Etam, Ain, Rimmon, Tochen, and Ashan – five towns. **4:33** They also lived in all the settlements that surrounded these towns as far as Baal. These were their settlements; they kept genealogical records.

4:34 Their clan leaders were:

Meshobab, Jamlech, Joshah son of Amaziah, **4:35** Joel, Jehu son of Joshibiah (son of Seraiah, son of Asiel), **4:36** Eleoenai, Jaakobah, Jeshohaiah, Asaiah, Adiel, Jesimiel, Benaiah, **4:37** Ziza son of Shipi (son of Allon, son of Jedaiah, son of Shimri, son of Shemaiah). **4:38** These who are named above were the leaders of their clans.

Their extended families increased greatly in numbers. **4:39** They went to the entrance of Gedor, to the east of the valley, looking for pasture for their sheep. **4:40** They found fertile and rich pasture; the land was very broad, undisturbed and peaceful. Indeed some Hamites had been living there prior to that. **4:41** The men whose names are listed came during the time of King Hezekiah of Judah and attacked the Hamites' settlements, as well as the Meunites they discovered there, and they wiped them out to this very day. They dispossessed them, for they found pasture for their sheep there. **4:42** Five hundred men of Simeon, led by Pelatiah, Neariah, Rephaiah, and Uzziel, the sons of Ishi, went to the hill country of Seir **4:43** and defeated the rest of the Amalekite refugees; they live there to this very day.

Reuben's Descendants

5:1 The sons of Reuben, Israel's firstborn –

(Now he was the firstborn, but when he defiled his father's bed, his rights as firstborn were given to the sons of Joseph, Israel's son. So Reuben is not listed as firstborn in the genealogical records. **5:2** Though Judah was the strongest among his brothers and a leader descended from him, the right of the firstborn belonged to Joseph.)
5:3 The sons of Reuben, Israel's firstborn:
Hanoch, Pallu, Hezron, and Carmi.
5:4 The descendants of Joel:
His son Shemaiah, his son Gog, his son Shimei, **5:5** his son Micah, his son Reaiah, his son Baal, **5:6** and his son Beerah, whom King Tiglath-pileser of Assyria carried into exile. Beerah was the tribal leader of Reuben.
5:7 His brothers by their clans, as listed in their genealogical records:
The leader Jeiel, Zechariah, **5:8** and Bela son of Azaz, son of Shema, son of Joel.
They lived in Aroer as far as Nebo and Baal Meon. **5:9** In the east they settled as far as the entrance to the desert that stretches to the Euphrates River, for their cattle had increased in numbers in the land of Gilead. **5:10** During the time of Saul they attacked the Hagrites and defeated them. They took over their territory in the entire eastern region of Gilead.
Gad's Descendants
5:11 The descendants of Gad lived near them in the land of Bashan, as far as Salecah.
5:12 They included Joel the leader, Shapham the second in command, Janai, and Shaphat in Bashan. **5:13** Their relatives, listed according to their families, included Michael, Meshullam, Sheba, Jorai, Jacan, Zia, and Eber – seven in all.
5:14 These were the sons of Abihail son of Huri, son of Jaroah, son of Gilead, son of Michael, son of Jeshishai, son of Jahdo, son of Buz. **5:15** Ahi son of Abdiel, son of Guni, was the leader of the family. **5:16** They lived in Gilead, in Bashan and its surrounding settlements, and in the pasturelands of Sharon to their very borders. **5:17** All of them were listed in the genealogical records in the time of King Jotham of Judah and in the time of King Jeroboam of Israel.
5:18 The Reubenites, Gadites, and the half-tribe of Manasseh had 44,760 men in their combined armies, warriors who carried shields and swords, were equipped with bows, and were trained for war. **5:19** They attacked the Hagrites, Jetur, Naphish, and Nodab. **5:20** They received divine help in fighting them, and the Hagrites and all their allies were handed over to them. They cried out to God during the battle; he responded to their prayers because they trusted in him. **5:21** They seized the Hagrites' animals, including 50,000 camels, 250,000 sheep, and 2,000 donkeys. They also took captive 100,000 people. **5:22** Because God fought for them, they killed many of the enemy. They dispossessed the Hagrites and lived in their land until the exile.
The Half-Tribe of Manasseh
5:23 The half-tribe of Manasseh settled in the land from Bashan as far as Baal Hermon, Senir, and Mount Hermon. They grew in number.
5:24 These were the leaders of their families:
Epher, Ishi, Eliel, Azriel, Jeremiah, Hodaviah, and Jahdiel. They were skilled warriors, men of reputation, and leaders of their families. **5:25** But they were unfaithful to the God of their ancestors and worshiped instead the gods of the native peoples whom God had destroyed before them. **5:26** So the God of Israel stirred up King Pul of Assyria (that is, King Tiglath-pileser of Assyria), and he carried away the Reubenites, Gadites, and half-tribe of Manasseh and took them to Halah, Habor, Hara, and the river of Gozan, where they remain to this very day.
Levi's Descendants
6:1 (5:27) The sons of Levi:
Gershon, Kohath, and Merari.
6:2 The sons of Kohath:
Amram, Izhar, Hebron, and Uzziel.
6:3 The children of Amram:
Aaron, Moses, and Miriam.
The sons of Aaron:
Nadab, Abihu, Eleazar, and Ithamar.
6:4 Eleazar was the father of Phinehas, and Phinehas was the father of Abishua. **6:5** Abishua was the father of Bukki, and Bukki was the father of Uzzi. **6:6** Uzzi was the father of Zerahiah, and Zerahiah was the father of Meraioth. **6:7** Meraioth was the father of Amariah, and Amariah was the father of Ahitub. **6:8** Ahitub was the father of Zadok, and Zadok was the father of Ahimaaz. **6:9** Ahimaaz was the father of Azariah, and Azariah was the father of Johanan. **6:10** Johanan was the father of Azariah, who served as a priest in the temple Solomon built in Jerusalem. **6:11** Azariah was the father of Amariah, and Amariah was the father of Ahitub. **6:12** Ahitub was the father of Zadok, and Zadok was the father of Shallum. **6:13** Shallum was the father of Hilkiah, and Hilkiah was the father of Azariah. **6:14** Azariah was the father of Seraiah, and Seraiah was the father of Jehozadak. **6:15** Jehozadak went into exile when the LORD sent the people of Judah and Jerusalem into exile by the hand of Nebuchadnezzar.
6:16 (6:1) The sons of Levi:
Gershom, Kohath, and Merari.

6:17 These are the names of the sons Gershom:
Libni and Shimei.
6:18 The sons of Kohath:
Amram, Izhar, Hebron, and Uzziel.
6:19 The sons of Merari:
Mahli and Mushi.
These are the clans of the Levites by their families.
6:20 To Gershom:
His son Libni, his son Jahath, his son Zimmah, **6:21** his son Joah, his son Iddo, his son Zerah, and his son Jeatherai.
6:22 The sons of Kohath:
His son Amminadab, his son Korah, his son Assir, **6:23** his son Elkanah, his son Ebiasaph, his son Assir, **6:24** his son Tahath, his son Uriel, his son Uzziah, and his son Shaul.
6:25 The sons of Elkanah:
Amasai, Ahimoth, **6:26** his son Elkanah, his son Zophai, his son Nahath, **6:27** his son Eliab, his son Jeroham, and his son Elkanah.
6:28 The sons of Samuel:
Joel the firstborn and Abijah the second oldest.
6:29 The descendants of Merari:
Mahli, his son Libni, his son Shimei, his son Uzzah, **6:30** his son Shimea, his son Haggiah, and his son Asaiah.
Professional Musicians
6:31 These are the men David put in charge of music in the LORD's sanctuary, after the ark was placed there. **6:32** They performed music before the sanctuary of the meeting tent until Solomon built the LORD's temple in Jerusalem. They carried out their tasks according to regulations.
6:33 These are the ones who served along with their sons:
From the Kohathites:
Heman the musician, son of Joel, son of Samuel, **6:34** son of Elkanah, son of Jeroham, son of Eliel, son of Toah, **6:35** son of Zuph, son of Elkanah, son of Mahath, son of Amasai, **6:36** son of Elkanah, son of Joel, son of Azariah, son of Zephaniah, **6:37** son of Tahath, son of Assir, son of Ebiasaph, son of Korah, **6:38** son of Izhar, son of Kohath, son of Levi, son of Israel.
6:39 Serving beside him was his fellow Levite Asaph, son of Berechiah, son of Shimea, **6:40** son of Michael, son of Baaseiah, son of Malkijah, **6:41** son of Ethni, son of Zerah, son of Adaiah, **6:42** son of Ethan, son of Zimmah, son of Shimei, **6:43** son of Jahath, son of Gershom, son of Levi.
6:44 Serving beside them were their fellow Levites, the descendants of Merari, led by Ethan, son of Kishi, son of Abdi, son of Malluch, **6:45** son of Hashabiah, son of Amaziah, son of Hilkiah, **6:46** son of Amzi, son of Bani, son of Shemer, **6:47** son of Mahli, son of Mushi, son of Merari, son of Levi.
6:48 The rest of their fellow Levites were assigned to perform the remaining tasks at God's sanctuary. **6:49** But Aaron and his descendants offered sacrifices on the altar for burnt offerings and on the altar for incense as they had been assigned to do in the most holy sanctuary. They made atonement for Israel, just as God's servant Moses had ordered.
6:50 These were the descendants of Aaron:
His son Eleazar, his son Phinehas, his son Abishua, **6:51** his son Bukki, his son Uzzi, his son Zerahiah, **6:52** his son Meraioth, his son Amariah, his son Ahitub, **6:53** his son Zadok, and his son Ahimaaz.
6:54 These were the areas where Aaron's descendants lived:
The following belonged to the Kohathite clan, for they received the first allotment:
6:55 They were allotted Hebron in the territory of Judah, as well as its surrounding pasturelands. **6:56** (But the city's land and nearby towns were allotted to Caleb son of Jephunneh.) **6:57** The descendants of Aaron were also allotted as cities of refuge Hebron, Libnah and its pasturelands, Jattir, Eshtemoa and its pasturelands, **6:58** Hilez and its pasturelands, Debir and its pasturelands, **6:59** Ashan and its pasturelands, and Beth Shemesh and its pasturelands.
6:60 Within the territory of the tribe of Benjamin they were allotted Geba and its pasturelands, Alemeth and its pasturelands, and Anathoth and its pasturelands. Their clans were allotted thirteen cities in all. **6:61** The rest of Kohath's descendants were allotted ten cities in the territory of the half-tribe of Manasseh.
6:62 The clans of Gershom's descendants received thirteen cities within the territory of the tribes of Issachar, Asher, Naphtali, and Manasseh (in Bashan).
6:63 The clans of Merari's descendants were allotted twelve cities within the territory of the tribes of Reuben, Gad, and Zebulun.
6:64 So the Israelites gave to the Levites these cities and their pasturelands. **6:65** They allotted these previously named cities from the territory of the tribes of Judah, Simeon, and Benjamin.
6:66 The clans of Kohath's descendants also received territory within the tribe of Ephraim. **6:67** They were allotted as cities of refuge Shechem and its pasturelands (in the hill country of Ephraim), Gezer and its pasturelands, **6:68** Jokmeam and its pasturelands, Beth Horon and its pasturelands, **6:69** Aijalon and its pasturelands, and Gath Rimmon and its pasturelands.

6:70 Within the territory of the half-tribe of Manasseh, the rest of Kohath's descendants received Aner and its pasturelands and Bileam and its pasturelands.

6:71 The following belonged to Gershom's descendants:
Within the territory of the half-tribe of Manasseh: Golan in Bashan and its pasturelands and Ashtaroth and its pasturelands.

6:72 Within the territory of the tribe of Issachar: Kedesh and its pasturelands, Daberath and its pasturelands, **6:73** Ramoth and its pasturelands, and Anem and its pasturelands.

6:74 Within the territory of the tribe of Asher: Mashal and its pasturelands, Abdon and its pasturelands, **6:75** Hukok and its pasturelands, and Rehob and its pasturelands.

6:76 Within the territory of the tribe of Naphtali: Kedesh in Galilee and its pasturelands, Hammon and its pasturelands, and Kiriathaim and its pasturelands.

6:77 The following belonged to the rest of Merari's descendants:
Within the territory of the tribe of Zebulun: Rimmono and its pasturelands, and Tabor and its pasturelands.

6:78 Within the territory of the tribe of Reuben across the Jordan River east of Jericho: Bezer in the desert and its pasturelands, Jahzah and its pasturelands, **6:79** Kedemoth and its pasturelands, and Mephaath and its pasturelands.

6:80 Within the territory of the tribe of Gad: Ramoth in Gilead and its pasturelands, Mahanaim and its pasturelands, **6:81** Heshbon and its pasturelands, and Jazer and its pasturelands.

Issachar's Descendants

7:1 The sons of Issachar:
Tola, Puah, Jashub, and Shimron – four in all.

7:2 The sons of Tola:
Uzzi, Rephaiah, Jeriel, Jahmai, Jibsam, and Samuel. They were leaders of their families. In the time of David there were 22,600 warriors listed in Tola's genealogical records.

7:3 The son of Uzzi:
Izrachiah.

The sons of Izrahiah:
Michael, Obadiah, Joel, and Isshiah. All five were leaders.

7:4 According to the genealogical records of their families, they had 36,000 warriors available for battle, for they had numerous wives and sons. **7:5** Altogether the genealogical records of the clans of Issachar listed 87,000 warriors.

Benjamin's Descendants

7:6 The sons of Benjamin:
Bela, Beker, and Jediael – three in all.

7:7 The sons of Bela:
Ezbon, Uzzi, Uzziel, Jerimoth, and Iri. The five of them were leaders of their families. There were 22,034 warriors listed in their genealogical records.

7:8 The sons of Beker:
Zemirah, Joash, Eliezer, Elioenai, Omri, Jeremoth, Abijah, Anathoth, and Alameth. All these were the sons of Beker. **7:9** There were 20,200 family leaders and warriors listed in their genealogical records.

7:10 The son of Jediael:
Bilhan.

The sons of Bilhan:
Jeush, Benjamin, Ehud, Kenaanah, Zethan, Tarshish, and Ahishahar. **7:11** All these were the sons of Jediael. Listed in their genealogical records were 17,200 family leaders and warriors who were capable of marching out to battle.

7:12 The Shuppites and Huppites were descendants of Ir; the Hushites were descendants of Aher.

Naphtali's Descendants

7:13 The sons of Naphtali:
Jahziel, Guni, Jezer, and Shallum – sons of Bilhah.

Manasseh's Descendants

7:14 The sons of Manasseh:
Asriel, who was born to Manasseh's Aramean concubine. She also gave birth to Makir the father of Gilead. **7:15** Now Makir married a wife from the Huppites and Shuppites. (His sister's name was Maacah.)
Zelophehad was Manasseh's second son; he had only daughters.

7:16 Maacah, Makir's wife, gave birth to a son, whom she named Peresh. His brother was Sheresh, and his sons were Ulam and Rekem.

7:17 The son of Ulam:
Bedan.

These were the sons of Gilead, son of Makir, son of Manasseh. **7:18** His sister Hammoleketh gave birth to Ishhod, Abiezer, and Mahlah.

7:19 The sons of Shemida were Ahian, Shechem, Likhi, and Aniam.

Ephraim's Descendants

7:20 The descendants of Ephraim:
Shuthelah, his son Bered, his son Tahath, his son Eleadah, his son Tahath, **7:21** his son Zabad, his son Shuthelah
(Ezer and Elead were killed by the men of Gath, who were natives of the land, when they went down to steal their cattle. **7:22** Their father Ephraim mourned for them many days and his brothers came to console him. **7:23**

He had sexual relations with his wife; she became pregnant and gave birth to a son. Ephraim named him Beriah because tragedy had come to his family. **7:24** His daughter was Sheerah, who built Lower and Upper Beth Horon, as well as Uzzen Sheerah),

7:25 his son Rephah, his son Resheph, his son Telah, his son Tahan, **7:26** his son Ladan, his son Ammihud, his son Elishama, **7:27** his son Nun, and his son Joshua.

7:28 Their property and settlements included Bethel and its surrounding towns, Naaran to the east, Gezer and its surrounding towns to the west, and Shechem and its surrounding towns as far as Ayyah and its surrounding towns. **7:29** On the border of Manasseh's territory were Beth-Shean and its surrounding towns, Taanach and its surrounding towns, Megiddo and its surrounding towns, and Dor and its surrounding towns. The descendants of Joseph, Israel's son, lived here.

Asher's Descendants

7:30 The sons of Asher:
Imnah, Ishvah, Ishvi, and Beriah. Serah was their sister.

7:31 The sons of Beriah:
Heber and Malkiel, who was the father of Birzaith.

7:32 Heber was the father of Japhlet, Shomer, Hotham, and Shua their sister.

7:33 The sons of Japhlet:
Pasach, Bimhal, and Ashvath. These were Japhlet's sons.

7:34 The sons of his brother Shemer:
Rohgah, Hubbah, and Aram.

7:35 The sons of his brother Helem:
Zophah, Imna, Shelesh, and Amal.

7:36 The sons of Zophah:
Suah, Harnepher, Shual, Beri, Imrah, **7:37** Bezer, Hod, Shamma, Shilshah, Ithran, and Beera.

7:38 The sons of Jether:
Jephunneh, Pispah, and Ara.

7:39 The sons of Ulla:
Arah, Hanniel, and Rizia.

7:40 All these were the descendants of Asher. They were the leaders of their families, the most capable men, who were warriors and served as head chiefs. There were 26,000 warriors listed in their genealogical records as capable of doing battle.

Benjamin's Descendants (Continued)

8:1 Benjamin was the father of Bela, his firstborn; Ashbel was born second, Aharah third, **8:2** Nohah fourth, and Rapha fifth.

8:3 Bela's sons were Addar, Gera, Abihud, **8:4** Abishua, Naaman, Ahoah, **8:5** Gera, Shephuphan, and Huram.

8:6 These were the descendants of Ehud who were leaders of the families living in Geba who were forced to move to Manahath: **8:7** Naaman, Ahijah, and Gera, who moved them. Gera was the father of Uzzah and Ahihud.

8:8 Shaharaim fathered sons in Moab after he divorced his wives Hushim and Baara. **8:9** By his wife Hodesh he fathered Jobab, Zibia, Mesha, Malkam, **8:10** Jeuz, Sakia, and Mirmah. These were his sons; they were family leaders. **8:11** By Hushim he fathered Abitub and Elpaal.

8:12 The sons of Elpaal:
Eber, Misham, Shemed (who built Ono and Lod, as well as its surrounding towns), **8:13** Beriah, and Shema. They were leaders of the families living in Aijalon and chased out the inhabitants of Gath.

8:14 Ahio, Shashak, Jeremoth, **8:15** Zebadiah, Arad, Eder, **8:16** Michael, Ishpah, and Joha were the sons of Beriah.

8:17 Zebadiah, Meshullam, Hizki, Heber, **8:18** Ishmerai, Izliah, and Jobab were the sons of Elpaal.

8:19 Jakim, Zikri, Zabdi, **8:20** Elienai, Zillethai, Eliel, **8:21** Adaiah, Beraiah, and Shimrath were the sons of Shimei.

8:22 Ishpan, Eber, Eliel, **8:23** Abdon, Zikri, Hanan, **8:24** Hananiah, Elam, Anthothijah, **8:25** Iphdeiah, and Penuel were the sons of Shashak.

8:26 Shamsherai, Shechariah, Athaliah, **8:27** Jaareshiah, Elijah, and Zikri were the sons of Jeroham. **8:28** These were the family leaders listed in the genealogical records; they lived in Jerusalem.

8:29 The father of Gibeon lived in Gibeon; his wife's name was Maacah. **8:30** His firstborn son was Abdon, followed by Zur, Kish, Baal, Nadab, **8:31** Gedor, Ahio, Zeker, and Mikloth. **8:32** Mikloth was the father of Shimeah. They also lived near their relatives in Jerusalem.

8:33 Ner was the father of Kish, and Kish was the father of Saul. Saul was the father of Jonathan, Malki-Shua, Abinadab, and Eshbaal.

8:34 The son of Jonathan:
Meribbaal.

Meribbaal was the father of Micah.

8:35 The sons of Micah:
Pithon, Melech, Tarea, and Ahaz.

8:36 Ahaz was the father of Jehoaddah, and Jehoaddah was the father of Alemeth, Azmaveth, and Zimri. Zimri was the father of Moza, **8:37** and Moza was the father of Binea. His son was Raphah, whose son was Eleasah, whose son was Azel.

8:38 Azel had six sons: Azrikam his firstborn, followed by Ishmael, Sheariah, Obadiah, and Hanan. All these were the sons of Azel.

8:39 The sons of his brother Eshek:

Ulam was his firstborn, Jeush second, and Eliphelet third. **8:40** The sons of Ulam were warriors who were adept archers. They had many sons and grandsons, a total of 150.

All these were the descendants of Benjamin.

9:1 Genealogical records were kept for all Israel; they are recorded in the Scroll of the Kings of Israel.

Exiles Who Resettled in Jerusalem

The people of Judah were carried away to Babylon because of their unfaithfulness. **9:2** The first to resettle on their property and in their cities were some Israelites, priests, Levites, and temple servants. **9:3** Some from the tribes of Judah, Benjamin, and Ephraim and Manasseh settled in Jerusalem.

9:4 The settlers included: Uthai son of Ammihud, son of Omri, son of Imri, son of Bani, who was a descendant of Perez son of Judah.

9:5 From the Shilonites: Asaiah the firstborn and his sons.

9:6 From the descendants of Zerah: Jeuel.

Their relatives numbered 690.

9:7 From the descendants of Benjamin:

Sallu son of Meshullam, son of Hodaviah, son of Hassenuah; **9:8** Ibneiah son of Jeroham; Elah son of Uzzi, son of Mikri; and Meshullam son of Shephatiah, son of Reuel, son of Ibnijah.

9:9 Their relatives, listed in their genealogical records, numbered 956. All these men were leaders of their families.

9:10 From the priests:

Jedaiah; Jehoiarib; Jakin; **9:11** Azariah son of Hilkiah, son of Meshullam, son of Zadok, son of Meraioth, son of Ahitub the leader in God's temple; **9:12** Adaiah son of Jeroham, son of Pashhur, son of Malkijah; and Maasai son of Adiel, son of Jahzerah, son of Meshullam, son of Meshillemith, son of Immer.

9:13 Their relatives, who were leaders of their families, numbered 1,760. They were capable men who were assigned to carry out the various tasks of service in God's temple.

9:14 From the Levites:

Shemaiah son of Hasshub, son of Azrikam, son of Hashabiah a descendant of Merari; **9:15** Bakbakkar; Heresh; Galal; Mattaniah son of Mika, son of Zikri, son of Asaph; **9:16** Obadiah son of Shemaiah, son of Galal, son of Jeduthun; and Berechiah son of Asa, son of Elkanah, who lived among the settlements of the Netophathites.

9:17 The gatekeepers were:

Shallum, Akkub, Talmon, Ahiman, and their brothers. Shallum was the leader; **9:18** he serves to this day at the King's Gate on the east. These were the gatekeepers from the camp of the descendants of Levi.

9:19 Shallum son of Kore, son of Ebiasaph, son of Korah, and his relatives from his family (the Korahites) were assigned to guard the entrance to the sanctuary. Their ancestors had guarded the entrance to the LORD's dwelling place. **9:20** Phinehas son of Eleazar had been their leader in earlier times, and the LORD was with him. **9:21** Zechariah son of Meshelemiah was the guard at the entrance to the meeting tent.

9:22 All those selected to be gatekeepers at the entrances numbered 212. Their names were recorded in the genealogical records of their settlements. David and Samuel the prophet had appointed them to their positions. **9:23** They and their descendants were assigned to guard the gates of the LORD's sanctuary (that is, the tabernacle). **9:24** The gatekeepers were posted on all four sides – east, west, north, and south. **9:25** Their relatives, who lived in their settlements, came from time to time and served with them for seven-day periods. **9:26** The four head gatekeepers, who were Levites, were assigned to guard the storerooms and treasuries in God's sanctuary. **9:27** They would spend the night in their posts all around God's sanctuary, for they were assigned to guard it and would open it with the key every morning. **9:28** Some of them were in charge of the articles used by those who served; they counted them when they brought them in and when they brought them out. **9:29** Some of them were in charge of the equipment and articles of the sanctuary, as well as the flour, wine, olive oil, incense, and spices. **9:30** (But some of the priests mixed the spices.) **9:31** Mattithiah, a Levite, the firstborn son of Shallum the Korahite, was in charge of baking the bread for offerings. **9:32** Some of the Kohathites, their relatives, were in charge of preparing the bread that is displayed each Sabbath.

9:33 The musicians and Levite family leaders stayed in rooms at the sanctuary and were exempt from other duties, for day and night they had to carry out their assigned tasks. **9:34** These were the family leaders of the Levites, as listed in their genealogical records. They lived in Jerusalem.

Jeiel's Descendants

9:35 Jeiel (the father of Gibeon) lived in Gibeon. His wife was Maacah. **9:36** His firstborn son was Abdon, followed by Zur, Kish, Baal, Ner, Nadab, **9:37** Gedor, Ahio, Zechariah, and Mikloth. **9:38** Mikloth was the father of Shimeam. They also lived near their relatives in Jerusalem. **9:39** Ner was the father of Kish, and Kish was the father of Saul. Saul was the father of Jonathan, Malki-Shua, Abinadab, and Eshbaal.

9:40 The son of Jonathan:

Meribbaal, who was the father of Micah.

9:41 The sons of Micah:

Pithon, Melech, Tahrea, and Ahaz.

9:42 Ahaz was the father of Jarah, and Jarah was the father of Alemeth, Azmaveth, and Zimri. Zimri was the father of Moza, **9:43** and Moza was the father of Binea. His son was Rephaiah, whose son was Eleasah, whose son was Azel.

9:44 Azel had six sons: Azrikam his firstborn, followed by Ishmael, Sheariah, Obadiah, and Hanan. These were the sons of Azel.

Saul's Death

10:1 Now the Philistines fought against Israel. The Israelites fled before the Philistines and many of them fell dead on Mount Gilboa. **10:2** The Philistines stayed right on the heels of Saul and his sons. They struck down Saul's sons Jonathan, Abinadab, and Malki-Shua. **10:3** The battle was thick around Saul; the archers spotted him and wounded him. **10:4** Saul told his armor bearer, "Draw your sword and stab me with it. Otherwise these uncircumcised people will come and torture me." But his armor bearer refused to do it, because he was very afraid. So Saul took the sword and fell on it. **10:5** When his armor bearer saw that Saul was dead, he also fell on his sword and died. **10:6** So Saul and his three sons died; his whole household died together. **10:7** When all the Israelites who were in the valley saw that the army had fled and that Saul and his sons were dead, they abandoned their cities and fled. The Philistines came and occupied them.

10:8 The next day, when the Philistines came to strip loot from the corpses, they discovered Saul and his sons lying dead on Mount Gilboa. **10:9** They stripped his corpse, and then carried off his head and his armor. They sent messengers throughout the land of the Philistines proclaiming the news to their idols and their people. **10:10** They placed his armor in the temple of their gods and hung his head in the temple of Dagon. **10:11** When all the residents of Jabesh Gilead heard about everything the Philistines had done to Saul, **10:12** all the warriors went and recovered the bodies of Saul and his sons and brought them to Jabesh. They buried their remains under the oak tree in Jabesh and fasted for seven days.

10:13 So Saul died because he was unfaithful to the LORD and did not obey the LORD's instructions; he even tried to conjure up underworld spirits. **10:14** He did not seek the LORD's guidance, so the LORD killed him and transferred the kingdom to David son of Jesse.

David Becomes King

11:1 All Israel joined David at Hebron and said, "Look, we are your very flesh and blood! **11:2** In the past, even when Saul was king, you were Israel's commanding general. The LORD your God said to you, 'You will shepherd my people Israel; you will rule over my people Israel.'" **11:3** When all the leaders of Israel came to the king at Hebron, David made an agreement with them in Hebron before the LORD. They anointed David king over Israel, just as the LORD had announced through Samuel.

David Conquers Jerusalem

11:4 David and the whole Israelite army advanced to Jerusalem (that is, Jebus). (The Jebusites, the land's original inhabitants, lived there.) **11:5** The residents of Jebus said to David, "You cannot invade this place!" But David captured the fortress of Zion (that is, the City of David). **11:6** David said, "Whoever attacks the Jebusites first will become commanding general!" So Joab son of Zeruiah attacked first and became commander. **11:7** David lived in the fortress; for this reason it is called the City of David. **11:8** He built up the city around it, from the terrace to the surrounding walls; Joab restored the rest of the city. **11:9** David's power steadily grew, for the LORD who commands armies was with him.

David's Warriors

11:10 These were the leaders of David's warriors who helped establish and stabilize his rule over all Israel, in accordance with the LORD's word. **11:11** This is the list of David's warriors:

Jashobeam, a Hacmonite, was head of the officers. He killed three hundred men with his spear in a single battle.

11:12 Next in command was Eleazar son of Dodo the Ahohite. He was one of the three elite warriors. **11:13** He was with David in Pas Dammim when the Philistines assembled there for battle. In an area of the field that was full of barley, the army retreated before the Philistines, **11:14** but then they made a stand in the middle of that area. They defended it and defeated the Philistines; the LORD gave them a great victory.

11:15 Three of the thirty leaders went down to David at the rocky cliff at the cave of Adullam, while a Philistine force was camped in the Valley of Rephaim. **11:16** David was in the stronghold at the time, while a Philistine garrison was in Bethlehem. **11:17** David was thirsty and said, "How I wish someone would give me some water to drink from the cistern in Bethlehem near the city gate!" **11:18** So the three elite warriors broke through the Philistine forces and drew some water from the cistern in Bethlehem near the city gate. They carried it back to David, but David refused to drink it. He poured it out as a drink offering to the LORD **11:19** and said, "God forbid that I should do this! Should I drink the blood of these men who risked their lives?" Because they risked their lives to bring it to him, he refused to drink it. Such were the exploits of the three elite warriors.

11:20 Abishai the brother of Joab was head of the three elite warriors. He killed three hundred men with his spear and gained fame along with the three elite warriors. **11:21** From the three he was given double honor and he became their officer, even though he was not one of them.

11:22 Benaiah son of Jehoiada was a brave warrior from Kabzeel who performed great exploits. He struck down the two sons of Ariel of Moab; he also went down and killed a lion inside a cistern on a snowy day. **11:23** He even killed an Egyptian who was seven and a half feet tall. The Egyptian had a spear as big as the crossbeam of a weaver's loom; Benaiah attacked him with a club. He grabbed the spear out of the Egyptian's hand and killed him with his own spear. **11:24** Such were the exploits of Benaiah son of Jehoiada, who gained fame along with the three elite warriors. **11:25** He received honor from the thirty warriors, though he was not one of the three elite warriors. David put him in charge of his bodyguard.

11:26 The mighty warriors were:

Asahel the brother of Joab,

Elhanan son of Dodo, from Bethlehem,

11:27 Shammoth the Harorite,

Helez the Pelonite,

11:28 Ira son of Ikkesh the Tekoite,

Abiezer the Anathothite,

11:29 Sibbekai the Hushathite,

Ilai the Ahohite,

11:30 Maharai the Netophathite,

Heled son of Baanah the Netophathite,

11:31 Ithai son of Ribai from Gibeah in Benjaminite territory,

Benaiah the Pirathonite,

11:32 Hurai from the valleys of Gaash,

Abiel the Arbathite,

11:33 Azmaveth the Baharumite,

Eliahba the Shaalbonite,

11:34 the sons of Hashem the Gizonite,

Jonathan son of Shageh the Hararite,

11:35 Ahiam son of Sakar the Hararite,

Eliphal son of Ur,

11:36 Hepher the Mekerathite,

Ahijah the Pelonite,

11:37 Hezro the Carmelite,

Naarai son of Ezbai,

11:38 Joel the brother of Nathan,

Mibhar son of Hagri,

11:39 Zelek the Ammonite,

Naharai the Beerothite, the armor-bearer of Joab son of Zeruiah,

11:40 Ira the Ithrite,

Gareb the Ithrite,

11:41 Uriah the Hittite,

Zabad son of Achli,

11:42 Adina son of Shiza the Reubenite, leader of the Reubenites and the thirty warriors with him,

11:43 Hanan son of Maacah,

Joshaphat the Mithnite,

11:44 Uzzia the Ashterathite,

Shama and Jeiel, the sons of Hotham the Aroerite,

11:45 Jediael son of Shimri,

and Joha his brother, the Tizite,

11:46 Eliel the Mahavite,

and Jeribai and Joshaviah, the sons of Elnaam,

and Ithmah the Moabite,

11:47 Eliel,

and Obed,

and Jaasiel the Mezobaite.

Warriors Who Joined David at Ziklag

12:1 These were the men who joined David in Ziklag, when he was banished from the presence of Saul son of Kish. (They were among the warriors who assisted him in battle. **12:2** They were armed with bows and could shoot arrows or sling stones right or left-handed. They were fellow tribesmen of Saul from Benjamin.) These were:

12:3 Ahiezer, the leader, and Joash, the sons of Shemaah the Gibeathite; Jeziel and Pelet, the sons of Azmaveth;

Berachah,

Jehu the Anathothite,

12:4 Ishmaiah the Gibeonite, one of the thirty warriors and their leader, (12:5) Jeremiah,

Jahaziel,

Johanan,

Jozabad the Gederathite,

12:5 (12:6) Eluzai,

Jerimoth,

Bealiah,

Shemariah,

Shephatiah the Haruphite,

12:6 Elkanah, Isshiah, Azarel, Joezer, and Jashobeam, who were Korahites,

12:7 and Joelah and Zebadiah, the sons of Jeroham from Gedor.

12:8 Some of the Gadites joined David at the stronghold in the desert. They were warriors who were trained for battle; they carried shields and spears. They were as fierce as lions and could run as quickly as gazelles across the hills. **12:9** Ezer was the leader, Obadiah the second in command, Eliab the third, **12:10** Mishmannah the fourth, Jeremiah the fifth, **12:11** Attai the sixth, Eliel the seventh, **12:12** Johanan the eighth, Elzabad the ninth, **12:13** Jeremiah the tenth, and Machbannai the eleventh. **12:14** These Gadites were military leaders; the least led a hundred men, the greatest a thousand. **12:15** They crossed the Jordan River in the first month, when it was overflowing its banks, and routed those living in all the valleys to the east and west.

12:16 Some from Benjamin and Judah also came to David's stronghold. **12:17** David went out to meet them and said, "If you come to me in peace and want to help me, then I will make an alliance with you. But if you come to betray me to my enemies when I have not harmed you, may the God of our ancestors take notice and judge!" **12:18** But a spirit empowered Amasai, the leader of the thirty warriors, and he said:

"We are yours, O David!

We support you, O son of Jesse!

May you greatly prosper!

May those who help you prosper!

Indeed your God helps you!"

So David accepted them and made them leaders of raiding bands.

12:19 Some men from Manasseh joined David when he went with the Philistines to fight against Saul. (But in the end they did not help the Philistines because, after taking counsel, the Philistine lords sent David away, saying: "It would be disastrous for us if he deserts to his master Saul.") **12:20** When David went to Ziklag, the men of Manasseh who joined him were Adnach, Jozabad, Jediael, Michael, Jozabad, Elihu, and Zillethai, leaders of a thousand soldiers each in the tribe of Manasseh. **12:21** They helped David fight against raiding bands, for all of them were warriors and leaders in the army. **12:22** Each day men came to help David until his army became very large.

Support for David in Hebron

12:23 The following is a record of the armed warriors who came with their leaders and joined David in Hebron in order to make David king in Saul's place, in accordance with the LORD's decree:

12:24 From Judah came 6,800 trained warriors carrying shields and spears.

12:25 From Simeon there were 7,100 warriors.

12:26 From Levi there were 4,600. **12:27** Jehoiada, the leader of Aaron's descendants, brought 3,700 men with him, **12:28** along with Zadok, a young warrior, and twenty-two leaders from his family.

12:29 From Benjamin, Saul's tribe, there were 3,000, most of whom, up to that time, had been loyal to Saul.

12:30 From Ephraim there were 20,800 warriors, who had brought fame to their families.

12:31 From the half tribe of Manasseh there were 18,000 who had been designated by name to come and make David king.

12:32 From Issachar there were 200 leaders and all their relatives at their command – they understood the times and knew what Israel should do.

12:33 From Zebulun there were 50,000 warriors who were prepared for battle, equipped with all kinds of weapons, and ready to give their undivided loyalty.

12:34 From Naphtali there were 1,000 officers, along with 37,000 men carrying shields and spears.

12:35 From Dan there were 28,600 men prepared for battle.

12:36 From Asher there were 40,000 warriors prepared for battle.

12:37 From the other side of the Jordan, from Reuben, Gad, and the half tribe of Manasseh, there were 120,000 men armed with all kinds of weapons.

12:38 All these men were warriors who were ready to march. They came to Hebron to make David king over all Israel by acclamation; all the rest of the Israelites also were in agreement that David should become king. **12:39** They spent three days feasting there with David, for their relatives had given them provisions. **12:40** Also their neighbors, from as far away as Issachar, Zebulun, and Naphtali, were bringing food on donkeys, camels, mules, and oxen. There were large supplies of flour, fig cakes, raisins, wine, olive oil, beef, and lamb, for Israel was celebrating.

Uzzah Meets Disaster

13:1 David consulted with his military officers, including those who led groups of a thousand and those who led groups of a hundred. **13:2** David said to the whole Israelite assembly, "If you so desire and the LORD our God approves, let's spread the word to our brothers who remain in all the regions of Israel, and to the priests and Levites in their cities, so they may join us. **13:3** Let's move the ark of our God back here, for we did not seek his will throughout Saul's reign." **13:4** The whole assembly agreed to do this, for the proposal seemed right to all the people. **13:5** So David assembled all Israel from the Shihor River in Egypt to Lebo Hamath, to bring the ark of God from Kiriath Jearim. **13:6** David and all Israel went up to Baalah (that is, Kiriath Jearim) in Judah to bring up from there the ark of God the LORD, who sits enthroned between the cherubim – the ark that is called by his name.

13:7 They transported the ark on a new cart from the house of Abinadab; Uzzah and Ahio were guiding the cart, **13:8** while David and all Israel were energetically celebrating before God, singing and playing various stringed instruments, tambourines, cymbals, and trumpets. **13:9** When they arrived at the threshing floor of Kidon, Uzzah reached out his hand to take hold of the ark, because the oxen stumbled. **13:10** The LORD was so furious with Uzzah, he killed him, because he reached out his hand and touched the ark. He died right there before God.

13:11 David was angry because the LORD attacked Uzzah; so he called that place Perez Uzzah, which remains its name to this very day. **13:12** David was afraid of God that day and said, "How will I ever be able to bring the ark of God up here?" **13:13** So David did not move the ark to the City of David; he left it in the house of Obed-Edom the Gittite. **13:14** The ark of God remained in Obed-Edom's house for three months; the LORD blessed Obed-Edom's family and everything that belonged to him.

David's Prestige Grows

14:1 King Hiram of Tyre sent messengers to David, along with cedar logs, stonemasons, and carpenters to build a palace for him. **14:2** David realized that the LORD had established him as king over Israel and that he had elevated his kingdom for the sake of his people Israel.

14:3 In Jerusalem David married more wives and fathered more sons and daughters. **14:4** These are the names of children born to him in Jerusalem: Shammua, Shobab, Nathan, Solomon, **14:5** Ibhar, Elishua, Elpelet, **14:6** Nogah, Nepheg, Japhia, **14:7** Elishama, Beeliada, and Eliphelet.

14:8 When the Philistines heard that David had been anointed king of all Israel, all the Philistines marched up to confront him. When David heard about it, he marched out against them. **14:9** Now the Philistines had come and raided the Valley of Rephaim. **14:10** David asked God, "Should I march up against the Philistines? Will you hand them over to me?" The LORD said to him, "March up! I will hand them over to you!" **14:11** So they marched against Baal Perazim and David defeated them there. David said, "Using me as his instrument, God has burst out against my enemies like water bursts out." So that place is called Baal Perazim. **14:12** The Philistines left their idols there, so David ordered that they be burned.

14:13 The Philistines again raided the valley. **14:14** So David again asked God what he should do. This time God told him, "Don't march up after them; circle around them and come against them in front of the trees. **14:15** When you hear the sound of marching in the tops of the trees, then attack. For at that moment the LORD is going before you to strike down the army of the Philistines." **14:16** David did just as God commanded him, and they struck down the Philistine army from Gibeon to Gezer.

14:17 So David became famous in all the lands; the LORD caused all the nations to fear him.

David Brings the Ark to Jerusalem

15:1 David constructed buildings in the City of David; he then prepared a place for the ark of God and pitched a tent for it. **15:2** Then David said, "Only the Levites may carry the ark of God, for the LORD chose them to carry the ark of the LORD and to serve before him perpetually. **15:3** David assembled all Israel at Jerusalem to bring the ark of the LORD up to the place he had prepared for it. **15:4** David gathered together the descendants of Aaron and the Levites:

15:5 From the descendants of Kohath: Uriel the leader and 120 of his relatives.

15:6 From the descendants of Merari: Asaiah the leader and 220 of his relatives.

15:7 From the descendants of Gershom: Joel the leader and 130 of his relatives.

15:8 From the descendants of Elizaphan: Shemaiah the leader and 200 of his relatives.

15:9 From the descendants of Hebron: Eliel the leader and 80 of his relatives.

15:10 From the descendants of Uzziel: Amminadab the leader and 112 of his relatives.

15:11 David summoned the priests Zadok and Abiathar, along with the Levites Uriel, Asaiah, Joel, Shemaiah, Eliel, and Amminadab. **15:12** He told them: "You are the leaders of the Levites' families. You and your relatives must consecrate yourselves and bring the ark of the LORD God of Israel up to the place I have prepared for it. **15:13** The first time you did not carry it; that is why the LORD God attacked us, because we did not ask him about the proper way to carry it." **15:14** The priests and Levites consecrated themselves so they could bring up the ark of the LORD God of Israel. **15:15** The descendants of Levi carried the ark of God on their shoulders with poles, just as Moses had ordered according to the divine command.

15:16 David told the leaders of the Levites to appoint some of their relatives as musicians; they were to play various instruments, including stringed instruments and cymbals, and to sing loudly and joyfully. **15:17** So the Levites appointed Heman son of Joel; one of his relatives, Asaph son of Berechiah; one of the descendants of Merari, Ethan son of Kushaiah; **15:18** along with some of their relatives who were second in rank, including Zechariah, Jaaziel, Shemiramoth, Jehiel, Unni, Eliab, Benaiah, Maaseiah, Mattithiah, Eliphelehu, Mikneiah, Obed-Edom, and Jeiel, the gatekeepers.

15:19 The musicians Heman, Asaph, and Ethan were to sound the bronze cymbals; **15:20** Zechariah, Aziel, Shemiramoth, Jehiel, Unni, Eliab, Maaseiah, and Benaiah were to play the harps according to the *alamoth* style; **15:21** Mattithiah, Eliphelehu, Mikneiah, Obed-Edom, Jeiel, and Azaziah were to play the lyres according to the *sheminith* style, as led by the director; **15:22** Kenaniah, the leader of the Levites, was in charge of transport, for he was well-informed on this matter; **15:23** Berechiah and Elkanah were guardians of the ark; **15:24** Shebaniah, Joshaphat, Nethanel, Amasai, Zechariah, Benaiah, and Eliezer the priests were to blow the trumpets before the ark of God; Obed-Edom and Jehiel were also guardians of the ark.

15:25 So David, the leaders of Israel, and the commanders of units of a thousand went to bring up the ark of the LORD's covenant from the house of Obed-Edom with celebration. **15:26** When God helped the Levites who were carrying the ark of the LORD's covenant, they sacrificed seven bulls and seven rams. **15:27** David was wrapped in a linen robe, as were all the Levites carrying the ark, the musicians, and Kenaniah the supervisor of transport and the musicians; David also wore a linen ephod. **15:28** All Israel brought up the ark of the LORD's covenant; they were shouting, blowing trumpets, sounding cymbals, and playing stringed instruments. **15:29** As the ark of the LORD's covenant entered the City of David, Michal, Saul's daughter, looked out the window. When she saw King David jumping and celebrating, she despised him.

David Leads in Worship

16:1 They brought the ark of God and put it in the middle of the tent David had pitched for it. Then they offered burnt sacrifices and peace offerings before God. **16:2** When David finished offering burnt sacrifices and peace offerings, he pronounced a blessing over the people in the LORD's name. **16:3** He then handed out to each Israelite man and woman a loaf of bread, a date cake, and a raisin cake. **16:4** He appointed some of the Levites to serve before the ark of the LORD, to offer prayers, songs of thanks, and hymns to the LORD God of Israel. **16:5** Asaph was the leader and Zechariah second in command, followed by Jeiel, Shemiramoth, Jehiel, Mattithiah, Eliab, Benaiah, Obed-Edom, and Jeiel. They were to play stringed instruments; Asaph was to sound the cymbals; **16:6** and the priests Benaiah and Jahaziel were to blow trumpets regularly before the ark of God's covenant.

David Thanks God

16:7 That day David first gave to Asaph and his colleagues this song of thanks to the LORD:

16:8 Give thanks to the LORD!
Call on his name!
Make known his accomplishments among the nations!
16:9 Sing to him! Make music to him!
Tell about all his miraculous deeds!
16:10 Boast about his holy name!
Let the hearts of those who seek the LORD rejoice!
16:11 Seek the LORD and the strength he gives!
Seek his presence continually!
16:12 Recall the miraculous deeds he performed,
his mighty acts and the judgments he decreed,

16:13 O children of Israel, God's servant,
you descendants of Jacob, God's chosen ones!
16:14 He is the LORD our God;
he carries out judgment throughout the earth.
16:15 Remember continually his covenantal decree,
the promise he made to a thousand generations –
16:16 the promise he made to Abraham,
the promise he made by oath to Isaac!
16:17 He gave it to Jacob as a decree,
to Israel as a lasting promise,
16:18 saying, "To you I will give the land of Canaan
as the portion of your inheritance."
16:19 When they were few in number,
just a very few, and foreign residents within it,
16:20 they wandered from nation to nation,
and from one kingdom to another.
16:21 He let no one oppress them,
he disciplined kings for their sake,
16:22 saying, "Don't touch my anointed ones!
Don't harm my prophets!"
16:23 Sing to the LORD, all the earth!
Announce every day how he delivers!
16:24 Tell the nations about his splendor,
tell all the nations about his miraculous deeds!
16:25 For the LORD is great and certainly worthy of praise,
he is more awesome than all gods.
16:26 For all the gods of the nations are worthless,
but the LORD made the heavens.

16:27 Majestic splendor emanates from him,
he is the source of strength and joy.
16:28 Ascribe to the LORD, O families of the nations,
ascribe to the LORD splendor and strength!
16:29 Ascribe to the LORD the splendor he deserves!
Bring an offering and enter his presence!
Worship the LORD in holy attire!
16:30 Tremble before him, all the earth!
The world is established, it cannot be moved.
16:31 Let the heavens rejoice, and the earth be happy!
Let the nations say, 'The LORD reigns!'
16:32 Let the sea and everything in it shout!
Let the fields and everything in them celebrate!
16:33 Then let the trees of the forest shout with joy before the LORD,
for he comes to judge the earth!
16:34 Give thanks to the LORD, for he is good
and his loyal love endures.
16:35 Say this prayer: "Deliver us, O God who delivers us!
Gather us! Rescue us from the nations!
Then we will give thanks to your holy name,
and boast about your praiseworthy deeds."
16:36 May the LORD God of Israel be praised,
in the future and forevermore.
Then all the people said, "We agree! Praise the LORD!"

David Appoints Worship Leaders

16:37 David left Asaph and his colleagues there before the ark of the LORD's covenant to serve before the ark regularly and fulfill each day's requirements, **16:38** including Obed-Edom and sixty-eight colleagues. Obed-Edom son of Jeduthun and Hosah were gatekeepers. **16:39** Zadok the priest and his fellow priests served before the LORD's tabernacle at the worship center in Gibeon, **16:40** regularly offering burnt sacrifices to the LORD on the altar for burnt sacrifice, morning and evening, according to what is prescribed in the law of the LORD which he charged Israel to observe. **16:41** Joining them were Heman, Jeduthun, and the rest of those chosen and designated by name to give thanks to the LORD. (For his loyal love endures!) **16:42** Heman and Jeduthun were in charge of the music, including the trumpets, cymbals, and the other musical instruments used in praising God. The sons of Jeduthun guarded the entrance.

16:43 Then all the people returned to their homes, and David went to pronounce a blessing on his family.

God Makes a Promise to David

17:1 When David had settled into his palace, he said to Nathan the prophet, "Look, I am living in a palace made from cedar, while the ark of the LORD's covenant is under a tent." **17:2** Nathan said to David, "You should do whatever you have in mind, for God is with you."

17:3 That night God told Nathan the prophet, **17:4** "Go, tell my servant David: 'This is what the LORD says: "You must not build me a house in which to live. **17:5** For I have not lived in a house from the time I brought Israel up from Egypt to the present day. I have lived in a tent that has been in various places. **17:6** Wherever I moved throughout Israel, I did not say to any of the leaders whom I appointed to care for my people Israel, 'Why have you not built me a house made from cedar?'"'

17:7 "So now, say this to my servant David: 'This is what the LORD who commands armies says: "I took you from the pasture and from your work as a shepherd to make you a leader of my people Israel. **17:8** I was with you wherever you went and I defeated all your enemies before you. Now I will make you as famous as the great men of the earth. **17:9** I will establish a place for my people Israel and settle them there; they will live there and not be disturbed anymore. Violent men will not oppress them again, as they did in the beginning **17:10** and during the time when I appointed judges to lead my people Israel. I will subdue all your enemies.

"""'I declare to you that the LORD will build a dynastic house for you! **17:11** When the time comes for you to die, I will raise up your descendant, one of your own sons, to succeed you, and I will establish his kingdom. **17:12** He will build me a house, and I will make his dynasty permanent. **17:13** I will become his father and he will become my son. I will never withhold my loyal love from him, as I withheld it from the one who ruled before you. **17:14** I will put him in permanent charge of my house and my kingdom; his dynasty will be permanent."'"' **17:15** Nathan told David all these words that were revealed to him.

David Praises God

17:16 David went in, sat before the LORD, and said: "Who am I, O LORD God, and what is my family, that you should have brought me to this point? **17:17** And you did not stop there, O God! You have also spoken about the future of your servant's family. You have revealed to me what men long to know, O LORD God. **17:18** What more can David say to you? You have honored your servant; you have given your servant special recognition. **17:19** O LORD, for the sake of your servant and according to your will, you have done this great thing in order to reveal your greatness. **17:20** O LORD, there is none like you; there is no God besides you! What we heard is true! **17:21** And who is like your people, Israel, a unique nation in the earth? Their God went to claim a nation for himself! You made a name for yourself by doing great and awesome deeds when you drove out nations before your people whom you had delivered from the Egyptian empire and its gods. **17:22** You made Israel your very own nation for all time. You, O LORD, became their God. **17:23** So now, O LORD, may the promise you made about your servant and his family become a permanent reality! Do as you promised, **17:24** so it may become a reality and you may gain lasting fame, as people say, 'The LORD who commands armies is the God of Israel.' David's dynasty will be established before you, **17:25** for you, my God, have revealed to your servant that you will build a dynasty for him. That is why your servant has had the courage to pray to you. **17:26** Now, O LORD, you are the true God; you have made this good promise to your servant. **17:27** Now you are willing to bless your servant's dynasty so that it may stand permanently before you, for you, O LORD, have blessed it and it will be blessed from now on into the future."

David Conquers the Neighboring Nations

18:1 Later David defeated the Philistines and subdued them. He took Gath and its surrounding towns away from the Philistines.

18:2 He defeated the Moabites; the Moabites became David's subjects and brought tribute.

18:3 David defeated King Hadadezer of Zobah as far as Hamath, when he went to extend his authority to the Euphrates River. **18:4** David seized from him 1,000 chariots, 7,000 charioteers, and 20,000 infantrymen. David cut the hamstrings of all but a hundred of Hadadezer's chariot horses. **18:5** The Arameans of Damascus came to help King Hadadezer of Zobah, but David killed 22,000 of the Arameans. **18:6** David placed garrisons in the territory of the Arameans of Damascus; the Arameans became David's subjects and brought tribute. The LORD protected David wherever he campaigned. **18:7** David took the golden shields which Hadadezer's servants had carried and brought them to Jerusalem. **18:8** From Tibhath and Kun, Hadadezer's cities, David took a great deal of bronze. (Solomon used it to make the big bronze basin called "The Sea," the pillars, and other bronze items.

18:9 When King Tou of Hamath heard that David had defeated the entire army of King Hadadezer of Zobah, **18:10** he sent his son Hadoram to King David to extend his best wishes and to pronounce a blessing on him for his victory over Hadadezer, for Tou had been at war with Hadadezer. He also sent various items made of gold, silver, and bronze. **18:11** King David dedicated these things to the LORD, along with the silver and gold which he had carried off from all the nations, including Edom, Moab, the Ammonites, the Philistines, and Amalek.

18:12 Abishai son of Zeruiah killed 18,000 Edomites in the Valley of Salt. **18:13** He placed garrisons in Edom, and all the Edomites became David's subjects. The LORD protected David wherever he campaigned.

David's Officials

18:14 David reigned over all Israel; he guaranteed justice for all his people. **18:15** Joab son of Zeruiah was commanding general of the army; Jehoshaphat son of Ahilud was secretary; **18:16** Zadok son of Ahitub and Abimelech son of Abiathar were priests; Shavsha was scribe; **18:17** Benaiah son of Jehoiada supervised the Kerethites and Pelethites; and David's sons were the king's leading officials.

David's Campaign against the Ammonites

19:1 Later King Nahash of the Ammonites died and his son succeeded him. **19:2** David said, "I will express my loyalty to Hanun son of Nahash, for his father was loyal to me." So David sent messengers to express his sympathy over his father's death. When David's servants entered Ammonite territory to visit Hanun and express the king's sympathy, **19:3** the Ammonite officials said to Hanun, "Do you really think David is trying to honor your father by sending these messengers to express his sympathy? No, his servants have come to you so they can get information and spy out the land!" **19:4** So Hanun seized David's servants and shaved their beards off. He cut off the lower part of their robes so that their buttocks were exposed and then sent them away. **19:5** Messengers came and told David what had happened to the men, so he summoned them, for the men were thoroughly humiliated. The king said, "Stay in Jericho until your beards grow again; then you may come back."

19:6 When the Ammonites realized that David was disgusted with them, Hanun and the Ammonites sent 1,000 talents of silver to hire chariots and charioteers from Aram Naharaim, Aram Maacah, and Zobah. **19:7** They hired 32,000 chariots, along with the king of Maacah and his army, who came and camped in front of Medeba. The Ammonites also assembled from their cities and marched out to do battle.

19:8 When David heard the news, he sent Joab and the entire army to meet them. **19:9** The Ammonites marched out and were deployed for battle at the entrance to the city, while the kings who had come were by themselves in the field. **19:10** When Joab saw that the battle would be fought on two fronts, he chose some of Israel's best men and deployed them against the Arameans. **19:11** He put his brother Abishai in charge of the rest of the army and they were deployed against the Ammonites. **19:12** Joab said, "If the Arameans start to overpower me, you come to my rescue. If the Ammonites start to overpower you, I will come to your rescue. **19:13** Be strong! Let's fight bravely for the sake of our people and the cities of our God! The LORD will do what he decides is best!" **19:14** So Joab and his men marched toward the Arameans to do battle, and they fled before him. **19:15** When the Ammonites saw the Arameans flee, they fled before Joab's brother Abishai and withdrew into the city. Joab went back to Jerusalem.

19:16 When the Arameans realized they had been defeated by Israel, they sent for reinforcements from beyond the Euphrates River, led by Shophach the commanding general of Hadadezer's army. **19:17** When David was informed, he gathered all Israel, crossed the Jordan River, and marched against them. David deployed his army against the Arameans for battle and they fought against him. **19:18** The Arameans fled before Israel. David killed 7,000 Aramean charioteers and 40,000 infantrymen; he also killed Shophach the commanding general. **19:19** When Hadadezer's subjects saw they were defeated by Israel, they made peace with David and became his subjects. The Arameans were no longer willing to help the Ammonites.

20:1 In the spring, at the time when kings normally conduct wars, Joab led the army into battle and devastated the land of the Ammonites. He went and besieged Rabbah, while David stayed in Jerusalem. Joab defeated Rabbah and tore it down. **20:2** David took the crown from the head of their king and wore it (its weight was a talent of gold and it was set with precious stones). He took a large amount of plunder from the city. **20:3** He removed the city's residents and made them do hard labor with saws, iron picks, and axes. This was his policy with all the Ammonite cities. Then David and all the army returned to Jerusalem.

Battles with the Philistines

20:4 Later there was a battle with the Philistines in Gezer. At that time Sibbekai the Hushathite killed Sippai, one of the descendants of the Rephaim, and the Philistines were subdued.

20:5 There was another battle with the Philistines in which Elhanan son of Jair the Bethlehemite killed the brother of Goliath the Gittite, whose spear had a shaft as big as the crossbeam of a weaver's loom.

20:6 In a battle in Gath there was a large man who had six fingers on each hand and six toes on each foot – twenty-four in all! He too was a descendant of Rapha. **20:7** When he taunted Israel, Jonathan son of Shimea, David's brother, killed him.

20:8 These were the descendants of Rapha who lived in Gath; they were killed by the hand of David and his soldiers.

The Lord Sends a Plague against Israel

21:1 An adversary opposed Israel, inciting David to count how many warriors Israel had. **21:2** David told Joab and the leaders of the army, "Go, count the number of warriors from Beer Sheba to Dan. Then bring back a report to me so I may know how many we have." **21:3** Joab replied, "May the LORD make his army a hundred times larger! My master, O king, do not all of them serve my master? Why does my master want to do this? Why bring judgment on Israel?"

21:4 But the king's edict stood, despite Joab's objections. So Joab left and traveled throughout Israel before returning to Jerusalem. **21:5** Joab reported to David the number of warriors. In all Israel there were 1,100,000 sword-wielding soldiers; Judah alone had 470,000 sword-wielding soldiers. **21:6** Now Joab did not number Levi and Benjamin, for the king's edict disgusted him. **21:7** God was also offended by it, so he attacked Israel.

21:8 David said to God, "I have sinned greatly by doing this! Now, please remove the guilt of your servant, for I have acted very foolishly." **21:9** The LORD told Gad, David's prophet, **21:10** "Go, tell David, 'This is what the LORD says: "I am offering you three forms of judgment from which to choose. Pick one of them."'" **21:11** Gad went to David and told him, "This is what the LORD says: 'Pick one of these: **21:12** three years of famine, or three months being chased by your enemies and struck down by their swords, or three days being struck down by the LORD, during which a plague will invade the land and the LORD's messenger will destroy throughout Israel's territory.' Now, decide what I should tell the one who sent me." **21:13** David said to Gad, "I am very upset! I prefer to be attacked by the LORD, for his mercy is very great; I do not want to be attacked by men!" **21:14** So the LORD sent a plague through Israel, and 70,000 Israelite men died.

21:15 God sent an angel to ravage Jerusalem. As he was doing so, the LORD watched and relented from his judgment. He told the angel who was destroying, "That's enough! Stop now!"

Now the LORD's angel was standing near the threshing floor of Ornan the Jebusite. **21:16** David looked up and saw the LORD's messenger standing between the earth and sky with his sword drawn and in his hand, stretched out over Jerusalem. David and the leaders, covered with sackcloth, threw themselves down with their faces to the ground. **21:17** David said to God, "Was I not the one who decided to number the army? I am the one who sinned and committed this awful deed! As for these sheep – what have they done? O LORD my God, attack me and my family, but remove the plague from your people!"

21:18 So the LORD's messenger told Gad to instruct David to go up and build an altar for the LORD on the threshing floor of Ornan the Jebusite. **21:19** So David went up as Gad instructed him to do in the name of the LORD. **21:20** While Ornan was threshing wheat, he turned and saw the messenger, and he and his four sons hid themselves. **21:21** When David came to Ornan, Ornan looked and saw David; he came out from the threshing floor and bowed to David with his face to the ground. **21:22** David said to Ornan, "Sell me the threshing floor so I can build on it an altar for the LORD – I'll pay top price – so that the plague may be removed from the people." **21:23** Ornan told David, "You can have it! My master, the king, may do what he wants. Look, I am giving you the oxen for burnt sacrifices, the threshing sledges for wood, and the wheat for an offering. I give it all to you." **21:24** King David replied to Ornan, "No, I insist on buying it for top price. I will not offer to the LORD what belongs to you or offer a burnt sacrifice that cost me nothing. **21:25** So David bought the place from Ornan for 600 pieces of gold. **21:26** David built there an altar to the LORD and offered burnt sacrifices and peace offerings. He called out to the LORD, and the LORD responded by sending fire from the sky and consuming the burnt sacrifice on the altar. **21:27** The LORD ordered the messenger to put his sword back into its sheath.

21:28 At that time, when David saw that the LORD responded to him at the threshing floor of Ornan the Jebusite, he sacrificed there. **21:29** Now the LORD's tabernacle (which Moses had made in the wilderness) and the altar for burnt sacrifices were at that time at the worship center in Gibeon. **21:30** But David could not go before it to seek God's will, for he was afraid of the sword of the LORD's messenger. **22:1** David then said, "This is the place where the temple of the LORD God will be, along with the altar for burnt sacrifices for Israel."

David Orders a Temple to Be Built

22:2 David ordered the resident foreigners in the land of Israel to be called together. He appointed some of them to be stonecutters to chisel stones for the building of God's temple. **22:3** David supplied a large amount of iron for the nails of the doors of the gates and for braces, more bronze than could be weighed, **22:4** and more cedar logs than could be counted. (The Sidonians and Tyrians had brought a large amount of cedar logs to David.)

22:5 David said, "My son Solomon is just an inexperienced young man, and the temple to be built for the LORD must be especially magnificent so it will become famous and be considered splendid by all the nations. Therefore I will make preparations for its construction." So David made extensive preparations before he died.

22:6 He summoned his son Solomon and charged him to build a temple for the LORD God of Israel. **22:7** David said to Solomon: "My son, I really wanted to build a temple to honor the LORD my God. **22:8** But the LORD said to me: 'You have spilled a great deal of blood and fought many battles. You must not build a temple to honor me, for you have spilled a great deal of blood on the ground before me. **22:9** Look, you will have a son, who will be a peaceful man. I will give him rest from all his enemies on every side. Indeed, Solomon will be his name; I will give Israel peace and quiet during his reign. **22:10** He will build a temple to honor me; he will become my son, and I will become his father. I will grant to his dynasty permanent rule over Israel.'

22:11 "Now, my son, may the LORD be with you! May you succeed and build a temple for the LORD your God, just as he announced you would. **22:12** Only may the LORD give you insight and understanding when he places you in charge of Israel, so you may obey the law of the LORD your God. **22:13** Then you will succeed, if you carefully obey the rules and regulations which the LORD ordered Moses to give to Israel. Be strong and brave! Don't be afraid and don't panic! **22:14** Now, look, I have made every effort to supply what is needed to build the LORD's temple. I have stored up 100,000 talents of gold, 1,000,000 talents of silver, and so much bronze and iron it cannot be weighed, as well as wood and stones. Feel free to add more! **22:15** You also have available many workers, including stonecutters, masons, carpenters, and an innumerable array of workers who are skilled **22:16** in using gold, silver, bronze, and iron. Get up and begin the work! May the LORD be with you!"

22:17 David ordered all the officials of Israel to support his son Solomon. **22:18** He told them, "The LORD your God is with you! He has made you secure on every side, for he handed over to me the inhabitants of the region and the region is subdued before the LORD and his people. **22:19** Now seek the LORD your God wholeheartedly and with your entire being! Get up and build the sanctuary of the LORD God! Then you can bring the ark of the LORD's covenant and the holy items dedicated to God's service into the temple that is built to honor the LORD."

David Organizes the Levites

23:1 When David was old and approaching the end of his life, he made his son Solomon king over Israel.

23:2 David assembled all the leaders of Israel, along with the priests and the Levites. **23:3** The Levites who were thirty years old and up were counted; there were 38,000 men. **23:4** David said, "Of these, 24,000 are to direct the work of the LORD's temple; 6,000 are to be officials and judges; **23:5** 4,000 are to be gatekeepers; and 4,000 are to praise the LORD with the instruments I supplied for worship." **23:6** David divided them into groups corresponding to the sons of Levi: Gershon, Kohath, and Merari.

23:7 The Gershonites included Ladan and Shimei.

23:8 The sons of Ladan:

Jehiel the oldest, Zetham, and Joel – three in all.

23:9 The sons of Shimei:

Shelomoth, Haziel, and Haran – three in all.
These were the leaders of the family of Ladan.
23:10 The sons of Shimei:
Jahath, Zina, Jeush, and Beriah. These were Shimei's sons – four in all.
23:11 Jahath was the oldest and Zizah the second oldest. Jeush and Beriah did not have many sons, so they were considered one family with one responsibility.
23:12 The sons of Kohath:
Amram, Izhar, Hebron, and Uzziel – four in all.
23:13 The sons of Amram:
Aaron and Moses.
Aaron and his descendants were chosen on a permanent basis to consecrate the most holy items, to offer sacrifices before the LORD, to serve him, and to praise his name. **23:14** The descendants of Moses the man of God were considered Levites.
23:15 The sons of Moses:
Gershom and Eliezer.
23:16 The son of Gershom:
Shebuel the oldest.
23:17 The son of Eliezer was Rehabiah, the oldest. Eliezer had no other sons, but Rehabiah had many descendants.
23:18 The son of Izhar:
Shelomith the oldest.
23:19 The sons of Hebron:
Jeriah the oldest, Amariah the second, Jahaziel the third, and Jekameam the fourth.
23:20 The sons of Uzziel:
Micah the oldest, and Isshiah the second.
23:21 The sons of Merari:
Mahli and Mushi.
The sons of Mahli:
Eleazar and Kish.
23:22 Eleazar died without having sons; he had only daughters. The sons of Kish, their cousins, married them.
23:23 The sons of Mushi:
Mahli, Eder, and Jeremoth – three in all.
23:24 These were the descendants of Levi according to their families, that is, the leaders of families as counted and individually listed who carried out assigned tasks in the LORD's temple and were twenty years old and up. **23:25** For David said, "The LORD God of Israel has given his people rest and has permanently settled in Jerusalem. **23:26** So the Levites no longer need to carry the tabernacle or any of the items used in its service." **23:27** According to David's final instructions, the Levites twenty years old and up were counted.
23:28 Their job was to help Aaron's descendants in the service of the LORD's temple. They were to take care of the courtyards, the rooms, ceremonial purification of all holy items, and other jobs related to the service of God's temple. **23:29** They also took care of the bread that is displayed, the flour for offerings, the unleavened wafers, the round cakes, the mixing, and all the measuring. **23:30** They also stood in a designated place every morning and offered thanks and praise to the LORD. They also did this in the evening **23:31** and whenever burnt sacrifices were offered to the LORD on the Sabbath and at new moon festivals and assemblies. A designated number were to serve before the LORD regularly in accordance with regulations. **23:32** They were in charge of the meeting tent and the holy place, and helped their relatives, the descendants of Aaron, in the service of the LORD's temple.

David Organizes the Priests

24:1 The divisions of Aaron's descendants were as follows:
The sons of Aaron:
Nadab, Abihu, Eleazar, and Ithamar.
24:2 Nadab and Abihu died before their father did; they had no sons. Eleazar and Ithamar served as priests.
24:3 David, Zadok (a descendant of Eleazar), and Ahimelech (a descendant of Ithamar) divided them into groups to carry out their assigned responsibilities. **24:4** The descendants of Eleazar had more leaders than the descendants of Ithamar, so they divided them up accordingly; the descendants of Eleazar had sixteen leaders, while the descendants of Ithamar had eight. **24:5** They divided them by lots, for there were officials of the holy place and officials designated by God among the descendants of both Eleazar and Ithamar. **24:6** The scribe Shemaiah son of Nethanel, a Levite, wrote down their names before the king, the officials, Zadok the priest, Ahimelech son of Abiathar, and the leaders of the priestly and Levite families. One family was drawn by lot from Eleazar, and then the next from Ithamar.
24:7 The first lot went to Jehoiarib,
the second to Jedaiah,
24:8 the third to Harim,
the fourth to Seorim,
24:9 the fifth to Malkijah,
the sixth to Mijamin,
24:10 the seventh to Hakkoz,
the eighth to Abijah,

24:11 the ninth to Jeshua,
the tenth to Shecaniah,
24:12 the eleventh to Eliashib,
the twelfth to Jakim,
24:13 the thirteenth to Huppah,
the fourteenth to Jeshebeab,
24:14 the fifteenth to Bilgah,
the sixteenth to Immer,
24:15 the seventeenth to Hezir,
the eighteenth to Happizzez,
24:16 the nineteenth to Pethahiah,
the twentieth to Jehezkel,
24:17 the twenty-first to Jakin,
the twenty-second to Gamul,
24:18 the twenty-third to Delaiah,
the twenty-fourth to Maaziah.
24:19 This was the order in which they carried out their assigned responsibilities when they entered the LORD's temple, according to the regulations given them by their ancestor Aaron, just as the LORD God of Israel had instructed him.

Remaining Levites

24:20 The rest of the Levites included:
Shubael from the sons of Amram,
Jehdeiah from the sons of Shubael,
24:21 the firstborn Isshiah from Rehabiah and the sons of Rehabiah,
24:22 Shelomoth from the Izharites,
Jahath from the sons of Shelomoth.
24:23 The sons of Hebron:
Jeriah, Amariah the second, Jahaziel the third, and Jekameam the fourth.
24:24 The son of Uzziel:
Micah;
Shamir from the sons of Micah.
24:25 The brother of Micah:
Isshiah.
Zechariah from the sons of Isshiah.
24:26 The sons of Merari:
Mahli and Mushi.
The son of Jaaziah:
Beno.
24:27 The sons of Merari, from Jaaziah:
Beno, Shoham, Zaccur, and Ibri.
24:28 From Mahli:
Eleazar, who had no sons.
24:29 From Kish:
Jerahmeel.
24:30 The sons of Mushi:
Mahli, Eder, and Jerimoth.
These were the Levites, listed by their families.
24:31 Just like their relatives, the descendants of Aaron, they also cast lots before King David, Zadok, Ahimelech, the leaders of families, the priests, and the Levites. The families of the oldest son cast lots along with the those of the youngest.

David Organizes the Musicians

25:1 David and the army officers selected some of the sons of Asaph, Heman, and Jeduthun to prophesy as they played stringed instruments and cymbals. The following men were assigned this responsibility:
25:2 From the sons of Asaph: Zaccur, Joseph, Nethaniah, and Asarelah. The sons of Asaph were supervised by Asaph, who prophesied under the king's supervision.
25:3 From the sons of Jeduthun: Gedaliah, Zeri, Jeshaiah, Hashabiah, and Mattithiah – six in all, under supervision of their father Jeduthun, who prophesied as he played a harp, giving thanks and praise to the LORD.
25:4 From the sons of Heman: Bukkiah, Mattaniah, Uzziel, Shebuel, Jerimoth, Hananiah, Hanani, Eliathah, Giddalti, Romamti-Ezer, Joshbekashah, Mallothi, Hothir, and Mahazioth. **25:5** All these were the sons of Heman, the king's prophet. God had promised him these sons in order to make him prestigious. God gave Heman fourteen sons and three daughters.
25:6 All of these were under the supervision of their fathers; they were musicians in the LORD's temple, playing cymbals and stringed instruments as they served in God's temple. Asaph, Jeduthun, and Heman were under the supervision of the king. **25:7** They and their relatives, all of them skilled and trained to make music to the LORD, numbered two hundred eighty-eight.
25:8 They cast lots to determine their responsibilities – oldest as well as youngest, teacher as well as student.
25:9 The first lot went to Asaph's son Joseph and his relatives and sons – twelve in all,
the second to Gedaliah and his relatives and sons – twelve in all,
25:10 the third to Zaccur and his sons and relatives – twelve in all,
25:11 the fourth to Izri and his sons and relatives – twelve in all,
25:12 the fifth to Nethaniah and his sons and relatives – twelve in all,
25:13 the sixth to Bukkiah and his sons and relatives – twelve in all,

25:14 the seventh to Jesharelah and his sons and relatives – twelve in all,

25:15 the eighth to Jeshaiah and his sons and relatives – twelve in all,

25:16 the ninth to Mattaniah and his sons and relatives – twelve in all,

25:17 the tenth to Shimei and his sons and relatives – twelve in all,

25:18 the eleventh to Azarel and his sons and relatives – twelve in all,

25:19 the twelfth to Hashabiah and his sons and relatives – twelve in all,

25:20 the thirteenth to Shubael and his sons and relatives – twelve in all,

25:21 the fourteenth to Mattithiah and his sons and relatives – twelve in all,

25:22 the fifteenth to Jerimoth and his sons and relatives – twelve in all,

25:23 the sixteenth to Hananiah and his sons and relatives – twelve in all,

25:24 the seventeenth to Joshbekashah and his sons and relatives – twelve in all,

25:25 the eighteenth to Hanani and his sons and relatives – twelve in all,

25:26 the nineteenth to Mallothi and his sons and relatives – twelve in all,

25:27 the twentieth to Eliathah and his sons and relatives – twelve in all,

25:28 the twenty-first to Hothir and his sons and relatives – twelve in all,

25:29 the twenty-second to Giddalti and his sons and relatives – twelve in all,

25:30 the twenty-third to Mahazioth and his sons and relatives – twelve in all,

25:31 the twenty-fourth to Romamti-Ezer and his sons and relatives – twelve in all.

Divisions of Gatekeepers

26:1 The divisions of the gatekeepers:

From the Korahites: Meshelemiah, son of Kore, one of the sons of Asaph. **26:2** Meshelemiah's sons:

The firstborn Zechariah, the second Jediael, the third Zebadiah, the fourth Jathniel, **26:3** the fifth Elam, the sixth Jehohanan, and the seventh Elihoenai.

26:4 Obed-Edom's sons:

The firstborn Shemaiah, the second Jehozabad, the third Joah, the fourth Sakar, the fifth Nethanel, **26:5** the sixth Ammiel, the seventh Issachar, and the eighth Peullethai. (Indeed, God blessed Obed-Edom.)

26:6 His son Shemaiah also had sons, who were leaders of their families, for they were highly respected. **26:7** The sons of Shemaiah:

Othni, Rephael, Obed, and Elzabad. His relatives Elihu and Semakiah were also respected.

26:8 All these were the descendants of Obed-Edom. They and their sons and relatives were respected men, capable of doing their responsibilities. There were sixty-two of them related to Obed-Edom.

26:9 Meshelemiah had sons and relatives who were respected – eighteen in all.

26:10 Hosah, one of the descendants of Merari, had sons:

The firstborn Shimri (he was not actually the firstborn, but his father gave him that status), **26:11** the second Hilkiah, the third Tebaliah, and the fourth Zechariah. All of Hosah's sons and relatives numbered thirteen.

26:12 These divisions of the gatekeepers, corresponding to their leaders, had assigned responsibilities, like their relatives, as they served in the LORD's temple.

26:13 They cast lots, both young and old, according to their families, to determine which gate they would be responsible for. **26:14** The lot for the east gate went to Shelemiah. They then cast lots for his son Zechariah, a wise adviser, and the lot for the north gate went to him. **26:15** Obed-Edom was assigned the south gate, and his sons were assigned the storehouses. **26:16** Shuppim and Hosah were assigned the west gate, along with the Shalleketh gate on the upper road. One guard was adjacent to another. **26:17** Each day there were six Levites posted on the east, four on the north, and four on the south. At the storehouses they were posted in pairs. **26:18** At the court on the west there were four posted on the road and two at the court. **26:19** These were the divisions of the gatekeepers who were descendants of Korah and Merari.

Supervisors of the Storehouses

26:20 Their fellow Levites were in charge of the storehouses in God's temple and the storehouses containing consecrated items. **26:21** The descendants of Ladan, who were descended from Gershon through Ladan and were leaders of the families of Ladan the Gershonite, included Jehieli **26:22** and the sons of Jehieli, Zetham and his brother Joel. They were in charge of the storehouses in the LORD's temple.

26:23 As for the Amramites, Izharites, Hebronites, and Uzzielites:

26:24 Shebuel son of Gershom, the son of Moses, was the supervisor of the storehouses. **26:25** His relatives through Eliezer included: Rehabiah his son, Jeshaiah his son, Joram his son, Zikri his son, and Shelomith his son. **26:26** Shelomith and his relatives were in charge of all the storehouses containing the consecrated items dedicated by King David, the family leaders who led units of a thousand and a hundred, and the army officers. **26:27** They had dedicated some of the plunder taken in battles to be used for repairs on the LORD's temple. **26:28** They were also in charge of everything dedicated by Samuel the prophet, Saul son of Kish, Abner son of Ner, and Joab son of Zeruiah; Shelomith and his relatives were in charge of everything that had been dedicated.

26:29 As for the Izharites: Kenaniah and his sons were given responsibilities outside the temple as officers and judges over Israel.

26:30 As for the Hebronites: Hashabiah and his relatives, 1,700 respected men, were assigned responsibilities in Israel west of the Jordan; they did the LORD's work and the king's service.

26:31 As for the Hebronites: Jeriah was the leader of the Hebronites according to the genealogical records. In the fortieth year of David's reign, they examined the records and discovered there were highly respected men in Jazer in Gilead. **26:32** Jeriah had 2,700 relatives who were respected family leaders. King David placed them in charge of the Reubenites, the Gadites, and the half-tribe of Manasseh; they took care of all matters pertaining to God and the king.

Leaders of the Army

27:1 What follows is a list of Israelite family leaders and commanders of units of a thousand and a hundred, as well as their officers who served the king in various matters. Each division was assigned to serve for one month during the year; each consisted of 24,000 men.

27:2 Jashobeam son of Zabdiel was in charge of the first division, which was assigned the first month. His division consisted of 24,000 men. **27:3** He was a descendant of Perez; he was in charge of all the army officers for the first month.

27:4 Dodai the Ahohite was in charge of the division assigned the second month; Mikloth was the next in rank. His division consisted of 24,000 men.

27:5 The third army commander, assigned the third month, was Benaiah son of Jehoiada the priest. He was the leader of his division, which consisted of 24,000 men. **27:6** Benaiah was the leader of the thirty warriors and his division; his son was Ammizabad.

27:7 The fourth, assigned the fourth month, was Asahel, brother of Joab; his son Zebadiah succeeded him. His division consisted of 24,000 men.

27:8 The fifth, assigned the fifth month, was the commander Shamhuth the Izrahite. His division consisted of 24,000 men.

27:9 The sixth, assigned the sixth month, was Ira son of Ikkesh the Tekoite. His division consisted of 24,000 men.

27:10 The seventh, assigned the seventh month, was Helez the Pelonite, an Ephraimite. His division consisted of 24,000 men.

27:11 The eighth, assigned the eighth month, was Sibbekai the Hushathite, a Zerahite. His division consisted of 24,000 men.

27:12 The ninth, assigned the ninth month, was Abiezer the Anathothite, a Benjaminite. His division consisted of 24,000 men.

27:13 The tenth, assigned the tenth month, was Maharai the Netophathite, a Zerahite. His division consisted of 24,000 men.

27:14 The eleventh, assigned the eleventh month, was Benaiah the Pirathonite, an Ephraimite. His division consisted of 24,000 men.

27:15 The twelfth, assigned the twelfth month, was Heldai the Netophathite, a descendant of Othniel. His division consisted of 24,000 men.

27:16 The officers of the Israelite tribes:

Eliezer son of Zikri was the leader of the Reubenites,

Shephatiah son of Maacah led the Simeonites,

27:17 Hashabiah son of Kemuel led the Levites,

Zadok led the descendants of Aaron,

27:18 Elihu, a brother of David, led Judah,

Omri son of Michael led Issachar,

27:19 Ishmaiah son of Obadiah led Zebulun,

Jerimoth son of Azriel led Naphtali,

27:20 Hoshea son of Azaziah led the Ephraimites,

Joel son of Pedaiah led the half-tribe of Manasseh,

27:21 Iddo son of Zechariah led the half-tribe of Manasseh in Gilead,

Jaasiel son of Abner led Benjamin,

27:22 Azarel son of Jeroham led Dan.

These were the commanders of the Israelite tribes.

27:23 David did not count the males twenty years old and under, for the LORD had promised to make Israel as numerous as the stars in the sky. **27:24** Joab son of Zeruiah started to count the men but did not finish. God was angry with Israel because of this, so the number was not recorded in the scroll called The Annals of King David.

Royal Officials

27:25 Azmaveth son of Adiel was in charge of the king's storehouses;

Jonathan son of Uzziah was in charge of the storehouses in the field, in the cities, in the towns, and in the towers.

27:26 Ezri son of Kelub was in charge of the field workers who farmed the land.

27:27 Shimei the Ramathite was in charge of the vineyards;

Zabdi the Shiphmite was in charge of the wine stored in the vineyards.

27:28 Baal-Hanan the Gederite was in charge of the olive and sycamore trees in the lowlands;

Joash was in charge of the storehouses of olive oil.

27:29 Shitrai the Sharonite was in charge of the cattle grazing in Sharon;

Shaphat son of Adlai was in charge of the cattle in the valleys.

27:30 Obil the Ishmaelite was in charge of the camels;

Jehdeiah the Meronothite was in charge of the donkeys.

27:31 Jaziz the Hagrite was in charge of the sheep.

All these were the officials in charge of King David's property.

27:32 Jonathan, David's uncle, was a wise adviser and scribe;

Jehiel son of Hacmoni cared for the king's sons. **27:33** Ahithophel was the king's adviser; Hushai the Arkite was the king's confidant. **27:34** Ahithophel was succeeded by Jehoiada son of Benaiah and by Abiathar.

Joab was the commanding general of the king's army.

David Commissions Solomon to Build the Temple

28:1 David assembled in Jerusalem all the officials of Israel, including the commanders of the tribes, the commanders of the army divisions that served the king, the commanders of units of a thousand and a hundred, the officials who were in charge of all the property and livestock of the king and his sons, the eunuchs, and the warriors, including the most skilled of them. **28:2** King David rose to his feet and said: "Listen to me, my brothers and my people. I wanted to build a temple where the ark of the LORD's covenant could be placed as a footstool for our God. I have made the preparations for building it. **28:3** But God said to me, 'You must not build a temple to honor me, for you are a warrior and have spilled blood.' **28:4** The LORD God of Israel chose me out of my father's entire family to become king over Israel and have a permanent dynasty. Indeed, he chose Judah as leader, and my father's family within Judah, and then he picked me out from among my father's sons and made me king over all Israel. **28:5** From all the many sons the LORD has given me, he chose Solomon my son to rule on his behalf over Israel. **28:6** He said to me, 'Solomon your son is the one who will build my temple and my courts, for I have chosen him to become my son and I will become his father. **28:7** I will establish his kingdom permanently, if he remains committed to obeying my commands and regulations, as you are doing this day.' **28:8** So now, in the sight of all Israel, the LORD's assembly, and in the hearing of our God, I say this: Carefully observe all the commands of the LORD your God, so that you may possess this good land and may leave it as a permanent inheritance for your children after you.

28:9 "And you, Solomon my son, obey the God of your father and serve him with a submissive attitude and a willing spirit, for the LORD examines all minds and understands every motive of one's thoughts. If you seek him, he will let you find him, but if you abandon him, he will reject you permanently. **28:10** Realize now that the LORD has chosen you to build a temple as his sanctuary. Be strong and do it!"

28:11 David gave to his son Solomon the blueprints for the temple porch, its buildings, its treasuries, its upper areas, its inner rooms, and the room for atonement. **28:12** He gave him the blueprints of all he envisioned for the courts of the LORD's temple, all the surrounding rooms, the storehouses of God's temple, and the storehouses for the holy items. **28:13** He gave him the regulations for the divisions of priests and Levites, for all the assigned responsibilities within the LORD's temple, and for all the items used in the service of the LORD's temple. **28:14** He gave him the prescribed weight for all the gold items to be used in various types of service in the LORD's temple, for all the silver items to be used in various types of service, **28:15** for the gold lampstands and their gold lamps, including the weight of each lampstand and its lamps, for the silver lampstands, including the weight of each lampstand and its lamps, according to the prescribed use of each lampstand, **28:16** for the gold used in the display tables, including the amount to be used in each table, for the silver to be used in the silver tables, **28:17** for the pure gold used for the meat forks, bowls, and jars, for the small gold bowls, including the weight for each bowl, for the small silver bowls, including the weight for each bowl, **28:18** and for the refined gold of the incense altar.

He gave him the blueprint for the seat of the gold cherubim that spread their wings and provide shelter for the ark of the LORD's covenant. **28:19** David said, "All of this I put in writing as the LORD directed me and gave me insight regarding the details of the blueprints."

28:20 David said to his son Solomon: "Be strong and brave! Do it! Don't be afraid and don't panic! For the LORD God, my God, is with you. He will not leave you or abandon you before all the work for the service of the LORD's temple is finished. **28:21** Here are the divisions of the priests and Levites who will perform all the service of God's temple. All the willing and skilled men are ready to assist you in all the work and perform their service. The officials and all the people are ready to follow your instructions."

The People Contribute to the Project

29:1 King David said to the entire assembly: "My son Solomon, the one whom God has chosen, is just an inexperienced young man, and the task is great, for this palace is not for man, but for the LORD God. **29:2** So I have made every effort to provide what is needed for the temple of my God, including the gold, silver, bronze, iron, wood, as well as a large amount of onyx, settings of antimony and other stones, all kinds of precious stones, and alabaster. **29:3** Now, to show my commitment to the temple of my God, I donate my personal treasure of gold and silver to the temple of my God, in addition to all that I have already supplied for this holy temple. **29:4** This includes 3,000 talents of gold from Ophir and 7,000 talents of refined silver for overlaying the walls of the buildings, **29:5** for gold and silver items, and for all the work of the craftsmen. Who else wants to contribute to the LORD today?"

29:6 The leaders of the families, the leaders of the Israelite tribes, the commanders of units of a thousand and a hundred, and the supervisors of the king's work contributed willingly. **29:7** They donated for the service of God's temple 5,000 talents and ten thousand darics of gold, 10,000 talents of silver, 18,000 talents of bronze, and 100,000 talents of iron. **29:8** All who possessed precious stones donated them to the treasury of the LORD's temple, which was under the supervision of Jehiel the Gershonite. **29:9** The people were delighted with their donations, for they contributed to the LORD with a willing attitude; King David was also very happy.

David Praises the Lord

29:10 David praised the LORD before the entire assembly:

"O LORD God of our father Israel, you deserve praise forevermore! **29:11** O LORD, you are great, mighty, majestic, magnificent, glorious, and sovereign over all the sky and earth! You have dominion and exalt yourself as the ruler of all. **29:12** You are the source of wealth and honor; you rule over all. You possess strength and might to magnify and give strength to all. **29:13** Now, our God, we give thanks to you and praise your majestic name!

29:14 "But who am I and who are my people, that we should be in a position to contribute this much? Indeed, everything comes from you, and we have simply given back to you what is yours. **29:15** For we are resident foreigners and nomads in your presence, like all our ancestors; our days are like a shadow on the earth, without security. **29:16** O LORD our God, all this wealth, which we have collected to build a temple for you to honor your holy name, comes from you; it all belongs to you. **29:17** I know, my God, that you examine thoughts and are pleased with integrity. With pure motives I contribute all this; and now I look with joy as your people who have gathered here contribute to you. **29:18** O LORD God of our ancestors Abraham, Isaac, and Israel, maintain the motives of your people and keep them devoted to you. **29:19** Make my son Solomon willing to obey your commands, rules, and regulations, and to complete building the palace for which I have made preparations."

29:20 David told the entire assembly: "Praise the LORD your God!" So the entire assembly praised the LORD God of their ancestors; they bowed down and stretched out flat on the ground before the LORD and the king.

David Designates Solomon King

29:21 The next day they made sacrifices and offered burnt sacrifices to the LORD (1,000 bulls, 1,000 rams, 1,000 lambs), along with their accompanying drink offerings and many other sacrifices for all Israel. **29:22** They held a feast before the LORD that day and celebrated.

Then they designated Solomon, David's son, as king a second time; before the LORD they anointed him as ruler and Zadok as priest. **29:23** Solomon sat on the LORD's throne as king in place of his father David; he was successful and all Israel was loyal to him. **29:24** All the officers and warriors, as well as all of King David's sons, pledged their allegiance to King Solomon. **29:25** The LORD greatly magnified Solomon before all Israel and bestowed on him greater majesty than any king of Israel before him.

David's Reign Comes to an End

29:26 David son of Jesse reigned over all Israel. **29:27** He reigned over Israel forty years; he reigned in Hebron seven years and in Jerusalem thirty-three years. **29:28** He died at a good old age, having enjoyed long life, wealth, and honor. His son Solomon succeeded him. **29:29** King David's accomplishments, from start to finish, are recorded in the Annals of Samuel the prophet, the Annals of Nathan the prophet, and the Annals of Gad the prophet. **29:30** Recorded there are all the facts about his reign and accomplishments, and an account of the events that involved him, Israel, and all the neighboring kingdoms.

Book 14. 2 Chronicles

The Lord Gives Solomon Wisdom

1:1 Solomon son of David solidified his royal authority, for the LORD his God was with him and magnified him greatly.

1:2 Solomon addressed all Israel, including those who commanded units of a thousand and a hundred, the judges, and all the leaders of all Israel who were heads of families. **1:3** Solomon and the entire assembly went to the worship center in Gibeon, for the tent where they met God was located there, which Moses the LORD's servant had made in the wilderness. **1:4** (Now David had brought up the ark of God from Kiriath Jearim to the place he had prepared for it, for he had pitched a tent for it in Jerusalem. **1:5** But the bronze altar made by Bezalel son of Uri, son of Hur, was in front of the LORD's tabernacle. Solomon and the entire assembly prayed to him there.) **1:6** Solomon went up to the bronze altar before the LORD which was at the meeting tent, and he offered up a thousand burnt sacrifices.

1:7 That night God appeared to Solomon and said to him, "Tell me what I should give you." **1:8** Solomon replied to God, "You demonstrated great loyalty to my father David and have made me king in his place. **1:9** Now, LORD God, may your promise to my father David be realized, for you have made me king over a great nation as numerous as the dust of the earth. **1:10** Now give me wisdom and discernment so I can effectively lead this nation. Otherwise no one is able to make judicial decisions for this great nation of yours."

1:11 God said to Solomon, "Because you desire this, and did not ask for riches, wealth, and honor, or for vengeance on your enemies, and because you did not ask for long life, but requested wisdom and discernment so you can make judicial decisions for my people over whom I have made you king, **1:12** you are granted wisdom and discernment. Furthermore I am giving you riches, wealth, and honor surpassing that of any king before or after you."

1:13 Solomon left the meeting tent at the worship center in Gibeon and went to Jerusalem, where he reigned over Israel.

Solomon's Wealth

1:14 Solomon accumulated chariots and horses. He had 1,400 chariots and 12,000 horses. He kept them in assigned cities and in Jerusalem. **1:15** The king made silver and gold as plentiful in Jerusalem as stones; cedar was as plentiful as sycamore fig trees are in the lowlands. **1:16** Solomon acquired his horses from Egypt and from Que; the king's traders purchased them from Que. **1:17** They paid 600 silver pieces for each chariot from Egypt, and 150 silver pieces for each horse. They also sold chariots and horses to all the kings of the Hittites and to the kings of Syria.

Solomon Gathers Building Materials for the Temple

2:1 (1:18) Solomon ordered a temple to be built to honor the LORD, as well as a royal palace for himself. **2:2** (2:1) Solomon had 70,000 common laborers and 80,000 stonecutters in the hills, in addition to 3,600 supervisors.

2:3 Solomon sent a message to King Huram of Tyre: "Help me as you did my father David, when you sent him cedar logs for the construction of his palace. **2:4** Look, I am ready to build a temple to honor the LORD my God and to dedicate it to him in order to burn fragrant incense before him, to set out the bread that is regularly displayed, and to offer burnt sacrifices each morning and evening, and on Sabbaths, new moon festivals, and at other times appointed by the LORD our God. This is something Israel must do on a permanent basis. **2:5** I will build a great temple, for our God is greater than all gods. **2:6** Of course, who can really build a temple for him, since the sky and the highest heavens cannot contain him? Who am I that I should build him a temple! It will really be only a place to offer sacrifices before him.

2:7 "Now send me a man who is skilled in working with gold, silver, bronze, and iron, as well as purple, crimson, and violet colored fabrics, and who knows how to engrave. He will work with my skilled craftsmen here in Jerusalem and Judah, whom my father David provided. **2:8** Send me cedars, evergreens, and algum trees from Lebanon, for I know your servants are adept at cutting down trees in Lebanon. My servants will work with your servants **2:9** to supply me with large quantities of timber, for I am building a great, magnificent temple. **2:10** Look, I will pay your servants who cut the timber 20,000 kors of ground wheat, 20,000 kors of barley, 120,000 gallons of wine, and 120,000 gallons of olive oil."

2:11 King Huram of Tyre sent this letter to Solomon: "Because the LORD loves his people, he has made you their king." **2:12** Huram also said, "Worthy of praise is the LORD God of Israel, who made the sky and the earth! He has given David a wise son who has discernment and insight and will build a temple for the LORD, as well as a royal palace for himself. **2:13** Now I am sending you Huram Abi, a skilled and capable man, **2:14** whose mother is a Danite and whose father is a Tyrian. He knows how to work with gold, silver, bronze, iron, stones, and wood, as well as purple, violet, white, and crimson fabrics. He knows how to do all kinds of engraving and understands any design given to him. He will work with your skilled craftsmen and the skilled craftsmen of my lord David your father. **2:15** Now let my lord send to his servants the wheat, barley, olive oil, and wine he has promised; **2:16** we will get all the timber you need from Lebanon and bring it in raft-like bundles by sea to Joppa. You can then haul it on up to Jerusalem."

2:17 Solomon took a census of all the male resident foreigners in the land of Israel, after the census his father David had taken. There were 153,600 in all. **2:18** He designated 70,000 as common laborers, 80,000 as stonecutters in the hills, and 3,600 as supervisors to make sure the people completed the work.

The Building of the Temple

3:1 Solomon began building the LORD's temple in Jerusalem on Mount Moriah, where the LORD had appeared to his father David. This was the place that David prepared at the threshing floor of Ornan the Jebusite. **3:2** He began building on the second day of the second month of the fourth year of his reign.

3:3 Solomon laid the foundation for God's temple; its length (determined according to the old standard of measure) was 90 feet, and its width 30 feet. **3:4** The porch in front of the main hall was 30 feet long, corresponding to the width of the temple, and its height was 30 feet. He plated the inside with pure gold. **3:5** He paneled the main hall with boards made from evergreen trees and plated it with fine gold, decorated with palm trees and chains. **3:6** He decorated the temple with precious stones; the gold he used came from Parvaim. **3:7** He overlaid the temple's rafters, thresholds, walls and doors with gold; he carved decorative cherubim on the walls.

3:8 He made the most holy place; its length was 30 feet, corresponding to the width of the temple, and its width 30 feet. He plated it with 600 talents of fine gold. **3:9** The gold nails weighed 50 shekels; he also plated the upper areas with gold. **3:10** In the most holy place he made two images of cherubim and plated them with gold. **3:11** The combined wing span of the cherubs was 30 feet. One of the first cherub's wings was seven and one-half feet long and touched one wall of the temple; its other wing was also seven and one-half feet long and touched one of the second cherub's wings. **3:12** Likewise one of the second cherub's wings was seven and one-half feet long and touched the other wall of the temple; its other wing was also seven and one-half feet long and touched one of the first cherub's wings. **3:13** The combined wingspan of these cherubim was 30 feet. They stood upright, facing inward. **3:14** He made the curtain out of violet, purple, crimson, and white fabrics, and embroidered on it decorative cherubim.

3:15 In front of the temple he made two pillars which had a combined length of 52½ feet, with each having a plated capital seven and one-half feet high. **3:16** He made ornamental chains and put them on top of the pillars. He also made one hundred pomegranate-shaped ornaments and arranged them within the chains. **3:17** He set up the pillars in front of the temple, one on the right side and the other on the left. He named the one on the right Jachin, and the one on the left Boaz.

4:1 He made a bronze altar, 30 feet long, 30 feet wide, and 15 feet high. **4:2** He also made the big bronze basin called "The Sea." It measured 15 feet from rim to rim, was circular in shape, and stood seven and one-half feet high. Its circumference was 45 feet. **4:3** Images of bulls were under it all the way around, ten every eighteen inches all the way around. The bulls were in two rows and had been cast with "The Sea." **4:4** "The Sea" stood on top of twelve bulls. Three faced northward, three westward, three southward, and three eastward. "The Sea" was placed on top of them, and they all faced outward. **4:5** It was four fingers thick and its rim was like that of a cup shaped like a lily blossom. It could hold 18,000 gallons. **4:6** He made ten washing basins; he put five on the south side and five on the north side. In them they rinsed the items used for burnt sacrifices; the priests washed in "The Sea."

4:7 He made ten gold lampstands according to specifications and put them in the temple, five on the right and five on the left. **4:8** He made ten tables and set them in the temple, five on the right and five on the left. He also made one hundred gold bowls. **4:9** He made the courtyard of the priests and the large enclosure and its doors; he plated their doors with bronze. **4:10** He put "The Sea" on the south side, in the southeast corner.

4:11 Huram Abi made the pots, shovels, and bowls. He finished all the work on God's temple he had been assigned by King Solomon. **4:12** He made the two pillars, the two bowl-shaped tops of the pillars, the latticework for the bowl-shaped tops of the two pillars, **4:13** the four hundred pomegranate-shaped ornaments for the latticework of the two pillars (each latticework had two rows of these ornaments at the bowl-shaped top of the pillar), **4:14** the ten movable stands with their ten basins, **4:15** the big bronze basin called "The Sea" with its twelve bulls underneath, **4:16** and the pots, shovels, and meat forks. All the items King Solomon assigned Huram Abi to make for the LORD's temple were made from polished bronze. **4:17** The king had them cast in earthen foundries in the region of the Jordan between Succoth and Zarethan. **4:18** Solomon made so many of these items they did not weigh the bronze.

4:19 Solomon also made these items for God's temple: the gold altar, the tables on which the Bread of the Presence was kept, **4:20** the pure gold lampstands and their lamps which burned as specified at the entrance to the inner sanctuary, **4:21** the pure gold flower-shaped ornaments, lamps, and tongs, **4:22** the pure gold trimming shears, basins, pans, and censers, and the gold door sockets for the inner sanctuary (the most holy place) and for the doors of the main hall of the temple. **5:1** When Solomon had finished constructing the LORD's temple, he put the holy items that belonged to his father David (the silver, gold, and all the other articles) in the treasuries of God's temple.

Solomon Moves the Ark into the Temple

5:2 Then Solomon convened Israel's elders – all the leaders of the Israelite tribes and families – in Jerusalem, so they could witness the transferal of the ark of the covenant of the LORD from the City of David (that is, Zion). **5:3** All the men of Israel assembled before the king during the festival in the seventh month. **5:4** When all Israel's elders had arrived, the Levites lifted the ark. **5:5** The priests and Levites carried the ark, the tent where God appeared to his people, and all the holy items in the tent. **5:6** Now King Solomon and all the Israelites who had assembled with him went on ahead of the ark and sacrificed more sheep and cattle than could be counted or numbered.

5:7 The priests brought the ark of the covenant of the LORD to its assigned place in the inner sanctuary of the temple, in the most holy place under the wings of the cherubs. **5:8** The cherubs' wings extended over the place where the ark sat; the cherubs overshadowed the ark and its poles. **5:9** The poles were so long their ends extending out from the ark were visible from in front of the inner sanctuary, but they could not be seen from beyond that point. They have remained there to this very day. **5:10** There was nothing in the ark except the two tablets Moses had placed there in Horeb. (It was there that the LORD made an agreement with the Israelites after he brought them out of the land of Egypt.) **5:11** The priests left the holy place. All the priests who participated had consecrated themselves, no matter which division they represented. **5:12** All the Levites who were musicians, including Asaph, Heman, Jeduthun, and their sons and relatives, wore linen. They played cymbals and stringed instruments as they stood east of the altar. They were accompanied by 120 priests who blew trumpets. **5:13** The trumpeters and musicians played together, praising and giving thanks to the LORD. Accompanied by trumpets, cymbals, and other instruments, they loudly praised the LORD, singing: "Certainly he is good; certainly his loyal love endures!" Then a cloud filled the LORD's temple. **5:14** The priests could not carry out their duties because of the cloud; the LORD's splendor filled God's temple.

6:1 Then Solomon said, "The LORD has said that he lives in thick darkness. **6:2** O LORD, I have built a lofty temple for you, a place where you can live permanently." **6:3** Then the king turned around and pronounced a blessing over the whole Israelite assembly as they stood there. **6:4** He said, "The LORD God of Israel is worthy of praise because he has fulfilled what he promised my father David. **6:5** He told David, 'Since the day I brought my people out of the land of Egypt, I have not chosen a city from all the tribes of Israel to build a temple in which to live. Nor did I choose a man as leader of my people Israel. **6:6** But now I have chosen Jerusalem as a place to live, and I have chosen David to lead my people Israel.' **6:7** Now my father David had a strong desire to build a temple to honor the LORD God of Israel. **6:8** The LORD told my father David, 'It is right for you to have a strong desire to build a temple to honor me. **6:9** But you will not build the temple; your very own son will build the temple for my honor.' **6:10** The LORD has kept the promise he made. I have taken my father David's place and have occupied the throne of Israel, as the LORD promised. I have built this temple for the honor of the LORD God of Israel **6:11** and set up in it a place for the ark containing the covenant the LORD made with the Israelites."

6:12 He stood before the altar of the LORD in front of the entire assembly of Israel and spread out his hands. **6:13** Solomon had made a bronze platform and had placed it in the middle of the enclosure. It was seven and one-half feet long, seven and one-half feet wide, and four and one-half feet high. He stood on it and then got down on his knees in front of the entire assembly of Israel. He spread out his hands toward the sky, **6:14** and prayed: "O LORD God of Israel, there is no god like you in heaven or on earth! You maintain covenantal loyalty to your servants who obey you with sincerity. **6:15** You have kept your word to your servant, my father David; this very day you have fulfilled what you promised. **6:16** Now, O LORD God of Israel, keep the promise you made to your servant, my father David, when you said, 'You will never fail to have a successor ruling before me on the throne of Israel, provided that your descendants watch their step and obey my law as you have done.' **6:17** Now, O LORD God of Israel, may the promise you made to your servant David be realized.

6:18 "God does not really live with humankind on the earth! Look, if the sky and the highest heaven cannot contain you, how much less this temple I have built! **6:19** But respond favorably to your servant's prayer and his request for help, O LORD my God. Answer the desperate prayer your servant is presenting to you. **6:20** Night and day may you watch over this temple, the place where you promised you would live. May you answer your servant's prayer for this place. **6:21** Respond to the requests of your servant and your people Israel for this place. Hear from your heavenly dwelling place and respond favorably and forgive.

6:22 "When someone is accused of sinning against his neighbor and the latter pronounces a curse on the alleged offender before your altar in this temple, **6:23** listen from heaven and make a just decision about your servants' claims. Condemn the guilty party, declare the other innocent, and give both of them what they deserve.

6:24 "If your people Israel are defeated by an enemy because they sinned against you, then if they come back to you, renew their allegiance to you, and pray for your help before you in this temple, **6:25** then listen from heaven, forgive the sin of your people Israel, and bring them back to the land you gave to them and their ancestors.

6:26 "The time will come when the skies are shut up tightly and no rain falls because your people sinned against you. When they direct their prayers toward this place, renew their allegiance to you, and turn away from their sin because you punish them, **6:27** then listen from heaven and forgive the sin of your servants, your people Israel. Certainly you will then teach them the right way to live and send rain on your land that you have given your people to possess.

6:28 "The time will come when the land suffers from a famine, a plague, blight, and disease, or a locust invasion, or when their enemy lays siege to the cities of the land, or when some other type of plague or epidemic occurs. **6:29** When all your people Israel pray and ask for help, as they acknowledge their intense pain and spread out their hands toward this temple, **6:30** then listen from your heavenly dwelling place, forgive their sin, and act favorably toward each one based on your evaluation of their motives. (Indeed you are the only one who can correctly evaluate the motives of all people.) **6:31** Then they will honor you by obeying you throughout their lifetimes as they live on the land you gave to our ancestors.

6:32 "Foreigners, who do not belong to your people Israel, will come from a distant land because of your great reputation and your ability to accomplish mighty deeds; they will come and direct their prayers toward this temple. **6:33** Then listen from your heavenly dwelling place and answer all the prayers of the foreigners. Then all the nations of the earth will acknowledge your reputation, obey you like your people Israel do, and recognize that this temple I built belongs to you.

6:34 "When you direct your people to march out and fight their enemies, and they direct their prayers to you toward this chosen city and this temple I built for your honor, **6:35** then listen from heaven to their prayers for help and vindicate them.

6:36 "The time will come when your people will sin against you (for there is no one who is sinless!) and you will be angry at them and deliver them over to their enemies, who will take them as prisoners to their land, whether far away or close by. **6:37** When your people come to their senses in the land where they are held prisoner, they will repent and beg for your mercy in the land of their imprisonment, admitting, 'We have sinned and gone astray, we have done evil!' **6:38** When they return to you with all their heart and being in the land where they are held prisoner and direct their prayers toward the land you gave to their ancestors, your chosen city, and the temple I built for your honor, **6:39** then listen from your heavenly dwelling place to their prayers for help, vindicate them, and forgive your sinful people.

6:40 "Now, my God, may you be attentive and responsive to the prayers offered in this place. **6:41** Now ascend, O LORD God, to your resting place, you and the ark of your strength! May your priests, O LORD God, experience your deliverance! May your loyal followers rejoice in the prosperity you give! **6:42** O LORD God, do not reject your chosen ones! Remember the faithful promises you made to your servant David!"

Solomon Dedicates the Temple

7:1 When Solomon finished praying, fire came down from heaven and consumed the burnt offering and the sacrifices, and the LORD's splendor filled the temple. **7:2** The priests were unable to enter the LORD's temple because the LORD's splendor filled the LORD's temple. **7:3** When all the Israelites saw the fire come down and the LORD's splendor over the temple, they got on their knees with their faces downward toward the pavement. They worshiped and gave thanks to the LORD, saying, "Certainly he is good; certainly his loyal love endures!"

7:4 The king and all the people were presenting sacrifices to the LORD. **7:5** King Solomon sacrificed 22,000 cattle and 120,000 sheep. Then the king and all the people dedicated God's temple. **7:6** The priests stood in their assigned spots, along with the Levites who had the musical instruments used for praising the LORD. (These were the ones King David made for giving thanks to the LORD and which were used by David when he offered praise, saying, "Certainly his loyal love endures.") Opposite the Levites, the priests were blowing the trumpets, while all Israel stood there. **7:7** Solomon consecrated the middle of the courtyard that is in front of the LORD's temple. He offered burnt sacrifices, grain offerings, and the fat from the peace offerings there, because the bronze altar that Solomon had made was too small to hold all these offerings. **7:8** At that time Solomon and all Israel with him celebrated a festival for seven days. This great assembly included people from Lebo Hamath in the north to the Brook of Egypt in the south. **7:9** On the eighth day they held an assembly, for they had dedicated the altar for seven days and celebrated the festival for seven more days. **7:10** On the twenty-third day of the seventh month, Solomon sent the people home. They left happy and contented because of the good the LORD had done for David, Solomon, and his people Israel.

The Lord Gives Solomon a Promise and a Warning

7:11 After Solomon finished building the LORD's temple and the royal palace, and accomplished all his plans for the LORD's temple and his royal palace, **7:12** the LORD appeared to Solomon at night and said to him: "I have answered your prayer and chosen this place to be my temple where sacrifices are to be made. **7:13** When I close up the sky so that it doesn't rain, or command locusts to devour the land's vegetation, or send a plague among my people, **7:14** if my people, who belong to me, humble themselves, pray, seek to please me, and repudiate their sinful practices, then I will respond from heaven, forgive their sin, and heal their land. **7:15** Now I will be attentive and responsive to the prayers offered in this place. **7:16** Now I have chosen and consecrated this temple by making it my permanent home; I will be constantly present there. **7:17** You must serve me as your father David did. Do everything I commanded and obey my rules and regulations. **7:18** Then I will establish your dynasty, just as I promised your father David, 'You will not fail to have a successor ruling over Israel.'

7:19 "But if you people ever turn away from me, fail to obey the regulations and rules I instructed you to keep, and decide to serve and worship other gods, **7:20** then I will remove you from my land I have given you, I will abandon this temple I have consecrated with my presence, and I will make you an object of mockery and ridicule among all the nations. **7:21**

As for this temple, which was once majestic, everyone who passes by it will be shocked and say, 'Why did the LORD do this to this land and this temple?' **7:22** Others will then answer, 'Because they abandoned the LORD God of their ancestors, who led them out of Egypt. They embraced other gods whom they worshiped and served. That is why he brought all this disaster down on them.'"

Building Projects and Commercial Efforts

8:1 After twenty years, during which Solomon built the LORD's temple and his royal palace, **8:2** Solomon rebuilt the cities that Huram had given him and settled Israelites there. **8:3** Solomon went to Hamath Zobah and seized it. **8:4** He built up Tadmor in the wilderness and all the storage cities he had built in Hamath. **8:5** He made upper Beth Horon and lower Beth Horon fortified cities with walls and barred gates, **8:6** and built up Baalath, all the storage cities that belonged to him, and all the cities where chariots and horses were kept. He built whatever he wanted in Jerusalem, Lebanon, and throughout his entire kingdom.

8:7 Now several non-Israelite peoples were left in the land after the conquest of Joshua, including the Hittites, Amorites, Perizzites, Hivites, and Jebusites. **8:8** Their descendants remained in the land (the Israelites were unable to wipe them out). Solomon conscripted them for his work crews and they continue in that role to this very day. **8:9** Solomon did not assign Israelites to these work crews; the Israelites served as his soldiers, officers, charioteers, and commanders of his chariot forces. **8:10** These men worked for Solomon as supervisors; there were a total of 250 of them who were in charge of the people.

8:11 Solomon moved Pharaoh's daughter up from the City of David to the palace he had built for her, for he said, "My wife must not live in the palace of King David of Israel, for the places where the ark of the LORD has entered are holy."

8:12 Then Solomon offered burnt sacrifices to the LORD on the altar of the LORD which he had built in front of the temple's porch. **8:13** He observed the daily requirements for sacrifices that Moses had specified for Sabbaths, new moon festivals, and the three annual celebrations – the Feast of Unleavened Bread, the Feast of Weeks, and the Feast of Temporary Shelters. **8:14** As his father David had decreed, Solomon appointed the divisions of the priests to do their assigned tasks, the Levitical orders to lead worship and help the priests with their daily tasks, and the divisions of the gatekeepers to serve at their assigned gates. This was what David the man of God had ordered. **8:15** They did not neglect any detail of the king's orders pertaining to the priests, Levites, and treasuries.

8:16 All the work ordered by Solomon was completed, from the day the foundation of the LORD's temple was laid until it was finished; the LORD's temple was completed.

8:17 Then Solomon went to Ezion Geber and to Elat on the coast in the land of Edom. **8:18** Huram sent him ships and some of his sailors, men who were well acquainted with the sea. They sailed with Solomon's men to Ophir, and took from there 450 talents of gold, which they brought back to King Solomon.

Solomon Entertains a Queen

9:1 When the queen of Sheba heard about Solomon, she came to challenge him with difficult questions. She arrived in Jerusalem with a great display of pomp, bringing with her camels carrying spices, a very large quantity of gold, and precious gems. She visited Solomon and discussed with him everything that was on her mind. **9:2** Solomon answered all her questions; there was no question too complex for the king. **9:3** When the queen of Sheba saw for herself Solomon's extensive wisdom, the palace he had built, **9:4** the food in his banquet hall, his servants and attendants in their robes, his cupbearers in their robes, and his burnt sacrifices which he presented in the LORD's temple, she was amazed. **9:5** She said to the king, "The report I heard in my own country about your wise sayings and insight was true! **9:6** I did not believe these things until I came and saw them with my own eyes. Indeed, I didn't hear even half the story! Your wisdom surpasses what was reported to me. **9:7** Your attendants, who stand before you at all times and hear your wise sayings, are truly happy! **9:8** May the LORD your God be praised because he favored you by placing you on his throne as the one ruling on his behalf! Because of your God's love for Israel and his lasting commitment to them, he made you king over them so you could make just and right decisions." **9:9** She gave the king 120 talents of gold and a very large quantity of spices and precious gems. The quantity of spices the queen of Sheba gave King Solomon has never been matched. **9:10** (Huram's servants, aided by Solomon's servants, brought gold from Ophir, as well as fine timber and precious gems. **9:11** With the timber the king made steps for the LORD's temple and royal palace as well as stringed instruments for the musicians. No one had seen anything like them in the land of Judah prior to that.) **9:12** King Solomon gave the queen of Sheba everything she requested, more than what she had brought him. Then she left and returned to her homeland with her attendants.

Solomon's Wealth

9:13 Solomon received 666 talents of gold per year, **9:14** besides what he collected from the merchants and traders. All the Arabian kings and the governors of the land also brought gold and silver to Solomon. **9:15** King Solomon made two hundred large shields of hammered gold; 600 measures of hammered gold were used for each shield. **9:16** He also made three hundred small shields of hammered gold; 300 measures of gold were used for each of those shields. The king placed them in the Palace of the Lebanon Forest.

9:17 The king made a large throne decorated with ivory and overlaid it with pure gold. **9:18** There were six steps leading up to the throne, and a gold footstool was attached to the throne. The throne had two armrests with a statue of a lion standing on each side. **9:19** There were twelve statues of lions on the six steps, one lion at each end of each step. There was nothing like it in any other kingdom.

9:20 All of King Solomon's cups were made of gold, and all the household items in the Palace of the Lebanon Forest were made of pure gold. There were no silver items, for silver was not considered very valuable in Solomon's time. **9:21** The king had a fleet of large merchant ships manned by Huram's men that sailed the sea. Once every three years the fleet came into port with cargoes of gold, silver, ivory, apes, and peacocks.

9:22 King Solomon was wealthier and wiser than any of the kings of the earth. **9:23** All the kings of the earth wanted to visit Solomon to see him display his God-given wisdom. **9:24** Year after year visitors brought their gifts, which included items of silver, items of gold, clothes, perfume, spices, horses, and mules.

9:25 Solomon had 4,000 stalls for his chariot horses and 12,000 horses. He kept them in assigned cities and in Jerusalem. **9:26** He ruled all the kingdoms from the Euphrates River to the land of the Philistines as far as the border of Egypt. **9:27** The king made silver as plentiful in Jerusalem as stones; cedar was as plentiful as sycamore fig trees are in the lowlands. **9:28** Solomon acquired horses from Egypt and from all the lands.

Solomon's Reign Ends

9:29 The rest of the events of Solomon's reign, from start to finish, are recorded in the Annals of Nathan the Prophet, the Prophecy of Ahijah the Shilonite, and the Vision of Iddo the Seer pertaining to Jeroboam son of Nebat. **9:30** Solomon ruled over all Israel from Jerusalem for forty years. **9:31** Then Solomon passed away and was buried in the city of his father David. His son Rehoboam replaced him as king.

The Northern Tribes Rebel

10:1 Rehoboam traveled to Shechem, for all Israel had gathered in Shechem to make Rehoboam king. **10:2** When Jeroboam son of Nebat heard the news, he was still in Egypt, where he had fled from King Solomon. Jeroboam returned from Egypt. **10:3** They sent for him and Jeroboam and all Israel came and spoke to Rehoboam, saying, **10:4** "Your father made us work too hard! Now if you lighten the demands he made and don't make us work as hard, we will serve you." **10:5** He said to them, "Go away for three days, then return to me." So the people went away.

10:6 King Rehoboam consulted with the older advisers who had served his father Solomon when he had been alive. He asked them, "How do you advise me to answer these people?" **10:7** They said to him, "If you are fair to these people, grant their request, and are cordial to them, they will be your servants from this time forward." **10:8** But Rehoboam rejected their advice and consulted the young advisers who served him, with whom he had grown up. **10:9** He asked them, "How do you advise me to respond to these people who said to me, 'Lessen the demands your father placed on us'?" **10:10** The young advisers with whom Rehoboam had grown up said to him, "Say this to these people who have said to you, 'Your father made us work hard, but now lighten our burden' – say this to them: 'I am a lot harsher than my father! **10:11** My father imposed heavy demands on you; I will make them even heavier. My father punished you with ordinary whips; I will punish you with whips that really sting your flesh.'"

10:12 Jeroboam and all the people reported to Rehoboam on the third day, just as the king had ordered when he said, "Return to me on the third day." **10:13** The king responded to the people harshly. He rejected the advice of the older men **10:14** and followed the advice of the younger ones. He said, "My father imposed heavy demands on you; I will make them even heavier. My father punished you with ordinary whips; I will punish you with whips that really sting your flesh." **10:15** The king refused to listen to the people, because God was instigating this turn of events so that he might bring to pass the prophetic announcement he had made through Ahijah the Shilonite to Jeroboam son of Nebat.

10:16 When all Israel saw that the king refused to listen to them, the people answered the king, "We have no portion in David – no share in the son of Jesse! Return to your homes, O Israel! Now, look after your own dynasty, O David!" So all Israel returned to their homes. **10:17** (Rehoboam continued to rule over the Israelites who lived in the cities of Judah.) **10:18** King Rehoboam sent Hadoram, the supervisor of the work crews, out after them, but the Israelites stoned him to death. King Rehoboam managed to jump into his chariot and escape to Jerusalem. **10:19** So Israel has been in rebellion against the Davidic dynasty to this very day.

11:1 When Rehoboam arrived in Jerusalem, he summoned 180,000 skilled warriors from Judah and Benjamin to attack Israel and restore the kingdom to Rehoboam. **11:2** But the LORD told Shemaiah the prophet, **11:3** "Say this to King Rehoboam son of Solomon of Judah and to all the Israelites in Judah and Benjamin, **11:4** 'The LORD says this: "Do not attack and make war with your brothers. Each of you go home, for I have caused this to happen.'"" They obeyed the LORD and called off the attack against Jeroboam.

Rehoboam's Reign

11:5 Rehoboam lived in Jerusalem; he built up these fortified cities throughout Judah: **11:6** Bethlehem, Etam, Tekoa, **11:7** Beth Zur, Soco, Adullam, **11:8** Gath, Mareshah, Ziph, **11:9** Adoraim, Lachish, Azekah, **11:10** Zorah, Aijalon, and Hebron. These were the fortified cities in Judah and Benjamin. **11:11** He fortified these cities and placed officers in them, as well as storehouses of food, olive oil, and wine. **11:12** In each city there were shields and spears; he strongly fortified them. Judah and Benjamin belonged to him.

11:13 The priests and Levites who lived throughout Israel supported him, no matter where they resided. **11:14** The Levites even left their pasturelands and their property behind and came to Judah and Jerusalem, for Jeroboam and his sons prohibited them from serving as the LORD's priests. **11:15** Jeroboam appointed his own priests to serve at the worship centers and to lead in the worship of the goat idols and calf idols he had made. **11:16** Those among all the Israelite tribes who were determined to worship the LORD God of Israel followed them to Jerusalem to sacrifice to the LORD God of their ancestors. **11:17** They supported the kingdom of Judah and were loyal to Rehoboam son of Solomon for three years; they followed the edicts of David and Solomon for three years.

11:18 Rehoboam married Mahalath the daughter of David's son Jerimoth and of Abihail, the daughter of Jesse's son Eliab. **11:19** She bore him sons named Jeush, Shemariah, and Zaham. **11:20** He later married Maacah the daughter of Absalom. She bore to him Abijah, Attai, Ziza, and Shelomith. **11:21** Rehoboam loved Maacah daughter of Absalom more than his other wives and concubines. He had eighteen wives and sixty concubines; he fathered twenty-eight sons and sixty daughters.

11:22 Rehoboam appointed Abijah son of Maacah as the leader over his brothers, for he intended to name him his successor. **11:23** He wisely placed some of his many sons throughout the regions of Judah and Benjamin in the various fortified cities. He supplied them with abundant provisions and acquired many wives for them.

12:1 After Rehoboam's rule was established and solidified, he and all Israel rejected the law of the LORD. **12:2** Because they were unfaithful to the LORD, in King Rehoboam's fifth year, King Shishak of Egypt attacked Jerusalem. **12:3** He had 1,200 chariots, 60,000 horsemen, and an innumerable number of soldiers who accompanied him from Egypt, including Libyans, Sukkites, and Cushites. **12:4** He captured the fortified cities of Judah and marched against Jerusalem.

12:5 Shemaiah the prophet visited Rehoboam and the leaders of Judah who were assembled in Jerusalem because of Shishak. He said to them, "This is what the LORD says: 'You have rejected me, so I have rejected you and will hand you over to Shishak.'" **12:6** The leaders of Israel and the king humbled themselves and said, "The LORD is just." **12:7** When the LORD saw that they humbled themselves, he gave this message to Shemaiah: "They have humbled themselves, so I will not destroy them. I will deliver them soon. My anger will not be unleashed against Jerusalem through Shishak. **12:8** Yet they will become his subjects, so they can experience how serving me differs from serving the surrounding nations."

12:9 King Shishak of Egypt attacked Jerusalem and took away the treasures of the LORD's temple and of the royal palace; he took everything, including the gold shields that Solomon had made. **12:10** King Rehoboam made bronze shields to replace them and assigned them to the officers of the royal guard who protected the entrance to the royal palace. **12:11** Whenever the king visited the LORD's temple, the royal guards carried them and then brought them back to the guardroom.

12:12 So when Rehoboam humbled himself, the LORD relented from his anger and did not annihilate him; Judah experienced some good things. **12:13** King Rehoboam solidified his rule in Jerusalem; he was forty-one years old when he became king and he ruled for seventeen years in Jerusalem, the city the LORD chose from all the tribes of Israel to be his home. Rehoboam's mother was an Ammonite named Naamah. **12:14** He did evil because he was not determined to follow the LORD.

12:15 The events of Rehoboam's reign, from start to finish, are recorded in the Annals of Shemaiah the prophet and of Iddo the seer that include genealogical records. **12:16** Then Rehoboam passed away and was buried in the City of David. His son Abijah replaced him as king.

Abijah's Reign

13:1 In the eighteenth year of the reign of King Jeroboam, Abijah became king over Judah. **13:2** He ruled for three years in Jerusalem. His mother was Michaiah, the daughter of Uriel from Gibeah.

There was war between Abijah and Jeroboam. **13:3** Abijah launched the attack with 400,000 well-trained warriors, while Jeroboam deployed against him 800,000 well-trained warriors.

13:4 Abijah ascended Mount Zemaraim, in the Ephraimite hill country, and said: "Listen to me, Jeroboam and all Israel! **13:5** Don't you realize that the LORD God of Israel has given David and his dynasty lasting dominion over Israel by a formal agreement? **13:6** Jeroboam son of Nebat, a servant of Solomon son of David, rose up and rebelled against his master. **13:7** Lawless good-for-nothing men gathered around him and conspired against Rehoboam son of Solomon, when Rehoboam was an inexperienced young man and could not resist them. **13:8** Now you are declaring that you will resist the LORD's rule through the Davidic dynasty. You have a huge army, and bring with you the gold calves that Jeroboam made for you as gods. **13:9** But you banished the LORD's priests, Aaron's descendants, and the Levites, and appointed your own priests just as the surrounding nations do! Anyone who comes to consecrate himself with a young bull or seven rams becomes a priest of these fake gods! **13:10** But as for us, the LORD is our God and we have not rejected him. Aaron's descendants serve as the LORD's priests and the Levites assist them with the work. **13:11** They offer burnt sacrifices to the LORD every morning and every evening, along with fragrant incense. They arrange the Bread of the Presence on a ritually clean table and light the lamps on the gold lampstand every evening. Certainly we are observing the LORD our God's regulations, but you have rejected him. **13:12** Now look, God is with us as our leader. His priests are ready to blow the trumpets to signal the attack against you. You Israelites, don't fight against the LORD God of your ancestors, for you will not win!"

13:13 Now Jeroboam had sent some men to ambush the Judahite army from behind. The main army was in front of the Judahite army; the ambushers were behind it. **13:14** The men of Judah turned around and realized they were being attacked from the front and the rear. So they cried out for help to the LORD. The priests blew their trumpets, **13:15** and the men of Judah gave the battle cry. As the men of Judah gave the battle cry, the LORD struck down Jeroboam and all Israel before Abijah and Judah. **13:16** The Israelites fled from before the Judahite army, and God handed them over to the men of Judah. **13:17** Abijah and his army thoroughly defeated them; 500,000 well-trained Israelite men fell dead. **13:18** That day the Israelites were defeated; the men of Judah prevailed because they relied on the LORD God of their ancestors.

13:19 Abijah chased Jeroboam; he seized from him these cities: Bethel and its surrounding towns, Jeshanah and its surrounding towns, and Ephron and its surrounding towns. **13:20** Jeroboam did not regain power during the reign of Abijah. The LORD struck him down and he died. **13:21** Abijah's power grew; he had fourteen wives and fathered twenty-two sons and sixteen daughters.

13:22 The rest of the events of Abijah's reign, including his deeds and sayings, are recorded in the writings of the prophet Iddo.

14:1 (13:23) Abijah passed away and was buried in the City of David. His son Asa replaced him as king. During his reign the land had rest for ten years.

Asa's Religious and Military Accomplishments

14:2 (14:1) Asa did what the LORD his God desired and approved. **14:3** He removed the pagan altars and the high places, smashed the sacred pillars, and cut down the Asherah poles. **14:4** He ordered Judah to seek the LORD God of their ancestors and to observe his law and commands. **14:5** He removed the high places and the incense altars from all the cities of Judah. The kingdom had rest under his rule.

14:6 He built fortified cities throughout Judah, for the land was at rest and there was no war during those years; the LORD gave him peace. **14:7** He said to the people of Judah: "Let's build these cities and fortify them with walls, towers, and barred gates. The land remains ours because we have followed the LORD our God and he has made us secure on all sides." So they built the cities and prospered.

14:8 Asa had an army of 300,000 men from Judah, equipped with large shields and spears. He also had 280,000 men from Benjamin who carried small shields and were adept archers; they were all skilled warriors. **14:9** Zerah the Cushite marched against them with an army of 1,000,000 men and 300 chariots. He arrived at Mareshah, **14:10** and Asa went out to oppose him. They deployed for battle in the Valley of Zephathah near Mareshah.

14:11 Asa prayed to the LORD his God: "O LORD, there is no one but you who can help the weak when they are vastly outnumbered. Help us, O LORD our God, for we rely on you and have marched on your behalf against this huge army. O LORD our God, don't let men prevail against you!" **14:12** The LORD struck down the Cushites before Asa and Judah. The Cushites fled, **14:13** and Asa and his army chased them as far as Gerar. The Cushites were wiped out; they were shattered before the LORD and his army. The men of Judah carried off a huge amount of plunder. **14:14** They defeated all the cities surrounding Gerar, for the LORD caused them to panic. The men of Judah looted all the cities, for they contained a huge amount of goods. **14:15** They also attacked the tents of the herdsmen in charge of the livestock. They carried off many sheep and camels and then returned to Jerusalem.

15:1 God's Spirit came upon Azariah son of Oded. **15:2** He met Asa and told him, "Listen to me, Asa and all Judah and Benjamin! The LORD is with you when you are loyal to him. If you seek him, he will respond to you, but if you reject him, he will reject you. **15:3** For a long time Israel had no true God, or priest to instruct them, or law. **15:4** Because of their distress, they turned back to the LORD God of Israel. They sought him and he responded to them. **15:5** In those days no one could travel safely, for total chaos had overtaken all the people of the surrounding lands. **15:6**

One nation was crushed by another, and one city by another, for God caused them to be in great turmoil. **15:7** But as for you, be strong and don't get discouraged, for your work will be rewarded."

15:8 When Asa heard these words and the prophecy of Oded the prophet, he was encouraged. He removed the detestable idols from the entire land of Judah and Benjamin and from the cities he had seized in the Ephraimite hill country. He repaired the altar of the LORD in front of the porch of the LORD's temple.

15:9 He assembled all Judah and Benjamin, as well as the settlers from Ephraim, Manasseh, and Simeon who had come to live with them. Many people from Israel had come there to live when they saw that the LORD his God was with him. **15:10** They assembled in Jerusalem in the third month of the fifteenth year of Asa's reign. **15:11** At that time they sacrificed to the LORD some of the plunder they had brought back, including 700 head of cattle and 7,000 sheep. **15:12** They solemnly agreed to seek the LORD God of their ancestors with their whole heart and being. **15:13** Anyone who would not seek the LORD God of Israel would be executed, whether they were young or old, male or female. **15:14** They swore their allegiance to the LORD, shouting their approval loudly and sounding trumpets and horns. **15:15** All Judah was happy about the oath, because they made the vow with their whole heart. They willingly sought the LORD and he responded to them. He made them secure on every side.

15:16 King Asa also removed Maacah his grandmother from her position as queen mother because she had made a loathsome Asherah pole. Asa cut down her Asherah pole and crushed and burned it in the Kidron Valley. **15:17** The high places were not eliminated from Israel, yet Asa was wholeheartedly devoted to the LORD throughout his lifetime. **15:18** He brought the holy items that his father and he had made into God's temple, including the silver, gold, and other articles.

Asa's Failures

15:19 There was no more war until the thirty-fifth year of Asa's reign. **16:1** In the thirty-sixth year of Asa's reign, King Baasha of Israel attacked Judah, and he established Ramah as a military outpost to prevent anyone from leaving or entering the land of King Asa of Judah. **16:2** Asa took all the silver and gold that was left in the treasuries of the LORD's temple and of the royal palace and sent it to King Ben Hadad of Syria, ruler in Damascus, along with this message: **16:3** "I want to make a treaty with you, like the one our fathers made. See, I have sent you silver and gold. Break your treaty with King Baasha of Israel, so he will retreat from my land." **16:4** Ben Hadad accepted King Asa's offer and ordered his army commanders to attack the cities of Israel. They conquered Ijon, Dan, Abel Maim, and all the storage cities of Naphtali. **16:5** When Baasha heard the news, he stopped fortifying Ramah and abandoned the project. **16:6** King Asa ordered all the men of Judah to carry away the stones and wood that Baasha had used to build Ramah. He used the materials to build up Geba and Mizpah.

16:7 At that time Hanani the prophet visited King Asa of Judah and said to him: "Because you relied on the king of Syria and did not rely on the LORD your God, the army of the king of Syria has escaped from your hand. **16:8** Did not the Cushites and Libyans have a huge army with chariots and a very large number of horsemen? But when you relied on the LORD, he handed them over to you! **16:9** Certainly the LORD watches the whole earth carefully and is ready to strengthen those who are devoted to him. You have acted foolishly in this matter; from now on you will have war. **16:10** Asa was so angry at the prophet, he put him in jail. Asa also oppressed some of the people at that time.

Asa's Reign Ends

16:11 The events of Asa's reign, from start to finish, are recorded in the Scroll of the Kings of Judah and Israel. **16:12** In the thirty-ninth year of his reign, Asa developed a foot disease. Though his disease was severe, he did not seek the LORD, but only the doctors. **16:13** Asa passed away in the forty-first year of his reign. **16:14** He was buried in the tomb he had carved out in the City of David. They laid him to rest on a bier covered with spices and assorted mixtures of ointments. They made a huge bonfire to honor him.

Jehoshaphat Becomes King

17:1 His son Jehoshaphat replaced him as king and solidified his rule over Israel. **17:2** He placed troops in all of Judah's fortified cities and posted garrisons throughout the land of Judah and in the cities of Ephraim that his father Asa had seized.

17:3 The LORD was with Jehoshaphat because he followed in his ancestor David's footsteps at the beginning of his reign. He did not seek the Baals, **17:4** but instead sought the God of his ancestors and obeyed his commands, unlike the Israelites. **17:5** The LORD made his kingdom secure; all Judah brought tribute to Jehoshaphat, and he became very wealthy and greatly respected. **17:6** He was committed to following the LORD; he even removed the high places and Asherah poles from Judah.

17:7 In the third year of his reign he sent his officials Ben-Hail, Obadiah, Zechariah, Nethanel, and Micaiah to teach in the cities of Judah. **17:8** They were accompanied by the Levites Shemaiah, Nethaniah, Zebadiah, Asahel, Shemiramoth, Jehonathan, Adonijah, Tobijah, and Tob-Adonijah, and by the priests Elishama and Jehoram. **17:9** They taught throughout Judah, taking with them the scroll of the law of the LORD. They traveled to all the cities of Judah and taught the people.

17:10 The LORD put fear into all the kingdoms surrounding Judah; they did not make war with Jehoshaphat. **17:11** Some of the Philistines brought Jehoshaphat tribute, including a load of silver. The Arabs brought him 7,700 rams and 7,700 goats from their flocks.

17:12 Jehoshaphat's power kept increasing. He built fortresses and storage cities throughout Judah. **17:13** He had many supplies stored in the cities of Judah and an army of skilled warriors stationed in Jerusalem. **17:14** These were their divisions by families:

There were a thousand officers from Judah. Adnah the commander led 300,000 skilled warriors, **17:15** Jehochanan the commander led 280,000, **17:16** and Amasiah son of Zikri, who volunteered to serve the LORD, led 200,000 skilled warriors.

17:17 From Benjamin, Eliada, a skilled warrior, led 200,000 men who were equipped with bows and shields, **17:18** and Jehozabad led 180,000 trained warriors.

17:19 These were the ones who served the king, besides those whom the king placed in the fortified cities throughout Judah.

Jehoshaphat Allies with Ahab

18:1 Jehoshaphat was very wealthy and greatly respected. He made an alliance by marriage with Ahab, **18:2** and after several years went down to visit Ahab in Samaria. Ahab slaughtered many sheep and cattle to honor Jehoshaphat and those who came with him. He persuaded him to join in an attack against Ramoth Gilead. **18:3** King Ahab of Israel said to Jehoshaphat, "Will you go with me to attack Ramoth Gilead?" Jehoshaphat replied to the king of Israel, "I will support you; my army is at your disposal and will support you in battle." **18:4** Then Jehoshaphat added, "First seek an oracle from the LORD." **18:5** So the king of Israel assembled 400 prophets and asked them, "Should we attack Ramoth Gilead or not?" They said, "Attack! God will hand it over to the king." **18:6** But Jehoshaphat asked, "Is there not a prophet of the LORD still here, that we may ask him?" **18:7** The king of Israel answered Jehoshaphat, "There is still one man through whom we can seek the LORD's will. But I despise him because he does not prophesy prosperity for me, but always disaster. His name is Micaiah son of Imlah. Jehoshaphat said, "The king should not say such things!" **18:8** The king of Israel summoned an officer and said, "Quickly bring Micaiah son of Imlah."

18:9 Now the king of Israel and King Jehoshaphat of Judah were sitting on their respective thrones, dressed in their royal robes, at the threshing floor at the entrance of the gate of Samaria. All the prophets were prophesying before them. **18:10** Zedekiah son of Kenaanah made iron horns and said, "This is what the LORD says, 'With these you will gore Syria until they are destroyed!'" **18:11** All the prophets were prophesying the same, saying, "Attack Ramoth Gilead! You will succeed; the LORD will hand it over to the king!" **18:12** Now the messenger who went to summon Micaiah said to him, "Look, the prophets are in complete agreement that the king will succeed. Your words must agree with theirs; you must predict success!" **18:13** But Micaiah said, "As certainly as the LORD lives, I will say what my God tells me to say!"

18:14 Micaiah came before the king and the king asked him, "Micaiah, should we attack Ramoth Gilead or not?" He answered him, "Attack! You will succeed; they will be handed over to you." **18:15** The king said to him, "How many times must I make you solemnly promise in the name of the LORD to tell me only the truth?" **18:16** Micaiah replied, "I saw all Israel scattered on the mountains like sheep that have no shepherd. Then the LORD said, 'They have no master. They should go home in peace.'" **18:17** The king of Israel said to Jehoshaphat, "Didn't I tell you he does not prophesy prosperity for me, but disaster?" **18:18** Micaiah said, "That being the case, hear the word of the LORD: I saw the LORD sitting on his throne, with all the heavenly assembly standing on his right and on his left. **18:19** The LORD said, 'Who will deceive King Ahab of Israel, so he will attack Ramoth Gilead and die there?' One said this and another that. **18:20** Then a spirit stepped forward and stood before the LORD. He said, 'I will deceive him.' The LORD asked him, 'How?' **18:21** He replied, 'I will go out and be a lying spirit in the mouths of all his prophets.' The LORD said, 'Deceive and overpower him. Go out and do as you have proposed.' **18:22** So now, look, the LORD has placed a lying spirit in the mouths of all these prophets of yours; but the LORD has decreed disaster for you." **18:23** Zedekiah son of Kenaanah approached, hit Micaiah on the jaw, and said, "Which way did the LORD's spirit go when he went from me to speak to you?" **18:24** Micaiah replied, "Look, you will see in the day when you go into an inner room to hide." **18:25** Then the king of Israel said, "Take Micaiah and return him to Amon the city official and Joash the king's son. **18:26** Say, 'This is what the king says: "Put this man in prison. Give him only a little bread and water until I return safely."'" **18:27** Micaiah said, "If you really do return safely, then the LORD has not spoken through me!" Then he added, "Take note, all you people."

18:28 The king of Israel and King Jehoshaphat of Judah attacked Ramoth Gilead. **18:29** The king of Israel said to Jehoshaphat, "I will disguise myself and then enter the battle; but you wear your royal attire." So the king of Israel disguised himself and they entered the battle. **18:30** Now the king of Syria had ordered his chariot commanders, "Do not fight common soldiers or high ranking officers; fight only the king of Israel!" **18:31** When the chariot commanders saw Jehoshaphat, they said, "He must be the king of Israel!" So they turned and attacked him, but Jehoshaphat cried out. The LORD helped him; God lured them away from him. **18:32** When the chariot commanders realized he was not the king of Israel, they turned away from him. **18:33** Now an archer shot an arrow at random and it struck the king of Israel between the plates of his armor. The king ordered his charioteer, "Turn around and take me from the battle line, for I am wounded." **18:34** While the battle raged throughout the day, the king stood propped up in his chariot opposite the Syrians. He died in the evening as the sun was setting.

19:1 When King Jehoshaphat of Judah returned home safely to Jerusalem, **19:2** the prophet Jehu son of Hanani confronted him; he said to King Jehoshaphat, "Is it right to help the wicked and be an ally of those who oppose the LORD? Because you have done this the LORD is angry with you! **19:3** Nevertheless you have done some good things; you removed the Asherah poles from the land and you were determined to follow the LORD."

Jehoshaphat Appoints Judges

19:4 Jehoshaphat lived in Jerusalem. He went out among the people from Beer Sheba to the hill country of Ephraim and encouraged them to follow the LORD God of their ancestors. **19:5** He appointed judges throughout the land and in each of the fortified cities of Judah. **19:6** He told the judges, "Be careful what you do, for you are not judging for men, but for the LORD, who will be with you when you make judicial decisions. **19:7** Respect the LORD and make careful decisions, for the LORD our God disapproves of injustice, partiality, and bribery."

19:8 In Jerusalem Jehoshaphat appointed some Levites, priests, and Israelite family leaders to judge on behalf of the LORD and to settle disputes among the residents of Jerusalem. **19:9** He commanded them: "Carry out your duties with respect for the LORD, with honesty, and with pure motives. **19:10** Whenever your countrymen who live in the cities bring a case before you (whether it involves a violent crime or other matters related to the law, commandments, rules, and regulations), warn them that they must not sin against the LORD. If you fail to do so, God will be angry with you and your colleagues; but if you obey, you will be free of guilt. **19:11** You will report to Amariah the chief priest in all matters pertaining to the LORD's law, and to Zebadiah son of Ishmael, the leader of the family of Judah, in all matters pertaining to the king. The Levites will serve as officials before you. Confidently carry out your duties! May the LORD be with those who do well!"

The Lord Gives Jehoshaphat Military Success

20:1 Later the Moabites and Ammonites, along with some of the Meunites, attacked Jehoshaphat. **20:2** Messengers arrived and reported to Jehoshaphat, "A huge army is attacking you from the other side of the Dead Sea, from the direction of Edom. Look, they are in Hazezon Tamar (that is, En Gedi)." **20:3** Jehoshaphat was afraid, so he decided to seek the LORD's advice. He decreed that all Judah should observe a fast. **20:4** The people of Judah assembled to ask for the LORD's help; they came from all the cities of Judah to ask for the LORD's help.

20:5 Jehoshaphat stood before the assembly of Judah and Jerusalem at the LORD's temple, in front of the new courtyard. **20:6** He prayed: "O LORD God of our ancestors, you are the God who lives in heaven and rules over all the kingdoms of the nations. You possess strength and power; no one can stand against you. **20:7** Our God, you drove out the inhabitants of this land before your people Israel and gave it as a permanent possession to the descendants of your friend Abraham. **20:8** They settled down in it and built in it a temple to honor you, saying, **20:9** 'If disaster comes on us in the form of military attack, judgment, plague, or famine, we will stand in front of this temple before you, for you are present in this temple. We will cry out to you for help in our distress, so that you will hear and deliver us.' **20:10** Now the Ammonites, Moabites, and men from Mount Seir are coming! When Israel came from the land of Egypt, you did not allow them to invade these lands. They bypassed them and did not destroy them. **20:11** Look how they are repaying us! They come to drive us out of our allotted land which you assigned to us! **20:12** Our God, will you not judge them? For we are powerless against this huge army that attacks us! We don't know what we should do; we look to you for help."

20:13 All the men of Judah were standing before the LORD, along with their infants, wives, and children. **20:14** Then in the midst of the assembly, the LORD's Spirit came upon Jachaziel son of Zechariah, son of Benaiah, son of Jeiel, son of Mattaniah, a Levite and descendant of Asaph. **20:15** He said: "Pay attention, all you people of Judah, residents of Jerusalem, and King Jehoshaphat! This is what the LORD says to you: 'Don't be afraid and don't panic because of this huge army! For the battle is not yours, but God's. **20:16** Tomorrow march down against them as they come up the Ascent of Ziz. You will find them at the end of the ravine in front of the Desert of Jeruel. **20:17** You will not fight in this battle. Take your positions, stand, and watch the LORD deliver you, O Judah and Jerusalem. Don't be afraid and don't panic! Tomorrow march out toward them; the LORD is with you!'"

20:18 Jehoshaphat bowed down with his face toward the ground, and all the people of Judah and the residents of Jerusalem fell down before the

LORD and worshiped him. **20:19** Then some Levites, from the Kohathites and Korahites, got up and loudly praised the LORD God of Israel.

20:20 Early the next morning they marched out to the Desert of Tekoa. When they were ready to march, Jehoshaphat stood up and said: "Listen to me, you people of Judah and residents of Jerusalem! Trust in the LORD your God and you will be safe! Trust in the message of his prophets and you will win." **20:21** He met with the people and appointed musicians to play before the LORD and praise his majestic splendor. As they marched ahead of the warriors they said: "Give thanks to the LORD, for his loyal love endures."

20:22 When they began to shout and praise, the LORD suddenly attacked the Ammonites, Moabites, and men from Mount Seir who were invading Judah, and they were defeated. **20:23** The Ammonites and Moabites attacked the men from Mount Seir and annihilated them. When they had finished off the men of Seir, they attacked and destroyed one another. **20:24** When the men of Judah arrived at the observation post overlooking the desert and looked at the huge army, they saw dead bodies on the ground; there were no survivors! **20:25** Jehoshaphat and his men went to gather the plunder; they found a huge amount of supplies, clothing and valuable items. They carried away everything they could. There was so much plunder, it took them three days to haul it off.

20:26 On the fourth day they assembled in the Valley of Berachah, where they praised the LORD. So that place is called the Valley of Berachah to this very day. **20:27** Then all the men of Judah and Jerusalem returned joyfully to Jerusalem with Jehoshaphat leading them; the LORD had given them reason to rejoice over their enemies. **20:28** They entered Jerusalem to the sound of stringed instruments and trumpets and proceeded to the temple of the LORD. **20:29** All the kingdoms of the surrounding lands were afraid of God when they heard how the LORD had fought against Israel's enemies. **20:30** Jehoshaphat's kingdom enjoyed peace; his God made him secure on every side.

Jehoshaphat's Reign Ends

20:31 Jehoshaphat reigned over Judah. He was thirty-five years old when he became king and he reigned for twenty-five years in Jerusalem. His mother was Azubah, the daughter of Shilhi. **20:32** He followed in his father Asa's footsteps and was careful to do what the LORD approved. **20:33** However, the high places were not eliminated; the people were still not devoted to the God of their ancestors.

20:34 The rest of the events of Jehoshaphat's reign, from start to finish, are recorded in the Annals of Jehu son of Hanani which are included in Scroll of the Kings of Israel.

20:35 Later King Jehoshaphat of Judah made an alliance with King Ahaziah of Israel, who did evil. **20:36** They agreed to make large seagoing merchant ships; they built the ships in Ezion Geber. **20:37** Eliezer son of Dodavahu from Mareshah prophesied against Jehoshaphat, "Because you made an alliance with Ahaziah, the LORD will shatter what you have made." The ships were wrecked and unable to go to sea.

21:1 Jehoshaphat passed away and was buried with his ancestors in the City of David. His son Jehoram replaced him as king.

Jehoram's Reign

21:2 His brothers, Jehoshaphat's sons, were Azariah, Jechiel, Zechariah, Azariahu, Michael, and Shephatiah. All of these were sons of King Jehoshaphat of Israel. **21:3** Their father gave them many presents, including silver, gold, and other precious items, along with fortified cities in Judah. But he gave the kingdom to Jehoram because he was the firstborn.

21:4 Jehoram took control of his father's kingdom and became powerful. Then he killed all his brothers, as well as some of the officials of Israel. **21:5** Jehoram was thirty-two years old when he became king and he reigned for eight years in Jerusalem. **21:6** He followed in the footsteps of the kings of Israel, just as Ahab's dynasty had done, for he married Ahab's daughter. He did evil in the sight of the LORD. **21:7** But the LORD was unwilling to destroy David's dynasty because of the promise he had made to give David a perpetual dynasty.

21:8 During Jehoram's reign Edom freed themselves from Judah's control and set up their own king. **21:9** Jehoram crossed over to Zair with his officers and all his chariots. The Edomites, who had surrounded him, attacked at night and defeated him and his chariot officers. **21:10** So Edom has remained free from Judah's control to this very day. At that same time Libnah also rebelled and freed themselves from Judah's control because Jehoram rejected the LORD God of his ancestors. **21:11** He also built high places on the hills of Judah; he encouraged the residents of Jerusalem to be unfaithful to the LORD and led Judah away from the LORD.

21:12 Jehoram received this letter from Elijah the prophet: "This is what the LORD God of your ancestor David says: 'You have not followed in the footsteps of your father Jehoshaphat and of King Asa of Judah, **21:13** but have instead followed in the footsteps of the kings of Israel. You encouraged the people of Judah and the residents of Jerusalem to be unfaithful to the LORD, just as the family of Ahab does in Israel. You also killed your brothers, members of your father's family, who were better than you. **21:14** So look, the LORD is about to severely afflict your people, your sons, your wives, and all you own. **21:15** And you will get a serious, chronic intestinal disease which will cause your intestines to come out."

21:16 The LORD stirred up against Jehoram the Philistines and the Arabs who lived beside the Cushites. **21:17** They attacked Judah and swept through it. They carried off everything they found in the royal palace, including his sons and wives. None of his sons was left, except for his youngest, Ahaziah. **21:18** After all this happened, the LORD afflicted him with an incurable intestinal disease. **21:19** After about two years his intestines came out because of the disease, so that he died a very painful death. His people did not make a bonfire to honor him, as they had done for his ancestors.

21:20 Jehoram was thirty-two years old when he became king and he reigned eight years in Jerusalem. No one regretted his death; he was buried in the City of David, but not in the royal tombs.

Ahaziah's Reign

22:1 The residents of Jerusalem made his youngest son Ahaziah king in his place, for the raiding party that invaded the city with the Arabs had killed all the older sons. So Ahaziah son of Jehoram became king of Judah. **22:2** Ahaziah was twenty-two years old when he became king and he reigned for one year in Jerusalem. His mother was Athaliah, the granddaughter of Omri. **22:3** He followed in the footsteps of Ahab's dynasty, for his mother gave him evil advice. **22:4** He did evil in the sight of the LORD like Ahab's dynasty because, after his father's death, they gave him advice that led to his destruction. **22:5** He followed their advice and joined Ahab's son King Joram of Israel in a battle against King Hazael of Syria at Ramoth Gilead in which the Syrians defeated Joram. **22:6** Joram returned to Jezreel to recover from the wounds he received from the Syrians in Ramah when he fought against King Hazael of Syria. Ahaziah son of King Jehoram of Judah went down to visit Joram son of Ahab in Jezreel, because he had been wounded.

22:7 God brought about Ahaziah's downfall through his visit to Joram. When Ahaziah arrived, he went out with Joram to meet Jehu son of Nimshi, whom the LORD had commissioned to wipe out Ahab's family. **22:8** While Jehu was dishing out punishment to Ahab's family, he discovered the officials of Judah and the sons of Ahaziah's relatives who were serving Ahaziah and killed them. **22:9** He looked for Ahaziah, who was captured while hiding in Samaria. They brought him to Jehu and then executed him. They did give him a burial, for they reasoned, "He is the son of Jehoshaphat, who sought the LORD with his whole heart." There was no one in Ahaziah's family strong enough to rule in his place.

Athaliah is Eliminated

22:10 When Athaliah the mother of Ahaziah saw that her son was dead, she was determined to destroy the entire royal line of Judah. **22:11** So Jehoshabeath, the daughter of King Jehoram, took Ahaziah's son Joash and sneaked him away from the rest of the royal descendants who were to be executed. She hid him and his nurse in the room where the bed covers were stored. So Jehoshabeath the daughter of King Jehoram, wife of Jehoiada the priest and sister of Ahaziah, hid him from Athaliah so she could not execute him. **22:12** He remained in hiding in God's temple for six years, while Athaliah was ruling over the land.

23:1 In the seventh year Jehoiada made a bold move. He made a pact with the officers of the units of hundreds: Azariah son of Jehoram, Ishmael son of Jehochanan, Azariah son of Obed, Maaseiah son of Adaiah, and Elishaphat son of Zikri. **23:2** They traveled throughout Judah and assembled the Levites from all the cities of Judah, as well as the Israelite family leaders.

They came to Jerusalem, **23:3** and the whole assembly made a covenant with the king in the temple of God. Jehoiada said to them, "The king's son will rule, just as the LORD promised David's descendants. **23:4** This is what you must do. One third of you priests and Levites who are on duty during the Sabbath will guard the doors. **23:5** Another third of you will be stationed at the royal palace and still another third at the Foundation Gate. All the others will stand in the courtyards of the LORD's temple. **23:6** No one must enter the LORD's temple except the priests and Levites who are on duty. They may enter because they are ceremonially pure. All the others should carry out their assigned service to the LORD. **23:7** The Levites must surround the king. Each of you must hold his weapon in his hand. Whoever tries to enter the temple must be killed. You must accompany the king wherever he goes."

23:8 The Levites and all the men of Judah did just as Jehoiada the priest ordered. Each of them took his men, those who were on duty during the Sabbath as well as those who were off duty on the Sabbath. Jehoiada the priest did not release his divisions from their duties. **23:9** Jehoiada the priest gave to the officers of the units of hundreds King David's spears and shields that were kept in God's temple. **23:10** He placed the men at their posts, each holding his weapon in his hand. They lined up from the south side of the temple to the north side and stood near the altar and the temple, surrounding the king. **23:11** Jehoiada and his sons led out the king's son and placed on him the crown and the royal insignia. They proclaimed him king and poured olive oil on his head. They declared, "Long live the king!"

23:12 When Athaliah heard the royal guard shouting and praising the king, she joined the crowd at the LORD's temple. **23:13** Then she saw the king standing by his pillar at the entrance. The officers and trumpeters stood beside the king and all the people of the land were celebrating and blowing trumpets, and the musicians with various instruments were leading the celebration. Athaliah tore her clothes and yelled, "Treason! Treason!" **23:14** Jehoiada the priest sent out the officers of the units of hundreds, who were in charge of the army, and ordered them, "Bring her outside the temple to the guards. Put the sword to anyone who follows her." The priest gave this order because he had decided she should not be executed in the LORD's temple. **23:15** They seized her and took her into the precincts of the royal palace through the horses' entrance. There they executed her.

23:16 Jehoiada then drew up a covenant stipulating that he, all the people, and the king should be loyal to the LORD. **23:17** All the people went and demolished the temple of Baal. They smashed its altars and idols. They killed Mattan the priest of Baal in front of the altars. **23:18** Jehoiada then assigned the duties of the LORD's temple to the priests, the Levites whom David had assigned to the LORD's temple. They were responsible for offering burnt sacrifices to the LORD with joy and music, according to the law of Moses and the edict of David. **23:19** He posted guards at the gates of the LORD's temple, so no one who was ceremonially unclean in any way could enter. **23:20** He summoned the officers of the units of hundreds, the nobles, the rulers of the people, and all the people of land, and he then led the king down from the LORD's temple. They entered the royal palace through the Upper Gate and seated the king on the royal throne. **23:21** All the people of the land celebrated, for the city had rest now that they had killed Athaliah.

Joash's Reign

24:1 Joash was seven years old when he began to reign. He reigned for forty years in Jerusalem. His mother was Zibiah, who was from Beer Sheba. **24:2** Joash did what the LORD approved throughout the lifetime of Jehoiada the priest. **24:3** Jehoiada chose two wives for him who gave him sons and daughters.

24:4 Joash was determined to repair the LORD's temple. **24:5** He assembled the priests and Levites and ordered them, "Go out to the cities of Judah and collect the annual quota of silver from all Israel for repairs on the temple of your God. Be quick about it!" But the Levites delayed.

24:6 So the king summoned Jehoiada the chief priest, and said to him, "Why have you not made the Levites collect from Judah and Jerusalem the tax authorized by Moses the LORD's servant and by the assembly of Israel at the tent containing the tablets of the law?" **24:7** (Wicked Athaliah and her sons had broken into God's temple and used all the holy items of the LORD's temple in their worship of the Baals.) **24:8** The king ordered a chest to be made and placed outside the gate of the LORD's temple. **24:9** An edict was sent throughout Judah and Jerusalem requiring the people to bring to the LORD the tax that Moses, God's servant, imposed on Israel in the wilderness. **24:10** All the officials and all the people gladly brought their silver and threw it into the chest until it was full. **24:11** Whenever the Levites brought the chest to the royal accountant and they saw there was a lot of silver, the royal scribe and the accountant of the high priest emptied the chest and then took it back to its place. They went through this routine every day and collected a large amount of silver.

24:12 The king and Jehoiada gave it to the construction foremen assigned to the LORD's temple. They hired carpenters and craftsmen to repair the LORD's temple, as well as those skilled in working with iron and bronze to restore the LORD's temple. **24:13** They worked hard and made the repairs. They followed the measurements specified for God's temple and restored it. **24:14** When they were finished, they brought the rest of the silver to the king and Jehoiada. They used it to make items for the LORD's temple, including items used in the temple service and for burnt sacrifices, pans, and various other gold and silver items. Throughout Jehoiada's lifetime, burnt sacrifices were offered regularly in the LORD's temple.

24:15 Jehoiada grew old and died at the age of 130. **24:16** He was buried in the City of David with the kings, because he had accomplished good in Israel and for God and his temple.

24:17 After Jehoiada died, the officials of Judah visited the king and declared their loyalty to him. The king listened to their advice. **24:18** They abandoned the temple of the LORD God of their ancestors, and worshiped the Asherah poles and idols. Because of this sinful activity, God was angry with Judah and Jerusalem. **24:19** The LORD sent prophets among them to lead them back to him. They warned the people, but they would not pay attention. **24:20** God's Spirit energized Zechariah son of Jehoiada the priest. He stood up before the people and said to them, "This is what God says: 'Why are you violating the commands of the LORD? You will not be prosperous! Because you have rejected the LORD, he has rejected you!'" **24:21** They plotted against him and by royal decree stoned him to death in the courtyard of the LORD's temple. **24:22** King Joash disregarded the loyalty his father Jehoiada had shown him and killed Jehoiada's son. As Zechariah was dying, he said, "May the LORD take notice and seek vengeance!"

24:23 At the beginning of the year the Syrian army attacked Joash and invaded Judah and Jerusalem. They wiped out all the leaders of the people and sent all the plunder they gathered to the king of Damascus. **24:24** Even though the invading Syrian army was relatively weak, the LORD handed over to them Judah's very large army, for the people of Judah had abandoned the LORD God of their ancestors. The Syrians gave Joash what he deserved. **24:25** When they withdrew, they left Joash badly wounded. His servants plotted against him because of what he had done to the son of Jehoiada the priest. They murdered him on his bed. Thus he died and was buried in the City of David, but not in the tombs of the kings. **24:26** The conspirators were Zabad son of Shimeath (an Ammonite woman) and Jehozabad son of Shimrith (a Moabite woman).

24:27 The list of Joash's sons, the many prophetic oracles pertaining to him, and the account of his building project on God's temple are included in the record of the Scroll of the Kings. His son Amaziah replaced him as king.

Amaziah's Reign

25:1 Amaziah was twenty-five years old when he began to reign, and he reigned for twenty-nine years in Jerusalem. His mother was Jehoaddan, who was from Jerusalem. **25:2** He did what the LORD approved, but not with wholehearted devotion.

25:3 When he had secured control of the kingdom, he executed the servants who had assassinated his father. **25:4** However, he did not execute their sons. He obeyed the LORD's commandment as recorded in the law scroll of Moses, "Fathers must not be executed for what their sons do, and sons must not be executed for what their fathers do. A man must be executed only for his own sin."

25:5 Amaziah assembled the people of Judah and assigned them by families to the commanders of units of a thousand and the commanders of units of a hundred for all Judah and Benjamin. He counted those twenty years old and up and discovered there were 300,000 young men of fighting age equipped with spears and shields. **25:6** He hired 100,000 Israelite warriors for a hundred talents of silver.

25:7 But a prophet visited him and said: "O king, the Israelite troops must not go with you, for the LORD is not with Israel or any of the Ephraimites. **25:8** Even if you go and fight bravely in battle, God will defeat you before the enemy. God is capable of helping or defeating." **25:9** Amaziah asked the prophet: "But what should I do about the hundred talents of silver I paid the Israelite troops?" The prophet replied, "The LORD is capable of giving you more than that." **25:10** So Amaziah dismissed the troops that had come to him from Ephraim and sent them home. They were very angry at Judah and returned home incensed. **25:11** Amaziah boldly led his army to the Valley of Salt, where he defeated 10,000 Edomites. **25:12** The men of Judah captured 10,000 men alive. They took them to the top of a cliff and threw them over. All the captives fell to their death. **25:13** Now the troops Amaziah had dismissed and had not allowed to fight in the battle raided the cities of Judah from Samaria to Beth Horon. They killed 3,000 people and carried off a large amount of plunder.

25:14 When Amaziah returned from defeating the Edomites, he brought back the gods of the people of Seir and made them his personal gods. He bowed down before them and offered them sacrifices. **25:15** The LORD was angry at Amaziah and sent a prophet to him, who said, "Why are you following these gods that could not deliver their own people from your power?" **25:16** While he was speaking, Amaziah said to him, "Did we appoint you to be a royal counselor? Stop prophesying or else you will be killed!" So the prophet stopped, but added, "I know that the LORD has decided to destroy you, because you have done this thing and refused to listen to my advice."

25:17 After King Amaziah of Judah consulted with his advisers, he sent this message to the king of Israel, Joash son of Jehoahaz, the son of Jehu, "Come, face me on the battlefield." **25:18** King Joash of Israel sent this message back to King Amaziah of Judah, "A thorn bush in Lebanon sent this message to a cedar in Lebanon, 'Give your daughter to my son as a wife.' Then a wild animal of Lebanon came by and trampled down the thorn bush. **25:19** You defeated Edom and it has gone to your head. Gloat over your success, but stay in your palace. Why bring calamity on yourself? Why bring down yourself and Judah along with you?"

25:20 But Amaziah did not heed the warning, for God wanted to hand them over to Joash because they followed the gods of Edom. **25:21** So King Joash of Israel attacked. He and King Amaziah of Judah faced each other on the battlefield in Beth Shemesh of Judah. **25:22** Judah was defeated by Israel, and each man ran back home. **25:23** King Joash of Israel captured King Amaziah of Judah, son of Joash son of Jehoahaz, in Beth Shemesh and brought him to Jerusalem. He broke down the wall of Jerusalem from the Gate of Ephraim to the Corner Gate – a distance of about six hundred feet. **25:24** He took away all the gold and silver, all the items found in God's temple that were in the care of Obed-Edom, the riches in the royal palace, and some hostages. Then he went back to Samaria.

25:25 King Amaziah son of Joash of Judah lived for fifteen years after the death of King Joash son of Jehoahaz of Israel. **25:26** The rest of the events of Amaziah's reign, from start to finish, are recorded in the Scroll of the Kings of Judah and Israel. **25:27** From the time Amaziah turned from following the LORD, conspirators plotted against him in Jerusalem, so he fled to Lachish. But they sent assassins after him and they killed

him there. **25:28** His body was carried back by horses, and he was buried in Jerusalem with his ancestors in the City of David.

Uzziah's Reign

26:1 All the people of Judah took Uzziah, who was sixteen years old, and made him king in his father Amaziah's place. **26:2** Uzziah built up Elat and restored it to Judah after King Amaziah had passed away.

26:3 Uzziah was sixteen years old when he began to reign, and he reigned for fifty-two years in Jerusalem. His mother's name was Jecoliah, who was from Jerusalem. **26:4** He did what the LORD approved, just as his father Amaziah had done. **26:5** He followed God during the lifetime of Zechariah, who taught him how to honor God. As long as he followed the LORD, God caused him to succeed.

26:6 Uzziah attacked the Philistines and broke down the walls of Gath, Jabneh, and Ashdod. He built cities in the region of Ashdod and throughout Philistine territory. **26:7** God helped him in his campaigns against the Philistines, the Arabs living in Gur Baal, and the Meunites. **26:8** The Ammonites paid tribute to Uzziah and his fame reached the border of Egypt, for he grew in power.

26:9 Uzziah built and fortified towers in Jerusalem at the Corner Gate, Valley Gate, and at the Angle. **26:10** He built towers in the desert and dug many cisterns, for he owned many herds in the lowlands and on the plain. He had workers in the fields and vineyards in the hills and in Carmel, for he loved agriculture.

26:11 Uzziah had an army of skilled warriors trained for battle. They were organized by divisions according to the muster rolls made by Jeiel the scribe and Maaseiah the officer under the authority of Hananiah, a royal official. **26:12** The total number of family leaders who led warriors was 2,600. **26:13** They commanded an army of 307,500 skilled and able warriors who were ready to defend the king against his enemies. **26:14** Uzziah supplied shields, spears, helmets, breastplates, bows, and slingstones for the entire army. **26:15** In Jerusalem he made war machines carefully designed to shoot arrows and large stones from the towers and corners of the walls. He became very famous, for he received tremendous support and became powerful.

26:16 But once he became powerful, his pride destroyed him. He disobeyed the LORD his God. He entered the LORD's temple to offer incense on the incense altar. **26:17** Azariah the priest and eighty other brave priests of the LORD followed him in. **26:18** They confronted King Uzziah and said to him, "It is not proper for you, Uzziah, to offer incense to the LORD. That is the responsibility of the priests, the descendants of Aaron, who are consecrated to offer incense. Leave the sanctuary, for you have disobeyed and the LORD God will not honor you!" **26:19** Uzziah, who had an incense censer in his hand, became angry. While he was ranting and raving at the priests, a skin disease appeared on his forehead right there in front of the priests in the LORD's temple near the incense altar. **26:20** When Azariah the high priest and the other priests looked at him, there was a skin disease on his forehead. They hurried him out of there; even the king himself wanted to leave quickly because the LORD had afflicted him. **26:21** King Uzziah suffered from a skin disease until the day he died. He lived in separate quarters, afflicted by a skin disease and banned from the LORD's temple. His son Jotham was in charge of the palace and ruled over the people of the land.

26:22 The rest of the events of Uzziah's reign, from start to finish, were recorded by the prophet Isaiah son of Amoz. **26:23** Uzziah passed away and was buried near his ancestors in a cemetery belonging to the kings. (This was because he had a skin disease.) His son Jotham replaced him as king.

Jotham's Reign

27:1 Jotham was twenty-five years old when he began to reign, and he reigned for sixteen years in Jerusalem. His mother was Jerusha the daughter of Zadok. **27:2** He did what the LORD approved, just as his father Uzziah had done. (He did not, however, have the audacity to enter the temple.) Yet the people were still sinning.

27:3 He built the Upper Gate to the LORD's temple and did a lot of work on the wall in the area known as Ophel. **27:4** He built cities in the hill country of Judah and fortresses and towers in the forests.

27:5 He launched a military campaign against the king of the Ammonites and defeated them. That year the Ammonites paid him 100 talents of silver, 10,000 kors of wheat, and 10,000 kors of barley. The Ammonites also paid this same amount of annual tribute the next two years.

27:6 Jotham grew powerful because he was determined to please the LORD his God. **27:7** The rest of the events of Jotham's reign, including all his military campaigns and his accomplishments, are recorded in the scroll of the kings of Israel and Judah. **27:8** He was twenty-five years old when he began to reign, and he reigned for sixteen years in Jerusalem. **27:9** Jotham passed away and was buried in the City of David. His son Ahaz replaced him as king.

Ahaz's Reign

28:1 Ahaz was twenty years old when he began to reign, and he reigned for sixteen years in Jerusalem. He did not do what pleased the LORD, in contrast to his ancestor David. **28:2** He followed in the footsteps of the kings of Israel; he also made images of the Baals. **28:3** He offered sacrifices in the Valley of Ben-Hinnom and passed his sons through the fire, a horrible sin practiced by the nations whom the LORD drove out before the Israelites. **28:4** He offered sacrifices and burned incense on the high places, on the hills, and under every green tree.

28:5 The LORD his God handed him over to the king of Syria. The Syrians defeated him and deported many captives to Damascus. He was also handed over to the king of Israel, who thoroughly defeated him. **28:6** In one day King Pekah son of Remaliah of Israel killed 120,000 warriors in Judah, because they had abandoned the LORD God of their ancestors. **28:7** Zikri, an Ephraimite warrior, killed the king's son Maaseiah, Azrikam, the supervisor of the palace, and Elkanah, the king's second-in-command. **28:8** The Israelites seized from their brothers 200,000 wives, sons, and daughters. They also carried off a huge amount of plunder and took it back to Samaria.

28:9 Oded, a prophet of the LORD, was there. He went to meet the army as they arrived in Samaria and said to them: "Look, because the LORD God of your ancestors was angry with Judah he handed them over to you. You have killed them so mercilessly that God has taken notice. **28:10** And now you are planning to enslave the people of Judah and Jerusalem. Yet are you not also guilty before the LORD your God? **28:11** Now listen to me! Send back those you have seized from your brothers, for the LORD is very angry at you!" **28:12** So some of the Ephraimite family leaders, Azariah son of Jehochanan, Berechiah son of Meshillemoth, Jechizkiah son of Shallum, and Amasa son of Hadlai confronted those returning from the battle. **28:13** They said to them, "Don't bring those captives here! Are you planning on making us even more sinful and guilty before the LORD? Our guilt is already great and the LORD is very angry at Israel." **28:14** So the soldiers released the captives and the plunder before the officials and the entire assembly. **28:15** Men were assigned to take the prisoners and find clothes among the plunder for those who were naked. So they clothed them, supplied them with sandals, gave them food and drink, and provided them with oil to rub on their skin. They put the ones who couldn't walk on donkeys. They brought them back to their brothers at Jericho, the city of the date palm trees, and then returned to Samaria.

28:16 At that time King Ahaz asked the king of Assyria for help. **28:17** The Edomites had again invaded and defeated Judah and carried off captives. **28:18** The Philistines had raided the cities of Judah in the lowlands and the Negev. They captured and settled in Beth Shemesh, Aijalon, Gederoth, Soco and its surrounding villages, Timnah and its surrounding villages, and Gimzo and its surrounding villages. **28:19** The LORD humiliated Judah because of King Ahaz of Israel, for he encouraged Judah to sin and was very unfaithful to the LORD. **28:20** King Tiglath-pileser of Assyria came, but he gave him more trouble than support. **28:21** Ahaz gathered riches from the LORD's temple, the royal palace, and the officials and gave them to the king of Assyria, but that did not help.

28:22 During his time of trouble King Ahaz was even more unfaithful to the LORD. **28:23** He offered sacrifices to the gods of Damascus whom he thought had defeated him. He reasoned, "Since the gods of the kings of Damascus helped them, I will sacrifice to them so they will help me." But they caused him and all Israel to stumble. **28:24** Ahaz gathered the items in God's temple and removed them. He shut the doors of the LORD's temple and erected altars on every street corner in Jerusalem. **28:25** In every city throughout Judah he set up high places to offer sacrifices to other gods. He angered the LORD God of his ancestors.

28:26 The rest of the events of Ahaz's reign, including his accomplishments from start to finish, are recorded in the Scroll of the Kings of Judah and Israel. **28:27** Ahaz passed away and was buried in the City of David; they did not bring him to the tombs of the kings of Israel. His son Hezekiah replaced him as king.

Hezekiah Consecrates the Temple

29:1 Hezekiah was twenty-five years old when he began to reign, and he reigned twenty-nine years in Jerusalem. His mother was Abijah, the daughter of Zechariah. **29:2** He did what the LORD approved, just as his ancestor David had done.

29:3 In the first month of the first year of his reign, he opened the doors of the LORD's temple and repaired them. **29:4** He brought in the priests and Levites and assembled them in the square on the east side. **29:5** He said to them: "Listen to me, you Levites! Now consecrate yourselves, so you can consecrate the temple of the LORD God of your ancestors! Remove from the sanctuary what is ceremonially unclean! **29:6** For our fathers were unfaithful; they did what is evil in the sight of the LORD our God and abandoned him! They turned away from the LORD's dwelling place and rejected him. **29:7** They closed the doors of the temple porch and put out the lamps; they did not offer incense or burnt sacrifices in the sanctuary of the God of Israel. **29:8** The LORD was angry at Judah and Jerusalem and made them an appalling object of horror at which people hiss out their scorn, as you can see with your own eyes. **29:9** Look, our fathers died violently and our sons, daughters, and wives were carried off because of this. **29:10** Now I intend to make a covenant with the LORD God of Israel, so that he may relent from his raging anger. **29:11** My sons, do not be negligent now, for the LORD has chosen you to serve in his presence and offer sacrifices."

29:12 The following Levites prepared to carry out the king's orders:
From the Kohathites: Mahath son of Amasai and Joel son of Azariah;

from the Merarites: Kish son of Abdi and Azariah son of Jehallelel;
from the Gershonites: Joah son of Zimmah and Eden son of Joah;
29:13 from the descendants of Elizaphan: Shimri and Jeiel;
from the descendants of Asaph: Zechariah and Mattaniah;
29:14 from the descendants of Heman: Jehiel and Shimei;
from the descendants of Jeduthun: Shemaiah and Uzziel.

29:15 They assembled their brothers and consecrated themselves. Then they went in to purify the LORD's temple, just as the king had ordered, in accordance with the word of the LORD. **29:16** The priests then entered the LORD's temple to purify it; they brought out to the courtyard of the LORD's temple every ceremonially unclean thing they discovered inside. The Levites took them out to the Kidron Valley. **29:17** On the first day of the first month they began consecrating; by the eighth day of the month they reached the porch of the LORD's temple. For eight more days they consecrated the LORD's temple. On the sixteenth day of the first month they were finished. **29:18** They went to King Hezekiah and said: "We have purified the entire temple of the LORD, including the altar of burnt sacrifice and all its equipment, and the table for the Bread of the Presence and all its equipment. **29:19** We have prepared and consecrated all the items that King Ahaz removed during his reign when he acted unfaithfully. They are in front of the altar of the LORD."

29:20 Early the next morning King Hezekiah assembled the city officials and went up to the LORD's temple. **29:21** They brought seven bulls, seven rams, seven lambs, and seven goats as a sin offering for the kingdom, the sanctuary, and Judah. The king told the priests, the descendants of Aaron, to offer burnt sacrifices on the altar of the LORD. **29:22** They slaughtered the bulls, and the priests took the blood and splashed it on the altar. Then they slaughtered the rams and splashed the blood on the altar; next they slaughtered the lambs and splashed the blood on the altar. **29:23** Finally they brought the goats for the sin offering before the king and the assembly, and they placed their hands on them. **29:24** Then the priests slaughtered them. They offered their blood as a sin offering on the altar to make atonement for all Israel, because the king had decreed that the burnt sacrifice and sin offering were for all Israel.

29:25 King Hezekiah stationed the Levites in the LORD's temple with cymbals and stringed instruments, just as David, Gad the king's prophet, and Nathan the prophet had ordered. (The LORD had actually given these orders through his prophets.) **29:26** The Levites had David's musical instruments and the priests had trumpets. **29:27** Hezekiah ordered the burnt sacrifice to be offered on the altar. As they began to offer the sacrifice, they also began to sing to the LORD, accompanied by the trumpets and the musical instruments of King David of Israel. **29:28** The entire assembly worshiped, as the singers sang and the trumpeters played. They continued until the burnt sacrifice was completed.

29:29 When the sacrifices were completed, the king and all who were with him bowed down and worshiped. **29:30** King Hezekiah and the officials told the Levites to praise the LORD, using the psalms of David and Asaph the prophet. So they joyfully offered praise and bowed down and worshiped. **29:31** Hezekiah said, "Now you have consecrated yourselves to the LORD. Come and bring sacrifices and thank offerings to the LORD's temple." So the assembly brought sacrifices and thank offerings, and whoever desired to do so brought burnt sacrifices.

29:32 The assembly brought a total of 70 bulls, 100 rams, and 200 lambs as burnt sacrifices to the LORD, **29:33** and 600 bulls and 3,000 sheep were consecrated. **29:34** But there were not enough priests to skin all the animals, so their brothers, the Levites, helped them until the work was finished and the priests could consecrate themselves. (The Levites had been more conscientious about consecrating themselves than the priests.) **29:35** There was a large number of burnt sacrifices, as well as fat from the peace offerings and drink offerings that accompanied the burnt sacrifices. So the service of the LORD's temple was reinstituted. **29:36** Hezekiah and all the people were happy about what God had done for them, for it had been done quickly.

Hezekiah Observes the Passover

30:1 Hezekiah sent messages throughout Israel and Judah; he even wrote letters to Ephraim and Manasseh, summoning them to come to the LORD's temple in Jerusalem and observe a Passover celebration for the LORD God of Israel. **30:2** The king, his officials, and the entire assembly in Jerusalem decided to observe the Passover in the second month. **30:3** They were unable to observe it at the regular time because not enough priests had consecrated themselves and the people had not assembled in Jerusalem. **30:4** The proposal seemed appropriate to the king and the entire assembly. **30:5** So they sent an edict throughout Israel from Beer Sheba to Dan, summoning the people to come and observe a Passover for the LORD God of Israel in Jerusalem, for they had not observed it on a nationwide scale as prescribed in the law. **30:6** Messengers delivered the letters from the king and his officials throughout Israel and Judah. This royal edict read: "O Israelites, return to the LORD God of Abraham, Isaac, and Israel, so he may return to you who have been spared from the kings of Assyria. **30:7** Don't be like your fathers and brothers who were unfaithful to the LORD God of their ancestors, provoking him to destroy them, as you can see. **30:8** Now, don't be stubborn like your fathers! Submit to the LORD and come to his sanctuary which he has permanently consecrated. Serve the LORD your God so that he might relent from his raging anger. **30:9** For if you return to the LORD, your brothers and sons will be shown mercy by their captors and return to this land. The LORD your God is merciful and compassionate; he will not reject you if you return to him."

30:10 The messengers journeyed from city to city through the land of Ephraim and Manasseh as far as Zebulun, but people mocked and ridiculed them. **30:11** But some men from Asher, Manasseh, and Zebulun humbled themselves and came to Jerusalem. **30:12** In Judah God moved the people to unite and carry out the edict the king and the officers had issued at the LORD's command. **30:13** A huge crowd assembled in Jerusalem to observe the Feast of Unleavened Bread in the second month. **30:14** They removed the altars in Jerusalem; they also removed all the incense altars and threw them into the Kidron Valley.

30:15 They slaughtered the Passover lamb on the fourteenth day of the second month. The priests and Levites were ashamed, so they consecrated themselves and brought burnt sacrifices to the LORD's temple. **30:16** They stood at their posts according to the regulations outlined in the law of Moses, the man of God. The priests were splashing the blood as the Levites handed it to them. **30:17** Because many in the assembly had not consecrated themselves, the Levites slaughtered the Passover lambs of all who were ceremonially unclean and could not consecrate their sacrifice to the LORD. **30:18** The majority of the many people from Ephraim, Manasseh, Issachar, and Zebulun were ceremonially unclean, yet they ate the Passover in violation of what is prescribed in the law. For Hezekiah prayed for them, saying: "May the LORD, who is good, forgive **30:19** everyone who has determined to follow God, the LORD God of his ancestors, even if he is not ceremonially clean according to the standards of the temple." **30:20** The LORD responded favorably to Hezekiah and forgave the people.

30:21 The Israelites who were in Jerusalem observed the Feast of Unleavened Bread for seven days with great joy. The Levites and priests were praising the LORD every day with all their might. **30:22** Hezekiah expressed his appreciation to all the Levites, who demonstrated great skill in serving the LORD. They feasted for the seven days of the festival, and were making peace offerings and giving thanks to the LORD God of their ancestors.

30:23 The entire assembly then decided to celebrate for seven more days; so they joyfully celebrated for seven more days. **30:24** King Hezekiah of Judah supplied 1,000 bulls and 7,000 sheep for the assembly, while the officials supplied them with 1,000 bulls and 10,000 sheep. Many priests consecrated themselves. **30:25** The celebration included the entire assembly of Judah, the priests, the Levites, the entire assembly of those who came from Israel, the resident foreigners who came from the land of Israel, and the residents of Judah. **30:26** There was a great celebration in Jerusalem, unlike anything that had occurred in Jerusalem since the time of King Solomon son of David of Israel. **30:27** The priests and Levites got up and pronounced blessings on the people. The LORD responded favorably to them as their prayers reached his holy dwelling place in heaven.

31:1 When all this was over, the Israelites who were in the cities of Judah went out and smashed the sacred pillars, cut down the Asherah poles, and demolished all the high places and altars throughout Judah, Benjamin, Ephraim, and Manasseh. Then all the Israelites returned to their own homes in their cities.

The People Contribute to the Temple

31:2 Hezekiah appointed the divisions of the priests and Levites to do their assigned tasks – to offer burnt sacrifices and present offerings and to serve, give thanks, and offer praise in the gates of the LORD's sanctuary.

31:3 The king contributed some of what he owned for burnt sacrifices, including the morning and evening burnt sacrifices and the burnt sacrifices made on Sabbaths, new moon festivals, and at other appointed times prescribed in the law of the LORD. **31:4** He ordered the people living in Jerusalem to contribute the portion prescribed for the priests and Levites so they might be obedient to the law of the LORD. **31:5** When the edict was issued, the Israelites freely contributed the initial portion of their grain, wine, olive oil, honey, and all the produce of their fields. They brought a tenth of everything, which added up to a huge amount. **31:6** The Israelites and people of Judah who lived in the cities of Judah also contributed a tenth of their cattle and sheep, as well as a tenth of the holy items consecrated to the LORD their God. They brought them and placed them in many heaps. **31:7** In the third month they began piling their contributions in heaps and finished in the seventh month. **31:8** When Hezekiah and the officials came and saw the heaps, they praised the LORD and pronounced blessings on his people Israel.

31:9 When Hezekiah asked the priests and Levites about the heaps, **31:10** Azariah, the head priest from the family of Zadok, said to him, "Since the contributions began arriving in the LORD's temple, we have had plenty to eat and have a large quantity left over. For the LORD has blessed his people, and this large amount remains." **31:11** Hezekiah ordered that storerooms be prepared in the LORD's temple. When this was done, **31:12** they brought in the contributions, tithes, and consecrated items that had been offered. Konaniah, a Levite, was in charge of all this, assisted by his

brother Shimei. **31:13** Jehiel, Azaziah, Nahath, Asahel, Jerimoth, Jozabad, Eliel, Ismakiah, Mahath, and Benaiah worked under the supervision of Konaniah and his brother Shimei, as directed by King Hezekiah and Azariah, the supervisor of God's temple.

31:14 Kore son of Imnah, a Levite and the guard on the east side, was in charge of the voluntary offerings made to God and disbursed the contributions made to the LORD and the consecrated items. **31:15** In the cities of the priests, Eden, Miniamin, Jeshua, Shemaiah, Amariah, and Shecaniah faithfully assisted him in making disbursements to their fellow priests according to their divisions, regardless of age. **31:16** They made disbursements to all the males three years old and up who were listed in the genealogical records – to all who would enter the LORD's temple to serve on a daily basis and fulfill their duties as assigned to their divisions. **31:17** They made disbursements to the priests listed in the genealogical records by their families, and to the Levites twenty years old and up, according to their duties as assigned to their divisions, **31:18** and to all the infants, wives, sons, and daughters of the entire assembly listed in the genealogical records, for they faithfully consecrated themselves. **31:19** As for the descendants of Aaron, the priests who lived in the outskirts of all their cities, men were assigned to disburse portions to every male among the priests and to every Levite listed in the genealogical records.

31:20 This is what Hezekiah did throughout Judah. He did what the LORD his God considered good and right and faithful. **31:21** He wholeheartedly and successfully reinstituted service in God's temple and obedience to the law, in order to follow his God.

Sennacherib Invades Judah

32:1 After these faithful deeds were accomplished, King Sennacherib of Assyria invaded Judah. He besieged the fortified cities, intending to seize them. **32:2** When Hezekiah saw that Sennacherib had invaded and intended to attack Jerusalem, **32:3** he consulted with his advisers and military officers about stopping up the springs outside the city, and they supported him. **32:4** A large number of people gathered together and stopped up all the springs and the stream that flowed through the district. They reasoned, "Why should the kings of Assyria come and find plenty of water?" **32:5** Hezekiah energetically rebuilt every broken wall. He erected towers and an outer wall, and fortified the terrace of the City of David. He made many weapons and shields.

32:6 He appointed military officers over the army and assembled them in the square at the city gate. He encouraged them, saying, **32:7** "Be strong and brave! Don't be afraid and don't panic because of the king of Assyria and this huge army that is with him! We have with us one who is stronger than those who are with him. **32:8** He has with him mere human strength, but the LORD our God is with us to help us and fight our battles!" The army was encouraged by the words of King Hezekiah of Judah.

32:9 Afterward King Sennacherib of Assyria, while attacking Lachish with all his military might, sent his messengers to Jerusalem. The message was for King Hezekiah of Judah and all the people of Judah who were in Jerusalem. It read: **32:10** "This is what King Sennacherib of Assyria says: 'Why are you so confident that you remain in Jerusalem while it is under siege? **32:11** Hezekiah says, "The LORD our God will rescue us from the power of the king of Assyria." But he is misleading you and you will die of hunger and thirst! **32:12** Hezekiah is the one who eliminated the LORD's high places and altars and then told Judah and Jerusalem, "At one altar you must worship and offer sacrifices." **32:13** Are you not aware of what I and my predecessors have done to all the nations of the surrounding lands? Have the gods of the surrounding lands actually been able to rescue their lands from my power? **32:14** Who among all the gods of these nations whom my predecessors annihilated was able to rescue his people from my power? **32:15** Now don't let Hezekiah deceive you or mislead you like this. Don't believe him, for no god of any nation or kingdom has been able to rescue his people from my power or the power of my predecessors. So how can your gods rescue you from my power?'"

32:16 Sennacherib's servants further insulted the LORD God and his servant Hezekiah. **32:17** He wrote letters mocking the LORD God of Israel and insulting him with these words: "The gods of the surrounding nations could not rescue their people from my power. Neither can Hezekiah's god rescue his people from my power." **32:18** They called out loudly in the Judahite dialect to the people of Jerusalem who were on the wall, trying to scare and terrify them so they could seize the city. **32:19** They talked about the God of Jerusalem as if he were one of the man-made gods of the nations of the earth.

32:20 King Hezekiah and the prophet Isaiah son of Amoz prayed about this and cried out to heaven. **32:21** The LORD sent a messenger and he wiped out all the soldiers, princes, and officers in the army of the king of Assyria. So Sennacherib returned home humiliated. When he entered the temple of his god, some of his own sons struck him down with the sword. **32:22** The LORD delivered Hezekiah and the residents of Jerusalem from the power of King Sennacherib of Assyria and from all the other nations. He made them secure on every side. **32:23** Many were bringing presents to the LORD in Jerusalem and precious gifts to King Hezekiah of Judah. From that time on he was respected by all the nations.

Hezekiah's Shortcomings and Accomplishments

32:24 In those days Hezekiah was stricken with a terminal illness. He prayed to the LORD, who answered him and gave him a sign confirming that he would be healed. **32:25** But Hezekiah was ungrateful; he had a proud attitude, provoking God to be angry at him, as well as Judah and Jerusalem. **32:26** But then Hezekiah and the residents of Jerusalem humbled themselves and abandoned their pride, and the LORD was not angry with them for the rest of Hezekiah's reign.

32:27 Hezekiah was very wealthy and greatly respected. He made storehouses for his silver, gold, precious stones, spices, and all his other valuable possessions. **32:28** He made storerooms for the harvest of grain, wine, and olive oil, and stalls for all his various kinds of livestock and his flocks. **32:29** He built royal cities and owned a large number of sheep and cattle, for God gave him a huge amount of possessions.

32:30 Hezekiah dammed up the source of the waters of the Upper Gihon and directed them down to the west side of the City of David. Hezekiah succeeded in all that he did. **32:31** So when the envoys arrived from the Babylonian officials to visit him and inquire about the sign that occurred in the land, God left him alone to test him, in order to know his true motives.

32:32 The rest of the events of Hezekiah's reign, including his faithful deeds, are recorded in the vision of the prophet Isaiah son of Amoz, included in the Scroll of the Kings of Judah and Israel. **32:33** Hezekiah passed away and was buried on the ascent of the tombs of the descendants of David. All the people of Judah and the residents of Jerusalem buried him with great honor. His son Manasseh replaced him as king.

Manasseh's Reign

33:1 Manasseh was twelve years old when he became king, and he reigned for fifty-five years in Jerusalem. **33:2** He did evil in the sight of the LORD and committed the same horrible sins practiced by the nations whom the LORD drove out ahead of the Israelites. **33:3** He rebuilt the high places that his father Hezekiah had destroyed; he set up altars for the Baals and made Asherah poles. He bowed down to all the stars in the sky and worshiped them. **33:4** He built altars in the LORD's temple, about which the LORD had said, "Jerusalem will be my permanent home." **33:5** In the two courtyards of the LORD's temple he built altars for all the stars in the sky. **33:6** He passed his sons through the fire in the Valley of Ben-Hinnom and practiced divination, omen reading, and sorcery. He set up a ritual pit to conjure up underworld spirits and appointed magicians to supervise it. He did a great amount of evil in the sight of the LORD and angered him. **33:7** He put an idolatrous image he had made in God's temple, about which God had said to David and to his son Solomon, "This temple in Jerusalem, which I have chosen out of all the tribes of Israel, will be my permanent home. **33:8** I will not make Israel again leave the land I gave to their ancestors, provided that they carefully obey all I commanded them, the whole law, the rules and regulations given to Moses." **33:9** But Manasseh misled the people of Judah and the residents of Jerusalem so that they sinned more than the nations whom the LORD had destroyed ahead of the Israelites.

33:10 The LORD confronted Manasseh and his people, but they paid no attention. **33:11** So the LORD brought against them the commanders of the army of the king of Assyria. They seized Manasseh, put hooks in his nose, bound him with bronze chains, and carried him away to Babylon. **33:12** In his pain Manasseh asked the LORD his God for mercy and truly humbled himself before the God of his ancestors. **33:13** When he prayed to the LORD, the LORD responded to him and answered favorably his cry for mercy. The LORD brought him back to Jerusalem to his kingdom. Then Manasseh realized that the LORD is the true God.

33:14 After this Manasseh built up the outer wall of the City of David on the west side of the Gihon in the valley to the entrance of the Fish Gate and all around the terrace; he made it much higher. He placed army officers in all the fortified cities in Judah.

33:15 He removed the foreign gods and images from the LORD's temple and all the altars he had built on the hill of the LORD's temple and in Jerusalem; he threw them outside the city. **33:16** He erected the altar of the LORD and offered on it peace offerings and thank offerings. He told the people of Judah to serve the LORD God of Israel. **33:17** The people continued to offer sacrifices at the high places, but only to the LORD their God.

33:18 The rest of the events of Manasseh's reign, including his prayer to his God and the words the prophets spoke to him in the name of the LORD God of Israel, are recorded in the Annals of the Kings of Israel. **33:19** The Annals of the Prophets include his prayer, give an account of how the LORD responded to it, record all his sins and unfaithful acts, and identify the sites where he built high places and erected Asherah poles and idols before he humbled himself. **33:20** Manasseh passed away and was buried in his palace. His son Amon replaced him as king.

Amon's Reign

33:21 Amon was twenty-two years old when he became king, and he reigned for two years in Jerusalem. **33:22** He did evil in the sight of the LORD, just like his father Manasseh had done. He offered sacrifices to all the idols his father Manasseh had made, and worshiped them. **33:23** He did not humble himself before the LORD as his father Manasseh had done. Amon was guilty of great sin. **33:24** His servants conspired against

him and killed him in his palace. **33:25** The people of the land executed all who had conspired against King Amon, and they made his son Josiah king in his place.

Josiah Institutes Religious Reforms

34:1 Josiah was eight years old when he became king, and he reigned for thirty-one years in Jerusalem. **34:2** He did what the LORD approved and followed in his ancestor David's footsteps; he did not deviate to the right or the left.

34:3 In the eighth year of his reign, while he was still young, he began to seek the God of his ancestor David. In his twelfth year he began ridding Judah and Jerusalem of the high places, Asherah poles, idols, and images. **34:4** He ordered the altars of the Baals to be torn down, and broke the incense altars that were above them. He smashed the Asherah poles, idols and images, crushed them up and sprinkled the dust over the tombs of those who had sacrificed to them. **34:5** He burned the bones of the pagan priests on their altars; he purified Judah and Jerusalem. **34:6** In the cities of Manasseh, Ephraim, and Simeon, as far as Naphtali, and in the ruins around them, **34:7** he tore down the altars and Asherah poles, demolished the idols, and smashed all the incense altars throughout the land of Israel. He returned to Jerusalem.

34:8 In the eighteenth year of his reign, he continued his policy of purifying the land and the temple. He sent Shaphan son of Azaliah, Maaseiah the city official, and Joah son of Joahaz the secretary to repair the temple of the LORD his God. **34:9** They went to Hilkiah the high priest and gave him the silver that had been brought to God's temple. The Levites who guarded the door had collected it from the people of Manasseh and Ephraim and from all who were left in Israel, as well as from all the people of Judah and Benjamin and the residents of Jerusalem. **34:10** They handed it over to the construction foremen assigned to the LORD's temple. They in turn paid the temple workers to restore and repair it. **34:11** They gave money to the craftsmen and builders to buy chiseled stone and wood for the braces and rafters of the buildings that the kings of Judah had allowed to fall into disrepair. **34:12** The men worked faithfully. Their supervisors were Jahath and Obadiah (Levites descended from Merari), as well as Zechariah and Meshullam (descendants of Kohath). The Levites, all of whom were skilled musicians, **34:13** supervised the laborers and all the foremen on their various jobs. Some of the Levites were scribes, officials, and guards.

34:14 When they took out the silver that had been brought to the LORD's temple, Hilkiah the priest found the law scroll the LORD had given to Moses. **34:15** Hilkiah informed Shaphan the scribe, "I found the law scroll in the LORD's temple." Hilkiah gave the scroll to Shaphan. **34:16** Shaphan brought the scroll to the king and reported, "Your servants are doing everything assigned to them. **34:17** They melted down the silver in the LORD's temple and handed it over to the supervisors of the construction foremen." **34:18** Then Shaphan the scribe told the king, "Hilkiah the priest has given me a scroll." Shaphan read it out loud before the king. **34:19** When the king heard the words of the law scroll, he tore his clothes. **34:20** The king ordered Hilkiah, Ahikam son of Shaphan, Abdon son of Micah, Shaphan the scribe, and Asaiah the king's servant, **34:21** "Go, seek an oracle from the LORD for me and those who remain in Israel and Judah. Find out about the words of this scroll that has been discovered. For the LORD's fury has been ignited against us, because our ancestors have not obeyed the word of the LORD by doing all that this scroll instructs!"

34:22 So Hilkiah and the others sent by the king went to Huldah the prophetess, the wife of Shallum son of Tokhath, the son of Hasrah, the supervisor of the wardrobe. (She lived in Jerusalem in the Mishneh district.) They stated their business, **34:23** and she said to them: "This is what the LORD God of Israel says: 'Say this to the man who sent you to me: **34:24** 'This is what the LORD says: 'I am about to bring disaster on this place and its residents, the details of which are recorded in the scroll which they read before the king of Judah. **34:25** This will happen because they have abandoned me and offered sacrifices to other gods, angering me with all the idols they have made. My anger will ignite against this place and will not be extinguished!'" **34:26** Say this to the king of Judah, who sent you to seek an oracle from the LORD: "This is what the LORD God of Israel says concerning the words you have heard: **34:27** 'You displayed a sensitive spirit and humbled yourself before God when you heard his words concerning this place and its residents. You humbled yourself before me, tore your clothes and wept before me, and I have heard you,' says the LORD. **34:28** 'Therefore I will allow you to die and be buried in peace. You will not have to witness all the disaster I will bring on this place and its residents.'"'" Then they reported back to the king.

34:29 The king summoned all the leaders of Judah and Jerusalem. **34:30** The king went up to the LORD's temple, accompanied by all the people of Judah, the residents of Jerusalem, the priests, and the Levites. All the people were there, from the oldest to the youngest. He read aloud all the words of the scroll of the covenant that had been discovered in the LORD's temple. **34:31** The king stood by his pillar and renewed the covenant before the LORD, agreeing to follow the LORD and to obey his commandments, laws, and rules with all his heart and being, by carrying out the terms of this covenant recorded on this scroll. **34:32** He made all who were in Jerusalem and Benjamin agree to it. The residents of Jerusalem acted in accordance with the covenant of God, the God of their ancestors. **34:33** Josiah removed all the detestable idols from all the areas belonging to the Israelites and encouraged all who were in Israel to worship the LORD their God. Throughout the rest of his reign they did not turn aside from following the LORD God of their ancestors.

Josiah Observes the Passover

35:1 Josiah observed a Passover festival for the LORD in Jerusalem. They slaughtered the Passover lambs on the fourteenth day of the first month. **35:2** He appointed the priests to fulfill their duties and encouraged them to carry out their service in the LORD's temple. **35:3** He told the Levites, who instructed all Israel about things consecrated to the LORD, "Place the holy ark in the temple which King Solomon son of David of Israel built. Don't carry it on your shoulders. Now serve the LORD your God and his people Israel! **35:4** Prepare yourselves by your families according to your divisions, as instructed by King David of Israel and his son Solomon. **35:5** Stand in the sanctuary and, together with the Levites, represent the family divisions of your countrymen. **35:6** Slaughter the Passover lambs, consecrate yourselves, and make preparations for your countrymen to do what the LORD commanded through Moses."

35:7 From his own royal flocks and herds, Josiah supplied the people with 30,000 lambs and goats for the Passover sacrifice, as well as 3,000 cattle. **35:8** His officials also willingly contributed to the people, priests, and Levites. Hilkiah, Zechariah, and Jehiel, the leaders of God's temple, supplied 2,600 Passover sacrifices and 300 cattle. **35:9** Konaniah and his brothers Shemaiah and Nethanel, along with Hashabiah, Jeiel, and Jozabad, the officials of the Levites, supplied the Levites with 5,000 Passover sacrifices and 500 cattle. **35:10** Preparations were made, and the priests stood at their posts and the Levites in their divisions as prescribed by the king. **35:11** They slaughtered the Passover lambs and the priests splashed the blood, while the Levites skinned the animals. **35:12** They reserved the burnt offerings and the cattle for the family divisions of the people to present to the LORD, as prescribed in the scroll of Moses. **35:13** They cooked the Passover sacrifices over the open fire as prescribed and cooked the consecrated offerings in pots, kettles, and pans. They quickly served them to all the people. **35:14** Afterward they made preparations for themselves and for the priests, because the priests, the descendants of Aaron, were offering burnt sacrifices and fat portions until evening. The Levites made preparations for themselves and for the priests, the descendants of Aaron. **35:15** The musicians, the descendants of Asaph, manned their posts, as prescribed by David, Asaph, Heman, and Jeduthun the king's prophet. The guards at the various gates did not need to leave their posts, for their fellow Levites made preparations for them. **35:16** So all the preparations for the LORD's service were made that day, as the Passover was observed and the burnt sacrifices were offered on the altar of the LORD, as prescribed by King Josiah. **35:17** So the Israelites who were present observed the Passover at that time, as well as the Feast of Unleavened Bread for seven days. **35:18** A Passover like this had not been observed in Israel since the days of Samuel the prophet. None of the kings of Israel had observed a Passover like the one celebrated by Josiah, the priests, the Levites, all the people of Judah and Israel who were there, and the residents of Jerusalem. **35:19** This Passover was observed in the eighteenth year of Josiah's reign.

Josiah's Reign Ends

35:20 After Josiah had done all this for the temple, King Necho of Egypt marched up to do battle at Carchemish on the Euphrates River. Josiah marched out to oppose him. **35:21** Necho sent messengers to him, saying, "Why are you opposing me, O king of Judah? I am not attacking you today, but the kingdom with which I am at war. God told me to hurry. Stop opposing God, who is with me, or else he will destroy you." **35:22** But Josiah did not turn back from him; he disguised himself for battle. He did not take seriously the words of Necho which he had received from God; he went to fight him in the Plain of Megiddo. **35:23** Archers shot King Josiah; the king ordered his servants, "Take me out of this chariot, for I am seriously wounded." **35:24** So his servants took him out of the chariot, put him in another chariot that he owned, and brought him to Jerusalem, where he died. He was buried in the tombs of his ancestors; all the people of Judah and Jerusalem mourned Josiah. **35:25** Jeremiah composed laments for Josiah which all the male and female singers use to mourn Josiah to this very day. It has become customary in Israel to sing these; they are recorded in the Book of Laments.

35:26 The rest of the events of Josiah's reign, including the faithful acts he did in obedience to what is written in the law of the LORD **35:27** and his accomplishments, from start to finish, are recorded in the Scroll of the Kings of Israel and Judah.

Jehoahaz's Reign

36:1 The people of the land took Jehoahaz son of Josiah and made him king in his father's place in Jerusalem. **36:2** Jehoahaz was twenty-three years old when he became king, and he reigned three months in Jerusalem. **36:3** The king of Egypt prevented him from ruling in Jerusalem and imposed on the land a special tax of one hundred talents of silver and a talent of gold. **36:4** The king of Egypt made Jehoahaz's brother Eliakim king over Judah and Jerusalem, and changed his name to Jehoiakim. Necho seized his brother Jehoahaz and took him to Egypt.

Jehoiakim's Reign

36:5 Jehoiakim was twenty-five years old when he became king, and he reigned for eleven years in Jerusalem. He did evil in the sight of the LORD his God. **36:6** King Nebuchadnezzar of Babylon attacked him, bound him with bronze chains, and carried him away to Babylon. **36:7** Nebuchadnezzar took some of the items in the LORD's temple to Babylon and put them in his palace there.

36:8 The rest of the events of Jehoiakim's reign, including the horrible sins he committed and his shortcomings, are recorded in the Scroll of the Kings of Israel and Judah. His son Jehoiachin replaced him as king.

Jehoiachin's Reign

36:9 Jehoiachin was eighteen years old when he became king, and he reigned three months and ten days in Jerusalem. He did evil in the sight of the LORD. **36:10** At the beginning of the year King Nebuchadnezzar ordered him to be brought to Babylon, along with the valuable items in the LORD's temple. In his place he made his relative Zedekiah king over Judah and Jerusalem.

Zedekiah's Reign

36:11 Zedekiah was twenty-one years old when he became king, and he ruled for eleven years in Jerusalem. **36:12** He did evil in the sight of the LORD his God. He did not humble himself before Jeremiah the prophet, the LORD's spokesman. **36:13** He also rebelled against King Nebuchadnezzar, who had made him vow allegiance in the name of God. He was stubborn and obstinate, and refused to return to the LORD God of Israel. **36:14** All the leaders of the priests and people became more unfaithful and committed the same horrible sins practiced by the nations. They defiled the LORD's temple which he had consecrated in Jerusalem.

The Babylonians Destroy Jerusalem

36:15 The LORD God of their ancestors continually warned them through his messengers, for he felt compassion for his people and his dwelling place. **36:16** But they mocked God's messengers, despised his warnings, and ridiculed his prophets. Finally the LORD got very angry at his people and there was no one who could prevent his judgment. **36:17** He brought against them the king of the Babylonians, who slaughtered their young men in their temple. He did not spare young men or women, or even the old and aging. God handed everyone over to him. **36:18** He carried away to Babylon all the items in God's temple, whether large or small, as well as what was in the treasuries of the LORD's temple and in the treasuries of the king and his officials. **36:19** They burned down the LORD's temple and tore down the wall of Jerusalem. They burned all its fortified buildings and destroyed all its valuable items. **36:20** He deported to Babylon all who escaped the sword. They served him and his sons until the Persian kingdom rose to power. **36:21** This took place to fulfill the LORD's message delivered

through Jeremiah. The land experienced its sabbatical years; it remained desolate for seventy years, as prophesied.

Cyrus Allows the Exiles to Go Home

36:22 In the first year of the reign of King Cyrus of Persia, in fulfillment of the promise he delivered through Jeremiah, the LORD moved King Cyrus of Persia to issue a written decree throughout his kingdom. **36:23** It read: "This is what King Cyrus of Persia says: 'The LORD God of the heavens has given to me all the kingdoms of the earth. He has appointed me to build for him a temple in Jerusalem in Judah. May the LORD your God energize you who belong to his people, so you may be able to go back there!'"

Book 15. Ezra

The Decree of Cyrus

1:1 In the first year of King Cyrus of Persia, in order to fulfill the LORD's message spoken through Jeremiah, the LORD stirred the mind of King Cyrus of Persia. He disseminated a proclamation throughout his entire kingdom, announcing in a written edict the following:

1:2 "Thus says King Cyrus of Persia:

"'The LORD God of heaven has given me all the kingdoms of the earth. He has instructed me to build a temple for him in Jerusalem, which is in Judah. **1:3** Anyone from his people among you (may his God be with him!) may go up to Jerusalem, which is in Judah, and may build the temple of the LORD God of Israel – he is the God who is in Jerusalem. **1:4** Anyone who survives in any of those places where he is a resident foreigner must be helped by his neighbors with silver, gold, equipment, and animals, along with voluntary offerings for the temple of God which is in Jerusalem.'"

The Exiles Prepare to Return to Jerusalem

1:5 Then the leaders of Judah and Benjamin, along with the priests and the Levites – all those whose mind God had stirred – got ready to go up in order to build the temple of the LORD in Jerusalem. **1:6** All their neighbors assisted them with silver utensils, gold, equipment, animals, and expensive gifts, not to mention all the voluntary offerings.

1:7 Then King Cyrus brought out the vessels of the LORD's temple which Nebuchadnezzar had brought from Jerusalem and had displayed in the temple of his gods. **1:8** King Cyrus of Persia entrusted them to Mithredath the treasurer, who counted them out to Sheshbazzar the leader of the Judahite exiles.

1:9 The inventory of these items was as follows:

30 gold basins,

1,000 silver basins,

29 silver utensils,

1:10 30 gold bowls,

410 other silver bowls,

and 1,000 other vessels.

1:11 All these gold and silver vessels totaled 5,400. Sheshbazzar brought them all along when the captives were brought up from Babylon to Jerusalem.

The Names of the Returning Exiles

2:1 These are the people of the province who were going up, from the captives of the exile whom King Nebuchadnezzar of Babylon had forced into exile in Babylon. They returned to Jerusalem and Judah, each to his own city. **2:2** They came with Zerubbabel, Jeshua, Nehemiah, Seraiah, Reelaiah, Mordecai, Bilshan, Mispar, Bigvai, Rehum, and Baanah.

The number of Israelites was as follows:

2:3 the descendants of Parosh: 2,172;

2:4 the descendants of Shephatiah: 372;

2:5 the descendants of Arah: 775;

2:6 the descendants of Pahath-Moab (from the line of Jeshua and Joab): 2,812;

2:7 the descendants of Elam: 1,254;

2:8 the descendants of Zattu: 945;

2:9 the descendants of Zaccai: 760;

2:10 the descendants of Bani: 642;

2:11 the descendants of Bebai: 623;

2:12 the descendants of Azgad: 1,222;

2:13 the descendants of Adonikam: 666;

2:14 the descendants of Bigvai: 2,056;

2:15 the descendants of Adin: 454;

2:16 the descendants of Ater (through Hezekiah): 98;

2:17 the descendants of Bezai: 323;

2:18 the descendants of Jorah: 112;

2:19 the descendants of Hashum: 223;

2:20 the descendants of Gibbar: 95.

2:21 The men of Bethlehem: 123;

2:22 the men of Netophah: 56;

2:23 the men of Anathoth: 128;

2:24 the men of the family of Azmaveth: 42;

2:25 the men of Kiriath Jearim, Kephirah and Beeroth: 743;

2:26 the men of Ramah and Geba: 621;

2:27 the men of Micmash: 122;

2:28 the men of Bethel and Ai: 223;

2:29 the descendants of Nebo: 52;

2:30 the descendants of Magbish: 156;

2:31 the descendants of the other Elam: 1,254;

2:32 the descendants of Harim: 320;

2:33 the men of Lod, Hadid, and Ono: 725;

2:34 the men of Jericho: 345;

2:35 the descendants of Senaah: 3,630.

2:36 The priests: the descendants of Jedaiah (through the family of Jeshua): 973;

2:37 the descendants of Immer: 1,052;

2:38 the descendants of Pashhur: 1,247;

2:39 the descendants of Harim: 1,017.

2:40 The Levites: the descendants of Jeshua and Kadmiel (through the line of Hodaviah): 74.

2:41 The singers: the descendants of Asaph: 128.

2:42 The gatekeepers: the descendants of Shallum, the descendants of Ater, the descendants of Talmon, the descendants of Akkub, the descendants of Hatita, and the descendants of Shobai: 139.

2:43 The temple servants: the descendants of Ziha, the descendants of Hasupha, the descendants of Tabbaoth, **2:44** the descendants of Keros, the descendants of Siaha, the descendants of Padon, **2:45** the descendants of Lebanah, the descendants of Hagabah, the descendants of Akkub, **2:46** the descendants of Hagab, the descendants of Shalmai, the descendants of Hanan, **2:47** the descendants of Giddel, the descendants of Gahar, the descendants of Reaiah, **2:48** the descendants of Rezin, the descendants of Nekoda, the descendants of Gazzam, **2:49** the descendants of Uzzah, the descendants of Paseah, the descendants of Besai, **2:50** the descendants of Asnah, the descendants of Meunim, the descendants of Nephussim, **2:51** the descendants of Bakbuk, the descendants of Hakupha, the descendants of Harhur, **2:52** the descendants of Bazluth, the descendants of Mehida, the descendants of Harsha, **2:53** the descendants of Barkos, the descendants of Sisera, the descendants of Temah, **2:54** the descendants of Neziah, and the descendants of Hatipha.

2:55 The descendants of the servants of Solomon: the descendants of Sotai, the descendants of Hassophereth, the descendants of Peruda, **2:56** the descendants of Jaala, the descendants of Darkon, the descendants of Giddel, **2:57** the descendants of Shephatiah, the descendants of Hattil, the descendants of Pokereth-Hazzebaim, and the descendants of Ami.

2:58 All the temple servants and the descendants of the servants of Solomon: 392.

2:59 These are the ones that came up from Tel Melah, Tel Harsha, Kerub, Addon, and Immer (although they were unable to certify their family connection or their ancestry, as to whether they really were from Israel):

2:60 the descendants of Delaiah, the descendants of Tobiah, and the descendants of Nekoda: 652.

2:61 And from among the priests: the descendants of Hobaiah, the descendants of Hakkoz, and the descendants of Barzillai (who had taken a wife from the daughters of Barzillai the Gileadite and was called by that name). **2:62** They searched for their records in the genealogical materials, but did not find them. They were therefore excluded from the priesthood. **2:63** The governor instructed them not to eat any of the sacred food until there was a priest who could consult the Urim and Thummim.

2:64 The entire group numbered 42,360, **2:65** not counting their male and female servants, who numbered 7,337. They also had 200 male and female singers **2:66** and 736 horses, 245 mules, **2:67** 435 camels, and 6,720 donkeys. **2:68** When they came to the LORD's temple in Jerusalem, some of the family leaders offered voluntary offerings for the temple of God in order to rebuild it on its site. **2:69** As they were able, they gave to the treasury for this work 61,000 drachmas of gold, 5,000 minas of silver, and 100 priestly robes.

2:70 The priests, the Levites, some of the people, the singers, the gatekeepers, and the temple servants lived in their towns, and all the rest of Israel lived in their towns.

The Altar is Rebuilt

3:1 When the seventh month arrived and the Israelites were living in their towns, the people assembled in Jerusalem. **3:2** Then Jeshua the son of Jozadak and his priestly colleagues and Zerubbabel son of Shealtiel and his colleagues started to build the altar of the God of Israel so they could offer burnt offerings on it as required by the law of Moses the man of God. **3:3** They established the altar on its foundations, even though they were in terror of the local peoples, and they offered burnt offerings on it to the LORD, both the morning and the evening offerings. **3:4** They observed the Festival of Temporary Shelters as required and offered the proper number of daily burnt offerings according to the requirement for each day. **3:5** Afterward they offered the continual burnt offerings and those for the new moons and those for all the holy assemblies of the LORD and all those that were being voluntarily offered to the LORD. **3:6** From the first day of the seventh month they began to offer burnt offerings to the LORD. However, the LORD's temple was not at that time established.

Preparations for Rebuilding the Temple

3:7 So they provided money for the masons and carpenters, and food, beverages, and olive oil for the people of Sidon and Tyre, so that they would bring cedar timber from Lebanon to the seaport at Joppa, in accord with the edict of King Cyrus of Persia. **3:8** In the second year after they had come to the temple of God in Jerusalem, in the second month, Zerubbabel the son of Shealtiel and Jeshua the son of Jozadak initiated the work, along with the rest of their associates, the priests and the Levites, and all those who were coming to Jerusalem from the exile. They appointed the Levites who were at least twenty years old to take charge of the work on the LORD's temple. **3:9** So Jeshua appointed both his sons and his relatives, Kadmiel and his sons (the sons of Yehudah), to take charge of the workers in the temple of God, along with the sons of Henadad, their sons, and their relatives the Levites. **3:10** When the builders established the LORD's temple, the priests, ceremonially attired and with their clarions, and the Levites (the sons of Asaph) with their cymbals, stood to praise the LORD according to the instructions left by King David of Israel. **3:11** With antiphonal response they sang, praising and glorifying the LORD:

"For he is good;

his loyal love toward Israel is forever."

All the people gave a loud shout as they praised the LORD when the temple of the LORD was established. **3:12** Many of the priests, the Levites, and the leaders – older people who had seen with their own eyes the former temple while it was still established – were weeping loudly, and many others raised their voice in a joyous shout. **3:13** People were unable to tell the difference between the sound of joyous shouting and the sound of the people's weeping, for the people were shouting so loudly that the sound was heard a long way off.

Opposition to the Building Efforts

4:1 When the enemies of Judah and Benjamin learned that the former exiles were building a temple for the LORD God of Israel, **4:2** they came to Zerubbabel and the leaders and said to them, "Let us help you build, for like you we seek your God and we have been sacrificing to him from the time of King Esarhaddon of Assyria, who brought us here." **4:3** But Zerubbabel, Jeshua, and the rest of the leaders of Israel said to them,

"You have no right to help us build the temple of our God. We will build it by ourselves for the LORD God of Israel, just as King Cyrus, the king of Persia, has commanded us." **4:4** Then the local people began to discourage the people of Judah and to dishearten them from building. **4:5** They were hiring advisers to oppose them, so as to frustrate their plans, throughout the time of King Cyrus of Persia until the reign of King Darius of Persia.

Official Complaints Are Lodged Against the Jews

4:6 At the beginning of the reign of Ahasuerus they filed an accusation against the inhabitants of Judah and Jerusalem. **4:7** And during the reign of Artaxerxes, Bishlam, Mithredath, Tabeel, and the rest of their colleagues wrote to King Artaxerxes of Persia. This letter was first written in Aramaic but then translated.

[Aramaic:]

4:8 Rehum the commander and Shimshai the scribe wrote a letter concerning Jerusalem to King Artaxerxes as follows: **4:9** From Rehum the commander, Shimshai the scribe, and the rest of their colleagues – the judges, the rulers, the officials, the secretaries, the Erechites, the Babylonians, the people of Susa (that is, the Elamites), **4:10** and the rest of nations whom the great and noble Ashurbanipal deported and settled in the cities of Samaria and other places in Trans-Euphrates. **4:11** (This is a copy of the letter they sent to him:)

"To King Artaxerxes, from your servants in Trans-Euphrates: **4:12** Now let the king be aware that the Jews who came up to us from you have gone to Jerusalem. They are rebuilding that rebellious and odious city. They are completing its walls and repairing its foundations. **4:13** Let the king also be aware that if this city is built and its walls are completed, no more tax, custom, or toll will be paid, and the royal treasury will suffer loss. **4:14** In light of the fact that we are loyal to the king, and since it does not seem appropriate to us that the king should sustain damage, we are sending the king this information **4:15** so that he may initiate a search of the records of his predecessors and discover in those records that this city is rebellious and injurious to both kings and provinces, producing internal revolts from long ago. It is for this very reason that this city was destroyed. **4:16** We therefore are informing the king that if this city is rebuilt and its walls are completed, you will not retain control of this portion of Trans-Euphrates."

4:17 The king sent the following response:

"To Rehum the commander, Shimshai the scribe, and the rest of their colleagues who live in Samaria and other parts of Trans-Euphrates: Greetings! **4:18** The letter you sent to us has been translated and read in my presence. **4:19** So I gave orders, and it was determined that this city from long ago has been engaging in insurrection against kings. It has continually engaged in rebellion and revolt. **4:20** Powerful kings have been over Jerusalem who ruled throughout the entire Trans-Euphrates and who were the beneficiaries of tribute, custom, and toll. **4:21** Now give orders that these men cease their work and that this city not be rebuilt until such time as I so instruct. **4:22** Exercise appropriate caution so that there is no negligence in this matter. Why should danger increase to the point that kings sustain damage?"

4:23 Then, as soon as the copy of the letter from King Artaxerxes was read in the presence of Rehum, Shimshai the scribe, and their colleagues, they proceeded promptly to the Jews in Jerusalem and stopped them with threat of armed force.

4:24 So the work on the temple of God in Jerusalem came to a halt. It remained halted until the second year of the reign of King Darius of Persia.

Tattenai Appeals to Darius

5:1 Then the prophets Haggai and Zechariah son of Iddo prophesied concerning the Jews who were in Judah and Jerusalem in the name of the God of Israel who was over them. **5:2** Then Zerubbabel the son of Shealtiel and Jeshua the son of Jozadak began to rebuild the temple of God in Jerusalem. The prophets of God were with them, supporting them. **5:3** At that time Tattenai governor of Trans-Euphrates, Shethar-Bozenai, and their colleagues came to them and asked, "Who gave you authority to rebuild this temple and to complete this structure?" **5:4** They also asked them, "What are the names of the men who are building this edifice?" **5:5** But God was watching over the elders of Judah, and they were not stopped until a report could be dispatched to Darius and a letter could be sent back concerning this.

5:6 This is a copy of the letter that Tattenai governor of Trans-Euphrates, Shethar Bozenai, and his colleagues who were the officials of Trans-Euphrates sent to King Darius. **5:7** The report they sent to him was written as follows:

"To King Darius: All greetings! **5:8** Let it be known to the king that we have gone to the province of Judah, to the temple of the great God. It is being built with large stones, and timbers are being placed in the walls. This work is being done with all diligence and is prospering in their hands. **5:9** We inquired of those elders, asking them, 'Who gave you the authority to rebuild this temple and to complete this structure?' **5:10** We also inquired of their names in order to inform you, so that we might write the names of the men who were their leaders. **5:11** They responded to us in the following way: 'We are servants of the God of heaven and earth. We are rebuilding the temple which was previously built many years ago. A great king of Israel built it and completed it. **5:12** But after our ancestors angered the God of heaven, he delivered them into the hands of King Nebuchadnezzar of Babylon, the Chaldean, who destroyed this temple and exiled the people to Babylon. **5:13** But in the first year of King Cyrus of Babylon, King Cyrus enacted a decree to rebuild this temple of God. **5:14** Even the gold and silver vessels of the temple of God that Nebuchadnezzar had taken from the temple in Jerusalem and had brought to the palace of Babylon – even those things King Cyrus brought from the palace of Babylon and presented to a man by the name of Sheshbazzar whom he had appointed as governor. **5:15** He said to him, "Take these vessels and go deposit them in the temple in Jerusalem, and let the house of God be rebuilt in its proper location." **5:16** Then this Sheshbazzar went and laid the foundations of the temple of God in Jerusalem. From that time to the present moment it has been in the process of being rebuilt, although it is not yet finished.'

5:17 "Now if the king is so inclined, let a search be conducted in the royal archives there in Babylon in order to determine whether King Cyrus did in fact issue orders for this temple of God to be rebuilt in Jerusalem. Then let the king send us a decision concerning this matter."

Darius Issues a Decree

6:1 So Darius the king issued orders, and they searched in the archives of the treasury which were deposited there in Babylon. **6:2** A scroll was found in the citadel of Ecbatana which is in the province of Media, and it was inscribed as follows:

"Memorandum: **6:3** In the first year of his reign, King Cyrus gave orders concerning the temple of God in Jerusalem: 'Let the temple be rebuilt as a place where sacrifices are offered. Let its foundations be set in place. Its height is to be ninety feet and its width ninety feet, **6:4** with three layers of large stones and one layer of timber. The expense is to be subsidized by the royal treasury. **6:5** Furthermore let the gold and silver vessels of the temple of God, which Nebuchadnezzar brought from the temple in Jerusalem and carried to Babylon, be returned and brought to their proper place in the temple in Jerusalem. Let them be deposited in the temple of God.'

6:6 "Now Tattenai governor of Trans-Euphrates, Shethar Bozenai, and their colleagues, the officials of Trans-Euphrates – all of you stay far away from there! **6:7** Leave the work on this temple of God alone. Let the governor of the Jews and the elders of the Jews rebuild this temple of God in its proper place.

6:8 "I also hereby issue orders as to what you are to do with those elders of the Jews in order to rebuild this temple of God. From the royal treasury, from the taxes of Trans-Euphrates the complete costs are to be given to these men, so that there may be no interruption of the work. **6:9** Whatever is needed – whether oxen or rams or lambs or burnt offerings for the God of heaven or wheat or salt or wine or oil, as required by the priests who are in Jerusalem – must be given to them daily without any neglect, **6:10** so that they may be offering incense to the God of heaven and may be praying for the good fortune of the king and his family.

6:11 "I hereby give orders that if anyone changes this directive a beam is to be pulled out from his house and he is to be raised up and impaled on it, and his house is to be reduced to a rubbish heap for this indiscretion. **6:12** May God who makes his name to reside there overthrow any king or nation who reaches out to cause such change so as to destroy this temple of God in Jerusalem. I, Darius, have given orders. Let them be carried out with precision!"

The Temple Is Finally Dedicated

6:13 Then Tattenai governor of Trans-Euphrates, Shethar-Bozenai, and their colleagues acted accordingly – with precision, just as Darius the king had given instructions. **6:14** The elders of the Jews continued building and prospering, while at the same time Haggai the prophet and Zechariah the son of Iddo continued prophesying. They built and brought it to completion by the command of the God of Israel and by the command of Cyrus and Darius and Artaxerxes king of Persia. **6:15** They finished this temple on the third day of the month Adar, which is the sixth year of the reign of King Darius.

6:16 The people of Israel – the priests, the Levites, and the rest of the exiles – observed the dedication of this temple of God with joy. **6:17** For the dedication of this temple of God they offered one hundred bulls, two hundred rams, four hundred lambs, and twelve male goats for the sin of all Israel, according to the number of the tribes of Israel. **6:18** They appointed the priests by their divisions and the Levites by their divisions over the worship of God at Jerusalem, in accord with the book of Moses. **6:19** The exiles observed the Passover on the fourteenth day of the first month. **6:20** The priests and the Levites had purified themselves, every last one, and they all were ceremonially pure. They sacrificed the Passover lamb for all the exiles, for their colleagues the priests, and for themselves. **6:21** The Israelites who were returning from the exile ate it, along with all those who had joined them in separating themselves from the uncleanness of the nations of the land to seek the LORD God of Israel. **6:22** They observed the Feast of Unleavened Bread for seven days with joy, for the LORD had given them joy and had changed the opinion of the king of Assyria toward them, so that he assisted them in the work on the temple of God, the God of Israel.

The Arrival of Ezra

7:1 Now after these things had happened, during the reign of King Artaxerxes of Persia, Ezra came up from Babylon. Ezra was the son of Seraiah, who was the son of Azariah, who was the son of Hilkiah, **7:2** who was the son of Shallum, who was the son of Zadok, who was the son of Ahitub, **7:3** who was the son of Amariah, who was the son of Azariah, who was the son of Meraioth, **7:4** who was the son of Zerahiah, who was the son of Uzzi, who was the son of Bukki, **7:5** who was the son of Abishua, who was the son of Phinehas, who was the son of Eleazar, who was the son of Aaron the chief priest. **7:6** This Ezra is the one who came up from Babylon. He was a scribe who was skilled in the law of Moses which the LORD God of Israel had given. The king supplied him with everything he requested, for the hand of the LORD his God was on him. **7:7** In the seventh year of King Artaxerxes, Ezra brought up to Jerusalem some of the Israelites and some of the priests, the Levites, the attendants, the gatekeepers, and the temple servants. **7:8** He entered Jerusalem in the fifth month of the seventh year of the king. **7:9** On the first day of the first month he had determined to make the ascent from Babylon, and on the first day of the fifth month he arrived at Jerusalem, for the good hand of his God was on him. **7:10** Now Ezra had dedicated himself to the study of the law of the LORD, to its observance, and to teaching its statutes and judgments in Israel.

Artaxerxes Gives Official Endorsement to Ezra's Mission

7:11 What follows is a copy of the letter that King Artaxerxes gave to Ezra the priestly scribe. Ezra was a scribe in matters pertaining to the commandments of the LORD and his statutes over Israel:

7:12 "Artaxerxes, king of kings, to Ezra the priest, a scribe of the perfect law of the God of heaven: **7:13** I have now issued a decree that anyone in my kingdom from the people of Israel – even the priests and Levites – who wishes to do so may go up with you to Jerusalem. **7:14** You are authorized by the king and his seven advisers to inquire concerning Judah and Jerusalem, according to the law of your God which is in your possession, **7:15** and to bring silver and gold which the king and his advisers have freely contributed to the God of Israel, who resides in Jerusalem, **7:16** along with all the silver and gold that you may collect throughout all the province of Babylon and the contributions of the people and the priests for the temple of their God which is in Jerusalem. **7:17** With this money you should be sure to purchase bulls, rams, and lambs, along with the appropriate meal offerings and libations. You should bring them to the altar of the temple of your God which is in Jerusalem. **7:18** You may do whatever seems appropriate to you and your colleagues with the rest of the silver and the gold, in keeping with the will of your God. **7:19** Deliver to the God of Jerusalem the vessels that are given to you for the service of the temple of your God. **7:20** The rest of the needs for the temple of your God that you may have to supply, you may do so from the royal treasury.

7:21 "I, King Artaxerxes, hereby issue orders to all the treasurers of Trans-Euphrates, that you precisely execute all that Ezra the priestly scribe of the law of the God of heaven may request of you – **7:22** up to 100 talents of silver, 100 cors of wheat, 100 baths of wine, 100 baths of olive oil, and unlimited salt. **7:23** Everything that the God of heaven has required should be precisely done for the temple of the God of heaven. Why should there be wrath against the empire of the king and his sons? **7:24** Furthermore, be aware of the fact that you have no authority to impose tax, tribute, or toll on any of the priests, the Levites, the musicians, the doorkeepers, the temple servants, or the attendants at the temple of this God.

7:25 "Now you, Ezra, in keeping with the wisdom of your God which you possess, appoint judges and court officials who can arbitrate cases on behalf of all the people who are in Trans-Euphrates who know the laws of your God. Those who do not know this law should be taught. **7:26** Everyone who does not observe both the law of your God and the law of the king will be completely liable to the appropriate penalty, whether it is death or banishment or confiscation of property or detainment in prison."

7:27 Blessed be the LORD God of our fathers, who so moved in the heart of the king to so honor the temple of the LORD which is in Jerusalem! **7:28** He has also conferred his favor on me before the king, his advisers, and all the influential leaders of the king. I gained strength as the hand of the LORD my God was on me, and I gathered leaders from Israel to go up with me.

The Leaders Who Returned with Ezra

8:1 These are the leaders and those enrolled with them by genealogy who were coming up with me from Babylon during the reign of King Artaxerxes:

8:2 from the descendants of Phinehas, Gershom;

from the descendants of Ithamar, Daniel;

from the descendants of David, Hattush **8:3** the son of Shecaniah;

from the descendants of Parosh, Zechariah, and with him were enrolled by genealogy 150 men;

8:4 from the descendants of Pahath-Moab, Eliehoenai son of Zerahiah, and with him 200 men;

8:5 from the descendants of Zattu, Shecaniah son of Jahaziel, and with him 300 men;

8:6 from the descendants of Adin, Ebed son of Jonathan, and with him 50 men;

8:7 from the descendants of Elam, Jeshaiah son of Athaliah, and with him 70 men;

8:8 from the descendants of Shephatiah, Zebadiah son of Michael, and with him 80 men;

8:9 from the descendants of Joab, Obadiah son of Jehiel, and with him 218 men;

8:10 from the descendants of Bani, Shelomith son of Josiphiah, and with him 160 men;

8:11 from the descendants of Bebai, Zechariah son of Bebai, and with him 28 men;

8:12 from the descendants of Azgad, Johanan son of Hakkatan, and with him 110 men;

8:13 from the descendants of Adonikam there were the latter ones. Their names were Eliphelet, Jeuel, and Shemaiah, and with them 60 men;

8:14 from the descendants of Bigvai, Uthai, and Zaccur, and with them 70 men.

The Exiles Travel to Jerusalem

8:15 I had them assemble at the canal that flows toward Ahava, and we camped there for three days. I observed that the people and the priests were present, but I found no Levites there. **8:16** So I sent for Eliezer, Ariel, Shemaiah, Elnathan, Jarib, Elnathan, Nathan, Zechariah, and Meshullam, who were leaders, and Joiarib and Elnathan, who were teachers. **8:17** I sent them to Iddo, who was the leader in the place called Casiphia. I told them what to say to Iddo and his relatives, who were the temple servants in Casiphia, so they would bring us attendants for the temple of our God.

8:18 Due to the fact that the good hand of our God was on us, they brought us a skilled man, from the descendants of Mahli the son of Levi son of Israel. This man was Sherebiah, who was accompanied by his sons and brothers, 18 men, **8:19** and Hashabiah, along with Jeshaiah from the descendants of Merari, with his brothers and their sons, 20 men, **8:20** and some of the temple servants that David and his officials had established for the work of the Levites – 220 of them. They were all designated by name.

8:21 I called for a fast there by the Ahava Canal, so that we might humble ourselves before our God and seek from him a safe journey for us, our children, and all our property. **8:22** I was embarrassed to request soldiers and horsemen from the king to protect us from the enemy along the way, because we had said to the king, "The good hand of our God is on everyone who is seeking him, but his great anger is against everyone who forsakes him." **8:23** So we fasted and prayed to our God about this, and he answered us.

8:24 Then I set apart twelve of the leading priests, together with Sherebiah, Hashabiah, and ten of their brothers, **8:25** and I weighed out to them the silver, the gold, and the vessels intended for the temple of our God – items that the king, his advisers, his officials, and all Israel who were present had contributed. **8:26** I weighed out to them 650 talents of silver, silver vessels worth 100 talents, 100 talents of gold, **8:27** 20 gold bowls worth 1,000 darics, and two exquisite vessels of gleaming bronze, as valuable as gold. **8:28** Then I said to them, "You are holy to the LORD, just as these vessels are holy. The silver and the gold are a voluntary offering to the LORD, the God of your fathers. **8:29** Be careful with them and protect them, until you weigh them out before the leading priests and the Levites and the family leaders of Israel in Jerusalem, in the storerooms of the temple of the LORD."

8:30 Then the priests and the Levites took charge of the silver, the gold, and the vessels that had been weighed out, to transport them to Jerusalem to the temple of our God.

8:31 On the twelfth day of the first month we began traveling from the Ahava Canal to go to Jerusalem. The hand of our God was on us, and he delivered us from our enemy and from bandits along the way. **8:32** So we came to Jerusalem, and we stayed there for three days. **8:33** On the fourth day we weighed out the silver, the gold, and the vessels in the house of our God into the care of Meremoth son of Uriah, the priest, and Eleazar son of Phinehas, who were accompanied by Jozabad son of Jeshua and Noadiah son of Binnui, who were Levites. **8:34** Everything was verified by number and by weight, and the total weight was written down at that time.

8:35 The exiles who were returning from the captivity offered burnt offerings to the God of Israel – twelve bulls for all Israel, ninety-six rams, seventy-seven male lambs, along with twelve male goats as a sin offering. All this was a burnt offering to the LORD. **8:36** Then they presented the decrees of the king to the king's satraps and to the governors of Trans-Euphrates, who gave help to the people and to the temple of God.

A Prayer of Ezra

9:1 Now when these things had been completed, the leaders approached me and said, "The people of Israel, the priests, and the Levites have not separated themselves from the local residents who practice detestable things similar to those of the Canaanites, the Hittites, the Perizzites, the

Jebusites, the Ammonites, the Moabites, the Egyptians, and the Amorites. **9:2** Indeed, they have taken some of their daughters as wives for themselves and for their sons, so that the holy race has become intermingled with the local residents. Worse still, the leaders and the officials have been at the forefront of all of this!"

9:3 When I heard this report, I tore my tunic and my robe and ripped out some of the hair from my head and beard. Then I sat down, quite devastated. **9:4** Everyone who held the words of the God of Israel in awe gathered around me because of the unfaithful acts of the people of the exile. Devastated, I continued to sit there until the evening offering.

9:5 At the time of the evening offering I got up from my self-abasement, with my tunic and robe torn, and then dropped to my knees and spread my hands to the LORD my God. **9:6** I prayed,

"O my God, I am ashamed and embarrassed to lift my face to you, my God! For our iniquities have climbed higher than our heads, and our guilt extends to the heavens. **9:7** From the days of our fathers until this very day our guilt has been great. Because of our iniquities we, along with our kings and priests, have been delivered over by the local kings to sword, captivity, plunder, and embarrassment – right up to the present time.

9:8 "But now briefly we have received mercy from the LORD our God, in that he has left us a remnant and has given us a secure position in his holy place. Thus our God has enlightened our eyes and has given us a little relief in our time of servitude. **9:9** Although we are slaves, our God has not abandoned us in our servitude. He has extended kindness to us in the sight of the kings of Persia, in that he has revived us to restore the temple of our God and to raise up its ruins and to give us a protective wall in Judah and Jerusalem.

9:10 "And now what are we able to say after this, our God? For we have forsaken your commandments **9:11** which you commanded us through your servants the prophets with these words: 'The land that you are entering to possess is a land defiled by the impurities of the local residents! With their abominations they have filled it from one end to the other with their filthiness. **9:12** Therefore do not give your daughters in marriage to their sons, and do not take their daughters in marriage for your sons. Do not ever seek their peace or welfare, so that you may be strong and may eat the good of the land and may leave it as an inheritance for your children forever.'

9:13 "Everything that has happened to us has come about because of our wicked actions and our great guilt. Even so, our God, you have exercised restraint toward our iniquities and have given us a remnant such as this. **9:14** Shall we once again break your commandments and intermarry with these abominable peoples? Would you not be so angered by us that you would wipe us out, with no survivor or remnant? **9:15** O LORD God of Israel, you are righteous, for we are left as a remnant this day. Indeed, we stand before you in our guilt. However, because of this guilt no one can really stand before you."

The People Confess Their Sins

10:1 While Ezra was praying and confessing, weeping and throwing himself to the ground before the temple of God, a very large crowd of Israelites – men, women, and children alike – gathered around him. The people wept loudly. **10:2** Then Shecaniah son of Jehiel, from the descendants of Elam, addressed Ezra:

"We have been unfaithful to our God by marrying foreign women from the local peoples. Nonetheless, there is still hope for Israel in this regard. **10:3** Therefore let us enact a covenant with our God to send away all these women and their offspring, in keeping with your counsel, my lord, and that of those who respect the commandments of our God. And let it be done according to the law. **10:4** Get up, for this matter concerns you. We are with you, so be strong and act decisively!"

10:5 So Ezra got up and made the leading priests and Levites and all Israel take an oath to carry out this plan. And they all took a solemn oath. **10:6** Then Ezra got up from in front of the temple of God and went to the room of Jehohanan son of Eliashib. While he stayed there, he did not eat food or drink water, for he was in mourning over the infidelity of the exiles.

10:7 A proclamation was circulated throughout Judah and Jerusalem that all the exiles were to be assembled in Jerusalem. **10:8** Everyone who did not come within three days would thereby forfeit all his property, in keeping with the counsel of the officials and the elders. Furthermore, he himself would be excluded from the assembly of the exiles.

10:9 All the men of Judah and Benjamin were gathered in Jerusalem within the three days. (It was in the ninth month, on the twentieth day of that month.) All the people sat in the square at the temple of God, trembling because of this matter and because of the rains.

10:10 Then Ezra the priest stood up and said to them, "You have behaved in an unfaithful manner by taking foreign wives! This has contributed to the guilt of Israel. **10:11** Now give praise to the LORD God of your fathers, and do his will. Separate yourselves from the local residents and from these foreign wives."

10:12 All the assembly replied in a loud voice: "We will do just as you have said! **10:13** However, the people are numerous and it is the rainy season. We are unable to stand here outside. Furthermore, this business cannot be resolved in a day or two, for we have sinned greatly in this matter. **10:14** Let our leaders take steps on behalf of all the assembly. Let all those in our towns who have married foreign women come at an appointed time, and with them the elders of each town and its judges, until the hot anger of our God is turned away from us in this matter."

10:15 Only Jonathan son of Asahel and Jahzeiah son of Tikvah were against this, assisted by Meshullam and Shabbethai the Levite. **10:16** So the exiles proceeded accordingly. Ezra the priest separated out by name men who were leaders in their family groups. They sat down to consider this matter on the first day of the tenth month, **10:17** and on the first day of the first month they finished considering all the men who had married foreign wives.

Those Who Had Taken Foreign Wives

10:18 It was determined that from the descendants of the priests, the following had taken foreign wives: from the descendants of Jeshua son of Jozadak, and his brothers: Maaseiah, Eliezer, Jarib, and Gedaliah. **10:19** (They gave their word to send away their wives; their guilt offering was a ram from the flock for their guilt.)

10:20 From the descendants of Immer: Hanani and Zebadiah.

10:21 From the descendants of Harim: Maaseiah, Elijah, Shemaiah, Jehiel, and Uzziah.

10:22 From the descendants of Pashhur: Elioenai, Maaseiah, Ishmael, Nethanel, Jozabad, and Elasah.

10:23 From the Levites: Jozabad, Shimei, Kelaiah (also known as Kelita), Pethahiah, Judah, and Eliezer.

10:24 From the singers: Eliashib. From the gatekeepers: Shallum, Telem, and Uri.

10:25 From the Israelites: from the descendants of Parosh: Ramiah, Izziah, Malkijah, Mijamin, Eleazar, Malkijah, and Benaiah.

10:26 From the descendants of Elam: Mattaniah, Zechariah, Jehiel, Abdi, Jeremoth, and Elijah.

10:27 From the descendants of Zattu: Elioenai, Eliashib, Mattaniah, Jeremoth, Zabad, and Aziza.

10:28 From the descendants of Bebai: Jehohanan, Hananiah, Zabbai, and Athlai.

10:29 From the descendants of Bani: Meshullam, Malluch, Adaiah, Jashub, Sheal, and Jeremoth.

10:30 From the descendants of Pahath-Moab: Adna, Kelal, Benaiah, Maaseiah, Mattaniah, Bezalel, Binnui, and Manasseh.

10:31 From the descendants of Harim: Eliezer, Ishijah, Malkijah, Shemaiah, Shimeon, **10:32** Benjamin, Malluch, and Shemariah.

10:33 From the descendants of Hashum: Mattenai, Mattattah, Zabad, Eliphelet, Jeremai, Manasseh, and Shimei.

10:34 From the descendants of Bani: Maadai, Amram, Uel, **10:35** Benaiah, Bedeiah, Keluhi, **10:36** Vaniah, Meremoth, Eliashib, **10:37** Mattaniah, Mattenai, and Jaasu.

10:38 From the descendants of Binnui: Shimei, **10:39** Shelemiah, Nathan, Adaiah, **10:40** Machnadebai, Shashai, Sharai, **10:41** Azarel, Shelemiah, Shemariah, **10:42** Shallum, Amariah, and Joseph.

10:43 From the descendants of Nebo: Jeiel, Mattithiah, Zabad, Zebina, Jaddai, Joel, and Benaiah.

10:44 All these had taken foreign wives, and some of them also had children by these women.

Book 16. Nehemiah

A Prayer of Nehemiah

1:1 These are the words of Nehemiah son of Hacaliah:

It so happened that in the month of Kislev, in the twentieth year, I was in Susa the citadel. **1:2** Hanani, who was one of my relatives, along with some of the men from Judah, came to me, and I asked them about the Jews who had escaped and had survived the exile, and about Jerusalem.

1:3 They said to me, "The remnant that remains from the exile there in the province are experiencing considerable adversity and reproach. The wall of Jerusalem lies breached, and its gates have been burned down!"

1:4 When I heard these things I sat down abruptly, crying and mourning for several days. I continued fasting and praying before the God of heaven. **1:5** Then I said, "Please, O LORD God of heaven, great and awesome God, who keeps his loving covenant with those who love him and obey his commandments, **1:6** may your ear be attentive and your eyes be open to hear the prayer of your servant that I am praying to you today throughout both day and night on behalf of your servants the Israelites. I am confessing the sins of the Israelites that we have committed against you – both I myself and my family have sinned. **1:7** We have behaved corruptly against you, not obeying the commandments, the statutes, and the judgments that you commanded your servant Moses. **1:8** Please recall the word you commanded your servant Moses: 'If you act unfaithfully, I will scatter you among the nations. **1:9** But if you repent and obey my commandments and do them, then even if your dispersed people are in the most remote location, I will gather them from there and bring them to the place I have chosen for my name to reside.' **1:10** They are your servants and your people, whom you have redeemed by your mighty strength and by your powerful hand. **1:11** Please, O Lord, listen attentively to the prayer of your servant and to the prayer of your servants who take pleasure in showing respect to your name. Grant your servant success today and show compassion to me in the presence of this man."

Now I was cupbearer for the king.

Nehemiah Is Permitted to Go to Jerusalem

2:1 Then in the month of Nisan, in the twentieth year of King Artaxerxes, when wine was brought to me, I took the wine and gave it to the king. Previously I had not been depressed in the king's presence. **2:2** So the king said to me, "Why do you appear to be depressed when you aren't sick? What can this be other than sadness of heart?" This made me very fearful.

2:3 I replied to the king, "O king, live forever! Why would I not appear dejected when the city with the graves of my ancestors lies desolate and its gates destroyed by fire?" **2:4** The king responded, "What is it you are seeking?" Then I quickly prayed to the God of heaven **2:5** and said to the king, "If the king is so inclined and if your servant has found favor in your sight, dispatch me to Judah, to the city with the graves of my ancestors, so that I can rebuild it." **2:6** Then the king, with his consort sitting beside him, replied, "How long would your trip take, and when would you return?" Since the king was amenable to dispatching me, I gave him a time. **2:7** I said to the king, "If the king is so inclined, let him give me letters for the governors of Trans-Euphrates that will enable me to travel safely until I reach Judah, **2:8** and a letter for Asaph the keeper of the king's nature preserve, so that he will give me timber for beams for the gates of the fortress adjacent to the temple and for the city wall and for the house to which I go." So the king granted me these requests, for the good hand of my God was on me. **2:9** Then I went to the governors of Trans-Euphrates, and I presented to them the letters from the king. The king had sent with me officers of the army and horsemen. **2:10** When Sanballat the Horonite and Tobiah the Ammonite official heard all this, they were very displeased that someone had come to seek benefit for the Israelites.

Nehemiah Arrives in Jerusalem

2:11 So I came to Jerusalem. When I had been there for three days, **2:12** I got up during the night, along with a few men who were with me. But I did not tell anyone what my God was putting on my heart to do for Jerusalem. There were no animals with me, except for the one I was riding. **2:13** I proceeded through the Valley Gate by night, in the direction of the Well of the Dragons and the Dung Gate, inspecting the walls of Jerusalem that had been breached and its gates that had been destroyed by fire. **2:14** I passed on to the Gate of the Well and the King's Pool, where there was not enough room for my animal to pass with me. **2:15** I continued up the valley during the night, inspecting the wall. Then I turned back and came to the Valley Gate, and so returned. **2:16** The officials did not know where I had gone or what I had been doing, for up to this point I had not told any of the Jews or the priests or the nobles or the officials or the rest of the workers. **2:17** Then I said to them, "You see the problem that we have: Jerusalem is desolate and its gates are burned. Come on! Let's rebuild the wall of Jerusalem so that this reproach will not continue." **2:18** Then I related to them how the good hand of my God was on me and what the king had said to me. Then they replied, "Let's begin rebuilding right away!" So they readied themselves for this good project. **2:19** But when Sanballat the Horonite, Tobiah the Ammonite official, and Geshem the Arab heard all this, they derided us and expressed contempt toward us. They said, "What is this you are doing? Are you rebelling against the king?" **2:20** I responded to them by saying, "The God of heaven will prosper us. We his servants will start the rebuilding. But you have no just or ancient right in Jerusalem."

The Names of the Builders

3:1 Then Eliashib the high priest and his priestly colleagues arose and built the Sheep Gate. They dedicated it and erected its doors, working as far as the Tower of the Hundred and the Tower of Hananel. **3:2** The men of Jericho built adjacent to it, and Zaccur son of Imri built adjacent to them.

3:3 The sons of Hassenaah rebuilt the Fish Gate. They laid its beams and positioned its doors, its bolts, and its bars. **3:4** Meremoth son of Uriah, the son of Hakoz, worked on the section adjacent to them. Meshullam son of Berechiah the son of Meshezabel worked on the section next to them. And Zadok son of Baana worked on the section adjacent to them. **3:5** The men of Tekoa worked on the section adjacent to them, but their town leaders would not assist with the work of their master.

3:6 Joiada son of Paseah and Meshullam son of Besodeiah worked on the Jeshanah Gate. They laid its beams and positioned its doors, its bolts, and its bars. **3:7** Adjacent to them worked Melatiah the Gibeonite and Jadon the Meronothite, who were men of Gibeon and Mizpah. These towns were under the jurisdiction of the governor of Trans-Euphrates. **3:8** Uzziel son of Harhaiah, a member of the goldsmiths' guild, worked on the section adjacent to him. Hananiah, a member of the perfumers' guild, worked on the section adjacent to him. They plastered the city wall of Jerusalem as far as the Broad Wall. **3:9** Rephaiah son of Hur, head of a half-district of Jerusalem, worked on the section adjacent to them. **3:10** Jedaiah son of Harumaph worked on the section adjacent to them opposite his house, and Hattush son of Hashabneiah worked on the section adjacent to him. **3:11** Malkijah son of Harim and Hasshub son of Pahath-Moab worked on another section and the Tower of the Fire Pots. **3:12** Shallum son of Hallohesh, head of a half-district of Jerusalem, worked on the section adjacent to him, assisted by his daughters.

3:13 Hanun and the residents of Zanoah worked on the Valley Gate. They rebuilt it and positioned its doors, its bolts, and its bars, in addition to working on fifteen hundred feet of the wall as far as the Dung Gate.

3:14 Malkijah son of Recab, head of the district of Beth Hakkerem, worked on the Dung Gate. He rebuilt it and positioned its doors, its bolts, and its bars.

3:15 Shallun son of Col-Hozeh, head of the district of Mizpah, worked on the Fountain Gate. He rebuilt it, put on its roof, and positioned its doors, its bolts, and its bars. In addition, he rebuilt the wall of the Pool of Siloam, by the royal garden, as far as the steps that go down from the City of David. **3:16** Nehemiah son of Azbuk, head of a half-district of Beth Zur, worked after him as far as the tombs of David and the artificial pool and the House of the Warriors.

3:17 After him the Levites worked – Rehum son of Bani and after him Hashabiah, head of half the district of Keilah, for his district. **3:18** After him their relatives worked – Binnui son of Henadad, head of a half-district of Keilah. **3:19** Adjacent to him Ezer son of Jeshua, head of Mizpah, worked on another section, opposite the ascent to the armory at the buttress. **3:20** After him Baruch son of Zabbai worked on another section, from the buttress to the door of the house of Eliashib the high priest. **3:21** After him Meremoth son of Uriah, the son of Hakkoz, worked on another section from the door of Eliashib's house to the end of it. **3:22** After him the priests worked, men of the nearby district. **3:23** After them Benjamin and Hasshub worked opposite their house. After them Azariah son of Maaseiah, the son of Ananiah, worked near his house. **3:24** After him Binnui son of Henadad worked on another section, from the house of Azariah to the buttress and the corner. **3:25** After him Palal son of Uzai worked opposite the buttress and the tower that protrudes from the upper palace of the court of the guard. After him Pedaiah son of Parosh **3:26** and the temple servants who were living on Ophel worked up to the area opposite the Water Gate toward the east and the protruding tower. **3:27** After them the men of Tekoa worked on another section, from opposite the great protruding tower to the wall of Ophel.

3:28 Above the Horse Gate the priests worked, each in front of his house. **3:29** After them Zadok son of Immer worked opposite his house, and after him Shemaiah son of Shecaniah, guard at the East Gate, worked. **3:30** After him Hananiah son of Shelemiah, and Hanun, the sixth son of Zalaph, worked on another section. After them Meshullam son of Berechiah worked opposite his quarters. **3:31** After him Malkijah, one of the goldsmiths, worked as far as the house of the temple servants and the traders, opposite the Inspection Gate, and up to the room above the corner. **3:32** And between the room above the corner and the Sheep Gate the goldsmiths and traders worked.

Opposition to the Work Continues

4:1 (3:33) Now when Sanballat heard that we were rebuilding the wall he became angry and was quite upset. He derided the Jews, **4:2** and in the presence of his colleagues and the army of Samaria he said, "What are these feeble Jews doing? Will they be left to themselves? Will they again offer sacrifice? Will they finish this in a day? Can they bring these burnt stones to life again from piles of dust?"

4:3 Then Tobiah the Ammonite, who was close by, said, "If even a fox were to climb up on what they are building, it would break down their wall of stones!"

4:4 Hear, O our God, for we are despised! Return their reproach on their own head! Reduce them to plunder in a land of exile!

4:5 Do not cover their iniquity, and do not wipe out their sin from before them. For they have bitterly offended the builders!

4:6 So we rebuilt the wall, and the entire wall was joined together up to half its height. The people were enthusiastic in their work.

4:7 (4:1) When Sanballat, Tobiah, the Arabs, the Ammonites, and the people of Ashdod heard that the restoration of the walls of Jerusalem had moved ahead and that the breaches had begun to be closed, they were very angry. **4:8** All of them conspired together to move with armed forces against Jerusalem and to create a disturbance in it. **4:9** So we prayed to our God and stationed a guard to protect against them both day and night. **4:10** Then those in Judah said, "The strength of the laborers has failed! The debris is so great that we are unable to rebuild the wall."

4:11 Our adversaries also boasted, "Before they are aware or anticipate anything, we will come in among them and kill them, and we will bring this work to a halt!"

4:12 So it happened that the Jews who were living near them came and warned us repeatedly about all the schemes they were plotting against us. **4:13** So I stationed people at the lower places behind the wall in the exposed places. I stationed the people by families, with their swords, spears, and bows. **4:14** When I had made an inspection, I stood up and said to the nobles, the officials, and the rest of the people, "Don't be afraid of them. Remember the great and awesome Lord, and fight on behalf of your brothers, your sons, your daughters, your wives, and your families!"

4:15 It so happened that when our adversaries heard that we were aware of these matters, God frustrated their intentions. Then all of us returned to the wall, each to his own work. **4:16** From that day forward, half of my men were doing the work and half of them were taking up spears, shields, bows, and body armor. Now the officers were behind all the people of Judah **4:17** who were rebuilding the wall. Those who were carrying loads did so by keeping one hand on the work and the other on their weapon. **4:18** The builders to a man had their swords strapped to their sides while they were building. But the trumpeter remained with me.

4:19 I said to the nobles, the officials, and the rest of the people, "The work is demanding and extensive, and we are spread out on the wall, far removed from one another. **4:20** Wherever you hear the sound of the trumpet, gather there with us. Our God will fight for us!"

4:21 So we worked on, with half holding spears, from dawn till dusk. **4:22** At that time I instructed the people, "Let every man and his coworker spend the night in Jerusalem and let them be guards for us by night and workers by day. **4:23** We did not change clothes – not I, nor my relatives, nor my workers, nor the watchmen who were with me. Each had his weapon, even when getting a drink of water.

Nehemiah Intervenes on behalf of the Oppressed

5:1 Then there was a great outcry from the people and their wives against their fellow Jews. **5:2** There were those who said, "With our sons and daughters, we are many. We must obtain grain in order to eat and stay alive." **5:3** There were others who said, "We are putting up our fields, our vineyards, and our houses as collateral in order to obtain grain during the famine." **5:4** Then there were those who said, "We have borrowed money to pay our taxes to the king on our fields and our vineyards. **5:5** And now, though we share the same flesh and blood as our fellow countrymen, and our children are just like their children, still we have found it necessary to subject our sons and daughters to slavery. Some of our daughters have been subjected to slavery, while we are powerless to help, since our fields and vineyards now belong to other people."

5:6 I was very angry when I heard their outcry and these complaints. **5:7** I considered these things carefully and then registered a complaint with the wealthy and the officials. I said to them, "Each one of you is seizing the collateral from your own countrymen!" Because of them I called for a great public assembly. **5:8** I said to them, "To the extent possible we have bought back our fellow Jews who had been sold to the Gentiles. But now you yourselves want to sell your own countrymen, so that we can then buy them back!" They were utterly silent, and could find nothing to say.

5:9 Then I said, "The thing that you are doing is wrong! Should you not conduct yourselves in the fear of our God in order to avoid the reproach of the Gentiles who are our enemies? **5:10** Even I and my relatives and my associates are lending them money and grain. But let us abandon this practice of seizing collateral! **5:11** This very day return to them their fields, their vineyards, their olive trees, and their houses, along with the interest that you are exacting from them on the money, the grain, the new wine, and the olive oil."

5:12 They replied, "We will return these things, and we will no longer demand anything from them. We will do just as you say." Then I called the priests and made the wealthy and the officials swear to do what had been promised. **5:13** I also shook out my garment, and I said, "In this way may God shake out from his house and his property every person who does not carry out this matter. In this way may he be shaken out and emptied!" All the assembly replied, "So be it!" and they praised the LORD. Then the people did as they had promised.

5:14 From the day that I was appointed governor in the land of Judah, that is, from the twentieth year until the thirty-second year of King Artaxerxes – twelve years in all – neither I nor my relatives ate the food allotted to the governor. **5:15** But the former governors who preceded me had burdened the people and had taken food and wine from them, in addition to forty shekels of silver. Their associates were also domineering over the people. But I did not behave in this way, due to my fear of God. **5:16** I gave myself to the work on this wall, without even purchasing a field. All my associates were gathered there for the work.

5:17 There were 150 Jews and officials who dined with me routinely, in addition to those who came to us from the nations all around us. **5:18** Every day one ox, six select sheep, and some birds were prepared for me, and every ten days all kinds of wine in abundance. Despite all this I did not require the food allotted to the governor, for the work was demanding on this people.

5:19 Please remember me for good, O my God, for all that I have done for this people.

Opposition to the Rebuilding Efforts Continues

6:1 When Sanballat, Tobiah, Geshem the Arab, and the rest of our enemies heard that I had rebuilt the wall and no breach remained in it (even though up to that time I had not positioned doors in the gates), **6:2** Sanballat and Geshem sent word to me saying, "Come on! Let's set up a time to meet together at Kephirim in the plain of Ono." Now they intended to do me harm.

6:3 So I sent messengers to them saying, "I am engaged in an important work, and I am unable to come down. Why should the work come to a halt when I leave it to come down to you?" **6:4** They contacted me four times in this way, and I responded the same way each time.

6:5 The fifth time that Sanballat sent his assistant to me in this way, he had an open letter in his hand. **6:6** Written in it were the following words: "Among the nations it is rumored (and Geshem has substantiated this) that you and the Jews have intentions of revolting, and for this reason you are building the wall. Furthermore, according to these rumors you are going to become their king. **6:7** You have also established prophets to announce in Jerusalem on your behalf, 'We have a king in Judah!' Now the king is going to hear about these rumors. So come on! Let's talk about this."

6:8 I sent word back to him, "We are not engaged in these activities you are describing. All of this is a figment of your imagination."

6:9 All of them were wanting to scare us, supposing, "Their hands will grow slack from the work, and it won't get done."

So now, strengthen my hands!

6:10 Then I went to the house of Shemaiah son of Delaiah, the son of Mehetabel. He was confined to his home. He said, "Let's set up a time to meet in the house of God, within the temple. Let's close the doors of the temple, for they are coming to kill you. It will surely be at night that they will come to kill you."

6:11 But I replied, "Should a man like me run away? Would someone like me flee to the temple in order to save his life? I will not go!" **6:12** I recognized the fact that God had not sent him, for he had spoken the prophecy against me as a hired agent of Tobiah and Sanballat. **6:13** He had been hired to scare me so that I would do this and thereby sin. They would thus bring reproach on me and I would be discredited.

6:14 Remember, O my God, Tobiah and Sanballat in light of these actions of theirs – also Noadiah the prophetess and the other prophets who were trying to scare me!

The Rebuilding of the Wall Is Finally Completed

6:15 So the wall was completed on the twenty-fifth day of Elul, in just fifty-two days. **6:16** When all our enemies heard and all the nations who were around us saw this, they were greatly disheartened. They knew that this work had been accomplished with the help of our God.

6:17 In those days the aristocrats of Judah repeatedly sent letters to Tobiah, and responses from Tobiah were repeatedly coming to them. **6:18** For many in Judah had sworn allegiance to him, because he was the son-in-law of Shecaniah son of Arah. His son Jonathan had married the daughter of Meshullam son of Berechiah. **6:19** They were telling me about his good deeds and then taking back to him the things I said. Tobiah, on the other hand, sent letters in order to scare me.

7:1 When the wall had been rebuilt and I had positioned the doors, and the gatekeepers, the singers, and the Levites had been appointed, **7:2** I then put in charge over Jerusalem my brother Hanani and Hananiah the chief of the citadel, for he was a faithful man and feared God more than many do. **7:3** I said to them, "The gates of Jerusalem must not be opened in the early morning, until those who are standing guard close the doors and lock them. Position residents of Jerusalem as guards, some at their guard stations and some near their homes." **7:4** Now the city was spread out and large, and there were not a lot of people in it. At that time houses had not been rebuilt. **7:5** My God placed it on my heart to gather the leaders, the officials, and the ordinary people so they could be enrolled on the basis of genealogy. I found the genealogical records of those who had formerly returned. Here is what I found written in that record:

7:6 These are the people of the province who returned from the captivity of the exiles, whom King Nebuchadnezzar of Babylon had forced into exile. They returned to Jerusalem and to Judah, each to his own city. **7:7** They came with Zerubbabel, Jeshua, Nehemiah, Azariah, Raamiah, Nahamani, Mordecai, Bilshan, Mispereth, Bigvai, Nehum, and Baanah.

The number of Israelite men was as follows:

7:8 the descendants of Parosh, 2,172;

7:9 the descendants of Shephatiah, 372;

7:10 the descendants of Arah, 652;

7:11 the descendants of Pahath-Moab (from the line of Jeshua and Joab), 2,818;

7:12 the descendants of Elam, 1,254;

7:13 the descendants of Zattu, 845;

7:14 the descendants of Zaccai, 760;

7:15 the descendants of Binnui, 648;

7:16 the descendants of Bebai, 628;

7:17 the descendants of Azgad, 2,322;

7:18 the descendants of Adonikam, 667;

7:19 the descendants of Bigvai, 2,067;

7:20 the descendants of Adin, 655;

7:21 the descendants of Ater (through Hezekiah), 98;

7:22 the descendants of Hashum, 328;

7:23 the descendants of Bezai, 324;

7:24 the descendants of Harif, 112;

7:25 the descendants of Gibeon, 95;

7:26 The men of Bethlehem and Netophah, 188;

7:27 the men of Anathoth, 128;

7:28 the men of the family of Azmaveth, 42;

7:29 the men of Kiriath Jearim, Kephirah, and Beeroth, 743;

7:30 the men of Ramah and Geba, 621;

7:31 the men of Micmash, 122;

7:32 the men of Bethel and Ai, 123;

7:33 the men of the other Nebo, 52;

7:34 the descendants of the other Elam, 1,254;

7:35 the descendants of Harim, 320;

7:36 the descendants of Jericho, 345;

7:37 the descendants of Lod, Hadid, and Ono, 721;

7:38 the descendants of Senaah, 3,930.

7:39 The priests:

the descendants of Jedaiah (through the family of Jeshua), 973;

7:40 the descendants of Immer, 1,052;

7:41 the descendants of Pashhur, 1,247;

7:42 the descendants of Harim, 1,017.

7:43 The Levites:

the descendants of Jeshua (through Kadmiel, through the line of Hodaviah), 74.

7:44 The singers:

the descendants of Asaph, 148.

7:45 The gatekeepers:

the descendants of Shallum, the descendants of Ater, the descendants of Talmon, the descendants of Akkub, the descendants of Hatita, and the descendants of Shobai, 138.

7:46 The temple servants:

the descendants of Ziha, the descendants of Hasupha, the descendants of Tabbaoth, **7:47** the descendants of Keros, the descendants of Sia, the descendants of Padon, **7:48** the descendants of Lebanah, the descendants of Hagabah, the descendants of Shalmai, **7:49** the descendants of Hanan, the descendants of Giddel, the descendants of Gahar, **7:50** the descendants of Reaiah, the descendants of Rezin, the descendants of Nekoda, **7:51** the descendants of Gazzam, the descendants of Uzzah, the descendants of Paseah, **7:52** the descendants of Besai, the descendants of Meunim, the descendants of Nephussim, **7:53** the descendants of Bakbuk, the descendants of Hakupha, the descendants of Harhur, **7:54** the descendants of Bazluth, the descendants of Mehida, the descendants of Harsha, **7:55** the descendants of Barkos, the descendants of Sisera, the descendants of Temah, **7:56** the descendants of Neziah, the descendants of Hatipha.

7:57 The descendants of the servants of Solomon:

the descendants of Sotai, the descendants of Sophereth, the descendants of Perida, **7:58** the descendants of Jaala, the descendants of Darkon, the descendants of Giddel, **7:59** the descendants of Shephatiah, the descendants of Hattil, the descendants of Pokereth-Hazzebaim, and the descendants of Amon.

7:60 All the temple servants and the descendants of the servants of Solomon, 392.

7:61 These are the ones who came up from Tel Melah, Tel Harsha, Kerub, Addon, and Immer (although they were unable to certify their family connection or their ancestry, as to whether they were really from Israel):

7:62 the descendants of Delaiah, the descendants of Tobiah, and the descendants of Nekoda, 642.

7:63 And from among the priests: the descendants of Hobaiah, the descendants of Hakkoz, and the descendants of Barzillai (who had married a woman from the daughters of Barzillai the Gileadite and was called by that name). **7:64** They searched for their records in the genealogical materials, but none were found. They were therefore excluded from the priesthood. **7:65** The governor instructed them not to eat any of the sacred food until there was a priest who could consult the Urim and Thummim.

7:66 The entire group numbered 42,360, **7:67** not counting their 7,337 male and female servants. They also had 245 male and female singers. **7:68** They had 736 horses, 245 mules, **7:69** (7:68) 435 camels, and 6,720 donkeys. **7:70** Some of the family leaders contributed to the work. The governor contributed to the treasury 1,000 gold drachmas, 50 bowls, and 530 priestly garments. **7:71** Some of the family leaders gave to the project treasury 20,000 gold drachmas and 2,200 silver minas. **7:72** What the rest of the people gave amounted to 20,000 gold drachmas, 2,000 silver minas, and 67 priestly garments.

7:73 The priests, the Levites, the gatekeepers, the singers, some of the people, the temple servants, and all the rest of Israel lived in their cities.

The People Respond to the Reading of the Law

When the seventh month arrived and the Israelites were settled in their cities, **8:1** all the people gathered together in the plaza which was in front of the Water Gate. They asked Ezra the scribe to bring the book of the law of Moses which the LORD had commanded Israel. **8:2** So Ezra the priest brought the law before the assembly which included men and women and all those able to understand what they heard. (This happened on the first day of the seventh month.) **8:3** So he read it before the plaza in front of the Water Gate from dawn till noon before the men and women and those children who could understand. All the people were eager to hear the book of the law.

8:4 Ezra the scribe stood on a towering wooden platform constructed for this purpose. Standing near him on his right were Mattithiah, Shema, Anaiah, Uriah, Hilkiah, and Maaseiah. On his left were Pedaiah, Mishael, Malkijah, Hashum, Hashbaddanah, Zechariah, and Meshullam. **8:5** Ezra opened the book in plain view of all the people, for he was elevated above all the people. When he opened the book, all the people stood up. **8:6** Ezra blessed the LORD, the great God, and all the people replied "Amen! Amen!" as they lifted their hands. Then they bowed down and worshiped the LORD with their faces to the ground.

8:7 Jeshua, Bani, Sherebiah, Jamin, Akkub, Shabbethai, Hodiah, Maaseiah, Kelita, Azariah, Jozabad, Hanan, and Pelaiah – all of whom were Levites – were teaching the people the law, as the people remained standing. **8:8** They read from the book of God's law, explaining it and imparting insight. Thus the people gained understanding from what was read.

8:9 Then Nehemiah the governor, Ezra the priestly scribe, and the Levites who were imparting understanding to the people said to all of them, "This day is holy to the LORD your God. Do not mourn or weep." For all the people had been weeping when they heard the words of the law. **8:10** He said to them, "Go and eat delicacies and drink sweet drinks and send portions to those for whom nothing is prepared. For this day is holy to our Lord. Do not grieve, for the joy of the LORD is your strength."

8:11 Then the Levites quieted all the people saying, "Be quiet, for this day is holy. Do not grieve." **8:12** So all the people departed to eat and drink and to share their food with others and to enjoy tremendous joy, for they had gained insight in the matters that had been made known to them.

8:13 On the second day of the month the family leaders met with Ezra the scribe, together with all the people, the priests, and the Levites, to consider the words of the law. **8:14** They discovered written in the law that the LORD had commanded through Moses that the Israelites should live in temporary shelters during the festival of the seventh month, **8:15** and that they should make a proclamation and disseminate this message in all their cities and in Jerusalem: "Go to the hill country and bring back olive branches and branches of wild olive trees, myrtle trees, date palms, and other leafy trees to construct temporary shelters, as it is written."

8:16 So the people went out and brought these things back and constructed temporary shelters for themselves, each on his roof and in his courtyard and in the courtyards of the temple of God and in the plaza of the Water Gate and the plaza of the Ephraim Gate. **8:17** So all the assembly which had returned from the exile constructed temporary shelters and lived in them. The Israelites had not done so from the days of Joshua son of Nun until that day. Everyone experienced very great joy. **8:18** Ezra read in the book of the law of God day by day, from the first day to the last. They observed the festival for seven days, and on the eighth day they held an assembly as was required.

The People Acknowledge Their Sin before God

9:1 On the twenty-fourth day of this same month the Israelites assembled; they were fasting and wearing sackcloth, their heads covered with dust. **9:2** Those truly of Israelite descent separated from all the foreigners, standing and confessing their sins and the iniquities of their ancestors. **9:3** For one-fourth of the day they stood in their place and read from the book of the law of the LORD their God, and for another fourth they were confessing their sins and worshiping the LORD their God. **9:4** Then the Levites – Jeshua, Binnui, Kadmiel, Shebaniah, Bunni, Sherebiah, Bani, and Kenani – stood on the steps and called out loudly to the LORD their God. **9:5** The Levites – Jeshua, Kadmiel, Bani, Hashabneiah, Sherebiah, Hodiah, Shebaniah, and Pethahiah – said, "Stand up and bless the LORD your God!"

"May you be blessed, O LORD our God, from age to age. May your glorious name be blessed; may it be lifted up above all blessing and praise. **9:6** You alone are the LORD. You made the heavens, even the highest heavens, along with all their multitude of stars, the earth and all that is on it, the seas and all that is in them. You impart life to them all, and the multitudes of heaven worship you.

9:7 "You are the LORD God who chose Abram and brought him forth from Ur of the Chaldeans. You changed his name to Abraham. **9:8** When you perceived that his heart was faithful toward you, you established a covenant with him to give his descendants the land of the Canaanites, the Hittites, the Amorites, the Perizzites, the Jebusites, and the Girgashites. You have fulfilled your promise, for you are righteous.

9:9 "You saw the affliction of our ancestors in Egypt, and you heard their cry at the Red Sea. **9:10** You performed awesome signs against Pharaoh, against his servants, and against all the people of his land, for you knew that the Egyptians had acted presumptuously against them. You made for yourself a name that is celebrated to this day. **9:11** You split the sea before them, and they crossed through the sea on dry ground! But you threw their pursuers into the depths, like a stone into surging waters. **9:12** You guided them with a pillar of cloud by day and with a pillar of fire by night to illumine for them the path they were to travel.

9:13 "You came down on Mount Sinai and spoke with them from heaven. You provided them with just judgments, true laws, and good statutes and commandments. **9:14** You made known to them your holy Sabbath; you issued commandments, statutes, and law to them through Moses your servant. **9:15** You provided bread from heaven for them in their time of hunger, and you brought forth water from the rock for them in their time of thirst. You told them to enter in order to possess the land that you had sworn to give them.

9:16 "But they – our ancestors – behaved presumptuously; they rebelled and did not obey your commandments. **9:17** They refused to obey and did not recall your miracles that you had performed among them. Instead, they rebelled and appointed a leader to return to their bondage in Egypt. But you are a God of forgiveness, merciful and compassionate, slow to get angry and unfailing in your loyal love. You did not abandon them, **9:18** even when they made a cast image of a calf for themselves and said, 'This is your God who brought you up from Egypt,' or when they committed atrocious blasphemies.

9:19 "Due to your great compassion you did not abandon them in the desert. The pillar of cloud did not stop guiding them in the path by day, nor did the pillar of fire stop illuminating for them by night the path on which they should travel. **9:20** You imparted your good Spirit to instruct them. You did not withhold your manna from their mouths; you provided water for their thirst. **9:21** For forty years you sustained them. Even in the desert they never lacked anything. Their clothes did not wear out and their feet did not swell.

9:22 "You gave them kingdoms and peoples, and you allocated them to every corner of the land. They inherited the land of King Sihon of Heshbon and the land of King Og of Bashan. **9:23** You multiplied their descendants like the stars of the sky. You brought them to the land you had told their ancestors to enter in order to possess. **9:24** Their descendants entered and possessed the land. You subdued before them the Canaanites who were the inhabitants of the land. You delivered them into their hand, together with their kings and the peoples of the land, to deal with as they pleased. **9:25** They captured fortified cities and fertile land. They took possession of houses full of all sorts of good things – wells previously dug, vineyards, olive trees, and fruit trees in abundance. They ate until they were full and grew fat. They enjoyed to the full your great goodness.

9:26 "Nonetheless they grew disobedient and rebelled against you; they disregarded your law. They killed your prophets who had solemnly admonished them in order to cause them to return to you. They committed atrocious blasphemies. **9:27** Therefore you delivered them into the hand of their adversaries, who oppressed them. But in the time of their distress they called to you, and you heard from heaven. In your abundant compassion you provided them with deliverers to rescue them from their adversaries.

9:28 "Then, when they were at rest again, they went back to doing evil before you. Then you abandoned them to their enemies, and they gained dominion over them. When they again cried out to you, in your compassion you heard from heaven and rescued them time and again. **9:29** And you solemnly admonished them in order to return them to your law, but they behaved presumptuously and did not obey your commandments. They sinned against your ordinances – those by which an individual, if he obeys them, will live. They boldly turned from you; they rebelled and did not obey. **9:30** You prolonged your kindness with them for many years, and you solemnly admonished them by your Spirit through your prophets. Still they paid no attention, so you delivered them into the hands of the neighboring peoples. **9:31** However, due to your abundant mercy you did not do away with them altogether; you did not abandon them. For you are a merciful and compassionate God.

9:32 "So now, our God – the great, powerful, and awesome God, who keeps covenant fidelity – do not regard as inconsequential all the hardship that has befallen us – our kings, our leaders, our priests, our prophets, our ancestors, and all your people – from the days of the kings of Assyria until this very day! **9:33** You are righteous with regard to all that has happened to us, for you have acted faithfully. It is we who have been in the wrong! **9:34** Our kings, our leaders, our priests, and our ancestors have not kept your law. They have not paid attention to your commandments or your testimonies by which you have solemnly admonished them. **9:35** Even when they were in their kingdom and benefiting from your incredible goodness that you had lavished on them in the spacious and fertile land you had set before them, they did not serve you, nor did they turn from their evil practices.

9:36 "So today we are slaves! In the very land you gave to our ancestors to eat its fruit and to enjoy its good things – we are slaves! **9:37** Its abundant produce goes to the kings you have placed over us due to our sins. They rule over our bodies and our livestock as they see fit, and we are in great distress.

The People Pledge to be Faithful

9:38 (10:1) "Because of all of this we are entering into a binding covenant in written form; our leaders, our Levites, and our priests have affixed their names on the sealed document."

10:1 On the sealed documents were the following names:
Nehemiah the governor, son of Hacaliah, along with Zedekiah,
10:2 Seraiah, Azariah, Jeremiah,
10:3 Pashhur, Amariah, Malkijah,
10:4 Hattush, Shebaniah, Malluch,
10:5 Harim, Meremoth, Obadiah,
10:6 Daniel, Ginnethon, Baruch,
10:7 Meshullam, Abijah, Mijamin,
10:8 Maaziah, Bilgai, and Shemaiah. These were the priests.
10:9 The Levites were as follows:

Jeshua son of Azaniah, Binnui of the sons of Henadad, Kadmiel.
10:10 Their colleagues were as follows:
Shebaniah, Hodiah, Kelita, Pelaiah, Hanan,
10:11 Mica, Rehob, Hashabiah,
10:12 Zaccur, Sherebiah, Shebaniah,
10:13 Hodiah, Bani, and Beninu.
10:14 The leaders of the people were as follows:
Parosh, Pahath-Moab, Elam, Zattu, Bani,
10:15 Bunni, Azgad, Bebai,
10:16 Adonijah, Bigvai, Adin,
10:17 Ater, Hezekiah, Azzur,
10:18 Hodiah, Hashum, Bezai,
10:19 Hariph, Anathoth, Nebai,
10:20 Magpiash, Meshullam, Hezir,
10:21 Meshezabel, Zadok, Jaddua,
10:22 Pelatiah, Hanan, Anaiah,
10:23 Hoshea, Hananiah, Hasshub,
10:24 Hallohesh, Pilha, Shobek,
10:25 Rehum, Hashabnah, Maaseiah,
10:26 Ahiah, Hanan, Anan,
10:27 Malluch, Harim, and Baanah.

10:28 "Now the rest of the people – the priests, the Levites, the gatekeepers, the singers, the temple attendants, and all those who have separated themselves from the neighboring peoples because of the law of God, along with their wives, their sons, and their daughters, all of whom are able to understand – **10:29** hereby participate with their colleagues the town leaders and enter into a curse and an oath to adhere to the law of God which was given through Moses the servant of God, and to obey carefully all the commandments of the LORD our Lord, along with his ordinances and his statutes.

10:30 "We will not give our daughters in marriage to the neighboring peoples, and we will not take their daughters in marriage for our sons. **10:31** We will not buy on the Sabbath or on a holy day from the neighboring peoples who bring their wares and all kinds of grain to sell on the Sabbath day. We will let the fields lie fallow every seventh year, and we will cancel every loan. **10:32** We accept responsibility for fulfilling the commands to give one third of a shekel each year for the work of the temple of our God, **10:33** for the loaves of presentation and for the regular grain offerings and regular burnt offerings, for the Sabbaths, for the new moons, for the appointed meetings, for the holy offerings, for the sin offerings to make atonement for Israel, and for all the work of the temple of our God.

10:34 "We – the priests, the Levites, and the people – have cast lots concerning the wood offerings, to bring them to the temple of our God according to our families at the designated times year by year to burn on the altar of the LORD our God, as is written in the law. **10:35** We also accept responsibility for bringing the first fruits of our land and the first fruits of every fruit tree year by year to the temple of the LORD. **10:36** We also accept responsibility, as is written in the law, for bringing the firstborn of our sons and our cattle and the firstborn of our herds and of our flocks to the temple of our God, to the priests who are ministering in the temple of our God. **10:37** We will also bring the first of our coarse meal, of our contributions, of the fruit of every tree, of new wine, and of olive oil to the priests at the storerooms of the temple of our God, along with a tenth of the produce of our land to the Levites, for the Levites are the ones who collect the tithes in all the cities where we work. **10:38** A priest of Aaron's line will be with the Levites when the Levites collect the tithes, and the Levites will bring up a tenth of the tithes to the temple of our God, to the storerooms of the treasury. **10:39** The Israelites and the Levites will bring the contribution of the grain, the new wine, and the olive oil to the storerooms where the utensils of the sanctuary are kept, and where the priests who minister stay, along with the gatekeepers and the singers. We will not neglect the temple of our God."

The Population of Jerusalem

11:1 So the leaders of the people settled in Jerusalem, while the rest of the people cast lots to bring one out of every ten to settle in Jerusalem, the holy city, while the other nine remained in other cities. **11:2** The people gave their blessing on all the men who volunteered to settle in Jerusalem.

11:3 These are the provincial leaders who settled in Jerusalem. (While other Israelites, the priests, the Levites, the temple attendants, and the sons of the servants of Solomon settled in the cities of Judah, each on his own property in their cities, **11:4** some of the descendants of Judah and some of the descendants of Benjamin settled in Jerusalem.)

Of the descendants of Judah:
Athaiah son of Uzziah, the son of Zechariah, the son of Amariah, the son of Shephatiah, the son of Mahalalel, from the descendants of Perez; **11:5** and Maaseiah son of Baruch, the son of Col-Hozeh, the son of Hazaiah, the son of Adaiah, the son of Joiarib, the son of Zechariah, from the descendants of Shelah. **11:6** The sum total of the descendants of Perez who were settling in Jerusalem was 468 exceptional men.

11:7 These are the descendants of Benjamin:

Sallu son of Meshullam, the son of Joed, the son of Pedaiah, the son of Kolaiah, the son of Maaseiah, the son of Ithiel, the son of Jeshaiah, **11:8** and his followers, Gabbai and Sallai – 928 in all. **11:9** Joel son of Zicri was the officer in charge of them, and Judah son of Hassenuah was second-in-command over the city.

11:10 From the priests:

Jedaiah son of Joiarib, Jakin, **11:11** Seraiah son of Hilkiah, the son of Meshullam, the son of Zadok, the son of Meraioth, the son of Ahitub, supervisor in the temple of God, **11:12** and their colleagues who were carrying out work for the temple – 822; and Adaiah son of Jeroham, the son of Pelaliah, the son of Amzi, the son of Zechariah, the son of Pashhur, the son of Malkijah, **11:13** and his colleagues who were heads of families – 242; and Amashsai son of Azarel, the son of Ahzai, the son of Meshillemoth, the son of Immer, **11:14** and his colleagues who were exceptional men – 128. The officer over them was Zabdiel the son of Haggedolim.

11:15 From the Levites:

Shemaiah son of Hasshub, the son of Azrikam, the son of Hashabiah, the son of Bunni; **11:16** Shabbethai and Jozabad, leaders of the Levites, were in charge of the external work for the temple of God; **11:17** Mattaniah son of Mica, the son of Zabdi, the son of Asaph, the praise leader who led in thanksgiving and prayer; Bakbukiah, second among his colleagues; and Abda son of Shammua, the son of Galal, the son of Jeduthun. **11:18** The sum total of the Levites in the holy city was 284.

11:19 And the gatekeepers:

Akkub, Talmon and their colleagues who were guarding the gates – 172.

11:20 And the rest of the Israelites, with the priests and the Levites, were in all the cities of Judah, each on his own property.

11:21 The temple attendants were living on Ophel, and Ziha and Gishpa were over them.

11:22 The overseer of the Levites in Jerusalem was Uzzi son of Bani, the son of Hashabiah, the son of Mattaniah, the son of Mica. He was one of Asaph's descendants who were the singers responsible for the service of the temple of God. **11:23** For they were under royal orders which determined their activity day by day.

11:24 Pethahiah son of Meshezabel, one of the descendants of Zerah son of Judah, was an adviser to the king in every matter pertaining to the people.

11:25 As for the settlements with their fields, some of the people of Judah settled in Kiriath Arba and its neighboring villages, in Dibon and its villages, in Jekabzeel and its settlements, **11:26** in Jeshua, in Moladah, in Beth Pelet, **11:27** in Hazar Shual, in Beer Sheba and its villages, **11:28** in Ziklag, in Meconah and its villages, **11:29** in En Rimmon, in Zorah, in Jarmuth, **11:30** Zanoah, Adullam and their settlements, in Lachish and its fields, and in Azekah and its villages. So they were encamped from Beer Sheba to the Valley of Hinnom.

11:31 Some of the descendants of Benjamin settled in Geba, Micmash, Aija, Bethel and its villages, **11:32** in Anathoth, Nob, and Ananiah, **11:33** in Hazor, Ramah, and Gittaim, **11:34** in Hadid, Zeboim, and Neballat, **11:35** in Lod, Ono, and the Valley of the Craftsmen. **11:36** Some of the Judean divisions of the Levites settled in Benjamin.

The Priests and the Levites Who Returned to Jerusalem

12:1 These are the priests and Levites who returned with Zerubbabel son of Shealtiel and Jeshua: Seraiah, Jeremiah, Ezra, **12:2** Amariah, Malluch, Hattush, **12:3** Shecaniah, Rehum, Meremoth, **12:4** Iddo, Ginnethon, Abijah, **12:5** Mijamin, Moadiah, Bilgah, **12:6** Shemaiah, Joiarib, Jedaiah, **12:7** Sallu, Amok, Hilkiah, and Jedaiah. These were the leaders of the priests and their colleagues in the days of Jeshua.

12:8 And the Levites: Jeshua, Binnui, Kadmiel, Sherebiah, Judah, and Mattaniah, who together with his colleagues was in charge of the songs of thanksgiving. **12:9** Bakbukiah and Unni, their colleagues, stood opposite them in the services.

12:10 Jeshua was the father of Joiakim, Joiakim was the father of Eliashib, Eliashib was the father of Joiada, **12:11** Joiada was the father of Jonathan, and Jonathan was the father of Jaddua.

12:12 In the days of Joiakim, these were the priests who were leaders of the families: of Seraiah, Meraiah; of Jeremiah, Hananiah; **12:13** of Ezra, Meshullam; of Amariah, Jehohanan; **12:14** of Malluch, Jonathan; of Shecaniah, Joseph; **12:15** of Harim, Adna; of Meremoth, Helkai; **12:16** of Iddo, Zechariah; of Ginnethon, Meshullam; **12:17** of Abijah, Zicri; of Miniamin and of Moadiah, Piltai; **12:18** of Bilgah, Shammua; of Shemaiah, Jehonathan; **12:19** of Joiarib, Mattenai; of Jedaiah, Uzzi; **12:20** of Sallu, Kallai; of Amok, Eber; **12:21** of Hilkiah, Hashabiah; of Jedaiah, Nethanel.

12:22 As for the Levites, in the days of Eliashib, Joiada, Johanan and Jaddua the heads of families were recorded, as were the priests during the reign of Darius the Persian. **12:23** The descendants of Levi were recorded in the Book of the Chronicles as heads of families up to the days of Johanan son of Eliashib. **12:24** And the leaders of the Levites were Hashabiah, Sherebiah, Jeshua son of Kadmiel, and their colleagues, who stood opposite them to offer praise and thanks, one contingent corresponding to the other, as specified by David the man of God.

12:25 Mattaniah, Bakbukiah, Obadiah, Meshullam, Talmon, and Akkub were gatekeepers who were guarding the storerooms at the gates. **12:26** These all served in the days of Joiakim son of Jeshua, the son of Jozadak, and in the days of Nehemiah the governor and of Ezra the priestly scribe.

The Wall of Jerusalem is Dedicated

12:27 At the dedication of the wall of Jerusalem, they sought out the Levites from all the places they lived to bring them to Jerusalem to celebrate the dedication joyfully with songs of thanksgiving and songs accompanied by cymbals, harps, and lyres. **12:28** The singers were also assembled from the district around Jerusalem and from the settlements of the Netophathites **12:29** and from Beth Gilgal and from the fields of Geba and Azmaveth, for the singers had built settlements for themselves around Jerusalem. **12:30** When the priests and Levites had purified themselves, they purified the people, the gates, and the wall.

12:31 I brought the leaders of Judah up on top of the wall, and I appointed two large choirs to give thanks. One was to proceed on the top of the wall southward toward the Dung Gate. **12:32** Going after them were Hoshaiah, half the leaders of Judah, **12:33** Azariah, Ezra, Meshullam, **12:34** Judah, Benjamin, Shemaiah, Jeremiah, **12:35** some of the priests with trumpets, Zechariah son of Jonathan, the son of Shemaiah, the son of Mattaniah, the son of Micaiah, the son of Zaccur, the son of Asaph, **12:36** and his colleagues – Shemaiah, Azarel, Milalai, Gilalai, Maai, Nethanel, Judah, and Hanani – with musical instruments of David the man of God. (Ezra the scribe led them.) **12:37** They went over the Fountain Gate and continued directly up the steps of the City of David on the ascent to the wall. They passed the house of David and continued on to the Water Gate toward the east.

12:38 The second choir was proceeding in the opposite direction. I followed them, along with half the people, on top of the wall, past the Tower of the Ovens to the Broad Wall, **12:39** over the Ephraim Gate, the Jeshanah Gate, the Fish Gate, the Tower of Hananel, and the Tower of the Hundred, to the Sheep Gate. They stopped at the Gate of the Guard.

12:40 Then the two choirs that gave thanks took their stations in the temple of God. I did also, along with half the officials with me, **12:41** and the priests – Eliakim, Maaseiah, Miniamin, Micaiah, Elioenai, Zechariah, Hananiah, with their trumpets – **12:42** and also Maaseiah, Shemaiah, Eleazar, Uzzi, Jehohanan, Malkijah, Elam, and Ezer. The choirs sang loudly under the direction of Jezrahiah. **12:43** And on that day they offered great sacrifices and rejoiced, for God had given them great joy. The women and children also rejoiced. The rejoicing in Jerusalem could be heard from far away.

12:44 On that day men were appointed over the storerooms for the contributions, first fruits, and tithes, to gather into them from the fields of the cities the portions prescribed by the law for the priests and the Levites, for the people of Judah took delight in the priests and Levites who were ministering. **12:45** They performed the service of their God and the service of purification, along with the singers and gatekeepers, according to the commandment of David and his son Solomon. **12:46** For long ago, in the days of David and Asaph, there had been directors for the singers and for the songs of praise and thanks to God. **12:47** So in the days of Zerubbabel and in the days of Nehemiah, all Israel was contributing the portions for the singers and gatekeepers, according to the daily need. They also set aside the portion for the Levites, and the Levites set aside the portion for the descendants of Aaron.

Further Reforms by Nehemiah

13:1 On that day the book of Moses was read aloud in the hearing of the people. They found written in it that no Ammonite or Moabite may ever enter the assembly of God, **13:2** for they had not met the Israelites with food and water, but instead had hired Balaam to curse them. (Our God, however, turned the curse into blessing.) **13:3** When they heard the law, they removed from Israel all who were of mixed ancestry.

13:4 But prior to this time, Eliashib the priest, a relative of Tobiah, had been appointed over the storerooms of the temple of our God. **13:5** He made for himself a large storeroom where previously they had been keeping the grain offering, the incense, and the vessels, along with the tithes of the grain, the new wine, and the olive oil as commanded for the Levites, the singers, the gate keepers, and the offering for the priests.

13:6 During all this time I was not in Jerusalem, for in the thirty-second year of King Artaxerxes of Babylon, I had gone back to the king. After some time I had requested leave of the king, **13:7** and I returned to Jerusalem. Then I discovered the evil that Eliashib had done for Tobiah by supplying him with a storeroom in the courts of the temple of God. **13:8** I was very upset, and I threw all of Tobiah's household possessions out of the storeroom. **13:9** Then I gave instructions that the storerooms should be purified, and I brought back the equipment of the temple of God, along with the grain offering and the incense.

13:10 I also discovered that the grain offerings for the Levites had not been provided, and that as a result the Levites and the singers who performed this work had all gone off to their fields. **13:11** So I registered a complaint with the leaders, asking "Why is the temple of God neglected?" Then I gathered them and reassigned them to their positions.

13:12 Then all of Judah brought the tithe of the grain, the new wine, and the olive oil to the storerooms. **13:13** I gave instructions that Shelemiah the priest, Zadok the scribe, and a certain Levite named Pedaiah be put in charge of the storerooms, and that Hanan son of Zaccur, the son of Mattaniah, be their assistant, for they were regarded as trustworthy. It was then their responsibility to oversee the distribution to their colleagues.

13:14 Please remember me for this, O my God, and do not wipe out the kindness that I have done for the temple of my God and for its services!

13:15 In those days I saw people in Judah treading winepresses on the Sabbath, bringing in heaps of grain and loading them onto donkeys, along with wine, grapes, figs, and all kinds of loads, and bringing them to Jerusalem on the Sabbath day. So I warned them on the day that they sold these provisions. **13:16** The people from Tyre who lived there were bringing fish and all kinds of merchandise and were selling it on the Sabbath to the people of Judah – and in Jerusalem, of all places! **13:17** So I registered a complaint with the nobles of Judah, saying to them, "What is this evil thing that you are doing, profaning the Sabbath day? **13:18** Isn't this the way your ancestors acted, causing our God to bring on them and on this city all this misfortune? And now you are causing even more wrath on Israel, profaning the Sabbath like this!"

13:19 When the evening shadows began to fall on the gates of Jerusalem before the Sabbath, I ordered the doors to be closed. I further directed that they were not to be opened until after the Sabbath. I positioned some of my young men at the gates so that no load could enter on the Sabbath day. **13:20** The traders and sellers of all kinds of merchandise spent the night outside Jerusalem once or twice. **13:21** But I warned them and said, "Why do you spend the night by the wall? If you repeat this, I will forcibly remove you!" From that time on they did not show up on the Sabbath. **13:22** Then I directed the Levites to purify themselves and come and guard the gates in order to keep the Sabbath day holy.

For this please remember me, O my God, and have pity on me in keeping with your great love.

13:23 Also in those days I saw the men of Judah who had married women from Ashdod, Ammon, and Moab. **13:24** Half of their children spoke the language of Ashdod (or the language of one of the other peoples mentioned) and were unable to speak the language of Judah. **13:25** So I entered a complaint with them. I called down a curse on them, and I struck some of the men and pulled out their hair. I had them swear by God saying, "You will not marry off your daughters to their sons, and you will not take any of their daughters as wives for your sons or for yourselves! **13:26** Was it not because of things like these that King Solomon of Israel sinned? Among the many nations there was no king like him. He was loved by his God, and God made him king over all Israel. But the foreign wives made even him sin! **13:27** Should we then in your case hear that you do all this great evil, thereby being unfaithful to our God by marrying foreign wives?"

13:28 Now one of the sons of Joiada son of Eliashib the high priest was a son-in-law of Sanballat the Horonite. So I banished him from my sight. **13:29** Please remember them, O my God, because they have defiled the priesthood, the covenant of the priesthood, and the Levites.

13:30 So I purified them of everything foreign, and I assigned specific duties to the priests and the Levites. **13:31** I also provided for the wood offering at the appointed times and also for the first fruits.

Please remember me for good, O my God.

Book 17. Esther

The King Throws a Lavish Party

1:1 The following events happened in the days of Ahasuerus. (I am referring to that Ahasuerus who used to rule over a hundred and twenty-seven provinces extending all the way from India to Ethiopia.) **1:2** In those days, as King Ahasuerus sat on his royal throne in Susa the citadel, **1:3** in the third year of his reign he provided a banquet for all his officials and his servants. The army of Persia and Media was present, as well as the nobles and the officials of the provinces.

1:4 He displayed the riches of his royal glory and the splendor of his majestic greatness for a lengthy period of time – a hundred and eighty days, to be exact! **1:5** When those days were completed, the king then provided a seven-day banquet for all the people who were present in Susa the citadel, for those of highest standing to the most lowly. It was held in the court located in the garden of the royal palace. **1:6** The furnishings included linen and purple curtains hung by cords of the finest linen and purple wool on silver rings, alabaster columns, gold and silver couches displayed on a floor made of valuable stones of alabaster, mother-of-pearl, and mineral stone. **1:7** Drinks were served in golden containers, all of which differed from one another. Royal wine was available in abundance at the king's expense. **1:8** There were no restrictions on the drinking, for the king had instructed all of his supervisors that they should do as everyone so desired. **1:9** Queen Vashti also gave a banquet for the women in King Ahasuerus' royal palace.

Queen Vashti is Removed from Her Royal Position

1:10 On the seventh day, as King Ahasuerus was feeling the effects of the wine, he ordered Mehuman, Biztha, Harbona, Bigtha, Abagtha, Zethar, and Carcas, the seven eunuchs who attended him, **1:11** to bring Queen Vashti into the king's presence wearing her royal high turban. He wanted

to show the people and the officials her beauty, for she was very attractive. **1:12** But Queen Vashti refused to come at the king's bidding conveyed through the eunuchs. Then the king became extremely angry, and his rage consumed him.

1:13 The king then inquired of the wise men who were discerners of the times – for it was the royal custom to confer with all those who were proficient in laws and legalities. **1:14** Those who were closest to him were Carshena, Shethar, Admatha, Tarshish, Meres, Marsena, and Memucan. These men were the seven officials of Persia and Media who saw the king on a regular basis and had the most prominent offices in the kingdom. **1:15** The king asked, "By law, what should be done to Queen Vashti in light of the fact that she has not obeyed the instructions of King Ahasuerus conveyed through the eunuchs?"

1:16 Memucan then replied to the king and the officials, "The wrong of Queen Vashti is not against the king alone, but against all the officials and all the people who are throughout all the provinces of King Ahasuerus. **1:17** For the matter concerning the queen will spread to all the women, leading them to treat their husbands with contempt, saying, 'When King Ahasuerus gave orders to bring Queen Vashti into his presence, she would not come.' **1:18** And this very day the noble ladies of Persia and Media who have heard the matter concerning the queen will respond in the same way to all the royal officials, and there will be more than enough contempt and anger! **1:19** If the king is so inclined, let a royal edict go forth from him, and let it be written in the laws of Persia and Media that cannot be repealed, that Vashti may not come into the presence of King Ahasuerus, and let the king convey her royalty to another who is more deserving than she. **1:20** And let the king's decision which he will enact be disseminated throughout all his kingdom, vast though it is. Then all the women will give honor to their husbands, from the most prominent to the lowly."

1:21 The matter seemed appropriate to the king and the officials. So the king acted on the advice of Memucan. **1:22** He sent letters throughout all the royal provinces, to each province according to its own script and to each people according to its own language, that every man should be ruling his family and should be speaking the language of his own people.

Esther Becomes Queen in Vashti's Place

2:1 When these things had been accomplished and the rage of King Ahasuerus had diminished, he remembered Vashti and what she had done and what had been decided against her. **2:2** The king's servants who attended him said, "Let a search be conducted in the king's behalf for attractive young women. **2:3** And let the king appoint officers throughout all the provinces of his kingdom to gather all the attractive young women to Susa the citadel, to the harem under the authority of Hegai, the king's eunuch who oversees the women, and let him provide whatever cosmetics they desire. **2:4** Let the young woman whom the king finds most attractive become queen in place of Vashti." This seemed like a good idea to the king, so he acted accordingly.

2:5 Now there happened to be a Jewish man in Susa the citadel whose name was Mordecai. He was the son of Jair, the son of Shimei, the son of Kish, a Benjaminite, **2:6** who had been taken into exile from Jerusalem with the captives who had been carried into exile with Jeconiah king of Judah, whom Nebuchadnezzar king of Babylon had taken into exile. **2:7** Now he was acting as the guardian of Hadassah (that is, Esther), the daughter of his uncle, for neither her father nor her mother was alive. This young woman was very attractive and had a beautiful figure. When her father and mother died, Mordecai had raised her as if she were his own daughter.

2:8 It so happened that when the king's edict and his law became known many young women were taken to Susa the citadel to be placed under the authority of Hegai. Esther also was taken to the royal palace to be under the authority of Hegai, who was overseeing the women. **2:9** This young woman pleased him, and she found favor with him. He quickly provided her with her cosmetics and her rations; he also provided her with the seven specially chosen young women who were from the palace. He then transferred her and her young women to the best quarters in the harem.

2:10 Now Esther had not disclosed her people or her lineage, for Mordecai had instructed her not to do so. **2:11** And day after day Mordecai used to walk back and forth in front of the court of the harem in order to learn how Esther was doing and what might happen to her.

2:12 At the end of the twelve months that were required for the women, when the turn of each young woman arrived to go to King Ahasuerus – for in this way they had to fulfill their time of cosmetic treatment: six months with oil of myrrh, and six months with perfume and various ointments used by women – **2:13** the woman would go to the king in the following way: Whatever she asked for would be provided for her to take with her from the harem to the royal palace. **2:14** In the evening she went, and in the morning she returned to a separate part of the harem, to the authority of Shaashgaz the king's eunuch who was overseeing the concubines. She would not go back to the king unless the king was pleased with her and she was requested by name.

2:15 When it became the turn of Esther daughter of Abihail the uncle of Mordecai (who had raised her as if she were his own daughter) to go to the king, she did not request anything except what Hegai the king's eunuch, who was overseer of the women, had recommended. Yet Esther met with the approval of all who saw her. **2:16** Then Esther was taken to King Ahasuerus at his royal residence in the tenth month (that is, the month of Tebeth) in the seventh year of his reign. **2:17** And the king loved Esther more than all the other women, and she met with his loving approval more than all the other young women. So he placed the royal high turban on her head and appointed her queen in place of Vashti. **2:18** Then the king prepared a large banquet for all his officials and his servants – it was actually Esther's banquet. He also set aside a holiday for the provinces, and he provided for offerings at the king's expense.

Mordecai Learns of a Plot against the King

2:19 Now when the young women were being gathered again, Mordecai was sitting at the king's gate. **2:20** Esther was still not divulging her lineage or her people, just as Mordecai had instructed her. Esther continued to do whatever Mordecai said, just as she had done when he was raising her.

2:21 In those days while Mordecai was sitting at the king's gate, Bigthan and Teresh, two of the king's eunuchs who protected the entrance, became angry and plotted to assassinate King Ahasuerus. **2:22** When Mordecai learned of the conspiracy, he informed Queen Esther, and Esther told the king in Mordecai's behalf. **2:23** The king then had the matter investigated and, finding it to be so, had the two conspirators hanged on a gallows. It was then recorded in the daily chronicles in the king's presence.

Haman Conspires to Destroy the Jews

3:1 Some time later King Ahasuerus promoted Haman the son of Hammedatha, the Agagite, exalting him and setting his position above that of all the officials who were with him. **3:2** As a result, all the king's servants who were at the king's gate were bowing and paying homage to Haman, for the king had so commanded. However, Mordecai did not bow, nor did he pay him homage.

3:3 Then the servants of the king who were at the king's gate asked Mordecai, "Why are you violating the king's commandment?" **3:4** And after they had spoken to him day after day without his paying any attention to them, they informed Haman to see whether this attitude on Mordecai's part would be permitted. Furthermore, he had disclosed to them that he was a Jew.

3:5 When Haman saw that Mordecai was not bowing or paying homage to him, he was filled with rage. **3:6** But the thought of striking out against Mordecai alone was repugnant to him, for he had been informed of the identity of Mordecai's people. So Haman sought to destroy all the Jews (that is, the people of Mordecai) who were in all the kingdom of Ahasuerus.

3:7 In the first month (that is, the month of Nisan), in the twelfth year of King Ahasuerus' reign, *pur* (that is, the lot) was cast before Haman in order to determine a day and a month. It turned out to be the twelfth month (that is, the month of Adar).

3:8 Then Haman said to King Ahasuerus, "There is a particular people that is dispersed and spread among the inhabitants throughout all the provinces of your kingdom whose laws differ from those of all other peoples. Furthermore, they do not observe the king's laws. It is not appropriate for the king to provide a haven for them. **3:9** If the king is so inclined, let an edict be issued to destroy them. I will pay ten thousand talents of silver to be conveyed to the king's treasuries for the officials who carry out this business."

3:10 So the king removed his signet ring from his hand and gave it to Haman the son of Hammedatha, the Agagite, who was hostile toward the Jews. **3:11** The king replied to Haman, "Keep your money, and do with those people whatever you wish."

3:12 So the royal scribes were summoned in the first month, on the thirteenth day of the month. Everything Haman commanded was written to the king's satraps and governors who were in every province and to the officials of every people, province by province according to its script and people by people according to its language. In the name of King Ahasuerus it was written and sealed with the king's signet ring. **3:13** Letters were sent by the runners to all the king's provinces stating that they should destroy, kill, and annihilate all the Jews, from youth to elderly, both women and children, on a particular day, namely the thirteenth day of the twelfth month (that is, the month of Adar), and to loot and plunder their possessions. **3:14** A copy of this edict was to be presented as law throughout every province; it was to be made known to all the inhabitants, so that they would be prepared for this day. **3:15** The messengers scurried forth with the king's order. The edict was issued in Susa the citadel. While the king and Haman sat down to drink, the city of Susa was in an uproar!

Esther Decides to Risk Everything in order to Help Her People

4:1 Now when Mordecai became aware of all that had been done, he tore his garments and put on sackcloth and ashes. He went out into the city, crying out in a loud and bitter voice. **4:2** But he went no further than the king's gate, for no one was permitted to enter the king's gate clothed in sackcloth. **4:3** Throughout each and every province where the king's edict and law were announced there was considerable mourning among the Jews, along with fasting, weeping, and sorrow. Sackcloth and ashes were

characteristic of many. **4:4** When Esther's female attendants and her eunuchs came and informed her about Mordecai's behavior, the queen was overcome with anguish. Although she sent garments for Mordecai to put on so that he could remove his sackcloth, he would not accept them. **4:5** So Esther called for Hathach, one of the king's eunuchs who had been placed at her service, and instructed him to find out the cause and reason for Mordecai's behavior. **4:6** So Hathach went to Mordecai at the plaza of the city in front of the king's gate. **4:7** Then Mordecai related to him everything that had happened to him, even the specific amount of money that Haman had offered to pay to the king's treasuries for the Jews to be destroyed. **4:8** He also gave him a written copy of the law that had been disseminated in Susa for their destruction so that he could show it to Esther and talk to her about it. He also gave instructions that she should go to the king to implore him and petition him on behalf of her people. **4:9** So Hathach returned and related Mordecai's instructions to Esther.

4:10 Then Esther replied to Hathach with instructions for Mordecai: **4:11** "All the servants of the king and the people of the king's provinces know that there is only one law applicable to any man or woman who comes uninvited to the king in the inner court – that person will be put to death, unless the king extends to him the gold scepter, permitting him to be spared. Now I have not been invited to come to the king for some thirty days!"

4:12 When Esther's reply was conveyed to Mordecai, **4:13** he said to take back this answer to Esther: **4:14** "Don't imagine that because you are part of the king's household you will be the one Jew who will escape. If you keep quiet at this time, liberation and protection for the Jews will appear from another source, while you and your father's household perish. It may very well be that you have achieved royal status for such a time as this!"

4:15 Then Esther sent this reply to Mordecai: **4:16** "Go, assemble all the Jews who are found in Susa and fast in my behalf. Don't eat and don't drink for three days, night or day. My female attendants and I will also fast in the same way. Afterward I will go to the king, even though it violates the law. If I perish, I perish!"

4:17 So Mordecai set out to do everything that Esther had instructed him.

Esther Appeals to the King for Help

5:1 It so happened that on the third day Esther put on her royal attire and stood in the inner court of the palace, opposite the king's quarters. The king was sitting on his royal throne in the palace, opposite the entrance. **5:2** When the king saw Queen Esther standing in the court, she met with his approval. The king extended to Esther the gold scepter that was in his hand, and Esther approached and touched the end of the scepter. **5:3** The king said to her, "What is on your mind, Queen Esther? What is your request? Even as much as half the kingdom will be given to you!" **5:4** Esther replied, "If the king is so inclined, let the king and Haman come today to the banquet that I have prepared for him." **5:5** The king replied, "Find Haman quickly so that we can do as Esther requests."

So the king and Haman went to the banquet that Esther had prepared. **5:6** While at the banquet of wine, the king said to Esther, "What is your request? It shall be given to you. What is your petition? Ask for as much as half the kingdom, and it shall be done!"

5:7 Esther responded, "My request and my petition is this: **5:8** If I have found favor in the king's sight and if the king is inclined to grant my request and perform my petition, let the king and Haman come tomorrow to the banquet that I will prepare for them. At that time I will do as the king wishes.

Haman Expresses His Hatred of Mordecai

5:9 Now Haman went forth that day pleased and very much encouraged. But when Haman saw Mordecai at the king's gate, and he did not rise nor tremble in his presence, Haman was filled with rage toward Mordecai. **5:10** But Haman restrained himself and went on to his home.

He then sent for his friends to join him, along with his wife Zeresh. **5:11** Haman then recounted to them his fabulous wealth, his many sons, and how the king had magnified him and exalted him over the king's other officials and servants. **5:12** Haman said, "Furthermore, Queen Esther invited only me to accompany the king to the banquet that she prepared! And also tomorrow I am invited along with the king. **5:13** Yet all of this fails to satisfy me so long as I have to see Mordecai the Jew sitting at the king's gate."

5:14 Haman's wife Zeresh and all his friends said to him, "Have a gallows seventy-five feet high built, and in the morning tell the king that Mordecai should be hanged on it. Then go with the king to the banquet contented."

It seemed like a good idea to Haman, so he had the gallows built.

The Turning Point: The King Honors Mordecai

6:1 Throughout that night the king was unable to sleep, so he asked for the book containing the historical records to be brought. As the records were being read in the king's presence, **6:2** it was found written that Mordecai had disclosed that Bigthana and Teresh, two of the king's eunuchs who guarded the entrance, had plotted to assassinate King Ahasuerus.

6:3 The king asked, "What great honor was bestowed on Mordecai because of this?" The king's attendants who served him responded, "Not a thing was done for him."

6:4 Then the king said, "Who is that in the courtyard?" Now Haman had come to the outer courtyard of the palace to suggest that the king hang Mordecai on the gallows that he had constructed for him. **6:5** The king's attendants said to him, "It is Haman who is standing in the courtyard." The king said, "Let him enter."

6:6 So Haman came in, and the king said to him, "What should be done for the man whom the king wishes to honor?" Haman thought to himself, "Who is it that the king would want to honor more than me?" **6:7** So Haman said to the king, "For the man whom the king wishes to honor, **6:8** let them bring royal attire which the king himself has worn and a horse on which the king himself has ridden – one bearing the royal insignia! **6:9** Then let this clothing and this horse be given to one of the king's noble officials. Let him then clothe the man whom the king wishes to honor, and let him lead him about through the plaza of the city on the horse, calling before him, 'So shall it be done to the man whom the king wishes to honor!'"

6:10 The king then said to Haman, "Go quickly! Take the clothing and the horse, just as you have described, and do as you just indicated to Mordecai the Jew who sits at the king's gate. Don't neglect a single thing of all that you have said."

6:11 So Haman took the clothing and the horse, and he clothed Mordecai. He led him about on the horse throughout the plaza of the city, calling before him, "So shall it be done to the man whom the king wishes to honor!"

6:12 Then Mordecai again sat at the king's gate, while Haman hurried away to his home, mournful and with a veil over his head. **6:13** Haman then related to his wife Zeresh and to all his friends everything that had happened to him. These wise men, along with his wife Zeresh, said to him, "If indeed this Mordecai before whom you have begun to fall is Jewish, you will not prevail against him. No, you will surely fall before him!"

6:14 While they were still speaking with him, the king's eunuchs arrived. They quickly brought Haman to the banquet that Esther had prepared.

The King Has Haman Executed

7:1 So the king and Haman came to dine with Queen Esther. **7:2** On the second day of the banquet of wine the king asked Esther, "What is your request, Queen Esther? It shall be granted to you. And what is your petition? Ask up to half the kingdom, and it shall be done!"

7:3 Queen Esther replied, "If I have met with your approval, O king, and if the king is so inclined, grant me my life as my request, and my people as my petition. **7:4** For we have been sold – both I and my people – to destruction and to slaughter and to annihilation! If we had simply been sold as male and female slaves, I would have remained silent, for such distress would not have been sufficient for troubling the king."

7:5 Then King Ahasuerus responded to Queen Esther, "Who is this individual? Where is this person to be found who is presumptuous enough to act in this way?"

7:6 Esther replied, "The oppressor and enemy is this evil Haman!"

Then Haman became terrified in the presence of the king and queen. **7:7** In rage the king arose from the banquet of wine and withdrew to the palace garden. Meanwhile, Haman stood to beg Queen Esther for his life, for he realized that the king had now determined a catastrophic end for him.

7:8 When the king returned from the palace garden to the banquet of wine, Haman was throwing himself down on the couch where Esther was lying. The king exclaimed, "Will he also attempt to rape the queen while I am still in the building!"

As these words left the king's mouth, they covered Haman's face. **7:9** Harbona, one of the king's eunuchs, said, "Indeed, there is the gallows that Haman made for Mordecai, who spoke out in the king's behalf. It stands near Haman's home and is seventy-five feet high."

The king said, "Hang him on it!" **7:10** So they hanged Haman on the very gallows that he had prepared for Mordecai. The king's rage then abated.

The King Acts to Protect the Jews

8:1 On that same day King Ahasuerus gave the estate of Haman, that adversary of the Jews, to Queen Esther. Now Mordecai had come before the king, for Esther had revealed how he was related to her. **8:2** The king then removed his signet ring (the very one he had taken back from Haman) and gave it to Mordecai. And Esther designated Mordecai to be in charge of Haman's estate.

8:3 Then Esther again spoke with the king, falling at his feet. She wept and begged him for mercy, that he might nullify the evil of Haman the Agagite which he had intended against the Jews. **8:4** When the king extended to Esther the gold scepter, she arose and stood before the king. **8:5** She said, "If the king is so inclined and if I have met with his approval and if the matter is agreeable to the king and if I am attractive to him, let an edict be written rescinding those recorded intentions of Haman the son of Hammedatha, the Agagite, which he wrote in order to destroy the Jews who are throughout all the king's provinces. **8:6** For how can I

watch the calamity that will befall my people, and how can I watch the destruction of my relatives?"

8:7 King Ahasuerus replied to Queen Esther and to Mordecai the Jew, "Look, I have already given Haman's estate to Esther, and he has been hanged on the gallows because he took hostile action against the Jews. **8:8** Now you write in the king's name whatever in your opinion is appropriate concerning the Jews and seal it with the king's signet ring. Any decree that is written in the king's name and sealed with the king's signet ring cannot be rescinded.

8:9 The king's scribes were quickly summoned – in the third month (that is, the month of Sivan), on the twenty-third day. They wrote out everything that Mordecai instructed to the Jews and to the satraps and the governors and the officials of the provinces all the way from India to Ethiopia – a hundred and twenty-seven provinces in all – to each province in its own script and to each people in their own language, and to the Jews according to their own script and their own language. **8:10** Mordecai wrote in the name of King Ahasuerus and sealed it with the king's signet ring. He then sent letters by couriers on horses, who rode royal horses that were very swift.

8:11 The king thereby allowed the Jews who were in every city to assemble and to stand up for themselves – to destroy, to kill, and to annihilate any army of whatever people or province that should become their adversaries, including their women and children, and to confiscate their property. **8:12** This was to take place on a certain day throughout all the provinces of King Ahasuerus – namely, on the thirteenth day of the twelfth month (that is, the month of Adar). **8:13** A copy of the edict was to be presented as law throughout each and every province and made known to all peoples, so that the Jews might be prepared on that day to avenge themselves from their enemies.

8:14 The couriers who were riding the royal horses went forth with the king's edict without delay. And the law was presented in Susa the citadel as well.

8:15 Now Mordecai went out from the king's presence in purple and white royal attire, with a large golden crown and a purple linen mantle. The city of Susa shouted with joy. **8:16** For the Jews there was radiant happiness and joyous honor. **8:17** Throughout every province and throughout every city where the king's edict and his law arrived, the Jews experienced happiness and joy, banquets and holidays. Many of the resident peoples pretended to be Jews, because the fear of the Jews had overcome them.

The Jews Prevail over Their Enemies

9:1 In the twelfth month (that is, the month of Adar), on its thirteenth day, the edict of the king and his law were to be executed. It was on this day that the enemies of the Jews had supposed that they would gain power over them. But contrary to expectations, the Jews gained power over their enemies. **9:2** The Jews assembled themselves in their cities throughout all the provinces of King Ahasuerus to strike out against those who were seeking their harm. No one was able to stand before them, for dread of them fell on all the peoples. **9:3** All the officials of the provinces, the satraps, the governors and those who performed the king's business were assisting the Jews, for the dread of Mordecai had fallen on them. **9:4** Mordecai was of high rank in the king's palace, and word about him was spreading throughout all the provinces. His influence continued to become greater and greater.

9:5 The Jews struck all their enemies with the sword, bringing death and destruction, and they did as they pleased with their enemies. **9:6** In Susa the citadel the Jews killed and destroyed five hundred men. **9:7** In addition, they also killed Parshandatha, Dalphon, Aspatha, **9:8** Poratha, Adalia, Aridatha, **9:9** Parmashta, Arisai, Aridai, and Vaizatha, **9:10** the ten sons of Haman son of Hammedatha, the enemy of the Jews. But they did not confiscate their property.

9:11 On that same day the number of those killed in Susa the citadel was brought to the king's attention. **9:12** Then the king said to Queen Esther, "In Susa the citadel the Jews have killed and destroyed five hundred men and the ten sons of Haman! What then have they done in the rest of the king's provinces? What is your request? It shall be given to you. What other petition do you have? It shall be done."

9:13 Esther replied, "If the king is so inclined, let the Jews who are in Susa be permitted to act tomorrow also according to today's law, and let them hang the ten sons of Haman on the gallows."

9:14 So the king issued orders for this to be done. A law was passed in Susa, and the ten sons of Haman were hanged. **9:15** The Jews who were in Susa then assembled on the fourteenth day of the month of Adar, and they killed three hundred men in Susa. But they did not confiscate their property.

9:16 The rest of the Jews who were throughout the provinces of the king assembled in order to stand up for themselves and to have rest from their enemies. They killed seventy-five thousand of their adversaries, but they did not confiscate their property. **9:17** All of this happened on the thirteenth day of the month of Adar. They then rested on the fourteenth day and made it a day for banqueting and happiness.

The Origins of the Feast of Purim

9:18 But the Jews who were in Susa assembled on the thirteenth and fourteenth days, and rested on the fifteenth, making it a day for banqueting and happiness. **9:19** This is why the Jews who are in the rural country – those who live in rural cities – set aside the fourteenth day of the month of Adar as a holiday for happiness, banqueting, holiday, and sending gifts to one another.
9:20 Mordecai wrote these matters down and sent letters to all the Jews who were throughout all the provinces of King Ahasuerus, both near and far, **9:21** to have them observe the fourteenth and the fifteenth day of the month of Adar each year **9:22** as the time when the Jews gave themselves rest from their enemies – the month when their trouble was turned to happiness and their mourning to a holiday. These were to be days of banqueting, happiness, sending gifts to one another, and providing for the poor.
9:23 So the Jews committed themselves to continue what they had begun to do and to what Mordecai had written to them. **9:24** For Haman the son of Hammedatha, the Agagite, the enemy of all the Jews, had devised plans against the Jews to destroy them. He had cast *pur* (that is, the lot) in order to afflict and destroy them. **9:25** But when the matter came to the king's attention, the king gave written orders that Haman's evil intentions that he had devised against the Jews should fall on his own head. He and his sons were hanged on the gallows. **9:26** For this reason these days are known as *Purim*, after the name of *pur*. **9:27** Therefore, because of the account found in this letter and what they had faced in this regard and what had happened to them, the Jews established as binding on themselves, their descendants, and all who joined their company that they should observe these two days without fail, just as written and at the appropriate time on an annual basis. **9:28** These days were to be remembered and to be celebrated in every generation and in every family, every province, and every city. The Jews were not to fail to observe these days of Purim; the remembrance of them was not to cease among their descendants.
9:29 So Queen Esther, the daughter of Abihail, and Mordecai the Jew wrote with full authority to confirm this second letter about Purim. **9:30** Letters were sent to all the Jews in the hundred and twenty-seven provinces of the empire of Ahasuerus – words of true peace – **9:31** to establish these days of Purim in their proper times, just as Mordecai the Jew and Queen Esther had established, and just as they had established both for themselves and their descendants, matters pertaining to fasting and lamentation. **9:32** Esther's command established these matters of Purim, and the matter was officially recorded.

Mordecai's Fame Increases
10:1 King Ahasuerus then imposed forced labor on the land and on the coastlands of the sea. **10:2** Now all the actions carried out under his authority and his great achievements, along with an exact statement concerning the greatness of Mordecai, whom the king promoted, are they not written in the Book of the Chronicles of the Kings of Media and Persia? **10:3** Mordecai the Jew was second only to King Ahasuerus. He was the highest-ranking Jew, and he was admired by his numerous relatives. He worked enthusiastically for the good of his people and was an advocate for the welfare of all his descendants.

Book 18. Job

I. The Prologue (1:1-2:13)
Job's Good Life
1:1 There was a man in the land of Uz whose name was Job. And that man was pure and upright, one who feared God and turned away from evil. **1:2** Seven sons and three daughters were born to him. **1:3** His possessions included 7,000 sheep, 3,000 camels, 500 yoke of oxen, and 500 female donkeys; in addition he had a very great household. Thus he was the greatest of all the people in the east.
1:4 Now his sons used to go and hold a feast in the house of each one in turn, and they would send and invite their three sisters to eat and to drink with them. **1:5** When the days of their feasting were finished, Job would send for them and sanctify them; he would get up early in the morning and offer burnt offerings according to the number of them all. For Job thought, "Perhaps my children have sinned and cursed God in their hearts." This was Job's customary practice.
Satan's Accusation of Job
1:6 Now the day came when the sons of God came to present themselves before the LORD – and Satan also arrived among them. **1:7** The LORD said to Satan, "Where have you come from?" And Satan answered the LORD, "From roving about on the earth, and from walking back and forth across it." **1:8** So the LORD said to Satan, "Have you considered my servant Job? There is no one like him on the earth, a pure and upright man, one who fears God and turns away from evil."
1:9 Then Satan answered the LORD, "Is it for nothing that Job fears God? **1:10** Have you not made a hedge around him and his household and all that he has on every side? You have blessed the work of his hands, and his livestock have increased in the land. **1:11** But extend your hand and strike everything he has, and he will no doubt curse you to your face!"

1:12 So the LORD said to Satan, "All right then, everything he has is in your power. Only do not extend your hand against the man himself!" So Satan went out from the presence of the LORD.
Job's Integrity in Adversity
1:13 Now the day came when Job's sons and daughters were eating and drinking wine in their oldest brother's house, **1:14** and a messenger came to Job, saying, "The oxen were plowing and the donkeys were grazing beside them, **1:15** and the Sabeans swooped down and carried them all away, and they killed the servants with the sword! And I – only I alone – escaped to tell you!"
1:16 While this one was still speaking, another messenger arrived and said, "The fire of God has fallen from heaven and has burned up the sheep and the servants – it has consumed them! And I – only I alone – escaped to tell you!"
1:17 While this one was still speaking another messenger arrived and said, "The Chaldeans formed three bands and made a raid on the camels and carried them all away, and they killed the servants with the sword! And I – only I alone – escaped to tell you!"
1:18 While this one was still speaking another messenger arrived and said, "Your sons and your daughters were eating and drinking wine in their oldest brother's house, **1:19** and suddenly a great wind swept across the wilderness and struck the four corners of the house, and it fell on the young people, and they died! And I – only I alone – escaped to tell you!"
1:20 Then Job got up and tore his robe. He shaved his head, and then he threw himself down with his face to the ground. **1:21** He said, "Naked I came from my mother's womb, and naked I will return there. The LORD gives, and the LORD takes away. May the name of the LORD be blessed!" **1:22** In all this Job did not sin, nor did he charge God with moral impropriety.
Satan's Additional Charge
2:1 Again the day came when the sons of God came to present themselves before the LORD, and Satan also arrived among them to present himself before the LORD. **2:2** And the LORD said to Satan, "Where do you come from?" Satan answered the LORD, "From roving about on the earth, and from walking back and forth across it." **2:3** Then the LORD said to Satan, "Have you considered my servant Job? For there is no one like him on the earth, a pure and upright man, one who fears God and turns away from evil. And he still holds firmly to his integrity, so that you stirred me up to destroy him without reason."
2:4 But Satan answered the LORD, "Skin for skin! Indeed, a man will give up all that he has to save his life! **2:5** But extend your hand and strike his bone and his flesh, and he will no doubt curse you to your face!"
2:6 So the LORD said to Satan, "All right, he is in your power; only preserve his life."
Job's Integrity in Suffering
2:7 So Satan went out from the presence of the LORD, and he afflicted Job with a malignant ulcer from the sole of his feet to the top of his head. **2:8** Job took a shard of broken pottery to scrape himself with while he was sitting among the ashes.
2:9 Then his wife said to him, "Are you still holding firmly to your integrity? Curse God, and die!" **2:10** But he replied, "You're talking like one of the godless women would do! Should we receive what is good from God, and not also receive what is evil?" In all this Job did not sin by what he said.
The Visit of Job's Friends
2:11 When Job's three friends heard about all this calamity that had happened to him, each of them came from his own country – Eliphaz the Temanite, Bildad the Shuhite, and Zophar the Naamathite. They met together to come to show sympathy for him and to console him. **2:12** But when they gazed intently from a distance but did not recognize him, they began to weep loudly. Each of them tore his robes, and they threw dust into the air over their heads. **2:13** Then they sat down with him on the ground for seven days and seven nights, yet no one spoke a word to him, for they saw that his pain was very great.
II. Job's Dialogue With His Friends (3:1-27:33)
Job Regrets His Birth
3:1 After this Job opened his mouth and cursed the day he was born. **3:2** Job spoke up and said:
3:3 "Let the day on which I was born perish,
and the night that said,
'A man has been conceived!'
3:4 That day – let it be darkness;
let not God on high regard it,
nor let light shine on it!
3:5 Let darkness and the deepest
shadow claim it;
let a cloud settle on it;
let whatever blackens the day terrify it!
3:6 That night – let darkness seize it;
let it not be included among the days of the year;
let it not enter among the number of the months!
3:7 Indeed, let that night be barren;
let no shout of joy penetrate it!

3:8 Let those who curse the day curse it –
those who are prepared to rouse Leviathan.
3:9 Let its morning stars be darkened;
let it wait for daylight but find none,
nor let it see the first rays of dawn,
3:10 because it did not shut the doors of my mother's womb on me,
nor did it hide trouble from my eyes!
Job Wishes He Had Died at Birth
3:11 "Why did I not die at birth,
and why did I not expire
as I came out of the womb?
3:12 Why did the knees welcome me,
and why were there two breasts
that I might nurse at them?
3:13 For now I would be lying down
and would be quiet,
I would be asleep and then at peace
3:14 with kings and counselors of the earth
who built for themselves places now desolate,
3:15 or with princes who possessed gold,
who filled their palaces with silver.
3:16 Or why was I not buried
like a stillborn infant,
like infants who have never seen the light?
3:17 There the wicked cease from
turmoil,
and there the weary are at rest.
3:18 There the prisoners relax together;
they do not hear the voice of the oppressor.
3:19 Small and great are there,
and the slave is free from his master.
Longing for Death
3:20 "Why does God give light to one who is in misery,
and life to those whose soul is bitter,
3:21 to those who wait for death that does not come,
and search for it
more than for hidden treasures,
3:22 who rejoice even to jubilation,
and are exultant when they find the grave?
3:23 Why is light given to a man
whose way is hidden,
and whom God has hedged in?
3:24 For my sighing comes in place of my food,
and my groanings flow forth like water.
3:25 For the very thing I dreaded has happened to me,
and what I feared has come upon me.
3:26 I have no ease, I have no quietness;
I cannot rest; turmoil has come upon me."
Eliphaz Begins to Speak
4:1 Then Eliphaz the Temanite answered:
4:2 "If someone should attempt a word with you,
will you be impatient?
But who can refrain from speaking?
4:3 Look, you have instructed many;
you have strengthened feeble hands.
4:4 Your words have supported those
who stumbled,
and you have strengthened the knees
that gave way.
4:5 But now the same thing comes to you,
and you are discouraged;
it strikes you,
and you are terrified.
4:6 Is not your piety your confidence,
and your blameless ways your hope?
4:7 Call to mind now:
Who, being innocent, ever perished?
And where were upright people ever destroyed?
4:8 Even as I have seen, those who plow iniquity
and those who sow trouble reap the same.
4:9 By the breath of God they perish,
and by the blast of his anger they are consumed.
4:10 There is the roaring of the lion
and the growling of the young lion,
but the teeth of the young lions are broken.
4:11 The mighty lion perishes for lack of prey,
and the cubs of the lioness are scattered.
Ungodly Complainers Provoke God's Wrath
4:12 "Now a word was secretly brought to me,
and my ear caught a whisper of it.
4:13 In the troubling thoughts of the dreams in the night
when a deep sleep falls on men,
4:14 a trembling gripped me – and a terror! –

and made all my bones shake.
4:15 Then a breath of air passes by my face;
it makes the hair of my flesh stand up.
4:16 It stands still,
but I cannot recognize its appearance;
an image is before my eyes,
and I hear a murmuring voice:
4:17 "Is a mortal man righteous before God?
Or a man pure before his Creator?
4:18 If God puts no trust in his servants
and attributes folly to his angels,
4:19 how much more to those who live in houses of clay,
whose foundation is in the dust,
who are crushed like a moth?
4:20 They are destroyed between morning and evening;
they perish forever without anyone regarding it.
4:21 Is not their excess wealth taken away from them?
They die, yet without attaining wisdom.
5:1 "Call now! Is there anyone who will answer you?
To which of the holy ones will you turn?
5:2 For wrath kills the foolish person,
and anger slays the silly one.
5:3 I myself have seen the fool taking root,
but suddenly I cursed his place of residence.
5:4 His children are far from safety,
and they are crushed at the place where judgment is rendered,
nor is there anyone to deliver them.
5:5 The hungry eat up his harvest,
and take it even from behind the thorns,
and the thirsty swallow up their fortune.
5:6 For evil does not come up from the dust,
nor does trouble spring up from the ground,
5:7 but people are born to trouble,
as surely as the sparks fly upward.
Blessings for the One Who Seeks God
5:8 "But as for me, I would seek God,
and to God I would set forth my case.
5:9 He does great and unsearchable things,
marvelous things without number;
5:10 he gives rain on the earth,
and sends water on the fields;
5:11 he sets the lowly on high,
that those who mourn are raised to safety.
5:12 He frustrates the plans of the crafty
so that their hands cannot accomplish
what they had planned!
5:13 He catches the wise in their own craftiness,
and the counsel of the cunning is brought to a quick end.
5:14 They meet with darkness in the daytime,
and grope about in the noontime as if it were night.
5:15 So he saves from the sword that comes from their mouth,
even the poor from the hand of the powerful.
5:16 Thus the poor have hope,
and iniquity shuts its mouth.

5:17 "Therefore, blessed is the man whom God corrects,
so do not despise the discipline of the Almighty.
5:18 For he wounds, but he also bandages;
he strikes, but his hands also heal.
5:19 He will deliver you from six calamities;
yes, in seven no evil will touch you.
5:20 In time of famine he will redeem you from death,
and in time of war from the power of the sword.
5:21 You will be protected from malicious gossip,
and will not be afraid of the destruction when it comes.
5:22 You will laugh at destruction and famine
and need not be afraid of the beasts of the earth.
5:23 For you will have a pact with the stones of the field,
and the wild animals will be at peace with you.
5:24 And you will know that your home
will be secure,
and when you inspect your domains,
you will not be missing anything.
5:25 You will also know that your children will be numerous,
and your descendants like the grass of the earth.
5:26 You will come to your grave in a full age,
As stacks of grain are harvested in their season.
5:27 Look, we have investigated this, so it is true.
Hear it, and apply it for your own good."
Job Replies to Eliphaz
6:1 Then Job responded:
6:2 "Oh, if only my grief could be weighed,
and my misfortune laid on the scales too!

6:3 But because it is heavier than the sand of the sea,
that is why my words have been wild.
6:4 For the arrows of the Almighty are within me;
my spirit drinks their poison;
God's sudden terrors are arrayed against me.
Complaints Reflect Suffering
6:5 "Does the wild donkey bray when it is near grass?
Or does the ox low near its fodder?
6:6 Can food that is tasteless be eaten without salt?
Or is there any taste in the white of an egg?
6:7 I have refused to touch such things;
they are like loathsome food to me.
A Cry for Death
6:8 "Oh that my request would be realized,
and that God would grant me what I long for!
6:9 And that God would be willing to crush me,
that he would let loose his hand
and kill me.
6:10 Then I would yet have my comfort,
then I would rejoice,
in spite of pitiless pain,
for I have not concealed the words of the Holy One.
6:11 What is my strength, that I should wait?
and what is my end,
that I should prolong my life?
6:12 Is my strength like that of stones?
or is my flesh made of bronze?
6:13 Is not my power to help myself nothing,
and has not every resource been driven from me?
Disappointing Friends
6:14 "To the one in despair, kindness should come from his friend
even if he forsakes the fear of the Almighty.
6:15 My brothers have been as treacherous as a seasonal stream,
and as the riverbeds of the intermittent streams
that flow away.
6:16 They are dark because of ice;
snow is piled up over them.
6:17 When they are scorched, they dry up,
when it is hot, they vanish from their place.
6:18 Caravans turn aside from their routes;
they go into the wasteland and perish.
6:19 The caravans of Tema looked intently for these streams;
the traveling merchants of Sheba hoped for them.
6:20 They were distressed,
because each one had been so confident;
they arrived there, but were disappointed.
6:21 For now you have become like these streams that are no help;
you see a terror, and are afraid.
Friends' Fears
6:22 "Have I ever said, 'Give me something,
and from your fortune make gifts in my favor'?
6:23 Or 'Deliver me from the enemy's power,
and from the hand of tyrants ransom me'?
No Sin Discovered
6:24 "Teach me and I, for my part, will be silent;
explain to me how I have been mistaken.
6:25 How painful are honest words!
But what does your reproof prove?
6:26 Do you intend to criticize mere words,
and treat the words of a despairing man as wind?
6:27 Yes, you would gamble for the fatherless,
and auction off your friend.
Other Explanation
6:28 "Now then, be good enough to look at me;
and I will not lie to your face!
6:29 Relent, let there be no falsehood;
reconsider, for my righteousness is intact!
6:30 Is there any falsehood on my lips?
Can my mouth not discern evil things?
The Brevity of Life
7:1 "Does not humanity have hard service on earth?
Are not their days also
like the days of a hired man?
7:2 Like a servant longing for the evening shadow,
and like a hired man looking for his wages,
7:3 thus I have been made to inherit
months of futility,
and nights of sorrow
have been appointed to me.
7:4 If I lie down, I say, 'When will I arise?',
and the night stretches on
and I toss and turn restlessly
until the day dawns.

7:5 My body is clothed with worms and dirty scabs;
my skin is broken and festering.
7:6 My days are swifter than a weaver's shuttle
and they come to an end without hope.
7:7 Remember that my life is but a breath,
that my eyes will never again see happiness.
7:8 The eye of him who sees me now will see me no more;
your eyes will look for me, but I will be gone.
7:9 As a cloud is dispersed and then disappears,
so the one who goes down to the grave
does not come up again.
7:10 He returns no more to his house,
nor does his place of residence know him any more.
Job Remonstrates with God
7:11 "Therefore, I will not refrain my mouth;
I will speak in the anguish of my spirit;
I will complain in the bitterness of my soul.
7:12 Am I the sea, or the creature of the deep,
that you must put me under guard?
7:13 If I say, "My bed will comfort me,
my couch will ease my complaint,"
7:14 then you scare me with dreams
and terrify me with visions,
7:15 so that I would prefer strangling,
and death more than life.
7:16 I loathe it; I do not want to live forever;
leave me alone, for my days are a vapor!
Insignificance of Humans
7:17 "What is mankind that you make so much of them,
and that you pay attention to them?
7:18 And that you visit them every morning,
and try them every moment?
7:19 Will you never look away from me,
will you not let me alone
long enough to swallow my spittle?
7:20 If I have sinned – what have I done to you,
O watcher of men?
Why have you set me as your target?
Have I become a burden to you?
7:21 And why do you not pardon my transgression,
and take away my iniquity?
For now I will lie down in the dust,
and you will seek me diligently,
but I will be gone."
Bildad's First Speech to Job
8:1 Then Bildad the Shuhite spoke up and said:
8:2 "How long will you speak these things,
seeing that the words of your mouth
are like a great wind?
8:3 Does God pervert justice?
Or does the Almighty pervert what is right?
8:4 If your children sinned against him,
he gave them over to the penalty of their sin.
8:5 But if you will look to God,
and make your supplication to the Almighty,
8:6 if you become pure and upright,
even now he will rouse himself for you,
and will restore your righteous abode.
8:7 Your beginning will seem so small,
since your future will flourish.

8:8 "For inquire now of the former generation,
and pay attention to the findings
of their ancestors;
8:9 For we were born yesterday and do not have knowledge,
since our days on earth are but a shadow.
8:10 Will they not instruct you and speak to you,
and bring forth words
from their understanding?
8:11 Can the papyrus plant grow tall where there is no marsh?
Can reeds flourish without water?
8:12 While they are still beginning to flower
and not ripe for cutting,
they can wither away
faster than any grass!
8:13 Such is the destiny of all who forget God;
the hope of the godless perishes,
8:14 whose trust is in something futile,
whose security is a spider's web.
8:15 He leans against his house but it does not hold up,
he takes hold of it but it does not stand.
8:16 He is a well-watered plant in the sun,
its shoots spread over its garden.

8:17 It wraps its roots around a heap of stones
and it looks for a place among stones.
8:18 If he is uprooted from his place,
then that place will disown him, saying,
'I have never seen you!'
8:19 Indeed, this is the joy of his way,
and out of the earth others spring up.

8:20 "Surely, God does not reject a blameless man,
nor does he grasp the hand
of the evildoers.
8:21 He will yet fill your mouth with laughter,
and your lips with gladness.
8:22 Those who hate you will be clothed with shame,
and the tent of the wicked will be no more."
Job's Reply to Bildad
9:1 Then Job answered:
9:2 "Truly, I know that this is so.
But how can a human be just before God?
9:3 If someone wishes to contend with him,
he cannot answer him one time in a thousand.
9:4 He is wise in heart and mighty in strength –
who has resisted him and remained safe?
9:5 He who removes mountains suddenly,
who overturns them in his anger;
9:6 he who shakes the earth out of its place
so that its pillars tremble;
9:7 he who commands the sun and it does not shine
and seals up the stars;
9:8 he alone spreads out the heavens,
and treads on the waves of the sea;
9:9 he makes the Bear, Orion, and the Pleiades,
and the constellations of the southern sky;
9:10 he does great and unsearchable things,
and wonderful things without number.
9:11 If he passes by me, I cannot see him,
if he goes by, I cannot perceive him.
9:12 If he snatches away, who can turn him back?
Who dares to say to him, 'What are you doing?'
9:13 God does not restrain his anger;
under him the helpers of Rahab lie crushed.
The Impossibility of Facing God in Court
9:14 "How much less, then, can I
answer him
and choose my words to argue with him!
9:15 Although I am innocent,
I could not answer him;
I could only plead with my judge for mercy.
9:16 If I summoned him, and he answered me,
I would not believe
that he would be listening to my voice –
9:17 he who crushes me with a tempest,
and multiplies my wounds for no reason.
9:18 He does not allow me to recover my breath,
for he fills me with bitterness.
9:19 If it is a matter of strength,
most certainly he is the strong one!
And if it is a matter of justice,
he will say, 'Who will summon me?'
9:20 Although I am innocent,
my mouth would condemn me;
although I am blameless,
it would declare me perverse.
9:21 I am blameless. I do not know myself.
I despise my life.
Accusation of God's Justice
9:22 "It is all one! That is why I say,
'He destroys the blameless and the guilty.'
9:23 If a scourge brings sudden death,
he mocks at the despair of the innocent.
9:24 If a land has been given
into the hand of a wicked man,
he covers the faces of its judges;
if it is not he, then who is it?
Renewed Complaint
9:25 "My days are swifter than a runner,
they speed by without seeing happiness.
9:26 They glide by like reed boats,
like an eagle that swoops down on its prey.
9:27 If I say, 'I will forget my complaint,
I will change my expression and be cheerful,'
9:28 I dread all my sufferings,
for I know that you do not hold me blameless.

9:29 If I am guilty,
why then weary myself in vain?
9:30 If I wash myself with snow water,
and make my hands clean with lye,
9:31 then you plunge me into a slimy pit
and my own clothes abhor me.
9:32 For he is not a human being like I am,
that I might answer him,
that we might come together in judgment.
9:33 Nor is there an arbiter between us,
who might lay his hand on us both,
9:34 who would take his rod away from me
so that his terror would not make me afraid.
9:35 Then would I speak and not fear him,
but it is not so with me.
An Appeal for Revelation
10:1 "I am weary of my life;
I will complain without restraint;
I will speak in the bitterness of my soul.
10:2 I will say to God, 'Do not condemn me;
tell me why you are contending with me.'
10:3 Is it good for you to oppress,
to despise the work of your hands,
while you smile
on the schemes of the wicked?
Motivations of God
10:4 "Do you have eyes of flesh,
or do you see as a human being sees?
10:5 Are your days like the days of a mortal,
or your years like the years of a mortal,
10:6 that you must search out my iniquity,
and inquire about my sin,
10:7 although you know that I am not guilty,
and that there is no one who can deliver
out of your hand?
Contradictions in God's Dealings
10:8 "Your hands have shaped me and made me,
but now you destroy me completely.
10:9 Remember that you have made me as with the clay;
will you return me to dust?
10:10 Did you not pour me out like milk,
and curdle me like cheese?
10:11 You clothed me with skin and flesh
and knit me together with bones and sinews.
10:12 You gave me life and favor,
and your intervention watched over my spirit.

10:13 "But these things you have concealed in your heart;
I know that this is with you:
10:14 If I sinned, then you would watch me
and you would not acquit me of my iniquity.
10:15 If I am guilty, woe to me,
and if I am innocent, I cannot lift my head;
I am full of shame,
and satiated with my affliction.
10:16 If I lift myself up,
you hunt me as a fierce lion,
and again you display your power against me.
10:17 You bring new witnesses against me,
and increase your anger against me;
relief troops come against me.
An Appeal for Relief
10:18 "Why then did you bring me out from the womb?
I should have died
and no eye would have seen me!
10:19 I should have been as though I had never existed;
I should have been carried
right from the womb to the grave!
10:20 Are not my days few?
Cease, then, and leave me alone,
that I may find a little comfort,
10:21 before I depart, never to return,
to the land of darkness
and the deepest shadow,
10:22 to the land of utter darkness,
like the deepest darkness,
and the deepest shadow and disorder,
where even the light is like darkness."
Zophar's First Speech to Job
11:1 Then Zophar the Naamathite spoke up and said:
11:2 "Should not this abundance of words be answered,
or should this talkative man
be vindicated?

11:3 Will your idle talk reduce people to silence,
and will no one rebuke you when you mock?
11:4 For you have said, 'My teaching is flawless,
and I am pure in your sight.'
11:5 But if only God would speak,
if only he would open his lips against you,
11:6 and reveal to you the secrets of wisdom –
for true wisdom has two sides –
so that you would know
that God has forgiven some of your sins.

11:7 "Can you discover the essence of God?
Can you find out
the perfection of the Almighty?
11:8 It is higher than the heavens – what can you do?
It is deeper than Sheol – what can you know?
11:9 Its measure is longer than the earth,
and broader than the sea.
11:10 If he comes by and confines you
and convenes a court,
then who can prevent him?
11:11 For he knows deceitful men;
when he sees evil, will he not consider it?
11:12 But an empty man will become wise,
when a wild donkey's colt is born a human being.
11:13 "As for you, if you prove faithful,
and if you stretch out your hands toward him,
11:14 if iniquity is in your hand – put it far away,
and do not let evil reside in your tents.
11:15 For then you will lift up your face
without blemish;
you will be securely established
and will not fear.
11:16 For you will forget your trouble;
you will remember it
like water that has flowed away.
11:17 And life will be brighter than the noonday;
though there be darkness,
it will be like the morning.
11:18 And you will be secure, because there is hope;
you will be protected
and will take your rest in safety.
11:19 You will lie down with no one to make you afraid,
and many will seek your favor.
11:20 But the eyes of the wicked fail,
and escape eludes them;
their one hope is to breathe their last."

Job's Reply to Zophar

12:1 Then Job answered:
12:2 "Without a doubt you are the people,
and wisdom will die with you.
12:3 I also have understanding as well as you;
I am not inferior to you.
Who does not know such things as these?
12:4 I am a laughingstock to my friends,
I, who called on God and whom he answered –
a righteous and blameless man
is a laughingstock!
12:5 For calamity, there is derision
(according to the ideas of the fortunate) –
a fate for those whose feet slip!
12:6 But the tents of robbers are peaceful,
and those who provoke God are confident –
who carry their god in their hands.

Knowledge of God's Wisdom

12:7 "But now, ask the animals and they will teach you,
or the birds of the sky and they will tell you.
12:8 Or speak to the earth and it will teach you,
or let the fish of the sea declare to you.
12:9 Which of all these does not know
that the hand of the LORD has done this,
12:10 in whose hand is the life of every creature
and the breath of all the human race.
12:11 Does not the ear test words,
as the tongue tastes food?
12:12 Is not wisdom found among the aged?
Does not long life bring understanding?

12:13 "With God are wisdom and power;
counsel and understanding are his.
12:14 If he tears down, it cannot be rebuilt;
if he imprisons a person, there is no escape.
12:15 If he holds back the waters, then they dry up;

if he releases them, they destroy the land.
12:16 With him are strength and prudence;
both the one who goes astray
and the one who misleads are his.
12:17 He leads counselors away stripped
and makes judges into fools.
12:18 He loosens the bonds of kings
and binds a loincloth around their waist.
12:19 He leads priests away stripped
and overthrows the potentates.
12:20 He deprives the trusted advisers of speech
and takes away the discernment of elders.
12:21 He pours contempt on noblemen
and disarms the powerful.
12:22 He reveals the deep things of darkness,
and brings deep shadows into the light.
12:23 He makes nations great, and destroys them;
he extends the boundaries of nations
and disperses them.
12:24 He deprives the leaders of the earth
of their understanding;
he makes them wander
in a trackless desert waste.
12:25 They grope about in darkness without light;
he makes them stagger like drunkards.

Job Pleads His Cause to God

13:1 "Indeed, my eyes have seen all this,
my ears have heard and understood it.
13:2 What you know, I know also;
I am not inferior to you!
13:3 But I wish to speak to the Almighty,
and I desire to argue my case with God.
13:4 But you, however, are inventors of lies;
all of you are worthless physicians!
13:5 If only you would keep completely silent!
For you, that would be wisdom.

13:6 "Listen now to my argument,
and be attentive to my lips' contentions.
13:7 Will you speak wickedly on God's behalf?
Will you speak deceitfully for him?
13:8 Will you show him partiality?
Will you argue the case for God?
13:9 Would it turn out well if he would examine you?
Or as one deceives a man would you deceive him?
13:10 He would certainly rebuke you
if you secretly showed partiality!
13:11 Would not his splendor terrify you
and the fear he inspires fall on you?
13:12 Your maxims are proverbs of ashes;
your defenses are defenses of clay.
13:13 "Refrain from talking with me so that I may speak;
then let come to me what may.
13:14 Why do I put myself in peril,
and take my life in my hands?
13:15 Even if he slays me, I will hope in him;
I will surely defend my ways to his face!
13:16 Moreover, this will become my deliverance,
for no godless person would come before him.
13:17 Listen carefully to my words;
let your ears be attentive to my explanation.
13:18 See now, I have prepared my case;
I know that I am right.
13:19 Who will contend with me?
If anyone can, I will be silent and die.
13:20 Only in two things spare me, O God,
and then I will not hide from your face:
13:21 Remove your hand far from me
and stop making me afraid with your terror.
13:22 Then call, and I will answer,
or I will speak, and you respond to me.
13:23 How many are my iniquities and sins?
Show me my transgression and my sin.
13:24 Why do you hide your face
and regard me as your enemy?
13:25 Do you wish to torment a windblown leaf
and chase after dry chaff?
13:26 For you write down bitter things against me
and cause me to inherit the sins of my youth.
13:27 And you put my feet in the stocks
and you watch all my movements;
you put marks on the soles of my feet.
13:28 So I waste away like something rotten,

like a garment eaten by moths.
The Brevity of Life
14:1 "Man, born of woman,
lives but a few days, and they are full of trouble.
14:2 He grows up like a flower and then withers away;
he flees like a shadow, and does not remain.
14:3 Do you fix your eye on such a one?
And do you bring me before you for judgment?
14:4 Who can make a clean thing come from an unclean?
No one!
14:5 Since man's days are determined,
the number of his months is under your control;
you have set his limit and he cannot pass it.
14:6 Look away from him and let him desist,
until he fulfills his time like a hired man.
The Inevitability of Death
14:7 "But there is hope for a tree:
If it is cut down, it will sprout again,
and its new shoots will not fail.
14:8 Although its roots may grow old in the ground
and its stump begins to die in the soil,
14:9 at the scent of water it will flourish
and put forth shoots like a new plant.
14:10 But man dies and is powerless;
he expires – and where is he?
14:11 As water disappears from the sea,
or a river drains away and dries up,
14:12 so man lies down and does not rise;
until the heavens are no more,
they will not awake
nor arise from their sleep.
The Possibility of Another Life
14:13 "O that you would hide me in Sheol,
and conceal me till your anger has passed!
O that you would set me a time
and then remember me!
14:14 If a man dies, will he live again?
All the days of my hard service I will wait
until my release comes.
14:15 You will call and I – I will answer you;
you will long for the creature you have made.
The Present Condition
14:16 "Surely now you count my steps;
then you would not mark my sin.
14:17 My offenses would be sealed up in a bag;
you would cover over my sin.
14:18 But as a mountain falls away and crumbles,
and as a rock will be removed from its place,
14:19 as water wears away stones,
and torrents wash away the soil,
so you destroy man's hope.
14:20 You overpower him once for all,
and he departs;
you change his appearance
and send him away.
14:21 If his sons are honored,
he does not know it;
if they are brought low,
he does not see it.
14:22 Only his flesh has pain for himself,
and he mourns for himself."
Eliphaz's Second Speech
15:1 Then Eliphaz the Temanite answered:
15:2 "Does a wise man answer with blustery knowledge,
or fill his belly with the east wind?
15:3 Does he argue with useless talk,
with words that have no value in them?
15:4 But you even break off piety,
and hinder meditation before God.
15:5 Your sin inspires your mouth;
you choose the language of the crafty.
15:6 Your own mouth condemns you, not I;
your own lips testify against you.

15:7 "Were you the first man ever born?
Were you brought forth before the hills?
15:8 Do you listen in on God's secret council?
Do you limit wisdom to yourself?
15:9 What do you know that we don't know?
What do you understand that we don't understand?
15:10 The gray-haired and the aged are on our side,
men far older than your father.
15:11 Are God's consolations too trivial for you;

or a word spoken in gentleness to you?
15:12 Why has your heart carried you away,
and why do your eyes flash,
15:13 when you turn your rage against God
and allow such words to escape from your mouth?
15:14 What is man that he should be pure,
or one born of woman, that he should be righteous?
15:15 If God places no trust in his holy ones,
if even the heavens are not pure in his eyes,
15:16 how much less man, who is abominable and corrupt,
who drinks in evil like water!

15:17 "I will explain to you;
listen to me,
and what I have seen, I will declare,
15:18 what wise men declare,
hiding nothing,
from the tradition of their ancestors,
15:19 to whom alone the land was given
when no foreigner passed among them.
15:20 All his days the wicked man suffers torment,
throughout the number of the years
that are stored up for the tyrant.
15:21 Terrifying sounds fill his ears;
in a time of peace marauders attack him.
15:22 He does not expect to escape from darkness;
he is marked for the sword;
15:23 he wanders about – food for vultures;
he knows that the day of darkness is at hand.
15:24 Distress and anguish terrify him;
they prevail against him
like a king ready to launch an attack,
15:25 for he stretches out his hand against God,
and vaunts himself against the Almighty,
15:26 defiantly charging against him
with a thick, strong shield!
15:27 Because he covered his face with fat,
and made his hips bulge with fat,
15:28 he lived in ruined towns
and in houses where no one lives,
where they are ready to crumble into heaps.
15:29 He will not grow rich,
and his wealth will not endure,
nor will his possessions spread over the land.
15:30 He will not escape the darkness;
a flame will wither his shoots
and he will depart
by the breath of God's mouth.
15:31 Let him not trust in what is worthless,
deceiving himself;
for worthlessness will be his reward.
15:32 Before his time he will be paid in full,
and his branches will not flourish.
15:33 Like a vine he will let his sour grapes fall,
and like an olive tree
he will shed his blossoms.
15:34 For the company of the godless is barren,
and fire consumes the tents of those who accept bribes.
15:35 They conceive trouble and bring forth evil;
their belly prepares deception."
Job's Reply to Eliphaz
16:1 Then Job replied:
16:2 "I have heard many things like these before.
What miserable comforters are you all!
16:3 Will there be an end to your windy words?
Or what provokes you that you answer?
16:4 I also could speak like you,
if you were in my place;
I could pile up words against you
and I could shake my head at you.
16:5 But I would strengthen you with my words;
comfort from my lips would bring you relief.
Abandonment by God and Man
16:6 "But if I speak, my pain is not relieved,
and if I refrain from speaking
– how much of it goes away?
16:7 Surely now he has worn me out,
you have devastated my entire household.
16:8 You have seized me,
and it has become a witness;
my leanness has risen up against me
and testifies against me.
16:9 His anger has torn me and persecuted me;

he has gnashed at me with his teeth;
my adversary locks his eyes on me.
16:10 People have opened their mouths against me,
they have struck my cheek in scorn;
they unite together against me.
16:11 God abandons me to evil men,
and throws me into the hands of wicked men.
16:12 I was in peace, and he has shattered me.
He has seized me by the neck and crushed me.
He has made me his target;
16:13 his archers surround me.
Without pity he pierces my kidneys
and pours out my gall on the ground.
16:14 He breaks through against me, time and time again;
he rushes against me like a warrior.
16:15 I have sewed sackcloth on my skin,
and buried my horn in the dust;
16:16 my face is reddened because of weeping,
and on my eyelids there is a deep darkness,
16:17 although there is no violence in my hands
and my prayer is pure.
An Appeal to God as Witness
16:18 "O earth, do not cover my blood,
nor let there be a secret place for my cry.
16:19 Even now my witness is in heaven;
my advocate is on high.
16:20 My intercessor is my friend
as my eyes pour out tears to God;
16:21 and he contends with God on behalf of man
as a man pleads for his friend.
16:22 For the years that lie ahead are few,
and then I will go on the way of no return.
17:1 My spirit is broken,
my days have faded out,
the grave awaits me.
17:2 Surely mockery is with me;
my eyes must dwell on their hostility.
17:3 Make then my pledge with you.
Who else will put up security for me?
17:4 Because you have closed their minds to understanding,
therefore you will not exalt them.
17:5 If a man denounces his friends for personal gain,
the eyes of his children will fail.
17:6 He has made me a byword to people,
I am the one in whose face they spit.
17:7 My eyes have grown dim with grief;
my whole frame is but a shadow.
17:8 Upright men are appalled at this;
the innocent man is troubled with the godless.
17:9 But the righteous man holds to his way,
and the one with clean hands grows stronger.
Anticipation of Death
17:10 "But turn, all of you, and come now!
I will not find a wise man among you.
17:11 My days have passed, my plans are shattered,
even the desires of my heart.
17:12 These men change night into day;
they say, 'The light is near
in the face of darkness.'
17:13 If I hope for the grave to be my home,
if I spread out my bed in darkness,
17:14 If I cry to corruption, 'You are my father,'
and to the worm, 'My Mother,' or 'My sister,'
17:15 where then is my hope?
And my hope, who sees it?
17:16 Will it go down to the barred gates of death?
Will we descend together into the dust?"
Bildad's Second Speech
18:1 Then Bildad the Shuhite answered:
18:2 "How long until you make an end of words?
You must consider, and then we can talk.
18:3 Why should we be regarded as beasts,
and considered stupid in your sight?
18:4 You who tear yourself to pieces in your anger,
will the earth be abandoned for your sake?
Or will a rock be moved from its place?

18:5 "Yes, the lamp of the wicked is extinguished;
his flame of fire does not shine.
18:6 The light in his tent grows dark;
his lamp above him is extinguished.
18:7 His vigorous steps are restricted,
and his own counsel throws him down.

18:8 For he has been thrown into a net by his feet
and he wanders into a mesh.
18:9 A trap seizes him by the heel;
a snare grips him.
18:10 A rope is hidden for him on the ground
and a trap for him lies on the path.
18:11 Terrors frighten him on all sides
and dog his every step.
18:12 Calamity is hungry for him,
and misfortune is ready at his side.
18:13 It eats away parts of his skin;
the most terrible death devours his limbs.
18:14 He is dragged from the security of his tent,
and marched off to the king of terrors.
18:15 Fire resides in his tent;
over his residence burning sulfur is scattered.
18:16 Below his roots dry up,
and his branches wither above.
18:17 His memory perishes from the earth,
he has no name in the land.
18:18 He is driven from light into darkness
and is banished from the world.
18:19 He has neither children nor descendants among his people,
no survivor in those places he once stayed.
18:20 People of the west are appalled at his fate;
people of the east are seized with horror, saying,
18:21 'Surely such is the residence of an evil man;
and this is the place of one who has not known God.'"
Job's Reply to Bildad
19:1 Then Job answered:
19:2 "How long will you torment me
and crush me with your words?
19:3 These ten times you have been reproaching me;
you are not ashamed to attack me!
19:4 But even if it were true that I have erred,
my error remains solely my concern!
19:5 If indeed you would exalt yourselves above me
and plead my disgrace against me,
19:6 know then that God has wronged me
and encircled me with his net.
Job's Abandonment and Affliction
19:7 "If I cry out, 'Violence!'
I receive no answer;
I cry for help,
but there is no justice.
19:8 He has blocked my way so I cannot pass,
and has set darkness over my paths.
19:9 He has stripped me of my honor
and has taken the crown off my head.
19:10 He tears me down on every side until I perish;
he uproots my hope like one uproots a tree.
19:11 Thus his anger burns against me,
and he considers me among his enemies.
19:12 His troops advance together;
they throw up a siege ramp against me,
and they camp around my tent.
Job's Forsaken State
19:13 "He has put my relatives far from me;
my acquaintances only turn away from me.
19:14 My kinsmen have failed me;
my friends have forgotten me.
19:15 My guests and my servant girls
consider me a stranger;
I am a foreigner in their eyes.
19:16 I summon my servant, but he does not respond,
even though I implore him with my own mouth.
19:17 My breath is repulsive to my wife;
I am loathsome to my brothers.
19:18 Even youngsters have scorned me;
when I get up, they scoff at me.
19:19 All my closest friends detest me;
and those whom I love have turned against me.
19:20 My bones stick to my skin and my flesh;
I have escaped alive with only the skin of my teeth.
19:21 Have pity on me, my friends, have pity on me,
for the hand of God has struck me.
19:22 Why do you pursue me like God does?
Will you never be satiated with my flesh?
Job's Assurance of Vindication
19:23 "O that my words were written down,
O that they were written on a scroll,
19:24 that with an iron chisel and with lead
they were engraved in a rock forever!

19:25 As for me, I know that my Redeemer lives,
and that as the last
he will stand upon the earth.
19:26 And after my skin has been destroyed,
yet in my flesh I will see God,
19:27 whom I will see for myself,
and whom my own eyes will behold,
and not another.
My heart grows faint within me.
19:28 If you say, 'How we will pursue him,
since the root of the trouble is found in him!'
19:29 Fear the sword yourselves,
for wrath brings the punishment by the sword,
so that you may know
that there is judgment."
Zophar's Second Speech
20:1 Then Zophar the Naamathite answered:
20:2 "This is why my troubled thoughts bring me back –
because of my feelings within me.
20:3 When I hear a reproof that dishonors me,
then my understanding prompts me to answer.
20:4 "Surely you know that it has been from old,
ever since humankind was placed on the earth,
20:5 that the elation of the wicked is brief,
the joy of the godless lasts but a moment.
20:6 Even though his stature reaches to the heavens
and his head touches the clouds,
20:7 he will perish forever, like his own excrement;
those who used to see him will say, 'Where is he?'
20:8 Like a dream he flies away, never again to be found,
and like a vision of the night he is put to flight.
20:9 People who had seen him will not see him again,
and the place where he was
will recognize him no longer.
20:10 His sons must recompense the poor;
his own hands must return his wealth.
20:11 His bones were full of his youthful vigor,
but that vigor will lie down with him in the dust.

20:12 "If evil is sweet in his mouth
and he hides it under his tongue,
20:13 if he retains it for himself
and does not let it go,
and holds it fast in his mouth,
20:14 his food is turned sour in his stomach;
it becomes the venom of serpents within him.
20:15 The wealth that he consumed he vomits up,
God will make him throw it out of his stomach.
20:16 He sucks the poison of serpents;
the fangs of a viper kill him.
20:17 He will not look on the streams,
the rivers, which are the torrents
of honey and butter.
20:18 He gives back the ill-gotten gain
without assimilating it;
he will not enjoy the wealth from his commerce.
20:19 For he has oppressed the poor and abandoned them;
he has seized a house which he did not build.
20:20 For he knows no satisfaction in his appetite;
he does not let anything he desires escape.

20:21 "Nothing is left for him to devour;
that is why his prosperity does not last.
20:22 In the fullness of his sufficiency,
distress overtakes him.
the full force of misery will come upon him.

20:23 "While he is filling his belly,
God sends his burning anger against him,
and rains down his blows upon him.
20:24 If he flees from an iron weapon,
then an arrow from a bronze bow pierces him.
20:25 When he pulls it out and it comes out of his back,
the gleaming point out of his liver,
terrors come over him.
20:26 Total darkness waits to receive his treasures;
a fire which has not been kindled
will consume him
and devour what is left in his tent.
20:27 The heavens reveal his iniquity;
the earth rises up against him.
20:28 A flood will carry off his house,
rushing waters on the day of God's wrath.

20:29 Such is the lot God allots the wicked,
and the heritage of his appointment from God."
Job's Reply to Zophar
21:1 Then Job answered:
21:2 "Listen carefully to my words;
let this be the consolation you offer me.
21:3 Bear with me and I will speak,
and after I have spoken you may mock.
21:4 Is my complaint against a man?
If so, why should I not be impatient?
21:5 Look at me and be appalled;
put your hands over your mouths.
21:6 For, when I think about this, I am terrified
and my body feels a shudder.
The Wicked Prosper
21:7 "Why do the wicked go on living,
grow old, even increase in power?
21:8 Their children are firmly established
in their presence,
their offspring before their eyes.
21:9 Their houses are safe and without fear;
and no rod of punishment from God is upon them.
21:10 Their bulls breed without fail;
their cows calve and do not miscarry.
21:11 They allow their children to run like a flock;
their little ones dance about.
21:12 They sing to the accompaniment of tambourine and harp,
and make merry to the sound of the flute.
21:13 They live out their years in prosperity
and go down to the grave in peace.
21:14 So they say to God, 'Turn away from us!
We do not want to know your ways.
21:15 Who is the Almighty, that we should serve him?
What would we gain
if we were to pray to him?'
21:16 But their prosperity is not their own doing.
The counsel of the wicked is far from me!
How Often Do the Wicked Suffer?
21:17 "How often is the lamp of the wicked extinguished?
How often does their misfortune come upon them?
How often does God apportion pain to them in his anger?
21:18 How often are they like straw before the wind,
and like chaff swept away by a whirlwind?
21:19 You may say, 'God stores up a man's punishment for his children!'
Instead let him repay the man himself
so that he may know it!
21:20 Let his own eyes see his destruction;
let him drink of the anger of the Almighty.
21:21 For what is his interest in his home
after his death,
when the number of his months
has been broken off?
21:22 Can anyone teach God knowledge,
since he judges those that are on high?
Death Levels Everything
21:23 "One man dies in his full vigor,
completely secure and prosperous,
21:24 his body well nourished,
and the marrow of his bones moist.
21:25 And another man dies in bitterness of soul,
never having tasted anything good.
21:26 Together they lie down in the dust,
and worms cover over them both.
Futile Words, Deceptive Answers
21:27 "Yes, I know what you are thinking,
the schemes by which you would wrong me.
21:28 For you say,
'Where now is the nobleman's house,
and where are the tents in which the wicked lived?'
21:29 Have you never questioned those who travel the roads?
Do you not recognize their accounts –
21:30 that the evil man is spared
from the day of his misfortune,
that he is delivered
from the day of God's wrath?
21:31 No one denounces his conduct to his face;
no one repays him for what he has done.
21:32 And when he is carried to the tombs,
and watch is kept over the funeral mound,
21:33 The clods of the torrent valley are sweet to him;
behind him everybody follows in procession,
and before him goes a countless throng.
21:34 So how can you console me with your futile words?

Nothing is left of your answers but deception!"
Eliphaz's Third Speech
22:1 Then Eliphaz the Temanite answered:
22:2 "Is it to God that a strong man is of benefit?
Is it to him that even a wise man is profitable?
22:3 Is it of any special benefit to the Almighty
that you should be righteous,
or is it any gain to him
that you make your ways blameless?
22:4 Is it because of your piety that he rebukes you
and goes to judgment with you?
22:5 Is not your wickedness great
and is there no end to your iniquity?

22:6 "For you took pledges from your brothers
for no reason,
and you stripped the clothing from the naked.
22:7 You gave the weary no water to drink
and from the hungry you withheld food.
22:8 Although you were a powerful man, owning land,
an honored man living on it,
22:9 you sent widows away empty-handed,
and the arms of the orphans you crushed.
22:10 That is why snares surround you,
and why sudden fear terrifies you,
22:11 why it is so dark you cannot see,
and why a flood of water covers you.

22:12 "Is not God on high in heaven?
And see the lofty stars, how high they are!
22:13 But you have said, 'What does God know?
Does he judge through such deep darkness?
22:14 Thick clouds are a veil for him, so he does not see us,
as he goes back and forth
in the vault of heaven.'
22:15 Will you keep to the old path
that evil men have walked –
22:16 men who were carried off before their time,
when the flood was poured out
on their foundations?
22:17 They were saying to God, 'Turn away from us,'
and 'What can the Almighty do to us?'
22:18 But it was he who filled their houses
with good things –
yet the counsel of the wicked
was far from me.
22:19 The righteous see their destruction and rejoice;
the innocent mock them scornfully, saying,
22:20 'Surely our enemies are destroyed,
and fire consumes their wealth.'

22:21 "Reconcile yourself with God,
and be at peace with him;
in this way your prosperity will be good.
22:22 Accept instruction from his mouth
and store up his words in your heart.
22:23 If you return to the Almighty, you will be built up;
if you remove wicked behavior far from your tent,
22:24 and throw your gold in the dust –
your gold of Ophir
among the rocks in the ravines –
22:25 then the Almighty himself will be your gold,
and the choicest silver for you.
22:26 Surely then you will delight yourself in the Almighty,
and will lift up your face toward God.
22:27 You will pray to him and he will hear you,
and you will fulfill your vows to him.
22:28 Whatever you decide on a matter,
it will be established for you,
and light will shine on your ways.
22:29 When people are brought low and you say
'Lift them up!'
then he will save the downcast;
22:30 he will deliver even someone who is not innocent,
who will escape through the cleanness of your hands."
Job's Reply to Eliphaz
23:1 Then Job answered:
23:2 "Even today my complaint is still bitter;
his hand is heavy despite my groaning.
23:3 O that I knew where I might find him,
that I could come to his place of residence!
23:4 I would lay out my case before him
and fill my mouth with arguments.

23:5 I would know with what words he would answer me,
and understand what he would say to me.
23:6 Would he contend with me with great power?
No, he would only pay attention to me.
23:7 There an upright person
could present his case before him,
and I would be delivered forever from my judge.
The Inaccessibility and Power of God
23:8 "If I go to the east, he is not there,
and to the west, yet I do not perceive him.
23:9 In the north when he is at work,
I do not see him;
when he turns to the south,
I see no trace of him.
23:10 But he knows the pathway that I take;
if he tested me, I would come forth like gold.
23:11 My feet have followed his steps closely;
I have kept to his way and have not turned aside.
23:12 I have not departed from the commands of his lips;
I have treasured the words of his mouth more than my allotted portion.
23:13 But he is unchangeable, and who can change him?
Whatever he has desired, he does.
23:14 For he fulfills his decree against me,
and many such things are his plans.
23:15 That is why I am terrified in his presence;
when I consider, I am afraid because of him.
23:16 Indeed, God has made my heart faint;
the Almighty has terrified me.
23:17 Yet I have not been silent because of the darkness,
because of the thick darkness
that covered my face.
The Apparent Indifference of God
24:1 "Why are times not appointed by the Almighty?
Why do those who know him not see his days?
24:2 Men move boundary stones;
they seize the flock and pasture them.
24:3 They drive away the orphan's donkey;
they take the widow's ox as a pledge.
24:4 They turn the needy from the pathway,
and the poor of the land hide themselves together.
24:5 Like wild donkeys in the desert
they go out to their labor,
seeking diligently for food;
the wasteland provides food for them
and for their children.
24:6 They reap fodder in the field,
and glean in the vineyard of the wicked.
24:7 They spend the night naked because they lack clothing;
they have no covering against the cold.
24:8 They are soaked by mountain rains
and huddle in the rocks because they lack shelter.
24:9 The fatherless child is snatched from the breast,
the infant of the poor is taken as a pledge.
24:10 They go about naked, without clothing,
and go hungry while they carry the sheaves.
24:11 They press out the olive oil between the rows of olive trees;
they tread the winepresses while they are thirsty.
24:12 From the city the dying groan,
and the wounded cry out for help,
but God charges no one with wrongdoing.
24:13 There are those who rebel against the light;
they do not know its ways
and they do not stay on its paths.
24:14 Before daybreak the murderer rises up;
he kills the poor and the needy;
in the night he is like a thief.
24:15 And the eye of the adulterer watches for the twilight,
thinking, 'No eye can see me,'
and covers his face with a mask.
24:16 In the dark the robber breaks into houses,
but by day they shut themselves in;
they do not know the light.
24:17 For all of them, the morning is to them
like deep darkness;
they are friends with the terrors of darkness.

24:18 "You say, 'He is foam on the face of the waters;
their portion of the land is cursed
so that no one goes to their vineyard.
24:19 The drought as well as the heat carry away
the melted snow;
so the grave takes away those who have sinned.
24:20 The womb forgets him,

the worm feasts on him,
no longer will he be remembered.
Like a tree, wickedness will be broken down.
24:21 He preys on the barren and childless woman,
and does not treat the widow well.
24:22 But God drags off the mighty by his power;
when God rises up against him, he has no faith in his life.
24:23 God may let them rest in a feeling of security,
but he is constantly watching all their ways.
24:24 They are exalted for a little while,
and then they are gone,
they are brought low like all others,
and gathered in,
and like a head of grain they are cut off.'

24:25 "If this is not so, who can prove me a liar
and reduce my words to nothing?"
Bildad's Third Speech
25:1 Then Bildad the Shuhite answered:
25:2 "Dominion and awesome might belong to God;
he establishes peace in his heights.
25:3 Can his armies be numbered?
On whom does his light not rise?
25:4 How then can a human being be righteous before God?
How can one born of a woman be pure?
25:5 If even the moon is not bright,
and the stars are not pure as far as he is concerned,
25:6 how much less a mortal man, who is but a maggot –
a son of man, who is only a worm!"
Job's Reply to Bildad
26:1 Then Job replied:
26:2 "How you have helped the powerless!
How you have saved the person who has no strength!
26:3 How you have advised the one without wisdom,
and abundantly revealed your insight!
26:4 To whom did you utter these words?
And whose spirit has come forth from your mouth?
A Better Description of God's Greatness
26:5 "The dead tremble –
those beneath the waters
and all that live in them.
26:6 The underworld is naked before God;
the place of destruction lies uncovered.
26:7 He spreads out the northern skies over empty space;
he suspends the earth on nothing.
26:8 He locks the waters in his clouds,
and the clouds do not burst with the weight of them.
26:9 He conceals the face of the full moon,
shrouding it with his clouds.
26:10 He marks out the horizon on the surface of the waters
as a boundary between light and darkness.
26:11 The pillars of the heavens tremble
and are amazed at his rebuke.
26:12 By his power he stills the sea;
by his wisdom he cut Rahab the great sea monster to pieces.
26:13 By his breath the skies became fair;
his hand pierced the fleeing serpent.
26:14 Indeed, these are but the outer fringes of his ways!
How faint is the whisper we hear of him!
But who can understand the thunder of his power?"
A Protest of Innocence
27:1 And Job took up his discourse again:
27:2 "As surely as God lives, who has denied me justice,
the Almighty, who has made my life bitter –
27:3 for while my spirit is still in me,
and the breath from God is in my nostrils,
27:4 my lips will not speak wickedness,
and my tongue will whisper no deceit.
27:5 I will never declare that you three are in the right;
until I die, I will not set aside my integrity!
27:6 I will maintain my righteousness
and never let it go;
my conscience will not reproach me
for as long as I live.
The Condition of the Wicked
27:7 "May my enemy be like the wicked,
my adversary like the unrighteous.
27:8 For what hope does the godless have when he is cut off,
when God takes away his life?
27:9 Does God listen to his cry
when distress overtakes him?
27:10 Will he find delight in the Almighty?
Will he call out to God at all times?

27:11 I will teach you about the power of God;
What is on the Almighty's mind I will not conceal.
27:12 If you yourselves have all seen this,
Why in the world do you continue this meaningless talk?
27:13 This is the portion of the wicked man
allotted by God,
the inheritance that evildoers receive
from the Almighty.
27:14 If his children increase – it is for the sword!
His offspring never have enough to eat.
27:15 Those who survive him are buried by the plague,
and their widows do not mourn for them.
27:16 If he piles up silver like dust
and stores up clothing like mounds of clay,
27:17 what he stores up a righteous man will wear,
and an innocent man will inherit his silver.
27:18 The house he builds is as fragile as a moth's cocoon,
like a hut that a watchman has made.
27:19 He goes to bed wealthy, but will do so no more.
When he opens his eyes, it is all gone.
27:20 Terrors overwhelm him like a flood;
at night a whirlwind carries him off.
27:21 The east wind carries him away, and he is gone;
it sweeps him out of his place.
27:22 It hurls itself against him without pity
as he flees headlong from its power.
27:23 It claps its hands at him in derision
and hisses him away from his place.
III. Job's Search for Wisdom (28:1-28)
No Known Road to Wisdom
28:1 "Surely there is a mine for silver,
and a place where gold is refined.
28:2 Iron is taken from the ground,
and rock is poured out as copper.
28:3 Man puts an end to the darkness;
he searches the farthest recesses
for the ore in the deepest darkness.
28:4 Far from where people live he sinks a shaft,
in places travelers have long forgotten,
far from other people he dangles and sways.
28:5 The earth, from which food comes,
is overturned below as though by fire;
28:6 a place whose stones are sapphires
and which contains dust of gold;
28:7 a hidden path no bird of prey knows –
no falcon's eye has spotted it.
28:8 Proud beasts have not set foot on it,
and no lion has passed along it.
28:9 On the flinty rock man has set to work with his hand;
he has overturned mountains at their bases.
28:10 He has cut out channels through the rocks;
his eyes have spotted every precious thing.
28:11 He has searched the sources of the rivers
and what was hidden he has brought into the light.
No Price Can Buy Wisdom
28:12 "But wisdom – where can it be found?
Where is the place of understanding?
28:13 Mankind does not know its place;
it cannot be found in the land of the living.
28:14 The deep says, 'It is not with me.'
And the sea says, 'It is not with me.'
28:15 Fine gold cannot be given in exchange for it,
nor can its price be weighed out in silver.
28:16 It cannot be measured out for purchase with the gold of Ophir,
with precious onyx or sapphires.
28:17 Neither gold nor crystal can be compared with it,
nor can a vase of gold match its worth.
28:18 Of coral and jasper no mention will be made;
the price of wisdom is more than pearls.
28:19 The topaz of Cush cannot be compared with it;
it cannot be purchased with pure gold.
God Alone Has Wisdom
28:20 "But wisdom – where does it come from?
Where is the place of understanding?
28:21 For it has been hidden
from the eyes of every living creature,
and from the birds of the sky it has been concealed.
28:22 Destruction and Death say,
'With our ears we have heard a rumor about where it can be found.'
28:23 God understands the way to it,
and he alone knows its place.
28:24 For he looks to the ends of the earth
and observes everything under the heavens.

28:25 When he made the force of the wind
and measured the waters with a gauge.
28:26 When he imposed a limit for the rain,
and a path for the thunderstorm,
28:27 then he looked at wisdom and assessed its value;
he established it and examined it closely.
28:28 And he said to mankind,
'The fear of the Lord – that is wisdom,
and to turn away from evil is understanding.'"
IV. Job's Concluding Soliloquy (29:1-31:40)
Job Recalls His Former Condition
29:1 Then Job continued his speech:
29:2 "O that I could be as I was
in the months now gone,
in the days when God watched over me,
29:3 when he caused his lamp
to shine upon my head,
and by his light
I walked through darkness;
29:4 just as I was in my most productive time,
when God's intimate friendship was experienced in my tent,
29:5 when the Almighty was still with me
and my children were around me;
29:6 when my steps were bathed with butter
and the rock poured out for me streams of olive oil!
29:7 When I went out to the city gate
and secured my seat in the public square,
29:8 the young men would see me and step aside,
and the old men would get up and remain standing;
29:9 the chief men refrained from talking
and covered their mouths with their hands;
29:10 the voices of the nobles fell silent,
and their tongues stuck to the roof of their mouths.
Job's Benevolence
29:11 "As soon as the ear heard these things, it blessed me,
and when the eye saw them, it bore witness to me,
29:12 for I rescued the poor who cried out for help,
and the orphan who had no one to assist him;
29:13 the blessing of the dying man descended on me,
and I made the widow's heart rejoice;
29:14 I put on righteousness and it clothed me,
my just dealing was like a robe and a turban;
29:15 I was eyes for the blind
and feet for the lame;
29:16 I was a father to the needy,
and I investigated the case of the person I did not know;
29:17 I broke the fangs of the wicked,
and made him drop his prey from his teeth.
Job's Confidence
29:18 "Then I thought, 'I will die in my own home,
my days as numerous as the grains of sand.
29:19 My roots reach the water,
and the dew lies on my branches all night long.
29:20 My glory will always be fresh in me,
and my bow ever new in my hand.'
Job's Reputation
29:21 "People listened to me and waited silently;
they kept silent for my advice.
29:22 After I had spoken, they did not respond;
my words fell on them drop by drop.
29:23 They waited for me as people wait for the rain,
and they opened their mouths
as for the spring rains.
29:24 If I smiled at them, they hardly believed it;
and they did not cause the light of my face to darken.
29:25 I chose the way for them
and sat as their chief;
I lived like a king among his troops;
I was like one who comforts mourners.
Job's Present Misery
30:1 "But now they mock me, those who are younger than I,
whose fathers I disdained too much
to put with my sheep dogs.
30:2 Moreover, the strength of their hands –
what use was it to me?
Men whose strength had perished;
30:3 gaunt with want and hunger,
they would gnaw the parched land,
in former time desolate and waste.
30:4 By the brush they would gather herbs from the salt marshes,
and the root of the broom tree was their food.
30:5 They were banished from the community –
people shouted at them

like they would shout at thieves –
30:6 so that they had to live
in the dry stream beds,
in the holes of the ground, and among the rocks.
30:7 They brayed like animals among the bushes
and were huddled together under the nettles.
30:8 Sons of senseless and nameless people,
they were driven out of the land with whips.
Job's Indignities
30:9 "And now I have become their taunt song;
I have become a byword among them.
30:10 They detest me and maintain their distance;
they do not hesitate to spit in my face.
30:11 Because God has untied my tent cord and afflicted me,
people throw off all restraint in my presence.
30:12 On my right the young rabble rise up;
they drive me from place to place,
and build up siege ramps against me.
30:13 They destroy my path;
they succeed in destroying me
without anyone assisting them.
30:14 They come in as through a wide breach;
amid the crash they come rolling in.
30:15 Terrors are turned loose on me;
they drive away my honor like the wind,
and like a cloud my deliverance has passed away.
Job's Despondency
30:16 "And now my soul pours itself out within me;
days of suffering take hold of me.
30:17 Night pierces my bones;
my gnawing pains never cease.
30:18 With great power God grasps my clothing;
he binds me like the collar of my tunic.
30:19 He has flung me into the mud,
and I have come to resemble dust and ashes.
30:20 I cry out to you, but you do not answer me;
I stand up, and you only look at me.
30:21 You have become cruel to me;
with the strength of your hand you attack me.
30:22 You pick me up on the wind and make me ride on it;
you toss me about in the storm.
30:23 I know that you are bringing me to death,
to the meeting place for all the living.
The Contrast With the Past
30:24 "Surely one does not stretch out his hand
against a broken man
when he cries for help in his distress.
30:25 Have I not wept for the unfortunate?
Was not my soul grieved for the poor?
30:26 But when I hoped for good, trouble came;
when I expected light, then darkness came.
30:27 My heart is in turmoil unceasingly;
the days of my affliction confront me.
30:28 I go about blackened, but not by the sun;
in the assembly I stand up and cry for help.
30:29 I have become a brother to jackals
and a companion of ostriches.
30:30 My skin has turned dark on me;
my body is hot with fever.
30:31 My harp is used for mourning
and my flute for the sound of weeping.
Job Vindicates Himself
31:1 "I made a covenant with my eyes;
how then could I entertain thoughts against a virgin?
31:2 What then would be one's lot from God above,
one's heritage from the Almighty on high?
31:3 Is it not misfortune for the unjust,
and disaster for those who work iniquity?
31:4 Does he not see my ways
and count all my steps?
31:5 If I have walked in falsehood,
and if my foot has hastened to deceit –
31:6 let him weigh me with honest scales;
then God will discover my integrity.
31:7 If my footsteps have strayed from the way,
if my heart has gone after my eyes,
or if anything has defiled my hands,
31:8 then let me sow and let another eat,
and let my crops be uprooted.
31:9 If my heart has been enticed by a woman,
and I have lain in wait at my neighbor's door,
31:10 then let my wife turn the millstone for another man,
and may other men have sexual relations with her.

31:11 For I would have committed a shameful act,
an iniquity to be judged.
31:12 For it is a fire that devours even to Destruction,
and it would uproot all my harvest.

31:13 "If I have disregarded the right of my male servants
or my female servants
when they disputed with me,
31:14 then what will I do when God confronts me in judgment;
when he intervenes,
how will I respond to him?
31:15 Did not the one who made me in the womb make them?
Did not the same one form us in the womb?
31:16 If I have refused to give the poor what they desired,
or caused the eyes of the widow to fail,
31:17 If I ate my morsel of bread myself,
and did not share any of it with orphans –
31:18 but from my youth I raised the orphan like a father,
and from my mother's womb
I guided the widow!
31:19 If I have seen anyone about to perish for lack of clothing,
or a poor man without a coat,
31:20 whose heart did not bless me
as he warmed himself with the fleece of my sheep,
31:21 if I have raised my hand to vote against the orphan,
when I saw my support in the court,
31:22 then let my arm fall from the shoulder,
let my arm be broken off at the socket.
31:23 For the calamity from God was a terror to me,
and by reason of his majesty I was powerless.

31:24 "If I have put my confidence in gold
or said to pure gold,
'You are my security!'
31:25 if I have rejoiced because of the extent of my wealth,
or because of the great wealth my hand had gained,
31:26 if I looked at the sun when it was shining,
and the moon advancing as a precious thing,
31:27 so that my heart was secretly enticed,
and my hand threw them a kiss from my mouth,
31:28 then this also would be iniquity to be judged,
for I would have been false to God above.
31:29 If I have rejoiced over the misfortune of my enemy
or exulted because calamity found him –
31:30 I have not even permitted my mouth to sin
by asking for his life through a curse –
31:31 if the members of my household have never said,
'If only there were someone
who has not been satisfied from Job's meat!' –
31:32 But no stranger had to spend the night outside,
for I opened my doors to the traveler –
31:33 if I have covered my transgressions as men do,
by hiding iniquity in my heart,
31:34 because I was terrified of the great multitude,
and the contempt of families terrified me,
so that I remained silent
and would not go outdoors –
Job's Appeal
31:35 "If only I had someone to hear me!
Here is my signature –
let the Almighty answer me!
If only I had an indictment
that my accuser had written.
31:36 Surely I would wear it proudly on my shoulder,
I would bind it on me like a crown;
31:37 I would give him an accounting of my steps;
like a prince I would approach him.
Job's Final Solemn Oath
31:38 "If my land cried out against me
and all its furrows wept together,
31:39 if I have eaten its produce without paying,
or caused the death of its owners,
31:40 then let thorns sprout up in place of wheat,
and in place of barley, weeds!"
The words of Job are ended.
V. The Speeches of Elihu (32:1-37:24)
Elihu's First Speech
32:1 So these three men refused to answer Job further, because he was righteous in his own eyes. **32:2** Then Elihu son of Barakel the Buzite, of the family of Ram, became very angry. He was angry with Job for justifying himself rather than God. **32:3** With Job's three friends he was also angry, because they could not find an answer, and so declared Job guilty. **32:4** Now Elihu had waited before speaking to Job, because the others were older than he was. **32:5** But when Elihu saw that the three men had no further reply, he became very angry.
Elihu Claims Wisdom
32:6 So Elihu son of Barakel the Buzite spoke up:
"I am young, but you are elderly;
that is why I was fearful,
and afraid to explain to you what I know.
32:7 I said to myself, 'Age should speak,
and length of years should make wisdom known.'
32:8 But it is a spirit in people,
the breath of the Almighty,
that makes them understand.
32:9 It is not the aged who are wise,
nor old men who understand what is right.
32:10 Therefore I say, 'Listen to me.
I, even I, will explain what I know.'
32:11 Look, I waited for you to speak;
I listened closely to your wise thoughts,while you were searching for words.
32:12 Now I was paying you close attention,
yet there was no one proving Job wrong,
not one of you was answering his statements!
32:13 So do not say, 'We have found wisdom!
God will refute him, not man!'
32:14 Job has not directed his words to me,
and so I will not reply to him with your arguments.
Job's Friends Failed to Answer
32:15 "They are dismayed and cannot answer any more;
they have nothing left to say.
32:16 And I have waited. But because they do not speak,
because they stand there and answer no more,
32:17 I too will answer my part,
I too will explain what I know.
32:18 For I am full of words,
and the spirit within me constrains me.
32:19 Inside I am like wine which has no outlet,
like new wineskins ready to burst!
32:20 I will speak, so that I may find relief;
I will open my lips, so that I may answer.
32:21 I will not show partiality to anyone,
nor will I confer a title on any man.
32:22 for I do not know how to give honorary titles,
if I did, my Creator would quickly do away with me.
Elihu Invites Job's Attention
33:1 "But now, O Job, listen to my words,
and hear everything I have to say!
33:2 See now, I have opened my mouth;
my tongue in my mouth has spoken.
33:3 My words come from the uprightness of my heart,
and my lips will utter knowledge sincerely.
33:4 The Spirit of God has made me,
and the breath of the Almighty gives me life.
33:5 Reply to me, if you can;
set your arguments in order before me
and take your stand!
33:6 Look, I am just like you in relation to God;
I too have been molded from clay.
33:7 Therefore no fear of me should terrify you,
nor should my pressure be heavy on you.
Elihu Rejects Job's Plea of Innocence
33:8 "Indeed, you have said in my hearing
(I heard the sound of the words!):
33:9 'I am pure, without transgression;
I am clean and have no iniquity.
33:10 Yet God finds occasions with me;
he regards me as his enemy!
33:11 He puts my feet in shackles;
he watches closely all my paths.'
33:12 Now in this, you are not right – I answer you,
for God is greater than a human being.
33:13 Why do you contend against him,
that he does not answer all a person's words?
Elihu Disagrees With Job's View of God
33:14 "For God speaks, the first time in one way,
the second time in another,
though a person does not perceive it.
33:15 In a dream, a night vision,
when deep sleep falls on people
as they sleep in their beds.
33:16 Then he gives a revelation to people,
and terrifies them with warnings,
33:17 to turn a person from his sin,
and to cover a person's pride.

33:18 He spares a person's life from corruption,
his very life from crossing over the river.
33:19 Or a person is chastened by pain on his bed,
and with the continual strife of his bones,
33:20 so that his life loathes food,
and his soul rejects appetizing fare.
33:21 His flesh wastes away from sight,
and his bones, which were not seen,
are easily visible.
33:22 He draws near to the place of corruption,
and his life to the messengers of death.
33:23 If there is an angel beside him,
one mediator out of a thousand,
to tell a person what constitutes his uprightness;
33:24 and if God is gracious to him and says,
'Spare him from going down
to the place of corruption,
I have found a ransom for him,'
33:25 then his flesh is restored like a youth's;
he returns to the days of his youthful vigor.
33:26 He entreats God, and God delights in him,
he sees God's face with rejoicing,
and God restores to him his righteousness.
33:27 That person sings to others, saying:
'I have sinned and falsified what is right,
but I was not punished according to what I deserved.
33:28 He redeemed my life
from going down to the place of corruption,
and my life sees the light!'
Elihu's Appeal to Job
33:29 "Indeed, God does all these things,
twice, three times, in his dealings with a person,
33:30 to turn back his life from the place of corruption,
that he may be enlightened with the light of life.
33:31 Pay attention, Job – listen to me;
be silent, and I will speak.
33:32 If you have any words, reply to me;
speak, for I want to justify you.
33:33 If not, you listen to me;
be silent, and I will teach you wisdom."
Elihu's Second Speech
34:1 Elihu answered:
34:2 "Listen to my words, you wise men;
hear me, you learned men.
34:3 For the ear assesses words
as the mouth tastes food.
34:4 Let us evaluate for ourselves what is right;
let us come to know among ourselves what is good.
34:5 For Job says, 'I am innocent,
but God turns away my right.
34:6 Concerning my right, should I lie?
My wound is incurable,
although I am without transgression.'
34:7 What man is like Job,
who drinks derision like water!
34:8 He goes about in company with evildoers,
he goes along with wicked men.
34:9 For he says, 'It does not profit a man
when he makes his delight with God.'
God is Not Unjust
34:10 "Therefore, listen to me, you men of understanding.
Far be it from God to do wickedness,
from the Almighty to do evil.
34:11 For he repays a person for his work,
and according to the conduct of a person,
he causes the consequences to find him.
34:12 Indeed, in truth, God does not act wickedly,
and the Almighty does not pervert justice.
34:13 Who entrusted to him the earth?
And who put him over the whole world?
34:14 If God were to set his heart on it,
and gather in his spirit and his breath,
34:15 all flesh would perish together
and human beings would return to dust.
God Is Impartial and Omniscient
34:16 "If you have understanding, listen to this,
hear what I have to say.
34:17 Do you really think
that one who hates justice can govern?
And will you declare guilty
the supremely righteous One,
34:18 who says to a king, 'Worthless man'
and to nobles, 'Wicked men,'

34:19 who shows no partiality to princes,
and does not take note of the rich more than the poor,
because all of them are the work of his hands?
34:20 In a moment they die, in the middle of the night,
people are shaken and they pass away.
The mighty are removed effortlessly.
34:21 For his eyes are on the ways of an individual,
he observes all a person's steps.
34:22 There is no darkness, and no deep darkness,
where evildoers can hide themselves.
34:23 For he does not still consider a person,
that he should come before God in judgment.
34:24 He shatters the great without inquiry,
and sets up others in their place.
34:25 Therefore, he knows their deeds,
he overthrows them in the night
and they are crushed.
34:26 He strikes them for their wickedness,
in a place where people can see,
34:27 because they have turned away from following him,
and have not understood any of his ways,
34:28 so that they caused the cry of the poor
to come before him,
so that he hears the cry of the needy.
34:29 But if God is quiet, who can condemn him?
If he hides his face, then who can see him?
Yet he is over the individual and the nation alike,
34:30 so that the godless man should not rule,
and not lay snares for the people.
Job Is Foolish to Rebel
34:31 "Has anyone said to God,
'I have endured chastisement,
but I will not act wrongly any more.
34:32 Teach me what I cannot see.
If I have done evil, I will do so no more.'
34:33 Is it your opinion that God should recompense it,
because you reject this?
But you must choose, and not I,
so tell us what you know.
34:34 Men of understanding say to me –
any wise man listening to me says –
34:35 that Job speaks without knowledge
and his words are without understanding.
34:36 But Job will be tested to the end,
because his answers are like those of wicked men.
34:37 For he adds transgression to his sin;
in our midst he claps his hands,
and multiplies his words against God."
Elihu's Third Speech
35:1 Then Elihu answered:
35:2 "Do you think this to be just:
when you say, 'My right before God.'
35:3 But you say, 'What will it profit you,'
and, 'What do I gain by not sinning?'
35:4 I will reply to you,
and to your friends with you.
35:5 Gaze at the heavens and see;
consider the clouds, which are higher than you!
35:6 If you sin, how does it affect God?
If your transgressions are many,
what does it do to him?
35:7 If you are righteous, what do you give to God,
or what does he receive from your hand?
35:8 Your wickedness affects only a person like yourself,
and your righteousness only other people.

35:9 "People cry out
because of the excess of oppression;
they cry out for help
because of the power of the mighty.
35:10 But no one says, 'Where is God, my Creator,
who gives songs in the night,
35:11 who teaches us more than the wild animals of the earth,
and makes us wiser than the birds of the sky?'
35:12 Then they cry out – but he does not answer –
because of the arrogance of the wicked.
35:13 Surely it is an empty cry – God does not hear it;
the Almighty does not take notice of it.
35:14 How much less, then,
when you say that you do not perceive him,
that the case is before him
and you are waiting for him!
35:15 And further, when you say

that his anger does not punish,
and that he does not know transgression!
35:16 So Job opens his mouth to no purpose;
without knowledge he multiplies words."
Elihu's Fourth Speech
36:1 Elihu said further:
36:2 "Be patient with me a little longer
and I will instruct you,
for I still have words to speak on God's behalf.
36:3 With my knowledge I will speak comprehensively,
and to my Creator I will ascribe righteousness.
36:4 For in truth, my words are not false;
it is one complete in knowledge
who is with you.
36:5 Indeed, God is mighty; and he does not despise people,
he is mighty, and firm in his intent.
36:6 He does not allow the wicked to live,
but he gives justice to the poor.
36:7 He does not take his eyes off the righteous;
but with kings on the throne
he seats the righteous and exalts them forever.
36:8 But if they are bound in chains,
and held captive by the cords of affliction,
36:9 then he reveals to them what they have done,
and their transgressions,
that they were behaving proudly.
36:10 And he reveals this for correction,
and says that they must turn from evil.
36:11 If they obey and serve him,
they live out their days in prosperity
and their years in pleasantness.
36:12 But if they refuse to listen,
they pass over the river of death,
and expire without knowledge.
36:13 The godless at heart nourish anger,
they do not cry out even when he binds them.
36:14 They die in their youth,
and their life ends among the male cultic prostitutes.
36:15 He delivers the afflicted by their afflictions,
he reveals himself to them by their suffering.
36:16 And surely, he drew you from the mouth of distress,
to a wide place, unrestricted,
and to the comfort of your table
filled with rich food.
36:17 But now you are preoccupied with the judgment due the wicked,
judgment and justice take hold of you.
36:18 Be careful that no one entices you with riches;
do not let a large bribe turn you aside.
36:19 Would your wealth sustain you,
so that you would not be in distress,
even all your mighty efforts?
36:20 Do not long for the cover of night
to drag people away from their homes.
36:21 Take heed, do not turn to evil,
for because of this you have been tested by affliction.
36:22 Indeed, God is exalted in his power;
who is a teacher like him?
36:23 Who has prescribed his ways for him?
Or said to him, 'You have done what is wicked'?
36:24 Remember to extol his work,
which people have praised in song.
36:25 All humanity has seen it;
people gaze on it from afar.
The Work and Wisdom of God
36:26 "Yes, God is great – beyond our knowledge!
The number of his years is unsearchable.
36:27 He draws up drops of water;
they distill the rain into its mist,
36:28 which the clouds pour down
and shower on humankind abundantly.
36:29 Who can understand the spreading of the clouds,
the thunderings of his pavilion?
36:30 See how he scattered his lightning about him;
he has covered the depths of the sea.
36:31 It is by these that he judges the nations
and supplies food in abundance.
36:32 With his hands he covers the lightning,
and directs it against its target.
36:33 His thunder announces the coming storm,
the cattle also, concerning the storm's approach.
37:1 At this also my heart pounds
and leaps from its place.
37:2 Listen carefully to the thunder of his voice,

to the rumbling that proceeds from his mouth.
37:3 Under the whole heaven he lets it go,
even his lightning to the far corners of the earth.
37:4 After that a voice roars;
he thunders with an exalted voice,
and he does not hold back his lightning bolts
when his voice is heard.
37:5 God thunders with his voice in marvelous ways;
he does great things beyond our understanding.
37:6 For to the snow he says, 'Fall to earth,'
and to the torrential rains, 'Pour down.'
37:7 He causes everyone to stop working,
so that all people may know his work.
37:8 The wild animals go to their lairs,
and in their dens they remain.
37:9 A tempest blows out from its chamber,
icy cold from the driving winds.
37:10 The breath of God produces ice,
and the breadth of the waters freeze solid.
37:11 He loads the clouds with moisture;
he scatters his lightning through the clouds.
37:12 The clouds go round in circles,
wheeling about according to his plans,
to carry out all that he commands them
over the face of the whole inhabited world.
37:13 Whether it is for punishment for his land,
or whether it is for mercy,
he causes it to find its mark.

37:14 "Pay attention to this, Job!
Stand still and consider the wonders God works.
37:15 Do you know how God commands them,
how he makes lightning flash in his storm cloud?
37:16 Do you know about the balancing of the clouds,
that wondrous activity of him who is perfect in knowledge?
37:17 You, whose garments are hot
when the earth is still because of the south wind,
37:18 will you, with him, spread out the clouds,
solid as a mirror of molten metal?
37:19 Tell us what we should say to him.
We cannot prepare a case
because of the darkness.
37:20 Should he be informed that I want to speak?
If a man speaks, surely he would be swallowed up!
37:21 But now, the sun cannot be looked at –
it is bright in the skies –
after a wind passed and swept the clouds away.
37:22 From the north he comes in golden splendor;
around God is awesome majesty.
37:23 As for the Almighty, we cannot attain to him!
He is great in power,
but justice and abundant righteousness he does not oppress.
37:24 Therefore people fear him,
for he does not regard all the wise in heart."
VI. The Divine Speeches (38:1-42:6)
The Lord's First Speech
38:1 Then the LORD answered Job out of the whirlwind:
38:2 "Who is this who darkens counsel
with words without knowledge?
38:3 Get ready for a difficult task like a man;
I will question you
and you will inform me!
God's questions to Job
38:4 "Where were you
when I laid the foundation of the earth?
Tell me, if you possess understanding!
38:5 Who set its measurements – if you know –
or who stretched a measuring line across it?
38:6 On what were its bases set,
or who laid its cornerstone –
38:7 when the morning stars sang in chorus,
and all the sons of God shouted for joy?

38:8 "Who shut up the sea with doors
when it burst forth, coming out of the womb,
38:9 when I made the storm clouds its garment,
and thick darkness its swaddling band,
38:10 when I prescribed its limits,
and set in place its bolts and doors,
38:11 when I said, 'To here you may come
and no farther,
here your proud waves will be confined'?

38:12 Have you ever in your life commanded the morning,
or made the dawn know its place,
38:13 that it might seize the corners of the earth,
and shake the wicked out of it?
38:14 The earth takes shape like clay under a seal;
its features are dyed like a garment.
38:15 Then from the wicked the light is withheld,
and the arm raised in violence is broken.
38:16 Have you gone to the springs that fill the sea,
or walked about in the recesses of the deep?
38:17 Have the gates of death been revealed to you?
Have you seen the gates of deepest darkness?
38:18 Have you considered the vast expanses of the earth?
Tell me, if you know it all!

38:19 "In what direction does light reside,
and darkness, where is its place,
38:20 that you may take them to their borders
and perceive the pathways to their homes?
38:21 You know, for you were born before them;
and the number of your days is great!
38:22 Have you entered the storehouse of the snow,
or seen the armory of the hail,
38:23 which I reserve for the time of trouble,
for the day of war and battle?
38:24 In what direction is lightning dispersed,
or the east winds scattered over the earth?
38:25 Who carves out a channel for the heavy rains,
and a path for the rumble of thunder,
38:26 to cause it to rain on an uninhabited land,
a desert where there are no human beings,
38:27 to satisfy a devastated and desolate land,
and to cause it to sprout with vegetation?
38:28 Does the rain have a father,
or who has fathered the drops of the dew?
38:29 From whose womb does the ice emerge,
and the frost from the sky, who gives birth to it,
38:30 when the waters become hard like stone,
when the surface of the deep is frozen solid?
38:31 Can you tie the bands of the Pleiades,
or release the cords of Orion?
38:32 Can you lead out
the constellations in their seasons,
or guide the Bear with its cubs?
38:33 Do you know the laws of the heavens,
or can you set up their rule over the earth?
38:34 Can you raise your voice to the clouds
so that a flood of water covers you?
38:35 Can you send out lightning bolts, and they go?
Will they say to you, 'Here we are'?
38:36 Who has put wisdom in the heart,
or has imparted understanding to the mind?
38:37 Who by wisdom can count the clouds,
and who can tip over the water jars of heaven,
38:38 when the dust hardens into a mass,
and the clumps of earth stick together?

38:39 "Do you hunt prey for the lioness,
and satisfy the appetite of the lions,
38:40 when they crouch in their dens,
when they wait in ambush in the thicket?
38:41 Who prepares prey for the raven,
when its young cry out to God
and wander about for lack of food?

39:1 "Are you acquainted with the way
the mountain goats give birth?
Do you watch as the wild deer give birth to their young?
39:2 Do you count the months they must fulfill,
and do you know the time they give birth?
39:3 They crouch, they bear their young,
they bring forth the offspring they have carried.
39:4 Their young grow strong, and grow up in the open;
they go off, and do not return to them.

39:5 Who let the wild donkey go free?
Who released the bonds of the donkey,
39:6 to whom I appointed the steppe for its home,
the salt wastes as its dwelling place?
39:7 It scorns the tumult in the town;
it does not hear the shouts of a driver.
39:8 It ranges the hills as its pasture,
and searches after every green plant.

39:9 Is the wild ox willing to be your servant?
Will it spend the night at your feeding trough?
39:10 Can you bind the wild ox to a furrow with its rope,
will it till the valleys, following after you?
39:11 Will you rely on it because its strength is great?
Will you commit your labor to it?
39:12 Can you count on it to bring in your grain,
and gather the grain to your threshing floor?

39:13 "The wings of the ostrich flap with joy,
but are they the pinions and plumage of a stork?
39:14 For she leaves her eggs on the ground,
and lets them be warmed on the soil.
39:15 She forgets that a foot might crush them,
or that a wild animal might trample them.
39:16 She is harsh with her young,
as if they were not hers;
she is unconcerned
about the uselessness of her labor.
39:17 For God deprived her of wisdom,
and did not impart understanding to her.
39:18 But as soon as she springs up,
she laughs at the horse and its rider.

39:19 "Do you give the horse its strength?
Do you clothe its neck with a mane?
39:20 Do you make it leap like a locust?
Its proud neighing is terrifying!
39:21 It paws the ground in the valley,
exulting mightily,
it goes out to meet the weapons.
39:22 It laughs at fear and is not dismayed;
it does not shy away from the sword.
39:23 On it the quiver rattles;
the lance and javelin flash.
39:24 In excitement and impatience it consumes the ground;
it cannot stand still when the trumpet is blown.
39:25 At the sound of the trumpet, it says, 'Aha!'
And from a distance it catches the scent of battle,
the thunderous shouting of commanders,
and the battle cries.

39:26 "Is it by your understanding that the hawk soars,
and spreads its wings toward the south?
39:27 Is it at your command that the eagle soars,
and builds its nest on high?
39:28 It lives on a rock and spends the night there,
on a rocky crag and a fortress.
39:29 From there it spots its prey,
its eyes gaze intently from a distance.
39:30 And its young ones devour the blood,
and where the dead carcasses are,
there it is."
Job's Reply to God's Challenge
40:1 Then the LORD answered Job:
40:2 "Will the one who contends with the Almighty correct him?
Let the person who accuses God give him an answer!"

40:3 Then Job answered the LORD:
40:4 "Indeed, I am completely unworthy – how could I reply to you?
I put my hand over my mouth to silence myself.
40:5 I have spoken once, but I cannot answer;
twice, but I will say no more."
The Lord's Second Speech
40:6 Then the LORD answered Job from the whirlwind:
40:7 "Get ready for a difficult task like a man.
I will question you and you will inform me!
40:8 Would you indeed annul my justice?
Would you declare me guilty so that you might be right?
40:9 Do you have an arm as powerful as God's,
and can you thunder with a voice like his?
40:10 Adorn yourself, then, with majesty and excellency,
and clothe yourself with glory and honor!
40:11 Scatter abroad the abundance of your anger.
Look at every proud man and bring him low;
40:12 Look at every proud man and abase him;
crush the wicked on the spot!
40:13 Hide them in the dust together,
imprison them in the grave.
40:14 Then I myself will acknowledge to you
that your own right hand can save you.
The Description of Behemoth

40:15 "Look now at Behemoth, which I made as I made you;
it eats grass like the ox.
40:16 Look at its strength in its loins,
and its power in the muscles of its belly.
40:17 It makes its tail stiff like a cedar,
the sinews of its thighs are tightly wound.
40:18 Its bones are tubes of bronze,
its limbs like bars of iron.
40:19 It ranks first among the works of God,
the One who made it
has furnished it with a sword.
40:20 For the hills bring it food,
where all the wild animals play.
40:21 Under the lotus trees it lies,
in the secrecy of the reeds and the marsh.
40:22 The lotus trees conceal it in their shadow;
the poplars by the stream conceal it.
40:23 If the river rages, it is not disturbed,
it is secure, though the Jordan
should surge up to its mouth.
40:24 Can anyone catch it by its eyes,
or pierce its nose with a snare?
The Description of Leviathan
41:1 (40:25) "Can you pull in Leviathan with a hook,
and tie down its tongue with a rope?
41:2 Can you put a cord through its nose,
or pierce its jaw with a hook?
41:3 Will it make numerous supplications to you,
will it speak to you with tender words?
41:4 Will it make a pact with you,
so you could take it as your slave for life?
41:5 Can you play with it, like a bird,
or tie it on a leash for your girls?
41:6 Will partners bargain for it?
Will they divide it up among the merchants?
41:7 Can you fill its hide with harpoons
or its head with fishing spears?
41:8 If you lay your hand on it,
you will remember the fight,
and you will never do it again!
41:9 (41:1) See, his expectation is wrong,
he is laid low even at the sight of it.
41:10 Is it not fierce when it is awakened?
Who is he, then, who can stand before it?
41:11 (Who has confronted me that I should repay?
Everything under heaven belongs to me!)
41:12 I will not keep silent about its limbs,
and the extent of its might,
and the grace of its arrangement.
41:13 Who can uncover its outer covering?
Who can penetrate to the inside of its armor?
41:14 Who can open the doors of its mouth?
Its teeth all around are fearsome.
41:15 Its back has rows of shields,
shut up closely together as with a seal;
41:16 each one is so close to the next
that no air can come between them.
41:17 They lock tightly together, one to the next;
they cling together and cannot be separated.
41:18 Its snorting throws out flashes of light;
its eyes are like the red glow of dawn.
41:19 Out of its mouth go flames,
sparks of fire shoot forth!
41:20 Smoke streams from its nostrils
as from a boiling pot over burning rushes.
41:21 Its breath sets coals ablaze
and a flame shoots from its mouth.
41:22 Strength lodges in its neck,
and despair runs before it.
41:23 The folds of its flesh are tightly joined;
they are firm on it, immovable.
41:24 Its heart is hard as rock,
hard as a lower millstone.
41:25 When it rises up, the mighty are terrified,
at its thrashing about they withdraw.
41:26 Whoever strikes it with a sword
will have no effect,
nor with the spear, arrow, or dart.
41:27 It regards iron as straw
and bronze as rotten wood.
41:28 Arrows do not make it flee;
slingstones become like chaff to it.
41:29 A club is counted as a piece of straw;

it laughs at the rattling of the lance.
41:30 Its underparts are the sharp points of potsherds,
it leaves its mark in the mud
like a threshing sledge.
41:31 It makes the deep boil like a cauldron
and stirs up the sea like a pot of ointment,
41:32 It leaves a glistening wake behind it;
one would think the deep had a head of white hair.
41:33 The likes of it is not on earth,
a creature without fear.
41:34 It looks on every haughty being;
it is king over all that are proud."
Job's Confession
42:1 Then Job answered the LORD:
42:2 "I know that you can do all things;
no purpose of yours can be thwarted;
42:3 you asked,
'Who is this who darkens counsel
without knowledge?'
But I have declared without understanding
things too wonderful for me to know.
42:4 You said,
'Pay attention, and I will speak;
I will question you, and you will answer me.'
42:5 I had heard of you by the hearing of the ear,
but now my eye has seen you.
42:6 Therefore I despise myself,
and I repent in dust and ashes!
VII. The Epilogue (42:7-17)
42:7 After the LORD had spoken these things to Job, he said to Eliphaz the Temanite, "My anger is stirred up against you and your two friends, because you have not spoken about me what is right, as my servant Job has. **42:8** So now take seven bulls and seven rams and go to my servant Job and offer a burnt offering for yourselves. And my servant Job will intercede for you, and I will respect him, so that I do not deal with you according to your folly, because you have not spoken about me what is right, as my servant Job has."
42:9 So they went, Eliphaz the Temanite, Bildad the Shuhite, and Zophar the Naamathite, and did just as the LORD had told them; and the LORD had respect for Job.
42:10 So the LORD restored what Job had lost after he prayed for his friends, and the LORD doubled all that had belonged to Job. **42:11** So they came to him, all his brothers and sisters and all who had known him before, and they dined with him in his house. They comforted him and consoled him for all the trouble the LORD had brought on him, and each one gave him a piece of silver and a gold ring.
42:12 So the LORD blessed the second part of Job's life more than the first. He had 14,000 sheep, 6,000 camels, 1,000 yoke of oxen, and
1,000 female donkeys. **42:13** And he also had seven sons and three daughters. **42:14** The first daughter he named Jemimah, the second Keziah, and the third Keren-Happuch. **42:15** Nowhere in all the land could women be found who were as beautiful as Job's daughters, and their father granted them an inheritance alongside their brothers.
42:16 After this Job lived 140 years; he saw his children and their children to the fourth generation. **42:17** And so Job died, old and full of days.

Book 19. Psalms

Book 1(Psalms 1-41)
Psalm 1
1:1 How blessed is the one who does not follow the advice of the wicked,
or stand in the pathway with sinners,
or sit in the assembly of scoffers!
1:2 Instead he finds pleasure in obeying the LORD's commands;
he meditates on his commands day and night.
1:3 He is like a tree planted by flowing streams;
it yields its fruit at the proper time,
and its leaves never fall off.
He succeeds in everything he attempts.
1:4 Not so with the wicked!
Instead they are like wind-driven chaff.
1:5 For this reason the wicked cannot withstand judgment,
nor can sinners join the assembly of the godly.
1:6 Certainly the LORD guards the way of the godly,
but the way of the wicked ends in destruction.
Psalm 2
2:1 Why do the nations rebel?
Why are the countries devising plots that will fail?
2:2 The kings of the earth form a united front;
the rulers collaborate
against the LORD and his anointed king.
2:3 They say, "Let's tear off the shackles they've put on us!
Let's free ourselves from their ropes!"

2:4 The one enthroned in heaven laughs in disgust;
the Lord taunts them.
2:5 Then he angrily speaks to them
and terrifies them in his rage, saying,
2:6 "I myself have installed my king
on Zion, my holy hill."
2:7 The king says, "I will announce the LORD's decree. He said to me:
'You are my son! This very day I have become your father!
2:8 Ask me,
and I will give you the nations as your inheritance,
the ends of the earth as your personal property.
2:9 You will break them with an iron scepter;
you will smash them like a potter's jar!'"
2:10 So now, you kings, do what is wise;
you rulers of the earth, submit to correction!
2:11 Serve the LORD in fear!
Repent in terror!
2:12 Give sincere homage!
Otherwise he will be angry,
and you will die because of your behavior,
when his anger quickly ignites.
How blessed are all who take shelter in him!

Psalm 3

A psalm of David, written when he fled from his son Absalom.
3:1 LORD, how numerous are my enemies!
Many attack me.
3:2 Many say about me,
"God will not deliver him." (Selah)
3:3 But you, LORD, are a shield that protects me;
you are my glory and the one who restores me.
3:4 To the LORD I cried out,
and he answered me from his holy hill. (Selah)
3:5 I rested and slept;
I awoke, for the LORD protects me.
3:6 I am not afraid of the multitude of people
who attack me from all directions.
3:7 Rise up, LORD!
Deliver me, my God!
Yes, you will strike all my enemies on the jaw;
you will break the teeth of the wicked.
3:8 The LORD delivers;
you show favor to your people. (Selah)

Psalm 4

For the music director, to be accompanied by stringed instruments; a psalm of David.
4:1 When I call out, answer me,
O God who vindicates me!
Though I am hemmed in, you will lead me into a wide, open place.
Have mercy on me and respond to my prayer!
4:2 You men, how long will you try to turn my honor into shame?
How long will you love what is worthless
and search for what is deceptive? (Selah)
4:3 Realize that the LORD shows the godly special favor;
the LORD responds when I cry out to him.
4:4 Tremble with fear and do not sin!
Meditate as you lie in bed, and repent of your ways! (Selah)
4:5 Offer the prescribed sacrifices
and trust in the LORD!
4:6 Many say, "Who can show us anything good?"
Smile upon us, LORD!
4:7 You make me happier
than those who have abundant grain and wine.
4:8 I will lie down and sleep peacefully,
for you, LORD, make me safe and secure.

Psalm 5

For the music director, to be accompanied by wind instruments; a psalm of David.
5:1 Listen to what I say, LORD!
Carefully consider my complaint!
5:2 Pay attention to my cry for help,
my king and my God,
for I am praying to you!
5:3 LORD, in the morning you will hear me;
in the morning I will present my case to you and then wait expectantly for an answer.
5:4 Certainly you are not a God who approves of evil;
evil people cannot dwell with you.
5:5 Arrogant people cannot stand in your presence;
you hate all who behave wickedly.
5:6 You destroy liars;
the LORD despises violent and deceitful people.
5:7 But as for me, because of your great faithfulness I will enter your house;
I will bow down toward your holy temple as I worship you.
5:8 LORD, lead me in your righteousness
because of those who wait to ambush me,
remove the obstacles in the way in which you are guiding me!
5:9 For they do not speak the truth;
their stomachs are like the place of destruction,
their throats like an open grave,
their tongues like a steep slope leading into it.
5:10 Condemn them, O God!
May their own schemes be their downfall!
Drive them away because of their many acts of insurrection,
for they have rebelled against you.
5:11 But may all who take shelter in you be happy!
May they continually shout for joy!
Shelter them so that those who are loyal to you may rejoice!
5:12 Certainly you reward the godly, LORD.
Like a shield you protect them in your good favor.

Psalm 6

For the music director, to be accompanied by stringed instruments, according to the *sheminith* style; a psalm of David.
6:1 LORD, do not rebuke me in your anger!
Do not discipline me in your raging fury!
6:2 Have mercy on me, LORD, for I am frail!
Heal me, LORD, for my bones are shaking!
6:3 I am absolutely terrified,
and you, LORD – how long will this continue?
6:4 Relent, LORD, rescue me!
Deliver me because of your faithfulness!
6:5 For no one remembers you in the realm of death,
In Sheol who gives you thanks?
6:6 I am exhausted as I groan;
all night long I drench my bed in tears;
my tears saturate the cushion beneath me.
6:7 My eyes grow dim from suffering;
they grow weak because of all my enemies.
6:8 Turn back from me, all you who behave wickedly,
for the LORD has heard the sound of my weeping!
6:9 The LORD has heard my appeal for mercy;
the LORD has accepted my prayer.
6:10 May all my enemies be humiliated and absolutely terrified!
May they turn back and be suddenly humiliated!

Psalm 7

A musical composition by David, which he sang to the LORD concerning a Benjaminite named Cush.
7:1 O LORD my God, in you I have taken shelter.
Deliver me from all who chase me! Rescue me!
7:2 Otherwise they will rip me to shreds like a lion;
they will tear me to bits and no one will be able to rescue me.
7:3 O LORD my God, if I have done what they say,
or am guilty of unjust actions,
7:4 or have wronged my ally,
or helped his lawless enemy,
7:5 may an enemy relentlessly chase me and catch me;
may he trample me to death
and leave me lying dishonored in the dust. (Selah)
7:6 Stand up angrily, LORD!
Rise up with raging fury against my enemies!
Wake up for my sake and execute the judgment you have decreed for them!
7:7 The countries are assembled all around you;
take once more your rightful place over them!
7:8 The LORD judges the nations.
Vindicate me, LORD, because I am innocent,
because I am blameless, O Exalted One!
7:9 May the evil deeds of the wicked come to an end!
But make the innocent secure,
O righteous God,
you who examine inner thoughts and motives!
7:10 The Exalted God is my shield,
the one who delivers the morally upright.
7:11 God is a just judge;
he is angry throughout the day.
7:12 If a person does not repent, God sharpens his sword
and prepares to shoot his bow.
7:13 He prepares to use deadly weapons against him;
he gets ready to shoot flaming arrows.
7:14 See the one who is pregnant with wickedness,
who conceives destructive plans,
and gives birth to harmful lies –
7:15 he digs a pit
and then falls into the hole he has made.
7:16 He becomes the victim of his own destructive plans
and the violence he intended for others falls on his own head.

7:17 I will thank the LORD for his justice;
I will sing praises to the sovereign LORD!

Psalm 8

For the music director, according to the *gittith* style; a psalm of David.
8:1 O LORD, our Lord,
how magnificent is your reputation throughout the earth!
You reveal your majesty in the heavens above!
8:2 From the mouths of children and nursing babies
you have ordained praise on account of your adversaries,
so that you might put an end to the vindictive enemy.
8:3 When I look up at the heavens, which your fingers made,
and see the moon and the stars, which you set in place,
8:4 Of what importance is the human race, that you should notice them?
Of what importance is mankind, that you should pay attention to them,
8:5 and make them a little less than the heavenly beings?
You grant mankind honor and majesty;
8:6 you appoint them to rule over your creation;
you have placed everything under their authority,
8:7 including all the sheep and cattle,
as well as the wild animals,
8:8 the birds in the sky, the fish in the sea
and everything that moves through the currents of the seas.
8:9 O LORD, our Lord,
how magnificent is your reputation throughout the earth!

Psalm 9

For the music director; according to the *alumoth-labben* style; a psalm of David.
9:1 I will thank the LORD with all my heart!
I will tell about all your amazing deeds!
9:2 I will be happy and rejoice in you!
I will sing praises to you, O sovereign One!
9:3 When my enemies turn back,
they trip and are defeated before you.
9:4 For you defended my just cause;
from your throne you pronounced a just decision.
9:5 You terrified the nations with your battle cry;
you destroyed the wicked;
you permanently wiped out all memory of them.
9:6 The enemy's cities have been reduced to permanent ruins;
you destroyed their cities;
all memory of the enemies has perished.
9:7 But the LORD rules forever;
he reigns in a just manner.
9:8 He judges the world fairly;
he makes just legal decisions for the nations.
9:9 Consequently the LORD provides safety for the oppressed;
he provides safety in times of trouble.
9:10 Your loyal followers trust in you,
for you, LORD, do not abandon those who seek your help.
9:11 Sing praises to the LORD, who rules in Zion!
Tell the nations what he has done!
9:12 For the one who takes revenge against murderers took notice of the oppressed;
he did not overlook their cry for help
9:13 when they prayed:
"Have mercy on me, LORD!
See how I am oppressed by those who hate me,
O one who can snatch me away from the gates of death!
9:14 Then I will tell about all your praiseworthy acts;
in the gates of Daughter Zion I will rejoice because of your deliverance."
9:15 The nations fell into the pit they had made;
their feet were caught in the net they had hidden.
9:16 The LORD revealed himself;
he accomplished justice;
the wicked were ensnared by their own actions. (Higgaion. Selah)
9:17 The wicked are turned back and sent to Sheol;
this is the destiny of all the nations that ignore God,
9:18 for the needy are not permanently ignored,
the hopes of the oppressed are not forever dashed.
9:19 Rise up, LORD!
Don't let men be defiant!
May the nations be judged in your presence!
9:20 Terrify them, LORD!
Let the nations know they are mere mortals! (Selah)

Psalm 10

10:1 Why, LORD, do you stand far off?
Why do you pay no attention during times of trouble?
10:2 The wicked arrogantly chase the oppressed;
the oppressed are trapped by the schemes the wicked have dreamed up.
10:3 Yes, the wicked man boasts because he gets what he wants;
the one who robs others curses and rejects the LORD.
10:4 The wicked man is so arrogant he always thinks,
"God won't hold me accountable; he doesn't care."

10:5 He is secure at all times.
He has no regard for your commands;
he disdains all his enemies.
10:6 He says to himself,
"I will never be upended,
because I experience no calamity."
10:7 His mouth is full of curses and deceptive, harmful words;
his tongue injures and destroys.
10:8 He waits in ambush near the villages;
in hidden places he kills the innocent.
His eyes look for some unfortunate victim.
10:9 He lies in ambush in a hidden place, like a lion in a thicket;
he lies in ambush, waiting to catch the oppressed;
he catches the oppressed by pulling in his net.
10:10 His victims are crushed and beaten down;
they are trapped in his sturdy nets.
10:11 He says to himself,
"God overlooks it;
he does not pay attention;
he never notices."
10:12 Rise up, LORD!
O God, strike him down!
Do not forget the oppressed!
10:13 Why does the wicked man reject God?
He says to himself, "You will not hold me accountable."
10:14 You have taken notice,
for you always see one who inflicts pain and suffering.
The unfortunate victim entrusts his cause to you;
you deliver the fatherless.
10:15 Break the arm of the wicked and evil man!
Hold him accountable for his wicked deeds,
which he thought you would not discover.
10:16 The LORD rules forever!
The nations are driven out of his land.
10:17 LORD, you have heard the request of the oppressed;
you make them feel secure because you listen to their prayer.
10:18 You defend the fatherless and oppressed,
so that mere mortals may no longer terrorize them.

Psalm 11

For the music director; by David.
11:1 In the LORD I have taken shelter.
How can you say to me,
"Flee to a mountain like a bird!
11:2 For look, the wicked prepare their bows,
they put their arrows on the strings,
to shoot in the darkness at the morally upright.
11:3 When the foundations are destroyed,
what can the godly accomplish?"
11:4 The LORD is in his holy temple;
the LORD's throne is in heaven.
His eyes watch;
his eyes examine all people.
11:5 The LORD approves of the godly,
but he hates the wicked and those who love to do violence.
11:6 May the LORD rain down burning coals and brimstone on the wicked!
A whirlwind is what they deserve!
11:7 Certainly the LORD is just;
he rewards godly deeds;
the upright will experience his favor.

Psalm 12

For the music director; according to the *sheminith* style; a psalm of David.
12:1 Deliver, LORD!
For the godly have disappeared;
people of integrity have vanished.
12:2 People lie to one another;
they flatter and deceive.
12:3 May the LORD cut off all flattering lips,
and the tongue that boasts!
12:4 They say, "We speak persuasively;
we know how to flatter and boast.
Who is our master?"
12:5 "Because of the violence done to the oppressed,
because of the painful cries of the needy,
I will spring into action," says the LORD.
"I will provide the safety they so desperately desire."
12:6 The LORD's words are absolutely reliable.
They are as untainted as silver purified in a furnace on the ground,
where it is thoroughly refined.
12:7 You, LORD, will protect them;
you will continually shelter each one from these evil people,
12:8 for the wicked seem to be everywhere,

when people promote evil.

Psalm 13

For the music director; a psalm of David.

13:1 How long, LORD, will you continue to ignore me?
How long will you pay no attention to me?
13:2 How long must I worry,
and suffer in broad daylight?
How long will my enemy gloat over me?
13:3 Look at me! Answer me, O LORD my God!
Revive me, or else I will die!
13:4 Then my enemy will say, "I have defeated him!"
Then my foes will rejoice because I am upended.
13:5 But I trust in your faithfulness.
May I rejoice because of your deliverance!
13:6 I will sing praises to the LORD
when he vindicates me.

Psalm 14

For the music director; by David.

14:1 Fools say to themselves, "There is no God."
They sin and commit evil deeds;
none of them does what is right.
14:2 The LORD looks down from heaven at the human race,
to see if there is anyone who is wise and seeks God.
14:3 Everyone rejects God;
they are all morally corrupt.
None of them does what is right,
not even one!
14:4 All those who behave wickedly do not understand –
those who devour my people as if they were eating bread,
and do not call out to the LORD.
14:5 They are absolutely terrified,
for God defends the godly.
14:6 You want to humiliate the oppressed,
even though the LORD is their shelter.
14:7 I wish the deliverance of Israel would come from Zion!
When the LORD restores the well-being of his people,
may Jacob rejoice,
may Israel be happy!

Psalm 15

A psalm of David.

15:1 LORD, who may be a guest in your home?
Who may live on your holy hill?
15:2 Whoever lives a blameless life,
does what is right,
and speaks honestly.
15:3 He does not slander,
or do harm to others,
or insult his neighbor.
15:4 He despises a reprobate,
but honors the LORD's loyal followers.
He makes firm commitments and does not renege on his promise.
15:5 He does not charge interest when he lends his money.
He does not take bribes to testify against the innocent.
The one who lives like this will never be upended.

Psalm 16

A prayer of David.

16:1 Protect me, O God, for I have taken shelter in you.
16:2 I say to the LORD, "You are the Lord,
my only source of well-being."
16:3 As for God's chosen people who are in the land,
and the leading officials I admired so much –
16:4 their troubles multiply,
they desire other gods.
I will not pour out drink offerings of blood to their gods,
nor will I make vows in the name of their gods.
16:5 LORD, you give me stability and prosperity;
you make my future secure.
16:6 It is as if I have been given fertile fields
or received a beautiful tract of land.
16:7 I will praise the LORD who guides me;
yes, during the night I reflect and learn.
16:8 I constantly trust in the LORD;
because he is at my right hand, I will not be upended.
16:9 So my heart rejoices
and I am happy;
My life is safe.
16:10 You will not abandon me to Sheol;
you will not allow your faithful follower to see the Pit.
16:11 You lead me in the path of life;
I experience absolute joy in your presence;
you always give me sheer delight.

Psalm 17

A prayer of David.

17:1 LORD, consider my just cause!
Pay attention to my cry for help!
Listen to the prayer
I sincerely offer!
17:2 Make a just decision on my behalf!
Decide what is right!
17:3 You have scrutinized my inner motives;
you have examined me during the night.
You have carefully evaluated me, but you find no sin.
I am determined I will say nothing sinful.
17:4 As for the actions of people –
just as you have commanded,
I have not followed in the footsteps of violent men.
17:5 I carefully obey your commands;
I do not deviate from them.
17:6 I call to you for you will answer me, O God.
Listen to me!
Hear what I say!
17:7 Accomplish awesome, faithful deeds,
you who powerfully deliver those who look to you for protection from their enemies.
17:8 Protect me as you would protect the pupil of your eye!
Hide me in the shadow of your wings!
17:9 Protect me from the wicked men who attack me,
my enemies who crowd around me for the kill.
17:10 They are calloused;
they speak arrogantly.
17:11 They attack me, now they surround me;
they intend to throw me to the ground.
17:12 He is like a lion that wants to tear its prey to bits,
like a young lion crouching in hidden places.
17:13 Rise up, LORD!
Confront him! Knock him down!
Use your sword to rescue me from the wicked man!
17:14 LORD, use your power to deliver me from these murderers,
from the murderers of this world!
They enjoy prosperity;
you overwhelm them with the riches they desire.
They have many children,
and leave their wealth to their offspring.
17:15 As for me, because I am innocent I will see your face;
when I awake you will reveal yourself to me.

Psalm 18

For the music director; by the LORD's servant David, who sang to the LORD the words of this song when the LORD rescued him from the power of all his enemies, including Saul.

18:1 He said:
"I love you, LORD, my source of strength!
18:2 The LORD is my high ridge, my stronghold, my deliverer.
My God is my rocky summit where I take shelter,
my shield, the horn that saves me, and my refuge.
18:3 I called to the LORD, who is worthy of praise,
and I was delivered from my enemies.
18:4 The waves of death engulfed me,
the currents of chaos overwhelmed me.
18:5 The ropes of Sheol tightened around me,
the snares of death trapped me.
18:6 In my distress I called to the LORD;
I cried out to my God.
From his heavenly temple he heard my voice;
he listened to my cry for help.
18:7 The earth heaved and shook;
the roots of the mountains trembled;
they heaved because he was angry.
18:8 Smoke ascended from his nose;
fire devoured as it came from his mouth;
he hurled down fiery coals.
18:9 He made the sky sink as he descended;
a thick cloud was under his feet.
18:10 He mounted a winged angel and flew;
he glided on the wings of the wind.
18:11 He shrouded himself in darkness,
in thick rain clouds.
18:12 From the brightness in front of him came
hail and fiery coals.
18:13 The LORD thundered in the sky;
the sovereign One shouted.
18:14 He shot his arrows and scattered them,
many lightning bolts and routed them.
18:15 The depths of the sea were exposed;
the inner regions of the world were uncovered
by your battle cry, LORD,
by the powerful breath from your nose.

18:16 He reached down from above and took hold of me;
he pulled me from the surging water.
18:17 He rescued me from my strong enemy,
from those who hate me,
for they were too strong for me.
18:18 They confronted me in my day of calamity,
but the LORD helped me.
18:19 He brought me out into a wide open place;
he delivered me because he was pleased with me.
18:20 The LORD repaid me for my godly deeds;
he rewarded my blameless behavior.
18:21 For I have obeyed the LORD's commands;
I have not rebelled against my God.
18:22 For I am aware of all his regulations,
and I do not reject his rules.
18:23 I was innocent before him,
and kept myself from sinning.
18:24 The LORD rewarded me for my godly deeds;
he took notice of my blameless behavior.
18:25 You prove to be loyal to one who is faithful;
you prove to be trustworthy to one who is innocent.
18:26 You prove to be reliable to one who is blameless,
but you prove to be deceptive to one who is perverse.
18:27 For you deliver oppressed people,
but you bring down those who have a proud look.
18:28 Indeed, you are my lamp, LORD.
My God illuminates the darkness around me.
18:29 Indeed, with your help I can charge against an army;
by my God's power I can jump over a wall.
18:30 The one true God acts in a faithful manner;
the LORD's promise is reliable;
he is a shield to all who take shelter in him.
18:31 Indeed, who is God besides the LORD?
Who is a protector besides our God?
18:32 The one true God gives me strength;
he removes the obstacles in my way.
18:33 He gives me the agility of a deer;
he enables me to negotiate the rugged terrain.
18:34 He trains my hands for battle;
my arms can bend even the strongest bow.
18:35 You give me your protective shield;
your right hand supports me;
your willingness to help enables me to prevail.
18:36 You widen my path;
my feet do not slip.
18:37 I chase my enemies and catch them;
I do not turn back until I wipe them out.
18:38 I beat them to death;
they fall at my feet.
18:39 You give me strength for battle;
you make my foes kneel before me.
18:40 You make my enemies retreat;
I destroy those who hate me.
18:41 They cry out, but there is no one to help them;
they cry out to the LORD, but he does not answer them.
18:42 I grind them as fine windblown dust;
I beat them underfoot like clay in the streets.
18:43 You rescue me from a hostile army;
you make me a leader of nations;
people over whom I had no authority are now my subjects.
18:44 When they hear of my exploits, they submit to me.
Foreigners are powerless before me;
18:45 foreigners lose their courage;
they shake with fear as they leave their strongholds.
18:46 The LORD is alive!
My protector is praiseworthy!
The God who delivers me is exalted as king!
18:47 The one true God completely vindicates me;
he makes nations submit to me.
18:48 He delivers me from my enemies;
you snatch me away from those who
attack me;
you rescue me from violent men.
18:49 So I will give you thanks before the nations, O LORD!
I will sing praises to you!
18:50 He gives his chosen king magnificent victories;
he is faithful to his chosen ruler,
to David and his descendants forever."
Psalm 19
For the music director; a psalm of David.
19:1 The heavens declare the glory of God;
the sky displays his handiwork.
19:2 Day after day it speaks out;

night after night it reveals his greatness.
19:3 There is no actual speech or word,
nor is its voice literally heard.
19:4 Yet its voice echoes throughout the earth;
its words carry to the distant horizon.
In the sky he has pitched a tent for the sun.
19:5 Like a bridegroom it emerges from its chamber;
like a strong man it enjoys running its course.
19:6 It emerges from the distant horizon,
and goes from one end of the sky to the other;
nothing can escape its heat.
19:7 The law of the LORD is perfect
and preserves one's life.
The rules set down by the LORD are reliable
and impart wisdom to the inexperienced.
19:8 The LORD's precepts are fair
and make one joyful.
The LORD's commands are pure
and give insight for life.
19:9 The commands to fear the LORD are right
and endure forever.
The judgments given by the LORD are trustworthy
and absolutely just.
19:10 They are of greater value than gold,
than even a great amount of pure gold;
they bring greater delight than honey,
than even the sweetest honey from a honeycomb.
19:11 Yes, your servant finds moral guidance there;
those who obey them receive a rich reward.
19:12 Who can know all his errors?
Please do not punish me for sins I am unaware of.
19:13 Moreover, keep me from committing flagrant sins;
do not allow such sins to control me.
Then I will be blameless,
and innocent of blatant rebellion.
19:14 May my words and my thoughts
be acceptable in your sight,
O LORD, my sheltering rock and my redeemer.
Psalm 20
For the music director; a psalm of David.
20:1 May the LORD answer you when you are in trouble;
may the God of Jacob make you secure!
20:2 May he send you help from his temple;
from Zion may he give you support!
20:3 May he take notice of your offerings;
may he accept your burnt sacrifice! (Selah)
20:4 May he grant your heart's desire;
may he bring all your plans to pass!
20:5 Then we will shout for joy over your victory;
we will rejoice in the name of our God!
May the LORD grant all your requests!
20:6 Now I am sure that the LORD will deliver his chosen king;
he will intervene for him from his holy heavenly temple,
and display his mighty ability to deliver.
20:7 Some trust in chariots and others in horses,
but we depend on the LORD our God.
20:8 They will fall down,
but we will stand firm.
20:9 The LORD will deliver the king;
he will answer us when we call to him for help!
Psalm 21
For the music director; a psalm of David.
21:1 O LORD, the king rejoices in the strength you give;
he takes great delight in the deliverance you provide.
21:2 You grant him his heart's desire;
you do not refuse his request. (Selah)
21:3 For you bring him rich blessings;
you place a golden crown on his head.
21:4 He asked you to sustain his life,
and you have granted him long life and an enduring dynasty.
21:5 Your deliverance brings him great honor;
you give him majestic splendor.
21:6 For you grant him lasting blessings;
you give him great joy by allowing him into your presence.
21:7 For the king trusts in the LORD,
and because of the sovereign LORD's faithfulness he is not upended.
21:8 You prevail over all your enemies;
your power is too great for those who hate you.
21:9 You burn them up like a fiery furnace when you appear;
the LORD angrily devours them;
the fire consumes them.
21:10 You destroy their offspring from the earth,
their descendants from among the human race.

21:11 Yes, they intend to do you harm;
they dream up a scheme, but they do not succeed.
21:12 For you make them retreat
when you shoot your arrows at them.
21:13 Rise up, O LORD, in strength!
We will sing and praise your power!
Psalm 22
For the music director; according to the tune "Morning Doe;" a psalm of
David.
22:1 My God, my God, why have you abandoned me?
I groan in prayer, but help seems far away.
22:2 My God, I cry out during the day,
but you do not answer,
and during the night my prayers do not let up.
22:3 You are holy;
you sit as king receiving the praises of Israel.
22:4 In you our ancestors trusted;
they trusted in you and you rescued them.
22:5 To you they cried out, and they were saved;
in you they trusted and they were not disappointed.
22:6 But I am a worm, not a man;
people insult me and despise me.
22:7 All who see me taunt me;
they mock me and shake their heads.
22:8 They say,
"Commit yourself to the LORD!
Let the LORD rescue him!
Let the LORD deliver him, for he delights in him."
22:9 Yes, you are the one who brought me out from the womb
and made me feel secure on my mother's breasts.
22:10 I have been dependent on you since birth;
from the time I came out of my mother's womb you have been my God.
22:11 Do not remain far away from me,
for trouble is near and I have no one to help me.
22:12 Many bulls surround me;
powerful bulls of Bashan hem me in.
22:13 They open their mouths to devour me
like a roaring lion that rips its prey.
22:14 My strength drains away like water;
all my bones are dislocated;
my heart is like wax;
it melts away inside me.
22:15 The roof of my mouth is as dry as a piece of pottery;
my tongue sticks to my gums.
You set me in the dust of death.
22:16 Yes, wild dogs surround me –
a gang of evil men crowd around me;
like a lion they pin my hands and feet.
22:17 I can count all my bones;
my enemies are gloating over me in triumph.
22:18 They are dividing up my clothes among themselves;
they are rolling dice for my garments.
22:19 But you, O LORD, do not remain far away!
You are my source of strength! Hurry and help me!
22:20 Deliver me from the sword!
Save my life from the claws of the wild dogs!
22:21 Rescue me from the mouth of the lion,
and from the horns of the wild oxen!
You have answered me!
22:22 I will declare your name to my countrymen!
In the middle of the assembly I will praise you!
22:23 You loyal followers of the LORD, praise him!
All you descendants of Jacob, honor him!
All you descendants of Israel, stand in awe of him!
22:24 For he did not despise or detest the suffering of the oppressed;
he did not ignore him;
when he cried out to him, he responded.
22:25 You are the reason I offer praise in the great assembly;
I will fulfill my promises before the LORD's loyal followers.
22:26 Let the oppressed eat and be filled!
Let those who seek his help praise the LORD!
May you live forever!
22:27 Let all the people of the earth acknowledge the LORD and turn to
him!
Let all the nations worship you!
22:28 For the LORD is king
and rules over the nations.
22:29 All of the thriving people of the earth will join the celebration and
worship;
all those who are descending into the grave will bow before him,
including those who cannot preserve their lives.
22:30 A whole generation will serve him;
they will tell the next generation about the sovereign Lord.

22:31 They will come and tell about his saving deeds;
they will tell a future generation what he has accomplished.
Psalm 23
A psalm of David.
23:1 The LORD is my shepherd,
I lack nothing.
23:2 He takes me to lush pastures,
he leads me to refreshing water.
23:3 He restores my strength.
He leads me down the right paths
for the sake of his reputation.
23:4 Even when I must walk through the darkest valley,
I fear no danger,
for you are with me;
your rod and your staff reassure me.
23:5 You prepare a feast before me
in plain sight of my enemies.
You refresh my head with oil;
my cup is completely full.
23:6 Surely your goodness and faithfulness will pursue me all my days,
and I will live in the LORD's house for the rest of my life.
Psalm 24
A psalm of David.
24:1 The LORD owns the earth and all it contains,
the world and all who live in it.
24:2 For he set its foundation upon the seas,
and established it upon the ocean currents.
24:3 Who is allowed to ascend the mountain of the LORD?
Who may go up to his holy dwelling place?
24:4 The one whose deeds are blameless
and whose motives are pure,
who does not lie,
or make promises with no intention of keeping them.
24:5 Such godly people are rewarded by the LORD,
and vindicated by the God who delivers them.
24:6 Such purity characterizes the people who seek his favor,
Jacob's descendants, who pray to him. (Selah)
24:7 Look up, you gates!
Rise up, you eternal doors!
Then the majestic king will enter!
24:8 Who is this majestic king?
The LORD who is strong and mighty!
The LORD who is mighty in battle!
24:9 Look up, you gates!
Rise up, you eternal doors!
Then the majestic king will enter!
24:10 Who is this majestic king?
The LORD who commands armies!
He is the majestic king! (Selah)
Psalm 25
By David.
25:1 O LORD, I come before you in prayer.
25:2 My God, I trust in you.
Please do not let me be humiliated;
do not let my enemies triumphantly rejoice over me!
25:3 Certainly none who rely on you will be humiliated.
Those who deal in treachery will be thwarted and humiliated.
25:4 Make me understand your ways, O LORD!
Teach me your paths!
25:5 Guide me into your truth and teach me.
For you are the God who delivers me;
on you I rely all day long.
25:6 Remember your compassionate and faithful deeds, O LORD,
for you have always acted in this manner.
25:7 Do not hold against me the sins of my youth or my rebellious acts!
Because you are faithful to me, extend to me your favor, O LORD!
25:8 The LORD is both kind and fair;
that is why he teaches sinners the right way to live.
25:9 May he show the humble what is right!
May he teach the humble his way!
25:10 The LORD always proves faithful and reliable
to those who follow the demands of his covenant.
25:11 For the sake of your reputation, O LORD,
forgive my sin, because it is great.
25:12 The LORD shows his faithful followers
the way they should live.
25:13 They experience his favor;
their descendants inherit the land.
25:14 The LORD's loyal followers receive his guidance,
and he reveals his covenantal demands to them.
25:15 I continually look to the LORD for help,
for he will free my feet from the enemy's net.
25:16 Turn toward me and have mercy on me,

for I am alone and oppressed!
25:17 Deliver me from my distress;
rescue me from my suffering!
25:18 See my pain and suffering!
Forgive all my sins!
25:19 Watch my enemies, for they outnumber me;
they hate me and want to harm me.
25:20 Protect me and deliver me!
Please do not let me be humiliated,
for I have taken shelter in you!
25:21 May integrity and godliness protect me,
for I rely on you!
25:22 O God, rescue Israel
from all their distress!
Psalm 26
By David.
26:1 Vindicate me, O LORD,
for I have integrity,
and I trust in the LORD without wavering.
26:2 Examine me, O LORD, and test me!
Evaluate my inner thoughts and motives!
26:3 For I am ever aware of your faithfulness,
and your loyalty continually motivates me.
26:4 I do not associate with deceitful men,
or consort with those who are dishonest.
26:5 I hate the mob of evil men,
and do not associate with the wicked.
26:6 I maintain a pure lifestyle,
so I can appear before your altar, O LORD,
26:7 to give you thanks,
and to tell about all your amazing deeds.
26:8 O LORD, I love the temple where you live,
the place where your splendor is revealed.
26:9 Do not sweep me away with sinners,
or execute me along with violent people,
26:10 who are always ready to do wrong
or offer a bribe.
26:11 But I have integrity!
Rescue me and have mercy on me!
26:12 I am safe,
and among the worshipers I will praise the LORD.
Psalm 27
By David.
27:1 The LORD delivers and vindicates me!
I fear no one!
The LORD protects my life!
I am afraid of no one!
27:2 When evil men attack me
to devour my flesh,
when my adversaries and enemies attack me,
they stumble and fall.
27:3 Even when an army is deployed against me,
I do not fear.
Even when war is imminent,
I remain confident.
27:4 I have asked the LORD for one thing –
this is what I desire!
I want to live in the LORD's house all the days of my life,
so I can gaze at the splendor of the LORD
and contemplate in his temple.
27:5 He will surely give me shelter in the day of danger;
he will hide me in his home;
he will place me on an inaccessible rocky summit.
27:6 Now I will triumph
over my enemies who surround me!
I will offer sacrifices in his dwelling place and shout for joy!
I will sing praises to the LORD!
27:7 Hear me, O LORD, when I cry out!
Have mercy on me and answer me!
27:8 My heart tells me to pray to you,
and I do pray to you, O LORD.
27:9 Do not reject me!
Do not push your servant away in anger!
You are my deliverer!
Do not forsake or abandon me,
O God who vindicates me!
27:10 Even if my father and mother abandoned me,
the LORD would take me in.
27:11 Teach me how you want me to live;
lead me along a level path because of those who wait to ambush me!
27:12 Do not turn me over to my enemies,
for false witnesses who want to destroy me testify against me.
27:13 Where would I be if I did not believe I would experience

the LORD's favor in the land of the living?
27:14 Rely on the LORD!
Be strong and confident!
Rely on the LORD!
Psalm 28
By David.
28:1 To you, O LORD, I cry out!
My protector, do not ignore me!
If you do not respond to me,
I will join those who are descending into the grave.
28:2 Hear my plea for mercy when I cry out to you for help,
when I lift my hands toward your holy temple!
28:3 Do not drag me away with evil men,
with those who behave wickedly,
who talk so friendly to their neighbors,
while they plan to harm them!
28:4 Pay them back for their evil deeds!
Pay them back for what they do!
Punish them!
28:5 For they do not understand the LORD's actions,
or the way he carries out justice.
The LORD will permanently demolish them.
28:6 The LORD deserves praise,
for he has heard my plea for mercy!
28:7 The LORD strengthens and protects me;
I trust in him with all my heart.
I am rescued and my heart is full of joy;
I will sing to him in gratitude.
28:8 The LORD strengthens his people;
he protects and delivers his chosen king.
28:9 Deliver your people!
Empower the nation that belongs to you!
Care for them like a shepherd and carry them in your arms at all times!
Psalm 29
A psalm of David.
29:1 Acknowledge the LORD, you heavenly beings,
acknowledge the LORD's majesty and power!
29:2 Acknowledge the majesty of the LORD's reputation!
Worship the LORD in holy attire!
29:3 The LORD's shout is heard over the water;
the majestic God thunders,
the LORD appears over the surging water.
29:4 The LORD's shout is powerful,
the LORD's shout is majestic.
29:5 The LORD's shout breaks the cedars,
the LORD shatters the cedars of Lebanon.
29:6 He makes Lebanon skip like a calf
and Sirion like a young ox.
29:7 The LORD's shout strikes with flaming fire.
29:8 The LORD's shout shakes the wilderness,
the LORD shakes the wilderness of Kadesh.
29:9 The LORD's shout bends the large trees
and strips the leaves from the forests.
Everyone in his temple says, "Majestic!"
29:10 The LORD sits enthroned over the engulfing waters,
the LORD sits enthroned as the eternal king.
29:11 The LORD gives his people strength;
the LORD grants his people security.
Psalm 30
A psalm – a song used at the dedication of the temple; by David.
30:1 I will praise you, O LORD, for you lifted me up,
and did not allow my enemies to gloat over me.
30:2 O LORD my God,
I cried out to you and you healed me.
30:3 O LORD, you pulled me up from Sheol;
you rescued me from among those descending into the grave.
30:4 Sing to the LORD, you faithful followers of his;
give thanks to his holy name.
30:5 For his anger lasts only a brief moment,
and his good favor restores one's life.
One may experience sorrow during the night,
but joy arrives in the morning.
30:6 In my self-confidence I said,
"I will never be upended."
30:7 O LORD, in your good favor you made me secure.
Then you rejected me and I was terrified.
30:8 To you, O LORD, I cried out;
I begged the Lord for mercy:
30:9 "What profit is there in taking my life,
in my descending into the Pit?
Can the dust of the grave praise you?
Can it declare your loyalty?
30:10 Hear, O LORD, and have mercy on me!

O Lord, deliver me!"
30:11 Then you turned my lament into dancing;
you removed my sackcloth and covered me with joy.
30:12 So now my heart will sing to you and not be silent;
O Lord my God, I will always give thanks to you.
Psalm 31
For the music director; a psalm of David.
31:1 In you, O Lord, I have taken shelter!
Never let me be humiliated!
Vindicate me by rescuing me!
31:2 Listen to me!
Quickly deliver me!
Be my protector and refuge,
a stronghold where I can be safe!
31:3 For you are my high ridge and my stronghold;
for the sake of your own reputation you lead me and guide me.
31:4 You will free me from the net they hid for me,
for you are my place of refuge.
31:5 Into your hand I entrust my life;
you will rescue me, O Lord, the faithful God.
31:6 I hate those who serve worthless idols,
but I trust in the Lord.
31:7 I will be happy and rejoice in your faithfulness,
because you notice my pain
and you are aware of how distressed I am.
31:8 You do not deliver me over to the power of the enemy;
you enable me to stand in a wide open place.
31:9 Have mercy on me, for I am in distress!
My eyes grow dim from suffering.
I have lost my strength.
31:10 For my life nears its end in pain;
my years draw to a close as I groan.
My strength fails me because of my sin,
and my bones become brittle.
31:11 Because of all my enemies, people disdain me;
my neighbors are appalled by my suffering –
those who know me are horrified by my condition;
those who see me in the street run away from me.
31:12 I am forgotten, like a dead man no one thinks about;
I am regarded as worthless, like a broken jar.
31:13 For I hear what so many are saying,
the terrifying news that comes from every direction.
When they plot together against me,
they figure out how they can take my life.
31:14 But I trust in you, O Lord!
I declare, "You are my God!"
31:15 You determine my destiny!
Rescue me from the power of my enemies and those who chase me.
31:16 Smile on your servant!
Deliver me because of your faithfulness!
31:17 O Lord, do not let me be humiliated,
for I call out to you!
May evil men be humiliated!
May they go wailing to the grave!
31:18 May lying lips be silenced –
lips that speak defiantly against the innocent
with arrogance and contempt!
31:19 How great is your favor,
which you store up for your loyal followers!
In plain sight of everyone you bestow it on those who take shelter in you.
31:20 You hide them with you, where they are safe from the attacks of men;
you conceal them in a shelter, where they are safe from slanderous attacks.
31:21 The Lord deserves praise
for he demonstrated his amazing faithfulness to me when I was besieged by enemies.
31:22 I jumped to conclusions and said,
"I am cut off from your presence!"
But you heard my plea for mercy when I cried out to you for help.
31:23 Love the Lord, all you faithful followers of his!
The Lord protects those who have integrity,
but he pays back in full the one who acts arrogantly.
31:24 Be strong and confident,
all you who wait on the Lord!
Psalm 32
By David; a well-written song.
32:1 How blessed is the one whose rebellious acts are forgiven,
whose sin is pardoned!
32:2 How blessed is the one whose wrongdoing the Lord does not punish,
in whose spirit there is no deceit.
32:3 When I refused to confess my sin,

my whole body wasted away,
while I groaned in pain all day long.
32:4 For day and night you tormented me;
you tried to destroy me in the intense heat of summer. (Selah)
32:5 Then I confessed my sin;
I no longer covered up my wrongdoing.
I said, "I will confess my rebellious acts to the Lord."
And then you forgave my sins. (Selah)
32:6 For this reason every one of your faithful followers should pray to you
while there is a window of opportunity.
Certainly when the surging water rises,
it will not reach them.
32:7 You are my hiding place;
you protect me from distress.
You surround me with shouts of joy from those celebrating deliverance. (Selah)
32:8 I will instruct and teach you about how you should live.
I will advise you as I look you in the eye.
32:9 Do not be like an unintelligent horse or mule,
which will not obey you
unless they are controlled by a bridle and bit.
32:10 An evil person suffers much pain,
but the Lord's faithfulness overwhelms the one who trusts in him.
32:11 Rejoice in the Lord and be happy, you who are godly!
Shout for joy, all you who are morally upright!
Psalm 33
33:1 You godly ones, shout for joy because of the Lord!
It is appropriate for the morally upright to offer him praise.
33:2 Give thanks to the Lord with the harp!
Sing to him to the accompaniment of a ten-stringed instrument!
33:3 Sing to him a new song!
Play skillfully as you shout out your praises to him!
33:4 For the Lord's decrees are just,
and everything he does is fair.
33:5 The Lord promotes equity and justice;
the Lord's faithfulness extends throughout the earth.
33:6 By the Lord's decree the heavens were made;
by a mere word from his mouth all the stars in the sky were created.
33:7 He piles up the water of the sea;
he puts the oceans in storehouses.
33:8 Let the whole earth fear the Lord!
Let all who live in the world stand in awe of him!
33:9 For he spoke, and it came into existence,
he issued the decree, and it stood firm.
33:10 The Lord frustrates the decisions of the nations;
he nullifies the plans of the peoples.
33:11 The Lord's decisions stand forever;
his plans abide throughout the ages.
33:12 How blessed is the nation whose God is the Lord,
the people whom he has chosen to be his special possession.
33:13 The Lord watches from heaven;
he sees all people.
33:14 From the place where he lives he looks carefully
at all the earth's inhabitants.
33:15 He is the one who forms every human heart,
and takes note of all their actions.
33:16 No king is delivered by his vast army;
a warrior is not saved by his great might.
33:17 A horse disappoints those who trust in it for victory;
despite its great strength, it cannot deliver.
33:18 Look, the Lord takes notice of his loyal followers,
those who wait for him to demonstrate his faithfulness
33:19 by saving their lives from death
and sustaining them during times of famine.
33:20 We wait for the Lord;
he is our deliverer and shield.
33:21 For our hearts rejoice in him,
for we trust in his holy name.
33:22 May we experience your faithfulness, O Lord,
for we wait for you.
Psalm 34
Written by David, when he pretended to be insane before Abimelech, causing the king to send him away.
34:1 I will praise the Lord at all times;
my mouth will continually praise him.
34:2 I will boast in the Lord;
let the oppressed hear and rejoice!
34:3 Magnify the Lord with me!
Let's praise his name together!
34:4 I sought the Lord's help and he answered me;
he delivered me from all my fears.
34:5 Those who look to him for help are happy;

their faces are not ashamed.
34:6 This oppressed man cried out and the LORD heard;
he saved him from all his troubles.
34:7 The LORD's angel camps around
the LORD's loyal followers and delivers them.
34:8 Taste and see that the LORD is good!
How blessed is the one who takes shelter in him!
34:9 Remain loyal to the LORD, you chosen people of his,
for his loyal followers lack nothing!
34:10 Even young lions sometimes lack food and are hungry,
but those who seek the LORD lack no good thing.
34:11 Come children! Listen to me!
I will teach you what it means to fear the LORD.
34:12 Do you want to really live?
Would you love to live a long, happy life?
34:13 Then make sure you don't speak evil words
or use deceptive speech!
34:14 Turn away from evil and do what is right!
Strive for peace and promote it!
34:15 The LORD pays attention to the godly
and hears their cry for help.
34:16 But the LORD opposes evildoers
and wipes out all memory of them from the earth.
34:17 The godly cry out and the LORD hears;
he saves them from all their troubles.
34:18 The LORD is near the brokenhearted;
he delivers those who are discouraged.
34:19 The godly face many dangers,
but the LORD saves them from each one of them.
34:20 He protects all his bones;
not one of them is broken.
34:21 Evil people self-destruct;
those who hate the godly are punished.
34:22 The LORD rescues his servants;
all who take shelter in him escape punishment.

Psalm 35
By David.
35:1 O LORD, fight those who fight with me!
Attack those who attack me!
35:2 Grab your small shield and large shield,
and rise up to help me!
35:3 Use your spear and lance against those who chase me!
Assure me with these words: "I am your deliverer!"
35:4 May those who seek my life be embarrassed and humiliated!
May those who plan to harm me be turned back and ashamed!
35:5 May they be like wind-driven chaff,
as the LORD's angel attacks them!
35:6 May their path be dark and slippery,
as the LORD's angel chases them!
35:7 I did not harm them, but they hid a net to catch me
and dug a pit to trap me.
35:8 Let destruction take them by surprise!
Let the net they hid catch them!
Let them fall into destruction!
35:9 Then I will rejoice in the LORD
and be happy because of his deliverance.
35:10 With all my strength I will say,
"O LORD, who can compare to you?
You rescue the oppressed from those who try to overpower them;
the oppressed and needy from those who try to rob them."
35:11 Violent men perjure themselves,
and falsely accuse me.
35:12 They repay me evil for the good I have done;
I am overwhelmed with sorrow.
35:13 When they were sick, I wore sackcloth,
and refrained from eating food.
(If I am lying, may my prayers go unanswered!)
35:14 I mourned for them as I would for a friend or my brother.
I bowed down in sorrow as if I were mourning for my mother.
35:15 But when I stumbled, they rejoiced and gathered together;
they gathered together to ambush me.
They tore at me without stopping to rest.
35:16 When I tripped, they taunted me relentlessly,
and tried to bite me.
35:17 O Lord, how long are you going to just stand there and watch this?
Rescue me from their destructive attacks;
guard my life from the young lions!
35:18 Then I will give you thanks in the great assembly;
I will praise you before a large crowd of people!
35:19 Do not let those who are my enemies for no reason gloat over me!
Do not let those who hate me without cause carry out their wicked schemes!
35:20 For they do not try to make peace with others,

but plan ways to deceive those who are unsuspecting.
35:21 They are ready to devour me;
they say, "Aha! Aha! We've got you!"
35:22 But you take notice, LORD!
O Lord, do not remain far away from me!
35:23 Rouse yourself, wake up and vindicate me!
My God and Lord, defend my just cause!
35:24 Vindicate me by your justice, O LORD my God!
Do not let them gloat over me!
35:25 Do not let them say to themselves, "Aha! We have what we wanted!"
Do not let them say, "We have devoured him!"
35:26 May those who want to harm me be totally embarrassed and ashamed!
May those who arrogantly taunt me be covered with shame and humiliation!
35:27 May those who desire my vindication shout for joy and rejoice!
May they continually say, "May the LORD be praised, for he wants his servant to be secure."
35:28 Then I will tell others about your justice,
and praise you all day long.

Psalm 36
For the music director; written by the LORD's servant, David; an oracle.
36:1 An evil man is rebellious to the core.
He does not fear God,
36:2 for he is too proud
to recognize and give up his sin.
36:3 The words he speaks are sinful and deceitful;
he does not care about doing what is wise and right.
36:4 He plans ways to sin while he lies in bed;
he is committed to a sinful lifestyle;
he does not reject what is evil.
36:5 O LORD, your loyal love reaches to the sky;
your faithfulness to the clouds.
36:6 Your justice is like the highest mountains,
your fairness like the deepest sea;
you preserve mankind and the animal kingdom.
36:7 How precious is your loyal love, O God!
The human race finds shelter under your wings.
36:8 They are filled with food from your house,
and you allow them to drink from the river of your delicacies.
36:9 For you are the one who gives
and sustains life.
36:10 Extend your loyal love to your faithful followers,
and vindicate the morally upright!
36:11 Do not let arrogant men overtake me,
or let evil men make me homeless!
36:12 I can see the evildoers! They have fallen!
They have been knocked down and are unable to get up!

Psalm 37
By David.
37:1 Do not fret when wicked men seem to succeed!
Do not envy evildoers!
37:2 For they will quickly dry up like grass,
and wither away like plants.
37:3 Trust in the LORD and do what is right!
Settle in the land and maintain your integrity!
37:4 Then you will take delight in the LORD,
and he will answer your prayers.
37:5 Commit your future to the LORD!
Trust in him, and he will act on your behalf.
37:6 He will vindicate you in broad daylight,
and publicly defend your just cause.
37:7 Wait patiently for the LORD!
Wait confidently for him!
Do not fret over the apparent success of a sinner,
a man who carries out wicked schemes!
37:8 Do not be angry and frustrated!
Do not fret! That only leads to trouble!
37:9 Wicked men will be wiped out,
but those who rely on the LORD are the ones who will possess the land.
37:10 Evil men will soon disappear;
you will stare at the spot where they once were, but they will be gone.
37:11 But the oppressed will possess the land
and enjoy great prosperity.
37:12 Evil men plot against the godly
and viciously attack them.
37:13 The Lord laughs in disgust at them,
for he knows that their day is coming.
37:14 Evil men draw their swords
and prepare their bows,
to bring down the oppressed and needy,
and to slaughter those who are godly.

37:15 Their swords will pierce their own hearts,
and their bows will be broken.
37:16 The little bit that a godly man owns is better than
the wealth of many evil men,
37:17 for evil men will lose their power,
but the LORD sustains the godly.
37:18 The LORD watches over the innocent day by day
and they possess a permanent inheritance.
37:19 They will not be ashamed when hard times come;
when famine comes they will have enough to eat.
37:20 But evil men will die;
the LORD's enemies will be incinerated –
they will go up in smoke.
37:21 Evil men borrow, but do not repay their debt,
but the godly show compassion and are generous.
37:22 Surely those favored by the LORD will possess the land,
but those rejected by him will be wiped out.
37:23 The LORD grants success to the one
whose behavior he finds commendable.
37:24 Even if he trips, he will not fall headlong,
for the LORD holds his hand.
37:25 I was once young, now I am old.
I have never seen a godly man abandoned,
or his children forced to search for food.
37:26 All day long he shows compassion and lends to others,
and his children are blessed.
37:27 Turn away from evil! Do what is right!
Then you will enjoy lasting security.
37:28 For the LORD promotes justice,
and never abandons his faithful followers.
They are permanently secure,
but the children of evil men are wiped out.
37:29 The godly will possess the land
and will dwell in it permanently.
37:30 The godly speak wise words
and promote justice.
37:31 The law of their God controls their thinking;
their feet do not slip.
37:32 Evil men set an ambush for the godly
and try to kill them.
37:33 But the LORD does not surrender the godly,
or allow them to be condemned in a court of law.
37:34 Rely on the LORD! Obey his commands!
Then he will permit you to possess the land;
you will see the demise of evil men.
37:35 I have seen ruthless evil men
growing in influence, like a green tree grows in its native soil.
37:36 But then one passes by, and suddenly they have disappeared!
I looked for them, but they could not be found.
37:37 Take note of the one who has integrity! Observe the godly!
For the one who promotes peace has a future.
37:38 Sinful rebels are totally destroyed;
evil men have no future.
37:39 But the LORD delivers the godly;
he protects them in times of trouble.
37:40 The LORD helps them and rescues them;
he rescues them from evil men and delivers them,
for they seek his protection.
Psalm 38
A psalm of David, written to get God's attention.
38:1 O LORD, do not continue to rebuke me in your anger!
Do not continue to punish me in your raging fury!
38:2 For your arrows pierce me,
and your hand presses me down.
38:3 My whole body is sick because of your judgment;
I am deprived of health because of my sin.
38:4 For my sins overwhelm me;
like a heavy load, they are too much for me to bear.
38:5 My wounds are infected and starting to smell,
because of my foolish sins.
38:6 I am dazed and completely humiliated;
all day long I walk around mourning.
38:7 For I am overcome with shame
and my whole body is sick.
38:8 I am numb with pain and severely battered;
I groan loudly because of the anxiety I feel.
38:9 O Lord, you understand my heart's desire;
my groaning is not hidden from you.
38:10 My heart beats quickly;
my strength leaves me;
I can hardly see.
38:11 Because of my condition, even my friends and acquaintances keep
their distance;

my neighbors stand far away.
38:12 Those who seek my life try to entrap me;
those who want to harm me speak destructive words;
all day long they say deceitful things.
38:13 But I am like a deaf man – I hear nothing;
I am like a mute who cannot speak.
38:14 I am like a man who cannot hear
and is incapable of arguing his defense.
38:15 Yet I wait for you, O LORD!
You will respond, O Lord, my God!
38:16 I have prayed for deliverance, because otherwise they will gloat
over me;
when my foot slips they will arrogantly taunt me.
38:17 For I am about to stumble,
and I am in constant pain.
38:18 Yes, I confess my wrongdoing,
and I am concerned about my sins.
38:19 But those who are my enemies for no reason are numerous;
those who hate me without cause outnumber me.
38:20 They repay me evil for the good I have done;
though I have tried to do good to them, they hurl accusations at me.
38:21 Do not abandon me, O LORD!
My God, do not remain far away from me!
38:22 Hurry and help me, O Lord, my deliverer!
Psalm 39
For the music director, Jeduthun; a psalm of David.
39:1 I decided, "I will watch what I say
and make sure I do not sin with my tongue.
I will put a muzzle over my mouth
while in the presence of an evil man."
39:2 I was stone silent;
I held back the urge to speak.
My frustration grew;
39:3 my anxiety intensified.
As I thought about it, I became impatient.
Finally I spoke these words:
39:4 "O LORD, help me understand my mortality
and the brevity of life!
Let me realize how quickly my life will pass!
39:5 Look, you make my days short-lived,
and my life span is nothing from your perspective.
Surely all people, even those who seem secure, are nothing but vapor.
39:6 Surely people go through life as mere ghosts.
Surely they accumulate worthless wealth
without knowing who will eventually haul it away."
39:7 But now, O Lord, upon what am I relying?
You are my only hope!
39:8 Deliver me from all my sins of rebellion!
Do not make me the object of fools' insults!
39:9 I am silent and cannot open my mouth
because of what you have done.
39:10 Please stop wounding me!
You have almost beaten me to death!
39:11 You severely discipline people for their sins;
like a moth you slowly devour their strength.
Surely all people are a mere vapor. (Selah)
39:12 Hear my prayer, O LORD!
Listen to my cry for help!
Do not ignore my sobbing!
For I am dependent on you, like one residing outside his native land;
I am at your mercy, just as all my ancestors were.
39:13 Turn your angry gaze away from me, so I can be happy
before I pass away.
Psalm 40
For the music director; By David, a psalm.
40:1 I relied completely on the LORD,
and he turned toward me
and heard my cry for help.
40:2 He lifted me out of the watery pit,
out of the slimy mud.
He placed my feet on a rock
and gave me secure footing.
40:3 He gave me reason to sing a new song,
praising our God.
May many see what God has done,
so that they might swear allegiance to him and trust in the LORD!
40:4 How blessed is the one who trusts in the LORD
and does not seek help from the proud or from liars!
40:5 O LORD, my God, you have accomplished many things;
you have done amazing things and carried out your purposes for us.
No one can thwart you!
I want to declare them and talk about them,
but they are too numerous to recount!

40:6 Receiving sacrifices and offerings are not your primary concern.
You make that quite clear to me!
You do not ask for burnt sacrifices and sin offerings.
40:7 Then I say,
"Look! I come!
What is written in the scroll pertains to me.
40:8 I want to do what pleases you, my God.
Your law dominates my thoughts."
40:9 I have told the great assembly about your justice.
Look! I spare no words!
O LORD, you know this is true.
40:10 I have not failed to tell about your justice;
I spoke about your reliability and deliverance;
I have not neglected to tell the great assembly about your loyal love and faithfulness.
40:11 O LORD, you do not withhold your compassion from me.
May your loyal love and faithfulness continually protect me!
40:12 For innumerable dangers surround me.
My sins overtake me
so I am unable to see;
they outnumber the hairs of my head
so my strength fails me.
40:13 Please be willing, O LORD, to rescue me!
O LORD, hurry and help me!
40:14 May those who are trying to snatch away my life
be totally embarrassed and ashamed!
May those who want to harm me
be turned back and ashamed!
40:15 May those who say to me, "Aha! Aha!"
be humiliated and disgraced!
40:16 May all those who seek you be happy and rejoice in you!
May those who love to experience your deliverance say continually,
"May the LORD be praised!"
40:17 I am oppressed and needy!
May the Lord pay attention to me!
You are my helper and my deliverer!
O my God, do not delay!

Psalm 41
For the music director; a psalm of David.
41:1 How blessed is the one who treats the poor properly!
When trouble comes, the LORD delivers him.
41:2 May the LORD protect him and save his life!
May he be blessed in the land!
Do not turn him over to his enemies!
41:3 The LORD supports him on his sickbed;
you completely heal him from his illness.
41:4 As for me, I said:
"O LORD, have mercy on me!
Heal me, for I have sinned against you!
41:5 My enemies ask this cruel question about me,
'When will he finally die and be forgotten?'
41:6 When someone comes to visit, he pretends to be friendly;
he thinks of ways to defame me,
and when he leaves he slanders me.
41:7 All who hate me whisper insults about me to one another;
they plan ways to harm me.
41:8 They say,
'An awful disease overwhelms him,
and now that he is bed-ridden he will never recover.'
41:9 Even my close friend whom I trusted,
he who shared meals with me, has turned against me.
41:10 As for you, O LORD, have mercy on me and raise me up,
so I can pay them back!"
41:11 By this I know that you are pleased with me,
for my enemy does not triumph over me.
41:12 As for me, you uphold me because of my integrity;
you allow me permanent access to your presence.
41:13 The LORD God of Israel deserves praise
in the future and forevermore!
We agree! We agree!
Book 2(Psalms 42-72)
Psalm 42
For the music director; a well-written song by the Korahites.
42:1 As a deer longs for streams of water,
so I long for you, O God!
42:2 I thirst for God,
for the living God.
I say, "When will I be able to go and appear in God's presence?"
42:3 I cannot eat, I weep day and night;
all day long they say to me, "Where is your God?"
42:4 I will remember and weep!
For I was once walking along with the great throng to the temple of God,

shouting and giving thanks along with the crowd as we celebrated the holy festival.
42:5 Why are you depressed, O my soul?
Why are you upset?
Wait for God!
For I will again give thanks
to my God for his saving intervention.
42:6 I am depressed,
so I will pray to you while I am trapped here in the region of the upper Jordan,
from Hermon, from Mount Mizar.
42:7 One deep stream calls out to another at the sound of your waterfalls;
all your billows and waves overwhelm me.
42:8 By day the LORD decrees his loyal love,
and by night he gives me a song,
a prayer to the living God.
42:9 I will pray to God, my high ridge:
"Why do you ignore me?
Why must I walk around mourning
because my enemies oppress me?"
42:10 My enemies' taunts cut into me to the bone,
as they say to me all day long, "Where is your God?"
42:11 Why are you depressed, O my soul?
Why are you upset?
Wait for God!
For I will again give thanks
to my God for his saving intervention.
Psalm 43
43:1 Vindicate me, O God!
Fight for me against an ungodly nation!
Deliver me from deceitful and evil men!
43:2 For you are the God who shelters me.
Why do you reject me?
Why must I walk around mourning
because my enemies oppress me?
43:3 Reveal your light and your faithfulness!
They will lead me,
they will escort me back to your holy hill,
and to the place where you live.
43:4 Then I will go to the altar of God,
to the God who gives me ecstatic joy,
so that I express my thanks to you, O God, my God, with a harp.
43:5 Why are you depressed, O my soul?
Why are you upset?
Wait for God!
For I will again give thanks
to my God for his saving intervention.
Psalm 44
For the music director; by the Korahites, a well-written song.
44:1 O God, we have clearly heard;
our ancestors have told us
what you did in their days,
in ancient times.
44:2 You, by your power, defeated nations and settled our fathers on their land;
you crushed the people living there and enabled our ancestors to occupy it.
44:3 For they did not conquer the land by their swords,
and they did not prevail by their strength,
but rather by your power, strength and good favor,
for you were partial to them.
44:4 You are my king, O God!
Decree Jacob's deliverance!
44:5 By your power we will drive back our enemies;
by your strength we will trample down our foes!
44:6 For I do not trust in my bow,
and I do not prevail by my sword.
44:7 For you deliver us from our enemies;
you humiliate those who hate us.
44:8 In God I boast all day long,
and we will continually give thanks to your name. (Selah)
44:9 But you rejected and embarrassed us!
You did not go into battle with our armies.
44:10 You made us retreat from the enemy.
Those who hate us take whatever they want from us.
44:11 You handed us over like sheep to be eaten;
you scattered us among the nations.
44:12 You sold your people for a pittance,
you did not ask a high price for them.
44:13 You made us an object of disdain to our neighbors;
those who live on our borders taunt and insult us.
44:14 You made us an object of ridicule among the nations;
foreigners treat us with contempt.

44:15 All day long I feel humiliated
and am overwhelmed with shame,
44:16 before the vindictive enemy
who ridicules and insults me.
44:17 All this has happened to us, even though we have not rejected you
or violated your covenant with us.
44:18 We have not been unfaithful,
nor have we disobeyed your commands.
44:19 Yet you have battered us, leaving us a heap of ruins overrun by wild dogs;
you have covered us with darkness.
44:20 If we had rejected our God,
and spread out our hands in prayer to another god,
44:21 would not God discover it,
for he knows one's thoughts?
44:22 Yet because of you we are killed all day long;
we are treated like sheep at the slaughtering block.
44:23 Rouse yourself! Why do you sleep, O Lord?
Wake up! Do not reject us forever!
44:24 Why do you look the other way,
and ignore the way we are oppressed and mistreated?
44:25 For we lie in the dirt,
with our bellies pressed to the ground.
44:26 Rise up and help us!
Rescue us because of your loyal love!

Psalm 45
For the music director; according to the tune of "Lilies;" by the Korahites, a well-written poem, a love song.
45:1 My heart is stirred by a beautiful song.
I say, "I have composed this special song for the king;
my tongue is as skilled as the stylus of an experienced scribe."
45:2 You are the most handsome of all men!
You speak in an impressive and fitting manner!
For this reason God grants you continual blessings.
45:3 Strap your sword to your thigh, O warrior!
Appear in your majestic splendor!
45:4 Appear in your majesty and be victorious!
Ride forth for the sake of what is right,
on behalf of justice!
Then your right hand will accomplish mighty acts!
45:5 Your arrows are sharp
and penetrate the hearts of the king's enemies.
Nations fall at your feet.
45:6 Your throne, O God, is permanent.
The scepter of your kingdom is a scepter of justice.
45:7 You love justice and hate evil.
For this reason God, your God has anointed you
with the oil of joy, elevating you above your companions.
45:8 All your garments are perfumed with myrrh, aloes, and cassia.
From the luxurious palaces comes the music of stringed instruments that makes you happy.
45:9 Princesses are among your honored guests,
your bride stands at your right hand, wearing jewelry made with gold from Ophir.
45:10 Listen, O princess!
Observe and pay attention!
Forget your homeland and your family!
45:11 Then the king will be attracted by your beauty.
After all, he is your master! Submit to him!
45:12 Rich people from Tyre
will seek your favor by bringing a gift.
45:13 The princess looks absolutely magnificent,
decked out in pearls and clothed in a brocade trimmed with gold.
45:14 In embroidered robes she is escorted to the king.
Her attendants, the maidens of honor who follow her,
are led before you.
45:15 They are bubbling with joy as they walk in procession
and enter the royal palace.
45:16 Your sons will carry on the dynasty of your ancestors;
you will make them princes throughout the land.
45:17 I will proclaim your greatness through the coming years,
then the nations will praise you forever.

Psalm 46
For the music director; by the Korahites; according to the *alamoth* style; a song.
46:1 God is our strong refuge;
he is truly our helper in times of trouble.
46:2 For this reason we do not fear when the earth shakes,
and the mountains tumble into the depths of the sea,
46:3 when its waves crash and foam,
and the mountains shake before the surging sea. (Selah)
46:4 The river's channels bring joy to the city of God,
the special, holy dwelling place of the sovereign One.

46:5 God lives within it, it cannot be moved.
God rescues it at the break of dawn.
46:6 Nations are in uproar, kingdoms are overthrown.
God gives a shout, the earth dissolves.
46:7 The LORD who commands armies is on our side!
The God of Jacob is our protector! (Selah)
46:8 Come! Witness the exploits of the LORD,
who brings devastation to the earth!
46:9 He brings an end to wars throughout the earth;
he shatters the bow and breaks the spear;
he burns the shields with fire.
46:10 He says, "Stop your striving and recognize that I am God!
I will be exalted over the nations! I will be exalted over the earth!"
46:11 The LORD who commands armies is on our side!
The God of Jacob is our protector! (Selah)

Psalm 47
For the music director; by the Korahites; a psalm.
47:1 All you nations, clap your hands!
Shout out to God in celebration!
47:2 For the sovereign LORD is awe-inspiring;
he is the great king who rules the whole earth!
47:3 He subdued nations beneath us
and countries under our feet.
47:4 He picked out for us a special land
to be a source of pride for Jacob, whom he loves. (Selah)
47:5 God has ascended his throne amid loud shouts;
the LORD has ascended his throne amid the blaring of ram's horns.
47:6 Sing to God! Sing!
Sing to our king! Sing!
47:7 For God is king of the whole earth!
Sing a well-written song!
47:8 God reigns over the nations!
God sits on his holy throne!
47:9 The nobles of the nations assemble,
along with the people of the God of Abraham,
for God has authority over the rulers of the earth.
He is highly exalted!

Psalm 48
A song, a psalm by the Korahites.
48:1 The LORD is great and certainly worthy of praise
in the city of our God, his holy hill.
48:2 It is lofty and pleasing to look at,
a source of joy to the whole earth.
Mount Zion resembles the peaks of Zaphon;
it is the city of the great king.
48:3 God is in its fortresses;
he reveals himself as its defender.
48:4 For look, the kings assemble;
they advance together.
48:5 As soon as they see, they are shocked;
they are terrified, they quickly retreat.
48:6 Look at them shake uncontrollably,
like a woman writhing in childbirth.
48:7 With an east wind
you shatter the large ships.
48:8 We heard about God's mighty deeds, now we have seen them,
in the city of the LORD, the invincible Warrior,
in the city of our God.
God makes it permanently secure. (Selah)
48:9 We reflect on your loyal love, O God,
within your temple.
48:10 The praise you receive as far away as the ends of the earth
is worthy of your reputation, O God.
You execute justice!
48:11 Mount Zion rejoices;
the towns of Judah are happy,
because of your acts of judgment.
48:12 Walk around Zion! Encircle it!
Count its towers!
48:13 Consider its defenses!
Walk through its fortresses,
so you can tell the next generation about it!
48:14 For God, our God, is our defender forever!
He guides us!

Psalm 49
For the music director, a psalm by the Korahites.
49:1 Listen to this, all you nations!
Pay attention, all you inhabitants of the world!
49:2 Pay attention, all you people,
both rich and poor!
49:3 I will declare a wise saying;
I will share my profound thoughts.
49:4 I will learn a song that imparts wisdom;

I will then sing my insightful song to the accompaniment of a harp.
49:5 Why should I be afraid in times of trouble,
when the sinful deeds of deceptive men threaten to overwhelm me?
49:6 They trust in their wealth
and boast in their great riches.
49:7 Certainly a man cannot rescue his brother;
he cannot pay God an adequate ransom price
49:8 (the ransom price for a human life is too high,
and people go to their final destiny),
49:9 so that he might continue to live forever
and not experience death.
49:10 Surely one sees that even wise people die;
fools and spiritually insensitive people all pass away
and leave their wealth to others.
49:11 Their grave becomes their permanent residence,
their eternal dwelling place.
They name their lands after themselves,
49:12 but, despite their wealth, people do not last,
they are like animals that perish.
49:13 This is the destiny of fools,
and of those who approve of their philosophy. (Selah)
49:14 They will travel to Sheol like sheep,
with death as their shepherd.
The godly will rule over them when the day of vindication dawns;
Sheol will consume their bodies and they will no longer live in impressive houses.
49:15 But God will rescue my life from the power of Sheol;
certainly he will pull me to safety. (Selah)
49:16 Do not be afraid when a man becomes rich
and his wealth multiplies!
49:17 For he will take nothing with him when he dies;
his wealth will not follow him down into the grave.
49:18 He pronounces this blessing on himself while he is alive:
"May men praise you, for you have done well!"
49:19 But he will join his ancestors;
they will never again see the light of day.
49:20 Wealthy people do not understand;
they are like animals that perish.

Psalm 50
A psalm by Asaph.
50:1 El, God, the LORD speaks,
and summons the earth to come from the east and west.
50:2 From Zion, the most beautiful of all places,
God comes in splendor.
50:3 Our God approaches and is not silent;
consuming fire goes ahead of him
and all around him a storm rages.
50:4 He summons the heavens above,
as well as the earth, so that he might judge his people.
50:5 He says:
"Assemble my covenant people before me,
those who ratified a covenant with me by sacrifice!"
50:6 The heavens declare his fairness,
for God is judge. (Selah)
50:7 He says:
"Listen my people! I am speaking!
Listen Israel! I am accusing you!
I am God, your God!
50:8 I am not condemning you because of your sacrifices,
or because of your burnt sacrifices that you continually offer me.
50:9 I do not need to take a bull from your household
or goats from your sheepfolds.
50:10 For every wild animal in the forest belongs to me,
as well as the cattle that graze on a thousand hills.
50:11 I keep track of every bird in the hills,
and the insects of the field are mine.
50:12 Even if I were hungry, I would not tell you,
for the world and all it contains belong to me.
50:13 Do I eat the flesh of bulls?
Do I drink the blood of goats?
50:14 Present to God a thank-offering!
Repay your vows to the sovereign One!
50:15 Pray to me when you are in trouble!
I will deliver you, and you will honor me!"
50:16 God says this to the evildoer:
"How can you declare my commands,
and talk about my covenant?
50:17 For you hate instruction
and reject my words.
50:18 When you see a thief, you join him;
you associate with men who are unfaithful to their wives.
50:19 You do damage with words,
and use your tongue to deceive.

50:20 You plot against your brother;
you slander your own brother.
50:21 When you did these things, I was silent,
so you thought I was exactly like you.
But now I will condemn you
and state my case against you!
50:22 Carefully consider this, you who reject God!
Otherwise I will rip you to shreds
and no one will be able to rescue you.
50:23 Whoever presents a thank-offering honors me.
To whoever obeys my commands, I will reveal my power to deliver."

Psalm 51
For the music director; a psalm of David, written when Nathan the prophet confronted him after David's affair with Bathsheba.
51:1 Have mercy on me, O God, because of your loyal love!
Because of your great compassion, wipe away my rebellious acts!
51:2 Wash away my wrongdoing!
Cleanse me of my sin!
51:3 For I am aware of my rebellious acts;
I am forever conscious of my sin.
51:4 Against you – you above all – I have sinned;
I have done what is evil in your sight.
So you are just when you confront me;
you are right when you condemn me.
51:5 Look, I was guilty of sin from birth,
a sinner the moment my mother conceived me.
51:6 Look, you desire integrity in the inner man;
you want me to possess wisdom.
51:7 Sprinkle me with water and I will be pure;
wash me and I will be whiter than snow.
51:8 Grant me the ultimate joy of being forgiven!
May the bones you crushed rejoice!
51:9 Hide your face from my sins!
Wipe away all my guilt!
51:10 Create for me a pure heart, O God!
Renew a resolute spirit within me!
51:11 Do not reject me!
Do not take your Holy Spirit away from me!
51:12 Let me again experience the joy of your deliverance!
Sustain me by giving me the desire to obey!
51:13 Then I will teach rebels your merciful ways,
and sinners will turn to you.
51:14 Rescue me from the guilt of murder, O God, the God who delivers me!
Then my tongue will shout for joy because of your deliverance.
51:15 O Lord, give me the words!
Then my mouth will praise you.
51:16 Certainly you do not want a sacrifice, or else I would offer it;
you do not desire a burnt sacrifice.
51:17 The sacrifices God desires are a humble spirit –
O God, a humble and repentant heart you will not reject.
51:18 Because you favor Zion, do what is good for her!
Fortify the walls of Jerusalem!
51:19 Then you will accept the proper sacrifices, burnt sacrifices and whole offerings;
then bulls will be sacrificed on your altar.

Psalm 52
For the music director; a well-written song by David. It was written when Doeg the Edomite went and informed Saul: "David has arrived at the home of Ahimelech."
52:1 Why do you boast about your evil plans, O powerful man?
God's loyal love protects me all day long!
52:2 Your tongue carries out your destructive plans;
it is as effective as a sharp razor, O deceiver.
52:3 You love evil more than good,
lies more than speaking the truth. (Selah)
52:4 You love to use all the words that destroy,
and the tongue that deceives.
52:5 Yet God will make you a permanent heap of ruins.
He will scoop you up and remove you from your home;
he will uproot you from the land of the living. (Selah)
52:6 When the godly see this, they will be filled with awe,
and will mock the evildoer, saying:
52:7 "Look, here is the man who would not make God his protector!
He trusted in his great wealth
and was confident about his plans to destroy others."
52:8 But I am like a flourishing olive tree in the house of God;
I continually trust in God's loyal love.
52:9 I will continually thank you when you execute judgment;
I will rely on you, for your loyal followers know you are good.

Psalm 53
For the music director; according to the *machalath* style; a well-written song by David.

53:1 Fools say to themselves, "There is no God."
They sin and commit evil deeds;
none of them does what is right.
53:2 God looks down from heaven at the human race,
to see if there is anyone who is wise and seeks God.
53:3 Everyone rejects God;
they are all morally corrupt.
None of them does what is right,
not even one!
53:4 All those who behave wickedly do not understand –
those who devour my people as if they were eating bread,
and do not call out to God.
53:5 They are absolutely terrified,
even by things that do not normally cause fear.
For God annihilates those who attack you.
You are able to humiliate them because God has rejected them.
53:6 I wish the deliverance of Israel would come from Zion!
When God restores the well-being of his people,
may Jacob rejoice,
may Israel be happy!

Psalm 54

For the music director, to be accompanied by stringed instruments; a well-written song by David. It was written when the Ziphites came and informed Saul: "David is hiding with us."
54:1 O God, deliver me by your name!
Vindicate me by your power!
54:2 O God, listen to my prayer!
Pay attention to what I say!
54:3 For foreigners attack me;
ruthless men, who do not respect God, seek my life. (Selah)
54:4 Look, God is my deliverer!
The Lord is among those who support me.
54:5 May those who wait to ambush me be repaid for their evil!
As a demonstration of your faithfulness, destroy them!
54:6 With a freewill offering I will sacrifice to you!
I will give thanks to your name, O LORD, for it is good!
54:7 Surely he rescues me from all trouble,
and I triumph over my enemies.

Psalm 55

For the music director, to be accompanied by stringed instruments; a well-written song by David.
55:1 Listen, O God, to my prayer!
Do not ignore my appeal for mercy!
55:2 Pay attention to me and answer me!
I am so upset and distressed, I am beside myself,
55:3 because of what the enemy says,
and because of how the wicked pressure me,
for they hurl trouble down upon me
and angrily attack me.
55:4 My heart beats violently within me;
the horrors of death overcome me.
55:5 Fear and panic overpower me;
terror overwhelms me.
55:6 I say, "I wish I had wings like a dove!
I would fly away and settle in a safe place!
55:7 Look, I will escape to a distant place;
I will stay in the wilderness. (Selah)
55:8 I will hurry off to a place that is safe
from the strong wind and the gale."
55:9 Confuse them, O Lord!
Frustrate their plans!
For I see violence and conflict in the city.
55:10 Day and night they walk around on its walls,
while wickedness and destruction are within it.
55:11 Disaster is within it;
violence and deceit do not depart from its public square.
55:12 Indeed, it is not an enemy who insults me,
or else I could bear it;
it is not one who hates me who arrogantly taunts me,
or else I could hide from him.
55:13 But it is you, a man like me,
my close friend in whom I confided.
55:14 We would share personal thoughts with each other;
in God's temple we would walk together among the crowd.
55:15 May death destroy them!
May they go down alive into Sheol!
For evil is in their dwelling place and in their midst.
55:16 As for me, I will call out to God,
and the LORD will deliver me.
55:17 During the evening, morning, and noontime
I will lament and moan,
and he will hear me.
55:18 He will rescue me and protect me from those who attack me,
even though they greatly outnumber me.
55:19 God, the one who has reigned as king from long ago,
will hear and humiliate them. (Selah)
They refuse to change,
and do not fear God.
55:20 He attacks his friends;
he breaks his solemn promises to them.
55:21 His words are as smooth as butter,
but he harbors animosity in his heart.
His words seem softer than oil,
but they are really like sharp swords.
55:22 Throw your burden upon the LORD,
and he will sustain you.
He will never allow the godly to be upended.
55:23 But you, O God, will bring them down to the deep Pit.
Violent and deceitful people will not live even half a normal lifespan.
But as for me, I trust in you.

Psalm 56

For the music director; according to the *yonath-elem-rechovim* style; a prayer of David, written when the Philistines captured him in Gath.
56:1 Have mercy on me, O God, for men are attacking me!
All day long hostile enemies are tormenting me.
56:2 Those who anticipate my defeat attack me all day long.
Indeed, many are fighting against me, O Exalted One.
56:3 When I am afraid,
I trust in you.
56:4 In God – I boast in his promise –
in God I trust, I am not afraid.
What can mere men do to me?
56:5 All day long they cause me trouble;
they make a habit of plotting my demise.
56:6 They stalk and lurk;
they watch my every step,
as they prepare to take my life.
56:7 Because they are bent on violence, do not let them escape!
In your anger bring down the nations, O God!
56:8 You keep track of my misery.
Put my tears in your leather container!
Are they not recorded in your scroll?
56:9 My enemies will turn back when I cry out to you for help;
I know that God is on my side.
56:10 In God – I boast in his promise –
in the LORD – I boast in his promise –
56:11 in God I trust, I am not afraid.
What can mere men do to me?
56:12 I am obligated to fulfill the vows I made to you, O God;
I will give you the thank-offerings you deserve,
56:13 when you deliver my life from death.
You keep my feet from stumbling,
so that I might serve God as I enjoy life.

Psalm 57

For the music director; according to the *al-tashcheth* style; a prayer of David, written when he fled from Saul into the cave.
57:1 Have mercy on me, O God! Have mercy on me!
For in you I have taken shelter.
In the shadow of your wings I take shelter
until trouble passes.
57:2 I cry out for help to the sovereign God,
to the God who vindicates me.
57:3 May he send help from heaven and deliver me
from my enemies who hurl insults! (Selah)
May God send his loyal love and faithfulness!
57:4 I am surrounded by lions;
I lie down among those who want to devour me;
men whose teeth are spears and arrows,
whose tongues are a sharp sword.
57:5 Rise up above the sky, O God!
May your splendor cover the whole earth!
57:6 They have prepared a net to trap me;
I am discouraged.
They have dug a pit for me.
They will fall into it! (Selah)
57:7 I am determined, O God! I am determined!
I will sing and praise you!
57:8 Awake, my soul!
Awake, O stringed instrument and harp!
I will wake up at dawn!
57:9 I will give you thanks before the nations, O Master!
I will sing praises to you before foreigners!
57:10 For your loyal love extends beyond the sky,
and your faithfulness reaches the clouds.
57:11 Rise up above the sky, O God!
May your splendor cover the whole earth!

Psalm 58

For the music director; according to the *al-tashcheth* style; a prayer of David.

58:1 Do you rulers really pronounce just decisions?
Do you judge people fairly?
58:2 No! You plan how to do what is unjust;
you deal out violence in the earth.
58:3 The wicked turn aside from birth;
liars go astray as soon as they are born.
58:4 Their venom is like that of a snake,
like a deaf serpent that does not hear,
58:5 that does not respond to the magicians,
or to a skilled snake-charmer.
58:6 O God, break the teeth in their mouths!
Smash the jawbones of the lions, O LORD!
58:7 Let them disappear like water that flows away!
Let them wither like grass!
58:8 Let them be like a snail that melts away as it moves along!
Let them be like stillborn babies that never see the sun!
58:9 Before the kindling is even placed under your pots,
he will sweep it away along with both the raw and cooked meat.
58:10 The godly will rejoice when they see vengeance carried out;
they will bathe their feet in the blood of the wicked.
58:11 Then observers will say,
"Yes indeed, the godly are rewarded!
Yes indeed, there is a God who judges in the earth!"

Psalm 59

For the music director; according to the *al-tashcheth* style; a prayer of David, written when Saul sent men to surround his house and murder him.

59:1 Deliver me from my enemies, my God!
Protect me from those who attack me!
59:2 Deliver me from evildoers!
Rescue me from violent men!
59:3 For look, they wait to ambush me;
powerful men stalk me,
but not because I have rebelled or sinned, O LORD.
59:4 Though I have done nothing wrong, they are anxious to attack.
Spring into action and help me! Take notice of me!
59:5 You, O LORD God, the invincible warrior, the God of Israel,
rouse yourself and punish all the nations!
Have no mercy on any treacherous evildoers! (Selah)
59:6 They return in the evening;
they growl like a dog
and prowl around outside the city.
59:7 Look, they hurl insults at me
and openly threaten to kill me,
for they say,
"Who hears?"
59:8 But you, O LORD, laugh in disgust at them;
you taunt all the nations.
59:9 You are my source of strength! I will wait for you!
For God is my refuge.
59:10 The God who loves me will help me;
God will enable me to triumph over my enemies.
59:11 Do not strike them dead suddenly,
because then my people might forget the lesson.
Use your power to make them homeless vagabonds and then bring them down,
O Lord who shields us!
59:12 They speak sinful words.
So let them be trapped by their own pride
and by the curses and lies they speak!
59:13 Angrily wipe them out! Wipe them out so they vanish!
Let them know that God rules
in Jacob and to the ends of the earth! (Selah)
59:14 They return in the evening;
they growl like a dog
and prowl around outside the city.
59:15 They wander around looking for something to eat;
they refuse to sleep until they are full.
59:16 As for me, I will sing about your strength;
I will praise your loyal love in the morning.
For you are my refuge
and my place of shelter when I face trouble.
59:17 You are my source of strength! I will sing praises to you!
For God is my refuge, the God who loves me.

Psalm 60

For the music director; according to the *shushan-eduth* style; a prayer of David written to instruct others. It was written when he fought against Aram Naharaim and Aram-Zobah. That was when Joab turned back and struck down 12,000 Edomites in the Valley of Salt.

60:1 O God, you have rejected us.

You suddenly turned on us in your anger.
Please restore us!
60:2 You made the earth quake; you split it open.
Repair its breaches, for it is ready to fall.
60:3 You have made your people experience hard times;
you have made us drink intoxicating wine.
60:4 You have given your loyal followers a rallying flag,
so that they might seek safety from the bow. (Selah)
60:5 Deliver by your power and answer me,
so that the ones you love may be safe.
60:6 God has spoken in his sanctuary:
"I will triumph! I will parcel out Shechem;
the Valley of Succoth I will measure off.
60:7 Gilead belongs to me,
as does Manasseh!
Ephraim is my helmet,
Judah my royal scepter.
60:8 Moab is my washbasin.
I will make Edom serve me.
I will shout in triumph over Philistia."
60:9 Who will lead me into the fortified city?
Who will bring me to Edom?
60:10 Have you not rejected us, O God?
O God, you do not go into battle with our armies.
60:11 Give us help against the enemy,
for any help men might offer is futile.
60:12 By God's power we will conquer;
he will trample down our enemies.

Psalm 61

For the music director; to be played on a stringed instrument; written by David.

61:1 O God, hear my cry for help!
Pay attention to my prayer!
61:2 From the most remote place on earth
I call out to you in my despair.
Lead me up to an inaccessible rocky summit!
61:3 Indeed, you are my shelter,
a strong tower that protects me from the enemy.
61:4 I will be a permanent guest in your home;
I will find shelter in the protection of your wings. (Selah)
61:5 For you, O God, hear my vows;
you grant me the reward that belongs to your loyal followers.
61:6 Give the king long life!
Make his lifetime span several generations!
61:7 May he reign forever before God!
Decree that your loyal love and faithfulness should protect him.
61:8 Then I will sing praises to your name continually,
as I fulfill my vows day after day.

Psalm 62

For the music director, Jeduthun; a psalm of David.

62:1 For God alone I patiently wait;
he is the one who delivers me.
62:2 He alone is my protector and deliverer.
He is my refuge; I will not be upended.
62:3 How long will you threaten a man?
All of you are murderers,
as dangerous as a leaning wall or an unstable fence.
62:4 They spend all their time planning how to bring him down.
They love to use deceit;
they pronounce blessings with their mouths,
but inwardly they utter curses. (Selah)
62:5 Patiently wait for God alone, my soul!
For he is the one who gives me confidence.
62:6 He alone is my protector and deliverer.
He is my refuge; I will not be upended.
62:7 God delivers me and exalts me;
God is my strong protector and my shelter.
62:8 Trust in him at all times, you people!
Pour out your hearts before him!
God is our shelter! (Selah)
62:9 Men are nothing but a mere breath;
human beings are unreliable.
When they are weighed in the scales,
all of them together are lighter than air.
62:10 Do not trust in what you can gain by oppression!
Do not put false confidence in what you can gain by robbery!
If wealth increases, do not become attached to it!
62:11 God has declared one principle;
two principles I have heard:
God is strong,
62:12 and you, O Lord, demonstrate loyal love.
For you repay men for what they do.

Psalm 63

A psalm of David, written when he was in the Judean wilderness.

63:1 O God, you are my God! I long for you!
My soul thirsts for you,
my flesh yearns for you,
in a dry and parched land where there is no water.
63:2 Yes, in the sanctuary I have seen you,
and witnessed your power and splendor.
63:3 Because experiencing your loyal love is better than life itself,
my lips will praise you.
63:4 For this reason I will praise you while I live;
in your name I will lift up my hands.
63:5 As if with choice meat you satisfy my soul.
My mouth joyfully praises you,
63:6 whenever I remember you on my bed,
and think about you during the nighttime hours.
63:7 For you are my deliverer;
under your wings I rejoice.
63:8 My soul pursues you;
your right hand upholds me.
63:9 Enemies seek to destroy my life,
but they will descend into the depths of the earth.
63:10 Each one will be handed over to the sword;
their corpses will be eaten by jackals.
63:11 But the king will rejoice in God;
everyone who takes oaths in his name will boast,
for the mouths of those who speak lies will be shut up.

Psalm 64

For the music director; a psalm of David.

64:1 Listen to me, O God, as I offer my lament!
Protect my life from the enemy's terrifying attacks.
64:2 Hide me from the plots of evil men,
from the crowd of evildoers.
64:3 They sharpen their tongues like a sword;
they aim their arrow, a slanderous charge,
64:4 in order to shoot down the innocent in secluded places.
They shoot at him suddenly and are unafraid of retaliation.
64:5 They encourage one another to carry out their evil deed.
They plan how to hide snares,
and boast, "Who will see them?"
64:6 They devise unjust schemes;
they disguise a well-conceived plot.
Man's inner thoughts cannot be discovered.
64:7 But God will shoot at them;
suddenly they will be wounded by an arrow.
64:8 Their slander will bring about their demise.
All who see them will shudder,
64:9 and all people will fear.
They will proclaim what God has done,
and reflect on his deeds.
64:10 The godly will rejoice in the LORD
and take shelter in him.
All the morally upright will boast.

Psalm 65

For the music director; a psalm of David, a song.

65:1 Praise awaits you, O God, in Zion.
Vows made to you are fulfilled.
65:2 You hear prayers;
all people approach you.
65:3 Our record of sins overwhelms me,
but you forgive our acts of rebellion.
65:4 How blessed is the one whom you choose,
and allow to live in your palace courts.
May we be satisfied with the good things of your house –
your holy palace.
65:5 You answer our prayers by performing awesome acts of deliverance,
O God, our savior.
All the ends of the earth trust in you,
as well as those living across the wide seas.
65:6 You created the mountains by your power,
and demonstrated your strength.
65:7 You calm the raging seas
and their roaring waves,
as well as the commotion made by the nations.
65:8 Even those living in the most remote areas are awestruck by your acts;
you cause those living in the east and west to praise you.
65:9 You visit the earth and give it rain;
you make it rich and fertile
with overflowing streams full of water.
You provide grain for them,
for you prepare the earth to yield its crops.
65:10 You saturate its furrows,
and soak its plowed ground.

With rain showers you soften its soil,
and make its crops grow.
65:11 You crown the year with your good blessings,
and you leave abundance in your wake.
65:12 The pastures in the wilderness glisten with moisture,
and the hills are clothed with joy.
65:13 The meadows are clothed with sheep,
and the valleys are covered with grain.
They shout joyfully, yes, they sing.

Psalm 66

For the music director; a song, a psalm.

66:1 Shout out praise to God, all the earth!
66:2 Sing praises about the majesty of his reputation!
Give him the honor he deserves!
66:3 Say to God:
"How awesome are your deeds!
Because of your great power your enemies cower in fear before you.
66:4 All the earth worships you
and sings praises to you!
They sing praises to your name!" (Selah)
66:5 Come and witness God's exploits!
His acts on behalf of people are awesome!
66:6 He turned the sea into dry land;
they passed through the river on foot.
Let us rejoice in him there!
66:7 He rules by his power forever;
he watches the nations.
Stubborn rebels should not exalt themselves. (Selah)
66:8 Praise our God, you nations!
Loudly proclaim his praise!
66:9 He preserves our lives
and does not allow our feet to slip.
66:10 For you, O God, tested us;
you purified us like refined silver.
66:11 You led us into a trap;
you caused us to suffer.
66:12 You allowed men to ride over our heads;
we passed through fire and water,
but you brought us out into a wide open place.
66:13 I will enter your temple with burnt sacrifices;
I will fulfill the vows I made to you,
66:14 which my lips uttered
and my mouth spoke when I was in trouble.
66:15 I will offer up to you fattened animals as burnt sacrifices,
along with the smell of sacrificial rams.
I will offer cattle and goats. (Selah)
66:16 Come! Listen, all you who are loyal to God!
I will declare what he has done for me.
66:17 I cried out to him for help
and praised him with my tongue.
66:18 If I had harbored sin in my heart,
the Lord would not have listened.
66:19 However, God heard;
he listened to my prayer.
66:20 God deserves praise,
for he did not reject my prayer
or abandon his love for me!

Psalm 67

For the music director; to be accompanied by stringed instruments; a psalm, a song.

67:1 May God show us his favor and bless us!
May he smile on us! (Selah)
67:2 Then those living on earth will know what you are like;
all nations will know how you deliver your people.
67:3 Let the nations thank you, O God!
Let all the nations thank you!
67:4 Let foreigners rejoice and celebrate!
For you execute justice among the nations,
and govern the people living on earth. (Selah)
67:5 Let the nations thank you, O God!
Let all the nations thank you!
67:6 The earth yields its crops.
May God, our God, bless us!
67:7 May God bless us!
Then all the ends of the earth will give him the honor he deserves.

Psalm 68

For the music director; by David, a psalm, a song.

68:1 God springs into action!
His enemies scatter;
his adversaries run from him.
68:2 As smoke is driven away by the wind, so you drive them away.
As wax melts before fire,
so the wicked are destroyed before God.

68:3 But the godly are happy;
they rejoice before God
and are overcome with joy.
68:4 Sing to God! Sing praises to his name!
Exalt the one who rides on the clouds!
For the LORD is his name!
Rejoice before him!
68:5 He is a father to the fatherless
and an advocate for widows.
God rules from his holy palace.
68:6 God settles those who have been deserted in their own homes;
he frees prisoners and grants them prosperity.
But sinful rebels live in the desert.
68:7 O God, when you lead your people into battle,
when you march through the desert, (Selah)
68:8 the earth shakes,
yes, the heavens pour down rain
before God, the God of Sinai,
before God, the God of Israel.
68:9 O God, you cause abundant showers to fall on your chosen people.
When they are tired, you sustain them,
68:10 for you live among them.
You sustain the oppressed with your good blessings, O God.
68:11 The Lord speaks;
many, many women spread the good news.
68:12 Kings leading armies run away – they run away!
The lovely lady of the house divides up the loot.
68:13 When you lie down among the sheepfolds,
the wings of the dove are covered with silver
and with glittering gold.
68:14 When the sovereign judge scatters kings,
let it snow on Zalmon!
68:15 The mountain of Bashan is a towering mountain;
the mountain of Bashan is a mountain with many peaks.
68:16 Why do you look with envy, O mountains with many peaks,
at the mountain where God has decided to live?
Indeed the LORD will live there permanently!
68:17 God has countless chariots;
they number in the thousands.
The Lord comes from Sinai in holy splendor.
68:18 You ascend on high,
you have taken many captives.
You receive tribute from men,
including even sinful rebels.
Indeed the LORD God lives there!
68:19 The Lord deserves praise!
Day after day he carries our burden,
the God who delivers us. (Selah)
68:20 Our God is a God who delivers;
the LORD, the sovereign Lord, can rescue from death.
68:21 Indeed God strikes the heads of his enemies,
the hairy foreheads of those who persist in rebellion.
68:22 The Lord says,
"I will retrieve them from Bashan,
I will bring them back from the depths of the sea,
68:23 so that your feet may stomp in their blood,
and your dogs may eat their portion of the enemies' corpses."
68:24 They see your processions, O God –
the processions of my God, my king, who marches along in holy splendor.
68:25 Singers walk in front;
musicians follow playing their stringed instruments,
in the midst of young women playing tambourines.
68:26 In your large assemblies praise God,
the LORD, in the assemblies of Israel!
68:27 There is little Benjamin, their ruler,
and the princes of Judah in their robes,
along with the princes of Zebulun and the princes of Naphtali.
68:28 God has decreed that you will be powerful.
O God, you who have acted on our behalf, demonstrate your power,
68:29 as you come out of your temple in Jerusalem!
Kings bring tribute to you.
68:30 Sound your battle cry against the wild beast of the reeds,
and the nations that assemble like a herd of calves led by bulls!
They humble themselves and offer gold and silver as tribute.
God scatters the nations that like to do battle.
68:31 They come with red cloth from Egypt,
Ethiopia voluntarily offers tribute to God.
68:32 O kingdoms of the earth, sing to God!
Sing praises to the Lord, (Selah)
68:33 to the one who rides through the sky from ancient times!
Look! He thunders loudly.
68:34 Acknowledge God's power,

his sovereignty over Israel,
and the power he reveals in the skies!
68:35 You are awe-inspiring, O God, as you emerge from your holy temple!
It is the God of Israel who gives the people power and strength.
God deserves praise!

Psalm 69
For the music director; according to the tune of "Lilies;" by David.
69:1 Deliver me, O God,
for the water has reached my neck.
69:2 I sink into the deep mire
where there is no solid ground;
I am in deep water,
and the current overpowers me.
69:3 I am exhausted from shouting for help;
my throat is sore;
my eyes grow tired of looking for my God.
69:4 Those who hate me without cause are more numerous than the hairs of my head.
Those who want to destroy me, my enemies for no reason, outnumber me.
They make me repay what I did not steal!
69:5 O God, you are aware of my foolish sins;
my guilt is not hidden from you.
69:6 Let none who rely on you be disgraced because of me,
O sovereign LORD and king!
Let none who seek you be ashamed because of me,
O God of Israel!
69:7 For I suffer humiliation for your sake
and am thoroughly disgraced.
69:8 My own brothers treat me like a stranger;
they act as if I were a foreigner.
69:9 Certainly zeal for your house consumes me;
I endure the insults of those who insult you.
69:10 I weep and refrain from eating food,
which causes others to insult me.
69:11 I wear sackcloth
and they ridicule me.
69:12 Those who sit at the city gate gossip about me;
drunkards mock me in their songs.
69:13 O LORD, may you hear my prayer and be favorably disposed to me!
O God, because of your great loyal love,
answer me with your faithful deliverance!
69:14 Rescue me from the mud! Don't let me sink!
Deliver me from those who hate me,
from the deep water!
69:15 Don't let the current overpower me!
Don't let the deep swallow me up!
Don't let the pit devour me!
69:16 Answer me, O LORD, for your loyal love is good!
Because of your great compassion, turn toward me!
69:17 Do not ignore your servant,
for I am in trouble! Answer me right away!
69:18 Come near me and redeem me!
Because of my enemies, rescue me!
69:19 You know how I am insulted, humiliated and disgraced;
you can see all my enemies.
69:20 Their insults are painful and make me lose heart;
I look for sympathy, but receive none,
for comforters, but find none.
69:21 They put bitter poison into my food,
and to quench my thirst they give me vinegar to drink.
69:22 May their dining table become a trap before them!
May it be a snare for that group of friends!
69:23 May their eyes be blinded!
Make them shake violently!
69:24 Pour out your judgment on them!
May your raging anger overtake them!
69:25 May their camp become desolate,
their tents uninhabited!
69:26 For they harass the one whom you discipline;
they spread the news about the suffering of those whom you punish.
69:27 Hold them accountable for all their sins!
Do not vindicate them!
69:28 May their names be deleted from the scroll of the living!
Do not let their names be listed with the godly!
69:29 I am oppressed and suffering!
O God, deliver and protect me!
69:30 I will sing praises to God's name!
I will magnify him as I give him thanks!
69:31 That will please the LORD more than an ox or a bull
with horns and hooves.
69:32 The oppressed look on – let them rejoice!

You who seek God, may you be encouraged!
69:33 For the LORD listens to the needy;
he does not despise his captive people.
69:34 Let the heavens and the earth praise him,
along with the seas and everything that swims in them!
69:35 For God will deliver Zion
and rebuild the cities of Judah,
and his people will again live in them and possess Zion.
69:36 The descendants of his servants will inherit it,
and those who are loyal to him will live in it.
Psalm 70
For the music director; by David; written to get God's attention.
70:1 O God, please be willing to rescue me!
O LORD, hurry and help me!
70:2 May those who are trying to take my life
be embarrassed and ashamed!
May those who want to harm me
be turned back and ashamed!
70:3 May those who say, "Aha! Aha!"
be driven back and disgraced!
70:4 May all those who seek you be happy and rejoice in you!
May those who love to experience your deliverance say continually,
"May God be praised!"
70:5 I am oppressed and needy!
O God, hurry to me!
You are my helper and my deliverer!
O LORD, do not delay!
Psalm 71
71:1 In you, O LORD, I have taken shelter!
Never let me be humiliated!
71:2 Vindicate me by rescuing me!
Listen to me! Deliver me!
71:3 Be my protector and refuge,
a stronghold where I can be safe!
For you are my high ridge and my stronghold.
71:4 My God, rescue me from the power of the wicked,
from the hand of the cruel oppressor!
71:5 For you give me confidence, O Lord;
O LORD, I have trusted in you since I was young.
71:6 I have leaned on you since birth;
you pulled me from my mother's womb.
I praise you continually.
71:7 Many are appalled when they see me,
but you are my secure shelter.
71:8 I praise you constantly
and speak of your splendor all day long.
71:9 Do not reject me in my old age!
When my strength fails, do not abandon me!
71:10 For my enemies talk about me;
those waiting for a chance to kill me plot my demise.
71:11 They say, "God has abandoned him.
Run and seize him, for there is no one who will rescue him!"
71:12 O God, do not remain far away from me!
My God, hurry and help me!
71:13 May my accusers be humiliated and defeated!
May those who want to harm me be covered with scorn and disgrace!
71:14 As for me, I will wait continually,
and will continue to praise you.
71:15 I will tell about your justice,
and all day long proclaim your salvation,
though I cannot fathom its full extent.
71:16 I will come and tell about the mighty acts of the sovereign LORD.
I will proclaim your justice – yours alone.
71:17 O God, you have taught me since I was young,
and I am still declaring your amazing deeds.
71:18 Even when I am old and gray,
O God, do not abandon me,
until I tell the next generation about your strength,
and those coming after me about your power.
71:19 Your justice, O God, extends to the skies above;
you have done great things.
O God, who can compare to you?
71:20 Though you have allowed me to experience much trouble and distress,
revive me once again!
Bring me up once again from the depths of the earth!
71:21 Raise me to a position of great honor!
Turn and comfort me!
71:22 I will express my thanks to you with a stringed instrument,
praising your faithfulness, O my God!
I will sing praises to you accompanied by a harp,
O Holy One of Israel!
71:23 My lips will shout for joy! Yes, I will sing your praises!

I will praise you when you rescue me!
71:24 All day long my tongue will also tell about your justice,
for those who want to harm me will be embarrassed and ashamed.
Psalm 72
For Solomon.
72:1 O God, grant the king the ability to make just decisions!
Grant the king's son the ability to make fair decisions!
72:2 Then he will judge your people fairly,
and your oppressed ones equitably.
72:3 The mountains will bring news of peace to the people,
and the hills will announce justice.
72:4 He will defend the oppressed among the people;
he will deliver the children of the poor
and crush the oppressor.
72:5 People will fear you as long as the sun and moon remain in the sky,
for generation after generation.
72:6 He will descend like rain on the mown grass,
like showers that drench the earth.
72:7 During his days the godly will flourish;
peace will prevail as long as the moon remains in the sky.
72:8 May he rule from sea to sea,
and from the Euphrates River to the ends of the earth!
72:9 Before him the coastlands will bow down,
and his enemies will lick the dust.
72:10 The kings of Tarshish and the coastlands will offer gifts;
the kings of Sheba and Seba will bring tribute.
72:11 All kings will bow down to him;
all nations will serve him.
72:12 For he will rescue the needy when they cry out for help,
and the oppressed who have no defender.
72:13 He will take pity on the poor and needy;
the lives of the needy he will save.
72:14 From harm and violence he will defend them;
he will value their lives.
72:15 May he live! May they offer him gold from Sheba!
May they continually pray for him!
May they pronounce blessings on him all day long!
72:16 May there be an abundance of grain in the earth;
on the tops of the mountains may it sway!
May its fruit trees flourish like the forests of Lebanon!
May its crops be as abundant as the grass of the earth!
72:17 May his fame endure!
May his dynasty last as long as the sun remains in the sky!
May they use his name when they formulate their blessings!
May all nations consider him to be favored by God!
72:18 The LORD God, the God of Israel, deserves praise!
He alone accomplishes amazing things!
72:19 His glorious name deserves praise forevermore!
May his majestic splendor fill the whole earth!
We agree! We agree!
72:20 This collection of the prayers of David son of Jesse ends here.
Book 3(Psalms 73-89)
Psalm 73
A psalm by Asaph.
73:1 Certainly God is good to Israel,
and to those whose motives are pure!
73:2 But as for me, my feet almost slipped;
my feet almost slid out from under me.
73:3 For I envied those who are proud,
as I observed the prosperity of the wicked.
73:4 For they suffer no pain;
their bodies are strong and well-fed.
73:5 They are immune to the trouble common to men;
they do not suffer as other men do.
73:6 Arrogance is their necklace,
and violence their clothing.
73:7 Their prosperity causes them to do wrong;
their thoughts are sinful.
73:8 They mock and say evil things;
they proudly threaten violence.
73:9 They speak as if they rule in heaven,
and lay claim to the earth.
73:10 Therefore they have more than enough food to eat,
and even suck up the water of the sea.
73:11 They say, "How does God know what we do?
Is the sovereign one aware of what goes on?"
73:12 Take a good look! This is what the wicked are like,
those who always have it so easy and get richer and richer.
73:13 I concluded, "Surely in vain I have kept my motives pure
and maintained a pure lifestyle.
73:14 I suffer all day long,
and am punished every morning."
73:15 If I had publicized these thoughts,

I would have betrayed your loyal followers.
73:16 When I tried to make sense of this,
it was troubling to me.
73:17 Then I entered the precincts of God's temple,
and understood the destiny of the wicked.
73:18 Surely you put them in slippery places;
you bring them down to ruin.
73:19 How desolate they become in a mere moment!
Terrifying judgments make their demise complete!
73:20 They are like a dream after one wakes up.
O Lord, when you awake you will despise them.
73:21 Yes, my spirit was bitter,
and my insides felt sharp pain.
73:22 I was ignorant and lacked insight;
I was as senseless as an animal before you.
73:23 But I am continually with you;
you hold my right hand.
73:24 You guide me by your wise advice,
and then you will lead me to a position of honor.
73:25 Whom do I have in heaven but you?
I desire no one but you on earth.
73:26 My flesh and my heart may grow weak,
but God always protects my heart and gives me stability.
73:27 Yes, look! Those far from you die;
you destroy everyone who is unfaithful to you.
73:28 But as for me, God's presence is all I need.
I have made the sovereign LORD my shelter,
as I declare all the things you have done.
Psalm 74
A well-written song by Asaph.
74:1 Why, O God, have you permanently rejected us?
Why does your anger burn against the sheep of your pasture?
74:2 Remember your people whom you acquired in ancient times,
whom you rescued so they could be your very own nation,
as well as Mount Zion, where you dwell!
74:3 Hurry and look at the permanent ruins,
and all the damage the enemy has done to the temple!
74:4 Your enemies roar in the middle of your sanctuary;
they set up their battle flags.
74:5 They invade like lumberjacks
swinging their axes in a thick forest.
74:6 And now they are tearing down all its engravings
with axes and crowbars.
74:7 They set your sanctuary on fire;
they desecrate your dwelling place by knocking it to the ground.
74:8 They say to themselves,
"We will oppress all of them."
They burn down all the places where people worship God in the land.
74:9 We do not see any signs of God's presence;
there are no longer any prophets
and we have no one to tell us how long this will last.
74:10 How long, O God, will the adversary hurl insults?
Will the enemy blaspheme your name forever?
74:11 Why do you remain inactive?
Intervene and destroy him!
74:12 But God has been my king from ancient times,
performing acts of deliverance on the earth.
74:13 You destroyed the sea by your strength;
you shattered the heads of the sea monster in the water.
74:14 You crushed the heads of Leviathan;
you fed him to the people who live along the coast.
74:15 You broke open the spring and the stream;
you dried up perpetually flowing rivers.
74:16 You established the cycle of day and night;
you put the moon and sun in place.
74:17 You set up all the boundaries of the earth;
you created the cycle of summer and winter.
74:18 Remember how the enemy hurls insults, O LORD,
and how a foolish nation blasphemes your name!
74:19 Do not hand the life of your dove over to a wild animal!
Do not continue to disregard the lives of your oppressed people!
74:20 Remember your covenant promises,
for the dark regions of the earth are full of places where violence rules.
74:21 Do not let the afflicted be turned back in shame!
Let the oppressed and poor praise your name!
74:22 Rise up, O God! Defend your honor!
Remember how fools insult you all day long!
74:23 Do not disregard what your enemies say,
or the unceasing shouts of those who defy you.
Psalm 75
For the music director; according to the *al-tashcheth* style; a psalm of Asaph; a song.
75:1 We give thanks to you, O God! We give thanks!

You reveal your presence;
people tell about your amazing deeds.
75:2 God says,
"At the appointed times,
I judge fairly.
75:3 When the earth and all its inhabitants dissolve in fear,
I make its pillars secure." (Selah)
75:4 I say to the proud, "Do not be proud,"
and to the wicked, "Do not be so confident of victory!
75:5 Do not be so certain you have won!
Do not speak with your head held so high!
75:6 For victory does not come from the east or west,
or from the wilderness.
75:7 For God is the judge!
He brings one down and exalts another.
75:8 For the LORD holds in his hand a cup full
of foaming wine mixed with spices,
and pours it out.
Surely all the wicked of the earth
will slurp it up and drink it to its very last drop."
75:9 As for me, I will continually tell what you have done;
I will sing praises to the God of Jacob!
75:10 God says,
"I will bring down all the power of the wicked;
the godly will be victorious."
Psalm 76
For the music director; to be accompanied by stringed instruments; a psalm of Asaph, a song.
76:1 God has revealed himself in Judah;
in Israel his reputation is great.

76:2 He lives in Salem;
he dwells in Zion.
76:3 There he shattered the arrows,
the shield, the sword, and the rest of the weapons of war. (Selah)
76:4 You shine brightly and reveal your majesty,
as you descend from the hills where you killed your prey.
76:5 The bravehearted were plundered;
they "fell asleep."
All the warriors were helpless.
76:6 At the sound of your battle cry, O God of Jacob,
both rider and horse "fell asleep."
76:7 You are awesome! Yes, you!
Who can withstand your intense anger?
76:8 From heaven you announced what their punishment would be.
The earth was afraid and silent
76:9 when God arose to execute judgment,
and to deliver all the oppressed of the earth. (Selah)
76:10 Certainly your angry judgment upon men will bring you praise;
you reveal your anger in full measure.
76:11 Make vows to the LORD your God and repay them!
Let all those who surround him bring tribute to the awesome one!
76:12 He humbles princes;
the kings of the earth regard him as awesome.
Psalm 77
For the music director, Jeduthun; a psalm of Asaph.
77:1 I will cry out to God and call for help!
I will cry out to God and he will pay attention to me.
77:2 In my time of trouble I sought the Lord.
I kept my hand raised in prayer throughout the night.
I refused to be comforted.
77:3 I said, "I will remember God while I groan;
I will think about him while my strength leaves me." (Selah)
77:4 You held my eyelids open;
I was troubled and could not speak.
77:5 I thought about the days of old,
about ancient times.
77:6 I said, "During the night I will remember the song I once sang;
I will think very carefully."
I tried to make sense of what was happening.
77:7 I asked, "Will the Lord reject me forever?
Will he never again show me his favor?
77:8 Has his loyal love disappeared forever?
Has his promise failed forever?
77:9 Has God forgotten to be merciful?
Has his anger stifled his compassion?"
77:10 Then I said, "I am sickened by the thought
that the sovereign One might become inactive.
77:11 I will remember the works of the LORD.
Yes, I will remember the amazing things you did long ago!
77:12 I will think about all you have done;
I will reflect upon your deeds!"
77:13 O God, your deeds are extraordinary!
What god can compare to our great God?
77:14 You are the God who does amazing things;
you have revealed your strength among the nations.
77:15 You delivered your people by your strength –
the children of Jacob and Joseph. (Selah)
77:16 The waters saw you, O God,
the waters saw you and trembled.
Yes, the depths of the sea shook with fear.
77:17 The clouds poured down rain;
the skies thundered.
Yes, your arrows flashed about.
77:18 Your thunderous voice was heard in the wind;
the lightning bolts lit up the world;
the earth trembled and shook.
77:19 You walked through the sea;
you passed through the surging waters,
but left no footprints.
77:20 You led your people like a flock of sheep,
by the hand of Moses and Aaron.
Psalm 78
A well-written song by Asaph.
78:1 Pay attention, my people, to my instruction!
Listen to the words I speak!
78:2 I will sing a song that imparts wisdom;
I will make insightful observations about the past.
78:3 What we have heard and learned –
that which our ancestors have told us –
78:4 we will not hide from their descendants.
We will tell the next generation
about the LORD's praiseworthy acts,
about his strength and the amazing things he has done.

78:5 He established a rule in Jacob;
he set up a law in Israel.
He commanded our ancestors
to make his deeds known to their descendants,
78:6 so that the next generation, children yet to be born,
might know about them.
They will grow up and tell their descendants about them.
78:7 Then they will place their confidence in God.
They will not forget the works of God,
and they will obey his commands.
78:8 Then they will not be like their ancestors,
who were a stubborn and rebellious generation,
a generation that was not committed
and faithful to God.
78:9 The Ephraimites were armed with bows,
but they retreated in the day of battle.
78:10 They did not keep their covenant with God,
and they refused to obey his law.
78:11 They forgot what he had done,
the amazing things he had shown them.
78:12 He did amazing things in the sight of their ancestors,
in the land of Egypt, in the region of Zoan.
78:13 He divided the sea and led them across it;
he made the water stand in a heap.
78:14 He led them with a cloud by day,
and with the light of a fire all night long.
78:15 He broke open rocks in the wilderness,
and gave them enough water to fill the depths of the sea.
78:16 He caused streams to flow from the rock,
and made the water flow like rivers.
78:17 Yet they continued to sin against him,
and rebelled against the sovereign One in the desert.
78:18 They willfully challenged God
by asking for food to satisfy their appetite.
78:19 They insulted God, saying,
"Is God really able to give us food in the wilderness?
78:20 Yes, he struck a rock and water flowed out,
streams gushed forth.
But can he also give us food?
Will he provide meat for his people?"
78:21 When the LORD heard this, he was furious.
A fire broke out against Jacob,
and his anger flared up against Israel,
78:22 because they did not have faith in God,
and did not trust his ability to deliver them.
78:23 He gave a command to the clouds above,
and opened the doors in the sky.
78:24 He rained down manna for them to eat;
he gave them the grain of heaven.
78:25 Man ate the food of the mighty ones.
He sent them more than enough to eat.
78:26 He brought the east wind through the sky,
and by his strength led forth the south wind.
78:27 He rained down meat on them like dust,
birds as numerous as the sand on the seashores.
78:28 He caused them to fall right in the middle of their camp,
all around their homes.
78:29 They ate until they were stuffed;
he gave them what they desired.
78:30 They were not yet filled up,
their food was still in their mouths,
78:31 when the anger of God flared up against them.
He killed some of the strongest of them;
he brought the young men of Israel to their knees.
78:32 Despite all this, they continued to sin,
and did not trust him to do amazing things.
78:33 So he caused them to die unsatisfied
and filled with terror.
78:34 When he struck them down, they sought his favor;
they turned back and longed for God.
78:35 They remembered that God was their protector,
and that the sovereign God was their deliverer.
78:36 But they deceived him with their words,
and lied to him.
78:37 They were not really committed to him,
and they were unfaithful to his covenant.
78:38 Yet he is compassionate.
He forgives sin and does not destroy.
He often holds back his anger,
and does not stir up his fury.
78:39 He remembered that they were made of flesh,
and were like a wind that blows past and does not return.
78:40 How often they rebelled against him in the wilderness,

and insulted him in the desert!
78:41 They again challenged God,
and offended the Holy One of Israel.
78:42 They did not remember what he had done,
how he delivered them from the enemy,
78:43 when he performed his awesome deeds in Egypt,
and his acts of judgment in the region of Zoan.
78:44 He turned their rivers into blood,
and they could not drink from their streams.
78:45 He sent swarms of biting insects against them,
as well as frogs that overran their land.
78:46 He gave their crops to the grasshopper,
the fruit of their labor to the locust.
78:47 He destroyed their vines with hail,
and their sycamore-fig trees with driving rain.
78:48 He rained hail down on their cattle,
and hurled lightning bolts down on their livestock.
78:49 His raging anger lashed out against them,
He sent fury, rage, and trouble
as messengers who bring disaster.
78:50 He sent his anger in full force;
he did not spare them from death;
he handed their lives over to destruction.
78:51 He struck down all the firstborn in Egypt,
the firstfruits of their reproductive power in the tents of Ham.
78:52 Yet he brought out his people like sheep;
he led them through the wilderness like a flock.
78:53 He guided them safely along,
while the sea covered their enemies.
78:54 He brought them to the border of his holy land,
to this mountainous land which his right hand acquired.
78:55 He drove the nations out from before them;
he assigned them their tribal allotments
and allowed the tribes of Israel to settle down.
78:56 Yet they challenged and defied the sovereign God,
and did not obey his commands.
78:57 They were unfaithful and acted as treacherously as their ancestors;
they were as unreliable as a malfunctioning bow.
78:58 They made him angry with their pagan shrines,
and made him jealous with their idols.
78:59 God heard and was angry;
he completely rejected Israel.
78:60 He abandoned the sanctuary at Shiloh,
the tent where he lived among men.
78:61 He allowed the symbol of his strong presence to be captured;
he gave the symbol of his splendor into the hand of the enemy.
78:62 He delivered his people over to the sword,
and was angry with his chosen nation.
78:63 Fire consumed their young men,
and their virgins remained unmarried.
78:64 Their priests fell by the sword,
but their widows did not weep.
78:65 But then the Lord awoke from his sleep;
he was like a warrior in a drunken rage.
78:66 He drove his enemies back;
he made them a permanent target for insults.
78:67 He rejected the tent of Joseph;
he did not choose the tribe of Ephraim.
78:68 He chose the tribe of Judah,
and Mount Zion, which he loves.
78:69 He made his sanctuary as enduring as the heavens above;
as secure as the earth, which he established permanently.
78:70 He chose David, his servant,
and took him from the sheepfolds.
78:71 He took him away from following the mother sheep,
and made him the shepherd of Jacob, his people,
and of Israel, his chosen nation.
78:72 David cared for them with pure motives;
he led them with skill.
Psalm 79
A psalm of Asaph.
79:1 O God, foreigners have invaded your chosen land;
they have polluted your holy temple
and turned Jerusalem into a heap of ruins.
79:2 They have given the corpses of your servants
to the birds of the sky;
the flesh of your loyal followers
to the beasts of the earth.
79:3 They have made their blood flow like water
all around Jerusalem, and there is no one to bury them.
79:4 We have become an object of disdain to our neighbors;
those who live on our borders taunt and insult us.
79:5 How long will this go on, O Lord?

Will you stay angry forever?
How long will your rage burn like fire?
79:6 Pour out your anger on the nations that do not acknowledge you,
on the kingdoms that do not pray to you!
79:7 For they have devoured Jacob
and destroyed his home.
79:8 Do not hold us accountable for the sins of earlier generations!
Quickly send your compassion our way,
for we are in serious trouble!
79:9 Help us, O God, our deliverer!
For the sake of your glorious reputation, rescue us!
Forgive our sins for the sake of your reputation!
79:10 Why should the nations say, "Where is their God?"
Before our very eyes may the shed blood of your servants
be avenged among the nations!
79:11 Listen to the painful cries of the prisoners!
Use your great strength to set free those condemned to die!
79:12 Pay back our neighbors in full!
May they be insulted the same way they insulted you, O Lord!
79:13 Then we, your people, the sheep of your pasture,
will continually thank you.
We will tell coming generations of your praiseworthy acts.
Psalm 80
For the music director; according to the *shushan-eduth* style; a psalm of Asaph.
80:1 O shepherd of Israel, pay attention,
you who lead Joseph like a flock of sheep!
You who sit enthroned above the winged angels, reveal your splendor!
80:2 In the sight of Ephraim, Benjamin, and Manasseh reveal your power!
Come and deliver us!
80:3 O God, restore us!
Smile on us! Then we will be delivered!
80:4 O Lord God, invincible warrior!
How long will you remain angry at your people while they pray to you?
80:5 You have given them tears as food;
you have made them drink tears by the measure.
80:6 You have made our neighbors dislike us,
and our enemies insult us.
80:7 O God, invincible warrior, restore us!
Smile on us! Then we will be delivered!
80:8 You uprooted a vine from Egypt;
you drove out nations and transplanted it.
80:9 You cleared the ground for it;
it took root,
and filled the land.
80:10 The mountains were covered by its shadow,
the highest cedars by its branches.
80:11 Its branches reached the Mediterranean Sea,
and its shoots the Euphrates River.
80:12 Why did you break down its walls,
so that all who pass by pluck its fruit?
80:13 The wild boars of the forest ruin it;
the insects of the field feed on it.
80:14 O God, invincible warrior, come back!
Look down from heaven and take notice!
Take care of this vine,
80:15 the root your right hand planted,
the shoot you made to grow!
80:16 It is burned and cut down.
They die because you are displeased with them.
80:17 May you give support to the one you have chosen,
to the one whom you raised up for yourself!
80:18 Then we will not turn away from you.
Revive us and we will pray to you!
80:19 O Lord God, invincible warrior, restore us!
Smile on us! Then we will be delivered!
Psalm 81
For the music director; according to the *gittith* style; by Asaph.
81:1 Shout for joy to God, our source of strength!
Shout out to the God of Jacob!
81:2 Sing a song and play the tambourine,
the pleasant sounding harp, and the ten-stringed instrument!
81:3 Sound the ram's horn on the day of the new moon,
and on the day of the full moon when our festival begins.
81:4 For observing the festival is a requirement for Israel;
it is an ordinance given by the God of Jacob.
81:5 He decreed it as a regulation in Joseph,
when he attacked the land of Egypt.
I heard a voice I did not recognize.
81:6 It said: "I removed the burden from his shoulder;
his hands were released from holding the basket.
81:7 In your distress you called out and I rescued you.

I answered you from a dark thundercloud.
I tested you at the waters of Meribah. (Selah)
81:8 I said, 'Listen, my people!
I will warn you!
O Israel, if only you would obey me!
81:9 There must be no other god among you.
You must not worship a foreign god.
81:10 I am the LORD, your God,
the one who brought you out of the land of Egypt.
Open your mouth wide and I will fill it!'
81:11 But my people did not obey me;
Israel did not submit to me.
81:12 I gave them over to their stubborn desires;
they did what seemed right to them.
81:13 If only my people would obey me!
If only Israel would keep my commands!
81:14 Then I would quickly subdue their enemies,
and attack their adversaries."
81:15 (May those who hate the LORD cower in fear before him!
May they be permanently humiliated!)
81:16 "I would feed Israel the best wheat,
and would satisfy your appetite with honey from the rocky cliffs."

Psalm 82

A psalm of Asaph.

82:1 God stands in the assembly of El;
in the midst of the gods he renders judgment.
82:2 He says, "How long will you make unjust legal decisions
and show favoritism to the wicked? (Selah)
82:3 Defend the cause of the poor and the fatherless!
Vindicate the oppressed and suffering!
82:4 Rescue the poor and needy!
Deliver them from the power of the wicked!
82:5 They neither know nor understand.
They stumble around in the dark,
while all the foundations of the earth crumble.
82:6 I thought, 'You are gods;
all of you are sons of the Most High.'
82:7 Yet you will die like mortals;
you will fall like all the other rulers."
82:8 Rise up, O God, and execute judgment on the earth!
For you own all the nations.

Psalm 83

A song, a psalm of Asaph.

83:1 O God, do not be silent!
Do not ignore us! Do not be inactive, O God!
83:2 For look, your enemies are making a commotion;
those who hate you are hostile.
83:3 They carefully plot against your people,
and make plans to harm the ones you cherish.
83:4 They say, "Come on, let's annihilate them so they are no longer a nation!
Then the name of Israel will be remembered no more."
83:5 Yes, they devise a unified strategy;
they form an alliance against you.
83:6 It includes the tents of Edom and the Ishmaelites,
Moab and the Hagrites,
83:7 Gebal, Ammon, and Amalek,
Philistia and the inhabitants of Tyre.
83:8 Even Assyria has allied with them,
lending its strength to the descendants of Lot. (Selah)
83:9 Do to them as you did to Midian –
as you did to Sisera and Jabin at the Kishon River!
83:10 They were destroyed at Endor;
their corpses were like manure on the ground.
83:11 Make their nobles like Oreb and Zeeb,
and all their rulers like Zebah and Zalmunna,
83:12 who said, "Let's take over the pastures of God!"
83:13 O my God, make them like dead thistles,
like dead weeds blown away by the wind!
83:14 Like the fire that burns down the forest,
or the flames that consume the mountainsides,
83:15 chase them with your gale winds,
and terrify them with your windstorm.
83:16 Cover their faces with shame,
so they might seek you, O LORD.
83:17 May they be humiliated and continually terrified!
May they die in shame!
83:18 Then they will know that you alone are the LORD,
the sovereign king over all the earth.

Psalm 84

For the music director; according to the *gittith* style; written by the Korahites, a psalm.

84:1 How lovely is the place where you live,
O LORD who rules over all!
84:2 I desperately want to be
in the courts of the LORD's temple.
My heart and my entire being shout for joy
to the living God.
84:3 Even the birds find a home there,
and the swallow builds a nest,
where she can protect her young
near your altars, O LORD who rules over all,
my king and my God.
84:4 How blessed are those who live in your temple
and praise you continually! (Selah)
84:5 How blessed are those who find their strength in you,
and long to travel the roads that lead to your temple!
84:6 As they pass through the Baca Valley,
he provides a spring for them.
The rain even covers it with pools of water.
84:7 They are sustained as they travel along;
each one appears before God in Zion.
84:8 O LORD, sovereign God,
hear my prayer!
Listen, O God of Jacob! (Selah)
84:9 O God, take notice of our shield!
Show concern for your chosen king!
84:10 Certainly spending just one day in your temple courts is better
than spending a thousand elsewhere.
I would rather stand at the entrance to the temple of my God
than live in the tents of the wicked.
84:11 For the LORD God is our sovereign protector.
The LORD bestows favor and honor;
he withholds no good thing from those who have integrity.
84:12 O LORD who rules over all,
how blessed are those who trust in you!

Psalm 85

For the music director; written by the Korahites, a psalm.

85:1 O LORD, you showed favor to your land;
you restored the well-being of Jacob.
85:2 You pardoned the wrongdoing of your people;
you forgave all their sin. (Selah)
85:3 You withdrew all your fury;
you turned back from your raging anger.
85:4 Restore us, O God our deliverer!
Do not be displeased with us!
85:5 Will you stay mad at us forever?
Will you remain angry throughout future generations?
85:6 Will you not revive us once more?
Then your people will rejoice in you!
85:7 O LORD, show us your loyal love!
Bestow on us your deliverance!
85:8 I will listen to what God the LORD says.
For he will make peace with his people, his faithful followers.
Yet they must not return to their foolish ways.
85:9 Certainly his loyal followers will soon experience his deliverance;
then his splendor will again appear in our land.
85:10 Loyal love and faithfulness meet;
deliverance and peace greet each other with a kiss.
85:11 Faithfulness grows from the ground,
and deliverance looks down from the sky.
85:12 Yes, the LORD will bestow his good blessings,
and our land will yield its crops.
85:13 Deliverance goes before him,
and prepares a pathway for him.

Psalm 86

A prayer of David.

86:1 Listen O LORD! Answer me!
For I am oppressed and needy.
86:2 Protect me, for I am loyal!
O my God, deliver your servant, who trusts in you!
86:3 Have mercy on me, O Lord,
for I cry out to you all day long!
86:4 Make your servant glad,
for to you, O Lord, I pray!
86:5 Certainly O Lord, you are kind and forgiving,
and show great faithfulness to all who cry out to you.
86:6 O LORD, hear my prayer!
Pay attention to my plea for mercy!
86:7 In my time of trouble I cry out to you,
for you will answer me.
86:8 None can compare to you among the gods, O Lord!
Your exploits are incomparable!
86:9 All the nations, whom you created,
will come and worship you, O Lord.
They will honor your name.

86:10 For you are great and do amazing things.
You alone are God.
86:11 O LORD, teach me how you want me to live!
Then I will obey your commands.
Make me wholeheartedly committed to you!
86:12 O Lord, my God, I will give you thanks with my whole heart!
I will honor your name continually!
86:13 For you will extend your great loyal love to me,
and will deliver my life from the depths of Sheol.
86:14 O God, arrogant men attack me;
a gang of ruthless men, who do not respect you, seek my life.
86:15 But you, O Lord, are a compassionate and merciful God.
You are patient and demonstrate great loyal love and faithfulness.
86:16 Turn toward me and have mercy on me!
Give your servant your strength!
Deliver your slave!
86:17 Show me evidence of your favor!
Then those who hate me will see it and be ashamed,
for you, O LORD, will help me and comfort me.
Psalm 87
Written by the Korahites; a psalm, a song.
87:1 The LORD's city is in the holy hills.
87:2 The LORD loves the gates of Zion
more than all the dwelling places of Jacob.
87:3 People say wonderful things about you,
O city of God. (Selah)
87:4 I mention Rahab and Babylon to my followers.
Here are Philistia and Tyre, along with Ethiopia.
It is said of them, "This one was born there."
87:5 But it is said of Zion's residents,
"Each one of these was born in her,
and the sovereign One makes her secure."
87:6 The LORD writes in the census book of the nations,
"This one was born there." (Selah)
87:7 As for the singers, as well as the pipers –
all of them sing within your walls.
Psalm 88
A song, a psalm written by the Korahites; for the music director; according to the *machalath-leannoth* style; a well-written song by Heman the Ezrachite.
88:1 O LORD God who delivers me!
By day I cry out
and at night I pray before you.
88:2 Listen to my prayer!
Pay attention to my cry for help!
88:3 For my life is filled with troubles
and I am ready to enter Sheol.
88:4 They treat me like those who descend into the grave.
I am like a helpless man,
88:5 adrift among the dead,
like corpses lying in the grave,
whom you remember no more,
and who are cut off from your power.
88:6 You place me in the lowest regions of the pit,
in the dark places, in the watery depths.
88:7 Your anger bears down on me,
and you overwhelm me with all your waves. (Selah)
88:8 You cause those who know me to keep their distance;
you make me an appalling sight to them.
I am trapped and cannot get free.
88:9 My eyes grow weak because of oppression.
I call out to you, O LORD, all day long;
I spread out my hands in prayer to you.
88:10 Do you accomplish amazing things for the dead?
Do the departed spirits rise up and give you thanks? (Selah)
88:11 Is your loyal love proclaimed in the grave,
or your faithfulness in the place of the dead?
88:12 Are your amazing deeds experienced in the dark region,
or your deliverance in the land of oblivion?
88:13 As for me, I cry out to you, O LORD;
in the morning my prayer confronts you.
88:14 O LORD, why do you reject me,
and pay no attention to me?
88:15 I am oppressed and have been on the verge of death since my youth.
I have been subjected to your horrors and am numb with pain.
88:16 Your anger overwhelms me;
your terrors destroy me.
88:17 They surround me like water all day long;
they join forces and encircle me.
88:18 You cause my friends and neighbors to keep their distance;
those who know me leave me alone in the darkness.
Psalm 89

A well-written song by Ethan the Ezrachite.
89:1 I will sing continually about the LORD's faithful deeds;
to future generations I will proclaim your faithfulness.
89:2 For I say, "Loyal love is permanently established;
in the skies you set up your faithfulness."
89:3 The LORD said,
"I have made a covenant with my chosen one;
I have made a promise on oath to David, my servant:
89:4 'I will give you an eternal dynasty
and establish your throne throughout future generations.'" (Selah)
89:5 O LORD, the heavens praise your amazing deeds,
as well as your faithfulness in the angelic assembly.
89:6 For who in the skies can compare to the LORD?
Who is like the LORD among the heavenly beings,
89:7 a God who is honored in the great angelic assembly,
and more awesome than all who surround him?
89:8 O LORD, sovereign God!
Who is strong like you, O LORD?
Your faithfulness surrounds you.
89:9 You rule over the proud sea.
When its waves surge, you calm them.
89:10 You crushed the Proud One and killed it;
with your strong arm you scattered your enemies.
89:11 The heavens belong to you, as does the earth.
You made the world and all it contains.
89:12 You created the north and the south.
Tabor and Hermon rejoice in your name.
89:13 Your arm is powerful,
your hand strong,
your right hand victorious.
89:14 Equity and justice are the foundation of your throne.
Loyal love and faithfulness characterize your rule.
89:15 How blessed are the people who worship you!
O LORD, they experience your favor.
89:16 They rejoice in your name all day long,
and are vindicated by your justice.
89:17 For you give them splendor and strength.
By your favor we are victorious.
89:18 For our shield belongs to the LORD,
our king to the Holy One of Israel.
89:19 Then you spoke through a vision to your faithful followers and said:
"I have energized a warrior;
I have raised up a young man from the people.
89:20 I have discovered David, my servant.
With my holy oil I have anointed him as king.
89:21 My hand will support him,
and my arm will strengthen him.
89:22 No enemy will be able to exact tribute from him;
a violent oppressor will not be able to humiliate him.
89:23 I will crush his enemies before him;
I will strike down those who hate him.
89:24 He will experience my faithfulness and loyal love,
and by my name he will win victories.
89:25 I will place his hand over the sea,
his right hand over the rivers.
89:26 He will call out to me,
'You are my father, my God, and the protector who delivers me.'
89:27 I will appoint him to be my firstborn son,
the most exalted of the earth's kings.
89:28 I will always extend my loyal love to him,
and my covenant with him is secure.
89:29 I will give him an eternal dynasty,
and make his throne as enduring as the skies above.
89:30 If his sons reject my law
and disobey my regulations,
89:31 if they break my rules
and do not keep my commandments,
89:32 I will punish their rebellion by beating them with a club,
their sin by inflicting them with bruises.
89:33 But I will not remove my loyal love from him,
nor be unfaithful to my promise.
89:34 I will not break my covenant
or go back on what I promised.
89:35 Once and for all I have vowed by my own holiness,
I will never deceive David.
89:36 His dynasty will last forever.
His throne will endure before me, like the sun,
89:37 it will remain stable, like the moon,
his throne will endure like the skies." (Selah)
89:38 But you have spurned and rejected him;
you are angry with your chosen king.
89:39 You have repudiated your covenant with your servant;

you have thrown his crown to the ground.
89:40 You have broken down all his walls;
you have made his strongholds a heap of ruins.
89:41 All who pass by have robbed him;
he has become an object of disdain to his neighbors.
89:42 You have allowed his adversaries to be victorious,
and all his enemies to rejoice.
89:43 You turn back his sword from the adversary,
and have not sustained him in battle.
89:44 You have brought to an end his splendor,
and have knocked his throne to the ground.
89:45 You have cut short his youth,
and have covered him with shame. (Selah)
89:46 How long, O LORD, will this last?
Will you remain hidden forever?
Will your anger continue to burn like fire?
89:47 Take note of my brief lifespan!
Why do you make all people so mortal?
89:48 No man can live on without experiencing death,
or deliver his life from the power of Sheol. (Selah)
89:49 Where are your earlier faithful deeds, O Lord,
the ones performed in accordance with your reliable oath to David?
89:50 Take note, O Lord, of the way your servants are taunted,
and of how I must bear so many insults from people!
89:51 Your enemies, O LORD, hurl insults;
they insult your chosen king as they dog his footsteps.
89:52 The LORD deserves praise forevermore!
We agree! We agree!
Book 4(Psalms 90-106)
Psalm 90
A prayer of Moses, the man of God.
90:1 O Lord, you have been our protector through all generations!
90:2 Even before the mountains came into existence,
or you brought the world into being,
you were the eternal God.
90:3 You make mankind return to the dust,
and say, "Return, O people!"
90:4 Yes, in your eyes a thousand years
are like yesterday that quickly passes,
or like one of the divisions of the nighttime.
90:5 You bring their lives to an end and they "fall asleep."
In the morning they are like the grass that sprouts up;
90:6 in the morning it glistens and sprouts up;
at evening time it withers and dries up.
90:7 Yes, we are consumed by your anger;
we are terrified by your wrath.
90:8 You are aware of our sins;
you even know about our hidden sins.
90:9 Yes, throughout all our days we experience your raging fury;
the years of our lives pass quickly, like a sigh.
90:10 The days of our lives add up to seventy years,
or eighty, if one is especially strong.
But even one's best years are marred by trouble and oppression.
Yes, they pass quickly and we fly away.
90:11 Who can really fathom the intensity of your anger?
Your raging fury causes people to fear you.
90:12 So teach us to consider our mortality,
so that we might live wisely.
90:13 Turn back toward us, O LORD!
How long must this suffering last?
Have pity on your servants!
90:14 Satisfy us in the morning with your loyal love!
Then we will shout for joy and be happy all our days!
90:15 Make us happy in proportion to the days you have afflicted us,
in proportion to the years we have experienced trouble!
90:16 May your servants see your work!
May their sons see your majesty!
90:17 May our sovereign God extend his favor to us!
Make our endeavors successful!
Yes, make them successful!
Psalm 91
91:1 As for you, the one who lives in the shelter of the sovereign One,
and resides in the protective shadow of the mighty king –
91:2 I say this about the LORD, my shelter and my stronghold,
my God in whom I trust –
91:3 he will certainly rescue you from the snare of the hunter
and from the destructive plague.
91:4 He will shelter you with his wings;
you will find safety under his wings.
His faithfulness is like a shield or a protective wall.
91:5 You need not fear the terrors of the night,
the arrow that flies by day,
91:6 the plague that comes in the darkness,
or the disease that comes at noon.
91:7 Though a thousand may fall beside you,
and a multitude on your right side,
it will not reach you.
91:8 Certainly you will see it with your very own eyes –
you will see the wicked paid back.
91:9 For you have taken refuge in the LORD,
my shelter, the sovereign One.
91:10 No harm will overtake you;
no illness will come near your home.
91:11 For he will order his angels
to protect you in all you do.
91:12 They will lift you up in their hands,
so you will not slip and fall on a stone.
91:13 You will subdue a lion and a snake;
you will trample underfoot a young lion and a serpent.
91:14 The LORD says,
"Because he is devoted to me, I will deliver him;
I will protect him because he is loyal to me.
91:15 When he calls out to me, I will answer him.
I will be with him when he is in trouble;
I will rescue him and bring him honor.
91:16 I will satisfy him with long life,
and will let him see my salvation.
Psalm 92
A psalm; a song for the Sabbath day.
92:1 It is fitting to thank the LORD,
and to sing praises to your name, O sovereign One!
92:2 It is fitting to proclaim your loyal love in the morning,
and your faithfulness during the night,
92:3 to the accompaniment of a ten-stringed instrument and a lyre,
to the accompaniment of the meditative tone of the harp.
92:4 For you, O LORD, have made me happy by your work.
I will sing for joy because of what you have done.
92:5 How great are your works, O LORD!
Your plans are very intricate!
92:6 The spiritually insensitive do not recognize this;
the fool does not understand this.
92:7 When the wicked sprout up like grass,
and all the evildoers glisten,
it is so that they may be annihilated.
92:8 But you, O LORD, reign forever!
92:9 Indeed, look at your enemies, O LORD!
Indeed, look at how your enemies perish!
All the evildoers are scattered!
92:10 You exalt my horn like that of a wild ox.
I am covered with fresh oil.
92:11 I gloat in triumph over those who tried to ambush me;
I hear the defeated cries of the evil foes who attacked me.
92:12 The godly grow like a palm tree;
they grow high like a cedar in Lebanon.
92:13 Planted in the LORD's house,
they grow in the courts of our God.
92:14 They bear fruit even when they are old;
they are filled with vitality and have many leaves.
92:15 So they proclaim that the LORD, my protector,
is just and never unfair.
Psalm 93
93:1 The LORD reigns!
He is robed in majesty,
the LORD is robed,
he wears strength around his waist.
Indeed, the world is established, it cannot be moved.
93:2 Your throne has been secure from ancient times;
you have always been king.
93:3 The waves roar, O LORD,
the waves roar,
the waves roar and crash.
93:4 Above the sound of the surging water,
and the mighty waves of the sea,
the LORD sits enthroned in majesty.
93:5 The rules you set down are completely reliable.
Holiness aptly adorns your house, O LORD, forever.
Psalm 94
94:1 O LORD, the God who avenges!
O God who avenges, reveal your splendor!
94:2 Rise up, O judge of the earth!
Pay back the proud!
94:3 O LORD, how long will the wicked,
how long will the wicked celebrate?
94:4 They spew out threats and speak defiantly;
all the evildoers boast.
94:5 O LORD, they crush your people;

they oppress the nation that belongs to you.
94:6 They kill the widow and the one residing outside his native land,
and they murder the fatherless.
94:7 Then they say, "The LORD does not see this;
the God of Jacob does not take notice of it."
94:8 Take notice of this, you ignorant people!
You fools, when will you ever understand?
94:9 Does the one who makes the human ear not hear?
Does the one who forms the human eye not see?
94:10 Does the one who disciplines the nations not punish?
He is the one who imparts knowledge to human beings!
94:11 The LORD knows that
peoples' thoughts are morally bankrupt.
94:12 How blessed is the one whom you instruct, O LORD,
the one whom you teach from your law,
94:13 in order to protect him from times of trouble,
until the wicked are destroyed.
94:14 Certainly the LORD does not forsake his people;
he does not abandon the nation that belongs to him.
94:15 For justice will prevail,
and all the morally upright will be vindicated.
94:16 Who will rise up to defend me against the wicked?
Who will stand up for me against the evildoers?
94:17 If the LORD had not helped me,
I would have laid down in the silence of death.
94:18 If I say, "My foot is slipping,"
your loyal love, O LORD, supports me.
94:19 When worries threaten to overwhelm me,
your soothing touch makes me happy.
94:20 Cruel rulers are not your allies,
those who make oppressive laws.
94:21 They conspire against the blameless,
and condemn to death the innocent.
94:22 But the LORD will protect me,
and my God will shelter me.
94:23 He will pay them back for their sin.
He will destroy them because of their evil;
the LORD our God will destroy them.
Psalm 95
95:1 Come! Let's sing for joy to the LORD!
Let's shout out praises to our protector who delivers us!
95:2 Let's enter his presence with thanksgiving!
Let's shout out to him in celebration!
95:3 For the LORD is a great God,
a great king who is superior to all gods.
95:4 The depths of the earth are in his hand,
and the mountain peaks belong to him.
95:5 The sea is his, for he made it.
His hands formed the dry land.
95:6 Come! Let's bow down and worship!
Let's kneel before the LORD, our creator!
95:7 For he is our God;
we are the people of his pasture,
the sheep he owns.
Today, if only you would obey him!
95:8 He says, "Do not be stubborn like they were at Meribah,
like they were that day at Massah in the wilderness,
95:9 where your ancestors challenged my authority,
and tried my patience, even though they had seen my work.
95:10 For forty years I was continually disgusted with that generation,
and I said, 'These people desire to go astray;
they do not obey my commands.'
95:11 So I made a vow in my anger,
'They will never enter into the resting place I had set aside for them.'"
Psalm 96
96:1 Sing to the LORD a new song!
Sing to the LORD, all the earth!
96:2 Sing to the LORD! Praise his name!
Announce every day how he delivers!
96:3 Tell the nations about his splendor!
Tell all the nations about his amazing deeds!
96:4 For the LORD is great and certainly worthy of praise;
he is more awesome than all gods.
96:5 For all the gods of the nations are worthless,
but the LORD made the sky.
96:6 Majestic splendor emanates from him;
his sanctuary is firmly established and beautiful.
96:7 Ascribe to the LORD, O families of the nations,
ascribe to the LORD splendor and strength!
96:8 Ascribe to the LORD the splendor he deserves!
Bring an offering and enter his courts!
96:9 Worship the LORD in holy attire!
Tremble before him, all the earth!

96:10 Say among the nations, "The LORD reigns!
The world is established, it cannot be moved.
He judges the nations fairly."
96:11 Let the sky rejoice, and the earth be happy!
Let the sea and everything in it shout!
96:12 Let the fields and everything in them celebrate!
Then let the trees of the forest shout with joy
96:13 before the LORD, for he comes!
For he comes to judge the earth!
He judges the world fairly,
and the nations in accordance with his justice.
Psalm 97
97:1 The LORD reigns!
Let the earth be happy!
Let the many coastlands rejoice!
97:2 Dark clouds surround him;
equity and justice are the foundation of his throne.
97:3 Fire goes before him;
on every side it burns up his enemies.
97:4 His lightning bolts light up the world;
the earth sees and trembles.
97:5 The mountains melt like wax before the LORD,
before the Lord of the whole earth.
97:6 The sky declares his justice,
and all the nations see his splendor.
97:7 All who worship idols are ashamed,
those who boast about worthless idols.
All the gods bow down before him.
97:8 Zion hears and rejoices,
the towns of Judah are happy,
because of your judgments, O LORD.
97:9 For you, O LORD, are the sovereign king over the whole earth;
you are elevated high above all gods.
97:10 You who love the LORD, hate evil!
He protects the lives of his faithful followers;
he delivers them from the power of the wicked.
97:11 The godly bask in the light;
the morally upright experience joy.
97:12 You godly ones, rejoice in the LORD!
Give thanks to his holy name.
Psalm 98
A psalm.
98:1 Sing to the LORD a new song,
for he performs amazing deeds!
His right hand and his mighty arm
accomplish deliverance.
98:2 The LORD demonstrates his power to deliver;
in the sight of the nations he reveals his justice.
98:3 He remains loyal and faithful to the family of Israel.
All the ends of the earth see our God deliver us.
98:4 Shout out praises to the LORD, all the earth!
Break out in a joyful shout and sing!
98:5 Sing to the LORD accompanied by a harp,
accompanied by a harp and the sound of music!
98:6 With trumpets and the blaring of the ram's horn,
shout out praises before the king, the LORD!
98:7 Let the sea and everything in it shout,
along with the world and those who live in it!
98:8 Let the rivers clap their hands!
Let the mountains sing in unison
98:9 before the LORD!
For he comes to judge the earth!
He judges the world fairly,
and the nations in a just manner.
Psalm 99
99:1 The LORD reigns!
The nations tremble.
He sits enthroned above the winged angels;
the earth shakes.
99:2 The LORD is elevated in Zion;
he is exalted over all the nations.
99:3 Let them praise your great and awesome name!
He is holy!
99:4 The king is strong;
he loves justice.
You ensure that legal decisions will be made fairly;
you promote justice and equity in Jacob.
99:5 Praise the LORD our God!
Worship before his footstool!
He is holy!
99:6 Moses and Aaron were among his priests;
Samuel was one of those who prayed to him.
They prayed to the LORD and he answered them.

99:7 He spoke to them from a pillar of cloud;
they obeyed his regulations and the ordinance he gave them.
99:8 O LORD our God, you answered them.
They found you to be a forgiving God,
but also one who punished their sinful deeds.
99:9 Praise the LORD our God!
Worship on his holy hill,
for the LORD our God is holy!
Psalm 100
A thanksgiving psalm.
100:1 Shout out praises to the LORD, all the earth!
100:2 Worship the LORD with joy!
Enter his presence with joyful singing!
100:3 Acknowledge that the LORD is God!
He made us and we belong to him;
we are his people, the sheep of his pasture.
100:4 Enter his gates with thanksgiving,
and his courts with praise!
Give him thanks!
Praise his name!
100:5 For the LORD is good.
His loyal love endures,
and he is faithful through all generations.
Psalm 101
A psalm of David.
101:1 I will sing about loyalty and justice!
To you, O LORD, I will sing praises!
101:2 I will walk in the way of integrity.
When will you come to me?
I will conduct my business with integrity in the midst of my palace.
101:3 I will not even consider doing what is dishonest.
I hate doing evil;
I will have no part of it.
101:4 I will have nothing to do with a perverse person;
I will not permit evil.
101:5 I will destroy anyone who slanders his neighbor in secret.
I will not tolerate anyone who has a cocky demeanor and an arrogant attitude.
101:6 I will favor the honest people of the land,
and allow them to live with me.
Those who walk in the way of integrity will attend me.
101:7 Deceitful people will not live in my palace.
Liars will not be welcome in my presence.
101:8 Each morning I will destroy all the wicked people in the land,
and remove all evildoers from the city of the LORD.
Psalm 102
The prayer of an oppressed man, as he grows faint and pours out his lament before the LORD.
102:1 O LORD, hear my prayer!
Pay attention to my cry for help!
102:2 Do not ignore me in my time of trouble!
Listen to me!
When I call out to you, quickly answer me!
102:3 For my days go up in smoke,
and my bones are charred like a fireplace.
102:4 My heart is parched and withered like grass,
for I am unable to eat food.
102:5 Because of the anxiety that makes me groan,
my bones protrude from my skin.
102:6 I am like an owl in the wilderness;
I am like a screech owl among the ruins.
102:7 I stay awake;
I am like a solitary bird on a roof.
102:8 All day long my enemies taunt me;
those who mock me use my name in their curses.
102:9 For I eat ashes as if they were bread,
and mix my drink with my tears,
102:10 because of your anger and raging fury.
Indeed, you pick me up and throw me away.
102:11 My days are coming to an end,
and I am withered like grass.
102:12 But you, O LORD, rule forever,
and your reputation endures.
102:13 You will rise up and have compassion on Zion.
For it is time to have mercy on her,
for the appointed time has come.
102:14 Indeed, your servants take delight in her stones,
and feel compassion for the dust of her ruins.
102:15 The nations will respect the reputation of the LORD,
and all the kings of the earth will respect his splendor,
102:16 when the LORD rebuilds Zion,
and reveals his splendor,
102:17 when he responds to the prayer of the destitute,

and does not reject their request.
102:18 The account of his intervention will be recorded for future generations;
people yet to be born will praise the LORD.
102:19 For he will look down from his sanctuary above;
from heaven the LORD will look toward earth,
102:20 in order to hear the painful cries of the prisoners,
and to set free those condemned to die,
102:21 so they may proclaim the name of the LORD in Zion,
and praise him in Jerusalem,
102:22 when the nations gather together,
and the kingdoms pay tribute to the LORD.
102:23 He has taken away my strength in the middle of life;
he has cut short my days.
102:24 I say, "O my God, please do not take me away in the middle of my life!
You endure through all generations.
102:25 In earlier times you established the earth;
the skies are your handiwork.
102:26 They will perish,
but you will endure.
They will wear out like a garment;
like clothes you will remove them and they will disappear.
102:27 But you remain;
your years do not come to an end.
102:28 The children of your servants will settle down here,
and their descendants will live securely in your presence."
Psalm 103
By David.
103:1 Praise the LORD, O my soul!
With all that is within me, praise his holy name!
103:2 Praise the LORD, O my soul!
Do not forget all his kind deeds!
103:3 He is the one who forgives all your sins,
who heals all your diseases,
103:4 who delivers your life from the Pit,
who crowns you with his loyal love and compassion,
103:5 who satisfies your life with good things,
so your youth is renewed like an eagle's.
103:6 The LORD does what is fair,
and executes justice for all the oppressed.
103:7 The LORD revealed his faithful acts to Moses,
his deeds to the Israelites.
103:8 The LORD is compassionate and merciful;
he is patient and demonstrates great loyal love.
103:9 He does not always accuse,
and does not stay angry.
103:10 He does not deal with us as our sins deserve;
he does not repay us as our misdeeds deserve.
103:11 For as the skies are high above the earth,
so his loyal love towers over his faithful followers.
103:12 As far as the eastern horizon is from the west,
so he removes the guilt of our rebellious actions from us.
103:13 As a father has compassion on his children,
so the LORD has compassion on his faithful followers.
103:14 For he knows what we are made of;
he realizes we are made of clay.
103:15 A person's life is like grass.
Like a flower in the field it flourishes,
103:16 but when the hot wind blows by, it disappears,
and one can no longer even spot the place where it once grew.
103:17 But the LORD continually shows loyal love to his faithful followers,
and is faithful to their descendants,
103:18 to those who keep his covenant,
who are careful to obey his commands.
103:19 The LORD has established his throne in heaven;
his kingdom extends over everything.
103:20 Praise the LORD, you angels of his,
you powerful warriors who carry out his decrees
and obey his orders!
103:21 Praise the LORD, all you warriors of his,
you servants of his who carry out his desires!
103:22 Praise the LORD, all that he has made,
in all the regions of his kingdom!
Praise the LORD, O my soul!
Psalm 104
104:1 Praise the LORD, O my soul!
O LORD my God, you are magnificent.
You are robed in splendor and majesty.
104:2 He covers himself with light as if it were a garment.
He stretches out the skies like a tent curtain,

104:3 and lays the beams of the upper rooms of his palace on the rain clouds.
He makes the clouds his chariot,
and travels along on the wings of the wind.
104:4 He makes the winds his messengers,
and the flaming fire his attendant.
104:5 He established the earth on its foundations;
it will never be upended.
104:6 The watery deep covered it like a garment;
the waters reached above the mountains.
104:7 Your shout made the waters retreat;
at the sound of your thunderous voice they hurried off –
104:8 as the mountains rose up,
and the valleys went down –
to the place you appointed for them.
104:9 You set up a boundary for them that they could not cross,
so that they would not cover the earth again.
104:10 He turns springs into streams;
they flow between the mountains.
104:11 They provide water for all the animals in the field;
the wild donkeys quench their thirst.
104:12 The birds of the sky live beside them;
they chirp among the bushes.
104:13 He waters the mountains from the upper rooms of his palace;
the earth is full of the fruit you cause to grow.
104:14 He provides grass for the cattle,
and crops for people to cultivate,
so they can produce food from the ground,
104:15 as well as wine that makes people feel so good,
and so they can have oil to make their faces shine,
as well as food that sustains people's lives.
104:16 The trees of the LORD receive all the rain they need,
the cedars of Lebanon which he planted,
104:17 where the birds make nests,
near the evergreens in which the herons live.
104:18 The wild goats live in the high mountains;
the rock badgers find safety in the cliffs.
104:19 He made the moon to mark the months,
and the sun sets according to a regular schedule.
104:20 You make it dark and night comes,
during which all the beasts of the forest prowl around.
104:21 The lions roar for prey,
seeking their food from God.
104:22 When the sun rises, they withdraw
and sleep in their dens.
104:23 Men then go out to do their work,
and labor away until evening.
104:24 How many living things you have made, O LORD!
You have exhibited great skill in making all of them;
the earth is full of the living things you have made.
104:25 Over here is the deep, wide sea,
which teems with innumerable swimming creatures,
living things both small and large.
104:26 The ships travel there,
and over here swims the whale you made to play in it.
104:27 All of your creatures wait for you
to provide them with food on a regular basis.
104:28 You give food to them and they receive it;
you open your hand and they are filled with food.
104:29 When you ignore them, they panic.
When you take away their life's breath, they die
and return to dust.
104:30 When you send your life-giving breath, they are created,
and you replenish the surface of the ground.
104:31 May the splendor of the LORD endure!
May the LORD find pleasure in the living things he has made!
104:32 He looks down on the earth and it shakes;
he touches the mountains and they start to smolder.
104:33 I will sing to the LORD as long as I live;
I will sing praise to my God as long as I exist!
104:34 May my thoughts be pleasing to him!
I will rejoice in the LORD.
104:35 May sinners disappear from the earth,
and the wicked vanish!
Praise the LORD, O my soul!
Praise the LORD!
Psalm 105
105:1 Give thanks to the LORD!
Call on his name!
Make known his accomplishments among the nations!
105:2 Sing to him!
Make music to him!
Tell about all his miraculous deeds!

105:3 Boast about his holy name!
Let the hearts of those who seek the LORD rejoice!
105:4 Seek the LORD and the strength he gives!
Seek his presence continually!
105:5 Recall the miraculous deeds he performed,
his mighty acts and the judgments he decreed,
105:6 O children of Abraham, God's servant,
you descendants of Jacob, God's chosen ones!
105:7 He is the LORD our God;
he carries out judgment throughout the earth.
105:8 He always remembers his covenantal decree,
the promise he made to a thousand generations –
105:9 the promise he made to Abraham,
the promise he made by oath to Isaac!
105:10 He gave it to Jacob as a decree,
to Israel as a lasting promise,
105:11 saying, "To you I will give the land of Canaan
as the portion of your inheritance."
105:12 When they were few in number,
just a very few, and resident aliens within it,
105:13 they wandered from nation to nation,
and from one kingdom to another.
105:14 He let no one oppress them;
he disciplined kings for their sake,
105:15 saying, "Don't touch my chosen ones!
Don't harm my prophets!"
105:16 He called down a famine upon the earth;
he cut off all the food supply.
105:17 He sent a man ahead of them –
Joseph was sold as a servant.
105:18 The shackles hurt his feet;
his neck was placed in an iron collar,
105:19 until the time when his prediction came true.
The LORD's word proved him right.
105:20 The king authorized his release;
the ruler of nations set him free.
105:21 He put him in charge of his palace,
and made him manager of all his property,
105:22 giving him authority to imprison his officials
and to teach his advisers.
105:23 Israel moved to Egypt;
Jacob lived for a time in the land of Ham.
105:24 The LORD made his people very fruitful,
and made them more numerous than their enemies.
105:25 He caused them to hate his people,
and to mistreat his servants.
105:26 He sent his servant Moses,
and Aaron, whom he had chosen.
105:27 They executed his miraculous signs among them,
and his amazing deeds in the land of Ham.
105:28 He made it dark;
they did not disobey his orders.
105:29 He turned their water into blood,
and killed their fish.
105:30 Their land was overrun by frogs,
which even got into the rooms of their kings.
105:31 He ordered flies to come;
gnats invaded their whole territory.
105:32 He sent hail along with the rain;
there was lightning in their land.
105:33 He destroyed their vines and fig trees,
and broke the trees throughout their territory.
105:34 He ordered locusts to come,
innumerable grasshoppers.
105:35 They ate all the vegetation in their land,
and devoured the crops of their fields.
105:36 He struck down all the firstborn in their land,
the firstfruits of their reproductive power.
105:37 He brought his people out enriched with silver and gold;
none of his tribes stumbled.
105:38 Egypt was happy when they left,
for they were afraid of them.
105:39 He spread out a cloud for a cover,
and provided a fire to light up the night.
105:40 They asked for food, and he sent quails;
he satisfied them with food from the sky.
105:41 He opened up a rock and water flowed out;
a river ran through dry regions.
105:42 Yes, he remembered the sacred promise
he made to Abraham his servant.
105:43 When he led his people out, they rejoiced;
his chosen ones shouted with joy.
105:44 He handed the territory of nations over to them,

and they took possession of what other peoples had produced,
105:45 so that they might keep his commands
and obey his laws.
Praise the LORD!
Psalm 106
106:1 Praise the LORD!
Give thanks to the LORD, for he is good,
and his loyal love endures!
106:2 Who can adequately recount the LORD's mighty acts,
or relate all his praiseworthy deeds?
106:3 How blessed are those who promote justice,
and do what is right all the time!
106:4 Remember me, O LORD, when you show favor to your people!
Pay attention to me, when you deliver,
106:5 so I may see the prosperity of your chosen ones,
rejoice along with your nation,
and boast along with the people who belong to you.
106:6 We have sinned like our ancestors;
we have done wrong, we have done evil.
106:7 Our ancestors in Egypt failed to appreciate your miraculous deeds,
they failed to remember your many acts of loyal love,
and they rebelled at the sea, by the Red Sea.
106:8 Yet he delivered them for the sake of his reputation,
that he might reveal his power.
106:9 He shouted at the Red Sea and it dried up;
he led them through the deep water as if it were a desert.
106:10 He delivered them from the power of the one who hated them,
and rescued them from the power of the enemy.
106:11 The water covered their enemies;
not even one of them survived.
106:12 They believed his promises;
they sang praises to him.
106:13 They quickly forgot what he had done;
they did not wait for his instructions.
106:14 In the wilderness they had an insatiable craving for meat;
they challenged God in the desert.
106:15 He granted their request,
then struck them with a disease.
106:16 In the camp they resented Moses,
and Aaron, the LORD's holy priest.
106:17 The earth opened up and swallowed Dathan;
it engulfed the group led by Abiram.
106:18 Fire burned their group;
the flames scorched the wicked.
106:19 They made an image of a calf at Horeb,
and worshiped a metal idol.
106:20 They traded their majestic God
for the image of an ox that eats grass.
106:21 They rejected the God who delivered them,
the one who performed great deeds in Egypt,
106:22 amazing feats in the land of Ham,
mighty acts by the Red Sea.
106:23 He threatened to destroy them,
but Moses, his chosen one, interceded with him
and turned back his destructive anger.
106:24 They rejected the fruitful land;
they did not believe his promise.
106:25 They grumbled in their tents;
they did not obey the LORD.
106:26 So he made a solemn vow
that he would make them die in the desert,
106:27 make their descendants die among the nations,
and scatter them among foreign lands.
106:28 They worshiped Baal of Peor,
and ate sacrifices offered to the dead.
106:29 They made the LORD angry by their actions,
and a plague broke out among them.
106:30 Phinehas took a stand and intervened,
and the plague subsided.
106:31 This brought him a reward,
an eternal gift.
106:32 They made him angry by the waters of Meribah,
and Moses suffered because of them,
106:33 for they aroused his temper,
and he spoke rashly.
106:34 They did not destroy the nations,
as the LORD had commanded them to do.
106:35 They mixed in with the nations
and learned their ways.
106:36 They worshiped their idols,
which became a snare to them.
106:37 They sacrificed their sons and daughters to demons.
106:38 They shed innocent blood –

the blood of their sons and daughters,
whom they sacrificed to the idols of Canaan.
The land was polluted by bloodshed.
106:39 They were defiled by their deeds,
and unfaithful in their actions.
106:40 So the LORD was angry with his people
and despised the people who belong to him.
106:41 He handed them over to the nations,
and those who hated them ruled over them.
106:42 Their enemies oppressed them;
they were subject to their authority.
106:43 Many times he delivered them,
but they had a rebellious attitude,
and degraded themselves by their sin.
106:44 Yet he took notice of their distress,
when he heard their cry for help.
106:45 He remembered his covenant with them,
and relented because of his great loyal love.
106:46 He caused all their conquerors
to have pity on them.
106:47 Deliver us, O LORD, our God!
Gather us from among the nations!
Then we will give thanks to your holy name,
and boast about your praiseworthy deeds.
106:48 The LORD God of Israel deserves praise,
in the future and forevermore.
Let all the people say, "We agree! Praise the LORD!"
Book 5(Psalms 107-150)
Psalm 107
107:1 Give thanks to the LORD, for he is good,
and his loyal love endures!
107:2 Let those delivered by the LORD speak out,
those whom he delivered from the power of the enemy,
107:3 and gathered from foreign lands,
from east and west,
from north and south.
107:4 They wandered through the wilderness on a desert road;
they found no city in which to live.
107:5 They were hungry and thirsty;
they fainted from exhaustion.
107:6 They cried out to the LORD in their distress;
he delivered them from their troubles.
107:7 He led them on a level road,
that they might find a city in which to live.
107:8 Let them give thanks to the LORD for his loyal love,
and for the amazing things he has done for people!
107:9 For he has satisfied those who thirst,
and those who hunger he has filled with food.
107:10 They sat in utter darkness,
bound in painful iron chains,
107:11 because they had rebelled against God's commands,
and rejected the instructions of the sovereign king.
107:12 So he used suffering to humble them;
they stumbled and no one helped them up.
107:13 They cried out to the LORD in their distress;
he delivered them from their troubles.
107:14 He brought them out of the utter darkness,
and tore off their shackles.
107:15 Let them give thanks to the LORD for his loyal love,
and for the amazing things he has done for people!
107:16 For he shattered the bronze gates,
and hacked through the iron bars.
107:17 They acted like fools in their rebellious ways,
and suffered because of their sins.
107:18 They lost their appetite for all food,
and they drew near the gates of death.
107:19 They cried out to the LORD in their distress;
he delivered them from their troubles.
107:20 He sent them an assuring word and healed them;
he rescued them from the pits where they were trapped.
107:21 Let them give thanks to the LORD for his loyal love,
and for the amazing things he has done for people!
107:22 Let them present thank offerings,
and loudly proclaim what he has done!
107:23 Some traveled on the sea in ships,
and carried cargo over the vast waters.
107:24 They witnessed the acts of the LORD,
his amazing feats on the deep water.
107:25 He gave the order for a windstorm,
and it stirred up the waves of the sea.
107:26 They reached up to the sky,
then dropped into the depths.
The sailors' strength left them because the danger was so great.

107:27 They swayed and staggered like a drunk,
and all their skill proved ineffective.
107:28 They cried out to the LORD in their distress;
he delivered them from their troubles.
107:29 He calmed the storm,
and the waves grew silent.
107:30 The sailors rejoiced because the waves grew quiet,
and he led them to the harbor they desired.
107:31 Let them give thanks to the LORD for his loyal love,
and for the amazing things he has done for people!
107:32 Let them exalt him in the assembly of the people!
Let them praise him in the place where the leaders preside!
107:33 He turned streams into a desert,
springs of water into arid land,
107:34 and a fruitful land into a barren place,
because of the sin of its inhabitants.
107:35 As for his people, he turned a desert into a pool of water,
and a dry land into springs of water.
107:36 He allowed the hungry to settle there,
and they established a city in which to live.
107:37 They cultivated fields,
and planted vineyards,
which yielded a harvest of fruit.
107:38 He blessed them so that they became very numerous.
He would not allow their cattle to decrease in number.
107:39 As for their enemies, they decreased in number and were beaten down,
because of painful distress and suffering.
107:40 He would pour contempt upon princes,
and he made them wander in a wasteland with no road.
107:41 Yet he protected the needy from oppression,
and cared for his families like a flock of sheep.
107:42 When the godly see this, they rejoice,
and every sinner shuts his mouth.
107:43 Whoever is wise, let him take note of these things!
Let them consider the LORD's acts of loyal love!

Psalm 108
A song, a psalm of David.
108:1 I am determined, O God!
I will sing and praise you with my whole heart.
108:2 Awake, O stringed instrument and harp!
I will wake up at dawn!
108:3 I will give you thanks before the nations, O LORD!
I will sing praises to you before foreigners!
108:4 For your loyal love extends beyond the sky,
and your faithfulness reaches the clouds.
108:5 Rise up above the sky, O God!
May your splendor cover the whole earth!
108:6 Deliver by your power and answer me,
so that the ones you love may be safe.
108:7 God has spoken in his sanctuary:
"I will triumph! I will parcel out Shechem,
the valley of Succoth I will measure off.
108:8 Gilead belongs to me,
as does Manasseh!
Ephraim is my helmet,
Judah my royal scepter.
108:9 Moab is my wash basin.
I will make Edom serve me.
I will shout in triumph over Philistia."
108:10 Who will lead me into the fortified city?
Who will bring me to Edom?
108:11 Have you not rejected us, O God?
O God, you do not go into battle with our armies.
108:12 Give us help against the enemy,
for any help men might offer is futile.
108:13 By God's power we will conquer;
he will trample down our enemies.

Psalm 109
For the music director, a psalm of David.
109:1 O God whom I praise, do not ignore me!
109:2 For they say cruel and deceptive things to me;
they lie to me.
109:3 They surround me and say hateful things;
they attack me for no reason.
109:4 They repay my love with accusations,
but I continue to pray.
109:5 They repay me evil for good,
and hate for love.
109:6 Appoint an evil man to testify against him!
May an accuser stand at his right side!
109:7 When he is judged, he will be found guilty!
Then his prayer will be regarded as sinful.

109:8 May his days be few!
May another take his job!
109:9 May his children be fatherless,
and his wife a widow!
109:10 May his children roam around begging,
asking for handouts as they leave their ruined home!
109:11 May the creditor seize all he owns!
May strangers loot his property!
109:12 May no one show him kindness!
May no one have compassion on his fatherless children!
109:13 May his descendants be cut off!
May the memory of them be wiped out by the time the next generation arrives!
109:14 May his ancestors' sins be remembered by the LORD!
May his mother's sin not be forgotten!
109:15 May the LORD be constantly aware of them,
and cut off the memory of his children from the earth!
109:16 For he never bothered to show kindness;
he harassed the oppressed and needy,
and killed the disheartened.
109:17 He loved to curse others, so those curses have come upon him.
He had no desire to bless anyone, so he has experienced no blessings.
109:18 He made cursing a way of life,
so curses poured into his stomach like water
and seeped into his bones like oil.
109:19 May a curse attach itself to him, like a garment one puts on,
or a belt one wears continually!
109:20 May the LORD repay my accusers in this way,
those who say evil things about me!
109:21 O sovereign LORD,
intervene on my behalf for the sake of your reputation!
Because your loyal love is good, deliver me!
109:22 For I am oppressed and needy,
and my heart beats violently within me.
109:23 I am fading away like a shadow at the end of the day;
I am shaken off like a locust.
109:24 I am so starved my knees shake;
I have turned into skin and bones.
109:25 I am disdained by them.
When they see me, they shake their heads.
109:26 Help me, O LORD my God!
Because you are faithful to me, deliver me!
109:27 Then they will realize this is your work,
and that you, LORD, have accomplished it.
109:28 They curse, but you will bless.
When they attack, they will be humiliated,
but your servant will rejoice.
109:29 My accusers will be covered with shame,
and draped in humiliation as if it were a robe.
109:30 I will thank the LORD profusely,
in the middle of a crowd I will praise him,
109:31 because he stands at the right hand of the needy,
to deliver him from those who threaten his life.

Psalm 110
A psalm of David.
110:1 Here is the LORD's proclamation to my lord:
"Sit down at my right hand until I make your enemies your footstool!"
110:2 The LORD extends your dominion from Zion.
Rule in the midst of your enemies!
110:3 Your people willingly follow you when you go into battle.
On the holy hills at sunrise the dew of your youth belongs to you.
110:4 The LORD makes this promise on oath and will not revoke it:
"You are an eternal priest after the pattern of Melchizedek."
110:5 O sovereign LORD, at your right hand
he strikes down kings in the day he unleashes his anger.
110:6 He executes judgment against the nations;
he fills the valleys with corpses;
he shatters their heads over the vast battlefield.
110:7 From the stream along the road he drinks;
then he lifts up his head.

Psalm 111
111:1 Praise the LORD!
I will give thanks to the LORD with my whole heart,
in the assembly of the godly and the congregation.
111:2 The LORD's deeds are great,
eagerly awaited by all who desire them.
111:3 His work is majestic and glorious,
and his faithfulness endures forever.
111:4 He does amazing things that will be remembered;
the LORD is merciful and compassionate.
111:5 He gives food to his faithful followers;
he always remembers his covenant.
111:6 He announced that he would do mighty deeds for his people,

giving them a land that belonged to other nations.
111:7 His acts are characterized by faithfulness and justice;
all his precepts are reliable.
111:8 They are forever firm,
and should be faithfully and properly carried out.
111:9 He delivered his people;
he ordained that his covenant be observed forever.
His name is holy and awesome.
111:10 To obey the LORD is the fundamental principle for wise living;
all who carry out his precepts acquire good moral insight.
He will receive praise forever.

Psalm 112

112:1 Praise the LORD!
How blessed is the one who obeys the LORD,
who takes great delight in keeping his commands.
112:2 His descendants will be powerful on the earth;
the godly will be blessed.
112:3 His house contains wealth and riches;
his integrity endures.
112:4 In the darkness a light shines for the godly,
for each one who is merciful, compassionate, and just.
112:5 It goes well for the one who generously lends money,
and conducts his business honestly.
112:6 For he will never be upended;
others will always remember one who is just.
112:7 He does not fear bad news.
He is confident; he trusts in the LORD.
112:8 His resolve is firm; he will not succumb to fear
before he looks in triumph on his enemies.
112:9 He generously gives to the needy;
his integrity endures.
He will be vindicated and honored.
112:10 When the wicked see this, they will worry;
they will grind their teeth in frustration and melt away;
the desire of the wicked will perish.

Psalm 113

113:1 Praise the LORD!
Praise, you servants of the LORD,
praise the name of the LORD!
113:2 May the LORD's name be praised
now and forevermore!
113:3 From east to west
the LORD's name is deserving of praise.
113:4 The LORD is exalted over all the nations;
his splendor reaches beyond the sky.
113:5 Who can compare to the LORD our God,
who sits on a high throne?
113:6 He bends down to look
at the sky and the earth.
113:7 He raises the poor from the dirt,
and lifts up the needy from the garbage pile,
113:8 that he might seat him with princes,
with the princes of his people.
113:9 He makes the barren woman of the family
a happy mother of children.
Praise the LORD!

Psalm 114

114:1 When Israel left Egypt,
when the family of Jacob left a foreign nation behind,
114:2 Judah became his sanctuary,
Israel his kingdom.
114:3 The sea looked and fled;
the Jordan River turned back.
114:4 The mountains skipped like rams,
the hills like lambs.
114:5 Why do you flee, O sea?
Why do you turn back, O Jordan River?
114:6 Why do you skip like rams, O mountains,
like lambs, O hills?
114:7 Tremble, O earth, before the Lord –
before the God of Jacob,
114:8 who turned a rock into a pool of water,
a hard rock into springs of water!

Psalm 115

115:1 Not to us, O LORD, not to us!
But to your name bring honor,
for the sake of your loyal love and faithfulness.
115:2 Why should the nations say,
"Where is their God?"
115:3 Our God is in heaven!
He does whatever he pleases!
115:4 Their idols are made of silver and gold –
they are man-made.

115:5 They have mouths, but cannot speak,
eyes, but cannot see,
115:6 ears, but cannot hear,
noses, but cannot smell,
115:7 hands, but cannot touch,
feet, but cannot walk.
They cannot even clear their throats.
115:8 Those who make them will end up like them,
as will everyone who trusts in them.
115:9 O Israel, trust in the LORD!
He is their deliverer and protector.
115:10 O family of Aaron, trust in the LORD!
He is their deliverer and protector.
115:11 You loyal followers of the LORD, trust in the LORD!
He is their deliverer and protector.
115:12 The LORD takes notice of us, he will bless –
he will bless the family of Israel,
he will bless the family of Aaron.
115:13 He will bless his loyal followers,
both young and old.
115:14 May he increase your numbers,
yours and your children's!
115:15 May you be blessed by the LORD,
the creator of heaven and earth!
115:16 The heavens belong to the LORD,
but the earth he has given to mankind.
115:17 The dead do not praise the LORD,
nor do any of those who descend into the silence of death.
115:18 But we will praise the LORD
now and forevermore.
Praise the LORD!

Psalm 116

116:1 I love the LORD
because he heard my plea for mercy,
116:2 and listened to me.
As long as I live, I will call to him when I need help.
116:3 The ropes of death tightened around me,
the snares of Sheol confronted me.
I was confronted with trouble and sorrow.
116:4 I called on the name of the LORD,
"Please LORD, rescue my life!"
116:5 The LORD is merciful and fair;
our God is compassionate.
116:6 The LORD protects the untrained;
I was in serious trouble and he delivered me.
116:7 Rest once more, my soul,
for the LORD has vindicated you.
116:8 Yes, LORD, you rescued my life from death,
and kept my feet from stumbling.
116:9 I will serve the LORD
in the land of the living.
116:10 I had faith when I said,
"I am severely oppressed."
116:11 I rashly declared,
"All men are liars."
116:12 How can I repay the LORD
for all his acts of kindness to me?
116:13 I will celebrate my deliverance,
and call on the name of the LORD.
116:14 I will fulfill my vows to the LORD
before all his people.
116:15 The LORD values
the lives of his faithful followers.
116:16 Yes, LORD! I am indeed your servant;
I am your lowest slave.
You saved me from death.
116:17 I will present a thank offering to you,
and call on the name of the LORD.
116:18 I will fulfill my vows to the LORD
before all his people,
116:19 in the courts of the LORD's temple,
in your midst, O Jerusalem.
Praise the LORD!

Psalm 117

117:1 Praise the LORD, all you nations!
Applaud him, all you foreigners!
117:2 For his loyal love towers over us,
and the LORD's faithfulness endures.
Praise the LORD!

Psalm 118

118:1 Give thanks to the LORD, for he is good
and his loyal love endures!
118:2 Let Israel say,

"Yes, his loyal love endures!"
118:3 Let the family of Aaron say,
"Yes, his loyal love endures!"
118:4 Let the loyal followers of the LORD say,
"Yes, his loyal love endures!"
118:5 In my distress I cried out to the LORD.
The LORD answered me and put me in a wide open place.
118:6 The LORD is on my side, I am not afraid!
What can people do to me?
118:7 The LORD is on my side as my helper.
I look in triumph on those who hate me.
118:8 It is better to take shelter in the LORD
than to trust in people.
118:9 It is better to take shelter in the LORD
than to trust in princes.
118:10 All the nations surrounded me.
Indeed, in the name of the LORD I pushed them away.
118:11 They surrounded me, yes, they surrounded me.
Indeed, in the name of the LORD I pushed them away.
118:12 They surrounded me like bees.
But they disappeared as quickly as a fire among thorns.
Indeed, in the name of the LORD I pushed them away.
118:13 "You aggressively attacked me and tried to knock me down,
but the LORD helped me.
118:14 The LORD gives me strength and protects me;
he has become my deliverer."
118:15 They celebrate deliverance in the tents of the godly.
The LORD's right hand conquers,
118:16 the LORD's right hand gives victory,
the LORD's right hand conquers.
118:17 I will not die, but live,
and I will proclaim what the LORD has done.
118:18 The LORD severely punished me,
but he did not hand me over to death.
118:19 Open for me the gates of the just king's temple!
I will enter through them and give thanks to the LORD.
118:20 This is the LORD's gate –
the godly enter through it.
118:21 I will give you thanks, for you answered me,
and have become my deliverer.
118:22 The stone which the builders discarded
has become the cornerstone.
118:23 This is the LORD's work.
We consider it amazing!
118:24 This is the day the LORD has brought about.
We will be happy and rejoice in it.
118:25 Please LORD, deliver!
Please LORD, grant us success!
118:26 May the one who comes in the name of the LORD be blessed!
We will pronounce blessings on you in the LORD's temple.
118:27 The LORD is God and he has delivered us.
Tie the offering with ropes
to the horns of the altar!
118:28 You are my God and I will give you thanks!
You are my God and I will praise you!
118:29 Give thanks to the LORD, for he is good
and his loyal love endures!
Psalm 119

א (Alef)
119:1 How blessed are those whose actions are blameless,
who obey the law of the LORD.
119:2 How blessed are those who observe his rules,
and seek him with all their heart,
119:3 who, moreover, do no wrong,
but follow in his footsteps.
119:4 You demand that your precepts
be carefully kept.
119:5 If only I were predisposed
to keep your statutes!
119:6 Then I would not be ashamed,
if I were focused on all your commands.
119:7 I will give you sincere thanks,
when I learn your just regulations.
119:8 I will keep your statutes.
Do not completely abandon me!

ב (Bet)
119:9 How can a young person maintain a pure life?
By guarding it according to your instructions!
119:10 With all my heart I seek you.
Do not allow me to stray from your commands!
119:11 In my heart I store up your words,
so I might not sin against you.

119:12 You deserve praise, O LORD!
Teach me your statutes!
119:13 With my lips I proclaim
all the regulations you have revealed.
119:14 I rejoice in the lifestyle prescribed by your rules
as if they were riches of all kinds.
119:15 I will meditate on your precepts
and focus on your behavior.
119:16 I find delight in your statutes;
I do not forget your instructions.

ג (Gimel)
119:17 Be kind to your servant!
Then I will live and keep your instructions.
119:18 Open my eyes so I can truly see
the marvelous things in your law!
119:19 I am like a foreigner in this land.
Do not hide your commands from me!
119:20 I desperately long to know
your regulations at all times.
119:21 You reprimand arrogant people.
Those who stray from your commands are doomed.
119:22 Spare me shame and humiliation,
for I observe your rules.
119:23 Though rulers plot and slander me,
your servant meditates on your statutes.
119:24 Yes, I find delight in your rules;
they give me guidance.

ד (Dalet)
119:25 I collapse in the dirt.
Revive me with your word!
119:26 I told you about my ways and you answered me.
Teach me your statutes!
119:27 Help me to understand what your precepts mean!
Then I can meditate on your marvelous teachings.
119:28 I collapse from grief.
Sustain me by your word!
119:29 Remove me from the path of deceit!
Graciously give me your law!
119:30 I choose the path of faithfulness;
I am committed to your regulations.
119:31 I hold fast to your rules.
O LORD, do not let me be ashamed!
119:32 I run along the path of your commands,
for you enable me to do so.

ה (He)
119:33 Teach me, O LORD, the lifestyle prescribed by your statutes,
so that I might observe it continually.
119:34 Give me understanding so that I might observe your law,
and keep it with all my heart.

119:35 Guide me in the path of your commands,
for I delight to walk in it.
119:36 Give me a desire for your rules,
rather than for wealth gained unjustly.
119:37 Turn my eyes away from what is worthless!
Revive me with your word!
119:38 Confirm to your servant your promise,
which you made to the one who honors you.
119:39 Take away the insults that I dread!
Indeed, your regulations are good.
119:40 Look, I long for your precepts.
Revive me with your deliverance!

ו (Vav)
119:41 May I experience your loyal love, O LORD,
and your deliverance, as you promised.
119:42 Then I will have a reply for the one who insults me,
for I trust in your word.
119:43 Do not completely deprive me of a truthful testimony,
for I await your justice.
119:44 Then I will keep your law continually
now and for all time.
119:45 I will be secure,
for I seek your precepts.
119:46 I will speak about your regulations before kings
and not be ashamed.
119:47 I will find delight in your commands,
which I love.
119:48 I will lift my hands to your commands,
which I love,
and I will meditate on your statutes.

ז (*Zayin*)

119:49 Remember your word to your servant,
for you have given me hope.
119:50 This is what comforts me in my trouble,
for your promise revives me.
119:51 Arrogant people do nothing but scoff at me.
Yet I do not turn aside from your law.
119:52 I remember your ancient regulations,
O LORD, and console myself.
119:53 Rage takes hold of me because of the wicked,
those who reject your law.
119:54 Your statutes have been my songs
in the house where I live.
119:55 I remember your name during the night, O LORD,
and I will keep your law.
119:56 This has been my practice,
for I observe your precepts.

ח (*Khet*)

119:57 The LORD is my source of security.
I have determined to follow your instructions.
119:58 I seek your favor with all my heart.
Have mercy on me as you promised!
119:59 I consider my actions
and follow your rules.
119:60 I keep your commands
eagerly and without delay.
119:61 The ropes of the wicked tighten around me,
but I do not forget your law.
119:62 In the middle of the night I arise to thank you
for your just regulations.
119:63 I am a friend to all your loyal followers,
and to those who keep your precepts.
119:64 O LORD, your loyal love fills the earth.
Teach me your statutes!

ט (*Tet*)

119:65 You are good to your servant,
O LORD, just as you promised.
119:66 Teach me proper discernment and understanding!
For I consider your commands to be reliable.
119:67 Before I was afflicted I used to stray off,
but now I keep your instructions.
119:68 You are good and you do good.
Teach me your statutes!
119:69 Arrogant people smear my reputation with lies,
but I observe your precepts with all my heart.
119:70 Their hearts are calloused,
but I find delight in your law.
119:71 It was good for me to suffer,
so that I might learn your statutes.
119:72 The law you have revealed is more important to me
than thousands of pieces of gold and silver.

י (*Yod*)

119:73 Your hands made me and formed me.
Give me understanding so that I might learn your commands.
119:74 Your loyal followers will be glad when they see me,
for I find hope in your word.
119:75 I know, LORD, that your regulations are just.
You disciplined me because of your faithful devotion to me.
119:76 May your loyal love console me,
as you promised your servant.
119:77 May I experience your compassion, so I might live!
For I find delight in your law.
119:78 May the arrogant be humiliated, for they have slandered me!
But I meditate on your precepts.
119:79 May your loyal followers turn to me,
those who know your rules.
119:80 May I be fully committed to your statutes,
so that I might not be ashamed.

כ (*Kaf*)

119:81 I desperately long for your deliverance.
I find hope in your word.
119:82 My eyes grow tired as I wait for your promise to be fulfilled.
I say, "When will you comfort me?"
119:83 For I am like a wineskin dried up in smoke.
I do not forget your statutes.
119:84 How long must your servant endure this?
When will you judge those who pursue me?
119:85 The arrogant dig pits to trap me,
which violates your law.
119:86 All your commands are reliable.

I am pursued without reason. Help me!
119:87 They have almost destroyed me here on the earth,
but I do not reject your precepts.
119:88 Revive me with your loyal love,
that I might keep the rules you have revealed.

ל (*Lamed*)

119:89 O LORD, your instructions endure;
they stand secure in heaven.
119:90 You demonstrate your faithfulness to all generations.
You established the earth and it stood firm.
119:91 Today they stand firm by your decrees,
for all things are your servants.
119:92 If I had not found encouragement in your law,
I would have died in my sorrow.
119:93 I will never forget your precepts,
for by them you have revived me.
119:94 I belong to you. Deliver me!
For I seek your precepts.
119:95 The wicked prepare to kill me,
yet I concentrate on your rules.
119:96 I realize that everything has its limits,
but your commands are beyond full comprehension.

מ (*Mem*)

119:97 O how I love your law!
All day long I meditate on it.
119:98 Your commandments make me wiser than my enemies,
for I am always aware of them.
119:99 I have more insight than all my teachers,
for I meditate on your rules.
119:100 I am more discerning than those older than I,
for I observe your precepts.
119:101 I stay away from the evil path,
so that I might keep your instructions.
119:102 I do not turn aside from your regulations,
for you teach me.
119:103 Your words are sweeter
in my mouth than honey!
119:104 Your precepts give me discernment.
Therefore I hate all deceitful actions.

נ (*Nun*)

119:105 Your word is a lamp to walk by,
and a light to illumine my path.
119:106 I have vowed and solemnly sworn
to keep your just regulations.
119:107 I am suffering terribly.
O LORD, revive me with your word!
119:108 O LORD, please accept the freewill offerings of my praise!
Teach me your regulations!
119:109 My life is in continual danger,
but I do not forget your law.
119:110 The wicked lay a trap for me,
but I do not wander from your precepts.
119:111 I claim your rules as my permanent possession,
for they give me joy.
119:112 I am determined to obey your statutes
at all times, to the very end.

ס (*Samek*)

119:113 I hate people with divided loyalties,
but I love your law.
119:114 You are my hiding place and my shield.
I find hope in your word.
119:115 Turn away from me, you evil men,
so that I can observe the commands of my God.
119:116 Sustain me as you promised, so that I will live.
Do not disappoint me!
119:117 Support me, so that I will be delivered.
Then I will focus on your statutes continually.
119:118 You despise all who stray from your statutes,
for they are deceptive and unreliable.
119:119 You remove all the wicked of the earth like slag.
Therefore I love your rules.
119:120 My body trembles because I fear you;
I am afraid of your judgments.

ע (*Ayin*)

119:121 I do what is fair and right.
Do not abandon me to my oppressors!
119:122 Guarantee the welfare of your servant!
Do not let the arrogant oppress me!
119:123 My eyes grow tired as I wait for your deliverance,
for your reliable promise to be fulfilled.

119:124 Show your servant your loyal love!
Teach me your statutes!
119:125 I am your servant. Give me insight,
so that I can understand your rules.
119:126 It is time for the LORD to act –
they break your law!
119:127 For this reason I love your commands
more than gold, even purest gold.
119:128 For this reason I carefully follow all your precepts.
I hate all deceitful actions.

 פ **(Pe)**

119:129 Your rules are marvelous.
Therefore I observe them.
119:130 Your instructions are a doorway through which light shines.
They give insight to the untrained.
119:131 I open my mouth and pant,
because I long for your commands.
119:132 Turn toward me and extend mercy to me,
as you typically do to your loyal followers.
119:133 Direct my steps by your word!
Do not let any sin dominate me!
119:134 Deliver me from oppressive men,
so that I can keep your precepts.
119:135 Smile on your servant!
Teach me your statutes!
119:136 Tears stream down from my eyes,
because people do not keep your law.

צ **(Tsade)**

119:137 You are just, O LORD,
and your judgments are fair.
119:138 The rules you impose are just,
and absolutely reliable.
119:139 My zeal consumes me,
for my enemies forget your instructions.
119:140 Your word is absolutely pure,
and your servant loves it!
119:141 I am insignificant and despised,
yet I do not forget your precepts.
119:142 Your justice endures,
and your law is reliable.
119:143 Distress and hardship confront me,
yet I find delight in your commands.
119:144 Your rules remain just.
Give me insight so that I can live.

ק **(Qof)**

119:145 I cried out with all my heart, "Answer me, O LORD!
I will observe your statutes."
119:146 I cried out to you, "Deliver me,
so that I can keep your rules."
119:147 I am up before dawn crying for help.
I find hope in your word.
119:148 My eyes anticipate the nighttime hours,
so that I can meditate on your word.
119:149 Listen to me because of your loyal love!
O LORD, revive me, as you typically do!
119:150 Those who are eager to do wrong draw near;
they are far from your law.
119:151 You are near, O LORD,
and all your commands are reliable.
119:152 I learned long ago that
you ordained your rules to last.

ר **(Resh)**

119:153 See my pain and rescue me!
For I do not forget your law.
119:154 Fight for me and defend me!
Revive me with your word!
119:155 The wicked have no chance for deliverance,
for they do not seek your statutes.
119:156 Your compassion is great, O LORD.
Revive me, as you typically do!
119:157 The enemies who chase me are numerous.
Yet I do not turn aside from your rules.
119:158 I take note of the treacherous and despise them,
because they do not keep your instructions.
119:159 See how I love your precepts!
O LORD, revive me with your loyal love!
119:160 Your instructions are totally reliable;
all your just regulations endure.

שׂ/שׁ **(Sin/Shin)**

119:161 Rulers pursue me for no reason,
yet I am more afraid of disobeying your instructions.
119:162 I rejoice in your instructions,
like one who finds much plunder.
119:163 I hate and despise deceit;
I love your law.
119:164 Seven times a day I praise you
because of your just regulations.
119:165 Those who love your law are completely secure;
nothing causes them to stumble.
119:166 I hope for your deliverance, O LORD,
and I obey your commands.
119:167 I keep your rules;
I love them greatly.
119:168 I keep your precepts and rules,
for you are aware of everything I do.

ת **(Tav)**

119:169 Listen to my cry for help, O LORD!
Give me insight by your word!
119:170 Listen to my appeal for mercy!
Deliver me, as you promised.
119:171 May praise flow freely from my lips,
for you teach me your statutes.
119:172 May my tongue sing about your instructions,
for all your commands are just.
119:173 May your hand help me,
for I choose to obey your precepts.
119:174 I long for your deliverance, O LORD;
I find delight in your law.
119:175 May I live and praise you!
May your regulations help me!
119:176 I have wandered off like a lost sheep.
Come looking for your servant,
for I do not forget your commands.
Psalm 120
A song of ascents.
120:1 In my distress I cried out
to the LORD and he answered me.
120:2 I said, "O LORD, rescue me
from those who lie with their lips
and those who deceive with their tongue.
120:3 How will he severely punish you,
you deceptive talker?
120:4 Here's how! With the sharp arrows of warriors,
with arrowheads forged over the hot coals.
120:5 How miserable I am!
For I have lived temporarily in Meshech;
I have resided among the tents of Kedar.
120:6 For too long I have had to reside
with those who hate peace.
120:7 I am committed to peace,
but when I speak, they want to make war.
Psalm 121
A song of ascents.
121:1 I look up toward the hills.
From where does my help come?
121:2 My help comes from the LORD,
the Creator of heaven and earth!
121:3 May he not allow your foot to slip!
May your protector not sleep!
121:4 Look! Israel's protector
does not sleep or slumber!
121:5 The LORD is your protector;
the LORD is the shade at your right hand.
121:6 The sun will not harm you by day,
or the moon by night.
121:7 The LORD will protect you from all harm;
he will protect your life.
121:8 The LORD will protect you in all you do,
now and forevermore.
Psalm 122
A song of ascents, by David.
122:1 I was glad because they said to me,
"We will go to the LORD's temple."
122:2 Our feet are standing
inside your gates, O Jerusalem.
122:3 Jerusalem is a city designed
to accommodate an assembly.
122:4 The tribes go up there,
the tribes of the LORD,
where it is required that Israel
give thanks to the name of the LORD.
122:5 Indeed, the leaders sit there on thrones and make legal decisions,

on the thrones of the house of David.
122:6 Pray for the peace of Jerusalem!
May those who love her prosper!
122:7 May there be peace inside your defenses,
and prosperity inside your fortresses!
122:8 For the sake of my brothers and my neighbors
I will say, "May there be peace in you!"
122:9 For the sake of the temple of the LORD our God
I will pray for you to prosper.
Psalm 123
A song of ascents.
123:1 I look up toward you,
the one enthroned in heaven.
123:2 Look, as the eyes of servants look to the hand of their master,
as the eyes of a female servant look to the hand of her mistress,
so my eyes will look to the LORD, our God, until he shows us favor.
123:3 Show us favor, O LORD, show us favor!
For we have had our fill of humiliation, and then some.
123:4 We have had our fill
of the taunts of the self-assured,
of the contempt of the proud.
Psalm 124
A song of ascents, by David.
124:1 "If the LORD had not been on our side" –
let Israel say this! –
124:2 if the LORD had not been on our side,
when men attacked us,
124:3 they would have swallowed us alive,
when their anger raged against us.
124:4 The water would have overpowered us;
the current would have overwhelmed us.
124:5 The raging water
would have overwhelmed us.
124:6 The LORD deserves praise,
for he did not hand us over as prey to their teeth.
124:7 We escaped with our lives, like a bird from a hunter's snare.
The snare broke, and we escaped.
124:8 Our deliverer is the LORD,
the Creator of heaven and earth.
Psalm 125
A song of ascents.
125:1 Those who trust in the LORD are like Mount Zion;
it cannot be upended and will endure forever.
125:2 As the mountains surround Jerusalem,
so the LORD surrounds his people,
now and forevermore.
125:3 Indeed, the scepter of a wicked king will not settle
upon the allotted land of the godly.
Otherwise the godly might
do what is wrong.
125:4 Do good, O LORD, to those who are good,
to the morally upright!
125:5 As for those who are bent on traveling a sinful path,
may the LORD remove them, along with those who behave wickedly!
May Israel experience peace!
Psalm 126
A song of ascents.
126:1 When the LORD restored the well-being of Zion,
we thought we were dreaming.
126:2 At that time we laughed loudly
and shouted for joy.
At that time the nations said,
"The LORD has accomplished great things for these people."
126:3 The LORD did indeed accomplish great things for us.
We were happy.
126:4 O LORD, restore our well-being,
just as the streams in the arid south are replenished.
126:5 Those who shed tears as they plant
will shout for joy when they reap the harvest.
126:6 The one who weeps as he walks along, carrying his bag of seed,
will certainly come in with a shout of joy, carrying his sheaves of grain.
Psalm 127
A song of ascents, by Solomon.
127:1 If the LORD does not build a house,
then those who build it work in vain.
If the LORD does not guard a city,
then the watchman stands guard in vain.
127:2 It is vain for you to rise early, come home late,
and work so hard for your food.
Yes, he can provide for those whom he loves even when they sleep.
127:3 Yes, sons are a gift from the LORD,
the fruit of the womb is a reward.
127:4 Sons born during one's youth

are like arrows in a warrior's hand.
127:5 How blessed is the man who fills his quiver with them!
They will not be put to shame when they confront enemies at the city gate.
Psalm 128
A song of ascents.
128:1 How blessed is every one of the LORD's loyal followers,
each one who keeps his commands!
128:2 You will eat what you worked so hard to grow.
You will be blessed and secure.
128:3 Your wife will be like a fruitful vine
in the inner rooms of your house;
your children will be like olive branches,
as they sit all around your table.
128:4 Yes indeed, the man who fears the LORD
will be blessed in this way.
128:5 May the LORD bless you from Zion,
that you might see Jerusalem prosper
all the days of your life,
128:6 and that you might see your grandchildren.
May Israel experience peace!
Psalm 129
A song of ascents.
129:1 "Since my youth they have often attacked me,"
let Israel say.
129:2 "Since my youth they have often attacked me,
but they have not defeated me.
129:3 The plowers plowed my back;
they made their furrows long.
129:4 The LORD is just;
he cut the ropes of the wicked."
129:5 May all who hate Zion
be humiliated and turned back!
129:6 May they be like the grass on the rooftops
which withers before one can even pull it up,
129:7 which cannot fill the reaper's hand,
or the lap of the one who gathers the grain!
129:8 Those who pass by will not say,
"May you experience the LORD's blessing!
We pronounce a blessing on you in the name of the LORD."
Psalm 130
A song of ascents.
130:1 From the deep water I cry out to you, O LORD.
130:2 O Lord, listen to me!
Pay attention to my plea for mercy!
130:3 If you, O LORD, were to keep track of sins,
O Lord, who could stand before you?
130:4 But you are willing to forgive,
so that you might be honored.
130:5 I rely on the LORD,
I rely on him with my whole being;
I wait for his assuring word.
130:6 I yearn for the Lord,
more than watchmen do for the morning,
yes, more than watchmen do for the morning.
130:7 O Israel, hope in the LORD,
for the LORD exhibits loyal love,
and is more than willing to deliver.
130:8 He will deliver Israel
from all the consequences of their sins.
Psalm 131
A song of ascents, by David.
131:1 O LORD, my heart is not proud,
nor do I have a haughty look.
I do not have great aspirations,
or concern myself with things that are beyond me.
131:2 Indeed I am composed and quiet,
like a young child carried by its mother;
I am content like the young child I carry.
131:3 O Israel, hope in the LORD
now and forevermore!
Psalm 132
A song of ascents.
132:1 O LORD, for David's sake remember
all his strenuous effort,
132:2 and how he made a vow to the LORD,
and swore an oath to the powerful ruler of Jacob.
132:3 He said, "I will not enter my own home,
or get into my bed.
132:4 I will not allow my eyes to sleep,
or my eyelids to slumber,
132:5 until I find a place for the LORD,
a fine dwelling place for the powerful ruler of Jacob."

132:6 Look, we heard about it in Ephrathah,
we found it in the territory of Jaar.
132:7 Let us go to his dwelling place!
Let us worship before his footstool!
132:8 Ascend, O LORD, to your resting place,
you and the ark of your strength!
132:9 May your priests be clothed with integrity!
May your loyal followers shout for joy!
132:10 For the sake of David, your servant,
do not reject your chosen king!
132:11 The LORD made a reliable promise to David;
he will not go back on his word.
He said, "I will place one of your descendants on your throne.
132:12 If your sons keep my covenant
and the rules I teach them,
their sons will also sit on your throne forever."
132:13 Certainly the LORD has chosen Zion;
he decided to make it his home.
132:14 He said, "This will be my resting place forever;
I will live here, for I have chosen it.
132:15 I will abundantly supply what she needs;
I will give her poor all the food they need.
132:16 I will protect her priests,
and her godly people will shout exuberantly.
132:17 There I will make David strong;
I have determined that my chosen king's dynasty will continue.
132:18 I will humiliate his enemies,
and his crown will shine.
Psalm 133
A song of ascents, by David.
133:1 Look! How good and how pleasant it is
when brothers live together!
133:2 It is like fine oil poured on the head
which flows down the beard –
Aaron's beard,
and then flows down his garments.
133:3 It is like the dew of Hermon,
which flows down upon the hills of Zion.
Indeed that is where the LORD has decreed
a blessing will be available – eternal life.
Psalm 134
A song of ascents.
134:1 Attention! Praise the LORD,
all you servants of the LORD,
who serve in the LORD's temple during the night.
134:2 Lift your hands toward the sanctuary
and praise the LORD!
134:3 May the LORD, the Creator of heaven and earth,
bless you from Zion!
Psalm 135
135:1 Praise the LORD!
Praise the name of the LORD!
Offer praise, you servants of the LORD,
135:2 who serve in the LORD's temple,
in the courts of the temple of our God.
135:3 Praise the LORD, for the LORD is good!
Sing praises to his name, for it is pleasant!
135:4 Indeed, the LORD has chosen Jacob for himself,
Israel to be his special possession.
135:5 Yes, I know the LORD is great,
and our Lord is superior to all gods.
135:6 He does whatever he pleases
in heaven and on earth,
in the seas and all the ocean depths.
135:7 He causes the clouds to arise from the end of the earth,
makes lightning bolts accompany the rain,
and brings the wind out of his storehouses.
135:8 He struck down the firstborn of Egypt,
including both men and animals.
135:9 He performed awesome deeds and acts of judgment
in your midst, O Egypt,
against Pharaoh and all his servants.
135:10 He defeated many nations,
and killed mighty kings –
135:11 Sihon, king of the Amorites,
and Og, king of Bashan,
and all the kingdoms of Canaan.
135:12 He gave their land as an inheritance,
as an inheritance to Israel his people.
135:13 O LORD, your name endures,
your reputation, O LORD, lasts.
135:14 For the LORD vindicates his people,
and has compassion on his servants.

135:15 The nations' idols are made of silver and gold,
they are man-made.
135:16 They have mouths, but cannot speak,
eyes, but cannot see,
135:17 and ears, but cannot hear.
Indeed, they cannot breathe.
135:18 Those who make them will end up like them,
as will everyone who trusts in them.
135:19 O family of Israel, praise the LORD!
O family of Aaron, praise the LORD!
135:20 O family of Levi, praise the LORD!
You loyal followers of the LORD, praise the LORD!
135:21 The LORD deserves praise in Zion –
he who dwells in Jerusalem.
Praise the LORD!
Psalm 136
136:1 Give thanks to the LORD, for he is good,
for his loyal love endures.
136:2 Give thanks to the God of gods,
for his loyal love endures.
136:3 Give thanks to the Lord of lords,
for his loyal love endures.
136:4 to the one who performs magnificent, amazing deeds all by himself,
for his loyal love endures,
136:5 to the one who used wisdom to make the heavens,
for his loyal love endures,
136:6 to the one who spread out the earth over the water,
for his loyal love endures,
136:7 to the one who made the great lights,
for his loyal love endures,
136:8 the sun to rule by day,
for his loyal love endures,
136:9 the moon and stars to rule by night,
for his loyal love endures,
136:10 to the one who struck down the firstborn of Egypt,
for his loyal love endures,
136:11 and led Israel out from their midst,
for his loyal love endures,
136:12 with a strong hand and an outstretched arm,
for his loyal love endures,
136:13 to the one who divided the Red Sea in two,
for his loyal love endures,
136:14 and led Israel through its midst,
for his loyal love endures,
136:15 and tossed Pharaoh and his army into the Red Sea,
for his loyal love endures,
136:16 to the one who led his people through the wilderness,
for his loyal love endures,
136:17 to the one who struck down great kings,
for his loyal love endures,
136:18 and killed powerful kings,
for his loyal love endures,
136:19 Sihon, king of the Amorites,
for his loyal love endures,
136:20 Og, king of Bashan,
for his loyal love endures,
136:21 and gave their land as an inheritance,
for his loyal love endures,
136:22 as an inheritance to Israel his servant,
for his loyal love endures,
136:23 to the one who remembered us when we were down,
for his loyal love endures,
136:24 and snatched us away from our enemies,
for his loyal love endures,
136:25 to the one who gives food to all living things,
for his loyal love endures.
136:26 Give thanks to the God of heaven,
for his loyal love endures!
Psalm 137
137:1 By the rivers of Babylon
we sit down and weep
when we remember Zion.
137:2 On the poplars in her midst
we hang our harps,
137:3 for there our captors ask us to compose songs;
those who mock us demand that we be happy, saying:
"Sing for us a song about Zion!"
137:4 How can we sing a song to the LORD
in a foreign land?
137:5 If I forget you, O Jerusalem,
may my right hand be crippled!
137:6 May my tongue stick to the roof of my mouth,

if I do not remember you,
and do not give Jerusalem priority
over whatever gives me the most joy.
137:7 Remember, O LORD, what the Edomites did
on the day Jerusalem fell.
They said, "Tear it down, tear it down,
right to its very foundation!"
137:8 O daughter Babylon, soon to be devastated!
How blessed will be the one who repays you
for what you dished out to us!
137:9 How blessed will be the one who grabs your babies
and smashes them on a rock!
Psalm 138
By David.
138:1 I will give you thanks with all my heart;
before the heavenly assembly I will sing praises to you.
138:2 I will bow down toward your holy temple,
and give thanks to your name,
because of your loyal love and faithfulness,
for you have exalted your promise above the entire sky.
138:3 When I cried out for help, you answered me.
You made me bold and energized me.
138:4 Let all the kings of the earth give thanks to you, O LORD,
when they hear the words you speak.
138:5 Let them sing about the LORD's deeds,
for the LORD's splendor is magnificent.
138:6 Though the LORD is exalted, he takes note of the lowly,
and recognizes the proud from far away.
138:7 Even when I must walk in the midst of danger, you revive me.
You oppose my angry enemies,
and your right hand delivers me.
138:8 The LORD avenges me.
O LORD, your loyal love endures.
Do not abandon those whom you have made!
Psalm 139
For the music director, a psalm of David.
139:1 O LORD, you examine me and know.
139:2 You know when I sit down and when I get up;
even from far away you understand my motives.
139:3 You carefully observe me when I travel or when I lie down to rest;
you are aware of everything I do.
139:4 Certainly my tongue does not frame a word
without you, O LORD, being thoroughly aware of it.
139:5 You squeeze me in from behind and in front;
you place your hand on me.
139:6 Your knowledge is beyond my comprehension;
it is so far beyond me, I am unable to fathom it.
139:7 Where can I go to escape your spirit?
Where can I flee to escape your presence?
139:8 If I were to ascend to heaven, you would be there.
If I were to sprawl out in Sheol, there you would be.
139:9 If I were to fly away on the wings of the dawn,
and settle down on the other side of the sea,
139:10 even there your hand would guide me,
your right hand would grab hold of me.
139:11 If I were to say, "Certainly the darkness will cover me,
and the light will turn to night all around me,"
139:12 even the darkness is not too dark for you to see,
and the night is as bright as day;
darkness and light are the same to you.
139:13 Certainly you made my mind and heart;
you wove me together in my mother's womb.
139:14 I will give you thanks because your deeds are awesome and amazing.
You knew me thoroughly;
139:15 my bones were not hidden from you,
when I was made in secret
and sewed together in the depths of the earth.
139:16 Your eyes saw me when I was inside the womb.
All the days ordained for me
were recorded in your scroll
before one of them came into existence.
139:17 How difficult it is for me to fathom your thoughts about me, O God!
How vast is their sum total!
139:18 If I tried to count them,
they would outnumber the grains of sand.
Even if I finished counting them,
I would still have to contend with you.
139:19 If only you would kill the wicked, O God!
Get away from me, you violent men!
139:20 They rebel against you and act deceitfully;
your enemies lie.

139:21 O LORD, do I not hate those who hate you,
and despise those who oppose you?
139:22 I absolutely hate them,
they have become my enemies!
139:23 Examine me, and probe my thoughts!
Test me, and know my concerns!
139:24 See if there is any idolatrous tendency in me,
and lead me in the reliable ancient path!
Psalm 140
For the music director; a psalm of David.
140:1 O LORD, rescue me from wicked men!
Protect me from violent men,
140:2 who plan ways to harm me.
All day long they stir up conflict.
140:3 Their tongues wound like a serpent;
a viper's venom is behind their lips. (Selah)
140:4 O LORD, shelter me from the power of the wicked!
Protect me from violent men,
who plan to knock me over.
140:5 Proud men hide a snare for me;
evil men spread a net by the path;
they set traps for me. (Selah)
140:6 I say to the LORD, "You are my God."
O LORD, pay attention to my plea for mercy!
140:7 O sovereign LORD, my strong deliverer,
you shield my head in the day of battle.
140:8 O LORD, do not let the wicked have their way!
Do not allow their plan to succeed when they attack! (Selah)
140:9 As for the heads of those who surround me –
may the harm done by their lips overwhelm them!
140:10 May he rain down fiery coals upon them!
May he throw them into the fire!
From bottomless pits they will not escape.
140:11 A slanderer will not endure on the earth;
calamity will hunt down a violent man and strike him down.
140:12 I know that the LORD defends the cause of the oppressed
and vindicates the poor.
140:13 Certainly the godly will give thanks to your name;
the morally upright will live in your presence.
Psalm 141
A psalm of David.
141:1 O LORD, I cry out to you. Come quickly to me!
Pay attention to me when I cry out to you!
141:2 May you accept my prayer like incense,
my uplifted hands like the evening offering!
141:3 O LORD, place a guard on my mouth!
Protect the opening of my lips!
141:4 Do not let me have evil desires,
or participate in sinful activities
with men who behave wickedly.
I will not eat their delicacies.
141:5 May the godly strike me in love and correct me!
May my head not refuse choice oil!
Indeed, my prayer is a witness against their evil deeds.
141:6 They will be thrown down the side of a cliff by their judges.
They will listen to my words, for they are pleasant.
141:7 As when one plows and breaks up the soil,
so our bones are scattered at the mouth of Sheol.
141:8 Surely I am looking to you, O sovereign LORD.
In you I take shelter.
Do not expose me to danger!
141:9 Protect me from the snare they have laid for me,
and the traps the evildoers have set.
141:10 Let the wicked fall into their own nets,
while I escape.
Psalm 142
A well-written song by David, when he was in the cave; a prayer.
142:1 To the LORD I cry out;
to the LORD I plead for mercy.
142:2 I pour out my lament before him;
I tell him about my troubles.
142:3 Even when my strength leaves me,
you watch my footsteps.
In the path where I walk
they have hidden a trap for me.
142:4 Look to the right and see!
No one cares about me.
I have nowhere to run;
no one is concerned about my life.
142:5 I cry out to you, O LORD;
I say, "You are my shelter,
my security in the land of the living."
142:6 Listen to my cry for help,

for I am in serious trouble!
Rescue me from those who chase me,
for they are stronger than I am.
142:7 Free me from prison,
that I may give thanks to your name.
Because of me the godly will assemble,
for you will vindicate me.
Psalm 143
A psalm of David.
143:1 O L ORD, hear my prayer!
Pay attention to my plea for help!
Because of your faithfulness and justice, answer me!
143:2 Do not sit in judgment on your servant,
for no one alive is innocent before you.
143:3 Certainly my enemies chase me.
They smash me into the ground.
They force me to live in dark regions,
like those who have been dead for ages.
143:4 My strength leaves me;
I am absolutely shocked.
143:5 I recall the old days;
I meditate on all you have done;
I reflect on your accomplishments.
143:6 I spread my hands out to you in prayer;
my soul thirsts for you in a parched land.
143:7 Answer me quickly, L ORD!
My strength is fading.
Do not reject me,
or I will join those descending into the grave.
143:8 May I hear about your loyal love in the morning,
for I trust in you.
Show me the way I should go,
because I long for you.
143:9 Rescue me from my enemies, O L ORD!
I run to you for protection.
143:10 Teach me to do what pleases you,
for you are my God.
May your kind presence
lead me into a level land.
143:11 O L ORD, for the sake of your reputation, revive me!
Because of your justice, rescue me from trouble!
143:12 As a demonstration of your loyal love, destroy my enemies!
Annihilate all who threaten my life,
for I am your servant.
Psalm 144
By David.
144:1 The L ORD, my protector, deserves praise –
the one who trains my hands for battle,
and my fingers for war,
144:2 who loves me and is my stronghold,
my refuge and my deliverer,
my shield and the one in whom I take shelter,
who makes nations submit to me.
144:3 O L ORD, of what importance is the human race, that you should notice them?
Of what importance is mankind, that you should be concerned about them?
144:4 People are like a vapor,
their days like a shadow that disappears.
144:5 O L ORD, make the sky sink and come down!
Touch the mountains and make them smolder!
144:6 Hurl lightning bolts and scatter them!
Shoot your arrows and rout them!
144:7 Reach down from above!
Grab me and rescue me from the surging water,
from the power of foreigners,
144:8 who speak lies,
and make false promises.
144:9 O God, I will sing a new song to you!
Accompanied by a ten-stringed instrument, I will sing praises to you,
144:10 the one who delivers kings,
and rescued David his servant from a deadly sword.
144:11 Grab me and rescue me from the power of foreigners,
who speak lies,
and make false promises.
144:12 Then our sons will be like plants,
that quickly grow to full size.
Our daughters will be like corner pillars,
carved like those in a palace.
144:13 Our storehouses will be full,
providing all kinds of food.
Our sheep will multiply by the thousands
and fill our pastures.

144:14 Our cattle will be weighted down with produce.
No one will break through our walls,
no one will be taken captive,
and there will be no terrified cries in our city squares.
144:15 How blessed are the people who experience these things!
How blessed are the people whose God is the L ORD!
Psalm 145
A psalm of praise, by David.
145:1 I will extol you, my God, O king!
I will praise your name continually!
145:2 Every day I will praise you!
I will praise your name continually!
145:3 The L ORD is great and certainly worthy of praise!
No one can fathom his greatness!
145:4 One generation will praise your deeds to another,
and tell about your mighty acts!
145:5 I will focus on your honor and majestic splendor,
and your amazing deeds!
145:6 They will proclaim the power of your awesome acts!
I will declare your great deeds!
145:7 They will talk about the fame of your great kindness,
and sing about your justice.
145:8 The L ORD is merciful and compassionate;
he is patient and demonstrates great loyal love.
145:9 The L ORD is good to all,
and has compassion on all he has made.
145:10 All he has made will give thanks to the L ORD.
Your loyal followers will praise you.
145:11 They will proclaim the splendor of your kingdom;
they will tell about your power,
145:12 so that mankind might acknowledge your mighty acts,
and the majestic splendor of your kingdom.
145:13 Your kingdom is an eternal kingdom,
and your dominion endures through all generations.
145:14 The L ORD supports all who fall,
and lifts up all who are bent over.
145:15 Everything looks to you in anticipation,
and you provide them with food on a regular basis.
145:16 You open your hand,
and fill every living thing with the food they desire.
145:17 The L ORD is just in all his actions,
and exhibits love in all he does.
145:18 The L ORD is near all who cry out to him,
all who cry out to him sincerely.
145:19 He satisfies the desire of his loyal followers;
he hears their cry for help and delivers them.
145:20 The L ORD protects those who love him,
but he destroys all the wicked.
145:21 My mouth will praise the L ORD.
Let all who live praise his holy name forever!
Psalm 146
146:1 Praise the L ORD!
Praise the L ORD, O my soul!
146:2 I will praise the L ORD as long as I live!
I will sing praises to my God as long as I exist!
146:3 Do not trust in princes,
or in human beings, who cannot deliver!
146:4 Their life's breath departs, they return to the ground;
on that day their plans die.
146:5 How blessed is the one whose helper is the God of Jacob,
whose hope is in the L ORD his God,
146:6 the one who made heaven and earth,
the sea, and all that is in them,
who remains forever faithful,
146:7 vindicates the oppressed,
and gives food to the hungry.
The L ORD releases the imprisoned.
146:8 The L ORD gives sight to the blind.
The L ORD lifts up all who are bent over.
The L ORD loves the godly.
146:9 The L ORD protects those residing outside their native land;
he lifts up the fatherless and the widow,
but he opposes the wicked.
146:10 The L ORD rules forever,
your God, O Zion, throughout the generations to come!
Praise the L ORD!
Psalm 147
147:1 Praise the L ORD,
for it is good to sing praises to our God!
Yes, praise is pleasant and appropriate!
147:2 The L ORD rebuilds Jerusalem,
and gathers the exiles of Israel.
147:3 He heals the brokenhearted,

and bandages their wounds.
147:4 He counts the number of the stars;
he names all of them.
147:5 Our Lord is great and has awesome power;
there is no limit to his wisdom.
147:6 The LORD lifts up the oppressed,
but knocks the wicked to the ground.
147:7 Offer to the LORD a song of thanks!
Sing praises to our God to the accompaniment of a harp!
147:8 He covers the sky with clouds,
provides the earth with rain,
and causes grass to grow on the hillsides.
147:9 He gives food to the animals,
and to the young ravens when they chirp.
147:10 He is not enamored with the strength of a horse,
nor is he impressed by the warrior's strong legs.
147:11 The LORD takes delight in his faithful followers,
and in those who wait for his loyal love.
147:12 Extol the LORD, O Jerusalem!
Praise your God, O Zion!
147:13 For he makes the bars of your gates strong.
He blesses your children within you.
147:14 He brings peace to your territory.
He abundantly provides for you the best grain.
147:15 He sends his command through the earth;
swiftly his order reaches its destination.
147:16 He sends the snow that is white like wool;
he spreads the frost that is white like ashes.
147:17 He throws his hailstones like crumbs.
Who can withstand the cold wind he sends?
147:18 He then orders it all to melt;
he breathes on it, and the water flows.
147:19 He proclaims his word to Jacob,
his statutes and regulations to Israel.
147:20 He has not done so with any other nation;
they are not aware of his regulations.
Praise the LORD!
Psalm 148
148:1 Praise the LORD!
Praise the LORD from the sky!
Praise him in the heavens!
148:2 Praise him, all his angels!
Praise him, all his heavenly assembly!
148:3 Praise him, O sun and moon!
Praise him, all you shiny stars!
148:4 Praise him, O highest heaven,
and you waters above the sky!
148:5 Let them praise the name of the LORD,
for he gave the command and they came into existence.
148:6 He established them so they would endure;
he issued a decree that will not be revoked.
148:7 Praise the LORD from the earth,
you sea creatures and all you ocean depths,
148:8 O fire and hail, snow and clouds,
O stormy wind that carries out his orders,
148:9 you mountains and all you hills,
you fruit trees and all you cedars,
148:10 you animals and all you cattle,
you creeping things and birds,
148:11 you kings of the earth and all you nations,
you princes and all you leaders on the earth,
148:12 you young men and young women,
you elderly, along with you children!
148:13 Let them praise the name of the LORD,
for his name alone is exalted;
his majesty extends over the earth and sky.
148:14 He has made his people victorious,
and given all his loyal followers reason to praise –
the Israelites, the people who are close to him.
Praise the LORD!
Psalm 149
149:1 Praise the LORD!
Sing to the LORD a new song!
Praise him in the assembly of the godly!
149:2 Let Israel rejoice in their Creator!
Let the people of Zion delight in their king!
149:3 Let them praise his name with dancing!
Let them sing praises to him to the accompaniment of the tambourine and
harp!
149:4 For the LORD takes delight in his people;
he exalts the oppressed by delivering them.
149:5 Let the godly rejoice because of their vindication!
Let them shout for joy upon their beds!

149:6 May they praise God
while they hold a two-edged sword in their hand,
149:7 in order to take revenge on the nations,
and punish foreigners.
149:8 They bind their kings in chains,
and their nobles in iron shackles,
149:9 and execute the judgment to which their enemies have been sentenced.
All his loyal followers will be vindicated.
Praise the LORD!
Psalm 150
150:1 Praise the LORD!
Praise God in his sanctuary!
Praise him in the sky, which testifies to his strength!
150:2 Praise him for his mighty acts!
Praise him for his surpassing greatness!
150:3 Praise him with the blast of the horn!
Praise him with the lyre and the harp!
150:4 Praise him with the tambourine and with dancing!
Praise him with stringed instruments and the flute!
150:5 Praise him with loud cymbals!
Praise him with clanging cymbals!
150:6 Let everything that has breath praise the LORD!
Praise the LORD!

Book 20. Proverbs

Introduction to the Book
1:1 The Proverbs of Solomon son of David, king of Israel:

1:2 To learn wisdom and moral instruction,
and to discern wise counsel.
1:3 To receive moral instruction in skillful living,
in righteousness, justice, and equity.
1:4 To impart shrewdness to the morally naive,
and a discerning plan to the young person.
1:5 (Let the wise also hear and gain instruction,
and let the discerning acquire guidance!)
1:6 To discern the meaning of a proverb and a parable,
the sayings of the wise and their riddles.
Introduction to the Theme of the Book
1:7 Fearing the LORD is the beginning of moral knowledge,
but fools despise wisdom and instruction.
1:8 Listen, my child, to the instruction from your father,
and do not forsake the teaching from your mother.
1:9 For they will be like an elegant garland on your head,
and like pendants around your neck.
Admonition to Avoid Easy but Unjust Riches
1:10 My child, if sinners try to entice you,
do not consent!
1:11 If they say, "Come with us!
We will lie in wait to shed blood;
we will ambush an innocent person capriciously.
1:12 We will swallow them alive like Sheol,
those full of vigor like those going down to the Pit.
1:13 We will seize all kinds of precious wealth;
we will fill our houses with plunder.
1:14 Join with us!
We will all share equally in what we steal."
1:15 My child, do not go down their way,
withhold yourself from their path;
1:16 for they are eager to inflict harm,
and they hasten to shed blood.
1:17 Surely it is futile to spread a net
in plain sight of any bird,
1:18 but these men lie in wait for their own blood,
they ambush their own lives!
1:19 Such are the ways of all who gain profit unjustly;
it takes away the life of those who obtain it!
Warning Against Disregarding Wisdom
1:20 Wisdom calls out in the street,
she shouts loudly in the plazas;
1:21 at the head of the noisy streets she calls,
in the entrances of the gates in the city she utters her words:
1:22 "How long will you simpletons love naiveté?
How long will mockers delight in mockery
and fools hate knowledge?
1:23 If only you will respond to my rebuke,
then I will pour out my thoughts to you
and I will make my words known to you.
1:24 However, because I called but you refused to listen,
because I stretched out my hand but no one paid attention,
1:25 because you neglected all my advice,

and did not comply with my rebuke,
1:26 so I myself will laugh when disaster strikes you,
I will mock when what you dread comes,
1:27 when what you dread comes like a whirlwind,
and disaster strikes you like a devastating storm,
when distressing trouble comes on you.
1:28 Then they will call to me, but I will not answer;
they will diligently seek me, but they will not find me.
1:29 Because they hated moral knowledge,
and did not choose to fear the LORD,
1:30 they did not comply with my advice,
they spurned all my rebuke.
1:31 Therefore they will eat from the fruit of their way,
and they will be stuffed full of their own counsel.
1:32 For the waywardness of the
simpletons will kill them,
and the careless ease of fools will destroy them.
1:33 But the one who listens to me will live in security,
and will be at ease from the dread of harm.
Benefits of Seeking Wisdom
2:1 My child, if you receive my words,
and store up my commands within you,
2:2 by making your ear attentive to wisdom,
and by turning your heart to understanding,
2:3 indeed, if you call out for discernment –
raise your voice for understanding –
2:4 if you seek it like silver,
and search for it like hidden treasure,
2:5 then you will understand how to fear the LORD,
and you will discover knowledge about God.
2:6 For the LORD gives wisdom,
and from his mouth comes knowledge and understanding.
2:7 He stores up effective counsel for the upright,
and is like a shield for those who live with integrity,
2:8 to guard the paths of the righteous
and to protect the way of his pious ones.
2:9 Then you will understand righteousness and justice
and equity – every good way.
2:10 For wisdom will enter your heart,
and moral knowledge will be attractive to you.
2:11 Discretion will protect you,
understanding will guard you,
2:12 to deliver you from the way of the wicked,
from those speaking perversity,
2:13 who leave the upright paths
to walk on the dark ways,
2:14 who delight in doing evil,
they rejoice in perverse evil;
2:15 whose paths are morally crooked,
and who are devious in their ways;
2:16 to deliver you from the adulteress,
from the sexually loose woman who speaks flattering words;
2:17 who leaves the husband from her younger days,
and forgets her marriage covenant made before God.
2:18 For her house sinks down to death,
and her paths lead to the place of the departed spirits.
2:19 None who go in to her will return,
nor will they reach the paths of life.

2:20 So you will walk in the way of good people,
and will keep on the paths of the righteous.
2:21 For the upright will reside in the land,
and those with integrity will remain in it,
2:22 but the wicked will be removed from the land,
and the treacherous will be torn away from it.
Exhortations to Seek Wisdom and Walk with the Lord
3:1 My child, do not forget my teaching,
but let your heart keep my commandments,
3:2 for they will provide a long and full life,
and they will add well-being to you.
3:3 Do not let truth and mercy leave you;
bind them around your neck,
write them on the tablet of your heart.
3:4 Then you will find favor and good understanding,
in the sight of God and people.

3:5 Trust in the LORD with all your heart,
and do not rely on your own understanding.
3:6 Acknowledge him in all your ways,
and he will make your paths straight.
3:7 Do not be wise in your own estimation;
fear the LORD and turn away from evil.
3:8 This will bring healing to your body,

and refreshment to your inner self.
3:9 Honor the LORD from your wealth
and from the first fruits of all your crops;
3:10 then your barns will be filled completely,
and your vats will overflow with new wine.

3:11 My child, do not despise discipline from the LORD,
and do not loathe his rebuke.
3:12 For the LORD disciplines those he loves,
just as a father disciplines the son in whom he delights.
Blessings of Obtaining Wisdom
3:13 Blessed is the one who finds wisdom,
and the one who obtains understanding.
3:14 For her benefit is more profitable than silver,
and her gain is better than gold.
3:15 She is more precious than rubies,
and none of the things you desire can compare with her.
3:16 Long life is in her right hand;
in her left hand are riches and honor.
3:17 Her ways are very pleasant,
and all her paths are peaceful.
3:18 She is like a tree of life to those who obtain her,
and everyone who grasps hold of her will be blessed.

3:19 By wisdom the LORD laid the foundation of the earth;
he established the heavens by understanding.
3:20 By his knowledge the primordial sea was broken open,
and the clouds drip down dew.

3:21 My child, do not let them escape from your sight;
safeguard sound wisdom and discretion.
3:22 So they will give life to you,
and grace to adorn your neck.
3:23 Then you will walk on your way with security,
and you will not stumble.
3:24 When you lie down you will not be filled with fear;
when you lie down your sleep will be pleasant.
3:25 You will not be afraid of sudden disaster,
or when destruction overtakes the wicked;
3:26 for the LORD will be the source of your confidence,
and he will guard your foot from being caught in a trap.
Wisdom Demonstrated in Relationships with People
3:27 Do not withhold good from those who need it,
when you have the ability to help.
3:28 Do not say to your neighbor, "Go! Return tomorrow
and I will give it," when you have it with you at the time.
3:29 Do not plot evil against your neighbor
when he dwells by you unsuspectingly.
3:30 Do not accuse anyone without legitimate cause,
if he has not treated you wrongly.
3:31 Do not envy a violent man,
and do not choose to imitate any of his ways;
3:32 for one who goes astray is an abomination to the LORD,
but he reveals his intimate counsel to the upright.
3:33 The LORD's curse is on the
household of the wicked,
but he blesses the home of the righteous.
3:34 Although he is scornful to arrogant scoffers,
yet he shows favor to the humble.
3:35 The wise inherit honor,
but he holds fools up to public contempt.
Admonition to Follow Righteousness and Avoid Wickedness
4:1 Listen, children, to a father's instruction,
and pay attention so that you may gain discernment.
4:2 Because I give you good instruction,
do not forsake my teaching.
4:3 When I was a son to my father,
a tender only child before my mother,
4:4 he taught me, and he said to me:
"Let your heart lay hold of my words;
keep my commands so that you will live.
4:5 Acquire wisdom, acquire understanding;
do not forget and do not turn aside from the words I speak.
4:6 Do not forsake wisdom, and she will protect you;
love her, and she will guard you.
4:7 Wisdom is supreme –
so acquire wisdom,
and whatever you acquire, acquire understanding!
4:8 Esteem her highly and she will exalt you;
she will honor you if you embrace her.
4:9 She will place a fair garland on your head;
she will bestow a beautiful crown on you."

4:10 Listen, my child, and accept my words,
so that the years of your life will be many.
4:11 I will guide you in the way of wisdom
and I will lead you in upright paths.
4:12 When you walk, your steps will not be hampered,
and when you run, you will not stumble.
4:13 Hold on to instruction, do not let it go;
protect it, because it is your life.
4:14 Do not enter the path of the wicked
or walk in the way of those who are evil.
4:15 Avoid it, do not go on it;
turn away from it, and go on.
4:16 For they cannot sleep unless they cause harm;
they are robbed of sleep until they make someone stumble.
4:17 For they eat bread gained from wickedness
and drink wine obtained from violence.
4:18 But the path of the righteous is like the bright morning light,
growing brighter and brighter until full day.
4:19 The way of the wicked is like gloomy darkness;
they do not know what causes them to stumble.

4:20 My child, pay attention to my words;
listen attentively to my sayings.
4:21 Do not let them depart from your sight,
guard them within your heart;
4:22 for they are life to those who find them
and healing to one's entire body.
4:23 Guard your heart with all vigilance,
for from it are the sources of life.
4:24 Remove perverse speech from your mouth;
keep devious talk far from your lips.
4:25 Let your eyes look directly in front of you
and let your gaze look straight before you.
4:26 Make the path for your feet level,
so that all your ways may be established.
4:27 Do not turn to the right or to the left;
turn yourself away from evil.
Admonition to Avoid Seduction to Evil
5:1 My child, be attentive to my wisdom,
pay close attention to my understanding,
5:2 in order to safeguard discretion,
and that your lips may guard knowledge.
5:3 For the lips of the adulterous woman drip honey,
and her seductive words are smoother than olive oil,
5:4 but in the end she is bitter as wormwood,
sharp as a two-edged sword.
5:5 Her feet go down to death;
her steps lead straight to the grave.
5:6 Lest she should make level the path leading to life,
her paths are unstable but she does not know it.

5:7 So now, children, listen to me;
do not turn aside from the words I speak.
5:8 Keep yourself far from her,
and do not go near the door of her house,
5:9 lest you give your vigor to others
and your years to a cruel person,
5:10 lest strangers devour your strength,
and your labor benefit another man's house.
5:11 And at the end of your life you will groan
when your flesh and your body are wasted away.
5:12 And you will say, "How I hated discipline!
My heart spurned reproof!
5:13 For I did not obey my teachers
and I did not heed my instructors.
5:14 I almost came to complete ruin
in the midst of the whole congregation!"

5:15 Drink water from your own cistern
and running water from your own well.
5:16 Should your springs be dispersed outside,
your streams of water in the wide plazas?
5:17 Let them be for yourself alone,
and not for strangers with you.
5:18 May your fountain be blessed,
and may you rejoice in your young wife –
5:19 a loving doe, a graceful deer;
may her breasts satisfy you at all times,
may you be captivated by her love always.
5:20 But why should you be captivated, my son, by an adulteress,
and embrace the bosom of a different woman?
5:21 For the ways of a person are in front of the LORD's eyes,
and the LORD weighs all that person's paths.

5:22 The wicked will be captured by his own iniquities,
and he will be held by the cords of his own sin.
5:23 He will die because there was no discipline;
because of the greatness of his folly he will reel.
Admonitions and Warnings against Dangerous and Destructive Acts
6:1 My child, if you have made a pledge for your neighbor,
and have become a guarantor for a stranger,
6:2 if you have been ensnared by the words you have uttered,
and have been caught by the words you have spoken,
6:3 then, my child, do this in order to deliver yourself,
because you have fallen into your neighbor's power:
go, humble yourself,
and appeal firmly to your neighbor.
6:4 Permit no sleep to your eyes
or slumber to your eyelids.
6:5 Deliver yourself like a gazelle from a snare,
and like a bird from the trap of the fowler.

6:6 Go to the ant, you sluggard;
observe its ways and be wise!
6:7 It has no commander,
overseer, or ruler,
6:8 yet it prepares its food in the summer;
it gathers at the harvest what it will eat.
6:9 How long, you sluggard, will you lie there?
When will you rise from your sleep?
6:10 A little sleep, a little slumber,
a little folding of the hands to relax,
6:11 and your poverty will come like a robber,
and your need like an armed man.

6:12 A worthless and wicked person
walks around saying perverse things;
6:13 he winks with his eyes,
signals with his feet,
and points with his fingers;
6:14 he plots evil with perverse thoughts in his heart,
he spreads contention at all times.
6:15 Therefore, his disaster will come suddenly;
in an instant he will be broken, and there will be no remedy.

6:16 There are six things that the LORD hates,
even seven things that are an abomination to him:
6:17 haughty eyes, a lying tongue,
and hands that shed innocent blood,
6:18 a heart that devises wicked plans,
feet that are swift to run to evil,
6:19 a false witness who pours out lies,
and a person who spreads discord among family members.

6:20 My child, guard the commands of your father
and do not forsake the instruction of your mother.
6:21 Bind them on your heart continually;
fasten them around your neck.
6:22 When you walk about, they will guide you;
when you lie down, they will watch over you;
when you wake up, they will talk to you.
6:23 For the commandments are like a lamp,
instruction is like a light,
and rebukes of discipline are like the road leading to life,
6:24 by keeping you from the evil woman,
from the smooth tongue of the loose woman.
6:25 Do not lust in your heart for her beauty,
and do not let her captivate you with her alluring eyes;
6:26 for on account of a prostitute one is brought down to a loaf of bread,
but the wife of another man preys on your precious life.
6:27 Can a man hold fire against his chest
without burning his clothes?
6:28 Can a man walk on hot coals
without scorching his feet?
6:29 So it is with the one who has sex with his neighbor's wife;
no one who touches her will escape punishment.
6:30 People do not despise a thief when he steals
to fulfill his need when he is hungry.
6:31 Yet if he is caught he must repay seven times over,
he might even have to give all the wealth of his house.
6:32 A man who commits adultery with a woman lacks wisdom,
whoever does it destroys his own life.
6:33 He will be beaten and despised,
and his reproach will not be wiped away;
6:34 for jealousy kindles a husband's rage,
and he will not show mercy when he takes revenge.
6:35 He will not consider any compensation;

he will not be willing, even if you multiply the compensation.

Admonition to Avoid the Wiles of the Adulteress

7:1 My child, keep my words
and treasure up my commands in your own keeping.
7:2 Keep my commands so that you may live,
and obey my instruction as your most prized possession.
7:3 Bind them on your forearm;
write them on the tablet of your heart.
7:4 Say to wisdom, "You are my sister,"
and call understanding a close relative,
7:5 so that they may keep you from the adulterous woman,
from the loose woman who flatters you with her words.

7:6 For at the window of my house
through my window lattice I looked out
7:7 and I saw among the naive –
I discerned among the youths –
a young man who lacked wisdom.
7:8 He was passing by the street near her corner,
making his way along the road to her house
7:9 in the twilight, the evening,
in the dark of the night.
7:10 Suddenly a woman came out to meet him!
She was dressed like a prostitute and with secret intent.
7:11 (She is loud and rebellious,
she does not remain at home –
7:12 at one time outside, at another in the wide plazas,
and by every corner she lies in wait.)
7:13 So she grabbed him and kissed him,
and with a bold expression she said to him,
7:14 "I have fresh meat at home;
today I have fulfilled my vows!
7:15 That is why I came out to meet you,
to look for you, and I found you!
7:16 I have spread my bed with elegant coverings,
with richly colored fabric from Egypt.
7:17 I have perfumed my bed
with myrrh, aloes, and cinnamon.
7:18 Come, let's drink deeply of lovemaking until morning,
let's delight ourselves with sexual intercourse.
7:19 For my husband is not at home;
he has gone on a journey of some distance.
7:20 He has taken a bag of money with him;
he will not return until the end of the month."
7:21 She persuaded him with persuasive words;
with her smooth talk she compelled him.
7:22 Suddenly he went after her
like an ox that goes to the slaughter,
like a stag prancing into a trapper's snare
7:23 till an arrow pierces his liver –
like a bird hurrying into a trap,
and he does not know that it will cost him his life.

7:24 So now, sons, listen to me,
and pay attention to the words I speak.
7:25 Do not let your heart turn aside to her ways –
do not wander into her pathways;
7:26 for she has brought down many fatally wounded,
and all those she has slain are many.
7:27 Her house is the way to the grave,
going down to the chambers of death.

The Appeal of Wisdom

8:1 Does not wisdom call out?
Does not understanding raise her voice?
8:2 At the top of the elevated places along the way,
at the intersection of the paths she takes her stand;
8:3 beside the gates opening into the city,
at the entrance of the doorways she cries out:
8:4 "To you, O people, I call out,
and my voice calls to all mankind.
8:5 You who are naive, discern wisdom!
And you fools, understand discernment!
8:6 Listen, for I will speak excellent things,
and my lips will utter what is right.
8:7 For my mouth speaks truth,
and my lips hate wickedness.
8:8 All the words of my mouth are righteous;
there is nothing in them twisted or crooked.
8:9 All of them are clear to the discerning
and upright to those who find knowledge.
8:10 Receive my instruction rather than silver,
and knowledge rather than choice gold.
8:11 For wisdom is better than rubies,

and desirable things cannot be compared to her.

8:12 "I, wisdom, live with prudence,
and I find knowledge and discretion.
8:13 The fear of the LORD is to hate evil;
I hate arrogant pride and the evil way
and perverse utterances.
8:14 Counsel and sound wisdom belong to me;
I possess understanding and might.
8:15 Kings reign by means of me,
and potentates decree righteousness;
8:16 by me princes rule,
as well as nobles and all righteous judges.
8:17 I love those who love me,
and those who seek me find me.
8:18 Riches and honor are with me,
long-lasting wealth and righteousness.
8:19 My fruit is better than the purest gold,
and what I produce is better than choice silver.
8:20 I walk in the path of righteousness,
in the pathway of justice,
8:21 that I may cause those who love me to inherit wealth,
and that I may fill their treasuries.
8:22 The LORD created me as the beginning of his works,
before his deeds of long ago.
8:23 From eternity I was appointed,
from the beginning, from before the world existed.
8:24 When there were no deep oceans I was born,
when there were no springs overflowing with water;
8:25 before the mountains were set in place –
before the hills – I was born,
8:26 before he made the earth and its fields,
or the beginning of the dust of the world.
8:27 When he established the heavens, I was there;
when he marked out the horizon over the face of the deep,
8:28 when he established the clouds above,
when the fountains of the deep grew strong,
8:29 when he gave the sea his decree
that the waters should not pass over his command,
when he marked out the foundations of the earth,
8:30 then I was beside him as a master craftsman,
and I was his delight day by day,
rejoicing before him at all times,
8:31 rejoicing in the habitable part of his earth,
and delighting in its people.

8:32 "So now, children, listen to me;
blessed are those who keep my ways.
8:33 Listen to my instruction so that you may be wise,
and do not neglect it.
8:34 Blessed is the one who listens to me,
watching at my doors day by day,
waiting beside my doorway.
8:35 For the one who finds me finds life
and receives favor from the LORD.
8:36 But the one who does not find me brings harm to himself;
all who hate me love death."

The Consequences of Accepting Wisdom or Folly

9:1 Wisdom has built her house;
she has carved out its seven pillars.
9:2 She has prepared her meat, she has mixed her wine;
she also has arranged her table.
9:3 She has sent out her female servants;
she calls out on the highest places of the city.
9:4 "Whoever is naive, let him turn in here,"
she says to those who lack understanding.
9:5 "Come, eat some of my food,
and drink some of the wine I have mixed.
9:6 Abandon your foolish ways so that you may live,
and proceed in the way of understanding."

9:7 Whoever corrects a mocker is asking for insult;
whoever reproves a wicked person receives abuse.
9:8 Do not reprove a mocker or he will hate you;
reprove a wise person and he will love you.
9:9 Give instruction to a wise person, and he will become wiser still;
teach a righteous person and he will add to his learning.
9:10 The beginning of wisdom is to fear the LORD,
and acknowledge the Holy One is understanding.
9:11 For because of me your days will be many,
and years will be added to your life.
9:12 If you are wise, you are wise to your own advantage,
but if you are a mocker, you alone must bear it.

9:13 The woman called Folly is brash,
she is naive and does not know anything.
9:14 So she sits at the door of her house,
on a seat at the highest point of the city,
9:15 calling out to those who are passing by her in the way,
who go straight on their way.
9:16 "Whoever is simple, let him turn in here,"
she says to those who lack understanding.
9:17 "Stolen waters are sweet,
and food obtained in secret is pleasant!"
9:18 But they do not realize that the dead are there,
that her guests are in the depths of the grave.
The First Collection of Solomonic Proverbs
10:1 The Proverbs of Solomon:

A wise child makes a father rejoice,
but a foolish child is a grief to his mother.
10:2 Treasures gained by wickedness do not profit,
but righteousness delivers from mortal danger.
10:3 The LORD satisfies the appetite of the righteous,
but he thwarts the craving of the wicked.
10:4 The one who is lazy becomes poor,
but the one who works diligently becomes wealthy.
10:5 The one who gathers crops in the summer is a wise son,
but the one who sleeps during the harvest
is a son who brings shame to himself.
10:6 Blessings are on the head of the righteous,
but the speech of the wicked conceals violence.
10:7 The memory of the righteous is a blessing,
but the reputation of the wicked will rot.
10:8 The wise person accepts instructions,
but the one who speaks foolishness will come to ruin.
10:9 The one who conducts himself in integrity will live securely,
but the one who behaves perversely will be found out.
10:10 The one who winks his eye causes trouble,
and the one who speaks foolishness will come to ruin.
10:11 The teaching of the righteous is a fountain of life,
but the speech of the wicked conceals violence.
10:12 Hatred stirs up dissension,
but love covers all transgressions.
10:13 Wisdom is found in the words of the discerning person,
but the one who lacks wisdom will be disciplined.
10:14 Those who are wise store up knowledge,
but foolish speech leads to imminent destruction.
10:15 The wealth of a rich person is like a fortified city,
but the poor are brought to ruin by their poverty.
10:16 The reward which the righteous receive is life;
the recompense which the wicked receive is judgment.
10:17 The one who heeds instruction is on the way to life,
but the one who rejects rebuke goes astray.
10:18 The one who conceals hatred utters lies,
and the one who spreads slander is certainly a fool.
10:19 When words abound, transgression is inevitable,
but the one who restrains his words is wise.
10:20 What the righteous say is like the best silver,
but what the wicked think is of little value.
10:21 The teaching of the righteous feeds many,
but fools die for lack of wisdom.
10:22 The blessing from the LORD makes a person rich,
and he adds no sorrow to it.
10:23 Carrying out a wicked scheme is enjoyable to a fool,
and so is wisdom for the one who has discernment.
10:24 What the wicked fears will come on him;
what the righteous desire will be granted.
10:25 When the storm passes through, the wicked are swept away,
but the righteous are an everlasting foundation.
10:26 Like vinegar to the teeth and like smoke to the eyes,
so is the sluggard to those who send him.
10:27 Fearing the LORD prolongs life,
but the life span of the wicked will be shortened.
10:28 The hope of the righteous is joy,
but the expectation of the wicked will remain unfulfilled.
10:29 The way of the LORD is like a stronghold for the upright,
but it is destruction to evildoers.
10:30 The righteous will never be moved,
but the wicked will not inhabit the land.
10:31 The speech of the righteous bears the fruit of wisdom,
but the one who speaks perversion will be destroyed.
10:32 The lips of the righteous know what is pleasing,
but the speech of the wicked is perverse.
11:1 The LORD abhors dishonest scales,
but an accurate weight is his elight.

11:2 When pride comes, then comes disgrace,
but with humility comes wisdom.
11:3 The integrity of the upright guides them,
but the crookedness of the unfaithful destroys them.
11:4 Wealth does not profit in the day of wrath,
but righteousness delivers from mortal danger.
11:5 The righteousness of the blameless will make straight their way,
but the wicked person will fall by his own wickedness.
11:6 The righteousness of the upright will deliver them,
but the faithless will be captured by their own desires.
11:7 When a wicked person dies, his expectation perishes,
and the hope of his strength perishes.
11:8 The righteous person is delivered out of trouble,
and the wicked turns up in his stead.
11:9 With his speech the godless person destroys his neighbor,
but by knowledge the righteous will be delivered.
11:10 When the righteous do well, the city rejoices;
when the wicked perish, there is joy.
11:11 A city is exalted by the blessing provided from the upright,
but it is destroyed by the counsel of the wicked.
11:12 The one who denounces his
neighbor lacks wisdom,
but the one who has discernment keeps silent.
11:13 The one who goes about slandering others reveals secrets,
but the one who is trustworthy conceals a matter.
11:14 When there is no guidance a nation falls,
but there is success in the abundance of counselors.
11:15 The one who puts up security for a stranger will surely have trouble,
but whoever avoids shaking hands will be secure.
11:16 A generous woman gains honor,
and ruthless men seize wealth.
11:17 A kind person benefits himself,
but a cruel person brings himself trouble.
11:18 The wicked person earns deceitful wages,
but the one who sows righteousness reaps a genuine reward.
11:19 True righteousness leads to life,
but the one who pursues evil pursues it to his own death.
11:20 The LORD abhors those who are perverse in heart,
but those who are blameless in their ways are his delight.
11:21 Be assured that the evil person will certainly be punished,
but the descendants of the righteous will not suffer unjust judgment.
11:22 Like a gold ring in a pig's snout
is a beautiful woman who rejects discretion.
11:23 What the righteous desire leads only to good,
but what the wicked hope for leads to wrath.
11:24 One person is generous and yet grows more wealthy,
but another withholds more than he should and comes to poverty.
11:25 A generous person will be enriched,
and the one who provides water for
others will himself be satisfied.
11:26 People will curse the one who withholds grain,
but they will praise the one who sells it.
11:27 The one who diligently seeks good seeks favor,
but the one who searches for evil – it will come to him.
11:28 The one who trusts in his riches will fall,
but the righteous will flourish like a green leaf.
11:29 The one who troubles his family will inherit nothing,
and the fool will be a servant to the wise person.
11:30 The fruit of the righteous is like a tree producing life,
and the one who wins souls is wise.
11:31 If the righteous are recompensed on earth,
how much more the wicked sinner!
12:1 The one who loves discipline loves knowledge,
but the one who hates reproof is stupid.
12:2 A good person obtains favor from the LORD,
but the LORD condemns a person with wicked schemes.
12:3 No one can be established through wickedness,
but a righteous root cannot be moved.
12:4 A noble wife is the crown of her husband,
but the wife who acts shamefully is like rottenness in his bones.
12:5 The plans of the righteous are just;
the counsels of the wicked are deceitful.
12:6 The words of the wicked lie in wait to shed innocent blood,
but the words of the upright will deliver them.
12:7 The wicked are overthrown and perish,
but the righteous household will stand.
12:8 A person is praised in accordance with his wisdom,
but the one who has a twisted mind is despised.
12:9 Better is a person of humble standing who nevertheless has a servant,
than one who pretends to be somebody important yet has no food.
12:10 A righteous person cares for the life of his animal,

but even the most compassionate acts of the wicked are cruel.
12:11 The one who works his field will have plenty of food,
but whoever chases daydreams lacks wisdom.
12:12 The wicked person desires a stronghold,
but the righteous root endures.
12:13 The evil person is ensnared by the transgression of his speech,
but the righteous person escapes out of trouble.
12:14 A person will be satisfied with good from the fruit of his words,
and the work of his hands will be rendered to him.
12:15 The way of a fool is right in his own opinion,
but the one who listens to advice is wise.
12:16 A fool's annoyance is known at once,
but the prudent overlooks an insult.
12:17 The faithful witness tells what is right,
but a false witness speaks deceit.
12:18 Speaking recklessly is like the thrusts of a sword,
but the words of the wise bring healing.
12:19 The one who tells the truth will endure forever,
but the one who lies will last only for a moment.
12:20 Deceit is in the heart of those who plot evil,
but those who promote peace have joy.
12:21 The righteous do not encounter any harm,
but the wicked are filled with calamity.
12:22 The LORD abhors a person who lies,
but those who deal truthfully are his delight.
12:23 The shrewd person conceals knowledge,
 but foolish people publicize folly.
12:24 The diligent person will rule,
but the slothful will become a slave.
12:25 Anxiety in a person's heart weighs him down,
but an encouraging word brings him joy.
12:26 The righteous person is cautious in his friendship,
but the way of the wicked leads them astray.
12:27 The lazy person does not roast his prey,
but personal possessions are precious to the diligent.
12:28 In the path of righteousness there is life,
but another path leads to death.
13:1 A wise son accepts his father's discipline,
but a scoffer does not listen to rebuke.
13:2 From the fruit of his speech a person eats good things,
but the faithless desire the fruit of violence.
13:3 The one who guards his words guards his life,
but whoever is talkative will come to ruin.
13:4 The appetite of the sluggard
craves but gets nothing,
but the desire of the diligent will be abundantly satisfied.
13:5 The righteous person hates anything false,
but the wicked person acts in shameful disgrace.
13:6 Righteousness guards the one who lives with integrity,
but wickedness overthrows the sinner.
13:7 There is one who pretends to be rich and yet has nothing;
another pretends to be poor and yet possesses great wealth.
13:8 The ransom of a person's life is his wealth,
but the poor person hears no threat.
13:9 The light of the righteous shines brightly,
but the lamp of the wicked goes out.
13:10 With pride comes only contention,
but wisdom is with the well-advised.
13:11 Wealth gained quickly will dwindle away,
but the one who gathers it little by little will become rich.
13:12 Hope deferred makes the heart sick,
but a longing fulfilled is like a tree of life.
13:13 The one who despises instruction will pay the penalty,
but whoever esteems instruction will be rewarded.
13:14 Instruction from the wise is like a life-giving fountain,
to turn a person from deadly snares.
13:15 Keen insight wins favor,
but the conduct of the unfaithful is harsh.
13:16 Every shrewd person acts with knowledge,
but a fool displays his folly.
13:17 An unreliable messenger falls into trouble,
but a faithful envoy brings healing.
13:18 The one who neglects discipline ends up in poverty and shame,
but the one who accepts reproof is honored.
13:19 A desire fulfilled is sweet to the soul,
but fools abhor turning away from evil.
13:20 The one who associates with the wise grows wise,
but a companion of fools suffers harm.
13:21 Calamity pursues sinners,
but prosperity rewards the righteous.
13:22 A benevolent person leaves an inheritance for his grandchildren,
but the wealth of a sinner is stored up for the righteous.
13:23 There is abundant food in the field of the poor,

but it is swept away by injustice.
13:24 The one who spares his rod hates his child,
but the one who loves his child is diligent in disciplining him.
13:25 The righteous has enough food to satisfy his appetite,
but the belly of the wicked lacks food.
14:1 Every wise woman builds her household,
but a foolish woman tears it down with her own hands.
14:2 The one who walks in his uprightness fears the LORD,
but the one who is perverted in his ways despises him.
14:3 In the speech of a fool is a rod for his back,
but the words of the wise protect them.
14:4 Where there are no oxen, the feeding trough is clean,
but an abundant harvest is produced by strong oxen.
14:5 A truthful witness does not lie,
but a false witness breathes out lies.
14:6 The scorner seeks wisdom but finds none,
but understanding is easy for a discerning person.
14:7 Leave the presence of a foolish person,
or you will not understand wise counsel.
14:8 The wisdom of the shrewd person is to discern his way,
but the folly of fools is deception.
14:9 Fools mock at reparation,
but among the upright there is favor.
14:10 The heart knows its own bitterness,
and with its joy no one else can share.
14:11 The household of the wicked will be destroyed,
but the tent of the upright will flourish.
14:12 There is a way that seems right to a person,
but its end is the way that leads to death.
14:13 Even in laughter the heart may ache,
and the end of joy may be grief.
14:14 The backslider will be paid back from his own ways,
but a good person will be rewarded for his.
14:15 A naive person believes everything,
but the shrewd person discerns his steps.
14:16 A wise person is cautious and turns from evil,
but a fool throws off restraint and is overconfident.
14:17 A person who has a quick temper does foolish things,
and a person with crafty schemes is hated.
14:18 The naive inherit folly,
but the shrewd are crowned with knowledge.
14:19 Those who are evil will bow before those who are good,
and the wicked will bow at the gates of the righteous.
14:20 A poor person is disliked even by his neighbors,
but those who love the rich are many.
14:21 The one who despises his neighbor sins,
but whoever is kind to the needy is blessed.
14:22 Do not those who devise evil go astray?
But those who plan good exhibit faithful covenant love.
14:23 In all hard work there is profit,
but merely talking about it only brings poverty.
14:24 The crown of the wise is their riches,
but the folly of fools is folly.
14:25 A truthful witness rescues lives,
but the one who breathes lies brings deception.
14:26 In the fear of the LORD one has strong confidence,
and it will be a refuge for his children.
14:27 The fear of the LORD is like a life-giving fountain,
to turn people from deadly snares.
14:28 A king's glory is the abundance of people,
but the lack of subjects is the ruin of a ruler.
14:29 The one who is slow to anger has great understanding,
but the one who has a quick temper exalts folly.
14:30 A tranquil spirit revives the body,
but envy is rottenness to the bones.
14:31 The one who oppresses the poor insults his Creator,
but whoever shows favor to the needy honors him.
14:32 The wicked will be thrown down in his trouble,
but the righteous have refuge even in the threat of death.
14:33 Wisdom rests in the heart of the discerning;
it is known even in the heart of fools.
14:34 Righteousness exalts a nation,
but sin is a disgrace to any people.
14:35 The king shows favor to a wise servant,
but his wrath falls on one who acts shamefully.
15:1 A gentle response turns away anger,
but a harsh word stirs up wrath.
15:2 The tongue of the wise treats knowledge correctly,
but the mouth of the fool spouts out folly.
15:3 The eyes of the LORD are in every place,
keeping watch on those who are evil and those who are good.
15:4 Speech that heals is like a life-giving tree,
but a perverse tongue breaks the spirit.

15:5 A fool rejects his father's discipline,
but whoever heeds reproof shows good sense.
15:6 In the house of the righteous is abundant wealth,
but the income of the wicked brings trouble.
15:7 The lips of the wise spread knowledge,
but not so the heart of fools.
15:8 The LORD abhors the sacrifices of the wicked,
but the prayer of the upright pleases him.
15:9 The LORD abhors the way of the wicked,
but he loves those who pursue righteousness.
15:10 Severe discipline is for the one who abandons the way;
the one who hates reproof will die.
15:11 Death and Destruction are before the LORD –
how much more the hearts of humans!
15:12 The scorner does not love one who corrects him;
he will not go to the wise.
15:13 A joyful heart makes the face cheerful,
but by a painful heart the spirit is broken.
15:14 The discerning heart seeks knowledge,
but the mouth of fools feeds on folly.
15:15 All the days of the afflicted are bad,
but one with a cheerful heart has a continual feast.
15:16 Better is little with the fear of the LORD
than great wealth and turmoil with it.
15:17 Better a meal of vegetables where there is love
than a fattened ox where there is hatred.
15:18 A quick-tempered person stirs up dissension,
but one who is slow to anger calms a quarrel.
15:19 The way of the sluggard is like a hedge of thorns,
but the path of the upright is like a highway.
15:20 A wise child brings joy to his father,
but a foolish person despises his mother.
15:21 Folly is a joy to one who lacks sense,
but one who has understanding follows an upright course.
15:22 Plans fail when there is no counsel,
but with abundant advisers they are established.
15:23 A person has joy in giving an appropriate answer,
and a word at the right time – how good it is!
15:24 The path of life is upward for the wise person,
to keep him from going downward to Sheol.
15:25 The LORD tears down the house of the proud,
but he maintains the boundaries of the widow.
15:26 The LORD abhors the plans of the wicked,
but pleasant words are pure.
15:27 The one who is greedy for gain troubles his household,
but whoever hates bribes will live.
15:28 The heart of the righteous considers how to answer,
but the mouth of the wicked pours out evil things.
15:29 The LORD is far from the wicked,
but he hears the prayer of the righteous.
15:30 A bright look brings joy to the heart,
and good news gives health to the body.
15:31 The person who hears the reproof that leads to life
is at home among the wise.
15:32 The one who refuses correction despises himself,
but whoever hears reproof acquires understanding.
15:33 The fear of the LORD provides wise instruction,
and before honor comes humility.
16:1 The intentions of the heart belong to a man,
but the answer of the tongue comes from the LORD.
16:2 All a person's ways seem right in his own opinion,
but the LORD evaluates the motives.
16:3 Commit your works to the LORD,
and your plans will be established.
16:4 The LORD works everything for its own ends –
even the wicked for the day of disaster.
16:5 The LORD abhors every arrogant person;
rest assured that they will not go unpunished.
16:6 Through loyal love and truth iniquity is appeased;
through fearing the LORD one avoids evil.
16:7 When a person's ways are pleasing to the LORD,
he even reconciles his enemies to himself.
16:8 Better to have a little with righteousness
than to have abundant income without justice.
16:9 A person plans his course,
but the LORD directs his steps.
16:10 The divine verdict is in the words of the king,
his pronouncements must not act treacherously against justice.
16:11 Honest scales and balances are from the LORD;
all the weights in the bag are his handiwork.
16:12 Doing wickedness is an abomination to kings,
because a throne is established in righteousness.
16:13 The delight of kings is righteous counsel,

and they love the one who speaks uprightly.
16:14 A king's wrath is like a messenger of death,
but a wise person appeases it.
16:15 In the light of the king's face there is life,
and his favor is like the clouds of the spring rain.
16:16 How much better it is to acquire wisdom than gold;
to acquire understanding is more desirable than silver.
16:17 The highway of the upright is to turn away from evil;
the one who guards his way safeguards his life.
16:18 Pride goes before destruction,
and a haughty spirit before a fall.
16:19 It is better to be lowly in spirit with the afflicted
than to share the spoils with the proud.
16:20 The one who deals wisely in a matter will find success,
and blessed is the one who trusts in the LORD.
16:21 The one who is wise in heart is called discerning,
and kind speech increases persuasiveness.
16:22 Insight is like a life-giving fountain to the one who possesses it,
but folly leads to the discipline of fools.
16:23 A wise person's heart makes his speech wise
and it adds persuasiveness to his words.
16:24 Pleasant words are like a honeycomb,
sweet to the soul and healing to the bones.
16:25 There is a way that seems right to a person,
but its end is the way that leads to death.
16:26 A laborer's appetite works on his behalf,
for his hunger urges him to work.
16:27 A wicked scoundrel digs up evil,
and his slander is like a scorching fire.
16:28 A perverse person spreads dissension,
and a gossip separates the closest friends.
16:29 A violent person entices his neighbor,
and leads him down a path that is terrible.
16:30 The one who winks his eyes devises perverse things,
and one who compresses his lips brings about evil.
16:31 Gray hair is like a crown of glory;
it is attained in the path of righteousness.
16:32 Better to be slow to anger than to be a mighty warrior,
and one who controls his temper is better than one who captures a city.
16:33 The dice are thrown into the lap,
but their every decision is from the LORD.
17:1 Better is a dry crust of bread where there is quietness
than a house full of feasting with strife.
17:2 A servant who acts wisely will rule
over an heir who behaves shamefully,
and will share the inheritance along with the relatives.
17:3 The crucible is for refining silver and the furnace is for gold,
likewise the LORD tests hearts.
17:4 One who acts wickedly pays attention to evil counsel;
a liar listens to a malicious tongue.
17:5 The one who mocks the poor insults his Creator;
whoever rejoices over disaster will not go unpunished.
17:6 Grandchildren are like a crown to the elderly,
and the glory of children is their parents.
17:7 Excessive speech is not becoming for a fool;
how much less are lies for a ruler!
17:8 A bribe works like a charm for the one who offers it;
in whatever he does he succeeds.
17:9 The one who forgives an offense seeks love,
but whoever repeats a matter separates close friends.
17:10 A rebuke makes a greater impression on a discerning person
than a hundred blows on a fool.
17:11 An evil person seeks only rebellion,
and so a cruel messenger will be sent against him.
17:12 It is better for a person to meet a mother bear being robbed of her cubs,
than to encounter a fool in his folly.
17:13 As for the one who repays evil for good,
evil will not leave his house.
17:14 Starting a quarrel is like letting out water;
stop it before strife breaks out!
17:15 The one who acquits the guilty and the one who condemns the innocent –
both of them are an abomination to the LORD.
17:16 Of what use is money in the hand of a fool,
since he has no intention of acquiring wisdom?
17:17 A friend loves at all times,
and a relative is born to help in adversity.
17:18 The one who lacks wisdom strikes hands in pledge,
and puts up financial security for his neighbor.
17:19 The one who loves a quarrel loves transgression;
whoever builds his gate high seeks destruction.
17:20 The one who has a perverse heart does not find good,

and the one who is deceitful in speech falls into trouble.
17:21 Whoever brings a fool into the world does so to his grief,
and the father of a fool has no joy.
17:22 A cheerful heart brings good healing,
but a crushed spirit dries up the bones.
17:23 A wicked person receives a bribe secretly
to pervert the ways of justice.
17:24 Wisdom is directly in front of the discerning person,
but the eyes of a fool run to the ends of the earth.
17:25 A foolish child is a grief to his father,
and bitterness to the mother who bore him.
17:26 It is terrible to punish a righteous person,
and to flog honorable men is wrong.
17:27 The truly wise person restrains his words,
and the one who stays calm is discerning.
17:28 Even a fool who remains silent is considered wise,
and the one who holds his tongue is deemed discerning.
18:1 One who has isolated himself seeks his own desires;
he rejects all sound judgment.
18:2 A fool takes no pleasure in understanding
but only in disclosing what is on his mind.
18:3 When a wicked person arrives, contempt shows up with him,
and with shame comes a reproach.
18:4 The words of a person's mouth are like deep waters,
and the fountain of wisdom is like a flowing brook.
18:5 It is terrible to show partiality to the wicked,
by depriving a righteous man of justice.

18:6 The lips of a fool enter into strife,
and his mouth invites a flogging.
18:7 The mouth of a fool is his ruin,
and his lips are a snare for his life.
18:8 The words of a gossip are like choice morsels;
they go down into the person's innermost being.
18:9 The one who is slack in his work
is a brother to one who destroys.
18:10 The name of the LORD is like a strong tower;
the righteous person runs to it and is set safely on high.
18:11 The wealth of a rich person is like a strong city,
and it is like a high wall in his imagination.
18:12 Before destruction the heart of a person is proud,
but humility comes before honor.
18:13 The one who gives an answer before he listens –
that is his folly and his shame.
18:14 A person's spirit sustains him through sickness –
but who can bear a crushed spirit?
18:15 The discerning person acquires knowledge,
and the wise person seeks knowledge.
18:16 A person's gift makes room for him,
and leads him before important people.
18:17 The first to state his case seems right,
until his opponent begins to cross-examine him.
18:18 A toss of a coin ends disputes,
and settles the issue between strong opponents.
18:19 A relative offended is harder to reach than a strong city,
and disputes are like the barred gates of a fortified citadel.
18:20 From the fruit of a person's mouth his stomach is satisfied,
with the product of his lips is he satisfied.
18:21 Death and life are in the power of the tongue,
and those who love its use will eat its fruit.
18:22 The one who finds a wife finds what is enjoyable,
and receives a pleasurable gift from the LORD.
18:23 A poor person makes supplications,
but a rich man answers harshly.
18:24 A person who has friends may be harmed by them,
but there is a friend who sticks closer than a brother.
19:1 Better is a poor person who walks in his integrity
than one who is perverse in his speech and is a fool.
19:2 It is dangerous to have zeal without knowledge,
and the one who acts hastily makes poor choices.
19:3 A person's folly subverts his way,
and his heart rages against the LORD.
19:4 Wealth adds many friends,
but a poor person is separated from his friend.
19:5 A false witness will not go unpunished,
and the one who spouts out lies will not escape punishment.
19:6 Many people entreat the favor of a generous person,
and everyone is the friend of the person who gives gifts.
19:7 All the relatives of a poor person hate him;
how much more do his friends avoid him –
he pursues them with words, but they do not respond.
19:8 The one who acquires wisdom loves himself;
the one who preserves understanding will prosper.

19:9 A false witness will not go unpunished,
and the one who spouts out lies will perish.
19:10 Luxury is not appropriate for a fool;
how much less for a servant to rule over princes!
19:11 A person's wisdom makes him slow to anger,
and it is his glory to overlook an offense.
19:12 A king's wrath is like the roar of a lion,
but his favor is like dew on the grass.
19:13 A foolish child is the ruin of his father,
and a contentious wife is like a constant dripping.
19:14 A house and wealth are inherited from parents,
but a prudent wife is from the LORD.
19:15 Laziness brings on a deep sleep,
and the idle person will go hungry.
19:16 The one who obeys commandments guards his life;
the one who despises his ways will die.
19:17 The one who is gracious to the poor lends to the LORD,
and the LORD will repay him for his good deed.
19:18 Discipline your child, for there is hope,
but do not set your heart on causing his death.
19:19 A person with great anger bears the penalty,
but if you deliver him from it once, you will have to do it again.
19:20 Listen to advice and receive discipline,
that you may become wise by the end of your life.
19:21 There are many plans in a person's mind,
but it is the counsel of the LORD which will stand.
19:22 What is desirable for a person is to show loyal love,
and a poor person is better than a liar.
19:23 Fearing the LORD leads to life,
and one who does so will live satisfied; he will not be afflicted by calamity.
19:24 The sluggard plunges his hand in the dish,
and he will not even bring it back to his mouth!
19:25 Flog a scorner, and as a result the simpleton will learn prudence;
correct a discerning person, and as a result he will understand knowledge.
19:26 The one who robs his father and chases away his mother
is a son who brings shame and disgrace.
19:27 If you stop listening to instruction, my child,
you will stray from the words of knowledge.
19:28 A crooked witness scorns justice,
and the mouth of the wicked devours iniquity.
19:29 Judgments are prepared for scorners,
and floggings for the backs of fools.
20:1 Wine is a mocker and strong drink is a brawler;
whoever goes astray by them is not wise.
20:2 The king's terrifying anger is like the roar of a lion;
whoever provokes him sins against himself.
20:3 It is an honor for a person to cease from strife,
but every fool quarrels.
20:4 The sluggard will not plow during the planting season,
so at harvest time he looks for the crop but has nothing.
20:5 Counsel in a person's heart is like deep water,
but an understanding person draws it out.
20:6 Many people profess their loyalty,
but a faithful person – who can find?
20:7 The righteous person behaves in integrity;
blessed are his children after him.
20:8 A king sitting on the throne to judge
separates out all evil with his eyes.
20:9 Who can say, "I have kept my heart clean;
I am pure from my sin"?
20:10 Diverse weights and diverse measures –
the LORD abhors both of them.
20:11 Even a young man is known by his actions,
whether his activity is pure and whether it is right.
20:12 The ear that hears and the eye that sees –
the LORD has made them both.
20:13 Do not love sleep, lest you become impoverished;
open your eyes so that you might be satisfied with food.
20:14 "It's worthless! It's worthless!" says the buyer,
but when he goes on his way, he boasts.
20:15 There is gold, and an abundance of rubies,
but words of knowledge are like a precious jewel.
20:16 Take a man's garment when he has given security for a stranger,
and when he gives surety for strangers, hold him in pledge.
20:17 Bread gained by deceit tastes sweet to a person,
but afterward his mouth will be filled with gravel.
20:18 Plans are established by counsel,
so make war with guidance.
20:19 The one who goes about gossiping reveals secrets;
therefore do not associate with someone who is always opening his mouth.
20:20 The one who curses his father and his mother,

his lamp will be extinguished in the blackest darkness.

20:21 An inheritance gained easily in the beginning
will not be blessed in the end.

20:22 Do not say, "I will pay back evil!"
Wait for the LORD, so that he may vindicate you.

20:23 The LORD abhors differing weights,
and dishonest scales are wicked.

20:24 The steps of a person are ordained by the LORD –
so how can anyone understand his own way?

20:25 It is a snare for a person to rashly cry, "Holy!"
and only afterward to consider what he has vowed.

20:26 A wise king separates out the wicked;
he turns the threshing wheel over them.

20:27 The human spirit is like the lamp of the LORD,
searching all his innermost parts.

20:28 Loyal love and truth preserve a king,
and his throne is upheld by loyal love.

20:29 The glory of young men is their strength,
and the splendor of old men is gray hair.

20:30 Beatings and wounds cleanse away evil,
and floggings cleanse the innermost being.

21:1 The king's heart is in the hand of the LORD like channels of water;
he turns it wherever he wants.

21:2 All of a person's ways seem right in his own opinion,
but the LORD evaluates the motives.

21:3 To do righteousness and justice
is more acceptable to the LORD than sacrifice.

21:4 Haughty eyes and a proud heart –
the agricultural product of the wicked is sin.

21:5 The plans of the diligent lead only to plenty,
but everyone who is hasty comes only to poverty.

21:6 Making a fortune by a lying tongue is like a vapor driven back and forth;
they seek death.

21:7 The violence done by the wicked will drag them away
because they refuse to do what is right.

21:8 The way of the guilty person is devious,
but as for the pure, his way is upright.

21:9 It is better to live on a corner of the housetop
than in a house in company with a quarrelsome wife.

21:10 The appetite of the wicked desires evil;
his neighbor is shown no favor in his eyes.

21:11 When a scorner is punished, the naive becomes wise;
when a wise person is instructed, he gains knowledge.

21:12 The Righteous One considers the house of the wicked;
he overthrows the wicked to their ruin.

21:13 The one who shuts his ears to the cry of the poor,
he too will cry out and will not be answered.

21:14 A gift given in secret subdues anger,
and a bribe given secretly subdues strong wrath.

21:15 Doing justice brings joy to the righteous
and terror to those who do evil.

21:16 The one who wanders from the way of wisdom
will end up in the company of the departed.

21:17 The one who loves pleasure will be a poor person;
whoever loves wine and anointing oil will not be rich.

21:18 The wicked become a ransom for the righteous,
and the faithless are taken in the place of the upright.

21:19 It is better to live in a desert land
than with a quarrelsome and easily-provoked woman.

21:20 There is desirable treasure and olive oil in the dwelling of the wise,
but a foolish person devours all he has.

21:21 The one who pursues righteousness and love
finds life, bounty, and honor.

21:22 The wise person can scale the city of the mighty
and bring down the stronghold in which they trust.

21:23 The one who guards his mouth and his tongue
keeps his life from troubles.

21:24 A proud and arrogant person, whose name is "Scoffer,"
acts with overbearing pride.

21:25 What the sluggard desires will kill him,
for his hands refuse to work.

21:26 All day long he craves greedily,
but the righteous gives and does not hold back.

21:27 The wicked person's sacrifice is an abomination;
how much more when he brings it with evil intent!

21:28 A lying witness will perish,
but the one who reports accurately speaks forever.

21:29 A wicked person shows boldness with his face,
but as for the upright, he discerns his ways.

21:30 There is no wisdom and there is no understanding,
and there is no counsel against the LORD.

21:31 A horse is prepared for the day of battle,
but the victory is from the LORD.

22:1 A good name is to be chosen rather than great wealth,
good favor more than silver or gold.

22:2 The rich and the poor meet together;
the LORD is the creator of them both.

22:3 A shrewd person sees danger and hides himself,
but the naive keep right on going and suffer for it.

22:4 The reward for humility and fearing the LORD
is riches and honor and life.

22:5 Thorns and snares are in the path of the perverse,
but the one who guards himself keeps far from them.

22:6 Train a child in the way that he
should go,
and when he is old he will not turn from it.

22:7 The rich rule over the poor,
and the borrower is servant to the lender.

22:8 The one who sows iniquity will reap trouble,
and the rod of his fury will end.

22:9 A generous person will be blessed,
for he gives some of his food to the poor.

22:10 Drive out the scorner and contention will leave;
strife and insults will cease.

22:11 The one who loves a pure heart
and whose speech is gracious – the king will be his friend.

22:12 The eyes of the LORD guard knowledge,
but he overthrows the words of the faithless person.

22:13 The sluggard says, "There is a lion outside!
I will be killed in the middle of the streets!"

22:14 The mouth of an adulteress is like a deep pit;
the one against whom the LORD is angry will fall into it.

22:15 Folly is bound up in the heart of a child,
but the rod of discipline will drive it far from him.

22:16 The one who oppresses the poor to increase his own gain
and the one who gives to the rich – both end up only in poverty.

The Sayings of the Wise

22:17 Incline your ear and listen to the words of the wise,
and apply your heart to my instruction.

22:18 For it is pleasing if you keep these sayings within you,
and they are ready on your lips.

22:19 So that your confidence may be in the LORD,
I am making them known to you today – even you.

22:20 Have I not written thirty sayings for you,
sayings of counsel and knowledge,

22:21 to show you true and reliable words,
so that you may give accurate answers to those who sent you?

22:22 Do not exploit a poor person because he is poor
and do not crush the needy in court,

22:23 for the LORD will plead their case
and will rob those who are robbing them.

22:24 Do not make friends with an angry person,
and do not associate with a wrathful person,

22:25 lest you learn his ways
and entangle yourself in a snare.

22:26 Do not be one who strikes hands in pledge
or who puts up security for debts.

22:27 If you do not have enough to pay,
your bed will be taken right out from under you!

22:28 Do not move an ancient boundary stone
which was put in place by your ancestors.

22:29 Do you see a person skilled in his work?
He will take his position before kings;
he will not take his position before obscure people.

23:1 When you sit down to eat with a ruler,
consider carefully what is before you,

23:2 and put a knife to your throat
if you possess a large appetite.

23:3 Do not crave that ruler's delicacies,
for that food is deceptive.

23:4 Do not wear yourself out to become rich;
be wise enough to restrain yourself.

23:5 When you gaze upon riches, they are gone,
for they surely make wings for themselves,
and fly off into the sky like an eagle!

23:6 Do not eat the food of a stingy person,
do not crave his delicacies;

23:7 for he is like someone calculating the cost in his mind.
"Eat and drink," he says to you,
but his heart is not with you;

23:8 you will vomit up the little bit you have eaten,
and will have wasted your pleasant words.

23:9 Do not speak in the ears of a fool,
for he will despise the wisdom of your words.

23:10 Do not move an ancient boundary stone,
or take over the fields of the fatherless,
23:11 for their Protector is strong;
he will plead their case against you.
23:12 Apply your heart to instruction
and your ears to the words of knowledge.
23:13 Do not withhold discipline from a child;
even if you strike him with the rod, he will not die.
 23:14 If you strike him with the rod,
you will deliver him from death.
23:15 My child, if your heart is wise,
then my heart also will be glad;
23:16 my soul will rejoice
when your lips speak what is right.
23:17 Do not let your heart envy sinners,
but rather be zealous in fearing the LORD all the time.
23:18 For surely there is a future,
and your hope will not be cut off.
23:19 Listen, my child, and be wise,
and guide your heart on the right way.
23:20 Do not spend time among drunkards,
among those who eat too much meat,
23:21 because drunkards and gluttons become impoverished,
and drowsiness clothes them with rags.
23:22 Listen to your father who begot you,
and do not despise your mother when she is old.
23:23 Acquire truth and do not sell it –
wisdom, and discipline, and understanding.
23:24 The father of a righteous person will rejoice greatly;
whoever fathers a wise child will have joy in him.
23:25 May your father and your mother have joy;
may she who bore you rejoice.
23:26 Give me your heart, my son,
and let your eyes observe my ways;
23:27 for a prostitute is like a deep pit;
a harlot is like a narrow well.
23:28 Indeed, she lies in wait like a robber,
and increases the unfaithful among men.

23:29 Who has woe? Who has sorrow?
Who has contentions? Who has complaints?
Who has wounds without cause? Who has dullness of the eyes?
23:30 Those who linger over wine,
those who go looking for mixed wine.
23:31 Do not look on the wine when it is red,
when it sparkles in the cup,
when it goes down smoothly.
23:32 Afterward it bites like a snake,
and stings like a viper.
23:33 Your eyes will see strange things,
and your mind will speak perverse things.
23:34 And you will be like one who lies down in the midst of the sea,
and like one who lies down on the top of the rigging.
23:35 You will say, "They have struck me, but I am not harmed!
They beat me, but I did not know it!
When will I awake? I will look for another drink."

24:1 Do not envy evil people,
do not desire to be with them;
24:2 for their hearts contemplate violence,
and their lips speak harm.
24:3 By wisdom a house is built,
and through understanding it is established;
24:4 by knowledge its rooms are filled
with all kinds of precious and pleasing treasures.

24:5 A wise warrior is strong,
and a man of knowledge makes his strength stronger;
24:6 for with guidance you wage your war,
and with numerous advisers there is victory.
24:7 Wisdom is unattainable for a fool;
in court he does not open his mouth.
24:8 The one who plans to do evil
will be called a scheming person.
24:9 A foolish scheme is sin,
and the scorner is an abomination to people.
24:10 If you faint in the day of trouble,
your strength is small!
24:11 Deliver those being taken away to death,
and hold back those slipping to the slaughter.
24:12 If you say, "But we did not know about this,"
does not the one who evaluates hearts consider?
Does not the one who guards your life know?

Will he not repay each person according to his deeds?
24:13 Eat honey, my child, for it is good,
and honey from the honeycomb is sweet to your taste.
24:14 Likewise, know that wisdom is sweet to your soul;
if you find it, you will have a future,
and your hope will not be cut off.
24:15 Do not lie in wait like the wicked against the place where the righteous live;
do not assault his home.
24:16 Although a righteous person may fall seven times, he gets up again,
but the wicked will be brought down by calamity.
24:17 Do not rejoice when your enemy falls,
and when he stumbles do not let your heart rejoice,
24:18 lest the LORD see it, and be displeased,
and turn his wrath away from him.
24:19 Do not fret because of evil people
or be envious of wicked people,
24:20 for the evil person has no future,
and the lamp of the wicked will be extinguished.
24:21 Fear the LORD, my child, as well as the king,
and do not associate with rebels,
24:22 for suddenly their destruction will overtake them,
and who knows the ruinous judgment both the LORD and the king can bring?
Further Sayings of the Wise
24:23 These sayings also are from the wise:
To show partiality in judgment is terrible:
24:24 The one who says to the guilty, "You are innocent,"
peoples will curse him, and nations will denounce him.
24:25 But there will be delight for those who convict the guilty,
and a pleasing blessing will come on them.
24:26 Like a kiss on the lips
is the one who gives an honest answer.
24:27 Establish your work outside and get your fields ready;
afterward build your house.
24:28 Do not be a witness against your neighbor without cause,
and do not deceive with your words.
24:29 Do not say, "I will do to him just as he has done to me;
I will pay him back according to what he has done."

24:30 I passed by the field of a sluggard,
by the vineyard of one who lacks wisdom.
24:31 I saw that thorns had grown up all over it,
the ground was covered with weeds,
and its stone wall was broken down.
24:32 When I saw this, I gave careful consideration to it;
I received instruction from what I saw:
24:33 "A little sleep, a little slumber,
a little folding of the hands to relax,
24:34 and your poverty will come like a bandit,
and your need like an armed robber."
Proverbs of Solomon Collected by Hezekiah
25:1 These also are proverbs of Solomon,
which the men of King Hezekiah of Judah copied:

25:2 It is the glory of God to conceal a matter,
and it is the glory of a king to search out a matter.
25:3 As the heaven is high and the earth is deep
so the hearts of kings are unsearchable.
25:4 Remove the dross from the silver,
and material for the silversmith will emerge;
25:5 remove the wicked from before the king,
and his throne will be established in righteousness.
25:6 Do not honor yourself before the king,
and do not stand in the place of great men;
25:7 for it is better for him to say to you, "Come up here,"
than to put you lower before a prince,
whom your eyes have seen.
25:8 Do not go out hastily to litigation,
or what will you do afterward
when your neighbor puts you to shame?
25:9 When you argue a case with your neighbor,
do not reveal the secret of another person,
25:10 lest the one who hears it put you to shame
and your infamy will never go away.
25:11 Like apples of gold in settings of silver,
so is a word skillfully spoken.
25:12 Like an earring of gold and an ornament of fine gold,
so is a wise reprover to the ear of the one who listens.
25:13 Like the cold of snow in the time of harvest,
so is a faithful messenger to those who send him,
for he refreshes the heart of his masters.
25:14 Like cloudy skies and wind that produce no rain,

so is the one who boasts of a gift not given.

25:15 Through patience a ruler can be persuaded,

and a soft tongue can break a bone.

25:16 When you find honey, eat only what is sufficient for you,

lest you become stuffed with it and vomit it up.

25:17 Don't set foot too frequently in your neighbor's house,

lest he become weary of you and hate you.

25:18 Like a club or a sword or a sharp arrow,

so is the one who testifies against his neighbor as a false witness.

25:19 Like a bad tooth or a foot out of joint,

so is confidence in an unfaithful person at the time of trouble.

25:20 Like one who takes off a garment on a cold day,

or like vinegar poured on soda,

so is one who sings songs to a heavy heart.

25:21 If your enemy is hungry, give him food to eat,

and if he is thirsty, give him water to drink,

25:22 for you will heap coals of fire on his head,

and the LORD will reward you.

25:23 The north wind brings forth rain,

and a gossiping tongue brings forth an angry look.

25:24 It is better to live on a corner of the housetop

than in a house in company with a quarrelsome wife.

25:25 Like cold water to a weary person,

so is good news from a distant land.

25:26 Like a muddied spring and a polluted well,

so is a righteous person who gives way before the wicked.

25:27 It is not good to eat too much honey,

nor is it honorable for people to seek their own glory.

25:28 Like a city that is broken down and without a wall,

so is a person who cannot control his temper.

26:1 Like snow in summer or rain in harvest,

so honor is not fitting for a fool.

26:2 Like a fluttering bird or like a flying swallow,

so a curse without cause does not come to rest.

26:3 A whip for the horse and a bridle for the donkey,

and a rod for the backs of fools!

26:4 Do not answer a fool according to his folly,

lest you yourself also be like him.

26:5 Answer a fool according to his folly,

lest he be wise in his own estimation.

26:6 Like cutting off the feet or drinking violence,

so is sending a message by the hand of a fool.

26:7 Like legs that hang limp from the lame,

so is a proverb in the mouth of fools.

26:8 Like tying a stone in a sling,

so is giving honor to a fool.

26:9 Like a thorn that goes into the hand of a drunkard,

so is a proverb in the mouth of a fool.

26:10 Like an archer who wounds at random,

so is the one who hires a fool or hires any passer-by.

26:11 Like a dog that returns to its vomit,

so a fool repeats his folly.

26:12 Do you see a man wise in his own eyes?

There is more hope for a fool than for him.

26:13 The sluggard says, "There is a lion in the road!

A lion in the streets!"

26:14 Like a door that turns on its hinges,

so a sluggard turns on his bed.

26:15 The sluggard plunges his hand in the dish;

he is too lazy to bring it back to his mouth.

26:16 The sluggard is wiser in his own estimation

than seven people who respond with good sense.

26:17 Like one who grabs a wild dog by the ears,

so is the person passing by who becomes furious over a quarrel not his own.

26:18 Like a madman who shoots

firebrands and deadly arrows,

26:19 so is a person who deceives his neighbor,

and says, "Was I not only joking?"

26:20 Where there is no wood, a fire goes out,

and where there is no gossip, contention ceases.

26:21 Like charcoal is to burning coals, and wood to fire,

so is a contentious person to kindle strife.

26:22 The words of a gossip are like delicious morsels;

they go down into a person's innermost being.

26:23 Like a coating of glaze over earthenware

are fervent lips with an evil heart.

26:24 The one who hates others disguises it with his lips,

but he stores up deceit within him.

26:25 When he speaks graciously, do not believe him,

for there are seven abominations within him.

26:26 Though his hatred may be concealed by deceit,

his evil will be uncovered in the assembly.

26:27 The one who digs a pit will fall into it;

the one who rolls a stone – it will come back on him.

26:28 A lying tongue hates those crushed by it,

and a flattering mouth works ruin.

27:1 Do not boast about tomorrow;

for you do not know what a day may bring forth.

27:2 Let another praise you, and not your own mouth;

someone else, and not your own lips.

27:3 A stone is heavy and sand is weighty,

but vexation by a fool is more burdensome than the two of them.

27:4 Wrath is cruel and anger is overwhelming,

but who can stand before jealousy?

27:5 Better is open rebuke

than hidden love.

27:6 Faithful are the wounds of a friend,

but the kisses of an enemy are excessive.

27:7 The one whose appetite is satisfied loathes honey,

but to the hungry mouth every bitter thing is sweet.

27:8 Like a bird that wanders from its nest,

so is a person who wanders from his home.

27:9 Ointment and incense make the heart rejoice,

likewise the sweetness of one's friend from sincere counsel.

27:10 Do not forsake your friend and your father's friend,

and do not enter your brother's house in the day of your disaster;

a neighbor nearby is better than a brother far away.

27:11 Be wise, my son, and make my heart glad,

so that I may answer anyone who taunts me.

27:12 A shrewd person sees danger and hides himself,

but the naive keep right on going and suffer for it.

27:13 Take a man's garment when he has given security for a stranger,

and when he gives surety for a stranger, hold him in pledge.

27:14 If someone blesses his neighbor with a loud voice early in the morning,

it will be counted as a curse to him.

27:15 A continual dripping on a rainy day

and a contentious wife are alike.

27:16 Whoever hides her hides the wind

or grasps oil with his right hand.

27:17 As iron sharpens iron,

so a person sharpens his friend.

27:18 The one who tends a fig tree will eat its fruit,

and whoever takes care of his master will be honored.

27:19 As in water the face is reflected as a face,

so a person's heart reflects the person.

27:20 As Death and Destruction are never satisfied,

so the eyes of a person are never satisfied.

27:21 As the crucible is for silver and the furnace is for gold,

so a person is proved by the praise he receives.

27:22 If you should pound the fool in the mortar

among the grain with the pestle,

his foolishness would not depart from him.

27:23 Pay careful attention to the condition of your flocks,

give careful attention to your herds,

27:24 for riches do not last forever,

nor does a crown last from generation to generation.

27:25 When the hay is removed and new grass appears,

and the grass from the hills is gathered in,

27:26 the lambs will be for your clothing,

and the goats will be for the price of a field.

27:27 And there will be enough goat's milk for your food,

for the food of your household,

and for the sustenance of your servant girls.

28:1 The wicked person flees when there is no one pursuing,

but the righteous person is as confident as a lion.

28:2 When a country is rebellious it has many princes,

but by someone who is discerning and knowledgeable order is maintained.

28:3 A poor person who oppresses the weak

is like a driving rain without food.

28:4 Those who forsake the law praise the wicked,

but those who keep the law contend with them.

28:5 Evil people do not understand justice,

but those who seek the LORD understand it all.

28:6 A poor person who walks in his integrity is better

than one who is perverse in his ways even though he is rich.

28:7 The one who keeps the law is a discerning child,

but a companion of gluttons brings shame to his parents.

28:8 The one who increases his wealth by increasing interest

gathers it for someone who is gracious to the needy.

28:9 The one who turns away his ear from hearing the law,

even his prayer is an abomination.

28:10 The one who leads the upright astray in an evil way

will himself fall into his own pit,
but the blameless will inherit what is good.
28:11 A rich person is wise in his own eyes,
but a discerning poor person can evaluate him properly.
28:12 When the righteous rejoice, great is the glory,
but when the wicked rise to power, people are sought out.
28:13 The one who covers his transgressions will not prosper,
but whoever confesses them and forsakes them will find mercy.
28:14 Blessed is the one who is always cautious,
but whoever hardens his heart will fall into evil.
28:15 Like a roaring lion or a roving bear,
so is a wicked ruler over a poor people.
28:16 The prince who is a great oppressor lacks wisdom,
but the one who hates unjust gain will prolong his days.
28:17 The one who is tormented by the murder of another will flee to the pit;
let no one support him.
28:18 The one who walks blamelessly will be delivered,
but whoever is perverse in his ways will fall at once.
28:19 The one who works his land will be satisfied with food,
but whoever chases daydreams will have his fill of poverty.
28:20 A faithful person will have an abundance of blessings,
but the one who hastens to gain riches will not go unpunished.
28:21 To show partiality is terrible,
for a person will transgress over the smallest piece of bread.
28:22 The stingy person hastens after riches
and does not know that poverty will overtake him.
28:23 The one who reproves another will in the end find more favor
than the one who flatters with the tongue.
28:24 The one who robs his father and mother and says, "There is no transgression,"
is a companion to the one who destroys.
28:25 The greedy person stirs up dissension,
but the one who trusts in the LORD will prosper.
28:26 The one who trusts in his own heart is a fool,
but the one who walks in wisdom will escape.
28:27 The one who gives to the poor will not lack,
but whoever shuts his eyes to them will receive many curses.
28:28 When the wicked gain control, people hide themselves,
but when they perish, the righteous increase.
29:1 The one who stiffens his neck after numerous rebukes
will suddenly be destroyed without remedy.
29:2 When the righteous become numerous, the people rejoice;
when the wicked rule, the people groan.
29:3 The man who loves wisdom brings joy to his father,
but whoever associates with prostitutes wastes his wealth.
29:4 A king brings stability to a land by justice,
but one who exacts tribute tears it down.
29:5 The one who flatters his neighbor
spreads a net for his steps.
29:6 In the transgression of an evil person there is a snare,
but a righteous person can sing and rejoice.
29:7 The righteous person cares for the legal rights of the poor;
the wicked does not understand such knowledge.
29:8 Scornful people inflame a city,
but those who are wise turn away wrath.
29:9 If a wise person goes to court with a foolish person,
there is no peace whether he is angry or laughs.
29:10 Bloodthirsty people hate someone with integrity;
as for the upright, they seek his life.
29:11 A fool lets fly with all his temper,
but a wise person keeps it back.
29:12 If a ruler listens to lies,
all his ministers will be wicked.
29:13 The poor person and the oppressor have this in common:
the LORD gives light to the eyes of them both.
29:14 If a king judges the poor in truth,
his throne will be established forever.
29:15 A rod and reproof impart wisdom,
but a child who is unrestrained brings shame to his mother.
29:16 When the wicked increase, transgression increases,
but the righteous will see their downfall.
29:17 Discipline your child, and he will give you rest;
he will bring you happiness.
29:18 When there is no prophetic vision the people cast off restraint,
but the one who keeps the law, blessed is he!
29:19 A servant cannot be corrected by words,
for although he understands, there is no answer.
29:20 Do you see someone who is hasty in his words?
There is more hope for a fool than for him.
29:21 If someone pampers his servant from youth,
he will be a weakling in the end.
29:22 An angry person stirs up dissension,

and a wrathful person is abounding in transgression.
29:23 A person's pride will bring him low,
but one who has a lowly spirit will gain honor.
29:24 Whoever shares with a thief is his own enemy;
he hears the oath to testify, but does not talk.
29:25 The fear of people becomes a snare,
but whoever trusts in the LORD will be set on high.
29:26 Many people seek the face of a ruler,
but it is from the LORD that one receives justice.
29:27 An unjust person is an abomination to the righteous,
and the one who lives an upright life is an abomination to the wicked.
The Words of Agur
30:1 The words of Agur, the son of Jakeh; an oracle:
This man says to Ithiel, to Ithiel and to Ukal:

30:2 Surely I am more brutish than any other human being,
and I do not have human understanding;
30:3 I have not learned wisdom,
nor do I have knowledge of the Holy One.
30:4 Who has ascended into heaven, and then descended?
Who has gathered up the winds in his fists?
Who has bound up the waters in his cloak?
Who has established all the ends of the earth?
What is his name, and what is his son's name? – if you know!

30:5 Every word of God is purified;
he is like a shield for those who take refuge in him.
30:6 Do not add to his words,
lest he reprove you, and prove you to be a liar.

30:7 Two things I ask from you;
do not refuse me before I die:
30:8 Remove falsehood and lies far from me;
do not give me poverty or riches,
feed me with my allotted portion of bread,
30:9 lest I become satisfied and act deceptively
and say, "Who is the LORD?"
Or lest I become poor and steal
and demean the name of my God.

30:10 Do not slander a servant to his master,
lest he curse you, and you are found guilty.
30:11 There is a generation who curse their fathers
and do not bless their mothers.
30:12 There is a generation who are pure in their own eyes
and yet are not washed from their filthiness.
30:13 There is a generation whose eyes are so lofty,
and whose eyelids are lifted up disdainfully.
30:14 There is a generation whose teeth are like swords
and whose molars are like knives
to devour the poor from the earth
and the needy from among the human race.

30:15 The leech has two daughters:
"Give! Give!"
There are three things that are never satisfied,
four that never say, "Enough" –
30:16 the grave, the barren womb,
land that is not satisfied with water,
and fire that never says, "Enough!"

30:17 The eye that mocks at a father
and despises obeying a mother –
the ravens of the valley will peck it out
and the young vultures will eat it.

30:18 There are three things that are too wonderful for me,
four that I do not understand:
30:19 the way of an eagle in the sky,
the way of a snake on a rock,
the way of a ship in the sea,
and the way of a man with a woman.
30:20 This is the way of an adulterous woman:
she eats and wipes her mouth
and says, "I have not done wrong."

30:21 Under three things the earth trembles,
and under four things it cannot bear up:
30:22 under a servant who becomes king,
under a fool who is stuffed with food,
30:23 under an unloved woman who is married,
and under a female servant who dispossesses her mistress.

30:24 There are four things on earth that are small,
but they are exceedingly wise:
30:25 ants are creatures with little strength,
but they prepare their food in the summer;
30:26 rock badgers are creatures with little power,
but they make their homes in the crags;
30:27 locusts have no king,
but they all go forward by ranks;
30:28 a lizard you can catch with the hand,
but it gets into the palaces of the king.

30:29 There are three things that are magnificent in their step,
four things that move about magnificently:
30:30 a lion, mightiest of the beasts,
who does not retreat from anything;
30:31 a strutting rooster, a male goat,
and a king with his army around him.

30:32 If you have done foolishly by exalting yourself
or if you have planned evil,
put your hand over your mouth!
30:33 For as the churning of milk produces butter
and as punching the nose produces blood,
so stirring up anger produces strife.
The Words of Lemuel
31:1 The words of King Lemuel,
an oracle that his mother taught him:

31:2 O my son, O son of my womb,
O son of my vows,
31:3 Do not give your strength to women,
nor your ways to that which ruins kings.
31:4 It is not for kings, O Lemuel,
it is not for kings to drink wine,
or for rulers to crave strong drink,
31:5 lest they drink and forget what is decreed,
and remove from all the poor their legal rights.
31:6 Give strong drink to the one who is perishing,
and wine to those who are bitterly distressed;
31:7 let them drink and forget their poverty,
and remember their misery no more.

31:8 Open your mouth on behalf of those unable to speak,
for the legal rights of all the dying.
31:9 Open your mouth, judge in righteousness,
and plead the cause of the poor and needy.
The Wife of Noble Character
31:10 Who can find a wife of noble character?
For her value is far more than rubies.
31:11 The heart of her husband has confidence in her,
and he has no lack of gain.
31:12 She brings him good and not evil
all the days of her life.
31:13 She obtains wool and flax,
and she is pleased to work with her hands.
31:14 She is like the merchant ships;
she brings her food from afar.
31:15 She also gets up while it is still night,
and provides food for her household and a portion to her female servants.
31:16 She considers a field and buys it;
from her own income she plants a vineyard.
31:17 She begins her work vigorously,
and she strengthens her arms.
31:18 She knows that her merchandise is good,
and her lamp does not go out in the night.
31:19 Her hands take hold of the distaff,
and her hands grasp the spindle.
31:20 She extends her hand to the poor,
and reaches out her hand to the needy.
31:21 She is not afraid of the snow for her household,
for all of her household are clothed with scarlet.
31:22 She makes for herself coverlets;
her clothing is fine linen and purple.
31:23 Her husband is well-known in the city gate
when he sits with the elders of the land.
31:24 She makes linen garments and sells them,
and supplies the merchants with sashes.
31:25 She is clothed with strength and honor,
and she can laugh at the time to come.
31:26 She opens her mouth with wisdom,
and loving instruction is on her tongue.
31:27 She watches over the ways of her household,
and does not eat the bread of idleness.

31:28 Her children rise up and call her blessed,
her husband also praises her:
31:29 "Many daughters have done valiantly,
but you surpass them all!"
31:30 Charm is deceitful and beauty is fleeting,
but a woman who fears the LORD will be praised.
31:31 Give her credit for what she has accomplished,
and let her works praise her in the city gates.

Book 21. Ecclesiastes

Title
1:1 The words of the Teacher, the son of David, king in Jerusalem:
Introduction: Utter Futility
1:2 "Futile! Futile!" laments the Teacher,
"Absolutely futile! Everything is futile!"
Futility Illustrated from Nature
1:3 What benefit do people get from all the effort
which they expend on
earth?
1:4 A generation comes and a generation goes,
but the earth remains the same through the ages.
1:5 The sun rises and the sun sets;
it hurries away to a place from which it rises again.
1:6 The wind goes to the south and circles around to the north;
round and round the wind goes and on its rounds it returns.
1:7 All the streams flow into the sea, but the sea is not full,
and to the place where the streams flow, there they will flow again.
1:8 All this monotony is tiresome; no one can bear to describe it:
The eye is never satisfied with seeing, nor is the ear ever content with hearing.
1:9 What exists now is what will be,
and what has been done is what will be done;
there is nothing truly new on earth.
1:10 Is there anything about which someone can say, "Look at this! It is new!"?
It was already done long ago, before
our time.
1:11 No one remembers the former events,
nor will anyone remember the events that are yet to happen;
they will not be remembered by the future generations.
Futility of Secular Accomplishment
1:12 I, the Teacher, have been king over Israel in Jerusalem.
1:13 I decided to carefully and thoroughly examine
all that has been accomplished on earth.
I concluded: God has given people a burdensome task
that keeps them occupied.
1:14 I reflected on everything that is accomplished by man on earth,
and I concluded: Everything he has accomplished is futile – like chasing the wind!
1:15 What is bent cannot be straightened,
and what is missing cannot be supplied.
Futility of Secular Wisdom
1:16 I thought to myself,
"I have become much wiser than any of my predecessors who ruled over Jerusalem;
I have acquired much wisdom and knowledge."
1:17 So I decided to discern the benefit of wisdom and knowledge over foolish behavior and ideas;
however, I concluded that even this endeavor is like trying to chase the wind!
1:18 For with great wisdom comes great frustration;
whoever increases his knowledge merely increases his heartache.
Futility of Self-Indulgent Pleasure
2:1 I thought to myself,
"Come now, I will try self-indulgent pleasure to see if it is worthwhile."
But I found that it also is futile.
2:2 I said of partying, "It is folly,"
and of self-indulgent pleasure, "It accomplishes nothing!"
2:3 I thought deeply about the effects of indulging myself with wine
(all the while my mind was guiding me with wisdom)
and the effects of behaving foolishly,
so that I might discover what is profitable
for people to do on earth during the few days of their lives.
Futility of Materialism
2:4 I increased my possessions:
I built houses for myself;
I planted vineyards for myself.
2:5 I designed royal gardens and parks for myself,
and I planted all kinds of fruit trees in them.
2:6 I constructed pools of water for myself,
to irrigate my grove of flourishing trees.
2:7 I purchased male and female slaves,

and I owned slaves who were born in my house;
I also possessed more livestock – both herds and flocks –
than any of my predecessors in Jerusalem.
2:8 I also amassed silver and gold for myself,
as well as valuable treasures taken from kingdoms and provinces.
I acquired male singers and female singers for myself,
and what gives a man sensual delight – a harem of beautiful concubines!
2:9 So I was far wealthier than all my predecessors in Jerusalem,
yet I maintained my objectivity:
2:10 I did not restrain myself from getting whatever I wanted;
I did not deny myself anything that would bring me pleasure.
So all my accomplishments gave me joy;
this was my reward for all my effort.
2:11 Yet when I reflected on everything I had accomplished
and on all the effort that I had expended to accomplish it,
I concluded: "All these achievements and possessions are ultimately profitless –
like chasing the wind!
There is nothing gained from them on earth."

Wisdom is Better than Folly

2:12 Next, I decided to consider wisdom, as well as foolish behavior and ideas.
For what more can the king's successor do than what the king has already done?
2:13 I realized that wisdom is preferable to folly,
just as light is preferable to darkness:
2:14 The wise man can see where he is going, but the fool walks in darkness.
Yet I also realized that the same fate happens to them both.
2:15 So I thought to myself, "The fate of the fool will happen even to me!
Then what did I gain by becoming so excessively wise?"
So I lamented to myself,
"The benefits of wisdom are ultimately meaningless!"
2:16 For the wise man, like the fool, will not be remembered for very long,
because in the days to come, both will already have been forgotten.
Alas, the wise man dies – just like the fool!
2:17 So I loathed life because what
happens on earth seems awful to me;
for all the benefits of wisdom are futile – like chasing the wind.

Futility of Being a Workaholic

2:18 So I loathed all the fruit of my effort,
for which I worked so hard on earth,
because I must leave it behind in the hands of my successor.
2:19 Who knows if he will be a wise man or a fool?
Yet he will be master over all the fruit of my labor
for which I worked so wisely on earth!
This also is futile!
2:20 So I began to despair about all the fruit of my labor
for which I worked so hard on earth.
2:21 For a man may do his work with wisdom, knowledge, and skill;
however, he must hand over the fruit of his labor as an inheritance
to someone else who did not work for it.
This also is futile, and an awful injustice!

Painful Days and Restless Nights

2:22 What does a man acquire from all his labor
and from the anxiety that accompanies his toil on earth?
2:23 For all day long his work produces pain and frustration,
and even at night his mind cannot relax!
This also is futile!

Enjoy Work and its Benefits

2:24 There is nothing better for people than to eat and drink,
and to find enjoyment in their work.
I also perceived that this ability to find enjoyment comes from God.
2:25 For no one can eat and drink
or experience joy apart from him.
2:26 For to the one who pleases him, God gives wisdom, knowledge, and joy,
but to the sinner, he gives the task of amassing wealth –
only to give it to the one who pleases God.
This task of the wicked is futile – like chasing the wind!

A Time for All Events in Life

3:1 For everything there is an appointed time,
and an appropriate time for every activity on earth:
3:2 A time to be born, and a time to die;
a time to plant, and a time to uproot what was planted;
3:3 A time to kill, and a time to heal;
a time to break down, and a time to build up;
3:4 A time to weep, and a time to laugh;
a time to mourn, and a time to dance.
3:5 A time to throw away stones, and a time to gather stones;
a time to embrace, and a time to refrain from embracing;
3:6 A time to search, and a time to give something up as lost;

a time to keep, and a time to throw away;
3:7 A time to rip, and a time to sew;
a time to keep silent, and a time to speak.
3:8 A time to love, and a time to hate;
a time for war, and a time for peace.

Man is Ignorant of God's Timing

3:9 What benefit can a worker gain from his toil?
3:10 I have observed the burden
that God has given to people to keep them occupied.
3:11 God has made everything fit beautifully in its appropriate time,
but he has also placed ignorance in the human heart
so that people cannot discover what God has ordained,
from the beginning to the end of their lives.

Enjoy Life in the Present

3:12 I have concluded that there is nothing better for people
than to be happy and to enjoy
themselves as long as they live,
3:13 and also that everyone should eat and drink, and find enjoyment in all his toil,
for these things are a gift from God.

God's Sovereignty

3:14 I also know that whatever God does will endure forever;
nothing can be added to it, and nothing taken away from it.
God has made it this way, so that men will fear him.
3:15 Whatever exists now has already been, and whatever will be has already been;
for God will seek to do again what has occurred in the past.

The Problem of Injustice and Oppression

3:16 I saw something else on earth:
In the place of justice, there was wickedness,
and in the place of fairness, there was wickedness.
3:17 I thought to myself, "God will judge both the righteous and the wicked;
for there is an appropriate time for every activity,
and there is a time of judgment for every deed.
3:18 I also thought to myself, "It is for the sake of people,
so God can clearly show them that they are like animals.
3:19 For the fate of humans and the fate of animals are the same:
As one dies, so dies the other; both have the same breath.
There is no advantage for humans over animals,
for both are fleeting.
3:20 Both go to the same place,
both come from the dust,
and to dust both return.
3:21 Who really knows if the human spirit ascends upward,
and the animal's spirit descends into the earth?
3:22 So I perceived there is nothing better than for people to enjoy their work,
because that is their reward;
for who can show them what the future holds?

Evil Oppression on Earth

4:1 So I again considered all the oppression that continually occurs on earth.
This is what I saw:
The oppressed were in tears, but no one was comforting them;
no one delivers them from the power of their oppressors.
4:2 So I considered those who are dead and gone
more fortunate than those who are still alive.
4:3 But better than both is the one who has not been born
and has not seen the evil things that are done on earth.

Labor Motivated by Envy

4:4 Then I considered all the skillful work that is done:
Surely it is nothing more than competition between one person and another.
This also is profitless – like chasing the wind.
4:5 The fool folds his hands and does no work,
so he has nothing to eat but his own flesh.
4:6 Better is one handful with some rest
than two hands full of toil and chasing the wind.

Labor Motivated by Greed

4:7 So I again considered another futile thing on earth:
4:8 A man who is all alone with no companion,
he has no children nor siblings;
yet there is no end to all his toil,
and he is never satisfied with riches.
He laments, "For whom am I toiling and depriving myself of pleasure?"
This also is futile and a burdensome task!

Labor is Beneficial When Its Rewards Are Shared

4:9 Two people are better than one,
because they can reap more benefit from their labor.
4:10 For if they fall, one will help his companion up,
but pity the person who falls down and has no one to help him up.

4:11 Furthermore, if two lie down together, they can keep each other warm,
but how can one person keep warm by himself?
4:12 Although an assailant may overpower one person,
two can withstand him.
Moreover, a three-stranded cord is not quickly broken.
Labor Motivated by Prestige-Seeking
4:13 A poor but wise youth is better than an old and foolish king
who no longer knows how to receive advice.
4:14 For he came out of prison to become king,
even though he had been born poor in what would become his kingdom.
4:15 I considered all the living who walk on earth,
as well as the successor who would arise in his place.
4:16 There is no end to all the people nor to the past generations,
yet future generations will not rejoice in him.
This also is profitless and like chasing the wind.
Rash Vows
5:1 Be careful what you do when you go to the temple of God;
draw near to listen rather than to offer a sacrifice like fools,
for they do not realize that they are doing wrong.
5:2 Do not be rash with your mouth or hasty in your heart to bring up a matter before God,
for God is in heaven and you are on earth!
Therefore, let your words be few.
5:3 Just as dreams come when there are many cares,
so the rash vow of a fool occurs when there are many words.
5:4 When you make a vow to God, do not delay in paying it.
For God takes no pleasure in fools:
Pay what you vow!
5:5 It is better for you not to vow
than to vow and not pay it.
5:6 Do not let your mouth cause you to sin,
and do not tell the priest, "It was a mistake!"
Why make God angry at you
so that he would destroy the work of your hands?"
5:7 Just as there is futility in many dreams,
so also in many words.
Therefore, fear God!
Government Corruption
5:8 If you see the extortion of the poor,
or the perversion of justice and fairness in the government,
do not be astonished by the matter.
For the high official is watched by a higher official,
and there are higher ones over them!
5:9 The produce of the land is seized by all of them,
even the king is served by the fields.
Covetousness
5:10 The one who loves money will never be satisfied with money,
he who loves wealth will never be
satisfied with his income.
This also is futile.
5:11 When someone's prosperity increases, those who consume it also increase;
so what does its owner gain, except that he gets to see it with his eyes?
5:12 The sleep of the laborer is pleasant – whether he eats little or much –
but the wealth of the rich will not allow him to sleep.
Materialism Thwarts Enjoyment of Life
5:13 Here is a misfortune on earth that I have seen:
Wealth hoarded by its owner to his own misery.
5:14 Then that wealth was lost through bad luck;
although he fathered a son, he has nothing left to give him.
5:15 Just as he came forth from his mother's womb, naked will he return as he came,
and he will take nothing in his hand that he may carry away from his toil.
5:16 This is another misfortune:
Just as he came, so will he go.
What did he gain from toiling for the wind?
5:17 Surely, he ate in darkness every day of his life,
and he suffered greatly with sickness and anger.
Enjoy the Fruit of Your Labor
5:18 I have seen personally what is the only beneficial and appropriate course of action for people:
to eat and drink, and find enjoyment in all their hard work on earth
during the few days of their life which God has given them,
for this is their reward.
5:19 To every man whom God has given wealth, and possessions,
he has also given him the ability
to eat from them, to receive his reward and to find enjoyment in his toil;
these things are the gift of God.
5:20 For he does not think much about the fleeting days of his life
because God keeps him preoccupied with the joy he derives from his activity.
Not Everyone Enjoys Life

6:1 Here is another misfortune that I have seen on earth,
and it weighs heavily on people:
6:2 God gives a man riches, property, and wealth
so that he lacks nothing that his heart desires,
yet God does not enable him to enjoy the fruit of his labor –
instead, someone else enjoys it!
This is fruitless and a grave misfortune.
6:3 Even if a man fathers a hundred children and lives many years –
even if he lives a long, long time, but cannot enjoy his prosperity –
even if he were to live forever –
I would say, "A stillborn child is better off than he is!"
6:4 Though the stillborn child came into the world for no reason and departed into darkness,
though its name is shrouded in darkness,
6:5 though it never saw the light of day nor knew anything,
yet it has more rest than that man –
6:6 if he should live a thousand years twice, yet does not enjoy his prosperity.
For both of them die!
6:7 All of man's labor is for nothing more than to fill his stomach –
yet his appetite is never satisfied!
6:8 So what advantage does a wise man have over a fool?
And what advantage does a pauper gain by knowing how to survive?
6:9 It is better to be content with what the eyes can see
than for one's heart always to crave more.
This continual longing is futile – like chasing the wind.
The Futile Way Life Works
6:10 Whatever has happened was foreordained,
and what happens to a person was also foreknown.
It is useless for him to argue with God about his fate
because God is more powerful than he is.
6:11 The more one argues with words, the less he accomplishes.
How does that benefit him?
6:12 For no one knows what is best for a person during his life –
during the few days of his fleeting life –
for they pass away like a shadow.
Nor can anyone tell him what the future will hold for him on earth.
Life is Brief and Death is Certain!
7:1 A good reputation is better than precious perfume;
likewise, the day of one's death is better than the day of one's birth.
7:2 It is better to go to a funeral
than a feast.
For death is the destiny of every person,
and the living should take this to heart.
7:3 Sorrow is better than laughter,
because sober reflection is good for the heart.
7:4 The heart of the wise is in the house of mourning,
but the heart of fools is in the house of merrymaking.
Frivolous Living Versus Wisdom
7:5 It is better for a person to receive a rebuke from those who are wise
than to listen to the song of fools.
7:6 For like the crackling of quick-burning thorns under a cooking pot,
so is the laughter of the fool.
This kind of folly also is useless.
Human Wisdom Overturned by Adversity
7:7 Surely oppression can turn a wise person into a fool;
likewise, a bribe corrupts the heart.
7:8 The end of a matter is better than its beginning;
likewise, patience is better than pride.
7:9 Do not let yourself be quickly provoked,
for anger resides in the lap of fools.
7:10 Do not say, "Why were the old days better than these days?"
for it is not wise to ask that.
Wisdom Can Lengthen One's Life
7:11 Wisdom, like an inheritance, is a good thing;
it benefits those who see the light of day.
7:12 For wisdom provides protection,
just as money provides protection.
But the advantage of knowledge is this:
Wisdom preserves the life of its owner.
Wisdom Acknowledges God's Orchestration of Life
7:13 Consider the work of God:
For who can make straight what he has bent?
7:14 In times of prosperity be joyful,
but in times of adversity consider this:
God has made one as well as the other,
so that no one can discover what the future holds.
Exceptions to the Law of Retribution
7:15 During the days of my fleeting life I have seen both of these things:
Sometimes a righteous person dies prematurely in spite of his righteousness,
and sometimes a wicked person lives long in spite of his evil deeds.
7:16 So do not be excessively righteous or excessively wise;

otherwise you might be disappointed.

7:17 Do not be excessively wicked and do not be a fool;
otherwise you might die before your time.

7:18 It is best to take hold of one warning without letting go of the other warning;
for the one who fears God will follow both warnings.

Wisdom Needed Because No One is Truly Righteous

7:19 Wisdom gives a wise person more protection
than ten rulers in a city.

7:20 For there is not one truly righteous person on the earth
who continually does good and never sins.

7:21 Also, do not pay attention to everything that people say;
otherwise, you might even hear your servant cursing you.

7:22 For you know in your own heart
that you also have cursed others many times.

Human Wisdom is Limited

7:23 I have examined all this by wisdom;
I said, "I am determined to comprehend this" – but it was beyond my grasp.

7:24 Whatever has happened is beyond human understanding;
it is far deeper than anyone can fathom.

True Righteousness and Wisdom are Virtually Nonexistent

7:25 I tried to understand, examine, and comprehend
the role of wisdom in the scheme of things,
and to understand the stupidity of wickedness and the insanity of folly.

7:26 I discovered this:
More bitter than death is the kind of woman who is like a hunter's snare;
her heart is like a hunter's net and her hands are like prison chains.
The man who pleases God escapes her,
but the sinner is captured by her.

7:27 The Teacher says:
I discovered this while trying to discover the scheme of things, item by item.

7:28 What I have continually sought, I have not found;
I have found only one upright man among a thousand,
but I have not found one upright woman among all of them.

7:29 This alone have I discovered: God made humankind upright,
but they have sought many evil schemes.

Human Government Demonstrates Limitations of Wisdom

8:1 Who is a wise person? Who knows the solution to a problem?
A person's wisdom brightens his appearance, and softens his harsh countenance.

8:2 Obey the king's command,
because you took an oath before God to be loyal to him.

8:3 Do not rush out of the king's presence in haste – do not delay when the matter is unpleasant,
for he can do whatever he pleases.

8:4 Surely the king's authority is absolute;
no one can say to him, "What are you doing?"

8:5 Whoever obeys his command will not experience harm,
and a wise person knows the proper time and procedure.

8:6 For there is a proper time and procedure for every matter,
for the oppression of the king is severe upon his victim.

8:7 Surely no one knows the future,
and no one can tell another person what will happen.

8:8 Just as no one has power over the wind to restrain it,
so no one has power over the day of his death.
Just as no one can be discharged during the battle,
so wickedness cannot rescue the wicked.

8:9 While applying my mind to everything that happens in this world, I have seen all this:
Sometimes one person dominates other people to their harm.

Contradictions to the Law of Retribution

8:10 Not only that, but I have seen the wicked approaching and entering the temple,
and as they left the holy temple, they
boasted in the city that they had done so.
This also is an enigma.

8:11 When a sentence is not executed at once against a crime,
the human heart is encouraged to do evil.

8:12 Even though a sinner might commit a hundred crimes and still live a long time,
yet I know that it will go well with God-fearing people – for they stand in fear before him.

8:13 But it will not go well with the wicked,
nor will they prolong their days like a shadow,
because they do not stand in fear before God.

8:14 Here is another enigma that occurs on earth:
Sometimes there are righteous people who get what the wicked deserve,
and sometimes there are wicked people who get what the righteous deserve.
I said, "This also is an enigma."

Enjoy Life In Spite of Its Injustices

8:15 So I recommend the enjoyment of life,
for there is nothing better on earth for a person to do except to eat, drink, and enjoy life.
So joy will accompany him in his toil
during the days of his life which God gives him on earth.

Limitations of Human Wisdom

8:16 When I tried to gain wisdom
and to observe the activity on earth –
even though it prevents anyone from sleeping day or night –

8:17 then I discerned all that God has done:
No one really comprehends what happens on earth.
Despite all human efforts to discover it, no one can ever grasp it.
Even if a wise person claimed that he understood,
he would not really comprehend it.

Everyone Will Die

9:1 So I reflected on all this, attempting to clear it all up.
I concluded that the righteous and the wise, as well as their works, are in the hand of God;
whether a person will be loved or hated –
no one knows what lies ahead.

9:2 Everyone shares the same fate –
the righteous and the wicked,
the good and the bad,
the ceremonially clean and unclean,
those who offer sacrifices and those who do not.
What happens to the good person, also happens to the sinner;
what happens to those who make vows, also happens to those who are afraid to make vows.

9:3 This is the unfortunate fact about everything that happens on earth:
the same fate awaits everyone.
In addition to this, the hearts of all people are full of evil,
and there is folly in their hearts during their lives – then they die.

Better to Be Poor but Alive than Rich but Dead

9:4 But whoever is among the living has hope;
a live dog is better than a dead lion.

9:5 For the living know that they will die, but the dead do not know anything;
they have no further reward – and even the memory of them disappears.

9:6 What they loved, as well as what they hated and envied, perished long ago,
and they no longer have a part in anything that happens on earth.

Life is Brief, so Cherish its Joys

9:7 Go, eat your food with joy,
and drink your wine with a happy heart,
because God has already approved your works.

9:8 Let your clothes always be white,
and do not spare precious ointment on your head.

9:9 Enjoy life with your beloved wife during all the days of your fleeting life
that God has given you on earth during all your fleeting days;
for that is your reward in life and in your burdensome work on earth.

9:10 Whatever you find to do with your hands,
do it with all your might,
because there is neither work nor planning nor knowledge nor wisdom in the grave,
the place where you will eventually go.

Wisdom Cannot Protect against Seemingly Chance Events

9:11 Again, I observed this on the earth:
the race is not always won by the swiftest,
the battle is not always won by the strongest;
prosperity does not always belong to those who are the wisest,
wealth does not always belong to those who are the most discerning,
nor does success always come to those with the most knowledge –
for time and chance may overcome them all.

9:12 Surely, no one knows his appointed time!
Like fish that are caught in a deadly net, and like birds that are caught in a snare –
just like them, all people are ensnared at an unfortunate time that falls upon them suddenly.

Most People Are Not Receptive to Wise Counsel

9:13 This is what I also observed about wisdom on earth,
and it is a great burden to me:

9:14 There was once a small city with a few men in it,
and a mighty king attacked it, besieging it and building strong siege works against it.

9:15 However, a poor but wise man lived in the city,
and he could have delivered the city by his wisdom,
but no one listened to that poor man.

9:16 So I concluded that wisdom is better than might,
but a poor man's wisdom is despised; no one ever listens to his advice.

Wisdom versus Fools, Sin, and Folly

9:17 The words of the wise are heard in quiet,
more than the shouting of a ruler is heard among fools.

9:18 Wisdom is better than weapons of war,
but one sinner can destroy much that is good.
10:1 One dead fly makes the perfumer's ointment give off a rancid stench,
so a little folly can outweigh much wisdom.
Wisdom Can Be Nullified By the Caprice of Rulers
10:2 A wise person's good sense protects him,
but a fool's lack of sense leaves him vulnerable.
10:3 Even when a fool walks along the road he lacks sense,
and shows everyone what a fool he is.
10:4 If the anger of the ruler flares up against you, do not resign from your position,
for a calm response can undo great offenses.
10:5 I have seen another misfortune on the earth:
It is an error a ruler makes.
10:6 Fools are placed in many positions of authority,
while wealthy men sit in lowly positions.
10:7 I have seen slaves on horseback
and princes walking on foot like slaves.
Wisdom is Needed to Avert Dangers in Everyday Life
10:8 One who digs a pit may fall into it,
and one who breaks through a wall may be bitten by a snake.
10:9 One who quarries stones may be injured by them;
one who splits logs may be endangered by them.
10:10 If an iron axhead is blunt and a workman does not sharpen its edge,
he must exert a great deal of effort;
so wisdom has the advantage of giving success.
10:11 If the snake should bite before it is charmed,
the snake charmer is in trouble.
Words and Works of Wise Men and Fools
10:12 The words of a wise person win him favor,
but the words of a fool are self-destructive.
10:13 At the beginning his words are foolish
and at the end his talk is wicked madness,
10:14 yet a fool keeps on babbling.
No one knows what will happen;
who can tell him what will happen in the future?
10:15 The toil of a stupid fool wears him out,
because he does not even know the way to the city.
The Problem with Foolish Rulers
10:16 Woe to you, O land, when your king is childish,
and your princes feast in the morning!
10:17 Blessed are you, O land, when your king is the son of nobility,
and your princes feast at the proper time – with self-control and not in drunkenness.
10:18 Because of laziness the roof caves in,
and because of idle hands the house leaks.
10:19 Feasts are made for laughter,
and wine makes life merry,
but money is the answer for everything.
10:20 Do not curse a king even in your thoughts,
and do not curse the rich while in your bedroom;
for a bird might report what you are thinking,
or some winged creature might repeat your words.
Ignorance of the Future Demands Diligence in the Present
11:1 Send your grain overseas,
for after many days you will get a return.
11:2 Divide your merchandise among seven or even eight investments,
for you do not know what calamity may happen on earth.
11:3 If the clouds are full of rain, they will empty themselves on the earth,
and whether a tree falls to the south or to the north, the tree will lie wherever it falls.
11:4 He who watches the wind will not sow,
and he who observes the clouds will not reap.
11:5 Just as you do not know the path of the wind,
or how the bones form in the womb of a pregnant woman,
so you do not know the work of God who makes everything.
11:6 Sow your seed in the morning,
and do not stop working until the evening;
for you do not know which activity will succeed –
whether this one or that one, or whether both will prosper equally.
Life Should Be Enjoyed Because Death is Inevitable
11:7 Light is sweet,
and it is pleasant for a person to see the sun.
11:8 So, if a man lives many years, let him rejoice in them all,
but let him remember that the days of darkness will be many – all that is about to come is obscure.
Enjoy Life to the Fullest under the Fear of God
11:9 Rejoice, young man, while you are young,
and let your heart cheer you in the days of your youth.
Follow the impulses of your heart and the desires of your eyes,
but know that God will judge your motives and actions.

11:10 Banish emotional stress from your mind.
and put away pain from your body;
for youth and the prime of life are fleeting.
Fear God Now Because Old Age and Death Come Quickly
12:1 So remember your Creator in the days of your youth –
before the difficult days come,
and the years draw near when you will say, "I have no pleasure in them";
12:2 before the sun and the light of the moon and the stars grow dark,
and the clouds disappear after the rain;
12:3 when those who keep watch over the house begin to tremble,
and the virile men begin to stoop over,
and the grinders begin to cease because they grow few,
and those who look through the windows grow dim,
12:4 and the doors along the street are shut;
when the sound of the grinding mill grows low,
and one is awakened by the sound of a bird,
and all their songs grow faint,
12:5 and they are afraid of heights and the dangers in the street;
the almond blossoms grow white,
and the grasshopper drags itself along,
and the caper berry shrivels up –
because man goes to his eternal home,
and the mourners go about in the streets –
12:6 before the silver cord is removed,
or the golden bowl is broken,
or the pitcher is shattered at the well,
or the water wheel is broken at the cistern –
12:7 and the dust returns to the earth as it was,
and the life's breath returns to God who gave it.
Concluding Refrain: Qoheleth Restates His Thesis
12:8 "Absolutely futile!" laments the Teacher,
"All of these things are futile!"
Concluding Epilogue: Qoheleth's Advice is Wise
12:9 Not only was the Teacher wise,
but he also taught knowledge to the people;
he carefully evaluated and arranged many proverbs.
12:10 The Teacher sought to find delightful words,
and to write accurately truthful
sayings.
12:11 The words of the sages are like prods,
and the collected sayings are like firmly fixed nails;
they are given by one shepherd.
Concluding Exhortation: Fear God and Obey His Commands!
12:12 Be warned, my son, of anything in addition to them.
There is no end to the making of many books,
and much study is exhausting to the body.
12:13 Having heard everything, I have reached this conclusion:
Fear God and keep his commandments,
because this is the whole duty of man.
12:14 For God will evaluate every deed,
including every secret thing, whether good or evil.

Book 22. The Song of Songs

Title/Superscription
1:1 Solomon's Most Excellent Love Song.
The Desire for Love
The Beloved to Her Lover:
1:2 Oh, how I wish you would kiss me passionately!
For your lovemaking is more delightful than wine.
1:3 The fragrance of your colognes is delightful;
your name is like the finest perfume.
No wonder the young women adore you!
1:4 Draw me after you; let us hurry!
May the king bring me into his bedroom chambers!
The Maidens to the Lover:
We will rejoice and delight in you;
we will praise your love more than wine.

The Beloved to Her Lover:

How rightly the young women adore you!
The Country Maiden and the Daughters of Jerusalem
The Beloved to the Maidens:
1:5 I am dark but lovely, O maidens of Jerusalem,
dark like the tents of Qedar,
lovely like the tent curtains of
Salmah.
1:6 Do not stare at me because I am dark,
for the sun has burned my skin.
My brothers were angry with me;
they made me the keeper of the vineyards.

Alas, my own vineyard I could not keep!
The Shepherd and the Shepherdess
The Beloved to Her Lover:
1:7 Tell me, O you whom my heart loves,
where do you pasture your sheep?
Where do you rest your sheep during the midday heat?
Tell me lest I wander around
beside the flocks of your companions!
The Lover to His Beloved:
1:8 If you do not know, O most beautiful of women,
simply follow the tracks of my flock,
and pasture your little lambs
beside the tents of the shepherds.
The Beautiful Mare and the Fragrant Myrrh
The Lover to His Beloved:
1:9 O my beloved, you are like a mare
among Pharaoh's stallions.
1:10 Your cheeks are beautiful with ornaments;
your neck is lovely with strings of jewels.
1:11 We will make for you gold ornaments
studded with silver.
The Beloved about Her Lover:
1:12 While the king was at his banqueting table,
my nard gave forth its fragrance.
1:13 My beloved is like a fragrant pouch of myrrh
spending the night between my breasts.
1:14 My beloved is like a cluster of henna blossoms
in the vineyards of En-Gedi.
Mutual Praise and Admiration
The Lover to His Beloved:
1:15 Oh, how beautiful you are, my beloved!
Oh, how beautiful you are!
Your eyes are like doves!
The Beloved to Her Lover:
1:16 Oh, how handsome you are, my lover!
Oh, how delightful you are!
The lush foliage is our canopied bed;
1:17 the cedars are the beams of our bedroom chamber;
the pines are the rafters of our bedroom.
The Lily among the Thorns and the Apple Tree in the Forest
The Beloved to Her Lover:
2:1 I am a meadow flower from Sharon,
a lily from the valleys.
The Lover to His Beloved:
2:2 Like a lily among the thorns,
so is my darling among the maidens.

The Beloved about Her Lover:
2:3 Like an apple tree among the trees of the forest,
so is my beloved among the young men.
I delight to sit in his shade,
and his fruit is sweet to my taste.
The Banquet Hall for the Love-Sick
The Beloved about Her Lover:
2:4 He brought me into the banquet hall,
and he looked at me lovingly.
2:5 Sustain me with raisin cakes,
refresh me with apples,
for I am faint with love.

The Double Refrain: Embracing and Adjuration

2:6 His left hand caresses my head,
and his right hand stimulates me.
The Beloved to the Maidens:
2:7 I adjure you, O maidens of Jerusalem,
by the gazelles and by the young does of the open fields:
Do not awaken or arouse love until it pleases!
The Arrival of the Lover
The Beloved about Her Lover:
2:8 Listen! My lover is approaching!
Look! Here he comes,
leaping over the mountains,
bounding over the hills!
2:9 My lover is like a gazelle or a young stag.
Look! There he stands behind our wall,
gazing through the window,
peering through the lattice.
The Season of Love and the Song of the Turtle-Dove
The Lover to His Beloved:
2:10 My lover spoke to me, saying:
"Arise, my darling;
My beautiful one, come away with me!

2:11 Look! The winter has passed,
the winter rains are over and gone.
2:12 The pomegranates have appeared in the land,
the time for pruning and singing has come;
the voice of the turtledove is heard in our land.
2:13 The fig tree has budded,
the vines have blossomed and give off their fragrance.
Arise, come away my darling;
my beautiful one, come away with me!"
The Dove in the Clefts of En-Gedi
The Lover to His Beloved:
2:14 O my dove, in the clefts of the rock,
in the hiding places of the mountain crags,
let me see your face,
let me hear your voice;
for your voice is sweet,
and your face is lovely.
The Foxes in the Vineyard
The Beloved to Her Lover:
2:15 Catch the foxes for us,
the little foxes,
that ruin the vineyards –
for our vineyard is in bloom.
Poetic Refrain: Mutual Possession
The Beloved about Her Lover:
2:16 My lover is mine and I am his;
he grazes among the lilies.
The Gazelle and the Rugged Mountains
The Beloved to Her Lover:
2:17 Until the dawn arrives and the shadows flee,
turn, my beloved –
be like a gazelle or a young stag
on the mountain gorges.
The Lost Lover is Found
The Beloved about Her Lover:
3:1 All night long on my bed
I longed for my lover.
I longed for him but he never appeared.
3:2 "I will arise and look all around throughout the town,
and throughout the streets and squares;
I will search for my beloved."
I searched for him but I did not find him.
3:3 The night watchmen found me – the ones who guard the city walls.
"Have you seen my beloved?"
3:4 Scarcely had I passed them by
when I found my beloved!
I held onto him tightly and would not let him go
until I brought him to my mother's house,
to the bedroom chamber of the one who conceived me.
The Adjuration Refrain
The Beloved to the Maidens:
3:5 I admonish you, O maidens of Jerusalem,
by the gazelles and by the young does of the open fields:
"Do not awake or arouse love until it pleases!"
The Royal Wedding Procession
The Speaker:
3:6 Who is this coming up from the desert
like a column of smoke,
like a fragrant billow of myrrh and frankincense,
every kind of fragrant powder of the traveling merchants?
3:7 Look! It is Solomon's portable couch!
It is surrounded by sixty warriors,
some of Israel's mightiest warriors.
3:8 All of them are skilled with a sword,
well-trained in the art of warfare.
Each has his sword at his side,
to guard against the terrors of the night.
3:9 King Solomon made a sedan chair for himself
of wood imported from Lebanon.
3:10 Its posts were made of silver;
its back was made of gold.
Its seat was upholstered with purple wool;
its interior was inlaid with leather by the
maidens of Jerusalem.
3:11 Come out, O maidens of Zion,
and gaze upon King Solomon!
He is wearing the crown with which his mother crowned him
on his wedding day,
on the most joyous day of his life!
The Wedding Night: Praise of the Bride
The Lover to His Beloved:
4:1 Oh, you are beautiful, my darling!
Oh, you are beautiful!

Your eyes behind your veil are like doves.
Your hair is like a flock of female goats
descending from Mount Gilead.
4:2 Your teeth are like a flock of newly-shorn sheep
coming up from the washing place;
each of them has a twin,
and not one of them is missing.
4:3 Your lips are like a scarlet thread;
your mouth is lovely.
Your forehead behind your veil
is like a slice of pomegranate.
4:4 Your neck is like the tower of David
built with courses of stones;
one thousand shields are hung on it –
all shields of valiant warriors.
4:5 Your two breasts are like two fawns,
twins of the gazelle
grazing among the lilies.
4:6 Until the dawn arrives
and the shadows flee,
I will go up to the mountain of myrrh,
and to the hill of frankincense.
4:7 You are altogether beautiful, my darling!
There is no blemish in you!
The Wedding Night: Beautiful as Lebanon
4:8 Come with me from Lebanon, my bride,
come with me from Lebanon.
Descend from the crest of Amana,
from the top of Senir, the summit of Hermon,
from the lions' dens
and the mountain haunts of the leopards.
4:9 You have stolen my heart, my sister, my bride!
You have stolen my heart with one glance of your eyes,
with one jewel of your necklace.
4:10 How delightful is your love, my sister, my bride!
How much better is your love than wine;
the fragrance of your perfume is better than any spice!
4:11 Your lips drip sweetness like the honeycomb, my bride,
honey and milk are under your tongue.
The fragrance of your garments is like the fragrance of Lebanon.
The Wedding Night: The Delightful Garden
The Lover to His Beloved:
4:12 You are a locked garden, my sister, my bride;
you are an enclosed spring, a sealed-up fountain.
4:13 Your shoots are a royal garden full of pomegranates
with choice fruits:
henna with nard,
4:14 nard and saffron;
calamus and cinnamon with every kind of spice,
myrrh and aloes with all the finest spices.
4:15 You are a garden spring,
a well of fresh water flowing down from Lebanon.
The Beloved to Her Lover:
4:16 Awake, O north wind; come, O south wind!
Blow on my garden so that its fragrant spices may send out their sweet smell.
May my beloved come into his garden
and eat its delightful fruit!
The Lover to His Beloved:
5:1 I have entered my garden, O my sister, my bride;
I have gathered my myrrh with my balsam spice.
I have eaten my honeycomb and my honey;
I have drunk my wine and my milk!
The Poet to the Couple:
Eat, friends, and drink!
Drink freely, O lovers!
The Trials of Love: The Beloved's Dream of Losing Her Lover
The Beloved about Her Lover:
5:2 I was asleep, but my mind was dreaming.
Listen! My lover is knocking at the door!
The Lover to His Beloved:
"Open for me, my sister, my darling,
my dove, my flawless one!
My head is drenched with dew,
my hair with the dampness of the night."
The Beloved to Her Lover:
5:3 "I have already taken off my robe – must I put it on again?
I have already washed my feet – must I soil them again?"
5:4 My lover thrust his hand through the hole,
and my feelings were stirred for him.
5:5 I arose to open for my beloved;
my hands dripped with myrrh –
my fingers flowed with myrrh

on the handles of the lock.
5:6 I opened for my beloved,
but my lover had already turned and gone away.
I fell into despair when he departed.
I looked for him but did not find him;
I called him but he did not answer me.
5:7 The watchmen found me as they made their rounds in the city.
They beat me, they bruised me;
they took away my cloak, those watchmen on the walls!
The Triumph of Love: The Beloved Praises Her Lover
The Beloved to the Maidens:
5:8 O maidens of Jerusalem, I command you –
If you find my beloved, what will you tell him?
Tell him that I am lovesick!
The Maidens to The Beloved:
5:9 Why is your beloved better than others,
O most beautiful of women?
Why is your beloved better than others,
that you would command us in this manner?
The Beloved to the Maidens:
5:10 My beloved is dazzling and ruddy;
he stands out in comparison to all other men.
5:11 His head is like the most pure gold.
His hair is curly – black like a raven.
5:12 His eyes are like doves by streams of water,
washed in milk, mounted like jewels.
5:13 His cheeks are like garden beds full of
balsam trees yielding perfume.
His lips are like lilies dripping with drops of myrrh.
5:14 His arms are like rods of gold set with chrysolite.
His abdomen is like polished ivory inlaid with sapphires.
5:15 His legs are like pillars of marble set on bases of pure gold.
His appearance is like Lebanon, choice as its cedars.
5:16 His mouth is very sweet;
he is totally desirable.
This is my beloved!
This is my companion, O maidens of Jerusalem!
The Lost Lover Found
The Maidens to the Beloved:
6:1 Where has your beloved gone,
O most beautiful among women?
Where has your beloved turned?
Tell us, that we may seek him with you.
The Beloved to the Maidens:
6:2 My beloved has gone down to his garden,
to the flowerbeds of balsam spices,
to graze in the gardens,
and to gather lilies.
Poetic Refrain: Mutual Possession
The Beloved about Her Lover:
6:3 I am my lover's and my lover is mine;
he grazes among the lilies.
The Renewal of Love
The Lover to His Beloved:
6:4 My darling, you are as beautiful as Tirzah,
as lovely as Jerusalem,
as awe-inspiring as bannered armies!
6:5 Turn your eyes away from me –
they overwhelm me!
Your hair is like a flock of goats
descending from Mount Gilead.
6:6 Your teeth are like a flock of sheep
coming up from the washing;
each has its twin;
not one of them is missing.
6:7 Like a slice of pomegranate
is your forehead behind your veil.
6:8 There may be sixty queens,
and eighty concubines,
and young women without number.
6:9 But she is unique!
My dove, my perfect one!
She is the special daughter of her mother,
she is the favorite of the one who bore her.
The maidens saw her and complimented her;
the queens and concubines praised her:
6:10 "Who is this who appears like the dawn?
Beautiful as the moon, bright as the sun,
awe-inspiring as the stars in procession?"
The Return to the Vineyards
The Lover to His Beloved:
6:11 I went down to the orchard of walnut trees,
to look for the blossoms of the valley,

to see if the vines had budded
or if the pomegranates were in bloom.
6:12 I was beside myself with joy!
There please give me your myrrh,
O daughter of my princely people.
The Love Song and Dance
The Lover to His Beloved:
6:13 (7:1) Turn, turn, O Perfect One!
Turn, turn, that I may stare at you!
The Beloved to Her Lover:
Why do you gaze upon the Perfect One
like the dance of the Mahanaim?
The Lover to His Beloved:
7:1 (7:2) How beautiful are your sandaled feet,
O nobleman's daughter!
The curves of your thighs are like jewels,
the work of the hands of a master craftsman.
7:2 Your navel is a round mixing bowl –
may it never lack mixed wine!
Your belly is a mound of wheat,
encircled by lilies.
7:3 Your two breasts are like two fawns,
twins of a gazelle.
7:4 Your neck is like a tower made of ivory.
Your eyes are the pools in Heshbon
by the gate of Bath-Rabbim.
Your nose is like the tower of Lebanon
overlooking Damascus.
7:5 Your head crowns you like Mount Carmel.
The locks of your hair are like royal tapestries –
the king is held captive in its tresses!
7:6 How beautiful you are! How lovely,
O love, with your delights!
The Palm Tree and the Palm Tree Climber
The Lover to His Beloved:
7:7 Your stature is like a palm tree,
and your breasts are like clusters of grapes.
7:8 I want to climb the palm tree,
and take hold of its fruit stalks.
May your breasts be like the clusters of grapes,
and may the fragrance of your breath be like apricots!
7:9 May your mouth be like the best wine,
flowing smoothly for my beloved,
gliding gently over our lips as we sleep together.
Poetic Refrain: Mutual Possession
The Beloved about Her Lover:
7:10 I am my beloved's,
and he desires me!
The Journey to the Countryside
The Beloved to Her Lover:
7:11 Come, my beloved, let us go to the countryside;
let us spend the night in the villages.
7:12 Let us rise early to go to the vineyards,
to see if the vines have budded,
to see if their blossoms have opened,
if the pomegranates are in bloom –
there I will give you my love.
7:13 The mandrakes send out their fragrance;
over our door is every delicacy,
both new and old, which I have stored up for you, my lover.
The Beloved's Wish Song
The Beloved to Her Lover:
8:1 Oh, how I wish you were my little brother,
nursing at my mother's breasts;
if I saw you outside, I could kiss you –
surely no one would despise me!
8:2 I would lead you and bring you to my mother's house,
the one who taught me.
I would give you spiced wine to drink,
the nectar of my pomegranates.
Double Refrain: Embracing and Adjuration
The Beloved about Her Lover:
8:3 His left hand caresses my head,
and his right hand stimulates me.

The Beloved to the Maidens:
8:4 I admonish you, O maidens of Jerusalem:
"Do not arouse or awaken love until it pleases!"
The Awakening of Love
The Maidens about His Beloved:
8:5 Who is this coming up from the desert,
leaning on her beloved?

The Beloved to Her Lover:
Under the apple tree I aroused you;
there your mother conceived you,
there she who bore you was in labor of childbirth.
The Nature of True Love
The Beloved to Her Lover:
8:6 Set me like a cylinder seal over your heart,
like a signet on your arm.
For love is as strong as death,
passion is as unrelenting as Sheol.
Its flames burst forth,
it is a blazing flame.
8:7 Surging waters cannot quench love;
floodwaters cannot overflow it.
If someone were to offer all his possessions to buy love,
the offer would be utterly despised.
The Brother's Plan and the Sister's Reward
The Beloved's Brothers:
8:8 We have a little sister,
and as yet she has no breasts.
What shall we do for our sister
on the day when she is spoken for?
8:9 If she is a wall,
we will build on her a battlement of silver;
but if she is a door,
we will barricade her with boards of cedar.
The Beloved:
8:10 I was a wall,
and my breasts were like fortress towers.
Then I found favor in his eyes.
Solomon's Vineyard and the Beloved's Vineyard
The Beloved to Her Lover:
8:11 Solomon had a vineyard at Baal-Hamon;
he leased out the vineyard to those who maintained it.
Each was to bring a thousand shekels of silver for its fruit.
8:12 My vineyard, which belongs to me, is at my disposal alone.
The thousand shekels belong to you, O Solomon,
and two hundred shekels belong to those who maintain it for its fruit.
Epilogue: The Lover's Request and His Beloved's Invitation
The Lover to His Beloved:
8:13 O you who stay in the gardens,
my companions are listening attentively for your voice;
let me be the one to hear it!
The Beloved to Her Lover:
8:14 Make haste, my beloved!
Be like a gazelle or a young stag
on the mountains of spices.

Book 23. Isaiah

Heading
1:1 Here is the message about Judah and Jerusalem that was revealed to Isaiah son of Amoz during the time when Uzziah, Jotham, Ahaz, and Hezekiah reigned over Judah.
Obedience, not Sacrifice
1:2 Listen, O heavens,
pay attention, O earth!
For the LORD speaks:
"I raised children, I brought them up,
but they have rebelled against me!
1:3 An ox recognizes its owner,
a donkey recognizes where its owner puts its food;
but Israel does not recognize me,
my people do not understand."
1:4 The sinful nation is as good as dead,
the people weighed down by evil deeds.
They are offspring who do wrong,
children who do wicked things.
They have abandoned the LORD,
and rejected the Holy One of Israel.
They are alienated from him.
1:5 Why do you insist on being battered?
Why do you continue to rebel?
Your head has a massive wound,
your whole body is weak.
1:6 From the soles of your feet to your head,
there is no spot that is unharmed.
There are only bruises, cuts,
and open wounds.
They have not been cleansed or bandaged,
nor have they been treated with olive oil.
1:7 Your land is devastated,
your cities burned with fire.

Right before your eyes your crops
are being destroyed by foreign invaders.
They leave behind devastation and destruction.
1:8 Daughter Zion is left isolated,
like a hut in a vineyard,
or a shelter in a cucumber field;
she is a besieged city.
1:9 If the LORD who commands armies had not left us a few survivors,
we would have quickly become like Sodom,
we would have become like Gomorrah.
1:10 Listen to the LORD's word,
you leaders of Sodom!
Pay attention to our God's rebuke,
people of Gomorrah!
1:11 "Of what importance to me are your many sacrifices?"
says the LORD.
"I am stuffed with burnt sacrifices
of rams and the fat from steers.
The blood of bulls, lambs, and goats
I do not want.
1:12 When you enter my presence,
do you actually think I want this –
animals trampling on my courtyards?
1:13 Do not bring any more meaningless offerings;
I consider your incense detestable!
You observe new moon festivals, Sabbaths, and convocations,
but I cannot tolerate sin-stained celebrations!
1:14 I hate your new moon festivals and assemblies;
they are a burden
that I am tired of carrying.
1:15 When you spread out your hands in prayer,
I look the other way;
when you offer your many prayers,
I do not listen,
because your hands are covered with blood.
1:16 Wash! Cleanse yourselves!
Remove your sinful deeds
from my sight.
Stop sinning!
1:17 Learn to do what is right!
Promote justice!
Give the oppressed reason to celebrate!
Take up the cause of the orphan!
Defend the rights of the widow!
1:18 Come, let's consider your options," says the LORD.
"Though your sins have stained you like the color red,
you can become white like snow;
though they are as easy to see as the color scarlet,
you can become white like wool.
1:19 If you have a willing attitude and obey,
then you will again eat the good crops of the land.
1:20 But if you refuse and rebel,
you will be devoured by the sword."
Know for certain that the LORD has spoken.
Purifying Judgment
1:21 How tragic that the once-faithful city
has become a prostitute!
She was once a center of justice,
fairness resided in her,
but now only murderers.
1:22 Your silver has become scum,
your beer is diluted with water.
1:23 Your officials are rebels,
they associate with thieves.
All of them love bribery,
and look for payoffs.
They do not take up the cause of the orphan,
or defend the rights of the widow.
1:24 Therefore, the sovereign LORD who commands armies,
the powerful ruler of Israel, says this:
"Ah, I will seek vengeance against my adversaries,
I will take revenge against my enemies.
1:25 I will attack you;
I will purify your metal with flux.
I will remove all your slag.
1:26 I will reestablish honest judges as in former times,
wise advisers as in earlier days.
Then you will be called, 'The Just City,
Faithful Town.'"
1:27 Zion will be freed by justice,
and her returnees by righteousness.
1:28 All rebellious sinners will be shattered,
those who abandon the LORD will perish.

1:29 Indeed, they will be ashamed of the sacred trees
you find so desirable;
you will be embarrassed because of the sacred orchards
where you choose to worship.
1:30 For you will be like a tree whose leaves wither,
like an orchard that is unwatered.
1:31 The powerful will be like a thread of yarn,
their deeds like a spark;
both will burn together,
and no one will put out the fire.
The Future Glory of Jerusalem
2:1 Here is the message about Judah and Jerusalem that was revealed to Isaiah son of Amoz.
2:2 In the future
the mountain of the LORD's temple will endure
as the most important of mountains,
and will be the most prominent of hills.
All the nations will stream to it,
2:3 many peoples will come and say,
"Come, let us go up to the LORD's mountain,
to the temple of the God of Jacob,
so he can teach us his requirements,
and we can follow his standards."
For Zion will be the center for moral instruction;
the LORD will issue edicts from Jerusalem.
2:4 He will judge disputes between nations;
he will settle cases for many peoples.
They will beat their swords into plowshares,
and their spears into pruning hooks.
Nations will not take up the sword against other nations,
and they will no longer train for war.
2:5 O descendants of Jacob,
come, let us walk in the LORD's guiding light.
The Lord's Day of Judgment
2:6 Indeed, O LORD, you have abandoned your people,
the descendants of Jacob.
For diviners from the east are everywhere;
they consult omen readers like the Philistines do.
Plenty of foreigners are around.
2:7 Their land is full of gold and silver;
there is no end to their wealth.
Their land is full of horses;
there is no end to their chariots.
2:8 Their land is full of worthless idols;
they worship the product of their own hands,
what their own fingers have fashioned.
2:9 Men bow down to them in homage,
they lie flat on the ground in worship.
Don't spare them!
2:10 Go up into the rocky cliffs,
hide in the ground.
Get away from the dreadful judgment of the LORD,
from his royal splendor!
2:11 Proud men will be brought low,
arrogant men will be humiliated;
the LORD alone will be exalted
in that day.
2:12 Indeed, the LORD who commands armies has planned a day of judgment,
for all the high and mighty,
for all who are proud – they will be humiliated;
2:13 for all the cedars of Lebanon,
that are so high and mighty,
for all the oaks of Bashan;
2:14 for all the tall mountains,
for all the high hills,
2:15 for every high tower,
for every fortified wall,
2:16 for all the large ships,
for all the impressive ships.
2:17 Proud men will be humiliated,
arrogant men will be brought low;
the LORD alone will be exalted
in that day.
2:18 The worthless idols will be completely eliminated.
2:19 They will go into caves in the rocky cliffs
and into holes in the ground,
trying to escape the dreadful judgment of the LORD
and his royal splendor,
when he rises up to terrify the earth.
2:20 At that time men will throw
their silver and gold idols,
which they made for themselves to worship,

into the caves where rodents and bats live,
2:21 so they themselves can go into the crevices of the rocky cliffs
and the openings under the rocky overhangs,
trying to escape the dreadful judgment of the LORD
and his royal splendor,
when he rises up to terrify the earth.
2:22 Stop trusting in human beings,
whose life's breath is in their nostrils.
For why should they be given special consideration?
A Coming Leadership Crisis
3:1 Look, the sovereign LORD who commands armies
is about to remove from Jerusalem and Judah
every source of security, including
all the food and water,
3:2 the mighty men and warriors,
judges and prophets,
omen readers and leaders,
3:3 captains of groups of fifty,
the respected citizens,
advisers and those skilled in magical arts,
and those who know incantations.
3:4 The LORD says, "I will make youths their officials;
malicious young men will rule over them.
3:5 The people will treat each other harshly;
men will oppose each other;
neighbors will fight.
Youths will proudly defy the elderly
and riffraff will challenge those who were once respected.
3:6 Indeed, a man will grab his brother
right in his father's house and say,
'You own a coat –
you be our leader!
This heap of ruins will be under your control.'
3:7 At that time the brother will shout,
'I am no doctor,
I have no food or coat in my house;
don't make me a leader of the people!'"
3:8 Jerusalem certainly stumbles,
Judah falls,
for their words and their actions offend the LORD;
they rebel against his royal authority.
3:9 The look on their faces testifies to their guilt;
like the people of Sodom they openly boast of their sin.
Too bad for them!
For they bring disaster on themselves.
3:10 Tell the innocent it will go well with them,
for they will be rewarded for what they have done.
3:11 Too bad for the wicked sinners!
For they will get exactly what they deserve.
3:12 Oppressors treat my people cruelly;
creditors rule over them.
My people's leaders mislead them;
they give you confusing directions.
3:13 The LORD takes his position to judge;
he stands up to pass sentence on his people.
3:14 The LORD comes to pronounce judgment
on the leaders of his people and their officials.
He says, "It is you who have ruined the vineyard!
You have stashed in your houses what you have stolen from the poor.
3:15 Why do you crush my people
and grind the faces of the poor?"
The sovereign LORD who commands armies has spoken.
Washing Away Impurity
3:16 The LORD says,
"The women of Zion are proud.
They walk with their heads high
and flirt with their eyes.
They skip along
and the jewelry on their ankles jingles.
3:17 So the sovereign master will afflict the foreheads of Zion's women
with skin diseases,
the LORD will make the front of their heads bald."

3:18 At that time the sovereign master will remove their beautiful ankle jewelry, neck ornaments, crescent shaped ornaments, **3:19** earrings, bracelets, veils, **3:20** headdresses, ankle ornaments, sashes, sachets, amulets, **3:21** rings, nose rings, **3:22** festive dresses, robes, shawls, purses, **3:23** garments, vests, head coverings, and gowns. **3:24** A putrid stench will replace the smell of spices,
a rope will replace a belt,
baldness will replace braided locks of hair,
a sackcloth garment will replace a fine robe,
and a prisoner's brand will replace beauty.

3:25 Your men will fall by the sword,
your strong men will die in battle.
3:26 Her gates will mourn and lament;
deprived of her people, she will sit on the ground.
4:1 Seven women will grab hold of
one man at that time.
They will say, "We will provide our own food,
we will provide our own clothes;
but let us belong to you –
take away our shame!"
The Branch of the Lord
4:2 At that time
the crops given by the LORD will bring admiration and honor;
the produce of the land will be a source of pride and delight
to those who remain in Israel.
4:3 Those remaining in Zion, those left in Jerusalem,
will be called "holy,"
all in Jerusalem who are destined to live.
4:4 At that time the sovereign master will wash the excrement from Zion's women,
he will rinse the bloodstains from Jerusalem's midst,
as he comes to judge
and to bring devastation.
4:5 Then the LORD will create
over all of Mount Zion
and over its convocations
a cloud and smoke by day
and a bright flame of fire by night;
indeed a canopy will accompany the LORD's glorious presence.
4:6 By day it will be a shelter to provide shade from the heat,
as well as safety and protection from the heavy downpour.
A Love Song Gone Sour
5:1 I will sing to my love –
a song to my lover about his vineyard.
My love had a vineyard
on a fertile hill.
5:2 He built a hedge around it, removed its stones,
and planted a vine.
He built a tower in the middle of it,
and constructed a winepress.
He waited for it to produce edible grapes,
but it produced sour ones instead.
5:3 So now, residents of Jerusalem,
people of Judah,
you decide between me and my vineyard!
5:4 What more can I do for my vineyard
beyond what I have already done?
When I waited for it to produce edible grapes,
why did it produce sour ones instead?
5:5 Now I will inform you
what I am about to do to my vineyard:
I will remove its hedge and turn it into pasture,
I will break its wall and allow animals to graze there.
5:6 I will make it a wasteland;
no one will prune its vines or hoe its ground,
and thorns and briers will grow there.
I will order the clouds
not to drop any rain on it.
5:7 Indeed Israel is the vineyard of the LORD who commands armies,
the people of Judah are the cultivated place in which he took delight.
He waited for justice, but look what he got – disobedience!
He waited for fairness, but look what he got – cries for help!
Disaster is Coming
5:8 Those who accumulate houses are as good as dead,
those who also accumulate landed property
until there is no land left,
and you are the only landowners remaining within the land.
5:9 The LORD who commands armies told me this:
"Many houses will certainly become desolate,
large, impressive houses will have no one living in them.
5:10 Indeed, a large vineyard will produce just a few gallons,
and enough seed to yield several bushels will produce less than a bushel."
5:11 Those who get up early to drink beer are as good as dead,
those who keep drinking long after dark
until they are intoxicated with wine.
5:12 They have stringed instruments, tambourines, flutes,
and wine at their parties.
So they do not recognize what the LORD is doing,
they do not perceive what he is bringing about.
5:13 Therefore my people will be deported
because of their lack of understanding.
Their leaders will have nothing to eat,
their masses will have nothing to drink.

5:14 So Death will open up its throat,
and open wide its mouth;
Zion's dignitaries and masses will descend into it,
including those who revel and celebrate within her.
5:15 Men will be humiliated,
they will be brought low;
the proud will be brought low.
5:16 The Lord who commands armies will be exalted when he punishes,
the sovereign God's authority will be recognized when he judges.
5:17 Lambs will graze as if in their pastures,
amid the ruins the rich sojourners will graze.
5:18 Those who pull evil along using cords of emptiness are as good as dead,
who pull sin as with cart ropes.
5:19 They say, "Let him hurry, let him act quickly,
so we can see;
let the plan of the Holy One of Israel take shape and come to pass,
then we will know it!"
5:20 Those who call evil good and good evil are as good as dead,
who turn darkness into light and light into darkness,
who turn bitter into sweet and sweet into bitter.
5:21 Those who think they are wise are as good as dead,
those who think they possess understanding.
5:22 Those who are champions at drinking wine are as good as dead,
who display great courage when mixing strong drinks.
5:23 They pronounce the guilty innocent for a payoff,
they ignore the just cause of the innocent.
5:24 Therefore, as flaming fire devours straw,
and dry grass disintegrates in the flames,
so their root will rot,
and their flower will blow away like dust.
For they have rejected the law of the Lord who commands armies,
they have spurned the commands of the Holy One of Israel.
5:25 So the Lord is furious with his people;
he lifts his hand and strikes them.
The mountains shake,
and corpses lie like manure in the middle of the streets.
Despite all this, his anger does not subside,
and his hand is ready to strike again.
5:26 He lifts a signal flag for a distant nation,
he whistles for it to come from the far regions of the earth.
Look, they come quickly and swiftly.
5:27 None tire or stumble,
they don't stop to nap or sleep.
They don't loosen their belts,
or unstrap their sandals to rest.
5:28 Their arrows are sharpened,
and all their bows are prepared.
The hooves of their horses are hard as flint,
and their chariot wheels are like a windstorm.
5:29 Their roar is like a lion's;
they roar like young lions.
They growl and seize their prey;
they drag it away and no one can come to the rescue.
5:30 At that time they will growl over their prey,
it will sound like sea waves crashing against rocks.
One will look out over the land and see the darkness of disaster,
clouds will turn the light into darkness.

Isaiah's Commission

6:1 In the year of King Uzziah's death, I saw the sovereign master seated on a high, elevated throne. The hem of his robe filled the temple. **6:2** Seraphs stood over him; each one had six wings. With two wings they covered their faces, with two they covered their feet, and they used the remaining two to fly. **6:3** They called out to one another, "Holy, holy, holy is the Lord who commands armies! His majestic splendor fills the entire earth!" **6:4** The sound of their voices shook the door frames, and the temple was filled with smoke. **6:5** I said, "Too bad for me! I am destroyed, for my lips are contaminated by sin, and I live among people whose lips are contaminated by sin. My eyes have seen the king, the Lord who commands armies." **6:6** But then one of the seraphs flew toward me. In his hand was a hot coal he had taken from the altar with tongs. **6:7** He touched my mouth with it and said, "Look, this coal has touched your lips. Your evil is removed; your sin is forgiven." **6:8** I heard the voice of the sovereign master say, "Whom will I send? Who will go on our behalf?" I answered, "Here I am, send me!" **6:9** He said, "Go and tell these people:

'Listen continually, but don't understand!
Look continually, but don't perceive!'
6:10 Make the hearts of these people calloused;
make their ears deaf and their eyes blind!
Otherwise they might see with their eyes and hear with their ears,
their hearts might understand and they might repent and be healed."

6:11 I replied, "How long, sovereign master?" He said,
"Until cities are in ruins and unpopulated,
and houses are uninhabited,
and the land is ruined and devastated,
6:12 and the Lord has sent the people off to a distant place,
and the very heart of the land is completely abandoned.
6:13 Even if only a tenth of the people remain in the land, it will again be destroyed, like one of the large sacred trees or an Asherah pole, when a sacred pillar on a high place is thrown down. That sacred pillar symbolizes the special chosen family."

Ahaz Receives a Sign

7:1 During the reign of Ahaz son of Jotham, son of Uzziah, king of Judah, King Rezin of Syria and King Pekah son of Remaliah of Israel marched up to Jerusalem to do battle, but they were unable to prevail against it. **7:2** It was reported to the family of David, "Syria has allied with Ephraim." They and their people were emotionally shaken, just as the trees of the forest shake before the wind. **7:3** So the Lord told Isaiah, "Go out with your son Shear-jashub and meet Ahaz at the end of the conduit of the upper pool which is located on the road to the field where they wash and dry cloth. **7:4** Tell him, 'Make sure you stay calm! Don't be afraid! Don't be intimidated by these two stubs of smoking logs, or by the raging anger of Rezin, Syria, and the son of Remaliah. **7:5** Syria has plotted with Ephraim and the son of Remaliah to bring about your demise. **7:6** They say, "Let's attack Judah, terrorize it, and conquer it. Then we'll set up the son of Tabeel as its king." **7:7** For this reason the sovereign master, the Lord, says:
"It will not take place;
it will not happen.
7:8 For Syria's leader is Damascus,
and the leader of Damascus is Rezin.
Within sixty-five years Ephraim will no longer exist as a nation.
7:9 Ephraim's leader is Samaria,
and Samaria's leader is the son of Remaliah.
If your faith does not remain firm,
then you will not remain secure."

7:10 The Lord again spoke to Ahaz: **7:11** "Ask for a confirming sign from the Lord your God. You can even ask for something miraculous." **7:12** But Ahaz responded, "I don't want to ask; I don't want to put the Lord to a test." **7:13** So Isaiah replied, "Pay attention, family of David. Do you consider it too insignificant to try the patience of men? Is that why you are also trying the patience of my God? **7:14** For this reason the sovereign master himself will give you a confirming sign. Look, this young woman is about to conceive and will give birth to a son. You, young woman, will name him Immanuel. **7:15** He will eat sour milk and honey, which will help him know how to reject evil and choose what is right. **7:16** Here is why this will be so: Before the child knows how to reject evil and choose what is right, the land whose two kings you fear will be desolate. **7:17** The Lord will bring on you, your people, and your father's family a time unlike any since Ephraim departed from Judah – the king of Assyria!"

7:18 At that time the Lord will whistle for flies from the distant streams of Egypt and for bees from the land of Assyria. **7:19** All of them will come and make their home in the ravines between the cliffs, and in the crevices of the cliffs, in all the thorn bushes, and in all the watering holes. **7:20** At that time the sovereign master will use a razor hired from the banks of the Euphrates River, the king of Assyria, to shave the head and the pubic hair; it will also shave off the beard. **7:21** At that time a man will keep alive a young cow from the herd and a couple of goats. **7:22** From the abundance of milk they produce, he will have sour milk for his meals. Indeed, everyone left in the heart of the land will eat sour milk and honey. **7:23** At that time every place where there had been a thousand vines worth a thousand shekels will be overrun with thorns and briers. **7:24** With bow and arrow men will hunt there, for the whole land will be covered with thorns and briers. **7:25** They will stay away from all the hills that were cultivated, for fear of the thorns and briers. Cattle will graze there and sheep will trample on them.

A Sign-Child is Born

8:1 The Lord told me, "Take a large tablet and inscribe these words on it with an ordinary stylus: 'Maher-Shalal-Hash-Baz.' **8:2** Then I will summon as my reliable witnesses Uriah the priest and Zechariah son of Jeberekiah." **8:3** I then had sexual relations with the prophetess; she conceived and gave birth to a son. The Lord told me, "Name him Maher-Shalal-Hash-Baz, **8:4** for before the child knows how to cry out, 'My father' or 'My mother,' the wealth of Damascus and the plunder of Samaria will be carried off by the king of Assyria."

8:5 The Lord spoke to me again: **8:6** "These people have rejected the gently flowing waters of Shiloah and melt in fear over Rezin and the son of Remaliah. **8:7** So look, the sovereign master is bringing up against them the turbulent and mighty waters of the Euphrates River – the king of Assyria and all his majestic power. It will reach flood stage and overflow its banks. **8:8** It will spill into Judah, flooding and engulfing, as it reaches to the necks of its victims. He will spread his wings out over your entire land, O Immanuel."

8:9 You will be broken, O nations;
you will be shattered!
Pay attention, all you distant lands of the earth!
Get ready for battle, and you will be shattered!
Get ready for battle, and you will be shattered!
8:10 Devise your strategy, but it will be thwarted!
Issue your orders, but they will not be executed!
For God is with us!
The Lord Encourages Isaiah
8:11 Indeed this is what the LORD told me. He took hold of me firmly and warned me not to act like these people:

8:12 "Do not say, 'Conspiracy,' every time these people say the word.
Don't be afraid of what scares them; don't be terrified.
8:13 You must recognize the authority of the LORD who commands armies.
He is the one you must respect;
he is the one you must fear.
8:14 He will become a sanctuary,
but a stone that makes a person trip,
and a rock that makes one stumble –
to the two houses of Israel.
He will become a trap and a snare
to the residents of Jerusalem.
8:15 Many will stumble over the stone and the rock,
and will fall and be seriously injured,
and will be ensnared and captured."
8:16 Tie up the scroll as legal evidence,
seal the official record of God's instructions and give it to my followers.
8:17 I will wait patiently for the LORD,
who has rejected the family of Jacob;
I will wait for him.
8:18 Look, I and the sons whom the LORD has given me are reminders and object lessons in Israel, sent from the LORD who commands armies, who lives on Mount Zion.
Darkness Turns to Light as an Ideal King Arrives
8:19 They will say to you, "Seek oracles at the pits used to conjure up underworld spirits, from the magicians who chirp and mutter incantations. Should people not seek oracles from their gods, by asking the dead about the destiny of the living?" **8:20** Then you must recall the LORD's instructions and the prophetic testimony of what would happen. Certainly they say such things because their minds are spiritually darkened. **8:21** They will pass through the land destitute and starving. Their hunger will make them angry, and they will curse their king and their God as they look upward. **8:22** When one looks out over the land, he sees distress and darkness, gloom and anxiety, darkness and people forced from the land. **9:1** (8:23) The gloom will be dispelled for those who were anxious.

In earlier times he humiliated
the land of Zebulun,
and the land of Naphtali;
but now he brings honor
to the way of the sea,
the region beyond the Jordan,
and Galilee of the nations.
9:2 (9:1) The people walking in darkness
see a bright light;
light shines
on those who live in a land of deep darkness.
9:3 You have enlarged the nation;
you give them great joy.
They rejoice in your presence
as harvesters rejoice;
as warriors celebrate when they divide up the plunder.
9:4 For their oppressive yoke
and the club that strikes their shoulders,
the cudgel the oppressor uses on them,
you have shattered, as in the day of Midian's defeat.
9:5 Indeed every boot that marches and shakes the earth
and every garment dragged through blood
is used as fuel for the fire.
9:6 For a child has been born to us,
a son has been given to us.
He shoulders responsibility
and is called:
Extraordinary Strategist,
Mighty God,
Everlasting Father,
Prince of Peace.
9:7 His dominion will be vast

and he will bring immeasurable prosperity.
He will rule on David's throne
and over David's kingdom,
establishing it and strengthening it
by promoting justice and fairness,
from this time forward and forevermore.
The LORD's intense devotion to his people will accomplish this.
God's Judgment Intensifies
9:8 The sovereign master decreed judgment on Jacob,
and it fell on Israel.
9:9 All the people were aware of it,
the people of Ephraim and those living in Samaria.
Yet with pride and an arrogant attitude, they said,
9:10 "The bricks have fallen,
but we will rebuild with chiseled stone;
the sycamore fig trees have been cut down,
but we will replace them with cedars."
9:11 Then the LORD provoked their adversaries to attack them,
he stirred up their enemies –
9:12 Syria from the east,
and the Philistines from the west,
they gobbled up Israelite territory.
Despite all this, his anger does not subside,
and his hand is ready to strike again.
9:13 The people did not return to the one who struck them,
they did not seek reconciliation with the LORD who commands armies.
9:14 So the LORD cut off Israel's head and tail,
both the shoots and stalk in one day.
9:15 The leaders and the highly respected people are the head,
the prophets who teach lies are the tail.
9:16 The leaders of this nation were misleading people,
and the people being led were destroyed.
9:17 So the sovereign master was not pleased with their young men,
he took no pity on their orphans and widows;
for the whole nation was godless and did wicked things,
every mouth was speaking disgraceful words.
Despite all this, his anger does not subside,
and his hand is ready to strike again.
9:18 For evil burned like a fire,
it consumed thorns and briers;
it burned up the thickets of the forest,
and they went up in smoke.
9:19 Because of the anger of the LORD who commands armies, the land was scorched,
and the people became fuel for the fire.
People had no compassion on one another.
9:20 They devoured on the right, but were still hungry,
they ate on the left, but were not satisfied.
People even ate the flesh of their own arm!
9:21 Manasseh fought against Ephraim,
and Ephraim against Manasseh;
together they fought against Judah.
Despite all this, his anger does not subside,
and his hand is ready to strike again.
10:1 Those who enact unjust policies are as good as dead,
those who are always instituting unfair regulations,
10:2 to keep the poor from getting fair treatment,
and to deprive the oppressed among my people of justice,
so they can steal what widows own,
and loot what belongs to orphans.
10:3 What will you do on judgment day,
when destruction arrives from a distant place?
To whom will you run for help?
Where will you leave your wealth?
10:4 You will have no place to go, except to kneel with the prisoners,
or to fall among those who have been killed.
Despite all this, his anger does not subside,
and his hand is ready to strike again.
The Lord Turns on Arrogant Assyria
10:5 Assyria, the club I use to vent my anger, is as good as dead,
a cudgel with which I angrily punish.
10:6 I sent him against a godless nation,
I ordered him to attack the people with whom I was angry,
to take plunder and to carry away loot,
to trample them down like dirt in the streets.
10:7 But he does not agree with this,
his mind does not reason this way,
for his goal is to destroy,
and to eliminate many nations.
10:8 Indeed, he says:
"Are not my officials all kings?
10:9 Is not Calneh like Carchemish?
Hamath like Arpad?

Samaria like Damascus?
10:10 I overpowered kingdoms ruled by idols,
whose carved images were more impressive than Jerusalem's or Samaria's.
10:11 As I have done to Samaria and its idols,
so I will do to Jerusalem and its idols."

10:12 But when the sovereign master finishes judging Mount Zion and Jerusalem, then I will punish the king of Assyria for what he has proudly planned and for the arrogant attitude he displays. **10:13** For he says:
"By my strong hand I have accomplished this,
by my strategy that I devised.
I invaded the territory of nations,
and looted their storehouses.
Like a mighty conqueror, I brought down rulers.
10:14 My hand discovered the wealth of the nations, as if it were in a nest,
as one gathers up abandoned eggs,
I gathered up the whole earth.
There was no wing flapping,
or open mouth chirping."
10:15 Does an ax exalt itself over the one who wields it,
or a saw magnify itself over the one who cuts with it?
As if a scepter should brandish the one who raises it,
or a staff should lift up what is not made of wood!
10:16 For this reason the sovereign master, the LORD who commands armies, will make his healthy ones emaciated. His majestic glory will go up in smoke.
10:17 The light of Israel will become a fire,
their Holy One will become a flame;
it will burn and consume the Assyrian king's briers
and his thorns in one day.
10:18 The splendor of his forest and his orchard
will be completely destroyed,
as when a sick man's life ebbs away.
10:19 There will be so few trees left in his forest,
a child will be able to count them.

10:20 At that time those left in Israel, those who remain of the family of Jacob, will no longer rely on a foreign leader that abuses them. Instead they will truly rely on the LORD, the Holy One of Israel. **10:21** A remnant will come back, a remnant of Jacob, to the mighty God. **10:22** For though your people, Israel, are as numerous as the sand on the seashore, only a remnant will come back. Destruction has been decreed; just punishment is about to engulf you. **10:23** The sovereign master, the LORD who commands armies, is certainly ready to carry out the decreed destruction throughout the land.
10:24 So here is what the sovereign master, the LORD who commands armies, says: "My people who live in Zion, do not be afraid of Assyria, even though they beat you with a club and lift their cudgel against you as Egypt did. **10:25** For very soon my fury will subside, and my anger will be directed toward their destruction." **10:26** The LORD who commands armies is about to beat them with a whip, similar to the way he struck down Midian at the rock of Oreb. He will use his staff against the sea, lifting it up as he did in Egypt.

10:27 At that time
the LORD will remove their burden from your shoulders,
and their yoke from your neck;
the yoke will be taken off because your neck will be too large.
10:28 They attacked Aiath,
moved through Migron,
depositing their supplies at Micmash.
10:29 They went through the pass,
spent the night at Geba.
Ramah trembled,
Gibeah of Saul ran away.
10:30 Shout out, daughter of Gallim!
Pay attention, Laishah!
Answer her, Anathoth!
10:31 Madmenah flees,
the residents of Gebim have hidden.
10:32 This very day, standing in Nob,
they shake their fist at Daughter Zion's mountain –
at the hill of Jerusalem.
10:33 Look, the sovereign master, the LORD who commands armies,
is ready to cut off the branches with terrifying power.
The tallest trees will be cut down,
the loftiest ones will be brought low.
10:34 The thickets of the forest will be chopped down with an ax,
and mighty Lebanon will fall.
An Ideal King Establishes a Kingdom of Peace
11:1 A shoot will grow out of Jesse's root stock,

a bud will sprout from his roots.
11:2 The LORD's spirit will rest on him –
a spirit that gives extraordinary wisdom,
a spirit that provides the ability to execute plans,
a spirit that produces absolute loyalty to the LORD.
11:3 He will take delight in obeying the LORD.
He will not judge by mere appearances,
or make decisions on the basis of hearsay.
11:4 He will treat the poor fairly,
and make right decisions for the downtrodden of the earth.
He will strike the earth with the rod of his mouth,
and order the wicked to be executed.
11:5 Justice will be like a belt around his waist,
integrity will be like a belt around his hips.
11:6 A wolf will reside with a lamb,
and a leopard will lie down with a young goat;
an ox and a young lion will graze together,
as a small child leads them along.
11:7 A cow and a bear will graze together,
their young will lie down together.
A lion, like an ox, will eat straw.
11:8 A baby will play
over the hole of a snake;
over the nest of a serpent
an infant will put his hand.
11:9 They will no longer injure or destroy
on my entire royal mountain.
For there will be universal submission to the LORD's sovereignty,
just as the waters completely cover the sea.
Israel is Reclaimed and Reunited
11:10 At that time a root from Jesse will stand like a signal flag for the nations. Nations will look to him for guidance, and his residence will be majestic. **11:11** At that time the sovereign master will again lift his hand to reclaim the remnant of his people from Assyria, Egypt, Pathros, Cush, Elam, Shinar, Hamath, and the seacoasts.

11:12 He will lift a signal flag for the nations;
he will gather Israel's dispersed people
and assemble Judah's scattered people
from the four corners of the earth.
11:13 Ephraim's jealousy will end,
and Judah's hostility will be eliminated.
Ephraim will no longer be jealous of Judah,
and Judah will no longer be hostile toward Ephraim.
11:14 They will swoop down on the Philistine hills to the west;
together they will loot the people of the east.
They will take over Edom and Moab,
and the Ammonites will be their subjects.
11:15 The LORD will divide the gulf of the Egyptian Sea;
he will wave his hand over the Euphrates River and send a strong wind,
he will turn it into seven dried-up streams,
and enable them to walk across in their sandals.
11:16 There will be a highway leading out of Assyria
for the remnant of his people,
just as there was for Israel,
when they went up from the land of Egypt.
12:1 At that time you will say:
"I praise you, O LORD,
for even though you were angry with me,
your anger subsided, and you consoled me.
12:2 Look, God is my deliverer!
I will trust in him and not fear.
For the LORD gives me strength and protects me;
he has become my deliverer."
12:3 Joyfully you will draw water
from the springs of deliverance.
12:4 At that time you will say:
"Praise the LORD!
Ask him for help!
Publicize his mighty acts among the nations!
Make it known that he is unique!
12:5 Sing to the LORD, for he has done magnificent things,
let this be known throughout the earth!
12:6 Cry out and shout for joy, O citizens of Zion,
for the Holy One of Israel acts mightily among you!"
The Lord Will Judge Babylon
13:1 This is a message about Babylon that God revealed to Isaiah son of Amoz:
13:2 On a bare hill raise a signal flag,
shout to them,
wave your hand,
so they might enter the gates of the princes!
13:3 I have given orders to my chosen soldiers;

I have summoned the warriors through whom I will vent my anger,
my boasting, arrogant ones.
13:4 There is a loud noise on the mountains –
it sounds like a large army!
There is great commotion among the kingdoms –
nations are being assembled!
The LORD who commands armies is mustering
forces for battle.
13:5 They come from a distant land,
from the horizon.
It is the LORD with his instruments of judgment,
coming to destroy the whole earth.
13:6 Wail, for the LORD's day of judgment is near;
it comes with all the destructive power of the sovereign judge.
13:7 For this reason all hands hang limp,
every human heart loses its courage.
13:8 They panic –
cramps and pain seize hold of them
like those of a woman who is straining to give birth.
They look at one another in astonishment;
their faces are flushed red.
13:9 Look, the LORD's day of judgment is coming;
it is a day of cruelty and savage, raging anger,
destroying the earth
and annihilating its sinners.
13:10 Indeed the stars in the sky and their constellations
no longer give out their light;
the sun is darkened as soon as it rises,
and the moon does not shine.
13:11 I will punish the world for its evil,
and wicked people for their sin.
I will put an end to the pride of the insolent,
I will bring down the arrogance of tyrants.
13:12 I will make human beings more scarce than pure gold,
and people more scarce than gold from Ophir.
13:13 So I will shake the heavens,
and the earth will shake loose from its foundation,
because of the fury of the LORD who commands armies,
in the day he vents his raging anger.
13:14 Like a frightened gazelle
or a sheep with no shepherd,
each will turn toward home,
each will run to his homeland.
13:15 Everyone who is caught will be stabbed;
everyone who is seized will die by the sword.
13:16 Their children will be smashed to pieces before their very eyes;
their houses will be looted
and their wives raped.
13:17 Look, I am stirring up the Medes to attack them;
they are not concerned about silver,
nor are they interested in gold.
13:18 Their arrows will cut young men to ribbons;
they have no compassion on a person's offspring,
they will not look with pity on children.
13:19 Babylon, the most admired of kingdoms,
the Chaldeans' source of honor and pride,
will be destroyed by God
just as Sodom and Gomorrah were.
13:20 No one will live there again;
no one will ever reside there again.
No bedouin will camp there,
no shepherds will rest their flocks there.
13:21 Wild animals will rest there,
the ruined houses will be full of hyenas.
Ostriches will live there,
wild goats will skip among the ruins.
13:22 Wild dogs will yip in her ruined fortresses,
jackals will yelp in the once-splendid palaces.
Her time is almost up,
her days will not be prolonged.

14:1 The LORD will certainly have compassion on Jacob; he will again choose Israel as his special people and restore them to their land. Resident foreigners will join them and unite with the family of Jacob. **14:2** Nations will take them and bring them back to their own place. Then the family of Jacob will make foreigners their servants as they settle in the LORD's land. They will make their captors captives and rule over the ones who oppressed them. **14:3** When the LORD gives you relief from your suffering and anxiety, and from the hard labor which you were made to perform, **14:4** you will taunt the king of Babylon with these words:
"Look how the oppressor has met his end!
Hostility has ceased!
14:5 The LORD has broken the club of the wicked,

the scepter of rulers.
14:6 It furiously struck down nations
with unceasing blows.
It angrily ruled over nations,
oppressing them without restraint.
14:7 The whole earth rests and is quiet;
they break into song.
14:8 The evergreens also rejoice over your demise,
as do the cedars of Lebanon, singing,
'Since you fell asleep,
no woodsman comes up to chop us down!'
14:9 Sheol below is stirred up about you,
ready to meet you when you arrive.
It rouses the spirits of the dead for you,
all the former leaders of the earth;
it makes all the former kings of the nations
rise from their thrones.
14:10 All of them respond to you, saying:
'You too have become weak like us!
You have become just like us!
14:11 Your splendor has been brought down to Sheol,
as well as the sound of your stringed instruments.
You lie on a bed of maggots,
with a blanket of worms over you.
14:12 Look how you have fallen from the sky,
O shining one, son of the dawn!
You have been cut down to the ground,
O conqueror of the nations!
14:13 You said to yourself,
"I will climb up to the sky.
Above the stars of El
I will set up my throne.
I will rule on the mountain of assembly
on the remote slopes of Zaphon.
14:14 I will climb up to the tops of the clouds;
I will make myself like the Most High!"
14:15 But you were brought down to Sheol,
to the remote slopes of the pit.
14:16 Those who see you stare at you,
they look at you carefully, thinking:
"Is this the man who shook the earth,
the one who made kingdoms tremble?
14:17 Is this the one who made the world like a desert,
who ruined its cities,
and refused to free his prisoners so they could return home?"'
14:18 As for all the kings of the nations,
all of them lie down in splendor,
each in his own tomb.
14:19 But you have been thrown out of your grave
like a shoot that is thrown away.
You lie among the slain,
among those who have been slashed by the sword,
among those headed for the stones of the pit,
as if you were a mangled corpse.
14:20 You will not be buried with them,
because you destroyed your land
and killed your people.
The offspring of the wicked
will never be mentioned again.
14:21 Prepare to execute his sons
for the sins their ancestors have committed.
They must not rise up and take possession of the earth,
or fill the surface of the world with cities."
14:22 "I will rise up against them,"
says the LORD who commands armies.
"I will blot out all remembrance of Babylon and destroy all her people,
including the offspring she produces,"
says the LORD.
14:23 "I will turn her into a place that is overrun with wild animals
and covered with pools of stagnant water.
I will get rid of her, just as one sweeps away dirt with a broom,"
says the LORD who commands armies.
14:24 The LORD who commands armies makes this solemn vow:
"Be sure of this:
Just as I have intended, so it will be;
just as I have planned, it will happen.
14:25 I will break Assyria in my land,
I will trample them underfoot on my hills.
Their yoke will be removed from my people,
the burden will be lifted from their shoulders.
14:26 This is the plan I have devised for the whole earth;
my hand is ready to strike all the nations."
14:27 Indeed, the LORD who commands armies has a plan,

and who can possibly frustrate it?
His hand is ready to strike,
and who can possibly stop it?

The Lord Will Judge the Philistines

14:28 In the year King Ahaz died, this message was revealed:

14:29 Don't be so happy, all you Philistines,
just because the club that beat you has been broken!
For a viper will grow out of the serpent's root,
and its fruit will be a darting adder.
14:30 The poor will graze in my pastures;
the needy will rest securely.
But I will kill your root by famine;
it will put to death all your survivors.
14:31 Wail, O city gate!
Cry out, O city!
Melt with fear, all you Philistines!
For out of the north comes a cloud of smoke,
and there are no stragglers in its ranks.
14:32 How will they respond to the messengers of this nation?
Indeed, the LORD has made Zion secure;
the oppressed among his people will find safety in her.

The Lord Will Judge Moab

15:1 Here is a message about Moab:

Indeed, in a night it is devastated,
Ar of Moab is destroyed!
Indeed, in a night it is devastated,
Kir of Moab is destroyed!
15:2 They went up to the temple,
the people of Dibon went up to the high places to lament.
Because of what happened to Nebo and Medeba, Moab wails.
Every head is shaved bare,
every beard is trimmed off.
15:3 In their streets they wear sackcloth;
on their roofs and in their town squares
all of them wail,
they fall down weeping.
15:4 The people of Heshbon and Elealeh cry out,
their voices are heard as far away as Jahaz.
For this reason Moab's soldiers shout in distress;
their courage wavers.
15:5 My heart cries out because of Moab's plight,
and for the fugitives stretched out as far as Zoar and Eglath Shelishiyah.
For they weep as they make their way up the ascent of Luhith;
they loudly lament their demise on the road to Horonaim.
15:6 For the waters of Nimrim are gone;
the grass is dried up,
the vegetation has disappeared,
and there are no plants.
15:7 For this reason what they have made and stored up,
they carry over the Stream of the Poplars.
15:8 Indeed, the cries of distress echo throughout Moabite territory;
their wailing can be heard in Eglaim and Beer Elim.
15:9 Indeed, the waters of Dimon are full of blood!
Indeed, I will heap even more trouble on Dimon.
A lion will attack the Moabite fugitives
and the people left in the land.
16:1 Send rams as tribute to the ruler of the land,
from Sela in the desert
to the hill of Daughter Zion.
16:2 At the fords of the Arnon
the Moabite women are like a bird
that flies about when forced from its nest.
16:3 "Bring a plan, make a decision!
Provide some shade in the middle of the day!
Hide the fugitives! Do not betray the one who tries to escape!
16:4 Please let the Moabite fugitives live among you.
Hide them from the destroyer!"

Certainly the one who applies pressure will cease,
the destroyer will come to an end,
those who trample will disappear from the earth.
16:5 Then a trustworthy king will be established;
he will rule in a reliable manner,
this one from David's family.
He will be sure to make just decisions
and will be experienced in executing justice.
16:6 We have heard about Moab's pride,
their great arrogance,
their boasting, pride, and excess.
But their boastful claims are empty!
16:7 So Moab wails over its demise –
they all wail!
Completely devastated, they moan

about what has happened to the raisin cakes of Kir Hareseth.
16:8 For the fields of Heshbon are dried up,
as well as the vines of Sibmah.
The rulers of the nations trample all over its vines,
which reach Jazer and spread to the desert;
their shoots spread out and cross the sea.
16:9 So I weep along with Jazer
over the vines of Sibmah.
I will saturate you with my tears, Heshbon and Elealeh,
for the conquering invaders shout triumphantly
over your fruit and crops.
16:10 Joy and happiness disappear from the orchards,
and in the vineyards no one rejoices or shouts;
no one treads out juice in the wine vats –
I have brought the joyful shouts to an end.
16:11 So my heart constantly sighs for Moab, like the strumming of a harp,
my inner being sighs for Kir Hareseth.
16:12 When the Moabites plead with all their might at their high places,
and enter their temples to pray, their prayers will be ineffective!
16:13 This is the message the LORD previously announced about Moab.
16:14 Now the LORD makes this announcement: "Within exactly three years Moab's splendor will disappear, along with all her many people; there will be just a few, insignificant survivors left."

The Lord Will Judge Damascus

17:1 Here is a message about Damascus:

"Look, Damascus is no longer a city,
it is a heap of ruins!
17:2 The cities of Aroer are abandoned.
They will be used for herds,
which will lie down there in peace.
17:3 Fortified cities will disappear from Ephraim,
and Damascus will lose its kingdom.
The survivors in Syria
will end up like the splendor of the Israelites,"
says the LORD who commands armies.
17:4 "At that time
Jacob's splendor will be greatly diminished,
and he will become skin and bones.
17:5 It will be as when one gathers the grain harvest,
and his hand gleans the ear of grain.
It will be like one gathering the ears of grain
in the Valley of Rephaim.
17:6 There will be some left behind,
like when an olive tree is beaten –
two or three ripe olives remain toward the very top,
four or five on its fruitful branches,"
says the LORD God of Israel.
17:7 At that time men will trust in their creator;
they will depend on the Holy One of Israel.
17:8 They will no longer trust in the altars their hands made,
or depend on the Asherah poles and incense altars their fingers made.
17:9 At that time their fortified cities will be
like the abandoned summits of the Amorites,
which they abandoned because of the Israelites;
there will be desolation.
17:10 For you ignore the God who rescues you;
you pay no attention to your strong protector.
So this is what happens:
You cultivate beautiful plants
and plant exotic vines.
17:11 The day you begin cultivating, you do what you can to make it grow;
the morning you begin planting, you do what you can to make it sprout.
Yet the harvest will disappear in the day of disease
and incurable pain.
17:12 The many nations massing together are as good as dead,
those who make a commotion as loud as the roaring of the sea's waves.
The people making such an uproar are as good as dead,
those who make an uproar as loud as the roaring of powerful waves.
17:13 Though these people make an uproar as loud as the roaring of powerful waves,
when he shouts at them, they will flee to a distant land,
driven before the wind like dead weeds on the hills,
or like dead thistles before a strong gale.
17:14 In the evening there is sudden terror;
by morning they vanish.
This is the fate of those who try to plunder us,
the destiny of those who try to loot us!

The Lord Will Judge a Distant Land in the South

18:1 The land of buzzing wings is as good as dead,
the one beyond the rivers of Cush,
18:2 that sends messengers by sea,

who glide over the water's surface in boats made of papyrus.
Go, you swift messengers,
to a nation of tall, smooth-skinned people,
to a people that are feared far and wide,
to a nation strong and victorious,
whose land rivers divide.
18:3 All you who live in the world,
who reside on the earth,
you will see a signal flag raised on the mountains;
you will hear a trumpet being blown.
18:4 For this is what the LORD has told me:
"I will wait and watch from my place,
like scorching heat produced by the sunlight,
like a cloud of mist in the heat of harvest."
18:5 For before the harvest, when the bud has sprouted,
and the ripening fruit appears,
he will cut off the unproductive shoots with pruning knives;
he will prune the tendrils.
18:6 They will all be left for the birds of the hills
and the wild animals;
the birds will eat them during the summer,
and all the wild animals will eat them during the winter.
18:7 At that time
tribute will be brought to the LORD who commands armies,
by a people that are tall and smooth-skinned,
a people that are feared far and wide,
a nation strong and victorious,
whose land rivers divide.
The tribute will be brought to the place where the LORD who commands armies has chosen to reside, on Mount Zion.
The Lord Will Judge Egypt
19:1 Here is a message about Egypt:
Look, the LORD rides on a swift-moving cloud
and approaches Egypt.
The idols of Egypt tremble before him;
the Egyptians lose their courage.
19:2 "I will provoke civil strife in Egypt,
brothers will fight with each other,
as will neighbors,
cities, and kingdoms.
19:3 The Egyptians will panic,
and I will confuse their strategy.
They will seek guidance from the idols and from the spirits of the dead,
from the pits used to conjure up underworld spirits, and from the magicians.
19:4 I will hand Egypt over to a harsh master;
a powerful king will rule over them,"
says the sovereign master, the LORD who commands armies.
19:5 The water of the sea will be dried up,
and the river will dry up and be empty.
19:6 The canals will stink;
the streams of Egypt will trickle and then dry up;
the bulrushes and reeds will decay,
19:7 along with the plants by the mouth of the river.
All the cultivated land near the river
will turn to dust and be blown away.
19:8 The fishermen will mourn and lament,
all those who cast a fishhook into the river,
and those who spread out a net on the water's surface will grieve.
19:9 Those who make clothes from combed flax will be embarrassed;
those who weave will turn pale.
19:10 Those who make cloth will be demoralized;
all the hired workers will be depressed.
19:11 The officials of Zoan are nothing but fools;
Pharaoh's wise advisers give stupid advice.
How dare you say to Pharaoh,
"I am one of the sages,
one well-versed in the writings of the ancient kings?"
19:12 But where, oh where, are your wise men?
Let them tell you, let them find out
what the LORD who commands armies has planned for Egypt.
19:13 The officials of Zoan are fools,
the officials of Memphis are misled;
the rulers of her tribes lead Egypt astray.
19:14 The LORD has made them undiscerning;
they lead Egypt astray in all she does,
so that she is like a drunk sliding around in his own vomit.
19:15 Egypt will not be able to do a thing,
head or tail, shoots and stalk.
19:16 At that time the Egyptians will be like women. They will tremble and fear because the LORD who commands armies brandishes his fist against them. **19:17** The land of Judah will humiliate Egypt. Everyone

who hears about Judah will be afraid because of what the LORD who commands armies is planning to do to them.
19:18 At that time five cities in the land of Egypt will speak the language of Canaan and swear allegiance to the LORD who commands armies. One will be called the City of the Sun. **19:19** At that time there will be an altar for the LORD in the middle of the land of Egypt, as well as a sacred pillar dedicated to the LORD at its border. **19:20** It will become a visual reminder in the land of Egypt of the LORD who commands armies. When they cry out to the LORD because of oppressors, he will send them a deliverer and defender who will rescue them. **19:21** The LORD will reveal himself to the Egyptians, and they will acknowledge the LORD's authority at that time. They will present sacrifices and offerings; they will make vows to the LORD and fulfill them. **19:22** The LORD will strike Egypt, striking and then healing them. They will turn to the LORD and he will listen to their prayers and heal them.
19:23 At that time there will be a highway from Egypt to Assyria. The Assyrians will visit Egypt, and the Egyptians will visit Assyria. The Egyptians and Assyrians will worship together. **19:24** At that time Israel will be the third member of the group, along with Egypt and Assyria, and will be a recipient of blessing in the earth. **19:25** The LORD who commands armies will pronounce a blessing over the earth, saying, "Blessed be my people, Egypt, and the work of my hands, Assyria, and my special possession, Israel!"
20:1 The LORD revealed the following message during the year in which King Sargon of Assyria sent his commanding general to Ashdod, and he fought against it and captured it. **20:2** At that time the LORD announced through Isaiah son of Amoz: "Go, remove the sackcloth from your waist and take your sandals off your feet." He did as instructed and walked around in undergarments and barefoot. **20:3** Later the LORD explained, "In the same way that my servant Isaiah has walked around in undergarments and barefoot for the past three years, as an object lesson and omen pertaining to Egypt and Cush, **20:4** so the king of Assyria will lead away the captives of Egypt and the exiles of Cush, both young and old. They will be in undergarments and barefoot, with the buttocks exposed; the Egyptians will be publicly humiliated. **20:5** Those who put their hope in Cush and took pride in Egypt will be afraid and embarrassed. **20:6** At that time those who live on this coast will say, 'Look what has happened to our source of hope to whom we fled for help, expecting to be rescued from the king of Assyria! How can we escape now?'"
The Lord Will Judge Babylon
21:1 Here is a message about the Desert by the Sea:
Like strong winds blowing in the south,
one invades from the desert,
from a land that is feared.
21:2 I have received a distressing message:
"The deceiver deceives,
the destroyer destroys.
Attack, you Elamites!
Lay siege, you Medes!
I will put an end to all the groaning!"
21:3 For this reason my stomach churns;
cramps overwhelm me
like the contractions of a woman in labor.
I am disturbed by what I hear,
horrified by what I see.
21:4 My heart palpitates,
I shake in fear;
the twilight I desired
has brought me terror.
21:5 Arrange the table,
lay out the carpet,
eat and drink!
Get up, you officers,
smear oil on the shields!
21:6 For this is what the sovereign master has told me:
"Go, post a guard!
He must report what he sees.
21:7 When he sees chariots,
teams of horses,
riders on donkeys,
riders on camels,
he must be alert,
very alert."
21:8 Then the guard cries out:
"On the watchtower, O sovereign master,
I stand all day long;
at my post
I am stationed every night.
21:9 Look what's coming!
A charioteer,
a team of horses."
When questioned, he replies,
"Babylon has fallen, fallen!

All the idols of her gods lie shattered on the ground!"
21:10 O my downtrodden people, crushed like stalks on the threshing floor,
what I have heard
from the LORD who commands armies,
the God of Israel,
I have reported to you.
Bad News for Seir
21:11 Here is a message about Dumah:
Someone calls to me from Seir,
"Watchman, what is left of the night?
Watchman, what is left of the night?"
21:12 The watchman replies,
"Morning is coming, but then night.
If you want to ask, ask;
come back again."
The Lord Will Judge Arabia
21:13 Here is a message about Arabia:
In the thicket of Arabia you spend the night,
you Dedanite caravans.
21:14 Bring out some water for the thirsty.
You who live in the land of Tema,
bring some food for the fugitives.
21:15 For they flee from the swords –
from the drawn sword
and from the battle-ready bow
and from the severity of the battle.
21:16 For this is what the sovereign master has told me: "Within exactly one year all the splendor of Kedar will come to an end.
21:17 Just a handful of archers, the warriors of Kedar, will be left." Indeed, the LORD God of Israel has spoken.
The Lord Will Judge Jerusalem
22:1 Here is a message about the Valley of Vision:
What is the reason
that all of you go up to the rooftops?
22:2 The noisy city is full of raucous sounds;
the town is filled with revelry.
Your slain were not cut down by the sword;
they did not die in battle.
22:3 All your leaders ran away together –
they fled to a distant place;
all your refugees were captured together –
they were captured without a single arrow being shot.
22:4 So I say:
"Don't look at me!
I am weeping bitterly.
Don't try to console me
concerning the destruction of my defenseless people."
22:5 For the sovereign master, the LORD who commands armies,
has planned a day of panic, defeat, and confusion.
In the Valley of Vision people shout
and cry out to the hill.
22:6 The Elamites picked up the quiver,
and came with chariots and horsemen;
the men of Kir prepared the shield.
22:7 Your very best valleys were full of chariots;
horsemen confidently took their positions at the gate.
22:8 They removed the defenses of Judah.
At that time you looked
for the weapons in the House of the Forest.
22:9 You saw the many breaks
in the walls of the city of David;
you stored up water in the lower pool.
22:10 You counted the houses in Jerusalem,
and demolished houses so you could have material to reinforce the wall.
22:11 You made a reservoir between the two walls
for the water of the old pool –
but you did not trust in the one who made it;
you did not depend on the one who formed it long ago!
22:12 At that time the sovereign master, the LORD who commands armies, called for weeping and mourning,
for shaved heads and sackcloth.
22:13 But look, there is outright celebration!
You say, "Kill the ox and slaughter the sheep,
eat meat and drink wine.
Eat and drink, for tomorrow we die!"
22:14 The LORD who commands armies told me this: "Certainly this sin will not be forgiven as long as you live," says the sovereign master, the LORD who commands armies.
22:15 This is what the sovereign master, the LORD who commands armies, says:
"Go visit this administrator, Shebna, who supervises the palace, and tell him:

22:16 'What right do you have to be here? What relatives do you have buried here?
Why do you chisel out a tomb for yourself here?
He chisels out his burial site in an elevated place,
he carves out his tomb on a cliff.
22:17 Look, the LORD will throw you far away, you mere man!
He will wrap you up tightly.
22:18 He will wind you up tightly into a ball
and throw you into a wide, open land.
There you will die,
and there with you will be your impressive chariots,
which bring disgrace to the house of your master.
22:19 I will remove you from your office;
you will be thrown down from your position.
22:20 "At that time I will summon my servant Eliakim, son of Hilkiah.
22:21 I will put your robe on him, tie your belt around him, and transfer your authority to him. He will become a protector of the residents of Jerusalem and of the people of Judah. **22:22** I will place the key to the house of David on his shoulder. When he opens the door, no one can close it; when he closes the door, no one can open it. **22:23** I will fasten him like a peg into a solid place; he will bring honor and respect to his father's family. **22:24** His father's family will gain increasing prominence because of him, including the offspring and the offshoots. All the small containers, including the bowls and all the jars will hang from this peg.'
22:25 "At that time," says the LORD who commands armies, "the peg fastened into a solid place will come loose. It will be cut off and fall, and the load hanging on it will be cut off." Indeed, the LORD has spoken.
The Lord Will Judge Tyre
23:1 Here is a message about Tyre:
Wail, you large ships,
for the port is too devastated to enter!
From the land of Cyprus this news is announced to them.
23:2 Lament, you residents of the coast,
you merchants of Sidon who travel over the sea,
whose agents sail over **23:3** the deep waters!
Grain from the Shihor region,
crops grown near the Nile she receives;
she is the trade center of the nations.
23:4 Be ashamed, O Sidon,
for the sea says this, O fortress of the sea:
"I have not gone into labor
or given birth;
I have not raised young men
or brought up young women."
23:5 When the news reaches Egypt,
they will be shaken by what has happened to Tyre.
23:6 Travel to Tarshish!
Wail, you residents of the coast!
23:7 Is this really your boisterous city
whose origins are in the distant past,
and whose feet led her to a distant land to reside?
23:8 Who planned this for royal Tyre,
whose merchants are princes,
whose traders are the dignitaries of the earth?
23:9 The LORD who commands armies planned it –
to dishonor the pride that comes from all her beauty,
to humiliate all the dignitaries of the earth.
23:10 Daughter Tarshish, travel back to your land, as one crosses the Nile;
there is no longer any marketplace in Tyre.
23:11 The LORD stretched out his hand over the sea,
he shook kingdoms;
he gave the order
to destroy Canaan's fortresses.
23:12 He said,
"You will no longer celebrate,
oppressed virgin daughter Sidon!
Get up, travel to Cyprus,
but you will find no relief there."
23:13 Look at the land of the Chaldeans,
these people who have lost their identity!
The Assyrians have made it a home for wild animals.
They erected their siege towers,
demolished its fortresses,
and turned it into a heap of ruins.
23:14 Wail, you large ships,
for your fortress is destroyed!
23:15 At that time Tyre will be forgotten for seventy years, the typical life span of a king. At the end of seventy years Tyre will try to attract attention again, like the prostitute in the popular song:
23:16 "Take the harp,
go through the city,
forgotten prostitute!

Play it well,
play lots of songs,
so you'll be noticed!"
23:17 At the end of seventy years the LORD will revive Tyre. She will start making money again by selling her services to all the earth's kingdoms. **23:18** Her profits and earnings will be set apart for the LORD. They will not be stored up or accumulated, for her profits will be given to those who live in the LORD's presence and will be used to purchase large quantities of food and beautiful clothes.

The Lord Will Judge the Earth

24:1 Look, the LORD is ready to devastate the earth
and leave it in ruins;
he will mar its surface
and scatter its inhabitants.
24:2 Everyone will suffer – the priest as well as the people,
the master as well as the servant,
the elegant lady as well as the female attendant,
the seller as well as the buyer,
the borrower as well as the lender,
the creditor as well as the debtor.
24:3 The earth will be completely devastated
and thoroughly ransacked.
For the LORD has decreed this judgment.
24:4 The earth dries up and withers,
the world shrivels up and withers;
the prominent people of the earth fade away.
24:5 The earth is defiled by its inhabitants,
for they have violated laws,
disregarded the regulation,
and broken the permanent treaty.
24:6 So a treaty curse devours the earth;
its inhabitants pay for their guilt.
This is why the inhabitants of the earth disappear,
and are reduced to just a handful of people.
24:7 The new wine dries up,
the vines shrivel up,
all those who like to celebrate groan.
24:8 The happy sound of the tambourines stops,
the revelry of those who celebrate comes to a halt,
the happy sound of the harp ceases.
24:9 They no longer sing and drink wine;
the beer tastes bitter to those who drink it.
24:10 The ruined town is shattered;
all of the houses are shut up tight.
24:11 They howl in the streets because of what happened to the wine;
all joy turns to sorrow;
celebrations disappear from the earth.
24:12 The city is left in ruins;
the gate is reduced to rubble.
24:13 This is what will happen throughout the earth,
among the nations.
It will be like when they beat an olive tree,
and just a few olives are left at the end of the harvest.
24:14 They lift their voices and shout joyfully;
they praise the majesty of the LORD in the west.
24:15 So in the east extol the LORD,
along the seacoasts extol the fame of the LORD God of Israel.
24:16 From the ends of the earth we hear songs –
the Just One is majestic.
But I say, "I'm wasting away! I'm wasting away! I'm doomed!
Deceivers deceive, deceivers thoroughly deceive!"
24:17 Terror, pit, and snare
are ready to overtake you inhabitants of the earth!
24:18 The one who runs away from the sound of the terror
will fall into the pit;
the one who climbs out of the pit,
will be trapped by the snare.
For the floodgates of the heavens are opened up
and the foundations of the earth shake.
24:19 The earth is broken in pieces,
the earth is ripped to shreds,
the earth shakes violently.
24:20 The earth will stagger around like a drunk;
it will sway back and forth like a hut in a windstorm.
Its sin will weigh it down,
and it will fall and never get up again.

The Lord Will Become King

24:21 At that time the LORD will punish
the heavenly forces in the heavens
and the earthly kings on the earth.
24:22 They will be imprisoned in a pit,
locked up in a prison,
and after staying there for a long time, they will be punished.

24:23 The full moon will be covered up,
the bright sun will be darkened;
for the LORD who commands armies will rule
on Mount Zion in Jerusalem
in the presence of his assembly, in majestic splendor.

25:1 O LORD, you are my God!
I will exalt you in praise, I will extol your fame.
For you have done extraordinary things,
and executed plans made long ago exactly as you decreed.
25:2 Indeed, you have made the city into a heap of rubble,
the fortified town into a heap of ruins;
the fortress of foreigners is no longer a city,
it will never be rebuilt.
25:3 So a strong nation will extol you;
the towns of powerful nations will fear you.
25:4 For you are a protector for the poor,
a protector for the needy in their distress,
a shelter from the rainstorm,
a shade from the heat.
Though the breath of tyrants is like a winter rainstorm,
25:5 like heat in a dry land,
you humble the boasting foreigners.
Just as the shadow of a cloud causes the heat to subside,
so he causes the song of tyrants to cease.
25:6 The LORD who commands armies will hold a banquet for all the nations on this mountain.
At this banquet there will be plenty of meat and aged wine –
tender meat and choicest wine.
25:7 On this mountain he will swallow up
the shroud that is over all the peoples,
the woven covering that is over all the nations;
25:8 he will swallow up death permanently.
The sovereign LORD will wipe away the tears from every face,
and remove his people's disgrace from all the earth.
Indeed, the LORD has announced it!
25:9 At that time they will say,
"Look, here is our God!
We waited for him and he delivered us.
Here is the LORD! We waited for him.
Let's rejoice and celebrate his deliverance!"
25:10 For the LORD's power will make this mountain secure.
Moab will be trampled down where it stands,
as a heap of straw is trampled down in a manure pile.
25:11 Moab will spread out its hands in the middle of it,
just as a swimmer spreads his hands to swim;
the LORD will bring down Moab's pride as it spreads its hands.
25:12 The fortified city (along with the very tops of your walls) he will knock down,
he will bring it down, he will throw it down to the dusty ground.

Judah Will Celebrate

26:1 At that time this song will be sung in the land of Judah:
"We have a strong city!
The LORD's deliverance, like walls and a rampart, makes it secure.
26:2 Open the gates so a righteous nation can enter –
one that remains trustworthy.
26:3 You keep completely safe the people who maintain their faith,
for they trust in you.
26:4 Trust in the LORD from this time forward,
even in Yah, the LORD, an enduring protector!
26:5 Indeed, the LORD knocks down those who live in a high place,
he brings down an elevated town;
he brings it down to the ground,
he throws it down to the dust.
26:6 It is trampled underfoot
by the feet of the oppressed,
by the soles of the poor."

God's People Anticipate Vindication

26:7 The way of the righteous is level,
the path of the righteous that you make is straight.
26:8 Yes, as your judgments unfold,
O LORD, we wait for you.
We desire your fame and reputation to grow.
26:9 I look for you during the night,
my spirit within me seeks you at dawn,
for when your judgments come upon the earth,
those who live in the world learn about justice.
26:10 If the wicked are shown mercy,
they do not learn about justice.
Even in a land where right is rewarded, they act unjustly;
they do not see the LORD's majesty revealed.
26:11 O LORD, you are ready to act,
but they don't even notice.

They will see and be put to shame by your angry judgment against humankind,
yes, fire will consume your enemies.
26:12 O LORD, you make us secure,
for even all we have accomplished, you have done for us.
26:13 O LORD, our God,
masters other than you have ruled us,
but we praise your name alone.
26:14 The dead do not come back to life,
the spirits of the dead do not rise.
That is because you came in judgment and destroyed them,
you wiped out all memory of them.
26:15 You have made the nation larger, O LORD,
you have made the nation larger and revealed your splendor,
you have extended all the borders of the land.
26:16 O LORD, in distress they looked for you;
they uttered incantations because of your discipline.
26:17 As when a pregnant woman gets ready to deliver
and strains and cries out because of her labor pains,
so were we because of you, O LORD.
26:18 We were pregnant, we strained,
we gave birth, as it were, to wind.
We cannot produce deliverance on the earth;
people to populate the world are not born.
26:19 Your dead will come back to life;
your corpses will rise up.
Wake up and shout joyfully, you who live in the ground!
For you will grow like plants drenched with the morning dew,
and the earth will bring forth its dead spirits.
26:20 Go, my people! Enter your inner rooms!
Close your doors behind you!
Hide for a little while,
until his angry judgment is over!
26:21 For look, the LORD is coming out of the place where he lives,
to punish the sin of those who live on the earth.
The earth will display the blood shed on it;
it will no longer cover up its slain.

27:1 At that time the LORD will punish
with his destructive, great, and powerful sword
Leviathan the fast-moving serpent,
Leviathan the squirming serpent;
he will kill the sea monster.
27:2 When that time comes,
sing about a delightful vineyard!
27:3 I, the LORD, protect it;
I water it regularly.
I guard it night and day,
so no one can harm it.
27:4 I am not angry.
I wish I could confront some thorns and briers!
Then I would march against them for battle;
I would set them all on fire,
27:5 unless they became my subjects
and made peace with me;
let them make peace with me.
27:6 The time is coming when Jacob will take root;
Israel will blossom and grow branches.
The produce will fill the surface of the world.
27:7 Has the LORD struck down Israel like he did their oppressors?
Has Israel been killed like their enemies?
27:8 When you summon her for divorce, you prosecute her;
he drives her away with his strong wind in the day of the east wind.
27:9 So in this way Jacob's sin will be forgiven,
and this is how they will show they are finished sinning:
They will make all the stones of the altars
like crushed limestone,
and the Asherah poles and the incense altars will no longer stand.
27:10 For the fortified city is left alone;
it is a deserted settlement
and abandoned like the desert.
Calves graze there;
they lie down there
and eat its branches bare.
27:11 When its branches get brittle, they break;
women come and use them for kindling.
For these people lack understanding,
therefore the one who made them has no compassion on them;
the one who formed them has no mercy on them.
27:12 At that time the LORD will shake the tree, from the Euphrates River to the Stream of Egypt. Then you will be gathered up one by one, O Israelites. **27:13** At that time a large trumpet will be blown, and the ones

lost in the land of Assyria will come, as well as the refugees in the land of Egypt. They will worship the LORD on the holy mountain in Jerusalem.

The Lord Will Judge Samaria

28:1 The splendid crown of Ephraim's drunkards is doomed,
the withering flower, its beautiful splendor,
situated at the head of a rich valley,
the crown of those overcome with wine.
28:2 Look, the sovereign master sends a strong, powerful one.
With the force of a hailstorm or a destructive windstorm,
with the might of a driving, torrential rainstorm,
he will knock that crown to the ground with his hand.
28:3 The splendid crown of Ephraim's drunkards
will be trampled underfoot.
28:4 The withering flower, its beautiful splendor,
situated at the head of a rich valley,
will be like an early fig before harvest –
as soon as someone notices it,
he grabs it and swallows it.
28:5 At that time the LORD who commands armies will become a beautiful crown
and a splendid diadem for the remnant of his people.
28:6 He will give discernment to the one who makes judicial decisions,
and strength to those who defend the city from attackers.
28:7 Even these men stagger because of wine,
they stumble around because of beer –
priests and prophets stagger because of beer,
they are confused because of wine,
they stumble around because of beer;
they stagger while seeing prophetic visions,
they totter while making legal decisions.
28:8 Indeed, all the tables are covered with vomit;
no place is untouched.
28:9 Who is the LORD trying to teach?
To whom is he explaining a message?
Those just weaned from milk!
Those just taken from their mother's breast!
28:10 Indeed, they will hear meaningless gibberish,
senseless babbling,
a syllable here, a syllable there.
28:11 For with mocking lips and a foreign tongue
he will speak to these people.
28:12 In the past he said to them,
"This is where security can be found.
Provide security for the one who is exhausted!
This is where rest can be found."
But they refused to listen.
28:13 So the LORD's word to them will sound like
meaningless gibberish,
senseless babbling,
a syllable here, a syllable there.
As a result, they will fall on their backsides when they try to walk,
and be injured, ensnared, and captured.

The Lord Will Judge Jerusalem

28:14 Therefore, listen to the LORD's word,
you who mock,
you rulers of these people
who reside in Jerusalem!
28:15 For you say,
"We have made a treaty with death,
with Sheol we have made an agreement.
When the overwhelming judgment sweeps by
it will not reach us.
For we have made a lie our refuge,
we have hidden ourselves in a deceitful word."
28:16 Therefore, this is what the sovereign master, the LORD, says:
"Look, I am laying a stone in Zion,
an approved stone,
set in place as a precious cornerstone for the foundation.
The one who maintains his faith will not panic.
28:17 I will make justice the measuring line,
fairness the plumb line;
hail will sweep away the unreliable refuge,
the floodwaters will overwhelm the hiding place.
28:18 Your treaty with death will be dissolved;
your agreement with Sheol will not last.
When the overwhelming judgment sweeps by,
you will be overrun by it.
28:19 Whenever it sweeps by, it will overtake you;
indeed, every morning it will sweep by,
it will come through during the day and the night."
When this announcement is understood,
it will cause nothing but terror.
28:20 For the bed is too short to stretch out on,

and the blanket is too narrow to wrap around oneself.
28:21 For the LORD will rise up, as he did at Mount Perazim,
he will rouse himself, as he did in the Valley of Gibeon,
to accomplish his work,
his peculiar work,
to perform his task,
his strange task.
28:22 So now, do not mock,
or your chains will become heavier!
For I have heard a message about decreed destruction,
from the sovereign master, the LORD who commands armies, against the entire land.
28:23 Pay attention and listen to my message!
Be attentive and listen to what I have to say!
28:24 Does a farmer just keep on plowing at planting time?
Does he keep breaking up and harrowing his ground?
28:25 Once he has leveled its surface,
does he not scatter the seed of the caraway plant,
sow the seed of the cumin plant,
and plant the wheat, barley, and grain in their designated places?
28:26 His God instructs him;
he teaches him the principles of agriculture.
28:27 Certainly caraway seed is not threshed with a sledge,
nor is the wheel of a cart rolled over cumin seed.
Certainly caraway seed is beaten with a stick,
and cumin seed with a flail.
28:28 Grain is crushed,
though one certainly does not thresh it forever.
The wheel of one's wagon rolls over it,
but his horses do not crush it.
28:29 This also comes from the LORD who commands armies,
who gives supernatural guidance and imparts great wisdom.
Ariel is Besieged
29:1 Ariel is as good as dead –
Ariel, the town David besieged!
Keep observing your annual rituals,
celebrate your festivals on schedule.
29:2 I will threaten Ariel,
and she will mourn intensely
and become like an altar hearth before me.
29:3 I will lay siege to you on all sides;
I will besiege you with troops;
I will raise siege works against you.
29:4 You will fall;
while lying on the ground you will speak;
from the dust where you lie, your words will be heard.
Your voice will sound like a spirit speaking from the underworld;
from the dust you will chirp as if muttering an incantation.
29:5 But the horde of invaders will be like fine dust,
the horde of tyrants like chaff that is blown away.
It will happen suddenly, in a flash.
29:6 Judgment will come from the LORD who commands armies,
accompanied by thunder, earthquake, and a loud noise,
by a strong gale, a windstorm, and a consuming flame of fire.
29:7 It will be like a dream, a night vision.
There will be a horde from all the nations that fight against Ariel,
those who attack her and her stronghold and besiege her.
29:8 It will be like a hungry man dreaming that he is eating,
only to awaken and find that his stomach is empty.
It will be like a thirsty man dreaming that he is drinking,
only to awaken and find that he is still weak and his thirst unquenched.
So it will be for the horde from all the nations
that fight against Mount Zion.
God's People are Spiritually Insensitive
29:9 You will be shocked and amazed!
You are totally blind!
They are drunk, but not because of wine;
they stagger, but not because of beer.
29:10 For the LORD has poured out on you
a strong urge to sleep deeply.
He has shut your eyes (the prophets),
and covered your heads (the seers).
29:11 To you this entire prophetic revelation is like words in a sealed scroll. When they hand it to one who can read and say, "Read this," he responds, "I can't, because it is sealed." **29:12** Or when they hand the scroll to one who can't read and say, "Read this," he says, "I can't read."
29:13 The sovereign master says,
"These people say they are loyal to me;
they say wonderful things about me,
but they are not really loyal to me.
Their worship consists of
nothing but man-made ritual.
29:14 Therefore I will again do an amazing thing for these people –

an absolutely extraordinary deed.
Wise men will have nothing to say,
the sages will have no explanations."
29:15 Those who try to hide their plans from the LORD are as good as dead,
who do their work in secret and boast,
"Who sees us? Who knows what we're doing?"
29:16 Your thinking is perverse!
Should the potter be regarded as clay?
Should the thing made say about its maker, "He didn't make me"?
Or should the pottery say about the potter, "He doesn't understand"?
Changes are Coming
29:17 In just a very short time
Lebanon will turn into an orchard,
and the orchard will be considered a forest.
29:18 At that time the deaf will be able to hear words read from a scroll,
and the eyes of the blind will be able to see through deep darkness.
29:19 The downtrodden will again rejoice in the LORD;
the poor among humankind will take delight in the Holy One of Israel.
29:20 For tyrants will disappear,
those who taunt will vanish,
and all those who love to do wrong will be eliminated –
29:21 those who bear false testimony against a person,
who entrap the one who arbitrates at the city gate
and deprive the innocent of justice by making false charges.
29:22 So this is what the LORD, the one who delivered Abraham, says to the family of Jacob:
"Jacob will no longer be ashamed;
their faces will no longer show their embarrassment.
29:23 For when they see their children,
whom I will produce among them,
they will honor my name.
They will honor the Holy One of Jacob;
they will respect the God of Israel.
29:24 Those who stray morally will gain understanding;
those who complain will acquire insight.
Egypt Will Prove Unreliable
30:1 "The rebellious children are as good as dead," says the LORD,
"those who make plans without consulting me,
who form alliances without consulting my Spirit,
and thereby compound their sin.
30:2 They travel down to Egypt
without seeking my will,
seeking Pharaoh's protection,
and looking for safety in Egypt's protective shade.
30:3 But Pharaoh's protection will bring you nothing but shame,
and the safety of Egypt's protective shade nothing but humiliation.
30:4 Though his officials are in Zoan
and his messengers arrive at Hanes,
30:5 all will be put to shame
because of a nation that cannot help them,
who cannot give them aid or help,
but only shame and disgrace."
30:6 This is a message about the animals in the Negev:
Through a land of distress and danger,
inhabited by lionesses and roaring lions,

by snakes and darting adders,
they transport their wealth on the backs of donkeys,
their riches on the humps of camels,
to a nation that cannot help them.
30:7 Egypt is totally incapable of helping.
For this reason I call her
'Proud one who is silenced.'"
30:8 Now go, write it down on a tablet in their presence,
inscribe it on a scroll,
so that it might be preserved for a future time
as an enduring witness.
30:9 For these are rebellious people –
they are lying children,
children unwilling to obey the LORD's law.
30:10 They say to the visionaries, "See no more visions!"
and to the seers, "Don't relate messages to us about what is right!
Tell us nice things,
relate deceptive messages.
30:11 Turn aside from the way,
stray off the path.
Remove from our presence the Holy One of Israel."
30:12 For this reason this is what the Holy One of Israel says:
"You have rejected this message;
you trust instead in your ability to oppress and trick,
and rely on that kind of behavior.

30:13 So this sin will become your downfall.
You will be like a high wall
that bulges and cracks and is ready to collapse;
it crumbles suddenly, in a flash.
30:14 It shatters in pieces like a clay jar,
so shattered to bits that none of it can be salvaged.
Among its fragments one cannot find a shard large enough
to scoop a hot coal from a fire
or to skim off water from a cistern."
30:15 For this is what the master, the LORD, the Holy One of Israel says:
"If you repented and patiently waited for me, you would be delivered;
if you calmly trusted in me you would find strength,
but you are unwilling.
30:16 You say, 'No, we will flee on horses,'
so you will indeed flee.
You say, 'We will ride on fast horses,'
so your pursuers will be fast.
30:17 One thousand will scurry at the battle cry of one enemy soldier;
at the battle cry of five enemy soldiers you will all run away,
until the remaining few are as isolated
as a flagpole on a mountaintop
or a signal flag on a hill."
The Lord Will Not Abandon His People
30:18 For this reason the LORD is ready to show you mercy;
he sits on his throne, ready to have compassion on you.
Indeed, the LORD is a just God;
all who wait for him in faith will be blessed.

30:19 For people will live in Zion;
in Jerusalem you will weep no more.
When he hears your cry of despair, he will indeed show you mercy;
when he hears it, he will respond to you.
30:20 The sovereign master will give you distress to eat
and suffering to drink;
but your teachers will no longer be hidden;
your eyes will see them.
30:21 You will hear a word spoken behind you, saying,
"This is the correct way, walk in it,"
whether you are heading to the right or the left.
30:22 You will desecrate your silver-plated idols
and your gold-plated images.
You will throw them away as if they were a menstrual rag,
saying to them, "Get out!"
30:23 He will water the seed you plant in the ground,
and the ground will produce crops in abundance.
At that time your cattle will graze in wide pastures.
30:24 The oxen and donkeys used in plowing
will eat seasoned feed winnowed with a shovel and pitchfork.
30:25 On every high mountain
and every high hill
there will be streams flowing with water,
at the time of great slaughter when the fortified towers collapse.
30:26 The light of the full moon will be like the sun's glare
and the sun's glare will be seven times brighter,
like the light of seven days,
when the LORD binds up his people's fractured bones
and heals their severe wound.
30:27 Look, the name of the LORD comes from a distant place
in raging anger and awesome splendor.
He speaks angrily
and his word is like destructive fire.
30:28 His battle cry overwhelms like a flooding river
that reaches one's neck.
He shakes the nations in a sieve that isolates the chaff;
he puts a bit into the mouth of the nations and leads them to destruction.
30:29 You will sing
as you do in the evening when you are celebrating a festival.
You will be happy like one who plays a flute
as he goes to the mountain of the LORD, the Rock who shelters Israel.
30:30 The LORD will give a mighty shout
and intervene in power,
with furious anger and flaming, destructive fire,
with a driving rainstorm and hailstones.
30:31 Indeed, the LORD's shout will shatter Assyria;
he will beat them with a club.
30:32 Every blow from his punishing cudgel,
with which the LORD will beat them,
will be accompanied by music from the tambourine and harp,
and he will attack them with his weapons.
30:33 For the burial place is already prepared;
it has been made deep and wide for the king.
The firewood is piled high on it.
The LORD's breath, like a stream flowing with brimstone,
will ignite it.
Egypt Will Disappoint
31:1 Those who go down to Egypt for help are as good as dead,
those who rely on war horses,
and trust in Egypt's many chariots
and in their many, many horsemen.
But they do not rely on the Holy One of Israel
and do not seek help from the LORD.
31:2 Yet he too is wise and he will bring disaster;
he does not retract his decree.
He will attack the wicked nation,
and the nation that helps those who commit sin.
31:3 The Egyptians are mere humans, not God;
their horses are made of flesh, not spirit.
The LORD will strike with his hand;
the one who helps will stumble
and the one being helped will fall.
Together they will perish.
The Lord Will Defend Zion
31:4 Indeed, this is what the LORD says to me:
"The LORD will be like a growling lion,
like a young lion growling over its prey.
Though a whole group of shepherds gathers against it,
it is not afraid of their shouts
or intimidated by their yelling.
In this same way the LORD who commands armies will descend
to do battle on Mount Zion and on its hill.
31:5 Just as birds hover over a nest,
so the LORD who commands armies will protect Jerusalem.
He will protect and deliver it;
as he passes over he will rescue it.
31:6 You Israelites! Return to the one against whom you have so blatantly rebelled! **31:7** For at that time everyone will get rid of the silver and gold idols your hands sinfully made.
31:8 Assyria will fall by a sword, but not one human-made;
a sword not made by humankind will destroy them.
They will run away from this sword
and their young men will be forced to do hard labor.
31:9 They will surrender their stronghold because of fear;
their officers will be afraid of the LORD's battle flag."
This is what the LORD says –
the one whose fire is in Zion,
whose firepot is in Jerusalem.
Justice and Wisdom Will Prevail
32:1 Look, a king will promote fairness;
officials will promote justice.
32:2 Each of them will be like a shelter from the wind
and a refuge from a rainstorm;
like streams of water in a dry region
and like the shade of a large cliff in a parched land.
32:3 Eyes will no longer be blind
and ears will be attentive.
32:4 The mind that acts rashly will possess discernment
and the tongue that stutters will speak with ease and clarity.
32:5 A fool will no longer be called honorable;
a deceiver will no longer be called principled.
32:6 For a fool speaks disgraceful things;
his mind plans out sinful deeds.
He commits godless deeds
and says misleading things about the LORD;
he gives the hungry nothing to satisfy their appetite
and gives the thirsty nothing to drink.
32:7 A deceiver's methods are evil;
he dreams up evil plans
to ruin the poor with lies,
even when the needy are in the right.
32:8 An honorable man makes honorable plans;
his honorable character gives him security.
The Lord Will Give True Security
32:9 You complacent women,
get up and listen to me!
You carefree daughters,
pay attention to what I say!
32:10 In a year's time
you carefree ones will shake with fear,
for the grape harvest will fail,
and the fruit harvest will not arrive.
32:11 Tremble, you complacent ones!
Shake with fear, you carefree ones!
Strip off your clothes and expose yourselves –
put sackcloth on your waist!
32:12 Mourn over the field,
over the delightful fields

and the fruitful vine!

32:13 Mourn over the land of my people,
which is overgrown with thorns and briers,
and over all the once-happy houses
in the city filled with revelry.
32:14 For the fortress is neglected;
the once-crowded city is abandoned.
Hill and watchtower
are permanently uninhabited.
Wild donkeys love to go there,
and flocks graze there.
32:15 This desolation will continue until new life is poured out on us from heaven.
Then the desert will become an orchard
and the orchard will be considered a forest.
32:16 Justice will settle down in the desert
and fairness will live in the orchard.
32:17 Fairness will produce peace
and result in lasting security.
32:18 My people will live in peaceful settlements,
in secure homes,
and in safe, quiet places.
32:19 Even if the forest is destroyed
and the city is annihilated,
32:20 you will be blessed,
you who plant seed by all the banks of the streams,
you who let your ox and donkey graze.

The Lord Will Restore Zion

33:1 The destroyer is as good as dead,
you who have not been destroyed!
The deceitful one is as good as dead,
the one whom others have not deceived!
When you are through destroying, you will be destroyed;
when you finish deceiving, others will deceive you!
33:2 LORD, be merciful to us! We wait for you.
Give us strength each morning!
Deliver us when distress comes.
33:3 The nations run away when they hear a loud noise;
the nations scatter when you spring into action!
33:4 Your plunder disappears as if locusts were eating it;
they swarm over it like locusts!
33:5 The LORD is exalted,
indeed, he lives in heaven;
he fills Zion with justice and fairness.
33:6 He is your constant source of stability;
he abundantly provides safety and great wisdom;
he gives all this to those who fear him.
33:7 Look, ambassadors cry out in the streets;
messengers sent to make peace weep bitterly.
33:8 Highways are empty,
there are no travelers.
Treaties are broken,
witnesses are despised,
human life is treated with disrespect.
33:9 The land dries up and withers away;
the forest of Lebanon shrivels up and decays.
Sharon is like the desert;
Bashan and Carmel are parched.
33:10 "Now I will rise up," says the LORD.
"Now I will exalt myself;
now I will magnify myself.
33:11 You conceive straw,
you give birth to chaff;
your breath is a fire that destroys you.
33:12 The nations will be burned to ashes;
like thorn bushes that have been cut down, they will be set on fire.
33:13 You who are far away, listen to what I have done!
You who are close by, recognize my strength!"
33:14 Sinners are afraid in Zion;
panic grips the godless.
They say, 'Who among us can coexist with destructive fire?
Who among us can coexist with unquenchable fire?'
33:15 The one who lives uprightly
and speaks honestly;
the one who refuses to profit from oppressive measures
and rejects a bribe;
the one who does not plot violent crimes
and does not seek to harm others –
33:16 This is the person who will live in a secure place;
he will find safety in the rocky, mountain strongholds;
he will have food
and a constant supply of water.
33:17 You will see a king in his splendor;

you will see a wide land.
33:18 Your mind will recall the terror you experienced,
and you will ask yourselves, "Where is the scribe?
Where is the one who weighs the money?
Where is the one who counts the towers?"
33:19 You will no longer see a defiant people
whose language you do not comprehend,
whose derisive speech you do not understand.
33:20 Look at Zion, the city where we hold religious festivals!
You will see Jerusalem,
a peaceful settlement,
a tent that stays put;
its stakes will never be pulled up;
none of its ropes will snap in two.
33:21 Instead the LORD will rule there as our mighty king.
Rivers and wide streams will flow through it;
no war galley will enter;
no large ships will sail through.
33:22 For the LORD, our ruler,
the LORD, our commander,
the LORD, our king –
he will deliver us.
33:23 Though at this time your ropes are slack,
the mast is not secured,
and the sail is not unfurled,
at that time you will divide up a great quantity of loot;
even the lame will drag off plunder.
33:24 No resident of Zion will say, "I am ill";
the people who live there will have their sin forgiven.

The Lord Will Judge Edom

34:1 Come near, you nations, and listen!
Pay attention, you people!
The earth and everything it contains must listen,
the world and everything that lives in it.
34:2 For the LORD is angry at all the nations
and furious with all their armies.
He will annihilate them and slaughter them.
34:3 Their slain will be left unburied,
their corpses will stink;
the hills will soak up their blood.
34:4 All the stars in the sky will fade away,
the sky will roll up like a scroll;
all its stars will wither,
like a leaf withers and falls from a vine
or a fig withers and falls from a tree.
34:5 He says, "Indeed, my sword has slaughtered heavenly powers.
Look, it now descends on Edom,
on the people I will annihilate in judgment."
34:6 The LORD's sword is dripping with blood,
it is covered with fat;
it drips with the blood of young rams and goats
and is covered with the fat of rams' kidneys.
For the LORD is holding a sacrifice in Bozrah,
a bloody slaughter in the land of Edom.
34:7 Wild oxen will be slaughtered along with them,
as well as strong bulls.
Their land is drenched with blood,
their soil is covered with fat.
34:8 For the LORD has planned a day of revenge,
a time when he will repay Edom for her hostility toward Zion.
34:9 Edom's streams will be turned into pitch
and her soil into brimstone;
her land will become burning pitch.
34:10 Night and day it will burn;
its smoke will ascend continually.
Generation after generation it will be a wasteland
and no one will ever pass through it again.
34:11 Owls and wild animals will live there,
all kinds of wild birds will settle in it.
The LORD will stretch out over her
the measuring line of ruin
and the plumb line of destruction.
34:12 Her nobles will have nothing left to call a kingdom
and all her officials will disappear.
34:13 Her fortresses will be overgrown with thorns;
thickets and weeds will grow in her fortified cities.
Jackals will settle there;
ostriches will live there.
34:14 Wild animals and wild dogs will congregate there;
wild goats will bleat to one another.
Yes, nocturnal animals will rest there
and make for themselves a nest.
34:15 Owls will make nests and lay eggs there;

they will hatch them and protect them.
Yes, hawks will gather there,
each with its mate.
34:16 Carefully read the scroll of the LORD!
Not one of these creatures will be missing,
none will lack a mate.
For the LORD has issued the decree,
and his own spirit gathers them.
34:17 He assigns them their allotment;
he measures out their assigned place.
They will live there permanently;
they will settle in it through successive generations.

The Land and Its People Are Transformed

35:1 Let the desert and dry region be happy;
let the wilderness rejoice and bloom like a lily!
35:2 Let it richly bloom;
let it rejoice and shout with delight!
It is given the grandeur of Lebanon,
the splendor of Carmel and Sharon.
They will see the grandeur of the LORD,
the splendor of our God.
35:3 Strengthen the hands that have gone limp,
steady the knees that shake!
35:4 Tell those who panic,
"Be strong! Do not fear!
Look, your God comes to avenge!
With divine retribution he comes to deliver you."
35:5 Then blind eyes will open,
deaf ears will hear.
35:6 Then the lame will leap like a deer,
the mute tongue will shout for joy;
for water will flow in the desert,
streams in the wilderness.
35:7 The dry soil will become a pool of water,
the parched ground springs of water.
Where jackals once lived and sprawled out,
grass, reeds, and papyrus will grow.
35:8 A thoroughfare will be there –
it will be called the Way of Holiness.
The unclean will not travel on it;
it is reserved for those authorized to use it –
fools will not stray into it.
35:9 No lions will be there,
no ferocious wild animals will be on it –
they will not be found there.
Those delivered from bondage will travel on it,
35:10 those whom the LORD has ransomed will return that way.
They will enter Zion with a happy shout.
Unending joy will crown them,
happiness and joy will overwhelm them;
grief and suffering will disappear.

Sennacherib Invades Judah

36:1 In the fourteenth year of King Hezekiah's reign, King Sennacherib of Assyria marched up against all the fortified cities of Judah and captured them. **36:2** The king of Assyria sent his chief adviser from Lachish to King Hezekiah in Jerusalem, along with a large army. The chief adviser stood at the conduit of the upper pool which is located on the road to the field where they wash and dry cloth. **36:3** Eliakim son of Hilkiah, the palace supervisor, accompanied by Shebna the scribe and Joah son of Asaph, the secretary, went out to meet him.
36:4 The chief adviser said to them, "Tell Hezekiah: 'This is what the great king, the king of Assyria, says: "What is your source of confidence? **36:5** Your claim to have a strategy and military strength is just empty talk. In whom are you trusting, that you would dare to rebel against me? **36:6** Look, you must be trusting in Egypt, that splintered reed staff. If someone leans on it for support, it punctures his hand and wounds him. That is what Pharaoh king of Egypt does to all who trust in him! **36:7** Perhaps you will tell me, 'We are trusting in the LORD our God.' But Hezekiah is the one who eliminated his high places and altars and then told the people of Judah and Jerusalem, 'You must worship at this altar.' **36:8** Now make a deal with my master the king of Assyria, and I will give you two thousand horses, provided you can find enough riders for them. **36:9** Certainly you will not refuse one of my master's minor officials and trust in Egypt for chariots and horsemen. **36:10** Furthermore it was by the command of the LORD that I marched up against this land to destroy it. The LORD told me, 'March up against this land and destroy it!'"'"
36:11 Eliakim, Shebna, and Joah said to the chief adviser, "Speak to your servants in Aramaic, for we understand it. Don't speak with us in the Judahite dialect in the hearing of the people who are on the wall." **36:12** But the chief adviser said, "My master did not send me to speak these words only to your master and to you. His message is also for the men who sit on the wall, for they will eat their own excrement and drink their own urine along with you!"
36:13 The chief adviser then stood there and called out loudly in the Judahite dialect, "Listen to the message of the great king, the king of Assyria. **36:14** This is what the king says: 'Don't let Hezekiah mislead you, for he is not able to rescue you! **36:15** Don't let Hezekiah talk you into trusting in the LORD by saying, "The LORD will certainly rescue us; this city will not be handed over to the king of Assyria." **36:16** Don't listen to Hezekiah!' For this is what the king of Assyria says, 'Send me a token of your submission and surrender to me. Then each of you may eat from his own vine and fig tree and drink water from his own cistern, **36:17** until I come and take you to a land just like your own – a land of grain and new wine, a land of bread and vineyards. **36:18** Hezekiah is misleading you when he says, "The LORD will rescue us." Has any of the gods of the nations rescued his land from the power of the king of Assyria? **36:19** Where are the gods of Hamath and Arpad? Where are the gods of Sepharvaim? Indeed, did any gods rescue Samaria from my power? **36:20** Who among all the gods of these lands have rescued their lands from my power? So how can the LORD rescue Jerusalem from my power?'" **36:21** They were silent and did not respond, for the king had ordered, "Don't respond to him."
36:22 Eliakim son of Hilkiah, the palace supervisor, accompanied by Shebna the scribe and Joah son of Asaph, the secretary, went to Hezekiah with their clothes torn in grief and reported to him what the chief adviser had said. **37:1** When King Hezekiah heard this, he tore his clothes, put on sackcloth, and went to the LORD's temple. **37:2** Eliakim the palace supervisor, Shebna the scribe, and the leading priests, clothed in sackcloth, sent this message to the prophet Isaiah son of Amoz: **37:3** "This is what Hezekiah says: 'This is a day of distress, insults, and humiliation, as when a baby is ready to leave the birth canal, but the mother lacks the strength to push it through. **37:4** Perhaps the LORD your God will hear all these things the chief adviser has spoken on behalf of his master, the king of Assyria, who sent him to taunt the living God. When the LORD your God hears, perhaps he will punish him for the things he has said. So pray for this remnant that remains.'"
37:5 When King Hezekiah's servants came to Isaiah, **37:6** Isaiah said to them, "Tell your master this: 'This is what the LORD says: "Don't be afraid because of the things you have heard – these insults the king of Assyria's servants have hurled against me. **37:7** Look, I will take control of his mind; he will receive a report and return to his own land. I will cut him down with a sword in his own land."'"
37:8 When the chief adviser heard the king of Assyria had departed from Lachish, he left and went to Libnah, where the king was campaigning. **37:9** The king heard that King Tirhakah of Ethiopia was marching out to fight him. He again sent messengers to Hezekiah, ordering them: **37:10** "Tell King Hezekiah of Judah this: 'Don't let your God in whom you trust mislead you when he says, "Jerusalem will not be handed over to the king of Assyria." **37:11** Certainly you have heard how the kings of Assyria have annihilated all lands. Do you really think you will be rescued? **37:12** Were the nations whom my predecessors destroyed – the nations of Gozan, Haran, Rezeph, and the people of Eden in Telassar – rescued by their gods? **37:13** Where are the king of Hamath, the king of Arpad, and the kings of Lair, Sepharvaim, Hena, and Ivvah?'"
37:14 Hezekiah took the letter from the messengers and read it. Then Hezekiah went up to the LORD's temple and spread it out before the LORD. **37:15** Hezekiah prayed before the LORD: **37:16** "O LORD who commands armies, O God of Israel, who is enthroned on the cherubim! You alone are God over all the kingdoms of the earth. You made the sky and the earth. **37:17** Pay attention, LORD, and hear! Open your eyes, LORD, and observe! Listen to this entire message Sennacherib sent and how he taunts the living God! **37:18** It is true, LORD, that the kings of Assyria have destroyed all the nations and their lands. **37:19** They have burned the gods of the nations, for they are not really gods, but only the product of human hands manufactured from wood and stone. That is why the Assyrians could destroy them. **37:20** Now, O LORD our God, rescue us from his power, so all the kingdoms of the earth may know that you alone are the LORD."
37:21 Isaiah son of Amoz sent this message to Hezekiah: "This is what the LORD God of Israel says: 'Because you prayed to me concerning King Sennacherib of Assyria, **37:22** this is what the LORD says about him:
"The virgin daughter Zion
despises you – she makes fun of you;
daughter Jerusalem
shakes her head after you.
37:23 Whom have you taunted and hurled insults at?
At whom have you shouted
and looked so arrogantly?
At the Holy One of Israel!
37:24 Through your messengers you taunted the sovereign master,
'With my many chariots I climbed up
the high mountains,
the slopes of Lebanon.

I cut down its tall cedars
and its best evergreens.
I invaded its most remote regions,
its thickest woods.
37:25 I dug wells
and drank water.
With the soles of my feet I dried up
all the rivers of Egypt.'
37:26 Certainly you must have heard!
Long ago I worked it out,
in ancient times I planned it,
and now I am bringing it to pass.
The plan is this:
Fortified cities will crash
into heaps of ruins.
37:27 Their residents are powerless;
they are terrified and ashamed.
They are as short-lived as plants in the field
or green vegetation.
They are as short-lived as grass on the rooftops
when it is scorched by the east wind.
37:28 I know where you live
and everything you do
and how you rage against me.
37:29 Because you rage against me
and the uproar you create has reached my ears,
I will put my hook in your nose,
and my bridle between your lips,
and I will lead you back
the way you came."

37:30 "This will be your reminder that I have spoken the truth: This year you will eat what grows wild, and next year what grows on its own. But the year after that you will plant seed and harvest crops; you will plant vines and consume their produce. **37:31** Those who remain in Judah will take root in the ground and bear fruit.
37:32 "For a remnant will leave Jerusalem;
survivors will come out of Mount Zion.
The intense devotion of the LORD who commands armies will accomplish this.
37:33 So this is what the LORD says about the king of Assyria:
'He will not enter this city,
nor will he shoot an arrow here.
He will not attack it with his shielded warriors,
nor will he build siege works against it.
37:34 He will go back the way he came –
he will not enter this city,' says the LORD.
37:35 I will shield this city and rescue it for the sake of my reputation and because of my promise to David my servant."'"

37:36 The LORD's messenger went out and killed 185,000 troops in the Assyrian camp. When they got up early the next morning, there were all the corpses! **37:37** So King Sennacherib of Assyria broke camp and went on his way. He went home and stayed in Nineveh. **37:38** One day, as he was worshiping in the temple of his god Nisroch, his sons Adrammelech and Sharezer struck him down with the sword. They ran away to the land of Ararat; his son Esarhaddon replaced him as king.
The Lord Hears Hezekiah's Prayer
38:1 In those days Hezekiah was stricken with a terminal illness. The prophet Isaiah son of Amoz visited him and told him, "This is what the LORD says, 'Give instructions to your household, for you are about to die; you will not get well.'" **38:2** Hezekiah turned his face to the wall and prayed to the LORD, **38:3** "Please, LORD. Remember how I have served you faithfully and with wholehearted devotion, and how I have carried out your will." Then Hezekiah wept bitterly.
38:4 The LORD told Isaiah, **38:5** "Go and tell Hezekiah: 'This is what the LORD God of your ancestor David says: "I have heard your prayer; I have seen your tears. Look, I will add fifteen years to your life, **38:6** and rescue you and this city from the king of Assyria. I will shield this city."'" **38:21** Isaiah ordered, "Let them take a fig cake and apply it to the ulcerated sore and he will get well." **38:22** Hezekiah said, "What is the confirming sign that I will go up to the LORD's temple?" **38:7** Isaiah replied, "This is your sign from the LORD confirming that the LORD will do what he has said: **38:8** Look, I will make the shadow go back ten steps on the stairs of Ahaz." And then the shadow went back ten steps.
Hezekiah's Song of Thanks
38:9 This is the prayer of King Hezekiah of Judah when he was sick and then recovered from his illness:
38:10 "I thought,
'In the middle of my life I must walk through the gates of Sheol,
I am deprived of the rest of my years.'
38:11 "I thought,
'I will no longer see the LORD in the land of the living,

I will no longer look on humankind with the inhabitants of the world.
38:12 My dwelling place is removed and taken away from me
like a shepherd's tent.
I rolled up my life like a weaver rolls cloth;
from the loom he cuts me off.
You turn day into night and end my life.
38:13 I cry out until morning;
like a lion he shatters all my bones;
you turn day into night and end my life.
38:14 Like a swallow or a thrush I chirp,
I coo like a dove;
my eyes grow tired from looking up to the sky.
O sovereign master, I am oppressed;
help me!
38:15 What can I say?
He has decreed and acted.
I will walk slowly all my years because I am overcome with grief.
38:16 O sovereign master, your decrees can give men life;
may years of life be restored to me.
Restore my health and preserve my life.'
38:17 "Look, the grief I experienced was for my benefit.
You delivered me from the pit of oblivion.
For you removed all my sins from your sight.
38:18 Indeed Sheol does not give you thanks;
death does not praise you.
Those who descend into the pit do not anticipate your faithfulness.
38:19 The living person, the living person, he gives you thanks,
as I do today.
A father tells his sons about your faithfulness.
38:20 The LORD is about to deliver me,
and we will celebrate with music
for the rest of our lives in the LORD's temple."
Messengers from Babylon Visit Hezekiah
39:1 At that time Merodach-Baladan son of Baladan, king of Babylon, sent letters and a gift to Hezekiah, for he heard that Hezekiah had been ill and had recovered. **39:2** Hezekiah welcomed them and showed them his storehouse with its silver, gold, spices, and high-quality olive oil, as well as his whole armory and everything in his treasuries. Hezekiah showed them everything in his palace and in his whole kingdom. **39:3** Isaiah the prophet visited King Hezekiah and asked him, "What did these men say? Where do they come from?" Hezekiah replied, "They come from the distant land of Babylon." **39:4** Isaiah asked, "What have they seen in your palace?" Hezekiah replied, "They have seen everything in my palace. I showed them everything in my treasuries." **39:5** Isaiah said to Hezekiah, "Listen to the word of the LORD who commands armies: **39:6** 'Look, a time is coming when everything in your palace and the things your ancestors have accumulated to this day will be carried away to Babylon; nothing will be left,' says the LORD. **39:7** 'Some of your very own descendants whom you father will be taken away and will be made eunuchs in the palace of the king of Babylon.'" **39:8** Hezekiah said to Isaiah, "The LORD's word which you have announced is appropriate." Then he thought, "For there will be peace and stability during my lifetime."
The Lord Returns to Jerusalem
40:1 "Comfort, comfort my people,"
says your God.
40:2 "Speak kindly to Jerusalem, and tell her
that her time of warfare is over,
that her punishment is completed.
For the LORD has made her pay double for all her sins."
40:3 A voice cries out,
"In the wilderness clear a way for the LORD;
construct in the desert a road for our God.
40:4 Every valley must be elevated,
and every mountain and hill leveled.
The rough terrain will become a level plain,
the rugged landscape a wide valley.
40:5 The splendor of the LORD will be revealed,
and all people will see it at the same time.
For the LORD has decreed it."
40:6 A voice says, "Cry out!"
Another asks, "What should I cry out?"
The first voice responds: "All people are like grass,
and all their promises are like the flowers in the field.
40:7 The grass dries up,
the flowers wither,
when the wind sent by the LORD blows on them.
Surely humanity is like grass.
40:8 The grass dries up,
the flowers wither,
but the decree of our God is forever reliable."
40:9 Go up on a high mountain, O herald Zion!
Shout out loudly, O herald Jerusalem!
Shout, don't be afraid!

Say to the towns of Judah,
"Here is your God!"
40:10 Look, the sovereign LORD comes as a victorious warrior;
his military power establishes his rule.
Look, his reward is with him;
his prize goes before him.
40:11 Like a shepherd he tends his flock;
he gathers up the lambs with his arm;
he carries them close to his heart;
he leads the ewes along.

The Lord is Incomparable

40:12 Who has measured out the waters in the hollow of his hand,
or carefully measured the sky,
or carefully weighed the soil of the earth,
or weighed the mountains in a balance,
or the hills on scales?
40:13 Who comprehends the mind of the LORD,
or gives him instruction as his counselor?
40:14 From whom does he receive directions?
Who teaches him the correct way to do things,
or imparts knowledge to him,
or instructs him in skillful design?
40:15 Look, the nations are like a drop in a bucket;
they are regarded as dust on the scales.
He lifts the coastlands as if they were dust.
40:16 Not even Lebanon could supply enough firewood for a sacrifice;
its wild animals would not provide enough burnt offerings.
40:17 All the nations are insignificant before him;
they are regarded as absolutely nothing.
40:18 To whom can you compare God?
To what image can you liken him?
40:19 A craftsman casts an idol;
a metalsmith overlays it with gold
and forges silver chains for it.
40:20 To make a contribution one selects wood that will not rot;
he then seeks a skilled craftsman
to make an idol that will not fall over.
40:21 Do you not know?
Do you not hear?
Has it not been told to you since the very beginning?
Have you not understood from the time the earth's foundations were made?
40:22 He is the one who sits on the earth's horizon;
its inhabitants are like grasshoppers before him.
He is the one who stretches out the sky like a thin curtain,
and spreads it out like a pitched tent.
40:23 He is the one who reduces rulers to nothing;
he makes the earth's leaders insignificant.
40:24 Indeed, they are barely planted;
yes, they are barely sown;
yes, they barely take root in the earth,
and then he blows on them, causing them to dry up,
and the wind carries them away like straw.
40:25 "To whom can you compare me? Whom do I resemble?"
says the Holy One.
40:26 Look up at the sky!
Who created all these heavenly lights?
He is the one who leads out their ranks;
he calls them all by name.
Because of his absolute power and awesome strength,
not one of them is missing.
40:27 Why do you say, Jacob,
Why do you say, Israel,
"The LORD is not aware of what is happening to me,
My God is not concerned with my vindication"?
40:28 Do you not know?
Have you not heard?
The LORD is an eternal God,
the creator of the whole earth.
He does not get tired or weary;
there is no limit to his wisdom.
40:29 He gives strength to those who are tired;
to the ones who lack power, he gives renewed energy.
40:30 Even youths get tired and weary;
even strong young men clumsily stumble.
40:31 But those who wait for the LORD's help find renewed strength;
they rise up as if they had eagles' wings,
they run without growing weary,
they walk without getting tired.

The Lord Challenges the Nations

41:1 "Listen to me in silence, you coastlands!
Let the nations find renewed strength!
Let them approach and then speak;
let us come together for debate!
41:2 Who stirs up this one from the east?
Who officially commissions him for service?
He hands nations over to him,
and enables him to subdue kings.
He makes them like dust with his sword,
like windblown straw with his bow.
41:3 He pursues them and passes by unharmed;
he advances with great speed.
41:4 Who acts and carries out decrees?
Who summons the successive generations from the beginning?
I, the LORD, am present at the very beginning,
and at the very end – I am the one.
41:5 The coastlands see and are afraid;
the whole earth trembles;
they approach and come.
41:6 They help one another;
one says to the other, 'Be strong!'
41:7 The craftsman encourages the metalsmith,
the one who wields the hammer encourages the one who pounds on the anvil.
He approves the quality of the welding,
and nails it down so it won't fall over."

The Lord Encourages His People

41:8 "You, my servant Israel,
Jacob whom I have chosen,
offspring of Abraham my friend,
41:9 you whom I am bringing back from the earth's extremities,
and have summoned from the remote regions –
I told you, "You are my servant."
I have chosen you and not rejected you.
41:10 Don't be afraid, for I am with you!
Don't be frightened, for I am your God!
I strengthen you –
yes, I help you –
yes, I uphold you with my saving right hand!
41:11 Look, all who were angry at you will be ashamed and humiliated;
your adversaries will be reduced to nothing and perish.
41:12 When you will look for your opponents, you will not find them;
your enemies will be reduced to absolutely nothing.
41:13 For I am the LORD your God,
the one who takes hold of your right hand,
who says to you, 'Don't be afraid, I am helping you.'
41:14 Don't be afraid, despised insignificant Jacob,
men of Israel.
I am helping you," says the LORD,
your protector, the Holy One of Israel.
41:15 "Look, I am making you like a sharp threshing sledge,
new and double-edged.
You will thresh the mountains and crush them;
you will make the hills like straw.
41:16 You will winnow them and the wind will blow them away;
the wind will scatter them.
You will rejoice in the LORD;
you will boast in the Holy One of Israel.
41:17 The oppressed and the poor look for water, but there is none;
their tongues are parched from thirst.
I, the LORD, will respond to their prayers;
I, the God of Israel, will not abandon them.
41:18 I will make streams flow down the slopes
and produce springs in the middle of the valleys.
I will turn the desert into a pool of water
and the arid land into springs.
41:19 I will make cedars, acacias, myrtles, and olive trees grow in the wilderness;
I will make evergreens, firs, and cypresses grow together in the desert.
41:20 I will do this so people will observe and recognize,
so they will pay attention and understand
that the LORD's power has accomplished this,
and that the Holy One of Israel has brought it into being."

The Lord Challenges the Pagan Gods

41:21 "Present your argument," says the LORD.
"Produce your evidence," says Jacob's king.
41:22 "Let them produce evidence! Let them tell us what will happen!
Tell us about your earlier predictive oracles,
so we may examine them and see how they were fulfilled.
Or decree for us some future events!
41:23 Predict how future events will turn out,
so we might know you are gods.
Yes, do something good or bad,
so we might be frightened and in awe.
41:24 Look, you are nothing, and your accomplishments are nonexistent;
the one who chooses to worship you is disgusting.

41:25 I have stirred up one out of the north and he advances,
one from the eastern horizon who prays in my name.
He steps on rulers as if they were clay,
like a potter treading the clay.
41:26 Who decreed this from the beginning, so we could know?
Who announced it ahead of time, so we could say, 'He's correct'?
Indeed, none of them decreed it!
Indeed, none of them announced it!
Indeed, no one heard you say anything!
41:27 I first decreed to Zion, 'Look, here's what will happen!'
I sent a herald to Jerusalem.
41:28 I look, but there is no one,
among them there is no one who serves as an adviser,
that I might ask questions and receive answers.
41:29 Look, all of them are nothing,
their accomplishments are nonexistent;
their metal images lack any real substance.

The Lord Commissions His Special Servant

42:1 "Here is my servant whom I support,
my chosen one in whom I take pleasure.
I have placed my spirit on him;
he will make just decrees for the nations.
42:2 He will not cry out or shout;
he will not publicize himself in the streets.
42:3 A crushed reed he will not break,
a dim wick he will not extinguish;
he will faithfully make just decrees.
42:4 He will not grow dim or be crushed
before establishing justice on the earth;
the coastlands will wait in anticipation for his decrees."
42:5 This is what the true God, the LORD, says –
the one who created the sky and stretched it out,
the one who fashioned the earth and everything that lives on it,
the one who gives breath to the people on it,
and life to those who live on it:
42:6 "I, the LORD, officially commission you;
I take hold of your hand.
I protect you and make you a covenant mediator for people,
and a light to the nations,
42:7 to open blind eyes,
to release prisoners from dungeons,
those who live in darkness from prisons.

The Lord Intervenes

42:8 I am the LORD! That is my name!
I will not share my glory with anyone else,
or the praise due me with idols.
42:9 Look, my earlier predictive oracles have come to pass;
now I announce new events.
Before they begin to occur,
I reveal them to you."
42:10 Sing to the LORD a brand new song!
Praise him from the horizon of the earth,
you who go down to the sea, and everything that lives in it,
you coastlands and those who live there!
42:11 Let the desert and its cities shout out,
the towns where the nomads of Kedar live!
Let the residents of Sela shout joyfully;
let them shout loudly from the mountaintops.
42:12 Let them give the LORD the honor he deserves;
let them praise his deeds in the coastlands.
42:13 The LORD emerges like a hero,
like a warrior he inspires himself for battle;
he shouts, yes, he yells,
he shows his enemies his power.
42:14 "I have been inactive for a long time;
I kept quiet and held back.
Like a woman in labor I groan;
I pant and gasp.
42:15 I will make the trees on the mountains and hills wither up;
I will dry up all their vegetation.
I will turn streams into islands,
and dry up pools of water.
42:16 I will lead the blind along an unfamiliar way;
I will guide them down paths they have never traveled.
I will turn the darkness in front of them into light,
and level out the rough ground.
This is what I will do for them.
I will not abandon them.
42:17 Those who trust in idols
will turn back and be utterly humiliated,
those who say to metal images, 'You are our gods.'"

The Lord Reasons with His People

42:18 "Listen, you deaf ones!
Take notice, you blind ones!
42:19 My servant is truly blind,
my messenger is truly deaf.
My covenant partner, the servant of the LORD, is truly blind.
42:20 You see many things, but don't comprehend;
their ears are open, but do not hear."
42:21 The LORD wanted to exhibit his justice
by magnifying his law and displaying it.
42:22 But these people are looted and plundered;
all of them are trapped in pits
and held captive in prisons.
They were carried away as loot with no one to rescue them;
they were carried away as plunder, and no one says, "Bring that back!"
42:23 Who among you will pay attention to this?
Who will listen attentively in the future?
42:24 Who handed Jacob over to the robber?
Who handed Israel over to the looters?
Was it not the LORD, against whom we sinned?
They refused to follow his commands;
they disobeyed his law.
42:25 So he poured out his fierce anger on them,
along with the devastation of war.
Its flames encircled them, but they did not realize it;
it burned against them, but they did notice.

The Lord Will Rescue His People

43:1 Now, this is what the LORD says,
the one who created you, O Jacob,
and formed you, O Israel:
"Don't be afraid, for I will protect you.
I call you by name, you are mine.
43:2 When you pass through the waters, I am with you;
when you pass through the streams, they will not overwhelm you.
When you walk through the fire, you will not be burned;
the flames will not harm you.
43:3 For I am the LORD your God,
the Holy One of Israel, your deliverer.
I have handed over Egypt as a ransom price,
Ethiopia and Seba in place of you.
43:4 Since you are precious and special in my sight,
and I love you,
I will hand over people in place of you,
nations in place of your life.
43:5 Don't be afraid, for I am with you.
From the east I will bring your descendants;
from the west I will gather you.
43:6 I will say to the north, 'Hand them over!'
and to the south, 'Don't hold any back!'
Bring my sons from distant lands,
and my daughters from the remote regions of the earth,
43:7 everyone who belongs to me,
whom I created for my glory,
whom I formed – yes, whom I made!

The Lord Declares His Sovereignty

43:8 Bring out the people who are blind, even though they have eyes,
those who are deaf, even though they have ears!
43:9 All nations gather together,
the peoples assemble.
Who among them announced this?
Who predicted earlier events for us?
Let them produce their witnesses to testify they were right;
let them listen and affirm, 'It is true.'
43:10 You are my witnesses," says the LORD,
"my servant whom I have chosen,
so that you may consider and believe in me,
and understand that I am he.
No god was formed before me,
and none will outlive me.
43:11 I, I am the LORD,
and there is no deliverer besides me.
43:12 I decreed and delivered and proclaimed,
and there was no other god among you.
You are my witnesses," says the LORD, "that I am God.
43:13 From this day forward I am he;
no one can deliver from my power;
I will act, and who can prevent it?"

The Lord Will Do Something New

43:14 This is what the LORD says,
your protector, the Holy One of Israel:
"For your sake I send to Babylon
and make them all fugitives,
turning the Babylonians' joyful shouts into mourning songs.
43:15 I am the LORD, your Holy One,
the one who created Israel, your king."

43:16 This is what the LORD says,
the one who made a road through the sea,
a pathway through the surging waters,
43:17 the one who led chariots and horses to destruction,
together with a mighty army.
They fell down, never to rise again;
they were extinguished, put out like a burning wick:
43:18 "Don't remember these earlier events;
don't recall these former events.

43:19 "Look, I am about to do something new.
Now it begins to happen! Do you not recognize it?
Yes, I will make a road in the desert
and paths in the wilderness.
43:20 The wild animals of the desert honor me,
the jackals and ostriches,
because I put water in the desert
and streams in the wilderness,
to quench the thirst of my chosen people,
43:21 the people whom I formed for myself,
so they might praise me."

The Lord Rebukes His People

43:22 "But you did not call for me, O Jacob;
you did not long for me, O Israel.
43:23 You did not bring me lambs for your burnt offerings;
you did not honor me with your sacrifices.
I did not burden you with offerings;
I did not make you weary by demanding incense.
43:24 You did not buy me aromatic reeds;
you did not present to me the fat of your sacrifices.
Yet you burdened me with your sins;
you made me weary with your evil deeds.
43:25 I, I am the one who blots out your rebellious deeds for my sake;
your sins I do not remember.
43:26 Remind me of what happened! Let's debate!
You, prove to me that you are right!
43:27 The father of your nation sinned;
your spokesmen rebelled against me.
43:28 So I defiled your holy princes,
and handed Jacob over to destruction,
and subjected Israel to humiliating abuse."

The Lord Will Renew Israel

44:1 "Now, listen, Jacob my servant,
Israel whom I have chosen!"
44:2 This is what the LORD, the one who made you, says –
the one who formed you in the womb and helps you:
"Don't be afraid, my servant Jacob,
Jeshurun, whom I have chosen!
44:3 For I will pour water on the parched ground
and cause streams to flow on the dry land.
I will pour my spirit on your offspring
and my blessing on your children.
44:4 They will sprout up like a tree in the grass,
like poplars beside channels of water.
44:5 One will say, 'I belong to the LORD,'
and another will use the name 'Jacob.'
One will write on his hand, 'The LORD's,'
and use the name 'Israel.'"

The Absurdity of Idolatry

44:6 This is what the LORD, Israel's king, says,
their protector, the LORD who commands armies:
"I am the first and I am the last,
there is no God but me.
44:7 Who is like me? Let him make his claim!
Let him announce it and explain it to me –
since I established an ancient people –
let them announce future events!
44:8 Don't panic! Don't be afraid!
Did I not tell you beforehand and decree it?
You are my witnesses! Is there any God but me?
There is no other sheltering rock; I know of none.
44:9 All who form idols are nothing;
the things in which they delight are worthless.
Their witnesses cannot see;
they recognize nothing, so they are put to shame.
44:10 Who forms a god and casts an idol
that will prove worthless?
44:11 Look, all his associates will be put to shame;
the craftsmen are mere humans.
Let them all assemble and take their stand!
They will panic and be put to shame.
44:12 A blacksmith works with his tool
and forges metal over the coals.

He forms it with hammers;
he makes it with his strong arm.
He gets hungry and loses his energy;
he drinks no water and gets tired.
44:13 A carpenter takes measurements;
he marks out an outline of its form;
he scrapes it with chisels,
and marks it with a compass.
He patterns it after the human form,
like a well-built human being,
and puts it in a shrine.
44:14 He cuts down cedars
and acquires a cypress or an oak.
He gets trees from the forest;
he plants a cedar and the rain makes it grow.
44:15 A man uses it to make a fire;
he takes some of it and warms himself.
Yes, he kindles a fire and bakes bread.
Then he makes a god and worships it;
he makes an idol and bows down to it.
44:16 Half of it he burns in the fire –
over that half he cooks meat;
he roasts a meal and fills himself.
Yes, he warms himself and says,
'Ah! I am warm as I look at the fire.'
44:17 With the rest of it he makes a god, his idol;
he bows down to it and worships it.
He prays to it, saying,
'Rescue me, for you are my god!'
44:18 They do not comprehend or understand,
for their eyes are blind and cannot see;
their minds do not discern.
44:19 No one thinks to himself,
nor do they comprehend or understand and say to themselves:
'I burned half of it in the fire –
yes, I baked bread over the coals;
I roasted meat and ate it.
With the rest of it should I make a disgusting idol?
Should I bow down to dry wood?'
44:20 He feeds on ashes;
his deceived mind misleads him.
He cannot rescue himself,
nor does he say, 'Is this not a false god I hold in my right hand?'
44:21 Remember these things, O Jacob,
O Israel, for you are my servant.
I formed you to be my servant;
O Israel, I will not forget you!
44:22 I remove the guilt of your rebellious deeds as if they were a cloud,
the guilt of your sins as if they were a cloud.
Come back to me, for I protect you."
44:23 Shout for joy, O sky, for the LORD intervenes;
shout out, you subterranean regions of the earth.
O mountains, give a joyful shout;
you too, O forest and all your trees!
For the LORD protects Jacob;
he reveals his splendor through Israel.

The Lord Empowers Cyrus

44:24 This is what the LORD, your protector, says,
the one who formed you in the womb:
"I am the LORD, who made everything,
who alone stretched out the sky,
who fashioned the earth all by myself,
44:25 who frustrates the omens of the empty talkers
and humiliates the omen readers,
who overturns the counsel of the wise men
and makes their advice seem foolish,
44:26 who fulfills the oracles of his prophetic servants
and brings to pass the announcements of his messengers,
who says about Jerusalem, 'She will be inhabited,'
and about the towns of Judah, 'They will be rebuilt,
her ruins I will raise up,'
44:27 who says to the deep sea, 'Be dry!
I will dry up your sea currents,'
44:28 who commissions Cyrus, the one I appointed as shepherd
to carry out all my wishes
and to decree concerning Jerusalem, 'She will be rebuilt,'
and concerning the temple, 'It will be reconstructed.'"

45:1 This is what the LORD says to his chosen one,
to Cyrus, whose right hand I hold
in order to subdue nations before him,
and disarm kings,
to open doors before him,

so gates remain unclosed:
45:2 "I will go before you
and level mountains.
Bronze doors I will shatter
and iron bars I will hack through.
45:3 I will give you hidden treasures,
riches stashed away in secret places,
so you may recognize that I am the LORD,
the one who calls you by name, the God of Israel.
45:4 For the sake of my servant Jacob,
Israel, my chosen one,
I call you by name
and give you a title of respect, even though you do not recognize me.
45:5 I am the LORD, I have no peer,
there is no God but me.
I arm you for battle, even though you do not recognize me.
45:6 I do this so people will recognize from east to west
that there is no God but me;
I am the LORD, I have no peer.
45:7 I am the one who forms light
and creates darkness;
the one who brings about peace
and creates calamity.
I am the LORD, who accomplishes all these things.
45:8 O sky, rain down from above!
Let the clouds send down showers of deliverance!
Let the earth absorb it so salvation may grow,
and deliverance may sprout up along with it.
I, the LORD, create it.

The Lord Gives a Warning

45:9 One who argues with his creator is in grave danger,
one who is like a mere shard among the other shards on the ground!
The clay should not say to the potter,
"What in the world are you doing?
Your work lacks skill!"
45:10 Danger awaits one who says to his father,
"What in the world are you fathering?"
and to his mother,
"What in the world are you bringing forth?"
45:11 This is what the LORD says,
the Holy One of Israel, the one who formed him,
concerning things to come:
"How dare you question me about my children!
How dare you tell me what to do with the work of my own hands!
45:12 I made the earth,
I created the people who live on it.
It was me – my hands stretched out the sky,
I give orders to all the heavenly lights.
45:13 It is me – I stir him up and commission him;
I will make all his ways level.
He will rebuild my city;
he will send my exiled people home,
but not for a price or a bribe,"
says the LORD who commands armies.

The Lord is the Nations' Only Hope

45:14 This is what the LORD says:
"The profit of Egypt and the revenue of Ethiopia,
along with the Sabeans, those tall men,
will be brought to you and become yours.
They will walk behind you, coming along in chains.
They will bow down to you
and pray to you:
'Truly God is with you; he has no peer;
there is no other God!'"
45:15 Yes, you are a God who keeps hidden,
O God of Israel, deliverer!
45:16 They will all be ashamed and embarrassed;
those who fashion idols will all be humiliated.
45:17 Israel will be delivered once and for all by the LORD;
you will never again be ashamed or humiliated.
45:18 For this is what the LORD says,
the one who created the sky –
he is the true God,
the one who formed the earth and made it;
he established it,
he did not create it without order,
he formed it to be inhabited –
"I am the LORD, I have no peer.
45:19 I have not spoken in secret,
in some hidden place.
I did not tell Jacob's descendants,
'Seek me in vain!'
I am the LORD,

the one who speaks honestly,
who makes reliable announcements.
45:20 Gather together and come!
Approach together, you refugees from the nations!
Those who carry wooden idols know nothing,
those who pray to a god that cannot deliver.
45:21 Tell me! Present the evidence!
Let them consult with one another!
Who predicted this in the past?
Who announced it beforehand?
Was it not I, the LORD?
I have no peer, there is no God but me,
a God who vindicates and delivers;
there is none but me.
45:22 Turn to me so you can be delivered,
all you who live in the earth's remote regions!
For I am God, and I have no peer.
45:23 I solemnly make this oath –
what I say is true and reliable:
'Surely every knee will bow to me,
every tongue will solemnly affirm;
45:24 they will say about me,
"Yes, the LORD is a powerful deliverer."'"
All who are angry at him will cower before him.
45:25 All the descendants of Israel will be vindicated by the LORD
and will boast in him.

The Lord Carries His People

46:1 Bel kneels down,
Nebo bends low.
Their images weigh down animals and beasts.
Your heavy images are burdensome to tired animals.
46:2 Together they bend low and kneel down;
they are unable to rescue the images;
they themselves head off into captivity.
46:3 "Listen to me, O family of Jacob,
all you who are left from the family of Israel,
you who have been carried from birth,
you who have been supported from the time you left the womb.
46:4 Even when you are old, I will take care of you,
even when you have gray hair, I will carry you.
I made you and I will support you;
I will carry you and rescue you.
46:5 To whom can you compare and liken me?
Tell me whom you think I resemble, so we can be compared!
46:6 Those who empty out gold from a purse
and weigh out silver on the scale
hire a metalsmith, who makes it into a god.
They then bow down and worship it.
46:7 They put it on their shoulder and carry it;
they put it in its place and it just stands there;
it does not move from its place.
Even when someone cries out to it, it does not reply;
it does not deliver him from his distress.
46:8 Remember this, so you can be brave!
Think about it, you rebels!
46:9 Remember what I accomplished in antiquity!
Truly I am God, I have no peer;
I am God, and there is none like me,
46:10 who announces the end from the beginning
and reveals beforehand what has not yet occurred,
who says, 'My plan will be realized,
I will accomplish what I desire,'
46:11 who summons an eagle from the east,
from a distant land, one who carries out my plan.
Yes, I have decreed,
yes, I will bring it to pass;
I have formulated a plan,
yes, I will carry it out.
46:12 Listen to me, you stubborn people,
you who distance yourself from doing what is right.
46:13 I am bringing my deliverance near, it is not far away;
I am bringing my salvation near, it does not wait.
I will save Zion;
I will adorn Israel with my splendor."

Babylon Will Fall

47:1 "Fall down! Sit in the dirt,
O virgin daughter Babylon!
Sit on the ground, not on a throne,
O daughter of the Babylonians!
Indeed, you will no longer be called delicate and pampered.
47:2 Pick up millstones and grind flour!
Remove your veil,
strip off your skirt,

expose your legs,
cross the streams!
47:3 Let your private parts be exposed!
Your genitals will be on display!
I will get revenge;
I will not have pity on anyone,"
47:4 says our protector –
the LORD who commands armies is his name,
the Holy One of Israel.
47:5 "Sit silently! Go to a hiding place,
O daughter of the Babylonians!
Indeed, you will no longer be called 'Queen of kingdoms.'
47:6 I was angry at my people;
I defiled my special possession
and handed them over to you.
You showed them no mercy;
you even placed a very heavy burden on old people.
47:7 You said,
'I will rule forever as permanent queen!'
You did not think about these things;
you did not consider how it would turn out.
47:8 So now, listen to this,
O one who lives so lavishly,
who lives securely,
who says to herself,
'I am unique! No one can compare to me!
I will never have to live as a widow;
I will never lose my children.'
47:9 Both of these will come upon you
suddenly, in one day!
You will lose your children and be widowed.
You will be overwhelmed by these tragedies,
despite your many incantations
and your numerous amulets.
47:10 You were complacent in your evil deeds;
you thought, 'No one sees me.'
Your self-professed wisdom and knowledge lead you astray,
when you say, 'I am unique! No one can compare to me!'
47:11 Disaster will overtake you;
you will not know how to charm it away.
Destruction will fall on you;
you will not be able to appease it.
Calamity will strike you suddenly,
before you recognize it.
47:12 Persist in trusting your amulets
and your many incantations,
which you have faithfully recited since your youth!
Maybe you will be successful –
maybe you will scare away disaster.
47:13 You are tired out from listening to so much advice.
Let them take their stand –
the ones who see omens in the sky,
who gaze at the stars,
who make monthly predictions –
let them rescue you from the disaster that is about to overtake you!
47:14 Look, they are like straw,
which the fire burns up;
they cannot rescue themselves
from the heat of the flames.
There are no coals to warm them,
no firelight to enjoy.
47:15 They will disappoint you,
those you have so faithfully dealt with since your youth.
Each strays off in his own direction,
leaving no one to rescue you."

The Lord Appeals to the Exiles

48:1 Listen to this, O family of Jacob,
you who are called by the name 'Israel,'
and are descended from Judah,
who take oaths in the name of the LORD,
and invoke the God of Israel –
but not in an honest and just manner.
48:2 Indeed, they live in the holy city;
they trust in the God of Israel,
whose name is the LORD who commands armies.
48:3 "I announced events beforehand,
I issued the decrees and made the predictions;
suddenly I acted and they came to pass.
48:4 I did this because I know how stubborn you are.
Your neck muscles are like iron
and your forehead like bronze.
48:5 I announced them to you beforehand;
before they happened, I predicted them for you,

so you could never say,
'My image did these things,
my idol, my cast image, decreed them.'
48:6 You have heard; now look at all the evidence!
Will you not admit that what I say is true?
From this point on I am announcing to you new events
that are previously unrevealed and you do not know about.
48:7 Now they come into being, not in the past;
before today you did not hear about them,
so you could not say,
'Yes, I know about them.'
48:8 You did not hear,
you do not know,
you were not told beforehand.
For I know that you are very deceitful;
you were labeled a rebel from birth.
48:9 For the sake of my reputation I hold back my anger;
for the sake of my prestige I restrain myself from destroying you.
48:10 Look, I have refined you, but not as silver;
I have purified you in the furnace of misery.
48:11 For my sake alone I will act,
for how can I allow my name to be defiled?
I will not share my glory with anyone else!
48:12 Listen to me, O Jacob,
Israel, whom I summoned!
I am the one;
I am present at the very beginning
and at the very end.
48:13 Yes, my hand founded the earth;
my right hand spread out the sky.
I summon them;
they stand together.
48:14 All of you, gather together and listen!
Who among them announced these things?
The LORD's ally will carry out his desire against Babylon;
he will exert his power against the Babylonians.
48:15 I, I have spoken –
yes, I have summoned him;
I lead him and he will succeed.
48:16 Approach me! Listen to this!
From the very first I have not spoken in secret;
when it happens, I am there."
So now, the sovereign LORD has sent me, accompanied by his spirit.
48:17 This is what the LORD, your protector, says,
the Holy One of Israel:
"I am the LORD your God,
who teaches you how to succeed,
who leads you in the way you should go.
48:18 If only you had obeyed my commandments,
prosperity would have flowed to you like a river,
deliverance would have come to you like the waves of the sea.
48:19 Your descendants would have been as numerous as sand,
and your children like its granules.
Their name would not have been cut off
and eliminated from my presence.
48:20 Leave Babylon!
Flee from the Babylonians!
Announce it with a shout of joy!
Make this known!
Proclaim it throughout the earth!
Say, 'The LORD protects his servant Jacob.
48:21 They do not thirst as he leads them through dry regions;
he makes water flow out of a rock for them;
he splits open a rock and water flows out.'
48:22 There will be no prosperity for the wicked," says the LORD.

Ideal Israel Delivers the Exiles

49:1 Listen to me, you coastlands!
Pay attention, you people who live far away!
The LORD summoned me from birth;
he commissioned me when my mother brought me into the world.
49:2 He made my mouth like a sharp sword,
he hid me in the hollow of his hand;
he made me like a sharpened arrow,
he hid me in his quiver.
49:3 He said to me, "You are my servant,
Israel, through whom I will reveal my splendor."
49:4 But I thought, "I have worked in vain;
I have expended my energy for absolutely nothing."
But the LORD will vindicate me;
my God will reward me.
49:5 So now the LORD says,
the one who formed me from birth to be his servant –
he did this to restore Jacob to himself,

so that Israel might be gathered to him;
and I will be honored in the LORD's sight,
for my God is my source of strength –
49:6 he says, "Is it too insignificant a task for you to be my servant,
to reestablish the tribes of Jacob,
and restore the remnant of Israel?
I will make you a light to the nations,
so you can bring my deliverance to the remote regions of the earth."
49:7 This is what the LORD,
the protector of Israel, their Holy One, says
to the one who is despised and rejected by nations,
a servant of rulers:
"Kings will see and rise in respect,
princes will bow down,
because of the faithful LORD,
the Holy One of Israel who has chosen you."
49:8 This is what the LORD says:
"At the time I decide to show my favor, I will respond to you;
in the day of deliverance I will help you;
I will protect you and make you a covenant mediator for people,
to rebuild the land
and to reassign the desolate property.
49:9 You will say to the prisoners, 'Come out,'
and to those who are in dark dungeons, 'Emerge.'
They will graze beside the roads;
on all the slopes they will find pasture.
49:10 They will not be hungry or thirsty;
the sun's oppressive heat will not beat down on them,
for one who has compassion on them will guide them;
he will lead them to springs of water.
49:11 I will make all my mountains into a road;
I will construct my roadways."
49:12 Look, they come from far away!
Look, some come from the north and west,
and others from the land of Sinim!
49:13 Shout for joy, O sky!
Rejoice, O earth!
Let the mountains give a joyful shout!
For the LORD consoles his people
and shows compassion to the oppressed.
The Lord Remembers Zion
49:14 "Zion said, 'The LORD has abandoned me,
the sovereign master has forgotten me.'
49:15 Can a woman forget her baby who nurses at her breast?
Can she withhold compassion from the child she has borne?
Even if mothers were to forget,
I could never forget you!
49:16 Look, I have inscribed your name on my palms;
your walls are constantly before me.
49:17 Your children hurry back,
while those who destroyed and devastated you depart.
49:18 Look all around you!
All of them gather to you.
As surely as I live," says the LORD,
"you will certainly wear all of them like jewelry;
you will put them on as if you were a bride.
49:19 Yes, your land lies in ruins;
it is desolate and devastated.
But now you will be too small to hold your residents,
and those who devoured you will be far away.
49:20 Yet the children born during your time of bereavement
will say within your hearing,
'This place is too cramped for us,
make room for us so we can live here.'
49:21 Then you will think to yourself,
'Who bore these children for me?
I was bereaved and barren,
dismissed and divorced.
Who raised these children?
Look, I was left all alone;
where did these children come from?'"
49:22 This is what the sovereign LORD says:
"Look I will raise my hand to the nations;
I will raise my signal flag to the peoples.
They will bring your sons in their arms
and carry your daughters on their shoulders.
49:23 Kings will be your children's guardians;
their princesses will nurse your children.
With their faces to the ground they will bow down to you
and they will lick the dirt on your feet.
Then you will recognize that I am the LORD;
those who wait patiently for me are not put to shame.
49:24 Can spoils be taken from a warrior,

or captives be rescued from a conqueror?
49:25 Indeed," says the LORD,
"captives will be taken from a warrior;
spoils will be rescued from a conqueror.
I will oppose your adversary
and I will rescue your children.
49:26 I will make your oppressors eat their own flesh;
they will get drunk on their own blood, as if it were wine.
Then all humankind will recognize that
I am the LORD, your deliverer,
your protector, the powerful ruler of Jacob."

50:1 This is what the LORD says:
"Where is your mother's divorce certificate
by which I divorced her?
Or to which of my creditors did I sell you?
Look, you were sold because of your sins;
because of your rebellious acts I divorced your mother.
50:2 Why does no one challenge me when I come?
Why does no one respond when I call?
Is my hand too weak to deliver you?
Do I lack the power to rescue you?
Look, with a mere shout I can dry up the sea;
I can turn streams into a desert,
so the fish rot away and die
from lack of water.
50:3 I can clothe the sky in darkness;
I can cover it with sackcloth."
The Servant Perseveres
50:4 The sovereign LORD has given me the capacity to be his spokesman,
so that I know how to help the weary.
He wakes me up every morning;
he makes me alert so I can listen attentively as disciples do.
50:5 The sovereign LORD has spoken to me clearly;
I have not rebelled,
I have not turned back.
50:6 I offered my back to those who attacked,
my jaws to those who tore out my beard;
I did not hide my face
from insults and spitting.
50:7 But the sovereign LORD helps me,
so I am not humiliated.
For that reason I am steadfastly resolved;
I know I will not be put to shame.
50:8 The one who vindicates me is close by.
Who dares to argue with me? Let us confront each other!
Who is my accuser? Let him challenge me!
50:9 Look, the sovereign LORD helps me.
Who dares to condemn me?
Look, all of them will wear out like clothes;
a moth will eat away at them.
50:10 Who among you fears the LORD?
Who obeys his servant?
Whoever walks in deep darkness,
without light,
should trust in the name of the LORD
and rely on his God.
50:11 Look, all of you who start a fire
and who equip yourselves with flaming arrows,
walk in the light of the fire you started
and among the flaming arrows you ignited!
This is what you will receive from me:
you will lie down in a place of pain.
There is Hope for the Future
51:1 "Listen to me, you who pursue godliness,
who seek the LORD!
Look at the rock from which you were chiseled,
at the quarry from which you were dug!
51:2 Look at Abraham, your father,
and Sarah, who gave you birth.
When I summoned him, he was a lone individual,
but I blessed him and gave him numerous descendants.
51:3 Certainly the LORD will console Zion;
he will console all her ruins.
He will make her wilderness like Eden,
her desert like the Garden of the LORD.
Happiness and joy will be restored to her,
thanksgiving and the sound of music.
51:4 Pay attention to me, my people!
Listen to me, my people!
For I will issue a decree,
I will make my justice a light to the nations.
51:5 I am ready to vindicate,

I am ready to deliver,
I will establish justice among the nations.
The coastlands wait patiently for me;
they wait in anticipation for the revelation of my power.
51:6 Look up at the sky!
Look at the earth below!
For the sky will dissipate like smoke,
and the earth will wear out like clothes;
its residents will die like gnats.
But the deliverance I give is permanent;
the vindication I provide will not disappear.
51:7 Listen to me, you who know what is right,
you people who are aware of my law!
Don't be afraid of the insults of men;
don't be discouraged because of their abuse!
51:8 For a moth will eat away at them like clothes;
a clothes moth will devour them like wool.
But the vindication I provide will be permanent;
the deliverance I give will last."
51:9 Wake up! Wake up!
Clothe yourself with strength, O arm of the LORD!
Wake up as in former times, as in antiquity!
Did you not smash the Proud One?
Did you not wound the sea monster?
51:10 Did you not dry up the sea,
the waters of the great deep?
Did you not make a path through the depths of the sea,
so those delivered from bondage could cross over?
51:11 Those whom the LORD has ransomed will return;
they will enter Zion with a happy shout.
Unending joy will crown them,
happiness and joy will overwhelm them;
grief and suffering will disappear.
51:12 "I, I am the one who consoles you.
Why are you afraid of mortal men,
of mere human beings who are as short-lived as grass?
51:13 Why do you forget the LORD, who made you,
who stretched out the sky
and founded the earth?
Why do you constantly tremble all day long
at the anger of the oppressor,
when he makes plans to destroy?
Where is the anger of the oppressor?
51:14 The one who suffers will soon be released;
he will not die in prison,
he will not go hungry.
51:15 I am the LORD your God,
who churns up the sea so that its waves surge.
The LORD who commands armies is his name!

Zion's Time to Celebrate

51:16 I commission you as my spokesman;
I cover you with the palm of my hand,
to establish the sky and to found the earth,
to say to Zion, 'You are my people.'"
51:17 Wake up! Wake up!
Get up, O Jerusalem!
You drank from the cup the LORD passed to you,
which was full of his anger!
You drained dry
the goblet full of intoxicating wine.
51:18 There was no one to lead her
among all the children she bore;
there was no one to take her by the hand
among all the children she raised.
51:19 These double disasters confronted you.
But who feels sorry for you?
Destruction and devastation,
famine and sword.
But who consoles you?
51:20 Your children faint;
they lie at the head of every street
like an antelope in a snare.
They are left in a stupor by the LORD's anger,
by the battle cry of your God.
51:21 So listen to this, oppressed one,
who is drunk, but not from wine!
51:22 This is what your sovereign master, the LORD your God, says:
"Look, I have removed from your hand
the cup of intoxicating wine,
the goblet full of my anger.
You will no longer have to drink it.
51:23 I will put it into the hand of your tormentors
who said to you, 'Lie down, so we can walk over you.'

You made your back like the ground,
and like the street for those who walked over you."

52:1 Wake up! Wake up!
Clothe yourself with strength, O Zion!
Put on your beautiful clothes,
O Jerusalem, holy city!
For uncircumcised and unclean pagans
will no longer invade you.
52:2 Shake off the dirt!
Get up, captive Jerusalem!
Take off the iron chains around your neck,
O captive daughter Zion!
52:3 For this is what the LORD says:
"You were sold for nothing,
and you will not be redeemed for money."
52:4 For this is what the sovereign LORD says:
"In the beginning my people went to live temporarily in Egypt;
Assyria oppressed them for no good reason.
52:5 And now, what do we have here?" says the LORD.
"Indeed my people have been carried away for nothing,
those who rule over them taunt," says the LORD,
"and my name is constantly slandered all day long.
52:6 For this reason my people will know my name,
for this reason they will know at that time that I am the one who says,
'Here I am.'"
52:7 How delightful it is to see approaching over the mountains
the feet of a messenger who announces peace,
a messenger who brings good news, who announces deliverance,
who says to Zion, "Your God reigns!"
52:8 Listen, your watchmen shout;
in unison they shout for joy,
for they see with their very own eyes
the LORD's return to Zion.
52:9 In unison give a joyful shout,
O ruins of Jerusalem!
For the LORD consoles his people;
he protects Jerusalem.
52:10 The LORD reveals his royal power
in the sight of all the nations;
the entire earth sees
our God deliver.
52:11 Leave! Leave! Get out of there!
Don't touch anything unclean!
Get out of it!
Stay pure, you who carry the LORD's holy items!
52:12 Yet do not depart quickly
or leave in a panic.
For the LORD goes before you;
the God of Israel is your rear guard.

The Lord Will Vindicate His Servant

52:13 "Look, my servant will succeed!
He will be elevated, lifted high, and greatly exalted –
52:14 (just as many were horrified by the sight of you)
he was so disfigured he no longer looked like a man;
52:15 his form was so marred he no longer looked human –
so now he will startle many nations.
Kings will be shocked by his exaltation,
for they will witness something unannounced to them,
and they will understand something they had not heard about.
53:1 Who would have believed what we just heard?
When was the LORD's power revealed through him?
53:2 He sprouted up like a twig before God,
like a root out of parched soil;
he had no stately form or majesty that might catch our attention,
no special appearance that we should want to follow him.
53:3 He was despised and rejected by people,
one who experienced pain and was acquainted with illness;
people hid their faces from him;
he was despised, and we considered him insignificant.
53:4 But he lifted up our illnesses,
he carried our pain;
even though we thought he was being punished,
attacked by God, and afflicted for something he had done.
53:5 He was wounded because of our rebellious deeds,
crushed because of our sins;
he endured punishment that made us well;
because of his wounds we have been healed.
53:6 All of us had wandered off like sheep;
each of us had strayed off on his own path,
but the LORD caused the sin of all of us to attack him.
53:7 He was treated harshly and afflicted,

but he did not even open his mouth.
Like a lamb led to the slaughtering block,
like a sheep silent before her shearers,
he did not even open his mouth.
53:8 He was led away after an unjust trial –
but who even cared?
Indeed, he was cut off from the land of the living;
because of the rebellion of his own people he was wounded.
53:9 They intended to bury him with criminals,
but he ended up in a rich man's tomb,
because he had committed no violent deeds,
nor had he spoken deceitfully.
53:10 Though the LORD desired to crush him and make him ill,
once restitution is made,
he will see descendants and enjoy long life,
and the LORD's purpose will be accomplished through him.
53:11 Having suffered, he will reflect on his work,
he will be satisfied when he understands what he has done.
"My servant will acquit many,
for he carried their sins.
53:12 So I will assign him a portion with the multitudes,
he will divide the spoils of victory with the powerful,
because he willingly submitted to death
and was numbered with the rebels,
when he lifted up the sin of many
and intervened on behalf of the rebels."
Zion Will Be Secure
54:1 "Shout for joy, O barren one who has not given birth!
Give a joyful shout and cry out, you who have not been in labor!
For the children of the desolate one are more numerous
than the children of the married woman," says the LORD.
54:2 Make your tent larger,
stretch your tent curtains farther out!
Spare no effort,
lengthen your ropes,
and pound your stakes deep.
54:3 For you will spread out to the right and to the left;
your children will conquer nations
and will resettle desolate cities.
54:4 Don't be afraid, for you will not be put to shame!
Don't be intimidated, for you will not be humiliated!
You will forget about the shame you experienced in your youth;
you will no longer remember the disgrace of your abandonment.
54:5 For your husband is the one who made you –
the LORD who commands armies is his name.
He is your protector, the Holy One of Israel.
He is called "God of the entire earth."
54:6 "Indeed, the LORD will call you back
like a wife who has been abandoned and suffers from depression,
like a young wife when she has been rejected," says your God.
54:7 "For a short time I abandoned you,
but with great compassion I will gather you.
54:8 In a burst of anger I rejected you momentarily,
but with lasting devotion I will have compassion on you,"
says your protector, the LORD.
54:9 "As far as I am concerned, this is like in Noah's time,
when I vowed that the waters of Noah's flood would never again cover the earth.
In the same way I have vowed that I will not be angry at you or shout at you.
54:10 Even if the mountains are removed
and the hills displaced,
my devotion will not be removed from you,
nor will my covenant of friendship be displaced,"
says the LORD, the one who has compassion on you.
54:11 "O afflicted one, driven away, and unconsoled!
Look, I am about to set your stones in antimony
and I lay your foundation with lapis-lazuli.
54:12 I will make your pinnacles out of gems,
your gates out of beryl,
and your outer wall out of beautiful stones.
54:13 All your children will be followers of the LORD,
and your children will enjoy great prosperity.
54:14 You will be reestablished when I vindicate you.
You will not experience oppression;
indeed, you will not be afraid.
You will not be terrified,
for nothing frightening will come near you.
54:15 If anyone dares to challenge you, it will not be my doing!
Whoever tries to challenge you will be defeated.
54:16 Look, I create the craftsman,
who fans the coals into a fire
and forges a weapon.

I create the destroyer so he might devastate.
54:17 No weapon forged to be used against you will succeed;
you will refute everyone who tries to accuse you.
This is what the LORD will do for his servants –
I will vindicate them,"
says the LORD.
The Lord Gives an Invitation
55:1 "Hey, all who are thirsty, come to the water!
You who have no money, come!
Buy and eat!
Come! Buy wine and milk
without money and without cost!
55:2 Why pay money for something that will not nourish you?
Why spend your hard-earned money on something that will not satisfy?
Listen carefully to me and eat what is nourishing!
Enjoy fine food!
55:3 Pay attention and come to me!
Listen, so you can live!
Then I will make an unconditional covenantal promise to you,
just like the reliable covenantal promises I made to David.
55:4 Look, I made him a witness to nations,
a ruler and commander of nations."
55:5 Look, you will summon nations you did not previously know;
nations that did not previously know you will run to you,
because of the LORD your God,
the Holy One of Israel,
for he bestows honor on you.
55:6 Seek the LORD while he makes himself available;
call to him while he is nearby!
55:7 The wicked need to abandon their lifestyle
and sinful people their plans.
They should return to the LORD, and he will show mercy to them,
and to their God, for he will freely forgive them.
55:8 "Indeed, my plans are not like your plans,
and my deeds are not like your deeds,
55:9 for just as the sky is higher than the earth,
so my deeds are superior to your deeds
and my plans superior to your plans.
55:10 The rain and snow fall from the sky
and do not return,
but instead water the earth
and make it produce and yield crops,
and provide seed for the planter and food for those who must eat.
55:11 In the same way, the promise that I make
does not return to me, having accomplished nothing.
No, it is realized as I desire
and is fulfilled as I intend."
55:12 Indeed you will go out with joy;
you will be led along in peace;
the mountains and hills will give a joyful shout before you,
and all the trees in the field will clap their hands.
55:13 Evergreens will grow in place of thorn bushes,
firs will grow in place of nettles;
they will be a monument to the LORD,
a permanent reminder that will remain.
The Lord Invites Outsiders to Enter
56:1 This is what the LORD says,
"Promote justice! Do what is right!
For I am ready to deliver you;
I am ready to vindicate you openly.
56:2 The people who do this will be blessed,
the people who commit themselves to obedience,
who observe the Sabbath and do not defile it,
who refrain from doing anything that is wrong.
56:3 No foreigner who becomes a follower of the LORD should say,
'The LORD will certainly exclude me from his people.'
The eunuch should not say,
'Look, I am like a dried-up tree.'"
56:4 For this is what the LORD says:
"For the eunuchs who observe my Sabbaths
and choose what pleases me
and are faithful to my covenant,
56:5 I will set up within my temple and my walls a monument
that will be better than sons and daughters.
I will set up a permanent monument for them that will remain.
56:6 As for foreigners who become followers of the LORD and serve him,
who love the name of the LORD and want to be his servants –
all who observe the Sabbath and do not defile it,
and who are faithful to my covenant –
56:7 I will bring them to my holy mountain;
I will make them happy in the temple where people pray to me.
Their burnt offerings and sacrifices will be accepted on my altar,
for my temple will be known as a temple where all nations may pray."

56:8 The sovereign LORD says this,
the one who gathers the dispersed of Israel:
"I will still gather them up."
The Lord Denounces Israel's Paganism
56:9 All you wild animals in the fields, come and devour,
all you wild animals in the forest!
56:10 All their watchmen are blind,
they are unaware.
All of them are like mute dogs,
unable to bark.
They pant, lie down,
and love to snooze.
56:11 The dogs have big appetites;
they are never full.
They are shepherds who have no understanding;
they all go their own way,
each one looking for monetary gain.
56:12 Each one says,
'Come on, I'll get some wine!
Let's guzzle some beer!
Tomorrow will be just like today!
We'll have everything we want!'
57:1 The godly perish,
but no one cares.
Honest people disappear,
when no one minds
that the godly disappear because of evil.
57:2 Those who live uprightly enter a place of peace;
they rest on their beds.
57:3 But approach, you sons of omen readers,
you offspring of adulteresses and prostitutes!
57:4 At whom are you laughing?
At whom are you opening your mouth
and sticking out your tongue?
You are the children of rebels,
the offspring of liars,
57:5 you who practice ritual sex under the oaks and every green tree,
who slaughter children near the streams under the rocky overhangs.
57:6 Among the smooth stones of the stream are the idols you love;
they, they are the object of your devotion.
You pour out liquid offerings to them,
you make an offering.
Because of these things I will seek vengeance.
57:7 On every high, elevated hill you prepare your bed;
you go up there to offer sacrifices.
57:8 Behind the door and doorpost you put your symbols.
Indeed, you depart from me and go up
and invite them into bed with you.
You purchase favors from them,
you love their bed,
and gaze longingly on their genitals.
57:9 You take olive oil as tribute to your king,
along with many perfumes.
You send your messengers to a distant place;
you go all the way to Sheol.
57:10 Because of the long distance you must travel, you get tired,
but you do not say, 'I give up.'
You get renewed energy,
so you don't collapse.
57:11 Whom are you worried about?
Whom do you fear, that you would act so deceitfully
and not remember me
or think about me?
Because I have been silent for so long,
you are not afraid of me.
57:12 I will denounce your so-called righteousness and your deeds,
but they will not help you.
57:13 When you cry out for help, let your idols help you!
The wind blows them all away,
a breeze carries them away.
But the one who looks to me for help will inherit the land
and will have access to my holy mountain."
57:14 He says,
"Build it! Build it! Clear a way!
Remove all the obstacles out of the way of my people!"
57:15 For this is what the high and exalted one says,
the one who rules forever, whose name is holy:
"I dwell in an exalted and holy place,
but also with the discouraged and humiliated,
in order to cheer up the humiliated
and to encourage the discouraged.
57:16 For I will not be hostile forever
or perpetually angry,

for then man's spirit would grow faint before me,
the life-giving breath I created.
57:17 I was angry because of their sinful greed;
I attacked them and angrily rejected them,
yet they remained disobedient and stubborn.
57:18 I have seen their behavior,
but I will heal them and give them rest,
and I will once again console those who mourn.
57:19 I am the one who gives them reason to celebrate.
Complete prosperity is available both to those who are far away and those
who are nearby,"
says the LORD, "and I will heal them.
57:20 But the wicked are like a surging sea
that is unable to be quiet;
its waves toss up mud and sand.
57:21 There will be no prosperity," says my God, "for the wicked."
The Lord Desires Genuine Devotion
58:1 "Shout loudly! Don't be quiet!
Yell as loud as a trumpet!
Confront my people with their rebellious deeds;
confront Jacob's family with their sin!
58:2 They seek me day after day;
they want to know my requirements,
like a nation that does what is right
and does not reject the law of their God.
They ask me for just decrees;
they want to be near God.
58:3 They lament, 'Why don't you notice when we fast?
Why don't you pay attention when we humble ourselves?'
Look, at the same time you fast, you satisfy your selfish desires,
you oppress your workers.
58:4 Look, your fasting is accompanied by arguments, brawls,
and fistfights.
Do not fast as you do today,
trying to make your voice heard in heaven.
58:5 Is this really the kind of fasting I want?
Do I want a day when people merely humble themselves,
bowing their heads like a reed
and stretching out on sackcloth and ashes?
Is this really what you call a fast,
a day that is pleasing to the LORD?
58:6 No, this is the kind of fast I want.
I want you to remove the sinful chains,
to tear away the ropes of the burdensome yoke,
to set free the oppressed,
and to break every burdensome yoke.
58:7 I want you to share your food with the hungry
and to provide shelter for homeless, oppressed people.
When you see someone naked, clothe him!
Don't turn your back on your own flesh and blood!
58:8 Then your light will shine like the sunrise;
your restoration will quickly arrive;
your godly behavior will go before you,
and the LORD's splendor will be your rear guard.
58:9 Then you will call out, and the LORD will respond;
you will cry out, and he will reply, 'Here I am.'
You must remove the burdensome yoke from among you
and stop pointing fingers and speaking sinfully.
58:10 You must actively help the hungry
and feed the oppressed.
Then your light will dispel the darkness,
and your darkness will be transformed into noonday.
58:11 The LORD will continually lead you;
he will feed you even in parched regions.
He will give you renewed strength,
and you will be like a well-watered garden,
like a spring that continually produces water.
58:12 Your perpetual ruins will be rebuilt;
you will reestablish the ancient foundations.
You will be called, 'The one who repairs broken walls,
the one who makes the streets inhabitable again.'
58:13 You must observe the Sabbath
rather than doing anything you please on my holy day.
You must look forward to the Sabbath
and treat the LORD's holy day with respect.
You must treat it with respect by refraining from your normal activities,
and by refraining from your selfish pursuits and from making business
deals.
58:14 Then you will find joy in your relationship to the LORD,
and I will give you great prosperity,
and cause crops to grow on the land I gave to your ancestor Jacob."
Know for certain that the LORD has spoken.
Injustice Brings Alienation from God

59:1 Look, the LORD's hand is not too weak to deliver you;
his ear is not too deaf to hear you.
59:2 But your sinful acts have alienated you from your God;
your sins have caused him to reject you and not listen to your prayers.
59:3 For your hands are stained with blood
and your fingers with sin;
your lips speak lies,
your tongue utters malicious words.
59:4 No one is concerned about justice;
no one sets forth his case truthfully.
They depend on false words and tell lies;
they conceive of oppression
and give birth to sin.
59:5 They hatch the eggs of a poisonous snake
and spin a spider's web.
Whoever eats their eggs will die,
a poisonous snake is hatched.
59:6 Their webs cannot be used for clothing;
they cannot cover themselves with what they make.
Their deeds are sinful;
they commit violent crimes.
59:7 They are eager to do evil,
quick to shed innocent blood.
Their thoughts are sinful;
they crush and destroy.
59:8 They are unfamiliar with peace;
their deeds are unjust.
They use deceitful methods,
and whoever deals with them is unfamiliar with peace.

Israel Confesses its Sin

59:9 For this reason deliverance is far from us
and salvation does not reach us.
We wait for light, but see only darkness;
we wait for a bright light, but live in deep darkness.
59:10 We grope along the wall like the blind,
we grope like those who cannot see;
we stumble at noontime as if it were evening.
Though others are strong, we are like dead men.
59:11 We all growl like bears,
we coo mournfully like doves;
we wait for deliverance, but there is none,
for salvation, but it is far from us.
59:12 For you are aware of our many rebellious deeds,
and our sins testify against us;
indeed, we are aware of our rebellious deeds;
we know our sins all too well.
59:13 We have rebelled and tried to deceive the LORD;
we turned back from following our God.
We stir up oppression and rebellion;
we tell lies we concocted in our minds.
59:14 Justice is driven back;
godliness stands far off.
Indeed, honesty stumbles in the city square
and morality is not even able to enter.
59:15 Honesty has disappeared;
the one who tries to avoid evil is robbed.
The LORD watches and is displeased,
for there is no justice.

The Lord Intervenes

59:16 He sees there is no advocate;
he is shocked that no one intervenes.
So he takes matters into his own hands;
his desire for justice drives him on.
59:17 He wears his desire for justice like body armor,
and his desire to deliver is like a helmet on his head.
He puts on the garments of vengeance
and wears zeal like a robe.
59:18 He repays them for what they have done,
dispensing angry judgment to his adversaries
and punishing his enemies.
He repays the coastlands.
59:19 In the west, people respect the LORD's reputation;
in the east they recognize his splendor.
For he comes like a rushing stream
driven on by wind sent from the LORD.
59:20 "A protector comes to Zion,
to those in Jacob who repent of their rebellious deeds," says the LORD.
59:21 "As for me, this is my promise to them," says the LORD. "My spirit, who is upon you, and my words, which I have placed in your mouth, will not depart from your mouth or from the mouths of your children and descendants from this time forward," says the LORD.

Zion's Future Splendor

60:1 "Arise! Shine! For your light arrives!

The splendor of the LORD shines on you!
60:2 For, look, darkness covers the earth
and deep darkness covers the nations,
but the LORD shines on you;
his splendor appears over you.
60:3 Nations come to your light,
kings to your bright light.
60:4 Look all around you!
They all gather and come to you –
your sons come from far away
and your daughters are escorted by guardians.
60:5 Then you will look and smile,
you will be excited and your heart will swell with pride.
For the riches of distant lands will belong to you
and the wealth of nations will come to you.
60:6 Camel caravans will cover your roads,
young camels from Midian and Ephah.
All the merchants of Sheba will come,
bringing gold and incense
and singing praises to the LORD.
60:7 All the sheep of Kedar will be gathered to you;
the rams of Nebaioth will be available to you as sacrifices.
They will go up on my altar acceptably,
and I will bestow honor on my majestic temple.
60:8 Who are these who float along like a cloud,
who fly like doves to their shelters?
60:9 Indeed, the coastlands look eagerly for me,
the large ships are in the lead,
bringing your sons from far away,
along with their silver and gold,
to honor the LORD your God,
the Holy One of Israel, for he has bestowed honor on you.
60:10 Foreigners will rebuild your walls;
their kings will serve you.
Even though I struck you down in my anger,
I will restore my favor and have compassion on you.
60:11 Your gates will remain open at all times;
they will not be shut during the day or at night,
so that the wealth of nations may be delivered,
with their kings leading the way.
60:12 Indeed, nations or kingdoms that do not serve you will perish;
such nations will be totally destroyed.
60:13 The splendor of Lebanon will come to you,
its evergreens, firs, and cypresses together,
to beautify my palace;
I will bestow honor on my throne room.
60:14 The children of your oppressors will come bowing to you;
all who treated you with disrespect will bow down at your feet.
They will call you, 'The City of the LORD,
Zion of the Holy One of Israel.'
60:15 You were once abandoned
and despised, with no one passing through,
but I will make you a permanent source of pride
and joy to coming generations.
60:16 You will drink the milk of nations;
you will nurse at the breasts of kings.
Then you will recognize that I, the LORD, am your deliverer,
your protector, the powerful ruler of Jacob.
60:17 Instead of bronze, I will bring you gold,
instead of iron, I will bring you silver,
instead of wood, I will bring you bronze,
instead of stones, I will bring you iron.
I will make prosperity your overseer,
and vindication your sovereign ruler.
60:18 Sounds of violence will no longer be heard in your land,
or the sounds of destruction and devastation within your borders.
You will name your walls, 'Deliverance,'
and your gates, 'Praise.'
60:19 The sun will no longer supply light for you by day,
nor will the moon's brightness shine on you;
the LORD will be your permanent source of light –
the splendor of your God will shine upon you.
60:20 Your sun will no longer set;
your moon will not disappear;
the LORD will be your permanent source of light;
your time of sorrow will be over.
60:21 All of your people will be godly;
they will possess the land permanently.
I will plant them like a shoot;
they will be the product of my labor,
through whom I reveal my splendor.
60:22 The least of you will multiply into a thousand;
the smallest of you will become a large nation.

When the right time comes, I the LORD will quickly do this!"

The Lord Will Rejuvenate His People

61:1 The spirit of the sovereign LORD is upon me,
because the LORD has chosen me.
He has commissioned me to encourage the poor,
to help the brokenhearted,
to decree the release of captives,
and the freeing of prisoners,
61:2 to announce the year when the LORD will show his favor,
the day when our God will seek vengeance,
to console all who mourn,
61:3 to strengthen those who mourn in Zion,
by giving them a turban, instead of ashes,
oil symbolizing joy, instead of mourning,
a garment symbolizing praise, instead of discouragement.
They will be called oaks of righteousness,
trees planted by the LORD to reveal his splendor.
61:4 They will rebuild the perpetual ruins
and restore the places that were desolate;
they will reestablish the ruined cities,
the places that have been desolate since ancient times.
61:5 "Foreigners will take care of your sheep;
foreigners will work in your fields and vineyards.
61:6 You will be called, 'the LORD's priests,
servants of our God.'
You will enjoy the wealth of nations
and boast about the riches you receive from them.
61:7 Instead of shame, you will get a double portion;
instead of humiliation, they will rejoice over the land they receive.
Yes, they will possess a double portion in their land
and experience lasting joy.
61:8 For I, the LORD, love justice
and hate robbery and sin.
I will repay them because of my faithfulness;
I will make a permanent covenant with them.
61:9 Their descendants will be known among the nations,
their offspring among the peoples.
All who see them will recognize that
the LORD has blessed them."
61:10 I will greatly rejoice in the LORD;
I will be overjoyed because of my God.
For he clothes me in garments of deliverance;
he puts on me a robe symbolizing vindication.
I look like a bridegroom when he wears a turban as a priest would;
I look like a bride when she puts on her jewelry.
61:11 For just as the ground produces its crops
and a garden yields its produce,
so the sovereign LORD will cause deliverance to grow,
and give his people reason to praise him in the sight of all the nations.

The Lord Takes Delight in Zion

62:1 "For the sake of Zion I will not be silent;
for the sake of Jerusalem I will not be quiet,
until her vindication shines brightly
and her deliverance burns like a torch."
62:2 Nations will see your vindication,
and all kings your splendor.
You will be called by a new name
that the LORD himself will give you.
62:3 You will be a majestic crown in the hand of the LORD,
a royal turban in the hand of your God.
62:4 You will no longer be called, "Abandoned,"
and your land will no longer be called "Desolate."
Indeed, you will be called "My Delight is in Her,"
and your land "Married."
For the LORD will take delight in you,
and your land will be married to him.
62:5 As a young man marries a young woman,
so your sons will marry you.
As a bridegroom rejoices over a bride,
so your God will rejoice over you.
62:6 I post watchmen on your walls, O Jerusalem;
they should keep praying all day and all night.
You who pray to the LORD, don't be silent!
62:7 Don't allow him to rest until he reestablishes Jerusalem,
until he makes Jerusalem the pride of the earth.
62:8 The LORD swears an oath by his right hand,
by his strong arm:
"I will never again give your grain
to your enemies as food,
and foreigners will not drink your wine,
which you worked hard to produce.
62:9 But those who harvest the grain will eat it,
and will praise the LORD.
Those who pick the grapes will drink the wine
in the courts of my holy sanctuary."
62:10 Come through! Come through the gates!
Prepare the way for the people!
Build it! Build the roadway!
Remove the stones!
Lift a signal flag for the nations!
62:11 Look, the LORD announces to the entire earth:
"Say to Daughter Zion,
'Look, your deliverer comes!
Look, his reward is with him
and his reward goes before him!'"
62:12 They will be called, "The Holy People,
the Ones Protected by the LORD."
You will be called, "Sought After,
City Not Abandoned."

The Victorious Divine Warrior

63:1 Who is this who comes from Edom,
dressed in bright red, coming from Bozrah?
Who is this one wearing royal attire,
who marches confidently because of his great strength?
"It is I, the one who announces vindication,
and who is able to deliver!"
63:2 Why are your clothes red?
Why do you look like someone who has stomped on grapes in a vat?
63:3 "I have stomped grapes in the winepress all by myself;
no one from the nations joined me.
I stomped on them in my anger;
I trampled them down in my rage.
Their juice splashed on my garments,
and stained all my clothes.
63:4 For I looked forward to the day of vengeance,
and then payback time arrived.
63:5 I looked, but there was no one to help;
I was shocked because there was no one offering support.
So my right arm accomplished deliverance;
my raging anger drove me on.
63:6 I trampled nations in my anger,
I made them drunk in my rage,
I splashed their blood on the ground."

A Prayer for Divine Intervention

63:7 I will tell of the faithful acts of the LORD,
of the LORD's praiseworthy deeds.
I will tell about all the LORD did for us,
the many good things he did for the family of Israel,
because of his compassion and great faithfulness.
63:8 He said, "Certainly they will be my people,
children who are not disloyal."
He became their deliverer.
63:9 Through all that they suffered, he suffered too.
The messenger sent from his very presence delivered them.
In his love and mercy he protected them;
he lifted them up and carried them throughout ancient times.
63:10 But they rebelled and offended his holy Spirit,
so he turned into an enemy
and fought against them.
63:11 His people remembered the ancient times.
Where is the one who brought them up out of the sea,
along with the shepherd of his flock?
Where is the one who placed his holy Spirit among them,
63:12 the one who made his majestic power available to Moses,
who divided the water before them,
gaining for himself a lasting reputation,
63:13 who led them through the deep water?
Like a horse running on flat land they did not stumble.
63:14 Like an animal that goes down into a valley to graze,
so the Spirit of the LORD granted them rest.
In this way you guided your people,
gaining for yourself an honored reputation.
63:15 Look down from heaven and take notice,
from your holy, majestic palace!
Where are your zeal and power?
Do not hold back your tender compassion!
63:16 For you are our father,
though Abraham does not know us
and Israel does not recognize us.
You, LORD, are our father;
you have been called our protector from ancient times.
63:17 Why, LORD, do you make us stray from your ways,
and make our minds stubborn so that we do not obey you?
Return for the sake of your servants,
the tribes of your inheritance!

63:18 For a short time your special nation possessed a land,
but then our adversaries knocked down your holy sanctuary.
63:19 We existed from ancient times,
but you did not rule over them,
they were not your subjects.
64:1 (63:19b) If only you would tear apart the sky and come down!
The mountains would tremble before you!
64:2 (64:1) As when fire ignites dry wood,
or fire makes water boil,
let your adversaries know who you are,
and may the nations shake at your presence!
64:3 When you performed awesome deeds that took us by surprise,
you came down, and the mountains trembled before you.
64:4 Since ancient times no one has heard or perceived,
no eye has seen any God besides you,
who intervenes for those who wait for him.
64:5 You assist those who delight in doing what is right,
who observe your commandments.
Look, you were angry because we violated them continually.
How then can we be saved?
64:6 We are all like one who is unclean,
all our so-called righteous acts are like a menstrual rag in your sight.
We all wither like a leaf;
our sins carry us away like the wind.
64:7 No one invokes your name,
or makes an effort to take hold of you.
For you have rejected us
and handed us over to our own sins.
64:8 Yet, LORD, you are our father.
We are the clay, and you are our potter;
we are all the product of your labor.
64:9 LORD, do not be too angry!
Do not hold our sins against us continually!
Take a good look at your people, at all of us!
64:10 Your chosen cities have become a desert;
Zion has become a desert,
Jerusalem is a desolate ruin.
64:11 Our holy temple, our pride and joy,
the place where our ancestors praised you,
has been burned with fire;
all our prized possessions have been destroyed.
64:12 In light of all this, how can you still hold back, LORD?
How can you be silent and continue to humiliate us?
The Lord Will Distinguish Between Sinners and the Godly
65:1 "I made myself available to those who did not ask for me;
I appeared to those who did not look for me.
I said, 'Here I am! Here I am!'
to a nation that did not invoke my name.
65:2 I spread out my hands all day long
to my rebellious people,
who lived in a way that is morally unacceptable,
and who did what they desired.
65:3 These people continually and blatantly offend me
as they sacrifice in their sacred orchards
and burn incense on brick altars.
65:4 They sit among the tombs
and keep watch all night long.
They eat pork,
and broth from unclean sacrificial meat is in their pans.
65:5 They say, 'Keep to yourself!
Don't get near me, for I am holier than you!'
These people are like smoke in my nostrils,
like a fire that keeps burning all day long.
65:6 Look, I have decreed:
I will not keep silent, but will pay them back;
I will pay them back exactly what they deserve,
65:7 for your sins and your ancestors' sins," says the LORD.
"Because they burned incense on the mountains
and offended me on the hills,
I will punish them in full measure."
65:8 This is what the LORD says:
"When juice is discovered in a cluster of grapes,
someone says, 'Don't destroy it, for it contains juice.'
So I will do for the sake of my servants –
I will not destroy everyone.
65:9 I will bring forth descendants from Jacob,
and from Judah people to take possession of my mountains.
My chosen ones will take possession of the land;
my servants will live there.
65:10 Sharon will become a pasture for sheep,
and the Valley of Achor a place where cattle graze;
they will belong to my people, who seek me.
65:11 But as for you who abandon the LORD

and forget about worshiping at my holy mountain,
who prepare a feast for the god called 'Fortune,'
and fill up wine jugs for the god called 'Destiny' –
65:12 I predestine you to die by the sword,
all of you will kneel down at the slaughtering block,
because I called to you, and you did not respond,
I spoke and you did not listen.
You did evil before me;
you chose to do what displeases me."
65:13 So this is what the sovereign LORD says:
"Look, my servants will eat, but you will be hungry!
Look, my servants will drink, but you will be thirsty!
Look, my servants will rejoice, but you will be humiliated!
65:14 Look, my servants will shout for joy as happiness fills their hearts!
But you will cry out as sorrow fills your hearts;
you will wail because your spirits will be crushed.
65:15 Your names will live on in the curse formulas of my chosen ones.
The sovereign LORD will kill you,
but he will give his servants another name.
65:16 Whoever pronounces a blessing in the earth
will do so in the name of the faithful God;
whoever makes an oath in the earth
will do so in the name of the faithful God.
For past problems will be forgotten;
I will no longer think about them.
65:17 For look, I am ready to create
new heavens and a new earth!
The former ones will not be remembered;
no one will think about them anymore.
65:18 But be happy and rejoice forevermore
over what I am about to create!
For look, I am ready to create Jerusalem to be a source of joy,
and her people to be a source of happiness.
65:19 Jerusalem will bring me joy,
and my people will bring me happiness.
The sound of weeping or cries of sorrow
will never be heard in her again.
65:20 Never again will one of her infants live just a few days
or an old man die before his time.
Indeed, no one will die before the age of a hundred,
anyone who fails to reach the age of a hundred will be considered cursed.
65:21 They will build houses and live in them;
they will plant vineyards and eat their fruit.
65:22 No longer will they build a house only to have another live in it,
or plant a vineyard only to have another eat its fruit,
for my people will live as long as trees,
and my chosen ones will enjoy to the fullest what they have produced.
65:23 They will not work in vain,
or give birth to children that will experience disaster.
For the LORD will bless their children
and their descendants.
65:24 Before they even call out, I will respond;
while they are still speaking, I will hear.
65:25 A wolf and a lamb will graze together;
a lion, like an ox, will eat straw,
and a snake's food will be dirt.
They will no longer injure or destroy
on my entire royal mountain," says the LORD.
66:1 This is what the LORD says:
"The heavens are my throne
and the earth is my footstool.
Where then is the house you will build for me?
Where is the place where I will rest?
66:2 My hand made them;
that is how they came to be," says the LORD.
I show special favor to the humble and contrite,
who respect what I have to say.
66:3 The one who slaughters a bull also strikes down a man;
the one who sacrifices a lamb also breaks a dog's neck;
the one who presents an offering includes pig's blood with it;
the one who offers incense also praises an idol.
They have decided to behave this way;
they enjoy these disgusting practices.
66:4 So I will choose severe punishment for them;
I will bring on them what they dread,
because I called, and no one responded,
I spoke and they did not listen.
They did evil before me;
they chose to do what displeases me."
66:5 Hear the word of the LORD,
you who respect what he has to say!
Your countrymen, who hate you
and exclude you, supposedly for the sake of my name,

say, "May the LORD be glorified,
then we will witness your joy."
But they will be put to shame.
66:6 The sound of battle comes from the city;
the sound comes from the temple!
It is the sound of the LORD paying back his enemies.
66:7 Before she goes into labor, she gives birth!
Before her contractions begin, she delivers a boy!
66:8 Who has ever heard of such a thing?
Who has ever seen this?
Can a country be brought forth in one day?
Can a nation be born in a single moment?
Yet as soon as Zion goes into labor she gives birth to sons!
66:9 "Do I bring a baby to the birth opening and then not deliver it?"
asks the LORD.
"Or do I bring a baby to the point of delivery and then hold it back?"
asks your God.
66:10 Be happy for Jerusalem
and rejoice with her, all you who love her!
Share in her great joy,
all you who have mourned over her!
66:11 For you will nurse from her satisfying breasts and be nourished;
you will feed with joy from her milk-filled breasts.
66:12 For this is what the LORD says:
"Look, I am ready to extend to her prosperity that will flow like a river,
the riches of nations will flow into her like a stream that floods its banks.
You will nurse from her breast and be carried at her side;
you will play on her knees.
66:13 As a mother consoles a child,
so I will console you,
and you will be consoled over Jerusalem."
66:14 When you see this, you will be happy,
and you will be revived.
The LORD will reveal his power to his servants
and his anger to his enemies.
66:15 For look, the LORD comes with fire,
his chariots come like a windstorm,
to reveal his raging anger,
his battle cry, and his flaming arrows.
66:16 For the LORD judges all humanity
with fire and his sword;
the LORD will kill many.
66:17 "As for those who consecrate and ritually purify themselves so they can follow their leader and worship in the sacred orchards, those who eat the flesh of pigs and other disgusting creatures, like mice – they will all be destroyed together," says the LORD. **66:18** "I hate their deeds and thoughts! So I am coming to gather all the nations and ethnic groups; they will come and witness my splendor. **66:19** I will perform a mighty act among them and then send some of those who remain to the nations – to Tarshish, Pul, Lud (known for its archers), Tubal, Javan, and to the distant coastlands that have not heard about me or seen my splendor. They will tell the nations of my splendor. **66:20** They will bring back all your countrymen from all the nations as an offering to the LORD. They will bring them on horses, in chariots, in wagons, on mules, and on camels to my holy hill Jerusalem," says the LORD, "just as the Israelites bring offerings to the LORD's temple in ritually pure containers. **66:21** And I will choose some of them as priests and Levites," says the LORD. **66:22** "For just as the new heavens and the new earth I am about to make will remain standing before me," says the LORD, "so your descendants and your name will remain. **66:23** From one month to the next and from one Sabbath to the next, all people will come to worship me," says the LORD. **66:24** "They will go out and observe the corpses of those who rebelled against me, for the maggots that eat them will not die, and the fire that consumes them will not die out. All people will find the sight abhorrent."

Book 24. Jeremiah

The Superscription
1:1 The following is a record of what Jeremiah son of Hilkiah prophesied. He was one of the priests who lived at Anathoth in the territory of the tribe of Benjamin. **1:2** The LORD began to speak to him in the thirteenth year that Josiah son of Amon ruled over Judah. **1:3** The LORD also spoke to him when Jehoiakim son of Josiah ruled over Judah, and he continued to speak to him until the fifth month of the eleventh year that Zedekiah son of Josiah ruled over Judah. That was when the people of Jerusalem were taken into exile.
Jeremiah's Call and Commission
1:4 The LORD said to me,
1:5 "Before I formed you in your mother's womb I chose you.
Before you were born I set you apart.
I appointed you to be a prophet to the nations."

1:6 I answered, "Oh, Lord GOD, I really do not know how to speak well enough for that, for I am too young." **1:7** The LORD said to me, "Do not say, 'I am too young.' But go to whomever I send you and say whatever I tell you. **1:8** Do not be afraid of those to whom I send you, for I will be with you to protect you," says the LORD. **1:9** Then the LORD reached out his hand and touched my mouth and said to me, "I will most assuredly give you the words you are to speak for me. **1:10** Know for certain that I hereby give you the authority to announce to nations and kingdoms that they will be uprooted and torn down, destroyed and demolished, rebuilt and firmly planted."
Visions Confirming Jeremiah's Call and Commission
1:11 Later the LORD asked me, "What do you see, Jeremiah?" I answered, "I see a branch of an almond tree." **1:12** Then the LORD said, "You have observed correctly. This means I am watching to make sure my threats are carried out."
1:13 The LORD again asked me, "What do you see?" I answered, "I see a pot of boiling water; it is tipped toward us from the north." **1:14** Then the LORD said, "This means destruction will break out from the north on all who live in the land. **1:15** For I will soon summon all the peoples of the kingdoms of the north," says the LORD. "They will come and their kings will set up their thrones near the entrances of the gates of Jerusalem. They will attack all the walls surrounding it, and all the towns in Judah. **1:16** In this way I will pass sentence on the people of Jerusalem and Judah because of all their wickedness. For they rejected me and offered sacrifices to other gods, worshiping what they made with their own hands."
1:17 "But you, Jeremiah, get yourself ready! Go and tell these people everything I instruct you to say. Do not be terrified of them, or I will give you good reason to be terrified of them. **1:18** I, the LORD, hereby promise to make you as strong as a fortified city, an iron pillar, and a bronze wall. You will be able to stand up against all who live in the land, including the kings of Judah, its officials, its priests and all the people of the land. **1:19** They will attack you but they will not be able to overcome you, for I will be with you to rescue you," says the LORD.
The Lord Recalls Israel's Earlier Faithfulness
2:1 The LORD spoke to me. He said: **2:2** "Go and declare in the hearing of the people of Jerusalem: 'This is what the LORD says: "I have fond memories of you, how devoted you were to me in your early years. I remember how you loved me like a new bride; you followed me through the wilderness, through a land that had never been planted. **2:3** Israel was set apart to the LORD; they were like the first fruits of a harvest to him. All who tried to devour them were punished; disaster came upon them," says the LORD.'"
The Lord Reminds Them of the Unfaithfulness of Their Ancestors
2:4 Now listen to what the Lord has to say, you descendants of Jacob,
all you family groups from the nation of Israel.
2:5 This is what the Lord says:
"What fault could your ancestors have possibly found in me
that they strayed so far from me?
They paid allegiance to worthless idols, and so became worthless to me.
2:6 They did not ask:
'Where is the LORD who delivered us out of Egypt,
who brought us through the wilderness,
through a land of desert sands and rift valleys,
through a land of drought and deep darkness,
through a land in which no one travels,
and where no one lives?'
2:7 I brought you into a fertile land
so you could enjoy its fruits and its rich bounty.
But when you entered my land, you defiled it;
you made the land I call my own loathsome to me.
2:8 Your priests did not ask, 'Where is the LORD?'
Those responsible for teaching my law did not really know me.
Your rulers rebelled against me.
Your prophets prophesied in the name of the god Baal.
They all worshiped idols that could not help them.
The Lord Charges Contemporary Israel with Spiritual Adultery
2:9 "So, once more I will state my case against you," says the LORD.
"I will also state it against your children and grandchildren.
2:10 Go west across the sea to the coasts of Cyprus and see.
Send someone east to Kedar and have them look carefully.
See if such a thing as this has ever happened:
2:11 Has a nation ever changed its gods
(even though they are not really gods at all)?
But my people have exchanged me, their glorious God,
for a god that cannot help them at all!
2:12 Be amazed at this, O heavens!
Be shocked and utterly dumbfounded,"
says the LORD.
2:13 "Do so because my people have committed a double wrong:
they have rejected me,
the fountain of life-giving water,
and they have dug cisterns for themselves,

cracked cisterns which cannot even hold water."
Israel's Reliance on Foreign Alliances (not on God)
2:14 "Israel is not a slave, is he?
He was not born into slavery, was he?
If not, why then is he being carried off?
2:15 Like lions his enemies roar victoriously over him;
they raise their voices in triumph.
They have laid his land waste;
his cities have been burned down and deserted.
2:16 Even the soldiers from Memphis and Tahpanhes
have cracked your skulls, people of Israel.
2:17 You have brought all this on yourself, Israel,
by deserting the LORD your God when he was leading you along the right path.
2:18 What good will it do you then to go down to Egypt
to seek help from the Egyptians?
What good will it do you to go over to Assyria
to seek help from the Assyrians?
2:19 Your own wickedness will bring about your punishment.
Your unfaithful acts will bring down discipline on you.
Know, then, and realize how utterly harmful
it was for you to reject me, the LORD your God,
to show no respect for me,"
says the Lord GOD who rules over all.
The Lord Expresses His Exasperation at Judah's Persistent Idolatry
2:20 "Indeed, long ago you threw off my authority
and refused to be subject to me.
You said, 'I will not serve you.'
Instead, you gave yourself to other gods on every high hill
and under every green tree,
like a prostitute sprawls out before her lovers.
2:21 I planted you in the land
like a special vine of the very best stock.
Why in the world have you turned into something like a wild vine
that produces rotten, foul-smelling grapes?
2:22 You can try to wash away your guilt with a strong detergent.
You can use as much soap as you want.
But the stain of your guilt is still there for me to see,"
says the Lord GOD.
2:23 "How can you say, 'I have not made myself unclean.
I have not paid allegiance to the gods called Baal.'
Just look at the way you have behaved in the Valley of Hinnom!
Think about the things you have done there!
You are like a flighty, young female camel
that rushes here and there, crisscrossing its path.
2:24 You are like a wild female donkey brought up in the wilderness.
In her lust she sniffs the wind to get the scent of a male.
No one can hold her back when she is in heat.
None of the males need wear themselves out chasing after her.
At mating time she is easy to find.
2:25 Do not chase after other gods until your shoes wear out
and your throats become dry.
But you say, 'It is useless for you to try and stop me
because I love those foreign gods and want to pursue them!'
2:26 Just as a thief has to suffer dishonor when he is caught,
so the people of Israel will suffer dishonor for what they have done.
So will their kings and officials,
their priests and their prophets.
2:27 They say to a wooden idol, 'You are my father.'
They say to a stone image, 'You gave birth to me.'
Yes, they have turned away from me instead of turning to me.
Yet when they are in trouble, they say, 'Come and save us!'
2:28 But where are the gods you made for yourselves?
Let them save you when you are in trouble.
The sad fact is that you have as many gods
as you have towns, Judah.

2:29 "Why do you try to refute me?
All of you have rebelled against me,"
says the LORD.
2:30 "It did no good for me to punish your people.
They did not respond to such correction.
You slaughtered your prophets
like a voracious lion."
2:31 You people of this generation,
listen to what the LORD says.
"Have I been like a wilderness to you, Israel?
Have I been like a dark and dangerous land to you?
Why then do you say, 'We are free to wander.
We will not come to you any more?'
2:32 Does a young woman forget to put on her jewels?
Does a bride forget to put on her bridal attire?
But my people have forgotten me

for more days than can even be counted.

2:33 "My, how good you have become
at chasing after your lovers!
Why, you could even teach prostitutes a thing or two!
2:34 Even your clothes are stained with
the lifeblood of the poor who had not done anything wrong;
you did not catch them breaking into your homes.
Yet, in spite of all these things you have done,
2:35 you say, 'I have not done anything wrong,
so the LORD cannot really be angry with me any more.'
But, watch out! I will bring down judgment on you
because you say, 'I have not committed any sin.'
2:36 Why do you constantly go about
changing your political allegiances?
You will get no help from Egypt
just as you got no help from Assyria.
2:37 Moreover, you will come away from Egypt
with your hands covering your faces in sorrow and shame
because the LORD will not allow your reliance on them to be successful
and you will not gain any help from them.

3:1 "If a man divorces his wife
and she leaves him and becomes another man's wife,
he may not take her back again.
Doing that would utterly defile the land.
But you, Israel, have given yourself as a prostitute to many gods.
So what makes you think you can return to me?"
says the LORD.
3:2 "Look up at the hilltops and consider this.
You have had sex with other gods on every one of them.
You waited for those gods like a thief lying in wait in the desert.
You defiled the land by your wicked prostitution to other gods.
3:3 That is why the rains have been withheld,
and the spring rains have not come.
Yet in spite of this you are obstinate as a prostitute.
You refuse to be ashamed of what you have done.
3:4 Even now you say to me, 'You are my father!
You have been my faithful companion ever since I was young.
3:5 You will not always be angry with me, will you?
You will not be mad at me forever, will you?'
That is what you say,
but you continually do all the evil that you can."

3:6 When Josiah was king of Judah, the LORD said to me, "Jeremiah, you have no doubt seen what wayward Israel has done. You have seen how she went up to every high hill and under every green tree to give herself like a prostitute to other gods. **3:7** Yet even after she had done all that, I thought that she might come back to me. But she did not. Her sister, unfaithful Judah, saw what she did. **3:8** She also saw that I gave wayward Israel her divorce papers and sent her away because of her adulterous worship of other gods. Even after her unfaithful sister Judah had seen this, she still was not afraid, and she too went and gave herself like a prostitute to other gods. **3:9** Because she took her prostitution so lightly, she defiled the land through her adulterous worship of gods made of wood and stone. **3:10** In spite of all this, Israel's sister, unfaithful Judah, has not turned back to me with any sincerity; she has only pretended to do so," says the LORD. **3:11** Then the LORD said to me, "Under the circumstances, wayward Israel could even be considered less guilty than unfaithful Judah.
The Lord Calls on Israel and Judah to Repent
3:12 "Go and shout this message to my people in the countries in the north. Tell them,
'Come back to me, wayward Israel,' says the LORD.
'I will not continue to look on you with displeasure.
For I am merciful,' says the LORD.
'I will not be angry with you forever.
3:13 However, you must confess that you have done wrong,
and that you have rebelled against the LORD your God.
You must confess that you have given yourself to foreign gods under every green tree,
and have not obeyed my commands,' says the LORD.

3:14 "Come back to me, my wayward sons," says the LORD, "for I am your true master. If you do, I will take one of you from each town and two of you from each family group, and I will bring you back to Zion. **3:15** I will give you leaders who will be faithful to me. They will lead you with knowledge and insight. **3:16** In those days, your population will greatly increase in the land. At that time," says the LORD, "people will no longer talk about having the ark that contains the LORD's covenant with us. They will not call it to mind, remember it, or miss it. No, that will not be done any more! **3:17** At that time the city of Jerusalem will be called the LORD's throne. All nations will gather there in Jerusalem to honor the

LORD's name. They will no longer follow the stubborn inclinations of their own evil hearts. **3:18** At that time the nation of Judah and the nation of Israel will be reunited. Together they will come back from a land in the north to the land that I gave to your ancestors as a permanent possession. "

3:19 "I thought to myself,
'Oh what a joy it would be for me to treat you like a son!
What a joy it would be for me to give you a pleasant land,
the most beautiful piece of property there is in all the world!'
I thought you would call me, 'Father'
and would never cease being loyal to me.
3:20 But, you have been unfaithful to me, nation of Israel,
like an unfaithful wife who has left her husband,"
says the LORD.
3:21 "A noise is heard on the hilltops.
It is the sound of the people of Israel crying and pleading to their gods.
Indeed they have followed sinful ways;
they have forgotten to be true to the LORD their God.
3:22 Come back to me, you wayward people.
I want to cure your waywardness.
Say, 'Here we are. We come to you
because you are the LORD our God.
3:23 We know our noisy worship of false gods
on the hills and mountains did not help us.
We know that the LORD our God
is the only one who can deliver Israel.
3:24 From earliest times our worship of that shameful god, Baal,
has taken away all that our ancestors worked for.
It has taken away our flocks and our herds,
and even our sons and daughters.
3:25 Let us acknowledge our shame.
Let us bear the disgrace that we deserve.
For we have sinned against the LORD our God,
both we and our ancestors.
From earliest times to this very day
we have not obeyed the LORD our God.'

4:1 "If you, Israel, want to come back," says the LORD,
"if you want to come back to me
you must get those disgusting idols out of my sight
and must no longer go astray.
4:2 You must be truthful, honest and upright
when you take an oath saying, 'As surely as the LORD lives!'
If you do, the nations will pray to be as blessed by him as you are
and will make him the object of their boasting."
4:3 Yes, the LORD has this to say
to the people of Judah and Jerusalem:
"Like a farmer breaking up hard unplowed ground,
you must break your rebellious will and make a new beginning;
just as a farmer must clear away thorns lest the seed is wasted,
you must get rid of the sin that is ruining your lives.
4:4 Just as ritual circumcision cuts away the foreskin
as an external symbol of dedicated covenant commitment,
you must genuinely dedicate yourselves to the LORD
and get rid of everything that hinders your commitment to me,
people of Judah and inhabitants of Jerusalem.
If you do not, my anger will blaze up like a flaming fire against you
that no one will be able to extinguish.
That will happen because of the evil you have done."
Warning of Coming Judgment
4:5 The LORD said,
"Announce this in Judah and proclaim it in Jerusalem:
'Sound the trumpet throughout the land!'
Shout out loudly,
'Gather together! Let us flee into the fortified cities!'
4:6 Raise a signal flag that tells people to go to Zion.
Run for safety! Do not delay!
For I am about to bring disaster out of the north.
It will bring great destruction.
4:7 Like a lion that has come up from its lair
the one who destroys nations has set out from his home base.
He is coming out to lay your land waste.
Your cities will become ruins and lie uninhabited.
4:8 So put on sackcloth!
Mourn and wail, saying,
'The fierce anger of the LORD
has not turned away from us!'"
4:9 "When this happens," says the LORD,
"the king and his officials will lose their courage.
The priests will be struck with horror,
and the prophets will be speechless in astonishment."

4:10 In response to all this I said, "Ah, Lord GOD, you have surely allowed the people of Judah and Jerusalem to be deceived by those who say, 'You will be safe!' But in fact a sword is already at our throats."

4:11 "At that time the people of Judah and Jerusalem will be told,
'A scorching wind will sweep down
from the hilltops in the desert on my dear people.
It will not be a gentle breeze
for winnowing the grain and blowing away the chaff.
4:12 No, a wind too strong for that will come at my bidding.
Yes, even now I, myself, am calling down judgment on them.'
4:13 Look! The enemy is approaching like gathering clouds.
The roar of his chariots is like that of a whirlwind.
His horses move more swiftly than eagles."

I cry out, "We are doomed, for we will be destroyed!"

4:14 "Oh people of Jerusalem, purify your hearts from evil
so that you may yet be delivered.
How long will you continue to harbor up
wicked schemes within you?
4:15 For messengers are coming, heralding disaster,
from the city of Dan and from the hills of Ephraim.
4:16 They are saying,
'Announce to the surrounding nations,
"The enemy is coming!"
Proclaim this message to Jerusalem:
"Those who besiege cities are coming from a distant land.
They are ready to raise the battle cry against the towns in Judah."'
4:17 They will surround Jerusalem
like men guarding a field
because they have rebelled against me,"
says the LORD.
4:18 "The way you have lived and the things you have done
will bring this on you.
This is the punishment you deserve, and it will be painful indeed.
The pain will be so bad it will pierce your heart."

4:19 I said,
"Oh, the feeling in the pit of my stomach!
I writhe in anguish.
Oh, the pain in my heart!
My heart pounds within me.
I cannot keep silent.
For I hear the sound of the trumpet;
the sound of the battle cry pierces my soul!
4:20 I see one destruction after another taking place,
so that the whole land lies in ruins.
I see our tents suddenly destroyed,
their curtains torn down in a mere instant.
4:21 How long must I see the enemy's battle flags
and hear the military signals of their bugles?"
4:22 The LORD answered,
"This will happen because my people are foolish.
They do not know me.
They are like children who have no sense.
They have no understanding.
They are skilled at doing evil.
They do not know how to do good."

4:23 "I looked at the land and saw that it was an empty wasteland.
I looked up at the sky, and its light had vanished.
4:24 I looked at the mountains and saw that they were shaking.
All the hills were swaying back and forth!
4:25 I looked and saw that there were no more people,
and that all the birds in the sky had flown away.
4:26 I looked and saw that the fruitful land had become a desert
and that all of the cities had been laid in ruins.
The LORD had brought this all about
because of his blazing anger.
4:27 All this will happen because the LORD said,
"The whole land will be desolate;
however, I will not completely destroy it.
4:28 Because of this the land will mourn
and the sky above will grow black.
For I have made my purpose known
and I will not relent or turn back from carrying it out."
4:29 At the sound of the approaching horsemen and archers
the people of every town will flee.
Some of them will hide in the thickets.
Others will climb up among the rocks.
All the cities will be deserted.
No one will remain in them.

4:30 And you, Zion, city doomed to destruction,
you accomplish nothing by wearing a beautiful dress,
decking yourself out in jewels of gold,
and putting on eye shadow!
You are making yourself beautiful for nothing.
Your lovers spurn you.
They want to kill you.
4:31 In fact, I hear a cry like that of a woman in labor,
a cry of anguish like that of a woman giving birth to her first baby.
It is the cry of Daughter Zion gasping for breath,
reaching out for help, saying, "I am done in!
My life is ebbing away before these murderers!"

Judah is Justly Deserving of Coming Judgment

5:1 The LORD said,
"Go up and down through the streets of Jerusalem.
Look around and see for yourselves.
Search through its public squares.
See if any of you can find a single person
who deals honestly and tries to be truthful.
If you can, then I will not punish this city.
5:2 These people make promises in the name of the LORD.
But the fact is, what they swear to is really a lie."
5:3 LORD, I know you look for faithfulness.
But even when you punish these people, they feel no remorse.
Even when you nearly destroy them, they refuse to be corrected.
They have become as hardheaded as a rock.
They refuse to change their ways.
5:4 I thought, "Surely it is only the ignorant poor who act this way.
They act like fools because they do not know what the LORD demands.
They do not know what their God requires of them.
5:5 I will go to the leaders
and speak with them.
Surely they know what the LORD demands.
Surely they know what their God requires of them."
Yet all of them, too, have rejected his authority
and refuse to submit to him.
5:6 So like a lion from the thicket their enemies will kill them.
Like a wolf from the desert they will destroy them.
Like a leopard they will lie in wait outside their cities
and totally destroy anyone who ventures out.
For they have rebelled so much
and done so many unfaithful things.

5:7 The LORD asked,
"How can I leave you unpunished, Jerusalem?
Your people have rejected me
and have worshiped gods that are not gods at all.
Even though I supplied all their needs, they were like an unfaithful wife to me.
They went flocking to the houses of prostitutes.
5:8 They are like lusty, well-fed stallions.
Each of them lusts after his neighbor's wife.
5:9 I will surely punish them for doing such things!" says the LORD.
"I will surely bring retribution on such a nation as this!"

5:10 The LORD commanded the enemy,
"March through the vineyards of Israel and Judah and ruin them.
But do not destroy them completely.
Strip off their branches
for these people do not belong to the LORD.
5:11 For the nations of Israel and Judah
have been very unfaithful to me,"
says the LORD.
5:12 "These people have denied what the LORD says.
They have said, 'That is not so!
No harm will come to us.
We will not experience war and famine.
5:13 The prophets will prove to be full of wind.
The LORD has not spoken through them.
So, let what they say happen to them.'"

5:14 Because of that, the LORD, the God who rules over all, said to me,
"Because these people have spoken like this,
I will make the words that I put in your mouth like fire.
And I will make this people like wood
which the fiery judgments you speak will burn up."
5:15 The LORD says, "Listen, nation of Israel!
I am about to bring a nation from far away to attack you.
It will be a nation that was founded long ago
and has lasted for a long time.
It will be a nation whose language you will not know.
Its people will speak words that you will not be able to understand.
5:16 All of its soldiers are strong and mighty.

Their arrows will send you to your grave.
5:17 They will eat up your crops and your food.
They will kill off your sons and your daughters.
They will eat up your sheep and your cattle.
They will destroy your vines and your fig trees.
Their weapons will batter down
the fortified cities you trust in.
5:18 Yet even then I will not completely destroy you," says the LORD.
5:19 "So then,
Jeremiah, when your people ask, 'Why has the LORD our God done all this to us?' tell them, 'It is because you rejected me and served foreign gods in your own land. So you must serve foreigners in a land that does not belong to you.'

5:20 "Proclaim this message among the descendants of Jacob.
Make it known throughout Judah.
5:21 Tell them: 'Hear this,
you foolish people who have no understanding,
who have eyes but do not discern,
who have ears but do not perceive:
5:22 "You should fear me!" says the LORD.
"You should tremble in awe before me!
I made the sand to be a boundary for the sea,
a permanent barrier that it can never cross.
Its waves may roll, but they can never prevail.
They may roar, but they can never cross beyond that boundary."
5:23 But these people have stubborn and rebellious hearts.
They have turned aside and gone their own way.
5:24 They do not say to themselves,
"Let us revere the LORD our God.
It is he who gives us the autumn rains and the spring rains at the proper time.
It is he who assures us of the regular weeks of harvest."
5:25 Your misdeeds have stopped these things from coming.
Your sins have deprived you of my bounty.'

5:26 "Indeed, there are wicked scoundrels among my people.
They lie in wait like bird catchers hiding in ambush.
They set deadly traps to catch people.
5:27 Like a cage filled with the birds that have been caught,
their houses are filled with the gains of their fraud and deceit.
That is how they have gotten so rich and powerful.
5:28 That is how they have grown fat and sleek.
There is no limit to the evil things they do.
They do not plead the cause of the fatherless in such a way as to win it.
They do not defend the rights of the poor.
5:29 I will certainly punish them for doing such things!" says the LORD.
"I will certainly bring retribution on such a nation as this!
5:30 "Something horrible and shocking
is going on in the land of Judah:
5:31 The prophets prophesy lies.
The priests exercise power by their own authority.
And my people love to have it this way.
But they will not be able to help you when the time of judgment comes!

The Destruction of Jerusalem Depicted

6:1 "Run for safety, people of Benjamin!
Get out of Jerusalem!
Sound the trumpet in Tekoa!
Light the signal fires at Beth Hakkerem!
For disaster lurks out of the north;
it will bring great destruction.
6:2 I will destroy Daughter Zion,
who is as delicate and defenseless as a young maiden.
6:3 Kings will come against it with their armies.
They will encamp in siege all around it.
Each of them will devastate the portion assigned to him.
6:4 They will say, 'Prepare to do battle against it!
Come on! Let's attack it at noon!'
But later they will say, 'Oh, oh! Too bad!
The day is almost over
and the shadows of evening are getting long.
6:5 So come on, let's go ahead and attack it by night
and destroy all its fortified buildings.'
6:6 All of this is because the LORD who rules over all has said:
'Cut down the trees around Jerusalem
and build up a siege ramp against its walls.
This is the city which is to be punished.
Nothing but oppression happens in it.
6:7 As a well continually pours out fresh water
so it continually pours out wicked deeds.
Sounds of violence and destruction echo throughout it.
All I see are sick and wounded people.'
6:8 So take warning, Jerusalem,

or I will abandon you in disgust
and make you desolate,
a place where no one can live."

6:9 This is what the LORD who rules over all said to me:
"Those who remain in Israel will be
like the grapes thoroughly gleaned from a vine.
So go over them again, as though you were a grape harvester
passing your hand over the branches one last time."

6:10 I answered,
"Who would listen
if I spoke to them and warned them?
Their ears are so closed
that they cannot hear!
Indeed, what the LORD says is offensive to them.
They do not like it at all.
6:11 I am as full of anger as you are, LORD,
I am tired of trying to hold it in."

The LORD answered,
"Vent it, then, on the children who play in the street
and on the young men who are gathered together.
Husbands and wives are to be included,
as well as the old and those who are advanced in years.
6:12 Their houses will be turned over to others
as will their fields and their wives.
For I will unleash my power
against those who live in this land,"
says the LORD.
6:13 "That is because, from the least important to the most important of them,
all of them are greedy for dishonest gain.
Prophets and priests alike,
all of them practice deceit.
6:14 They offer only superficial help
for the harm my people have suffered.
They say, 'Everything will be all right!'
But everything is not all right!
6:15 Are they ashamed because they have done such shameful things?
No, they are not at all ashamed.
They do not even know how to blush!
So they will die, just like others have died.
They will be brought to ruin when I punish them,"
says the LORD.
6:16 The LORD said to his people:
"You are standing at the crossroads. So consider your path.
Ask where the old, reliable paths are.
Ask where the path is that leads to blessing and follow it.
If you do, you will find rest for your souls."
But they said, "We will not follow it!"
6:17 The LORD said,
"I appointed prophets as watchmen to warn you, saying:
'Pay attention to the warning sound of the trumpet!'"
But they said, "We will not pay attention!"
6:18 So the LORD said,
"Hear, you nations!
Be witnesses and take note of what will happen to these people.
6:19 Hear this, you peoples of the earth:
'Take note! I am about to bring disaster on these people.
It will come as punishment for their scheming.
For they have paid no attention to what I have said,
and they have rejected my law.
6:20 I take no delight when they offer up to me
frankincense that comes from Sheba
or sweet-smelling cane imported from a faraway land.
I cannot accept the burnt offerings they bring me.
I get no pleasure from the sacrifices they offer to me.'
6:21 So, this is what the LORD says:
'I will assuredly make these people stumble to their doom.
Parents and children will stumble and fall to their destruction.
Friends and neighbors will die.'

6:22 "This is what the LORD says:
'Beware! An army is coming from a land in the north.
A mighty nation is stirring into action in faraway parts of the earth.
6:23 Its soldiers are armed with bows and spears.
They are cruel and show no mercy.
They sound like the roaring sea
as they ride forth on their horses.
Lined up in formation like men going into battle
to attack you, Daughter Zion.'"

6:24 The people cry out, "We have heard reports about them!
We have become helpless with fear!
Anguish grips us,
agony like that of a woman giving birth to a baby!
6:25 Do not go out into the countryside.
Do not travel on the roads.
For the enemy is there with sword in hand.
They are spreading terror everywhere."
6:26 So I said, "Oh, my dear people, put on sackcloth
and roll in ashes.
Mourn with painful sobs
as though you had lost your only child.
For any moment now that destructive army
will come against us."

6:27 The LORD said to me,
"I have made you like a metal assayer
to test my people like ore.
You are to observe them
and evaluate how they behave."

6:28 I reported,
"All of them are the most stubborn of rebels!
They are as hard as bronze or iron.
They go about telling lies.
They all deal corruptly.
6:29 The fiery bellows of judgment burn fiercely.
But there is too much dross to be removed.
The process of refining them has proved useless.
The wicked have not been purged.
6:30 They are regarded as 'rejected silver'
because the LORD rejects them."

Faulty Religion and Unethical Behavior Will Lead to Judgment

7:1 The LORD said to Jeremiah: **7:2** "Stand in the gate of the LORD's temple and proclaim this message: 'Listen, all you people of Judah who have passed through these gates to worship the LORD. Hear what the LORD has to say. **7:3** The LORD God of Israel who rules over all says: Change the way you have been living and do what is right. If you do, I will allow you to continue to live in this land. **7:4** Stop putting your confidence in the false belief that says, "We are safe! The temple of the LORD is here! The temple of the LORD is here! The temple ofthe LORD is here!" **7:5** You must change the way you have been living and do what is right. You must treat one another fairly. **7:6** Stop oppressing foreigners who live in your land, children who have lost their fathers, and women who have lost their husbands. Stop killing innocent people in this land. Stop paying allegiance to other gods. That will only bring about your ruin. **7:7** If you stop doing these things, I will allow you to continue to live in this land which I gave to your ancestors as a lasting possession.
7:8 "'But just look at you! You are putting your confidence in a false belief that will not deliver you. **7:9** You steal. You murder. You commit adultery. You lie when you swear on oath. You sacrifice to the god Baal. You pay allegiance to other gods whom you have not previously known. **7:10** Then you come and stand in my presence in this temple I have claimed as my own and say, "We are safe!" You think you are so safe that you go on doing all those hateful sins! **7:11** Do you think this temple I have claimed as my own is to be a hideout for robbers? You had better take note! I have seen for myself what you have done! says the LORD. **7:12** So, go to the place in Shiloh where I allowed myself to be worshiped in the early days. See what I did to it because of the wicked things my people Israel did. **7:13** You also have done all these things, says the LORD, and I have spoken to you over and over again. But you have not listened! You have refused to respond when I called you to repent! **7:14** So I will destroy this temple which I have claimed as my own, this temple that you are trusting to protect you. I will destroy this place that I gave to you and your ancestors, just like I destroyed Shiloh. **7:15** And I will drive you out of my sight just like I drove out your relatives, the people of Israel.'"

7:16 Then the LORD said, "As for you, Jeremiah, do not pray for these people! Do not cry out to me or petition me on their behalf! Do not plead with me to save them, because I will not listen to you. **7:17** Do you see what they are doing in the towns of Judah and in the streets of Jerusalem? **7:18** Children are gathering firewood, fathers are building fires with it, and women are mixing dough to bake cakes to offer to the goddess they call the Queen of Heaven. They are also pouring out drink offerings to other gods. They seem to do all this just to trouble me. **7:19** But I am not really the one being troubled!" says the LORD. "Rather they are bringing trouble on themselves to their own shame! **7:20** So," the Lord GOD says, "my raging fury will be poured out on this land. It will be poured out on human beings and animals, on trees and crops. And it will burn like a fire which cannot be extinguished."

7:21 The LORD said to the people of Judah, "The LORD God of Israel who rules over all says: 'You might as well go ahead and add the meat of your burnt offerings to that of the other sacrifices and eat it, too! **7:22**

Consider this: When I spoke to your ancestors after I brought them out of Egypt, I did not merely give them commands about burnt offerings and sacrifices. 7:23 I also explicitly commanded them: "Obey me. If you do, I will be your God and you will be my people. Live exactly the way I tell you and things will go well with you." 7:24 But they did not listen to me or pay any attention to me. They followed the stubborn inclinations of their own wicked hearts. They acted worse and worse instead of better. 7:25 From the time your ancestors departed the land of Egypt until now, I sent my servants the prophets to you again and again, day after day. 7:26 But your ancestors did not listen to me nor pay attention to me. They became obstinate and were more wicked than even their own forefathers.'"

7:27 Then the LORD said to me, "When you tell them all this, they will not listen to you. When you call out to them, they will not respond to you. 7:28 So tell them: 'This is a nation that has not obeyed the LORD their God and has not accepted correction. Faithfulness is nowhere to be found in it. These people do not even profess it anymore. 7:29 So, mourn, you people of this nation. Cut off your hair and throw it away. Sing a song of mourning on the hilltops. For the LORD has decided to reject and forsake this generation that has provoked his wrath!'"

7:30 The LORD says, "I have rejected them because the people of Judah have done what I consider evil. They have set up their disgusting idols in the temple which I have claimed for my own and have defiled it. 7:31 They have also built places of worship in a place called Topheth in the Valley of Ben Hinnom so that they can sacrifice their sons and daughters by fire. That is something I never commanded them to do! Indeed, it never even entered my mind to command such a thing! 7:32 So, watch out!" says the LORD. "The time will soon come when people will no longer call those places Topheth or the Valley of Ben Hinnom. But they will call that valley the Valley of Slaughter and they will bury so many people in Topheth they will run out of room. 7:33 Then the dead bodies of these people will be left on the ground for the birds and wild animals to eat. There will not be any survivors to scare them away. 7:34 I will put an end to the sounds of joy and gladness, or the glad celebration of brides and grooms throughout the towns of Judah and the streets of Jerusalem. For the whole land will become a desolate wasteland."

8:1 The LORD says, "When that time comes, the bones of the kings of Judah and its leaders, the bones of the priests and prophets and of all the other people who lived in Jerusalem will be dug up from their graves. 8:2 They will be spread out and exposed to the sun, the moon and the stars. These are things they adored and served, things to which they paid allegiance, from which they sought guidance, and worshiped. The bones of these people will never be regathered and reburied. They will be like manure used to fertilize the ground. 8:3 However, I will leave some of these wicked people alive and banish them to other places. But wherever these people who survive may go, they will wish they had died rather than lived," says the LORD who rules over all.

Willful Disregard of God Will Lead to Destruction

8:4 The LORD said to me,
"Tell them, 'The LORD says,
Do people not get back up when they fall down?
Do they not turn around when they go the wrong way?
8:5 Why, then, do these people of Jerusalem
continually turn away from me in apostasy?
They hold fast to their deception.
They refuse to turn back to me.
8:6 I have listened to them very carefully,
but they do not speak honestly.
None of them regrets the evil he has done.
None of them says, "I have done wrong!"
All of them persist in their own wayward course
like a horse charging recklessly into battle.
8:7 Even the stork knows
when it is time to move on.
The turtledove, swallow, and crane
recognize the normal times for their migration.
But my people pay no attention
to what I, the LORD, require of them.
8:8 How can you say, "We are wise!
We have the law of the LORD"?
The truth is, those who teach it have used their writings
to make it say what it does not really mean.
8:9 Your wise men will be put to shame.
They will be dumbfounded and be brought to judgment.
Since they have rejected the word of the LORD,
what wisdom do they really have?
8:10 So I will give their wives to other men
and their fields to new owners.
For from the least important to the most important of them,
all of them are greedy for dishonest gain.
Prophets and priests alike,
all practice deceit.
8:11 They offer only superficial help

for the hurt my dear people have suffered.
They say, "Everything will be all right!"
But everything is not all right!
8:12 Are they ashamed because they have done such disgusting things?
No, they are not at all ashamed!
They do not even know how to blush!
So they will die just like others have died.
They will be brought to ruin when I punish them,
says the LORD.
8:13 I will take away their harvests, says the LORD.
There will be no grapes on their vines.
There will be no figs on their fig trees.
Even the leaves on their trees will wither.
The crops that I gave them will be taken away.'"

Jeremiah Laments over the Coming Destruction

8:14 The people say,
"Why are we just sitting here?
Let us gather together inside the fortified cities.
Let us at least die there fighting,
since the LORD our God has condemned us to die.
He has condemned us to drink the poison waters of judgment
because we have sinned against him.
8:15 We hoped for good fortune, but nothing good has come of it.
We hoped for a time of relief, but instead we experience terror.
8:16 The snorting of the enemy's horses
is already being heard in the city of Dan.
The sound of the neighing of their stallions
causes the whole land to tremble with fear.
They are coming to destroy the land and everything in it!
They are coming to destroy the cities and everyone who lives in them!"

8:17 The LORD says,
"Yes indeed, I am sending an enemy against you
that will be like poisonous snakes which cannot be charmed away.
And they will inflict fatal wounds on you."

8:18 Then I said,
"There is no cure for my grief!
I am sick at heart!
8:19 I hear my dear people crying out
throughout the length and breadth of the land.
They are crying, 'Is the LORD no longer in Zion?
Is her divine King no longer there?'"
The LORD answers,
"Why then do they provoke me to anger with their images,
with their worthless foreign idols?"
8:20 "They cry, 'Harvest time has come and gone, and the summer is over,
and still we have not been delivered.'
8:21 My heart is crushed because my dear people are being crushed.
I go about crying and grieving. I am overwhelmed with dismay.
8:22 There is still medicinal ointment available in Gilead!
There is still a physician there!
Why then have my dear people
not been restored to health?
9:1 (8:23) I wish that my head were a well full of water
and my eyes were a fountain full of tears!
If they were, I could cry day and night
for those of my dear people who have been killed.
9:2 (9:1) I wish I had a lodging place in the desert
where I could spend some time like a weary traveler.
Then I would desert my people
and walk away from them
because they are all unfaithful to God,
a congregation of people that has been disloyal to him.

The Lord Laments That He Has No Choice But to Judge Them

9:3 The LORD says,
"These people are like soldiers who have readied their bows.
Their tongues are always ready to shoot out lies.
They have become powerful in the land,
but they have not done so by honest means.
Indeed, they do one evil thing after another
and do not pay attention to me.
9:4 Everyone must be on his guard around his friends.
He must not even trust any of his relatives.
For every one of them will find some way to cheat him.
And all of his friends will tell lies about him.
9:5 One friend deceives another
and no one tells the truth.
These people have trained themselves to tell lies.
They do wrong and are unable to repent
9:6 They do one act of violence after another,
and one deceitful thing after another.

They refuse to pay attention to me,"
says the LORD.

9:7 Therefore the LORD who rules over all says,
"I will now purify them in the fires of affliction and test them.
The wickedness of my dear people has left me no choice.
What else can I do?
9:8 Their tongues are like deadly arrows.
They are always telling lies.
Friendly words for their neighbors come from their mouths.
But their minds are thinking up ways to trap them.
9:9 I will certainly punish them for doing such things!" says the LORD.
"I will certainly bring retribution on such a nation as this!"
The Coming Destruction Calls For Mourning
9:10 I said,
"I will weep and mourn for the grasslands on the mountains,
I will sing a mournful song for the pastures in the wilderness
because they are so scorched no one travels through them.
The sound of livestock is no longer heard there.
Even the birds in the sky and the wild animals in the fields
have fled and are gone."
9:11 The LORD said,
"I will make Jerusalem a heap of ruins.
Jackals will make their home there.
I will destroy the towns of Judah
so that no one will be able to live in them."
9:12 I said,
"Who is wise enough to understand why this has happened?
Who has a word from the LORD that can explain it?
Why does the land lie in ruins?
Why is it as scorched as a desert through which no one travels?"

9:13 The LORD answered, "This has happened because these people have rejected my laws which I gave them. They have not obeyed me or followed those laws. **9:14** Instead they have followed the stubborn inclinations of their own hearts. They have paid allegiance to the gods called Baal, as their fathers taught them to do. **9:15** So then, listen to what I, the LORD God of Israel who rules over all, say. 'I will make these people eat the bitter food of suffering and drink the poison water of judgment. **9:16** I will scatter them among nations that neither they nor their ancestors have known anything about. I will send people chasing after them with swords until I have destroyed them.'"

9:17 The LORD who rules over all told me to say to this people,
"Take note of what I say.
Call for the women who mourn for the dead!
Summon those who are the most skilled at it!"
9:18 I said, "Indeed, let them come quickly and sing a song of mourning for us.
Let them wail loudly until tears stream from our own eyes
and our eyelids overflow with water.
9:19 For the sound of wailing is soon to be heard in Zion.
They will wail, 'We are utterly ruined! We are completely disgraced!
For our houses have been torn down
and we must leave our land.'"
9:20 I said,
"So now, you wailing women, hear what the LORD says.
Open your ears to the words from his mouth.
Teach your daughters this mournful song,
and each of you teach your neighbor this lament.
9:21 'Death has climbed in through our windows.
It has entered into our fortified houses.
It has taken away our children who play in the streets.
It has taken away our young men who gather in the city squares.'
9:22 Tell your daughters and neighbors, 'The LORD says,
"The dead bodies of people will lie scattered everywhere
like manure scattered on a field.
They will lie scattered on the ground
like grain that has been cut down but has not been gathered."'"
9:23 The LORD says,
"Wise people should not boast that they are wise.
Powerful people should not boast that they are powerful.
Rich people should not boast that they are rich.
9:24 If people want to boast, they should boast about this:
They should boast that they understand and know me.
They should boast that they know and understand
that I, the LORD, act out of faithfulness, fairness, and justice in the earth
and that I desire people to do these things,"
says the LORD.

9:25 The LORD says, "Watch out! The time is soon coming when I will punish all those who are circumcised only in the flesh. **9:26** That is, I will punish the Egyptians, the Judeans, the Edomites, the Ammonites, the Moabites, and all the desert people who cut their hair short at the temples. I will do so because none of the people of those nations are really circumcised in the LORD's sight. Moreover, none of the people of Israel are circumcised when it comes to their hearts."
The Lord, not Idols, is the Only Worthy Object of Worship
10:1 You people of Israel, listen to what the LORD has to say to you.
10:2 The LORD says,
"Do not start following pagan religious practices.
Do not be in awe of signs that occur in the sky
even though the nations hold them in awe.
10:3 For the religion of these people is worthless.
They cut down a tree in the forest,
and a craftsman makes it into an idol with his tools.
10:4 He decorates it with overlays of silver and gold.
He uses hammer and nails to fasten it together
so that it will not fall over.
10:5 Such idols are like scarecrows in a cucumber field.
They cannot talk.
They must be carried
because they cannot walk.
Do not be afraid of them
because they cannot hurt you.
And they do not have any power to help you."
10:6 I said,
"There is no one like you, LORD.
You are great.
And you are renowned for your power.
10:7 Everyone should revere you, O King of all nations,
because you deserve to be revered.
For there is no one like you
among any of the wise people of the nations nor among any of their kings.
10:8 The people of those nations are both stupid and foolish.
Instruction from a wooden idol is worthless!
10:9 Hammered-out silver is brought from Tarshish
and gold is brought from Uphaz to cover those idols.
They are the handiwork of carpenters and goldsmiths.
They are clothed in blue and purple clothes.
They are all made by skillful workers.
10:10 The LORD is the only true God.
He is the living God and the everlasting King.
When he shows his anger the earth shakes.
None of the nations can stand up to his fury.

10:11 You people of Israel should tell those nations this:
'These gods did not make heaven and earth.
They will disappear from the earth and from under the heavens.'
10:12 The LORD is the one who by his power made the earth.
He is the one who by his wisdom established the world.
And by his understanding he spread out the skies.
10:13 When his voice thunders, the heavenly ocean roars.
He makes the clouds rise from the far-off horizons.
He makes the lightning flash out in the midst of the rain.
He unleashes the wind from the places where he stores it.
10:14 All these idolaters will prove to be stupid and ignorant.
Every goldsmith will be disgraced by the idol he made.
For the image he forges is merely a sham.
There is no breath in any of those idols.
10:15 They are worthless, mere objects to be mocked.
When the time comes to punish them, they will be destroyed.
10:16 The LORD, who is the inheritance of Jacob's descendants, is not like them.
He is the one who created everything.
And the people of Israel are those he claims as his own.
He is known as the LORD who rules over all."
Jeremiah Laments for and Prays for the Soon-to-be-Judged People
10:17 Gather your belongings together and prepare to leave the land,
you people of Jerusalem who are being besieged.
10:18 For the LORD says, "I will now throw out
those who live in this land.
I will bring so much trouble on them
that they will actually feel it."
10:19 And I cried out, "We are doomed!
Our wound is severe!
We once thought, 'This is only an illness.
And we will be able to bear it!'
10:20 But our tents have been destroyed.
The ropes that held them in place have been ripped apart.
Our children are gone and are not coming back.
There is no survivor to put our tents back up,
no one left to hang their tent curtains in place.
10:21 For our leaders are stupid.
They have not sought the LORD's advice.

So they do not act wisely,
and the people they are responsible for have all been scattered.
10:22 Listen! News is coming even now.
The rumble of a great army is heard approaching from a land in the north.
It is coming to turn the towns of Judah into rubble,
places where only jackals live.
10:23 LORD, we know that people do not control their own destiny.
It is not in their power to determine what will happen to them.
10:24 Correct us, LORD, but only in due measure.
Do not punish us in anger or you will reduce us to nothing.
10:25 Vent your anger on the nations that do not acknowledge you.
Vent it on the peoples who do not worship you.
For they have destroyed the people of Jacob.
They have completely destroyed them
and left their homeland in utter ruin.

The People Have Violated Their Covenant with God

11:1 The LORD said to Jeremiah: **11:2** "Hear the terms of the covenant I made with Israel and pass them on to the people of Judah and the citizens of Jerusalem. **11:3** Tell them that the LORD, the God of Israel, says, 'Anyone who does not keep the terms of the covenant will be under a curse. **11:4** Those are the terms that I charged your ancestors to keep when I brought them out of Egypt, that place which was like an iron-smelting furnace. I said at that time, "Obey me and carry out the terms of the agreement exactly as I commanded you. If you do, you will be my people and I will be your God. **11:5** Then I will keep the promise I swore on oath to your ancestors to give them a land flowing with milk and honey." That is the very land that you still live in today.'" And I responded, "Amen! Let it be so, LORD!"

11:6 The LORD said to me, "Announce all the following words in the towns of Judah and in the streets of Jerusalem: 'Listen to the terms of my covenant with you and carry them out! **11:7** For I solemnly warned your ancestors to obey me. I warned them again and again, ever since I delivered them out of Egypt until this very day. **11:8** But they did not listen to me or pay any attention to me! Each one of them followed the stubborn inclinations of his own wicked heart. So I brought on them all the punishments threatened in the covenant because they did not carry out its terms as I commanded them to do.'"

11:9 The LORD said to me, "The people of Judah and the citizens of Jerusalem have plotted rebellion against me! **11:10** They have gone back to the evil ways of their ancestors of old who refused to obey what I told them. They, too, have paid allegiance to other gods and worshiped them. Both the nation of Israel and the nation of Judah have violated the covenant I made with their ancestors. **11:11** So I, the LORD, say this: 'I will soon bring disaster on them which they will not be able to escape! When they cry out to me for help, I will not listen to them. **11:12** Then those living in the towns of Judah and in Jerusalem will go and cry out for help to the gods to whom they have been sacrificing. However, those gods will by no means be able to save them when disaster strikes them. **11:13** This is in spite of the fact that the people of Judah have as many gods as they have towns and the citizens of Jerusalem have set up as many altars to sacrifice to that disgusting god, Baal, as they have streets in the city!' **11:14** So, Jeremiah, do not pray for these people. Do not cry out to me or petition me on their behalf. Do not plead with me to save them. For I will not listen to them when they call out to me for help when disaster strikes them."

11:15 The LORD says to the people of Judah,
"What right do you have to be in my temple, my beloved people?
Many of you have done wicked things.
Can your acts of treachery be so easily canceled by sacred offerings
that you take joy in doing evil even while you make them?
11:16 I, the LORD, once called you a thriving olive tree,
one that produced beautiful fruit.
But I will set you on fire,
fire that will blaze with a mighty roar.
Then all your branches will be good for nothing.
11:17 For though I, the LORD who rules over all, planted you in the land,
I now decree that disaster will come on you
because the nations of Israel and Judah have done evil
and have made me angry by offering sacrifices to the god Baal."

A Plot Against Jeremiah is Revealed and He Complains of Injustice

11:18 The LORD gave me knowledge, that I might have understanding.
Then he showed me what the people were doing.
11:19 Before this I had been like a docile lamb ready to be led to the slaughter.
I did not know they were making plans to kill me.
I did not know they were saying,
"Let's destroy the tree along with its fruit!
Let's remove Jeremiah from the world of the living
so people will not even be reminded of him any more."
11:20 So I said to the LORD,
"O LORD who rules over all, you are a just judge!
You examine people's hearts and minds.
I want to see you pay them back for what they have done

because I trust you to vindicate my cause."

11:21 Then the LORD told me about some men from Anathoth who were threatening to kill me. They had threatened, "Stop prophesying in the name of the LORD or we will kill you!" **11:22** So the LORD who rules over all said, "I will surely punish them! Their young men will be killed in battle. Their sons and daughters will die of starvation. **11:23** Not one of them will survive. I will bring disaster on those men from Anathoth who threatened you. A day of reckoning is coming for them."

12:1 LORD, you have always been fair
whenever I have complained to you.
However, I would like to speak with you about the disposition of justice.
Why are wicked people successful?
Why do all dishonest people have such easy lives?
12:2 You plant them like trees and they put down their roots.
They grow prosperous and are very fruitful.
They always talk about you,
but they really care nothing about you.
12:3 But you, LORD, know all about me.
You watch me and test my devotion to you.
Drag these wicked men away like sheep to be slaughtered!
Appoint a time when they will be killed!
12:4 How long must the land be parched
and the grass in every field be withered?
How long must the animals and the birds die
because of the wickedness of the people who live in this land?
For these people boast,
"God will not see what happens to us."
12:5 The LORD answered,
"If you have raced on foot against men and they have worn you out,
how will you be able to compete with horses?
And if you feel secure only in safe and open country,
how will you manage in the thick undergrowth along the Jordan River?
12:6 As a matter of fact, even your own brothers
and the members of your own family have betrayed you too.
Even they have plotted to do away with you.
So do not trust them even when they say kind things to you.

12:7 "I will abandon my nation.
I will forsake the people I call my own.
I will turn my beloved people
over to the power of their enemies.
12:8 The people I call my own have turned on me
like a lion in the forest.
They have roared defiantly at me.
So I will treat them as though I hate them.
12:9 The people I call my own attack me like birds of prey or like hyenas.
But other birds of prey are all around them.
Let all the nations gather together like wild beasts.
Let them come and destroy these people I call my own.
12:10 Many foreign rulers will ruin the land where I planted my people.
They will trample all over my chosen land.
They will turn my beautiful land
into a desolate wasteland.
12:11 They will lay it waste.
It will lie parched and empty before me.
The whole land will be laid waste.
But no one living in it will pay any heed.
12:12 A destructive army will come marching
over the hilltops in the desert.
For the LORD will use them as his destructive weapon
against everyone from one end of the land to the other.
No one will be safe.
12:13 My people will sow wheat, but will harvest weeds.
They will work until they are exhausted, but will get nothing from it.
They will be disappointed in their harvests
because the LORD will take them away in his fierce anger.

12:14 "I, the LORD, also have something to say concerning the wicked nations who surround my land and have attacked and plundered the land that I gave to my people as a permanent possession. I say: 'I will uproot the people of those nations from their lands and I will free the people of Judah who have been taken there. **12:15** But after I have uprooted the people of those nations, I will relent and have pity on them. I will restore the people of each of those nations to their own lands and to their own country. **12:16** But they must make sure you learn to follow the religious practices of my people. Once they taught my people to swear their oaths using the name of the god Baal. But then, they must swear oaths using my name, saying, "As surely as the LORD lives, I swear." If they do these things, then they will be included among the people I call my own. **12:17** But I will completely uproot and destroy any of those nations that will not pay heed,'" says the LORD.

An Object Lesson from Ruined Linen Shorts

13:1 The LORD said to me, "Go and buy some linen shorts and put them on. Do not put them in water." **13:2** So I bought the shorts as the LORD had told me to do and put them on. **13:3** Then the LORD spoke to me again and said, **13:4** "Take the shorts that you bought and are wearing and go at once to Perath. Bury the shorts there in a crack in the rocks." **13:5** So I went and buried them at Perath as the LORD had ordered me to do. **13:6** Many days later the LORD said to me, "Go at once to Perath and get the shorts I ordered you to bury there." **13:7** So I went to Perath and dug up the shorts from the place where I had buried them. I found that they were ruined; they were good for nothing.

13:8 Then the LORD said to me, **13:9** "I, the LORD, say: 'This shows how I will ruin the highly exalted position in which Judah and Jerusalem take pride. **13:10** These wicked people refuse to obey what I have said. They follow the stubborn inclinations of their own hearts and pay allegiance to other gods by worshiping and serving them. So they will become just like these linen shorts which are good for nothing. **13:11** For,' I say, 'just as shorts cling tightly to a person's body, so I bound the whole nation of Israel and the whole nation of Judah tightly to me.' I intended for them to be my special people and to bring me fame, honor, and praise. But they would not obey me.

13:12 "So tell them, 'The LORD, the God of Israel, says, "Every wine jar is made to be filled with wine."' And they will probably say to you, 'Do you not think we know that every wine jar is supposed to be filled with wine?' **13:13** Then tell them, 'The LORD says, "I will soon fill all the people who live in this land with stupor. I will also fill the kings from David's dynasty, the priests, the prophets, and the citizens of Jerusalem with stupor. **13:14** And I will smash them like wine bottles against one another, children and parents alike. I will not show any pity, mercy, or compassion. Nothing will keep me from destroying them,' says the LORD."

13:15 Then I said to the people of Judah,
"Listen and pay attention! Do not be arrogant!
For the LORD has spoken.
13:16 Show the LORD your God the respect that is due him.
Do it before he brings the darkness of disaster.
Do it before you stumble into distress
like a traveler on the mountains at twilight.
Do it before he turns the light of deliverance you hope for
into the darkness and gloom of exile.
13:17 But if you will not pay attention to this warning,
I will weep alone because of your arrogant pride.
I will weep bitterly and my eyes will overflow with tears
because you, the LORD's flock, will be carried into exile."

13:18 The LORD told me,
"Tell the king and the queen mother,
'Surrender your thrones,
for your glorious crowns
will be removed from your heads.
13:19 The gates of the towns in southern Judah will be shut tight.
No one will be able to go in or out of them.
All Judah will be carried off into exile.
They will be completely carried off into exile.'"

13:20 Then I said,
"Look up, Jerusalem, and see
the enemy that is coming from the north.
Where now is the flock of people that were entrusted to your care?
Where now are the 'sheep' that you take such pride in?
13:21 What will you say when the LORD appoints as rulers over you those allies
that you, yourself, had actually prepared as such?
Then anguish and agony will grip you
like that of a woman giving birth to a baby.
13:22 You will probably ask yourself,
'Why have these things happened to me?
Why have I been treated like a disgraced adulteress
whose skirt has been torn off and her limbs exposed?'
It is because you have sinned so much.
13:23 But there is little hope for you ever doing good,
you who are so accustomed to doing evil.
Can an Ethiopian change the color of his skin?
Can a leopard remove its spots?

13:24 "The LORD says,
'That is why I will scatter your people like chaff
that is blown away by a desert wind.
13:25 This is your fate,

the destiny to which I have appointed you,
because you have forgotten me
and have trusted in false gods.
13:26 So I will pull your skirt up over your face
and expose you to shame like a disgraced adulteress!
13:27 People of Jerusalem, I have seen your adulterous worship,
your shameless prostitution to, and your lustful pursuit of, other gods.
I have seen your disgusting acts of worship
on the hills throughout the countryside.
You are doomed to destruction!
How long will you continue to be unclean?'"

A Lament over the Ravages of Drought

14:1 The LORD spoke to Jeremiah about the drought.
14:2 "The people of Judah are in mourning.
The people in her cities are pining away.
They lie on the ground expressing their sorrow.
Cries of distress come up to me from Jerusalem.
14:3 The leading men of the cities send their servants for water.
They go to the cisterns, but they do not find any water there.
They return with their containers empty.
Disappointed and dismayed, they bury their faces in their hands.
14:4 They are dismayed because the ground is cracked
because there has been no rain in the land.
The farmers, too, are dismayed
and bury their faces in their hands.
14:5 Even the doe abandons her newborn fawn in the field
because there is no grass.
14:6 Wild donkeys stand on the hilltops
and pant for breath like jackals.
Their eyes are strained looking for food,
because there is none to be found."
14:7 Then I said,
"O LORD, intervene for the honor of your name
even though our sins speak out against us.
Indeed, we have turned away from you many times.
We have sinned against you.
14:8 You have been the object of Israel's hopes.
You have saved them when they were in trouble.
Why have you become like a resident foreigner in the land?
Why have you become like a traveler who only stops in to spend the night?
14:9 Why should you be like someone who is helpless,
like a champion who cannot save anyone?
You are indeed with us,
and we belong to you.
Do not abandon us!"

14:10 Then the LORD spoke about these people.
"They truly love to go astray.
They cannot keep from running away from me.
So I am not pleased with them.
I will now call to mind the wrongs they have done
and punish them for their sins."

Judgment for Believing the Misleading Lies of the False Prophets

14:11 Then the LORD said to me, "Do not pray for good to come to these people! **14:12** Even if they fast, I will not hear their cries for help. Even if they offer burnt offerings and grain offerings, I will not accept them. Instead, I will kill them through wars, famines, and plagues." **14:13** Then I said, "Oh, Lord GOD, look! The prophets are telling them that you said, 'You will not experience war or suffer famine. I will give you lasting peace and prosperity in this land.'"
14:14 Then the LORD said to me, "Those prophets are prophesying lies while claiming my authority! I did not send them. I did not commission them. I did not speak to them. They are prophesying to these people false visions, worthless predictions, and the delusions of their own mind. **14:15** I did not send those prophets, though they claim to be prophesying in my name. They may be saying, 'No war or famine will happen in this land.' But I, the LORD, say this about them: 'War and starvation will kill those prophets.' **14:16** The people to whom they are prophesying will die through war and famine. Their bodies will be thrown out into the streets of Jerusalem and there will be no one to bury them. This will happen to the men and their wives, their sons, and their daughters. For I will pour out on them the destruction they deserve."

Lament over Present Destruction and Threat of More to Come

14:17 "Tell these people this, Jeremiah:
'My eyes overflow with tears
day and night without ceasing.
For my people, my dear children, have suffered a crushing blow.
They have suffered a serious wound.
14:18 If I go out into the countryside,
I see those who have been killed in battle.
If I go into the city,
I see those who are sick because of starvation.

For both prophet and priest go about their own business
in the land without having any real understanding.'"
14:19 Then I said,
"LORD, have you completely rejected the nation of Judah?
Do you despise the city of Zion?
Why have you struck us with such force
that we are beyond recovery?
We hope for peace, but nothing good has come of it.
We hope for a time of relief from our troubles, but experience terror.
14:20 LORD, we confess that we have been wicked.
We confess that our ancestors have done wrong.
We have indeed sinned against you.
14:21 For the honor of your name, do not treat Jerusalem with contempt.
Do not treat with disdain the place where your glorious throne sits.
Be mindful of your covenant with us. Do not break it!
14:22 Do any of the worthless idols of the nations cause rain to fall?
Do the skies themselves send showers?
Is it not you, O Lord our God, who does this?
So we put our hopes in you
because you alone do all this."

15:1 Then the LORD said to me, "Even if Moses and Samuel stood before me pleading for these people, I would not feel pity for them! Get them away from me! Tell them to go away! **15:2** If they ask you, 'Where should we go?' tell them the LORD says this:
"Those who are destined to die of disease will go to death by disease.
Those who are destined to die in war will go to death in war.
Those who are destined to die of starvation will go to death by starvation.
Those who are destined to go into exile will go into exile."

15:3 "I will punish them in four different ways: I will have war kill them. I will have dogs drag off their dead bodies. I will have birds and wild beasts devour and destroy their corpses. **15:4** I will make all the people in all the kingdoms of the world horrified at what has happened to them because of what Hezekiah's son Manasseh, king of Judah, did in Jerusalem."

15:5 The LORD cried out,
"Who in the world will have pity on you, Jerusalem?
Who will grieve over you?
Who will stop long enough
to inquire about how you are doing?
15:6 I, the LORD, say: 'You people have deserted me!
You keep turning your back on me.'
So I have unleashed my power against you and have begun to destroy you.
I have grown tired of feeling sorry for you!"
15:7 The LORD continued,
"In every town in the land I will purge them
like straw blown away by the wind.
I will destroy my people.
I will kill off their children.
I will do so because they did not change their behavior.
15:8 Their widows will become in my sight more numerous
than the grains of sand on the seashores.
At noontime I will bring a destroyer
against the mothers of their young men.
I will cause anguish and terror
to fall suddenly upon them.
15:9 The mother who had seven children will grow faint.
All the breath will go out of her.
Her pride and joy will be taken from her in the prime of their life.
It will seem as if the sun had set while it was still day.
She will suffer shame and humiliation.
I will cause any of them who are still left alive
to be killed in war by the onslaughts of their enemies,"
says the LORD.
Jeremiah Complains about His Lot and The Lord Responds
15:10 I said,
"Oh, mother, how I regret that you ever gave birth to me!
I am always starting arguments and quarrels with the people of this land.
I have not lent money to anyone and I have not borrowed from anyone.
Yet all of these people are treating me with contempt."
15:11 The LORD said,
"Jerusalem, I will surely send you away for your own good.
I will surely bring the enemy upon you in a time of trouble and distress.
15:12 Can you people who are like iron and bronze
break that iron fist from the north?
15:13 I will give away your wealth and your treasures as plunder.
I will give it away free of charge for the sins you have committed throughout your land.
15:14 I will make you serve your enemies in a land that you know nothing about.

For my anger is like a fire that will burn against you."
15:15 I said,
"LORD, you know how I suffer.
Take thought of me and care for me.
Pay back for me those who have been persecuting me.
Do not be so patient with them that you allow them to kill me.
Be mindful of how I have put up with their insults for your sake.
15:16 As your words came to me I drank them in,
and they filled my heart with joy and happiness
because I belong to you.
15:17 I did not spend my time in the company of other people,
laughing and having a good time.
I stayed to myself because I felt obligated to you
and because I was filled with anger at what they had done.
15:18 Why must I continually suffer such painful anguish?
Why must I endure the sting of their insults like an incurable wound?
Will you let me down when I need you
like a brook one goes to for water, but that cannot be relied on?"
15:19 Because of this, the LORD said,
"You must repent of such words and thoughts!
If you do, I will restore you to the privilege of serving me.
If you say what is worthwhile instead of what is worthless,
I will again allow you to be my spokesman.
They must become as you have been.
You must not become like them.
15:20 I will make you as strong as a wall to these people,
a fortified wall of bronze.
They will attack you,
but they will not be able to overcome you.
For I will be with you to rescue you and deliver you,"
says the LORD.
15:21 "I will deliver you from the power of the wicked.
I will free you from the clutches of violent people."
Jeremiah Forbidden to Marry, to Mourn, or to Feast
16:1 The LORD said to me, **16:2** "Do not get married and do not have children here in this land. **16:3** For I, the LORD, tell you what will happen to the children who are born here in this land and to the men and women who are their mothers and fathers. **16:4** They will die of deadly diseases. No one will mourn for them. They will not be buried. Their dead bodies will lie like manure spread on the ground. They will be killed in war or die of starvation. Their corpses will be food for the birds and wild animals.
16:5 "Moreover I, the LORD, tell you: 'Do not go into a house where they are having a funeral meal. Do not go there to mourn and express your sorrow for them. For I have stopped showing them my good favor, my love, and my compassion. I, the LORD, so affirm it! **16:6** Rich and poor alike will die in this land. They will not be buried or mourned. People will not cut their bodies or shave off their hair to show their grief for them. **16:7** No one will take any food to those who mourn for the dead to comfort them. No one will give them any wine to drink to console them for the loss of their father or mother.
16:8 "'Do not go to a house where people are feasting and sit down to eat and drink with them either. **16:9** For I, the LORD God of Israel who rules over all, tell you what will happen. I will put an end to the sounds of joy and gladness, to the glad celebration of brides and grooms in this land. You and the rest of the people will live to see this happen.'"
The Lord Promises Exile (But Also Restoration)
16:10 "When you tell these people about all this, they will undoubtedly ask you, 'Why has the LORD threatened us with such great disaster? What wrong have we done? What sin have we done to offend the LORD our God?' **16:11** Then tell them that the LORD says, 'It is because your ancestors rejected me and paid allegiance to other gods. They have served them and worshiped them. But they have rejected me and not obeyed my law. **16:12** And you have acted even more wickedly than your ancestors! Each one of you has followed the stubborn inclinations of your own wicked heart and not obeyed me. **16:13** So I will throw you out of this land into a land that neither you nor your ancestors have ever known. There you must worship other gods day and night, for I will show you no mercy.'"
16:14 Yet I, the LORD, say: "A new time will certainly come. People now affirm their oaths with 'I swear as surely as the LORD lives who delivered the people of Israel out of Egypt.' **16:15** But in that time they will affirm them with 'I swear as surely as the LORD lives who delivered the people of Israel from the land of the north and from all the other lands where he had banished them.' At that time I will bring them back to the land I gave their ancestors."
16:16 But for now I, the LORD, say: "I will send many enemies who will catch these people like fishermen. After that I will send others who will hunt them out like hunters from all the mountains, all the hills, and the crevices in the rocks. **16:17** For I see everything they do. Their wicked ways are not hidden from me. Their sin is not hidden away where I cannot see it. **16:18** Before I restore them I will punish them in full for their sins and the wrongs they have done. For they have polluted my land with

the lifeless statues of their disgusting idols. They have filled the land I have claimed as my own with their detestable idols."
16:19 Then I said,
"LORD, you give me strength and protect me.
You are the one I can run to for safety when I am in trouble.
Nations from all over the earth
will come to you and say,
'Our ancestors had nothing but false gods –
worthless idols that could not help them at all.
16:20 Can people make their own gods?
No, what they make are not gods at all."
16:21 The LORD said,
"So I will now let this wicked people know –
I will let them know my mighty power in judgment.
Then they will know that my name is the LORD."
17:1 The sin of Judah is engraved with an iron chisel
on their stone-hard hearts.
It is inscribed with a diamond point
on the horns of their altars.
17:2 Their children are always thinking about their altars
and their sacred poles dedicated to the goddess Asherah,
set up beside the green trees on the high hills
17:3 and on the mountains and in the fields.
I will give your wealth and all your treasures away as plunder.
I will give it away as the price for the sins you have committed throughout your land.
17:4 You will lose your hold on the land
which I gave to you as a permanent possession.
I will make you serve your enemies in a land that you know nothing about.
For you have made my anger burn like a fire that will never be put out."
Individuals Are Challenged to Put Their Trust in the Lord
17:5 The LORD says,
"I will put a curse on people
who trust in mere human beings,
who depend on mere flesh and blood for their strength,
and whose hearts have turned away from the LORD.
17:6 They will be like a shrub in the desert.
They will not experience good things even when they happen.
It will be as though they were growing in the desert,
in a salt land where no one can live.
17:7 My blessing is on those people who trust in me,
who put their confidence in me.
17:8 They will be like a tree planted near a stream
whose roots spread out toward the water.
It has nothing to fear when the heat comes.
Its leaves are always green.
It has no need to be concerned in a year of drought.
It does not stop bearing fruit.
17:9 The human mind is more deceitful than anything else.
It is incurably bad. Who can understand it?
17:10 I, the LORD, probe into people's minds.
I examine people's hearts.
I deal with each person according to how he has behaved.
I give them what they deserve based on what they have done.
17:11 The person who gathers wealth by unjust means
is like the partridge that broods over eggs but does not hatch them.
Before his life is half over he will lose his ill-gotten gains.
At the end of his life it will be clear he was a fool."
Jeremiah Appeals to the Lord for Vindication
17:12 Then I said,
"LORD, from the very beginning
you have been seated on your glorious throne on high.
You are the place where we can find refuge.
17:13 You are the one in whom Israel may find hope.
All who leave you will suffer shame.
Those who turn away from you will be consigned to the nether world.
For they have rejected you, the LORD, the fountain of life.
17:14 LORD, grant me relief from my suffering
so that I may have some relief.
Rescue me from those who persecute me
so that I may be rescued.
17:15 Listen to what they are saying to me.
They are saying, "Where are the things the LORD threatens us with?
Come on! Let's see them happen!"
17:16 But I have not pestered you to bring disaster.
I have not desired the time of irreparable devastation.
You know that.
You are fully aware of every word that I have spoken.
17:17 Do not cause me dismay!
You are my source of safety in times of trouble.
17:18 May those who persecute me be disgraced.
Do not let me be disgraced.

May they be dismayed.
Do not let me be dismayed.
Bring days of disaster on them.
Bring on them the destruction they deserve."
Observance of the Sabbath Day Is a Key to the Future
17:19 The LORD told me, "Go and stand in the People's Gate through which the kings of Judah enter and leave the city. Then go and stand in all the other gates of the city of Jerusalem. **17:20** As you stand in those places announce, 'Listen, all you people who pass through these gates. Listen, all you kings of Judah, all you people of Judah and all you citizens of Jerusalem. Listen to what the LORD says. **17:21** The LORD says, 'Be very careful if you value your lives! Do not carry any loads in through the gates of Jerusalem on the Sabbath day. **17:22** Do not carry any loads out of your houses or do any work on the Sabbath day. But observe the Sabbath day as a day set apart to the LORD, as I commanded your ancestors. **17:23** Your ancestors, however, did not listen to me or pay any attention to me. They stubbornly refused to pay attention or to respond to any discipline.' **17:24** The LORD says, 'You must make sure to obey me. You must not bring any loads through the gates of this city on the Sabbath day. You must set the Sabbath day apart to me. You must not do any work on that day. **17:25** If you do this, then the kings and princes who follow in David's succession and ride in chariots or on horses will continue to enter through these gates, as well as their officials and the people of Judah and the citizens of Jerusalem. This city will always be filled with people. **17:26** Then people will come here from the towns in Judah, from the villages surrounding Jerusalem, from the territory of Benjamin, from the western foothills, from the southern hill country, and from the southern part of Judah. They will come bringing offerings to the temple of the LORD: burnt offerings, sacrifices, grain offerings, and incense along with their thank offerings. **17:27** But you must obey me and set the Sabbath day apart to me. You must not carry any loads in through the gates of Jerusalem on the Sabbath day. If you disobey, I will set the gates of Jerusalem on fire. It will burn down all the fortified dwellings in Jerusalem and no one will be able to put it out.'"
An Object Lesson from the Making of Pottery
18:1 The LORD said to Jeremiah: **18:2** "Go down at once to the potter's house. I will speak to you further there." **18:3** So I went down to the potter's house and found him working at his wheel. **18:4** Now and then there would be something wrong with the pot he was molding from the clay with his hands. So he would rework the clay into another kind of pot as he saw fit.
18:5 Then the LORD said to me, **18:6** "I, the LORD, say: 'O nation of Israel, can I not deal with you as this potter deals with the clay? In my hands, you, O nation of Israel, are just like the clay in this potter's hand.' **18:7** There are times, Jeremiah, when I threaten to uproot, tear down, and destroy a nation or kingdom. **18:8** But if that nation I threatened stops doing wrong, I will cancel the destruction I intended to do to it. **18:9** And there are times when I promise to build up and establish a nation or kingdom. **18:10** But if that nation does what displeases me and does not obey me, then I will cancel the good I promised to do to it. **18:11** So now, tell the people of Judah and the citizens of Jerusalem this: The LORD says, 'I am preparing to bring disaster on you! I am making plans to punish you. So, every one of you, stop the evil things you have been doing. Correct the way you have been living and do what is right.' **18:12** But they just keep saying, 'We do not care what you say! We will do whatever we want to do! We will continue to behave wickedly and stubbornly!'"

18:13 Therefore, the LORD says,
"Ask the people of other nations
whether they have heard of anything like this.
Israel should have been like a virgin.
But she has done something utterly revolting!
18:14 Does the snow ever completely vanish from the rocky slopes of Lebanon?
Do the cool waters from those distant mountains ever cease to flow?
18:15 Yet my people have forgotten me
and offered sacrifices to worthless idols!
This makes them stumble along in the way they live
and leave the old reliable path of their fathers.
They have left them to walk in bypaths,
in roads that are not smooth and level.
18:16 So their land will become an object of horror.
People will forever hiss out their scorn over it.
All who pass that way will be filled with horror
and will shake their heads in derision.
18:17 I will scatter them before their enemies
like dust blowing in front of a burning east wind.
I will turn my back on them and not look favorably on them
when disaster strikes them."
Jeremiah Petitions the Lord to Punish Those Who Attack Him
18:18 Then some people said, "Come on! Let us consider how to deal with Jeremiah! There will still be priests to instruct us, wise men to give us advice, and prophets to declare God's word. Come on! Let's bring

charges against him and get rid of him! Then we will not need to pay attention to anything he says."

18:19 Then I said,
"LORD, pay attention to me.
Listen to what my enemies are saying.
18:20 Should good be paid back with evil?
Yet they are virtually digging a pit to kill me.
Just remember how I stood before you
pleading on their behalf
to keep you from venting your anger on them.
18:21 So let their children die of starvation.
Let them be cut down by the sword.
Let their wives lose their husbands and children.
Let the older men die of disease
and the younger men die by the sword in battle.
18:22 Let cries of terror be heard in their houses
when you send bands of raiders unexpectedly to plunder them.
For they have virtually dug a pit to capture me
and have hidden traps for me to step into.
18:23 But you, LORD, know
all their plots to kill me.
Do not pardon their crimes!
Do not ignore their sins as though you had erased them!
Let them be brought down in defeat before you!
Deal with them while you are still angry!

An Object Lesson from a Broken Clay Jar

19:1 The LORD told Jeremiah, "Go and buy a clay jar from a potter. Take with you some of the leaders of the people and some of the leaders of the priests. **19:2** Go out to the part of the Hinnom Valley which is near the entrance of the Potsherd Gate. Announce there what I tell you. **19:3** Say, 'Listen to what the LORD says, you kings of Judah and citizens of Jerusalem! The LORD God of Israel who rules over all says, "I will bring a disaster on this place that will make the ears of everyone who hears about it ring! **19:4** I will do so because these people have rejected me and have defiled this place. They have offered sacrifices in it to other gods which neither they nor their ancestors nor the kings of Judah knew anything about. They have filled it with the blood of innocent children. **19:5** They have built places here for worship of the god Baal so that they could sacrifice their children as burnt offerings to him in the fire. Such sacrifices are something I never commanded them to make! They are something I never told them to do! Indeed, such a thing never even entered my mind! **19:6** So I, the LORD, say: "The time will soon come that people will no longer call this place Topheth or the Hinnom Valley. But they will call this valley the Valley of Slaughter! **19:7** In this place I will thwart the plans of the people of Judah and Jerusalem. I will deliver them over to the power of their enemies who are seeking to kill them. They will die by the sword at the hands of their enemies. I will make their dead bodies food for the birds and wild beasts to eat. **19:8** I will make this city an object of horror, a thing to be hissed at. All who pass by it will be filled with horror and will hiss out their scorn because of all the disasters that have happened to it. **19:9** I will reduce the people of this city to desperate straits during the siege imposed on it by their enemies who are seeking to kill them. I will make them so desperate that they will eat the flesh of their own sons and daughters and the flesh of one another."'"

19:10 The LORD continued, "Now break the jar in front of those who have come here with you. **19:11** Tell them the LORD who rules over all says, 'I will do just as Jeremiah has done. I will smash this nation and this city as though it were a potter's vessel which is broken beyond repair. The dead will be buried here in Topheth until there is no more room to bury them.' **19:12** I, the LORD, say: 'That is how I will deal with this city and its citizens. I will make it like Topheth. **19:13** The houses in Jerusalem and the houses of the kings of Judah will be defiled by dead bodies just like this place, Topheth. For they offered sacrifice to the stars and poured out drink offerings to other gods on the roofs of those houses.'"

19:14 Then Jeremiah left Topheth where the LORD had sent him to give that prophecy. He went to the LORD's temple and stood in its courtyard and called out to all the people. **19:15** "The LORD God of Israel who rules over all says, 'I will soon bring on this city and all the towns surrounding it all the disaster I threatened to do to it. I will do so because they have stubbornly refused to pay any attention to what I have said!'"

Jeremiah is Flogged and Put in A Cell

20:1 Now Pashhur son of Immer heard Jeremiah prophesy these things. He was the priest who was chief of security in the LORD's temple. **20:2** When he heard Jeremiah's prophecy, he had the prophet flogged. Then he put him in the stocks which were at the Upper Gate of Benjamin in the LORD's temple. **20:3** But the next day Pashhur released Jeremiah from the stocks. When he did, Jeremiah said to him, "The LORD's name for you is not 'Pashhur' but 'Terror is Everywhere.' **20:4** For the LORD says, 'I will make both you and your friends terrified of what will happen to you. You will see all of them die by the swords of their enemies. I will hand all the people of Judah over to the king of Babylon. He will carry some of them away into exile in Babylon and he will kill others of them with the sword.

20:5 I will hand over all the wealth of this city to their enemies. I will hand over to them all the fruits of the labor of the people of this city and all their prized possessions, as well as all the treasures of the kings of Judah. Their enemies will seize it all as plunder and carry it off to Babylon. **20:6** You, Pashhur, and all your household will go into exile in Babylon. You will die there and you will be buried there. The same thing will happen to all your friends to whom you have prophesied lies.'"

Jeremiah Complains about the Reaction to His Ministry

20:7 LORD, you coerced me into being a prophet,
and I allowed you to do it.
You overcame my resistance and prevailed over me.
Now I have become a constant laughingstock.
Everyone ridicules me.
20:8 For whenever I prophesy, I must cry out,
"Violence and destruction are coming!"
This message from the LORD has made me
an object of continual insults and derision.
20:9 Sometimes I think, "I will make no mention of his message.
I will not speak as his messenger any more."
But then his message becomes like a fire
locked up inside of me, burning in my heart and soul.
I grow weary of trying to hold it in;
I cannot contain it.
20:10 I hear many whispering words of intrigue against me.
Those who would cause me terror are everywhere!
They are saying, "Come on, let's publicly denounce him!"
All my so-called friends are just watching for
something that would lead to my downfall.
They say, "Perhaps he can be enticed into slipping up,
so we can prevail over him and get our revenge on him.
20:11 But the LORD is with me to help me like an awe-inspiring warrior.
Therefore those who persecute me will fail and will not prevail over me.
They will be thoroughly disgraced because they did not succeed.
Their disgrace will never be forgotten.
20:12 O LORD who rules over all, you test and prove the righteous.
You see into people's hearts and minds.
Pay them back for what they have done
because I trust you to vindicate my cause.
20:13 Sing to the LORD! Praise the LORD!
For he rescues the oppressed from the clutches of evildoers.
20:14 Cursed be the day I was born!
May that day not be blessed when my mother gave birth to me.
20:15 Cursed be the man
who made my father very glad
when he brought him the news
that a baby boy had been born to him!
20:16 May that man be like the cities
that the LORD destroyed without showing any mercy.
May he hear a cry of distress in the morning
and a battle cry at noon.
20:17 For he did not kill me before I came from the womb,
making my pregnant mother's womb my grave forever.
20:18 Why did I ever come forth from my mother's womb?
All I experience is trouble and grief,
and I spend my days in shame.

The Lord Will Hand Jerusalem over to Enemies

21:1 The LORD spoke to Jeremiah when King Zedekiah sent to him Pashhur son of Malkijah and the priest Zephaniah son of Maaseiah. Zedekiah sent them to Jeremiah to ask, **21:2** "Please ask the LORD to come and help us, because King Nebuchadnezzar of Babylon is attacking us. Maybe the LORD will perform one of his miracles as in times past and make him stop attacking us and leave." **21:3** Jeremiah answered them, "Tell Zedekiah **21:4** that the LORD, the God of Israel, says, 'The forces at your disposal are now outside the walls fighting against King Nebuchadnezzar of Babylon and the Babylonians who have you under siege. I will gather those forces back inside the city. **21:5** In anger, in fury, and in wrath I myself will fight against you with my mighty power and great strength! **21:6** I will kill everything living in Jerusalem, people and animals alike! They will die from terrible diseases. **21:7** Then I, the LORD, promise that I will hand over King Zedekiah of Judah, his officials, and any of the people who survive the war, starvation, and disease. I will hand them over to King Nebuchadnezzar of Babylon and to their enemies who want to kill them. He will slaughter them with the sword. He will not show them any mercy, compassion, or pity.'

21:8 "But tell the people of Jerusalem that the LORD says, 'I will give you a choice between two courses of action. One will result in life; the other will result in death. **21:9** Those who stay in this city will die in battle or of starvation or disease. Those who leave the city and surrender to the Babylonians who are besieging it will live. They will escape with their lives. **21:10** For I, the LORD, say that I am determined not to deliver this city but to bring disaster on it. It will be handed over to the king of Babylon and he will destroy it with fire.'"

Warnings to the Royal Court

21:11 The LORD told me to say to the royal court of Judah,
"Listen to what the LORD says,
21:12 O royal family descended from David.
The LORD says:
'See to it that people each day are judged fairly.
Deliver those who have been robbed from those who oppress them.
Otherwise, my wrath will blaze out against you.
It will burn like a fire that cannot be put out
because of the evil that you have done.
21:13 Listen, you who sit enthroned above the valley on a rocky plateau.
I am opposed to you,' says the LORD.
'You boast, "No one can swoop down on us.
No one can penetrate into our places of refuge."
21:14 But I will punish you as your deeds deserve,'
says the LORD.
'I will set fire to your palace;
it will burn up everything around it.'"

22:1 The LORD told me, "Go down to the palace of the king of Judah. Give him a message from me there. **22:2** Say: 'Listen, O king of Judah who follows in David's succession. You, your officials, and your subjects who pass through the gates of this palace must listen to what the LORD says. **22:3** The LORD says, "Do what is just and right. Deliver those who have been robbed from those who oppress them. Do not exploit or mistreat foreigners who live in your land, children who have no fathers, or widows. Do not kill innocent people in this land. **22:4** If you are careful to obey these commands, then the kings who follow in David's succession and ride in chariots or on horses will continue to come through the gates of this palace, as will their officials and their subjects. **22:5** But, if you do not obey these commands, I solemnly swear that this palace will become a pile of rubble. I, the LORD, affirm it!"

22:6 "'For the LORD says concerning the palace of the king of Judah,
"This place looks like a veritable forest of Gilead to me.
It is like the wooded heights of Lebanon in my eyes.
But I swear that I will make it like a wilderness
whose towns have all been deserted.
22:7 I will send men against it to destroy it
with their axes and hatchets.
They will hack up its fine cedar panels and columns
and throw them into the fire.
22:8 "'People from other nations will pass by this city. They will ask one another, "Why has the LORD done such a thing to this great city?" **22:9** The answer will come back, "It is because they broke their covenant with the LORD their God and worshiped and served other gods."

Judgment on Jehoahaz
22:10 "'Do not weep for the king who was killed.
Do not grieve for him.
But weep mournfully for the king who has gone into exile.
For he will never return to see his native land again.
22:11 "'For the LORD has spoken about Shallum son of Josiah, who succeeded his father as king of Judah but was carried off into exile. He has said, "He will never return to this land. **22:12** For he will die in the country where they took him as a captive. He will never see this land again."

Judgment on Jehoiakim
22:13 "'Sure to be judged is the king who builds his palace using injustice
and treats people unfairly while adding its upper rooms.
He makes his countrymen work for him for nothing.
He does not pay them for their labor.
22:14 He says, "I will build myself a large palace
with spacious upper rooms."
He cuts windows in its walls,
panels it with cedar, and paints its rooms red.
22:15 Does it make you any more of a king
that you outstrip everyone else in building with cedar?
Just think about your father.
He was content that he had food and drink.
He did what was just and right.
So things went well with him.
22:16 He upheld the cause of the poor and needy.
So things went well for Judah.'
The LORD says,
'That is a good example of what it means to know me.'
22:17 But you are always thinking and looking
for ways to increase your wealth by dishonest means.
Your eyes and your heart are set
on killing some innocent person
and committing fraud and oppression.
22:18 So the LORD has this to say about Josiah's son, King Jehoiakim of Judah:
People will not mourn for him, saying,
"This makes me sad, my brother!
This makes me sad, my sister!"

They will not mourn for him, saying,
"Poor, poor lord! Poor, poor majesty!"
22:19 He will be left unburied just like a dead donkey.
His body will be dragged off and thrown outside the gates of Jerusalem.'"

Warning to Jerusalem
22:20 People of Jerusalem, go up to Lebanon and cry out in mourning.
Go to the land of Bashan and cry out loudly.
Cry out in mourning from the mountains of Moab.
For your allies have all been defeated.
22:21 While you were feeling secure I gave you warning.
But you said, "I refuse to listen to you."
That is the way you have acted from your earliest history onward.
Indeed, you have never paid attention to me.
22:22 My judgment will carry off all your leaders like a storm wind!
Your allies will go into captivity.
Then you will certainly be disgraced and put to shame
because of all the wickedness you have done.
22:23 You may feel as secure as a bird
nesting in the cedars of Lebanon.
But oh how you will groan when the pains of judgment come on you.
They will be like those of a woman giving birth to a baby.

Jeconiah Will Be Permanently Exiled
22:24 The LORD says,
"As surely as I am the living God, you, Jeconiah, king of Judah, son of Jehoiakim, will not be the earthly representative of my authority. Indeed, I will take that right away from you. **22:25** I will hand you over to those who want to take your life and of whom you are afraid. I will hand you over to King Nebuchadnezzar of Babylon and his Babylonian soldiers. **22:26** I will force you and your mother who gave you birth into exile. You will be exiled to a country where neither of you were born, and you will both die there. **22:27** You will never come back to this land to which you will long to return!"
22:28 This man, Jeconiah, will be like a broken pot someone threw away.
He will be like a clay vessel that no one wants.
Why will he and his children be forced into exile?
Why will they be thrown out into a country they know nothing about?
22:29 O land of Judah, land of Judah, land of Judah!
Listen to what the LORD has to say!
22:30 The LORD says,
"Enroll this man in the register as though he were childless.
Enroll him as a man who will not enjoy success during his lifetime.
For none of his sons will succeed in occupying the throne of David
or ever succeed in ruling over Judah."

New Leaders over a Regathered Remnant
23:1 The LORD says, "The leaders of my people are sure to be judged. They were supposed to watch over my people like shepherds watch over their sheep. But they are causing my people to be destroyed and scattered. **23:2** So the LORD God of Israel has this to say about the leaders who are ruling over his people: "You have caused my people to be dispersed and driven into exile. You have not taken care of them. So I will punish you for the evil that you have done. I, the LORD, affirm it! **23:3** Then I myself will regather those of my people who are still alive from all the countries where I have driven them. I will bring them back to their homeland. They will greatly increase in number. **23:4** I will install rulers over them who will care for them. Then they will no longer need to fear or be terrified. None of them will turn up missing. I, the LORD, promise it!
23:5 "I, the LORD, promise that a new time will certainly come
when I will raise up for them a righteous branch, a descendant of David.
He will rule over them with wisdom and understanding
and will do what is just and right in the land.
23:6 Under his rule Judah will enjoy safety
and Israel will live in security.
This is the name he will go by:
'The LORD has provided us with justice.'
23:7 "So I, the LORD, say: 'A new time will certainly come. People now affirm their oaths with "I swear as surely as the LORD lives who delivered the people of Israel out of Egypt." **23:8** But at that time they will affirm them with "I swear as surely as the LORD lives who delivered the descendants of the former nation of Israel from the land of the north and from all the other lands where he had banished them." At that time they will live in their own land.'"

Oracles Against the False Prophets
23:9 Here is what the LORD says concerning the false prophets:
My heart and my mind are deeply disturbed.
I tremble all over.
I am like a drunk person,
like a person who has had too much wine,
because of the way the LORD
and his holy word are being mistreated.
23:10 For the land is full of people unfaithful to him.
They live wicked lives and they misuse their power.
So the land is dried up because it is under his curse.
The pastures in the wilderness are withered.

23:11 Moreover, the LORD says,
"Both the prophets and priests are godless.
I have even found them doing evil in my temple!
23:12 So the paths they follow will be dark and slippery.
They will stumble and fall headlong.
For I will bring disaster on them.
A day of reckoning is coming for them."
The LORD affirms it!

23:13 The LORD says, "I saw the prophets of Samaria
doing something that was disgusting.
They prophesied in the name of the god Baal
and led my people Israel astray.
23:14 But I see the prophets of Jerusalem
doing something just as shocking.
They are unfaithful to me
and continually prophesy lies.
So they give encouragement to people who are doing evil,
with the result that they do not stop their evildoing.
I consider all of them as bad as the people of Sodom,
and the citizens of Jerusalem as bad as the people of Gomorrah.
23:15 So then I, the LORD who rules over all,
have something to say concerning the prophets of Jerusalem:
'I will make these prophets eat the bitter food of suffering
and drink the poison water of judgment.
For the prophets of Jerusalem are the reason
that ungodliness has spread throughout the land.'"

23:16 The LORD who rules over all says to the people of Jerusalem:
"Do not listen to what
those prophets are saying to you.
They are filling you with false hopes.
They are reporting visions of their own imaginations,
not something the LORD has given them to say.
23:17 They continually say to those who reject what the LORD has said,
'Things will go well for you!'
They say to all those who follow the stubborn inclinations of their own hearts,
'Nothing bad will happen to you!'
23:18 Yet which of them has ever stood in the LORD's inner circle
so they could see and hear what he has to say?
Which of them have ever paid attention or listened to what he has said?
23:19 But just watch! The wrath of the LORD
will come like a storm!
Like a raging storm it will rage down
on the heads of those who are wicked.
23:20 The anger of the LORD will not turn back
until he has fully carried out his intended purposes.
In days to come
you people will come to understand this clearly.
23:21 I did not send those prophets.
Yet they were in a hurry to give their message.
I did not tell them anything.
Yet they prophesied anyway.
23:22 But if they had stood in my inner circle,
they would have proclaimed my message to my people.
They would have caused my people to turn from their wicked ways
and stop doing the evil things they are doing.
23:23 Do you people think that I am some local deity
and not the transcendent God?" the LORD asks.
23:24 "Do you really think anyone can hide himself
where I cannot see him?" the LORD asks.
"Do you not know that I am everywhere?"
the LORD asks.

23:25 The LORD says, "I have heard what those prophets who are prophesying lies in my name are saying. They are saying, 'I have had a dream! I have had a dream!' **23:26** Those prophets are just prophesying lies. They are prophesying the delusions of their own minds. **23:27** How long will they go on plotting to make my people forget who I am through the dreams they tell one another? That is just as bad as what their ancestors did when they forgot who I am by worshiping the god Baal. **23:28** Let the prophet who has had a dream go ahead and tell his dream. Let the person who has received my message report that message faithfully. What is like straw cannot compare to what is like grain! I, the LORD, affirm it! **23:29** My message is like a fire that purges dross! It is like a hammer that breaks a rock in pieces! I, the LORD, so affirm it! **23:30** So I, the LORD, affirm that I am opposed to those prophets who steal messages from one another that they claim are from me. **23:31** I, the LORD, affirm that I am opposed to those prophets who are using their own tongues to declare, 'The LORD declares....' **23:32** I, the LORD, affirm that I am opposed to those prophets who dream up lies and report them. They are misleading

my people with their reckless lies. I did not send them. I did not commission them. They are not helping these people at all. I, the LORD, affirm it!"

23:33 The LORD said to me, "Jeremiah, when one of these people, or a prophet, or a priest asks you, 'What burdensome message do you have from the LORD?' Tell them, 'You are the burden, and I will cast you away. I, the LORD, affirm it! **23:34** I will punish any prophet, priest, or other person who says "The LORD's message is burdensome." I will punish both that person and his whole family.'"

23:35 So I, Jeremiah, tell you, "Each of you people should say to his friend or his relative, 'How did the LORD answer? Or what did the LORD say?' **23:36** You must no longer say that the LORD's message is burdensome. For what is 'burdensome' really pertains to what a person himself says. You are misrepresenting the words of our God, the living God, the LORD who rules over all. **23:37** Each of you should merely ask the prophet, 'What answer did the LORD give you? Or what did the LORD say?' **23:38** But just suppose you continue to say, 'The message of the LORD is burdensome.' Here is what the LORD says will happen: 'I sent word to you that you must not say, "The LORD's message is burdensome." But you used the words "The LORD's message is burdensome" anyway. **23:39** So I will carry you far off and throw you away. I will send both you and the city I gave to you and to your ancestors out of my sight. **23:40** I will bring on you lasting shame and lasting disgrace which will never be forgotten!'"

Good Figs and Bad Figs
24:1 The LORD showed me two baskets of figs sitting before his temple. This happened after King Nebuchadnezzar of Babylon deported Jehoiakim's son, King Jeconiah of Judah. He deported him and the leaders of Judah, along with the craftsmen and metal workers, and took them to Babylon. **24:2** One basket had very good-looking figs in it. They looked like those that had ripened early. The other basket had very bad-looking figs in it, so bad they could not be eaten. **24:3** The LORD said to me, "What do you see, Jeremiah?" I answered, "I see figs. The good ones look very good. But the bad ones look very bad, so bad that they cannot be eaten."

24:4 The LORD said to me, **24:5** "I, the LORD, the God of Israel, say: 'The exiles whom I sent away from here to the land of Babylon are like those good figs. I consider them to be good. **24:6** I will look after their welfare and will restore them to this land. There I will build them up and will not tear them down. I will plant them firmly in the land and will not uproot them. **24:7** I will give them the desire to acknowledge that I am the LORD. I will be their God and they will be my people. For they will wholeheartedly return to me.'

24:8 "I, the LORD, also solemnly assert: 'King Zedekiah of Judah, his officials, and the people who remain in Jerusalem or who have gone to live in Egypt are like those bad figs. I consider them to be just like those bad figs that are so bad they cannot be eaten. **24:9** I will bring such disaster on them that all the kingdoms of the earth will be horrified. I will make them an object of reproach, a proverbial example of disaster. I will make them an object of ridicule, an example to be used in curses. That is how they will be remembered wherever I banish them. **24:10** I will bring war, starvation, and disease on them until they are completely destroyed from the land I gave them and their ancestors.'"

Seventy Years of Servitude for Failure to Give Heed
25:1 In the fourth year that Jehoiakim son of Josiah was king of Judah, the LORD spoke to Jeremiah concerning all the people of Judah. (That was the same as the first year that Nebuchadnezzar was king of Babylon.) **25:2** So the prophet Jeremiah spoke to all the people of Judah and to all the people who were living in Jerusalem. **25:3** "For the last twenty-three years, from the thirteenth year that Josiah son of Amon was ruling in Judah until now, the LORD has been speaking to me. I told you over and over again what he said. But you would not listen. **25:4** Over and over again the LORD has sent his servants the prophets to you. But you have not listened or paid attention. **25:5** He said through them, 'Each of you must turn from your wicked ways and stop doing the evil things you are doing. If you do, I will allow you to continue to live here in the land that I gave to you and your ancestors as a lasting possession. **25:6** Do not pay allegiance to other gods and worship and serve them. Do not make me angry by the things that you do. Then I will not cause you any harm.' **25:7** So, now the LORD says, 'You have not listened to me. But you have made me angry by the things that you have done. Thus you have brought harm on yourselves.'

25:8 "Therefore, the LORD who rules over all says, 'You have not listened to what I said. **25:9** So I, the LORD, affirm that I will send for all the peoples of the north and my servant, King Nebuchadnezzar of Babylon. I will bring them against this land and its inhabitants and all the nations that surround it. I will utterly destroy this land, its inhabitants, and all the nations that surround it and make them everlasting ruins. I will make them objects of horror and hissing scorn. **25:10** I will put an end to the sounds of joy and gladness, to the glad celebration of brides and grooms in these lands. I will put an end to the sound of people grinding meal. I will put an end to lamps shining in their houses. **25:11** This whole area will become a desolate wasteland. These nations will be subject to the king of Babylon for seventy years.'

25:12 "'But when the seventy years are over, I will punish the king of Babylon and his nation for their sins. I will make the land of Babylon an everlasting ruin. I, the LORD, affirm it! **25:13** I will bring on that land everything that I said I would. I will bring on it everything that is written in this book. I will bring on it everything that Jeremiah has prophesied against all the nations. **25:14** For many nations and great kings will make slaves of the king of Babylon and his nation too. I will repay them for all they have done!'"

Judah and the Nations Will Experience God's Wrath

25:15 So the LORD, the God of Israel, spoke to me in a vision. "Take this cup from my hand. It is filled with the wine of my wrath. Take it and make the nations to whom I send you drink it. **25:16** When they have drunk it, they will stagger to and fro and act insane. For I will send wars sweeping through them."

25:17 So I took the cup from the LORD's hand. I made all the nations to whom he sent me drink the wine of his wrath. **25:18** I made Jerusalem and the cities of Judah, its kings and its officials drink it. I did it so Judah would become a ruin. I did it so Judah, its kings, and its officials would become an object of horror and of hissing scorn, an example used in curses. Such is already becoming the case! **25:19** I made all of these other people drink it: Pharaoh, king of Egypt; his attendants, his officials, his people, **25:20** the foreigners living in Egypt; all the kings of the land of Uz; all the kings of the land of the Philistines, the people of Ashkelon, Gaza, Ekron, the people who had been left alive from Ashdod; **25:21** all the people of Edom, Moab, Ammon; **25:22** all the kings of Tyre, all the kings of Sidon; all the kings of the coastlands along the sea; **25:23** the people of Dedan, Tema, Buz, all the desert people who cut their hair short at the temples; **25:24** all the kings of Arabia who live in the desert; **25:25** all the kings of Zimri; all the kings of Elam; all the kings of Media; **25:26** all the kings of the north, whether near or far from one another; and all the other kingdoms which are on the face of the earth. After all of them have drunk the wine of the LORD's wrath, the king of Babylon must drink it.

25:27 Then the LORD said to me, "Tell them that the LORD God of Israel who rules over all says, 'Drink this cup until you get drunk and vomit. Drink until you fall down and can't get up. For I will send wars sweeping through you.' **25:28** If they refuse to take the cup from your hand and drink it, tell them that the LORD who rules over all says 'You most certainly must drink it! **25:29** For take note, I am already beginning to bring disaster on the city that I call my own. So how can you possibly avoid being punished? You will not go unpunished! For I am proclaiming war against all who live on the earth. I, the LORD who rules over all, affirm it!'

25:30 "Then, Jeremiah, make the following prophecy against them:
'Like a lion about to attack, the LORD will roar from the heights of heaven;
from his holy dwelling on high he will roar loudly.
He will roar mightily against his land.
He will shout in triumph like those stomping juice from the grapes
against all those who live on the earth.
25:31 The sounds of battle will resound to the ends of the earth.
For the LORD will bring charges against the nations.
He will pass judgment on all humankind
and will hand the wicked over to be killed in war.'
The LORD so affirms it!
25:32 The LORD who rules over all says,
'Disaster will soon come on one nation after another.
A mighty storm of military destruction is rising up
from the distant parts of the earth.'
25:33 Those who have been killed by the LORD at that time
will be scattered from one end of the earth to the other.
They will not be mourned over, gathered up, or buried.
Their dead bodies will lie scattered over the ground like manure.
25:34 Wail and cry out in anguish, you rulers!
Roll in the dust, you who shepherd flocks of people!
The time for you to be slaughtered has come.
You will lie scattered and fallen like broken pieces of fine pottery.
25:35 The leaders will not be able to run away and hide.
The shepherds of the flocks will not be able to escape.
25:36 Listen to the cries of anguish of the leaders.
Listen to the wails of the shepherds of the flocks.
They are wailing because the LORD
is about to destroy their lands.
25:37 Their peaceful dwelling places will be laid waste
by the fierce anger of the LORD.
25:38 The LORD is like a lion who has left his lair.
So their lands will certainly be laid waste
by the warfare of the oppressive nation
and by the fierce anger of the LORD."

Jeremiah Is Put on Trial as a False Prophet

26:1 The LORD spoke to Jeremiah at the beginning of the reign of Josiah's son, King Jehoiakim of Judah. **26:2** The LORD said, "Go stand in the courtyard of the LORD's temple. Speak out to all the people who are coming from the towns of Judah to worship in the LORD's temple. Tell them everything I command you to tell them. Do not leave out a single word! **26:3** Maybe they will pay attention and each of them will stop living the evil way they do. If they do that, then I will forgo destroying them as I had intended to do because of the wicked things they have been doing. **26:4** Tell them that the LORD says, 'You must obey me! You must live according to the way I have instructed you in my laws. **26:5** You must pay attention to the exhortations of my servants the prophets. I have sent them to you over and over again. But you have not paid any attention to them. **26:6** If you do not obey me, then I will do to this temple what I did to Shiloh. And I will make this city an example to be used in curses by people from all the nations on the earth.'"

26:7 The priests, the prophets, and all the people heard Jeremiah say these things in the LORD's temple. **26:8** Jeremiah had just barely finished saying all the LORD had commanded him to say to all the people. All at once some of the priests, the prophets, and the people grabbed him and shouted, "You deserve to die! **26:9** How dare you claim the LORD's authority to prophesy such things! How dare you claim his authority to prophesy that this temple will become like Shiloh and that this city will become an uninhabited ruin!" Then all the people crowded around Jeremiah.

26:10 However, some of the officials of Judah heard about what was happening and they rushed up to the LORD's temple from the royal palace. They set up court at the entrance of the New Gate of the LORD's temple. **26:11** Then the priests and the prophets made their charges before the officials and all the people. They said, "This man should be condemned to die because he prophesied against this city. You have heard him do so with your own ears."

26:12 Then Jeremiah made his defense before all the officials and all the people. "The LORD sent me to prophesy everything you have heard me say against this temple and against this city. **26:13** But correct the way you have been living and do what is right. Obey the LORD your God. If you do, the LORD will forgo destroying you as he threatened he would. **26:14** As to my case, I am in your power. Do to me what you deem fair and proper. **26:15** But you should take careful note of this: If you put me to death, you will bring on yourselves and this city and those who live in it the guilt of murdering an innocent man. For the LORD has sent me to speak all this where you can hear it. That is the truth!"

26:16 Then the officials and all the people rendered their verdict to the priests and the prophets. They said, "This man should not be condemned to die. For he has spoken to us under the authority of the LORD our God." **26:17** Then some of the elders of Judah stepped forward and spoke to all the people gathered there. They said, **26:18** "Micah from Moresheth prophesied during the time Hezekiah was king of Judah. He told all the people of Judah,
'The LORD who rules over all says,
"Zion will become a plowed field.
Jerusalem will become a pile of rubble.
The temple mount will become a mere wooded ridge."'
26:19 King Hezekiah and all the people of Judah did not put him to death, did they? Did not Hezekiah show reverence for the LORD and seek the LORD's favor? Did not the LORD forgo destroying them as he threatened he would? But we are on the verge of bringing great disaster on ourselves."

26:20 Now there was another man who prophesied as the LORD's representative against this city and this land just as Jeremiah did. His name was Uriah son of Shemaiah from Kiriath Jearim. **26:21** When the king and all his bodyguards and officials heard what he was prophesying, the king sought to have him executed. But Uriah found out about it and fled to Egypt out of fear. **26:22** However, King Jehoiakim sent some men to Egypt, including Elnathan son of Achbor, **26:23** and they brought Uriah back from there. They took him to King Jehoiakim, who had him executed and had his body thrown into the burial place of the common people.

26:24 However, Ahikam son of Shaphan used his influence to keep Jeremiah from being handed over and executed by the people.

Jeremiah Counsels Submission to Babylon

27:1 The LORD spoke to Jeremiah early in the reign of Josiah's son, King Zedekiah of Judah. **27:2** The LORD told me, "Make a yoke out of leather straps and wooden crossbars and put it on your neck. **27:3** Use it to send messages to the kings of Edom, Moab, Ammon, Tyre, and Sidon. Send them through the envoys who have come to Jerusalem to King Zedekiah of Judah. **27:4** Charge them to give their masters a message from me. Tell them, 'The LORD God of Israel who rules over all says to give your masters this message. **27:5** "I made the earth and the people and animals on it by my mighty power and great strength, and I give it to whomever I see fit. **27:6** I have at this time placed all these nations of yours under the power of my servant, King Nebuchadnezzar of Babylon. I have even made all the wild animals subject to him. **27:7** All nations must serve him and his son and grandson until the time comes for his own nation to fall. Then many nations and great kings will in turn subjugate Babylon. **27:8** But suppose a nation or a kingdom will not be subject to King Nebuchadnezzar of Babylon. Suppose it will not submit to the yoke of servitude to him. I, the LORD, affirm that I will punish that nation. I will use the king of Babylon to punish it with war, starvation, and disease until I have destroyed it. **27:9** So do not listen to your prophets or to those who claim to predict the future by divination, by dreams, by consulting the dead, or by practicing magic. They keep telling you, 'You do not need to be subject to the king of Babylon.' **27:10** Do not listen to them, because their prophecies are lies. Listening to them will only cause you to be taken far away from your native land. I will drive you out of your country and you will die in exile. **27:11** Things will go better for the nation that submits to the yoke of servitude to the king of Babylon and is subject to him. I will leave that nation in its native land. Its people can continue to farm it and live in it. I, the LORD, affirm it!'"'

27:12 I told King Zedekiah of Judah the same thing. I said, "Submit to the yoke of servitude to the king of Babylon. Be subject to him and his people. Then you will continue to live. **27:13** There is no reason why you and your people should die in war or from starvation or disease! That's what the LORD says will happen to any nation that will not be subject to the king of Babylon. **27:14** Do not listen to the prophets who are telling you that you do not need to serve the king of Babylon. For they are prophesying lies to you. **27:15** For I, the LORD, affirm that I did not send them. They are prophesying lies to you. If you listen to them, I will drive you and the prophets who are prophesying lies out of the land and you will all die in exile."

27:16 I also told the priests and all the people, "The LORD says, 'Do not listen to what your prophets are saying. They are prophesying to you that the valuable articles taken from the LORD's temple will be brought back from Babylon very soon. But they are prophesying a lie to you. **27:17** Do not listen to them. Be subject to the king of Babylon. Then you will continue to live. Why should this city be made a pile of rubble?'" **27:18** I also told them, "If they are really prophets and the LORD is speaking to them, let them pray earnestly to the LORD who rules over all. Let them plead with him not to let the valuable articles that are still left in the LORD's temple, in the royal palace, and in Jerusalem be taken away to Babylon. **27:19** For the LORD who rules over all has already spoken about the two bronze pillars, the large bronze basin called 'The Sea,' and the movable bronze stands. He has already spoken about the rest of the valuable articles that are left in this city. **27:20** He has already spoken about these things that King Nebuchadnezzar of Babylon did not take away when he carried Jehoiakim's son King Jeconiah of Judah and the nobles of Judah and Jerusalem away as captives. **27:21** Indeed, the LORD God of Israel who rules over all has already spoken about the valuable articles that are left in the LORD's temple, in the royal palace of Judah, and in Jerusalem. **27:22** He has said, 'They will be carried off to Babylon. They will remain there until it is time for me to show consideration for them again. Then I will bring them back and restore them to this place.' I, the LORD, affirm this!"

Jeremiah Confronted by a False Prophet

28:1 The following events occurred in that same year, early in the reign of King Zedekiah of Judah. To be more precise, it was the fifth month of the fourth year of his reign. The prophet Hananiah son of Azzur, who was from Gibeon, spoke to Jeremiah in the LORD's temple in the presence of the priests and all the people. **28:2** "The LORD God of Israel who rules over all says, 'I will break the yoke of servitude to the king of Babylon. **28:3** Before two years are over, I will bring back to this place everything that King Nebuchadnezzar of Babylon took from it and carried away to Babylon. **28:4** I will also bring back to this place Jehoiakim's son King Jeconiah of Judah and all the exiles who were taken to Babylon.' Indeed, the LORD affirms, 'I will break the yoke of servitude to the king of Babylon.'"

28:5 Then the prophet Jeremiah responded to the prophet Hananiah in the presence of the priests and all the people who were standing in the LORD's temple. **28:6** The prophet Jeremiah said, "Amen! May the LORD do all this! May the LORD make your prophecy come true! May he bring back to this place from Babylon all the valuable articles taken from the LORD's temple and the people who were carried into exile. **28:7** But listen to what I say to you and to all these people. **28:8** From earliest times, the prophets who preceded you and me invariably prophesied war, disaster, and plagues against many countries and great kingdoms. **28:9** So if a prophet prophesied peace and prosperity, it was only known that the LORD truly sent him when what he prophesied came true."

28:10 The prophet Hananiah then took the yoke off the prophet Jeremiah's neck and broke it. **28:11** Then he spoke up in the presence of all the people. "The LORD says, 'In the same way I will break the yoke of servitude of all the nations to King Nebuchadnezzar of Babylon before two years are over.'" After he heard this, the prophet Jeremiah departed and went on his way.

28:12 But shortly after the prophet Hananiah had broken the yoke off the prophet Jeremiah's neck, the LORD spoke to Jeremiah. **28:13** "Go and tell Hananiah that the LORD says, 'You have indeed broken the wooden yoke. But you have only succeeded in replacing it with an iron one! **28:14** For the LORD God of Israel who rules over all says, "I have put an irresistible yoke of servitude on all these nations so they will serve King Nebuchad-

nezzar of Babylon. And they will indeed serve him. I have even given him control over the wild animals."'" **28:15** Then the prophet Jeremiah told the prophet Hananiah, "Listen, Hananiah! The LORD did not send you! You are making these people trust in a lie! **28:16** So the LORD says, 'I will most assuredly remove you from the face of the earth. You will die this very year because you have counseled rebellion against the LORD.'" **28:17** In the seventh month of that very same year the prophet Hananiah died.

Jeremiah's Letter to the Exiles

29:1 The prophet Jeremiah sent a letter to the exiles Nebuchadnezzar had carried off from Jerusalem to Babylon. It was addressed to the elders who were left among the exiles, to the priests, to the prophets, and to all the other people who were exiled in Babylon. **29:2** He sent it after King Jeconiah, the queen mother, the palace officials, the leaders of Judah and Jerusalem, the craftsmen, and the metal workers had been exiled from Jerusalem. **29:3** He sent it with Elasah son of Shaphan and Gemariah son of Hilkiah. King Zedekiah of Judah had sent these men to Babylon to King Nebuchadnezzar of Babylon. The letter said:

29:4 "The LORD God of Israel who rules over all says to all those he sent into exile to Babylon from Jerusalem, **29:5** 'Build houses and settle down. Plant gardens and eat what they produce. **29:6** Marry and have sons and daughters. Find wives for your sons and allow your daughters get married so that they too can have sons and daughters. Grow in number; do not dwindle away. **29:7** Work to see that the city where I sent you as exiles enjoys peace and prosperity. Pray to the LORD for it. For as it prospers you will prosper.'

29:8 "For the LORD God of Israel who rules over all says, 'Do not let the prophets or those among you who claim to be able to predict the future by divination deceive you. And do not pay any attention to the dreams that you are encouraging them to dream. **29:9** They are prophesying lies to you and claiming my authority to do so. But I did not send them. I, the LORD, affirm it!'

29:10 "For the LORD says, 'Only when the seventy years of Babylonian rule are over will I again take up consideration for you. Then I will fulfill my gracious promise to you and restore you to your homeland. **29:11** For I know what I have planned for you,' says the LORD. 'I have plans to prosper you, not to harm you. I have plans to give you a future filled with hope. **29:12** When you call out to me and come to me in prayer, I will hear your prayers. **29:13** When you seek me in prayer and worship, you will find me available to you. If you seek me with all your heart and soul, **29:14** I will make myself available to you,' says the LORD. 'Then I will reverse your plight and will regather you from all the nations and all the places where I have exiled you,' says the LORD. 'I will bring you back to the place from which I exiled you.'

29:15 "You say, 'The LORD has raised up prophets of good news for us here in Babylon.' **29:16** But just listen to what the LORD has to say about the king who occupies David's throne and all your fellow countrymen who are still living in this city of Jerusalem and were not carried off into exile with you. **29:17** The LORD who rules over all says, 'I will bring war, starvation, and disease on them. I will treat them like figs that are so rotten they cannot be eaten. **29:18** I will chase after them with war, starvation, and disease. I will make all the kingdoms of the earth horrified at what happens to them. I will make them examples of those who are cursed, objects of horror, hissing scorn, and ridicule among all the nations where I exile them. **29:19** For they have not paid attention to what I said to them through my servants the prophets whom I sent to them over and over again,' says the LORD. 'And you exiles have not paid any attention to them either,' says the LORD. **29:20** 'So pay attention to what I, the LORD, have said, all you exiles whom I have sent to Babylon from Jerusalem.'

29:21 "The LORD God of Israel who rules over all also has something to say about Ahab son of Kolaiah and Zedekiah son of Maaseiah, who are prophesying lies to you and claiming my authority to do so. 'I will hand them over to King Nebuchadnezzar of Babylon and he will execute them before your very eyes. **29:22** And all the exiles of Judah who are in Babylon will use them as examples when they put a curse on anyone. They will say, "May the LORD treat you like Zedekiah and Ahab whom the king of Babylon roasted to death in the fire!" **29:23** This will happen to them because they have done what is shameful in Israel. They have committed adultery with their neighbors' wives and have spoken lies while claiming my authority. They have spoken words that I did not command them to speak. I know what they have done. I have been a witness to it,' says the LORD."

A Response to the Letter and a Subsequent Letter

29:24 The LORD told Jeremiah, "Tell Shemaiah the Nehelamite **29:25** that the LORD God of Israel who rules over all has a message for him. Tell him, 'On your own initiative you sent a letter to the priest Zephaniah son of Maaseiah and to all the other priests and to all the people in Jerusalem. In your letter you said to Zephaniah, **29:26** "The LORD has made you priest in place of Jehoiada. He has put you in charge in the LORD's temple of controlling any lunatic who pretends to be a prophet. And it is your duty to put any such person in the stocks with an iron collar around his neck. **29:27** You should have reprimanded Jeremiah from Anathoth who is pretending to be a prophet among you! **29:28** For he has even sent a message to us here in Babylon. He wrote and told us, "You will be there a long time. Build houses and settle down. Plant gardens and eat what they produce."'"

29:29 Zephaniah the priest read that letter to the prophet Jeremiah. **29:30** Then the LORD spoke to Jeremiah. **29:31** "Send a message to all the exiles in Babylon. Tell them, 'The LORD has spoken about Shemaiah the Nehelamite. "Shemaiah has spoken to you as a prophet even though I did not send him. He is making you trust in a lie. **29:32** Because he has done this," the LORD says, "I will punish Shemaiah the Nehelamite and his whole family. There will not be any of them left to experience the good things that I will do for my people. I, the LORD, affirm it! For he counseled rebellion against the LORD."'"

Introduction to the Book of Consolation

30:1 The LORD spoke to Jeremiah. **30:2** "The LORD God of Israel says, 'Write everything that I am about to tell you in a scroll. **30:3** For I, the LORD, affirm that the time will come when I will reverse the plight of my people, Israel and Judah,' says the LORD. 'I will bring them back to the land I gave their ancestors and they will take possession of it once again.'"

Israel and Judah Will Be Delivered after a Time of Deep Distress

30:4 So here is what the LORD has to say about Israel and Judah.

30:5 Yes, here is what he says:

"You hear cries of panic and of terror;
there is no peace in sight.
30:6 Ask yourselves this and consider it carefully:
Have you ever seen a man give birth to a baby?
Why then do I see all these strong men
grabbing their stomachs in pain like a woman giving birth?
And why do their faces
turn so deathly pale?
30:7 Alas, what a terrible time of trouble it is!
There has never been any like it.
It is a time of trouble for the descendants of Jacob,
but some of them will be rescued out of it.
30:8 When the time for them to be rescued comes,"
says the LORD who rules over all,
"I will rescue you from foreign subjugation.
I will deliver you from captivity.
Foreigners will then no longer subjugate them.
30:9 But they will be subject to the LORD their God
and to the Davidic ruler whom I will raise up as king over them.
30:10 So I, the LORD, tell you not to be afraid,
you descendants of Jacob, my servants.
Do not be terrified, people of Israel.
For I will rescue you and your descendants
from a faraway land where you are captives.
The descendants of Jacob will return to their land and enjoy peace.
They will be secure and no one will terrify them.
30:11 For I, the LORD, affirm that
I will be with you and will rescue you.
I will completely destroy all the nations where I scattered you.
But I will not completely destroy you.
I will indeed discipline you, but only in due measure.
I will not allow you to go entirely unpunished."

The Lord Will Heal the Wounds of Judah

30:12 Moreover, the LORD says to the people of Zion,
"Your injuries are incurable;
your wounds are severe.
30:13 There is no one to plead your cause.
There are no remedies for your wounds.
There is no healing for you.
30:14 All your allies have abandoned you.
They no longer have any concern for you.
For I have attacked you like an enemy would.
I have chastened you cruelly.
For your wickedness is so great
and your sin is so much.
30:15 Why do you complain about your injuries,
that your pain is incurable?
I have done all this to you
because your wickedness is so great
and your sin is so much.
30:16 But all who destroyed you will be destroyed.
All your enemies will go into exile.
Those who plundered you will be plundered.
I will cause those who pillaged you to be pillaged.
30:17 Yes, I will restore you to health.
I will heal your wounds.
I, the LORD, affirm it!
For you have been called an outcast,
Zion, whom no one cares for."

The Lord Will Restore Israel and Judah

30:18 The LORD says,
"I will restore the ruined houses of the descendants of Jacob.
I will show compassion on their ruined homes.
Every city will be rebuilt on its former ruins.
Every fortified dwelling will occupy its traditional site.
30:19 Out of those places you will hear songs of thanksgiving
and the sounds of laughter and merriment.
I will increase their number and they will not dwindle away.
I will bring them honor and they will no longer be despised.
30:20 The descendants of Jacob will enjoy their former privileges.
Their community will be reestablished in my favor
and I will punish all who try to oppress them.
30:21 One of their own people will be their leader.
Their ruler will come from their own number.
I will invite him to approach me, and he will do so.
For no one would dare approach me on his own.
I, the LORD, affirm it!
30:22 Then you will again be my people
and I will be your God.
30:23 Just watch! The wrath of the LORD
will come like a storm.
Like a raging storm it will rage down
on the heads of those who are wicked.
30:24 The anger of the LORD will not turn back
until he has fully carried out his intended purposes.
In days to come you will come to understand this.
31:1 At that time I will be the God of all the clans of Israel
and they will be my people.
I, the LORD, affirm it!"

Israel Will Be Restored and Join Judah in Worship

31:2 The LORD says,
"The people of Israel who survived
death at the hands of the enemy
will find favor in the wilderness
as they journey to find rest for themselves.
31:3 In a far-off land the LORD will manifest himself to them.
He will say to them, 'I have loved you with an everlasting love.
That is why I have continued to be faithful to you.
31:4 I will rebuild you, my dear children Israel,
so that you will once again be built up.
Once again you will take up the tambourine
and join in the happy throng of dancers.
31:5 Once again you will plant vineyards
on the hills of Samaria.
Those who plant them
will once again enjoy their fruit.
31:6 Yes, a time is coming
when watchmen will call out on the mountains of Ephraim,
"Come! Let us go to Zion
to worship the LORD our God!"'"
31:7 Moreover, the LORD says,
"Sing for joy for the descendants of Jacob.
Utter glad shouts for that foremost of the nations.
Make your praises heard.
Then say, 'LORD, rescue your people.
Deliver those of Israel who remain alive.'
31:8 Then I will reply, 'I will bring them back from the land of the north.
I will gather them in from the distant parts of the earth.
Blind and lame people will come with them,
so will pregnant women and women about to give birth.
A vast throng of people will come back here.
31:9 They will come back shedding tears of contrition.
I will bring them back praying prayers of repentance.
I will lead them besides streams of water,
along smooth paths where they will never stumble.
I will do this because I am Israel's father;
Ephraim is my firstborn son.'"
31:10 Hear what the LORD has to say, O nations.
Proclaim it in the faraway lands along the sea.
Say, "The one who scattered Israel will regather them.
He will watch over his people like a shepherd watches over his flock."
31:11 For the LORD will rescue the descendants of Jacob.
He will secure their release from those who had overpowered them.
31:12 They will come and shout for joy on Mount Zion.
They will be radiant with joy over the good things the LORD provides,
the grain, the fresh wine, the olive oil,
the young sheep and calves he has given to them.
They will be like a well-watered garden
and will not grow faint or weary any more.
31:13 The LORD says, "At that time young women will dance and be glad.
Young men and old men will rejoice.
I will turn their grief into gladness.

I will give them comfort and joy in place of their sorrow.
31:14 I will provide the priests with abundant provisions.
My people will be filled to the full with the good things I provide."
31:15 The LORD says,
"A sound is heard in Ramah,
a sound of crying in bitter grief.
It is the sound of Rachel weeping for her children
and refusing to be comforted, because her children are gone."
31:16 The LORD says to her,
"Stop crying! Do not shed any more tears!
For your heartfelt repentance will be rewarded.
Your children will return from the land of the enemy.
I, the LORD, affirm it!
31:17 Indeed, there is hope for your posterity.
Your children will return to their own territory.
I, the LORD, affirm it!
31:18 I have indeed heard the people of Israel say mournfully,
'We were like a calf untrained to the yoke.
You disciplined us and we learned from it.
Let us come back to you and we will do so,
for you are the LORD our God.
31:19 For after we turned away from you we repented.
After we came to our senses we beat our breasts in sorrow.
We are ashamed and humiliated
because of the disgraceful things we did previously.'
31:20 Indeed, the people of Israel are my dear children.
They are the children I take delight in.
For even though I must often rebuke them,
I still remember them with fondness.
So I am deeply moved with pity for them
and will surely have compassion on them.
I, the LORD, affirm it!
31:21 I will say, 'My dear children of Israel, keep in mind
the road you took when you were carried off.
Mark off in your minds the landmarks.
Make a mental note of telltale signs marking the way back.
Return, my dear children of Israel.
Return to these cities of yours.
31:22 How long will you vacillate,
you who were once like an unfaithful daughter?
For I, the LORD, promise to bring about something new on the earth,
something as unique as a woman protecting a man!'"
Judah Will Be Restored
31:23 The LORD God of Israel who rules over all says,
"I will restore the people of Judah to their land and to their towns.
When I do, they will again say of Jerusalem,
'May the LORD bless you, you holy mountain,
the place where righteousness dwells.'
31:24 The land of Judah will be inhabited by people who live in its towns
as well as by farmers and shepherds with their flocks.
31:25 I will fully satisfy the needs of those who are weary
and fully refresh the souls of those who are faint.
31:26 Then they will say, 'Under these conditions I can enjoy sweet sleep
when I wake up and look around.'"
Israel and Judah Will Be Repopulated
31:27 "Indeed, a time is coming," says the LORD, "when I will cause people and animals to sprout up in the lands of Israel and Judah. **31:28** In the past I saw to it that they were uprooted and torn down, that they were destroyed and demolished. But now I will see to it that they are built up and firmly planted. I, the LORD, affirm it!"
The Lord Will Make a New Covenant with Israel and Judah
31:29 "When that time comes, people will no longer say, 'The parents have eaten sour grapes, but the children's teeth have grown numb.' **31:30** Rather, each person will die for his own sins. The teeth of the person who eats the sour grapes will themselves grow numb.
31:31 "Indeed, a time is coming," says the LORD, "when I will make a new covenant with the people of Israel and Judah. **31:32** It will not be like the old covenant that I made with their ancestors when I delivered them from Egypt. For they violated that covenant, even though I was like a faithful husband to them," says the LORD. **31:33** "But I will make a new covenant with the whole nation of Israel after I plant them back in the land," says the LORD. "I will put my law within them and write it on their hearts and minds. I will be their God and they will be my people.
31:34 "People will no longer need to teach their neighbors and relatives to know me. For all of them, from the least important to the most important, will know me," says the LORD. "For I will forgive their sin and will no longer call to mind the wrong they have done."
The Lord Guarantees Israel's Continuance
31:35 The LORD has made a promise to Israel.
He promises it as the one who fixed the sun to give light by day
and the moon and stars to give light by night.
He promises it as the one who stirs up the sea so that its waves roll.
He promises it as the one who is known as the LORD who rules over all.

31:36 The LORD affirms, "The descendants of Israel will not
cease forever to be a nation in my sight.
That could only happen if the fixed ordering of the heavenly lights
were to cease to operate before me."
31:37 The LORD says, "I will not reject all the descendants of Israel
because of all that they have done.
That could only happen if the heavens above could be measured
or the foundations of the earth below could all be explored,"
says the LORD.
Jerusalem Will Be Enlarged
31:38 "Indeed a time is coming," says the LORD, "when the city of Jerusalem will be rebuilt as my special city. It will be built from the Tower of Hananel westward to the Corner Gate. **31:39** The boundary line will extend beyond that, straight west from there to the Hill of Gareb and then turn southward to Goah. **31:40** The whole valley where dead bodies and sacrificial ashes are thrown and all the terraced fields out to the Kidron Valley on the east as far north as the Horse Gate will be included within this city that is sacred to the LORD. The city will never again be torn down or destroyed."
Jeremiah Buys a Field
32:1 In the tenth year that Zedekiah was ruling over Judah the LORD spoke to Jeremiah. That was the same as the eighteenth year of Nebuchadnezzar.
32:2 Now at that time, the armies of the king of Babylon were besieging Jerusalem. The prophet Jeremiah was confined in the courtyard of the guardhouse attached to the royal palace of Judah. **32:3** For King Zedekiah had confined Jeremiah there after he had reproved him for prophesying as he did. He had asked Jeremiah, "Why do you keep prophesying these things? Why do you keep saying that the LORD says, 'I will hand this city over to the king of Babylon? I will let him capture it. **32:4** King Zedekiah of Judah will not escape from the Babylonians. He will certainly be handed over to the king of Babylon. He must answer personally to the king of Babylon and confront him face to face. **32:5** Zedekiah will be carried off to Babylon and will remain there until I have fully dealt with him. I, the LORD, affirm it! Even if you continue to fight against the Babylonians, you cannot win.'"
32:6 So now, Jeremiah said, "The LORD told me, **32:7** 'Hanamel, the son of your uncle Shallum, will come to you soon. He will say to
you, "Buy my field at Anathoth because you are entitled as my closest relative to buy it."' **32:8** Now it happened just as the LORD had said! My cousin Hanamel came to me in the courtyard of the guardhouse. He said to me, 'Buy my field which is at Anathoth in the territory of the tribe of Benjamin. Buy it for yourself since you are entitled as my closest relative to take possession of it for yourself.' When this happened, I recognized that the LORD had indeed spoken to me. **32:9** So I bought the field at Anathoth from my cousin Hanamel. I weighed out seven ounces of silver and gave it to him to pay for it. **32:10** I signed the deed of purchase, sealed it, and had some men serve as witnesses to the purchase. I weighed out the silver for him on a scale. **32:11** There were two copies of the deed of purchase. One was sealed and contained the order of transfer and the conditions of purchase. The other was left unsealed. **32:12** I took both copies of the deed of purchase and gave them to Baruch son of Neriah, the son of Mahseiah. I gave them to him in the presence of my cousin Hanamel, the witnesses who had signed the deed of purchase, and all the Judeans who were housed in the courtyard of the guardhouse. **32:13** In the presence of all these people I instructed Baruch, **32:14** 'The LORD God of Israel who rules over all says, "Take these documents, both the sealed copy of the deed of purchase and the unsealed copy. Put them in a clay jar so that they may be preserved for a long time to come."' **32:15** For the LORD God of Israel who rules over all says, "Houses, fields, and vineyards will again be bought in this land."'
Jeremiah's Prayer of Praise and Bewilderment
32:16 "After I had given the copies of the deed of purchase to Baruch son of Neriah, I prayed to the LORD, **32:17** 'Oh, Lord GOD, you did indeed make heaven and earth by your mighty power and great strength. Nothing is too hard for you! **32:18** You show unfailing love to thousands. But you also punish children for the sins of their parents. You are the great and powerful God who is known as the LORD who rules over all. **32:19** You plan great things and you do mighty deeds. You see everything people do. You reward each of them for the way they live and for the things they do. **32:20** You did miracles and amazing deeds in the land of Egypt which have had lasting effect. By this means you gained both in Israel and among humankind a renown that lasts to this day. **32:21** You used your mighty power and your great strength to perform miracles and amazing deeds and to bring great terror on the Egyptians. By this means you brought your people Israel out of the land of Egypt. **32:22** You kept the promise that you swore on oath to their ancestors. You gave them a land flowing with milk and honey. **32:23** But when they came in and took possession of it, they did not obey you or live as you had instructed them. They did not do anything that you commanded them to do. So you brought all this disaster on them. **32:24** Even now siege ramps have been built up around the city in order to capture it. War, starvation, and disease are sure to make the city fall into the hands of the Babylonians who are

attacking it. LORD, you threatened that this would happen. Now you can see that it is already taking place. **32:25** The city is sure to fall into the hands of the Babylonians. Yet, in spite of this, you, Lord GOD, have said to me, "Buy that field with silver and have the transaction legally witnessed."'"

The Lord Answers Jeremiah's Prayer

32:26 The LORD answered Jeremiah. **32:27** "I am the LORD, the God of all humankind. There is, indeed, nothing too difficult for me. **32:28** Therefore I, the LORD, say: 'I will indeed hand this city over to King Nebuchadnezzar of Babylon and the Babylonian army. They will capture it. **32:29** The Babylonian soldiers that are attacking this city will break into it and set it on fire. They will burn it down along with the houses where people have made me angry by offering sacrifices to the god Baal and by pouring out drink offerings to other gods on their rooftops. **32:30** This will happen because the people of Israel and Judah have repeatedly done what displeases me from their earliest history until now and because they have repeatedly made me angry by the things they have done. I, the LORD, affirm it! **32:31** This will happen because the people of this city have aroused my anger and my wrath since the time they built it until now. They have made me so angry that I am determined to remove it from my sight. **32:32** I am determined to do so because the people of Israel and Judah have made me angry with all their wickedness – they, their kings, their officials, their priests, their prophets, and especially the people of Judah and the citizens of Jerusalem have done this wickedness. **32:33** They have turned away from me instead of turning to me. I tried over and over again to instruct them, but they did not listen and respond to correction. **32:34** They set up their disgusting idols in the temple which I have claimed for my own and defiled it. **32:35** They built places of worship for the god Baal in the Valley of Ben Hinnom so that they could sacrifice their sons and daughters to the god Molech. Such a disgusting practice was not something I commanded them to do! It never even entered my mind to command them to do such a thing! So Judah is certainly liable for punishment.'

32:36 "You and your people are right in saying, 'War, starvation, and disease are sure to make this city fall into the hands of the king of Babylon.' But now I, the LORD God of Israel, have something further to say about this city: **32:37** 'I will certainly regather my people from all the countries where I will have exiled them in my anger, fury, and great wrath. I will bring them back to this place and allow them to live here in safety. **32:38** They will be my people, and I will be their God. **32:39** I will give them a single-minded purpose to live in a way that always shows respect for me. They will want to do that for their own good and the good of the children who descend from them. **32:40** I will make a lasting covenant with them that I will never stop doing good to them. I will fill their hearts and minds with respect for me so that they will never again turn away from me. **32:41** I will take delight in doing good to them. I will faithfully and wholeheartedly plant them firmly in the land.'

32:42 "For I, the LORD, say: 'I will surely bring on these people all the good fortune that I am hereby promising them. I will be just as sure to do that as I have been in bringing all this great disaster on them. **32:43** You and your people are saying that this land will become desolate, uninhabited by either people or animals. You are saying that it will be handed over to the Babylonians. But fields will again be bought in this land. **32:44** Fields will again be bought with silver, and deeds of purchase signed, sealed, and witnessed. This will happen in the territory of Benjamin, the villages surrounding Jerusalem, the towns in Judah, the southern hill country, the western foothills, and southern Judah. For I will restore them to their land. I, the LORD, affirm it!'"

The Lord Promises a Second Time to Restore Israel and Judah

33:1 The LORD spoke to Jeremiah a second time while he was still confined in the courtyard of the guardhouse. **33:2** "I, the LORD, do these things. I, the LORD, form the plan to bring them about. I am known as the LORD. I say to you, **33:3** 'Call on me in prayer and I will answer you. I will show you great and mysterious things which you still do not know about.' **33:4** For I, the LORD God of Israel, have something more to say about the houses in this city and the royal buildings which have been torn down for defenses against the siege ramps and military incursions of the Babylonians: **33:5** 'The defenders of the city will go out and fight with the Babylonians. But they will only fill those houses and buildings with the dead bodies of the people that I will kill in my anger and my wrath. That will happen because I have decided to turn my back on this city on account of the wicked things they have done. **33:6** But I will most surely heal the wounds of this city and restore it and its people to health. I will show them abundant peace and security. **33:7** I will restore Judah and Israel and will rebuild them as they were in days of old. **33:8** I will purify them from all the sin that they committed against me. I will forgive all their sins which they committed in rebelling against me. **33:9** All the nations will hear about all the good things which I will do to them. This city will bring me fame, honor, and praise before them for the joy that I bring it. The nations will tremble in awe at all the peace and prosperity that I will provide for it.'

33:10 "I, the LORD, say: 'You and your people are saying about this place, "It lies in ruins. There are no people or animals in it." That is true.

The towns of Judah and the streets of Jerusalem will soon be desolate, uninhabited either by people or by animals. But happy sounds will again be heard in these places. **33:11** Once again there will be sounds of joy and gladness and the glad celebrations of brides and grooms. Once again people will bring their thank offerings to the temple of the LORD and will say, "Give thanks to the LORD who rules over all. For the LORD is good and his unfailing love lasts forever." For I, the LORD, affirm that I will restore the land to what it was in days of old.'

33:12 "I, the LORD who rules over all, say: 'This place will indeed lie in ruins. There will be no people or animals in it. But there will again be in it and in its towns sheepfolds where shepherds can rest their sheep. **33:13** I, the LORD, say that shepherds will once again count their sheep as they pass into the fold. They will do this in all the towns in the southern hill country, the western foothills, the southern hill country, the territory of Benjamin, the villages surrounding Jerusalem, and the towns of Judah.'

The Lord Reaffirms His Covenant with David, Israel, and Levi

33:14 "I, the LORD, affirm: 'The time will certainly come when I will fulfill my gracious promise concerning the nations of Israel and Judah. **33:15** In those days and at that time I will raise up for them a righteous descendant of David.

"'He will do what is just and right in the land. **33:16** Under his rule Judah will enjoy safety and Jerusalem will live in security. At that time Jerusalem will be called "The LORD has provided us with justice." **33:17** For I, the LORD, promise: "David will never lack a successor to occupy the throne over the nation of Israel. **33:18** Nor will the Levitical priests ever lack someone to stand before me and continually offer up burnt offerings, sacrifice cereal offerings, and offer the other sacrifices."'"

33:19 The LORD spoke further to Jeremiah. **33:20** "I, LORD, make the following promise: 'I have made a covenant with the day and with the night that they will always come at their proper times. Only if you people could break that covenant **33:21** could my covenant with my servant David and my covenant with the Levites ever be broken. So David will by all means always have a descendant to occupy his throne as king and the Levites will by all means always have priests who will minister before me. **33:22** I will make the children who follow one another in the line of my servant David very numerous. I will also make the Levites who minister before me very numerous. I will make them all as numerous as the stars in the sky and as the sands which are on the seashore.'"

33:23 The LORD spoke still further to Jeremiah. **33:24** "You have surely noticed what these people are saying, haven't you? They are saying, 'The LORD has rejected the two families of Israel and Judah that he chose.' So they have little regard that my people will ever again be a nation. **33:25** But I, the LORD, make the following promise: I have made a covenant governing the coming of day and night. I have established the fixed laws governing heaven and earth. **33:26** Just as surely as I have done this, so surely will I never reject the descendants of Jacob. Nor will I ever refuse to choose one of my servant David's descendants to rule over the descendants of Abraham, Isaac, and Jacob. Indeed, I will restore them and show mercy to them."

The Lord Makes an Ominous Promise to Zedekiah

34:1 The LORD spoke to Jeremiah while King Nebuchadnezzar of Babylon was attacking Jerusalem and the towns around it with a large army. This army consisted of troops from his own army and from the kingdoms and peoples of the lands under his dominion. **34:2** The LORD God of Israel told Jeremiah to go and give King Zedekiah of Judah a message. He told Jeremiah to tell him, "The LORD says, 'I am going to hand this city over to the king of Babylon and he will burn it down. **34:3** You yourself will not escape his clutches, but will certainly be captured and handed over to him. You must confront the king of Babylon face to face and answer to him personally. Then you must go to Babylon. **34:4** However, listen to what I, the LORD, promise you, King Zedekiah of Judah. I, the LORD, promise that you will not die in battle or be executed. **34:5** You will die a peaceful death. They will burn incense at your burial just as they did at the burial of your ancestors, the former kings who preceded you. They will mourn for you, saying, "Poor, poor master!" Indeed, you have my own word on this. I, the LORD, affirm it!'"

34:6 The prophet Jeremiah told all this to King Zedekiah of Judah in Jerusalem. **34:7** He did this while the army of the king of Babylon was attacking Jerusalem and the cities of Lachish and Azekah. He was attacking these cities because they were the only fortified cities of Judah which were still holding out.

The Lord Threatens to Destroy Those Who Wronged Their Slaves

34:8 The LORD spoke to Jeremiah after King Zedekiah had made a covenant with all the people in Jerusalem to grant their slaves their freedom. **34:9** Everyone was supposed to free their male and female Hebrew slaves. No one was supposed to keep a fellow Judean enslaved. **34:10** All the people and their leaders had agreed to this. They had agreed to free their male and female slaves and not keep them enslaved any longer. They originally complied with the covenant and freed them. **34:11** But later they had changed their minds. They had taken back their male and female slaves that they had freed and forced them to be slaves again. **34:12** That was when the LORD spoke to Jeremiah, **34:13** "The LORD God of Israel has a message for you. 'I made a covenant with your ancestors when I brought them out of Egypt where they had been slaved. It stipulated, **34:14** "Every seven years each of you must free any fellow Hebrews who have sold themselves to you. After they have served you for six years, you shall set them free." But your ancestors did not obey me or pay any attention to me. **34:15** Recently, however, you yourselves showed a change of heart and did what is pleasing to me. You granted your fellow countrymen their freedom and you made a covenant to that effect in my presence in the house that I have claimed for my own. **34:16** But then you turned right around and showed that you did not honor me. Each of you took back your male and female slaves whom you had freed as they desired, and you forced them to be your slaves again. **34:17** So I, the LORD, say: "You have not really obeyed me and granted freedom to your neighbor and fellow countryman. Therefore, I will grant you freedom, the freedom to die in war, or by starvation or disease. I, the LORD, affirm it! I will make all the kingdoms of the earth horrified at what happens to you. **34:18** I will punish those people who have violated their covenant with me. I will make them like the calf they cut in two and passed between its pieces. I will do so because they did not keep the terms of the covenant they made in my presence. **34:19** I will punish the leaders of Judah and Jerusalem, the court officials, the priests, and all the other people of the land who passed between the pieces of the calf. **34:20** I will hand them over to their enemies who want to kill them. Their dead bodies will become food for the birds and the wild animals. **34:21** I will also hand King Zedekiah of Judah and his officials over to their enemies who want to kill them. I will hand them over to the army of the king of Babylon, even though they have temporarily withdrawn from attacking you. **34:22** For I, the LORD, affirm that I will soon give the order and bring them back to this city. They will fight against it and capture it and burn it down. I will also make the towns of Judah desolate so that there will be no one living in them.""'

Judah's Unfaithfulness Contrasted with the Rechabites' Faithfulness

35:1 The LORD spoke to Jeremiah when Jehoiakim son of Josiah was ruling over Judah. **35:2** "Go to the Rechabite community. Invite them to come into one of the side rooms of the LORD's temple and offer them some wine to drink." **35:3** So I went and got Jaazaniah son of Jeremiah the grandson of Habazziniah, his brothers, all his sons, and all the rest of the Rechabite community. **35:4** I took them to the LORD's temple. I took them into the room where the disciples of the prophet Hanan son of Igdaliah stayed. That room was next to the one where the temple officers stayed and above the room where Maaseiah son of Shallum, one of the doorkeepers of the temple, stayed. **35:5** Then I set cups and pitchers full of wine in front of the members of the Rechabite community and said to them, "Have some wine." **35:6** But they answered, "We do not drink wine because our ancestor Jonadab son of Rechab commanded us not to. He told us, 'You and your children must never drink wine. **35:7** Do not build houses. Do not plant crops. Do not plant a vineyard or own one. Live in tents all your lives. If you do these things you will live a long time in the land that you wander about on.' **35:8** We and our wives and our sons and daughters have obeyed everything our ancestor Jonadab commanded us. We have never drunk wine. **35:9** We have not built any houses to live in. We do not own any vineyards, fields, or crops. **35:10** We have lived in tents. We have obeyed our ancestor Jonadab and done exactly as he commanded us. **35:11** But when King Nebuchadnezzar of Babylon invaded the land we said, 'Let's get up and go to Jerusalem to get away from the Babylonian and Aramean armies.' That is why we are staying here in Jerusalem."

35:12 Then the LORD spoke to Jeremiah. **35:13** The LORD God of Israel who rules over all told him, "Go and speak to the people of Judah and the citizens of Jerusalem. Tell them, 'I, the LORD, say: "You must learn a lesson from this about obeying what I say! **35:14** Jonadab son of Rechab ordered his descendants not to drink wine. His orders have been carried out. To this day his descendants have drunk no wine because they have obeyed what their ancestor commanded them. But I have spoken to you over and over again, but you have not obeyed me! **35:15** I sent all my servants the prophets to warn you over and over again. They said, "Every one of you, stop doing the evil things you have been doing and do what is right. Do not pay allegiance to other gods and worship them. Then you can continue to live in this land that I gave to you and your ancestors." But you did not pay any attention or listen to me. **35:16** Yes, the descendants of Jonadab son of Rechab have carried out the orders that their ancestor gave them. But you people have not obeyed me! **35:17** So I, the LORD, the God who rules over all, the God of Israel, say: "I will soon bring on Judah and all the citizens of Jerusalem all the disaster that I threatened to bring on them. I will do this because I spoke to them but they did not listen. I called out to them but they did not answer."''

35:18 Then Jeremiah spoke to the Rechabite community, "The LORD God of Israel who rules over all says, 'You have obeyed the orders of your ancestor Jonadab. You have followed all his instructions. You have done exactly as he commanded you.' **35:19** So the LORD God of Israel who rules over all says, 'Jonadab son of Rechab will never lack a male descendant to serve me.'"

Jehoiakim Burns the Scroll Containing the Lord's Messages

36:1 The LORD spoke to Jeremiah in the fourth year that Jehoiakim son of Josiah was ruling over Judah. **36:2** "Get a scroll. Write on it everything I have told you to say about Israel, Judah, and all the other nations since I began to speak to you in the reign of Josiah until now. **36:3** Perhaps when the people of Judah hear about all the disaster I intend to bring on them, they will all stop doing the evil things they have been doing. If they do, I will forgive their sins and the wicked things they have done."

36:4 So Jeremiah summoned Baruch son of Neriah. Then Jeremiah dictated to Baruch everything the LORD had told him to say and Baruch wrote it all down in a scroll. **36:5** Then Jeremiah told Baruch, "I am no longer allowed to go into the LORD's temple. **36:6** So you go there the next time all the people of Judah come in from their towns to fast in the LORD's temple. Read out loud where all of them can hear you what I told you the LORD said, which you wrote in the scroll. **36:7** Perhaps then they will ask the LORD for mercy and will all stop doing the evil things they have been doing. For the LORD has threatened to bring great anger and wrath against these people."

36:8 So Baruch son of Neriah did exactly what the prophet Jeremiah had told him to do. He read what the LORD had said from the scroll in the temple of the LORD. **36:9** All the people living in Jerusalem and all the people who came into Jerusalem from the towns of Judah came to observe a fast before the LORD. The fast took place in the ninth month of the fifth year that Jehoiakim son of Josiah was ruling over Judah. **36:10** At that time Baruch went into the temple of the LORD. He stood in the entrance of the room of Gemariah the son of Shaphan who had been the royal secretary. That room was in the upper court near the entrance of the New Gate. There, where all the people could hear him, he read from the scroll what Jeremiah had said.

36:11 Micaiah, who was the son of Gemariah and the grandson of Shaphan, heard Baruch read from the scroll everything the LORD had said. **36:12** He went down to the chamber of the royal secretary in the king's palace and found all the court officials in session there. Elishama the royal secretary, Delaiah son of Shemaiah, Elnathan son of Achbor, Gemariah son of Shaphan, Zedekiah son of Hananiah, and all the other officials were seated there. **36:13** Micaiah told them everything he had heard Baruch read from the scroll in the hearing of the people. **36:14** All the officials sent Jehudi, who was the son of Nethaniah and the grandson of Cushi, to Baruch. They ordered him to tell Baruch, "Come here and bring with you the scroll you read in the hearing of the people." So Baruch son of Neriah went to them, carrying the scroll in his hand. **36:15** They said to him, "Please sit down and read it to us." So Baruch sat down and read it to them. **36:16** When they had heard it all, they expressed their alarm to one another. Then they said to Baruch, "We must certainly give the king a report about everything you have read!" **36:17** Then they asked Baruch, "How did you come to write all these words? Do they actually come from Jeremiah's mouth?" **36:18** Baruch answered, "Yes, they came from his own mouth. He dictated all these words to me and I wrote them down in ink on this scroll." **36:19** Then the officials said to Baruch, "You and Jeremiah must go and hide. You must not let anyone know where you are."

36:20 The officials put the scroll in the room of Elishama, the royal secretary, for safekeeping. Then they went to the court and reported everything to the king. **36:21** The king sent Jehudi to get the scroll. He went and got it from the room of Elishama, the royal secretary. Then he himself read it to the king and all the officials who were standing around him. **36:22** Since it was the ninth month of the year, the king was sitting in his winter quarters. A fire was burning in the firepot in front of him. **36:23** As soon as Jehudi had read three or four columns of the scroll, the king would cut them off with a penknife and throw them on the fire in the firepot. He kept doing so until the whole scroll was burned up in the fire. **36:24** Neither he nor any of his attendants showed any alarm when they heard all that had been read. Nor did they tear their clothes to show any grief or sorrow. **36:25** The king did not even listen to Elnathan, Delaiah, and Gemariah, who had urged him not to burn the scroll. **36:26** He also ordered Jerahmeel, who was one of the royal princes, Seraiah son of Azriel, and Shelemiah son of Abdeel to arrest the scribe Baruch and the prophet Jeremiah. However, the LORD hid them.

Baruch and Jeremiah Write Another Scroll

36:27 The LORD spoke to Jeremiah after Jehoiakim had burned the scroll containing what Jeremiah had spoken and Baruch had written down. **36:28** "Get another scroll and write on it everything that was written on the original scroll that King Jehoiakim of Judah burned. **36:29** Tell King Jehoiakim of Judah, 'The LORD says, "You burned the scroll. You asked Jeremiah, 'How dare you write in this scroll that the king of Babylon will certainly come and destroy this land and wipe out all the people and animals on it?'" **36:30** So the LORD says concerning King Jehoiakim of Judah, "None of his line will occupy the throne of David. His dead body will be thrown out to be exposed to scorching heat by day and frost by night. **36:31** I will punish him and his descendants and the officials who serve him for the wicked things they have done. I will bring on them, the citizens of Jerusalem, and the people of Judah all the disaster that I threatened to do to them. I will punish them because I threatened them but they still paid no heed."'" **36:32** Then Jeremiah got another scroll and gave it to the scribe Baruch son of Neriah. As Jeremiah dictated, Baruch wrote on this scroll everything that had been on the scroll that King Jehoiakim of Judah burned in the fire. They also added on this scroll several other messages of the same kind.

Introduction to Incidents During the Reign of Zedekiah

37:1 Zedekiah son of Josiah succeeded Jeconiah son of Jehoiakim as king. He was elevated to the throne of the land of Judah by King Nebuchadnezzar of Babylon. **37:2** Neither he nor the officials who served him nor the people of Judah paid any attention to what the LORD said through the prophet Jeremiah.

The Lord Responds to Zedekiah's Hope for Help

37:3 King Zedekiah sent Jehucal son of Shelemiah and the priest Zephaniah son of Maaseiah to the prophet Jeremiah. He told them to say, "Please pray to the LORD our God on our behalf." **37:4** (Now Jeremiah had not yet been put in prison. So he was still free to come and go among the people as he pleased. **37:5** At that time the Babylonian forces had temporarily given up their siege against Jerusalem. They had had it under siege, but withdrew when they heard that the army of Pharaoh had set out from Egypt.) **37:6** The LORD gave the prophet Jeremiah a message for them. He told him to tell them, **37:7** "The LORD God of Israel says, 'Give a message to the king of Judah who sent you to ask me to help him. Tell him, "The army of Pharaoh that was on its way to help you will go back home to Egypt. **37:8** Then the Babylonian forces will return. They will attack the city and will capture it and burn it down. **37:9** Moreover, I, the LORD, warn you not to deceive yourselves into thinking that the Babylonian forces will go away and leave you alone. For they will not go away. **37:10** For even if you were to defeat all the Babylonian forces fighting against you so badly that only wounded men were left lying in their tents, they would get up and burn this city down."'"

Jeremiah is Charged with Deserting, Arrested, and Imprisoned

37:11 The following events also occurred while the Babylonian forces had temporarily withdrawn from Jerusalem because the army of Pharaoh was coming. **37:12** Jeremiah started to leave Jerusalem to go to the territory of Benjamin. He wanted to make sure he got his share of the property that was being divided up among his family there. **37:13** But he only got as far as the Benjamin Gate. There an officer in charge of the guards named Irijah, who was the son of Shelemiah and the grandson of Hananiah, stopped him. He seized Jeremiah and said, "You are deserting to the Babylonians!" **37:14** Jeremiah answered, "That's a lie! I am not deserting to the Babylonians." But Irijah would not listen to him. Irijah put Jeremiah under arrest and took him to the officials. **37:15** The officials were very angry at Jeremiah. They had him flogged and put in prison in the house of Jonathan, the royal secretary, which they had converted into a place for confining prisoners.

37:16 So Jeremiah was put in prison in a cell in the dungeon in Jonathan's house. He was kept there for a long time. **37:17** Then King Zedekiah had him brought to the palace. There he questioned him privately and asked him, "Is there any message from the LORD?" Jeremiah answered, "Yes, there is." Then he announced, "You will be handed over to the king of Babylon." **37:18** Then Jeremiah asked King Zedekiah, "What crime have I committed against you, or the officials who serve you, or the people of Judah? What have I done to make you people throw me into prison? **37:19** Where now are the prophets who prophesied to you that the king of Babylon would not attack you or this land? **37:20** But now please listen, your royal Majesty, and grant my plea for mercy. Do not send me back to the house of Jonathan, the royal secretary. If you do, I will die there." **37:21** Then King Zedekiah ordered that Jeremiah be committed to the courtyard of the guardhouse. He also ordered that a loaf of bread be given to him every day from the baker's street until all the bread in the city was gone. So Jeremiah was kept in the courtyard of the guardhouse.

Jeremiah Is Charged with Treason and Put in a Cistern to Die

38:1 Now Shephatiah son of Mattan, Gedaliah son of Pashhur, Jehucal son of Shelemiah, and Pashhur son of Malkijah had heard the things that Jeremiah had been telling the people. They had heard him say, **38:2** "The LORD says, 'Those who stay in this city will die in battle or of starvation or disease. Those who leave the city and surrender to the Babylonians will live. They will escape with their lives.'" **38:3** They had also heard him say, "The LORD says, 'This city will certainly be handed over to the army of the king of Babylon. They will capture it.'" **38:4** So these officials said to the king, "This man must be put to death. For he is demoralizing the soldiers who are left in the city as well as all the other people there by these things he is saying. This man is not seeking to help these people but is trying to harm them." **38:5** King Zedekiah said to them, "Very well, you can do what you want with him. For I cannot do anything to stop you." **38:6** So the officials took Jeremiah and put him in the cistern of Malkijah, one of the royal princes, that was in the courtyard of the guardhouse. There was no water in the cistern, only mud. So when they lowered Jeremiah into the cistern with ropes he sank in the mud.

An Ethiopian Official Rescues Jeremiah from the Cistern

38:7 An Ethiopian, Ebed Melech, a court official in the royal palace, heard that Jeremiah had been put in the cistern. While the king was holding court at the Benjamin Gate, **38:8** Ebed Melech departed the palace and went to speak to the king. He said to him, **38:9** "Your royal Majesty, those men have been very wicked in all that they have done to the prophet Jeremiah. They have thrown him into a cistern and he is sure to die of starvation there because there is no food left in the city. **38:10** Then the king gave Ebed Melech the Ethiopian the following order: "Take thirty men with you from here and go pull the prophet Jeremiah out of the cistern before he dies." **38:11** So Ebed Melech took the men with him and went to a room under the treasure room in the palace. He got some worn-out clothes and old rags from there and let them down by ropes to Jeremiah in the cistern. **38:12** Ebed Melech called down to Jeremiah, "Put these rags and worn-out clothes under your armpits to pad the ropes. Jeremiah did as Ebed Melech instructed. **38:13** So they pulled Jeremiah up from the cistern with ropes. Jeremiah, however, still remained confined to the courtyard of the guardhouse.

Jeremiah Responds to Zedekiah's Request for Secret Advice

38:14 Some time later Zedekiah sent and had Jeremiah brought to him at the third entrance of the LORD's temple. The king said to Jeremiah, "I would like to ask you a question. Do not hide anything from me when you answer." **38:15** Jeremiah said to Zedekiah, "If I answer you, you will certainly kill me. If I give you advice, you will not listen to me." **38:16** So King Zedekiah made a secret promise to Jeremiah and sealed it with an oath. He promised, "As surely as the LORD lives who has given us life and breath, I promise you this: I will not kill you or hand you over to those men who want to kill you." **38:17** Then Jeremiah said to Zedekiah, "The LORD, the God who rules over all, the God of Israel, says, 'You must surrender to the officers of the king of Babylon. If you do, your life will be spared and this city will not be burned down. Indeed, you and your whole family will be spared. **38:18** But if you do not surrender to the officers of the king of Babylon, this city will be handed over to the Babylonians and they will burn it down. You yourself will not escape from them.'" **38:19** Then King Zedekiah said to Jeremiah, "I am afraid of the Judeans who have deserted to the Babylonians. The Babylonians might hand me over to them and they will torture me." **38:20** Then Jeremiah answered, "You will not be handed over to them. Please obey the LORD by doing what I have been telling you. Then all will go well with you and your life will be spared. **38:21** But if you refuse to surrender, the LORD has shown me a vision of what will happen. Here is what I saw: **38:22** All the women who are left in the royal palace of Judah will be led out to the officers of the king of Babylon. They will taunt you saying,

'Your trusted friends misled you;
they have gotten the best of you.
Now that your feet are stuck in the mud,
they have turned their backs on you.'

38:23 "All your wives and your children will be turned over to the Babylonians. You yourself will not escape from them but will be captured by the king of Babylon. This city will be burned down."

38:24 Then Zedekiah told Jeremiah, "Do not let anyone know about the conversation we have had. If you do, you will die. **38:25** The officials may hear that I have talked with you. They may come to you and say, 'Tell us what you said to the king and what the king said to you. Do not hide anything from us. If you do, we will kill you.' **38:26** If they do this, tell them, 'I was pleading with the king not to send me back to die in the dungeon of Jonathan's house.'" **38:27** All the officials did indeed come and question Jeremiah. He told them exactly what the king had instructed him to say. They stopped questioning him any further because no one had actually heard their conversation. **38:28** So Jeremiah remained confined in the courtyard of the guardhouse until the day Jerusalem was captured.

The Fall of Jerusalem and Its Aftermath

The following events occurred when Jerusalem was captured.

39:1 King Nebuchadnezzar of Babylon came against Jerusalem with his whole army and laid siege to it. The siege began in the tenth month of the ninth year that Zedekiah ruled over Judah. **39:2** It lasted until the ninth day of the fourth month of Zedekiah's eleventh year. On that day they broke through the city walls. **39:3** Then Nergal-Sharezer of Samgar, Nebo-Sarsekim, who was a chief officer, Nergal-Sharezer, who was a high official, and all the other officers of the king of Babylon came and set up quarters in the Middle Gate. **39:4** When King Zedekiah of Judah and all his soldiers saw them, they tried to escape. They departed from the city during the night. They took a path through the king's garden and passed out through the gate between the two walls. Then they headed for the Jordan Valley. **39:5** But the Babylonian army chased after them. They caught up with Zedekiah in the plains of Jericho and captured him. They took him to King Nebuchadnezzar of Babylon at Riblah in the territory of Hamath and Nebuchadnezzar passed sentence on him there. **39:6** There at Riblah the king of Babylon had Zedekiah's sons put to death while Zedekiah was forced to watch. The king of Babylon also had all the nobles of Judah put to death. **39:7** Then he had Zedekiah's eyes put out and had him bound in chains to be led off to Babylon. **39:8** The Babylonians burned down the royal palace, the temple of the LORD, and the people's homes, and they tore down the wall of Jerusalem. **39:9** Then Nebuzaradan, the captain of the royal guard, took captive the rest of the people who were left in the city. He carried them off to Babylon along with the people who had deserted to him. **39:10** But he left behind in the land of

Judah some of the poor people who owned nothing. He gave them fields and vineyards at that time.

39:11 Now King Nebuchadnezzar of Babylon had issued orders concerning Jeremiah. He had passed them on through Nebuzaradan, the captain of his royal guard, **39:12** "Find Jeremiah and look out for him. Do not do anything to harm him, but do with him whatever he tells you." **39:13** So Nebuzaradan, the captain of the royal guard, Nebushazban, who was a chief officer, Nergal-Sharezer, who was a high official, and all the other officers of the king of Babylon **39:14** sent and had Jeremiah brought from the courtyard of the guardhouse. They turned him over to Gedaliah, the son of Ahikam and the grandson of Shaphan, to take him home with him. But Jeremiah stayed among the people.

Ebed Melech Is Promised Deliverance because of His Faith

39:15 Now the LORD had spoken to Jeremiah while he was still confined in the courtyard of the guardhouse, **39:16** "Go and tell Ebed-Melech the Ethiopian, 'The LORD God of Israel who rules over all says, "I will carry out against this city what I promised. It will mean disaster and not good fortune for it. When that disaster happens, you will be there to see it. **39:17** But I will rescue you when it happens. I, the LORD, affirm it! You will not be handed over to those whom you fear. **39:18** I will certainly save you. You will not fall victim to violence. You will escape with your life because you trust in me. I, the LORD, affirm it!"'"

Jeremiah Is Set Free A Second Time

40:1 The LORD spoke to Jeremiah after Nebuzaradan the captain of the royal guard had set him free at Ramah. He had taken him there in chains along with all the people from Jerusalem and Judah who were being carried off to exile to Babylon. **40:2** The captain of the royal guard took Jeremiah aside and said to him, "The LORD your God threatened this place with this disaster. **40:3** Now he has brought it about. The LORD has done just as he threatened to do. This disaster has happened because you people sinned against the LORD and did not obey him. **40:4** But now, Jeremiah, today I will set you free from the chains on your wrists. If you would like to come to Babylon with me, come along and I will take care of you. But if you prefer not to come to Babylon with me, you are not required to do so. You are free to go anywhere in the land you want to go. Go wherever you choose." **40:5** Before Jeremiah could turn to leave, the captain of the guard added, "Go back to Gedaliah, the son of Ahikam and grandson of Shaphan, whom the king of Babylon appointed to govern the towns of Judah. Go back and live with him among the people. Or go wherever else you choose." Then the captain of the guard gave Jeremiah some food and a present and let him go. **40:6** So Jeremiah went to Gedaliah son of Ahikam at Mizpah and lived there with him. He stayed there to live among the people who had been left in the land of Judah.

A Small Judean Province is Established at Mizpah

40:7 Now some of the officers of the Judean army and their troops had been hiding in the countryside. They heard that the king of Babylon had appointed Gedaliah son of Ahikam to govern the country. They also heard that he had been put in charge over the men, women, and children from the poorer classes of the land who had not been carried off into exile in Babylon. **40:8** So all these officers and their troops came to Gedaliah at Mizpah. The officers who came were Ishmael son of Nethaniah, Johanan and Jonathan the sons of Kareah, Seraiah son of Tanhumeth, the sons of Ephai the Netophathite, and Jezaniah son of the Maacathite. **40:9** Gedaliah, the son of Ahikam and grandson of Shaphan, took an oath so as to give them and their troops some assurance of safety. "Do not be afraid to submit to the Babylonians. Settle down in the land and submit to the king of Babylon. Then things will go well for you. **40:10** I for my part will stay at Mizpah to represent you before the Babylonians whenever they come to us. You for your part go ahead and harvest the wine, the dates, the figs, and the olive oil, and store them in jars. Go ahead and settle down in the towns that you have taken over." **40:11** Moreover, all the Judeans who were in Moab, Ammon, Edom, and all the other countries heard what had happened. They heard that the king of Babylon had allowed some people to stay in Judah and that he had appointed Gedaliah, the son of Ahikam and grandson of Shaphan, to govern them. **40:12** So all these Judeans returned to the land of Judah from the places where they had been scattered. They came to Gedaliah at Mizpah. Thus they harvested a large amount of wine and dates and figs.

Ishmael Murders Gedaliah and Carries the Judeans at Mizpah off as Captives

40:13 Johanan and all the officers of the troops that had been hiding in the open country came to Gedaliah at Mizpah. **40:14** They said to him, "Are you at all aware that King Baalis of Ammon has sent Ishmael son of Nethaniah to kill you?" But Gedaliah son of Ahikam would not believe them. **40:15** Then Johanan son of Kareah spoke privately to Gedaliah there at Mizpah, "Let me go and kill Ishmael the son of Nethaniah before anyone knows about it. Otherwise he will kill you and all the Judeans who have rallied around you will be scattered. Then what remains of Judah will disappear." **40:16** But Gedaliah son of Ahikam said to Johanan son of Kareah, "Do not do that because what you are saying about Ishmael is not true."

41:1 But in the seventh month Ishmael, the son of Nethaniah and grandson of Elishama who was a member of the royal family and had been one of Zedekiah's chief officers, came with ten of his men to Gedaliah son of Ahikam at Mizpah. While they were eating a meal together with him there at Mizpah, **41:2** Ishmael son of Nethaniah and the ten men who were with him stood up, pulled out their swords, and killed Gedaliah, the son of Ahikam and grandson of Shaphan. Thus Ishmael killed the man that the king of Babylon had appointed to govern the country. **41:3** Ishmael also killed all the Judeans who were with Gedaliah at Mizpah and the Babylonian soldiers who happened to be there.

41:4 On the day after Gedaliah had been murdered, before anyone even knew about it, **41:5** eighty men arrived from Shechem, Shiloh, and Samaria. They had shaved off their beards, torn their clothes, and cut themselves to show they were mourning. They were carrying grain offerings and incense to present at the temple of the LORD in Jerusalem. **41:6** Ishmael son of Nethaniah went out from Mizpah to meet them. He was pretending to cry as he walked along. When he met them, he said to them, "Come with me to meet Gedaliah son of Ahikam." **41:7** But as soon as they were inside the city, Ishmael son of Nethaniah and the men who were with him slaughtered them and threw their bodies in a cistern. **41:8** But there were ten men among them who said to Ishmael, "Do not kill us. For we will give you the stores of wheat, barley, olive oil, and honey we have hidden in a field. So he spared their lives and did not kill them along with the rest. **41:9** Now the cistern where Ishmael threw all the dead bodies of those he had killed was a large one that King Asa had constructed as part of his defenses against King Baasha of Israel. Ishmael son of Nethaniah filled it with dead bodies. **41:10** Then Ishmael took captive all the people who were still left alive in Mizpah. This included the royal princesses and all the rest of the people in Mizpah that Nebuzaradan, the captain of the royal guard, had put under the authority of Gedaliah son of Ahikam. Ishmael son of Nethaniah took all these people captive and set out to cross over to the Ammonites.

Johanan Rescues the People Ishmael Had Carried Off

41:11 Johanan son of Kareah and all the army officers who were with him heard about all the atrocities that Ishmael son of Nethaniah had committed. **41:12** So they took all their troops and went to fight against Ishmael son of Nethaniah. They caught up with him near the large pool at Gibeon. **41:13** When all the people that Ishmael had taken captive saw Johanan son of Kareah and all the army officers with him, they were glad. **41:14** All those people that Ishmael had taken captive from Mizpah turned and went over to Johanan son of Kareah. **41:15** But Ishmael son of Nethaniah managed to escape from Johanan along with eight of his men, and he went on over to Ammon.

41:16 Johanan son of Kareah and all the army officers who were with him led off all the people who had been left alive at Mizpah. They had rescued them from Ishmael son of Nethaniah after he killed Gedaliah son of Ahikam. They led off the men, women, children, soldiers, and court officials whom they had brought away from Gibeon. **41:17** They set out to go to Egypt to get away from the Babylonians, but stopped at Geruth Kimham near Bethlehem. **41:18** They were afraid of what the Babylonians might do because Ishmael son of Nethaniah had killed Gedaliah son of Ahikam, whom the king of Babylon had appointed to govern the country.

The Survivors Ask the Lord for Advice but Refuse to Follow It

42:1 Then all the army officers, including Johanan son of Kareah and Jezaniah son of Hoshaiah and all the people of every class, went to the prophet Jeremiah. **42:2** They said to him, "Please grant our request and pray to the LORD your God for all those of us who are still left alive here. For, as you yourself can see, there are only a few of us left out of the many there were before. **42:3** Pray that the LORD your God will tell us where we should go and what we should do." **42:4** The prophet Jeremiah answered them, "Agreed! I will indeed pray to the LORD your God as you have asked. I will tell you everything the LORD replies in response to you. I will not keep anything back from you." **42:5** They answered Jeremiah, "May the LORD be a true and faithful witness against us if we do not do just as the LORD sends you to tell us to do. **42:6** We will obey what the LORD our God to whom we are sending you tells us to do. It does not matter whether we like what he tells us or not. We will obey what he tells us to do so that things will go well for us."

42:7 Ten days later the LORD spoke to Jeremiah. **42:8** So Jeremiah summoned Johanan son of Kareah and all the army officers who were with him and all the people of every class. **42:9** Then Jeremiah said to them, "You sent me to the LORD God of Israel to make your request known to him. Here is what he says to you: **42:10** 'If you will just stay in this land, I will build you up. I will not tear you down. I will firmly plant you. I will not uproot you. For I am filled with sorrow because of the disaster that I have brought on you. **42:11** Do not be afraid of the king of Babylon whom you now fear. Do not be afraid of him because I will be with you to save you and to rescue you from his power. I, the LORD, affirm it! **42:12** I will have compassion on you so that he in turn will have mercy on you and allow you to return to your land.' **42:13** "You must not disobey the LORD your God by saying, 'We will not stay in this land.' **42:14** You must not say, 'No, we will not stay. Instead we will go and live in the land of Egypt where we will not face war, or hear the enemy's trumpet calls, or starve for lack of food.' **42:15** If you people who remain in Judah do that, then listen to what the LORD says. The LORD God of Israel who rules over all says, 'If you are so determined to go to Egypt that you go and settle there, **42:16** the wars you fear will catch up with you there in the land of Egypt. The starvation you are worried about will follow you there to Egypt. You will die there. **42:17** All the people who are determined to go and settle in Egypt will die from war, starvation, or disease. No one will survive or escape the disaster I will bring on them.' **42:18** For the LORD God of Israel who rules over all says, 'If you go to Egypt, I will pour out my wrath on you just as I poured out my anger and wrath on the citizens of Jerusalem. You will become an object of horror and ridicule, an example of those who have been cursed and that people use in pronouncing a curse. You will never see this place again.'

42:19 "The LORD has told you people who remain in Judah, 'Do not go to Egypt.' Be very sure of this: I warn you here and now. **42:20** You are making a fatal mistake. For you sent me to the LORD your God and asked me, 'Pray to the LORD our God for us. Tell us what the LORD our God says and we will do it.' **42:21** This day I have told you what he said. But you do not want to obey the LORD by doing what he sent me to tell you. **42:22** So now be very sure of this: You will die from war, starvation, or disease in the place where you want to go and live."

43:1 Jeremiah finished telling all the people all these things the LORD their God had sent him to tell them. **43:2** Then Azariah son of Hoshaiah, Johanan son of Kareah, and other arrogant men said to Jeremiah, "You are telling a lie! The LORD our God did not send you to tell us, 'You must not go to Egypt and settle there.' **43:3** But Baruch son of Neriah is stirring you up against us. He wants to hand us over to the Babylonians so that they will kill us or carry us off into exile in Babylon." **43:4** So Johanan son of Kareah, all the army officers, and all the rest of the people did not obey the LORD's command to stay in the land. **43:5** Instead Johanan son of Kareah and all the army officers led off all the Judean remnant who had come back to live in the land of Judah from all the nations where they had been scattered. **43:6** They also led off all the men, women, children, and royal princesses that Nebuzaradan, the captain of the royal guard, had left with Gedaliah, the son of Ahikam and grandson of Shaphan. This included the prophet Jeremiah and Baruch son of Neriah. **43:7** They went on to Egypt because they refused to obey the LORD, and came to Tahpanhes.

Jeremiah Predicts that Nebuchadnezzar Will Plunder Egypt and Its Gods

43:8 At Tahpanhes the LORD spoke to Jeremiah. **43:9** "Take some large stones and bury them in the mortar of the clay pavement at the entrance of Pharaoh's residence here in Tahpanhes. Do it while the people of Judah present there are watching. **43:10** Then tell them, 'The LORD God of Israel who rules over all says, "I will bring my servant King Nebuchadnezzar of Babylon. I will set his throne over these stones which I have buried. He will pitch his royal tent over them. **43:11** He will come and attack Egypt. Those who are destined to die of disease will die of disease. Those who are destined to be carried off into exile will be carried off into exile. Those who are destined to die in war will die in war. **43:12** He will set fire to the temples of the gods of Egypt. He will burn their gods or carry them off as captives. He will pick Egypt clean like a shepherd picks the lice from his clothing. He will leave there unharmed. **43:13** He will demolish the sacred pillars in the temple of the sun in Egypt and will burn down the temples of the gods of Egypt.""'

The Lord Will Punish the Judean Exiles in Egypt for Their Idolatry

44:1 The LORD spoke to Jeremiah concerning all the Judeans who were living in the land of Egypt, those in Migdol, Tahpanhes, Memphis, and in the region of southern Egypt. **44:2** "The LORD God of Israel who rules over all says, 'You have seen all the disaster I brought on Jerusalem and all the towns of Judah. Indeed, they now lie in ruins and are deserted. **44:3** This happened because of the wickedness the people living there did. They made me angry by worshiping and offering sacrifice to other gods whom neither they nor you nor your ancestors previously knew. **44:4** I sent my servants the prophets to you people over and over again warning you not to do this disgusting thing I hate. **44:5** But the people of Jerusalem and Judah would not listen or pay any attention. They would not stop the wickedness they were doing nor quit sacrificing to other gods. **44:6** So my anger and my wrath were poured out and burned like a fire through the towns of Judah and the streets of Jerusalem. That is why they have become the desolate ruins that they are today.'

44:7 "So now the LORD, the God who rules over all, the God of Israel, asks, 'Why will you do such great harm to yourselves? Why should every man, woman, child, and baby of yours be destroyed from the midst of Judah? Why should you leave yourselves without a remnant? **44:8** That is what will result from your making me angry by what you are doing. You are making me angry by sacrificing to other gods here in the land of Egypt where you live. You will be destroyed for doing that! You will become an example used in curses and an object of ridicule among all the nations of the earth. **44:9** Have you forgotten all the wicked things that have been done in the towns of Judah and in the streets of Jerusalem by your ancestors, by the kings of Judah and their wives, by you and your wives? **44:10** To this day your people have shown no contrition! They

have not revered me nor followed the laws and statutes I commanded you and your ancestors.'

44:11 "Because of this, the LORD God of Israel who rules over all says, 'I am determined to bring disaster on you, even to the point of destroying all the Judeans here. **44:12** I will see to it that all the Judean remnant that was determined to go and live in the land of Egypt will be destroyed. Here in the land of Egypt they will fall in battle or perish from starvation. People of every class will die in war or from starvation. They will become an object of horror and ridicule, an example of those who have been cursed and that people use in pronouncing a curse. **44:13** I will punish those who live in the land of Egypt with war, starvation, and disease just as I punished Jerusalem. **44:14** None of the Judean remnant who have come to live in the land of Egypt will escape or survive to return to the land of Judah. Though they long to return and live there, none of them shall return except a few fugitives.'"

44:15 Then all the men who were aware that their wives were sacrificing to other gods, as well as all their wives, answered Jeremiah. There was a great crowd of them representing all the people who lived in northern and southern Egypt. They answered, **44:16** "We will not listen to what you claim the LORD has spoken to us! **44:17** Instead we will do everything we vowed we would do. We will sacrifice and pour out drink offerings to the goddess called the Queen of Heaven just as we and our ancestors, our kings, and our leaders previously did in the towns of Judah and in the streets of Jerusalem. For then we had plenty of food, were well-off, and had no troubles. **44:18** But ever since we stopped sacrificing and pouring out drink offerings to the Queen of Heaven, we have been in great need. Our people have died in wars or of starvation." **44:19** The women added, "We did indeed sacrifice and pour out drink offerings to the Queen of Heaven. But it was with the full knowledge and approval of our husbands that we made cakes in her image and poured out drink offerings to her."

44:20 Then Jeremiah replied to all the people, both men and women, who responded to him in this way. **44:21** "The LORD did indeed remember and call to mind what you did! He remembered the sacrifices you and your ancestors, your kings, your leaders, and all the rest of the people of the land offered to other gods in the towns of Judah and in the streets of Jerusalem. **44:22** Finally the LORD could no longer endure your wicked deeds and the disgusting things you did. That is why your land has become the desolate, uninhabited ruin that it is today. That is why it has become a proverbial example used in curses. **44:23** You have sacrificed to other gods! You have sinned against the LORD! You have not obeyed the LORD! You have not followed his laws, his statutes, and his decrees! That is why this disaster that is evident to this day has happened to you."

44:24 Then Jeremiah spoke to all the people, particularly to all the women. "Listen to what the LORD has to say all you people of Judah who are in Egypt. **44:25** The LORD God of Israel who rules over all says, 'You women have confirmed by your actions what you vowed with your lips! You said, "We will certainly carry out our vows to sacrifice and pour out drink offerings to the Queen of Heaven." Well, then fulfill your vows! Carry them out!' **44:26** But listen to what the LORD has to say, all you people of Judah who are living in the land of Egypt. The LORD says, 'I hereby swear by my own great name that none of the people of Judah who are living anywhere in Egypt will ever again invoke my name in their oaths! Never again will any of them use it in an oath saying, "As surely as the Lord GOD lives...." **44:27** I will indeed see to it that disaster, not prosperity, happens to them. All the people of Judah who are in the land of Egypt will die in war or from starvation until not one of them is left. **44:28** Some who survive in battle will return to the land of Judah from the land of Egypt. But they will be very few indeed! Then the Judean remnant who have come to live in the land of Egypt will know whose word proves true, mine or theirs.' **44:29** Moreover the LORD says, 'I will make something happen to prove that I will punish you in this place. I will do it so that you will know that my threats to bring disaster on you will prove true. **44:30** I, the LORD, promise that I will hand Pharaoh Hophra king of Egypt over to his enemies who are seeking to kill him. I will do that just as surely as I handed King Zedekiah of Judah over to King Nebuchadnezzar of Babylon, his enemy who was seeking to kill him.'"

Baruch is Rebuked but also Comforted

45:1 The prophet Jeremiah spoke to Baruch son of Neriah while he was writing down in a scroll the words that Jeremiah spoke to him. This happened in the fourth year that Jehoiakim son of Josiah was ruling over Judah. **45:2** "The LORD God of Israel has a message for you, Baruch. **45:3** 'You have said, "I feel so hopeless! For the LORD has added sorrow to my suffering. I am worn out from groaning. I can't find any rest."'"

45:4 The LORD told Jeremiah, "Tell Baruch, 'The LORD says, "I am about to tear down what I have built and to uproot what I have planted. I will do this throughout the whole earth. **45:5** Are you looking for great things for yourself? Do not look for such things. For I, the LORD, affirm that I am about to bring disaster on all humanity. But I will allow you to escape with your life wherever you go.""'

Prophecies Against Foreign Nations

46:1 The LORD spoke to Jeremiah about the nations.

The Prophecy about Egypt's Defeat at Carchemish

46:2 He spoke about Egypt and the army of Pharaoh Necho king of Egypt which was encamped along the Euphrates River at Carchemish. Now this was the army that King Nebuchadnezzar of Babylon defeated in the fourth year that Jehoiakim son of Josiah was ruling over Judah.
46:3 "Fall into ranks with your shields ready!
Prepare to march into battle!
46:4 Harness the horses to the chariots!
Mount your horses!
Put on your helmets and take your positions!
Sharpen you spears!
Put on your armor!
46:5 What do I see?" says the LORD.
"The soldiers are terrified.
They are retreating.
They have been defeated.
They are overcome with terror;
they desert quickly
without looking back.
46:6 But even the swiftest cannot get away.
Even the strongest cannot escape.
There in the north by the Euphrates River
they stumble and fall in defeat.

46:7 "Who is this that rises like the Nile,
like its streams turbulent at flood stage?
46:8 Egypt rises like the Nile,
like its streams turbulent at flood stage.
Egypt says, 'I will arise and cover the earth.
I will destroy cities and the people who inhabit them.'
46:9 Go ahead and charge into battle, you horsemen!
Drive furiously, you charioteers!
Let the soldiers march out into battle,
those from Ethiopia and Libya who carry shields,
and those from Lydia who are armed with the bow.
46:10 But that day belongs to the Lord God who rules over all.
It is the day when he will pay back his enemies.
His sword will devour them until its appetite is satisfied!
It will drink their blood until it is full!
For the Lord GOD who rules over all will offer them up as a sacrifice
in the land of the north by the Euphrates River.
46:11 Go up to Gilead and get medicinal ointment,
you dear poor people of Egypt.
But it will prove useless no matter how much medicine you use;
there will be no healing for you.
46:12 The nations will hear of your devastating defeat.
your cries of distress will echo throughout the earth.
In the panic of their flight one soldier will trip over another
and both of them will fall down defeated."
The Lord Predicts that Nebuchadnezzar Will Attack and Plunder Egypt
46:13 The LORD spoke to the prophet Jeremiah about Nebuchadnezzar coming to attack the land of Egypt.
46:14 "Make an announcement throughout Egypt.
Proclaim it in Migdol, Memphis, and Tahpanhes.
'Take your positions and prepare to do battle.
For the enemy army is destroying all the nations around you.'
46:15 Why will your soldiers be defeated?
They will not stand because I, the LORD, will thrust them down.
46:16 I will make many stumble.
They will fall over one another in their hurry to flee.
They will say, 'Get up!
Let's go back to our own people.
Let's go back to our homelands
because the enemy is coming to destroy us.'
46:17 There at home they will say, 'Pharaoh king of Egypt is just a big noise!
He has let the most opportune moment pass by.'
46:18 I the King, whose name is the LORD who rules over all, swear this:
I swear as surely as I live that a conqueror is coming.
He will be as imposing as Mount Tabor is among the mountains,
as Mount Carmel is against the backdrop of the sea.
46:19 Pack your bags for exile,
you inhabitants of poor dear Egypt.
For Memphis will be laid waste.
It will lie in ruins and be uninhabited.
46:20 Egypt is like a beautiful young cow.
But northern armies will attack her like swarms of stinging flies.
46:21 Even her mercenaries
will prove to be like pampered, well-fed calves.
For they too will turn and run away.
They will not stand their ground
when the time for them to be destroyed comes,
the time for them to be punished.
46:22 Egypt will run away, hissing like a snake,

as the enemy comes marching up in force.
They will come against her with axes
as if they were woodsmen chopping down trees.
46:23 The population of Egypt is like a vast, impenetrable forest.
But I, the LORD, affirm that the enemy will cut them down.
For those who chop them down will be more numerous than locusts.
They will be too numerous to count.
46:24 Poor dear Egypt will be put to shame.
She will be handed over to the people from the north."
46:25 The LORD God of Israel who rules over all says, "I will punish Amon, the god of Thebes. I will punish Egypt, its gods, and its kings. I will punish Pharaoh and all who trust in him. **46:26** I will hand them over to Nebuchadnezzar and his troops, who want to kill them. But later on, people will live in Egypt again as they did in former times. I, the LORD, affirm it!"
A Promise of Hope for Israel
46:27 "You descendants of Jacob, my servants, do not be afraid;
do not be terrified, people of Israel.
For I will rescue you and your descendants
from the faraway lands where you are captives.
The descendants of Jacob will return to their land and enjoy peace.
They will be secure and no one will terrify them.
46:28 I, the LORD, tell you not to be afraid,
you descendants of Jacob, my servant,
for I am with you.
Though I completely destroy all the nations where I scatter you,
I will not completely destroy you.
I will indeed discipline you but only in due measure.
I will not allow you to go entirely unpunished."
Judgment on the Philistine Cities
47:1 The LORD spoke to the prophet Jeremiah about the Philistines before Pharaoh attacked Gaza.
47:2 "Look! Enemies are gathering in the north like water rising in a river.
They will be like an overflowing stream.
They will overwhelm the whole country and everything in it like a flood.
They will overwhelm the cities and their inhabitants.
People will cry out in alarm.
Everyone living in the country will cry out in pain.
47:3 Fathers will hear the hoofbeats of the enemies' horses,
the clatter of their chariots and the rumbling of their wheels.
They will not turn back to save their children
because they will be paralyzed with fear.
47:4 For the time has come
to destroy all the Philistines.
The time has come to destroy all the help
that remains for Tyre and Sidon.
For I, the LORD, will destroy the Philistines,
that remnant that came from the island of Crete.
47:5 The people of Gaza will shave their heads in mourning.
The people of Ashkelon will be struck dumb.
How long will you gash yourselves to show your sorrow,
you who remain of Philistia's power?
47:6 How long will you cry out, 'Oh, sword of the LORD,
how long will it be before you stop killing?
Go back into your sheath!
Stay there and rest!'
47:7 But how can it rest
when I, the LORD, have given it orders?
I have ordered it to attack
the people of Ashkelon and the seacoast.
Judgment Against Moab
48:1 The LORD God of Israel who rules over all spoke about Moab.
"Sure to be judged is Nebo! Indeed, it will be destroyed!
Kiriathaim will suffer disgrace. It will be captured!
Its fortress will suffer disgrace. It will be torn down!
48:2 People will not praise Moab any more.
The enemy will capture Heshbon and plot how to destroy Moab,
saying, 'Come, let's put an end to that nation!'
City of Madmen, you will also be destroyed.
A destructive army will march against you.
48:3 Cries of anguish will arise in Horonaim,
'Oh, the ruin and great destruction!'
48:4 "Moab will be crushed.
Her children will cry out in distress.
48:5 Indeed they will climb the slopes of Luhith,
weeping continually as they go.
For on the road down to Horonaim
they will hear the cries of distress over the destruction.
48:6 They will hear, 'Run! Save yourselves!
Even if you must be like a lonely shrub in the desert!'
48:7 "Moab, you trust in the things you do and in your riches.
So you too will be conquered.

Your god Chemosh will go into exile
along with his priests and his officials.
48:8 The destroyer will come against every town.
Not one town will escape.
The towns in the valley will be destroyed.
The cities on the high plain will be laid waste.
I, the LORD, have spoken!
48:9 Set up a gravestone for Moab,
for it will certainly be laid in ruins!
Its cities will be laid waste
and become uninhabited."
48:10 A curse on anyone who is lax in doing the LORD's work!
A curse on anyone who keeps from carrying out his destruction!
48:11 "From its earliest days Moab has lived undisturbed.
It has never been taken into exile.
Its people are like wine allowed to settle undisturbed on its dregs,
never poured out from one jar to another.
They are like wine which tastes like it always did,
whose aroma has remained unchanged.
48:12 But the time is coming when I will send
men against Moab who will empty it out.
They will empty the towns of their people,
then will lay those towns in ruins.
I, the LORD, affirm it!
48:13 The people of Moab will be disappointed by their god Chemosh.
They will be as disappointed as the people of Israel were
when they put their trust in the calf god at Bethel.
48:14 How can you men of Moab say, 'We are heroes,
men who are mighty in battle?'
48:15 Moab will be destroyed. Its towns will be invaded.
Its finest young men will be slaughtered.
I, the King, the LORD who rules over all, affirm it!
48:16 Moab's destruction is at hand.
Disaster will come on it quickly.
48:17 Mourn for that nation, all you nations living around it,
all of you nations that know of its fame.
Mourn and say, 'Alas, its powerful influence has been broken!
Its glory and power have been done away!'
48:18 Come down from your place of honor;
sit on the dry ground, you who live in Dibon.
For the one who will destroy Moab will attack you;
he will destroy your fortifications.
48:19 You who live in Aroer,
stand by the road and watch.
Question the man who is fleeing and the woman who is escaping.
Ask them, 'What has happened?'
48:20 They will answer, 'Moab is disgraced, for it has fallen!
Wail and cry out in mourning!
Announce along the Arnon River
that Moab has been destroyed.'

48:21 "Judgment will come on the cities on the high plain: on Holon, Jahzah, and Mephaath, **48:22** on Dibon, Nebo, and Beth Diblathaim, **48:23** on Kiriathaim, Beth Gamul, and Beth Meon, **48:24** on Kerioth and Bozrah. It will come on all the towns of Moab, both far and near. **48:25** Moab's might will be crushed. Its power will be broken. I, the LORD, affirm it!

48:26 "Moab has vaunted itself against me.
So make him drunk with the wine of my wrath
until he splashes around in his own vomit,
until others treat him as a laughingstock.
48:27 For did not you people of Moab laugh at the people of Israel?
Did you think that they were nothing but thieves,
that you shook your head in contempt
every time you talked about them?
48:28 Leave your towns, you inhabitants of Moab.
Go and live in the cliffs.
Be like a dove that makes its nest
high on the sides of a ravine.
48:29 I have heard how proud the people of Moab are,
I know how haughty they are.
I have heard how arrogant, proud, and haughty they are,
what a high opinion they have of themselves.
48:30 I, the LORD, affirm that I know how arrogant they are.
But their pride is ill-founded.
Their boastings will prove to be false.
48:31 So I will weep with sorrow for Moab.
I will cry out in sadness for all of Moab.
I will moan for the people of Kir Heres.
48:32 I will weep for the grapevines of Sibmah
just like the town of Jazer weeps over them.
Their branches once spread as far as the Dead Sea.

They reached as far as the town of Jazer.
The destroyer will ravage
her fig, date, and grape crops.
48:33 Joy and gladness will disappear
from the fruitful land of Moab.
I will stop the flow of wine from the winepresses.
No one will stomp on the grapes there and shout for joy.
The shouts there will be shouts of soldiers,
not the shouts of those making wine.
48:34 Cries of anguish raised from Heshbon and Elealeh
will be sounded as far as Jahaz.
They will be sounded from Zoar as far as Horonaim and Eglath Shelish-iyah.
For even the waters of Nimrim will be dried up.
48:35 I will put an end in Moab
to those who make offerings at her places of worship.
I will put an end to those who sacrifice to other gods.
I, the LORD, affirm it!
48:36 So my heart moans for Moab
like a flute playing a funeral song.
Yes, like a flute playing a funeral song,
my heart moans for the people of Kir Heres.
For the wealth they have gained will perish.
48:37 For all of them will shave their heads in mourning.
They will all cut off their beards to show their sorrow.
They will all make gashes in their hands.
They will all put on sackcloth.
48:38 On all the housetops in Moab
and in all its public squares
there will be nothing but mourning.
For I will break Moab like an unwanted jar.
I, the LORD, affirm it!

48:39 Oh, how shattered Moab will be!
Oh, how her people will wail!
Oh, how she will turn away in shame!
Moab will become an object of ridicule,
a terrifying sight to all the nations that surround her."
48:40 For the LORD says,
"Look! Like an eagle with outspread wings
a nation will swoop down on Moab.
48:41 Her towns will be captured.
Her fortresses will be taken.
At that time the soldiers of Moab will be frightened
like a woman in labor.
48:42 Moab will be destroyed and no longer be a nation,
because she has vaunted herself against the LORD.
48:43 Terror, pits, and traps are in store
for the people who live in Moab.
I, the LORD, affirm it!
48:44 Anyone who flees at the sound of terror
will fall into a pit.
Anyone who climbs out of the pit
will be caught in a trap.
For the time is coming
when I will punish the people of Moab.
I, the LORD, affirm it!
48:45 In the shadows of the walls of Heshbon
those trying to escape will stand helpless.
For a fire will burst forth from Heshbon.
Flames will shoot out from the former territory of Sihon.
They will burn the foreheads of the people of Moab,
the skulls of those war-loving people.
48:46 Moab, you are doomed!
You people who worship Chemosh will be destroyed.
Your sons will be taken away captive.
Your daughters will be carried away into exile.
48:47 Yet in days to come
I will reverse Moab's ill fortune."
says the LORD.
The judgment against Moab ends here.

Judgment Against Ammon

49:1 The LORD spoke about the Ammonites.
"Do you think there are not any people of the nation of Israel remaining?
Do you think there are not any of them remaining to reinherit their land?
Is that why you people who worship the god Milcom
have taken possession of the territory of Gad and live in his cities?
49:2 Because you did that,
I, the LORD, affirm that a time is coming
when I will make Rabbah, the capital city of Ammon,
hear the sound of the battle cry.
It will become a mound covered with ruins.
Its villages will be burned to the ground.

Then Israel will take back its land
from those who took their land from them.
I, the Lord, affirm it!
49:3 Wail, you people in Heshbon, because Ai in Ammon is destroyed.
Cry out in anguish, you people in the villages surrounding Rabbah.
Put on sackcloth and cry out in mourning.
Run about covered with gashes.
For your god Milcom will go into exile
along with his priests and officials.
49:4 Why do you brag about your great power?
Your power is ebbing away, you rebellious people of Ammon,
who trust in your riches and say,
'Who would dare to attack us?'
49:5 I will bring terror on you from every side,"
says the Lord GOD who rules over all.
"You will be scattered in every direction.
No one will gather the fugitives back together.
49:6 Yet in days to come
I will reverse Ammon's ill fortune."
says the LORD.
Judgment Against Edom
49:7 The LORD who rules over all spoke about Edom.
"Is wisdom no longer to be found in Teman?
Can Edom's counselors not give her any good advice?
Has all of their wisdom turned bad?
49:8 Turn and flee! Take up refuge in remote places,
you people who live in Dedan.
For I will bring disaster on the descendants of Esau.
I have decided it is time for me to punish them.
49:9 If grape pickers came to pick your grapes,
would they not leave a few grapes behind?
If robbers came at night,
would they not pillage only what they needed?
49:10 But I will strip everything away from Esau's descendants.
I will uncover their hiding places so they cannot hide.
Their children, relatives, and neighbors will all be destroyed.
Not one of them will be left!
49:11 Leave your orphans behind and I will keep them alive.
Your widows too can depend on me."

49:12 For the LORD says, "If even those who did not deserve to drink
from the cup of my wrath must drink from it, do you think you will go
unpunished? You will not go unpunished, but must certainly drink from
the cup of my wrath. **49:13** For I solemnly swear," says the LORD, "that
Bozrah will become a pile of ruins. It will become an object of horror and
ridicule, an example to be used in curses. All the towns around it will lie
in ruins forever."

49:14 I said, "I have heard a message from the LORD.
A messenger has been sent among the nations to say,
'Gather your armies and march out against her!
Prepare to do battle with her!'"
49:15 The LORD says to Edom,
"I will certainly make you small among nations.
I will make you despised by all humankind.
49:16 The terror you inspire in others
and the arrogance of your heart have deceived you.
You may make your home in the clefts of the rocks;
you may occupy the highest places in the hills.
But even if you made your home where the eagles nest,
I would bring you down from there,"
says the LORD.
49:17 "Edom will become an object of horror.
All who pass by it will be filled with horror;
they will hiss out their scorn
because of all the disasters that have happened to it.
49:18 Edom will be destroyed like Sodom and Gomorrah
and the towns that were around them.
No one will live there.
No human being will settle in it,"
says the LORD.
49:19 "A lion coming up from the thick undergrowth along the Jordan
scatters the sheep in the pastureland around it.
So too I will chase the Edomites off their land.
Then I will appoint over it whomever I choose.
For there is no one like me, and there is no one who can call me to account.
There is no ruler who can stand up against me.
49:20 So listen to what I, the LORD, have planned against Edom,
what I intend to do to the people who live in Teman.
Their little ones will be dragged off.
I will completely destroy their land because of what they have done.

49:21 The people of the earth will quake when they hear of their downfall.
Their cries of anguish will be heard all the way to the Gulf of Aqaba.
49:22 Look! Like an eagle with outspread wings,
a nation will soar up and swoop down on Bozrah.
At that time the soldiers of Edom will be as fearful
as a woman in labor."
Judgment Against Damascus
49:23 The LORD spoke about Damascus.
"The people of Hamath and Arpad will be dismayed
because they have heard bad news.
Their courage will melt away because of worry.
Their hearts will not be able to rest.
49:24 The people of Damascus will lose heart and turn to flee.
Panic will grip them.
Pain and anguish will seize them
like a woman in labor.
49:25 How deserted will that once-famous city be,
that city that was once filled with joy!
49:26 For her young men will fall in her city squares.
All her soldiers will be destroyed at that time,"
says the LORD who rules over all.
49:27 "I will set fire to the walls of Damascus;
it will burn up the palaces of Ben Hadad."
Judgment Against Kedar and Hazor
49:28 The LORD spoke about Kedar and the kingdoms of Hazor that King
Nebuchadnezzar of Babylon conquered.
"Army of Babylon, go and attack Kedar.
Lay waste those who live in the eastern desert.
49:29 Their tents and their flocks will be taken away.
Their tent curtains, equipment, and camels will be carried off.
People will shout to them,
'Terror is all around you!'"
49:30 The LORD says, "Flee quickly, you who live in Hazor.
Take up refuge in remote places.
For King Nebuchadnezzar of Babylon has laid out plans to attack you.
He has formed his strategy on how to defeat you."
49:31 The LORD says, "Army of Babylon, go and attack
a nation that lives in peace and security.
They have no gates or walls to protect them.
They live all alone.
49:32 Their camels will be taken as plunder.
Their vast herds will be taken as spoil.
I will scatter to the four winds
those desert peoples who cut their hair short at the temples.
I will bring disaster against them
from every direction," says the LORD.
49:33 "Hazor will become a permanent wasteland,
a place where only jackals live.
No one will live there.
No human being will settle in it."
Judgment Against Elam
49:34 Early in the reign of King Zedekiah of Judah, the LORD spoke to
the prophet Jeremiah about Elam.
49:35 The LORD who rules over all said,
"I will kill all the archers of Elam,
who are the chief source of her military might.
49:36 I will cause enemies to blow through Elam from every direction
like the winds blowing in from the four quarters of heaven.
I will scatter the people of Elam to the four winds.
There will not be any nation where the refugees of Elam will not go.
49:37 I will make the people of Elam terrified of their enemies,
who are seeking to kill them.
I will vent my fierce anger
and bring disaster upon them," says the LORD.
"I will send armies chasing after them
until I have completely destroyed them.
49:38 I will establish my sovereignty over Elam.
I will destroy their king and their leaders," says the LORD.
49:39 "Yet in days to come
I will reverse Elam's ill fortune."
says the LORD.
Judgment Against Babylon
50:1 The LORD spoke concerning Babylon and the land of Babylonia
through the prophet Jeremiah.
50:2 "Announce the news among the nations! Proclaim it!
Signal for people to pay attention!
Declare the news! Do not hide it! Say:
'Babylon will be captured.
Bel will be put to shame.
Marduk will be dismayed.
Babylon's idols will be put to shame.
Her disgusting images will be dismayed.

50:3 For a nation from the north will attack Babylon.
It will lay her land waste.
People and animals will flee out of it.
No one will inhabit it.'

50:4 "When that time comes," says the LORD,
"the people of Israel and Judah will return to the land together.
They will come back with tears of repentance
as they seek the LORD their God.
50:5 They will ask the way to Zion;
they will turn their faces toward it.
They will come and bind themselves to the LORD
in a lasting covenant that will never be forgotten.

50:6 "My people have been lost sheep.
Their shepherds have allow them to go astray.
They have wandered around in the mountains.
They have roamed from one mountain and hill to another.
They have forgotten their resting place.
50:7 All who encountered them devoured them.
Their enemies who did this said, 'We are not liable for punishment!
For those people have sinned against the LORD, their true pasture.
They have sinned against the LORD in whom their ancestors trusted.'

50:8 "People of Judah, get out of Babylon quickly!
Leave the land of Babylonia!
Be the first to depart!
Be like the male goats that lead the herd.
50:9 For I will rouse into action and bring against Babylon
a host of mighty nations from the land of the north.
They will set up their battle lines against her.
They will come from the north and capture her.
Their arrows will be like a skilled soldier
who does not return from the battle empty-handed.
50:10 Babylonia will be plundered.
Those who plunder it will take all they want,"
says the LORD.
50:11 "People of Babylonia, you plundered my people.
That made you happy and glad.
You frolic about like calves in a pasture.
Your joyous sounds are like the neighs of a stallion.
50:12 But Babylonia will be put to great shame.
The land where you were born will be disgraced.
Indeed, Babylonia will become the least important of all nations.
It will become a dry and barren desert.
50:13 After I vent my wrath on it Babylon will be uninhabited.
It will be totally desolate.
All who pass by will be filled with horror and will hiss out their scorn
because of all the disasters that have happened to it.

50:14 "Take up your battle positions all around Babylon,
all you soldiers who are armed with bows.
Shoot all your arrows at her! Do not hold any back!
For she has sinned against the LORD.
50:15 Shout the battle cry from all around the city.
She will throw up her hands in surrender.
Her towers will fall.
Her walls will be torn down.
Because I, the LORD, am wreaking revenge,
take out your vengeance on her!
Do to her as she has done!
50:16 Kill all the farmers who sow the seed in the land of Babylon.
Kill all those who wield the sickle at harvest time.
Let all the foreigners return to their own people.
Let them hurry back to their own lands
to escape destruction by that enemy army.

50:17 "The people of Israel are like scattered sheep
which lions have chased away.
First the king of Assyria devoured them.
Now last of all King Nebuchadnezzar of Babylon has gnawed their
bones.
50:18 So I, the LORD God of Israel who rules over all, say:
'I will punish the king of Babylon and his land
just as I punished the king of Assyria.
50:19 But I will restore the flock of Israel to their own pasture.
They will graze on Mount Carmel and the land of Bashan.
They will eat until they are full
on the hills of Ephraim and the land of Gilead.
50:20 When that time comes,
no guilt will be found in Israel.
No sin will be found in Judah.
For I will forgive those of them I have allowed to survive.

I, the LORD, affirm it!'"

50:21 The LORD says,
"Attack the land of Merathaim
and the people who live in Pekod!
Pursue, kill, and completely destroy them!
Do just as I have commanded you!
50:22 The noise of battle can be heard in the land of Babylonia.
There is the sound of great destruction.
50:23 Babylon hammered the whole world to pieces.
But see how that 'hammer' has been broken and shattered!
See what an object of horror
Babylon has become among the nations!
50:24 I set a trap for you, Babylon;
you were caught before you knew it.
You fought against me.
So you were found and captured.
50:25 I have opened up the place where my weapons are stored.
I have brought out the weapons for carrying out my wrath.
For I, the Lord GOD who rules over all,
have work to carry out in the land of Babylonia.
50:26 Come from far away and attack Babylonia!
Open up the places where she stores her grain!
Pile her up in ruins! Destroy her completely!
Do not leave anyone alive!
50:27 Kill all her soldiers!
Let them be slaughtered!
They are doomed, for their day of reckoning has come,
the time for them to be punished."
50:28 Listen! Fugitives and refugees are coming from the land of Baby-
lon.
They are coming to Zion to declare there
how the LORD our God is getting revenge,
getting revenge for what they have done to his temple.
50:29 "Call for archers to come against Babylon!
Summon against her all who draw the bow!
Set up camp all around the city!
Do not allow anyone to escape!
Pay her back for what she has done.
Do to her what she has done to others.
For she has proudly defied me,
the Holy One of Israel.
50:30 So her young men will fall in her city squares.
All her soldiers will be destroyed at that time,"
says the LORD.
50:31 "Listen! I am opposed to you, you proud city,"
says the Lord GOD who rules over all.
"Indeed, your day of reckoning has come,
the time when I will punish you.
50:32 You will stumble and fall, you proud city;
no one will help you get up.
I will set fire to your towns;
it will burn up everything that surrounds you."

50:33 The LORD who rules over all says,
"The people of Israel are oppressed.
So too are the people of Judah.
All those who took them captive are holding them prisoners.
They refuse to set them free.
50:34 But the one who will rescue them is strong.
He is known as the LORD who rules over all.
He will strongly champion their cause.
As a result he will bring peace and rest to the earth,
but trouble and turmoil to the people who inhabit Babylonia.

50:35 "Destructive forces will come against the Babylonians," says the
LORD.
"They will come against the people who inhabit Babylonia,
against her leaders and her men of wisdom.
50:36 Destructive forces will come against her false prophets;
they will be shown to be fools!
Destructive forces will come against her soldiers;
they will be filled with terror!
50:37 Destructive forces will come against her horses and her chariots.
Destructive forces will come against all the foreign troops within her;
they will be as frightened as women!
Destructive forces will come against her treasures;
they will be taken away as plunder!
50:38 A drought will come upon her land;
her rivers and canals will be dried up.
All of this will happen because her land is filled with idols.
Her people act like madmen because of those idols they fear.
50:39 Therefore desert creatures and jackals will live there.

Ostriches will dwell in it too.
But no people will ever live there again.
No one will dwell there for all time to come.
50:40 I will destroy Babylonia just like I did
Sodom and Gomorrah and the neighboring towns.
No one will live there.
No human being will settle in it,"
says the LORD.

50:41 "Look! An army is about to come from the north.
A mighty nation and many kings are stirring into action
in faraway parts of the earth.
50:42 Its soldiers are armed with bows and spears.
They are cruel and show no mercy.
They sound like the roaring sea
as they ride forth on their horses.
Lined up in formation like men going into battle,
they are coming against you, fair Babylon!
50:43 The king of Babylon will become paralyzed with fear
when he hears news of their coming.
Anguish will grip him,
agony like that of a woman giving birth to a baby.

50:44 "A lion coming up from the thick undergrowth along the Jordan
scatters the sheep in the pastureland around it.
So too I will chase the Babylonians off of their land.
Then I will appoint over it whomever I choose.
For there is no one like me.
There is no one who can call me to account.
There is no ruler that can stand up against me.
50:45 So listen to what I, the LORD, have planned against Babylon,
what I intend to do to the people who inhabit the land of Babylonia.
Their little ones will be dragged off.
I will completely destroy their land because of what they have done.
50:46 The people of the earth will quake when they hear Babylon has been captured.
Her cries of anguish will be heard by the other nations."

51:1 The LORD says,
"I will cause a destructive wind to blow
against Babylon and the people who inhabit Babylonia.
51:2 I will send people to winnow Babylonia like a wind blowing away chaff.
They will winnow her and strip her land bare.
This will happen when they come against her from every direction,
when it is time to destroy her.
51:3 Do not give her archers time to string their bows
or to put on their coats of armor.
Do not spare any of her young men.
Completely destroy her whole army.
51:4 Let them fall slain in the land of Babylonia,
mortally wounded in the streets of her cities.

51:5 "For Israel and Judah will not be forsaken
by their God, the LORD who rules over all.
For the land of Babylonia is full of guilt
against the Holy One of Israel.
51:6 Get out of Babylonia quickly, you foreign people.
Flee to save your lives.
Do not let yourselves be killed because of her sins.
For it is time for the LORD to wreak his revenge.
He will pay Babylonia back for what she has done.
51:7 Babylonia had been a gold cup in the LORD's hand.
She had made the whole world drunk.
The nations had drunk from the wine of her wrath.
So they have all gone mad.
51:8 But suddenly Babylonia will fall and be destroyed.
Cry out in mourning over it!
Get medicine for her wounds!
Perhaps she can be healed!
51:9 Foreigners living there will say,
'We tried to heal her, but she could not be healed.
Let's leave Babylonia and each go back to his own country.
For judgment on her will be vast in its proportions.
It will be like it is piled up to heaven, stacked up into the clouds.'
51:10 The exiles from Judah will say,
'The LORD has brought about a great deliverance for us!
Come on, let's go and proclaim in Zion
what the LORD our God has done!'

51:11 "Sharpen your arrows!
Fill your quivers!
The LORD will arouse a spirit of hostility in the kings of Media.

For he intends to destroy Babylonia.
For that is how the LORD will get his revenge –
how he will get his revenge for the Babylonians' destruction of his temple.
51:12 Give the signal to attack Babylon's wall!
Bring more guards!
Post them all around the city!
Put men in ambush!
For the LORD will do what he has planned.
He will do what he said he would do to the people of Babylon.

51:13 "You who live along the rivers of Babylon,
the time of your end has come.
You who are rich in plundered treasure,
it is time for your lives to be cut off.
51:14 The LORD who rules over all has solemnly sworn,
'I will fill your land with enemy soldiers.
They will swarm over it like locusts.
They will raise up shouts of victory over it.'
51:15 He is the one who by his power made the earth.
He is the one who by his wisdom fixed the world in place,
by his understanding he spread out the heavens.
51:16 When his voice thunders, the waters in the heavens roar.
He makes the clouds rise from the far-off horizons.
He makes the lightning flash out in the midst of the rain.
He unleashes the wind from the places where he stores it.
51:17 All idolaters will prove to be stupid and ignorant.
Every goldsmith will be disgraced by the idol he made.
For the image he forges is merely a sham.
There is no breath in any of those idols.
51:18 They are worthless, objects to be ridiculed.
When the time comes to punish them, they will be destroyed.
51:19 The LORD, who is the portion of the descendants of Jacob, is not like them.
For he is the one who created everything,
including the people of Israel whom he claims as his own.
He is known as the LORD who rules over all.

51:20 "Babylon, you are my war club,
my weapon for battle.
I used you to smash nations.
I used you to destroy kingdoms.
51:21 I used you to smash horses and their riders.
I used you to smash chariots and their drivers.
51:22 I used you to smash men and women.
I used you to smash old men and young men.
I used you to smash young men and young women.
51:23 I used you to smash shepherds and their flocks.
I used you to smash farmers and their teams of oxen.
I used you to smash governors and leaders."
51:24 "But I will repay Babylon
and all who live in Babylonia
for all the wicked things they did in Zion
right before the eyes of you Judeans,"
says the LORD.

51:25 The LORD says, "Beware! I am opposed to you, Babylon!
You are like a destructive mountain that destroys all the earth.
I will unleash my power against you;
I will roll you off the cliffs and make you like a burned-out mountain.
51:26 No one will use any of your stones as a cornerstone.
No one will use any of them in the foundation of his house.
For you will lie desolate forever,"
says the LORD.
51:27 "Raise up battle flags throughout the lands.
Sound the trumpets calling the nations to do battle.
Prepare the nations to do battle against Babylonia.
Call for these kingdoms to attack her:
Ararat, Minni, and Ashkenaz.
Appoint a commander to lead the attack.
Send horses against her like a swarm of locusts.
51:28 Prepare the nations to do battle against her.
Prepare the kings of the Medes.
Prepare their governors and all their leaders.
Prepare all the countries they rule to do battle against her.
51:29 The earth will tremble and writhe in agony.
For the LORD will carry out his plan.
He plans to make the land of Babylonia
a wasteland where no one lives.
51:30 The soldiers of Babylonia will stop fighting.
They will remain in their fortified cities.
They will lose their strength to do battle.
They will be as frightened as women.

The houses in her cities will be set on fire.
The gates of her cities will be broken down.
51:31 One runner after another will come to the king of Babylon.
One messenger after another will come bringing news.
They will bring news to the king of Babylon
that his whole city has been captured.
51:32 They will report that the fords have been captured,
the reed marshes have been burned,
the soldiers are terrified.
51:33 For the LORD God of Israel who rules over all says,
'Fair Babylon will be like a threshing floor
which has been trampled flat for harvest.
The time for her to be cut down and harvested
will come very soon.'

51:34 "King Nebuchadnezzar of Babylon
devoured me and drove my people out.
Like a monster from the deep he swallowed me.
He filled his belly with my riches.
He made me an empty dish.
He completely cleaned me out."
51:35 The person who lives in Zion says,
"May Babylon pay for the violence done to me and to my relatives."
Jerusalem says,
"May those living in Babylonia pay for the bloodshed of my people."
51:36 Therefore the LORD says,
"I will stand up for your cause.
I will pay the Babylonians back for what they have done to you.
I will dry up their sea.
I will make their springs run dry.
51:37 Babylon will become a heap of ruins.
Jackals will make their home there.
It will become an object of horror and of hissing scorn,
a place where no one lives.
51:38 The Babylonians are all like lions roaring for prey.
They are like lion cubs growling for something to eat.
51:39 When their appetites are all stirred up,
I will set out a banquet for them.
I will make them drunk
so that they will pass out,
they will fall asleep forever,
they will never wake up,"
says the LORD.
51:40 "I will lead them off to be slaughtered
like lambs, rams, and male goats."

51:41 "See how Babylon has been captured!
See how the pride of the whole earth has been taken!
See what an object of horror
Babylon has become among the nations!
51:42 The sea has swept over Babylon.
She has been covered by a multitude of its waves.
51:43 The towns of Babylonia have become heaps of ruins.
She has become a dry and barren desert.
No one lives in those towns any more.
No one even passes through them.
51:44 I will punish the god Bel in Babylon.
I will make him spit out what he has swallowed.
The nations will not come streaming to him any longer.
Indeed, the walls of Babylon will fall."

51:45 "Get out of Babylon, my people!
Flee to save your lives
from the fierce anger of the LORD!
51:46 Do not lose your courage or become afraid
because of the reports that are heard in the land.
For a report will come in one year.
Another report will follow it in the next.
There will be violence in the land
with ruler fighting against ruler."

51:47 "So the time will certainly come
when I will punish the idols of Babylon.
Her whole land will be put to shame.
All her mortally wounded will collapse in her midst.
51:48 Then heaven and earth and all that is in them
will sing for joy over Babylon.
For destroyers from the north will attack it,"
says the LORD.
51:49 "Babylon must fall
because of the Israelites she has killed,
just as the earth's mortally wounded fell
because of Babylon.

51:50 You who have escaped the sword,
go, do not delay.
Remember the LORD in a faraway land.
Think about Jerusalem.
51:51 'We are ashamed because we have been insulted.
Our faces show our disgrace.
For foreigners have invaded
the holy rooms in the LORD's temple.'
51:52 Yes, but the time will certainly come," says the LORD,
"when I will punish her idols.
Throughout her land the mortally wounded will groan.
51:53 Even if Babylon climbs high into the sky
and fortifies her elevated stronghold,
I will send destroyers against her,"
says the LORD.

51:54 Cries of anguish will come from Babylon,
the sound of great destruction from the land of the Babylonians.
51:55 For the LORD is ready to destroy Babylon,
and put an end to her loud noise.
Their waves will roar like turbulent waters.
They will make a deafening noise.
51:56 For a destroyer is attacking Babylon.
Her warriors will be captured;
their bows will be broken.
For the LORD is a God who punishes;
he pays back in full.

51:57 "I will make her officials and wise men drunk,
along with her governors, leaders, and warriors.
They will fall asleep forever and never wake up,"
says the King whose name is the LORD who rules over all.
51:58 This is what the LORD who rules over all says,
"Babylon's thick wall will be completely demolished.
Her high gates will be set on fire.
The peoples strive for what does not satisfy.
The nations grow weary trying to get what will be destroyed."

51:59 This is the order Jeremiah the prophet gave to Seraiah son of Neriah, son of Mahseiah, when he went to King Zedekiah of Judah in Babylon during the fourth year of his reign. (Seraiah was a quartermaster.) **51:60** Jeremiah recorded on one scroll all the judgments that would come upon Babylon – all these prophecies written about Babylon. **51:61** Then Jeremiah said to Seraiah, "When you arrive in Babylon, make sure you read aloud all these prophecies. **51:62** Then say, 'O LORD, you have announced that you will destroy this place so that no people or animals live in it any longer. Certainly it will lie desolate forever!' **51:63** When you finish reading this scroll aloud, tie a stone to it and throw it into the middle of the Euphrates River. **51:64** Then say, 'In the same way Babylon will sink and never rise again because of the judgments I am ready to bring upon her; they will grow faint.'"
The prophecies of Jeremiah end here.
The Fall of Jerusalem
52:1 Zedekiah was twenty-one years old when he became king, and he ruled in Jerusalem for eleven years. His mother's name was Hamutal daughter of Jeremiah, from Libnah. **52:2** He did what displeased the LORD just as Jehoiakim had done.
52:3 What follows is a record of what happened to Jerusalem and Judah because of the LORD's anger when he drove them out of his sight. Zedekiah rebelled against the king of Babylon. **52:4** King Nebuchadnezzar of Babylon came against Jerusalem with his whole army and set up camp outside it. They built siege ramps all around it. He arrived on the tenth day of the tenth month in the ninth year that Zedekiah ruled over Judah. **52:5** The city remained under siege until Zedekiah's eleventh year. **52:6** By the ninth day of the fourth month the famine in the city was so severe the residents had no food. **52:7** They broke through the city walls, and all the soldiers tried to escape. They left the city during the night. They went through the gate between the two walls that is near the king's garden. (The Babylonians had the city surrounded.) Then they headed for the Jordan Valley. **52:8** But the Babylonian army chased after the king. They caught up with Zedekiah in the plains of Jericho, and his entire army deserted him. **52:9** They captured him and brought him up to the king of Babylon at Riblah in the territory of Hamath and he passed sentence on him there. **52:10** The king of Babylon had Zedekiah's sons put to death while Zedekiah was forced to watch. He also had all the nobles of Judah put to death there at Riblah. **52:11** He had Zedekiah's eyes put out and had him bound in chains. Then the king of Babylon had him led off to Babylon and he was imprisoned there until the day he died.
52:12 On the tenth day of the fifth month, in the nineteenth year of King Nebuchadnezzar of Babylon, Nebuzaradan, the captain of the royal guard who served the king of Babylon, arrived in Jerusalem. **52:13** He burned down the LORD's temple, the royal palace, and all the houses in Jerusalem, including every large house. **52:14** The whole Babylonian army that

came with the captain of the royal guard tore down the walls that surrounded Jerusalem. **52:15** Nebuzaradan, the captain of the royal guard, took into exile some of the poor, the rest of the people who remained in the city, those who had deserted to him, and the rest of the craftsmen. **52:16** But he left behind some of the poor and gave them fields and vineyards. **52:17** The Babylonians broke the two bronze pillars in the temple of the LORD, as well as the movable stands and the large bronze basin called the "The Sea." They took all the bronze to Babylon. **52:18** They also took the pots, shovels, trimming shears, basins, pans, and all the bronze utensils used by the priests. **52:19** The captain of the royal guard took the gold and silver bowls, censers, basins, pots, lampstands, pans, and vessels. **52:20** The bronze of the items that King Solomon made for the LORD's temple (including the two pillars, the large bronze basin called "The Sea," the twelve bronze bulls under "The Sea," and the movable stands) was too heavy to be weighed. **52:21** Each of the pillars was about 27 feet high, about 18 feet in circumference, three inches thick, and hollow. **52:22** The bronze top of one pillar was about seven and one-half feet high and had bronze latticework and pomegranate-shaped ornaments all around it. The second pillar with its pomegranate-shaped ornaments was like it. **52:23** There were ninety-six pomegranate-shaped ornaments on the sides; in all there were one hundred pomegranate-shaped ornaments over the latticework that went around it.

52:24 The captain of the royal guard took Seraiah the chief priest, Zephaniah the priest who was second in rank, and the three doorkeepers. **52:25** From the city he took an official who was in charge of the soldiers, seven of the king's advisers who were discovered in the city, an official army secretary who drafted citizens for military service, and sixty citizens who were discovered in the middle of the city. **52:26** Nebuzaradan, the captain of the royal guard, took them and brought them to the king of Babylon at Riblah. **52:27** The king of Babylon ordered them to be executed at Riblah in the territory of Hamath.

So Judah was taken into exile away from its land. **52:28** Here is the official record of the number of people Nebuchadnezzar carried into exile: In the seventh year, 3,023 Jews; **52:29** in Nebuchadnezzar's eighteenth year, 832 people from Jerusalem; **52:30** in Nebuchadnezzar's twenty-third year, Nebuzaradan, the captain of the royal guard, carried into exile 745 Judeans. In all 4,600 people went into exile.

Jehoiachin in Exile

52:31 In the thirty-seventh year of the exile of King Jehoiachin of Judah, on the twenty-fifth day of the twelfth month, Evil-Merodach, in the first year of his reign, pardoned King Jehoiachin of Judah and released him from prison. **52:32** He spoke kindly to him and gave him a more prestigious position than the other kings who were with him in Babylon. **52:33** Jehoiachin took off his prison clothes and ate daily in the king's presence for the rest of his life. **52:34** He was given daily provisions by the king of Babylon for the rest of his life until the day he died.

Book 25. Lamentations

The Prophet Speaks:

א (*Alef*)

1:1 Alas! The city once full of people
now sits all alone!
The prominent lady among the nations
has become a widow!
The princess who once ruled the provinces
has become a forced laborer!

ב (*Bet*)

1:2 She weeps bitterly at night;
tears stream down her cheeks.
She has no one to comfort her
among all her lovers.
All her friends have betrayed her;
they have become her enemies.

ג (*Gimel*)

1:3 Judah has departed into exile
under affliction and harsh oppression.
She lives among the nations;
she has found no resting place.
All who pursued her overtook her
in narrow straits.

ד (*Dalet*)

1:4 The roads to Zion mourn
because no one travels to the festivals.
All her city gates are deserted;
her priests groan.
Her virgins grieve;
she is in bitter anguish!

ה (*He*)

1:5 Her foes subjugated her;
her enemies are at ease.
For the LORD afflicted her
because of her many acts of rebellion.
Her children went away
captive before the enemy.

ו (*Vav*)

1:6 All of Daughter Zion's splendor
has departed.
Her leaders became like deer;
they found no pasture,
so they were too exhausted to escape
from the hunter.

ז (*Zayin*)

1:7 Jerusalem remembers,
when she became a poor homeless person,
all her treasures
that she owned in days of old.
When her people fell into an enemy's grip,
none of her allies came to her rescue.
Her enemies gloated over her;
they sneered at her downfall.

ח (*Khet*)

1:8 Jerusalem committed terrible sin;
therefore she became an object of scorn.
All who admired her have despised her
because they have seen her nakedness.
She groans aloud
and turns away in shame.

ט (*Tet*)

1:9 Her menstrual flow has soiled her clothing;
she did not consider the consequences of her sin.
Her demise was astonishing,
and there was no one to comfort her.
She cried, "Look, O LORD, on my affliction
because my enemy boasts!"

י (*Yod*)

1:10 An enemy grabbed
all her valuables.
Indeed she watched in horror as Gentiles
invaded her holy temple –
those whom you had commanded:
"They must not enter your assembly place."

כ (*Kaf*)

1:11 All her people groaned
as they searched for a morsel of bread.
They exchanged their valuables
for just enough food
to stay alive.
Jerusalem Speaks:
"Look, O LORD! Consider
that I have become worthless!"

ל (*Lamed*)

1:12 Is it nothing to you, all you who pass by on the road?
Look and see!
Is there any pain like mine?
The LORD has afflicted me,
he has inflicted it on me
when he burned with anger.

מ (*Mem*)

1:13 He sent down fire
into my bones, and it overcame them.
He spread out a trapper's net for my feet;
he made me turn back.
He has made me desolate;
I am faint all day long.

נ (*Nun*)

1:14 My sins are bound around my neck like a yoke;
they are fastened together by his hand.
He has placed his yoke on my neck;
he has sapped my strength.
The Lord has handed me over
to those whom I cannot resist.

ס (*Samek*)

1:15 He rounded up all my mighty ones;
The Lord did this in my midst.
He summoned an assembly against me
to shatter my young men.

The Lord has stomped like grapes
the virgin daughter, Judah.

ע (Ayin)

1:16 I weep because of these things;
my eyes flow with tears.
For there is no one in sight who can comfort me
or encourage me.
My children are desolated
because an enemy has prevailed.
The Prophet Speaks:

פ (Pe)

1:17 Zion spread out her hands,
but there is no one to comfort her.
The LORD has issued a decree against Jacob;
his neighbors have become his enemies.
Jerusalem has become
like filthy garbage in their midst.
Jerusalem Speaks:

צ (Tsade)

1:18 The LORD is right to judge me!
Yes, I rebelled against his commands.
Please listen, all you nations,
and look at my suffering!
My young women and men
have gone into exile.

ק (Qof)

1:19 I called for my lovers,
but they had deceived me.
My priests and my elders
perished in the city.
Truly they had searched for food
to keep themselves alive.

ר (Resh)

1:20 Look, O LORD! I am distressed;
my stomach is in knots!
My heart is pounding inside me.
Yes, I was terribly rebellious!
Out in the street the sword bereaves a mother of her children;
Inside the house death is present.

ש (Sin/Shin)

1:21 They have heard that I groan,
yet there is no one to comfort me.
All my enemies have heard of my trouble;
they are glad that you have brought it about.
Bring about the day of judgment that you promised
so that they may end up like me!

ת (Tav)

1:22 Let all their wickedness come before you;
afflict them
just as you have afflicted me
because of all my acts of rebellion.
For my groans are many,
and my heart is sick with sorrow.
The Prophet Speaks:

א (Alef)

2:1 Alas! The Lord has covered
Daughter Zion with his anger.
He has thrown down the splendor of Israel
from heaven to earth;
he did not protect his temple
when he displayed his anger.

ב (Bet)

2:2 The Lord destroyed mercilessly
all the homes of Jacob's descendants.
In his anger he tore down
the fortified cities of Daughter Judah.
He knocked to the ground and humiliated
the kingdom and its rulers.

ג (Gimel)

2:3 In fierce anger he destroyed
the whole army of Israel.
He withdrew his right hand
as the enemy attacked.
He was like a raging fire in the land of Jacob;
it consumed everything around it.

ד (Dalet)

2:4 He prepared his bow like an enemy;

his right hand was ready to shoot.
Like a foe he killed everyone,
even our strong young men;
he has poured out his anger like fire
on the tent of Daughter Zion.

ה (He)

2:5 The Lord, like an enemy,
destroyed Israel.
He destroyed all her palaces;
he ruined her fortified cities.
He made everyone in Daughter Judah
mourn and lament.

ו (Vav)

2:6 He destroyed his temple as if it were a vineyard;
he destroyed his appointed meeting place.
The LORD has made those in Zion forget
both the festivals and the Sabbaths.
In his fierce anger he has spurned
both king and priest.

ז (Zayin)

2:7 The Lord rejected his altar
and abhorred his temple.
He handed over to the enemy
her palace walls;
the enemy shouted in the LORD's temple
as if it were a feast day.

ח (Khet)

2:8 The LORD was determined to tear down
Daughter Zion's wall.
He prepared to knock it down;
he did not withdraw his hand from destroying.
He made the ramparts and fortified walls lament;
together they mourned their ruin.

ט (Tet)

2:9 Her city gates have fallen to the ground;
he smashed to bits the bars that lock her gates.
Her king and princes were taken into exile;
there is no more guidance available.
As for her prophets,
they no longer receive a vision from the LORD.

י (Yod)

2:10 The elders of Daughter Zion
sit on the ground in silence.
They have thrown dirt on their heads;
They have dressed in sackcloth.
Jerusalem's young women stare down at the ground.

כ (Kaf)

2:11 My eyes are worn out from weeping;
my stomach is in knots.
My heart is poured out on the ground
due to the destruction of my helpless people;
children and infants faint
in the town squares.

ל (Lamed)

2:12 Children say to their mothers,
"Where are food and drink?" They faint like a wounded warrior
in the city squares.
They die slowly
in their mothers' arms.

מ (Mem)

2:13 With what can I equate you?
To what can I compare you, O Daughter Jerusalem?
To what can I liken you
so that I might comfort you, O Virgin Daughter Zion?
Your wound is as deep as the sea.
Who can heal you?

נ (Nun)

2:14 Your prophets saw visions for you
that were worthless lies.
They failed to expose your sin
so as to restore your fortunes.
They saw oracles for you
that were worthless lies.

ס (Samek)

2:15 All who passed by on the road
clapped their hands to mock you.
They sneered and shook their heads
at Daughter Jerusalem.
"Ha! Is this the city they called
'The perfection of beauty,
the source of joy of the whole earth!'?"

פ (Pe)

2:16 All your enemies
gloated over you.
They sneered and gnashed their teeth;
they said, "We have destroyed her!
Ha! We have waited a long time for this day.
We have lived to see it!"

ע (Ayin)

2:17 The LORD has done what he planned;
he has fulfilled his promise
that he threatened long ago:
He has overthrown you without mercy
and has enabled the enemy to gloat over you;
he has exalted your adversaries' power.

צ (Tsade)

2:18 Cry out from your heart to the Lord,
O wall of Daughter Zion!
Make your tears flow like a river
all day and all night long!
Do not rest;
do not let your tears stop!

ק (Qof)

2:19 Get up! Cry out in the night
when the night watches start!
Pour out your heart like water
before the face of the Lord!
Lift up your hands to him
for your children's lives;
they are fainting
at every street corner.
Jerusalem Speaks:

ר (Resh)

2:20 Look, O LORD! Consider!
Whom have you ever afflicted like this?
Should women eat their offspring,
their healthy infants?
Should priest and prophet
be killed in the Lord's sanctuary?

ש (Sin/Shin)

2:21 The young boys and old men
lie dead on the ground in the streets.
My young women and my young men
have fallen by the sword.
You killed them when you were angry;
you slaughtered them without mercy.

ת (Tav)

2:22 As if it were a feast day, you call
enemies to terrify me on every side.
On the day of the LORD's anger
no one escaped or survived.
My enemy has finished off
those healthy infants whom I bore and raised.
The Prophet Speaks:

א (Alef)

3:1 I am the man who has experienced affliction
from the rod of his wrath.
3:2 He drove me into captivity and made me walk
in darkness and not light.
3:3 He repeatedly attacks me,
he turns his hand against me all day long.

ב (Bet)

3:4 He has made my mortal skin waste away;
he has broken my bones.
3:5 He has besieged and surrounded me
with bitter hardship.
3:6 He has made me reside in deepest darkness
like those who died long ago.

ג (Gimel)

3:7 He has walled me in so that I cannot get out;
he has weighted me down with heavy prison chains.
3:8 Also, when I cry out desperately for help,

he has shut out my prayer.
3:9 He has blocked every road I take with a wall of hewn stones;
he has made every path impassable.

ד (Dalet)

3:10 To me he is like a bear lying in ambush,
like a hidden lion stalking its prey.
3:11 He has obstructed my paths and torn me to pieces;
he has made me desolate.
3:12 He drew his bow and made me
the target for his arrow.

ה (He)

3:13 He shot his arrows
into my heart.
3:14 I have become the laughingstock of all people,
their mocking song all day long.
3:15 He has given me my fill of bitter herbs
and made me drunk with bitterness.

ו (Vav)

3:16 He ground my teeth in gravel;
he trampled me in the dust.
3:17 I am deprived of peace;
I have forgotten what happiness is.
3:18 So I said, "My endurance has expired;
I have lost all hope of deliverance from the LORD."

ז (Zayin)

3:19 Remember my impoverished and homeless condition,
which is a bitter poison.
3:20 I continually think about this,
and I am depressed.
3:21 But this I call to mind;
therefore I have hope:

ח (Khet)

3:22 The LORD's loyal kindness never ceases;
his compassions never end.
3:23 They are fresh every morning;
your faithfulness is abundant!
3:24 "My portion is the LORD," I have said to myself,
so I will put my hope in him.

ט (Tet)

3:25 The LORD is good to those who trust in him,
to the one who seeks him.
3:26 It is good to wait patiently
for deliverance from the LORD.
3:27 It is good for a man
to bear the yoke while he is young.

י (Yod)

3:28 Let a person sit alone in silence,
when the LORD is disciplining him.
3:29 Let him bury his face in the dust;
perhaps there is hope.
3:30 Let him offer his cheek to the one who hits him;
let him have his fill of insults.

כ (Kaf)

3:31 For the Lord will not
reject us forever.
3:32 Though he causes us grief, he then has compassion on us
according to the abundance of his loyal kindness.
3:33 For he is not predisposed to afflict
or to grieve people.

ל (Lamed)

3:34 To crush underfoot
all the earth's prisoners,
3:35 to deprive a person of his rights
in the presence of the Most High,
3:36 to defraud a person in a lawsuit –
the Lord does not approve of such things!

מ (Mem)

3:37 Whose command was ever fulfilled
unless the Lord decreed it?
3:38 Is it not from the mouth of the Most High that everything comes –
both calamity and blessing?
3:39 Why should any living person complain
when punished for his sins?

נ (Nun)

3:40 Let us carefully examine our ways,
and let us return to the LORD.
3:41 Let us lift up our hearts and our hands

to God in heaven:
3:42 "We have blatantly rebelled;
you have not forgiven."

ס (Samek)
3:43 You shrouded yourself with anger and then pursued us;
you killed without mercy.
3:44 You shrouded yourself with a cloud
so that no prayer can get through.
3:45 You make us like filthy scum
in the estimation of the nations.

פ (Pe)
3:46 All our enemies have gloated over us;
3:47 Panic and pitfall have come upon us,
devastation and destruction.
3:48 Streams of tears flow from my eyes
because my people are destroyed.

ע (Ayin)
3:49 Tears flow from my eyes and will not stop;
there will be no break
3:50 until the LORD looks down from heaven
and sees what has happened.
3:51 What my eyes see grieves me –
all the suffering of the daughters in my city.

צ (Tsade)
3:52 For no good reason my enemies
hunted me down like a bird.
3:53 They shut me up in a pit
and threw stones at me.
3:54 The waters closed over my head;
I thought I was about to die.

ק (Qof)
3:55 I have called on your name, O LORD,
from the deepest pit.
3:56 You heard my plea:
"Do not close your ears to my cry for relief!"
3:57 You came near on the day I called to you;
you said, "Do not fear!"

ר (Resh)
3:58 O Lord, you championed my cause,
you redeemed my life.
3:59 You have seen the wrong done to me, O LORD;
pronounce judgment on my behalf!
3:60 You have seen all their vengeance,
all their plots against me.

שׁ (Sin/Shin)
3:61 You have heard their taunts, O LORD,
all their plots against me.
3:62 My assailants revile and conspire
against me all day long.
3:63 Watch them from morning to evening;
I am the object of their mocking songs.

ת (Tav)
3:64 Pay them back what they deserve, O LORD,
according to what they have done.
3:65 Give them a distraught heart;
may your curse be on them!
3:66 Pursue them in anger and eradicate them
from under the LORD's heaven.
The Prophet Speaks:

א (Alef)
4:1 Alas! Gold has lost its luster;
pure gold loses value.
Jewels are scattered
on every street corner.

ב (Bet)
4:2 The precious sons of Zion
were worth their weight in gold –
Alas! – but now they are treated like broken clay pots,
made by a potter.

ג (Gimel)
4:3 Even the jackals nurse their young
at their breast,
but my people are cruel,
like ostriches in the desert.

ד (Dalet)
4:4 The infant's tongue sticks
to the roof of its mouth due to thirst;
little children beg for bread,
but no one gives them even a morsel.

ה (He)
4:5 Those who once feasted on delicacies
are now starving to death in the streets.
Those who grew up wearing expensive clothes
are now dying amid garbage.

ו (Vav)
4:6 The punishment of my people
exceeded that of of Sodom,
which was overthrown in a moment
with no one to help her.

ז (Zayin)
4:7 Her consecrated ones were brighter than snow,
whiter than milk;
their bodies more ruddy than corals,
their hair like lapis lazuli.

ח (Khet)
4:8 Now their appearance is darker than soot;
they are not recognized in the streets.
Their skin has shriveled on their bones;
it is dried up, like tree bark.

ט (Tet)
4:9 Those who died by the sword are better off
than those who die of hunger,
those who waste away,
struck down from lack of food.

י (Yod)
4:10 The hands of tenderhearted women
cooked their own children,
who became their food,
when my people were destroyed.

כ (Kaf)
4:11 The LORD fully vented his wrath;
he poured out his fierce anger.
He started a fire in Zion;
it consumed her foundations.

ל (Lamed)
4:12 Neither the kings of the earth
nor the people of the lands ever thought
that enemy or foe would enter
the gates of Jerusalem.

מ (Mem)
4:13 But it happened due to the sins of her prophets
and the iniquities of her priests,
who poured out in her midst
the blood of the righteous.

נ (Nun)
4:14 They wander blindly through the streets,
defiled by the blood they shed,
while no one dares
to touch their garments.

ס (Samek)
4:15 People cry to them, "Turn away! You are unclean!
Turn away! Turn away! Don't touch us!"
So they have fled and wander about;
but the nations say, "They may not stay here any longer."

פ (Pe)
4:16 The LORD himself has scattered them;
he no longer watches over them.
They did not honor the priests;
they did not show favor to the elders.
The People of Jerusalem Lament:

ע (Ayin)
4:17 Our eyes continually failed us
as we looked in vain for help.
From our watchtowers we watched
for a nation that could not rescue us.

צ (Tsade)
4:18 Our enemies hunted us down at every step
so that we could not walk about in our streets.
Our end drew near, our days were numbered,
for our end had come!

ק (Qof)

4:19 Those who pursued us were swifter
than eagles in the sky.
They chased us over the mountains;
they ambushed us in the wilderness.

ר *(Resh)*

4:20 Our very life breath – the LORD's anointed king –
was caught in their traps,
of whom we thought,
"Under his protection we will survive among the nations."
The Prophet Speaks:

שׁ *(Sin/Shin)*

4:21 Rejoice and be glad for now, O people of Edom,
who reside in the land of Uz.
But the cup of judgment will pass to you also;
you will get drunk and take off your clothes.

ת *(Tav)*

4:22 O people of Zion, your punishment will come to an end;
he will not prolong your exile.
But, O people of Edom, he will punish your sin
and reveal your offenses!
The People of Jerusalem Pray:

5:1 O LORD, reflect on what has happened to us;
consider and look at our disgrace.
5:2 Our inheritance is turned over to strangers;
foreigners now occupy our homes.
5:3 We have become fatherless orphans;
our mothers have become widows.
5:4 We must pay money for our own water;
we must buy our own wood at a steep price.
5:5 We are pursued – they are breathing down our necks;
we are weary and have no rest.
5:6 We have submitted to Egypt and Assyria
in order to buy food to eat.
5:7 Our forefathers sinned and are dead,
but we suffer their punishment.
5:8 Slaves rule over us;
there is no one to rescue us from their power.
5:9 At the risk of our lives we get our food
because robbers lurk in the countryside.
5:10 Our skin is hot as an oven
due to a fever from hunger.
5:11 They raped women in Zion,
virgins in the towns of Judah.
5:12 Princes were hung by their hands;
elders were mistreated.
5:13 The young men perform menial labor;
boys stagger from their labor.
5:14 The elders are gone from the city gate;
the young men have stopped playing their music.
5:15 Our hearts no longer have any joy;
our dancing is turned to mourning.
5:16 The crown has fallen from our head;
woe to us, for we have sinned!
5:17 Because of this, our hearts are sick;
because of these things, we can hardly see through our tears.
5:18 For wild animals are prowling over Mount Zion,
which lies desolate.
5:19 But you, O LORD, reign forever;
your throne endures from generation to generation.
5:20 Why do you keep on forgetting us?
Why do you forsake us so long?
5:21 Bring us back to yourself, O LORD, so that we may return to you;
renew our life as in days before,
5:22 unless you have utterly rejected us
and are angry with us beyond measure.

Book 26. Ezekiel

A Vision of God's Glory

1:1 In the thirtieth year, on the fifth day of the fourth month, while I was among the exiles at the Kebar River, the heavens opened and I saw a divine vision. 1:2 (On the fifth day of the month – it was the fifth year of King Jehoiachin's exile – 1:3 the word of the LORD came to the priest Ezekiel the son of Buzi, at the Kebar River in the land of the Babylonians. The hand of the LORD came on him there). 1:4 As I watched, I noticed a windstorm coming from the north – an enormous cloud, with lightning flashing, such that bright light rimmed it and came from it like glowing amber from the middle of a fire. 1:5 In the fire were what looked like four living beings. In their appearance they had human form, 1:6 but each had four faces and four wings. 1:7 Their legs were straight, but the soles of their feet were like calves' feet. They gleamed like polished bronze. 1:8 They had human hands under their wings on their four sides. As for the faces and wings of the four of them, 1:9 their wings touched each other; they did not turn as they moved, but went straight ahead.

1:10 Their faces had this appearance: Each of the four had the face of a man, with the face of a lion on the right, the face of an ox on the left and also the face of an eagle. 1:11 Their wings were spread out above them; each had two wings touching the wings of one of the other beings on either side and two wings covering their bodies. 1:12 Each moved straight ahead – wherever the spirit would go, they would go, without turning as they went. 1:13 In the middle of the living beings was something like burning coals of fire or like torches. It moved back and forth among the living beings. It was bright, and lightning was flashing out of the fire. 1:14 The living beings moved backward and forward as quickly as flashes of lightning.

1:15 Then I looked, and I saw one wheel on the ground beside each of the four beings. 1:16 The appearance of the wheels and their construction was like gleaming jasper, and all four wheels looked alike. Their structure was like a wheel within a wheel. 1:17 When they moved they would go in any of the four directions they faced without turning as they moved. 1:18 Their rims were high and awesome, and the rims of all four wheels were full of eyes all around.

1:19 When the living beings moved, the wheels beside them moved; when the living beings rose up from the ground, the wheels rose up too. 1:20 Wherever the spirit would go, they would go, and the wheels would rise up beside them because the spirit of the living being was in the wheel. 1:21 When the living beings moved, the wheels moved, and when they stopped moving, the wheels stopped. When they rose up from the ground, the wheels rose up from the ground; the wheels rose up beside them because the spirit of the living being was in the wheel.

1:22 Over the heads of the living beings was something like a platform, glittering awesomely like ice, stretched out over their heads. 1:23 Under the platform their wings were stretched out, each toward the other. Each of the beings also had two wings covering its body. 1:24 When they moved, I heard the sound of their wings – it was like the sound of rushing waters, or the voice of the Almighty, or the tumult of an army. When they stood still, they lowered their wings.

1:25 Then there was a voice from above the platform over their heads when they stood still. 1:26 Above the platform over their heads was something like a sapphire shaped like a throne. High above on the throne was a form that appeared to be a man. 1:27 I saw an amber glow like a fire enclosed all around from his waist up. From his waist down I saw something that looked like fire. There was a brilliant light around it, 1:28 like the appearance of a rainbow in the clouds after the rain. This was the appearance of the surrounding brilliant light; it looked like the glory of the LORD. When I saw it, I threw myself face down, and I heard a voice speaking.

Ezekiel's Commission

2:1 He said to me, "Son of man, stand on your feet and I will speak with you." 2:2 As he spoke to me, a wind came into me and stood me on my feet, and I heard the one speaking to me.

2:3 He said to me, "Son of man, I am sending you to the house of Israel, to rebellious nations who have rebelled against me; both they and their fathers have revolted against me to this very day. 2:4 The people to whom I am sending you are obstinate and hard-hearted, and you must say to them, 'This is what the sovereign LORD says.' 2:5 And as for them, whether they listen or not – for they are a rebellious house – they will know that a prophet has been among them. 2:6 But you, son of man, do not fear them, and do not fear their words – even though briers and thorns surround you and you live among scorpions – do not fear their words and do not be terrified of the looks they give you, for they are a rebellious house! 2:7 You must speak my words to them whether they listen or not, for they are rebellious. 2:8 As for you, son of man, listen to what I am saying to you: Do not rebel like that rebellious house! Open your mouth and eat what I am giving you."

2:9 Then I looked and realized a hand was stretched out to me, and in it was a written scroll. 2:10 He unrolled it before me, and it had writing on the front and back; written on it were laments, mourning, and woe.

3:1 He said to me, "Son of man, eat what you see in front of you – eat this scroll – and then go and speak to the house of Israel." 3:2 So I opened my mouth and he fed me the scroll.

3:3 He said to me, "Son of man, feed your stomach and fill your belly with this scroll I am giving to you." So I ate it, and it was sweet like honey in my mouth.

3:4 He said to me, "Son of man, go to the house of Israel and speak my words to them. 3:5 For you are not being sent to a people of unintelligible speech and difficult language, but to the house of Israel – 3:6 not to many peoples of unintelligible speech and difficult language, whose words you cannot understand – surely if I had sent you to them, they would listen to you! 3:7 But the house of Israel is unwilling to listen to you, because they are not willing to listen to me, for the whole house of Israel is hard-headed and hard-hearted.

3:8 "I have made your face adamant to match their faces, and your forehead hard to match their foreheads. **3:9** I have made your forehead harder than flint – like diamond! Do not fear them or be terrified of the looks they give you, for they are a rebellious house."

3:10 And he said to me, "Son of man, take all my words that I speak to you to heart and listen carefully. **3:11** Go to the exiles, to your fellow countrymen, and speak to them – say to them, 'This is what the sovereign LORD says,' whether they pay attention or not."

Ezekiel Before the Exiles

3:12 Then a wind lifted me up and I heard a great rumbling sound behind me as the glory of the LORD rose from its place, **3:13** and the sound of the living beings' wings brushing against each other, and the sound of the wheels alongside them, a great rumbling sound. **3:14** A wind lifted me up and carried me away. I went bitterly, my spirit full of fury, and the hand of the LORD rested powerfully on me. **3:15** I came to the exiles at Tel Abib, who lived by the Kebar River. I sat dumbfounded among them there, where they were living, for seven days.

3:16 At the end of seven days the word of the LORD came to me: **3:17** "Son of man, I have appointed you a watchman for the house of Israel. Whenever you hear a word from my mouth, you must give them a warning from me. **3:18** When I say to the wicked, "You will certainly die," and you do not warn him – you do not speak out to warn the wicked to turn from his wicked deed and wicked lifestyle so that he may live – that wicked person will die for his iniquity, but I will hold you accountable for his death. **3:19** But as for you, if you warn the wicked and he does not turn from his wicked deed and from his wicked lifestyle, he will die for his iniquity but you will have saved your own life.

3:20 "When a righteous person turns from his righteousness and commits iniquity, and I set an obstacle before him, he will die. If you have not warned him, he will die for his sin. The righteous deeds he performed will not be considered, but I will hold you accountable for his death. **3:21** However, if you warn the righteous person not to sin, and he does not sin, he will certainly live because he was warned, and you will have saved your own life."

Isolated and Silenced

3:22 The hand of the LORD rested on me there, and he said to me, "Get up, go out to the valley, and I will speak with you there." **3:23** So I got up and went out to the valley, and the glory of the LORD was standing there, just like the glory I had seen by the Kebar River, and I threw myself face down.

3:24 Then a wind came into me and stood me on my feet. The LORD spoke to me and said, "Go shut yourself in your house. **3:25** As for you, son of man, they will put ropes on you and tie you up with them, so you cannot go out among them. **3:26** I will make your tongue stick to the roof of your mouth so that you will be silent and unable to reprove them, for they are a rebellious house. **3:27** But when I speak with you, I will loosen your tongue and you must say to them, 'This is what the sovereign LORD says.' Those who listen will listen, but the indifferent will refuse, for they are a rebellious house.

Ominous Object Lessons

4:1 "And you, son of man, take a brick and set it in front of you. Inscribe a city on it – Jerusalem. **4:2** Lay siege to it! Build siege works against it. Erect a siege ramp against it! Post soldiers outside it and station battering rams around it. **4:3** Then for your part take an iron frying pan and set it up as an iron wall between you and the city. Set your face toward it. It is to be under siege; you are to besiege it. This is a sign for the house of Israel.

4:4 "Also for your part lie on your left side and place the iniquity of the house of Israel on it. For the number of days you lie on your side you will bear their iniquity. **4:5** I have determined that the number of the years of their iniquity are to be the number of days for you – 390 days. So bear the iniquity of the house of Israel.

4:6 "When you have completed these days, then lie down a second time, but on your right side, and bear the iniquity of the house of Judah 40 days – I have assigned one day for each year. **4:7** You must turn your face toward the siege of Jerusalem with your arm bared and prophesy against it. **4:8** Look here, I will tie you up with ropes, so you cannot turn from one side to the other until you complete the days of your siege.

4:9 "As for you, take wheat, barley, beans, lentils, millet, and spelt, put them in a single container, and make food from them for yourself. For the same number of days that you lie on your side – 390 days – you will eat it. **4:10** The food you eat will be eight ounces a day by weight; you must eat it at fixed times. **4:11** And you must drink water by measure, a pint and a half; you must drink it at fixed times. **4:12** And you must eat the food like you would a barley cake. You must bake it in front of them over a fire made with dried human excrement." **4:13** And the LORD said, "This is how the people of Israel will eat their unclean food among the nations where I will banish them."

4:14 And I said, "Ah, sovereign LORD, I have never been ceremonially defiled before. I have never eaten a carcass or an animal torn by wild beasts; from my youth up, unclean meat has never entered my mouth."

4:15 So he said to me, "All right then, I will substitute cow's manure instead of human excrement. You will cook your food over it."

4:16 Then he said to me, "Son of man, I am about to remove the bread supply in Jerusalem. They will eat their bread ration anxiously, and they will drink their water ration in terror **4:17** because they will lack bread and water. Each one will be terrified, and they will rot for their iniquity.

5:1 "As for you, son of man, take a sharp sword and use it as a barber's razor. Shave off some of the hair from your head and your beard. Then take scales and divide up the hair you cut off. **5:2** Burn a third of it in the fire inside the city when the days of your siege are completed. Take a third and slash it with a sword all around the city. Scatter a third to the wind, and I will unleash a sword behind them. **5:3** But take a few strands of hair from those and tie them in the ends of your garment. **5:4** Again, take more of them and throw them into the fire, and burn them up. From there a fire will spread to all the house of Israel.

5:5 "This is what the sovereign LORD says: This is Jerusalem; I placed her in the center of the nations with countries all around her. **5:6** Then she defied my regulations and my statutes, becoming more wicked than the nations and the countries around her. Indeed, they have rejected my regulations, and they do not follow my statutes.

5:7 "Therefore this is what the sovereign LORD says: Because you are more arrogant than the nations around you, you have not followed my statutes and have not carried out my regulations. You have not even carried out the regulations of the nations around you!

5:8 "Therefore this is what the sovereign LORD says: I – even I – am against you, and I will execute judgment among you while the nations watch. **5:9** I will do to you what I have never done before and will never do again because of all your abominable practices. **5:10** Therefore fathers will eat their sons within you, Jerusalem, and sons will eat their fathers. I will execute judgments on you, and I will scatter any survivors to the winds.

5:11 "Therefore, as surely as I live, says the sovereign LORD, because you defiled my sanctuary with all your detestable idols and with all your abominable practices, I will withdraw; my eye will not pity you, nor will I spare you. **5:12** A third of your people will die of plague or be overcome by the famine within you. A third of your people will fall by the sword surrounding you, and a third I will scatter to the winds. I will unleash a sword behind them. **5:13** Then my anger will be fully vented; I will exhaust my rage on them, and I will be appeased. Then they will know that I, the LORD, have spoken in my jealousy when I have fully vented my rage against them.

5:14 "I will make you desolate and an object of scorn among the nations around you, in the sight of everyone who passes by. **5:15** You will be an object of scorn and taunting, a prime example of destruction among the nations around you when I execute judgments against you in anger and raging fury. I, the LORD, have spoken! **5:16** I will shoot against them deadly, destructive arrows of famine, which I will shoot to destroy you. I will prolong a famine on you and will remove the bread supply. **5:17** I will send famine and wild beasts against you and they will take your children from you. Plague and bloodshed will overwhelm you, and I will bring a sword against you. I, the LORD, have spoken!"

Judgment on the Mountains of Israel

6:1 The word of the LORD came to me: **6:2** "Son of man, turn toward the mountains of Israel and prophesy against them: **6:3** Say, 'Mountains of Israel, Hear the word of the sovereign LORD! This is what the sovereign LORD says to the mountains and the hills, to the ravines and the valleys: I am bringing a sword against you, and I will destroy your high places. **6:4** Your altars will be ruined and your incense altars will be broken. I will throw down your slain in front of your idols. **6:5** I will place the corpses of the people of Israel in front of their idols, and I will scatter your bones around your altars. **6:6** In all your dwellings, the cities will be laid waste and the high places ruined so that your altars will be laid waste and ruined, your idols will be shattered and demolished, your incense altars will be broken down, and your works wiped out. **6:7** The slain will fall among you and then you will know that I am the LORD.

6:8 "'But I will spare some of you. Some will escape the sword when you are scattered in foreign lands. **6:9** Then your survivors will remember me among the nations where they are exiled. They will realize how I was crushed by their unfaithful heart which turned from me and by their eyes which lusted after their idols. They will loathe themselves because of the evil they have done and because of all their abominable practices. **6:10** They will know that I am the LORD; my threats to bring this catastrophe on them were not empty.'

6:11 "'This is what the sovereign LORD says: Clap your hands, stamp your feet, and say, "Ah!" because of all the evil, abominable practices of the house of Israel, for they will fall by the sword, famine, and pestilence. **6:12** The one far away will die by pestilence, the one close by will fall by the sword, and whoever is left and has escaped these will die by famine. I will fully vent my rage against them. **6:13** Then you will know that I am the LORD – when their dead lie among their idols around their altars, on every high hill and all the mountaintops, under every green tree and every leafy oak, the places where they have offered fragrant incense to all their idols. **6:14** I will stretch out my hand against them and make the land a desolate waste from the wilderness to Riblah, in all the places where they live. Then they will know that I am the LORD!"

The End Arrives

7:1 The word of the LORD came to me: **7:2** "You, son of man – this is what the sovereign LORD says to the land of Israel: An end! The end is coming on the four corners of the land! **7:3** The end is now upon you, and I will release my anger against you; I will judge you according to your behavior, I will hold you accountable for all your abominable practices. **7:4** My eye will not pity you; I will not spare you. For I will hold you responsible for your behavior, and you will suffer the consequences of your abominable practices. Then you will know that I am the LORD! **7:5** "This is what the sovereign LORD says: A disaster – a one-of-a-kind disaster – is coming! **7:6** An end comes – the end comes! It has awakened against you – the end is upon you! Look, it is coming! **7:7** Doom is coming upon you who live in the land! The time is coming, the day is near. There are sounds of tumult, not shouts of joy, on the mountains. **7:8** Soon now I will pour out my rage on you; I will fully vent my anger against you. I will judge you according to your behavior. I will hold you accountable for all your abominable practices. **7:9** My eye will not pity you; I will not spare you. For your behavior I will hold you accountable, and you will suffer the consequences of your abominable practices. Then you will know that it is I, the LORD, who is striking you.

7:10 "Look, the day! Look, it is coming! Doom has gone out! The staff has budded, pride has blossomed! **7:11** Violence has grown into a staff that supports wickedness. Not one of them will be left – not from their crowd, not from their wealth, not from their prominence. **7:12** The time has come; the day has struck! The customer should not rejoice, nor the seller mourn; for divine wrath comes against their whole crowd. **7:13** The customer will no longer pay the seller while both parties are alive, for the vision against their whole crowd will not be revoked. Each person, for his iniquity, will fail to preserve his life.

7:14 "They have blown the trumpet and everyone is ready, but no one goes to battle, because my anger is against their whole crowd. **7:15** The sword is outside; pestilence and famine are inside the house. Whoever is in the open field will die by the sword, and famine and pestilence will consume everyone in the city. **7:16** Their survivors will escape to the mountains and become like doves of the valleys; all of them will moan – each one for his iniquity. **7:17** All of their hands will hang limp; their knees will be wet with urine. **7:18** They will wear sackcloth, terror will cover them; shame will be on all their faces, and all of their heads will be shaved bald. **7:19** They will discard their silver in the streets, and their gold will be treated like filth. Their silver and gold will not be able to deliver them on the day of the LORD's fury. They will not satisfy their hunger or fill their stomachs because their wealth was the obstacle leading to their iniquity. **7:20** They rendered the beauty of his ornaments into pride, and with it they made their abominable images – their detestable idols. Therefore I will render it filthy to them. **7:21** I will give it to foreigners as loot, to the world's wicked ones as plunder, and they will desecrate it. **7:22** I will turn my face away from them and they will desecrate my treasured place. Vandals will enter it and desecrate it. **7:23** (Make the chain, because the land is full of murder and the city is full of violence.) **7:24** I will bring the most wicked of the nations and they will take possession of their houses. I will put an end to the arrogance of the strong, and their sanctuaries will be desecrated. **7:25** Terror is coming! They will seek peace, but find none. **7:26** Disaster after disaster will come, and one rumor after another. They will seek a vision from a prophet; priestly instruction will disappear, along with counsel from the elders. **7:27** The king will mourn and the prince will be clothed with shuddering; the hands of the people of the land will tremble. Based on their behavior I will deal with them, and by their standard of justice I will judge them. Then they will know that I am the LORD!"

A Desecrated Temple

8:1 In the sixth year, in the sixth month, on the fifth of the month, as I was sitting in my house with the elders of Judah sitting in front of me, the hand of the sovereign LORD seized me. **8:2** As I watched, I noticed a form that appeared to be a man. From his waist downward was something like fire, and from his waist upward something like a brightness, like an amber glow. **8:3** He stretched out the form of a hand and grabbed me by a lock of hair on my head. Then a wind lifted me up between the earth and sky and brought me to Jerusalem by means of divine visions, to the door of the inner gate which faces north where the statue which provokes to jealousy was located. **8:4** Then I perceived that the glory of the God of Israel was there, as in the vision I had seen earlier in the valley.

8:5 He said to me, "Son of man, look up toward the north." So I looked up toward the north, and I noticed to the north of the altar gate was this statue of jealousy at the entrance.

8:6 He said to me, "Son of man, do you see what they are doing – the great abominations that the people of Israel are practicing here, to drive me far from my sanctuary? But you will see greater abominations than these!"

8:7 He brought me to the entrance of the court, and as I watched, I noticed a hole in the wall. **8:8** He said to me, "Son of man, dig into the wall." So I dug into the wall and discovered a doorway.

8:9 He said to me, "Go in and see the evil abominations they are practicing here." **8:10** So I went in and looked. I noticed every figure of creeping thing and beast – detestable images – and every idol of the house of Israel, engraved on the wall all around. **8:11** Seventy men from the elders of the house of Israel (with Jaazaniah son of Shaphan standing among them) were standing in front of them, each with a censer in his hand, and fragrant vapors from a cloud of incense were swirling upward.

8:12 He said to me, "Do you see, son of man, what the elders of the house of Israel are doing in the dark, each in the chamber of his idolatrous images? For they think, 'The LORD does not see us! The LORD has abandoned the land!'" **8:13** He said to me, "You will see them practicing even greater abominations!"

8:14 Then he brought me to the entrance of the north gate of the LORD's house. I noticed women sitting there weeping for Tammuz. **8:15** He said to me, "Do you see this, son of man? You will see even greater abominations than these!"

8:16 Then he brought me to the inner court of the LORD's house. Right there at the entrance to the LORD's temple, between the porch and the altar, were about twenty-five men with their backs to the LORD's temple, facing east – they were worshiping the sun toward the east!

8:17 He said to me, "Do you see, son of man? Is it a trivial thing that the house of Judah commits these abominations they are practicing here? For they have filled the land with violence and provoked me to anger still further. Look, they are putting the branch to their nose! **8:18** Therefore I will act with fury! My eye will not pity them nor will I spare them. When they have shouted in my ears, I will not listen to them."

The Execution of Idolaters

9:1 Then he shouted in my ears, "Approach, you who are to visit destruction on the city, each with his destructive weapon in his hand!" **9:2** Next, I noticed six men coming from the direction of the upper gate which faces north, each with his war club in his hand. Among them was a man dressed in linen with a writing kit at his side. They came and stood beside the bronze altar.

9:3 Then the glory of the God of Israel went up from the cherub where it had rested to the threshold of the temple. He called to the man dressed in linen who had the writing kit at his side. **9:4** The LORD said to him, "Go through the city of Jerusalem and put a mark on the foreheads of the people who moan and groan over all the abominations practiced in it."

9:5 While I listened, he said to the others, "Go through the city after him and strike people down; do no let your eye pity nor spare anyone! **9:6** Old men, young men, young women, little children, and women – wipe them out! But do not touch anyone who has the mark. Begin at my sanctuary!" So they began with the elders who were at the front of the temple.

9:7 He said to them, "Defile the temple and fill the courtyards with corpses. Go!" So they went out and struck people down throughout the city. **9:8** While they were striking them down, I was left alone, and I threw myself face down and cried out, "Ah, sovereign LORD! Will you destroy the entire remnant of Israel when you pour out your fury on Jerusalem?"

9:9 He said to me, "The sin of the house of Israel and Judah is extremely great; the land is full of murder, and the city is full of corruption, for they say, 'The LORD has abandoned the land, and the LORD does not see!' **9:10** But as for me, my eye will not pity them nor will I spare them; I hereby repay them for what they have done."

9:11 Next I noticed the man dressed in linen with the writing kit at his side bringing back word: "I have done just as you commanded me."

God's Glory Leaves the Temple

10:1 As I watched, I saw on the platform above the top of the cherubim something like a sapphire, resembling the shape of a throne, appearing above them. **10:2** The LORD said to the man dressed in linen, "Go between the wheelwork underneath the cherubim. Fill your hands with burning coals from among the cherubim and scatter them over the city." He went as I watched.

10:3 (The cherubim were standing on the south side of the temple when the man went in, and a cloud filled the inner court.) **10:4** Then the glory of the LORD arose from the cherub and moved to the threshold of the temple. The temple was filled with the cloud while the court was filled with the brightness of the LORD's glory. **10:5** The sound of the wings of the cherubim could be heard from the outer court, like the sound of the sovereign God when he speaks.

10:6 When the LORD commanded the man dressed in linen, "Take fire from within the wheelwork, from among the cherubim," the man went in and stood by one of the wheels. **10:7** Then one of the cherubim stretched out his hand toward the fire which was among the cherubim. He took some and put it into the hands of the man dressed in linen, who took it and left. **10:8** (The cherubim appeared to have the form of human hands under their wings.)

10:9 As I watched, I noticed four wheels by the cherubim, one wheel beside each cherub; the wheels gleamed like jasper. **10:10** As for their appearance, all four of them looked the same, something like a wheel within a wheel. **10:11** When they moved, they would go in any of the four directions they faced without turning as they moved; in the direction the head would turn they would follow without turning as they moved, **10:12** along with their entire bodies, their backs, their hands, and their wings. The wheels of the four of them were full of eyes all around. **10:13** As for their wheels, they were called "the wheelwork" as I listened. **10:14** Each of the cherubim had four faces: The first was the face of a cherub, the second that of a man, the third that of a lion, and the fourth that of an eagle.

10:15 The cherubim rose up; these were the living beings I saw at the Kebar River. **10:16** When the cherubim moved, the wheels moved beside them; when the cherubim spread their wings to rise from the ground, the wheels did not move from their side. **10:17** When the cherubim stood still, the wheels stood still, and when they rose up, the wheels rose up with them, for the spirit of the living beings was in the wheels.

10:18 Then the glory of the LORD moved away from the threshold of the temple and stopped above the cherubim. **10:19** The cherubim spread their wings, and they rose up from the earth while I watched (when they went the wheels went alongside them). They stopped at the entrance to the east gate of the LORD's temple as the glory of the God of Israel hovered above them.

10:20 These were the living creatures which I saw at the Kebar River underneath the God of Israel; I knew that they were cherubim. **10:21** Each had four faces; each had four wings and the form of human hands under the wings. **10:22** As for the form of their faces, they were the faces whose appearance I had seen at the Kebar River. Each one moved straight ahead.

The Fall of Jerusalem

11:1 A wind lifted me up and brought me to the east gate of the Lord's temple that faces the east. There, at the entrance of the gate, I noticed twenty-five men. Among them I saw Jaazaniah son of Azzur and Pelatiah son of Benaiah, officials of the people. **11:2** The LORD said to me, "Son of man, these are the men who plot evil and give wicked advice in this city. **11:3** They say, 'The time is not near to build houses; the city is a cooking pot and we are the meat in it.' **11:4** Therefore, prophesy against them! Prophesy, son of man!"

11:5 Then the Spirit of the Lord came upon me and said to me, "Say: This is what the Lord says: 'This is what you are thinking, O house of Israel; I know what goes through your minds. **11:6** You have killed many people in this city; you have filled its streets with corpses.' **11:7** Therefore, this is what the sovereign Lord says: 'The corpses you have dumped in the midst of the city are the meat, and this city is the cooking pot, but I will take you out of it. **11:8** You fear the sword, so the sword I will bring against you,' declares the sovereign Lord. **11:9** 'But I will take you out of the city. And I will hand you over to foreigners. I will execute judgments on you. **11:10** You will die by the sword; I will judge you at the border of Israel. Then you will know that I am the Lord. **11:11** This city will not be a cooking pot for you, and you will not be meat within it; I will judge you at the border of Israel. **11:12** Then you will know that I am the Lord, whose statutes you have not followed and whose regulations you have not carried out. Instead you have behaved according to the regulations of the nations around you!'"

11:13 Now, while I was prophesying, Pelatiah son of Benaiah died. Then I threw myself face down and cried out with a loud voice, "Alas, sovereign Lord! You are completely wiping out the remnant of Israel!"

11:14 Then the word of the LORD came to me: **11:15** "Son of man, your brothers, your relatives, and the whole house of Israel, all of them are those to whom the inhabitants of Jerusalem have said, 'They have gone far away from the LORD; to us this land has been given as a possession.'

11:16 "Therefore say: 'This is what the sovereign LORD says: Although I have removed them far away among the nations and have dispersed them among the countries, I have been a little sanctuary for them among the lands where they have gone.'

11:17 "Therefore say: 'This is what the sovereign LORD says: When I regather you from the peoples and assemble you from the lands where you have been dispersed, I will give you back the country of Israel.'

11:18 "When they return to it, they will remove from it all its detestable things and all its abominations. **11:19** I will give them one heart and I will put a new spirit within them; I will remove the hearts of stone from their bodies and I will give them tender hearts, **11:20** so that they may follow my statutes and observe my regulations and carry them out. Then they will be my people, and I will be their God. **11:21** But those whose hearts are devoted to detestable things and abominations, I hereby repay them for what they have done, says the sovereign LORD."

11:22 Then the cherubim spread their wings with their wheels alongside them while the glory of the God of Israel hovered above them. **11:23** The glory of the LORD rose up from within the city and stopped over the mountain east of it. **11:24** Then a wind lifted me up and carried me to the exiles in Babylonia, in the vision given to me by the Spirit of God. Then the vision I had seen went up from me. **11:25** So I told the exiles everything the LORD had shown me.

Previewing the Exile

12:1 The word of the LORD came to me: **12:2** "Son of man, you are living in the midst of a rebellious house. They have eyes to see, but do not see, and ears to hear, but do not hear, because they are a rebellious house.

12:3 "Therefore, son of man, pack up your belongings as if for exile. During the day, while they are watching, pretend to go into exile. Go from where you live to another place. Perhaps they will understand, alt-

hough they are a rebellious house. **12:4** Bring out your belongings packed for exile during the day while they are watching. And go out at evening, while they are watching, as if for exile. **12:5** While they are watching, dig a hole in the wall and carry your belongings out through it. **12:6** While they are watching, raise your baggage onto your shoulder and carry it out in the dark. You must cover your face so that you cannot see the ground because I have made you an object lesson to the house of Israel."

12:7 So I did just as I was commanded. I carried out my belongings packed for exile during the day, and at evening I dug myself a hole through the wall with my hands. I went out in the darkness, carrying my baggage on my shoulder while they watched.

12:8 The word of the LORD came to me in the morning: **12:9** "Son of man, has not the house of Israel, that rebellious house, said to you, 'What are you doing?' **12:10** Say to them, 'This is what the sovereign LORD says: The prince will raise this burden in Jerusalem, and all the house of Israel within it.' **12:11** Say, 'I am an object lesson for you. Just as I have done, it will be done to them; they will go into exile and captivity.'

12:12 "The prince who is among them will raise his belongings onto his shoulder in darkness, and will go out. He will dig a hole in the wall to leave through. He will cover his face so that he cannot see the land with his eyes. **12:13** But I will throw my net over him, and he will be caught in my snare. I will bring him to Babylon, the land of the Chaldeans (but he will not see it), and there he will die. **12:14** All his retinue – his attendants and his troops – I will scatter to every wind; I will unleash a sword behind them.

12:15 "Then they will know that I am the LORD when I disperse them among the nations and scatter them among foreign countries. **12:16** But I will let a small number of them survive the sword, famine, and pestilence, so that they can confess all their abominable practices to the nations where they go. Then they will know that I am the LORD."

12:17 The word of the LORD came to me: **12:18** "Son of man, eat your bread with trembling, and drink your water with anxious shaking. **12:19** Then say to the people of the land, 'This is what the sovereign LORD says about the inhabitants of Jerusalem and of the land of Israel: They will eat their bread with anxiety and drink their water in fright, for their land will be stripped bare of all it contains because of the violence of all who live in it. **12:20** The inhabited towns will be left in ruins and the land will be devastated. Then you will know that I am the LORD.'"

12:21 The word of the LORD came to me: **12:22** "Son of man, what is this proverb you have in the land of Israel, 'The days pass slowly, and every vision fails'? **12:23** Therefore tell them, 'This is what the sovereign LORD says: I hereby end this proverb; they will not recite it in Israel any longer.' But say to them, 'The days are at hand when every vision will be fulfilled. **12:24** For there will no longer be any false visions or flattering omens amidst the house of Israel. **12:25** For I, the LORD, will speak. Whatever word I speak will be accomplished. It will not be delayed any longer. Indeed in your days, O rebellious house, I will speak the word and accomplish it, declares the sovereign LORD.'"

12:26 The word of the LORD came to me: **12:27** "Take note, son of man, the house of Israel is saying, 'The vision that he sees is for distant days; he is prophesying about the far future.' **12:28** Therefore say to them, 'This is what the sovereign LORD says: None of my words will be delayed any longer! The word I speak will come to pass, declares the sovereign LORD.'"

False Prophets Denounced

13:1 Then the word of the LORD came to me: **13:2** "Son of man, prophesy against the prophets of Israel who are now prophesying. Say to the prophets who prophesy from their imagination: 'Hear the word of the LORD! **13:3** This is what the sovereign LORD says: Woe to the foolish prophets who follow their own spirit but have seen nothing! **13:4** Your prophets have become like jackals among the ruins, O Israel. **13:5** You have not gone up in the breaks in the wall, nor repaired a wall for the house of Israel that it would stand strong in the battle on the day of the LORD. **13:6** They see delusion and their omens are a lie. They say, "the LORD declares," though the LORD has not sent them; yet they expect their word to be confirmed. **13:7** Have you not seen a false vision and announced a lying omen when you say, "the LORD declares," although I myself never spoke?

13:8 "'Therefore, this is what the sovereign LORD says: Because you have spoken false words and forecast delusion, look, I am against you, declares the sovereign LORD. **13:9** My hand will be against the prophets who see delusion and announce lying omens. They will not be included in the council of my people, nor be written in the registry of the house of Israel, nor enter the land of Israel. Then you will know that I am the sovereign LORD.

13:10 "'This is because they have led my people astray saying, "All is well," when things are not well. When anyone builds a wall without mortar, they coat it with whitewash. **13:11** Tell the ones who coat it with whitewash that it will fall. When there is a deluge of rain, hailstones will fall and a violent wind will break out. **13:12** When the wall has collapsed, people will ask you, "Where is the whitewash you coated it with?"

13:13 "'Therefore this is what the sovereign LORD says: In my rage I will make a violent wind break out. In my anger there will be a deluge of rain and hailstones in destructive fury. **13:14** I will break down the wall you coated with whitewash and knock it to the ground so that its foundation is exposed. When it falls you will be destroyed beneath it, and you will know that I am the LORD. **13:15** I will vent my rage against the wall, and against those who coated it with whitewash. Then I will say to you, "The wall is no more and those who whitewashed it are no more – **13:16** those prophets of Israel who would prophesy about Jerusalem and would see visions of peace for it, when there was no peace," declares the sovereign LORD.'

13:17 "As for you, son of man, turn toward the daughters of your people who are prophesying from their imagination. Prophesy against them **13:18** and say 'This is what the sovereign LORD says: Woe to those who sew bands on all their wrists and make headbands for heads of every size to entrap people's lives! Will you entrap my people's lives, yet preserve your own lives? **13:19** You have profaned me among my people for handfuls of barley and scraps of bread. You have put to death people who should not die and kept alive those who should not live by your lies to my people, who listen to lies!

13:20 "'Therefore, this is what the sovereign LORD says: Take note that I am against your wristbands with which you entrap people's lives like birds. I will tear them from your arms and will release the people's lives, which you hunt like birds. **13:21** I will tear off your headbands and rescue my people from your power; they will no longer be prey in your hands. Then you will know that I am the LORD. **13:22** This is because you have disheartened the righteous person with lies (although I have not grieved him), and because you have encouraged the wicked person not to turn from his evil conduct and preserve his life. **13:23** Therefore you will no longer see false visions and practice divination. I will rescue my people from your power, and you will know that I am the LORD.'"

Well-Deserved Judgment

14:1 Then some men from Israel's elders came to me and sat down in front of me. **14:2** The word of the LORD came to me: **14:3** "Son of man, these men have erected their idols in their hearts and placed the obstacle leading to their iniquity right before their faces. Should I really allow them to seek me? **14:4** Therefore speak to them and say to them, 'This is what the sovereign LORD says: When any one from the house of Israel erects his idols in his heart and sets the obstacle leading to his iniquity before his face, and then consults a prophet, I the LORD am determined to answer him personally according to the enormity of his idolatry. **14:5** I will do this in order to capture the hearts of the house of Israel, who have alienated themselves from me on account of all their idols.'

14:6 "Therefore say to the house of Israel, 'This is what the sovereign LORD says: Return! Turn from your idols, and turn your faces away from your abominations. **14:7** For when anyone from the house of Israel, or the foreigner who lives in Israel, separates himself from me and erects his idols in his heart and sets the obstacle leading to his iniquity before his face, and then consults a prophet to seek something from me, I the LORD am determined to answer him personally. **14:8** I will set my face against that person and will make him an object lesson and a byword and will cut him off from among my people. Then you will know that I am the LORD.

14:9 "'As for the prophet, if he is made a fool by being deceived into speaking a prophetic word – I, the LORD, have made a fool of that prophet, and I will stretch out my hand against him and destroy him from among my people Israel. **14:10** They will bear their punishment; the punishment of the one who sought an oracle will be the same as the punishment of the prophet who gave it **14:11** so that the house of Israel will no longer go astray from me, nor continue to defile themselves by all their sins. They will be my people and I will be their God, declares the sovereign LORD.'"

14:12 The word of the LORD came to me: **14:13** "Son of man, suppose a country sins against me by being unfaithful, and I stretch out my hand against it, cut off its bread supply, cause famine to come on it, and kill both people and animals. **14:14** Even if these three men, Noah, Daniel, and Job, were in it, they would save only their own lives by their righteousness, declares the sovereign LORD.

14:15 "Suppose I were to send wild animals through the land and kill its children, leaving it desolate, without travelers due to the wild animals. **14:16** Even if these three men were in it, as surely as I live, declares the sovereign LORD, they could not save their own sons or daughters; they would save only their own lives, and the land would become desolate.

14:17 "Or suppose I were to bring a sword against that land and say, 'Let a sword pass through the land,' and I were to kill both people and animals. **14:18** Even if these three men were in it, as surely as I live, declares the sovereign LORD, they could not save their own sons or daughters – they would save only their own lives.

14:19 "Or suppose I were to send a plague into that land, and pour out my rage on it with bloodshed, killing both people and animals. **14:20** Even if Noah, Daniel, and Job were in it, as surely as I live, declares the sovereign LORD, they could not save their own son or daughter; they would save only their own lives by their righteousness.

14:21 "For this is what the sovereign LORD says: How much worse will it be when I send my four terrible judgments – sword, famine, wild animals, and plague – to Jerusalem to kill both people and animals! **14:22**

Yet some survivors will be left in it, sons and daughters who will be brought out. They will come out to you, and when you see their behavior and their deeds, you will be consoled about the catastrophe I have brought on Jerusalem – for everything I brought on it. **14:23** They will console you when you see their behavior and their deeds, because you will know that it was not without reason that I have done everything which I have done in it, declares the sovereign LORD."

Burning a Useless Vine

15:1 The word of the LORD came to me: **15:2** "Son of man, of all the woody branches among the trees of the forest, what happens to the wood of the vine? **15:3** Can wood be taken from it to make anything useful? Or can anyone make a peg from it to hang things on? **15:4** No! It is thrown in the fire for fuel; when the fire has burned up both ends of it and it is charred in the middle, will it be useful for anything? **15:5** Indeed! If it was not made into anything useful when it was whole, how much less can it be made into anything when the fire has burned it up and it is charred?

15:6 "Therefore, this is what the sovereign LORD says: Like the wood of the vine is among the trees of the forest which I have provided as fuel for the fire – so I will provide the residents of Jerusalem as fuel. **15:7** I will set my face against them – although they have escaped from the fire, the fire will still consume them! Then you will know that I am the LORD, when I set my face against them. **15:8** I will make the land desolate because they have acted unfaithfully, declares the sovereign LORD."

God's Unfaithful Bride

16:1 The word of the LORD came to me: **16:2** "Son of man, confront Jerusalem with her abominable practices **16:3** and say, 'This is what the sovereign LORD says to Jerusalem: Your origin and your birth were in the land of the Canaanites; your father was an Amorite and your mother a Hittite. **16:4** As for your birth, on the day you were born your umbilical cord was not cut, nor were you washed in water; you were certainly not rubbed down with salt, nor wrapped with blankets. **16:5** No eye took pity on you to do even one of these things for you to spare you; you were thrown out into the open field because you were detested on the day you were born.

16:6 "'I passed by you and saw you kicking around helplessly in your blood. I said to you as you lay there in your blood, "Live!" I said to you as you lay there in your blood, "Live!" **16:7** I made you plentiful like sprouts in a field; you grew tall and came of age so that you could wear jewelry. Your breasts had formed and your hair had grown, but you were still naked and bare.

16:8 "'Then I passed by you and watched you, noticing that you had reached the age for love. I spread my cloak over you and covered your nakedness. I swore a solemn oath to you and entered into a marriage covenant with you, declares the sovereign LORD, and you became mine.

16:9 "'Then I bathed you in water, washed the blood off you, and anointed you with fragrant oil. **16:10** I dressed you in embroidered clothing and put fine leather sandals on your feet. I wrapped you with fine linen and covered you with silk. **16:11** I adorned you with jewelry. I put bracelets on your hands and a necklace around your neck. **16:12** I put a ring in your nose, earrings on your ears, and a beautiful crown on your head. **16:13** You were adorned with gold and silver, while your clothing was of fine linen, silk, and embroidery. You ate the finest flour, honey, and olive oil. You became extremely beautiful and attained the position of royalty. **16:14** Your fame spread among the nations because of your beauty; your beauty was perfect because of the splendor which I bestowed on you, declares the sovereign LORD.

16:15 "'But you trusted in your beauty and capitalized on your fame by becoming a prostitute. You offered your sexual favors to every man who passed by so that your beauty became his. **16:16** You took some of your clothing and made for yourself decorated high places; you engaged in prostitution on them. You went to him to become his. **16:17** You also took your beautiful jewelry, made of my gold and my silver I had given to you, and made for yourself male images and engaged in prostitution with them. **16:18** You took your embroidered clothing and used it to cover them; you offered my olive oil and my incense to them. **16:19** As for my food that I gave you – the fine flour, olive oil, and honey I fed you – you placed it before them as a soothing aroma. That is exactly what happened, declares the sovereign LORD.

16:20 "'You took your sons and your daughters whom you bore to me and you sacrificed them as food for the idols to eat. As if your prostitution not enough, **16:21** you slaughtered my children and sacrificed them to the idols. **16:22** And with all your abominable practices and prostitution you did not remember the days of your youth when you were naked and bare, kicking around in your blood.

16:23 "'After all of your evil – "Woe! Woe to you!" declares the sovereign LORD – **16:24** you built yourself a chamber and put up a pavilion in every public square. **16:25** At the head of every street you erected your pavilion and you disgraced your beauty when you spread your legs to every passerby and multiplied your promiscuity. **16:26** You engaged in prostitution with the Egyptians, your sexually aroused neighbors, multiplying your promiscuity and provoking me to anger. **16:27** So see here, I have stretched out my hand against you and cut off your rations. I have delivered you into the power of those who hate you, the daughters of the

Philistines, who were ashamed by your obscene conduct. **16:28** You engaged in prostitution with the Assyrians because your sexual desires were insatiable; you prostituted yourself with them and yet you were still not satisfied. **16:29** Then you multiplied your promiscuity to the land of merchants, Babylonia, but you were not satisfied there either.

16:30 '"How sick is your heart, declares the sovereign LORD, when you perform all of these acts, the deeds of a bold prostitute. **16:31** When you built your chamber at the head of every street and put up your pavilion in every public square, you were not like a prostitute, because you scoffed at payment.

16:32 '"Adulterous wife, who prefers strangers instead of her own husband! **16:33** All prostitutes receive payment, but instead you give gifts to every one of your lovers. You bribe them to come to you from all around for your sexual favors! **16:34** You were different from other prostitutes because no one solicited you. When you gave payment and no payment was given to you, you became the opposite!

16:35 '"Therefore O prostitute, hear the word of the LORD: **16:36** This is what the sovereign LORD says: Because your lust was poured out and your nakedness was uncovered in your prostitution with your lovers, and because of all your detestable idols, and because of the blood of your children you have given to them, **16:37** therefore, take note: I am about to gather all your lovers whom you enjoyed, both all those you loved and all those you hated. I will gather them against you from all around, and I will expose your nakedness to them, and they will see all your nakedness. **16:38** I will punish you as an adulteress and murderer deserves. I will avenge your bloody deeds with furious rage. **16:39** I will give you into their hands and they will destroy your chambers and tear down your pavilions. They will strip you of your clothing and take your beautiful jewelry and leave you naked and bare. **16:40** They will summon a mob who will stone you and hack you in pieces with their swords. **16:41** They will burn down your houses and execute judgments on you in front of many women. Thus I will put a stop to your prostitution, and you will no longer give gifts to your clients. **16:42** I will exhaust my rage on you, and then my fury will turn from you. I will calm down and no longer be angry.

16:43 '"Because you did not remember the days of your youth and have enraged me with all these deeds, I hereby repay you for what you have done, declares the sovereign LORD. Have you not engaged in prostitution on top of all your other abominable practices?

16:44 '"Observe – everyone who quotes proverbs will quote this proverb about you: "Like mother, like daughter." **16:45** You are the daughter of your mother, who detested her husband and her sons, and you are the sister of your sisters who detested their husbands and their sons. Your mother was a Hittite and your father an Amorite. **16:46** Your older sister was Samaria, who lived north of you with her daughters, and your younger sister, who lived south of you, was Sodom with her daughters. **16:47** Have you not copied their behavior and practiced their abominable deeds? In a short time you became even more depraved in all your conduct than they were! **16:48** As surely as I live, declares the sovereign LORD, your sister Sodom and her daughters never behaved as wickedly as you and your daughters have behaved.

16:49 '"See here – this was the iniquity of your sister Sodom: She and her daughters had majesty, abundance of food, and enjoyed carefree ease, but they did not help the poor and needy. **16:50** They were haughty and practiced abominable deeds before me. Therefore when I saw it I removed them. **16:51** Samaria has not committed half the sins you have; you have done more abominable deeds than they did. You have made your sisters appear righteous with all the abominable things you have done. **16:52** So now, bear your disgrace, because you have given your sisters reason to justify their behavior. Because the sins you have committed were more abominable than those of your sisters; they have become more righteous than you. So now, be ashamed and bear the disgrace of making your sisters appear righteous.

16:53 '"I will restore their fortunes, the fortunes of Sodom and her daughters, and the fortunes of Samaria and her daughters (along with your fortunes among them), **16:54** so that you may bear your disgrace and be ashamed of all you have done in consoling them. **16:55** As for your sisters, Sodom and her daughters will be restored to their former status, Samaria and her daughters will be restored to their former status, and you and your daughters will be restored to your former status. **16:56** In your days of majesty, was not Sodom your sister a byword in your mouth, **16:57** before your evil was exposed? Now you have become an object of scorn to the daughters of Aram and all those around her and to the daughters of the Philistines – those all around you who despise you. **16:58** You must bear your punishment for your obscene conduct and your abominable practices, declares the LORD.

16:59 '"For this is what the sovereign LORD says: I will deal with you according to what you have done when you despised your oath by breaking your covenant. **16:60** Yet I will remember the covenant I made with you in the days of your youth, and I will establish a lasting covenant with you. **16:61** Then you will remember your conduct, and be ashamed when you receive your older and younger sisters. I will give them to you as daughters, but not on account of my covenant with you. **16:62** I will

establish my covenant with you, and then you will know that I am the LORD. **16:63** Then you will remember, be ashamed, and remain silent when I make atonement for all you have done, declares the sovereign LORD.'"

A Parable of Two Eagles and a Vine

17:1 The word of the LORD came to me: **17:2** "Son of man, offer a riddle, and tell a parable to the house of Israel. **17:3** Say to them: 'This is what the sovereign LORD says:

"'A great eagle with broad wings, long feathers,
with full plumage which was multi-hued,
came to Lebanon and took the top of the cedar.
17:4 He plucked off its topmost shoot;
he brought it to a land of merchants
and planted it in a city of traders.
17:5 He took one of the seedlings of the land,
placed it in a cultivated plot;
a shoot by abundant water,
like a willow he planted it.
17:6 It sprouted and became a vine,
spreading low to the ground;
its branches turning toward him, its roots were under itself.
So it became a vine; it produced shoots and sent out branches.
17:7 "There was another great eagle
with broad wings and thick plumage.
Now this vine twisted its roots toward him
and sent its branches toward him
to be watered from the soil where it was planted.
17:8 In a good field, by abundant waters, it was planted
to grow branches, bear fruit, and become a beautiful vine.
17:9 "Say to them: This is what the sovereign LORD says:
"'Will it prosper?
Will he not rip out its roots
and cause its fruit to rot and wither?
All its foliage will wither.
No strong arm or large army
will be needed to pull it out by its roots.
17:10 Consider! It is planted, but will it prosper?
Will it not wither completely when the east wind blows on it?
Will it not wither in the soil where it sprouted?'"

17:11 Then the word of the LORD came to me: **17:12** "Say to the rebellious house of Israel: 'Don't you know what these things mean?' Say: 'See here, the king of Babylon came to Jerusalem and took her king and her officials prisoner and brought them to himself in Babylon. **17:13** He took one from the royal family, made a treaty with him, and put him under oath. He then took the leaders of the land **17:14** so it would be a lowly kingdom which could not rise on its own but must keep its treaty with him in order to stand. **17:15** But this one from Israel's royal family rebelled against the king of Babylon by sending his emissaries to Egypt to obtain horses and a large army. Will he prosper? Will the one doing these things escape? Can he break the covenant and escape?

17:16 '"As surely as I live, declares the sovereign LORD, surely in the city of the king who crowned him, whose oath he despised and whose covenant he broke – in the middle of Babylon he will die! **17:17** Pharaoh with his great army and mighty horde will not help him in battle, when siege ramps are erected and siege-walls are built to kill many people. **17:18** He despised the oath by breaking the covenant. Take note – he gave his promise and did all these things – he will not escape!

17:19 '"Therefore this is what the sovereign LORD says: As surely as I live, I will certainly repay him for despising my oath and breaking my covenant! **17:20** I will throw my net over him and he will be caught in my snare; I will bring him to Babylon and judge him there because of the unfaithfulness he committed against me. **17:21** All the choice men among his troops will die by the sword and the survivors will be scattered to every wind. Then you will know that I, the LORD, have spoken!

17:22 '"This is what the sovereign LORD says:
"'I will take a sprig from the lofty top of the cedar and plant it.
I will pluck from the top one of its tender twigs;
I myself will plant it on a high and lofty mountain.
17:23 I will plant it on a high mountain of Israel,
and it will raise branches and produce fruit and become a beautiful cedar.
Every bird will live under it;
Every winged creature will live in the shade of its branches.
17:24 All the trees of the field will know that I am the LORD.
I make the high tree low; I raise up the low tree.
I make the green tree wither, and I make the dry tree sprout.
I, the LORD, have spoken, and I will do it!'"

Individual Retribution

18:1 The word of the LORD came to me: **18:2** "What do you mean by quoting this proverb concerning the land of Israel,
"'The fathers eat sour grapes
And the children's teeth become numb?'
18:3 "As surely as I live, declares the sovereign LORD, you will not quote this proverb in Israel anymore! **18:4** Indeed! All lives are mine – the life

of the father as well as the life of the son is mine. The one who sins will die.

18:5 "Suppose a man is righteous. He practices what is just and right, **18:6** does not eat pagan sacrifices on the mountains or pray to the idols of the house of Israel, does not defile his neighbor's wife, does not have sexual relations with a woman during her period, **18:7** does not oppress anyone, but gives the debtor back whatever was given in pledge, does not commit robbery, but gives his bread to the hungry and clothes the naked, **18:8** does not engage in usury or charge interest, but refrains from wrongdoing, promotes true justice between men, **18:9** and follows my statutes and observes my regulations by carrying them out. That man is righteous; he will certainly live, declares the sovereign LORD.

18:10 "Suppose such a man has a violent son who sheds blood and does any of these things mentioned previously **18:11** (though the father did not do any of them). He eats pagan sacrifices on the mountains, defiles his neighbor's wife, **18:12** oppresses the poor and the needy, commits robbery, does not give back what was given in pledge, prays to idols, performs abominable acts, **18:13** engages in usury and charges interest. Will he live? He will not! Because he has done all these abominable deeds he will certainly die. He will bear the responsibility for his own death.

18:14 "But suppose he in turn has a son who notices all the sins his father commits, considers them, and does not follow his father's example. **18:15** He does not eat pagan sacrifices on the mountains, does not pray to the idols of the house of Israel, does not defile his neighbor's wife, **18:16** does not oppress anyone or keep what has been given in pledge, does not commit robbery, gives his food to the hungry, and clothes the naked, **18:17** refrains from wrongdoing, does not engage in usury or charge interest, carries out my regulations and follows my statutes. He will not die for his father's iniquity; he will surely live. **18:18** As for his father, because he practices extortion, robs his brother, and does what is not good among his people, he will die for his iniquity.

18:19 "Yet you say, 'Why should the son not suffer for his father's iniquity?' When the son does what is just and right, and observes all my statutes and carries them out, he will surely live. **18:20** The person who sins is the one who will die. A son will not suffer for his father's iniquity, and a father will not suffer for his son's iniquity; the righteous person will be judged according to his righteousness, and the wicked person according to his wickedness.

18:21 "But if the wicked person turns from all the sin he has committed and observes all my statutes and does what is just and right, he will surely live; he will not die. **18:22** None of the sins he has committed will be held against him; because of the righteousness he has done, he will live. **18:23** Do I actually delight in the death of the wicked, declares the sovereign LORD? Do I not prefer that he turn from his wicked conduct and live?

18:24 "But if a righteous man turns away from his righteousness and practices wrongdoing according to all the abominable practices the wicked carry out, will he live? All his righteous acts will not be remembered; because of the unfaithful acts he has done and the sin he has committed, he will die.

18:25 "Yet you say, 'The Lord's conduct is unjust!' Hear, O house of Israel: Is my conduct unjust? Is it not your conduct that is unjust? **18:26** When a righteous person turns back from his righteousness and practices wrongdoing, he will die for it; because of the wrongdoing he has done, he will die. **18:27** When a wicked person turns from the wickedness he has committed and does what is just and right, he will preserve his life. **18:28** Because he considered and turned from all the sins he had done, he will surely live; he will not die. **18:29** Yet the house of Israel says, 'The Lord's conduct is unjust!' Is my conduct unjust, O house of Israel? Is it not your conduct that is unjust?

18:30 "Therefore I will judge each person according to his conduct, O house of Israel, declares the sovereign LORD. Repent and turn from all your wickedness; then it will not be an obstacle leading to iniquity. **18:31** Throw away all your sins you have committed and fashion yourselves a new heart and a new spirit! Why should you die, O house of Israel? **18:32** For I take no delight in the death of anyone, declares the sovereign LORD. Repent and live!

Lament for the Princes of Israel

19:1 "And you, sing a lament for the princes of Israel, **19:2** and say:

"'What a lioness was your mother among the lions!
She lay among young lions; she reared her cubs.
19:3 She reared one of her cubs; he became a young lion.
He learned to tear prey; he devoured people.
19:4 The nations heard about him; he was trapped in their pit.
They brought him with hooks to the land of Egypt.

19:5 "'When she realized that she waited in vain, her hope was lost.
She took another of her cubs and made him a young lion.
19:6 He walked about among the lions; he became a young lion.
He learned to tear prey; he devoured people.
19:7 He broke down their strongholds and devastated their cities.
The land and everything in it was frightened at the sound of his roaring.
19:8 The nations – the surrounding regions – attacked him.
They threw their net over him; he was caught in their pit.

19:9 They put him in a collar with hooks;
they brought him to the king of Babylon;
they brought him to prison
so that his voice would not be heard
any longer on the mountains of Israel.

19:10 "'Your mother was like a vine in your vineyard, planted by water.
It was fruitful and full of branches because it was well-watered.
19:11 Its boughs were strong, fit for rulers' scepters; it reached up into the clouds.
It stood out because of its height and its many branches.
19:12 But it was plucked up in anger; it was thrown down to the ground.
The east wind dried up its fruit;
its strong branches broke off and withered –
a fire consumed them.
19:13 Now it is planted in the wilderness,
in a dry and thirsty land.
19:14 A fire has gone out from its branch; it has consumed its shoot and its fruit.
No strong branch was left in it, nor a scepter to rule.'
This is a lament song, and has become a lament song."

Israel's Rebellion

20:1 In the seventh year, in the fifth month, on the tenth of the month, some of the elders of Israel came to seek the LORD, and they sat down in front of me. **20:2** The word of the LORD came to me: **20:3** "Son of man, speak to the elders of Israel, and tell them: 'This is what the sovereign LORD says: Are you coming to seek me? As surely as I live, I will not allow you to seek me, declares the sovereign LORD.' **20:4** "Are you willing to pronounce judgment? Are you willing to pronounce judgment, son of man? Then confront them with the abominable practices of their fathers, **20:5** and say to them:

"'This is what the sovereign LORD says: On the day I chose Israel I swore to the descendants of the house of Jacob and made myself known to them in the land of Egypt. I swore to them, "I am the LORD your God." **20:6** On that day I swore to bring them out of the land of Egypt to a land which I had picked out for them, a land flowing with milk and honey, the most beautiful of all lands. **20:7** I said to them, "Each of you must get rid of the detestable idols you keep before you, and do not defile yourselves with the idols of Egypt; I am the LORD your God." **20:8** But they rebelled against me, and refused to listen to me; no one got rid of their detestable idols, nor did they abandon the idols of Egypt. Then I decided to pour out my rage on them and fully vent my anger against them in the midst of the land of Egypt. **20:9** I acted for the sake of my reputation, so that I would not be profaned before the nations among whom they lived, before whom I revealed myself by bringing them out of the land of Egypt.

20:10 "'So I brought them out of the land of Egypt and led them to the wilderness. **20:11** I gave them my statutes and revealed my regulations to them. The one who carries them out will live by them! **20:12** I also gave them my Sabbaths as a reminder of our relationship, so that they would know that I, the LORD, sanctify them. **20:13** But the house of Israel rebelled against me in the wilderness; they did not follow my statutes and they rejected my regulations (the one who obeys them will live by them), and they utterly desecrated my Sabbaths. So I decided to pour out my rage on them in the wilderness and destroy them. **20:14** I acted for the sake of my reputation, so that I would not be profaned before the nations in whose sight I had brought them out. **20:15** I also swore to them in the wilderness that I would not bring them to the land I had given them – a land flowing with milk and honey, the most beautiful of all lands. **20:16** I did this because they rejected my regulations, did not follow my statutes, and desecrated my Sabbaths; for their hearts followed their idols. **20:17** Yet I had pity on them and did not destroy them, so I did not make an end of them in the wilderness.

20:18 "'But I said to their children in the wilderness, "Do not follow the practices of your fathers; do not observe their regulations, nor defile yourselves with their idols. **20:19** I am the LORD your God; follow my statutes, observe my regulations, and carry them out. **20:20** Treat my Sabbaths as holy and they will be a reminder of our relationship, and then you will know that I am the LORD your God." **20:21** "'But the children rebelled against me, did not follow my statutes, did not observe my regulations by carrying them out (the one who obeys them will live by them), and desecrated my Sabbaths. I decided to pour out my rage on them and fully vent my anger against them in the wilderness. **20:22** But I refrained from doing so, and acted instead for the sake of my reputation, so that I would not be profaned before the nations in whose sight I had brought them out. **20:23** I also swore to them in the wilderness that I would scatter them among the nations and disperse them throughout the lands. **20:24** I did this because they did not observe my regulations, they rejected my statutes, they desecrated my Sabbaths, and their eyes were fixed on their fathers' idols. **20:25** I also gave them decrees which were not good and regulations by which they could not live. **20:26** I declared them to be defiled because of their sacrifices – they caused all their first born to pass through the fire – so that I would devastate them, so that they will know that I am the LORD.'

20:27 "Therefore, speak to the house of Israel, son of man, and tell them, 'This is what the sovereign LORD says: In this way too your fathers blasphemed me when they were unfaithful to me. **20:28** I brought them to the land which I swore to give them, but whenever they saw any high hill or leafy tree, they offered their sacrifices there and presented the offerings that provoke me to anger. They offered their soothing aroma there and poured out their drink offerings. **20:29** So I said to them, What is this high place you go to?'" (So it is called "High Place" to this day.)

20:30 "Therefore say to the house of Israel, 'This is what the sovereign LORD says: Will you defile yourselves like your fathers and engage in prostitution with detestable idols? **20:31** When you present your sacrifices – when you make your sons pass through the fire – you defile yourselves with all your idols to this very day. Will I allow you to seek me, O house of Israel? As surely as I live, declares the sovereign LORD, I will not allow you to seek me!

20:32 "What you plan will never happen. You say, "We will be like the nations, like the clans of the lands, who serve gods of wood and stone." **20:33** As surely as I live, declares the sovereign LORD, with a powerful hand and an outstretched arm, and with an outpouring of rage, I will be king over you. **20:34** I will bring you out from the nations, and will gather you from the lands where you are scattered, with a powerful hand and an outstretched arm and with an outpouring of rage! **20:35** I will bring you into the wilderness of the nations, and there I will enter into judgment with you face to face. **20:36** Just as I entered into judgment with your fathers in the wilderness of the land of Egypt, so I will enter into judgment with you, declares the sovereign LORD. **20:37** I will make you pass under the shepherd's staff, and I will bring you into the bond of the covenant. **20:38** I will eliminate from among you the rebels and those who revolt against me. I will bring them out from the land where they have been residing, but they will not come to the land of Israel. Then you will know that I am the LORD.

20:39 "As for you, O house of Israel, this is what the sovereign LORD says: Each of you go and serve your idols, if you will not listen to me. But my holy name will not be profaned again by your sacrifices and your idols. **20:40** For there on my holy mountain, the high mountain of Israel, declares the sovereign LORD, all the house of Israel will serve me, all of them in the land. I will accept them there, and there I will seek your contributions and your choice gifts, with all your holy things. **20:41** When I bring you out from the nations and gather you from the lands where you are scattered, I will accept you along with your soothing aroma. I will display my holiness among you in the sight of the nations. **20:42** Then you will know that I am the LORD when I bring you to the land of Israel, to the land I swore to give to your fathers. **20:43** And there you will remember your conduct and all your deeds by which you defiled yourselves. You will despise yourselves because of all the evil deeds you have done. **20:44** Then you will know that I am the LORD, when I deal with you for the sake of my reputation and not according to your wicked conduct and corrupt deeds, O house of Israel, declares the sovereign LORD.'"

Prophecy Against the South

20:45 (21:1) The word of the LORD came to me: **20:46** "Son of man, turn toward the south, and speak out against the south. Prophesy against the open scrub land of the Negev, **20:47** and say to the scrub land of the Negev, 'Hear the word of the LORD: This is what the sovereign LORD says: Look here, I am about to start a fire in you, and it will devour every green tree and every dry tree in you. The flaming fire will not be extinguished, and the whole surface of the ground from the Negev to the north will be scorched by it. **20:48** And everyone will see that I, the LORD, have burned it; it will not be extinguished.'"

20:49 Then I said, "O sovereign LORD! They are saying of me, 'Does he not simply speak in eloquent figures of speech?'"

The Sword of Judgment

21:1 (21:6) The word of the LORD came to me: **21:2** "Son of man, turn toward Jerusalem and speak out against the sanctuaries. Prophesy against the land of Israel **21:3** and say to them, 'This is what the LORD says: Look, I am against you. I will draw my sword from its sheath and cut off from you both the righteous and the wicked. **21:4** Because I will cut off from you both the righteous and the wicked, my sword will go out from its sheath against everyone from the south to the north. **21:5** Then everyone will know that I am the LORD, who drew my sword from its sheath – it will not be sheathed again!'

21:6 "And you, son of man, groan with an aching heart and bitterness; groan before their eyes. **21:7** When they ask you, 'Why are you groaning?' you will reply, 'Because of the report that has come. Every heart will melt with fear and every hand will be limp; everyone will faint and every knee will be wet with urine.' Pay attention – it is coming and it will happen, declares the sovereign LORD."

21:8 The word of the LORD came to me: **21:9** "Son of man, prophesy and say: 'This is what the Lord says:

"'A sword, a sword is sharpened,
and also polished.
21:10 It is sharpened for slaughter,

it is polished to flash like lightning!

"'Should we rejoice in the scepter of my son? No! The sword despises every tree!

21:11 "'He gave it to be polished,
to be grasped in the hand –
the sword is sharpened, it is polished –
giving it into the hand of the executioner.
21:12 Cry out and moan, son of man,
for it is wielded against my people;
against all the princes of Israel.
They are delivered up to the sword, along with my people.
Therefore, strike your thigh.

21:13 "'For testing will come, and what will happen when the scepter, which the sword despises, is no more? declares the sovereign LORD.'

21:14 "And you, son of man, prophesy,
and clap your hands together.
Let the sword strike twice, even three times!
It is a sword for slaughter,
a sword for the great slaughter surrounding them.
21:15 So hearts melt with fear and many stumble.
At all their gates I have stationed the sword for slaughter.
Ah! It is made to flash, it is drawn for slaughter!
21:16 Cut sharply on the right!
Swing to the left,
wherever your edge is appointed to strike.
21:17 I too will clap my hands together,
I will exhaust my rage;
I the LORD have spoken."

21:18 The word of the LORD came to me: **21:19** "You, son of man, mark out two routes for the king of Babylon's sword to take; both of them will originate in a single land. Make a signpost and put it at the beginning of the road leading to the city. **21:20** Mark out the routes for the sword to take: "Rabbah of the Ammonites" and "Judah with Jerusalem in it." **21:21** For the king of Babylon stands at the fork in the road at the head of the two routes. He looks for omens: He shakes arrows, he consults idols, he examines animal livers. **21:22** Into his right hand comes the portent for Jerusalem – to set up battering rams, to give the signal for slaughter, to shout out the battle cry, to set up battering rams against the gates, to erect a siege ramp, to build a siege wall. **21:23** But those in Jerusalem will view it as a false omen. They have sworn solemn oaths, but the king of Babylon will accuse them of violations in order to seize them.

21:24 "Therefore this is what the sovereign LORD says: 'Because you have brought up your own guilt by uncovering your transgressions and revealing your sins through all your actions, for this reason you will be taken by force.

21:25 "'As for you, profane and wicked prince of Israel,
whose day has come, the time of final punishment,
21:26 this is what the sovereign LORD says:
Tear off the turban,
take off the crown!
Things must change!
Exalt the lowly,
bring down the proud!
21:27 A total ruin I will make it!
It will come to an end
when the one arrives to whom I have assigned judgment.'

21:28 "As for you, son of man, prophesy and say, 'This is what the sovereign LORD says concerning the Ammonites and their coming humiliation; say:

"'A sword, a sword drawn for slaughter,
polished to consume, to flash like lightning –
21:29 while seeing false visions for you
and reading lying omens for you –
to place that sword on the necks of the profane wicked,
whose day has come,
the time of final punishment.
21:30 Return it to its sheath!
In the place where you were created,
in your native land, I will judge you.
21:31 I will pour out my anger on you;
the fire of my fury I will blow on you.
I will hand you over to brutal men,
who are skilled in destruction.
21:32 You will become fuel for the fire –
your blood will stain the middle of the land;
you will no longer be remembered,
for I, the LORD, have spoken.'"

The Sins of Jerusalem
22:1 The word of the LORD came to me: **22:2** "As for you, son of man, are you willing to pronounce judgment, are you willing to pronounce judgment on the bloody city? Then confront her with all her abominable deeds! **22:3** Then say, 'This is what the sovereign LORD says: O city, who spills blood within herself (which brings on her doom), and who makes herself idols (which results in impurity), **22:4** you are guilty because of the blood you shed and defiled by the idols you made. You have hastened the day of your doom; the end of your years has come. Therefore I will make you an object of scorn to the nations, an object to be mocked by all lands. **22:5** Those both near and far from you will mock you, you with your bad reputation, full of turmoil.
22:6 "'See how each of the princes of Israel living within you has used his authority to shed blood. **22:7** They have treated father and mother with contempt within you; they have oppressed the foreigner among you; they have wronged the orphan and the widow within you. **22:8** You have despised my holy things and desecrated my Sabbaths! **22:9** Slanderous men shed blood within you. Those who live within you eat pagan sacrifices on the mountains; they commit obscene acts among you. **22:10** They have sex with their father's wife within you; they violate women during their menstrual period within you. **22:11** One commits an abominable act with his neighbor's wife; another obscenely defiles his daughter-in-law; another violates his sister – his father's daughter – within you. **22:12** They take bribes within you to shed blood. You engage in usury and charge interest; you extort money from your neighbors. You have forgotten me, declares the sovereign LORD.
22:13 "'See, I strike my hands together at the dishonest profit you have made, and at the bloodshed they have done among you. **22:14** Can your heart endure, or can your hands be strong when I deal with you? I, the LORD, have spoken, and I will do it! **22:15** I will scatter you among the nations and disperse you among various countries; I will remove your impurity from you. **22:16** You will be profaned within yourself in the sight of the nations; then you will know that I am the LORD.'"
22:17 The word of the LORD came to me: **22:18** "Son of man, the house of Israel has become slag to me. All of them are like bronze, tin, iron, and lead in the furnace; they are the worthless slag of silver. **22:19** Therefore this is what the sovereign LORD says: 'Because all of you have become slag, look out! – I am about to gather you in the middle of Jerusalem. **22:20** As silver, bronze, iron, lead, and tin are gathered in a furnace so that the fire can melt them, so I will gather you in my anger and in my rage. I will deposit you there and melt you. **22:21** I will gather you and blow on you with the fire of my fury, and you will be melted in it. **22:22** As silver is melted in a furnace, so you will be melted in it, and you will know that I, the LORD, have poured out my anger on you.'"
22:23 The word of the LORD came to me: **22:24** "Son of man, say to her: 'You are a land that receives no rain or showers in the day of my anger.' **22:25** Her princes within her are like a roaring lion tearing its prey; they have devoured lives. They take away riches and valuable things; they have made many women widows within it. **22:26** Her priests abuse my law and have desecrated my holy things. They do not distinguish between the holy and the profane, or recognize any distinction between the unclean and the clean. They ignore my Sabbaths and I am profaned in their midst. **22:27** Her officials are like wolves in her midst rending their prey – shedding blood and destroying lives – so they can get dishonest profit. **22:28** Her prophets coat their messages with whitewash. They see false visions and announce lying omens for them, saying, 'This is what the sovereign LORD says,' when the LORD has not spoken. **22:29** The people of the land have practiced extortion and committed robbery. They have wronged the poor and needy; they have oppressed the foreigner who lives among them and denied them justice.
22:30 "I looked for a man from among them who would repair the wall and stand in the gap before me on behalf of the land, so that I would not destroy it, but I found no one. **22:31** So I have poured my anger on them, and destroyed them with the fire of my fury. I hereby repay them for what they have done, declares the sovereign LORD."
Two Sisters
23:1 The word of the LORD came to me: **23:2** "Son of man, there were two women who were daughters of the same mother. **23:3** They engaged in prostitution in Egypt; in their youth they engaged in prostitution. Their breasts were squeezed there; lovers fondled their virgin nipples there. **23:4** Oholah was the name of the older and Oholibah the name of her younger sister. They became mine, and gave birth to sons and daughters. Oholah is Samaria and Oholibah is Jerusalem.
23:5 "Oholah engaged in prostitution while she was mine. She lusted after her lovers, the Assyrians – warriors **23:6** clothed in blue, governors and officials, all of them desirable young men, horsemen riding on horses. **23:7** She bestowed her sexual favors on them; all of them were the choicest young men of Assyria. She defiled herself with all whom she desired – with all their idols. **23:8** She did not abandon the prostitution she had practiced in Egypt; for in her youth men had sex with her, fondled her virgin breasts, and ravished her. **23:9** Therefore I handed her over to her lovers, the Assyrians for whom she lusted. **23:10** They exposed her nakedness, seized her sons and daughters, and killed her with

the sword. She became notorious among women, and they executed judgments against her.
23:11 "Her sister Oholibah watched this, but she became more corrupt in her lust than her sister had been, and her acts of prostitution were more numerous than those of her sister. **23:12** She lusted after the Assyrians – governors and officials, warriors in full armor, horsemen riding on horses, all of them desirable young men. **23:13** I saw that she was defiled; both of them followed the same path. **23:14** But she increased her prostitution. She saw men carved on the wall, images of the Chaldeans carved in bright red, **23:15** wearing belts on their waists and flowing turbans on their heads, all of them looking like officers, the image of Babylonians whose native land is Chaldea. **23:16** When she saw them, she lusted after them and sent messengers to them in Chaldea. **23:17** The Babylonians crawled into bed with her. They defiled her with their lust; after she was defiled by them, she became disgusted with them. **23:18** When she lustfully exposed her nakedness, I was disgusted with her, just as I had been disgusted with her sister. **23:19** Yet she increased her prostitution, remembering the days of her youth when she engaged in prostitution in the land of Egypt. **23:20** She lusted after their genitals – as large as those of donkeys, and their seminal emission was as strong as that of stallions. **23:21** This is how you assessed the obscene conduct of your youth, when the Egyptians fondled your nipples and squeezed your young breasts.
23:22 "Therefore, Oholibah, this is what the sovereign LORD says: Look here, I am about to stir up against you the lovers with whom you were disgusted; I will bring them against you from every side: **23:23** the Babylonians and all the Chaldeans, Pekod, Shoa, and Koa, and all the Assyrians with them, desirable young men, all of them governors and officials, officers and nobles, all of them riding on horses. **23:24** They will attack you with weapons, chariots, wagons, and with a huge army; they will array themselves against you on every side with large shields, small shields, and helmets. I will assign them the task of judgment; they will punish you according to their laws. **23:25** I will direct my jealous anger against you, and they will deal with you in rage. They will cut off your nose and your ears, and your survivors will die by the sword. They will seize your sons and daughters, and your survivors will be consumed by fire. **23:26** They will strip your clothes off you and take away your beautiful jewelry. **23:27** So I will put an end to your obscene conduct and your prostitution which you have practiced in the land of Egypt. You will not seek their help or remember Egypt anymore.
23:28 "For this is what the sovereign LORD says: Look here, I am about to deliver you over to those whom you hate, to those with whom you were disgusted. **23:29** They will treat you with hatred, take away all you have labored for, and leave you naked and bare. Your nakedness will be exposed, just as when you engaged in prostitution and obscene conduct. **23:30** I will do these things to you because you engaged in prostitution with the nations, polluting yourself with their idols. **23:31** You have followed the ways of your sister, so I will place her cup of judgment in your hand. **23:32** "This is what the sovereign LORD says: "You will drink your sister's deep and wide cup; you will be scorned and derided, for it holds a great deal. **23:33** You will be overcome by drunkenness and sorrow. The cup of your sister Samaria is a cup of horror and desolation. **23:34** You will drain it dry, gnaw its pieces, and tear out your breasts, for I have spoken, declares the sovereign LORD.
23:35 "Therefore this is what the sovereign LORD says: Because you have forgotten me and completely disregarded me, you must bear now the punishment for your obscene conduct and prostitution."
23:36 The LORD said to me: "Son of man, are you willing to pronounce judgment on Oholah and Oholibah? Then declare to them their abominable deeds! **23:37** For they have committed adultery and blood is on their hands. They have committed adultery with their idols, and their sons, whom they bore to me, they have passed through the fire as food to their idols. **23:38** Moreover, they have done this to me: In the very same day they desecrated my sanctuary and profaned my Sabbaths. **23:39** On the same day they slaughtered their sons for their idols, they came to my sanctuary to desecrate it. This is what they have done in the middle of my house.
23:40 "They even sent for men from far away; when the messenger arrived, those men set out. For them you bathed, painted your eyes, and decorated yourself with jewelry. **23:41** You sat on a magnificent couch, with a table arranged in front of it where you placed my incense and my olive oil. **23:42** The sound of a carefree crowd accompanied her, including all kinds of men; even Sabeans were brought from the desert. The sisters put bracelets on their wrists and beautiful crowns on their heads. **23:43** Then I said about the one worn out by adultery, 'Now they will commit immoral acts with her.' **23:44** They had sex with her as one does with a prostitute. In this way they had sex with Oholah and Oholibah, promiscuous women. **23:45** But upright men will punish them appropriately for their adultery and bloodshed, because they are adulteresses and blood is on their hands.
23:46 "For this is what the sovereign LORD says: Bring up an army against them and subject them to terror and plunder. **23:47** That army will pelt them with stones and slash them with their swords; they will kill their sons and daughters and burn their houses. **23:48** I will put an end to

the obscene conduct in the land; all the women will learn a lesson from this and not engage in obscene conduct. **23:49** They will repay you for your obscene conduct, and you will be punished for idol worship. Then you will know that I am the sovereign LORD."

The Boiling Pot

24:1 The word of the LORD came to me in the ninth year, in the tenth month, on the tenth day of the month: **24:2** "Son of man, write down the name of this day, this very day. The king of Babylon has laid siege to Jerusalem this very day. **24:3** Recite a proverb to this rebellious house and say to them, 'This is what the sovereign LORD says:

"'Set on the pot, set it on,
pour water in it too;
24:4 add the pieces of meat to it,
every good piece,
the thigh and the shoulder;
fill it with choice bones.
24:5 Take the choice bone of the flock,
heap up bones under it;
boil rapidly,
and boil its bones in it.

24:6 "'Therefore this is what the sovereign LORD says:
Woe to the city of bloodshed,
the pot whose rot is in it,
whose rot has not been removed from it!
Empty it piece by piece.
No lot has fallen on it.
24:7 For her blood was in it;
she poured it on an exposed rock;
she did not pour it on the ground to cover it up with dust.
24:8 To arouse anger, to take vengeance,
I have placed her blood on an exposed rock so that it cannot be covered up.

24:9 "'Therefore this is what the sovereign LORD says:
Woe to the city of bloodshed!
I will also make the pile high.
24:10 Pile up the bones, kindle the fire;
cook the meat well, mix in the spices,
let the bones be charred.
24:11 Set the empty pot on the coals,
until it becomes hot and its copper glows,
until its uncleanness melts within it and its rot is consumed.
24:12 It has tried my patience;
yet its thick rot is not removed from it.
Subject its rot to the fire!
24:13 You mix uncleanness with obscene conduct.
I tried to cleanse you, but you are not clean.
You will not be cleansed from your uncleanness
until I have exhausted my anger on you.
24:14 "'I the LORD have spoken; judgment is coming and I will act! I will not relent, or show pity, or be sorry! I will judge you according to your conduct and your deeds, declares the sovereign LORD.'"

Ezekiel's Wife Dies

24:15 The word of LORD came to me: **24:16** "Son of man, realize that I am about to take the delight of your eyes away from you with a jolt, but you must not mourn or weep or shed tears. **24:17** Groan in silence for the dead, but do not perform mourning rites. Bind on your turban and put your sandals on your feet. Do not cover your lip and do not eat food brought by others."

24:18 So I spoke to the people in the morning, and my wife died in the evening. In the morning I acted just as I was commanded. **24:19** Then the people said to me, "Will you not tell us what these things you are doing mean for us?"

24:20 So I said to them: "The word of the LORD came to me: **24:21** Say to the house of Israel, 'This is what the sovereign LORD says: Realize I am about to desecrate my sanctuary – the source of your confident pride, the object in which your eyes delight, and your life's passion. Your very own sons and daughters whom you have left behind will die by the sword. **24:22** Then you will do as I have done: You will not cover your lip or eat food brought by others. **24:23** Your turbans will be on your heads and your sandals on your feet; you will not mourn or weep, but you will rot for your iniquities and groan among yourselves. **24:24** Ezekiel will be an object lesson for you; you will do all that he has done. When it happens, then you will know that I am the sovereign LORD.'

24:25 "And you, son of man, this is what will happen on the day I take from them their stronghold – their beautiful source of joy, the object in which their eyes delight, and the main concern of their lives, as well as their sons and daughters: **24:26** On that day a fugitive will come to you to report the news. **24:27** On that day you will be able to speak again; you will talk with the fugitive and be silent no longer. You will be an object lesson for them, and they will know that I am the LORD."

A Prophecy Against Ammon

25:1 The word of the LORD came to me: **25:2** "Son of man, turn toward the Ammonites and prophesy against them. **25:3** Say to the Ammonites, 'Hear the word of the sovereign LORD: This is what the sovereign LORD says: You said "Aha!" about my sanctuary when it was desecrated, about the land of Israel when it was made desolate, and about the house of Judah when they went into exile. **25:4** So take note, I am about to make you slaves of the tribes of the east. They will make camps among you and pitch their tents among you. They will eat your fruit and drink your milk. **25:5** I will make Rabbah a pasture for camels and Ammon a resting place for sheep. Then you will know that I am the LORD. **25:6** For this is what the sovereign LORD says: Because you clapped your hands, stamped your feet, and rejoiced with intense scorn over the land of Israel, **25:7** take note, I have stretched out my hand against you, and I will hand you over as plunder to the nations. I will cut you off from the peoples and make you perish from the lands. I will destroy you; then you will know that I am the LORD.'"

A Prophecy Against Moab

25:8 "This is what the sovereign LORD says: 'Moab and Seir say, "Look, the house of Judah is like all the other nations." **25:9** So look, I am about to open up Moab's flank, eliminating the cities, including its frontier cities, the beauty of the land – Beth Jeshimoth, Baal Meon, and Kiriathaim. **25:10** I will hand it over, along with the Ammonites, to the tribes of the east, so that the Ammonites will no longer be remembered among the nations. **25:11** I will execute judgments against Moab. Then they will know that I am the LORD.'"

A Prophecy Against Edom

25:12 "This is what the sovereign LORD says: 'Edom has taken vengeance against the house of Judah; they have made themselves fully culpable by taking vengeance on them. **25:13** So this is what the sovereign LORD says: I will stretch out my hand against Edom, and I will kill the people and animals within her, and I will make her desolate; from Teman to Dedan they will die by the sword. **25:14** I will exact my vengeance upon Edom by the hand of my people Israel. They will carry out in Edom my anger and rage; they will experience my vengeance, declares the sovereign LORD.'"

A Prophecy Against Philistia

25:15 "This is what the sovereign LORD says: 'The Philistines have exacted merciless revenge, showing intense scorn in their effort to destroy Judah with unrelenting hostility. **25:16** So this is what the sovereign LORD says: Take note, I am about to stretch out my hand against the Philistines. I will kill the Cherethites and destroy those who remain on the seacoast. **25:17** I will exact great vengeance upon them with angry rebukes. Then they will know that I am the LORD, when I exact my vengeance upon them.'"

A Prophecy Against Tyre

26:1 In the eleventh year, on the first day of the month, the word of the LORD came to me: **26:2** "Son of man, because Tyre has said about Jerusalem, 'Aha, the gateway of the peoples is broken; it has swung open to me. I will become rich, now that she has been destroyed,' **26:3** therefore this is what the sovereign LORD says: Look, I am against you, O Tyre! I will bring up many nations against you, as the sea brings up its waves. **26:4** They will destroy the walls of Tyre and break down her towers. I will scrape her soil from her and make her a bare rock. **26:5** She will be a place where fishing nets are spread, surrounded by the sea. For I have spoken, declares the sovereign LORD. She will become plunder for the nations, **26:6** and her daughters who are in the field will be slaughtered by the sword. Then they will know that I am the LORD.

26:7 "For this is what the sovereign LORD says: Take note that I am about to bring King Nebuchadrezzar of Babylon, king of kings, against Tyre from the north, with horses, chariots, and horsemen, an army and hordes of people. **26:8** He will kill your daughters in the field with the sword. He will build a siege wall against you, erect a siege ramp against you, and raise a great shield against you. **26:9** He will direct the blows of his battering rams against your walls and tear down your towers with his weapons. **26:10** He will cover you with the dust kicked up by his many horses. Your walls will shake from the noise of the horsemen, wheels, and chariots when he enters your gates like those who invade through a city's broken walls. **26:11** With his horses' hoofs he will trample all your streets. He will kill your people with the sword, and your strong pillars will tumble down to the ground. **26:12** They will steal your wealth and loot your merchandise. They will tear down your walls and destroy your luxurious homes. Your stones, your trees, and your soil he will throw into the water. **26:13** I will silence the noise of your songs; the sound of your harps will be heard no more. **26:14** I will make you a bare rock; you will be a place where fishing nets are spread. You will never be built again, for I, the LORD, have spoken, declares the sovereign LORD.

26:15 "This is what the sovereign LORD says to Tyre: Oh, how the coastlands will shake at the sound of your fall, when the wounded groan, at the massive slaughter in your midst! **26:16** All the princes of the sea will vacate their thrones. They will remove their robes and strip off their embroidered clothes; they will clothe themselves with trembling. They will sit on the ground; they will tremble continually and be shocked at what has happened to you. **26:17** They will sing this lament over you:

"'How you have perished – you have vanished from the seas,
O renowned city, once mighty in the sea,
she and her inhabitants, who spread their terror!
26:18 Now the coastlands will tremble on the day of your fall;
the coastlands by the sea will be terrified by your passing.'
26:19 "For this is what the sovereign LORD says: When I make you desolate like the uninhabited cities, when I bring up the deep over you and the surging waters overwhelm you, **26:20** then I will bring you down to bygone people, to be with those who descend to the pit. I will make you live in the lower parts of the earth, among the primeval ruins, with those who descend to the pit, so that you will not be inhabited or stand in the land of the living. **26:21** I will bring terrors on you, and you will be no more! Though you are sought after, you will never be found again, declares the sovereign LORD."

A Lament for Tyre

27:1 The word of the LORD came to me: **27:2** "You, son of man, sing a lament for Tyre. **27:3** Say to Tyre, who sits at the entrance of the sea, merchant to the peoples on many coasts, 'This is what the sovereign LORD says:
"'O Tyre, you have said, "I am perfectly beautiful."
27:4 Your borders are in the heart of the seas;
your builders have perfected your beauty.
27:5 They crafted all your planks out of fir trees from Senir;
they took a cedar from Lebanon to make your mast.
27:6 They made your oars from oaks of Bashan;
they made your deck with cypresses from the Kittean isles.
27:7 Fine linen from Egypt, woven with patterns, was used for your sail
to serve as your banner;
blue and purple from the coastlands of Elishah was used for your deck's awning.
27:8 The leaders of Sidon and Arvad were your rowers;
your skilled men, O Tyre, were your captains.
27:9 The elders of Gebal and her skilled men were within you, mending cracks;
all the ships of the sea and their mariners were within you to trade for your merchandise.
27:10 Men of Persia, Lud, and Put were in your army, men of war.
They hung shield and helmet on you; they gave you your splendor.
27:11 The Arvadites joined your army on your walls all around,
and the Gammadites were in your towers.
They hung their quivers on your walls all around;
they perfected your beauty.
27:12 "'Tarshish was your trade partner because of your abundant wealth; they exchanged silver, iron, tin, and lead for your products. **27:13** Javan, Tubal, and Meshech were your clients; they exchanged slaves and bronze items for your merchandise. **27:14** Beth Togarmah exchanged horses, chargers, and mules for your products. **27:15** The Dedanites were your clients. Many coastlands were your customers; they paid you with ivory tusks and ebony. **27:16** Edom was your trade partner because of the abundance of your goods; they exchanged turquoise, purple, embroidered work, fine linen, coral, and rubies for your products. **27:17** Judah and the land of Israel were your clients; they traded wheat from Minnith, millet, honey, olive oil, and balm for your merchandise. **27:18** Damascus was your trade partner because of the abundance of your goods and of all your wealth: wine from Helbon, white wool from Zahar, **27:19** and casks of wine from Izal they exchanged for your products. Wrought iron, cassia, and sweet cane were among your merchandise. **27:20** Dedan was your client in saddlecloths for riding. **27:21** Arabia and all the princes of Kedar were your trade partners; for lambs, rams, and goats they traded with you. **27:22** The merchants of Sheba and Raamah engaged in trade with you; they traded the best kinds of spices along with precious stones and gold for your products. **27:23** Haran, Kanneh, Eden, merchants from Sheba, Asshur, and Kilmad were your clients. **27:24** They traded with you choice garments, purple clothes and embroidered work, and multicolored carpets, bound and reinforced with cords; these were among your merchandise. **27:25** The ships of Tarshish were the transports for your merchandise.
"'So you were filled and weighed down in the heart of the seas.
27:26 Your rowers have brought you into surging waters.
The east wind has wrecked you in the heart of the seas.
27:27 Your wealth, products, and merchandise, your sailors and captains,
your ship's carpenters, your merchants,
and all your fighting men within you,
along with all your crew who are in you,
will fall into the heart of the seas on the day of your downfall.
27:28 At the sound of your captains' cry the waves will surge;
27:29 They will descend from their ships – all who handle the oar,
the sailors and all the sea captains – they will stand on the land.
27:30 They will lament loudly over you and cry bitterly.
They will throw dust on their heads and roll in the ashes;
27:31 they will tear out their hair because of you and put on sackcloth,
and they will weep bitterly over you with intense mourning.
27:32 As they wail they will lament over you, chanting:

"Who was like Tyre, like a tower in the midst of the sea?"
27:33 When your products went out from the seas,
you satisfied many peoples;
with the abundance of your wealth and merchandise
you enriched the kings of the earth.
27:34 Now you are wrecked by the seas, in the depths of the waters;
your merchandise and all your company have sunk along with you.
27:35 All the inhabitants of the coastlands are shocked at you,
and their kings are horribly afraid – their faces are troubled.
27:36 The traders among the peoples hiss at you;
you have become a horror, and will be no more.'"

A Prophecy Against the King of Tyre

28:1 The word of the LORD came to me: **28:2** "Son of man, say to the prince of Tyre, 'This is what the sovereign LORD says:
"'Your heart is proud and you said, "I am a god;
I sit in the seat of gods, in the heart of the seas" –
yet you are a man and not a god,
though you think you are godlike.
28:3 Look, you are wiser than Daniel;
no secret is hidden from you.
28:4 By your wisdom and understanding you have gained wealth for yourself;
you have amassed gold and silver in your treasuries.
28:5 By your great skill in trade you have increased your wealth,
and your heart is proud because of your wealth.

28:6 "'Therefore this is what the sovereign LORD says:
Because you think you are godlike,
28:7 I am about to bring foreigners against you, the most terrifying of nations.
They will draw their swords against the grandeur made by your wisdom,
and they will defile your splendor.
28:8 They will bring you down to the pit, and you will die violently in the heart of the seas.
28:9 Will you still say, "I am a god," before the one who kills you –
though you are a man and not a god –
when you are in the power of those who wound you?
28:10 You will die the death of the uncircumcised by the hand of foreigners;
for I have spoken, declares the sovereign LORD.'"

28:11 The word of the LORD came to me: **28:12** "Son of man, sing a lament for the king of Tyre, and say to him, 'This is what the sovereign LORD says:
"'You were the sealer of perfection,
full of wisdom, and perfect in beauty.
28:13 You were in Eden, the garden of God.
Every precious stone was your covering,
the ruby, topaz, and emerald,
the chrysolite, onyx, and jasper,
the sapphire, turquoise, and beryl;
your settings and mounts were made of gold.
On the day you were created they were prepared.
28:14 I placed you there with an anointed guardian cherub;
you were on the holy mountain of God;
you walked about amidst fiery stones.
28:15 You were blameless in your behavior from the day you were created,
until sin was discovered in you.
28:16 In the abundance of your trade you were filled with violence, and you sinned;
so I defiled you and banished you from the mountain of God –
the guardian cherub expelled you from the midst of the stones of fire.
28:17 Your heart was proud because of your beauty;
you corrupted your wisdom on account of your splendor.
I threw you down to the ground;
I placed you before kings, that they might see you.
28:18 By the multitude of your iniquities, through the sinfulness of your trade,
you desecrated your sanctuaries.
So I drew fire out from within you;
it consumed you,
and I turned you to ashes on the earth
before the eyes of all who saw you.
28:19 All who know you among the peoples are shocked at you;
you have become terrified and will be no more.'"

A Prophecy Against Sidon

28:20 The word of the LORD came to me: **28:21** "Son of man, turn toward Sidon and prophesy against it. **28:22** Say, 'This is what the sovereign LORD says:
"'Look, I am against you, Sidon,
and I will magnify myself in your midst.
Then they will know that I am the LORD

when I execute judgments on her
and reveal my sovereign power in her.
28:23 I will send a plague into the city and bloodshed into its streets;
the slain will fall within it, by the sword that attacks it from every side.
Then they will know that I am the LORD.

28:24 "'No longer will Israel suffer from the sharp briers or painful thorns of all who surround and scorn them. Then they will know that I am the sovereign LORD.
28:25 "'This is what the sovereign LORD says: When I regather the house of Israel from the peoples where they are dispersed, I will reveal my sovereign power over them in the sight of the nations, and they will live in their land that I gave to my servant Jacob. **28:26** They will live securely in it; they will build houses and plant vineyards. They will live securely when I execute my judgments on all those who scorn them and surround them. Then they will know that I am the LORD their God.'"

A Prophecy Against Egypt
29:1 In the tenth year, in the tenth month, on the twelfth day of the month, the word of the LORD came to me: **29:2** "Son of man, turn toward Pharaoh king of Egypt, and prophesy against him and against all Egypt.
29:3 Tell them, 'This is what the sovereign LORD says:
"'Look, I am against you, Pharaoh king of Egypt,
the great monster lying in the midst of its waterways,
who has said, "My Nile is my own, I made it for myself."
29:4 I will put hooks in your jaws
and stick the fish of your waterways to your scales.
I will haul you up from the midst of your waterways,
and all the fish of your waterways will stick to your scales.
29:5 I will leave you in the wilderness,
you and all the fish of your waterways;
you will fall in the open field and will not be gathered up or collected.
I have given you as food to the beasts of the earth and the birds of the skies.
29:6 Then all those living in Egypt will know that I am the LORD
because they were a reed staff for the house of Israel;
29:7 when they grasped you with their hand, you broke and tore their shoulders,
and when they leaned on you, you splintered and caused their legs to be unsteady.
29:8 "'Therefore, this is what the sovereign LORD says: Look, I am about to bring a sword against you, and I will kill every person and every animal. **29:9** The land of Egypt will become a desolate ruin. Then they will know that I am the LORD.
Because he said, "The Nile is mine and I made it," **29:10** I am against you and your waterways. I will turn the land of Egypt into an utter desolate ruin from Migdol to Syene, as far as the border with Ethiopia. **29:11** No human foot will pass through it, and no animal's foot will pass through it; it will be uninhabited for forty years. **29:12** I will turn the land of Egypt into a desolation in the midst of desolate lands; for forty years her cities will lie desolate in the midst of ruined cities. I will scatter Egypt among the nations and disperse them among foreign countries.
29:13 "'For this is what the sovereign LORD says: At the end of forty years I will gather Egypt from the peoples where they were scattered. **29:14** I will restore the fortunes of Egypt, and will bring them back to the land of Pathros, to the land of their origin; there they will be an insignificant kingdom. **29:15** It will be the most insignificant of the kingdoms; it will never again exalt itself over the nations. I will make them so small that they will not rule over the nations. **29:16** It will never again be Israel's source of confidence, but a reminder of how they sinned by turning to Egypt for help. Then they will know that I am the sovereign LORD.'"
29:17 In the twenty-seventh year, in the first month, on the first day of the month, the word of the LORD came to me: **29:18** "Son of man, King Nebuchadrezzar of Babylon made his army labor hard against Tyre. Every head was rubbed bald and every shoulder rubbed bare; yet he and his army received no wages from Tyre for the work he carried out against it. **29:19** Therefore this is what the sovereign LORD says: Look, I am about to give the land of Egypt to King Nebuchadrezzar of Babylon. He will carry off her wealth, capture her loot, and seize her plunder; it will be his army's wages. **29:20** I have given him the land of Egypt as his compensation for attacking Tyre, because they did it for me, declares the sovereign LORD. **29:21** On that day I will make Israel powerful, and I will give you the right to be heard among them. Then they will know that I am the LORD."

A Lament Over Egypt
30:1 The word of the LORD came to me: **30:2** "Son of man, prophesy and say, 'This is what the sovereign LORD says:
"'Wail, "Alas, the day is here!"
30:3 For the day is near,
the day of the LORD is near;
it will be a day of storm clouds,
it will be a time of judgment for the nations.
30:4 A sword will come against Egypt
and panic will overtake Ethiopia

when the slain fall in Egypt
and they carry away her wealth
and dismantle her foundations.
30:5 Ethiopia, Put, Lud, all the foreigners, Libya, and the people of the covenant land will die by the sword along with them.
30:6 "'This is what the LORD says:
Egypt's supporters will fall;
her confident pride will crumble.
From Migdol to Syene they will die by the sword within her,
declares the sovereign LORD.
30:7 They will be desolate among desolate lands,
and their cities will be among ruined cities.
30:8 They will know that I am the LORD
when I ignite a fire in Egypt
and all her allies are defeated.
30:9 On that day messengers will go out from me in ships to frighten overly confident Ethiopia; panic will overtake them on the day of Egypt's doom; for beware – it is coming!
30:10 "'This is what the sovereign LORD says:
I will put an end to the hordes of Egypt,
by the hand of King Nebuchadrezzar of Babylon.
30:11 He and his people with him,
the most terrifying of the nations,
will be brought there to destroy the land.
They will draw their swords against Egypt,
and fill the land with corpses.
30:12 I will dry up the waterways
and hand the land over to evil men.
I will make the land and everything in it desolate by the hand of foreigners.
I, the LORD, have spoken!
30:13 "'This is what the sovereign LORD says:
I will destroy the idols,
and put an end to the gods of Memphis.
There will no longer be a prince from the land of Egypt;
so I will make the land of Egypt fearful.
30:14 I will desolate Pathros,
I will ignite a fire in Zoan,
and I will execute judgments on Thebes.
30:15 I will pour out my anger upon Pelusium,
the stronghold of Egypt;
I will cut off the hordes of Thebes.
30:16 I will ignite a fire in Egypt;
Syene will writhe in agony,
Thebes will be broken down,
and Memphis will face enemies every day.
30:17 The young men of On and of Pi-beseth will die by the sword;
and the cities will go into captivity.
30:18 In Tahpanhes the day will be dark
when I break the yoke of Egypt there.
Her confident pride will cease within her;
a cloud will cover her, and her daughters will go into captivity.
30:19 I will execute judgments on Egypt.
Then they will know that I am the LORD.'"

30:20 In the eleventh year, in the first month, on the seventh day of the month, the word of the LORD came to me: **30:21** "Son of man, I have broken the arm of Pharaoh king of Egypt. Look, it has not been bandaged for healing or set with a dressing so that it might become strong enough to grasp a sword. **30:22** Therefore this is what the sovereign LORD says: Look, I am against Pharaoh king of Egypt, and I will break his arms, the strong arm and the broken one, and I will make the sword drop from his hand. **30:23** I will scatter the Egyptians among the nations, and disperse them among foreign countries. **30:24** I will strengthen the arms of the king of Babylon, and I will place my sword in his hand, but I will break the arms of Pharaoh, and he will groan like the fatally wounded before the king of Babylon. **30:25** I will strengthen the arms of the king of Babylon, but the arms of Pharaoh will fall limp. Then they will know that I am the LORD when I place my sword in the hand of the king of Babylon and he extends it against the land of Egypt. **30:26** I will scatter the Egyptians among the nations and disperse them among foreign countries. Then they will know that I am the LORD."

A Cedar in Lebanon
31:1 In the eleventh year, in the third month, on the first day of the month, the word of the LORD came to me: **31:2** "Son of man, say to Pharaoh king of Egypt and his hordes:
"'Who are you like in your greatness?
31:3 Consider Assyria, a cedar in Lebanon,
with beautiful branches, like a forest giving shade,
and extremely tall;
its top reached into the clouds.
31:4 The water made it grow;
underground springs made it grow tall.

Rivers flowed all around the place it was planted,
while smaller channels watered all the trees of the field.
31:5 Therefore it grew taller than all the trees of the field;
its boughs grew large and its branches grew long,
because of the plentiful water in its shoots.
31:6 All the birds of the sky nested in its boughs;
under its branches all the beasts of the field gave birth,
in its shade all the great nations lived.
31:7 It was beautiful in its loftiness, in the length of its branches;
for its roots went down deep to plentiful waters.
31:8 The cedars in the garden of God could not eclipse it,
nor could the fir trees match its boughs;
the plane trees were as nothing compared to its branches;
no tree in the garden of God could rival its beauty.
31:9 I made it beautiful with its many branches;
all the trees of Eden, in the garden of God, envied it.

31:10 "'Therefore this is what the sovereign LORD says: Because it was tall in stature, and its top reached into the clouds, and it was proud of its height, **31:11** I gave it over to the leader of the nations. He has judged it thoroughly, as its sinfulness deserves. I have thrown it out. **31:12** Foreigners from the most terrifying nations have cut it down and left it to lie there on the mountains. In all the valleys its branches have fallen, and its boughs lie broken in the ravines of the land. All the peoples of the land have departed from its shade and left it. **31:13** On its ruins all the birds of the sky will live, and all the wild animals will walk on its branches. **31:14** For this reason no watered trees will grow so tall; their tops will not reach into the clouds, nor will the well-watered ones grow that high. For all of them have been appointed to die in the lower parts of the earth; they will be among mere mortals, with those who descend to the pit.
31:15 "'This is what the sovereign LORD says: On the day it went down to Sheol I caused observers to lament. I covered it with the deep and held back its rivers; its plentiful water was restrained. I clothed Lebanon in black for it, and all the trees of the field wilted because of it. **31:16** I made the nations shake at the sound of its fall, when I threw it down to Sheol, along with those who descend to the pit. Then all the trees of Eden, the choicest and the best of Lebanon, all that were well-watered, were comforted in the earth below. **31:17** Those who lived in its shade, its allies among the nations, also went down with it to Sheol, to those killed by the sword. **31:18** Which of the trees of Eden was like you in majesty and loftiness? You will be brought down with the trees of Eden to the lower parts of the earth; you will lie among the uncircumcised, with those killed by the sword! This is what will happen to Pharaoh and all his hordes, declares the sovereign LORD.'"

Lamentation over Pharaoh and Egypt

32:1 In the twelfth year, in the twelfth month, on the first of the month, the word of the LORD came to me: **32:2** "Son of man, sing a lament for Pharaoh king of Egypt, and say to him:
"'You were like a lion among the nations,
but you are a monster in the seas;
you thrash about in your streams,
stir up the water with your feet,
and muddy your streams.

32:3 "'This is what the sovereign LORD says:
"'I will throw my net over you in the assembly of many peoples;
and they will haul you up in my dragnet.
32:4 I will leave you on the ground,
I will fling you on the open field,
I will allow all the birds of the sky to settle on you,
and I will permit all the wild animals to gorge themselves on you.
32:5 I will put your flesh on the mountains,
and fill the valleys with your maggot-infested carcass.
32:6 I will drench the land with the flow
of your blood up to the mountains,
and the ravines will be full of your blood.
32:7 When I extinguish you, I will cover the sky;
I will darken its stars.
I will cover the sun with a cloud,
and the moon will not shine.
32:8 I will darken all the lights in the sky over you,
and I will darken your land,
declares the sovereign LORD.
32:9 I will disturb many peoples,
when I bring about your destruction among the nations,
among countries you do not know.
32:10 I will shock many peoples with you,
and their kings will shiver with horror because of you.
When I brandish my sword before them,
every moment each one will tremble for his life, on the day of your fall.

32:11 "'For this is what the sovereign LORD says:
"'The sword of the king of Babylon will attack you.

32:12 By the swords of the mighty warriors I will cause your hordes to fall –
all of them are the most terrifying among the nations.
They will devastate the pride of Egypt,
and all its hordes will be destroyed.
32:13 I will destroy all its cattle beside the plentiful waters;
and no human foot will disturb the waters again,
nor will the hooves of cattle disturb them.
32:14 Then I will make their waters calm,
and will make their streams flow like olive oil, declares the sovereign LORD.
32:15 When I turn the land of Egypt into desolation
and the land is destitute of everything that fills it,
when I strike all those who live in it,
then they will know that I am the LORD.'
32:16 This is a lament; they will chant it.
The daughters of the nations will chant it.
They will chant it over Egypt and over all her hordes,
declares the sovereign LORD."

32:17 In the twelfth year, on the fifteenth day of the month, the word of the LORD came to me: **32:18** "Son of man, wail over the horde of Egypt. Bring it down; bring her and the daughters of powerful nations down to the lower parts of the earth, along with those who descend to the pit. **32:19** Say to them, 'Whom do you surpass in beauty? Go down and be laid to rest with the uncircumcised!' **32:20** They will fall among those killed by the sword. The sword is drawn; they carry her and all her hordes away. **32:21** The bravest of the warriors will speak to him from the midst of Sheol along with his allies, saying: 'The uncircumcised have come down; they lie still, killed by the sword.'
32:22 "Assyria is there with all her assembly around her grave, all of them struck down by the sword. **32:23** Their graves are located in the remote slopes of the pit. Her assembly is around her grave, all of them struck down by the sword, those who spread terror in the land of the living.
32:24 "Elam is there with all her hordes around her grave; all of them struck down by the sword. They went down uncircumcised to the lower parts of the earth, those who spread terror in the land of the living. Now they will bear their shame with those who descend to the pit. **32:25** Among the dead they have made a bed for her, along with all her hordes around her grave. All of them are uncircumcised, killed by the sword, for their terror had spread in the land of the living. They bear their shame along with those who descend to the pit; they are placed among the dead.
32:26 "Meshech-Tubal is there, along with all her hordes around her grave. All of them are uncircumcised, killed by the sword, for they spread their terror in the land of the living. **32:27** They do not lie with the fallen warriors of ancient times, who went down to Sheol with their weapons of war, having their swords placed under their heads and their shields on their bones, when the terror of these warriors was in the land of the living.
32:28 "But as for you, in the midst of the uncircumcised you will be broken, and you will lie with those killed by the sword.
32:29 "Edom is there with her kings and all her princes. Despite their might they are laid with those killed by the sword; they lie with the uncircumcised and those who descend to the pit.
32:30 "All the leaders of the north are there, along with all the Sidonians; despite their might they have gone down in shameful terror with the dead. They lie uncircumcised with those killed by the sword, and bear their shame with those who descend to the pit.
32:31 "Pharaoh will see them and be consoled over all his hordes who were killed by the sword, Pharaoh and all his army, declares the sovereign LORD. **32:32** Indeed, I terrified him in the land of the living, yet he will lie in the midst of the uncircumcised with those killed by the sword, Pharaoh and all his hordes, declares the sovereign LORD."

Ezekiel Israel's Watchman

33:1 The word of the LORD came to me: **33:2** "Son of man, speak to your people, and say to them, 'Suppose I bring a sword against the land, and the people of the land take one man from their borders and make him their watchman. **33:3** He sees the sword coming against the land, blows the trumpet, and warns the people, **33:4** but there is one who hears the sound of the trumpet yet does not heed the warning. Then the sword comes and sweeps him away. He will be responsible for his own death. **33:5** He heard the sound of the trumpet but did not heed the warning, so he is responsible for himself. If he had heeded the warning, he would have saved his life. **33:6** But suppose the watchman sees the sword coming and does not blow the trumpet to warn the people. Then the sword comes and takes one of their lives. He is swept away for his iniquity, but I will hold the watchman accountable for that person's death.'
33:7 "As for you, son of man, I have made you a watchman for the house of Israel. Whenever you hear a word from my mouth, you must warn them on my behalf. **33:8** When I say to the wicked, 'O wicked man, you must certainly die,' and you do not warn the wicked about his behavior, the wicked man will die for his iniquity, but I will hold you accountable

for his death. **33:9** But if you warn the wicked man to change his behavior, and he refuses to change, he will die for his iniquity, but you have saved your own life.

33:10 "And you, son of man, say to the house of Israel, 'This is what you have said: "Our rebellious acts and our sins have caught up with us, and we are wasting away because of them. How then can we live?"' **33:11** Say to them, 'As surely as I live, declares the sovereign LORD, I take no pleasure in the death of the wicked, but prefer that the wicked change his behavior and live. Turn back, turn back from your evil deeds! Why should you die, O house of Israel?'

33:12 "And you, son of man, say to your people, 'The righteousness of the righteous will not deliver him if he rebels. As for the wicked, his wickedness will not make him stumble if he turns from it. The righteous will not be able to live by his righteousness if he sins.' **33:13** Suppose I tell the righteous that he will certainly live, but he becomes confident in his righteousness and commits iniquity. None of his righteous deeds will be remembered; because of the iniquity he has committed he will die. **33:14** Suppose I say to the wicked, 'You must certainly die,' but he turns from his sin and does what is just and right. **33:15** He returns what was taken in pledge, pays back what he has stolen, and follows the statutes that give life, committing no iniquity. He will certainly live – he will not die. **33:16** None of the sins he has committed will be counted against him. He has done what is just and right; he will certainly live.

33:17 "Yet your people say, 'The behavior of the Lord is not right,' when it is their behavior that is not right. **33:18** When a righteous man turns from his godliness and commits iniquity, he will die for it. **33:19** When the wicked turns from his sin and does what is just and right, he will live because of it. **33:20** Yet you say, 'The behavior of the Lord is not right.' House of Israel, I will judge each of you according to his behavior."

The Fall of Jerusalem

33:21 In the twelfth year of our exile, in the tenth month, on the fifth of the month, a refugee came to me from Jerusalem saying, "The city has been defeated!" **33:22** Now the hand of the LORD had been on me the evening before the refugee reached me, but the LORD opened my mouth by the time the refugee arrived in the morning; he opened my mouth and I was no longer unable to speak. **33:23** The word of the LORD came to me: **33:24** "Son of man, the ones living in these ruins in the land of Israel are saying, 'Abraham was only one man, yet he possessed the land, but we are many; surely the land has been given to us for a possession.' **33:25** Therefore say to them, 'This is what the sovereign LORD says: You eat the meat with the blood still in it, pray to your idols, and shed blood. Do you really think you will possess the land? **33:26** You rely on your swords and commit abominable deeds; each of you defiles his neighbor's wife. Will you possess the land?'

33:27 "This is what you must say to them, 'This is what the sovereign LORD says: As surely as I live, those living in the ruins will die by the sword, those in the open field I will give to the wild beasts for food, and those who are in the strongholds and caves will die of disease. **33:28** I will turn the land into a desolate ruin; her confident pride will come to an end. The mountains of Israel will be so desolate no one will pass through them. **33:29** Then they will know that I am the LORD when I turn the land into a desolate ruin because of all the abominable deeds they have committed.'

33:30 "But as for you, son of man, your people (who are talking about you by the walls and at the doors of the houses) say to one another, 'Come hear the word that comes from the LORD.' **33:31** They come to you in crowds, and they sit in front of you as my people. They hear your words, but do not obey them. For they talk lustfully, and their heart is set on their own advantage. **33:32** Realize that to them you are like a sensual song, a beautiful voice and skilled musician. They hear your words, but they do not obey them. **33:33** When all this comes true – and it certainly will – then they will know that a prophet was among them."

A Prophecy Against False Shepherds

34:1 The word of the LORD came to me: **34:2** "Son of man, prophesy against the shepherds of Israel; prophesy, and say to them – to the shepherds: 'This is what the sovereign LORD says: Woe to the shepherds of Israel who have been feeding themselves! Should not shepherds feed the flock? **34:3** You eat the fat, you clothe yourselves with the wool, you slaughter the choice animals, but you do not feed the sheep! **34:4** You have not strengthened the weak, healed the sick, bandaged the injured, brought back the strays, or sought the lost, but with force and harshness you have ruled over them. **34:5** They were scattered because they had no shepherd, and they became food for every wild beast. **34:6** My sheep wandered over all the mountains and on every high hill. My sheep were scattered over the entire face of the earth with no one looking or searching for them.

34:7 "'Therefore, you shepherds, hear the word of the LORD: **34:8** As surely as I live, declares the sovereign LORD, my sheep have become prey and have become food for all the wild beasts. There was no shepherd, and my shepherds did not search for my flock, but fed themselves and did not feed my sheep, **34:9** Therefore, you shepherds, hear the word of the LORD: **34:10** This is what the sovereign LORD says: Look, I am against the shepherds, and I will demand my sheep from their hand. I will

no longer let them be shepherds; the shepherds will not feed themselves anymore. I will rescue my sheep from their mouth, so that they will no longer be food for them.

34:11 "'For this is what the sovereign LORD says: Look, I myself will search for my sheep and seek them out. **34:12** As a shepherd seeks out his flock when he is among his scattered sheep, so I will seek out my flock. I will rescue them from all the places where they have been scattered on a cloudy, dark day. **34:13** I will bring them out from among the peoples and gather them from foreign countries; I will bring them to their own land. I will feed them on the mountains of Israel, by the streams and all the inhabited places of the land. **34:14** In a good pasture I will feed them; the mountain heights of Israel will be their pasture. There they will lie down in a lush pasture, and they will feed on rich grass on the mountains of Israel. **34:15** I myself will feed my sheep and I myself will make them lie down, declares the sovereign LORD. **34:16** I will seek the lost and bring back the strays; I will bandage the injured and strengthen the sick, but the fat and the strong I will destroy. I will feed them – with judgment!

34:17 "'As for you, my sheep, this is what the sovereign LORD says: Look, I am about to judge between one sheep and another, between rams and goats. **34:18** Is it not enough for you to feed on the good pasture, that you must trample the rest of your pastures with your feet? When you drink clean water, must you muddy the rest of the water by trampling it with your feet? **34:19** As for my sheep, they must eat what you trampled with your feet, and drink what you have muddied with your feet!

34:20 "'Therefore, this is what the sovereign LORD says to them: Look, I myself will judge between the fat sheep and the lean sheep. **34:21** Because you push with your side and your shoulder, and thrust your horns at all the weak sheep until you scatter them abroad, **34:22** I will save my sheep; they will no longer be prey. I will judge between one sheep and another.

34:23 I will set one shepherd over them, and he will feed them – namely, my servant David. He will feed them and will be their shepherd. **34:24** I, the LORD, will be their God, and my servant David will be prince among them; I, the LORD, have spoken!

34:25 "'I will make a covenant of peace with them and will rid the land of wild beasts, so that they can live securely in the wilderness and even sleep in the woods. **34:26** I will turn them and the regions around my hill into a blessing. I will make showers come down in their season; they will be showers that bring blessing. **34:27** The trees of the field will yield their fruit and the earth will yield its crops. They will live securely on their land; they will know that I am the LORD, when I break the bars of their yoke and rescue them from the hand of those who enslaved them. **34:28** They will no longer be prey for the nations and the wild beasts will not devour them. They will live securely and no one will make them afraid. **34:29** I will prepare for them a healthy planting. They will no longer be victims of famine in the land and will no longer bear the insults of the nations. **34:30** Then they will know that I, the LORD their God, am with them, and that they are my people, the house of Israel, declares the sovereign LORD. **34:31** And you, my sheep, the sheep of my pasture, are my people, and I am your God, declares the sovereign LORD.'"

Prophecy Against Mount Seir

35:1 The word of the LORD came to me: **35:2** "Son of man, turn toward Mount Seir, and prophesy against it. **35:3** Say to it, 'This is what the sovereign LORD says:

"'Look, I am against you, Mount Seir;
I will stretch out my hand against you
and turn you into a desolate ruin.
35:4 I will lay waste your cities;
and you will become desolate.
Then you will know that I am the LORD!

35:5 "'You have shown unrelenting hostility and poured the people of Israel onto the blades of a sword at the time of their calamity, at the time of their final punishment. **35:6** Therefore, as surely as I live, declares the sovereign LORD, I will subject you to bloodshed, and bloodshed will pursue you. Since you did not hate bloodshed, bloodshed will pursue you. **35:7** I will turn Mount Seir into a desolate ruin; I will cut off from it the one who passes through or returns. **35:8** I will fill its mountains with its dead; on your hills and in your valleys and in all your ravines, those killed by the sword will fall. **35:9** I will turn you into a perpetual desolation, and your cities will not be inhabited. Then you will know that I am the LORD.

35:10 "'You said, "These two nations, these two lands will be mine, and we will possess them," – although the LORD was there – **35:11** therefore, as surely as I live, declares the sovereign LORD, I will deal with you according to your anger, and according to your envy, by which you acted spitefully against them. I will reveal myself to them when I judge you. **35:12** Then you will know that I, the LORD, have heard all the insults you spoke against the mountains of Israel, saying, "They are desolate, they have been given to us for food." **35:13** You exalted yourselves against me with your speech and hurled many insults against me – I have heard them all! **35:14** This is what the sovereign LORD says: While the whole earth rejoices, I will turn you into a desolation. **35:15** As you rejoiced over the inheritance of the house of Israel because it was desolate, so will I deal with you – you will be desolate, Mount Seir, and all of Edom – all of it! Then they will know that I am the LORD.'"

Blessings on the Mountains of Israel

36:1 "As for you, son of man, prophesy to the mountains of Israel, and say: 'O mountains of Israel, hear the word of the LORD! **36:2** This is what the sovereign LORD says: The enemy has spoken against you, saying "Aha!" and, "The ancient heights have become our property!"' **36:3** So prophesy and say: 'This is what the sovereign LORD says: Surely because they have made you desolate and crushed you from all directions, so that you have become the property of the rest of the nations, and have become the subject of gossip and slander among the people, **36:4** therefore, O mountains of Israel, hear the word of the sovereign LORD: This is what the sovereign LORD says to the mountains and hills, the ravines and valleys, and to the desolate ruins and the abandoned cities that have become prey and an object of derision to the rest of the nations round about – **36:5** therefore this is what the sovereign LORD says: Surely I have spoken in the fire of my zeal against the rest of the nations, and against all Edom, who with great joy and utter contempt have made my land their property and prey, because of its pasture.'

36:6 "Therefore prophesy concerning the land of Israel, and say to the mountains and hills, the ravines and valleys, 'This is what the sovereign LORD says: Look, I have spoken in my zeal and in my anger, because you have endured the insults of the nations. **36:7** So this is what the sovereign LORD says: I vow that the nations around you will endure insults as well. **36:8** 'But you, mountains of Israel, will grow your branches, and bear your fruit for my people Israel; for they will arrive soon. **36:9** For indeed, I am on your side; I will turn to you, and you will be plowed and planted. **36:10** I will multiply your people – the whole house of Israel, all of it. The cities will be populated and the ruins rebuilt. **36:11** I will increase the number of people and animals on you; they will increase and be fruitful. I will cause you to be inhabited as in ancient times, and will do more good for you than at the beginning of your history. Then you will know that I am the LORD. **36:12** I will lead people, my people Israel, across you; they will possess you and you will become their inheritance. No longer will you bereave them of their children.

36:13 "'This is what the sovereign LORD says: Because they are saying to you, "You are a devourer of men, and bereave your nation of children," **36:14** therefore you will no longer devour people and no longer bereave your nation of children, declares the sovereign LORD. **36:15** I will no longer subject you to the nations' insults; no longer will you bear the shame of the peoples, and no longer will you bereave your nation, declares the sovereign LORD.'"

36:16 The word of the LORD came to me: **36:17** "Son of man, when the house of Israel was living on their own land, they defiled it by their behavior and their deeds. In my sight their behavior was like the uncleanness of a woman having her monthly period. **36:18** So I poured my anger on them because of the blood they shed on the land and because of the idols with which they defiled it. **36:19** I scattered them among the nations; they were dispersed throughout foreign countries. In accordance with their behavior and their deeds I judged them. **36:20** But when they arrived in the nations where they went, they profaned my holy name. It was said of them, 'These are the people of the LORD, yet they have departed from his land.' **36:21** I was concerned for my holy reputation which the house of Israel profaned among the nations where they went.

36:22 "Therefore say to the house of Israel, 'This is what the sovereign LORD says: It is not for your sake that I am about to act, O house of Israel, but for the sake of my holy reputation which you profaned among the nations where you went. **36:23** I will magnify my great name that has been profaned among the nations, that you have profaned among them. The nations will know that I am the LORD, declares the sovereign LORD, when I magnify myself among you in their sight.

36:24 "'I will take you from the nations and gather you from all the countries; then I will bring you to your land. **36:25** I will sprinkle you with pure water and you will be clean from all your impurities. I will purify you from all your idols. **36:26** I will give you a new heart, and I will put a new spirit within you. I will remove the heart of stone from your body and give you a heart of flesh. **36:27** I will put my Spirit within you; I will take the initiative and you will obey my statutes and carefully observe my regulations. **36:28** Then you will live in the land I gave to your fathers; you will be my people, and I will be your God. **36:29** I will save you from all your uncleanness. I will call for the grain and multiply it; I will not bring a famine on you. **36:30** I will multiply the fruit of the trees and the produce of the fields, so that you will never again suffer the disgrace of famine among the nations. **36:31** Then you will remember your evil behavior and your deeds which were not good; you will loathe yourselves on account of your sins and your abominable deeds. **36:32** Understand that it is not for your sake I am about to act, declares the sovereign LORD. Be ashamed and embarrassed by your behavior, O house of Israel.

36:33 "'This is what the sovereign LORD says: In the day I cleanse you from all your sins, I will populate the cities and the ruins will be rebuilt. **36:34** The desolate land will be plowed, instead of being desolate in the sight of everyone who passes by. **36:35** They will say, "This desolate land

has become like the garden of Eden; the ruined, desolate, and destroyed cities are now fortified and inhabited." **36:36** Then the nations which remain around you will know that I, the LORD, have rebuilt the ruins and replanted what was desolate. I, the LORD, have spoken – and I will do it!' **36:37** "This is what the sovereign LORD says: I will allow the house of Israel to ask me to do this for them: I will multiply their people like sheep. **36:38** Like the sheep for offerings, like the sheep of Jerusalem during her appointed feasts, so will the ruined cities be filled with flocks of people. Then they will know that I am the LORD."

The Valley of Dry Bones

37:1 The hand of the LORD was on me, and he brought me out by the Spirit of the LORD and placed me in the midst of the valley, and it was full of bones. **37:2** He made me walk all around among them. I realized there were a great many bones in the valley and they were very dry. **37:3** He said to me, "Son of man, can these bones live?" I said to him, "Sovereign Lord, you know." **37:4** Then he said to me, "Prophesy over these bones, and tell them: 'Dry bones, hear the word of the LORD. **37:5** This is what the sovereign LORD says to these bones: Look, I am about to infuse breath into you and you will live. **37:6** I will put tendons on you and muscles over you and will cover you with skin; I will put breath in you and you will live. Then you will know that I am the LORD.'"

37:7 So I prophesied as I was commanded. There was a sound when I prophesied – I heard a rattling, and the bones came together, bone to bone. **37:8** As I watched, I saw tendons on them, then muscles appeared, and skin covered over them from above, but there was no breath in them. **37:9** He said to me, "Prophesy to the breath, – prophesy, son of man – and say to the breath: 'This is what the sovereign LORD says: Come from the four winds, O breath, and breathe on these corpses so that they may live.'" **37:10** So I prophesied as I was commanded, and the breath came into them; they lived and stood on their feet, an extremely great army.

37:11 Then he said to me, "Son of man, these bones are all the house of Israel. Look, they are saying, 'Our bones are dry, our hope has perished; we are cut off.' **37:12** Therefore prophesy, and tell them, 'This is what the sovereign LORD says: Look, I am about to open your graves and will raise you from your graves, my people. I will bring you to the land of Israel. **37:13** Then you will know that I am the LORD, when I open your graves and raise you from your graves, my people. **37:14** I will place my breath in you and you will live; I will give you rest in your own land. Then you will know that I am the LORD – I have spoken and I will act, declares the LORD.'"

37:15 The word of the LORD came to me: **37:16** "As for you, son of man, take one branch, and write on it, 'For Judah, and for the Israelites associated with him.' Then take another branch and write on it, 'For Joseph, the branch of Ephraim and all the house of Israel associated with him.' **37:17** Join them as one stick; they will be as one in your hand. **37:18** When your people say to you, 'Will you not tell us what these things mean?' **37:19** tell them, 'This is what the sovereign LORD says: Look, I am about to take the branch of Joseph which is in the hand of Ephraim and the tribes of Israel associated with him, and I will place them on the stick of Judah, and make them into one stick – they will be one in my hand.' **37:20** The sticks you write on will be in your hand in front of them. **37:21** Then tell them, 'This is what the sovereign LORD says: Look, I am about to take the Israelites from among the nations where they have gone. I will gather them from round about and bring them to their land. **37:22** I will make them one nation in the land, on the mountains of Israel, and one king will rule over them all. They will never again be two nations and never again be divided into two kingdoms. **37:23** They will not defile themselves with their idols, their detestable things, and all their rebellious deeds. I will save them from all their unfaithfulness by which they sinned. I will purify them; they will become my people and I will become their God.

37:24 "'My servant David will be king over them; there will be one shepherd for all of them. They will follow my regulations and carefully observe my statutes. **37:25** They will live in the land I gave to my servant Jacob, in which your fathers lived; they will live in it – they and their children and their grandchildren forever. David my servant will be prince over them forever. **37:26** I will make a covenant of peace with them; it will be a perpetual covenant with them. I will establish them, increase their numbers, and place my sanctuary among them forever. **37:27** My dwelling place will be with them; I will be their God, and they will be my people. **37:28** Then, when my sanctuary is among them forever, the nations will know that I, the LORD, sanctify Israel.'"

A Prophecy Against Gog

38:1 The word of the LORD came to me: **38:2** "Son of man, turn toward Gog, of the land of Magog, the chief prince of Meshech and Tubal. Prophesy against him **38:3** and say: 'This is what the sovereign LORD says: Look, I am against you, Gog, chief prince of Meshech and Tubal. **38:4** I will turn you around, put hooks into your jaws, and bring you out with all your army, horses and horsemen, all of them fully armed, a great company with shields of different types, all of them armed with swords. **38:5** Persia, Ethiopia, and Put are with them, all of them with shields and helmets. **38:6** They are joined by Gomer with all its troops, and by Beth Togarmah from the remote parts of the north with all its troops – many peoples are with you.

38:7 "'Be ready and stay ready, you and all your companies assembled around you, and be a guard for them. **38:8** After many days you will be summoned; in the latter years you will come to a land restored from the ravages of war, with many peoples gathered on the mountains of Israel that had long been in ruins. Its people were brought out from the peoples, and all of them will be living securely. **38:9** You will advance; you will come like a storm. You will be like a cloud covering the earth, you, all your troops, and the many other peoples with you.

38:10 "'This is what the sovereign LORD says: On that day thoughts will come into your mind, and you will devise an evil plan. **38:11** You will say, "I will invade a land of unwalled towns; I will advance against those living quietly in security – all of them living without walls and barred gates – **38:12** to loot and plunder, to attack the inhabited ruins and the people gathered from the nations, who are acquiring cattle and goods, who live at the center of the earth." **38:13** Sheba and Dedan and the traders of Tarshish with all its young warriors will say to you, "Have you come to loot? Have you assembled your armies to plunder, to carry away silver and gold, to take away cattle and goods, to haul away a great amount of spoils?"'

38:14 "Therefore, prophesy, son of man, and say to Gog: 'This is what the sovereign LORD says: On that day when my people Israel are living securely, you will take notice **38:15** and come from your place, from the remote parts of the north, you and many peoples with you, all of them riding on horses, a great company and a vast army. **38:16** You will advance against my people Israel like a cloud covering the earth. In the latter days I will bring you against my land so that the nations may acknowledge me, when before their eyes I magnify myself through you, O Gog.

38:17 "'This is what the sovereign LORD says: Are you the one of whom I spoke in former days by my servants the prophets of Israel, who prophesied in those days that I would bring you against them? **38:18** On that day, when Gog invades the land of Israel, declares the sovereign LORD, my rage will mount up in my anger. **38:19** In my zeal, in the fire of my fury, I declare that on that day there will be a great earthquake in the land of Israel. **38:20** The fish of the sea, the birds of the sky, the wild beasts, all the things that creep on the ground, and all people who live on the face of the earth will shake at my presence. The mountains will topple, the cliffs will fall, and every wall will fall to the ground. **38:21** I will call for a sword to attack Gog on all my mountains, declares the sovereign LORD; every man's sword will be against his brother. **38:22** I will judge him with plague and bloodshed. I will rain down on him, his troops and the many peoples who are with him a torrential downpour, hailstones, fire, and brimstone. **38:23** I will exalt and magnify myself; I will reveal myself before many nations. Then they will know that I am the LORD.'

39:1 "As for you, son of man, prophesy against Gog, and say: 'This is what the sovereign LORD says: Look, I am against you, O Gog, chief prince of Meshech and Tubal! **39:2** I will turn you around and drag you along; I will lead you up from the remotest parts of the north and bring you against the mountains of Israel. **39:3** I will knock your bow out of your left hand and make your arrows fall from your right hand. **39:4** You will fall dead on the mountains of Israel, you and all your troops and the people who are with you. I give you as food to every kind of bird and every wild beast. **39:5** You will fall dead in the open field; for I have spoken, declares the sovereign LORD. **39:6** I will send fire on Magog and those who live securely in the coastlands; then they will know that I am the LORD.

39:7 "'I will make my holy name known in the midst of my people Israel; I will not let my holy name be profaned anymore. Then the nations will know that I am the LORD, the Holy One of Israel. **39:8** Realize that it is coming and it will be done, declares the sovereign LORD. It is the day I have spoken about.

39:9 "'Then those who live in the cities of Israel will go out and use the weapons for kindling – the shields, bows and arrows, war clubs and spears – they will burn them for seven years. **39:10** They will not need to take wood from the field or cut down trees from the forests, because they will make fires with the weapons. They will take the loot from those who looted them and seize the plunder of those who plundered them, declares the sovereign LORD.

39:11 "'On that day I will assign Gog a grave in Israel. It will be the valley of those who travel east of the sea; it will block the way of the travelers. There they will bury Gog and all his horde; they will call it the valley of Hamon-Gog. **39:12** For seven months Israel will bury them, in order to cleanse the land. **39:13** All the people of the land will bury them, and it will be a memorial for them on the day I magnify myself, declares the sovereign LORD. **39:14** They will designate men to scout continually through the land, burying those who remain on the surface of the ground, in order to cleanse it. They will search for seven full months. **39:15** When the scouts survey the land and see a human bone, they will place a sign by it, until those assigned to burial duty have buried it in the valley of Hamon-Gog. **39:16** (A city by the name of Hamonah will also be there.) They will cleanse the land.'

39:17 "As for you, son of man, this is what the sovereign LORD says: Tell every kind of bird and every wild beast: 'Assemble and come! Gather from all around to my slaughter which I am going to make for you, a great slaughter on the mountains of Israel! You will eat flesh and drink blood. **39:18** You will eat the flesh of warriors and drink the blood of the princes of the earth – the rams, lambs, goats, and bulls, all of them fattened animals of Bashan. **39:19** You will eat fat until you are full, and drink blood until you are drunk, at my slaughter which I have made for you. **39:20** You will fill up at my table with horses and charioteers, with warriors and all the soldiers,' declares the sovereign LORD.

39:21 "I will display my majesty among the nations. All the nations will witness the judgment I have executed, and the power I have exhibited among them. **39:22** Then the house of Israel will know that I am the LORD their God, from that day forward. **39:23** The nations will know that the house of Israel went into exile due to their iniquity, for they were unfaithful to me. So I hid my face from them and handed them over to their enemies; all of them died by the sword. **39:24** According to their uncleanness and rebellion I have dealt with them, and I hid my face from them.

39:25 "Therefore this is what the sovereign LORD says: Now I will restore the fortunes of Jacob, and I will have mercy on the entire house of Israel. I will be zealous for my holy name. **39:26** They will bear their shame for all their unfaithful acts against me, when they live securely on their land with no one to make them afraid. **39:27** When I have brought them back from the peoples and gathered them from the countries of their enemies, I will magnify myself among them in the sight of many nations. **39:28** Then they will know that I am the LORD their God, because I sent them into exile among the nations, and then gathered them into their own land. I will not leave any of them in exile any longer. **39:29** I will no longer hide my face from them, when I pour out my Spirit on the house of Israel, declares the sovereign LORD."

Vision of the New Temple

40:1 In the twenty-fifth year of our exile, at the beginning of the year, on the tenth day of the month, in the fourteenth year after the city was struck down, on this very day, the hand of the LORD was on me, and he brought me there. **40:2** By means of divine visions he brought me to the land of Israel and placed me on a very high mountain, and on it was a structure like a city, to the south. **40:3** When he brought me there, I saw a man whose appearance was like bronze, with a linen cord and a measuring stick in his hand. He was standing in the gateway. **40:4** The man said to me, "Son of man, watch closely, listen carefully, and pay attention to everything I show you, for you have been brought here so that I can show it to you. Tell the house of Israel everything you see."

40:5 I saw a wall all around the outside of the temple. In the man's hand was a measuring stick 10½ feet long. He measured the thickness of the wall as 10½ feet, and its height as 10½ feet. **40:6** Then he went to the gate facing east. He climbed its steps and measured the threshold of the gate as 10½ feet deep. **40:7** The alcoves were 10½ feet long and 10½ feet wide; between the alcoves were 8¾ feet. The threshold of the gate by the porch of the gate facing inward was 10½ feet. **40:8** Then he measured the porch of the gate facing inward as 10½ feet. **40:9** He measured the porch of the gate as 14 feet, and its jambs as 3½ feet; the porch of the gate faced inward. **40:10** There were three alcoves on each side of the east gate; the three had the same measurement, and the jambs on either side had the same measurement. **40:11** He measured the width of the entrance of the gateway as 17½ feet, and the length of the gateway as 22¾ feet. **40:12** There was a barrier in front of the alcoves, 1¾ feet on either side; the alcoves were 10½ feet on either side. **40:13** He measured the gateway from the roof of one alcove to the roof of the other, a width of 43¾ feet from one entrance to the opposite one. **40:14** He measured the porch at 105 feet high; the gateway went all around to the jamb of the courtyard. **40:15** From the front of the entrance gate to the porch of the inner gate was 87½ feet. **40:16** There were closed windows toward the alcoves and toward their jambs within the gate all around, and likewise for the porches. There were windows all around the inside, and on each jamb were decorative palm trees.

40:17 Then he brought me to the outer court. I saw chambers there, and a pavement made for the court all around; thirty chambers faced the pavement. **40:18** The pavement was beside the gates, corresponding to the length of the gates; this was the lower pavement. **40:19** Then he measured the width from before the lower gate to the front of the exterior of the inner court as 175 feet on the east and on the north.

40:20 He measured the length and width of the gate of the outer court which faces north. **40:21** Its alcoves, three on each side, and its jambs and porches had the same measurement as the first gate; 87½ feet long and 43¾ feet wide. **40:22** Its windows, its porches, and its decorative palm trees had the same measurement as the gate which faced east. Seven steps led up to it, and its porch was in front of them. **40:23** Opposite the gate on the north and the east was a gate of the inner court; he measured the distance from gate to gate at 175 feet.

40:24 Then he led me toward the south. I saw a gate on the south. He measured its jambs and its porches; they had the same dimensions as the others. **40:25** There were windows all around it and its porches, like the windows of the others; 87½ feet long and 43¾ feet wide. **40:26** There were seven steps going up to it; its porches were in front of them. It had decorative palm trees on its jambs, one on either side. **40:27** The inner court had a gate toward the south; he measured it from gate to gate toward the south as 175 feet.

40:28 Then he brought me to the inner court by the south gate. He measured the south gate; it had the same dimensions as the others. **40:29** Its alcoves, its jambs, and its porches had the same dimensions as the others, and there were windows all around it and its porches; its length was 87½ feet and its width 43¾ feet. **40:30** There were porches all around, 43¾ feet long and 8¾ feet wide. **40:31** Its porches faced the outer court, and decorative palm trees were on its jambs, and its stairway had eight steps.

40:32 Then he brought me to the inner court on the east side. He measured the gate; it had the same dimensions as the others. **40:33** Its alcoves, its jambs, and its porches had the same dimensions as the others, and there were windows all around it and its porches; its length was 87½ feet and its width 43¾ feet. **40:34** Its porches faced the outer court, it had decorative palm trees on its jambs, and its stairway had eight steps.

40:35 Then he brought me to the north gate, and he measured it; it had the same dimensions as the others – **40:36** its alcoves, its jambs, and its porches. It had windows all around it; its length was 87½ feet and its width 43¾ feet. **40:37** Its jambs faced the outer court, and it had decorative palm trees on its jambs, on either side, and its stairway had eight steps.

40:38 There was a chamber with its door by the porch of the gate; there they washed the burnt offering. **40:39** In the porch of the gate were two tables on either side on which to slaughter the burnt offering, the sin offering, and the guilt offering. **40:40** On the outside of the porch as one goes up at the entrance of the north gate were two tables, and on the other side of the porch of the gate were two tables. **40:41** Four tables were on each side of the gate, eight tables on which the sacrifices were to be slaughtered. **40:42** The four tables for the burnt offering were of carved stone, 32 inches long, 32 inches wide, and 21 inches high. They would put the instruments which they used to slaughter the burnt offering and the sacrifice on them. **40:43** There were hooks three inches long, fastened in the house all around, and on the tables was the flesh of the offering.

40:44 On the outside of the inner gate were chambers for the singers of the inner court, one at the side of the north gate facing south, and the other at the side of the south gate facing north. **40:45** He said to me, "This chamber which faces south is for the priests who keep charge of the temple, **40:46** and the chamber which faces north is for the priests who keep charge of the altar. These are the descendants of Zadok, from the descendants of Levi, who may approach the LORD to minister to him." **40:47** He measured the court as a square 175 feet long and 175 feet wide; the altar was in front of the temple.

40:48 Then he brought me to the porch of the temple and measured the jambs of the porch as 8¾ feet on either side, and the width of the gate was 24½ feet and the sides were 5¼ feet on each side. **40:49** The length of the porch was 35 feet and the width 19¼ feet; steps led up to it, and there were pillars beside the jambs on either side.

The Inner Temple

41:1 Then he brought me to the outer sanctuary, and measured the jambs; the jambs were 10½ feet wide on each side. **41:2** The width of the entrance was 17½ feet, and the sides of the entrance were 8¾ feet on each side. He measured the length of the outer sanctuary as 70 feet, and its width as 35 feet.

41:3 Then he went into the inner sanctuary and measured the jambs of the entrance as 3½ feet, the entrance as 10½ feet, and the width of the entrance as 12¼ feet **41:4** Then he measured its length as 35 feet, and its width as 35 feet, before the outer sanctuary. He said to me, "This is the most holy place."

41:5 Then he measured the wall of the temple as 10½ feet, and the width of the side chambers as 7 feet, all around the temple. **41:6** The side chambers were in three stories, one above the other, thirty in each story. There were offsets in the wall all around to serve as supports for the side chambers, so that the supports were not in the wall of the temple. **41:7** The side chambers surrounding the temple were wider at each successive story; for the structure surrounding the temple went up story by story all around the temple. For this reason the width of the temple increased as it went up, and one went up from the lowest story to the highest by the way of the middle story.

41:8 I saw that the temple had a raised platform all around; the foundations of the side chambers were a full measuring stick of 10½ feet high. **41:9** The width of the outer wall of the side chambers was 8¾ feet, and the open area between the side chambers of the temple **41:10** and the chambers of the court was 35 feet in width all around the temple on every side. **41:11** There were entrances from the side chambers toward the open area, one entrance toward the north, and another entrance toward the south; the width of the open area was 8¾ feet all around. **41:12** The building that was facing the temple courtyard at the west side was 122½ feet wide; the wall of the building was 8¾ feet all around, and its length 157½ feet.

41:13 Then he measured the temple as 175 feet long, the courtyard of the temple and the building and its walls as 175 feet long, **41:14** and also the width of the front of the temple and the courtyard on the east as 175 feet.

41:15 Then he measured the length of the building facing the courtyard at the rear of the temple, with its galleries on either side as 175 feet.

The interior of the outer sanctuary and the porch of the court, **41:16** as well as the thresholds, narrow windows and galleries all around on three sides facing the threshold were paneled with wood all around, from the ground up to the windows (now the windows were covered), **41:17** to the space above the entrance, to the inner room, and on the outside, and on all the walls in the inner room and outside, by measurement. **41:18** It was made with cherubim and decorative palm trees, with a palm tree between each cherub. Each cherub had two faces: **41:19** a human face toward the palm tree on one side and a lion's face toward the palm tree on the other side. They were carved on the whole temple all around; **41:20** from the ground to the area above the entrance, cherubim and decorative palm trees were carved on the wall of the outer sanctuary. **41:21** The doorposts of the outer sanctuary were square. In front of the sanctuary one doorpost looked just like the other. **41:22** The altar was of wood, 5¼ feet high, with its length 3½ feet; its corners, its length, and its walls were of wood. He said to me, "This is the table that is before the LORD." **41:23** The outer sanctuary and the inner sanctuary each had a double door. **41:24** Each of the doors had two leaves, two swinging leaves; two leaves for one door and two leaves for the other. **41:25** On the doors of the outer sanctuary were carved cherubim and palm trees, like those carved on the walls, and there was a canopy of wood on the front of the outside porch. **41:26** There were narrow windows and decorative palm trees on either side of the side walls of the porch; this is what the side chambers of the temple and the canopies were like.

Chambers for the Temple

42:1 Then he led me out to the outer court, toward the north, and brought me to the chamber which was opposite the courtyard and opposite the building on the north. **42:2** Its length was 175 feet on the north side, and its width 87½ feet. **42:3** Opposite the 35 feet that belonged to the inner court, and opposite the pavement which belonged to the outer court, gallery faced gallery in the three stories. **42:4** In front of the chambers was a walkway on the inner side, 17½ feet wide at a distance of 1¾ feet, and their entrances were on the north. **42:5** Now the upper chambers were narrower, because the galleries took more space from them than from the lower and middle chambers of the building. **42:6** For they were in three stories and had no pillars like the pillars of the courts; therefore the upper chambers were set back from the ground more than the lower and upper ones. **42:7** As for the outer wall by the side of the chambers, toward the outer court facing the chambers, it was 87½ feet long. **42:8** For the chambers on the outer court were 87½ feet long, while those facing the temple were 175 feet long. **42:9** Below these chambers was a passage on the east side as one enters from the outer court.

42:10 At the beginning of the wall of the court toward the south, facing the courtyard and the building, were chambers **42:11** with a passage in front of them. They looked like the chambers on the north. Of the same length and width, and all their exits according to their arrangements and entrances **42:12** were the chambers which were toward the south. There was an opening at the head of the passage, the passage in front of the corresponding wall toward the east when one enters.

42:13 Then he said to me, "The north chambers and the south chambers which face the courtyard are holy chambers where the priests who approach the LORD will eat the most holy offerings. There they will place the most holy offerings – the grain offering, the sin offering, and the guilt offering, because the place is holy. **42:14** When the priests enter, then they will not go out from the sanctuary to the outer court without taking off their garments in which they minister, for these are holy; they will put on other garments, then they will go near the places where the people are."

42:15 Now when he had finished measuring the interior of the temple, he led me out by the gate which faces east and measured all around. **42:16** He measured the east side with the measuring stick as 875 feet by the measuring stick. **42:17** He measured the north side as 875 feet by the measuring stick. **42:18** He measured the south side as 875 feet by the measuring stick. **42:19** He turned to the west side and measured 875 feet by the measuring stick. **42:20** He measured it on all four sides. It had a wall around it, 875 feet long and 875 feet wide, to separate the holy and common places.

The Glory Returns to the Temple

43:1 Then he brought me to the gate that faced toward the east. **43:2** I saw the glory of the God of Israel coming from the east; the sound was like that of rushing water; and the earth radiated his glory. **43:3** It was like the vision I saw when he came to destroy the city, and the vision I saw by the Kebar River. I threw myself face down. **43:4** The glory of the LORD came into the temple by way of the gate that faces east. **43:5** Then a wind lifted me up and brought me to the inner court; I watched the glory of the LORD filling the temple.

43:6 I heard someone speaking to me from the temple, while the man was standing beside me. **43:7** He said to me: "Son of man, this is the place of my throne and the place for the soles of my feet, where I will live among the people of Israel forever. The house of Israel will no longer profane my holy name, neither they nor their kings, by their spiritual prostitution or by the pillars of their kings set up when they die. **43:8** When they placed their threshold by my threshold and their doorpost by my doorpost, with only the wall between me and them, they profaned my holy name by the abominable deeds they committed. So I consumed them in my anger. **43:9** Now they must put away their spiritual prostitution and the pillars of their kings far from me, and then I will live among them forever.

43:10 "As for you, son of man, describe the temple to the house of Israel, so that they will be ashamed of their sins and measure the pattern. **43:11** When they are ashamed of all that they have done, make known to them the design of the temple, its pattern, its exits and entrances, and its whole design – all its statutes, its entire design, and all its laws; write it all down in their sight, so that they may observe its entire design and all its statutes and do them.

43:12 "This is the law of the temple: The entire area on top of the mountain all around will be most holy. Indeed, this is the law of the temple.

The Altar

43:13 "And these are the measurements of the altar: Its base is 1¾ feet high, and 1¾ feet wide, and its border nine inches on its edge. This is to be the height of the altar. **43:14** From the base of the ground to the lower edge is 3½ feet, and the width 1¾ feet; and from the smaller ledge to the larger edge, 7 feet, and the width 1¾ feet; **43:15** and the altar hearth, 7 feet, and from the altar hearth four horns projecting upward. **43:16** Now the altar hearth is a perfect square, 21 feet long and 21 feet wide. **43:17** The ledge is 24½ feet long and 24½ feet wide on four sides; the border around it is 10½ inches, and its surrounding base 1¾ feet. Its steps face east."

43:18 Then he said to me: "Son of man, this is what the sovereign LORD says: These are the statutes of the altar: On the day it is built to offer up burnt offerings on it and to sprinkle blood on it, **43:19** you will give a young bull for a sin offering to the Levitical priests who are descended from Zadok, who approach me to minister to me, declares the sovereign LORD. **43:20** You will take some of its blood, and place it on the four horns of the altar, on the four corners of the ledge, and on the border all around; you will cleanse it and make atonement for it. **43:21** You will also take the bull for the sin offering, and it will be burned in the appointed place in the temple, outside the sanctuary.

43:22 "On the second day, you will offer a male goat without blemish for a sin offering. They will purify the altar just as they purified it with the bull. **43:23** When you have finished purifying it, you will offer an unblemished young bull and an unblemished ram from the flock. **43:24** You will present them before the LORD, and the priests will scatter salt on them and offer them up as a burnt offering to the LORD.

43:25 "For seven days you will provide every day a goat for a sin offering; a young bull and a ram from the flock, both without blemish, will be provided. **43:26** For seven days they will make atonement for the altar and cleanse it, so they will consecrate it. **43:27** When the prescribed period is over, on the eighth day and thereafter the priests will offer up on the altar your burnt offerings and your peace offerings; I will accept you, declares the sovereign LORD."

The Closed Gate

44:1 Then he brought me back by way of the outer gate of the sanctuary which faces east, but it was shut. **44:2** The LORD said to me: "This gate will be shut; it will not be opened, and no one will enter by it. For the LORD, the God of Israel, has entered by it; therefore it will remain shut. **44:3** Only the prince may sit in it to eat a sacrificial meal before the LORD; he will enter by way of the porch of the gate and will go out by the same way."

44:4 Then he brought me by way of the north gate to the front of the temple. As I watched, I noticed the glory of the LORD filling the LORD's temple, and I threw myself face down. **44:5** The LORD said to me: "Son of man, pay attention, watch closely and listen carefully to everything I tell you concerning all the statutes of the LORD's house and all its laws. Pay attention to the entrances to the temple with all the exits of the sanctuary. **44:6** Say to the rebellious, to the house of Israel, 'This is what the sovereign LORD says: Enough of all your abominable practices, O house of Israel! **44:7** When you bring foreigners, those uncircumcised in heart and in flesh, into my sanctuary, you desecrate it – even my house – when you offer my food, the fat and the blood. You have broken my covenant by all your abominable practices. **44:8** You have not kept charge of my holy things, but you have assigned foreigners to keep charge of my sanctuary for you. **44:9** This is what the sovereign LORD says: No foreigner, who is uncircumcised in heart and flesh among all the foreigners who are among the people of Israel, will enter into my sanctuary.

44:10 "But the Levites who went far from me, straying off from me after their idols when Israel went astray, will be responsible for their sin. **44:11** Yet they will be ministers in my sanctuary, having oversight at the gates of the temple, and serving the temple. They will slaughter the burnt offerings and the sacrifices for the people, and they will stand before them to minister to them. **44:12** Because they used to minister to them before their idols, and became a sinful obstacle to the house of Israel, consequently I have made a vow concerning them, declares the sovereign LORD, that they will be responsible for their sin. **44:13** They will not

come near me to serve me as priest, nor will they come near any of my holy things, the things which are most sacred. They will bear the shame of the abominable deeds they have committed. **44:14** Yet I will appoint them to keep charge of the temple, all of its service and all that will be done in it.

The Levitical Priests

44:15 "But the Levitical priests, the descendants of Zadok who kept the charge of my sanctuary when the people of Israel went astray from me, will approach me to minister to me; they will stand before me to offer me the fat and the blood, declares the sovereign LORD. **44:16** They will enter my sanctuary, and approach my table to minister to me; they will keep my charge.

44:17 "When they enter the gates of the inner court, they must wear linen garments; they must not have any wool on them when they minister in the inner gates of the court and in the temple. **44:18** Linen turbans will be on their heads and linen undergarments will be around their waists; they must not bind themselves with anything that causes sweat. **44:19** When they go out to the outer court to the people, they must remove the garments they were ministering in, and place them in the holy chambers; they must put on other garments so that they will not transmit holiness to the people with their garments.

44:20 "They must not shave their heads nor let their hair grow long; they must only trim their heads. **44:21** No priest may drink wine when he enters the inner court. **44:22** They must not marry a widow or a divorcee, but they may marry a virgin from the house of Israel or a widow who is a priest's widow. **44:23** Moreover, they will teach my people the difference between the holy and the common, and show them how to distinguish between the ceremonially unclean and the clean.

44:24 "In a controversy they will act as judges; they will judge according to my ordinances. They will keep my laws and my statutes regarding all my appointed festivals and will observe my Sabbaths.

44:25 "They must not come near a dead person or they will be defiled; however, for father, mother, son, daughter, brother or sister, they may defile themselves. **44:26** After a priest has become ceremonially clean, they must count off a period of seven days for him. **44:27** On the day he enters the sanctuary, into the inner court to serve in the sanctuary, he must offer his sin offering, declares the sovereign LORD.

44:28 "This will be their inheritance: I am their inheritance, and you must give them no property in Israel; I am their property. **44:29** They may eat the grain offering, the sin offering, and the guilt offering, and every devoted thing in Israel will be theirs. **44:30** The first of all the first fruits and all contributions of any kind will be for the priests; you will also give to the priest the first portion of your dough, so that a blessing may rest on your house. **44:31** The priests will not eat any bird or animal that has died a natural death or was torn to pieces by a wild animal.

The Lord's Portion of the Land

45:1 "When you allot the land as an inheritance, you will offer an allotment to the LORD, a holy portion from the land; the length will be eight and a quarter miles and the width three and one-third miles. This entire area will be holy. **45:2** Of this area a square 875 feet by 875 feet will be designated for the sanctuary, with 87½ feet set aside for its open space round about. **45:3** From this measured area you will measure a length of eight and a quarter miles and a width of three and one-third miles; in it will be the sanctuary, the most holy place. **45:4** It will be a holy portion of the land; it will be for the priests, the ministers of the sanctuary who approach the LORD to minister to him. It will be a place for their houses and a holy place for the sanctuary. **45:5** An area eight and a quarter miles in length and three and one-third miles in width will be for the Levites, who minister at the temple, as the place for the cities in which they will live.

45:6 "Alongside the portion set apart as the holy allotment, you will allot for the city an area one and two-thirds miles wide and eight and a quarter miles long; it will be for the whole house of Israel.

45:7 "For the prince there will be land on both sides of the holy allotment and the allotted city, alongside the holy allotment and the allotted city, on the west side and on the east side; it will be comparable in length to one of the portions, from the west border to the east border **45:8** of the land. This will be his property in Israel. My princes will no longer oppress my people, but the land will be allotted to the house of Israel according to their tribes.

45:9 "This is what the sovereign LORD says: Enough, you princes of Israel! Put away violence and destruction, and do what is just and right. Put an end to your evictions of my people, declares the sovereign LORD. **45:10** You must use just balances, a just dry measure (an ephah), and a just liquid measure (a bath). **45:11** The dry and liquid measures will be the same, the bath will contain a tenth of a homer, and the ephah a tenth of a homer; the homer will be the standard measure. **45:12** The shekel will be twenty gerahs. Sixty shekels will be a mina for you.

45:13 "This is the offering you must offer: a sixth of an ephah from a homer of wheat; a sixth of an ephah from a homer of barley, **45:14** and as the prescribed portion of olive oil, one tenth of a bath from each kor (which is ten baths or a homer, for ten baths make a homer); **45:15** and one sheep from each flock of two hundred, from the watered places of

Israel, for a grain offering, burnt offering, and peace offering, to make atonement for them, declares the sovereign LORD. **45:16** All the people of the land will contribute to this offering for the prince of Israel. **45:17** It will be the duty of the prince to provide the burnt offerings, the grain offering, and the drink offering at festivals, on the new moons and Sabbaths, at all the appointed feasts of the house of Israel; he will provide the sin offering, the grain offering, the burnt offering, and the peace offerings to make atonement for the house of Israel.

45:18 "'This is what the sovereign LORD says: In the first month, on the first day of the month, you must take an unblemished young bull and purify the sanctuary. **45:19** The priest will take some of the blood of the sin offering and place it on the doorpost of the temple, on the four corners of the ledge of the altar, and on the doorpost of the gate of the inner court. **45:20** This is what you must do on the seventh day of the month for anyone who sins inadvertently or through ignorance; so you will make atonement for the temple.

45:21 "'In the first month, on the fourteenth day of the month, you will celebrate the Passover, and for seven days bread made without yeast will be eaten. **45:22** On that day the prince will provide for himself and for all the people of the land a bull for a sin offering. **45:23** And during the seven days of the feast he will provide as a burnt offering to the LORD seven bulls and seven rams, all without blemish, on each of the seven days, and a male goat daily for a sin offering. **45:24** He will provide as a grain offering an ephah for each bull, an ephah for each ram, and a gallon of olive oil for each ephah of grain. **45:25** In the seventh month, on the fifteenth day of the month, at the feast, he will make the same provisions for the sin offering, burnt offering, and grain offering, and for the olive oil, for the seven days.

The Prince's Offerings

46:1 "'This is what the sovereign LORD says: The gate of the inner court that faces east will be closed six working days, but on the Sabbath day it will be opened and on the day of the new moon it will be opened. **46:2** The prince will enter by way of the porch of the gate from the outside, and will stand by the doorpost of the gate. The priests will provide his burnt offering and his peace offerings, and he will bow down at the threshold of the gate and then go out. But the gate will not be closed until evening. **46:3** The people of the land will bow down at the entrance of that gate before the LORD on the Sabbaths and on the new moons. **46:4** The burnt offering which the prince will offer to the LORD on the Sabbath day will be six unblemished lambs and one unblemished ram. **46:5** The grain offering will be an ephah with the ram, and the grain offering with the lambs will be as much as he is able to give, and a gallon of olive oil with an ephah. **46:6** On the day of the new moon he will offer an unblemished young bull, and six lambs and a ram, all without blemish. **46:7** He will provide a grain offering: an ephah with the bull and an ephah with the ram, and with the lambs as much as he wishes, and a gallon of olive oil with each ephah of grain. **46:8** When the prince enters, he will come by way of the porch of the gate and will go out the same way.

46:9 "'When the people of the land come before the LORD at the appointed feasts, whoever enters by way of the north gate to worship will go out by way of the south gate; whoever enters by way of the south gate will go out by way of the north gate. No one will return by way of the gate they entered but will go out straight ahead. **46:10** When they come in, the prince will come in with them, and when they go out, he will go out.

46:11 "'At the festivals and at the appointed feasts the grain offering will be an ephah with the bull and an ephah with the ram, and with the lambs as much as one is able, and a gallon of olive oil with each ephah of grain. **46:12** When the prince provides a freewill offering, a burnt offering, or peace offerings as a voluntary offering to the LORD, the gate facing east will be opened for him, and he will provide his burnt offering and his peace offerings just as he did on the Sabbath. Then he will go out, and the gate will be closed after he goes out.

46:13 "'You will provide a lamb a year old without blemish for a burnt offering daily to the LORD; morning by morning he will provide it. **46:14** And you will provide a grain offering with it morning by morning, a sixth of an ephah, and a third of a gallon of olive oil to moisten the choice flour, as a grain offering to the LORD; this is a perpetual statute. **46:15** Thus they will provide the lamb, the grain offering, and the olive oil morning by morning, as a perpetual burnt offering.

46:16 "'This is what the sovereign LORD says: If the prince should give a gift to one of his sons as his inheritance, it will belong to his sons, it is their property by inheritance. **46:17** But if he gives a gift from his inheritance to one of his servants, it will be his until the year of liberty; then it will revert to the prince. His inheritance will only remain with his sons. **46:18** The prince will not take away any of the people's inheritance by oppressively removing them from their property. He will give his sons an inheritance from his own possessions so that my people will not be scattered, each from his own property.'"

46:19 Then he brought me through the entrance, which was at the side of the gate, into the holy chambers for the priests which faced north. There I saw a place at the extreme western end. **46:20** He said to me, "This is the place where the priests will boil the guilt offering and the sin offering,

and where they will bake the grain offering, so that they do not bring them out to the outer court to transmit holiness to the people."

46:21 Then he brought me out to the outer court and led me past the four corners of the court, and I noticed that in every corner of the court there was a court. **46:22** In the four corners of the court were small courts, 70 feet in length and 52½ feet in width; the four were all the same size. **46:23** There was a row of masonry around each of the four courts, and places for boiling offerings were made under the rows all around. **46:24** Then he said to me, "These are the houses for boiling, where the ministers of the temple boil the sacrifices of the people."

Water from the Temple

47:1 Then he brought me back to the entrance of the temple. I noticed that water was flowing from under the threshold of the temple toward the east (for the temple faced east). The water was flowing down from under the right side of the temple, from south of the altar. **47:2** He led me out by way of the north gate and brought me around the outside of the outer gate that faces toward the east; I noticed that the water was trickling out from the south side.

47:3 When the man went out toward the east with a measuring line in his hand, he measured 1,750 feet, and then he led me through water, which was ankle deep. **47:4** Again he measured 1,750 feet and led me through the water, which was now knee deep. Once more he measured 1,750 feet and led me through the water, which was waist deep. **47:5** Again he measured 1,750 feet and it was a river I could not cross, for the water had risen; it was deep enough to swim in, a river that could not be crossed. **47:6** He said to me, "Son of man, have you seen this?"

Then he led me back to the bank of the river. **47:7** When I had returned, I noticed a vast number of trees on the banks of the river, on both sides. **47:8** He said to me, "These waters go out toward the eastern region and flow down into the Arabah; when they enter the Dead Sea, where the sea is stagnant, the waters become fresh. **47:9** Every living creature which swarms where the river flows will live; there will be many fish, for these waters flow there. It will become fresh and everything will live where the river flows. **47:10** Fishermen will stand beside it; from Engedi to Eneglaim they will spread nets. They will catch many kinds of fish, like the fish of the Great Sea. **47:11** But its swamps and its marshes will not become fresh; they will remain salty. **47:12** On both sides of the river's banks, every kind of tree will grow for food. Their leaves will not wither nor will their fruit fail, but they will bear fruit every month, because their water source flows from the sanctuary. Their fruit will be for food and their leaves for healing."

Boundaries for the Land

47:13 This is what the sovereign LORD says: "Here are the borders you will observe as you allot the land to the twelve tribes of Israel. (Joseph will have two portions.) **47:14** You must divide it equally just as I vowed to give it to your forefathers; this land will be assigned as your inheritance.

47:15 "This will be the border of the land: On the north side, from the Great Sea by way of Hethlon to the entrance of Zedad; **47:16** Hamath, Berothah, Sibraim, which is between the border of Damascus and the border of Hamath, as far as Hazer-hattikon, which is on the border of Hauran. **47:17** The border will run from the sea to Hazar-enan, at the border of Damascus, and on the north is the border of Hamath. This is the north side. **47:18** On the east side, between Hauran and Damascus, and between Gilead and the land of Israel, will be the Jordan. You will measure from the border to the eastern sea. This is the east side. **47:19** On the south side it will run from Tamar to the waters of Meribath Kadesh, the river, to the Great Sea. This is the south side. **47:20** On the west side the Great Sea will be the boundary to a point opposite Lebo-hamath. This is the west side.

47:21 "This is how you will divide this land for yourselves among the tribes of Israel. **47:22** You must allot it as an inheritance among yourselves and for the foreigners who reside among you, who have fathered sons among you. You must treat them as native-born among the people of Israel; they will be allotted an inheritance with you among the tribes of Israel. **47:23** In whatever tribe the foreigner resides, there you will give him his inheritance," declares the sovereign LORD.

The Tribal Portions

48:1 "These are the names of the tribes: From the northern end beside the road of Hethlon to Lebo-hamath, as far as Hazar-enan (which is on the border of Damascus, toward the north beside Hamath), extending from the east side to the west, Dan will have one portion. **48:2** Next to the border of Dan, from the east side to the west, Asher will have one portion. **48:3** Next to the border of Asher from the east side to the west, Naphtali will have one portion. **48:4** Next to the border of Naphtali from the east side to the west, Manasseh will have one portion. **48:5** Next to the border of Manasseh from the east side to the west, Ephraim will have one portion. **48:6** Next to the border of Ephraim from the east side to the west, Reuben will have one portion. **48:7** Next to the border of Reuben from the east side to the west, Judah will have one portion.

48:8 "Next to the border of Judah from the east side to the west will be the allotment you must set apart. It is to be eight and a quarter miles wide, and the same length as one of the tribal portions, from the east side

to the west; the sanctuary will be in the middle of it. **48:9** The allotment you set apart to the LORD will be eight and a quarter miles in length and three and one-third miles in width. **48:10** These will be the allotments for the holy portion: for the priests, toward the north eight and a quarter miles in length, toward the west three and one-third miles in width, toward the east three and one-third miles in width, and toward the south eight and a quarter miles in length; the sanctuary of the LORD will be in the middle. **48:11** This will be for the priests who are set apart from the descendants of Zadok who kept my charge and did not go astray when the people of Israel strayed off, like the Levites did. **48:12** It will be their portion from the allotment of the land, a most holy place, next to the border of the Levites.
48:13 "Alongside the border of the priests, the Levites will have an allotment eight and a quarter miles in length and three and one-third miles in width. The whole length will be eight and a quarter miles and the width three and one-third miles. **48:14** They must not sell or exchange any of it; they must not transfer this choice portion of land, for it is set apart to the LORD.
48:15 "The remainder, one and two-thirds miles in width and eight and a quarter miles in length, will be for common use by the city, for houses and for open space. The city will be in the middle of it; **48:16** these will be its measurements: The north side will be one and one-half miles, the south side one and one-half miles, the east side one and one-half miles, and the west side one and one-half miles. **48:17** The city will have open spaces: On the north there will be 437½ feet, on the south 437½ feet, on the east 437½ feet, and on the west 437½ feet. **48:18** The remainder of the length alongside the
holy allotment will be three and one-third miles to the east and three and one-third miles toward the west, and it will be beside the holy allotment. Its produce will be for food for the workers of the city. **48:19** The workers of the city from all the tribes of Israel will cultivate it. **48:20** The whole allotment will be eight and a quarter miles square, you must set apart the holy allotment with the possession of the city.
48:21 "The rest, on both sides of the holy allotment and the property of the city, will belong to the prince. Extending from the eight and a quarter miles of the holy allotment to the east border, and westward from the eight and a quarter miles to the west border, alongside the portions, it will belong to the prince. The holy allotment and the sanctuary of the temple will be in the middle of it. **48:22** The property of the Levites and of the city will be in the middle of that which belongs to the prince. The portion between the border of Judah and the border of Benjamin will be for the prince.
48:23 "As for the rest of the tribes: From the east side to the west side, Benjamin will have one portion. **48:24** Next to the border of Benjamin, from the east side to the west side, Simeon will have one portion. **48:25** Next to the border of Simeon, from the east side to the west side, Issachar will have one portion. **48:26** Next to the border of Issachar, from the east side to the
west side, Zebulun will have one portion. **48:27** Next to the border of Zebulun, from the east side to the west side, Gad will have one portion. **48:28** Next to the border of Gad, at the south side, the border will run from Tamar to the waters of Meribath Kadesh, to the Stream of Egypt and on to the Great Sea. **48:29** This is the land which you will allot to the tribes of Israel, and these are their portions, declares the sovereign LORD.
48:30 "These are the exits of the city: On the north side, one and one-half miles by measure, **48:31** the gates of the city will be named for the tribes of Israel; there will be three gates to the north: one gate for Reuben, one gate for Judah, and one gate for Levi. **48:32** On the east side, one and one-half miles in length, there will be three gates: one gate for Joseph, one gate for Benjamin, and one gate for Dan. **48:33** On the south side, one and one-half miles by measure, there will be three gates: one gate for Simeon, one gate for Issachar, and one gate for Zebulun. **48:34** On the west side, one and one-half miles in length, there will be three gates: one gate for Gad, one gate for Asher, and one gate for Naphtali. **48:35** The circumference of the city will be six miles. The name of the city from that day forward will be: 'The LORD Is There.'"

Book 27. Daniel

Daniel Finds Favor in Babylon

1:1 In the third year of the reign of King Jehoiakim of Judah, King Nebuchadnezzar of Babylon advanced against Jerusalem and laid it under siege. **1:2** Now the Lord delivered King Jehoiakim of Judah into his power, along with some of the vessels of the temple of God. He brought them to the land of Babylonia to the temple of his god and put the vessels in the treasury of his god. **1:3** The king commanded Ashpenaz, who was in charge of his court officials, to choose some of the Israelites who were of royal and noble descent – **1:4** young men in whom there was no physical defect and who were handsome, well versed in all kinds of wisdom, well educated and having keen insight, and who were capable of entering the king's royal service – and to teach them the literature and language of the Babylonians. **1:5** So the king assigned them a daily ration from his royal delicacies

and from the wine he himself drank. They were to be trained for the next three years. At the end of that time they were to enter the king's service. **1:6** As it turned out, among these young men were some from Judah: Daniel, Hananiah, Mishael, and Azariah. **1:7** But the overseer of the court officials renamed them. He gave Daniel the name Belteshazzar, Hananiah he named Shadrach, Mishael he named Meshach, and Azariah he named Abednego.
1:8 But Daniel made up his mind that he would not defile himself with the royal delicacies or the royal wine. He therefore asked the overseer of the court officials for permission not to defile himself. **1:9** Then God made the overseer of the court officials sympathetic to Daniel. **1:10** But he responded to Daniel, "I fear my master the king. He is the one who has decided your food and drink. What would happen if he saw that you looked malnourished in comparison to the other young men your age? If that happened, you would endanger my life with the king!" **1:11** Daniel then spoke to the warden whom the overseer of the court officials had appointed over Daniel, Hananiah, Mishael, and Azariah: **1:12** "Please test your servants for ten days by providing us with some vegetables to eat and water to drink. **1:13** Then compare our appearance with that of the young men who are eating the royal delicacies; deal with us in light of what you see." **1:14** So the warden agreed to their proposal and tested them for ten days.
1:15 At the end of the ten days their appearance was better and their bodies were healthier than all the young men who had been eating the royal delicacies. **1:16** So the warden removed the delicacies and the wine from their diet and gave them a diet of vegetables instead. **1:17** Now as for these four young men, God endowed them with knowledge and skill in all sorts of literature and wisdom – and Daniel had insight into all kinds of visions and dreams.
1:18 When the time appointed by the king arrived, the overseer of the court officials brought them into Nebuchadnezzar's presence. **1:19** When the king spoke with them, he did not find among the entire group anyone like Daniel, Hananiah, Mishael, or Azariah. So they entered the king's service. **1:20** In every matter of wisdom and insight the king asked them about, he found them to be ten times better than any of the magicians and astrologers that were in his entire empire. **1:21** Now Daniel lived on until the first year of Cyrus the king.

Nebuchadnezzar Has a Disturbing Dream

2:1 In the second year of his reign Nebuchadnezzar had many dreams. His mind was disturbed and he suffered from insomnia. **2:2** The king issued an order to summon the magicians, astrologers, sorcerers, and wise men in order to explain his dreams to him. So they came and awaited the king's instructions.
2:3 The king told them, "I have had a dream, and I am anxious to understand the dream." **2:4** The wise men replied to the king: [What follows is in Aramaic] "O king, live forever! Tell your servants the dream, and we will disclose its interpretation." **2:5** The king replied to the wise men, "My decision is firm. If you do not inform me of both the dream and its interpretation, you will be dismembered and your homes reduced to rubble! **2:6** But if you can disclose the dream and its interpretation, you will receive from me gifts, a reward, and considerable honor. So disclose to me the dream and its interpretation!" **2:7** They again replied, "Let the king inform us of the dream; then we will disclose its interpretation." **2:8** The king replied, "I know for sure that you are attempting to gain time, because you see that my decision is firm. **2:9** If you don't inform me of the dream, there is only one thing that is going to happen to you. For you have agreed among yourselves to report to me something false and deceitful until such time as things might change. So tell me the dream, and I will have confidence that you can disclose its interpretation."
2:10 The wise men replied to the king, "There is no man on earth who is able to disclose the king's secret, for no king, regardless of his position and power, has ever requested such a thing from any magician, astrologer, or wise man. **2:11** What the king is asking is too difficult, and no one exists who can disclose it to the king, except for the gods – but they don't live among mortals!"
2:12 Because of this the king got furiously angry and gave orders to destroy all the wise men of Babylon. **2:13** So a decree went out, and the wise men were about to be executed. They also sought Daniel and his friends so that they could be executed.
2:14 Then Daniel spoke with prudent counsel to Arioch, who was in charge of the king's executioners and who had gone out to execute the wise men of Babylon. **2:15** He inquired of Arioch the king's deputy, "Why is the decree from the king so urgent?" Then Arioch informed Daniel about the matter. **2:16** So Daniel went in and requested the king to grant him time, that he might disclose the interpretation to the king. **2:17** Then Daniel went to his home and informed his friends Hananiah, Mishael, and Azariah of the matter. **2:18** He asked them to pray for mercy from the God of heaven concerning this mystery so that he and his friends would not be destroyed along with the rest of the wise men of Babylon. **2:19** Then in a night vision the mystery was revealed to Daniel. So Daniel praised the God of heaven, **2:20** saying,
"Let the name of God be praised forever and ever,
for wisdom and power belong to him.

2:21 He changes times and seasons,
deposing some kings
and establishing others.
He gives wisdom to the wise;
he imparts knowledge to those with understanding;
2:22 he reveals deep and hidden things.
He knows what is in the darkness,
and light resides with him.
2:23 O God of my fathers, I acknowledge and glorify you,
for you have bestowed wisdom and power on me.
Now you have enabled me to understand what I requested from you.
For you have enabled me to understand the king's dilemma."
2:24 Then Daniel went in to see Arioch (whom the king had appointed to destroy the wise men of Babylon). He came and said to him, "Don't destroy the wise men of Babylon! Escort me to the king, and I will disclose the interpretation to him!"
2:25 So Arioch quickly ushered Daniel into the king's presence, saying to him, "I have found a man from the captives of Judah who can make known the interpretation to the king." 2:26 The king then asked Daniel (whose name was also Belteshazzar), "Are you able to make known to me the dream that I saw, as well as its interpretation?" 2:27 Daniel replied to the king, "The mystery that the king is asking about is such that no wise men, astrologers, magicians, or diviners can possibly disclose it to the king. 2:28 However, there is a God in heaven who reveals mysteries, and he has made known to King Nebuchadnezzar what will happen in the times to come. The dream and the visions you had while lying on your bed are as follows.
2:29 "As for you, O king, while you were in your bed your thoughts turned to future things. The revealer of mysteries has made known to you what will take place. 2:30 As for me, this mystery was revealed to me not because I possess more wisdom than any other living person, but so that the king may understand the interpretation and comprehend the thoughts of your mind.
2:31 "You, O king, were watching as a great statue – one of impressive size and extraordinary brightness – was standing before you. Its appearance caused alarm. 2:32 As for that statue, its head was of fine gold, its chest and arms were of silver, its belly and thighs were of bronze. 2:33 Its legs were of iron; its feet were partly of iron and partly of clay. 2:34 You were watching as a stone was cut out, but not by human hands. It struck the statue on its iron and clay feet, breaking them in pieces. 2:35 Then the iron, clay, bronze, silver, and gold were broken in pieces without distinction and became like chaff from the summer threshing floors that the wind carries away. Not a trace of them could be found. But the stone that struck the statue became a large mountain that filled the entire earth. 2:36 This was the dream. Now we will set forth before the king its interpretation.

Daniel Interprets Nebuchadnezzar's Dream

2:37 "You, O king, are the king of kings. The God of heaven has granted you sovereignty, power, strength, and honor. 2:38 Wherever human beings, wild animals, and birds of the sky live – he has given them into your power. He has given you authority over them all. You are the head of gold. 2:39 Now after you another kingdom will arise, one inferior to yours. Then a third kingdom, one of bronze, will rule in all the earth. 2:40 Then there will be a fourth kingdom, one strong like iron. Just like iron breaks in pieces and shatters everything, and as iron breaks in pieces all of these metals, so it will break in pieces and crush the others. 2:41 In that you were seeing feet and toes partly of wet clay and partly of iron, so this will be a divided kingdom. Some of the strength of iron will be in it, for you saw iron mixed with wet clay. 2:42 In that the toes of the feet were partly of iron and partly of clay, the latter stages of this kingdom will be partly strong and partly fragile. 2:43 And in that you saw iron mixed with wet clay, so people will be mixed with one another without adhering to one another, just as iron does not mix with clay. 2:44 In the days of those kings the God of heaven will raise up an everlasting kingdom that will not be destroyed and a kingdom that will not be left to another people. It will break in pieces and bring about the demise of all these kingdoms. But it will stand forever. 2:45 You saw that a stone was cut from a mountain, but not by human hands; it smashed the iron, bronze, clay, silver, and gold into pieces. The great God has made known to the king what will occur in the future. The dream is certain, and its interpretation is reliable."
2:46 Then King Nebuchadnezzar bowed down with his face to the ground and paid homage to Daniel. He gave orders to offer sacrifice and incense to him. 2:47 The king replied to Daniel, "Certainly your God is a God of gods and Lord of kings and revealer of mysteries, for you were able to reveal this mystery!" 2:48 Then the king elevated Daniel to high position and bestowed on him many marvelous gifts. He granted him authority over the entire province of Babylon and made him the main prefect over all the wise men of Babylon. 2:49 And at Daniel's request, the king appointed Shadrach, Meshach, and Abednego over the administration of the province of Babylon. Daniel himself served in the king's court.

Daniel's Friends Are Tested

3:1 King Nebuchadnezzar had a golden statue made. It was ninety feet tall and nine feet wide. He erected it on the plain of Dura in the province of Babylon. 3:2 Then King Nebuchadnezzar sent out a summons to assemble the satraps, prefects, governors, counselors, treasurers, judges, magistrates, and all the other authorities of the province to attend the dedication of the statue that he had erected. 3:3 So the satraps, prefects, governors, counselors, treasurers, judges, magistrates, and all the other provincial authorities assembled for the dedication of the statue that King Nebuchadnezzar had erected. They were standing in front of the statue that Nebuchadnezzar had erected.
3:4 Then the herald made a loud proclamation: "To you, O peoples, nations, and language groups, the following command is given: 3:5 When you hear the sound of the horn, flute, zither, trigon, harp, pipes, and all kinds of music, you must bow down and pay homage to the golden statue that King Nebuchadnezzar has erected. 3:6 Whoever does not bow down and pay homage will immediately be thrown into the midst of a furnace of blazing fire!" 3:7 Therefore when they all heard the sound of the horn, flute, zither, trigon, harp, pipes, and all kinds of music, all the peoples, nations, and language groups began bowing down and paying homage to the golden statue that King Nebuchadnezzar had erected.
3:8 Now at that time certain Chaldeans came forward and brought malicious accusations against the Jews. 3:9 They said to King Nebuchadnezzar, "O king, live forever! 3:10 You have issued an edict, O king, that everyone must bow down and pay homage to the golden statue when they hear the sound of the horn, flute, zither, trigon, harp, pipes, and all kinds of music. 3:11 And whoever does not bow down and pay homage must be thrown into the midst of a furnace of blazing fire. 3:12 But there are Jewish men whom you appointed over the administration of the province of Babylon – Shadrach, Meshach, and Abednego – and these men have not shown proper respect to you, O king. They don't serve your gods and they don't pay homage to the golden statue that you have erected."
3:13 Then Nebuchadnezzar in a fit of rage demanded that they bring Shadrach, Meshach, and Abednego before him. So they brought them before the king. 3:14 Nebuchadnezzar said to them, "Is it true, Shadrach, Meshach, and Abednego, that you don't serve my gods and that you don't pay homage to the golden statue that I erected? 3:15 Now if you are ready, when you hear the sound of the horn, flute, zither, trigon, harp, pipes, and all kinds of music, you must bow down and pay homage to the statue that I had made. If you don't pay homage to it, you will immediately be thrown into the midst of the furnace of blazing fire. Now, who is that god who can rescue you from my power?" 3:16 Shadrach, Meshach, and Abednego replied to King Nebuchadnezzar, "We do not need to give you a reply concerning this. 3:17 If our God whom we are serving exists, he is able to rescue us from the furnace of blazing fire, and he will rescue us, O king, from your power as well. 3:18 But if not, let it be known to you, O king, that we don't serve your gods, and we will not pay homage to the golden statue that you have erected."
3:19 Then Nebuchadnezzar was filled with rage, and his disposition changed toward Shadrach, Meshach, and Abednego. He gave orders to heat the furnace seven times hotter than it was normally heated. 3:20 He ordered strong soldiers in his army to tie up Shadrach, Meshach, and Abednego and to throw them into the furnace of blazing fire. 3:21 So those men were tied up while still wearing their cloaks, trousers, turbans, and other clothes, and were thrown into the furnace of blazing fire. 3:22 But since the king's command was so urgent, and the furnace was so excessively hot, the men who escorted Shadrach, Meshach, and Abednego were killed by the leaping flames. 3:23 But those three men, Shadrach, Meshach, and Abednego, fell into the furnace of blazing fire while still securely bound.

God Delivers His Servants

3:24 Then King Nebuchadnezzar was startled and quickly got up. He said to his ministers, "Wasn't it three men that we tied up and threw into the fire?" They replied to the king, "For sure, O king." 3:25 He answered, "But I see four men, untied and walking around in the midst of the fire! No harm has come to them! And the appearance of the fourth is like that of a god!" 3:26 Then Nebuchadnezzar approached the door of the furnace of blazing fire. He called out, "Shadrach, Meshach, and Abednego, servants of the most high God, come out! Come here!"
Then Shadrach, Meshach, and Abednego emerged from the fire. 3:27 Once the satraps, prefects, governors, and ministers of the king had gathered around, they saw that those men were physically unharmed by the fire. The hair of their heads was not singed, nor were their trousers damaged. Not even the smell of fire was to be found on them!
3:28 Nebuchadnezzar exclaimed, "Praised be the God of Shadrach, Meshach, and Abednego, who has sent forth his angel and has rescued his servants who trusted in him, ignoring the edict of the king and giving up their bodies rather than serve or pay homage to any god other than their God! 3:29 I hereby decree that any people, nation, or language group that blasphemes the god of Shadrach, Meshach, or Abednego will be dismembered and his home reduced to rubble! For there exists no other god who can deliver in this way." 3:30 Then Nebuchadnezzar promoted Shadrach, Meshach, and Abednego in the province of Babylon.

4:1 (3:31) "King Nebuchadnezzar, to all peoples, nations, and language groups that live in all the land: Peace and prosperity! **4:2** I am delighted to tell you about the signs and wonders that the most high God has done for me.

4:3 "How great are his signs!
How mighty are his wonders!
His kingdom will last forever,
and his authority continues from one generation to the next."

Nebuchadnezzar Dreams of a Tree Chopped Down

4:4 (4:1) I, Nebuchadnezzar, was relaxing in my home, living luxuriously in my palace. **4:5** I saw a dream that frightened me badly. The things I imagined while lying on my bed – these visions of my mind – were terrifying me. **4:6** So I issued an order for all the wise men of Babylon to be brought before me so that they could make known to me the interpretation of the dream. **4:7** When the magicians, astrologers, wise men, and diviners entered, I recounted the dream for them. But they were unable to make known its interpretation to me. **4:8** Later Daniel entered (whose name is Belteshazzar after the name of my god, and in whom there is a spirit of the holy gods). I recounted the dream for him as well, **4:9** saying, "Belteshazzar, chief of the magicians, in whom I know there to be a spirit of the holy gods and whom no mystery baffles, consider my dream that I saw and set forth its interpretation! **4:10** Here are the visions of my mind while I was on my bed.

While I was watching,
there was a tree in the middle of the land.
It was enormously tall.
4:11 The tree grew large and strong.
Its top reached far into the sky;
it could be seen from the borders of all the land.
4:12 Its foliage was attractive and its fruit plentiful;
on it there was food enough for all.
Under it the wild animals used to seek shade,
and in its branches the birds of the sky used to nest.
All creatures used to feed themselves from it.
4:13 While I was watching in my mind's visions on my bed,
a holy sentinel came down from heaven.
4:14 He called out loudly as follows:
'Chop down the tree and lop off its branches!
Strip off its foliage
and scatter its fruit!
Let the animals flee from under it
and the birds from its branches!
4:15 But leave its taproot in the ground,
with a band of iron and bronze around it
surrounded by the grass of the field.
Let it become damp with the dew of the sky,
and let it live with the animals in the grass of the land.
4:16 Let his mind be altered from that of a human being,
and let an animal's mind be given to him,
and let seven periods of time go by for him.
4:17 This announcement is by the decree of the sentinels;
this decision is by the pronouncement of the holy ones,
so that those who are alive may understand
that the Most High has authority over human kingdoms,
and he bestows them on whomever he wishes.
He establishes over them even the lowliest of human beings.'

4:18 "This is the dream that I, King Nebuchadnezzar, saw. Now you, Belteshazzar, declare its interpretation, for none of the wise men in my kingdom are able to make known to me the interpretation. But you can do so, for a spirit of the holy gods is in you."

Daniel Interprets Nebuchadnezzar's Dream

4:19 Then Daniel (whose name is also Belteshazzar) was upset for a brief time; his thoughts were alarming him. The king said, "Belteshazzar, don't let the dream and its interpretation alarm you." But Belteshazzar replied, "Sir, if only the dream were for your enemies and its interpretation applied to your adversaries! **4:20** The tree that you saw that grew large and strong, whose top reached to the sky, and which could be seen in all the land, **4:21** whose foliage was attractive and its fruit plentiful, and from which there was food available for all, under whose branches wild animals used to live, and in whose branches birds of the sky used to nest – **4:22** it is you, O king! For you have become great and strong. Your greatness is such that it reaches to heaven, and your authority to the ends of the earth. **4:23** As for the king seeing a holy sentinel coming down from heaven and saying, 'Chop down the tree and destroy it, but leave its taproot in the ground, with a band of iron and bronze around it, surrounded by the grass of the field. Let it become damp with the dew of the sky, and let it live with the wild animals, until seven periods of time go by for him' – **4:24** this is the interpretation, O king! It is the decision of the Most High that this has happened to my lord the king. **4:25** You will be driven from human society, and you will live with the wild animals. You will be fed grass like oxen, and you will become damp with the dew of the sky. Seven periods of time will pass by for you, before you under-stand that the Most High is ruler over human kingdoms and gives them to whomever he wishes. **4:26** They said to leave the taproot of the tree, for your kingdom will be restored to you when you come to understand that heaven rules. **4:27** Therefore, O king, may my advice be pleasing to you. Break away from your sins by doing what is right, and from your iniquities by showing mercy to the poor. Perhaps your prosperity will be prolonged."

4:28 Now all of this happened to King Nebuchadnezzar. **4:29** After twelve months, he happened to be walking around on the battlements of the royal palace of Babylon. **4:30** The king uttered these words: "Is this not the great Babylon that I have built for a royal residence by my own mighty strength and for my majestic honor?" **4:31** While these words were still on the king's lips, a voice came down from heaven: "It is hereby announced to you, King Nebuchadnezzar, that your kingdom has been removed from you! **4:32** You will be driven from human society, and you will live with the wild animals. You will be fed grass like oxen, and seven periods of time will pass by for you before you understand that the Most High is ruler over human kingdoms and gives them to whomever he wishes."

4:33 Now in that very moment this pronouncement about Nebuchadnezzar came true. He was driven from human society, he ate grass like oxen, and his body became damp with the dew of the sky, until his hair became long like an eagle's feathers, and his nails like a bird's claws.

4:34 But at the end of the appointed time I, Nebuchadnezzar, looked up toward heaven, and my sanity returned to me.
I extolled the Most High,
and I praised and glorified the one who lives forever.
For his authority is an everlasting authority,
and his kingdom extends from one generation to the next.
4:35 All the inhabitants of the earth are regarded as nothing.
He does as he wishes with the army of heaven
and with those who inhabit the earth.
No one slaps his hand
and says to him, 'What have you done?'

4:36 At that time my sanity returned to me. I was restored to the honor of my kingdom, and my splendor returned to me. My ministers and my nobles were seeking me out, and I was reinstated over my kingdom. I became even greater than before. **4:37** Now I, Nebuchadnezzar, praise and exalt and glorify the King of heaven, for all his deeds are right and his ways are just. He is able to bring down those who live in pride.

Belshazzar Sees Mysterious Handwriting on a Wall

5:1 King Belshazzar prepared a great banquet for a thousand of his nobles, and he was drinking wine in front of them all. **5:2** While under the influence of the wine, Belshazzar issued an order to bring in the gold and silver vessels – the ones that Nebuchadnezzar his father had confiscated from the temple in Jerusalem – so that the king and his nobles, together with his wives and his concubines, could drink from them. **5:3** So they brought the gold and silver vessels that had been confiscated from the temple, the house of God in Jerusalem, and the king and his nobles, together with his wives and concubines, drank from them. **5:4** As they drank wine, they praised the gods of gold and silver, bronze, iron, wood, and stone.

5:5 At that very moment the fingers of a human hand appeared and wrote on the plaster of the royal palace wall, opposite the lampstand. The king was watching the back of the hand that was writing. **5:6** Then all the color drained from the king's face and he became alarmed. The joints of his hips gave way, and his knees began knocking together. **5:7** The king called out loudly to summon the astrologers, wise men, and diviners. The king proclaimed to the wise men of Babylon that anyone who could read this inscription and disclose its interpretation would be clothed in purple and have a golden collar placed on his neck and be third ruler in the kingdom.

5:8 So all the king's wise men came in, but they were unable to read the writing or to make known its interpretation to the king. **5:9** Then King Belshazzar was very terrified, and he was visibly shaken. His nobles were completely dumbfounded.

5:10 Due to the noise caused by the king and his nobles, the queen mother then entered the banquet room. She said, "O king, live forever! Don't be alarmed! Don't be shaken! **5:11** There is a man in your kingdom who has within him a spirit of the holy gods. In the days of your father, he proved to have insight, discernment, and wisdom like that of the gods. King Nebuchadnezzar your father appointed him chief of the magicians, astrologers, wise men, and diviners. **5:12** Thus there was found in this man Daniel, whom the king renamed Belteshazzar, an extraordinary spirit, knowledge, and skill to interpret dreams, solve riddles, and decipher knotty problems. Now summon Daniel, and he will disclose the interpretation."

5:13 So Daniel was brought in before the king. The king said to Daniel, "Are you that Daniel who is one of the captives of Judah, whom my father the king brought from Judah? **5:14** I have heard about you, how there is a spirit of the gods in you, and how you have insight, discernment, and extraordinary wisdom. **5:15** Now the wise men and astrologers were brought before me to read this writing and make known to me its interpretation. But they were unable to disclose the interpretation of the message. **5:16** However, I have heard that you are able to provide interpretations and to decipher knotty problems. Now if you are able to read this writing and make known to me its interpretation, you will wear purple and have a golden collar around your neck and be third ruler in the kingdom."

Daniel Interprets the Handwriting on the Wall

5:17 But Daniel replied to the king, "Keep your gifts, and give your rewards to someone else! However, I will read the writing for the king and make known its interpretation. **5:18** As for you, O king, the most high God bestowed on your father Nebuchadnezzar a kingdom, greatness, honor, and majesty. **5:19** Due to the greatness that he bestowed on him, all peoples, nations, and language groups were trembling with fear before him. He killed whom he wished, he spared whom he wished, he exalted whom he wished, and he brought low whom he wished. **5:20** And when his mind became arrogant and his spirit filled with pride, he was deposed from his royal throne and his honor was removed from him. **5:21** He was driven from human society, his mind was changed to that of an animal, he lived with the wild donkeys, he was fed grass like oxen, and his body became damp with the dew of the sky, until he came to understand that the most high God rules over human kingdoms, and he appoints over them whomever he wishes.

5:22 "But you, his son Belshazzar, have not humbled yourself, although you knew all this. **5:23** Instead, you have exalted yourself against the Lord of heaven. You brought before you the vessels from his temple, and you and your nobles, together with your wives and concubines, drank wine from them. You praised the gods of silver, gold, bronze, iron, wood, and stone – gods that cannot see or hear or comprehend! But you have not glorified the God who has in his control your very breath and all your ways! **5:24** Therefore the palm of a hand was sent from him, and this writing was inscribed.

5:25 "This is the writing that was inscribed: MENE, MENE, TEQEL, and PHARSIN. **5:26** This is the interpretation of the words: As for *mene* – God has numbered your kingdom's days and brought it to an end. **5:27** As for *teqel* – you are weighed on the balances and found to be lacking. **5:28** As for *peres* – your kingdom is divided and given over to the Medes and Persians."

5:29 Then, on Belshazzar's orders, Daniel was clothed in purple, a golden collar was placed around his neck, and he was proclaimed third ruler in the kingdom. **5:30** And in that very night Belshazzar, the Babylonian king, was killed. **5:31** (6:1) So Darius the Mede took control of the kingdom when he was about sixty-two years old.

Daniel is Thrown into a Lions' Den

6:1 It seemed like a good idea to Darius to appoint over the kingdom 120 satraps who would be in charge of the entire kingdom. **6:2** Over them would be three supervisors, one of whom was Daniel. These satraps were accountable to them, so that the king's interests might not incur damage. **6:3** Now this Daniel was distinguishing himself above the other supervisors and the satraps, for he had an extraordinary spirit. In fact, the king intended to appoint him over the entire kingdom. **6:4** Consequently the supervisors and satraps were trying to find some pretext against Daniel in connection with administrative matters. But they were unable to find any such damaging evidence, because he was trustworthy and guilty of no negligence or corruption. **6:5** So these men concluded, "We won't find any pretext against this man Daniel unless it is in connection with the law of his God."

6:6 So these supervisors and satraps came by collusion to the king and said to him, "O King Darius, live forever! **6:7** To all the supervisors of the kingdom, the prefects, satraps, counselors, and governors it seemed like a good idea for a royal edict to be issued and an interdict to be enforced. For the next thirty days anyone who prays to any god or human other than you, O king, should be thrown into a den of lions. **6:8** Now let the king issue a written interdict so that it cannot be altered, according to the law of the Medes and Persians, which cannot be changed. **6:9** So King Darius issued the written interdict.

6:10 When Daniel realized that a written decree had been issued, he entered his home, where the windows in his upper room opened toward Jerusalem. Three times daily he was kneeling and offering prayers and thanks to his God just as he had been accustomed to do previously. **6:11** Then those officials who had gone to the king came by collusion and found Daniel praying and asking for help before his God. **6:12** So they approached the king and said to him, "Did you not issue an edict to the effect that for the next thirty days anyone who prays to any god or human other than to you, O king, would be thrown into a den of lions?" The king replied, "That is correct, according to the law of the Medes and Persians, which cannot be changed." **6:13** Then they said to the king, "Daniel, who is one of the captives from Judah, pays no attention to you, O king, or to the edict that you issued. Three times daily he offers his prayer." **6:14** When the king heard this, he was very upset and began thinking about how he might rescue Daniel. Until late afternoon he was struggling to find a way to rescue him. **6:15** Then those men came by collusion to the king and said to him, "Recall, O king, that it is a law of the Medes and Persians that no edict or decree that the king issues can be changed." **6:16** So the king gave the order, and Daniel was brought and thrown into a den of lions. The king consoled Daniel by saying, "Your God whom you continually serve will rescue you!" **6:17** Then a stone was brought and placed over the opening to the den. The king sealed it with his signet ring and with those of his nobles so that nothing could be changed with regard to Daniel. **6:18** Then the king departed to his palace. But he spent the night without eating, and no diversions were brought to him. He was unable to sleep.

God Rescues Daniel from the Lions

6:19 In the morning, at the earliest sign of daylight, the king got up and rushed to the lions' den. **6:20** As he approached the den, he called out to Daniel in a worried voice, "Daniel, servant of the living God, was your God whom you continually serve able to rescue you from the lions?" **6:21** Then Daniel spoke to the king, "O king, live forever! **6:22** My God sent his angel and closed the lions' mouths so that they have not harmed me, because I was found to be innocent before him. Nor have I done any harm to you, O king."

6:23 Then the king was delighted and gave an order to haul Daniel up from the den. So Daniel was hauled up out of the den. He had no injury of any kind, because he had trusted in his God. **6:24** The king gave another order, and those men who had maliciously accused Daniel were brought and thrown into the lions' den – they, their children, and their wives. They did not even reach the bottom of the den before the lions overpowered them and crushed all their bones.

6:25 Then King Darius wrote to all the peoples, nations, and language groups who were living in all the land: "Peace and prosperity! **6:26** I have issued an edict that throughout all the dominion of my kingdom people are to revere and fear the God of Daniel.

"For he is the living God;
he endures forever.
His kingdom will not be destroyed;
his authority is forever.
6:27 He rescues and delivers
and performs signs and wonders
in the heavens and on the earth.
He has rescued Daniel from the power of the lions!"

6:28 So this Daniel prospered during the reign of Darius and the reign of Cyrus the Persian.

Daniel has a Vision of Four Animals Coming up from the Sea

7:1 In the first year of King Belshazzar of Babylon, Daniel had a dream filled with visions while he was lying on his bed. Then he wrote down the dream in summary fashion. **7:2** Daniel explained: "I was watching in my vision during the night as the four winds of the sky were stirring up the great sea. **7:3** Then four large beasts came up from the sea; they were different from one another.

7:4 "The first one was like a lion with eagles' wings. As I watched, its wings were pulled off and it was lifted up from the ground. It was made to stand on two feet like a human being, and a human mind was given to it.

7:5 "Then a second beast appeared, like a bear. It was raised up on one side, and there were three ribs in its mouth between its teeth. It was told, 'Get up and devour much flesh!'

7:6 "After these things, as I was watching, another beast like a leopard appeared, with four bird-like wings on its back. This beast had four heads, and ruling authority was given to it.

7:7 "After these things, as I was watching in the night visions a fourth beast appeared – one dreadful, terrible, and very strong. It had two large rows of iron teeth. It devoured and crushed, and anything that was left it trampled with its feet. It was different from all the beasts that came before it, and it had ten horns.

7:8 "As I was contemplating the horns, another horn – a small one – came up between them, and three of the former horns were torn out by the roots to make room for it. This horn had eyes resembling human eyes and a mouth speaking arrogant things.

7:9 "While I was watching,
thrones were set up,
and the Ancient of Days took his seat.
His attire was white like snow;
the hair of his head was like lamb's wool.
His throne was ablaze with fire
and its wheels were all aflame.
7:10 A river of fire was streaming forth
and proceeding from his presence.
Many thousands were ministering to him;
Many tens of thousands stood ready to serve him.
The court convened
and the books were opened.

7:11 "Then I kept on watching because of the arrogant words of the horn that was speaking. I was watching until the beast was killed and its body destroyed and thrown into the flaming fire. **7:12** As for the rest of the beasts, their ruling authority had already been removed, though they were permitted to go on living for a time and a season. **7:13** I was watching in the night visions,

"And with the clouds of the sky
one like a son of man was approaching.
He went up to the Ancient of Days
and was escorted before him.
7:14 To him was given ruling authority, honor, and sovereignty.
All peoples, nations, and language groups were serving him.
His authority is eternal and will not pass away.
His kingdom will not be destroyed.

An Angel Interprets Daniel's Vision

7:15 "As for me, Daniel, my spirit was distressed, and the visions of my mind were alarming me. **7:16** I approached one of those standing nearby and asked him about the meaning of all this. So he spoke with me and revealed to me the interpretation of the vision: **7:17** 'These large beasts, which are four in number, represent four kings who will arise from the earth. **7:18** The holy ones of the Most High will receive the kingdom and will take possession of the kingdom forever and ever.'

7:19 "Then I wanted to know the meaning of the fourth beast, which was different from all the others. It was very dreadful, with two rows of iron teeth and bronze claws, and it devoured, crushed, and trampled anything that was left with its feet. **7:20** I also wanted to know the meaning of the ten horns on its head, and of that other horn which came up and before which three others fell. This was the horn that had eyes and a mouth speaking arrogant things, whose appearance was more formidable than the others. **7:21** While I was watching, that horn began to wage war against the holy ones and was defeating them, **7:22** until the Ancient of Days arrived and judgment was rendered in favor of the holy ones of the Most High. Then the time came for the holy ones to take possession of the kingdom.

7:23 "This is what he told me:
'The fourth beast means that there will be a fourth kingdom on earth that will differ from all the other kingdoms.
It will devour all the earth
and will trample and crush it.
7:24 The ten horns
mean that ten kings will arise from that kingdom.
Another king will arise after them,
but he will be different from the earlier ones.
He will humiliate three kings.
7:25 He will speak words against the Most High.
He will harass the holy ones of the Most High continually.
His intention will be to change times established by law.
They will be delivered into his hand
For a time, times, and half a time.
7:26 But the court will convene, and his ruling authority will be removed –
destroyed and abolished forever!
7:27 Then the kingdom, authority,
and greatness of the kingdoms under all of heaven
will be delivered to the people of the holy ones of the Most High.
His kingdom is an eternal kingdom;
all authorities will serve him and obey him.'

7:28 "This is the conclusion of the matter. As for me, Daniel, my thoughts troubled me greatly, and the color drained from my face. But I kept the matter to myself."

Daniel Has a Vision of a Goat and a Ram

8:1 In the third year of King Belshazzar's reign, a vision appeared to me, Daniel, after the one that had appeared to me previously. **8:2** In this vision I saw myself in Susa the citadel, which is located in the province of Elam. In the vision I saw myself at the Ulai Canal. **8:3** I looked up and saw a ram with two horns standing at the canal. Its two horns were both long, but one was longer than the other. The longer one was coming up after the shorter one. **8:4** I saw that the ram was butting westward, northward, and southward. No animal was able to stand before it, and there was none who could deliver from its power. It did as it pleased and acted arrogantly.

8:5 While I was contemplating all this, a male goat was coming from the west over the surface of all the land without touching the ground. This goat had a conspicuous horn between its eyes. **8:6** It came to the two-horned ram that I had seen standing beside the canal and rushed against it with raging strength. **8:7** I saw it approaching the ram. It went into a fit of rage against the ram and struck it and broke off its two horns. The ram had no ability to resist it. The goat hurled the ram to the ground and trampled it. No one could deliver the ram from its power. **8:8** The male goat acted even more arrogantly. But no sooner had the large horn become strong than it was broken, and there arose four conspicuous horns in its place, extending toward the four winds of the sky.

8:9 From one of them came a small horn. But it grew to be very big, toward the south and the east and toward the beautiful land. **8:10** It grew so big it reached the army of heaven, and it brought about the fall of some of the army and some of the stars to the ground, where it trampled them. **8:11** It also acted arrogantly against the Prince of the army, from whom

the daily sacrifice was removed and whose sanctuary was thrown down. **8:12** The army was given over, along with the daily sacrifice, in the course of his sinful rebellion. It hurled truth to the ground and enjoyed success.

8:13 Then I heard a holy one speaking. Another holy one said to the one who was speaking, "To what period of time does the vision pertain – this vision concerning the daily sacrifice and the destructive act of rebellion and the giving over of both the sanctuary and army to be trampled?" **8:14** He said to me, "To 2,300 evenings and mornings; then the sanctuary will be put right again."

An Angel Interprets Daniel's Vision

8:15 While I, Daniel, was watching the vision, I sought to understand it. Now one who appeared to be a man was standing before me. **8:16** Then I heard a human voice coming from between the banks of the Ulai. It called out, "Gabriel, enable this person to understand the vision." **8:17** So he approached the place where I was standing. As he came, I felt terrified and fell flat on the ground. Then he said to me, "Understand, son of man, that the vision pertains to the time of the end." **8:18** As he spoke with me, I fell into a trance with my face to the ground. But he touched me and stood me upright.

8:19 Then he said, "I am going to inform you about what will happen in the latter time of wrath, for the vision pertains to the appointed time of the end. **8:20** The ram that you saw with the two horns stands for the kings of Media and Persia. **8:21** The male goat is the king of Greece, and the large horn between its eyes is the first king. **8:22** The horn that was broken and in whose place there arose four others stands for four kingdoms that will arise from his nation, though they will not have his strength. **8:23** Toward the end of their rule, when rebellious acts are complete, a rash and deceitful king will arise. **8:24** His power will be great, but it will not be by his strength alone. He will cause terrible destruction. He will be successful in what he undertakes. He will destroy powerful people and the people of the holy ones. **8:25** By his treachery he will succeed through deceit. He will have an arrogant attitude, and he will destroy many who are unaware of his schemes. He will rise up against the Prince of princes, yet he will be broken apart – but not by human agency. **8:26** The vision of the evenings and mornings that was told to you is correct. But you should seal up the vision, for it refers to a time many days from now."

8:27 I, Daniel, was exhausted and sick for days. Then I got up and again carried out the king's business. But I was astonished at the vision, and there was no one to explain it.

Daniel Prays for His People

9:1 In the first year of Darius son of Ahasuerus, who was of Median descent and who had been appointed king over the Babylonian empire – **9:2** in the first year of his reign I, Daniel, came to understand from the sacred books that, according to the word of the LORD disclosed to the prophet Jeremiah, the years for the fulfilling of the desolation of Jerusalem were seventy in number. **9:3** So I turned my attention to the Lord God to implore him by prayer and requests, with fasting, sackcloth, and ashes. **9:4** I prayed to the LORD my God, confessing in this way:

"O Lord, great and awesome God who is faithful to his covenant with those who love him and keep his commandments, **9:5** we have sinned! We have done what is wrong and wicked; we have rebelled by turning away from your commandments and standards. **9:6** We have not paid attention to your servants the prophets, who spoke by your authority to our kings, our leaders, and our ancestors, and to all the inhabitants of the land as well.

9:7 "You are righteous, O Lord, but we are humiliated this day – the people of Judah and the inhabitants of Jerusalem and all Israel, both near and far away in all the countries in which you have scattered them, because they have behaved unfaithfully toward you. **9:8** O LORD, we have been humiliated – our kings, our leaders, and our ancestors – because we have sinned against you. **9:9** Yet the Lord our God is compassionate and forgiving, even though we have rebelled against him. **9:10** We have not obeyed the LORD our God by living according to his laws that he set before us through his servants the prophets.

9:11 "All Israel has broken your law and turned away by not obeying you. Therefore you have poured out on us the judgment solemnly threatened in the law of Moses the servant of God, for we have sinned against you. **9:12** He has carried out his threats against us and our rulers who were over us by bringing great calamity on us – what has happened to Jerusalem has never been equaled under all heaven! **9:13** Just as it is written in the law of Moses, so all this calamity has come on us. Still we have not tried to pacify the LORD our God by turning back from our sin and by seeking wisdom from your reliable moral standards. **9:14** The LORD was mindful of the calamity, and he brought it on us. For the LORD our God is just in all he has done, and we have not obeyed him.

9:15 "Now, O Lord our God, who brought your people out of the land of Egypt with great power and made a name for yourself that is remembered to this day – we have sinned and behaved wickedly. **9:16** O Lord, according to all your justice, please turn your raging anger away from your city Jerusalem, your holy mountain. For due to our sins and the iniquities of our ancestors, Jerusalem and your people are mocked by all our neighbors.

9:17 "So now, our God, accept the prayer and requests of your servant, and show favor to your devastated sanctuary for your own sake. **9:18** Listen attentively, my God, and hear! Open your eyes and look on our desolated ruins and the city called by your name. For it is not because of our own righteous deeds that we are praying to you, but because your compassion is abundant. **9:19** O Lord, hear! O Lord, forgive! O Lord, pay attention, and act! Don't delay, for your own sake, O my God! For your city and your people are called by your name."

Gabriel Gives to Daniel a Prophecy of Seventy Weeks

9:20 While I was still speaking and praying, confessing my sin and the sin of my people Israel and presenting my request before the LORD my God concerning his holy mountain – **9:21** yes, while I was still praying, the man Gabriel, whom I had seen previously in a vision, was approaching me in my state of extreme weariness, around the time of the evening offering. **9:22** He spoke with me, instructing me as follows: "Daniel, I have now come to impart understanding to you. **9:23** At the beginning of your requests a message went out, and I have come to convey it to you, for you are of great value in God's sight. Therefore consider the message and understand the vision:

9:24 "Seventy weeks have been determined
concerning your people and your holy city
to put an end to rebellion,
to bring sin to completion,
to atone for iniquity,
to bring in perpetual righteousness,
to seal up the prophetic vision,
and to anoint a most holy place.
9:25 So know and understand:
From the issuing of the command to restore and rebuild
Jerusalem until an anointed one, a prince arrives,
there will be a period of seven weeks and sixty-two weeks.
It will again be built, with plaza and moat,
but in distressful times.
9:26 Now after the sixty-two weeks,
an anointed one will be cut off and have nothing.
As for the city and the sanctuary,
the people of the coming prince will destroy them.
But his end will come speedily like a flood.
Until the end of the war that has been decreed
there will be destruction.
9:27 He will confirm a covenant with many for one week.
But in the middle of that week
he will bring sacrifices and offerings to a halt.
On the wing of abominations will come one who destroys,
until the decreed end is poured out on the one who destroys."

An Angel Appears to Daniel

10:1 In the third year of King Cyrus of Persia a message was revealed to Daniel (who was also called Belteshazzar). This message was true and concerned a great war. He understood the message and gained insight by the vision.

10:2 In those days I, Daniel, was mourning for three whole weeks. **10:3** I ate no choice food; no meat or wine came to my lips, nor did I anoint myself with oil until the end of those three weeks. **10:4** On the twenty-fourth day of the first month I was beside the great river, the Tigris. **10:5** I looked up and saw a man clothed in linen; around his waist was a belt made of gold from Upaz. **10:6** His body resembled yellow jasper, and his face had an appearance like lightning. His eyes were like blazing torches; his arms and feet had the gleam of polished bronze. His voice thundered forth like the sound of a large crowd.

10:7 Only I, Daniel, saw the vision; the men who were with me did not see it. On the contrary, they were overcome with fright and ran away to hide. **10:8** I alone was left to see this great vision. My strength drained from me, and my vigor disappeared; I was without energy. **10:9** I listened to his voice, and as I did so I fell into a trance-like sleep with my face to the ground. **10:10** Then a hand touched me and set me on my hands and knees. **10:11** He said to me, "Daniel, you are of great value. Understand the words that I am about to speak to you. So stand up, for I have now been sent to you." When he said this to me, I stood up shaking. **10:12** Then he said to me, "Don't be afraid, Daniel, for from the very first day you applied your mind to understand and to humble yourself before your God, your words were heard. I have come in response to your words. **10:13** However, the prince of the kingdom of Persia was opposing me for twenty-one days. But Michael, one of the leading princes, came to help me, because I was left there with the kings of Persia. **10:14** Now I have come to help you understand what will happen to your people in the latter days, for the vision pertains to future days."

10:15 While he was saying this to me, I was flat on the ground and unable to speak. **10:16** Then one who appeared to be a human being was touching my lips. I opened my mouth and started to speak, saying to the one who was standing before me, "Sir, due to the vision, anxiety has gripped me and I have no strength. **10:17** How, sir, am I able to speak with you? My strength is gone, and I am breathless." **10:18** Then the one who appeared to be a human being touched me again and strengthened me. **10:19** He said to me, "Don't be afraid, you who are valued. Peace be to you! Be strong! Be really strong!" When he spoke to me, I was strengthened. I said, "Sir, you may speak now, for you have given me strength." **10:20** He said, "Do you know why I have come to you? Now I am about to return to engage in battle with the prince of Persia. When I go, the prince of Greece is coming. **10:21** However, I will first tell you what is written in a dependable book. (There is no one who strengthens me against these princes, except Michael your prince. **11:1** And in the first year of Darius the Mede, I stood to strengthen him and to provide protection for him.) **11:2** Now I will tell you the truth.

The Angel Gives a Message to Daniel

"Three more kings will arise for Persia. Then a fourth king will be unusually rich, more so than all who preceded him. When he has amassed power through his riches, he will stir up everyone against the kingdom of Greece. **11:3** Then a powerful king will arise, exercising great authority and doing as he pleases. **11:4** Shortly after his rise to power, his kingdom will be broken up and distributed toward the four winds of the sky – but not to his posterity or with the authority he exercised, for his kingdom will be uprooted and distributed to others besides these.

11:5 "Then the king of the south and one of his subordinates will grow strong. His subordinate will resist him and will rule a kingdom greater than his. **11:6** After some years have passed, they will form an alliance. Then the daughter of the king of the south will come to the king of the north to make an agreement, but she will not retain her power, nor will he continue in his strength. She, together with the one who brought her, her child, and her benefactor will all be delivered over at that time.

11:7 "There will arise in his place one from her family line who will come against their army and will enter the stronghold of the king of the north and will move against them successfully. **11:8** He will also take their gods into captivity to Egypt, along with their cast images and prized utensils of silver and gold. Then he will withdraw for some years from the king of the north. **11:9** Then the king of the north will advance against the empire of the king of the south, but will withdraw to his own land.

11:10 His sons will wage war, mustering a large army which will advance like an overflowing river and carrying the battle all the way to the enemy's fortress.

11:11 "Then the king of the south will be enraged and will march out to fight against the king of the north, who will also muster a large army, but that army will be delivered into his hand. **11:12** When the army is taken away, the king of the south will become arrogant. He will be responsible for the death of thousands and thousands of people, but he will not continue to prevail. **11:13** For the king of the north will again muster an army, one larger than before. At the end of some years he will advance with a huge army and enormous supplies.

11:14 "In those times many will oppose the king of the south. Those who are violent among your own people will rise up in confirmation of the vision, but they will falter. **11:15** Then the king of the north will advance and will build siege mounds and capture a well-fortified city. The forces of the south will not prevail, not even his finest contingents. They will have no strength to prevail. **11:16** The one advancing against him will do as he pleases, and no one will be able to stand before him. He will prevail in the beautiful land, and its annihilation will be within his power. **11:17** His intention will be to come with the strength of his entire kingdom, and he will form alliances. He will give the king of the south a daughter in marriage in order to destroy the kingdom, but it will not turn out to his advantage. **11:18** Then he will turn his attention to the coastal regions and will capture many of them. But a commander will bring his shameful conduct to a halt; in addition, he will make him pay for his shameful conduct. **11:19** He will then turn his attention to the fortresses of his own land, but he will stumble and fall, not to be found again. **11:20** There will arise after him one who will send out an exactor of tribute to enhance the splendor of the kingdom, but after a few days he will be destroyed, though not in anger or battle.

11:21 "Then there will arise in his place a despicable person to whom the royal honor has not been rightfully conferred. He will come on the scene in a time of prosperity and will seize the kingdom through deceit. **11:22** Armies will be suddenly swept away in defeat before him; both they and a covenant leader will be destroyed. **11:23** After entering into an alliance with him, he will behave treacherously; he will ascend to power with only a small force. **11:24** In a time of prosperity for the most productive areas of the province he will come and accomplish what neither his fathers nor their fathers accomplished. He will distribute loot, spoils, and property to his followers, and he will devise plans against fortified cities, but not for long. **11:25** He will rouse his strength and enthusiasm against the king of the south with a large army.

The king of the south will wage war with a large and very powerful army, but he will not be able to prevail because of the plans devised against him. **11:26** Those who share the king's fine food will attempt to destroy him, and his army will be swept away; many will be killed in battle. **11:27** These two kings, their minds filled with evil intentions, will trade lies with one another at the same table. But it will not succeed, for there is still an end at the appointed time. **11:28** Then the king of the north will return to his own land with much property. His mind will be set against the holy covenant. He will take action, and then return to his own land. **11:29** At an appointed time he will again invade the south, but this latter visit will not turn out the way the former one did. **11:30** The ships of Kittim will come against him, leaving him disheartened. He will turn back and direct his indignation against the holy covenant. He will return and honor those who forsake the holy covenant. **11:31** His forces will rise up and profane the fortified sanctuary, stopping the daily sacrifice. In its place they will set up the abomination that causes desolation. **11:32** Then with smooth words he will defile those who have rejected the covenant. But the people who are loyal to their God will act valiantly. **11:33** These who are wise among the people will teach the masses. However, they will fall by the sword and by the flame, and they will be imprisoned and plundered for some time. **11:34** When they stumble, they will be granted some help. But many will unite with them deceitfully. **11:35** Even some of the wise will stumble, resulting in their refinement, purification, and cleansing until the time of the end, for it is still for the appointed time.

11:36 "Then the king will do as he pleases. He will exalt and magnify himself above every deity and he will utter presumptuous things against the God of gods. He will succeed until the time of wrath is completed, for what has been decreed must occur. **11:37** He will not respect the gods of his fathers – not even the god loved by women. He will not respect any god; he will elevate himself above them all. **11:38** What he will honor is a god of fortresses – a god his fathers did not acknowledge he will honor with gold, silver, valuable stones, and treasured commodities. **11:39** He will attack mighty fortresses, aided by a foreign deity. To those who recognize him he will grant considerable honor. He will place them in authority over many people, and he will parcel out land for a price.

11:40 "At the time of the end the king of the south will attack him. Then the king of the north will storm against him with chariots, horsemen, and a large armada of ships. He will invade lands, passing through them like an overflowing river. **11:41** Then he will enter the beautiful land. Many will fall, but these will escape: Edom, Moab, and the Ammonite leadership. **11:42** He will extend his power against other lands; the land of Egypt will not escape. **11:43** He will have control over the hidden stores of gold and silver, as well as all the treasures of Egypt. Libyans and Ethiopians will submit to him. **11:44** But reports will trouble him from the east and north, and he will set out in a tremendous rage to destroy and wipe out many. **11:45** He will pitch his royal tents between the seas toward the beautiful holy mountain. But he will come to his end, with no one to help him.

12:1 "At that time Michael,
the great prince who watches over your people,
will arise.
There will be a time of distress
unlike any other from the nation's beginning
up to that time.
But at that time your own people,
all those whose names are found written in the book,
will escape.
12:2 Many of those who sleep
in the dusty ground will awake –
some to everlasting life,
and others to shame and everlasting abhorrence.
12:3 But the wise will shine
like the brightness of the heavenly expanse.
And those bringing many to righteousness
will be like the stars forever and ever.

12:4 "But you, Daniel, close up these words and seal the book until the time of the end. Many will dash about, and knowledge will increase." **12:5** I, Daniel, watched as two others stood there, one on each side of the river. **12:6** One said to the man clothed in linen who was above the waters of the river, "When will the end of these wondrous events occur?" **12:7** Then I heard the man clothed in linen who was over the waters of the river as he raised both his right and left hands to the sky and made an oath by the one who lives forever: "It is for a time, times, and half a time. Then, when the power of the one who shatters the holy people has been exhausted, all these things will be finished." **12:8** I heard, but I did not understand. So I said, "Sir, what will happen after these things?" **12:9** He said, "Go, Daniel. For these matters are closed and sealed until the time of the end. **12:10** Many will be purified, made clean, and refined, but the wicked will go on being wicked. None of the wicked will understand, though the wise will understand. **12:11** From the time that the daily sacrifice is removed and the abomination that causes desolation is set in place, there are 1,290 days. **12:12** Blessed is the one who waits and attains to the 1,335 days. **12:13** But you should go your way until the end. You will rest and then at the end of the days you will arise to receive what you have been allotted."

Book 28. Hosea

Superscription

1:1 This is the word of the LORD which was revealed to Hosea son of Beeri during the time when Uzziah, Jotham, Ahaz, and Hezekiah ruled Judah, and during the time when Jeroboam son of Joash ruled Israel.

Symbols of Sin and Judgment: The Prostitute and Her Children

1:2 When the LORD first spoke through Hosea, he said to him, "Go marry a prostitute who will bear illegitimate children conceived through prostitution, because the nation continually commits spiritual prostitution by turning away from the LORD." **1:3** So Hosea married Gomer, the daughter of Diblaim. Then she conceived and gave birth to a son for him. **1:4** Then the LORD said to Hosea, "Name him 'Jezreel,' because in a little while I will punish the dynasty of Jehu on account of the bloodshed in the valley of Jezreel, and I will put an end to the kingdom of Israel. **1:5** At that time, I will destroy the military power of Israel in the valley of Jezreel."

1:6 She conceived again and gave birth to a daughter. Then the LORD said to him, "Name her 'No Pity' (Lo-Ruhamah) because I will no longer have pity on the nation of Israel. For I will certainly not forgive their guilt. **1:7** But I will have pity on the nation of Judah. I will deliver them by the LORD their God; I will not deliver them by the warrior's bow, by sword, by military victory, by chariot horses, or by chariots."

1:8 When she had weaned 'No Pity' (Lo-Ruhamah) she conceived again and gave birth to another son. **1:9** Then the LORD said: "Name him 'Not My People' (Lo-Ammi), because you are not my people and I am not your God."

The Restoration of Israel

1:10 (2:1) However, in the future the number of the people of Israel will be like the sand of the sea which can be neither measured nor numbered. Although it was said to them, "You are not my people," it will be said to them, "You are children of the living God!" **1:11** Then the people of Judah and the people of Israel will be gathered together. They will appoint for themselves one leader, and will flourish in the land. Certainly, the day of Jezreel will be great! **2:1** Then you will call your brother, "My People" (Ammi)! You will call your sister, "Pity" (Ruhamah)!

Idolatrous Israel Will Be Punished Like a Prostitute

2:2 Plead earnestly with your mother
(for she is not my wife, and I am not her husband),
so that she might put an end to her adulterous lifestyle,
and turn away from her sexually immoral behavior.
2:3 Otherwise, I will strip her naked,
and expose her like she was when she was born.
I will turn her land into a wilderness
and make her country a parched land,
so that I might kill her with thirst.
2:4 I will have no pity on her children,
because they are children conceived in adultery.
2:5 For their mother has committed adultery;
she who conceived them has acted shamefully.
For she said, "I will seek out my lovers;
they are the ones who give me my bread and my water,
my wool, my flax, my olive oil, and my wine.

The Lord's Discipline Will Bring Israel Back

2:6 Therefore, I will soon fence her in with thorns;
I will wall her in so that she cannot find her way.
2:7 Then she will pursue her lovers, but she will not catch them;
she will seek them, but she will not find them.
Then she will say,
"I will go back to my husband,
because I was better off then than I am now."

Agricultural Fertility Withdrawn from Israel

2:8 Yet until now she has refused to acknowledge that I was the one
who gave her the grain, the new wine, and the olive oil;
and that it was I who lavished on her the silver and gold –
which they used in worshiping Baal!
2:9 Therefore, I will take back my grain during the harvest time
and my new wine when it ripens;
I will take away my wool and my flax
which I had provided in order to clothe her.
2:10 Soon I will expose her lewd nakedness in front of her lovers,
and no one will be able to rescue her from me!
2:11 I will put an end to all her celebration:
her annual religious festivals,
monthly new moon celebrations,
and weekly Sabbath festivities –
all her appointed festivals.

2:12 I will destroy her vines and fig trees,
about which she said, "These are my wages for prostitution
that my lovers gave to me!"
I will turn her cultivated vines and fig trees into an uncultivated thicket,
so that wild animals will devour them.

2:13 "I will punish her for the festival days
when she burned incense to the Baal idols;
she adorned herself with earrings and jewelry,

and went after her lovers,
but she forgot me!" says the LORD.
Future Repentance and Restoration of Israel
2:14 However, in the future I will allure her;
I will lead her back into the wilderness,
and speak tenderly to her.
2:15 From there I will give back her vineyards to her,
and turn the "Valley of Trouble" into an "Opportunity for Hope."
There she will sing as she did when she was young,
when she came up from the land of Egypt.

2:16 "At that time," declares the LORD,
"you will call, 'My husband';
you will never again call me, 'My master.'
2:17 For I will remove the names of the Baal idols from your lips,
so that you will never again utter their names!"
 New Covenant Relationship with Repentant Israel
2:18 "At that time I will make a covenant for them with the wild animals,
the birds of the air, and the creatures that crawl on the ground.
I will abolish the warrior's bow and sword
 – that is, every weapon of warfare – from the land,
and I will allow them to live securely."
2:19 I will commit myself to you forever;
I will commit myself to you in righteousness and justice,
in steadfast love and tender compassion.
2:20 I will commit myself to you in faithfulness;
then you will acknowledge the LORD."
Agricultural Fertility Restored to the Repentant Nation
2:21 "At that time, I will willingly respond," declares the LORD.
"I will respond to the sky,
and the sky will respond to the ground;
2:22 then the ground will respond to the grain, the new wine, and the olive oil;
and they will respond to 'God Plants' (Jezreel)!
2:23 Then I will plant her as my own in the land.
I will have pity on 'No Pity' (Lo-Ruhamah).
I will say to 'Not My People' (Lo-Ammi), 'You are my people!'
And he will say, 'You are my God!'"
An Illustration of God's Love for Idolatrous Israel
3:1 The LORD said to me, "Go, show love to your wife again, even though she loves another man and continually commits adultery. Likewise, the LORD loves the Israelites although they turn to other gods and love to offer raisin cakes to idols." **3:2** So I paid fifteen shekels of silver and about seven bushels of barley to purchase her. **3:3** Then I told her, "You must live with me many days; you must not commit adultery or have sexual intercourse with another man, and I also will wait for you." **3:4** For the Israelites must live many days without a king or prince, without sacrifice or sacred fertility pillar, without ephod or idols. **3:5** Afterward, the Israelites will turn and seek the LORD their God and their Davidic king. Then they will submit to the LORD in fear and receive his blessings in the future.
The Lord's Covenant Lawsuit against the Nation Israel
4:1 Hear the word of the LORD, you Israelites!
For the LORD has a covenant lawsuit against the people of Israel.
For there is neither faithfulness nor loyalty in the land,
nor do they acknowledge God.
4:2 There is only cursing, lying, murder, stealing, and adultery.
They resort to violence and bloodshed.
4:3 Therefore the land will mourn,
and all its inhabitants will perish.
The wild animals, the birds of the sky,
and even the fish in the sea will perish.
The Lord's Dispute against the Sinful Priesthood
4:4 Do not let anyone accuse or contend against anyone else:
for my case is against you priests!
4:5 You stumble day and night,
and the false prophets stumble with you;
You have destroyed your own people!
4:6 You have destroyed my people
by failing to acknowledge me!
Because you refuse to acknowledge me,
I will reject you as my priests.
Because you reject the law of your God,
I will reject your descendants.
4:7 The more the priests increased in numbers,
the more they rebelled against me.
They have turned their glorious calling
into a shameful disgrace!
4:8 They feed on the sin offerings of my people;
their appetites long for their iniquity!
4:9 I will deal with the people and priests together:
I will punish them both for their ways,
and I will repay them for their deeds.

4:10 They will eat, but not be satisfied;
they will engage in prostitution, but not increase in numbers;
because they have abandoned the LORD
by pursuing other gods.
Judgment of Pagan Idolatry and Cultic Prostitution
4:11 Old and new wine
take away the understanding of my people.
4:12 They consult their wooden idols,
and their diviner's staff answers with an oracle.
The wind of prostitution blows them astray;
they commit spiritual adultery against their God.
4:13 They sacrifice on the mountaintops,
and burn offerings on the hills;
they sacrifice under oak, poplar, and terebinth,
because their shade is so pleasant.
As a result, your daughters have become cult prostitutes,
and your daughters-in-law commit adultery!
4:14 I will not punish your daughters when they commit prostitution,
nor your daughters-in-law when they commit adultery.
For the men consort with harlots,
they sacrifice with temple prostitutes.
It is true: "A people that lacks understanding will come to ruin!"
Warning to Judah: Do Not Join in Israel's Apostasy!
4:15 Although you, O Israel, commit adultery,
do not let Judah become guilty!
Do not journey to Gilgal!
Do not go up to Beth Aven!
Do not swear, "As surely as the LORD lives!"

4:16 Israel has rebelled like a stubborn heifer!
Soon the LORD will put them out to pasture
like a lamb in a broad field!
4:17 Ephraim has attached himself to idols;
Do not go near him!
The Shameful Sinners Will Be Brought to Shame
4:18 They consume their alcohol,
then engage in cult prostitution;
they dearly love their shameful behavior.
4:19 A whirlwind has wrapped them in its wings;
they will be brought to shame because of their idolatrous worship.
Announcement of Sin and Judgment
5:1 Hear this, you priests!
Pay attention, you Israelites!
Listen closely, O king!
For judgment is about to overtake you!
For you were like a trap to Mizpah,
like a net spread out to catch Tabor.
5:2 Those who revolt are knee-deep in slaughter,
but I will discipline them all.
5:3 I know Ephraim all too well;
the evil of Israel is not hidden from me.
For you have engaged in prostitution, O Ephraim;
Israel has defiled itself.
5:4 Their wicked deeds do not allow them to return to their God;
because a spirit of idolatry controls their heart,
and they do not acknowledge the LORD.
5:5 The arrogance of Israel testifies against it;
Israel and Ephraim will be overthrown because of their iniquity.
Even Judah will be brought down with them.
The Futility of Sacrificial Ritual without Moral Obedience
5:6 Although they bring their flocks and herds
to seek the favor of the LORD,
They will not find him –
he has withdrawn himself from them!
5:7 They have committed treason against the LORD,
because they bore illegitimate children.
Soon the new moon festival will devour them and their fields.
The Prophet's Declaration of Judgment
5:8 Blow the ram's horn in Gibeah!
Sound the trumpet in Ramah!
Sound the alarm in Beth Aven!
Tremble in fear, O Benjamin!
5:9 Ephraim will be ruined in the day of judgment!
What I am declaring to the tribes of Israel will certainly take place!
The Oppressors of the Helpless Will Be Oppressed
5:10 The princes of Judah are like those who move boundary markers.
I will pour out my rage on them like a torrential flood!
5:11 Ephraim will be oppressed, crushed under judgment,
because he was determined to pursue worthless idols.
The Curse of the Incurable Wound
5:12 I will be like a moth to Ephraim,
like wood rot to the house of Judah.

5:13 When Ephraim saw his sickness
and Judah saw his wound,
then Ephraim turned to Assyria,
and begged its great king for help.
But he will not be able to heal you!
He cannot cure your wound!

The Lion Will Carry Israel Off Into Exile

5:14 I will be like a lion to Ephraim,
like a young lion to the house of Judah.
I myself will tear them to pieces,
then I will carry them off, and no one will be able to rescue them!
5:15 Then I will return again to my lair
until they have suffered their punishment.
Then they will seek me;
in their distress they will earnestly seek me.

Superficial Repentance Breeds False Assurance of God's Forgiveness

6:1 "Come on! Let's return to the LORD!
He himself has torn us to pieces,
but he will heal us!
He has injured us,
but he will bandage our wounds!
6:2 He will restore us in a very short time;
he will heal us in a little while,
so that we may live in his presence.
6:3 So let us acknowledge him!
Let us seek to acknowledge the LORD!
He will come to our rescue as certainly as the appearance of the dawn,
as certainly as the winter rain comes,
as certainly as the spring rain that waters the land."

Transitory Faithfulness and Imminent Judgment

6:4 What am I going to do with you, O Ephraim?
What am I going to do with you, O Judah?
For your faithfulness is as fleeting as the morning mist;
it disappears as quickly as dawn's dew!
6:5 Therefore, I will certainly cut you into pieces at the hands of the prophets;
I will certainly kill you in fulfillment of my oracles of judgment;
for my judgment will come forth like the light of the dawn.
6:6 For I delight in faithfulness, not simply in sacrifice;
I delight in acknowledging God, not simply in whole burnt offerings.

Indictments Against the Cities of Israel and Judah

6:7 At Adam they broke the covenant;
Oh how they were unfaithful to me!
6:8 Gilead is a city full of evildoers;
its streets are stained with bloody footprints!
6:9 The company of priests is like a gang of robbers,
lying in ambush to pounce on a victim.
They commit murder on the road to Shechem;
they have done heinous crimes!
6:10 I have seen a disgusting thing in the temple of Israel:
there Ephraim practices temple prostitution
and Judah defiles itself.
6:11 I have appointed a time to reap judgment for you also, O Judah!

If Israel Would Repent of Sin, God Would Relent of Judgment

Whenever I want to restore the fortunes of my people,
7:1 whenever I want to heal Israel,
the sin of Ephraim is revealed,
and the evil deeds of Samaria are exposed.
For they do what is wrong;
thieves break into houses,
and gangs rob people out in the streets.
7:2 They do not realize
that I remember all of their wicked deeds.
Their evil deeds have now surrounded them;
their sinful deeds are always before me.

Political Intrigue and Conspiracy in the Palace

7:3 The royal advisers delight the king with their evil schemes,
the princes make him glad with their lies.
7:4 They are all like bakers,
they are like a smoldering oven;
they are like a baker who does not stoke the fire
until the kneaded dough is ready for baking.
7:5 At the celebration of their king,
his princes become inflamed with wine;
they conspire with evildoers.
7:6 They approach him, all the while plotting against him.
Their hearts are like an oven;
their anger smolders all night long,
but in the morning it bursts into a flaming fire.
7:7 All of them are blazing like an oven;
they devour their rulers.
All of their kings fall –
and none of them call on me!

Israel Lacks Discernment and Refuses to Repent

7:8 Ephraim has mixed itself like flour among the nations;
Ephraim is like a ruined cake of bread that is scorched on one side.
7:9 Foreigners are consuming what his strenuous labor produced,
but he does not recognize it!
His head is filled with gray hair,
but he does not realize it!
7:10 The arrogance of Israel testifies against him,
yet they refuse to return to the LORD their God!
In spite of all this they refuse to seek him!

Israel Turns to Assyria and Egypt for Help

7:11 Ephraim has been like a dove,
easily deceived and lacking discernment.
They called to Egypt for help;
they turned to Assyria for protection.
7:12 I will throw my bird net over them while they are flying,
I will bring them down like birds in the sky;
I will discipline them when I hear them flocking together.

Israel Has Turned Away from the Lord

7:13 Woe to them! For they have fled from me!
Destruction to them! For they have rebelled against me!
I want to deliver them,
but they have lied to me.
7:14 They do not pray to me,
but howl in distress on their beds;
They slash themselves for grain and new wine,
but turn away from me.

7:15 Although I trained and strengthened them,
they plot evil against me!
7:16 They turn to Baal;
they are like an unreliable bow.
Their leaders will fall by the sword
because their prayers to Baal have made me angry.
So people will disdain them in the land of Egypt.

God Will Raise Up the Assyrians to Attack Israel

8:1 Sound the alarm!
An eagle looms over the temple of the LORD!
For they have broken their covenant with me,
and have rebelled against my law.
8:2 Israel cries out to me,
"My God, we acknowledge you!"
8:3 But Israel has rejected what is morally good;
so an enemy will pursue him.

The Political and Cultic Sin of Israel

8:4 They enthroned kings without my consent!
They appointed princes without my approval!
They made idols out of their silver and gold,
but they will be destroyed!
8:5 O Samaria, he has rejected your calf idol!
My anger burns against them!
They will not survive much longer without being punished,
even though they are Israelites!
8:6 That idol was made by a workman – it is not God!
The calf idol of Samaria will be broken to bits.

The Fertility Cultists Will Become Infertile

8:7 They sow the wind,
and so they will reap the whirlwind!
The stalk does not have any standing grain;
it will not produce any flour.
Even if it were to yield grain,
foreigners would swallow it all up.
8:8 Israel will be swallowed up among the nations;
they will be like a worthless piece of pottery.

The Willful Donkey and the Wanton Harlot

8:9 They have gone up to Assyria,
like a wild donkey that wanders off.
Ephraim has hired prostitutes as lovers.

8:10 Even though they have hired lovers among the nations,
I will soon gather them together for judgment.
Then they will begin to waste away
under the oppression of a mighty king.

Sacrifices Ineffective without Moral Obedience

8:11 Although Ephraim has built many altars for sin offerings,
these have become altars for sinning!
8:12 I spelled out my law for him in great detail,
but they regard it as something totally unknown to them!
8:13 They offer up sacrificial gifts to me,
and eat the meat,
but the LORD does not accept their sacrifices.
Soon he will remember their wrongdoing,
he will punish their sins,

and they will return to Egypt.
8:14 Israel has forgotten his Maker and built royal palaces,
and Judah has built many fortified cities.
But I will send fire on their cities;
it will consume their royal citadels.

Fertility Cult Festivals Have Intoxicated Israel
9:1 O Israel, do not rejoice jubilantly like the nations,
for you are unfaithful to your God.
You love to receive a prostitute's wages
on all the floors where you thresh your grain.
9:2 Threshing floors and wine vats will not feed the people,
and new wine only deceives them.

Assyrian Exile Will Reverse the Egyptian Exodus
9:3 They will not remain in the LORD's land.
Ephraim will return to Egypt;
they will eat ritually unclean food in Assyria.
9:4 They will not pour out drink offerings of wine to the LORD;
they will not please him with their sacrifices.
Their sacrifices will be like bread eaten while in mourning;
all those who eat them will make themselves ritually unclean.
For their bread will be only to satisfy their appetite;
it will not come into the temple of the LORD.
9:5 So what will you do on the festival day,
on the festival days of the LORD?

No Escape for the Israelites This Time!
9:6 Look! Even if they flee from the destruction,
Egypt will take hold of them,
and Memphis will bury them.
The weeds will inherit the silver they treasure –
thorn bushes will occupy their homes.
9:7 The time of judgment is about to arrive!
The time of retribution is imminent!
Let Israel know!

Israel Rejects Hosea's Prophetic Exhortations
The prophet is considered a fool –
the inspired man is viewed as a madman –
because of the multitude of your sins
and your intense animosity.
9:8 The prophet is a watchman over Ephraim on behalf of God,
yet traps are laid for him along all of his paths;
animosity rages against him in the land of his God.

The Best of Times, the Worst of Times
9:9 They have sunk deep into corruption
as in the days of Gibeah.
He will remember their wrongdoing.
He will repay them for their sins.
9:10 When I found Israel, it was like finding grapes in the wilderness.
I viewed your ancestors like an early fig on a fig tree in its first season.
Then they came to Baal-Peor and they dedicated themselves to shame –
they became as detestable as what they loved.

The Fertility Worshipers Will Become Infertile
9:11 Ephraim will be like a bird;
what they value will fly away.
They will not bear children –
they will not enjoy pregnancy –
they will not even conceive!
9:12 Even if they raise their children,
I will take away every last one of them.
Woe to them!
For I will turn away from them.
9:13 Just as lion cubs are born predators,
so Ephraim will bear his sons for slaughter.
9:14 Give them, O LORD –
what will you give them?
Give them wombs that miscarry,
and breasts that cannot nurse!
9:15 Because of all their evil in Gilgal,
I hate them there.
On account of their evil deeds,
I will drive them out of my land.
I will no longer love them;
all their rulers are rebels.
9:16 Ephraim will be struck down –
their root will be dried up;
they will not yield any fruit.
Even if they do bear children,
I will kill their precious offspring.
9:17 My God will reject them,
for they have not obeyed him;
so they will be fugitives among the nations.

Israel is Guilty of Fertility Cult Worship
10:1 Israel was a fertile vine
that yielded fruit.

As his fruit multiplied,
he multiplied altars to Baal.
As his land prospered,
they adorned the fertility pillars.
10:2 Their heart is slipping;
soon they will be punished for their guilt.
The LORD will break their altars;
he will completely destroy their fertility pillars.

The Lord Will Punish Israel by Removing Its Kings
10:3 Very soon they will say, "We have no king
since we did not fear the LORD.
But what can a king do for us anyway?"
10:4 They utter empty words,
taking false oaths and making empty agreements.
Therefore legal disputes sprout up
like poisonous weeds in the furrows of a plowed field.

The Calf Idol and Idolaters of Samaria Will Be Exiled
10:5 The inhabitants of Samaria will lament over the calf idol of Beth Aven.
Its people will mourn over it;
its idolatrous priests will wail over it,
because its splendor will be taken from them into exile.
10:6 Even the calf idol will be carried to Assyria,
as tribute for the great king.
Ephraim will be disgraced;
Israel will be put to shame because of its wooden idol.
10:7 Samaria and its king will be carried off
like a twig on the surface of the waters.
10:8 The high places of the "House of Wickedness" will be destroyed;
it is the place where Israel sins.
Thorns and thistles will grow up over its altars.
Then they will say to the mountains, "Cover us!"
and to the hills, "Fall on us!"

Failure to Learn from the Sin and Judgment of Gibeah
10:9 O Israel, you have sinned since the time of Gibeah,
and there you have remained.
Did not war overtake the evildoers in Gibeah?
10:10 When I please, I will discipline them;
I will gather nations together to attack them,
to bind them in chains for their two sins.

Fertility Imagery: Plowing, Sowing, and Reaping
10:11 Ephraim was a well-trained heifer who loved to thresh grain;
I myself put a fine yokeon her neck.
I will harness Ephraim.
Let Judah plow!
Let Jacob break up the unplowed ground for himself!
10:12 Sow righteousness for yourselves,
reap unfailing love.
Break up the unplowed ground for yourselves,
for it is time to seek the LORD,
until he comes and showers deliverance on you.
10:13 But you have plowed wickedness;
you have reaped injustice;
you have eaten the fruit of deception.
Because you have depended on your chariots;
you have relied on your many warriors.

Bethel Will Be Destroyed Like Beth Arbel
10:14 The roar of battle will rise against your people;
all your fortresses will be devastated,
just as Shalman devastated Beth Arbel on the day of battle,
when mothers were dashed to the ground with their children.
10:15 So will it happen to you, O Bethel,
because of your great wickedness!
When that day dawns,
the king of Israel will be destroyed.

Reversal of the Exodus: Return to Egypt and Exile in Assyria
11:1 When Israel was a young man, I loved him like a son,
and I summoned my son out of Egypt.
11:2 But the more I summoned them,
the farther they departed from me.
They sacrificed to the Baal idols
and burned incense to images.

11:3 Yet it was I who led Ephraim,
I took them by the arm;
but they did not acknowledge
that I had healed them.
11:4 I led them with leather cords,
with leather ropes;
I lifted the yoke from their neck,
and gently fed them.

11:5 They will return to Egypt!

Assyria will rule over them
because they refuse to repent!
11:6 A sword will flash in their cities,
it will destroy the bars of their city gates,
and will devour them in their fortresses.
11:7 My people are obsessed with turning away from me;
they call to Baal, but he will never exalt them!
The Divine Dilemma: Judgment or Mercy?
11:8 How can I give you up, O Ephraim?
How can I surrender you, O Israel?
How can I treat you like Admah?
How can I make you like Zeboiim?
I have had a change of heart!
All my tender compassions are aroused!
11:9 I cannot carry out my fierce anger!
I cannot totally destroy Ephraim!
Because I am God, and not man – the Holy One among you –
I will not come in wrath!
God Will Restore the Exiles to Israel
11:10 He will roar like a lion,
and they will follow the LORD;
when he roars,
his children will come trembling from the west.
11:11 They will return in fear and trembling
like birds from Egypt,
like doves from Assyria,
and I will settle them in their homes," declares the LORD.
God's Lawsuit against Israel: Breach of Covenant
11:12 (12:1) Ephraim has surrounded me with lies;
the house of Israel has surrounded me with deceit.
But Judah still roams about with God;
he remains faithful to the Holy One.
12:1 Ephraim continually feeds on the wind;
he chases the east wind all day;
he multiplies lies and violence.
They make treaties with Assyria,
and send olive oil as tribute to Egypt.
12:2 The LORD also has a covenant lawsuit against Judah;
he will punish Jacob according to his ways
and repay him according to his deeds.
Israel Must Return to the God of Jacob
12:3 In the womb he attacked his brother;
in his manly vigor he struggled with God.
12:4 He struggled with an angel and prevailed;
he wept and begged for his favor.
He found God at Bethel,
and there he spoke with him!
12:5 As for the LORD God Almighty,
the LORD is the name by which he is remembered!
12:6 But you must return to your God,
by maintaining love and justice,
and by waiting for your God to return to you.
The Lord Refutes Israel's False Claim of Innocence
12:7 The businessmen love to cheat;
they use dishonest scales.
12:8 Ephraim boasts, "I am very rich!
I have become wealthy!
In all that I have done to gain my wealth,
no one can accuse me of any offense that is actually sinful."
12:9 "I am the LORD your God who brought you out of Egypt;
I will make you live in tents again as in the days of old.
12:10 I spoke to the prophets;
I myself revealed many visions;
I spoke in parables through the prophets."

12:11 Is there idolatry in Gilead?
Certainly its inhabitants will come to nothing!
Do they sacrifice bulls in Gilgal?
Surely their altars will be like stones heaped up on a plowed field!
Jacob in Aram, Israel in Egypt, and Ephraim in Trouble
12:12 Jacob fled to the country of Aram,
then Israel worked to acquire a wife;
he tended sheep to pay for her.
12:13 The LORD brought Israel out of Egypt by a prophet,
and due to a prophet Israel was preserved alive.
12:14 But Ephraim bitterly provoked him to anger;
so he will hold him accountable for the blood he has shed,
his Lord will repay him for the contempt he has shown.
Baal Worshipers and Calf Worshipers to be Destroyed
13:1 When Ephraim spoke, there was terror;
he was exalted in Israel,
but he became guilty by worshiping Baal and died.
13:2 Even now they persist in sin!

They make metal images for themselves,
idols that they skillfully fashion from their own silver;
all of them are nothing but the work of craftsmen!
There is a saying about them:
"Those who sacrifice to the calf idol are calf kissers!"
13:3 Therefore they will disappear like the morning mist,
like early morning dew that evaporates,
like chaff that is blown away from a threshing floor,
like smoke that disappears through an open window.
Well-Fed Israel Will Be Fed to Wild Animals
13:4 But I am the LORD your God,
who brought you out of Egypt.
Therefore, you must not acknowledge any God but me;
except me there is no Savior.

13:5 I cared for you in the wilderness,
in the dry desert where no water was.
13:6 When they were fed, they became satisfied;
when they were satisfied, they became proud;
as a result, they forgot me!
13:7 So I will pounce on them like a lion;
like a leopard I will lurk by the path.
13:8 I will attack them like a bear robbed of her cubs –
I will rip open their chests.
I will devour them there like a lion –
like a wild animal would tear them apart.
Israel's King Unable to Deliver the Nation
13:9 I will destroy you, O Israel!
Who is there to help you?
13:10 Where then is your king,
that he may save you in all your cities?
Where are your rulers for whom you asked, saying,
"Give me a king and princes"?
13:11 I granted you a king in my anger,
and I will take him away in my wrath!
Israel's Punishment Will Not Be Withheld Much Longer
13:12 The punishment of Ephraim has been decreed;
his punishment is being stored up for the future.
13:13 The labor pains of a woman will overtake him,
but the baby will lack wisdom;
when the time arrives,
he will not come out of the womb!
The Lord Will Not Relent from the Threatened Judgment
13:14 Will I deliver them from the power of Sheol? No, I will not!
Will I redeem them from death? No, I will not!
O Death, bring on your plagues!
O Sheol, bring on your destruction!
My eyes will not show any compassion!
The Capital of the Northern Empire Will Be Destroyed
13:15 Even though he flourishes like a reed plant,
a scorching east wind will come,
a wind from the LORD rising up from the desert.
As a result, his spring will dry up;
his well will become dry.
That wind will spoil all his delightful foods
in the containers in his storehouse.

13:16 (14:1) Samaria will be held guilty,
because she rebelled against her God.
They will fall by the sword,
their infants will be dashed to the ground –
their pregnant women will be ripped open.
Prophetic Call to Genuine Repentance
14:1 Return, O Israel, to the LORD your God,
for your sin has been your downfall!
14:2 Return to the LORD and repent!
Say to him: "Completely forgive our iniquity;
accept our penitential prayer,
that we may offer the praise of our lips as sacrificial bulls.
14:3 Assyria cannot save us;
we will not ride warhorses.
We will never again say, 'Our gods'
to what our own hands have made.
For only you will show compassion to Orphan Israel!"
Divine Promise to Relent from Judgment and to Restore Blessings
14:4 "I will heal their waywardness
and love them freely,
for my anger will turn away from them.

14:5 I will be like the dew to Israel;
he will blossom like a lily,
he will send down his roots like a cedar of Lebanon.
14:6 His young shoots will grow;

his splendor will be like an olive tree,
his fragrance like a cedar of Lebanon.
14:7 People will reside again in his shade;
they will plant and harvest grain in abundance.
They will blossom like a vine,
and his fame will be like the wine from Lebanon.

14:8 O Ephraim, I do not want to have anything to do with idols anymore!
I will answer him and care for him.
I am like a luxuriant cypress tree;
your fruitfulness comes from me!
Concluding Exhortation
14:9 Who is wise?
Let him discern these things!
Who is discerning?
Let him understand them!
For the ways of the LORD are right;
the godly walk in them,
but in them the rebellious stumble.

Book 29. Joel

Introduction
1:1 This is the LORD's message that was given
to Joel the son of Pethuel:
A Locust Plague Foreshadows the Day of the Lord
1:2 Listen to this, you elders;
pay attention, all inhabitants of the land.
Has anything like this ever happened in your whole life
or in the lifetime of your ancestors?
1:3 Tell your children about it,
have your children tell their children,
and their children the following generation.
1:4 What the *gazam*-locust left the *'arbeh*-locust consumed,
what the *'arbeh*-locust left the *yeleq*-locust consumed,
and what the *yeleq*-locust left the *hasil*-locust consumed!
1:5 Wake up, you drunkards, and weep!
Wail, all you wine drinkers,
because the sweet wine has been taken away from you.
1:6 For a nation has invaded our land.
There are so many of them they are too numerous to count.
Their teeth are like those of a lion;
they tear apart their prey like a lioness.
1:7 They have destroyed our vines;
they have turned our fig trees into mere splinters.
They have completely stripped off the bark and thrown them aside;
the twigs are stripped bare.
A Call to Lament
1:8 Wail like a young virgin clothed in sackcloth,
lamenting the death of her husband-to-be.
1:9 No one brings grain offerings or drink offerings
to the temple of the LORD anymore.
So the priests, those who serve the LORD, are in mourning.
1:10 The crops of the fields have been destroyed.
The ground is in mourning because the grain has perished.
The fresh wine has dried up;
the olive oil languishes.

1:11 Be distressed, farmers;
wail, vinedressers, over the wheat and the barley.
For the harvest of the field has perished.
1:12 The vine has dried up;
the fig tree languishes –
the pomegranate, date, and apple as well.
In fact, all the trees of the field have dried up.
Indeed, the joy of the people has dried up!

1:13 Get dressed and lament, you priests!
Wail, you who minister at the altar!
Come, spend the night in sackcloth, you servants of my God,
because no one brings grain offerings or drink offerings
to the temple of your God anymore.
1:14 Announce a holy fast;
proclaim a sacred assembly.
Gather the elders and all the inhabitants of the land
to the temple of the LORD your God,
and cry out to the LORD.

1:15 How awful that day will be!
For the day of the LORD is near;
it will come as destruction from the Divine Destroyer.

1:16 Our food has been cut off right before our eyes!
There is no longer any joy or gladness in the temple of our God!
1:17 The grains of seed have shriveled beneath their shovels.
Storehouses have been decimated
and granaries have been torn down, for the grain has dried up.
1:18 Listen to the cattle groan!
The herds of livestock wander around in confusion
because they have no pasture.
Even the flocks of sheep are suffering.

1:19 To you, O LORD, I call out for help,
for fire has burned up the grassy pastures,
flames have razed all the trees in the fields.
1:20 Even the wild animals cry out to you;
for the river beds have dried up;
fire has destroyed the grassy pastures.
The Locusts' Devastation
2:1 Blow the trumpet in Zion;
sound the alarm signal on my holy mountain!
Let all the inhabitants of the land shake with fear,
for the day of the LORD is about to come.
Indeed, it is near!
2:2 It will be a day of dreadful darkness,
a day of foreboding storm clouds,
like blackness spread over the mountains.
It is a huge and powerful army –
there has never been anything like it ever before,
and there will not be anything like it for many generations to come!
2:3 Like fire they devour everything in their path;
a flame blazes behind them.
The land looks like the Garden of Eden before them,
but behind them there is only a desolate wilderness –
for nothing escapes them!
2:4 They look like horses;
they charge ahead like war horses.
2:5 They sound like chariots rumbling over mountain tops,
like the crackling of blazing fire consuming stubble,
like the noise of a mighty army being drawn up for battle.
2:6 People writhe in fear when they see them.
All of their faces turn pale with fright.
2:7 They charge like warriors;
they scale walls like soldiers.
Each one proceeds on his course;
they do not alter their path.
2:8 They do not jostle one another;
each of them marches straight ahead.
They burst through the city defenses
and do not break ranks.
2:9 They rush into the city;
they scale its walls.
They climb up into the houses;
they go in through the windows like a thief.
2:10 The earth quakes before them;
the sky reverberates.
The sun and the moon grow dark;
the stars refuse to shine.
2:11 The voice of the LORD thunders as he leads his army.
Indeed, his warriors are innumerable;
Surely his command is carried out!
Yes, the day of the LORD is awesome
and very terrifying – who can survive it?
An Appeal for Repentance
2:12 "Yet even now," the LORD says,
"return to me with all your heart –
with fasting, weeping, and mourning.
Tear your hearts,
not just your garments!"
2:13 Return to the LORD your God,
for he is merciful and compassionate,
slow to anger and boundless in loyal love – often relenting from calamitous punishment.
2:14 Who knows?
Perhaps he will be compassionate and grant a reprieve,
and leave blessing in his wake –
a meal offering and a drink offering for you to offer to the LORD your God!
2:15 Blow the trumpet in Zion.
Announce a holy fast;
proclaim a sacred assembly!
2:16 Gather the people;
sanctify an assembly!

Gather the elders;
gather the children and the nursing infants.
Let the bridegroom come out from his bedroom
and the bride from her private quarters.
2:17 Let the priests, those who serve the LORD, weep
from the vestibule all the way back to the altar.
Let them say, "Have pity, O LORD, on your people;
please do not turn over your inheritance to be mocked,
to become a proverb among the nations.
Why should it be said among the peoples,
"Where is their God?"
The LORD's Response
2:18 Then the LORD became zealous for his land;
he had compassion on his people.
2:19 The LORD responded to his people,
"Look! I am about to restore your grain
as well as fresh wine and olive oil.
You will be fully satisfied.
I will never again make you an object of mockery among the nations.
2:20 I will remove the one from the north far from you.
I will drive him out to a dry and desolate place.
Those in front will be driven eastward into the Dead Sea,
and those in back westward into the Mediterranean Sea.
His stench will rise up as a foul smell."
Indeed, the LORD has accomplished great things.
2:21 Do not fear, my land!
Rejoice and be glad,
because the LORD has accomplished great things!
2:22 Do not fear, wild animals!
For the pastures of the wilderness are again green with grass.
Indeed, the trees bear their fruit;
the fig tree and the vine yield to their fullest.
2:23 Citizens of Zion, rejoice!
Be glad because of what the LORD your God has done!
For he has given to you the early rains as vindication.
He has sent to you the rains –
both the early and the late rains as formerly.
2:24 The threshing floors are full of grain;
the vats overflow with fresh wine and olive oil.
2:25 I will make up for the years
that the *'arbeh*-locust consumed your crops –
the *yeleq*-locust, the *hasil*-locust, and the *gazam*-locust –
my great army that I sent against you.
2:26 You will have plenty to eat,
and your hunger will be fully satisfied;
you will praise the name of the LORD your God,
who has acted wondrously in your behalf.
My people will never again be put to shame.
2:27 You will be convinced that I am in the midst of Israel.
I am the LORD your God; there is no other.
My people will never again be put to shame.
An Outpouring of the Spirit
2:28 (3:1) After all of this
I will pour out my Spirit on all kinds of people.
Your sons and daughters will prophesy.
Your elderly will have revelatory dreams;
your young men will see prophetic visions.
2:29 Even on male and female servants
I will pour out my Spirit in those days.
2:30 I will produce portents both in the sky and on the earth –
blood, fire, and columns of smoke.
2:31 The sunlight will be turned to darkness
and the moon to the color of blood,
before the day of the LORD comes –
that great and terrible day!
2:32 It will so happen that
everyone who calls on the name of the LORD will be delivered.
For on Mount Zion and in Jerusalem there will be those who survive,
just as the LORD has promised;
the remnant will be those whom the LORD will call.
The LORD Plans to Judge the Nations
3:1 (4:1) For look! In those days and at that time
I will return the exiles to Judah and Jerusalem.
3:2 Then I will gather all the nations,
and bring them down to the valley of Jehoshaphat.
I will enter into judgment against them there
concerning my people Israel who are my inheritance,
whom they scattered among the nations.
They partitioned my land,
3:3 and they cast lots for my people.
They traded a boy for a prostitute;
they sold a little girl for wine so they could drink.

3:4 Why are you doing these things to me, Tyre and Sidon?
Are you trying to get even with me, land of Philistia?
I will very quickly repay you for what you have done!
3:5 For you took my silver and my gold
and brought my precious valuables to your own palaces.
3:6 You sold Judeans and Jerusalemites to the Greeks,
removing them far from their own country.
3:7 Look! I am rousing them from that place to which you sold them.
I will repay you for what you have done!
3:8 I will sell your sons and daughters to the people of Judah.
They will sell them to the Sabeans, a nation far away.
Indeed, the LORD has spoken!
Judgment in the Valley of Jehoshaphat
3:9 Proclaim this among the nations:
"Prepare for a holy war!
Call out the warriors!
Let all these fighting men approach and attack!
3:10 Beat your plowshares into swords,
and your pruning hooks into spears!
Let the weak say, 'I too am a warrior!'
3:11 Lend your aid and come,
all you surrounding nations,
and gather yourselves to that place."
Bring down, O LORD, your warriors!
3:12 Let the nations be roused and let them go up
to the valley of Jehoshaphat,
for there I will sit in judgment on all the surrounding nations.
3:13 Rush forth with the sickle, for the harvest is ripe!
Come, stomp the grapes, for the winepress is full!
The vats overflow.
Indeed, their evil is great!
3:14 Crowds, great crowds are in the valley of decision,
for the day of the LORD is near in the valley of decision!
3:15 The sun and moon are darkened;
the stars withhold their brightness.
3:16 The LORD roars from Zion;
from Jerusalem his voice bellows out.
The heavens and the earth shake.
But the LORD is a refuge for his people;
he is a stronghold for the citizens of Israel.
The LORD's Presence in Zion
3:17 You will be convinced that I the LORD am your God,
dwelling on Zion, my holy mountain.
Jerusalem will be holy –
conquering armies will no longer pass through it.
3:18 On that day the mountains will drip with sweet wine,
and the hills will flow with milk.
All the dry stream beds of Judah will flow with water.
A spring will flow out from the temple of the LORD,
watering the Valley of Acacia Trees.
3:19 Egypt will be desolate
and Edom will be a desolate wilderness,
because of the violence they did to the people of Judah,
in whose land they shed innocent blood.
3:20 But Judah will reside securely forever,
and Jerusalem will be secure from one generation to the next.
3:21 I will avenge their blood which I had not previously acquitted.
It is the LORD who dwells in Zion!

Book 30. Amos

Introduction
1:1 The following is a record of what Amos prophesied. He was one of the herdsmen from Tekoa. These prophecies about Israel were revealed to him during the time of King Uzziah of Judah and King Jeroboam son of Joash of Israel, two years before the earthquake.
God Will Judge the Surrounding Nations
1:2 Amos said:
"The LORD comes roaring out of Zion;
from Jerusalem he comes bellowing!
The shepherds' pastures wilt;
the summit of Carmel withers."

1:3 This is what the LORD says:
"Because Damascus has committed three crimes –
make that four! – I will not revoke my
decree of judgment.
They ripped through Gilead like threshing sledges with iron teeth.
1:4 So I will set Hazael's house on fire;
fire will consume Ben Hadad's fortresses.
1:5 I will break the bar on the gate of Damascus.
I will remove the ruler from Wicked Valley,

the one who holds the royal scepter from Beth Eden.
The people of Aram will be deported to Kir."
The LORD has spoken!

1:6 This is what the LORD says:
"Because Gaza has committed three crimes –
make that four! – I will not revoke my decree of judgment.
They deported a whole community and sold them to Edom.
1:7 So I will set Gaza's city wall on fire;
fire will consume her fortresses.
1:8 I will remove the ruler from Ashdod,
the one who holds the royal scepter from Ashkelon.
I will strike Ekron with my hand;
the rest of the Philistines will also die."
The sovereign LORD has spoken!

1:9 This is what the LORD says:
"Because Tyre has committed three crimes –
make that four! – I will not revoke my decree of judgment.
They sold a whole community to Edom;
they failed to observe a treaty of brotherhood.
1:10 So I will set fire to Tyre's city wall;
fire will consume her fortresses."

1:11 This is what the LORD says:
"Because Edom has committed three crimes –
make that four! – I will not revoke my decree of judgment.
He chased his brother with a sword;
he wiped out his allies.
In his anger he tore them apart without stopping to rest;
in his fury he relentlessly attacked them.
1:12 So I will set Teman on fire;
fire will consume Bozrah's fortresses."

1:13 This is what the LORD says:
"Because the Ammonites have committed three crimes –
make that four! – I will not revoke my decree of judgment.
They ripped open Gilead's pregnant women
so they could expand their territory.
1:14 So I will set fire to Rabbah's city wall;
fire will consume her fortresses.
War cries will be heard on the day of battle;
a strong gale will blow on the day of the windstorm.
1:15 Ammon's king will be deported;
he and his officials will be carried off together."
The LORD has spoken!

2:1 This is what the LORD says:
"Because Moab has committed three crimes –
make that four! – I will not revoke my decree of judgment.
They burned the bones of Edom's king into lime.
2:2 So I will set Moab on fire,
and it will consume Kerioth's fortresses.
Moab will perish in the heat of battle
amid war cries and the blaring of the ram's horn.
2:3 I will remove Moab's leader;
I will kill all Moab's officials with him."
The LORD has spoken!

2:4 This is what the LORD says:
"Because Judah has committed three covenant transgressions –
make that four! – I will not revoke my decree of judgment.
They rejected the LORD's law;
they did not obey his commands.
Their false gods,
to which their fathers were loyal,
led them astray.
2:5 So I will set Judah on fire,
and it will consume Jerusalem's fortresses."
God Will Judge Israel
2:6 This is what the LORD says:
"Because Israel has committed three covenant transgressions –
make that four! – I will not revoke my decree of judgment.
They sold the innocent for silver,
the needy for a pair of sandals.
2:7 They trample on the dirt-covered heads of the poor;
they push the destitute away.
A man and his father go to the same girl;
in this way they show disrespect for my moral purity.
2:8 They stretch out on clothing seized as collateral;
they do so right beside every altar!
They drink wine bought with the fines they have levied;
they do so right in the temple of their God!

2:9 For Israel's sake I destroyed the Amorites.
They were as tall as cedars
and as strong as oaks,
but I destroyed the fruit on their branches
and their roots in the ground.
2:10 I brought you up from the land of Egypt;
I led you through the wilderness for forty years
so you could take the Amorites' land as your own.
2:11 I made some of your sons prophets
and some of your young men Nazirites.
Is this not true, you Israelites?"
The LORD is speaking!

2:12 "But you made the Nazirites drink wine;
you commanded the prophets, 'Do not prophesy!'
2:13 Look! I will press you down,
like a cart loaded down with grain presses down.
2:14 Fast runners will find no place to hide;
strong men will have no strength left;
warriors will not be able to save their lives.
2:15 Archers will not hold their ground;
fast runners will not save their lives,
nor will those who ride horses.
2:16 Bravehearted warriors will run away naked in that day."
The LORD is speaking!
Every Effect has its Cause
3:1 Listen, you Israelites, to this message which the LORD is proclaiming against you! This message is for the entire clan I brought up from the land of Egypt: **3:2** "I have chosen you alone from all the clans of the earth. Therefore I will punish you for all your sins."

3:3 Do two walk together without having met?
3:4 Does a lion roar in the woods if he has not cornered his prey?
Does a young lion bellow from his den if he has not caught something?
3:5 Does a bird swoop down into a trap on the ground if there is no bait?
Does a trap spring up from the ground unless it has surely caught something?
3:6 If an alarm sounds in a city, do people not fear?
If disaster overtakes a city, is the LORD not responsible?
3:7 Certainly the sovereign LORD does nothing without first revealing his plan to his servants the prophets.
3:8 A lion has roared! Who is not afraid?
The sovereign LORD has spoken! Who can refuse to prophesy?
Samaria Will Fall
3:9 Make this announcement in the fortresses of Ashdod
and in the fortresses in the land of Egypt.
Say this:
"Gather on the hills around Samaria!
Observe the many acts of violence taking place within the city,
the oppressive deeds occurring in it."

3:10 "They do not know how to do what is right." (The LORD is speaking.)
"They store up the spoils of destructive violence in their fortresses.
3:11 Therefore," says the sovereign LORD, "an enemy will encircle the land.
He will take away your power;
your fortresses will be looted."

3:12 This is what the LORD says:
"Just as a shepherd salvages from the lion's mouth a couple of leg bones or a piece of an ear,
so the Israelites who live in Samaria will be salvaged.
They will be left with just a corner of a bed,
and a part of a couch."
3:13 Listen and warn the family of Jacob!
The sovereign LORD, the God who commands armies, is speaking!

3:14 "Certainly when I punish Israel for their covenant transgressions,
I will destroy Bethel's altars.
The horns of the altar will be cut off and fall to the ground.
3:15 I will destroy both the winter and summer houses.
The houses filled with ivory will be ruined,
the great houses will be swept away."
The LORD is speaking!

4:1 Listen to this message, you cows of Bashan who live on Mount Samaria!
You oppress the poor;
you crush the needy.
You say to your husbands,
"Bring us more to drink!"
4:2 The sovereign LORD confirms this oath by his own holy character:

"Certainly the time is approaching
when you will be carried away in baskets,
every last one of you in fishermen's pots.
4:3 Each of you will go straight through the gaps in the walls;
you will be thrown out toward Harmon."
The LORD is speaking!

Israel has an Appointment with God
4:4 "Go to Bethel and rebel!
At Gilgal rebel some more!
Bring your sacrifices in the morning,
your tithes on the third day!
4:5 Burn a thank offering of bread made with yeast!
Make a public display of your voluntary offerings!
For you love to do this, you Israelites."
The sovereign LORD is speaking!

4:6 "But surely I gave you no food to eat in any of your cities;
you lacked food everywhere you live.
Still you did not come back to me."
The LORD is speaking!

4:7 "I withheld rain from you three months before the harvest.
I gave rain to one city, but not to another.
One field would get rain, but the field that received no rain dried up.
4:8 People from two or three cities staggered into one city to get water,
but remained thirsty.
Still you did not come back to me."
The LORD is speaking!

4:9 "I destroyed your crops with blight and disease.
Locusts kept devouring your orchards, vineyards, fig trees, and olive trees.
Still you did not come back to me."
The LORD is speaking!

4:10 "I sent against you a plague like one of the Egyptian plagues.
I killed your young men with the sword,
along with the horses you had captured.
I made the stench from the corpses rise up into your nostrils.
Still you did not come back to me."
The LORD is speaking!

4:11 "I overthrew some of you the way God overthrew Sodom and Gomorrah.
You were like a burning stick snatched from the flames.
Still you did not come back to me."
The LORD is speaking!

4:12 "Therefore this is what I will do to you, Israel.
Because I will do this to you,
prepare to meet your God, Israel!
4:13 For here he is!
He formed the mountains and created the wind.
He reveals his plans to men.
He turns the dawn into darkness
and marches on the heights of the earth.
The LORD, the God who commands armies, is his name!"

Death is Imminent
5:1 Listen to this funeral song I am ready to sing about you, family of Israel:
5:2 "The virgin Israel has fallen down and will not get up again.
She is abandoned on her own land
with no one to help her get up."

5:3 The sovereign LORD says this:
"The city that marches out with a thousand soldiers will have only a hundred left;
the town that marches out with a hundred soldiers will have only ten left
for the family of Israel."

5:4 The LORD says this to the family of Israel:
"Seek me so you can live!
5:5 Do not seek Bethel!
Do not visit Gilgal!
Do not journey down to Beer Sheba!
For the people of Gilgal will certainly be carried into exile;
and Bethel will become a place where disaster abounds."
5:6 Seek the LORD so you can live!
Otherwise he will break out like fire against Joseph's family;
the fire will consume
and no one will be able to quench it and save Bethel.
5:7 The Israelites turn justice into bitterness;
they throw what is fair and right to the ground.

5:8 (But there is one who made the constellations Pleiades and Orion;
he can turn the darkness into morning
and daylight into night.
He summons the water of the seas
and pours it out on the earth's surface.
The LORD is his name!
5:9 He flashes destruction down upon the strong
so that destruction overwhelms the fortified places.)

5:10 The Israelites hate anyone who arbitrates at the city gate;
they despise anyone who speaks honestly.
5:11 Therefore, because you make the poor pay taxes on their crops
and exact a grain tax from them,
you will not live in the houses you built with chiseled stone,
nor will you drink the wine from the fine vineyards you planted.
5:12 Certainly I am aware of your many rebellious acts
and your numerous sins.
You torment the innocent, you take bribes,
and you deny justice to the needy at the city gate.
5:13 For this reason whoever is smart keeps quiet in such a time,
for it is an evil time.
5:14 Seek good and not evil so you can live!
Then the LORD, the God who commands armies, just might be with you,
as you claim he is.
5:15 Hate what is wrong, love what is right!
Promote justice at the city gate!
Maybe the LORD, the God who commands armies, will have mercy on those who are left from Joseph.
5:16 Because of Israel's sins this is what the LORD, the God who commands armies, the sovereign One, says:
"In all the squares there will be wailing,
in all the streets they will mourn the dead.
They will tell the field workers to lament
and the professional mourners to wail.
5:17 In all the vineyards there will be wailing,
for I will pass through your midst," says the LORD.

The Lord Demands Justice
5:18 Woe to those who wish for the day of the LORD!
Why do you want the LORD's day of judgment to come?
It will bring darkness, not light.
5:19 Disaster will be inescapable,
as if a man ran from a lion only to meet a bear,
then escaped into a house,
leaned his hand against the wall,
and was bitten by a poisonous snake.
5:20 Don't you realize the LORD's day of judgment will bring darkness, not light –
gloomy blackness, not bright light?
5:21 "I absolutely despise your festivals!
I get no pleasure from your religious assemblies!
5:22 Even if you offer me burnt and grain offerings, I will not be satisfied;
I will not look with favor on your peace offerings of fattened calves.
5:23 Take away from me your noisy songs;
I don't want to hear the music of your stringed instruments.
5:24 Justice must flow like torrents of water,
righteous actions like a stream that never dries up.
5:25 You did not bring me sacrifices and grain offerings during the forty years you spent in the wilderness, family of Israel.
5:26 You will pick up your images of Sikkuth, your king,
and Kiyyun, your star god, which you made for yourselves,
5:27 and I will drive you into exile beyond Damascus," says the LORD.
He is called the God who commands armies!

The Party is over for the Rich
6:1 Woe to those who live in ease in Zion,
to those who feel secure on Mount Samaria.
They think of themselves as the elite class of the best nation.
The family of Israel looks to them for leadership.
6:2 They say to the people:
"Journey over to Calneh and look at it!
Then go from there to Hamath-Rabbah!
Then go down to Gath of the Philistines!
Are they superior to our two kingdoms?
Is their territory larger than yours?"
6:3 You refuse to believe a day of disaster will come,
but you establish a reign of violence.
6:4 They lie around on beds decorated with ivory,
and sprawl out on their couches.
They eat lambs from the flock,
and calves from the middle of the pen.
6:5 They sing to the tune of stringed instruments;
like David they invent musical instruments.

6:6 They drink wine from sacrificial bowls,
and pour the very best oils on themselves.
Yet they are not concerned over the ruin of Joseph.
6:7 Therefore they will now be the first to go into exile,
and the religious banquets where they sprawl on couches will end.
6:8 The sovereign LORD confirms this oath by his very own life.

The LORD, the God who commands armies, is speaking:
"I despise Jacob's arrogance;
I hate their fortresses.
I will hand over to their enemies the city of Samaria and everything in it."

6:9 If ten men are left in one house, they too will die. **6:10** When their close relatives, the ones who will burn the corpses, pick up their bodies to remove the bones from the house, they will say to anyone who is in the inner rooms of the house, "Is anyone else with you?" He will respond, "Be quiet! Don't invoke the LORD's name!"
6:11 Indeed, look! The LORD is giving the command.
He will smash the large house to bits,
and the small house into little pieces.
6:12 Can horses run on rocky cliffs?
Can one plow the sea with oxen?
Yet you have turned justice into a poisonous plant,
and the fruit of righteous actions into a bitter plant.
6:13 You are happy because you conquered Lo-Debar.
You say, "Did we not conquer Karnaim by our own power?"

6:14 "Look! I am about to bring a nation against you, family of Israel."
The LORD, the God who commands armies, is speaking.
"They will oppress you all the way from Lebo-Hamath to the Stream of the Arabah."

Symbolic Visions of Judgment

7:1 The sovereign LORD showed me this: I saw him making locusts just as the crops planted late were beginning to sprout. (The crops planted late sprout after the royal harvest.) **7:2** When they had completely consumed the earth's vegetation, I said,
"Sovereign LORD, forgive Israel!
How can Jacob survive?
He is too weak!"
7:3 The LORD decided not to do this. "It will not happen," the LORD said.

7:4 The sovereign LORD showed me this: I saw the sovereign LORD summoning a shower of fire. It consumed the great deep and devoured the fields.
7:5 I said, "Sovereign LORD, stop!
How can Jacob survive?
He is too weak!"
7:6 The LORD decided not to do this. The sovereign LORD said, "This will not happen either."

7:7 He showed me this: I saw the sovereign One standing by a tin wall holding tin in his hand. **7:8** The LORD said to me, "What do you see, Amos?" I said, "Tin." The sovereign One then said,
"Look, I am about to place tin among my people Israel.
I will no longer overlook their sin.
7:9 Isaac's centers of worship will become desolate;
Israel's holy places will be in ruins.
I will attack Jeroboam's dynasty with the sword."

Amos Confronts a Priest

7:10 Amaziah the priest of Bethel sent this message to King Jeroboam of Israel: "Amos is conspiring against you in the very heart of the kingdom of Israel! The land cannot endure all his prophecies. **7:11** As a matter of fact, Amos is saying this: 'Jeroboam will die by the sword and Israel will certainly be carried into exile away from its land.'"
7:12 Amaziah then said to Amos, "Leave, you visionary! Run away to the land of Judah! Earn your living and prophesy there! **7:13** Don't prophesy at Bethel any longer, for a royal temple and palace are here!"
7:14 Amos replied to Amaziah, "I was not a prophet by profession. No, I was a herdsman who also took care of sycamore fig trees. **7:15** Then the LORD took me from tending flocks and gave me this commission, 'Go! Prophesy to my people Israel!' **7:16** So now listen to the LORD's message! You say, 'Don't prophesy against Israel! Don't preach against the family of Isaac!'
7:17 "Therefore this is what the LORD says:
'Your wife will become a prostitute in the streets
and your sons and daughters will die violently.
Your land will be given to others
and you will die in a foreign land.
Israel will certainly be carried into exile away from its land.'"

More Visions and Messages of Judgment

8:1 The sovereign LORD showed me this: I saw a basket of summer fruit.

8:2 He said, "What do you see, Amos?" I replied, "A basket of summer fruit." Then the LORD said to me, "The end has come for my people Israel! I will no longer overlook their sins.
8:3 The women singing in the temple will wail in that day."
The sovereign LORD is speaking.
"There will be many corpses littered everywhere! Be quiet!"
8:4 Listen to this, you who trample the needy,
and do away with the destitute in the land.
8:5 You say,
"When will the new moon festival be over, so we can sell grain?
When will the Sabbath end, so we can open up the grain bins?"
We're eager to sell less for a higher price,
and to cheat the buyer with rigged scales!
8:6 We're eager to trade silver for the poor,
a pair of sandals for the needy!
We want to mix in some chaff with the grain!"
8:7 The LORD confirms this oath by the arrogance of Jacob:
"I swear I will never forget all you have done!
8:8 Because of this the earth will quake,
and all who live in it will mourn.
The whole earth will rise like the River Nile,
it will surge upward and then grow calm, like the Nile in Egypt.
8:9 In that day," says the sovereign LORD, "I will make the sun set at noon,
and make the earth dark in the middle of the day.
8:10 I will turn your festivals into funerals,
and all your songs into funeral dirges.
I will make everyone wear funeral clothes
and cause every head to be shaved bald.
I will make you mourn as if you had lost your only son;
when it ends it will indeed have been a bitter day.
8:11 Be certain of this, the time is coming," says the sovereign LORD,
"when I will send a famine through the land –
not a shortage of food or water
but an end to divine revelation!
8:12 People will stagger from sea to sea,
and from the north around to the east.
They will wander about looking for a revelation from the LORD,
but they will not find any.
8:13 In that day your beautiful young women and your young men will faint from thirst. **8:14** These are the ones who now take oaths in the name of the sinful idol goddess of Samaria.
They vow, 'As surely as your god lives, O Dan,' or 'As surely as your beloved one lives, O Beer Sheba!'
But they will fall down and not get up again."

9:1 I saw the sovereign One standing by the altar and he said, "Strike the tops of the support pillars, so the thresholds shake!
Knock them down on the heads of all the people,
and I will kill the survivors with the sword.
No one will be able to run away;
no one will be able to escape.
9:2 Even if they could dig down into the netherworld,
my hand would pull them up from there.
Even if they could climb up to heaven,
I would drag them down from there.
9:3 Even if they were to hide on the top of Mount Carmel,
I would hunt them down and take them from there.
Even if they tried to hide from me at the bottom of the sea,
from there I would command the Sea Serpent to bite them.
9:4 Even when their enemies drive them into captivity,
from there I will command the sword to kill them.
I will not let them out of my sight;
they will experience disaster, not prosperity."
9:5 The sovereign LORD who commands armies will do this.
He touches the earth and it dissolves;
all who live on it mourn.
The whole earth rises like the River Nile,
and then grows calm like the Nile in Egypt.
9:6 He builds the upper rooms of his palace in heaven
and sets its foundation supports on the earth.
He summons the water of the sea
and pours it out on the earth's surface.
The LORD is his name.

9:7 "You Israelites are just like the Ethiopians in my sight," says the LORD.
"Certainly I brought Israel up from the land of Egypt,
but I also brought the Philistines from Caphtor and the Arameans from Kir.
9:8 Look, the sovereign LORD is watching the sinful nation,
and I will destroy it from the face of the earth.
But I will not completely destroy the family of Jacob," says the LORD.

9:9 "For look, I am giving a command
and I will shake the family of Israel together with all the nations.
It will resemble a sieve being shaken,
when not even a pebble falls to the ground.
9:10 All the sinners among my people will die by the sword –
the ones who say, 'Disaster will not come near, it will not confront us.'
The Restoration of the Davidic Dynasty
9:11 "In that day I will rebuild the collapsing hut of David.
I will seal its gaps,
repair its ruins,
and restore it to what it was like in days gone by.
9:12 As a result they will conquer those left in Edom
and all the nations subject to my rule."
The LORD, who is about to do this, is speaking!

9:13 "Be sure of this, the time is coming," says the LORD,
"when the plowman will catch up to the reaper
and the one who stomps the grapes will overtake the planter.
Juice will run down the slopes,
it will flow down all the hillsides.
9:14 I will bring back my people, Israel;
they will rebuild the cities lying in rubble and settle down.
They will plant vineyards and drink the wine they produce;
they will grow orchards and eat the fruit they produce.
9:15 I will plant them on their land
and they will never again be uprooted from the land I have given them,"
says the LORD your God.

Book 31. Obadiah

God's Judgment on Edom
1:1 The vision that Obadiah saw.
The Lord GOD says this concerning Edom:
Edom's Approaching Destruction
We have heard a report from the LORD.
An envoy was sent among the nations, saying,
"Arise! Let us make war against Edom!"
1:2 The LORD says, "Look! I will make you a weak nation;
you will be greatly despised!
1:3 Your presumptuous heart has deceived you –
you who reside in the safety of the rocky cliffs,
whose home is high in the mountains.
You think to yourself,
'No one can bring me down to the ground!'
1:4 Even if you were to soar high like an eagle,
even if you were to make your nest among the stars,
I can bring you down even from there!" says the LORD.
1:5 "If thieves came to rob you during the night,
they would steal only as much as they wanted!
If grape pickers came to harvest your vineyards,
they would leave some behind for the poor!
But you will be totally destroyed!
1:6 How the people of Esau will be thoroughly plundered!
Their hidden valuables will be ransacked!
1:7 All your allies will force you from your homeland!
Your treaty partners will deceive you and overpower you.
Your trusted friends will set an ambush for you
that will take you by surprise!
1:8 At that time," the LORD says,
"I will destroy the wise sages of Edom!
the advisers from Esau's mountain!
1:9 Your warriors will be shattered, O Teman,
so that everyone will be destroyed from Esau's mountain!
Edom's Treachery Against Judah
1:10 "Because you violently slaughtered your relatives, the people of Jacob,
shame will cover you, and you will be destroyed forever.
1:11 You stood aloof while strangers took his army captive,
and foreigners advanced to his gates.
When they cast lots over Jerusalem,
you behaved as though you were in league with them.
1:12 You should not have gloated when your relatives suffered calamity.
You should not have rejoiced over the people of Judah when they were destroyed.
You should not have boasted when they suffered adversity.
1:13 You should not have entered the city of my people when they experienced distress.
You should not have joined in gloating over their misfortune when they suffered distress.
You should not have looted their wealth when they endured distress.
1:14 You should not have stood at the fork in the road to slaughter those trying to escape.

You should not have captured their refugees when they suffered adversity.
The Coming Day of the Lord
1:15 "For the day of the LORD is approaching for all the nations!
Just as you have done, so it will be done to you.
You will get exactly what your deeds deserve.
1:16 For just as you have drunk on my holy mountain,
so all the nations will drink continually.
They will drink, and they will gulp down;
they will be as though they had never been.
1:17 But on Mount Zion there will be a remnant of those who escape,
and it will be a holy place once again.
The descendants of Jacob will conquer
those who had conquered them.
1:18 The descendants of Jacob will be a fire,
and the descendants of Joseph a flame.
The descendants of Esau will be like stubble.
They will burn them up and devour them.
There will not be a single survivor of the descendants of Esau!"
Indeed, the LORD has spoken it.
1:19 The people of the Negev will take possession of Esau's mountain,
and the people of the Shephelah will take
possession of the land of the Philistines.
They will also take possession of the territory of Ephraim and the territory of Samaria,
and the people of Benjamin will take possession of Gilead.
1:20 The exiles of this fortress of the people of Israel
will take possession of what belongs to
the people of Canaan, as far as Zarephath,
and the exiles of Jerusalem who are in Sepharad
will take possession of the towns of the Negev.
1:21 Those who have been delivered will go up on Mount Zion
in order to rule over Esau's mountain.
Then the LORD will reign as King!

Book 32. Jonah

Jonah Tries to Run from the Lord
1:1 The LORD said to Jonah son of Amittai, **1:2** "Go immediately to Nineveh, that large capital city, and announce judgment against its people because their wickedness has come to my attention." **1:3** Instead, Jonah immediately headed off to Tarshish to escape from the commission of the LORD. He traveled to Joppa and found a merchant ship heading to Tarshish. So he paid the fare and went aboard it to go with them to Tarshish far away from the LORD. **1:4** But the LORD hurled a powerful wind on the sea. Such a violent tempest arose on the sea that the ship threatened to break up! **1:5** The sailors were so afraid that each cried out to his own god and they flung the ship's cargo overboard to make the ship lighter. Jonah, meanwhile, had gone down into the hold below deck, had lain down, and was sound asleep. **1:6** The ship's captain approached him and said, "What are you doing asleep? Get up! Cry out to your god! Perhaps your god might take notice of us so that we might not die!" **1:7** The sailors said to one another, "Come on, let's cast lots to find out whose fault it is that this disaster has overtaken us." So they cast lots, and Jonah was singled out. **1:8** They said to him, "Tell us, whose fault is it that this disaster has overtaken us? What's your occupation? Where do you come from? What's your country? And who are your people?" **1:9** He said to them, "I am a Hebrew! And I worship the LORD, the God of heaven, who made the sea and the dry land." **1:10** Hearing this, the men became even more afraid and said to him, "What have you done?" (The men said this because they knew that he was trying to escape from the LORD, because he had previously told them.) **1:11** Because the storm was growing worse and worse, they said to him, "What should we do to you to make the sea calm down for us?" **1:12** He said to them, "Pick me up and throw me into the sea to make the sea quiet down, because I know it's my fault you are in this severe storm." **1:13** Instead, they tried to row back to land, but they were not able to do so because the storm kept growing worse and worse. **1:14** So they cried out to the LORD, "Oh, please, LORD, don't let us die on account of this man! Don't hold us guilty of shedding innocent blood. After all, you, LORD, have done just as you pleased." **1:15** So they picked Jonah up and threw him into the sea, and the sea stopped raging. **1:16** The men feared the LORD greatly, and earnestly vowed to offer lavish sacrifices to the LORD.
Jonah Prays
1:17 (2:1) The LORD sent a huge fish to swallow Jonah, and Jonah was in the stomach of the fish three days and three nights. **2:1** Jonah prayed to the LORD his God from the stomach of the fish **2:2** and said,

"I called out to the LORD from my distress,
and he answered me;
from the belly of Sheol I cried out for help,
and you heard my prayer.
2:3 You threw me into the deep waters,

into the middle of the sea;
the ocean current engulfed me;
all the mighty waves you sent swept over me.
2:4 I thought I had been banished from your sight,
that I would never again see your holy temple!
2:5 Water engulfed me up to my neck;
the deep ocean surrounded me;
seaweed was wrapped around my head.
2:6 I went down to the very bottoms of
the mountains;
the gates of the netherworld barred me in forever;
but you brought me up from the Pit, O LORD, my God.
2:7 When my life was ebbing away, I called out to the LORD,
and my prayer came to your holy temple.
2:8 Those who worship worthless idols forfeit the mercy that could be theirs.
2:9 But as for me, I promise to offer a sacrifice to you with a public declaration of praise;
I will surely do what I have promised.
Salvation belongs to the LORD!”

2:10 Then the LORD commanded the fish and it disgorged Jonah on dry land.
The People of Nineveh Respond to Jonah's Warning
3:1 The LORD said to Jonah a second time, **3:2** “Go immediately to Nineveh, that large city, and proclaim to it the message that I tell you.” **3:3** So Jonah went immediately to Nineveh, as the LORD had said. (Now Nineveh was an enormous city – it required three days to walk through it!) **3:4** When Jonah began to enter the city one day's walk, he announced, “At the end of forty days, Nineveh will be overthrown!”
3:5 The people of Nineveh believed in God, and they declared a fast and put on sackcloth, from the greatest to the least of them. **3:6** When the news reached the king of Nineveh, he got up from his throne, took off his royal robe, put on sackcloth, and sat on ashes. **3:7** He issued a proclamation and said, “In Nineveh, by the decree of the king and his nobles: No human or animal, cattle or sheep, is to taste anything; they must not eat and they must not drink water. **3:8** Every person and animal must put on sackcloth and must cry earnestly to God, and everyone must turn from their evil way of living and from the violence that they do. **3:9** Who knows? Perhaps God might be willing to change his mind and relent and turn from his fierce anger so that we might not die.” **3:10** When God saw their actions – they turned from their evil way of living! – God relented concerning the judgment he had threatened them with and he did not destroy them.
Jonah Responds to God's Kindness
4:1 This displeased Jonah terribly and he became very angry. **4:2** He prayed to the LORD and said, “Oh, LORD, this is just what I thought would happen when I was in my own country. This is what I tried to prevent by attempting to escape to Tarshish! – because I knew that you are gracious and compassionate, slow to anger and abounding in mercy, and one who relents concerning threatened judgment. **4:3** So now, LORD, kill me instead, because I would rather die than live!” **4:4** The LORD said, “Are you really so very angry?”
4:5 Jonah left the city and sat down east of it. He made a shelter for himself there and sat down under it in the shade to see what would happen to the city. **4:6** The LORD God appointed a little plant and caused it to grow up over Jonah to be a shade over his head to rescue him from his misery. Now Jonah was very delighted about the little plant.
4:7 So God sent a worm at dawn the next day, and it attacked the little plant so that it dried up. **4:8** When the sun began to shine, God sent a hot east wind. So the sun beat down on Jonah's head, and he grew faint. So he despaired of life, and said, “I would rather die than live!” **4:9** God said to Jonah, “Are you really so very angry about the little plant?” And he said, “I am as angry as I could possibly be!”**4:10** The LORD said, “You were upset about this little plant, something for which you have not worked nor did you do anything to make it grow. It grew up overnight and died the next day. **4:11** Should I not be even more concerned about Nineveh, this enormous city? There are more than one hundred twenty thousand people in it who do not know right from wrong, as well as many animals!”

Book 33. Micah

Introduction
1:1 This is the prophetic message that the LORD gave to Micah of Moresheth. He delivered this message during the reigns of Jotham, Ahaz, and Hezekiah, kings of Judah. The prophecies pertain to Samaria and Jerusalem.
The Judge is Coming
1:2 Listen, all you nations!
Pay attention, all inhabitants of earth!
The sovereign LORD will testify against you;
the LORD will accuse you from his majestic palace.

1:3 Look, the LORD is coming out of his dwelling place!
He will descend and march on the earth's mountaintops!
1:4 The mountains will disintegrate beneath him,
and the valleys will be split in two.
The mountains will melt like wax in a fire,
the rocks will slide down like water cascading down a steep slope.
1:5 All this is because of Jacob's rebellion
and the sins of the nation of Israel.
How has Jacob rebelled, you ask?
Samaria epitomizes their rebellion!
Where are Judah's pagan worship centers, you ask?
They are right in Jerusalem!

1:6 “I will turn Samaria into a heap of ruins in an open field –
vineyards will be planted there!
I will tumble the rubble of her stone walls down into the valley,
and tear down her fortifications to their foundations.
1:7 All her carved idols will be smashed to pieces;
all her metal cult statues will be destroyed by fire.
I will make a waste heap of all her images.
Since she gathered the metal as a prostitute collects her wages,
the idols will become a prostitute's wages again.”

1:8 For this reason I will mourn and wail;
I will walk around barefoot and without my outer garments.
I will howl like a wild dog,
and screech like an owl.
1:9 For Samaria's disease is incurable.
It has infected Judah;
it has spread to the leadership of my people
and has even contaminated Jerusalem!
1:10 Don't spread the news in Gath!
Don't shed even a single tear!
In Beth Leaphrah sit in the dust!
1:11 Residents of Shaphir, pass by in nakedness and humiliation!
The residents of Zaanan can't leave their city.
Beth Ezel mourns,
“He takes from you what he desires.”
1:12 Indeed, the residents of Maroth hope for something good to happen,
though the LORD has sent disaster against the city of Jerusalem.
1:13 Residents of Lachish, hitch the horses to the chariots!
You influenced Daughter Zion to sin,
for Israel's rebellious deeds can be traced back to you!
1:14 Therefore you will have to say farewell to Moresheth Gath.
The residents of Achzib will be as disappointing
as a dried up well to the kings of Israel.
1:15 Residents of Mareshah, a conqueror will attack you,
the leaders of Israel shall flee to Adullam.
1:16 Shave your heads bald as you mourn for the children you love;
shave your foreheads as bald as an eagle,
for they are taken from you into exile.
Land Robbers Will Lose their Land
2:1 Those who devise sinful plans are as good as dead,
those who dream about doing evil as they lie in bed.
As soon as morning dawns they carry out their plans,
because they have the power to do so.
2:2 They confiscate the fields they desire,
and seize the houses they want.
They defraud people of their homes,
and deprive people of the land they have inherited.

2:3 Therefore the LORD says this: “Look, I am devising disaster for this nation!
It will be like a yoke from which you cannot free your neck.
You will no longer walk proudly,
for it will be a time of catastrophe.
2:4 In that day people will sing this taunt song to you –
they will mock you with this lament:
'We are completely destroyed;
they sell off the property of my people.
How they remove it from me!
They assign our fields to the conqueror.'
2:5 Therefore no one will assign you land in the LORD's community.

2:6 'Don't preach with such impassioned rhetoric,' they say excitedly.
'These prophets should not preach of such things;
we will not be overtaken by humiliation.'
2:7 Does the family of Jacob say,
'The LORD's patience can't be exhausted –
he would never do such things'?
To be sure, my commands bring a reward
for those who obey them,
2:8 but you rise up as an enemy against my people.

You steal a robe from a friend,
from those who pass by peacefully as if returning from a war.
2:9 You wrongly evict widows among my people from their cherished homes.
You defraud their children of their prized inheritance.
2:10 But you are the ones who will be forced to leave!
For this land is not secure!
Sin will thoroughly destroy it!
2:11 If a lying windbag should come and say,
'I'll promise you blessings of wine and beer,'
he would be just the right preacher for these people!
The Lord Will Restore His People
2:12 I will certainly gather all of you, O Jacob,
I will certainly assemble those Israelites who remain.
I will bring them together like sheep in a fold,
like a flock in the middle of a pasture;
they will be so numerous that they will make a lot of noise.
2:13 The one who can break through barriers will lead them out
they will break out, pass through the gate, and leave.
Their king will advance before them,
The LORD himself will lead them.
God Will Judge Judah's Sinful Leaders
3:1 I said,
"Listen, you leaders of Jacob,
you rulers of the nation of Israel!
You ought to know what is just,
3:2 yet you hate what is good,
and love what is evil.
You flay my people's skin
and rip the flesh from their bones.
3:3 You devour my people's flesh,
strip off their skin,
and crush their bones.
You chop them up like flesh in a pot –
like meat in a kettle.
3:4 Someday these sinners will cry to the LORD for help,
but he will not answer them.
He will hide his face from them at that time,
because they have done such wicked deeds."

3:5 This is what the LORD says: "The prophets who mislead my people
are as good as dead.
If someone gives them enough to eat,
they offer an oracle of peace.
But if someone does not give them food,
they are ready to declare war on him.
3:6 Therefore night will fall, and you will receive no visions;
it will grow dark, and you will no longer be able to read the omens.
The sun will set on these prophets,
and the daylight will turn to darkness over their heads.
3:7 The prophets will be ashamed;
the omen readers will be humiliated.
All of them will cover their mouths,
for they will receive no divine oracles."

3:8 But I am full of the courage that the LORD's Spirit gives,
and have a strong commitment to justice.
This enables me to confront Jacob with its rebellion,
and Israel with its sin.

3:9 Listen to this, you leaders of the family of Jacob,
you rulers of the nation of Israel!
You hate justice
and pervert all that is right.
3:10 You build Zion through bloody crimes,
Jerusalem through unjust violence.
3:11 Her leaders take bribes when they decide legal cases,
her priests proclaim rulings for profit,
and her prophets read omens for pay.
Yet they claim to trust the LORD and say,
"The LORD is among us.
Disaster will not overtake us!"
3:12 Therefore, because of you, Zion will be plowed up like a field,
Jerusalem will become a heap of ruins,
and the Temple Mount will become a hill overgrown with brush!
Better Days Ahead for Jerusalem
4:1 In the future the LORD's Temple Mount will be the most important mountain of all;
it will be more prominent than other hills.
People will stream to it.
4:2 Many nations will come, saying,
"Come on! Let's go up to the LORD's mountain,
to the temple of Jacob's God,

so he can teach us his commands
and we can live by his laws."
For Zion will be the source of instruction;
the LORD's teachings will proceed from Jerusalem.
4:3 He will arbitrate between many peoples
and settle disputes between many distant nations.
They will beat their swords into plowshares,
and their spears into pruning hooks.
Nations will not use weapons against other nations,
and they will no longer train for war.
4:4 Each will sit under his own grapevine
or under his own fig tree without any fear.
The LORD who commands armies has decreed it.
4:5 Though all the nations follow their respective gods,
we will follow the LORD our God forever.
Restoration Will Follow Crisis
4:6 "In that day," says the LORD, "I will gather the lame,
and assemble the outcasts whom I injured.
4:7 I will transform the lame into the nucleus of a new nation,
and those far off into a mighty nation.
The LORD will reign over them on Mount Zion,
from that day forward and forevermore."
4:8 As for you, watchtower for the flock,
fortress of Daughter Zion –
your former dominion will be restored,
the sovereignty that belongs to Daughter Jerusalem.
4:9 Jerusalem, why are you now shouting so loudly?
Has your king disappeared?
Has your wise leader been destroyed?
Is this why pain grips you as if you were a woman in labor?
4:10 Twist and strain, Daughter Zion, as if you were in labor!
For you will leave the city
and live in the open field.
You will go to Babylon,
but there you will be rescued.
There the LORD will deliver you
from the power of your enemies.
4:11 Many nations have now assembled against you.
They say, "Jerusalem must be desecrated,
so we can gloat over Zion!"
4:12 But they do not know what the LORD is planning;
they do not understand his strategy.
He has gathered them like stalks of grain to be threshed at the threshing floor.
4:13 "Get up and thresh, Daughter Zion!
For I will give you iron horns;
I will give you bronze hooves,
and you will crush many nations."
You will devote to the LORD the spoils you take from them,
and dedicate their wealth to the sovereign Ruler of the whole earth.
5:1 (4:14) But now slash yourself, daughter surrounded by soldiers!
We are besieged!
With a scepter they strike Israel's ruler
on the side of his face.
A King Will Come and a Remnant Will Prosper
5:2 (5:1) As for you, Bethlehem Ephrathah,
seemingly insignificant among the clans of Judah –
from you a king will emerge who will rule over Israel on my behalf,
one whose origins are in the distant past.
5:3 So the LORD will hand the people of Israel over to their enemies
until the time when the woman in labor gives birth.
Then the rest of the king's countrymen will return
to be reunited with the people of Israel.
5:4 He will assume his post and shepherd the people by the LORD's strength,
by the sovereign authority of the LORD his God.
They will live securely, for at that time he will be honored
even in the distant regions of the earth.
5:5 He will give us peace.
Should the Assyrians try to invade our land
and attempt to set foot in our fortresses,
we will send against them seven shepherd-rulers,
make that eight commanders.
5:6 They will rule the land of Assyria with the sword,
the land of Nimrod with a drawn sword.
Our king will rescue us from the Assyrians
should they attempt to invade our land
and try to set foot in our territory.
5:7 Those survivors from Jacob will live
in the midst of many nations.
They will be like the dew the LORD sends,
like the rain on the grass,
that does not hope for men to come

or wait around for humans to arrive.
5:8 Those survivors from Jacob will live among the nations,
in the midst of many peoples.
They will be like a lion among the animals of the forest,
like a young lion among the flocks of sheep,
which attacks when it passes through;
it rips its prey and there is no one to stop it.
5:9 Lift your hand triumphantly against your adversaries;
may all your enemies be destroyed!

The Lord Will Purify His People

5:10 "In that day," says the LORD,
"I will destroy your horses from your midst,
and smash your chariots.
5:11 I will destroy the cities of your land,
and tear down all your fortresses.
5:12 I will remove the sorcery that you practice,
and you will no longer have omen readers living among you.
5:13 I will remove your idols and sacred pillars from your midst;
you will no longer worship what your own hands made.
5:14 I will uproot your images of Asherah from your midst,
and destroy your idols.
5:15 I will angrily seek vengeance
on the nations that do not obey me."

The Lord Demands Justice, not Ritual

6:1 Listen to what the LORD says:
"Get up! Defend yourself before the mountains!
Present your case before the hills!"
6:2 Hear the LORD's accusation, you mountains,
you enduring foundations of the earth!
For the LORD has a case against his people;
he has a dispute with Israel!
6:3 "My people, how have I wronged you?
How have I wearied you? Answer me!
6:4 In fact, I brought you up from the land of Egypt,
I delivered you from that place of slavery.
I sent Moses, Aaron, and Miriam to lead you.
6:5 My people, recall how King Balak of Moab planned to harm you,
how Balaam son of Beor responded to him.
Recall how you journeyed from Shittim to Gilgal,
so you might acknowledge that the LORD has treated you fairly."

6:6 With what should I enter the LORD's presence?
With what should I bow before the sovereign God?
Should I enter his presence with burnt offerings,
with year-old calves?
6:7 Will the LORD accept a thousand rams,
or ten thousand streams of olive oil?
Should I give him my firstborn child as payment for my rebellion,
my offspring – my own flesh and blood – for my sin?
6:8 He has told you, O man, what is good,
and what the LORD really wants from you:
He wants you to promote justice, to be faithful,
and to live obediently before your God.

6:9 Listen! The LORD is calling to the city!
It is wise to respect your authority, O LORD!
Listen, O nation, and those assembled in the city!

6:10 "I will not overlook, O sinful house, the dishonest gain you have hoarded away,
or the smaller-than-standard measure I hate so much.
6:11 I do not condone the use of rigged scales,
or a bag of deceptive weights.
6:12 The city's rich men think nothing of resorting to violence;
her inhabitants lie,
their tongues speak deceptive words.
6:13 I will strike you brutally
and destroy you because of your sin.
6:14 You will eat, but not be satisfied.
Even if you have the strength to overtake some prey,
you will not be able to carry it away;
if you do happen to carry away something,
I will deliver it over to the sword.
6:15 You will plant crops, but will not harvest them;
you will squeeze oil from the olives, but you will have no oil to rub on your bodies;
you will squeeze juice from the grapes, but you will have no wine to drink.
6:16 You implement the regulations of Omri,
and all the practices of Ahab's dynasty;
you follow their policies.
Therefore I will make you an appalling sight,
the city's inhabitants will be taunted derisively,

and nations will mock all of you."

Micah Laments Judah's Sin

7:1 I am depressed!
Indeed, it is as if the summer fruit has been gathered,
and the grapes have been harvested.
There is no grape cluster to eat,
no fresh figs that I crave so much.
7:2 Faithful men have disappeared from the land;
there are no godly men left.
They all wait in ambush so they can shed blood;
they hunt their own brother with a net.
7:3 They are determined to be experts at doing evil;
government officials and judges take bribes,
prominent men make demands,
and they all do what is necessary to satisfy them.
7:4 The best of them is like a thorn;
the most godly among them are more dangerous than a row of thorn bushes.
The day you try to avoid by posting watchmen –
your appointed time of punishment – is on the way,
and then you will experience confusion.
7:5 Do not rely on a friend;
do not trust a companion!
Don't even share secrets with the one who lies in your arms!
7:6 For a son thinks his father is a fool,
a daughter challenges her mother,
and a daughter-in-law her mother-in-law;
a man's enemies are his own servants.
7:7 But I will keep watching for the LORD;
I will wait for the God who delivers me.
My God will hear my lament.

Jerusalem Will Be Vindicated

7:8 My enemies, do not gloat over me!
Though I have fallen, I will get up.
Though I sit in darkness, the LORD will be my light.
7:9 I must endure the LORD's anger,
for I have sinned against him.
But then he will defend my cause,
and accomplish justice on my behalf.
He will lead me out into the light;
I will experience firsthand his deliverance.
7:10 When my enemies see this, they will be covered with shame.
They say to me, "Where is the LORD your God?"
I will gloat over them.
Then they will be trampled down
like mud in the streets.
7:11 It will be a day for rebuilding your walls;
in that day your boundary will be extended.

A Closing Prayer

7:12 In that day people will come to you
from Assyria as far as Egypt,
from Egypt as far as the Euphrates River,
from the seacoasts and the mountains.
7:13 The earth will become desolate
because of what its inhabitants have done.
7:14 Shepherd your people with your shepherd's rod,
the flock that belongs to you,
the one that lives alone in a thicket,
in the midst of a pastureland.
Allow them to graze in Bashan and Gilead,
as they did in the old days.
7:15 "As in the days when you departed from the land of Egypt,
I will show you miraculous deeds."
7:16 Nations will see this and be disappointed by all their strength,
they will put their hands over their mouths,
and act as if they were deaf.
7:17 They will lick the dust like a snake,
like serpents crawling on the ground.
They will come trembling from their strongholds
to the LORD our God;
they will be terrified of you.
7:18 There is no other God like you!
You forgive sin
and pardon the rebellion
of those who remain among your people.
You do not remain angry forever,
but delight in showing loyal love.
7:19 You will once again have mercy on us;
you will conquer our evil deeds;
you will hurl our sins into the depths of the sea.
7:20 You will be loyal to Jacob
and extend your loyal love to Abraham,
which you promised on oath to our ancestors

in ancient times.

Book 34. Nahum

Introduction
1:1 The oracle against Nineveh;
the book of the vision of Nahum the Elkoshite:
God Takes Vengeance against His Enemies
1:2 The LORD is a zealous and avenging God;
the LORD is avenging and very angry.
The LORD takes vengeance against his foes;
he sustains his rage against his enemies.
1:3 The LORD is slow to anger but great in power;
the LORD will certainly not allow the wicked to go unpunished.
The Divine Warrior Destroys His Enemies but Protects His People
He marches out in the whirlwind and the raging storm;
dark storm clouds billow like dust under his feet.
1:4 He shouts a battle cry against the sea and makes it dry up;
he makes all the rivers run dry.
Bashan and Carmel wither;
the blossom of Lebanon withers.
1:5 The mountains tremble before him,
the hills convulse;
the earth is laid waste before him,
the world and all its inhabitants are laid waste.
1:6 No one can withstand his indignation!
No one can resist his fierce anger!
His wrath is poured out like volcanic fire,
boulders are broken up as he approaches.
1:7 The LORD is good –
indeed, he is a fortress in time of distress,
and he protects those who seek refuge in him.
1:8 But with an overwhelming flood
he will make a complete end of Nineveh;
he will drive his enemies into darkness.
Denunciation and Destruction of Nineveh
1:9 Whatever you plot against the LORD, he will completely destroy!
Distress will not arise a second time.
1:10 Surely they will be totally consumed
like entangled thorn bushes,
like the drink of drunkards,
like very dry stubble.
1:11 From you, O Nineveh, one has marched forth who plots evil against the LORD,
a wicked military strategist.
Oracle of Deliverance to Judah
1:12 This is what the LORD says:
"Even though they are powerful –
and what is more, even though their army is numerous –
nevertheless, they will be destroyed and trickle away!
Although I afflicted you,
I will afflict you no more.
1:13 And now, I will break Assyria's yoke bar from your neck;
I will tear apart the shackles that are on you."
Oracle of Judgment against the King of Nineveh
1:14 The LORD has issued a decree against you:
"Your dynasty will come to an end.
I will destroy the idols and images in the temples of your gods.
I will desecrate your grave – because you are accursed!"
Proclamation of the Deliverance of Judah
1:15 (2:1) Look! A herald is running on the mountains!
A messenger is proclaiming deliverance:
"Celebrate your sacred festivals, O Judah!
Fulfill your sacred vows to praise God!
For never again will the wicked Assyrians invade you,
they have been completely destroyed."
Proclamation of the Destruction of Nineveh
2:1 (2:2) The watchmen of Nineveh shout:
"An enemy who will scatter you is marching out to attack you!"
"Guard the rampart!
Watch the road!
Prepare yourselves for battle!
Muster your mighty strength!"

2:2 For the LORD will restore the majesty of Jacob,
as well as the majesty of Israel,
though their enemies have plundered them
and have destroyed their fields.
Prophetic Vision of the Fall of Nineveh
2:3 The shields of his warriors are dyed red;
the mighty soldiers are dressed in scarlet garments.
The metal fittings of the chariots shine
like fire on the day of battle;
the soldiers brandish their spears.

2:4 The chariots race madly through the streets,
they rush back and forth in the broad plazas;
they look like lightning bolts,
they dash here and there like flashes of lightning.

2:5 The commander orders his officers;
they stumble as they advance;
they rush to the city wall
and they set up the covered siege tower.

2:6 The sluice gates are opened;
the royal palace is deluged and dissolves.
2:7 Nineveh is taken into exile and is led away;
her slave girls moan like doves while they beat their breasts.

2:8 Nineveh was like a pool of water throughout her days,
but now her people are running away;
she cries out: "Stop! Stop!" –
but no one turns back.

2:9 Her conquerors cry out:
"Plunder the silver! Plunder the gold!"
There is no end to the treasure;
riches of every kind of precious thing.

2:10 Destruction, devastation, and desolation!
Their hearts faint,
their knees tremble,
each stomach churns, each face turns pale!
Taunt against the Once-Mighty Lion
2:11 Where now is the den of the lions,
the feeding place of the young lions,
where the lion, lioness, and lion cub once prowled
and no one disturbed them?
2:12 The lion tore apart as much prey as his cubs needed
and strangled prey to provide food for his lionesses;
he filled his lairs with prey
and his dens with torn flesh.
Battle Cry of the Divine Warrior
2:13 "I am against you!" declares the LORD who commands armies:
"I will burn your chariots with fire;
the sword will devour your young lions;
you will no longer prey upon the land;
the voices of your messengers will no longer be heard."
Reason for Judgment: Sins of Nineveh
3:1 Woe to the city guilty of bloodshed!
She is full of lies;
she is filled with plunder;
she has hoarded her spoil!
Portrayal of the Destruction of Nineveh
3:2 The chariot drivers will crack their whips;
the chariot wheels will shake the ground;
the chariot horses will gallop;
the war chariots will bolt forward!
3:3 The charioteers will charge ahead;
their swords will flash
and their spears will glimmer!
There will be many people slain;
there will be piles of the dead,
and countless casualties –
so many that people will stumble over the corpses.
Taunt against the Harlot City
3:4 "Because you have acted like a wanton prostitute –
a seductive mistress who practices sorcery,
who enslaves nations by her harlotry,
and entices peoples by her sorcery –
3:5 I am against you," declares the LORD who commands armies.
"I will strip off your clothes!
I will show your nakedness to the nations
and your shame to the kingdoms;
3:6 I will pelt you with filth;
I will treat you with contempt;
I will make you a public spectacle.
3:7 Everyone who sees you will turn away from you in disgust;
they will say, 'Nineveh has been devastated!
Who will lament for her?'
There will be no one to comfort you!"
Nineveh Will Suffer the Same Fate as Thebes
3:8 You are no more secure than Thebes –

she was located on the banks of the Nile;
the waters surrounded her,
her rampart was the sea,
the water was her wall.
3:9 Cush and Egypt had limitless strength;
Put and the Libyans were among her allies.
3:10 Yet she went into captivity as an exile;
even her infants were smashed to pieces at the head of every street.
They cast lots for her nobility;
all her dignitaries were bound with chains.
3:11 You too will act like drunkards;
you will go into hiding;
you too will seek refuge from the enemy.
The Assyrian Defenses Will Fail
3:12 All your fortifications will be like fig trees with first-ripe fruit:
If they are shaken, their figs will fall into the mouth of the eater!
3:13 Your warriors will be like women in your midst;
the gates of your land will be wide open to your enemies;
fire will consume the bars of your gates.
3:14 Draw yourselves water for a siege!
Strengthen your fortifications!
Trample the mud and tread the clay!
Make mud bricks to strengthen your walls!
3:15 There the fire will consume you;
the sword will cut you down;
it will devour you like the young locust would.
The Assyrian Defenders Will Flee
Multiply yourself like the young locust;
multiply yourself like the flying locust!
3:16 Increase your merchants more than the stars of heaven!
They are like the young locust which sheds its skin and flies away.
3:17 Your courtiers are like locusts,
your officials are like a swarm of locusts!
They encamp in the walls on a cold day,
yet when the sun rises, they fly away;
and no one knows where they are.
Concluding Dirge
3:18 Your shepherds are sleeping, O king of Assyria!
Your officers are slumbering!
Your people are scattered like sheep on the mountains
and there is no one to regather them!
3:19 Your destruction is like an incurable wound;
your demise is like a fatal injury!
All who hear what has happened to you will clap their hands for joy,
for no one ever escaped your endless cruelty!

Book 35. Habakkuk

Habakkuk Complains to the Lord
1:1 The following is the message which God revealed to Habakkuk the prophet:
1:2 How long, LORD, must I cry for help?
But you do not listen!
I call out to you, "Violence!"
But you do not intervene!
1:3 Why do you force me to witness injustice?
Why do you put up with wrongdoing?
Destruction and violence confront me;
conflict is present and one must endure strife.
1:4 For this reason the law lacks power,
and justice is never carried out.
Indeed, the wicked intimidate the innocent.
For this reason justice is perverted.
The Lord Reveals Some Startling News
1:5 "Look at the nations and pay attention!
You will be shocked and amazed!
For I will do something in your lifetime
that you will not believe even though you are forewarned.
1:6 Look, I am about to empower the Babylonians,
that ruthless and greedy nation.
They sweep across the surface of the earth,
seizing dwelling places that do not belong to them.
1:7 They are frightening and terrifying;
they decide for themselves what is right.
1:8 Their horses are faster than leopards
and more alert than wolves in the desert.
Their horses gallop,
their horses come a great distance;
like a vulture they swoop down quickly to devour their prey.
1:9 All of them intend to do violence;
every face is determined.
They take prisoners as easily as one scoops up sand.
1:10 They mock kings

and laugh at rulers.
They laugh at every fortified city;
they build siege ramps and capture them.
1:11 They sweep like by the wind and pass on.
But the one who considers himself a god will be held guilty."
Habakkuk Voices Some Concerns
1:12 LORD, you have been active from ancient times;
my sovereign God, you are immortal.
LORD, you have made them your instrument of judgment.
Protector, you have appointed them as your instrument of punishment.
1:13 You are too just to tolerate evil;
you are unable to condone wrongdoing.
So why do you put up with such treacherous people?
Why do you say nothing when the wicked devour those more righteous than they are?
1:14 You made people like fish in the sea,
like animals in the sea that have no ruler.
1:15 The Babylonian tyrant pulls them all up with a fishhook;
he hauls them in with his throw net.
When he catches them in his dragnet,
he is very happy.
1:16 Because of his success he offers sacrifices to his throw net
and burns incense to his dragnet;
for because of them he has plenty of food,
and more than enough to eat.
1:17 Will he then continue to fill and empty his throw net?
Will he always destroy nations and spare none?
2:1 I will stand at my watch post;
I will remain stationed on the city wall.
I will keep watching, so I can see what he says to me
and can know how I should answer
when he counters my argument.
The Lord Assures Habakkuk
2:2 The LORD responded:
"Write down this message! Record it legibly on tablets,
so the one who announces it may read it easily.
2:3 For the message is a witness to what is decreed;
it gives reliable testimony about how matters will turn out.
Even if the message is not fulfilled right away, wait patiently;
for it will certainly come to pass – it will not arrive late.
2:4 Look, the one whose desires are not upright will faint from exhaustion,
but the person of integrity will live because of his faithfulness.
2:5 Indeed, wine will betray the proud, restless man!
His appetite is as big as Sheol's;
like death, he is never satisfied.
He gathers all the nations;
he seizes all peoples.
The Proud Babylonians are as Good as Dead
2:6 "But all these nations will someday taunt him
and ridicule him with proverbial sayings:
'The one who accumulates what does not belong to him is as good as dead
(How long will this go on?) –
he who gets rich by extortion!'
2:7 Your creditors will suddenly attack;
those who terrify you will spring into action,
and they will rob you.
2:8 Because you robbed many countries,
all who are left among the nations will rob you.
You have shed human blood
and committed violent acts against lands, cities, and those who live in them.
2:9 The one who builds his house by unjust gain is as good as dead.
He does this so he can build his nest way up high
and escape the clutches of disaster.
2:10 Your schemes will bring shame to your house.
Because you destroyed many nations, you will self-destruct.
2:11 For the stones in the walls will cry out,
and the wooden rafters will answer back.
2:12 The one who builds a city by bloodshed is as good as dead –
he who starts a town by unjust deeds.
2:13 Be sure of this! The LORD who commands armies has decreed:
The nations' efforts will go up in smoke;
their exhausting work will be for nothing.
2:14 For recognition of the LORD's sovereign majesty will fill the earth
just as the waters fill up the sea.

2:15 "You who force your neighbor to drink wine are as good as dead –
you who make others intoxicated by forcing them to drink from the bowl of your furious anger,
so you can look at their genitals.
2:16 But you will become drunk with shame, not majesty.

Now it is your turn to drink and expose your uncircumcised foreskin!
The cup of wine in the LORD's right hand is coming to you,
and disgrace will replace your majestic glory!
2:17 For you will pay in full for your violent acts against Lebanon;
terrifying judgment will come upon you because of the way you destroyed the wild animals living there.
You have shed human blood
and committed violent acts against lands, cities, and those who live in them.
2:18 What good is an idol? Why would a craftsman make it?
What good is a metal image that gives misleading oracles?
Why would its creator place his trust in it
and make such mute, worthless things?
2:19 The one who says to wood, 'Wake up!' is as good as dead –
he who says to speechless stone, 'Awake!'
Can it give reliable guidance?
It is overlaid with gold and silver;
it has no life's breath inside it.
2:20 But the LORD is in his majestic palace.
The whole earth is speechless in his presence!"
Habakkuk's Vision of the Divine Warrior
3:1 This is a prayer of Habakkuk the prophet:
3:2 LORD, I have heard the report of what you did;
I am awed, LORD, by what you accomplished.
In our time repeat those deeds;
in our time reveal them again.
But when you cause turmoil, remember to show us mercy!
3:3 God comes from Teman,
the sovereign one from Mount Paran. *Selah*.
His splendor covers the skies,
his glory fills the earth.
3:4 He is as bright as lightning;
a two-pronged lightning bolt flashes from his hand.
This is the outward display of his power.
3:5 Plague goes before him;
pestilence marches right behind him.
3:6 He takes his battle position and shakes the earth;
with a mere look he frightens the nations.
The ancient mountains disintegrate;
the primeval hills are flattened.
He travels on the ancient roads.
3:7 I see the tents of Cushan overwhelmed by trouble;
the tent curtains of the land of Midian are shaking.
3:8 Is the LORD mad at the rivers?
Are you angry with the rivers?
Are you enraged at the sea?
Is this why you climb into your horse-drawn chariots,
your victorious chariots?
3:9 Your bow is ready for action;
you commission your arrows. *Selah*.
You cause flash floods on the earth's surface.
3:10 When the mountains see you, they shake.
The torrential downpour sweeps through.
The great deep shouts out;
it lifts its hands high.
3:11 The sun and moon stand still in their courses;
the flash of your arrows drives them away,
the bright light of your lightning-quick spear.
3:12 You furiously stomp on the earth,
you angrily trample down the nations.
3:13 You march out to deliver your people,
to deliver your special servant.
You strike the leader of the wicked nation,
laying him open from the lower body to the neck. *Selah*.
3:14 You pierce the heads of his warriors with a spear.
They storm forward to scatter us;
they shout with joy as if they were plundering the poor with no opposition.
3:15 But you trample on the sea with your horses,
on the surging, raging waters.
Habakkuk Declares His Confidence
3:16 I listened and my stomach churned;
the sound made my lips quiver.
My frame went limp, as if my bones were decaying,
and I shook as I tried to walk.
I long for the day of distress
to come upon the people who attack us.
3:17 When the fig tree does not bud,
and there are no grapes on the vines;
when the olive trees do not produce,
and the fields yield no crops;
when the sheep disappear from the pen,
and there are no cattle in the stalls,

3:18 I will rejoice because of the LORD;
I will be happy because of the God who delivers me!
3:19 The sovereign LORD is my source of strength.
He gives me the agility of a deer;
he enables me to negotiate the rugged terrain.
(This prayer is for the song leader. It is to be accompanied by stringed instruments.)

Book 36. Zephaniah

Introduction
1:1 This is the prophetic message that the LORD gave to Zephaniah son of Cushi, son of Gedaliah, son of Amariah, son of Hezekiah. Zephaniah delivered this message during the reign of King Josiah son of Amon of Judah:
The Lord's Day of Judgment is Approaching
1:2 "I will destroy everything from the face of the earth," says the LORD.
1:3 "I will destroy people and animals;
I will destroy the birds in the sky
and the fish in the sea.
(The idolatrous images of these creatures will be destroyed along with evil people.)
I will remove humanity from the face of the earth," says the LORD.
1:4 "I will attack Judah
and all who live in Jerusalem.
I will remove from this place every trace of Baal worship,
as well as the very memory of the pagan priests.
1:5 I will remove those who worship the stars in the sky from their rooftops,
those who swear allegiance to the LORD while taking oaths in the name of their 'king,'
1:6 and those who turn their backs on the LORD
and do not want the LORD's help or guidance."
1:7 Be silent before the Lord GOD,
for the LORD's day of judgment is almost here.
The LORD has prepared a sacrificial meal;
he has ritually purified his guests.
1:8 "On the day of the LORD's sacrificial meal,
I will punish the princes and the king's sons,
and all who wear foreign styles of clothing.
1:9 On that day I will punish all who leap over the threshold,
who fill the house of their master with wealth taken by violence and deceit.
1:10 On that day," says the LORD,
"a loud cry will go up from the Fish Gate,
wailing from the city's newer district,
and a loud crash from the hills.
1:11 Wail, you who live in the market district,
for all the merchants will disappear
and those who count money will be removed.
1:12 At that time I will search through Jerusalem with lamps.
I will punish the people who are entrenched in their sin,
those who think to themselves,
'The LORD neither rewards nor punishes.'
1:13 Their wealth will be stolen
and their houses ruined!
They will not live in the houses they have built,
nor will they drink the wine from the vineyards they have planted.
1:14 The LORD's great day of judgment is almost here;
it is approaching very rapidly!
There will be a bitter sound on the LORD's day of judgment;
at that time warriors will cry out in battle.
1:15 That day will be a day of God's anger,
a day of distress and hardship,
a day of devastation and ruin,
a day of darkness and gloom,
a day of clouds and dark skies,
1:16 a day of trumpet blasts and battle cries.
Judgment will fall on the fortified cities and the high corner towers.
1:17 I will bring distress on the people
and they will stumble like blind men,
for they have sinned against the LORD.
Their blood will be poured out like dirt;
their flesh will be scattered like manure.
1:18 Neither their silver nor their gold will be able to deliver them
in the day of the LORD's angry judgment.
The whole earth will be consumed by his fiery wrath.
Indeed, he will bring terrifying destruction on all who live on the earth."
The Prophet Warns the People
2:1 Bunch yourselves together like straw, you undesirable nation,
2:2 before God's decree becomes reality and the day of opportunity disappears like windblown chaff,
before the LORD's raging anger overtakes you –

before the day of the LORD's angry judgment overtakes you!
2:3 Seek the LORD's favor, all you humble people of the land who have obeyed his commands!
Strive to do what is right! Strive to be humble!
Maybe you will be protected on the day of the LORD's angry judgment.
Judgment on Surrounding Nations
2:4 Indeed, Gaza will be deserted
and Ashkelon will become a heap of ruins.
Invaders will drive away the people of Ashdod by noon,
and Ekron will be overthrown.
2:5 Those who live by the sea, the people who came from Crete, are as good as dead.
The LORD has decreed your downfall, Canaan, land of the Philistines:
"I will destroy everyone who lives there!"
2:6 The seacoast will be used as pasture lands by the shepherds
and as pens for their flocks.
2:7 Those who are left from the kingdom of Judah will take possession of it.
By the sea they will graze,
in the houses of Ashkelon they will lie down in the evening,
for the LORD their God will intervene for them and restore their prosperity.

2:8 "I have heard Moab's taunts
and the Ammonites' insults.
They taunted my people
and verbally harassed those living in Judah.
2:9 Therefore, as surely as I live," says the LORD who commands armies, the God of Israel,
"be certain that Moab will become like Sodom
and the Ammonites like Gomorrah.
They will be overrun by weeds,
filled with salt pits,
and permanently desolate.
Those of my people who are left will plunder their belongings;
those who are left in Judah will take possession of their land."
2:10 This is how they will be repaid for their arrogance,
for they taunted and verbally harassed the people of the LORD who commands armies.
2:11 The LORD will terrify them,
for he will weaken all the gods of the earth.
All the distant nations will worship the LORD in their own lands.
2:12 "You Ethiopians will also die by my sword!"
2:13 The LORD will attack the north
and destroy Assyria.
He will make Nineveh a heap of ruins;
it will be as barren as the desert.
2:14 Flocks and herds will lie down in the middle of it,
as well as every kind of wild animal.
Owls will sleep in the tops of its support pillars;
they will hoot through the windows.
Rubble will cover the thresholds;
even the cedar work will be exposed to the elements.
2:15 This is how the once-proud city will end up –
the city that was so secure.
She thought to herself, "I am unique! No one can compare to me!"
What a heap of ruins she has become, a place where wild animals live!
Everyone who passes by her taunts her and shakes his fist.
Jerusalem is Corrupt
3:1 The filthy, stained city is as good as dead;
the city filled with oppressors is finished!
3:2 She is disobedient;
she refuses correction.
She does not trust the LORD;
she does not seek the advice of her God.
3:3 Her princes are as fierce as roaring lions;
her rulers are as hungry as wolves in the desert,
who completely devour their prey by morning.
3:4 Her prophets are proud;
they are deceitful men.
Her priests defile what is holy;
they break God's laws.
3:5 The just LORD resides within her;
he commits no unjust acts.
Every morning he reveals his justice.
At dawn he appears without fail.
Yet the unjust know no shame.
The Lord's Judgment will Purify
3:6 "I destroyed nations;
their walled cities are in ruins.
I turned their streets into ruins;
no one passes through them.
Their cities are desolate;

no one lives there.
3:7 I thought, 'Certainly you will respect me!
Now you will accept correction.'
If she had done so, her home would not be destroyed
by all the punishments I have threatened.
But they eagerly sinned
in everything they did.
3:8 Therefore you must wait patiently for me," says the LORD,
"for the day when I attack and take plunder.
I have decided to gather nations together
and assemble kingdoms,
so I can pour out my fury on them –
all my raging anger.
For the whole earth will be consumed
by my fiery anger.
3:9 Know for sure that I will then enable
the nations to give me acceptable praise.
All of them will invoke the LORD's name when they pray,
and will worship him in unison.
3:10 From beyond the rivers of Ethiopia,
those who pray to me will bring me tribute.
3:11 In that day you will not be ashamed of all your rebelliousness against me,
for then I will remove from your midst those who proudly boast,
and you will never again be arrogant on my holy hill.
3:12 I will leave in your midst a humble and meek group of people,
and they will find safety in the LORD's presence.
3:13 The Israelites who remain will not act deceitfully.
They will not lie,
and a deceitful tongue will not be found in their mouth.
Indeed, they will graze peacefully like sheep and lie down;
no one will terrify them."
3:14 Shout for joy, Daughter Zion!
Shout out, Israel!
Be happy and boast with all your heart, Daughter Jerusalem!
3:15 The LORD has removed the judgment against you;
he has turned back your enemy.
Israel's king, the LORD, is in your midst!
You no longer need to fear disaster.
3:16 On that day they will say to Jerusalem,
"Don't be afraid, Zion!
Your hands must not be paralyzed from panic!
3:17 The LORD your God is in your midst;
he is a warrior who can deliver.
He takes great delight in you;
he renews you by his love;
he shouts for joy over you."
3:18 "As for those who grieve because they cannot attend the festivals –
I took them away from you;
they became tribute and were a source of shame to you.
3:19 Look, at that time I will deal with those who mistreated you.
I will rescue the lame sheep
and gather together the scattered sheep.
I will take away their humiliation
and make the whole earth admire and respect them.
3:20 At that time I will lead you –
at the time I gather you together.
Be sure of this! I will make all the nations of the earth respect and admire you
when you see me restore you," says the LORD.

Book 37. Haggai

Introduction
1:1 On the first day of the sixth month of King Darius' second year, the LORD spoke this message through the prophet Haggai to Zerubbabel son of Shealtiel, governor of Judah, and to the high priest Joshua son of Jehozadak:
The Indifference of the People
1:2 The LORD who rules over all says this: "These people have said, 'The time for rebuilding the LORD's temple has not yet come.'" **1:3** So the LORD spoke through the prophet Haggai as follows: **1:4** "Is it right for you to live in richly paneled houses while my temple is in ruins? **1:5** Here then is what the LORD who rules over all says: 'Think carefully about what you are doing. **1:6** You have planted much, but have harvested little. You eat, but are never filled. You drink, but are still thirsty. You put on clothes, but are not warm. Those who earn wages end up with holes in their money bags.'"
The Instruction of the People
1:7 "Moreover, the LORD who rules over all says: 'Pay close attention to these things also. **1:8** Go up to the hill country and bring back timber to build the temple. Then I will be pleased and honored,' says the LORD. **1:9** 'You expected a large harvest, but instead there was little, and when you

brought it home it disappeared right away. Why?' asks the LORD who rules over all. 'Because my temple remains in ruins, thanks to each of you favoring his own house! **1:10** This is why the sky has held back its dew and the earth its produce. **1:11** Moreover, I have called for a drought that will affect the fields, the hill country, the grain, new wine, fresh olive oil, and everything that grows from the ground; it also will harm people, animals, and everything they produce.'"

The Response of the People

1:12 Then Zerubbabel son of Shealtiel and the high priest Joshua son of Jehozadak, along with the whole remnant of the people, obeyed the LORD their God. They responded favorably to the message of the prophet Haggai, who spoke just as the LORD their God had instructed him, and the people began to respect the LORD. **1:13** Then Haggai, the LORD's messenger, spoke the LORD's word to the people: "I am with you!" says the LORD. **1:14** So the LORD energized and encouraged Zerubbabel son of Shealtiel, governor of Judah, the high priest Joshua son of Jehozadak, and the whole remnant of the people. They came and worked on the temple of their God, the LORD who rules over all. **1:15** This took place on the twenty-fourth day of the sixth month of King Darius' second year.

The Glory to Come

2:1 On the twenty-first day of the seventh month, the LORD spoke again through the prophet Haggai: **2:2** "Ask the following questions to Zerubbabel son of Shealtiel, governor of Judah, the high priest Joshua son of Jehozadak, and the remnant of the people: **2:3** 'Who among you survivors saw the former splendor of this temple? How does it look to you now? Isn't it nothing by comparison? **2:4** Even so, take heart, Zerubbabel,' says the LORD. 'Take heart, Joshua son of Jehozadak, the high priest, and all you citizens of the land,' says the LORD, 'and begin to work. For I am with you,' says the LORD who rules over all. **2:5** 'Do not fear, because I made a promise to your ancestors when they left Egypt, and my spirit even now testifies to you.' **2:6** Moreover, the LORD who rules over all says: 'In just a little while I will once again shake the sky and the earth, the sea and the dry ground. **2:7** I will also shake up all the nations, and they will offer their treasures; then I will fill this temple with glory,' says the LORD who rules over all. **2:8** 'The silver and gold will be mine,' says the LORD who rules over all. **2:9** 'The future splendor of this temple will be greater than that of former times,' the LORD who rules over all declares, 'and in this place I will give peace.'"

The Promised Blessing

2:10 On the twenty-fourth day of the ninth month of Darius' second year, the LORD spoke again to the prophet Haggai: **2:11** "The LORD who rules over all says, 'Ask the priests about the law. **2:12** If someone carries holy meat in a fold of his garment and that fold touches bread, a boiled dish, wine, olive oil, or any other food, will that item become holy?'" The priests answered, "It will not." **2:13** Then Haggai asked, "If a person who is ritually unclean because of touching a dead body comes in contact with one of these items, will it become unclean?" The priests answered, "It will be unclean."

2:14 Then Haggai responded, "'The people of this nation are unclean in my sight,' says the LORD. 'And so is all their effort; everything they offer is also unclean. **2:15** Now therefore reflect carefully on the recent past, before one stone was laid on another in the LORD's temple. **2:16** From that time when one came expecting a heap of twenty measures, there were only ten; when one came to the wine vat to draw out fifty measures from it, there were only twenty. **2:17** I struck all the products of your labor with blight, disease, and hail, and yet you brought nothing to me,' says the LORD. **2:18** 'Think carefully about the past: from today, the twenty-fourth day of the ninth month, to the day work on the temple of the LORD was resumed, think about it. **2:19** The seed is still in the storehouse, isn't it? And the vine, fig tree, pomegranate, and olive tree have not produced. Nevertheless, from today on I will bless you.'"

Zerubbabel the Chosen One

2:20 Then the LORD spoke again to Haggai on the twenty-fourth day of the month: **2:21** Tell Zerubbabel governor of Judah: 'I am ready to shake the sky and the earth. **2:22** I will overthrow royal thrones and shatter the might of earthly kingdoms. I will overthrow chariots and those who ride them, and horses and their riders will fall as people kill one another. **2:23** On that day,' says the LORD who rules over all, 'I will take you, Zerubbabel son of Shealtiel, my servant,' says the LORD, 'and I will make you like a signet ring, for I have chosen you,' says the LORD who rules over all."

Book 38. Zechariah

Introduction

1:1 In the eighth month of Darius' second year, the word of the LORD came to the prophet Zechariah, son of Berechiah son of Iddo, as follows:
1:2 The LORD was very angry with your ancestors. **1:3** Therefore say to the people: The LORD who rules over all says, "Turn to me," says the LORD who rules over all, "and I will turn to you," says the LORD who rules over all. **1:4** "Do not be like your ancestors, to whom the former prophets called out, saying, 'The LORD who rules over all says, "Turn now from your evil wickedness,"' but they would by no means obey me,"

says the LORD. **1:5** "As for your ancestors, where are they? And did the prophets live forever? **1:6** But have my words and statutes, which I commanded my servants the prophets, not outlived your fathers? Then they paid attention and confessed, 'The LORD who rules over all has indeed done what he said he would do to us, because of our sinful ways.'"

The Introduction to the Visions

1:7 On the twenty-fourth day of the eleventh month, the month *Shebat*, in Darius' second year, the word of the LORD came to the prophet Zechariah son of Berechiah son of Iddo, as follows:

The Content of the First Vision

1:8 I was attentive that night and saw a man seated on a red horse that stood among some myrtle trees in the ravine. Behind him were red, sorrel, and white horses.

The Interpretation of the First Vision

1:9 Then I asked one nearby, "What are these, sir?" The angelic messenger who replied to me said, "I will show you what these are." **1:10** Then the man standing among the myrtle trees spoke up and said, "These are the ones whom the LORD has sent to walk about on the earth." **1:11** The riders then agreed with the angel of the LORD, who was standing among the myrtle trees, "We have been walking about on the earth, and now everything is at rest and quiet." **1:12** The angel of the LORD then asked, "LORD who rules over all, how long before you have compassion on Jerusalem and the other cities of Judah which you have been so angry with for these seventy years?" **1:13** The LORD then addressed good, comforting words to the angelic messenger who was speaking to me. **1:14** Turning to me, the messenger then said, "Cry out that the LORD who rules over all says, 'I am very much moved for Jerusalem and for Zion. **1:15** But I am greatly displeased with the nations that take my grace for granted. I was a little displeased with them, but they have only made things worse for themselves.

The Oracle of Response

1:16 "'Therefore,' says the LORD, 'I have become compassionate toward Jerusalem and will rebuild my temple in it,' says the LORD who rules over all. 'Once more a surveyor's measuring line will be stretched out over Jerusalem.' **1:17** Speak up again with the message of the LORD who rules over all: 'My cities will once more overflow with prosperity, and once more the LORD will comfort Zion and validate his choice of Jerusalem.'"

Vision Two: The Four Horns

1:18 (2:1) Once again I looked and this time I saw four horns. **1:19** So I asked the angelic messenger who spoke with me, "What are these?" He replied, "These are the horns that have scattered Judah, Israel, and Jerusalem." **1:20** Next the LORD showed me four blacksmiths. **1:21** I asked, "What are these going to do?" He answered, "These horns are the ones that have scattered Judah so that there is no one to be seen. But the blacksmiths have come to terrify Judah's enemies and cut off the horns of the nations that have thrust themselves against the land of Judah in order to scatter its people."

Vision Three: The Surveyor

2:1 (2:5) I looked again, and there was a man with a measuring line in his hand. **2:2** I asked, "Where are you going?" He replied, "To measure Jerusalem in order to determine its width and its length." **2:3** At this point the angelic messenger who spoke to me went out, and another messenger came to meet him **2:4** and said to him, "Hurry, speak to this young man as follows: 'Jerusalem will no longer be enclosed by walls because of the multitude of people and animals there. **2:5** But I (the LORD says) will be a wall of fire surrounding Jerusalem and the source of glory in her midst.'"
2:6 "You there! Flee from the northland!" says the LORD, "for like the four winds of heaven I have scattered you," says the LORD. **2:7** "Escape, Zion, you who live among the Babylonians!" **2:8** For the LORD who rules over all says to me that for his own glory he has sent me to the nations that plundered you – for anyone who touches you touches the pupil of his eye. **2:9** "I am about to punish them in such a way," he says, "that they will be looted by their own slaves." Then you will know that the LORD who rules over all has sent me.
2:10 "Sing out and be happy, Zion my daughter! For look, I have come; I will settle in your midst," says the LORD. **2:11** "Many nations will join themselves to the LORD on the day of salvation, and they will also be my people. Indeed, I will settle in the midst of you all." Then you will know that the LORD who rules over all has sent me to you. **2:12** The LORD will take possession of Judah as his portion in the holy land and he will choose Jerusalem once again. **2:13** Be silent in the LORD's presence, all people everywhere, for he is being moved to action in his holy dwelling place.

Vision Four: The Priest

3:1 Next I saw Joshua the high priest standing before the angel of the LORD, with Satan standing at his right hand to accuse him. **3:2** The LORD said to Satan, "May the LORD rebuke you, Satan! May the LORD, who has chosen Jerusalem, rebuke you! Isn't this man like a burning stick snatched from the fire?" **3:3** Now Joshua was dressed in filthy clothes as he stood there before the angel. **3:4** The angel spoke up to those standing all around, "Remove his filthy clothes." Then he said to Joshua, "I have freely forgiven your iniquity and will dress you in fine clothing." **3:5**

Then I spoke up, "Let a clean turban be put on his head." So they put a clean turban on his head and clothed him, while the angel of the LORD stood nearby. **3:6** Then the angel of the LORD exhorted Joshua solemnly: **3:7** "The LORD who rules over all says, 'If you live and work according to my requirements, you will be able to preside over my temple and attend to my courtyards, and I will allow you to come and go among these others who are standing by you. **3:8** Listen now, Joshua the high priest, both you and your colleagues who are sitting before you, all of you are a symbol that I am about to introduce my servant, the Branch. **3:9** As for the stone I have set before Joshua – on the one stone there are seven eyes. I am about to engrave an inscription on it,' says the LORD who rules over all, 'to the effect that I will remove the iniquity of this land in a single day. **3:10** In that day,' says the LORD who rules over all, 'everyone will invite his friend to fellowship under his vine and under his fig tree.'"

Vision Five: The Menorah

4:1 The angelic messenger who had been speaking with me then returned and woke me, as a person is wakened from sleep. **4:2** He asked me, "What do you see?" I replied, "I see a menorah of pure gold with a receptacle at the top and seven lamps, with fourteen pipes going to the lamps. **4:3** There are also two olive trees beside it, one on the right of the receptacle and the other on the left." **4:4** Then I asked the messenger who spoke with me, "What are these, sir?" **4:5** He replied, "Don't you know what these are?" So I responded, "No, sir." **4:6** Therefore he told me, "These signify the word of the LORD to Zerubbabel: 'Not by strength and not by power, but by my Spirit,' says the LORD who rules over all."

Oracle of Response

4:7 "What are you, you great mountain? Because of Zerubbabel you will become a level plain! And he will bring forth the temple capstone with shoutings of 'Grace! Grace!' because of this." **4:8** Moreover, the word of the LORD came to me as follows: **4:9** "The hands of Zerubbabel have laid the foundations of this temple, and his hands will complete it." Then you will know that the LORD who rules over all has sent me to you. **4:10** For who dares make light of small beginnings? These seven eyes will joyfully look on the tin tablet in Zerubbabel's hand. (These are the eyes of the LORD, which constantly range across the whole earth.)

4:11 Next I asked the messenger, "What are these two olive trees on the right and the left of the menorah?" **4:12** Before he could reply I asked again, "What are these two extensions of the olive trees, which are emptying out the golden oil through the two golden pipes?" **4:13** He replied, "Don't you know what these are?" And I said, "No, sir." **4:14** So he said, "These are the two anointed ones who stand by the Lord of the whole earth."

Vision Six: The Flying Scroll

5:1 Then I turned to look, and there was a flying scroll! **5:2** Someone asked me, "What do you see?" I replied, "I see a flying scroll thirty feet long and fifteen feet wide." **5:3** The speaker went on to say, "This is a curse traveling across the whole earth. For example, according to the curse whoever steals will be removed from the community; or on the other hand (according to the curse) whoever swears falsely will suffer the same fate." **5:4** "I will send it out," says the LORD who rules over all, "and it will enter the house of the thief and of the person who swears falsely in my name. It will land in the middle of his house and destroy both timber and stones."

Vision Seven: The Ephah

5:5 After this the angelic messenger who had been speaking to me went out and said, "Look, see what is leaving." **5:6** I asked, "What is it?" And he replied, "It is a basket for measuring grain that is moving away from here." Moreover, he said, "This is their 'eye' throughout all the earth." **5:7** Then a round lead cover was raised up, revealing a woman sitting inside the basket. **5:8** He then said, "This woman represents wickedness," and he pushed her down into the basket and placed the lead cover on top. **5:9** Then I looked again and saw two women going forth with the wind in their wings (they had wings like those of a stork) and they lifted up the basket between the earth and the sky. **5:10** I asked the messenger who was speaking to me, "Where are they taking the basket?" **5:11** He replied, "To build a temple for her in the land of Babylonia. When it is finished, she will be placed there in her own residence."

Vision Eight: The Chariots

6:1 Once more I looked, and this time I saw four chariots emerging from between two mountains of bronze. **6:2** Harnessed to the first chariot were red horses, to the second black horses, **6:3** to the third white horses, and to the fourth spotted horses, all of them strong. **6:4** Then I asked the angelic messenger who was speaking with me, "What are these, sir?" **6:5** The messenger replied, "These are the four spirits of heaven that have been presenting themselves before the Lord of all the earth. **6:6** The chariot with the black horses is going to the north country and the white ones are going after them, but the spotted ones are going to the south country. **6:7** All these strong ones are scattering; they have sought permission to go and walk about over the earth." The Lord had said, "Go! Walk about over the earth!" So they are doing so. **6:8** Then he cried out to me, "Look! The ones going to the northland have brought me peace about the northland."

A Concluding Oracle

6:9 The word of the LORD came to me as follows: **6:10** "Choose some people from among the exiles, namely, Heldai, Tobijah, and Jedaiah, all of whom have come from Babylon, and when you have done so go to the house of Josiah son of Zephaniah. **6:11** Then take some silver and gold to make a crown and set it on the head of Joshua son of Jehozadak, the high priest. **6:12** Then say to him, 'The LORD who rules over all says, "Look – here is the man whose name is Branch, who will sprout up from his place and build the temple of the LORD. **6:13** Indeed, he will build the temple of the LORD, and he will be clothed in splendor, sitting as king on his throne. Moreover, there will be a priest with him on his throne and they will see eye to eye on everything. **6:14** The crown will then be turned over to Helem, Tobijah, Jedaiah, and Hen son of Zephaniah as a memorial in the temple of the LORD. **6:15** Then those who are far away will come and build the temple of the LORD so that you may know that the LORD who rules over all has sent me to you. This will all come to pass if you completely obey the voice of the LORD your God."'"

The Hypocrisy of False Fasting

7:1 In King Darius' fourth year, on the fourth day of *Kislev*, the ninth month, the word of the LORD came to Zechariah. **7:2** Now the people of Bethel had sent Sharezer and Regem-Melech and their companions to seek the LORD's favor **7:3** by asking both the priests of the temple of the LORD who rules over all and the prophets, "Should we weep in the fifth month, fasting as we have done over the years?" **7:4** The word of the LORD who rules over all then came to me, **7:5** "Speak to all the people and priests of the land as follows: 'When you fasted and lamented in the fifth and seventh months through all these seventy years, did you truly fast for me – for me, indeed? **7:6** And now when you eat and drink, are you not doing so for yourselves?'" **7:7** Should you not have obeyed the words that the LORD cried out through the former prophets when Jerusalem was peacefully inhabited and her surrounding cities, the Negev, and the Shephelah were also populated?

7:8 Again the word of the LORD came to Zechariah: **7:9** "The LORD who rules over all said, 'Exercise true judgment and show brotherhood and compassion to each other. **7:10** You must not oppress the widow, the orphan, the foreigner, or the poor, nor should anyone secretly plot evil against his fellow human being.'

7:11 "But they refused to pay attention, turning away stubbornly and stopping their ears so they could not hear. **7:12** Indeed, they made their heart as hard as diamond, so that they could not obey the Torah and the other words the LORD who rules over all had sent by his Spirit through the former prophets. Therefore, the LORD who rules over all had poured out great wrath.

7:13 "'It then came about that just as I cried out, but they would not obey, so they will cry out, but I will not listen,' the LORD LORD who rules over all had said. **7:14** 'Rather, I will sweep them away in a storm into all the nations they are not familiar with.' Thus the land had become desolate because of them, with no one crossing through or returning, for they had made the fruitful land a waste."

The Blessing of True Fasting

8:1 Then the word of the LORD who rules over all came to me as follows: **8:2** "The LORD who rules over all says, 'I am very much concerned for Zion; indeed, I am so concerned for her that my rage will fall on those who hurt her.' **8:3** The LORD says, 'I have returned to Zion and will live within Jerusalem. Now Jerusalem will be called "truthful city," "mountain of the LORD who rules over all," "holy mountain."' **8:4** Moreover, the LORD who rules over all says, 'Old men and women will once more live in the plazas of Jerusalem, each one leaning on a cane because of advanced age. **8:5** And the streets of the city will be full of boys and girls playing. **8:6** And,' says the LORD who rules over all, 'though such a thing may seem to be difficult in the opinion of the small community of those days, will it also appear difficult to me?' asks the LORD who rules over all.

8:7 "The LORD who rules over all asserts, 'I am about to save my people from the lands of the east and the west. **8:8** And I will bring them to settle within Jerusalem. They will be my people, and I will be their God, in truth and righteousness.'

8:9 "The LORD who rules over all also says, 'Gather strength, you who are listening to these words today from the mouths of the prophets who were there at the founding of the house of the LORD who rules over all, so that the temple might be built. **8:10** Before that time there was no compensation for man or animal, nor was there any relief from adversity for those who came and went, because I had pitted everybody – each one – against everyone else. **8:11** But I will be different now to this remnant of my people from the way I was in those days,' says the LORD who rules over all, **8:12** 'for there will be a peaceful time of sowing, the vine will produce its fruit and the ground its yield, and the skies will rain down dew. Then I will allow the remnant of my people to possess all these things. **8:13** And it will come about that just as you (both Judah and Israel) were a curse to the nations, so I will save you and you will be a blessing. Do not be afraid! Instead, be strong!'

8:14 "For the LORD who rules over all says, 'As I had planned to hurt you when your fathers made me angry,' says the LORD who rules over all, 'and I was not sorry, **8:15** so, to the contrary, I have planned in these days to do good to Jerusalem and Judah – do not fear! **8:16** These are the things you must do: Speak the truth, each of you, to one another. Practice true and righteous judgment in your courts. **8:17** Do not plan evil in your hearts against one another. Do not favor a false oath – these are all things that I hate,' says the LORD."

8:18 The word of the LORD who rules over all came to me as follows: **8:19** "The LORD who rules over all says, 'The fast of the fourth, fifth, seventh, and tenth months will become joyful and happy, pleasant feasts for the house of Judah, so love truth and peace.' **8:20** The LORD who rules over all says, 'It will someday come to pass that people – residents of many cities – will come. **8:21** The inhabitants of one will go to another and say, "Let's go up at once to ask the favor of the LORD, to seek the LORD who rules over all. Indeed, I'll go with you." **8:22** Many peoples and powerful nations will come to Jerusalem to seek the LORD who rules over all and to ask his favor. **8:23** The LORD who rules over all says, 'In those days ten people from all languages and nations will grasp hold of – indeed, grab – the robe of one Jew and say, "Let us go with you, for we have heard that God is with you."'"

The Coming of the True King

9:1 An oracle of the word of the LORD concerning the land of Hadrach, with its focus on Damascus:

The eyes of all humanity, especially of the tribes of Israel, are toward the LORD, **9:2** as are those of Hamath also, which adjoins Damascus, and Tyre and Sidon, though they consider themselves to be very wise. **9:3** Tyre built herself a fortification and piled up silver like dust and gold like the mud of the streets! **9:4** Nevertheless the Lord will evict her and shove her fortifications into the sea – she will be consumed by fire. **9:5** Ashkelon will see and be afraid; Gaza will be in great anguish, as will Ekron, for her hope will have been dried up. Gaza will lose her king, and Ashkelon will no longer be inhabited. **9:6** A mongrel people will live in Ashdod, for I will greatly humiliate the Philistines. **9:7** I will take away their abominable religious practices; then those who survive will become a community of believers in our God, like a clan in Judah, and Ekron will be like the Jebusites. **9:8** Then I will surround my temple to protect it like a guard from anyone crossing back and forth; so no one will cross over against them anymore as an oppressor, for now I myself have seen it.

9:9 Rejoice greatly, daughter of Zion!
Shout, daughter of Jerusalem!
Look! Your king is coming to you:
he is legitimate and victorious,
humble and riding on a donkey –
on a young donkey, the foal of a female donkey.
9:10 I will remove the chariot from Ephraim
and the warhorse from Jerusalem,
and the battle bow will be removed.
Then he will announce peace to the nations.
His dominion will be from sea to sea
and from the Euphrates River to the ends of the earth.
9:11 Moreover, as for you, because of our covenant relationship secured with blood, I will release your prisoners from the waterless pit. **9:12** Return to the stronghold, you prisoners, with hope; today I declare that I will return double what was taken from you. **9:13** I will bend Judah as my bow; I will load the bow with Ephraim, my arrow! I will stir up your sons, Zion, against yours, Greece, and I will make you, Zion, like a warrior's sword.

9:14 Then the LORD will appear above them, and his arrow will shoot forth like lightning; the Lord GOD will blow the trumpet and will sally forth on the southern storm winds. **9:15** The LORD who rules over all will guard them, and they will prevail and overcome with sling stones. Then they will drink, and will become noisy like drunkards, full like the sacrificial basin or like the corners of the altar. **9:16** On that day the LORD their God will deliver them as the flock of his people, for they are the precious stones of a crown sparkling over his land. **9:17** How precious and fair! Grain will make the young men flourish and new wine the young women.

The Restoration of the True People

10:1 Ask the LORD for rain in the season of the late spring rains – the LORD who causes thunderstorms – and he will give everyone showers of rain and green growth in the field. **10:2** For the household gods have spoken wickedness, the soothsayers have seen a lie, and as for the dreamers, they have disclosed emptiness and give comfort in vain. Therefore the people set out like sheep and become scattered because they have no shepherd. **10:3** I am enraged at the shepherds and will punish the leadgoats.

For the LORD who rules over all has brought blessing to his flock, the house of Judah, and will transform them into his majestic warhorse. **10:4** From him will come the cornerstone, the wall peg, the battle bow, and every ruler. **10:5** And they will be like warriors trampling the mud of the streets in battle. They will fight, for the LORD will be with them, and will defeat the enemy cavalry.

10:6 "I (says the LORD) will strengthen the kingdom of Judah and deliver the people of Joseph and will bring them back because of my compassion for them. They will be as though I had never rejected them, for I am the LORD their God and therefore I will hear them. **10:7** The Ephraimites will be like warriors and will rejoice as if they had drunk wine. Their children will see it and rejoice; they will celebrate in the things of the LORD. **10:8** I will signal for them and gather them, for I have already redeemed them; then they will become as numerous as they were before. **10:9** Though I scatter them among the nations, they will remember in far-off places – they and their children will sprout forth and return. **10:10** I will bring them back from Egypt and gather them from Assyria. I will bring them to the lands of Gilead and Lebanon, for there will not be enough room for them in their own land. **10:11** The LORD will cross the sea of storms and will calm its turbulence. The depths of the Nile will dry up, the pride of Assyria will be humbled, and the domination of Egypt will be no more. **10:12** Thus I will strengthen them by my power, and they will walk about in my name," says the LORD.

The History and Future of Judah's Wicked Kings

11:1 Open your gates, Lebanon,
so that the fire may consume your cedars.
11:2 Howl, fir tree,
because the cedar has fallen;
the majestic trees have been destroyed.
Howl, oaks of Bashan,
because the impenetrable forest has fallen.
11:3 Listen to the howling of shepherds,
because their magnificence has been destroyed.
Listen to the roaring of young lions,
because the thickets of the Jordan have been devastated.

11:4 The LORD my God says this: "Shepherd the flock set aside for slaughter. **11:5** Those who buy them slaughter them and are not held guilty; those who sell them say, 'Blessed be the LORD, for I am rich.' Their own shepherds have no compassion for them. **11:6** Indeed, I will no longer have compassion on the people of the land," says the LORD, "but instead I will turn every last person over to his neighbor and his king. They will devastate the land, and I will not deliver it from them."

11:7 So I began to shepherd the flock destined for slaughter, the most afflicted of all the flock. Then I took two staffs, calling one "Pleasantness" and the other "Binders," and I tended the flock. **11:8** Next I eradicated the three shepherds in one month, for I ran out of patience with them and, indeed, they detested me as well. **11:9** I then said, "I will not shepherd you. What is to die, let it die, and what is to be eradicated, let it be eradicated. As for those who survive, let them eat each other's flesh!" **11:10** Then I took my staff "Pleasantness" and cut it in two to annul my covenant that I had made with all the people. **11:11** So it was annulled that very day, and then the most afflicted of the flock who kept faith with me knew that that was the word of the LORD.

11:12 Then I said to them, "If it seems good to you, pay me my wages, but if not, forget it." So they weighed out my payment – thirty pieces of silver. **11:13** The LORD then said to me, "Throw to the potter that exorbitant sum at which they valued me!" So I took the thirty pieces of silver and threw them to the potter at the temple of the LORD. **11:14** Then I cut the second staff "Binders" in two in order to annul the covenant of brotherhood between Judah and Israel.

11:15 Again the LORD said to me, "Take up once more the equipment of a foolish shepherd. **11:16** Indeed, I am about to raise up a shepherd in the land who will not take heed to the sheep headed to slaughter, will not seek the scattered, and will not heal the injured. Moreover, he will not nourish the one that is healthy but instead will eat the meat of the fat sheep and tear off their hooves.

11:17 Woe to the worthless shepherd
who abandons the flock!
May a sword fall on his arm and his right eye!
May his arm wither completely away,
and his right eye become completely blind!"

The Repentance of Judah

12:1 The revelation of the word of the LORD concerning Israel: The LORD – he who stretches out the heavens and lays the foundations of the earth, who forms the human spirit within a person – says, **12:2** "I am about to make Jerusalem a cup that brings dizziness to all the surrounding nations; indeed, Judah will also be included when Jerusalem is besieged. **12:3** Moreover, on that day I will make Jerusalem a heavy burden for all the nations, and all who try to carry it will be seriously injured; yet all the peoples of the earth will be assembled against it. **12:4** In that day," says the LORD, "I will strike every horse with confusion and its rider with madness. I will pay close attention to the house of Judah, but will strike all the horses of the nations with blindness. **12:5** Then the leaders of Judah will say to themselves, 'The inhabitants of Jerusalem are a means of strength to us through their God, the LORD who rules over all.' **12:6** On that day I will make the leaders of Judah like an igniter among sticks and a burning torch among sheaves, and they will burn up all the surrounding nations right and left. Then the people of Jerusalem will settle once more in their place, the city of Jerusalem. **12:7** The LORD also will deliver the homes of Judah first, so that the splendor of the kingship of David and of the people of Jerusalem may not exceed that of Judah. **12:8** On that day the LORD himself will defend the inhabitants of Jerusalem, so that the weakest among them will be like mighty David, and the dynasty of David will be like God, like the angel of the LORD before them. **12:9** So on that day I will set out to destroy all the nations that come against Jerusalem."

12:10 "I will pour out on the kingship of David and the population of Jerusalem a spirit of grace and supplication so that they will look to me, the one they have pierced. They will lament for him as one laments for an only son, and there will be a bitter cry for him like the bitter cry for a firstborn. **12:11** On that day the lamentation in Jerusalem will be as great as the lamentation at Hadad-Rimmon in the plain of Megiddo. **12:12** The land will mourn, clan by clan – the clan of the royal household of David by itself and their wives by themselves; the clan of the family of Nathan by itself and their wives by themselves; **12:13** the clan of the descendants of Levi by itself and their wives by themselves; and the clan of the Shimeites by itself and their wives by themselves – **12:14** all the clans that remain, each separately with their wives."

The Refinement of Judah

13:1 "In that day there will be a fountain opened up for the dynasty of David and the people of Jerusalem to cleanse them from sin and impurity. **13:2** And also on that day," says the LORD who rules over all, "I will remove the names of the idols from the land and they will never again be remembered. Moreover, I will remove the prophets and the unclean spirit from the land. **13:3** Then, if anyone prophesies in spite of this, his father and mother to whom he was born will say to him, 'You cannot live, for you lie in the name of the LORD.' Then his father and mother to whom he was born will run him through with a sword when he prophesies.

13:4 "Therefore, on that day each prophet will be ashamed of his vision when he prophesies and will no longer wear the hairy garment of a prophet to deceive the people. **13:5** Instead he will say, 'I am no prophet – indeed, I am a farmer, for a man has made me his indentured servant since my youth.' **13:6** Then someone will ask him, 'What are these wounds on your chest?' and he will answer, 'Some that I received in the house of my friends.'

13:7 "Awake, sword, against my shepherd,
against the man who is my associate,"
says the LORD who rules over all.
Strike the shepherd that the flock may be scattered;
I will turn my hand against the insignificant ones.

13:8 It will happen in all the land, says the LORD,
that two-thirds of the people in it will be cut off and die,
but one-third will be left in it.

13:9 Then I will bring the remaining third into the fire;
I will refine them like silver is refined
and will test them like gold is tested.
They will call on my name and I will answer;
I will say, 'These are my people,'
and they will say, 'The LORD is my God.'"

The Sovereignty of the Lord

14:1 A day of the LORD is about to come when your possessions will be divided as plunder in your midst. **14:2** For I will gather all the nations against Jerusalem to wage war; the city will be taken, its houses plundered, and the women raped. Then half of the city will go into exile, but the remainder of the people will not be taken away.

14:3 Then the LORD will go to battle and fight against those nations, just as he fought battles in ancient days. **14:4** On that day his feet will stand on the Mount of Olives which lies to the east of Jerusalem, and the Mount of Olives will be split in half from east to west, leaving a great valley. Half the mountain will move northward and the other half southward. **14:5** Then you will escape through my mountain valley, for the mountains will extend to Azal. Indeed, you will flee as you fled from the earthquake in the days of King Uzziah of Judah. Then the LORD my God will come with all his holy ones with him. **14:6** On that day there will be no light – the sources of light in the heavens will congeal. **14:7** It will happen in one day (a day known to the LORD); not in the day or the night, but in the evening there will be light. **14:8** Moreover, on that day living waters will flow out from Jerusalem, half of them to the eastern sea and half of them to the western sea; it will happen both in summer and in winter.

14:9 The LORD will then be king over all the earth. In that day the LORD will be seen as one with a single name. **14:10** All the land will change and become like the Arabah from Geba to Rimmon, south of Jerusalem; and Jerusalem will be raised up and will stay in its own place from the Benjamin Gate to the site of the First Gate and on to the Corner Gate, and from the Tower of Hananel to the royal winepresses. **14:11** And people will settle there, and there will no longer be the threat of divine extermination – Jerusalem will dwell in security.

14:12 But this will be the nature of the plague with which the LORD will strike all the nations that have fought against Jerusalem: Their flesh will decay while they stand on their feet, their eyes will rot away in their sockets, and their tongues will dissolve in their mouths. **14:13** On that day there will be great confusion from the LORD among them; they will seize each other and attack one another violently. **14:14** Moreover, Judah will fight at Jerusalem, and the wealth of all the surrounding nations will be gathered up – gold, silver, and clothing in great abundance. **14:15** This is the kind of plague that will devastate horses, mules, camels, donkeys, and all the other animals in those camps.

14:16 Then all who survive from all the nations that came to attack Jerusalem will go up annually to worship the King, the LORD who rules over all, and to observe the Feast of Tabernacles. **14:17** But if any of the nations anywhere on earth refuse to go up to Jerusalem to worship the King, the LORD who rules over all, they will get no rain. **14:18** If the Egyptians will not do so, they will get no rain – instead there will be the kind of plague which the LORD inflicts on any nations that do not go up to celebrate the Feast of Tabernacles. **14:19** This will be the punishment of Egypt and of all nations that do not go up to celebrate the Feast of Tabernacles.

14:20 On that day the bells of the horses will bear the inscription "HOLY TO THE LORD." The cooking pots in the LORD's temple will be as holy as the bowls in front of the altar. **14:21** Every cooking pot in Jerusalem and Judah will become holy in the sight of the LORD who rules over all, so that all who offer sacrifices may come and use some of them to boil their sacrifices in them. On that day there will no longer be a Canaanite in the house of the LORD who rules over all.

Book 39. Malachi

Introduction and God's Election of Israel

1:1 What follows is divine revelation. The word of the LORD came to Israel through Malachi:

1:2 "I have shown love to you," says the LORD, but you say, "How have you shown love to us?"

"Esau was Jacob's brother," the LORD explains, "yet I chose Jacob **1:3** and rejected Esau. I turned Esau's mountains into a deserted wasteland and gave his territory to the wild jackals."

1:4 Edom says, "Though we are devastated, we will once again build the ruined places." So the LORD who rules over all responds, "They indeed may build, but I will overthrow. They will be known as the land of evil, the people with whom the LORD is permanently displeased. **1:5** Your eyes will see it, and then you will say, 'May the LORD be magnified even beyond the border of Israel!'"

The Sacrilege of Priestly Service

1:6 "A son naturally honors his father and a slave respects his master. If I am your father, where is my honor? If I am your master, where is my respect? The LORD who rules over all asks you this, you priests who make light of my name! But you reply, 'How have we made light of your name?' **1:7** You are offering improper sacrifices on my altar, yet you ask, 'How have we offended you?' By treating the table of the LORD as if it is of no importance! **1:8** For when you offer blind animals as a sacrifice, is that not wrong? And when you offer the lame and sick, is that not wrong as well? Indeed, try offering them to your governor! Will he be pleased with you or show you favor?" asks the LORD who rules over all. **1:9** But now plead for God's favor that he might be gracious to us. "With this kind of offering in your hands, how can he be pleased with you?" asks the LORD who rules over all.

1:10 "I wish that one of you would close the temple doors, so that you no longer would light useless fires on my altar. I am not pleased with you," says the LORD who rules over all, "and I will no longer accept an offering from you. **1:11** For from the east to the west my name will be great among the nations. Incense and pure offerings will be offered in my name everywhere, for my name will be great among the nations," says the LORD who rules over all. **1:12** "But you are profaning it by saying that the table of the Lord is common and its offerings despicable. **1:13** You also say, 'How tiresome it is.' You turn up your nose at it," says the LORD who rules over all, "and instead bring what is stolen, lame, or sick. You bring these things for an offering! Should I accept this from you?" asks the LORD. **1:14** "There will be harsh condemnation for the hypocrite who has a valuable male animal in his flock but vows and sacrifices something inferior to the Lord. For I am a great king," says the LORD who rules over all, "and my name is awesome among the nations."

The Sacrilege of the Priestly Message

2:1 "Now, you priests, this commandment is for you. **2:2** If you do not listen and take seriously the need to honor my name," says the LORD who rules over all, "I will send judgment on you and turn your blessings into curses – indeed, I have already done so because you are not taking it to heart. **2:3** I am about to discipline your children and will spread offal on your faces, the very offal produced at your festivals, and you will be carried away along with it. **2:4** Then you will know that I sent this commandment to you so that my covenant may continue to be with Levi," says the LORD who rules over all. **2:5** "My covenant with him was designed to bring life and peace. I gave its statutes to him to fill him with awe, and he indeed revered me and stood in awe before me. **2:6** He taught what was true; sinful words were not found on his lips. He walked with me in peace and integrity, and he turned many people away from sin. **2:7** For the lips of a priest should preserve knowledge of sacred things, and people should seek instruction from him because he is the messenger of the LORD who rules over all. **2:8** You, however, have turned from the way. You have caused many to violate the law; you have corrupted the covenant with Levi," says the LORD who rules over all. **2:9** "Therefore, I have caused you to be ignored and belittled before all people to the extent to which you are not following after me and are showing partiality in your instruction."

The Rebellion of the People

2:10 Do we not all have one father? Did not one God create us? Why do we betray one another, in this way making light of the covenant of our ancestors? **2:11** Judah has become disloyal, and unspeakable sins have been committed in Israel and Jerusalem. For Judah has profaned the holy things that the LORD loves and

has turned to a foreign god! **2:12** May the LORD cut off from the community of Jacob every last person who does this, as well as the person who presents improper offerings to the LORD who rules over all!

2:13 You also do this: You cover the altar of the LORD with tears as you weep and groan, because he no longer pays any attention to the offering nor accepts it favorably from you. **2:14** Yet you ask, "Why?" The LORD is testifying against you on behalf of the wife you married when you were young, to whom you have become unfaithful even though she is your companion and wife by law. **2:15** No one who has even a small portion of the Spirit in him does this. What did our ancestor do when seeking a child from God? Be attentive, then, to your own spirit, for one should not be disloyal to the wife he took in his youth.

2:16 "I hate divorce," says the LORD God of Israel, "and the one who is guilty of violence," says the LORD who rules over all. "Pay attention to your conscience, and do not be unfaithful."

Resistance to the Lord through Self-deceit

2:17 You have wearied the LORD with your words. But you say, "How have we wearied him?" Because you say, "Everyone who does evil is good in the Lord's opinion, and he delights in them," or "Where is the God of justice?" **3:1** "I am about to send my messenger, who will clear the way before me. Indeed, the Lord you are seeking will suddenly come to his temple, and the messenger of the covenant, whom you long for, is certainly coming," says the LORD who rules over all.

3:2 Who can endure the day of his coming? Who can keep standing when he appears? For he will be like a refiner's fire, like a launderer's soap. **3:3** He will act like a refiner and purifier of silver and will cleanse the Levites and refine them like gold and silver. Then they will offer the LORD a proper offering. **3:4** The offerings of Judah and Jerusalem will be pleasing to the LORD as in former times and years past.

3:5 "I will come to you in judgment. I will be quick to testify against those who practice divination, those who commit adultery, those who break promises, and those who exploit workers, widows, and orphans, who refuse to help the immigrant and in this way show they do not fear me," says the LORD who rules over all.

Resistance to the Lord through Selfishness

3:6 "Since, I, the LORD, do not go back on my promises, you, sons of Jacob, have not perished. **3:7** From the days of your ancestors you have ignored my commandments and have not kept them! Return to me, and I will return to you," says the LORD who rules over all. "But you say, 'How should we return?' **3:8** Can a person rob God? You indeed are robbing me, but you say, 'How are we robbing you?' In tithes and contributions! **3:9** You are bound for judgment because you are robbing me – this whole nation is guilty.

3:10 "Bring the entire tithe into the storehouse so that there may be food in my temple. Test me in this matter," says the LORD who rules over all, "to see if I will not open for you the windows of heaven and pour out for you a blessing until there is no room for it all. **3:11** Then I will stop the plague from ruining your crops, and the vine will not lose its fruit before harvest," says the LORD who rules over all. **3:12** "All nations will call you happy, for you indeed will live in a delightful land," says the LORD who rules over all.

Resistance to the Lord through Self-sufficiency

3:13 "You have criticized me sharply," says the LORD, "but you ask, 'How have we criticized you?' **3:14** You have said, 'It is useless to serve God. How have we been helped by keeping his requirements and going about like mourners before the LORD who rules over all? **3:15** So now we consider the arrogant to be happy; indeed, those who practice evil are successful. In fact, those who challenge God escape!'"

3:16 Then those who respected the LORD spoke to one another, and the LORD took notice. A scroll was prepared before him in which were recorded the names of those who respected the LORD and honored his name. **3:17** "They will belong to me," says the LORD who rules over all, "in the day when I prepare my own special property. I will spare them as a man spares his son who serves him. **3:18** Then once more you will see that I make a distinction between the righteous and the wicked, between the one who serves God and the one who does not.

4:1 (3:19) "For indeed the day is coming, burning like a furnace, and all the arrogant evildoers will be chaff. The coming day will burn them up,"

says the LORD who rules over all. "It will not leave even a root or branch. **4:2** But for you who respect my name, the sun of vindication will rise with healing wings, and you will skip about like calves released from the stall. **4:3** You will trample on the wicked, for they will be like ashes under the soles of your feet on the day which I am preparing," says the LORD who rules over all.

Restoration through the Lord

4:4 "Remember the law of my servant Moses, to whom at Horeb I gave rules and regulations for all Israel to obey. **4:5** Look, I will send you Elijah the prophet before the great and terrible day of the LORD arrives. **4:6** He will encourage fathers and their children to return to me, so that I will not come and strike the earth with judgment."

The New Testament

Book 40. Matthew

The Genealogy of Jesus Christ

1:1 This is the record of the genealogy of Jesus Christ, the son of David, the son of Abraham.

1:2 Abraham was the father of Isaac, Isaac the father of Jacob, Jacob the father of Judah and his brothers, **1:3** Judah the father of Perez and Zerah (by Tamar), Perez the father of Hezron, Hezron the father of Ram, **1:4** Ram the father of Amminadab, Amminadab the father of Nahshon, Nahshon the father of Salmon, **1:5** Salmon the father of Boaz (by Rahab), Boaz the father of Obed (by Ruth), Obed the father of Jesse, **1:6** and Jesse the father of David the king.

David was the father of Solomon (by the wife of Uriah), **1:7** Solomon the father of Rehoboam, Rehoboam the father of Abijah, Abijah the father of Asa, **1:8** Asa the father of Jehoshaphat, Jehoshaphat the father of Joram, Joram the father of Uzziah, **1:9** Uzziah the father of Jotham, Jotham the father of Ahaz, Ahaz the father of Hezekiah, **1:10** Hezekiah the father of Manasseh, Manasseh the father of Amon, Amon the father of Josiah, **1:11** and Josiah the father of Jeconiah and his brothers, at the time of the deportation to Babylon.

1:12 After the deportation to Babylon, Jeconiah became the father of Shealtiel, Shealtiel the father of Zerubbabel, **1:13** Zerubbabel the father of Abiud, Abiud the father of Eliakim, Eliakim the father of Azor, **1:14** Azor the father of Zadok, Zadok the father of Achim, Achim the father of Eliud, **1:15** Eliud the father of Eleazar, Eleazar the father of Matthan, Matthan the father of Jacob, **1:16** and Jacob the father of Joseph, the husband of Mary, by whom Jesus was born, who is called Christ.

1:17 So all the generations from Abraham to David are fourteen generations, and from David to the deportation to Babylon, fourteen generations, and from the deportation to Babylon to Christ, fourteen generations.

The Birth of Jesus Christ

1:18 Now the birth of Jesus Christ happened this way. While his mother Mary was engaged to Joseph, but before they came together, she was found to be pregnant through the Holy Spirit. **1:19** Because Joseph, her husband to be, was a righteous man, and because he did not want to disgrace her, he intended to divorce her privately. **1:20** When he had contemplated this, an angel of the Lord appeared to him in a dream and said, "Joseph, son of David, do not be afraid to take Mary as your wife, because the child conceived in her is from the Holy Spirit. **1:21** She will give birth to a son and you will name him Jesus, because he will save his people from their sins." **1:22** This all happened so that what was spoken by the Lord through the prophet would be fulfilled: **1:23** *Look! The virgin will conceive and bear a son, and they will call him Emmanuel,*" which means "*God with us.*" **1:24** When Joseph awoke from sleep he did what the angel of the Lord told him. He took his wife, **1:25** but did not have marital relations with her until she gave birth to a son, whom he named Jesus.

The Visit of the Wise Men

2:1 After Jesus was born in Bethlehem in Judea, in the time of King Herod, wise men from the East came to Jerusalem **2:2** saying, "Where is the one who is born king of the Jews? For we saw his star when it rose and have come to worship him." **2:3** When King Herod heard this he was alarmed, and all Jerusalem with him. **2:4** After assembling all the chief priests and experts in the law, he asked them where the Christ was to be born. **2:5** "In Bethlehem of Judea," they said, "for it is written this way by the prophet:

2:6 'And you, Bethlehem, **in the land of Judah,**

are in no way least among the rulers of Judah,

for out of you will come a ruler who will shepherd my people Israel.'"

2:7 Then Herod privately summoned the wise men and determined from them when the star had appeared. **2:8** He sent them to Bethlehem and said, "Go and look carefully for the child. When you find him, inform me so that I can go and worship him as well." **2:9** After listening to the king they left, and once again the star they saw when it rose led them until it stopped above the place where the child was. **2:10** When they saw the star they shouted joyfully. **2:11** As they came into the house and saw the child with Mary his mother, they bowed down and worshiped him. They opened their treasure boxes and gave him gifts of gold, frankincense, and myrrh. **2:12** After being warned in a dream not to return to Herod, they went back by another route to their own country.

The Escape to Egypt

2:13 After they had gone, an angel of the Lord appeared to Joseph in a dream and said, "Get up, take the child and his mother and flee to Egypt, and stay there until I tell you, for Herod is going to look for the child to kill him." **2:14** Then he got up, took the child and his mother during the night, and went to Egypt. **2:15** He stayed there until Herod died. In this way what was spoken by the Lord through the prophet was fulfilled: "*I called my Son out of Egypt.*"

2:16 When Herod saw that he had been tricked by the wise men, he became enraged. He sent men to kill all the children in Bethlehem and throughout the surrounding region from the age of two and under, according to the time he had learned from the wise men. **2:17** Then what was spoken by Jeremiah the prophet was fulfilled:

2:18 "A voice was heard in Ramah,

weeping and loud wailing,

Rachel weeping for her children,

and she did not want to be comforted, because they were gone."

The Return to Nazareth

2:19 After Herod had died, an angel of the Lord appeared in a dream to Joseph in Egypt **2:20** saying, "Get up, take the child and his mother, and go to the land of Israel, for those who were seeking the child's life are dead." **2:21** So he got up and took the child and his mother and returned to the land of Israel. **2:22** But when he heard that Archelaus was reigning over Judea in place of his father Herod, he was afraid to go there. After being warned in a dream, he went to the regions of Galilee. **2:23** He came to a town called Nazareth and lived there. Then what had been spoken by the prophets was fulfilled, that Jesus would be called a Nazarene.

The Ministry of John the Baptist

3:1 In those days John the Baptist came into the wilderness of Judea proclaiming,

3:2 "Repent, for the kingdom of heaven is near." **3:3** For he is the one about whom Isaiah the prophet had spoken:

"The voice of one shouting in the wilderness,

'Prepare the way for the Lord, make his paths straight.'"

3:4 Now John wore clothing made from camel's hair with a leather belt around his waist, and his diet consisted of locusts and wild honey. **3:5** Then people from Jerusalem, as well as all Judea and all the region around the Jordan, were going out to him, **3:6** and he was baptizing them in the Jordan River as they confessed their sins.

3:7 But when he saw many Pharisees and Sadducees coming to his baptism, he said to them, "You offspring of vipers! Who warned you to flee from the coming wrath? **3:8** Therefore produce fruit that proves your repentance, **3:9** and don't think you can say to yourselves, 'We have Abraham as our father.' For I tell you that God can raise up children for Abraham from these stones! **3:10** Even now the ax is laid at the root of the trees, and every tree that does not produce good fruit will be cut down and thrown into the fire.

3:11 "I baptize you with water, for repentance, but the one coming after me is more powerful than I am – I am not worthy to carry his sandals. He will baptize you with the Holy Spirit and fire. **3:12** His winnowing fork is in his hand, and he will clean out his threshing floor and will gather his wheat into the storehouse, but the chaff he will burn up with inextinguishable fire."

The Baptism of Jesus

3:13 Then Jesus came from Galilee to John to be baptized by him in the Jordan River. **3:14** But John tried to prevent him, saying, "I need to be baptized by you, and yet you come to me?" **3:15** So Jesus replied to him, "Let it happen now, for it is right for us to fulfill all righteousness." Then John yielded to him. **3:16** After Jesus was baptized, just as he was coming up out of the water, the heavens opened and he saw the Spirit of God descending like a dove and coming on him. **3:17** And a voice from heaven said, "This is my one dear Son; in him I take great delight."

The Temptation of Jesus

4:1 Then Jesus was led by the Spirit into the wilderness to be tempted by the devil. **4:2** After he fasted forty days and forty nights he was famished. **4:3** The tempter came and said to him, "If you are the Son of God, command these stones to become bread." **4:4** But he answered, "It is written, '*Man does not live by bread alone, but by every word that comes from the mouth of God.*'" **4:5** Then the devil took him to the holy city, had him stand on the highest point of the temple, **4:6** and said to him, "If you are the Son of God, throw yourself down. For it is written, '*He will command his angels concerning you*' and '*with their hands they will lift you up, so that you will not strike your foot against a stone.*'" **4:7** Jesus said to him, "Once again it is written: '*You are not to put the Lord your God to the test.*'" **4:8** Again, the devil took him to a very high mountain, and showed him all the kingdoms of the world and their grandeur. **4:9** And he said to him, "I will give you all these things if you throw yourself to the ground and worship me." **4:10** Then Jesus said to him, "Go away, Satan! For it is written: '*You are to worship the Lord your God and serve* only *him.*'" **4:11** Then the devil left him, and angels came and began ministering to his needs.

Preaching in Galilee

4:12 Now when Jesus heard that John had been imprisoned, he went into Galilee. **4:13** While in Galilee, he moved from Nazareth to make his home in Capernaum by the sea, in the region of Zebulun and Naphtali, **4:14** so that what was spoken by Isaiah the prophet would be fulfilled:

4:15 "Land of Zebulun and land of Naphtali,

the way by the sea, beyond the Jordan, Galilee of the Gentiles –

4:16 the people who sit in darkness have seen a great light,

and on those who sit in the region and shadow of death a light has dawned."

4:17 From that time Jesus began to preach this message: "Repent, for the kingdom of heaven is near."

The Call of the Disciples

4:18 As he was walking by the Sea of Galilee he saw two brothers, Simon (called Peter) and Andrew his brother, casting a net into the sea (for they were fishermen). **4:19** He said to them, "Follow me, and I will turn you into fishers of people." **4:20** They left their nets immediately and followed him. **4:21** Going on from there he saw two other brothers, James the son of Zebedee and John his brother, in a boat with Zebedee their father, mending their nets. Then he called them. **4:22** They immediately left the boat and their father and followed him.

Jesus' Healing Ministry

4:23 Jesus went throughout all of Galilee, teaching in their synagogues, preaching the gospel of the kingdom, and healing all kinds of disease and sickness among the people. **4:24** So a report about him spread throughout Syria. People brought to him all who suffered with various illnesses and afflictions, those who had seizures, paralytics, and those possessed by demons, and he healed them. **4:25** And large crowds followed him from Galilee, the Decapolis, Jerusalem, Judea, and beyond the Jordan River.

The Beatitudes

5:1 When he saw the crowds, he went up the mountain. After he sat down his disciples came to him. **5:2** Then he began to teach them by saying:

5:3 "Blessed are the poor in spirit, for the kingdom of heaven belongs to them.

5:4 "Blessed are those who mourn, for they will be comforted.

5:5 "Blessed are the meek, for they will inherit the earth.

5:6 "Blessed are those who hunger and thirst for righteousness, for they will be satisfied.

5:7 "Blessed are the merciful, for they will be shown mercy.

5:8 "Blessed are the pure in heart, for they will see God.

5:9 "Blessed are the peacemakers, for they will be called the children of God.

5:10 "Blessed are those who are persecuted for righteousness, for the kingdom of heaven belongs to them.

5:11 "Blessed are you when people insult you and persecute you and say all kinds of evil things about you falsely on account of me. **5:12** Rejoice and be glad because your reward is great in heaven, for they persecuted the prophets before you in the same way.

Salt and Light

5:13 "You are the salt of the earth. But if salt loses its flavor, how can it be made salty again? It is no longer good for anything except to be thrown out and trampled on by people. **5:14** You are the light of the world. A city located on a hill cannot be hidden. **5:15** People do not light a lamp and put it under a basket but on a lampstand, and it gives light to all in the house. **5:16** In the same way, let your light shine before people, so that they can see your good deeds and give honor to your Father in heaven.

Fulfillment of the Law and Prophets

5:17 "Do not think that I have come to abolish the law or the prophets. I have not come to abolish these things but to fulfill them. **5:18** I tell you the truth, until heaven and earth pass away not the smallest letter or stroke of a letter will pass from the law until everything takes place. **5:19** So anyone who breaks one of the least of these commands and teaches others to do so will be called least in the kingdom of heaven, but whoever obeys them and teaches others to do so will be called great in the kingdom of heaven. **5:20** For I tell you, unless your righteousness goes beyond that of the experts in the law and the Pharisees, you will never enter the kingdom of heaven.

Anger and Murder

5:21 "You have heard that it was said to an older generation, '*Do not murder*,' and 'whoever murders will be subjected to judgment.' **5:22** But I say to you that anyone who is angry with a brother will be subjected to judgment. And whoever insults a brother will be brought before the council, and whoever says 'Fool' will be sent to fiery hell. **5:23** So then, if you bring your gift to the altar and there remember that your brother has something against you, **5:24** leave your gift there in front of the altar. First go and be reconciled to your brother and then come and present your gift. **5:25** Reach agreement quickly with your accuser while on the way to court, or he may hand you over to the judge, and the judge hand you over to the warden, and you will be thrown into prison. **5:26** I tell you the truth, you will never get out of there until you have paid the last penny!

Adultery

5:27 "You have heard that it was said, '*Do not commit adultery*.' **5:28** But I say to you that whoever looks at a woman to desire her has already committed adultery with her in his heart. **5:29** If your right eye causes you to sin, tear it out and throw it away! It is better to lose one of your members than to have your whole body thrown into hell. **5:30** If your right hand causes you to sin, cut it off and throw it away! It is better to lose one of your members than to have your whole body go into hell.

Divorce

5:31 "It was said, '*Whoever divorces his wife must give her a legal document*.' **5:32** But I say to you that everyone who divorces his wife, except for immorality, makes her commit adultery, and whoever marries a divorced woman commits adultery.

Oaths

5:33 "Again, you have heard that it was said to an older generation, '*Do not break an oath, but fulfill your vows to the Lord*.' **5:34** But I say to you, do not take oaths at all – not by heaven, because it is the throne of God, **5:35** not by earth, because it is his footstool, and not by Jerusalem, because it is the city of the great King. **5:36** Do not take an oath by your head, because you are not able to make one hair white or black. **5:37** Let your word be 'Yes, yes' or 'No, no.' More than this is from the evil one.

Retaliation

5:38 "You have heard that it was said, '*An eye for an eye and a tooth for a tooth*.' **5:39** But I say to you, do not resist the evildoer. But whoever strikes you on the right cheek, turn the other to him as well. **5:40** And if someone wants to sue you and to take your tunic, give him your coat also. **5:41** And if anyone forces you to go one mile, go with him two. **5:42** Give to the one who asks you, and do not reject the one who wants to borrow from you.

Love for Enemies

5:43 "You have heard that it was said, '*Love your neighbor*' and 'hate your enemy.' **5:44** But I say to you, love your enemy and pray for those who persecute you, **5:45** so that you may be like your Father in heaven, since he causes the sun to rise on the evil and the good, and sends rain on the righteous and the unrighteous. **5:46** For if you love those who love you, what reward do you have? Even the tax collectors do the same, don't they? **5:47** And if you only greet your brothers, what more do you do? Even the Gentiles do the same, don't they? **5:48** So then, be perfect, as your heavenly Father is perfect.

Pure-hearted Giving

6:1 "Be careful not to display your righteousness merely to be seen by people. Otherwise you have no reward with your Father in heaven. **6:2** Thus whenever you do charitable giving, do not blow a trumpet before you, as the hypocrites do in synagogues and on streets so that people will praise them. I tell you the truth, they have their reward. **6:3** But when you do your giving, do not let your left hand know what your right hand is doing, **6:4** so that your gift may be in secret. And your Father, who sees in secret, will reward you.

Private Prayer

6:5 "Whenever you pray, do not be like the hypocrites, because they love to pray while standing in synagogues and on street corners so that people can see them. Truly I say to you, they have their reward. **6:6** But whenever you pray, go into your room, close the door, and pray to your Father in secret. And your Father, who sees in secret, will reward you. **6:7** When you pray, do not babble repetitiously like the Gentiles, because they think that by their many words they will be heard. **6:8** Do not be like them, for your Father knows what you need before you ask him. **6:9** So pray this way:

Our Father in heaven, may your name be honored,
6:10 may your kingdom come,
may your will be done on earth as it is in heaven.
6:11 Give us today our daily bread,
6:12 and forgive us our debts, as we ourselves have forgiven our debtors.
6:13 And do not lead us into temptation, but deliver us from the evil one.
6:14 "For if you forgive others their sins, your heavenly Father will also forgive you. **6:15** But if you do not forgive others, your Father will not forgive you your sins.

Proper Fasting

6:16 "When you fast, do not look sullen like the hypocrites, for they make their faces unattractive so that people will see them fasting. I tell you the truth, they have their reward. **6:17** When you fast, put oil on your head and wash your face, **6:18** so that it will not be obvious to others when you are fasting, but only to your Father who is in secret. And your Father, who sees in secret, will reward you.

Lasting Treasure

6:19 "Do not accumulate for yourselves treasures on earth, where moth and rust destroy and where thieves break in and steal. **6:20** But accumulate for yourselves treasures in heaven, where moth and rust do not destroy, and thieves do not break in and steal. **6:21** For where your treasure is, there your heart will be also.

6:22 "The eye is the lamp of the body. If then your eye is healthy, your whole body will be full of light. **6:23** But if your eye is diseased, your whole body will be full of darkness. If then the light in you is darkness, how great is the darkness!

6:24 "No one can serve two masters, for either he will hate the one and love the other, or he will be devoted to the one and despise the other. You cannot serve God and money.

Do Not Worry

6:25 "Therefore I tell you, do not worry about your life, what you will eat or drink, or about your body, what you will wear. Isn't there more to life than food and more to the body than clothing? **6:26** Look at the birds in the sky: They do not sow, or reap, or gather into barns, yet your heavenly Father feeds them. Aren't you more valuable than they are? **6:27** And which of you by worrying can add even one hour to his life? **6:28** Why do you worry about clothing? Think about how the flowers of the field grow; they do not work or spin. **6:29** Yet I tell you that not even Solomon in all his glory was clothed like one of these! **6:30** And if this is how God clothes the wild grass, which is here today and tomorrow is tossed into the fire to heat the oven, won't he clothe you even more, you people of little faith? **6:31** So then, don't worry saying, 'What will we eat?' or 'What will we drink?' or 'What will we wear?' **6:32** For the unconverted pursue these things, and your heavenly Father knows that you need them. **6:33** But above all pursue his kingdom and righteousness, and all these things will be given to you as well. **6:34** So then, do not worry about tomorrow, for tomorrow will worry about itself. Today has enough trouble of its own.

Do Not Judge

7:1 "Do not judge so that you will not be judged. **7:2** For by the standard you judge you will be judged, and the measure you use will be the measure you receive. **7:3** Why do you see the speck in your brother's eye, but fail to see the beam of wood in your own? **7:4** Or how can you say to your brother, 'Let me remove the speck from your eye,' while there is a beam in your own? **7:5** You hypocrite! First remove the beam from your own eye, and then you can see clearly to remove the speck from your brother's eye. **7:6** Do not give what is holy to dogs or throw your pearls before pigs; otherwise they will trample them under their feet and turn around and tear you to pieces.

Ask, Seek, Knock

7:7 "Ask and it will be given to you; seek and you will find; knock and the door will be opened for you. **7:8** For everyone who asks receives, and the one who seeks finds, and to the one who knocks, the door will be opened. **7:9** Is there anyone among you who, if his son asks for bread, will give him a stone? **7:10** Or if he asks for a fish, will give him a snake? **7:11** If you then, although you are evil, know how to give good gifts to your children, how much more will your Father in heaven give good gifts to those who ask him! **7:12** In everything, treat others as you would want them to treat you, for this fulfills the law and the prophets.

The Narrow Gate

7:13 "Enter through the narrow gate, because the gate is wide and the way is spacious that leads to destruction, and there are many who enter through it. **7:14** But the gate is narrow and the way is difficult that leads to life, and there are few who find it.

A Tree and Its Fruit

7:15 "Watch out for false prophets, who come to you in sheep's clothing but inwardly are voracious wolves. **7:16** You will recognize them by their fruit. Grapes are not gathered from thorns or figs from thistles, are they? **7:17** In the same way, every good tree bears good fruit, but the bad tree bears bad fruit. **7:18** A good tree is not able to bear bad fruit, nor a bad tree to bear good fruit. **7:19** Every tree that does not bear good fruit is cut down and thrown into the fire. **7:20** So then, you will recognize them by their fruit.

Judgment of Pretenders

7:21 "Not everyone who says to me, 'Lord, Lord,' will enter into the kingdom of heaven – only the one who does the will of my Father in heaven. **7:22** On that day, many will say to me, 'Lord, Lord, didn't we prophesy in your name, and in your name cast out demons and do many powerful deeds?' **7:23** Then I will declare to them, 'I never knew you. Go away from me, you lawbreakers!'

Hearing and Doing

7:24 "Everyone who hears these words of mine and does them is like a wise man who built his house on rock. **7:25** The rain fell, the flood came, and the winds beat against that house, but it did not collapse because it had been founded on rock. **7:26** Everyone who hears these words of mine and does not do them is like a foolish man who built his house on sand. **7:27** The rain fell, the flood came, and the winds beat against that house, and it collapsed; it was utterly destroyed!"

7:28 When Jesus finished saying these things, the crowds were amazed by his teaching, **7:29** because he taught them like one who had authority, not like their experts in the law.

Cleansing a Leper

8:1 After he came down from the mountain, large crowds followed him. **8:2** And a leper approached, and bowed low before him, saying, "Lord, if you are willing, you can make me clean." **8:3** He stretched out his hand and touched him saying, "I am willing. Be clean!" Immediately his leprosy was cleansed. **8:4** Then Jesus said to him, "See that you do not speak to anyone, but go, show yourself to a priest, and bring the offering that Moses commanded, as a testimony to them."

Healing the Centurion's Servant

8:5 When he entered Capernaum, a centurion came to him asking for help: **8:6** "Lord, my servant is lying at home paralyzed, in terrible anguish." **8:7** Jesus said to him, "I will come and heal him." **8:8** But the centurion replied, "Lord, I am not worthy to have you come under my roof. Instead, just say the word and my servant will be healed. **8:9** For I too am a man under authority, with soldiers under me. I say to this one, 'Go' and he goes, and to another 'Come' and he comes, and to my slave 'Do this' and he does it." **8:10** When Jesus heard this he was amazed and said to those who followed him, "I tell you the truth, I have not found such faith in anyone in Israel! **8:11** I tell you, many will come from the east and west to share the banquet with Abraham, Isaac, and Jacob in the kingdom of heaven, **8:12** but the sons of the kingdom will be thrown out

into the outer darkness, where there will be weeping and gnashing of teeth." **8:13** Then Jesus said to the centurion, "Go; just as you believed, it will be done for you." And the servant was healed at that hour.

Healings at Peter's House

8:14 Now when Jesus entered Peter's house, he saw his mother-in-law lying down, sick with a fever. **8:15** He touched her hand, and the fever left her. Then she got up and began to serve them. **8:16** When it was evening, many demon-possessed people were brought to him. He drove out the spirits with a word, and healed all who were sick. **8:17** In this way what was spoken by Isaiah the prophet was fulfilled:

"He took our weaknesses and carried our diseases."

Challenging Professed Followers

8:18 Now when Jesus saw a large crowd around him, he gave orders to go to the other side of the lake. **8:19** Then an expert in the law came to him and said, "Teacher, I will follow you wherever you go." **8:20** Jesus said to him, "Foxes have dens, and the birds in the sky have nests, but the Son of Man has no place to lay his head." **8:21** Another of the disciples said to him, "Lord, let me first go and bury my father." **8:22** But Jesus said to him, "Follow me, and let the dead bury their own dead."

Stilling of a Storm

8:23 As he got into the boat, his disciples followed him. **8:24** And a great storm developed on the sea so that the waves began to swamp the boat. But he was asleep. **8:25** So they came and woke him up saying, "Lord, save us! We are about to die!" **8:26** But he said to them, "Why are you cowardly, you people of little faith?" Then he got up and rebuked the winds and the sea, and it was dead calm. **8:27** And the men were amazed and said, "What sort of person is this? Even the winds and the sea obey him!"

Healing the Gadarene Demoniacs

8:28 When he came to the other side, to the region of the Gadarenes, two demon-possessed men coming from the tombs met him. They were extremely violent, so that no one was able to pass by that way. **8:29** They cried out, "Son of God, leave us alone! Have you come here to torment us before the time?" **8:30** A large herd of pigs was feeding some distance from them. **8:31** Then the demons begged him, "If you drive us out, send us into the herd of pigs." **8:32** And he said, "Go!" So they came out and went into the pigs, and the herd rushed down the steep slope into the lake and drowned in the water. **8:33** The herdsmen ran off, went into the town, and told everything that had happened to the demon-possessed men. **8:34** Then the entire town came out to meet Jesus. And when they saw him, they begged him to leave their region.

Healing and Forgiving a Paralytic

9:1 After getting into a boat he crossed to the other side and came to his own town. **9:2** Just then some people brought to him a paralytic lying on a stretcher. When Jesus saw their faith, he said to the paralytic, "Have courage, son! Your sins are forgiven." **9:3** Then some of the experts in the law said to themselves, "This man is blaspheming!" **9:4** When Jesus saw their reaction he said, "Why do you respond with evil in your hearts? **9:5** Which is easier, to say, 'Your sins are forgiven' or to say, 'Stand up and walk'? **9:6** But so that you may know that the Son of Man has authority on earth to forgive sins" – then he said to the paralytic – "Stand up, take your stretcher, and go home." **9:7** And he stood up and went home. **9:8** When the crowd saw this, they were afraid and honored God who had given such authority to men.

The Call of Matthew; Eating with Sinners

9:9 As Jesus went on from there, he saw a man named Matthew sitting at the tax booth. "Follow me," he said to him. And he got up and followed him. **9:10** As Jesus was having a meal in Matthew's house, many tax collectors and sinners came and ate with Jesus and his disciples. **9:11** When the Pharisees saw this they said to his disciples, "Why does your teacher eat with tax collectors and sinners?" **9:12** When Jesus heard this he said, "Those who are healthy don't need a physician, but those who are sick do. **9:13** Go and learn what this saying means: '*I want mercy and not sacrifice.*' For I did not come to call the righteous, but sinners."

The Superiority of the New

9:14 Then John's disciples came to Jesus and asked, "Why do we and the Pharisees fast often, but your disciples don't fast?" **9:15** Jesus said to them, "The wedding guests cannot mourn while the bridegroom is with them, can they? But the days are coming when the bridegroom will be taken from them, and then they will fast. **9:16** No one sews a patch of unshrunk cloth on an old garment, because the patch will pull away from the garment and the tear will be worse. **9:17** And no one pours new wine into old wineskins; otherwise the skins burst and the wine is spilled out and the skins are destroyed. Instead they put new wine into new wineskins and both are preserved."

Restoration and Healing

9:18 As he was saying these things, a ruler came, bowed low before him, and said, "My daughter has just died, but come and lay your hand on her and she will live." **9:19** Jesus and his disciples got up and followed him. **9:20** But a woman who had been suffering from a hemorrhage for twelve years came up behind him and touched the edge of his cloak. **9:21** For she kept saying to herself, "If only I touch his cloak, I will be healed." **9:22** But when Jesus turned and saw her he said, "Have courage, daughter!

Your faith has made you well." And the woman was healed from that hour. **9:23** When Jesus entered the ruler's house and saw the flute players and the disorderly crowd, **9:24** he said, "Go away, for the girl is not dead but asleep." And they began making fun of him. **9:25** But when the crowd had been put outside, he went in and gently took her by the hand, and the girl got up. **9:26** And the news of this spread throughout that region.

Healing the Blind and Mute

9:27 As Jesus went on from there, two blind men followed him, shouting, "Have mercy on us, Son of David!" **9:28** When he went into the house, the blind men came to him. Jesus said to them, "Do you believe that I am able to do this?" They said to him, "Yes, Lord." **9:29** Then he touched their eyes saying, "Let it be done for you according to your faith." **9:30** And their eyes were opened. Then Jesus sternly warned them, "See that no one knows about this." **9:31** But they went out and spread the news about him throughout that entire region.

9:32 As they were going away, a man who could not talk and was demon-possessed was brought to him. **9:33** After the demon was cast out, the man who had been mute spoke. The crowds were amazed and said, "Never has anything like this been seen in Israel!" **9:34** But the Pharisees said, "By the ruler of demons he casts out demons."

Workers for the Harvest

9:35 Then Jesus went throughout all the towns and villages, teaching in their synagogues, preaching the good news of the kingdom, and healing every kind of disease and sickness. **9:36** When he saw the crowds, he had compassion on them because they were bewildered and helpless, like sheep without a shepherd. **9:37** Then he said to his disciples, "The harvest is plentiful, but the workers are few. **9:38** Therefore ask the Lord of the harvest to send out workers into his harvest."

Sending Out the Twelve Apostles

10:1 Jesus called his twelve disciples and gave them authority over unclean spirits so they could cast them out and heal every kind of disease and sickness. **10:2** Now these are the names of the twelve apostles: first, Simon (called Peter), and Andrew his brother; James son of Zebedee and John his brother; **10:3** Philip and Bartholomew; Thomas and Matthew the tax collector; James the son of Alphaeus, and Thaddaeus; **10:4** Simon the Zealot and Judas Iscariot, who betrayed him.

10:5 Jesus sent out these twelve, instructing them as follows: "Do not go to Gentile regions and do not enter any Samaritan town. **10:6** Go instead to the lost sheep of the house of Israel. **10:7** As you go, preach this message: 'The kingdom of heaven is near!' **10:8** Heal the sick, raise the dead, cleanse lepers, cast out demons. Freely you received, freely give. **10:9** Do not take gold, silver, or copper in your belts, **10:10** no bag for the journey, or an extra tunic, or sandals or staff, for the worker deserves his provisions. **10:11** Whenever you enter a town or village, find out who is worthy there and stay with them until you leave. **10:12** As you enter the house, give it greetings. **10:13** And if the house is worthy, let your peace come on it, but if it is not worthy, let your peace return to you. **10:14** And if anyone will not welcome you or listen to your message, shake the dust off your feet as you leave that house or that town. **10:15** I tell you the truth, it will be more bearable for the region of Sodom and Gomorrah on the day of judgment than for that town!

Persecution of Disciples

10:16 "I am sending you out like sheep surrounded by wolves, so be wise as serpents and innocent as doves. **10:17** Beware of people, because they will hand you over to councils and flog you in their synagogues. **10:18** And you will be brought before governors and kings because of me, as a witness to them and the Gentiles. **10:19** Whenever they hand you over for trial, do not worry about how to speak or what to say, for what you should say will be given to you at that time. **10:20** For it is not you speaking, but the Spirit of your Father speaking through you. **10:21** "Brother will hand over brother to death, and a father his child. Children will rise against parents and have them put to death. **10:22** And you will be hated by everyone because of my name. But the one who endures to the end will be saved. **10:23** Whenever they persecute you in one place, flee to another. I tell you the truth, you will not finish going through all the towns of Israel before the Son of Man comes.

10:24 "A disciple is not greater than his teacher, nor a slave greater than his master. **10:25** It is enough for the disciple to become like his teacher, and the slave like his master. If they have called the head of the house 'Beelzebul,' how much more will they defame the members of his household!

Fear God, Not Man

10:26 "Do not be afraid of them, for nothing is hidden that will not be revealed, and nothing is secret that will not be made known. **10:27** What I say to you in the dark, tell in the light, and what is whispered in your ear, proclaim from the housetops. **10:28** Do not be afraid of those who kill the body but cannot kill the soul. Instead, fear the one who is able to destroy both soul and body in hell. **10:29** Aren't two sparrows sold for a penny? Yet not one of them falls to the ground apart from your Father's will. **10:30** Even all the hairs on your head are numbered. **10:31** So do not be afraid; you are more valuable than many sparrows.

10:32 "Whoever, then, acknowledges me before people, I will acknowledge before my Father in heaven. **10:33** But whoever denies me before people, I will deny him also before my Father in heaven.

Not Peace, but a Sword

10:34 "Do not think that I have come to bring peace to the earth. I have not come to bring peace but a sword. **10:35** For I have come to set *a man against his father, a daughter against her mother, and a daughter-in-law against her mother-in-law,* **10:36** and *a man's enemies will be the members of his household.*

10:37 "Whoever loves father or mother more than me is not worthy of me, and whoever loves son or daughter more than me is not worthy of me. **10:38** And whoever does not take up his cross and follow me is not worthy of me. **10:39** Whoever finds his life will lose it, and whoever loses his life because of me will find it.

Rewards

10:40 "Whoever receives you receives me, and whoever receives me receives the one who sent me. **10:41** Whoever receives a prophet in the name of a prophet will receive a prophet's reward. Whoever receives a righteous person in the name of a righteous person will receive a righteous person's reward. **10:42** And whoever gives only a cup of cold water to one of these little ones in the name of a disciple, I tell you the truth, he will never lose his reward."

11:1 When Jesus had finished instructing his twelve disciples, he went on from there to teach and preach in their towns.

Jesus and John the Baptist

11:2 Now when John heard in prison about the deeds Christ had done, he sent his disciples to ask a question: **11:3** "Are you the one who is to come, or should we look for another?" **11:4** Jesus answered them, "Go tell John what you hear and see: **11:5** The blind see, the lame walk, lepers are cleansed, the deaf hear, the dead are raised, and the poor have good news proclaimed to them. **11:6** Blessed is anyone who takes no offense at me."

11:7 While they were going away, Jesus began to speak to the crowd about John: "What did you go out into the wilderness to see? A reed shaken by the wind? **11:8** What did you go out to see? A man dressed in fancy clothes? Look, those who wear fancy clothes are in the homes of kings! **11:9** What did you go out to see? A prophet? Yes, I tell you, and more than a prophet. **11:10** This is the one about whom it is written:

'Look, I am sending my messenger ahead of you,
who will prepare your way before you.'

11:11 "I tell you the truth, among those born of women, no one has arisen greater than John the Baptist. Yet the one who is least in the kingdom of heaven is greater than he is. **11:12** From the days of John the Baptist until now the kingdom of heaven has suffered violence, and forceful people lay hold of it. **11:13** For all the prophets and the law prophesied until John appeared. **11:14** And if you are willing to accept it, he is Elijah, who is to come. **11:15** The one who has ears had better listen!

11:16 "To what should I compare this generation? They are like children sitting in the marketplaces who call out to one another,

11:17 'We played the flute for you, yet you did not dance;
we wailed in mourning, yet you did not weep.'

11:18 For John came neither eating nor drinking, and they say, 'He has a demon!' **11:19** The Son of Man came eating and drinking, and they say, 'Look at him, a glutton and a drunk, a friend of tax collectors and sinners!' But wisdom is vindicated by her deeds."

Woes on Unrepentant Cities

11:20 Then Jesus began to criticize openly the cities in which he had done many of his miracles, because they did not repent. **11:21** "Woe to you, Chorazin! Woe to you, Bethsaida! If the miracles done in you had been done in Tyre and Sidon, they would have repented long ago in sackcloth and ashes. **11:22** But I tell you, it will be more bearable for Tyre and Sidon on the day of judgment than for you! **11:23** And you, Capernaum, will you be exalted to heaven? No, you will be thrown down to Hades! For if the miracles done among you had been done in Sodom, it would have continued to this day. **11:24** But I tell you, it will be more bearable for the region of Sodom on the day of judgment than for you!"

Jesus' Invitation

11:25 At that time Jesus said, "I praise you, Father, Lord of heaven and earth, because you have hidden these things from the wise and intelligent, and revealed them to little children. **11:26** Yes, Father, for this was your gracious will. **11:27** All things have been handed over to me by my Father. No one knows the Son except the Father, and no one knows the Father except the Son and anyone to whom the Son decides to reveal him. **11:28** Come to me, all you who are weary and burdened, and I will give you rest. **11:29** Take my yoke on you and learn from me, because I am gentle and humble in heart, and you will find rest for your souls. **11:30** For my yoke is easy to bear, and my load is not hard to carry."

Lord of the Sabbath

12:1 At that time Jesus went through the grain fields on a Sabbath. His disciples were hungry, and they began to pick heads of wheat and eat them. **12:2** But when the Pharisees saw this they said to him, "Look, your disciples are doing what is against the law to do on the Sabbath." **12:3** He said to them, "Haven't you read what David did when he and his companions were hungry – **12:4** how he entered the house of God and they ate the sacred bread, which was against the law for him or his companions to eat, but only for the priests? **12:5** Or have you not read in the law that the priests in the temple desecrate the Sabbath and yet are not guilty? **12:6** I tell you that something greater than the temple is here. **12:7** If you had known what this means: '*I want mercy and not sacrifice*,' you would not have condemned the innocent. **12:8** For the Son of Man is lord of the Sabbath."

12:9 Then Jesus left that place and entered their synagogue. **12:10** A man was there who had a withered hand. And they asked Jesus, "Is it lawful to heal on the Sabbath?" so that they could accuse him. **12:11** He said to them, "Would not any one of you, if he had one sheep that fell into a pit on the Sabbath, take hold of it and lift it out? **12:12** How much more valuable is a person than a sheep! So it is lawful to do good on the Sabbath." **12:13** Then he said to the man, "Stretch out your hand." He stretched it out and it was restored, as healthy as the other. **12:14** But the Pharisees went out and plotted against him, as to how they could assassinate him.

God's Special Servant

12:15 Now when Jesus learned of this, he went away from there. Great crowds followed him, and he healed them all. **12:16** But he sternly warned them not to make him known. **12:17** This fulfilled what was spoken by Isaiah the prophet:

12:18 "Here is my servant whom I have chosen,
the one I love, in whom I take great delight.
I will put my Spirit on him, and he will proclaim justice to the nations.
12:19 He will not quarrel or cry out,
nor will anyone hear his voice in the streets.
12:20 He will not break a bruised reed or extinguish a smoldering wick,
until he brings justice to victory.
12:21 And in his name the Gentiles will hope."

Jesus and Beelzebul

12:22 Then they brought to him a demon-possessed man who was blind and mute. Jesus healed him so that he could speak and see. **12:23** All the crowds were amazed and said, "Could this one be the Son of David?" **12:24** But when the Pharisees heard this they said, "He does not cast out demons except by the power of Beelzebul, the ruler of demons!" **12:25** Now when Jesus realized what they were thinking, he said to them, "Every kingdom divided against itself is destroyed, and no town or house divided against itself will stand. **12:26** So if Satan casts out Satan, he is divided against himself. How then will his kingdom stand? **12:27** And if I cast out demons by Beelzebul, by whom do your sons cast them out? For this reason they will be your judges. **12:28** But if I cast out demons by the Spirit of God, then the kingdom of God has already overtaken you. **12:29** How else can someone enter a strong man's house and steal his property, unless he first ties up the strong man? Then he can thoroughly plunder the house. **12:30** Whoever is not with me is against me, and whoever does not gather with me scatters. **12:31** For this reason I tell you, people will be forgiven for every sin and blasphemy, but the blasphemy against the Spirit will not be forgiven. **12:32** Whoever speaks a word against the Son of Man will be forgiven. But whoever speaks against the Holy Spirit will not be forgiven, either in this age or in the age to come.

Trees and Their Fruit

12:33 "Make a tree good and its fruit will be good, or make a tree bad and its fruit will be bad, for a tree is known by its fruit. **12:34** Offspring of vipers! How are you able to say anything good, since you are evil? For the mouth speaks from what fills the heart. **12:35** The good person brings good things out of his good treasury, and the evil person brings evil things out of his evil treasury. **12:36** I tell you that on the day of judgment, people will give an account for every worthless word they speak. **12:37** For by your words you will be justified, and by your words you will be condemned."

The Sign of Jonah

12:38 Then some of the experts in the law along with some Pharisees answered him, "Teacher, we want to see a sign from you." **12:39** But he answered them, "An evil and adulterous generation asks for a sign, but no sign will be given to it except the sign of the prophet Jonah. **12:40** For just as Jonah was *in the belly of the huge fish for three days and three nights*, so the Son of Man will be in the heart of the earth for three days and three nights. **12:41** The people of Nineveh will stand up at the judgment with this generation and condemn it, because they repented when Jonah preached to them – and now, something greater than Jonah is here! **12:42** The queen of the South will rise up at the judgment with this generation and condemn it, because she came from the ends of the earth to hear the wisdom of Solomon – and now, something greater than Solomon is here!

The Return of the Unclean Spirit

12:43 "When an unclean spirit goes out of a person, it passes through waterless places looking for rest but does not find it. **12:44** Then it says, 'I will return to the home I left.' When it returns, it finds the house empty, swept clean, and put in order. **12:45** Then it goes and brings with it seven other spirits more evil than itself, and they go in and live there, so

the last state of that person is worse than the first. It will be that way for this evil generation as well!"

Jesus' True Family

12:46 While Jesus was still speaking to the crowds, his mother and brothers came and stood outside, asking to speak to him. **12:47** Someone told him, "Look, your mother and your brothers are standing outside wanting to speak to you." **12:48** To the one who had said this, Jesus replied, "Who is my mother and who are my brothers?" **12:49** And pointing toward his disciples he said, "Here are my mother and my brothers! **12:50** For whoever does the will of my Father in heaven is my brother and sister and mother."

The Parable of the Sower

13:1 On that day after Jesus went out of the house, he sat by the lake. **13:2** And such a large crowd gathered around him that he got into a boat to sit while the whole crowd stood on the shore. **13:3** He told them many things in parables, saying: "Listen! A sower went out to sow. **13:4** And as he sowed, some seeds fell along the path, and the birds came and devoured them. **13:5** Other seeds fell on rocky ground where they did not have much soil. They sprang up quickly because the soil was not deep. **13:6** But when the sun came up, they were scorched, and because they did not have sufficient root, they withered. **13:7** Other seeds fell among the thorns, and they grew up and choked them. **13:8** But other seeds fell on good soil and produced grain, some a hundred times as much, some sixty, and some thirty. **13:9** The one who has ears had better listen!"

13:10 Then the disciples came to him and said, "Why do you speak to them in parables?" **13:11** He replied, "You have been given the opportunity to know the secrets of the kingdom of heaven, but they have not. **13:12** For whoever has will be given more, and will have an abundance. But whoever does not have, even what he has will be taken from him. **13:13** For this reason I speak to them in parables: Although they see they do not see, and although they hear they do not hear nor do they understand. **13:14** And concerning them the prophecy of Isaiah is fulfilled that says:

'You will listen carefully yet will never understand,
you will look closely yet will never comprehend.
13:15 For the heart of this people has become dull;
they are hard of hearing,
and they have shut their eyes,
so that they would not see with their eyes
and hear with their ears
and understand with their hearts
and turn, and I would heal them.'

13:16 "But your eyes are blessed because they see, and your ears because they hear. **13:17** For I tell you the truth, many prophets and righteous people longed to see what you see but did not see it, and to hear what you hear but did not hear it.

13:18 "So listen to the parable of the sower: **13:19** When anyone hears the word about the kingdom and does not understand it, the evil one comes and snatches what was sown in his heart; this is the seed sown along the path. **13:20** The seed sown on rocky ground is the person who hears the word and immediately receives it with joy. **13:21** But he has no root in himself and does not endure; when trouble or persecution comes because of the word, immediately he falls away. **13:22** The seed sown among thorns is the person who hears the word, but worldly cares and the seductiveness of wealth choke the word, so it produces nothing. **13:23** But as for the seed sown on good soil, this is the person who hears the word and understands. He bears fruit, yielding a hundred, sixty, or thirty times what was sown."

The Parable of the Weeds

13:24 He presented them with another parable: "The kingdom of heaven is like a person who sowed good seed in his field. **13:25** But while everyone was sleeping, an enemy came and sowed weeds among the wheat and went away. **13:26** When the plants sprouted and bore grain, then the weeds also appeared. **13:27** So the slaves of the owner came and said to him, 'Sir, didn't you sow good seed in your field? Then where did the weeds come from?' **13:28** He said, 'An enemy has done this.' So the slaves replied, 'Do you want us to go and gather them?' **13:29** But he said, 'No, since in gathering the weeds you may uproot the wheat with them. **13:30** Let both grow together until the harvest. At harvest time I will tell the reapers, "First collect the weeds and tie them in bundles to be burned, but then gather the wheat into my barn."'"

The Parable of the Mustard Seed

13:31 He gave them another parable: "The kingdom of heaven is like a mustard seed that a man took and sowed in his field. **13:32** It is the smallest of all the seeds, but when it has grown it is the greatest garden plant and becomes a tree, so that the wild birds come and nest in its branches."

The Parable of the Yeast

13:33 He told them another parable: "The kingdom of heaven is like yeast that a woman took and mixed with three measures of flour until all the dough had risen."

The Purpose of Parables

13:34 Jesus spoke all these things in parables to the crowds; he did not speak to them without a parable. **13:35** This fulfilled what was spoken by the prophet:

"I will open my mouth in parables,
I will announce what has been hidden from the foundation of the world."

Explanation for the Disciples

13:36 Then he left the crowds and went into the house. And his disciples came to him saying, "Explain to us the parable of the weeds in the field." **13:37** He answered, "The one who sowed the good seed is the Son of Man. **13:38** The field is the world and the good seed are the people of the kingdom. The weeds are the people of the evil one, **13:39** and the enemy who sows them is the devil. The harvest is the end of the age, and the reapers are angels. **13:40** As the weeds are collected and burned with fire, so it will be at the end of the age. **13:41** The Son of Man will send his angels, and they will gather from his kingdom everything that causes sin as well as all lawbreakers. **13:42** They will ***throw them into the fiery furnace***, where there will be weeping and gnashing of teeth. **13:43** Then *the righteous will shine like the sun in the kingdom of their Father.* The one who has ears had better listen!

Parables on the Kingdom of Heaven

13:44 "The kingdom of heaven is like a treasure, hidden in a field, that a person found and hid. Then because of joy he went and sold all that he had and bought that field.

13:45 "Again, the kingdom of heaven is like a merchant searching for fine pearls. **13:46** When he found a pearl of great value, he went out and sold everything he had and bought it.

13:47 "Again, the kingdom of heaven is like a net that was cast into the sea that caught all kinds of fish. **13:48** When it was full, they pulled it ashore, sat down, and put the good fish into containers and threw the bad away. **13:49** It will be this way at the end of the age. Angels will come and separate the evil from the righteous **13:50** and *throw them into the fiery furnace*, where there will be weeping and gnashing of teeth.

13:51 "Have you understood all these things?" They replied, "Yes." **13:52** Then he said to them, "Therefore every expert in the law who has been trained for the kingdom of heaven is like the owner of a house who brings out of his treasure what is new and old."

Rejection at Nazareth

13:53 Now when Jesus finished these parables, he moved on from there. **13:54** Then he came to his hometown and began to teach the people in their synagogue. They were astonished and said, "Where did this man get such wisdom and miraculous powers? **13:55** Isn't this the carpenter's son? Isn't his mother named Mary? And aren't his brothers James, Joseph, Simon, and Judas? **13:56** And aren't all his sisters here with us? Where did he get all this?" **13:57** And so they took offense at him. But Jesus said to them, "A prophet is not without honor except in his hometown and in his own house." **13:58** And he did not do many miracles there because of their unbelief.

The Death of John the Baptist

14:1 At that time Herod the tetrarch heard reports about Jesus, **14:2** and he said to his servants, "This is John the Baptist. He has been raised from the dead! And because of this, miraculous powers are at work in him." **14:3** For Herod had arrested John, bound him, and put him in prison on account of Herodias, his brother Philip's wife, **14:4** because John had repeatedly told him, "It is not lawful for you to have her." **14:5** Although Herod wanted to kill John, he feared the crowd because they accepted John as a prophet. **14:6** But on Herod's birthday, the daughter of Herodias danced before them and pleased Herod, **14:7** so much that he promised with an oath to give her whatever she asked. **14:8** Instructed by her mother, she said, "Give me the head of John the Baptist here on a platter." **14:9** Although it grieved the king, because of his oath and the dinner guests he commanded it to be given. **14:10** So he sent and had John beheaded in the prison. **14:11** His head was brought on a platter and given to the girl, and she brought it to her mother. **14:12** Then John's disciples came and took the body and buried it and went and told Jesus.

The Feeding of the Five Thousand

14:13 Now when Jesus heard this he went away from there privately in a boat to an isolated place. But when the crowd heard about it, they followed him on foot from the towns. **14:14** As he got out he saw the large crowd, and he had compassion on them and healed their sick. **14:15** When evening arrived, his disciples came to him saying, "This is an isolated place and the hour is already late. Send the crowds away so that they can go into the villages and buy food for themselves." **14:16** But he replied, "They don't need to go. You give them something to eat." **14:17** They said to him, "We have here only five loaves and two fish." **14:18** "Bring them here to me," he replied. **14:19** Then he instructed the crowds to sit down on the grass. He took the five loaves and two fish, and looking up to heaven he gave thanks and broke the loaves. He gave them to the disciples, who in turn gave them to the crowds. **14:20** They all ate and were satisfied, and they picked up the broken pieces left over, twelve baskets full. **14:21** Not counting women and children, there were about five thousand men who ate.

Walking on Water

14:22 Immediately Jesus made the disciples get into the boat and go ahead of him to the other side, while he dispersed the crowds. **14:23** And after he sent the crowds away, he went up the mountain by himself to pray. When evening came, he was there alone. **14:24** Meanwhile the boat, already far from land, was taking a beating from the waves because the wind was against it. **14:25** As the night was ending, Jesus came to them walking on the sea. **14:26** When the disciples saw him walking on the water they were terrified and said, "It's a ghost!" and cried out with fear. **14:27** But immediately Jesus spoke to them: "Have courage! It is I. Do not be afraid." **14:28** Peter said to him, "Lord, if it is you, order me to come to you on the water." **14:29** So he said, "Come." Peter got out of the boat, walked on the water, and came toward Jesus. **14:30** But when he saw the strong wind he became afraid. And starting to sink, he cried out, "Lord, save me!" **14:31** Immediately Jesus reached out his hand and caught him, saying to him, "You of little faith, why did you doubt?" **14:32** When they went up into the boat, the wind ceased. **14:33** Then those who were in the boat worshiped him, saying, "Truly you are the Son of God."

14:34 After they had crossed over, they came to land at Gennesaret. **14:35** When the people there recognized him, they sent word into all the surrounding area, and they brought all their sick to him. **14:36** They begged him if they could only touch the edge of his cloak, and all who touched it were healed.

Breaking Human Traditions

15:1 Then Pharisees and experts in the law came from Jerusalem to Jesus and said, **15:2** "Why do your disciples disobey the tradition of the elders? For they don't wash their hands when they eat." **15:3** He answered them, "And why do you disobey the commandment of God because of your tradition? **15:4** For God said, '***Honor your father and mother***' and '***Whoever insults his father or mother must be put to death***.' **15:5** But you say, 'If someone tells his father or mother, "Whatever help you would have received from me is given to God," **15:6** he does not need to honor his father.' You have nullified the word of God on account of your tradition. **15:7** Hypocrites! Isaiah prophesied correctly about you when he said,

15:8 'This people honors me with their lips,
but their heart is far from me,
15:9 and they worship me in vain,
teaching as doctrines the commandments of men.'"

True Defilement

15:10 Then he called the crowd to him and said, "Listen and understand. **15:11** What defiles a person is not what goes into the mouth; it is what comes out of the mouth that defiles a person." **15:12** Then the disciples came to him and said, "Do you know that when the Pharisees heard this saying they were offended?" **15:13** And he replied, "Every plant that my heavenly Father did not plant will be uprooted. **15:14** Leave them! They are blind guides. If someone who is blind leads another who is blind, both will fall into a pit." **15:15** But Peter said to him, "Explain this parable to us." **15:16** Jesus said, "Even after all this, are you still so foolish? **15:17** Don't you understand that whatever goes into the mouth enters the stomach and then passes out into the sewer? **15:18** But the things that come out of the mouth come from the heart, and these things defile a person. **15:19** For out of the heart come evil ideas, murder, adultery, sexual immorality, theft, false testimony, slander. **15:20** These are the things that defile a person; it is not eating with unwashed hands that defiles a person."

A Canaanite Woman's Faith

15:21 After going out from there, Jesus went to the region of Tyre and Sidon. **15:22** A Canaanite woman from that area came and cried out, "Have mercy on me, Lord, Son of David! My daughter is horribly demon-possessed!" **15:23** But he did not answer her a word. Then his disciples came and begged him, "Send her away, because she keeps on crying out after us." **15:24** So he answered, "I was sent only to the lost sheep of the house of Israel." **15:25** But she came and bowed down before him and said, "Lord, help me!" **15:26** "It is not right to take the children's bread and throw it to the dogs," he said. **15:27** "Yes, Lord," she replied, "but even the dogs eat the crumbs that fall from their masters' table." **15:28** Then Jesus answered her, "Woman, your faith is great! Let what you want be done for you." And her daughter was healed from that hour.

Healing Many Others

15:29 When he left there, Jesus went along the Sea of Galilee. Then he went up a mountain, where he sat down. **15:30** Then large crowds came to him bringing with them the lame, blind, crippled, mute, and many others. They laid them at his feet, and he healed them. **15:31** As a result, the crowd was amazed when they saw the mute speaking, the crippled healthy, the lame walking, and the blind seeing, and they praised the God of Israel.

The Feeding of the Four Thousand

15:32 Then Jesus called the disciples and said, "I have compassion on the crowd, because they have already been here with me three days and they have nothing to eat. I don't want to send them away hungry since they may faint on the way." **15:33** The disciples said to him, "Where can we get enough bread in this desolate place to satisfy so great a crowd?" **15:34**

Jesus said to them, "How many loaves do you have?" They replied, "Seven – and a few small fish." **15:35** After instructing the crowd to sit down on the ground, **15:36** he took the seven loaves and the fish, and after giving thanks, he broke them and began giving them to the disciples, who then gave them to the crowds. **15:37** They all ate and were satisfied, and they picked up the broken pieces left over, seven baskets full. **15:38** Not counting children and women, there were four thousand men who ate. **15:39** After sending away the crowd, he got into the boat and went to the region of Magadan.

The Demand for a Sign

16:1 Now when the Pharisees and Sadducees came to test Jesus, they asked him to show them a sign from heaven. **16:2** He said, "When evening comes you say, 'It will be fair weather, because the sky is red,' **16:3** and in the morning, 'It will be stormy today, because the sky is red and darkening.' You know how to judge correctly the appearance of the sky, but you cannot evaluate the signs of the times. **16:4** A wicked and adulterous generation asks for a sign, but no sign will be given to it except the sign of Jonah." Then he left them and went away.

The Yeast of the Pharisees and Sadducees

16:5 When the disciples went to the other side, they forgot to take bread. **16:6** "Watch out," Jesus said to them, "beware of the yeast of the Pharisees and Sadducees." **16:7** So they began to discuss this among themselves, saying, "It is because we brought no bread." **16:8** When Jesus learned of this, he said, "You who have such little faith! Why are you arguing among yourselves about having no bread? **16:9** Do you still not understand? Don't you remember the five loaves for the five thousand, and how many baskets you took up? **16:10** Or the seven loaves for the four thousand and how many baskets you took up? **16:11** How could you not understand that I was not speaking to you about bread? But beware of the yeast of the Pharisees and Sadducees!" **16:12** Then they understood that he had not told them to be on guard against the yeast in bread, but against the teaching of the Pharisees and Sadducees.

Peter's Confession

16:13 When Jesus came to the area of Caesarea Philippi, he asked his disciples, "Who do people say that the Son of Man is?" **16:14** They answered, "Some say John the Baptist, others Elijah, and others Jeremiah or one of the prophets." **16:15** He said to them, "But who do you say that I am?" **16:16** Simon Peter answered, "You are the Christ, the Son of the living God." **16:17** And Jesus answered him, "You are blessed, Simon son of Jonah, because flesh and blood did not reveal this to you, but my Father in heaven! **16:18** And I tell you that you are Peter, and on this rock I will build my church, and the gates of Hades will not overpower it. **16:19** I will give you the keys of the kingdom of heaven. Whatever you bind on earth will have been bound in heaven, and whatever you release on earth will have been released in heaven." **16:20** Then he instructed his disciples not to tell anyone that he was the Christ.

First Prediction of Jesus' Death and Resurrection

16:21 From that time on Jesus began to show his disciples that he must go to Jerusalem and suffer many things at the hands of the elders, chief priests, and experts in the law, and be killed, and on the third day be raised. **16:22** So Peter took him aside and began to rebuke him: "God forbid, Lord! This must not happen to you!" **16:23** But he turned and said to Peter, "Get behind me, Satan! You are a stumbling block to me, because you are not setting your mind on God's interests, but on man's." **16:24** Then Jesus said to his disciples, "If anyone wants to become my follower, he must deny himself, take up his cross, and follow me. **16:25** For whoever wants to save his life will lose it, but whoever loses his life for my sake will find it. **16:26** For what does it benefit a person if he gains the whole world but forfeits his life? Or what can a person give in exchange for his life? **16:27** For the Son of Man will come with his angels in the glory of his Father, and then *he will reward each person according to what he has done.* **16:28** I tell you the truth, there are some standing here who will not experience death before they see the Son of Man coming in his kingdom."

The Transfiguration

17:1 Six days later Jesus took with him Peter, James, and John the brother of James, and led them privately up a high mountain. **17:2** And he was transfigured before them. His face shone like the sun, and his clothes became white as light. **17:3** Then Moses and Elijah also appeared before them, talking with him. **17:4** So Peter said to Jesus, "Lord, it is good for us to be here. If you want, I will make three shelters – one for you, one for Moses, and one for Elijah." **17:5** While he was still speaking, a bright cloud overshadowed them, and a voice from the cloud said, "This is my one dear Son, in whom I take great delight. Listen to him!" **17:6** When the disciples heard this, they were overwhelmed with fear and threw themselves down with their faces to the ground. **17:7** But Jesus came and touched them. "Get up," he said. "Do not be afraid." **17:8** When they looked up, all they saw was Jesus alone.

17:9 As they were coming down from the mountain, Jesus commanded them, "Do not tell anyone about the vision until the Son of Man is raised from the dead." **17:10** The disciples asked him, "Why then do the experts in the law say that Elijah must come first?" **17:11** He answered, "Elijah does indeed come first and will restore all things. **17:12** And I tell you that Elijah has already come. Yet they did not recognize him, but did to him whatever they wanted. In the same way, the Son of Man will suffer at their hands." **17:13** Then the disciples understood that he was speaking to them about John the Baptist.

The Disciples' Failure to Heal

17:14 When they came to the crowd, a man came to him, knelt before him, **17:15** and said, "Lord, have mercy on my son, because he has seizures and suffers terribly, for he often falls into the fire and into the water. **17:16** I brought him to your disciples, but they were not able to heal him." **17:17** Jesus answered, "You unbelieving and perverse generation! How much longer must I be with you? How much longer must I endure you? Bring him here to me." **17:18** Then Jesus rebuked the demon and it came out of him, and the boy was healed from that moment. **17:19** Then the disciples came to Jesus privately and said, "Why couldn't we cast it out?" **17:20** He told them, "It was because of your little faith. I tell you the truth, if you have faith the size of a mustard seed, you will say to this mountain, 'Move from here to there,' and it will move; nothing will be impossible for you."

Second Prediction of Jesus' Death and Resurrection

17:22 When they gathered together in Galilee, Jesus told them, "The Son of Man is going to be betrayed into the hands of men. **17:23** They will kill him, and on the third day he will be raised." And they became greatly distressed.

The Temple Tax

17:24 After they arrived in Capernaum, the collectors of the temple tax came to Peter and said, "Your teacher pays the double drachma tax, doesn't he?" **17:25** He said, "Yes." When Peter came into the house, Jesus spoke to him first, "What do you think, Simon? From whom do earthly kings collect tolls or taxes – from their sons or from foreigners?" **17:26** After he said, "From foreigners," Jesus said to him, "Then the sons are free. **17:27** But so that we don't offend them, go to the lake and throw out a hook. Take the first fish that comes up, and when you open its mouth, you will find a four drachma coin. Take that and give it to them for me and you."

Questions About the Greatest

18:1 At that time the disciples came to Jesus saying, "Who is the greatest in the kingdom of heaven?" **18:2** He called a child, had him stand among them, **18:3** and said, "I tell you the truth, unless you turn around and become like little children, you will never enter the kingdom of heaven! **18:4** Whoever then humbles himself like this little child is the greatest in the kingdom of heaven. **18:5** And whoever welcomes a child like this in my name welcomes me.

18:6 "But if anyone causes one of these little ones who believe in me to sin, it would be better for him to have a huge millstone hung around his neck and to be drowned in the open sea. **18:7** Woe to the world because of stumbling blocks! It is necessary that stumbling blocks come, but woe to the person through whom they come. **18:8** If your hand or your foot causes you to sin, cut it off and throw it away. It is better for you to enter life crippled or lame than to have two hands or two feet and be thrown into eternal fire. **18:9** And if your eye causes you to sin, tear it out and throw it away. It is better for you to enter into life with one eye than to have two eyes and be thrown into fiery hell.

The Parable of the Lost Sheep

18:10 "See that you do not disdain one of these little ones. For I tell you that their angels in heaven always see the face of my Father in heaven. **18:12** What do you think? If someone owns a hundred sheep and one of them goes astray, will he not leave the ninety-nine on the mountains and go look for the one that went astray? **18:13** And if he finds it, I tell you the truth, he will rejoice more over it than over the ninety-nine that did not go astray. **18:14** In the same way, your Father in heaven is not willing that one of these little ones be lost.

Restoring Christian Relationships

18:15 "If your brother sins, go and show him his fault when the two of you are alone. If he listens to you, you have regained your brother. **18:16** But if he does not listen, take one or two others with you, so that *at the testimony of two or three witnesses every matter may be established.* **18:17** If he refuses to listen to them, tell it to the church. If he refuses to listen to the church, treat him like a Gentile or a tax collector. **18:18** "I tell you the truth, whatever you bind on earth will have been bound in heaven, and whatever you release on earth will have been released in heaven. **18:19** Again, I tell you the truth, if two of you on earth agree about whatever you ask, my Father in heaven will do it for you. **18:20** For where two or three are assembled in my name, I am there among them."

18:21 Then Peter came to him and said, "Lord, how many times must I forgive my brother who sins against me? As many as seven times?" **18:22** Jesus said to him, "Not seven times, I tell you, but seventy-seven times!

The Parable of the Unforgiving Slave

18:23 "For this reason, the kingdom of heaven is like a king who wanted to settle accounts with his slaves. **18:24** As he began settling his accounts, a man who owed ten thousand talents was brought to him. **18:25** Because he was not able to repay it, the lord ordered him to be sold, along with his wife, children, and whatever he possessed, and repayment to be made.

18:26 Then the slave threw himself to the ground before him, saying, 'Be patient with me, and I will repay you everything.' **18:27** The lord had compassion on that slave and released him, and forgave him the debt. **18:28** After he went out, that same slave found one of his fellow slaves who owed him one hundred silver coins. So he grabbed him by the throat and started to choke him, saying, 'Pay back what you owe me!' **18:29** Then his fellow slave threw himself down and begged him, 'Be patient with me, and I will repay you.' **18:30** But he refused. Instead, he went out and threw him in prison until he repaid the debt. **18:31** When his fellow slaves saw what had happened, they were very upset and went and told their lord everything that had taken place. **18:32** Then his lord called the first slave and said to him, 'Evil slave! I forgave you all that debt because you begged me! **18:33** Should you not have shown mercy to your fellow slave, just as I showed it to you?' **18:34** And in anger his lord turned him over to the prison guards to torture him until he repaid all he owed. **18:35** So also my heavenly Father will do to you, if each of you does not forgive your brother from your heart."

Questions About Divorce

19:1 Now when Jesus finished these sayings, he left Galilee and went to the region of Judea beyond the Jordan River. **19:2** Large crowds followed him, and he healed them there.

19:3 Then some Pharisees came to him in order to test him. They asked, "Is it lawful to divorce a wife for any cause?" **19:4** He answered, "Have you not read that from the beginning the Creator *made them male and female*, **19:5** and said, '*For this reason a man will leave his father and mother and will be united with his wife, and the two will become one flesh*'? **19:6** So they are no longer two, but one flesh. Therefore what God has joined together, let no one separate." **19:7** They said to him, "Why then did Moses command us *to give a certificate of dismissal and to divorce* her?" **19:8** Jesus said to them, "Moses permitted you to divorce your wives because of your hard hearts, but from the beginning it was not this way. **19:9** Now I say to you that whoever divorces his wife, except for immorality, and marries another commits adultery." **19:10** The disciples said to him, "If this is the case of a husband with a wife, it is better not to marry!" **19:11** He said to them, "Not everyone can accept this statement, except those to whom it has been given. **19:12** For there are some eunuchs who were that way from birth, and some who were made eunuchs by others, and some who became eunuchs for the sake of the kingdom of heaven. The one who is able to accept this should accept it."

Jesus and Little Children

19:13 Then little children were brought to him for him to lay his hands on them and pray. But the disciples scolded those who brought them. **19:14** But Jesus said, "Let the little children come to me and do not try to stop them, for the kingdom of heaven belongs to such as these." **19:15** And he placed his hands on them and went on his way.

The Rich Young Man

19:16 Now someone came up to him and said, "Teacher, what good thing must I do to gain eternal life?" **19:17** He said to him, "Why do you ask me about what is good? There is only one who is good. But if you want to enter into life, keep the commandments." **19:18** "Which ones?" he asked. Jesus replied, "*Do not murder, do not commit adultery, do not steal, do not give false testimony,* **19:19** *honor your father and mother,* and *love your neighbor as yourself.*" **19:20** The young man said to him, "I have wholeheartedly obeyed all these laws. What do I still lack?" **19:21** Jesus said to him, "If you wish to be perfect, go sell your possessions and give the money to the poor, and you will have treasure in heaven. Then come, follow me." **19:22** But when the young man heard this he went away sorrowful, for he was very rich.

19:23 Then Jesus said to his disciples, "I tell you the truth, it will be hard for a rich person to enter the kingdom of heaven! **19:24** Again I say, it is easier for a camel to go through the eye of a needle than for a rich person to enter into the kingdom of God." **19:25** The disciples were greatly astonished when they heard this and said, "Then who can be saved?" **19:26** Jesus looked at them and replied, "This is impossible for mere humans, but for God all things are possible." **19:27** Then Peter said to him, "Look, we have left everything to follow you! What then will there be for us?" **19:28** Jesus said to them, "I tell you the truth: In the age when all things are renewed, when the Son of Man sits on his glorious throne, you who have followed me will also sit on twelve thrones, judging the twelve tribes of Israel. **19:29** And whoever has left houses or brothers or sisters or father or mother or children or fields for my sake will receive a hundred times as much and will inherit eternal life. **19:30** But many who are first will be last, and the last first.

Workers in the Vineyard

20:1 "For the kingdom of heaven is like a landowner who went out early in the morning to hire workers for his vineyard. **20:2** And after agreeing with the workers for the standard wage, he sent them into his vineyard. **20:3** When it was about nine o'clock in the morning, he went out again and saw others standing around in the marketplace without work. **20:4** He said to them, 'You go into the vineyard too, and I will give you whatever is right.' **20:5** So they went. When he went out again about noon and three o'clock that afternoon, he did the same thing. **20:6** And about five o'clock that afternoon he went out and found others standing around, and

said to them, 'Why are you standing here all day without work?' **20:7** They said to him, 'Because no one hired us.' He said to them, 'You go and work in the vineyard too.' **20:8** When it was evening the owner of the vineyard said to his manager, 'Call the workers and give the pay starting with the last hired until the first.' **20:9** When those hired about five o'clock came, each received a full day's pay. **20:10** And when those hired first came, they thought they would receive more. But each one also received the standard wage. **20:11** When they received it, they began to complain against the landowner, **20:12** saying, 'These last fellows worked one hour, and you have made them equal to us who bore the hardship and burning heat of the day.' **20:13** And the landowner replied to one of them, 'Friend, I am not treating you unfairly. Didn't you agree with me to work for the standard wage? **20:14** Take what is yours and go. I want to give to this last man the same as I gave to you. **20:15** Am I not permitted to do what I want with what belongs to me? Or are you envious because I am generous?' **20:16** So the last will be first, and the first last."

Third Prediction of Jesus' Death and Resurrection

20:17 As Jesus was going up to Jerusalem, he took the twelve aside privately and said to them on the way, **20:18** "Look, we are going up to Jerusalem, and the Son of Man will be handed over to the chief priests and the experts in the law. They will condemn him to death, **20:19** and will turn him over to the Gentiles to be mocked and flogged severely and crucified. Yet on the third day, he will be raised."

A Request for James and John

20:20 Then the mother of the sons of Zebedee came to him with her sons, and kneeling down she asked him for a favor. **20:21** He said to her, "What do you want?" She replied, "Permit these two sons of mine to sit, one at your right hand and one at your left, in your kingdom." **20:22** Jesus answered, "You don't know what you are asking! Are you able to drink the cup I am about to drink?" They said to him, "We are able." **20:23** He told them, "You will drink my cup, but to sit at my right and at my left is not mine to give. Rather, it is for those for whom it has been prepared by my Father."

20:24 Now when the other ten heard this, they were angry with the two brothers. **20:25** But Jesus called them and said, "You know that the rulers of the Gentiles lord it over them, and those in high positions use their authority over them. **20:26** It must not be this way among you! Instead whoever wants to be great among you must be your servant, **20:27** and whoever wants to be first among you must be your slave – **20:28** just as the Son of Man did not come to be served but to serve, and to give his life as a ransom for many."

Two Blind Men Healed

20:29 As they were leaving Jericho, a large crowd followed them. **20:30** Two blind men were sitting by the road. When they heard that Jesus was passing by, they shouted, "Have mercy on us, Lord, Son of David!" **20:31** The crowd scolded them to get them to be quiet. But they shouted even more loudly, "Lord, have mercy on us, Son of David!" **20:32** Jesus stopped, called them, and said, "What do you want me to do for you?" **20:33** They said to him, "Lord, let our eyes be opened." **20:34** Moved with compassion, Jesus touched their eyes. Immediately they received their sight and followed him.

The Triumphal Entry

21:1 Now when they approached Jerusalem and came to Bethphage, at the Mount of Olives, Jesus sent two disciples, **21:2** telling them, "Go to the village ahead of you. Right away you will find a donkey tied there, and a colt with her. Untie them and bring them to me. **21:3** If anyone says anything to you, you are to say, 'The Lord needs them,' and he will send them at once." **21:4** This took place to fulfill what was spoken by the prophet:

21:5 "Tell the people of Zion,
'Look, your king is coming to you,
unassuming and seated on a donkey,
and on a colt, the foal of a donkey.'"

21:6 So the disciples went and did as Jesus had instructed them. **21:7** They brought the donkey and the colt and placed their cloaks on them, and he sat on them. **21:8** A very large crowd spread their cloaks on the road. Others cut branches from the trees and spread them on the road. **21:9** The crowds that went ahead of him and those following kept shouting, "*Hosanna* to the Son of David! *Blessed is the one who comes in the name of the Lord! Hosanna* in the highest!" **21:10** As he entered Jerusalem the whole city was thrown into an uproar, saying, "Who is this?" **21:11** And the crowds were saying, "This is the prophet Jesus, from Nazareth in Galilee."

Cleansing the Temple

21:12 Then Jesus entered the temple area and drove out all those who were selling and buying in the temple courts, and turned over the tables of the money changers and the chairs of those selling doves. **21:13** And he said to them, "It is written, '*My house will be called a house of prayer,*' but you are turning it into *a den of robbers*!"

21:14 The blind and lame came to him in the temple courts, and he healed them. **21:15** But when the chief priests and the experts in the law saw the wonderful things he did and heard the children crying out in the temple courts, "Hosanna to the Son of David," they became indignant

21:16 and said to him, "Do you hear what they are saying?" Jesus said to them, "Yes. Have you never read, '*Out of the mouths of children and nursing infants you have prepared praise for yourself*'?" **21:17** And leaving them, he went out of the city to Bethany and spent the night there.

The Withered Fig Tree

21:18 Now early in the morning, as he returned to the city, he was hungry. **21:19** After noticing a fig tree by the road he went to it, but found nothing on it except leaves. He said to it, "Never again will there be fruit from you!" And the fig tree withered at once. **21:20** When the disciples saw it they were amazed, saying, "How did the fig tree wither so quickly?" **21:21** Jesus answered them, "I tell you the truth, if you have faith and do not doubt, not only will you do what was done to the fig tree, but even if you say to this mountain, 'Be lifted up and thrown into the sea,' it will happen. **21:22** And whatever you ask in prayer, if you believe, you will receive."

The Authority of Jesus

21:23 Now after Jesus entered the temple courts, the chief priests and elders of the people came up to him as he was teaching and said, "By what authority are you doing these things, and who gave you this authority?" **21:24** Jesus answered them, "I will also ask you one question. If you answer me then I will also tell you by what authority I do these things. **21:25** Where did John's baptism come from? From heaven or from people?" They discussed this among themselves, saying, "If we say, 'From heaven,' he will say, 'Then why did you not believe him?' **21:26** But if we say, 'From people,' we fear the crowd, for they all consider John to be a prophet." **21:27** So they answered Jesus, "We don't know." Then he said to them, "Neither will I tell you by what authority I am doing these things.

The Parable of the Two Sons

21:28 "What do you think? A man had two sons. He went to the first and said, 'Son, go and work in the vineyard today.' **21:29** The boy answered, 'I will not.' But later he had a change of heart and went. **21:30** The father went to the other son and said the same thing. This boy answered, 'I will, sir,' but did not go. **21:31** Which of the two did his father's will?" They said, "The first." Jesus said to them, "I tell you the truth, tax collectors and prostitutes will go ahead of you into the kingdom of God! **21:32** For John came to you in the way of righteousness, and you did not believe him. But the tax collectors and prostitutes did believe. Although you saw this, you did not later change your minds and believe him.

The Parable of the Tenants

21:33 "Listen to another parable: There was a landowner who planted a vineyard. He put a fence around it, dug a pit for its winepress, and built a watchtower. Then he leased it to tenant farmers and went on a journey. **21:34** When the harvest time was near, he sent his slaves to the tenants to collect his portion of the crop. **21:35** But the tenants seized his slaves, beat one, killed another, and stoned another. **21:36** Again he sent other slaves, more than the first, and they treated them the same way. **21:37** Finally he sent his son to them, saying, 'They will respect my son.' **21:38** But when the tenants saw the son, they said to themselves, 'This is the heir. Come, let's kill him and get his inheritance!' **21:39** So they seized him, threw him out of the vineyard, and killed him. **21:40** Now when the owner of the vineyard comes, what will he do to those tenants?" **21:41** They said to him, "He will utterly destroy those evil men! Then he will lease the vineyard to other tenants who will give him his portion at the harvest."

21:42 Jesus said to them, "Have you never read in the scriptures:

'The stone the builders rejected has become the cornerstone.

This is from the Lord, and it is marvelous in our eyes'?

21:43 For this reason I tell you that the kingdom of God will be taken from you and given to a people who will produce its fruit. **21:44** The one who falls on this stone will be broken to pieces, and the one on whom it falls will be crushed." **21:45** When the chief priests and the Pharisees heard his parables, they realized that he was speaking about them. **21:46** They wanted to arrest him, but they were afraid of the crowds, because the crowds regarded him as a prophet.

The Parable of the Wedding Banquet

22:1 Jesus spoke to them again in parables, saying: **22:2** "The kingdom of heaven can be compared to a king who gave a wedding banquet for his son. **22:3** He sent his slaves to summon those who had been invited to the banquet, but they would not come. **22:4** Again he sent other slaves, saying, 'Tell those who have been invited, "Look! The feast I have prepared for you is ready. My oxen and fattened cattle have been slaughtered, and everything is ready. Come to the wedding banquet."' **22:5** But they were indifferent and went away, one to his farm, another to his business. **22:6** The rest seized his slaves, insolently mistreated them, and killed them. **22:7** The king was furious! He sent his soldiers, and they put those murderers to death and set their city on fire. **22:8** Then he said to his slaves, 'The wedding is ready, but the ones who had been invited were not worthy. **22:9** So go into the main streets and invite everyone you find to the wedding banquet.' **22:10** And those slaves went out into the streets and gathered all they found, both bad and good, and the wedding hall was filled with guests. **22:11** But when the king came in to see the wedding guests, he saw a man there who was not wearing wedding clothes. **22:12**

And he said to him, 'Friend, how did you get in here without wedding clothes?' But he had nothing to say. **22:13** Then the king said to his attendants, 'Tie him up hand and foot and throw him into the outer darkness, where there will be weeping and gnashing of teeth!' **22:14** For many are called, but few are chosen."

Paying Taxes to Caesar

22:15 Then the Pharisees went out and planned together to entrap him with his own words. **22:16** They sent to him their disciples along with the Herodians, saying, "Teacher, we know that you are truthful, and teach the way of God in accordance with the truth. You do not court anyone's favor because you show no partiality. **22:17** Tell us then, what do you think? Is it right to pay taxes to Caesar or not?" **22:18** But Jesus realized their evil intentions and said, "Hypocrites! Why are you testing me? **22:19** Show me the coin used for the tax." So they brought him a denarius. **22:20** Jesus said to them, "Whose image is this, and whose inscription?" **22:21** They replied, "Caesar's." He said to them, "Then give to Caesar the things that are Caesar's, and to God the things that are God's." **22:22** Now when they heard this they were stunned, and they left him and went away.

Marriage and the Resurrection

22:23 The same day Sadducees (who say there is no resurrection) came to him and asked him, **22:24** "Teacher, Moses said, '*If a man dies without having children, his brother must marry the widow and father children for his brother.*' **22:25** Now there were seven brothers among us. The first one married and died, and since he had no children he left his wife to his brother. **22:26** The second did the same, and the third, down to the seventh. **22:27** Last of all, the woman died. **22:28** In the resurrection, therefore, whose wife of the seven will she be? For they all had married her." **22:29** Jesus answered them, "You are deceived, because you don't know the scriptures or the power of God. **22:30** For in the resurrection they neither marry nor are given in marriage, but are like angels in heaven. **22:31** Now as for the resurrection of the dead, have you not read what was spoken to you by God, **22:32** '*I am the God of Abraham, the God of Isaac, and the God of Jacob*'? He is not the God of the dead but of the living!" **22:33** When the crowds heard this, they were amazed at his teaching.

The Greatest Commandment

22:34 Now when the Pharisees heard that he had silenced the Sadducees, they assembled together. **22:35** And one of them, an expert in religious law, asked him a question to test him: **22:36** "Teacher, which commandment in the law is the greatest?" **22:37** Jesus said to him, "'*Love the Lord your God with all your heart, with all your soul, and with all your mind.*' **22:38** This is the first and greatest commandment. **22:39** The second is like it: '*Love your neighbor as yourself.*' **22:40** All the law and the prophets depend on these two commandments."

The Messiah: David's Son and Lord

22:41 While the Pharisees were assembled, Jesus asked them a question: **22:42** "What do you think about the Christ? Whose son is he?" They said, "The son of David." **22:43** He said to them, "How then does David by the Spirit call him 'Lord,' saying,

22:44 'The Lord said to my lord,

"Sit at my right hand,

until I put your enemies under your feet"'?

22:45 If David then calls him 'Lord,' how can he be his son?" **22:46** No one was able to answer him a word, and from that day on no one dared to question him any longer.

Seven Woes

23:1 Then Jesus said to the crowds and to his disciples, **23:2** "The experts in the law and the Pharisees sit on Moses' seat. **23:3** Therefore pay attention to what they tell you and do it. But do not do what they do, for they do not practice what they teach. **23:4** They tie up heavy loads, hard to carry, and put them on men's shoulders, but they themselves are not willing even to lift a finger to move them. **23:5** They do all their deeds to be seen by people, for they make their phylacteries wide and their tassels long. **23:6** They love the place of honor at banquets and the best seats in the synagogues **23:7** and elaborate greetings in the marketplaces, and to have people call them 'Rabbi.' **23:8** But you are not to be called 'Rabbi,' for you have one Teacher and you are all brothers. **23:9** And call no one your 'father' on earth, for you have one Father, who is in heaven. **23:10** Nor are you to be called 'teacher,' for you have one teacher, the Christ. **23:11** The greatest among you will be your servant. **23:12** And whoever exalts himself will be humbled, and whoever humbles himself will be exalted.

23:13 "But woe to you, experts in the law and you Pharisees, hypocrites! You keep locking people out of the kingdom of heaven! For you neither enter nor permit those trying to enter to go in.

23:15 "Woe to you, experts in the law and you Pharisees, hypocrites! You cross land and sea to make one convert, and when you get one, you make him twice as much a child of hell as yourselves!

23:16 "Woe to you, blind guides, who say, 'Whoever swears by the temple is bound by nothing. But whoever swears by the gold of the temple is bound by the oath.' **23:17** Blind fools! Which is greater, the gold or the temple that makes the gold sacred? **23:18** And, 'Whoever swears by the altar is bound by nothing. But if anyone swears by the gift on it he is bound by the oath.' **23:19** You are blind! For which is greater, the gift or the altar that makes the gift sacred? **23:20** So whoever swears by the altar swears by it and by everything on it. **23:21** And whoever swears by the temple swears by it and the one who dwells in it. **23:22** And whoever swears by heaven swears by the throne of God and the one who sits on it. **23:23** "Woe to you, experts in the law and you Pharisees, hypocrites! You give a tenth of mint, dill, and cumin, yet you neglect what is more important in the law – justice, mercy, and faithfulness! You should have done these things without neglecting the others. **23:24** Blind guides! You strain out a gnat yet swallow a camel!

23:25 "Woe to you, experts in the law and you Pharisees, hypocrites! You clean the outside of the cup and the dish, but inside they are full of greed and self-indulgence. **23:26** Blind Pharisee! First clean the inside of the cup, so that the outside may become clean too!

23:27 "Woe to you, experts in the law and you Pharisees, hypocrites! You are like whitewashed tombs that look beautiful on the outside but inside are full of the bones of the dead and of everything unclean. **23:28** In the same way, on the outside you look righteous to people, but inside you are full of hypocrisy and lawlessness.

23:29 "Woe to you, experts in the law and you Pharisees, hypocrites! You build tombs for the prophets and decorate the graves of the righteous. **23:30** And you say, 'If we had lived in the days of our ancestors, we would not have participated with them in shedding the blood of the prophets.' **23:31** By saying this you testify against yourselves that you are descendants of those who murdered the prophets. **23:32** Fill up then the measure of your ancestors! **23:33** You snakes, you offspring of vipers! How will you escape being condemned to hell?

23:34 "For this reason I am sending you prophets and wise men and experts in the law, some of whom you will kill and crucify, and some you will flog in your synagogues and pursue from town to town, **23:35** so that on you will come all the righteous blood shed on earth, from the blood of righteous Abel to the blood of Zechariah son of Barachiah, whom you murdered between the temple and the altar. **23:36** I tell you the truth, this generation will be held responsible for all these things!

Judgment on Israel

23:37 "O Jerusalem, Jerusalem, you who kill the prophets and stone those who are sent to you! How often I have longed to gather your children together as a hen gathers her chicks under her wings, but you would have none of it! **23:38** Look, your house is left to you desolate! **23:39** For I tell you, you will not see me from now until you say, '*Blessed is the one who comes in the name of the Lord!*'"

The Destruction of the Temple

24:1 Now as Jesus was going out of the temple courts and walking away, his disciples came to show him the temple buildings. **24:2** And he said to them, "Do you see all these things? I tell you the truth, not one stone will be left on another. All will be torn down!"

Signs of the End of the Age

24:3 As he was sitting on the Mount of Olives, his disciples came to him privately and said, "Tell us, when will these things happen? And what will be the sign of your coming and of the end of the age?" **24:4** Jesus answered them, "Watch out that no one misleads you. **24:5** For many will come in my name, saying, 'I am the Christ,' and they will mislead many. **24:6** You will hear of wars and rumors of wars. Make sure that you are not alarmed, for this must happen, but the end is still to come. **24:7** For nation will rise up in arms against nation, and kingdom against kingdom. And there will be famines and earthquakes in various places. **24:8** All these things are the beginning of birth pains.

Persecution of Disciples

24:9 "Then they will hand you over to be persecuted and will kill you. You will be hated by all the nations because of my name. **24:10** Then many will be led into sin, and they will betray one another and hate one another. **24:11** And many false prophets will appear and deceive many, **24:12** and because lawlessness will increase so much, the love of many will grow cold. **24:13** But the person who endures to the end will be saved. **24:14** And this gospel of the kingdom will be preached throughout the whole inhabited earth as a testimony to all the nations, and then the end will come.

The Abomination of Desolation

24:15 "So when you see *the abomination of desolation* – spoken about by Daniel the prophet – standing in the holy place (let the reader understand), **24:16** then those in Judea must flee to the mountains. **24:17** The one on the roof must not come down to take anything out of his house, **24:18** and the one in the field must not turn back to get his cloak. **24:19** Woe to those who are pregnant and to those who are nursing their babies in those days! **24:20** Pray that your flight may not be in winter or on a Sabbath. **24:21** For then there will be great suffering unlike anything that has happened from the beginning of the world until now, or ever will happen. **24:22** And if those days had not been cut short, no one would be saved. But for the sake of the elect those days will be cut short. **24:23** Then if anyone says to you, 'Look, here is the Christ!' or 'There he is!' do not believe him. **24:24** For false messiahs and false prophets will appear and perform great signs and wonders to deceive, if possible, even

the elect. **24:25** Remember, I have told you ahead of time. **24:26** So then, if someone says to you, 'Look, he is in the wilderness,' do not go out, or 'Look, he is in the inner rooms,' do not believe him. **24:27** For just like the lightning comes from the east and flashes to the west, so the coming of the Son of Man will be. **24:28** Wherever the corpse is, there the vultures will gather.

The Arrival of the Son of Man

24:29 "Immediately after the suffering of those days, *the sun will be darkened, and the moon will not give its light; the stars will fall from heaven, and the powers of heaven will be shaken.* **24:30** Then the sign of the Son of Man will appear in heaven, and all the tribes of the earth will mourn. They will see *the Son of Man arriving on the clouds of heaven* with power and great glory. **24:31** And he will send his angels with a loud trumpet blast, and they will gather his elect from the four winds, from one end of heaven to the other.

The Parable of the Fig Tree

24:32 "Learn this parable from the fig tree: Whenever its branch becomes tender and puts out its leaves, you know that summer is near. **24:33** So also you, when you see all these things, know that he is near, right at the door. **24:34** I tell you the truth, this generation will not pass away until all these things take place. **24:35** Heaven and earth will pass away, but my words will never pass away.

Be Ready!

24:36 "But as for that day and hour no one knows it – not even the angels in heaven – except the Father alone. **24:37** For just like the days of Noah were, so the coming of the Son of Man will be. **24:38** For in those days before the flood, people were eating and drinking, marrying and giving in marriage, until the day Noah entered the ark. **24:39** And they knew nothing until the flood came and took them all away. It will be the same at the coming of the Son of Man. **24:40** Then there will be two men in the field; one will be taken and one left. **24:41** There will be two women grinding grain with a mill; one will be taken and one left.

24:42 "Therefore stay alert, because you do not know on what day your Lord will come. **24:43** But understand this: If the owner of the house had known at what time of night the thief was coming, he would have been alert and would not have let his house be broken into. **24:44** Therefore you also must be ready, because the Son of Man will come at an hour when you do not expect him.

The Faithful and Wise Slave

24:45 "Who then is the faithful and wise slave, whom the master has put in charge of his household, to give the other slaves their food at the proper time? **24:46** Blessed is that slave whom the master finds at work when he comes. **24:47** I tell you the truth, the master will put him in charge of all his possessions. **24:48** But if that evil slave should say to himself, 'My master is staying away a long time,' **24:49** and he begins to beat his fellow slaves and to eat and drink with drunkards, **24:50** then the master of that slave will come on a day when he does not expect him and at an hour he does not foresee, **24:51** and will cut him in two, and assign him a place with the hypocrites, where there will be weeping and gnashing of teeth.

The Parable of the Ten Virgins

25:1 "At that time the kingdom of heaven will be like ten virgins who took their lamps and went out to meet the bridegroom. **25:2** Five of the virgins were foolish, and five were wise. **25:3** When the foolish ones took their lamps, they did not take extra olive oil with them. **25:4** But the wise ones took flasks of olive oil with their lamps. **25:5** When the bridegroom was delayed a long time, they all became drowsy and fell asleep. **25:6** But at midnight there was a shout, 'Look, the bridegroom is here! Come out to meet him.' **25:7** Then all the virgins woke up and trimmed their lamps. **25:8** The foolish ones said to the wise, 'Give us some of your oil, because our lamps are going out.' **25:9** 'No,' they replied. 'There won't be enough for you and for us. Go instead to those who sell oil and buy some for yourselves.' **25:10** But while they had gone to buy it, the bridegroom arrived, and those who were ready went inside with him to the wedding banquet. Then the door was shut. **25:11** Later, the other virgins came too, saying, 'Lord, lord! Let us in!' **25:12** But he replied, 'I tell you the truth, I do not know you!' **25:13** Therefore stay alert, because you do not know the day or the hour.

The Parable of the Talents

25:14 "For it is like a man going on a journey, who summoned his slaves and entrusted his property to them. **25:15** To one he gave five talents, to another two, and to another one, each according to his ability. Then he went on his journey. **25:16** The one who had received five talents went off right away and put his money to work and gained five more. **25:17** In the same way, the one who had two gained two more. **25:18** But the one who had received one talent went out and dug a hole in the ground and hid his master's money in it. **25:19** After a long time, the master of those slaves came and settled his accounts with them. **25:20** The one who had received the five talents came and brought five more, saying, 'Sir, you entrusted me with five talents. See, I have gained five more.' **25:21** His master answered, 'Well done, good and faithful slave! You have been faithful in a few things. I will put you in charge of many things. Enter into the joy of your master.' **25:22** The one with the two talents also came and said, 'Sir, you entrusted two talents to me. See, I have gained two more.' **25:23** His master answered, 'Well done, good and faithful slave! You have been faithful with a few things. I will put you in charge of many things. Enter into the joy of your master.' **25:24** Then the one who had received the one talent came and said, 'Sir, I knew that you were a hard man, harvesting where you did not sow, and gathering where you did not scatter seed, **25:25** so I was afraid, and I went and hid your talent in the ground. See, you have what is yours.' **25:26** But his master answered, 'Evil and lazy slave! So you knew that I harvest where I didn't sow and gather where I didn't scatter? **25:27** Then you should have deposited my money with the bankers, and on my return I would have received my money back with interest! **25:28** Therefore take the talent from him and give it to the one who has ten. **25:29** For the one who has will be given more, and he will have more than enough. But the one who does not have, even what he has will be taken from him. **25:30** And throw that worthless slave into the outer darkness, where there will be weeping and gnashing of teeth.'

The Judgment

25:31 "When the Son of Man comes in his glory and all the angels with him, then he will sit on his glorious throne. **25:32** All the nations will be assembled before him, and he will separate people one from another like a shepherd separates the sheep from the goats. **25:33** He will put the sheep on his right and the goats on his left. **25:34** Then the king will say to those on his right, 'Come, you who are blessed by my Father, inherit the kingdom prepared for you from the foundation of the world. **25:35** For I was hungry and you gave me food, I was thirsty and you gave me something to drink, I was a stranger and you invited me in, **25:36** I was naked and you gave me clothing, I was sick and you took care of me, I was in prison and you visited me.' **25:37** Then the righteous will answer him, 'Lord, when did we see you hungry and feed you, or thirsty and give you something to drink? **25:38** When did we see you a stranger and invite you in, or naked and clothe you? **25:39** When did we see you sick or in prison and visit you?' **25:40** And the king will answer them, 'I tell you the truth, just as you did it for one of the least of these brothers or sisters of mine, you did it for me.'

25:41 "Then he will say to those on his left, 'Depart from me, you accursed, into the eternal fire that has been prepared for the devil and his angels! **25:42** For I was hungry and you gave me nothing to eat, I was thirsty and you gave me nothing to drink. **25:43** I was a stranger and you did not receive me as a guest, naked and you did not clothe me, sick and in prison and you did not visit me.' **25:44** Then they too will answer, 'Lord, when did we see you hungry or thirsty or a stranger or naked or sick or in prison, and did not give you whatever you needed?' **25:45** Then he will answer them, 'I tell you the truth, just as you did not do it for one of the least of these, you did not do it for me.' **25:46** And these will depart into eternal punishment, but the righteous into eternal life."

The Plot Against Jesus

26:1 When Jesus had finished saying all these things, he told his disciples, **26:2** "You know that after two days the Passover is coming, and the Son of Man will be handed over to be crucified." **26:3** Then the chief priests and the elders of the people met together in the palace of the high priest, who was named Caiaphas. **26:4** They planned to arrest Jesus by stealth and kill him. **26:5** But they said, "Not during the feast, so that there won't be a riot among the people."

Jesus' Anointing

26:6 Now while Jesus was in Bethany at the house of Simon the leper, **26:7** a woman came to him with an alabaster jar of expensive perfumed oil, and she poured it on his head as he was at the table. **26:8** When the disciples saw this, they became indignant and said, "Why this waste? **26:9** It could have been sold at a high price and the money given to the poor!" **26:10** When Jesus learned of this, he said to them, "Why are you bothering this woman? She has done a good service for me. **26:11** For you will always have the poor with you, but you will not always have me! **26:12** When she poured this oil on my body, she did it to prepare me for burial. **26:13** I tell you the truth, wherever this gospel is proclaimed in the whole world, what she has done will also be told in memory of her."

The Plan to Betray Jesus

26:14 Then one of the twelve, the one named Judas Iscariot, went to the chief priests **26:15** and said, "What will you give me to betray him into your hands?" So they set out thirty silver coins for him. **26:16** From that time on, Judas began looking for an opportunity to betray him.

The Passover

26:17 Now on the first day of the feast of Unleavened Bread the disciples came to Jesus and said, "Where do you want us to prepare for you to eat the Passover?" **26:18** He said, "Go into the city to a certain man and tell him, 'The Teacher says, "My time is near. I will observe the Passover with my disciples at your house."'" **26:19** So the disciples did as Jesus had instructed them, and they prepared the Passover. **26:20** When it was evening, he took his place at the table with the twelve. **26:21** And while they were eating he said, "I tell you the truth, one of you will betray me." **26:22** They became greatly distressed and each one began to say to him, "Surely not I, Lord?" **26:23** He answered, "The one who has dipped his hand into the bowl with me will betray me. **26:24** The Son of Man will go as it is written about him, but woe to that man by whom the Son of Man

is betrayed! It would be better for him if he had never been born." **26:25** Then Judas, the one who would betray him, said, "Surely not I, Rabbi?" Jesus replied, "You have said it yourself."

The Lord's Supper

26:26 While they were eating, Jesus took bread, and after giving thanks he broke it, gave it to his disciples, and said, "Take, eat, this is my body." **26:27** And after taking the cup and giving thanks, he gave it to them, saying, "Drink from it, all of you, **26:28** for this is my blood, the blood of the covenant, that is poured out for many for the forgiveness of sins. **26:29** I tell you, from now on I will not drink of this fruit of the vine until that day when I drink it new with you in my Father's kingdom." **26:30** After singing a hymn, they went out to the Mount of Olives.

The Prediction of Peter's Denial

26:31 Then Jesus said to them, "This night you will all fall away because of me, for it is written:

'I will strike the shepherd,
and the sheep of the flock will be scattered.'

26:32 But after I am raised, I will go ahead of you into Galilee." **26:33** Peter said to him, "If they all fall away because of you, I will never fall away!" **26:34** Jesus said to him, "I tell you the truth, on this night, before the rooster crows, you will deny me three times." **26:35** Peter said to him, "Even if I must die with you, I will never deny you." And all the disciples said the same thing.

Gethsemane

26:36 Then Jesus went with them to a place called Gethsemane, and he said to the disciples, "Sit here while I go over there and pray." **26:37** He took with him Peter and the two sons of Zebedee, and became anguished and distressed. **26:38** Then he said to them, "My soul is deeply grieved, even to the point of death. Remain here and stay awake with me." **26:39** Going a little farther, he threw himself down with his face to the ground and prayed, "My Father, if possible, let this cup pass from me! Yet not what I will, but what you will." **26:40** Then he came to the disciples and found them sleeping. He said to Peter, "So, couldn't you stay awake with me for one hour? **26:41** Stay awake and pray that you will not fall into temptation. The spirit is willing, but the flesh is weak." **26:42** He went away a second time and prayed, "My Father, if this cup cannot be taken away unless I drink it, your will must be done." **26:43** He came again and found them sleeping; they could not keep their eyes open. **26:44** So leaving them again, he went away and prayed for the third time, saying the same thing once more. **26:45** Then he came to the disciples and said to them, "Are you still sleeping and resting? Look, the hour is approaching, and the Son of Man is betrayed into the hands of sinners. **26:46** Get up, let us go. Look! My betrayer is approaching!"

Betrayal and Arrest

26:47 While he was still speaking, Judas, one of the twelve, arrived. With him was a large crowd armed with swords and clubs, sent by the chief priests and elders of the people. **26:48** (Now the betrayer had given them a sign, saying, "The one I kiss is the man. Arrest him!") **26:49** Immediately he went up to Jesus and said, "Greetings, Rabbi," and kissed him. **26:50** Jesus said to him, "Friend, do what you are here to do." Then they came and took hold of Jesus and arrested him. **26:51** But one of those with Jesus grabbed his sword, drew it out, and struck the high priest's slave, cutting off his ear. **26:52** Then Jesus said to him, "Put your sword back in its place! For all who take hold of the sword will die by the sword. **26:53** Or do you think that I cannot call on my Father, and that he would send me more than twelve legions of angels right now? **26:54** How then would the scriptures that say it must happen this way be fulfilled?" **26:55** At that moment Jesus said to the crowd, "Have you come out with swords and clubs to arrest me like you would an outlaw? Day after day I sat teaching in the temple courts, yet you did not arrest me. **26:56** But this has happened so that the scriptures of the prophets would be fulfilled." Then all the disciples left him and fled.

Condemned by the Sanhedrin

26:57 Now the ones who had arrested Jesus led him to Caiaphas, the high priest, in whose house the experts in the law and the elders had gathered. **26:58** But Peter was following him from a distance, all the way to the high priest's courtyard. After going in, he sat with the guards to see the outcome. **26:59** The chief priests and the whole Sanhedrin were trying to find false testimony against Jesus so that they could put him to death. **26:60** But they did not find anything, though many false witnesses came forward. Finally two came forward **26:61** and declared, "This man said, 'I am able to destroy the temple of God and rebuild it in three days.'" **26:62** So the high priest stood up and said to him, "Have you no answer? What is this that they are testifying against you?" **26:63** But Jesus was silent. The high priest said to him, "I charge you under oath by the living God, tell us if you are the Christ, the Son of God." **26:64** Jesus said to him, "You have said it yourself. But I tell you, from now on you will see the Son of Man *sitting at the right hand* of the Power and *coming on the clouds of heaven.*" **26:65** Then the high priest tore his clothes and declared, "He has blasphemed! Why do we still need witnesses? Now you have heard the blasphemy! **26:66** What is your verdict?" They answered, "He is guilty and deserves death." **26:67** Then they spat in his face and struck him with their fists. And some slapped him, **26:68** saying, "Prophesy for us, you Christ! Who hit you?"

Peter's Denials

26:69 Now Peter was sitting outside in the courtyard. A slave girl came to him and said, "You also were with Jesus the Galilean." **26:70** But he denied it in front of them all: "I don't know what you're talking about!" **26:71** When he went out to the gateway, another slave girl saw him and said to the people there, "This man was with Jesus the Nazarene." **26:72** He denied it again with an oath, "I do not know the man!" **26:73** After a little while, those standing there came up to Peter and said, "You really are one of them too – even your accent gives you away!" **26:74** At that he began to curse, and he swore with an oath, "I do not know the man!" At that moment a rooster crowed. **26:75** Then Peter remembered what Jesus had said: "Before the rooster crows, you will deny me three times." And he went outside and wept bitterly.

Jesus Brought Before Pilate

27:1 When it was early in the morning, all the chief priests and the elders of the people plotted against Jesus to execute him. **27:2** They tied him up, led him away, and handed him over to Pilate the governor.

Judas' Suicide

27:3 Now when Judas, who had betrayed him, saw that Jesus had been condemned, he regretted what he had done and returned the thirty silver coins to the chief priests and the elders, **27:4** saying, "I have sinned by betraying innocent blood!" But they said, "What is that to us? You take care of it yourself!" **27:5** So Judas threw the silver coins into the temple and left. Then he went out and hanged himself. **27:6** The chief priests took the silver and said, "It is not lawful to put this into the temple treasury, since it is blood money." **27:7** After consulting together they bought the Potter's Field with it, as a burial place for foreigners. **27:8** For this reason that field has been called the "Field of Blood" to this day. **27:9** Then what was spoken by Jeremiah the prophet was fulfilled: "*They took the thirty silver coins, the price of the one whose price had been set by the people of Israel,* **27:10** *and they gave them for the potter's field, as the Lord commanded me.*"

Jesus and Pilate

27:11 Then Jesus stood before the governor, and the governor asked him, "Are you the king of the Jews?" Jesus said, "You say so." **27:12** But when he was accused by the chief priests and the elders, he did not respond. **27:13** Then Pilate said to him, "Don't you hear how many charges they are bringing against you?" **27:14** But he did not answer even one accusation, so that the governor was quite amazed.

27:15 During the feast the governor was accustomed to release one prisoner to the crowd, whomever they wanted. **27:16** At that time they had in custody a notorious prisoner named Jesus Barabbas. **27:17** So after they had assembled, Pilate said to them, "Whom do you want me to release for you, Jesus Barabbas or Jesus who is called the Christ?" **27:18** (For he knew that they had handed him over because of envy.) **27:19** As he was sitting on the judgment seat, his wife sent a message to him: "Have nothing to do with that innocent man; I have suffered greatly as a result of a dream about him today." **27:20** But the chief priests and the elders persuaded the crowds to ask for Barabbas and to have Jesus killed. **27:21** The governor asked them, "Which of the two do you want me to release for you?" And they said, "Barabbas!" **27:22** Pilate said to them, "Then what should I do with Jesus who is called the Christ?" They all said, "Crucify him!" **27:23** He asked, "Why? What wrong has he done?" But they shouted more insistently, "Crucify him!"

Jesus is Condemned and Mocked

27:24 When Pilate saw that he could do nothing, but that instead a riot was starting, he took some water, washed his hands before the crowd and said, "I am innocent of this man's blood. You take care of it yourselves!" **27:25** In reply all the people said, "Let his blood be on us and on our children!" **27:26** Then he released Barabbas for them. But after he had Jesus flogged, he handed him over to be crucified. **27:27** Then the governor's soldiers took Jesus into the governor's residence and gathered the whole cohort around him. **27:28** They stripped him and put a scarlet robe around him, **27:29** and after braiding a crown of thorns, they put it on his head. They put a staff in his right hand, and kneeling down before him, they mocked him: "Hail, king of the Jews!" **27:30** They spat on him and took the staff and struck him repeatedly on the head. **27:31** When they had mocked him, they stripped him of the robe and put his own clothes back on him. Then they led him away to crucify him.

The Crucifixion

27:32 As they were going out, they found a man from Cyrene named Simon, whom they forced to carry his cross. **27:33** They came to a place called Golgotha (which means "Place of the Skull") **27:34** and offered Jesus wine mixed with gall to drink. But after tasting it, he would not drink it. **27:35** When they had crucified him, *they divided his clothes by throwing dice.* **27:36** Then they sat down and kept guard over him there. **27:37** Above his head they put the charge against him, which read: "This is Jesus, the king of the Jews." **27:38** Then two outlaws were crucified with him, one on his right and one on his left. **27:39** Those who passed by defamed him, shaking their heads **27:40** and saying, "You who can destroy the temple and rebuild it in three days, save yourself! If you are God's Son, come down from the cross!" **27:41** In the same way even the chief priests – together with the experts in the law and elders – were mocking him: **27:42** "He saved others, but he cannot save himself! He is the king of Israel! If he comes down now from the cross, we will believe in him! **27:43** He *trusts in God – let God, if he wants to, deliver him now* because he said, 'I am God's Son'!" **27:44** The robbers who were crucified with him also spoke abusively to him.

Jesus' Death

27:45 Now from noon until three, darkness came over all the land. **27:46** At about three o'clock Jesus shouted with a loud voice, "*Eli, Eli, lema sabachthani?*" that is, "**My God, my God, why have you forsaken me?**" **27:47** When some of the bystanders heard it, they said, "This man is calling for Elijah." **27:48** Immediately one of them ran and got a sponge, filled it with sour wine, put it on a stick, and gave it to him to drink. **27:49** But the rest said, "Leave him alone! Let's see if Elijah will come to save him." **27:50** Then Jesus cried out again with a loud voice and gave up his spirit. **27:51** Just then the temple curtain was torn in two, from top to bottom. The earth shook and the rocks were split apart. **27:52** And tombs were opened, and the bodies of many saints who had died were raised. **27:53** (They came out of the tombs after his resurrection and went into the holy city and appeared to many people.) **27:54** Now when the centurion and those with him who were guarding Jesus saw the earthquake and what took place, they were extremely terrified and said, "Truly this one was God's Son!" **27:55** Many women who had followed Jesus from Galilee and given him support were also there, watching from a distance. **27:56** Among them were Mary Magdalene, Mary the mother of James and Joseph, and the mother of the sons of Zebedee.

Jesus' Burial

27:57 Now when it was evening, there came a rich man from Arimathea, named Joseph, who was also a disciple of Jesus. **27:58** He went to Pilate and asked for the body of Jesus. Then Pilate ordered that it be given to him. **27:59** Joseph took the body, wrapped it in a clean linen cloth, **27:60** and placed it in his own new tomb that he had cut in the rock. Then he rolled a great stone across the entrance of the tomb and went away. **27:61** (Now Mary Magdalene and the other Mary were sitting there, opposite the tomb.)

The Guard at the Tomb

27:62 The next day (which is after the day of preparation) the chief priests and the Pharisees assembled before Pilate **27:63** and said, "Sir, we remember that while that deceiver was still alive he said, 'After three days I will rise again.' **27:64** So give orders to secure the tomb until the third day. Otherwise his disciples may come and steal his body and say to the people, 'He has been raised from the dead,' and the last deception will be worse than the first." **27:65** Pilate said to them, "Take a guard of soldiers. Go and make it as secure as you can." **27:66** So they went with the soldiers of the guard and made the tomb secure by sealing the stone.

The Resurrection

28:1 Now after the Sabbath, at dawn on the first day of the week, Mary Magdalene and the other Mary went to look at the tomb. **28:2** Suddenly there was a severe earthquake, for an angel of the Lord descending from heaven came and rolled away the stone and sat on it. **28:3** His appearance was like lightning, and his clothes were white as snow. **28:4** The guards were shaken and became like dead men because they were so afraid of him. **28:5** But the angel said to the women, "Do not be afraid; I know that you are looking for Jesus, who was crucified. **28:6** He is not here, for he has been raised, just as he said. Come and see the place where he was lying. **28:7** Then go quickly and tell his disciples, 'He has been raised from the dead. He is going ahead of you into Galilee. You will see him there.' Listen, I have told you!" **28:8** So they left the tomb quickly, with fear and great joy, and ran to tell his disciples. **28:9** But Jesus met them, saying, "Greetings!" They came to him, held on to his feet and worshiped him. **28:10** Then Jesus said to them, "Do not be afraid. Go and tell my brothers to go to Galilee. They will see me there."

The Guards' Report

28:11 While they were going, some of the guard went into the city and told the chief priests everything that had happened. **28:12** After they had assembled with the elders and formed a plan, they gave a large sum of money to the soldiers, **28:13** telling them, "You are to say, 'His disciples came at night and stole his body while we were asleep.' **28:14** If this matter is heard before the governor, we will satisfy him and keep you out of trouble." **28:15** So they took the money and did as they were instructed. And this story is told among the Jews to this day.

The Great Commission

28:16 So the eleven disciples went to Galilee to the mountain Jesus had designated. **28:17** When they saw him, they worshiped him, but some doubted. **28:18** Then Jesus came up and said to them, "All authority in heaven and on earth has been given to me. **28:19** Therefore go and make disciples of all nations, baptizing them in the name of the Father and the Son and the Holy Spirit, **28:20** teaching them to obey everything I have commanded you. And remember, I am with you always, to the end of the age."

Book 41. Mark

The Ministry of John the Baptist

1:1 The beginning of the gospel of Jesus Christ, the Son of God. **1:2** As it is written in Isaiah the prophet,

"Look, I am sending my messenger ahead of you,
who will prepare your way,
1:3 the voice of one shouting in the wilderness,
'Prepare the way for the Lord,
make his paths straight.'"

1:4 In the wilderness John the baptizer began preaching a baptism of repentance for the forgiveness of sins. **1:5** People from the whole Judean countryside and all of Jerusalem were going out to him, and he was baptizing them in the Jordan River as they confessed their sins. **1:6** John wore a garment made of camel's hair with a leather belt around his waist, and he ate locusts and wild honey. **1:7** He proclaimed, "One more powerful than I am is coming after me; I am not worthy to bend down and untie the strap of his sandals. **1:8** I baptize you with water, but he will baptize you with the Holy Spirit."

The Baptism and Temptation of Jesus

1:9 Now in those days Jesus came from Nazareth in Galilee and was baptized by John in the Jordan River. **1:10** And just as Jesus was coming up out of the water, he saw the heavens splitting apart and the Spirit descending on him like a dove. **1:11** And a voice came from heaven: "You are my one dear Son; in you I take great delight." **1:12** The Spirit immediately drove him into the wilderness. **1:13** He was in the wilderness forty days, enduring temptations from Satan. He was with wild animals, and angels were ministering to his needs.

Preaching in Galilee and the Call of the Disciples

1:14 Now after John was imprisoned, Jesus went into Galilee and proclaimed the gospel of God. **1:15** He said, "The time is fulfilled and the kingdom of God is near. Repent and believe the gospel!" **1:16** As he went along the Sea of Galilee, he saw Simon and Andrew, Simon's brother, casting a net into the sea (for they were fishermen). **1:17** Jesus said to them, "Follow me, and I will turn you into fishers of people." **1:18** They left their nets immediately and followed him. **1:19** Going on a little farther, he saw James, the son of Zebedee, and John his brother in their boat mending nets. **1:20** Immediately he called them, and they left their father Zebedee in the boat with the hired men and followed him.

Jesus' Authority

1:21 Then they went to Capernaum. When the Sabbath came, Jesus went into the synagogue and began to teach. **1:22** The people there were amazed by his teaching, because he taught them like one who had authority, not like the experts in the law. **1:23** Just then there was a man in their synagogue with an unclean spirit, and he cried out, **1:24** "Leave us alone, Jesus the Nazarene! Have you come to destroy us? I know who you are – the Holy One of God!" **1:25** But Jesus rebuked him: "Silence! Come out of him!" **1:26** After throwing him into convulsions, the unclean spirit cried out with a loud voice and came out of him. **1:27** They were all amazed so that they asked each other, "What is this? A new teaching with authority! He even commands the unclean spirits and they obey him." **1:28** So the news about him spread quickly throughout all the region around Galilee.

Healings at Simon's House

1:29 Now as soon as they left the synagogue, they entered Simon and Andrew's house, with James and John. **1:30** Simon's mother-in-law was lying down, sick with a fever, so they spoke to Jesus at once about her. **1:31** He came and raised her up by gently taking her hand. Then the fever left her and she began to serve them. **1:32** When it was evening, after sunset, they brought to him all who were sick and demon-possessed. **1:33** The whole town gathered by the door. **1:34** So he healed many who were sick with various diseases and drove out many demons. But he would not permit the demons to speak, because they knew him.

Praying and Preaching

1:35 Then Jesus got up early in the morning when it was still very dark, departed, and went out to a deserted place, and there he spent time in prayer. **1:36** Simon and his companions searched for him. **1:37** When they found him, they said, "Everyone is looking for you." **1:38** He replied, "Let us go elsewhere, into the surrounding villages, so that I can preach there too. For that is what I came out here to do." **1:39** So he went into all of Galilee preaching in their synagogues and casting out demons.

Cleansing a Leper

1:40 Now a leper came to him and fell to his knees, asking for help. "If you are willing, you can make me clean," he said. **1:41** Moved with compassion, Jesus stretched out his hand and touched him, saying, "I am willing. Be clean!" **1:42** The leprosy left him at once, and he was clean. **1:43** Immediately Jesus sent the man away with a very strong warning. **1:44** He told him, "See that you do not say anything to anyone, but go, show yourself to a priest, and bring the offering that Moses commanded for your cleansing, as a testimony to them." **1:45** But as the man went out he began to announce it publicly and spread the story widely, so that Jesus was no longer able to enter any town openly but stayed outside in remote places.

Still they kept coming to him from everywhere.

Healing and Forgiving a Paralytic

2:1 Now after some days, when he returned to Capernaum, the news spread that he was at home. **2:2** So many gathered that there was no longer any room, not even by the door, and he preached the word to them. **2:3** Some people came bringing to him a paralytic, carried by four of them. **2:4** When they were not able to bring him in because of the crowd, they removed the roof above Jesus. Then, after tearing it out, they lowered the stretcher the paralytic was lying on. **2:5** When Jesus saw their faith, he said to the paralytic, "Son, your sins are forgiven." **2:6** Now some of the experts in the law were sitting there, turning these things over in their minds: **2:7** "Why does this man speak this way? He is blaspheming! Who can forgive sins but God alone?" **2:8** Now immediately, when Jesus realized in his spirit that they were contemplating such thoughts, he said to them, "Why are you thinking such things in your hearts? **2:9** Which is easier, to say to the paralytic, 'Your sins are forgiven,' or to say, 'Stand up, take your stretcher, and walk'? **2:10** But so that you may know that the Son of Man has authority on earth to forgive sins," – he said to the paralytic – **2:11** "I tell you, stand up, take your stretcher, and go home." **2:12** And immediately the man stood up, took his stretcher, and went out in front of them all. They were all amazed and glorified God, saying, "We have never seen anything like this!"

The Call of Levi; Eating with Sinners

2:13 Jesus went out again by the sea. The whole crowd came to him, and he taught them. **2:14** As he went along, he saw Levi, the son of Alphaeus, sitting at the tax booth. "Follow me," he said to him. And he got up and followed him. **2:15** As Jesus was having a meal in Levi's home, many tax collectors and sinners were eating with Jesus and his disciples, for there were many who followed him. **2:16** When the experts in the law and the Pharisees saw that he was eating with sinners and tax collectors, they said to his disciples, "Why does he eat with tax collectors and sinners?" **2:17** When Jesus heard this he said to them, "Those who are healthy don't need a physician, but those who are sick do. I have not come to call the righteous, but sinners."

The Superiority of the New

2:18 Now John's disciples and the Pharisees were fasting. So they came to Jesus and said, "Why do the disciples of John and the disciples of the Pharisees fast, but your disciples don't fast?" **2:19** Jesus said to them, "The wedding guests cannot fast while the bridegroom is with them, can they? As long as they have the bridegroom with them they do not fast. **2:20** But the days are coming when the bridegroom will be taken from them, and at that time they will fast. **2:21** No one sews a patch of unshrunk cloth on an old garment; otherwise, the patch pulls away from it, the new from the old, and the tear becomes worse. **2:22** And no one pours new wine into old wineskins; otherwise, the wine will burst the skins, and both the wine and the skins will be destroyed. Instead new wine is poured into new wineskins."

Lord of the Sabbath

2:23 Jesus was going through the grain fields on a Sabbath, and his disciples began to pick some heads of wheat as they made their way. **2:24** So the Pharisees said to him, "Look, why are they doing what is against the law on the Sabbath?" **2:25** He said to them, "Have you never read what David did when he was in need and he and his companions were hungry – **2:26** how he entered the house of God when Abiathar was high priest and ate the sacred bread, which is against the law for any but the priests to eat, and also gave it to his companions?" **2:27** Then he said to them, "The Sabbath was made for people, not people for the Sabbath. **2:28** For this reason the Son of Man is lord even of the Sabbath."

Healing a Withered Hand

3:1 Then Jesus entered the synagogue again, and a man was there who had a withered hand. **3:2** They watched Jesus closely to see if he would heal him on the Sabbath, so that they could accuse him. **3:3** So he said to the man who had the withered hand, "Stand up among all these people." **3:4** Then he said to them, "Is it lawful to do good on the Sabbath, or evil, to save a life or destroy it?" But they were silent. **3:5** After looking around at them in anger, grieved by the hardness of their hearts, he said to the man, "Stretch out your hand." He stretched it out, and his hand was restored. **3:6** So the Pharisees went out immediately and began plotting with the Herodians, as to how they could assassinate him.

Crowds by the Sea

3:7 Then Jesus went away with his disciples to the sea, and a great multitude from Galilee followed him. And from Judea, **3:8** Jerusalem, Idumea, beyond the Jordan River, and around Tyre and Sidon a great multitude came to him when they heard about the things he had done. **3:9** Because of the crowd, he told his disciples to have a small boat ready for him so the crowd would not press toward him. **3:10** For he had healed many, so that all who were afflicted with diseases pressed toward him in order to touch him. **3:11** And whenever the unclean spirits saw him, they fell down before him and cried out, "You are the Son of God." **3:12** But he sternly ordered them not to make him known.

Appointing the Twelve Apostles

3:13 Now Jesus went up the mountain and called for those he wanted, and they came to him. **3:14** He appointed twelve (whom he named apostles), so that they would be with him and he could send them to preach **3:15** and to have authority to cast out demons. **3:16** He appointed twelve: To Simon he gave the name Peter; **3:17** to James and his brother John, the sons of Zebedee, he gave the name Boanerges (that is, "sons of thunder"); **3:18** and Andrew, Philip, Bartholomew, Matthew, Thomas, James the son of Alphaeus, Thaddaeus, Simon the Zealot, **3:19** and Judas Iscariot, who betrayed him.

Jesus and Beelzebul

3:20 Now Jesus went home, and a crowd gathered so that they were not able to eat. **3:21** When his family heard this they went out to restrain him, for they said, "He is out of his mind." **3:22** The experts in the law who came down from Jerusalem said, "He is possessed by Beelzebul," and, "By the ruler of demons he casts out demons." **3:23** So he called them and spoke to them in parables: "How can Satan cast out Satan? **3:24** If a kingdom is divided against itself, that kingdom will not be able to stand. **3:25** If a house is divided against itself, that house will not be able to stand. **3:26** And if Satan rises against himself and is divided, he is not able to stand and his end has come. **3:27** But no one is able to enter a strong man's house and steal his property unless he first ties up the strong man. Then he can thoroughly plunder his house. **3:28** I tell you the truth, people will be forgiven for all sins, even all the blasphemies they utter. **3:29** But whoever blasphemes against the Holy Spirit will never be forgiven, but is guilty of an eternal sin" **3:30** (because they said, "He has an unclean spirit").

Jesus' True Family

3:31 Then Jesus' mother and his brothers came. Standing outside, they sent word to him, to summon him. **3:32** A crowd was sitting around him and they said to him, "Look, your mother and your brothers are outside looking for you." **3:33** He answered them and said, "Who are my mother and my brothers?" **3:34** And looking at those who were sitting around him in a circle, he said, "Here are my mother and my brothers! **3:35** For whoever does the will of God is my brother and sister and mother."

The Parable of the Sower

4:1 Again he began to teach by the lake. Such a large crowd gathered around him that he got into a boat on the lake and sat there while the whole crowd was on the shore by the lake. **4:2** He taught them many things in parables, and in his teaching said to them: **4:3** "Listen! A sower went out to sow. **4:4** And as he sowed, some seed fell along the path, and the birds came and devoured it. **4:5** Other seed fell on rocky ground where it did not have much soil. It sprang up at once because the soil was not deep. **4:6** When the sun came up it was scorched, and because it did not have sufficient root, it withered. **4:7** Other seed fell among the thorns, and they grew up and choked it, and it did not produce grain. **4:8** But other seed fell on good soil and produced grain, sprouting and growing; some yielded thirty times as much, some sixty, and some a hundred times." **4:9** And he said, "Whoever has ears to hear had better listen!"

The Purpose of Parables

4:10 When he was alone, those around him with the twelve asked him about the parables. **4:11** He said to them, "The secret of the kingdom of God has been given to you. But to those outside, everything is in parables,

4:12 so that although they look they may look but not see,
and although they hear they may hear but not understand,
so they may not repent and be forgiven.*"*

4:13 He said to them, "Don't you understand this parable? Then how will you understand any parable? **4:14** The sower sows the word. **4:15** These are the ones on the path where the word is sown: Whenever they hear, immediately Satan comes and snatches the word that was sown in them. **4:16** These are the ones sown on rocky ground: As soon as they hear the word, they receive it with joy. **4:17** But they have no root in themselves and do not endure. Then, when trouble or persecution comes because of the word, immediately they fall away. **4:18** Others are the ones sown among thorns: They are those who hear the word, **4:19** but worldly cares, the seductiveness of wealth, and the desire for other things come in and choke the word, and it produces nothing. **4:20** But these are the ones sown on good soil: They hear the word and receive it and bear fruit, one thirty times as much, one sixty, and one a hundred."

The Parable of the Lamp

4:21 He also said to them, "A lamp isn't brought to be put under a basket or under a bed, is it? Isn't it to be placed on a lampstand? **4:22** For nothing is hidden except to be revealed, and nothing concealed except to be brought to light. **4:23** If anyone has ears to hear, he had better listen!" **4:24** And he said to them, "Take care about what you hear. The measure you use will be the measure you receive, and more will be added to you. **4:25** For whoever has will be given more, but whoever does not have, even what he has will be taken from him."

The Parable of the Growing Seed

4:26 He also said, "The kingdom of God is like someone who spreads seed on the ground. **4:27** He goes to sleep and gets up, night and day, and the seed sprouts and grows, though he does not know how. **4:28** By itself the soil produces a crop, first the stalk, then the head, then the full grain in the head. **4:29** And when the grain is ripe, he sends in the sickle because the harvest has come."

The Parable of the Mustard Seed

4:30 He also asked, "To what can we compare the kingdom of God, or what parable can we use to present it? **4:31** It is like a mustard seed that when sown in the ground, even though it is the smallest of all the seeds in the ground – **4:32** when it is sown, it grows up, becomes the greatest of all garden plants, and grows large branches so that the wild birds can nest in its shade."

The Use of Parables

4:33 So with many parables like these, he spoke the word to them, as they were able to hear. **4:34** He did not speak to them without a parable. But privately he explained everything to his own disciples.

Stilling of a Storm

4:35 On that day, when evening came, Jesus said to his disciples, "Let's go across to the other side of the lake." **4:36** So after leaving the crowd, they took him along, just as he was, in the boat, and other boats were with him. **4:37** Now a great windstorm developed and the waves were breaking into the boat, so that the boat was nearly swamped. **4:38** But he was in the stern, sleeping on a cushion. They woke him up and said to him, "Teacher, don't you care that we are about to die?" **4:39** So he got up and rebuked the wind, and said to the sea, "Be quiet! Calm down!" Then the wind stopped, and it was dead calm. **4:40** And he said to them, "Why are you cowardly? Do you still not have faith?" **4:41** They were overwhelmed by fear and said to one another, "Who then is this? Even the wind and sea obey him!"

Healing of a Demoniac

5:1 So they came to the other side of the lake, to the region of the Gerasenes. **5:2** Just as Jesus was getting out of the boat, a man with an unclean spirit came from the tombs and met him. **5:3** He lived among the tombs, and no one could bind him anymore, not even with a chain. **5:4** For his hands and feet had often been bound with chains and shackles, but he had torn the chains apart and broken the shackles in pieces. No one was strong enough to subdue him. **5:5** Each night and every day among the tombs and in the mountains, he would cry out and cut himself with stones. **5:6** When he saw Jesus from a distance, he ran and bowed down before him. **5:7** Then he cried out with a loud voice, "Leave me alone, Jesus, Son of the Most High God! I implore you by God – do not torment me!" **5:8** (For Jesus had said to him, "Come out of that man, you unclean spirit!") **5:9** Jesus asked him, "What is your name?" And he said, "My name is Legion, for we are many." **5:10** He begged Jesus repeatedly not to send them out of the region. **5:11** There on the hillside, a great herd of pigs was feeding. **5:12** And the demonic spirits begged him, "Send us into the pigs. Let us enter them." **5:13** Jesus gave them permission. So the unclean spirits came out and went into the pigs. Then the herd rushed down the steep slope into the lake, and about two thousand were drowned in the lake.

5:14 Now the herdsmen ran off and spread the news in the town and countryside, and the people went out to see what had happened. **5:15** They came to Jesus and saw the demon-possessed man sitting there, clothed and in his right mind – the one who had the "Legion" – and they were afraid. **5:16** Those who had seen what had happened to the demon-possessed man reported it, and they also told about the pigs. **5:17** Then they asked Jesus to leave their region. **5:18** As he was getting into the boat the man who had been demon-possessed asked if he could go with him. **5:19** But Jesus did not permit him to do so. Instead, he said to him, "Go to your home and to your people and tell them what the Lord has done for you, that he had mercy on you." **5:20** So he went away and began to proclaim in the Decapolis what Jesus had done for him, and all were amazed.

Restoration and Healing

5:21 When Jesus had crossed again in a boat to the other side, a large crowd gathered around him, and he was by the sea. **5:22** Then one of the synagogue rulers, named Jairus, came up, and when he saw Jesus, he fell at his feet. **5:23** He asked him urgently, "My little daughter is near death. Come and lay your hands on her so that she may be healed and live." **5:24** Jesus went with him, and a large crowd followed and pressed around him.

5:25 Now a woman was there who had been suffering from a hemorrhage for twelve years. **5:26** She had endured a great deal under the care of many doctors and had spent all that she had. Yet instead of getting better, she grew worse. **5:27** When she heard about Jesus, she came up behind him in the crowd and touched his cloak, **5:28** for she kept saying, "If only I touch his clothes, I will be healed." **5:29** At once the bleeding stopped, and she felt in her body that she was healed of her disease. **5:30** Jesus knew at once that power had gone out from him. He turned around in the crowd and said, "Who touched my clothes?" **5:31** His disciples said to him, "You see the crowd pressing against you and you say, 'Who touched me?'" **5:32** But he looked around to see who had done it. **5:33** Then the woman, with fear and trembling, knowing what had happened to her, came and fell down before him and told him the whole truth. **5:34** He said to her, "Daughter, your faith has made you well. Go in peace, and be healed of your disease."

5:35 While he was still speaking, people came from the synagogue ruler's house saying, "Your daughter has died. Why trouble the teacher any longer?" **5:36** But Jesus, paying no attention to what was said, told the synagogue ruler, "Do not be afraid; just believe." **5:37** He did not let anyone follow him except Peter, James, and John, the brother of James. **5:38** They came to the house of the synagogue ruler where he saw noisy confusion and people weeping and wailing loudly. **5:39** When he entered he said to them, "Why are you distressed and weeping? The child is not dead but asleep." **5:40** And they began making fun of him. But he put them all outside and he took the child's father and mother and his own companions and went into the room where the child was. **5:41** Then, gently taking the child by the hand, he said to her, "*Talitha koum*," which means, "Little girl, I say to you, get up." **5:42** The girl got up at once and began to walk around (she was twelve years old). They were completely astonished at this. **5:43** He strictly ordered that no one should know about this, and told them to give her something to eat.

Rejection at Nazareth

6:1 Now Jesus left that place and came to his hometown, and his disciples followed him. **6:2** When the Sabbath came, he began to teach in the synagogue. Many who heard him were astonished, saying, "Where did he get these ideas? And what is this wisdom that has been given to him? What are these miracles that are done through his hands? **6:3** Isn't this the carpenter, the son of Mary and brother of James, Joses, Judas, and Simon? And aren't his sisters here with us?" And so they took offense at him. **6:4** Then Jesus said to them, "A prophet is not without honor except in his hometown, and among his relatives, and in his own house." **6:5** He was not able to do a miracle there, except to lay his hands on a few sick people and heal them. **6:6** And he was amazed because of their unbelief. Then he went around among the villages and taught.

Sending Out the Twelve Apostles

6:7 Jesus called the twelve and began to send them out two by two. He gave them authority over the unclean spirits. **6:8** He instructed them to take nothing for the journey except a staff – no bread, no bag, no money in their belts – **6:9** and to put on sandals but not to wear two tunics. **6:10** He said to them, "Wherever you enter a house, stay there until you leave the area. **6:11** If a place will not welcome you or listen to you, as you go out from there, shake the dust off your feet as a testimony against them." **6:12** So they went out and preached that all should repent. **6:13** They cast out many demons and anointed many sick people with oil and healed them.

The Death of John the Baptist

6:14 Now King Herod heard this, for Jesus' name had become known. Some were saying, "John the baptizer has been raised from the dead, and because of this, miraculous powers are at work in him." **6:15** Others said, "He is Elijah." Others said, "He is a prophet, like one of the prophets from the past." **6:16** But when Herod heard this, he said, "John, whom I beheaded, has been raised!" **6:17** For Herod himself had sent men, arrested John, and bound him in prison on account of Herodias, his brother Philip's wife, because Herod had married her. **6:18** For John had repeatedly told Herod, "It is not lawful for you to have your brother's wife." **6:19** So Herodias nursed a grudge against him and wanted to kill him. But she could not **6:20** because Herod stood in awe of John and protected him, since he knew that John was a righteous and holy man. When Herod heard him, he was thoroughly baffled, and yet he liked to listen to John.

6:21 But a suitable day came, when Herod gave a banquet on his birthday for his court officials, military commanders, and leaders of Galilee. **6:22** When his daughter Herodias came in and danced, she pleased Herod and his dinner guests. The king said to the girl, "Ask me for whatever you want and I will give it to you." **6:23** He swore to her, "Whatever you ask I will give you, up to half my kingdom." **6:24** So she went out and said to her mother, "What should I ask for?" Her mother said, "The head of John the baptizer." **6:25** Immediately she hurried back to the king and made her request: "I want the head of John the Baptist on a platter immediately." **6:26** Although it grieved the king deeply, he did not want to reject her request because of his oath and his guests. **6:27** So the king sent an executioner at once to bring John's head, and he went and beheaded John in prison. **6:28** He brought his head on a platter and gave it to the girl, and the girl gave it to her mother. **6:29** When John's disciples heard this, they came and took his body and placed it in a tomb.

The Feeding of the Five Thousand

6:30 Then the apostles gathered around Jesus and told him everything they had done and taught. **6:31** He said to them, "Come with me privately to an isolated place and rest a while" (for many were coming and going, and there was no time to eat). **6:32** So they went away by themselves in a boat to some remote place. **6:33** But many saw them leaving and recognized them, and they hurried on foot from all the towns and arrived there ahead of them. **6:34** As Jesus came ashore he saw the large crowd and he had compassion on them, because they were like sheep without a shepherd. So he taught them many things. **6:35** When it was already late, his disciples came to him and said, "This is an isolated place and it is already very late. **6:36** Send them away so that they can go into the surrounding countryside and villages and buy something for themselves to eat." **6:37** But he answered them, "You give them something to eat." And they said, "Should we go and buy bread for two hundred silver coins and give it to them to eat?" **6:38** He said to

them, "How many loaves do you have? Go and see." When they found out, they said, "Five – and two fish." **6:39** Then he directed them all to sit down in groups on the green grass. **6:40** So they reclined in groups of hundreds and fifties. **6:41** He took the five loaves and the two fish, and looking up to heaven, he gave thanks and broke the loaves. He gave them to his disciples to serve the people, and he divided the two fish among them all. **6:42** They all ate and were satisfied, **6:43** and they picked up the broken pieces and fish that were left over, twelve baskets full. **6:44** Now there were five thousand men who ate the bread.

Walking on Water

6:45 Immediately Jesus made his disciples get into the boat and go on ahead to the other side, to Bethsaida, while he dispersed the crowd. **6:46** After saying good-bye to them, he went to the mountain to pray. **6:47** When evening came, the boat was in the middle of the sea and he was alone on the land. **6:48** He saw them straining at the oars, because the wind was against them. As the night was ending, he came to them walking on the sea, for he wanted to pass by them. **6:49** When they saw him walking on the water they thought he was a ghost. They cried out, **6:50** for they all saw him and were terrified. But immediately he spoke to them: "Have courage! It is I. Do not be afraid." **6:51** Then he went up with them into the boat, and the wind ceased. They were completely astonished, **6:52** because they did not understand about the loaves, but their hearts were hardened.

Healing the Sick

6:53 After they had crossed over, they came to land at Gennesaret and anchored there. **6:54** As they got out of the boat, people immediately recognized Jesus. **6:55** They ran through that whole region and began to bring the sick on mats to wherever he was rumored to be. **6:56** And wherever he would go – into villages, towns, or countryside – they would place the sick in the marketplaces, and would ask him if they could just touch the edge of his cloak, and all who touched it were healed.

Breaking Human Traditions

7:1 Now the Pharisees and some of the experts in the law who came from Jerusalem gathered around him. **7:2** And they saw that some of Jesus' disciples ate their bread with unclean hands, that is, unwashed. **7:3** (For the Pharisees and all the Jews do not eat unless they perform a ritual washing, holding fast to the tradition of the elders. **7:4** And when they come from the marketplace, they do not eat unless they wash. They hold fast to many other traditions: the washing of cups, pots, kettles, and dining couches.) **7:5** The Pharisees and the experts in the law asked him, "Why do your disciples not live according to the tradition of the elders, but eat with unwashed hands?" **7:6** He said to them, "Isaiah prophesied correctly about you hypocrites, as it is written:

'This people honors me with their lips,

but their heart is far from me.

7:7 They worship me in vain,

teaching as doctrine the commandments of men.'

7:8 Having no regard for the command of God, you hold fast to human tradition." **7:9** He also said to them, "You neatly reject the commandment of God in order to set up your tradition. **7:10** For Moses said, '*Honor your father and your mother*,' and, '*Whoever insults his father or mother must be put to death*.' **7:11** But you say that if anyone tells his father or mother, 'Whatever help you would have received from me is *corban*' (that is, a gift for God), **7:12** then you no longer permit him to do anything for his father or mother. **7:13** Thus you nullify the word of God by your tradition that you have handed down. And you do many things like this."

7:14 Then he called the crowd again and said to them, "Listen to me, everyone, and understand. **7:15** There is nothing outside of a person that can defile him by going into him. Rather, it is what comes out of a person that defiles him."

7:17 Now when Jesus had left the crowd and entered the house, his disciples asked him about the parable. **7:18** He said to them, "Are you so foolish? Don't you understand that whatever goes into a person from outside cannot defile him? **7:19** For it does not enter his heart but his stomach, and then goes out into the sewer." (This means all foods are clean.) **7:20** He said, "What comes out of a person defiles him. **7:21** For from within, out of the human heart, come evil ideas, sexual immorality, theft, murder, **7:22** adultery, greed, evil, deceit, debauchery, envy, slander, pride, and folly. **7:23** All these evils come from within and defile a person."

A Syrophoenician Woman's Faith

7:24 After Jesus left there, he went to the region of Tyre. When he went into a house, he did not want anyone to know, but he was not able to escape notice. **7:25** Instead, a woman whose young daughter had an unclean spirit immediately heard about him and came and fell at his feet. **7:26** The woman was a Greek, of Syrophoenician origin. She asked him to cast the demon out of her daughter. **7:27** He said to her, "Let the children be satisfied first, for it is not right to take the children's bread and to throw it to the dogs." **7:28** She answered, "Yes, Lord, but even the dogs under the table eat the children's crumbs." **7:29** Then he said to her, "Because you said this, you may go. The demon has left your daughter." **7:30**

She went home and found the child lying on the bed, and the demon gone.

Healing a Deaf Mute

7:31 Then Jesus went out again from the region of Tyre and came through Sidon to the Sea of Galilee in the region of the Decapolis. **7:32** They brought to him a deaf man who had difficulty speaking, and they asked him to place his hands on him. **7:33** After Jesus took him aside privately, away from the crowd, he put his fingers in the man's ears, and after spitting, he touched his tongue. **7:34** Then he looked up to heaven and said with a sigh, "*Ephphatha*" (that is, "Be opened"). **7:35** And immediately the man's ears were opened, his tongue loosened, and he spoke plainly. **7:36** Jesus ordered them not to tell anything. But as much as he ordered them not to do this, they proclaimed it all the more. **7:37** People were completely astounded and said, "He has done everything well. He even makes the deaf hear and the mute speak."

The Feeding of the Four Thousand

8:1 In those days there was another large crowd with nothing to eat. So Jesus called his disciples and said to them, **8:2** "I have compassion on the crowd, because they have already been here with me three days, and they have nothing to eat. **8:3** If I send them home hungry, they will faint on the way, and some of them have come from a great distance." **8:4** His disciples answered him, "Where can someone get enough bread in this desolate place to satisfy these people?" **8:5** He asked them, "How many loaves do you have?" They replied, "Seven." **8:6** Then he directed the crowd to sit down on the ground. After he took the seven loaves and gave thanks, he broke them and began giving them to the disciples to serve. So they served the crowd. **8:7** They also had a few small fish. After giving thanks for these, he told them to serve these as well. **8:8** Everyone ate and was satisfied, and they picked up the broken pieces left over, seven baskets full. **8:9** There were about four thousand who ate. Then he dismissed them. **8:10** Immediately he got into a boat with his disciples and went to the district of Dalmanutha.

The Demand for a Sign

8:11 Then the Pharisees came and began to argue with Jesus, asking for a sign from heaven to test him. **8:12** Sighing deeply in his spirit he said, "Why does this generation look for a sign? I tell you the truth, no sign will be given to this generation." **8:13** Then he left them, got back into the boat, and went to the other side.

The Yeast of the Pharisees and Herod

8:14 Now they had forgotten to take bread, except for one loaf they had with them in the boat. **8:15** And Jesus ordered them, "Watch out! Beware of the yeast of the Pharisees and the yeast of Herod!" **8:16** So they began to discuss with one another about having no bread. **8:17** When he learned of this, Jesus said to them, "Why are you arguing about having no bread? Do you still not see or understand? Have your hearts been hardened? **8:18** Though you have eyes, don't you see? And though you have ears, can't you hear? Don't you remember? **8:19** When I broke the five loaves for the five thousand, how many baskets full of pieces did you pick up?" They replied, "Twelve." **8:20** "When I broke the seven loaves for the four thousand, how many baskets full of pieces did you pick up?" They replied, "Seven." **8:21** Then he said to them, "Do you still not understand?"

A Two-stage Healing

8:22 Then they came to Bethsaida. They brought a blind man to Jesus and asked him to touch him. **8:23** He took the blind man by the hand and brought him outside of the village. Then he spit on his eyes, placed his hands on his eyes and asked, "Do you see anything?" **8:24** Regaining his sight he said, "I see people, but they look like trees walking." **8:25** Then Jesus placed his hands on the man's eyes again. And he opened his eyes, his sight was restored, and he saw everything clearly. **8:26** Jesus sent him home, saying, "Do not even go into the village."

Peter's Confession

8:27 Then Jesus and his disciples went to the villages of Caesarea Philippi. On the way he asked his disciples, "Who do people say that I am?" **8:28** They said, "John the Baptist, others say Elijah, and still others, one of the prophets." **8:29** He asked them, "But who do you say that I am?" Peter answered him, "You are the Christ." **8:30** Then he warned them not to tell anyone about him.

First Prediction of Jesus' Death and Resurrection

8:31 Then Jesus began to teach them that the Son of Man must suffer many things and be rejected by the elders, chief priests, and experts in the law, and be killed, and after three days rise again. **8:32** He spoke openly about this. So Peter took him aside and began to rebuke him. **8:33** But after turning and looking at his disciples, he rebuked Peter and said, "Get behind me, Satan. You are not setting your mind on God's interests, but on man's."

Following Jesus

8:34 Then Jesus called the crowd, along with his disciples, and said to them, "If anyone wants to become my follower, he must deny himself, take up his cross, and follow me. **8:35** For whoever wants to save his life will lose it, but whoever loses his life for my sake and for the gospel will save it. **8:36** For what benefit is it for a person to gain the whole world, yet forfeit his life? **8:37** What can a person give in exchange for his life?

8:38 For if anyone is ashamed of me and my words in this adulterous and sinful generation, the Son of Man will also be ashamed of him when he comes in the glory of his Father with the holy angels." **9:1** And he said to them, "I tell you the truth, there are some standing here who will not experience death before they see the kingdom of God come with power."

The Transfiguration

9:2 Six days later Jesus took with him Peter, James, and John and led them alone up a high mountain privately. And he was transfigured before them, **9:3** and his clothes became radiantly white, more so than any launderer in the world could bleach them. **9:4** Then Elijah appeared before them along with Moses, and they were talking with Jesus. **9:5** So Peter said to Jesus, "Rabbi, it is good for us to be here. Let us make three shelters – one for you, one for Moses, and one for Elijah." **9:6** (For they were afraid, and he did not know what to say.) **9:7** Then a cloud overshadowed them, and a voice came from the cloud, "This is my one dear Son. Listen to him!" **9:8** Suddenly when they looked around, they saw no one with them any more except Jesus.

9:9 As they were coming down from the mountain, he gave them orders not to tell anyone what they had seen until after the Son of Man had risen from the dead. **9:10** They kept this statement to themselves, discussing what this rising from the dead meant.

9:11 Then they asked him, "Why do the experts in the law say that Elijah must come first?" **9:12** He said to them, "Elijah does indeed come first, and restores all things. And why is it written that the Son of Man must suffer many things and be despised? **9:13** But I tell you that Elijah has certainly come, and they did to him whatever they wanted, just as it is written about him."

The Disciples' Failure to Heal

9:14 When they came to the disciples, they saw a large crowd around them and experts in the law arguing with them. **9:15** When the whole crowd saw him, they were amazed and ran at once and greeted him. **9:16** He asked them, "What are you arguing about with them?" **9:17** A member of the crowd said to him, "Teacher, I brought you my son, who is possessed by a spirit that makes him mute. **9:18** Whenever it seizes him, it throws him down, and he foams at the mouth, grinds his teeth, and becomes rigid. I asked your disciples to cast it out, but they were not able to do so." **9:19** He answered them, "You unbelieving generation! How much longer must I be with you? How much longer must I endure you? Bring him to me." **9:20** So they brought the boy to him. When the spirit saw him, it immediately threw the boy into a convulsion. He fell on the ground and rolled around, foaming at the mouth. **9:21** Jesus asked his father, "How long has this been happening to him?" And he said, "From childhood. **9:22** It has often thrown him into fire or water to destroy him. But if you are able to do anything, have compassion on us and help us." **9:23** Then Jesus said to him, "'If you are able?' All things are possible for the one who believes." **9:24** Immediately the father of the boy cried out and said, "I believe; help my unbelief!"

9:25 Now when Jesus saw that a crowd was quickly gathering, he rebuked the unclean spirit, saying to it, "Mute and deaf spirit, I command you, come out of him and never enter him again." **9:26** It shrieked, threw him into terrible convulsions, and came out. The boy looked so much like a corpse that many said, "He is dead!" **9:27** But Jesus gently took his hand and raised him to his feet, and he stood up.

9:28 Then, after he went into the house, his disciples asked him privately, "Why couldn't we cast it out?" **9:29** He told them, "This kind can come out only by prayer."

Second Prediction of Jesus' Death and Resurrection

9:30 They went out from there and passed through Galilee. But Jesus did not want anyone to know, **9:31** for he was teaching his disciples and telling them, "The Son of Man will be betrayed into the hands of men. They will kill him, and after three days he will rise." **9:32** But they did not understand this statement and were afraid to ask him.

Questions About the Greatest

9:33 Then they came to Capernaum. After Jesus was inside the house he asked them, "What were you discussing on the way?" **9:34** But they were silent, for on the way they had argued with one another about who was the greatest. **9:35** After he sat down, he called the twelve and said to them, "If anyone wants to be first, he must be last of all and servant of all." **9:36** He took a little child and had him stand among them. Taking him in his arms, he said to them, **9:37** "Whoever welcomes one of these little children in my name welcomes me, and whoever welcomes me does not welcome me but the one who sent me."

On Jesus' Side

9:38 John said to him, "Teacher, we saw someone casting out demons in your name, and we tried to stop him because he was not following us." **9:39** But Jesus said, "Do not stop him, because no one who does a miracle in my name will be able soon afterward to say anything bad about me. **9:40** For whoever is not against us is for us. **9:41** For I tell you the truth, whoever gives you a cup of water because you bear Christ's name will never lose his reward.

9:42 "If anyone causes one of these little ones who believe in me to sin, it would be better for him to have a huge millstone tied around his neck and to be thrown into the sea. **9:43** If your hand causes you to sin, cut it off! It is better for you to enter into life crippled than to have two hands and go into hell, to the unquenchable fire. **9:45** If your foot causes you to sin, cut it off! It is better to enter life lame than to have two feet and be thrown into hell. **9:47** If your eye causes you to sin, tear it out! It is better to enter into the kingdom of God with one eye than to have two eyes and be thrown into hell, **9:48** where their worm never dies and the fire is never quenched. **9:49** Everyone will be salted with fire. **9:50** Salt is good, but if it loses its saltiness, how can you make it salty again? Have salt in yourselves, and be at peace with each other."

Divorce

10:1 Then Jesus left that place and went to the region of Judea and beyond the Jordan River. Again crowds gathered to him, and again, as was his custom, he taught them. **10:2** Then some Pharisees came, and to test him they asked, "Is it lawful for a man to divorce his wife?" **10:3** He answered them, "What did Moses command you?" **10:4** They said, "Moses permitted a man *to write* **a certificate of dismissal** *and to divorce* her." **10:5** But Jesus said to them, "He wrote this commandment for you because of your hard hearts. **10:6** But from the beginning of creation *he made them male and female*. **10:7** *For this reason a man will leave his father and mother,* **10:8** *and the two will become one flesh*. So they are no longer two, but one flesh. **10:9** Therefore what God has joined together, let no one separate."

10:10 In the house once again, the disciples asked him about this. **10:11** So he told them, "Whoever divorces his wife and marries another commits adultery against her. **10:12** And if she divorces her husband and marries another, she commits adultery."

Jesus and Little Children

10:13 Now people were bringing little children to him for him to touch, but the disciples scolded those who brought them. **10:14** But when Jesus saw this, he was indignant and said to them, "Let the little children come to me and do not try to stop them, for the kingdom of God belongs to such as these. **10:15** I tell you the truth, whoever does not receive the kingdom of God like a child will never enter it." **10:16** After he took the children in his arms, he placed his hands on them and blessed them.

The Rich Man

10:17 Now as Jesus was starting out on his way, someone ran up to him, fell on his knees, and said, "Good teacher, what must I do to inherit eternal life?" **10:18** Jesus said to him, "Why do you call me good? No one is good except God alone. **10:19** You know the commandments: '*Do not murder, do not commit adultery, do not steal, do not give false testimony,* do not defraud, *honor your father and mother*.'" **10:20** The man said to him, "Teacher, I have wholeheartedly obeyed all these laws since my youth." **10:21** As Jesus looked at him, he felt love for him and said, "You lack one thing. Go, sell whatever you have and give the money to the poor, and you will have treasure in heaven. Then come, follow me." **10:22** But at this statement, the man looked sad and went away sorrowful, for he was very rich.

10:23 Then Jesus looked around and said to his disciples, "How hard it is for the rich to enter the kingdom of God!" **10:24** The disciples were astonished at these words. But again Jesus said to them, "Children, how hard it is to enter the kingdom of God! **10:25** It is easier for a camel to go through the eye of a needle than for a rich person to enter the kingdom of God." **10:26** They were even more astonished and said to one another, "Then who can be saved?" **10:27** Jesus looked at them and replied, "This is impossible for mere humans, but not for God; all things are possible for God."

10:28 Peter began to speak to him, "Look, we have left everything to follow you!" **10:29** Jesus said, "I tell you the truth, there is no one who has left home or brothers or sisters or mother or father or children or fields for my sake and for the sake of the gospel **10:30** who will not receive in this age a hundred times as much – homes, brothers, sisters, mothers, children, fields, all with persecutions – and in the age to come, eternal life. **10:31** But many who are first will be last, and the last first."

Third Prediction of Jesus' Death and Resurrection

10:32 They were on the way, going up to Jerusalem. Jesus was going ahead of them, and they were amazed, but those who followed were afraid. He took the twelve aside again and began to tell them what was going to happen to him. **10:33** "Look, we are going up to Jerusalem, and the Son of Man will be handed over to the chief priests and experts in the law. They will condemn him to death and will turn him over to the Gentiles. **10:34** They will mock him, spit on him, flog him severely, and kill him. Yet after three days, he will rise again."

The Request of James and John

10:35 Then James and John, the sons of Zebedee, came to him and said, "Teacher, we want you to do for us whatever we ask." **10:36** He said to them, "What do you want me to do for you?" **10:37** They said to him, "Permit one of us to sit at your right hand and the other at your left in your glory." **10:38** But Jesus said to them, "You don't know what you are asking! Are you able to drink the cup I drink or be baptized with the baptism I experience?" **10:39** They said to him, "We are able." Then Jesus said to them, "You will drink the cup I drink, and you will be baptized with the baptism I experience, **10:40** but to sit at my right or at my left is not mine to give. It is for those for whom it has been prepared."

10:41 Now when the other ten heard this, they became angry with James and John. **10:42** Jesus called them and said to them, "You know that those who are recognized as rulers of the Gentiles lord it over them, and those in high positions use their authority over them. **10:43** But it is not this way among you. Instead whoever wants to be great among you must be your servant, **10:44** and whoever wants to be first among you must be the slave of all. **10:45** For even the Son of Man did not come to be served but to serve, and to give his life as a ransom for many."

Healing Blind Bartimaeus

10:46 They came to Jericho. As Jesus and his disciples and a large crowd were leaving Jericho, Bartimaeus the son of Timaeus, a blind beggar, was sitting by the road. **10:47** When he heard that it was Jesus the Nazarene, he began to shout, "Jesus, Son of David, have mercy on me!" **10:48** Many scolded him to get him to be quiet, but he shouted all the more, "Son of David, have mercy on me!" **10:49** Jesus stopped and said, "Call him." So they called the blind man and said to him, "Have courage! Get up! He is calling you." **10:50** He threw off his cloak, jumped up, and came to Jesus. **10:51** Then Jesus said to him, "What do you want me to do for you?" The blind man replied, "Rabbi, let me see again." **10:52** Jesus said to him, "Go, your faith has healed you." Immediately he regained his sight and followed him on the road.

The Triumphal Entry

11:1 Now as they approached Jerusalem, near Bethphage and Bethany, at the Mount of Olives, Jesus sent two of his disciples **11:2** and said to them, "Go to the village ahead of you. As soon as you enter it, you will find a colt tied there that has never been ridden. Untie it and bring it here. **11:3** If anyone says to you, 'Why are you doing this?' say, 'The Lord needs it and will send it back here soon.'" **11:4** So they went and found a colt tied at a door, outside in the street, and untied it. **11:5** Some people standing there said to them, "What are you doing, untying that colt?" **11:6** They replied as Jesus had told them, and the bystanders let them go. **11:7** Then they brought the colt to Jesus, threw their cloaks on it, and he sat on it. **11:8** Many spread their cloaks on the road and others spread branches they had cut in the fields. **11:9** Both those who went ahead and those who followed kept shouting, "*Hosanna! Blessed is the one who comes in the name of the Lord!* **11:10** Blessed is the coming kingdom of our father David! Hosanna in the highest!" **11:11** Then Jesus entered Jerusalem and went to the temple. And after looking around at everything, he went out to Bethany with the twelve since it was already late.

Cursing of the Fig Tree

11:12 Now the next day, as they went out from Bethany, he was hungry. **11:13** After noticing in the distance a fig tree with leaves, he went to see if he could find any fruit on it. When he came to it he found nothing but leaves, for it was not the season for figs. **11:14** He said to it, "May no one ever eat fruit from you again." And his disciples heard it.

Cleansing the Temple

11:15 Then they came to Jerusalem. Jesus entered the temple area and began to drive out those who were selling and buying in the temple courts. He turned over the tables of the money changers and the chairs of those selling doves, **11:16** and he would not permit anyone to carry merchandise through the temple courts. **11:17** Then he began to teach them and said, "Is it not written: '*My house will be called a house of prayer for all nations*'? But you have turned it into *a den of robbers*!" **11:18** The chief priests and the experts in the law heard it and they considered how they could assassinate him, for they feared him, because the whole crowd was amazed by his teaching. **11:19** When evening came, Jesus and his disciples went out of the city.

The Withered Fig Tree

11:20 In the morning as they passed by, they saw the fig tree withered from the roots. **11:21** Peter remembered and said to him, "Rabbi, look! The fig tree you cursed has withered." **11:22** Jesus said to them, "Have faith in God. **11:23** I tell you the truth, if someone says to this mountain, 'Be lifted up and thrown into the sea,' and does not doubt in his heart but believes that what he says will happen, it will be done for him. **11:24** For this reason I tell you, whatever you pray and ask for, believe that you have received it, and it will be yours. **11:25** Whenever you stand praying, if you have anything against anyone, forgive him, so that your Father in heaven will also forgive you your sins."

The Authority of Jesus

11:27 They came again to Jerusalem. While Jesus was walking in the temple courts, the chief priests, the experts in the law, and the elders came up to him **11:28** and said, "By what authority are you doing these things? Or who gave you this authority to do these things?" **11:29** Jesus said to them, "I will ask you one question. Answer me and I will tell you by what authority I do these things: **11:30** John's baptism – was it from heaven or from people? Answer me." **11:31** They discussed with one another, saying, "If we say, 'From heaven,' he will say, 'Then why did you not believe him?' **11:32** But if we say, 'From people – '" (they feared the crowd, for they all considered John to be truly a prophet). **11:33** So they answered Jesus, "We don't know." Then Jesus said to them, "Neither will I tell you by what authority I am doing these things."

The Parable of the Tenants

12:1 Then he began to speak to them in parables: "A man planted a vineyard. He put a fence around it, dug a pit for its winepress, and built a watchtower. Then he leased it to tenant farmers and went on a journey. **12:2** At harvest time he sent a slave to the tenants to collect from them his portion of the crop. **12:3** But those tenants seized his slave, beat him, and sent him away empty-handed. **12:4** So he sent another slave to them again. This one they struck on the head and treated outrageously. **12:5** He sent another, and that one they killed. This happened to many others, some of whom were beaten, others killed. **12:6** He had one left, his one dear son. Finally he sent him to them, saying, 'They will respect my son.' **12:7** But those tenants said to one another, 'This is the heir. Come, let's kill him and the inheritance will be ours!' **12:8** So they seized him, killed him, and threw his body out of the vineyard. **12:9** What then will the owner of the vineyard do? He will come and destroy those tenants and give the vineyard to others. **12:10** Have you not read this scripture:

'The stone the builders rejected has become the cornerstone.

12:11 This is from the Lord, and it is marvelous in our eyes*'?"*

12:12 Now they wanted to arrest him (but they feared the crowd), because they realized that he told this parable against them. So they left him and went away.

Paying Taxes to Caesar

12:13 Then they sent some of the Pharisees and Herodians to trap him with his own words. **12:14** When they came they said to him, "Teacher, we know that you are truthful and do not court anyone's favor, because you show no partiality but teach the way of God in accordance with the truth. Is it right to pay taxes to Caesar or not? Should we pay or shouldn't we?" **12:15** But he saw through their hypocrisy and said to them, "Why are you testing me? Bring me a denarius and let me look at it." **12:16** So they brought one, and he said to them, "Whose image is this, and whose inscription?" They replied, "Caesar's." **12:17** Then Jesus said to them, "Give to Caesar the things that are Caesar's, and to God the things that are God's." And they were utterly amazed at him.

Marriage and the Resurrection

12:18 Sadducees (who say there is no resurrection) also came to him and asked him, **12:19** "Teacher, Moses wrote for us: *'If a man's brother dies and leaves a wife but no children, that man must marry the widow and father children for his brother.'* **12:20** There were seven brothers. The first one married, and when he died he had no children. **12:21** The second married her and died without any children, and likewise the third. **12:22** None of the seven had children. Finally, the woman died too. **12:23** In the resurrection, when they rise again, whose wife will she be? For all seven had married her." **12:24** Jesus said to them, "Aren't you deceived for this reason, because you don't know the scriptures or the power of God? **12:25** For when they rise from the dead, they neither marry nor are given in marriage, but are like angels in heaven. **12:26** Now as for the dead being raised, have you not read in the book of Moses, in the passage about the bush, how God said to him, *'I am the God of Abraham, the God of Isaac, and the God of Jacob'*? **12:27** He is not the God of the dead but of the living. You are badly mistaken!"

The Greatest Commandment

12:28 Now one of the experts in the law came and heard them debating. When he saw that Jesus answered them well, he asked him, "Which commandment is the most important of all?" **12:29** Jesus answered, "The most important is: *'Listen, Israel, the Lord our God, the Lord is one.* **12:30** *Love the Lord your God with all your heart, with all your soul, with all your mind, and with all your strength.'* **12:31** The second is: *'Love your neighbor as yourself.'* There is no other commandment greater than these." **12:32** The expert in the law said to him, "That is true, Teacher; you are right to say that *he is one, and there is no one else besides him.* **12:33** And *to love him with all your heart, with all your mind, and with all your strength* and *to love your neighbor as yourself* is more important than all burnt offerings and sacrifices." **12:34** When Jesus saw that he had answered thoughtfully, he said to him, "You are not far from the kingdom of God." Then no one dared any longer to question him.

The Messiah: David's Son and Lord

12:35 While Jesus was teaching in the temple courts, he said, "How is it that the experts in the law say that the Christ is David's son? **12:36** David himself, by the Holy Spirit, said,

'The Lord said to my lord,

"Sit at my right hand,

until I put your enemies under your feet.*"'*

12:37 If David himself calls him 'Lord,' how can he be his son?" And the large crowd was listening to him with delight.

Warnings About Experts in the Law

12:38 In his teaching Jesus also said, "Watch out for the experts in the law. They like walking around in long robes and elaborate greetings in the marketplaces, **12:39** and the best seats in the synagogues and the places of honor at banquets. **12:40** They devour widows' property, and as a show make long prayers. These men will receive a more severe punishment."

The Widow's Offering

12:41 Then he sat down opposite the offering box, and watched the crowd putting coins into it. Many rich people were throwing in large amounts. **12:42** And a poor widow came and put in two small copper coins, worth less than a penny. **12:43** He called his disciples and said to them, "I tell you the truth, this poor widow has put more into the offering box than all the others. **12:44** For they all gave out of their wealth. But she, out of her poverty, put in what she had to live on, everything she had."

The Destruction of the Temple

13:1 Now as Jesus was going out of the temple courts, one of his disciples said to him, "Teacher, look at these tremendous stones and buildings!" **13:2** Jesus said to him, "Do you see these great buildings? Not one stone will be left on another. All will be torn down!"

Signs of the End of the Age

13:3 So while he was sitting on the Mount of Olives opposite the temple, Peter, James, John, and Andrew asked him privately, **13:4** "Tell us, when will these things happen? And what will be the sign that all these things are about to take place?" **13:5** Jesus began to say to them, "Watch out that no one misleads you. **13:6** Many will come in my name, saying, 'I am he,' and they will mislead many. **13:7** When you hear of wars and rumors of wars, do not be alarmed. These things must happen, but the end is still to come. **13:8** For nation will rise up in arms against nation, and kingdom against kingdom. There will be earthquakes in various places, and there will be famines. These are but the beginning of birth pains.

Persecution of Disciples

13:9 "You must watch out for yourselves. You will be handed over to councils and beaten in the synagogues. You will stand before governors and kings because of me, as a witness to them. **13:10** First the gospel must be preached to all nations. **13:11** When they arrest you and hand you over for trial, do not worry about what to speak. But say whatever is given you at that time, for it is not you speaking, but the Holy Spirit. **13:12** Brother will hand over brother to death, and a father his child. Children will rise against parents and have them put to death. **13:13** You will be hated by everyone because of my name. But the one who endures to the end will be saved.

The Abomination of Desolation

13:14 "But when you see *the abomination of desolation* standing where it should not be (let the reader understand), then those in Judea must flee to the mountains. **13:15** The one on the roof must not come down or go inside to take anything out of his house. **13:16** The one in the field must not turn back to get his cloak. **13:17** Woe to those who are pregnant and to those who are nursing their babies in those days! **13:18** Pray that it may not be in winter. **13:19** For in those days there will be suffering unlike anything that has happened from the beginning of the creation that God created until now, or ever will happen. **13:20** And if the Lord had not cut short those days, no one would be saved. But because of the elect, whom he chose, he has cut them short. **13:21** Then if anyone says to you, 'Look, here is the Christ!' or 'Look, there he is!' do not believe him. **13:22** For false messiahs and false prophets will appear and perform signs and wonders to deceive, if possible, the elect. **13:23** Be careful! I have told you everything ahead of time.

The Arrival of the Son of Man

13:24 "But in those days, after that suffering, *the sun will be darkened and the moon will not give its light;* **13:25** *the stars will be falling from heaven, and the powers in the heavens will be shaken.* **13:26** Then everyone will see *the Son of Man arriving in the clouds* with great power and glory. **13:27** Then he will send angels and they will gather his elect from the four winds, from the ends of the earth to the ends of heaven.

The Parable of the Fig Tree

13:28 "Learn this parable from the fig tree: Whenever its branch becomes tender and puts out its leaves, you know that summer is near. **13:29** So also you, when you see these things happening, know that he is near, right at the door. **13:30** I tell you the truth, this generation will not pass away until all these things take place. **13:31** Heaven and earth will pass away, but my words will never pass away.

Be Ready!

13:32 "But as for that day or hour no one knows it – neither the angels in heaven, nor the Son – except the Father. **13:33** Watch out! Stay alert! For you do not know when the time will come. **13:34** It is like a man going on a journey. He left his house and put his slaves in charge, assigning to each his work, and commanded the doorkeeper to stay alert. **13:35** Stay alert, then, because you do not know when the owner of the house will return – whether during evening, at midnight, when the rooster crows, or at dawn – **13:36** or else he might find you asleep when he returns suddenly. **13:37** What I say to you I say to everyone: Stay alert!"

The Plot Against Jesus

14:1 Two days before the Passover and the Feast of Unleavened Bread, the chief priests and the experts in the law were trying to find a way to arrest Jesus by stealth and kill him. **14:2** For they said, "Not during the feast, so there won't be a riot among the people."

Jesus' Anointing

14:3 Now while Jesus was in Bethany at the house of Simon the leper, reclining at the table, a woman came with an alabaster jar of costly aromatic oil from pure nard. After breaking open the jar, she poured it on his head. **14:4** But some who were present indignantly said to one another, "Why this waste of expensive ointment? **14:5** It could have been sold for more than three hundred silver coins and the money given to the poor!" So they spoke angrily to her. **14:6** But Jesus said, "Leave her alone. Why are you bothering her? She has done a good service for me. **14:7** For you will always have the poor with you, and you can do good for them whenever you want. But you will not always have me! **14:8** She did what she could. She anointed my body beforehand for burial. **14:9** I tell you the truth, wherever the gospel is proclaimed in the whole world, what she has done will also be told in memory of her."

The Plan to Betray Jesus

14:10 Then Judas Iscariot, one of the twelve, went to the chief priests to betray Jesus into their hands. **14:11** When they heard this, they were delighted and promised to give him money. So Judas began looking for an opportunity to betray him.

The Passover

14:12 Now on the first day of the feast of Unleavened Bread, when the Passover lamb is sacrificed, Jesus' disciples said to him, "Where do you want us to prepare for you to eat the Passover?" **14:13** He sent two of his disciples and told them, "Go into the city, and a man carrying a jar of water will meet you. Follow him. **14:14** Wherever he enters, tell the owner of the house, 'The Teacher says, "Where is my guest room where I may eat the Passover with my disciples?"' **14:15** He will show you a large room upstairs, furnished and ready. Make preparations for us there." **14:16** So the disciples left, went into the city, and found things just as he had told them, and they prepared the Passover.

14:17 Then, when it was evening, he came to the house with the twelve. **14:18** While they were at the table eating, Jesus said, "I tell you the truth, one of you eating with me will betray me." **14:19** They were distressed, and one by one said to him, "Surely not I?" **14:20** He said to them, "It is one of the twelve, one who dips his hand with me into the bowl. **14:21** For the Son of Man will go as it is written about him, but woe to that man by whom the Son of Man is betrayed! It would be better for him if he had never been born."

The Lord's Supper

14:22 While they were eating, he took bread, and after giving thanks he broke it, gave it to them, and said, "Take it. This is my body." **14:23** And after taking the cup and giving thanks, he gave it to them, and they all drank from it. **14:24** He said to them, "This is my blood, the blood of the covenant, that is poured out for many. **14:25** I tell you the truth, I will no longer drink of the fruit of the vine until that day when I drink it new in the kingdom of God." **14:26** After singing a hymn, they went out to the Mount of Olives.

The Prediction of Peter's Denial

14:27 Then Jesus said to them, "You will all fall away, for it is written,

'I will strike the shepherd,
and the sheep will be scattered.'

14:28 But after I am raised, I will go ahead of you into Galilee." **14:29** Peter said to him, "Even if they all fall away, I will not!" **14:30** Jesus said to him, "I tell you the truth, today – this very night – before a rooster crows twice, you will deny me three times." **14:31** But Peter insisted emphatically, "Even if I must die with you, I will never deny you." And all of them said the same thing.

Gethsemane

14:32 Then they went to a place called Gethsemane, and Jesus said to his disciples, "Sit here while I pray." **14:33** He took Peter, James, and John with him, and became very troubled and distressed. **14:34** He said to them, "My soul is deeply grieved, even to the point of death. Remain here and stay alert." **14:35** Going a little farther, he threw himself to the ground and prayed that if it were possible the hour would pass from him. **14:36** He said, "Abba, Father, all things are possible for you. Take this cup away from me. Yet not what I will, but what you will." **14:37** Then he came and found them sleeping, and said to Peter, "Simon, are you sleeping? Couldn't you stay awake for one hour? **14:38** Stay awake and pray that you will not fall into temptation. The spirit is willing, but the flesh is weak." **14:39** He went away again and prayed the same thing. **14:40** When he came again he found them sleeping; they could not keep their eyes open. And they did not know what to tell him. **14:41** He came a third time and said to them, "Are you still sleeping and resting? Enough of that! The hour has come. Look, the Son of Man is betrayed into the hands of sinners. **14:42** Get up, let us go. Look! My betrayer is approaching!"

Betrayal and Arrest

14:43 Right away, while Jesus was still speaking, Judas, one of the twelve, arrived. With him came a crowd armed with swords and clubs, sent by the chief priests and experts in the law and elders. **14:44** (Now the betrayer had given them a sign, saying, "The one I kiss is the man. Arrest him and lead him away under guard.") **14:45** When Judas arrived, he went up to Jesus immediately and said, "Rabbi!" and kissed him. **14:46** Then they took hold of him and arrested him. **14:47** One of the bystanders drew his sword and struck the high priest's slave, cutting off his ear. **14:48** Jesus said to them, "Have you come with swords and clubs to arrest me like you would an outlaw? **14:49** Day after day I was with you, teaching in the temple courts, yet you did not arrest me. But this has happened so that the scriptures would be fulfilled." **14:50** Then all the disciples left him and fled. **14:51** A young man was following him, wearing only a linen cloth. They tried to arrest him, **14:52** but he ran off naked, leaving his linen cloth behind.

Condemned by the Sanhedrin

14:53 Then they led Jesus to the high priest, and all the chief priests and elders and experts in the law came together. **14:54** And Peter had followed him from a distance, up to the high priest's courtyard. He was sitting with the guards and warming himself by the fire. **14:55** The chief priests and the whole Sanhedrin were looking for evidence against Jesus so that they could put him to death, but they did not find anything. **14:56** Many gave false testimony against him, but their testimony did not agree. **14:57** Some stood up and gave this false testimony against him: **14:58** "We heard him say, 'I will destroy this temple made with hands and in three days build another not made with hands.'" **14:59** Yet even on this point their testimony did not agree. **14:60** Then the high priest stood up before them and asked Jesus, "Have you no answer? What is this that they are testifying against you?" **14:61** But he was silent and did not answer. Again the high priest questioned him, "Are you the Christ, the Son of the Blessed One?" **14:62** "I am," said Jesus, "and you will see *the Son of Man sitting at the right hand* of the Power and *coming with the clouds of heaven*." **14:63** Then the high priest tore his clothes and said, "Why do we still need witnesses? **14:64** You have heard the blasphemy! What is your verdict?" They all condemned him as deserving death. **14:65** Then some began to spit on him, and to blindfold him, and to strike him with their fists, saying, "Prophesy!" The guards also took him and beat him.

Peter's Denials

14:66 Now while Peter was below in the courtyard, one of the high priest's slave girls came by. **14:67** When she saw Peter warming himself, she looked directly at him and said, "You also were with that Nazarene, Jesus." **14:68** But he denied it: "I don't even understand what you're talking about!" Then he went out to the gateway, and a rooster crowed. **14:69** When the slave girl saw him, she began again to say to the bystanders, "This man is one of them." **14:70** But he denied it again. A short time later the bystanders again said to Peter, "You must be one of them, because you are also a Galilean." **14:71** Then he began to curse, and he swore with an oath, "I do not know this man you are talking about!" **14:72** Immediately a rooster crowed a second time. Then Peter remembered what Jesus had said to him: "Before a rooster crows twice, you will deny me three times." And he broke down and wept.

Jesus Brought Before Pilate

15:1 Early in the morning, after forming a plan, the chief priests with the elders and the experts in the law and the whole Sanhedrin tied Jesus up, led him away, and handed him over to Pilate. **15:2** So Pilate asked him, "Are you the king of the Jews?" He replied, "You say so." **15:3** Then the chief priests began to accuse him repeatedly. **15:4** So Pilate asked him again, "Have you nothing to say? See how many charges they are bringing against you!" **15:5** But Jesus made no further reply, so that Pilate was amazed.

Jesus and Barabbas

15:6 During the feast it was customary to release one prisoner to the people, whomever they requested. **15:7** A man named Barabbas was imprisoned with rebels who had committed murder during an insurrection. **15:8** Then the crowd came up and began to ask Pilate to release a prisoner for them, as was his custom. **15:9** So Pilate asked them, "Do you want me to release the king of the Jews for you?" **15:10** (For he knew that the chief priests had handed him over because of envy.) **15:11** But the chief priests stirred up the crowd to have him release Barabbas instead. **15:12** So Pilate spoke to them again, "Then what do you want me to do with the one you call king of the Jews?" **15:13** They shouted back, "Crucify him!" **15:14** Pilate asked them, "Why? What has he done wrong?" But they shouted more insistently, "Crucify him!" **15:15** Because he wanted to satisfy the crowd, Pilate released Barabbas for them. Then, after he had Jesus flogged, he handed him over to be crucified.

Jesus is Mocked

15:16 So the soldiers led him into the palace (that is, the governor's residence) and called together the whole cohort. **15:17** They put a purple cloak on him and after braiding a crown of thorns, they put it on him. **15:18** They began to salute him: "Hail, king of the Jews!" **15:19** Again and again they struck him on the head with a staff and spit on him. Then they knelt down and paid homage to him. **15:20** When they had finished mocking him, they stripped him of the purple cloak and put his own clothes back on him. Then they led him away to crucify him.

The Crucifixion

15:21 The soldiers forced a passerby to carry his cross, Simon of Cyrene, who was coming in from the country (he was the father of Alexander and Rufus). **15:22** They brought Jesus to a place called Golgotha (which is translated, "Place of the Skull"). **15:23** They offered him wine mixed with myrrh, but he did not take it. **15:24** Then they crucified him and *divided his clothes, throwing dice* for them, to decide what each would take. **15:25** It was nine o'clock in the morning when they crucified him. **15:26** The inscription of the charge against him read, "The king of the Jews." **15:27** And they crucified two outlaws with him, one on his right and one on his left. **15:29** Those who passed by defamed him, shaking their heads and saying, "Aha! You who can destroy the temple and rebuild it in three days, **15:30** save yourself and come down from the cross!" **15:31** In the same way even the chief priests – together with the experts in the law – were mocking him among themselves: "He saved others, but he cannot save himself! **15:32** Let the Christ, the king of Israel, come down from the cross now, that we may see and believe!" Those who were crucified with him also spoke abusively to him.

Jesus' Death

15:33 Now when it was noon, darkness came over the whole land until three in the afternoon. **15:34** Around three o'clock Jesus cried out with a loud voice, "*Eloi, Eloi, lema sabachthani?*" which means, "*My God, my God, why have you forsaken me?*" **15:35** When some of the bystanders heard it they said, "Listen, he is calling for Elijah!" **15:36** Then someone ran, filled a sponge with sour wine, put it on a stick, and gave it to him to drink, saying, "Leave him alone! Let's see if Elijah will come to take him down!" **15:37** But Jesus cried out with a loud voice and breathed his last. **15:38** And the temple curtain was torn in two, from top to bottom. **15:39** Now when the centurion, who stood in front of him, saw how he died, he said, "Truly this man was God's Son!" **15:40** There were also women, watching from a distance. Among them were Mary Magdalene, and Mary the mother of James the younger and of Joses, and Salome. **15:41** When he was in Galilee, they had followed him and given him support. Many other women who had come up with him to Jerusalem were there too.

Jesus' Burial

15:42 Now when evening had already come, since it was the day of preparation (that is, the day before the Sabbath), **15:43** Joseph of Arimathea, a highly regarded member of the council, who was himself looking forward to the kingdom of God, went boldly to Pilate and asked for the body of Jesus. **15:44** Pilate was surprised that he was already dead. He called the centurion and asked him if he had been dead for some time. **15:45** When Pilate was informed by the centurion, he gave the body to Joseph. **15:46** After Joseph bought a linen cloth and took down the body, he wrapped it in the linen and placed it in a tomb cut out of the rock. Then he rolled a stone across the entrance of the tomb. **15:47** Mary Magdalene and Mary the mother of Joses saw where the body was placed.

The Resurrection

16:1 When the Sabbath was over, Mary Magdalene, Mary the mother of James, and Salome bought aromatic spices so that they might go and anoint him. **16:2** And very early on the first day of the week, at sunrise, they went to the tomb. **16:3** They had been asking each other, "Who will roll away the stone for us from the entrance to the tomb?" **16:4** But when they looked up, they saw that the stone, which was very large, had been rolled back. **16:5** Then as they went into the tomb, they saw a young man dressed in a white robe sitting on the right side; and they were alarmed. **16:6** But he said to them, "Do not be alarmed. You are looking for Jesus the Nazarene, who was crucified. He has been raised! He is not here. Look, there is the place where they laid him. **16:7** But go, tell his disciples, even Peter, that he is going ahead of you into Galilee. You will see him there, just as he told you." **16:8** Then they went out and ran from the tomb, for terror and bewilderment had seized them. And they said nothing to anyone, because they were afraid.

The Longer Ending of Mark

[[**16:9** Early on the first day of the week, after he arose, he appeared first to Mary Magdalene, from whom he had driven out seven demons. **16:10** She went out and told those who were with him, while they were mourning and weeping. **16:11** And when they heard that he was alive and had been seen by her, they did not believe.

16:12 After this he appeared in a different form to two of them while they were on their way to the country. **16:13** They went back and told the rest, but they did not believe them. **16:14** Then he appeared to the eleven themselves, while they were eating, and he rebuked them for their unbelief and hardness of heart, because they did not believe those who had seen him resurrected. **16:15** He

said to them, "Go into all the world and preach the gospel to every creature. **16:16** The one who believes and is baptized will be saved, but the one who does not believe will be condemned. **16:17** These signs will accompany those who believe: In my name they will drive out demons; they will speak in new languages; **16:18** they will pick up snakes with their hands, and whatever poison they drink will not harm them; they will place their hands on the sick and they will be well." **16:19** After the Lord Jesus had spoken to them, he was taken up into heaven and sat down at the right hand of God. **16:20** They went out and proclaimed everywhere, while the Lord worked with them and confirmed the word through the accompanying signs.]]

Book 42. Luke

Explanatory Preface

1:1 Now many have undertaken to compile an account of the things that have been fulfilled among us, **1:2** like the accounts passed on to us by those who were eyewitnesses and servants of the word from the beginning. **1:3** So it seemed good to me as well, because I have followed all things carefully from the beginning, to write an orderly account for you, most excellent Theophilus, **1:4** so that you may know for certain the things you were taught.

Birth Announcement of John the Baptist

1:5 During the reign of Herod king of Judea, there lived a priest named Zechariah who belonged to the priestly division of Abijah, and he had a wife named Elizabeth, who was a descendant of Aaron. **1:6** They were both righteous in the sight of God, following all the commandments and ordinances of the Lord blamelessly. **1:7** But they did not have a child, because Elizabeth was barren, and they were both very old.

1:8 Now while Zechariah was serving as priest before God when his division was on duty, **1:9** he was chosen by lot, according to the custom of the priesthood, to enter the holy place of the Lord and burn incense. **1:10** Now the whole crowd of people were praying outside at the hour of the incense offering. **1:11** An angel of the Lord, standing on the right side of the altar of incense, appeared to him. **1:12** And Zechariah, visibly shaken when he saw the angel, was seized with fear. **1:13** But the angel said to him, "Do not be afraid, Zechariah, for your prayer has been heard, and your wife Elizabeth will bear you a son; you will name him John. **1:14** Joy and gladness will come to you, and many will rejoice at his birth, **1:15** for he will be great in the sight of the Lord. He must never drink wine or strong drink, and he will be filled with the Holy Spirit, even before his birth. **1:16** He will turn many of the people of Israel to the Lord their God. **1:17** And he will go as forerunner before the Lord in the spirit and power of Elijah, to turn the hearts of the fathers back to their children and the disobedient to the wisdom of the just, to make ready for the Lord a people prepared for him."

1:18 Zechariah said to the angel, "How can I be sure of this? For I am an old man, and my wife is old as well." **1:19** The angel answered him, "I am Gabriel, who stands in the presence of God, and I was sent to speak to you and to bring you this good news. **1:20** And now, because you did not believe my words, which will be fulfilled in their time, you will be silent, unable to speak, until the day these things take place."

1:21 Now the people were waiting for Zechariah, and they began to wonder why he was delayed in the holy place. **1:22** When he came out, he was not able to speak to them. They realized that he had seen a vision in the holy place, because he was making signs to them and remained unable to speak. **1:23** When his time of service was over, he went to his home.

1:24 After some time his wife Elizabeth became pregnant, and for five months she kept herself in seclusion. She said, **1:25** "This is what the Lord has done for me at the time when he has been gracious to me, to take away my disgrace among people."

Birth Announcement of Jesus the Messiah

1:26 In the sixth month of Elizabeth's pregnancy, the angel Gabriel was sent by God to a town of Galilee called Nazareth, **1:27** to a virgin engaged to a man whose name was Joseph, a descendant of David, and the virgin's name was Mary. **1:28** The angel came to her and said, "Greetings, favored one, the Lord is with you!" **1:29** But she was greatly troubled by his words and began to wonder about the meaning of this greeting. **1:30** So the angel said to her, "Do not be afraid, Mary, for you have found favor with God! **1:31** Listen: You will become pregnant and give birth to a son, and you will name him Jesus. **1:32** He will be great, and will be called the Son of the Most High, and the Lord God will give him the throne of his father David. **1:33** He will reign over the house of Jacob forever, and his kingdom will never end." **1:34** Mary said to the angel, "How will this be, since I have not had sexual relations with a man?" **1:35** The angel replied, "The Holy Spirit will come upon you, and the power of the Most High will overshadow you. Therefore the child to be born will be holy; he will be called the Son of God.

1:36 "And look, your relative Elizabeth has also become pregnant with a son in her old age – although she was called barren, she is now in her sixth month! **1:37** For nothing will be impossible with God." **1:38** So Mary said, "Yes, I am a servant of the Lord; let this happen to me according to your word." Then the angel departed from her.

Mary and Elizabeth

1:39 In those days Mary got up and went hurriedly into the hill country, to a town of Judah, **1:40** and entered Zechariah's house and greeted Elizabeth. **1:41** When Elizabeth heard Mary's greeting, the baby leaped in her womb, and Elizabeth was filled with the Holy Spirit. **1:42** She exclaimed with a loud voice, "Blessed are you among women, and blessed is the child in your womb! **1:43** And who am I that the mother of my Lord should come and visit me? **1:44** For the instant the sound of your greeting reached my ears, the baby in my womb leaped for joy. **1:45** And blessed is she who believed that what was spoken to her by the Lord would be fulfilled."

Mary's Hymn of Praise

1:46 And Mary said,

"My soul exalts the Lord,

1:47 and my spirit has begun to rejoice in God my Savior,
1:48 because he has looked upon the humble state of his servant.
For from now on all generations will call me blessed,
1:49 because he who is mighty has done great things for me, and holy is his name;
1:50 from generation to generation he is merciful to those who fear him.
1:51 He has demonstrated power with his arm; he has scattered those whose pride wells up from the sheer arrogance of their hearts.
1:52 He has brought down the mighty from their thrones, and has lifted up those of lowly position;
1:53 he has filled the hungry with good things, and has sent the rich away empty.
1:54 He has helped his servant Israel, remembering his mercy,
1:55 as he promised to our ancestors, to Abraham and to his descendants forever."
1:56 So Mary stayed with Elizabeth about three months and then returned to her home.

The Birth of John

1:57 Now the time came for Elizabeth to have her baby, and she gave birth to a son. **1:58** Her neighbors and relatives heard that the Lord had shown great mercy to her, and they rejoiced with her. **1:59** On the eighth day they came to circumcise the child, and they wanted to name him Zechariah after his father. **1:60** But his mother replied, "No! He must be named John." **1:61** They said to her, "But none of your relatives bears this name." **1:62** So they made signs to the baby's father, inquiring what he wanted to name his son. **1:63** He asked for a writing tablet and wrote, "His name is John." And they were all amazed. **1:64** Immediately Zechariah's mouth was opened and his tongue released, and he spoke, blessing God. **1:65** All their neighbors were filled with fear, and throughout the entire hill country of Judea all these things were talked about. **1:66** All who heard these things kept them in their hearts, saying, "What then will this child be?" For the Lord's hand was indeed with him.

Zechariah's Praise and Prediction

1:67 Then his father Zechariah was filled with the Holy Spirit and prophesied,
1:68 "Blessed be the Lord God of Israel,
because he has come to help and has redeemed his people.
1:69 For he has raised up a horn of salvation for us in the house of his servant David,
1:70 as he spoke through the mouth of his holy prophets from long ago,
1:71 that we should be saved from our enemies,
and from the hand of all who hate us.
1:72 He has done this to show mercy to our ancestors,
and to remember his holy covenant –
1:73 the oath that he swore to our ancestor Abraham.
This oath grants
1:74 that we, being rescued from the hand of our enemies,
may serve him without fear,
1:75 in holiness and righteousness before him for as long as we live.
1:76 And you, child, will be called the
prophet of the Most High.
For you will go before the Lord to prepare his ways,
1:77 to give his people knowledge of salvation through the forgiveness of their sins.
1:78 Because of our God's tender mercy
the dawn will break upon us from on high
1:79 to give light to those who sit in darkness and in the shadow of death,
to guide our feet into the way of peace."
1:80 And the child kept growing and becoming strong in spirit, and he was in the wilderness until the day he was revealed to Israel.

The Census and the Birth of Jesus

2:1 Now in those days a decree went out from Caesar Augustus to register all the empire for taxes. **2:2** This was the first registration, taken when Quirinius was governor of Syria. **2:3** Everyone went to his own town to be registered. **2:4** So Joseph also went up from the town of Nazareth in Galilee to Judea, to the city of David called Bethlehem, because he was of the house and family line of David. **2:5** He went to be registered with Mary, who was promised in marriage to him, and who was expecting a child. **2:6** While they were there, the time came for her to deliver her child. **2:7** And she gave birth to her firstborn son and wrapped him in strips of cloth and laid him in a manger, because there was no place for them in the inn.

The Shepherds' Visit

2:8 Now there were shepherds nearby living out in the field, keeping guard over their flock at night. **2:9** An angel of the Lord appeared to them, and the glory of the Lord shone around them, and they were absolutely terrified. **2:10** But the angel said to them, "Do not be afraid! Listen carefully, for I proclaim to you good news that brings great joy to all the people: **2:11** Today your Savior is born in the city of David. He is Christ the Lord. **2:12** This will be a sign for you: You will find a baby wrapped in strips of cloth and lying in a manger." **2:13** Suddenly a vast, heavenly army appeared with the angel, praising God and saying,
2:14 "Glory to God in the highest,
and on earth peace among people with whom he is pleased!"
2:15 When the angels left them and went back to heaven, the shepherds said to one another, "Let us go over to Bethlehem and see this thing that has taken place, that the Lord has made known to us." **2:16** So they hurried off and located Mary and Joseph, and found the baby lying in a manger. **2:17** When they saw him, they related what they had been told about this child, **2:18** and all who heard it were astonished at what the shepherds said. **2:19** But Mary treasured up all these words, pondering in her heart what they might mean. **2:20** So the shepherds returned, glorifying and praising God for all they had heard and seen; everything was just as they had been told.
2:21 At the end of eight days, when he was circumcised, he was named Jesus, the name given by the angel before he was conceived in the womb.

Jesus' Presentation at the Temple

2:22 Now when the time came for their purification according to the law of Moses, Joseph and Mary brought Jesus up to Jerusalem to present him to the Lord **2:23** (just as it is written in the law of the Lord, "*Every firstborn male will be set apart to the Lord*"), **2:24** and to offer a sacrifice according to what is specified in the law of the Lord, *a pair of doves or two young pigeons*.

The Prophecy of Simeon

2:25 Now there was a man in Jerusalem named Simeon who was righteous and devout, looking for the restoration of Israel, and the Holy Spirit was upon him. **2:26** It had been revealed to him by the Holy Spirit that he would not die before he had seen the Lord's Christ. **2:27** So Simeon, directed by the Spirit, came into the temple courts, and when the parents brought in the child Jesus to do for him what was customary according to the law, **2:28** Simeon took him in his arms and blessed God, saying,
2:29 "Now, according to your word, Sovereign Lord, permit your servant to depart in peace.
2:30 For my eyes have seen your salvation
2:31 that you have prepared in the presence of all peoples:
2:32 a light,
for revelation to the Gentiles,
and for glory to your people Israel."
2:33 So the child's father and mother were amazed at what was said about him. **2:34** Then Simeon blessed them and said to his mother Mary, "Listen carefully: This child is destined to be the cause of the falling and rising of many in Israel and to be a sign that will be rejected. **2:35** Indeed, as a result of him the thoughts of many hearts will be revealed – and a sword will pierce your own soul as well!"

The Testimony of Anna

2:36 There was also a prophetess, Anna the daughter of Phanuel, of the tribe of Asher. She was very old, having been married to her husband for seven years until his death. **2:37** She had lived as a widow since then for eighty-four years. She never left the temple, worshiping with fasting and prayer night and day. **2:38** At that moment, she came up to them and began to give thanks to God and to speak about the child to all who were waiting for the redemption of Jerusalem.
2:39 So when Joseph and Mary had performed everything according to the law of the Lord, they returned to Galilee, to their own town of Nazareth. **2:40** And the child grew and became strong, filled with wisdom, and the favor of God was upon him.

Jesus in the Temple

2:41 Now Jesus' parents went to Jerusalem every year for the feast of the Passover. **2:42** When he was twelve years old, they went up according to custom. **2:43** But when the feast was over, as they were returning home, the boy Jesus stayed behind in Jerusalem. His parents did not know it, **2:44** but (because they assumed that he was in their group of travelers) they went a day's journey. Then they began to look for him among their relatives and acquaintances. **2:45** When they did not find him, they returned to Jerusalem to look for him. **2:46** After three days they found him in the temple courts, sitting among the teachers, listening to them and asking them questions. **2:47** And all who heard Jesus were astonished at his understanding and his answers. **2:48** When his parents saw him, they were overwhelmed. His mother said to him, "Child, why have you treated us like this? Look, your father and I have been looking for you anxiously." **2:49** But he replied, "Why were you looking for me? Didn't you know that I must be in my Father's house?" **2:50** Yet his parents did not understand the remark he made to them. **2:51** Then he went down with them and came to Nazareth, and was obedient to them. But his mother kept all these things in her heart. **2:52** And Jesus increased in wisdom and in stature, and in favor with God and with people.

The Ministry of John the Baptist

3:1 In the fifteenth year of the reign of Tiberius Caesar, when Pontius Pilate was governor of Judea, and Herod was tetrarch of Galilee, and his brother Philip was tetrarch of the region of Iturea and Trachonitis, and Lysanias was tetrarch of Abilene, **3:2** during the high priesthood of Annas and Caiaphas, the word of God came to John the son of Zechariah in the wilderness. **3:3** He went into all the region around the Jordan River, preaching a baptism of repentance for the forgiveness of sins.

3:4 As it is written in the book of the words of Isaiah the prophet,

"The voice of one shouting in the wilderness:

'Prepare the way for the Lord,

make his paths straight.

3:5 Every valley will be filled,

and every mountain and hill will be brought low,

and the crooked will be made straight,

and the rough ways will be made smooth,

3:6 and all humanity will see the salvation of God.'"

3:7 So John said to the crowds that came out to be baptized by him, "You offspring of vipers! Who warned you to flee from the coming wrath? **3:8** Therefore produce fruit that proves your repentance, and don't begin to say to yourselves, 'We have Abraham as our father.' For I tell you that God can raise up children for Abraham from these stones! **3:9** Even now the ax is laid at the root of the trees, and every tree that does not produce good fruit will be cut down and thrown into the fire."

3:10 So the crowds were asking him, "What then should we do?" **3:11** John answered them, "The person who has two tunics must share with the person who has none, and the person who has food must do likewise." **3:12** Tax collectors also came to be baptized, and they said to him, "Teacher, what should we do?" **3:13** He told them, "Collect no more than you are required to." **3:14** Then some soldiers also asked him, "And as for us – what should we do?" He told them, "Take money from no one by violence or by false accusation, and be content with your pay."

3:15 While the people were filled with anticipation and they all wondered whether perhaps John could be the Christ, **3:16** John answered them all, "I baptize you with water,

but one more powerful than I am is coming – I am not worthy to untie the strap of his sandals. He will baptize you with the Holy Spirit and fire. **3:17** His winnowing fork is in his hand to clean out his threshing floor and to gather the wheat into his storehouse, but the chaff he will burn up with inextinguishable fire."

3:18 And in this way, with many other exhortations, John proclaimed good news to the people. **3:19** But when John rebuked Herod the tetrarch because of Herodias, his brother's

wife, and because of all the evil deeds that he had done, **3:20** Herod added this to them all: He locked up John in prison.

The Baptism of Jesus

3:21 Now when all the people were baptized, Jesus also was baptized. And while he was praying, the heavens opened, **3:22** and the Holy Spirit descended on him in bodily form like a dove. And a voice came from heaven, "You are my one dear Son; in you I take great delight."

The Genealogy of Jesus

3:23 So Jesus, when he began his ministry, was about thirty years old. He was the son (as was supposed) of Joseph, the son of Heli, **3:24** the son of Matthat, the son of Levi, the son of Melchi, the son of Jannai, the son of Joseph, **3:25** the son of Mattathias, the son of Amos, the son of Nahum, the son of Esli, the son of Naggai, **3:26** the son of Maath, the son of Mattathias, the son of Semein, the son of Josech, the son of Joda, **3:27** the son of Joanan, the son of Rhesa, the son of Zerubbabel, the son of Shealtiel, the son of Neri, **3:28** the son of Melchi, the son of Addi, the son of Cosam, the son of Elmadam, the son of Er, **3:29** the son of Joshua, the son of Eliezer, the son of Jorim, the son of Matthat, the son of Levi, **3:30** the son of Simeon, the son of Judah, the son of Joseph, the son of Jonam, the son of Eliakim, **3:31** the son of Melea, the son of Menna, the son of Mattatha, the son of Nathan, the son of David, **3:32** the son of Jesse, the son of Obed, the son of Boaz, the son of Sala, the son of Nahshon, **3:33** the son of Amminadab, the son of Admin, the son of Arni, the son of Hezron, the son of Perez, the son of Judah, **3:34** the son of Jacob, the son of Isaac, the son of Abraham, the son of Terah, the son of Nahor, **3:35** the son of Serug, the son of Reu, the son of Peleg, the son of Eber, the son of Shelah, **3:36** the son of Cainan, the son of Arphaxad, the son of Shem, the son of Noah, the son of Lamech, **3:37** the son of Methuselah, the son of Enoch, the son of Jared, the son of Mahalalel, the son of Kenan, **3:38** the son of Enosh, the son of Seth, the son of Adam, the son of God.

The Temptation of Jesus

4:1 Then Jesus, full of the Holy Spirit, returned from the Jordan River and was led by the Spirit in the wilderness, **4:2** where for forty days he endured temptations from the devil. He ate nothing during those days, and when they were completed, he was famished. **4:3** The devil said to him, "If you are the Son of God, command this stone to become bread." **4:4** Jesus answered him, "It is written, '*Man does not live by bread alone.*'"

4:5 Then the devil led him up to a high place and showed him in a flash all the kingdoms of the world. **4:6** And he said to him, "To you I will grant this whole realm – and the glory that goes along with it, for it has been relinquished to me, and I can give it to anyone I wish. **4:7** So then, if you will worship me, all this will be yours." **4:8** Jesus answered him, "It is written, '*You are to worship the Lord your God and serve* only *him.*'" **4:9** Then the devil brought him to Jerusalem, had him stand on the highest point of the temple, and said to him, "If you are the Son of God, throw

yourself down from here, **4:10** for it is written, '*He will command his angels concerning you, to protect you,*' **4:11** and '*with their hands they will lift you up, so that you will not strike your foot against a stone.*'" **4:12** Jesus answered him, "It is said, '*You are not to put the Lord your God to the test.*'" **4:13** So when the devil had completed every temptation, he departed from him until a more opportune time.

The Beginning of Jesus' Ministry in Galilee

4:14 Then Jesus, in the power of the Spirit, returned to Galilee, and news about him spread throughout the surrounding countryside. **4:15** He began to teach in their synagogues and was praised by all.

Rejection at Nazareth

4:16 Now Jesus came to Nazareth, where he had been brought up, and went into the synagogue on the Sabbath day, as was his custom. He stood up to read, **4:17** and the scroll of the prophet Isaiah was given to him. He unrolled the scroll and found the place where it was written,

4:18 "The Spirit of the Lord is upon me,

because he has anointed me to proclaim good news to the poor.

He has sent me to proclaim release to the captives

and the regaining of sight to the blind,

to set free those who are oppressed,

4:19 to proclaim the year of the Lord's favor."

4:20 Then he rolled up the scroll, gave it back to the attendant, and sat down. The eyes of everyone in the synagogue were fixed on him. **4:21** Then he began to tell them, "Today this scripture has been fulfilled even as you heard it being read." **4:22** All were speaking well of him, and were amazed at the gracious words coming out of his mouth. They said, "Isn't this Joseph's son?" **4:23** Jesus said to them, "No doubt you will quote to me the proverb, 'Physician, heal yourself!' and say, 'What we have heard that you did in Capernaum, do here in your hometown too.'" **4:24** And he added, "I tell you the truth, no prophet is acceptable in his hometown. **4:25** But in truth I tell you, there were many widows in Israel in Elijah's days, when the sky was shut up three and a half years, and there was a great famine over all the land. **4:26** Yet Elijah was sent to none of them, but only to a woman who was a widow at Zarephath in Sidon. **4:27** And there were many lepers in Israel in the time of the prophet Elisha, yet none of them was cleansed except Naaman the Syrian." **4:28** When they heard this, all the people in the synagogue were filled with rage. **4:29** They got up, forced him out of the town, and brought him to the brow of the hill on which their town was built, so that they could throw him down the cliff. **4:30** But he passed through the crowd and went on his way.

Ministry in Capernaum

4:31 So he went down to Capernaum, a town in Galilee, and on the Sabbath he began to teach the people. **4:32** They were amazed at his teaching, because he spoke with authority.

4:33 Now in the synagogue there was a man who had the spirit of an unclean demon, and he cried out with a loud voice, **4:34** "Ha! Leave us alone, Jesus the Nazarene! Have you come to destroy us? I know who you are – the Holy One of God." **4:35** But Jesus rebuked him: "Silence! Come out of him!" Then, after the demon threw the man down in their midst, he came out of him without hurting him. **4:36** They were all amazed and began to say to one another, "What's happening here? For with authority and power he commands the unclean spirits, and they come out!" **4:37** So the news about him spread into all areas of the region.

4:38 After Jesus left the synagogue, he entered Simon's house. Now Simon's mother-in-law was suffering from a high fever, and they asked Jesus to help her. **4:39** So he stood over her, commanded the fever, and it left her. Immediately she got up and began to serve them.

4:40 As the sun was setting, all those who had any relatives sick with various diseases brought them to Jesus. He placed his hands on every one of them and healed them. **4:41** Demons also came out of many, crying out, "You are the Son of God!" But he rebuked them, and would not allow them to speak, because they knew that he was the Christ.

4:42 The next morning Jesus departed and went to a deserted place. Yet the crowds were seeking him, and they came to him and tried to keep him from leaving them. **4:43** But Jesus said to them, "I must proclaim the good news of the kingdom of God to the other towns too, for that is what I was sent to do." **4:44** So he continued to preach in the synagogues of Judea.

The Call of the Disciples

5:1 Now Jesus was standing by the Lake of Gennesaret, and the crowd was pressing around him to hear the word of God. **5:2** He saw two boats by the lake, but the fishermen had gotten out of them and were washing their nets. **5:3** He got into one of the boats, which was Simon's, and asked him to put out a little way from the shore. Then Jesus sat down and taught the crowds from the boat. **5:4** When he had finished speaking, he said to Simon, "Put out into the deep water and lower your nets for a catch." **5:5** Simon answered, "Master, we worked hard all night and caught nothing! But at your word I will lower the nets." **5:6** When they had done this, they caught so many fish that their nets started to tear. **5:7** So they motioned to their partners in the other boat to come and help them. And they came and filled both boats, so that they were about to sink. **5:8** But when Simon Peter saw it, he fell down at Jesus' knees, saying, "Go away from me, Lord, for I am a sinful man!" **5:9** For Peter and all who were with him were astonished at the catch of fish that they had taken, **5:10** and so were James and John, Zebedee's sons, who were Simon's business partners. Then Jesus said to Simon, "Do not be afraid; from now on you will be catching people." **5:11** So when they had brought their boats to shore, they left everything and followed him.

Healing a Leper

5:12 While Jesus was in one of the towns, a man came to him who was covered with leprosy. When he saw Jesus, he bowed down with his face to the ground and begged him, "Lord, if you are willing, you can make me clean." **5:13** So he stretched out his hand and touched him, saying, "I am willing. Be clean!" And immediately the leprosy left him. **5:14** Then he ordered the man to tell no one, but commanded him, "Go and show yourself to a priest, and bring the offering for your cleansing, as Moses commanded, as a testimony to them." **5:15** But the news about him spread even more, and large crowds were gathering together to hear him and to be healed of their illnesses. **5:16** Yet Jesus himself frequently withdrew to the wilderness and prayed.

Healing and Forgiving a Paralytic

5:17 Now on one of those days, while he was teaching, there were Pharisees and teachers of the law sitting nearby (who had come from every village of Galilee and Judea and from Jerusalem), and the power of the Lord was with him to heal. **5:18** Just then some men showed up, carrying a paralyzed man on a stretcher. They were trying to bring him in and place him before Jesus. **5:19** But since they found no way to carry him in because of the crowd, they went up on the roof and let him down on the stretcher through the roof tiles right in front of Jesus. **5:20** When Jesus saw their faith he said, "Friend, your sins are forgiven." **5:21** Then the experts in the law and the Pharisees began to think to themselves, "Who is this man who is uttering blasphemies? Who can forgive sins but God alone?" **5:22** When Jesus perceived their hostile thoughts, he said to them, "Why are you raising objections within yourselves? **5:23** Which is easier, to say, 'Your sins are forgiven,' or to say, 'Stand up and walk'? **5:24** But so that you may know that the Son of Man has authority on earth to forgive sins" – he said to the paralyzed man – "I tell you, stand up, take your stretcher and go home." **5:25** Immediately he stood up before them, picked up the stretcher he had been lying on, and went home, glorifying God. **5:26** Then astonishment seized them all, and they glorified God. They were filled with awe, saying, "We have seen incredible things today."

The Call of Levi; Eating with Sinners

5:27 After this, Jesus went out and saw a tax collector named Levi sitting at the tax booth. "Follow me," he said to him. **5:28** And he got up and followed him, leaving everything behind.

5:29 Then Levi gave a great banquet in his house for Jesus, and there was a large crowd of tax collectors and others sitting at the table with them. **5:30** But the Pharisees and their experts in the law complained to his disciples, saying, "Why do you eat and drink with tax collectors and sinners?" **5:31** Jesus answered them, "Those who are well don't need a physician, but those who are sick do. **5:32** I have not come to call the righteous, but sinners to repentance."

The Superiority of the New

5:33 Then they said to him, "John's disciples frequently fast and pray, and so do the disciples of the Pharisees, but yours continue to eat and drink." **5:34** So Jesus said to them, "You cannot make the wedding guests fast while the bridegroom is with them, can you? **5:35** But those days are coming, and when the bridegroom is taken from them, at that time they will fast." **5:36** He also told them a parable: "No one tears a patch from a new garment and sews it on an old garment. If he does, he will have torn the new, and the piece from the new will not match the old. **5:37** And no one pours new wine into old wineskins. If he does, the new wine will burst the skins and will be spilled, and the skins will be destroyed. **5:38** Instead new wine must be poured into new wineskins. **5:39** No one after drinking old wine wants the new, for he says, 'The old is good enough.'"

Lord of the Sabbath

6:1 Jesus was going through the grain fields on a Sabbath, and his disciples picked some heads of wheat, rubbed them in their hands, and ate them. **6:2** But some of the Pharisees said, "Why are you doing what is against the law on the Sabbath?" **6:3** Jesus answered them, "Haven't you read what David did when he and his companions were hungry – **6:4** how he entered the house of God, took and ate the sacred bread, which is not lawful for any to eat but the priests alone, and gave it to his companions?" **6:5** Then he said to them, "The Son of Man is lord of the Sabbath."

Healing a Withered Hand

6:6 On another Sabbath, Jesus entered the synagogue and was teaching. Now a man was there whose right hand was withered. **6:7** The experts in the law and the Pharisees watched Jesus closely to see if he would heal on the Sabbath, so that they could find a reason to accuse him. **6:8** But he knew their thoughts, and said to the man who had the withered hand, "Get up and stand here." So he rose and stood there. **6:9** Then Jesus said to them, "I ask you, is it lawful to do good on the Sabbath or to do evil, to save a life or to destroy it?" **6:10** After looking around at them all, he said

to the man, "Stretch out your hand." The man did so, and his hand was restored. **6:11** But they were filled with mindless rage and began debating with one another what they would do to Jesus.

Choosing the Twelve Apostles

6:12 Now it was during this time that Jesus went out to the mountain to pray, and he spent all night in prayer to God. **6:13** When morning came, he called his disciples and chose twelve of them, whom he also named apostles: **6:14** Simon (whom he named Peter), and his brother Andrew; and James, John, Philip, Bartholomew, **6:15** Matthew, Thomas, James the son of Alphaeus, Simon who was called the Zealot, **6:16** Judas the son of James, and Judas Iscariot, who became a traitor.

The Sermon on the Plain

6:17 Then he came down with them and stood on a level place. And a large number of his disciples had gathered along with a vast multitude from all over Judea, from Jerusalem, and from the seacoast of Tyre and Sidon. They came to hear him and to be healed of their diseases, **6:18** and those who suffered from unclean spirits were cured. **6:19** The whole crowd was trying to touch him, because power was coming out from him and healing them all.

6:20 Then he looked up at his disciples and said:

"Blessed are you who are poor, for the kingdom of God belongs to you.

6:21 "Blessed are you who hunger now, for you will be satisfied.

"Blessed are you who weep now, for you will laugh.

6:22 "Blessed are you when people hate you, and when they exclude you and insult you and reject you as evil on account of the Son of Man! **6:23** Rejoice in that day, and jump for joy, because your reward is great in heaven. For their ancestors did the same things to the prophets.

6:24 "But woe to you who are rich, for you have received your comfort already.

6:25 "Woe to you who are well satisfied with food now, for you will be hungry.

"Woe to you who laugh now, for you will mourn and weep.

6:26 "Woe to you when all people speak well of you, for their ancestors did the same things to the false prophets.

6:27 "But I say to you who are listening: Love your enemies, do good to those who hate you, **6:28** bless those who curse you, pray for those who mistreat you. **6:29** To the person who strikes you on the cheek, offer the other as well, and from the person who takes away your coat, do not withhold your tunic either. **6:30** Give to everyone who asks you, and do not ask for your possessions back from the person who takes them away. **6:31** Treat others in the same way that you would want them to treat you. **6:32** "If you love those who love you, what credit is that to you? For even sinners love those who love them. **6:33** And if you do good to those who do good to you, what credit is that to you? Even sinners do the same. **6:34** And if you lend to those from whom you hope to be repaid, what credit is that to you? Even sinners lend to sinners, so that they may be repaid in full. **6:35** But love your enemies, and do good, and lend, expecting nothing back. Then your reward will be great, and you will be sons of the Most High, because he is kind to ungrateful and evil people. **6:36** Be merciful, just as your Father is merciful.

Do Not Judge Others

6:37 "Do not judge, and you will not be judged; do not condemn, and you will not be condemned; forgive, and you will be forgiven. **6:38** Give, and it will be given to you: A good measure, pressed down, shaken together, running over, will be poured into your lap. For the measure you use will be the measure you receive."

6:39 He also told them a parable: "Someone who is blind cannot lead another who is blind, can he? Won't they both fall into a pit? **6:40** A disciple is not greater than his teacher, but everyone when fully trained will be like his teacher. **6:41** Why do you see the speck in your brother's eye, but fail to see the beam of wood in your own? **6:42** How can you say to your brother, 'Brother, let me remove the speck from your eye,' while you yourself don't see the beam in your own? You hypocrite! First remove the beam from your own eye, and then you can see clearly to remove the speck from your brother's eye.

6:43 "For no good tree bears bad fruit, nor again does a bad tree bear good fruit, **6:44** for each tree is known by its own fruit. For figs are not gathered from thorns, nor are grapes picked from brambles. **6:45** The good person out of the good treasury of his heart produces good, and the evil person out of his evil treasury produces evil, for his mouth speaks from what fills his heart.

6:46 "Why do you call me 'Lord, Lord,' and don't do what I tell you? **6:47** "Everyone who comes to me and listens to my words and puts them into practice – I will show you what he is like: **6:48** He is like a man building a house, who dug down deep, and laid the foundation on bedrock. When a flood came, the river burst against that house but could not shake it, because it had been well built. **6:49** But the person who hears and does not put my words into practice is like a man who built a house on the ground without a foundation. When the river burst against that house, it collapsed immediately, and was utterly destroyed!"

Healing the Centurion's Slave

7:1 After Jesus had finished teaching all this to the people, he entered Capernaum. **7:2** A centurion there had a slave who was highly regarded, but who was sick and at the point of death. **7:3** When the centurion heard about Jesus, he sent some Jewish elders to him, asking him to come and heal his slave. **7:4** When they came to Jesus, they urged him earnestly, "He is worthy to have you do this for him, **7:5** because he loves our nation, and even built our synagogue." **7:6** So Jesus went with them. When he was not far from the house, the centurion sent friends to say to him, "Lord, do not trouble yourself, for I am not worthy to have you come under my roof. **7:7** That is why I did not presume to come to you. Instead, say the word, and my servant must be healed. **7:8** For I too am a man set under authority, with soldiers under me. I say to this one, 'Go,' and he goes, and to another, 'Come,' and he comes, and to my slave, 'Do this,' and he does it." **7:9** When Jesus heard this, he was amazed at him. He turned and said to the crowd that followed him, "I tell you, not even in Israel have I found such faith!" **7:10** So when those who had been sent returned to the house, they found the slave well.

Raising a Widow's Son

7:11 Soon afterward Jesus went to a town called Nain, and his disciples and a large crowd went with him. **7:12** As he approached the town gate, a man who had died was being carried out, the only son of his mother (who was a widow), and a large crowd from the town was with her. **7:13** When the Lord saw her, he had compassion for her and said to her, "Do not weep." **7:14** Then he came up and touched the bier, and those who carried it stood still. He said, "Young man, I say to you, get up!" **7:15** So the dead man sat up and began to speak, and Jesus gave him back to his mother. **7:16** Fear seized them all, and they began to glorify God, saying, "A great prophet has appeared among us!" and "God has come to help his people!" **7:17** This report about Jesus circulated throughout Judea and all the surrounding country.

Jesus and John the Baptist

7:18 John's disciples informed him about all these things. So John called two of his disciples **7:19** and sent them to Jesus to ask, "Are you the one who is to come, or should we look for another?" **7:20** When the men came to Jesus, they said, "John the Baptist has sent us to you to ask, 'Are you the one who is to come, or should we look for another?'" **7:21** At that very time Jesus cured many people of diseases, sicknesses, and evil spirits, and granted sight to many who were blind. **7:22** So he answered them, "Go tell John what you have seen and heard: The blind see, the lame walk, lepers are cleansed, the deaf hear, the dead are raised, the poor have good news proclaimed to them. **7:23** Blessed is anyone who takes no offense at me."

7:24 When John's messengers had gone, Jesus began to speak to the crowds about John: "What did you go out into the wilderness to see? A reed shaken by the wind? **7:25** What did you go out to see? A man dressed in fancy clothes? Look, those who wear fancy clothes and live in luxury are in kings' courts! **7:26** What did you go out to see? A prophet? Yes, I tell you, and more than a prophet. **7:27** This is the one about whom it is written, '*Look, I am sending my messenger ahead of you, who will prepare your way before you.*' **7:28** I tell you, among those born of women no one is greater than John. Yet the one who is least in the kingdom of God is greater than he is." **7:29** (Now all the people who heard this, even the tax collectors, acknowledged God's justice, because they had been baptized with John's baptism. **7:30** However, the Pharisees and the experts in religious law rejected God's purpose for themselves, because they had not been baptized by John.)

7:31 "To what then should I compare the people of this generation, and what are they like? **7:32** They are like children sitting in the marketplace and calling out to one another,

'We played the flute for you, yet you did not dance;
we wailed in mourning, yet you did not weep.'

7:33 For John the Baptist has come eating no bread and drinking no wine, and you say, 'He has a demon!' **7:34** The Son of Man has come eating and drinking, and you say, 'Look at him, a glutton and a drunk, a friend of tax collectors and sinners!' **7:35** But wisdom is vindicated by all her children."

Jesus' Anointing

7:36 Now one of the Pharisees asked Jesus to have dinner with him, so he went into the Pharisee's house and took his place at the table. **7:37** Then when a woman of that town, who was a sinner, learned that Jesus was dining at the Pharisee's house, she brought an alabaster jar of perfumed oil. **7:38** As she stood behind him at his feet, weeping, she began to wet his feet with her tears. She wiped them with her hair, kissed them, and anointed them with the perfumed oil. **7:39** Now when the Pharisee who had invited him saw this, he said to himself, "If this man were a prophet, he would know who and what kind of woman this is who is touching him, that she is a sinner." **7:40** So Jesus answered him, "Simon, I have something to say to you." He replied, "Say it, Teacher." **7:41** "A certain creditor had two debtors; one owed him five hundred silver coins, and the other fifty. **7:42** When they could not pay, he canceled the debts of both. Now which of them will love him more?" **7:43** Simon answered, "I suppose the one who had the bigger debt canceled." Jesus said to him, "You have judged rightly." **7:44** Then, turning toward the woman, he said to Simon, "Do you see this woman? I entered your house. You gave me no water for my feet, but she has wet my feet with her tears and wiped them

with her hair. **7:45** You gave me no kiss of greeting, but from the time I entered she has not stopped kissing my feet. **7:46** You did not anoint my head with oil, but she has anointed my feet with perfumed oil. **7:47** Therefore I tell you, her sins, which were many, are forgiven, thus she loved much; but the one who is forgiven little loves little." **7:48** Then Jesus said to her, "Your sins are forgiven." **7:49** But those who were at the table with him began to say among themselves, "Who is this, who even forgives sins?" **7:50** He said to the woman, "Your faith has saved you; go in peace."

Jesus' Ministry and the Help of Women

8:1 Some time afterward he went on through towns and villages, preaching and proclaiming the good news of the kingdom of God. The twelve were with him, **8:2** and also some women who had been healed of evil spirits and disabilities: Mary (called Magdalene), from whom seven demons had gone out, **8:3** and Joanna the wife of Cuza (Herod's household manager), Susanna, and many others who provided for them out of their own resources.

The Parable of the Sower

8:4 While a large crowd was gathering and people were coming to Jesus from one town after another, he spoke to them in a parable: **8:5** "A sower went out to sow his seed. And as he sowed, some fell along the path and was trampled on, and the wild birds devoured it. **8:6** Other seed fell on rock, and when it came up, it withered because it had no moisture. **8:7** Other seed fell among the thorns, and they grew up with it and choked it. **8:8** But other seed fell on good soil and grew, and it produced a hundred times as much grain." As he said this, he called out, "The one who has ears to hear had better listen!"

8:9 Then his disciples asked him what this parable meant. **8:10** He said, "You have been given the opportunity to know the secrets of the kingdom of God, but for others they are in parables, so that *although they see they may not see, and although they hear they may not understand.*

8:11 "Now the parable means this: The seed is the word of God. **8:12** Those along the path are the ones who have heard; then the devil comes and takes away the word from their hearts, so that they may not believe and be saved. **8:13** Those on the rock are the ones who receive the word with joy when they hear it, but they have no root. They believe for a while, but in a time of testing fall away. **8:14** As for the seed that fell among thorns, these are the ones who hear, but as they go on their way they are choked by the worries and riches and pleasures of life, and their fruit does not mature. **8:15** But as for the seed that landed on good soil, these are the ones who, after hearing the word, cling to it with an honest and good heart, and bear fruit with steadfast endurance.

Showing the Light

8:16 "No one lights a lamp and then covers it with a jar or puts it under a bed, but puts it on a lampstand so that those who come in can see the light. **8:17** For nothing is hidden that will not be revealed, and nothing concealed that will not be made known and brought to light. **8:18** So listen carefully, for whoever has will be given more, but whoever does not have, even what he thinks he has will be taken from him."

Jesus' True Family

8:19 Now Jesus' mother and his brothers came to him, but they could not get near him because of the crowd. **8:20** So he was told, "Your mother and your brothers are standing outside, wanting to see you." **8:21** But he replied to them, "My mother and my brothers are those who hear the word of God and do it."

Stilling of a Storm

8:22 One day Jesus got into a boat with his disciples and said to them, "Let's go across to the other side of the lake." So they set out, **8:23** and as they sailed he fell asleep. Now a violent windstorm came down on the lake, and the boat started filling up with water, and they were in danger. **8:24** They came and woke him, saying, "Master, Master, we are about to die!" So he got up and rebuked the wind and the raging waves; they died down, and it was calm. **8:25** Then he said to them, "Where is your faith?" But they were afraid and amazed, saying to one another, "Who then is this? He commands even the winds and the water, and they obey him!"

Healing of a Demoniac

8:26 So they sailed over to the region of the Gerasenes, which is opposite Galilee. **8:27** As Jesus stepped ashore, a certain man from the town met him who was possessed by demons. For a long time this man had worn no clothes and had not lived in a house, but among the tombs. **8:28** When he saw Jesus, he cried out, fell down before him, and shouted with a loud voice, "Leave me alone, Jesus, Son of the Most High God! I beg you, do not torment me!" **8:29** For Jesus had started commanding the evil spirit to come out of the man. (For it had seized him many times, so he would be bound with chains and shackles and kept under guard. But he would break the restraints and be driven by the demon into deserted places.) **8:30** Jesus then asked him, "What is your name?" He said, "Legion," because many demons had entered him. **8:31** And they began to beg him not to order them to depart into the abyss. **8:32** Now a large herd of pigs was feeding there on the hillside, and the demonic spirits begged Jesus to let them go into them. He gave them permission. **8:33** So the demons came out of the man and went into the pigs, and the herd of pigs rushed down the steep slope into the lake and drowned. **8:34** When the herdsmen saw what had happened, they ran off and spread the news in the town and countryside. **8:35** So the people went out to see what had happened, and they came to Jesus. They found the man from whom the demons had gone out, sitting at Jesus' feet, clothed and in his right mind, and they were afraid. **8:36** Those who had seen it told them how the man who had been demon-possessed had been healed. **8:37** Then all the people of the Gerasenes and the surrounding region asked Jesus to leave them alone, for they were seized with great fear. So he got into the boat and left. **8:38** The man from whom the demons had gone out begged to go with him, but Jesus sent him away, saying, **8:39** "Return to your home, and declare what God has done for you." So he went away, proclaiming throughout the whole town what Jesus had done for him.

Restoration and Healing

8:40 Now when Jesus returned, the crowd welcomed him, because they were all waiting for him. **8:41** Then a man named Jairus, who was a ruler of the synagogue, came up. Falling at Jesus' feet, he pleaded with him to come to his house, **8:42** because he had an only daughter, about twelve years old, and she was dying.

As Jesus was on his way, the crowds pressed around him. **8:43** Now a woman was there who had been suffering from a hemorrhage for twelve years but could not be healed by anyone. **8:44** She came up behind Jesus and touched the edge of his cloak, and at once the bleeding stopped. **8:45** Then Jesus asked, "Who was it who touched me?" When they all denied it, Peter said, "Master, the crowds are surrounding you and pressing against you!" **8:46** But Jesus said, "Someone touched me, for I know that power has gone out from me." **8:47** When the woman saw that she could not escape notice, she came trembling and fell down before him. In the presence of all the people, she explained why she had touched him and how she had been immediately healed. **8:48** Then he said to her, "Daughter, your faith has made you well. Go in peace."

8:49 While he was still speaking, someone from the synagogue ruler's house came and said, "Your daughter is dead; do not trouble the teacher any longer." **8:50** But when Jesus heard this, he told him, "Do not be afraid; just believe, and she will be healed." **8:51** Now when he came to the house, Jesus did not let anyone go in with him except Peter, John, and James, and the child's father and mother. **8:52** Now they were all wailing and mourning for her, but he said, "Stop your weeping; she is not dead but asleep." **8:53** And they began making fun of him, because they knew that she was dead. **8:54** But Jesus gently took her by the hand and said, "Child, get up." **8:55** Her spirit returned, and she got up immediately. Then he told them to give her something to eat. **8:56** Her parents were astonished, but he ordered them to tell no one what had happened.

The Sending of the Twelve Apostles

9:1 After Jesus called the twelve together, he gave them power and authority over all demons and to cure diseases, **9:2** and he sent them out to proclaim the kingdom of God and to heal the sick. **9:3** He said to them, "Take nothing for your journey – no staff, no bag, no bread, no money, and do not take an extra tunic. **9:4** Whatever house you enter, stay there until you leave the area. **9:5** Wherever they do not receive you, as you leave that town, shake the dust off your feet as a testimony against them." **9:6** Then they departed and went throughout the villages, proclaiming the good news and healing people everywhere.

Herod's Confusion about Jesus

9:7 Now Herod the tetrarch heard about everything that was happening, and he was thoroughly perplexed, because some people were saying that John had been raised from the dead, **9:8** while others were saying that Elijah had appeared, and still others that one of the prophets of long ago had risen. **9:9** Herod said, "I had John beheaded, but who is this about whom I hear such things?" So Herod wanted to learn about Jesus.

The Feeding of the Five Thousand

9:10 When the apostles returned, they told Jesus everything they had done. Then he took them with him and they withdrew privately to a town called Bethsaida. **9:11** But when the crowds found out, they followed him. He welcomed them, spoke to them about the kingdom of God, and cured those who needed healing. **9:12** Now the day began to draw to a close, so the twelve came and said to Jesus, "Send the crowd away, so they can go into the surrounding villages and countryside and find lodging and food, because we are in an isolated place." **9:13** But he said to them, "You give them something to eat." They replied, "We have no more than five loaves and two fish – unless we go and buy food for all these people." **9:14** (Now about five thousand men were there.) Then he said to his disciples, "Have them sit down in groups of about fifty each." **9:15** So they did as Jesus directed, and the people all sat down. **9:16** Then he took the five loaves and the two fish, and looking up to heaven he gave thanks and broke them. He gave them to the disciples to set before the crowd. **9:17** They all ate and were satisfied, and what was left over was picked up – twelve baskets of broken pieces.

Peter's Confession

9:18 Once when Jesus was praying by himself, and his disciples were nearby, he asked them, "Who do the crowds say that I am?" **9:19** They answered, "John the Baptist; others say Elijah; and still others that one of

the prophets of long ago has risen." **9:20** Then he said to them, "But who do you say that I am?" Peter answered, "The Christ of God." **9:21** But he forcefully commanded them not to tell this to anyone, **9:22** saying, "The Son of Man must suffer many things and be rejected by the elders, chief priests, and experts in the law, and be killed, and on the third day be raised."

A Call to Discipleship

9:23 Then he said to them all, "If anyone wants to become my follower, he must deny himself, take up his cross daily, and follow me. **9:24** For whoever wants to save his life will lose it, but whoever loses his life for my sake will save it. **9:25** For what does it benefit a person if he gains the whole world but loses or forfeits himself? **9:26** For whoever is ashamed of me and my words, the Son of Man will be ashamed of that person when he comes in his glory and in the glory of the Father and of the holy angels. **9:27** But I tell you most certainly, there are some standing here who will not experience death before they see the kingdom of God."

The Transfiguration

9:28 Now about eight days after these sayings, Jesus took with him Peter, John, and James, and went up the mountain to pray. **9:29** As he was praying, the appearance of his face was transformed, and his clothes became very bright, a brilliant white. **9:30** Then two men, Moses and Elijah, began talking with him. **9:31** They appeared in glorious splendor and spoke about his departure that he was about to carry out at Jerusalem. **9:32** Now Peter and those with him were quite sleepy, but as they became fully awake, they saw his glory and the two men standing with him. **9:33** Then as the men were starting to leave, Peter said to Jesus, "Master, it is good for us to be here. Let us make three shelters, one for you and one for Moses and one for Elijah" – not knowing what he was saying. **9:34** As he was saying this, a cloud came and overshadowed them, and they were afraid as they entered the cloud. **9:35** Then a voice came from the cloud, saying, "This is my Son, my Chosen One. Listen to him!" **9:36** After the voice had spoken, Jesus was found alone. So they kept silent and told no one at that time anything of what they had seen.

Healing a Boy with an Unclean Spirit

9:37 Now on the next day, when they had come down from the mountain, a large crowd met him. **9:38** Then a man from the crowd cried out, "Teacher, I beg you to look at my son – he is my only child! **9:39** A spirit seizes him, and he suddenly screams; it throws him into convulsions and causes him to foam at the mouth. It hardly ever leaves him alone, torturing him severely. **9:40** I begged your disciples to cast it out, but they could not do so." **9:41** Jesus answered, "You unbelieving and perverse generation! How much longer must I be with you and endure you? Bring your son here." **9:42** As the boy was approaching, the demon threw him to the ground and shook him with convulsions. But Jesus rebuked the unclean spirit, healed the boy, and gave him back to his father. **9:43** Then they were all astonished at the mighty power of God.

Another Prediction of Jesus' Suffering

But while the entire crowd was amazed at everything Jesus was doing, he said to his disciples, **9:44** "Take these words to heart, for the Son of Man is going to be betrayed into the hands of men." **9:45** But they did not understand this statement; its meaning had been concealed from them, so that they could not grasp it. Yet they were afraid to ask him about this statement.

Concerning the Greatest

9:46 Now an argument started among the disciples as to which of them might be the greatest. **9:47** But when Jesus discerned their innermost thoughts, he took a child, had him stand by his side, **9:48** and said to them, "Whoever welcomes this child in my name welcomes me, and whoever welcomes me welcomes the one who sent me, for the one who is least among you all is the one who is great."

On the Right Side

9:49 John answered, "Master, we saw someone casting out demons in your name, and we tried to stop him because he is not a disciple along with us." **9:50** But Jesus said to him, "Do not stop him, for whoever is not against you is for you."

Rejection in Samaria

9:51 Now when the days drew near for him to be taken up, Jesus set out resolutely to go to Jerusalem. **9:52** He sent messengers on ahead of him. As they went along, they entered a Samaritan village to make things ready in advance for him, **9:53** but the villagers refused to welcome him, because he was determined to go to Jerusalem. **9:54** Now when his disciples James and John saw this, they said, "Lord, do you want us *to call fire to come down from heaven and consume them*?" **9:55** But Jesus turned and rebuked them, **9:56** and they went on to another village.

Challenging Professed Followers

9:57 As they were walking along the road, someone said to him, "I will follow you wherever you go." **9:58** Jesus said to him, "Foxes have dens and the birds in the sky have nests, but the Son of Man has no place to lay his head." **9:59** Jesus said to another, "Follow me." But he replied, "Lord, first let me go and bury my father." **9:60** But Jesus said to him, "Let the dead bury their own dead, but as for you, go and proclaim the kingdom of God." **9:61** Yet another said, "I will follow you, Lord, but first let me say goodbye to my family." **9:62** Jesus said to him, "No one who puts his hand to the plow and looks back is fit for the kingdom of God."

The Mission of the Seventy-Two

10:1 After this the Lord appointed seventy-two others and sent them on ahead of him two by two into every town and place where he himself was about to go. **10:2** He said to them, "The harvest is plentiful, but the workers are few. Therefore ask the Lord of the harvest to send out workers into his harvest. **10:3** Go! I am sending you out like lambs surrounded by wolves. **10:4** Do not carry a money bag, a traveler's bag, or sandals, and greet no one on the road. **10:5** Whenever you enter a house, first say, 'May peace be on this house!' **10:6** And if a peace-loving person is there, your peace will remain on him, but if not, it will return to you. **10:7** Stay in that same house, eating and drinking what they give you, for the worker deserves his pay. Do not move around from house to house. **10:8** Whenever you enter a town and the people welcome you, eat what is set before you. **10:9** Heal the sick in that town and say to them, 'The kingdom of God has come upon you!' **10:10** But whenever you enter a town and the people do not welcome you, go into its streets and say, **10:11** 'Even the dust of your town that clings to our feet we wipe off against you. Nevertheless know this: The kingdom of God has come.' **10:12** I tell you, it will be more bearable on that day for Sodom than for that town!

10:13 "Woe to you, Chorazin! Woe to you, Bethsaida! For if the miracles done in you had been done in Tyre and Sidon, they would have repented long ago, sitting in sackcloth and ashes. **10:14** But it will be more bearable for Tyre and Sidon in the judgment than for you! **10:15** And you, Capernaum, will you be exalted to heaven? No, you will be thrown down to Hades!

10:16 "The one who listens to you listens to me, and the one who rejects you rejects me, and the one who rejects me rejects the one who sent me."

10:17 Then the seventy-two returned with joy, saying, "Lord, even the demons submit to us in your name!" **10:18** So he said to them, "I saw Satan fall like lightning from heaven. **10:19** Look, I have given you authority to tread on snakes and scorpions and on the full force of the enemy, and nothing will hurt you. **10:20** Nevertheless, do not rejoice that the spirits submit to you, but rejoice that your names stand written in heaven."

10:21 On that same occasion Jesus rejoiced in the Holy Spirit and said, "I praise you, Father, Lord of heaven and earth, because you have hidden these things from the wise and intelligent, and revealed them to little children. Yes, Father, for this was your gracious will. **10:22** All things have been given to me by my Father. No one knows who the Son is except the Father, or who the Father is except the Son and anyone to whom the Son decides to reveal him."

10:23 Then Jesus turned to his disciples and said privately, "Blessed are the eyes that see what you see! **10:24** For I tell you that many prophets and kings longed to see what you see but did not see it, and to hear what you hear but did not hear it."

The Parable of the Good Samaritan

10:25 Now an expert in religious law stood up to test Jesus, saying, "Teacher, what must I do to inherit eternal life?" **10:26** He said to him, "What is written in the law? How do you understand it?" **10:27** The expert answered, "*Love the Lord your God with all your heart, with all your soul, with all your strength, and with all your mind*, and *love your neighbor as yourself*." **10:28** Jesus said to him, "You have answered correctly; do this, and you will live."

10:29 But the expert, wanting to justify himself, said to Jesus, "And who is my neighbor?" **10:30** Jesus replied, "A man was going down from Jerusalem to Jericho, and fell into the hands of robbers, who stripped him, beat him up, and went off, leaving him half dead. **10:31** Now by chance a priest was going down that road, but when he saw the injured man he passed by on the other side. **10:32** So too a Levite, when he came up to the place and saw him, passed by on the other side. **10:33** But a Samaritan who was traveling came to where the injured man was, and when he saw him, he felt compassion for him. **10:34** He went up to him and bandaged his wounds, pouring oil and wine on them. Then he put him on his own animal, brought him to an inn, and took care of him. **10:35** The next day he took out two silver coins and gave them to the innkeeper, saying, 'Take care of him, and whatever else you spend, I will repay you when I come back this way.' **10:36** Which of these three do you think became a neighbor to the man who fell into the hands of the robbers?" **10:37** The expert in religious law said, "The one who showed mercy to him." So Jesus said to him, "Go and do the same."

Jesus and Martha

10:38 Now as they went on their way, Jesus entered a certain village where a woman named Martha welcomed him as a guest. **10:39** She had a sister named Mary, who sat at the Lord's feet and listened to what he said. **10:40** But Martha was distracted with all the preparations she had to make, so she came up to him and said, "Lord, don't you care that my sister has left me to do all the work alone? Tell her to help me." **10:41** But the Lord answered her, "Martha, Martha, you are worried and troubled about many things, **10:42** but one thing is needed. Mary has chosen the best part; it will not be taken away from her."

Instructions on Prayer

11:1 Now Jesus was praying in a certain place. When he stopped, one of his disciples said to him, "Lord, teach us to pray, just as John taught his disciples." **11:2** So he said to them, "When you pray, say:
Father, may your name be honored;
may your kingdom come.
11:3 Give us each day our daily bread,
11:4 and forgive us our sins,
for we also forgive everyone who sins against us.
And do not lead us into temptation."

11:5 Then he said to them, "Suppose one of you has a friend, and you go to him at midnight and say to him, 'Friend, lend me three loaves of bread, **11:6** because a friend of mine has stopped here while on a journey, and I have nothing to set before him.' **11:7** Then he will reply from inside, 'Do not bother me. The door is already shut, and my children and I are in bed. I cannot get up and give you anything.' **11:8** I tell you, even though the man inside will not get up and give him anything because he is his friend, yet because of the first man's sheer persistence he will get up and give him whatever he needs.

11:9 "So I tell you: Ask, and it will be given to you; seek, and you will find; knock, and the door will be opened for you. **11:10** For everyone who asks receives, and the one who seeks finds, and to the one who knocks, the door will be opened. **11:11** What father among you, if your son asks for a fish, will give him a snake instead of a fish? **11:12** Or if he asks for an egg, will give him a scorpion? **11:13** If you then, although you are evil, know how to give good gifts to your children, how much more will the heavenly Father give the Holy Spirit to those who ask him!"

Jesus and Beelzebul

11:14 Now he was casting out a demon that was mute. When the demon had gone out, the man who had been mute began to speak, and the crowds were amazed. **11:15** But some of them said, "By the power of Beelzebul, the ruler of demons, he casts out demons." **11:16** Others, to test him, began asking for a sign from heaven. **11:17** But Jesus, realizing their thoughts, said to them, "Every kingdom divided against itself is destroyed, and a divided household falls. **11:18** So if Satan too is divided against himself, how will his kingdom stand? I ask you this because you claim that I cast out demons by Beelzebul. **11:19** Now if I cast out demons by Beelzebul, by whom do your sons cast them out? Therefore they will be your judges. **11:20** But if I cast out demons by the finger of God, then the kingdom of God has already overtaken you. **11:21** When a strong man, fully armed, guards his own palace, his possessions are safe. **11:22** But when a stronger man attacks and conquers him, he takes away the first man's armor on which the man relied and divides up his plunder. **11:23** Whoever is not with me is against me, and whoever does not gather with me scatters.

Response to Jesus' Work

11:24 "When an unclean spirit goes out of a person, it passes through waterless places looking for rest but not finding any. Then it says, 'I will return to the home I left.' **11:25** When it returns, it finds the house swept clean and put in order. **11:26** Then it goes and brings seven other spirits more evil than itself, and they go in and live there, so the last state of that person is worse than the first."

11:27 As he said these things, a woman in the crowd spoke out to him, "Blessed is the womb that bore you and the breasts at which you nursed!" **11:28** But he replied, "Blessed rather are those who hear the word of God and obey it!"

The Sign of Jonah

11:29 As the crowds were increasing, Jesus began to say, "This generation is a wicked generation; it looks for a sign, but no sign will be given to it except the sign of Jonah. **11:30** For just as Jonah became a sign to the people of Nineveh, so the Son of Man will be a sign to this generation. **11:31** The queen of the South will rise up at the judgment with the people of this generation and condemn them, because she came from the ends of the earth to hear the wisdom of Solomon – and now, something greater than Solomon is here! **11:32** The people of Nineveh will stand up at the judgment with this generation and condemn it, because they repented when Jonah preached to them – and now, something greater than Jonah is here!

Internal Light

11:33 "No one after lighting a lamp puts it in a hidden place or under a basket, but on a lampstand, so that those who come in can see the light. **11:34** Your eye is the lamp of your body. When your eye is healthy, your whole body is full of light, but when it is diseased, your body is full of darkness. **11:35** Therefore see to it that the light in you is not darkness. **11:36** If then your whole body is full of light, with no part in the dark, it will be as full of light as when the light of a lamp shines on you."

Rebuking the Pharisees and Experts in the Law

11:37 As he spoke, a Pharisee invited Jesus to have a meal with him, so he went in and took his place at the table. **11:38** The Pharisee was astonished when he saw that Jesus did not first wash his hands before the meal. **11:39** But the Lord said to him, "Now you Pharisees clean the outside of the cup and the plate, but inside you are full of greed and wickedness. **11:40** You fools! Didn't the one who made the outside make the inside as well? **11:41** But give from your heart to those in need, and then everything will be clean for you.

11:42 "But woe to you Pharisees! You give a tenth of your mint, rue, and every herb, yet you neglect justice and love for God! But you should have done these things without neglecting the others. **11:43** Woe to you Pharisees! You love the best seats in the synagogues and elaborate greetings in the marketplaces! **11:44** Woe to you! You are like unmarked graves, and people walk over them without realizing it!"

11:45 One of the experts in religious law answered him, "Teacher, when you say these things you insult us too." **11:46** But Jesus replied, "Woe to you experts in religious law as well! You load people down with burdens difficult to bear, yet you yourselves refuse to touch the burdens with even one of your fingers! **11:47** Woe to you! You build the tombs of the prophets whom your ancestors killed. **11:48** So you testify that you approve of the deeds of your ancestors, because they killed the prophets and you build their tombs! **11:49** For this reason also the wisdom of God said, 'I will send them prophets and apostles, some of whom they will kill and persecute,' **11:50** so that this generation may be held accountable for the blood of all the prophets that has been shed since the beginning of the world, **11:51** from the blood of Abel to the blood of Zechariah, who was killed between the altar and the sanctuary. Yes, I tell you, it will be charged against this generation. **11:52** Woe to you experts in religious law! You have taken away the key to knowledge! You did not go in yourselves, and you hindered those who were going in."

11:53 When he went out from there, the experts in the law and the Pharisees began to oppose him bitterly, and to ask him hostile questions about many things, **11:54** plotting against him, to catch him in something he might say.

Fear God, Not People

12:1 Meanwhile, when many thousands of the crowd had gathered so that they were trampling on one another, Jesus began to speak first to his disciples, "Be on your guard against the yeast of the Pharisees, which is hypocrisy. **12:2** Nothing is hidden that will not be revealed, and nothing is secret that will not be made known. **12:3** So then whatever you have said in the dark will be heard in the light, and what you have whispered in private rooms will be proclaimed from the housetops.

12:4 "I tell you, my friends, do not be afraid of those who kill the body, and after that have nothing more they can do. **12:5** But I will warn you whom you should fear: Fear the one who, after the killing, has authority to throw you into hell. Yes, I tell you, fear him! **12:6** Aren't five sparrows sold for two pennies? Yet not one of them is forgotten before God. **12:7** In fact, even the hairs on your head are all numbered. Do not be afraid; you are more valuable than many sparrows.

12:8 "I tell you, whoever acknowledges me before men, the Son of Man will also acknowledge before God's angels. **12:9** But the one who denies me before men will be denied before God's angels. **12:10** And everyone who speaks a word against the Son of Man will be forgiven, but the person who blasphemes against the Holy Spirit will not be forgiven. **12:11** But when they bring you before the synagogues, the rulers, and the authorities, do not worry about how you should make your defense or what you should say, **12:12** for the Holy Spirit will teach you at that moment what you must say."

The Parable of the Rich Landowner

12:13 Then someone from the crowd said to him, "Teacher, tell my brother to divide the inheritance with me." **12:14** But Jesus said to him, "Man, who made me a judge or arbitrator between you two?" **12:15** Then he said to them, "Watch out and guard yourself from all types of greed, because one's life does not consist in the abundance of his possessions." **12:16** He then told them a parable: "The land of a certain rich man produced an abundant crop, **12:17** so he thought to himself, 'What should I do, for I have nowhere to store my crops?' **12:18** Then he said, 'I will do this: I will tear down my barns and build bigger ones, and there I will store all my grain and my goods. **12:19** And I will say to myself, "You have plenty of goods stored up for many years; relax, eat, drink, celebrate!"' **12:20** But God said to him, 'You fool! This very night your life will be demanded back from you, but who will get what you have prepared for yourself?' **12:21** So it is with the one who stores up riches for himself, but is not rich toward God."

Exhortation Not to Worry

12:22 Then Jesus said to his disciples, "Therefore I tell you, do not worry about your life, what you will eat, or about your body, what you will wear. **12:23** For there is more to life than food, and more to the body than clothing. **12:24** Consider the ravens: They do not sow or reap, they have no storeroom or barn, yet God feeds them. How much more valuable are you than the birds! **12:25** And which of you by worrying can add an hour to his life? **12:26** So if you cannot do such a very little thing as this, why do you worry about the rest? **12:27** Consider how the flowers grow; they do not work or spin. Yet I tell you, not even Solomon in all his glory was clothed like one of these! **12:28** And if this is how God clothes the wild grass, which is here today and tomorrow is tossed into the fire to heat the oven, how much more will he clothe you, you people of little faith! **12:29** So do not be overly concerned about what you will eat and what you will drink, and do not worry about such things. **12:30** For all the nations of the

world pursue these things, and your Father knows that you need them. **12:31** Instead, pursue his kingdom, and these things will be given to you as well.

12:32 "Do not be afraid, little flock, for your Father is well pleased to give you the kingdom. **12:33** Sell your possessions and give to the poor. Provide yourselves purses that do not wear out – a treasure in heaven that never decreases, where no thief approaches and no moth destroys. **12:34** For where your treasure is, there your heart will be also.

Call to Faithful Stewardship

12:35 "Get dressed for service and keep your lamps burning; **12:36** be like people waiting for their master to come back from the wedding celebration, so that when he comes and knocks they can immediately open the door for him. **12:37** Blessed are those slaves whom their master finds alert when he returns! I tell you the truth, he will dress himself to serve, have them take their place at the table, and will come and wait on them! **12:38** Even if he comes in the second or third watch of the night and finds them alert, blessed are those slaves! **12:39** But understand this: If the owner of the house had known at what hour the thief was coming, he would not have let his house be broken into. **12:40** You also must be ready, because the Son of Man will come at an hour when you do not expect him."

12:41 Then Peter said, "Lord, are you telling this parable for us or for everyone?" **12:42** The Lord replied, "Who then is the faithful and wise manager, whom the master puts in charge of his household servants, to give them their allowance of food at the proper time? **12:43** Blessed is that slave whom his master finds at work when he returns. **12:44** I tell you the truth, the master will put him in charge of all his possessions. **12:45** But if that slave should say to himself, 'My master is delayed in returning,' and he begins to beat the other slaves, both men and women, and to eat, drink, and get drunk, **12:46** then the master of that slave will come on a day when he does not expect him and at an hour he does not foresee, and will cut him in two, and assign him a place with the unfaithful. **12:47** That servant who knew his master's will but did not get ready or do what his master asked will receive a severe beating. **12:48** But the one who did not know his master's will and did things worthy of punishment will receive a light beating. From everyone who has been given much, much will be required, and from the one who has been entrusted with much, even more will be asked.

Not Peace, but Division

12:49 "I have come to bring fire on the earth – and how I wish it were already kindled! **12:50** I have a baptism to undergo, and how distressed I am until it is finished! **12:51** Do you think I have come to bring peace on earth? No, I tell you, but rather division! **12:52** For from now on there will be five in one household divided, three against two and two against three. **12:53** They will be divided, father against son and son against father, mother against daughter and daughter against mother, mother-in-law against her daughter-in-law and daughter-in-law against mother-in-law."

Reading the Signs

12:54 Jesus also said to the crowds, "When you see a cloud rising in the west, you say at once, 'A rainstorm is coming,' and it does. **12:55** And when you see the south wind blowing, you say, 'There will be scorching heat,' and there is. **12:56** You hypocrites! You know how to interpret the appearance of the earth and the sky, but how can you not know how to interpret the present time?

Clear the Debts

12:57 "And why don't you judge for yourselves what is right? **12:58** As you are going with your accuser before the magistrate, make an effort to settle with him on the way, so that he will not drag you before the judge, and the judge hand you over to the officer, and the officer throw you into prison. **12:59** I tell you, you will never get out of there until you have paid the very last cent!"

A Call to Repent

13:1 Now there were some present on that occasion who told him about the Galileans whose blood Pilate had mixed with their sacrifices. **13:2** He answered them, "Do you think these Galileans were worse sinners than all the other Galileans, because they suffered these things? **13:3** No, I tell you! But unless you repent, you will all perish as well! **13:4** Or those eighteen who were killed when the tower in Siloam fell on them, do you think they were worse offenders than all the others who live in Jerusalem? **13:5** No, I tell you! But unless you repent you will all perish as well!"

Warning to Israel to Bear Fruit

13:6 Then Jesus told this parable: "A man had a fig tree planted in his vineyard, and he came looking for fruit on it and found none. **13:7** So he said to the worker who tended the vineyard, 'For three years now, I have come looking for fruit on this fig tree, and each time I inspect it I find none. Cut it down! Why should it continue to deplete the soil?' **13:8** But the worker answered him, 'Sir, leave it alone this year too, until I dig around it and put fertilizer on it. **13:9** Then if it bears fruit next year, very well, but if not, you can cut it down.'"

Healing on the Sabbath

13:10 Now he was teaching in one of the synagogues on the Sabbath, **13:11** and a woman was there who had been disabled by a spirit for eighteen years. She was bent over and could not straighten herself up completely. **13:12** When Jesus saw her, he called her to him and said, "Woman, you are freed from your infirmity." **13:13** Then he placed his hands on her, and immediately she straightened up and praised God. **13:14** But the president of the synagogue, indignant because Jesus had healed on the Sabbath, said to the crowd, "There are six days on which work should be done! So come and be healed on those days, and not on the Sabbath day." **13:15** Then the Lord answered him, "You hypocrites! Does not each of you on the Sabbath untie his ox or his donkey from its stall, and lead it to water? **13:16** Then shouldn't this woman, a daughter of Abraham whom Satan bound for eighteen long years, be released from this imprisonment on the Sabbath day?" **13:17** When he said this all his adversaries were humiliated, but the entire crowd was rejoicing at all the wonderful things he was doing.

On the Kingdom of God

13:18 Thus Jesus asked, "What is the kingdom of God like? To what should I compare it? **13:19** It is like a mustard seed that a man took and sowed in his garden. It grew and became a tree, and the wild birds nested in its branches."

13:20 Again he said, "To what should I compare the kingdom of God? **13:21** It is like yeast that a woman took and mixed with three measures of flour until all the dough had risen."

The Narrow Door

13:22 Then Jesus traveled throughout towns and villages, teaching and making his way toward Jerusalem. **13:23** Someone asked him, "Lord, will only a few be saved?" So he said to them, **13:24** "Exert every effort to enter through the narrow door, because many, I tell you, will try to enter and will not be able to. **13:25** Once the head of the house gets up and shuts the door, then you will stand outside and start to knock on the door and beg him, 'Lord, let us in!' But he will answer you, 'I don't know where you come from.' **13:26** Then you will begin to say, 'We ate and drank in your presence, and you taught in our streets.' **13:27** But he will reply, 'I don't know where you come from! Go away from me, all you evildoers!' **13:28** There will be weeping and gnashing of teeth when you see Abraham, Isaac, Jacob, and all the prophets in the kingdom of God but you yourselves thrown out. **13:29** Then people will come from east and west, and from north and south, and take their places at the banquet table in the kingdom of God. **13:30** But indeed, some are last who will be first, and some are first who will be last."

Going to Jerusalem

13:31 At that time, some Pharisees came up and said to Jesus, "Get away from here, because Herod wants to kill you." **13:32** But he said to them, "Go and tell that fox, 'Look, I am casting out demons and performing healings today and tomorrow, and on the third day I will complete my work. **13:33** Nevertheless I must go on my way today and tomorrow and the next day, because it is impossible that a prophet should be killed outside Jerusalem.' **13:34** O Jerusalem, Jerusalem, you who kill the prophets and stone those who are sent to you! How often I have longed to gather your children together as a hen gathers her chicks under her wings, but you would have none of it! **13:35** Look, your house is forsaken! And I tell you, you will not see me until you say, '*Blessed is the one who comes in the name of the Lord!*'"

Healing Again on the Sabbath

14:1 Now one Sabbath when Jesus went to dine at the house of a leader of the Pharisees, they were watching him closely. **14:2** There right in front of him was a man suffering from dropsy. **14:3** So Jesus asked the experts in religious law and the Pharisees, "Is it lawful to heal on the Sabbath or not?" **14:4** But they remained silent. So Jesus took hold of the man, healed him, and sent him away. **14:5** Then he said to them, "Which of you, if you have a son or an ox that has fallen into a well on a Sabbath day, will not immediately pull him out?" **14:6** But they could not reply to this.

On Seeking Seats of Honor

14:7 Then when Jesus noticed how the guests chose the places of honor, he told them a parable. He said to them, **14:8** "When you are invited by someone to a wedding feast, do not take the place of honor, because a person more distinguished than you may have been invited by your host. **14:9** So the host who invited both of you will come and say to you, 'Give this man your place.' Then, ashamed, you will begin to move to the least important place. **14:10** But when you are invited, go and take the least important place, so that when your host approaches he will say to you, 'Friend, move up here to a better place.' Then you will be honored in the presence of all who share the meal with you. **14:11** For everyone who exalts himself will be humbled, but the one who humbles himself will be exalted."

14:12 He said also to the man who had invited him, "When you host a dinner or a banquet, don't invite your friends or your brothers or your relatives or rich neighbors so you can be invited by them in return and get repaid. **14:13** But when you host an elaborate meal, invite the poor, the crippled, the lame, and the blind. **14:14** Then you will be blessed, because they cannot repay you, for you will be repaid at the resurrection of the righteous."

The Parable of the Great Banquet

14:15 When one of those at the meal with Jesus heard this, he said to him, "Blessed is everyone who will feast in the kingdom of God!" **14:16** But Jesus said to him, "A man once gave a great banquet and invited many guests. **14:17** At the time for the banquet he sent his slave to tell those who had been invited, 'Come, because everything is now ready.' **14:18** But one after another they all began to make excuses. The first said to him, 'I have bought a field, and I must go out and see it. Please excuse me.' **14:19** Another said, 'I have bought five yoke of oxen, and I am going out to examine them. Please excuse me.' **14:20** Another said, 'I just got married, and I cannot come.' **14:21** So the slave came back and reported this to his master. Then the master of the household was furious and said to his slave, 'Go out quickly to the streets and alleys of the city, and bring in the poor, the crippled, the blind, and the lame.' **14:22** Then the slave said, 'Sir, what you instructed has been done, and there is still room.' **14:23** So the master said to his slave, 'Go out to the highways and country roads and urge people to come in, so that my house will be filled. **14:24** For I tell you, not one of those individuals who were invited will taste my banquet!'"

Counting the Cost

14:25 Now large crowds were accompanying Jesus, and turning to them he said, **14:26** "If anyone comes to me and does not hate his own father and mother, and wife and children, and brothers and sisters, and even his own life, he cannot be my disciple. **14:27** Whoever does not carry his own cross and follow me cannot be my disciple. **14:28** For which of you, wanting to build a tower, doesn't sit down first and compute the cost to see if he has enough money to complete it? **14:29** Otherwise, when he has laid a foundation and is not able to finish the tower, all who see it will begin to make fun of him. **14:30** They will say, 'This man began to build and was not able to finish!' **14:31** Or what king, going out to confront another king in battle, will not sit down first and determine whether he is able with ten thousand to oppose the one coming against him with twenty thousand? **14:32** If he cannot succeed, he will send a representative while the other is still a long way off and ask for terms of peace. **14:33** In the same way therefore not one of you can be my disciple if he does not renounce all his own possessions.

14:34 "Salt is good, but if salt loses its flavor, how can its flavor be restored? **14:35** It is of no value for the soil or for the manure pile; it is to be thrown out. The one who has ears to hear had better listen!"

The Parable of the Lost Sheep and Coin

15:1 Now all the tax collectors and sinners were coming to hear him. **15:2** But the Pharisees and the experts in the law were complaining, "This man welcomes sinners and eats with them."

15:3 So Jesus told them this parable: **15:4** "Which one of you, if he has a hundred sheep and loses one of them, would not leave the ninety-nine in the open pasture and go look for the one that is lost until he finds it? **15:5** Then when he has found it, he places it on his shoulders, rejoicing. **15:6** Returning home, he calls together his friends and neighbors, telling them, 'Rejoice with me, because I have found my sheep that was lost.' **15:7** I tell you, in the same way there will be more joy in heaven over one sinner who repents than over ninety-nine righteous people who have no need to repent.

15:8 "Or what woman, if she has ten silver coins and loses one of them, does not light a lamp, sweep the house, and search thoroughly until she finds it? **15:9** Then when she has found it, she calls together her friends and neighbors, saying, 'Rejoice with me, for I have found the coin that I had lost.' **15:10** In the same way, I tell you, there is joy in the presence of God's angels over one sinner who repents."

The Parable of the Compassionate Father

15:11 Then Jesus said, "A man had two sons. **15:12** The younger of them said to his father, 'Father, give me the share of the estate that will belong to me.' So he divided his assets between them. **15:13** After a few days, the younger son gathered together all he had and left on a journey to a distant country, and there he squandered his wealth with a wild lifestyle. **15:14** Then after he had spent everything, a severe famine took place in that country, and he began to be in need. **15:15** So he went and worked for one of the citizens of that country, who sent him to his fields to feed pigs. **15:16** He was longing to eat the carob pods the pigs were eating, but no one gave him anything. **15:17** But when he came to his senses he said, 'How many of my father's hired workers have food enough to spare, but here I am dying from hunger! **15:18** I will get up and go to my father and say to him, "Father, I have sinned against heaven and against you. **15:19** I am no longer worthy to be called your son; treat me like one of your hired workers."' **15:20** So he got up and went to his father. But while he was still a long way from home his father saw him, and his heart went out to him; he ran and hugged his son and kissed him. **15:21** Then his son said to him, 'Father, I have sinned against heaven and against you; I am no longer worthy to be called your son.' **15:22** But the father said to his slaves, 'Hurry! Bring the best robe, and put it on him! Put a ring on his finger and sandals on his feet! **15:23** Bring the fattened calf and kill it!

Let us eat and celebrate, **15:24** because this son of mine was dead, and is alive again – he was lost and is found!' So they began to celebrate. **15:25** "Now his older son was in the field. As he came and approached the house, he heard music and dancing. **15:26** So he called one of the slaves and asked what was happening. **15:27** The slave replied, 'Your brother has returned, and your father has killed the fattened calf because he got his son back safe and sound.' **15:28** But the older son became angry and refused to go in. His father came out and appealed to him, **15:29** but he answered his father, 'Look! These many years I have worked like a slave for you, and I never disobeyed your commands. Yet you never gave me even a goat so that I could celebrate with my friends! **15:30** But when this son of yours came back, who has devoured your assets with prostitutes, you killed the fattened calf for him!' **15:31** Then the father said to him, 'Son, you are always with me, and everything that belongs to me is yours. **15:32** It was appropriate to celebrate and be glad, for your brother was dead, and is alive; he was lost and is found.'"

The Parable of the Clever Steward

16:1 Jesus also said to the disciples, "There was a rich man who was informed of accusations that his manager was wasting his assets. **16:2** So he called the manager in and said to him, 'What is this I hear about you? Turn in the account of your administration, because you can no longer be my manager.' **16:3** Then the manager said to himself, 'What should I do, since my master is taking my position away from me? I'm not strong enough to dig, and I'm too ashamed to beg. **16:4** I know what to do so that when I am put out of management, people will welcome me into their homes.' **16:5** So he contacted his master's debtors one by one. He asked the first, 'How much do you owe my master?' **16:6** The man replied, 'A hundred measures of olive oil.' The manager said to him, 'Take your bill, sit down quickly, and write fifty.' **16:7** Then he said to another, 'And how much do you owe?' The second man replied, 'A hundred measures of wheat.' The manager said to him, 'Take your bill, and write eighty.' **16:8** The master commended the dishonest manager because he acted shrewdly. For the people of this world are more shrewd in dealing with their contemporaries than the people of light. **16:9** And I tell you, make friends for yourselves by how you use worldly wealth, so that when it runs out you will be welcomed into the eternal homes.

16:10 "The one who is faithful in a very little is also faithful in much, and the one who is dishonest in a very little is also dishonest in much. **16:11** If then you haven't been trustworthy in handling worldly wealth, who will entrust you with the true riches? **16:12** And if you haven't been trustworthy with someone else's property, who will give you your own? **16:13** No servant can serve two masters, for either he will hate the one and love the other, or he will be devoted to the one and despise the other. You cannot serve God and money."

More Warnings about the Pharisees

16:14 The Pharisees (who loved money) heard all this and ridiculed him. **16:15** But Jesus said to them, "You are the ones who justify yourselves in men's eyes, but God knows your hearts. For what is highly prized among men is utterly detestable in God's sight.

16:16 "The law and the prophets were in force until John; since then, the good news of the kingdom of God has been proclaimed, and everyone is urged to enter it. **16:17** But it is easier for heaven and earth to pass away than for one tiny stroke of a letter in the law to become void.

16:18 "Everyone who divorces his wife and marries someone else commits adultery, and the one who marries a woman divorced from her husband commits adultery.

The Rich Man and Lazarus

16:19 "There was a rich man who dressed in purple and fine linen and who feasted sumptuously every day. **16:20** But at his gate lay a poor man named Lazarus whose body was covered with sores, **16:21** who longed to eat what fell from the rich man's table. In addition, the dogs came and licked his sores.

16:22 "Now the poor man died and was carried by the angels to Abraham's side. The rich man also died and was buried. **16:23** And in hell, as he was in torment, he looked up and saw Abraham far off with Lazarus at his side. **16:24** So he called out, 'Father Abraham, have mercy on me, and send Lazarus to dip the tip of his finger in water and cool my tongue, because I am in anguish in this fire.' **16:25** But Abraham said, 'Child, remember that in your lifetime you received your good things and Lazarus likewise bad things, but now he is comforted here and you are in anguish. **16:26** Besides all this, a great chasm has been fixed between us, so that those who want to cross over from here to you cannot do so, and no one can cross from there to us.' **16:27** So the rich man said, 'Then I beg you, father – send Lazarus to my father's house **16:28** (for I have five brothers) to warn them so that they don't come into this place of torment.' **16:29** But Abraham said, 'They have Moses and the prophets; they must respond to them.' **16:30** Then the rich man said, 'No, father Abraham, but if someone from the dead goes to them, they will repent.' **16:31** He replied to him, 'If they do not respond to Moses and the prophets, they will not be convinced even if someone rises from the dead.'"

Sin, Forgiveness, Faith, and Service

17:1 Jesus said to his disciples, "Stumbling blocks are sure to come, but woe to the one through whom they come! **17:2** It would be better for him to have a millstone tied around his neck and be thrown into the sea than for him to cause one of these little ones to sin. **17:3** Watch yourselves! If your brother sins, rebuke him. If he repents, forgive him. **17:4** Even if he sins against you seven times in a day, and seven times returns to you saying, 'I repent,' you must forgive him."

17:5 The apostles said to the Lord, "Increase our faith!" **17:6** So the Lord replied, "If you had faith the size of a mustard seed, you could say to this black mulberry tree, 'Be pulled out by the roots and planted in the sea,' and it would obey you.

17:7 "Would any one of you say to your slave who comes in from the field after plowing or shepherding sheep, 'Come at once and sit down for a meal'? **17:8** Won't the master instead say to him, 'Get my dinner ready, and make yourself ready to serve me while I eat and drink. Then you may eat and drink'? **17:9** He won't thank the slave because he did what he was told, will he? **17:10** So you too, when you have done everything you were commanded to do, should say, 'We are slaves undeserving of special praise; we have only done what was our duty.'"

The Grateful Leper

17:11 Now on the way to Jerusalem, Jesus was passing along between Samaria and Galilee. **17:12** As he was entering a village, ten men with leprosy met him. They stood at a distance, **17:13** raised their voices and said, "Jesus, Master, have mercy on us." **17:14** When he saw them he said, "Go and show yourselves to the priests." And as they went along, they were cleansed. **17:15** Then one of them, when he saw he was healed, turned back, praising God with a loud voice. **17:16** He fell with his face to the ground at Jesus' feet and thanked him. (Now he was a Samaritan.) **17:17** Then Jesus said, "Were not ten cleansed? Where are the other nine? **17:18** Was no one found to turn back and give praise to God except this foreigner?" **17:19** Then he said to the man, "Get up and go your way. Your faith has made you well."

The Coming of the Kingdom

17:20 Now at one point the Pharisees asked Jesus when the kingdom of God was coming, so he answered, "The kingdom of God is not coming with signs to be observed, **17:21** nor will they say, 'Look, here it is!' or 'There!' For indeed, the kingdom of God is in your midst."

The Coming of the Son of Man

17:22 Then he said to the disciples, "The days are coming when you will desire to see one of the days of the Son of Man, and you will not see it. **17:23** Then people will say to you, 'Look, there he is!' or 'Look, here is!' Do not go out or chase after them. **17:24** For just like the lightning flashes and lights up the sky from one side to the other, so will the Son of Man be in his day. **17:25** But first he must suffer many things and be rejected by this generation. **17:26** Just as it was in the days of Noah, so too it will be in the days of the Son of Man. **17:27** People were eating, they were drinking, they were marrying, they were being given in marriage – right up to the day Noah entered the ark. Then the flood came and destroyed them all. **17:28** Likewise, just as it was in the days of Lot, people were eating, drinking, buying, selling, planting, building; **17:29** but on the day Lot went out from Sodom, fire and sulfur rained down from heaven and destroyed them all. **17:30** It will be the same on the day the Son of Man is revealed. **17:31** On that day, anyone who is on the roof, with his goods in the house, must not come down to take them away, and likewise the person in the field must not turn back. **17:32** Remember Lot's wife! **17:33** Whoever tries to keep his life will lose it, but whoever loses his life will preserve it. **17:34** I tell you, in that night there will be two people in one bed; one will be taken and the other left. **17:35** There will be two women grinding grain together; one will be taken and the other left."

17:37 Then the disciples said to him, "Where, Lord?" He replied to them, "Where the dead body is, there the vultures will gather."

Prayer and the Parable of the Persistent Widow

18:1 Then Jesus told them a parable to show them they should always pray and not lose heart. **18:2** He said, "In a certain city there was a judge who neither feared God nor respected people. **18:3** There was also a widow in that city who kept coming to him and saying, 'Give me justice against my adversary.' **18:4** For a while he refused, but later on he said to himself, 'Though I neither fear God nor have regard for people, **18:5** yet because this widow keeps on bothering me, I will give her justice, or in the end she will wear me out by her unending pleas.'" **18:6** And the Lord said, "Listen to what the unrighteous judge says! **18:7** Won't God give justice to his chosen ones, who cry out to him day and night? Will he delay long to help them? **18:8** I tell you, he will give them justice speedily. Nevertheless, when the Son of Man comes, will he find faith on earth?"

The Parable of the Pharisee and Tax Collector

18:9 Jesus also told this parable to some who were confident that they were righteous and looked down on everyone else. **18:10** "Two men went up to the temple to pray, one a Pharisee and the other a tax collector. **18:11** The Pharisee stood and prayed about himself like this: 'God, I thank you that I am not like other people: extortionists, unrighteous people, adulterers – or even like this tax collector. **18:12** I fast twice a week; I give a tenth of everything I get.' **18:13** The tax collector, however, stood far off and would not even look up to heaven, but beat his breast and said,

'God, be merciful to me, sinner that I am!' **18:14** I tell you that this man went down to his home justified rather than the Pharisee. For everyone who exalts himself will be humbled, but he who humbles himself will be exalted."

Jesus and Little Children

18:15 Now people were even bringing their babies to him for him to touch. But when the disciples saw it, they began to scold those who brought them. **18:16** But Jesus called for the children, saying, "Let the little children come to me and do not try to stop them, for the kingdom of God belongs to such as these. **18:17** I tell you the truth, whoever does not receive the kingdom of God like a child will never enter it."

The Wealthy Ruler

18:18 Now a certain ruler asked him, "Good teacher, what must I do to inherit eternal life?" **18:19** Jesus said to him, "Why do you call me good? No one is good except God alone. **18:20** You know the commandments: '*Do not commit adultery, do not murder, do not steal, do not give false testimony, honor your father and mother*.'" **18:21** The man replied, "I have wholeheartedly obeyed all these laws since my youth." **18:22** When Jesus heard this, he said to him, "One thing you still lack. Sell all that you have and give the money to the poor, and you will have treasure in heaven. Then come, follow me." **18:23** But when the man heard this he became very sad, for he was extremely wealthy. **18:24** When Jesus noticed this, he said, "How hard it is for the rich to enter the kingdom of God! **18:25** In fact, it is easier for a camel to go through the eye of a needle than for a rich person to enter the kingdom of God." **18:26** Those who heard this said, "Then who can be saved?" **18:27** He replied, "What is impossible for mere humans is possible for God." **18:28** And Peter said, "Look, we have left everything we own to follow you!" **18:29** Then Jesus said to them, "I tell you the truth, there is no one who has left home or wife or brothers or parents or children for the sake of God's kingdom **18:30** who will not receive many times more in this age – and in the age to come, eternal life."

Another Prediction of Jesus' Passion

18:31 Then Jesus took the twelve aside and said to them, "Look, we are going up to Jerusalem, and everything that is written about the Son of Man by the prophets will be accomplished. **18:32** For he will be handed over to the Gentiles; he will be mocked, mistreated, and spat on. **18:33** They will flog him severely and kill him. Yet on the third day he will rise again." **18:34** But the twelve understood none of these things. This saying was hidden from them, and they did not grasp what Jesus meant.

Healing a Blind Man

18:35 As Jesus approached Jericho, a blind man was sitting by the road begging. **18:36** When he heard a crowd going by, he asked what was going on. **18:37** They told him, "Jesus the Nazarene is passing by." **18:38** So he called out, "Jesus, Son of David, have mercy on me!" **18:39** And those who were in front scolded him to get him to be quiet, but he shouted even more, "Son of David, have mercy on me!" **18:40** So Jesus stopped and ordered the beggar to be brought to him. When the man came near, Jesus asked him, **18:41** "What do you want me to do for you?" He replied, "Lord, let me see again." **18:42** Jesus said to him, "Receive your sight; your faith has healed you." **18:43** And immediately he regained his sight and followed Jesus, praising God. When all the people saw it, they too gave praise to God.

Jesus and Zacchaeus

19:1 Jesus entered Jericho and was passing through it. **19:2** Now a man named Zacchaeus was there; he was a chief tax collector and was rich. **19:3** He was trying to get a look at Jesus, but being a short man he could not see over the crowd. **19:4** So he ran on ahead and climbed up into a sycamore tree to see him, because Jesus was going to pass that way. **19:5** And when Jesus came to that place, he looked up and said to him, "Zacchaeus, come down quickly, because I must stay at your house today." **19:6** So he came down quickly and welcomed Jesus joyfully. **19:7** And when the people saw it, they all complained, "He has gone in to be the guest of a man who is a sinner." **19:8** But Zacchaeus stopped and said to the Lord, "Look, Lord, half of my possessions I now give to the poor, and if I have cheated anyone of anything, I am paying back four times as much!" **19:9** Then Jesus said to him, "Today salvation has come to this household, because he too is a son of Abraham! **19:10** For the Son of Man came to seek and to save the lost."

The Parable of the Ten Minas

19:11 While the people were listening to these things, Jesus proceeded to tell a parable, because he was near to Jerusalem, and because they thought that the kingdom of God was going to appear immediately. **19:12** Therefore he said, "A nobleman went to a distant country to receive for himself a kingdom and then return. **19:13** And he summoned ten of his slaves, gave them ten minas, and said to them, 'Do business with these until I come back.' **19:14** But his citizens hated him and sent a delegation after him, saying, 'We do not want this man to be king over us!' **19:15** When he returned after receiving the kingdom, he summoned these slaves to whom he had given the money. He wanted to know how much they had earned by trading. **19:16** So the first one came before him and said, 'Sir, your mina has made ten minas more.' **19:17** And the king said to him, 'Well done, good slave! Because you have been faithful in a very

small matter, you will have authority over ten cities.' **19:18** Then the second one came and said, 'Sir, your mina has made five minas.' **19:19** So the king said to him, 'And you are to be over five cities.' **19:20** Then another slave came and said, 'Sir, here is your mina that I put away for safekeeping in a piece of cloth. **19:21** For I was afraid of you, because you are a severe man. You withdraw what you did not deposit and reap what you did not sow.' **19:22** The king said to him, 'I will judge you by your own words, you wicked slave! So you knew, did you, that I was a severe man, withdrawing what I didn't deposit and reaping what I didn't sow? **19:23** Why then didn't you put my money in the bank, so that when I returned I could have collected it with interest?' **19:24** And he said to his attendants, 'Take the mina from him, and give it to the one who has ten.' **19:25** But they said to him, 'Sir, he has ten minas already!' **19:26** 'I tell you that everyone who has will be given more, but from the one who does not have, even what he has will be taken away. **19:27** But as for these enemies of mine who did not want me to be their king, bring them here and slaughter them in front of me!'"

The Triumphal Entry

19:28 After Jesus had said this, he continued on ahead, going up to Jerusalem. **19:29** Now when he approached Bethphage and Bethany, at the place called the Mount of Olives, he sent two of the disciples, **19:30** telling them, "Go to the village ahead of you. When you enter it, you will find a colt tied there that has never been ridden. Untie it and bring it here. **19:31** If anyone asks you, 'Why are you untying it?' just say, 'The Lord needs it.'" **19:32** So those who were sent ahead found it exactly as he had told them. **19:33** As they were untying the colt, its owners asked them, "Why are you untying that colt?" **19:34** They replied, "The Lord needs it." **19:35** Then they brought it to Jesus, threw their cloaks on the colt, and had Jesus get on it. **19:36** As he rode along, they spread their cloaks on the road. **19:37** As he approached the road leading down from the Mount of Olives, the whole crowd of his disciples began to rejoice and praise God with a loud voice for all the mighty works they had seen: **19:38** "*Blessed is the king who comes in the name of the Lord!* Peace in heaven and glory in the highest!" **19:39** But some of the Pharisees in the crowd said to him, "Teacher, rebuke your disciples." **19:40** He answered, "I tell you, if they keep silent, the very stones will cry out!"

Jesus Weeps for Jerusalem under Judgment

19:41 Now when Jesus approached and saw the city, he wept over it, **19:42** saying, "If you had only known on this day, even you, the things that make for peace! But now they are hidden from your eyes. **19:43** For the days will come upon you when your enemies will build an embankment against you and surround you and close in on you from every side. **19:44** They will demolish you – you and your children within your walls – and they will not leave within you one stone on top of another, because you did not recognize the time of your visitation from God."

Cleansing the Temple

19:45 Then Jesus entered the temple courts and began to drive out those who were selling things there, **19:46** saying to them, "It is written, '*My house will be a house of prayer*,' but you have turned it into *a den of robbers*!"

19:47 Jesus was teaching daily in the temple courts. The chief priests and the experts in the law and the prominent leaders among the people were seeking to assassinate him, **19:48** but they could not find a way to do it, for all the people hung on his words.

The Authority of Jesus

20:1 Now one day, as Jesus was teaching the people in the temple courts and proclaiming the gospel, the chief priests and the experts in the law with the elders came up **20:2** and said to him, "Tell us: By what authority are you doing these things? Or who it is who gave you this authority?" **20:3** He answered them, "I will also ask you a question, and you tell me: **20:4** John's baptism – was it from heaven or from people?" **20:5** So they discussed it with one another, saying, "If we say, 'From heaven,' he will say, 'Why did you not believe him?' **20:6** But if we say, 'From people,' all the people will stone us, because they are convinced that John was a prophet." **20:7** So they replied that they did not know where it came from. **20:8** Then Jesus said to them, "Neither will I tell you by whose authority I do these things."

The Parable of the Tenants

20:9 Then he began to tell the people this parable: "A man planted a vineyard, leased it to tenant farmers, and went on a journey for a long time. **20:10** When harvest time came, he sent a slave to the tenants so that they would give him his portion of the crop. However, the tenants beat his slave and sent him away empty-handed. **20:11** So he sent another slave. They beat this one too, treated him outrageously, and sent him away empty-handed. **20:12** So he sent still a third. They even wounded this one, and threw him out. **20:13** Then the owner of the vineyard said, 'What should I do? I will send my one dear son; perhaps they will respect him.' **20:14** But when the tenants saw him, they said to one another, 'This is the heir; let's kill him so the inheritance will be ours!' **20:15** So they threw him out of the vineyard and killed him. What then will the owner of the vineyard do to them? **20:16** He will come and destroy those tenants and give the vineyard to others." When the people heard this, they said, "May this never happen!" **20:17** But Jesus looked straight at them and said, "Then what is the meaning of that which is written: '*The stone the builders rejected has become the cornerstone*'? **20:18** Everyone who falls on this stone will be broken to pieces, and the one on whom it falls will be crushed." **20:19** Then the experts in the law and the chief priests wanted to arrest him that very hour, because they realized he had told this parable against them. But they were afraid of the people.

Paying Taxes to Caesar

20:20 Then they watched him carefully and sent spies who pretended to be sincere. They wanted to take advantage of what he might say so that they could deliver him up to the authority and jurisdiction of the governor. **20:21** Thus they asked him, "Teacher, we know that you speak and teach correctly, and show no partiality, but teach the way of God in accordance with the truth. **20:22** Is it right for us to pay the tribute tax to Caesar or not?" **20:23** But Jesus perceived their deceit and said to them, **20:24** "Show me a denarius. Whose image and inscription are on it?" They said, "Caesar's." **20:25** So he said to them, "Then give to Caesar the things that are Caesar's, and to God the things that are God's." **20:26** Thus they were unable in the presence of the people to trap him with his own words. And stunned by his answer, they fell silent.

Marriage and the Resurrection

20:27 Now some Sadducees (who contend that there is no resurrection) came to him. **20:28** They asked him, "Teacher, Moses wrote for us that *if a man's brother dies leaving* a wife but *no children, that man must marry the widow and father children for his brother*. **20:29** Now there were seven brothers. The first one married a woman and died without children. **20:30** The second **20:31** and then the third married her, and in this same way all seven died, leaving no children. **20:32** Finally the woman died too. **20:33** In the resurrection, therefore, whose wife will the woman be? For all seven had married her."

20:34 So Jesus said to them, "The people of this age marry and are given in marriage. **20:35** But those who are regarded as worthy to share in that age and in the resurrection from the dead neither marry nor are given in marriage. **20:36** In fact, they can no longer die, because they are equal to angels and are sons of God, since they are sons of the resurrection. **20:37** But even Moses revealed that the dead are raised in the passage about the bush, where he calls the Lord *the God of Abraham and the God of Isaac and the God of Jacob*. **20:38** Now he is not God of the dead, but of the living, for all live before him." **20:39** Then some of the experts in the law answered, "Teacher, you have spoken well!" **20:40** For they did not dare any longer to ask him anything.

The Messiah: David's Son and Lord

20:41 But he said to them, "How is it that they say that the Christ is David's son? **20:42** For David himself says in the book of Psalms,

'The Lord said to my lord,

"Sit at my right hand,

20:43 until I make your enemies a footstool for your feet."'

20:44 If David then calls him 'Lord,' how can he be his son?"

Jesus Warns the Disciples against Pride

20:45 As all the people were listening, Jesus said to his disciples, **20:46** "Beware of the experts in the law. They like walking around in long robes, and they love elaborate greetings in the marketplaces and the best seats in the synagogues and the places of honor at banquets. **20:47** They devour widows' property, and as a show make long prayers. They will receive a more severe punishment."

The Widow's Offering

21:1 Jesus looked up and saw the rich putting their gifts into the offering box. **21:2** He also saw a poor widow put in two small copper coins. **21:3** He said, "I tell you the truth, this poor widow has put in more than all of them. **21:4** For they all offered their gifts out of their wealth. But she, out of her poverty, put in everything she had to live on."

The Signs of the End of the Age

21:5 Now while some were speaking about the temple, how it was adorned with beautiful stones and offerings, Jesus said, **21:6** "As for these things that you are gazing at, the days will come when not one stone will be left on another. All will be torn down!" **21:7** So they asked him, "Teacher, when will these things happen? And what will be the sign that these things are about to take place?" **21:8** He said, "Watch out that you are not misled. For many will come in my name, saying, 'I am he,' and, 'The time is near.' Do not follow them! **21:9** And when you hear of wars and rebellions, do not be afraid. For these things must happen first, but the end will not come at once."

Persecution of Disciples

21:10 Then he said to them, "Nation will rise up in arms against nation, and kingdom against kingdom. **21:11** There will be great earthquakes, and famines and plagues in various places, and there will be terrifying sights and great signs from heaven. **21:12** But before all this, they will seize you and persecute you, handing you over to the synagogues and prisons. You will be brought before kings and governors because of my name. **21:13** This will be a time for you to serve as witnesses. **21:14** Therefore be resolved not to rehearse ahead of time how to make your defense. **21:15** For I will give you the words along with the wisdom that none of your adversaries will be able to withstand or contradict. **21:16** You will be betrayed even by parents, brothers, relatives, and friends, and they will have some of you put to death. **21:17** You will be hated by everyone because of my name. **21:18** Yet not a hair of your head will perish. **21:19** By your endurance you will gain your lives.

The Desolation of Jerusalem

21:20 "But when you see Jerusalem surrounded by armies, then know that its desolation has come near. **21:21** Then those who are in Judea must flee to the mountains. Those who are inside the city must depart. Those who are out in the country must not enter it, **21:22** because these are days of vengeance, to fulfill all that is written. **21:23** Woe to those who are pregnant and to those who are nursing their babies in those days! For there will be great distress on the earth and wrath against this people. **21:24** They will fall by the edge of the sword and be led away as captives among all nations. Jerusalem will be trampled down by the Gentiles until the times of the Gentiles are fulfilled.

The Arrival of the Son of Man

21:25 "And there will be signs in the sun and moon and stars, and on the earth nations will be in distress, anxious over the roaring of the sea and the surging waves. **21:26** People will be fainting from fear and from the expectation of what is coming on the world, for *the powers of the heavens will be shaken*. **21:27** Then they will see *the Son of Man arriving in a cloud* with power and great glory. **21:28** But when these things begin to happen, stand up and raise your heads, because your redemption is drawing near."

The Parable of the Fig Tree

21:29 Then he told them a parable: "Look at the fig tree and all the other trees. **21:30** When they sprout leaves, you see for yourselves and know that summer is now near. **21:31** So also you, when you see these things happening, know that the kingdom of God is near. **21:32** I tell you the truth, this generation will not pass away until all these things take place. **21:33** Heaven and earth will pass away, but my words will never pass away.

Be Ready!

21:34 "But be on your guard so that your hearts are not weighed down with dissipation and drunkenness and the worries of this life, and that day close down upon you suddenly like a trap. **21:35** For it will overtake all who live on the face of the whole earth. **21:36** But stay alert at all times, praying that you may have strength to escape all these things that must happen, and to stand before the Son of Man."

21:37 So every day Jesus was teaching in the temple courts, but at night he went and stayed on the Mount of Olives. **21:38** And all the people came to him early in the morning to listen to him in the temple courts.

Judas' Decision to Betray Jesus

22:1 Now the Feast of Unleavened Bread, which is called the Passover, was approaching. **22:2** The chief priests and the experts in the law were trying to find some way to execute Jesus, for they were afraid of the people.

22:3 Then Satan entered Judas, the one called Iscariot, who was one of the twelve. **22:4** He went away and discussed with the chief priests and officers of the temple guard how he might betray Jesus, handing him over to them. **22:5** They were delighted and arranged to give him money. **22:6** So Judas agreed and began looking for an opportunity to betray Jesus when no crowd was present.

The Passover

22:7 Then the day for the feast of Unleavened Bread came, on which the Passover lamb had to be sacrificed. **22:8** Jesus sent Peter and John, saying, "Go and prepare the Passover for us to eat." **22:9** They said to him, "Where do you want us to prepare it?" **22:10** He said to them, "Listen, when you have entered the city, a man carrying a jar of water will meet you. Follow him into the house that he enters, **22:11** and tell the owner of the house, 'The Teacher says to you, "Where is the guest room where I may eat the Passover with my disciples?"' **22:12** Then he will show you a large furnished room upstairs. Make preparations there." **22:13** So they went and found things just as he had told them, and they prepared the Passover.

The Lord's Supper

22:14 Now when the hour came, Jesus took his place at the table and the apostles joined him. **22:15** And he said to them, "I have earnestly desired to eat this Passover with you before I suffer. **22:16** For I tell you, I will not eat it again until it is fulfilled in the kingdom of God." **22:17** Then he took a cup, and after giving thanks he said, "Take this and divide it among yourselves. **22:18** For I tell you that from now on I will not drink of the fruit of the vine until the kingdom of God comes." **22:19** Then he took bread, and after giving thanks he broke it and gave it to them, saying, "This is my body which is given for you. Do this in remembrance of me." **22:20** And in the same way he took the cup after they had eaten, saying, "This cup that is poured out for you is the new covenant in my blood.

A Final Discourse

22:21 "But look, the hand of the one who betrays me is with me on the table. **22:22** For the Son of Man is to go just as it has been determined, but woe to that man by whom he is betrayed!" **22:23** So they began to question one another as to which of them it could possibly be who would do this.

22:24 A dispute also started among them over which of them was to be regarded as the greatest. **22:25** So Jesus said to them, "The kings of the Gentiles lord it over them, and those in authority over them are called 'benefactors.' **22:26** Not so with you; instead the one who is greatest among you must become like the youngest, and the leader like the one who serves. **22:27** For who is greater, the one who is seated at the table, or the one who serves? Is it not the one who is seated at the table? But I am among you as one who serves.

22:28 "You are the ones who have remained with me in my trials. **22:29** Thus I grant to you a kingdom, just as my Father granted to me, **22:30** that you may eat and drink at my table in my kingdom, and you will sit on thrones judging the twelve tribes of Israel.

22:31 "Simon, Simon, pay attention! Satan has demanded to have you all, to sift you like wheat, **22:32** but I have prayed for you, Simon, that your faith may not fail. When you have turned back, strengthen your brothers." **22:33** But Peter said to him, "Lord, I am ready to go with you both to prison and to death!" **22:34** Jesus replied, "I tell you, Peter, the rooster will not crow today until you have denied three times that you know me." **22:35** Then Jesus said to them, "When I sent you out with no money bag, or traveler's bag, or sandals, you didn't lack anything, did you?" They replied, "Nothing." **22:36** He said to them, "But now, the one who has a money bag must take it, and likewise a traveler's bag too. And the one who has no sword must sell his cloak and buy one. **22:37** For I tell you that this scripture must be fulfilled in me, '*And he was counted with the transgressors.*' For what is written about me is being fulfilled." **22:38** So they said, "Look, Lord, here are two swords." Then he told them, "It is enough."

On the Mount of Olives

22:39 Then Jesus went out and made his way, as he customarily did, to the Mount of Olives, and the disciples followed him. **22:40** When he came to the place, he said to them, "Pray that you will not fall into temptation." **22:41** He went away from them about a stone's throw, knelt down, and prayed, **22:42** "Father, if you are willing, take this cup away from me. Yet not my will but yours be done." [**22:43** Then an angel from heaven appeared to him and strengthened him. **22:44** And in his anguish he prayed more earnestly, and his sweat was like drops of blood falling to the ground.] **22:45** When he got up from prayer, he came to the disciples and found them sleeping, exhausted from grief. **22:46** So he said to them, "Why are you sleeping? Get up and pray that you will not fall into temptation!"

Betrayal and Arrest

22:47 While he was still speaking, suddenly a crowd appeared, and the man named Judas, one of the twelve, was leading them. He walked up to Jesus to kiss him. **22:48** But Jesus said to him, "Judas, would you betray the Son of Man with a kiss?" **22:49** When those who were around him saw what was about to happen, they said, "Lord, should we use our swords?" **22:50** Then one of them struck the high priest's slave, cutting off his right ear. **22:51** But Jesus said, "Enough of this!" And he touched the man's ear and healed him. **22:52** Then Jesus said to the chief priests, the officers of the temple guard, and the elders who had come out to get him, "Have you come out with swords and clubs like you would against an outlaw? **22:53** Day after day when I was with you in the temple courts, you did not arrest me. But this is your hour, and that of the power of darkness!"

Jesus' Condemnation and Peter's Denials

22:54 Then they arrested Jesus, led him away, and brought him into the high priest's house. But Peter was following at a distance. **22:55** When they had made a fire in the middle of the courtyard and sat down together, Peter sat down among them. **22:56** Then a slave girl, seeing him as he sat in the firelight, stared at him and said, "This man was with him too!" **22:57** But Peter denied it: "Woman, I don't know him!" **22:58** Then a little later someone else saw him and said, "You are one of them too." But Peter said, "Man, I am not!" **22:59** And after about an hour still another insisted, "Certainly this man was with him, because he too is a Galilean." **22:60** But Peter said, "Man, I don't know what you're talking about!" At that moment, while he was still speaking, a rooster crowed. **22:61** Then the Lord turned and looked straight at Peter, and Peter remembered the word of the Lord, how he had said to him, "Before a rooster crows today, you will deny me three times." **22:62** And he went outside and wept bitterly.

22:63 Now the men who were holding Jesus under guard began to mock him and beat him. **22:64** They blindfolded him and asked him repeatedly, "Prophesy! Who hit you?" **22:65** They also said many other things against him, reviling him.

22:66 When day came, the council of the elders of the people gathered together, both the chief priests and the experts in the law. Then they led Jesus away to their council **22:67** and said, "If you are the Christ, tell us." But he said to them, "If I tell you, you will not believe, **22:68** and if I ask you, you will not answer. **22:69** But from now on *the Son of Man will be seated at the right hand* of the power of God." **22:70** So they all said, "Are you the Son of God, then?" He answered them, "You say that I am." **22:71** Then they said, "Why do we need further testimony? We have heard it ourselves from his own lips!"

Jesus Brought Before Pilate

23:1 Then the whole group of them rose up and brought Jesus before Pilate. **23:2** They began to accuse him, saying, "We found this man subverting our nation, forbidding us to pay the tribute tax to Caesar and claiming that he himself is Christ, a king." **23:3** So Pilate asked Jesus, "Are you the king of the Jews?" He replied, "You say so." **23:4** Then Pilate said to the chief priests and the crowds, "I find no basis for an accusation against this man." **23:5** But they persisted in saying, "He incites the people by teaching throughout all Judea. It started in Galilee and ended up here!"

Jesus Brought Before Herod

23:6 Now when Pilate heard this, he asked whether the man was a Galilean. **23:7** When he learned that he was from Herod's jurisdiction, he sent him over to Herod, who also happened to be in Jerusalem at that time. **23:8** When Herod saw Jesus, he was very glad, for he had long desired to see him, because he had heard about him and was hoping to see him perform some miraculous sign. **23:9** So Herod questioned him at considerable length; Jesus gave him no answer. **23:10** The chief priests and the experts in the law were there, vehemently accusing him. **23:11** Even Herod with his soldiers treated him with contempt and mocked him. Then, dressing him in elegant clothes, Herod sent him back to Pilate. **23:12** That very day Herod and Pilate became friends with each other, for prior to this they had been enemies.

Jesus Brought Before the Crowd

23:13 Then Pilate called together the chief priests, the rulers, and the people, **23:14** and said to them, "You brought me this man as one who was misleading the people. When I examined him before you, I did not find this man guilty of anything you accused him of doing. **23:15** Neither did Herod, for he sent him back to us. Look, he has done nothing deserving death. **23:16** I will therefore have him flogged and release him."

23:18 But they all shouted out together, "Take this man away! Release Barabbas for us!" **23:19** (This was a man who had been thrown into prison for an insurrection started in the city, and for murder.) **23:20** Pilate addressed them once again because he wanted to release Jesus. **23:21** But they kept on shouting, "Crucify, crucify him!" **23:22** A third time he said to them, "Why? What wrong has he done? I have found him guilty of no crime deserving death. I will therefore flog him and release him." **23:23** But they were insistent, demanding with loud shouts that he be crucified. And their shouts prevailed. **23:24** So Pilate decided that their demand should be granted. **23:25** He released the man they asked for, who had been thrown in prison for insurrection and murder. But he handed Jesus over to their will.

The Crucifixion

23:26 As they led him away, they seized Simon of Cyrene, who was coming in from the country. They placed the cross on his back and made him carry it behind Jesus. **23:27** A great number of the people followed him, among them women who were mourning and wailing for him. **23:28** But Jesus turned to them and said, "Daughters of Jerusalem, do not weep for me, but weep for yourselves and for your children. **23:29** For this is certain: The days are coming when they will say, 'Blessed are the barren, the wombs that never bore children, and the breasts that never nursed!' **23:30** Then they will begin *to say to the mountains, 'Fall on us!' and to the hills, 'Cover us!'* **23:31** For if such things are done when the wood is green, what will happen when it is dry?"

23:32 Two other criminals were also led away to be executed with him. **23:33** So when they came to the place that is called "The Skull," they crucified him there, along with the criminals, one on his right and one on his left. **23:34** [But Jesus said, "Father, forgive them, for they don't know what they are doing."] Then *they threw dice to divide his clothes.* **23:35** The people also stood there watching, but the rulers ridiculed him, saying, "He saved others. Let him save himself if he is the Christ of God, his chosen one!" **23:36** The soldiers also mocked him, coming up and offering him sour wine, **23:37** and saying, "If you are the king of the Jews, save yourself!" **23:38** There was also an inscription over him, "This is the king of the Jews."

23:39 One of the criminals who was hanging there railed at him, saying, "Aren't you the Christ? Save yourself and us!" **23:40** But the other rebuked him, saying, "Don't you fear God, since you are under the same sentence of condemnation? **23:41** And we rightly so, for we are getting what we deserve for what we did, but this man has done nothing wrong." **23:42** Then he said, "Jesus, remember me when you come in your kingdom." **23:43** And Jesus said to him, "I tell you the truth, today you will be with me in paradise."

23:44 It was now about noon, and darkness came over the whole land until three in the afternoon, **23:45** because the sun's light failed. The temple curtain was torn in two. **23:46** Then Jesus, calling out with a loud voice, said, "Father, *into your hands I commit my spirit!*" And after he said this he breathed his last.

23:47 Now when the centurion saw what had happened, he praised God and said, "Certainly this man was innocent!" **23:48** And all the crowds that had assembled for this spectacle, when they saw what had taken place, returned home beating their breasts. **23:49** And all those who knew

Jesus stood at a distance, and the women who had followed him from Galilee saw these things.

Jesus' Burial

23:50 Now there was a man named Joseph who was a member of the council, a good and righteous man. **23:51** (He had not consented to their plan and action.) He was from the Judean town of Arimathea, and was looking forward to the kingdom of God. **23:52** He went to Pilate and asked for the body of Jesus. **23:53** Then he took it down, wrapped it in a linen cloth, and placed it in a tomb cut out of the rock, where no one had yet been buried. **23:54** It was the day of preparation and the Sabbath was beginning. **23:55** The women who had accompanied Jesus from Galilee followed, and they saw the tomb and how his body was laid in it. **23:56** Then they returned and prepared aromatic spices and perfumes.

On the Sabbath they rested according to the commandment.

The Resurrection

24:1 Now on the first day of the week, at early dawn, the women went to the tomb, taking the aromatic spices they had prepared. **24:2** They found that the stone had been rolled away from the tomb, **24:3** but when they went in, they did not find the body of the Lord Jesus. **24:4** While they were perplexed about this, suddenly two men stood beside them in dazzling attire. **24:5** The women were terribly frightened and bowed their faces to the ground, but the men said to them, "Why do you look for the living among the dead? **24:6** He is not here, but has been raised! Remember how he told you, while he was still in Galilee, **24:7** that the Son of Man must be delivered into the hands of sinful men, and be crucified, and on the third day rise again." **24:8** Then the women remembered his words, **24:9** and when they returned from the tomb they told all these things to the eleven and to all the rest. **24:10** Now it was Mary Magdalene, Joanna, Mary the mother of James, and the other women with them who told these things to the apostles. **24:11** But these words seemed like pure nonsense to them, and they did not believe them. **24:12** But Peter got up and ran to the tomb. He bent down and saw only the strips of linen cloth; then he went home, wondering what had happened.

Jesus Walks the Road to Emmaus

24:13 Now that very day two of them were on their way to a village called Emmaus, about seven miles from Jerusalem. **24:14** They were talking to each other about all the things that had happened. **24:15** While they were talking and debating these things, Jesus himself approached and began to accompany them **24:16** (but their eyes were kept from recognizing him). **24:17** Then he said to them, "What are these matters you are discussing so intently as you walk along?" And they stood still, looking sad. **24:18** Then one of them, named Cleopas, answered him, "Are you the only visitor to Jerusalem who doesn't know the things that have happened there in these days?" **24:19** He said to them, "What things?" "The things concerning Jesus the Nazarene," they replied, "a man who, with his powerful deeds and words, proved to be a prophet before God and all the people; **24:20** and how our chief priests and rulers handed him over to be condemned to death, and crucified him. **24:21** But we had hoped that he was the one who was going to redeem Israel. Not only this, but it is now the third day since these things happened. **24:22** Furthermore, some women of our group amazed us. They were at the tomb early this morning, **24:23** and when they did not find his body, they came back and said they had seen a vision of angels, who said he was alive. **24:24** Then some of those who were with us went to the tomb, and found it just as the women had said, but they did not see him." **24:25** So he said to them, "You foolish people – how slow of heart to believe all that the prophets have spoken! **24:26** Wasn't it necessary for the Christ to suffer these things and enter into his glory?" **24:27** Then beginning with Moses and all the prophets, he interpreted to them the things written about himself in all the scriptures.

24:28 So they approached the village where they were going. He acted as though he wanted to go farther, **24:29** but they urged him, "Stay with us, because it is getting toward evening and the day is almost done." So he went in to stay with them.

24:30 When he had taken his place at the table with them, he took the bread, blessed and broke it, and gave it to them. **24:31** At this point their eyes were opened and they recognized him. Then he vanished out of their sight. **24:32** They said to each other, "Didn't our hearts burn within us while he was speaking with us on the road, while he was explaining the scriptures to us?" **24:33** So they got up that very hour and returned to Jerusalem. They found the eleven and those with them gathered together **24:34** and saying, "The Lord has really risen, and has appeared to Simon!" **24:35** Then they told what had happened on the road, and how they recognized him when he broke the bread.

Jesus Makes a Final Appearance

24:36 While they were saying these things, Jesus himself stood among them and said to them, "Peace be with you." **24:37** But they were startled and terrified, thinking they saw a ghost. **24:38** Then he said to them, "Why are you frightened, and why do doubts arise in your hearts? **24:39** Look at my hands and my feet; it's me! Touch me and see; a ghost does not have flesh and bones like you see I have." **24:40** When he had said this, he showed them his hands and his feet. **24:41** And while they still could not believe it (because of their joy) and were amazed, he said to them, "Do you have anything here to eat?" **24:42** So they gave him a piece of broiled fish, **24:43** and he took it and ate it in front of them.

Jesus' Final Commission

24:44 Then he said to them, "These are my words that I spoke to you while I was still with you, that everything written about me in the law of Moses and the prophets and the psalms must be fulfilled." **24:45** Then he opened their minds so they could understand the scriptures, **24:46** and said to them, "Thus it stands written that the Christ would suffer and would rise from the dead on the third day, **24:47** and repentance for the forgiveness of sins would be proclaimed in his name to all nations, beginning from Jerusalem. **24:48** You are witnesses of these things. **24:49** And look, I am sending you what my Father promised. But stay in the city until you have been clothed with power from on high."

Jesus' Departure

24:50 Then Jesus led them out as far as Bethany, and lifting up his hands, he blessed them. **24:51** Now during the blessing he departed and was taken up into heaven. **24:52** So they worshiped him and returned to Jerusalem with great joy, **24:53** and were continually in the temple courts blessing God.

Book 43. John

The Prologue to the Gospel

1:1 In the beginning was the Word, and the Word was with God, and the Word was fully God. **1:2** The Word was with God in the beginning. **1:3** All things were created by him, and apart from him not one thing was created that has been created. **1:4** *In him was life*, and the life was the light of mankind. **1:5** And the light shines on in the darkness, but the darkness has not mastered it.

1:6 A man came, sent from God, whose name was John. **1:7** He came as a witness to testify about the light, so that everyone might believe through him. **1:8** He himself was not the light, but he came to testify about the light. **1:9** The true light, who gives light to everyone, was coming into the world. **1:10** He was in the world, and the world was created by him, but the world did not recognize him. **1:11** He came to what was his own, but his own people did not receive him. **1:12** But to all who have received him – those who believe in his name – he has given the right to become God's children **1:13** – children not born by human parents or by human desire or a husband's decision, but by God.

1:14 Now the Word became flesh and took up residence among us. We saw his glory – the glory of the one and only, full of grace and truth, who came from the Father. **1:15** John testified about him and shouted out, "This one was the one about whom I said, 'He who comes after me is greater than I am, because he existed before me.'" **1:16** For we have all received from his fullness one gracious gift after another. **1:17** For the law was given through Moses, but grace and truth came about through Jesus Christ. **1:18** No one has ever seen God. The only one, himself God, who is in closest fellowship with the Father, has made God known.

The Testimony of John the Baptist

1:19 Now this was John's testimony when the Jewish leaders sent priests and Levites from Jerusalem to ask him, "Who are you?" **1:20** He confessed – he did not deny but confessed – "I am not the Christ!" **1:21** So they asked him, "Then who are you? Are you Elijah?" He said, "I am not!" "Are you the Prophet?" He answered, "No!" **1:22** Then they said to him, "Who are you? Tell us so that we can give an answer to those who sent us. What do you say about yourself?"

1:23 John said, "I am *the voice of one shouting in the wilderness, 'Make straight the way for the Lord,'* as Isaiah the prophet said." **1:24** (Now they had been sent from the Pharisees.) **1:25** So they asked John, "Why then are you baptizing if you are not the Christ, nor Elijah, nor the Prophet?"

1:26 John answered them, "I baptize with water. Among you stands one whom you do not recognize, **1:27** who is coming after me. I am not worthy to untie the strap of his sandal!" **1:28** These things happened in Bethany across the Jordan River where John was baptizing.

1:29 On the next day John saw Jesus coming toward him and said, "Look, the Lamb of God who takes away the sin of the world! **1:30** This is the one about whom I said, 'After me comes a man who is greater than I am, because he existed before me.' **1:31** I did not recognize him, but I came baptizing with water so that he could be revealed to Israel."

1:32 Then John testified, "I saw the Spirit descending like a dove from heaven, and it remained on him. **1:33** And I did not recognize him, but the one who sent me to baptize with water said to me, 'The one on whom you see the Spirit descending and remaining – this is the one who baptizes with the Holy Spirit.' **1:34** I have both seen and testified that this man is the Chosen One of God."

1:35 Again the next day John was standing there with two of his disciples. **1:36** Gazing at Jesus as he walked by, he said, "Look, the Lamb of God!" **1:37** When John's two disciples heard him say this, they followed Jesus. **1:38** Jesus turned around and saw them following and said to them, "What do you want?" So they said to him, "Rabbi" (which is translated Teacher), "where are you staying?" **1:39** Jesus answered, "Come and you will see." So they came and saw where he was staying, and they stayed with him that day. Now it was about four o'clock in the afternoon.

Andrew's Declaration

1:40 Andrew, the brother of Simon Peter, was one of the two disciples who heard what John said and followed Jesus. **1:41** He first found his own brother Simon and told him, "We have found the Messiah!" (which is translated Christ). **1:42** Andrew brought Simon to Jesus. Jesus looked at him and said, "You are Simon, the son of John. You will be called Cephas" (which is translated Peter).

The Calling of More Disciples

1:43 On the next day Jesus wanted to set out for Galilee. He found Philip and said to him, "Follow me." **1:44** (Now Philip was from Bethsaida, the town of Andrew and Peter.) **1:45** Philip found Nathanael and told him, "We have found the one Moses wrote about in the law, and the prophets also wrote about – Jesus of Nazareth, the son of Joseph." **1:46** Nathanael replied, "Can anything good come out of Nazareth?" Philip replied, "Come and see."

1:47 Jesus saw Nathanael coming toward him and exclaimed, "Look, a true Israelite *in whom there is no deceit!*" **1:48** Nathanael asked him, "How do you know me?" Jesus replied, "Before Philip called you, when you were under the fig tree, I saw you." **1:49** Nathanael answered him, "Rabbi, you are the Son of God; you are the king of Israel!" **1:50** Jesus said to him, "Because I told you that I saw you under the fig tree, do you believe? You will see greater things than these." **1:51** He continued, "I tell all of you the solemn truth – you will see heaven opened and the angels of God ascending and descending on the Son of Man."

Turning Water into Wine

2:1 Now on the third day there was a wedding at Cana in Galilee. Jesus' mother was there, **2:2** and Jesus and his disciples were also invited to the wedding. **2:3** When the wine ran out, Jesus' mother said to him, "They have no wine left." **2:4** Jesus replied, "Woman, why are you saying this to me? My time has not yet come." **2:5** His mother told the servants, "Whatever he tells you, do it."

2:6 Now there were six stone water jars there for Jewish ceremonial washing, each holding twenty or thirty gallons. **2:7** Jesus told the servants, "Fill the water jars with water." So they filled them up to the very top. **2:8** Then he told them, "Now draw some out and take it to the head steward," and they did. **2:9** When the head steward tasted the water that had been turned to wine, not knowing where it came from (though the servants who had drawn the water knew), he called the bridegroom **2:10** and said to him, "Everyone serves the good wine first, and then the cheaper wine when the guests are drunk. You have kept the good wine until now!" **2:11** Jesus did this as the first of his miraculous signs, in Cana of Galilee. In this way he revealed his glory, and his disciples believed in him.

Cleansing the Temple

2:12 After this he went down to Capernaum with his mother and brothers and his disciples, and they stayed there a few days. **2:13** Now the Jewish feast of Passover was near, so Jesus went up to Jerusalem.

2:14 He found in the temple courts those who were selling oxen and sheep and doves, and the money changers sitting at tables. **2:15** So he made a whip of cords and drove them all out of the temple courts, with the sheep and the oxen. He scattered the coins of the money changers and overturned their tables. **2:16** To those who sold the doves he said, "Take these things away from here! Do not make my Father's house a marketplace!" **2:17** His disciples remembered that it was written, "***Zeal for your house will devour me.***"

2:18 So then the Jewish leaders responded, "What sign can you show us, since you are doing these things?" **2:19** Jesus replied, "Destroy this temple and in three days I will raise it up again." **2:20** Then the Jewish leaders said to him, "This temple has been under construction for forty-six years, and are you going to raise it up in three days?" **2:21** But Jesus was speaking about the temple of his body. **2:22** So after he was raised from the dead, his disciples remembered that he had said this, and they believed the scripture and the saying that Jesus had spoken.

Jesus at the Passover Feast

2:23 Now while Jesus was in Jerusalem at the feast of the Passover, many people believed in his name because they saw the miraculous signs he was doing. **2:24** But Jesus would not entrust himself to them, because he knew all people. **2:25** He did not need anyone to testify about man, for he knew what was in man.

Conversation with Nicodemus

3:1 Now a certain man, a Pharisee named Nicodemus, who was a member of the Jewish ruling council, **3:2** came to Jesus at night and said to him, "Rabbi, we know that you are a teacher who has come from God. For no one could perform the miraculous signs that you do unless God is with him." **3:3** Jesus replied, "I tell you the solemn truth, unless a person is born from above, he cannot see the kingdom of God." **3:4** Nicodemus said to him, "How can a man be born when he is old? He cannot enter his mother's womb and be born a second time, can he?"

3:5 Jesus answered, "I tell you the solemn truth, unless a person is born of water and spirit, he cannot enter the kingdom of God. **3:6** What is born of the flesh is flesh, and what is born of the Spirit is spirit. **3:7** Do not be amazed that I said to you, 'You must all be born from above.' **3:8** The wind blows wherever it will, and you hear the sound it makes, but do not know where it comes from and where it is going. So it is with everyone who is born of the Spirit."

3:9 Nicodemus replied, "How can these things be?" **3:10** Jesus answered, "Are you the teacher of Israel and yet you don't understand these things? **3:11** I tell you the solemn truth, we speak about what we know and testify about what we have seen, but you people do not accept our testimony. **3:12** If I have told you people about earthly things and you don't believe, how will you believe if I tell you about heavenly things? **3:13** No one has ascended into heaven except the one who descended from heaven – the Son of Man. **3:14** Just as Moses *lifted up the serpent in the wilderness*, so must the Son of Man be lifted up, **3:15** so that everyone who believes in him may have eternal life."

3:16 For this is the way God loved the world: He gave his one and only Son, so that everyone who believes in him will not perish but have eternal life. **3:17** For God did not send his Son into the world to condemn the world, but that the world should be saved through him. **3:18** The one who believes in him is not condemned. The one who does not believe has been condemned already, because he has not believed in the name of the one and only Son of God. **3:19** Now this is the basis for judging: that the light has come into the world and people loved the darkness rather than the light, because their deeds were evil. **3:20** For everyone who does evil deeds hates the light and does not come to the light, so that their deeds will not be exposed. **3:21** But the one who practices the truth comes to the light, so that it may be plainly evident that his deeds have been done in God.

Further Testimony About Jesus by John the Baptist

3:22 After this, Jesus and his disciples came into Judean territory, and there he spent time with them and was baptizing. **3:23** John was also baptizing at Aenon near Salim, because water was plentiful there, and people were coming to him and being baptized. **3:24** (For John had not yet been thrown into prison.)

3:25 Now a dispute came about between some of John's disciples and a certain Jew concerning ceremonial washing. **3:26** So they came to John and said to him, "Rabbi, the one who was with you on the other side of the Jordan River, about whom you testified – see, he is baptizing, and everyone is flocking to him!"

3:27 John replied, "No one can receive anything unless it has been given to him from heaven. **3:28** You yourselves can testify that I said, 'I am not the Christ,' but rather, 'I have been sent before him.' **3:29** The one who has the bride is the bridegroom. The friend of the bridegroom, who stands by and listens for him, rejoices greatly when he hears the bridegroom's voice. This then is my joy, and it is complete. **3:30** He must become more important while I become less important."

3:31 The one who comes from above is superior to all. The one who is from the earth belongs to the earth and speaks about earthly things. The one who comes from heaven is superior to all. **3:32** He testifies about what he has seen and heard, but no one accepts his testimony. **3:33** The one who has accepted his testimony has confirmed clearly that God is truthful. **3:34** For the one whom God has sent speaks the words of God, for he does not give the Spirit sparingly. **3:35** The Father loves the Son and has placed all things under his authority. **3:36** The one who believes in the Son has eternal life. The one who rejects the Son will not see life, but God's wrath remains on him.

Departure From Judea

4:1 Now when Jesus knew that the Pharisees had heard that he was winning and baptizing more disciples than John **4:2** (although Jesus himself was not baptizing, but his disciples were), **4:3** he left Judea and set out once more for Galilee.

Conversation With a Samaritan Woman

4:4 But he had to pass through Samaria. **4:5** Now he came to a Samaritan town called Sychar, near the plot of land that Jacob had given to his son Joseph. **4:6** Jacob's well was there, so Jesus, since he was tired from the journey, sat right down beside the well. It was about noon.

4:7 A Samaritan woman came to draw water. Jesus said to her, "Give me some water to drink." **4:8** (For his disciples had gone off into the town to buy supplies.) **4:9** So the Samaritan woman said to him, "How can you – a Jew – ask me, a Samaritan woman, for water to drink?" (For Jews use nothing in common with Samaritans.)

4:10 Jesus answered her, "If you had known the gift of God and who it is who said to you, 'Give me some water to drink,' you would have asked him, and he would have given you living water." **4:11** "Sir," the woman said to him, "you have no bucket and the well is deep; where then do you get this living water? **4:12** Surely you're not greater than our ancestor Jacob, are you? For he gave us this well and drank from it himself, along with his sons and his livestock."

4:13 Jesus replied, "Everyone who drinks some of this water will be thirsty again. **4:14** But whoever drinks some of the water that I will give him will never be thirsty again, but the water that I will give him will become in him a fountain of water springing up to eternal life." **4:15** The woman said to him, "Sir, give me this water, so that I will not be thirsty or have to come here to draw water." **4:16** He said to her, "Go call your husband and come back here." **4:17** The woman replied, "I have no husband." Jesus said to her, "Right you are when you said, 'I have no husband,' **4:18** for you have had five husbands, and the man you are living with now is not your husband. This you said truthfully!"

4:19 The woman said to him, "Sir, I see that you are a prophet. **4:20** Our fathers worshiped on this mountain, and you people say that the place where people must worship is in Jerusalem." **4:21** Jesus said to her, "Believe me, woman, a time is coming when you will worship the Father neither on this mountain nor in Jerusalem. **4:22** You people worship what you do not know. We worship what we know, because salvation is from the Jews. **4:23** But a time is coming – and now is here – when the true worshipers will worship the Father in spirit and truth, for the Father seeks such people to be his worshipers. **4:24** God is spirit, and the people who worship him must worship in spirit and truth." **4:25** The woman said to him, "I know that Messiah is coming" (the one called Christ); "whenever he comes, he will tell us everything." **4:26** Jesus said to her, "I, the one speaking to you, am he."

The Disciples Return

4:27 Now at that very moment his disciples came back. They were shocked because he was speaking with a woman. However, no one said, "What do you want?" or "Why are you speaking with her?" **4:28** Then the woman left her water jar, went off into the town and said to the people, **4:29** "Come, see a man who told me everything I ever did. Surely he can't be the Messiah, can he?" **4:30** So they left the town and began coming to him.

Workers for the Harvest

4:31 Meanwhile the disciples were urging him, "Rabbi, eat something." **4:32** But he said to them, "I have food to eat that you know nothing about." **4:33** So the disciples began to say to one another, "No one brought him anything to eat, did they?" **4:34** Jesus said to them, "My food is to do the will of the one who sent me and to complete his work. **4:35** Don't you say, 'There are four more months and then comes the harvest?' I tell you, look up and see that the fields are already white for harvest! **4:36** The one who reaps receives pay and gathers fruit for eternal life, so that the one who sows and the one who reaps can rejoice together. **4:37** For in this instance the saying is true, 'One sows and another reaps.' **4:38** I sent you to reap what you did not work for; others have labored and you have entered into their labor."

The Samaritans Respond

4:39 Now many Samaritans from that town believed in him because of the report of the woman who testified, "He told me everything I ever did." **4:40** So when the Samaritans came to him, they began asking him to stay with them. He stayed there two days, **4:41** and because of his word many more believed. **4:42** They said to the woman, "No longer do we believe because of your words, for we have heard for ourselves, and we know that this one really is the Savior of the world."

Onward to Galilee

4:43 After the two days he departed from there to Galilee. **4:44** (For Jesus himself had testified that a prophet has no honor in his own country.) **4:45** So when he came to Galilee, the Galileans welcomed him because they had seen all the things he had done in Jerusalem at the feast (for they themselves had gone to the feast).

Healing the Royal Official's Son

4:46 Now he came again to Cana in Galilee where he had made the water wine. In Capernaum there was a certain royal official whose son was sick. **4:47** When he heard that Jesus had come back from Judea to Galilee, he went to him and begged him to come down and heal his son, who was about to die. **4:48** So Jesus said to him, "Unless you people see signs and wonders you will never believe!" **4:49** "Sir," the official said to him, "come down before my child dies." **4:50** Jesus told him, "Go home; your son will live." The man believed the word that Jesus spoke to him, and set off for home.

4:51 While he was on his way down, his slaves met him and told him that his son was going to live. **4:52** So he asked them the time when his condition began to improve, and they told him, "Yesterday at one o'clock in the afternoon the fever left him." **4:53** Then the father realized that it was the very time Jesus had said to him, "Your son will live," and he himself believed along with his entire household. **4:54** Jesus did this as his second miraculous sign when he returned from Judea to Galilee.

Healing a Paralytic at the Pool of Bethesda

5:1 After this there was a Jewish feast, and Jesus went up to Jerusalem. **5:2** Now there is in Jerusalem by the Sheep Gate a pool called *Bethzatha* in Aramaic, which has five covered walkways. **5:3** A great number of sick, blind, lame, and paralyzed people were lying in these walkways. **5:5** Now a man was there who had been disabled for thirty-eight years. **5:6** When Jesus saw him lying there and when he realized that the man had been disabled a long time already, he said to him, "Do you want to become well?" **5:7** The sick man answered him, "Sir, I have no one to put me into the pool when the water is stirred up. While I am trying to get into the water, someone else goes down there before me." **5:8** Jesus said to him, "Stand up! Pick up your mat and walk." **5:9** Immediately the man was healed, and he picked up his mat and started walking. (Now that day was a Sabbath.)

5:10 So the Jewish leaders said to the man who had been healed, "It is the Sabbath, and you are not permitted to carry your mat." **5:11** But he answered them, "The man who made me well said to me, 'Pick up your mat and walk.'" **5:12** They asked him, "Who is the man who said to you, 'Pick up your mat and walk'?" **5:13** But the man who had been healed did not know who it was, for Jesus had slipped out, since there was a crowd in that place.

5:14 After this Jesus found him at the temple and said to him, "Look, you have become well. Don't sin any more, lest anything worse happen to you." **5:15** The man went away and informed the Jewish leaders that Jesus was the one who had made him well.

Responding to Jewish Leaders

5:16 Now because Jesus was doing these things on the Sabbath, the Jewish leaders began persecuting him. **5:17** So he told them, "My Father is working until now, and I too am working." **5:18** For this reason the Jewish leaders were trying even harder to kill him, because not only was he breaking the Sabbath, but he was also calling God his own Father, thus making himself equal with God.

5:19 So Jesus answered them, "I tell you the solemn truth, the Son can do nothing on his own initiative, but only what he sees the Father doing. For whatever the Father does, the Son does likewise. **5:20** For the Father loves the Son and shows him everything he does, and will show him greater deeds than these, so that you will be amazed. **5:21** For just as the Father raises the dead and gives them life, so also the Son gives life to whomever he wishes. **5:22** Furthermore, the Father does not judge anyone, but has assigned all judgment to the Son, **5:23** so that all people will honor the Son just as they honor the Father. The one who does not honor the Son does not honor the Father who sent him.

5:24 "I tell you the solemn truth, the one who hears my message and believes the one who sent me has eternal life and will not be condemned, but has crossed over from death to life. **5:25** I tell you the solemn truth, a time is coming – and is now here – when the dead will hear the voice of the Son of God, and those who hear will live. **5:26** For just as the Father has life in himself, thus he has granted the Son to have life in himself, **5:27** and he has granted the Son authority to execute judgment, because he is the Son of Man.

5:28 "Do not be amazed at this, because a time is coming when all who are in the tombs will hear his voice **5:29** and will come out – the ones who have done what is good to the resurrection resulting in life, and the ones who have done what is evil to the resurrection resulting in condemnation. **5:30** I can do nothing on my own initiative. Just as I hear, I judge, and my judgment is just, because I do not seek my own will, but the will of the one who sent me.

More Testimony About Jesus

5:31 "If I testify about myself, my testimony is not true. **5:32** There is another who testifies about me, and I know the testimony he testifies about me is true. **5:33** You have sent to John, and he has testified to the truth. **5:34** (I do not accept human testimony, but I say this so that you may be saved.) **5:35** He was a lamp that was burning and shining, and you wanted to rejoice greatly for a short time in his light.

5:36 "But I have a testimony greater than that from John. For the deeds that the Father has assigned me to complete – the deeds I am now doing – testify about me that the Father has sent me. **5:37** And the Father who sent me has himself testified about me. You people have never heard his voice nor seen his form at any time, **5:38** nor do you have his word residing in you, because you do not believe the one whom he sent. **5:39** You study the scriptures thoroughly because you think in them you possess eternal life, and it is these same scriptures that testify about me, **5:40** but you are not willing to come to me so that you may have life.

5:41 "I do not accept praise from people, **5:42** but I know you, that you do not have the love of God within you. **5:43** I have come in my Father's name, and you do not accept me. If someone else comes in his own name, you will accept him. **5:44** How can you believe, if you accept praise from one another and don't seek the praise that comes from the only God?

5:45 "Do not suppose that I will accuse you before the Father. The one who accuses you is Moses, in whom you have placed your hope. **5:46** If you believed Moses, you would believe me, because he wrote about me. **5:47** But if you do not believe what Moses wrote, how will you believe my words?"

The Feeding of the Five Thousand

6:1 After this Jesus went away to the other side of the Sea of Galilee (also called the Sea of Tiberias). **6:2** A large crowd was following him because they were observing the miraculous signs he was performing on the sick. **6:3** So Jesus went on up the mountainside and sat down there with his disciples. **6:4** (Now the Jewish feast of the Passover was near.) **6:5** Then Jesus, when he looked up and saw that a large crowd was coming to him, said to Philip, "Where can we buy bread so that these people may eat?" **6:6** (Now Jesus said this to test him, for he knew what he was going to do.) **6:7** Philip replied, "Two hundred silver coins worth of bread would not be enough for each one to get a little." **6:8** One of Jesus' disciples, Andrew, Simon Peter's brother, said to him, **6:9** "Here is a boy who has five barley loaves and two fish, but what good are these for so many people?"

6:10 Jesus said, "Have the people sit down." (Now there was a lot of grass in that place.) So the men sat down, about five thousand in number. **6:11** Then Jesus took the loaves, and when he had given thanks, he distributed the bread to those who were seated. He then did the same with the fish, as much as they wanted. **6:12** When they were all satisfied, Jesus said to his disciples, "Gather up the broken pieces that are left over, so that nothing is wasted." **6:13** So they gathered them up and filled twelve baskets with broken pieces from the five barley loaves left over by the people who had eaten.

6:14 Now when the people saw the miraculous sign that Jesus performed, they began to say to one another, "This is certainly *the Prophet who is to come into the world.*" **6:15** Then Jesus, because he knew they were going to come and seize him by force to make him king, withdrew again up the mountainside alone.

Walking on Water

6:16 Now when evening came, his disciples went down to the lake, **6:17** got into a boat, and started to cross the lake to Capernaum. (It had already become dark, and Jesus had not yet come to them.) **6:18** By now a strong wind was blowing and the sea was getting rough. **6:19** Then, when they had rowed about three or four miles, they caught sight of Jesus walking on the lake, approaching the boat, and they were frightened. **6:20** But he said to them, "It is I. Do not be afraid." **6:21** Then they wanted to take him into the boat, and immediately the boat came to the land where they had been heading.

6:22 The next day the crowd that remained on the other side of the lake realized that only one small boat had been there, and that Jesus had not boarded it with his disciples, but that his disciples had gone away alone. **6:23** But some boats from Tiberias came to shore near the place where they had eaten the bread after the Lord had given thanks. **6:24** So when the crowd realized that neither Jesus nor his disciples were there, they got into the boats and came to Capernaum looking for Jesus.

Jesus' Discourse About the Bread of Life

6:25 When they found him on the other side of the lake, they said to him, "Rabbi, when did you get here?" **6:26** Jesus replied, "I tell you the solemn truth, you are looking for me not because you saw miraculous signs, but because you ate all the loaves of bread you wanted. **6:27** Do not work for the food that disappears, but for the food that remains to eternal life – the food which the Son of Man will give to you. For God the Father has put his seal of approval on him."

6:28 So then they said to him, "What must we do to accomplish the deeds God requires?" **6:29** Jesus replied, "This is the deed God requires – to believe in the one whom he sent." **6:30** So they said to him, "Then what miraculous sign will you perform, so that we may see it and believe you? What will you do? **6:31** Our ancestors ate the manna in the wilderness, just as it is written, '*He gave them bread from heaven to eat.*'"

6:32 Then Jesus told them, "I tell you the solemn truth, it is not Moses who has given you the bread from heaven, but my Father is giving you the true bread from heaven. **6:33** For the bread of God is the one who comes down from heaven and gives life to the world." **6:34** So they said to him, "Sir, give us this bread all the time!"

6:35 Jesus said to them, "I am the bread of life. The one who comes to me will never go hungry, and the one who believes in me will never be thirsty. **6:36** But I told you that you have seen me and still do not believe. **6:37** Everyone whom the Father gives me will come to me, and the one who comes to me I will never send away. **6:38** For I have come down from heaven not to do my own will but the will of the one who sent me. **6:39** Now this is the will of the one who sent me – that I should not lose one person of every one he has given me, but raise them all up at the last day. **6:40** For this is the will of my Father – for everyone who looks on the Son and believes in him to have eternal life, and I will raise him up at the last day."

6:41 Then the Jews who were hostile to Jesus began complaining about him because he said, "I am the bread that came down from heaven," **6:42** and they said, "Isn't this Jesus the son of Joseph, whose father and mother we know? How can he now say, 'I have come down from heaven'?" **6:43** Jesus replied, "Do not complain about me to one another. **6:44** No one can come to me unless the Father who sent me draws him, and I will raise him up at the last day. **6:45** It is written in the prophets, '*And they will all be taught by God.*' Everyone who hears and learns from the Father comes to me. **6:46** (Not that anyone has seen the Father except the one who is from God – he has seen the Father.) **6:47** I tell you the solemn truth, the one who believes has eternal life. **6:48** I am the bread of life. **6:49** Your ancestors ate the manna in the wilderness, and they died. **6:50** This is the bread that has come down from heaven, so that a person may eat from it and not die. **6:51** I am the living bread that came down from heaven. If anyone eats from this bread he will live forever. The bread that I will give for the life of the world is my flesh."

6:52 Then the Jews who were hostile to Jesus began to argue with one another, "How can this man give us his flesh to eat?" **6:53** Jesus said to them, "I tell you the solemn truth, unless you eat the flesh of the Son of Man and drink his blood, you have no life in yourselves. **6:54** The one who eats my flesh and drinks my blood has eternal life, and I will raise him up on the last day. **6:55** For my flesh is true food, and my blood is true drink. **6:56** The one who eats my flesh and drinks my blood resides in me, and I in him. **6:57** Just as the living Father sent me, and I live because of the Father, so the one who consumes me will live because of me. **6:58** This is the bread that came down from heaven; it is not like the bread your ancestors ate, but then later died. The one who eats this bread will live forever."

Many Followers Depart

6:59 Jesus said these things while he was teaching in the synagogue in Capernaum. **6:60** Then many of his disciples, when they heard these things, said, "This is a difficult saying! Who can understand it?" **6:61** When Jesus was aware that his disciples were complaining about this, he said to them, "Does this cause you to be offended? **6:62** Then what if you see the Son of Man ascending where he was before? **6:63** The Spirit is the one who gives life; human nature is of no help! The words that I have spoken to you are spirit and are life. **6:64** But there are some of you who do not believe." (For Jesus had already known from the beginning who those were who did not believe, and who it was who would betray him.) **6:65** So Jesus added, "Because of this I told you that no one can come to me unless the Father has allowed him to come."

Peter's Confession

6:66 After this many of his disciples quit following him and did not accompany him any longer. **6:67** So Jesus said to the twelve, "You don't want to go away too, do you?" **6:68** Simon Peter answered him, "Lord, to whom would we go? You have the words of eternal life. **6:69** We have come to believe and to know that you are the Holy One of God!" **6:70** Jesus replied, "Didn't I choose you, the twelve, and yet one of you is the devil?" **6:71** (Now he said this about Judas son of Simon Iscariot, for Judas, one of the twelve, was going to betray him.)

The Feast of Tabernacles

7:1 After this Jesus traveled throughout Galilee. He stayed out of Judea because the Jewish leaders wanted to kill him. **7:2** Now the Jewish feast of Tabernacles was near. **7:3** So Jesus' brothers advised him, "Leave here and go to Judea so your disciples may see your miracles that you are performing. **7:4** For no one who seeks to make a reputation for himself does anything in secret. If you are doing these things, show yourself to the world." **7:5** (For not even his own brothers believed in him.) **7:6** So Jesus replied, "My time has not yet arrived, but you are ready at any opportunity! **7:7** The world cannot hate you, but it hates me, because I am testifying about it that its deeds are evil. **7:8** You go up to the feast yourselves. I am not going up to this feast because my time has not yet fully arrived." **7:9** When he had said this, he remained in Galilee.

7:10 But when his brothers had gone up to the feast, then Jesus himself also went up, not openly but in secret. **7:11** So the Jewish leaders were looking for him at the feast, asking, "Where is he?" **7:12** There was a lot of grumbling about him among the crowds. Some were saying, "He is a good man," but others, "He deceives the common people." **7:13** However, no one spoke openly about him for fear of the Jewish leaders.

Teaching in the Temple

7:14 When the feast was half over, Jesus went up to the temple courts and began to teach. **7:15** Then the Jewish leaders were astonished and said, "How does this man know so much when he has never had formal instruction?" **7:16** So Jesus replied, "My teaching is not from me, but from the one who sent me. **7:17** If anyone wants to do God's will, he will know about my teaching, whether it is from God or whether I speak from my own authority. **7:18** The person who speaks on his own authority desires to receive honor for himself; the one who desires the honor of the one who sent him is a man of integrity, and there is no unrighteousness in him. **7:19** Hasn't Moses given you the law? Yet not one of you keeps the law! Why do you want to kill me?"

7:20 The crowd answered, "You're possessed by a demon! Who is trying to kill you?" **7:21** Jesus replied, "I performed one miracle and you are all amazed. **7:22** However, because Moses gave you the practice of circumcision (not that it came from Moses, but from the forefathers), you circumcise a male child on the Sabbath. **7:23** But if a male child is circumcised on the Sabbath so that the law of Moses is not broken, why are you angry with me because I made a man completely well on the Sabbath? **7:24** Do not judge according to external appearance, but judge with proper judgment."

Questions About Jesus' Identity

7:25 Then some of the residents of Jerusalem began to say, "Isn't this the man they are trying to kill? **7:26** Yet here he is, speaking publicly, and they are saying nothing to him. Do the rulers really know that this man is the Christ? **7:27** But we know where this man comes from. Whenever the Christ comes, no one will know where he comes from."

7:28 Then Jesus, while teaching in the temple courts, cried out, "You both know me and know where I come from! And I have not come on my own initiative, but the one who sent me is true. You do not know him, **7:29** but I know him, because I have come from him and he sent me." **7:30** So then they tried to seize Jesus, but no one laid a hand on him, because his time had not yet come. **7:31** Yet many of the crowd believed in him and said, "Whenever the Christ comes, he won't perform more miraculous signs than this man did, will he?"

7:32 The Pharisees heard the crowd murmuring these things about Jesus, so the chief priests and the Pharisees sent officers to arrest him. **7:33** Then Jesus said, "I will be with you for only a little while longer, and then I am going to the one who sent me. **7:34** You will look for me but will not find me, and where I am you cannot come."

7:35 Then the Jewish leaders said to one another, "Where is he going to go that we cannot find him? He is not going to go to the Jewish people dispersed among the Greeks and teach the Greeks, is he? **7:36** What did he mean by saying, 'You will look for me but will not find me, and where I am you cannot come'?"

Teaching About the Spirit

7:37 On the last day of the feast, the greatest day, Jesus stood up and shouted out, "If anyone is thirsty, let him come to me, and **7:38** let the one who believes in me drink. Just as the scripture says, '*From within him will flow rivers of living water.*'" **7:39** (Now he said this about the Spirit, whom those who believed in him were going to receive, for the Spirit had not yet been given, because Jesus was not yet glorified.)

Differing Opinions About Jesus

7:40 When they heard these words, some of the crowd began to say, "This really is the Prophet!" **7:41** Others said, "This is the Christ!" But still others said, "No, for the Christ doesn't come from Galilee, does he? **7:42** Don't the scriptures say that the Christ is *a descendant of David* and *comes from Bethlehem*, the village where David lived?" **7:43** So there was a division in the crowd because of Jesus. **7:44** Some of them were wanting to seize him, but no one laid a hand on him.

Lack of Belief

7:45 Then the officers returned to the chief priests and Pharisees, who said to them, "Why didn't you bring him back with you?" **7:46** The officers replied, "No one ever spoke like this man!" **7:47** Then the Pharisees answered, "You haven't been deceived too, have you? **7:48** None of the rulers or the Pharisees have believed in him, have they? **7:49** But this rabble who do not know the law are accursed!"

7:50 Nicodemus, who had gone to Jesus before and who was one of the rulers, said, **7:51** "Our law doesn't condemn a man unless it first hears from him and learns what he is doing, does it?" **7:52** They replied, "You aren't from Galilee too, are you? Investigate carefully and you will see that no prophet comes from Galilee!"

A Woman Caught in Adultery

[[**7:53** And each one departed to his own house. **8:1** But Jesus went to the Mount of Olives. **8:2** Early in the morning he came to the temple courts again. All the people came to him, and he sat down and began to teach them. **8:3** The experts in the law and the Pharisees brought a woman who had been caught committing adultery. They made her stand in front of them **8:4** and said to Jesus, "Teacher, this woman was caught in the very act of adultery. **8:5** In the law *Moses commanded us to stone to death* such women. What then do you say?" **8:6** (Now they were asking this in an attempt to trap him, so that they could bring charges against him.) Jesus bent down and wrote on the ground with his finger. **8:7** When they persisted in asking him, he stood up straight and replied, "Whoever among you is guiltless may be the first to throw a stone at her." **8:8** Then he bent over again and wrote on the ground.

8:9 Now when they heard this, they began to drift away one at a time, starting with the older ones, until Jesus was left alone with the woman standing before him. **8:10** Jesus stood up straight and said to her, "Woman, where are they? Did no one condemn you?" **8:11** She replied, "No one, Lord." And Jesus said, "I do not condemn you either. Go, and from now on do not sin any more."]]

Jesus as the Light of the World

8:12 Then Jesus spoke out again, "I am the light of the world. The one who follows me will never walk in darkness, but will have the light of life." **8:13** So the Pharisees objected, "You testify about yourself; your testimony is not true!" **8:14** Jesus answered, "Even if I testify about myself, my testimony is true, because I know where I came from and where I am going. But you people do not know where I came from or where I am going. **8:15** You people judge by outward appearances; I do not judge anyone. **8:16** But if I judge, my evaluation is accurate, because I am not alone when I judge, but I and the Father who sent me do so together. **8:17** It is written in your law that *the testimony of two men is true.* **8:18** I testify about myself and the Father who sent me testifies about me."

8:19 Then they began asking him, "Who is your father?" Jesus answered, "You do not know either me or my Father. If you knew me you would know my Father too." **8:20** (Jesus spoke these words near the offering box while he was teaching in the temple courts. No one seized him because his time had not yet come.)

Where Jesus Came From and Where He is Going

8:21 Then Jesus said to them again, "I am going away, and you will look for me but will die in your sin. Where I am going you cannot come." **8:22** So the Jewish leaders began to say, "Perhaps he is going to kill himself, because he says, 'Where I am going you cannot come.'" **8:23** Jesus replied, "You people are from below; I am from above. You people are from this world; I am not from this world. **8:24** Thus I told you that you will die in your sins. For unless you believe that I am he, you will die in your sins."

8:25 So they said to him, "Who are you?" Jesus replied, "What I have told you from the beginning. **8:26** I have many things to say and to judge about you, but the Father who sent me is truthful, and the things I have heard from him I speak to the world." **8:27** (They did not understand that he was telling them about his Father.)

8:28 Then Jesus said, "When you lift up the Son of Man, then you will know that I am he, and I do nothing on my own initiative, but I speak just what the Father taught me. **8:29** And the one who sent me is with me. He has not left me alone, because I always do those things that please him." **8:30** While he was saying these things, many people believed in him.

Abraham's Children and the Devil's Children

8:31 Then Jesus said to those Judeans who had believed him, "If you continue to follow my teaching, you are really my disciples **8:32** and you will know the truth, and the truth will set you free." **8:33** "We are descendants of Abraham," they replied, "and have never been anyone's slaves! How can you say, 'You will become free'?" **8:34** Jesus answered them, "I tell you the solemn truth, everyone who practices sin is a slave of sin. **8:35** The slave does not remain in the family forever, but the son remains forever. **8:36** So if the son sets you free, you will be really free. **8:37** I know that you are Abraham's descendants. But you want to kill me, because my teaching makes no progress among you. **8:38** I am telling you the things I have seen while with the Father; as for you, practice the things you have heard from the Father!"

8:39 They answered him, "Abraham is our father!" Jesus replied, "If you are Abraham's children, you would be doing the deeds of Abraham. **8:40** But now you are trying to kill me, a man who has told you the truth I heard from God. Abraham did not do this! **8:41** You people are doing the deeds of your father."

Then they said to Jesus, "We were not born as a result of immorality! We have only one Father, God himself." **8:42** Jesus replied, "If God were your Father, you would love me, for I have come from God and am now here. I have not come on my own initiative, but he sent me. **8:43** Why don't you understand what I am saying? It is because you cannot accept my teaching. **8:44** You people are from your father the devil, and you want to do what your father desires. He was a murderer from the beginning, and does not uphold the truth, because there is no truth in him. Whenever he lies, he speaks according to his own nature, because he is a liar and the father of lies. **8:45** But because I am telling you the truth, you do not believe me. **8:46** Who among you can prove me guilty of any sin? If I am telling you the truth, why don't you believe me? **8:47** The one who belongs to God listens and responds to God's words. You don't listen and respond, because you don't belong to God."

8:48 The Judeans replied, "Aren't we correct in saying that you are a Samaritan and are possessed by a demon?" **8:49** Jesus answered, "I am not possessed by a demon, but I honor my Father – and yet you dishonor me. **8:50** I am not trying to get praise for myself. There is one who demands it, and he also judges. **8:51** I tell you the solemn truth, if anyone obeys my teaching, he will never see death."

8:52 Then the Judeans responded, "Now we know you're possessed by a demon! Both Abraham and the prophets died, and yet you say, 'If anyone obeys my teaching, he will never experience death.' **8:53** You aren't greater than our father Abraham who died, are you? And the prophets died too! Who do you claim to be?" **8:54** Jesus replied, "If I glorify myself, my glory is worthless. The one who glorifies me is my Father, about whom you people say, 'He is our God.' **8:55** Yet you do not know him, but I know him. If I were to say that I do not know him, I would be a liar like you. But I do know him, and I obey his teaching. **8:56** Your father Abraham was overjoyed to see my day, and he saw it and was glad."

8:57 Then the Judeans replied, "You are not yet fifty years old! Have you seen Abraham?" **8:58** Jesus said to them, "I tell you the solemn truth, before Abraham came into existence, I am!" **8:59** Then they picked up stones to throw at him, but Jesus hid himself and went out from the temple area.

Healing a Man Born Blind

9:1 Now as Jesus was passing by, he saw a man who had been blind from birth. **9:2** His disciples asked him, "Rabbi, who committed the sin that caused him to be born blind, this man or his parents?" **9:3** Jesus answered, "Neither this man nor his parents sinned, but he was born blind so that the acts of God may be revealed through what happens to him. **9:4** We must perform the deeds of the one who sent me as long as it is daytime. Night is coming when no one can work. **9:5** As long as I am in the world, I am the light of the world." **9:6** Having said this, he spat on the ground and made some mud with the saliva. He smeared the mud on the blind man's eyes **9:7** and said to him, "Go wash in the pool of Siloam" (which is translated "sent"). So the blind man went away and washed, and came back seeing.

9:8 Then the neighbors and the people who had seen him previously as a beggar began saying, "Is this not the man who used to sit and beg?" **9:9** Some people said, "This is the man!" while others said, "No, but he looks like him." The man himself kept insisting, "I am the one!" **9:10** So they asked him, "How then were you made to see?" **9:11** He replied, "The man called Jesus made mud, smeared it on my eyes and told me, 'Go to

Siloam and wash.' So I went and washed, and was able to see." **9:12** They said to him, "Where is that man?" He replied, "I don't know."

The Pharisees' Reaction to the Healing

9:13 They brought the man who used to be blind to the Pharisees. **9:14** (Now the day on which Jesus made the mud and caused him to see was a Sabbath.) **9:15** So the Pharisees asked him again how he had gained his sight. He replied, "He put mud on my eyes and I washed, and now I am able to see."

9:16 Then some of the Pharisees began to say, "This man is not from God, because he does not observe the Sabbath." But others said, "How can a man who is a sinner perform such miraculous signs?" Thus there was a division among them. **9:17** So again they asked the man who used to be blind, "What do you say about him, since he caused you to see?" "He is a prophet," the man replied.

9:18 Now the Jewish religious leaders refused to believe that he had really been blind and had gained his sight until at last they summoned the parents of the man who had become able to see. **9:19** They asked the parents, "Is this your son, whom you say was born blind? Then how does he now see?" **9:20** So his parents replied, "We know that this is our son and that he was born blind. **9:21** But we do not know how he is now able to see, nor do we know who caused him to see. Ask him, he is a mature adult. He will speak for himself." **9:22** (His parents said these things because they were afraid of the Jewish religious leaders. For the Jewish leaders had already agreed that anyone who confessed Jesus to be the Christ would be put out of the synagogue. **9:23** For this reason his parents said, "He is a mature adult, ask him.")

9:24 Then they summoned the man who used to be blind a second time and said to him, "Promise before God to tell the truth. We know that this man is a sinner." **9:25** He replied, "I do not know whether he is a sinner. I do know one thing – that although I was blind, now I can see." **9:26** Then they said to him, "What did he do to you? How did he cause you to see?" **9:27** He answered, "I told you already and you didn't listen. Why do you want to hear it again? You people don't want to become his disciples too, do you?"

9:28 They heaped insults on him, saying, "You are his disciple! We are disciples of Moses! **9:29** We know that God has spoken to Moses! We do not know where this man comes from!" **9:30** The man replied, "This is a remarkable thing, that you don't know where he comes from, and yet he caused me to see! **9:31** We know that God doesn't listen to sinners, but if anyone is devout and does his will, God listens to him. **9:32** Never before has anyone heard of someone causing a man born blind to see. **9:33** If this man were not from God, he could do nothing." **9:34** They replied, "You were born completely in sinfulness, and yet you presume to teach us?" So they threw him out.

The Man's Response to Jesus

9:35 Jesus heard that they had thrown him out, so he found the man and said to him, "Do you believe in the Son of Man?" **9:36** The man replied, "And who is he, sir, that I may believe in him?" **9:37** Jesus told him, "You have seen him; he is the one speaking with you." [**9:38** He said, "Lord, I believe," and he worshiped him. **9:39** Jesus said,] "For judgment I have come into this world, so that those who do not see may gain their sight, and the ones who see may become blind."

9:40 Some of the Pharisees who were with him heard this and asked him, "We are not blind too, are we?" **9:41** Jesus replied, "If you were blind, you would not be guilty of sin, but now because you claim that you can see, your guilt remains."

Jesus as the Good Shepherd

10:1 "I tell you the solemn truth, the one who does not enter the sheepfold by the door, but climbs in some other way, is a thief and a robber. **10:2** The one who enters by the door is the shepherd of the sheep. **10:3** The doorkeeper opens the door for him, and the sheep hear his voice. He calls his own sheep by name and leads them out. **10:4** When he has brought all his own sheep out, he goes ahead of them, and the sheep follow him because they recognize his voice. **10:5** They will never follow a stranger, but will run away from him, because they do not recognize the stranger's voice." **10:6** Jesus told them this parable, but they did not understand what he was saying to them.

10:7 So Jesus said to them again, "I tell you the solemn truth, I am the door for the sheep. **10:8** All who came before me were thieves and robbers, but the sheep did not listen to them. **10:9** I am the door. If anyone enters through me, he will be saved, and will come in and go out, and find pasture. **10:10** The thief comes only to steal and kill and destroy; I have come so that they may have life, and may have it abundantly.

10:11 "I am the good shepherd. The good shepherd lays down his life for the sheep. **10:12** The hired hand, who is not a shepherd and does not own sheep, sees the wolf coming and abandons the sheep and runs away. So the wolf attacks the sheep and scatters them. **10:13** Because he is a hired hand and is not concerned about the sheep, he runs away.

10:14 "I am the good shepherd. I know my own and my own know me – **10:15** just as the Father knows me and I know the Father – and I lay down my life for the sheep. **10:16** I have other sheep that do not come from this sheepfold. I must bring them too, and they will listen to my voice, so that there will be one flock and one shepherd. **10:17** This is why the Father

loves me – because I lay down my life, so that I may take it back again. **10:18** No one takes it away from me, but I lay it down of my own free will. I have the authority to lay it down, and I have the authority to take it back again. This commandment I received from my Father."

10:19 Another sharp division took place among the Jewish people because of these words. **10:20** Many of them were saying, "He is possessed by a demon and has lost his mind! Why do you listen to him?" **10:21** Others said, "These are not the words of someone possessed by a demon. A demon cannot cause the blind to see, can it?"

Jesus at the Feast of Dedication

10:22 Then came the feast of the Dedication in Jerusalem. **10:23** It was winter, and Jesus was walking in the temple area in Solomon's Portico. **10:24** The Jewish leaders surrounded him and asked, "How long will you keep us in suspense? If you are the Christ, tell us plainly." **10:25** Jesus replied, "I told you and you do not believe. The deeds I do in my Father's name testify about me. **10:26** But you refuse to believe because you are not my sheep. **10:27** My sheep listen to my voice, and I know them, and they follow me. **10:28** I give them eternal life, and they will never perish; no one will snatch them from my hand. **10:29** My Father, who has given them to me, is greater than all, and no one can snatch them from my Father's hand. **10:30** The Father and I are one."

10:31 The Jewish leaders picked up rocks again to stone him to death. **10:32** Jesus said to them, "I have shown you many good deeds from the Father. For which one of them are you going to stone me?" **10:33** The Jewish leaders replied, "We are not going to stone you for a good deed but for blasphemy, because you, a man, are claiming to be God."

10:34 Jesus answered, "Is it not written in your law, '*I said, you are gods*'? **10:35** If those people to whom the word of God came were called 'gods' (and the scripture cannot be broken), **10:36** do you say about the one whom the Father set apart and sent into the world, 'You are blaspheming,' because I said, 'I am the Son of God'? **10:37** If I do not perform the deeds of my Father, do not believe me. **10:38** But if I do them, even if you do not believe me, believe the deeds, so that you may come to know and understand that I am in the Father and the Father is in me." **10:39** Then they attempted again to seize him, but he escaped their clutches.

10:40 Jesus went back across the Jordan River again to the place where John had been baptizing at an earlier time, and he stayed there. **10:41** Many came to him and began to say, "John performed no miraculous sign, but everything John said about this man was true!" **10:42** And many believed in Jesus there.

The Death of Lazarus

11:1 Now a certain man named Lazarus was sick. He was from Bethany, the village where Mary and her sister Martha lived. **11:2** (Now it was Mary who anointed the Lord with perfumed oil and wiped his feet dry with her hair, whose brother Lazarus was sick.) **11:3** So the sisters sent a message to Jesus, "Lord, look, the one you love is sick." **11:4** When Jesus heard this, he said, "This sickness will not lead to death, but to God's glory, so that the Son of God may be glorified through it." **11:5** (Now Jesus loved Martha and her sister and Lazarus.)

11:6 So when he heard that Lazarus was sick, he remained in the place where he was for two more days. **11:7** Then after this, he said to his disciples, "Let us go to Judea again." **11:8** The disciples replied, "Rabbi, the Jewish leaders were just now trying to stone you to death! Are you going there again?" **11:9** Jesus replied, "Are there not twelve hours in a day? If anyone walks around in the daytime, he does not stumble, because he sees the light of this world. **11:10** But if anyone walks around at night, he stumbles, because the light is not in him."

11:11 After he said this, he added, "Our friend Lazarus has fallen asleep. But I am going there to awaken him." **11:12** Then the disciples replied, "Lord, if he has fallen asleep, he will recover." **11:13** (Now Jesus had been talking about his death, but they thought he had been talking about real sleep.)

11:14 Then Jesus told them plainly, "Lazarus has died, **11:15** and I am glad for your sake that I was not there, so that you may believe. But let us go to him." **11:16** So Thomas (called Didymus) said to his fellow disciples, "Let us go too, so that we may die with him."

Speaking with Martha and Mary

11:17 When Jesus arrived, he found that Lazarus had been in the tomb four days already. **11:18** (Now Bethany was less than two miles from Jerusalem, **11:19** so many of the Jewish people of the region had come to Martha and Mary to console them over the loss of their brother.) **11:20** So when Martha heard that Jesus was coming, she went out to meet him, but Mary was sitting in the house. **11:21** Martha said to Jesus, "Lord, if you had been here, my brother would not have died. **11:22** But even now I know that whatever you ask from God, God will grant you."

11:23 Jesus replied, "Your brother will come back to life again." **11:24** Martha said, "I know that he will come back to life again in the resurrection at the last day." **11:25** Jesus said to her, "I am the resurrection and the life. The one who believes in me will live even if he dies, **11:26** and the one who lives and believes in me will never die. Do you believe this?" **11:27** She replied, "Yes, Lord, I believe that you are the Christ, the Son of God who comes into the world."

11:28 And when she had said this, Martha went and called her sister Mary, saying privately, "The Teacher is here and is asking for you." **11:29** So when Mary heard this, she got up quickly and went to him. **11:30** (Now Jesus had not yet entered the village, but was still in the place where Martha had come out to meet him.) **11:31** Then the people who were with Mary in the house consoling her saw her get up quickly and go out. They followed her, because they thought she was going to the tomb to weep there. **11:32** Now when Mary came to the place where Jesus was and saw him, she fell at his feet and said to him, "Lord, if you had been here, my brother would not have died." **11:33** When Jesus saw her weeping, and the people who had come with her weeping, he was intensely moved in spirit and greatly distressed. **11:34** He asked, "Where have you laid him?" They replied, "Lord, come and see." **11:35** Jesus wept. **11:36** Thus the people who had come to mourn said, "Look how much he loved him!" **11:37** But some of them said, "This is the man who caused the blind man to see! Couldn't he have done something to keep Lazarus from dying?"

Lazarus Raised from the Dead

11:38 Jesus, intensely moved again, came to the tomb. (Now it was a cave, and a stone was placed across it.) **11:39** Jesus said, "Take away the stone." Martha, the sister of the deceased, replied, "Lord, by this time the body will have a bad smell, because he has been buried four days." **11:40** Jesus responded, "Didn't I tell you that if you believe, you would see the glory of God?" **11:41** So they took away the stone. Jesus looked upward and said, "Father, I thank you that you have listened to me. **11:42** I knew that you always listen to me, but I said this for the sake of the crowd standing around here, that they may believe that you sent me." **11:43** When he had said this, he shouted in a loud voice, "Lazarus, come out!" **11:44** The one who had died came out, his feet and hands tied up with strips of cloth, and a cloth wrapped around his face. Jesus said to them, "Unwrap him and let him go."

The Response of the Jewish Leaders

11:45 Then many of the people, who had come with Mary and had seen the things Jesus did, believed in him. **11:46** But some of them went to the Pharisees and reported to them what Jesus had done. **11:47** So the chief priests and the Pharisees called the council together and said, "What are we doing? For this man is performing many miraculous signs. **11:48** If we allow him to go on in this way, everyone will believe in him, and the Romans will come and take away our sanctuary and our nation." **11:49** Then one of them, Caiaphas, who was high priest that year, said, "You know nothing at all! **11:50** You do not realize that it is more to your advantage to have one man die for the people than for the whole nation to perish." **11:51** (Now he did not say this on his own, but because he was high priest that year, he prophesied that Jesus was going to die for the Jewish nation, **11:52** and not for the Jewish nation only, but to gather together into one the children of God who are scattered.) **11:53** So from that day they planned together to kill him.

11:54 Thus Jesus no longer went around publicly among the Judeans, but went away from there to the region near the wilderness, to a town called Ephraim, and stayed there with his disciples. **11:55** Now the Jewish feast of Passover was near, and many people went up to Jerusalem from the rural areas before the Passover to cleanse themselves ritually. **11:56** Thus they were looking for Jesus, and saying to one another as they stood in the temple courts, "What do you think? That he won't come to the feast?" **11:57** (Now the chief priests and the Pharisees had given orders that anyone who knew where Jesus was should report it, so that they could arrest him.)

Jesus' Anointing

12:1 Then, six days before the Passover, Jesus came to Bethany, where Lazarus lived, whom he had raised from the dead. **12:2** So they prepared a dinner for Jesus there. Martha was serving, and Lazarus was among those present at the table with him. **12:3** Then Mary took three quarters of a pound of expensive aromatic oil from pure nard and anointed the feet of Jesus. She then wiped his feet dry with her hair. (Now the house was filled with the fragrance of the perfumed oil.) **12:4** But Judas Iscariot, one of his disciples (the one who was going to betray him) said, **12:5** "Why wasn't this oil sold for three hundred silver coins and the money given to the poor?" **12:6** (Now Judas said this not because he was concerned about the poor, but because he was a thief. As keeper of the money box, he used to steal what was put into it.) **12:7** So Jesus said, "Leave her alone. She has kept it for the day of my burial. **12:8** For you will always have the poor with you, but you will not always have me!"

12:9 Now a large crowd of Judeans learned that Jesus was there, and so they came not only because of him but also to see Lazarus whom he had raised from the dead. **12:10** So the chief priests planned to kill Lazarus too, **12:11** for on account of him many of the Jewish people from Jerusalem were going away and believing in Jesus.

The Triumphal Entry

12:12 The next day the large crowd that had come to the feast heard that Jesus was coming to Jerusalem. **12:13** So they took branches of palm trees and went out to meet him. They began to shout, "*Hosanna! Blessed is the one who comes in the name of the Lord!* Blessed is the king of Israel!" **12:14** Jesus found a young donkey and sat on it, just as it is writ-ten, **12:15** "*Do not be afraid, people of Zion; look, your king is coming, seated on a donkey's colt!*" **12:16** (His disciples did not understand these things when they first happened, but when Jesus was glorified, then they remembered that these things were written about him and that these things had happened to him.)

12:17 So the crowd who had been with him when he called Lazarus out of the tomb and raised him from the dead were continuing to testify about it. **12:18** Because they had heard that Jesus had performed this miraculous sign, the crowd went out to meet him. **12:19** Thus the Pharisees said to one another, "You see that you can do nothing. Look, the world has run off after him!"

Seekers

12:20 Now some Greeks were among those who had gone up to worship at the feast. **12:21** So these approached Philip, who was from Bethsaida in Galilee, and requested, "Sir, we would like to see Jesus." **12:22** Philip went and told Andrew, and they both went and told Jesus. **12:23** Jesus replied, "The time has come for the Son of Man to be glorified. **12:24** I tell you the solemn truth, unless a kernel of wheat falls into the ground and dies, it remains by itself alone. But if it dies, it produces much grain. **12:25** The one who loves his life destroys it, and the one who hates his life in this world guards it for eternal life. **12:26** If anyone wants to serve me, he must follow me, and where I am, my servant will be too. If anyone serves me, the Father will honor him.

12:27 "Now my soul is greatly distressed. And what should I say? 'Father, deliver me from this hour'? No, but for this very reason I have come to this hour. **12:28** Father, glorify your name." Then a voice came from heaven, "I have glorified it, and I will glorify it again." **12:29** The crowd that stood there and heard the voice said that it had thundered. Others said that an angel had spoken to him. **12:30** Jesus said, "This voice has not come for my benefit but for yours. **12:31** Now is the judgment of this world; now the ruler of this world will be driven out. **12:32** And I, when I am lifted up from the earth, will draw all people to myself." **12:33** (Now he said this to indicate clearly what kind of death he was going to die.)

12:34 Then the crowd responded, "We have heard from the law that *the Christ will remain forever*. How can you say, 'The Son of Man must be lifted up'? Who is this Son of Man?" **12:35** Jesus replied, "The light is with you for a little while longer. Walk while you have the light, so that the darkness may not overtake you. The one who walks in the darkness does not know where he is going. **12:36** While you have the light, believe in the light, so that you may become sons of light." When Jesus had said these things, he went away and hid himself from them.

The Outcome of Jesus' Public Ministry Foretold

12:37 Although Jesus had performed so many miraculous signs before them, they still refused to believe in him, **12:38** so that the word of Isaiah the prophet would be fulfilled. He said, "*Lord, who has believed our message, and to whom has the arm of the Lord been revealed?*" **12:39** For this reason they could not believe, because again Isaiah said,

12:40 "He has blinded their eyes
and hardened their heart,
so that they would not see with their eyes
and understand with their heart,
and turn to me, and I would heal them*."*

12:41 Isaiah said these things because he saw Christ's glory, and spoke about him.

12:42 Nevertheless, even among the rulers many believed in him, but because of the Pharisees they would not confess Jesus to be the Christ, so that they would not be put out of the synagogue. **12:43** For they loved praise from men more than praise from God.

Jesus' Final Public Words

12:44 But Jesus shouted out, "The one who believes in me does not believe in me, but in the one who sent me, **12:45** and the one who sees me sees the one who sent me. **12:46** I have come as a light into the world, so that everyone who believes in me should not remain in darkness. **12:47** If anyone hears my words and does not obey them, I do not judge him. For I have not come to judge the world, but to save the world. **12:48** The one who rejects me and does not accept my words has a judge; the word I have spoken will judge him at the last day. **12:49** For I have not spoken from my own authority, but the Father himself who sent me has commanded me what I should say and what I should speak. **12:50** And I know that his commandment is eternal life. Thus the things I say, I say just as the Father has told me."

Washing the Disciples' Feet

13:1 Just before the Passover feast, Jesus knew that his time had come to depart from this world to the Father. Having loved his own who were in the world, he now loved them to the very end. **13:2** The evening meal was in progress, and the devil had already put into the heart of Judas Iscariot, Simon's son, that he should betray Jesus. **13:3** Because Jesus knew that the Father had handed all things over to him, and that he had come from God and was going back to God, **13:4** he got up from the meal, removed his outer clothes, took a towel and tied it around himself. **13:5** He poured water into the washbasin and began to wash the disciples' feet and to dry them with the towel he had wrapped around himself.

13:6 Then he came to Simon Peter. Peter said to him, "Lord, are you going to wash my feet?" **13:7** Jesus replied, "You do not understand what I am doing now, but you will understand after these things." **13:8** Peter said to him, "You will never wash my feet!" Jesus replied, "If I do not wash you, you have no share with me." **13:9** Simon Peter said to him, "Lord, wash not only my feet, but also my hands and my head!" **13:10** Jesus replied, "The one who has bathed needs only to wash his feet, but is completely clean. And you disciples are clean, but not every one of you." **13:11** (For Jesus knew the one who was going to betray him. For this reason he said, "Not every one of you is clean.")

13:12 So when Jesus had washed their feet and put his outer clothing back on, he took his place at the table again and said to them, "Do you understand what I have done for you? **13:13** You call me 'Teacher' and 'Lord,' and do so correctly, for that is what I am. **13:14** If I then, your Lord and Teacher, have washed your feet, you too ought to wash one another's feet. **13:15** For I have given you an example – you should do just as I have done for you. **13:16** I tell you the solemn truth, the slave is not greater than his master, nor is the one who is sent as a messenger greater than the one who sent him. **13:17** If you understand these things, you will be blessed if you do them.

The Announcement of Jesus' Betrayal

13:18 "What I am saying does not refer to all of you. I know the ones I have chosen. But this is to fulfill the scripture, '*The one who eats my bread has turned against me.*' **13:19** I am telling you this now, before it happens, so that when it happens you may believe that I am he. **13:20** I tell you the solemn truth, whoever accepts the one I send accepts me, and whoever accepts me accepts the one who sent me."

13:21 When he had said these things, Jesus was greatly distressed in spirit, and testified, "I tell you the solemn truth, one of you will betray me." **13:22** The disciples began to look at one another, worried and perplexed to know which of them he was talking about. **13:23** One of his disciples, the one Jesus loved, was at the table to the right of Jesus in a place of honor. **13:24** So Simon Peter gestured to this disciple to ask Jesus who it was he was referring to. **13:25** Then the disciple whom Jesus loved leaned back against Jesus' chest and asked him, "Lord, who is it?" **13:26** Jesus replied, "It is the one to whom I will give this piece of bread after I have dipped it in the dish." Then he dipped the piece of bread in the dish and gave it to Judas Iscariot, Simon's son. **13:27** And after Judas took the piece of bread, Satan entered into him. Jesus said to him, "What you are about to do, do quickly." **13:28** (Now none of those present at the table understood why Jesus said this to Judas. **13:29** Some thought that, because Judas had the money box, Jesus was telling him to buy whatever they needed for the feast, or to give something to the poor.) **13:30** Judas took the piece of bread and went out immediately. (Now it was night.)

The Prediction of Peter's Denial

13:31 When Judas had gone out, Jesus said, "Now the Son of Man is glorified, and God is glorified in him. **13:32** If God is glorified in him, God will also glorify him in himself, and he will glorify him right away. **13:33** Children, I am still with you for a little while. You will look for me, and just as I said to the Jewish religious leaders, 'Where I am going you cannot come,' now I tell you the same. **13:34** "I give you a new commandment – to love one another. Just as I have loved you, you also are to love one another. **13:35** Everyone will know by this that you are my disciples – if you have love for one another."

13:36 Simon Peter said to him, "Lord, where are you going?" Jesus replied, "Where I am going, you cannot follow me now, but you will follow later." **13:37** Peter said to him, "Lord, why can't I follow you now? I will lay down my life for you!" **13:38** Jesus answered, "Will you lay down your life for me? I tell you the solemn truth, the rooster will not crow until you have denied me three times!

Jesus' Parting Words to His Disciples

14:1 "Do not let your hearts be distressed. You believe in God; believe also in me. **14:2** There are many dwelling places in my Father's house. Otherwise, I would have told you, because I am going away to make ready a place for you. **14:3** And if I go and make ready a place for you, I will come again and take you to be with me, so that where I am you may be too. **14:4** And you know the way where I am going."

14:5 Thomas said, "Lord, we don't know where you are going. How can we know the way?" **14:6** Jesus replied, "I am the way, and the truth, and the life. No one comes to the Father except through me. **14:7** If you have known me, you will know my Father too. And from now on you do know him and have seen him."

14:8 Philip said, "Lord, show us the Father, and we will be content." **14:9** Jesus replied, "Have I been with you for so long, and you have not known me, Philip? The person who has seen me has seen the Father! How can you say, 'Show us the Father'? **14:10** Do you not believe that I am in the Father, and the Father is in me? The words that I say to you, I do not speak on my own initiative, but the Father residing in me performs his miraculous deeds. **14:11** Believe me that I am in the Father, and the Father is in me, but if you do not believe me, believe because of the miraculous deeds themselves. **14:12** I tell you the solemn truth, the person who believes in me will perform the miraculous deeds that I am doing, and

will perform greater deeds than these, because I am going to the Father. **14:13** And I will do whatever you ask in my name, so that the Father may be glorified in the Son. **14:14** If you ask me anything in my name, I will do it.

Teaching on the Holy Spirit

14:15 "If you love me, you will obey my commandments. **14:16** Then I will ask the Father, and he will give you another Advocate to be with you forever – **14:17** the Spirit of truth, whom the world cannot accept, because it does not see him or know him. But you know him, because he resides with you and will be in you.

14:18 "I will not abandon you as orphans, I will come to you. **14:19** In a little while the world will not see me any longer, but you will see me; because I live, you will live too. **14:20** You will know at that time that I am in my Father and you are in me and I am in you. **14:21** The person who has my commandments and obeys them is the one who loves me. The one who loves me will be loved by my Father, and I will love him and will reveal myself to him."

14:22 "Lord," Judas (not Judas Iscariot) said, "what has happened that you are going to reveal yourself to us and not to the world?" **14:23** Jesus replied, "If anyone loves me, he will obey my word, and my Father will love him, and we will come to him and take up residence with him. **14:24** The person who does not love me does not obey my words. And the word you hear is not mine, but the Father's who sent me.

14:25 "I have spoken these things while staying with you. **14:26** But the Advocate, the Holy Spirit, whom the Father will send in my name, will teach you everything, and will cause you to remember everything I said to you.

14:27 "Peace I leave with you; my peace I give to you; I do not give it to you as the world does. Do not let your hearts be distressed or lacking in courage. **14:28** You heard me say to you, 'I am going away and I am coming back to you.' If you loved me, you would be glad that I am going to the Father, because the Father is greater than I am. **14:29** I have told you now before it happens, so that when it happens you may believe. **14:30** I will not speak with you much longer, for the ruler of this world is coming. He has no power over me, **14:31** but I am doing just what the Father commanded me, so that the world may know that I love the Father. Get up, let us go from here."

The Vine and the Branches

15:1 "I am the true vine and my Father is the gardener. **15:2** He takes away every branch that does not bear fruit in me. He prunes every branch that bears fruit so that it will bear more fruit. **15:3** You are clean already because of the word that I have spoken to you. **15:4** Remain in me, and I will remain in you. Just as the branch cannot bear fruit by itself, unless it remains in the vine, so neither can you unless you remain in me.

15:5 "I am the vine; you are the branches. The one who remains in me – and I in him – bears much fruit, because apart from me you can accomplish nothing. **15:6** If anyone does not remain in me, he is thrown out like a branch, and dries up; and such branches are gathered up and thrown into the fire, and are burned up. **15:7** If you remain in me and my words remain in you, ask whatever you want, and it will be done for you. **15:8** My Father is honored by this, that you bear much fruit and show that you are my disciples.

15:9 "Just as the Father has loved me, I have also loved you; remain in my love. **15:10** If you obey my commandments, you will remain in my love, just as I have obeyed my Father's commandments and remain in his love. **15:11** I have told you these things so that my joy may be in you, and your joy may be complete. **15:12** My commandment is this – to love one another just as I have loved you. **15:13** No one has greater love than this – that one lays down his life for his friends. **15:14** You are my friends if you do what I command you. **15:15** I no longer call you slaves, because the slave does not understand what his master is doing. But I have called you friends, because I have revealed to you everything I heard from my Father. **15:16** You did not choose me, but I chose you and appointed you to go and bear fruit, fruit that remains, so that whatever you ask the Father in my name he will give you. **15:17** This I command you – to love one another.

The World's Hatred

15:18 "If the world hates you, be aware that it hated me first. **15:19** If you belonged to the world, the world would love you as its own. However, because you do not belong to the world, but I chose you out of the world, for this reason the world hates you. **15:20** Remember what I told you, 'A slave is not greater than his master.' If they persecuted me, they will also persecute you. If they obeyed my word, they will obey yours too. **15:21** But they will do all these things to you on account of my name, because they do not know the one who sent me. **15:22** If I had not come and spoken to them, they would not be guilty of sin. But they no longer have any excuse for their sin. **15:23** The one who hates me hates my Father too. **15:24** If I had not performed among them the miraculous deeds that no one else did, they would not be guilty of sin. But now they have seen the deeds and have hated both me and my Father. **15:25** Now this happened to fulfill the word that is written in their law, '*They hated me without reason.*' **15:26** When the Advocate comes, whom I will send you from the Father – the Spirit of truth who goes out from the Father – he will testify about me, **15:27** and you also will testify, because you have been with me from the beginning.

16:1 "I have told you all these things so that you will not fall away. **16:2** They will put you out of the synagogue, yet a time is coming when the one who kills you will think he is offering service to God. **16:3** They will do these things because they have not known the Father or me. **16:4** But I have told you these things so that when their time comes, you will remember that I told you about them.

"I did not tell you these things from the beginning because I was with you. **16:5** But now I am going to the one who sent me, and not one of you is asking me, 'Where are you going?' **16:6** Instead your hearts are filled with sadness because I have said these things to you. **16:7** But I tell you the truth, it is to your advantage that I am going away. For if I do not go away, the Advocate will not come to you, but if I go, I will send him to you. **16:8** And when he comes, he will prove the world wrong concerning sin and righteousness and judgment – **16:9** concerning sin, because they do not believe in me; **16:10** concerning righteousness, because I am going to the Father and you will see me no longer; **16:11** and concerning judgment, because the ruler of this world has been condemned.

16:12 "I have many more things to say to you, but you cannot bear them now. **16:13** But when he, the Spirit of truth, comes, he will guide you into all truth. For he will not speak on his own authority, but will speak whatever he hears, and will tell you what is to come. **16:14** He will glorify me, because he will receive from me what is mine and will tell it to you. **16:15** Everything that the Father has is mine; that is why I said the Spirit will receive from me what is mine and will tell it to you. **16:16** In a little while you will see me no longer; again after a little while, you will see me."

16:17 Then some of his disciples said to one another, "What is the meaning of what he is saying, 'In a little while you will not see me; again after a little while, you will see me,' and, 'because I am going to the Father'?" **16:18** So they kept on repeating, "What is the meaning of what he says, 'In a little while'? We do not understand what he is talking about."

16:19 Jesus could see that they wanted to ask him about these things, so he said to them, "Are you asking each other about this – that I said, 'In a little while you will not see me; again after a little while, you will see me'? **16:20** I tell you the solemn truth, you will weep and wail, but the world will rejoice; you will be sad, but your sadness will turn into joy. **16:21** When a woman gives birth, she has distress because her time has come, but when her child is born, she no longer remembers the suffering because of her joy that a human being has been born into the world. **16:22** So also you have sorrow now, but *I will see you again, and your hearts will rejoice, and no one will take your joy away from you.* **16:23** At that time you will ask me nothing. I tell you the solemn truth, whatever you ask the Father in my name he will give you. **16:24** Until now you have not asked for anything in my name. Ask and you will receive it, so that your joy may be complete.

16:25 "I have told you these things in obscure figures of speech; a time is coming when I will no longer speak to you in obscure figures, but will tell you plainly about the Father. **16:26** At that time you will ask in my name, and I do not say that I will ask the Father on your behalf. **16:27** For the Father himself loves you, because you have loved me and have believed that I came from God. **16:28** I came from the Father and entered into the world, but in turn, I am leaving the world and going back to the Father."

16:29 His disciples said, "Look, now you are speaking plainly and not in obscure figures of speech! **16:30** Now we know that you know everything and do not need anyone to ask you anything. Because of this we believe that you have come from God."

16:31 Jesus replied, "Do you now believe? **16:32** Look, a time is coming – and has come – when you will be scattered, each one to his own home, and I will be left alone. Yet I am not alone, because my Father is with me. **16:33** I have told you these things so that in me you may have peace. In the world you have trouble and suffering, but take courage – I have conquered the world."

Jesus Prays for the Father to Glorify Him

17:1 When Jesus had finished saying these things, he looked upward to heaven and said, "Father, the time has come. Glorify your Son, so that your Son may glorify you – **17:2** just as you have given him authority over all humanity, so that he may give eternal life to everyone you have given him. **17:3** Now this is eternal life – that they know you, the only true God, and Jesus Christ, whom you sent. **17:4** I glorified you on earth by completing the work you gave me to do. **17:5** And now, Father, glorify me at your side with the glory I had with you before the world was created.

Jesus Prays for the Disciples

17:6 "I have revealed your name to the men you gave me out of the world. They belonged to you, and you gave them to me, and they have obeyed your word. **17:7** Now they understand that everything you have given me comes from you, **17:8** because I have given them the words you have given me. They accepted them and really understand that I came from you, and they believed that you sent me. **17:9** I am praying on behalf of them. I am not praying on behalf of the world, but on behalf of those you have given me, because they belong to you. **17:10** Everything I have belongs to you, and everything you have belongs to me, and I have been glorified by them. **17:11** I am no longer in the world, but they are in the world, and I am coming to you. Holy Father, keep them safe in your name that you have given me, so that they may be one just as we are one. **17:12** When I was with them I kept them safe and watched over them in your name that you have given me. Not one of them was lost except the one destined for destruction, so that the scripture could be fulfilled. **17:13** But now I am coming to you, and I am saying these things in the world, so they may experience my joy completed in themselves. **17:14** I have given them your word, and the world has hated them, because they do not belong to the world, just as I do not belong to the world. **17:15** I am not asking you to take them out of the world, but that you keep them safe from the evil one. **17:16** They do not belong to the world just as I do not belong to the world. **17:17** Set them apart in the truth; your word is truth. **17:18** Just as you sent me into the world, so I sent them into the world. **17:19** And I set myself apart on their behalf, so that they too may be truly set apart.

Jesus Prays for Believers Everywhere

17:20 "I am not praying only on their behalf, but also on behalf of those who believe in me through their testimony, **17:21** that they will all be one, just as you, Father, are in me and I am in you. I pray that they will be in us, so that the world will believe that you sent me. **17:22** The glory you gave to me I have given to them, that they may be one just as we are one – **17:23** I in them and you in me – that they may be completely one, so that the world will know that you sent me, and you have loved them just as you have loved me.

17:24 "Father, I want those you have given me to be with me where I am, so that they can see my glory that you gave me because you loved me before the creation of the world. **17:25** Righteous Father, even if the world does not know you, I know you, and these men know that you sent me. **17:26** I made known your name to them, and I will continue to make it known, so that the love you have loved me with may be in them, and I may be in them."

Betrayal and Arrest

18:1 When he had said these things, Jesus went out with his disciples across the Kidron Valley. There was an orchard there, and he and his disciples went into it. **18:2** (Now Judas, the one who betrayed him, knew the place too, because Jesus had met there many times with his disciples.) **18:3** So Judas obtained a squad of soldiers and some officers of the chief priests and Pharisees. They came to the orchard with lanterns and torches and weapons.

18:4 Then Jesus, because he knew everything that was going to happen to him, came and asked them, "Who are you looking for?" **18:5** They replied, "Jesus the Nazarene." He told them, "I am he." (Now Judas, the one who betrayed him, was standing there with them.) **18:6** So when Jesus said to them, "I am he," they retreated and fell to the ground. **18:7** Then Jesus asked them again, "Who are you looking for?" And they said, "Jesus the Nazarene." **18:8** Jesus replied, "I told you that I am he. If you are looking for me, let these men go." **18:9** He said this to fulfill the word he had spoken, "I have not lost a single one of those whom you gave me."

18:10 Then Simon Peter, who had a sword, pulled it out and struck the high priest's slave, cutting off his right ear. (Now the slave's name was Malchus.) **18:11** But Jesus said to Peter, "Put your sword back into its sheath! Am I not to drink the cup that the Father has given me?"

Jesus Before Annas

18:12 Then the squad of soldiers with their commanding officer and the officers of the Jewish leaders arrested Jesus and tied him up. **18:13** They brought him first to Annas, for he was the father-in-law of Caiaphas, who was high priest that year. **18:14** (Now it was Caiaphas who had advised the Jewish leaders that it was to their advantage that one man die for the people.)

Peter's First Denial

18:15 Simon Peter and another disciple followed them as they brought Jesus to Annas. (Now the other disciple was acquainted with the high priest, and he went with Jesus into the high priest's courtyard.) **18:16** But Simon Peter was left standing outside by the door. So the other disciple who was acquainted with the high priest came out and spoke to the slave girl who watched the door, and brought Peter inside. **18:17** The girl who was the doorkeeper said to Peter, "You're not one of this man's disciples too, are you?" He replied, "I am not." **18:18** (Now the slaves and the guards were standing around a charcoal fire they had made, warming themselves because it was cold. Peter also was standing with them, warming himself.)

Jesus Questioned by Annas

18:19 While this was happening, the high priest questioned Jesus about his disciples and about his teaching. **18:20** Jesus replied, "I have spoken publicly to the world. I always taught in the synagogues and in the temple courts, where all the Jewish people assemble together. I have said nothing in secret. **18:21** Why do you ask me? Ask those who heard what I said. They know what I said." **18:22** When Jesus had said this, one of the high priest's officers who stood nearby struck him on the face and said, "Is that the way you answer the high priest?" **18:23** Jesus replied, "If I have said something wrong, confirm what is wrong. But if I spoke correctly, why strike me?" **18:24** Then Annas sent him, still tied up, to Caiaphas the high priest.

Peter's Second and Third Denials
18:25 Meanwhile Simon Peter was standing in the courtyard warming himself. They said to him, "You aren't one of his disciples too, are you?" Peter denied it: "I am not!" **18:26** One of the high priest's slaves, a relative of the man whose ear Peter had cut off, said, "Did I not see you in the orchard with him?" **18:27** Then Peter denied it again, and immediately a rooster crowed.

Jesus Brought Before Pilate
18:28 Then they brought Jesus from Caiaphas to the Roman governor's residence. (Now it was very early morning.) They did not go into the governor's residence so they would not be ceremonially defiled, but could eat the Passover meal. **18:29** So Pilate came outside to them and said, "What accusation do you bring against this man?" **18:30** They replied, "If this man were not a criminal, we would not have handed him over to you." **18:31** Pilate told them, "Take him yourselves and pass judgment on him according to your own law!" The Jewish leaders replied, "We cannot legally put anyone to death." **18:32** (This happened to fulfill the word Jesus had spoken when he indicated what kind of death he was going to die.)

Pilate Questions Jesus
18:33 So Pilate went back into the governor's residence, summoned Jesus, and asked him, "Are you the king of the Jews?" **18:34** Jesus replied, "Are you saying this on your own initiative, or have others told you about me?" **18:35** Pilate answered, "I am not a Jew, am I? Your own people and your chief priests handed you over to me. What have you done?" **18:36** Jesus replied, "My kingdom is not from this world. If my kingdom were from this world, my servants would be fighting to keep me from being handed over to the Jewish authorities. But as it is, my kingdom is not from here." **18:37** Then Pilate said, "So you are a king!" Jesus replied, "You say that I am a king. For this reason I was born, and for this reason I came into the world – to testify to the truth. Everyone who belongs to the truth listens to my voice." **18:38** Pilate asked, "What is truth?"

When he had said this he went back outside to the Jewish leaders and announced, "I find no basis for an accusation against him. **18:39** But it is your custom that I release one prisoner for you at the Passover. So do you want me to release for you the king of the Jews?" **18:40** Then they shouted back, "Not this man, but Barabbas!" (Now Barabbas was a revolutionary.)

Pilate Tries to Release Jesus
19:1 Then Pilate took Jesus and had him flogged severely. **19:2** The soldiers braided a crown of thorns and put it on his head, and they clothed him in a purple robe. **19:3** They came up to him again and again and said, "Hail, king of the Jews!" And they struck him repeatedly in the face. **19:4** Again Pilate went out and said to the Jewish leaders, "Look, I am bringing him out to you, so that you may know that I find no reason for an accusation against him." **19:5** So Jesus came outside, wearing the crown of thorns and the purple robe. Pilate said to them, "Look, here is the man!" **19:6** When the chief priests and their officers saw him, they shouted out, "Crucify him! Crucify him!" Pilate said, "You take him and crucify him! Certainly I find no reason for an accusation against him!" **19:7** The Jewish leaders replied, "We have a law, and according to our law he ought to die, because he claimed to be the Son of God!" **19:8** When Pilate heard what they said, he was more afraid than ever, **19:9** and he went back into the governor's residence and said to Jesus, "Where do you come from?" But Jesus gave him no answer. **19:10** So Pilate said, "Do you refuse to speak to me? Don't you know I have the authority to release you, and to crucify you?" **19:11** Jesus replied, "You would have no authority over me at all, unless it was given to you from above. Therefore the one who handed me over to you is guilty of greater sin." **19:12** From this point on, Pilate tried to release him. But the Jewish leaders shouted out, "If you release this man, you are no friend of Caesar! Everyone who claims to be a king opposes Caesar!" **19:13** When Pilate heard these words he brought Jesus outside and sat down on the judgment seat in the place called "The Stone Pavement" (*Gabbatha* in Aramaic). **19:14** (Now it was the day of preparation for the Passover, about noon.) Pilate said to the Jewish leaders, "Look, here is your king!" **19:15** Then they shouted out, "Away with him! Away with him! Crucify him!" Pilate asked, "Shall I crucify your king?" The high priests replied, "We have no king except Caesar!" **19:16** Then Pilate handed him over to them to be crucified.

The Crucifixion
So they took Jesus, **19:17** and carrying his own cross he went out to the place called "The Place of the Skull" (called in Aramaic *Golgotha*). **19:18** There they crucified him along with two others, one on each side, with Jesus in the middle. **19:19** Pilate also had a notice written and fastened to

the cross, which read: "Jesus the Nazarene, the king of the Jews." **19:20** Thus many of the Jewish residents of Jerusalem read this notice, because the place where Jesus was crucified was near the city, and the notice was written in Aramaic, Latin, and Greek. **19:21** Then the chief priests of the Jews said to Pilate, "Do not write, 'The king of the Jews,' but rather, 'This man said, I am king of the Jews.'" **19:22** Pilate answered, "What I have written, I have written."

19:23 Now when the soldiers crucified Jesus, they took his clothes and made four shares, one for each soldier, and the tunic remained. (Now the tunic was seamless, woven from top to bottom as a single piece.) **19:24** So the soldiers said to one another, "Let's not tear it, but throw dice to see who will get it." This took place to fulfill the scripture that says, "*They divided my garments among them, and for my clothing they threw dice*." So the soldiers did these things.

19:25 Now standing beside Jesus' cross were his mother, his mother's sister, Mary the wife of Clopas, and Mary Magdalene. **19:26** So when Jesus saw his mother and the disciple whom he loved standing there, he said to his mother, "Woman, look, here is your son!" **19:27** He then said to his disciple, "Look, here is your mother!" From that very time the disciple took her into his own home.

Jesus' Death
19:28 After this Jesus, realizing that by this time everything was completed, said (in order to fulfill the scripture), "I am thirsty!" **19:29** A jar full of sour wine was there, so they put a sponge soaked in sour wine on a branch of hyssop and lifted it to his mouth. **19:30** When he had received the sour wine, Jesus said, "It is completed!" Then he bowed his head and gave up his spirit.

19:31 Then, because it was the day of preparation, so that the bodies should not stay on the crosses on the Sabbath (for that Sabbath was an especially important one), the Jewish leaders asked Pilate to have the victims' legs broken and the bodies taken down. **19:32** So the soldiers came and broke the legs of the two men who had been crucified with Jesus, first the one and then the other. **19:33** But when they came to Jesus and saw that he was already dead, they did not break his legs. **19:34** But one of the soldiers pierced his side with a spear, and blood and water flowed out immediately. **19:35** And the person who saw it has testified (and his testimony is true, and he knows that he is telling the truth), so that you also may believe. **19:36** For these things happened so that the scripture would be fulfilled, "*Not a bone of his will be broken*." **19:37** And again another scripture says, "*They will look on the one whom they have pierced*."

Jesus' Burial
19:38 After this, Joseph of Arimathea, a disciple of Jesus (but secretly, because he feared the Jewish leaders), asked Pilate if he could remove the body of Jesus. Pilate gave him permission, so he went and took the body away. **19:39** Nicodemus, the man who had previously come to Jesus at night, accompanied Joseph, carrying a mixture of myrrh and aloes weighing about seventy-five pounds. **19:40** Then they took Jesus' body and wrapped it, with the aromatic spices, in strips of linen cloth according to Jewish burial customs. **19:41** Now at the place where Jesus was crucified there was a garden, and in the garden was a new tomb where no one had yet been buried. **19:42** And so, because it was the Jewish day of preparation and the tomb was nearby, they placed Jesus' body there.

The Resurrection
20:1 Now very early on the first day of the week, while it was still dark, Mary Magdalene came to the tomb and saw that the stone had been moved away from the entrance. **20:2** So she went running to Simon Peter and the other disciple whom Jesus loved and told them, "They have taken the Lord from the tomb, and we don't know where they have put him!" **20:3** Then Peter and the other disciple set out to go to the tomb. **20:4** The two were running together, but the other disciple ran faster than Peter and reached the tomb first. **20:5** He bent down and saw the strips of linen cloth lying there, but he did not go in. **20:6** Then Simon Peter, who had been following him, arrived and went right into the tomb. He saw the strips of linen cloth lying there, **20:7** and the face cloth, which had been around Jesus' head, not lying with the strips of linen cloth but rolled up in a place by itself. **20:8** Then the other disciple, who had reached the tomb first, came in, and he saw and believed. **20:9** (For they did not yet understand the scripture that Jesus must rise from the dead.)

Jesus' Appearance to Mary Magdalene
20:10 So the disciples went back to their homes. **20:11** But Mary stood outside the tomb weeping. As she wept, she bent down and looked into the tomb. **20:12** And she saw two angels in white sitting where Jesus' body had been lying, one at the head and one at the feet. **20:13** They said to her, "Woman, why are you weeping?" Mary replied, "They have taken my Lord away, and I do not know where they have put him!" **20:14** When she had said this, she turned around and saw Jesus standing there, but she did not know that it was Jesus.

20:15 Jesus said to her, "Woman, why are you weeping? Who are you looking for?" Because she thought he was the gardener, she said to him, "Sir, if you have carried him away, tell me where you have put him, and I will take him." **20:16** Jesus said to her, "Mary." She turned and said to him in Aramaic, "*Rabboni*" (which means Teacher). **20:17** Jesus replied,

"Do not touch me, for I have not yet ascended to my Father. Go to my brothers and tell them, 'I am ascending to my Father and your Father, to my God and your God.'" **20:18** Mary Magdalene came and informed the disciples, "I have seen the Lord!" And she told them what Jesus had said to her.

Jesus' Appearance to the Disciples

20:19 On the evening of that day, the first day of the week, the disciples had gathered together and locked the doors of the place because they were afraid of the Jewish leaders. Jesus came and stood among them and said to them, "Peace be with you." **20:20** When he had said this, he showed them his hands and his side. Then the disciples rejoiced when they saw the Lord. **20:21** So Jesus said to them again, "Peace be with you. Just as the Father has sent me, I also send you." **20:22** And after he said this, he breathed on them and said, "Receive the Holy Spirit. **20:23** If you forgive anyone's sins, they are forgiven; if you retain anyone's sins, they are retained."

The Response of Thomas

20:24 Now Thomas (called Didymus), one of the twelve, was not with them when Jesus came. **20:25** The other disciples told him, "We have seen the Lord!" But he replied, "Unless I see the wounds from the nails in his hands, and put my finger into the wounds from the nails, and put my hand into his side, I will never believe it!"

20:26 Eight days later the disciples were again together in the house, and Thomas was with them. Although the doors were locked, Jesus came and stood among them and said, "Peace be with you!" **20:27** Then he said to Thomas, "Put your finger here, and examine my hands. Extend your hand and put it into my side. Do not continue in your unbelief, but believe." **20:28** Thomas replied to him, "My Lord and my God!" **20:29** Jesus said to him, "Have you believed because you have seen me? Blessed are the people who have not seen and yet have believed."

20:30 Now Jesus performed many other miraculous signs in the presence of the disciples, which are not recorded in this book. **20:31** But these are recorded so that you may believe that Jesus is the Christ, the Son of God, and that by believing you may have life in his name.

Jesus' Appearance to the Disciples in Galilee

21:1 After this Jesus revealed himself again to the disciples by the Sea of Tiberias. Now this is how he did so. **21:2** Simon Peter, Thomas (called Didymus), Nathanael (who was from Cana in Galilee), the sons of Zebedee, and two other disciples of his were together. **21:3** Simon Peter told them, "I am going fishing." "We will go with you," they replied. They went out and got into the boat, but that night they caught nothing. **21:4** When it was already very early morning, Jesus stood on the beach, but the disciples did not know that it was Jesus. **21:5** So Jesus said to them, "Children, you don't have any fish, do you?" They replied, "No." **21:6** He told them, "Throw your net on the right side of the boat, and you will find some." So they threw the net, and were not able to pull it in because of the large number of fish.

21:7 Then the disciple whom Jesus loved said to Peter, "It is the Lord!" So Simon Peter, when he heard that it was the Lord, tucked in his outer garment (for he had nothing on underneath it), and plunged into the sea. **21:8** Meanwhile the other disciples came with the boat, dragging the net full of fish, for they were not far from land, only about a hundred yards. **21:9** When they got out on the beach, they saw a charcoal fire ready with a fish placed on it, and bread. **21:10** Jesus said, "Bring some of the fish you have just now caught." **21:11** So Simon Peter went aboard and pulled the net to shore. It was full of large fish, one hundred fifty-three, but although there were so many, the net was not torn. **21:12** "Come, have breakfast," Jesus said. But none of the disciples dared to ask him, "Who are you?" because they knew it was the Lord. **21:13** Jesus came and took the bread and gave it to them, and did the same with the fish. **21:14** This was now the third time Jesus was revealed to the disciples after he was raised from the dead.

Peter's Restoration

21:15 Then when they had finished breakfast, Jesus said to Simon Peter, "Simon, son of John, do you love me more than these do?" He replied, "Yes, Lord, you know I love you." Jesus told him, "Feed my lambs." **21:16** Jesus said a second time, "Simon, son of John, do you love me?" He replied, "Yes, Lord, you know I love you." Jesus told him, "Shepherd my sheep." **21:17** Jesus said a third time, "Simon, son of John, do you love me?" Peter was distressed that Jesus asked him a third time, "Do you love me?" and said, "Lord, you know everything. You know that I love you." Jesus replied, "Feed my sheep. **21:18** I tell you the solemn truth, when you were young, you tied your clothes around you and went wherever you wanted, but when you are old, you will stretch out your hands, and others will tie you up and bring you where you do not want to go." **21:19** (Now Jesus said this to indicate clearly by what kind of death Peter was going to glorify God.) After he said this, Jesus told Peter, "Follow me."

Peter and the Disciple Jesus Loved

21:20 Peter turned around and saw the disciple whom Jesus loved following them. (This was the disciple who had leaned back against Jesus' chest at the meal and asked, "Lord, who is the one who is going to betray you?") **21:21** So when Peter saw him, he asked Jesus, "Lord, what about him?" **21:22** Jesus replied, "If I want him to live until I come back, what concern is that of yours? You follow me!" **21:23** So the saying circulated among the brothers and sisters that this disciple was not going to die. But Jesus did not say to him that he was not going to die, but rather, "If I want him to live until I come back, what concern is that of yours?"

A Final Note

21:24 This is the disciple who testifies about these things and has written these things, and we know that his testimony is true. **21:25** There are many other things that Jesus did. If every one of them were written down, I suppose the whole world would not have room for the books that would be written.

Book 44. Acts

Jesus Ascends to Heaven

1:1 I wrote the former account, Theophilus, about all that Jesus began to do and teach **1:2** until the day he was taken up to heaven, after he had given orders by the Holy Spirit to the apostles he had chosen. **1:3** To the same apostles also, after his suffering, he presented himself alive with many convincing proofs. He was seen by them over a forty-day period and spoke about matters concerning the kingdom of God. **1:4** While he was with them, he declared, "Do not leave Jerusalem, but wait there for what my Father promised, which you heard about from me. **1:5** For John baptized with water, but you will be baptized with the Holy Spirit not many days from now."

1:6 So when they had gathered together, they began to ask him, "Lord, is this the time when you are restoring the kingdom to Israel?" **1:7** He told them, "You are not permitted to know the times or periods that the Father has set by his own authority. **1:8** But you will receive power when the Holy Spirit has come upon you, and you will be my witnesses in Jerusalem, and in all Judea and Samaria, and to the farthest parts of the earth." **1:9** After he had said this, while they were watching, he was lifted up and a cloud hid him from their sight. **1:10** As they were still staring into the sky while he was going, suddenly two men in white clothing stood near them **1:11** and said, "Men of Galilee, why do you stand here looking up into the sky? This same Jesus who has been taken up from you into heaven will come back in the same way you saw him go into heaven."

A Replacement for Judas Is Chosen

1:12 Then they returned to Jerusalem from the mountain called the Mount of Olives (which is near Jerusalem, a Sabbath day's journey away). **1:13** When they had entered Jerusalem, they went to the upstairs room where they were staying. Peter and John, and James, and Andrew, Philip and Thomas, Bartholomew and Matthew, James son of Alphaeus and Simon the Zealot, and Judas son of James were there. **1:14** All these continued together in prayer with one mind, together with the women, along with Mary the mother of Jesus, and his brothers. **1:15** In those days Peter stood up among the believers (a gathering of about one hundred and twenty people) and said, **1:16** "Brothers, the scripture had to be fulfilled that the Holy Spirit foretold through David concerning Judas – who became the guide for those who arrested Jesus – **1:17** for he was counted as one of us and received a share in this ministry." **1:18** (Now this man Judas acquired a field with the reward of his unjust deed, and falling headfirst he burst open in the middle and all his intestines gushed out. **1:19** This became known to all who lived in Jerusalem, so that in their own language they called that field *Hakeldama*, that is, "Field of Blood.") **1:20** "For it is written in the book of Psalms, '*Let his house become deserted, and let there be no one to live in it*,' and '*Let another take his position of responsibility.*' **1:21** Thus one of the men who have accompanied us during all the time the Lord Jesus associated with us, **1:22** beginning from his baptism by John until the day he was taken up from us – one of these must become a witness of his resurrection together with us." **1:23** So they proposed two candidates: Joseph called Barsabbas (also called Justus) and Matthias. **1:24** Then they prayed, "Lord, you know the hearts of all. Show us which one of these two you have chosen **1:25** to assume the task of this service and apostleship from which Judas turned aside to go to his own place." **1:26** Then they cast lots for them, and the one chosen was Matthias; so he was counted with the eleven apostles.

The Holy Spirit and the Day of Pentecost

2:1 Now when the day of Pentecost had come, they were all together in one place. **2:2** Suddenly a sound like a violent wind blowing came from heaven and filled the entire house where they were sitting. **2:3** And tongues spreading out like a fire appeared to them and came to rest on each one of them. **2:4** All of them were filled with the Holy Spirit, and they began to speak in other languages as the Spirit enabled them.

2:5 Now there were devout Jews from every nation under heaven residing in Jerusalem. **2:6** When this sound occurred, a crowd gathered and was in confusion, because each one heard them speaking in his own language. **2:7** Completely baffled, they said, "Aren't all these who are speaking Galileans? **2:8** And how is it that each one of us hears them in our own native language? **2:9** Parthians, Medes, Elamites, and residents of Mesopotamia, Judea and Cappadocia, Pontus and the province of Asia, **2:10** Phrygia and Pamphylia, Egypt and the parts of Libya near Cyrene, and visitors from Rome, **2:11** both Jews and proselytes, Cretans and Arabs –

we hear them speaking in our own languages about the great deeds God has done!" **2:12** All were astounded and greatly confused, saying to one another, "What does this mean?" **2:13** But others jeered at the speakers, saying, "They are drunk on new wine!"

Peter's Address on the Day of Pentecost

2:14 But Peter stood up with the eleven, raised his voice, and addressed them: "You men of Judea and all you who live in Jerusalem, know this and listen carefully to what I say. **2:15** In spite of what you think, these men are not drunk, for it is only nine o'clock in the morning. **2:16** But this is what was spoken about through the prophet Joel:

2:17 'And *in the last days* it will be,' God says,
'that I will pour out my Spirit on all people,
and your sons and your daughters will prophesy,
and your young men will see visions,
and your old men will dream dreams.

2:18 Even on my servants, both men and women,
I will pour out my Spirit in those days, and they will prophesy.

2:19 And I will perform wonders in the sky above
and miraculous signs on the earth below,
blood and fire and clouds of smoke.

2:20 The sun will be changed to darkness
and the moon to blood
before the great and glorious day of the Lord comes.

2:21 And then everyone who calls on the name of the Lord will be saved.'

2:22 "Men of Israel, listen to these words: Jesus the Nazarene, a man clearly attested to you by God with powerful deeds, wonders, and miraculous signs that God performed among you through him, just as you yourselves know – **2:23** this man, who was handed over by the predetermined plan and foreknowledge of God, you executed by nailing him to a cross at the hands of Gentiles. **2:24** But God raised him up, having released him from the pains of death, because it was not possible for him to be held in its power. **2:25** For David says about him,

'I saw the Lord always in front of me,
for he is at my right hand so that I will not be shaken.

2:26 Therefore my heart was glad and my tongue rejoiced;
my body also will live in hope,

2:27 because you will not leave my soul in Hades,
nor permit your Holy One to experience decay.

2:28 You have made known to me the paths of life;
you will make me full of joy with your presence.'

2:29 "Brothers, I can speak confidently to you about our forefather David, that he both died and was buried, and his tomb is with us to this day. **2:30** So then, because he was a prophet and knew that God *had sworn to him with an oath to seat one of his descendants on his throne*, **2:31** David by foreseeing this spoke about the resurrection of the Christ, that *he was neither abandoned to Hades*, nor did his body *experience decay*. **2:32** This Jesus God raised up, and we are all witnesses of it. **2:33** So then, exalted to the right hand of God, and having received the promise of the Holy Spirit from the Father, he has poured out what you both see and hear. **2:34** For David did not ascend into heaven, but he himself says,

'The Lord said to my lord,
"Sit at my right hand

2:35 until I make your enemies a footstool for your feet."'

2:36 Therefore let all the house of Israel know beyond a doubt that God has made this Jesus whom you crucified both Lord and Christ."

The Response to Peter's Address

2:37 Now when they heard this, they were acutely distressed and said to Peter and the rest of the apostles, "What should we do, brothers?" **2:38** Peter said to them, "Repent, and each one of you be baptized in the name of Jesus Christ for the forgiveness of your sins, and you will receive the gift of the Holy Spirit. **2:39** For the promise is for you and your children, and for all who are far away, as many as the Lord our God will call to himself." **2:40** With many other words he testified and exhorted them saying, "Save yourselves from this perverse generation!" **2:41** So those who accepted his message were baptized, and that day about three thousand people were added.

The Fellowship of the Early Believers

2:42 They were devoting themselves to the apostles' teaching and to fellowship, to the breaking of bread and to prayer. **2:43** Reverential awe came over everyone, and many wonders and miraculous signs came about by the apostles. **2:44** All who believed were together and held everything in common, **2:45** and they began selling their property and possessions and distributing the proceeds to everyone, as anyone had need. **2:46** Every day they continued to gather together by common consent in the temple courts, breaking bread from house to house, sharing their food with glad and humble hearts, **2:47** praising God and having the good will of all the people. And the Lord was adding to their number every day those who were being saved.

Peter and John Heal a Lame Man at the Temple

3:1 Now Peter and John were going up to the temple at the time for prayer, at three o'clock in the afternoon. **3:2** And a man lame from birth was being carried up, who was placed at the temple gate called "the Beautiful Gate" every day so he could beg for money from those going into the temple courts. **3:3** When he saw Peter and John about to go into the temple courts, he asked them for money. **3:4** Peter looked directly at him (as did John) and said, "Look at us!" **3:5** So the lame man paid attention to them, expecting to receive something from them. **3:6** But Peter said, "I have no silver or gold, but what I do have I give you. In the name of Jesus Christ the Nazarene, stand up and walk!" **3:7** Then Peter took hold of him by the right hand and raised him up, and at once the man's feet and ankles were made strong. **3:8** He jumped up, stood and began walking around, and he entered the temple courts with them, walking and leaping and praising God. **3:9** All the people saw him walking and praising God, **3:10** and they recognized him as the man who used to sit and ask for donations at the Beautiful Gate of the temple, and they were filled with astonishment and amazement at what had happened to him.

Peter Addresses the Crowd

3:11 While the man was hanging on to Peter and John, all the people, completely astounded, ran together to them in the covered walkway called Solomon's Portico. **3:12** When Peter saw this, he declared to the people, "Men of Israel, why are you amazed at this? Why do you stare at us as if we had made this man walk by our own power or piety? **3:13** The God of Abraham, Isaac, and Jacob, the God of our forefathers, has glorified his servant Jesus, whom you handed over and rejected in the presence of Pilate after he had decided to release him. **3:14** But you rejected the Holy and Righteous One and asked that a man who was a murderer be released to you. **3:15** You killed the Originator of life, whom God raised from the dead. To this fact we are witnesses! **3:16** And on the basis of faith in Jesus' name, his very name has made this man – whom you see and know – strong. The faith that is through Jesus has given him this complete health in the presence of you all. **3:17** And now, brothers, I know you acted in ignorance, as your rulers did too. **3:18** But the things God foretold long ago through all the prophets – that his Christ would suffer – he has fulfilled in this way. **3:19** Therefore repent and turn back so that your sins may be wiped out, **3:20** so that times of refreshing may come from the presence of the Lord, and so that he may send the Messiah appointed for you – that is, Jesus. **3:21** This one heaven must receive until the time all things are restored, which God declared from times long ago through his holy prophets. **3:22** Moses said, '*The Lord your God will raise up for you a prophet like me from among your brothers. You must obey him in everything he tells you. 3:23 Every person who does not obey that prophet will be destroyed and thus removed from the people.*' **3:24** And all the prophets, from Samuel and those who followed him, have spoken about and announced these days. **3:25** You are the sons of the prophets and of the covenant that God made with your ancestors, saying to Abraham, '*And in your descendants all the nations of the earth will be blessed.*' **3:26** God raised up his servant and sent him first to you, to bless you by turning each one of you from your iniquities."

The Arrest and Trial of Peter and John

4:1 While Peter and John were speaking to the people, the priests and the commander of the temple guard and the Sadducees came up to them, **4:2** angry because they were teaching the people and announcing in Jesus the resurrection of the dead. **4:3** So they seized them and put them in jail until the next day (for it was already evening). **4:4** But many of those who had listened to the message believed, and the number of the men came to about five thousand.

4:5 On the next day, their rulers, elders, and experts in the law came together in Jerusalem. **4:6** Annas the high priest was there, and Caiaphas, John, Alexander, and others who were members of the high priest's family. **4:7** After making Peter and John stand in their midst, they began to inquire, "By what power or by what name did you do this?" **4:8** Then Peter, filled with the Holy Spirit, replied, "Rulers of the people and elders, **4:9** if we are being examined today for a good deed done to a sick man – by what means this man was healed – **4:10** let it be known to all of you and to all the people of Israel that by the name of Jesus Christ the Nazarene whom you crucified, whom God raised from the dead, this man stands before you healthy. **4:11** This Jesus is *the stone that was rejected by* you, *the builders, that has become the cornerstone*. **4:12** And there is salvation in no one else, for there is no other name under heaven given among people by which we must be saved."

4:13 When they saw the boldness of Peter and John, and discovered that they were uneducated and ordinary men, they were amazed and recognized these men had been with Jesus. **4:14** And because they saw the man who had been healed standing with them, they had nothing to say against this. **4:15** But when they had ordered them to go outside the council, they began to confer with one another, **4:16** saying, "What should we do with these men? For it is plain to all who live in Jerusalem that a notable miraculous sign has come about through them, and we cannot deny it. **4:17** But to keep this matter from spreading any further among the people, let us warn them to speak no more to anyone in this name." **4:18** And they called them in and ordered them not to speak or teach at all in the name of Jesus. **4:19** But Peter and John replied, "Whether it is right before God to obey you rather than God, you decide, **4:20** for it is impossible for us not to speak about what we have seen and heard." **4:21** After threatening them further, they released them, for they could not find how to punish them on account of the people, because they were all praising God for what had happened. **4:22** For the man, on whom this miraculous sign of healing had been performed, was over forty years old.

The Followers of Jesus Pray for Boldness

4:23 When they were released, Peter and John went to their fellow believers and reported everything the high priests and the elders had said to them. **4:24** When they heard this, they raised their voices to God with one mind and said, "Master of all, you who made the heaven, the earth, the sea, and everything that is in them, **4:25** who said by the Holy Spirit through your servant David our forefather,

'Why do the nations rage,

and the peoples plot foolish things?

4:26 The kings of the earth stood together,

and the rulers assembled together,

against the Lord and against his Christ.'

4:27 "For indeed both Herod and Pontius Pilate, with the Gentiles and the people of Israel, assembled together in this city against your holy servant Jesus, whom you anointed, **4:28** to do as much as your power and your plan had decided beforehand would happen. **4:29** And now, Lord, pay attention to their threats, and grant to your servants to speak your message with great courage, **4:30** while you extend your hand to heal, and to bring about miraculous signs and wonders through the name of your holy servant Jesus." **4:31** When they had prayed, the place where they were assembled together was shaken, and they were all filled with the Holy Spirit and began to speak the word of God courageously.

Conditions Among the Early Believers

4:32 The group of those who believed were of one heart and mind, and no one said that any of his possessions was his own, but everything was held in common. **4:33** With great power the apostles were giving testimony to the resurrection of the Lord Jesus, and great grace was on them all. **4:34** For there was no one needy among them, because those who were owners of land or houses were selling them and bringing the proceeds from the sales **4:35** and placing them at the apostles' feet. The proceeds were distributed to each, as anyone had need. **4:36** So Joseph, a Levite who was a native of Cyprus, called by the apostles Barnabas (which is translated "son of encouragement"), **4:37** sold a field that belonged to him and brought the money and placed it at the apostles' feet.

The Judgment on Ananias and Sapphira

5:1 Now a man named Ananias, together with Sapphira his wife, sold a piece of property. **5:2** He kept back for himself part of the proceeds with his wife's knowledge; he brought only part of it and placed it at the apostles' feet. **5:3** But Peter said, "Ananias, why has Satan filled your heart to lie to the Holy Spirit and keep back for yourself part of the proceeds from the sale of the land? **5:4** Before it was sold, did it not belong to you? And when it was sold, was the money not at your disposal? How have you thought up this deed in your heart? You have not lied to people but to God!"

5:5 When Ananias heard these words he collapsed and died, and great fear gripped all who heard about it. **5:6** So the young men came, wrapped him up, carried him out, and buried him. **5:7** After an interval of about three hours, his wife came in, but she did not know what had happened. **5:8** Peter said to her, "Tell me, were the two of you paid this amount for the land?" Sapphira said, "Yes, that much." **5:9** Peter then told her, "Why have you agreed together to test the Spirit of the Lord? Look! The feet of those who have buried your husband are at the door, and they will carry you out!" **5:10** At once she collapsed at his feet and died. So when the young men came in, they found her dead, and they carried her out and buried her beside her husband. **5:11** Great fear gripped the whole church and all who heard about these things.

The Apostles Perform Miraculous Signs and Wonders

5:12 Now many miraculous signs and wonders came about among the people through the hands of the apostles. By common consent they were all meeting together in Solomon's Portico. **5:13** None of the rest dared to join them, but the people held them in high honor. **5:14** More and more believers in the Lord were added to their number, crowds of both men and women. **5:15** Thus they even carried the sick out into the streets, and put them on cots and pallets, so that when Peter came by at least his shadow would fall on some of them. **5:16** A crowd of people from the towns around Jerusalem also came together, bringing the sick and those troubled by unclean spirits. They were all being healed.

Further Trouble for the Apostles

5:17 Now the high priest rose up, and all those with him (that is, the religious party of the Sadducees), and they were filled with jealousy. **5:18** They laid hands on the apostles and put them in a public jail. **5:19** But during the night an angel of the Lord opened the doors of the prison, led them out, and said, **5:20** "Go and stand in the temple courts and proclaim to the people all the words of this life." **5:21** When they heard this, they entered the temple courts at daybreak and began teaching.

Now when the high priest and those who were with him arrived, they summoned the Sanhedrin – that is, the whole high council of the Israelites – and sent to the jail to have the apostles brought before them. **5:22** But the officers who came for them did not find them in the prison, so they returned and reported, **5:23** "We found the jail locked securely and

the guards standing at the doors, but when we opened them, we found no one inside." **5:24** Now when the commander of the temple guard and the chief priests heard this report, they were greatly puzzled concerning it, wondering what this could be. **5:25** But someone came and reported to them, "Look! The men you put in prison are standing in the temple courts and teaching the people!" **5:26** Then the commander of the temple guard went with the officers and brought the apostles without the use of force (for they were afraid of being stoned by the people).

5:27 When they had brought them, they stood them before the council, and the high priest questioned them, **5:28** saying, "We gave you strict orders not to teach in this name. Look, you have filled Jerusalem with your teaching, and you intend to bring this man's blood on us!" **5:29** But Peter and the apostles replied, "We must obey God rather than people. **5:30** The God of our forefathers raised up Jesus, whom you seized and killed by hanging him on a tree. **5:31** God exalted him to his right hand as Leader and Savior, to give repentance to Israel and forgiveness of sins. **5:32** And we are witnesses of these events, and so is the Holy Spirit whom God has given to those who obey him."

5:33 Now when they heard this, they became furious and wanted to execute them. **5:34** But a Pharisee whose name was Gamaliel, a teacher of the law who was respected by all the people, stood up in the council and ordered the men to be put outside for a short time. **5:35** Then he said to the council, "Men of Israel, pay close attention to what you are about to do to these men. **5:36** For some time ago Theudas rose up, claiming to be somebody, and about four hundred men joined him. He was killed, and all who followed him were dispersed and nothing came of it. **5:37** After him Judas the Galilean arose in the days of the census, and incited people to follow him in revolt. He too was killed, and all who followed him were scattered. **5:38** So in this case I say to you, stay away from these men and leave them alone, because if this plan or this undertaking originates with people, it will come to nothing, **5:39** but if it is from God, you will not be able to stop them, or you may even be found fighting against God." He convinced them, **5:40** and they summoned the apostles and had them beaten. Then they ordered them not to speak in the name of Jesus and released them. **5:41** So they left the council rejoicing because they had been considered worthy to suffer dishonor for the sake of the name. **5:42** And every day both in the temple courts and from house to house, they did not stop teaching and proclaiming the good news that Jesus was the Christ.

The Appointment of the First Seven Deacons

6:1 Now in those days, when the disciples were growing in number, a complaint arose on the part of the Greek-speaking Jews against the native Hebraic Jews, because their widows were being overlooked in the daily distribution of food. **6:2** So the twelve called the whole group of the disciples together and said, "It is not right for us to neglect the word of God to wait on tables. **6:3** But carefully select from among you, brothers, seven men who are well-attested, full of the Spirit and of wisdom, whom we may put in charge of this necessary task. **6:4** But we will devote ourselves to prayer and to the ministry of the word." **6:5** The proposal pleased the entire group, so they chose Stephen, a man full of faith and of the Holy Spirit, with Philip, Prochorus, Nicanor, Timon, Parmenas, and Nicolas, a Gentile convert to Judaism from Antioch. **6:6** They stood these men before the apostles, who prayed and placed their hands on them. **6:7** The word of God continued to spread, the number of disciples in Jerusalem increased greatly, and a large group of priests became obedient to the faith.

Stephen is Arrested

6:8 Now Stephen, full of grace and power, was performing great wonders and miraculous signs among the people. **6:9** But some men from the Synagogue of the Freedmen (as it was called), both Cyrenians and Alexandrians, as well as some from Cilicia and the province of Asia, stood up and argued with Stephen. **6:10** Yet they were not able to resist the wisdom and the Spirit with which he spoke. **6:11** Then they secretly instigated some men to say, "We have heard this man speaking blasphemous words against Moses and God." **6:12** They incited the people, the elders, and the experts in the law; then they approached Stephen, seized him, and brought him before the council. **6:13** They brought forward false witnesses who said, "This man does not stop saying things against this holy place and the law. **6:14** For we have heard him saying that Jesus the Nazarene will destroy this place and change the customs that Moses handed down to us." **6:15** All who were sitting in the council looked intently at Stephen and saw his face was like the face of an angel.

Stephen's Defense Before the Council

7:1 Then the high priest said, "Are these things true?" **7:2** So he replied, "Brothers and fathers, listen to me. The God of glory appeared to our forefather Abraham when he was in Mesopotamia, before he settled in Haran, **7:3** and said to him, '*Go out from your country and from your relatives, and come to the land I will show you.*' **7:4** Then he went out from the country of the Chaldeans and settled in Haran. After his father died, God made him move to this country where you now live. **7:5** He did not give any of it to him for an inheritance, not even a foot of ground, yet God promised *to give it to him as his possession, and to his descendants after him,* even though Abraham as yet had no child. **7:6** But God spoke as follows: 'Your **descendants will be foreigners in a foreign country, whose citizens will enslave them and mistreat them for four hundred years. 7:7 But I will punish the nation they serve as slaves,**' said God, '**and after these things they will come out of there** and worship me in this place.' **7:8** Then God gave Abraham the covenant of circumcision, and so he became the father of Isaac and circumcised him when he was eight days old, and Isaac became the father of Jacob, and Jacob of the twelve patriarchs. **7:9** The patriarchs, because they were jealous of Joseph, sold him into Egypt. But God was with him, **7:10** and rescued him from all his troubles, and granted him favor and wisdom in the presence of Pharaoh, king of Egypt, who made him ruler over Egypt and over all his household. **7:11** Then a famine occurred throughout Egypt and Canaan, causing great suffering, and our ancestors could not find food. **7:12** So when Jacob heard that there was grain in Egypt, he sent our ancestors there the first time. **7:13** On their second visit Joseph made himself known to his brothers again, and Joseph's family became known to Pharaoh. **7:14** So Joseph sent a message and invited his father Jacob and all his relatives to come, seventy-five people in all. **7:15** So Jacob went down to Egypt and died there, along with our ancestors, **7:16** and their bones were later moved to Shechem and placed in the tomb that Abraham had bought for a certain sum of money from the sons of Hamor in Shechem.

7:17 "But as the time drew near for God to fulfill the promise he had declared to Abraham, the people increased greatly in number in Egypt, **7:18** until **another king who did not know about Joseph ruled over Egypt. 7:19** This was the one who exploited our people and was cruel to our ancestors, forcing them to abandon their infants so they would die. **7:20** At that time Moses was born, and he was beautiful to God. For three months he was brought up in his father's house, **7:21** and when he had been abandoned, Pharaoh's daughter adopted him and brought him up as her own son. **7:22** So Moses was trained in all the wisdom of the Egyptians and was powerful in his words and deeds. **7:23** But when he was about forty years old, it entered his mind to visit his fellow countrymen the Israelites. **7:24** When he saw one of them being hurt unfairly, Moses came to his defense and avenged the person who was mistreated by striking down the Egyptian. **7:25** He thought his own people would understand that God was delivering them through him, but they did not understand. **7:26** The next day Moses saw two men fighting, and tried to make peace between them, saying, 'Men, you are brothers; why are you hurting one another?' **7:27** But the man who was unfairly hurting his neighbor pushed Moses aside, saying, '**Who made you a ruler and judge over us? 7:28 You don't want to kill me the way you killed the Egyptian yesterday, do you?**' **7:29** When the man said this, Moses fled and became a foreigner in the land of Midian, where he became the father of two sons. **7:30** "After forty years had passed, *an angel appeared to him in the desert of Mount Sinai, in the flame of a burning bush.* **7:31** When Moses saw it, he was amazed at the sight, and when he approached to investigate, there came the voice of the Lord, **7:32** '*I am the God of your forefathers, the God of Abraham, Isaac, and Jacob.*' Moses began to tremble and did not dare to look more closely. **7:33** *But the Lord said to him, 'Take the sandals off your feet, for the place where you are standing is holy ground. 7:34 I have certainly seen the suffering of my people who are in Egypt and have heard their groaning, and I have come down to rescue them. Now come, I will send you to Egypt.*' **7:35** This same Moses they had rejected, saying, '*Who made you a ruler and judge?*' God sent as both ruler and deliverer through the hand of the angel who appeared to him in the bush. **7:36** This man led them out, performing wonders and miraculous signs in the land of Egypt, at the Red Sea, and in the wilderness for forty years. **7:37** This is the Moses who said to the Israelites, '*God will raise up for you a prophet like me from among your brothers.*' **7:38** This is the man who was in the congregation in the wilderness with the angel who spoke to him at Mount Sinai, and with our ancestors, and he received living oracles to give to you. **7:39** Our ancestors were unwilling to obey him, but pushed him aside and turned back to Egypt in their hearts, **7:40** saying to Aaron, '*Make us gods who will go in front of us, for this Moses, who led us out of the land of Egypt – we do not know what has happened to him!*' **7:41** At that time they made an idol in the form of a calf, brought a sacrifice to the idol, and began rejoicing in the works of their hands. **7:42** But God turned away from them and gave them over to worship the host of heaven, as it is written in the book of the prophets: '*It was not to me that you offered slain animals and sacrifices forty years in the wilderness, was it, house of Israel? 7:43 But you took along the tabernacle of Moloch and the star of the god Rephan, the images you made to worship, but I will deport you beyond Babylon.*' **7:44** Our ancestors had the tabernacle of testimony in the wilderness, just as God who spoke to Moses ordered him to make it according to the design he had seen. **7:45** Our ancestors received possession of it and brought it in with Joshua when they dispossessed the nations that God drove out before our ancestors, until the time of David. **7:46** He found favor with God and asked that he could find a dwelling place for the house of Jacob. **7:47** But Solomon built a house for him. **7:48** Yet the Most High does not live in houses made by human hands, as the prophet says,

7:49 'Heaven is my throne,
and earth is the footstool for my feet.
What kind of house will you build for me, says the Lord,
or what is my resting place?
7:50 Did my hand not make all these things?'
7:51 "You stubborn people, with uncircumcised hearts and ears! You are always resisting the Holy Spirit, like your ancestors did! **7:52** Which of the prophets did your ancestors not persecute? They killed those who foretold long ago the coming of the Righteous One, whose betrayers and murderers you have now become! **7:53** You received the law by decrees given by angels, but you did not obey it."

Stephen is Killed
7:54 When they heard these things, they became furious and ground their teeth at him. **7:55** But Stephen, full of the Holy Spirit, looked intently toward heaven and saw the glory of God, and Jesus standing at the right hand of God. **7:56** "Look!" he said. "I see the heavens opened, and the Son of Man standing at the right hand of God!" **7:57** But they covered their ears, shouting out with a loud voice, and rushed at him with one intent. **7:58** When they had driven him out of the city, they began to stone him, and the witnesses laid their cloaks at the feet of a young man named Saul. **7:59** They continued to stone Stephen while he prayed, "Lord Jesus, receive my spirit!" **7:60** Then he fell to his knees and cried out with a loud voice, "Lord, do not hold this sin against them!" When he had said this, he died. **8:1** And Saul agreed completely with killing him.

Saul Begins to Persecute the Church
Now on that day a great persecution began against the church in Jerusalem, and all except the apostles were forced to scatter throughout the regions of Judea and Samaria. **8:2** Some devout men buried Stephen and made loud lamentation over him. **8:3** But Saul was trying to destroy the church; entering one house after another, he dragged off both men and women and put them in prison.

Philip Preaches in Samaria
8:4 Now those who had been forced to scatter went around proclaiming the good news of the word. **8:5** Philip went down to the main city of Samaria and began proclaiming the Christ to them. **8:6** The crowds were paying attention with one mind to what Philip said, as they heard and saw the miraculous signs he was performing. **8:7** For unclean spirits, crying with loud shrieks, were coming out of many who were possessed, and many paralyzed and lame people were healed. **8:8** So there was great joy in that city.
8:9 Now in that city was a man named Simon, who had been practicing magic and amazing the people of Samaria, claiming to be someone great. **8:10** All the people, from the least to the greatest, paid close attention to him, saying, "This man is the power of God that is called 'Great.'" **8:11** And they paid close attention to him because he had amazed them for a long time with his magic. **8:12** But when they believed Philip as he was proclaiming the good news about the kingdom of God and the name of Jesus Christ, they began to be baptized, both men and women. **8:13** Even Simon himself believed, and after he was baptized, he stayed close to Philip constantly, and when he saw the signs and great miracles that were occurring, he was amazed.
8:14 Now when the apostles in Jerusalem heard that Samaria had accepted the word of God, they sent Peter and John to them. **8:15** These two went down and prayed for them so that they would receive the Holy Spirit. **8:16** (For the Spirit had not yet come upon any of them, but they had only been baptized in the name of the Lord Jesus.) **8:17** Then Peter and John placed their hands on the Samaritans, and they received the Holy Spirit.
8:18 Now Simon, when he saw that the Spirit was given through the laying on of the apostles' hands, offered them money, **8:19** saying, "Give me this power too, so that everyone I place my hands on may receive the Holy Spirit." **8:20** But Peter said to him, "May your silver perish with you, because you thought you could acquire God's gift with money! **8:21** You have no share or part in this matter because your heart is not right before God! **8:22** Therefore repent of this wickedness of yours, and pray to the Lord that he may perhaps forgive you for the intent of your heart. **8:23** For I see that you are bitterly envious and in bondage to sin." **8:24** But Simon replied, "You pray to the Lord for me so that nothing of what you have said may happen to me."
8:25 So after Peter and John had solemnly testified and spoken the word of the Lord, they started back to Jerusalem, proclaiming the good news to many Samaritan villages as they went.

Philip and the Ethiopian Eunuch
8:26 Then an angel of the Lord said to Philip, "Get up and go south on the road that goes down from Jerusalem to Gaza." (This is a desert road.) **8:27** So he got up and went. There he met an Ethiopian eunuch, a court official of Candace, queen of the Ethiopians, who was in charge of all her treasury. He had come to Jerusalem to worship, **8:28** and was returning home, sitting in his chariot, reading the prophet Isaiah. **8:29** Then the Spirit said to Philip, "Go over and join this chariot." **8:30** So Philip ran up to it and heard the man reading Isaiah the prophet. He asked him, "Do you understand what you're reading?" **8:31** The man replied, "How in the world can I, unless someone guides me?" So he invited Philip to come up

and sit with him. **8:32** Now the passage of scripture the man was reading was this:

"He was led like a sheep to slaughter,
and like a lamb before its shearer is silent,
so he did not open his mouth.
8:33 In humiliation justice was taken from him.
Who can describe his posterity?
For his life was taken away from the earth.*"*

8:34 Then the eunuch said to Philip, "Please tell me, who is the prophet saying this about – himself or someone else?" **8:35** So Philip started speaking, and beginning with this scripture proclaimed the good news about Jesus to him. **8:36** Now as they were going along the road, they came to some water, and the eunuch said, "Look, there is water! What is to stop me from being baptized?" **8:38** So he ordered the chariot to stop, and both Philip and the eunuch went down into the water, and Philip baptized him. **8:39** Now when they came up out of the water, the Spirit of the Lord snatched Philip away, and the eunuch did not see him any more, but went on his way rejoicing. **8:40** Philip, however, found himself at Azotus, and as he passed through the area, he proclaimed the good news to all the towns until he came to Caesarea.

The Conversion of Saul
9:1 Meanwhile Saul, still breathing out threats to murder the Lord's disciples, went to the high priest **9:2** and requested letters from him to the synagogues in Damascus, so that if he found any who belonged to the Way, either men or women, he could bring them as prisoners to Jerusalem. **9:3** As he was going along, approaching Damascus, suddenly a light from heaven flashed around him. **9:4** He fell to the ground and heard a voice saying to him, "Saul, Saul, why are you persecuting me?" **9:5** So he said, "Who are you, Lord?" He replied, "I am Jesus whom you are persecuting! **9:6** But stand up and enter the city and you will be told what you must do." **9:7** (Now the men who were traveling with him stood there speechless, because they heard the voice but saw no one.) **9:8** So Saul got up from the ground, but although his eyes were open, he could see nothing. Leading him by the hand, his companions brought him into Damascus. **9:9** For three days he could not see, and he neither ate nor drank anything.
9:10 Now there was a disciple in Damascus named Ananias. The Lord said to him in a vision, "Ananias," and he replied, "Here I am, Lord." **9:11** Then the Lord told him, "Get up and go to the street called 'Straight,' and at Judas' house look for a man from Tarsus named Saul. For he is praying, **9:12** and he has seen in a vision a man named Ananias come in and place his hands on him so that he may see again." **9:13** But Ananias replied, "Lord, I have heard from many people about this man, how much harm he has done to your saints in Jerusalem, **9:14** and here he has authority from the chief priests to imprison all who call on your name!" **9:15** But the Lord said to him, "Go, because this man is my chosen instrument to carry my name before Gentiles and kings and the people of Israel. **9:16** For I will show him how much he must suffer for the sake of my name." **9:17** So Ananias departed and entered the house, placed his hands on Saul and said, "Brother Saul, the Lord Jesus, who appeared to you on the road as you came here, has sent me so that you may see again and be filled with the Holy Spirit." **9:18** Immediately something like scales fell from his eyes, and he could see again. He got up and was baptized, **9:19** and after taking some food, his strength returned.
For several days he was with the disciples in Damascus, **9:20** and immediately he began to proclaim Jesus in the synagogues, saying, "This man is the Son of God." **9:21** All who heard him were amazed and were saying, "Is this not the man who in Jerusalem was ravaging those who call on this name, and who had come here to bring them as prisoners to the chief priests?" **9:22** But Saul became more and more capable, and was causing consternation among the Jews who lived in Damascus by proving that Jesus is the Christ.

Saul's Escape from Damascus
9:23 Now after some days had passed, the Jews plotted together to kill him, **9:24** but Saul learned of their plot against him. They were also watching the city gates day and night so that they could kill him. **9:25** But his disciples took him at night and let him down through an opening in the wall by lowering him in a basket.

Saul Returns to Jerusalem
9:26 When he arrived in Jerusalem, he attempted to associate with the disciples, and they were all afraid of him, because they did not believe that he was a disciple. **9:27** But Barnabas took Saul, brought him to the apostles, and related to them how he had seen the Lord on the road, that the Lord had spoken to him, and how in Damascus he had spoken out boldly in the name of Jesus. **9:28** So he was staying with them, associating openly with them in Jerusalem, speaking out boldly in the name of the Lord. **9:29** He was speaking and debating with the Greek-speaking Jews, but they were trying to kill him. **9:30** When the brothers found out about this, they brought him down to Caesarea and sent him away to Tarsus.

9:31 Then the church throughout Judea, Galilee, and Samaria experienced peace and thus was strengthened. Living in the fear of the Lord and in the encouragement of the Holy Spirit, the church increased in numbers.

Peter Heals Aeneas
9:32 Now as Peter was traveling around from place to place, he also came down to the saints who lived in Lydda. **9:33** He found there a man named Aeneas who had been confined to a mattress for eight years because he was paralyzed. **9:34** Peter said to him, "Aeneas, Jesus the Christ heals you. Get up and make your own bed!" And immediately he got up. **9:35** All those who lived in Lydda and Sharon saw him, and they turned to the Lord.

Peter Raises Dorcas
9:36 Now in Joppa there was a disciple named Tabitha (which in translation means Dorcas). She was continually doing good deeds and acts of charity. **9:37** At that time she became sick and died. When they had washed her body, they placed it in an upstairs room. **9:38** Because Lydda was near Joppa, when the disciples heard that Peter was there, they sent two men to him and urged him, "Come to us without delay." **9:39** So Peter got up and went with them, and when he arrived they brought him to the upper room. All the widows stood beside him, crying and showing him the tunics and other clothing Dorcas used to make while she was with them. **9:40** But Peter sent them all outside, knelt down, and prayed. Turning to the body, he said, "Tabitha, get up." Then she opened her eyes, and when she saw Peter, she sat up. **9:41** He gave her his hand and helped her get up. Then he called the saints and widows and presented her alive. **9:42** This became known throughout all Joppa, and many believed in the Lord. **9:43** So Peter stayed many days in Joppa with a man named Simon, a tanner.

Peter Visits Cornelius
10:1 Now there was a man in Caesarea named Cornelius, a centurion of what was known as the Italian Cohort. **10:2** He was a devout, God-fearing man, as was all his household; he did many acts of charity for the people and prayed to God regularly. **10:3** About three o'clock one afternoon he saw clearly in a vision an angel of God who came in and said to him, "Cornelius." **10:4** Staring at him and becoming greatly afraid, Cornelius replied, "What is it, Lord?" The angel said to him, "Your prayers and your acts of charity have gone up as a memorial before God. **10:5** Now send men to Joppa and summon a man named Simon, who is called Peter. **10:6** This man is staying as a guest with a man named Simon, a tanner, whose house is by the sea." **10:7** When the angel who had spoken to him departed, Cornelius called two of his personal servants and a devout soldier from among those who served him, **10:8** and when he had explained everything to them, he sent them to Joppa.
10:9 About noon the next day, while they were on their way and approaching the city, Peter went up on the roof to pray. **10:10** He became hungry and wanted to eat, but while they were preparing the meal, a trance came over him. **10:11** He saw heaven opened and an object something like a large sheet descending, being let down to earth by its four corners. **10:12** In it were all kinds of four-footed animals and reptiles of the earth and wild birds. **10:13** Then a voice said to him, "Get up, Peter; slaughter and eat!" **10:14** But Peter said, "Certainly not, Lord, for I have never eaten anything defiled and ritually unclean!" **10:15** The voice spoke to him again, a second time, "What God has made clean, you must not consider ritually unclean!" **10:16** This happened three times, and immediately the object was taken up into heaven.
10:17 Now while Peter was puzzling over what the vision he had seen could signify, the men sent by Cornelius had learned where Simon's house was and approached the gate. **10:18** They called out to ask if Simon, known as Peter, was staying there as a guest. **10:19** While Peter was still thinking seriously about the vision, the Spirit said to him, "Look! Three men are looking for you. **10:20** But get up, go down, and accompany them without hesitation, because I have sent them." **10:21** So Peter went down to the men and said, "Here I am, the person you're looking for. Why have you come?" **10:22** They said, "Cornelius the centurion, a righteous and God-fearing man, well spoken of by the whole Jewish nation, was directed by a holy angel to summon you to his house and to hear a message from you." **10:23** So Peter invited them in and entertained them as guests.
On the next day he got up and set out with them, and some of the brothers from Joppa accompanied him. **10:24** The following day he entered Caesarea. Now Cornelius was waiting anxiously for them and had called together his relatives and close friends. **10:25** So when Peter came in, Cornelius met him, fell at his feet, and worshiped him. **10:26** But Peter helped him up, saying, "Stand up. I too am a mere mortal." **10:27** Peter continued talking with him as he went in, and he found many people gathered together. **10:28** He said to them, "You know that it is unlawful for a Jew to associate with or visit a Gentile, yet God has shown me that I should call no person defiled or ritually unclean. **10:29** Therefore when you sent for me, I came without any objection. Now may I ask why you sent for me?" **10:30** Cornelius replied, "Four days ago at this very hour, at three o'clock in the afternoon, I was praying in my house, and suddenly a man in shining clothing stood before me **10:31** and said, 'Cornelius, your prayer has been heard and your acts of charity have been remem-

bered before God. **10:32** Therefore send to Joppa and summon Simon, who is called Peter. This man is staying as a guest in the house of Simon the tanner, by the sea.' **10:33** Therefore I sent for you at once, and you were kind enough to come. So now we are all here in the presence of God to listen to everything the Lord has commanded you to say to us."

10:34 Then Peter started speaking: "I now truly understand that God does not show favoritism in dealing with people, **10:35** but in every nation the person who fears him and does what is right is welcomed before him. **10:36** You know the message he sent to the people of Israel, proclaiming the good news of peace through Jesus Christ (he is Lord of all) – **10:37** you know what happened throughout Judea, beginning from Galilee after the baptism that John announced: **10:38** with respect to Jesus from Nazareth, that God anointed him with the Holy Spirit and with power. He went around doing good and healing all who were oppressed by the devil, because God was with him. **10:39** We are witnesses of all the things he did both in Judea and in Jerusalem. They killed him by hanging him on a tree, **10:40** but God raised him up on the third day and caused him to be seen, **10:41** not by all the people, but by us, the witnesses God had already chosen, who ate and drank with him after he rose from the dead. **10:42** He commanded us to preach to the people and to warn them that he is the one appointed by God as judge of the living and the dead. **10:43** About him all the prophets testify, that everyone who believes in him receives forgiveness of sins through his name."

The Gentiles Receive the Holy Spirit

10:44 While Peter was still speaking these words, the Holy Spirit fell on all those who heard the message. **10:45** The circumcised believers who had accompanied Peter were greatly astonished that the gift of the Holy Spirit had been poured out even on the Gentiles, **10:46** for they heard them speaking in tongues and praising God. Then Peter said, **10:47** "No one can withhold the water for these people to be baptized, who have received the Holy Spirit just as we did, can he?" **10:48** So he gave orders to have them baptized in the name of Jesus Christ. Then they asked him to stay for several days.

Peter Defends His Actions to the Jerusalem Church

11:1 Now the apostles and the brothers who were throughout Judea heard that the Gentiles too had accepted the word of God. **11:2** So when Peter went up to Jerusalem, the circumcised believers took issue with him, **11:3** saying, "You went to uncircumcised men and shared a meal with them." **11:4** But Peter began and explained it to them point by point, saying, **11:5** "I was in the city of Joppa praying, and in a trance I saw a vision, an object something like a large sheet descending, being let down from heaven by its four corners, and it came to me. **11:6** As I stared I looked into it and saw four-footed animals of the earth, wild animals, reptiles, and wild birds. **11:7** I also heard a voice saying to me, 'Get up, Peter; slaughter and eat!' **11:8** But I said, 'Certainly not, Lord, for nothing defiled or ritually unclean has ever entered my mouth!' **11:9** But the voice replied a second time from heaven, 'What God has made clean, you must not consider ritually unclean!' **11:10** This happened three times, and then everything was pulled up to heaven again. **11:11** At that very moment, three men sent to me from Caesarea approached the house where we were staying. **11:12** The Spirit told me to accompany them without hesitation. These six brothers also went with me, and we entered the man's house. **11:13** He informed us how he had seen an angel standing in his house and saying, 'Send to Joppa and summon Simon, who is called Peter, **11:14** who will speak a message to you by which you and your entire household will be saved.' **11:15** Then as I began to speak, the Holy Spirit fell on them just as he did on us at the beginning. **11:16** And I remembered the word of the Lord, as he used to say, 'John baptized with water, but you will be baptized with the Holy Spirit.' **11:17** Therefore if God gave them the same gift as he also gave us after believing in the Lord Jesus Christ, who was I to hinder God?" **11:18** When they heard this, they ceased their objections and praised God, saying, "So then, God has granted the repentance that leads to life even to the Gentiles."

Activity in the Church at Antioch

11:19 Now those who had been scattered because of the persecution that took place over Stephen went as far as Phoenicia, Cyprus, and Antioch, speaking the message to no one but Jews. **11:20** But there were some men from Cyprus and Cyrene among them who came to Antioch and began to speak to the Greeks too, proclaiming the good news of the Lord Jesus. **11:21** The hand of the Lord was with them, and a great number who believed turned to the Lord. **11:22** A report about them came to the attention of the church in Jerusalem, and they sent Barnabas to Antioch. **11:23** When he came and saw the grace of God, he rejoiced and encouraged them all to remain true to the Lord with devoted hearts, **11:24** because he was a good man, full of the Holy Spirit and of faith, and a significant number of people were brought to the Lord. **11:25** Then Barnabas departed for Tarsus to look for Saul, **11:26** and when he found him, he brought him to Antioch. So for a whole year Barnabas and Saul met with the church and taught a significant number of people. Now it was in Antioch that the disciples were first called Christians.

Famine Relief for Judea

11:27 At that time some prophets came down from Jerusalem to Antioch. **11:28** One of them, named Agabus, got up and predicted by the Spirit that a severe famine was about to come over the whole inhabited world. (This took place during the reign of Claudius.) **11:29** So the disciples, each in accordance with his financial ability, decided to send relief to the brothers living in Judea. **11:30** They did so, sending their financial aid to the elders by Barnabas and Saul.

James is Killed and Peter Imprisoned

12:1 About that time King Herod laid hands on some from the church to harm them. **12:2** He had James, the brother of John, executed with a sword. **12:3** When he saw that this pleased the Jews, he proceeded to arrest Peter too. (This took place during the feast of Unleavened Bread.) **12:4** When he had seized him, he put him in prison, handing him over to four squads of soldiers to guard him. Herod planned to bring him out for public trial after the Passover. **12:5** So Peter was kept in prison, but those in the church were earnestly praying to God for him. **12:6** On that very night before Herod was going to bring him out for trial, Peter was sleeping between two soldiers, bound with two chains, while guards in front of the door were keeping watch over the prison. **12:7** Suddenly an angel of the Lord appeared, and a light shone in the prison cell. He struck Peter on the side and woke him up, saying, "Get up quickly!" And the chains fell off Peter's wrists. **12:8** The angel said to him, "Fasten your belt and put on your sandals." Peter did so. Then the angel said to him, "Put on your cloak and follow me." **12:9** Peter went out and followed him; he did not realize that what was happening through the angel was real, but thought he was seeing a vision. **12:10** After they had passed the first and second guards, they came to the iron gate leading into the city. It opened for them by itself, and they went outside and walked down one narrow street, when at once the angel left him. **12:11** When Peter came to himself, he said, "Now I know for certain that the Lord has sent his angel and rescued me from the hand of Herod and from everything the Jewish people were expecting to happen."

12:12 When Peter realized this, he went to the house of Mary, the mother of John Mark, where many people had gathered together and were praying. **12:13** When he knocked at the door of the outer gate, a slave girl named Rhoda answered. **12:14** When she recognized Peter's voice, she was so overjoyed she did not open the gate, but ran back in and told them that Peter was standing at the gate. **12:15** But they said to her, "You've lost your mind!" But she kept insisting that it was Peter, and they kept saying, "It is his angel!" **12:16** Now Peter continued knocking, and when they opened the door and saw him, they were greatly astonished. **12:17** He motioned to them with his hand to be quiet and then related how the Lord had brought him out of the prison. He said, "Tell James and the brothers these things," and then he left and went to another place.

12:18 At daybreak there was great consternation among the soldiers over what had become of Peter. **12:19** When Herod had searched for him and did not find him, he questioned the guards and commanded that they be led away to execution. Then Herod went down from Judea to Caesarea and stayed there.

12:20 Now Herod was having an angry quarrel with the people of Tyre and Sidon. So they joined together and presented themselves before him. And after convincing Blastus, the king's personal assistant, to help them, they asked for peace, because their country's food supply was provided by the king's country. **12:21** On a day determined in advance, Herod put on his royal robes, sat down on the judgment seat, and made a speech to them. **12:22** But the crowd began to shout, "The voice of a god, and not of a man!" **12:23** Immediately an angel of the Lord struck Herod down because he did not give the glory to God, and he was eaten by worms and died. **12:24** But the word of God kept on increasing and multiplying.

12:25 So Barnabas and Saul returned to Jerusalem when they had completed their mission, bringing along with them John Mark.

The Church at Antioch Commissions Barnabas and Saul

13:1 Now there were these prophets and teachers in the church at Antioch: Barnabas, Simeon called Niger, Lucius the Cyrenian, Manaen (a close friend of Herod the tetrarch from childhood) and Saul. **13:2** While they were serving the Lord and fasting, the Holy Spirit said, "Set apart for me Barnabas and Saul for the work to which I have called them." **13:3** Then, after they had fasted and prayed and placed their hands on them, they sent them off.

Paul and Barnabas Preach in Cyprus

13:4 So Barnabas and Saul, sent out by the Holy Spirit, went down to Seleucia, and from there they sailed to Cyprus. **13:5** When they arrived in Salamis, they began to proclaim the word of God in the Jewish synagogues. (Now they also had John as their assistant.) **13:6** When they had crossed over the whole island as far as Paphos, they found a magician, a Jewish false prophet named Bar-Jesus, **13:7** who was with the proconsul Sergius Paulus, an intelligent man. The proconsul summoned Barnabas and Saul and wanted to hear the word of God. **13:8** But the magician Elymas (for that is the way his name is translated) opposed them, trying to turn the proconsul away from the faith. **13:9** But Saul (also known as Paul), filled with the Holy Spirit, stared straight at him **13:10** and said, "You who are full of all deceit and all wrongdoing, you son of the devil, you enemy of all righteousness – will you not stop making crooked the straight paths of the Lord? **13:11** Now look, the hand of the Lord is against you, and you will be blind, unable to see the sun for a time!"

Immediately mistiness and darkness came over him, and he went around seeking people to lead him by the hand. **13:12** Then when the proconsul saw what had happened, he believed, because he was greatly astounded at the teaching about the Lord.

Paul and Barnabas at Pisidian Antioch

13:13 Then Paul and his companions put out to sea from Paphos and came to Perga in Pamphylia, but John left them and returned to Jerusalem. **13:14** Moving on from Perga, they arrived at Pisidian Antioch, and on the Sabbath day they went into the synagogue and sat down. **13:15** After the reading from the law and the prophets, the leaders of the synagogue sent them a message, saying, "Brothers, if you have any message of exhortation for the people, speak it." **13:16** So Paul stood up, gestured with his hand and said,

"Men of Israel, and you Gentiles who fear God, listen: **13:17** The God of this people Israel chose our ancestors and made the people great during their stay as foreigners in the country of Egypt, and with uplifted arm he led them out of it. **13:18** For a period of about forty years he put up with them in the wilderness. **13:19** After he had destroyed seven nations in the land of Canaan, he gave his people their land as an inheritance. **13:20** All this took about four hundred fifty years. After this he gave them judges until the time of Samuel the prophet. **13:21** Then they asked for a king, and God gave them Saul son of Kish, a man from the tribe of Benjamin, who ruled forty years. **13:22** After removing him, God raised up David their king. He testified about him: *'I have found David* the son of Jesse *to be a man after my heart*, who will accomplish everything I want him to do.' **13:23** From the descendants of this man God brought to Israel a Savior, Jesus, just as he promised. **13:24** Before Jesus arrived, John had proclaimed a baptism for repentance to all the people of Israel. **13:25** But while John was completing his mission, he said repeatedly, 'What do you think I am? I am not he. But look, one is coming after me. I am not worthy to untie the sandals on his feet!' **13:26** Brothers, descendants of Abraham's family, and those Gentiles among you who fear God, the message of this salvation has been sent to us. **13:27** For the people who live in Jerusalem and their rulers did not recognize him, and they fulfilled the sayings of the prophets that are read every Sabbath by condemning him. **13:28** Though they found no basis for a death sentence, they asked Pilate to have him executed. **13:29** When they had accomplished everything that was written about him, they took him down from the cross and placed him in a tomb. **13:30** But God raised him from the dead, **13:31** and for many days he appeared to those who had accompanied him from Galilee to Jerusalem. These are now his witnesses to the people. **13:32** And we proclaim to you the good news about the promise to our ancestors, **13:33** that this promise God has fulfilled to us, their children, by raising Jesus, as also it is written in the second psalm, *'You are my Son; today I have fathered you.'* **13:34** But regarding the fact that he has raised Jesus from the dead, never again to be in a state of decay, God has spoken in this way: *'I will give you the holy and trustworthy promises made to David.'* **13:35** Therefore he also says in another psalm, *'You will not permit your Holy One to experience decay.'* **13:36** For David, after he had served God's purpose in his own generation, died, was buried with his ancestors, and experienced decay, **13:37** but the one whom God raised up did not experience decay. **13:38** Therefore let it be known to you, brothers, that through this one forgiveness of sins is proclaimed to you, **13:39** and by this one everyone who believes is justified from everything from which the law of Moses could not justify you. **13:40** Watch out, then, that what is spoken about by the prophets does not happen to you:

13:41 'Look, you scoffers; be amazed and perish!

For I am doing a work in your days,

a work you would never believe, even if someone tells you.'"

13:42 As Paul and Barnabas were going out, the people were urging them to speak about these things on the next Sabbath. **13:43** When the meeting of the synagogue had broken up, many of the Jews and God-fearing proselytes followed Paul and Barnabas, who were speaking with them and were persuading them to continue in the grace of God.

13:44 On the next Sabbath almost the whole city assembled together to hear the word of the Lord. **13:45** But when the Jews saw the crowds, they were filled with jealousy, and they began to contradict what Paul was saying by reviling him. **13:46** Both Paul and Barnabas replied courageously, "It was necessary to speak the word of God to you first. Since you reject it and do not consider yourselves worthy of eternal life, we are turning to the Gentiles. **13:47** For this is what the Lord has commanded us: *'I have appointed you to be a light for the Gentiles, to bring salvation to the ends of the earth.'"* **13:48** When the Gentiles heard this, they began to rejoice and praise the word of the Lord, and all who had been appointed for eternal life believed. **13:49** So the word of the Lord was spreading through the entire region. **13:50** But the Jews incited the God-fearing women of high social standing and the prominent men of the city, stirred up persecution against Paul and Barnabas, and threw them out of their region. **13:51** So after they shook the dust off their feet in protest against them, they went to Iconium. **13:52** And the disciples were filled with joy and with the Holy Spirit.

Paul and Barnabas at Iconium

14:1 The same thing happened in Iconium when Paul and Barnabas went into the Jewish synagogue and spoke in such a way that a large group of both Jews and Greeks believed. **14:2** But the Jews who refused to believe stirred up the Gentiles and poisoned their minds against the brothers. **14:3** So they stayed there for a considerable time, speaking out courageously for the Lord, who testified to the message of his grace, granting miraculous signs and wonders to be performed through their hands. **14:4** But the population of the city was divided; some sided with the Jews, and some with the apostles. **14:5** When both the Gentiles and the Jews (together with their rulers) made an attempt to mistreat them and stone them, **14:6** Paul and Barnabas learned about it and fled to the Lycaonian cities of Lystra and Derbe and the surrounding region. **14:7** There they continued to proclaim the good news.

Paul and Barnabas at Lystra

14:8 In Lystra sat a man who could not use his feet, lame from birth, who had never walked. **14:9** This man was listening to Paul as he was speaking. When Paul stared intently at him and saw he had faith to be healed, **14:10** he said with a loud voice, "Stand upright on your feet." And the man leaped up and began walking. **14:11** So when the crowds saw what Paul had done, they shouted in the Lycaonian language, "The gods have come down to us in human form!" **14:12** They began to call Barnabas Zeus and Paul Hermes, because he was the chief speaker. **14:13** The priest of the temple of Zeus, located just outside the city, brought bulls and garlands to the city gates; he and the crowds wanted to offer sacrifices to them. **14:14** But when the apostles Barnabas and Paul heard about it, they tore their clothes and rushed out into the crowd, shouting, **14:15** "Men, why are you doing these things? We too are men, with human natures just like you! We are proclaiming the good news to you, so that you should turn from these worthless things to the living God, who made the heaven, the earth, the sea, and everything that is in them. **14:16** In past generations he allowed all the nations to go their own ways, **14:17** yet he did not leave himself without a witness by doing good, by giving you rain from heaven and fruitful seasons, satisfying you with food and your hearts with joy." **14:18** Even by saying these things, they scarcely persuaded the crowds not to offer sacrifice to them.

14:19 But Jews came from Antioch and Iconium, and after winning the crowds over, they stoned Paul and dragged him out of the city, presuming him to be dead. **14:20** But after the disciples had surrounded him, he got up and went back into the city. On the next day he left with Barnabas for Derbe.

Paul and Barnabas Return to Antioch in Syria

14:21 After they had proclaimed the good news in that city and made many disciples, they returned to Lystra, to Iconium, and to Antioch. **14:22** They strengthened the souls of the disciples and encouraged them to continue in the faith, saying, "We must enter the kingdom of God through many persecutions." **14:23** When they had appointed elders for them in the various churches, with prayer and fasting they entrusted them to the protection of the Lord in whom they had believed. **14:24** Then they passed through Pisidia and came into Pamphylia, **14:25** and when they had spoken the word in Perga, they went down to Attalia. **14:26** From there they sailed back to Antioch, where they had been commended to the grace of God for the work they had now completed. **14:27** When they arrived and gathered the church together, they reported all the things God had done with them, and that he had opened a door of faith for the Gentiles. **14:28** So they spent considerable time with the disciples.

The Jerusalem Council

15:1 Now some men came down from Judea and began to teach the brothers, "Unless you are circumcised according to the custom of Moses, you cannot be saved." **15:2** When Paul and Barnabas had a major argument and debate with them, the church appointed Paul and Barnabas and some others from among them to go up to meet with the apostles and elders in Jerusalem about this point of disagreement. **15:3** So they were sent on their way by the church, and as they passed through both Phoenicia and Samaria, they were relating at length the conversion of the Gentiles and bringing great joy to all the brothers. **15:4** When they arrived in Jerusalem, they were received by the church and the apostles and the elders, and they reported all the things God had done with them. **15:5** But some from the religious party of the Pharisees who had believed stood up and said, "It is necessary to circumcise the Gentiles and to order them to observe the law of Moses."

15:6 Both the apostles and the elders met together to deliberate about this matter. **15:7** After there had been much debate, Peter stood up and said to them, "Brothers, you know that some time ago God chose me to preach to the Gentiles so they would hear the message of the gospel and believe. **15:8** And God, who knows the heart, has testified to them by giving them the Holy Spirit just as he did to us, **15:9** and he made no distinction between us and them, cleansing their hearts by faith. **15:10** So now why are you putting God to the test by placing on the neck of the disciples a yoke that neither our ancestors nor we have been able to bear? **15:11** On the contrary, we believe that we are saved through the grace of the Lord Jesus, in the same way as they are."

15:12 The whole group kept quiet and listened to Barnabas and Paul while they explained all the miraculous signs and wonders God had done among the Gentiles through them. **15:13** After they stopped speaking, James replied, "Brothers, listen to me. **15:14** Simeon has explained how God first concerned himself to select from among the Gentiles a people for his name. **15:15** The words of the prophets agree with this, as it is written,

15:16 'After this I will return,
and I will rebuild the fallen tent of David;
I will rebuild its ruins and restore it,
15:17 so that the rest of humanity may seek the Lord,
namely, all the Gentiles I have called to be my own,' says the Lord, **who makes these things** *15:18* **known from long ago.**

15:19 "Therefore I conclude that we should not cause extra difficulty for those among the Gentiles who are turning to God, **15:20** but that we should write them a letter telling them to abstain from things defiled by idols and from sexual immorality and from what has been strangled and from blood. **15:21** For Moses has had those who proclaim him in every town from ancient times, because he is read aloud in the synagogues every Sabbath."

15:22 Then the apostles and elders, with the whole church, decided to send men chosen from among them, Judas called Barsabbas and Silas, leaders among the brothers, to Antioch with Paul and Barnabas. **15:23** They sent this letter with them:

From the apostles and elders, your brothers, to the Gentile brothers and sisters in Antioch, Syria, and Cilicia, greetings! **15:24** Since we have heard that some have gone out from among us with no orders from us and have confused you, upsetting your minds by what they said, **15:25** we have unanimously decided to choose men to send to you along with our dear friends Barnabas and Paul, **15:26** who have risked their lives for the name of our Lord Jesus Christ. **15:27** Therefore we are sending Judas and Silas who will tell you these things themselves in person. **15:28** For it seemed best to the Holy Spirit and to us not to place any greater burden on you than these necessary rules: **15:29** that you abstain from meat that has been sacrificed to idols and from blood and from what has been strangled and from sexual immorality. If you keep yourselves from doing these things, you will do well. Farewell.

15:30 So when they were dismissed, they went down to Antioch, and after gathering the entire group together, they delivered the letter. **15:31** When they read it aloud, the people rejoiced at its encouragement. **15:32** Both Judas and Silas, who were prophets themselves, encouraged and strengthened the brothers with a long speech. **15:33** After they had spent some time there, they were sent off in peace by the brothers to those who had sent them. **15:35** But Paul and Barnabas remained in Antioch, teaching and proclaiming (along with many others) the word of the Lord.

Paul and Barnabas Part Company

15:36 After some days Paul said to Barnabas, "Let's return and visit the brothers in every town where we proclaimed the word of the Lord to see how they are doing." **15:37** Barnabas wanted to bring John called Mark along with them too, **15:38** but Paul insisted that they should not take along this one who had left them in Pamphylia and had not accompanied them in the work. **15:39** They had a sharp disagreement, so that they parted company. Barnabas took along Mark and sailed away to Cyprus, **15:40** but Paul chose Silas and set out, commended to the grace of the Lord by the brothers and sisters. **15:41** He passed through Syria and Cilicia, strengthening the churches.

Timothy Joins Paul and Silas

16:1 He also came to Derbe and to Lystra. A disciple named Timothy was there, the son of a Jewish woman who was a believer, but whose father was a Greek. **16:2** The brothers in Lystra and Iconium spoke well of him. **16:3** Paul wanted Timothy to accompany him, and he took him and circumcised him because of the Jews who were in those places, for they all knew that his father was Greek. **16:4** As they went through the towns, they passed on the decrees that had been decided on by the apostles and elders in Jerusalem for the Gentile believers to obey. **16:5** So the churches were being strengthened in the faith and were increasing in number every day.

Paul's Vision of the Macedonian Man

16:6 They went through the region of Phrygia and Galatia, having been prevented by the Holy Spirit from speaking the message in the province of Asia. **16:7** When they came to Mysia, they attempted to go into Bithynia, but the Spirit of Jesus did not allow them to do this, **16:8** so they passed through Mysia and went down to Troas. **16:9** A vision appeared to Paul during the night: A Macedonian man was standing there urging him, "Come over to Macedonia and help us!" **16:10** After Paul saw the vision, we attempted immediately to go over to Macedonia, concluding that God had called us to proclaim the good news to them.

Arrival at Philippi

16:11 We put out to sea from Troas and sailed a straight course to Samothrace, the next day to Neapolis, **16:12** and from there to Philippi, which is a leading city of that district of Macedonia, a Roman colony. We stayed in this city for some days. **16:13** On the Sabbath day we went outside the city gate to the side of the river, where we thought there would be a place of prayer, and we sat down and began to speak to the women who had assembled there. **16:14** A woman named Lydia, a dealer

in purple cloth from the city of Thyatira, a God-fearing woman, listened to us. The Lord opened her heart to respond to what Paul was saying. **16:15** After she and her household were baptized, she urged us, "If you consider me to be a believer in the Lord, come and stay in my house." And she persuaded us.

Paul and Silas Are Thrown Into Prison

16:16 Now as we were going to the place of prayer, a slave girl met us who had a spirit that enabled her to foretell the future by supernatural means. She brought her owners a great profit by fortune-telling. **16:17** She followed behind Paul and us and kept crying out, "These men are servants of the Most High God, who are proclaiming to you the way of salvation." **16:18** She continued to do this for many days. But Paul became greatly annoyed, and turned and said to the spirit, "I command you in the name of Jesus Christ to come out of her!" And it came out of her at once. **16:19** But when her owners saw their hope of profit was gone, they seized Paul and Silas and dragged them into the marketplace before the authorities. **16:20** When they had brought them before the magistrates, they said, "These men are throwing our city into confusion. They are Jews **16:21** and are advocating customs that are not lawful for us to accept or practice, since we are Romans."

16:22 The crowd joined the attack against them, and the magistrates tore the clothes off Paul and Silas and ordered them to be beaten with rods. **16:23** After they had beaten them severely, they threw them into prison and commanded the jailer to guard them securely. **16:24** Receiving such orders, he threw them in the inner cell and fastened their feet in the stocks.

16:25 About midnight Paul and Silas were praying and singing hymns to God, and the rest of the prisoners were listening to them. **16:26** Suddenly a great earthquake occurred, so that the foundations of the prison were shaken. Immediately all the doors flew open, and the bonds of all the prisoners came loose. **16:27** When the jailer woke up and saw the doors of the prison standing open, he drew his sword and was about to kill himself, because he assumed the prisoners had escaped. **16:28** But Paul called out loudly, "Do not harm yourself, for we are all here!" **16:29** Calling for lights, the jailer rushed in and fell down trembling at the feet of Paul and Silas. **16:30** Then he brought them outside and asked, "Sirs, what must I do to be saved?" **16:31** They replied, "Believe in the Lord Jesus and you will be saved, you and your household." **16:32** Then they spoke the word of the Lord to him, along with all those who were in his house. **16:33** At that hour of the night he took them and washed their wounds; then he and all his family were baptized right away. **16:34** The jailer brought them into his house and set food before them, and he rejoiced greatly that he had come to believe in God, together with his entire household. **16:35** At daybreak the magistrates sent their police officers, saying, "Release those men." **16:36** The jailer reported these words to Paul, saying, "The magistrates have sent orders to release you. So come out now and go in peace." **16:37** But Paul said to the police officers, "They had us beaten in public without a proper trial – even though we are Roman citizens – and they threw us in prison. And now they want to send us away secretly? Absolutely not! They themselves must come and escort us out!" **16:38** The police officers reported these words to the magistrates. They were frightened when they heard Paul and Silas were Roman citizens **16:39** and came and apologized to them. After they brought them out, they asked them repeatedly to leave the city. **16:40** When they came out of the prison, they entered Lydia's house, and when they saw the brothers, they encouraged them and then departed.

Paul and Silas at Thessalonica

17:1 After they traveled through Amphipolis and Apollonia, they came to Thessalonica, where there was a Jewish synagogue. **17:2** Paul went to the Jews in the synagogue, as he customarily did, and on three Sabbath days he addressed them from the scriptures, **17:3** explaining and demonstrating that the Christ had to suffer and to rise from the dead, saying, "This Jesus I am proclaiming to you is the Christ." **17:4** Some of them were persuaded and joined Paul and Silas, along with a large group of God-fearing Greeks and quite a few prominent women. **17:5** But the Jews became jealous, and gathering together some worthless men from the rabble in the marketplace, they formed a mob and set the city in an uproar. They attacked Jason's house, trying to find Paul and Silas to bring them out to the assembly. **17:6** When they did not find them, they dragged Jason and some of the brothers before the city officials, screaming, "These people who have stirred up trouble throughout the world have come here too, **17:7** and Jason has welcomed them as guests! They are all acting against Caesar's decrees, saying there is another king named Jesus!" **17:8** They caused confusion among the crowd and the city officials who heard these things. **17:9** After the city officials had received bail from Jason and the others, they released them.

Paul and Silas at Berea

17:10 The brothers sent Paul and Silas off to Berea at once, during the night. When they arrived, they went to the Jewish synagogue. **17:11** These Jews were more open-minded than those in Thessalonica, for they eagerly received the message, examining the scriptures carefully every day to see if these things were so. **17:12** Therefore many of them believed, along with quite a few prominent Greek women and men. **17:13**

But when the Jews from Thessalonica heard that Paul had also proclaimed the word of God in Berea, they came there too, inciting and disturbing the crowds. **17:14** Then the brothers sent Paul away to the coast at once, but Silas and Timothy remained in Berea. **17:15** Those who accompanied Paul escorted him as far as Athens, and after receiving an order for Silas and Timothy to come to him as soon as possible, they left.
Paul at Athens
17:16 While Paul was waiting for them in Athens, his spirit was greatly upset because he saw the city was full of idols. **17:17** So he was addressing the Jews and the God-fearing Gentiles in the synagogue, and in the marketplace every day those who happened to be there. **17:18** Also some of the Epicurean and Stoic philosophers were conversing with him, and some were asking, "What does this foolish babbler want to say?" Others said, "He seems to be a proclaimer of foreign gods." (They said this because he was proclaiming the good news about Jesus and the resurrection.) **17:19** So they took Paul and brought him to the Areopagus, saying, "May we know what this new teaching is that you are proclaiming? **17:20** For you are bringing some surprising things to our ears, so we want to know what they mean." **17:21** (All the Athenians and the foreigners who lived there used to spend their time in nothing else than telling or listening to something new.)
17:22 So Paul stood before the Areopagus and said, "Men of Athens, I see that you are very religious in all respects. **17:23** For as I went around and observed closely your objects of worship, I even found an altar with this inscription: 'To an unknown god.' Therefore what you worship without knowing it, this I proclaim to you. **17:24** The God who made the world and everything in it, who is Lord of heaven and earth, does not live in temples made by human hands, **17:25** nor is he served by human hands, as if he needed anything, because he himself gives life and breath and everything to everyone. **17:26** From one man he made every nation of the human race to inhabit the entire earth, determining their set times and the fixed limits of the places where they would live, **17:27** so that they would search for God and perhaps grope around for him and find him, though he is not far from each one of us. **17:28** For in him we live and move about and exist, as even some of your own poets have said, 'For we too are his offspring.' **17:29** So since we are God's offspring, we should not think the deity is like gold or silver or stone, an image made by human skill and imagination. **17:30** Therefore, although God has overlooked such times of ignorance, he now commands all people everywhere to repent, **17:31** because he has set a day on which he is going to judge the world in righteousness, by a man whom he designated, having provided proof to everyone by raising him from the dead."
17:32 Now when they heard about the resurrection from the dead, some began to scoff, but others said, "We will hear you again about this." **17:33** So Paul left the Areopagus. **17:34** But some people joined him and believed. Among them were Dionysius, who was a member of the Areopagus, a woman named Damaris, and others with them.
Paul at Corinth
18:1 After this Paul departed from Athens and went to Corinth. **18:2** There he found a Jew named Aquila, a native of Pontus, who had recently come from Italy with his wife Priscilla, because Claudius had ordered all the Jews to depart from Rome. Paul approached them, **18:3** and because he worked at the same trade, he stayed with them and worked with them (for they were tentmakers by trade). **18:4** He addressed both Jews and Greeks in the synagogue every Sabbath, attempting to persuade them.
18:5 Now when Silas and Timothy arrived from Macedonia, Paul became wholly absorbed with proclaiming the word, testifying to the Jews that Jesus was the Christ. **18:6** When they opposed him and reviled him, he protested by shaking out his clothes and said to them, "Your blood be on your own heads! I am guiltless! From now on I will go to the Gentiles!" **18:7** Then Paul left the synagogue and went to the house of a person named Titius Justus, a Gentile who worshiped God, whose house was next door to the synagogue. **18:8** Crispus, the president of the synagogue, believed in the Lord together with his entire household, and many of the Corinthians who heard about it believed and were baptized. **18:9** The Lord said to Paul by a vision in the night, "Do not be afraid, but speak and do not be silent, **18:10** because I am with you, and no one will assault you to harm you, because I have many people in this city." **18:11** So he stayed there a year and six months, teaching the word of God among them.
Paul Before the Proconsul Gallio
18:12 Now while Gallio was proconsul of Achaia, the Jews attacked Paul together and brought him before the judgment seat, **18:13** saying, "This man is persuading people to worship God in a way contrary to the law!" **18:14** But just as Paul was about to speak, Gallio said to the Jews, "If it were a matter of some crime or serious piece of villainy, I would have been justified in accepting the complaint of you Jews, **18:15** but since it concerns points of disagreement about words and names and your own law, settle it yourselves. I will not be a judge of these things!" **18:16** Then he had them forced away from the judgment seat. **18:17** So they all seized Sosthenes, the president of the synagogue, and began to beat him in front of the judgment seat. Yet none of these things were of any concern to Gallio.

Paul Returns to Antioch in Syria
18:18 Paul, after staying many more days in Corinth, said farewell to the brothers and sailed away to Syria accompanied by Priscilla and Aquila. He had his hair cut off at Cenchrea because he had made a vow. **18:19** When they reached Ephesus, Paul left Priscilla and Aquila behind there, but he himself went into the synagogue and addressed the Jews. **18:20** When they asked him to stay longer, he would not consent, **18:21** but said farewell to them and added, "I will come back to you again if God wills." Then he set sail from Ephesus, **18:22** and when he arrived at Caesarea, he went up and greeted the church at Jerusalem and then went down to Antioch. **18:23** After he spent some time there, Paul left and went through the region of Galatia and Phrygia, strengthening all the disciples.
Apollos Begins His Ministry
18:24 Now a Jew named Apollos, a native of Alexandria, arrived in Ephesus. He was an eloquent speaker, well-versed in the scriptures. **18:25** He had been instructed in the way of the Lord, and with great enthusiasm he spoke and taught accurately the facts about Jesus, although he knew only the baptism of John. **18:26** He began to speak out fearlessly in the synagogue, but when Priscilla and Aquila heard him, they took him aside and explained the way of God to him more accurately. **18:27** When Apollos wanted to cross over to Achaia, the brothers encouraged him and wrote to the disciples to welcome him. When he arrived, he assisted greatly those who had believed by grace, **18:28** for he refuted the Jews vigorously in public debate, demonstrating from the scriptures that the Christ was Jesus.
Disciples of John the Baptist at Ephesus
19:1 While Apollos was in Corinth, Paul went through the inland regions and came to Ephesus. He found some disciples there **19:2** and said to them, "Did you receive the Holy Spirit when you believed?" They replied, "No, we have not even heard that there is a Holy Spirit." **19:3** So Paul said, "Into what then were you baptized?" "Into John's baptism," they replied. **19:4** Paul said, "John baptized with a baptism of repentance, telling the people to believe in the one who was to come after him, that is, in Jesus." **19:5** When they heard this, they were baptized in the name of the Lord Jesus, **19:6** and when Paul placed his hands on them, the Holy Spirit came upon them, and they began to speak in tongues and to prophesy. **19:7** (Now there were about twelve men in all.)
Paul Continues to Minister at Ephesus
19:8 So Paul entered the synagogue and spoke out fearlessly for three months, addressing and convincing them about the kingdom of God. **19:9** But when some were stubborn and refused to believe, reviling the Way before the congregation, he left them and took the disciples with him, addressing them every day in the lecture hall of Tyrannus. **19:10** This went on for two years, so that all who lived in the province of Asia, both Jews and Greeks, heard the word of the Lord.
The Seven Sons of Sceva
19:11 God was performing extraordinary miracles by Paul's hands, **19:12** so that when even handkerchiefs or aprons that had touched his body were brought to the sick, their diseases left them and the evil spirits went out of them. **19:13** But some itinerant Jewish exorcists tried to invoke the name of the Lord Jesus over those who were possessed by evil spirits, saying, "I sternly warn you by Jesus whom Paul preaches." **19:14** (Now seven sons of a man named Sceva, a Jewish high priest, were doing this.) **19:15** But the evil spirit replied to them, "I know about Jesus and I am acquainted with Paul, but who are you?" **19:16** Then the man who was possessed by the evil spirit jumped on them and beat them all into submission. He prevailed against them so that they fled from that house naked and wounded. **19:17** This became known to all who lived in Ephesus, both Jews and Greeks; fear came over them all, and the name of the Lord Jesus was praised. **19:18** Many of those who had believed came forward, confessing and making their deeds known. **19:19** Large numbers of those who had practiced magic collected their books and burned them up in the presence of everyone. When the value of the books was added up, it was found to total fifty thousand silver coins. **19:20** In this way the word of the Lord continued to grow in power and to prevail.
A Riot in Ephesus
19:21 Now after all these things had taken place, Paul resolved to go to Jerusalem, passing through Macedonia and Achaia. He said, "After I have been there, I must also see Rome." **19:22** So after sending two of his assistants, Timothy and Erastus, to Macedonia, he himself stayed on for a while in the province of Asia.
19:23 At that time a great disturbance took place concerning the Way. **19:24** For a man named Demetrius, a silversmith who made silver shrines of Artemis, brought a great deal of business to the craftsmen. **19:25** He gathered these together, along with the workmen in similar trades, and said, "Men, you know that our prosperity comes from this business. **19:26** And you see and hear that this Paul has persuaded and turned away a large crowd, not only in Ephesus but in practically all of the province of Asia, by saying that gods made by hands are not gods at all. **19:27** There is danger not only that this business of ours will come into disrepute, but also that the temple of the great goddess Artemis will be regarded as nothing, and she whom all the province of Asia and the world worship will suffer the loss of her greatness."

19:28 When they heard this they became enraged and began to shout, "Great is Artemis of the Ephesians!" **19:29** The city was filled with the uproar, and the crowd rushed to the theater together, dragging with them Gaius and Aristarchus, the Macedonians who were Paul's traveling companions. **19:30** But when Paul wanted to enter the public assembly, the disciples would not let him. **19:31** Even some of the provincial authorities who were his friends sent a message to him, urging him not to venture into the theater. **19:32** So then some were shouting one thing, some another, for the assembly was in confusion, and most of them did not know why they had met together. **19:33** Some of the crowd concluded it was about Alexander because the Jews had pushed him to the front. Alexander, gesturing with his hand, was wanting to make a defense before the public assembly. **19:34** But when they recognized that he was a Jew, they all shouted in unison, "Great is Artemis of the Ephesians!" for about two hours. **19:35** After the city secretary quieted the crowd, he said, "Men of Ephesus, what person is there who does not know that the city of the Ephesians is the keeper of the temple of the great Artemis and of her image that fell from heaven? **19:36** So because these facts are indisputable, you must keep quiet and not do anything reckless. **19:37** For you have brought these men here who are neither temple robbers nor blasphemers of our goddess. **19:38** If then Demetrius and the craftsmen who are with him have a complaint against someone, the courts are open and there are proconsuls; let them bring charges against one another there. **19:39** But if you want anything in addition, it will have to be settled in a legal assembly. **19:40** For we are in danger of being charged with rioting today, since there is no cause we can give to explain this disorderly gathering." **19:41** After he had said this, he dismissed the assembly.

Paul Travels Through Macedonia and Greece
20:1 After the disturbance had ended, Paul sent for the disciples, and after encouraging them and saying farewell, he left to go to Macedonia. **20:2** After he had gone through those regions and spoken many words of encouragement to the believers there, he came to Greece, **20:3** where he stayed for three months. Because the Jews had made a plot against him as he was intending to sail for Syria, he decided to return through Macedonia. **20:4** Paul was accompanied by Sopater son of Pyrrhus from Berea, Aristarchus and Secundus from Thessalonica, Gaius from Derbe, and Timothy, as well as Tychicus and Trophimus from the province of Asia. **20:5** These had gone on ahead and were waiting for us in Troas. **20:6** We sailed away from Philippi after the days of Unleavened Bread, and within five days we came to the others in Troas, where we stayed for seven days. **20:7** On the first day of the week, when we met to break bread, Paul began to speak to the people, and because he intended to leave the next day, he extended his message until midnight. **20:8** (Now there were many lamps in the upstairs room where we were meeting.) **20:9** A young man named Eutychus, who was sitting in the window, was sinking into a deep sleep while Paul continued to speak for a long time. Fast asleep, he fell down from the third story and was picked up dead. **20:10** But Paul went down, threw himself on the young man, put his arms around him, and said, "Do not be distressed, for he is still alive!" **20:11** Then Paul went back upstairs, and after he had broken bread and eaten, he talked with them a long time, until dawn. Then he left. **20:12** They took the boy home alive and were greatly comforted.

The Voyage to Miletus
20:13 We went on ahead to the ship and put out to sea for Assos, intending to take Paul aboard there, for he had arranged it this way. He himself was intending to go there by land. **20:14** When he met us in Assos, we took him aboard and went to Mitylene. **20:15** We set sail from there, and on the following day we arrived off Chios. The next day we approached Samos, and the day after that we arrived at Miletus. **20:16** For Paul had decided to sail past Ephesus so as not to spend time in the province of Asia, for he was hurrying to arrive in Jerusalem, if possible, by the day of Pentecost. **20:17** From Miletus he sent a message to Ephesus, telling the elders of the church to come to him.
20:18 When they arrived, he said to them, "You yourselves know how I lived the whole time I was with you, from the first day I set foot in the province of Asia, **20:19** serving the Lord with all humility and with tears, and with the trials that happened to me because of the plots of the Jews. **20:20** You know that I did not hold back from proclaiming to you anything that would be helpful, and from teaching you publicly and from house to house, **20:21** testifying to both Jews and Greeks about repentance toward God and faith in our Lord Jesus. **20:22** And now, compelled by the Spirit, I am going to Jerusalem without knowing what will happen to me there, **20:23** except that the Holy Spirit warns me in town after town that imprisonment and persecutions are waiting for me. **20:24** But I do not consider my life worth anything to myself, so that I may finish my task and the ministry that I received from the Lord Jesus, to testify to the good news of God's grace.
20:25 "And now I know that none of you among whom I went around proclaiming the kingdom will see me again. **20:26** Therefore I declare to you today that I am innocent of the blood of you all. **20:27** For I did not hold back from announcing to you the whole purpose of God. **20:28** Watch out for yourselves and for all the flock of which the Holy Spirit has made you overseers, to shepherd the church of God that he obtained with the blood of his own Son. **20:29** I know that after I am gone fierce wolves will come in among you, not sparing the flock. **20:30** Even from among your own group men will arise, teaching perversions of the truth to draw the disciples away after them. **20:31** Therefore be alert, remembering that night and day for three years I did not stop warning each one of you with tears. **20:32** And now I entrust you to God and to the message of his grace. This message is able to build you up and give you an inheritance among all those who are sanctified. **20:33** I have desired no one's silver or gold or clothing. **20:34** You yourselves know that these hands of mine provided for my needs and the needs of those who were with me. **20:35** By all these things, I have shown you that by working in this way we must help the weak, and remember the words of the Lord Jesus that he himself said, 'It is more blessed to give than to receive.'"
20:36 When he had said these things, he knelt down with them all and prayed. **20:37** They all began to weep loudly, and hugged Paul and kissed him, **20:38** especially saddened by what he had said, that they were not going to see him again. Then they accompanied him to the ship.

Paul's Journey to Jerusalem
21:1 After we tore ourselves away from them, we put out to sea, and sailing a straight course, we came to Cos, on the next day to Rhodes, and from there to Patara. **21:2** We found a ship crossing over to Phoenicia, went aboard, and put out to sea. **21:3** After we sighted Cyprus and left it behind on our port side, we sailed on to Syria and put in at Tyre, because the ship was to unload its cargo there. **21:4** After we located the disciples, we stayed there seven days. They repeatedly told Paul through the Spirit not to set foot in Jerusalem. **21:5** When our time was over, we left and went on our way. All of them, with their wives and children, accompanied us outside of the city. After kneeling down on the beach and praying, **21:6** we said farewell to one another. Then we went aboard the ship, and they returned to their own homes. **21:7** We continued the voyage from Tyre and arrived at Ptolemais, and when we had greeted the brothers, we stayed with them for one day. **21:8** On the next day we left and came to Caesarea, and entered the house of Philip the evangelist, who was one of the seven, and stayed with him. **21:9** (He had four unmarried daughters who prophesied.)
21:10 While we remained there for a number of days, a prophet named Agabus came down from Judea. **21:11** He came to us, took Paul's belt, tied his own hands and feet with it, and said, "The Holy Spirit says this: 'This is the way the Jews in Jerusalem will tie up the man whose belt this is, and will hand him over to the Gentiles.'" **21:12** When we heard this, both we and the local people begged him not to go up to Jerusalem. **21:13** Then Paul replied, "What are you doing, weeping and breaking my heart? For I am ready not only to be tied up, but even to die in Jerusalem for the name of the Lord Jesus." **21:14** Because he could not be persuaded, we said no more except, "The Lord's will be done."
21:15 After these days we got ready and started up to Jerusalem. **21:16** Some of the disciples from Caesarea came along with us too, and brought us to the house of Mnason of Cyprus, a disciple from the earliest times, with whom we were to stay. **21:17** When we arrived in Jerusalem, the brothers welcomed us gladly. **21:18** The next day Paul went in with us to see James, and all the elders were there. **21:19** When Paul had greeted them, he began to explain in detail what God had done among the Gentiles through his ministry. **21:20** When they heard this, they praised God. Then they said to him, "You see, brother, how many thousands of Jews there are who have believed, and they are all ardent observers of the law. **21:21** They have been informed about you – that you teach all the Jews now living among the Gentiles to abandon Moses, telling them not to circumcise their children or live according to our customs. **21:22** What then should we do? They will no doubt hear that you have come. **21:23** So do what we tell you: We have four men who have taken a vow; **21:24** take them and purify yourself along with them and pay their expenses, so that they may have their heads shaved. Then everyone will know there is nothing in what they have been told about you, but that you yourself live in conformity with the law. **21:25** But regarding the Gentiles who have believed, we have written a letter, having decided that they should avoid meat that has been sacrificed to idols and blood and what has been strangled and sexual immorality." **21:26** Then Paul took the men the next day, and after he had purified himself along with them, he went to the temple and gave notice of the completion of the days of purification, when the sacrifice would be offered for each of them. **21:27** When the seven days were almost over, the Jews from the province of Asia who had seen him in the temple area stirred up the whole crowd and seized him, **21:28** shouting, "Men of Israel, help! This is the man who teaches everyone everywhere against our people, our law, and this sanctuary! Furthermore he has brought Greeks into the inner courts of the temple and made this holy place ritually unclean!" **21:29** (For they had seen Trophimus the Ephesian in the city with him previously, and they assumed Paul had brought him into the inner temple courts.) **21:30** The whole city was stirred up, and the people rushed together. They seized Paul and dragged him out of the temple courts, and immediately the doors were shut. **21:31** While they were trying to kill him, a report was sent up to the commanding officer of the cohort that all Jerusalem was in confusion. **21:32** He immediately took soldiers and centurions and ran down to the crowd.

When they saw the commanding officer and the soldiers, they stopped beating Paul. **21:33** Then the commanding officer came up and arrested him and ordered him to be tied up with two chains; he then asked who he was and what he had done. **21:34** But some in the crowd shouted one thing, and others something else, and when the commanding officer was unable to find out the truth because of the disturbance, he ordered Paul to be brought into the barracks. **21:35** When he came to the steps, Paul had to be carried by the soldiers because of the violence of the mob, **21:36** for a crowd of people followed them, screaming, "Away with him!" **21:37** As Paul was about to be brought into the barracks, he said to the commanding officer, "May I say something to you?" The officer replied, "Do you know Greek? **21:38** Then you're not that Egyptian who started a rebellion and led the four thousand men of the 'Assassins' into the wilderness some time ago?" **21:39** Paul answered, "I am a Jew from Tarsus in Cilicia, a citizen of an important city. Please allow me to speak to the people." **21:40** When the commanding officer had given him permission, Paul stood on the steps and gestured to the people with his hand. When they had become silent, he addressed them in Aramaic,

Paul's Defense

22:1 "Brothers and fathers, listen to my defense that I now make to you." **22:2** (When they heard that he was addressing them in Aramaic, they became even quieter.) Then Paul said, **22:3** "I am a Jew, born in Tarsus in Cilicia, but brought up in this city, educated with strictness under Gamaliel according to the law of our ancestors, and was zealous for God just as all of you are today. **22:4** I persecuted this Way even to the point of death, tying up both men and women and putting them in prison, **22:5** as both the high priest and the whole council of elders can testify about me. From them I also received letters to the brothers in Damascus, and I was on my way to make arrests there and bring the prisoners to Jerusalem to be punished. **22:6** As I was en route and near Damascus, about noon a very bright light from heaven suddenly flashed around me. **22:7** Then I fell to the ground and heard a voice saying to me, 'Saul, Saul, why are you persecuting me?' **22:8** I answered, 'Who are you, Lord?' He said to me, 'I am Jesus the Nazarene, whom you are persecuting.' **22:9** Those who were with me saw the light, but did not understand the voice of the one who was speaking to me. **22:10** So I asked, 'What should I do, Lord?' The Lord said to me, 'Get up and go to Damascus; there you will be told about everything that you have been designated to do.' **22:11** Since I could not see because of the brilliance of that light, I came to Damascus led by the hand of those who were with me. **22:12** A man named Ananias, a devout man according to the law, well spoken of by all the Jews who live there, **22:13** came to me and stood beside me and said to me, 'Brother Saul, regain your sight!' And at that very moment I looked up and saw him. **22:14** Then he said, 'The God of our ancestors has already chosen you to know his will, to see the Righteous One, and to hear a command from his mouth, **22:15** because you will be his witness to all people of what you have seen and heard. **22:16** And now what are you waiting for? Get up, be baptized, and have your sins washed away, calling on his name.' **22:17** When I returned to Jerusalem and was praying in the temple, I fell into a trance **22:18** and saw the Lord saying to me, 'Hurry and get out of Jerusalem quickly, because they will not accept your testimony about me.' **22:19** I replied, 'Lord, they themselves know that I imprisoned and beat those in the various synagogues who believed in you. **22:20** And when the blood of your witness Stephen was shed, I myself was standing nearby, approving, and guarding the cloaks of those who were killing him.' **22:21** Then he said to me, 'Go, because I will send you far away to the Gentiles.'"

The Roman Commander Questions Paul

22:22 The crowd was listening to him until he said this. Then they raised their voices and shouted, "Away with this man from the earth! For he should not be allowed to live!" **22:23** While they were screaming and throwing off their cloaks and tossing dust in the air, **22:24** the commanding officer ordered Paul to be brought back into the barracks. He told them to interrogate Paul by beating him with a lash so that he could find out the reason the crowd was shouting at Paul in this way. **22:25** When they had stretched him out for the lash, Paul said to the centurion standing nearby, "Is it legal for you to lash a man who is a Roman citizen without a proper trial?" **22:26** When the centurion heard this, he went to the commanding officer and reported it, saying, "What are you about to do? For this man is a Roman citizen." **22:27** So the commanding officer came and asked Paul, "Tell me, are you a Roman citizen?" He replied, "Yes." **22:28** The commanding officer answered, "I acquired this citizenship with a large sum of money." "But I was even born a citizen," Paul replied. **22:29** Then those who were about to interrogate him stayed away from him, and the commanding officer was frightened when he realized that Paul was a Roman citizen and that he had had him tied up.

Paul Before the Sanhedrin

22:30 The next day, because the commanding officer wanted to know the true reason Paul was being accused by the Jews, he released him and ordered the chief priests and the whole council to assemble. He then brought Paul down and had him stand before them.

23:1 Paul looked directly at the council and said, "Brothers, I have lived my life with a clear conscience before God to this day." **23:2** At that the high priest Ananias ordered those standing near Paul to strike him on the mouth. **23:3** Then Paul said to him, "God is going to strike you, you whitewashed wall! Do you sit there judging me according to the law, and in violation of the law you order me to be struck?" **23:4** Those standing near him said, "Do you dare insult God's high priest?" **23:5** Paul replied, "I did not realize, brothers, that he was the high priest, for it is written, '***You must not speak evil about a ruler of your people.***'"

23:6 Then when Paul noticed that part of them were Sadducees and the others Pharisees, he shouted out in the council, "Brothers, I am a Pharisee, a son of Pharisees. I am on trial concerning the hope of the resurrection of the dead!" **23:7** When he said this, an argument began between the Pharisees and the Sadducees, and the assembly was divided. **23:8** (For the Sadducees say there is no resurrection, or angel, or spirit, but the Pharisees acknowledge them all.) **23:9** There was a great commotion, and some experts in the law from the party of the Pharisees stood up and protested strongly, "We find nothing wrong with this man. What if a spirit or an angel has spoken to him?" **23:10** When the argument became so great the commanding officer feared that they would tear Paul to pieces, he ordered the detachment to go down, take him away from them by force, and bring him into the barracks.

23:11 The following night the Lord stood near Paul and said, "Have courage, for just as you have testified about me in Jerusalem, so you must also testify in Rome."

The Plot to Kill Paul

23:12 When morning came, the Jews formed a conspiracy and bound themselves with an oath not to eat or drink anything until they had killed Paul. **23:13** There were more than forty of them who formed this conspiracy. **23:14** They went to the chief priests and the elders and said, "We have bound ourselves with a solemn oath not to partake of anything until we have killed Paul. **23:15** So now you and the council request the commanding officer to bring him down to you, as if you were going to determine his case by conducting a more thorough inquiry. We are ready to kill him before he comes near this place."

23:16 But when the son of Paul's sister heard about the ambush, he came and entered the barracks and told Paul. **23:17** Paul called one of the centurions and said, "Take this young man to the commanding officer, for he has something to report to him." **23:18** So the centurion took him and brought him to the commanding officer and said, "The prisoner Paul called me and asked me to bring this young man to you because he has something to tell you." **23:19** The commanding officer took him by the hand, withdrew privately, and asked, "What is it that you want to report to me?" **23:20** He replied, "The Jews have agreed to ask you to bring Paul down to the council tomorrow, as if they were going to inquire more thoroughly about him. **23:21** So do not let them persuade you to do this, because more than forty of them are lying in ambush for him. They have bound themselves with an oath not to eat or drink anything until they have killed him, and now they are ready, waiting for you to agree to their request." **23:22** Then the commanding officer sent the young man away, directing him, "Tell no one that you have reported these things to me." **23:23** Then he summoned two of the centurions and said, "Make ready two hundred soldiers to go to Caesarea along with seventy horsemen and two hundred spearmen by nine o'clock tonight, **23:24** and provide mounts for Paul to ride so that he may be brought safely to Felix the governor." **23:25** He wrote a letter that went like this:

23:26 Claudius Lysias to His Excellency Governor Felix, greetings. **23:27** This man was seized by the Jews and they were about to kill him, when I came up with the detachment and rescued him, because I had learned that he was a Roman citizen. **23:28** Since I wanted to know what charge they were accusing him of, I brought him down to their council. **23:29** I found he was accused with reference to controversial questions about their law, but no charge against him deserved death or imprisonment. **23:30** When I was informed there would be a plot against this man, I sent him to you at once, also ordering his accusers to state their charges against him before you.

23:31 So the soldiers, in accordance with their orders, took Paul and brought him to Antipatris during the night. **23:32** The next day they let the horsemen go on with him, and they returned to the barracks. **23:33** When the horsemen came to Caesarea and delivered the letter to the governor, they also presented Paul to him. **23:34** When the governor had read the letter, he asked what province he was from. When he learned that he was from Cilicia, **23:35** he said, "I will give you a hearing when your accusers arrive too." Then he ordered that Paul be kept under guard in Herod's palace.

The Accusations Against Paul

24:1 After five days the high priest Ananias came down with some elders and an attorney named Tertullus, and they brought formal charges against Paul to the governor. **24:2** When Paul had been summoned, Tertullus began to accuse him, saying, "We have experienced a lengthy time of peace through your rule, and reforms are being made in this nation through your foresight. **24:3** Most excellent Felix, we acknowledge this everywhere and in every way with all gratitude. **24:4** But so that I may not delay you any further, I beg you to hear us briefly with your customary graciousness. **24:5** For we have found this man to be a troublemaker, one who stirs up riots among all the Jews throughout the world, and a ringleader of the sect of the Nazarenes. **24:6** He even tried to desecrate the temple, so we arrested him. **24:8** When you examine him yourself, you will be able to learn from him about all these things we are accusing him of doing." **24:9** The Jews also joined in the verbal attack, claiming that these things were true.

Paul's Defense Before Felix

24:10 When the governor gestured for him to speak, Paul replied, "Because I know that you have been a judge over this nation for many years, I confidently make my defense. **24:11** As you can verify for yourself, not more than twelve days ago I went up to Jerusalem to worship. **24:12** They did not find me arguing with anyone or stirring up a crowd in the temple courts or in the synagogues or throughout the city, **24:13** nor can they prove to you the things they are accusing me of doing. **24:14** But I confess this to you, that I worship the God of our ancestors according to the Way (which they call a sect), believing everything that is according to the law and that is written in the prophets. **24:15** I have a hope in God (a hope that these men themselves accept too) that there is going to be a resurrection of both the righteous and the unrighteous. **24:16** This is the reason I do my best to always have a clear conscience toward God and toward people. **24:17** After several years I came to bring to my people gifts for the poor and to present offerings, **24:18** which I was doing when they found me in the temple, ritually purified, without a crowd or a disturbance. **24:19** But there are some Jews from the province of Asia who should be here before you and bring charges, if they have anything against me. **24:20** Or these men here should tell what crime they found me guilty of when I stood before the council, **24:21** other than this one thing I shouted out while I stood before them: 'I am on trial before you today concerning the resurrection of the dead.'"

24:22 Then Felix, who understood the facts concerning the Way more accurately, adjourned their hearing, saying, "When Lysias the commanding officer comes down, I will decide your case." **24:23** He ordered the centurion to guard Paul, but to let him have some freedom, and not to prevent any of his friends from meeting his needs.

Paul Speaks Repeatedly to Felix

24:24 Some days later, when Felix arrived with his wife Drusilla, who was Jewish, he sent for Paul and heard him speak about faith in Christ Jesus. **24:25** While Paul was discussing righteousness, self-control, and the coming judgment, Felix became frightened and said, "Go away for now, and when I have an opportunity, I will send for you." **24:26** At the same time he was also hoping that Paul would give him money, and for this reason he sent for Paul as often as possible and talked with him. **24:27** After two years had passed, Porcius Festus succeeded Felix, and because he wanted to do the Jews a favor, Felix left Paul in prison.

Paul Appeals to Caesar

25:1 Now three days after Festus arrived in the province, he went up to Jerusalem from Caesarea. **25:2** So the chief priests and the most prominent men of the Jews brought formal charges against Paul to him. **25:3** Requesting him to do them a favor against Paul, they urged Festus to summon him to Jerusalem, planning an ambush to kill him along the way. **25:4** Then Festus replied that Paul was being kept at Caesarea, and he himself intended to go there shortly. **25:5** "So," he said, "let your leaders go down there with me, and if this man has done anything wrong, they may bring charges against him."

25:6 After Festus had stayed not more than eight or ten days among them, he went down to Caesarea, and the next day he sat on the judgment seat and ordered Paul to be brought. **25:7** When he arrived, the Jews who had come down from Jerusalem stood around him, bringing many serious charges that they were not able to prove. **25:8** Paul said in his defense, "I have committed no offense against the Jewish law or against the temple or against Caesar." **25:9** But Festus, wanting to do the Jews a favor, asked Paul, "Are you willing to go up to Jerusalem and be tried before me there on these charges?" **25:10** Paul replied, "I am standing before Caesar's judgment seat, where I should be tried. I have done nothing wrong to the Jews, as you also know very well. **25:11** If then I am in the wrong and have done anything that deserves death, I am not trying to escape dying, but if not one of their charges against me is true, no one can hand me over to them. I appeal to Caesar!" **25:12** Then, after conferring with his council, Festus replied, "You have appealed to Caesar; to Caesar you will go!"

Festus Asks King Agrippa for Advice

25:13 After several days had passed, King Agrippa and Bernice arrived at Caesarea to pay their respects to Festus. **25:14** While they were staying there many days, Festus explained Paul's case to the king to get his opinion, saying, "There is a man left here as a prisoner by Felix. **25:15** When I was in Jerusalem, the chief priests and the elders of the Jews informed me about him, asking for a sentence of condemnation against him. **25:16** I answered them that it was not the custom of the Romans to hand over anyone before the accused had met his accusers face to face and had been given an opportunity to make a defense against the accusation. **25:17** So

after they came back here with me, I did not postpone the case, but the next day I sat on the judgment seat and ordered the man to be brought. **25:18** When his accusers stood up, they did not charge him with any of the evil deeds I had suspected. **25:19** Rather they had several points of disagreement with him about their own religion and about a man named Jesus who was dead, whom Paul claimed to be alive. **25:20** Because I was at a loss how I could investigate these matters, I asked if he were willing to go to Jerusalem and be tried there on these charges. **25:21** But when Paul appealed to be kept in custody for the decision of His Majesty the Emperor, I ordered him to be kept under guard until I could send him to Caesar." **25:22** Agrippa said to Festus, "I would also like to hear the man myself." "Tomorrow," he replied, "you will hear him."

Paul Before King Agrippa and Bernice

25:23 So the next day Agrippa and Bernice came with great pomp and entered the audience hall, along with the senior military officers and the prominent men of the city. When Festus gave the order, Paul was brought in. **25:24** Then Festus said, "King Agrippa, and all you who are present here with us, you see this man about whom the entire Jewish populace petitioned me both in Jerusalem and here, shouting loudly that he ought not to live any longer. **25:25** But I found that he had done nothing that deserved death, and when he appealed to His Majesty the Emperor, I decided to send him. **25:26** But I have nothing definite to write to my lord about him. Therefore I have brought him before you all, and especially before you, King Agrippa, so that after this preliminary hearing I may have something to write. **25:27** For it seems unreasonable to me to send a prisoner without clearly indicating the charges against him."

Paul Offers His Defense

26:1 So Agrippa said to Paul, "You have permission to speak for yourself." Then Paul held out his hand and began his defense:

26:2 "Regarding all the things I have been accused of by the Jews, King Agrippa, I consider myself fortunate that I am about to make my defense before you today, **26:3** because you are especially familiar with all the customs and controversial issues of the Jews. Therefore I ask you to listen to me patiently. **26:4** Now all the Jews know the way I lived from my youth, spending my life from the beginning among my own people and in Jerusalem. **26:5** They know, because they have known me from time past, if they are willing to testify, that according to the strictest party of our religion, I lived as a Pharisee. **26:6** And now I stand here on trial because of my hope in the promise made by God to our ancestors, **26:7** a promise that our twelve tribes hope to attain as they earnestly serve God night and day. Concerning this hope the Jews are accusing me, Your Majesty! **26:8** Why do you people think it is unbelievable that God raises the dead? **26:9** Of course, I myself was convinced that it was necessary to do many things hostile to the name of Jesus the Nazarene. **26:10** And that is what I did in Jerusalem: Not only did I lock up many of the saints in prisons by the authority I received from the chief priests, but I also cast my vote against them when they were sentenced to death. **26:11** I punished them often in all the synagogues and tried to force them to blaspheme. Because I was so furiously enraged at them, I went to persecute them even in foreign cities.

26:12 "While doing this very thing, as I was going to Damascus with authority and complete power from the chief priests, **26:13** about noon along the road, Your Majesty, I saw a light from heaven, brighter than the sun, shining everywhere around me and those traveling with me. **26:14** When we had all fallen to the ground, I heard a voice saying to me in Aramaic, 'Saul, Saul, why are you persecuting me? You are hurting yourself by kicking against the goads.' **26:15** So I said, 'Who are you, Lord?' And the Lord replied, 'I am Jesus whom you are persecuting. **26:16** But get up and stand on your feet, for I have appeared to you for this reason, to designate you in advance as a servant and witness to the things you have seen and to the things in which I will appear to you. **26:17** I will rescue you from your own people and from the Gentiles, to whom I am sending you **26:18** to open their eyes so that they turn from darkness to light and from the power of Satan to God, so that they may receive forgiveness of sins and a share among those who are sanctified by faith in me.'

26:19 "Therefore, King Agrippa, I was not disobedient to the heavenly vision, **26:20** but I declared to those in Damascus first, and then to those in Jerusalem and in all Judea, and to the Gentiles, that they should repent and turn to God, performing deeds consistent with repentance. **26:21** For this reason the Jews seized me in the temple courts and were trying to kill me. **26:22** I have experienced help from God to this day, and so I stand testifying to both small and great, saying nothing except what the prophets and Moses said was going to happen: **26:23** that the Christ was to suffer and be the first to rise from the dead, to proclaim light both to our people and to the Gentiles."

26:24 As Paul was saying these things in his defense, Festus exclaimed loudly, "You have lost your mind, Paul! Your great learning is driving you insane!" **26:25** But Paul replied, "I have not lost my mind, most excellent Festus, but am speaking true and rational words. **26:26** For the king knows about these things, and I am speaking freely to him, because I cannot believe that any of these things has escaped his notice, for this was not done in a corner. **26:27** Do you believe the prophets, King Agrippa? I know that you believe." **26:28** Agrippa said to Paul, "In such a short time are you persuading me to become a Christian?" **26:29** Paul replied, "I pray to God that whether in a short or a long time not only you but also all those who are listening to me today could become such as I am, except for these chains."

26:30 So the king got up, and with him the governor and Bernice and those sitting with them, **26:31** and as they were leaving they said to one another, "This man is not doing anything deserving death or imprisonment." **26:32** Agrippa said to Festus, "This man could have been released if he had not appealed to Caesar."

Paul and Company Sail for Rome

27:1 When it was decided we would sail to Italy, they handed over Paul and some other prisoners to a centurion of the Augustan Cohort named Julius. **27:2** We went on board a ship from Adramyttium that was about to sail to various ports along the coast of the province of Asia and put out to sea, accompanied by Aristarchus, a Macedonian from Thessalonica. **27:3** The next day we put in at Sidon, and Julius, treating Paul kindly, allowed him to go to his friends so they could provide him with what he needed. **27:4** From there we put out to sea and sailed under the lee of Cyprus because the winds were against us. **27:5** After we had sailed across the open sea off Cilicia and Pamphylia, we put in at Myra in Lycia. **27:6** There the centurion found a ship from Alexandria sailing for Italy, and he put us aboard it. **27:7** We sailed slowly for many days and arrived with difficulty off Cnidus. Because the wind prevented us from going any farther, we sailed under the lee of Crete off Salmone. **27:8** With difficulty we sailed along the coast of Crete and came to a place called Fair Havens that was near the town of Lasea.

Caught in a Violent Storm

27:9 Since considerable time had passed and the voyage was now dangerous because the fast was already over, Paul advised them, **27:10** "Men, I can see the voyage is going to end in disaster and great loss not only of the cargo and the ship, but also of our lives." **27:11** But the centurion was more convinced by the captain and the ship's owner than by what Paul said. **27:12** Because the harbor was not suitable to spend the winter in, the majority decided to put out to sea from there. They hoped that somehow they could reach Phoenix, a harbor of Crete facing southwest and northwest, and spend the winter there. **27:13** When a gentle south wind sprang up, they thought they could carry out their purpose, so they weighed anchor and sailed close along the coast of Crete. **27:14** Not long after this, a hurricane-force wind called the northeaster blew down from the island. **27:15** When the ship was caught in it and could not head into the wind, we gave way to it and were driven along. **27:16** As we ran under the lee of a small island called Cauda, we were able with difficulty to get the ship's boat under control. **27:17** After the crew had hoisted it aboard, they used supports to undergird the ship. Fearing they would run aground on the Syrtis, they lowered the sea anchor, thus letting themselves be driven along. **27:18** The next day, because we were violently battered by the storm, they began throwing the cargo overboard, **27:19** and on the third day they threw the ship's gear overboard with their own hands. **27:20** When neither sun nor stars appeared for many days and a violent storm continued to batter us, we finally abandoned all hope of being saved.

27:21 Since many of them had no desire to eat, Paul stood up among them and said, "Men, you should have listened to me and not put out to sea from Crete, thus avoiding this damage and loss. **27:22** And now I advise you to keep up your courage, for there will be no loss of life among you, but only the ship will be lost. **27:23** For last night an angel of the God to whom I belong and whom I serve came to me **27:24** and said, 'Do not be afraid, Paul! You must stand before Caesar, and God has graciously granted you the safety of all who are sailing with you.' **27:25** Therefore keep up your courage, men, for I have faith in God that it will be just as I have been told. **27:26** But we must run aground on some island."

27:27 When the fourteenth night had come, while we were being driven across the Adriatic Sea, about midnight the sailors suspected they were approaching some land. **27:28** They took soundings and found the water was twenty fathoms deep; when they had sailed a little farther they took soundings again and found it was fifteen fathoms deep. **27:29** Because they were afraid that we would run aground on the rocky coast, they threw out four anchors from the stern and wished for day to appear. **27:30** Then when the sailors tried to escape from the ship and were lowering the ship's boat into the sea, pretending that they were going to put out anchors from the bow, **27:31** Paul said to the centurion and the soldiers, "Unless these men stay with the ship, you cannot be saved." **27:32** Then the soldiers cut the ropes of the ship's boat and let it drift away.

27:33 As day was about to dawn, Paul urged them all to take some food, saying, "Today is the fourteenth day you have been in suspense and have gone without food; you have eaten nothing. **27:34** Therefore I urge you to take some food, for this is important for your survival. For not one of you will lose a hair from his head." **27:35** After he said this, Paul took bread and gave thanks to God in front of them all, broke it, and began to eat. **27:36** So all of them were encouraged and took food themselves. **27:37** (We were in all two hundred seventy-six persons on the ship.) **27:38** When they had eaten enough to be satisfied, they lightened the ship by throwing the wheat into the sea.

Paul is Shipwrecked

27:39 When day came, they did not recognize the land, but they noticed a bay with a beach, where they decided to run the ship aground if they could. **27:40** So they slipped the anchors and left them in the sea, at the same time loosening the linkage that bound the steering oars together. Then they hoisted the foresail to the wind and steered toward the beach. **27:41** But they encountered a patch of crosscurrents and ran the ship aground; the bow stuck fast and could not be moved, but the stern was being broken up by the force of the waves. **27:42** Now the soldiers' plan was to kill the prisoners so that none of them would escape by swimming away. **27:43** But the centurion, wanting to save Paul's life, prevented them from carrying out their plan. He ordered those who could swim to jump overboard first and get to land, **27:44** and the rest were to follow, some on planks and some on pieces of the ship. And in this way all were brought safely to land.

Paul on Malta

28:1 After we had safely reached shore, we learned that the island was called Malta. **28:2** The local inhabitants showed us extraordinary kindness, for they built a fire and welcomed us all because it had started to rain and was cold. **28:3** When Paul had gathered a bundle of brushwood and was putting it on the fire, a viper came out because of the heat and fastened itself on his hand. **28:4** When the local people saw the creature hanging from Paul's hand, they said to one another, "No doubt this man is a murderer! Although he has escaped from the sea, Justice herself has not allowed him to live!" **28:5** However, Paul shook the creature off into the fire and suffered no harm. **28:6** But they were expecting that he was going to swell up or suddenly drop dead. So after they had waited a long time and had seen nothing unusual happen to him, they changed their minds and said he was a god.

28:7 Now in the region around that place were fields belonging to the chief official of the island, named Publius, who welcomed us and entertained us hospitably as guests for three days. **28:8** The father of Publius lay sick in bed, suffering from fever and dysentery. Paul went in to see him and after praying, placed his hands on him and healed him. **28:9** After this had happened, many of the people on the island who were sick also came and were healed. **28:10** They also bestowed many honors, and when we were preparing to sail, they gave us all the supplies we needed.

Paul Finally Reaches Rome

28:11 After three months we put out to sea in an Alexandrian ship that had wintered at the island and had the "Heavenly Twins" as its figurehead. **28:12** We put in at Syracuse and stayed there three days. **28:13** From there we cast off and arrived at Rhegium, and after one day a south wind sprang up and on the second day we came to Puteoli. **28:14** There we found some brothers and were invited to stay with them seven days. And in this way we came to Rome. **28:15** The brothers there, when they heard about us, came as far as the Forum of Appius and Three Taverns to meet us. When he saw them, Paul thanked God and took courage. **28:16** When we entered Rome, Paul was allowed to live by himself, with the soldier who was guarding him.

Paul Addresses the Jewish Community in Rome

28:17 After three days Paul called the local Jewish leaders together. When they had assembled, he said to them, "Brothers, although I had done nothing against our people or the customs of our ancestors, from Jerusalem I was handed over as a prisoner to the Romans. **28:18** When they had heard my case, they wanted to release me, because there was no basis for a death sentence against me. **28:19** But when the Jews objected, I was forced to appeal to Caesar – not that I had some charge to bring against my own people. **28:20** So for this reason I have asked to see you and speak with you, for I am bound with this chain because of the hope of Israel." **28:21** They replied, "We have received no letters from Judea about you, nor have any of the brothers come from there and reported or said anything bad about you. **28:22** But we would like to hear from you what you think, for regarding this sect we know that people everywhere speak against it."

28:23 They set a day to meet with him, and they came to him where he was staying in even greater numbers. From morning until evening he explained things to them, testifying about the kingdom of God and trying to convince them about Jesus from both the law of Moses and the prophets. **28:24** Some were convinced by what he said, but others refused to believe. **28:25** So they began to leave, unable to agree among themselves, after Paul made one last statement: "The Holy Spirit spoke rightly to your ancestors through the prophet Isaiah **28:26** when he said,

'Go to this people and say,

"You will keep on hearing, but will never understand,
and you will keep on looking, but will never perceive.
28:27 For the heart of this people has become dull,
and their ears are hard of hearing,
and they have closed their eyes,
so that they would not see with their eyes
and hear with their ears
and understand with their heart

and turn, and I would heal them.*'*

28:28 "Therefore be advised that this salvation from God has been sent to the Gentiles; they will listen!"

28:30 Paul lived there two whole years in his own rented quarters and welcomed all who came to him, **28:31** proclaiming the kingdom of God and teaching about the Lord Jesus Christ with complete boldness and without restriction.

Book 45. Romans

Salutation

1:1 From Paul, a slave of Christ Jesus, called to be an apostle, set apart for the gospel of God. **1:2** This gospel he promised beforehand through his prophets in the holy scriptures, **1:3** concerning his Son who was a descendant of David with reference to the flesh, **1:4** who was appointed the Son-of-God-in-power according to the Holy Spirit by the resurrection from the dead, Jesus Christ our Lord. **1:5** Through him we have received grace and our apostleship to bring about the obedience of faith among all the Gentiles on behalf of his name. **1:6** You also are among them, called to belong to Jesus Christ. **1:7** To all those loved by God in Rome, called to be saints: Grace and peace to you from God our Father and the Lord Jesus Christ!

Paul's Desire to Visit Rome

1:8 First of all, I thank my God through Jesus Christ for all of you, because your faith is proclaimed throughout the whole world. **1:9** For God, whom I serve in my spirit by preaching the gospel of his Son, is my witness that I continually remember you **1:10** and I always ask in my prayers, if perhaps now at last I may succeed in visiting you according to the will of God. **1:11** For I long to see you, so that I may impart to you some spiritual gift to strengthen you, **1:12** that is, that we may be mutually comforted by one another's faith, both yours and mine. **1:13** I do not want you to be unaware, brothers and sisters, that I often intended to come to you (and was prevented until now), so that I may have some fruit even among you, just as I already have among the rest of the Gentiles. **1:14** I am a debtor both to the Greeks and to the barbarians, both to the wise and to the foolish. **1:15** Thus I am eager also to preach the gospel to you who are in Rome.

The Power of the Gospel

1:16 For I am not ashamed of the gospel, for it is God's power for salvation to everyone who believes, to the Jew first and also to the Greek. **1:17** For the righteousness of God is revealed in the gospel from faith to faith, just as it is written, "*The righteous by faith will live.*"

The Condemnation of the Unrighteous

1:18 For the wrath of God is revealed from heaven against all ungodliness and unrighteousness of people who suppress the truth by their unrighteousness, **1:19** because what can be known about God is plain to them, because God has made it plain to them. **1:20** For since the creation of the world his invisible attributes – his eternal power and divine nature – have been clearly seen, because they are understood through what has been made. So people are without excuse. **1:21** For although they knew God, they did not glorify him as God or give him thanks, but they became futile in their thoughts and their senseless hearts were darkened. **1:22** Although they claimed to be wise, they became fools **1:23** and exchanged the glory of the immortal God for an image resembling mortal human beings or birds or four-footed animals or reptiles.

1:24 Therefore God gave them over in the desires of their hearts to impurity, to dishonor their bodies among themselves. **1:25** They exchanged the truth of God for a lie and worshiped and served the creation rather than the Creator, who is blessed forever! Amen.

1:26 For this reason God gave them over to dishonorable passions. For their women exchanged the natural sexual relations for unnatural ones, **1:27** and likewise the men also abandoned natural relations with women and were inflamed in their passions for one another. Men committed shameless acts with men and received in themselves the due penalty for their error.

1:28 And just as they did not see fit to acknowledge God, God gave them over to a depraved mind, to do what should not be done. **1:29** They are filled with every kind of unrighteousness, wickedness, covetousness, malice. They are rife with envy, murder, strife, deceit, hostility. They are gossips, **1:30** slanderers, haters of God, insolent, arrogant, boastful, contrivers of all sorts of evil, disobedient to parents, **1:31** senseless, covenant-breakers, heartless, ruthless. **1:32** Although they fully know God's righteous decree that those who practice such things deserve to die, they not only do them but also approve of those who practice them.

The Condemnation of the Moralist

2:1 Therefore you are without excuse, whoever you are, when you judge someone else. For on whatever grounds you judge another, you condemn yourself, because you who judge practice the same things. **2:2** Now we know that God's judgment is in accordance with truth against those who practice such things. **2:3** And do you think, whoever you are, when you judge those who practice such things and yet do them yourself, that you will escape God's judgment? **2:4** Or do you have contempt for the wealth of his kindness, forbearance, and patience, and yet do not know that

God's kindness leads you to repentance? **2:5** But because of your stubbornness and your unrepentant heart, you are storing up wrath for yourselves in the day of wrath, when God's righteous judgment is revealed! **2:6** He *will reward each one according to his works*: **2:7** eternal life to those who by perseverance in good works seek glory and honor and immortality, **2:8** but wrath and anger to those who live in selfish ambition and do not obey the truth but follow unrighteousness. **2:9** There will be affliction and distress on everyone who does evil, on the Jew first and also the Greek, **2:10** but glory and honor and peace for everyone who does good, for the Jew first and also the Greek. **2:11** For there is no partiality with God. **2:12** For all who have sinned apart from the law will also perish apart from the law, and all who have sinned under the law will be judged by the law. **2:13** For it is not those who hear the law who are righteous before God, but those who do the law will be declared righteous. **2:14** For whenever the Gentiles, who do not have the law, do by nature the things required by the law, these who do not have the law are a law to themselves. **2:15** They show that the work of the law is written in their hearts, as their conscience bears witness and their conflicting thoughts accuse or else defend them, **2:16** on the day when God will judge the secrets of human hearts, according to my gospel through Christ Jesus.

The Condemnation of the Jew

2:17 But if you call yourself a Jew and rely on the law and boast of your relationship to God **2:18** and know his will and approve the superior things because you receive instruction from the law, **2:19** and if you are convinced that you yourself are a guide to the blind, a light to those who are in darkness, **2:20** an educator of the senseless, a teacher of little children, because you have in the law the essential features of knowledge and of the truth – **2:21** therefore you who teach someone else, do you not teach yourself? You who preach against stealing, do you steal? **2:22** You who tell others not to commit adultery, do you commit adultery? You who abhor idols, do you rob temples? **2:23** You who boast in the law dishonor God by transgressing the law! **2:24** For just as it is written, "*the name of God is being blasphemed among the Gentiles because of you.*" **2:25** For circumcision has its value if you practice the law, but if you break the law, your circumcision has become uncircumcision. **2:26** Therefore if the uncircumcised man obeys the righteous requirements of the law, will not his uncircumcision be regarded as circumcision? **2:27** And will not the physically uncircumcised man who keeps the law judge you who, despite the written code and circumcision, transgress the law? **2:28** For a person is not a Jew who is one outwardly, nor is circumcision something that is outward in the flesh, **2:29** but someone is a Jew who is one inwardly, and circumcision is of the heart by the Spirit and not by the written code. This person's praise is not from people but from God.

3:1 Therefore what advantage does the Jew have, or what is the value of circumcision? **3:2** Actually, there are many advantages. First of all, the Jews were entrusted with the oracles of God. **3:3** What then? If some did not believe, does their unbelief nullify the faithfulness of God? **3:4** Absolutely not! Let God be proven true, and every human being shown up as a liar, just as it is written: "*so that you will be justified in your words and will prevail when you are judged.*"

3:5 But if our unrighteousness demonstrates the righteousness of God, what shall we say? The God who inflicts wrath is not unrighteous, is he? (I am speaking in human terms.) **3:6** Absolutely not! For otherwise how could God judge the world? **3:7** For if by my lie the truth of God enhances his glory, why am I still actually being judged as a sinner? **3:8** And why not say, "Let us do evil so that good may come of it"? – as some who slander us allege that we say. (Their condemnation is deserved!)

The Condemnation of the World

3:9 What then? Are we better off? Certainly not, for we have already charged that Jews and Greeks alike are all under sin, **3:10** just as it is written:

"There is no one righteous, not even one,

3:11 there is no one who understands,

there is no one who seeks God.

3:12 All have turned away,

together they have become worthless;

there is no one who shows kindness, not even one."

3:13 "Their throats are open graves,

they deceive with their tongues,

the poison of asps is under their lips."

3:14 "Their mouths are full of cursing and bitterness."

3:15 "Their feet are swift to shed blood,

3:16 ruin and misery are in their paths,

3:17 and the way of peace they have not known."

3:18 "There is no fear of God before their eyes."

3:19 Now we know that whatever the law says, it says to those who are under the law, so that every mouth may be silenced and the whole world may be held accountable to God. **3:20** For *no one is declared righteous before him* by the works of the law, for through the law comes the knowledge of sin. **3:21** But now apart from the law the righteousness of God (which is attested by the law and the prophets) has been disclosed – **3:22** namely, the righteousness of God through the faithfulness of Jesus

Christ for all who believe. For there is no distinction, **3:23** for all have sinned and fall short of the glory of God. **3:24** But they are justified freely by his grace through the redemption that is in Christ Jesus. **3:25** God publicly displayed him at his death as the mercy seat accessible through faith. This was to demonstrate his righteousness, because God in his forbearance had passed over the sins previously committed. **3:26** This was also to demonstrate his righteousness in the present time, so that he would be just and the justifier of the one who lives because of Jesus' faithfulness.

3:27 Where, then, is boasting? It is excluded! By what principle? Of works? No, but by the principle of faith! **3:28** For we consider that a person is declared righteous by faith apart from the works of the law. **3:29** Or is God the God of the Jews only? Is he not the God of the Gentiles too? Yes, of the Gentiles too! **3:30** Since God is one, he will justify the circumcised by faith and the uncircumcised through faith. **3:31** Do we then nullify the law through faith? Absolutely not! Instead we uphold the law.

The Illustration of Justification

4:1 What then shall we say that Abraham, our ancestor according to the flesh, has discovered regarding this matter? **4:2** For if Abraham was declared righteous by the works of the law, he has something to boast about – but not before God. **4:3** For what does the scripture say? *"Abraham believed God, and it was credited to him as righteousness."* **4:4** Now to the one who works, his pay is not credited due to grace but due to obligation. **4:5** But to the one who does not work, but believes in the one who declares the ungodly righteous, his faith is credited as righteousness. **4:6** So even David himself speaks regarding the blessedness of the man to whom God credits righteousness apart from works:

4:7 "Blessed are those whose lawless deeds are forgiven, and whose sins are covered;

4:8 blessed is the one against whom the Lord will never count sin.*"*

4:9 Is this blessedness then for the circumcision or also for the uncircumcision? For we say, *"faith was credited to Abraham as righteousness."* **4:10** How then was it credited to him? Was he circumcised at the time, or not? No, he was not circumcised but uncircumcised! **4:11** And he received the sign of circumcision as a seal of the righteousness that he had by faith while he was still uncircumcised, so that he would become the father of all those who believe but have never been circumcised, that they too could have righteousness credited to them. **4:12** And he is also the father of the circumcised, who are not only circumcised, but who also walk in the footsteps of the faith that our father Abraham possessed when he was still uncircumcised.

4:13 For the promise to Abraham or to his descendants that he would inherit the world was not fulfilled through the law, but through the righteousness that comes by faith. **4:14** For if they become heirs by the law, faith is empty and the promise is nullified. **4:15** For the law brings wrath, because where there is no law there is no transgression either. **4:16** For this reason it is by faith so that it may be by grace, with the result that the promise may be certain to all the descendants – not only to those who are under the law, but also to those who have the faith of Abraham, who is the father of us all **4:17** (as it is written, *"I have made you the father of many nations"*). He is our father in the presence of God whom he believed – the God who makes the dead alive and summons the things that do not yet exist as though they already do. **4:18** Against hope Abraham believed in hope with the result that he became *the father of many nations* according to the pronouncement, *"so will your descendants be."* **4:19** Without being weak in faith, he considered his own body as dead (because he was about one hundred years old) and the deadness of Sarah's womb. **4:20** He did not waver in unbelief about the promise of God but was strengthened in faith, giving glory to God. **4:21** He was fully convinced that what God promised he was also able to do. **4:22** So indeed it was credited to Abraham as righteousness.

4:23 But the statement *it was credited to him* was not written only for Abraham's sake, **4:24** but also for our sake, to whom it will be credited, those who believe in the one who raised Jesus our Lord from the dead. **4:25** He was given over because of our transgressions
and was raised for the sake of our justification.

The Expectation of Justification

5:1 Therefore, since we have been declared righteous by faith, we have peace with God through our Lord Jesus Christ, **5:2** through whom we have also obtained access by faith into this grace in which we stand, and we rejoice in the hope of God's glory. **5:3** Not only this, but we also rejoice in sufferings, knowing that suffering produces endurance, **5:4** and endurance, character, and character, hope. **5:5** And hope does not disappoint, because the love of God has been poured out in our hearts through the Holy Spirit who was given to us.

5:6 For while we were still helpless, at the right time Christ died for the ungodly. **5:7** (For rarely will anyone die for a righteous person, though for a good person perhaps someone might possibly dare to die.) **5:8** But God demonstrates his own love for us, in that while we were still sinners, Christ died for us. **5:9** Much more then, because we have now been declared righteous by his blood, we will be saved through him from God's wrath. **5:10** For if while we were enemies we were reconciled to God through the death of his Son, how much more, since we have been reconciled, will we be saved by his life? **5:11** Not only this, but we also rejoice in God through our Lord Jesus Christ, through whom we have now received this reconciliation.

The Amplification of Justification

5:12 So then, just as sin entered the world through one man and death through sin, and so death spread to all people because all sinned – **5:13** for before the law was given, sin was in the world, but there is no accounting for sin when there is no law. **5:14** Yet death reigned from Adam until Moses even over those who did not sin in the same way that Adam (who is a type of the coming one) transgressed. **5:15** But the gracious gift is not like the transgression. For if the many died through the transgression of the one man, how much more did the grace of God and the gift by the grace of the one man Jesus Christ multiply to the many! **5:16** And the gift is not like the one who sinned. For judgment, resulting from the one transgression, led to condemnation, but the gracious gift from the many failures led to justification. **5:17** For if, by the transgression of the one man, death reigned through the one, how much more will those who receive the abundance of grace and of the gift of righteousness reign in life through the one, Jesus Christ!

5:18 Consequently, just as condemnation for all people came through one transgression, so too through the one righteous act came righteousness leading to life for all people. **5:19** For just as through the disobedience of the one man many were made sinners, so also through the obedience of one man many will be made righteous. **5:20** Now the law came in so that the transgression may increase, but where sin increased, grace multiplied all the more, **5:21** so that just as sin reigned in death, so also grace will reign through righteousness to eternal life through Jesus Christ our Lord.

The Believer's Freedom from Sin's Domination

6:1 What shall we say then? Are we to remain in sin so that grace may increase? **6:2** Absolutely not! How can we who died to sin still live in it? **6:3** Or do you not know that as many as were baptized into Christ Jesus were baptized into his death? **6:4** Therefore we have been buried with him through baptism into death, in order that just as Christ was raised from the dead through the glory of the Father, so we too may live a new life.

6:5 For if we have become united with him in the likeness of his death, we will certainly also be united in the likeness of his resurrection. **6:6** We know that our old man was crucified with him so that the body of sin would no longer dominate us, so that we would no longer be enslaved to sin. **6:7** (For someone who has died has been freed from sin.) **6:8** Now if we died with Christ, we believe that we will also live with him. **6:9** We know that since Christ has been raised from the dead, he is never going to die again; death no longer has mastery over him. **6:10** For the death he died, he died to sin once for all, but the life he lives, he lives to God. **6:11** So you too consider yourselves dead to sin, but alive to God in Christ Jesus.

6:12 Therefore do not let sin reign in your mortal body so that you obey its desires, **6:13** and do not present your members to sin as instruments to be used for unrighteousness, but present yourselves to God as those who are alive from the dead and your members to God as instruments to be used for righteousness. **6:14** For sin will have no mastery over you, because you are not under law but under grace.

The Believer's Enslavement to God's Righteousness

6:15 What then? Shall we sin because we are not under law but under grace? Absolutely not! **6:16** Do you not know that if you present yourselves as obedient slaves, you are slaves of the one you obey, either of sin resulting in death, or obedience resulting in righteousness? **6:17** But thanks be to God that though you were slaves to sin, you obeyed from the heart that pattern of teaching you were entrusted to, **6:18** and having been freed from sin, you became enslaved to righteousness. **6:19** (I am speaking in human terms because of the weakness of your flesh.) For just as you once presented your members as slaves to impurity and lawlessness leading to more lawlessness, so now present your members as slaves to righteousness leading to sanctification. **6:20** For when you were slaves of sin, you were free with regard to righteousness.

6:21 So what benefit did you then reap from those things that you are now ashamed of? For the end of those things is death. **6:22** But now, freed from sin and enslaved to God, you have your benefit leading to sanctification, and the end is eternal life. **6:23** For the payoff of sin is death, but the gift of God is eternal life in Christ Jesus our Lord.

The Believer's Relationship to the Law

7:1 Or do you not know, brothers and sisters (for I am speaking to those who know the law), that the law is lord over a person as long as he lives? **7:2** For a married woman is bound by law to her husband as long as he lives, but if her husband dies, she is released from the law of the marriage. **7:3** So then, if she is joined to another man while her husband is alive, she will be called an adulteress. But if her husband dies, she is free from that law, and if she is joined to another man, she is not an adulteress. **7:4** So, my brothers and sisters, you also died to the law through the body of Christ, so that you could be joined to another, to the one who was raised from the dead, to bear fruit to God. **7:5** For when we were in the flesh, the sinful desires, aroused by the law, were active in the members of our body to bear fruit for death. **7:6** But now we have been released from the law, because we have died to what controlled us, so that we may serve in the new life of the Spirit and not under the old written code.

7:7 What shall we say then? Is the law sin? Absolutely not! Certainly, I would not have known sin except through the law. For indeed I would not have known what it means to desire something belonging to someone else if the law had not said, "*Do not covet*." **7:8** But sin, seizing the opportunity through the commandment, produced in me all kinds of wrong desires. For apart from the law, sin is dead. **7:9** And I was once alive apart from the law, but with the coming of the commandment sin became alive **7:10** and I died. So I found that the very commandment that was intended to bring life brought death! **7:11** For sin, seizing the opportunity through the commandment, deceived me and through it I died. **7:12** So then, the law is holy, and the commandment is holy, righteous, and good. **7:13** Did that which is good, then, become death to me? Absolutely not! But sin, so that it would be shown to be sin, produced death in me through what is good, so that through the commandment sin would become utterly sinful. **7:14** For we know that the law is spiritual – but I am unspiritual, sold into slavery to sin. **7:15** For I don't understand what I am doing. For I do not do what I want – instead, I do what I hate. **7:16** But if I do what I don't want, I agree that the law is good. **7:17** But now it is no longer me doing it, but sin that lives in me. **7:18** For I know that nothing good lives in me, that is, in my flesh. For I want to do the good, but I cannot do it. **7:19** For I do not do the good I want, but I do the very evil I do not want! **7:20** Now if I do what I do not want, it is no longer me doing it but sin that lives in me.

7:21 So, I find the law that when I want to do good, evil is present with me. **7:22** For I delight in the law of God in my inner being. **7:23** But I see a different law in my members waging war against the law of my mind and making me captive to the law of sin that is in my members. **7:24** Wretched man that I am! Who will rescue me from this body of death? **7:25** Thanks be to God through Jesus Christ our Lord! So then, I myself serve the law of God with my mind, but with my flesh I serve the law of sin.

The Believer's Relationship to the Holy Spirit

8:1 There is therefore now no condemnation for those who are in Christ Jesus. **8:2** For the law of the life-giving Spirit in Christ Jesus has set you free from the law of sin and death. **8:3** For God achieved what the law could not do because it was weakened through the flesh. By sending his own Son in the likeness of sinful flesh and concerning sin, he condemned sin in the flesh, **8:4** so that the righteous requirement of the law may be fulfilled in us, who do not walk according to the flesh but according to the Spirit.

8:5 For those who live according to the flesh have their outlook shaped by the things of the flesh, but those who live according to the Spirit have their outlook shaped by the things of the Spirit. **8:6** For the outlook of the flesh is death, but the outlook of the Spirit is life and peace, **8:7** because the outlook of the flesh is hostile to God, for it does not submit to the law of God, nor is it able to do so. **8:8** Those who are in the flesh cannot please God. **8:9** You, however, are not in the flesh but in the Spirit, if indeed the Spirit of God lives in you. Now if anyone does not have the Spirit of Christ, this person does not belong to him. **8:10** But if Christ is in you, your body is dead because of sin, but the Spirit is your life because of righteousness. **8:11** Moreover if the Spirit of the one who raised Jesus from the dead lives in you, the one who raised Christ from the dead will also make your mortal bodies alive through his Spirit who lives in you.

8:12 So then, brothers and sisters, we are under obligation, not to the flesh, to live according to the flesh **8:13** (for if you live according to the flesh, you will die), but if by the Spirit you put to death the deeds of the body you will live. **8:14** For all who are led by the Spirit of God are the sons of God. **8:15** For you did not receive the spirit of slavery leading again to fear, but you received the Spirit of adoption, by whom we cry, "Abba, Father." **8:16** The Spirit himself bears witness to our spirit that we are God's children. **8:17** And if children, then heirs (namely, heirs of God and also fellow heirs with Christ) – if indeed we suffer with him so we may also be glorified with him.

8:18 For I consider that our present sufferings cannot even be compared to the glory that will be revealed to us. **8:19** For the creation eagerly waits for the revelation of the sons of God. **8:20** For the creation was subjected to futility – not willingly but because of God who subjected it – in hope **8:21** that the creation itself will also be set free from the bondage of decay into the glorious freedom of God's children. **8:22** For we know that the whole creation groans and suffers together until now. **8:23** Not only this, but we ourselves also, who have the firstfruits of the Spirit, groan inwardly as we eagerly await our adoption, the redemption of our bodies. **8:24** For in hope we were saved. Now hope that is seen is not hope, because who hopes for what he sees? **8:25** But if we hope for what we do not see, we eagerly wait for it with endurance.

8:26 In the same way, the Spirit helps us in our weakness, for we do not know how we should pray, but the Spirit himself intercedes for us with inexpressible groanings. **8:27** And he who searches our hearts knows the mind of the Spirit, because the Spirit intercedes on behalf of the saints according to God's will. **8:28** And we know that all things work together for good for those who love God, who are called according to his purpose, **8:29** because those whom he foreknew he also predestined to be conformed to the image of his Son, that his Son would be the firstborn among many brothers and sisters. **8:30** And those he predestined, he also called; and those he called, he also justified; and those he justified, he also glorified.

8:31 What then shall we say about these things? If God is for us, who can be against us? **8:32** Indeed, he who did not spare his own Son, but gave him up for us all – how will he not also, along with him, freely give us all things? **8:33** Who will bring any charge against God's elect? It is God who justifies. **8:34** Who is the one who will condemn? Christ is the one who died (and more than that, he was raised), who is at the right hand of God, and who also is interceding for us. **8:35** Who will separate us from the love of Christ? Will trouble, or distress, or persecution, or famine, or nakedness, or danger, or sword? **8:36** As it is written, "*For your sake we encounter death all day long; we were considered as sheep to be slaughtered*." **8:37** No, in all these things we have complete victory through him who loved us! **8:38** For I am convinced that neither death, nor life, nor angels, nor heavenly rulers, nor things that are present, nor things to come, nor powers, **8:39** nor height, nor depth, nor anything else in creation will be able to separate us from the love of God in Christ Jesus our Lord.

Israel's Rejection Considered

9:1 I am telling the truth in Christ (I am not lying!), for my conscience assures me in the Holy Spirit – **9:2** I have great sorrow and unceasing anguish in my heart. **9:3** For I could wish that I myself were accursed – cut off from Christ – for the sake of my people, my fellow countrymen, **9:4** who are Israelites. To them belong the adoption as sons, the glory, the covenants, the giving of the law, the temple worship, and the promises. **9:5** To them belong the patriarchs, and from them, by human descent, came the Christ, who is God over all, blessed forever! Amen.

9:6 It is not as though the word of God had failed. For not all those who are descended from Israel are truly Israel, **9:7** nor are all the children Abraham's true descendants; rather "*through Isaac will your descendants be counted*." **9:8** This means it is not the children of the flesh who are the children of God; rather, the children of promise are counted as descendants. **9:9** For this is what the promise declared: "*About a year from now I will return and Sarah will have a son*." **9:10** Not only that, but when Rebekah had conceived children by one man, our ancestor Isaac – **9:11** even before they were born or had done anything good or bad (so that God's purpose in election would stand, not by works but by his calling) – **9:12** it was said to her, "*The older will serve the younger*," **9:13** just as it is written: "*Jacob I loved, but Esau I hated*."

9:14 What shall we say then? Is there injustice with God? Absolutely not! **9:15** For he says to Moses: "*I will have mercy on whom I have mercy, and I will have compassion on whom I have compassion*." **9:16** So then, it does not depend on human desire or exertion, but on God who shows mercy. **9:17** For the scripture says to Pharaoh: "*For this very purpose I have raised you up, that I may demonstrate my power in you, and that my name may be proclaimed in all the earth*." **9:18** So then, God has mercy on whom he chooses to have mercy, and he hardens whom he chooses to harden.

9:19 You will say to me then, "Why does he still find fault? For who has ever resisted his will?" **9:20** But who indeed are you – a mere human being – to talk back to God? *Does what is molded say to the molder,* "*Why have you made me like this?*" **9:21** Has the potter no right to make from the same lump of clay one vessel for special use and another for ordinary use? **9:22** But what if God, willing to demonstrate his wrath and to make known his power, has endured with much patience the objects of wrath prepared for destruction? **9:23** And what if he is willing to make known the wealth of his glory on the objects of mercy that he has prepared beforehand for glory – **9:24** even us, whom he has called, not only from the Jews but also from the Gentiles? **9:25** As he also says in Hosea:
"I will call those who were not my people, 'My people,' and I will call her who was unloved, 'My beloved.'"
9:26 "And in the very place where it was said to them, 'You are not my people,'
there they will be called 'sons of the living God.'"

9:27 And Isaiah cries out on behalf of Israel, "*Though the number of the children of Israel are as the sand of the sea, only the remnant will be saved, 9:28 for the Lord will execute his sentence on the earth completely and quickly*." **9:29** Just as Isaiah predicted,
"If the Lord of armies had not left us descendants,
we would have become like Sodom,
and we would have resembled Gomorrah."

Israel's Rejection Culpable

9:30 What shall we say then? – that the Gentiles who did not pursue righteousness obtained it, that is, a righteousness that is by faith, **9:31** but Israel even though pursuing a law of righteousness did not attain it. **9:32** Why not? Because they pursued it not by faith but (as if it were possible) by works. They stumbled over the stumbling stone, **9:33** just as it is written,

"Look, I am laying in Zion a stone that will cause people to stumble
and a rock that will make them fall,
yet the one who believes in him will not be put to shame."
10:1 Brothers and sisters, my heart's desire and prayer to God on behalf of my fellow Israelites is for their salvation. **10:2** For I can testify that they are zealous for God, but their zeal is not in line with the truth. **10:3** For ignoring the righteousness that comes from God, and seeking instead to establish their own righteousness, they did not submit to God's righteousness. **10:4** For Christ is the end of the law, with the result that there is righteousness for everyone who believes.
10:5 For Moses writes about the righteousness that is by the law: "*The one who does these things will live by them.*" **10:6** But the righteousness that is by faith says: "*Do not say in your heart*, 'Who will ascend into heaven?'" (that is, to bring Christ down) **10:7** or "*Who will descend into the abyss?*" (that is, to bring Christ up from the dead). **10:8** But what does it say? "*The word is near you, in your mouth and in your heart*" (that is, the word of faith that we preach), **10:9** because if you confess with your mouth that Jesus is Lord and believe in your heart that God raised him from the dead, you will be saved. **10:10** For with the heart one believes and thus has righteousness and with the mouth one confesses and thus has salvation. **10:11** For the scripture says, "*Everyone who believes in him will not be put to shame.*" **10:12** For there is no distinction between the Jew and the Greek, for the same Lord is Lord of all, who richly blesses all who call on him. **10:13** For *everyone who calls on the name of the Lord will be saved*.
10:14 How are they to call on one they have not believed in? And how are they to believe in one they have not heard of? And how are they to hear without someone preaching to them? **10:15** And how are they to preach unless they are sent? As it is written, "*How timely is the arrival of those who proclaim the good news.*" **10:16** But not all have obeyed the good news, for Isaiah says, "*Lord, who has believed our report?*" **10:17** Consequently faith comes from what is heard, and what is heard comes through the preached word of Christ.
10:18 But I ask, have they not heard? Yes, they have: *Their voice has gone out to all the earth, and their words to the ends of the world*. **10:19** But again I ask, didn't Israel understand? First Moses says, "*I will make you jealous by those who are not a nation; with a senseless nation I will provoke you to anger.*" **10:20** And Isaiah is even bold enough to say, "*I was found by those who did not seek me; I became well known to those who did not ask for me.*" **10:21** But about Israel he says, "*All day long I held out my hands to this disobedient and stubborn people!*"

Israel's Rejection not Complete nor Final
11:1 So I ask, God has not rejected his people, has he? Absolutely not! For I too am an Israelite, a descendant of Abraham, from the tribe of Benjamin. **11:2** God has not rejected his people whom he foreknew! Do you not know what the scripture says about Elijah, how he pleads with God against Israel? **11:3** "Lord, *they have killed your prophets, they have demolished your altars; I alone am left and they are seeking my life!*" **11:4** But what was the divine response to him? "*I have kept* for myself *seven thousand people who have not bent the knee to Baal.*" **11:5** So in the same way at the present time there is a remnant chosen by grace. **11:6** And if it is by grace, it is no longer by works, otherwise grace would no longer be grace. **11:7** What then? Israel failed to obtain what it was diligently seeking, but the elect obtained it. The rest were hardened, **11:8** as it is written,
"God gave them a spirit of stupor,
eyes that would not see and ears that would not hear,
to this very day."
11:9 And David says,
"Let their table become a snare and trap,
a stumbling block and a retribution for them;
11:10 let their eyes be darkened so that they may not see,
and make their backs bend continually."
11:11 I ask then, they did not stumble into an irrevocable fall, did they? Absolutely not! But by their transgression salvation has come to the Gentiles, to make Israel jealous. **11:12** Now if their transgression means riches for the world and their defeat means riches for the Gentiles, how much more will their full restoration bring?
11:13 Now I am speaking to you Gentiles. Seeing that I am an apostle to the Gentiles, I magnify my ministry, **11:14** if somehow I could provoke my people to jealousy and save some of them. **11:15** For if their rejection is the reconciliation of the world, what will their acceptance be but life from the dead? **11:16** If the first portion of the dough offered is holy, then the whole batch is holy, and if the root is holy, so too are the branches.
11:17 Now if some of the branches were broken off, and you, a wild olive shoot, were grafted in among them and participated in the richness of the olive root, **11:18** do not boast over the branches. But if you boast, remember that you do not support the root, but the root supports you. **11:19** Then you will say, "The branches were broken off so that I could be grafted in." **11:20** Granted! They were broken off because of their unbelief, but you stand by faith. Do not be arrogant, but fear! **11:21** For if God did not spare the natural branches, perhaps he will not spare you. **11:22** Notice therefore the kindness and harshness of God – harshness toward those who have fallen, but God's kindness toward you, provided you continue in his kindness; otherwise you also will be cut off. **11:23** And even they – if they do not continue in their unbelief – will be grafted in, for God is able to graft them in again. **11:24** For if you were cut off from what is by nature a wild olive tree, and grafted, contrary to nature, into a cultivated olive tree, how much more will these natural branches be grafted back into their own olive tree?
11:25 For I do not want you to be ignorant of this mystery, brothers and sisters, so that you may not be conceited: A partial hardening has happened to Israel until the full number of the Gentiles has come in. **11:26** And so all Israel will be saved, as it is written:
"The Deliverer will come out of Zion;
he will remove ungodliness from Jacob.
11:27 And this is my covenant with them,
when I take away their sins."
11:28 In regard to the gospel they are enemies for your sake, but in regard to election they are dearly loved for the sake of the fathers. **11:29** For the gifts and the call of God are irrevocable. **11:30** Just as you were formerly disobedient to God, but have now received mercy due to their disobedience, **11:31** so they too have now been disobedient in order that, by the mercy shown to you, they too may now receive mercy. **11:32** For God has consigned all people to disobedience so that he may show mercy to them all.
11:33 Oh, the depth of the riches and wisdom and knowledge of God! How unsearchable are his judgments and how fathomless his ways!
11:34 For who has known the mind of the Lord,
or who has been his counselor?
11:35 Or who has first given to God,
that God needs to repay him?
11:36 For from him and through him and to him are all things. To him be glory forever! Amen.

Consecration of the Believer's Life
12:1 Therefore I exhort you, brothers and sisters, by the mercies of God, to present your bodies as a sacrifice – alive, holy, and pleasing to God – which is your reasonable service. **12:2** Do not be conformed to this present world, but be transformed by the renewing of your mind, so that you may test and approve what is the will of God – what is good and well-pleasing and perfect.

Conduct in Humility
12:3 For by the grace given to me I say to every one of you not to think more highly of yourself than you ought to think, but to think with sober discernment, as God has distributed to each of you a measure of faith. **12:4** For just as in one body we have many members, and not all the members serve the same function, **12:5** so we who are many are one body in Christ, and individually we are members who belong to one another. **12:6** And we have different gifts according to the grace given to us. If the gift is prophecy, that individual must use it in proportion to his faith. **12:7** If it is service, he must serve; if it is teaching, he must teach; **12:8** if it is exhortation, he must exhort; if it is contributing, he must do so with sincerity; if it is leadership, he must do so with diligence; if it is showing mercy, he must do so with cheerfulness.

Conduct in Love
12:9 Love must be without hypocrisy. Abhor what is evil, cling to what is good. **12:10** Be devoted to one another with mutual love, showing eagerness in honoring one another. **12:11** Do not lag in zeal, be enthusiastic in spirit, serve the Lord. **12:12** Rejoice in hope, endure in suffering, persist in prayer. **12:13** Contribute to the needs of the saints, pursue hospitality. **12:14** Bless those who persecute you, bless and do not curse. **12:15** Rejoice with those who rejoice, weep with those who weep. **12:16** Live in harmony with one another; do not be haughty but associate with the lowly. Do not be conceited. **12:17** Do not repay anyone evil for evil; consider what is good before all people. **12:18** If possible, so far as it depends on you, live peaceably with all people. **12:19** Do not avenge yourselves, dear friends, but give place to God's wrath, for it is written, "*Vengeance is mine, I will repay,*" says the Lord. **12:20** Rather, *if your enemy is hungry, feed him; if he is thirsty, give him a drink; for in doing this you will be heaping burning coals on his head*. **12:21** Do not be overcome by evil, but overcome evil with good.

Submission to Civil Government
13:1 Let every person be subject to the governing authorities. For there is no authority except by God's appointment, and the authorities that exist have been instituted by God. **13:2** So the person who resists such authority resists the ordinance of God, and those who resist will incur judgment **13:3** (for rulers cause no fear for good conduct but for bad). Do you desire not to fear authority? Do good and you will receive its commendation, **13:4** for it is God's servant for your good. But if you do wrong, be in fear, for it does not bear the sword in vain. It is God's servant to administer retribution on the wrongdoer. **13:5** Therefore it is necessary to be in subjection, not only because of the wrath of the authorities but also because of your conscience. **13:6** For this reason you also pay taxes, for the authorities are God's servants devoted to governing. **13:7** Pay everyone what is owed: taxes to whom taxes are due, revenue to whom revenue is due, respect to whom respect is due, honor to whom honor is due.

Exhortation to Love Neighbors

13:8 Owe no one anything, except to love one another, for the one who loves his neighbor has fulfilled the law. **13:9** For the commandments, "*Do not commit adultery, do not murder, do not steal, do not covet,*" (and if there is any other commandment) are summed up in this, "*Love your neighbor as yourself.*" **13:10** Love does no wrong to a neighbor. Therefore love is the fulfillment of the law.

Motivation to Godly Conduct

13:11 And do this because we know the time, that it is already the hour for us to awake from sleep, for our salvation is now nearer than when we became believers. **13:12** The night has advanced toward dawn; the day is near. So then we must lay aside the works of darkness, and put on the weapons of light. **13:13** Let us live decently as in the daytime, not in carousing and drunkenness, not in sexual immorality and sensuality, not in discord and jealousy. **13:14** Instead, put on the Lord Jesus Christ, and make no provision for the flesh to arouse its desires.

Exhortation to Mutual Forbearance

14:1 Now receive the one who is weak in the faith, and do not have disputes over differing opinions. **14:2** One person believes in eating everything, but the weak person eats only vegetables. **14:3** The one who eats everything must not despise the one who does not, and the one who abstains must not judge the one who eats everything, for God has accepted him. **14:4** Who are you to pass judgment on another's servant? Before his own master he stands or falls. And he will stand, for the Lord is able to make him stand.

14:5 One person regards one day holier than other days, and another regards them all alike. Each must be fully convinced in his own mind. **14:6** The one who observes the day does it for the Lord. The one who eats, eats for the Lord because he gives thanks to God, and the one who abstains from eating abstains for the Lord, and he gives thanks to God. **14:7** For none of us lives for himself and none dies for himself. **14:8** If we live, we live for the Lord; if we die, we die for the Lord. Therefore, whether we live or die, we are the Lord's. **14:9** For this reason Christ died and returned to life, so that he may be the Lord of both the dead and the living.

14:10 But you who eat vegetables only – why do you judge your brother or sister? And you who eat everything – why do you despise your brother or sister? For we will all stand before the judgment seat of God. **14:11** For it is written, "*As I live, says the Lord, every knee will bow to me, and every tongue will give praise to God.*" **14:12** Therefore, each of us will give an account of himself to God.

Exhortation for the Strong not to Destroy the Weak

14:13 Therefore we must not pass judgment on one another, but rather determine never to place an obstacle or a trap before a brother or sister. **14:14** I know and am convinced in the Lord Jesus that there is nothing unclean in itself; still, it is unclean to the one who considers it unclean. **14:15** For if your brother or sister is distressed because of what you eat, you are no longer walking in love. Do not destroy by your food someone for whom Christ died. **14:16** Therefore do not let what you consider good be spoken of as evil. **14:17** For the kingdom of God does not consist of food and drink, but righteousness, peace, and joy in the Holy Spirit. **14:18** For the one who serves Christ in this way is pleasing to God and approved by people.

14:19 So then, let us pursue what makes for peace and for building up one another. **14:20** Do not destroy the work of God for the sake of food. For although all things are clean, it is wrong to cause anyone to stumble by what you eat. **14:21** It is good not to eat meat or drink wine or to do anything that causes your brother to stumble. **14:22** The faith you have, keep to yourself before God. Blessed is the one who does not judge himself by what he approves. **14:23** But the man who doubts is condemned if he eats, because he does not do so from faith, and whatever is not from faith is sin.

Exhortation for the Strong to Help the Weak

15:1 But we who are strong ought to bear with the failings of the weak, and not just please ourselves. **15:2** Let each of us please his neighbor for his good to build him up. **15:3** For even Christ did not please himself, but just as it is written, "*The insults of those who insult you have fallen on me.*" **15:4** For everything that was written in former times was written for our instruction, so that through endurance and through encouragement of the scriptures we may have hope. **15:5** Now may the God of endurance and comfort give you unity with one another in accordance with Christ Jesus, **15:6** so that together you may with one voice glorify the God and Father of our Lord Jesus Christ.

Exhortation to Mutual Acceptance

15:7 Receive one another, then, just as Christ also received you, to God's glory. **15:8** For I tell you that Christ has become a servant of the circumcised on behalf of God's truth to confirm the promises made to the fathers, **15:9** and thus the Gentiles glorify God for his mercy. As it is written, "*Because of this I will confess you among the Gentiles, and I will sing praises to your name.*" **15:10** And again it says: "*Rejoice, O Gentiles, with his people.*" **15:11** And again, "*Praise the Lord all you Gentiles, and let all the peoples praise him.*" **15:12** And again Isaiah says, "*The root of Jesse will come, and the one who rises to rule over the*

Gentiles, in him will the Gentiles hope." **15:13** Now may the God of hope fill you with all joy and peace as you believe in him, so that you may abound in hope by the power of the Holy Spirit.

Paul's Motivation for Writing the Letter

15:14 But I myself am fully convinced about you, my brothers and sisters, that you yourselves are full of goodness, filled with all knowledge, and able to instruct one another. **15:15** But I have written more boldly to you on some points so as to remind you, because of the grace given to me by God **15:16** to be a minister of Christ Jesus to the Gentiles. I serve the gospel of God like a priest, so that the Gentiles may become an acceptable offering, sanctified by the Holy Spirit. **15:17** So I boast in Christ Jesus about the things that pertain to God. **15:18** For I will not dare to speak of anything except what Christ has accomplished through me in order to bring about the obedience of the Gentiles, by word and deed, **15:19** in the power of signs and wonders, in the power of the Spirit of God. So from Jerusalem even as far as Illyricum I have fully preached the gospel of Christ. **15:20** And in this way I desire to preach where Christ has not been named, so as not to build on another person's foundation, **15:21** but as it is written: "*Those who were not told about him will see, and those who have not heard will understand.*"

Paul's Intention of Visiting the Romans

15:22 This is the reason I was often hindered from coming to you. **15:23** But now there is nothing more to keep me in these regions, and I have for many years desired to come to you **15:24** when I go to Spain. For I hope to visit you when I pass through and that you will help me on my journey there, after I have enjoyed your company for a while. **15:25** But now I go to Jerusalem to minister to the saints. **15:26** For Macedonia and Achaia are pleased to make some contribution for the poor among the saints in Jerusalem. **15:27** For they were pleased to do this, and indeed they are indebted to the Jerusalem saints. For if the Gentiles have shared in their spiritual things, they are obligated also to minister to them in material things. **15:28** Therefore after I have completed this and have safely delivered this bounty to them, I will set out for Spain by way of you, **15:29** and I know that when I come to you I will come in the fullness of Christ's blessing.

15:30 Now I urge you, brothers and sisters, through our Lord Jesus Christ and through the love of the Spirit, to join fervently with me in prayer to God on my behalf. **15:31** Pray that I may be rescued from those who are disobedient in Judea and that my ministry in Jerusalem may be acceptable to the saints, **15:32** so that by God's will I may come to you with joy and be refreshed in your company. **15:33** Now may the God of peace be with all of you. Amen.

Personal Greetings

16:1 Now I commend to you our sister Phoebe, who is a servant of the church in Cenchrea, **16:2** so that you may welcome her in the Lord in a way worthy of the saints and provide her with whatever help she may need from you, for she has been a great help to many, including me.

16:3 Greet Prisca and Aquila, my fellow workers in Christ Jesus, **16:4** who risked their own necks for my life. Not only I, but all the churches of the Gentiles are grateful to them. **16:5** Also greet the church in their house. Greet my dear friend Epenetus, who was the first convert to Christ in the province of Asia. **16:6** Greet Mary, who has worked very hard for you. **16:7** Greet Andronicus and Junia, my compatriots and my fellow prisoners. They are well known to the apostles, and they were in Christ before me. **16:8** Greet Ampliatus, my dear friend in the Lord. **16:9** Greet Urbanus, our fellow worker in Christ, and my good friend Stachys. **16:10** Greet Apelles, who is approved in Christ. Greet those who belong to the household of Aristobulus. **16:11** Greet Herodion, my compatriot. Greet those in the household of Narcissus who are in the Lord. **16:12** Greet Tryphena and Tryphosa, laborers in the Lord. Greet my dear friend Persis, who has worked hard in the Lord. **16:13** Greet Rufus, chosen in the Lord, and his mother who was also a mother to me. **16:14** Greet Asyncritus, Phlegon, Hermes, Patrobas, Hermas, and the brothers and sisters with them. **16:15** Greet Philologus and Julia, Nereus and his sister, and Olympas, and all the believers who are with them. **16:16** Greet one another with a holy kiss. All the churches of Christ greet you.

16:17 Now I urge you, brothers and sisters, to watch out for those who create dissensions and obstacles contrary to the teaching that you learned. Avoid them! **16:18** For these are the kind who do not serve our Lord Christ, but their own appetites. By their smooth talk and flattery they deceive the minds of the naive. **16:19** Your obedience is known to all and thus I rejoice over you. But I want you to be wise in what is good and innocent in what is evil. **16:20** The God of peace will quickly crush Satan under your feet. The grace of our Lord Jesus be with you.

16:21 Timothy, my fellow worker, greets you; so do Lucius, Jason, and Sosipater, my compatriots. **16:22** I, Tertius, who am writing this letter, greet you in the Lord. **16:23** Gaius, who is host to me and to the whole church, greets you. Erastus the city treasurer and our brother Quartus greet you.

16:25 Now to him who is able to strengthen you according to my gospel and the proclamation of Jesus Christ, according to the revelation of the mystery that had been kept secret for long ages, **16:26** but now is disclosed, and through the prophetic scriptures has been made known to all the nations, according to the command of the eternal God, to bring about the obedience of faith – **16:27** to the only wise God, through Jesus Christ, be glory forever! Amen.

Book 46. 1 Corinthians

Salutation

1:1 From Paul, called to be an apostle of Christ Jesus by the will of God, and Sosthenes, our brother, **1:2** to the church of God that is in Corinth, to those who are sanctified in Christ Jesus, and called to be saints, with all those in every place who call on the name of our Lord Jesus Christ, their Lord and ours. **1:3** Grace and peace to you from God our Father and the Lord Jesus Christ!

Thanksgiving

1:4 I always thank my God for you because of the grace of God that was given to you in Christ Jesus. **1:5** For you were made rich in every way in him, in all your speech and in every kind of knowledge – **1:6** just as the testimony about Christ has been confirmed among you – **1:7** so that you do not lack any spiritual gift as you wait for the revelation of our Lord Jesus Christ. **1:8** He will also strengthen you to the end, so that you will be blameless on the day of our Lord Jesus Christ. **1:9** God is faithful, by whom you were called into fellowship with his son, Jesus Christ our Lord.

Divisions in the Church

1:10 I urge you, brothers and sisters, by the name of our Lord Jesus Christ, to agree together, to end your divisions, and to be united by the same mind and purpose. **1:11** For members of Chloe's household have made it clear to me, my brothers and sisters, that there are quarrels among you. **1:12** Now I mean this, that each of you is saying, "I am with Paul," or "I am with Apollos," or "I am with Cephas," or "I am with Christ." **1:13** Is Christ divided? Paul wasn't crucified for you, was he? Or were you in fact baptized in the name of Paul? **1:14** I thank God that I did not baptize any of you except Crispus and Gaius, **1:15** so that no one can say that you were baptized in my name! **1:16** (I also baptized the household of Stephanus. Otherwise, I do not remember whether I baptized anyone else.) **1:17** For Christ did not send me to baptize, but to preach the gospel – and not with clever speech, so that the cross of Christ would not become useless.

The Message of the Cross

1:18 For the message about the cross is foolishness to those who are perishing, but to us who are being saved it is the power of God. **1:19** For it is written, "*I will destroy the wisdom of the wise, and I will thwart the cleverness of the intelligent.*" **1:20** Where is the wise man? Where is the expert in the Mosaic law? Where is the debater of this age? Has God not made the wisdom of the world foolish? **1:21** For since in the wisdom of God the world by its wisdom did not know God, God was pleased to save those who believe by the foolishness of preaching. **1:22** For Jews demand miraculous signs and Greeks ask for wisdom, **1:23** but we preach about a crucified Christ, a stumbling block to Jews and foolishness to Gentiles. **1:24** But to those who are called, both Jews and Greeks, Christ is the power of God and the wisdom of God. **1:25** For the foolishness of God is wiser than human wisdom, and the weakness of God is stronger than human strength.

1:26 Think about the circumstances of your call, brothers and sisters. Not many were wise by human standards, not many were powerful, not many were born to a privileged position. **1:27** But God chose what the world thinks foolish to shame the wise, and God chose what the world thinks weak to shame the strong. **1:28** God chose what is low and despised in the world, what is regarded as nothing, to set aside what is regarded as something, **1:29** so that no one can boast in his presence. **1:30** He is the reason you have a relationship with Christ Jesus, who became for us wisdom from God, and righteousness and sanctification and redemption, **1:31** so that, as it is written, "*Let the one who boasts, boast in the Lord.*" **2:1** When I came to you, brothers and sisters, I did not come with superior eloquence or wisdom as I proclaimed the testimony of God. **2:2** For I decided to be concerned about nothing among you except Jesus Christ, and him crucified. **2:3** And I was with you in weakness and in fear and with much trembling. **2:4** My conversation and my preaching were not with persuasive words of wisdom, but with a demonstration of the Spirit and of power, **2:5** so that your faith would not be based on human wisdom but on the power of God.

Wisdom from God

2:6 Now we do speak wisdom among the mature, but not a wisdom of this age or of the rulers of this age, who are perishing. **2:7** Instead we speak the wisdom of God, hidden in a mystery, that God determined before the ages for our glory. **2:8** None of the rulers of this age understood it. If they had known it, they would not have crucified the Lord of glory. **2:9** But just as it is written, "*Things that no eye has seen, or ear heard, or mind imagined, are the things God has prepared for those who love him.*" **2:10** God has revealed these to us by the Spirit. For the Spirit searches all things, even the deep things of God. **2:11** For who among men knows the things of a man except the man's spirit within

him? So too, no one knows the things of God except the Spirit of God. **2:12** Now we have not received the spirit of the world, but the Spirit who is from God, so that we may know the things that are freely given to us by God. **2:13** And we speak about these things, not with words taught us by human wisdom, but with those taught by the Spirit, explaining spiritual things to spiritual people. **2:14** The unbeliever does not receive the things of the Spirit of God, for they are foolishness to him. And he cannot understand them, because they are spiritually discerned. **2:15** The one who is spiritual discerns all things, yet he himself is understood by no one. **2:16** *For who has known the mind of the Lord, so as to advise him?* But we have the mind of Christ.

Immaturity and Self-deception

3:1 So, brothers and sisters, I could not speak to you as spiritual people, but instead as people of the flesh, as infants in Christ. **3:2** I fed you milk, not solid food, for you were not yet ready. In fact, you are still not ready, **3:3** for you are still influenced by the flesh. For since there is still jealousy and dissension among you, are you not influenced by the flesh and behaving like unregenerate people? **3:4** For whenever someone says, "I am with Paul," or "I am with Apollos," are you not merely human?

3:5 What is Apollos, really? Or what is Paul? Servants through whom you came to believe, and each of us in the ministry the Lord gave us. **3:6** I planted, Apollos watered, but God caused it to grow. **3:7** So neither the one who plants counts for anything, nor the one who waters, but God who causes the growth. **3:8** The one who plants and the one who waters work as one, but each will receive his reward according to his work. **3:9** We are coworkers belonging to God. You are God's field, God's building. **3:10** According to the grace of God given to me, like a skilled master-builder I laid a foundation, but someone else builds on it. And each one must be careful how he builds. **3:11** For no one can lay any foundation other than what is being laid, which is Jesus Christ. **3:12** If anyone builds on the foundation with gold, silver, precious stones, wood, hay, or straw, **3:13** each builder's work will be plainly seen, for the Day will make it clear, because it will be revealed by fire. And the fire will test what kind of work each has done. **3:14** If what someone has built survives, he will receive a reward. **3:15** If someone's work is burned up, he will suffer loss. He himself will be saved, but only as through fire.

3:16 Do you not know that you are God's temple and that God's Spirit lives in you? **3:17** If someone destroys God's temple, God will destroy him. For God's temple is holy, which is what you are.

3:18 Guard against self-deception, each of you. If someone among you thinks he is wise in this age, let him become foolish so that he can become wise. **3:19** For the wisdom of this age is foolishness with God. As it is written, "*He catches the wise in their craftiness.*" **3:20** And again, "*The Lord knows that the thoughts of the wise are futile.*" **3:21** So then, no more boasting about mere mortals! For everything belongs to you, **3:22** whether Paul or Apollos or Cephas or the world or life or death or the present or the future. Everything belongs to you, **3:23** and you belong to Christ, and Christ belongs to God.

The Apostles' Ministry

4:1 One should think about us this way – as servants of Christ and stewards of the mysteries of God. **4:2** Now what is sought in stewards is that one be found faithful. **4:3** So for me, it is a minor matter that I am judged by you or by any human court. In fact, I do not even judge myself. **4:4** For I am not aware of anything against myself, but I am not acquitted because of this. The one who judges me is the Lord. **4:5** So then, do not judge anything before the time. Wait until the Lord comes. He will bring to light the hidden things of darkness and reveal the motives of hearts. Then each will receive recognition from God.

4:6 I have applied these things to myself and Apollos because of you, brothers and sisters, so that through us you may learn "not to go beyond what is written," so that none of you will be puffed up in favor of the one against the other. **4:7** For who concedes you any superiority? What do you have that you did not receive? And if you received it, why do you boast as though you did not? **4:8** Already you are satisfied! Already you are rich! You have become kings without us! I wish you had become kings so that we could reign with you! **4:9** For, I think, God has exhibited us apostles last of all, as men condemned to die, because we have become a spectacle to the world, both to angels and to people. **4:10** We are fools for Christ, but you are wise in Christ! We are weak, but you are strong! You are distinguished, we are dishonored! **4:11** To the present hour we are hungry and thirsty, poorly clothed, brutally treated, and without a roof over our heads. **4:12** We do hard work, toiling with our own hands. When we are verbally abused, we respond with a blessing, when persecuted, we endure, **4:13** when people lie about us, we answer in a friendly manner. We are the world's dirt and scum, even now.

A Father's Warning

4:14 I am not writing these things to shame you, but to correct you as my dear children. **4:15** For though you may have ten thousand guardians in Christ, you do not have many fathers, because I became your father in Christ Jesus through the gospel. **4:16** I encourage you, then, be imitators of me. **4:17** For this reason, I have sent Timothy to you, who is my dear and faithful son in the Lord. He will remind you of my ways in Christ, as I teach them everywhere in every church. **4:18** Some have become arrogant, as if I were not coming to you. **4:19** But I will come to you soon, if the Lord is willing, and I will find out not only the talk of these arrogant people, but also their power. **4:20** For the kingdom of God is demonstrated not in idle talk but with power. **4:21** What do you want? Shall I come to you with a rod of discipline or with love and a spirit of gentleness?

Church Discipline

5:1 It is actually reported that sexual immorality exists among you, the kind of immorality that is not permitted even among the Gentiles, so that someone is cohabiting with his father's wife. **5:2** And you are proud! Shouldn't you have been deeply sorrowful instead and removed the one who did this from among you? **5:3** For even though I am absent physically, I am present in spirit. And I have already judged the one who did this, just as though I were present. **5:4** When you gather together in the name of our Lord Jesus, and I am with you in spirit, along with the power of our Lord Jesus, **5:5** turn this man over to Satan for the destruction of the flesh, so that his spirit may be saved in the day of the Lord.

5:6 Your boasting is not good. Don't you know that a little yeast affects the whole batch of dough? **5:7** Clean out the old yeast so that you may be a new batch of dough – you are, in fact, without yeast. For Christ, our Passover lamb, has been sacrificed. **5:8** So then, let us celebrate the festival, not with the old yeast, the yeast of vice and evil, but with the bread without yeast, the bread of sincerity and truth.

5:9 I wrote you in my letter not to associate with sexually immoral people. **5:10** In no way did I mean the immoral people of this world, or the greedy and swindlers and idolaters, since you would then have to go out of the world. **5:11** But now I am writing to you not to associate with anyone who calls himself a Christian who is sexually immoral, or greedy, or an idolater, or verbally abusive, or a drunkard, or a swindler. Do not even eat with such a person. **5:12** For what do I have to do with judging those outside? Are you not to judge those inside? **5:13** But God will judge those outside. *Remove the evil person from among you.*

Lawsuits

6:1 When any of you has a legal dispute with another, does he dare go to court before the unrighteous rather than before the saints? **6:2** Or do you not know that the saints will judge the world? And if the world is to be judged by you, are you not competent to settle trivial suits? **6:3** Do you not know that we will judge angels? Why not ordinary matters! **6:4** So if you have ordinary lawsuits, do you appoint as judges those who have no standing in the church? **6:5** I say this to your shame! Is there no one among you wise enough to settle disputes between fellow Christians? **6:6** Instead, does a Christian sue a Christian, and do this before unbelievers? **6:7** The fact that you have lawsuits among yourselves demonstrates that you have already been defeated. Why not rather be wronged? Why not rather be cheated? **6:8** But you yourselves wrong and cheat, and you do this to your brothers and sisters!

6:9 Do you not know that the unrighteous will not inherit the kingdom of God? Do not be deceived! The sexually immoral, idolaters, adulterers, passive homosexual partners, practicing homosexuals, **6:10** thieves, the greedy, drunkards, the verbally abusive, and swindlers will not inherit the kingdom of God. **6:11** Some of you once lived this way. But you were washed, you were sanctified, you were justified in the name of the Lord Jesus Christ and by the Spirit of our God.

Flee Sexual Immorality

6:12 "All things are lawful for me" – but not everything is beneficial. "All things are lawful for me" – but I will not be controlled by anything. **6:13** "Food is for the stomach and the stomach is for food, but God will do away with both." The body is not for sexual immorality, but for the Lord, and the Lord for the body. **6:14** Now God indeed raised the Lord and he will raise us by his power. **6:15** Do you not know that your bodies are members of Christ? Should I take the members of Christ and make them members of a prostitute? Never! **6:16** Or do you not know that anyone who is united with a prostitute is one body with her? For it is said, "***The two will become one flesh.***" **6:17** But the one united with the Lord is one spirit with him. **6:18** Flee sexual immorality! "Every sin a person commits is outside of the body" – but the immoral person sins against his own body. **6:19** Or do you not know that your body is the temple of the Holy Spirit who is in you, whom you have from God, and you are not your own? **6:20** For you were bought at a price. Therefore glorify God with your body.

Celibacy and Marriage

7:1 Now with regard to the issues you wrote about: "It is good for a man not to have sexual relations with a woman." **7:2** But because of immoralities, each man should have relations with his own wife and each woman with her own husband. **7:3** A husband should give to his wife her sexual rights, and likewise a wife to her husband. **7:4** It is not the wife who has the rights to her own body, but the husband. In the same way, it is not the husband who has the rights to his own body, but the wife. **7:5** Do not deprive each other, except by mutual agreement for a specified time, so that you may devote yourselves to prayer. Then resume your relationship, so that Satan may not tempt you because of your lack of self-control. **7:6** I say this as a concession, not as a command. **7:7** I wish that everyone was as I am. But each has his own gift from God, one this way, another that.

7:8 To the unmarried and widows I say that it is best for them to remain as I am. **7:9** But if they do not have self-control, let them get married. For it is better to marry than to burn with sexual desire.

7:10 To the married I give this command – not I, but the Lord – a wife should not divorce a husband **7:11** (but if she does, let her remain unmarried, or be reconciled to her husband), and a husband should not divorce his wife.

7:12 To the rest I say – I, not the Lord – if a brother has a wife who is not a believer and she is happy to live with him, he should not divorce her. **7:13** And if a woman has a husband who is not a believer and he is happy to live with her, she should not divorce him. **7:14** For the unbelieving husband is sanctified because of the wife, and the unbelieving wife because of her husband. Otherwise your children are unclean, but now they are holy. **7:15** But if the unbeliever wants a divorce, let it take place. In these circumstances the brother or sister is not bound. God has called you in peace. **7:16** For how do you know, wife, whether you will bring your husband to salvation? Or how do you know, husband, whether you will bring your wife to salvation?

The Circumstances of Your Calling

7:17 Nevertheless, as the Lord has assigned to each one, as God has called each person, so must he live. I give this sort of direction in all the churches. **7:18** Was anyone called after he had been circumcised? He should not try to undo his circumcision. Was anyone called who is uncircumcised? He should not get circumcised. **7:19** Circumcision is nothing and uncircumcision is nothing. Instead, keeping God's commandments is what counts. **7:20** Let each one remain in that situation in life in which he was called. **7:21** Were you called as a slave? Do not worry about it. But if indeed you are able to be free, make the most of the opportunity. **7:22** For the one who was called in the Lord as a slave is the Lord's freedman. In the same way, the one who was called as a free person is Christ's slave. **7:23** You were bought with a price. Do not become slaves of men. **7:24** In whatever situation someone was called, brothers and sisters, let him remain in it with God.

Remaining Unmarried

7:25 With regard to the question about people who have never married, I have no command from the Lord, but I give my opinion as one shown mercy by the Lord to be trustworthy. **7:26** Because of the impending crisis I think it best for you to remain as you are. **7:27** The one bound to a wife should not seek divorce. The one released from a wife should not seek marriage. **7:28** But if you marry, you have not sinned. And if a virgin marries, she has not sinned. But those who marry will face difficult circumstances, and I am trying to spare you such problems. **7:29** And I say this, brothers and sisters: The time is short. So then those who have wives should be as those who have none, **7:30** those with tears like those not weeping, those who rejoice like those not rejoicing, those who buy like those without possessions, **7:31** those who use the world as though they were not using it to the full. For the present shape of this world is passing away.

7:32 And I want you to be free from concern. An unmarried man is concerned about the things of the Lord, how to please the Lord. **7:33** But a married man is concerned about the things of the world, how to please his wife, **7:34** and he is divided. An unmarried woman or a virgin is concerned about the things of the Lord, to be holy both in body and spirit. But a married woman is concerned about the things of the world, how to please her husband. **7:35** I am saying this for your benefit, not to place a limitation on you, but so that without distraction you may give notable and constant service to the Lord.

7:36 If anyone thinks he is acting inappropriately toward his virgin, if she is past the bloom of youth and it seems necessary, he should do what he wishes; he does not sin. Let them marry. **7:37** But the man who is firm in his commitment, and is under no necessity but has control over his will, and has decided in his own mind to keep his own virgin, does well. **7:38** So then, the one who marries his own virgin does well, but the one who does not, does better.

7:39 A wife is bound as long as her husband is living. But if her husband dies, she is free to marry anyone she wishes (only someone in the Lord). **7:40** But in my opinion, she will be happier if she remains as she is – and I think that I too have the Spirit of God!

Food Sacrificed to Idols

8:1 With regard to food sacrificed to idols, we know that "we all have knowledge." Knowledge puffs up, but love builds up. **8:2** If someone thinks he knows something, he does not yet know to the degree that he needs to know. **8:3** But if someone loves God, he is known by God.

8:4 With regard then to eating food sacrificed to idols, we know that "an idol in this world is nothing," and that "there is no God but one." **8:5** If after all there are so-called gods, whether in heaven or on earth (as there are many gods and many lords), **8:6** yet for us there is one God, the Father, from whom are all things and for whom we live, and one Lord, Jesus Christ, through whom are all things and through whom we live.

8:7 But this knowledge is not shared by all. And some, by being accustomed to idols in former times, eat this food as an idol sacrifice, and their conscience, because it is weak, is defiled. **8:8** Now food will not bring us close to God. We are no worse if we do not eat and no better if we do. **8:9**

But be careful that this liberty of yours does not become a hindrance to the weak. **8:10** For if someone weak sees you who possess knowledge dining in an idol's temple, will not his conscience be "strengthened" to eat food offered to idols? **8:11** So by your knowledge the weak brother or sister, for whom Christ died, is destroyed. **8:12** If you sin against your brothers or sisters in this way and wound their weak conscience, you sin against Christ. **8:13** For this reason, if food causes my brother or sister to sin, I will never eat meat again, so that I may not cause one of them to sin.

The Rights of an Apostle

9:1 Am I not free? Am I not an apostle? Have I not seen Jesus our Lord? Are you not my work in the Lord? **9:2** If I am not an apostle to others, at least I am to you, for you are the confirming sign of my apostleship in the Lord. **9:3** This is my defense to those who examine me. **9:4** Do we not have the right to financial support? **9:5** Do we not have the right to the company of a believing wife, like the other apostles and the Lord's brothers and Cephas? **9:6** Or do only Barnabas and I lack the right not to work? **9:7** Who ever serves in the army at his own expense? Who plants a vineyard and does not eat its fruit? Who tends a flock and does not consume its milk? **9:8** Am I saying these things only on the basis of common sense, or does the law not say this as well? **9:9** For it is written in the law of Moses, "***Do not muzzle an ox while it is treading out the grain.***" God is not concerned here about oxen, is he? **9:10** Or is he not surely speaking for our benefit? It was written for us, because the one plowing and threshing ought to work in hope of enjoying the harvest. **9:11** If we sowed spiritual blessings among you, is it too much to reap material things from you? **9:12** If others receive this right from you, are we not more deserving?

But we have not made use of this right. Instead we endure everything so that we may not be a hindrance to the gospel of Christ. **9:13** Don't you know that those who serve in the temple eat food from the temple, and those who serve at the altar receive a part of the offerings? **9:14** In the same way the Lord commanded those who proclaim the gospel to receive their living by the gospel. **9:15** But I have not used any of these rights. And I am not writing these things so that something will be done for me. In fact, it would be better for me to die than – no one will deprive me of my reason for boasting! **9:16** For if I preach the gospel, I have no reason for boasting, because I am compelled to do this. Woe to me if I do not preach the gospel! **9:17** For if I do this voluntarily, I have a reward. But if I do it unwillingly, I am entrusted with a responsibility. **9:18** What then is my reward? That when I preach the gospel I may offer the gospel free of charge, and so not make full use of my rights in the gospel.

9:19 For since I am free from all I can make myself a slave to all, in order to gain even more people. **9:20** To the Jews I became like a Jew to gain the Jews. To those under the law I became like one under the law (though I myself am not under the law) to gain those under the law. **9:21** To those free from the law I became like one free from the law (though I am not free from God's law but under the law of Christ) to gain those free from the law. **9:22** To the weak I became weak in order to gain the weak. I have become all things to all people, so that by all means I may save some.

9:23 I do all these things because of the gospel, so that I can be a participant in it.

9:24 Do you not know that all the runners in a stadium compete, but only one receives the prize? So run to win. **9:25** Each competitor must exercise self-control in everything. They do it to receive a perishable crown, but we an imperishable one.

9:26 So I do not run uncertainly or box like one who hits only air. **9:27** Instead I subdue my body and make it my slave, so that after preaching to others I myself will not be disqualified.

Learning from Israel's Failures

10:1 For I do not want you to be unaware, brothers and sisters, that our fathers were all under the cloud and all passed through the sea, **10:2** and all were baptized into Moses in the cloud and in the sea, **10:3** and all ate the same spiritual food, **10:4** and all drank the same spiritual drink. For they were all drinking from the spiritual rock that followed them, and the rock was Christ. **10:5** But God was not pleased with most of them, for they were cut down in the wilderness. **10:6** These things happened as examples for us, so that we will not crave evil things as they did. **10:7** So do not be idolaters, as some of them were. As it is written, "***The people sat down to eat and drink and rose up to play.***" **10:8** And let us not be immoral, as some of them were, and twenty-three thousand died in a single day. **10:9** And let us not put Christ to the test, as some of them did, and were destroyed by snakes. **10:10** And do not complain, as some of them did, and were killed by the destroying angel. **10:11** These things happened to them as examples and were written for our instruction, on whom the ends of the ages have come. **10:12** So let the one who thinks he is standing be careful that he does not fall. **10:13** No trial has overtaken you that is not faced by others. And God is faithful: He will not let you be tried beyond what you are able to bear, but with the trial will also provide a way out so that you may be able to endure it.

Avoid Idol Feasts

10:14 So then, my dear friends, flee from idolatry. **10:15** I am speaking to thoughtful people. Consider what I say. **10:16** Is not the cup of blessing that we bless a sharing in the blood of Christ? Is not the bread that we break a sharing in the body of Christ? **10:17** Because there is one bread, we who are many are one body, for we all share the one bread. **10:18** Look at the people of Israel. Are not those who eat the sacrifices partners in the altar? **10:19** Am I saying that idols or food sacrificed to them amount to anything? **10:20** No, I mean that what the pagans sacrifice is to demons and not to God. I do not want you to be partners with demons. **10:21** You cannot drink the cup of the Lord and the cup of demons. You cannot take part in the table of the Lord and the table of demons. **10:22** Or are we trying to provoke the Lord to jealousy? Are we really stronger than he is?

Live to Glorify God

10:23 "Everything is lawful," but not everything is beneficial. "Everything is lawful," but not everything builds others up. **10:24** Do not seek your own good, but the good of the other person. **10:25** Eat anything that is sold in the marketplace without questions of conscience, **10:26** for *the earth and its abundance are the Lord's.* **10:27** If an unbeliever invites you to dinner and you want to go, eat whatever is served without asking questions of conscience. **10:28** But if someone says to you, "This is from a sacrifice," do not eat, because of the one who told you and because of conscience – **10:29** I do not mean yours but the other person's. For why is my freedom being judged by another's conscience? **10:30** If I partake with thankfulness, why am I blamed for the food that I give thanks for? **10:31** So whether you eat or drink, or whatever you do, do everything for the glory of God. **10:32** Do not give offense to Jews or Greeks or to the church of God, **10:33** just as I also try to please everyone in all things. I do not seek my own benefit, but the benefit of many, so that they may be saved. **11:1** Be imitators of me, just as I also am of Christ.

Women's Head Coverings

11:2 I praise you because you remember me in everything and maintain the traditions just as I passed them on to you. **11:3** But I want you to know that Christ is the head of every man, and the man is the head of a woman, and God is the head of Christ. **11:4** Any man who prays or prophesies with his head covered disgraces his head. **11:5** But any woman who prays or prophesies with her head uncovered disgraces her head, for it is one and the same thing as having a shaved head. **11:6** For if a woman will not cover her head, she should cut off her hair. But if it is disgraceful for a woman to have her hair cut off or her head shaved, she should cover her head. **11:7** For a man should not have his head covered, since he is the image and glory of God. But the woman is the glory of the man. **11:8** For man did not come from woman, but woman from man. **11:9** Neither was man created for the sake of woman, but woman for man. **11:10** For this reason a woman should have a symbol of authority on her head, because of the angels. **11:11** In any case, in the Lord woman is not independent of man, nor is man independent of woman. **11:12** For just as woman came from man, so man comes through woman. But all things come from God. **11:13** Judge for yourselves: Is it proper for a woman to pray to God with her head uncovered? **11:14** Does not nature itself teach you that if a man has long hair, it is a disgrace for him, **11:15** but if a woman has long hair, it is her glory? For her hair is given to her for a covering. **11:16** If anyone intends to quarrel about this, we have no other practice, nor do the churches of God.

The Lord's Supper

11:17 Now in giving the following instruction I do not praise you, because you come together not for the better but for the worse. **11:18** For in the first place, when you come together as a church I hear there are divisions among you, and in part I believe it. **11:19** For there must in fact be divisions among you, so that those of you who are approved may be evident. **11:20** Now when you come together at the same place, you are not really eating the Lord's Supper. **11:21** For when it is time to eat, everyone proceeds with his own supper. One is hungry and another becomes drunk. **11:22** Do you not have houses so that you can eat and drink? Or are you trying to show contempt for the church of God by shaming those who have nothing? What should I say to you? Should I praise you? I will not praise you for this!

11:23 For I received from the Lord what I also passed on to you, that the Lord Jesus on the night in which he was betrayed took bread, **11:24** and after he had given thanks he broke it and said, "This is my body, which is for you. Do this in remembrance of me." **11:25** In the same way, he also took the cup after supper, saying, "This cup is the new covenant in my blood. Do this, every time you drink it, in remembrance of me." **11:26** For every time you eat this bread and drink the cup, you proclaim the Lord's death until he comes.

11:27 For this reason, whoever eats the bread or drinks the cup of the Lord in an unworthy manner will be guilty of the body and blood of the Lord. **11:28** A person should examine himself first, and in this way let him eat the bread and drink of the cup. **11:29** For the one who eats and drinks without careful regard for the body eats and drinks judgment against himself. **11:30** That is why many of you are weak and sick, and quite a few are dead. **11:31** But if we examined ourselves, we would not be judged. **11:32** But when we are judged by the Lord, we are disciplined so that we may not be condemned with the world. **11:33** So then, my brothers and sisters, when you come together to eat, wait for one another. **11:34** If anyone is hungry, let him eat at home, so that when you assemble it does not lead to judgment. I will give directions about other matters when I come.

Spiritual Gifts

12:1 With regard to spiritual gifts, brothers and sisters, I do not want you to be uninformed. **12:2** You know that when you were pagans you were often led astray by speechless idols, however you were led. **12:3** So I want you to understand that no one speaking by the Spirit of God says, "Jesus is cursed," and no one can say, "Jesus is Lord," except by the Holy Spirit.

12:4 Now there are different gifts, but the same Spirit. **12:5** And there are different ministries, but the same Lord. **12:6** And there are different results, but the same God who produces all of them in everyone. **12:7** To each person the manifestation of the Spirit is given for the benefit of all. **12:8** For one person is given through the Spirit the message of wisdom, and another the message of knowledge according to the same Spirit, **12:9** to another faith by the same Spirit, and to another gifts of healing by the one Spirit, **12:10** to another performance of miracles, to another prophecy, and to another discernment of spirits, to another different kinds of tongues, and to another the interpretation of tongues. **12:11** It is one and the same Spirit, distributing as he decides to each person, who produces all these things.

Different Members in One Body

12:12 For just as the body is one and yet has many members, and all the members of the body – though many – are one body, so too is Christ. **12:13** For in one Spirit we were all baptized into one body. Whether Jews or Greeks or slaves or free, we were all made to drink of the one Spirit. **12:14** For in fact the body is not a single member, but many. **12:15** If the foot says, "Since I am not a hand, I am not part of the body," it does not lose its membership in the body because of that. **12:16** And if the ear says, "Since I am not an eye, I am not part of the body," it does not lose its membership in the body because of that. **12:17** If the whole body were an eye, what part would do the hearing? If the whole were an ear, what part would exercise the sense of smell? **12:18** But as a matter of fact, God has placed each of the members in the body just as he decided. **12:19** If they were all the same member, where would the body be? **12:20** So now there are many members, but one body. **12:21** The eye cannot say to the hand, "I do not need you," nor in turn can the head say to the foot, "I do not need you." **12:22** On the contrary, those members that seem to be weaker are essential, **12:23** and those members we consider less honorable we clothe with greater honor, and our unpresentable members are clothed with dignity, **12:24** but our presentable members do not need this. Instead, God has blended together the body, giving greater honor to the lesser member, **12:25** so that there may be no division in the body, but the members may have mutual concern for one another. **12:26** If one member suffers, everyone suffers with it. If a member is honored, all rejoice with it.

12:27 Now you are Christ's body, and each of you is a member of it. **12:28** And God has placed in the church first apostles, second prophets, third teachers, then miracles, gifts of healing, helps, gifts of leadership, different kinds of tongues. **12:29** Not all are apostles, are they? Not all are prophets, are they? Not all are teachers, are they? Not all perform miracles, do they? **12:30** Not all have gifts of healing, do they? Not all speak in tongues, do they? Not all interpret, do they? **12:31** But you should be eager for the greater gifts.

And now I will show you a way that is beyond comparison.

The Way of Love

13:1 If I speak in the tongues of men and of angels, but I do not have love, I am a noisy gong or a clanging cymbal. **13:2** And if I have prophecy, and know all mysteries and all knowledge, and if I have all faith so that I can remove mountains, but do not have love, I am nothing. **13:3** If I give away everything I own, and if I give over my body in order to boast, but do not have love, I receive no benefit.

13:4 Love is patient, love is kind, it is not envious. Love does not brag, it is not puffed up. **13:5** It is not rude, it is not self-serving, it is not easily angered or resentful. **13:6** It is not glad about injustice, but rejoices in the truth. **13:7** It bears all things, believes all things, hopes all things, endures all things.

13:8 Love never ends. But if there are prophecies, they will be set aside; if there are tongues, they will cease; if there is knowledge, it will be set aside. **13:9** For we know in part, and we prophesy in part, **13:10** but when what is perfect comes, the partial will be set aside. **13:11** When I was a child, I talked like a child, I thought like a child, I reasoned like a child. But when I became an adult, I set aside childish ways. **13:12** For now we see in a mirror indirectly, but then we will see face to face. Now I know in part, but then I will know fully, just as I have been fully known. **13:13** And now these three remain: faith, hope, and love. But the greatest of these is love.

Prophecy and Tongues

14:1 Pursue love and be eager for the spiritual gifts, especially that you may prophesy. **14:2** For the one speaking in a tongue does not speak to

people but to God, for no one understands; he is speaking mysteries by the Spirit. **14:3** But the one who prophesies speaks to people for their strengthening, encouragement, and consolation. **14:4** The one who speaks in a tongue builds himself up, but the one who prophesies builds up the church. **14:5** I wish you all spoke in tongues, but even more that you would prophesy. The one who prophesies is greater than the one who speaks in tongues, unless he interprets so that the church may be strengthened.

14:6 Now, brothers and sisters, if I come to you speaking in tongues, how will I help you unless I speak to you with a revelation or with knowledge or prophecy or teaching? **14:7** It is similar for lifeless things that make a sound, like a flute or harp. Unless they make a distinction in the notes, how can what is played on the flute or harp be understood? **14:8** If, for example, the trumpet makes an unclear sound, who will get ready for battle? **14:9** It is the same for you. If you do not speak clearly with your tongue, how will anyone know what is being said? For you will be speaking into the air. **14:10** There are probably many kinds of languages in the world, and none is without meaning. **14:11** If then I do not know the meaning of a language, I will be a foreigner to the speaker and the speaker a foreigner to me. **14:12** It is the same with you. Since you are eager for manifestations of the Spirit, seek to abound in order to strengthen the church.

14:13 So then, one who speaks in a tongue should pray that he may interpret. **14:14** If I pray in a tongue, my spirit prays, but my mind is unproductive. **14:15** What should I do? I will pray with my spirit, but I will also pray with my mind. I will sing praises with my spirit, but I will also sing praises with my mind. **14:16** Otherwise, if you are praising God with your spirit, how can someone without the gift say "Amen" to your thanksgiving, since he does not know what you are saying? **14:17** For you are certainly giving thanks well, but the other person is not strengthened. **14:18** I thank God that I speak in tongues more than all of you, **14:19** but in the church I want to speak five words with my mind to instruct others, rather than ten thousand words in a tongue.

14:20 Brothers and sisters, do not be children in your thinking. Instead, be infants in evil, but in your thinking be mature. **14:21** It is written in the law: "***By people with strange tongues and by the lips of strangers I will speak to this people, yet not even in this way will they listen to me***," says the Lord. **14:22** So then, tongues are a sign not for believers but for unbelievers. Prophecy, however, is not for unbelievers but for believers. **14:23** So if the whole church comes together and all speak in tongues, and unbelievers or uninformed people enter, will they not say that you have lost your minds? **14:24** But if all prophesy, and an unbeliever or uninformed person enters, he will be convicted by all, he will be called to account by all. **14:25** The secrets of his heart are disclosed, and in this way he will fall down with his face to the ground and worship God, declaring, "God is really among you."

Church Order

14:26 What should you do then, brothers and sisters? When you come together, each one has a song, has a lesson, has a revelation, has a tongue, has an interpretation. Let all these things be done for the strengthening of the church. **14:27** If someone speaks in a tongue, it should be two, or at the most three, one after the other, and someone must interpret. **14:28** But if there is no interpreter, he should be silent in the church. Let him speak to himself and to God. **14:29** Two or three prophets should speak and the others should evaluate what is said. **14:30** And if someone sitting down receives a revelation, the person who is speaking should conclude. **14:31** For you can all prophesy one after another, so all can learn and be encouraged. **14:32** Indeed, the spirits of the prophets are subject to the prophets, **14:33** for God is not characterized by disorder but by peace.

As in all the churches of the saints, **14:34** the women should be silent in the churches, for they are not permitted to speak. Rather, let them be in submission, as in fact the law says. **14:35** If they want to find out about something, they should ask their husbands at home, because it is disgraceful for a woman to speak in church. **14:36** Did the word of God begin with you, or did it come to you alone?

14:37 If anyone considers himself a prophet or spiritual person, he should acknowledge that what I write to you is the Lord's command. **14:38** If someone does not recognize this, he is not recognized. **14:39** So then, brothers and sisters, be eager to prophesy, and do not forbid anyone from speaking in tongues. **14:40** And do everything in a decent and orderly manner.

Christ's Resurrection

15:1 Now I want to make clear for you, brothers and sisters, the gospel that I preached to you, that you received and on which you stand, **15:2** and by which you are being saved, if you hold firmly to the message I preached to you – unless you believed in vain. **15:3** For I passed on to you as of first importance what I also received – that Christ died for our sins according to the scriptures, **15:4** and that he was buried, and that he was raised on the third day according to the scriptures, **15:5** and that he appeared to Cephas, then to the twelve. **15:6** Then he appeared to more than five hundred of the brothers and sisters at one time, most of whom are still alive, though some have fallen asleep. **15:7** Then he appeared to James, then to all the apostles. **15:8** Last of all, as though to one born at the wrong time, he appeared to me also. **15:9** For I am the least of the apostles, unworthy to be called an apostle, because I persecuted the church of God. **15:10** But by the grace of God I am what I am, and his grace to me has not been in vain. In fact, I worked harder than all of them – yet not I, but the grace of God with me. **15:11** Whether then it was I or they, this is the way we preach and this is the way you believed.

No Resurrection?

15:12 Now if Christ is being preached as raised from the dead, how can some of you say there is no resurrection of the dead? **15:13** But if there is no resurrection of the dead, then not even Christ has been raised. **15:14** And if Christ has not been raised, then our preaching is futile and your faith is empty. **15:15** Also, we are found to be false witnesses about God, because we have testified against God that he raised Christ from the dead, when in reality he did not raise him, if indeed the dead are not raised. **15:16** For if the dead are not raised, then not even Christ has been raised. **15:17** And if Christ has not been raised, your faith is useless; you are still in your sins. **15:18** Furthermore, those who have fallen asleep in Christ have also perished. **15:19** For if only in this life we have hope in Christ, we should be pitied more than anyone.

15:20 But now Christ has been raised from the dead, the firstfruits of those who have fallen asleep. **15:21** For since death came through a man, the resurrection of the dead also came through a man. **15:22** For just as in Adam all die, so also in Christ all will be made alive. **15:23** But each in his own order: Christ, the firstfruits; then when Christ comes, those who belong to him. **15:24** Then comes the end, when he hands over the kingdom to God the Father, when he has brought to an end all rule and all authority and power. **15:25** For he must reign until he has put all his enemies under his feet. **15:26** The last enemy to be eliminated is death. **15:27** For *he has put everything in subjection under his feet*. But when it says "everything" has been put in subjection, it is clear that this does not include the one who put everything in subjection to him. **15:28** And when all things are subjected to him, then the Son himself will be subjected to the one who subjected everything to him, so that God may be all in all.

15:29 Otherwise, what will those do who are baptized for the dead? If the dead are not raised at all, then why are they baptized for them? **15:30** Why too are we in danger every hour? **15:31** Every day I am in danger of death! This is as sure as my boasting in you, which I have in Christ Jesus our Lord. **15:32** If from a human point of view I fought with wild beasts at Ephesus, what did it benefit me? If the dead are not raised, *let us eat and drink, for tomorrow we die*. **15:33** Do not be deceived: "Bad company corrupts good morals." **15:34** Sober up as you should, and stop sinning! For some have no knowledge of God – I say this to your shame!

The Resurrection Body

15:35 But someone will say, "How are the dead raised? With what kind of body will they come?" **15:36** Fool! What you sow will not come to life unless it dies. **15:37** And what you sow is not the body that is to be, but a bare seed – perhaps of wheat or something else. **15:38** But God gives it a body just as he planned, and to each of the seeds a body of its own. **15:39** All flesh is not the same: People have one flesh, animals have another, birds and fish another. **15:40** And there are heavenly bodies and earthly bodies. The glory of the heavenly body is one sort and the earthly another. **15:41** There is one glory of the sun, and another glory of the moon and another glory of the stars, for star differs from star in glory.

15:42 It is the same with the resurrection of the dead. What is sown is perishable, what is raised is imperishable. **15:43** It is sown in dishonor, it is raised in glory; it is sown in weakness, it is raised in power; **15:44** it is sown a natural body, it is raised a spiritual body. If there is a natural body, there is also a spiritual body. **15:45** So also it is written, "*The first man, Adam, became a living person*"; the last Adam became a life-giving spirit. **15:46** However, the spiritual did not come first, but the natural, and then the spiritual. **15:47** The first man is from the earth, made of dust; the second man is from heaven. **15:48** Like the one made of dust, so too are those made of dust, and like the one from heaven, so too those who are heavenly. **15:49** And just as we have borne the image of the man of dust, let us also bear the image of the man of heaven.

15:50 Now this is what I am saying, brothers and sisters: Flesh and blood cannot inherit the kingdom of God, nor does the perishable inherit the imperishable. **15:51** Listen, I will tell you a mystery: We will not all sleep, but we will all be changed – **15:52** in a moment, in the blinking of an eye, at the last trumpet. For the trumpet will sound, and the dead will be raised imperishable, and we will be changed. **15:53** For this perishable body must put on the imperishable, and this mortal body must put on immortality. **15:54** Now when this perishable puts on the imperishable, and this mortal puts on immortality, then the saying that is written will happen,

"Death has been swallowed up in victory."

15:55 "Where, O death, is your victory?
Where, O death, is your sting?"

15:56 The sting of death is sin, and the power of sin is the law. **15:57** But thanks be to God, who gives us the victory through our Lord Jesus Christ! **15:58** So then, dear brothers and sisters, be firm. Do not be moved! Always be outstanding in the work of the Lord, knowing that your labor is not in vain in the Lord.

A Collection to Aid Jewish Christians

16:1 With regard to the collection for the saints, please follow the directions that I gave to the churches of Galatia: **16:2** On the first day of the week, each of you should set aside some income and save it to the extent that God has blessed you, so that a collection will not have to be made when I come. **16:3** Then, when I arrive, I will send those whom you approve with letters of explanation to carry your gift to Jerusalem. **16:4** And if it seems advisable that I should go also, they will go with me.

Paul's Plans to Visit

16:5 But I will come to you after I have gone through Macedonia – for I will be going through Macedonia – **16:6** and perhaps I will stay with you, or even spend the winter, so that you can send me on my journey, wherever I go. **16:7** For I do not want to see you now in passing, since I hope to spend some time with you, if the Lord allows. **16:8** But I will stay in Ephesus until Pentecost, **16:9** because a door of great opportunity stands wide open for me, but there are many opponents.

16:10 Now if Timothy comes, see that he has nothing to fear among you, for he is doing the Lord's work, as I am too. **16:11** So then, let no one treat him with contempt. But send him on his way in peace so that he may come to me. For I am expecting him with the brothers.

16:12 With regard to our brother Apollos: I strongly encouraged him to visit you with the other brothers, but it was simply not his intention to come now. He will come when he has the opportunity.

Final Challenge and Blessing

16:13 Stay alert, stand firm in the faith, show courage, be strong. **16:14** Everything you do should be done in love.

16:15 Now, brothers and sisters, you know about the household of Stephanus, that as the first converts of Achaia, they devoted themselves to ministry for the saints. I urge you **16:16** also to submit to people like this, and to everyone who cooperates in the work and labors hard. **16:17** I was glad about the arrival of Stephanus, Fortunatus, and Achaicus because they have supplied the fellowship with you that I lacked. **16:18** For they refreshed my spirit and yours. So then, recognize people like this.

16:19 The churches in the province of Asia send greetings to you. Aquila and Prisca greet you warmly in the Lord, with the church that meets in their house. **16:20** All the brothers and sisters send greetings. Greet one another with a holy kiss.

16:21 I, Paul, send this greeting with my own hand.

16:22 Let anyone who has no love for the Lord be accursed. Our Lord, come!

16:23 The grace of the Lord Jesus be with you.

16:24 My love be with all of you in Christ Jesus.

Book 47. 2 Corinthians

Salutation

1:1 From Paul, an apostle of Christ Jesus by the will of God, and Timothy our brother, to the church of God that is in Corinth, with all the saints who are in all Achaia. **1:2** Grace and peace to you from God our Father and the Lord Jesus Christ!

Thanksgiving for God's Comfort

1:3 Blessed is the God and Father of our Lord Jesus Christ, the Father of mercies and God of all comfort, **1:4** who comforts us in all our troubles so that we may be able to comfort those experiencing any trouble with the comfort with which we ourselves are comforted by God. **1:5** For just as the sufferings of Christ overflow toward us, so also our comfort through Christ overflows to you. **1:6** But if we are afflicted, it is for your comfort and salvation; if we are comforted, it is for your comfort that you experience in your patient endurance of the same sufferings that we also suffer. **1:7** And our hope for you is steadfast because we know that as you share in our sufferings, so also you will share in our comfort. **1:8** For we do not want you to be unaware, brothers and sisters, regarding the affliction that happened to us in the province of Asia, that we were burdened excessively, beyond our strength, so that we despaired even of living. **1:9** Indeed we felt as if the sentence of death had been passed against us, so that we would not trust in ourselves but in God who raises the dead. **1:10** He delivered us from so great a risk of death, and he will deliver us. We have set our hope on him that he will deliver us yet again, **1:11** as you also join in helping us by prayer, so that many people may give thanks to God on our behalf for the gracious gift given to us through the help of many.

Paul Defends His Changed Plans

1:12 For our reason for confidence is this: the testimony of our conscience, that with pure motives and sincerity which are from God – not by human wisdom but by the grace of God – we conducted ourselves in the world, and all the more toward you. **1:13** For we do not write you anything other than what you can read and also understand. But I hope that you will understand completely **1:14** just as also you have partly understood us, that we are your source of pride just as you also are ours in the day of the Lord Jesus. **1:15** And with this confidence I intended to come to you first so that you would get a second opportunity to see us, **1:16** and through your help to go on into Macedonia and then from Macedonia to come back to you and be helped on our way into Judea by you.

1:17 Therefore when I was planning to do this, I did not do so without thinking about what I was doing, did I? Or do I make my plans according to mere human standards that I would be saying both "Yes, yes" and "No, no" at the same time? **1:18** But as God is faithful, our message to you is not "Yes" and "No." **1:19** For the Son of God, Jesus Christ, the one who was proclaimed among you by us – by me and Silvanus and Timothy – was not "Yes" and "No," but it has always been "Yes" in him. **1:20** For every one of God's promises are "Yes" in him; therefore also through him the "Amen" is spoken, to the glory we give to God. **1:21** But it is God who establishes us together with you in Christ and who anointed us, **1:22** who also sealed us and gave us the Spirit in our hearts as a down payment.

Why Paul Postponed His Visit

1:23 Now I appeal to God as my witness, that to spare you I did not come again to Corinth. **1:24** I do not mean that we rule over your faith, but we are workers with you for your joy, because by faith you stand firm. **2:1** So I made up my own mind not to pay you another painful visit. **2:2** For if I make you sad, who would be left to make me glad but the one I caused to be sad? **2:3** And I wrote this very thing to you, so that when I came I would not have sadness from those who ought to make me rejoice, since I am confident in you all that my joy would be yours. **2:4** For out of great distress and anguish of heart I wrote to you with many tears, not to make you sad, but to let you know the love that I have especially for you. **2:5** But if anyone has caused sadness, he has not saddened me alone, but to some extent (not to exaggerate) he has saddened all of you as well. **2:6** This punishment on such an individual by the majority is enough for him, **2:7** so that now instead you should rather forgive and comfort him. This will keep him from being overwhelmed by excessive grief to the point of despair. **2:8** Therefore I urge you to reaffirm your love for him. **2:9** For this reason also I wrote you: to test you to see if you are obedient in everything. **2:10** If you forgive anyone for anything, I also forgive him – for indeed what I have forgiven (if I have forgiven anything) I did so for you in the presence of Christ, **2:11** so that we may not be exploited by Satan (for we are not ignorant of his schemes). **2:12** Now when I arrived in Troas to proclaim the gospel of Christ, even though the Lord had opened a door of opportunity for me, **2:13** I had no relief in my spirit, because I did not find my brother Titus there. So I said good-bye to them and set out for Macedonia.

Apostolic Ministry

2:14 But thanks be to God who always leads us in triumphal procession in Christ and who makes known through us the fragrance that consists of the knowledge of him in every place. **2:15** For we are a sweet aroma of Christ to God among those who are being saved and among those who are perishing – **2:16** to the latter an odor from death to death, but to the former a fragrance from life to life. And who is adequate for these things? **2:17** For we are not like so many others, hucksters who peddle the word of God for profit, but we are speaking in Christ before God as persons of sincerity, as persons sent from God.

A Living Letter

3:1 Are we beginning to commend ourselves again? We don't need letters of recommendation to you or from you as some other people do, do we? **3:2** You yourselves are our letter, written on our hearts, known and read by everyone, **3:3** revealing that you are a letter of Christ, delivered by us, written not with ink but by the Spirit of the living God, not *on stone tablets* but on tablets of human hearts.

3:4 Now we have such confidence in God through Christ. **3:5** Not that we are adequate in ourselves to consider anything as if it were coming from ourselves, but our adequacy is from God, **3:6** who made us adequate to be servants of a new covenant not based on the letter but on the Spirit, for the letter kills, but the Spirit gives life.

The Greater Glory of the Spirit's Ministry

3:7 But if the ministry that produced death – carved in letters on stone tablets – came with glory, so that the Israelites could not keep their eyes fixed on the face of Moses because of the glory of his face (a glory which was made ineffective), **3:8** how much more glorious will the ministry of the Spirit be? **3:9** For if there was glory in the ministry that produced condemnation, how much more does the ministry that produces righteousness excel in glory! **3:10** For indeed, what had been glorious now has no glory because of the tremendously greater glory of what replaced it. **3:11** For if what was made ineffective came with glory, how much more has what remains come in glory! **3:12** Therefore, since we have such a hope, we behave with great boldness, **3:13** and not like Moses who used to put a veil over his face to keep the Israelites from staring at the result of the glory that was made ineffective. **3:14** But their minds were closed. For to this very day, the same veil remains when they hear the old covenant read. It has not been removed because only in Christ is it taken away. **3:15** But until this very day whenever Moses is read, a veil lies over their minds, **3:16** but when one turns to the Lord, *the veil is removed.* **3:17** Now the Lord is the Spirit, and where the Spirit of the Lord is present, there is freedom. **3:18** And we all, with unveiled faces reflecting the glory of the Lord, are being transformed into the same image from one degree of glory to another, which is from the Lord, who is the Spirit.

Paul's Perseverance in Ministry

4:1 Therefore, since we have this ministry, just as God has shown us mercy, we do not become discouraged. **4:2** But we have rejected shameful hidden deeds, not behaving with deceptiveness or distorting the word of God, but by open proclamation of the truth we commend ourselves to everyone's conscience before God. **4:3** But even if our gospel is veiled, it is veiled only to those who are perishing, **4:4** among whom the god of this age has blinded the minds of those who do not believe so they would not see the light of the glorious gospel of Christ, who is the image of God. **4:5** For we do not proclaim ourselves, but Jesus Christ as Lord, and ourselves as your slaves for Jesus' sake. **4:6** For God, who said "*Let light shine out of darkness,*" is the one who shined in our hearts to give us the light of the glorious knowledge of God in the face of Christ.

An Eternal Weight of Glory

4:7 But we have this treasure in clay jars, so that the extraordinary power belongs to God and does not come from us. **4:8** We are experiencing trouble on every side, but are not crushed; we are perplexed, but not driven to despair; **4:9** we are persecuted, but not abandoned; we are knocked down, but not destroyed, **4:10** always carrying around in our body the death of Jesus, so that the life of Jesus may also be made visible in our body. **4:11** For we who are alive are constantly being handed over to death for Jesus' sake, so that the life of Jesus may also be made visible in our mortal body. **4:12** As a result, death is at work in us, but life is at work in you. **4:13** But since we have the same spirit of faith as that shown in what has been written, "*I believed; therefore I spoke,*" we also believe, therefore we also speak. **4:14** We do so because we know that the one who raised up Jesus will also raise us up with Jesus and will bring us with you into his presence. **4:15** For all these things are for your sake, so that the grace that is including more and more people may cause thanksgiving to increase to the glory of God. **4:16** Therefore we do not despair, but even if our physical body is wearing away, our inner person is being renewed day by day. **4:17** For our momentary, light suffering is producing for us an eternal weight of glory far beyond all comparison **4:18** because we are not looking at what can be seen but at what cannot be seen. For what can be seen is temporary, but what cannot be seen is eternal.

Living by Faith, Not by Sight

5:1 For we know that if our earthly house, the tent we live in, is dismantled, we have a building from God, a house not built by human hands, that is eternal in the heavens. **5:2** For in this earthly house we groan, because we desire to put on our heavenly dwelling, **5:3** if indeed, after we have put on our heavenly house, we will not be found naked. **5:4** For we groan while we are in this tent, since we are weighed down, because we do not want to be unclothed, but clothed, so that what is mortal may be swallowed up by life. **5:5** Now the one who prepared us for this very purpose is God, who gave us the Spirit as a down payment. **5:6** Therefore we are always full of courage, and we know that as long as we are alive here on earth we are absent from the Lord – **5:7** for we live by faith, not by sight. **5:8** Thus we are full of courage and would prefer to be away from the body and at home with the Lord. **5:9** So then whether we are alive or away, we make it our ambition to please him. **5:10** For we must all appear before the judgment seat of Christ, so that each one may be paid back according to what he has done while in the body, whether good or evil.

The Message of Reconciliation

5:11 Therefore, because we know the fear of the Lord, we try to persuade people, but we are well known to God, and I hope we are well known to your consciences too. **5:12** We are not trying to commend ourselves to you again, but are giving you an opportunity to be proud of us, so that you may be able to answer those who take pride in outward appearance and not in what is in the heart. **5:13** For if we are out of our minds, it is for God; if we are of sound mind, it is for you. **5:14** For the love of Christ controls us, since we have concluded this, that Christ died for all; therefore all have died. **5:15** And he died for all so that those who live should no longer live for themselves but for him who died for them and was raised. **5:16** So then from now on we acknowledge no one from an outward human point of view. Even though we have known Christ from such a human point of view, now we do not know him in that way any longer. **5:17** So then, if anyone is in Christ, he is a new creation; what is old has passed away – look, what is new has come! **5:18** And all these things are from God who reconciled us to himself through Christ, and who has given us the ministry of reconciliation. **5:19** In other words, in Christ God was reconciling the world to himself, not counting people's trespasses against them, and he has given us the message of reconciliation. **5:20** Therefore we are ambassadors for Christ, as though God were making His plea through us. We plead with you on Christ's behalf, "Be reconciled to God!" **5:21** God made the one who did not know sin to be sin for us, so that in him we would become the righteousness of God.

God's Suffering Servants

6:1 Now because we are fellow workers, we also urge you not to receive the grace of God in vain. **6:2** For he says, "*I heard you at the acceptable time, and in the day of salvation I helped you.*" Look, now is *the acceptable time*; look, now is *the day of salvation*! **6:3** We do not give anyone an occasion for taking an offense in anything, so that no fault may be found with our ministry. **6:4** But as God's servants, we have commended ourselves in every

way, with great endurance, in persecutions, in difficulties, in distresses, **6:5** in beatings, in imprisonments, in riots, in troubles, in sleepless nights, in hunger, **6:6** by purity, by knowledge, by patience, by benevolence, by the Holy Spirit, by genuine love, **6:7** by truthful teaching, by the power of God, with weapons of righteousness both for the right hand and for the left, **6:8** through glory and dishonor, through slander and praise; regarded as impostors, and yet true; **6:9** as unknown, and yet well-known; as dying and yet – see! – we continue to live; as those who are scourged and yet not executed; **6:10** as sorrowful, but always rejoicing, as poor, but making many rich, as having nothing, and yet possessing everything.

6:11 We have spoken freely to you, Corinthians; our heart has been opened wide to you. **6:12** Our affection for you is not restricted, but you are restricted in your affections for us. **6:13** Now as a fair exchange – I speak as to my children – open wide your hearts to us also.

Unequal Partners

6:14 Do not become partners with those who do not believe, for what partnership is there between righteousness and lawlessness, or what fellowship does light have with darkness? **6:15** And what agreement does Christ have with Beliar? Or what does a believer share in common with an unbeliever? **6:16** And what mutual agreement does the temple of God have with idols? For we are the temple of the living God, just as God said, "*I will live in them and will walk among them, and I will be their God, and they will be my people.*" **6:17** Therefore "*come out from their midst, and be separate*," says the Lord, "*and touch no unclean thing, and I will welcome you,* **6:18** *and I will be a father to you, and you will be my sons and daughters*," says the All-Powerful Lord.

Self-Purification

7:1 Therefore, since we have these promises, dear friends, let us cleanse ourselves from everything that could defile the body and the spirit, and thus accomplish holiness out of reverence for God. **7:2** Make room for us in your hearts; we have wronged no one, we have ruined no one, we have exploited no one. **7:3** I do not say this to condemn you, for I told you before that you are in our hearts so that we die together and live together with you.

A Letter That Caused Sadness

7:4 I have great confidence in you; I take great pride on your behalf. I am filled with encouragement; I am overflowing with joy in the midst of all our suffering. **7:5** For even when we came into Macedonia, our body had no rest at all, but we were troubled in every way – struggles from the outside, fears from within. **7:6** But God, who encourages the downhearted, encouraged us by the arrival of Titus. **7:7** We were encouraged not only by his arrival, but also by the encouragement you gave him, as he reported to us your longing, your mourning, your deep concern for me, so that I rejoiced more than ever. **7:8** For even if I made you sad by my letter, I do not regret having written it (even though I did regret it, for I see that my letter made you sad, though only for a short time). **7:9** Now I rejoice, not because you were made sad, but because you were made sad to the point of repentance. For you were made sad as God intended, so that you were not harmed in any way by us. **7:10** For sadness as intended by God produces a repentance that leads to salvation, leaving no regret, but worldly sadness brings about death. **7:11** For see what this very thing, this sadness as God intended, has produced in you: what eagerness, what defense of yourselves, what indignation, what alarm, what longing, what deep concern, what punishment! In everything you have proved yourselves to be innocent in this matter. **7:12** So then, even though I wrote to you, it was not on account of the one who did wrong, or on account of the one who was wronged, but to reveal to you your eagerness on our behalf before God. **7:13** Therefore we have been encouraged. And in addition to our own encouragement, we rejoiced even more at the joy of Titus, because all of you have refreshed his spirit. **7:14** For if I have boasted to him about anything concerning you, I have not been embarrassed by you, but just as everything we said to you was true, so our boasting to Titus about you has proved true as well. **7:15** And his affection for you is much greater when he remembers the obedience of you all, how you welcomed him with fear and trembling. **7:16** I rejoice because in everything I am fully confident in you.

Completing the Collection for the Saints

8:1 Now we make known to you, brothers and sisters, the grace of God given to the churches of Macedonia, **8:2** that during a severe ordeal of suffering, their abundant joy and their extreme poverty have overflowed in the wealth of their generosity. **8:3** For I testify, they gave according to their means and beyond their means. They did so voluntarily, **8:4** begging us with great earnestness for the blessing and fellowship of helping the saints. **8:5** And they did this not just as we had hoped, but they gave themselves first to the Lord and to us by the will of God. **8:6** Thus we urged Titus that, just as he had previously begun this work, so also he should complete this act of kindness for you. **8:7** But as you excel in everything – in faith, in speech, in knowledge, and in all eagerness and in the love from us that is in you – make sure that you excel in this act of kindness too. **8:8** I am not saying this as a command, but I am testing the genuineness of your love by comparison with the eagerness of others. **8:9** For you know the grace of our Lord Jesus Christ, that although he was rich, he became poor for your sakes, so that you by his poverty could become rich. **8:10** So here is my opinion on this matter: It is to your advantage, since you made a good start last year both in your giving and your desire to give, **8:11** to finish what you started, so that just as you wanted to do it eagerly, you can also complete it according to your means. **8:12** For if the eagerness is present, the gift itself is acceptable according to whatever one has, not according to what he does not have. **8:13** For I do not say this so there would be relief for others and suffering for you, but as a matter of equality. **8:14** At the present time, your abundance will meet their need, so that one day their abundance may also meet your need, and thus there may be equality, **8:15** as it is written: "*The one who gathered much did not have too much, and the one who gathered little did not have too little.*"

The Mission of Titus

8:16 But thanks be to God who put in the heart of Titus the same devotion I have for you, **8:17** because he not only accepted our request, but since he was very eager, he is coming to you of his own accord. **8:18** And we are sending along with him the brother who is praised by all the churches for his work in spreading the gospel. **8:19** In addition, this brother has also been chosen by the churches as our traveling companion as we administer this generous gift to the glory of the Lord himself and to show our readiness to help. **8:20** We did this as a precaution so that no one should blame us in regard to this generous gift we are administering. **8:21** For we are *concerned about what is right not only before the Lord but also before men.* **8:22** And we are sending with them our brother whom we have tested many times and found eager in many matters, but who now is much more eager than ever because of the great confidence he has in you. **8:23** If there is any question about Titus, he is my partner and fellow worker among you; if there is any question about our brothers, they are messengers of the churches, a glory to Christ. **8:24** Therefore show them openly before the churches the proof of your love and of our pride in you.

Preparing the Gift

9:1 For it is not necessary for me to write you about this service to the saints, **9:2** because I know your eagerness to help. I keep boasting to the Macedonians about this eagerness of yours, that Achaia has been ready to give since last year, and your zeal to participate has stirred up most of them. **9:3** But I am sending these brothers so that our boasting about you may not be empty in this case, so that you may be ready just as I kept telling them. **9:4** For if any of the Macedonians should come with me and find that you are not ready to give, we would be humiliated (not to mention you) by this confidence we had in you. **9:5** Therefore I thought it necessary to urge these brothers to go to you in advance and to arrange ahead of time the generous contribution you had promised, so this may be ready as a generous gift and not as something you feel forced to do. **9:6** My point is this: The person who sows sparingly will also reap sparingly, and the person who sows generously will also reap generously. **9:7** Each one of you should give just as he has decided in his heart, not reluctantly or under compulsion, because God loves a cheerful giver. **9:8** And God is able to make all grace overflow to you so that because you have enough of everything in every way at all times, you will overflow in every good work. **9:9** Just as it is written, "*He has scattered widely, he has given to the poor; his righteousness remains forever.*" **9:10** Now God who provides seed for the sower and bread for food will provide and multiply your supply of seed and will cause the harvest of your righteousness to grow. **9:11** You will be enriched in every way so that you may be generous on every occasion, which is producing through us thanksgiving to God, **9:12** because the service of this ministry is not only providing for the needs of the saints but is also overflowing with many thanks to God. **9:13** Through the evidence of this service they will glorify God because of your obedience to your confession in the gospel of Christ and the generosity of your sharing with them and with everyone. **9:14** And in their prayers on your behalf they long for you because of the extraordinary grace God has shown to you. **9:15** Thanks be to God for his indescribable gift!

Paul's Authority from the Lord

10:1 Now I, Paul, appeal to you personally by the meekness and gentleness of Christ (I who am meek when present among you, but am full of courage toward you when away!) – **10:2** now I ask that when I am present I may not have to be bold with the confidence that (I expect) I will dare to use against some who consider us to be behaving according to human standards. **10:3** For though we live as human beings, we do not wage war according to human standards, **10:4** for the weapons of our warfare are not human weapons, but are made powerful by God for tearing down strongholds. We tear down arguments **10:5** and every arrogant obstacle that is raised up against the knowledge of God, and we take every thought captive to make it obey Christ. **10:6** We are also ready to punish every act of disobedience, whenever your obedience is complete. **10:7** You are looking at outward appearances. If anyone is confident that he belongs to Christ, he should reflect on this again: Just as he himself belongs to Christ, so too do we. **10:8** For if I boast somewhat more about our authority that the Lord gave us for building you up and not for tearing you down, I will not be ashamed of doing so. **10:9** I do not want to seem as though I am trying to terrify you with my letters, **10:10** because some say, "His letters are weighty and forceful, but his physical presence is weak and his speech is of no account." **10:11** Let such a person consider this: What we say by letters when we are absent, we also are in actions when we are present.

Paul's Mission

10:12 For we would not dare to classify or compare ourselves with some of those who recommend themselves. But when they measure themselves by themselves and compare themselves with themselves, they are without understanding. **10:13** But we will not boast beyond certain limits, but will confine our boasting according to the limits of the work to which God has appointed us, that reaches even as far as you. **10:14** For we were not overextending ourselves, as though we did not reach as far as you, because we were the first to reach as far as you with the gospel about Christ. **10:15** Nor do we boast beyond certain limits in the work done by others, but we hope that as your faith continues to grow, our work may be greatly expanded among you according to our limits, **10:16** so that we may preach the gospel in the regions that lie beyond you, and not boast of work already done in another person's area. **10:17** But *the one who boasts must boast in the Lord*. **10:18** For it is not the person who commends himself who is approved, but the person the Lord commends.

Paul and His Opponents

11:1 I wish that you would be patient with me in a little foolishness, but indeed you are being patient with me! **11:2** For I am jealous for you with godly jealousy, because I promised you in marriage to one husband, to present you as a pure virgin to Christ. **11:3** But I am afraid that just as the serpent deceived Eve by his treachery, your minds may be led astray from a sincere and pure devotion to Christ. **11:4** For if someone comes and proclaims another Jesus different from the one we proclaimed, or if you receive a different spirit than the one you received, or a different gospel than the one you accepted, you put up with it well enough! **11:5** For I consider myself not at all inferior to those "super-apostles." **11:6** And even if I am unskilled in speaking, yet I am certainly not so in knowledge. Indeed, we have made this plain to you in everything in every way. **11:7** Or did I commit a sin by humbling myself so that you could be exalted, because I proclaimed the gospel of God to you free of charge? **11:8** I robbed other churches by receiving support from them so that I could serve you! **11:9** When I was with you and was in need, I was not a burden to anyone, for the brothers who came from Macedonia fully supplied my needs. I kept myself from being a burden to you in any way, and will continue to do so. **11:10** As the truth of Christ is in me, this boasting of mine will not be stopped in the regions of Achaia. **11:11** Why? Because I do not love you? God knows I do! **11:12** And what I am doing I will continue to do, so that I may eliminate any opportunity for those who want a chance to be regarded as our equals in the things they boast about. **11:13** For such people are false apostles, deceitful workers, disguising themselves as apostles of Christ. **11:14** And no wonder, for even Satan disguises himself as an angel of light. **11:15** Therefore it is not surprising his servants also disguise themselves as servants of righteousness, whose end will correspond to their actions.

Paul's Sufferings for Christ

11:16 I say again, let no one think that I am a fool. But if you do, then at least accept me as a fool, so that I too may boast a little. **11:17** What I am saying with this boastful confidence I do not say the way the Lord would. Instead it is, as it were, foolishness. **11:18** Since many are boasting according to human standards, I too will boast. **11:19** For since you are so wise, you put up with fools gladly. **11:20** For you put up with it if someone makes slaves of you, if someone exploits you, if someone takes advantage of you, if someone behaves arrogantly toward you, if someone strikes you in the face. **11:21** (To my disgrace I must say that we were too weak for that!) But whatever anyone else dares to boast about (I am speaking foolishly), I also dare to boast about the same thing. **11:22** Are they Hebrews? So am I. Are they Israelites? So am I. Are they descendants of Abraham? So am I. **11:23** Are they servants of Christ? (I am talking like I am out of my mind!) I am even more so: with much greater labors, with far more imprisonments, with more severe beatings, facing death many times. **11:24** Five times I received from the Jews forty lashes less one. **11:25** Three times I was beaten with a rod. Once I received a stoning. Three times I suffered shipwreck. A night and a day I spent adrift in the open sea. **11:26** I have been on journeys many times, in dangers from rivers, in dangers from robbers, in dangers from my own countrymen, in dangers from Gentiles, in dangers in the city, in dangers in the wilderness, in dangers at sea, in dangers from false brothers, **11:27** in hard work and toil, through many sleepless nights, in hunger and thirst, many times without food, in cold and without enough clothing. **11:28** Apart from other things, there is the daily pressure on me of my anxious concern for all the churches. **11:29** Who is weak, and I am not weak? Who is led into sin, and I do not burn with indignation? **11:30** If I must boast, I will boast about the things that show my weakness. **11:31** The God and Father of the Lord Jesus, who is blessed forever, knows I am not lying. **11:32** In Damascus, the governor under King Aretas was guarding the city of Damascus in order to arrest me, **11:33** but I was let down in a rope-basket through a window in the city wall, and escaped his hands.

Paul's Thorn in the Flesh

12:1 It is necessary to go on boasting. Though it is not profitable, I will go on to visions and revelations from the Lord. **12:2** I know a man in Christ who fourteen years ago (whether in the body or out of the body I do not know, God knows) was caught up to the third heaven. **12:3** And I know that this man (whether in the body or apart from the body I do not know, God knows) **12:4** was caught up into paradise and heard things too sacred to be put into words, things that a person is not permitted to speak. **12:5** On behalf of such an individual I will boast, but on my own behalf I will not boast, except about my weaknesses. **12:6** For even if I wish to boast, I will not be a fool, for I would be telling the truth, but I refrain from this so that no one may regard me beyond what he sees in me or what he hears from me, **12:7** even because of the extraordinary character of the revelations. Therefore, so that I would not become arrogant, a thorn in the flesh was given to me, a messenger of Satan to trouble me – so that I would not become arrogant. **12:8** I asked the Lord three times about this, that it would depart from me. **12:9** But he said to me, "My grace is enough for you, for my power is made perfect in weakness." So then, I will boast most gladly about my weaknesses, so that the power of Christ may reside in me. **12:10** Therefore I am content with weaknesses, with insults, with troubles, with persecutions and difficulties for the sake of Christ, for whenever I am weak, then I am strong.

The Signs of an Apostle

12:11 I have become a fool. You yourselves forced me to do it, for I should have been commended by you. For I lack nothing in comparison to those "super-apostles," even though I am nothing. **12:12** Indeed, the signs of an apostle were performed among you with great perseverance by signs and wonders and powerful deeds. **12:13** For how were you treated worse than the other churches, except that I myself was not a burden to you? Forgive me this injustice! **12:14** Look, for the third time I am ready to come to you, and I will not be a burden to you, because I do not want your possessions, but you. For children should not have to save up for their parents, but parents for their children. **12:15** Now I will most gladly spend and be spent for your lives! If I love you more, am I to be loved less? **12:16** But be that as it may, I have not burdened you. Yet because I was a crafty person, I took you in by deceit! **12:17** I have not taken advantage of you through anyone I have sent to you, have I? **12:18** I urged Titus to visit you and I sent our brother along with him. Titus did not take advantage of you, did he? Did we not conduct ourselves in the same spirit? Did we not behave in the same way? **12:19** Have you been thinking all this time that we have been defending ourselves to you? We are speaking in Christ before God, and everything we do, dear friends, is to build you up. **12:20** For I am afraid that somehow when I come I will not find you what I wish, and you will find me not what you wish. I am afraid that somehow there may be quarreling, jealousy, intense anger, selfish ambition, slander, gossip, arrogance, and disorder. **12:21** I am afraid that when I come again, my God may humiliate me before you, and I will grieve for many of those who previously sinned and have not repented of the impurity, sexual immorality, and licentiousness that they have practiced.

Paul's Third Visit to Corinth

13:1 This is the third time I am coming to visit you. *By the testimony of two or three witnesses every matter will be established*. **13:2** I said before when I was present the second time and now, though absent, I say again to those who sinned previously and to all the rest, that if I come again, I will not spare anyone, **13:3** since you are demanding proof that Christ is speaking through me. He is not weak toward you but is powerful among you. **13:4** For indeed he was crucified by reason of weakness, but he lives because of God's power. For we also are weak in him, but we will live together with him, because of God's power toward you. **13:5** Put yourselves to the test to see if you are in the faith; examine yourselves! Or do you not recognize regarding yourselves that Jesus Christ is in you – unless, indeed, you fail the test! **13:6** And I hope that you will realize that we have not failed the test! **13:7** Now we pray to God that you may not do anything wrong, not so that we may appear to have passed the test, but so that you may do what is right even if we may appear to have failed the test. **13:8** For we cannot do anything against the truth, but only for the sake of the truth. **13:9** For we rejoice whenever we are weak, but you are strong. And we pray for this: that you may become fully qualified. **13:10** Because of this I am writing these things while absent, so that when I arrive I may not have to deal harshly with you by using my authority – the Lord gave it to me for building up, not for tearing down!

Final Exhortations and Greetings

13:11 Finally, brothers and sisters, rejoice, set things right, be encouraged, agree with one another, live in peace, and the God of love and peace will be with you. **13:12** Greet one another with a holy kiss. All the saints greet you. **13:13** The grace of the Lord Jesus Christ and the love of God and the fellowship of the Holy Spirit be with you all.

Book 48. Galatians

Salutation

1:1 From Paul, an apostle (not from men, nor by human agency, but by Jesus Christ and God the Father who raised him from the dead) **1:2** and all the brothers with me, to the churches of Galatia. **1:3** Grace and peace to you from God the Father and our Lord Jesus Christ, **1:4** who gave himself for our sins to rescue us from this present evil age according to the will of our God and Father, **1:5** to whom be glory forever and ever! Amen.

Occasion of the Letter

1:6 I am astonished that you are so quickly deserting the one who called you by the grace of Christ and are following a different gospel – **1:7** not that there really is another gospel, but there are some who are disturbing you and wanting to distort the gospel of Christ. **1:8** But even if we (or an angel from heaven) should preach a gospel contrary to the one we preached to you, let him be condemned to hell! **1:9** As we have said before, and now I say again, if any one is preaching to you a gospel contrary to what you received, let him be condemned to hell! **1:10** Am I now trying to gain the approval of people, or of God? Or am I trying to please people? If I were still trying to

please people, I would not be a slave of Christ!

Paul's Vindication of His Apostleship

1:11 Now I want you to know, brothers and sisters, that the gospel I preached is not of human origin. **1:12** For I did not receive it or learn it from any human source; instead I received it by a revelation of Jesus Christ.

1:13 For you have heard of my former way of life in Judaism, how I was savagely persecuting the church of God and trying to destroy it. **1:14** I was advancing in Judaism beyond many of my contemporaries in my nation, and was extremely zealous for the traditions of my ancestors. **1:15** But when the one who set me apart from birth and called me by his grace was pleased **1:16** to reveal his Son in me so that I could preach him among the Gentiles, I did not go to ask advice from any human being, **1:17** nor did I go up to Jerusalem to see those who were apostles before me, but right away I departed to Arabia, and then returned to Damascus. **1:18** Then after three years I went up to Jerusalem to visit Cephas and get information from him, and I stayed with him fifteen days. **1:19** But I saw none of the other apostles except James the Lord's brother. **1:20** I assure you that, before God, I am not lying about what I am writing to you! **1:21** Afterward I went to the regions of Syria and Cilicia. **1:22** But I was personally unknown to the churches of Judea that are in Christ. **1:23** They were only hearing, "The one who once persecuted us is now proclaiming the good news of the faith he once tried to destroy." **1:24** So they glorified God because of me.

Confirmation from the Jerusalem Apostles

2:1 Then after fourteen years I went up to Jerusalem again with Barnabas, taking Titus along too. **2:2** I went there because of a revelation and presented to them the gospel that I preach among the Gentiles. But I did so only in a private meeting with the influential people, to make sure that I was not running – or had not run – in vain. **2:3** Yet not even Titus, who was with me, was compelled to be circumcised, although he was a Greek. **2:4** Now this matter arose because of the false brothers with false pretenses who slipped in unnoticed to spy on our freedom that we have in Christ Jesus, to make us slaves. **2:5** But we did not surrender to them even for a moment, in order that the truth of the gospel would remain with you.

2:6 But from those who were influential (whatever they were makes no difference to me; God shows no favoritism between people) – those influential leaders added nothing to my message. **2:7** On the contrary, when they saw that I was entrusted with the gospel to the uncircumcised just as Peter was to the circumcised **2:8** (for he who empowered Peter for his apostleship to the circumcised also empowered me for my apostleship to the Gentiles) **2:9** and when James, Cephas, and John, who had a

reputation as pillars, recognized the grace that had been given to me, they gave to Barnabas and me the right hand of fellowship, agreeing that we would go to the Gentiles and they to the circumcised. **2:10** They requested only that we remember the poor, the very thing I also was eager to do.

Paul Rebukes Peter

2:11 But when Cephas came to Antioch, I opposed him to his face, because he had clearly done wrong. **2:12** Until certain people came from James, he had been eating with the Gentiles. But when they arrived, he stopped doing this and separated himself because he was afraid of those who were pro-circumcision. **2:13** And the rest of the Jews also joined with him in this hypocrisy, so that even Barnabas was led astray with them by their hypocrisy. **2:14** But when I saw that they were not behaving consistently with the truth of the gospel, I said to Cephas in front of them all, "If you, although you are a Jew, live like a Gentile and not like a Jew, how can you try to force the Gentiles to live like Jews?"

Jews and Gentiles are Justified by Faith

2:15 We are Jews by birth and not Gentile sinners, **2:16** yet we know that no one is justified by the works of the law but by the faithfulness of Jesus Christ. And we have come to believe in Christ Jesus, so that we may be

justified by the faithfulness of Christ and not by the works of the law, because by the works of the law no one will be justified. **2:17** But if while seeking to be justified in Christ we ourselves have also been found to be sinners, is Christ then one who encourages sin? Absolutely not! **2:18** But if I build up again those things I once destroyed, I demonstrate that I am one who breaks God's law. **2:19** For through the law I died to the law so that I may live to God. **2:20** I have been crucified with Christ, and it is no longer I who live, but Christ lives in me. So the life I now live in the body, I live because of the faithfulness of the Son of God, who loved me and gave himself for me. **2:21** I do not set aside God's grace, because if righteousness could come through the law, then Christ died for nothing!

Justification by Law or by Faith?

3:1 You foolish Galatians! Who has cast a spell on you? Before your eyes Jesus Christ was vividly portrayed as crucified! **3:2** The only thing I want to learn from you is this: Did you receive the Spirit by doing the works of the law or by believing what you heard? **3:3** Are you so foolish? Although you began with the Spirit, are you now trying to finish by human effort? **3:4** Have you suffered so many things for nothing? – if indeed it was for nothing. **3:5** Does God then give you the Spirit and work miracles among you by your doing the works of the law or by your believing what you heard?

3:6 Just as Abraham *believed God, and it was credited to him as righteousness*, **3:7** so then, understand that those who believe are the sons of Abraham. **3:8** And the scripture, foreseeing that God would justify the Gentiles by faith, proclaimed the gospel to Abraham ahead of time, saying, "*All the nations will be blessed in you.*" **3:9** So then those who believe are blessed along with Abraham the believer. **3:10** For all who rely on doing the works of the law are under a curse, because it is written, "*Cursed is everyone who does not keep on doing everything written in the book of the law.*" **3:11** Now it is clear no one is justified before God by the law, because *the righteous one will live by faith*. **3:12** But the law is not based on faith, but *the one who does* the works of the law *will live by them*. **3:13** Christ redeemed us from the curse of the law by becoming a curse for us (because it is written, "*Cursed is everyone who hangs on a tree*") **3:14** in order that in Christ Jesus the blessing of Abraham would come to the Gentiles, so that we could receive the promise of the Spirit by faith.

Inheritance Comes from Promises and not Law

3:15 Brothers and sisters, I offer an example from everyday life: When a covenant has been ratified, even though it is only a human contract, no one can set it aside or add anything to it. **3:16** Now the promises were spoken to Abraham and to his descendant. Scripture does not say, "and to the descendants," referring to many, but "*and to your descendant*," referring to one, who is Christ. **3:17** What I am saying is this: The law that came four hundred thirty years later does not cancel a covenant previously ratified by God, so as to invalidate the promise. **3:18** For if the inheritance is based on the law, it is no longer based on the promise, but God graciously gave it to Abraham through the promise.

3:19 Why then was the law given? It was added because of transgressions, until the arrival of the descendant to whom the promise had been made. It was administered through angels by an intermediary. **3:20** Now an intermediary is not for one party alone, but God is one. **3:21** Is the law therefore opposed to the promises of God? Absolutely not! For if a law had been given that was able to give life, then righteousness would certainly have come by the law. **3:22** But the scripture imprisoned everything and everyone under sin so that the promise could be given – because of the faithfulness of Jesus Christ – to those who believe.

Sons of God Are Heirs of Promise

3:23 Now before faith came we were held in custody under the law, being kept as prisoners until the coming faith would be revealed.

3:24 Thus the law had become our guardian until Christ, so that we could be declared righteous by faith. **3:25** But now that faith has come, we are no longer under a guardian. **3:26** For in Christ Jesus you are all sons of God through faith. **3:27** For all of you who were baptized into Christ have clothed yourselves with Christ. **3:28** There is neither Jew nor Greek, there is neither slave nor free, there is neither male nor female – for all of you are one in Christ Jesus. **3:29** And if you belong to Christ, then you are Abraham's descendants, heirs according to the promise.

4:1 Now I mean that the heir, as long as he is a minor, is no different from a slave, though he is the owner of everything. **4:2** But he is under guardians and managers until the date set by his father. **4:3** So also we, when we were minors, were enslaved under the basic forces of the world. **4:4** But when the appropriate time had come, God sent out his Son, born of a

woman, born under the law, **4:5** to redeem those who were under the law, so that we may be adopted as sons with full rights. **4:6** And because you are sons, God sent the Spirit of his Son into our hearts, who calls "*Abba! Father!*" **4:7** So you are no longer a slave but a son, and if you are a son, then you are also an heir through God.

Heirs of Promise Are Not to Return to Law

4:8 Formerly when you did not know God, you were enslaved to beings that by nature are not gods at all. **4:9** But now that you have come to know God (or rather to be known by God), how can you turn back again to the weak and worthless basic forces? Do you want to be enslaved to them all over again? **4:10** You are observing religious days and months and seasons and years. **4:11** I fear for you that my work for you may have been in vain. **4:12** I beg you, brothers and sisters, become like me, because I have become like you. You have done me no wrong!

Personal Appeal of Paul

4:13 But you know it was because of a physical illness that I first proclaimed the gospel to you, **4:14** and though my physical condition put you to the test, you did not despise or reject me. Instead, you welcomed me as though I were an angel of God, as though I were Christ Jesus himself! **4:15** Where then is your sense of happiness now? For I testify about you that if it were possible, you would have pulled out your eyes and given them to me! **4:16** So then, have I become your enemy by telling you the truth?

4:17 They court you eagerly, but for no good purpose; they want to exclude you, so that you would seek them eagerly. **4:18** However, it is good to be sought eagerly for a good purpose at all times, and not only when I am present with you. **4:19** My children – I am again undergoing birth pains until Christ is formed in you! **4:20** I wish I could be with you now and change my tone of voice, because I am perplexed about you.

An Appeal from Allegory

4:21 Tell me, you who want to be under the law, do you not understand the law? **4:22** For it is written that Abraham had two sons, one by the slave woman and the other by the free woman. **4:23** But one, the son by the slave woman, was born by natural descent, while the other, the son by the free woman, was born through the promise. **4:24** These things may be treated as an allegory, for these women represent two covenants. One is from Mount Sinai bearing children for slavery; this is Hagar. **4:25** Now Hagar represents Mount Sinai in Arabia and corresponds to the present Jerusalem, for she is in slavery with her children. **4:26** But the Jerusalem above is free, and she is our mother. **4:27** For it is written:

"*Rejoice, O barren woman who does not bear children;*
break forth and shout, you who have no birth pains,
because the children of the desolate woman are more numerous
than those of the woman who has a husband."

4:28 But you, brothers and sisters, are children of the promise like Isaac. **4:29** But just as at that time the one born by natural descent persecuted the one born according to the Spirit, so it is now. **4:30** But what does the scripture say? "*Throw out the slave woman and her son, for the son of the slave woman will not share the inheritance with the son*" of the free woman. **4:31** Therefore, brothers and sisters, we are not children of the slave woman but of the free woman.

Freedom of the Believer

5:1 For freedom Christ has set us free. Stand firm, then, and do not be subject again to the yoke of slavery. **5:2** Listen! I, Paul, tell you that if you let yourselves be circumcised, Christ will be of no benefit to you at all! **5:3** And I testify again to every man who lets himself be circumcised that he is obligated to obey the whole law. **5:4** You who are trying to be declared righteous by the law have been alienated from Christ; you have fallen away from grace! **5:5** For through the Spirit, by faith, we wait expectantly for the hope of righteousness. **5:6** For in Christ Jesus neither circumcision nor uncircumcision carries any weight – the only thing that matters is faith working through love.

5:7 You were running well; who prevented you from obeying the truth? **5:8** This persuasion does not come from the one who calls you! **5:9** A little yeast makes the whole batch of dough rise! **5:10** I am confident in the Lord that you will accept no other view. But the one who is confusing you will pay the penalty, whoever he may be. **5:11** Now, brothers and sisters, if I am still preaching circumcision, why am I still being persecuted? In that case the offense of the cross has been removed. **5:12** I wish those agitators would go so far as to castrate themselves!

Practice Love

5:13 For you were called to freedom, brothers and sisters; only do not use your freedom as an opportunity to indulge your flesh, but through love serve one another. **5:14** For the whole law can be summed up in a single commandment, namely, "*You must love your neighbor as yourself.*" **5:15** However, if you continually bite and devour one another, beware that you are not consumed by one another. **5:16** But I say, live by the Spirit and you will not carry out the desires of the flesh. **5:17** For the flesh has desires that are opposed to the Spirit, and the Spirit has desires that are opposed to the flesh, for these are in opposition to each other, so that you cannot do what you want. **5:18** But if you are led by the Spirit, you are not under the law. **5:19** Now the works of the flesh are obvious: sexual immorality, impurity, depravity, **5:20** idolatry, sorcery, hostilities, strife, jealousy, outbursts of anger, selfish rivalries, dissensions, factions, **5:21** envying, murder, drunkenness, carousing, and similar things. I am warning you, as I had warned you before: Those who practice such things will not inherit the kingdom of God!

5:22 But the fruit of the Spirit is love, joy, peace, patience, kindness, goodness, faithfulness, **5:23** gentleness, and self-control. Against such things there is no law. **5:24** Now those who belong to Christ have crucified the flesh with its passions and desires. **5:25** If we live by the Spirit, let us also behave in accordance with the Spirit. **5:26** Let us not become conceited, provoking one another, being jealous of one another.

Support One Another

6:1 Brothers and sisters, if a person is discovered in some sin, you who are spiritual restore such a person in a spirit of gentleness. Pay close attention to yourselves, so that you are not tempted too. **6:2** Carry one another's burdens, and in this way you will fulfill the law of Christ. **6:3** For if anyone thinks he is something when he is nothing, he deceives himself. **6:4** Let each one examine his own work. Then he can take pride in himself and not compare himself with someone else. **6:5** For each one will carry his own load.

6:6 Now the one who receives instruction in the word must share all good things with the one who teaches it. **6:7** Do not be deceived. God will not be made a fool. For a person will reap what he sows, **6:8** because the person who sows to his own flesh will reap corruption from the flesh, but the one who sows to the Spirit will reap eternal life from the Spirit. **6:9** So we must not grow weary in doing good, for in due time we will reap, if we do not give up. **6:10** So then, whenever we have an opportunity, let us do good to all people, and especially to those who belong to the family of faith.

Final Instructions and Benediction

6:11 See what big letters I make as I write to you with my own hand! **6:12** Those who want to make a good showing in external matters are trying to force you to be circumcised. They do so only to avoid being persecuted for the cross of Christ. **6:13** For those who are circumcised do not obey the law themselves, but they want you to be circumcised so that they can boast about your flesh. **6:14** But may I never boast except in the cross of our Lord Jesus Christ, through which the world has been crucified to me, and I to the world. **6:15** For neither circumcision nor uncircumcision counts for anything; the only thing that matters is a new creation! **6:16** And all who will behave in accordance with this rule, peace and mercy be on them, and on the Israel of God.

6:17 From now on let no one cause me trouble, for I bear the marks of Jesus on my body.

6:18 The grace of our Lord Jesus Christ be with your spirit, brothers and sisters. Amen.

Book 49. Ephesians

Salutation

1:1 From Paul, an apostle of Christ Jesus by the will of God, to the saints [in Ephesus], the faithful in Christ Jesus. **1:2** Grace and peace to you from God our Father and the Lord Jesus Christ!

Spiritual Blessings in Christ

1:3 Blessed is the God and Father of our Lord Jesus Christ, who has blessed us with every spiritual blessing in the heavenly realms in Christ. **1:4** For he chose us in Christ before the foundation of the world that we may be holy and unblemished in his sight in love. **1:5** He did this by predestining us to adoption as his sons through Jesus Christ, according to the pleasure of his will – **1:6** to the praise of the glory of his grace that he has freely bestowed on us in his dearly loved Son. **1:7** In him we have redemption through his blood, the forgiveness of our trespasses, according to the riches of his grace **1:8** that he lavished on us in all wisdom and insight. **1:9** He did this when he revealed to us the secret of his will, according to his good pleasure that he set forth in Christ, **1:10** toward the administration of the fullness of the times, to head up all things in Christ – the things in heaven and the things on earth. **1:11** In Christ we too have been claimed as God's own possession, since we were predestined according to the one purpose of him who accomplishes all things according to the counsel of his will **1:12** so that we, who were the first to set our hope on Christ, would be to the praise of his glory. **1:13** And when you heard the word of truth (the gospel of your salvation) – when you believed in Christ – you were marked with the seal of the promised Holy Spirit, **1:14** who is the down payment of our inheritance, until the redemption of God's own possession, to the praise of his glory.

Prayer for Wisdom and Revelation

1:15 For this reason, because I have heard of your faith in the Lord Jesus and your love for all the saints, **1:16** I do not cease to give thanks for you when I remember you in my prayers. **1:17** I pray that the God of our Lord Jesus Christ, the Father of glory, may give you spiritual wisdom and revelation in your growing knowledge of him, **1:18** – since the eyes of your heart have been enlightened – so that you may know what is the hope of his calling, what is the wealth of his glorious inheritance in the saints, **1:19** and what is the incomparable greatness of his power toward us who believe, as displayed in the exercise of his immense strength. **1:20** This power he exercised in Christ when he raised him from the dead and seated him at his right hand in the heavenly realms **1:21** far above every rule and authority and power and dominion and every name that is named, not only in this age but also in the one to come. **1:22** And God *put all things under* Christ's *feet*, and he gave him to the church as head over all things. **1:23** Now the church is his body, the fullness of him who fills all in all.

New Life Individually

2:1 And although you were dead in your transgressions and sins, **2:2** in which you formerly lived according to this world's present path, according to the ruler of the kingdom of the air, the ruler of the spirit that is now energizing the sons of disobedience, **2:3** among whom all of us also formerly lived out our lives in the cravings of our flesh, indulging the desires of the flesh and the mind, and were by nature children of wrath even as the rest…

2:4 But God, being rich in mercy, because of his great love with which he loved us, **2:5** even though we were dead in transgressions, made us alive together with Christ – by grace you are saved! – **2:6** and he raised us up with him and seated us with him in the heavenly realms in Christ Jesus, **2:7** to demonstrate in the coming ages the surpassing wealth of his grace in kindness toward us in Christ Jesus. **2:8** For by grace you are saved through faith, and this is not from yourselves, it is the gift of God; **2:9** it is not from works, so that no one can boast. **2:10** For we are his workmanship, having been created in Christ Jesus for good works that God prepared beforehand so we may do them.

New Life Corporately

2:11 Therefore remember that formerly you, the Gentiles in the flesh – who are called "uncircumcision" by the so-called "circumcision" that is performed on the body by human hands – **2:12** that you were at that time without the Messiah, alienated from the citizenship of Israel and strangers to the covenants of promise, having no hope and without God in the world. **2:13** But now in Christ Jesus you who used to be far away have been brought near by the blood of Christ. **2:14** For he is our peace, the one who made both groups into one and who destroyed the middle wall of partition, the hostility, **2:15** when he nullified in his flesh the law of commandments in decrees. He did this to create in himself one new man out of two, thus making peace, **2:16** and to reconcile them both in one body to God through the cross, by which the hostility has been killed. **2:17** And he came and preached peace to you who were far off and peace to those who were near, **2:18** so that through him we both have access in one Spirit to the Father. **2:19** So then you are no longer foreigners and noncitizens, but you are fellow citizens with the saints and members of God's household, **2:20** because you have been built on the foundation of the apostles and prophets, with Christ Jesus himself as the cornerstone. **2:21** In him the whole building, being joined together, grows into a holy temple in the Lord, **2:22** in whom you also are being built together into a dwelling place of God in the Spirit.

Paul's Relationship to the Divine Mystery

3:1 For this reason I, Paul, the prisoner of Christ Jesus for the sake of you Gentiles – **3:2** if indeed you have heard of the stewardship of God's grace that was given to me for you, **3:3** that by revelation the divine secret was made known to me, as I wrote before briefly. **3:4** When reading this, you will be able to understand my insight into this secret of Christ. **3:5** Now this secret was not disclosed to people in former generations as it has now been revealed to his holy apostles and prophets by the Spirit, **3:6** namely, that through the gospel the Gentiles are fellow heirs, fellow members of the body, and fellow partakers of the promise in Christ Jesus. **3:7** I became a servant of this gospel according to the gift of God's grace that was given to me by the exercise of his power. **3:8** To me – less than the least of all the saints – this grace was given, to proclaim to the Gentiles the unfathomable riches of Christ **3:9** and to enlighten everyone about God's secret plan – a secret that has been hidden for ages in God who has created all things. **3:10** The purpose of this enlightenment is that through the church the multifaceted wisdom of God should now be disclosed to the rulers and the authorities in the heavenly realms. **3:11** This was according to the eternal purpose that he accomplished in Christ Jesus our Lord, **3:12** in whom we have boldness and confident access to God because of Christ's faithfulness. **3:13** For this reason I ask you not to lose heart because of what I am suffering for you, which is your glory.

Prayer for Strengthened Love

3:14 For this reason I kneel before the Father, **3:15** from whom every family in heaven and on the earth is named. **3:16** I pray that according to the wealth of his glory he may grant you to be strengthened with power through his Spirit in the inner person, **3:17** that Christ may dwell in your hearts through faith, so that, because you have been rooted and grounded in love, **3:18** you may be able to comprehend with all the saints what is the breadth and length and height and depth, **3:19** and thus to know the love of Christ that surpasses knowledge, so that you may be filled up to all the fullness of God.

3:20 Now to him who by the power that is working within us is able to do far beyond all that we ask or think, **3:21** to him be the glory in the church and in Christ Jesus to all generations, forever and ever. Amen.

Live in Unity

4:1 I, therefore, the prisoner for the Lord, urge you to live worthily of the calling with which you have been called, **4:2** with all humility and gentleness, with patience, bearing with one another in love, **4:3** making every effort to keep the unity of the Spirit in the bond of peace. **4:4** There is one body and one Spirit, just as you too were called to the one hope of your calling, **4:5** one Lord, one faith, one baptism, **4:6** one God and Father of all, who is over all and through all and in all.

4:7 But to each one of us grace was given according to the measure of the gift of Christ. **4:8** Therefore it says, *"When he ascended on high he captured captives; he gave gifts to men."* **4:9** Now what is the meaning of *"he ascended,"* except that he also descended to the lower regions, namely, the earth? **4:10** He, the very one who descended, is also the one who ascended above all the heavens, in order to fill all things. **4:11** It was he who gave some as apostles, some as prophets, some as evangelists, and some as pastors and teachers, **4:12** to equip the saints for the work of ministry, that is, to build up the body of Christ, **4:13** until we all attain to the unity of the faith and of the knowledge of the Son of God – a mature person, attaining to the measure of Christ's full stature. **4:14** So we are no longer to be children, tossed back and forth by waves and carried about by every wind of teaching by the trickery of people who craftily carry out their deceitful schemes. **4:15** But practicing the truth in love, we will in all things grow up into Christ, who is the head. **4:16** From him the whole body grows, fitted and held together through every supporting ligament. As each one does its part, the body grows in love.

Live in Holiness

4:17 So I say this, and insist in the Lord, that you no longer live as the Gentiles do, in the futility of their thinking. **4:18** They are darkened in their understanding, being alienated from the life of God because of the ignorance that is in them due to the hardness of their hearts. **4:19** Because they are callous, they have given themselves over to indecency for the practice of every kind of impurity with greediness. **4:20** But you did not learn about Christ like this, **4:21** if indeed you heard about him and were taught in him, just as the truth is in Jesus. **4:22** You were taught with reference to your former way of life to lay aside the old man who is being corrupted in accordance with deceitful desires, **4:23** to be renewed in the spirit of your mind, **4:24** and to put on the new man who has been created in God's image – in righteousness and holiness that comes from truth. **4:25** Therefore, having laid aside falsehood, *each one of you speak the truth with his neighbor,* for we are members of one another. **4:26** *Be angry and do not sin;* do not let the sun go down on the cause of your anger. **4:27** Do not give the devil an opportunity. **4:28** The one who steals must steal no longer; rather he must labor, doing good with his own hands, so that he may have something to share with the one who has need. **4:29** You must let no unwholesome word come out of your mouth, but only what is beneficial for the building up of the one in need, that it may give grace to those who hear. **4:30** And do not grieve the Holy Spirit of God, by whom you were sealed for the day of redemption. **4:31** You must put away every kind of bitterness, anger, wrath, quarreling, and evil, slanderous talk. **4:32** Instead, be kind to one another, compassionate, forgiving one another, just as God in Christ also forgave you.

Live in Love

5:1 Therefore, be imitators of God as dearly loved children **5:2** and live in love, just as Christ also loved us and gave himself for us, a sacrificial and fragrant offering to God. **5:3** But among you there must not be either sexual immorality, impurity of any kind, or greed, as these are not fitting for the saints. **5:4** Neither should there be vulgar speech, foolish talk, or coarse jesting – all of which are out of character – but rather thanksgiving. **5:5** For you can be confident of this one thing: that no person who is immoral, impure, or greedy (such a person is an idolater) has any inheritance in the kingdom of Christ and God.

Live in the Light

5:6 Let nobody deceive you with empty words, for because of these things God's wrath comes on the sons of disobedience. **5:7** Therefore do not be partakers with them, **5:8** for you were at one time darkness, but now you are light in the Lord. Walk as children of the light – **5:9** for the fruit of the light consists in all goodness, righteousness, and truth – **5:10** trying to learn what is pleasing to the Lord. **5:11** Do not participate in the unfruitful deeds of darkness, but rather expose them. **5:12** For the things they do in secret are shameful even to mention. **5:13** But all things being exposed by the light are made evident. **5:14** For everything made evident is light, and for this reason it says:

"Awake, O sleeper!
Rise from the dead,
and Christ will shine on you!"

Live Wisely

5:15 Therefore be very careful how you live – not as unwise but as wise, **5:16** taking advantage of every opportunity, because the days are evil. **5:17** For this reason do not be foolish, but be wise by understanding what the Lord's will is. **5:18** And do not get drunk with wine, which is debauchery, but be filled by the Spirit, **5:19** speaking to one another in psalms, hymns, and spiritual songs, singing and making music in your hearts to the Lord, **5:20** always giving thanks to God the Father for each other in the name of our Lord Jesus Christ, **5:21** and submitting to one another out of reverence for Christ.

Exhortations to Households

5:22 Wives, submit to your husbands as to the Lord, **5:23** because the husband is the head of the wife as also Christ is the head of the church – he himself being the savior of the body. **5:24** But as the church submits to Christ, so also wives should submit to their husbands in everything. **5:25** Husbands, love your wives just as Christ loved the church and gave himself for her **5:26** to sanctify her by cleansing her with the washing of the water by the word, **5:27** so that he may present the church to himself as glorious – not having a stain or wrinkle, or any such blemish, but holy and blameless. **5:28** In the same way husbands ought to love their wives as their own bodies. He who loves his wife loves himself. **5:29** For no one has ever hated his own body but he feeds it and takes care of it, just as Christ also does the church, **5:30** for we are members of his body. **5:31** *For this reason a man will leave his father and mother and will be joined to his wife, and the two will become one flesh.* **5:32** This mystery is great – but I am actually speaking with reference to Christ and the church. **5:33** Nevertheless, each one of you must also love his own wife as he loves himself, and the wife must respect her husband.

6:1 Children, obey your parents in the Lord for this is right. **6:2** "*Honor your father and mother,*" which is the first commandment accompanied by a promise, namely, **6:3** "*that it may go well with you and that you will live a long time on the earth.*"

6:4 Fathers, do not provoke your children to anger, but raise them up in the discipline and instruction of the Lord.

6:5 Slaves, obey your human masters with fear and trembling, in the sincerity of your heart as to Christ, **6:6** not like those who do their work only when someone is watching – as people-pleasers – but as slaves of Christ doing the will of God from the heart. **6:7** Obey with enthusiasm, as though serving the Lord and not people, **6:8** because you know that each person, whether slave or free, if he does something good, this will be rewarded by the Lord.

6:9 Masters, treat your slaves the same way, giving up the use of threats, because you know that both you and they have the same master in heaven, and there is no favoritism with him.

Exhortations for Spiritual Warfare

6:10 Finally, be strengthened in the Lord and in the strength of his power. **6:11** Clothe yourselves with the full armor of God so that you may be able to stand against the schemes of the devil. **6:12** For our struggle is not against flesh and blood, but against the rulers, against the powers, against the world rulers of this darkness, against the spiritual forces of evil in the heavens. **6:13** For this reason, take up the full armor of God so that you may be able to stand your ground on the evil day, and having done everything, to stand. **6:14** Stand firm therefore, by fastening the belt of truth around your waist, by putting on the breastplate of righteousness, **6:15** by fitting your feet with the preparation that comes from the good news of peace, **6:16** and in all of this, by taking up the shield of faith with which you can extinguish all the flaming arrows of the evil one. **6:17** And take *the helmet of salvation* and the sword of the Spirit, which is the word of God. **6:18** With every prayer and petition, pray at all times in the Spirit, and to this end be alert, with all perseverance and requests for all the saints. **6:19** Pray for me also, that I may be given the message when I begin to speak – that I may confidently make known the mystery of the gospel, **6:20** for which I am an ambassador in chains. Pray that I may be able to speak boldly as I ought to speak.

Farewell Comments

6:21 Tychicus, my dear brother and faithful servant in the Lord, will make everything known to you, so that you too may know about my circumstances, how I am doing. **6:22** I have sent him to you for this very purpose, that you may know our circumstances and that he may encourage your hearts.

6:23 Peace to the brothers and sisters, and love with faith, from God the Father and the Lord Jesus Christ. **6:24** Grace be with all of those who love our Lord Jesus Christ with an undying love.

Book 50. Philippians

Salutation

1:1 From Paul and Timothy, slaves of Christ Jesus, to all the saints in Christ Jesus who are in Philippi, with the overseers and deacons. **1:2** Grace and peace to you from God our Father and the Lord Jesus Christ!

Prayer for the Church

1:3 I thank my God every time I remember you. **1:4** I always pray with joy in my every prayer for all of you **1:5** because of your participation in the gospel from the first day until now. **1:6** For I am sure of this very thing, that the one who began a good work in you will perfect it until the day of Christ Jesus. **1:7** For it is right for me to think this about all of you, because I have you in my heart, since both in my imprisonment and in the defense and confirmation of the gospel all of you became partners in God's grace together with me. **1:8** For God is my witness that I long for all of you with the affection of Christ Jesus. **1:9** And I pray this, that your love may abound even more and more in knowledge and every kind of insight **1:10** so that you can decide what is best, and thus be sincere and blameless for the day of Christ, **1:11** filled with the fruit of righteousness that comes through Jesus Christ to the glory and praise of God.

Ministry as a Prisoner

1:12 I want you to know, brothers and sisters, that my situation has actually turned out to advance the gospel: **1:13** The whole imperial guard and everyone else knows that I am in prison for the sake of Christ, **1:14** and most of the brothers and sisters, having confidence in the Lord because of my imprisonment, now more than ever dare to speak the word fearlessly. **1:15** Some, to be sure, are preaching Christ from envy and rivalry, but others from goodwill. **1:16** The latter do so from love because they know that I am placed here for the defense of the gospel. **1:17** The former proclaim Christ from selfish ambition, not sincerely, because they think they can cause trouble for me in my imprisonment. **1:18** What is the result? Only that in every way, whether in pretense or in truth, Christ is being proclaimed, and in this I rejoice.

Yes, and I will continue to rejoice, **1:19** for I know that this will turn out for my deliverance through your prayers and the help of the Spirit of Jesus Christ. **1:20** My confident hope is that I will in no way be ashamed but that with complete boldness, even now as always, Christ will be exalted in my body, whether I live or die. **1:21** For to me, living is Christ and dying is gain. **1:22** Now if I am to go on living in the body, this will mean productive work for me, yet I don't know which I prefer: **1:23** I feel torn between the two, because I have a desire to depart and be with Christ, which is better by far, **1:24** but it is more vital for your sake that I remain in the body. **1:25** And since I am sure of this, I know that I will remain and continue with all of you for the sake of your progress and joy in the faith, **1:26** so that what you can be proud of may increase because of me in Christ Jesus, when I come back to you.

1:27 Only conduct yourselves in a manner worthy of the gospel of Christ so that – whether I come and see you or whether I remain absent – I should hear that you are standing firm in one spirit, with one mind, by contending side by side for the faith of the gospel, **1:28** and by not being intimidated in any way by your opponents. This is a sign of their destruction, but of your salvation – a sign which is from God. **1:29** For it has been granted to you not only to believe in Christ but also to suffer for him, **1:30** since you are encountering the same conflict that you saw me face and now hear that I am facing.

Christian Unity and Christ's Humility

2:1 Therefore, if there is any encouragement in Christ, any comfort provided by love, any fellowship in the Spirit, any affection or mercy, **2:2** complete my joy and be of the same mind, by having the same love, being united in spirit, and having one purpose. **2:3** Instead of being motivated by selfish ambition or vanity, each of you should, in humility, be moved to treat one another as more important than yourself. **2:4** Each of you should be concerned not only about your own interests, but about the interests of others as well. **2:5** You should have the same attitude toward one another that Christ Jesus had,

2:6 who though he existed in the form of God
did not regard equality with God
as something to be grasped,
2:7 but emptied himself
by taking on the form of a slave,
by looking like other men,
and by sharing in human nature.
2:8 He humbled himself,
by becoming obedient to the point of death
– even death on a cross!
2:9 As a result God exalted him
and gave him the name
that is above every name,
2:10 so that at the name of Jesus
every knee will bow
– in heaven and on earth and under the earth –
2:11 and every tongue confess
that Jesus Christ is Lord
to the glory of God the Father.

Lights in the World

2:12 So then, my dear friends, just as you have always obeyed, not only in my presence but even more in my absence, continue working out your salvation with awe and reverence, **2:13** for the one bringing forth in you both the desire and the effort – for the sake of his good pleasure – is God. **2:14** Do everything without grumbling or arguing, **2:15** so that you may be blameless and pure, children of God without blemish though you live in a crooked and perverse society, in which you shine as lights in the world **2:16** by holding on to the word of life so that on the day of Christ I will have a reason to boast that I did not run in vain nor labor in vain. **2:17** But even if I am being poured out like a drink offering on the sacrifice and service of your faith, I am glad and rejoice together with all of you. **2:18** And in the same way you also should be glad and rejoice together with me.

Models for Ministry

2:19 Now I hope in the Lord Jesus to send Timothy to you soon, so that I too may be encouraged by hearing news about you. **2:20** For there is no one here like him who will readily demonstrate his deep concern for you. **2:21** Others are busy with their own concerns, not those of Jesus Christ. **2:22** But you know his qualifications, that like a son working with his father, he served with me in advancing the gospel. **2:23** So I hope to send him as soon as I know more about my situation, **2:24** though I am confident in the Lord that I too will be coming to see you soon.

2:25 But for now I have considered it necessary to send Epaphroditus to you. For he is my brother, coworker and fellow soldier, and your messenger and minister to me in my need. 2:26 Indeed, he greatly missed all of you and was distressed because you heard that he had been ill. 2:27 In fact he became so ill that he nearly died. But God showed mercy to him – and not to him only, but also to me – so that I would not have grief on top of grief. 2:28 Therefore I am all the more eager to send him, so that when you see him again you can rejoice and I can be free from anxiety. 2:29 So welcome him in the Lord with great joy, and honor people like him, 2:30 since it was because of the work of Christ that he almost died. He risked his life so that he could make up for your inability to serve me.

True and False Righteousness

3:1 Finally, my brothers and sisters, rejoice in the Lord! To write this again is no trouble to me, and it is a safeguard for you.

3:2 Beware of the dogs, beware of the evil workers, beware of those who mutilate the flesh! 3:3 For we are the circumcision, the ones who worship by the Spirit of God, exult in Christ Jesus, and do not rely on human credentials 3:4 – though mine too are significant. If someone thinks he has good reasons to put confidence in human credentials, I have more: 3:5 I was circumcised on the eighth day, from the people of Israel and the tribe of Benjamin, a Hebrew of Hebrews. I lived according to the law as a Pharisee. 3:6 In my zeal for God I persecuted the church. According to the righteousness stipulated in the law I was blameless. 3:7 But these assets I have come to regard as liabilities because of Christ. 3:8 More than that, I now regard all things as liabilities compared to the far greater value of knowing Christ Jesus my Lord, for whom I have suffered the loss of all things – indeed, I regard them as dung! – that I may gain Christ, 3:9 and be found in him, not because I have my own righteousness derived from the law, but because I have the righteousness that comes by way of Christ's faithfulness – a righteousness from God that is in fact based on Christ's faithfulness. 3:10 My aim is to know him, to experience the power of his resurrection, to share in his sufferings, and to be like him in his death, 3:11 and so, somehow, to attain to the resurrection from the dead.

Keep Going Forward

3:12 Not that I have already attained this – that is, I have not already been perfected – but I strive to lay hold of that for which Christ Jesus also laid hold of me. 3:13 Brothers and sisters, I do not consider myself to have attained this. Instead I am single-minded: Forgetting the things that are behind and reaching out for the things that are ahead, 3:14 with this goal in mind, I strive toward the prize of the upward call of God in Christ Jesus. 3:15 Therefore let those of us who are "perfect" embrace this point of view. If you think otherwise, God will reveal to you the error of your ways. 3:16 Nevertheless, let us live up to the standard that we have already attained.

3:17 Be imitators of me, brothers and sisters, and watch carefully those who are living this way, just as you have us as an example. 3:18 For many live, about whom I have often told you, and now, with tears, I tell you that they are the enemies of the cross of Christ. 3:19 Their end is destruction, their god is the belly, they exult in their shame, and they think about earthly things. 3:20 But our citizenship is in heaven – and we also await a savior from there, the Lord Jesus Christ, 3:21 who will transform these humble bodies of ours into the likeness of his glorious body by means of that power by which he is able to subject all things to himself.

Christian Practices

4:1 So then, my brothers and sisters, dear friends whom I long to see, my joy and crown, stand in the Lord in this way, my dear friends!

4:2 I appeal to Euodia and to Syntyche to agree in the Lord. 4:3 Yes, I say also to you, true companion, help them. They have struggled together in the gospel ministry along with me and Clement and my other coworkers, whose names are in the book of life. 4:4 Rejoice in the Lord always. Again I say, rejoice! 4:5 Let everyone see your gentleness. The Lord is near! 4:6 Do not be anxious about anything. Instead, in every situation, through prayer and petition with thanksgiving, tell your requests to God. 4:7 And the peace of God that surpasses all understanding will guard your hearts and minds in Christ Jesus.

4:8 Finally, brothers and sisters, whatever is true, whatever is worthy of respect, whatever is just, whatever is pure, whatever is lovely, whatever is commendable, if something is excellent or praiseworthy, think about these things. 4:9 And what you learned and received and heard and saw in me, do these things. And the God of peace will be with you.

Appreciation for Support

4:10 I have great joy in the Lord because now at last you have again expressed your concern for me. (Now I know you were concerned before but had no opportunity to do anything.) 4:11 I am not saying this because I am in need, for I have learned to be content in any circumstance. 4:12 I have experienced times of need and times of abundance. In any and every circumstance I have learned the secret of contentment, whether I go satisfied or hungry, have plenty or nothing. 4:13 I am able to do all things through the one who strengthens me. 4:14 Nevertheless, you did well to share with me in my trouble.

4:15 And as you Philippians know, at the beginning of my gospel ministry, when I left Macedonia, no church shared with me in this matter of giving and receiving except you alone. 4:16 For even in Thessalonica on more than one occasion you sent something for my need. 4:17 I do not say this because I am seeking a gift. Rather, I seek the credit that abounds to your account. 4:18 For I have received everything, and I have plenty. I have all I need because I received from Epaphroditus what you sent – a fragrant offering, an acceptable sacrifice, very pleasing to God. 4:19 And my God will supply your every need according to his glorious riches in Christ Jesus. 4:20 May glory be given to God our Father forever and ever. Amen.

Final Greetings

4:21 Give greetings to all the saints in Christ Jesus. The brothers with me here send greetings. 4:22 All the saints greet you, especially those who belong to Caesar's household. 4:23 The grace of the Lord Jesus Christ be with your spirit.

Book 51. Colossians

Salutation

1:1 From Paul, an apostle of Christ Jesus by the will of God, and Timothy our brother, 1:2 to the saints, the faithful brothers and sisters in Christ, at Colossae. Grace and peace to you from God our Father!

Paul's Thanksgiving and Prayer for the Church

1:3 We always give thanks to God, the Father of our Lord Jesus Christ, when we pray for you, 1:4 since we heard about your faith in Christ Jesus and the love that you have for all the saints. 1:5 Your faith and love have arisen from the hope laid up for you in heaven, which you have heard about in the message of truth, the gospel 1:6 that has come to you. Just as in the entire world this gospel is bearing fruit and growing, so it has also been bearing fruit and growing among you from the first day you heard it and understood the grace of God in truth. 1:7 You learned the gospel from Epaphras, our dear fellow slave – a faithful minister of Christ on our behalf – 1:8 who also told us of your love in the Spirit.

Paul's Prayer for the Growth of the Church

1:9 For this reason we also, from the day we heard about you, have not ceased praying for you and asking God to fill you with the knowledge of his will in all spiritual wisdom and understanding, 1:10 so that you may live worthily of the Lord and please him in all respects – bearing fruit in every good deed, growing in the knowledge of God, 1:11 being strengthened with all power according to his glorious might for the display of all patience and steadfastness, joyfully 1:12 giving thanks to the Father who has qualified you to share in the saints' inheritance in the light. 1:13 He delivered us from the power of darkness and transferred us to the kingdom of the Son he loves, 1:14 in whom we have redemption, the forgiveness of sins.

The Supremacy of Christ

1:15 He is the image of the invisible God, the firstborn over all creation,

1:16 for all things in heaven and on earth were created by him – all things, whether visible or invisible, whether thrones or dominions, whether principalities or powers – all things were created through him and for him.

1:17 He himself is before all things and all things are held together in him.

1:18 He is the head of the body, the church, as well as the beginning, the firstborn from among the dead, so that he himself may become first in all things.

1:19 For God was pleased to have all his fullness dwell in the Son

1:20 and through him to reconcile all things to himself by making peace through the blood of his cross – through him, whether things on earth or things in heaven.

Paul's Goal in Ministry

1:21 And you were at one time strangers and enemies in your minds as expressed through your evil deeds, 1:22 but now he has reconciled you by his physical body through death to present you holy, without blemish, and blameless before him – 1:23 if indeed you remain in the faith, established and firm, without shifting from the hope of the gospel that you heard. This gospel has also been preached in all creation under heaven, and I, Paul, have become its servant.

1:24 Now I rejoice in my sufferings for you, and I fill up in my physical body – for the sake of his body, the church – what is lacking in the sufferings of Christ. 1:25 I became a servant of the church according to the stewardship from God – given to me for you – in order to complete the word of God, 1:26 that is, the mystery that has been kept hidden from ages and generations, but has now been revealed to his saints. 1:27 God wanted to make known to them the glorious riches of this mystery among the Gentiles, which is Christ in you, the hope of glory. 1:28 We proclaim him by instructing and teaching all people with all wisdom so that we may present every person mature in Christ. 1:29 Toward this goal I also labor, struggling according to his power that powerfully works in me.

2:1 For I want you to know how great a struggle I have for you, and for those in Laodicea, and for those who have not met me face to face. 2:2

My goal is that their hearts, having been knit together in love, may be encouraged, and that they may have all the riches that assurance brings in their understanding of the knowledge of the mystery of God, namely, Christ, **2:3** in whom are hidden all the treasures of wisdom and knowledge. **2:4** I say this so that no one will deceive you through arguments that sound reasonable. **2:5** For though I am absent from you in body, I am present with you in spirit, rejoicing to see your morale and the firmness of your faith in Christ.

Warnings Against the Adoption of False Philosophies

2:6 Therefore, just as you received Christ Jesus as Lord, continue to live your lives in him, **2:7** rooted and built up in him and firm in your faith just as you were taught, and overflowing with thankfulness. **2:8** Be careful not to allow anyone to captivate you through an empty, deceitful philosophy that is according to human traditions and the elemental spirits of the world, and not according to Christ. **2:9** For in him all the fullness of deity lives in bodily form, **2:10** and you have been filled in him, who is the head over every ruler and authority. **2:11** In him you also were circumcised – not, however, with a circumcision performed by human hands, but by the removal of the fleshly body, that is, through the circumcision done by Christ. **2:12** Having been buried with him in baptism, you also have been raised with him through your faith in the power of God who raised him from the dead. **2:13** And even though you were dead in your transgressions and in the uncircumcision of your flesh, he nevertheless made you alive with him, having forgiven all your transgressions. **2:14** He has destroyed what was against us, a certificate of indebtedness expressed in decrees opposed to us. He has taken it away by nailing it to the cross. **2:15** Disarming the rulers and authorities, he has made a public disgrace of them, triumphing over them by the cross.

2:16 Therefore do not let anyone judge you with respect to food or drink, or in the matter of a feast, new moon, or Sabbath days – **2:17** these are only the shadow of the things to come, but the reality is Christ! **2:18** Let no one who delights in humility and the worship of angels pass judgment on you. That person goes on at great lengths about what he has supposedly seen, but he is puffed up with empty notions by his fleshly mind. **2:19** He has not held fast to the head from whom the whole body, supported and knit together through its ligaments and sinews, grows with a growth that is from God.

2:20 If you have died with Christ to the elemental spirits of the world, why do you submit to them as though you lived in the world? **2:21** "Do not handle! Do not taste! Do not touch!" **2:22** These are all destined to perish with use, founded as they are on human commands and teachings. **2:23** Even though they have the appearance of wisdom with their self-imposed worship and false humility achieved by an unsparing treatment of the body – a wisdom with no true value – they in reality result in fleshly indulgence.

Exhortations to Seek the Things Above

3:1 Therefore, if you have been raised with Christ, keep seeking the things above, where Christ is, seated at the right hand of God. **3:2** Keep thinking about things above, not things on the earth, **3:3** for you have died and your life is hidden with Christ in God. **3:4** When Christ (who is your life) appears, then you too will be revealed in glory with him. **3:5** So put to death whatever in your nature belongs to the earth: sexual immorality, impurity, shameful passion, evil desire, and greed which is idolatry. **3:6** Because of these things the wrath of God is coming on the sons of disobedience. **3:7** You also lived your lives in this way at one time, when you used to live among them. **3:8** But now, put off all such things as anger, rage, malice, slander, abusive language from your mouth. **3:9** Do not lie to one another since you have put off the old man with its practices **3:10** and have been clothed with the new man that is being renewed in knowledge according to the image of the one who created it. **3:11** Here there is neither Greek nor Jew, circumcised or uncircumcised, barbarian, Scythian, slave or free, but Christ is all and in all.

Exhortation to Unity and Love

3:12 Therefore, as the elect of God, holy and dearly loved, clothe yourselves with a heart of mercy, kindness, humility, gentleness, and patience, **3:13** bearing with one another and forgiving one another, if someone happens to have a complaint against anyone else. Just as the Lord has forgiven you, so you also forgive others. **3:14** And to all these virtues add love, which is the perfect bond. **3:15** Let the peace of Christ be in control in your heart (for you were in fact called as one body to this peace), and be thankful. **3:16** Let the word of Christ dwell in you richly, teaching and exhorting one another with all wisdom, singing psalms, hymns, and spiritual songs, all with grace in your hearts to God. **3:17** And whatever you do in word or deed, do it all in the name of the Lord Jesus, giving thanks to God the Father through him.

Exhortation to Households

3:18 Wives, submit to your husbands, as is fitting in the Lord. **3:19** Husbands, love your wives and do not be embittered against them. **3:20** Children, obey your parents in everything, for this is pleasing in the Lord. **3:21** Fathers, do not provoke your children, so they will not become disheartened. **3:22** Slaves, obey your earthly masters in every respect, not only when they are watching – like those who are strictly people-pleasers – but with a sincere heart, fearing the Lord. **3:23** Whatever you are doing, work at it with enthusiasm, as to the Lord and not for people, **3:24** because you know that you will receive your inheritance from the Lord as the reward. Serve the Lord Christ.

3:25 For the one who does wrong will be repaid for his wrong, and there are no exceptions. **4:1** Masters, treat your slaves with justice and fairness, because you know that you also have a master in heaven.

Exhortation to Pray for the Success of Paul's Mission

4:2 Be devoted to prayer, keeping alert in it with thanksgiving. **4:3** At the same time pray for us too, that God may open a door for the message so that we may proclaim the mystery of Christ, for which I am in chains. **4:4** Pray that I may make it known as I should. **4:5** Conduct yourselves with wisdom toward outsiders, making the most of the opportunities. **4:6** Let your speech always be gracious, seasoned with salt, so that you may know how you should answer everyone.

Personal Greetings and Instructions

4:7 Tychicus, a dear brother, faithful minister, and fellow slave in the Lord, will tell you all the news about me. **4:8** I sent him to you for this very purpose, that you may know how we are doing and that he may encourage your hearts. **4:9** I sent him with Onesimus, the faithful and dear brother, who is one of you. They will tell you about everything here. **4:10** Aristarchus, my fellow prisoner, sends you greetings, as does Mark, the cousin of Barnabas (about whom you received instructions; if he comes to you, welcome him). **4:11** And Jesus who is called Justus also sends greetings. In terms of Jewish converts, these are the only fellow workers for the kingdom of God, and they have been a comfort to me. **4:12** Epaphras, who is one of you and a slave of Christ, greets you. He is always struggling in prayer on your behalf, so that you may stand mature and fully assured in all the will of God. **4:13** For I can testify that he has worked hard for you and for those in Laodicea and Hierapolis. **4:14** Our dear friend Luke the physician and Demas greet you. **4:15** Give my greetings to the brothers and sisters who are in Laodicea and to Nympha and the church that meets in her house. **4:16** And after you have read this letter, have it read to the church of Laodicea. In turn, read the letter from Laodicea as well. **4:17** And tell Archippus, "See to it that you complete the ministry you received in the Lord."

4:18 I, Paul, write this greeting by my own hand. Remember my chains. Grace be with you.

Book 52. 1 Thessalonians

Salutation

1:1 From Paul and Silvanus and Timothy, to the church of the Thessalonians in God the Father and the Lord Jesus Christ. Grace and peace to you!

Thanksgiving for Response to the Gospel

1:2 We thank God always for all of you as we mention you constantly in our prayers, **1:3** because we recall in the presence of our God and Father your work of faith and labor of love and endurance of hope in our Lord Jesus Christ. **1:4** We know, brothers and sisters loved by God, that he has chosen you, **1:5** in that our gospel did not come to you merely in words, but in power and in the Holy Spirit and with deep conviction (surely you recall the character we displayed when we came among you to help you). **1:6** And you became imitators of us and of the Lord, when you received the message with joy that comes from the Holy Spirit, despite great affliction. **1:7** As a result you became an example to all the believers in Macedonia and in Achaia. **1:8** For from you the message of the Lord has echoed forth not just in Macedonia and Achaia, but in every place reports of your faith in God have spread, so that we do not need to say anything. **1:9** For people everywhere report how you welcomed us and how you turned to God from idols to serve the living and true God **1:10** and to wait for his Son from heaven, whom he raised from the dead, Jesus our deliverer from the coming wrath.

Paul's Ministry in Thessalonica

2:1 For you yourselves know, brothers and sisters, about our coming to you – it has not proven to be purposeless. **2:2** But although we suffered earlier and were mistreated in Philippi, as you know, we had the courage in our God to declare to you the gospel of God in spite of much opposition. **2:3** For the appeal we make does not come from error or impurity or with deceit, **2:4** but just as we have been approved by God to be entrusted with the gospel, so we declare it, not to please people but God, who examines our hearts. **2:5** For we never appeared with flattering speech, as you know, nor with a pretext for greed – God is our witness – **2:6** nor to seek glory from people, either from you or from others, **2:7** although we could have imposed our weight as apostles of Christ; instead we became little children among you. Like a nursing mother caring for her own children, **2:8** with such affection for you we were happy to share with you not only the gospel of God but also our own lives, because you had become dear to us. **2:9** For you recall, brothers and sisters, our toil and drudgery: By working night and day so as not to impose a burden on any of you, we preached to you the gospel of God. **2:10** You are witnesses, and so is

God, as to how holy and righteous and blameless our conduct was toward you who believe. **2:11** As you know, we treated each one of you as a father treats his own children, **2:12** exhorting and encouraging you and insisting that you live in a way worthy of God who calls you to his own kingdom and his glory. **2:13** And so we too constantly thank God that when you received God's message that you heard from us, you accepted it not as a human message, but as it truly is, God's message, which is at work among you who believe. **2:14** For you became imitators, brothers and sisters, of God's churches in Christ Jesus that are in Judea, because you too suffered the same things from your own countrymen as they in fact did from the Jews, **2:15** who killed both the Lord Jesus and the prophets and persecuted us severely. They

are displeasing to God and are opposed to all people, **2:16** because they hinder us from speaking to the Gentiles so that they may be saved. Thus they constantly fill up their measure of sins, but wrath has come upon them completely.

Forced Absence from Thessalonica

2:17 But when we were separated from you, brothers and sisters, for a short time (in presence, not in affection) we became all the more fervent in our great desire to see you in person. **2:18** For we wanted to come to you (I, Paul, in fact tried again and again) but Satan thwarted us. **2:19** For who is our hope or joy or crown to boast of before our Lord Jesus at his coming? Is it not of course you? **2:20** For you are our glory and joy!

3:1 So when we could bear it no longer, we decided to stay on in Athens alone. **3:2** We sent Timothy, our brother and fellow worker for God in the gospel of Christ, to strengthen you and encourage you about your faith, **3:3** so that no one would be shaken by these afflictions. For you yourselves know that we are destined for this. **3:4** For in fact when we were with you, we were telling you in advance that we would suffer affliction, and so it has happened, as you well know. **3:5** So when I could bear it no longer, I sent to find out about your faith, for fear that the tempter somehow tempted you and our toil had proven useless.

3:6 But now Timothy has come to us from you and given us the good news of your faith and love and that you always think of us with affection and long to see us just as we also long to see you! **3:7** So in all our distress and affliction, we were reassured about you, brothers and sisters, through your faith. **3:8** For now we are alive again, if you stand firm in the Lord. **3:9** For how can we thank God enough for you, for all the joy we feel because of you before our God? **3:10** We pray earnestly night and day to see you in person and make up what may be lacking in your faith. **3:11** Now may God our Father himself and our Lord Jesus direct our way to you. **3:12** And may the Lord cause you to increase and abound in love for one another and for all, just as we do for you, **3:13** so that your hearts are strengthened in holiness to be blameless before our God and Father at the coming of our Lord Jesus with all his saints.

A Life Pleasing to God

4:1 Finally then, brothers and sisters, we ask you and urge you in the Lord Jesus, that as you received instruction from us about how you must live and please God (as you are in fact living) that you do so more and more. **4:2** For you know what commands we gave you through the Lord Jesus. **4:3** For this is God's will: that you become holy, that you keep away from sexual immorality, **4:4** that each of you know how to possess his own body in holiness and honor, **4:5** not in lustful passion like the Gentiles who do not know God. **4:6** In this matter no one should violate the rights of his brother or take advantage of him, because the Lord is the avenger in all these cases, as we also told you earlier and warned you solemnly. **4:7** For God did not call us to impurity but in holiness. **4:8** Consequently the one who rejects this is not rejecting human authority but God, who gives his Holy Spirit to you.

4:9 Now on the topic of brotherly love you have no need for anyone to write you, for you yourselves are taught by God to love one another. **4:10** And indeed you are practicing it toward all the brothers and sisters in all of Macedonia. But we urge you, brothers and sisters, to do so more and more, **4:11** to aspire to lead a

quiet life, to attend to your own business, and to work with your hands, as we commanded you. **4:12** In this way you will live a decent life before outsiders and not be in need.

The Lord Returns for Believers

4:13 Now we do not want you to be uninformed, brothers and sisters, about those who are asleep, so that you will not grieve like the rest who have no hope. **4:14** For if we believe that Jesus died and rose again, so also we believe that God will bring with him those who have fallen asleep as Christians. **4:15** For we tell you this by the word of the Lord, that we who are alive, who are left until the coming of the Lord, will surely not go ahead of those who have fallen asleep. **4:16** For the Lord himself will come down from heaven with a shout of command, with the voice of the archangel, and with the trumpet of God, and the dead in Christ

will rise first. **4:17** Then we who are alive, who are left, will be suddenly caught up together with them in the clouds to meet the Lord in the air. And so we will always be with the Lord. **4:18** Therefore encourage one another with these words.

The Day of the Lord

5:1 Now on the topic of times and seasons, brothers and sisters, you have no need for anything to be written to you. **5:2** For you know quite well that the day of the Lord will come in the same way as a thief in the night. **5:3** Now when they are saying, "There is peace and security," then sudden destruction comes on them, like labor pains on a pregnant woman, and they will surely not escape. **5:4** But you, brothers and sisters, are not in the darkness for the day to overtake you like a thief would. **5:5** For you all are sons of the light and sons of the day. We are not of the night nor of the darkness. **5:6** So then we must not sleep as the rest, but must stay alert and sober. **5:7** For those who sleep, sleep at night and those who get drunk are drunk at night. **5:8** But since we are of the day, we must stay sober *by putting on the breastplate* of faith and love and as *a helmet* our hope *for salvation*. **5:9** For God did not destine us for wrath but for gaining salvation through our Lord Jesus Christ. **5:10** He died for us so that whether we are alert or asleep we will come to life together with him. **5:11** Therefore encourage one another and build up each other, just as you are in fact doing.

Final Instructions

5:12 Now we ask you, brothers and sisters, to acknowledge those who labor among you and preside over you in the Lord and admonish you, **5:13** and to esteem them most highly in love because of their work. Be at peace among yourselves. **5:14** And we urge you, brothers and sisters, admonish the undisciplined, comfort the discouraged, help the weak, be patient toward all. **5:15** See that no one pays back evil for evil to anyone, but always pursue what is good for one another and for all. **5:16** Always rejoice, **5:17** constantly pray, **5:18** in everything give thanks. For this is God's will for you in Christ Jesus. **5:19** Do not extinguish the Spirit. **5:20** Do not treat prophecies with contempt. **5:21** But examine all things; hold fast to what is good. **5:22** Stay away from every form of evil.

Conclusion

5:23 Now may the God of peace himself make you completely holy and may your spirit and soul and body be kept entirely blameless at the coming of our Lord Jesus Christ. **5:24** He who calls you is trustworthy, and he will in fact do this. **5:25** Brothers and sisters, pray for us too. **5:26** Greet all the brothers and sisters with a holy kiss. **5:27** I call on you solemnly in the Lord to have this letter read to all the brothers and sisters. **5:28** The grace of our Lord Jesus Christ be with you.

Book 53. 2 Thessalonians

Salutation

1:1 From Paul and Silvanus and Timothy, to the church of the Thessalonians in God our Father and the Lord Jesus Christ. **1:2** Grace and peace to you from God the Father and the Lord Jesus Christ!

Thanksgiving

1:3 We ought to thank God always for you, brothers and sisters, and rightly so, because your faith flourishes more and more and the love of each one of you all for one another is ever greater. **1:4** As a result we ourselves boast about you in the churches of God for your perseverance and faith in all the persecutions and afflictions you are enduring.

Encouragement in Persecution

1:5 This is evidence of God's righteous judgment, to make you worthy of the kingdom of God, for which in fact you are suffering. **1:6** For it is right for God to repay with affliction those who afflict you, **1:7** and to you who are being afflicted to give rest together with us when the Lord Jesus is revealed from heaven with his mighty angels. **1:8** *With flaming fire he will mete out punishment on those who do not know God* and do not obey the gospel of our Lord Jesus. **1:9** They will undergo the penalty of eternal destruction, *away from the presence of the Lord and from the glory of his strength*, **1:10** when he comes to be glorified among his saints and admired on that day among all who have believed – and you did in fact believe our testimony. **1:11** And in this regard we pray for you always, that our God will make you worthy of his calling and fulfill by his power your every desire for goodness and every work of faith, **1:12** that the name of our Lord Jesus may be glorified in you, and you in him, according to the grace of our God and the Lord Jesus Christ.

The Day of the Lord

2:1 Now regarding the arrival of our Lord Jesus Christ and our being gathered to be with him, we ask you, brothers and sisters, **2:2** not to be easily shaken from your composure or disturbed by any kind of spirit or message or letter allegedly from us, to the effect that the day of the Lord is already here. **2:3** Let no one deceive you in any way. For that day will not arrive until the rebellion comes and the man of

lawlessness is revealed, the son of destruction. **2:4** He opposes *and exalts himself above every* so-called *god* or object of worship, and as a result *he takes his seat* in God's temple, displaying himself as God. **2:5** Surely you recall that I used to tell you these things while I was still with you. **2:6** And so you know what holds him back, so that he will be revealed in his own time. **2:7** For the hidden power of lawlessness is already at work. However, the one who holds him back will do so until he is taken out of the way, **2:8** and then the lawless one will be

revealed, whom the Lord will destroy by the breath of his mouth and wipe out by the manifestation of his arrival. **2:9** The arrival of the lawless one will be by Satan's working with all kinds of miracles and signs and false wonders, **2:10** and with every kind of evil deception directed against those who are perishing, because they found no place in their hearts for the truth so as to be saved. **2:11** Consequently God sends on them a deluding influence so that they will believe what is false. **2:12** And so all of them who have not believed the truth but have delighted in evil will be condemned.

Call to Stand Firm

2:13 But we ought to thank God always for you, brothers and sisters loved by the Lord, because God chose you from the beginning for salvation through sanctification by the Spirit and faith in the truth. **2:14** He called you to this salvation through our gospel, so that you may possess the glory of our Lord Jesus Christ. **2:15** Therefore, brothers and sisters, stand firm and hold on to the traditions that we taught you, whether by speech or by letter. **2:16** Now may our Lord Jesus Christ himself and God our Father, who loved us and by grace gave us eternal comfort and good hope, **2:17** encourage your hearts and strengthen you in every good thing you do or say.

Request for Prayer

3:1 Finally, pray for us, brothers and sisters, that the Lord's message may spread quickly and be honored as in fact it was among you, **3:2** and that we may be delivered from perverse and evil people. For not all have faith. **3:3** But the Lord is faithful, and he will strengthen you and protect you from the evil one. **3:4** And we are confident about you in the Lord that you are both doing – and will do – what we are commanding. **3:5** Now may the Lord direct your hearts toward the love of God and the endurance of Christ.

Response to the Undisciplined

3:6 But we command you, brothers and sisters, in the name of our Lord Jesus Christ, to keep away from any brother who lives an undisciplined life and not according to the tradition they received from us. **3:7** For you know yourselves how you must imitate us, because we did not behave without discipline among you, **3:8** and we did not eat anyone's food without paying. Instead, in toil and drudgery we worked night and day in order not to burden any of you. **3:9** It was not because we do not have that right, but to give ourselves as an example for you to imitate. **3:10** For even when we were with you, we used to give you this command: "If anyone is not willing to work, neither should he eat." **3:11** For we hear that some among you are living an undisciplined life, not doing their own work but meddling in the work of others. **3:12** Now such people we command and urge in the Lord Jesus Christ to work quietly and so provide their own food to eat. **3:13** But you, brothers and sisters, do not grow weary in doing what is right. **3:14** But if anyone does not obey our message through this letter, take note of him and do not associate closely with him, so that he may be ashamed. **3:15** Yet do not regard him as an enemy, but admonish him as a brother.

Conclusion

3:16 Now may the Lord of peace himself give you peace at all times and in every way. The Lord be with you all. **3:17** I, Paul, write this greeting with my own hand, which is how I write in every letter. **3:18** The grace of our Lord Jesus Christ be with you all.

Book 54. 1 Timothy

Salutation

1:1 From Paul, an apostle of Christ Jesus by the command of God our Savior and of Christ Jesus our hope, **1:2** to Timothy, my genuine child in the faith. Grace, mercy, and peace from God the Father and Christ Jesus our Lord!

Timothy's Task in Ephesus

1:3 As I urged you when I was leaving for Macedonia, stay on in Ephesus to instruct certain people not to spread false teachings, **1:4** nor to occupy themselves with myths and interminable genealogies. Such things promote useless speculations rather than God's redemptive plan that operates by faith. **1:5** But the aim of our instruction is love that comes from a pure heart, a good conscience, and a sincere faith. **1:6** Some have strayed from these and turned away to empty discussion. **1:7** They want to be teachers of the law, but they do not understand what they are saying or the things they insist on so confidently.

1:8 But we know that the law is good if someone uses it legitimately, **1:9** realizing that law is not intended for a righteous person, but for lawless and rebellious people, for the ungodly and sinners, for the unholy and profane, for those who kill their fathers or mothers, for murderers, **1:10** sexually immoral people, practicing homosexuals, kidnappers, liars, perjurers – in fact, for any who live contrary to sound teaching. **1:11** This accords with the glorious gospel of the blessed God that was entrusted to me.

1:12 I am grateful to the one who has strengthened me, Christ Jesus our Lord, because he considered me faithful in putting me into ministry, **1:13** even though I was formerly a blasphemer and a persecutor, and an arrogant man. But I was treated with mercy because I acted ignorantly in unbelief, **1:14** and our Lord's grace was abundant, bringing faith and love in Christ Jesus. **1:15** This saying is trustworthy and deserves full acceptance: "Christ Jesus came into the world to save sinners" – and I am the worst of them! **1:16** But here is why I was treated with mercy: so that in me as the worst, Christ Jesus could demonstrate his utmost patience, as an example for those who are going to believe in him for eternal life. **1:17** Now to the eternal king, immortal, invisible, the only God, be honor and glory forever and ever! Amen.

1:18 I put this charge before you, Timothy my child, in keeping with the prophecies once spoken about you, in order that with such encouragement you may fight the good fight. **1:19** To do this you must hold firmly to faith and a good conscience, which some have rejected and so have suffered shipwreck in regard to the faith. **1:20** Among these are Hymenaeus and Alexander, whom I handed over to Satan to be taught not to blaspheme.

Prayer for All People

2:1 First of all, then, I urge that requests, prayers, intercessions, and thanks be offered on behalf of all people, **2:2** even for kings and all who are in authority, that we may lead a peaceful and quiet life in all godliness and dignity. **2:3** Such prayer for all is good and welcomed before God our Savior, **2:4** since he wants all people to be saved and to come to a knowledge of the truth. **2:5** For there is one God and one intermediary between God and humanity, Christ Jesus, himself human, **2:6** who gave himself as a ransom for all, revealing God's purpose at his appointed time. **2:7** For this I was appointed a preacher and apostle – I am telling the truth; I am not lying – and a teacher of the Gentiles in faith and truth. **2:8** So I want the men to pray in every place, lifting up holy hands without anger or dispute.

Conduct of Women

2:9 Likewise the women are to dress in suitable apparel, with modesty and self-control. Their adornment must not be with braided hair and gold or pearls or expensive clothing, **2:10** but with good deeds, as is proper for women who profess reverence for God. **2:11** A woman must learn quietly with all submissiveness. **2:12** But I do not allow a woman to teach or exercise authority over a man. She must remain quiet. **2:13** For Adam was formed first and then Eve. **2:14** And Adam was not deceived, but the woman, because she was fully deceived, fell into transgression. **2:15** But she will be delivered through childbearing, if she continues in faith and love and holiness with self-control.

Qualifications for Overseers and Deacons

3:1 This saying is trustworthy: "If someone aspires to the office of overseer, he desires a good work." **3:2** The overseer then must be above reproach, the husband of one wife, temperate, self-controlled, respectable, hospitable, an able teacher, **3:3** not a drunkard, not violent, but gentle, not contentious, free from the love of money. **3:4** He must manage his own household well and keep his children in control without losing his dignity. **3:5** But if someone does not know how to manage his own household, how will he care for the church of God? **3:6** He must not be a recent convert or he may become arrogant and fall into the punishment that the devil will exact. **3:7** And he must be well thought of by those outside the faith, so that he may not fall into disgrace and be caught by the devil's trap.

3:8 Deacons likewise must be dignified, not two-faced, not given to excessive drinking, not greedy for gain, **3:9** holding to the mystery of the faith with a clear conscience. **3:10** And these also must be tested first and then let them serve as deacons if they are found blameless. **3:11** Likewise also their wives must be dignified, not slanderous, temperate, faithful in every respect. **3:12** Deacons must be husbands of one wife and good managers of their children and their own households. **3:13** For those who have served well as deacons gain a good standing for themselves and great boldness in the faith that is in Christ Jesus.

Conduct in God's Church

3:14 I hope to come to you soon, but I am writing these instructions to you **3:15** in case I am delayed, to let you know how people ought to conduct themselves in the household of God, because it is the church of the living God, the support and bulwark of the truth. **3:16** And we all agree, our religion contains amazing revelation:

He was revealed in the flesh,

vindicated by the Spirit,

seen by angels,

proclaimed among Gentiles,

believed on in the world,

taken up in glory.

Timothy's Ministry in the Later Times

4:1 Now the Spirit explicitly says that in the later times some will desert the faith and occupy themselves with deceiving spirits and demonic teachings, **4:2** influenced by the hypocrisy of liars whose consciences are seared. **4:3** They will prohibit marriage and require abstinence from foods that God created to be received with thanksgiving by those who believe and know the truth. **4:4** For every creation of God is good and no food is to be rejected if it is received with thanksgiving. **4:5** For it is sanctified by God's word and by prayer.

4:6 By pointing out such things to the brothers and sisters, you will be a good servant of Christ Jesus, having nourished yourself on the words of the faith and of the good teaching that you have followed. **4:7** But reject those myths fit only for the godless and gullible, and train yourself for godliness. **4:8** For "physical exercise has some value, but godliness is valuable in every way. It holds promise for the present life and for the life to come." **4:9** This saying is trustworthy and deserves full acceptance. **4:10** In fact this is why we work hard and struggle, because we have set our hope on the living God, who is the Savior of all people, especially of believers.

4:11 Command and teach these things. **4:12** Let no one look down on you because you are young, but set an example for the believers in your speech, conduct, love, faithfulness, and purity. **4:13** Until I come, give attention to the public reading of scripture, to exhortation, to teaching. **4:14** Do not neglect the spiritual gift you have, given to you and confirmed by prophetic words when the elders laid hands on you. **4:15** Take pains with these things; be absorbed in them, so that everyone will see your progress. **4:16** Be conscientious about how you live and what you teach. Persevere in this, because by doing so you will save both yourself and those who listen to you.

Instructions about Specific Groups

5:1 Do not address an older man harshly but appeal to him as a father. Speak to younger men as brothers, **5:2** older women as mothers, and younger women as sisters – with complete purity.

5:3 Honor widows who are truly in need. **5:4** But if a widow has children or grandchildren, they should first learn to fulfill their duty toward their own household and so repay their parents what is owed them. For this is what pleases God. **5:5** But the widow who is truly in need, and completely on her own, has set her hope on God and continues in her pleas and prayers night and day. **5:6** But the one who lives for pleasure is dead even while she lives. **5:7** Reinforce these commands, so that they will be beyond reproach. **5:8** But if someone does not provide for his own, especially his own family, he has denied the faith and is worse than an unbeliever.

5:9 No widow should be put on the list unless she is at least sixty years old, was the wife of one husband, **5:10** and has a reputation for good works: as one who has raised children, practiced hospitality, washed the feet of the saints, helped those in distress – as one who has exhibited all kinds of good works. **5:11** But do not accept younger widows on the list, because their passions may lead them away from Christ and they will desire to marry, **5:12** and so incur judgment for breaking their former pledge. **5:13** And besides that, going around from house to house they learn to be lazy, and they are not only lazy, but also gossips and busybodies, talking about things they should not. **5:14** So I want younger women to marry, raise children, and manage a household, in order to give the adversary no opportunity to vilify us. **5:15** For some have already wandered away to follow Satan. **5:16** If a believing woman has widows in her family, let her help them. The church should not be burdened, so that it may help the widows who are truly in need.

5:17 Elders who provide effective leadership must be counted worthy of double honor, especially those who work hard in speaking and teaching. **5:18** For the scripture says, "***Do not muzzle an ox while it is treading out the grain***," and, "The worker deserves his pay." **5:19** Do not accept an accusation against an elder unless it can be confirmed *by two or three witnesses*. **5:20** Those guilty of sin must be rebuked before all, as a warning to the rest. **5:21** Before God and Christ Jesus and the elect angels, I solemnly charge you to carry out these commands without prejudice or favoritism of any kind. **5:22** Do not lay hands on anyone hastily and so identify with the sins of others. Keep yourself pure. **5:23** (Stop drinking just water, but use a little wine for your digestion and your frequent illnesses.) **5:24** The sins of some people are obvious, going before them into judgment, but for others, they show up later. **5:25** Similarly good works are also obvious, and the ones that are not cannot remain hidden.

6:1 Those who are under the yoke as slaves must regard their own masters as deserving of full respect. This will prevent the name of God and Christian teaching from being discredited. **6:2** But those who have believing masters must not show them less respect because they are brothers. Instead they are to serve all the more, because those who benefit from their service are believers and dearly loved.

Summary of Timothy's Duties

Teach them and exhort them about these things. **6:3** If someone spreads false teachings and does not agree with sound words (that is, those of our Lord Jesus Christ) and with the teaching that accords with godliness, **6:4** he is conceited and understands nothing, but has an unhealthy interest in controversies and verbal disputes. This gives rise to envy, dissension, slanders, evil suspicions, **6:5** and constant bickering by people corrupted in their minds and deprived of the truth, who suppose that godliness is a way of making a profit. **6:6** Now godliness combined with contentment brings great profit. **6:7** For we have brought nothing into this world and so we cannot take a single thing out either. **6:8** But if we have food and shelter, we will be satisfied with that. **6:9** Those who long to be rich, however, stumble into temptation and a trap and many senseless and harmful desires that plunge people into ruin and destruction. **6:10** For the love of money is the root of all evils. Some people in reaching for it have strayed from the faith and stabbed themselves with many pains.

6:11 But you, as a person dedicated to God, keep away from all that. Instead pursue righteousness, godliness, faithfulness, love, endurance, and gentleness. **6:12** Compete well for the faith and lay hold of that eternal life you were called for and made your good confession for in the presence of many witnesses. **6:13** I charge you before God who gives life to all things and Christ Jesus who made his good confession before Pontius Pilate, **6:14** to obey this command without fault or failure until the appearing of our Lord Jesus Christ **6:15** – whose appearing the blessed and only Sovereign, the King of kings and Lord of lords, will reveal at the right time. **6:16** He alone possesses immortality and lives in unapproachable light, whom no human has ever seen or is able to see. To him be honor and eternal power! Amen.

6:17 Command those who are rich in this world's goods not to be haughty or to set their hope on riches, which are uncertain, but on God who richly provides us with all things for our enjoyment. **6:18** Tell them to do good, to be rich in good deeds, to be generous givers, sharing with others. **6:19** In this way they will save up a treasure for themselves as a firm foundation for the future and so lay hold of what is truly life.

Conclusion

6:20 O Timothy, protect what has been entrusted to you. Avoid the profane chatter and absurdities of so-called "knowledge." **6:21** By professing it, some have strayed from the faith. Grace be with you all.

Book 55. 2 Timothy

Salutation

1:1 From Paul, an apostle of Christ Jesus by the will of God, to further the promise of life in Christ Jesus, **1:2** to Timothy, my dear child. Grace, mercy, and peace from God the Father and Christ Jesus our Lord!

Thanksgiving and Charge to Timothy

1:3 I am thankful to God, whom I have served with a clear conscience as my ancestors did, when I remember you in my prayers as I do constantly night and day. **1:4** As I remember your tears, I long to see you, so that I may be filled with joy. **1:5** I recall your sincere faith that was alive first in your grandmother Lois and in your mother Eunice, and I am sure is in you.

1:6 Because of this I remind you to rekindle God's gift that you possess through the laying on of my hands. **1:7** For God did not give us a Spirit of fear but of power and love and self-control. **1:8** So do not be ashamed of the testimony about our Lord or of me, a prisoner for his sake, but by God's power accept your share of suffering for the gospel. **1:9** He is the one who saved us and called us with a holy calling, not based on our works but on his own purpose and grace, granted to us in Christ Jesus before time began, **1:10** but now made visible through the appearing of our Savior Christ Jesus. He has broken the power of death and brought life and immortality to light through the gospel! **1:11** For this gospel I was appointed a preacher and apostle and teacher. **1:12** Because of this, in fact, I suffer as I do. But I am not ashamed, because I know the one in whom my faith is set and I am convinced that he is able to protect what has been entrusted to me until that day. **1:13** Hold to the standard of sound words that you heard from me and do so with the faith and love that are in Christ Jesus. **1:14** Protect that good thing entrusted to you, through the Holy Spirit who lives within us.

1:15 You know that everyone in the province of Asia deserted me, including Phygelus and Hermogenes. **1:16** May the Lord grant mercy to the family of Onesiphorus, because he often refreshed me and was not ashamed of my imprisonment. **1:17** But when he arrived in Rome, he eagerly searched for me and found me. **1:18** May the Lord grant him to find mercy from the Lord on that day! And you know very well all the ways he served me in Ephesus.

Serving Faithfully Despite Hardship

2:1 So you, my child, be strong in the grace that is in Christ Jesus. **2:2** And entrust what you heard me say in the presence of many others as witnesses to faithful people who will be competent to teach others as well. **2:3** Take your share of suffering as a good soldier of Christ Jesus. **2:4** No one in military service gets entangled in matters of everyday life; otherwise he will not please the one who recruited him. **2:5** Also, if anyone competes as an athlete, he will not be crowned as the winner unless he competes according to the rules. **2:6** The farmer who works hard ought to have the first share of the crops. **2:7** Think about what I am saying and the Lord will give you understanding of all this.

2:8 Remember Jesus Christ, raised from the dead, a descendant of David; such is my gospel, **2:9** for which I suffer hardship to the point of imprisonment as a criminal, but God's message is not imprisoned! **2:10** So I endure all things for the sake of those chosen by God, that they too may obtain salvation in Christ Jesus and its eternal glory. **2:11** This saying is trustworthy:

If we died with him, we will also live with him.

2:12 If we endure, we will also reign with him.

If we deny him, he will also deny us.

2:13 If we are unfaithful, he remains faithful, since he cannot deny himself.

Dealing with False Teachers

2:14 Remind people of these things and solemnly charge them before the Lord not to wrangle over words. This is of no benefit; it just brings ruin on those who listen. **2:15** Make every effort to present yourself before God as a proven worker who does not need to be ashamed, teaching the message of truth accurately. **2:16** But avoid profane chatter, because those occupied with it will stray further and further into ungodliness, **2:17** and their message will spread its infection like gangrene. Hymenaeus and Philetus are in this group. **2:18** They have strayed from the truth by saying that the resurrection has already occurred, and they are undermining some people's faith. **2:19** However, God's solid foundation remains standing, bearing this seal: "*The Lord knows those who are his*," and "Everyone who confesses the name of the Lord must turn away from evil."

2:20 Now in a wealthy home there are not only gold and silver vessels, but also ones made of wood and of clay, and some are for honorable use, but others for ignoble use. **2:21** So if someone cleanses himself of such behavior, he will be a vessel for honorable use, set apart, useful for the Master, prepared for every good work. **2:22** But keep away from youthful passions, and pursue righteousness, faithfulness, love, and peace, in company with others who call on the Lord from a pure heart. **2:23** But reject foolish and ignorant controversies, because you know they breed infighting. **2:24** And the Lord's slave must not engage in heated disputes but be kind toward all, an apt teacher, patient, **2:25** correcting opponents with gentleness. Perhaps God will grant them repentance and then knowledge of the truth **2:26** and they will come to their senses and escape the devil's trap where they are held captive to do his will.

Ministry in the Last Days

3:1 But understand this, that in the last days difficult times will come. **3:2** For people will be lovers of themselves, lovers of money, boastful, arrogant, blasphemers, disobedient to parents, ungrateful, unholy, **3:3** unloving, irreconcilable, slanderers, without self-control, savage, opposed to what is good, **3:4** treacherous, reckless, conceited, loving pleasure rather than loving God. **3:5** They will maintain the outward appearance of religion but will have repudiated its power. So avoid people like these. **3:6** For some of these insinuate themselves into households and captivate weak women who are overwhelmed with sins and led along by various passions, **3:7** Such women are always seeking instruction, yet never able to arrive at a knowledge of the truth. **3:8** And just as Jannes and Jambres opposed Moses, so these people – who have warped minds and are disqualified in the faith – also oppose the truth. **3:9** But they will not go much further, for their foolishness will be obvious to everyone, just like it was with Jannes and Jambres.

Continue in What You Have Learned

3:10 You, however, have followed my teaching, my way of life, my purpose, my faith, my patience, my love, my endurance, **3:11** as well as the persecutions and sufferings that happened to me in Antioch, in Iconium, and in Lystra. I endured these persecutions and the Lord delivered me from them all. **3:12** Now in fact all who want to live godly lives in Christ Jesus will be persecuted. **3:13** But evil people and charlatans will go from bad to worse, deceiving others and being deceived themselves. **3:14** You, however, must continue in the things you have learned and are confident about. You know who taught you **3:15** and how from infancy you have known the holy writings, which are able to give you wisdom for salvation

through faith in Christ Jesus. **3:16** Every scripture is inspired by God and useful for teaching, for reproof, for correction, and for training in righteousness, **3:17** that the person dedicated to God may be capable and equipped for every good work.

Charge to Timothy Repeated

4:1 I solemnly charge you before God and Christ Jesus, who is going to judge the living and the dead, and by his appearing and his kingdom: **4:2** Preach the message, be ready whether it is convenient or not, reprove, rebuke, exhort with complete patience and instruction. **4:3** For there will be a time when people will not tolerate sound teaching. Instead, following their own desires, they will accumulate teachers for themselves, because they have an insatiable curiosity to hear new things. **4:4** And they will turn away from hearing the truth, but on the other hand they will turn aside to myths. **4:5** You, however, be self-controlled in all things, endure hardship, do an evangelist's work, fulfill your ministry. **4:6** For I am already being poured out as an offering, and the time for me to depart is at hand. **4:7** I have competed

well; I have finished the race; I have kept the faith! **4:8** Finally the crown of righteousness is reserved for me. The Lord, the righteous Judge, will award it to me in that day – and not to me only, but also to all who have set their affection on his appearing.

Travel Plans and Concluding Greetings

4:9 Make every effort to come to me soon. **4:10** For Demas deserted me, since he loved the present age, and he went to Thessalonica. Crescens went to Galatia and Titus to Dalmatia. **4:11** Only Luke is with me. Get Mark and bring him with you, because he is a great help to me in ministry. **4:12** Now I have sent Tychicus to Ephesus. **4:13** When you come, bring with you the cloak I left in Troas with Carpas and the scrolls, especially the parchments. **4:14** Alexander the coppersmith did me a great

deal of harm. *The Lord will repay him in keeping with his deeds.* **4:15** You be on guard against him too, because he vehemently opposed our words. **4:16** At my first defense no one appeared in my support; instead they all deserted me – may they not be held accountable for it. **4:17** But the Lord stood by me and strengthened me, so that through me the message would be fully proclaimed for all the Gentiles to hear. And so I was delivered from the lion's mouth! **4:18** The Lord will deliver me from every evil deed and will bring me safely into his heavenly kingdom. To him be glory for ever and ever! Amen.

4:19 Greetings to Prisca and Aquila and the family of Onesiphorus. **4:20** Erastus stayed in Corinth. Trophimus I left ill in Miletus. **4:21** Make every effort to come before winter. Greetings to you from Eubulus, Pudens, Linus, Claudia, and all the brothers and sisters. **4:22** The Lord be with your spirit. Grace be with you.

Book 56. *Titus*

Salutation

1:1 From Paul, a slave of God and apostle of Jesus Christ, to further the faith of God's chosen ones and the knowledge of the truth that is in keeping with godliness, **1:2** in hope of eternal life, which God, who does not lie, promised before the ages began. **1:3** But now in his own time he has made his message evident through the preaching I was entrusted with according to the command of God our Savior. **1:4** To Titus, my genuine son in a common faith. Grace and peace from God the Father and Christ Jesus our Savior!

Titus' Task on Crete

1:5 The reason I left you in Crete was to set in order the remaining matters and to appoint elders in every town, as I directed you. **1:6** An elder must be blameless, the husband of one wife, with faithful children who cannot be charged with dissipation or rebellion. **1:7** For the overseer must be blameless as one entrusted with God's work, not arrogant, not prone to anger, not a drunkard, not violent, not greedy for gain. **1:8** Instead he must be hospitable, devoted to what is good, sensible, upright, devout, and self-controlled. **1:9** He must hold firmly to the faithful message as it has been taught, so that he will be able to give exhortation in such healthy teaching and correct those who speak against it.

1:10 For there are many rebellious people, idle talkers, and deceivers, especially those with Jewish connections, **1:11** who must be silenced because they mislead whole families by teaching for dishonest gain what ought not to be taught. **1:12** A certain one of them, in fact, one of their own prophets, said, "Cretans are always liars, evil beasts, lazy gluttons." **1:13** Such testimony is true. For this reason rebuke them sharply that they may be healthy in the faith **1:14** and not pay attention to Jewish myths and commands of people who reject the truth. **1:15** All is pure to those who are pure. But to those who are corrupt and unbelieving, nothing is pure, but both their minds and consciences are corrupted. **1:16** They profess to know God but with their deeds they deny him, since they are detestable, disobedient, and unfit for any good deed.

Conduct Consistent with Sound Teaching

2:1 But as for you, communicate the behavior that goes with sound teaching. **2:2** Older men are to be temperate, dignified, self-controlled, sound in faith, in love, and in endurance. **2:3** Older women likewise are to exhibit behavior fitting for those who are holy, not slandering, not slaves to excessive drinking, but teaching what is good. **2:4** In this way they will train the younger women to love their husbands, to love their children, **2:5** to be self-controlled, pure, fulfilling their duties at home, kind, being subject to their own husbands, so that the message of God may not be discredited. **2:6** Encourage younger men likewise to be self-controlled, **2:7** showing yourself to be an example of good works in every way. In your teaching show integrity, dignity, **2:8** and a sound message that cannot be criticized, so that any opponent will be at a loss, because he has nothing evil to say about us. **2:9** Slaves are to be subject to their own masters in everything, to do what is wanted and not talk back, **2:10** not pilfering, but showing all good faith, in order to bring credit to the teaching of God our Savior in everything.

2:11 For the grace of God has appeared, bringing salvation to all people. **2:12** It trains us to reject godless ways and worldly desires and to live self-controlled, upright, and godly lives in the present age, **2:13** as we wait for the happy fulfillment of our hope in the glorious appearing of our great God and Savior, Jesus Christ. **2:14** He gave himself for us to set us free from every kind of lawlessness and to purify for himself a people who are truly his, who are eager to do good. **2:15** So communicate these things with the sort of exhortation or rebuke that carries full authority. Don't let anyone look down on you.

Conduct Toward Those Outside the Church

3:1 Remind them to be subject to rulers and authorities, to be obedient, to be ready for every good work. **3:2** They must not slander anyone, but be peaceable, gentle, showing complete courtesy to all people. **3:3** For we too were once foolish, disobedient, misled, enslaved to various passions and desires, spending our lives in evil and envy, hateful and hating one another. **3:4** But "when the kindness of God our Savior and his love for mankind appeared, **3:5** he saved us not by works of righteousness that we have done but on the basis of his mercy, through the washing of the new birth and the renewing of the Holy Spirit, **3:6** whom he poured out on us in full measure through Jesus Christ our Savior. **3:7** And so, since we have been justified by his grace, we become heirs with the confident expectation of eternal life."

Summary of the Letter

3:8 This saying is trustworthy, and I want you to insist on such truths, so that those who have placed their faith in God may be intent on engaging in good works. These things are good and beneficial for all people. **3:9** But avoid foolish controversies, genealogies, quarrels, and fights about the law, because they are useless and empty. **3:10** Reject a divisive person after one or two warnings. **3:11** You know that such a person is twisted by sin and is conscious of it himself.

Final Instructions and Greeting

3:12 When I send Artemas or Tychicus to you, do your best to come to me at Nicopolis, for I have decided to spend the winter there. **3:13** Make every effort to help Zenas the lawyer and Apollos on their way; make sure they have what they need. **3:14** Here is another way that our people can learn to engage in good works to meet pressing needs and so not be unfruitful. **3:15** Everyone with me greets you. Greet those who love us in the faith. Grace be with you all.

Book 57. Philemon

Salutation

1:1 From Paul, a prisoner of Christ Jesus, and Timothy our brother, to Philemon, our dear friend and colaborer, **1:2** to Apphia our sister, to Archippus our fellow soldier, and to the church that meets in your house. **1:3** Grace and peace to you from God our Father and the Lord Jesus Christ!

Thanks for Philemon's Love and Faith

1:4 I always thank my God as I remember you in my prayers, **1:5** because I hear of your faith in the Lord Jesus and your love for all the saints. **1:6** I pray that the faith you share with us may deepen your understanding of every blessing that belongs to you in Christ. **1:7** I have had great joy and encouragement because of your love, for the hearts of the saints have been refreshed through you, brother.

Paul's Request for Onesimus

1:8 So, although I have quite a lot of confidence in Christ and could command you to do what is proper, **1:9** I would rather appeal to you on the basis of love – I, Paul, an old man and even now a prisoner for the sake of Christ Jesus – **1:10** I am appealing to you concerning my child, whose spiritual father I have become during my imprisonment, that is, Onesimus, **1:11** who was formerly useless to you, but is now useful to you and me. **1:12** I have sent him (who is my very heart) back to you. **1:13** I wanted to keep him so that he could serve me in your place during my imprisonment for the sake of the gospel. **1:14** However, without your consent I did not want to do anything, so that your good deed would not be out of compulsion, but from your own willingness. **1:15** For perhaps it was for this reason that he was separated from you for a little while, so that you would have him back eternally, **1:16** no longer as a slave, but more than a slave, as a dear brother. He is especially so to me, and even more so to you now, both humanly speaking and in the Lord. **1:17** Therefore if you regard me as a partner, accept him as you would me. **1:18** Now if he has defrauded you of anything or owes you anything, charge what he owes to me. **1:19** I, Paul, have written this letter with my own hand: I will repay it. I could also mention that you owe me your very self. **1:20** Yes, brother, let me have some benefit from you in the Lord. Refresh my heart in Christ. **1:21** Since I was confident that you would obey, I wrote to you, because I knew that you would do even more than what I am asking you to do. **1:22** At the same time also, prepare a place for me to stay, for I hope that through your prayers I will be given back to you.

Concluding Greetings

1:23 Epaphras, my fellow prisoner in Christ Jesus, greets you. **1:24** Mark, Aristarchus, Demas and Luke, my colaborers, greet you too. **1:25** May the grace of the Lord Jesus Christ be with your spirit.

Book 58. Hebrews

Introduction: God Has Spoken Fully and Finally in His Son

1:1 After God spoke long ago in various portions and in various ways to our ancestors through the prophets, **1:2** in these last days he has spoken to us in a son, whom he appointed heir of all things, and through whom he created the world. **1:3** The Son is the radiance of his glory and the representation of his essence, and he sustains all things by his powerful word, and so when he had accomplished cleansing for sins, *he sat down at the right hand of the Majesty on high.* **1:4** Thus he became so far better than the angels as he has inherited a name superior to theirs.

The Son Is Superior to Angels

1:5 For to which of the angels did God ever say, "*You are my son! Today I have fathered you*"? And in another place he says, "*I will be his father and he will be my son.*" **1:6** But when he again brings his firstborn into the world, he says, "*Let all the angels of God worship him!*" **1:7** And he says of the angels, "*He makes his angels spirits and his ministers a flame of fire,*" **1:8** but of the Son he says,

"Your throne, O God, is forever and ever,
and a righteous scepter is the scepter of your kingdom.
1:9 You have loved righteousness and hated lawlessness.
So God, your God, has anointed you over your companions with the oil of rejoicing."

1:10 And,

"You founded the earth in the beginning, Lord,
and the heavens are the works of your hands.
1:11 They will perish, but you continue.
And they will all grow old like a garment,
1:12 and like a robe you will fold them up
and *like a garment* they will be changed,
but you are the same and your years will never run out."

1:13 But to which of the angels has he ever said, "*Sit at my right hand until I make your enemies a footstool for your feet*"? **1:14** Are they not all ministering spirits, sent out to serve those who will inherit salvation?

Warning Against Drifting Away

2:1 Therefore we must pay closer attention to what we have heard, so that we do not drift away. **2:2** For if the message spoken through angels proved to be so firm that every violation or disobedience received its just penalty, **2:3** how will we escape if we neglect such a great salvation? It was first communicated through the Lord and was confirmed to us by those who heard him, **2:4** while God confirmed their witness with signs and wonders and various miracles and gifts of the Holy Spirit distributed according to his will. Exposition of Psalm 8: Jesus and the Destiny of Humanity

2:5 For he did not put the world to come, about which we are speaking, under the control of angels. **2:6** Instead someone testified somewhere:

"What is man that you think of him or the son of man that you care for him?
2:7 You made him lower than the angels for a little while.
You crowned him with glory and honor.
2:8 You put all things under his control."

For when he *put all things under his control*, he left nothing outside of his control. At present we do not yet see *all things under his control*, **2:9** but we see Jesus, who was made *lower than the angels for a little while*, now crowned with glory and honor because he suffered death, so that by God's grace he would experience death on behalf of everyone. **2:10** For it was fitting for him, for whom and through whom all things exist, in bringing many sons to glory, to make the pioneer of their salvation perfect through sufferings. **2:11** For indeed he who makes holy and those being made holy all have the same origin, and so he is not ashamed to call them brothers and sisters, **2:12** saying, "*I will proclaim your name to my brothers; in the midst of the assembly I will praise you.*" **2:13** Again he says, "I will be confident in him," and again, "*Here I am, with the children God has given me.*" **2:14** Therefore, since the children share in flesh and blood, he likewise shared in their humanity, so that through death he could destroy the one who holds the power of death (that is, the devil), **2:15** and set free those who were held in slavery all their lives by their fear of death. **2:16** For surely his concern is not for angels, but he is concerned for Abraham's descendants. **2:17** Therefore he had to be made like his brothers and sisters in every respect, so that he could become a merciful and faithful high priest in things relating to God, to make atonement for the sins of the people. **2:18** For since he himself suffered when he was tempted, he is able to help those who are tempted.

Jesus and Moses

3:1 Therefore, holy brothers and sisters, partners in a heavenly calling, take note of Jesus, the apostle and high priest whom we confess, **3:2** who is faithful to the one who appointed him, as Moses was also in God's house. **3:3** For he has come to deserve greater glory than Moses, just as the builder of a house deserves greater honor than the house itself! **3:4** For every house is built by someone, but the builder of all things is God. **3:5** Now Moses was *faithful in all God's house* as a servant, to testify to the things that would be spoken. **3:6** But Christ is faithful as a son over God's house. We are of his house, if in fact we hold firmly to our confidence and the hope we take pride in.

Exposition of Psalm 95: Hearing God's Word in Faith

3:7 Therefore, as the Holy Spirit says,

"Oh, that today you would listen as he speaks!
3:8 "Do not harden your hearts as in the rebellion, in the day of testing in the wilderness.
3:9 "There your fathers tested me and tried me, and they saw my works for forty years.
3:10 "Therefore, I became provoked at that generation and said, 'Their hearts are always wandering and they have not known my ways.'
3:11 "As I swore in my anger, 'They will never enter my rest!'"

3:12 See to it, brothers and sisters, that none of you has an evil, unbelieving heart that forsakes the living God. **3:13** But exhort one another each day, as long as it is called "Today," that none of you may become hardened by sin's deception. **3:14** For we have become partners with Christ, if in fact we hold our initial confidence firm until the end. **3:15** As it says, *"Oh, that today you would listen as he speaks! Do not harden your hearts as in the rebellion."* **3:16** For which ones heard and rebelled? Was it not all who came out of Egypt under Moses' leadership? **3:17** And against whom was God provoked for forty years? Was it not those who sinned, *whose dead bodies fell in the wilderness*? **3:18** And to whom did he swear they would never enter into his rest, except those who were disobedient? **3:19** So we see that they could not enter because of unbelief.

God's Promised Rest

4:1 Therefore we must be wary that, while the promise of entering his rest remains open, none of you may seem to have come short of it. **4:2** For we had good news proclaimed to us just as they did. But the message they heard did them no good, since they did not join in with those who heard it in faith. **4:3** For we who have believed enter that rest, as he has said, "*As I swore in my anger, 'They will never enter my rest!'*" And yet God's works were accomplished from the foundation of the world. **4:4** For he has spoken somewhere about the seventh day in this way: "*And God rested on the seventh day from all his works,*" **4:5** but to repeat the text cited earlier: "*They will never enter my rest!*" **4:6** Therefore it remains for some to enter it, yet those to whom it was previously proclaimed did not enter because of disobedience. **4:7** So God again ordains a certain day, "Today," speaking through David after so long a time, as in the words quoted before, "*O, that today you would listen as he speaks! Do not harden your hearts.*" **4:8** For if Joshua had given them rest, God would not have spoken afterward about another day. **4:9** Consequently a Sabbath rest remains for the people of God. **4:10** For the one who enters God's rest has also rested from his works, just as God did from his own works. **4:11** Thus we must make every effort to enter that rest, so that no one may fall by following the same pattern of disobedience. **4:12** For the word of God is living and active and sharper than any double-edged sword, piercing even to the point of dividing soul from spirit, and joints from marrow; it is able to judge the desires and thoughts of the heart. **4:13** And no creature is hidden from God, but everything is naked and exposed to the eyes of him to whom we must render an account.

Jesus Our Compassionate High Priest

4:14 Therefore since we have a great high priest who has passed through the heavens, Jesus the Son of God, let us hold fast to our confession. **4:15** For we do not have a high priest incapable of sympathizing with our weaknesses, but one who has been tempted in every way just as we are, yet without sin. **4:16** Therefore let us confidently approach the throne of grace to receive mercy and find grace whenever we need help.

5:1 For every high priest is taken from among the people and appointed to represent them before God, to offer both gifts and sacrifices for sins. **5:2** He is able to deal compassionately with those who are ignorant and erring, since he also is subject to weakness, **5:3** and for this reason he is obligated to make sin offerings for himself as well as for the people. **5:4** And no one assumes this honor on his own initiative, but only when called to it by God, as in fact Aaron was. **5:5** So also Christ did not glorify himself in becoming high priest, but the one who glorified him was God, who said to him, "*You are my Son! Today I have fathered you,*" **5:6** as also in another place God says, "*You are a priest forever in the order of Melchizedek.*" **5:7** During his earthly life Christ offered both requests and supplications, with loud cries and tears, to the one who was able to save him from death and he was heard because of his devotion. **5:8** Although he was a son, he learned obedience through the things he suffered. **5:9** And by being perfected in this way, he became the source of eternal salvation to all who obey him, **5:10** and he was designated by God as high priest *in the order of Melchizedek*.

The Need to Move on to Maturity

5:11 On this topic we have much to say and it is difficult to explain, since you have become sluggish in hearing. **5:12** For though you should in fact be teachers by this time, you need someone to teach you the beginning elements of God's utterances. You have gone back to needing milk, not solid food. **5:13** For everyone who lives on milk is inexperienced in the message of righteousness, because he is an infant. **5:14** But solid food is for the mature, whose perceptions are trained by practice to discern both good and evil.

6:1 Therefore we must progress beyond the elementary instructions about Christ and move on to maturity, not laying this foundation again: repentance from dead works and faith in God, **6:2** teaching about baptisms, laying on of hands, resurrection of the dead, and eternal judgment. **6:3** And this is what we intend to do, if God permits. **6:4** For it is impossible in the case of those who have once been enlightened, tasted the heavenly gift, become partakers of the Holy Spirit, **6:5** tasted the good word of God and the miracles of the coming age, **6:6** and then have committed apostasy, to renew them again to repentance, since they are crucifying the Son of God for themselves all over again and holding him up to contempt. **6:7** For the ground that has soaked up the rain that frequently falls on it and yields useful vegetation for those who tend it receives a blessing from God. **6:8** But if it produces thorns and thistles, it is useless and about to be cursed; its fate is to be burned. **6:9** But in your case, dear friends, even though we speak like this, we are convinced of better things relating to salvation. **6:10** For God is not unjust so as to forget your work

and the love you have demonstrated for his name, in having served and continuing to serve the saints. **6:11** But we passionately want each of you to demonstrate the same eagerness for the fulfillment of your hope until the end, **6:12** so that you may not be sluggish, but imitators of those who through faith and perseverance inherit the promises.

6:13 Now when God made his promise to Abraham, since he could swear by no one greater, he swore by himself, **6:14** saying, "*Surely I will bless you greatly and multiply your descendants abundantly*." **6:15** And so by persevering, Abraham inherited the promise. **6:16** For people swear by something greater than themselves, and the oath serves as a confirmation to end all dispute. **6:17** In the same way God wanted to demonstrate more clearly to the heirs of the promise that his purpose was unchangeable, and so he intervened with an oath, **6:18** so that we who have found refuge in him may find strong encouragement to hold fast to the hope set before us through two unchangeable things, since it is impossible for God to lie. **6:19** We have this hope as an anchor for the soul, sure and steadfast, which reaches inside behind the curtain, **6:20** where Jesus our forerunner entered on our behalf, since he became *a priest forever in the order of Melchizedek*.

The Nature of Melchizedek's Priesthood

7:1 Now this *Melchizedek, king of Salem, priest of the most high God, met Abraham as he was returning from defeating the kings and blessed him*. **7:2** To him also *Abraham apportioned a tithe of everything*. His name first means king of righteousness, then *king of Salem*, that is, king of peace. **7:3** Without father, without mother, without genealogy, he has neither beginning of days nor end of life but is like the son of God, and he remains a priest for all time. **7:4** But see how great he must be, if Abraham the patriarch gave him a tithe of his plunder. **7:5** And those of the sons of Levi who receive the priestly office have authorization according to the law to collect a tithe from the people, that is, from their fellow countrymen, although they too are descendants of Abraham. **7:6** But Melchizedek who does not share their ancestry collected a tithe from Abraham and blessed the one who possessed the promise. **7:7** Now without dispute the inferior is blessed by the superior, **7:8** and in one case tithes are received by mortal men, while in the other by him who is affirmed to be alive. **7:9** And it could be said that Levi himself, who receives tithes, paid a tithe through Abraham. **7:10** For he was still in his ancestor Abraham's loins when Melchizedek met him.

Jesus and the Priesthood of Melchizedek

7:11 So if perfection had in fact been possible through the Levitical priesthood – for on that basis the people received the law – what further need would there have been for another priest to arise, said to be in the order of Melchizedek and not in Aaron's order? **7:12** For when the priesthood changes, a change in the law must come as well. **7:13** Yet the one these things are spoken about belongs to a different tribe, and no one from that tribe has ever officiated at the altar. **7:14** For it is clear that our Lord is descended from Judah, yet Moses said nothing about priests in connection with that tribe. **7:15** And this is even clearer if another priest arises in the likeness of Melchizedek, **7:16** who has become a priest not by a legal regulation about physical descent but by the power of an indestructible life. **7:17** For here is the testimony about him: "*You are a priest forever in the order of Melchizedek.*" **7:18** On the one hand a former command is set aside because it is weak and useless, **7:19** for the law made nothing perfect. On the other hand a better hope is introduced, through which we draw near to God. **7:20** And since this was not done without a sworn affirmation – for the others have become priests without a sworn affirmation, **7:21** but Jesus did so with a sworn affirmation by the one who said to him, "*The Lord has sworn and will not change his mind, 'You are a priest forever'*" – **7:22** accordingly Jesus has become the guarantee of a better covenant. **7:23** And the others who became priests were numerous, because death prevented them from continuing in office, **7:24** but he holds his priesthood permanently since he lives forever. **7:25** So he is able to save completely those who come to God through him, because he always lives to intercede for them. **7:26** For it is indeed fitting for us to have such a high priest: holy, innocent, undefiled, separate from sinners, and exalted above the heavens. **7:27** He has no need to do every day what those priests do, to offer sacrifices first for their own sins and then for the sins of the people, since he did this in offering himself once for all. **7:28** For the law appoints as high priests men subject to weakness, but the word of solemn affirmation that came after the law appoints a son made perfect forever.

The High Priest of a Better Covenant

8:1 Now the main point of what we are saying is this: We have such a high priest, one who *sat down at the right hand of the throne of the Majesty in heaven*, **8:2** a minister in the sanctuary and the true tabernacle that the Lord, not man, set up. **8:3** For every high priest is appointed to offer both gifts and sacrifices. So this one too had to have something to offer. **8:4** Now if he were on earth, he would not be a priest, since there are already priests who offer the gifts prescribed by the law. **8:5** The place where they serve is a sketch and shadow of the heavenly sanctuary, just as Moses was warned by God as he was about to complete the tabernacle. For he says, "*See that you make everything according to the design shown to you on the mountain.*" **8:6** But now Jesus has obtained a superior ministry, since the covenant that he mediates is also better and is enacted on better promises.

8:7 For if that first covenant had been faultless, no one would have looked for a second one. **8:8** But showing its fault, God says to them,

"Look, the days are coming, says the Lord, when I will complete a new covenant with the house of Israel and with the house of Judah.

8:9 "It will not be like the covenant that I made with their fathers, on the day when I took them by the hand to lead them out of Egypt, because they did not continue in my covenant and I had no regard for them, says the Lord.

8:10 "For this is the covenant that I will establish with the house of Israel after those days, says the Lord. I will put my laws in their minds and I will inscribe them on their hearts. And I will be their God and they will be my people.

8:11 "And there will be no need at all for each one to teach his countryman or each one to teach his brother saying, 'Know the Lord,' since they will all know me, from the least to the greatest.

8:12 "For I will be merciful toward their evil deeds, and their sins I will remember no longer."

8:13 When he speaks of a new covenant, he makes the first obsolete. Now what is growing obsolete and aging is about to disappear.

The Arrangement and Ritual of the Earthly Sanctuary

9:1 Now the first covenant, in fact, had regulations for worship and its earthly sanctuary. **9:2** For a tent was prepared, the outer one, which contained the lampstand, the table, and the presentation of the loaves; this is called the holy place. **9:3** And after the second curtain there was a tent called the holy of holies. **9:4** It contained the golden altar of incense and the ark of the covenant covered entirely with gold. In this ark were the golden urn containing the manna, Aaron's rod that budded, and the stone tablets of the covenant. **9:5** And above the ark were the cherubim of glory overshadowing the mercy seat. Now is not the time to speak of these things in detail. **9:6** So with these things prepared like this, the priests enter continually into the outer tent as they perform their duties. **9:7** But only the high priest enters once a year into the inner tent, and not without blood that he offers for himself and for the sins of the people committed in ignorance. **9:8** The Holy Spirit is making clear that the way into the holy place had not yet appeared as long as the old tabernacle was standing. **9:9** This was a symbol for the time then present, when gifts and sacrifices were offered that could not perfect the conscience of the worshiper. **9:10** They served only for matters of food and drink and various washings; they are external regulations imposed until the new order came.

Christ's Service in the Heavenly Sanctuary

9:11 But now Christ has come as the high priest of the good things to come. He passed through the greater and more perfect tent not made with hands, that is, not of this creation, **9:12** and he entered once for all into the most holy place not by the blood of goats and calves but by his own blood, and so he himself secured eternal redemption. **9:13** For if the blood of goats and bulls and the ashes of a young cow sprinkled on those who are defiled consecrated them and provided ritual purity, **9:14** how much more will the blood of Christ, who through the eternal Spirit offered himself without blemish to God, purify our consciences from dead works to worship the living God.

9:15 And so he is the mediator of a new covenant, so that those who are called may receive the eternal inheritance he has promised, since he died to set them free from the violations committed under the first covenant. **9:16** For where there is a will, the death of the one who made it must be proven. **9:17** For a will takes effect only at death, since it carries no force while the one who made it is alive. **9:18** So even the first covenant was inaugurated with blood. **9:19** For when Moses had spoken every command to all the people according to the law, he took the blood of calves and goats with water and scarlet wool and hyssop and sprinkled both the book itself and all the people, **9:20** and said, "*This is the blood of the covenant that God has commanded you to keep.*" **9:21** And both the tabernacle and all the utensils of worship he likewise sprinkled with blood. **9:22** Indeed according to the law almost everything was purified with blood, and without the shedding of blood there is no forgiveness. **9:23** So it was necessary for the sketches of the things in heaven to be purified with these sacrifices, but the heavenly things themselves required better sacrifices than these. **9:24** For Christ did not enter a sanctuary made with hands – the representation of the true sanctuary – but into heaven itself, and he appears now in God's presence for us. **9:25** And he did not enter to offer himself again and again, the way the high priest enters the sanctuary year after year with blood that is not his own, **9:26** for then he would have had to suffer again and again since the foundation of the world. But now he has appeared once for all at the consummation of the ages to put away sin by his sacrifice. **9:27** And just as people are appointed to die once, and then to face judgment, **9:28** so also, after Christ was offered once to *bear the sins of many*, to those who eagerly await him he will appear a second time, not to bear sin but to bring salvation.

Concluding Exposition: Old and New Sacrifices Contrasted

10:1 For the law possesses a shadow of the good things to come but not the reality itself, and is therefore completely unable, by the same sacrifices offered continually, year after year, to perfect those who come to worship. **10:2** For otherwise would they not have ceased to be offered, since the worshipers would have been purified once for all and so have no further consciousness of sin? **10:3** But in those sacrifices there is a reminder of sins year after year. **10:4** For the blood of bulls and goats cannot take away sins. **10:5** So when he came into the world, he said,

"Sacrifice and offering you did not desire, but a body you prepared for me.

10:6 "Whole burnt offerings and sin-offerings you took no delight in.

10:7 "Then I said, 'Here I am: I have come – it is written of me in the scroll of the book – to do your will, O God.'"

10:8 When he says above, "*Sacrifices and offerings* and *whole burnt offerings and sin-offerings you did not desire nor did you take delight* in them" (which are offered according to the law), **10:9** then he says, "*Here I am: I have come to do your will.*" He does away with the first to establish the second. **10:10** By his will we have been made holy through the offering of the body of Jesus Christ once for all. **10:11** And every priest stands day after day serving and offering the same sacrifices again and again – sacrifices that can never take away sins. **10:12** But when this priest had offered one sacrifice for sins for all time, *he sat down at the right hand* of God, **10:13** where he is now waiting *until his enemies are made a footstool for his feet.* **10:14** For by one offering he has perfected for all time those who are made holy. **10:15** And the Holy Spirit also witnesses to us, for after saying, **10:16** "*This is the covenant that I will establish with them after those days, says the Lord. I will put my laws on their hearts and I will inscribe them on their minds,*" **10:17** then he says, "*Their sins and their lawless deeds I will remember no longer.*" **10:18** Now where there is forgiveness of these, there is no longer any offering for sin.

Drawing Near to God in Enduring Faith

10:19 Therefore, brothers and sisters, since we have confidence to enter the sanctuary by the blood of Jesus, **10:20** by the fresh and living way that he inaugurated for us through the curtain, that is, through his flesh, **10:21** and since we have a great priest over the house of God, **10:22** let us draw near with a sincere heart in the assurance that faith brings, because we have had our hearts sprinkled clean from an evil conscience and our bodies washed in pure water. **10:23** And let us hold unwaveringly to the hope that we confess, for the one who made the promise is trustworthy. **10:24** And let us take thought of how to spur one another on to love and good works, **10:25** not abandoning our own meetings, as some are in the habit of doing, but encouraging each other, and even more so because you see the day drawing near.

10:26 For if we deliberately keep on sinning after receiving the knowledge of the truth, no further sacrifice for sins is left for us, **10:27** but only a certain fearful expectation of judgment and *a fury of fire that will consume God's enemies.* **10:28** Someone who rejected the law of Moses was put to death without mercy *on the testimony of two or three witnesses.* **10:29** How much greater punishment do you think that person deserves who has contempt for the Son of God, and profanes the blood of the covenant that made him holy, and insults the Spirit of grace? **10:30** For we know the one who said, "*Vengeance is mine, I will repay,*" and again, "*The Lord will judge his people.*" **10:31** It is a terrifying thing to fall into the hands of the living God.

10:32 But remember the former days when you endured a harsh conflict of suffering after you were enlightened. **10:33** At times you were publicly exposed to abuse and afflictions, and at other times you came to share with others who were treated in that way. **10:34** For in fact you shared the sufferings of those in prison, and you accepted the confiscation of your belongings with joy, because you knew that you certainly had a better and lasting possession. **10:35** So do not throw away your confidence, because it has great reward. **10:36** But for you need endurance in order to do God's will and so receive what is promised. **10:37** For *just a little longer* and *he who is coming will arrive and not delay.* **10:38** *But my righteous one will live by faith, and if he shrinks back, I take no pleasure in him.* **10:39** But we are not among those who shrink back and thus perish, but are among those who have faith and preserve their souls.

People Commended for Their Faith

11:1 Now faith is being sure of what we hope for, being convinced of what we do not see. **11:2** For by it the people of old received God's commendation. **11:3** By faith we understand that the worlds were set in order at God's command, so that the visible has its origin in the invisible. **11:4** By faith Abel offered God a greater sacrifice than Cain, and through his faith he was commended as righteous, because God commended him for his offerings. And through his faith he still speaks, though he is dead. **11:5** By faith Enoch was taken up so that he did not see death, and he was not to be found because God took him up. For before his removal he had been commended as having pleased God. **11:6** Now without faith it is impossible to please him, for the one who approaches God must believe that he exists and that he rewards those who seek him. **11:7** By faith Noah, when he was warned about things not yet seen, with reverent regard constructed an ark for the deliverance of his family. Through faith he condemned the world and became an heir of the righteousness that comes by faith.

11:8 By faith Abraham obeyed when he was called to go out to a place he would later receive as an inheritance, and he went out without understanding where he was going. **11:9** By faith he lived as a foreigner in the promised land as though it were a foreign country, living in tents with Isaac and Jacob, who were fellow heirs of the same promise. **11:10** For he was looking forward to the city with firm foundations, whose architect and builder is God. **11:11** By faith, even though Sarah herself was barren and he was too old, he received the ability to procreate, because he regarded the one who had given the promise to be trustworthy. **11:12** So in fact children were fathered by one man – and this one as good as dead – *like the number of stars in the sky and like the innumerable grains of sand on the seashore.* **11:13** These all died in faith without receiving the things promised, but they saw them in the distance and welcomed them and acknowledged that they were strangers and foreigners on the earth. **11:14** For those who speak in such a way make it clear that they are seeking a homeland. **11:15** In fact, if they had been thinking of the land that they had left, they would have had opportunity to return. **11:16** But as it is, they aspire to a better land, that is, a heavenly one. Therefore, God is not ashamed to be called their God, for he has prepared a city for them. **11:17** By faith Abraham, when he was tested, offered up Isaac. He had received the promises, yet he was ready to offer up his only son. **11:18** God had told him, "*Through Isaac descendants will carry on your name,*" **11:19** and he reasoned that God could even raise him from the dead, and in a sense he received him back from there. **11:20** By faith also Isaac blessed Jacob and Esau concerning the future. **11:21** By faith Jacob, as he was dying, blessed each of the sons of Joseph and *worshiped as he leaned on his staff.* **11:22** By faith Joseph, at the end of his life, mentioned the exodus of the sons of Israel and gave instructions about his burial.

11:23 By faith, when Moses was born, his parents hid him for three months, because they saw the child was beautiful and they were not afraid of the king's edict. **11:24** By faith, when he grew up, Moses refused to be called the son of Pharaoh's daughter, **11:25** choosing rather to be ill-treated with the people of God than to enjoy sin's fleeting pleasure. **11:26** He regarded abuse suffered for Christ to be greater wealth than the treasures of Egypt, for his eyes were fixed on the reward. **11:27** By faith he left Egypt without fearing the king's anger, for he persevered as though he could see the one who is invisible. **11:28** By faith he kept the Passover and the sprinkling of the blood, so that the one who destroyed the firstborn would not touch them. **11:29** By faith they crossed the Red Sea as if on dry ground, but when the Egyptians tried it, they were swallowed up. **11:30** By faith the walls of Jericho fell after the people marched around them for seven days. **11:31** By faith Rahab the prostitute escaped the destruction of the disobedient, because she welcomed the spies in peace.

11:32 And what more shall I say? For time will fail me if I tell of Gideon, Barak, Samson, Jephthah, of David and Samuel and the prophets. **11:33** Through faith they conquered kingdoms, administered justice, gained what was promised, shut the mouths of lions, **11:34** quenched raging fire, escaped the edge of the sword, gained strength in weakness, became mighty in battle, put foreign armies to flight, **11:35** and women received back their dead raised to life. But others were tortured, not accepting release, to obtain resurrection to a better life. **11:36** And others experienced mocking and flogging, and even chains and imprisonment. **11:37** They were stoned, sawed apart, murdered with the sword; they went about in sheepskins and goatskins; they were destitute, afflicted, ill-treated **11:38** (the world was not worthy of them); they wandered in deserts and mountains and caves and openings in the earth. **11:39** And these all were commended for their faith, yet they did not receive what was promised. **11:40** For God had provided something better for us, so that they would be made perfect together with us.

The Lord's Discipline

12:1 Therefore, since we are surrounded by such a great cloud of witnesses, we must get rid of every weight and the sin that clings so closely, and run with endurance the race set out for us, **12:2** keeping our eyes fixed on Jesus, the pioneer and perfecter of our faith. For the joy set out for him he endured the cross, disregarding its shame, and *has taken his seat at the right hand of the throne* of God. **12:3** Think of him who endured such opposition against himself by sinners, so that you may not grow weary in your souls and give up. **12:4** You have not yet resisted to the point of bloodshed in your struggle against sin. **12:5** And have you forgotten the exhortation addressed to you as sons?

"My son, do not scorn the Lord's discipline
or give up when he corrects you.
12:6 "For the Lord disciplines the one he loves and chastises every son he accepts."

12:7 Endure your suffering as discipline; God is treating you as sons. For what son is there that a father does not discipline? **12:8** But if you do not experience discipline, something all sons have shared in, then you are illegitimate and are not sons. **12:9** Besides, we have experienced discipline from our earthly fathers and we respected them; shall we not submit ourselves all the more to the Father of spirits and receive life? **12:10** For they disciplined us for a little while as seemed good to them, but he does so for our benefit, that we may share his holiness. **12:11** Now all discipline seems painful at the time, not joyful. But later it produces the fruit of peace and righteousness for those trained by it. **12:12** Therefore, *strengthen your listless hands and your weak knees,* **12:13** and *make straight paths for your feet,* so that what is lame may not be put out of joint but be healed.

Do Not Reject God's Warning

12:14 Pursue peace with everyone, and holiness, for without it no one will see the Lord. **12:15** See to it that no one comes short of the grace of God, that no one be like *a bitter root springing up* and causing trouble, and through him many become defiled. **12:16** And see to it that no one becomes an immoral or godless person like Esau, who *sold his own birthright for a single meal.* **12:17** For you know that later when he wanted to inherit the blessing, he was rejected, for he found no opportunity for repentance, although he sought the blessing with tears. **12:18** For you have not come to something that can be touched, to a burning fire and darkness and gloom and a whirlwind **12:19** and the blast of a trumpet and a voice uttering words such that those who heard begged to hear no more. **12:20** For they could not bear what was commanded: "*If even an animal touches the mountain, it must be stoned.*" **12:21** In fact, the scene was so terrifying that Moses said, "*I shudder with fear.*" **12:22** But you have come to Mount Zion, the city of the living God, the heavenly Jerusalem, and to myriads of angels, to the assembly **12:23** and congregation of the firstborn, who are enrolled in heaven, and to God, the judge of all, and to the spirits of the righteous, who have been made perfect, **12:24** and to Jesus, the mediator of a new covenant, and to the sprinkled blood that speaks of something better than Abel's does.

12:25 Take care not to refuse the one who is speaking! For if they did not escape when they refused the one who warned them on earth, how much less shall we, if we reject the one who warns from heaven? **12:26** Then his voice shook the earth, but now he has promised, "*I will once more shake not only the earth but heaven too.*" **12:27** Now this phrase "*once more*" indicates the removal of what is shaken, that is, of created things, so that what is unshaken may remain. **12:28** So since we are receiving an unshakable kingdom, let us give thanks, and through this let us offer worship pleasing to God in devotion and awe. **12:29** For our *God is indeed a devouring fire.*

Final Exhortations

13:1 Brotherly love must continue. **13:2** Do not neglect hospitality, because through it some have entertained angels without knowing it. **13:3** Remember those in prison as though you were in prison with them, and those ill-treated as though you too felt their torment. **13:4** Marriage must be honored among all and the marriage bed kept undefiled, for God will judge sexually immoral people and adulterers. **13:5** Your conduct must be free from the love of money and you must be content with what you have, for he has said, "*I will never leave you and I will never abandon you.*" **13:6** So we can say with confidence, "*The Lord is my helper, and I will not be afraid. What can man do to me?*" **13:7** Remember your leaders, who spoke God's message to you; reflect on the outcome of their lives and imitate their faith. **13:8** Jesus Christ is the same yesterday and today and forever! **13:9** Do not be carried away by all sorts of strange teachings. For it is good for the heart to be strengthened by grace, not ritual meals, which have never benefited those who participated in them. **13:10** We have an altar that those who serve in the tabernacle have no right to eat from. **13:11** For the bodies of those animals whose blood the high priest brings into the sanctuary as an offering for sin are burned outside the camp. **13:12** Therefore, to sanctify the people by his own blood, Jesus also suffered outside the camp. **13:13** We must go out to him, then, outside the camp, bearing the abuse he experienced. **13:14** For here we have no lasting city, but we seek the city that is to come. **13:15** Through him then let us continually offer up a sacrifice of praise to God, that is, the fruit of our lips, acknowledging his name. **13:16** And do not neglect to do good and to share what you have, for God is pleased with such sacrifices.

13:17 Obey your leaders and submit to them, for they keep watch over your souls and will give an account for their work. Let them do this with joy and not with complaints, for this would be no advantage for you. **13:18** Pray for us, for we are sure that we have a clear conscience and desire to conduct ourselves rightly in every respect. **13:19** I especially ask you to pray that I may be restored to you very soon.

Benediction and Conclusion

13:20 Now may the God of peace who by the blood of the eternal covenant brought back from the dead the great shepherd of the sheep, our Lord Jesus Christ, **13:21** equip you with every good thing to do his will, working in us what is pleasing before him through Jesus Christ, to whom be glory forever. Amen.

13:22 Now I urge you, brothers and sisters, bear with my message of exhortation, for in fact I have written to you briefly. **13:23** You should know that our brother Timothy has been released. If he comes soon, he will be with me when I see you. **13:24** Greetings to all your leaders and all the saints. Those from Italy send you greetings. **13:25** Grace be with you all.

Book 59. James

Salutation

1:1 From James, a slave of God and the Lord Jesus Christ, to the twelve tribes dispersed abroad. Greetings!

Joy in Trials

1:2 My brothers and sisters, consider it nothing but joy when you fall into all sorts of trials, **1:3** because you know that the testing of your faith produces endurance. **1:4** And let endurance have its perfect effect, so that you will be perfect and complete, not deficient in anything. **1:5** But if anyone is deficient in wisdom, he should ask God, who gives to all generously and without reprimand, and it will be given to him. **1:6** But he must ask in faith without doubting, for the one who doubts is like a wave of the sea, blown and tossed around by the wind. **1:7** For that person must not suppose that he will receive anything from the Lord, **1:8** since he is a double-minded individual, unstable in all his ways.

1:9 Now the believer of humble means should take pride in his high position. **1:10** But the rich person's pride should be in his humiliation, because he will pass away like a wildflower in the meadow. **1:11** For the sun rises with its heat and dries up the meadow; the petal of the flower falls off and its beauty is lost forever. So also the rich person in the midst of his pursuits will wither away. **1:12** Happy is the one who endures testing, because when he has proven to be genuine, he will receive the crown of life that God promised to those who love him. **1:13** Let no one say when he is tempted, "I am tempted by God," for God cannot be tempted by evil, and he himself tempts no one. **1:14** But each one is tempted when he is lured and enticed by his own desires. **1:15** Then when desire conceives, it gives birth to sin, and when sin is full grown, it gives birth to death. **1:16** Do not be led astray, my dear brothers and sisters. **1:17** All generous giving and every perfect gift is from above, coming down from the Father of lights, with whom there is no variation or the slightest hint of change. **1:18** By his sovereign plan he gave us birth through the message of truth, that we would be a kind of firstfruits of all he created.

Living Out the Message

1:19 Understand this, my dear brothers and sisters! Let every person be quick to listen, slow to speak, slow to anger. **1:20** For human anger does not accomplish God's righteousness. **1:21** So put away all filth and evil excess and humbly welcome the message implanted within you, which is able to save your souls. **1:22** But be sure you live out the message and do not merely listen to it and so deceive yourselves. **1:23** For if someone merely listens to the message and does not live it out, he is like someone who gazes at his own face in a mirror. **1:24** For he gazes at himself and then goes out and immediately forgets what sort of person he was. **1:25** But the one who peers into the perfect law of liberty and fixes his attention there, and does not become a forgetful listener but one who lives it out – he will be blessed in what he does. **1:26** If someone thinks he is religious yet does not bridle his tongue, and so deceives his heart, his religion is futile. **1:27** Pure and undefiled religion before God the Father is this: to care for orphans and widows in their misfortune and to keep oneself unstained by the world.

Prejudice and the Law of Love

2:1 My brothers and sisters, do not show prejudice if you possess faith in our glorious Lord Jesus Christ. **2:2** For if someone comes into your assembly wearing a gold ring and fine clothing, and a poor person enters in filthy clothes, **2:3** do you pay attention to the one who is finely dressed and say, "You sit here in a good place," and to the poor person, "You stand over there," or "Sit on the floor"? **2:4** If so, have you not made distinctions among yourselves and become judges with evil motives? **2:5** Listen, my dear brothers and sisters! Did not God choose the poor in the world to be rich in faith and heirs of the kingdom that he promised to those who love him? **2:6** But you have dishonored the poor! Are not the rich oppressing you and dragging you into the courts? **2:7** Do they not blaspheme the good name of the one you belong to? **2:8** But if you fulfill the royal law as expressed in this scripture, "*You shall love your neighbor as yourself*," you are doing well. **2:9** But if you show prejudice, you are committing sin and are convicted by the law as violators. **2:10** For the one who obeys the whole law but fails in one point has become guilty of all of it. **2:11** For he who said, "*Do not commit adultery*," also said, "*Do not murder*." Now if you do not commit adultery but do commit murder, you have become a violator of the law. **2:12** Speak and act as those who will be judged by a law that gives freedom. **2:13** For judgment is merciless for the one who has shown no mercy. But mercy triumphs over judgment.

Faith and Works Together

2:14 What good is it, my brothers and sisters, if someone claims to have faith but does not have works? Can this kind of faith save him? **2:15** If a brother or sister is poorly clothed and lacks daily food, **2:16** and one of you says to them, "Go in peace, keep warm and eat well," but you do not give them what the body needs, what good is it? **2:17** So also faith, if it does not have works, is dead being by itself. **2:18** But someone will say, "You have faith and I have works." Show me your faith without works and I will show you faith by my works. **2:19** You believe that God is one; well and good. Even the demons believe that – and tremble with fear. **2:20** But would you like evidence, you empty fellow, that faith without works is useless? **2:21** Was not Abraham our father justified by works when he offered Isaac his son on the altar? **2:22** You see that his faith was working together with his works and his faith was perfected by works. **2:23** And the scripture was fulfilled that says, "*Now Abraham believed God and it was counted to him for righteousness*," and *he was called God's friend*. **2:24** You see that a person is justified by works and not by faith alone. **2:25** And similarly, was not Rahab the prostitute also justified by works when she welcomed the messengers and sent them out by another way? **2:26** For just as the body without the spirit is dead, so also faith without works is dead.

The Power of the Tongue

3:1 Not many of you should become teachers, my brothers and sisters, because you know that we will be judged more strictly. **3:2** For we all stumble in many ways. If someone does not stumble in what he says, he is a perfect individual, able to control the entire body as well. **3:3** And if we put bits into the mouths of horses to get them to obey us, then we guide their entire bodies. **3:4** Look at ships too: Though they are so large and driven by harsh winds, they are steered by a tiny rudder wherever the pilot's inclination directs. **3:5** So too the tongue is a small part of the body, yet it has great pretensions. Think how small a flame sets a huge forest ablaze. **3:6** And the tongue is a fire! The tongue represents the world of wrongdoing among the parts of our bodies. It pollutes the entire body and sets fire to the course of human existence – and is set on fire by hell.

3:7 For every kind of animal, bird, reptile, and sea creature is subdued and has been subdued by humankind. **3:8** But no human being can subdue the tongue; it is a restless evil, full of deadly poison. **3:9** With it we bless the Lord and Father, and with it we curse people made in God's image. **3:10** From the same mouth come blessing and cursing. These things should not be so, my brothers and sisters. **3:11** A spring does not pour out fresh water and bitter water from the same opening, does it? **3:12** Can a fig tree produce olives, my brothers and sisters, or a vine produce figs? Neither can a salt water spring produce fresh water.

True Wisdom

3:13 Who is wise and understanding among you? By his good conduct he should show his works done in the gentleness that wisdom brings. **3:14** But if you have bitter jealousy and selfishness in your hearts, do not boast and tell lies against the truth. **3:15** Such wisdom does not come from above but is earthly, natural, demonic. **3:16** For where there is jealousy and selfishness, there is disorder and every evil practice. **3:17** But the wisdom from above is first pure, then peaceable, gentle, accommodating, full of mercy and good fruit, impartial, and not hypocritical. **3:18** And the fruit that consists of righteousness is planted in peace among those who make peace.

Passions and Pride

4:1 Where do the conflicts and where do the quarrels among you come from? Is it not from this, from your passions that battle inside you? **4:2** You desire and you do not have; you murder and envy and you cannot obtain; you quarrel and fight. You do not have because you do not ask; **4:3** you ask and do not receive because you ask wrongly, so you can spend it on your passions.

4:4 Adulterers, do you not know that friendship with the world means hostility toward God? So whoever decides to be the world's friend makes himself God's enemy. **4:5** Or do you think the scripture means nothing when it says, "The spirit that God caused to live within us has an envious yearning"? **4:6** But he gives greater grace. Therefore it says, "*God opposes the proud, but he gives grace to the humble*." **4:7** So submit to God. But resist the devil and he will flee from you. **4:8** Draw near to God and he will draw near to you. Cleanse your hands, you sinners, and make your hearts pure, you double-minded. **4:9** Grieve, mourn, and weep. Turn your laughter into mourning and your joy into despair. **4:10** Humble yourselves before the Lord and he will exalt you.

4:11 Do not speak against one another, brothers and sisters. He who speaks against a fellow believer or judges a fellow believer speaks against the law and judges the law. But if you judge the law, you are not a doer of the law but its judge. **4:12** But there is only one who is lawgiver and judge – the one who is able to save and destroy. On the other hand, who are you to judge your neighbor?

4:13 Come now, you who say, "Today or tomorrow we will go into this or that town and spend a year there and do business and make a profit." **4:14** You do not know about tomorrow. What is your life like? For you are a puff of smoke that appears for a short time and then vanishes. **4:15** You ought to say instead, "If the Lord is willing, then we will live and do this or that." **4:16** But as it is, you boast in your arrogance. All such boasting is evil. **4:17** So whoever knows what is good to do and does not do it is guilty of sin.

Warning to the Rich

5:1 Come now, you rich! Weep and cry aloud over the miseries that are coming on you. **5:2** Your riches have rotted and your clothing has become moth-eaten. **5:3** Your gold and silver have rusted and their rust will be a witness against you. It will consume your flesh like fire. It is in the last days that you have hoarded treasure! **5:4** Look, the pay you have held back from the workers who mowed your fields cries out against you, and the cries of the reapers have reached the ears of the Lord of hosts. **5:5** You have lived indulgently and luxuriously on the earth. You have fattened your hearts in a day of slaughter. **5:6** You have condemned and murdered the righteous person, although he does not resist you.

Patience in Suffering

5:7 So be patient, brothers and sisters, until the Lord's return. Think of how the farmer waits for the precious fruit of the ground and is patient for it until it receives the early and late rains. **5:8** You also be patient and strengthen your hearts, for the Lord's return is near. **5:9** Do not grumble against one another, brothers and sisters, so that you may not be judged. See, the judge stands before the gates! **5:10** As an example of suffering and patience, brothers and sisters, take the prophets who spoke in the Lord's name. **5:11** Think of how we regard as blessed those who have endured. You have heard of Job's endurance and you have seen the Lord's purpose, that *the Lord is full of compassion and mercy*. **5:12** And above all, my brothers and sisters, do not swear, either by heaven or by earth or by any other oath. But let your "Yes" be yes and your "No" be no, so that you may not fall into judgment.

Prayer for the Sick

5:13 Is anyone among you suffering? He should pray. Is anyone in good spirits? He should sing praises. **5:14** Is anyone among you ill? He should summon the elders of the church, and they should pray for him and anoint him with oil in the name of the Lord. **5:15** And the prayer of faith will save the one who is sick and the Lord will raise him up – and if he has committed sins, he will be forgiven. **5:16** So confess your sins to one another and pray for one another so that you may be healed. The prayer of a righteous person has great effectiveness. **5:17** Elijah was a human being like us, and he prayed earnestly that it would not rain and there was no rain on the land for three years and six months! **5:18** Then he prayed again, and the sky gave rain and the land sprouted with a harvest. **`5:19** My brothers and sisters, if anyone among you wanders from the truth and someone turns him back, **5:20** he should know that the one who turns a sinner back from his wandering path will save that person's soul from death and will cover a multitude of sins.

Book 60. 1 Peter

Salutation

1:1 From Peter, an apostle of Jesus Christ, to those temporarily residing abroad (in Pontus, Galatia, Cappadocia, the province of Asia, and Bithynia) who are chosen **1:2** according to the foreknowledge of God the Father by being set apart by the Spirit for obedience and for sprinkling with Jesus Christ's blood. May grace and peace be yours in full measure!

New Birth to Joy and Holiness

1:3 Blessed be the God and Father of our Lord Jesus Christ! By his great mercy he gave us new birth into a living hope through the resurrection of Jesus Christ from the dead, **1:4** that is, into an inheritance imperishable, undefiled, and unfading. It is reserved in heaven for you, **1:5** who by God's power are protected through faith for a salvation ready to be revealed in the last time. **1:6** This brings you great joy, although you may have to suffer for a short time in various trials. **1:7** Such trials show the proven character of your faith, which is much more valuable than gold – gold that is tested by fire, even though it is passing away – and will bring praise and glory and honor when Jesus Christ is revealed. **1:8** You have not seen him, but you love him. You do not see him now but you believe in him, and so you rejoice with an indescribable and glorious joy, **1:9** because you are attaining the goal of your faith – the salvation of your souls.

1:10 Concerning this salvation, the prophets who predicted the grace that would come to you searched and investigated carefully. **1:11** They probed into what person or time the Spirit of Christ within them was indicating when he testified beforehand about the sufferings appointed for Christ and his subsequent glory. **1:12** They were shown that they were serving not themselves but you, in regard to the things now announced to you through those who proclaimed the gospel to you by the Holy Spirit sent from heaven – things angels long to catch a glimpse of.

1:13 Therefore, get your minds ready for action by being fully sober, and set your hope completely on the grace that will be brought to you when Jesus Christ is revealed. **1:14** Like obedient children, do not comply with the evil urges you used to follow in your ignorance, **1:15** but, like the Holy One who called you, become holy yourselves in all of your conduct, **1:16** for it is written, "*You shall be holy, because I am holy*." **1:17** And if you address as Father the one who impartially judges according to each one's work, live out the time of your temporary residence here in reverence. **1:18** You know that from your empty way of life inherited from your ancestors you were ransomed – not by perishable things like silver or gold, **1:19** but by precious blood like that of an unblemished and spot-less lamb, namely Christ. **1:20** He was foreknown before the foundation of the world but was manifested in these last times for your sake. **1:21** Through him you now trust in God, who raised him from the dead and gave him glory, so that your faith and hope are in God.

1:22 You have purified your souls by obeying the truth in order to show sincere mutual love. So love one another earnestly from a pure heart. **1:23** You have been born anew, not from perishable but from imperishable seed, through the living and enduring word of God. **1:24** For

all flesh is like grass
and all its glory like the flower of the grass;
the grass withers and the flower falls off,
1:25 but the word of the Lord endures forever.

And this is the word that was proclaimed to you.

2:1 So get rid of all evil and all deceit and hypocrisy and envy and all slander. **2:2** And yearn like newborn infants for pure, spiritual milk, so that by it you may grow up to salvation, **2:3** if *you have experienced the Lord's kindness*.

A Living Stone, a Chosen People

2:4 So as you come to him, a living stone rejected by men but chosen and priceless in God's sight, **2:5** you yourselves, as living stones, are built up as a spiritual house to be a holy priesthood and to offer spiritual sacrifices that are acceptable to God through Jesus Christ. **2:6** For it says in scripture, "*Look, I lay in Zion a stone, a chosen and priceless cornerstone, and whoever believes in him will never be put to shame*." **2:7** So you who believe see his value, but for those who do not believe, *the stone that the builders rejected has become the cornerstone*, **2:8** and *a stumbling-stone and a rock to trip over*. They stumble because they disobey the word, as they were destined to do. **2:9** But you are *a chosen race, a royal priesthood, a holy nation, a people of his own*, so that you may *proclaim the virtues* of the one who called you out of darkness into his marvelous light. **2:10** You once were *not a people*, but now you are God's people. You were *shown no mercy,* but now you have received mercy.

2:11 Dear friends, I urge you as foreigners and exiles to keep away from fleshly desires that do battle against the soul, **2:12** and maintain good conduct among the non-Christians, so that though they now malign you as wrongdoers, they may see your good deeds and glorify God when he appears.

Submission to Authorities

2:13 Be subject to every human institution for the Lord's sake, whether to a king as supreme **2:14** or to governors as those he commissions to punish wrongdoers and praise those who do good. **2:15** For God wants you to silence the ignorance of foolish people by doing good. **2:16** Live as free people, not using your freedom as a pretext for evil, but as God's slaves. **2:17** Honor all people, love the family of believers, fear God, honor the king.

2:18 Slaves, be subject to your masters with all reverence, not only to those who are good and gentle, but also to those who are perverse. **2:19** For this finds God's favor, if because of conscience toward God someone endures hardships in suffering unjustly. **2:20** For what credit is it if you sin and are mistreated and endure it? But if you do good and suffer and so endure, this finds favor with God. **2:21** For to this you were called, since Christ also suffered for you, leaving an example for you to follow in his steps.

2:22 He *committed no* sin *nor was deceit found in his mouth*. **2:23** When he was maligned, he did not answer back; when he suffered, he threatened no retaliation, but committed himself to God who judges justly. **2:24** He *himself bore our sins* in his body on the tree, that we may cease from sinning and live for righteousness. *By* his *wounds you were healed*. **2:25** For you were *going astray like sheep* but now you have turned back to the shepherd and guardian of your souls.

Wives and Husbands

3:1 In the same way, wives, be subject to your own husbands. Then, even if some are disobedient to the word, they will be won over without a word by the way you live, **3:2** when they see your pure and reverent conduct. **3:3** Let your beauty not be external – the braiding of hair and wearing of gold jewelry or fine clothes – **3:4** but the inner person of the heart, the lasting beauty of a gentle and tranquil spirit, which is precious in God's sight. **3:5** For in the same way the holy women who hoped in God long ago adorned themselves by being subject to their husbands, **3:6** like Sarah who obeyed Abraham, calling him lord. You become her children when you do what is good and have no fear in doing so. **3:7** Husbands, in the same way, treat your wives with consideration as the weaker partners and show them honor as fellow heirs of the grace of life. In this way nothing will hinder your prayers.

Suffering for Doing Good

3:8 Finally, all of you be harmonious, sympathetic, affectionate, compassionate, and humble. **3:9** Do not return evil for evil or insult for insult, but instead bless others because you were called to inherit a blessing. **3:10** For

the one who wants to love life and see good days must keep his tongue from evil and his lips from uttering deceit.

3:11 And he must turn away from evil and do good;

he must seek peace and pursue it.

3:12 For the eyes of the Lord are upon the righteous and his ears are open to their prayer.

But the Lord's face is against those who do evil.

3:13 For who is going to harm you if you are devoted to what is good? **3:14** But in fact, if you happen to suffer for doing what is right, you are blessed. ***But do not be terrified of them or be shaken.*** **3:15** But set Christ apart as Lord in your hearts and always be ready to give an answer to anyone who asks about the hope you possess. **3:16** Yet do it with courtesy and respect, keeping a good conscience, so that those who slander your good conduct in Christ may be put to shame when they accuse you. **3:17** For it is better to suffer for doing good, if God wills it, than for doing evil.

3:18 Because Christ also suffered once for sins,

the just for the unjust,

to bring you to God,

by being put to death in the flesh

but by being made alive in the spirit.

3:19 In it he went and preached to the spirits in prison, **3:20** after they were disobedient long ago when God patiently waited in the days of Noah as an ark was being constructed. In the ark a few, that is eight souls, were delivered through water. **3:21** And this prefigured baptism, which now saves you – not the washing off of physical dirt but the pledge of a good conscience to God – through the resurrection of Jesus Christ, **3:22** who went into heaven and is at the right hand of God with angels and authorities and powers subject to him.

4:1 So, since Christ suffered in the flesh, you also arm yourselves with the same attitude, because the one who has suffered in the flesh has finished with sin, **4:2** in that he spends the rest of his time on earth concerned about the will of God and not human desires. **4:3** For the time that has passed was sufficient for you to do what the non-Christians desire. You lived then in debauchery, evil desires, drunkenness, carousing, drinking bouts, and wanton idolatries. **4:4** So they are astonished when you do not rush with them into the same flood of wickedness, and they vilify you. **4:5** They will face a reckoning before Jesus Christ who stands ready to judge the living and the dead. **4:6** Now it was for this very purpose that the gospel was preached to those who are now dead, so that though they were judged in the flesh by human standards they may live spiritually by God's standards.

Service, Suffering, and Judgment

4:7 For the culmination of all things is near. So be self-controlled and sober-minded for the sake of prayer. **4:8** Above all keep your love for one another fervent, because ***love covers a multitude of sins***. **4:9** Show hospitality to one another without complaining. **4:10** Just as each one has received a gift, use it to serve one another as good stewards of the varied grace of God. **4:11** Whoever speaks, let it be with God's words. Whoever serves, do so with the strength that God supplies, so that in everything God will be glorified through Jesus Christ. To him belong the glory and the power forever and ever. Amen.

4:12 Dear friends, do not be astonished that a trial by fire is occurring among you, as though something strange were happening to you. **4:13** But rejoice in the degree that you have shared in the sufferings of Christ, so that when his glory is revealed you may also rejoice and be glad. **4:14** If you are insulted for the name of Christ, you are blessed, because the Spirit of glory, who is ***the Spirit of God, rests*** on you. **4:15** But let none of you suffer as a murderer or thief or criminal or as a troublemaker. **4:16** But if you suffer as a Christian, do not be ashamed, but glorify God that you bear such a name. **4:17** For it is time for judgment to begin, starting with the house of God. And if it starts with us, what will be the fate of those who are disobedient to the gospel of God? **4:18** And ***if the righteous are barely saved, what will become of the ungodly and sinners?*** **4:19** So then let those who suffer according to the will of God entrust their souls to a faithful Creator as they do good.

Leading and Living in God's Flock

5:1 So as your fellow elder and a witness of Christ's sufferings and as one who shares in the glory that will be revealed, I urge the elders among you: **5:2** Give a shepherd's care to God's flock among you, exercising oversight not merely as a duty but willingly under God's direction, not for shameful profit but eagerly. **5:3** And do not lord it over those entrusted to you, but be examples to the flock. **5:4** Then when the Chief Shepherd appears, you will receive the crown of glory that never fades away.

5:5 In the same way, you who are younger, be subject to the elders. And all of you, clothe yourselves with humility toward one another, because God ***opposes the proud but gives grace to the humble***. **5:6** And God will exalt you in due time, if you humble yourselves under his mighty hand **5:7** by casting all your cares on him because he cares for you. **5:8** Be sober and alert. Your enemy the devil, *like a roaring lion,* is on the prowl looking for someone to devour. **5:9** Resist him, strong in your faith, because you know that your brothers and sisters throughout the world are enduring the same kinds of suffering. **5:10** And, after you have suffered for a little while, the God of all grace who called you to his eternal glory in Christ will himself restore, confirm, strengthen, and establish you. **5:11** To him belongs the power forever. Amen.

Final Greetings

5:12 Through Silvanus, whom I know to be a faithful brother, I have written to you briefly, in order to encourage you and testify that this is the true grace of God. Stand fast in it. **5:13** The church in Babylon, chosen together with you, greets you, and so does Mark, my son. **5:14** Greet one another with a loving kiss. Peace to all of you who are in Christ.

Book 61. 2 Peter

Salutation

1:1 From Simeon Peter, a slave and apostle of Jesus Christ, to those who through the righteousness of our God and Savior, Jesus Christ, have been granted a faith just as precious as ours. **1:2** May grace and peace be lavished on you as you grow in the rich knowledge of God and of Jesus our Lord!

Believers' Salvation and the Work of God

1:3 I can pray this because his divine power has bestowed on us everything necessary for life and godliness through the rich knowledge of the one who called us by his own glory and excellence. **1:4** Through these things he has bestowed on us his precious and most magnificent promises, so that by means of what was promised you may become partakers of the divine nature, after escaping the worldly corruption that is produced by evil desire. **1:5** For this very reason, make every effort to add to your faith excellence, to excellence, knowledge; **1:6** to knowledge, self-control; to self-control, perseverance; to perseverance, godliness; **1:7** to godliness, brotherly affection; to brotherly affection, unselfish love. **1:8** For if these things are really yours and are continually increasing, they will keep you from becoming ineffective and unproductive in your pursuit of knowing our Lord Jesus Christ more intimately. **1:9** But concerning the one who lacks such things – he is blind. That is to say, he is nearsighted, since he has forgotten about the cleansing of his past sins. **1:10** Therefore, brothers and sisters, make every effort to be sure of your calling and election. For by doing this you will never stumble into sin. **1:11** For thus an entrance into the eternal kingdom of our Lord and Savior, Jesus Christ, will be richly provided for you.

Salvation Based on the Word of God

1:12 Therefore, I intend to remind you constantly of these things even though you know them and are well established in the truth that you now have. **1:13** Indeed, as long as I am in this tabernacle, I consider it right to stir you up by way of a reminder, **1:14** since I know that my tabernacle will soon be removed, because our Lord Jesus Christ revealed this to me. **1:15** Indeed, I will also make every effort that, after my departure, you have a testimony of these things.

1:16 For we did not follow cleverly concocted fables when we made known to you the power and return of our Lord Jesus Christ; no, we were eyewitnesses of his grandeur. **1:17** For he received honor and glory from God the Father, when that voice was conveyed to him by the Majestic Glory: "This is my dear Son, in whom I am delighted." **1:18** When this voice was conveyed from heaven, we ourselves heard it, for we were with him on the holy mountain. **1:19** Moreover, we possess the prophetic word as an altogether reliable thing. You do well if you pay attention to this as you would to a light shining in a murky place, until the day dawns and the morning star rises in your hearts. **1:20** Above all, you do well if you recognize this: No prophecy of scripture ever comes about by the prophet's own imagination. **1:21** for no prophecy was ever borne of human impulse; rather, men carried along by the Holy Spirit spoke from God.

The False Teachers' Ungodly Lifestyle

2:1 But false prophets arose among the people, just as there will be false teachers among you. These false teachers will infiltrate your midst with destructive heresies, even to the point of denying the Master who bought them. As a result, they will bring swift destruction on themselves. **2:2** And many will follow their debauched lifestyles. Because of these false teachers, the way of truth will be slandered. **2:3** And in their greed they will exploit you with deceptive words. Their condemnation pronounced long ago is not sitting idly by; their destruction is not asleep.

2:4 For if God did not spare the angels who sinned, but threw them into hell and locked them up in chains in utter darkness, to be kept until the judgment, **2:5** and if he did not spare the ancient world, but did protect Noah, a herald of righteousness, along with seven others, when God brought a flood on an ungodly world, **2:6** and if he turned to ashes the cities of Sodom and Gomorrah when he condemned them to destruction, having appointed them to serve as an example to future generations of the ungodly, **2:7** and if he rescued Lot, a righteous man in anguish over the debauched lifestyle of lawless men, **2:8** (for while he lived among them day after day, that righteous man was tormented in his righteous soul by the lawless deeds he saw and heard) **2:9** – if so, then the Lord knows how to rescue the godly from their trials, and to reserve the unrighteous for punishment at the day of judgment, **2:10** especially those who indulge their fleshly desires and who despise authority.

Brazen and insolent, they are not afraid to insult the glorious ones, **2:11** yet even angels, who are much more powerful, do not bring a slanderous judgment against them before the Lord. **2:12** But these men, like irrational animals – creatures of instinct, born to be caught and destroyed – do not understand whom they are insulting, and consequently in their destruction they will be destroyed, **2:13** suffering harm as the wages for their harmful ways. By considering it a pleasure to carouse in broad daylight, they are stains and blemishes, indulging in their deceitful pleasures when they feast together with you. **2:14** Their eyes, full of adultery, never stop sinning; they entice unstable people. They have trained their hearts for greed, these cursed children! **2:15** By forsaking the right path they have gone astray, because they followed the way of Balaam son of Bosor, who loved the wages of unrighteousness, **2:16** yet was rebuked for his own transgression (a dumb donkey, speaking with a human voice, restrained the prophet's madness).

2:17 These men are waterless springs and mists driven by a storm, for whom the utter depths of darkness have been reserved. **2:18** For by speaking high-sounding but empty words they are able to entice, with fleshly desires and with debauchery, people who have just escaped from those who reside in error. **2:19** Although these false teachers promise such people freedom, they themselves are enslaved to immorality. For whatever a person succumbs to, to that he is enslaved. **2:20** For if after they have escaped the filthy things of the world through the rich knowledge of our Lord and Savior Jesus Christ, they again get entangled in them and succumb to

them, their last state has become worse for them than their first. **2:21** For it would have been better for them never to have known the way of righteousness than, having known it, to turn back from the holy commandment that had been delivered to them. **2:22** They are illustrations of this true proverb: "*A dog returns to its own vomit*," and "A sow, after washing herself, wallows in the mire."

The False Teachers' Denial of the Lord's Return

3:1 Dear friends, this is already the second letter I have written you, in which I am trying to stir up your pure mind by way of reminder: **3:2** I want you to recall both the predictions foretold by the holy prophets and the commandment of the Lord and Savior through your apostles. **3:3** Above all, understand this: In the last days blatant scoffers will come, being propelled by their own evil urges **3:4** and saying, "Where is his promised return? For ever since our ancestors died, all things have continued as they were from the beginning of creation." **3:5** For they deliberately suppress this fact, that by the word of God heavens existed long ago and an earth was formed out of water and by means of water. **3:6** Through these things the world existing at that time was destroyed when it was deluged with water. **3:7** But by the same word the present heavens and earth have been reserved for fire, by being kept for the day of judgment and destruction of the ungodly.

3:8 Now, dear friends, do not let this one thing escape your notice, that a single day is like a thousand years with the Lord and a thousand years are like a single day. **3:9** The Lord is not slow concerning his promise, as some regard slowness, but is being patient toward you, because he does not wish for any to perish but for all to come to repentance. **3:10** But the day of the Lord will come like a thief; when it comes, the heavens will disappear with a horrific noise, and the celestial bodies will melt away in a blaze, and the earth and every deed done on it will be laid bare. **3:11** Since all these things are to melt away in this manner, what sort of people must we be, conducting our lives in holiness and godliness, **3:12** while waiting for and hastening the coming of the day of God? Because of this day, the heavens will be burned up and dissolve, and the celestial bodies will melt away in a blaze! **3:13** But, according to his promise, we are waiting for new heavens and a new earth, in which righteousness truly resides.

Exhortation to the Faithful

3:14 Therefore, dear friends, since you are waiting for these things, strive to be found at peace, without spot or blemish, when you come into his presence. **3:15** And regard the patience of our Lord as salvation, just as also our dear brother Paul wrote to you, according to the wisdom given to him, **3:16** speaking of these things in all his letters. Some things in these letters are hard to understand, things the ignorant and unstable twist to their own destruction, as they also do to the rest of the scriptures. **3:17** Therefore, dear friends, since you have been forewarned, be on your guard that you do not get led astray by the error of these unprincipled men and fall from your firm grasp on the truth. **3:18** But grow in the grace and knowledge of our Lord and Savior Jesus Christ. To him be the honor both now and on that eternal day.

Book 62. 1 John

The Prologue to the Letter

1:1 This is what we proclaim to you: what was from the beginning, what we have heard, what we have seen with our eyes, what we have looked at and our hands have touched (concerning the word of life – **1:2** and the life was revealed, and we have seen and testify and announce to you the eternal life that was with the Father and was revealed to us). **1:3** What we have seen and heard we announce to you too, so that you may have fellowship with us (and indeed our fellowship is with the Father and with his Son Jesus Christ). **1:4** Thus we are writing these things so that our joy may be complete.

God Is Light, So We Must Walk in the Light

1:5 Now this is the gospel message we have heard from him and announce to you: God is light, and in him there is no darkness at all. **1:6** If we say we have fellowship with him and yet keep on walking in the darkness, we are lying and not practicing the truth. **1:7** But if we walk in the light as he himself is in the light, we have fellowship with one another and the blood of Jesus his Son cleanses us from all sin. **1:8** If we say we do not bear the guilt of sin, we are deceiving ourselves and the truth is not in us. **1:9** But if we confess our sins, he is faithful and righteous, forgiving us our sins and cleansing us from all unrighteousness. **1:10** If we say we have not sinned, we make him a liar and his word is not in us. **2:1** (My little children, I am writing these things to you so that you may not sin.) But if anyone does sin, we have an advocate with the Father, Jesus Christ the righteous One, **2:2** and he himself is the atoning sacrifice for our sins, and not only for our sins but also for the whole world.

Keeping God's Commandments

2:3 Now by this we know that we have come to know God: if we keep his commandments. **2:4** The one who says "I have come to know God" and yet does not keep his commandments is a liar, and the truth is not in such a person. **2:5** But whoever obeys his word, truly in this person the love of God has been perfected. By this we know that we are in him. **2:6** The one who says he resides in God ought himself to walk just as Jesus walked.

2:7 Dear friends, I am not writing a new commandment to you, but an old commandment which you have had from the beginning. The old commandment is the word that you have already heard. **2:8** On the other hand, I am writing a new commandment to you which is true in him and in you, because the darkness is passing away and the true light is already shining. **2:9** The one who says he is in the light but still hates his fellow Christian is still in the darkness. **2:10** The one who loves his fellow Christian resides in the light, and there is no cause for stumbling in him. **2:11** But the one who hates his fellow Christian is in the darkness, walks in the darkness, and does not know where he is going, because the darkness has blinded his eyes.

Words of Reassurance

2:12 I am writing to you, little children, that your sins have been forgiven because of his name. **2:13** I am writing to you, fathers, that you have known him who has been from the beginning. I am writing to you, young people, that you have conquered the evil one. **2:14** I have written to you, children, that you have known the Father. I have written to you, fathers, that you have known him who has been from the beginning. I have written to you, young people, that you are strong, and the word of God resides in you, and you have conquered the evil one.

2:15 Do not love the world or the things in the world. If anyone loves the world, the love of the Father is not in him, **2:16** because all that is in the world (the desire of the flesh and the desire of the eyes and the arrogance produced by material possessions) is not from the Father, but is from the world. **2:17** And the world is passing away with all its desires, but the person who does the will of God remains forever.

Warning About False Teachers

2:18 Children, it is the last hour, and just as you heard that the antichrist is coming, so now many antichrists have appeared. We know from this that it is the last hour. **2:19** They went out from us, but they did not really belong to us, because if they had belonged to us, they would have remained with us. But they went out from us to demonstrate that all of them do not belong to us.

2:20 Nevertheless you have an anointing from the Holy One, and you all know. **2:21** I have not written to you that you do not know the truth, but that you do know it, and that no lie is of the truth. **2:22** Who is the liar but the person who denies that Jesus is the Christ? This one is the antichrist: the person who denies the Father and the Son. **2:23** Everyone who denies the Son does not have the Father either. The person who confesses the Son has the Father also.

2:24 As for you, what you have heard from the beginning must remain in you. If what you heard from the beginning remains in you, you also will remain in the Son and in the Father. **2:25** Now this is the promise that he himself made to us: eternal life. **2:26** These things I have written to you about those who are trying to deceive you.

2:27 Now as for you, the anointing that you received from him resides in you, and you have no need for anyone to teach you. But as his anointing teaches you about all things, it is true and is not a lie. Just as it has taught you, you reside in him.

Children of God

2:28 And now, little children, remain in him, so that when he appears we may have confidence and not shrink away from him in shame when he comes back. **2:29** If you know that he is righteous, you also know that everyone who practices righteousness has been fathered by him.

3:1 (See what sort of love the Father has given to us: that we should be called God's children – and indeed we are! For this reason the world does not know us: because it did not know him. **3:2** Dear friends, we are God's children now, and what we will be has not yet been revealed. We know that whenever it is revealed we will be like him, because we will see him just as he is. **3:3** And everyone who has this hope focused on him purifies himself, just as Jesus is pure).

3:4 Everyone who practices sin also practices lawlessness; indeed, sin is lawlessness. **3:5** And you know that Jesus was revealed to take away sins, and in him there is no sin. **3:6** Everyone who resides in him does not sin; everyone who sins has neither seen him nor known him. **3:7** Little children, let no one deceive you: The one who practices righteousness is righteous, just as Jesus is righteous. **3:8** The one who practices sin is of the devil, because the devil has been sinning from the beginning. For this purpose the Son of God was revealed: to destroy the works of the devil. **3:9** Everyone who has been fathered by God does not practice sin, because God's seed resides in him, and thus he is not able to sin, because he has been fathered by God. **3:10** By this the children of God and the children of the devil are revealed: Everyone who does not practice righteousness – the one who does not love his fellow Christian – is not of God.

God Is Love, So We Must Love One Another

3:11 For this is the gospel message that you have heard from the beginning: that we should love one another, **3:12** not like Cain who was of the evil one and brutally murdered his brother. And why did he murder him? Because his deeds were evil, but his brother's were righteous.
3:13 Therefore do not be surprised, brothers and sisters, if the world hates you. **3:14** We know that we have crossed over from death to life because we love our fellow Christians. The one who does not love remains in death. **3:15** Everyone who hates his fellow Christian is a murderer, and you know that no murderer has eternal life residing in him. **3:16** We have come to know love by this: that Jesus laid down his life for us; thus we ought to lay down our lives for our fellow Christians. **3:17** But whoever has the world's possessions and sees his fellow Christian in need and shuts off his compassion against him, how can the love of God reside in such a person?
3:18 Little children, let us not love with word or with tongue but in deed and truth. **3:19** And by this we will know that we are in the truth and will convince our conscience in his presence, **3:20** that if our conscience condemns us, that God is greater than our conscience and knows all things. **3:21** Dear friends, if our conscience does not condemn us, we have confidence in the presence of God, **3:22** and whatever we ask we receive from him, because we keep his commandments and do the things that are pleasing to him. **3:23** Now this is his commandment: that we believe in the name of his Son Jesus Christ and love one another, just as he gave us the commandment. **3:24** And the person who keeps his commandments resides in God, and God in him. Now by this we know that God resides in us: by the Spirit he has given us.

Testing the Spirits

4:1 Dear friends, do not believe every spirit, but test the spirits to determine if they are from God, because many false prophets have gone out into the world. **4:2** By this you know the Spirit of God: Every spirit that confesses Jesus as the Christ who has come in the flesh is from God, **4:3** but every spirit that does not confess Jesus is not from God, and this is the spirit of the antichrist, which you have heard is coming, and now is already in the world.
4:4 You are from God, little children, and have conquered them, because the one who is in you is greater than the one who is in the world. **4:5** They are from the world; therefore they speak from the world's perspective and the world listens to them. **4:6** We are from God; the person who knows God listens to us, but whoever is not from God does not listen to us. By this we know the Spirit of truth and the spirit of deceit.

God is Love

4:7 Dear friends, let us love one another, because love is from God, and everyone who loves has been fathered by God and knows God. **4:8** The person who does not love does not know God, because God is love. **4:9** By this the love of God is revealed in us: that God has sent his one and only Son into the world so that we may live through him. **4:10** In this is love: not that we have loved God, but that he loved us and sent his Son to be the atoning sacrifice for our sins.
4:11 Dear friends, if God so loved us, then we also ought to love one another. **4:12** No one has seen God at any time. If we love one another, God resides in us, and his love is perfected in us. **4:13** By this we know that we reside in God and he in us: in that he has given us of his Spirit. **4:14** And we have seen and testify that the Father has sent the Son to be the Savior of the world.
4:15 If anyone confesses that Jesus is the Son of God, God resides in him and he in God. **4:16** And we have come to know and to believe the love that God has in us. God is love, and the one who resides in love resides in God, and God resides in him. **4:17** By this love is perfected with us, so that we may have confidence in the day of judgment, because just as Jesus is, so also are we in this world. **4:18** There is no fear in love, but perfect love drives out fear, because fear has to do with punishment. The one who fears punishment has not been perfected in love. **4:19** We love because he loved us first.
4:20 If anyone says "I love God" and yet hates his fellow Christian, he is a liar, because the one who does not love his fellow Christian whom he has seen cannot love God whom he has not seen. **4:21** And the commandment we have from him is this: that the one who loves God should love his fellow Christian too. **5:1** Everyone who believes that Jesus is the Christ has been fathered by God, and everyone who loves the father loves

the child fathered by him. **5:2** By this we know that we love the children of God: whenever we love God and obey his commandments. **5:3** For this is the love of God: that we keep his commandments. And his commandments do not weigh us down, **5:4** because everyone who has been fathered by God conquers the world.

Testimony About the Son

This is the conquering power that has conquered the world: our faith. **5:5** Now who is the person who has conquered the world except the one who believes that Jesus is the Son of God? **5:6** Jesus Christ is the one who came by water and blood – not by the water only, but by the water and the blood. And the Spirit is the one who testifies, because the Spirit is the truth.
5:7 For there are three that testify, **5:8** the Spirit and the water and the blood, and these three are in agreement.
5:9 If we accept the testimony of men, the testimony of God is greater, because this is the testimony of God that he has testified concerning his Son. **5:10** (The one who believes in the Son of God has the testimony in himself; the one who does not believe God has made him a liar, because he has not believed in the testimony that God has testified concerning his Son.) **5:11** And this is the testimony: God has given us eternal life, and this life is in his Son. **5:12** The one who has the Son has this eternal life; the one who does not have the Son of God does not have this eternal life.

Assurance of Eternal Life

5:13 I have written these things to you who believe in the name of the Son of God so that you may know that you have eternal life.
5:14 And this is the confidence that we have before him: that whenever we ask anything according to his will, he hears us. **5:15** And if we know that he hears us in regard to whatever we ask, then we know that we have the requests that we have asked from him. **5:16** If anyone sees his fellow Christian committing a sin not resulting in death, he should ask, and God will grant life to the person who commits a sin not resulting in death. There is a sin resulting in death. I do not say that he should ask about that. **5:17** All unrighteousness is sin, but there is sin not resulting in death.
5:18 We know that everyone fathered by God does not sin, but God protects the one he has fathered, and the evil one cannot touch him. **5:19** We know that we are from God, and the whole world lies in the power of the evil one. **5:20** And we know that the Son of God has come and has given us insight to know him who is true, and we are in him who is true, in his Son Jesus Christ. This one is the true God and eternal life. **5:21** Little children, guard yourselves from idols.

Book 63. 2 John

Introduction and Thanksgiving

1:1 From the elder, to an elect lady and her children, whom I love in truth (and not I alone, but also all those who know the truth), **1:2** because of the truth that resides in us and will be with us forever. **1:3** Grace, mercy, and peace will be with us from God the Father and from Jesus Christ the Son of the Father, in truth and love.
1:4 I rejoiced greatly because I have found some of your children living according to the truth, just as the Father commanded us.

Warning Against False Teachers

1:5 But now I ask you, lady (not as if I were writing a new commandment to you, but the one we have had from the beginning), that we love one another. **1:6** (Now this is love: that we walk according to his commandments.) This is the commandment, just as you have heard from the beginning; thus you should walk in it. **1:7** For many deceivers have gone out into the world, people who do not confess Jesus as Christ coming in the flesh. This person is the deceiver and the antichrist! **1:8** Watch out, so that you do not lose the things we have worked for, but receive a full reward.
1:9 Everyone who goes on ahead and does not remain in the teaching of Christ does not have God. The one who remains in this teaching has both the Father and the Son. **1:10** If anyone comes to you and does not bring this teaching, do not receive him into your house and do not give him any greeting, **1:11** because the person who gives him a greeting shares in his evil deeds.

Conclusion

1:12 Though I have many other things to write to you, I do not want to do so with paper and ink, but I hope to come visit you and speak face to face, so that our joy may be complete.
1:13 The children of your elect sister greet you.

Book 64. 3 John

Introduction and Thanksgiving

1:1 From the elder, to Gaius my dear brother, whom I love in truth. **1:2** Dear friend, I pray that all may go well with you and that you may be in good health, just as it is well with your soul. **1:3** For I rejoiced greatly when the brothers came and testified to your truth, just as you are living according to the truth.

1:4 I have no greater joy than this: to hear that my children are living according to the truth.

The Charge to Gaius

1:5 Dear friend, you demonstrate faithfulness by whatever you do for the brothers (even though they are strangers). **1:6** They have testified to your love before the church. You will do well to send them on their way in a manner worthy of God. **1:7** For they have gone forth on behalf of "The Name," accepting nothing from the pagans. **1:8** Therefore we ought to support such people, so that we become coworkers in cooperation with the truth.

Diotrephes the Troublemaker

1:9 I wrote something to the church, but Diotrephes, who loves to be first among them, does not acknowledge us. **1:10** Therefore, if I come, I will call attention to the deeds he is doing – the bringing of unjustified charges against us with evil words! And not being content with that, he not only refuses to welcome the brothers himself, but hinders the people who want to do so and throws them out of the church! **1:11** Dear friend, do not imitate what is bad but what is good. The one who does good is of God; the one who does what is bad has not seen God.

Worthy Demetrius

1:12 Demetrius has been testified to by all, even by the truth itself. We also testify to him, and you know that our testimony is true.

Conclusion

1:13 I have many things to write to you, but I do not wish to write to you with pen and ink. **1:14** But I hope to see you right away, and we will speak face to face. **1:15** Peace be with you. The friends here greet you. Greet the friends there by name.

Book 65. Jude

Salutation

1:1 From Jude, a slave of Jesus Christ and brother of James, to those who are called, wrapped in the love of God the Father and kept for Jesus Christ. **1:2** May mercy, peace, and love be lavished on you!

Condemnation of the False Teachers

1:3 Dear friends, although I have been eager to write to you about our common salvation, I now feel compelled instead to write to encourage you to contend earnestly for the faith that was once for all entrusted to the saints. **1:4** For certain men have secretly slipped in among you – men who long ago were marked out for the condemnation I am about to describe – ungodly men who have turned the grace of our God into a license for evil and who deny our only Master and Lord, Jesus Christ.

1:5 Now I desire to remind you (even though you have been fully informed of these facts once for all) that Jesus, having saved the people out of the land of Egypt, later destroyed those who did not believe. **1:6** You also know that the angels who did not keep within their proper domain but abandoned their own place of residence, he has kept in eternal chains in utter darkness, locked up for the judgment of the great Day. **1:7** So also Sodom and Gomorrah and the neighboring towns, since they indulged in sexual immorality and pursued unnatural desire in a way similar to these angels, are now displayed as an example by suffering the punishment of eternal fire.

1:8 Yet these men, as a result of their dreams, defile the flesh, reject authority, and insult the glorious ones. **1:9** But even when Michael the archangel was arguing with the devil and debating with him concerning Moses' body, he did not dare to bring a slanderous judgment, but said, "May the Lord rebuke you!" **1:10** But these men do not understand the things they slander, and they are being destroyed by the very things that, like irrational animals, they instinctively comprehend. **1:11** Woe to them! For they have traveled down Cain's path, and because of greed have abandoned themselves to Balaam's error; hence, they will certainly perish in Korah's rebellion. **1:12** These men are dangerous reefs at your love feasts, feasting without reverence, feeding only themselves. They are waterless clouds, carried along by the winds; autumn trees without fruit – twice dead, uprooted; **1:13** wild sea waves, spewing out the foam of their shame; wayward stars for whom the utter depths of eternal darkness have been reserved.

1:14 Now Enoch, the seventh in descent beginning with Adam, even prophesied of them, saying, "Look! The Lord is coming with thousands and thousands of his holy ones, **1:15** to execute judgment on all, and to convict every person of all their thoroughly ungodly deeds that they have committed, and of all the harsh words that ungodly sinners have spoken against him." **1:16** These people are grumblers and fault-finders who go wherever their desires lead them, and they give bombastic speeches, enchanting folks for their own gain.

Exhortation to the Faithful

1:17 But you, dear friends – recall the predictions foretold by the apostles of our Lord Jesus Christ. **1:18** For they said to you, "In the end time there will come scoffers, propelled by their own ungodly desires." **1:19** These people are divisive, worldly, devoid of the Spirit. **1:20** But you, dear friends, by building yourselves up in your most holy faith, by praying in the Holy Spirit, **1:21** maintain yourselves in the love of God, while anticipating the mercy of our Lord

Jesus Christ that brings eternal life. **1:22** And have mercy on those who waver; **1:23** save others by snatching them out of the fire; have mercy on others, coupled with a fear of God, hating even the clothes stained by the flesh.

Final Blessing

1:24 Now to the one who is able to keep you from falling, and to cause you to stand, rejoicing, without blemish before his glorious presence, **1:25** to the only God our Savior through Jesus Christ our Lord, be glory, majesty, power, and authority, before all time, and now, and for all eternity. Amen.

Book 66. Revelation

The Prologue

1:1 The revelation of Jesus Christ, which God gave him to show his servants what must happen very soon. He made it clear by sending his angel to his servant John, **1:2** who then testified to everything that he saw concerning the word of God and the testimony about Jesus Christ. **1:3** Blessed is the one who reads the words of this prophecy aloud, and blessed are those who hear and obey the things written in it, because the time is near!

1:4 From John, to the seven churches that are in the province of Asia: Grace and peace to you from "he who is," and who was, and who is still to come, and from the seven spirits who are before his throne, **1:5** and from Jesus Christ – the faithful witness, the firstborn from among the dead, the ruler over the kings of the earth. To the one who loves us and has set us free from our sins at the cost of his own blood **1:6** and has appointed us as a kingdom, as priests serving his God and Father – to him be the glory and the power for ever and ever! Amen.

1:7 (Look! *He is returning with the clouds,*
and *every eye will see him,*
even those who pierced him,
and all the tribes on the earth will mourn because of him.
This will certainly come to pass! Amen.)

1:8 "I am the Alpha and the Omega," says the Lord God – the one who is, and who was, and who is still to come – the All-Powerful!

1:9 I, John, your brother and the one who shares with you in the persecution, kingdom, and endurance that are in Jesus, was on the island called Patmos because of the word of God and the testimony about Jesus. **1:10** I was in the Spirit on the Lord's Day when I heard behind me a loud voice like a trumpet, **1:11** saying: "Write in a book what you see and send it to the seven churches – to Ephesus, Smyrna, Pergamum, Thyatira, Sardis, Philadelphia, and Laodicea."

1:12 I turned to see whose voice was speaking to me, and when I did so, I saw seven golden lampstands, **1:13** and in the midst of the lampstands was one *like a son of man.* He was dressed in a robe extending down to his feet and he wore a wide golden belt around his chest. **1:14** His head and hair were as white as wool, even as white as snow, and his eyes were like a fiery flame. **1:15** His feet were like polished bronze refined in a furnace, and his voice was like the roar of many waters. **1:16** He held seven stars in his right hand, and a sharp double-edged sword extended out of his mouth. His face shone like the sun shining at full strength. **1:17** When I saw him I fell down at his feet as though I were dead, but he placed his right hand on me and said: "Do not be afraid! I am the first and the last, **1:18** and the one who lives! I was dead, but look, now I am alive – forever and ever – and I hold the keys of death and of Hades! **1:19** Therefore write what you saw, what is, and what will be after these things. **1:20** The mystery of the seven stars that you saw in my right hand and the seven golden lampstands is this: The seven stars are the angels of the seven churches and the seven lampstands are the seven churches.

To the Church in Ephesus

2:1 "To the angel of the church in Ephesus, write the following:

"This is the solemn pronouncement of the one who has a firm grasp on the seven stars in his right hand – the one who walks among the seven golden lampstands: **2:2** 'I know your works as well as your labor and steadfast endurance, and that you cannot tolerate evil. You have even put to the test those who refer to themselves as apostles (but are not), and have discovered that they are false. **2:3** I am also aware that you have persisted steadfastly, endured much for the sake of my name, and have not grown weary. **2:4** But I have this against you: You have departed from your first love! **2:5** Therefore, remember from what high state you have fallen and repent! Do the deeds you did at the first; if not, I will come to you and remove your lampstand from its place – that is, if you do not repent. **2:6** But you do have this going for you: You hate what the Nicolaitans practice – practices I also hate. **2:7** The one who has an ear had better hear what the Spirit says to the churches. To the one who conquers, I will permit him to eat from the tree of life that is in the paradise of God.'

To the Church in Smyrna

2:8 "To the angel of the church in Smyrna write the following:

"This is the solemn pronouncement of the one who is the first and the last, the one who was dead, but came to life: **2:9** 'I know the distress you are suffering and your poverty (but you are rich). I also know the slander against you by those who call themselves Jews and really are not, but are a synagogue of Satan. **2:10** Do not be afraid of the things you are about to suffer. The devil is about to have some of you thrown into prison so you may be tested, and you will experience suffering for ten days. Remain faithful even to the point of death, and I will give you the crown that is life itself. **2:11** The one who has an ear had better hear what the Spirit says to the churches. The one who conquers will in no way be harmed by the second death.'

To the Church in Pergamum

2:12 "To the angel of the church in Pergamum write the following:
"This is the solemn pronouncement of the one who has the sharp double-edged sword: **2:13** 'I know where you live – where Satan's throne is. Yet you continue to cling to my name and you have not denied your faith in me, even in the days of Antipas, my faithful witness, who was killed in your city where Satan lives. **2:14** But I have a few things against you: You have some people there who follow the teaching of Balaam, who instructed Balak to put a stumbling block before the people of Israel so they would eat food sacrificed to idols and commit sexual immorality. **2:15** In the same way, there are also some among you who follow the teaching of the Nicolaitans. **2:16** Therefore, repent! If not, I will come against you quickly and make war against those people with the sword of my mouth. **2:17** The one who has an ear had better hear what the Spirit says to the churches. To the one who conquers, I will give him some of the hidden manna, and I will give him a white stone, and on that stone will be written a new name that no one can understand except the one who receives it.'

To the Church in Thyatira

2:18 "To the angel of the church in Thyatira write the following:
"This is the solemn pronouncement of the Son of God, the one who has eyes like a fiery flame and whose feet are like polished bronze: **2:19** 'I know your deeds: your love, faith, service, and steadfast endurance. In fact, your more recent deeds are greater than your earlier ones. **2:20** But I have this against you: You tolerate that woman Jezebel, who calls herself a prophetess, and by her teaching deceives my servants to commit sexual immorality and to eat food sacrificed to idols. **2:21** I have given her time to repent, but she is not willing to repent of her sexual immorality. **2:22** Look! I am throwing her onto a bed of violent illness, and those who commit adultery with her into terrible suffering, unless they repent of her deeds. **2:23** Furthermore, I will strike her followers with a deadly disease, and then all the churches will know that I am the one who searches minds and hearts. I will repay each one of you what your deeds deserve. **2:24** But to the rest of you in Thyatira, all who do not hold to this teaching (who have not learned the so-called "deep secrets of Satan"), to you I say: I do not put any additional burden on you. **2:25** However, hold on to what you have until I come. **2:26** And to the one who conquers and who continues in my deeds until the end, I will give him authority over the nations –

2:27 *he will rule them with an iron rod*

and like clay jars he will break them to pieces,

2:28 just as I have received the right to rule from my Father – and I will give him the morning star. **2:29** The one who has an ear had better hear what the Spirit says to the churches.'

To the Church in Sardis

3:1 "To the angel of the church in Sardis write the following:
"This is the solemn pronouncement of the one who holds the seven spirits of God and the seven stars: 'I know your deeds, that you have a reputation that you are alive, but in reality you are dead. **3:2** Wake up then, and strengthen what remains that was about to die, because I have not found your deeds complete in the sight of my God. **3:3** Therefore, remember what you received and heard, and obey it, and repent. If you do not wake up, I will come like a thief, and you will never know at what hour I will come against you. **3:4** But you have a few individuals in Sardis who have not stained their clothes, and they will walk with me dressed in white, because they are worthy. **3:5** The one who conquers will be dressed like them in white clothing, and I will never erase his name from the book of life, but will declare his name before my Father and before his angels. **3:6** The one who has an ear had better hear what the Spirit says to the churches.'

To the Church in Philadelphia

3:7 "To the angel of the church in Philadelphia write the following:
"This is the solemn pronouncement of the Holy One, the True One, who holds the key of David, who opens doors no one can shut, and shuts doors no one can open: **3:8** 'I know your deeds. (Look! I have put in front of you an open door that no one can shut.) I know that you have little strength, but you have obeyed my word and have not denied my name. **3:9** Listen! I am going to make those people from the synagogue of Satan – who say they are Jews yet are not, but are lying – Look, I will make them come and bow down at your feet and acknowledge that I have loved you. **3:10** Because you have kept my admonition to endure steadfastly, I will also keep you from the hour of testing that is about to come on the whole world to test those who live on the earth. **3:11** I am coming soon. Hold on to what you have so that no one can take away your crown. **3:12** The one who conquers I will make a pillar in the temple of my God, and

he will never depart from it. I will write on him the name of my God and the name of the city of my God (the new Jerusalem that comes down out of heaven from my God), and my new name as well. **3:13** The one who has an ear had better hear what the Spirit says to the churches.'

To the Church in Laodicea

3:14 "To the angel of the church in Laodicea write the following:
"This is the solemn pronouncement of the Amen, the faithful and true witness, the originator of God's creation: **3:15** 'I know your deeds, that you are neither cold nor hot. I wish you were either cold or hot! **3:16** So because you are lukewarm, and neither hot nor cold, I am going to vomit you out of my mouth! **3:17** Because you say, "I am rich and have acquired great wealth, and need nothing," but do not realize that you are wretched, pitiful, poor, blind, and naked, **3:18** take my advice and buy gold from me refined by fire so you can become rich! Buy from me white clothing so you can be clothed and your shameful nakedness will not be exposed, and buy eye salve to put on your eyes so you can see! **3:19** All those I love, I rebuke and discipline. So be earnest and repent! **3:20** Listen! I am standing at the door and knocking! If anyone hears my voice and opens the door I will come into his home and share a meal with him, and he with me. **3:21** I will grant the one who conquers permission to sit with me on my throne, just as I too conquered and sat down with my Father on his throne. **3:22** The one who has an ear had better hear what the Spirit says to the churches.'"

The Amazing Scene in Heaven

4:1 After these things I looked, and there was a door standing open in heaven! And the first voice I had heard speaking to me like a trumpet said: "Come up here so that I can show you what must happen after these things." **4:2** Immediately I was in the Spirit, and a throne was standing in heaven with someone seated on it! **4:3** And the one seated on it was like jasper and carnelian in appearance, and a rainbow looking like it was made of emerald encircled the throne. **4:4** In a circle around the throne were twenty-four other thrones, and seated on those thrones were twenty-four elders. They were dressed in white clothing and had golden crowns on their heads. **4:5** From the throne came out flashes of lightning and roaring and crashes of thunder. Seven flaming torches, which are the seven spirits of God, were burning in front of the throne **4:6** and in front of the throne was something like a sea of glass, like crystal.

In the middle of the throne and around the throne were four living creatures full of eyes in front and in back. **4:7** The first living creature was like a lion, the second creature like an ox, the third creature had a face like a man's, and the fourth creature looked like an eagle flying. **4:8** Each one of the four living creatures had six wings and was full of eyes all around and inside. They never rest day or night, saying:

"*Holy Holy Holy is the Lord God, the All-Powerful*,
Who was and who is, and who is still to come!"

4:9 And whenever the living creatures give glory, honor, and thanks to the one who sits on the throne, who lives forever and ever, **4:10** the twenty-four elders throw themselves to the ground before the one who sits on the throne and worship the one who lives forever and ever, and they offer their crowns before his throne, saying:

4:11 "You are worthy, our Lord and God,
to receive glory and honor and power,
since you created all things,
and because of your will they existed and were created!"

The Opening of the Scroll

5:1 Then I saw in the right hand of the one who was seated on the throne a scroll written on the front and back and sealed with seven seals. **5:2** And I saw a powerful angel proclaiming in a loud voice: "Who is worthy to open the scroll and to break its seals?" **5:3** But no one in heaven or on earth or under the earth was able to open the scroll or look into it. **5:4** So I began weeping bitterly because no one was found who was worthy to open the scroll or to look into it. **5:5** Then one of the elders said to me, "Stop weeping! Look, the Lion of the tribe of Judah, the root of David, has conquered; thus he can open the scroll and its seven seals."
5:6 Then I saw standing in the middle of the throne and of the four living creatures, and in the middle of the elders, a Lamb that appeared to have been killed. He had seven horns and seven eyes, which are the seven spirits of God sent out into all the earth. **5:7** Then he came and took the scroll from the right hand of the one who was seated on the throne, **5:8** and when he had taken the scroll, the four living creatures and the twenty-four elders threw themselves to the ground before the Lamb. Each of them had a harp and golden bowls full of incense (which are the prayers of the saints). **5:9** They were singing a new song:

"You are worthy to take the scroll
and to open its seals
because you were killed,
and at the cost of your own blood you have purchased for God
persons from every tribe, language, people, and nation.
5:10 You have appointed them as a kingdom and priests to serve our God, and they will reign on the earth."
5:11 Then I looked and heard the voice of many angels in a circle around the throne, as well as the living creatures and the elders. Their number

was ten thousand times ten thousand – thousands times thousands – **5:12** all of whom were singing in a loud voice:

"Worthy is the lamb who was killed
to receive power and wealth
and wisdom and might
and honor and glory and praise!"

5:13 Then I heard every creature – in heaven, on earth, under the earth, in the sea, and all that is in them – singing:

"To the one seated on the throne and to the Lamb
be praise, honor, glory, and ruling power forever and ever!"

5:14 And the four living creatures were saying "Amen," and the elders threw themselves to the ground and worshiped.

The Seven Seals

6:1 I looked on when the Lamb opened one of the seven seals, and I heard one of the four living creatures saying with a thunderous voice, "Come!" **6:2** So I looked, and here came a white horse! The one who rode it had a bow, and he was given a crown, and as a conqueror he rode out to conquer.

6:3 Then when the Lamb opened the second seal, I heard the second living creature saying, "Come!" **6:4** And another horse, fiery red, came out, and the one who rode it was granted permission to take peace from the earth, so that people would butcher one another, and he was given a huge sword.

6:5 Then when the Lamb opened the third seal I heard the third living creature saying, "Come!" So I looked, and here came a black horse! The one who rode it had a balance scale in his hand. **6:6** Then I heard something like a voice from among the four living creatures saying, "A quart of wheat will cost a day's pay and three quarts of barley will cost a day's pay. But do not damage the olive oil and the wine!"

6:7 Then when the Lamb opened the fourth seal I heard the voice of the fourth living creature saying, "Come!" **6:8** So I looked and here came a pale green horse! The name of the one who rode it was Death, and Hades followed right behind. They were given authority over a fourth of the earth, to kill its population with the sword, famine, and disease, and by the wild animals of the earth.

6:9 Now when the Lamb opened the fifth seal, I saw under the altar the souls of those who had been violently killed because of the word of God and because of the testimony they had given. **6:10** They cried out with a loud voice, "How long, Sovereign Master, holy and true, before you judge those who live on the earth and avenge our blood?" **6:11** Each of them was given a long white robe and they were told to rest for a little longer, until the full number was reached of both their fellow servants and their brothers who were going to be killed just as they had been.

6:12 Then I looked when the Lamb opened the sixth seal, and a huge earthquake took place; the sun became as black as sackcloth made of hair, and the full moon became blood red; **6:13** and the stars in the sky fell to the earth like a fig tree dropping its unripe figs when shaken by a fierce wind. **6:14** The sky was split apart like a scroll being rolled up, and every mountain and island was moved from its place. **6:15** Then the kings of the earth, the very important people, the generals, the rich, the powerful, and everyone, slave and free, hid themselves in the caves and among the rocks of the mountains. **6:16** They said to the mountains and to the rocks, "Fall on us and hide us from the face of the one who is seated on the throne and from the wrath of the Lamb, **6:17** because the great day of their wrath has come, and who is able to withstand it?"

The Sealing of the 144,000

7:1 After this I saw four angels standing at the four corners of the earth, holding back the four winds of the earth so no wind could blow on the earth, on the sea, or on any tree. **7:2** Then I saw another angel ascending from the east, who had the seal of the living God. He shouted out with a loud voice to the four angels who had been given permission to damage the earth and the sea: **7:3** "Do not damage the earth or the sea or the trees until we have put a seal on the foreheads of the servants of our God." **7:4** Now I heard the number of those who were marked with the seal, one hundred and forty-four thousand, sealed from all the tribes of the people of Israel:

7:5 From the tribe of Judah, twelve thousand were sealed,
from the tribe of Reuben, twelve thousand,
from the tribe of Gad, twelve thousand,
7:6 from the tribe of Asher, twelve thousand,
from the tribe of Naphtali, twelve thousand,
from the tribe of Manasseh, twelve thousand,
7:7 from the tribe of Simeon, twelve thousand,
from the tribe of Levi, twelve thousand,
from the tribe of Issachar, twelve thousand,
7:8 from the tribe of Zebulun, twelve thousand,
from the tribe of Joseph, twelve thousand,
from the tribe of Benjamin, twelve thousand were sealed.

7:9 After these things I looked, and here was an enormous crowd that no one could count, made up of persons from every nation, tribe, people, and language, standing before the throne and before the Lamb dressed in long white robes, and with palm branches in their hands. **7:10** They were shouting out in a loud voice,

"Salvation belongs to our God,
to the one seated on the throne, and to the Lamb!"

7:11 And all the angels stood there in a circle around the throne and around the elders and the four living creatures, and they threw themselves down with their faces to the ground before the throne and worshiped God, **7:12** saying,

"Amen! Praise and glory,
and wisdom and thanksgiving,
and honor and power and strength
be to our God for ever and ever. Amen!"

7:13 Then one of the elders asked me, "These dressed in long white robes – who are they and where have they come from?" **7:14** So I said to him, "My lord, you know the answer." Then he said to me, "These are the ones who have come out of the great tribulation. They have washed their robes and made them white in the blood of the Lamb! **7:15** For this reason they are before the throne of God, and they serve him day and night in his temple, and the one seated on the throne will shelter them. **7:16** *They will never go hungry or be thirsty again, and the sun will not beat down on them, nor any burning heat,* **7:17** because the Lamb in the middle of the throne will shepherd them and lead them to springs of living water, *and God will wipe away every tear from their eyes.*"

The Seventh Seal

8:1 Now when the Lamb opened the seventh seal there was silence in heaven for about half an hour. **8:2** Then I saw the seven angels who stand before God, and seven trumpets were given to them. **8:3** Another angel holding a golden censer came and was stationed at the altar. A large amount of incense was given to him to offer up, with the prayers of all the saints, on the golden altar that is before the throne. **8:4** The smoke coming from the incense, along with the prayers of the saints, ascended before God from the angel's hand. **8:5** Then the angel took the censer, filled it with fire from the altar, and threw it on the earth, and there were crashes of thunder, roaring, flashes of lightning, and an earthquake.

8:6 Now the seven angels holding the seven trumpets prepared to blow them.

8:7 The first angel blew his trumpet, and there was hail and fire mixed with blood, and it was thrown at the earth so that a third of the earth was burned up, a third of the trees were burned up, and all the green grass was burned up.

8:8 Then the second angel blew his trumpet, and something like a great mountain of burning fire was thrown into the sea. A third of the sea became blood, **8:9** and a third of the creatures living in the sea died, and a third of the ships were completely destroyed.

8:10 Then the third angel blew his trumpet, and a huge star burning like a torch fell from the sky; it landed on a third of the rivers and on the springs of water. **8:11** (Now the name of the star is Wormwood.) So a third of the waters became wormwood, and many people died from these waters because they were poisoned.

8:12 Then the fourth angel blew his trumpet, and a third of the sun was struck, and a third of the moon, and a third of the stars, so that a third of them were darkened. And there was no light for a third of the day and for a third of the night likewise. **8:13** Then I looked, and I heard an eagle flying directly overhead, proclaiming with a loud voice, "Woe! Woe! Woe to those who live on the earth because of the remaining sounds of the trumpets of the three angels who are about to blow them!"

9:1 Then the fifth angel blew his trumpet, and I saw a star that had fallen from the sky to the earth, and he was given the key to the shaft of the abyss. **9:2** He opened the shaft of the abyss and smoke rose out of it like smoke from a giant furnace. The sun and the air were darkened with smoke from the shaft. **9:3** Then out of the smoke came locusts onto the earth, and they were given power like that of the scorpions of the earth. **9:4** They were told not to damage the grass of the earth, or any green plant or tree, but only those people who did not have the seal of God on their forehead. **9:5** The locusts were not given permission to kill them, but only to torture them for five months, and their torture was like that of a scorpion when it stings a person. **9:6** In those days people will seek death, but will not be able to find it; they will long to die, but death will flee from them.

9:7 Now the locusts looked like horses equipped for battle. On their heads were something like crowns similar to gold, and their faces looked like men's faces. **9:8** They had hair like women's hair, and their teeth were like lions' teeth. **9:9** They had breastplates like iron breastplates, and the sound of their wings was like the noise of many horse-drawn chariots charging into battle. **9:10** They have tails and stingers like scorpions, and their ability to injure people for five months is in their tails. **9:11** They have as king over them the angel of the abyss, whose name in Hebrew is *Abaddon*, and in Greek, *Apollyon*.

9:12 The first woe has passed, but two woes are still coming after these things!

9:13 Then the sixth angel blew his trumpet, and I heard a single voice coming from the horns on the golden altar that is before God, **9:14** saying to the sixth angel, the one holding the trumpet, "Set free the four angels who are bound at the great river Euphrates!" **9:15** Then the four angels who had been prepared for this hour, day, month, and year were set free to kill a third of humanity. **9:16** The number of soldiers on horseback was two hundred million; I heard their number. **9:17** Now this is what the horses and their riders looked like in my vision: The riders had breastplates that were fiery red, dark blue, and sulfurous yellow in color. The heads of the horses looked like lions' heads, and fire, smoke, and sulfur came out of their mouths. **9:18** A third of humanity was killed by these three plagues, that is, by the fire, the smoke, and the sulfur that came out of their mouths. **9:19** For the power of the horses resides in their mouths and in their tails, because their tails are like snakes, having heads that inflict injuries. **9:20** The rest of humanity, who had not been killed by these plagues, did not repent of the works of their hands, so that they did not stop worshiping demons and idols made of gold, silver, bronze, stone, and wood – idols that cannot see or hear or walk about. **9:21** Furthermore, they did not repent of their murders, of their magic spells, of their sexual immorality, or of their stealing.

The Angel with the Little Scroll

10:1 Then I saw another powerful angel descending from heaven, wrapped in a cloud, with a rainbow above his head; his face was like the sun and his legs were like pillars of fire. **10:2** He held in his hand a little scroll that was open, and he put his right foot on the sea and his left on the land. **10:3** Then he shouted in a loud voice like a lion roaring, and when he shouted, the seven thunders sounded their voices. **10:4** When the seven thunders spoke, I was preparing to write, but just then I heard a voice from heaven say, "Seal up what the seven thunders spoke and do not write it down." **10:5** Then the angel I saw standing on the sea and on the land raised his right hand to heaven **10:6** and swore by the one who lives forever and ever, who created heaven and what is in it, and the earth and what is in it, and the sea and what is in it, "There will be no more delay! **10:7** But in the days when the seventh angel is about to blow his trumpet, the mystery of God is completed, just as he has proclaimed to his servants the prophets." **10:8** Then the voice I had heard from heaven began to speak to me again, "Go and take the open scroll in the hand of the angel who is standing on the sea and on the land." **10:9** So I went to the angel and asked him to give me the little scroll. He said to me, "Take the scroll and eat it. It will make your stomach bitter, but it will be as sweet as honey in your mouth." **10:10** So I took the little scroll from the angel's hand and ate it, and it did taste as sweet as honey in my mouth, but when I had eaten it, my stomach became bitter. **10:11** Then they told me: "You must prophesy again about many peoples, nations, languages, and kings."

The Fate of the Two Witnesses

11:1 Then a measuring rod like a staff was given to me, and I was told, "Get up and measure the temple of God, and the altar, and the ones who worship there. **11:2** But do not measure the outer courtyard of the temple; leave it out, because it has been given to the Gentiles, and they will trample on the holy city for forty-two months. **11:3** And I will grant my two witnesses authority to prophesy for 1,260 days, dressed in sackcloth. **11:4** (These are the two olive trees and the two lampstands that stand before the Lord of the earth.) **11:5** If anyone wants to harm them, fire comes out of their mouths and completely consumes their enemies. If anyone wants to harm them, they must be killed this way. **11:6** These two have the power to close up the sky so that it does not rain during the time they are prophesying. They have power to turn the waters to blood and to strike the earth with every kind of plague whenever they want. **11:7** When they have completed their testimony, the beast that comes up from the abyss will make war on them and conquer them and kill them. **11:8** Their corpses will lie in the street of the great city that is symbolically called Sodom and Egypt, where their Lord was also crucified. **11:9** For three and a half days those from every people, tribe, nation, and language will look at their corpses, because they will not permit them to be placed in a tomb. **11:10** And those who live on the earth will rejoice over them and celebrate, even sending gifts to each other, because these two prophets had tormented those who live on the earth. **11:11** But after three and a half days a breath of life from God entered them, and they stood on their feet, and tremendous fear seized those who were watching them. **11:12** Then they heard a loud voice from heaven saying to them: "Come up here!" So the two prophets went up to heaven in a cloud while their enemies stared at them. **11:13** Just then a major earthquake took place and a tenth of the city collapsed; seven thousand people were killed in the earthquake, and the rest were terrified and gave glory to the God of heaven.

11:14 The second woe has come and gone; the third is coming quickly.

The Seventh Trumpet

11:15 Then the seventh angel blew his trumpet, and there were loud voices in heaven saying:
"The kingdom of the world
has become the kingdom of our Lord
and of his Christ,
and he will reign for ever and ever."
11:16 Then the twenty-four elders who are seated on their thrones before God threw themselves down with their faces to the ground and worshiped God **11:17** with these words:
"We give you thanks, Lord God, the All-Powerful,

the one who is and who was,
because you have taken your great power
and begun to reign.
11:18 The nations were enraged,
but your wrath has come,
and the time has come for the dead to be judged,
and the time has come to give to your servants,
the prophets, their reward,
as well as to the saints
and to those who revere your name, both small and great,
and the time has come to destroy those who destroy the earth."
11:19 Then the temple of God in heaven was opened and the ark of his covenant was visible within his temple. And there were flashes of lightning, roaring, crashes of thunder, an earthquake, and a great hailstorm.

The Woman, the Child, and the Dragon

12:1 Then a great sign appeared in heaven: a woman clothed with the sun, and with the moon under her feet, and on her head was a crown of twelve stars. **12:2** She was pregnant and was screaming in labor pains, struggling to give birth. **12:3** Then another sign appeared in heaven: a huge red dragon that had seven heads and ten horns, and on its heads were seven diadem crowns. **12:4** Now the dragon's tail swept away a third of the stars in heaven and hurled them to the earth. Then the dragon stood before the woman who was about to give birth, so that he might devour her child as soon as it was born. **12:5** So the woman gave birth to a son, a male child, who is going *to rule over all the nations with an iron rod*. Her child was suddenly caught up to God and to his throne, **12:6** and she fled into the wilderness where a place had been prepared for her by God, so she could be taken care of for 1,260 days.

War in Heaven

12:7 Then war broke out in heaven: Michael and his angels fought against the dragon, and the dragon and his angels fought back. **12:8** But the dragon was not strong enough to prevail, so there was no longer any place left in heaven for him and his angels. **12:9** So that huge dragon – the ancient serpent, the one called the devil and Satan, who deceives the whole world – was thrown down to the earth, and his angels along with him. **12:10** Then I heard a loud voice in heaven saying,
"The salvation and the power
and the kingdom of our God,
and the ruling authority of his Christ, have now come,
because the accuser of our brothers and sisters,
the one who accuses them day and night before our God,
has been thrown down.
12:11 But they overcame him
by the blood of the Lamb
and by the word of their testimony,
and they did not love their lives so much that they were afraid to die.
12:12 Therefore you heavens rejoice, and all who reside in them!
But woe to the earth and the sea
because the devil has come down to you!
He is filled with terrible anger,
for he knows that he only has a little time!"
12:13 Now when the dragon realized that he had been thrown down to the earth, he pursued the woman who had given birth to the male child. **12:14** But the woman was given the two wings of a giant eagle so that she could fly out into the wilderness, to the place God prepared for her, where she is taken care of – away from the presence of the serpent – for a time, times, and half a time. **12:15** Then the serpent spouted water like a river out of his mouth after the woman in an attempt to sweep her away by a flood, **12:16** but the earth came to her rescue; the ground opened up and swallowed the river that the dragon had spewed from his mouth. **12:17** So the dragon became enraged at the woman and went away to make war on the rest of her children, those who keep God's commandments and hold to the testimony about Jesus. **12:18** And the dragon stood on the sand of the seashore.

The Two Beasts

13:1 Then I saw a beast coming up out of the sea. It had ten horns and seven heads, and on its horns were ten diadem crowns, and on its heads a blasphemous name. **13:2** Now the beast that I saw was like a leopard, but its feet were like a bear's, and its mouth was like a lion's mouth. The dragon gave the beast his power, his throne, and great authority to rule. **13:3** One of the beast's heads appeared to have been killed, but the lethal wound had been healed. And the whole world followed the beast in amazement; **13:4** they worshiped the dragon because he had given ruling authority to the beast, and they worshiped the beast too, saying: "Who is like the beast?" and "Who is able to make war against him?" **13:5** The beast was given a mouth speaking proud words and blasphemies, and he was permitted to exercise ruling authority for forty-two months. **13:6** So the beast opened his mouth to blaspheme against God – to blaspheme both his name and his dwelling place, that is, those who dwell in heaven. **13:7** The beast was permitted to go to war against the saints and conquer them. He was given ruling authority over every tribe, people, language, and nation, **13:8** and all those who live on the earth will worship the beast, everyone whose name has not been written since the foundation of

the world in the book of life belonging to the Lamb who was killed. **13:9** If anyone has an ear, he had better listen!
13:10 If anyone is meant for captivity,
into captivity he will go.
If anyone is to be killed by the sword,
then by the sword he must be killed.
This requires steadfast endurance and faith from the saints.
13:11 Then I saw another beast coming up from the earth. He had two horns like a lamb, but was speaking like a dragon. **13:12** He exercised all the ruling authority of the first beast on his behalf, and made the earth and those who inhabit it worship the first beast, the one whose lethal wound had been healed. **13:13** He performed momentous signs, even making fire come down from heaven in front of people **13:14** and, by the signs he was permitted to perform on behalf of the beast, he deceived those who live on the earth. He told those who live on the earth to make an image to the beast who had been wounded by the sword, but still lived. **13:15** The second beast was empowered to give life to the image of the first beast so that it could speak, and could cause all those who did not worship the image of the beast to be killed. **13:16** He also caused everyone (small and great, rich and poor, free and slave) to obtain a mark on their right hand or on their forehead. **13:17** Thus no one was allowed to buy or sell things unless he bore the mark of the beast – that is, his name or his number. **13:18** This calls for wisdom: Let the one who has insight calculate the beast's number, for it is man's number, and his number is 666.

An Interlude: The Song of the 144,000
14:1 Then I looked, and here was the Lamb standing on Mount Zion, and with him were one hundred and forty-four thousand, who had his name and his Father's name written on their foreheads. **14:2** I also heard a sound coming out of heaven like the sound of many waters and like the sound of loud thunder. Now the sound I heard was like that made by harpists playing their harps, **14:3** and they were singing a new song before the throne and before the four living creatures and the elders. No one was able to learn the song except the one hundred and forty-four thousand who had been redeemed from the earth.
14:4 These are the ones who have not defiled themselves with women, for they are virgins. These are the ones who follow the Lamb wherever he goes. These were redeemed from humanity as firstfruits to God and to the Lamb, **14:5** and no lie was found on their lips; they are blameless.
Three Angels and Three Messages
14:6 Then I saw another angel flying directly overhead, and he had an eternal gospel to proclaim to those who live on the earth – to every nation, tribe, language, and people. **14:7** He declared in a loud voice: "Fear God and give him glory, because the hour of his judgment has arrived, and worship the one who made heaven and earth, the sea and the springs of water!"
14:8 A second angel followed the first, declaring: "Fallen, fallen is Babylon the great city! She made all the nations drink of the wine of her immoral passion."
14:9 A third angel followed the first two, declaring in a loud voice: "If anyone worships the beast and his image, and takes the mark on his forehead or his hand, **14:10** that person will also drink of the wine of God's anger that has been mixed undiluted in the cup of his wrath, and he will be tortured with fire and sulfur in front of the holy angels and in front of the Lamb. **14:11** And the smoke from their torture will go up forever and ever, and those who worship the beast and his image will have no rest day or night, along with anyone who receives the mark of his name."
14:12 This requires the steadfast endurance of the saints – those who obey God's commandments and hold to their faith in Jesus.
14:13 Then I heard a voice from heaven say, "Write this:
'Blessed are the dead,
those who die in the Lord from this moment on!'"
"Yes," says the Spirit, "so they can rest from their hard work, because their deeds will follow them."
14:14 Then I looked, and a white cloud appeared, and seated *on the cloud was one like a son of man!* He had a golden crown on his head and a sharp sickle in his hand. **14:15** Then another angel came out of the temple, shouting in a loud voice to the one seated on the cloud, "Use your sickle and start to reap, because the time to reap has come, since the earth's harvest is ripe!" **14:16** So the one seated on the cloud swung his sickle over the earth, and the earth was reaped.
14:17 Then another angel came out of the temple in heaven, and he too had a sharp sickle. **14:18** Another angel, who was in charge of the fire, came from the altar and called in a loud voice to the angel who had the sharp sickle, "Use your sharp sickle and gather the clusters of grapes off the vine of the earth, because its grapes are now ripe." **14:19** So the angel swung his sickle over the earth and gathered the grapes from the vineyard of the earth and tossed them into the great winepress of the wrath of God. **14:20** Then the winepress was stomped outside the city, and blood poured out of the winepress up to the height of horses' bridles for a distance of almost two hundred miles.
The Final Plagues

15:1 Then I saw another great and astounding sign in heaven: seven angels who have seven final plagues (they are final because in them God's anger is completed).
15:2 Then I saw something like a sea of glass mixed with fire, and those who had conquered the beast and his image and the number of his name. They were standing by the sea of glass, holding harps given to them by God. **15:3** They sang the song of Moses the servant of God and the song of the Lamb:
"Great and astounding are your deeds,
Lord God, the All-Powerful!
Just and true are your ways,
King over the nations!
15:4 Who will not fear you, O Lord,
and glorify your name, because you alone are holy?
All nations will come and worship before you
for your righteous acts have been revealed."
15:5 After these things I looked, and the temple (the tent of the testimony) was opened in heaven, **15:6** and the seven angels who had the seven plagues came out of the temple, dressed in clean bright linen, wearing wide golden belts around their chests. **15:7** Then one of the four living creatures gave the seven angels seven golden bowls filled with the wrath of God who lives forever and ever, **15:8** and the temple was filled with smoke from God's glory and from his power. Thus no one could enter the temple until the seven plagues from the seven angels were completed.
The Bowls of God's Wrath
16:1 Then I heard a loud voice from the temple declaring to the seven angels: "Go and pour out on the earth the seven bowls containing God's wrath." **16:2** So the first angel went and poured out his bowl on the earth. Then ugly and painful sores appeared on the people who had the mark of the beast and who worshiped his image.
16:3 Next, the second angel poured out his bowl on the sea and it turned into blood, like that of a corpse, and every living creature that was in the sea died.
16:4 Then the third angel poured out his bowl on the rivers and the springs of water, and they turned into blood. **16:5** Now I heard the angel of the waters saying:
"You are just – the one who is and who was,
the Holy One – because you have passed these judgments,
16:6 because they poured out the blood of your saints and prophets,
so you have given them blood to drink. They got what they deserved!"
16:7 Then I heard the altar reply, "Yes, Lord God, the All-Powerful, your judgments are true and just!"
16:8 Then the fourth angel poured out his bowl on the sun, and it was permitted to scorch people with fire. **16:9** Thus people were scorched by the terrible heat, yet they blasphemed the name of God, who has ruling authority over these plagues, and they would not repent and give him glory.
16:10 Then the fifth angel poured out his bowl on the throne of the beast so that darkness covered his kingdom, and people began to bite their tongues because of their pain. **16:11** They blasphemed the God of heaven because of their sufferings and because of their sores, but nevertheless they still refused to repent of their deeds.
16:12 Then the sixth angel poured out his bowl on the great river Euphrates and dried up its water to prepare the way for the kings from the east. **16:13** Then I saw three unclean spirits that looked like frogs coming out of the mouth of the dragon, out of the mouth of the beast, and out of the mouth of the false prophet. **16:14** For they are the spirits of the demons performing signs who go out to the kings of the earth to bring them together for the battle that will take place on the great day of God, the All-Powerful.
16:15 (Look! I will come like a thief!
Blessed is the one who stays alert and does not lose his clothes so that he will not have to walk around naked and his shameful condition be seen.)
16:16 Now the spirits gathered the kings and their armies to the place that is called Armageddon in Hebrew.
16:17 Finally the seventh angel poured out his bowl into the air and a loud voice came out of the temple from the throne, saying: "It is done!" **16:18** Then there were flashes of lightning, roaring, and crashes of thunder, and there was a tremendous earthquake – an earthquake unequaled since humanity has been on the earth, so tremendous was that earthquake. **16:19** The great city was split into three parts and the cities of the nations collapsed. So Babylon the great was remembered before God, and was given the cup filled with the wine made of God's furious wrath. **16:20** Every island fled away and no mountains could be found. **16:21** And gigantic hailstones, weighing about a hundred pounds each, fell from heaven on people, but they blasphemed God because of the plague of hail, since it was so horrendous.
The Great Prostitute and the Beast
17:1 Then one of the seven angels who had the seven bowls came and spoke to me. "Come," he said, "I will show you the condemnation and punishment of the great prostitute who sits on many waters, **17:2** with whom the kings of the earth committed sexual immorality and the earth's inhabitants got drunk with the wine of her immorality." **17:3** So he car-

ried me away in the Spirit to a wilderness, and there I saw a woman sitting on a scarlet beast that was full of blasphemous names and had seven heads and ten horns. **17:4** Now the woman was dressed in purple and scarlet clothing, and adorned with gold, precious stones, and pearls. She held in her hand a golden cup filled with detestable things and unclean things from her sexual immorality. **17:5** On her forehead was written a name, a mystery: "Babylon the Great, the Mother of prostitutes and of the detestable things of the earth." **17:6** I saw that the woman was drunk with the blood of the saints and the blood of those who testified to Jesus. I was greatly astounded when I saw her. **17:7** But the angel said to me, "Why are you astounded? I will interpret for you the mystery of the woman and of the beast with the seven heads and ten horns that carries her. **17:8** The beast you saw was, and is not, but is about to come up from the abyss and then go to destruction. The inhabitants of the earth – all those whose names have not been written in the book of life since the foundation of the world – will be astounded when they see that the beast was, and is not, but is to come. **17:9** (This requires a mind that has wisdom.) The seven heads are seven mountains the woman sits on. They are also seven kings: **17:10** five have fallen; one is, and the other has not yet come, but whenever he does come, he must remain for only a brief time. **17:11** The beast that was, and is not, is himself an eighth king and yet is one of the seven, and is going to destruction. **17:12** The ten horns that you saw are ten kings who have not yet received a kingdom, but will receive ruling authority as kings with the beast for one hour. **17:13** These kings have a single intent, and they will give their power and authority to the beast. **17:14** They will make war with the Lamb, but the Lamb will conquer them, because he is Lord of lords and King of kings, and those accompanying the Lamb are the called, chosen, and faithful."

17:15 Then the angel said to me, "The waters you saw (where the prostitute is seated) are peoples, multitudes, nations, and languages. **17:16** The ten horns that you saw, and the beast – these will hate the prostitute and make her desolate and naked. They will consume her flesh and burn her up with fire. **17:17** For God has put into their minds to carry out his purpose by making a decision to give their royal power to the beast until the words of God are fulfilled. **17:18** As for the woman you saw, she is the great city that has sovereignty over the kings of the earth."

Babylon is Destroyed

18:1 After these things I saw another angel, who possessed great authority, coming down out of heaven, and the earth was lit up by his radiance. **18:2** He shouted with a powerful voice:
"Fallen, fallen, is Babylon the great!
She has become a lair for demons,
a haunt for every unclean spirit,
a haunt for every unclean bird,
a haunt for every unclean and detested beast.
18:3 For all the nations have fallen from
the wine of her immoral passion,
and the kings of the earth have committed sexual immorality with her,
and the merchants of the earth have gotten rich from the power of her sensual behavior."

18:4 Then I heard another voice from heaven saying, "Come out of her, my people, so you will not take part in her sins and so you will not receive her plagues, **18:5** because her sins have piled up all the way to heaven and God has remembered her crimes. **18:6** Repay her the same way she repaid others; pay her back double corresponding to her deeds. In the cup she mixed, mix double the amount for her. **18:7** As much as she exalted herself and lived in sensual luxury, to this extent give her torment and grief because she said to herself, 'I rule as queen and am no widow; I will never experience grief!' **18:8** For this reason, she will experience her plagues in a single day: disease, mourning, and famine, and she will be burned down with fire, because the Lord God who judges her is powerful!"

18:9 Then the kings of the earth who committed immoral acts with her and lived in sensual luxury with her will weep and wail for her when they see the smoke from the fire that burns her up. **18:10** They will stand a long way off because they are afraid of her torment, and will say,
"Woe, woe, O great city,
Babylon the powerful city!
For in a single hour your doom has come!"

18:11 Then the merchants of the earth will weep and mourn for her because no one buys their cargo any longer – **18:12** cargo such as gold, silver, precious stones, pearls, fine linen, purple cloth, silk, scarlet cloth, all sorts of things made of citron wood, all sorts of objects made of ivory, all sorts of things made of expensive wood, bronze, iron and marble, **18:13** cinnamon, spice, incense, perfumed ointment, frankincense, wine, olive oil and costly flour, wheat, cattle and sheep, horses and four-wheeled carriages, slaves and human lives.
18:14 (The ripe fruit you greatly desired
has gone from you,
and all your luxury and splendor
have gone from you –
they will never ever be found again!)

18:15 The merchants who sold these things, who got rich from her, will stand a long way off because they are afraid of her torment. They will weep and mourn, **18:16** saying,
"Woe, woe, O great city –
dressed in fine linen, purple and scarlet clothing,
and adorned with gold, precious stones, and pearls –
18:17 because in a single hour such great wealth has been destroyed!"
And every ship's captain, and all who sail along the coast – seamen, and all who make their living from the sea, stood a long way off **18:18** and began to shout when they saw the smoke from the fire that burned her up, "Who is like the great city?" **18:19** And they threw dust on their heads and were shouting with weeping and mourning,
"Woe, Woe, O great city –
in which all those who had ships on the sea got rich from her wealth –
because in a single hour she has been destroyed!"
18:20 (Rejoice over her, O heaven,
and you saints and apostles and prophets,
for God has pronounced judgment against her on your behalf!)
18:21 Then one powerful angel picked up a stone like a huge millstone, threw it into the sea, and said,
"With this kind of sudden violent force
Babylon the great city will be thrown down
and it will never be found again!
18:22 And the sound of the harpists, musicians,
flute players, and trumpeters
will never be heard in you again.
No craftsman who practices any trade
will ever be found in you again;
the noise of a mill will never be heard in you again.
18:23 Even the light from a lamp
will never shine in you again!
The voices of the bridegroom and his bride
will never be heard in you again.
For your merchants were the tycoons of the world,
because all the nations were deceived by your magic spells!
18:24 The blood of the saints and prophets was found in her,
along with the blood of all those who had been killed on the earth."

19:1 After these things I heard what sounded like the loud voice of a vast throng in heaven, saying,
"Hallelujah! Salvation and glory and power belong to our God,
19:2 because his judgments are true and just.
For he has judged the great prostitute
who corrupted the earth with her sexual immorality,
and has avenged the blood of his servants poured out by her own hands!"
19:3 Then a second time the crowd shouted, "Hallelujah!" The smoke rises from her forever and ever. **19:4** The twenty-four elders and the four living creatures threw themselves to the ground and worshiped God, who was seated on the throne, saying: "Amen! Hallelujah!"
19:5 Then a voice came from the throne, saying:
"Praise our God
all you his servants,
and all you who fear Him,
both the small and the great!"

The Wedding Celebration of the Lamb

19:6 Then I heard what sounded like the voice of a vast throng, like the roar of many waters and like loud crashes of thunder. They were shouting:
"Hallelujah!
For the Lord our God, the All-Powerful, reigns!
19:7 Let us rejoice and exult
and give him glory,
because the wedding celebration of the Lamb has come,
and his bride has made herself ready.
19:8 She was permitted to be dressed in bright, clean, fine linen" (for the fine linen is the righteous deeds of the saints).

19:9 Then the angel said to me, "Write the following: Blessed are those who are invited to the banquet at the wedding celebration of the Lamb!" He also said to me, "These are the true words of God." **19:10** So I threw myself down at his feet to worship him, but he said, "Do not do this! I am only a fellow servant with you and your brothers who hold to the testimony about Jesus. Worship God, for the testimony about Jesus is the spirit of prophecy."

The Son of God Goes to War

19:11 Then I saw heaven opened and here came a white horse! The one riding it was called "Faithful" and "True," and with justice he judges and goes to war. **19:12** His eyes are like a fiery flame and there are many diadem crowns on his head. He has a name written that no one knows except himself. **19:13** He is dressed in clothing dipped in blood, and he is called the Word of God. **19:14** The armies that are in heaven, dressed in white, clean, fine linen, were following him on white horses. **19:15** From his mouth extends a sharp sword, so that with it he can strike the nations. *He will rule them with an iron rod*, and he stomps the winepress of the furious wrath of God, the All-Powerful. **19:16** He has a name written on his clothing and on his thigh: "King of kings and Lord of lords."

19:17 Then I saw one angel standing in the sun, and he shouted in a loud voice to all the birds flying high in the sky:

"Come, gather around for the great banquet of God,

19:18 to eat your fill of the flesh of kings,

the flesh of generals,

the flesh of powerful people,

the flesh of horses and those who ride them,

and the flesh of all people, both free and slave,

and small and great!"

19:19 Then I saw the beast and the kings of the earth and their armies assembled to do battle with the one who rode the horse and with his army. **19:20** Now the beast was seized, and along with him the false prophet who had performed the signs on his behalf – signs by which he deceived those who had received the mark of the beast and those who worshiped his image. Both of them were thrown alive into the lake of fire burning with sulfur. **19:21** The others were killed by the sword that extended from the mouth of the one who rode the horse, and all the birds gorged themselves with their flesh.

The Thousand Year Reign

20:1 Then I saw an angel descending from heaven, holding in his hand the key to the abyss and a huge chain. **20:2** He seized the dragon – the ancient serpent, who is the devil and Satan – and tied him up for a thousand years. **20:3** The angel then threw him into the abyss and locked and sealed it so that he could not deceive the nations until the one thousand years were finished. (After these things he must be released for a brief period of time.)

20:4 Then I saw thrones and seated on them were those who had been given authority to judge. I also saw the souls of those who had been beheaded because of the testimony about Jesus and because of the word of God. These had not worshiped the beast or his image and had refused to receive his mark on their forehead or hand. They came to life and reigned with Christ for a thousand years. **20:5** (The rest of the dead did not come to life until the thousand years were finished.) This is the first resurrection. **20:6** Blessed and holy is the one who takes part in the first resurrection. The second death has no power over them, but they will be priests of God and of Christ, and they will reign with him for a thousand years.

Satan's Final Defeat

20:7 Now when the thousand years are finished, Satan will be released from his prison **20:8** and will go out to deceive the nations at the four corners of the earth, Gog and Magog, to bring them together for the battle. They are as numerous as the grains of sand in the sea. **20:9** They went up on the broad plain of the earth and encircled the camp of the saints and the beloved city, but fire came down from heaven and devoured them completely. **20:10** And the devil who deceived them was thrown into the lake of fire and sulfur, where the beast and the false prophet are too, and they will be tormented there day and night forever and ever.

The Great White Throne

20:11 Then I saw a large white throne and the one who was seated on it; the earth and the heaven fled from his presence, and no place was found for them. **20:12** And I saw the dead, the great and the small, standing before the throne. Then books were opened, and another book was opened – the book of life. So the dead were judged by what was written in the books, according to their deeds. **20:13** The sea gave up the dead that were in it, and Death and Hades gave up the dead that were in them, and each one was judged according to his deeds. **20:14** Then Death and Hades were thrown into the lake of fire. This is the second death – the lake of fire. **20:15** If anyone's name was not found written in the book of life, that person was thrown into the lake of fire.

A New Heaven and a New Earth

21:1 Then I saw a new heaven and a new earth, for the first heaven and earth had ceased to exist, and the sea existed no more. **21:2** And I saw the holy city – the new Jerusalem – descending out of heaven from God, made ready like a bride adorned for her husband. **21:3** And I heard a loud voice from the throne saying: "Look! The residence of God is among human beings. He will live among them, and they will be his people, and God himself will be with them. **21:4** He will wipe away every tear from their eyes, and death will not exist any more – or mourning, or crying, or pain, for the former things have ceased to exist."

21:5 And the one seated on the throne said: "Look! I am making all things new!" Then he said to me, "Write it down, because these words are reliable and true." **21:6** He also said to me, "It is done! I am the Alpha and the Omega, the beginning and the end. To the one who is thirsty I will give water free of charge from the spring of the water of life. **21:7** The one who conquers will inherit these things, and I will be his God and he will be my son. **21:8** But to the cowards, unbelievers, detestable persons, murderers, the sexually immoral, and those who practice magic spells, idol worshipers, and all those who lie, their place will be in the lake that burns with fire and sulfur. That is the second death."

The New Jerusalem Descends

21:9 Then one of the seven angels who had the seven bowls full of the seven final plagues came and spoke to me, saying, "Come, I will show

you the bride, the wife of the Lamb!" **21:10** So he took me away in the Spirit to a huge, majestic mountain and showed me the holy city, Jerusalem, descending out of heaven from God. **21:11** The city possesses the glory of God; its brilliance is like a precious jewel, like a stone of crystal-clear jasper. **21:12** It has a massive, high wall with twelve gates, with twelve angels at the gates, and the names of the twelve tribes of the nation of Israel are written on the gates. **21:13** There are three gates on the east side, three gates on the north side, three gates on the south side and three gates on the

west side. **21:14** The wall of the city has twelve foundations, and on them are the twelve names of the twelve apostles of the Lamb.

21:15 The angel who spoke to me had a golden measuring rod with which to measure the city and its foundation stones and wall. **21:16** Now the city is laid out as a square, its length and width the same. He measured the city with the measuring rod at fourteen hundred miles (its length and width and height are equal). **21:17** He also measured its wall, one hundred forty-four cubits according to human measurement, which is also the angel's. **21:18** The city's wall is made of jasper and the city is pure gold, like transparent glass. **21:19** The foundations of the city's wall are decorated with every kind of precious stone. The first foundation is jasper, the second sapphire, the third agate, the fourth emerald, **21:20** the fifth onyx, the sixth carnelian, the seventh chrysolite, the eighth beryl, the ninth topaz, the tenth chrysoprase, the eleventh jacinth, and the twelfth amethyst. **21:21** And the twelve gates are twelve pearls – each one of the gates is made from just one pearl! The main street of the city is pure gold, like transparent glass.

21:22 Now I saw no temple in the city, because the Lord God – the All-Powerful – and the Lamb are its temple. **21:23** The city does not need the sun or the moon to shine on it, because the glory of God lights it up, and its lamp is the Lamb. **21:24** The nations will walk by its light and the kings of the earth will bring their grandeur into it. **21:25** Its gates will never be closed during the day (and there will be no night there). **21:26** They will bring the grandeur and the wealth of the nations into it,

21:27 but nothing ritually unclean will ever enter into it, nor anyone who does what is detestable or practices falsehood, but only those whose names are written in the Lamb's book of life.

22:1 Then the angel showed me the river of the water of life – water as clear as crystal – pouring out from the throne of God and of the Lamb, **22:2** flowing down the middle of the city's main street. On each side of the river is the tree of life producing twelve kinds of fruit, yielding its fruit every month of the year. Its leaves are for the healing of the nations. **22:3** And there will no longer be any curse, and the throne of God and the Lamb will be in the city. His servants will worship him, **22:4** and they will see his face, and his name will be on their foreheads. **22:5** Night will be no more, and they will not need the light of a lamp or the light of the sun, because the Lord God will shine on them, and they will reign forever and ever.

A Final Reminder

22:6 Then the angel said to me, "These words are reliable and true. The Lord, the God of the spirits of the prophets, has sent his angel to show his servants what must happen soon."

22:7 (Look! I am coming soon!

Blessed is the one who keeps the words of the prophecy expressed in this book.)

22:8 I, John, am the one who heard and saw these things, and when I heard and saw them, I threw myself down to worship at the feet of the angel who was showing them to me. **22:9** But he said to me, "Do not do this! I am a fellow servant with you and with your brothers the prophets, and with those who obey the words of this book. Worship God!" **22:10** Then he said to me, "Do not seal up the words of the prophecy contained in this book, because the time is near. **22:11** The evildoer must continue to do evil, and the one who is morally filthy must continue to be filthy. The one who is righteous must continue to act righteously, and the one who is holy must continue to be holy."

22:12 (Look! I am coming soon,

and my reward is with me to pay each one according to what he has done!

22:13 I am the Alpha and the Omega,

the first and the last,

the beginning and the end!)

22:14 Blessed are those who wash their robes so they can have access to the tree of life and can enter into the city by the gates. **22:15** Outside are the dogs and the sorcerers and the sexually immoral, and the murderers, and the idolaters and everyone who loves and practices falsehood!

22:16 "I, Jesus, have sent my angel to testify to you about these things for the churches. I am the root and the descendant of David, the bright morning star!" **22:17** And the Spirit and the bride say, "Come!" And let the one who hears say: "Come!" And let the one who is thirsty come; let the one who wants it take the water of life free of charge.

22:18 I testify to the one who hears the words of the prophecy contained in this book: If anyone adds to them, God will add to him the plagues described in this book. **22:19** And if anyone takes away from the words of this book of prophecy, God will take away his share in the tree of life and in the holy city that are described in this book.

22:20 The one who testifies to these things says, "Yes, I am coming soon!" Amen! Come, Lord Jesus! **22:21** The grace of the Lord Jesus be with all.

Discover Over 100 Hours of Video Content.
Scan the QR code or enter the following link to access a collection of documentaries and lectures exploring the sacred texts of the Ethiopian Bible, apocryphal books, and the history of Christianity.

https://t.ly/dkL4u

Deuterocanonical and Apocryphal Books

Book 67. The Wisdom Of Solomon

Wis.1 [1] Love righteousness, ye that be judges of the earth: think of the Lord with a good heart, and in simplicity of heart seek him. [2] For he will be found of them that tempt him not; and sheweth himself unto such as do not distrust him. [3] For froward thoughts separate from God: and his power, when it is tried, reproveth the unwise. [4] For into a malicious soul wisdom shall not enter; nor dwell in the body that is subject unto sin. [5] For the holy spirit of discipline will flee deceit, and remove from thoughts that are without understanding, and will not abide when unrighteousness cometh in. [6] For wisdom is a loving spirit; and will not acquit a blasphemer of his words: for God is witness of his reins, and a true beholder of his heart, and a hearer of his tongue. [7] For the Spirit of the Lord filleth the world: and that which containeth all things hath knowledge of the voice. [8] Therefore he that speaketh unrighteous things cannot be hid: neither shall vengeance, when it punisheth, pass by him. [9] For inquisition shall be made into the counsels of the ungodly: and the sound of his words shall come unto the Lord for the manifestation of his wicked deeds. [10] For the ear of jealousy heareth all things: and the noise of murmurings is not hid. [11] Therefore beware of murmuring, which is unprofitable; and refrain your tongue from backbiting: for there is no word so secret, that shall go for nought: and the mouth that belieth slayeth the soul. [12] Seek not death in the error of your life: and pull not upon yourselves destruction with the works of your hands. [13] For God made not death: neither hath he pleasure in the destruction of the living. [14] For he created all things, that they might have their being: and the generations of the world were healthful; and there is no poison of destruction in them, nor the kingdom of death upon the earth: [15] For righteousness is immortal: [16] But ungodly men with their works and words called it to them: for when they thought to have it their friend, they consumed to nought, and made a covenant with it, because they are worthy to take part with it. Wis.2 [1] For the ungodly said, reasoning with themselves, but not aright, Our life is short and tedious, and in the death of a man there is no remedy: neither was there any man known to have returned from the grave. [2] For we are born at all adventure: and we shall be hereafter as though we had never been: for the breath in our nostrils is as smoke, and a little spark in the moving of our heart: [3] Which being extinguished, our body shall be turned into ashes, and our spirit shall vanish as the soft air, [4] And our name shall be forgotten in time, and no man shall have our works in remembrance, and our life shall pass away as the trace of a cloud, and shall be dispersed as a mist, that is driven away with the beams of the sun, and overcome with the heat thereof. [5] For our time is a very shadow that passeth away; and after our end there is no returning: for it is fast sealed, so that no man cometh again. [6] Come on therefore, let us enjoy the good things that are present: and let us speedily use the creatures like as in youth. [7] Let us fill ourselves with costly wine and ointments: and let no flower of the spring pass by us: [8] Let us crown ourselves with rosebuds, before they be withered: [9] Let none of us go without his part of our voluptuousness: let us leave tokens of our joyfulness in every place: for this is our portion, and our lot is this. [10] Let us oppress the poor righteous man, let us not spare the widow, nor reverence the ancient gray hairs of the aged. [11] Let our strength be the law of justice: for that which is feeble is found to be nothing worth. [12] Therefore let us lie in wait for the righteous; because he is not for our turn, and he is clean contrary to our doings: he upbraideth us with our offending the law, and objecteth to our infamy the transgressings of our education. [13] He professeth to have the knowledge of God: and he calleth himself the child of the Lord. [14] He was made to reprove our thoughts. [15] He is grievous unto us even to behold: for his life is not like other men's, his ways are of another fashion. [16] We are esteemed of him as counterfeits: he abstaineth from our ways as from filthiness: he pronounceth the end of the just to be blessed, and maketh his boast that God is his father. [17] Let us see if his words be true: and let us prove what shall happen in the end of him. [18] For if the just man be the son of God, he will help him, and deliver him from the hand of his enemies. [19] Let us examine him with despitefulness and torture, that we may know his meekness, and prove his patience. [20] Let us condemn him with a shameful death: for by his own saying he shall be respected. [21] Such things they did imagine, and were deceived: for their own wickedness hath blinded them. [22] As for the mysteries of God, they kn ew them not: neither hoped they for the wages of righteousness, nor discerned a reward for blameless souls. [23] For God created man to be immortal, and made him to be an image of his own eternity. [24] Nevertheless through envy of the devil came death into the world: and they that do hold of his side do find it. Wis.3 [1] But the souls of the righteous are in the hand of God, and there shall no torment touch them. [2] In the sight of the unwise they seemed to die: and their departure is taken for misery, [3] And their going from us to be utter destruction: but they are in peace. [4] For though they be punished in the sight of men, yet is their hope full of immortality. [5] And having

been a little chastised, they shall be greatly rewarded: for God proved them, and found them worthy for himself. [6] As gold in the furnace hath he tried them, and received them as a burnt offering. [7] And in the time of their visitation they shall shine, and run to and fro like sparks among the stubble. [8] They shall judge the nations, and have dominion over the people, and their Lord shall reign for ever. [9] They that put their trust in him shall understand the truth: and such as be faithful in love shall abide with him: for grace and mercy is to his saints, and he hath care for his elect. [10] But the ungodly shall be punished according to their own imaginations, which have neglected the righteous, and forsaken the Lord. [11] For whoso despiseth wisdom and nurture, he is miserable, and their hope is vain, their labours unfruitful, and their works unprofitable: [12] Their wives are foolish, and their children wicked: [13] Their offspring is cursed. Wherefore blessed is the barren that is undefiled, which hath not known the sinful bed: she shall have fruit in the visitation of souls. [14] And blessed is the eunuch, which with his hands hath wrought no iniquity, nor imagined wicked things against God: for unto him shall be given the special gift of faith, and an inheritance in the temple of the Lord more acceptable to his mind. [15] For glorious is the fruit of good labours: and the root of wisdom shall never fall away. [16] As for the children of adulterers, they shall not come to their perfection, and the seed of an unrighteous bed shall be rooted out. [17] For though they live long, yet shall they be nothing regarded: and their last age shall be without honour. [18] Or, if they die quickly, they have no hope, neither comfort in the day of trial. [19] For horrible is the end of the unrighteous generation. Wis.4 [1] Better it is to have no children, and to have virtue: for the memorial thereof is immortal: because it is known with God, and with men. [2] When it is present, men take example at it; and when it is gone, they desire it: it weareth a crown, and triumpheth for ever, having gotten the victory, striving for undefiled rewards. [3] But the multiplying brood of the ungodly shall not thrive, nor take deep rooting from bastard slips, nor lay any fast foundation. [4] For though they flourish in branches for a time; yet standing not last, they shall be shaken with the wind, and through the force of winds they shall be rooted out. [5] The imperfect branches shall be broken off, their fruit unprofitable, not ripe to eat, yea, meet for nothing. [6] For children begotten of unlawful beds are witnesses of wickedness against their parents in their trial. [7] But though the righteous be prevented with death, yet shall he be in rest. [8] For honourable age is not that which standeth in length of time, nor that is measured by number of years. [9] But wisdom is the gray hair unto men, and an unspotted life is old age. [10] He pleased God, and was beloved of him: so that living among sinners he was translated. [11] Yea speedily was he taken away, lest that wickedness should alter his understanding, or deceit beguile his soul. [12] For the bewitching of naughtiness doth obscure things that are honest; and the wandering of concupiscence doth undermine the simple mind. [13] He, being made perfect in a short time, fulfilled a long time: [14] For his soul pleased the Lord: therefore hasted he to take him away from among the wicked. [15] This the people saw, and understood it not, neither laid they up this in their minds, That his grace and mercy is with his saints, and that he hath respect unto his chosen. [16] Thus the righteous that is dead shall condemn the ungodly which are living; and youth that is soon perfected the many years and old age of the unrighteous. [17] For they shall see the end of the wise, and shall not understand what God in his counsel hath decreed of him, and to what end the Lord hath set him in safety. [18] They shall see him, and despise him; but God shall laugh them to scorn: and they shall hereafter be a vile carcase, and a reproach among the dead for evermore. [19] For he shall rend them, and cast them down headlong, that they shall be speechless; and he shall shake them from the foundation; and they shall be utterly laid waste, and be in sorrow; and their memorial shall perish. [20] And when they cast up the accounts of their sins, they shall come with fear: and their own iniquities shall convince them to their face. Wis.5 [1] Then shall the righteous man stand in great boldness before the face of such as have afflicted him, and made no account of his labours. [2] When they see it, they shall be troubled with terrible fear, and shall be amazed at the strangeness of his salvation, so far beyond all that they looked for. [3] And they repenting and groaning for anguish of spirit shall say within themselves, This was he, whom we had sometimes in derision, and a proverb of reproach: [4] We fools accounted his life madness, and his end to be without honour: [5] How is he numbered among the children of God, and his lot is among the saints! [6] Therefore have we erred from the way of truth, and the light of righteousness hath not shined unto us, and the sun of righteousness rose not upon us. [7] We wearied ourselves in the way of wickedness and destruction: yea, we have gone through deserts, where there lay no way: but as for the way of the Lord, we have not known it. [8] What hath pride profited us? or what good hath riches with our vaunting brought us? [9] All those things are passed away like a shadow, and as a post that hasted by; [10] And as a ship that passeth over the waves of the water, which when it is gone by, the trace thereof cannot be found, neither the pathway of the keel in the waves; [11] Or as when a bird hath flown through the air, there is no token of her way to be found, but the light air being beaten with the stroke of her wings and parted with the violent noise and motion of them, is passed through, and therein afterwards no sign where she went is to be found; [12] Or like as when an arrow is shot at a mark, it parteth the air, which immediately cometh together again, so that a man cannot know where it went through: [13] Even so we in like manner, as soon as we were born, began to draw to our end, and had no sign of virtue to shew; but were consumed in our own wickedness. [14] For the hope of the Godly is like dust that is blown away with the wind; like a thin froth that is driven away with the storm; like as the smoke which is dispersed here and there with a tempest, and passeth away as the remembrance of a guest that tarrieth but a day. [15] But the righteous live for evermore; their reward also is with the Lord, and the care of them is with the most High. [16] Therefore shall they receive a glorious kingdom, and a beautiful crown from the Lord's hand: for with his right hand shall he cover them, and with his arm shall he protect them. [17] He shall take to him his jealousy for complete armour, and make the creature his weapon for the revenge of his enemies. [18] He shall put on righteousness as a breastplate, and true judgment instead of an helmet. [19] He shall take holiness for an invincible shield. [20] His severe wrath shall he sharpen for a sword, and the world shall fight with him against the unwise. [21] Then shall the right aiming thunderbolts go abroad; and from the clouds, as from a well drawn bow, shall they fly to the mark. [22] And hailstones full of wrath shall be cast as out of a stone bow, and the water of the sea shall rage against them, and the floods shall cruelly drown them. [23] Yea, a mighty wind shall stand up against them, and like a storm shall blow them away: thus iniquity shall lay waste the whole earth, and ill dealing shall overthrow the thrones of the mighty. Wis.6 [1] Hear therefore, O ye kings, and understand; learn, ye that be judges of the ends of the earth. [2] Give ear, ye that rule the people, and glory in the multitude of nations. [3] For power is given you of the Lord, and sovereignty from the Highest, who shall try your works, and search out your counsels. [4] Because, being ministers of his kingdom, ye have not judged aright, nor kept the law, nor walked after the counsel of God; [5] Horribly and speedily shall he come upon you: for a sharp judgment shall be to them that be in high places. [6] For mercy will soon pardon the meanest: but mighty men shall be mightily tormented. [7] For he which is Lord over all shall fear no man's person, neither shall he stand in awe of any man's greatness: for he hath made the small and great, and careth for all alike. [8] But a sore trial shall come upon the mighty. [9] Unto you therefore, O kings, do I speak, that ye may learn wisdom, and not fall away. [10] For they that keep holiness holily shall be judged holy: and they that have learned such things shall find what to answer. [11] Wherefore set your affection upon my words; desire them, and ye shall be instructed. [12] Wisdom is glorious, and never fadeth away: yea, she is easily seen of them that love her, and found of such as seek her. [13] She preventeth them that desire her, in making herself first known unto them. [14] Whoso seeketh her early shall have no great travail: for he shall find her sitting at his doors. [15] To think therefore upon her is perfection of wisdom: and whoso watcheth for her shall quickly be without care. [16] For she goeth about seeking such as are worthy of her, sheweth herself favourably unto them in the ways, and meeteth them in every thought. [17] For the very true beginning of her is the desire of discipline; and the care of discipline is love; [18] And love is the keeping of her laws; and the giving heed unto her laws is the assurance of incorruption; [19] And incorruption maketh us near unto God: [20] Therefore the desire of wisdom bringeth to a kingdom. [21] If your delight be then in thrones and sceptres, O ye kings of the people, honour wisdom, that ye may reign for evermore. [22] As for wisdom, what she is, and how she came up, I will tell you, and will not hide mysteries from you: but will seek her out from the beginning of her nativity, and bring the knowledge of her into light, and will not pass over the truth. [23] Neither will I go with consuming envy; for such a man shall have no fellowship with wisdom. [24] But the multitude of the wise is the welfare of the world: and a wise king is the upholding of the people. [25] Receive therefore instruction through my words, and it shall do you good. Wis.7 [1] I myself also am a mortal man, like to all, and the offspring of him that was first made of the earth, [2] And in my mother's womb was fashioned to be flesh in the time of ten months, being compacted in blood, of the seed of man, and the pleasure that came with sleep. [3] And when I was born, I drew in the common air, and fell upon the earth, which is of like nature, and the first voice which I uttered was crying, as all others do. [4] I was nursed in swaddling clothes, and that with cares. [5] For there is no king that had any other beginning of birth. [6] For all men have one entrance into life, and the like going out. [7] Wherefore I prayed, and understanding was given me: I called upon God, and the spirit of wisdom came to me [8] I preferred her before sceptres and thrones, and esteemed riches nothing in comparison of her. [9] Neither compared I unto her any precious stone, because all gold in respect of her is as a little sand, and silver shall be counted as clay before her. [10] I loved her above health and beauty, and chose to have her instead of light: for the light that cometh from her never goeth out. [11] All good things together came to me with her, and innumerable riches in her hands. [12] And I rejoiced in them all, because wisdom goeth before them: and I knew not that she was the mother of them. [13] I learned diligently, and do communicate her liberally: I do not hide her riches. [14] For she is a treasure unto men that never faileth: which they that use become the friends of God, being commended for the gifts that come from learning. [15] God hath granted me to speak as I would, and to conceive as is meet for the things that are given me: because it is he that leadeth unto wisdom, and directeth the wise. [16] For in his hand are both we and our words; all wisdom also, and knowledge of workmanship. [17] For he hath given me certain knowledge of the things that are, namely, to know how the world was made, and the operation of the elements: [18] The beginning, ending, and midst of the times: the alterations of the turning of the sun, and the change of seasons: [19] The circuits of years, and the positions of stars: [20] The natures of living creatures, and the furies of wild beasts: the violence of winds, and the reasonings of men: the diversities of plants and the virtues of roots: [21] And all such things as are either secret or manifest, them I know. [22] For wisdom, which is the worker of all things, taught me: for in her is an understanding spirit holy, one only, manifold, subtil, lively, clear, undefiled, plain, not subject to hurt, loving the thing that is good quick, which cannot be letted, ready to do good, [23] Kind to man, steadfast, sure, free from care, having all power, overseeing all things, and going through all understanding, pure, and most subtil, spirits. [24] For wisdom is more moving than any motion: she passeth and goeth through all things by reason of her pureness. [25] For she is the breath of the power of God, and a pure influence flowing from the glory of the Almighty: therefore can no defiled thing fall into her. [26] For she is the brightness of the everlasting light, the unspotted mirror of the power of God, and the image of his goodness. [27] And being but one, she can do all things: and remaining in herself, she maketh all things new: and in all ages entering into holy souls, she maketh them friends of God, and prophets. [28] For God loveth none but him that dwelleth with wisdom. [29] For she is more beautiful than the sun, and above all the order of stars: being compared with the light, she is found before it. [30] For after this cometh night: but vice shall not prevail against wisdom. Wis.8 [1] Wisdom reacheth from one end to another mightily: and sweetly doth she order all things. [2] I loved her, and sought her out from my youth, I desired to make her my spouse, and I was a lover of her beauty. [3] In that she is conversant with God, she magnifieth her nobility: yea, the Lord of all things himself loved her. [4] For she is privy to the mysteries of the knowledge of God, and a lover of his works. [5] If riches be a possession to be desired in this life; what is richer than wisdom, that worketh all things? [6] And if prudence work; who of all that are is a more cunning workman than she? [7] And if a man love righteousness her labours are virtues: for she teacheth temperance and prudence, justice and fortitude: which are such things, as en can have nothing more profitable in their life. [8] If a man desire much experience, she knoweth things of old, and conjectureth aright what is to come: she knoweth the subtilties of speeches, and can expound dark sentences: she foreseeth signs and wonders, and the events of seasons and times. [9] Therefore I purposed to take her to me to live with me, knowing that she would be a counsellor of good things, and a comfort in cares and grief. [10] For her sake I shall have estimation among the multitude, and honour with the elders, though I be young. [11] I shall be found of a quick conceit in judgment, and shall be admired in the sight of great men. [12] When I hold my tongue, they shall bide my leisure, and when I speak, they shall give good ear unto me: if I talk much, they shall lay their hands upon their mouth. [13] Moreover by the means of her I shall obtain immortality, and leave behind me an everlasting memorial to them that come after me. [14] I shall set the people in order, and the nations shall be subject unto me. [15] Horrible tyrants shall be afraid, when they do but hear of me; I shall be found good among the multitude, and valiant in war. [16] After I am come into mine house, I will repose myself with her: for her conversation hath no bitterness; and to live with her hath no sorrow, but mirth and joy. [17] Now when I considered these things in myself, and pondered them in my heart, how that to be allied unto wisdom is immortality; [18] And great pleasure it is to have her friendship; and in the works of her hands are infinite riches; and in the exercise of conference with her, prudence; and in talking with her, a good report; I went about seeking how to take her to me. [19] For I was a witty child, and had a good spirit. [20] Yea rather, being good, I came into a body undefiled. [21] Nevertheless, when I perceived that I could not otherwise obtain her, except God gave her me; and that was a point of wisdom also to know whose gift she was; I prayed unto the Lord, and besought him, and with my whole heart I said, Wis.9 [1] O God of my fathers, and Lord of mercy, who hast made all things with thy word, [2] And ordained man through thy wisdom, that he should have dominion over the creatures which thou hast made, [3] And order the world according to equity and righteousness, and execute judgment with an upright heart: [4] Give me wisdom, that sitteth by thy throne; and reject me not from among thy children: [5] For I thy servant and son of thine handmaid am a feeble person, and of a short time, and too young for the understanding of judgment and laws. [6] For though a man be never so perfect among the children of men, yet if thy wisdom be not with him, he shall be nothing regarded. [7] Thou hast chosen me to be a king of thy people, and a judge of thy sons and daughters: [8] Thou hast commanded me to build a temple upon thy holy mount, and an altar in the city wherein thou dwellest, a resemblance of the holy tabernacle, which thou hast prepared from the beginning. [9] And wisdom was with thee: which knoweth thy works, and was present when thou madest the world, and knew what was acceptable in thy sight, and right in thy commandments. [10] O send her out of thy holy heavens, and from the throne of thy glory, that being present she may labour with me, that I may know what is pleasing unto thee. [11] For she knoweth and understandeth all things, and she shall lead me soberly in my doings, and preserve me in her power. [12] So shall my works be acceptable, and then shall I judge thy people righteously, and be worthy to sit in my father's seat. [13] For what man is he that can know the counsel of God? or who can think what the will of the Lord is? [14] For the thoughts of mortal men are miserable, and our devices are but uncertain. [15] For the corruptible body presseth down the soul, and the earthy tabernacle weigheth down the mind that museth upon many things. [16] And hardly do we guess aright at things that are upon earth, and with labour do we find the things that are before us: but the things that are in heaven who hath searched out? [17] And thy counsel who hath known, except thou give wisdom, and send thy Holy Spirit from above? [18] For so the ways of them which lived on the earth were reformed, and men were taught the things that are pleasing unto thee, and were saved through wisdom. Wis.10 [1] She preserved the first formed father of the world, that was created alone, and brought him out of his fall, [2] And gave him power to rule all things. [3] But when the unrighteous went away from her in his anger, he perished also in the fury wherewith he murdered his brother. [4] For whose cause the earth being drowned with the flood, wisdom again preserved it, and directed the course of the righteous in a piece of wood of small value. [5] Moreover, the nations in their wicked conspiracy being confounded, she found out the righteous, and preserved him blameless unto God, and kept him strong against his tender compassion toward his son. [6] When the ungodly perished, she delivered the righteous man, who fled from the fire which fell down upon the five cities. [7] Of whose wickedness even to this day the waste land that smoketh is a testimony, and plants bearing fruit that never come to ripeness: and a standing pillar of salt is a monument of an unbelieving soul. [8] For regarding not wisdom, they gat not only this hurt, that they knew not the things which were good; but also left behind them to the world a memorial of their foolishness: so that in the things wherein they offended they could not so much as be hid. [9] Rut wisdom delivered from pain those that attended upon her. [10] When the righteous fled from his brother's wrath she guided him in right paths, shewed him the kingdom of God, and gave him knowledge of holy things, made him rich in his travels, and multiplied the fruit of his labours. [11] In the covetousness of such as oppressed him she stood by him, and made him rich. [12] She defended him from his enemies, and kept him safe from those that lay in wait, and in a sore conflict she gave him the victory; that he might know that goodness is stronger than all. [13] When the righteous was sold, she forsook him not, but delivered him from sin: she went down with him into the pit, [14] And left him not in bonds, till she brought him the sceptre of the kingdom, and power against those that oppressed him: as for them that had accused him, she shewed them to be liars, and gave him perpetual glory. [15] She delivered the righteous people and blameless seed from the nation that oppressed them. [16] She entered into the soul of the servant of the Lord, and withstood dreadful kings in wonders and signs; [17] Rendered to the righteous a reward of their labours, guided them in a marvellous way, and was unto them for a cover by day, and a light of stars in the night season; [18] Brought them through the Red sea, and led them through much water: [19] But she drowned their enemies, and cast them up out of the bottom of the deep. [20] Therefore the righteous spoiled the ungodly, and praised thy holy name, O Lord, and magnified with one accord thine hand, that fought for them. [21] For wisdom opened the mouth of the dumb, and made the tongues of them that cannot speak eloquent. Wis.11 [1] She prospered their works in the hand of the holy prophet. [2] They went through the wilderness that was not inhabited, and pitched tents in places where there lay no way. [3] They stood against their enemies, and were avenged of their adversaries. [4] When they were thirsty, they called upon thee, and water was given them out of the flinty rock, and their thirst was quenched out of the hard stone. [5] For by what things their enemies were punished, by the same they in their need were benefited. [6] For instead of of a perpetual running river troubled with foul blood, [7] For a manifest reproof of that commandment, whereby the infants were slain, thou gavest unto them abundance of water by a means which they hoped not for: [8] Declaring by that thirst then how thou hadst punished their adversaries. [9] For when they were tried albeit but in mercy chastised, they knew how the ungodly were judged in wrath and tormented, thirsting in another manner than the just. [10] For these thou didst admonish and try, as a father: but the other, as a severe king, thou didst condemn and punish. [11] Whether they were absent or present, they were vexed alike. [12] For a double grief came upon them, and a groaning for the remembrance of things past. [13] For when they heard by their own punishments the other to be benefited, they had some feel-

ing of the Lord. [14] For whom they respected with scorn, when he was long before thrown out at the casting forth of the infants, him in the end, when they saw what came to pass, they admired. [15] But for the foolish devices of their wickedness, wherewith being deceived they worshipped serpents void of reason, and vile beasts, thou didst send a multitude of unreasonable beasts upon them for vengeance; [16] That they might know, that wherewithal a man sinneth, by the same also shall he be punished. [17] For thy Almighty hand, that made the world of matter without form, wanted not means to send among them a multitude of bears or fierce lions, [18] Or unknown wild beasts, full of rage, newly created, breathing out either a fiery vapour, or filthy scents of scattered smoke, or shooting horrible sparkles out of their eyes: [19] Whereof not only the harm might dispatch them at once, but also the terrible sight utterly destroy them. [20] Yea, and without these might they have fallen down with one blast, being persecuted of vengeance, and scattered abroad through the breath of thy power: but thou hast ordered all things in measure and number and weight. [21] For thou canst shew thy great strength at all times when thou wilt; and who may withstand the power of thine arm? [22] For the whole world before thee is as a little grain of the balance, yea, as a drop of the morning dew that falleth down upon the earth. [23] But thou hast mercy upon all; for thou canst do all things, and winkest at the sins of men, because they should amend. [24] For thou lovest all the things that are, and abhorrest nothing which thou hast made: for never wouldest thou have made any thing, if thou hadst hated it. [25] And how could any thing have endured, if it had not been thy will? or been preserved, if not called by thee? [26] But thou sparest all: for they are thine, O Lord, thou lover of souls. Wis.12 [1] For thine incorruptible Spirit is in all things. [2] Therefore chastenest thou them by little and little that offend, and warnest them by putting them in remembrance wherein they have offended, that leaving their wickedness they may believe on thee, O Lord. [3] For it was thy will to destroy by the hands of our fathers both those old inhabitants of thy holy land, [4] Whom thou hatedst for doing most odious works of witchcrafts, and wicked sacrifices; [5] And also those merciless murderers of children, and devourers of man's flesh, and the feasts of blood, [6] With their priests out of the midst of their idolatrous crew, and the parents, that killed with their own hands souls destitute of help: [7] That the land, which thou esteemedst above all other, might receive a worthy colony of God's children. [8] Nevertheless even those thou sparedst as men, and didst send wasps, forerunners of thine host, to destroy them by little and little. [9] Not that thou wast unable to bring the ungodly under the hand of the righteous in battle, or to destroy them at once with cruel beasts, or with one rough word: [10] But executing thy judgments upon them by little and little, thou gavest them place of repentance, not being ignorant that they were a naughty generation, and that their malice was bred in them, and that their cogitation would never be changed. [11] For it was a cursed seed from the beginning; neither didst thou for fear of any man give them pardon for those things wherein they sinned. [12] For who shall say, What hast thou done? or who shall withstand thy judgment? or who shall accuse thee for the nations that perish, whom thou made? or who shall come to stand against thee, to be revenged for the unrighteous men? [13] For neither is there any God but thou that careth for all, to whom thou mightest shew that thy judgment is not unright. [14] Neither shall king or tyrant be able to set his face against thee for any whom thou hast punished. [15] Forsomuch then as thou art righteous thyself, thou orderest all things righteously: thinking it not agreeable with thy power to condemn him that hath not deserved to be punished. [16] For thy power is the beginning of righteousness, and because thou art the Lord of all, it maketh thee to be gracious unto all. [17] For when men will not believe that thou art of a full power, thou shewest thy strength, and among them that know it thou makest their boldness manifest. [18] But thou, mastering thy power, judgest with equity, and orderest us with great favour: for thou mayest use power when thou wilt. [19] But by such works hast thou taught thy people that the just man should be merciful, and hast made thy children to be of a good hope that thou givest repentance for sins. [20] For if thou didst punish the enemies of thy children, and the condemned to death, with such deliberation, giving them time and place, whereby they might be delivered from their malice: [21] With how great circumspection didst thou judge thine own sons, unto whose fathers thou hast sworn, and made covenants of good promises? [22] Therefore, whereas thou dost chasten us, thou scourgest our enemies a thousand times more, to the intent that, when we judge, we should carefully think of thy goodness, and when we ourselves are judged, we should look for mercy. [23] Wherefore, whereas men have lived dissolutely and unrighteously, thou hast tormented them with their own abominations. [24] For they went astray very far in the ways of error, and held them for gods, which even among the beasts of their enemies were despised, being deceived, as children of no understanding. [25] Therefore unto them, as to children without the use of reason, thou didst send a judgment to mock them. [26] But they that would not be reformed by that correction, wherein he dallied with them, shall feel a judgment worthy of God. [27] For, look, for what things they grudged, when they were punished, that is, for them whom they thought to be gods; [now] being punished in them, when they saw it, they acknowledged him to be the true God, whom before they denied to know: and therefore came extreme damnation upon them. Wis.13 [1] Surely vain are all men by nature, who are ignorant of God, and could not out of the good things that are seen know him that is: neither by considering the works did they acknowledge the workmaster; [2] But deemed either fire, or wind, or the swift air, or the circle of the stars, or the violent water, or the lights of heaven, to be the gods which govern the world. [3] With whose beauty if they being delighted took them to be gods; let them know how much better the Lord of them is: for the first author of beauty hath created them. [4] But if they were astonished at their power and virtue, let them understand by them, how much mightier he is that made them. [5] For by the greatness and beauty of the creatures proportionably the maker of them is seen. [6] But yet for this they are the less to be blamed: for they peradventure err, seeking God, and desirous to find him. [7] For being conversant in his works they search him diligently, and believe their sight: because the things are beautiful that are seen. [8] Howbeit neither are they to be pardoned. [9] For if they were able to know so much, that they could aim at the world; how did they not sooner find out the Lord thereof? [10] But miserable are they, and in dead things is their hope, who call them gods, which are the works of men's hands, gold and silver, to shew art in, and resemblances of beasts, or a stone good for nothing, the work of an ancient hand. [11] Now a carpenter that felleth timber, after he hath sawn down a tree meet for the purpose, and taken off all the bark skilfully round about, and hath wrought it handsomely, and made a vessel thereof fit for the service of man's life; [12] And after spending the refuse of his work to dress his meat, hath filled himself; [13] And taking the very refuse among those which served to no use, being a crooked piece of wood, and full of knots, hath carved it diligently, when he had nothing else to do, and formed it by the skill of his understanding, and fashioned it to the image of a man; [14] Or made it like some vile beast, laying it over with vermilion, and with paint colouring it red, and covering every spot therein; [15] And when he had made a convenient room for it, set it in a wall, and made it fast with iron: [16] For he provided for it that it might not fall, knowing that it was unable to help itself; for it is an image, and hath need of help: [17] Then maketh he prayer for his goods, for his wife and children, and is not ashamed to speak to that which hath no life. [18] For health he calleth upon that which is weak: for life prayeth to that which is dead; for aid humbly beseecheth that which hath least means to help: and for a good journey he asketh of that which cannot set a foot forward: [19] And for gaining and getting, and for good success of his hands, asketh ability to do of him, that is most unable to do any thing. Wis.14 [1] Again, one preparing himself to sail, and about to pass through the raging waves, calleth upon a piece of wood more rotten than the vessel that carrieth him. [2] For verily desire of gain devised that, and the workman built it by his skill. [3] But thy providence, O Father, governeth it: for thou hast made a way in the sea, and a safe path in the waves; [4] Shewing that thou canst save from all danger: yea, though a man went to sea without art. [5] Nevertheless thou wouldest not that the works of thy wisdom should be idle, and therefore do men commit their lives to a small piece of wood, and passing the rough sea in a weak vessel are saved. [6] For in the old time also, when the proud giants perished, the hope of the world governed by thy hand escaped in a weak vessel, and left to all ages a seed of generation. [7] For blessed is the wood whereby righteousness cometh. [8] But that which is made with hands is cursed, as well it, as he that made it: he, because he made it; and it, because, being corruptible, it was called god. [9] For the ungodly and his ungodliness are both alike hateful unto God. [10] For that which is made shall be punished together with him that made it. [11] Therefore even upon the idols of the Gentiles shall there be a visitation: because in the creature of God they are become an abomination, and stumblingblocks to the souls of men, and a snare to the feet of the unwise. [12] For the devising of idols was the beginning of spiritual fornication, and the invention of them the corruption of life. [13] For neither were they from the beginning, neither shall they be for ever. [14] For by the vain glory of men they entered into the world, and therefore shall they come shortly to an end. [15] For a father afflicted with untimely mourning, when he hath made an image of his child soon taken away, now honoured him as a god, which was then a dead man, and delivered to those that were under him ceremonies and sacrifices. [16] Thus in process of time an ungodly custom grown strong was kept as a law, and graven images were worshipped by the commandments of kings. [17] Whom men could not honour in presence, because they dwelt far off, they took the counterfeit of his visage from far, and made an express image of a king whom they honoured, to the end that by this their forwardness they might flatter him that was absent, as if he were present. [18] Also the singular diligence of the artificer did help to set forward the ignorant to more superstition. [19] For he, peradventure willing to please one in authority, forced all his skill to make the resemblance of the best fashion. [20] And so the multitude, allured by the grace of the work, took him now for a god, which a little before was but honoured. [21] And this was an occasion to deceive the world: for men, serving either calamity or tyranny, did ascribe unto stones and stocks the incommunicable name. [22] Moreover this was not enough for them, that they erred in the knowledge of God; but whereas they lived in the great war of ignorance, those so great plagues called they peace. [23] For whilst they slew their children in sacrifices, or used secret ceremonies, or made revellings of strange rites; [24] They kept neither lives nor marriages any longer undefiled: but either one slew another traiterously, or grieved him by adultery. [25] So that there reigned in all men without exception blood, manslaughter, theft, and dissimulation, corruption, unfaithfulness, tumults, perjury, [26] Disquieting of good men, forgetfulness of good turns, defiling of souls, changing of kind, disorder in marriages, adultery, and shameless uncleanness. [27] For the worshipping of idols not to be named is the beginning, the cause, and the end, of all evil. [28] For either they are mad when they be merry, or prophesy lies, or live unjustly, or else lightly forswear themselves. [29] For insomuch as their trust is in idols, which have no life; though they swear falsely, yet they look not to be hurt. [30] Howbeit for both causes shall they be justly punished: both because they thought not well of God, giving heed unto idols, and also unjustly swore in deceit, despising holiness. [31] For it is not the power of them by whom they swear: but it is the just vengeance of sinners, that punisheth always the offence of the ungodly. Wis.15 [1] But thou, O God, art gracious and true, longsuffering, and in mercy ordering all things, [2] For if we sin, we are thine, knowing thy power: but we will not sin, knowing that we are counted thine. [3] For to know thee is perfect righteousness: yea, to know thy power is the root of immortality. [4] For neither did the mischievous invention of men deceive us, nor an image spotted with divers colours, the painter's fruitless labour; [5] The sight whereof enticeth fools to lust after it, and so they desire the form of a dead image, that hath no breath. [6] Both they that make them, they that desire them, and they that worship them, are lovers of evil things, and are worthy to have such things to trust upon. [7] For the potter, tempering soft earth, fashioneth every vessel with much labour for our service: yea, of the same clay he maketh both the vessels that serve for clean uses, and likewise also all such as serve to the contrary: but what is the use of either sort, the potter himself is the judge. [8] And employing his labours lewdly, he maketh a vain god of the same clay, even he which a little before was made of earth himself, and within a little while after returneth to the same, out when his life which was lent him shall be demanded. [9] Notwithstanding his care is, not that he shall have much labour, nor that his life is short: but striveth to excel goldsmiths and silversmiths, and endeavoureth to do like the workers in brass, and counteth it his glory to make counterfeit things. [10] His heart is ashes, his hope is more vile than earth, and his life of less value than clay: [11] Forasmuch as he knew not his Maker, and him that inspired into him an active soul, and breathed in a living spirit. [12] But they counted our life a pastime, and our time here a market for gain: for, say they, we must be getting every way, though it be by evil means. [13] For this man, that of earthly matter maketh brittle vessels and graven images, knoweth himself to offend above all others. [14] And all the enemies of thy people, that hold them in subjection, are most foolish, and are more miserable than very babes. [15] For they counted all the idols of the heathen to be gods: which neither have the use of eyes to see, nor noses to draw breath, nor ears to hear, nor fingers of hands to handle; and as for their feet, they are slow to go. [16] For man made them, and he that borrowed his own spirit fashioned them: but no man can make a god like unto himself. [17] For being mortal, he worketh a dead thing with wicked hands: for he himself is better than the things which he worshippeth: whereas he lived once, but they never. [18] Yea, they worshipped those beasts also that are most hateful: for being compared together, some are worse than others. [19] Neither are they beautiful, so much as to be desired in respect of beasts: but they went without the praise of God and his blessing. Wis.16 [1] Therefore by the like were they punished worthily, and by the multitude of beasts tormented. [2] Instead of which punishment, dealing graciously with thine own people, thou preparedst for them meat of a strange taste, even quails to stir up their appetite: [3] To the end that they, desiring food, might for the ugly sight of the beasts sent among them lothe even that, which they must needs desire; but these, suffering penury for a short space, might be made partakers of a strange taste. [4] For it was requisite, that upon them exercising tyranny should come penury, which they could not avoid: but to these it should only be shewed how their enemies were tormented. [5] For when the horrible fierceness of beasts came upon these, and they perished with the stings of crooked serpents, thy wrath endured not for ever: [6] But they were troubled for a small season, that they might be admonished, having a sign of salvation, to put them in remembrance of the commandment of thy law. [7] For he that turned himself toward it was not saved by the thing that he saw, but by thee, that art the Saviour of all. [8] And in this thou madest thine enemies confess, that it is thou who deliverest from all evil: [9] For them the bitings of grasshoppers and flies killed, neither was there found any remedy for their life: for they were worthy to be punished by such. [10] But thy sons not the very teeth of venomous dragons overcame: for thy mercy was ever by them, and healed them. [11] For they were pricked, that they should remember thy words; and were quickly saved, that not falling into deep forgetfulness, they might be continually mindful of thy goodness. [12] For it was neither herb, nor mollifying plaister, that restored them to health: but thy word, O Lord, which healeth all things. [13] For thou hast power of life and death: thou leadest to the gates of hell, and bringest up again. [14] A man indeed killeth through his malice: and the spirit, when it is gone forth, returneth not; neither the soul received up cometh again. [15] But it is not possible to escape thine hand. [16] For the ungodly, that denied to know thee, were scourged by the strength of thine arm: with strange rains, hails, and showers, were they persecuted, that they could not avoid, and through fire were they consumed. [17] For, which is most to be wondered at, the fire had more force in the water, that quencheth all things: for the world fighteth for the righteous. [18] For sometime the flame was mitigated, that it might not burn up the beasts that were sent against the ungodly; but themselves might see and perceive that they were persecuted with the judgment of God. [19] And at another time it burneth even in the midst of water above the power of fire, that it might destroy the fruits of an unjust land. [20] Instead whereof thou feddest thine own people with angels' food, and didst send them from heaven bread prepared without their labour, able to content every man's delight, and agreeing to every taste. [21] For thy sustenance declared thy sweetness unto thy children, and serving to the appetite of the eater, tempered itself to every man's liking. [22] But snow and ice endured the fire, and melted not, that they might know that fire burning in the hail, and sparkling in the rain, did destroy the fruits of the enemies. [23] But this again did even forget his own strength, that the righteous might be nourished. [24] For the creature that serveth thee, who art the Maker increaseth his strength against the unrighteous for their punishment, and abateth his strength for the benefit of such as put their trust in thee. [25] Therefore even then was it altered into all fashions, and was obedient to thy grace, that nourisheth all things, according to the desire of them that had need: [26] That thy children, O Lord, whom thou lovest, might know, that it is not the growing of fruits that nourisheth man: but that it is thy word, which preserveth them that put their trust in thee. [27] For that which was not destroyed of the fire, being warmed with a little sunbeam, soon melted away: [28] That it might be known, that we must prevent the sun to give thee thanks, and at the dayspring pray unto thee. [29] For the hope of the unthankful shall melt away as the winter's hoar frost, and shall run away as unprofitable water. Wis.17 [1] For great are thy judgments, and cannot be expressed: therefore unnurtured souls have erred. [2] For when unrighteous men thought to oppress the holy nation; they being shut up in their houses, the prisoners of darkness, and fettered with the bonds of a long night, lay there exiled from the eternal providence. [3] For while they supposed to lie hid in their secret sins, they were scattered under a dark veil of forgetfulness, being horribly astonished, and troubled with [strange] apparitions. [4] For neither might the corner that held them keep them from fear: but noises [as of waters] falling down sounded about them, and sad visions appeared unto them with heavy countenances. [5] No power of the fire might give them light: neither could the bright flames of the stars endure to lighten that horrible night. [6] Only there appeared unto them a fire kindled of itself, very dreadful: for being much terrified, they thought the things which they saw to be worse than the sight they saw not. [7] As for the illusions of art magick, they were put down, and their vaunting in wisdom was reproved with disgrace. [8] For they, that promised to drive away terrors and troubles from a sick soul, were sick themselves of fear, worthy to be laughed at. [9] For though no terrible thing did fear them; yet being scared with beasts that passed by, and hissing of serpents, [10] They died for fear, denying that they saw the air, which could of no side be avoided. [11] For wickedness, condemned by her own witness, is very timorous, and being pressed with conscience, always forecasteth grievous things. [12] For fear is nothing else but a betraying of the succours which reason offereth. [13] And the expectation from within, being less, counteth the ignorance more than the cause which bringeth the torment. [14] But they sleeping the same sleep that night, which was indeed intolerable, and which came upon them out of the bottoms of inevitable hell, [15] Were partly vexed with monstrous apparitions, and partly fainted, their heart failing them: for a sudden fear, and not looked for, came upon them. [16] So then whosoever there fell down was straitly kept, shut up in a prison without iron bars, [17] For whether he were husbandman, or shepherd, or a labourer in the field, he was overtaken, and endured that necessity, which could not be avoided: for they were all bound with one chain of darkness. [18] Whether it were a whistling wind, or a melodious noise of birds among the spreading branches, or a pleasing fall of water running violently, [19] Or a terrible sound of stones cast down, or a running that could not be seen of skipping beasts, or a roaring voice of most savage wild beasts, or a rebounding echo from the hollow mountains; these things made them to swoon for fear. [20] For the whole world shined with clear light, and none were hindered in their labour: [21] Over them only was spread an heavy night, an image of that darkness which should afterward receive them: but yet were they unto themselves more grievous than the darkness. Wis.18 [1] Nevertheless thy saints had a very great light, whose voice they hearing, and not seeing their shape, because they also had not suffered the same things, they counted them happy. [2] But for that they did not hurt them now, of whom they had been wronged before, they thanked them, and besought them pardon for that they had been enemies. [3] Instead whereof thou gavest them a burning pillar of fire, both to be a guide of the unknown journey, and an harmless sun to entertain them honourably. [4] For they were worthy to be deprived of light and imprisoned in darkness, who had kept thy sons shut up, by whom the uncorrupt light of the law was to be given unto the world. [5] And when they had determined to slay the babes of the saints, one child being cast forth, and saved, to reprove them, thou tookest away the multitude of their children, and destroyedst them altogether in a mighty water. [6] Of that night were our fathers certified afore, that assuredly knowing unto what oaths they had given credence, they might afterwards be of good cheer. [7] So of thy people was accepted both the salvation of the righteous, and destruction of the enemies. [8] For wherewith thou didst punish our adversaries, by the same thou didst glorify us, whom thou hadst called. [9] For the righteous children of good men did sacrifice secretly, and with one consent made a holy law, that the saints should be like partakers of the same good and evil, the fathers now singing out the songs of praise. [10] But on the other side there sounded an ill according cry of the enemies, and a lamentable noise was carried abroad for children that were bewailed. [11] The master and the servant were punished after one manner; and like as the king, so suffered the common person. [12] So they all together had innumerable dead with one kind of death; neither were the living sufficient to bury them: for in one moment the noblest offspring of them was destroyed. [13] For whereas they would not believe any thing by reason of the enchantments; upon the destruction of the firstborn, they acknowledged this people to be the sons of God. [14] For while all things were in quiet silence, and that night was in the midst of her swift course, [15] Thine Almighty word leaped down from heaven out of thy royal throne, as a fierce man of war into the midst of a land of destruction, [16] And brought thine unfeigned commandment as a sharp sword, and standing up filled all things with death; and it touched the heaven, but it stood upon the earth. [17] Then suddenly visions of horrible dreams troubled them sore, and terrors came upon them unlooked for [18] And one thrown here, and another there, half dead, shewed the cause of his death. [19] For the dreams that troubled them did foreshew this, lest they should perish, and not know why they were afflicted. [20] Yea, the tasting of death touched the righteous also, and there was a destruction of the multitude in the wilderness: but the wrath endured not long. [21] For then the blameless man made haste, and stood forth to defend them; and bringing the shield of his proper ministry, even prayer, and the propitiation of incense, set himself against the wrath, and so brought the calamity to an end, declaring that he was thy servant. [22] So he overcame the destroyer, not with strength of body, nor force of arms, but with a word subdued him that punished, alleging the oaths and covenants made with the fathers. [23] For when the dead were now fallen down by heaps one upon another, standing between, he stayed the wrath, and parted the way to the living. [24] For in the long garment was the whole world, and in the four rows of the stones was the glory of the fathers graven, and thy Majesty upon the daidem of his head. [25] Unto these the destroyer gave place, and was afraid of them: for it was enough that they only tasted of the wrath. Wis.19 [1] As for the ungodly, wrath came upon them without mercy unto the end: for he knew before what they would do; [2] How that having given them leave to depart, and sent them hastily away, they would repent and pursue them. [3] For whilst they were yet mourning and making lamentation at the graves of the dead, they added another foolish device, and pursued them as fugitives, whom they had intreated to be gone. [4] For the destiny, whereof they were worthy, drew them unto this end, and made them forget the things that had already happened, that they might fulfil the punishment which was wanting to their torments: [5] And that thy people might pass a wonderful way: but they might find a strange death. [6] For the whole creature in his proper kind was fashioned again anew, serving the peculiar commandments that were given unto them, that thy children might be kept without hurt: [7] As namely, a cloud shadowing the camp; and where water stood before, dry land appeared; and out of the Red sea a way without impediment; and out of the violent stream a green field: [8] Wherethrough all the people went that were defended with thy hand, seeing thy marvellous strange wonders. [9] For they went at large like horses, and leaped like lambs, praising thee, O Lord, who hadst delivered them. [10] For they were yet mindful of the things that were done while they sojourned in the strange land, how the ground brought forth flies instead of cattle, and how the river cast up a multitude of frogs instead of fishes. [11] But afterwards they saw a new generation of fowls, when, being led with their appetite, they asked delicate meats. [12] For quails came up unto them from the sea for their contentment. [13] And punishments came upon the sinners not without former signs by the force of thunders: for they suffered justly according to their own wickedness, insomuch as they used a more hard and hateful behaviour toward strangers. [14] For the Sodomites did not receive those, whom they knew not when they came: but these brought friends into bondage, that had well deserved of them. [15] And not only so, but peradventure some respect shall be had of those, because they used strangers not friendly: [16] But these very grievously afflicted them, whom they had received with feastings, and were already made partakers of the same laws with them. [17] Therefore even with blindness were these stricken, as those were at the doors of the righteous man: when, being compassed about with horrible great darkness, every one sought the passage of his own doors. [18] For the elements were changed in themselves by a kind of harmony, like as in a psaltery notes change the name of the tune, and yet are always sounds; which may well be perceived by the sight of the things that have been done. [19] For earthly things were turned into watery, and the things, that before swam in the water, now went upon the ground. [20] The fire had power in the water, forgetting his own virtue: and the water forgat his own quenching nature. [21] On the other side, the flames wasted not the flesh of the corruptible living things, though they walked therein; neither melted they the icy kind of heavenly meat that was of nature apt to melt. [22] For in all things, O Lord, thou didst magnify thy people, and glorify them, neither didst thou lightly regard them: but didst assist them in every time and place.

Book 68. I Meqabyan

Chapter 1 [1] There were one man whose name are called Tseerutsaydan an who love sin ~ him would boast ina him horses abundance an him troops firmness beneath him authority. [2] Him had many priests who serve him idols whom him worship an fe whom him bow an sacrifice sacrifice by night an by daylight. [3] But ina him heart dullness it would seem fe him that them give him firmness an Power. [4] An ina him heart it would seem fe him that them give him authority ina all him Rule. [5] An again ina formation time it would seem fe him that them give him all the desired authority also. [6] An him would sacrifice sacrifice fe them day an night. [7] Him appointed priests who serve him idols. [8] While them ate from that defouled sacrifice - them would tell him pretendin that the idols eat night an day. [9] Again them would mek other persons diligent like unto them - that them might sacrifice sacrifice an eat. An again them would mek other persons diligent that them might sacrifice sacrifice - an sacrifice sacrifice like unto them. [10] But him would trust ina him idols that don't profit nor benefit. [11] By him timeframe bein small - an ina him heart dullness - it would seem fe him that them Irated him - that them feed him an that them crown him ~ it would seem fe him that them Irated him - fe Seythan have deafened him reasonin lest him know him Irator Who Irated him bringin from not livin toward livin - or lest him with him kindreds know him Irator Who Irated him bringin from not livin toward livin - that them might go toward Gehannem of Fiyah foriva - it bein judged pon them with him who call them gods without them bein gods. [12] As them aren't never well whenever - it are due that him might call them dead ones. [13] As Seythan authority that mislead them will lodge ina that idol image - an as him will tell them them reasonin accord - an as him will reveal fe them like unto them loved - him will judge pon the idols wherein them believed an wherein 'Adam childran trust - whose reasonin were like unto ashes. [14] An them will marvel pon the time them sight up that him fulfilled what them thought fe them - an them will do him accord fe him reachin up til them sacrifice them dawta childran an them male childran birthed from them nature - up til them spill dawta dawta childran an male childran blood that were clean. [15] Them didn't sadden them - fe Seythan have savoured him sacrifice fe them fe fulfill them evil accord - that him might lower them toward Gehannem like unto him - where there are no exits up til Iternity - where him will raceive tribulation. [16] But that Tseerutsaydan were arrogant ~ him had fifty idols worked ina males pattern an twenty worked ina dawtaz pattern. [17] An him would boast ina those idols that have no benefit ~ him would totally glorify them while him sacrificed sacrifice mornin an evenin. [18] An him would command persons that them might sacrifice sacrifice fe the idols - an him would eat from that defouled sacrifice - an him would command other persons that them might eat from the sacrifice ~ him would especially provoke fe evil. [19] Him had five houses worked fe him beaten worked idols that were iron an brass an lead. [20] An him ornamanted them ina silver an gold ~ him veiled curtains around the houses fe them an planted a tent fe them. [21] Him appointed keepers fe them there ~ him would Itinually sacrifice forty fe him idols - ten fattened oxen - ten sterile cows - ten fattened sheep ewes - ten barren goats - with birds that have wings. [22] But it would seem fe him that him idols ate ~ him would present fe them fifty feeqen of grapes an fifty dishes of wheat kneaded with oil. [23] An him told him priests: - "Tek an give them ~ mek mi irators eat what mi slaughtered fe them - an mek them drink the grape mi presented fe them ~ as fe if it aren't enough fe them - mi will add fe them." [24] An him would command all that them might eat an drink from that defouled sacrifice. [25] But ina him evil malice him would send him troops who visit ina all the kingdom - that as it were there were one who neither sacrifice nor bow - them might separate an know an bring him - an might punish him by fiyah an by sword before him - that them might plunder him money an might burn him house ina fiyah - that them might downstroy all him money him had pon him. [26] "Fe them are kind an great ones - an fe them have Irated wi ina them

charity - an mi will show punishmant an tribulation fe him unless him worshipped mi irators an sacrificed sacrifice fe mi irators. [27] An mi will show him punishmant an tribulation - fe them have Irated Earth an Heaven an the sea that were wide an moon an Sun an stars an rains an winds an all that live ina this world fe be food an fe be satiety fe wi." [28] But persons who worship them shall be punished ina firm tribulation - an them won't be nice fe them. Chapter 2 [1] There were one man birthed from the tribe of Binyam whose name are called Meqabees; [2] him had three childran who were handsome an totally warriors ~ them had bein iloved alongside all persons ina that Midyam an Miedon country that are Tseerutsaydan Rule. [3] An like unto the king commanded them pon the time him found them: - "Don't unu bow fe Tseerutsaydan irators? How about don't unu sacrifice sacrifice? [4] But if unu refuse - wi will seize an tek unu toward the king - an wi will downstroy all your money like unto the king commanded." [5] These youts who were handsome replied fe him sayin - "As fe Him fe Whom InI bow - there are InI Faada Irator Who Irated Earth an Heaven an what are within she - an the sea - moon an Sun an clouds an stars ~ Him are the True Irator Whom InI worship an ina Whom InI believe." [6] An these the king youts are four - an them servants who carry shield an spear are a hundred. [7] An pon the time them loved that them might seize these hola ones - them escaped from them hands and there are none who touched them ~ as those youts are totally warriors ina Power - them went seizin shields an them spears. [8] An there were from them one who strangle an kill panther - an at that time him would strangle it like unto a chicken. [9] An there were one from them who kill a lion with one rock or strikin at one time with a stick. [10] An there were one from them who kill a hundred persons - strikin ina formation time with one sword - an them name an them hunt were thus ~ it were called ina all Babilon an Mo`ab countries. [11] An them were warriors ina Power - an them had a thing bein iloved an comeliness. [12] An again them features comeliness were wondrous - however becau them worshipped JAH an becau them didn't fear death - it are them reasonin comeliness that surpass all. [13] An pon the time them frightened the troops - there are none who could able fe seize them - but them who were warriors escaped proceedin toward a lofty mountain. [14] An those troops returned toward the city an shut the fortress gate ~ them terrorized the people sayin - "Unless unu brought those warriors the Meqabyans - wi will burn your city ina fiyah - an wi will send toward the king an downstroy your country." [15] An at that time the country persons - rich an poor ones an dawtaz an males - a child whose faada an mother dead pon him an old dawtaz - everyone proceeded an shouted together - an them straightened them necks toward the mountain an shouted toward them sayin - "Don't downstroy InI - an don't downstroy InI country pon InI." [16] At that time them wept together - an them feared - arisin from JAH. [17] Returnin them faces Eastward an streachin forth them hands them begged toward JAH together - "Lord - should InI refuse these men who demolished Thy Command an Thy LAW? [18] Yet him believed ina silver an gold an ina the stone an wood that a person hands worked - but InI don't love that InI might hear that criminal word - who didn't believe Thy LAW" them said. [19] When Thou are the Irator Who save an Who kill - him mek him ras self like unto them Irated him also ~ as fe him - him are who spill a person blood an who eat a person flesh. [20] But InI don't love that InI might sight up that criminal face nor hear him word" them said. [21] "However if Thou commanded InI - InI will go toward him ~ becau InI believe ina Thee-I - InI will pass an give InI bodies fe death - an pon the time him said 'Sacrifice sacrifice fe mi irators' - InI won't hear that criminal word. [22] But InI believed Thee-I - Lord Who examine kidneys an reasonins - InI Faadas Irator - 'Abriham an Yis'haq an Ya`iqob who did Thy Accord an lived firmed up ina Thy LAW. [23] Thou examine a person reasonin an help the sinner an the righteous one - an there be none hidden from Thee-I - an him who took refuge are revealed alongside Thee-I. [24] But InI have no other Irator apart from Thee-I. [25] That InI might give InI bodies fe death becau Thy glorified Name - however be Power an Firmness an a Shelter fe InI ina this Work that InI are ruled fe Thee-I. [26] An pon the time 'Isra'iel entered toward Gibts country Thou heard Ya`iqob plea - an now glorified God - InI beg Thee-I." [27] An pon the time the two men whose features were quite handsome were sight up fe them standin before them - pon the time fiyah swords that frighten like unto lightnin alit an cut them necks an killed them - at that time them arose bein well like unto formerly. [28] Them features comeliness became totally handsome an them shone more than Sun - an them became more handsome than formerly. Chapter 3 [1] Like unto unu sight up before unu these the Most I JAH slaves - 'Abya - Seela - Fentos who dead an arose - unu have that unu might arise likewise after unu dead - an your faces shall shine like unto the Sun ina the Kingdom of Heaven. [2] An them went with those men an raceived martyrdom there. [3] At that time them begged - them praised - an them bowed fe JAH ~ death didn't frighten them an the king punishmant didn't frighten them. [4] An them went toward those youts an became like unto a sheep that have no evil - yet them didn't frighten them - an pon the time them arrived toward them - them seized an beat them an bound an whipped them - an them delivered them toward the king an stood them before him. [5] An the king answered fe them sayin - "How won't unu stubborn ones sacrifice sacrifice an bow fe mi irators?" [6] Those bredren who were cleansed from sin - who were honoured an chosen an Irie - an who shine like unto a jewel whose value were wondrous - Seela an 'Abya an Fentos answered fe him ina one word. [7] Them told that king who were a plague - "As fe InI - InI won't bow nor sacrifice fe defouled idols that have no knowledge nor reasonin." [8] An again them told him - "InI won't bow fe idols that were silver an gold that a person hand worked - that were stone an wood - that have no reasonin nor soul nor knowledge - that don't benefit them friends nor harm them enemies." [9] An the king answered fe them sayin - "Why do unu do thus - an as them know who insult them an who wrong them - why do unu insult the glorified irators?" [10] Them answered fe him sayin - "As them are like unto a trifle alongside InI - as fe InI - InI will insult them an won't glorify them." [11] An the king answered fe them sayin - "Mi will punish unu like unto your Work evil measure ~ mi will downstroy your features comeliness with whippin an firm tribulation an fiyah. [12] An now tell mi whether unu will give or won't give sacrifice fe mi irators - as fe if this didn't happen - mi will punish unu by sword an by whippin." [13] Them answered fe him sayin - "As fe InI - InI won't sacrifice sacrifice nor bow fe defouled idols" - an the king commanded them that them might beat them with a fat stick - an again that them might whip them with a whip - an after it - that them might splinter them up til them inner organs were sight up. [14] An after this them bound an made them while ina jail house up til him counsel by money that punish an kill them. [15] Without niceness them took an bound them a firm imprisonmant ina prison house - an them sat ina prison house three nights an three daylights. [16] An after this third day the king commanded that a Proclamation speaker might turn an that counselors an nobles - country elders an officials - might be gathered. [17] An pon the time the king Tseerutsaydan sat ina square - him commanded that them might bring those honoured ones - Seela an 'Abya an Fentos ~ them stood before him bein wounded an bound. [18] An the king told them - "When unu sat these three days - are there really the returnin that unu returned - or are unu ina your former evil?" [19] An those honoured JAH Souljahs answered fe him sayin - "As fe that InI were cruel - InI won't agree that InI might worship the idols filled of sin an evil that thou check up." [20] An that criminal vexed an commanded that them might stand them up ina lofty place an might renew them wounds ~ them blood flowed pon Earth. [21] An again him commanded that them might burn them with a torch lamp an might char them flesh - an him servants did like unto him commanded them - an those honoured men told him - "Thou who forgot JAH LAW - speak ~ InI reward shall abound ina the measure whereby thou multiply InI punishmant." [22] An again him commanded that them might bring an send pon them bears an tigers an lions that were evil beasts before them eat them food that them might totally eat them flesh with them bones. [23] An him commanded persons who keep the beasts that them might send the beasts pon them - an them did like unto him commanded them - an them bound those honoured martyrs feet - an again them maliciously beat an bound them with tent-stakes. [24] An those beasts were flung over them while them roared - an pon the time them arrived toward the martyrs them hailed an bowed fe them. [25] Them returned toward them keepers while them roared - an them frightened them keepers ~ them took them toward the square up til them delivered them toward before the king. [26] An them killed seventy five men from the criminals army there. [27] Many persons panicked - the one anguishin pon the one ina fear - up til the king quit him throne an fled - an them seized the beasts with difficulty an took them toward them lodgin. [28] Seela an 'Abya an Fentos two bredren came an released them from the imprisonmant them bound an told them - "Come mek InI flee lest these skeptics an criminals find InI. [29] An those martyrs answered them bredren sayin - "It aren't procedure that InI might flee after InI set up fe testimony ~ as it were unu had feared - go fleein." [30] An those them likkle bredren said - "InI will stand with unu before the king - an if unu dead InI will dead with unu." [31] An after this the king were pon him lordship hall balcany an sight up that these honoured men were released an that all the five bredren stood together ~ those chiefs who work an punish troops questioned that them were bredren an told the king - an the king vexed an shouted like unto a wilderness boar. [32] An up til the king counseled by money that punish all the five bredren - him commanded that them might seize an add them ina prison house ~ them placed them ina prison house bindin ina firm imprisonmant without niceness with a hollow stalk. [33] An the king Tseerutsaydan said - "These youts who erred wearied mi ~ what should these men reasonin firm up? an them Work evil are like unto them Power firmness ~ if mi say - "Them will return" - them will mek them reasonin evil. [34] An mi will bring the hardship pon them like unto them Work evil measure - an mi will burn them flesh ina fiyah that it might be charred ash - an pon that mi will scattar them flesh ash like unto dust pon mountains." [35] An after him spoke this him waited three days an commanded that them might bring those honoured men - an pon the time those honoured men approached him commanded that them might burn a fiyah within the great pit oven - an that them might add within it a malice Work that flame the fiyah an whereby them boil a yat - the fat an soapberries - sea foam an resin an the sulfur. [36] An pon the time fiyah flamed ina the pit the messengers went toward the king when them said - "Wi did what thou commanded wi - send the men who will be added." [37] An him commanded that them might receive an cast them ina the fiyah pit - an the youts did like unto the king commanded them - an pon the time those honoured men entered toward the fiyah them gave them souls fe JAH. [38] An when the persons who cast them sight up - Angels received an took them souls toward the Garden where Yis'haq an 'Abriham an Ya`iqob are - where Irie Ites are found. Chapter 4 [1] An pon the time that criminal sight up that them dead - him commanded that them might burn them flesh ina fiyah up til it are ash an that them might scattar them ina wind - but the fiyah couldn't able fe burn the corpse hair from them corpses side - an them sent them forth from the pit. [2] An again them flamed fiyah over them iginnin from mornin up til evenin ~ it didn't burn them ~ them said - "An now come mek wi cast them corpses seaward." [3] An them did like unto the king commanded them ~ them cast them pon the sea ~ even if them cast them seaward addin great stones an iron hearthstones an a millstone whereby a donkey grind by turnin - there are no sinkin that the sea sank them ~ as JAH Spirit of Support have lodged ina them - them floated pon the sea yet them didn't sink ~ it failed him fe downstroy them by all the malice that were provoked pon them. [4] "As this them death have made weary more than them Life - mek mi cast them corpses fe beasts that them might eat them - yet what will mi do?" him said. [5] An the youts did like unto him commanded them ~ vultures an beasts didn't touch them corpses ~ birds an vultures veiled them with them wings from burnin ina Sun an the five martyrs corpses sat fourteen days. [6] An pon the time them sight them up - them bodies shone up like unto Sun - an Angels incircled them corpses like unto light incircle the Tent. [7] Him counseled counsel ~ him lacked what him do - an after this him dug a grave an buried the five martyrs corpses. [8] An when that king who forgot JAH LAW had reclined pon a bed at night the five martyrs were sight up fe him standin before him at night vexin an seizin swords. [9] As it have seemed fe him that them entered toward him house at night ina crime - pon the time him awoke from him slumber him feared an loved that him might flee from the bedchamber toward the hall - an as it have seemed fe him that them kill him seemin that them committed crime pon him - him feared an him knees trembled. [10] Becaudis thing him said - "Mi lords - what do unu love? as fe mi - what should mi do fe unu?" [11] Them answered fe him sayin - "Aren't InI whom thou killed burnin ina fiyah an InI whom thou commanded that them might cast pon the sea? As JAH have kept InI bodies becau InI believed ina Him - it failed thee fe downstroy InI ~ as a person who believed ina Him won't perish - mek glory an praise due fe JAH - an InI also who believed ina Him didn't shame ina the tribulation. [12] "As mi didn't know that a punishmant like unto this will find mi - what reward should mi give unu becau the stead wherefore mi did a evil thing pon unu? [13] An now separate fe mi the reward mi give unu - lest unu tek mi body ina death an lest unu lower mi body toward See'ol when mi are ina Life. [14] As mi have wronged unu - forgive mi mi sin - becau it were your Faada JAH LAW Niceness" him told them. [15] An those honoured martyrs answered fe him sayin - "Becau the stead wherefore thou did a evil thing pon InI - as fe InI - InI won't pay thee a evil thing ~ as JAH are Who bring hardship pon a soul - as fe Him Who will pay thee hardship - there are JAH. [16] However InI were sight up fe thee bein revealed that InI were well fe thy timeframe bein small an becau thy reasonin deafness ~ as fe it seemin fe thee that thou killed InI - thou prepared welfare fe InI. [17] But thy idols priests an thou will downscend toward Gehannem where are no exits foriva. [18] Woe fe thy idols fe whom thou bow havin quit bowin fe JAH Who Irated unu when unu were scorned like unto spit - an fe unu who worship them - an unu don't know JAH Who Irated unu bringin from not livin toward livin ~ aren't unu who are sight up today like unto smoke an tomorrow who perish?" [19] An the king answered fe them sayin - "What will unu command mi that mi might do fe unu all that unu loved?" [20] "It are fe save thy ras self lest thou enter toward the Gehannem of Fiyah - yet it aren't fe save InI ras selves who teach thee. [21] Fe your idols are silver an gold - stone an wood - that have no reasonin nor soul knowledge - that a person hand worked. [22] But them don't kill ~ them don't save ~ them don't benefit them friend ~ them don't harm them enemy ~ them don't downbase ~ them don't honour ~ them don't mek wealthy ~ them don't impoverish ~ them mislead unu by demons authority - who don't love that the one from persons might be saved - yet them don't uproot nor plant. [23] Them especially don't love that the persons like unto unu might be saved from death - unu dull-hearted ones fe whom them seem that them irated unu - when unu are who worked them. [24] As Seythans an demons authority have lodged ina them - them shall return a thing fe unu like unto unu loved - that it might drown unu within the sea of Gehannem . [25] But thou - quit this thy error an mek this also be InI reward becau InI dead stead - that InI might benefit InI souls worshippin InI Irator JAH" them told him. [26] But him were alarmed an would totally astony - an as all five have been sight up fe him drawin them swords - him feared - an becaudis thing him bowed fe them. [27] "Hence mi knew that after dead ones who were dust dead them will really arise ~ as fe mi - only a likkle had remained fe mi fe dead." [28] After this them were hidden from before that king face ~ from that day onward that Tseerutsaydan who are totally arrogant quit burnin them corpses. [29] As them have misled them many eras - him would be Irie ina him idols an him reasonin error - an him misled many persons like unto him up til them quit followin ina Worship JAH Who Irated them - yet it aren't only him who erred. [30] An them would sacrifice them dawta childran an them male childran fe demons - yet them work a seducin an downsturbance that are them reasonin accord - that them faada Seythan taught them that him might mek the seducin an downsturbance that JAH don't love. [31] Them marry them mothers - an them abuse them aunts an them sistren ~ them abuse them bodies while them worked all that resemble this filthy Work ~ as Seythan have firmed up those crooked persons reasonin - them said - "Wi won't return." [32] But that Tseerutsaydan - who don't know him Irator - were totally arrogant - an him would boast ina him idols. [33] If them say - "How will JAH give the Kingdom fe persons who don't know Him ina LAW an ina Worship?" - them will totally return toward Him ina repentance ~ as Him test them thus - it are becaudis. [34] But if them totally return ina repentance Him would love them - an Him would keep them Kingdom - but if them refuse a fiyah will punish them ina Fiyah of Gehannem foriva. [35] But it would be due a king fe fear him Irator JAH like unto him lordship fame - an it would be due a judge fe be ruled fe him Irator while him judged goodly judgemant like unto him Rule fame. [36] An it would be due chiefs an chiefs an envoys an petty kings fe be commanded fe them Irator like unto them lordship abundance measure. [37] As Him are Heaven an Earth Lord Who Irated all the Iration - becau there are no other Irator ina Heavan nor Earth who impoverish an mek rich - Him are Who honour an downbase. Chapter 5 [1] "The one warrior from the sixty warriors were proud ~ JAH made him body Iginnin from him foot up til him head fe swell with one spoon of sulphur ~ him dead ina one plague. [2] An again Keeram who built a iron bed were proud arisin from him powerfulness abundance - an JAH hid him ina death. [3] An again Nabukedenetsor were proud sayin - 'There are no other king without mi - an mi are Irator who mek the Sun rise ina this world' - an him said thus arisin from him arrogance abundance. [4] An JAH separated from persons an sent him toward a wilderness seven years - an him made him fortune with Heaven birds an wilderness beasts up til him knew that JAH were Who Irated him. [5] An pon the time him knew Him ina worship - Him again returned him toward him kingdom ~ who are it who weren't of Earth - bein boldly proud pon JAH Who Irated him? [6] How about who are it demolished HIM LAW an Him Order an whom Earth didn't swallow? [7] An thou Tseerutsaydan love that thou might be proud pon thy Irator - an again thou have that Him might downstroy thee like unto them - an might lower thee toward a grave arisin from thy arrogance. [8] An again after them entered toward See'ol where are tooth grindin an mournin - that were darkness fulfillmant - thou have that Him might lower thee toward the deep pit Gehannem where are no exits foriva. [9] As fe thou - thou are a man who will dead an be demolished tomorrow like unto arrogant kings who were like unto thee - who quit this world livin. [10] As fe InI - InI say - 'Thou are demolished ruins - but thou aren't JAH - fe JAH are Who Irated Earth an Heaven an thee.' [11] Him downbase arrogant ones ~ Him honour them who were downbased ~ Him give firmness fe persons who wearied. [12] Him kill well ones ~ Him raise up the persons who were Earth - who dead buried ina grave. [13] An Him send slaves forth free ina Life from sin rulership. [14] O king Tseerutsaydan - why do thou boast ina thy defouled idols who have no benefit? [15] But JAH Irated Earth an Heaven an great seas ~ Him Irated moon an Sun - an Him prepared eras. [16] Man graze toward him field - an him while when him plough up til it dusk - an Heaven stars live firmed up by Him Word. [17] An Him call all ina Heaven ~ there are nothing done without JAH knowin it. [18] Him commanded Heaven Angels that them might serve Him an might praise Him glorified Name - an Angels are sent toward all persons who inherit Life. [19] Rufa'iel who were a servant were sent toward Thobeet - an him saved Thobya from death ina Ragu'iel country. [20] Hola Meeka'iel were sent toward Giediewon that him might draw him attention by money that him downstroy 'Iloflee persons; an him were sent toward the prophet Mussie pon the time him made 'Isra'iel cross 'Eritra sea. [21] As only JAH have said him led them - there were no different idol with them. [22] An Him sent them forth toward crops pon Earth. [23] An Him fed them Him plantation grain ~ as Him have totally loved them - Him cherished them feedin the honey that firmed up like unto a rock. [24] An that thou might totally keep Him kindreds by what are due - an that thou might do JAH Accord Who Irated thee - Him crowned thee givin Itority pon the four kingdoms. [25] Fe Him have crowned thee makin loftier than all - an thy Irator totally crowned thee that thou might love JAH. [26] An it are procedure that thou might love thy Irator JAH like unto Him loved thee - like unto Him trusted thee pon all the people - an thou - do JAH Accord that thy era might abound ina this world an that Him might live with thee ina Support. [27] An do JAH Accord that Him might stand fe thee bein a Guardian pon thy enemies - an that Him might seat thee pon thy throne - an that Him might hide thee ina him Wing of Support. [28] As fe if thou don't know - JAH chose an crowned thee pon 'Isra'iel like unto Him chose Sa'ol fron 'Isra'iel childran when him kept him faada donkeys - an Him crowned him pon him kindreds 'Isra'iel - an him sat with 'Isra'iel pon

him throne. [29] An Him gave him a lofty fortune separatin from him kindreds ~ JAH crowned thee pon Him kindreds ~ as fe henceforth onward - check - keep Him kindreds. [30] As JAH have Ipointed thee over them that thou might kill an might save - keep them ina evil thing - them who work a goodly thing an them who work a evil thing pon a goodly thing" him told him. [31] "An as JAH have Ipointed thee pon all that thou might do Him Accord be it while thou whipped or while thou saved - pay them evil Work - them who work goodly Work an them who work goodly Work an evil Work. [32] Fe thou are a slave of JAH Who rule all ina Heaven - an thou - do JAH Accord that Him might do thy accord fe thee ina all thou thought an ina all thou begged while thou wheedled before Him. [33] There are none who rule Him - but Him rule all. [34] There are none who Ipointed Him - but Him Ipoint all. [35] There are none who dismiss Him - but Him dismiss all. [36] There are none who reproach Him - but Him reproach all. [37] There are none who mek Him diligent - but Him mek all diligent ~ as Heaven an Earth rulership are fe Him - there are none who escape from Him Itority; all are revealed alongside Him - yet there are none hidden from Him Face. [38] Him sight up all - but there are none who sight Him up ~ Him hear the person priah who pray toward Him sayin 'Save I' - fe Him have Irated man ina Him Pattern - an Him accept him plea. [39] As Him are a King Who live up til the Iternity - Him feed all from Him unchangin Nature. Chapter 6 [1] Him crown fe true the kings who do Him Accord - the kings wrote a straight thing becau Him. [2] As them have done JAH Accord - Him shall shine up ina Light that aren't examined Yis'haq an 'Abriham an Ya`iqob - Selomon an Daweet an Hiziqyas lodgins ina the Garden where are all beautiful kings whose lodgin were Light. [3] Heaven Hall are what totally shone - yet Earth halls aren't like unto Heaven Hall ~ it floor - whose features are silver an gold an jewel features - are clean. [4] An it features that totally shine are unexamined by a person reasonin ~ Heaven Hall are what shine like unto jewels. [5] Like unto JAH knew - Who were a Nature Knower - the Heaven Hall that Him Irated are what a person reasonin don't examine an what shine ina total Light ~ it floor - that were worked ina silver an gold - ina jewels - ina white silk an ina blue silk - are clean. [6] It are quite totally beautiful like unto this. [7] Righteous ones who firmed up ina religion an virtue are who shall inherit it ina JAH Charity an fe Pardon. [8] An there are welfare Water that flow from it - an it totally shine like unto Sun - an there are a Light tent within it - an it are incircled by grace perfume. [9] A Garden fruit that were beautiful an Iloved - whose features an taste were different - are around the house - an there are a oil an grape place there - an it are totally beautiful - an it fruit fragrance are sweet. [10] When a fleshly bloodly person enter toward it - him soul would have separated from him flesh from the Irie Ites abundance that are ina it arisin from it fragrance flavour. [11] Beautiful kings who did JAH Accord shall be Irie there ~ them honour an them place are known ina the Kingdom of Heaven that live firmed ina him foriva - where welfare are found. [12] Him showed that them lordship pon Earth were famed an honoured - an that them lordship ina Heaven were famed an honoured; them shall be honoured an lofty ina Heaven like unto them honour them an bow fe them ina this world ~ if them work goodly Work ina this world them shall be Irie. [13] But kings who were evil ina them Rule an them kingdoms that JAH gave them - them don't judge fe true by what are due ~ as them have ignored the destitute an poor ones cries - them don't judge Truth an save the refugee an the wronged child whose faada an mother dead pon him. [14] Them don't save destitute an poor ones from the wealthy hand that rob them ~ them don't divide an give from them food an satta them who hungered - an them don't divide an give from them drink an give fe drink the persons who thirsted - an them didn't return them ears toward the poor one cry. [15] An Him shall tek them toward Gehannem that were a dark endin ~ pon the time that lofty Day arrived pon them when JAH shall come - an pon the time Him wrath were done pon them like unto Daweet spoke ina him Praises 'Lord - don't chastise I ina Thy Judgemant an don't admonish I ina Thy chastisemant' - them problems an them downbasemant shall abound like unto them fame abundance measure. [16] When nobles an kings are who rule this world ina this world - there are persons who didn't keep thy law. [17] But JAH Who rule all are there ina Heaven ~ all persons souls an all persons welfare have been seized by Him Itority ~ Him are Who give honour fe persons who glorify Him - fe Him totally rule all - an Him love the persons who love Him. [18] As them are Earth an Heaven Lord - Him examine an know what kidneys transported an what a reasonin thought - an fe a person who begged toward Him with a pure reasonin - Him shall give him him plea reward. [19] Him shall downstroy powerful ones arrogance - who work evil Work pon the child whose mother an faada dead pon him - an pon old dawtaz. [20] It aren't by thy Power that thou seized this kingdom ~ it aren't by thy bein able that thou sat pon this throne ~ Him loved fe test thee thus that it be possible fe thee fe rule like unto Sa'ol who ruled him kindreds ina that season - an Him seated thee pon a kingdom throne - yet it aren't by thy Power that thou seized this kingdom ~ it are when Him test thee like unto Sa'ol who ignored the prophet Samu'iel word an JAH Word an didn't serve him army nor 'Amalieq king - yet it aren't by thy bein able that thou seized this kingdom. [21] An JAH told the prophet Samu'iel - Go - an as them have saddened I by demolishin

LAW an worshippin the idols an bowin fe the idol an by them mosques an by all them hated Works without benefit - tell Sa'ol - 'Go toward 'Amalieq country an downstroy them hosts an all the kings Iginnin from persons up til livestock.' [22] Pon them who saddened JAH - becaudis thing Him sent Sa'ol that him might downstroy them. [23] But him saved them king from death - an him saved many livestock an beauties an dawtaz an handsome youts from death ~ As him have scorned I thing an as him didn't hear I Command - becaudis thing - JAH told the prophet Samu'iel - Go an divide him kingdom. [24] Becau him stead - Inoint `Issiey child Daweet that him might reign pon 'Isra'iel. [25] But pon him adjourn a demon who will strangle an cast him. [26] As him have refused if I-man gave him a kingdom that him might do I Accord - pon the time him refused I fe do I Accord I-man dismissed him from him kingdom that are due him - but thou - go an tell him sayin - 'Will thou thus ignore JAH Who crowned thee pon Him kindreds 'Isra'iel - Who seated thee pon Him Lordship Throne?' [27] But thou - tell him - 'Thou didn't know JAH Who gave around this much honour an famousness' Him told him. [28] An the prophet Samu'iel went toward the king Sa'ol an entered toward him sittin at a dinnertable - an when 'Amalieq king 'Agag had sat pon him left. [29] 'Why did thou totally ignore JAH Who commanded thee that thou might downstroy the livestock an persons?' him told him. [30] An at that time the king feared an arose from him throne an tellin Samu'iel 'Return fe wi' him seized him clothes - an Samu'iel refused fe return ~ Samu'iel clothes were torn. [31] An Samu'iel told Sa'ol - 'JAH divided thy kingdom.' [32] An again Sa'ol told Samu'iel before the people - 'Honour mi an atone mi sin fe mi before JAH that Him might forgive mi' ~ an as him have feared JAH Word Who Irated him - but as him didn't fear the king who dead - Samu'iel refused fe return ina him word. [33] Becaudis thing him pierced 'Amalieq king 'Agag before him swallowed what him chewed. [34] An a demon seized that Sa'ol who demolished the LAW of JAH - an becau Him were the King of Kings Who rule all - JAH struck pon him head a king who worked sin - fe it don't shame him. [35] Fe Him are all the Iration Lord Who dismiss all the nobles an kings Itority who don't fear Him - but there are none who rule Him. [36] Like unto Him spoke sayin - Daweet kindred shall go while it were famed an honoured - but Sa'ol kindred shall go while it were downbased - Him downstroyed kingdom from him child an from Sa'ol. [37] Becau it saddened Him - an becau Him downstroyed the criminals who saddened Him by them evil Work - JAH revenged an downstroyed Sa'ol kindred childran - fe a person who don't revenge JAH enemy - him are JAH enemy. [38] When it are possible fe him fe revenge an downstroy - an when him have Itority - a person who don't revenge an downstroy the sinner an don't revenge an downstroy a person who don't keep JAH LAW - as him are JAH enemy - Him downstroyed Sa'ol kindred childran. Chapter 7 [1] An whether thou be a king or a ruler - what important thing are thou? [2] Aren't it JAH Who Irated thee bringin from not livin toward livin - that thou might do Him Accord an might live firmed up by Him Command an might fear Him Judgemant? Like unto thou vex pon thy slaves an governed over them - all likewise there are also JAH Who vex pon thee an govern over thee. [3] Like unto thou beat without niceness persons who worked sin - all likewise there are also JAH Who will strike thee an lower thee toward Gehannem where are no exits up til Iternity. [4] Like unto thou whip him who weren't ruled fe thee an didn't bring a tribute fe thee - fe what are it that thou don't introduce a tribute fe JAH? [5] As Him are Who Irated thee in order that thou love that them might fear thee - an Who crowned thee pon all the Iration that thou might keep Him kindreds fe true - fe what are it that thou don't fear thy Irator JAH? [6] Judge by what are due an fe true like unto JAH Ipointed thee - yet don't sight up a face an favour fe small nor great ~ whom will thou fear without Him? keep Him Worship an the Nine Commands. [7] Like unto Mussie commanded 'Isra'iel childran sayin - 'I-man presented Water an fiyah fe thee-I ~ add thy hand toward what thou loved' - don't go neither rightward nor leftward. [8] Hear Him Word that I-man tell thee - that thou might hear Him Word an might do Him Command - lest thou say - 'She are beyond the sea or beyond the deep or beyond the river ~ who will bring fe mi that mi might sight she up an might hear Him Word an might do Him Command?' [9] Lest thou say - 'Who will proceed toward Heaven again an lower that JAH Word fe mi that mi might hear an do she?' - JAH Word are what approached - check - fe thou fe teach she with thy mouth an give alms by she with thy hand. [10] An thou didn't hear thy Irator JAH unless thou heard Him Book - an thou didn't love Him nor keep Him Command unless thou kept Him LAW. [11] An thou have that thou might enter toward Gehannem foriva - an unless thou loved Him Command - an unless thou did JAH Accord - Who honoured an famed thee separatin from all thy kindreds that thou might keep them fe true - thou have that thou might enter toward Gehannem foriva. [12] Him made thee above all - an Him crowned thee pon all Him kindreds that thou might rule Him kindreds fe true by what are due while thou thought of thy Irator Name Who Irated thee an gave thee a kingdom. [13] There are them whom thou whip from persons who wronged thee - an there are him whom thou pardon while thou thought of JAH Work - an there are him fe whom thou judge by what are due straightenin up thy reasonin. [14] An don't favour havin sight up a face pon the time them argued before thee ~ as Earth

physique are thy money - don't accept a bribe that thou might pardon the sinner person an wrong the clean person. [15] If thou did Him Accord - JAH shall multiply thy era ina this world fe thee - but if thou sadden Him - Him will diminish thy era. [16] Think that thou will rise after thou dead - an that thou will be examined standin before Him pon all the Work thou worked whether it be goodly or evil. [17] If thou work goodly Work - thou will live ina Garden ina the Kingdom of Heaven - ina houses where kind kings live an where Light filled. Fe JAH don't shame thy lordship authority - but if thou work evil Work - thou will live ina See'ol Gehannem where evil kings live. [18] But pon the time thou sight up thy bein feared famousness - thy warriors award - thy hangin shield an spear - an pon the time thou sight up thy horses an thy troops beneath thy authority an them who beat drum an persons who play pon a harp before thee... [19] But pon the time thou sight up all this - thou mek thy reasonin lofty - an thou firm up thy collar of reasonin - an thou don't think of JAH Who gave thee all this honour - however pon the time Him told thee - Quit all this - thou aren't who quit it. [20] Fe thou have totally neglected the Ipointmant Him Ipointed thee - an Him shall give thy lordship fe another. [21] As death shall suddenly come pon thee - an as Judgemant shall be done ina Resurrection time - an as all man Work shall be examined - Him shall totally investigate an judge pon thee. [22] There are none who will honour this world kings - fe becau Him were Truth Judge - ina Judgemant time poor an wealthy will stand together. This world nobles crowns wherein them boast shall fall. [23] Judgemant are prepared - an a soul shall quake ~ at that time sinners an righteous ones Work shall be examined. [24] An there are none who shall be hidden. Pon the time a dawta arrived fe birthin - an pon the time the fetus ina she belly arrived fe bein birthed - like unto she cyaan prevent she womb - Earth also cyaan prevent she lodgers that are pon she ~ she will return. [25] An like unto clouds cyaan prevent rain lest them tek an rain toward the place JAH commanded them - fe JAH Word have Irated all bringin from not livin toward livin - an fe JAH Word again have introduced all toward a grave; an all likewise - after Resurrection time arrived - it aren't possible fe be that dead persons won't rise. [26] Like unto Mussie spoke sayin - 'It are by Words that proceed from JAH Tongue - yet it aren't only by grain that a person are saved'; an JAH Word again shall arouse all persons from graves. [27] Check - it were known that dead persons shall arise by JAH Word. [28] An again JAH said thus ina Repeatin Law becau persons who were nobles an kings who do Him Accord - As the day have arrived when them are counted fe downstruction - I-man shall revenge an downstroy them pon the day when Judgemant are judged an at the time when them feet stumble Him said. [29] An again JAH told persons who know Him Judgemant - Know know that I-man were your Irator JAH - an that I-man kill an I-man save. [30] I-man chastise ina the tribulation an I-man pardon ~ I-man lower toward See'ol an again I-man send forth toward the Garden - an there are none who shall escape from I Itority Him told them. [31] JAH said thus becau nobles an kings who didn't keep Him LAW - As Earthly kingdoms are a passin - an as them pass from mornin up til evenin - keep I Order an I LAW that unu might enter toward the Kingdom of Heaven that live firmed up foriva Him said. [32] Fe JAH callin Righteous ones are fe glory - an sinners fe tribulation ~ Him will mek the sinner wretched but will honour righteous ones. [33] Him will dismiss the person who didn't do Him Accord - but Him will Ipoint the person who did Him Accord. Chapter 8 [1] Hear I - mek I tell thee the thing whereby dead persons shall arise ~ them shall plant a plant an be fertile an grapes shall send forth vines ~ as JAH shall bring the fruit 'imhibe 'albo ~ them shall cast wine from it. [2] Overstand that that plant thou planted were small - but that she sent forth tips fruit an leaves today. [3] JAH give she root fe drink from Earth an Water - from both. [4] But Him feed she wood from fiyah an wind ~ roots give leaves Water fe drink - an Earth give firmness fe woods. [5] But the soul that JAH Irated mek them bear fruit amidst them - an dead persons arisin are likewise. [6] Pon the time soul were separated from flesh - as each of them ras selves have gone - Him said - Gather souls from the four natures - from Earth an Water - wind an fiyah. [7] But Earth nature lived firmed up ina she nature an became Earth - an Water nature lived firmed up ina she nature an became Water. [8] An wind nature lived firmed up ina she nature an became wind - an fiyah nature lived firmed up ina she nature an became a hot fiyah. [9] But a soul that JAH separated from flesh returned toward she Irator ~ up til Him raise she up inited with flesh pon the time Him loved - Him place she ina Garden ina the place Him loved. [10] Him place righteous souls ina Light house ina Garden - but that Him might send way sinners souls - Him also place them ina darkness house ina See'ol up til the time when Him loved. [11] JAH told the prophet Hiziq'iel - Call souls from the four corners - that them might be gathered an be one limb. [12] Pon the time Him spoke ina one Word sayin thus - the souls were gathered from the four corners. [13] An Water nature brought verdure - an again fiyah nature brought fiyah. [14] An again Earth nature brought Earth - an wind nature brought wind. [15] An JAH brought a soul from the Garden place where Him placed it ~ them were gathered by one Word - an a Resurrection were made. [16] An again I-man shall show thee the example that are alongside thee ~ the day dusk ~ thou sleep ~ the night dawn - an thou rise from thy beddin - but pon the time thou slept it are thy death example.

[17] An pon the time thou awoke it are thy arisin example - but the night when all persons sleep whose physiques were dark - fe darkness have covered them - are this world example. [18] But the mornin light - when darkness are eliminated an when light are ina all the world an when persons arise an graze toward the field - are dead persons example. [19] An this Kingdom of Heaven where man are renewed are like unto this ~ dead persons Resurrection are like unto this ~ as this world are passin - it are the night example. [20] An like unto Daweet spoke sayin - 'Him placed Him example ina Sun' - as Sun shine pon the time it rose - it are a Kingdom of Heaven example. [21] An like unto Sun shine ina this world today - pon the time Kristos come Him shall shine like unto Sun in Kingdom of Heaven that are new ~ as Him have said - Him won't set an a Torch that aren't extinguished - Him JAH are she Light. [22] An Him shall quickly arouse the dead persons again ~ I-man shall bring one example fe thee again from thy food that thou sow an whereby thou are saved - an whether it be a wheat kernel or a barley kernel or a lentil kernel or all man seeds sown pon Earth - there are none that grow unless it were demolished an rotten. [23] An like unto the person flesh thou sight up - pon the time it were demolished an rotten - Earth eat stoutness with the hide. [24] An pon the time Earth ate it stoutness it grow bein around a kernel seventh ~ JAH give a cloud that seized rain like unto Him loved - an roots grow pon Earth an send forth leaves. [25] An if she were demolished an rotten she cyaan grow - but after she grew she send forth many buds. [26] An by JAH Accord fruit are given fe those buds that grew - an Him clothe it stoutness ina straw. [27] Sight up like unto the measure that the seed kernel thou sowed abounded - yet the silver an the leaf - the ear an the straw aren't counted fe thee. [28] Don't be a dull one who don't know - an sight up thy seed that it abounded - an all likewise - think that dead persons shall raceive the arisin that them will arise - an them hardship like unto them Work. [29] Hear I - that if thou sow wheat - it won't grow bein barley - nor bein wheat if thou sow barley - an mek I tell thee again that it won't grow ~ if thou sow wheat will thou gather barley? If thou sow watercress will thou gather linseed? [30] How about from plants kind - if thou plant figs will it really grow fe thee bein nuts? How about if thou plant almonds - will it grow fe thee bein grapes? [31] If thou plant the sweet fruit will it grow fe thee bein bitter? How about if thou plant the bitter fruit - are it possible fe it fe be sweet? [32] How about all likewise - if a sinner dead are it possible fe arise bein righteous ina Resurrection time? How about if a righteous person dead - are it possible fe arise bein a sinner ina Resurrection time? Every one shall raceive him hardship like unto him Work - yet him will raceive him hardship like unto him sin an him hand Work - yet there are none who will be canvicted by him companion sin. [33] A highland tree are planted an it send forth long branches ~ it will totally dry up ~ yet unless Heaven rained rain it leaves won't be verdant. [34] An the cedar will be uprooted from it roots unless summer rain alit pon it. [35] An all likewise - dead persons won't arise unless welfare dew alit fe them bein commanded from JAH. Chapter 9 [1] Unless highland mountains an Gielabuhie regions rained a pardon rain fe them bein commanded from JAH - them won't grow grass fe beasts an animals. [2] An 'Elam mountains an Gele`ad mountains won't give verdant leaves fe sheeps an goats - nor fe oribi an animals ina wilderness - nor fe ibexes an hartebeest. [3] An likewise - pardon an dew bein commanded from JAH didn't alight fe doubters an criminals who made error an crime a money beforehand ~ dead persons won't arise ~ an Deemas an Qophros who worship idols an dig roots an work an instigate a thing... [4] An them who dig roots an practice sorcery an mek persons battle... [5] An them who lust havin departed from LAW - an Miedon an 'Atiena persons who believe ina them idols - an them who play an sing fe them while them beat violins an drums an strummed harps - them won't arise unless pardon dew alit fe them bein commanded from JAH. [6] These are them who will be canvicted pon the day when dead persons arise an when Definite Judgemant are done - yet persons who save them ras selves an who lust ina them hands Work - them err by them idols. [7] Thou wasteful of heart dull one - do it seem fe thee that dead persons won't arise? [8] Pon the time a trumpet were blown by the Angels Chief Hola Meeka'iel tongue - that dead ones arise then - as thou won't remain ina grave without arisin - don't think a thing that are thus. [9] Hills an mountains shall be level an shall be a cleared path. [10] An Resurrection shall be done fe all fleshly ones. Chapter 10 [1] However if it weren't thus - it are that former persons might be buried ina them faadas grave Iginnin from 'Adam - Iginnin from Siet an 'Abiel - Siem an Noh - Yis'haq an 'Abriham - Yosief an Ya`iqob - an 'Aron an Mussie - yet fe what are it that them didn't love that them might be buried ina another place? [2] Aren't it fe them fe arise together with them cousins ina Resurrection time? How about aren't it lest them bones be counted with evil ones an pagans bones - them who worship idols? Fe what are it that them didn't love that them might be buried ina another place? [3] But thou - don't mislead thy reasonin while thou said - 'How will dead persons arise after them dead - them who were buried ina one grave bein tens of thousands an whose bodies were demolished an rotten?' [4] An pon the time thou sight up toward a grave - thou speak this ina thy reasonin dullness while thou said - 'A whole fistful of Earth won't be found ~ how will dead persons arise?' [5] Will thou say the seed thou sowed won't grow? Even

the seed thou sowed shall grow. [6] An all likewise - the souls JAH sowed shall quickly arise - as Him have Irated man ina Him Truth bringin from not livin toward livin - Him shall arouse them quickly by Him Word that save ~ Him won't delay Him arousin. [7] An as Him have again returned him from livin - toward a grave ina death - what about aren't it possible fe Him again fe return from death toward Life? [8] Savin an liftin up are possible fe JAH. Chapter 11 [1] 'Armon perished an she fortress were demolished ~ as JAH have brought the hardship pon them like unto them evil an the Work them worked by them hands - persons who worship the idols ina 'Edomyas an Zablon shall be downbased at that time ~ as JAH have approached - Who shall canvict them who worked ina them infancy an didn't quit up til them aged - becau them idols an them evil - Seedona an Theeros shall weep.. [2] Becau them worked sin an seducin fornication an worshipped idols - becaudis thing JAH shall revenge an downstroy them ~ fe them didn't live firmed up ina them Irator JAH Command - an Yihuda dawta childran shall be wretched. [3] She lived firmed up ina killin prophets an ina Irie Ites - yet as she didn't live firmed up ina the Nine Laws an the Worship - pon the time when dead ones arise - 'Iyerusaliem sin shall be revealed. [4] At that time JAH shall examine she ina Him Nature Wisdom ~ Him will revenge an downstroy she pon all she sin that she worked ina she infancy era ~ she didn't quit workin she sin Iginnin from she beauty era up til she age. [5] She entered toward a grave an became dust like unto she former faadas who lived firmed up ina them sin - an ina Resurrection time Him shall revenge an downstroy persons who demolished JAH LAW. [6] It shall be judged pon them - fe Mussie have spoken becau them sayin - 'Them LAW lodgin - them reasonins - became Sedom law lodgin.' [7] An them kindred are Gemorra kindred - an them law are what downstroy - an them Work are evil. [8] An them law are snake poison that downstroy - an viper poison that downstroy from alongside them. Chapter 12 [1] 'Iyerusaliem child - as this thy sin are like unto Gemorra an Sedom sin - 'Iyerusaliem child - this are thy tribulation that were spoken by a prophet. [2] An thy tribulation are like unto Gemorra an Sedom tribulation - an them law lodgin reasonin firmed up ina adultery an arrogance. [3] Aside from adultery an arrogance rain - pardon an humility rain didn't rain from them reasonins by money that them Law reasonin lodgin are fertile - apart from spillin man blood an robbin an forgettin them Irator JAH. [4] An them didn't know them Irator JAH - apart from them evil Work an them idols - an them are Irie ina them hands Work - an them lust pon males an pon livestock. [5] As them eye of reasonin have been blinded lest them sight up secrets - an as them ears have deafened lest them hear or do JAH Accord that Him love - them didn't know JAH ina them Work - an them reasonins are like unto Sedom law lodgin. An them kindred - Gemorra grapes kindred that bear sweet fruit. [6] An if them examine them Work - it are poison that kill - fe it have firmed up ina curse Iginnin from the day when it were worked - an fe it grounation have been ina downstruction era. [7] As them Law lodgin - them reasonins - have firmed up ina sin Work - as them bodies have firmed up ina Seythan burnin Work fe build sin - them Law lodgin - them reasonins - have no goodly Work everytime. [8] An pon the time him shame an were baptise (by one who is led) it were fe chastisemant an downstruction - an him will firm up the persons who drank an them reasonins - an him will mek them who downstroy I - disgustin persons who distanced from JAH. [9] Fe them have lived firmed up ina them Work that were evil - an him will mek them Deeyablos lodgin - an eatin what were sacrificed fe the idols have been begun ina the House of 'Isra'iel - an she proceed toward the mountains an the trees. [10] An she worship the idols that peoples ina she area worship - an she dawta childran an she male childran fe demons who don't know goodly Work separatin from evil. [11] An them spill clean blood ~ them gush an spill grapes from Sedom fe the idols foriva. [12] An she glorify an worship the Dagwon that the 'Iloflans worship - an she sacrifice fe him from she flocks an she fattened cows - that she might be Irie ina demons laziness that them taught she fe sacrifice fe them - an ina them gushin an spillin the grapes - an that she might do them accord. [13] She sacrifice fe him that she might be Irie in demons laziness that them taught she lest she know she Irator JAH Who feed she at each time an Who cherished an raised she Iginnin from she infancy up til she beauty - an again up til she age - an again up til she age day when she dead. [14] An again I-man shall revenge an canvict him ina Resurrection time - an as she didn't return toward I LAW - an as she didn't live firmed up ina I Command - she time when she live ina Gehannem shall be up til Iternity. [15] If were Irators fe true - mek she idols arise with she an downscend toward Gehannem an save she pon the time I-man vexed an downstroyed she - an pon the time I-man distanced all the priests of the idols who lust with she. [16] Like unto she made sin an insult pon the Hola Items an pon I Lodgin the Temple - I-man made she wretched by all this. [17] When them told she - 'Check - this are JAH kindred - an she are 'Isra'iel Irator JAH Lodgin - an the famous King country 'Iyerusaliem who were separate from them who were separate - she are the Most I JAH Name Lodgin' - I-man made she wretched like unto she saddened I Name that were called ina she. [18] She boast ina I that she were I slave an that I-man were she Lord ~ she wink pon I like unto a criminal - yet she aren't who fear I an do I Accord like unto I bein she Lord. [19] Them became a obstacle pon she fe mislead that them might distance she from I - yet she are ruled fe other idols who don't feed she nor clothe she. [20] She sacrifice sacrifice fe them - an she eat the sacrifice - an she spill blood fe them - an she gush an drink from the grapes fe them ~ she smoke up ishence fe them - an she mek the ishence fragrance smell fe them ~ she idols command she - an she are commanded fe them. [21] An again she sacrifice she dawta childran an she male childran fe them - an as she present praises fe them becau them Love - she are Irie ina the thing she spoke by she tongue an ina she hands Work. [22] Woe fe she pon the day when Definite Judgemant are done - an woe fe she idols whom she love an inite; an she shall downscend with them toward Gehannem beneath See'ol - where the worm don't slumber an the fiyah aren't extinguished. [23] Woe fe thee wretched 'Iyerusaliem child - fe thou have quit I Who Irated thee an have worshipped different idols. [24] An I-man shall bring the hardship pon thee like unto thy Work ~ as thou have saddened I - an as thou have ignored I Word - an as thou didn't work goodly Work - I-man shall canvict thee toward thy pretensions. [25] Fe thou have saddened I Word - an fe thou didn't live firmed up ina I LAW whereby thou swore with I - that thou might keep I LAW an that I man might live with thee ina Support an might save thee from all who fight thee - an also that thou might keep I Order that I-man commanded thee - an I-man shall ignore thee an won't quickly save thee from the tribulation. [26] Thou didn't keep all this - an I-man ignored thee ~ as I-man have created thee - an as thou didn't keep I Command nor I Word - I-man shall canvict thee ina Judgemant time - an I-man honoured thee that thou might be I kin. [27] An like unto Gemorra an Sedom were separated from I - thou were separated from I. [28] An I-man judged an downstroyed them - an like unto Sedom an Gemorra were separated from I - thou separated from I - an now like unto I man vexed an downstroyed them - I-man vexed an downstroyed thee ~ as thou are from Sedom an Gemorra kindred whom I-man downstroyed - I man downstroyed thee ~ as them whom I-man Irated have saddened I by goin toward a youtmon wife an by lustin without LAW - with animals an males like unto arrivin with dawtaz - I-man downstroyed them name invocation from this world lest them live ina them Irie Ites. [29] There are no fearin JAH ina them faces Iginnin from a infant up til a elder ~ them help him ina all them evil Work - yet Him don't vex pon each one that them might quit workin she ~ as them Work are evil - them are sated of sin an iniquity. [30] All evil Work - robbery an arrogance an greed - are prepared ina them reasonins. [31] An becaudis thing JAH ignored them an downstroyed them countries - an them are there that Him might burn them with fiyah up til them root grounation perish ~ them totally perished up til the Iternity - yet Him didn't mek even one from them remain. [32] As them have firmed up ina sin - them shall wait ina downstruction foriva up til the Day of Advent when Definite Judgemant are done - fe them have saddened I with them evil Work - an I-man won't pardon them nor forgive them. [33] An I-man ignored them ~ fe thou won't find a reason pon the time I man vexed an seized thee becau all thy Work were robbery an sin - adultery an greed an speakin lies - all error Work an the obstacle that I-man don't love - an thou 'Iyerusaliem child who were wretched - pon the day when Judgemant are done thou will be seized ina Judgemant like unto them. [34] I-man had made thee fe honour - but thou downbased thy ras self ~ I man had called thee I money - but thou became fe another. [35] I-man had betrothed thee fe honour - but thou became fe Deeyablos - an I-man shall revenge an downstroy thee like unto thy evil Work. [36] Becau thou didn't hear all I Word - an becau thou didn't keep the Command I-man commanded thee pon the time I-man loved thee - I-man shall multiply an bring firm vengeance pon thee - fe I-man am JAH Who Irated thee - an I-man shall judge pon all sinners like unto thee - an pon the day when Judgemant are done I-man shall bring the hardship pon them like unto them evil Work. [37] As thou didn't keep I Word - an as thou have ignored I Judgemant - I man shall canvict thee with them. [38] Woe fe unu - Gemorra an Sedom - who have no fearin JAH ina your reasonin. [39] All likewise - woe fe thy sista 'Iyerusaliem child pon whom it shall be judged together with thee ina Fiyah of Gehannem - fe unu will downscend together toward Gehannem that were prepared fe unu - where are no exits foriva - an woe fe all sinners who worked thy sin. [40] As unu didn't keep I Command nor I Word - thou an she who didn't keep I Command nor I Word shall downscend toward See'ol together pon the day when Judgemant are judged. [41] But kind persons who kept I Command an I Word shall eat the money that sinner persons accumulated - an like unto JAH commanded - kind persons shall share the loot that evil persons captured - an kind persons shall be totally Irie. [42] But wrongdoers an sinner persons shall weep - an them shall be sad becau all them sin that them wronged havin departed from I Command. [43] Him who keep I Word an live firmed up ina I Command - him are who find I blessin an are honoured alongside I. [44] All person who keep I Word an live firmed up ina I Command shall eat the fatness found from Earth - an shall live havin entered toward the Garden where enter kind kings who have straight reasonins. Chapter 13 [1] As them shall be wretched an perish by I wrath pon the time I-man seized them - woe fe Theeros an Seedona an all Yihuda country regions who mek them ras selves arrogant today. [2] Conquerin JAH said thus ~ Him have said - Deeyablos child who are totally arrogant shall be birthed

from them - the False Messeeh who fe a Truth thing are she enemy - who firm up him collar of reasonin - who boast an don't know him Irator - an Him said - Woe fe them - an JAH Who rule all said - I-man made him fe I anger pattern that I-man might be revealed ina him Power. [3] An this Qifirnahom Semarya an Geleela an Demasqo an Sorya an 'Akeya an Qophros an all Yordanos region are kindreds who firmed up them collars of reasonin - who live firmed up ina them sin - an whom death shadow an darkness covered - fe Deeyablos have covered them reasonins ina sin - an fe them are commanded fe that arrogant Deeyablos - an them didn't return toward fearin JAH. [4] At that time woe fe persons who are commanded fe demons an who sacrifice sacrifice ina them name fe them ~ as them have denied JAH Who Irated them - them resemble animals without minds - fe the False Messeeh who forgot JAH LAW an are Deeyablos child shall set up him image ina all the places (fe him have said 'Mi are a god') - an him shall be Irie ina him reasonin accord - ina him hand Work an ina robbery an all the sins an perfidy an iniquity - ina robbery an all the adulteries that a person work. [5] Fe becau it were counted alongside JAH that him work this - the era are known that them work sin. [6] Sun shall darken an moon shall be blood - an stars shall be shaken from Heaven - all the Work shall pass by the miracles that JAH shall bring ina Fulfillmant Era that Him might mek Earth pass - an that Him might mek all pass who live ina sin of persons who live within she. [7] As JAH have been proud pon the Iration Him Irated - an as Him have quickly made all Him loved ina one iwa - the Lord death shall downstroy a small enemy Deeyablos. [8] Fe JAH Who rule all have said - I-man shall judge an downstroy - but after Advent - Deeyablos have no authority. [9] An pon the day when him were seized by I anger - him shall downscend toward Gehannem - fe which him mek application an where firm tribulation are ~ as him will tek all who are with him toward chastisemant an downstruction an perfidy - becau I-man were Who send forth from Gehannem an Who introduce toward Gehannem - him will downscend toward Gehannem. [10] As Him give firmness an Power fe weak persons - an again as Him give weakness fe powerful an firm persons - mek a powerful one not boast ina him Power. [11] As Him are a Ruler - an as Him judge an save the wronged persons from the persons hands who wrong them - Him will return the grudge of the widows an the child whose faada an mother dead pon him. [12] Woe fe thee who boast an firm up thy collar of reasonin - fe whom it seem that I-man won't rule thee nor judge an downstroy thee - fe ina him boastin an him arrogance him have said - 'Mi will streach mi throne ina stars an Heaven - an mi will be like unto JAH Who are lofty.' [13] An like unto Him spoke sayin - How Deeyablos fell from Heaven - him who shine like unto a mornin star that were Irated precedin all - woe fe thee. [14] An thou dared an spoke this ina thy arrogance - an thou didn't think of JAH Who totally Irated thee by Him Itority ~ why did thou boast thy ras self that thou downscend toward Gehannem ina thy reasonin firmness? [15] Thou were downbased separate from all Angels like unto thee - fe them praise them Irator with a humbled reasonin becau them knew that Him were Who Irated them from fiyah an wind - an fe them don't depart from Him Command - an fe them keep them reasonins from perfidy lest them totally depart from Him Command. [16] But thou did a firm perfidy ina thy reasonin arrogance ~ thou became a wretched man separate from thy companions - fe thou have cherished all the sin an iniquity - robbery an perfidy whereby persons who forgot JAH LAW an sinners like unto thee live firmed up - them who are from thy kindred an commit crime like unto thee - an who live firmed up by thy command an thy accord whereby thou teach sin. [17] Woe fe thee - fe the demons thou misled ina thy malice an thou will downscend toward Gehannem together. [18] O unu JAH childran who erred by that misleadin criminal Deeyablos - woe fe unu ~ as unu have erred like unto him by the money that him taught unu an that him hosts taught unu - unu will downscend toward Gehannem together - where are no exits foriva. [19] An formerly when JAH slave Mussie were there - unu saddened JAH by the Water where argumant were made an pon Korieb - an by 'Amalieq an pon Mount Seena. [20] An moreover pon the time unu sent scouts toward Kene`an - pon the time them told unu this sayin 'The path are far - an them ramparts an them fortresses that reach up til Heaven are firm - an warriors live there' - unu vexed that unu might return towad Gibts country where unu work worrisome Work - an unu saddened JAH Word. [21] Unu didn't think of JAH Who firmed unu up from the tribulation - an Who did great miracles ina Gibts - an Who led unu by Him Angel Itority. Him would veil unu ina cloud by day lest the Sun burn unu an Him would shine a column of fiyah fe unu by night lest your feet stumble ina darkness. [22] An pon the time the army an Fer`on frightened unu - unu totally cried toward Mussie - an Mussie totally cried toward JAH - an Him lodged ina Him Angel an kept unu lest unu meet with Fer`on. [23] But Him introduced them toward 'Eritra ina tribulation ~ JAH led only 'Isra'iel - fe Him have said - An there were no different idol with them - but Him buried them enemies ina sea at one time - an Him didn't preserve none who flee from them. [24] An Him made 'Isra'iel cross amidst the sea by foot ~ there are no tribulation that found them arisin from the Gibtsans ~ Him delivered them toward Mount Seena - an there Him fed them menna forty eras. [25] As 'Isra'iel childran sadden JAH everytime - Him did all this goodly thing fe them an them neglected fe worship JAH. [26] Them placed evil ina them reasonins Iginnin from them childhood up til them age - fe JAH Mouth have spoken thus ina 'Oreet where the faadas birth were written ~ as Him have spoken sayin - 'Adam childran reasonin are ash - an all them Work are toward robbery an them run toward evil ~ there are none from them who love straight Work - apart from gatherin a person money ina violence an swearin ina lie an wrongin companions an robbin an stealin - them placed evil ina them reasonins. [27] An all go toward evil Work ina the era when them live ina Life ~ 'Isra'iel childran who demolished JAH LAW totally saddened JAH Iginnin from Antiquity up til fufillmant era. Chapter 14 [1] An pon the time JAH downstroyed Qayen childran - kindreds who preceded - ina downstruction Water becau them sin - Him baptised Earth ina Water of Downstruction - an Him cleansed she from all Qayel childran sin. [2] As Him have said - I-man were sad becau I-man Irated man - Him downstroyed all wrongdoers ~ Him didn't preserve apart from eight persons ~ Him downstroyed all ~ after this Him multiplied them an them filled Earth ~ them shared them faada 'Adam inheritance. [3] But Noh swore with JAH a oath ~ them swore a oath with JAH lest JAH again downstroy Earth ina Downstruction Water - an lest Noh childran eat what deceased nor what lodged dead - lest them worship different idols apart from JAH Who Irated them - an that Him might be a Love Faada fe them - an lest Him downstroy them at one time ina them vain sin - an lest Him prevent them the first an the spring rain - an that Him might give fe livestock an persons them food at each time - an that Him might give them the grass an the grain fruit an plants - an that them might work goodly Work ina all that JAH love. [4] An after Him gave them this Order - 'Isra'iel childran saddened JAH by them sin ~ them didn't live firmed up ina Him LAW like unto them faadas Yis'haq an 'Abriham an Ya`iqob who didn't demolish them Irator JAH LAW. [5] An Iginnin from the small up til the great - those 'Isra'iel childran who didn't keep JAH LAW are crooked ina them Work. [6] An whether them be them priests or them chiefs or them scribes - everyone demolish JAH LAW. [7] Them don't live firmed up ina JAH Order an Him LAW that Mussie commanded them ina Repeatin Law sayin - 'Love thy Irator JAH ina thy complete body an thy complete reasonin.' [8] Them don't firm up ina JAH Order an Him LAW that Mussie commanded them ina book where LAW were written sayin - 'Love thy companion like unto thy body - an don't worship him idols that were different - an don't go toward a youtmon wife ~ don't kill a soul ~ don't steal. [9] An don't witness ina lie - an be it him donkey or be it him ox - don't love thy companion money nor all that thy bredda bought.' [10] However after him commanded them all this - 'Isra'iel childran who were evil return toward treachery an sin - robbery an iniquity - toward a youtmon wife an toward lies an stealin an worshippin idols. [11] 'Isra'iel childran saddened JAH pon Korieb by workin a cow that graze toward grass ~ them bowed sayin - 'Check - these are wi irators who sent wi forth from Gibts.' [12] An them were Irie ina them hand Work ~ if them ate an drank an satta - them arose fe sing. [13] As JAH have told him sayin - Thy kindreds whom thou sent forth from Gibts country where rulership are - them have proceeded from LAW an wronged - an them worked a cow image an bowed fe the idol - becaudis thing Mussie vexed an alit from Seena mountain. [14] While Mussie vexed pon him kindreds - him alit with him canfidante 'Iyasu - an pon the time 'Iyasu heard - him said - 'Check - I-man hear warriors voice ina 'Isra'iel camp.' [15] An Mussie told 'Iyasu - 'It are when 'Isra'iel play havin drunk the unboiled wine - yet as fe a warrior voice - it aren't' - an him alit an broke them image an totally crushed it up til it were like unto dust ~ him mixed it within the Water that 'Isra'iel childran drink beside the mountain. [16] An after this him commanded the priests that them might slay one another becau the sin them worked before JAH. [17] Them knew that defyin JAH surpass killin them an killin them faadas - an them did like unto him commanded them. [18] An Mussie told them - 'Becau unu saddened JAH Who fed unu an cherished unu an Who sent unu forth from a rulership house an Who bequeathed fe unu the inheritance that Him swore fe your faadas that Him might give fe them an fe them childran after them - becaudis thing unu made JAH Irie.' [19] Fe them go toward sin an a evil thing - an them didn't quit saddenin JAH there. [20] Them aren't like unto them faadas Yis'haq an 'Abriham an Ya`iqob who made JAH Irie with them goodly Work that Him might give them what are pon Earth an what Him prepared fe persons who love Him ina Heaven Iginnin from them infancy up til them youthood an up til them age ~ them aren't like unto 'Abriham an Yis'haq an Ya`iqob who made Him Irie with them Work that Him might give them a Earth of inheritance where Irie Ites are found ina this world - an a garden that mek Irie - prepared fe kind persons ina hereafter world - what Him prepared fe 'Abriham an Yis'haq an Ya`iqob who made JAH Irie when them were ina Life an who love Him - Whom a eye didn't sight up nor a ear hear an Who aren't thought of ina reasonin. [21] An them childran who denied JAH an were evil an who live firmed up ina them reasonin accord - them didn't hear JAH Command - Him Who fed them an cherished them an kept them Iginnin from them infancy. [22] Them didn't think of JAH - Who sent them forth from Gibts land an saved them from brick Work an a firm rulership. [23] But them totally saddened Him - an Him would arouse peoples ina them area pon them - an them would arise pon them ina enmity an also tax them like unto them

loved. Chapter 15 [1] An at that time Midyam persons arose pon them ina enmity - an them aroused them armies pon 'Isra'iel that them might fight them - an them king name are called 'Akrandis ~ him quickly gathered many armies ina Keeliqyas an Sorya an Demasqo. [2] An campin beyond Yordanos him sent messengers sayin - 'An that mi might capture your money - pay tax toward 'Isra'iel fe mi' ~ him told them - 'But if unu don't pay tax - mi came that mi might punish unu an might capture your livestocks an tek your mares an capture your childran.' [3] 'Mi will capture unu tek unu toward the country unu don't know - an there mi will mek unu Water pourers an wood pickers' him told them. [4] 'Don't boast while unu said - "InI are JAH kindreds an there are nothing able fe InI" - aren't JAH Who sent mi that mi might downstroy unu an plunder your money? an aren't mi whom JAH sent that mi might gather all your kindreds? [5] Are there really a savin that them different idols saved the other kins that mi downstroyed? Mi captured them mares an them horses an mi killed them an captured them childran. [6] An unless unu introduced the tax that mi commanded unu - mi will downstroy unu like unto them' him said - an him crossed Yordanos that him might plunder them livestocks an them money an capture them wives. [7] An after this 'Isra'iel childran wept a firm mournin toward JAH - an them totally cried - however them lacked one who help them. [8] An becaudis thing JAH gave firmness fe the three bredren - an them names are like unto this: - an them are Yihuda an Mebikyas an Meqabees - whose features were handsome an who were warriors ina them Power. [9] An 'Isra'iel childran totally wept there ~ pon the time them heard - it saddened them ina them heart arisin from all 'Isra'iel childran shout ~ the child whose mother an faada dead pon him - an widows - an them officials an them priests - all 'Isra'iel kindred - both dawtaz an males - an all childran - would weep sprinklin ash pon them heads - an them nobles had worn sackcloth. [10] But those bredren - who were attractive an comely - went an agreed that them might save them ~ them counseled sayin - 'Mek InI go an give InI bodies fe death becau these persons.' [11] Tellin one another - 'Tek heart - tek heart' - them went girdin them swords pon them waists an seizin them spears ina them hands - an them went prepared that them might incriminate the warrior. [12] An them arrived toward them camp ~ Mebikyus attacked the warrior (the king) when him had sat at a dinnertable ~ him cut him neck ina one blow when food were ina him mouth; an Meqabyus an Yihuda struck him armies pon the king left an right by sword an killed them. [13] An pon the time them king were defeated - them entered toward them spears ina them companions hearts - an them all totally fled an them bows were broken an them were defeated. [14] But those bredren who are attractive an comely were saved from death ~ there are no evil thing that found them - but as JAH have returned chastisemant toward them - them sliced up one another an were depleted. [15] Them were defeated an dead an them crossed Yordanos - an up til them crossed them cast way all them money - an all them money remained - an pom the time 'Isra'iel childran sight up that them enemies fled - them went toward them camp an took both what them plundered an them money fe them ras selves. [16] JAH saved 'Isra'iel doin thus by the bredren an Mebikyu hand. [17] 'Isra'iel sat a few days while them made JAH Irie. [18] But after that them again returned toward them sin ~ 'Isra'iel childran neglected worshippin JAH by what are due. [19] An Him shall again sadden them by kins who don't know them an who will gather them field crops an downstroy them grape places an plunder them flocks an slaughter an feed them them livestocks before them... [20] an who will capture them wives an them dawta childran an them male childran ~ becau it were that them sadden JAH everytime; as themare kindreds who demolished the LAW - them will hammer them childran before them pon each of them heads ~ them won't save them. Chapter 16 [1] Them who do this are Theeros an Seedona an them who live beyond Yordanos river an pon the sea edge - Keran an Gele`ad - 'Iyabuseewon an Kenaniewon - 'Edom an Giegiesiewon an 'Amalieq persons. [2] All peoples do thus - who live firmed up ina each of them tribes an countries an regions an ina each of them Works an country languages - an all live firmed up like unto JAH worked them. [3] An there are persons from them who know JAH - an whose Work were beautiful. [4] An there are persons from them whose Work were evil an who don't know JAH Who Irated them - an like unto them worked sin - Him ruled them ina Sorya king Silminasor hand. [5] As him plunder an tek Demasqo money - an as him share Semarya loot that are before Gibts king - Him ruled them ina Silminasor hand. [6] Gielabuhie region an also persons ina Fars an Miedon - Qephedoqya an Sewseegya - who live ina the West mountains - ina Gele`ad fortress an Phasthos that are part of Yihuda land... [7] an these are who live in them region - an them are kindreds who don't know JAH nor keep Him Command - an whose collar of reasonin were firm. [8] An Him shall pay them them hardship like unto them Work evil an them hands Work. [9] Fe Gele`ad kindreds an Qeesarya region an 'Amalieq have become one there - that them might downstroy JAH country that were filled of a Truth thing - an within which 'Isra'iel Irator are praised - Him Who are Most Glorified an Conquerin - an Whom Angels who are many many ina Keerubiel chariots - them who stand before Him - serve fearin an tremblin - an Him shall pay them them hardship like unto them Work evil an them hands Work. Chapter 17 [1] 'Amalieq an 'Edomyas persons don't worship JAH by Whose Itority Earth an Heaven rulership were seized ~ as them are criminals who don't live firmed up ina Truth Work - them don't fear fe demolish Him Lodgin - the Temple. [2] An there are no fearin JAH before them - apart from sheddin blood an adultery an eatin what were beaten an sacrificed fe a idol an all that resemble what lodged dead - an these are scorned sinners. [3] Them have no virtue nor religion ~ as them are who hated goodly Work - an as them don't know JAH - an as them don't know Love Work - apart from robbin a person money an from sin - an apart from downsturbin a person an all hated Work - apart from games an song like unto them faada Deeyablos taught them - them have no virtue nor religion. [4] As him have ruled them with him host - demons - him teach them all evil Work that were fe each of them ras selves - all robbery an sin - theft an falsehood - robbin money an eatin what were beaten an what lodged dead - an adultery Work. [5] An him teach them all that resemble this - an goin toward a youtman wife - an sheddin blood - eatin what were sacrificed fe idol an what lodged dead - an killin a person soul ina violence - an envy an winkin an greed an all evil Work that JAH don't love ~ Deeyablos who were them enemy teach them this teachin that him might distance them from JAH LAW Who rule all the world. [6] But JAH Work are innocence an humility - not annoyin a bredren an lovin a companion - harmonisin an lovin with all persons. [7] Don't be hypocrites fe favour fe a person face - an don't be wrongdoers nor totally robbers nor persons who go toward a youtman wife - nor persons who work iniquity an evil Work pon them companion - nor who cajole that them might wrong them companion ina violence. [8] Them wink an shake them heads an provoke fe evil ~ them discourage fe mislead that them might lower them toward Iternity Definite Judgemant. Chapter 18 [1] Think that thou will go ina death toward JAH ina Whose Hand all are - an thou will stand before Him that Him might canvict thee before Him pon all the sin thou Worked. [2] As them who are arrogant an evil - an powerful ones children who aren't strengthenin more than them - were likewise formerly - becau them sight up them stature an them Power an them firm authority - them didn't mek JAH before them - an them didn't know that Him were them Irator Who Irated them bringin from not livin toward livin. [3] An when them faadas bein like unto "Angels" praised pon Mount Hola with Angels - pon the time them accord misled them - them alit toward this world where Definite Judgemant shall be done foriva. [4] As JAH ina the Antiquity have Irated human flesh fe them - that it might mislead them becau them reasonin arrogance an might test them as it were them kept Him LAW an Him Command - them married wives from Qayel children. [5] But them didn't keep Him LAW ~ Him lowered them toward Gehannem fiyah with them faada Deeyablos; fe JAH have vexed pon the offspring of Siet who wronged like unto persons - an persons era diminished becau them sin. [6] An them took 'Adam children toward sin with them ~ Him lowered them toward See'ol where them shall raceive a verdict. [7] As persons era have been divided becau Siet children erred by Qayel children - when a person eras were nine hundred ina the Antiquity - them returned toward livin a hundred twenty eras. [8] An as them are flesh an blood - JAH said - I Spirit of Support won't live firmed up pon them. [9] An becaudis thing InI era were divided - fe becau InI sin an InI iniquity - InI era have been divided from InI faadas who preceded - an when them are ina them infancy again - them are dyin. [10] But InI faadas era had abounded - becau them kept Him LAW an becau them didn't sadden JAH. [11] But InI faadas era had abounded - becau them vexed pon them dawta children that them might teach them - an becau them vexed pon them male children lest them demolish JAH LAW. [12] Becau them didn't demolish JAH LAW with them dawta children an them male children - becaudis thing them era had abounded fe true. Chapter 19 [1] Pon the time Qayen children abounded them worked drums an harps - santee an violins - an them made songs an all the games. [2] Children who are attractive an comely were birthed fe Qayen from the wife of the kind man 'Abiel - whom him killed becau she - fe she were attractive - an after him killed him bredda him took that an she who were him money. [3] An separatin from him faada - him seized them an went toward Qiefaz region that are toward the West - an that attractive one children were attractive like unto them mother. [4] An becaudis thing Siet children downscended toward Qayen children - an after them sight them up them didn't wait one iwa - an them made the dawtaz whom them chose wives fe them ras selves. [5] As them have taken InI toward error together with them becau them error - becaudis thing JAH vexed pon InI an vexed pon them. [6] An Deeyablos havin cajoled sayin - 'Unu will become irators like unto your Irator JAH' - him took InI mother Hiewan an InI faada 'Adam toward him error. [7] But it seemin Truth fe them ina them dullness - them demolished JAH LAW - Him Who Irated them bringin from not-livin toward livin that them might bow an praise Him glorified Name. [8] But Him - them Irator - downbased those 'Adam an Hiewan who made godhood fe them ras selves - an Him downbased him who are arrogant. [9] Like unto Daweet spoke sayin - ' 'Adam perish by the sinner Deeyablos arrogance' - him abused them - fe InI faada 'Adam have been canvicted pon Deeyablos arrogance by Him true Judgemant. [10] An Siet children who erred by Qayel children took InI toward them sin thus ~ becaudis thing InI era that JAH gave InI were less than InI faadas eras. [11] But them had worked goodly Work - fe them had firmed up them reasonins ina JAH - fe them

had taught them dawta children an them male children lest them depart from JAH LAW that them taught them - an there were no evil enemy who approach them. [12] But if them worked goodly Work - there are nothing that benefit them if them didn't tell nor teach fe them children. [13] Like unto Daweet spoke sayin - 'Them didn't hide from them children fe another child - an teach JAH praise - the wondrous miracles Him did - an Him Power' - there are nothing that benefit them if them didn't teach fe them children that them might teach fe them children fe mek heart like unto them knew - an that them might know an do Him Accord - an that them might tell them JAH LAW Trust - an that them might keep Him LAW like unto them faadas who made JAH Irie with them beautiful Work. [14] An them who told them Trust from them faadas ina them infancy didn't demolish Him Command - like unto them faadas learned JAH Worship an the Nine Laws from them faadas. [15] Them children learned from them faadas that them might work goodly Work an might present praise fe them Irator - fe them have kept Him LAW - an fe them have loved Him. [16] An Him shall hear them ina them priah - an Him won't ignore them plea - but Him are a Forgiver. [17] Havin multiplied Him wrath - Him shall return it fe them - an Him wouldn't downstroy all ina Him chastisemant. Chapter 20 [1] InI bredren - think - don't forget what them told unu formerly - that JAH keep the true Work of persons who work goodly Work. [2] An Him multiply them children ina this world - an them name invocation shall live firmed up fe a goodly thing up til the Iternity - an them children won't be troubled fe grain ina this world. [3] As Him shall dispute fe them becau them - an as Him won't cast them ina them enemy hand - Him shall save them from them enemies hand who hate them. [4] An fe persons who love Him Name - Him shall be them Helper ina them tribulation time ~ Him shall guard them an pardon them all them sin. Chapter 21 [1] Daweet believed ina JAH - fe Him have believed ina him - an Him saved him bein a Refuge from the king Sa'ol hand. [2] An as him have believed ina Him an kept Him LAW pon the time when him child 'Abiesielom arose - an pon the time when the 'Iloflans arose - an pon the time when the 'Edomyans an the 'Amalieqans arose - pon the time when the one from the four Rafayn arose - JAH saved Daweet from all this tribulation that enemies who disputed him brought pon him. [3] As prevailin are by JAH Accord - them were defeated by them enemies hand - yet but JAH didn't save the evil kings who didn't believe ina Him. [4] An Hiziqyas believed ina JAH ~ Him saved him from Senakriem hand who were arrogant. [5] But him child Minassie were defeated by him enemy hand - fe him didn't mek him trustin ina JAH ~ as him didn't mek him trustin ina JAH an as him didn't fear JAH Who totally honoured an famed him - them bound an took him toward them country - yet but those enemies who defeated Minassie weren't like unto him. [6] At that time Him denied him the kingdom Him gave him - fe him didn't work goodly Work before him Irator JAH - that him era might abound an that Him might dispute him enemy fe him an that him might have Power an firmness behind an in front. [7] Fe it are better fe believe ina JAH than ina many armies - than believin ina horses an bows an shields. [8] Believin ina JAH surpass ~ a person who believed ina Him shall firm up an be honoured an totally lofty. [9] Fe JAH don't favour fe a face - but persons who didn't believe ina JAH - who believed ina them money abundance - became them who departed from the grace an honour that Him gave them. [10] Him shall guard the persons who believe ina Him - but Him shall mek the persons ignorant who call Him ignorant - an as them didn't discipline them reasonins fe follow JAH nor keep Him LAW - Him won't quickly help them ina them tribulation time nor ina the time them enemies disputed with them. [11] But fe a person who were disciplined ina worshippin JAH an fe keep Him LAW - Him shall be a Refuge ina him tribulation time. [12] By downstroyin him enemy - an by plunderin him enemy livestock - an by capturin him enemy country persons - an by rainin eras rain - an by growin sprouts - an by introducin the grain pile - ina the plant fruit... [13] An by rainin the first an the spring rains - an by makin the grass verdant - an by givin the rain that rain at each time that thy kindreds beneath thy Itority might be Irie - Him shall mek him Irie. [14] Him shall mek him Irie - that them might eat the other one money - that them might satta havin eaten the money them plundered from them enemy - that them might plunder animals an sheeps an cows - an that them might eat the other one dinnertable - an that them might tek them enemies children captive. [15] JAH shall do all this fe the person whom Him love - but Him will mek the person who hate Him fe him enemy ransackery. [16] An Him shall bind him feet an him hands an shall cast him ina him enemy hand - an Him shall mek him fe him enemies derision - an as him have become a blood shedder who demolished JAH LAW - Him won't mek him Irie ina him house seed. [17] An him won't firm up ina Judgemant time - an that Him might bring the hardship fe persons who work sin - Him will also give persons who work evil Work them sin hardship. [18] But it were commanded from alongside JAH fe give persons who work goodly Work them reward - that Him might keep them ina Him Itority. [19] Fe Him are empowered pon all the Iration Him Irated that Him might do goodly Work an might give them Iternal welfare an that them might praise JAH Who Irated them - an Him commanded that him might keep Him LAW ~ apart from only man there are none from all the Irations Him Irated that departed from Him Command. [20]

Like unto JAH commanded all who live firmed up ina each of them Works - them all know an are kept ina Him LAW. [21] But man are emboldened pon JAH Who crowned all pon each of them inventions - pon animal an beasts an pon Heaven birds. [22] Be it what are ina sea or all pon land - JAH gave all the Iration Him Irated fe them faada 'Adam ~ JAH gave them that him might do what him loved - an that them might eat them like unto grain that grew pon Earth - an that them might rule an tax them - an that be them beasts or animals them might be commanded fe man - an Him Ipointed them pon all Him Irated that persons who reigned might be commanded fe JAH Who gave them honour an that them might favour Him. [23] But if them depart from Him LAW Him will separate them from the lordship Him gave them ~ as Him are Who rule Earth an Heaven - Him will give it fe him who do Him Accord. [24] Him Ipoint whom Him loved fe Ipoint - but Him dismiss whom Him loved fc dismiss ~ Him kill ~ Him save ~ Him whip ina tribulation ~ Him forgive. [25] There are no other Irator like unto Him ~ as Him are Ruler fe all the Iration Him Irated - as there are no other without Him - the Irator - ina Heaven above Earth nor pon Earth beneath Heaven - there are none who shall criticise Him. [26] Him Ipoint ~ Him dismiss ~ Him kill ~ Him save ~ Him whip ina tribulation ~ Him forgive ~ Him impoverish ~ Him honour. [27] Him hear persons who beg Him ina them plea ~ Him accept a person plea who do Him Accord with a clean reasonin; an Him hear them ina them priah - an Him do them accord fe them ina all that them begged Him. [28] An Him mek the great an the small fe be commanded fe them ~ all this are them money pon hills an mountains an at trees roots an ina caves an Earth wells an all them kindreds pon both dry an sea. [29] An fe persons who do them Irator Accord all this are them money - an Him won't trouble them from them plenty - an Him shall give them them praise reward. [30] An Him shall give them the honour Him prepared ina Heaven fe them faadas Yis'haq an 'Abriham an Ya`iqob ~ Him shall give them what Him prepared fe Hiziqyas an Daweet an Samu-'iel who didn't depart from Him LAW an Him Command. [31] That them might be Irie ina Him Lordship - Him shall give them who served Him Iginnin from Antiquity the honour Him prepared fe them faadas Yis'haq an 'Abriham an Ya`iqob - fe whom Him swore fe give them a inheritance. Chapter 22 [1] Please - think of persons name who work goodly Work - an don't forget them Work. [2] Straighten up that thy name be called like unto them name - that thou might be Irie with them ina the Kingdom of Heaven - that were Light Lodgin that Him prepared fe nobles an kings who did JAH Accord an were kind persons. [3] An again - know an be canvinced of evil nobles an kings names - that Him shall canvict them an revile them alongside man after them dead. [4] Fe them didn't line up them Work while them sight up an heard - an know an be canvinced that unless them did JAH Accord - Him shall judge pon them ina the King-dom of Heaven more than criminals an persons who forgot JAH LAW. [5] Be kindly - innocent - honest - yet don't thou also go pon persons path who forgot JAH LAW - pon whom JAH vexed becau them evil Work. [6] Judge Truth an save the child whose mother an faada dead pon him - an the widow from sinner persons hand who rob them. [7] Be a guardian like unto him faada fe the child whose mother an faada dead pon him - that thou might save him from the wealthy one hand who rob him - an stand fe him - an be alarmed pon the time the child - whose mother an faada dead pon him - tears flowed before thee-I - lest thou be alarmed ina fiyah sea where sinner persons who didn't enter repentance are punished. [8] An straighten up thy feet toward Love an Inity path ~ as JAH Eyes check up Him friends - an as Him Ears hear them plea - seek Love an follow she. [9] But JAH Face of Him Wrath are toward persons who work evil Work - that Him might downstroy them name invocation from this world - an Him won't preserve a person who near pon ramparts nor mountains. [10] As I-man am JAH Who am jealous pon I Godhood - as I-man am a Irator who revenge an downstroy persons who hate I an don't keep I Word - I-man won't return I Face of Support reachin up til I-man down-stroy the person who don't keep I Word. [11] An I-man shall honour persons who honour I an keep I Word. Chapter 23 [1] Don't live firmed up ina Qayel order - who killed him bredda who followed him ina inno-cence - it seemin fe him that him bredda love him. [2] An him killed him bredda envyin pon a dawta ~ persons who mek envy an iniquity an be-trayal pon them companion are like unto him. [3] But as 'Abiel are inno-cent like unto a sheep - an as him blood are like unto the clean sheep blood that them sacrificed fe JAH by a clean reasonin - them went pon Qayel path that aren't pon 'Abiel path. [4] Fe becau all the persons who live ina innocence were persons whom JAH love - like unto a kind man 'Abiel - them have been innocent ones like unto 'Abiel - but those persons who live firmed up ina 'Abiel Work love JAH. [5] But JAH neglect evil ones - an them Definite Judgemant mek application fe them pon them bodies - an it are written pon the record of them reasonins - an pon the time when Judgemant are judged - them shall read she before man an Angels an before all the Iration. [6] At that time them shall shame ~ wrongdoers an refusers who didn't do JAH Accord shall shame. [7] An a alarmin Word shall be given them that say - Place them ina Gehannem where are no exit up til Iternity. Chapter 24 [1] But pon the time Giedie-won trusted JAH - him defeated uncircumcise peoples armies who were many many ina army of a few tens of thousands an without number like

unto locusts. [2] As there are no Irator without I - o nobles an kings - don't believe ina the different idols. [3] As I-man am your Irator JAH Who sent unu forth from your mothers wombs an raised unu an fed unu an clothed unu - why do unu pretext? How about why do unu worship other idols without I? [4] I-man did all this fe unu ~ what did unu give I? It are that unu might live firmed up ina I LAW an I Order an I Command an that I-man might give unu your bodies welfare - yet what will I-man want from unu? [5] JAH Who rule all said thus ~ Him said - Save your ras selves from worshippin idols an practisin sorcery an discouragin pessimism. [6] As JAH chastisemant shall come pon these who do this - an pon them who hear them an do them accord an are them friends an who live firmed up ina them command - save your ras selves from wor-shippin idols. [7] As peoples - who don't know unu an aren't nice fe unu - shall arise pon unu - unless unu who feared did JAH Accord - them will eat the money wherefor unu wearied ~ like unto Him servants the proph-ets spoke an like unto Hienok spoke an like unto 'Asaf spoke - unless unu did JAH Accord - them will eat the money wherefor unu wearied. [8] Evil persons will come havin changed them clothes Him said ~ there are no other law alongside them apart from eatin an drinkin an adornin ina silver an gold - an livin havin firmed up ina sin all the Work JAH don't love. [9] But them are prepared fe go toward drink an food ~ after them were aroused from them slumber Iginnin from mornin up til evenin them go toward evil Work; there are misery an tribulation ina them path - yet them feet have no Love path. [10] An them don't know Love an Inity Work - an there are no fearin JAH ina them faces ~ them are crooked evil ones without religion nor virtue ~ them are greedy ones who eat an drink alone ~ them are drunkards - an them sin are without LAW an without measure ~ them are who go toward seducin - sheddin blood - theft an perfidy an violently robbin him money who don't have it. [11] An them are who criticise without Love an without LAW - fe them don't fear JAH Who Irated them - an there are no fear ina them faces. [12] Them don't shame ina the person face that them sight up - an them don't shame a grey-hair nor a elder face ~ pon the time them heard when them said - 'An there are money ina this world' - them mek it them ras self money before them sight it up with them eyes - fe there are no fearin JAH ina them faces - an pon the time them sight it up with them eyes it seem fe them that them ate it. [13] An them nobles eat trust money ~ them are who eat ~ as them are negativists an as there are no straight thing ina them tongues - them don't repeat ina evenin what them spoke ina mornin. [14] Fe them ignore sufferahs an poor ones cries - an them kings hasten fe evil - them who downsturb a person - him havin saved refugees from wealthy ones hands who rob them. [15] Mek them save him who were wronged an the refugee - yet mek the kings not be them who begrudge justice becaudis thing. [16] But them are who exact tribute ~ them are who rob a person money - an them are criminals - an as them Work are evil - them aren't nice when them eat the newborn calf with she mother an a bird with she egg ~ them mek all them sight up an heard them ras self money. [17] Them love that them might gather fe them ras selves - yet them aren't nice fe sick an poor ones - an them violently rob the mon-ey of a person who don't have it - an them gather all them found that them might be fattened an be Irie ina it. [18] Fe them shall perish quickly like unto a scarab that proceeded from it pit an whose track aren't found an that don't return toward it house - an becau them didn't work goodly Work when them are ina them Life - woe fe them bodies pon the time JAH vexed an seized them. [19] Pon the time JAH neglected them - them will perish at one time like unto them are ina one chastisemant - fe Him indure them meanin as it were them returned toward repentance - yet Him don't quickly downstroy them - an them shall perish pon the time when them shall perish. [20] But if them don't return toward repentance - Him will quickly downstroy them like unto former persons who were precedin them - who didn't keep JAH LAW by what are due. [21] Them are who eat a person flesh an drink a person blood ~ as them gird an work vio-lence fe go toward sin - there are no fearin JAH ina them faces everytime - an after them arose from them beddin them don't rest fe work sin. [22] An them Work are drink an food - goin toward downstruction an sin - that them might downstroy many persons bodies ina this world. Chapter 25 [1] As them Work are crooked - an as all are who live firmed up ina Seythan Work that mislead - JAH Who rule all said - Woe fe your body pon the time I-man vexed an seized she. [2] But fe them don't know JAH Work - fe them have returned it toward them rear - an fe them have ne-glected I LAW. [3] An later ina fulfillmant era I-man shall bring the hardship pon them like unto them evil measure ~ like unto them sin were written alongside I - I- man shall revenge an downstroy them pon the day when Judgemant are judged. [4] As I-man JAH am full from horizon up til horizon - an as all the Iration have been seized ina I Itority - there are none who escape from I Itority ina Heaven nor Earth nor depth nor sea. [5] I-man command a snake that are beneath Earth - an I-man command a fish that are within sea - an I-man command birds ina Heaven - an I-man command the desert donkey ina wilderness - fe it are I money Iginnin from horizon up til horizon. [6] As I-man am Who work wondrous Work an do miracles before I - there are none who escape from I Itority pon Earth nor ina Heaven ~ there are none who tell I - 'Where do Thou go? How about what do thou Work?' [7] An I-man command pon Angels chiefs an hosts ~ all Irations whose name are called are I money - an beasts ina wilderness an all birds ina Heaven an livestocks are I moneys. [8] It arise from 'Azieb wind an firm up ina drought ina Mesi` ~ later ina fulfillment era 'Eritra sea shall perish bein heard - arisin from JAH - Who shall come toward she - bein feared an famousness. [9] Fe Him rule them who dead an persons who are there - an she shall perish bein heard with Saba an Noba an Hindekie an 'Ityopphya limits an all them regions. [10] An Him watch all ina lofty Itority an innocence - fe Him Itority surpass all the itority - an Him keep cangregations ina Him Itority. [11] An fe Him Itority firm up more than all the itority - an fe Him Kingdom surpass all the kingdoms - an fe Him Itority are what rule all the world - fe Him able fe all - an fe there are nothing that fail Him. [12] Him rule all clouds ina Heaven ~ Him grow grass fe livestocks pon Earth - an Him give fruit pon the buds. [13] Him feed fe all each of the kinds like unto Him loved ~ Him feed all that Him Irated by each of the fruits an each of the foods - an Him feed ants an locusts beneath Earth an livestocks pon Earth an beasts - an fe a person who prayed Him give him him priah - an Him don't ignore the plea of the child whose mother an faada dead pon him - nor widows. [14] As evil persons rebellion are like unto a swirlin wind an wrongdoers council like unto misty urine - Him shall rather accept the plea of them who beg toward Him at each time an clean ones. [15] An as them body are like unto a flyin bird - an as them features comeliness that are silver an gold are perishable ina this world - examination will benefit persons who forgot JAH LAW yet not them gold - an moths shall eat them clothes. [16] An weevils shall totally eat the wheat an the barley fatness - an all shall pass like unto the day that passed yesterday - an like unto a word that proceeded from a mouth don't return - sinner persons money also are like unto it - an them 'beautiful lifestyle' are like unto a passin shadow ~ sinner persons money before JAH are like unto a lie clothes. [17] But if kind persons are honoured JAH won't ignore them - fe them have been honoured while them were nice fe poor ones - an them hear justice of sufferahs an a child whose mother an faada dead pon him ~ JAH won't ignore them - fe without neglectin them house childran - them honour Him while them clothe the naked from the clothes JAH gave them that them might give fe the refugee sufferah. [18] Them don't favour loyal persons judgemant - an them don't mek a hireling salary lodge ~ as JAH thing are Truth an honoured like unto a sword whose mouths were two - them won't do iniquity ina them seasons number an ina them balance measurement. Chapter 26 [1] But poor ones will think again pon them beddin - but if wealthy ones don't accept them - them will be like unto dry wood that have no verdure - an a root won't be fertile from alongside where no moisture are - an the leaf won't be fertile if there are no root. [2] As a leaf serve a flower fe be a ornamant fe fruit - unless the leaf were fertile it won't bear fruit ~ as man fulfillmant are religion - a person without religion have no virtue. [3] If him firmed up religion him worked virtue - an JAH are Irie by a person who work Truth an straight Work. [4] An fe the person who begged Him - Him shall give him him plea an him tongue reward - an Him won't wrong the true person becau him true Work that him worked. [5] As JAH are true - an as Him have loved a Truth thing - Him won't justify the sinner person without repentance becau the Work evil him worked - an as all persons souls have been seized ina Him Itority becau Him were Who ruled Earth an Heaven - as Him won't favour for the wealthy more than the poor ina Judgemant time - Him won't justify him without repentance. Chapter 27 [1] Him Irated havin brought all the world from not livin toward livin - an Him totally prepared hills an mountains - an Him firmed up Earth pon Water - an lest sea be shaken Him delineated she by sand - fe ina Him first Word JAH have said Mek Light be Irated. [2] Light were Irated when this world had been covered ina darkness ~ JAH Irated all the Iration - an Him prepared this world - an Him firmed up this world by what are due an by money that are straight ~ Him said - Mek evenin be dark. [3] An again JAH said Mek Light be Irated ~ it dawned an there were Light - an Him Ilivated the upper Water toward Heaven. [4] An Him streached it forth like unto a tent - an Him firmed it up by a wind - an Him placed the lower Water within a pit. [5] An Him shut the sea lock ina sand - an Him firmed them up ina Him Itority lest them drown ina Water - an Him placed animals an beasts within she - an Him placed within she Liewatan an Biehiemot who were great beasts - an Him placed within she the beasts without number - sight up an not sight up. [6] Pon the third day JAH Irated pon Earth plants - all the roots an woods an fruits that bear forth ina each of them kinds - an a welfare wood beautiful fe them fe sight it up.. [7] An Him Irated a welfare wood that were both beautiful fe them fe sight it up an sweet fe them fe eat it - an Him Irated grass - an all plants whose seeds are found from within them - fe be food fe birds an livestocks an beasts. [8] It dusked ~ it dawned - an pon the fourth day Him said - Mek Light be Irated ina Heaven called cosmos ~ JAH havin Irated moon an Sun an stars - Him placed them ina Heaven called cosmos that them might shine ina this world an that them might feed them daylight an night. [9] An after this moon an Sun an stars alternated ina night an daylight. [10] An pon the fifth day JAH Irated all animals an beasts that live within Water an all birds that fly pon Heaven - all that are sight up an not sight up - all this. [11] An pon the sixth day Him Irated livestocks an beasts an others - an havin Irated an prepared all - Him Irated 'Adam ina Him Example an

Him Appearance. [12] Him gave him all animals an beasts Him Irated that him might reign pon them - an again - all animals an beasts an all fishes - an Liewatan an Biehiemot that are ina sea. [13] An Him gave him all cows that live ina this world an sheeps - the animals not sight up an them that are sight up. [14] An Him placed ina Garden 'Adam whom Him Irated ina Him Example an Him Appearance - that him might eat an might cultivate plants an might praise JAH there. [15] An fe lest him demolish Him Command - Him have said - Pon the time when unu ate from this Herb of Fig unu will dead death. [16] An Him commanded him lest him eat from the Herb of Fig that bring death - that draw attention fe evil an good - that bring death. [17] InI mother Hiewan were cajoled by a snake misleadin an she ate from that Herb of Fig an gave it fe InI faada 'Adam. [18] An 'Adam havin eaten from that Herb of Fig brought death pon him childran an pon him ras self. [19] As him have demolished Him Command - an as him have eaten from that Herb of Fig that JAH commanded sayin - Don't eat from she - JAH vexed pon InI faada 'Adam an expelled an sent him way from the Garden - an Him gave him that Earth that grow thistle an thorn - that Him cursed becau him pon the time him demolished Him Command - that him might eat him weariness reward havin toiled an laboured that him might plow she. [20] An pon the time JAH sent him forth toward this land - 'Adam returned toward complete sadness - an havin toiled an laboured that him might plow Earth - him began fe eat ina weariness an also ina struggles. Chapter 28 [1] An after him childran lived havin abounded - there were from them ones who praise an honour JAH an don't demolish Him Command. [2] There were prophets who spoke what were done an what will be done henceforth - an from him childran there were sinners who speak lies an who wrong persons ~ 'Adam firstborn child Qayel became evil an killed him bredda 'Abiel. [3] JAH judged Judgemant pon Qayel becau him killed him bredda 'Abiel - an JAH vexed pon Earth becau she drank him blood. [4] An JAH told Qayel - Where are thy bredda 'Abiel? - an Qayel ina him heart arrogance said - 'Are mi mi bredda 'Abiel keeper?' [5] 'Abiel became a clean man - but Qayel became a sinner man by killin a kind man - him bredda 'Abiel. [6] Again a kind child Siet were birthed ~ 'Adam birthed sixty childran ~ there are kind persons an evil persons from them. [7] An there are kind persons from them ~ an there are persons who were prophets an them who were traitors an sinners. [8] There are blessed persons who were kind persons - who fulfill them faada 'Adam accord an all him told fe him child Siet - Iginnin from 'Adam up til Noh who are a kind man who kept JAH LAW. [9] An him sanctioned JAH LAW fe him childran ~ him told them - 'Guard' - lest them demolish JAH LAW - an that them might tell fe them childran like unto them faada Noh told them - an that them might keep JAH LAW. [10] An them lived while them taught them childran - persons birthed after them. [11] But Seythan lived when him spoke fe them faadas - havin lodged ina idols that reached fe a grave an that have vows pon them - an havin defeated the persons who told him alright - an when them did all that Seythan - who are sin teacher - commanded them. [12] An them lived when them worshipped the idols like unto them order - up til a kind man 'Abriham who fulfill JAH Accord. [13] Fe him have lived firmed up ina the LAW beforehand separate from him cousins - an JAH swore a oath with him - havin lodged ina wind an fiyah. [14] JAH swore fe him that Him might give him a land of inheritance an that Him might give fe him childran up til the Iternity. [15] An Him swore fe Yis'haq like unto him that Him might give him him faada 'Abriham inheritance - an Him swore fe Ya`iqob that Him might give him him faada Yis'haq inheritance ~ Him swore fe him like into Yis'haq. [16] An Him separated them childran - who were birthed after them from Ya`iqob - from the twelve tribes of 'Isra'iel - an made them priests an kings ~ Him blessed them sayin - Abound an totally be many many. [17] An Him gave them them faada inheritance - however while Him fed them an loved them - them didn't quit saddenin JAH ina all. [18] An pon the time Him downstroyed them - at that time them will seek Him ina worship - an them will return from sin an go toward JAH - fe Him love them - an JAH shall pardon them. [19] Fe bein nice fe all Him Irated - Him shall pardon them - an it are becau them faadas Work that Him love them - yet it aren't becau them ras selves Work. [20] An Him streach forth Him Right Hand ina plenty that Him might satta a hungry body - an Him reveal Him Eye fe pardonin that Him might multiply grain fe food. [21] Him give food fe crows chicks an fe beasts that beg Him ~ pon the time them cried toward Him - Him will save 'Isra'iel childran from them enemies hands who delayed from the time. [22] An them will return toward sin again that them might sadden Him - an Him will arouse them enemies peoples ina them area pon them ~ them will downstroy them an kill them an capture them. [23] An again them will shout toward JAH ina mournin an sadness - an there are the time when Him sent help an saved them by prophets hands. [24] An there are the time when Him saved them by princes hands - an pon the time them saddened JAH them enemies taxed them an captured them. [25] An Daweet arose an saved them from the 'Iloflans hands; an again them saddened JAH - an JAH aroused pon them peoples who worry them. [26] An there are the time when Him saved them by Yoftahie hand - an again them forgot JAH Who saved them ina them tribulation time. As JAH have brought the hardship pon them - Him will arouse pon them enemies who were evil who will firm up tribulation pon them an totally capture them. [27] An pon the time them were worried by tribulation them were seized an again cried toward Him - an Him saved them by Giediewon hand - an again them saddened JAH by them hands Work. [28] An again Him aroused pon them peoples who firm up tribulation pon them - an them returned an wept an cried toward JAH. [29] An again Him saved them from peoples by Somson hand - an them rested a likkle from the tribulation. An them arose that them might sadden JAH by them former sin. [30] An again Him aroused pon them other peoples who worry them - an again them cried an wept toward JAH that Him might send help fe them - an Him saved them from peoples by Bariq an Deebora hands. [31] Again them lived a likkle season while them worshipped JAH - an again them forgot JAH ina them former sin an saddened Him. [32] An Him aroused pon them other peoples who worry them - an again Him saved them by Yodeet hand; an havin sat again a likkle season them arose that them might sadden JAH by them sin like unto formerly. [33] An Him aroused pon them peoples who rule them - an them cried an wept toward JAH; fe Him have struck pon him head 'Abiemieliek who were a warrior who came that him might fight Yihuda country. [34] An Him saved them by the childran ina the area an by Matatyu hand - an pon the time that warrior dead him army fled an were scattared - an 'Isra'iel childran followed an fought them up til 'Iyabboq - an them didn't preserve even one person from them. [35] After this them waited a likkle an arose that them might sadden JAH - an Him aroused pon them peoples who rule them - an again them totally cried toward JAH; an JAH ignored them cryin an them mournin - fe them have saddened JAH everytime - an fe them have demolished Him LAW. [36] An them captured an took them with them priests toward Babilon persons country. [37] An then 'Isra'iel childran who were traitors didn't quit saddenin JAH while them worked sin an worshipped idols. [38] JAH vexed that Him might downstroy them one time ina them sin - Hama havin introduced ten thousand gold ina the king box - pon the day when it were known - him lodged anger ina the king 'Arthieksis reasonin - lest him preserve them childran ina Fars country Iginnin from Hindekie an up til 'Ityopphya pon the time him told him that him might downstroy them. [39] Him did thus - an him wrote a letter where a message were written by the king authority - an him gave him a seal ina him hand that him might deliver toward Fars country. [40] Him gave him a seal that him might downstroy them pon one day when him loved them fe downstroy them like unto the king commanded - but him commanded that him might introduce them money - the gold an the silver - toward the king box. [41] An pon the time 'Isra'iel childran heard this thing them totally cried an wept toward JAH - an them told it fe Merdokyos - an Merdokyos told fe 'Astier. [42] An 'Astier said - 'Fast - beg - an all 'Isra'iel childran kindreds - cry toward JAH ina the place where unu are.' [43] An Merdokyos wore sackcloth an sprinkled dust pon him ras self - an 'Isra'iel childran fasted - begged - an entered repentance ina the country where them were. [44] An 'Astier were totally sad - an bein a queen she wore sackcloth ~ she sprinkled dust an shaved she head - she didn't anoint perfume like unto Fars queens anoint perfume - an ina she deep reasonin she cried an wept toward she faadas Irator JAH. [45] An becaudis thing Him gave she bein loved alongside Fars king 'Arthieksis - an she made a kind lunch fe she faadas Irator. [46] An Hama an the king entered toward the lunch that 'Astier prepared - an like unto him loved that him might do pon Merdokyos - JAH paid the hardship pon that Hama - an them hanged him pon a tall wood. [47] The king letter were commanded that them might quit 'Isra'iel like unto them were ina all them accord - an lest them tax them nor rob them nor wrong them nor tek them money pon them. [48] As JAH shall pardon 'Isra'iel doin thus pon the time them cried enterin repentance - it are that them might love them an honour them ina Fars country where them lived - yet a king letter were commanded lest them downstroy them country nor plunder them livestocks. [49] An pon them time them saddened Him - Him will arouse pon them peoples who worry them ~ at that time them will totally weep an cry that Him might send them help fe them an that Him might save them from peoples hand who firm up tribulation pon them. Chapter 29 [1] An pon the time Gibts persons also made 'Isra'iel childran work by makin them work bricks ina difficulty - an pon the time them worried them all the Work by kickin mud without straw an heatin bricks... [2] An pon the time them made them work havin appointed chiefs pon them who rush workers - them cried toward JAH that Him might save them from workin all Gibts bricks. [3] At that time Him sent fe them 'Aron an Mussie who help them - fe JAH have sent them that them might send forth Him kindreds from Fer'on rulership house - an Him saved them from brick Work ~ becau ina him arrogance him refused fe adjourn 'Isra'iel lest them be ruled an sacrifice sacrifice fe JAH ina wilderness - JAH have sent them that them might send forth Him kindreds 'Isra'iel from Gibts king Fer'on rulership house - an them saved them. [4] Fe JAH neglect arrogant ones - an Him drowned Fer'on ina 'Eritra sea with him army becau him arrogance. [5] An like unto him - Him shall downstroy them who didn't work goodly Work ina all the kingdoms that Him I-pointed an crowned them - that them who ignore JAH Word when them are nobles an kings might fulfill Him Accord fe Him - an that them might give persons who serve ina a goodly thing them wage - an that them might honour Him famous Name.

[6] JAH Who rule all said - But if them will straighten up I Kingdom - I man will straighten up them kingdom fe them. [7] Work goodly Work fe I - an I-man shall work goodly Work fe unu ~ keep I LAW - an I-man shall keep unu your bodies ~ live firmed up ina I LAW - an I-man shall live lodgin honesty ina unu like unto your reasonin. [8] Love I - an I-man shall love your welfare ~ near toward I - an I-man shall heal unu. [9] JAH Who rule all said - Believe ina I - an I-man shall save unu from the tribulation. [10] Don't live side by side ~ as JAH Who rule all love straight Work - Him said - Unu - approach toward I - an I-man shall approach toward unu ~ unu persons who are sinners an traitors - cleanse your hands from sin - an distance your reasonins from evil. [11] An I-man shall distance I anger from unu - an I-man shall return fe unu ina Charity an Forgiveness. [12] I-man shall distance criminals an enemies who work iniquity from unu - like unto I-man saved I slave Daweet from him enemies who met him - from them much malice - an from Gwolyad who were a warrior - an also from Sa'ol hand who sought that him might kill him - an from him child 'Abiesielom hand who loved that him might tek him kingdom. [13] I-man shall save persons who keep I LAW an fulfill I Accord like unto him ~ I-man shall bequeath them honour - an them shall be Irie ina the present world an yonder ina the world that shall come ~ I-man shall crown them pon all that them might be Irie. [14] Them shall be one with kings who served JAH an were honoured ina them beautiful way of Life - like unto the prophet Samu'iel served Him ina him beautiful way of Life Iginnin from him infancy - whom JAH - Him bein LAW - chose. [15] Him told him that him might tell 'Elee who were a servant elder - an when him served ina JAH Lodgin the Temple - Samu'iel Work also were merciful an I-loved. [16] An pon the time him grew when him served ina JAH Lodgin the Temple - Him made him fe be Ipointed an Inointed - that him might Ipoint him people an that kings might be Inointed by JAH Accord. As JAH have loved him that the kindred him chose from 'Isra'iel childran might be Ipointed - pon the time him fulfilled JAH Accord Who Irated him - Him gave him the Inointin of the Kingdom ina him hand. [17] An when Sa'ol were ina him kingdom JAH told Him prophet Samu'iel - Go - an as I-man have loved `Issiey child Daweet who were birthed from Yihuda kin - Inoint him. Chapter 30 [1] I-man have hated Sa'ol kin - fe him have saddened I becau him violated I Word. [2] An I-man neglected him - fe him didn't keep I LAW - an I-man won't crown from him kin again. [3] An persons who didn't keep I LAW an I Word an I Order like unto him - I-man shall downstroy I Kingdom an I gift from them childran up til the Iternity. [4] An as them didn't mek I famous pon the time I-man made them famous - I-man shall downstroy them - yet I-man won't again return fe lift them up ~ though I-man honour them - as them didn't honour I - I-man won't mek them famous. [5] Fe them didn't do a goodly thing fe I pon the time I-man did a goodly thing fe them - an fe them didn't forgive I pon the time I-man forgave them. [6] An as them didn't mek I a Ruler pon the time I-man made them rulers pon all - as them didn't honour I pon the time I-man honoured them more than all - I-man won't mek them famous again nor honour them - an fe them didn't keep I LAW. [7] An I-man withheld the gift I-man gave them - an I-man won't return the money I-man withheld from them like unto the measure I-man vexed an swore ~ JAH Who rule all said thus ~ Him said - I-man shall honour them who honoured I - an love them who loved I. [8] I-man shall separate them who didn't honour I nor keep I LAW from the gift I-man gave them. [9] JAH Who rule all said; I-man love them who loved I - an mek famous him who made I famous - Him said.. [10] As I-man JAH am Who rule all - there are none who escape I Itority ina Earth nor Heaven - fe I-man am JAH Who kill an Who save an Who sadden an Who forgive. [11] As famousness an honour are I money - I-man honour him whom I man loved - fe I-man am Who judge an Who revenge an downstroy - an I man mek wretched him whom I-man hated. [12] Fe I-man am Who forgive them who love I an call I Name everytime - fe I-man am Who feed food fe the wealthy an fe the poor. [13] An I-man feed birds an animals - fishes ina sea an beasts an flowers - yet I-man aren't Who feed only man. [14] I-man feed crocodiles an whales - gophers an hippos - an badgers... [15] an all that live within Water - all that fly pon wind - yet I-man aren't Who feed only man ~ all this are I money. [16] I-man am Who feed all that seek I by all that are due an I-loved. Chapter 31 [1] An the kings don't reign without I Accord - an sufferahs are by I Command - yet them aren't poor without I Command - an powerful ones are by I Accord - yet them aren't strong without I Accord. [2] I-man gave bein I-loved fe Daweet an Wisdom fe Selomon - an I-man added eras fe Hiziqyas. [3] I-man diminished Gwolyad era - an I-man gave Power fe Somson - an again I-man weakened him Power. [4] An I-man saved I slave Daweet from Gwolyad hand who were a warrior. [5] An again I-man saved him from the king Sa'ol hand an from the secand warrior who disputed him - an fe him have kept I Command - an I-man saved him from the persons hand who dispute him an fight him. [6] An I-man loved him - an I-man love all the nobles an the kings who keep I LAW ~ as them have made I Irie - I-man shall give them prevailin an Power pon them enemies. [7] An again that them might inherit them faadas land - I-man shall give them the cleansed an shinin land of inheritance that I-man swore fe them faadas. Chapter 32 [1] JAH Who rule all said - An unu the nobles an also the kings - hear I ina I Word - an keep I

Command ~ lest unu sadden I an worship like unto 'Isra'iel childran saddened I an worshipped different idols - them whom I man kept an saved when I-man JAH am them Irator - JAH Who rule all said - Hear I ina I Word; an all whom I-man raised an loved an fed Iginnin that them were birthed from them mother an faada. [2] An whom I-man sent forth toward Earth crops - an whom I-man fed the fatness found from Earth makin like unto are due - an whom I-man gave the grape vine an the oil-tree fruit that them didn't plant an the clear Water well that them didn't dig. [3] Hear I ina I Word lest unu sadden I like unto 'Isra'iel childran saddened I worshippin other idols when I-man JAH am them Irator - Him told them - Who fed them the sheep milk an the honey comb with the hulled wheat - an Who clothed them clothes where ornamant are - an Who gave them all them love. [4] An without it livin that I-man deprived them all them begged I. Chapter 33 [1] Like unto Daweet spoke sayin - "Isra'iel childran were fed the menna that Angels lowered' - an again hear I ina I Word lest unu sadden I like unto 'Isra'iel childran saddened I worshippin the idols when I-man am them Irator JAH Who fed them sweet menna ina wilderness - Him said ~ I-man did all this fe them that them might worship I by what are due an fe true. [2] JAH Who rule all said - But them didn't worship I - an I-man neglected them ~ them saddened I an lived firmed up ina law of idols that weren't I LAW. [3] An I-man shall bring the hardship pon them like unto them sin ~ as them have neglected I Worship an as them didn't firm up ina I counsel an I Order - I-man neglected them ina the sin measure that them worked by them hands - an I-man shall lower them toward Gehannem ina Definite Judgemant that are done ina Heaven. [4] Fe them didn't keep I LAW - an fe I-man vex pon them - an I-man shall diminish them era ina this world. [5] If thou be a king - aren't thou a man who shall dead an be demolished an tomorrow who shall be worms an dust? [6] But today thou boast an are proud like unto a man who won't dead foriva. [7] JAH Who rule all said - But thou who are sight up bein well today are a man who will dead tomorrow. [8] But if unu keep I Command an I Word - I-man shall bequeath thee-I a honoured country with honoured kings who did I Accord - whose lodgin were Light an whose crowns were beautiful - an whose thrones were silver an gold an whom persons who sit pon them adorned - Him said. [9] An them shall be Irie within Him country that are a place that approached fe persons who worked goodly Work. [10] But fe persons who work sin - as them didn't keep I LAW - said JAH Who rule all... [11] it aren't due them that them might enter toward that country where honoured kings shall enter. Chapter 34 [1] Miedon kingdom shall perish - but Rom kingdom shall totally firm up pon Meqiedonya kingdom - an Nenewie kingdom shall firm up pon Fars kingdom. [2] An 'Ityopphya kingdom shall firm up pon 'Iskindriya kingdom ~ as peoples shall arise - Mo`ab kingdom shall firm up pon 'Amalieq kingdom. [3] An bredda shall arise pon him bredda - an JAH shall revenge a downstroy like unto Him spoke that it might perish. [4] Kingdom shall arise pon kingdom - an the people pon the people an country pon country - Him said. [5] An arguments shall be done an there shall be formations - famine - plague - earthquake - drought ~ as Love have perished from this world - JAH chastisemant downscended pon she. [6] Fe the day have arrived suddenly when JAH shall come - Who frighten like unto lightnin that are sight up from East up til West. [7] Pon the day when HIM JAH judge Judgemant - at that time everyone shall raceive him hardship like unto him hand weakness an him sin firmness - fe Him have said I-man shall revenge them pon the day when HIM JAH judge Judgemant an pon the day when them feet are hindered - fe the day when them are counted fe downstruction have arrived. [8] At that time JAH shall downstroy ina Gehannem foriva persons who won't live firmed up in Him LAW - who work sin. [9] An them who live ina the West ilands an Noba an Hindekie - Saba an 'Ityopphya an Gibts persons - all persons who live ina them... [10] at that time shall know I that I-man were JAH Who rule Earth an Heaven - an Who give bein I-loved an honour - an Who save an Who kill. [11] I-man am Who send forth Sun - Who send it toward it settin - Who bring the evil an the good. [12] I-man am Who bring peoples whom unu don't know - who slaughter an eat the money whereby unu wearied - your sheeps an your cows flocks. [13] An them shall capture your childran while them hammer them before unu - an unu cyaan save them. Becau JAH Spirit of Support didn't lodge ina unu - as unu didn't fear JAH Command that unu heard - Him shall downstroy your lavishmants an your assignmants. [14] But a person ina whom JAH Spirit of Support lodged will know all - like unto Nabukedenetsor told Dan'iel sayin - 'Mi sight up JAH Spirit of Support that lodged ina thee-I.' [15] An a person ina whom JAH Spirit of Support lodged will know all - an what were hidden will be revealed fe him - an him will know all that were revealed an that were hidden - yet there are nothing hidden from a person ina whom JAH Spirit of Support lodged. [16] But as InI are persons who will dead tomorrow - InI sins that InI hid an worked shall be revealed. [17] An like unto them test silver an gold ina fiyah - like unto them are sinners - later pon the Day of Advent them shall be examined - fe them didn't keep JAH Command. [18] At that time all peoples an all 'Isra'iel childran Works shall be examined. Chapter 35 [1] As JAH vex pon unu becau unu didn't judge a Truth Judgemant fe the child whose mother an faada dead pon him - woe fe unu 'Isra'iel nobles. [2] Woe fe unu persons who go toward a drinkin house mornin an evenin

an get drunk - who are partial ina judgemant - an who don't hear the widow justice nor the child whose mother an faada dead pon him - who live ina sin an seducin. [3] JAH told 'Isra'iel nobles sayin thus: - Unless unu lived firmed up ina I Command an kept I LAW an loved what I-man love - woe fe unu - Him told them. [4] An I-man shall bring downstruction an chastisemant an tribulation pon unu - an unu will perish like unto what weevils an moths ate - an your tracks an your region won't be found - Him told them. [5] An your country will be a wilderness - an all persons who sight she up formerly shall clap them hands ~ them shall marvel pon she while them said - 'Weren't this country filled of she plenty an all who love it?; JAH made she thus by persons sin who live ina she.' [6] Them shall say - 'As she have made she heart proud - an as she have ilivated she ras self - an as she have firmed up she collar of reasonin up til JAH mek she wretched pon Earth - an as she shall be a desert by persons arrogance who live ina she - an as thorns have grown pon she with thistles - woe fe she.' [7] An she grow weeds an nettles - an she became a wilderness an a desert - an beasts shall live within she. [8] Fe JAH Judgemant have firmed up pon she - an fe she shall raceive JAH Judgemant Chalice becau she reasonin arrogance by persons sin who live ina she - an she became frightenin fe persons who go toward she. Chapter 36 [1] Meqiedon persons - don't boast ~ as JAH are there Who shall downstroy unu - 'Amalieqans - don't firm up your collar of reasonin. [2] Fe unu will be lofty up til Heaven an unu will downscend up til Gehannem. [3] Pon the time 'Isra'iel formerly entered toward Gibts country ina Mo`ab an Miedon kingdom Him said - Don't boast - fe it aren't due fe pretend pon JAH that unu might pretend pon Him. [4] Thou Yisma'iel kindred - slave child - why do thou firm up thy collar of reasonin by what weren't thy money? How about don't thou think that JAH shall judge pon thee pon the time Him arose that it might be judged pon Earth - pon the day when it are judged pon thee? [5] JAH Who rule all said - At that time thou will raceive thy hardship like unto thy hand Work - how about why do thou ilivate thy reasonin? How about why do thou firm up thy collar of reasonin? [6] An I-man shall pretend pon thee like unto thou pretended pon persons who weren't thy kindreds - fe thou do what thou love that thou might work sin - an I-man shall neglect thee ina the place where them sent thee. [7] JAH Who rule all said - An I-man shall do thus pon thee ~ Him said - But if thou worked goodly Work an if thou love what I-man loved - I-man also shall hear thee-I ina all that thou begged. [8] An if thou fulfill I Accord fe I - I-man shall fulfill thy accord fe thee-I - an I-man shall dispute thy enemies fe thee-I - an I-man shall bless thy children an thy seed fe thee-I. [9] An I-man shall multiply thy sheeps an thy cows flocks fe thee-I - an if thou lived firmed up ina I Command an also if thou did what I-man love - JAH Who rule all said - I-man shall bless fe thee-I all thou seized ina thy hand. [10] But if thou don't do I Accord - if thou don't live firmed up ina I LAW an I Command - all this tribulation that were told formerly shall find thee - fe thou didn't indure tribulation firmed up ina I Command - an fe thou didn't live firmed up ina I LAW - an thou cyaan escape from I anger that will come pon thee everytime. [11] An as thou didn't love what I-man loved - when I-man am Who Irated thee bringin from not livin toward livin... [12] all this were thy money - that thou might kill an heal fe do all that thou loved - that thou might work an demolish - that thou might honour an abuse - that thou might ilivate an downbase - an as thou have neglected I Worship an I praise when I-man am Who gave thee lordship an also honour alongside persons who are beneath thy authority - thou cyaan escape from I anger that will come pon thee. [13] An if thou did JAH Accord an if thou lived frmed up ina Him Command - Him will love thee-I that thou might be Irie with Him ina Him Lordship - an that thou might be a partaker with persons who inherited a honoured country. [14] Fe Him have said - If them indure I - I-man will bequeath them bein I loved an honour - fe I-man shall mek them Irie ina the Temple where priah are prayed - fe JAH Who rule all have said - An them shall be I-loved an chosen like unto a sacrifice. [15] Don't neglect fe do Work whereby welfare are done an a goodly thing that unu might cross from death toward Life. [16] But persons who work goodly Work - JAH shall keep them ina all Him goodly Work - that them might be Him slaves like unto 'Iyob whom JAH kept from all the tribulation [17] JAH shall keep them ina all goodly Work - that them might be Him slaves fe Him like unto 'Abriham whom Him saved pon the time him killed the kings - an like unto Mussie whom Him saved from Kenaniewon hand an Fer`on hand - ina whom 'Abriham lived - an who were also downsturbin him body evenin an mornin night an day that them might mek him worship idols. [18] But when them took him toward the idols that were them money - him would indure the tribulation while him refused. [19] Fe 'Abriham who believed Him Iginnin from him childhood were fe JAH Him trusted friend - an while him refused him would worship JAH Who Irated him. [20] As him totally love JAH - him didn't quit worshippin JAH up til him dead - an him didn't depart from Him LAW up til when him dead - an him taught him childran that might keep JAH LAW. [21] An like unto them faada 'Abriham kept Him LAW - them didn't depart from JAH LAW ~ like unto Him told fe Angels sayin - I-man have a friend ina this world called 'Abriham - 'Abriham childran Ya`iqob an Yis'haq - who are Him slaves becau whom JAH spoke - didn't depart from JAH LAW. [22] JAH Who were praised alongside them an Who rule all said - 'Abriham are I friend ~ Yis'haq are I canfidante - an Ya`iqob are I friend whom I Reasonin loved. [23] But when Him totally loved 'Isra'iel childran - them lived when them Itinually saddened Him - an Him lived when Him indured them an when Him fed them menna ina wilderness. [24] Them clothes didn't age - fe them have been fed menna that are knowledge 'injera - an them feet didn't awaken. [25] But them reasonins would distance from JAH everytime ~ as them were who work sin Iginnin from Antiquity - them had no hope fe be saved. [26] Them became like unto a crooked bow - yet them didn't become like unto them faadas Yis'haq an 'Abriham an Ya`iqob who served JAH ina them beautiful way of Life ~ them would sadden Him everytime by them idols pon the mountains an the hills ~ them would eat pon the mountain an at the caves an the trees roots. [27] Them would slaughter a steer ~ them would sacrifice a sacrifice - an them would be Irie ina them hands Work ~ them would eat the rest of the sacrifice ~ them would drink of them sacrifice - an them would play with demons while them sang. [28] An demons would admire all them games an them songs fe them - an them would work them drunkenness an adultery without measure - an them would do the robbery an greed that JAH don't love. [29] Fe Kene`an idols - an fe Midyam idols an fe Be`al - an fe 'Aphlon an Dagon an Seraphyon an 'Arthiemadies who are 'Eloflee idols... [30] an fe all peoples idols ina them area - them would sacrifice sacrifice; an all 'Isra'iel would worship idols like unto peoples worship idols by money that them sight up an heard ~ them would mek them games an them songs an them bluster that peoples mek. [31] All 'Isra'iel kindreds do likewise - who say 'Wi will worship JAH' - without keepin Him Command an Him LAW that Mussie told them ina 'Oreet that them might keep JAH LAW an might distance from worshippin idols. [32] Lest them worship separated idols - apart from them faadas Irator Who fed them the honey found from Maga who fed them the plantation grain an sent them forth toward the Earth crops - an Who fed them the menna ... [33] Mussie commanded them sayin 'Don't worship' - fe Him are them Irator - an fe Him feed them who loved Him - an Him won't deprive them who loved Him an desired Him. [34] But them didn't quit saddenin JAH - an them would sadden JAH pon the time Him made them Irie. [35] An pon the time Him saddened them - them would cry toward Him - an Him would save them from the tribulation that found them - an them would again be totally Irie an would live many eras. [36] An at that time them would totally return them heart toward sin that them might sadden JAH like unto formerly - an Him would arouse pon them peoples ina them area that them might downstroy them - an them would worry an tax them. [37] An again them would totally return an cry toward them Irator JAH. [38] An Him would forgive them ~ it are becau them faadas - Noh - Yis'haq an 'Abriham an Ya`iqob - who served JAH ina them beautiful way of Life Iginnnin from Antiquity - fe whom Him firmed up Him Oath - yet it aren't becau them ras selves Work that Him forgive them. [39] An Him loved persons who kept Him LAW lovin that them might multiply them childran like unto Heaven stars an sea sand. [40] But pon the time dead ones arose that them have like unto sea sand - them are sinner persons souls that will separate from 'Isra'iel childran an enter toward Gehannem. [41] As JAH have told 'Abriham - Sight up toward Heaven at night an count Heaven stars as it were thou could count - likewise as Him have told him - Thy childran an righteous ones shall shine ina Heaven like unto Heaven stars - them are like unto stars that shine ina Heaven - but what them have are kind persons souls birthed from 'Isra'iel. [42] An again as Him have told him - Overstand toward the river edge an the sea - an sight up what are amidst the sand ~ count as it were thou could count - an thy sinner childran are likewise - who will downscend toward Gehannem pon the time dead ones arose - them are sinner persons souls. [43] An 'Abriham believed ina JAH ~ becaudis thing it were counted fe him bein Truth ~ him found him morale ina this world - an after him wife Sora aged she birthed a child called Yis'haq. [44] Fe him have believed that persons who worked goodly Work shall arise an go toward the Kingdom of Heaven that live firmed up foriva - an again him shall find a Kingdom ina Heaven. [45] But fe him have believed that persons who worked sin shall go toward Gehannem that live firmed up foriva pon the time dead ones arose - but that righteous ones who worked goodly Work shall reign with Him foriva. [46] But fe him have believed that it shall be judged foriva fe true without falsehood pon persons who worked sin - fe him shall find Life Kingdom ina Heaven." Mek glory an praise enter fe JAH fe true without falsehood - an the first book that speak the Meqabyans thing were filled an fulfilled.

Book 69. II Meqabyan

Chapter 1 [1] This are a book that speak that Meqabees found 'Isra'iel ina Mesphiethomya that are Sorya part an killed them ina them region iginnin from 'Iyabboq up til 'Iyerusaliem square - an that him downstroyed the country. [2] Becau Sorya an 'Edomyas persons an the 'Amalieqans were one with the Mo`ab man Meqabees who downstroyed 'Iyerusaliem country - as them have camped iginnin from Semarya up til 'Iyerusaliem square an up til all she region - them killed ina war without

preservin persons who fled apart from a few persons. [3] An pon the time 'Isra'iel childran wronged - Him aroused Mo`ab man Meqabees pon them - an him killed them by a sword. [4] An becaudis thing JAH enemies the peoples bragged pon Him honoured country - an them swore ina them crime. [5] An 'Iloflee an 'Idomyas persons camped - as Him have sent them becau them pretended JAH Word - them began fe revenge an downstroy JAH country. [6] An that Meqabees country are Riemat that are Mo`ab part - an him arose from him country ina Power an them swore also with persons with him. [7] An them camped ina Gielabuhie region that are Mesphiethomya lot up til Sorya that them might downstroy JAH country - an there him begged the 'Amalieqans an 'Iloflans ~ him gave them much silver an gold an chariots an horses that them might be one with him ina crime. [8] Them came together an crushed the fortress ~ persons who lived ina she shed blood like unto Water. [9] An them made 'Iyerusaliem like unto a plant keepin hut - an him made a voice heard within she ~ him worked all the sin Work that JAH don't love - an them also defouled JAH country that were filled of praise an honour. [10] Them made thy friends flesh an thy slaves corpses food fe wilderness beasts an Heaven birds. [11] An them robbed childran whose mother an faada dead pon them an widows - fe without fearin JAH them have done like unto Seythan taught them - an up til JAH Who examine kidneys an reasonins vexed - them took out the fetus ina pregnant dawtaz belly. [12] Them returned toward them country while them were Irie becau them worked evil Work pon JAH kindreds - an them took the plunder that them captured from a honoured country. [13] Pon the time them returned an entered toward them houses them made Ites an song an clappin. Chapter 2 [1] The prophet whom them call Re`ay told him thus: - "Today be Irie a likkle pon the time when Irie Ites were made ~ JAH Whom 'Isra'iel glorified have that Him might revenge an downstroy thee ina the chastisemant thou didn't doubt. [2] Will thou say - 'Mi horses are swift ~ becaudis mi will escape by runnin'? [3] As fe I - I-man tell thee - Persons who will follow thee are swifter than vultures ~ thou won't escape from JAH Judgemant an downstruction that shall come pon thee. [4] Will thou say - 'Mi wear iron clothes - an spear flingin an bow stingin aren't able fe mi'?; JAH Who honour 'Isra'iel said - It aren't by spear flingin that I-man will revenge an downstroy thee" Him told him ~ "I-man shall bring pon thee heart sickness an itch an rheumatism sickness that were worse an firmer than spear flingin an bow stingin - yet it aren't by this that I-man shall revenge an downstroy thee. [5] Thou have aroused I anger ~ I-man shall bring heart sickness pon thee - an thou will lack one who help thee - an thou won't escape from I Itority up til I-man downstroy thy name invocation from this world. [6] As thou have firmed up thy collar of reasonin - an as thou have ilivated thy ras self pon I country - pon the time I-man quickly did this thing like unto a eye wink - thou will know I that I-man were thy Irator ~ as thou are before I like unto grass before the wind that fiyah eat - an as thou are like unto the dust that winds spill an scattar from Earth - thou are like unto them alongside I. [7] Fe thou have aroused I anger - an fe thou didn't know thy Irator - an I man shall neglect all thy kindred - an neither will I-man preserve him who neared pon thy fortress. [8] An now return from all thy sin that thou worked ~ if thou return from thy sin an totally appease ina mournin an sadness before JAH - an if thou beg toward him ina clean reasonin - JAH will forgive thee all thy sin that thou worked before Him" - him told him. [9] At that time Meqabees wore dust an mourned before JAH becau him sin - fe JAH have vexed pon him. [10] Fe Him eyes are revealed - fe Him don't withhold - an fe Him ears are opened - fe Him don't neglect - an fe Him don't mek the word Him spoke false - an fe Him quickly do she at one time - fe JAH knew lest Him preserve the chastisemant Him spoke by the prophet Word. [11] Him cast him clothes an wore sackcloth an sprinkled dust pon him head an cried an wept before him Irator JAH becau him sin that him worked. Chapter 3 [1] An the prophet came from Riemat an told him - fe Riemat that are Mo`ab part are near fe Sorya. [2] Him dug a pit an entered up til him neck an wept firm tears - an him entered repentance becau him sin that him worked before JAH. [3] An JAH told the prophet thus: - Return from Yihuda country Riemat toward the Mo`ab official Meqabees Him told him. Tell him - "JAH told thee thus" - Tell him - "Him told thee - I-man JAH Who am thy Irator sent thee by I Accord that thou might downstroy I country - lest thou say - 'Mi destroyed the honoured country 'Iyerusaliem by mi Power firmness an mi army abundance' - yet it aren't thou who did this thing. [4] Fe she have saddened I by all she greed an she perfidy an she lustfulness. [5] An I-man neglected an cast she by thy hand - an now JAH forgave thy sin becau thy childran whom thou birthed ~ it aren't becau thou who firmed up thy collar of reasonin an say 'Mi incircled the country 'Iyerusaliem by mi authority firmness.' [6] As persons who doubt aren't disciplined fe enter repentance - don't be a doubter - an now enter repentance bein disciplined ina thy complete reasonin." [7] However persons are admired who enter repentance ina them complete reasonins an who don't again return toward thirst an sin by all that entered toward repentance becau them sin. [8] Persons are admired who return toward them Irator JAH bein disciplined ina mournin an sadness - ina bowin an many pleas. Persons are admired who are disciplined an enter repentance - fe Him have told them - Unu are I moneys who entered repentance after unu misled persons who entered repentance. [9] Him told arrogant Meqabees pon the time him returned toward Him ina repentance after him misled - I-man forgive thee thy sin becau thy fright an thy alarm; fe I-man am JAH thy Irator Who bring hardship pon childran by a faada sin up til seven generations if the child work the sin that the faada worked - an Who do Charity up til ten thousand generations fe persons who love I an keep I LAW. [10] An now I-man will firm up I Oath with thee becau these thy childran whom thou birthed - an JAH Who rule all an Who honoured 'Isra'iel said - I-man will accept the repentance thou made becau thy sin that thou worked. [11] At that time him proceeded from the pit an bowed fe the prophet ~ him swore sayin - "As mi have saddened JAH - mek mi what thou loved - yet mek JAH do mi thus thus lest mi separate from thee-I ~ as wi have no Law - mi didn't live firmed up ina Him Command like unto mi faadas ~ thou know that wi faadas taught wi an that wi worship idols. [12] Fe mi are a sinner who lived firmed up ina mi sin - who firmed up ina mi collar of reasonin firmness an mi reasonin arrogance whereby mi saddened JAH Command - but up til now mi hadn't heard JAH servants the prophets Word - an mi didn't live firmed up ina Him LAW an Him Command that Him commanded mi." [13] Him told him sayin - "As there are none from your kindred precedin unu who trusted him sin - mi knew that the prophet raceived repentance today." [14] "But now quit thy worshippin idols an return toward knowin JAH that thou might have true repentance" him told him ~ him fell an bowed at the prophet feet - an the prophet lifted up an commanded him all the goodly Work that are due him. [15] An him returned toward him house doin also like unto JAH commanded him. [16] An that Meqabees returned him body toward worshippin JAH - an him downstroyed from him house the idols an also the sorcery - persons who worship idols as pessimists an magicians. [17] An mornin an evenin like unto them faadas do - him would examine the childran him captured an brought from 'Iyerusaliem ina all JAH Commands an Him Order an Him LAW. [18] An from the childran him captured - him appointed knowin ones pon him house. [19] An again from the infants him appointed knowin childran who keep levelled childran who were small - who enter toward the beddin that them might teach them JAH LAW that 'Isra'iel childran do ~ him would hear from captured 'Isra'iel childran the Order an the LAW an the Nine Laws - that Mo`ab persons order an them mosques that them mek were vain. [20] Him downstroyed them mosques - them idols an them sorcery - an the sacrifice an the grapes sacrificed fe the idols mornin an evenin from the goat kids an fattened sheeps flocks. [21] An him downstroyed him idols whom him worship an beg an believe ina all him Work while him sacrificed sacrifice afternoon an at noon - an fe all priests told him - an him idols fe whom him do them accord. [22] As it would seem fe him that them save him ina all that them told - him wouldn't scorn all the thing them told him. [23] But that Meqabees quit them Work. [24] After him heard the Ra`ay thing - whom them call a prophet - him accomplished him Work ina repentance ~ as 'Isra'iel childran would sadden Him at one time - an pon the time Him chastised them ina the tribulation - as them know an also cry toward JAH - all Him kindreds worked goodly Work more than 'Isra'iel childran ina that season. [25] Pon the time Him heard that them were seized an abused by peoples hand who firm up tribulation pon them an that them cried toward Him - Him thought of them faadas oath an at that time Him would forgive them becau them faadas Yis'haq - 'Abriham - an Ya`iqob. [26] An pon the time Him saved them - them would forget JAH Who saved them from tribulation - an them would return toward worshippin the idols. [27] An at that time Him would arouse pon them peoples who firm up tribulation pon them - an pon the time them firmed up tribulation pon them an saddened them - them would cry toward JAH ~ as Him love them becau them were Him Itority Iration - at that time Him would be nice an forgive them. [28] An pon the time Him kept them - them again returned toward sin that them might sadden Him by them hands Work that were firm an by worshippin idols ina them councils. [29] But Him would arouse pon them Mo`ab an 'Iloflee - Sorya - Midyam an Gibts persons; an pon the time them enemies defeated them - them would cry an weep ~ pon the time them firmed up pon them an taxed them an ruled them - JAH would arouse princes fe them that Him might save them pon the time Him loved. Chapter 4 [1] An ina 'Iyasu time are a day when Him saved them. [2] An ina Giediewon time are a day when Him saved them. [3] An ina Somson time an ina Deebora an Bariq an Yodeet time are a day when Him saved them - an lodgin whether pon male or pon dawta - Him would arouse princes fe them that them might save them from them enemies hands who firm up tribulation pon them. [4] An like unto JAH loved - Him would save them from persons who firm up tribulation pon them. [5] An them would be totally Irie ina all the Work that Him accomplished fe them ~ them would be Irie ina them land seed an ina multiplyin all them flocks ina wilderness an them livestock. [6] An Him would bless them plants an them livestock fe them - fe Him sight them up ina Eye of Mercy - an fe Him wouldn't diminish them livestock pon them - fe them are kind persons childran an Him would totally love them. [7] But pon the time them were evil ina them Work - Him would cast them ina them enemies hands. [8] An pon the time Him downstroyed them - them would seek Him ina worship - an them would return from sin an march toward JAH ina repentance. [9] An pon the time them returned ina them complete

reasonin - Him would atone them sin fe them ~ Him wouldn't think of them former sin pon them - fe Him know them that them were flesh an blood - fe them have this world misleadin thoughts pon them - an fe them have demons ina them. [10] But pon the time that Meqabees heard this Order that JAH worked ina Him worshippin place the Temple - him were slain ina repentance. [11] After him sight up an heard this - him didn't scorn workin goodly Work; him didn't scorn workin all the goodly Work that 'Isra'iel childran work pon the time JAH forgave them - an after them trespassed from Him LAW - them weep an would cry pon the time JAH whipped them - an again Him would forgive them - an them would keep Him LAW. [12] An Meqabees likewise would straighten up him Work - an him would keep Him LAW - an him would live firmed up ina 'Isra'iel Irator JAH Command. [13] At that time after him heard all the Work whereby 'Isra'iel childran boast - Him would boast like unto them ina keepin JAH LAW. [14] Him would urge him kindred an childran that them might live firmed up ina JAH Command an all Him LAW. [15] An him would forbid the order that 'Isra'iel forbid - an him would hear an keep the Law that 'Isra'iel keep - an when him kindred are another Mo`ab man - him would forbid the food that 'Isra'iel forbid. [16] An him would send forth tithes ~ him would give all that were first birthed an that him owned from him cows an him sheeps an him donkeys - an returnin him face toward 'Iyerusaliem him would sacrifice the sacrifice that 'Isra'iel sacrifice. [17] Him would sacrifice sin an vow sacrifices - a sacrifice whereby welfare are done an a accord sacrifice - an the Itinual sacrifice. [18] An him would give him first crops - an him would gush an pour the grapes that 'Isra'iel pour - an him would give this fe him priest whom him I pointed - an likewise him would do all that 'Isra'iel do - an him would sweeten him ishence. [19] Him built a candlestick an a bowl an a seat an a tent an the four links of rings - an diluted oil fe the Hola of Holas lamps - an the curtain that 'Isra'iel mek ina the Hola of Holas pon the time them served JAH. [20] An like unto them worked goodly Work pon the time them lived firmed up ina Him Order an Him LAW an pon the time JAH didn't neglect an cast them ina them enemies hands - Meqabees also would work goodly Work like unto them. [21] Him would beg toward 'Isra'iel Irator JAH everytime that Him might be him Teacher an lest Him separate him from 'Isra'iel childran whom Him chose an who did Him Accord. [22] An again him would beg Him that Him might give him childran ina Tsiyon an a house ina 'Iyerusaliem - that Him might give them Heavenly Seed of Virtue ina Tsiyon an a Heavenly House of Soul ina 'Iyerusaliem - an that Him might save him from the downstruction spoken by the prophet tongue - that Him might accept him repentance ina all the mournin him wept before JAH bein sad an enterin repentance... [23] an lest Him downstroy childran ina this world pon him - an that Him might keep him ina him proceedin an enterin. [24] Kindreds from Mo`ab peoples beneath Meqabees Itority were Irie fe them that them might believe - fe them chief live firmed up ina straight Work - an them would check up him judgemant an fulfill him accord - an them would scorn them country language an them country justice ~ them would overstand that Meqabees Work surpassed an were straight. [25] An them would come an hear Meqabees charity an Truth judgemants. [26] Him had much money ~ him had dawta slaves an male slaves an camels an donkeys - an him had five hundred horses that wear breastplates ~ him would totally defeat the 'Amalieqans an 'Iloflans an Sorya persons - but formerly when him worshipped idols him lived when them defeated him. [27] Him prevailed - yet but from him worshippin JAH onward - when him went toward battle there are none who defeated him. [28] But them would come ina them idols Power that them might fight him - an them would call them idols names an curse him - however there were none who defeat him - fe him have made him faith pon him Irator JAH. [29] An when him did thus an when him defeated him enemies - him lived when him ruled peoples ina him Itority. [30] Him would revenge an downstroy wronged persons enemy fe them ~ him would judge Truth fe a child whose mother an faada dead pon him. [31] An him would raceive widows ina them trouble time - an him would give from him food an satta them who hungered - an him would clothe the naked from him clothes. [32] An him would be Irie ina him hands Work - an him would give from the money him had without begrudgin - an him would give tithes fe the Temple ~ Meqabees dead havin lived ina Irie Ites when him did this. Chapter 5 [1] An him dead quittin him childran who were small - an them grew up like unto them faada taught them ~ them kept them house Order - an them would keep all them kindred - an them wouldn't mek poor ones cry - nor widows nor a child whose mother an faada dead pon him. [2] Them would fear JAH - an them would give them money alms fe poor ones - an them would keep all the trust them faada told them - an them would calm the child whose mother an faada dead pon them an widows ina them trouble time - an them would be them mother an faada ~ them would mek them cast from persons hand who wrong them - an calm them from all the downsturbance an sadness that found them. [3] Them lived five years while them did thus. [4] After this the Keledans king Tseerutsaydan came ~ him downstroyed all them country - an him captured Meqabees childran an downstroyed all them villages. [5] An him plundered all them money ~ them lived firmed up ina all evil Work an sin - ina adultery - insult an greed an not thinkin of them Irator - yet persons who don't live firmed up ina JAH LAW an Him Command an who worship idols seized them also an took them toward them country. [6] Them eat what a beast bit an the blood an the carcass - an what a scavenger beat an cast - all that JAH don't love - yet them have no order from all the true Commands written ina 'Oreet . [7] Them don't know JAH them Irator - Who sent them forth from them mothers wombs an fed them by what are due - were them Medicine. [8] Them marry from them aunt an them faada wife - them step mother - an them go toward robbery an evil thing an sin an adultery - yet them have no order ina Judgemant time - an them work all evil Work an them marry them aunts an them sistren an them have no LAW. [9] An all them roads are dark an slippery - an them Work are sin an adultery. [10] But those Meqabees childran would keep ina all them Order ~ them wouldn't eat what a scavenger beat nor what dead an lodged ~ them wouldn't work all the Work that the Keledans childran work - fe them many Works are evil that weren't written ina this book - that sinners work - an doubters an criminals - betrayers totally filled of robbery an sin an pagans childran. [11] All the Work them Irator JAH love aren't there alongside them. [12] An again them would worship a idol called Bi'iel Fiegor ~ them would trust it like unto them Irator JAH when it were deaf an dumb. Fe it are the idol that a person hand worked - fe it are the person hand Work that a smith would worked who work silver an gold - that have no breath nor knowledge - an it had nothing that it sight up nor hear. [13] It don't eat nor drink. [14] It don't kill nor save. [15] It don't plant nor uproot. [16] It don't harm it enemy nor benefit it friend. [17] It don't impoverish nor honour. [18] It will be a hindrance fe mislead the Keledans persons who were lazy - yet it don't chastise nor forgive. Chapter 6 [1] JAH enemy Tseerutsaydan who were arrogant appointed them who veil an falsehood priests fe him idols. [2] Him would sacrifice sacrifice fe them an pour the grapes fe them. [3] An it would seem fe him that them eat an drink. [4] An while it dawned him would give them cows an donkeys an heifers - an him would sacrifice sacrifice mornin an evenin - an him would eat from that defouled sacrifice. [5] An again him would downsturb an obligate other persons that them might sacrifice fe him idols - yet it weren't that only them do it. [6] Pon the time them sight up Meqabees childran that them were handsome an that them worship them Irator JAH - the idols priests loved that them might mislead them fe sacrifice sacrifice an fe eat from that hated sacrifice - but these honoured Meqabees childran refused them. [7] As them keep them faada command - an as them have firmed up ina workin goodly Work - an as them totally fear JAH - it failed them fe agree... [8] pon the time them bound them an insulted them an robbed them. [9] Them told fe the king Tseerutsaydan that them refused sacrifice an bowin fe him idols. [10] An becaudis thing the king vexed ~ him were sad an commanded that them might bring them - an them brought an stood them before him - an the king told them fe him idols - "Sacrifice a sacrifice fe mi idols." [11] An them spoke an told him - "An InI won't answer thee ina this thing - an InI won't sacrifice sacrifice fe thy defouled idols." [12] Him frightened them by Works that abounded - yet him couldn't able fe them - fe them have disciplined them reasonins believin ina JAH. [13] Him flamed a fiyah an cast them ina fiyah - an them gave them bodies fe JAH. [14] After them dead them arose an were sight up fe him at night drawin them swords when him had reclined pon him lordship throne - an him totally feared. [15] "Mi sirs - tell mi alright - what should mi do fe unu? Don't tek mi body ina death - that mi might do all thou commanded mi." [16] Them told him all that are due fe him while them said - "Think that JAH were thy Irator - an JAH are there Who shall dismiss from this thy kingdom where thou are arrogant - an Who shall lower thee toward Gehannem of Fiyah with thy faada Deeyablos ~ when InI worshipped InI Irator JAH without a iniquity livin that InI wronged thee - an when InI bowed fe Him ina fearin Him JAHness - like unto thou burned InI ina fiyah - thou will finish all thy hardship by that also. [17] Fe Him are Who Irated all - Earth an Heaven an sea an all that are within she. [18] An fe Him are Who Irated moon an Sun an stars - an fe Him Who Irated all the Iration are JAH. [19] Fe there are no other irator withou Him ina Earth nor Heaven - fe Him are Who able fe all - an fe there are nothing that fail Him. As Him are Who kill an Who save - Who whip ina tribulation an Who forgive - when InI bowed fe Him ina fearin JAH - like unto thou burned InI ina fiyah - thou will finish thy hardship by that" them told him. [20] "As Him are Who rule Earth an Heaven - there are none who escape from Him Itority. [21] There are none from the Iration Him Irated who departed from Him Command - apart from thou who are a criminal - an criminals like unto thee whose reasonins thy faada Seythan hid - an thou an those thy priests an thy idols will downscend together toward Gehannem where are no exits up til Iternity. [22] Thy teacher are Seythan who taught thee this evil Work that thou might do a evil thing pon InI - yet as it aren't only thou who do this - unu will downscend toward Gehannem together. [23] Fe thou mek thy ras self like unto thy Irator JAH - yet thou didn't know JAH Who Irated thee. [24] An thou are arrogant ina thy idols an thy hand Work up til JAH mek thee wretched ~ Him shall canvict thee pon all thy sin an iniquity that thou worked ina this world. Chapter 7 [1] Woe fe unu who don't know JAH Who Irated unu - fe thy idols who are like unto thee - an fe thee - an fe unu have that unu might regret a regrets that won't profit pon the time unu were sad bein seized ina See'ol difficulty - an woe

fe thee - fe unu who don't keep Him Word an Him LAW. [2] Unu will have no exit from she up til Iternity - thy priests an thou who sacrifice fe them like unto your Irator JAH - fe thy idols who have no breath nor soul - who won't revenge an downstroy him who did a evil thing pon them - nor do a goodly thing fe him who did a goodly thing fe them. [3] Woe fe unu who sacrifice fe them - fe them are a person hands Work where Seythan live - lodgin there fe mislead lazy ones reasonin like unto thee - that him might lower unu toward Gehannem of Fiyah - an the priests who serve demons commanded fe unu an your idols. [4] As unu don't know that there are nothing that will profit unu - unu wrong an err. [5] As fe the animals that JAH Irated fe be food fe unu - an dogs an beasts - them are better than unu - fe besides one death there are no more condemnation pon them. [6] But as unu will dead an receive hardship ina Gehannem Fiyah where are no exits up til Iternity - animals are better." [7] Havin spoken this - them went an were hidden from him. [8] But that Tseerutsaydan lodged when him trembled - seized by a firm fright - an fright didn't quit him up til it dawned. Chapter 8 [1] An him lived firmed up ina reasonin malice an arrogance. [2] An as iron have been called firm - like unto Dan'iel sight it up pon him kingdom - him turned ina peoples countries ina him area. [3] Him lived firmed up ina evil an all him laziness an ina downsturbin persons. [4] An him totally downstroy what InI spoke formerly - an him eat a person money. [5] Fe him are diligent fe evil like unto him faada Deeyablos who firmed up him collar of reasonin - an him downstroy what remained with him army. [6] Him say - "Mi era became like unto the Sun era" - yet him don't know JAH that Him were him Irator. [7] An ina him reasonin him think that the Sun are found from him. [8] Him arise in Power - him camp ina Tribe of Zablon lot an begin a formation ina Meqiedonya - an him receive him food from Semarya - an them give him presents from Semarya. [9] Him camp ina nomads region - an him reach up til Seedona - an him cast a tax pon 'Akayya - an him elevate him collar of reasonin up til the flowin sea - an him return an send messengers up til Hindekie sea. [10] An likewise him elevate him collar of reasonin up til Heaven. [11] An him live firmed up ina bein arrogant an ina evil - yet him don't have humblin him ras self. [12] An him path are toward darkness an slipperiness - an toward crime an bein arrogant - an toward sheddin blood an tribulation. [13] An all him Work are what JAH hate ~ him do like unto robbery an evil an sin teacher Deeyablos taught him ~ him mek a child cry whose mother an faada dead pon him - an him aren't nice fe a poor one. [14] An him defeated an downstroyed peoples kings by him authority. [15] An him ruled enemies chiefs - an him ruled many peoples - an him taxed them like unto him loved. [16] Even if him downstroyed - him didn't quit ~ there are no person whom him didn't snatch Iginnin from Tersies sea up til 'Iyareeko sea. [17] Him would bow fe idols ~ him would eat what dead an lodged - the blood - what a sword bloated an cut - an what were sacrificed fe idols ~ all him Work are without justice - yet him have no justice ~ as him have been who alarm peoples beneath him authority - him would tax them tax like unto him loved. [18] As him do all that him loved before him - there are no fearin JAH before him - an him live ina malice before JAH Who Irated him. [19] Him didn't do it like unto him Irator - an like unto him did a evil thing pon him companion pon the time him vexed an seized him - JAH shall also pay him him hardship. [20] As JAH have said - I-man shall revenge an downstroy sinner persons who don't live by I Command - that I-man might downstroy them name invocation from this world - like unto Him downstroyed peoples who were precedin him - Him shall revenge an downstroy him pon the time when Him downstroy. [21] An like unto evil persons did evil things - them shall receive them hardship. [22] But bein commanded from JAH - goodly Work shall follow persons who work goodly Work. [23] Fe like unto 'Iyasu downstroyed the five Kene`an kings ina cave ina one day - an like unto him made Sun stand ina Geba`on by him priah that him might downstroy them armies - Sun have stood amidst Heaven up til him downstroyed 'Ewiewon an Kenaniewon - Fierziewon an Kiethiewon an 'Iyabusiewon armies - an like unto him killed around twenty thousand persons at one time - an like unto him killed them - an like unto him bound them makin foot from neck - an like unto him killed them ina cave by spear - an like unto him fitted a stone pon them... [24] Tribulation like unto this shall find all persons who sadden JAH ina them evil Work. Chapter 9 [1] "O thou weak man who aren't LAW - why are thou proud? thou who are sight up today bein a man are Earth ashes tomorrow - an thou will totally be worms ina thy grave. [2] Fe thy teacher are Deeyablos who return all persons sin hardship toward him ras self becau him misled InI faada 'Adam - an See'ol will find thee again - an she will find persons who work thy sin. [3] Fe ina firmin up him collar of reasonin an makin him ras self proud - like unto him refused fe bow fe 'Adam whom the Irator Irated... [4] thou also have refused fe bow fe thy Irator JAH like unto thy teacher Deeyablos did. [5] Like unto thy precedin faadas - who don't know them Irator JAH ina worship - will go toward Gehannem - thou also will go toward Gehannem . [6] Like unto Him revenged an downstroyed them becau them evil Work that them worked ina this world - an like unto them downscended toward Gehannem ... [7] thou also will downscend toward Gehannem like unto them. [8] As thou have aroused Him anger - an as thou have neglected fe worship JAH Who gave thee Itority pon the five kingdoms - do it seem fe thee that thou will escape from JAH Itority? [9] Thou don't do thus that thou do Him Accord - thus Him examined thee - but if thou work goodly Work ina this world - JAH will accomplish all thy Work fe thee-I - an Him will accomplish an bless all the Work thou seized ina thy hand fe thee-I - an Him will subject thy Antiquity of enemies an thy day enemies fe thee-I [10] Thou will be Irie ina thy enterins an thy proceedins an ina thy child birthed from thy nature - an ina thy flocks an thy fatnesses - an ina all Work where thou placed thy hand - an ina all that thou thought ina thy heart ~ as Itority have been given thee-I from alongside JAH that thou might do thus an might work an plant an demolish - all will be commanded fe thee-I. [11] However if thou won't hear JAH Word nor live firmed up ina Him LAW - like unto criminals who were precedin thee - an who don't worship JAH by what are due - an who didn't believe firmed up ina HIM straight LAW - there are nothing whereby thou will escape from JAH Itority - fe JAH Judgemant are Truth. [12] All are totally revealed before Him - yet there are nothing hidden from before Him. [13] Him are Who seize the kings Itority an Who overturn powerful ones thrones. [14] Him are Who Ilivate them who were downbased an Who lift up them who fell. [15] Him are Who loose them who were bound an Who arouse them who dead ~ as pardon dew are found from alongside Him - pon the time Him loved Him shall arouse persons whose flesh were demolished an rotten an were like unto dust. [16] An havin aroused an judged persons who worked evil Work - Him will tek them toward Gehannem - fe them have saddened Him. [17] Fe them are who demolished JAH Order an Him LAW - an Him will downstroy them child from this world. [18] As kind persons Work are more difficult than sinner persons Work - sinner persons don't love that them might live ina kind persons counsel. [19] Like unto Heavens were distanced from Earth - likewise kind persons Work were distanced from evil persons Work. [20] But sinner persons Work are robbery an sin - adultery an iniquity - greed an perfidy Work ~ it are bein drunk ina iniquity an robbin a person money. [21] It are quickly goin toward sheddin a person blood - an it are goin toward downstruction that don't benefit - an it are makin a child weep whose mother an faada dead pon him ~ it are eatin blood an what dead an lodged - an it are eatin camel an boar flesh - an it are goin toward a dawta ina she blood before she are cleansed - an toward a dawta ina childbirth. [22] All this are sinner persons Work ~ she are Seythan trap that were a wide an prepared path - an that tek toward Gehannem that live firmed up foriva - an toward See'ol . [23] But righteous ones path that were totally narrow are what tek toward welfare - an innocence an humbleness - an Inity an Love - an priah an fast - an flesh purity - toward keepin from what don't benefit - from eatin what a sword bloated an cut an what dead an lodged - an from goin toward a youtmon wife an from adultery. [24] Them keep from what weren't commanded by LAW - from eatin disgustin food an from all hated Work - an from all the Work that JAH don't love - fe sinner persons do all this. [25] As fe kind persons - them distance from all the Work that JAH don't love. [26] Him love them an shall keep them from all them tribulation like unto Trust money. [27] Fe them keep Him Order an Him LAW an all that Him love - but Seythan rule sinner persons. Chapter 10 [1] Fear JAH Who Irated unu an kept unu up til today - yet unu the nobles an the kings - don't go pon Seythan path. [2] Live ina the LAW an Command of JAH Who rule all - yet don't go pon Seythan path. [3] As pon the time 'Isra'iel childran came toward 'Amalieq that them might inherit Kiethiewon an Kenaniewon an Fierziewon country - Siefor child Balaq an Bele`am... [4] whom thou cursed are cursed - an him whom thou blessed blessed ~ don't go pon Seythan road - fe him have said - "An mi will give thee much silver an gold that honour thee - that thou might curse fe mi an - an havin cursed - that thou might downstroy fe mi." [5] An fe Bele`am have come makin him sorcery reward a morale - an fe Siefor child Balaq have shown him the place where 'Isra'iel childran camped. [6] Fe him have done him pessimism - an fe him have sacrificed him sacrifice - an fe him have slaughtered from him fattened cows an sheeps - an fe him have loved that him might curse an downstroy 'Isra'iel childran. [7] Him returned a curse toward a bless - yet but as JAH didn't love that him might curse them by Him Word - don't go pon Seythan road. [8] "As thou are the kindred that JAH chose - as thou are JAH Lodgin that shall come from Heaven - mek persons be cursed who curse thee-I - an mek persons who bless thee-I be blessed" him said. [9] Pon the time him blessed them before him - after this Siefor child Balaq were sad - an him totally vexed an commanded that him might curse them. [10] Fe the kindred that JAH blessed have come toward this country - an Bele`am told him - "Mi won't curse 'Isra'iel whom JAH blessed." [11] An Siefor child Balaq told Bele`am - "As fe mi - mi had loved that thou might curse fe mi ~ thou blessed them before mi - yet but thou didn't curse them ~ if thou had cursed fe mi an told mi 'Give mi' - as fe mi - mi would have given thee a house full of silver an gold - but thou totally blessed them - an thou didn't do a goodly thing fe mi - an mi won't do a goodly thing fe thee." [12] Bele`am said - "What JAH told mi Speak with mi tongue - mi will speak it - yet as fe mi - mi cyaan dare fe ignore JAH thing. [13] Lest mi curse a blessed kindred - as JAH shall vex pon mi if mi love money - as fe mi - mi don't love money more than mi soul. [14] As JAH have told them faada Ya`iqob - Mek persons who bless thee-I be blessed an mek persons who curse thee-I be cursed - lest mi curse blessed Ya`iqob - as fe

mi - mi don't love money more than mi soul" him said - an as JAH have told him - Him who bless thee-I are blessed... [15] an a person who curse thee-I unjustly are cursed - accomplish thy path an thy Work that JAH might love thee. [16] An don't be like unto former persons who saddened JAH ina them sin an whom Him neglected - an there are them whom Him downstroyed ina Downstruction Water. [17] An there are them whom Him downstroyed by them haters hands ~ there are them whom Him downstroyed by them enemies hands - bringin enemies who were evil persons who firmed up tribulation pon them - an them captured them lords with them priests an them prophets. [18] An them delivered them toward the foreign country them don't know ~ them totally captured them - an them plundered them livestocks pon them an downstroyed them country. [19] Fe them have demolished the honoured country 'Iyerusaliem fences an ramparts - an them made 'Iyerusaliem like unto a field. [20] An the priests were capture - an the LAW were demolished - an warriors fought ina war an fell. [21] An widows were capture ~ as them have been capture - them wept fe them ras selves - yet them didn't weep fe them husbands who dead. [22] An the childran wept - an elders shamed - an them weren't nice fe neither a grey haired person nor a elder. [23] Them downstroyed all them found ina the country - yet them weren't nice fe beauties nor fe them ina LAW ~ as JAH have vexed pon Him kindreds pon the time Him loved that Him might beforehand downstroy Him Lodgin the Temple - them captured an took them toward the country them don't know an toward peoples. [24] As them sadden them Irator everytime - becaudis thing pon the time JAH neglected 'Isra'iel childran - JAH made 'Iyerusaliem fe be ploughed like unto a field. [25] Fe Him are nice fe them becau them faadas - but Him didn't downstroy them at one time ~ as Him love them faadas Yis'haq an 'Abriham an Ya`iqob who reigned fe true an lived firmed up ina straight LAW before them Irator - it are becau them faadas kindness - yet it aren't becau them ras selves kindness that him forgive them. [26] An Him I-pointed them pon honours that were twofold - an them found two Kingdoms - pon Earth an ina Heaven. [27] An unu the kings an the nobles who live ina this passin world - like unto your faadas who lived firmed up ina Work that are due an who were precedin unu likewise inherited the Kingdom of Heaven - an like unto them names were beautiful fe a child childran - think of them. [28] An thou - straighten up thy Work - that Him might straighten up thy Kingdom fe thee - an that thy name might be called ina goodly invocation like unto the kind kings who were precedin thee who served JAH ina them beautiful lifestyle. Chapter 11 [1] Think of JAH slave Mussie who weren't annoyed when him kept around this kindred ina him humbleness an him priah an whom not even one person downstroyed - an him begged toward JAH ina him innocence fe him sista an bredda who backbit him an loved that JAH might downstroy them while him said - "As them have wronged Thee-I - Lord - pardon an don't neglect thy kindreds" - an him atoned them sin fe them - yet Him thought of JAH servant Mussie who weren't annoyed. [2] "Fe I-man have wronged Thee-I - an forgive I Thy slave who am a sinner - fe Thou are Merciful - an fe Thou are a Pardoner - an forgive them him sin." [3] An Mussie likewise atoned them sin fe him sista an bredda who backbit him. [4] An becaudis thing him were called innocent. [5] An JAH totally loved him more than all the priests childran who were him bredren - fe Him I-point the priests - an JAH made him like unto Him Ras Self alongside them. [6] But Him also sank beneath Earth Qorie childran who challenged ~ Him lowered them toward See'ol with them livestocks an them tents when them said "Wi are there - wi are there ina flesh an soul" ~ as him Irator JAH have loved him - an as him didn't depart from Him Command - all the word him spoke would be done fe him like unto JAH Word. [7] An unless thou demolished JAH Command likewise - JAH will do thy accord fe thee-I an will love thy thing fe thee-I - an Him will keep thy Kingdom fe thee-I. [8] An 'Asaf an Qorie childran who departed from Mussie command grumbled pon him becau him told them - "Straighten up your reasonins fe be ruled fe JAH." [9] Them grumbled sayin - "How about aren't wi Liewee childran who work priesthood Work ina Tent that were special?" [10] Them went an smoked up ishence seizin them censers that them might smoke up - but JAH didn't accept them plea - an them were burnt by the fiyah ina them censers - an them melted like unto the wax that fiyah melt - an not even one person remained from them ~ as Him have said - Them censers were honoured by them bodies bein burnt - apart from them censers that entered toward JAH Lodgin fe JAH Command - neither them clothes nor them bones remained. [11] Becaudis thing JAH told 'Aron an Mussie - Gather them censers toward the Tent ~ mek it be a instrumant fe I Lodgin wherefor I-man prepared all I-ginnin from outside up til within. [12] An him prepared the honoured Tent instrumants ~ him prepared the rings an the joiners - Keerubiel picture sea. [13] Him worked the cups - the curtains - the Tent area grounds fe the mobilisation - the altar an the jugs whereby them sacrifice ina the Tent that were special. [14] Them sacrificed the sacrifice that them sacrifice by them accord - the sacrifice whereby welfare are made - the sacrifice whereby Him atone sin - an the vow sacrifice an the mornin an the evenin sacrifice. [15] All that Him commanded fe Mussie - him commanded them ina the Tent that were special - that them might work Work ina she. [16] Them didn't scorn bein ruled fe them Irator JAH - that Him Name might be praised by them ina the LAW Lodgin Tent of them Irator JAH Who gave them a promise that Him might give them fe give them them faadas inheritance that produce honey an milk that Him swore fe 'Abriham. [17] Them didn't scorn bein ruled fe them Irator JAH - Who swore fe Yis'haq an firmed up Him Worship fe Ya`iqob... [18] an Who firmed up fe 'Aron an Mussie the Tent where Him Worship are kept... [19] an Who firmed up Him Worship fe both 'Elyas an Samu'iel ina the Temple an Tent that Selomon worked up til it became JAH Lodgin ina 'Iyerusaliem - an up til JAH Name Lodgin became JAH Lodgin that honoured 'Isra'iel. [20] Fe she are a supplication - an fe she are a sin atonemant where it are overturned fe them who live ina innocence an fe the priests. [21] An fe she are a place fe persons who do Him Accord where Him will hear them pleas... [22] an JAH LAW Canstruction that honoured 'Isra'iel. [23] Fe she are where sacrifice are sacrificed an where Ishence are smoked up that JAH Who honoured 'Isra'iel be ina goodly Fragrance. [24] An Him would speak bein pon the joiner where Him forgive ina the Tent that were special ~ JAH Light would be revealed fe Ya`iqob childran whom Him chose an fe friends who live firmed up ina Him LAW an Him Command. [25] But persons who ignored JAH LAW will be like unto Qorie childran whom Earth sank - an likewise sinner persons have that them might enter toward Gehannem that have no exits up til Iternity. Chapter 12 [1] Unu who didn't keep the LAW Him commanded unu ina Tent - woe fe unu 'Isra'iel nobles who also didn't do Him Accord - yet unu did your ras selves accord - an this are bein arrogant an pride - greed an adultery - drink an bein drunk - an swearin ina lie. [2] An becaudis thing I anger - like unto chaff are burnt before a fiyah - an like unto fiyah burn the mountain - an like unto a whirl wind spill the crushed chaff from Earth an scattar it toward Heaven - lest it trace be found ina it place - I anger will downstroy unu like unto that. [3] JAH Who honoured 'Isra'iel said - I-man shall likewise downstroy all persons who work sin - an think of JAH Who rule all an fe Whom nothing fail. [4] Him love persons who love Him - an fe persons who live firmed up ina Him Command - Him will atone them iniquity an them sin fe them ~ don't be dull an stingy of heart by not believin. [5] An mek your reasonins straight fe be ruled fe JAH - an believe ina Him that unu might firm up your bodies - an I-man shall save unu from your enemy hand ina your tribulation day. [6] An ina your plea time I-man tell unu - Check - I-man am there with unu ina Support ~ I-man shall save unu from your enemy hand ~ as unu have believed ina I - an as unu have done I Command - an as unu didn't depart from I LAW - an as unu have loved what I-man love - JAH Who rule all said - I-man won't neglect unu pon your tribulation day. [7] Him love them who love Him - fe Him are a Pardoner - an fe Him are nice - an Him keep persons who keep Him LAW - like unto a trust money. [8] Him return Him anger fe them many times ~ becau Him were who know them that them are flesh an blood - as Him are a Pardoner - Him didn't downstroy all ina Him chastisemant - an pon the time them souls were separated from them flesh - them will return toward them Earthliness. [9] As Him have Irated them bringin from not livin toward livin - them won't know the place where them live up til JAH love that Him might bring them from not livin toward livin ~ again Him separated them souls from them flesh - an Earth nature returned toward it Earthliness. [10] An again Him Accord shall bring them from not livin toward livin." [11] But Tseerutsaydan who denied JAH multiplied bein arrogant before JAH ~ him made him ras self lofty up til the day that him loved pon the time him quit Him. [12] "An mi era became like unto Heaven era - an mi are who send forth Sun - an mi won't dead up til Iternity" him said. [13] An before him finished speakin this thing the Angel of Death whose name are called Thilimyakos alit an struck him heart ~ him dead ina that iwa ~ as him didn't praise him Irator - him were separated from him beautiful lifestyle an him perished arisin from him arrogance abundance an him Work evil. [14] But when the Keledans king army had camped ina the city an the country squares lovin fe fight him - pon the time him dead - them proceeded an downstroyed him country ~ them plundered all him livestock - an them didn't preserve a elder who near an sight up ramparts. [15] Them plundered all him money - an them took him tiny money - an them burned him country ina fiyah an returned toward them country. Chapter 13 [1] But these five Meqabees childran who believed gave them bodies fe death refusin fe eat the sacrifice sacrificed fe idols. [2] Fe them have known that pretendin with JAH surpass from pretendin with persons - an JAH anger from the king anger. [3] Havin known that this world will totally pass an that the Irie Ites won't live firmed up foriva - them gave them bodies fe fiyah that them might be saved from fiyah ina Heaven. [4] An as them have known that bein made Irie ina Garden one day are better than livin many eras ina this world - an that findin Thy Pardon one iwa Lord - are better than many eras - them gave them bodies fe fiyah. [5] What are InI era? Like unto a shadow - like unto passin wax melt an perish pon a fiyah edge - aren't it like unto that? [6] But Thou Lord live foriva - an Thy Era aren't fulfilled - an Thy Name invocation are fe a child childran. [7] An Meqabees childran thought that it seemed all this ~ refusin fe eat a disgustin sacrifice them chose believin ina JAH. [8] Knowin that them will arise with persons who dead - an meanin becau JAH - knowin that Judgemant shall be judged after Resurrection of Council - becaudis thing them gave them bodies fe martyrdom. [9] Unu persons who don't know nor believe

persons who dead risin - knowin that the Life them find later will surpass from this them passin Earthly Life - arisin from these five Meqabees childran who gave them bodies together fe the death and whose appearance were handsome - after this them knew Resurrection. [10] Becau them believed ina Him knowin that all shall pass - an becau them didn't bow fe idols - becau them didn't eat a disgustin sacrifice that don't give Support - them gave them bodies fe death that them might find thanks from JAH. [11] Fe becaudis thing knowin that Him will mek them Irie ina flesh an soul ina later era - them didn't know this world flavour an death tribulation a serious thing fe them who have child an wife - an knowin that Resurrection be made ina flesh an soul pon the Day of Advent - them gave them bodies fe death. [12] An knowin that persons who kept JAH LAW - with the nobles an the kings who believed JAH Word an were nice... [13] shall live reignin fe a child childran many eras ina Kingdom of Heaven where are no sadness an tribulation nor death - an knowin ina them reasonins what will be done later - like unto wax melt amidst a fiyah - becaudis thing them gave them bodies fe death. [14] Believin that them faces will shine seven hands more than the Sun - an that them will be Irie ina Him Love pon the time all arose ina flesh an soul - them gave them bodies fe death. Chapter 14 [1] But the Samrans an 'Ayhuds thing - the Seduqans who don't believe persons who dead risin - an the Fereesans thing quite totally sadden I - an it help I fe I reasonin ~ "Wi will dead tomorrow" 'Ayhuds say - "Mek wi eat an drink ~ wi will dead tomorrow ~ there are no Irie Ites wi will sight up ina grave." [2] But the Samrans say - "As wi flesh will be dust - it won't arise. [3] Becau she were invisible like unto wind an like unto iyunder voice - check - she are here - an becau she were what them don't call an invisible - as soul won't arise if flesh dead - pon the time Resurrection are done wi will believe wi souls arisin. [4] But as beasts will eat she an as worms will eat she ina the grave - wi flesh are sight up alongside all ~ she will become dust an ashes. [5] An those beasts who ate she will become dust - fe them have been like unto grass - an fe them have become dust like unto them weren't irated - an fe them trace won't be found - but wi flesh won't arise." [6] An the Fereesans say - "Wi believe as fe persons who dead arisin - however Him will bring an Inite souls with another flesh that are ina Heaven - that aren't pon Earth ~ where will demolished an rotten fleshes be found?" [7] But the Seduqans say - "After wi soul proceeded from wi flesh - wi won't arise with persons who dead - an flesh an soul have no arisin after them dead - an after wi dead wi won't arise." [8] An becaudis thing them totally err - an as them speak insult pon JAH Lordship - them thing sadden I. [9] As them didn't believe JAH Who honour them - them have no hope fe be saved - however them have no hope fe dead an arise an be saved. [10] O 'Ayhudan who are blind of reasonin - when thou are whom Him Irated bringin from not livin toward livin - an scorned like unto spit - will thou mek JAH ignorant - Who made thee a person? Will it fail JAH Who Irated thee ina Him Example an Him Appearance fe arouse Initin thy flesh an thy soul? [11] As thou won't escape from JAH Itority - don't think a thing that are thus ~ thou will arise without thou lovin - fe there are the hardship thou will raceive ina See'ol where thou were seized pon the time thou dead - an it shall be judged pon thee without thou lovin. [12] Fe the sin found from demons that demons place ina thy reasonin are worked alongside thee after thou were birthed from thy mother womb - an fe she are worked abundantly pon the time thou grew up. [13] Them place she ina thy body pon the time thou dead - an she will bring hardship pon them pon the time them worked she. [14] Like unto there are sin ina them collar of reasonin - as there are persons who work sin bein seized by she - she kindreds will present demons. [15] All sinner persons souls shall come from Heaven edge where them are - an thy sin likewise shall introduce thee toward Gehannem pullin an bringin thy soul from where thou are. [16] An after thy flesh lived separate from thy soul - JAH Charity dew shall arouse thee bein seven fold like unto InI faada 'Adam flesh. [17] Thou who live ina grave - thou also err ina thy error - yet mek it not seem fe thee that thou only mislead the others ~ thou say - "The arisin that persons who dead shall arise aren't there" - that them might depart from JAH Command an err. [18] Him shall arouse thee that Him might give thee thy hardship like unto thy Work that thou worked - yet who shall quit thee that thou might remain bein dust? [19] But at that time - whether wind ina wind be thy nature - or if Water ina Water be thy nature - or if Earth ina Earth be thy nature - or if fiyah ina fiyah be thy nature - it shall come. [20] An if a soul that lodged ina thee be what lived ina See'ol - she shall come. [21] An righteous ones souls that live ina Garden ina Ites shall come. [22] But thou 'Ayhudan - Samran - Fereesan - Seduqan - will live ina See'ol up til it are judged pon thee. [23] At that time thou will sight up that JAH shall pay thee the hardship like unto thy sin becau thou misled persons. [24] "Persons who dead won't arise ~ as wi will dead - mek wi eat an drink" - an becau thou sat ina Mussie chair an misled by thy words while thou said - "Persons who dead won't arise" - thou will sight up that Him shall pay thee thy hardship. [25] An without thy knowin 'Oreet Book - an when thou teach the books word - becaudis thing thou erred ~ it would be better had thou remained without learnin from thy misleadin a person. [26] It would have been better if thou didn't know the books word - when thou promulgate JAH kindreds ina thy evil teachin an thy worthless words. [27] Fe JAH don't favour havin sight up a face - an fe Him shall give the grace an glory Him prepared fe Him friends - persons who teach goodly Work - but thou have that thou might raceive thy reward like unto thy Work an the things that thou spoke. [28] But there are nothing whereby thou will escape from JAH Itority Who shall judge pon thee - an Him have that Him might pay thee like unto thy Work - fe them whom thou taught an thou together will raceive a sentance. [29] Know that persons who dead shall arise - an if them are persons who kept Him LAW them shall arise - an like unto Earth send forth grass pon the time rain rained - as Him Command shall send them forth from a grave - it aren't possible fe it fe remain demolished an rotten. [30] Like unto moist wood drink dew an send forth leaves pon the time Him satta she rain fe Earth - like unto wheat bear forth fruit - an like unto grain produce buds - like unto it aren't possible fe she fe withhold that she might prevent she fruit if JAH loved... [31] an like unto it aren't possible fe a dawta who canceived fe close an prevent she womb pon the time labour seized she - like unto it aren't possible fe she fe escape without birthin... [32] as dew have alit toward she bein commanded from JAH - at that time she shall produce them at one time - yet after she heard JAH Word - a grave also likewise cyaan prevent the persons gathered alongside she from arisin. [33] An fleshes shall be gathered ina the place where them corpses fell - an them places where souls live shall be opened - an souls shall return toward the flesh where them were formerly separated. [34] An pon the time a drum were beaten - persons who dead shall quickly arise like unto a eye wink - an havin arisen them shall stand before JAH - an Him shall give them them reward like unto them hand Work. [35] At that time thou will sight up that thou arise with dead ones - an thou will marvel at all the Work thou worked ina this world - an pon the time thou sight up all thy sins written before thee - at that time thou will regret a useless regret. [36] Thou know that thou will arise with dead ones an that thou will raceive thy hardship like unto the Work that thou worked. Chapter 15 [1] But persons who found them reward by them goodly Work shall be Irie at that time ~ persons who ignored while them said - "Persons who dead won't arise" shall be sad at that time pon the time them sight up that persons who dead arose with them evil Work that don't benefit. [2] That - them Work that them worked shall canvict them - an them ras selves shall know that it canvict them without one livin who will dispute them. [3] Pon the day when Judgemant an mournin are done - pon the day when JAH shall come - pon the day when Definite Judgemant are judged - persons who forgot JAH LAW shall stand ina the place where them stand. [4] Pon the day when there shall be total darkness - an pon the day when mist are pulled - pon the day when flashes are sight up an when lightnin are heard... [5] an pon the day when quakes an fright an heatwave an sleet frost are made... [6] pon the day when a evil person who worked evil Work raceive hardship - an pon the day when a clean person raceive him reward like unto him worked clean Work - an pon the day when persons who forgot JAH LAW raceive the hardship like unto a sinner person worked sin - them shall stand ina the place where them stand. [7] Fe pon the day when a master aren't more honoured than him slave - an pon the time when a mistress aren't more honoured than she slave... [8] an pon the time when the king aren't more honoured than a poor one - an pon the time when a elder aren't more honoured than a infant - pon the time when a faada aren't more honoured than him child - an pon the time when a mother aren't more honoured than she child... [9] pon the time when a wealthy one aren't more honoured than a poor one - an pon the time when a arrogant one aren't more honoured than a downbased one - an pon the time when the great aren't more honoured than the small - she are the day when Judgemant are judged - fe she are the day when them raceive sentance an hardship - an fe she are the day when all will raceive hardship like unto them worked sin. [10] An fe she are the day when persons who worked goodly Work raceive them reward - an fe she are the day when persons who worked sin raceive hardship. [11] An as she are the day when persons who found them reward are made Irie - persons who forgot JAH LAW shall stand ina the place where them stand. Persons who mek liars - who digest books while them said - "Persons who dead won't arise" - them shall sight up Resurrection. [12] At that time this world sinners - who didn't work goodly Work ina this world - shall weep pon them sin that them worked - becau sadness found them without calmin. [13] An all likewise - kind persons who worked goodly Work - them Irie Ites won't be fulfilled up til Iternity - fe them have worked goodly Work when them were ina this world. [14] Fe them have known that them will arise after them dead - an them didn't depart from them Irator LAW. [15] Becau them didn't depart from Him LAW - them shall inherit two welfares ~ Him multiplied them seed ina this world - an Him honoured them childran. [16] Him bequeathed them the Kingdom of Heaven where shall be found the welfare him swore fe them faadas pon the time when persons who dead arise - an pon the time when rich ones become poor. [17] Persons shall weep who worked sin - who don't believe persons who dead arisin - who don't keep JAH LAW - an who don't think of Arisin Day. [18] At that time them will sight up the tribulation that shall find them an shall have no endin - an where are no calmin nor welfare - an it have the sadness that have no rest nor calmin ina them reasonin. [19] An a fiyah that don't perish an worms that don't sleep shall find them. [20] An ina the place where are them flesh are fiyah - sulphur - whirl wind - frost - hail - sleet ~ all this shall rain over them. [21] Fe persons who don't believe persons who dead arisin - there are fiyah of Gehannem pon them. Chapter 16 [1] Thou - please think of what are pon thy flesh - an thy feet an thy hands nails - an thy head hair - fe them proceed quickly pon the time thou cut them ~ know Resurrection by this - that thou have a reasonin - an that thou have religion an knowledge. [2] Thy feet an thy hands nails an thy head hair - thou say - "Where do these come from?" ~ aren't it JAH Who prepared it that them might proceed - that thou know arisin that shall be done pon thy flesh that aren't pon another flesh - that thou might know that thou will arise after thou dead? [3] Becau thou misled persons while thou said - "There are no Resurrection of the dead ones" - pon the time when dead ones arise thou will raceive thy hardship like unto thou worked sin an iniquity. [4] An as even what thou planted now won't remain refusin that it might grow - whether it be wheat or barley - thou will sight she up pon the time the day arrived when thou raceive thy hardship. [5] An again - the plant thou planted won't say - "I-man won't grow" - an be it a fig wood or a grape vine - it fruit an it leaf won't be changed. [6] If thou plant grapes - it won't be changed that it might be a fig - an if thou plant figs - it won't be changed that it might be grapes - an if thou sow wheat it won't be changed that it might be barley. [7] All - ina each of the seeds - ina each of it kinds - each of the fruits - each of the woods - each of the leaves - each of the roots - send forth fruit havin raceived Pardon Dew blessin by what are found from JAH - yet if thou sow barley also it won't be changed that it might be wheat. [8] An all likewise - that a grave might produce flesh an soul - she shall produce persons like unto JAH sowed pon she ~ the flesh an soul that JAH sowed shall arise bein Inited - yet persons who worked goodly Work won't be changed ina persons who worked evil Work - an persons who worked evil Work also won't be changed ina persons who worked goodly Work. [9] Pon pon the time the iwa arrived when a drum are beaten - persons who dead shall arise by the Pardon Dew found from JAH ~ persons who worked goodly Work shall arise ina Life Resurrection - an them reward are the Garden where are Irie Ites that JAH prepared fe kind persons - where are no tribulation nor disease - an that are clean ones lodgin where them won't again dead after this. [10] But persons who worked evil Work shall arise a Definite Judgement arisin - an with Deeyablos who misled them... [11] an with him armies - demons who don't love that even one person might be saved from all 'Adam childran... [12] them shall downscend toward Gehannem that were darkness edge - where are tooth grindin an mournin - where are no charity nor pardon - an where are no exits up til Iternity - that are beneath See'ol foriva. Fe them didn't work goodly Work ina them Life ina this world when them were ina them flesh. [13] Becaudis thing it shall be judged pon them pon the time when flesh an soul arise bein Inited. [14] Woe fe persons who don't believe the flesh an soul arisin whereby JAH show Him miracles abundance together. [15] An all an each one shall raceive him reward like unto him Work an him hands weariness. Chapter 17 [1] A wheat kernel won't grow nor bear fruit unless she were demolished. But if a wheat kernel are demolished she will send roots toward Earth ~ she will send forth leaves ~ there will be buds ~ it will bear fruit. [2] Unu know that the one wheat kernel will become many kernels. [3] An all likewise - this kernel grow risin up from Water an wind an Earth dew - fe wheat cyaan bear fruit without Sun - but Sun are becau fiyah stead. [4] An wind are becau a soul stead - an wheat cyaan bear fruit without wind - an the Water give Earth fe drink an satta she. [5] An after Earth that are ashes drank Water - she produce roots - an she tips are lofty upward ~ she bear fruit around what JAH blessed she. [6] But a wheat kernel are 'Adam example - ina whom lodged a resonatin soul that JAH Irated - an likewise a grape wood drink Water an send forth roots - an the thin root kinds drink Water. [7] Fe Pardon Dew found from JAH give fe drink vines tips that were long - an it send the Water upward toward the leaf tips ~ it bud up from the Sun heat - an by JAH Accord it bear fruit. [8] It shall be a goodly fragrance that mek a reasonin Irie - an pon the time them ate it - it shall satta like unto Water that don't mek thirsty an grain that don't mek hungry - an pon the time them immersed it - it will be the cluster blood. [9] An like unto it were told ina Psalm sayin - "Grapes mek a person reasonin Irie" - pon the time them drank it - it mek a person heart Irie - an pon the time a person who came loose opened him mouth an drank it - him are drunk ~ him drink an fill ina him lungs - an the blood flow toward him heart. [10] As grapes drunkenness totally mislead - an as it deprive him him mind - it mek the pit an the cliff like unto a wide meadow - an him don't know obstacles an thorns pon him feet an hands. [11] JAH did thus pon she fruit an grape wood that Him Name might be praised by persons who believe dead persons arisin an who do Him Accord. [12] Ina the Kingdom of Heaven Him shall mek persons Irie who believe persons who dead arisin. Chapter 18 [1] Unu persons who don't believe persons who dead arisin - around what error unu err! An pon the time them took unu toward the place unu don't know - unu will regret a useless regrets - an becau unu didn't believe the arisin that persons who dead shall arise Inited ina soul an flesh - an pon the time persons cast unu toward Gehannem ... [2] if unu work whether the good or the evil - unu will raceive your reward like unto your Work - fe unu have misled them companions reasonin while unu said - "Wi know that persons who dead -

who were dust an ashes - won't arise." [3] As them death have no exit - an as them have no Power fe them chastisemant that shall come pon them - an as them weren't firm ina them tribulation - becaudis thing them mislead them companions ~ fe them have that them might stand ina JAH Square. [4] Pon the time Him vexed pon them ina Him wrath them will totally fear ~ becau them didn't know that them were Irated bringin from not livin toward livin - as them speak JAH LAW without knowin - it shall be judged pon them all becau them worked evil. [5] Them don't know Gehannem where them will go - fe becau them were angry an becau them were crooked ina them Work - them teach fe them companions like unto them reasonin thirst measure - an fe them are evil ones who teach a crooked thing while them said - "There are no Resurrection of dead ones." [6] At that time them shall know that persons who dead shall arise - an them shall know that it shall be judged pon them becau them didn't believe the persons who dead arisin that are fe all 'Adam childran. [7] Fe all InI are 'Adam childran - an fe InI have dead becau 'Adam - an fe death judgemant have found InI all from alongside JAH becau InI faada 'Adam error. [8] InI will again arise there with InI faada 'Adam that InI might raceive InI hardship by InI Work that InI worked - fe the world have been ruled fe death by InI faada 'Adam ignorance. [9] By 'Adam infringin JAH Command - becaudis thing InI raceived hardship ~ InI flesh ina grave melted like unto wax - an InI bodies perished. [10] An Earth drank InI marrow ~ InI perished an InI comeliness perished ina grave - an InI flesh were buried ina grave - an InI beautiful words were buried ina Earth. [11] An worms proceeded from InI shinin eyes - an InI features perished ina grave an became dust. [12] Where are youtmons features comeliness - who were attractive - whose stance were handsome an whose word thing succeeded? How about where are warriors firmness? [13] Where are the kings armies - or how about the nobles lordship? Where are adornin ina horses an adornin ina silver an gold an adornin ina shinin weapons? Didn't it perish? [14] Where are sweet grape drink - an how about food flavour? Chapter 19 [1] O Earth who gathered the nobles an the kings an rich ones an elders an dawtaz who were attractive an beauties who were attractive - woe arisin from thee-I. [2] O Earth who gathered persons who were warriors - them who have comeliness - an them who were fine of leg - an them who have reasonin an knowledge - an them whose words have words that were beautiful like unto a hummin harp an like unto a lyre an a violin beat... [3] an them who have a tune that mek Irie like unto grape drink mek Irie - an them whose eyes shine like unto a mornin star... [4] an them who sketch what were firm like unto them right hands lift up what are given an withheld an like unto them were - an them whose feet were beautiful fe sight up - an them who run like unto rushin wheels - woe arisin from thee-I. [5] O death who separated attractive persons souls from them flesh - woe arisin from thee-I - fe thou have been sent by JAH Accord. [6] As thou have gathered many persons whom JAH produced from thee-I an returned toward thee-I - thou Earth - woe arisin from thee-I ~ InI were found from thee-I ~ InI returned toward thee-I by Accord of JAH ~ InI were Irie over thee-I by JAH Accord. [7] Thou became a carpet fe InI corpses ~ InI recurred over thee-I - an InI were buried within thee-I ~ InI ate thy fruit - an thou ate InI flesh. [8] An InI drank the Water found from thy springs - an thou drank InI blood springs ~ InI ate the fruit found from thy Earthliness - an thou ate InI body flesh. [9] Like unto JAH commanded thee-I fe be InI food - InI ate grain from thy Earthliness that have beautiful dew - an thou raceived InI fleh comeliness an made it dust fe thy food like unto JAH commanded thee-I. [10] O death who gathered the nobles an the kings who were powerful - woe arisin from thee-I ~ thou didn't fear arisin from them famousness an them frightenin - like unto JAH Who Irated them commanded thee-I ~ o death - woe arisin from thee-I - an thou didn't scorn the sufferah. [11] An thou weren't nice fe persons whose features are beautiful - an thou didn't quit powerful ones an warriors ~ thou didn't quit poor nor rich ones - neither kind nor evil ones - neither childran nor elders - neither dawtaz nor males. [12] Thou didn't quit persons who think a goodly thing an who didn't depart from the LAW - an thou didn't quit them who were like unto animals ina them Work - who think a evil thing - who were totally beautiful ina them features comeliness - ina them thing flavour an ina them words ~ o death - woe arisin from thee-I. [13] Thou didn't quit persons whose words were angry an whose mouths were full of curses ~ thou gathered persons who live in darkness an ina light an them souls ina thy places ~ o death - woe arisin from thee-I. [14] An Earth gathered the persons flesh who live whether ina cave or ina Earth - up til a drum are beaten an persons who dead arise. [15] As persons who dead shall arise quickly like unto a eye wink by JAH Command an pon a drum bein beaten - persons who worked evil Work shall raceive them hardship ina them sin abundance measure that them worked it - an persons who worked goodly Work shall be Irie. Chapter 20 [1] An believe I that all InI Work that InI worked ina this world won't remain nor be hidden pon the time InI stood before Him fearin an tremblin. [2] An pon the time InI didn't seize provisions fe InI path - an pon the time InI won't have clothes fe InI bodies... [3] pon the time InI won't have a staff fe InI hands nor shoes fe InI feet... [4] an pon the time InI won't know the paths where demons tek InI - whether it be slippery or smooth - or be it dark - an whether it be thorns or nettles - or whether it be a Water depth or a pit depth - believe I that InI Work that InI worked ina this world won't remain nor be hidden. [5] InI won't know the demons who tek InI - an InI won't hear them thing. [6] As them are black ones - an as them lead InI toward darkness - InI don't sight up them faces. [7] An like unto the prophet spoke sayin - "Pon the time I soul were separated from I flesh - Lord I Lord - Thou know I path - an them hid a trap pon that path where I-man went - an I-man sight up returnin toward the right ~ I-man lacked one who know I - an I-man have nothing there whereby I-man will escape" - as them tek InI toward darkness - InI won't sight up them faces. [8] As him know that demons ridicule pon him - an as them will lead him toward the path him don't know - him speakin this are becaudis - an if him return leftward an rightward - there are no person who know him. [9] Him are alone amidst demons - an yet there are none who know him. [10] Angels of Light who are subtle are who are sent toward kind persons that them might raceive righteous ones souls - an might tek toward a Light place - toward the Garden - where welfare are found. [11] Demons an Angels of darkness are who are sent that them might raceive them an might tek them toward Gehannem that were prepared fe them that them might raceive them hardship by them sin that them worked. [12] Woe fe sinner persons souls who tek them toward downstruction - who have no welfare nor rest - nor escapin from the tribulation that found them - nor proceedin from Gehannem up til Iternity. [13] As them have lived firmed up ina Qayel Work - an as them have perished by Bele`am iniquity price - an as them have lacked what them will do - woe fe sinner persons - fe them pretext fe receive interest an presents that ina downgression them might tek a foreigner money that weren't them money. [14] Them shall raceive them hardship ina Gehannem by them sin that them worked. Chapter 21 [1] Where are persons who gather a foreigner money that weren't them Work nor them money? [2] Fe them tek a person money for free - an fe them shll be gathered without knowin the day when them dead that shall arrive pon them - however them quit them money for a foreigner. [3] Fe like unto them faadas - them are sinners kindreds who worry an seize sinners like unto them whether it be by theft or by robbery - an them childran won't be Irie by them faadas money. [4] As them have gathered fe them ina downgression - an as it are like unto misty urine an like unto the smoke that wind scattar an like unto wiltin grass - an like unto wax that melt arisin from before a fiyah - as sinners glory shall perish like unto that - there are none whom them faadas money will benefit ~ like unto Daweet spoke sayin - "I-man sight up a sinner man... [5] bein honoured an famed like unto a cordia an like unto a cypress - but pon the time I-man returned I-man lacked him ~ I-man searched an didn't find him place" - there are none whom them faadas money will profit nor benefit. [6] Becau them gathered a person money ina downgression - it seemin fe them that them won't dead - like unto persons who wrong them companions won't boast - sinner persons downstruction are likewise at one time. [7] Unu lazy ones - think that unu will perish an that your money will perish with unu - an if your silver an your gold abound it shall be rusted. [8] An if unu birth many childran them shall be fe many graves - an if unu work many houses them shall be demolished. [9] Fe unu didn't fulfill your Irator JAH Accord - an if unu multiply livestock them shall be for your enemies capture - an all the money unu seized ina your hands won't be found - fe it have been what weren't blessed. [10] Whether it be ina house or ina forest - an be it ina wilderness or a pasture place - an be it ina grape threshinfloor or ina grain threshinfloor - it won't be found. [11] Becau unu didn't keep JAH Command - as JAH won't save unu with all your house hold from the tribulation - there shall be sadness pon unu arisin from all your enemies - yet unu won't be Irie ina your childran birthed from your nature. [12] But from Him plenty - Him won't trouble persons who kept Him Order an Him LAW ~ Him give all who begged Him - yet Him bless them childran birthed from them nature an also them land fruit fe them. [13] An Him mek them rulers pon all peoples ina them area that them might rule lest them be who are ruled - an Him give them all Him plenty ina them pasture place. [14] Him bless fe them all them seized ina them hand - all them field fruit - an all them livestocks places - an Him mek them Irie in them childran birthed from them nature. [15] An Him don't diminish them livestocks pon them ~ Him save them from all them tribulation an from weariness an illness an downstruction - an from them enemy them don't know an from him them know. [16] An Him will dispute fe them ina Judgemant time - an Him shall save them from a evil thing an from tribulation an from all who dispute them ~ ina the first era if a priest lived who work the Tent Work - who keep the LAW an keep the Tent Order an live firmed up ina JAH Accord - by the first Order an all the LAW as them would give him the tithe an what were birthed first Iginnin from man up til livestock - Him would save them from all the tribulation. [17] Like unto Mussie commanded Newie child 'Iyasu - there was a country of sanctuary ina all them country ~ by not knowin an by knowin up til them judged judgemant pon whom them canvicted an fe whom them acquitted... [18] if a person lived who killed a soul - him would be measured there that him might be saved. [19] Him told them - "Examine ina your reasonins that him have a quarrel with him formerly - an be it by axe or be it by a stone or be it by wood - as it have fallen from him hand by not knowin - if him say "That person pon whom it fell dead pon mi" - examine an save him ~ if him did it ina not knowin mek him be saved. [20] But if him do it knowin - him will raceive him hardship like unto him sin - an there are none who will pardon him; but if him kill him ina not knowin - as him have done it ina not knowin - examine an save him lest him dead. [21] Him worked fe them that them might distance from all the sin - yet Mussie would work like unto this fe 'Isra'iel childran lest them depart from JAH LAW. [22] Him commanded them that 'Adam childran - who live firmed up ina JAH Command from worshippin idols an eatin what dead an lodged an what a sword bloated an cut - an who distance from all evil work like unto him worked fe them - that them might work it an might totally distance from all that aren't due. [23] Him commanded them lest them depart from the Command Him worked fe them ina the Tent example ina Heaven - that them might save them bodies an might find them lodgin with them faadas. [24] As them have been birthed from Siet an 'Adam who did JAH Accord - persons who believed ina JAH Word an lived firmed up ina Him Command will be called kind persons childran. [25] As InI are 'Adam childran - as Him have Irated InI ina Him Example an Him Appearance that InI might work all goodly Work that mek JAH Irie - Him won't scorn it. [26] As Him totally won't separate Him friends - if InI work goodly Work - InI shall inherit the Kingdom of Heaven where are welfare with persons who work goodly Work. [27] Him totally love persons who beg him cleanly - an Him hear them ina them priah - an Him accept the repentance of persons who are disciplined an enter repentance ~ Him give firmness an Power fe persons who keep Him Order an Him LAW an Him Command. [28] Persons who did Him Accord shall be Irie with Him ina Him Kingdom foriva - an whether them be persons who preceded or who arose later - them will present praise fe Him Iginnin from today up til Iternity. Mek glory due fe JAH foriva - an the secand Meqabyan arrived an were fulfilled.

Book 70. III Meqabyan

Chapter 1 [1] Kristos shall rejoice Gibts persons - becau Him shall come toward them ina later era that Him will revenge an downstroy Deeyablos - who wronged them who were kindly an innocent - an who misled persons - an who hate him Irator Work. [2] Him shall revenge an downstroy him ~ Him shall return him lordship toward wretchedness an bein downbased - fe him have been arrogant ina him reasonin. [3] Him shall return him lordship toward bein downbased - fe him have said - "As mi will enter toward the sea midst - an as mi will proceed toward Heaven - an as mi will sight up depths - an as mi will grasp an seize 'Adam childran like unto bird chicks - who are it who are loftier than mi? [4] Becau mi became by them reason that mi might distance them from the straight LAW of JAH - as mi will strengthen pon persons who live ina this world unless them did JAH Accord - there are none who will depose mi from mi authority" him said. [5] "Fe mi will be a reason fe return them toward a path that were smooth fe go toward Gehannem with mi. [6] Persons who loved Him an kept Him LAW hate mi becaudis thing - but persons who departed from them Lord LAW an who erred will come toward mi an love mi an keep mi oath ~ as mi will mek them reasonin evil an change them thoughts lest them return toward them Irator JAH - them will do mi command like unto mi commanded them. [7] An pon the time mi showed them this world money - mi will mislead them reasonin from straight LAW - an pon the time mi showed them beautiful an attractive dawtaz - mi will distance them by these from straight LAW. [8] An pon the time mi showed them shinin Hindekie jewels an silver an gold - mi will distance them by this also from straight LAW that them might return toward mi Work. [9] An pon the time mi showed them thin clothes an red silk an white silk - an linens an white silk - mi will distance them by this also from straight LAW - an mi will return them toward mi thoughts ~ pon the time mi multiplied money an livestocks like unto sand an showed them - by this also mi will return them toward mi Work. [10] An pon the time mi showed them jealousy done in arrogance becau dawtaz an becau anger an quarrels - by all this mi will return them toward mi Work. [11] An pon the time mi showed them signs - mi will lodge ina them companions reasonin - an mi will lodge a sign thing that were fe each of the ras selves ina them reasonin - an mi showed them words signs an misled them. [12] An fe persons ina whom mi lodged mi lodgin - mi will show them signs - an be it ina stars gait - or be it ina cloud proceedin or ina fiyah flickerin - or be it ina beasts an birds cries - as them are mi lodgins - mi will lodge signs ina them reasonin pon them by all this. [13] Them will speak an give signs fe them companions - an like unto those them naysayers told them - mi will precede an be a sign fe them. [14] Mi will do them words signs fe them - that persons who examined them might be misled - an that them might give a wage fe magicians - an that them might tell fe them companions sayin - 'There are no savants like unto so-an-so an so-an-so fe whom it are done like unto them spoke - an who know prophecy - an who separate good an evil - an fe whom all are like unto them spoke - an fe whom it are done like unto them word.' [15] Mi will be Irie pon the time them spoke this - that persons who perish an err by mi might totally abound an that 'Adam childran might perish - fe JAH have downbased mi from mi rank becau them faada 'Adam - pon mi sayin 'Mi won't bow fe 'Adam who are downbased fe mi.' [16] An mi will tek toward downstruc-

tion all him childran who live firmed up ina mi command ~ mi have a Oath from JAH Who Irated mi - that all persons whom mi misled might downscend toward Gehannem with mi. [17] An pon the time Him multiplied Him anger pon mi - an pon the time Him commanded that them might bind an cast mi toward Gehannem - pon the time mi Irator commanded sayin thus - mi interceded with mi Lord ~ mi interceded before Him while mi said - 'As Thou have vexed pon mi - an as Thou have admonished mi by Thy chastisemant - an as Thou have chastised mi by Thy wrath - Lord mi Lord - adjourn mi that mi might speak one thing before Thee-I.' [18] An mi Lord answered fe mi sayin - Speak - I-man will hear thee ~ at that time mi began mi plea toward Him sayin - 'After mi were downbased from mi rank - mek the persons whom mi misled be like unto mi ina Gehannem where mi will raceive tribulation. [19] An mek them be fe Thy Lordship who refused mi - who didn't err by mi - who didn't keep mi command - that them might do Thy Command an might fulfill Thy Accord an might keep Thy Word - pon the time them didn't err by mi like unto mi misled them havin refused like unto mi taught them - an pon the time Thou loved mi - mek them tek the crown Thou gave fe mi. [20] Give them the crown of the authorities called Seythans who were sent with mi ~ seat them pon mi throne pon Thy Right that were a wilderness from mi an mi hosts. [21] An mek them praise Thee-I like unto Thou loved - an mek them be like unto mi hosts an like unto mi ~ becau Thou hated mi an loved them who were Irated from ashes an Earth - as mi authority have perished - an as them authority have been lofty - mek them praise Thee-I like unto Thou loved.' [22] Mi Lord answered fe mi sayin - As thou have misled them while them sight up an while them heard - if thou misled them without them lovin I Order - mek them be fe thee like unto thy accord an like unto thy word. [23] If them quit the Books Word an I Command an came toward thee - an if thou misled them while them downstruction also saddened mi - mek them raceive tribulation ina Gehannem like unto thee - Him told mi. [24] Unu will raceive tribulation ina Gehannem up til the Iternity - yet unu will have no exits from Gehannem up til the Iternity - fe them whom thou misled nor fe thee. Chapter 2 [1] But I-man will bequeath thy throne ina lordship fe them whom it failed thee fe mislead - like unto I slave 'Iyob ~ JAH Who rule all said - I-man will give the Kingdom of Heaven fe persons whom it failed thee fe mislead. [2] An mi provoke pon 'Adam childran ina all ~ if it were possible fe mi fe mislead them - mi won't quit them that them might firm up ina goodly Work ~ fe mi provoke pon all 'Adam childran - an mi sweeten this world Irie Ites fe them. [3] Be it by lovin drink an food an clothes - or by lovin things - or by withholdin an givin... [4] or be it by lovin fe hear an sight up - or be it by lovin fe caress an go - or be it by multiplyin arrogance an things - or be it by lovin dreams an slumber... [5] or be it by multiplyin drunkenness an drink - or be it by multiplyin insults an anger - be it by speakin games an useless things... [6] or be it by quarrels an by backbitin them companion - or be it by sightin up this world dawtaz who were attractive - be it by smellin perfumes fragrance that mislead them... [7] mi hate them by all this lest them able fe be saved ~ mi distance them from JAH LAW that them might enter with mi toward the downstruction whereby mi were downbased from mi rank." [8] An the prophet told him - "Thou who downstroy persons - perish ~ pon the time thou departed from JAH LAW an committed crime ina thy reasonin firmness an thy arrogance - an by saddenin thy Irator an not worshippin thy Irator ina thy reasonin firmness - will thou thus be arrogant pon JAH Iration? [9] Pon the time thy Irator vexed pon thee - Him downbased thee from thy rank becau thy evil Work ~ why do thou tek 'Adam toward sin - him whom him Irator Irated from Earth - whom Him made like unto Him loved - an whom Him placed fe Him praise?" him told him. [10] "Pon the time thou - who are subtle an were Irated from wind an fiyah - were arrogant ina sayin 'Mi are the Irator'... [11] pon the time thou boasted - as JAH have sight up thy evil Work an thou have denied JAH with thy hosts - Him Irated 'Adam who will praise becau thy stead - that him might praise Him Name without diminishin. [12] As thou have made thy ras self prouder than all Angels hosts who are like unto thee - becau thy arrogance JAH Irated 'Adam with him childran that them might praise JAH Name becau the praise that thou praise with thy hosts whom Him scorned. [13] An becaudis thing JAH downstroyed thee separatin from all Angels chiefs like unto thee - an thy hosts Irated ina one counsel with thee - an thou - unu proceeded an erred from JAH praise becau your useless reasonin arrogance an becau your reasonin firmness - an unu were arrogant pon your Irator - that aren't pon another. [14] Becaudis thing Him Irated 'Adam from Earth that Him might be praised by downbased persons - an Him gave him a Command an Law sayin Don't eat lest him eat from fig fruit. [15] An Him I-pointed him pon all the Iration Him Irated ~ Him notified him sayin - Don't eat from one fig fruit that bring death - lest thou bring death pon thy ras self - yet eat fruit from all the woods amidst the Garden. [16] An pon the time thou heard this Word - thou lodged perfidy ina him arisin from the thing thou spoke ina thy tongue fe Hiewan who were found from 'Adam side bone. [17] Thou misled 'Adam who were clean - ina firm perfidy that thou might mek him a Law demolisher like unto thee. [18] Pon the time thou misled Hiewan - who were Irated bein like unto a innocent dove an who don't know thy malice - thou made she betray by thy thing that succeeded an thy crooked word - an after thou misled that Hiewan who were Irated beforehand - she also went an misled JAH Iration 'Adam who were Irated from Earth beforehand. [19] An thou made him betray a downsturbance that aren't by thy arrogance - an thou made him fe deny that him might deny him Irator Word - an thou downstroyed 'Adam ina thy arrogance. [20] An ina thy malice thou distanced him from him Irator Love - an by thy reason thou sent him way from the Garden where Irie Ites are - an by thy hindrance thou made him quit the Garden food. [21] Fe Iginnin from Antiquity thou have quarreled with the innocent Iration 'Adam that thou might lower him toward See'ol where thou will raiceive hardship - an that thou might send him way from the Love that brought him an Irated him from not livin toward true livin - an by thy false thing thou made him thirst a drink from the Garden. [22] An when him are Earthly - Him made him a subtle Angel who totally praise him Irator ina him flesh an him soul an him reasonin. [23] An Him Irated many thoughts fe him - like unto harps praise ina each of them styles. Chapter 3 [1] But Him Irated one thought fe thee - that thou might totally praise while thou were sent toward where thy Irator sent thee. [2] But fe 'Adam were given five thoughts that were evil an five thoughts that were goodly - ten thoughts. [3] An again him have many thoughts like unto sea waves - an like unto a whirl wind that scattar dust liftin up from Earth - an like unto the sea waves that shake - an arisin from him unnumbered thoughts abundance ina him heart like unto unnumbered rain drops - 'Adam thoughts are like unto that. [4] But thy thought are one ~ as thou aren't fleshly - thou have no other thought. [5] But thou lodged ina snake reasonin ~ ina evil perfidy thou downstroyed 'Adam who were one limb - an Hiewan heard the snake thing - an havin heard - she did like unto she commanded she. [6] After she ate a fig fruit - she came an misled JAH first Iration 'Adam - an she brought death pon him an pon she childran becau she infringed she Irator Command. [7] Them proceeded from the Garden fe JAH by Him true Judgemant ~ Him calmed them ina the land where them were sent by them childran birthed from them nature an by them crops found from Earth - yet Him didn't distance them from the Garden quarrelin. [8] An pon the time thou expelled them straight from the Garden - that them might plant plants an childran fe be calmed an fe renew them reasonin ina the Earth fruit that Earth prepared from she Earthliness - an that them might be calmed by Earth fruit an the Garden fruit that JAH gave them... [9] JAH gave them woods more verdant than the Garden woods - an Hiewan an 'Adam - whom thou sent way from the Garden pon them eatin it - were totally calmed from sadness. [10] As JAH know fe calm Him Iration - them reasonins are calmed becau them childran an becau the crops found from Earth. [11] As them have been sent toward this world that grow nettles an thorns - them firm up them reasonins ina Water an grain. Chapter 4 [1] The Lord have that Him might ransom 'Adam - an Him shall shame thee ~ Him will save a sheep from a wolf mouth ('Adam from Deeyablos). [2] However thou will go toward Gehannem seizin with thee the persons whom thou ruled. [3] Persons who kept them Irator JAH LAW shall be Irie with them Irator JAH Who hid them from evil Work that Him might mek them Him fortune - an that them might praise Him with honoured Angels who didn't infringe them Irator JAH LAW like unto thee. [4] But JAH - Who chose an gave thee more than all Angels like unto thee that thou might praise Him with Him servant Angels - withheld from thee a lofty throne ina thy arrogance. [5] But thou became famous an were called one who love godhood - an thy hosts were called demons. [6] But persons who loved JAH shall be Him kindreds like unto honoured Angels - an the Surafiel an Keerubiel who praise Him streach forth them wings an praise without slackness. [7] But ina thy arrogance an thy laziness thou downstroyed thy praise that thou might praise Him everytime with thy host an thy kindreds Irated ina thy features. [8] Lest the praise of JAH - Who Irated thee makin a tenth tribe - be diminished pon the time thou forgot the praise of JAH Who Irated thee - it havin seemed fe thee that it aren't posssible fe Him fe Irate a Iration like unto thee - an lest the praise of JAH - Who Irated thee - be diminished pon the time thou were separated from thy bredren Inity - Him Irated 'Adam becau thy stead. [9] But ina thy reasonin arrogance thou neglected the praise of JAH Who Irated thee - an Him vexed pon thee ~ Him ridiculed thee - an Him bound an banished thee ina Gehannem with thy hosts also. [10] Him brought Soil from Earth with Him glorified Hands - an addin fiyah an Water an wind - Him Irated 'Adam ina Him Example an Him Features. [11] Him I-pointed him pon all the Iration Him Irated ina Him Itority - that Him praise might be filled by the praise thou would praise Him ~ 'Adam praise became one with Angels praise - an them praise were level. [12] But ina thy collar of reasonin firmness an thy arrogance thou were downbased from thy rank - an havin departed from JAH Lordship - Who Irated thee - thou downstroyed thy ras self. [13] Know that Him praise weren't diminished - fe JAH have Irated 'Adam who praised Him ina him reasonin counsel lest Him JAHness praise be diminished. [14] Fe Him know all before it are done - an Him knew thee before Him Irated thee that thou will demolish Him Command ~ as there are a counsel hidden alongside Him before Him Irated the world - pon the time thou denied Him - Him Irated Him slave 'Adam ina Him Features an Him Example. [15] Like unto Selomon spoke sayin - 'Before hills were Irated an before the world succeeded bein Irated - an before winds that are Earth grounations were Irated... [16] an before

Him firmed up hills an mountains grounations - an before this world Work firmed up - an before moon an Sun light shone - before eras an stars caretakin were known... [17] an before daylight an night alternated - an before the sea were delineated by sand - before all the Irated Iration were Irated... [18] an before all sight up today were sight up - before all the names called today were called - Him Irated I Selomon' - Angels like unto unu an thou an Him slave 'Adam were ina JAH Reasonin. [19] Him Irated 'Adam that Him glorified Name might be praised pon the time thou mutinied - an that Him might be praised by Him downbased slave 'Adam who were Irated from Earth pon the time thou were arrogant. [20] Fe bein ina Heaven JAH hear poor ones plea - an Him love downbased persons praise. [21] Him love fe save havin lodged ina persons who fear Him - yet as Him don't love horse Power - an as Him don't step meanin fe the lap of a concubine - JAH shall ignore arrogant ones thing. [22] An them shall weep while them cried becau them sin that them worked. [23] It failed thee fe plead ina repentance. [24] But 'Adam who were Irated from Earth returned ina repentance while him totally wept before JAH becau him sin. [25] But ina thy collar of reasonin firmness an thy heart arrogance thou didn't know Love Work an thou didn't know repentance ~ it failed thee fe plead before thy Irator JAH ina repentance an mournin an sadness. [26] But that 'Adam who are ashes an Earth returned toward repentance ina mournin an sadness - an him returned toward humbleness an Love Work. [27] But thou didn't downbase thy reasonin an thy ras self fe JAH Who Irated thee. [28] As fe 'Adam - him downbased him ras self an pleaded pon the iniquity him wronged ~ him weren't proud. [29] As thou have totally produced crime - it were found from thee - yet it aren't him who produced that error ~ ina thy arrogance thou took him with thee toward thy downstruction. [30] Before him Irated unu both - as Him have known unu that unu were sinners - an as Him have known your Works - Him know that this that were done were ina thy heart arrogance. [31] But Him returned that 'Adam - who were without arrogance or malice - ina repentance mournin an sadness. [32] Fe a person who wrong an don't plead ina repentance have multiplied him iniquity more than him earlier iniquity - but ina thy heart arrogance it failed thee fe plead ina repentance - but a person who plead an weep enterin repentance before Him Irator JAH... [33] him entered repentance fe true - an him found Work whereby him will be saved that him might fear him Lord Heart - an him pleaded before him Irator - fe him have pleaded before Him ina bowin an much repentance - an arisin from the earlier tribulation the Lord shall lighten him sin fe him lest Him vex pon Him slave - an Him will forgive him him former sin. [34] If him didn't return toward him former sin an if him did this - this are perfect repentance ~ 'Adam didn't forget fe think of him Irator nor fe implore him Irator JAH ina repentance. [35] An thou - plea ina repentance toward thy Irator JAH - an don't wrong them becau them were flesh an blood - fe JAH Who Irated them know them weakness - an don't wrong the persons Him Irated by Him Itority. [36] An after them soul were separated from them flesh - them flesh shall be dust up til the day that JAH love. Chapter 5 [1] Know JAH WHo Irated thee-I ~ as JAH have Irated thee-I ina Him Features an Him Example when thou are Earth - don't forget JAH Who firmed thee-I up an saved thee-I an Whom 'Is-ra'iel glorified ~ Him placed thee-I ina Garden that thou might be Irie an might dig Earth. [2] Pon the time thou demolished Him Command - Him sent thee way from the Garden toward this world that Him cursed becau thee - that grow nettles an thorns. [3] Fe thou are Earth - an fe she are Earth - fe thou are dust - an fe she are dust - fe thou are Soil - an fe she are Soil - fe thou are fed the grain found from she - an fe thou will return toward she - fe thou will be Soil up til Him love that Him might raise thee - an fe Him shall examine thee the sin thou worked an all the iniquity. [4] Know what thou will answer Him at that time ~ think of the good an evil thou worked ina this world ~ examine whether the evil would abound or whether the good would abound ~ try. [5] If thou work a goodly thing - it are a goodly thing fe thee-I that thou might be Irie pon the day when persons who dead will arise. [6] But if thou work evil Work - woe fe thee - fe thou will raiceive thy hardship like unto thy hands Work an like unto thy reasonin evil ~ fe if thou work a evil thing pon thy companion an if thou didn't fear JAH - thou will raiceive thy hardship. [7] An if thou betray thy companion an if thou call JAH Name an swear ina lie - as thou will raiceive thy hardship like unto thy Work - woe fe thee. [8] An thou tell thy false thing fe thy companion simulatin Truth - but thou know that thou spoke a lie. [9] An thou persuade the persons with thee thy false thing simulatin Truth - an thou multiply false things that weren't Truth - an thou will raiceive thy hardship like unto thy sin ~ thou deny thy companion while thou tell thy companion 'mi will give thee' what thou won't give him. [10] An pon the time thou said 'Mi will give' ina thy pure reasonin - demons mek application fe thee like unto dogs - an them mek thee forget all - an if thou withhold or if thou love that thou might give - them don't know the person fe whom them gather - yet as Him have said - Them shall fatten - this world money appetise thee that thou might fatten the money that won't benefit thee an that thou won't eat. [11] An again - as Him have said - 'Adam liar childran mek a balance false ~ as fe them - them go from robbery toward robbery - this world money appetise thee. [12] O persons - don't mek hope ina distortin scales an balances - an ina stealin a person money - an ina makin a person money one ina downgression - an ina infringin your companions money - an ina stealin him field - ina all the lies unu do fe your ras selves profit that aren't fe your companions. [13] If unu do this unu will raceive your hardship like unto your Work. [14] O persons - be fed by your hands Work that were straight - yet don't desire robbery ~ don't love that unu might totally rob an eat a person money without justice by what aren't due. [15] An if unu eat it - it won't satta unu ~ pon the time unu dead unu will quit it fe another - yet even if unu fatten - it won't benefit unu. [16] An if your money abound - don't distort your reasonins ~ as sinner persons money are like unto the smoke that proceed from a griddle an the wind tek it - better than sinner persons money are the likkle money them accumulated ina Truth. Chapter 6 [1] Think of the day when unu will dead ~ pon the time your souls were separated from your flesh - an pon the time unu quit your money fe another - an pon the time unu went pon the path unu don't know - think of the tribulation that shall come pon unu. [2] An the demons that will raceive unu are evil - an them features are ugly - an them are frightenin ina them splendour - an them won't hear your words - an unu won't hear them words. [3] An becau unu didn't do your Irator JAH Accord - them won't hear unu ina your plea pon the time unu begged them ~ becaudis thing them will totally frighten unu. [4] But persons who fulfilled JAH Accord have no fear - fe demons fear them. But demons shall ridicule sinner persons souls pon them. [5] But kind persons souls shall be Irie pon Angels ina Irie Ites - fe them shall totally mek them Irie becau them scorned this world - but angels who are evil shall raceive sinner persons souls. [6] Pardon Angels shall raceive kind persons an righteous ones souls - fe them are sent from JAH that them might calm righteous ones souls ~ as Angels that were evil are sent from Deeyablos that them might ridicule pon sinner persons souls - demons shall raceive sinner persons souls. [7] Sinner persons - woe fe unu ~ weep fe your ras selves before the day when unu dead arrive pon unu ~ pon the time unu reach toward JAH... [8] enter repentance ina your era that are there before your era pass - that unu might live ina Irieness an Ites without tribulation nor disease - yet as after unu dead your era won't return that passed - weep. [9] Lest it be pon unu toward a vain accord that distance from JAH - ina your firm criticism mek lovin fe be lavished an food an Irie Ites not be found ina unu ~ as a body that are sated without measure won't think of JAH Name - Deeyablos wealth shall lodge pon it - yet as the Hola Spirit won't lodge ina it - mek lovin the Irie Ites not be found ina unu. [10] Like unto Mussie spoke - Mussie havin said - "Ya`iqob ate an were sated an fattened an tall an wide - an JAH Who Irated him were separated from him. [11] An him lifestyle distanced from JAH" - as a body that were sated without measure nor moderation won't think of JAH Name - mek lovin Irie Ites not be found alongside unu ~ as belly satiety without measure are bein like unto a boar an like unto a wanderin horse - mek drinkin an eatin without measure an adultery not be found ina unu. [12] But a person who eat ina measure shall live firmed up ina JAH Support - an him shall live firmed up like unto the horizon an like unto a tower that have a stone fence; a person who forgot JAH LAW shall flee without one livin who chase him. [13] A kind person shall live ina bein raspected like unto a lion. [14] But persons who don't love JAH won't keep Him LAW - an them reasonins aren't straight. [15] An JAH shall bring sadness an alarm pon them when them are ina this world - an bein seized ina tremblin an fright - an bein seized ina the tribulations without number by them money bein snatched - bein bound by them hands ina chains from them masters hands... [16] lest them be who rested from the tribulation - an lest them lifestyle be ina Irie Ites - lest them rest when them are ina alarmin tribulations that are pon each of them ras selves - Him shall bring sadness an alarm pon them. Chapter 7 [1] But like unto Daweet spoke sayin - "I-man believed ina JAH ~ I-man won't fear havin said - 'What would a person mek I?'" - there are no fright an alarm pon persons who believed ina JAH. [2] An again like unto him spoke sayin - "If warriors surround I - I-man believed ina Him ~ I-man begged JAH one thing ~ I-man seek that" - persons who believed ina Him have no fright pon them ~ a person who believed ina Him shall live ina Life foriva - an him won't fear arisin from a evil thing. [3] Who are a person who shamed believin in JAH? how about who ignored Him fe a desire? [4] As Him have said - I-man love him who loved I - an I-man shall honour him who glorified I ~ I-man shall keep him who returned toward I ina repentance - who are a person who shamed believin ina Him? [5] Judge Truth an save the widow body ~ save them that JAH might save unu from all that oppose unu ina evil thing ~ keep them ~ as kind persons chidran are honoured - them are given makin a profit - an yet Him shall save your chidran after unu - fe them won't be troubled fe grain. Chapter 8 [1] 'Iyob believed ina JAH ~ as him didn't neglect fe praise him Irator JAH - JAH saved him from all the tribulation that 'Adam chidran enemy Deeyablos brought pon him ~ him said - "JAH gave ~ JAH withheld ~ it happened like unto JAH loved pon I - an mek JAH Name be praised by all pon Earth an ina Heaven" - yet as him didn't sadden him reasonin - JAH saved him. [2] An pon the time JAH sight up 'Iyob that him heart were cleansed from sin - Him raceived him ina much honour. [3] An Him gave him money that abounded more than him money that preceded ~ fe him have totally indured him tribulation - an Him cured him from him wounds becau him indurin all the tribulation that arrived pon him. [4] An if unu like unto

him indure the tribulation arisin from demons sent toward unu - unu will be admired. [5] Indure the tribulation ~ that JAH might be fe unu a fortress Refuge from persons who hate unu - an that Him might be a fortress Refuge fe your chidran chidran an fe your chidran after unu - don't sadden your reasonins arisin from the tribulation that came pon unu ~ believe ina Him - an Him shall be a fortress Refuge fe unu. [6] Beg Him ~ Him will hear unu ~ mek hope - an Him will forgive unu ~ beg Him - an Him will be a Faada fe unu; [7] Think of Merdokyos an 'Astier - Yodeet an Giediewon an Deebora an Bariq an Yoftahie an Somson... [8] an other persons like unto them who were disciplined fe believe ina JAH an whose enemies didn't defeat them. [9] Fe JAH are True - an fe Him don't favour havin sight up a face - but persons raceived hardship who love that them might work sin pon them ras selves ~ all persons who fear Him an keep Him LAW shall keep bodies - an Him shall give them bein I-loved an honour. [10] Him shall mek them Irie ina them proceedin an them enterin - ina them Life an them death - an ina them arisin an sittin ~ Fe Him save - an Him seclude. [11] Fe Him sadden - an Him pardon. [12] Fe Him mek poor - an Him honour ~ Him mek wretched - an as Him honour - Him mek them Irie. Chapter 9 [1] An whether it be what are ina Heaven - or whether it be what are pon Earth - an be it either subtle or stout - everything n all Him money live bein firmed up ina Him Order. [2] There are nothing that departed from JAH LAW an Him Order - Who Irated all the world ~ be it a vulture track that fly ina Heaven - Him command toward it destination where Him loved. [3] An Him command a Earth snake path that live ina cave toward where Him loved - an a boat path that go pon sea - apart from only JAH there are none who know it path. [4] An apart from only JAH - there are none who know the path where a soul go pon the time it were separated from it flesh - be it a righteous or a sinner soul. [5] Who know where it will turn - that it would turn ina wilderness or pon a mountain? or that it would fly like unto a bird - that it would be like unto Heaven dew that alight pon a mountain... [6] or that it would be like unto deep wind - or that it would be like unto lightnin that straighten up it path... [7] or that it would be like unto stars that shine amidst the deep - or that it would be like unto sand pon a sea shore that are piled amidst the deep... [8] or that it would be like unto a horizon stone that firmed up pon the sea deep edge - or like unto a wood that give she beautiful fruit that grew by a Water spout... [9] or that it would be that I likened unto the reed that heat of the Sun burnt - an that wind lift an tek toward another place where it didn't grow - an whose trace aren't found... [10] or that it would be like unto misty urine whose trace aren't found - who know JAH Work? who are Him counsellors? how about with whom did Him counsel? [11] As JAH Thoughts are hidden from persons - who will examine an know Him Work? [12] As Him have Irated Earth pon Water - an as Him have firmed she up without stakes - there are none who examine an know JAH Counsel or Him Wisdom - an Him Irated Heaven ina Him perfect Wisdom an firmed it up ina winds - an Him streached forth a lofty cosmos like unto a tent. [13] Him commanded clouds that them might rain rain pon Earth - an Him grow grass - an Him grow fruits without number fe be food fe persons - that InI might believe ina JAH an be Irie ina Inity. [14] JAH are Who give 'Adam chidran the Irie Ites an all the fatness an all the satiety ~ JAH are Who give that them might satta an praise JAH Who gave them fruit from Earth... [15] an Who dressed them ina beautiful robes - Who gave them all the I loved plenty - the Irieness an the Ites that are given fe persons who fulfill JAH Accord. [16] Him give bein I-loved an honour ina the house Him prepared an ina the Kingdom of Heaven fe them faadas who keep JAH LAW. [17] Him give bein I-loved an honour ina the place Him prepared an ina the Kingdom of Heaven fe them faadas who lived firmed up ina Him Worship an Him LAW - an who didn't depart from Him LAW - whom Him famed an raised that them might keep Him Order an Him LAW - an I-man sight up what JAH do fe Him friends ina this world by weakenin them enemies an by keepin them bodies. [18] I-man sight up that Him give them all them begged Him an that Him fulfill them accord fe them - don't depart from JAH - an fulfill JAH Accord. [19] Don't depart from Him Command an Him LAW - lest Him vex pon unu an lest Him downstroy unu at one time - an lest Him vex an whip unu ina the tribulation from where unu lived formerly - lest unu depart from your faadas Order where unu were formerly - an lest uour lodgin be ina Gehannem where are no exits up til the Iternity. [20] Keep your Irator JAH LAW when your soul are separated from your flesh that Him might do goodly Work fe unu pon the time unu stood before JAH. [21] Fe Earth an Heaven Kingdoms are fe Him - an fe Kingdom an capability are fe Him - an fe bein nice an pardonin are only fe Him. [22] As Him mek rich an Him mek poor - as Him mek wretched an Him honour - keep JAH LAW. [23] An Daweet spoke becau Him while him said - "Man seem vain - an him era pass like unto a shadow." [24] Him spoke becau Him sayin - "But Lord - Thou live foriva - an Thy Name Invocation are fe a child chidran." [25] An again him said - "Thy Kingdom are all the world Kingdom - an Thy Rulership are fe a child chidran" ~ Thou returned a kingdom fe Daweet bringin from Sa'ol. [26] But there are none who will I-point Thee-I ~ there are none who can dismiss ~ Thou sight up all - yet there are none who can sight up Thee-I. [27] An Thy kingdom won't perish foriva fe a child chidran ~ there are none who will rule Him - but Him rule all ~ Him sight up all - but there are none who sight Him up. [28] As Him have Irated man ina Him Features an ina Him example that them might praise Him an might know Him Worship ina straight reasonin without doubt - Him examine an know what kidneys smoked up an what a reasonin transported. [29] Yet them bow fe stone - fe wood - an fe silver an gold that a person hand worked. [30] An them sacrifice sacrifice fe them up til them sacrifice smoke proceed toward Heaven - that them sin might live firmed up before JAH - but yet them refused fe worship JAH Who Irated them ~ Him shall downcuse them becau all them sin that them worked ina worshippin them idols. [31] Them learned bowin fe idols an all stained Work that aren't due - naysayin by stars - sorcery - worshippin idols - evil accord - an all the Work that JAH don't love - yet them didn't keep JAH Command that them learned. [32] Them didn't love fe worship JAH that them might save them bodies from sin an iniquity by Him servants the Angels an by money that them praise before JAH - them work all this ina lackin goodly Work. [33] An pon the time them all arose together from the graves where them were buried an where them bodies perished - them souls shall stand empty before JAH - an them souls lived ina the Kingdom of Heaven prepared fe kind persons. [34] But sinner persons souls shall live ina Gehannem - an pon the time graves were opened - persons who dead shall arise - an souls shall return toward the flesh that them were separated formerly. [35] Like unto them were bithed ina them nakedness from them mother belly - them shall stand ina them nakedness before JAH - an them sins that them worked Iginnin from them infancy up til that time shall be revealed. [36] Them shall raceive them sin hardship pon them bodies - an whether them likkle or much sin - them shall raceive them hardship like unto them sin. Chapter 10 [1] Fe the blood of soul found from JAH shall lodge ina them like unto it lodged ina them formerly - an if unu didn't believe persons who dead arisin - hear that Irations shall arise ina rainy season without bein birthed from them mother nor faada. [2] An Him command them formerly by Him Word that them dead. [3] An them flesh bein demolished an rotten an again renewed - them shall arise like unto Him loved. [4] An again pon the time rain alit an pon the time it sated Earth - them shall live havin arisin like unto them were Irated formerly. [5] As them who are everlivin ina bloodly soul an who live ina this world an them whom Water produce have been Irated - Him havin said Mek them be Irated - an as JAH Itority lodge pon the Water - she give them a bloodly soul by Him Itority an by Him Word. [6] As them are Irated by Him Itority an by Him Word without a faada nor mother - thou blind of reasonin who say "Persons who dead won't arise" - if thou have knowledge or Wisdom - how will thou say persons who dead won't arise by them Irator JAH Word? [7] As persons who dead - who were ashes an dust ina grave - shall arise by JAH Word - as fe thou - enter repentance an return toward thy religion. [8] Like unto Him Word spoke formerly - them shall arise by the Pardon Dew found from JAH - an that Word shall turn all the world an arouse the persons who dead like unto Him loved. [9] An know that thou will arise an stand before Him - an mek it not seem fe thee ina thy reasonin dullness that thou will remain ina grave. [10] It aren't thus ~ thou will arise an raceive thy hardship like unto the Work measure that thou worked - whether it be goodly or evil - yet mek it not seem fe thee that thou will remain - fe this Day are the day when them will raceive hardship. [11] An ina Resurrection time thou will raceive thy hardship by all thy sin that thou worked ~ thou will finish thy sin hardship that were written Iginnin from thy infancy up til that time - an thou have no reason that thou will pretext pon thy sin like unto this world Work that thou might deny thy sin. [12] Like unto thou mek thy false word truth before thee - an like unto thou mek the lie thing that thou spoke truth - thou have no reason that thou will pretext like unto this world Work. [13] Becau it were that she know pon thee all thy evil Work thou worked - an becau it were that she will reveal pon thee before she Irator JAH - as JAH Word shall lodge pon thee an speak pon thee - thou have no reason pon what thou pretext. [14] Thou will shame there becau thy sin that thou worked ~ it are that thou might be thanked with persons who are thanke pon them beautiful Work - yet lest thou shame before man an Angels pon the day when Judgemant are judged - quickly enter repentance ina this world before thou arrive toward there. [15] Persons who praise JAH with Angels shall raceive them reward from them Irator without shamin - an them shall be Irie ina the Kingdom of Heaven - however unless thou worked goodly Work when thou are ina thy flesh ina Life - thou have no fortune with righteous ones. [16] As thou weren't prepared when thou have knowledge an when thou have this world where thou enter repentance - there shall be a useless regret pon thee - an fe thou didn't give a morsel fe the hungry when thou have money. [17] An fe thou didn't clothe the naked when thou have clothes - an fe thou didn't save the wronged when thou have Itority. [18] Fe thou didn't teach the sinner person when thou have knowledge - that him might return an enter repentance - an that JAH might forgive him him sin that him formerly worked ina ignorance - an fe thou didn't fight with demons who quarrel with thee when thou have Power that thou able fe prevail. [19] An fe thou didn't fast nor pray when thou have firmness that thou might weaken thy infancy Power that are pon flesh - an that thou might subject thy ras self fe Rightness that aren't favorin pon flesh... [20] that aren't favorin Irie Ites when it are ina this world ina beautiful drink an sweet food - an that aren't

adornin ina thin clothes an silver an gold... [21] an as thou didn't fast nor pray when thou have firmness that thou might subject thy ras self fe Rightness that aren't adornin ina honoured Hindekie jewels called emerald an phazyon - there shall be a useless regret pon thee ~ this aren't a person ornamant that are due. [22] As fe a person ornamant - it are purity - Wisdom - knowledge - lovin one another by what are due without envyin nor jealousy nor doubtin nor quarrels ~ while thou loved thy companion like unto thy ras self... [23] an without thy doin a evil thing pon a person who did a evil thing pon thee-I - it are lovin one another by what are due - that thou might enter toward the Kingdom of Heaven that are given fe person who indured the tribulation - that Him might give thee the honoured Kingdom of Heaven an thy reward pon makin hope ina the Kingdom of Heaven ina Resurrection time with honoured persons ina knowledge an Wisdom. [24] An don't say "After wi dead wi won't arise" - fe Deeyablos cut off hope of persons who speak an think this lest them be saved in Resurrection time ~ them will know that them have hardship pon them pon the time Advent arrived pon them ~ ina Resurrection time persons will be totally sad who worked sin ina not knowin that Him might think of them sin pon them - fe them didn't believe ina Him that them will arise pon that Day. [25] Becaudis thing them shall be reproached like unto them Work evil measure that them worked ina this world - an them shall sight up the Resurrection that them denied whereby them will arise together ina flesh. [26] Them shall weep at that time becau them didn't work goodly Work ~ it would have been better fe them if them wept ina this world if it are possible fe them lest them be who weep ina Gehannem. [27] If InI didn't weep ina this world by InI accord - demons will mek InI weep without InI accord ina Gehannem ~ if InI didn't enter repentance ina this world - InI prepare worthless an useless cries an mournin ina Gehannem . [28] Prepare goodly Work - that unu might cross from death toward Life - an that unu might go from this passin world toward the Kingdom of Heaven - an that unu might sight up the Kingdom of Heaven Light that surpass light ina this world. [29] Refuse Irie Ites that are ina this world - that thou might be Irie without measure ina the Kingdom of Heaven ina Irie Ites that aren't fulfilled Iginnin from today up til the Iternity with persons who believe persons who dead arisin. Mek Glory an praise due JAH foriva - an the third book that speak the Meqabyans thing were fulfilled.

Book 71. 1. Enoch

Chapter 1 [1] Who will be living in the day of tribulation, when all the wicked and godless are to be removed. [2] And he took up his parable and said -Enoch a righteous man, whose eyes were opened by God, saw the vision of the Holy One in the heavens, which the angels showed me, and from them I heard everything, and from them I understood as I saw, but not for this generation, but for a remote one which is for to come. [3] Concerning the elect I said, and took up my parable concerning them: The Holy Great One will come forth from His dwelling, [4] And the eternal God will tread upon the earth, even on Mount Sinai, and appear from His camp. And appear in the strength of His might from the heaven of heavens. [5] And all shall be smitten with fear and the watchers shall quake, and great fear and trembling shall seize them unto the ends of the earth. [6] And the high mountains shall be shaken, and the high hills shall be made low, and shall melt like wax before the flame, [7] And the earth shall be wholly rent in sunder, and all that is upon the earth shall perish, and there shall be a judgement upon all men. [8] But with the righteous He will make peace, and will protect the elect, and mercy shall be upon them. And they shall all belong to God, and they shall be prospered, and they shall all be blessed. And He will help them all, and light shall appear unto them, and He will make peace with them'. [9] And behold! He cometh with ten thousands of His holy ones to execute judgement upon all, and to destroy all the ungodly: and to convict all flesh of all the works of their ungodliness which they have ungodly committed, and of all the hard things which ungodly sinners have spoken against Him. Chapter 2 [1] Observe ye everything that takes place in the heaven, how they do not change their orbits, and the luminaries which are in the heaven, how they all rise and set in order each in its season, [2] And transgress not against their appointed order. Behold ye the earth, and give heed to the things which take place upon it from first to last, how steadfast they are, how none of the things upon earth change, [3] But all the works of God appear to you. Behold the summer and the winter, how the whole earth is filled with water, and clouds and dew and rain lie upon it. Chapter 3 [1] Observe and see how, in the winter, all the trees seem as though they had withered and shed all their leaves, except fourteen trees, which do not lose their foliage but retain the old foliage from two to three years till the new comes. Chapter 4 [1] And again, observe ye the days of summer how the sun is above the earth over against it. [2] And you seek shade and shelter by reason of the heat of the sun, and the earth also burns with growing heat, and so you cannot tread on the earth, or on a rock by reason of its heat. Chapter 5 [1] Observe ye how the trees cover themselves with green leaves and bear fruit: wherefore give ye heed and know with regard to all His works, and recognize how He that liveth for ever hath made them so. [2] And all His works go on thus from year to year for ever, and all the tasks which they accomplish for Him, and their tasks change not, but according as God hath ordained so is it done. [3] And behold how the sea and the rivers in like manner accomplish and change not their tasks from His commandments'. [4] But ye - ye have not been steadfast, nor done the commandments of the Lord, but ye have turned away and spoken proud and hard words with your impure mouths against His greatness. Oh, ye hard-hearted, ye shall find no peace. [5] Therefore shall ye execrate your days, and the years of your life shall perish, and the years of your destruction shall be multiplied in eternal execration, and ye shall find no mercy. [6] In those days ye shall make your names an eternal execration unto all the righteous, and by you shall all who curse, curse, and all the sinners and godless shall imprecate by you, and for you the godless there shall be a curse. And all shall rejoice, and there shall be forgiveness of sins, and every mercy and peace and forbearance: There shall be salvation unto them, a goodly light. And for all of you sinners there shall be no salvation, but on you all shall abide a curse. [7] But for the elect there shall be light and joy and peace, and they shall inherit the earth. [8] And then there shall be bestowed upon the elect wisdom, and they shall all live and never again sin, either through ungodliness or through pride: but they who are wise shall be humble. [9] And they shall not again transgress, nor shall they sin all the days of their life, nor shall they die of the divine anger or wrath, but they shall complete the number of the days of their life. And their lives shall be increased in peace, and the years of their joy shall be multiplied, in eternal gladness and peace, all the days of their life. Chapter 6 [1] And it came to pass when the children of men had multiplied that in those days were born unto them beautiful and comely daughters. [2] And the angels, the children of the heaven, saw and lusted after them, and said to one another: 'Come, let us choose us wives from among the children of men, [3] And beget us children.' And Semjaza, who was their leader, said unto them: 'I fear ye will not, [4] Indeed agree to do this deed, and I alone shall have to pay the penalty of a great sin.' And they all answered him and said: 'Let us all swear an oath, and all bind ourselves by mutual imprecations, [5] Not to abandon this plan but to do this thing.' Then sware they all together and bound themselves by mutual imprecations upon it. [6] And they were in all two hundred; who descended in the days of Jared on the summit of Mount Hermon, and they called it Mount Hermon, because they had sworn, [7] And bound themselves by mutual imprecations upon it. And these are the names of their leaders: Samlazaz, their leader, Araklba, Rameel, Kokablel, Tamlel, Ramlel, Danel, Ezeqeel, Baraqijal, [8] Asael, Armaros, Batarel, Ananel, Zaq1el, Samsapeel, Satarel, Turel, Jomjael, Sariel. These are their chiefs of tens. Chapter 7 [1] And all the others together with them took unto themselves wives, and each chose for himself one, and they began to go in unto them and to defile themselves with them, and they taught them charms, [2] And enchantments, and the cutting of roots, and made them acquainted with plants. [3] And they became pregnant, and they bare great giants, whose height was three thousand ells: [4] Who consumed all the acquisitions of men. And when men could no longer sustain the m, the giants turned against them, [5] And devoured mankind. And they began to sin against birds, and beasts, and reptiles, [6] And fish, and to devour one another's flesh, and drink the blood. Then the earth laid accusation against the lawless ones. Chapter 8 [1] And Azazel taught men to make swords, and knives, and shields, and breastplates, and made known to them the metals of the earth and the art of working them, and bracelets, and ornaments, and the use of antimony, and the beautifying of the eyelids, and all kinds of costly stones, [2] And all colouring tinctures. And there arose much godlessness, and they committed fornication, [3] And theywere led astray, and became corrupt in all their ways. Semjaza taught enchantments, and root-cuttings, 'Armaros the resolving of enchantments, Baraqijal (taught) astrology, Kokabel the constellations, Ezeqeel the knowledge of the clouds, Araqiel the signs of the earth, Shamsiel the signs of the sun, and Sariel the course of the moon. And as men perished, they cried, and their cry went up to heaven. Chapter 9 [1] And then Michael, Uriel, Raphael, and Gabriel looked down from heaven, [2] And saw much blood being shed upon the earth, and all lawlessness being wrought upon the earth. And they said one to another: 'The earth made without inhabitant cries the voice of their cryingst up to the gates of heaven. [3] And now to you, the holy ones of heaven, the souls of men make their suit, saying, "Bring our cause, [4] Before the Most High."' And they said to the Lord of the ages: 'Lord of lords, God of gods, king of kings, and God of the ages, the throne of Thy glory standeth unto all the generations of the ages, [5] And Thy name holy and glorious and blessed unto all the ages! Thou hast made all things, and power over all things hast Thou: and all things are naked and open in Thy sight, and Thou seest all things, [6] And nothing can hide itself from Thee. Thou seest what Azazel hath done, who hath taught all unrighteousness on earth and revealed the eternal secrets which were preserved in heaven, [7] Which men were striving to learn: And Semjaza, to whom Thou hast given authority to bear rule over his associates. And they have gone to the daughters of men upon the earth, and have slept with the women, [8] And have defiled themselves, and revealed to them all kinds of sins. And the women have borne giants, [9] And the whole earth has thereby been filled with blood and unrighteousness. [10] And now, behold, the souls of those who have died are crying and making their suit to the gates of heaven, and the ir lamentations have ascended: and cannot cease because of the lawless deeds which are wrought on the earth. [11] And Thou knowest all things before they come to pass, and Thou seest these things and Thou dost suffer them, and Thou dost not say to us what we are to do to them in regard to these.' Chapter 10 [1] Then said the Most High, the Holy and Great One spake, and sent Uriel to the son of Lamech, [2] And said to him: Go to Noah and tell him in my name "Hide thyself!" and reveal to him the end that is approaching: that the whole earth will be destroyed, and a deluge is about to come upon the whole earth, [3] And will destroy all that is on it. And now instruct him that he may escape, [4] And his seed may be preserved for all the generations of the world. And again the Lord said to Raphael: Bind Azazel hand and foot, and cast him into the darkness: and make an opening in the desert, [5] Which is in Dudael, and cast him therein. And place upon him rough and jagged rocks, and cover him with darkness, and let him abide there for ever, and cover his face that he may not see light. [6] And on the day of the great judgement he shall be cast into the fire. [7] And heal the earth which the angels have corrupted, and proclaim the healing of the earth, that they may heal the plague, and that all the children of men may not perish through all the secret things that the Watchers have disclosed and have taught their sons. [8] And the whole earth has been corrupted through the works that were taught by Azazel: to him ascribe all sin. [9] And to Gabriel said the Lord: Proceed against the bastards and the reprobates, and against the children of fornication: and destroy the children of fornication and the children of the Watchers from amongst men and cause them to go forth: send them one against the other that they may destroy each other in [10] battle: for length of days shall they not have. And no request that they make of thee shall be granted unto their fathers on their behalf; for they hope to live an eternal life, [11] And that each one of them will live five hundred years. And the Lord said unto Michael: Go, bind Semjaza and his associates who have united themselves with women so as to have defiled themselves, [12] with them in all their uncleanness. And when their sons have slain one another, and they have seen the destruction of their beloved ones, bind them fast for seventy generations in the valleys of the earth, till the day of their judgement and of their consummation, [13] Till the judgement that is forever and ever is consummated. In those days they shall be led off to the abyss of fire: [14] And to the torment and the prison in which they shall be confined for ever. And whosoever shall be condemned and destroyed will from thenceforth be bound together with them to the end of all generations. [15] And destroy all the spirits of the reprobate and the children of the Watchers, [16] Because they have wronged mankind. Destroy all wrong from the face of the earth and let every evil work come to an end: and let the plant of righteousness and truth appear: and it shall prove a blessing; the works of righteousness and truth shall be planted in truth and joy for evermore. [17] And then shall all the righteous escape, and shall live till they beget thousands of children, and all the days of their youth and their old age shall they complete in peace. [18] And then shall the whole earth be tilled in righteousness, and shall all be planted with trees and be full of blessing. [19] And all desirable trees shall be planted on it, and they sha ll plant vines on it: and the vine which they plant thereon shall yield wine in abundance, and as for all the seed which is sown thereon each measure of it shall bear a thousand, and each measure of olives shall yield ten presses of oil. [20] And cleanse thou the earth from all oppression, and from all unrighteousness, and from all sin, and from all godlessness: and all the uncleanness that is wrought upon the earth destroy from off the earth. And all the children of men shall become righteous, [21] And all nations shall offer adoration and shall praise Me, and all shall worship Me. And the earth shall be cleansed from all defilement, and from all sin, and from all punishment, and from all torment, and I will never again send them upon it from generation to generation and for ever. Chapter 11 [1] And in those days I will open the store chambers of blessing which are in the heaven, [2] So as to send 2 them down upon the earth over the work and labour of the children of men. And truth and peace shall be associated together throughout all the days of the world and throughout all the generations of men. Chapter 12 [3] Before these things Enoch was hidden, and no one of the children of men knew where he was hidden, [4] And where he abode, and what had become of him. And his activities had to do with the Watchers, and his days were with the holy ones. [5] And I Enoch was blessing the Lord of majesty and the King of the ages, and lo! [6] The Watchers called me - Enoch the scribe- and said to me: 'Enoch, thou scribe of righteousness, go, declare to the Watchers of the heaven who have left the high heaven, the holy eternal place, and have defiled themselves with women, and have done as the children of earth do, [7] And have taken unto themselves wives: "Ye have wrought great destruction on the earth: And ye shall have no peace nor forgiveness of sin: [8] And inasmuch as they delight themselves in their children, The murder of their beloved ones shall they see, and over the destruction of their children shall they lament, and shall make supplication unto eternity, but mercy and peace shall ye not attain." Chapter 13 [1] And Enoch went and said: Azazel, thou shalt have no peace: a severe sentence has gone forth,

[2] Against thee to put thee in bonds: And thou shalt not have toleration nor request granted to thee, because of the unrighteousness which thou hast taught, and because of all the works of godlessness, [3] And unrighteousness and sin which thou hast shown to men. Then I went and spoke to them all together, [4] And they were all afraid, and fear and trembling seized them. And they besought me to draw up a petition for them that they might find forgiveness, and to read their petition in the presence of the Lord of heaven. [5] For from thenceforward they could not speak with Him nor lift up their eyes to heaven for shame of their sins for which they had been condemned. Then I wrote out their petition, and the prayer in regard to their spirits and their deeds individually and in regard to their requests that they should have forgiveness and length. [6] And I went off and sat down at the waters of Dan, in the land of Dan, to the south of the west of Hermon: I read their petition till I fell asleep. [7] And behold a dream came to me, and visions fell down upon me, and I saw visions of chastisement, and a voice came bidding me I to tell it to the sons of heaven, and reprimand them. [8] And when I awaked, I came unto them, and they were all sitting gathered together, weeping in Abelsjail, [9] Which is between Lebanon and Seneser, with their faces covered. And I recounted before them all the visions which I had seen in sleep, and I began to speak the words of righteousness, and to reprimand the heavenly Watchers. Chapter 14 [1] The book of the words of righteousness, and of the reprimand of the eternal Watchers, [2] In accordance with the command of the Holy Great One in that vision. I saw in my sleep what I will now say with a tongue of flesh and with the breath of my mouth: which the Great One has given to men to converse therewith and understand with the heart. [3] As He has created and given to man the power of understanding the word of wisdom, so hath He created me also and given me the power of reprimanding the Watchers, [4] The children of heaven. I wrote out your petition, and in my vision it appeared thus, that your petition will not be granted unto you throughout all the days of eternity, [5] And that judgement has been finally passed upon you: yea (your petition) will not be granted unto you. And from henceforth you shall not ascend into heaven unto all eternity, and in bonds of the earth the decree has gone forth to bind you for all the days of the world. [6] And (that) previously you shall have seen the destruction of your beloved sons and ye shall have no pleasure in them, but they shall fall before you by the sword. [7] And your petition on their behalf shall not be granted, nor yet on your own: even though you weep and pray and speak all the words contained in the writing which I have written. [8] And the vision was shown to me thus: Behold, in the vision clouds invited me and a mist summoned me, and the course of the stars and the lightnings sped and hastened me, [9] And the winds in the vision caused me to fly and lifted me upward, and bore me into heaven. And I went in till I drew nigh to a wall which is built of crystals and surrounded by tongues of fire: and it began to affright me. [10] And I went into the tongues of fire and drew nigh to a large house which was built of crystals: and the walls of the house were like a tesselated floor made of crystals, and its groundwork was of crystal. [11] Its ceiling was like the path of the stars and the lightnings, and between them were fiery cherubim, and their heaven was (clear as) water. A flaming fire surrounded the walls, and its portals blazed with fire. [12] And I entered into that house, and it was hot as fire and cold as ice: [13] There were no delights of life therein: fear covered me, and trembling got hold upon me. [14] And as I quaked and trembled, I fell upon my face. [15] And I beheld a vision, And lo! There was a second house, greater than the former, [16] And the entire portal stood open before me, and it was built of flames of fire. And in every respect it so excelled in splendour and magnificence and extent that I cannot describe to you its splendour and its extent. [17] And its floor was of fire, and above it were lightnings and the path of the stars, [18] And its ceiling also was flaming fire. And I looked and saw therein a lofty throne: its appearance was as crystal, and the wheels thereof as the shining sun, and there was the vision of cherubim. [19] And from underneath the throne came streams of flaming fire so that I could not look thereon. [20] And the Great Glory sat thereon, and His raiment shone more brightly than the sun and was whiter than any snow. [21] None of the angels could enter and could behold His face by reason of the magnificence and glory and no flesh could behold Him. [22] The flaming fire was round about Him, and a great fire stood before Him, and none around could draw nigh Him: ten thousand times ten thousand stood before Him, [23] Yet He needed no counselor. And the most holy ones who were nigh to Him did not leave by night nor depart from Him. [24] And until then I had been prostrate on my face, trembling: and the Lord called me with His own mouth, and said to me: 'Come hither, [25] Enoch, and hear my word.' And one of the holy ones came to me and waked me, and He made me rise up and approach the door: and I bowed my face downwards. Chapter 15 [1] And He answered and said to me, and I heard His voice: 'Fear not, Enoch, thou righteous man and scribe of righteousness: [2] Approach hither and hear my voice. And go, say to the Watchers of heaven, who have sent thee to intercede for them: "You should intercede" for men, and not men for you: [3] Wherefore have ye left the high, holy, and eternal heaven, and lain with women, and defiled yourselves with the daughters of men and taken to yourselves wives, and done like the children of earth, [4]

And begotten giants as your sons? And though ye were holy, spiritual, living the eternal life, you have defiled yourselves with the blood of women, and have begotten children with the blood of flesh, and, as the children of men, have lusted after flesh and blood as those also do who die and perish. [5] Therefore have I given them wives also that they might impregnate them, and beget children by them, [6] That thus nothing might be wanting to them on earth. But you were formerly spiritual, [7] Living the eternal life, and immortal for all generations of the world. And therefore I have not appointed wives for you; for as for the spiritual ones of the heaven, in heaven is their dwelling. [8] And now, the giants, who are produced from the spirits and flesh, shall be called evil spirits upon the earth, [9] And on the earth shall be their dwelling. Evil spirits have proceeded from their bodies; because they are born from men and from the holy Watchers is their beginning and primal origin; [10] They shall be evil spirits on earth, and evil spirits shall they be called. As for the spirits of heaven, in heaven shall be their dwelling, but as for the spirits of the earth which were born upon the earth, on the earth shall be their dwelling. [11] And the spirits of the giants afflict, oppress, destroy, attack, do battle, and work destruction on the earth, and cause trouble: they take no food, but nevertheless hunger and thirst, [12] And cause offences. And these spirits shall rise up against the children of men and against the women, because they have proceeded from them. Chapter 16 [1] From the days of the slaughter and destruction and death of the giants, from the souls of whose flesh the spirits, having gone forth, shall destroy without incurring judgement –thus shall they destroy until the day of the consummation, the great judgement in which the age shall be consummated, [2] Over the Watchers and the godless, yea, shall be wholly consummated." And now as to the Watchers who have sent thee to intercede for them, who had been aforetime in heaven, say to them: [3] "You have been in heaven, but all the mysteries had not yet been revealed to you, and you knew worthless ones, and these in the hardness of your hearts you have made known to the women, and through these mysteries women and men work much evil on earth." [4] Say to them therefore: " You have no peace."' Chapter 17 [1] And they took and brought me to a place in which those who were there were like flaming fire, [2] And, when they wished, they appeared as men. And they brought me to the place of darkness, and to a mountain the point of whose summit reached to heaven. [3] And I saw the places of the luminaries and the treasuries of the stars and of the thunder and in the uttermost depths, [4] Where were a fiery bow and arrows and their quiver, and a fiery sword and all the lightnings. And they took me to the living waters, [5] And to the fire of the west, which receives every setting of the sun. [6] And I came to a river of fire in which the fire flows like water and discharges itself into the great sea towards the west. I saw the great rivers and came to the great river and to the great darkness, [7] And went to the place where no flesh walks. I saw the mountains of the darkness of winter and the place, [8] Whence all the waters of the deep flow. I saw the mouths of all the rivers of the earth and the mouth of the deep. Chapter 18 [1] I saw the treasuries of all the winds: I saw how He had furnished with them the whole creation, [2] And the firm foundations of the earth. And I saw the corner-stone of the earth: I saw the four winds, [3] Which bear the earth and the firmament of the heaven. And I saw how the winds stretch out the vaults of heaven, and have their station between heaven and earth: these are the pillars of the heaven. [4] I saw the winds of heaven which turn and bring the circumference of the sun, [5] And all the stars to their setting. I saw the winds on the earth carrying the clouds: I saw the paths of the angels. [6] I saw at the end of the earth the firmament of the heaven above. And I proceeded and saw a place which burns day and night, where there are seven mountains of magnificent stones, [7] Three towards the east, and three towards the south. And as for those towards the east, was of coloured stone, and one of pearl, and one of jacinth, and those towards the south of red stone. [8] But the middle one reached to heaven like the throne of God, of alabaster, and the summit of the throne was of sapphire. [9] And I saw a flaming fire. [10] And beyond these mountains Is a region the end of the great earth: there the heavens were completed. [11] And I saw a deep abyss, with columns of heavenly fire, and among them I saw columns of fire fall, which were beyond measure alike towards [12] the height and towards the depth. And beyond that abyss I saw a place which had no firmament of the heaven above, and no firmly founded earth beneath it: there was no water upon it, [13] And no birds, but it was a waste and horrible place. I saw there seven stars like great burning mountains, [14] And to me, when I inquired regarding them, The angel said: 'This place is the end of heaven and earth: this has become a prison for the stars and the host of heaven. [15] And the stars which roll over the fire are they which have transgressed the commandment of the Lord in the beginning of their rising, [16] Because they did not come forth at their appointed times. And He was wroth with them, and bound them till the time when their guilt should be consummated even for ten thousand years.' Chapter 19 [1] And Uriel said to me: 'Here shall stand the angels who have connected themselves with women, and their spirits assuming many different forms are defiling mankind and shall lead them astray into sacrificing to demons as gods, here shall they stand, till the day of the great judgement in [2] Which they shall be judged till they are made an end of. And the women also of the angels, [3] who went astray shall become sirens.' And I, Enoch, alone saw the vision, the ends of all things: and no man shall see as I have seen. Chapter 20 [1] And these are the names of the holy angels who watch. [2] Uriel, one of the holy angels, [3] Who is over the world and over Tartarus. Raphael, one of the holy angels, who is over the spirits of men. [4] Raguel, one of the holy angels who takes vengeance on the world of the luminaries. [5] Michael, one of the holy angels, to wit, he that is set over the best part of ma nkind and over chaos. [6] Saraqael, one of the holy angels, who is set over the spirits, who sin in the spirit. [7] Gabriel, one of the holy angels, who is over Paradise and the serpents and the Cherubim. [8] Remiel, one of the holy angels, whom God set over those who rise. Chapter 21 [1] And I proceeded to where things were chaotic. [2] And I saw there something horrible: I saw neither [3] Heaven above nor a firmly founded earth, but a place chaotic and horrible. [4] And there I saw seven stars of the heaven bound together in it, like great mountains and burning with fire. [5] Then I said: 'For what sin are they bound, and on what account have they been cast in hither?' Then said Uriel, one of the holy angels, who was with me, and was chief over them, and said: 'Enoch, why dost thou ask, [6] And why art thou eager for the truth? These are of the number of the stars of heaven, which have transgressed the commandment of the Lord, and are bound here till ten thousand years, [7] The time entailed by their sins, are consummated.' And from thence I went to another place, which was still more horrible than the former, and I saw a horrible thing: a great fire there which burnt and blazed, and the place was cleft as far as the abyss, being full of great descending columns of fire: [8] Neither its extent or magnitude could I see, nor could I conjecture. [9] Then I said: 'How fearful is the place and how terrible to look upon!' Then Uriel answered me, one of the holy angels who was with me, and said unto me: 'Enoch, why hast thou such fear and affright?' [10] And I answered: 'Because of this fearful place, and because of the spectacle of the pain.' And he said unto me: 'This place is the prison of the angels, and here they will be imprisoned for ever.' Chapter 22 [1] And thence I went to another place, and he mountain and of hard rock. [2] And there was in it four hollow places, deep and wide and very smooth. How smooth are the hollow places and deep and dark to look at. [3] Then Raphael answered, one of the holy angels who was with me, and said unto me: 'These hollow places have been created for this very purpose, that the spirits of the souls of the dead should assemble therein, [4] Yea that all the souls of the children of men should assemble here. And these places have been made to receive them till the day of their judgement and till their appointed period [till the period appointed], till the great judgement (comes) upon them.' I saw (the spirit of) a dead man making suit, [5] And his voice went forth to heaven and made suit. And I asked Raphael the angel who was with me, [6] And I said unto him: 'This spirit which maketh suit, whose is it, whose voice goeth forth and maketh suit to heaven ?' [7] And he answered me saying: 'This is the spirit which went forth from Abel, whom his brother Cain slew, and he makes his suit against him till his seed is destroyed from the face of the earth, and his seed is annihilated from amongst the seed of men.' [8] The I asked regarding it, and regarding all the hollow places: 'Why is one separated from the other?' [9] And he answered me and said unto me: 'These three have been made that the spirits of the dead might be separated. And such a division has been make for the spirits of the righteous, in which there is the bright spring of water. [10] And such has been made for sinners when they die and are buried in the earth and judgement has not been executed on them in their lifetime. [11] Here their spirits shall be set apart in this great pain till the great day of judgement and punishment and torment of those who curse for ever and retribution for their spirits. [12] There He shall bind them for ever. And such a division has been made for the spirits of those who make their suit, who make disclosures concerning their destruction, when they were slain in the days of the sinners. [13] Such has been made for the spirits of men who were not righteous but sinners, who were complete in transgression, and of the transgressors they shall be companions: but their spirits shall not be slain in the day of judgement nor shall they be raised from thence.' [14] The I blessed the Lord of glory and said: 'Blessed be my Lord, the Lord of righteousness, who ruleth for ever.' Chapter 23 [1] From thence I went to another place to the west of the ends of the earth. [2] And I saw a burning fire which ran without resting, [3] And paused not from its course day or night but ran regularly. [4] And I asked saying: 'What is this which rests not?' Then Raguel, one of the holy angels who was with me, answered me and said unto me: 'This course of fire which thou hast seen is the fire in the west which persecutes all the luminaries of heaven.' Chapter 24 [1] And from thence I went to another place of the earth, and he showed me a mountain range of fire, [2] Which burnt day and night. And I went beyond it and saw seven magnificent mountains all differing each from the other, and the stones thereof were magnificent and beautiful, magnificent as a whole, of glorious appearance and fair exterior: three towards the east, one founded on the other, and three towards the south, one upon the other, and deep rough ravines, no one of which joined with any other. [3] And the seventh mountain was in the midst of these, and it excelled them in height, [4] Resembling the seat of a throne: and fragrant trees encircled the throne. And amongst them was a tree such as I had never yet smelt, neither was any amongst them nor were others like it: it had a fragrance beyond all fragrance, and its leaves and blooms and wood wither not for ever: [5] And its fruit is beautiful, and its fruit n resembles the dates of a palm. Then I said: 'How beautiful is this tree, and fragrant, and its leaves are fair, and its blooms very delightful in appearance.' [6] Then answered Michael, one of the holy and honoured angels who was with me, and was their leader. Chapter 25 [1] And he said unto me: 'Enoch, why dost thou ask me regarding the fragrance of the tree, [2] And why dost thou wish to learn the truth?' Then I answered him saying: 'I wish to know about everything, [3] But especially about this tree.' And he answered saying: 'This high mountain which thou hast seen, whose summit is like the throne of God, is His throne, where the Holy Great One, the Lord of Glory, the Eternal King, will sit, when He shall come down to visit the earth with goodness. [4] And as for this fragrant tree no mortal is permitted to touch it till the great judgement, when He shall take vengeance on all and bring everything to its consummation for ever. [5] It shall then be given to the righteous and holy. Its fruit shall be for food to the elect: it shall be transplanted to the holy place, to the temple of the Lord, the Eternal King. [6] Then shall they rejoice with joy and be glad, and into the holy place shall they enter; And its fragrance shall be in their bones, and they shall live a long life on earth, Such as thy fathers lived: And in their days shall no sorrow or plague or torment or calamity touch them.' [7] Then blessed I the God of Glory, the Eternal King, who hath prepared such things for the righteous, and hath created them and promised to give to them. Chapter 26 [1] And I went from thence to the middle of the earth, and I saw a blessed place, [2] In which there were trees with branches abiding and blooming of a dismembered tree. And there I saw a holy mountain, [3] And underneath the mountain to the east there was a stream and it flowed towards the south. And I saw towards the east another mountain higher than this, and between them a deep and narrow ravine: [4] In it also ran a stream underneath the mountain. And to the west thereof there was another mountain, lower than the former and of small elevation, and a ravine deep and dry between them: and another deep and dry ravine was at the extremities of the three mountains. [5] And all the ravines were deep rand narrow, being formed of hard rock, and trees were not planted upon them. And I marveled at the rocks, and I marveled at the ravine, yea, I marveled very much. Chapter 27 [1] Then said I: 'For what object is this blessed land, which is entirely filled with trees, [2] And this accursed valley between?' Then Uriel, one of the holy angels who was with me, answered and said: 'This accursed valley is for those who are accursed for ever: Here shall all the accursed be gathered together who utter with their lips against the Lord unseemly words and of His glory speak hard things. Here shall they be gathered together, [3] And here shall be their place of judgement. In the last days there shall be upon them the spectacle of righteous judgement in the presence of the righteous for ever: here shall the merciful bless the Lord of glory, the Eternal King. [4] In the days of judgement over the former, they shall bless Him for the mercy in accordance with [5] Which He has assigned them (their lot).' Then I blessed the Lord of Glory and set forth His glory and lauded Him gloriously. Chapter 28 [1] And thence I went towards the east, into the midst of the mountain range of the desert, [2] And I saw a wilderness and it was solitary, full of trees and plants. And water gushed forth from above. [3] Rushing like a copious watercourse which flowed towards the north west it caused clouds and dew to ascend on every side. Chapter 29 [1] And thence I went to another place in the desert, and approached to the east of this mountain range. [2] And there I saw aromatic trees exhaling the fragrance of frankincense and myrrh, and the trees also were similar to the almond tree. Chapter 30 [1] And beyond these, I went afar to the east, [2] And I saw another place, a valley full of water. [3] And therein there was a tree, the colour of fragrant trees such as the mastic. And on the sides of those valleys I saw fragrant cinnamon. And beyond these I proceeded to the east. Chapter 31 [1] And I saw other mountains, and amongst them were groves of trees, and there flowed forth from them nectar, [2] Which is named sarara and galbanum. And beyond these mountains I saw another mountain to the east of the ends of the earth, whereon were aloe-trees, and all the trees were full of stacte, being like almond-trees. [3] And when one burnt it, it smelt sweeter than any fragrant odour. Chapter 32 [1] And after these fragrant odours, as I looked towards the north over the mountains I saw seven mountains full of choice nard and fragrant trees and cinnamon and pepper. [2] And thence I went over the summits of all these mountains, far towards the east of the earth, and passed above the Erythraean sea and went far from it, and passed over the angel Zotiel. And I came to the Garden of Righteousness, [3] I and from afar off trees more numerous than I these trees and great-two trees there, very great, beautiful, and glorious, and magnificent, and the tree of knowledge, whose holy fruit they eat and know great wisdom. [4] That tree is in height like the fir, and its leaves are like (those of) the Carob tree: [5] And its fruit is like the clusters of the vine, very beautiful: and the fragrance of the tree penetrates afar. [6] Then I said: 'How beautiful is the tree, and how attractive is its look!' Then Raphael the holy angel, who was with me, answered me and said: 'This is the tree of wisdom, of which thy father old (in years) and thy aged mother, who were before thee, have eaten, and they learnt wisdom and their eyes were opened, and they knew that they were naked and they were driven out of the garden.' Chapter 33 [1] And from thence I went to the ends of the earth And saw there great beasts, and each differed from the other; and I saw birds also differing in appearance and beauty and voice, the one differing from the other. And to the east of those beasts I saw the ends of the earth whereon the heaven rests, [2] And the portals of the heaven open. And I saw how the stars of heaven come forth, [3] And I counted the portals out of which they proceed, and wrote down all their outlets, of each individual star by itself, according to their number and their names, their courses and their positions, and their times and their months, [4] As Uriel the holy angel who was with me showed me. He showed all things to me and wrote them down for me: also their names he wrote for me, and their laws and their companies. Chapter 34 [1] And from thence I went towards the north to the ends of the earth, and there I saw a great and glorious device at the ends of the whole earth. And here I saw three portals of heaven open in the heaven: through each of them proceed north winds: when they blow there is cold, hail, frost, snow, dew, and rain. [2] And out of one portal they blow for good: but when they blow through the other two portals, it is with violence and affliction on the earth, and they blow with violence. Chapter 35 [1] And from thence I went towards the west to the ends of the earth, and saw there three portals of the heaven open such as I had seen in the east, the same number of portals, and the same number of outlets. Chapter 36 [1] And from thence I went to the south to the ends of the earth, and saw there three open portals of the heaven: [2] And thence there come dew, rain, and wind. And from thence I went to the east to the ends of the heaven, and saw here the three eastern portals of heaven open and small portals above them. [3] Through each of these small portals pass the stars of heaven and run their course to the west on the path which is shown to them. And as often as I saw I blessed always the Lord of Glory, and I continued to bless the Lord of Glory who has wrought great and glorious wonders, to show the greatness of His work to the angels and to spirits and to men, that they might praise His work and all His creation: that they might see the work of His might and praise the great work of His hands and bless Him for ever.

Book 72. 2. Enoch

Chapter 37 [1] The second vision which he saw, the vision of wisdom - which Enoch the son of Jared, [2] The son of Mahalalel, the son of Cainan, the son of Enos, the son of Seth, the son of Adam, saw. And this is the beginning of the words of wisdom which I lifted up my voice to speak and say to those which dwell on earth: Hear, ye men of old time, and see, ye that come after, [3] The words of the Holy one which I will speak before the Lord of Spirits. It were better to declare, them only, to the men of old time, but even from those that come after we will not withhold the beginning of wisdom. [4] Till the present day such wisdom has never been given by the Lord of Spirits as I have received according to my insight, according to the good pleasure of the Lord of Spirits by whom the lot of eternal life has been given to me. [5] Now three Parables were imparted to me, and I lifted up my voice and recounted them to those that dwell on the earth. Chapter 38 [1] The first Parable. When the congregation of the righteous shall appear, and sinners shall be judged for their sins, and shall be driven from the face of the earth: [2] And when the Righteous One shall appear before the eyes of the righteous, whose elect works hang upon the Lord of Spirits, and light shall appear to the righteous and the elect who dwell on the earth, where then will be the dwelling of the sinners, and where the resting-place of those who have denied the Lord of Spirits? It had been good for them if they had not been born. [3] When the secrets of the righteous shall be revealed and the sinners judged, and the godless driven from the presence of the righteous and elect, [4] From that time those that possess the earth shall no longer be powerful and exalted: And they shall not be able to behold the face of the holy, For the Lord of Spirits has caused His light to appear on the face of the holy, righteous, and elect. [5] Then shall the kings and the mighty perish and be given into the hands of the righteous and holy. [6] And thenceforward none shall seek for themselves mercy from the Lord of Spirits for their life is at an end. Chapter 39 [1] And it shall come to pass in those days that elect and holy children will descend from the high heaven, [2] And their seed will become one with the children of men. And in those days Enoch received books of zeal and wrath, and books of disquiet and expulsion. And mercy shall not be accorded to them, saith the Lord of Spirits. [3] And in those days a whirlwind carried me off from the earth, and set me down at the end of the heavens. [4] And there I saw another vision, the dwelling-places of the holy, and the resting-places of the righteous. [5] Here mine eyes saw their dwellings with His righteous angels, and their resting-places with the holy. And they petitioned and interceded and prayed for the children of men, and righteousness flowed before them as water, and mercy like dew upon the earth: Thus it is amongst them for ever and ever. [6] And in that place mine eyes saw the Elect One of righteousness and of faith, and I saw his dwelling-place under the wings of the Lord of Spirits. And righteousness shall prevail in

his days, and the righteous and elect shall be without number before Him for ever and ever. [7] And all the righteous and elect before Him shall be strong as fiery lights, and their mouth shall be full of blessing, and their lips extol the name of the Lord of Spirits, and righteousness before Him shall never fail, and uprightness shall never fail before Him. [8] There I wished to dwell, and my spirit longed for that dwelling-place: And there heretofore hath been my portion, For so has it been established concerning me before the Lord of Spirits. [9] In those days I praised and extolled the name of the Lord of Spirits with blessings and praises, because He hath destined me for blessing and glory according to the good pleasure of the Lord of Spirits. [10] For a long time my eyes regarded that place, and I blessed Him and praised Him, saying: Blessed is He, and may He be blessed from the beginning and for evermo re. And before Him there is no ceasing. He knows before the world was created what is for ever and what will he from generation unto generation. [11] Those who sleep not bless Thee: they stand before Thy glory and bless, praise, and extol, saying: "Holy, holy, holy, is the Lord of Spirits: [12] He filleth the earth with 12 spirits." And here my eyes saw all those who sleep not: they stand before Him and bless and say: Blessed be Thou, and blessed be the name of the Lord for ever and ever. And my face was changed; for I could no longer behold. Chapter 40 [1] And after that I saw thousands of thousands and ten thousand times ten thousand, I saw a multitude beyond number and reckoning, [2] Who stood before the Lord of Spirits. And on the four sides of the Lord of Spirits I saw four presences, different from those that sleep not, and I learnt their names: for the angel that went with me made known to me their names, and showed me all the hidden things. [3] And I heard the voices of those four presences as they uttered praises before the Lord of glory. [4] The first voice blesses the Lord of Spirits for ever and ever. [5] And the second voice I heard blessing the Elect One, [6] And the elect ones who hang upon the Lord of Spirits. And the third voice I heard pray and intercede for those who dwell on the earth and supplicate in the name of the Lord of Spirits. [7] And I heard the fourth voice fending off the Satans and forbidding them to come before the Lord of Spirits to accuse them who dwell on the earth. [8] After that I asked the angel of peace who went with me, who showed me everything that is hidden: Who are these four presences which I have seen and whose words I have heard and written down? [9] And he said to me: This first is Michael, the merciful and long suffering: and the second, who is set over all the diseases and all the wounds of the children of men, is Raphael: and the third, who is set over all the powers, is Gabriel: and the fourth, who is set over the repentance unto hope of those who inherit eternal life, is named Phanuel. [10] And these are the four angels of the Lord of Spirits and the four voices I heard in those days. Chapter 41 [1] And after that I saw all the secrets of the heavens, and how the kingdom is divided, [2] And how the actions of men are weighed in the balance. And there I saw the mansions of the elect and the mansions of the holy, and mine eyes saw there all the sinners being driven from thence which deny the name of the Lord of Spirits, and being dragged off: and they could not abide because of the punishment which proceeds from the Lord of Spirits. [3] And there mine eyes saw the secrets of the lightning and of the thunder, and the secrets of the winds, how they are divided to blow over the earth, and the secrets of the clouds and dew, [4] And these I saw from whence they proceed in that place and from whence they saturate the dusty earth. And there I saw closed chambers out of which the winds are divided, the chamber of the hail and winds, the chamber of the mist, and of the clouds, and the cloud thereof hovers over the earth from the beginning of the world. [5] And I saw the chambers of the sun and moon, whence they proceed, and whither they come again, and their glorious return, and how one is superior to the other, and their stately orbit, and how they do not leave their orbit, and they add nothing to their orbit, and they take nothing from it, and they keep faith with each other, in accordance with the oath by which they are bound together. [6] And first the sun goes forth and traverses his path according to the commandment of the Lord of Spirits, [7] And mighty is His name for ever and ever. And after that I saw the hidden and the visible path of the moon, and she accomplishes the course of her path in that place by day and by night-the one holding a position opposite to the other before the Lord of Spirits. And they give thanks and praise and rest not; For unto them is their thanksgiving rest. [8] For the sun changes oft for a blessing or a curse, and the course of the path of the moon is light to the righteous. And darkness to the sinners in the name of the Lord, who made a separation between the light and the darkness, and divided the spirits of men, and strengthened the spirits of the righteous, in the name of His righteousness. [9] For no angel hinders and no power is able to hinder; for He appoints a judge for them all and He judges them all before Him. Chapter 42 [1] Wisdom found no place where she might dwell; Then a dwelling-place was assigned her in the heavens. [2] Wisdom went forth to make her dwelling among the children of men, and found no dwelling-place: Wisdom returned to her place, and took her seat among the angels. [3] And unrighteousness went forth from her chambers: Whom she sought not she found, and dwelt with them, as rain in a desert, and dew on a thirsty land. Chapter 43 [1] And I saw other lightnings and the stars of heaven, and I saw how He called them all by their names and they hearkened unto Him. [2] And I saw how they are weighed in a righteous balance according to their proportions of light: I saw the width of their spaces and the day of their appearing, and how their revolution produces lightning: and I saw their revolution according to the number of the angels, [3] And how they keep faith with each other. And I asked the angel who went with me who showed me what was hidden: What are these? And he said to me: The Lord of Spirits hath showed thee their parabolic meaning: these are the names of the holy who dwell on the earth and believe in the name of the Lord of Spirits for ever and ever. Chapter 44 [1] Also another phenomenon I saw in regard to the lightnings: how some of the stars arise and become lightnings and cannot part with their new form. Chapter 45 [1] And this is the second Parable concerning those who deny the name of the dwelling of the holy ones and the Lord of Spirits. [2] And into the heaven they shall not ascend, and on the earth they shall not come: Such shall be the lot of the sinners who have denied the name of the Lord of Spirits, who are thus preserved for the day of suffering and tribulation. [3] On that day Mine Elect One shall sit on the throne of glory, and shall try their works, and their places of rest shall be innumerable. And their souls shall grow strong within them when they see Mine Elect Ones, and those who have called upon My glorious name: [4] Then will I cause Mine Elect One to dwell among them. And I will transform the heaven and make it an eternal blessing and light, [5] And I will transform the earth and make it a blessing: And I will cause Mine elect ones to dwell upon it: But the sinners and evil-doers shall not set foot thereon. [6] For I have provided and satisfied with peace My righteous ones, and have caused them to dwell before Me: But for the sinners there is judgement impending with Me, so that I shall destroy them from the face of the earth. Chapter 46 [1] And there I saw one who had a head of days, and His head was white like wool, and with Him was another being whose countenance had the appearance of a man, and his face was full of graciousness, like one of the holy angels. [2] And I asked the angel who went with me and showed me all the hidden things, concerning that Son of Man, [3] who he was, and whence he was, and why he went with the Head of Days? And he answered and said unto me: This is the son of Man who hath righteousness, with whom dwelleth righteousness, and who revealeth all the treasures of that which is hidden, because the Lord of Spirits hath chosen him, and whose lot hath the pre-eminence before the Lord of Spirits in uprightness for ever. [4] And this Son of Man whom thou hast seen shall raise up the kings and the mighty from their seats, and the strong from their thrones, and shall loosen the reins of the strong, and break the teeth of the sinners. [5] And he shall put down the kings from their thrones and kingdoms because they do not extol and praise Him, nor humbly acknowledge whence the kingdom was bestowed upon them. [6] And he shall put down the countenance of the strong, and shall fill them with shame. And darkness shall be their dwelling, and worms shall be their bed, and they shall have no hope of rising from their beds, because they do not extol the name of the Lord of Spirits. [7] And these are they who judge the stars of heaven, and raise their hands against the Most High, and tread upon the earth and dwell upon it. And all their deeds manifest unrighteousness, and their power rests upon their riches, and their faith is in the gods which they have made with their hands, and they deny the name of the Lord of Spirits, [8] And they persecute the houses of His congregations, and the faithful who hang upon the name of the Lord of Spirits. Chapter 47 [1] And in those days shall have ascended the prayer of the righteous, and the blood of the righteous from the earth before the Lord of Spirits. [2] In those days the holy ones who dwell above in the heavens shall unite with one voice and supplicate and pray and praise, and give thanks and bless the name of the Lord of Spirits on behalf of the blood of the righteous which has been shed, and that the prayer of the righteous may not be in vain before the Lord of Spirits, that judgement may be done unto them, and that they may not have to suffer for ever. [3] In those days I saw the Head of Days when He seated himself upon the throne of His glory, and the books of the living were opened before Him: And all His host which is in heaven above and His counselors stood before Him, [4] And the hearts of the holy were filled with joy; Because the number of the righteous had been offered, and the prayer of the righteous had been heard, and the blood of the righteous been required before the Lord of Spirits. Chapter 48 [1] And in that place I saw the fountain of righteousness which was inexhaustible: And around it were many fountains of wisdom: And all the thirsty drank of them, and were filled with wisdom, and their dwellings were with the righteous and holy and elect. [2] And at that hour that Son of Man was named In the presence of the Lord of Spirits, and his name before the Head of Days. [3] Yea, before the sun and the signs were created, before the stars of the heaven were made, his name was named before the Lord of Spirits. [4] He shall be a staff to the righteous whereon to stay themselves and not fall, and he shall be the light of the Gentiles, and the hope of those who are troubled of heart. [5] All who dwell on earth shall fall down and worship before him, and will praise and bless and celebrate with song the Lord of Spirits. [6] And for this reason hath he been chosen and hidden before Him, before the creation of the world and for evermore. [7] And the wisdom of the Lord of Spirits hath revealed him to the holy and righteous; For he hath preserved the lot of the righteous, because they have hated and despised this world of unrighteousness, and have hated all its works and ways in the name of the Lord of Spirits: For in his name they are saved, and according to his good pleasure hath it been in regard to their life. [8] In these days downcast in countenance shall the kings of the earth have become, and the strong who possess the land because of the works of their hands, for on the day of their anguish and affliction they shall not (be able to) save themselves. And I will give them over into the hands of Mine elect: [9] As straw in the fire so shall they bur n before the face of the holy: As lead in the water shall they sink before the face of the righteous, and no trace of them shall any more be found. [10] And on the day of their affliction there shall be rest on the earth, and before them they shall fall and not rise again: And there shall be no one to take them with his hands and raise them: For they have denied the Lord of Spirits and His Anointed. The name of the Lord of Spirits be blessed. Chapter 49 [1] For wisdom is poured out like water, and glory faileth not before him for evermore. [2] For he is mighty in all the secrets of righteousness, and unrighteousness shall disappear as a shadow, and have no continuance; Because the Elect One standeth before the Lord of Spirits, and his glory is for ever and ever, and his might unto all generations. [3] And in him dwells the spirit of wisdom, and the spirit which gives insight, and the spirit of understanding and of might, and the spirit of those who have fallen asleep in righteousness. [4] And he shall judge the secret things, and none shall be able to utter a lying word before him; For he is the Elect One before the Lord of Spirits according to His good pleasure. Chapter 50 [1] And in those days a change shall take place for the holy and elect, and the light of days shall abide upon them, and glory and honour shall turn to the holy, [2] On the day of affliction on which evil shall have been treasured up against the sinners. And the righteous shall be victorious in the name of the Lord of Spirits: And He will cause the others to witness this that they may repent, and forgot the works of their hands. [3] They shall have no honour through the name of the Lord of Spirits, yet through His name shall they be saved, and the Lord of Spirits will have compassion on them, for His compassion is great. [4] And He is righteous also in His judgement, and in the presence of His glory unrighteousness also shall not maintain itself: At His judgement the unrepentant shall perish before Him. [5] And from henceforth I will have no mercy on them, saith the Lord of Spirits. Chapter 51 [1] And in those days shall the earth also give back that which has been entrusted to it, and Sheol also shall give back that which it has received, and hell shall give back that which it owes. For in those days the Elect One shall arise, [2] And he shall choose the righteous and holy from among them: For the day has drawn nigh that they should be saved. [3] And the Elect One shall in those days sit on My throne, and his mouth shall pour forth all the secrets of wisdom and counsel: For the Lord of Spirits hath given (them) to him and hath glorified him. [4] And in those days shall the mountains leap like rams, and the hills also shall skip like lambs satisfied with milk, [5] And the faces of all the angels in heaven shall be lighted up with joy. And the earth shall rejoice, and the righteous shall dwell upon it, and the elect shall walk thereon. Chapter 52 [1] And after those days in that place where I had seen all the visions of that which is hidden, [2] For I had been carried off in a whirlwind and they had borne me towards the west-there mine eyes saw all the secret things of heaven that shall be, a mountain of iron, and a mountain of copper, and a mountain of silver, and a mountain of gold, and a mountain of soft metal, and a mountain of lead. [3] And I asked the angel who went with me, saying, What things are these which I have seen in secret? [4] And he said unto me: All these things which thou hast seen shall serve the dominion of His Anointed that he may be potent and mighty on the earth. [5] And that angel of peace answered, saying unto me: Wait a little, and there shall be revealed unto thee all the secret things which surround the Lord of Spirits. [6] And these mountains which thine eyes have seen, the mountain of iron, and the mountain of copper, and the mountain of silver, and the mountain of gold, and the mountain of soft metal, and the mountain of lead, all these shall be in the presence of the Elect One as wax: before the fire, and like the water which streams down from above upon those mountains, and they shall become powerless before his feet. [7] And it shall come to pass in those days that none shall be saved, either by gold or by silver, and none be able to escape. [8] And there shall be no iron for war, nor shall one clothe oneself with a breastplate. Bronze shall be of no service, and tin [shall be of no service and] shall not be esteemed, and lead shall not be desired. [9] And all these things shall be [denied and] destroyed from the surface of the earth, when the Elect One shall appear before the face of the Lord of Spirits. Chapter 53 [1] There mine eyes saw a deep valley with open mouths, and all who dwell on the earth and sea and islands shall bring to him gifts and presents and tokens of homage, but that deep valley shall not become full. [2] And their hands commit lawless deeds, and the sinners devour all whom they lawlessly oppress: Yet the sinners shall be destroyed before the face of the Lord of Spirits, and they shall be banished from off the face of His earth, and they shall perish for ever and ever. [3] For I saw all the angels of punishment abiding there and preparing all the instruments of Satan. [4] And I asked the angel of peace who went with me: For whom are they preparing these instruments? [5] And he said unto me: They prepare these for the kings and the mighty of this earth, that they may thereby be destroyed. [6] And after this the Righteous and Elect One shall cause the house of his congregation to appear: henceforth they shall be no more hindered in the name of the Lord of Spirits. [7] And these mountains shall not stand as the earth before his righteousness, but the hills shall be as a fountain of water, and the righteous shall have rest from the oppression of sinners. Chapter 54 [1] And I looked and turned to another part of the earth, and saw there a deep valley with burning fire. [2] And they brought the kings and the mighty, and began to cast them into this deep valley. [3] And there mine eyes saw how they made these their instruments, iron chains of immeasurable weight. [4] And I asked the angel of peace who went with me, saying: For whom are these chains being prepared? [5] And he said unto me: These are being prepared for the hosts of Azazel, so that they may take them and cast them into the abyss of complete condemnation, and they shall cover their jaws with rough stones as the Lord of Spirits commanded. [6] And Michael, and Gabriel, and Raphael, and Phanuel shall take hold of them on that great day, and cast them on that day into the burning furnace, that the Lord of Spirits may take vengeance on them for their unrighteousness in becoming subject to Satan and leading astray those who dwell on the earth. [7] And in those days shall punishment come from the Lord of Spirits, and he will open all the chambers of waters which are above the heavens, and of the fountains which are beneath the earth. [8] And all the waters shall be joined with the waters: that which is above the heavens is the masculine, [9] And the water which is beneath the earth is the feminine. And they shall destroy all who dwell on the earth, [10] And those who dwell under the ends of the heaven. And when they have recognized their unrighteousness which they have wrought on the earth, then by these shall they perish. Chapter 55 [1] And after that the Head of Days repented and said: In vain have I destroyed all who dwell on the earth. [2] And He sware by His great name: Henceforth I will not do so to all who dwell on the earth, and I will set a sign in the heaven: and this shall be a pledge of good faith between Me and them for ever, so long as heaven is above the earth. And this is in accordance with My command. [3] When I have desired to take hold of them by the hand of the angels on the day of tribulation and pain because of this, I will cause My chastisement and My wrath to abide upon them, saith God, the Lord of Spirits. [4] Ye mighty kings who dwell on the earth, ye shall have to behold Mine Elect One, how he sits on the throne of glory and judges Azazel, and all his associates, and all his hosts in the name of the Lord of Spirits. Chapter 56 [1] And I saw there the hosts of the angels of punishment going, and they held scourges and chains of iron and bronze. And I asked the angel of peace who went with me, saying: [2] To whom are these who hold the scourges going? And he said unto me: [3] To their elect and beloved ones, that they may be cast into the chasm of the abyss of the valley. [4] And then that valley shall be filled with their elect and beloved, And the days of their lives shall be at an end, And the days of their leading astray shall not thenceforward be reckoned. [5] And in those days the angels shall return, and hurl themselves to the east upon the Parthians and Medes: They shall stir up the kings, so that a spirit of unrest shall come upon them, and they shall rouse them from their thrones, that they may break forth as lions from their lairs, and as hungry wolves among their flocks. [6] And they shall go up and tread under foot the land of His elect ones, and the land of His elect ones shall be before the m a threshing-floor and a highway : [7] But the city of my righteous shall be a hindrance to their horses. And they shall begin to fight among themselves, and their right hand shall be strong against themselves, and a man shall not know his brother, nor a son his father or his mother, till there be no number of the corpses through their slaughter, and their punishment be not in vain. [8] In those days Sheol shall open its jaws, and they shall be swallowed up therein, and their destruction shall be at an end; Sheol shall devour the sinners in the presence of the elect. Chapter 57 [1] And it came to pass after this that I saw another host of wagons, and men riding thereon, [2] And coming on the winds from the east, and from the west to the south. And the noise of their wagons was heard, and when this turmoil took place the holy ones from heaven remarked it, and the pillars of the earth were moved from their place, and the sound thereof was heard from the one end of heaven to the other, in one day. [3] And they shall all fall down and worship the Lord of Spirits. And this is the end of the second Parable. Chapter 58 [1] And I began to speak the third Parable concerning the righteous and elect. [2] Blessed are ye, ye righteous and elect, for glorious shall be your lot. [3] And the righteous shall be in the light of the sun. And the elect in the light of eternal life: The days of their life shall be unending, and the days of the holy without number. [4] And they shall seek the light and find righteousness with the Lord of Spirits: There shall be peace to the righteous in the name of the Eternal Lord. [5] And after this it shall be said to the holy in heaven that they should seek out the secrets of righteousness, the heritage of faith: For it has become bright as the sun upon earth, and the darkness is past. [6] And there shall be a light that never endeth, and to a limit of days they shall not come, for the darkness shall first have been destroyed, and the light established before the Lord of Spirits, and the light of uprightness established for ever before the Lord of Spirits. Chapter 59 [1] In those days mine eyes saw the secrets of the lightnings, and of the lights, and the judgements they execute and they lighten for a blessing or a curse as the Lord of

Spirits willeth. [2] And there I saw the secrets of the thunder, and how when it resounds above in the heaven, the sound thereof is heard, and he caused me to see the judgements executed on the earth, whether they be for well-being and blessing, or for a curse according to the word of the Lord of Spirits. [3] And after that all the secrets of the lights and lightnings were shown to me, and they lighten for blessing and for satisfying.

Book 73. Noah

Chapter 60 [1] In the year 500, in the seventh month, on the fourteenth day of the month in the life of Enoch. In that Parable I saw how a mighty quaking made the heaven of heavens to quake, and the host of the Most High, and the angels, a thousand thousands and ten thousand times ten thousand, [2] Were disquieted with a great disquiet. And the Head of Days sat on the throne of His glory, and the angels and the righteous stood around Him. [3] And a great trembling seized me, and fear took hold of me, and my loins gave way, and dissolved were my reins, and I fell upon my face. [4] And Michael sent another angel from among the holy ones and he raised me up, and when he had raised me up my spirit returned; for I had not been able to endure the look of this host, [5] And the commotion and the quaking of the heaven. And Michael said unto me: Why art thou disquieted with such a vision ? Until this day lasted the day of His mercy; and He hath been merciful, [6] And long-suffering towards those who dwell on the earth. And when the day, and the power, and the punishment, and the judgement come, which the Lord of Spirits hath prepared for those who worship not the righteous law, and for those who deny the righteous judgement, and for those who take His name in vain- that day is prepared, for the elect a covenant, but for sinners an inquisition. [7] When the punishment of the Lord of Spirits shall rest upon them, it shall rest in order that the punishment of the Lord of Spirits may not come, in vain, and it shall slay the children with their mothers and the children with their fathers. Afterwards the judgement shall take place according to His mercy and His patience. And on that day were two monsters parted, a female monster named Leviathan, [8] To dwell in the abysses of the ocean over the fountains of the waters. But the male is named Behemoth, who occupied with his breast a waste wilderness named Duidain, on the east of the garden where the elect and righteous dwell, where my grandfather was taken up, the seventh from Adam, [9] The first man whom the Lord of Spirits created. And I besought the other angel that he should show me the might of those monsters, how they were parted on one day and cast, the one into the abysses of the sea, [10] And the other unto the dry land of the wilderness. And he said to me: Thou son of man, herein thou dost seek to know what is hidden. [11] And the other angel who went with me and showed me what was hidden told me what is first and last in the heaven in the height, and beneath the earth in the depth, and at the ends of the heaven, [12] And on the foundation of the heaven. And the chambers of the winds, and how the winds are divided, and how they are weighed, and how the portals of the winds are reckoned, each according to the power of the wind, and the power of the lights of the moon, and according to the power that is fitting: and the divisions of the stars according to their names, and how all the divisions are divided. [13] And the thunders according to the places where they fall, and all the divisions that are made among the lightnings that it may lighten, and their host that they may at once obey. [14] For the thunder has places of rest (which are assigned (to it) while it is waiting for its peal; And the thunder and lightning are inseparable, and although not one and undivided, they both go together through the spirit and separate not. [15] For when the lightning lightens, the thunder utters its voice, and the spirit enforces a pause during the peal, and divides equally between them; for the treasury of their peals is like the sand, and each one of them as it peals is held in with a bridle, and turned back by the power of the spirit, and pushed forward according to the many quarters of the earth. [16] And the spirit of the sea is masculine and strong, and according to the might of his strength he draws it back with a rein, and in like manner it is driven forward and disperses amid all the mountains of the earth. [17] And the spirit of the hoar-frost is his own angel, and the spirit of the hail is a good angel. [18] And the spirit of the snow has forsaken his chambers on account of his strength - There is a special spirit therein, and that which ascends from it is like smoke, and its name is frost. [19] And the spirit of the mist is not united with them in their chambers, but it has a special chamber; for its course is glorious both in light and in darkness, and in winter and in summer, and in its chamber is an angel. [20] And the spirit of the dew has its dwelling at the ends of the heaven, and is connected with the chambers of the rain, and its course is in winter and summer: and its clouds and the clouds of the mist are connected, [21] And the one gives to the other. And when the spirit of the rain goes forth from its chamber, the angels come and open the chamber and lead it out, and when it is diffused over the whole earth it unites with the water on the earth. And whensoever it unites with the water on the earth. [22] For the waters are for those who dwell on the earth; for they are nourishment for the earthfrom the Most High who is in heaven: therefore there is a measure for the rain, and the angels take it in charge. And these things I saw towards the Garden of the Righteous. [23] And the angel of peace who was with me said to me: These two monsters, prepared conformably to the greatness of God, shall feed. Chapter 61 [1] And I saw in those days how long cords were given to those angels, and they took to themselves wings and flew, and they went towards the north. [2] And I asked the angel, saying unto him: Why have those (angels) taken these cords and gone off? And he said unto me: They have gone to measure. [3] And the angel who went with me said unto me: These shall bring the measures of the righteous, and the ropes of the righteous to the righteous, that they may stay themselves on the name of the Lord of Spirits for ever and ever. [4] The elect shall begin to dwell with the elect, and those are the measures which shall be given to faith, and which shall strengthen righteousness. [5] And these measures shall reveal all the secrets of the depths of the earth, and those who have been destroyed by the desert, and those who have been devoured by the beasts, and those who have been devoured by the fish of the sea, that they may return and stay themselves on the day of the Elect One; For none shall be destroyed before the Lord of Spirits, and none can be destroyed. [6] And all who dwell above in the heaven received a command and power and one voice and one light like unto fire. [7] And that One with their first words they blessed, and extolled and lauded with wisdom, and they were wise in utterance and in the spirit of life. [8] And the Lord of Spirits placed the Elect one on the throne of glory. And he shall judge all the works of the holy above in the heaven, and in the balance shall their deeds be weighed. Chapter 62 [1] And thus the Lord commanded the kings and the mighty and the exalted, and those who dwell on the earth, and said: Open your eyes and lift up your horns if ye are able to recognize the Elect One. [2] And the Lord of Spirits seated him on the throne of His glory, and the spirit of righteousness was poured out upon him, and the word of his mouth slays all the sinners, and all the unrighteous are destroyed from before his face. [3] And there shall stand up in that day all the kings and the mighty, and the exalted and those who hold the earth, and they shall see and recognize How he sits on the throne of his glory, and righteousness is judged before him, and no lying word is spoken before him. [4] Then shall pain come upon them as on a woman in trava il, and she has pain in bringing forth, when her child enters the mouth of the womb, and she has pain in bringing forth. [5] And one portion of them shall look on the other, and they shall be terrified, and they shall be downcast of countenance, and pain shall seize them, when they see that Son of Man Sitting on the throne of his glory. [6] And the kings and the mighty and all who possess the earth shall bless and glorify and extol him who rules over all, who was hidden. [7] For from the beginning the Son of Man was hidden, and the most High preserved him in the presence of His might, and revealed him to the elect. [8] And the congregation of the elect and holy shall be sown, and all the elect shall stand before him on that day. [9] And all the kings and the mighty and the exalted and those who rule the eart. Shall fall down before him on their faces, and worship and set their hope upon that Son of Man, and petition him and supplicate for mercy at his hands. [10] Nevertheless that Lord of Spirits will so press them that they shall hastily go forth from His presence, and their faces shall be filled with shame, and the darkness grow deeper on their faces. [11] And He will deliver them to the angels for punishment, to execute vengeance on them because they have oppressed His children and His elect, [12] And they shall be a spectacle for the righteous and for His elect: They shall rejoice over them, because the wrath of the Lord of Spirits resteth upon them, and His sword is drunk with their blood. [13] And the righteous and elect shall be saved on that day, and they shall never thenceforward see the face of the sinners and unrighteous. [14] And the Lord of Spirits will abide over them, and with that Son of Man shall they eat and lie down and rise up for ever and ever. [15] And the righteous and elect shall have risen from the earth, and ceased to be of downcast countenance. And they shall have been clothed with garments of glory, [16] And these shall be the garments of life from the Lord of Spirits: And your garments shall not grow old, nor your glory pass away before the Lord of Spirits. Chapter 63 [1] In those days shall the mighty and the kings who possess the earth implore Him to grant them a little respite from His angels of punishment to whom they were delivered, [2] That they might fall down and worship before the Lord of Spirits, and confess their sins before Him. And they shall bless and glorify the Lord of Spirits, and say: Blessed is the Lord of Spirits and the Lord of kings, And the Lord of the mighty and the Lord of the rich, And the Lord of glory and the Lord of wisdom, [3] And splendid in every secret thing is Thy power from generation to generation, and Thy glory for ever and ever: Deep are all Thy secrets and innumerable, and Thy righteousness is beyond reckoning. [4] We have now learnt that we should glorify and bless the Lord of kings and Him who is king over all kings. [5] And they shall say: Would that we had rest to glorify and give thanks and confess our faith before His glory ! [6] And now we long for a little rest but find it not: We follow hard upon and obtain (it) not: And light has vanished from before us, and darkness is our dwelling-place for ever and ever: [7] For we have not believed before Him nor glorified the name of the Lord of Spirits, nor glorified our Lord but our hope was in the sceptre of our kingdom, and in our glory. [8] And in the day of our suffering and tribulation He saves us not, and we find no respite for confession that our

Lord is true in all His works, and in His judgements and His justice, and His judgements have no respect of persons. [9] And we pass away from before His face on account of our works, and all our sins are reckoned up in righteousness. [10] Now they shall say unto themselves: Our souls are full of unrighteous gain, but it does not prevent us from descending from the midst thereof into the burden of Sheol. [11] And after that their faces shall be filled with darkness, and shame before that Son of Man, and they shall be driven from his presence, and the sword shall abide before his face in their midst. [12] Thus spake the Lord of Spirits: This is the ordinance and judgement with respect to the mighty and the kings and the exalted and those who possess the earth before the Lord of Spirits. Chapter 64 [1] And other forms I saw hidden in that place. I heard the voice of the angel saying: These are the angels who descended to the earth, [2] And revealed what was hidden to the children of men and seduced the children of men into committing sin. Chapter 65 [1] And in those days Noah saw the earth that it had sunk down and its destruction was nigh. [2] And he arose from thence and went to the ends of the earth, and cried aloud to his grandfather Enoch: [3] And Noah said three times with an embittered voice: Hear me, hear me, hear me. And I said unto him: Tell me what it is that is falling out on the earth that the earth is in such evil plight, [4] And shaken, lest perchance I shall perish with it? And thereupon there was a great commotion , on the earth, and a voice was heard from heaven, and I fell on my face. [5] And Enoch my grandfather came and stood by me, and said unto me: Why hast thou cried unto me with a bitter cry and weeping, [6] And a command has gone forth from the presence of the Lord concerning those who dwell on the earth that their ruin is accomplished because they have learnt all the secrets of the angels, and all the violence of the Satans, and all their powers -the most secret ones- and all the power of those who practice sorcery, and the power of witchcraft, and the power of those who make molten images for the whole earth: [7] And how silver is produced from the dust of the earth, and how soft metal originates in the earth. [8] For lead and tin are not produced from the earth like the first: it is a fountain that produces them, [9] And an angel stands therein, and that angel is pre-eminent. And after that my grandfather Enoch took hold of me by my hand and raised me up, and said unto me: [10] Go, for I have asked the Lord of Spirits as touching this commotion on the earth. And He said unto me: "Because of their unrighteousness their judgement has been determined upon and shall not be withheld by Me for ever. Because of the sorceries which they have searched out and learnt, the earth, [11] and those who dwell upon it shall be destroyed." And these-they have no place of repentance forever, because they have shown them what was hidden, and they are the damned: but as for thee, my son, the Lord of Spirits knows that thou art pure, and guiltless of this reproach concerning the secrets. [12] And He has destined thy name to be among the holy, And will preserve thee amongst those who dwell on the earth, and has destined thy righteous seed both for kingship and for great honours, and from thy seed shall proceed a fountain of the righteous and holy witho ut number forever. Chapter 66 [1] And after that he showed me the angels of punishment who are prepared to come and let loose all the powers of the waters which are beneath in the earth in order to bring judgement and destruction on all who abide and dwell on the earth. [2] And the Lord of Spirits gave commandment to the angels who were going forth, that they should not cause the waters to rise but should hold them in check; [3] For those angels were over the powers of the waters. And I went away from the presence of Enoch. Chapter 67 [1] And in those days the word of God came unto me, and He said unto me: Noah, thy lot has come up before Me, [2] A lot without blame, a lot of love and uprightness. And now the angels are making a wooden building, and when they have completed that task I will place My hand upon it and preserve it, and there shall come forth from it the seed of life, and a change shall set in so that the earth will not remain without inhabitant. [3] And I will make fast thy seed before me for ever and ever, and I will spread abroad those who dwell with thee: it shall not be unfruitful on the face of the earth, but it shall be blessed and multiply on the earth in the name of the Lord. [4] And He will imprison those angels, who have shown unrighteousness, in that burning valley which my grandfather Enoch had formerly shown to me in the west among the mountains of gold and silver and iron and soft metal and tin. [5] And I saw that valley in which there was a great convulsion and a convulsion of the waters. [6] And when all this took place, from that fiery molten metal and from the convulsion thereof in that place, there was produced a smell of sulphur, and it was connected with those waters, and that valley of the angels who had led astray mankind burned beneath that land. [7] And through its valleys proceed streams of fire, where these angels are punished who had led astray those who dwell upon the earth. [8] But those waters shall in those days serve for the kings and the mighty and the exalted, and those who dwell on the earth, for the healing of the body, but for the punishment of the spirit; Now their spirit is full of lust, that they may be punished in their body, for they have denied the Lord of Spirits and see their punishment daily, [9] And yet believe not in His name. And in proportion as the burning of their bodies becomes severe, a corresponding change shall take place in their spirit for ever and ever; [10] For before the Lord of Spirits none shall utter an idle word. For the judgement shall come upon them, [11] Because they believe in the lust of their body and deny the Spirit of the Lord. And those same waters will undergo a change in those days; for when those angels are punished in these waters, these water-springs shall change their temperature, and when the angels ascend, this water of the springs shall change and become cold. [12] And I heard Michael answering and saying: This judgement wherewith the angels are judged is a testimony for the kings and the mighty who possess the earth. [13] Because these waters of judgement minister to the healing of the body of the kings and the lust of their body; therefore they will not see and will not believe that those waters will change and become a fire which burns for ever. Chapter 68 [1] And after that my grandfather Enoch gave me the teaching of all the secrets in the book in the Parables which had been given to him, and he put them together for me in the words of the book of the Parables. [2] And on that day Michael answered Raphael and said: The power of the spirit transports and makes me to tremble because of the severity of the judgement of the secrets, the judgement of the angels: who can endure the severe judgement which has been executed, [3] And before which they melt away ? And Michael answered again, and said to Raphael: Who is he whose heart is not softened concerning it, and whose reins are not troubled by this word of judgement that has gone forth upon them because of those who have thus led them out ? [4] And it came to pass when he stood before the Lord of Spirits, Michael said thus to Raphael: I will not take their part under the eye of the Lord; for the Lord of Spirits has been angry with them because they do as if they were the Lord. [5] Therefore all that is hidden shall come upon them forever and ever; for neither angel nor man shall have his portion in it, but alone they have received their judgement for ever and ever. Chapter 69 [1] And after this judgement they shall terrify and make them to tremble because they have shown this to those who dwell on the earth. [2] And behold the names of those angels [and these are their names: the first of them is Samjaza, the second Artaqifa, and the third Armen, the fourth Kokabel, the fifth Turael, the sixth Rumjal, the seventh Danjal, the eighth Neqael, the ninth Baraqel, the tenth Azazel, the eleventh Armaros, the twelfth Batarjal, the thirteenth Busasejal, the fourteenth Hananel, the fifteenth Turel, and the sixteenth Simapesiel, the seventeenth Jetrel, the eighteenth Tumael, the nineteenth Turel, the twentieth Rumael, the twenty first Azazel. [3] And these are the chiefs of their angels and their names, and their chief ones over hundreds and over fifties and over tens. [4] The name of the first Jeqon: that is, the one who led astray [all] the sons of God, and brought them down to the earth, and led them astray through the daughters of men. [5] And the second was named Asbeel: he imparted to the holy sons of God evil counsel, and led them astray so that they defiled their bodies with the daughters of men. And the third was named Gadreel: he it is who showed the children of men all the blows of death, and he led astray Eve, [6] And showed the weapons of death to the sons of men the shield and the coat of mail, and the sword for battle, and all the weapons of death to the children of men. [7] And from his hand they have proceeded against those who dwell on the earth from that day and for evermore. [8] And the fourth was named Penemue: he taught the children of men the bitter and the sweet, [9] And he taught them all the secrets of their wisdom. And he instructed mankind in writing with ink and paper, and thereby many sinned from eternity to eternity and until this day. [10] For men were not created for such a purpose, to give confirmation to their good faith with pen and ink. [11] For me n were created exactly like the angels, to the intent that they should continue pure and righteous, and death, which destroys everything, could not have taken hold of them, but through this their knowledge they are perishing, and through this power it is consuming me. [12] And the fifth was named Kasdeja: this is he who showed the children of men all the wicked smitings of spirits and demons, and the smitings of the embryo in the womb, that it may pass away, and the smitings of the soul the bites of the serpent, and the smitings, [13] Which befall through the noontide heat, the son of the serpent named Tabaet. And this is the task of Kasbeel, the chief of the oath which he showed to the holy ones when he dwelt high above in glory, and its name is Biqa. [14] This angel requested Michael to show him the hidden name, that he might enunciate it in the oath, so that those might quake before that name and oath who revealed all that was in secret to the children of men. [15] And this is the power of this oath, for it is powerful and strong, and he placed this oath Akae in the hand of Michael. [16] And these are the secrets of this oath , And they are strong through his oath: And the heaven was suspended before the world was created, and forever. [17] And through it the earth was founded upon the water, and from the secret recesses of the mountains come beautiful waters, from the creation of the world and unto eternity. [18] And through that oath the sea was created, and as its foundation He set for it the sand against the time of its anger, and it dare not pass beyond it from the creation of the world unto eternity. [19] And through that oath are the depths made fast, and abide and stir not from their place from eternity to eternity. [20] And through that oath the sun and moon complete their course, and deviate not from their ordinance from eternity to eternity. [21] And through that oath the stars complete their course, and He calls them by their names, and they answer Him from eternity to eternity. [22] And in like manner the spirits of the

water, and of the winds, and of all zephyrs, andtheir paths from all the quarters of the winds. [23] And there are preserved the voices of the thunder and the light of the lightnings: and there are preserved the chambers of the hail and the chambers of the hoarfrost, [24] And the chambers of the mist, and the chambers of the rain and the dew. And all these believe and give thanks before the Lord of Spirits, and glorify Him with all their power, and their food is in every act of thanksgiving: they thank and glorify and extol the name of the Lord of Spirits for ever and ever. [25] And this oath is mighty over them and through it they are preserved and their paths are preserved, And their course is not destroyed. [26] And there was great joy amongst them, and they blessed and glorified and extolled because the name of that Son of Man had been revealed unto them. [27] And he sat on the throne of his glory, and the sum of judgement was given unto the Son of Man, and he caused the sinners to pass away and be destroyed from off the face of the earth, and those who have led the world astray. [28] With chains shall they be bound, and in their assemblage-place of destruction shall they be imprisoned, and all their works vanish from the face of the earth. [29] And from henceforth there shall be nothing corruptible; For that Son of Man has appeared, and has seated himself on the throne of his glory, and all evil shall pass away before his face, and the word of that Son of Man shall go forth and be strong before the Lord of Spirits. Chapter 70 [1] And it came to pass after this that his name during his lifetime was raised aloft to that Son of Man, [2] And to the Lord of Spirits from amongst those who dwell on the earth. [3] And he was raised aloft on the chariots of the spirit and his name vanished among them. And from that day I was no longer numbered amongst them: and he set me between the two winds, between the North and the West, [4] Where the angels took the cords to measure for me the place for the elect and righteous. And there I saw the first fathers and the righteous who from the beginning dwell in that place. Chapter 71 [1] And it came to pass after this that my spirit was translated and it ascended into the heavens: And I saw the holy sons of God. They were stepping on flames of fire: Their garments were white and their raiment, and their faces shone like snow. [2] And I saw two streams of fire, and the light of that fire shone like hyacinth, and I fell on my face before the Lord of Spirits. [3] And the angel Michael[one of the archangels] seized me by my right hand, and lifted me up and led me forth into all the secrets, and he showed me all the secrets of righteousness. [4] And he showed me all the secrets of the ends of the heaven, and all the chambers of all the stars, and all the luminaries, whence they proceed before the face of the holy ones. [5] And he translated my spirit into the heaven of heavens, and I saw there as it were a structure built of crystals, and between those crystals tongues of living fire. [6] And my spirit saw the girdle which girt that house of fire, and on its four sides were streams full of living fire, and they girt that house. [7] And round about were Seraphin, Cherubic, and Ophannin: And these are they who sleep not and guard the throne of His glory. [8] And I saw angels who could not be counted, a thousand thousands, and ten thousand times ten thousand, encircling that house. And Michael, and Raphael, and Gabriel, and Phanuel, and the holy angels who are above the heavens, go in and out of that house. [9] And they came forth from that house, and Michael and Gabriel, Raphael and Phanuel, and many holy angels without number. [10] And with them the Head of Days, His head white and pure as wool, and His raiment indescribable. [11] And I fell on my face, and my whole body became relaxed, and my spirit was transfigured; and I cried with a loud voice, with the spirit of power, and blessed and glorified and extolled. [12] And these blessings which went forth out of my mouth were well pleasing before that Head of Days. And that Head of Days came with Michael and Gabriel, Raphael and Phanuel, thousands and ten thousands of angels without number. [13] Lost passage where in the Son of Man was described as accompanying the Head of Days, and Enoch asked one of the angels concerning the Son of Man as to who he was. [14] And he, the angel, came to me and greeted me with His voice, and said unto me this is the Son of Man who is born unto righteousness, and righteousness abides over him, and the righteousness of the Head of Days forsakes him not. [15] And he said unto me: He proclaims unto thee peace in the name of the world to come; For from hence has proceeded peace since the creation of the world, and so shall it be unto thee for ever and for ever and ever. [16] And all shall walk in his ways since righteousness never forsaketh him: With him will be their dwelling-places, and with him their heritage, and they shall not be separated from him for ever and ever and ever. And so there shall be length of days with that Son of Man, and the righteous shall have peace and an upright way in the name of the Lord of Spirits for ever and ever.

Book 74. The Book Of The Luminaries Of The Heaven – Enoch's Ethiopic Book 3

Chapter 72 [1] The book of the courses of the luminaries of the heaven, the relations of each, according to their classes, their dominion and their seasons, according to their names and places of origin, and according to their months, which Uriel, the holy angel, who was with me, who is their guide, showed me; and he showed me all their laws exactly as they are, and how it is with regard to all the years of the world and unto eternity, [2] Till the new creation is accomplished which dureth till eternity. And this is the first law of the luminaries: the luminary the Sun has its rising in the eastern portals of the heaven, [3] And its setting in the western portals of the heaven. And I saw six portals in which the sun rises, and six portals in which the sun sets and the moon rises and sets in these portals, and the leaders of the stars and those whom they lead: six in the east and six in the west, and all following each other in accurately corresponding order: [4] also many windows to the right and left of these portals. And first there goes forth the great luminary, named the Sun, and his circumference is like the circumference of the heaven, [5] And he is quite filled with illuminating and heating fire. The chariot on which he ascends, the wind drives, and the sun goes down from the heaven and returns through the north in order to reach the east, and is so guided that he comes to the appropriate portal and shines in the face of the heaven. [6] In this way he rises in the first month in the great portal, [7] Which is the fourth [those six portals in the cast]. And in that fourth portal from which the sun rises in the first month are twelve window openings, from which proceed a flame when they are opened in their season. [8] When the sun rises in the heaven, he comes forth through that fourth portal thirty, [9] Mornings in succession, and sets accurately in the fourth portal in the west of the heaven. And during this period the day becomes daily longer and the night nightly shorter to the thirtieth morning. [10] On that day the day is longer than the night by a ninth part, and the day amounts exactly to ten parts and the night to eight parts. And the sun rises from that fourth portal, and sets in the fourth and returns to the fifth portal of the east thirty mornings, and rises from it and sets in the fifth portal. [11] And then the day becomes longer by two parts and amounts to eleven parts, and the night becomes shorter and amounts to seven parts. [12] And it returns to the east and enters into the sixth portal, [13] And rises and sets in the sixth portal one-and-thirty mornings on account of its sign. [14] On that day the day becomes longer than the night, and the day becomes double the night, and the day becomes twelve parts, [15] And the night is shortened and becomes six parts. And the sun mounts up to make the day shorter and the night longer, and the sun returns to the east and enters into the sixth portal, [16] And rises from it and sets thirty mornings. And when thirty mornings are accomplished, [17] The day decreases by exactly one part, and becomes eleven parts, and the night seven. And the sun goes forth from that sixth portal in the west, and goes to the east and rises in the fifth portal for thirty mornings, [18] And sets in the west again in the fifth western portal. On that day the day decreases by two parts, and amounts to ten parts and the night to eight parts. [19] And the sun goes forth from that fifth portal and sets in the fifth portal of the west, and rises in the fourth portal for one-and-thirty mornings on account of its sign, and sets in the west. [20] On that day the day is equalized with the night, and becomes of equal length, and the night amounts to nine parts and the day to nine parts. [21] And the sun rises from that portal and sets in the west, and returns to the east and rises thirty mornings in the third portal and sets in the west in the third portal. [22] And on that day the night becomes longer than the day, and night becomes longer than night, and day shorter than day till thhe thirtieth morning, and the night amounts exactly to ten parts and the day to eight parts. [23] And the sun rises from that third portal and sets in the third portal in the west and returns to the east, and for thirty mornings rises in the second portal in the east, [24] And in like manner sets in the second portal in the west of the heaven. And on that day the night amounts to eleven parts and the day to seven parts. [25] And the sun rises on that day from that second portal and sets in the west in the second portal, and returns to the east into the first portal for one and thirty mornings, [26] And sets in the first portal in the west of the heaven. And on that day the night becomes longer and amounts to the double of the day: and the night amounts exactly to twelve parts and the day to six. [27] And the sun has therewith traversed the divisions of his orbit and turns again on those divisions of his orbit, and enters that portal thirty mornings and sets also in the west opposite to it. [28] And on that night has the night decreased in length by a ninth part, and the night has become eleven parts and the day seven parts. And the sun has returned and entered into the second portal in the east, and returns on those his divisions of his orbit for thirty mornings, rising and setting. [29] And on that day the night decreases in length, and the night amounts to ten parts and the day to eight. [30] And on that day the sun rises from that portal, and sets in the west, [31] And returns to the east, and rises in the third portal for one-and-thirty mornings, and sets in the west of the heaven. [32] On that day the night decreases and amounts to nine parts, and the day to nine parts, and the night is equal to the day and the year is exactly as to its days three hundred and sixty-four. And the length of the day and of the night, [33] And the shortness of the day and of the night arisethrough the course of the sun these distinctions are made. [34] So it comes that its course becomes daily longer, and its course nightly shorter. [35] And this is the law and the course of the sun, and his return as often as he returns sixty times and rises, i.e. the great luminary which is named the sun, forever and ever. [36] And that which, thus, rises is the great luminary, and is so named according to its appearance, according as the Lord commanded. As he rises, so he sets and decreases not, and rests not, but runs day and night, and his light is sevenfold brighter than that of the moon; but as regards size they are both equal. Chapter 73 [1] And after this law I saw another law dealing with the smaller luminary, which is named the Moon. [2] And her circumference is like the circumference of the heaven, and her chariot in which she rides is driven by the wind, and light is given to her in definite measure. And her rising and setting change every month: [3] And her days are like the days of the sun, and when her light is uniform it amounts to the seventh part of the light of the sun. [4] And thus she rises. And her first phase in the east comes forth on the thirtieth morning: and on that day she becomes visible, and constitutes for you the first phase of the moon on the thirtieth day together with the sun in the portal where the sun rises. [5] And the one half of her goes forth by a seventh part, and her whole circumference is empty, without light, with the exception of one-seventh part of it, and the fourteenth part of her light. [6] And when she receives one-seventh part of the half of her light, her light amounts to one-seventh part and the half thereof. [7] And she sets with the sun, and when the sun rises the moon rises with him and receives the half of one part of light, and in that night in the beginning of her morning in the commencement of the lunar day the moon sets with the sun, [8] And is invisible that night with the fourteen parts and the half of one of them. And she rises on that day with exactly a seventh part, and comes forth and recedes from the rising of the sun, [9] And in her remaining days she becomes bright in the remaining thirteen parts. Chapter 74 [1] And I saw another course, a law for her, (and) how according to that law she performs her monthly revolution. [2] And all these Uriel, the holy angel who is the leader of them all, showed to me, and their positions, and I wrote down their positions as he showed them to me, and I wrote down their months as they were, [3] And the appearance of their lights till fifteen days were accomplished. In single seventh parts she accomplishes all her light in the east, and in single seventh parts accomplishes all her darkness in the west. [4] And in certain months she alters her settings, and in certain months she pursues her own peculiar course. [5] In two months the moon sets with the sun: in those two middle portals the third and the fourth. [6] She goes forth for seven days, and turns about and returns again through the portal where the sun rises, and accomplishes all her light: and she recedes from the sun, and in eight days enters the sixth portal from which the sun goes forth. [7] And when the sun goes forth from the fourth portal she goes forth seven days, until she goes forth from the fifth and turns back again in seven days into the fourth portal and accomplishes all her light: and she recedes and enters into the first portal in eight days. [8] And she returns again in seven days into the fourth portal from which the sun goes forth. [9] Thus I saw their position how the moons rose and the sun set in those days. [10] And if five years are added together the sun has an overplus of thirty days, and all the days which accrue to it for one of those five years, [11] When they are full, amount to 364 days. And the overplus of the sun and of the stars amounts to six days: in 5 years 6 days every year come to 30 days: and the moon falls behind the sun and stars to the number of 30 days. [12] And the sun and the stars bring in all the years exactly, so that they do not advance or delay their position by a single day unto eternity; but complete the years with perfect justice in 364 days. [13] In 3 years there are 1,092 days, and in 5 years 1,820 days, so that in 8 years there are 2,912 days. [14] For the moon alone the days amount in 3 years to 1,062 days, and in 5 years she falls 50 days behind:i.e. to the sum (of 1,770) there is 5 to be added (1,000 and) 62 days. [15] And in 5 years there are 1,770 days, so that for the moon the days 6 in 8 years amount to 21,832 days. [16] For in 8 years she falls behind to the amount of 80 days, all the 17 days she falls behind in 8 years are 80. And the year is accurately completed in conformity with their world stations and the stations of the sun, which rise from the portals through which it the sun rises and sets 30 days. Chapter 75 [1] And the leaders of the heads of the thousands, who are placed over the whole creation and over all the stars, have also to do with the four intercalary days, being inseparable from their office, according to the reckoning of the year, and these render service on the four days which are not reckoned in the reckoning of the year. [2] And owing to them men go wrong therein, for those luminaries truly render service on the world-stations, one in the first portal, one in the third portal of the heaven, one in the fourth portal, and one in the sixth portal, and the exactness of the year is accomplished through its separate three hundred and sixty- four stations. [3] For the signs and the times and the years and the days the angel Uriel showed to me, whom the Lord of glory hath set for ever over all the luminaries of the heaven, in the heaven and in the world, that they should rule on the face of the heaven and be seen on the earth, and be leaders for the day and the night, i.e. the sun, moon, and stars, and all the ministering creatures which make their revolution in all the chariots of the heaven. [4] In like manner twelve doors Uriel showed me, open in the circumference of the suns chariot in the heaven, through which the rays of the sun break forth: and from them is warmth diffused over the earth, when they are opened at their appointed seasons. And for the winds and the spirit of the dew when they are opened, [5] Standing open in the heavens at the ends. As for the twelve portals in the heaven, at the ends of the earth, out of which go forth the sun, moon, and stars, and all the works of heaven in the east and in the west, [6] There are many windows open to the left and right of them, and one window at its appointed season produces warmth, corresponding as these do to those doors from which the stars come forth according as He has commanded them, and where in they set corresponding to their number. And I saw chariots in the heaven, running in the world, above those portals in which revolve the stars that never set. And one is larger than all the rest, and it is that that makes its course through the entire world. Chapter 76 [1] And at the ends of the earth I saw twelve portals open to all the quarters of the heaven, [2] From which the winds go forth and blow over the earth. Three of them are open on the face of the heavens, and three in the west, and three on the right of the heaven, and three on the left. [3] And the three first are those of the east, and three are of the north, [4] And three after those on the left of the south, and three of the west. Through four of these come winds of blessing and prosperity, and from those eight come hurtful winds: when they are sent, the y bring destruction on all the earth and on the water upon it, and on all who dwell thereon, and on everything which is in the water and on the land. [5] And the first wind from those portals, called the east wind, comes forth through the first portal which is in the east, inclining towards the south: from it come forth desolation, drought, heat, and destruction. [6] And through the second portal in the middle comes what is fitting, and from it there come rain and fruitfulness and prosperity and dew; and through the third portal which lies toward the north come cold and drought. [7] And after these come forth the south winds through three portals: through the first portal of them inclining to the east comes forth a hot wind. [8] And through the middle portal next to it there come forth fragrant smells, [9] And dew and rain, and prosperity and health. And through the third portal lying to the west come forth dew and rain, locusts and desolation. [10] And after these the north winds: from the seventh portal in the east come dew and rain, locusts and desolation. [11] And from the middle portal come in a direct direction health and rain and dew and prosperity; and through the third portal in the west come cloud and hoar-frost, and snow and rain, and dew and locusts. [12] And after thesefour are the west winds: through the first portal adjoining the north come forth dew and hoar- frost, and cold and snow and frost. And from the middle portal come forth dew and rain, and prosperity and blessing; and through the last portal which adjoins the south come forth drought and desolation, and burning and destruction. And the twelve portals of the four quarters of the heaven are therewith completed, and all their laws and all their plagues and all their benefactions have I shown to thee, my son Methuselah. Chapter 77 [1] And the first quarter is called the east, because it is the first: and the second, the south, because the Most High will descend there, yea, there in quite a special sense will He who is blessed for ever descend. [2] And the west quarter is named the diminished, because there all the luminaries of the heaven wane and go down. [3] And the fourth quarter, named the north, is divided into three parts: the first of them is for the dwelling of men: and the second contains seas of water, and the abysses and forests and rivers, and darkness and clouds; and the third part contains the garden of righteousness. [4] I saw seven high mountains, higher than all the mountains which are on the earth: and thence comes forth hoar frost, [5] And days, seasons, and years pass away. I saw seven rivers on the earth larger than all the rivers: one of them coming from the west pours its waters into the Great Sea. [6] And these two come from the north to the sea and pour their waters into the Erythraean Sea in the east. [7] And the remaining, four come forth on the side of the north to their own sea, two of them to the Erythraean Sea, and two into the Great Sea and discharge themselves thereand some say: into the desert. [8] Seven great islands I saw in the sea and in the mainland: two in the mainland and five in the Great Sea. Chapter 78 [1] And the names of the sun are the following: the first Orjares, and the second Tomas. [2] And the moon has four names: the first name is Asonja, the second Ebla, the third Benase, and the fourth Erae. [3] These are the two great luminaries: their circumference is like the circumference of the heaven, and the size of the circumference of both is alike. [4] In the circumference of the sun there are seven portions of light which are added to it more than to the moon, and in definite measures it is s transferred till the seventh portion of the sun is exhausted. [5] And they set and enter the portals of the west, and make their revolution by the north, and come forth through the eastern portals on the face of the heaven. [6] And when the moon rises one- fourteenth part appears in the heaven: [7] The light becomes full in her: on the fourteenth day she accomplishes her light. And fifteen parts of light are transferred to her till the fifteenth day when her light is accomplished, according to the sign of the year, and she becomes fifteen parts, and the moon grows by (the addition of) fourteenth parts. [8] And in her waning (the moon) decreases on the first day to fourteen parts of her light, on the second to thirteen parts of light, on the third to twelve, on the fourth to eleven, on the fifth to ten, on the sixth to nine, on the seventh to eight, on the eighth to seven, on the ninth to six, on the tenth to five, on the eleventh to four, on the twelfth to three, on the thirteenth to two, on the fourteenth to the half of a seventh, [9] And all her remaining light disappears wholly on the fifteenth. [10] And in certain months the month has twenty-nine days and once twenty-eight. And Uriel showed me another law: when light is transferred to the moon, and on which side it is transferred to her by the sun. [11] During all the period during which the moon is growing in her light, she is transferring it to herself when opposite to the sun during fourteen daysher light is accomplished in the heaven, [12] And when she is illumined throughout, her light is accomplished full in the heaven. And on the first day she is called the new moon, [13] For on that day the light rises upon her. She becomes full moon exactly on the day when the sun sets in the west, and from the east she rises at night, and the moon shines the whole night through till the sun rises over against her and the moon is seen over against the sun. [14] On the side whence the light of the moon comes forth, there again she wanes till all the light vanishes and all the days of the month are at an end, and her circumference is empty, void of light. [15] And three months she makes of thirty days, and at her time she makes three months of twenty nine days each, in which she accomplishes her waning in the first period of time, [16] And in the first portal for one hundred and seventy-seven days. And in the time of her going out she appears for three months of thirty days each, and for three months she appears of twentynine each. At night she appears like a man for twenty days each time, and by day she appears like the heaven, and there is nothing else in her save her light. Chapter 79 [1] And now, my son, I have shown thee everything, and the law of all the stars of the heaven is completed. [2] And he showed me all the laws of these for every day, and for every season of bearing rule, and for every year, and for its going forth, and for the order prescribed to it every month and every week: [3] And the waning of the moon which takes place in the sixth portal: for in this sixth portal her light is accomplished, [4] And after that there is the beginning of the waning: And the waning which takes place in the first portal in its season, till one hundred and seventy seven days are accomplished: [5] Reckoned according to weeks, twenty five weeks and two days. She falls behind the sun and the order of the stars exactly five days in the course of one period, [6] And when this place which thou seest has been traversed. Such is the picture and sketch of every luminary which Uriel the archangel, who is their leader, showed unto me. Chapter 80 [1] And in those days the angel Uriel answered and said to me: Behold, I have shown thee everything, Enoch, and I have revealed everything to thee that thou shouldst see this sun and this moon, and the leaders of the stars of the heaven and all those who turn them, their tasks and times and departures. [2] And in the days of the sinners the years shall be shortened, and their seed shall be tardy on their lands and fields, and all things on the earth shall alter, and shall not appear in their time: And the rain shall be kept back and the heaven shall withhold it. [3] And in those times the fruits of the earth shall be backward, and shall not grow in their time, and the fruits of the trees shall be withheld in their time. [4] And the moon shall alter her order, and not appear at her time. [5] And in those days the sun shall be seen and he shall journey in the evening on the extremity of the great chariot in the west and shall shine more brightly than accords with the order of light. [6] And many chiefs of the stars shall transgress the order prescribed. And these shall alter their orbits and tasks, and not appear at the seasons prescribed to them. [7] And the whole order of the stars shall be concealed from the sinners, and the thoughts of those on the earth shall err concerning them, and they shall be altered from all their ways, Yea, they shall err and take them to be gods. [8] And evil shall be multiplied upon them, and punishment shall come upon them So as to destroy all. Chapter 81 [1] And he said unto me: Observe, Enoch, these heavenly tablets, and read what is written thereon, and mark every individual fact. [2] And I observed the heavenly tablets, and read everything whic h was written thereon and understood everything, and read the book of all the deeds of mankind, and of all the children of flesh that shall be upon the earth to the remotest generations. [3] And forthwith I blessed the great Lord the King of glory for ever, in that He has made all the works of the world, and I extolled the Lord because of His patience, and blessed Him because of the children of men. [4] And after that I said: Blessed is the man who dies in righteousness and goodness, Concerning whom there is no book of unrighteousness written, And against whom no day of judgement shall be found. [5] And those seven holy ones brought me and placed me on the earth before the door of my house, and said to me: Declare everything to thy son Methuselah, and show to all thy children that no flesh is righteous in the sight of the Lord, [6] For He is their Creator. One year we will leave thee with thy son, till thou givest thy last commands, that thou mayest teach thy children and record it for them, and testify to all thy children; and in the second year they shall take thee from their midst. [7] Let thy heart be strong, for the good shall announce righteousness to the good; The righteous with the righteous shall rejoice, And shall offer congratulation to one another. [8] But the sinners shall die with the sinners, And the apostate go down with the apostate. [9] And those who practice righteousness shall die on account of the deeds of men, And be taken away on account of the doings of the godless. [10] And in those days they ceased to speak to me, and I came to my people, blessing the Lord of the world. Chapter 82 [1] And now, my son Methuselah, all these things I am recounting to thee and writing down for thee! and I have revealed to thee everything, and given thee books concerning all these: so preserve, my son Methuselah, the books from thy fathers hand, and see that thou deliver them to the generations of the world. [2] I have given Wisdom to thee and to thy children, And thy children that shall be to thee, That they may give it to their children for generations, This wisdom (namely) that passeth their thought. [3] And those who understand it shall not sleep, but shall listen with the ear that they may learn this wisdom, And it shall please those that eat thereof better than good food. [4] Blessed are all the righteous, blessed are all those who walk In the way of righteousness and sin not as the sinners, in the reckoning of all their days in which the sun traverses the heaven, entering into and departing from the portals for thirty days with the heads of thousands of the order of the stars, together with the four which are intercalated which divide the four portions of the year, [5] Which lead them and enter with them four days. Owing to them men shall be at fault and not reckon them in the whole reckoning of the year: yea, men shall be at fault, and not recognize them accurately. [6] For they belong to the reckoning of the year and are truly recorded thereon for ever, one in the first portal and one in the third, and one in the fourth and one in the sixth, and the year is completed in three hundred and sixty-four days. [7] And the account thereof is accurate and the recorded reckoning thereof exact; for the luminaries, and months and festivals, and years and days, has Uriel shown and revealed to me, to whom the Lord of the whole creation of the world hath subjected the host of heaven. [8] And he has power over night and day in the heaven to cause the light to give light to men -sun, moon, and stars, [9] And all the powers of the heaven which revolve in their circular chariots. And these are the orders of the stars, which set in their places, and in their seasons and festivals and months. [10] And these are the names of those who lead them, who watch that they enter at their times, in their orders, in their seasons, in their months, in their periods of dominion, and in their positions. Their four leaders who divide the four parts of the year enter first; and after them the twelve leaders of the orders who divide the months; [11] And for the three hundred and sixty (days) there are heads over thousands who divide the days; and for the four intercalary days there are the leaders which sunder the four parts of the year. [12] And these heads over thousands are intercalated between leader and leader, each behind a station, but their leaders make the division. [13] And these are the names of the leaders who divide the four parts of the year which are ordained: Milkiel, Helemmelek, and Melejal, and Narel. [14] And the names of those who lead them: Ad narel, and Ijasusael, and Elomeelthese three follow the leaders of the orders, [15] And there is one that follows the three leaders of the orders which follow those leaders of stations that divide the four parts of the year. In the beginning of the year Melkejal rises first and rules, who is named Tamaini and sun, [16] And all the days of his dominion whilst he bears rule are ninety-one days. And these are the signs of the days which are to be seen on earth in the days of his dominion: sweat, and heat, and calms; and all the trees bear fruit, and leaves are produced on all the trees, and the harvest of wheat, and the rose- flowers, and all the flowers which come forth in the field, [17] But the trees of the winter season become withered. And these are the names of the leaders which are under them: Berkael, Zelebsel, and another who is added a head of a thousand, called Hilujaseph: and the days of the dominion of this leader are at an end. [18] The next leader after him is Helemmelek, whom one names the shining sun, and all the days of his light are ninety-one days. [19] And these are the signs of (his) days on the earth: glowing heat and dryness, and the trees ripen their fruits and produce all their fruits ripe and ready, and the sheep pair and become pregnant, and all the fruits of the earth are gathered in, and everything that is in the fields, [20] And the winepress: these things take place in the days of his dominion. These are the names, and the orders, and the leaders of those heads of thousands: Gidaljal, Keel, and Heel, and the name of the head of a thousand which is added to them, Asfael: and the days of his dominion are at an end.

Book 75. The Book Of Dream And Vision – Enoch's Ethiopic Book 4

Chapter 83 [1] And now, my son Methuselah, I will show thee all my visions which I have seen, recounting them before thee. [2] Two visions I saw before I took a wife, and the one was quite unlike the other: the first when I was learning to write: the second before I took thy mother, when I saw a terrible vision. [3] And regarding them I prayed to the Lord. I had laid me down in the house of my grandfather Mahalalel, when I saw in a vision how the heaven collapsed and was borne off and fell to the earth. [4] And when it fell to the earth I saw how the earth was swallowed up in a great abyss, and mountains were suspended on mountains, and hills sank down on hills, and high trees were rent from their stems, [5] And hurled down and sunk in the abyss. And thereupon a word fell into my mouth, [6] And I lifted up my voice to cry aloud, and said: The earth is destroyed. And my grandfather Mahalalel waked me as I lay near him, and said unto me: Why dost thou cry so, my son, [7] And why dost thou make such lamentation? And I recounted to him the whole vision which I had seen, and he said unto me: A terrible thing hast thou seen, my son,

and of grave moment is thy dream- vision as to the secrets if all the sin of the earth: it must sink into the abyss and be destroyed with a great destruction. [8] And now, my son, arise and make petition to the Lord of glory, since thou art a believer, that a remnant may remain on the earth, and that He may not destroy the whole earth. [9] My son, from heaven all this will come upon the earth, and upon the earth there will be great destruction. [10] After that I arose and prayed and implored and besought, and wrote down my prayer for the generations of the world, and I will show everything to thee, my son Methuselah. And when I had gone forth below and seen the heaven, and the sun rising in the east, and the moon setting in the west, and a few stars, and the whole earth, and everything as He had known it in the beginning, then I blessed the Lord of judgement and extolled Him because He had made the sun to go forth from the windows of the east, and he ascended and rose on the face of the heaven, and set out and kept traversing the path shown unto him. Chapter 84 [1] And I lifted up my hands in righteousness and blessed the Holy and Great One, and spake with the breath of my mouth, and with the tongue of flesh, which God has made for the children of the flesh of men, that they should speak therewith, and He gave them breath and a tongue and a mouth that they should speak therewith: [2] Blessed be Thou, O Lord, King, Great and mighty in Thy greatness, Lord of the whole creation of the heaven, King of kings and God of the whole world. And Thy power and kingship and greatness abide for ever and ever, And throughout all generations Thy dominion; And all the heavens are Thy throne for ever, And the whole earth Thy footstool for ever and ever. [3] For Thou hast made and Thou rule st all things, And nothing is too hard for Thee, Wisdom departs not from the place of Thy throne, Nor turns away from Thy presence. And Thou knowest and seest and hearest everything, And there is nothing hidden from Theefor Thou seest everything. [4] And now the angels of Thy heavens are guilty of trespass, And upon the flesh of men abideth Thy wrath until the great day of judgement. [5] And now, O God and Lord and Great King, I implore and beseech Thee to fulfil my prayer, To leave me a posterity on earth, And not destroy all the flesh of man, And make the earth without inhabitant, So that there should be an eternal destruction. [6] And now, my Lord, destroy from the earth the flesh which has aroused Thy wrath, But the flesh of righteousness and uprightness establish as a plant of the eternal seed, And hide not Thy face from the prayer of Thy servant, O Lord. Chapter 85 [1] And after this I saw another dream, and I will show the whole dream to thee, my son. [2] And Enoch lifted up his voice and spake to his son Methuselah: To thee, my son, will I speak: hear my words- incline thine ear to the dream- vision of thy father. [3] Before I took thy mother Edna, I saw in a vision on my bed, and behold a bull came forth from the earth, and that bull was white; and after it came forth a heifer, and along with this latter came forth two bulls, one of them black and the other red. [4] And that black bull gored the red one and pursued him over the earth, and thereupon I could no longer see that red bull. [5] But that black bull grew and that heifer went with him, and I saw that many oxen proceeded from him which resembled and followed him. [6] And that cow, that first one, went from the presence of that first bull in order to seek that red one, but found him not, [7] And lamented with a great lamentation over him and sought him. And I looked till that first bull came to her and quieted her, [8] And from that time onward she cried no more. And after that she bore another white bull, and after him she bore many bulls and black cows. [9] And I saw in my sleep that white bull likewise grow and become a great white bull, and from Him proceeded many white bulls, and they resembled him. And they began to beget many white bulls, which resembled them, one following the other, even many. Chapter 86 [1] And again I saw with mine eyes as I slept, and I saw the heaven above, and behold a star fell from heaven, and it arose and eat and pastured amongst those oxen. [2] And after that I saw the large and the black oxen, and behold they all changed their stalls and pastures and their cattle, and began to live with each other. [3] And again I saw in the vision, and looked towards the heaven, and behold I saw many stars descend and cast themselves down from heaven to that first star, and they became bulls amongst those cattle and pastured with themamongst them. [4] And I looked at them and saw, and behold they all let out their privy members, like horses, and began to cover the cows of the oxen, and they all became pregnant and bare elephants, camels, and asses. [5] And all the oxen feared them and were affrighted at them, and began to bite with their teeth and to devour, and to gore with their horns. [6] And they began, moreover, to devour those oxen; and behold all the children of the earth began to tremble and quake before them and to flee from them. Chapter 87 [1] And again I saw how they began to gore each other and to devour each other, and the earth began to cry aloud. [2] And I raised mine eyes again to heaven, and I saw in the vision, and behold there came forth from heaven beings who were like white men: and four went forth from that place and three with them. [3] And those three that had last come forth grasped me by my hand and took me up, away from the generations of the earth, and raised me up to a lofty place, and showed me a tower raised high above the earth, and all the hills were lower. [4] And one said unto me: Remain here till thou seest everything that befalls those elephants, camels, and asses, and the stars and the oxen, and all of them. Chapter 88 [1] And I saw one of those four who had come forth first, and he seized that first star which had fallen from the heaven, and bound it hand and foot and cast it into an abyss: now that abyss was narrow and deep, [2] And horrible and dark. And one of them drew a sword, and gave it to those elephants and camels and asses: then they began to smite each other, and the whole earth quaked because of them. [3] And as I was beholding in the vision, lo, one of those four who had come forth stoned (them) from heaven, and gathered and took all the great stars whose privy members were like those of horses, and bound them all hand and foot, and cast them in an abyss of the earth. Chapter 89 [1] And one of those four went to that white bull and instructed him in a secret, without his being terrified: he was born a bull and became a man, and built for himself a great vessel and dwelt thereon; [2] And three bulls dwelt with him in that vessel and they were covered in. And again I raised mine eyes towards heaven and saw a lofty roof, with seven water torrents thereon, and those torrents flowed with much water into an enclosure. [3] And I saw again, and behold fountains were opened on the surface of that great enclosure, and that water began to swell and rise upon the surface, [4] And I saw that enclosure till all its surface was covered with water. And the water, the darkness, and mist increased upon it; and as I looked at the height of that water, that water had risen above the height of that enclosure, and was streaming over that enclosure, and it stood upon the earth. [5] And all the cattle of that enclosure were gathered together until I saw how they sank and were swallowed up and perished in that water. [6] But that vessel floated on the water, while all the oxen and elephants and camels and asses sank to the bottom with all the animals, so that I could no longer see them, [7] And they were not able to escape, but perished and sank into the depths. And again I saw in the vision till those water torrents were removed from that high roof, and the chasms of the earth were leveled up and other abysses were opened. [8] Then the water began to run down into these, till the earth became visible; but that vessel settled on the earth, and the darkness retired and light appeared. [9] But that white bull which had become a man came out of that vessel, and the three bulls with him, and one of those three was white like that bull, and one of them was red as blood, and one black: and that white bull departed from them. [10] And they began to bring forth beasts of the field and birds, so that there arose different genera: lions, tigers, wolves, dogs, hyenas, wild boars, foxes, squirrels, swine, falcons, vultures, kites, eagles, and ravens; [11] And among them was born a white bull. And they began to bite one another; but that white bull which was born amongst them begat a wild ass and a white bull with it, [12] And the wild asses multiplied. But that bull which was born from him begat a black wild boar and a white sheep; [13] And the former begat many boars, but that sheep begat twelve sheep. And when those twelve sheep had grown, they gave up one of them to the asses, and those asses again gave up that sheep to the wolves, [14] And that sheep grew up among the wolves. And the Lord brought the eleven sheep to live with it and to pasture with it among the wolves: and they multiplied and became many flocks of sheep. [15] And the wolves began to fear them, and they oppressed them until they destroyed cry aloud on account of their little ones, [16] And to complain unto their Lord. And a sheep which had been saved from the wolves fled and escaped to the wild asses; and I saw the sheep how they lamented and cried, and besought their Lord with all their might, till that Lord of the sheep descended at the voice of the sheep from a lofty abode, and came to them and pastured them. [17] And He called that sheep which had escaped the wolves, and spake with it concerning the wolves that it should admonish them not to touch the sheep. [18] And the sheep went to the wolves according to the word of the Lord, and another sheep met it and went with it, and the two went and entered together into the assembly of those wolves, and spake with them and admonished them not to touch the sheep from henceforth. [19] And thereupon I saw the wolves, and how they oppressed the sheep exceedingly with all their power; and the sheep cried aloud. And the Lord came to the sheep and they began to smite those wolves: [20] And the wolves began to make lamentation; but the sheep became quiet and forthwith ceased to cry out. [21] And I saw the sheep till they departed from amongst the wolves; but the eyes of the wolves were blinded, and those wolves departed in pursuit of the sheep with all their power. [22] And the Lord of the sheep went with them, as their leader, and all His sheep followed Him: [23] And his face was dazzling and glorious and terrible to behold. But the wolves began to pursue those sheep till they reached a sea of water. [24] And that sea was divided, and the water stood on this side and on that before their face, and their Lord led them and placed Himself between them and the wolves. [25] And as those wolves did not yet see the sheep, they proceeded into the midst of that sea, and the wolves followed the sheep, and those wolves ran after them into that sea. [26] And when they saw the Lord of the sheep, they turned to flee before His face, but that sea gathered itself together, and became as it had been created, and the water swelled and rose till it covered those wolves. [27] And I saw till all the wolves who pursued those sheep perished and were drowned. [28] But the sheep escaped from that water and went forth into a wilderness, where there was no water and no grass; and they began to open their eyes and to see; and I saw the Lord of the sheep pasturing them and giving them water and grass, [28] And that sheep

going and leading them. And that sheep ascended to the summit of that lofty rock, and the Lord of the sheep sent it to them. [29] And after that I saw the Lord of the sheep who stood before them, and His appearance was great and terrible and majestic, [30] And all those sheep saw Him and were afraid before His face. And they all feared and trembled because of Him, and they cried to that sheep with them which was amongst them: [31] We are not able to stand before our Lord or to behold Him. And that sheep which led them again ascended to the summit of that rock, but the sheep began to be blinded and to wander from the way which he had showed them, but that sheep wot not thereof. [32] And the Lord of the sheep was wrathful exceedingly against them, and that sheep discovered it, and went down from the summit of the rock, and came to the sheep, and found the greatest part of them blinded and fallen away. [33] And when they saw it they feared and trembled at its presence, and desired to return to their folds. [34] And that sheep took other sheep with it, and came to those sheep which had fallen away, and began to slay them; and the sheep feared its presence, and thus that sheep brought back those sheep that had fallen away, and they returned to their folds. [35] And I saw in this vision till that sheep became a man and built a house for the Lord of the sheep, and placed all the sheep in that house. And I saw till this sheep which had met that sheep which led them fell asleep: and I saw till all the great sheep perished and little ones arose in their place, and they came to a pasture, and approached a stream of water. [36] Then that sheep, their leader which had become a man, withdrew from them and fell asleep, [37] And all the sheep sought it and cried over it with a great crying. [38] And I saw till they left off crying for that sheep and crossed that stream of water, and there arose the two sheep as leaders in the place of those which had led them and fallen asleep. [39] And I saw till the sheep came to a goodly place, and a pleasant and glorious land, and I saw till those sheep were satisfied; and that house stood amongst them in the pleasant land. [40] And sometimes their eyes were opened, and sometimes blinded, till another sheep arose and led them and brought them all back, and their eyes were opened. [41] And the dogs and the foxes and the wild boars began to devour those sheep till the Lord of the sheep raised up another sheep a ram from their midst, which led them. And that ram began to butt on either side those dogs, foxes, and wild boars till he had destroyed them all. And that sheep whose eyes were opened saw that ram, which was amongst the sheep, till it forsook its glory and began to butt those sheep, and trampled upon the m, and behaved itself unseemly. [42] And the Lord of the sheep sent the lamb to another lamb and raised it to being a ram and leader of the sheep instead of that ram which had forsaken its glory. [43] And it went to it and spake to it alone, and raised it to being a ram, [44] And made it the prince and leader of the sheep; but during all these things those dogs oppressed the sheep. [45] And the first ram pursued that second ram, and that second ram arose and fled before it; and I saw till those dogs pulled down the first ram. [46] And that second ram arose and led the little sheep. [47] And those sheep grew and multiplied; but all the dogs, and foxes, and wild boars feared and fled before it, and that ram butted and killed the wild beasts, and those wild beasts had no longer any power among the sheep and robbed them no more of ought. [48] And that ram begat many sheep and fell asleep; and a little sheep became ram in its stead, and became prince and leader of those sheep, [49] And that house became great and broad, and it was built for those sheep: and a tower lofty and great was built on the house for the Lord of the sheep, and that house was low, but the tower was elevated and lofty, and the Lord of the sheep stood on that tower and they offered a full table before Him. [50] And again I saw those sheep that they again erred and went many ways, and forsook that their house, and the Lord of the sheep called some from amongst the sheep and sent them to the sheep, [51] But the sheep began to slay them. And one of them was saved and was not slain, and it sped away and cried aloud over the sheep; and they sought to slay it, but the Lord of the sheep saved it from the sheep, and brought it up to me, and caused it to dwell there. [52] And many other sheep He sent to those sheep to testify unto them and lament over them. [53] And after that I saw that when they forsook the house of the Lord and His tower they fell away entirely, and their eyes were blinded; and I saw the Lord of the sheep how He wrought much slaughter amongst them in their herds until those sheep invited that slaughter and betrayed His place. [54] And He gave them over into the hands of the lions and tigers, and wolves and hyenas, and into the hand of the foxes, and to all the wild beasts, [55] And those wild beasts began to tear in pieces those sheep. And I saw that He forsook that their house and their tower and gave them all into the hand of the lions, to tear and devour them, [56] Into the hand of all the wild beasts. And I began to cry aloud with all my power, and to appeal to the Lord of the sheep, and to represent to Him in regard to the sheep that they were devoured by all the wild beasts. [57] But He remained unmoved, though He saw it, and rejoiced that they were devoured and swallowed and robbed, and left them to be devoured in the hand of all the beasts. [58] And He called seventy shepherds, and cast those sheep to them that they might pasture them, and He spake to the shepherds and their companions: Let each individual of you pasture the sheep henceforward, [59] And everything that I shall command you that do ye. And I will deliver them over unto you duly numbered, and tell you which of them are to be destroyed-and them destroy ye. [60] And He gave over unto them those sheep. And He called another and spake unto him: Observe and mark everything that the shepherds will do to those sheep; for they will destroy more of them than I have commanded them. [61] And every excess and the destruction which will be wrought through the shepherds, record namely how many they destroy according to my command, and how many according to their own caprice: record against every individual shepherd all the destruction he effects. [62] And read out before me by number how many they destroy, and how many they deliver over for destruction, that I may have this as a testimony against them, and know every deed of the shepherds, that I may comprehend and see what they do, whether or not they abide by my command which I have commanded them. [63] But they shall not know it, and thou shalt not declare it to them, [64] Nor admonish them, but only record against each individual all the destruction which the shepherds effect each in his time and lay it all before me. And I saw till those shepherds pastured in their season, and they began to slay and to destroy more than they were bidden, and they delivered those sheep into the hand of the lions. [65] And the lions and tigers eat and devoured the greater part of those sheep, and the wild boars eat along with them; and they burnt that tower and demolished that house. [66] And I became exceedingly sorrowful over that tower because that house of the sheep was demolished, and afterwards I was unable to see if those sheep entered that house. [67] And the shepherds and their associates delivered over those sheep to all the wild beasts, to devour them, and each one of them received in his time a definite number: it was written by the other in a book how many each one of them destroyed of them. [68] And each one slew and destroyed many more than was prescribed; [69] And I began to weep and lament on account of those sheep. And thus in the vision I saw that one who wrote, how he wrote down every one that was destroyed by those shepherds, day by day, and carried up and laid down and showed actually the whole book to the Lord of the sheep-(even) everything that they had done, and all that each one of them had made away with, [70] And all that they had given over to destruction. And the book was read before the Lord of the sheep, and He took the book from his hand and read it and sealed it and laid it down. [71] And forthwith I saw how the shepherds pastured for twelve hours, and behold three of those sheep turned back and came and entered and began to build up all that had fallen down of that house; [72] But the wild boars tried to hinder them, but they were not able. And they began again to build as before, and they reared up that tower, and it was named the high tower; and they began again to place a table before the tower, but all the bread on it was polluted and not pure. [73] And as touching all this the eyes of those sheep were blinded so that they saw not, and the eyes of their shepherds likewise; and they delivered them in large numbers to their shepherds for destruction, [74] And they trampled the sheep with their feet and devoured them. And the Lord of the sheep remained unmoved till all the sheep were dispersed over the field and mingled with them the beasts, [75] And they the shepherds did not save them out of the hand of the beasts. And this one who wrote the book carried it up, and showed it and read it before the Lord of the sheep, and implored Him on their account, and besought Him on their account as he showed Him all the doings of the shepherds, [76] And gave testimony before Him against all the shepherds. And he took the actual book and laid it down beside Him and departed. Chapter 90 [1] And I saw till that in this manner thirty- five shepherds undertook the pasturing of the sheep, and they severally completed their periods as did the first; and others receive them into their hands, [2] To pasture them for their period, each shepherd in his own period. And after that I saw in my vision all the birds of heaven coming, the eagles, the vultures, the kites, the ravens; but the eagles led all the birds; and they began to devour those sheep, and to pick out their eyes and to devour their flesh. [3] And the sheep cried out because their flesh was being devoured by the birds, [4] And as for me I looked and lamented in my sleep over that shepherd who pastured the sheep. And I saw until those sheep were devo ured by the dogs and eagles and kites, and they left neither flesh nor skin nor sinew remaining on them till only their bones stood there: and their bones too fell to the earth and the sheep became few. [5] And I saw until that twenty-three had undertaken the pasturing and completed in their several periods fifty-eight times. [6] But behold lambs were borne by those white sheep, and they began to open their eyes and to see, [7] And to cry to the sheep. Yea, they cried to them, but they did not hearken to what the y said to them, [8] But were exceedingly deaf, and their eyes were very exceedingly blinded. And I saw in the vision how the ravens flew upon those lambs and took one of those lambs, and dashed the sheep in pieces and devoured them. [9] And I saw till horns grew upon those lambs, and the ravens cast down their horns; and I saw till there sprouted a great horn of one of those sheep, and their eyes were opened. [10] And it looked at themand their eyes opened, and it cried to the sheep, [11] And the rams saw it and all ran to it. [12] And notwithstanding all this those eagles and vultures and ravens, [13] And kites still kept tearing the sheep and swooping down upon them and devouring them: [14] Still the sheep remained silent, but the rams lamented and cried out. [15] And those ravens fought and battled with it and sought to lay low its horn, but they had no power over it. [16] All the

eagles and vultures and ravens and kites were gathered together, [17] And there came with them all the sheep of the field, [18] Yea, they all came together, and helped each other to break that horn of the ram. [19] And I saw till a great sword was given to the sheep, and the sheep proceeded against all the beasts of the field to slay them, and all the beasts and the birds of the heaven fled before their face. And I saw that man, who wrote the book according to the command of the Lord, till he opened that book concerning the destruction which those twelve last shepherds had wrought, and showed that they had destroyed much more than their predecessors, before the Lord of the sheep. And I saw till the Lord of the sheep came unto them and took in His hand the staff of His wrath, and smote the earth, and the earth clave asunder, and all the beasts and all the birds of the heaven fell from among those sheep, and were swallowed up in the earth and it covered them. [20] And I saw till a throne was erected in the pleasant land, and the Lord of the sheep sat Himself thereon, and the other took the sealed books and opened those books before the Lord of the sheep. [21] And the Lord called those men the seven first white ones, and commanded that they should bring before Him, beginning with the first star which led the way, all the stars whose privy members were like those of horses, [22] And they brought them all before Him. And He said to that man who wrote before Him, being one of those seven white ones, and said unto him: Take those seventy shepherds to whom I delivered the sheep, and who taking them on their own authority slew more than I commanded them. [23] And behold they were all bound, I saw, and they all stood before Him. [24] And the judgement was held first over the stars, and they were judged and found guilty, and went to the place of condemnation, and they were cast into an abyss, full of fire and flaming, and full of pillars of fire. [25] And those seventy shepherds were judged and found guilty, and they were cast into that fiery abyss. [26] And I saw at that time how a like abyss was opened in the midst of the earth, full of fire, and they brought those blinded sheep, and they were all judged and found guilty, [27] And cast into this fiery abyss, and they burned; now this abyss was to the right of that house. And I saw those sheep burning and their bones burning. [28] And I stood up to see till they folded up that old house; and carried off all the pillars, and all the beams and ornaments of the house were at the same time folded up with it, and they carried it off and laid it in a place in the south of the land. [29] And I saw till the Lord of the sheep brought a new house greater and loftier than that first, and set it up in the place of the first which had beer folded up: all its pillars were new, and its ornaments were new and larger than those of the first, the old one which He had taken away, and all the sheep were within it. [30] And I saw all the sheep which had been left, and all the beasts on the earth, and all the birds of the heaven, falling down and doing homage to those sheep and making petition to and obeying them in every thing. [31] And thereafter those three who were clothed in white and had seized me by my handwho had taken me up before, and the hand of that ram also seizing hold of me, [32] They took me up and set me down in the midst of those sheep before the judgement took place. And those sheep were all white, [33] And their wool was abundant and clean. And all that had been destroyed and dispersed, and all the beasts of the field, and all the birds of the heaven, assembled in that house, and the Lord of the sheep rejoiced with great joy because they were all good and had returned to His house. [34] And I saw till they laid down that sword, which had been given to the sheep, and they brought it back into the house, and it was sealed before the presence of the Lord, and all the sheep were invited into that house, [35] But it held them not. And the eyes of them all were opened, and they saw the good, [36] And there was not one among them that did not see. And I saw that that house was large and broad and very full. [37] And I saw that a white bull was born, with large horns and all the beasts of the field and all the birds of the air feared him and made petition to him all the time of and I saw till all their generations were transformed, [38] And they all became white bulls; and the first among them became a lamb, and that lamb became a great animal and had great black horns on its head; and the Lord of the sheep rejoiced over it and over all the oxen. [39] And I slept in their midst: and I awoke and saw everything. [40] This is the vision which I saw while I slept, and I awoke and blessed the Lord of righteousness and gave Him glory. [41] Then I wept with a great weeping and my tears stayed not till I could no longer endure it: when I saw, they flowed on account of what I had seen; for everything shall come and be fulfilled, [42] And all the deeds of men in their order were shown to me. On that night I remembered the first dream, and because of it I wept and was troubled-because I had seen that vision. The Epistle Of Enoch – Enoch's Ethiopic Book 5 Chapter 91 [1] And now, my son Methuselah, call to me all thy brothers and gather together to me all the sons of thy mother; For the word calls me, And the spirit is poured out upon me, That I may show you everything that shall befall you for ever. [2] And there upon Methuselah went and summoned to him all his brothers and assembled his relatives. [3] And he spake unto all the children of righteousness and said: Hear, ye sons of Enoch, all the words of your father, And hearken aright to the voice of my mouth; For I exhort you and say unto you, beloved: [4] Love uprightness and walk therein. And draw not nigh to uprightness with a double heart, And associate not with those of a double heart, But walk in righteousness, my sons. And it shall guide you on good paths, And righteousness shall be your companion. [5] For I know that violence must increase on the earth, And a great chastisement be executed on the earth, And all unrighteousness come to an end: Yea, it shall be cut off from its roots, And its whole structure be destroyed. [6] And unrighteousness shall again be consummated on the earth, And all the deeds of unrighteousness and of violence and transgression shall prevail in a twofold degree. [7] And when sin and unrighteousness and blasphemy and violence in all kinds of deeds increase, and apostasy and transgression and uncleanness increase, a great chastisement shall come from heaven upon all these, and the holy Lord will come forth with wrath and chastisement to execute judgement on earth. [8] In those days violence shall be cut off from its roots, and the roots of unrighteousness together with deceit, and they shall be destroyed from under heaven. [9] And all the idols of the heathen shall be abandoned, and the temples burned with fire, And they shall remove them from the whole earth, And they the heathen shall be cast into the judgement of fire, And shall perish in wrath and in grievous judgement for ever. [10] And the righteous shall arise from their sleep, and wisdom shall arise and be given unto them. [11] And after that the roots of unrighteousness shall be cut off, and the sinners shall bedestroyed by the sword and the blasphemers destroyed in every place, [12] And those who plan violence and those who commit blasphemy shall perish by the sword. [13] And now I tell you, my sons, and show you the paths of righteousness and the paths of violence. Yea, I will show them to you again that ye may know what will come to pass. [14] And now, hearken unto me, my sons, and walk in the paths of righteousness, and walk not in the paths of violence; For all who walk in the paths of unrighteousness shall perish for ever. Chapter 92 [1] The book written by Enoch indeed wrote this complete doctrine of wisdom, which is praised of all men and a judge of all the earth for all my children who shall dwell on the earth. And for the future generations who shall observe uprightness and peace. [2] Let not your spirit be troubled on account of the times; For the Holy and Great One has appointed days for all things. [3] And the righteous one shall arise from sleep, shall arise and walk in the paths of righteousness, And all his path and conversation shall be in eternal goodness and grace. [4] He will be gracious to the righteous and give him eternal uprightness, And He will give him power so that he shall be endowed with goodness and righteousness. And he shall walk in eternal light. [5] And sin shall perish in darkness for ever, And shall no more be seen from that day for evermore. Chapter 93 [1] And after that Enoch both gave and began to recount from the books. And Enoch said: Concerning the children of righteousness and concerning the elect of the world, And concerning the plant of uprightness, I will speak these things, Yea, I Enoch will declare (them) unto you, my sons: According to that which appeared to me in the heavenly vision, [2] And which I have known through the word of the holy angels, And have learnt from the heavenly tablets. [3] And Enoch began to recount from the books and said: I was born the seventh in the first week, while judgement and righteousness still endured. [4] And after me there shall arise in the second week great wickedness, And deceit shall have sprung up; And in it there shall be the first end. And in it a man shall be saved; And after it is ended unrighteousness shall grow up, [5] And a law shall be made for the sinners. And after that in the third week at its close a man shall be elected as the plant of righteous judgement, And his posterity shall become the plant of righteousness for evermore. [6] And after that in the fourth week, at its close, Visions of the holy and righteous shall be seen, And a law for all generations and an enclosure shall be made for them. And after that in the fifth week, at its close, The house of glory and dominion shall be built for ever. [7] And after that in the sixth week all who live in it shall be blinded, And the hearts of all of them shall godlessly forsake wisdom. And in it a man shall ascend; [8] And at its close the house of dominion shall be burnt with fire, And the whole race of the chosen root shall be dispersed. [9] And after that in the seventh week shall an apostate generation arise, And many shall be its deeds, And all its deeds shall be apostate. [10] And at its close shall be elected the elect righteous of the eternal plant of righteousness, to receive sevenfold instruction concerning all His creation. [11] For who is there of all the children of men that is able to hear the voice of the Holy One without being troubled? And who can think His thoughts? and who is there that can behold all the works of heaven? [12] And how should there be one who could behold the heaven, and who is there that could understand the things of heaven and see a soul or a spirit and could tell thereof, or ascend and see all their ends and think them or do like them? [13] And who is there of all men that could know what is the breadth and the length of the earth, and to whom has been shown the measure of all of them? Or is there any one who could discern the length of the heaven and how great is its height, [14] and upon what it is founded, and how great is the number of the stars, and where all the luminaries rest? Chapter 94 [1] And now I say unto you, my sons, love righteousness and walk therein; For the paths of righteousness are worthy of acceptation, but the paths of unrighteousness shall suddenly be destroyed and vanish. [2] And to certain men of a generation shall the paths of violence and of death be revealed, And they shall hold themselves afar from them, And shall not follow them. [3] And now I say unto you the

righteous: Walk not in the paths of wickedness, nor in the paths of death, And draw not nigh to them, lest ye be destroyed. [4] But seek and choose for yourselves righteousness and an elect life, And walk in the paths of peace, And ye shall live and prosper. [5] And hold fast my words in the thoughts of your hearts, And suffer them not to be effaced from your hearts; For I know that sinners will tempt men to evilly-entreat wisdom, So that no place may be found for her, And no manner of temptation may minish. [6] Woe to those who build unrighteousness and oppression and lay deceit as a foundation; For they shall be suddenly overthrown, And they shall have no peace. [7] Woe to those who build their houses with sin; For from all their foundations shall they be overthrown, And by the sword shall they fall. And those who acquire gold and silver in judgement suddenly shall perish. [8] Woe to you, ye rich, for ye have trusted in your riches, And from your riches shall ye depart, Because ye have not remembered the Most High in the days of your riches. [9] Ye have committed blasphemy and unrighteousness, And have become ready for the day of slaughter, And the day of darkness and the day of the great judgement. [10] Thus I speak and declare unto you: He who hath created you will overthrow you, And for your fall there shall be no compassion, And your Creator will rejoice at your destruction. [11] And your righteous ones in those days shall be a reproach to the sinners and the godless. Chapter 95 [1] Oh that mine eyes were a cloud of waters that I might weep over you, And pour down my tears as a cloud of waters: That so I might rest from my trouble of heart! [2] Who has permitted you to practice reproaches and wickedness? And so judgement shall overtake you, sinners. [3] Fear not the sinners, ye righteous; For again will the Lord deliver them into your hands, that ye may execute judgement upon them according to your desires. [4] Woe to you who fulminate anathemas which cannot be reversed: Healing shall therefore be far from you because of your sins. [5] Woe to you who requite your neighbour with evil; For ye shall be requited according to your works. [6] Woe to you, lying witnesses, And to those who weigh out injustice, For suddenly shall ye perish. [7] Woe to you, sinners, for ye persecute the righteous; For ye shall be delivered up and persecuted because of injustice, And heavy shall its yoke be upon you. Chapter 96 [1] Be hopeful, ye righteous; for suddenly shall the sinners perish before you, And ye shall have lordship over them according to your desires. [2] And in the day of the tribulation of the sinners, Your children shall mount and rise as eagles, And higher than the vultures will be your nest, And ye shall ascend and enter the crevices of the earth, And the clefts of the rock for ever as coneys before the unrighteous, And the sirens shall sigh because of you-and weep wherefore fear not, ye that have suffered; [3] For healing shall be your portion, And a bright light shall enlighten you, And the voice of rest ye shall hear from heaven. [4] Woe unto you, ye sinners, for your riches make you appear like the righteous, But your hearts convict you of being sinners, And this fact shall be a testimony against you for a memorial of (your) evil deeds. [5] Woe to you who devour the finest of the wheat, And drink wine in large bowls, And tread under foot the lowly with your might. [6] Woe to you who drink water from every fountain, For suddenly shall ye be consumed and wither away, Because ye have forsaken the fountain of life. [7] Woe to you who work unrighteousness and deceit and blasphemy: It shall be a memorial against you for evil. [8] Woe to you, ye mighty, Who with might oppress the righteous; For the day of your destruction is coming. In those days many and good days shall come to the righteous- in the day of your judgement. Chapter 97 [1] Believe, ye righteous, that the sinners will become a shame and perish in the day of unrighteousness. [2] Be it known unto you (ye sinners) that the Most High is mindful of your destruction, And the angels of heaven rejoice over your destruction. [3] What will ye do, ye sinners, And whither will ye flee on that day of judgement, when ye hear the voice of the prayer of the righteous? [4] Yea, ye shall fare like unto them, against whom this word shall be a testimony: " Ye have been companions of sinners." [5] And in those days the prayer of the righteous shall reach unto the Lord, And for you the days of your judgement shall come. [6] And all the words of your unrighteousness shall be read out before the Great Holy One, And your faces shall be covered with shame, And He will reject every work which is grounded on unrighteousness. [7] Woe to you, ye sinners, who live on the mid ocean and on the dry land, Whose remembrance is evil against you. [8] Woe to you who acquire silver and gold in unrighteousness and say: " We have become rich with riches and have possessions; And have acquired everything we have desired. [9] And now let us do what we purposed: For we have gathered silver, And many are the husbandmen in our houses." And our granaries are (brim) full as with water, Yea and like water your lies shall flow away; For your riches shall not abide but speedily ascend from you; For ye have acquired it all in unrighteousness, And ye shall be given over to a great curse. Chapter 98 [1] And now I swear unto you, to the wise and to the foolish, For ye shall have manifold experiences on the earth. [2] For ye men shall put on more adornments than a woman, And coloured garments more than a virgin: In royalty and in grandeur and in power, And in silver and in gold and in purple, And in splendour and in food they shall be poured out as water. [3] Therefore they shall be wanting in doctrine and wisdom, And they shall perish thereby together with their possessions; And with all their glory and their splendour, And in shame and in slaughter and in great destitution, Their spirits shall be cast into the furnace of fire. [4] I have sworn unto you, ye sinners, as a mountain has not become a slave, And a hill does not become the handmaid of a woman, Even so sin has not been sent upon the earth, But man of himself has created it, And under a great curse shall they fall who commit it. [5] And barrenness has not been given to the woman, but on account of the deeds of her own hands she dies without children. [6] I have sworn unto you, ye sinners, by the Holy Great One, that all your evil deeds are revealed in the heavens, And that none of your deeds of oppression are covered and hidden. [7] And do not think in your spirit nor say in your heart that ye do not know and that ye do not see that every sin is every day recorded in heaven in the presence of the Most High. [8] From henceforth ye know that all your oppression wherewith ye oppress is written down every day till the day of your judgement woe to you, ye fools, for through your folly shall ye perish: [9] And ye transgress against the wise, [10] And so good hap shall not be your portion. And now, know ye that ye are prepared for the day of destruction: wherefore do not hope to live, ye sinners, but ye shall depart and die; for ye know no ransom; for ye are prepared for the day of the great judgement, for the day of tribulation and great shame for your spirits. [11] Woe to you, ye obstinate of heart, who work wickedness and eat blood: Whence have ye good things to eat and to drink and to be filled? From all the good things which the Lord the Most High has placed in abundance on the earth; therefore ye shall have no peace. [12] Woe to you who love the deeds of unrighteousness: wherefore do ye hope for good hap unto yourselves? know that ye shall be delivered into the hands of the righteous, and they shall cut off your necks and slay you, [13] And have no mercy upon you. Woe to you who rejoice in the tribulation of the righteous; for no grave shall be dug for you. Woe to you who set at nought the words of the righteous; [14] For ye shall have no hope of life. Woe to you who write down lying and godless words; for they write down their lies that men may hear them and act godlessly towards their neighbour. [15] Therefore they shall have no peace but die a sudden death. Chapter 99 [16] Woe to you who work godlessness, And glory in lying and extol them: Ye shall perish, and no happy life shall be yours. [17] Woe to them who pervert the words of uprightness, And transgress the eternal law, And transform themselves into what they were notinto sinners: They shall be trodden under foot upon the earth. [18] In those days make ready, ye righteous, to raise your prayers as a memorial, And place them as a testimony before the angels, that they may place the sin of the sinners for a memorial before the Most High. [19] In those days the nations shall be stirred up, And the families of the nations shall arise on the day of destruction. [20] And in those days the destitute shall go forth and carry off their children, And they shall abandon them, so that their children shall perish through them: Yea, they shall abandon their children (that are still) sucklings, and not return to them, And shall have no pity on their beloved ones. [21] And again I swear to you, ye sinners, that sin is prepared for a day of unceasing bloodshed. [22] And they who worship stones, and grave images of gold and silver and wood and stone and clay, and those who worship impure spirits and demons, and all kinds of idols not according to knowledge, shall get no manner of help from them. [23] And they shall become godless by reason of the folly of their hearts, And their eyes shall be blinded through the fear of their hearts and through visions in their dreams. [24] Through these they shall become godless and fearful; For they sha ll have wrought all their work in a lie, And shall have worshiped a stone: Therefore in an instant shall they perish. [25] But in those days blessed are all they who accept the words of wisdom, and understand them, And observe the paths of the Most High, and walk in the path of His righteousness, And become not godless with the godless; For they shall be saved. [26] Woe to you who spread evil to your neighbours; For you shall be slain in Sheol. [27] Woe to you who make deceitful and false measures, And who cause bitterness on the earth; For they shall thereby be utterly consumed. [28] Woe to you who build your houses through the grievous toil of others, And all their building materials are the bricks and stones of sin; I tell you ye shall have no peace. [29] Woe to them who reject the measure and eternal heritage of their fathers and whose souls follow after idols; For they shall have no rest. [30] Woe to them who work unrighteousness and help oppression, And slay their neighbours until the day of the great judgement. [31] For He shall cast down your glory, And bring affliction on your hearts, And shall arouse His fierce indignation and destroy you all with the sword; And all the holy and righteous shall remember your sins. Chapter 100 [1] And in those days in one place the fathers together with their sons shall be smitten and brothers one with another shall fall in death till the streams flow with their blood. [2] For a man shall not withhold his hand from slaying his sons and his sons sons, And the sinner shall not withhold his hand from his honoured brother: From dawn till sunset they shall slay one another. [3] And the horse shall walk up to the breast in the blood of sinners, And the chariot shall be submerged to its height. [4] In those days the angels shall descend into the secret places and gather together into one place all those who brought down sin and the Most High will arise on that day of judgement to execute great judgement amongst sinners. [5] And over all the righteous and holy He will appoint guardians from amongst the holy angels to guard them as the apple of an eye, until He makes an end of all wickedness and all sin, And though the righteous sleep a long sleep, they have nought to fear. [6] And then the children of the earth shall see the wise in security, And shall understand all the words of this book, And recognize that their riches shall not be able to save them in the overthrow of their sins. [7] Woe to you, Sinners, on the day of strong anguish, Ye who afflict the righteous and burn them with fire: Ye shall be requited according to your works. [8] Woe to you, ye obstinate of heart, who watch in order to devise wickedness: Therefore shall fear come upon you and there shall be none to help you. [9] Woe to you, ye sinners, on account of the words of your mouth, And on account of the deeds of your hands which your godlessness as wrought, in blazing flames burning worse than fire shall ye burn. [10] And now, know ye that from the angels He will inquire as to your deeds in heaven, from the sun and from the moon and from the stars in reference to your sins because upon the earth ye execute judgement on the righteous. And He will summon to testify against you every cloud and mist and dew and rain; for they shall all be withheld because of you from descending upon you, and they shall be mindful of your sins. And now give presents to the rain that it be not with held from descending upon you, nor yet the dew, when it has received gold and silver from you that it may descend. When the hoar-frost and snow with their chilliness, and all the snowstorms with all their plagues fall upon you, in those days ye shall not be able to stand before them. Chapter 101 [1] Observe the heaven, ye children of heaven, and every work of the Most High, and fear ye Him and work no evil in His presence. [2] If He closes the windows of heaven, and withholds the rain and the dew from descending on the earth on your account, what will ye do then? [3] And if He sends His anger upon you because of yoour deeds, ye cannot petition Him; for ye spake proud and insolent words against His righteousness: therefore ye shall have no peace. [4] And see ye not the sailors of the ships, how their ships are tossed to and fro by the waves, and are shaken by the winds, and are in sore trouble? [5] And therefore do they fear because all their goodly possessions go upon the sea with them, and they have evil forebodings of heart that the sea will swallow them and they will perish therein. [6] Are not the entire sea and all its waters, and all its movements, the work of the Most High, and has He not set limits to its doings, and confined it throughout by the sand? [7] And at His reproof it is afraid and dries up, and all its fish die and all that is in it; But ye sinners that are on the earth fear Him not. [8] Has He not made the heaven and the earth, and all that is therein? Who has given understanding and wisdom to everything that moves on the earth and in the sea. [9] Do not the sailors of the ships fear the sea ? Yet sinners fear not the Most High. Chapter 102 [1] In those days when He hath brought a grievous fire upon you, Whither will ye flee, and where will ye find deliverance? And when He launches forth His Word against you Will you not be affrighted and fear? [2] And all the luminaries shall be affrighted with great fear, And all the earth shall be affrighted and tremble and be alarmed. [3] And all the angels shall execute their commandst and shall seek to hide themselves from the presence of the Great Glory, And the children of earth shall tremble and quake; And ye sinners shall be cursed for ever, And ye shall have no peace. [4] Fear ye not, ye souls of the righteous, And be hopeful ye that have died in righteousness. [5] And grieve not if your soul into Sheol has descended in grief, And that in your life your body fared not according to your goodness, but wait for the day of the judgement of sinners and for the day of cursing and chastisement. [6] And yet when ye die the sinners speak over you:" As we die, so die the righteous, And what benefit do they reap for their deeds? Behold, even as we, so do they die in grief and darkness, And what have they more than we? [7] From henceforth we are equal. And what will they receive and what will they see for ever? [8] Behold, they too have died, And henceforth for ever shall they see no light." [9] I tell you, ye sinners, ye are content to eat and drink, and rob and sin, and strip men naked, and acquire wealth and see good days. [10] Have ye seen the righteous how their end falls out, that no manner of violence is found in them till their death? "Nevertheless they perished and became as though they had not been, and their spirits descended into Sheol in tribulation." Chapter 103 [1] Now, therefore, I swear to you, the righteous, by the glory of the Great and Honoured and Mighty One in dominion, and by His greatness I swear to you. [2] I know a mystery and have read the heavenly tablets, And have seen the holy books, And have found written therein and inscribed regarding them: [3] That all goodness and joy and glory are prepared for them, And written down for the spirits of those who have died in righteousness, And that manifold good shall be given to you in recompense for your labours, And that your lot is abundantly beyond the lot of the living. [4] And the spirits of you who have died in righteousness shall live and rejoice, And their spirits shall not perish, nor their memorial from before the face of the Great One unto all the generations of the world: wherefore no longer fear their contumely. [5] Woe to you, ye sinners, whe n ye have died, If ye die in the wealth of your sins, And those who are like you say regarding you: Blessed are the sinners: they have seen all their days. [6] And how they have died in prosperity and in wealth, And have not seen tribulation or murder in their life; And they have died in honour, And judgement has not been executed on them during their life. [7] "Know ye, that their souls will be made to descend into Sheol and they shall be wretched in their great tribulation. [8] And into darkness and chains and a burning flame where there is grievous judgement shall your spirits enter; And the great judgement shall be for all the generations of the world. Woe to you, for ye shall have no peace. [9] Say not in regard to the righteous and good who are in life: "In our troubled days we have toiled laboriously and experienced every trouble, And met with much evil and been consumed, And have become few and our spirit small. [10] And we have been destroyed and have not found any to help us even with a word: We have been torturedand destroyed, and not hoped to see life from day to day. [11] We hoped to be the head and have become the tail: We have toiled laboriously and had no satisfaction in our toil; And we have become the food of the sinners and the unrighteous, And they have laid their yoke heavily upon us. [12] They have had dominion over us that hated us and smote us; And to those that hated us we have bowed our necks But they pitied us not. [13] We desired to get away from them that we might escape and be at rest, but found no place whereunto we should flee and be safe from them. [14] And are complained to the rulers in our tribulation, And cried out against those who devoured us, but they did not attend to our cries and would not hearken to our voice. [15] And they helped those who robbed us and devoured us and those who made us few; and they concealed their oppression, and they did not remove from us the yoke of those that devoured us and dispersed us and murdered us, and they concealed their murder, and remembered not that they had lifted up their hands against us. Chapter 104 [1] I swear unto you, that in heaven the angels remember you for good before the glory of the Great One: and your names are written before the glory of the Great One. [2] Be hopeful; for aforetime ye were put to shame through ill and affliction; but now ye shall shine as the lights of heaven, ye shall shine and ye shalll be seen, and the portals of heaven shall be opened to you. [3] And in your cry, cry for judgement, and it shall appear to you; for all your tribulation shall be visited on the rulers, and on all who helped those who plundered you. [4] Be hopeful, and cast not away your hopes for ye shall have great joy as the angels of heaven. What shall ye be obliged to do? [5] Ye shall not have to hide on the day of the great judgement and ye shall not be found as sinners, and the eternal judgement shall be far from you for all the generations of the world. [6] And now fear not, ye righteous, when ye see the sinners growing strong and prospering in their ways: be not companions with them, [7] But keep afar from their violence; for ye shall become companions of the hosts of heaven. And, although ye sinners say: "All our sins shall not be searched out and be written down", nevertheless they shall write down all your sins every day. [8] And now I show unto you that light and darkness, day and night, see all your sins. [9] Be not godless in your hearts, and lie not and alter not the words of uprightness, nor charge with lying the words of the Holy Great One, nor take account of your idols; [10] For all your lying and all your godlessness issue not in righteousness but in great sin. And now I know this mystery, that sinners will alter and pervert the words of righteousness in many ways, and will speak wicked words, and lie, and practice great deceits, and write books concerning their words. [11] But when they write down truthfully all my words in their languages, and do not change or minish ought from my words but write them all down truthfully all that I first testified concerning them. [12] Then, I know another mystery, that books will be given to the righteous and the wise to become a cause of joy and uprightness and much wisdom. And to them shall the books be given, and they shall believe in them and rejoice over them, and then shall all the righteous who have learnt therefrom all the paths of uprightness be recompensed. Chapter 105 [1] In those days the Lord bade them to summon and testify to the children of earth concerning their wisdom: Show it unto them; for ye are their guides, and a recompense over the whole earth. [2] For I and My son will be united with them for ever in the paths of uprightness in their lives; and ye shall have peace: rejoice, ye children of uprightness. Amen. Chapter 106 [1] And after some days my son Methuselah took a wife for his son Lamech, and she became pregnant by him and bore a son. [2] And his body was white as snow and red as the blooming of a rose, and the hair of his head and his long locks were white as wool, and his eyes beautiful. And when he opened his eyes, he lighted up the whole house like the sun, and the whole house was very bright. [3] And thereupon he arose in the hands of the midwife, opened his mouth, and conversed with the Lord of righteousness. [4] And his father Lamech was afraid of him and fled, and came to his father Methuselah. [5] And he said unto him: I have begotten a strange son, diverse from and unlike man, and resembling the sons of the God of heaven; and his nature is different and he is not like us, and his eyes are as the rays of the sun, and his countenance is glorious. [6] And it seems to me that he is not sprung from me but from the angels, and I fear that in his days a wonder may be wrought on the earth. [7] And now, my father, I am here to petition thee and implore thee that thou mayest go to Enoch, our father, and learn from him the truth, for his dwelling place is amongst the angels. [8] And when Methuselah heard the words of his son, he came to me to the ends of the earth; for he had heard that I was there, [9] And he cried aloud, and I heard his voice and I came to him. And I said unto him: Behold, here am I, my son, wherefore hast thou come to me? And he answered and said: Because of a great cause of anxiety have I come to thee, and because of a disturbing vision have I approached. [10] And now, my father, hear me: unto Lamech my son there hath been born a son, the like of whom there is none, and his nature is not like mans nature, and the colour of his body is whiter than snow and redder than the bloom of a rose, and the hair of his head is whiter than white wool, and his eyes are like the rays of the sun, and he opened his eyes and thereupon lighted up the whole house. [11] And he arose in the hands of the midwife, and opened his mouth and blessed the Lord of heaven. [12] And his father Lamech became afraid and fled to me, and did not believe that he was sprung from him, but that he was in the likeness of the angels of heaven; and behold I have come to thee that thou mayest make known to me the truth. [13] And I, Enoch, answered and said unto him: The Lord will do a new thing on the earth, and this I have already seen in a vision, and make known to thee that in the generation of my father Jared some of the angels of heaven transgressed the word of the Lord. [14] And behold they commit sin and transgress the law, and have united themselves with women and commit sin with them, and have married some of them, and have begot children by them. [15] And they shall produce on the earth giants not according to the spirit, but according to the flesh, and there shall be a great punishment on the earth, and the earth shall be cleansed from all impurity. Yea, there shall come a great destruction over the whole earth, and there shall be a deluge and a great destruction for one year. [16] And this son who has been born unto you shall be left on the earth, and his three children shall be saved with him: when all mankind that are on the earth shall diehe and his sons shall be saved. [17] And now make known to thy son Lamech that he who has been born is in truth his son, and call his name Noah; for he shall be left to you, and he and his sons shall be saved from the destruction, which shall come upon the earth on account of all the sin and all the unrighteousness, which shall be consummated on the earth in his days. And after that there shall be still more unrighteousness than that which was first consummated on the earth; for I know the mysteries of the holy ones; for He, the Lord, has showed me and informed me, and I have read them in the heavenly tablets. Chapter 107 [1] And I saw written on them that generation upon generation shall transgress, till a generation of righteousness arises, and transgression is destroyed and sin passes away from the earth, and all manner of good comes upon it. [2] And now, my son, go and make known to thy son Lamech that this son, which has been born, is in truth his son, and that this is no lie. [3] And when Methuselah had heard the words of his father Enoch for he had shown to him everything in secret he returned and showed them to him and called the name of that son Noah; for he will comfort the earth after all the destruction. Chapter 108 [1] Another book which Enoch wrote for his son Methuselah and for those who will come after him, and keep the law in the last days. [2] Ye who have done good shall wait for those days till an end is made of those who work evil; and an end of the might of the transgressors. And wait ye indeed till sin has passed away, [3] For their names shall be blotted out of the book of life and out of the holy books, and their seed shall be destroyed for ever, [4] And their spirits shall be slain, and they shall cry and make lamentation in a place that is a chaotic wilderness, and in the fire shall they burn; for there is no earth there. And I saw there something like an invisible cloud; for by reason of its depth I could not look over, and I saw a flame of fire blazing brightly, and things like shining mountains circling and sweeping to and fro. [5] And I asked one of the holy angels who was with me and said unto him: What is this shining thing? for it is not a heaven but only the flame of a blazing fire, [6] And the voice of weeping and crying and lamentation and strong pain. And he said unto me: This place which thou seest here are cast the spirits of sinners and blasphemers, and of those who work wickedness, and of those who pervert everything that the Lord hath spoken through the mouth of the prophets even the things that shall be. [7] For some of them are written and inscribed above in the heaven, in order tha t the angels may read them and know that which shall befall the sinners, and the spirits of the humble, and of those who have afflicted their bodies, and been recompensed by God; [8] And of those who have been put to shame by wicked men: Who love God and loved neither gold nor silver nor any of the good things which are in the world, but gave over their bodies to torture. [9] Who, since they came into being, longed not after earthly food, but regarded everything as a passing breath, and lived accordingly, and the Lord tried them much, and their spirits were found pure so that they should bless His name. [10] And all the blessings destined for them I have recounted in the books. And he hath assigned them their recompense, because they have been found to be such as loved heaven more than their life in the world, and though they were trodden under foot of wicked men, and experienced abuse and reviling from them and were put to shame, [11] Yet they blessed Me. And now I will summon the spirits of the good who belong to the generation of light, and I will transform those who were born in darkness, who in the flesh were not recompensed with such honour as their faithfulness deserved. [12] And I will bring forth in shining light those who have loved My holy name, and I will seat each on the throne of his honour. [13] And they shall be resplendent for times without number; for righteousness is the judgement of God; for to the faithful He will give faithfulness in the habitation of upright paths. And they shall see those who were, born in darkness led into darkness, while the righteous shall be resplendent. [14] And the sinners shall cry aloud and see them resplendent, and they indeed will go where days and seasons are prescribed for them.

Book 76. Esdras

1Esdr.1 [1] And Josias held the feast of the passover in Jerusalem unto his Lord, and offered the passover the fourteenth day of the first month; [2] Having set the priests according to their daily courses, being arrayed in long garments, in the temple of the Lord. [3] And he spake unto the Levites, the holy ministers of Israel, that they should hallow themselves unto the Lord, to set the holy ark of the Lord in the house that king Solomon the son of David had built: [4] And said, Ye shall no more bear the ark upon your shoulders: now therefore serve the Lord your God, and minister unto his people Israel, and prepare you after your families and kindreds, [5] According as David the king of Israel prescribed, and according to the magnificence of Solomon his son: and standing in the temple according to the several dignity of the families of you the Levites, who minister in the presence of your brethren the children of Israel, [6] Offer the passover in order, and make ready the sacrifices for your brethren, and keep the passover according to the commandment of the Lord, which was given unto Moses. [7] And unto the people that was found there Josias gave thirty thousand lambs and kids, and three thousand calves: these things were given of the king's allowance, according as he promised, to the people, to the priests, and to the Levites. [8] And Helkias, Zacharias, and Syelus, the governors of the temple, gave to the priests for the passover two thousand and six hundred sheep, and three hundred calves. [9] And Jeconias, and Samaias, and Nathanael his brother, and Assabias, and Ochiel, and Joram, captains over thousands, gave to the Levites for the passover five thousand sheep, and seven hundred calves. [10] And when these things were done, the priests and Levites, having the unleavened bread, stood in very comely order according to the kindreds, [11] And according to the several dignities of the fathers, before the people, to offer to the Lord, as it is written in the book of Moses: and thus did they in the morning. [12] And they roasted the passover with fire, as apperttaineth: as for the sacrifices, they sod them in brass pots and pans with a good savour, [13] And set them before all the people: and afterward they prepared for themselves, and for the priests their brethren, the sons of Aaron. [14] For the priests offered the fat until night: and the Levites prepared for themselves, and the priests their brethren, the sons of Aaron. [15] The holy singers also, the sons of Asaph, were in their order, according to the appointment of David, to wit, Asaph, Zacharias, and Jeduthun, who was of the king's retinue. [16] Moreover the porters were at every gate; it was not lawful for any to go from his ordinary service: for their brethren the Levites prepared for them. [17] Thus were the things that belonged to the sacrifices of the Lord accomplished in that day, that they might hold the passover, [18] And offer sacrifices upon the altar of the Lord, according to the commandment of king Josias. [19] So the children of Israel which were present held the passover at that time, and the feast of sweet bread seven days. [20] And such a passover was not kept in Israel since the time of the prophet Samuel. [21] Yea, all the kings of Israel held not such a passover as Josias, and the priests, and the Levites, and the Jews, held with all Israel that were found dwelling at Jerusalem. [22] In the eighteenth year of the reign of Josias was this passover kept. [23] And the works or Josias were upright before his Lord with an heart full of godliness. [24] As for the things that came to pass in his time, they were written in former times, concerning those that sinned, and did wickedly against the Lord above all people and kingdoms, and how they grieved him exceedingly, so that the words of the Lord rose up against Israel. [25] Now after all these acts of Josias it came to pass, that Pharaoh the king of Egypt came to raise war at Carchamis upon Euphrates: and Josias went out against him. [26] But the king of Egypt sent to him, saying, What have I to do with thee, O king of Judea? [27] I am not sent out from the Lord God against thee; for my war is upon Euphrates: and now the Lord is with me, yea, the Lord is with me hasting me forward: depart from me, and be not against the Lord. [28] Howbeit Josias did not turn back his chariot from him, but undertook to fight with him, not regarding the words of the prophet Jeremy spoken by the mouth of the Lord: [29] But joined battle with him in the plain of Magiddo, and the princes came against king Josias. [30] Then said the king unto his servants, Carry me away out of the battle; for I am very weak. And immediately his servants took him away out of the battle. [31] Then gat he up upon his second chariot; and being brought back to Jerusalem died, and was buried in his father's sepulchre. [32] And in all Jewry they mourned for Josias, yea, Jeremy the prophet lamented for Josias, and the chief men with the women made lamentation for him unto this day: and this was given out for an ordinance to be done continually in all the nation of Israel. [33] These things are written in the book of the stories of the kings of Judah, and every one of the acts that Josias did, and his glory, and his understanding in the law of the Lord, and the things that he had done before, and the things now recited, are reported in the book of the kings of Israel and Judea. [34] And the people took Joachaz the son of Josias, and made him king instead of Josias his father, when he was twenty and three years old. [35] And he reigned in Judea and in Jerusalem three months: and then the king of Egypt deposed him from reigning in Jerusalem. [36] And he set a tax upon the land of an hundred talents of silver and one talent of gold. [37] The king of Egypt also made king Joacim his brother king of Judea and Jerusalem. [38] And he bound Joacim and the nobles: but Zaraces his brother he apprehended, and brought him out of Egypt. [39] Five and twenty years old was Joacim when he was made king in the land of Judea and Jerusalem; and he did evil before the Lord. [40] Wherefore against him Nabuchodonosor the king of Babylon came up, and bound him with a chain of brass, and carried him into Babylon. [41] Nabuchodonosor also took of the holy vessels of the Lord, and carried them away, and set them in his own temple at Babylon. [42] But those things that are recorded of him, and of his uncleanness and impiety, are written in the chronicles of the kings. [43] And Joacim his son reigned in his stead: he was made king being eighteen years old; [44] And reigned but three months and ten days in Jerusalem; and did evil before the Lord. [45] So after a year Nabuchodonosor sent and caused him to be brought into Babylon with the holy vessels of the Lord; [46] And made Zedechias king of Judea and Jerusalem, when he was one and twenty years old; and he reigned eleven years: [47] And he did evil also in the sight of the Lord, and cared not for the words that were spoken unto him by the prophet Jeremy from the mouth of the Lord. [48] And after that king Nabuchodonosor had made him to swear by the name of the Lord, he forswore himself, and rebelled; and hardening his neck, his heart, he transgressed the laws of the Lord God of Israel. [49] The governors also of the people and of the priests did many things against the laws, and passed all the pollutions of all nations, and defiled the temple of the Lord, which was sanctified in Jerusalem. [50] Nevertheless the God of their fathers sent by his messenger to call them back, because he spared them and his tabernacle also. [51] But they had his messengers in derision; and, look, when the Lord spake unto them, they made a sport of his prophets: [52] So far forth, that he, being wroth with his people for their great ungodliness, commanded the kings of the Chaldees to come up against them; [53] Who slew their young men with the sword, yea, even within the compass of their holy temple, and spared neither young man nor maid, old man nor child, among them; for he delivered all into their hands. [54] And they took all the holy vessels of the Lord, both great and small, with the vessels of the ark of God, and the king's treasures, and carried them away into Babylon. [55] As for the house of the Lord, they burnt it, and brake down the walls of Jerusalem, and set fire upon her towers: [56] And as for her glorious things, they never ceased till they had consumed and brought them all to nought: and the people that were not slain with the sword he carried unto Babylon: [57] Who became servants to him and his children, till the Persians reigned, to fulfil the word of the Lord spoken by the mouth of Jeremy: [58] Until the land had enjoyed her sabbaths, the whole time of her desolation shall she rest, until the full term of seventy years. 1Esdr.2 [1] In the first year of Cyrus king of the Persians, that the word of the Lord might be accomplished, that he had promised by the mouth of Jeremy; [2] The Lord raised up the spirit of Cyrus the king of the Persians, and he made proclamation through all his kingdom, and also by writing, [3] Saying, Thus saith Cyrus king of the Persians; The Lord of Israel, the most high Lord, hath made me king of the whole world, [4] And commanded me to build him an house at Jerusalem in Jewry. [5] If therefore there be any of you that are of his people, let the Lord, even his Lord, be with him, and let him go up to Jerusalem that is in Judea, and build the house of the Lord of Israel: for he is the Lord that dwelleth in Jerusalem. [6] Whosoever then dwell in the places about, let them help him, those, I say, that are his neighbours, with gold, and with silver, [7] With gifts, with horses, and with cattle, and other things, which have been set forth by vow, for the temple of the Lord at Jerusalem. [8] Then the chief of the families of Judea and of the tribe of Benjamin stood up; the priests also, and the Levites, and all they whose mind the Lord had moved to go up, and to build an house for the Lord at Jerusalem, [9] And they that dwelt round about them, and helped them in all things with silver and gold, with horses and cattle, and with very many free gifts of a great number whose minds were stirred up thereto. [10] King Cyrus also brought forth the holy vessels, which Nabuchodonosor had carried away from Jerusalem, and had set up in his temple of idols. [11] Now when Cyrus king of the Persians had brought them forth, he delivered them to Mithridates his treasurer: [12] And by him they were delivered to Sanabassar the governor of Judea. [13] And this was the number of them; A thousand golden cups, and a thousand of silver, censers of silver twenty nine, vials of gold thirty, and of silver two thousand four hundred and ten, and a thousand other vessels. [14] So all the vessels of gold and of silver, which were carried away, were five thousand four hundred threescore and nine. [15] These were brought back by Sanabassar, together with them of the captivity, from Babylon to Jerusalem. [16] But in the time of Artexerxes king of the Persians Belemus, and Mithridates, and Tabellius, and Rathumus, and Beeltethmus, and Semellius the secretary, with others that were in commission with them, dwelling in Samaria and other places, wrote unto him against them that dwelt in Judea and Jerusalem these letters following; [17] To king Artexerxes our lord, Thy servants, Rathumus the storywriter, and Semellius the scribe, and the rest of their council, and the judges that are in Celosyria and Phenice. [18] Be it now known to the lord king, that the Jews that are up from you to us, being come into Jerusalem, that rebellious and wicked city, do build the marketplaces, and repair the walls of it and do lay the foundation of the temple. [19] Now if this city and the walls thereof be made up again, they will not only refuse to give tribute, but also rebel against kings. [20] And forasmuch as the things pertaining to the temple are now in hand, we think it meet not to neglect such a matter, [21] But to speak unto our lord the king, to the intent that, if it be thy pleasure it may be sought out in the books of thy fathers: [22] And thou shalt find in the chronicles what is written concerning these things, and shalt understand that that city was rebellious, troubling both kings and cities: [23] And that the Jews were rebellious, and raised always wars therein; for the which cause even this city was made desolate. [24] Wherefore now we do declare unto thee, O lord the king, that if this city be built again, and the walls thereof set up anew, thou shalt from henceforth have no passage into Celosyria and Phenice. [25] Then the king wrote back again to Rathumus the storywriter, to Beeltethmus, to Semellius the scribe, and to the rest that were in commission, and dwellers in Samaria and Syria and Phenice, after this manner; [26] I have read the epistle which ye have sent unto me: therefore I commanded to make diligent search, and it hath been found that that city was from the beginning practising against kings; [27] And the men therein were given to rebellion and war: and that mighty kings and fierce were in Jerusalem, who reigned and exacted tributes in Celosyria and Phenice. [28] Now therefore I have commanded to hinder those men from building the city, and heed to be taken that there be no more done in it; [29] And that those wicked workers proceed no further to the annoyance of kings; [30] Then king Artexerxes his letters being read, Rathumus, and Semellius the scribe, and the rest that were in commission with them, removing in haste toward Jerusalem with a troop of horsemen and a multitude of people in battle array, began to hinder the builders; and the building of the temple in Jerusalem ceased until the second year of the reign of Darius king of the Persians. 1Esdr.3 [1] Now when Darius reigned, he made a great feast unto all his subjects, and unto all his household, and unto all the princes of Media and Persia, [2] And to all the governors and captains and lieutenants that were under him, from India unto Ethiopia, of an hundred twenty and seven provinces. [3] And when they had eaten and drunken, and being satisfied were gone home, then Darius the king went into his bedchamber, and slept, and soon after awaked. [4] Then three young men, that were of the guard that kept the king's body, spake one to another; [5] Let every one of us speak a sentence: he that shall overcome, and whose sentence shall seem wiser than the others, unto him shall the king Darius give great gifts, and great things in token of victory: [6] As, to be clothed in purple, to drink in gold, and to sleep upon gold, and a chariot with bridles of gold, and an headtire of fine linen, and a chain about his neck: [7] And he shall sit next to Darius because of his wisdom, and shall be called Darius his cousin. [8] And then every one wrote his sentence, sealed it, and laid it under king Darius his pillow; [9] And said that, when the king is risen, some will give him the writings; and of whose side the king and the three princes of Persia shall judge that his sentence is the wisest, to him shall the victory be given, as was appointed. [10] The first wrote, Wine is the strongest. [11] The second wrote, The king is strongest. [12] The third wrote, Women are strongest: but above all things Truth beareth away the victory. [13] Now when the king was risen up, they took their writings, and delivered them unto him, and so he read them: [14] And sending forth he called all the princes of Persia and Media, and the governors, and the captains, and the lieutenants, and the chief officers; [15] And sat him down in the royal seat of judgment; and the writings were read before them. [16] And he said, Call the young men, and they shall declare their own sentences. So they were called, and came in. [17] And he said unto them, Declare unto us your mind concerning the writings. Then began the first, who had spoken of the strength of wine; [18] And he said thus, O ye men, how exceeding strong is wine! it causeth all men to err that drink it: [19] It maketh the mind of the king and of the fatherless child to be all one; of the bondman and of the freeman, of the poor man and of the rich: [20] It turneth also every thought into jollity and mirth, so that a man remembereth neither sorrow nor debt: [21] And it maketh every heart rich, so that a man remembereth neither king nor governor; and it maketh to speak all things by talents: [22] And when they are in their cups, they forget their love both to friends and brethren, and a little after draw out swords: [23] But when they are from the wine, they remember not what they have done. [24] O ye men, is not wine the strongest, that enforceth to do thus? And when he had so spoken, he held his peace. 1Esdr.4 [1] Then the second, that had spoken of the strength of the king, began to say, [2] O ye men, do not men excel in strength that bear rule over sea and land and all things in them? [3] But yet the king is more mighty: for he is lord of all these things, and hath dominion over them; and whatsoever he commandeth them they do. [4] If he bid them make war the one against the other, they do it: if he send them out against the enemies, they go, and break down mountains walls and towers. [5] They slay and are slain, and transgress not the king's commandment: if they get the victory, they bring all to the king, as well the spoil, as all things else. [6] Likewise for those that are no soldiers, and have not to do with wars, but use husbundry, when they have reaped again that which they had sown, they bring it to the king, and compel one another to pay tribute unto the king. [7] And yet he is but one man: if he command to kill, they kill; if he command to spare, they spare; [8] If he command to smite, they smite; if he command to make desolate, they make desolate; if he command to build, they build; [9] If he command to cut down, they cut down; if he command to plant, they plant. [10] So all his people and his armies obey him: furthermore he lieth down, he eateth and drinketh, and taketh his rest: [11] And these keep watch round about him, neither may any one depart, and do his own business, neither disobey they him in any thing. [12] O ye men, how should not the king be mightiest, when in such sort he is obeyed? And he held his tongue. [13] Then the third, who had spoken of women, and of the truth, (this was Zorobabel) began to speak. [14] O ye men, it is not the great king, nor the multitude of men, neither is it wine, that excelleth; who is it then that ruleth them, or hath the lordship over them? are they not women? [15] Women have borne the king and all the people that bear rule by sea and land. [16] Even of them came they: and they nourished them up that planted the vineyards, from whence the wine cometh. [17] These also make garments for men; these bring glory unto men; and without women cannot men be. [18] Yea, and if men have gathered together gold and silver, or any other goodly thing, do they not love a woman which is comely in favour and beauty? [19] And letting all those things go, do they not gape, and even with open mouth fix their eyes fast on her; and have not all men more desire unto her than unto silver or gold, or any goodly thing whatsoever? [20] A man leaveth his own father that brought him up, and his own country, and cleaveth unto his wife. [21] He sticketh not to spend his life with his wife. and remembereth neither father, nor mother, nor country. [22] By this also ye must know that women have dominion over you: do ye not labour and toil, and give and bring all to the woman? [23] Yea, a man taketh his sword, and goeth his way to rob and to steal, to sail upon the sea and upon rivers; [24] And looketh upon a lion, and goeth in the darkness; and when he hath stolen, spoiled, and robbed, he bringeth it to his love. [25] Wherefore a man loveth his wife better than father or mother. [26] Yea, many there be that have run out of their wits for women, and become servants for their sakes. [27] Many also have perished, have erred, and sinned, for women. [28] And now do ye not believe me? is not the king great in his power? do not all regions fear to touch him? [29] Yet did I see him and Apame the king's concubine, the daughter of the admirable Bartacus, sitting at the right hand of the king, [30] And taking the crown from the king's head, and setting it upon her own head; she also struck the king with her left hand. [31] And yet for all this the king gaped and gazed upon her with open mouth: if she laughed upon him, he laughed also: but if she took any displeasure at him, the king was fain to flatter, that she might be reconciled to him again. [32] O ye men, how can it be but women should be strong, seeing they do thus? [33] Then the king and the princes looked one upon another: so he began to speak of the truth. [34] O ye men, are not women strong? great is the earth, high is the heaven, swift is the sun in his course, for he compasseth the heavens round about, and fetcheth his course again to his own place in one day. [35] Is he not great that maketh these things? therefore great is the truth, and stronger than all things. [36] All the earth crieth upon the truth, and the heaven blesseth it: all works shake and tremble at it, and with it is no unrighteous thing. [37] Wine is wicked, the king is wicked, women are wicked, all the children of men are wicked, and such are all their wicked works; and there is no truth in them; in their unrighteousness also they shall perish. [38] As for the truth, it endureth, and is alwaYs strong; it liveth and conquereth for evermore. [39] With her there is no accepting of persons or rewards; but she doeth the things that are just, and refraineth from all unjust and wicked things; and all men do well like of her works. [40] Neither in her judgment is any unrighteousness; and she is the strength, kingdom, power, and majesty, of all ages. Blessed be the God of truth. [41] And with that he held his peace. And all the people then shouted, and said, Great is Truth, and mighty above all things. [42] Then said the king unto him, Ask what thou wilt more than is appointed in the writing, and we will give it thee, because thou art found wisest; and thou shalt sit next me, and shalt be called my cousin. [43] Then said he unto the king, Remember thy vow, which thou hast vowed to build Jerusalem, in the day when thou camest to thy kingdom, [44] And to send away all the vessels that were taken away out of Jerusalem, which Cyrus set apart, when he vowed to destroy Babylon, and to send them again thither. [45] Thou also hast vowed to build up the temple, which the Edomites burned when Judea was made desolate by the Chaldees. [46] And now, O lord the king, this is that which I require, and which I desire of thee, and this is the princely liberality proceeding from thyself: I desire therefore that thou make good the vow, the performance whereof with thine own mouth thou hast vowed to the King of heaven. [47] Then Darius the king stood up, and kissed him, and wrote letters for him unto all the treasurers and lieutenants and captains and governors, that they should safely convey on their way both him, and all those that go up with him to build Jerusalem. [48] He wrote letters also unto the lieutenants that were in Celosyria and Phenice, and unto them in Libanus, that they should bring cedar wood from Libanus unto Jerusalem, and that they should build the city with him. [49] Moreover he wrote for all the Jews that went out of his realm up into Jewry, concerning their freedom, that no officer, no ruler, no lieutenant, nor treasurer, should forcibly enter into their doors; [50] And that all the country which they hold should be free without tribute; and that the Edomites should give over the villages of the Jews which then they held: [51] Yea, that there should be yearly given twenty talents to the building of the temple, until the time that it were built; [52] And other ten talents yearly, to maintain the burnt offerings upon the altar every day, as they had a commandment to offer seventeen: [53] And that all they that went from Babylon to build the city should have free liberty, as well they as their posterity, and all the priests that went away. [54] He wrote also concerning. the charges, and the priests' vestments wherein they minister; [55] And likewise for the charges of the Levites, to be given them until the day that the house were finished, and Jerusalem builded up. [56] And he commanded to give to all that kept the city pensions and wages. [57] He sent away also all the vessels from Babylon, that Cyrus had set apart; and all that Cyrus had given in commandment, the same charged he also to be done, and sent unto Jerusalem. [58] Now when this young man was gone forth, he lifted up his face to heaven toward Jerusalem, and praised the King of heaven, [59] And said, From thee cometh victory, from thee cometh wisdom, and thine is the glory, and I am thy servant. [60] Blessed art thou, who hast given me wisdom: for to thee I give thanks, O Lord of our fathers. [61] And so he took the letters, and went out, and came unto Babylon, and told it all his brethren. [62] And they praised the God of their fathers, because he had given them freedom and liberty [63] To go up, and to build Jerusalem, and the temple which is called by his name: and they feasted with instruments of musick and gladness seven days. 1Esdr.5 [1] After this were the principal men of the families chosen according to their tribes, to go up with their wives and sons and daughters, with their menservants and maidservants, and their cattle. [2] And Darius sent with them a thousand horsemen, till they had brought them back to Jerusalem safely, and with musical [instruments] tabrets and flutes. [3] And all their brethren played, and he made them go up together with them. [4] And these are the names of the men which went up, according to their families among their tribes, after their several heads. [5] The priests, the sons of Phinees the son of Aaron: Jesus the son of Josedec, the son of Saraias, and Joacim the son of Zorobabel, the son of Salathiel, of the house of David, out of the kindred of Phares, of the tribe of Judah; [6] Who spake wise sentences before Darius the king of Persia in the second year of his reign, in the month Nisan, which is the first month. [7] And these are they of Jewry that came up from the captivity, where they dwelt as strangers, whom Nabuchodonosor the king of Babylon had carried away unto Babylon. [8] And they returned unto Jerusalem, and to the other parts of Jewry, every man to his own city, who came with Zorobabel, with Jesus, Nehemias, and Zacharias, and Reesaias, Enenius, Mardocheus. Beelsarus, Aspharasus, Reelius, Roimus, and Baana, their guides. [9] The number of them of the nation, and their governors, sons of Phoros, two thousand an hundred seventy and two; the sons of Saphat, four hundred seventy and two: [10] The sons of Ares, seven hundred fifty and six: [11] The sons of Phaath Moab, two thousand eight hundred and twelve: [12] The sons of Elam, a thousand two hundred fifty and four: the sons of Zathul, nine hundred forty and five: the sons of Corbe, seven hundred and five: the sons of Bani, six hundred forty and eight: [13] The sons of Bebai, six hundred twenty and three: the sons of Sadas, three thousand two hundred twenty and two: [14] The sons of Adonikam, six hundred sixty and seven: the sons of Bagoi, two thousand sixty and six: the sons of Adin, four hundred fifty and four: [15] The sons of Aterezias, ninety and two: the sons of Ceilan and Azetas threescore and seven: the sons of Azuran, four hundred thirty and two: [16] The sons of Ananias, an hundred and one: the sons of Arom, thirty two: and the sons of Bassa, three hundred twenty and three: the sons of Azephurith, an hundred and two: [17] The sons of Meterus, three thousand and five: the sons of Bethlomon, an hundred twenty and three: [18] They of Netophah, fifty and five: they of Anathoth, an hundred fifty and eight: they of Bethsamos, forty and two: [19] They of Kiriathiarius, twenty and five: they of Caphira and Beroth, seven hundred forty and three: they of Pira, seven hundred: [20] They of Chadias and Ammidoi, four hundred twenty and two: they of Cirama and Gabdes, six hundred twenty and one: [21] They of Macalon, an hundred twenty and two: they of Betolius, fifty and two: the sons of Nephis, an hundred fifty and six: [22] The sons of Calamolalus and Onus, seven hundred twenty and five: the sons of Jerechus, two hundred forty and five: [23] The sons of Annas, three thousand three hundred and thirty. [24] The priests: the sons of Jeddu, the son of Jesus among the sons of Sanasib, nine hundred seventy and two: the sons of Meruth, a thousand fifty and two: [25] The sons of Phassaron, a thousand forty and seven: the sons of Carme, a thousand and seventeen. [26] The Levites: the sons of Jessue, and Cadmiel, and Banuas, and Sudias, seventy and four. [27] The holy singers: the sons of Asaph, an hundred twenty and eight. [28] The porters: the sons of Salum, the sons of Jatal, the sons of Talmon, the sons of Dacobi, the sons of Teta, the sons of Sami, in all an hundred thirty and nine. [29] The servants of the temple: the sons of Esau, the sons of Asipha, the sons of Tabaoth, the sons of Ceras, the sons of Sud, the sons of Phaleas, the sons of Labana, the sons of Graba, [30] The sons of Acua, the sons of Uta, the sons of Cetab, the sons of Agaba, the sons of Subai, the sons of Anan, the sons of Cathua, the sons of Geddur, [31] The sons of Airus, the sons of Daisan, the sons of Noeba, the sons of Chaseba, the sons of Gazera, the sons of Azia, the sons of Phinees, the sons of Azare, the sons of Bastai, the sons of Asana, the sons of Meani, the sons of Naphisi, the sons of Acub, the sons of Acipha, the sons of Assur, the sons of Pharacim, the sons of Basaloth, [32] The sons of Meeda, the sons of Coutha, the sons of Charea, the sons of Charcus, the sons of Aserer, the sons of Thomoi, the sons of Nasith, the sons of Atipha. [33] The sons of the servants of Solomon: the sons of Azaphion, the sons of Pharira, the sons of Jeeli, the sons of Lozon, the sons of Israel, the sons of Sapheth, [34] The sons of Hagia, the sons of Pharacareth, the sons of Sabi, the sons of Sarothie, the sons of Masias, the sons of Gar, the sons of Addus, the sons of Suba, the sons of Apherra, the sons of Barodis, the sons of Sabat, the sons of Allom. [35] All the ministers of the temple, and the sons of the servants of Solomon, were three hundred seventy and two. [36] These came up from Thermeleth and Thelersas, Charaathalar leading them, and Aalar; [37] Neither could they shew their families, nor their stock, how they were of Israel: the sons of Ladan, the son of Ban, the sons of Necodan, six hundred fifty and two. [38] And of the priests that usurped the office of the priesthood, and were not found: the sons of Obdia, the sons of Accoz, the sons of Addus, who married Augia one of the daughters of Barzelus, and was named after his name. [39] And when the description of the kindred of these men was sought in the register, and was not found, they were removed from executing the office of the priesthood: [40] For unto them said Nehemias and Atharias, that they should not be partakers of the holy things, till there arose up an high priest clothed with doctrine and truth. [41] So of Israel, from them of twelve years old and upward, they were all in number forty thousand, beside menservants and women-servants two thousand three hundred and sixty. [42] Their menservants and handmaids were seven thousand three hundred forty and seven: the singing men and singing women, two hundred forty and five: [43] Four hundred thirty and five camels, seven thousand thirty and six horses, two hundred forty and five mules, five thousand five hundred twenty and five beasts used to the yoke. [44] And certain of the chief of their families, when they came to the temple of God that is in Jerusalem, vowed to set up the house again in his own place according to their ability, [45] And to give into the holy treasury of the works a thousand pounds of gold, five thousand of silver, and an hundred priestly vestments. [46] And so dwelt the priests and the Levites and the people in Jerusalem, and in the country, the singers also and the porters; and all Israel in their villages. [47] But when the seventh month was at hand, and when the children of Israel were every man in his own place, they came all together with one consent into the open place of the first gate which is toward the east. [48] Then stood up Jesus the son of Josedec, and his brethren the priests and Zorobabel the son of Salathiel, and his brethren, and made ready the altar of the God of Israel, [49] To offer burnt sacrifices upon it, according as it is expressly commanded in the book of Moses the man of God. [50] And there were gathered unto them out of the other nations of the land, and they erected the altar upon his own place, because all the nations of the land were at enmity with them, and oppressed them; and they offered sacrifices according to the time, and burnt offerings to the Lord both morning and evening. [51] Also they held the feast of tabernacles, as it is commanded in the law, and offered sacrifices daily, as was meet: [52] And after that, the continual oblations, and the sacrifice of the sabbaths, and of the new moons, and of all holy feasts. [53] And all they that had made any vow to God began to offer sacrifices to God from the first day of the seventh month, although the temple of the Lord was not yet built. [54] And they gave unto the masons and carpenters money, meat, and drink, with cheerfulness. [55] Unto them of Zidon also and Tyre they gave carrs, that they should bring cedar trees from Libanus, which should be brought by floats to the haven of Joppa, according as it was commanded them by Cyrus king of the Persians. [56] And in the second year and second month after his coming to the temple of God at Jerusalem began Zorobabel the son of Salathiel, and Jesus the son of Josedec, and their brethren, and the priests, and the Levites, and all they that were come unto Jerusalem out of the captivity: [57] And they laid the foundation of the house of God in the first day of the second month, in the second year after they were come to Jewry and Jerusalem. [58] And they appointed the Levites from twenty years old over the works of the Lord. Then stood up Jesus, and his sons and brethren, and Cadmiel his brother, and the sons of Madiabun, with the sons of Joda the son of Eliadun, with their sons and brethren, all Levites, with one accord setters forward of the business, labouring to advance the works in the house of God. So the workmen built the temple of the Lord. [59] And the priests stood arrayed in their vestments with musical instruments and trumpets; and the Levites the sons of Asaph had cymbals, [60] Singing songs of thanksgiving, and praising the Lord, according as David the king of Israel had ordained. [61] And they sung with loud voices songs to the praise of the Lord, because his mercy and glory is for ever in all Israel. [62] And all the people sounded trumpets, and shouted with a loud voice, singing songs of thanksgiving unto the Lord for the rearing up of the house of the Lord. [63] Also of the priests and Levites, and of the chief of their families, the ancients who had seen the former house came to the building of this with weeping and great crying. [64] But many with trumpets and joy shouted with loud voice, [65] Insomuch that the trumpets might not be heard for the weeping of the people: yet the multitude sounded marvellously, so that it was heard afar off. [66] Wherefore when the enemies of the tribe of Judah and Benjamin heard it, they came to know what that noise of trumpets should mean. [67] And they perceived that they that were of the captivity did build the temple unto the Lord God of Israel. [68] So they went to Zorobabel and Jesus, and to the chief of the families, and said unto them, We will build together with you. [69] For we likewise, as ye, do obey your Lord, and do sacrifice unto him from the days of Azbazareth the king of the Assyrians, who brought us hither. [70] Then Zorobabel and Jesus and the chief of the families of Israel said unto them, It is not for us and you to build together an house unto the Lord our God. [71] We ourselves alone will build unto the Lord of Israel, according as Cyrus the king of the Persians hath commanded us. [72] But the heathen of the land lying heavy upon the inhabitants of Judea, and holding them strait, hindered their building; [73] And by their secret plots, and popular persuasions and commotions, they hindered the finishing of the building all the time that king Cyrus lived: so they were hindered from building for the space of two years, until the reign of Darius. 1Esdr.6 [1] Now in the second year of the reign of Darius Aggeus and Zacharias the son of Addo, the prophets, prophesied unto the Jews in Jewry and Jerusalem in the name of the Lord God of Israel, which was upon them. [2] Then stood up Zorobabel the son of Salatiel, and Jesus the son of Josedec, and began to build the house of the Lord at Jerusalem, the prophets of the Lord being with them, and helping them. [3] At the same time came unto them Sisinnes the governor of Syria and Phenice, with Sathrabuzanes and his companions, and said unto them, [4] By whose appointment do ye build this house and this roof, and perform all the other things? and who are the workmen that perform these things? [5] Nevertheless the elders of the Jews obtained favour, because the Lord had visited the captivity; [6] And they were not hindered from building, until such time as signification was given unto Darius concerning them, and an answer received. [7] The copy of the letters which Sisinnes, governor of Syria and Phenice, and Sathrabuzanes, with their companions, rulers in Syria and Phenice, wrote and sent unto Darius; To king Darius, greeting: [8] Let all things be known unto our lord the king, that being come into the country of Judea, and entered into the city of Jerusalem we found in the city of Jerusalem the ancients of the Jews that were of the captivity [9] Building an house unto the Lord, great and new, of hewn and costly stones, and the timber already laid upon the walls. [10] And those works are done with great speed, and the work goeth on prosperously in their hands, and with all glory and diligence is it made. [11] Then asked we these elders, saying, By whose commandment build ye this house, and lay the foundations of these works? [12] Therefore to the intent that we might give knowledge unto thee by writing, we demanded of them who were the chief doers, and we required of them the names in writing of their principal men. [13] So they gave us this answer, We are the servants of the Lord which made heaven and earth. [14] And as for this house, it was builded many years ago by a king of Israel great and strong, and was finished. [15] But when our fathers provoked God unto wrath, and sinned against the Lord of Israel which is in heaven, he gave them over into the power of Nabuchodonosor king of Babylon, of the Chaldees; [16] Who pulled down the house, and burned it, and carried away the people captives unto Babylon. [17] But in the first year that king Cyrus reigned over the country of Babylon Cyrus the king wrote to build up this house. [18] And the holy vessels of gold and of silver, that Nabuchodonosor had carried away out of the house at Jerusalem, and had set them in his own temple those Cyrus the king brought forth again out of the temple at Babylon, and they were delivered to Zorobabel and to Sanabassarus the ruler, [19] With commandment that he should carry away the same vessels, and put them in the temple at Jerusalem; and that the temple of the Lord should be built in his place. [20] Then the same Sanabassarus, being come hither, laid the foundations of the house of the Lord at Jerusalem; and from that time to this being still a building, it is not yet fully ended. [21] Now therefore, if it seem good unto the king, let search be made among the records of king Cyrus: [22] And if it be found that the building of the house of the Lord at Jerusalem hath been done with the consent of king Cyrus, and if our lord the king be so minded, let him signify unto us thereof. [23] Then commanded king Darius to seek among the records at Babylon: and so at Ecbatane the palace, which is in the country of Media, there was found a roll wherein these things were recorded. [24] In the first year of the reign of Cyrus king Cyrus commanded that the house of the Lord at Jerusalem should be built again, where they do sacrifice with continual fire: [25] Whose height shall be sixty cubits and the breadth sixty cubits, with three rows of hewn stones, and one row of new wood of that country; and the expences thereof to be given out of the house of king Cyrus: [26] And that the holy vessels of the house of the Lord, both of gold and silver, that Nabuchodonosor took out of the house at Jerusalem, and brought to Babylon, should be restored to the house at Jerusalem, and be set in the place where they were before. [27] And also he commanded that Sisinnes the governor of Syria and Phenice, and Sathrabuzanes, and their companions, and those which were appointed rulers in Syria and Phenice, should be careful not to meddle with the place, but suffer Zorobabel, the servant of the Lord, and governor of Judea, and the elders of the Jews, to build the house of the Lord in that place. [28] I have commanded also to have it built up whole again; and that they look diligently to help those that be of the captivity of the Jews, till the house of the Lord be finished: [29] And out of the tribute of Celosyria and Phenice a portion carefully to be given these men for the sacrifices of the Lord, that is, to Zorobabel the governor, for bullocks, and rams, and lambs; [30] And also corn, salt, wine, and oil, and that continually every year without further question, according as the priests that be in Jerusalem shall signify to be daily spent: [31] That offerings may be made to the most high God for the king and for his children, and that they may pray for their lives. [32] And he commanded that whosoever should transgress, yea, or make light of any thing afore spoken or written, out of his own house should a tree be taken, and he thereon be hanged, and all his goods seized for the king. [33] The Lord therefore, whose name is there called upon, utterly destroy every king and nation, that stretcheth out his hand to hinder or endamage that house of the Lord in Jerusalem. [34] I Darius the king have ordained that according unto these things it be done with diligence. 1Esdr.7 [1] Then Sisinnes the governor of Celosyria and Phenice, and Sathrabuzanes, with their companions following the commandments of king Darius, [2] Did very carefully oversee the holy works, assisting the ancients of the Jews and governors of the temple. [3] And so the holy works prospered, when Aggeus and Zacharias the prophets prophesied. [4] And they finished these things by the commandment of the Lord God of Israel, and with the consent of Cyrus, Darius, and Artexerxes, kings of Persia. [5] And thus was the holy house finished in the three and twentieth day of the month Adar, in the sixth year of Darius king of the Persians [6] And the children of Israel, the priests, and the Levites, and others that were of the captivity, that were added unto them, did according to the things written in the book of Moses. [7] And to the dedication of the temple of the Lord they offered an hundred bullocks two hundred rams, four hundred lambs; [8] And twelve goats for the sin of all Israel, according to the number of the chief of the tribes of Israel. [9] The priests also and the Levites stood arrayed in their vestments, according to their kindreds, in the service of the Lord God of Israel, according to the book of Moses: and the porters at every gate. [10] And the children of Israel that were of the captivity held the passover the fourteenth day of the first month, after that the priests and the Levites were sanctified. [11] They that were of the captivity were not all sanctified together: but the Levites were all sanctified together. [12] And so they offered the passover for all them of the captivity, and for their brethren the priests, and for themselves. [13] And the children of Israel that came out of the captivity did eat, even all they that had separated themselves from the abominations of the people of the land, and sought the Lord. [14] And they kept the feast of unleavened bread seven days, making merry before the Lord, [15] For that he had turned the counsel of the king of Assyria toward them, to strengthen their hands in the works of the Lord God of Israel. 1Esdr.8 [1] And after these things, when Artexerxes the king of the Persians reigned came Esdras the son of Saraias, the son of Ezerias, the son of Helchiah, the son of Salum, [2] The son of Sadduc, the son of Achitob, the son of Amarias, the son of Ezias, the son of Meremoth, the son of Zaraias, the son of Savias, the son of Boccas, the son of Abisum, the son of Phinees, the son of Eleazar, the son of Aaron the chief priest. [3] This Esdras went up from Babylon, as a scribe, being very ready in the law of Moses, that was given by the God of Israel. [4] And the king did him honour: for he found grace in his sight in all his requests. [5] There went up with him also certain of the children of Israel, of the priest of the Levites, of the holy singers, porters, and ministers of the temple, unto Jerusalem, [6] In the seventh year of the reign of Artexerxes, in the fifth month, this was the king's seventh year; for they went from Babylon in the first day of the first month, and came to Jerusalem, according to the prosperous journey which the Lord gave them. [7] For Esdras had very great skill, so that he omitted nothing of the law and commandments of the Lord, but taught all Israel the ordinances and judgments. [8] Now the copy of the commission, which was written from Artexerxes the king, and came to Esdras the priest and reader of the law of the Lord, is this that followeth; [9] King Artexerxes unto Esdras the priest and reader of the law of the Lord sendeth greeting: [10] Having determined to deal graciously, I have given order, that such of the nation of the Jews, and of the priests and Levites being within our realm, as are willing and desirous should go with thee unto Jerusalem. [11] As many therefore as have a mind thereunto, let them depart with thee, as it hath seemed good both to me and my seven friends the counsellors; [12] That they may look unto the affairs of Judea and Jerusalem, agreeably to that which is in the law of the Lord; [13] And carry the gifts unto the Lord of Israel to Jerusalem, which I and my friends have vowed, and all the gold and silver that in the country of Babylon can be found, to the Lord in Jerusalem, [14] With that also which is given of the people for the temple of the Lord their God at Jerusalem: and that silver and gold may be collected for bullocks, rams, and lambs, and things thereunto appertaining; [15] To the end that they may offer sacrifices unto the Lord upon the altar of the Lord their God, which is in Jerusalem. [16] And whatsoever thou and thy brethren will do with the silver and gold, that do, according to the will of thy God. [17] And the holy vessels of the Lord, which are given thee for the use of the temple of thy God, which is in Jerusalem, thou shalt set before thy God in Jerusalem. [18] And whatsoever thing else thou shalt remember for the use of the temple of thy God, thou shalt give it out of the king's treasury. [19] And I king Artexerxes have also commanded the keepers of the treasures in Syria and Phenice, that whatsoever Esdras the priest and the reader of the law of the most high God shall send for, they should give it him with speed, [20] To the sum of an hundred talents of silver, likewise also of wheat even to an hundred cors, and an hundred pieces of wine, and other things in abundance. [21] Let all things be performed after the law of God diligently unto the most high God, that wrath come not upon the kingdom of the king and his sons. [22] I command you also, that ye require no tax, nor any other imposition, of any of the priests, or Levites, or holy singers, or porters, or ministers of the temple, or of any that have doings in this temple, and that no man have authority to impose any thing upon them. [23] And thou, Esdras, according to the wisdom of God ordain judges and justices, that they may judge in all Syria and Phenice all those that know the law of thy God; and those that know it not thou shalt teach. [24] And whosoever shall transgress the law of thy God, and of the king, shall be punished diligently, whether it be by death, or other punishment, by penalty of money, or by imprisonment. [25] Then said Esdras the scribe, Blessed be the only Lord God of my fathers, who hath put these things into the heart of the king, to glorify his house that is in Jerusalem: [26] And hath honoured me in the sight of the king, and his counsellors, and all his friends and nobles. [27] Therefore was I encouraged by the help of the Lord my God, and gathered together men of Israel to go up with me. [28] And these are the chief according to their families and several dignities, that went up with me from Babylon in the reign of king Artexerxes: [29] Of the sons of Phinees, Gerson: of the sons of Ithamar, Gamael: of the sons of David, Lettus the son of Sechenias: [30] Of the sons of Pharez, Zacharias; and with him were counted an hundred and fifty men: [31] Of the sons of Pahath Moab, Eliaonias, the son of Zaraias, and with him two hundred men: [32] Of the sons of Zathoe, Sechenias the son of Jezelus, and with him three hundred men: of the sons of Adin, Obeth the son of Jonathan, and with him two hundred and fifty men: [33] Of the sons of Elam, Josias son of Gotholias, and with him seventy men: [34] Of the sons of Saphatias, Zaraias son of Michael, and with him threescore and ten men: [35] Of the sons of Joab, Abadias son of Jezelus, and with him two hundred and twelve men: [36] Of the sons of Banid, Assalimoth son of Josaphias, and with him an hundred and threescore men: [37] Of the sons of Babi, Zacharias son of Bebai, and with him twenty and eight men: [38] Of the sons of Astath, Johannes son of Acatan, and with him an hundred and ten men: [39] Of the sons of Adonikam the last, and these are the names of them, Eliphalet, Jewel, and Samaias, and with them seventy men: [40] Of the sons of Bago, Uthi the son of Istalcurus, and with him seventy men. [41] And these I gathered together to the river called Theras, where we pitched our tents three days: and then I surveyed them. [42] But when I had found there none of the priests and Levites, [43] Then sent I unto Eleazar, and Iduel, and Masman, [44] And Alnathan, and Mamaias, and Joribas, and Nathan, Eunatan, Zacharias, and Mosollamon, principal men and learned. [45] And I bade them that they should go unto Saddeus the captain, who was in the place of the treasury: [46] And commanded them that they should speak unto Daddeus, and to his brethren, and to the treasurers in that place, to send us such men as might execute the priests' office in the house of the Lord. [47] And by the mighty hand of our Lord they brought unto us skilful men of the sons of Moli the son of Levi, the son of Israel, Asebebia, and his sons, and his brethren, who were eighteen. [48] And Asebia, and Annus, and Osaias his brother, of the sons of Channuneus, and their sons, were twenty men. [49] And of the servants of the temple whom David had ordained, and the principal men for the service of the Levites to wit, the servants of the temple two hundred and twenty, the catalogue of whose names were shewed. [50] And there I vowed a fast unto the young men before our Lord, to desire of him a prosperous journey both for us and them that were with us, for our children, and for the cattle: [51] For I was ashamed to ask the king footmen, and horsemen, and conduct for safeguard against our adversaries. [52] For we had said unto the king, that the power of the Lord our God should be with them that seek him, to support them in all ways. [53] And again we besought our Lord as touching these things, and found him favourable unto us. [54] Then I separated twelve of the chief of the priests, Esebrias, and Assanias, and ten men of their brethren with them: [55] And I weighed them the gold, and the silver, and the holy vessels of the house of our Lord, which the king, and his council, and the princes, and all Israel, had given. [56] And when I had weighed it, I delivered unto them six hundred and fifty talents of silver, and silver vessels of an hundred talents, and an hundred talents of gold, [57] And twenty golden vessels, and twelve vessels of brass, even of fine brass, glittering like gold. [58] And I said unto them, Both ye are holy unto the Lord, and the vessels are holy, and the gold and the silver is a vow unto the Lord, the Lord of our fathers. [59] Watch ye, and keep them till ye deliver them to the chief of the priests and Levites, and to the principal men of the families of Israel, in Jerusalem, into the chambers of the house of our God. [60] So the priests and the Levites, who had received the silver and the gold and the vessels, brought them unto Jerusalem, into the temple of the Lord. [61] And from the river Theras we departed the twelfth day of the first month, and came to Jerusalem by the mighty hand of our Lord, which was with us: and from the beginning of our journey the Lord delivered us from every enemy, and so we came to Jerusalem. [62] And when we had been there three days, the gold and silver that was weighed was delivered in the house of our Lord on the fourth day unto Marmoth the priest the son of Iri. [63] And with him was Eleazar the son of Phinees, and with them were Josabad the son of Jesu and Moeth the son of Sabban, Levites: all was delivered them by number and weight. [64] And all the weight of them was written up the same hour. [65] Moreover they that were come out of the captivity offered sacrifice unto the Lord God of Israel, even twelve bullocks for all Israel, fourscore and sixteen rams, [66] Threescore and twelve lambs, goats for a peace offering, twelve; all of them a sacrifice to the Lord. [67] And they delivered the king's commandments unto the king's stewards' and to the governors of Celosyria and Phenice; and they honoured the people and the temple of God. [68] Now when these things were done, the rulers came unto me, and said, [69] The nation of Israel, the princes, the priests and Levites, have not put away from them the strange people of the land, nor the pollutions of the Gentiles to wit, of the Canaanites, Hittites, Pheresites, Jebusites, and the Moabites, Egyptians, and Edomites. [70] For both they and their sons have married with their daughters, and the holy seed is mixed with the strange people of the land; and from the beginning of this matter the rulers and the great men have been partakers of this iniquity. [71] And as soon as I had heard these things, I rent my clothes, and the holy garment, and pulled off the hair from off my head and beard, and sat me down sad and very heavy. [72] So all they that were then moved at the word of the Lord God of Israel assembled unto me, whilst I mourned for the iniquity: but I sat still full of heaviness until the evening sacrifice. [73] Then rising up from the fast with my clothes and the holy garment rent, and bowing my knees, and stretching forth my hands unto the Lord, [74] I said, O Lord, I am confounded and ashamed before thy face; [75] For our sins are multiplied above our heads, and our ignorances have reached up unto heaven. [76] For ever since the time of our fathers we have been and are in great sin, even unto this day. [77] And for our sins and our fathers' we with our brethren and our kings and our priests were given up unto the kings of the earth, to the sword, and to captivity, and for a prey with shame, unto this day. [78] And now in some measure hath mercy been shewed unto us from thee, O Lord, that there should be left us a root and a name in the place of thy sanctuary; [79] And to discover unto us a light in the house of the Lord our God, and to give us food in the time of our servitude. [80] Yea, when we were in bondage, we were not forsaken of our Lord; but he made us gracious before the kings of Persia, so that they gave us food; [81] Yea, and honoured the temple of our Lord, and raised up the desolate Sion, that they have given us a sure abiding in Jewry and Jerusalem. [82] And now, O Lord, what shall we say, having these things? for we have transgressed thy commandments, which thou gavest by the hand of thy servants the prophets, saying, [83] That the land, which ye enter into to possess as an heritage, is a land polluted with the pollutions of the strangers of the land, and they have filled it with their uncleanness. [84] Therefore now shall ye not join your daughters unto their sons, neither shall ye take their daughters unto your sons. [85] Moreover ye shall never seek to have peace with them, that ye may be strong, and eat the good things of the land, and that ye may leave the inheritance of the land unto your children for evermore. [86] And all that is befallen is done unto us for our wicked works and great sins; for thou, O Lord, didst make our sins light, [87] And didst give unto us such a root: but we have turned back again to transgress thy law, and to mingle ourselves with the uncleanness of the nations of the land. [88] Mightest not thou be angry with us to destroy us, till thou hadst left us neither root, seed, nor name? [89] O Lord of Israel, thou art true: for we are left a root this day. [90] Behold, now are we before thee in our iniquities, for we cannot stand any longer by reason of these things before thee. [91] And as Esdras in his prayer made his confession, weeping, and lying flat upon the ground before the temple, there gathered unto him from Jerusalem a very great multitude of men and women and children: for there was great weeping among the multitude. [92] Then Jechonias the son of Jeelus, one of the sons of Israel, called out, and said, O Esdras, we have sinned against the Lord God, we have married strange women of the nations of the land, and now is all Israel aloft. [93] Let us make an oath to the Lord, that we will put away all our wives, which we have taken of the heathen, with their children, [94] Like as thou hast decreed, and as many as do obey the law of the Lord. [95] Arise and put in execution: for to thee doth this matter appertain, and we will be with thee: do valiantly. [96] So Esdras arose, and took an oath of the chief of the priests and Levites of all Israel to do after these things; and so they sware. 1Esdr.9 [1] Then Esdras rising from the court of the temple went to the chamber of Joanan the son of Eliasib, [2] And remained there, and did eat no meat nor drink water, mourning for the great iniquities of the multitude. [3] And there was a proclamation in all Jewry and Jerusalem to all them that were of the captivity, that they should be gathered together at Jerusalem: [4] And that whosoever met not there within two or three days according as the elders that bare rule appointed, their cattle should be seized to the use of the temple, and himself cast out from them that were of the captivity. [5] And in three days were all they of the tribe of Judah and Benjamin gathered together at Jerusalem the twentieth day of the ninth month. [6] And all the multitude sat trembling in the broad court of the temple because of the present foul weather. [7] So Esdras arose up, and said unto them, Ye have transgressed the law in marrying strange wives, thereby to increase the sins of Israel. [8] And now by confessing give glory unto the Lord God of our fathers, [9] And do his will, and separate yourselves from the heathen of the land, and from the strange women. [10] Then cried the whole multitude, and said with a loud voice, Like as thou hast spoken, so will we do. [11] But forasmuch as the people are many, and it is foul weather, so that we cannot stand without, and this is not a work of a day or two, seeing our sin in these things is spread far: [12] Therefore let the rulers of the multitude stay, and let all them of our habitations that have strange wives come at the time appointed, [13] And with them the rulers and judges of every place, till we turn away the wrath of the Lord from us for this matter. [14] Then Jonathan the son of Azael and Ezechias the son of Theocanus accordingly took this matter upon them: and Mosollam and Levis and Sabbatheus helped them. [15] And they that were of the captivity did according to all these things. [16] And Esdras the priest chose unto him the principal men of their families, all by name: and in the first day of the tenth month they sat together to examine the matter. [17] So their cause that held strange wives was brought to an end in the first day of the first month. [18] And of the priests that were come together, and had strange wives, there were found: [19] Of the sons of Jesus the son of Josedec, and his brethren; Matthelas and Eleazar, and Joribus and Joadanus. [20] And they gave their hands to put away their wives and to offer rams to make reconcilement for their errors. [21] And of the sons of Emmer; Ananias, and Zabdeus, and Eanes, and Sameius, and Hiereel, and Azarias. [22] And of the sons of Phaisur; Elionas, Massias Israel, and Nathanael, and Ocidelus and Talsas. [23] And of the Levites; Jozabad, and Semis, and Colius, who was called Calitas, and Patheus, and Judas, and Jonas. [24] Of the holy singers; Eleazurus, Bacchurus. [25] Of the porters; Sallumus, and Tolbanes. [26] Of them of Israel, of the sons of Phoros; Hiermas, and Eddias, and Melchias, and Maelus, and Eleazar, and Asibias, and Baanias. [27] Of the sons of Ela; Matthanias, Zacharias, and Hierielus, and Hieremoth, and Aedias. [28] And of the sons of Zamoth; Eliadas, Elisimus, Othonias, Jarimoth, and Sabatus, and Sardeus. [29] Of the sons of Babai; Johannes, and Ananias and Josabad, and Amatheis. [30] Of the sons of Mani; Olamus, Mamuchus, Jedeus, Jasubus, Jasael, and Hieremoth. [31] And of the sons of Addi; Naathus, and Moosias, Lacunus, and Naidus, and Mathanias, and Sesthel, Balnuus, and Manasseas. [32] And of the sons of Annas; Elionas and Aseas, and Melchias, and Sabbeus, and Simon Chosameus. [33] And of the sons of Asom; Altaneus, and Matthias, and Baanaia, Eliphalet, and Manasses, and Semei. [34] And of the sons of Maani; Jeremias, Momdis, Omaerus, Juel, Mabdai, and Pelias, and Anos, Carabasion, and Enasibus, and Mamnitanaimus, Eliasis, Bannus, Eliali, Samis, Selemias, Nathanias: and of the sons of Ozora; Sesis, Esril, Azaelus, Samatus, Zambis, Josephus. [35] And of the sons of Ethma; Mazitias, Zabadaias, Edes, Juel, Banaias. [36] All these had taken strange wives, and they put them away with their children. [37] And the priests and Levites, and they that were of Israel, dwelt in Jerusalem, and in the country, in the first day of the seventh month: so the children of Israel were in their habitations. [38] And the whole multitude came together with one accord into the broad place of the holy porch toward the east: [39] And they spake unto Esdras the priest and reader, that he would bring the law of Moses, that was given of the Lord God of Israel. [40] So Esdras the chief priest brought the law unto the whole multitude from man to woman, and to all the priests, to hear law in the first day of the seventh month. [41] And he read in the broad court before the holy porch from morning unto midday, before both men and women; and the multitude gave heed unto the law. [42] And Esdras the priest and reader of the law stood up upon a pulpit of wood, which was made for that purpose. [43] And there stood up by him Mattathias, Sammus, Ananias, Azarias, Urias, Ezecias, Balasamus, upon the right hand: [44] And upon his left hand stood Phaldaius, Misael, Melchias, Lothasubus, and Nabarias. [45] Then took Esdras the book of the law before the multitude: for he sat honourably in the first place in the sight of them all. [46] And when he opened the law, they stood all straight up. So Esdras blessed the Lord God most High, the God of hosts, Almighty. [47] And all the people answered, Amen; and lifting up their hands they fell to the ground, and worshipped the Lord. [48] Also Jesus, Anus, Sarabias, Adinus, Jacubus, Sabateas, Auteas, Maianeas, and Calitas, Asrias, and Joazabdus, and Ananias, Biatas, the Levites, taught the law of the Lord, making them withal to understand it. [49] Then spake Attharates unto Esdras the chief priest. and reader, and to the Levites that taught the multitude, even to all, saying, [50] This day is holy unto the Lord; (for they all wept when they heard the law:) [51] Go then, and eat the fat, and drink the sweet, and send part to them that have nothing; [52] For this day is holy unto the Lord: and be not sorrowful; for the Lord will bring you to honour. [53] So the Levites published all things to the people, saying, This day is holy to the Lord; be not sorrowful. [54] Then went they their way, every one to eat and drink, and make merry, and to give part to them that had nothing, and to make great cheer; [55] Because they understood the words wherein they were instructed, and for the which they had been assembled. 2Ezra.1 [1] The second book of the prophet Esdras, the son of Saraias, the son of Azarias, the son of Helchias, the son of Sadamias, the sou of Sadoc, the son of Achitob, [2] The son of Achias, the son of Phinees, the son of Heli, the son of Amarias, the son of Aziei, the son of Marimoth, the son of And he spake unto the of Borith, the son of Abisei, the son of Phinees, the son of Eleazar, [3] The son of Aaron, of the tribe of Levi; which was captive in the land of the Medes, in the reign of Artexerxes king of the Persians. [4] And the word of the Lord came unto me, saying, [5] Go thy way, and shew my people their sinful deeds, and their children their wickedness which they have done against me; that they may tell their children's children: [6] Because the sins of their fathers are increased in them: for they have forgotten me, and have offered unto strange gods. [7] Am not I even he that brought them out of the land of Egypt, from the house of bondage? but they have provoked me unto wrath, and despised my counsels. [8] Pull thou off then the hair of thy head, and cast all evil upon them, for they have not been obedient unto my law, but it is a rebellious people. [9] How long shall I forbear them, into whom I have done so much good? [10] Many kings have I destroyed for their sakes; Pharaoh with his servants and all his power have I smitten down. [11] All the nations have I destroyed before them, and in the east I have scattered the people of two provinces, even of Tyrus and Sidon, and have slain all their enemies. [12] Speak thou therefore unto them, saying, Thus saith the Lord, [13] I led you through the sea and in the beginning gave you a large and safe passage; I gave you Moses for a leader, and Aaron for a priest. [14] I gave you light in a pillar of fire, and great wonders have I done among you; yet have ye forgotten me, saith the Lord. [15] Thus saith the Almighty Lord, The quails were as a token to you; I gave you tents for your safeguard: nevertheless ye murmured there, [16] And triumphed not in my name for the destruction of your enemies, but ever to this day do ye yet murmur. [17] Where are the benefits that I have done for you? When ye were hungry and thirsty in the wilderness, did ye not cry unto me, [18] Saying, Why hast thou brought us into this wilderness to kill us? it had been better for us to have served the Egyptians, than to die in this wilderness. [19] Then had I pity upon your mournings, and gave you manna to eat; so ye did eat angels' bread. [20] When ye were thirsty, did I not cleave the rock, and waters flowed out to your fill? for the heat I covered you with the leaves of the trees. [21] I divided among you a fruitful land, I cast out the Canaanites, the Pherezites, and the Philistines, before you: what shall I yet do more for you? saith the Lord. [22] Thus saith the Almighty Lord, When ye were in the wilderness, in the river of the Amorites, being athirst, and blaspheming my name, [23] I gave you not fire for your blasphemies, but cast a tree in the water, and made the river sweet. [24] What shall I do unto thee, O Jacob? thou, Juda, wouldest not obey me: I will turn me to other nations, and unto those will I give my name, that they may keep my statutes. [25] Seeing ye have forsaken me, I will forsake you also; when ye desire me to be gracious unto you, I shall have no mercy upon you. [26] Whensoever ye shall call upon me, I will not hear you: for ye have defiled your hands with blood, and your feet are swift to commit manslaughter. [27] Ye have not as it were forsaken me, but your own selves, saith the Lord. [28] Thus saith the Almighty Lord, Have I not prayed you as a father his sons, as a mother her daughters, and a nurse her young babes, [29] That ye would be my people, and I should be your God; that ye would be my children, and I should be your father? [30] I gathered you together, as a hen gathereth her chickens under her wings: but now, what shall I do unto you? I will cast you out from my face. [31] When ye offer unto me, I will turn my face from you: for your solemn feastdays, your new moons, and your circumcisions, have I forsaken. [32] I sent unto you my servants the prophets, whom ye have taken and slain, and torn their bodies in pieces, whose blood I will require of your hands, saith the Lord. [33] Thus saith the Almighty Lord, Your house is desolate, I will cast you out as the wind doth stubble. [34] And your children shall not be fruitful; for they have despised my commandment, and done the thing that is an evil before me. [35] Your houses will I give to a people that shall come; which not having heard of me yet shall believe me; to whom I have shewed no signs, yet they shall do that I have commanded them. [36] They have seen no prophets, yet they shall call their sins to remembrance, and acknowledge them. [37] I take to witness the grace of the people to come, whose little ones rejoice in gladness: and though they have not seen me with bodily eyes, yet in spirit they believe the thing that I say. [38] And now, brother, behold what glory; and see the people that come from the east: [39] Unto whom I will give for leaders, Abraham, Isaac, and Jacob, Oseas, Amos, and Micheas, Joel, Abdias, and Jonas, [40] Nahum, and Abacuc, Sophonias, Aggeus, Zachary, and Malachy, which is called also an angel of the Lord. 2Ezra.2 [1] Thus saith the Lord, I brought this people out of bondage, and I gave them my commandments by menservants the prophets; whom they would not hear, but despised my counsels. [2] The mother that bare them saith unto them, Go your way, ye children; for I am a widow and forsaken. [3] I brought you up with gladness; but with sorrow and heaviness have I lost you: for ye have sinned before the Lord your God, and done that thing that is evil before him. [4] But what shall I now do unto you? I am a widow and forsaken: go your way, O my children, and ask mercy of the Lord. [5] As for me, O father, I call upon thee for a witness over the mother of these children, which would not keep my covenant, [6] That thou bring them to confusion, and their mother to a spoil, that there may be no offspring of them. [7] Let them be scattered abroad among the heathen, let their names be put out of the earth: for they have despised my covenant. [8] Woe be unto thee, Assur, thou that hidest the unrighteous in thee! O thou wicked people, remember what I did unto Sodom and Gomorrha; [9] Whose land lieth in clods of pitch and heaps of ashes: even so also will I do unto them that hear me not, saith the Almighty Lord. [10] Thus saith the Lord unto Esdras, Tell my people that I will give them the kingdom of Jerusalem, which I would have given unto Israel. [11] Their glory also will I take unto me, and give these the everlasting tabernacles, which I had prepared for them. [12] They shall have the tree of life for an ointment of sweet savour; they shall neither labour, nor be weary. [13] Go, and ye shall receive: pray for few days unto you, that they may be shortened: the kingdom is already prepared for you: watch. [14] Take heaven and earth to witness; for I have broken the evil in pieces, and created the good: for I live, saith the Lord. [15] Mother, embrace thy children, and bring them up with gladness, make their feet as fast as a pillar: for I have chosen thee, saith the Lord. [16] And those that be dead will I raise up again from their places, and bring them out of the graves: for I have known my name in Israel. [17] Fear not, thou mother of the children: for I have chosen thee, saith the Lord. [18] For thy help will I send my servants Esau and Jeremy, after whose counsel I have sanctified and prepared for thee twelve trees laden with divers fruits, [19] And as many fountains flowing with milk and honey, and seven mighty mountains, whereupon there grow roses and lilies, whereby I will fill thy children with joy. [20] Do right to the widow, judge for the fatherless, give to the poor, defend the orphan, clothe the naked, [21] Heal the broken and the weak, laugh not a lame man to scorn, defend the maimed, and let the blind man come into the sight of my clearness. [22] Keep the old and young within thy walls. [23] Wheresoever thou findest the dead, take them and bury them, and I will give thee the first place in my resurrection. [24] Abide still, O my people, and take thy rest, for thy quietness still come. [25] Nourish thy children, O thou good nurse; stablish their feet. [26] As for the servants whom I have given thee, there shall not one of them perish; for I will require them from among thy number. [27] Be not weary: for when the day of trouble and heaviness cometh, others shall weep and be sorrowful, but thou shalt be merry and have abundance. [28] The heathen shall envy thee, but they shall be able to do nothing against thee, saith the Lord. [29] My hands shall cover thee, so that thy children shall not see hell. [30] Be joyful, O thou mother, with thy children; for I will deliver thee, saith the Lord. [31] Remember thy children that sleep, for I shall bring them out of the sides of the earth, and shew mercy unto them: for I am merciful, saith the Lord Almighty. [32] Embrace thy children until I come and shew mercy unto them: for my wells run over, and my grace shall not fail. [33] I Esdras received a charge of the Lord upon the mount Oreb, that I should go unto Israel; but when I came unto them, they set me at nought, and despised the commandment of the Lord. [34] And therefore I say unto you, O ye heathen, that hear and understand, look for your Shepherd, he shall give you everlasting rest; for he is nigh at hand, that shall come in the end of the world. [35] Be ready to the reward of the kingdom, for the everlasting light shall shine upon you for evermore. [36] Flee the shadow of this world, receive the joyfulness of your glory: I testify my Saviour openly. [37] O receive the gift that is given you, and be glad, giving thanks unto him that hath led you to the heavenly kingdom. [38] Arise up and stand, behold the number of those that be sealed in the feast of the Lord; [39] Which are departed from the shadow of the world, and have received glorious garments of the Lord. [40] Take thy number, O Sion, and shut up those of thine that are clothed in white, which have fulfilled the law of the Lord. [41] The number of thy children, whom thou longedst for, is fulfilled: beseech the power of the Lord, that thy people, which have been called from the beginning, may be hallowed. [42] I Esdras saw upon the mount Sion a great people, whom I could not number, and they all praised the Lord with songs. [43] And in the midst of them there was a young man of a high stature, taller than all the rest, and upon every one of their heads he set crowns, and was more exalted; which I marvelled at greatly. [44] So I asked the angel, and said, Sir, what are these? [45] He answered and said unto me, These be they that have put off the mortal clothing, and put on the immortal, and have confessed the name of God: now are they crowned, and receive palms. [46] Then said I unto the angel, What young person is it that crowneth them, and giveth them palms in their hands? [47] So he answered and said unto me, It is the Son of God, whom they have confessed in the world. Then began I greatly to commend them that stood so stiffly for the name of the Lord. [48] Then the angel said unto me, Go thy way, and tell my people what manner of things, and how great wonders of the Lord thy God, thou hast seen. 2Ezra.3 [1] In the thirtieth year after the ruin of the city I was in Babylon, and lay troubled upon my bed, and my thoughts came up over my heart: [2] For I saw the desolation of Sion, and the wealth of them that dwelt at Babylon. [3] And my spirit was sore moved, so that I began to speak words full of fear to the most High, and said, [4] O Lord, who bearest rule, thou spakest at the beginning, when thou didst plant the earth, and that thyself alone, and commandedst the people, [5] And gavest a body unto Adam without soul, which was the workmanship of thine hands, and didst breathe into him the breath of life, and he was made living before thee. [6] And thou leadest him into paradise, which thy right hand had planted, before ever the earth came forward. [7] And unto him thou gavest commandment to love thy way: which he transgressed, and immediately thou appointedst death in him and in his generations, of whom came nations, tribes, people, and kindreds, out of number. [8] And every people walked after their own will, and did wonderful things before thee, and despised thy commandments. [9] And again in process of time thou broughtest the flood upon those that dwelt in the world, and destroyedst them. [10] And it came to pass in every of them, that as death was to Adam, so was the flood to these. [11] Nevertheless one of them thou leftest, namely, Noah with his household, of whom came all righteous men. [12] And it happened, that when they that dwelt upon the earth began to multiply, and had gotten them many children, and were a great people, they began again to be more ungodly than the first. [13] Now when they lived so wickedly before thee, thou didst choose thee a man from among them, whose name was Abraham. [14] Him thou lovedst, and unto him only thou shewedst thy will: [15] And madest an everlasting covenant with him, promising him that thou wouldest never forsake his seed. [16] And unto him thou gavest Isaac, and unto Isaac also thou gavest Jacob and Esau. As for Jacob, thou didst choose him to thee, and put by Esau: and so Jacob became a great multitude . [17] And it came to pass, that when thou leadest his seed out of Egypt, thou broughtest them up to the mount Sinai. [18] And bowing the heavens, thou didst set fast the earth, movedst the whole world, and madest the depths to tremble, and troubledst the men of that age. [19] And thy glory went through four gates, of fire, and of earthquake, and of wind, and of cold; that thou mightest give the law unto the seed of Jacob, and diligence unto the generation of Israel. [20] And yet tookest thou not away from them a wicked heart, that thy law might bring forth fruit in them. [21] For the first Adam bearing a wicked heart transgressed, and was overcome; and so be all they that are born of him. [22] Thus infirmity was made permanent; and the law (also) in the heart of the people with the malignity of the root; so that the good departed away, and the evil abode still. [23] So the times passed away, and the years were brought to an end: then didst thou raise thee up a servant, called David: [24] Whom thou commandedst to build a city unto thy name, and to offer incense and oblations unto thee therein. [25] When this was done many years, then they that inhabited the city forsook thee, [26] And in all things did even as Adam and all his generations had done: for they also had a wicked heart: [27] And so thou gavest thy city over into the hands of thine enemies. [28] Are their deeds then any better that inhabit Babylon, that they should therefore have the dominion over Sion? [29] For when I came thither, and had seen impieties without number, then my soul saw many evildoers in this thirtieth year, so that my heart failed me. [30] For I have seen how thou sufferest them sinning, and hast spared wicked doers: and hast destroyed thy people, and hast preserved thine enemies, and hast not signified it. [31] I do not remember how this way may be left: Are they then of Babylon better than they of Sion? [32] Or is there any other people that knoweth thee beside Israel? or what generation hath so believed thy covenants as Jacob? [33] And yet their reward appeareth not, and their labour hath no fruit: for I have gone here and there through the heathen, and I see that they flow in wealth, and think not upon thy commandments. [34] Weigh thou therefore our wickedness now in the balance, and their's also that dwell the world; and so shall thy name no where be found but in Israel. [35] Or when was it that they which dwell upon the earth have not sinned in thy sight? or what people have so kept thy commandments? [36] Thou shalt find that Israel by name hath kept thy precepts; but not the heathen. 2Ezra.4 [1] And the angel that was sent unto me, whose name was Uriel, gave me an answer, [2] And said, Thy heart hath gone to far in this world, and thinkest thou to comprehend the way of the most High? [3] Then said I, Yea, my lord. And he answered me, and said, I am sent to shew thee three ways, and to set forth three similitudes before thee: [4] Whereof if thou canst declare me one,

I will shew thee also the way that thou desirest to see, and I shall shew thee from whence the wicked heart cometh. [5] And I said, Tell on, my lord. Then said he unto me, Go thy way, weigh me the weight of the fire, or measure me the blast of the wind, or call me again the day that is past. [6] Then answered I and said, What man is able to do that, that thou shouldest ask such things of me? [7] And he said unto me, If I should ask thee how great dwellings are in the midst of the sea, or how many springs are in the beginning of the deep, or how many springs are above the firmament, or which are the outgoings of paradise: [8] Peradventure thou wouldest say unto me, I never went down into the deep, nor as yet into hell, neither did I ever climb up into heaven. [9] Nevertheless now have I asked thee but only of the fire and wind, and of the day wherethrough thou hast passed, and of things from which thou canst not be separated, and yet canst thou give me no answer of them. [10] He said moreover unto me, Thine own things, and such as are grown up with thee, canst thou not know; [11] How should thy vessel then be able to comprehend the way of the Highest, and, the world being now outwardly corrupted to understand the corruption that is evident in my sight? [12] Then said I unto him, It were better that we were not at all, than that we should live still in wickedness, and to suffer, and not to know wherefore. [13] He answered me, and said, I went into a forest into a plain, and the trees took counsel, [14] And said, Come, let us go and make war against the sea that it may depart away before us, and that we may make us more woods. [15] The floods of the sea also in like manner took counsel, and said, Come, let us go up and subdue the woods of the plain, that there also we may make us another country. [16] The thought of the wood was in vain, for the fire came and consumed it. [17] The thought of the floods of the sea came likewise to nought, for the sand stood up and stopped them. [18] If thou wert judge now betwixt these two, whom wouldest thou begin to justify? or whom wouldest thou condemn? [19] I answered and said, Verily it is a foolish thought that they both have devised, for the ground is given unto the wood, and the sea also hath his place to bear his floods. [20] Then answered he me, and said, Thou hast given a right judgment, but why judgest thou not thyself also? [21] For like as the ground is given unto the wood, and the sea to his floods: even so they that dwell upon the earth may understand nothing but that which is upon the earth: and he that dwelleth above the heavens may only understand the things that are above the height of the heavens. [22] Then answered I and said, I beseech thee, O Lord, let me have understanding: [23] For it was not my mind to be curious of the high things, but of such as pass by us daily, namely, wherefore Israel is given up as a reproach to the heathen, and for what cause the people whom thou hast loved is given over unto ungodly nations, and why the law of our forefathers is brought to nought, and the written covenants come to none effect, [24] And we pass away out of the world as grasshoppers, and our life is astonishment and fear, and we are not worthy to obtain mercy. [25] What will he then do unto his name whereby we are called? of these things have I asked. [26] Then answered he me, and said, The more thou searchest, the more thou shalt marvel; for the world hasteth fast to pass away, [27] And cannot comprehend the things that are promised to the righteous in time to come: for this world is full of unrighteousness and infirmities. [28] But as concerning the things whereof thou askest me, I will tell thee; for the evil is sown, but the destruction thereof is not yet come. [29] If therefore that which is sown be not turned upside down, and if the place where the evil is sown pass not away, then cannot it come that is sown with good. [30] For the grain of evil seed hath been sown in the heart of Adam from the beginning, and how much ungodliness hath it brought up unto this time? and how much shall it yet bring forth until the time of threshing come? [31] Ponder now by thyself, how great fruit of wickedness the grain of evil seed hath brought forth. [32] And when the ears shall be cut down, which are without number, how great a floor shall they fill? [33] Then I answered and said, How, and when shall these things come to pass? wherefore are our years few and evil? [34] And he answered me, saying, Do not thou hasten above the most Highest: for thy haste is in vain to be above him, for thou hast much exceeded. [35] Did not the souls also of the righteous ask question of these things in their chambers, saying, How long shall I hope on this fashion? when cometh the fruit of the floor of our reward? [36] And unto these things Uriel the archangel gave them answer, and said, Even when the number of seeds is filled in you: for he hath weighed the world in the balance. [37] By measure hath he measured the times; and by number hath he numbered the times; and he doth not move nor stir them, until the said measure be fulfilled. [38] Then answered I and said, O Lord that bearest rule, even we all are full of impiety. [39] And for our sakes peradventure it is that the floors of the righteous are not filled, because of the sins of them that dwell upon the earth. [40] So he answered me, and said, Go thy way to a woman with child, and ask of her when she hath fulfilled her nine months, if her womb may keep the birth any longer within her. [41] Then said I, No, Lord, that can she not. And he said unto me, In the grave the chambers of souls are like the womb of a woman: [42] For like as a woman that travaileth maketh haste to escape the necessity of the travail: even so do these places haste to deliver those things that are committed unto them. [43] From the beginning, look, what thou desirest to see, it shall be shewed thee. [44] Then answered I and said, If I have found favour in thy sight, and if it be possible, and if I be meet therefore, [45] Shew me then whether there be more to come than is past, or more past than is to come. [46] What is past I know, but what is for to come I know not. [47] And he said unto me, Stand up upon the right side, and I shall expound the similitude unto thee. [48] So I stood, and saw, and, behold, an hot burning oven passed by before me: and it happened that when the flame was gone by I looked, and, behold, the smoke remained still. [49] After this there passed by before me a watery cloud, and sent down much rain with a storm; and when the stormy rain was past, the drops remained still. [50] Then said he unto me, Consider with thyself; as the rain is more than the drops, and as the fire is greater than the smoke; but the drops and the smoke remain behind: so the quantity which is past did more exceed. [51] Then I prayed, and said, May I live, thinkest thou, until that time? or what shall happen in those days? [52] He answered me, and said, As for the tokens whereof thou askest me, I may tell thee of them in part: but as touching thy life, I am not sent to shew thee; for I do not know it. 2Ezra.5 [1] Nevertheless as coming the tokens, behold, the days shall come, that they which dwell upon earth shall be taken in a great number, and the way of truth shall be hidden, and the land shall be barren of faith. [2] But iniquity shall be increased above that which now thou seest, or that thou hast heard long ago. [3] And the land, that thou seest now to have root, shalt thou see wasted suddenly. [4] But if the most High grant thee to live, thou shalt see after the third trumpet that the sun shall suddenly shine again in the night, and the moon thrice in the day: [5] And blood shall drop out of wood, and the stone shall give his voice, and the people shall be troubled: [6] And even he shall rule, whom they look not for that dwell upon the earth, and the fowls shall take their flight away together: [7] And the Sodomitish sea shall cast out fish, and make a noise in the night, which many have not known: but they shall all hear the voice thereof. [8] There shall be a confusion also in many places, and the fire shall be oft sent out again, and the wild beasts shall change their places, and menstruous women shall bring forth monsters: [9] And salt waters shall be found in the sweet, and all friends shall destroy one another; then shall wit hide itself, and understanding withdraw itself into his secret chamber, [10] And shall be sought of many, and yet not be found: then shall unrighteousness and incontinency be multiplied upon earth. [11] One land also shall ask another, and say, Is righteousness that maketh a man righteous gone through thee? And it shall say, No. [12] At the same time shall men hope, but nothing obtain: they shall labour, but their ways shall not prosper. [13] To shew thee such tokens I have leave; and if thou wilt pray again, and weep as now, and fast even days, thou shalt hear yet greater things. [14] Then I awaked, and an extreme fearfulness went through all my body, and my mind was troubled, so that it fainted. [15] So the angel that was come to talk with me held me, comforted me, and set me up upon my feet. [16] And in the second night it came to pass, that Salathiel the captain of the people came unto me, saying, Where hast thou been? and why is thy countenance so heavy? [17] Knowest thou not that Israel is committed unto thee in the land of their captivity? [18] Up then, and eat bread, and forsake us not, as the shepherd that leaveth his flock in the hands of cruel wolves. [19] Then said I unto him, Go thy ways from me, and come not nigh me. And he heard what I said, and went from me. [20] And so I fasted seven days, mourning and weeping, like as Uriel the angel commanded me. [21] And after seven days so it was, that the thoughts of my heart were very grievous unto me again, [22] And my soul recovered the spirit of understanding, and I began to talk with the most High again, [23] And said, O Lord that bearest rule, of every wood of the earth, and of all the trees thereof, thou hast chosen thee one only vine: [24] And of all lands of the whole world thou hast chosen thee one pit: and of all the flowers thereof one lily: [25] And of all the depths of the sea thou hast filled thee one river: and of all builded cities thou hast hallowed Sion unto thyself: [26] And of all the fowls that are created thou hast named thee one dove: and of all the cattle that are made thou hast provided thee one sheep: [27] And among all the multitudes of people thou hast gotten thee one people: and unto this people, whom thou lovedst, thou gavest a law that is approved of all. [28] And now, O Lord, why hast thou given this one people over unto many? and upon the one root hast thou prepared others, and why hast thou scattered thy only one people among many? [29] And they which did gainsay thy promises, and believed not thy covenants, have trodden them down. [30] If thou didst so much hate thy people, yet shouldest thou punish them with thine own hands. [31] Now when I had spoken these words, the angel that came to me the night afore was sent unto me, [32] And said unto me, Hear me, and I will instruct thee; hearken to the thing that I say, and I shall tell thee more. [33] And I said, Speak on, my Lord. Then said he unto me, Thou art sore troubled in mind for Israel's sake: lovest thou that people better than he that made them? [34] And I said, No, Lord: but of very grief have I spoken: for my reins pain me every hour, while I labour to comprehend the way of the most High, and to seek out part of his judgment. [35] And he said unto me, Thou canst not. And I said, Wherefore, Lord? whereunto was I born then? or why was not my mother's womb then my grave, that I might not have seen the travail of Jacob, and the wearisome toil of the stock of Israel? [36] And he said unto me, Number me the things that are not yet come, gather me together the dross that are scattered abroad, make me the flowers green again that are withered, [37] Open me the places that are closed, and bring me forth the winds that in them are shut up, shew me the image of a voice: and then I will declare to thee the thing that thou labourest to know. [38] And I said, O Lord that bearest rule, who may know these things, but he that hath not his dwelling with men? [39] As for me, I am unwise: how may I then speak of these things whereof thou askest me? [40] Then said he unto me, Like as thou canst do none of these things that I have spoken of, even so canst thou not find out my judgment, or in the end the love that I have promised unto my people. [41] And I said, Behold, O Lord, yet art thou nigh unto them that be reserved till the end: and what shall they do that have been before me, or we that be now, or they that shall come after us? [42] And he said unto me, I will liken my judgment unto a ring: like as there is no slackness of the last, even so there is no swiftness of the first. [43] So I answered and said, Couldest thou not make those that have been made, and be now, and that are for to come, at once; that thou mightest shew thy judgment the sooner? [44] Then answered he me, and said, The creature may not haste above the maker; neither may the world hold them at once that shall be created therein. [45] And I said, As thou hast said unto thy servant, that thou, which givest life to all, hast given life at once to the creature that thou hast created, and the creature bare it: even so it might now also bear them that now be present at once. [46] And he said unto me, Ask the womb of a woman, and say unto her, If thou bringest forth children, why dost thou it not together, but one after another? pray her therefore to bring forth ten children at once. [47] And I said, She cannot: but must do it by distance of time. [48] Then said he unto me, Even so have I given the womb of the earth to those that be sown in it in their times. [49] For like as a young child may not bring forth the things that belong to the aged, even so have I disposed the world which I created. [50] And I asked, and said, Seeing thou hast now given me the way, I will proceed to speak before thee: for our mother, of whom thou hast told me that she is young, draweth now nigh unto age. [51] He answered me, and said, Ask a woman that beareth children, and she shall tell thee. [52] Say unto her, Wherefore are unto they whom thou hast now brought forth like those that were before, but less of stature? [53] And she shall answer thee, They that be born in the strength of youth are of one fashion, and they that are born in the time of age, when the womb faileth, are otherwise. [54] Consider thou therefore also, how that ye are less of stature than those that were before you. [55] And so are they that come after you less than ye, as the creatures which now begin to be old, and have passed over the strength of youth. [56] Then said I, Lord, I beseech thee, if I have found favour in thy sight, shew thy servant by whom thou visitest thy creature. 2Ezra.6 [1] And he said unto me, In the beginning, when the earth was made, before the borders of the world stood, or ever the winds blew, [2] Before it thundered and lightened, or ever the foundations of paradise were laid, [3] Before the fair flowers were seen, or ever the moveable powers were established, before the innumerable multitude of angels were gathered together, [4] Or ever the heights of the air were lifted up, before the measures of the firmament were named, or ever the chimneys in Sion were hot, [5] And ere the present years were sought out, and or ever the inventions of them that now sin were turned, before they were sealed that have gathered faith for a treasure: [6] Then did I consider these things, and they all were made through me alone, and through none other: by me also they shall be ended, and by none other. [7] Then answered I and said, What shall be the parting asunder of the times? or when shall be the end of the first, and the beginning of it that followeth? [8] And he said unto me, From Abraham unto Isaac, when Jacob and Esau were born of him, Jacob's hand held first the heel of Esau. [9] For Esau is the end of the world, and Jacob is the beginning of it that followeth. [10] The hand of man is betwixt the heel and the hand: other question, Esdras, ask thou not. [11] I answered then and said, O Lord that bearest rule, if I have found favour in thy sight, [12] I beseech thee, shew thy servant the end of thy tokens, whereof thou shewedst me part the last night. [13] So he answered and said unto me, Stand up upon thy feet, and hear a mighty sounding voice. [14] And it shall be as it were a great motion; but the place where thou standest shall not be moved. [15] And therefore when it speaketh be not afraid: for the word is of the end, and the foundation of the earth is understood. [16] And why? because the speech of these things trembleth and is moved: for it knoweth that the end of these things must be changed. [17] And it happened, that when I had heard it I stood up upon my feet, and hearkened, and, behold, there was a voice that spake, and the sound of it was like the sound of many waters. [18] And it said, Behold, the days come, that I will begin to draw nigh, and to visit them that dwell upon the earth, [19] And will begin to make inquisition of them, what they be that have hurt unjustly with their unrighteousness, and when the affliction of Sion shall be fulfilled; [20] And when the world, that shall begin to vanish away, shall be finished, then will I shew these tokens: the books shall be opened before the firmament, and they shall see all together: [21] And the children of a year old shall speak with their voices, the women with child shall bring forth untimely children of three or four months old, and they shall live, and be raised up. [22] And suddenly shall the sown places appear unsown, the full storehouses shall suddenly be found empty: [23] And tha trumpet shall give a sound, which when every man heareth, they shall be suddenly afraid. [24] At that time shall friends fight one against another like enemies, and the earth shall stand in fear with those that dwell therein, the springs of the fountains shall stand still, and in three hours they shall not run. [25] Whosoever remaineth from all these that I have told thee shall escape, and see my salvation, and the end of your world. [26] And the men that are received shall see it, who have not tasted death from their birth: and the heart of the inhabitants shall be changed, and turned into another meaning. [27] For evil shall be put out, and deceit shall be quenched. [28] As for faith, it shall flourish, corruption shall be overcome, and the truth, which hath been so long without fruit, shall be declared. [29] And when he talked with me, behold, I looked by little and little upon him before whom I stood. [30] And these words said he unto me; I am come to shew thee the time of the night to come. [31] If thou wilt pray yet more, and fast seven days again, I shall tell thee greater things by day than I have heard. [32] For thy voice is heard before the most High: for the Mighty hath seen thy righteous dealing, he hath seen also thy chastity, which thou hast had ever since thy youth. [33] And therefore hath he sent me to shew thee all these things, and to say unto thee, Be of good comfort and fear not [34] And hasten not with the times that are past, to think vain things, that thou mayest not hasten from the latter times. [35] And it came to pass after this, that I wept again, and fasted seven days in like manner, that I might fulfil the three weeks which he told me. [36] And in the eighth night was my heart vexed within me again, and I began to speak before the most High. [37] For my spirit was greatly set on fire, and my soul was in distress. [38] And I said, O Lord, thou spakest from the beginning of the creation, even the first day, and saidst thus; Let heaven and earth be made; and thy word was a perfect work. [39] And then was the spirit, and darkness and silence were on every side; the sound of man's voice was not yet formed. [40] Then commandedst thou a fair light to come forth of thy treasures, that thy work might appear. [41] Upon the second day thou madest the spirit of the firmament, and commandedst it to part asunder, and to make a division betwixt the waters, that the one part might go up, and the other remain beneath. [42] Upon the third day thou didst command that the waters should be gathered in the seventh part of the earth: six pats hast thou dried up, and kept them, to the intent that of these some being planted of God and tilled might serve thee. [43] For as soon as thy word went forth the work was made. [44] For immediately there was great and innumerable fruit, and many and divers pleasures for the taste, and flowers of unchangeable colour, and odours of wonderful smell: and this was done the third day. [45] Upon the fourth day thou commandedst that the sun should shine, and the moon give her light, and the stars should be in order: [46] And gavest them a charge to do service unto man, that was to be made. [47] Upon the fifth day thou saidst unto the seventh part, where the waters were gathered that it should bring forth living creatures, fowls and fishes: and so it came to pass. [48] For the dumb water and without life brought forth living things at the commandment of God, that all people might praise thy wondrous works. [49] Then didst thou ordain two living creatures, the one thou calledst Enoch, and the other Leviathan; [50] And didst separate the one from the other: for the seventh part, namely, where the water was gathered together, might not hold them both. [51] Unto Enoch thou gavest one part, which was dried up the third day, that he should dwell in the same part, wherein are a thousand hills: [52] But unto Leviathan thou gavest the seventh part, namely, the moist; and hast kept him to be devoured of whom thou wilt, and when. [53] Upon the sixth day thou gavest commandment unto the earth, that before thee it should bring forth beasts, cattle, and creeping things: [54] And after these, Adam also, whom thou madest lord of all thy creatures: of him come we all, and the people also whom thou hast chosen. [55] All this have I spoken before thee, O Lord, because thou madest the world for our sakes [56] As for the other people, which also come of Adam, thou hast said that they are nothing, but be like unto spittle: and hast likened the abundance of them unto a drop that falleth from a vessel. [57] And now, O Lord, behold, these heathen, which have ever been reputed as nothing, have begun to be lords over us, and to devour us. [58] But we thy people, whom thou hast called thy firstborn, thy only begotten, and thy fervent lover, are given into their hands. [59] If the world now be made for our sakes, why do we not possess an inheritance with the world? how long shall this endure? 4Ezra.7 [1] And when I had made an end of speaking these words, there was sent unto me the angel which had been sent unto me the nights afore: [2] And he said unto me, Up, Esdras, and hear the words that I am come to tell thee. [3] And I said, Speak on, my God. Then said he unto me, The sea is set in a wide place, that it might be deep and great. [4] But put the case the entrance were narrow, and like a river; [5] Who then could go into the sea to look upon it, and to rule it? if he went not through the narrow, how could he come into the broad? [6] There is also another thing; A city is builded, and set upon a broad field, and is full of all good things: [7] The entrance thereof is narrow, and is set in a dangerous place to fall, like as if there were a fire on the right hand, and on the left a deep water: [8] And one only path between them both, even between the fire and the water, so small that there could but one man go there at once. [9] If this city now were given unto a man for an inheritance, if he never shall pass the danger set before it, how shall he receive this inheritance? [10] And I said, It is so, Lord. Then said he unto me, Even so also is Israel's portion. [11] Because for their sakes I made the world: and when Adam transgressed my statutes, then was decreed that now is done. [12] Then were the entrances of this world made narrow, full of sorrow and travail: they are but few and evil, full of perils,: and very painful. [13] For the entrances of the elder world were wide and sure, and brought immortal fruit. [14] If then they that live labour not to enter these strait and vain things, they can never receive those that are laid up for them. [15] Now therefore why disquietest thou thyself, seeing thou art but a corruptible man? and why art thou moved, whereas thou art but mortal? [16] Why hast thou not considered in thy mind this thing that is to come, rather than that which is present? [17] Then answered I and said, O Lord that bearest rule, thou hast ordained in thy law, that the righteous should inherit these things, but that the ungodly should perish. [18] Nevertheless the righteous shall suffer strait things, and hope for wide: for they that have done wickedly have suffered the strait things, and yet shall not see the wide. [19] And he said unto me. There is no judge above God, and none that hath understanding above the Highest. [20] For there be many that perish in this life, because they despise the law of God that is set before them. [21] For God hath given strait commandment to such as came, what they should do to live, even as they came, and what they should observe to avoid punishment. [22] Nevertheless they were not obedient unto him; but spake against him, and imagined vain things; [23] And deceived themselves by their wicked deeds; and said of the most High, that he is not; and knew not his ways: [24] But his law have they despised, and denied his covenants; in his statutes have they not been faithful, and have not performed his works. [25] And therefore, Esdras, for the empty are empty things, and for the full are the full things. [26] Behold, the time shall come, that these tokens which I have told thee shall come to pass, and the bride shall appear, and she coming forth shall be seen, that now is withdrawn from the earth. [27] And whosoever is delivered from the foresaid evils shall see my wonders. [28] For my son Jesus shall be revealed with those that be with him, and they that remain shall rejoice within four hundred years. [29] After these years shall my son Christ die, and all men that have life. [30] And the world shall be turned into the old silence seven days, like as in the former judgments: so that no man shall remain. [31] And after seven days the world, that yet awaketh not, shall be raised up, and that shall die that is corrupt [32] And the earth shall restore those that are asleep in her, and so shall the dust those that dwell in silence, and the secret places shall deliver those souls that were committed unto them. [33] And the most High shall appear upon the seat of judgment, and misery shall pass away, and the long suffering shall have an end: [34] But judgment only shall remain, truth shall stand, and faith shall wax strong: [35] And the work shall follow, and the reward shall be shewed, and the good deeds shall be of force, and wicked deeds shall bear no rule. [36] Then said I, Abraham prayed first for the Sodomites, and Moses for the fathers that sinned in the wilderness: [37] And Jesus after him for Israel in the time of Achan: [38] And Samuel and David for the destruction: and Solomon for them that should come to the sanctuary: [39] And Helias for those that received rain; and for the dead, that he might live: [40] And Ezechias for the people in the time of Sennacherib: and many for many. [41] Even so now, seeing corruption is grown up, and wickedness increased, and the righteous have prayed for the ungodly: wherefore shall it not be so now also? [42] He answered me, and said, This present life is not the end where much glory doth abide; therefore have they prayed for the weak. [43] But the day of doom shall be the end of this time, and the beginning of the immortality for to come, wherein corruption is past, [44] Intemperance is at an end, infidelity is cut off, righteousness is grown, and truth is sprung up. [45] Then shall no man be able to save him that is destroyed, nor to oppress him that hath gotten the victory. [46] I answered then and said, This is my first and last saying, that it had been better not to have given the earth unto Adam: or else, when it was given him, to have restrained him from sinning. [47] For what profit is it for men now in this present time to live in heaviness, and after death to look for punishment? [48] O thou Adam, what hast thou done? for though it was thou that sinned, thou art not fallen alone, but we all that come of thee. [49] For what profit is it unto us, if there be promised us an immortal time, whereas we have done the works that bring death? [50] And that there is promised us an everlasting hope, whereas ourselves being most wicked are made vain? [51] And that there are laid up for us dwellings of health and safety, whereas we have lived wickedly? [52] And that the glory of the most High is kept to defend them which have led a wary life, whereas we have walked in the most wicked ways of all? [53] And that there should be shewed a paradise, whose fruit endureth for ever, wherein is security and medicine, since we shall not enter into it? [54] (For we have walked in unpleasant places.) [55] And that the faces of them which have used abstinence shall shine above the stars, whereas our faces shall be blacker than darkness? [56] For while we lived and committed iniquity, we considered not that we should begin to suffer for it after death. [57] Then answered he me, and said, This is the condition of the battle, which man that is born upon the earth shall fight; [58] That, if he be overcome, he shall suffer as thou hast said: but if he get the victory, he shall receive the thing that I say. [59] For this is the life whereof Moses spake unto the people while he lived, saying, Choose thee life, that thou mayest live. [60] Nevertheless they believed not him, nor yet the prophets after him, no nor me which have spoken unto them, [61] That there should not be such heaviness in their destruction, as shall be joy over them that are persuaded to salvation. [62] I answered then, and said, I know, Lord, that the most High is called merciful, in that he hath mercy upon them which are not yet come into the world, [63] And upon those also that turn to his law; [64] And that he is patient, and long suffereth those that have sinned, as his creatures; [65] And that he is bountiful, for he is ready to give where it needeth; [66] And that he is of great mercy, for he multiplieth more and more mercies to them that are present, and that are past, and also to them which are to come. [67] For if he shall not multiply his mercies, the world would not continue with them that inherit therein. [68] And he pardoneth; for if he did not so of his goodness, that they which have committed iniquities might be eased of them, the ten thousandth part of men should not remain living. [69] And being judge, if he should not forgive them that are cured with his word, and put out the multitude of contentions, [70] There should be very few left peradventure in an innumerable multitude. 2Ezra.8 [1] And he answered me, saying, The most High hath made this world for many, but the world to come for few. [2] I will tell thee a similitude, Esdras; As when thou askest the earth, it shall say unto thee, that it giveth much mould whereof earthen vessels are made, but little dust that gold cometh of: even so is the course of this present world. [3] There be many created, but few shall be saved. [4] So answered I and said, Swallow then down, O my soul, understanding, and devour wisdom. [5] For thou hast agreed to give ear, and art willing to prophesy: for thou hast no longer space than only to live. [6] O Lord, if thou suffer not thy servant, that we may pray before thee, and thou give us seed unto our heart, and culture to our understanding, that there may come fruit of it; how shall each man live that is corrupt, who beareth the place of a man? [7] For thou art alone, and we all one workmanship of thine hands, like as thou hast said. [8] For when the body is fashioned now in the mother's womb, and thou givest it members, thy creature is preserved in fire and water, and nine months doth thy workmanship endure thy creature which is created in her. [9] But that which keepeth and is kept shall both be preserved: and when the time cometh, the womb preserved delivereth up the things that grew in it. [10] For thou hast commanded out of the parts of the body, that is to say, out of the breasts, milk to be given, which is the fruit of the breasts, [11] That the thing which is fashioned may be nourished for a time, till thou disposest it to thy mercy. [12] Thou broughtest it up with thy righteousness, and nurturedst it in thy law, and reformedst it with thy judgment. [13] And thou shalt mortify it as thy creature, and quicken it as thy work. [14] If therefore thou shalt destroy him which with so great labour was fashioned, it is an easy thing to be ordained by thy commandment, that the thing which was made might be preserved. [15] Now therefore, Lord, I will speak; touching man in general, thou knowest best; but touching thy people, for whose sake I am sorry; [16] And for thine inheritance, for whose cause I mourn; and for Israel, for whom I am heavy; and for Jacob, for whose sake I am troubled; [17] Therefore will I begin to pray before thee for myself and for them: for I see the falls of us that dwell in the land. [18] But I have heard the swiftness of the judge which is to come. [19] Therefore hear my voice, and understand my words, and I shall speak before thee. This is the beginning of the words of Esdras, before he was taken up: and I said, [20] O Lord, thou that dwellest in everlastingness which beholdest from above things in the heaven and in the air; [21] Whose throne is inestimable; whose glory may not be comprehended; before whom the hosts of angels stand with trembling, [22] Whose service is conversant in wind and fire; whose word is true, and sayings constant; whose commandment is strong, and ordinance fearful; [23] Whose look drieth up the depths, and indignation maketh the mountains to melt away; which the truth witnesseth: [24] O hear the prayer of thy servant, and give ear to the petition of thy creature. [25] For while I live I will speak, and so long as I have understanding I will answer. [26] O look not upon the sins of thy people; but on them which serve thee in truth. [27] Regard not the wicked inventions of the heathen, but the desire of those that keep thy testimonies in afflictions. [28] Think not upon those that have walked feignedly before thee: but remember them, which according to thy will have known thy fear. [29] Let it not be thy will to destroy them which have lived like beasts; but to look upon them that have clearly taught thy law. [30] Take thou no indignation at them which are deemed worse than beasts; but love them that always put their trust in thy righteousness and glory. [31] For we and our fathers do languish of such diseases: but because of us sinners thou shalt be called merciful. [32] For if thou hast a desire to have mercy upon us, thou shalt be called merciful, to us namely, that have no works of righteousness. [33] For the just, which have many good works laid up with thee, shall out of their own deeds receive reward. [34] For what is man, that thou shouldest take displeasure at him? or what is a corruptible generation, that thou shouldest be so bitter toward it? [35] For in truth them is no man among them that be born, but he hath dealt wickedly; and among the faithful there is none which hath not done amiss. [36] For in this, O Lord, thy righteousness and thy goodness shall be declared, if thou be merciful unto them which have not the confidence of good works. [37] Then answered he me, and said, Some things hast thou spoken aright, and according unto thy words it shall be. [38] For indeed I will not think on the disposition of them which have sinned before death, before judgment, before destruction: [39] But I will rejoice over the disposition of the righteous, and I will remember also their pilgrimage, and the salvation, and the reward, that they shall have. [40] Like as I have spoken now, so shall it come to pass. [41] For as the husbandman soweth much seed upon the ground, and planteth many trees, and yet the thing that is sown good in his season cometh not up, neither doth all that is planted take root: even so is it of them that are sown in the world; they shall not all be saved. [42] I answered then and said, If I have found grace, let me speak. [43] Like as the husbandman's seed perisheth, if it come not up, and receive not thy rain in due season; or if there come too much rain, and corrupt it: [44] Even so perisheth man also, which is formed with thy hands, and is called thine own image, because thou art like unto him, for whose sake thou hast made all things, and likened him unto the husbandman's seed. [45] Be not wroth with us but spare thy people, and have mercy upon thine own inheritance: for thou art merciful unto thy creature. [46] Then answered he me, and said, Things present are for the present, and things to cometh for such as be to come. [47] For thou comest far short that thou shouldest be able to love my creature more than I: but I have ofttimes drawn nigh unto thee, and unto it, but never to the unrighteous. [48] In this also thou art marvellous before the most High: [49] In that thou hast humbled thyself, as it becometh thee, and hast not judged thyself worthy to be much glorified among the righteous. [50] For many great miseries shall be done to them that in the latter time shall dwell in the world, because they have walked in great pride. [51] But understand thou for thyself, and seek out the glory for such as be like thee. [52] For unto you is paradise opened, the tree of life is planted, the time to come is prepared, plenteousness is made ready, a city is builded, and rest is allowed, yea, perfect goodness and wisdom. [53] The root of evil is sealed up from you, weakness and the moth is hid from you, and corruption is fled into hell to be forgotten: [54] Sorrows are passed, and in the end is shewed the treasure of immortality. [55] And therefore ask thou no more questions concerning the multitude of them that perish. [56] For when they had taken liberty, they despised the most High, thought scorn of his law, and forsook his ways. [57] Moreover they have trodden down his righteous, [58] And said in their heart, that there is no God; yea, and that knowing they must die. [59] For as the things aforesaid shalt receive you, so thirst and pain are prepared for them: for it was not his will that men should come to nought: [60] But they which be created have defiled the name of him that made them, and were unthankful unto him which prepared life for them. [61] And therefore is my judgment now at hand. [62] These things have I not shewed unto all men, but unto thee, and a few like thee. Then answered I and said, [63] Behold, O Lord, now hast thou shewed me the multitude of the wonders, which thou wilt begin to do in the last times: but at what time, thou hast not shewed me. 2Ezra.9 [1] He answered me then, and said, Measure thou the time diligently in itself: and when thou seest part of the signs past, which I have told thee before, [2] Then shalt thou understand, that it is the very same time, wherein the Highest will begin to visit the world which he made. [3] Therefore when there shall be seen earthquakes and uproars of the people in the world: [4] Then shalt thou well understand, that the most High spake of those things from the days that were before thee, even from the beginning. [5] For like as all that is made in the world hath a beginning and an end, and the end is manifest: [6] Even so the times also of the Highest have plain beginnings in wonder and powerful works, and endings in effects and signs. [7] And every one that shall be saved, and shall be able to escape by his works, and by faith, whereby ye have believed, [8] Shall be preserved from the said perils, and shall see my salvation in my land, and within my borders: for I have sanctified them for me from the beginning. [9] Then shall they be in pitiful case, which now have abused my ways: and they that have cast them away despitefully shall dwell in torments. [10] For such as in their life have received benefits, and have not known me; [11] And they that have loathed my law, while they had yet liberty, and, when as yet place of repentance was open unto them, understood not, but despised it; [12] The same must know it after death by pain. [13] And therefore be thou not curious how the ungodly shall be punished, and when: but enquire how the righteous shall be saved, whose the world is, and for whom the world is created. [14] Then answered I and said, [15] I have said before, and now do speak, and will speak it also hereafter, that there be many more of them which perish, than of them which shall be saved: [16] Like as a wave is greater than a drop. [17] And he answered me, saying, Like as the field is, so is also the seed; as the flowers be, such are the colours also; such as the workman is, such also is the work; and as the husbandman ls himself, so is his husbandry also: for it was the time of the world. [18] And now when I prepared the world, which was not yet made, even for them to dwell in that now live, no man spake against me. [19] For then every one obeyed: but now the manners of them which are created in this world that is made are corrupted by a perpetual seed, and by a law which is unsearchable rid themselves. [20] So I considered the world, and, behold, there was peril because of the devices that were come into it. [21] And I saw, and spared it greatly, and have kept me a grape of the cluster, and a plant of a great people. [22] Let the multitude perish then, which was born in vain; and let my grape be kept, and my plant; for with great labour have I made it perfect. [23] Nevertheless, if thou wilt cease yet seven days more, (but thou shalt not fast in them, [24] But go into a field of flowers, where no house is builded, and eat only the flowers of the field; taste no flesh, drink no wine, but eat flowers only; [25] And pray unto the Highest continually, then will I come and talk with thee. [26] So I went my way into the field which is called Ardath, like as he commanded me; and there I sat among the flowers, and did eat of the herbs of the field, and the meat of the same satisfied me. [27] After seven days I sat upon the grass, and my heart was vexed within me, like as before: [28] And I opened my mouth, and began to talk before the most High, and said, [29] O Lord, thou that shewest thyself unto us, thou wast shewed unto our fathers in the wilderness, in a place where no man treadeth, in a barren place, when they came out of Egypt. [30] And thou spakest saying, Hear me, O Israel; and mark my words, thou seed of Jacob. [31] For, behold, I sow my law in you, and it shall bring fruit in you, and ye shall be honoured in it for ever. [32] But our fathers, which received the law, kept it not, and observed not thy ordinances: and though the fruit of thy law did not perish, neither could it, for it was thine; [33] Yet they that received it perished, because they kept not the thing that was sown in them. [34] And, lo, it ls a custom, when the ground hath received seed, or the sea a ship, or any vessel meat or drink, that, that being perished wherein it was sown or cast into, [35] That thing also which was sown, or cast therein, or received, doth perish, and remaineth not with us: but with us it hath not happened so. [36] For we that have received the law perish by sin, and our heart also which received it [37] Notwithstanding the law perisheth not, but remaineth in his force. [38] And when I spake these things in my heart, I looked back with mine eyes, and upon the right side I saw a woman, and, behold, she mourned and wept with a loud voice, and was much grieved in heart, and her clothes were rent, and she had ashes upon her head. [39] Then let I my thoughts go that I was in, and turned me unto her, [40] And said unto her, Wherefore weepest thou? why art thou so grieved in thy mind? [41] And she said unto me, Sir, let me alone, that I may bewail myself, and add unto my sorrow, for I am sore vexed in my mind, and brought very low. [42] And I said unto her, What aileth thee? tell me. [43] She said unto me, I thy servant have been barren, and had no child, though I had an husband thirty years, [44] And those thirty years I did nothing else day and night, and every hour, but make my, prayer to the Highest. [45] After thirty years God heard me thine handmaid, looked upon my misery, considered my trouble, and gave me a son: and I was very glad of him, so was my husband also, and all my neighbours: and we gave great honour unto the Almighty. [46] And I nourished him with great travail. [47] So when he grew up, and came to the time that he should have a wife, I made a feast. 2Ezra.10 [1] And it so came to pass, that when my son was entered into his wedding chamber, he fell down, and died. [2] Then we all overthrew the lights, and all my neighbours rose up to comfort me: so I took my rest unto the second day at night. [3] And it came to pass, when they had all left off to comfort me, to the end I might be quiet; then rose I up by night and fled, and came hither into this field, as thou seest. [4] And I do now purpose not to return into the city, but here to stay, and neither to eat nor drink, but continually to mourn and to fast until I die. [5] Then left I the meditations wherein I was, and spake to her in anger, saying, [6] Thou foolish woman above all other, seest thou not our mourning, and what happeneth unto us? [7] How that Sion our mother is full of all heaviness, and much humbled, mourning very sore? [8] And now, seeing we all mourn and are sad, for we are all in heaviness, art thou grieved for one son? [9] For ask the earth, and she shall tell thee, that it is she which ought to mourn for the fall of so many that grow upon her. [10] For out of her came all at the first, and out of her shall all others come, and, behold, they walk almost all into destruction, and a multitude of them is utterly rooted out. [11] Who then should make more mourning than she, that hath lost so great a multitude; and not thou, which art sorry but for one? [12] But if thou sayest unto me, My lamentation is not like the earth's, because I have lost the fruit of my womb, which I brought forth with pains, and bare with sorrows; [13] But the earth not so: for the multitude present in it according to the course of the earth is gone, as it came: [14] Then say I unto thee, Like as thou hast brought forth with labour; even so the earth also hath given her fruit, namely, man, ever since the beginning unto him that made her. [15] Now therefore keep thy sorrow to thyself, and bear with a good courage that which hath befallen thee. [16] For if thou shalt acknowledge the determination of God to be just, thou shalt both receive thy son in time, and shalt be commended among women. [17] Go thy way then into the city to thine husband. [18] And she said unto me, That will I not do: I will not go into the city, but here will I die. [19] So I proceeded to speak further unto her, and said, [20] Do not so, but be counselled. by me: for how many are the adversities of Sion? be comforted in regard of the sorrow of Jerusalem. [21] For thou seest that our sanctuary is laid waste, our altar broken down, our temple destroyed; [22] Our psaltery is laid on the ground, our song is put to silence, our rejoicing is at an end, the light of our candlestick is put out, the ark of our covenant is spoiled, our holy things are defiled, and the name that is called upon us is almost profaned: our children are put to shame, our priests are burnt, our Levites are gone into captivity, our virgins are defiled, and our wives ravished; our righteous men carried away, our little ones destroyed, our young men are brought in bondage, and our strong men are become weak; [23] And, which is the greatest of all, the seal of Sion hath now lost her honour; for she is delivered into the hands of them that hate us. [24] And therefore shake off thy great heaviness, and put away the multitude of sorrows, that the Mighty may be merciful unto thee again, and the Highest shall give thee rest and ease from thy labour. [25] And it came to pass while I was talking with her, behold, her face upon a sudden shined exceedingly, and her countenance glistered, so that I was afraid of her, and mused what it might be. [26] And, behold, suddenly she made a great cry very fearful: so that the earth shook at the noise of the woman. [27] And I looked, and, behold, the woman appeared unto me no more, but there was a city builded, and a large place shewed itself from the foundations: then was I afraid, and cried with a loud voice, and said, [28] Where is Uriel the angel, who came unto me at the first? for he hath caused me to fall into many trances, and mine end is turned into corruption, and my prayer to rebuke. [29] And as I was speaking these words behold, he came unto me, and looked upon me. [30] And, lo, I lay as one that had been dead, and mine understanding was taken from me: and he took me by the right hand, and comforted me, and set me upon my feet, and said unto me, [31] What aileth thee? and why art thou so disquieted? and why is thine understanding troubled, and the thoughts of thine heart? [32] And I said, Because thou hast forsaken me, and yet I did according to thy words, and I went into the field, and, lo, I have seen, and yet see, that I am not able to express. [33] And he said unto me, Stand up manfully, and I will advise thee. [34] Then said I, Speak on, my lord, in me; only forsake me not, lest I die frustrate of my hope. [35] For I have seen that I knew not, and hear that I do not know. [36] Or is my sense deceived, or my soul in a dream? [37] Now therefore I beseech thee that thou wilt shew thy servant of this vision. [38] He answered me then, and said, Hear me, and I shall inform thee, and tell thee wherefore thou art afraid: for the Highest will reveal many secret things unto thee. [39] He hath seen that thy way is right: for that thou sorrowest continually for thy people, and makest great lamentation for Sion. [40] This therefore is the meaning of the vision which thou lately sawest: [41] Thou sawest a woman mourning, and thou begannest to comfort her: [42] But now seest thou the likeness of the woman no more, but there appeared unto thee a city builded. [43] And whereas she told thee of the death of her son, this is the solution: [44] This woman, whom thou sawest is Sion: and whereas she said unto thee, even she whom thou seest as a city builded, [45] Whereas, I say, she said unto thee, that she hath been thirty years barren: those are the thirty years wherein there was no offering made in her. [46] But after thirty years Solomon builded the city and offered offerings: and then bare the barren a son. [47] And whereas she told thee that she nourished him with labour: that was the dwelling in Jerusalem. [48] But whereas she said unto thee, That my son coming into his marriage chamber happened to have a fail, and died: this was the destruction that came to Jerusalem. [49] And, behold, thou sawest her likeness, and because she mourned for her son, thou begannest to comfort her: and of these things which have chanced, these are to be opened unto thee. [50] For now the most High seeth that thou art grieved unfeignedly, and sufferest from thy whole heart for her, so hath he shewed thee the brightness of her glory, and the comeliness of her beauty: [51] And therefore I bade thee remain in the field where no house was builded: [52] For I knew that the Highest would shew this unto thee. [53] Therefore I commanded thee to go into the field, where no foundation of any building was. [54] For in the place wherein the Highest beginneth to shew his city, there can no man's building be able to stand. [55] And therefore fear not, let not thine heart be affrighted, but go thy way in, and see the beauty and greatness of the building, as much as thine eyes be able to see: [56] And then shalt thou hear as much as thine ears may comprehend. [57] For thou art blessed above many other, and art called with the Highest; and so are but few. [58] But to morrow at night thou shalt remain here; [59] And so shall the Highest shew thee visions of the high things, which the most High will do unto them that dwell upon the earth in the last days. So I slept that night and another, like as he commanded me. 2Ezra.11 [1] Then saw I a dream, and, behold, there came up from the sea an eagle, which had twelve feathered wings, and three heads. [2] And I saw, and, behold, she spread her wings over all the earth, and all the winds of the air blew on her, and were gathered together. [3] And I beheld, and out of her feathers there grew other contrary feathers; and they became little feathers and small. [4] But her heads were at rest: the head in the midst was greater than the other, yet rested it with the residue. [5] Moreover I beheld, and, lo, the eagle flew with her feathers, and reigned upon earth, and over them that dwelt therein. [6] And I saw that all things under heaven were subject unto her, and no man spake against her, no, not one creature upon earth. [7] And I beheld, and, lo, the eagle rose upon her talons, and spake to her feathers, saying, [8] Watch not all at once: sleep every one in his own place, and watch by course: [9] But let the heads be preserved for the last. [10] And I beheld, and, lo, the voice went not out of her heads, but from the midst of her body. [11] And I numbered her contrary feathers, and, behold, there were eight of them. [12] And I looked, and, behold, on the right side there arose one feather, and reigned over all the earth; [13] And so it was, that when it reigned, the end of it came, and the place thereof appeared no more: so the next following stood up. and reigned, and had a great time; [14] And it happened, that when it reigned, the end of it came also, like as the first, so that it appeared no more. [15] Then came there a voice unto it, and said, [16] Hear thou that hast borne rule over the earth so long: this I say unto thee, before thou beginnest to appear no more, [17] There shall none after thee attain unto thy time, neither unto the half thereof. [18] Then arose the third, and reigned as the other before, and appeared no more also. [19] So went it with all the residue one after another, as that every one reigned, and then appeared no more. [20] Then I beheld, and, lo, in process of time the feathers that followed stood up upon the right side, that they might rule also; and some of them ruled, but within a while they appeared no more: [21] For some of them were set up, but ruled not. [22] After this I looked, and, behold, the twelve feathers appeared no more, nor the two little feathers: [23] And there was no more upon the eagle's body, but three heads that rested, and six little wings. [24] Then saw I also that two little feathers divided themselves from the six, and remained under the head that was upon the right side: for the four continued in their place. [25] And I beheld, and, lo, the feathers that were under the wing thought to set up themselves and to have the rule. [26] And I beheld, and, lo, there was one set up, but shortly it appeared no more. [27] And the second was sooner away than the first. [28] And I beheld, and, lo, the two that remained thought also in themselves to reign: [29] And when they so thought, behold, there awaked one of the heads that were at rest, namely, it that was in the midst; for that was greater than the two other heads. [30] And then I saw that the two other heads were joined with it. [31] And, behold, the head was turned with them that were with it, and did eat up the two feathers under the wing that would have reigned. [32] But this head put the whole earth in fear, and bare rule in it over all those that dwelt upon the earth with much oppression; and it had the governance of the world more than all the wings that had been. [33] And after this I beheld, and, lo, the head that was in the midst suddenly appeared no more, like as the wings. [34] But there remained the two heads, which also in like sort ruled upon the earth, and over those that dwelt therein. [35] And I beheld, and, lo, the head upon the right side devoured it that was upon the left side. [36] Then I head a voice, which said unto me, Look before thee, and consider the thing that thou seest. [37] And I beheld, and lo, as it were a roaring lion chased out of the wood: and I saw that he sent out a man's voice unto the eagle, and said, [38] Hear thou, I will talk with thee, and the Highest shall say unto thee, [39] Art not thou it that remainest of the four beasts, whom I made to reign in my world, that the end of their times might come through them? [40] And the fourth came, and overcame all the beasts that were past, and had power over the world with great fearfulness, and over the whole compass of the earth with much wicked oppression; and so long time dwelt he upon the earth with deceit. [41] For the earth hast thou not judged with truth. [42] For thou hast afflicted the meek, thou hast hurt the peaceable, thou hast loved liars, and destroyed the dwellings of them that brought forth fruit, and hast cast down the walls of such as did thee no harm. [43] Therefore is thy wrongful dealing come up unto the Highest, and thy pride unto the Mighty. [44] The Highest also hath looked upon the proud times, and, behold, they are ended, and his abominations are fulfilled. [45] And therefore appear no more, thou eagle, nor thy horrible wings, nor thy wicked feathers nor thy malicious heads, nor thy hurtful claws, nor all thy vain body: [46] That all the earth may be refreshed, and may return, being delivered from thy violence, and that she may hope for the judgment and mercy of him that made her. 4Ezra.12 [1] And it came to pass, whiles the lion spake these words unto the eagle, I saw, [2] And, behold, the head that remained and the four wings appeared no more, and the two went unto it and set themselves up to reign, and their kingdom was small, and fill of uproar. [3] And I saw, and, behold, they appeared no more, and the whole body of the eagle was burnt so that the earth was in great fear: then awaked I out of the trouble and trance of my mind, and from great fear, and said unto my spirit, [4] Lo, this hast thou done unto me, in that thou searchest out the ways of the Highest. [5] Lo, yet am I weary in my mind, and very weak in my spirit; and little strength is there in me, for the great fear wherewith I was afflicted this night. [6] Therefore will I now beseech the Highest, that he will comfort me unto the end. [7] And I said, Lord that bearest rule, if I have found grace before thy sight, and if I am justified with thee before many others, and if my prayer indeed be come up before thy face; [8] Comfort me then, and shew me thy servant the interpretation and plain difference of this fearful vision, that thou mayest perfectly comfort my soul. [9] For thou hast judged me worthy to shew me the last times. [10] And he said unto me, This is the interpretation of the vision: [11] The eagle, whom thou sawest come up from the sea, is the kingdom which was seen in the vision of thy brother Daniel. [12] But it was not expounded unto him, therefore now I declare it unto thee. [13] Behold, the days will come, that there shall rise up a kingdom upon earth, and it shall be feared above all the kingdoms that were before it. [14] In the same shall twelve kings reign, one after another: [15] Whereof the second shall begin to reign, and shall have more time than any of the twelve. [16] And this do the twelve wings signify, which thou sawest. [17] As for the voice which thou heardest speak, and that thou sawest not to go out from the heads but from the midst of the body thereof, this is the interpretation: [18] That after the time of that kingdom there shall arise great strivings, and it shall stand in peril of failing: nevertheless it shall not then fall, but shall be restored again to his beginning. [19] And whereas thou sawest the eight small under feathers sticking to her wings, this is the interpretation: [20] That in him there shall arise eight kings, whose times shall be but small, and their years swift. [21] And two of them shall perish, the middle time approaching: four shall be kept until their end begin to approach: but two shall be kept unto the end. [22] And whereas thou sawest three heads resting, this is the interpretation: [23] In his last days shall the most High raise up three kingdoms, and renew many things therein, and they shall have the dominion of the earth, [24] And of those that dwell therein, with much oppression, above all those that were before them: therefore are they called the heads of the eagle. [25] For these are they that shall accomplish his wickedness, and that shall finish his last end. [26] And whereas thou sawest that the great head appeared no more, it signifieth that one of them shall die upon his bed, and yet with pain. [27] For the two that remain shall be slain with the sword. [28] For the sword of the one shall devour the other: but at the last shall he fall through the sword himself. [29] And whereas thou sawest two feathers under the wings passing over the head that is on the right side; [30] It signifieth that these are they, whom the Highest hath kept unto their end: this is the small kingdom and full of trouble, as thou sawest. [31] And the lion, whom thou sawest rising up out of the wood, and roaring, and speaking to the eagle, and rebuking her for her unrighteousness with all the words which thou hast heard; [32] This is the anointed, which the Highest hath kept for them and for their wickedness unto the end: he shall reprove them, and shall upbraid them with their cruelty. [33] For he shall set them before him alive in judgment, and shall rebuke them, and correct them. [34] For the rest of my people shall he deliver with mercy, those that have been pressed upon my borders, and he shall make them joyful until the coming of the day of judgment, whereof I have spoken unto thee from the the beginning. [35] This is the dream that thou sawest, and these are the interpretations. [36] Thou only hast been meet to know this secret of the Highest. [37] Therefore write all these things that thou hast seen in a book, and hide them: [38] And teach them to the wise of the people, whose hearts thou knowest may comprehend and keep these secrets. [39] But wait thou here thyself yet seven days more, that it may be shewed thee, whatsoever it pleaseth the Highest to declare unto thee. And with that he went his way. [40] And it came to pass, when all the people saw that the seven days were past, and I not come again into the city, they gathered them all together, from the least unto the greatest, and came unto me, and said, [41] What have we offended thee? and what evil have we done against thee, that thou forsakest us, and sittest here in this place? [42] For of all the prophets thou only art left us, as a cluster of the vintage, and as a candle in a dark place, and as a haven or ship preserved from the tempest. [43] Are not the evils which are come to us sufficient? [44] If thou shalt forsake us, how much better had it been for us, if we also had been burned in the midst of Sion? [45] For we are not better than they that died there. And they wept with a loud voice. Then answered I them, and said, [46] Be of good comfort, O Israel; and be not heavy, thou house of Jacob: [47] For the Highest hath you in remembrance, and the Mighty hath not forgotten you in temptation. [48] As for me, I have not forsaken you, neither am I departed from you: but am come into this place, to pray for the desolation of Sion, and that I might seek mercy for the low estate of your sanctuary. [49] And now go your way home every man, and after these days will I come unto you. [50] So the people went their way into the city, like as I commanded them: [51] But I remained still in the field seven days, as the angel commanded me; and did eat only in those days of the flowers of the field, and had my meat of the herbs 2Ezra.13 [1] And it came to pass after seven days, I dreamed a dream by night: [2] And, lo, there arose a wind from the sea, that it moved all the waves thereof. [3] And I beheld, and, lo, that man waxed strong with the thousands of heaven: and when he turned his countenance to look, all the things trembled that were seen under him. [4] And whensoever the voice went out of his mouth, all they burned that heard his voice, like as the earth faileth when it feeleth the fire. [5] And after this I beheld, and, lo, there was gathered together a multitude of men, out of number, from the four winds of the heaven, to subdue the man that came out of the sea [6] But I beheld, and, lo, he had graved himself a great mountain, and flew up upon it. [7] But I would have seen the region or place whereout the hill was graven, and I could not. [8] And after this I beheld, and, lo, all they which were gathered together to subdue him were sore afraid, and yet durst fight. [9] And, lo, as he saw the violence of the multitude that came, he neither lifted up his hand, nor held sword, nor any instrument of war: [10] But only I saw that he sent out of his mouth as it had been a blast of fire, and out of his lips a flaming breath, and out of his tongue he cast out sparks and tempests. [11] And they were all mixed together; the blast of fire, the flaming breath, and the great tempest; and fell with violence upon the multitude which was prepared to fight, and burned them up every one, so that upon a sudden of an innumerable multitude nothing was to be perceived, but only dust and smell of smoke: when I saw this I was afraid. [12] Afterward saw I the same man come down from the mountain, and call unto him another peaceable Multitude. [13] And there came much people unto him, whereof some were glad, some were sorry, and some of them were bound, and other some brought of them that were offered: then was I sick through great fear, and I awaked, and said, [14] Thou hast shewed thy servant these wonders from the beginning, and hast counted me worthy that thou shouldest receive my prayer: [15] Shew me now yet the interpretation of this dream. [16] For as I conceive in mine understanding, woe unto them that shall be left in those days and much more woe unto them that are not left behind! [17] For they that were not left were in heaviness. [18] Now understand I the things that are laid up in the latter days, which shall happen unto them, and to those that are left behind. [19] Therefore are they come into great perils and many necessities, like as these dreams declare. [20] Yet is it easier for him that is in danger to come into these things, than to pass away as a cloud out of the world, and not to see the things that happen in the last days. And he answered unto me, and said, [21] The interpretation of the vision shall I shew thee, and I will open unto thee the thing that thou hast required. [22] Whereas thou hast spoken of them that are left behind, this is the interpretation: [23] He that shall endure the peril in that time hath kept himself: they that be fallen into danger are such as have works, and faith toward the Almighty. [24] Know this therefore, that they which be left behind are more blessed than they that be dead. [25] This is the meaning of the vision: Whereas thou sawest a man coming up from the midst of the sea: [26] The same is he whom God the Highest hath kept a great season, which by his own self shall deliver his creature: and he shall order them that are left behind. [27] And whereas thou sawest, that out of his mouth there came as a blast of wind, and fire, and storm; [28] And that he held neither sword, nor any instrument of war, but that the rushing in of him destroyed the whole multitude that came to subdue him; this is the interpretation: [29] Behold, the days come, when the most High will begin to deliver them that are upon the earth. [30] And he shall come to the astonishment of them that dwell on the earth. [31] And one shall undertake to fight against another, one city against another, one place against another, one people against another, and one realm against another. [32] And the time shall be when these things shall come to pass, and the signs shall happen which I shewed thee before, and then shall my Son be declared, whom thou sawest as a man ascending. [33] And when all the people hear his voice, every man shall in their own land leave the battle they have one against another. [34] And an innumerable multitude shall be gathered together, as thou sawest them, willing to come, and to overcome him by fighting. [35] But he shall stand upon the top of the mount Sion. [36] And Sion shall come, and shall be shewed to all men, being prepared and builded, like as thou sawest the hill graven without hands. [37] And this my Son shall rebuke the wicked inventions of those nations, which for their wicked life are fallen into the tempest; [38] And shall lay before them their evil thoughts, and the torments wherewith they shall begin to be tormented, which are like unto a flame: and he shall destroy them without labour by the law which is like unto me. [39] And whereas thou sawest that he gathered another peaceable multitude unto him; [40] Those are the ten tribes, which were carried away prisoners out of their own land in the time of Osea the king, whom Salmanasar the king of Assyria led away captive, and he carried them over the waters, and so came they into another land. [41] But they took this counsel among themselves, that they would leave the multitude of the heathen, and go forth into a further country, where never mankind dwelt, [42] That they might there keep their statutes, which they never kept in their own land. [43] And they entered into Euphrates by the narrow places of the river. [44] For the most High then shewed signs for them, and held still the flood, till they were passed over. [45] For through that country there was a great way to go, namely, of a year and a half: and the same region is called Arsareth. [46] Then dwelt they there until the latter time; and now when they shall begin to come, [47] The Highest shall stay the springs of the stream again, that they may go through: therefore sawest thou the multitude with peace. [48] But those that be left behind of thy people are they that are found within my borders. [49] Now when he destroyeth the multitude of the nations that are gathered together, he shall defend his people that remain. [50] And then shall he shew them great wonders. [51] Then said I, O Lord that bearest rule, shew me this: Wherefore have I seen the man coming up from the midst of the sea? [52] And he said unto me, Like as thou canst neither seek out nor know the things that are in the deep of the sea: even so can no man upon earth see my Son, or those that be with him, but in the day time. [53] This is the interpretation of the dream which thou sawest, and whereby thou only art here lightened. [54] For thou hast forsaken thine own way, and applied thy diligence unto my law, and sought it. [55] Thy life hast thou ordered in wisdom, and hast called understanding thy mother. [56] And therefore have I shewed thee the treasures of the Highest: after other three days I will speak other things unto thee, and declare unto thee mighty and wondrous things. [57] Then went I forth into the field, giving praise and thanks greatly unto the most High because of his wonders which he did in time; [58] And because he governeth the same, and such things as fall in their seasons: and there I sat three days. 2Ezra.14 [1] And it came to pass upon the third day, I sat under an oak, and, behold, there came a voice out of a bush over against me, and said, Esdras, Esdras. [2] And I said, Here am I, Lord And I stood up upon my feet. [3] Then said he unto me, In the bush I did manifestly reveal myself unto Moses, and talked with him, when my people served in Egypt: [4] And I sent him and led my people out of Egypt, and brought him up to the mount of where I held him by me a long season, [5] And told him many wondrous things, and shewed him the secrets of the times, and the end; and commanded him, saying, [6] These words shalt thou declare, and these shalt thou hide. [7] And now I say unto thee, [8] That thou lay up in thy heart the signs that I have shewed, and the dreams that thou hast seen, and the interpretations which thou hast heard: [9] For thou shalt be taken away from all, and from henceforth thou shalt remain with my Son, and with such as be like thee, until the times be ended. [10] For the world hath lost his youth, and the times begin to wax old. [11] For the world is divided into twelve parts, and the ten parts of it are gone already, and half of a tenth part: [12] And there remaineth that which is after the half of the tenth part. [13] Now therefore set thine house in order, and reprove thy people, comfort such of them as be in trouble, and now renounce corruption, [14] Let go from thee mortal thoughts, cast away the burdens of man, put off now the weak nature, [15] And set aside the thoughts that are most heavy unto thee, and haste thee to flee from these times. [16] For yet greater evils than those which thou hast seen happen shall be done hereafter. [17] For look how much the world shall be weaker through age, so much the more shall evils increase upon them that dwell therein. [18] For the time is fled far away, and leasing is hard at hand: for now hasteth the vision to come, which thou hast seen. [19] Then answered I before thee, and said, [20] Behold, Lord, I will go, as thou hast commanded me, and reprove the people which are present: but they that shall be born afterward, who shall admonish them? thus the world is set in darkness, and they that dwell therein are without light. [21] For thy law is burnt, therefore no man knoweth the things that are done of thee, or the work that shall begin. [22] But if I have found grace before thee, send the Holy Ghost into me, and I shall write all that hath been done in the world since the beginning, which were written in thy law, that men may find thy path, and that they which will live in the latter days may live. [23] And he answered me, saying, Go thy way, gather the people together, and say unto them, that they seek thee not for forty days. [24] But look thou prepare thee many box trees, and take with thee Sarea, Dabria, Selemia, Ecanus, and Asiel, these five which are ready to write swiftly; [25] And come hither, and I shall light a candle of understanding in thine heart, which shall not be put out, till the things be performed which thou shalt begin to write. [26] And when thou hast done, some things shalt thou publish, and some things shalt thou shew secretly to the wise: to morrow this hour shalt thou begin to write. [27] Then went I forth, as he commanded, and gathered all the people together, and said, [28] Hear these words, O Israel. [29] Our fathers at the beginning were strangers in Egypt, from whence they were delivered: [30] And received the law of life, which they kept not, which ye also have transgressed after them. [31] Then was the land, even the land of Sion, parted among you by lot: but your fathers, and ye yourselves, have done unrighteousness, and have not kept the ways which the Highest commanded you. [32] And forasmuch as he is a righteous judge, he took from you in time the thing that he had given you. [33] And now are ye here, and your brethren among you. [34] Therefore if so be that ye will subdue your own understanding, and reform your hearts, ye shall be kept alive and after death ye shall obtain mercy. [35] For after death shall the judgment come, when we shall live again: and then shall the names of the righteous be manifest, and the works of the ungodly shall be declared. [36] Let no man therefore come unto me now, nor seek after me these forty days. [37] So I took the five men, as he commanded me, and we went into the field, and remained there. [38] And the next day, behold, a voice called me, saying, Esdras, open thy mouth, and drink that I give thee to drink. [39] Then opened I my mouth, and, behold, he reached me a full cup, which was full as it were with water, but the colour of it was like fire. [40] And I took it, and drank: and when I had drunk of it, my heart uttered understanding, and wisdom grew in my breast, for my spirit strengthened my memory: [41] And my mouth was opened, and shut no more. [42] The Highest gave understanding unto the five men, and they wrote the wonderful visions of the night that were told, which they knew not: and they sat forty days, and they wrote in the day, and at night they ate bread. [43] As for me. I spake in the day, and I held not my tongue by night. [44] In forty days they wrote two hundred and four books. [45] And it came to pass, when the forty days were filled, that the Highest spake, saying, The first that thou hast written publish openly, that the worthy and unworthy may read it: [46] But keep the seventy last, that thou mayest deliver them only to such as be wise among the people: [47] For in them is the spring of understanding, the fountain of wisdom, and the stream of knowledge. [48] And I did so. 2Ezra.15 [1] Behold, speak thou in the ears of my people the words of prophecy, which I will put in thy mouth, saith the Lord: [2] And cause them to be written in paper: for they are faithful and true. [3] Fear not the imaginations against thee, let not the incredulity of them trouble thee, that speak against thee. [4] For all the unfaithful shall die in their unfaithfulness. [5] Behold, saith the Lord, I will bring plagues upon the world; the sword, famine, death, and destruction. [6] For wickedness hath exceedingly polluted the whole earth, and their hurtful works are fulfilled. [7] Therefore saith the Lord, [8] I will hold my tongue no more as touching their wickedness, which they profanely commit, neither will I suffer them in those things, in which they wickedly exercise themselves: behold, the innocent and righteous blood crieth unto me, and the souls of the just complain continually. [9] And therefore, saith the Lord, I will surely avenge them, and receive unto me all the innocent blood from among them. [10] Behold, my people is led as a flock to the slaughter: I will not suffer them now to dwell in the land of Egypt: [11] But I will bring them with a mighty hand and a stretched out arm, and smite Egypt with plagues, as before, and will destroy all the land thereof. [12] Egypt shall mourn, and the foundation of it shall be smitten with the plague and punishment that God shall bring upon it. [13] They that till the ground shall mourn: for their seeds shall fail through the blasting and hail, and with a fearful constellation. [14] Woe to the world and them that dwell therein! [15] For the sword and their destruction draweth nigh, and one people shall stand up and fight against another, and swords in their hands. [16] For there shall be sedition among men, and invading one another; they shall not regard their kings nor princes, and the course of their actions shall stand in their power. [17] A man shall desire to go into a city, and shall not be able. [18] For because of their pride the cities shall be troubled, the houses shall be destroyed, and men shall be afraid. [19] A man shall have no pity upon his neighbour, but shall destroy their houses with the sword, and spoil their goods, because of the lack of bread, and for great tribulation. [20] Behold, saith God, I will call together all the kings of the earth to reverence me, which are from the rising of the sun, from the south, from the east, and Libanus; to turn themselves one against another, and repay the things that they have done to them. [21] Like as they do yet this day unto my chosen, so will I do also, and recompense in their bosom. Thus saith the Lord God; [22] My right hand shall not spare the sinners, and my sword shall not cease over them that shed innocent blood upon the earth. [23] The fire is gone forth from his wrath, and hath consumed the foundations of the earth, and the sinners, like the straw that is kindled. [24] Woe to them that sin, and keep not my commandments! saith the Lord. [25] I will not spare them: go your way, ye children, from the power, defile not my sanctuary. [26] For the Lord knoweth all them that sin against him, and therefore delivereth he them unto death and destruction. [27] For now are the plagues come upon the whole earth and ye shall remain in them: for God shall not deliver you, because ye have sinned against him. [28] Behold an horrible vision, and the appearance thereof from the east: [29] Where the nations of the dragons of Arabia shall come out with many chariots, and the multitude of them shall be carried as the wind upon earth, that all they which hear them may fear and tremble. [30] Also the Carmanians raging in wrath shall go forth as the wild boars of the wood, and with great power shall they come, and join battle with them, and shall waste a portion of the land of the Assyrians. [31] And then shall the dragons have the upper hand, remembering their nature; and if they shall turn themselves, conspiring together in great power to persecute them, [32] Then these shall be troubled bled, and keep silence through their power, and shall flee. [33] And from the land of the Assyrians shall the enemy besiege them, and consume some of them, and in their host shall be fear and dread, and strife among their kings. [34] Behold clouds from the east and from the north unto the south, and they are very horrible to look upon, full of wrath and storm. [35] They shall smite one upon another, and they shall smite down a great multitude of stars upon the earth, even their own star; and blood shall be from the sword unto the belly, [36] And dung of men unto the camel's hough. [37] And there shall be great fearfulness and trembling upon earth: and they that see the wrath shall be afraid, and trembling shall come upon them. [38] And then shall there come great storms from the south, and from the north, and another part from the west. [39] And strong winds shall arise from the east, and shall open it; and the cloud which he raised up in wrath, and the star stirred to cause fear toward the east and west wind, shall be destroyed. [40] The great and mighty clouds shall be puffed up full of wrath, and the star, that they may make all the earth afraid, and them that dwell therein; and they shall pour out over every high and eminent place an horrible star, [41] Fire, and hail, and flying swords, and many waters, that all fields may be full, and all rivers, with the abundance of great waters. [42] And they shall break down the cities and walls, mountains and hills, trees of the wood, and grass of the meadows, and their corn. [43] And they shall go stedfastly unto Babylon, and make her afraid. [44] They shall come to her, and besiege her, the star and all wrath shall they pour out upon her: then shall the dust and smoke go up unto the heaven, and all they that be about her shall bewail her. [45] And they that remain under her shall do service unto them that have put her in fear. [46] And thou, Asia, that art partaker of the hope of Babylon, and art the glory of her person: [47] Woe be unto thee, thou wretch, because thou hast made thyself like unto her; and hast decked thy daughters in whoredom, that they might please and glory in thy lovers, which have always desired to commit whoredom with thee. [48] Thou hast followed her that is hated in all her works and inventions: therefore saith God, [49] I will send plagues upon thee; widowhood, poverty, famine, sword, and pestilence, to waste thy houses with destruction and death. [50] And the glory of thy Power shall be dried up as a flower, the heat shall arise that is sent over thee. [51] Thou shalt be weakened as a poor woman with stripes, and as one chastised with wounds, so that the mighty and lovers shall not be able to receive thee. [52] Would I with jealousy have so proceeded against thee, saith the Lord, [53] If thou hadst not always slain my chosen, exalting the stroke of thine hands, and saying over their dead, when thou wast drunken, [54] Set forth the beauty of thy countenance? [55] The reward of thy whoredom shall be in thy bosom, therefore shalt thou receive recompence. [56] Like as thou hast done unto my chosen, saith the Lord, even so shall God do unto thee, and shall deliver thee into mischief [57] Thy children shall die of hunger, and thou shalt fall through the sword: thy cities shall be broken down, and all thine shall perish with the sword in the field. [58] They that be in the mountains shall die of hunger, and eat their own flesh, and drink their own blood, for very hunger of bread, and thirst of water. [59] Thou as unhappy shalt come through the sea, and receive plagues again. [60] And in the passage they shall rush on the idle city, and shall destroy some portion of thy land, and consume part of thy glory, and shall return to Babylon that was destroyed. [61] And thou shalt be cast down by them as stubble, and they shall be unto thee as fire; [62] And shall consume thee, and thy cities, thy land, and thy mountains; all thy woods and thy fruitful trees shall they burn up with fire. [63] Thy children shall they carry away captive, and, look, what thou hast, they shall spoil it, and mar the beauty of thy face. 2Ezra.16 [1] Woe be unto thee, Babylon, and Asia! woe be unto thee, Egypt and Syria! [2] Gird up yourselves with cloths of sack and hair, bewail your children, and be sorry; for your destruction is at hand. [3] A sword is sent upon you, and who may turn it back? [4] A fire is sent among you, and who may quench it? [5] Plagues are sent unto you, and what is he that may drive them away? [6] May any man drive away an hungry lion in the wood? or may any one quench the fire in stubble, when it hath begun to burn? [7] May one turn again the arrow that is shot of a strong archer? [8] The mighty Lord sendeth the plagues and who is he that can drive them away? [9] A fire shall go forth from his wrath, and who is he that may quench it? [10] He shall cast lightnings, and who shall not fear? he shall thunder, and who shall not be afraid? [11] The Lord shall threaten, and who shall not be utterly beaten to powder at his presence? [12] The earth quaketh, and the foundations thereof; the sea ariseth up with waves from the deep, and the waves of it are troubled, and the fishes thereof also, before the Lord, and before the glory of his power: [13] For strong is his right hand that bendeth the bow, his arrows that he shooteth are sharp, and shall not miss, when they begin to be shot into the ends of the world. [14] Behold, the plagues are sent, and shall not return again, until they come upon the earth. [15] The fire is kindled, and shall not be put out, till it consume the foundation of the earth. [16] Like as an arrow which is shot of a mighty archer returneth not backward: even so the plagues that shall be sent upon earth shall not return again. [17] Woe is me! woe is me! who will deliver me in those days? [18] The beginning of sorrows and great mournings; the beginning of famine and great death; the beginning of wars, and the powers shall stand in fear; the beginning of evils! what shall I do when these evils shall come? [19] Behold, famine and plague, tribulation and anguish, are sent as scourges for amendment. [20] But for all these things they shall not turn from their wickedness, nor be always mindful of the scourges. [21] Behold, victuals shall be so good cheap upon earth, that they shall think themselves to be in good case, and even then shall evils grow upon earth, sword, famine, and great confusion. [22] For many of them that dwell upon earth shall perish of famine; and the other, that escape the hunger, shall the sword destroy. [23] And the dead shall be cast out as dung, and there shall be no man to comfort them: for the earth shall be wasted, and the cities shall be cast down. [24] There shall be no man left to till the earth, and to sow it [25] The trees shall give fruit, and who shall gather them? [26] The grapes shall ripen, and who shall tread them? for all places shall be desolate of men: [27] So that one man shall desire to see another, and to hear his voice. [28] For of a city there shall be ten left, and two of the field, which shall hide themselves in the thick groves, and in the clefts of the rocks. [29] As in an orchard of Olives upon every tree there are left three or four olives; [30] Or as when a vineyard is gath-

ered, there are left some clusters of them that diligently seek through the vineyard: [31] Even so in those days there shall be three or four left by them that search their houses with the sword. [32] And the earth shall be laid waste, and the fields thereof shall wax old, and her ways and all her paths shall grow full of thorns, because no man shall travel therethrough. [33] The virgins shall mourn, having no bridegrooms; the women shall mourn, having no husbands; their daughters shall mourn, having no helpers. [34] In the wars shall their bridegrooms be destroyed, and their husbands shall perish of famine. [35] Hear now these things and understand them, ye servants of the Lord. [36] Behold, the word of the Lord, receive it: believe not the gods of whom the Lord spake. [37] Behold, the plagues draw nigh, and are not slack. [38] As when a woman with child in the ninth month bringeth forth her son, with two or three hours of her birth great pains compass her womb, which pains, when the child cometh forth, they slack not a moment: [39] Even so shall not the plagues be slack to come upon the earth, and the world shall mourn, and sorrows shall come upon it on every side. [40] O my people, hear my word: make you ready to thy battle, and in those evils be even as pilgrims upon the earth. [41] He that selleth, let him be as he that fleeth away: and he that buyeth, as one that will lose: [42] He that occupieth merchandise, as he that hath no profit by it: and he that buildeth, as he that shall not dwell therein: [43] He that soweth, as if he should not reap: so also he that planteth the vineyard, as he that shall not gather the grapes: [44] They that marry, as they that shall get no children; and they that marry not, as the widowers. [45] And therefore they that labour labour in vain: [46] For strangers shall reap their fruits, and spoil their goods, overthrow their houses, and take their children captives, for in captivity and famine shall they get children. [47] And they that occupy their merchandise with robbery, the more they deck their cities, their houses, their possessions, and their own persons: [48] The more will I be angry with them for their sin, saith the Lord. [49] Like as a whore envieth a right honest and virtuous woman: [50] So shall righteousness hate iniquity, when she decketh herself, and shall accuse her to her face, when he cometh that shall defend him that diligently searcheth out every sin upon earth. [51] And therefore be ye not like thereunto, nor to the works thereof. [52] For yet a little, and iniquity shall be taken away out of the earth, and righteousness shall reign among you. [53] Let not the sinner say that he hath not sinned: for God shall burn coals of fire upon his head, which saith before the Lord God and his glory, I have not sinned. [54] Behold, the Lord knoweth all the works of men, their imaginations, their thoughts, and their hearts: [55] Which spake but the word, Let the earth be made; and it was made: Let the heaven be made; and it was created. [56] In his word were the stars made, and he knoweth the number of them. [57] He searcheth the deep, and the treasures thereof; he hath measured the sea, and what it containeth. [58] He hath shut the sea in the midst of the waters, and with his word hath he hanged the earth upon the waters. [59] He spreadeth out the heavens like a vault; upon the waters hath he founded it. [60] In the desert hath he made springs of water, and pools upon the tops of the mountains, that the floods might pour down from the high rocks to water the earth. [61] He made man, and put his heart in the midst of the body, and gave him breath, life, and understanding. [62] Yea and the Spirit of Almighty God, which made all things, and searcheth out all hidden things in the secrets of the earth, [63] Surely he knoweth your inventions, and what ye think in your hearts, even them that sin, and would hide their sin. [64] Therefore hath the Lord exactly searched out all your works, and he will put you all to shame. [65] And when your sins are brought forth, ye shall be ashamed before men, and your own sins shall be your accusers in that day. [66] What will ye do? or how will ye hide your sins before God and his angels? [67] Behold, God himself is the judge, fear him: leave off from your sins, and forget your iniquities, to meddle no more with them for ever: so shall God lead you forth, and deliver you from all trouble. [68] For, behold, the burning wrath of a great multitude is kindled over you, and they shall take away certain of you, and feed you, being idle, with things offered unto idols. [69] And they that consent unto them shall be had in derision and in reproach, and trodden under foot. [70] For there shall be in every place, and in the next cities, a great insurrection upon those that fear the Lord. [71] They shall be like mad men, sparing none, but still spoiling and destroying those that fear the Lord. [72] For they shall waste and take away their goods, and cast them out of their houses. [73] Then shall they be known, who are my chosen; and they shall be tried as the gold in the fire. [74] Hear, O ye my beloved, saith the Lord: behold, the days of trouble are at hand, but I will deliver you from the same. [75] Be ye not afraid neither doubt; for God is your guide, [76] And the guide of them who keep my commandments and precepts, saith the Lord God: let not your sins weigh you down, and let not your iniquities lift up themselves. [77] Woe be unto them that are bound with their sins, and covered with their iniquities like as a field is covered over with bushes, and the path thereof covered with thorns, that no man may travel through! [78] It is left undressed, and is cast into the fire to be consumed therewith.

Book 77. The Prophecy Of Jeremiah

EpJer.1 [1] Because of the sins which ye have committed before God, ye shall be led away captives into Babylon by Nabuchodonosor king of the Babylonians. [2] So when ye be come unto Babylon, ye shall remain there many years, and for a long season, namely, seven generations: and after that I will bring you away peaceably from thence. [3] Now shall ye see in Babylon gods of silver, and of gold, and of wood, borne upon shoulders, which cause the nations to fear. [4] Beware therefore that ye in no wise be like to strangers, neither be ye and of them, when ye see the multitude before them and behind them, worshipping them. [5] But say ye in your hearts, O Lord, we must worship thee. [6] For mine angel is with you, and I myself caring for your souls. [7] As for their tongue, it is polished by the workman, and they themselves are gilded and laid over with silver; yet are they but false, and cannot speak. [8] And taking gold, as it were for a virgin that loveth to go gay, they make crowns for the heads of their gods. [9] Sometimes also the priests convey from their gods gold and silver, and bestow it upon themselves. [10] Yea, they will give thereof to the common harlots, and deck them as men with garments, [being] gods of silver, and gods of gold, and wood. [11] Yet cannot these gods save themselves from rust and moth, though they be covered with purple raiment. [12] They wipe their faces because of the dust of the temple, when there is much upon them. [13] And he that cannot put to death one that offendeth him holdeth a sceptre, as though he were a judge of the country. [14] He hath also in his right hand a dagger and an ax: but cannot deliver himself from war and thieves. [15] Whereby they are known not to be gods: therefore fear them not. [16] For like as a vessel that a man useth is nothing worth when it is broken; even so it is with their gods: when they be set up in the temple, their eyes be full of dust through the feet of them that come in. [17] And as the doors are made sure on every side upon him that offendeth the king, as being committed to suffer death: even so the priests make fast their temples with doors, with locks, and bars, lest their gods be spoiled with robbers. [18] They light them candles, yea, more than for themselves, whereof they cannot see one. [19] They are as one of the beams of the temple, yet they say their hearts are gnawed upon by things creeping out of the earth; and when they eat them and their clothes, they feel it not. [20] Their faces are blacked through the smoke that cometh out of the temple. [21] Upon their bodies and heads sit bats, swallows, and birds, and the cats also. [22] By this ye may know that they are no gods: therefore fear them not. [23] Notwithstanding the gold that is about them to make them beautiful, except they wipe off the rust, they will not shine: for neither when they were molten did they feel it. [24] The things wherein there is no breath are bought for a most high price. [25] They are borne upon shoulders, having no feet whereby they declare unto men that they be nothing worth. [26] They also that serve them are ashamed: for if they fall to the ground at any time, they cannot rise up again of themselves: neither, if one set them upright, can they move of themselves: neither, if they be bowed down, can they make themselves straight: but they set gifts before them as unto dead men. [27] As for the things that are sacrificed unto them, their priests sell and abuse; in like manner their wives lay up part thereof in salt; but unto the poor and impotent they give nothing of it. [28] Menstruous women and women in childbed eat their sacrifices: by these things ye may know that they are no gods: fear them not. [29] For how can they be called gods? because women set meat before the gods of silver, gold, and wood. [30] And the priests sit in their temples, having their clothes rent, and their heads and beards shaven, and nothing upon their heads. [31] They roar and cry before their gods, as men do at the feast when one is dead. [32] The priests also take off their garments, and clothe their wives and children. [33] Whether it be evil that one doeth unto them, or good, they are not able to recompense it: they can neither set up a king, nor put him down. [34] In like manner, they can neither give riches nor money: though a man make a vow unto them, and keep it not, they will not require it. [35] They can save no man from death, neither deliver the weak from the mighty. [36] They cannot restore a blind man to his sight, nor help any man in his distress. [37] They can shew no mercy to the widow, nor do good to the fatherless. [38] Their gods of wood, and which are overlaid with gold and silver, are like the stones that be hewn out of the mountain: they that worship them shall be confounded. [39] How should a man then think and say that they are gods, when even the Chaldeans themselves dishonour them? [40] Who if they shall see one dumb that cannot speak, they bring him, and intreat Bel that he may speak, as though he were able to understand. [41] Yet they cannot understand this themselves, and leave them: for they have no knowledge. [42] The women also with cords about them, sitting in the ways, burn bran for perfume: but if any of them, drawn by some that passeth by, lie with him, she reproacheth her fellow, that she was not thought as worthy as herself, nor her cord broken. [43] Whatsoever is done among them is false: how may it then be thought or said that they are gods? [44] They are made of carpenters and goldsmiths: they can be nothing else than the workmen will have them to be. [45] And they themselves that made them can never continue long; how should then the things that are made of them be gods? [46] For they left

lies and reproaches to them that come after. [47] For when there cometh any war or plague upon them, the priests consult with themselves, where they may be hidden with them. [48] How then cannot men perceive that they be no gods, which can neither save themselves from war, nor from plague? [49] For seeing they be but of wood, and overlaid with silver and gold, it shall be known hereafter that they are false: [50] And it shall manifestly appear to all nations and kings that they are no gods, but the works of men's hands, and that there is no work of God in them. [51] Who then may not know that they are no gods? [52] For neither can they set up a king in the land, nor give rain unto men. [53] Neither can they judge their own cause, nor redress a wrong, being unable: for they are as crows between heaven and earth. [54] Whereupon when fire falleth upon the house of gods of wood, or laid over with gold or silver, their priests will flee away, and escape; but they themselves shall be burned asunder like beams. [55] Moreover they cannot withstand any king or enemies: how can it then be thought or said that they be gods? [56] Neither are those gods of wood, and laid over with silver or gold, able to escape either from thieves or robbers. [57] Whose gold, and silver, and garments wherewith they are clothed, they that are strong take, and go away withal: neither are they able to help themselves. [58] Therefore it is better to be a king that sheweth his power, or else a profitable vessel in an house, which the owner shall have use of, than such false gods; or to be a door in an house, to keep such things therein, than such false gods. or a pillar of wood in a a palace, than such false gods. [59] For sun, moon, and stars, being bright and sent to do their offices, are obedient. [60] In like manner the lightning when it breaketh forth is easy to be seen; and after the same manner the wind bloweth in every country. [61] And when God commandeth the clouds to go over the whole world, they do as they are bidden. [62] And the fire sent from above to consume hills and woods doeth as it is commanded: but these are like unto them neither in shew nor power. [63] Wherefore it is neither to be supposed nor said that they are gods, seeing, they are able neither to judge causes, nor to do good unto men. [64] Knowing therefore that they are no gods, fear them not, [65] For they can neither curse nor bless kings: [66] Neither can they shew signs in the heavens among the heathen, nor shine as the sun, nor give light as the moon. [67] The beasts are better than they: for they can get under a cover and help themselves. [68] It is then by no means manifest unto us that they are gods: therefore fear them not. [69] For as a scarecrow in a garden of cucumbers keepeth nothing: so are their gods of wood, and laid over with silver and gold. [70] And likewise their gods of wood, and laid over with silver and gold, are like to a white thorn in an orchard, that every bird sitteth upon; as also to a dead body, that is east into the dark. [71] And ye shall know them to be no gods by the bright purple that rotteth upon then: and they themselves afterward shall be eaten, and shall be a reproach in the country. [72] Better therefore is the just man that hath none idols: for he shall be far from reproach.

Book 78. Baruc

Bar.1 [1] And these are the words of the book, which Baruch the son of Nerias, the son of Maasias, the son of Sedecias, the son of Asadias, the son of Chelcias, wrote in Babylon, [2] In the fifth year, and in the seventh day of the month, what time as the Chaldeans took Jerusalem, and burnt it with fire. [3] And Baruch did read the words of this book in the hearing of Jechonias the son of Joachim king of Juda, and in the ears of all the people that came to hear the book, [4] And in the hearing of the nobles, and of the king's sons, and in the hearing of the elders, and of all the people, from the lowest unto the highest, even of all them that dwelt at Babylon by the river Sud. [5] Whereupon they wept, fasted, and prayed before the Lord. [6] They made also a collection of money according to every man's power: [7] And they sent it to Jerusalem unto Joachim the high priest, the son of Chelcias, son of Salom, and to the priests, and to all the people which were found with him at Jerusalem, [8] At the same time when he received the vessels of the house of the Lord, that were carried out of the temple, to return them into the land of Juda, the tenth day of the month Sivan, namely, silver vessels, which Sedecias the son of Josias king of Jada had made, [9] After that Nabuchodonosor king of Babylon had carried away Jechonias, and the princes, and the captives, and the mighty men, and the people of the land, from Jerusalem, and brought them unto Babylon. [10] And they said, Behold, we have sent you money to buy you burnt offerings, and sin offerings, and incense, and prepare ye manna, and offer upon the altar of the Lord our God; [11] And pray for the life of Nabuchodonosor king of Babylon, and for the life of Balthasar his son, that their days may be upon earth as the days of heaven: [12] And the Lord will give us strength, and lighten our eyes, and we shall live under the shadow of Nabuchodonosor king of Babylon, and under the shadow of Balthasar his son, and we shall serve them many days, and find favour in their sight. [13] Pray for us also unto the Lord our God, for we have sinned against the Lord our God; and unto this day the fury of the Lord and his wrath is not turned from us. [14] And ye shall read this book which we have sent unto you, to make confession in the house of the Lord, upon the feasts and solemn days. [15

] And ye shall say, To the Lord our God belongeth righteousness, but unto us the confusion of faces, as it is come to pass this day, unto them of Juda, and to the inhabitants of Jerusalem, [16] And to our kings, and to our princes, and to our priests, and to our prophets, and to our fathers: [17] For we have sinned before the Lord, [18] And disobeyed him, and have not hearkened unto the voice of the Lord our God, to walk in the commandments that he gave us openly: [19] Since the day that the Lord brought our forefathers out of the land of Egypt, unto this present day, we have been disobedient unto the Lord our God, and we have been negligent in not hearing his voice. [20] Wherefore the evils cleaved unto us, and the curse, which the Lord appointed by Moses his servant at the time that he brought our fathers out of the land of Egypt, to give us a land that floweth with milk and honey, like as it is to see this day. [21] Nevertheless we have not hearkened unto the voice of the Lord our God, according unto all the words of the prophets, whom he sent unto us: [22] But every man followed the imagination of his own wicked heart, to serve strange gods, and to do evil in the sight of the Lord our God. Bar.2 [1] Therefore the Lord hath made good his word, which he pronounced against us, and against our judges that judged Israel, and against our kings, and against our princes, and against the men of Israel and Juda, [2] To bring upon us great plagues, such as never happened under the whole heaven, as it came to pass in Jerusalem, according to the things that were written in the law of Moses; [3] That a man should eat the flesh of his own son, and the flesh of his own daughter. [4] Moreover he hath delivered them to be in subjection to all the kingdoms that are round about us, to be as a reproach and desolation among all the people round about, where the Lord hath scattered them. [5] Thus we were cast down, and not exalted, because we have sinned against the Lord our God, and have not been obedient unto his voice. [6] To the Lord our God appertaineth righteousness: but unto us and to our fathers open shame, as appeareth this day. [7] For all these plagues are come upon us, which the Lord hath pronounced against us [8] Yet have we not prayed before the Lord, that we might turn every one from the imaginations of his wicked heart. [9] Wherefore the Lord watched over us for evil, and the Lord hath brought it upon us: for the Lord is righteous in all his works which he hath commanded us. [10] Yet we have not hearkened unto his voice, to walk in the commandments of the Lord, that he hath set before us. [11] And now, O Lord God of Israel, that hast brought thy people out of the land of Egypt with a mighty hand, and high arm, and with signs, and with wonders, and with great power, and hast gotten thyself a name, as appeareth this day: [12] O Lord our God, we have sinned, we have done ungodly, we have dealt unrighteously in all thine ordinances. [13] Let thy wrath turn from us: for we are but a few left among the heathen, where thou hast scattered us. [14] Hear our prayers, O Lord, and our petitions, and deliver us for thine own sake, and give us favour in the sight of them which have led us away: [15] That all the earth may know that thou art the Lord our God, because Israel and his posterity is called by thy name. [16] O Lord, look down from thine holy house, and consider us: bow down thine ear, O Lord, to hear us. [17] Open thine eyes, and behold; for the dead that are in the graves, whose souls are taken from their bodies, will give unto the Lord neither praise nor righteousness: [18] But the soul that is greatly vexed, which goeth stooping and feeble, and the eyes that fail, and the hungry soul, will give thee praise and righteousness, O Lord. [19] Therefore we do not make our humble supplication before thee, O Lord our God, for the righteousness of our fathers, and of our kings. [20] For thou hast sent out thy wrath and indignation upon us, as thou hast spoken by thy servants the prophets, saying, [21] Thus saith the Lord, Bow down your shoulders to serve the king of Babylon: so shall ye remain in the land that I gave unto your fathers. [22] But if ye will not hear the voice of the Lord, to serve the king of Babylon, [23] I will cause to cease out of the cites of Judah, and from without Jerusalem, the voice of mirth, and the voice of joy, the voice of the bridegroom, and the voice of the bride: and the whole land shall be desolate of inhabitants. [24] But we would not hearken unto thy voice, to serve the king of Babylon: therefore hast thou made good the words that thou spakest by thy servants the prophets, namely, that the bones of our kings, and the bones of our fathers, should be taken out of their place. [25] And, lo, they are cast out to the heat of the day, and to the frost of the night, and they died in great miseries by famine, by sword, and by pestilence. [26] And the house which is called by thy name hast thou laid waste, as it is to be seen this day, for the wickedness of the house of Israel and the house of Juda. [27] O Lord our God, thou hast dealt with us after all thy goodness, and according to all that great mercy of thine, [28] As thou spakest by thy servant Moses in the day when thou didst command him to write the law before the children of Israel, saying, [29] If ye will not hear my voice, surely this very great multitude shall be turned into a small number among the nations, where I will scatter them. [30] For I knew that they would not hear me, because it is a stiffnecked people: but in the land of their captivities they shall remember themselves. [31] And shall know that I am the Lord their God: for I will give them an heart, and ears to hear: [32] And they shall praise me in the land of their captivity, and think upon my name, [33] And return from their stiff neck, and from their wicked deeds: for they shall remember the way of their fathers, which sinned before the Lord. [34] And I will bring them again into the land which I promised with an oath unto their fathers, Abraham, Isaac, and Jacob, and they shall be lords of it: and I will increase them, and they shall not be diminished. [35] And I will make an everlasting covenant with them to be their God, and they shall be my people: and I will no more drive my people of Israel out of the land that I have given them. Bar.3 [1] O Lord Almighty, God of Israel, the soul in anguish the troubled spirit, crieth unto thee. [2] Hear, O Lord, and have mercy; ar thou art merciful: and have pity upon us, because we have sinned before thee. [3] For thou endurest for ever, and we perish utterly. [4] O Lord Almighty, thou God of Israel, hear now the prayers of the dead Israelites, and of their children, which have sinned before thee, and not hearkened unto the voice of thee their God: for the which cause these plagues cleave unto us. [5] Remember not the iniquities of our forefathers: but think upon thy power and thy name now at this time. [6] For thou art the Lord our God, and thee, O Lord, will we praise. [7] And for this cause thou hast put thy fear in our hearts, to the intent that we should call upon thy name, and praise thee in our captivity: for we have called to mind all the iniquity of our forefathers, that sinned before thee. [8] Behold, we are yet this day in our captivity, where thou hast scattered us, for a reproach and a curse, and to be subject to payments, according to all the iniquities of our fathers, which departed from the Lord our God. [9] Hear, Israel, the commandments of life: give ear to understand wisdom. [10] How happeneth it Israel, that thou art in thine enemies' land, that thou art waxen old in a strange country, that thou art defiled with the dead, [11] That thou art counted with them that go down into the grave? [12] Thou hast forsaken the fountain of wisdom. [13] For if thou hadst walked in the way of God, thou shouldest have dwelled in peace for ever. [14] Learn where is wisdom, where is strength, where is understanding; that thou mayest know also where is length of days, and life, where is the light of the eyes, and peace. [15] Who hath found out her place? or who hath come into her treasures ? [16] Where are the princes of the heathen become, and such as ruled the beasts upon the earth; [17] They that had their pastime with the fowls of the air, and they that hoarded up silver and gold, wherein men trust, and made no end of their getting? [18] For they that wrought in silver, and were so careful, and whose works are unsearchable, [19] They are vanished and gone down to the grave, and others are come up in their steads. [20] Young men have seen light, and dwelt upon the earth: but the way of knowledge have they not known, [21] Nor understood the paths thereof, nor laid hold of it: their children were far off from that way. [22] It hath not been heard of in Chanaan, neither hath it been seen in Theman. [23] The Agarenes that seek wisdom upon earth, the merchants of Meran and of Theman, the authors of fables, and searchers out of understanding; none of these have known the way of wisdom, or remember her paths. [24] O Israel, how great is the house of God! and how large is the place of his possession! [25] Great, and hath none end; high, and unmeasurable. [26] There were the giants famous from the beginning, that were of so great stature, and so expert in war. [27] Those did not the Lord choose, neither gave he the way of knowledge unto them: [28] But they were destroyed, because they had no wisdom, and perished through their own foolishness. [29] Who hath gone up into heaven, and taken her, and brought her down from the clouds? [30] Who hath gone over the sea, and found her, and will bring her for pure gold? [31] No man knoweth her way, nor thinketh of her path. [32] But he that knoweth all things knoweth her, and hath found her out with his understanding: he that prepared the earth for evermore hath filled it with fourfooted beasts: [33] He that sendeth forth light, and it goeth, calleth it again, and it obeyeth him with fear. [34] The stars shined in their watches, and rejoiced: when he calleth them, they say, Here we be; and so with cheerfulness they shewed light unto him that made them. [35] This is our God, and there shall none other be accounted of in comparison of him [36] He hath found out all the way of knowledge, and hath given it unto Jacob his servant, and to Israel his beloved. [37] Afterward did he shew himself upon earth, and conversed with men. Bar.4 [1] This is the book of the commandments of God, and the law that endureth for ever: all they that keep it shall come to life; but such as leave it shall die. [2] Turn thee, O Jacob, and take hold of it: walk in the presence of the light thereof, that thou mayest be illuminated. [3] Give not thine honour to another, nor the things that are profitable unto thee to a strange nation. [4] O Israel, happy are we: for things that are pleasing to God are made known unto us. [5] Be of good cheer, my people, the memorial of Israel. [6] Ye were sold to the nations, not for [your] destruction: but because ye moved God to wrath, ye were delivered unto the enemies. [7] For ye provoked him that made you by sacrificing unto devils, and not to God. [8] Ye have forgotten the everlasting God, that brought you up; and ye have grieved Jerusalem, that nursed you. [9] For when she saw the wrath of God coming upon you, she said, Hearken, O ye that dwell about Sion: God hath brought upon me great mourning; [10] For I saw the captivity of my sons and daughters, which the Everlasting brought upon them. [11] With joy did I nourish them; but sent them away with weeping and mourning. [12] Let no man rejoice over me, a widow, and forsaken of many, who for the sins of my children am left desolate; because they departed from the law of God. [

13] They knew not his statutes, nor walked in the ways of his commandments, nor trod in the paths of discipline in his righteousness. [14] Let them that dwell about Sion come, and remember ye the captivity of my sons and daughters, which the Everlasting hath brought upon them. [15] For he hath brought a nation upon them from far, a shameless nation, and of a strange language, who neither reverenced old man, nor pitied child. [16] These have carried away the dear beloved children of the widow, and left her that was alone desolate without daughters. [17] But what can I help you? [18] For he that brought these plagues upon you will deliver you from the hands of your enemies. [19] Go your way, O my children, go your way: for I am left desolate. [20] I have put off the clothing of peace, and put upon me the sackcloth of my prayer: I will cry unto the Everlasting in my days. [21] Be of good cheer, O my children, cry unto the Lord, and he will deliver you from the power and hand of the enemies. [22] For my hope is in the Everlasting, that he will save you; and joy is come unto me from the Holy One, because of the mercy which shall soon come unto you from the Everlasting our Saviour. [23] For I sent you out with mourning and weeping: but God will give you to me again with joy and gladness for ever. [24] Like as now the neighbours of Sion have seen your captivity: so shall they see shortly your salvation from our God which shall come upon you with great glory, and brightness of the Everlasting. [25] My children, suffer patiently the wrath that is come upon you from God: for thine enemy hath persecuted thee; but shortly thou shalt see his destruction, and shalt tread upon his neck. [26] My delicate ones have gone rough ways, and were taken away as a flock caught of the enemies. [27] Be of good comfort, O my children, and cry unto God: for ye shall be remembered of him that brought these things upon you. [28] For as it was your mind to go astray from God: so, being returned, seek him ten times more. [29] For he that hath brought these plagues upon you shall bring you everlasting joy with your salvation. [30] Take a good heart, O Jerusalem: for he that gave thee that name will comfort thee. [31] Miserable are they that afflicted thee, and rejoiced at thy fall. [32] Miserable are the cities which thy children served: miserable is she that received thy sons. [33] For as she rejoiced at thy ruin, and was glad of thy fall: so shall she be grieved for her own desolation. [34] For I will take away the rejoicing of her great multitude, and her pride shall be turned into mourning. [35] For fire shall come upon her from the Everlasting, long to endure; and she shall be inhabited of devils for a great time. [36] O Jerusalem, look about thee toward the east, and behold the joy that cometh unto thee from God. [37] Lo, thy sons come, whom thou sentest away, they come gathered together from the east to the west by the word of the Holy One, rejoicing in the glory of God. Bar.5 [1] Put off, O Jerusalem, the garment of mourning and affliction, and put on the comeliness of the glory that cometh from God for ever. [2] Cast about thee a double garment of the righteousness which cometh from God; and set a diadem on thine head of the glory of the Everlasting. [3] For God will shew thy brightness unto every country under heaven. [4] For thy name shall be called of God for ever The peace of righteousness, and The glory of God's worship. [5] Arise, O Jerusalem, and stand on high, and look about toward the east, and behold thy children gathered from the west unto the east by the word of the Holy One, rejoicing in the remembrance of God. [6] For they departed from thee on foot, and were led away of their enemies: but God bringeth them unto thee exalted with glory, as children of the kingdom. [7] For God hath appointed that every high hill, and banks of long continuance, should be cast down, and valleys filled up, to make even the ground, that Israel may go safely in the glory of God, [8] Moreover even the woods and every sweetsmelling tree shall overshadow Israel by the commandment of God. [9] For God shall lead Israel with joy in the light of his glory with the mercy and righteousness that cometh from him.

Book 79. Additions Of The Book Of Esther

AddEsth.1 [1] Then Mardocheus said, God hath done these things. [2] For I remember a dream which I saw concerning these matters, and nothing thereof hath failed. [3] A little fountain became a river, and there was light, and the sun, and much water: this river is Esther, whom the king married, and made queen: [4] And the two dragons are I and Aman. [5] And the nations were those that were assembled to destroy the name of the Jews: [6] And my nation is this Israel, which cried to God, and were saved: for the Lord hath saved his people, and the Lord hath delivered us from all those evils, and God hath wrought signs and great wonders, which have not been done among the Gentiles. [7] Therefore hath he made two lots, one for the people of God, and another for all the Gentiles. [8] And these two lots came at the hour, and time, and day of judgment, before God among all nations. [9] So God remembered his people, and justified his inheritance. [10] Therefore those days shall be unto them in the month Adar, the fourteenth and fifteenth day of the same month, with an assembly, and joy, and with gladness before God, according to the generations for ever among his people. AddEsth.2 [1] In the fourth year of the reign of Ptolemeus and Cleopatra, Dositheus, who said he was a priest and Levite, and Ptolemeus his son, brought this

epistle of Phurim, which they said was the same, and that Lysimachus the son of Ptolemeus, that was in Jerusalem, had interpreted it. [2] In the second year of the reign of Artexerxes the great, in the first day of the month Nisan, Mardocheus the son of Jairus, the son of Semei, the son of Cisai, of the tribe of Benjamin, had a dream; [3] Who was a Jew, and dwelt in the city of Susa, a great man, being a servitor in the king's court. [4] He was also one of the captives, which Nabuchodonosor the king of Babylon carried from Jerusalem with Jechonias king of Judea; and this was his dream: [5] Behold a noise of a tumult, with thunder, and earthquakes, and uproar in the land: [6] And, behold, two great dragons came forth ready to fight, and their cry was great. [7] And at their cry all nations were prepared to battle, that they might fight against the righteous people. [8] And lo a day of darkness and obscurity, tribulation and anguish, affliction and great uproar, upon earth. [9] And the whole righteous nation was troubled, fearing their own evils, and were ready to perish. [10] Then they cried unto God, and upon their cry, as it were from a little fountain, was made a great flood, even much water. [11] The light and the sun rose up, and the lowly were exalted, and devoured the glorious. [12] Now when Mardocheus, who had seen this dream, and what God had determined to do, was awake, he bare this dream in mind, and until night by all means was desirous to know it. AddEsth.3 [1] And Mardocheus took his rest in the court with Gabatha and Tharra, the two eunuchs of the king, and keepers of the palace. [2] And he heard their devices, and searched out their purposes, and learned that they were about to lay hands upon Artexerxes the king; and so he certified the king of them. [3] Then the king examined the two eunuchs, and after that they had confessed it, they were strangled. [4] And the king made a record of these things, and Mardocheus also wrote thereof. [5] So the king commanded, Mardocheus to serve in the court, and for this he rewarded him. [6] Howbeit Aman the son of Amadathus the Agagite, who was in great honour with the king, sought to molest Mardocheus and his people because of the two eunuchs of the king. AddEsth.4 [1] The copy of the letters was this: The great king Artexerxes writeth these things to the princes and governors that are under him from India unto Ethiopia in an hundred and seven and twenty provinces. [2] After that I became lord over many nations and had dominion over the whole world, not lifted up with presumption of my authority, but carrying myself always with equity and mildness, I purposed to settle my subjects continually in a quiet life, and making my kingdom peaceable, and open for passage to the utmost coasts, to renew peace, which is desired of all men. [3] Now when I asked my counsellors how this might be brought to pass, Aman, that excelled in wisdom among us, and was approved for his constant good will and steadfast fidelity, and had the honour of the second place in the kingdom, [4] Declared unto us, that in all nations throughout the world there was scattered a certain malicious people, that had laws contrary to all nations, and continually despised the commandments of kings, so as the uniting of our kingdoms, honourably intended by us cannot go forward. [5] Seeing then we understand that this people alone is continually in opposition unto all men, differing in the strange manner of their laws, and evil affected to our state, working all the mischief they can that our kingdom may not be firmly established: [6] Therefore have we commanded, that all they that are signified in writing unto you by Aman, who is ordained over the affairs, and is next unto us, shall all, with their wives and children, be utterly destroyed by the sword of their enemies, without all mercy and pity, the fourteenth day of the twelfth month Adar of this present year: [7] That they, who of old and now also are malicious, may in one day with violence go into the grave, and so ever hereafter cause our affairs to be well settled, and without trouble. [8] Then Mardocheus thought upon all the works of the Lord, and made his prayer unto him, [9] Saying, O Lord, Lord, the King Almighty: for the whole world is in thy power, and if thou hast appointed to save Israel, there is no man that can gainsay thee: [10] For thou hast made heaven and earth, and all the wondrous things under the heaven. [11] Thou art Lord of all things, and and there is no man that can resist thee, which art the Lord. [12] Thou knowest all things, and thou knowest, Lord, that it was neither in contempt nor pride, nor for any desire of glory, that I did not bow down to proud Aman. [13] For I could have been content with good will for the salvation of Israel to kiss the soles of his feet. [14] But I did this, that I might not prefer the glory of man above the glory of God: neither will I worship any but thee, O God, neither will I do it in pride. [15] And now, O Lord God and King, spare thy people: for their eyes are upon us to bring us to nought; yea, they desire to destroy the inheritance, that hath been thine from the beginning. [16] Despise not the portion, which thou hast delivered out of Egypt for thine own self. [17] Hear my prayer, and be merciful unto thine inheritance: turn our sorrow into joy, that we may live, O Lord, and praise thy name: and destroy not the mouths of them that praise thee, O Lord. [18] All Israel in like manner cried most earnestly unto the Lord, because their death was before their eyes. AddEsth.5 [1] Queen Esther also, being in fear of death, resorted unto the Lord: [2] And laid away her glorious apparel, and put on the garments of anguish and mourning: and instead of precious ointments, she covered her head with ashes and dung, and she humbled her body greatly, and all the places of her joy she filled with her torn hair. [3] And she prayed unto the Lord God of Israel, saying, O my Lord, thou only art our King: help me, desolate woman, which have no helper but thee: [4] For my danger is in mine hand. [5] From my youth up I have heard in the tribe of my family that thou, O Lord, tookest Israel from among all people, and our fathers from all their predecessors, for a perpetual inheritance, and thou hast performed whatsoever thou didst promise them. [6] And now we have sinned before thee: therefore hast thou given us into the hands of our enemies, [7] Because we worshipped their gods: O Lord, thou art righteous. [8] Nevertheless it satisfieth them not, that we are in bitter captivity: but they have stricken hands with their idols, [9] That they will abolish the thing that thou with thy mouth hast ordained, and destroy thine inheritance, and stop the mouth of them that praise thee, and quench the glory of thy house, and of thine altar, [10] And open the mouths of the heathen to set forth the praises of the idols, and to magnify a fleshly king for ever. [11] O Lord, give not thy sceptre unto them that be nothing, and let them not laugh at our fall; but turn their device upon themselves, and make him an example, that hath begun this against us. [12] Remember, O Lord, make thyself known in time of our affliction, and give me boldness, O King of the nations, and Lord of all power. [13] Give me eloquent speech in my mouth before the lion: turn his heart to hate him that fighteth against us, that there may be an end of him, and of all that are likeminded to him: [14] But deliver us with thine hand, and help me that am desolate, which have no other help but thee. [15] Thou knowest all things, O Lord; thou knowest that I hate the glory of the unrighteous, and abhor the bed of the uncircumcised, and of all the heathen. [16] Thou knowest my necessity: for I abhor the sign of my high estate, which is upon mine head in the days wherein I shew myself, and that I abhor it as a menstruous rag, and that I wear it not when I am private by myself. [17] And that thine handmaid hath not eaten at Aman's table, and that I have not greatly esteemed the king's feast, nor drunk the wine of the drink offerings. [18] Neither hath thine handmaid any joy since the day that I was brought hither to this present, but in thee, O Lord God of Abraham. [19] O thou mighty God above all, hear the voice of the forlorn and deliver us out of the hands of the mischievous, and deliver me out of my fear. AddEsth.6 [1] And upon the third day, when she had ended her prayers, she laid away her mourning garments, and put on her glorious apparel. [2] And being gloriously adorned, after she had called upon God, who is the beholder and saviour of all things, she took two maids with her: [3] And upon the one she leaned, as carrying herself daintily; [4] And the other followed, bearing up her train. [5] And she was ruddy through the perfection of her beauty, and her countenance was cheerful and very amiable: but her heart was in anguish for fear. [6] Then having passed through all the doors, she stood before the king, who sat upon his royal throne, and was clothed with all his robes of majesty, all glittering with gold and precious stones; and he was very dreadful. [7] Then lifting up his countenance that shone with majesty, he looked very fiercely upon her: and the queen fell down, and was pale, and fainted, and bowed herself upon the head of the maid that went before her. [8] Then God changed the spirit of the king into mildness, who in a fear leaped from his throne, and took her in his arms, till she came to herself again, and comforted her with loving words and said unto her, [9] Esther, what is the matter? I am thy brother, be of good cheer: [10] Thou shalt not die, though our our commandment be general: come near. [11] And so be held up his golden sceptre, and laid it upon her neck, [12] And embraced her, and said, Speak unto me. [13] Then said she unto him, I saw thee, my lord, as an angel of God, and my heart was troubled for fear of thy majesty. [14] For wonderful art thou, lord, and thy countenance is full of grace. [15] And as she was speaking, she fell down for faintness. [16] Then the king was troubled, and ail his servants comforted her. AddEsth.7 [1] The great king Artexerxes unto the princes and governors of an hundred and seven and twenty provinces from India unto Ethiopia, and unto all our faithful subjects, greeting. [2] Many, the more often they are honoured with the great bounty of their gracious princes, the more proud they are waxen, [3] And endeavour to hurt not our subjects only, but not being able to bear abundance, do take in hand to practise also against those that do them good: [4] And take not only thankfulness away from among men, but also lifted up with the glorious words of lewd persons, that were never good, they think to escape the justice of God, that seeth all things and hateth evil. [5] Oftentimes also fair speech of those, that are put in trust to manage their friends' affairs, hath caused many that are in authority to be partakers of innocent blood, and hath enwrapped them in remediless calamities: [6] Beguiling with the falsehood and deceit of their lewd disposition the innocency and goodness of princes. [7] Now ye may see this, as we have declared, not so much by ancient histories, as ye may, if ye search what hath been wickedly done of late through the pestilent behaviour of them that are unworthily placed in authority. [8] And we must take care for the time to come, that our kingdom may be quiet and peaceable for all men, [9] Both by changing our purposes, and always judging things that are evident with more equal proceeding. [10] For Aman, a Macedonian, the son of Amadatha, being indeed a stranger from the Persian blood, and far distant from our goodness, and as a stranger received of us, [11] Had so far forth obtained the favour that we shew toward every nation, as that he was called our father,

and was continually honoured of all the next person unto the king. [12] But he, not bearing his great dignity, went about to deprive us of our kingdom and life: [13] Having by manifold and cunning deceits sought of us the destruction, as well of Mardocheus, who saved our life, and continually procured our good, as also of blameless Esther, partaker of our kingdom, with their whole nation. [14] For by these means he thought, finding us destitute of friends to have translated the kingdom of the Persians to the Macedonians. [15] But we find that the Jews, whom this wicked wretch hath delivered to utter destruction, are no evildoers, but live by most just laws: [16] And that they be children of the most high and most mighty, living God, who hath ordered the kingdom both unto us and to our progenitors in the most excellent manner. [17] Wherefore ye shall do well not to put in execution the letters sent unto you by Aman the son of Amadatha. [18] For he that was the worker of these things, is hanged at the gates of Susa with all his family: God, who ruleth all things, speedily rendering vengeance to him according to his deserts. [19] Therefore ye shall publish the copy of this letter in all places, that the Jews may freely live after their own laws. [20] And ye shall aid them, that even the same day, being the thirteenth day of the twelfth month Adar, they may be avenged on them, who in the time of their affliction shall set upon them. [21] For Almighty God hath turned to joy unto them the day, wherein the chosen people should have perished. [22] Ye shall therefore among your solemn feasts keep it an high day with all feasting: [23] That both now and hereafter there may be safety to us and the well affected Persians; but to those which do conspire against us a memorial of destruction. [24] Therefore every city and country whatsoever, which shall not do according to these things, shall be destroyed without mercy with fire and sword, and shall be made not only unpassable for men, but also most hateful to wild beasts and fowls for ever.

Book 80. Psalm 151

151A (Hebrew) A Hallelujah of David, Jesse's son. [1] I was the smallest of my brothers, the youngest of my father's sons. He made me shepherd of his flock, ruler over their young. [2] My hands made a flute, my fingers a lyre. Let me give glory to the Lord, I thought to myself. [3] The mountains cannot witness to God; the hills cannot proclaim him. But the trees have cherished my words, the flocks my deeds. [4] Who can proclaim, who can announce, who can declare the Lord's deeds? God has seen everything; God has heard everything; God has listened. [5] God sent his prophet to anoint me; Samuel to make me great. My brothers went out to meet him, handsome in form and appearance: [6] Their stature tall, their hair beautiful, but the Lord God did not choose them. [7] Instead, he sent and took me from following the flock. God anointed me with holy oil; God made me leader for his people, ruler over the children of his covenant. 151B (Hebrew and Syriac) At the beginning of David's power after the prophet of God anointed him. [1] I went out to attack the Philistine, who cursed me by his idols. [2] But after I uncovered his own sword, I cut off his head. So I removed the shame from the Israelites. 151C (Greek) This additional psalm is said to have been written by David when he fought Goliath in single combat. [1] I was small among my brothers, and the youngest of my father's sons. I was shepherd of my father's sheep. [2] My hands made a musical instrument; my fingers strung a lap harp. [3] Who will tell my Lord? The Lord himself, the Lord hears me. [4] The Lord himself sent his messenger, and took me away from my father's sheep. He put special oil on my forehead to anoint me. [5] My brothers were good-looking and tall, but the Lord didn't take special pleasure in them. [6] I went out to meet the Philistine, who cursed me by his idols. [7] But I took his own sword out of its sheath and cut off his head. So I removed the shame from the Israelites.

Book 81. The Wisdom Of Jesus Son Of Sirach

Sir.1 [1] All wisdom cometh from the Lord, and is with him for ever. [2] Who can number the sand of the sea, and the drops of rain, and the days of eternity? [3] Who can find out the height of heaven, and the breadth of the earth, and the deep, and wisdom? [4] Wisdom hath been created before all things, and the understanding of prudence from everlasting. [5] The word of God most high is the fountain of wisdom; and her ways are everlasting commandments. [6] To whom hath the root of wisdom been revealed? or who hath known her wise counsels? [7] Unto whom hath the knowledge of wisdom been made manifest? and who hath understood her great experience? [8] There is one wise and greatly to be feared, the Lord sitting upon his throne. [9] He created her, and saw her, and numbered her, and poured her out upon all his works. [10] She is with all flesh according to his gift, and he hath given her to them that love him. [11] The fear of the Lord is honour, and glory, and gladness, and a crown of rejoicing. [12] The fear of the Lord maketh a merry heart, and giveth joy, and gladness, and a long life. [13] Whoso feareth the Lord, it shall go well with him at the last, and he shall find favour in the day of his death. [14] To fear the Lord is the beginning of wisdom: and it was created with the faithful in the womb. [15] She hath built an everlasting foundation with men, and she shall continue with their seed. [16] To fear the Lord is fulness of wisdom, and filleth men with her fruits. [17] She filleth all their house with things desirable, and the garners with her increase. [18] The fear of the Lord is a crown of wisdom, making peace and perfect health to flourish; both which are the gifts of God: and it enlargeth their rejoicing that love him. [19] Wisdom raineth down skill and knowledge of understanding standing, and exalteth them to honour that hold her fast. [20] The root of wisdom is to fear the Lord, and the branches thereof are long life. [21] The fear of the Lord driveth away sins: and where it is present, it turneth away wrath. [22] A furious man cannot be justified; for the sway of his fury shall be his destruction. [23] A patient man will tear for a time, and afterward joy shall spring up unto him. [24] He will hide his words for a time, and the lips of many shall declare his wisdom. [25] The parables of knowledge are in the treasures of wisdom: but godliness is an abomination to a sinner. [26] If thou desire wisdom, keep the commandments, and the Lord shall give her unto thee. [27] For the fear of the Lord is wisdom and instruction: and faith and meekness are his delight. [28] Distrust not the fear of the Lord when thou art poor: and come not unto him with a double heart. [29] Be not an hypocrite in the sight of men, and take good heed what thou speakest. [30] Exalt not thyself, lest thou fall, and bring dishonour upon thy soul, and so God discover thy secrets, and cast thee down in the midst of the congregation, because thou camest not in truth to the fear of the Lord, but thy heart is full of deceit. Sir.2 [1] My son, if thou come to serve the Lord, prepare thy soul for temptation. [2] Set thy heart aright, and constantly endure, and make not haste in time of trouble. [3] Cleave unto him, and depart not away, that thou mayest be increased at thy last end. [4] Whatsoever is brought upon thee take cheerfully, and be patient when thou art changed to a low estate. [5] For gold is tried in the fire, and acceptable men in the furnace of adversity. [6] Believe in him, and he will help thee; order thy way aright, and trust in him. [7] Ye that fear the Lord, wait for his mercy; and go not aside, lest ye fall. [8] Ye that fear the Lord, believe him; and your reward shall not fail. [9] Ye that fear the Lord, hope for good, and for everlasting joy and mercy. [10] Look at the generations of old, and see; did ever any trust in the Lord, and was confounded? or did any abide in his fear, and was forsaken? or whom did he ever despise, that called upon him? [11] For the Lord is full of compassion and mercy, longsuffering, and very pitiful, and forgiveth sins, and saveth in time of affliction. [12] Woe be to fearful hearts, and faint hands, and the sinner that goeth two ways! [13] Woe unto him that is fainthearted! for he believeth not; therefore shall he not be defended. [14] Woe unto you that have lost patience! and what will ye do when the Lord shall visit you? [15] They that fear the Lord will not disobey his Word; and they that love him will keep his ways. [16] They that fear the Lord will seek that which is well, pleasing unto him; and they that love him shall be filled with the law. [17] They that fear the Lord will prepare their hearts, and humble their souls in his sight, [18] Saying, We will fall into the hands of the Lord, and not into the hands of men: for as his majesty is, so is his mercy. Sir.3 [1] Hear me your father, O children, and do thereafter, that ye may be safe. [2] For the Lord hath given the father honour over the children, and hath confirmed the authority of the mother over the sons. [3] Whoso honoureth his father maketh an atonement for his sins: [4] And he that honoureth his mother is as one that layeth up treasure. [5] Whoso honoureth his father shall have joy of his own children; and when he maketh his prayer, he shall be heard. [6] He that honoureth his father shall have a long life; and he that is obedient unto the Lord shall be a comfort to his mother. [7] He that feareth the Lord will honour his father, and will do service unto his parents, as to his masters. [8] Honour thy father and mother both in word and deed, that a blessing may come upon thee from them. [9] For the blessing of the father establisheth the houses of children; but the curse of the mother rooteth out foundations. [10] Glory not in the dishonour of thy father; for thy father's dishonour is no glory unto thee. [11] For the glory of a man is from the honour of his father; and a mother in dishonour is a reproach to the children. [12] My son, help thy father in his age, and grieve him not as long as he liveth. [13] And if his understanding fail, have patience with him; and despise him not when thou art in thy full strength. [14] For the relieving of thy father shall not be forgotten: and instead of sins it shall be added to build thee up. [15] In the day of thine affliction it shall be remembered; thy sins also shall melt away, as the ice in the fair warm weather. [16] He that forsaketh his father is as a blasphemer; and he that angereth his mother is cursed: of God. [17] My son, go on with thy business in meekness; so shalt thou be beloved of him that is approved. [18] The greater thou art, the more humble thyself, and thou shalt find favour before the Lord. [19] Many are in high place, and of renown: but mysteries are revealed unto the meek. [20] For the power of the Lord is great, and he is honoured of the lowly. [21] Seek not out things that are too hard for thee, neither search the things that are above thy strength. [22] But what is commanded thee, think thereupon with reverence, for it is not needful for thee to see with thine eyes the things that are in secret. [23] Be not curious in unnecessary matters: for more things are shewed unto thee than men understand. [24] For many are deceived by their own vain opinion; and an evil suspicion hath overthrown their judgment. [25] Without eyes thou shalt want light: profess not the knowledge therefore that thou hast not. [26] A stubborn heart shall fare evil at the last; and he that loveth danger shall perish therein. [27] An obstinate heart shall be laden with sorrows; and the wicked man shall heap sin upon sin. [28] In the punishment of the proud there is no remedy; for the plant of wickedness hath taken root in him. [29] The heart of the prudent will understand a parable; and an attentive ear is the desire of a wise man. [30] Water will quench a flaming fire; and alms maketh an atonement for sins. [31] And he that requiteth good turns is mindful of that which may come hereafter; and when he falleth, he shall find a stay. Sir.4 [1] My son, defraud not the poor of his living, and make not the needy eyes to wait long. [2] Make not an hungry soul sorrowful; neither provoke a man in his distress. [3] Add not more trouble to an heart that is vexed; and defer not to give to him that is in need. [4] Reject not the supplication of the afflicted; neither turn away thy face from a poor man. [5] Turn not away thine eye from the needy, and give him none occasion to curse thee: [6] For if he curse thee in the bitterness of his soul, his prayer shall be heard of him that made him. [7] Get thyself the love of the congregation, and bow thy head to a great man. [8] Let it not grieve thee to bow down thine ear to the poor, and give him a friendly answer with meekness. [9] Deliver him that suffereth wrong from the hand of the oppressor; and be not fainthearted when thou sittest in judgment. [10] Be as a father unto the fatherless, and instead of an husband unto their mother: so shalt thou be as the son of the most High, and he shall love thee more than thy mother doth. [11] Wisdom exalteth her children, and layeth hold of them that seek her. [12] He that loveth her loveth life; and they that seek to her early shall be filled with joy. [13] He that holdeth her fast shall inherit glory; and wheresoever she entereth, the Lord will bless. [14] They that serve her shall minister to the Holy One: and them that love her the Lord doth love. [15] Whoso giveth ear unto her shall judge the nations: and he that attendeth unto her shall dwell securely. [16] If a man commit himself unto her, he shall inherit her; and his generation shall hold her in possession. [17] For at the first she will walk with him by crooked ways, and bring fear and dread upon him, and torment him with her discipline, until she may trust his soul, and try him by her laws. [18] Then will she return the straight way unto him, and comfort him, and shew him her secrets. [19] But if he go wrong, she will forsake him, and give him over to his own ruin. [20] Observe the opportunity, and beware of evil; and be not ashamed when it concerneth thy soul. [21] For there is a shame that bringeth sin; and there is a shame which is glory and grace. [22] Accept no person against thy soul, and let not the reverence of any man cause thee to fall. [23] And refrain not to speak, when there is occasion to do good, and hide not thy wisdom in her beauty. [24] For by speech wisdom shall be known: and learning by the word of the tongue. [25] In no wise speak against the truth; but be abashed of the error of thine ignorance. [26] Be not ashamed to confess thy sins; and force not the course of the river. [27] Make not thyself an underling to a foolish man; neither accept the person of the mighty. [28] Strive for the truth unto death, and the Lord shall fight for thee. [29] Be not hasty in thy tongue, and in thy deeds slack and remiss. [30] Be not as a lion in thy house, nor frantick among thy servants. [31] Let not thine hand be stretched out to receive, and shut when thou shouldest repay. Sir.5 [1] Set thy heart upon thy goods; and say not, I have enough for my life. [2] Follow not thine own mind and thy strength, to walk in the ways of thy heart: [3] And say not, Who shall controul me for my works? for the Lord will surely revenge thy pride. [4] Say not, I have sinned, and what harm hath happened unto me? for the Lord is longsuffering, he will in no wise let thee go. [5] Concerning propitiation, be not without fear to add sin unto sin: [6] And say not His mercy is great; he will be pacified for the multitude of my sins: for mercy and wrath come from him, and his indignation resteth upon sinners. [7] Make no tarrying to turn to the Lord, and put not off from day to day: for suddenly shall the wrath of the Lord come forth, and in thy security thou shalt be destroyed, and perish in the day of vengeance. [8] Set not thine heart upon goods unjustly gotten, for they shall not profit thee in the day of calamity. [9] Winnow not with every wind, and go not into every way: for so doth the sinner that hath a double tongue. [10] Be stedfast in thy understanding; and let thy word be the same. [11] Be swift to hear; and let thy life be sincere; and with patience give answer. [12] If thou hast understanding, answer thy neighbour; if not, lay thy hand upon thy mouth. [13] Honour and shame is in talk: and the tongue of man is his fall. [14] Be not called a whisperer, and lie not in wait with thy tongue: for a foul shame is upon the thief, and an evil condemnation upon the double tongue. [15] Be not ignorant of any thing in a great matter or a small. Sir.6 [1] Instead of a friend become not an enemy; for [thereby] thou shalt inherit an ill name, shame, and reproach: even so shall a sinner that hath a double tongue. [2] Extol not thyself in the counsel of thine own heart; that thy soul be not torn in pieces as a bull [straying alone.] [3] Thou shalt eat up thy leaves, and lose thy fruit, and leave thyself as a dry tree. [4] A wicked soul shall destroy him that hath it, and shall make him to be laughed to scorn of his enemies. [5] Sweet language will multiply friends: and a fairspeaking tongue will increase kind greetings. [6] Be in peace with many: nevertheless have but one counsellor of a thousand. [7] If thou wouldest get a friend, prove him first and be not hasty to credit him. [8] For some man is a friend for his own occasion, and will not abide in the day of thy trouble. [9] And there is a friend, who being turned to enmity, and strife will discover thy reproach. [10] Again, some friend is a companion at the table, and will not continue in the day of thy affliction. [11] But in thy prosperity he will be as thyself, and will be bold over thy servants. [12] If thou be brought low, he will be against thee, and will hide himself from thy face. [13] Separate thyself from thine enemies, and take heed of thy friends. [14] A faithfull friend is a strong defence: and he that hath found such an one hath found a treasure. [15] Nothing doth countervail a faithful friend, and his excellency is invaluable. [16] A faithful friend is the medicine of life; and they that fear the Lord shall find him. [17] Whoso feareth the Lord shall direct his friendship aright: for as he is, so shall his neighbour be also. [18] My son, gather instruction from thy youth up: so shalt thou find wisdom till thine old age. [19] Come unto her as one that ploweth and soweth, and wait for her good fruits: for thou shalt not toil much in labouring about her, but thou shalt eat of her fruits right soon. [20] She is very unpleasant to the unlearned: he that is without understanding will not remain with her. [21] She will lie upon him as a mighty stone of trial; and he will cast her from him ere it be long. [22] For wisdom is according to her name, and she is not manifest unto many. [23] Give ear, my son, receive my advice, and refuse not my counsel, [24] And put thy feet into her fetters, and thy neck into her chain. [25] Bow down thy shoulder, and bear her, and be not grieved with her bonds. [26] Come unto her with thy whole heart, and keep her ways with all thy power. [27] Search, and seek, and she shall be made known unto thee: and when thou hast got hold of her, let her not go. [28] For at the last thou shalt find her rest, and that shall be turned to thy joy. [29] Then shall her fetters be a strong defence for thee, and her chains a robe of glory. [30] For there is a golden ornament upon her, and her bands are purple lace. [31] Thou shalt put her on as a robe of honour, and shalt put her about thee as a crown of joy. [32] My son, if thou wilt, thou shalt be taught: and if thou wilt apply thy mind, thou shalt be prudent. [33] If thou love to hear, thou shalt receive understanding: and if thou bow thine ear, thou shalt be wise, [34] Stand in the multitude of the elders; and cleave unto him that is wise. [35] Be willing to hear every godly discourse; and let not the parables of understanding escape thee. [36] And if thou seest a man of understanding, get thee betimes unto him, and let thy foot wear the steps of his door. [37] Let thy mind be upon the ordinances of the Lord and meditate continually in his commandments: he shall establish thine heart, and give thee wisdom at thine owns desire. Sir.7 [1] Do no evil, so shall no harm come unto thee. [2] Depart from the unjust, and iniquity shall turn away from thee. [3] My son, sow not upon the furrows of unrighteousness, and thou shalt not reap them sevenfold. [4] Seek not of the Lord preeminence, neither of the king the seat of honour. [5] justify not thyself before the Lord; and boast not of thy wisdom before the king. [6] Seek not to be judge, being not able to take away iniquity; lest at any time thou fear the person of the mighty, an stumblingblock in the way of thy uprightness. [7] Offend not against the multitude of a city, and then thou shalt not cast thyself down among the people. [8] Bind not one sin upon another; for in one thou shalt not be unpunished. [9] Say not, God will look upon the multitude of my oblations, and when I offer to the most high God, he will accept it. [10] Be not fainthearted when thou makest thy prayer, and neglect not to give alms. [11] Laugh no man to scorn in the bitterness of his soul: for there is one which humbleth and exalteth. [12] Devise not a lie against thy brother; neither do the like to thy friend. [13] Use not to make any manner of lie: for the custom thereof is not good. [14] Use not many words in a multitude of elders, and make not much babbling when thou prayest. [15] Hate not laborious work, neither husbandry, which the most High hath ordained. [16] Number not thyself among the multitude of sinners, but remember that wrath will not tarry long. [17] Humble thyself greatly: for the vengeance of the ungodly is fire and worms. [18] Change not a friend for any good by no means; neither a faithful brother for the gold of Ophir. [19] Forego not a wise and good woman: for her grace is above gold. [20] Whereas thy servant worketh truly, entreat him not evil. nor the hireling that bestoweth himself wholly for thee. [21] Let thy soul love a good servant, and defraud him not of liberty. [22] Hast thou cattle? have an eye to them: and if they be for thy profit, keep them with thee. [23] Hast thou children? instruct them, and bow down their neck from their youth. [24] Hast thou daughters? have a care of their body, and shew not thyself cheerful toward them. [25] Marry thy daughter, and so shalt thou have performed a weighty matter: but give her to a man of understanding. [26] Hast thou a wife after thy mind? forsake her not: but give not thyself over to a light woman. [27] Honour thy father with thy whole heart, and forget not the sorrows of thy mother. [28] Remember that thou wast begotten of them; and how canst thou recompense them the things that they have done for thee? [29] Fear the Lord with all thy soul, and reverence his priests. [30] Love him that made thee with all thy strength, and forsake not his ministers. [31] Fear the Lord, and honor the priest; and give him his portion, as it is commanded thee; the firstfruits, and the trespass offering, and the gift of the shoulders, and the sacrifice of sanctification, and the firstfruits of the holy things. [32] And stretch thine hand unto the poor, that thy blessing may be perfected. [33] A gift hath grace in the sight of every man living; and for the dead detain it not. [34] Fail not to be with them that weep, and mourn with them that mourn. [35] Be not slow to visit the sick: fir that shall make thee to be beloved. [36] Whatsoever thou takest in hand, remember the end, and thou shalt never do amiss. Sir.8 [1] Strive not with a mighty man' lest thou fall into his hands. [2] Be not at variance with a rich man, lest he overweigh thee: for gold hath destroyed many, and perverted the hearts of kings. [3] Strive not with a man that is full of tongue, and heap not wood upon his fire. [4] Jest not with a rude man, lest thy ancestors be disgraced. [5] Reproach not a man that turneth from sin, but remember that we are all worthy of punishment. [6] Dishonour not a man in his old age: for even some of us wax old. [7] Rejoice not over thy greatest enemy being dead, but remember that we die all. [8] Despise not the discourse of the wise, but acquaint thyself with their proverbs: for of them thou shalt learn instruction, and how to serve great men with ease. [9] Miss not the discourse of the elders: for they also learned of their fathers, and of them thou shalt learn understanding, and to give answer as need requireth. [10] Kindle not the coals of a sinner, lest thou be burnt with the flame of his fire. [11] Rise not up [in anger] at the presence of an injurious person, lest he lie in wait to entrap thee in thy words [12] Lend not unto him that is mightier than thyself; for if thou lendest him, count it but lost. [13] Be not surety above thy power: for if thou be surety, take care to pay it. [14] Go not to law with a judge; for they will judge for him according to his honour. [15] Travel not by the way with a bold fellow, lest he become grievous unto thee: for he will do according to his own will, and thou shalt perish with him through his folly. [16] Strive not with an angry man, and go not with him into a solitary place: for blood is as nothing in his sight, and where there is no help, he will overthrow thee. [17] Consult not with a fool; for he cannot keep counsel. [18] Do no secret thing before a stranger; for thou knowest not what he will bring forth. [19] Open not thine heart to every man, lest he requite thee with a shrewd turn. Sir.9 [1] Be not jealous over the wife of thy bosom, and teach her not an evil lesson against thyself. [2] Give not thy soul unto a woman to set her foot upon thy substance. [3] Meet not with an harlot, lest thou fall into her snares. [4] Use not much the company of a woman that is a singer, lest thou be taken with her attempts. [5] Gaze not on a maid, that thou fall not by those things that are precious in her. [6] Give not thy soul unto harlots, that thou lose not thine inheritance. [7] Look not round about thee in the streets of the city, neither wander thou in the solitary place thereof. [8] Turn away thine eye from a beautiful woman, and look not upon another's beauty; for many have been deceived by the beauty of a woman; for herewith love is kindled as a fire. [9] Sit not at all with another man's wife, nor sit down with her in thine arms, and spend not thy money with her at the wine; lest thine heart incline unto her, and so through thy desire thou fall into destruction. [10] Forsake not an old friend; for the new is not comparable to him: a new friend is as new wine; when it is old, thou shalt drink it with pleasure. [11] Envy not the glory of a sinner: for thou knowest not what shall be his end. [12] Delight not in the thing that the ungodly have pleasure in; but remember they shall not go unpunished unto their grave. [13] Keep thee far from the man that hath power to kill; so shalt thou not doubt the fear of death: and if thou come unto him, make no fault, lest he take away thy life presently: remember that thou goest in the midst of snares, and that thou walkest upon the battlements of the city. [14] As near as thou canst, guess at thy neighbour, and consult with the wise. [15] Let thy talk be with the wise, and all thy communication in the law of the most High. [16] And let just men eat and drink with thee; and let thy glorying be in the fear of the Lord. [17] For the hand of the artificer the work shall be commended: and the wise ruler of the people for his speech. [18] A man of an ill tongue is dangerous in his city; and he that is rash in his talk shall be hated. Sir.10 [1] A wise judge will instruct his people; and the government of a prudent man is well ordered. [2] As the judge of the people is himself, so are his officers; and what manner of man the ruler of the city is, such are all they that dwell therein. [3] An unwise king destroyeth his people; but through the prudence of them which are in authority the city shall be inhabited. [4] The power of the earth is in the hand of the Lord, and in due time he will set over it one that is profitable. [5] In the hand of God is the prosperity of man: and upon the person of the scribe shall he lay his honour. [6] Bear not hatred to thy neighbour for every wrong; and do nothing at all by injurious practices. [7] Pride is hateful before God and man: and by both doth one commit iniquity. [8] Because of unrighteous dealings, injuries, and riches got by deceit, the kingdom is translated from one people to another. [9] Why is earth and ashes proud? There is not a more wicked thing than a covetous man: for such an one setteth his own soul to sale; because while he liveth he casteth away his bowels. [10] The physician cutteth off a long disease; and he that is to day a king to morrow shall die. [11] For when a man is dead, he shall inherit creeping things, beasts, and worms. [12] The beginning of pride is when one departeth from God, and his heart is turned away from his Maker. [13] For pride is the beginning of sin, and he that hath it shall pour out abomination: and therefore the Lord brought upon them strange calamities, and overthrew them utterly. [14] The Lord hath cast down the thrones of proud princes, and set up the meek in their stead. [15] The Lord hath plucked up the roots of the proud nations, and planted the lowly in their place. [16] The Lord overthrew countries of the heathen, and destroyed them to the foundations of the earth. [17] He took some of them away, and destroyed them, and hath made their memorial to cease from the earth. [18] Pride was not made for men, nor furious anger for them that are born of a woman. [19] They that fear the Lord are a sure seed, and they that love him an honourable plant: they that regard not the law are a dishonourable seed; they that transgress the commandments are a deceivable seed. [20] Among brethren he that is chief is honorable; so are they that fear the Lord in his eyes. [21] The fear of the Lord goeth before the obtaining of authority: but roughness and pride is the losing thereof. [22] Whether he be rich, noble, or poor, their glory is the fear of the Lord. [23] It is not meet to despise the poor man that hath understanding; neither is it convenient to magnify a sinful man. [24] Great men, and judges, and potentates, shall be honoured; yet is there none of them greater than he that feareth the Lord. [25] Unto the servant that is wise shall they that are free do service: and he that hath knowledge will not grudge when he is reformed. [26] Be not overwise in doing thy business; and boast not thyself in the time of thy distress. [27] Better is he that laboureth, and aboundeth in all things, than he that boasteth himself, and wanteth bread. [28] My son, glorify thy soul in meekness, and give it honour according to the dignity thereof. [29] Who will justify him that sinneth against his own soul? and who will honour him that dishonoureth his own life? [30] The poor man is honoured for his skill, and the rich man is honoured for his riches. [31] He that is honoured in poverty, how much more in riches? and he that is dishonourable in riches, how much more in poverty? Sir.11 [1] Wisdom lifteth up the head of him that is of low degree, and maketh him to sit among great men. [2] Commend not a man for his beauty; neither abhor a man for his outward appearance. [3] The bee is little among such as fly; but her fruit is the chief of sweet things. [4] Boast not of thy clothing and raiment, and exalt not thyself in the day of honour: for the works of the Lord are wonderful, and his works among men are hidden. [5] Many kings have sat down upon the ground; and one that was never thought of hath worn the crown. [6] Many mighty men have been greatly disgraced; and the honourable delivered into other men's hands. [7] Blame not before thou hast examined the truth: understand first, and then rebuke. [8] Answer not before thou hast heard the cause: neither interrupt men in the midst of their talk. [9] Strive not in a matter that concerneth thee not; and sit not in judgment with sinners. [10] My son, meddle not with many matters: for if thou meddle much, thou shalt not be innocent; and if thou follow after, thou shalt not obtain, neither shalt thou escape by fleeing. [11] There is one that laboureth, and taketh pains, and maketh haste, and is so much the more behind. [12] Again, there is another that is slow, and hath need of help, wanting ability, and full of poverty; yet the eye of the Lord looked upon him for good, and set him up from his low estate, [13] And lifted up his head from misery; so that many that saw from him is peace over all the [14] Prosperity and adversity, life and death, poverty and riches, come of the Lord. [15] Wisdom, knowledge, and understanding of the law, are of the Lord: love, and the way of good works, are from him. [16] Error and darkness had their beginning together with sinners: and evil shall wax old with them that glory therein. [17] The gift of the Lord remaineth with the ungodly, and his favour bringeth prosperity for ever. [18] There is that waxeth rich by his wariness and pinching, and this his the portion of his reward: [19] Whereas he saith, I have found rest, and now will eat continually of my goods; and yet he knoweth not what time shall come upon him, and that he must leave those things to others, and die. [20] Be stedfast in thy covenant, and be conversant therein, and wax old in thy work. [21] Marvel not at the works of sinners; but trust in the Lord, and abide in thy labour: for it is an easy thing in the sight of the Lord on the sudden to make a poor man rich. [22] The blessing of the Lord is in the reward of the godly, and suddenly he maketh his blessing flourish. [23] Say not, What profit is there of my service? and what good things shall I have hereafter? [24] Again, say not, I have enough, and possess many things, and what evil shall I have hereafter? [25] In the day of prosperity there is a forgetfulness of affliction: and in the day of affliction there is no more remembrance of prosperity. [26] For it is an easy thing unto the Lord in the day of death to reward a man according to his ways. [27] The affliction of an hour maketh a man forget pleasure: and in his end his deeds shall be discovered. [28] Judge none blessed before his death: for a man shall be known in his children. [29] Bring not every man into thine house: for the deceitful man hath many trains. [30] Like as a partridge taken [and kept] in a cage, so is the heart of the proud; and like as a spy, watcheth he for thy fall: [31] For he lieth in wait, and turneth good into evil, and in things worthy praise will lay blame upon thee. [32] Of a spark of fire a heap of coals is kindled: and a sinful man layeth wait for blood. [33] Take heed of a mischievous man, for he worketh wickedness; lest he bring upon thee a perpetual blot. [34] Receive a stranger into thine house, and he will disturb thee, and turn thee out of thine own. Sir.12 [1] When thou wilt do good know to whom thou doest it; so shalt thou be thanked for thy benefits. [2] Do good to the godly man, and thou shalt find a recompence; and if not from him, yet from the most High. [3] There can no good come to him that is always occupied in evil, nor to him that giveth no alms. [4] Give to the godly man, and help not a sinner. [5] Do well unto him that is lowly, but give not to the ungodly: hold back thy bread, and give it not unto him, lest he overmaster thee thereby: for [else] thou shalt receive twice as much evil for all the good thou shalt have done unto him. [6] For the most High hateth sinners, and will repay vengeance unto the ungodly, and keepeth them against the mighty day of their punishment. [7] Give unto the good, and help not the sinner. [8] A friend cannot be known in prosperity: and an enemy cannot be hidden in adversity. [9] In the prosperity of a man enemies will be grieved: but in his adversity even a friend will depart. [10] Never trust thine enemy: for like as iron rusteth, so is his wickedness. [11] Though he humble himself, and go crouching, yet take good heed and beware of him, and thou shalt be unto him as if thou hadst wiped a lookingglass, and thou shalt know that his rust hath not been altogether wiped away. [12] Set him not by thee, lest, when he hath overthrown thee, he stand up in thy place; neither let him sit at thy right hand, lest he seek to take thy seat, and thou at the last remember my words, and be pricked therewith. [13] Who will pity a charmer that is bitten with a serpent, or any such as come nigh wild beasts? [14] So one that goeth to a sinner, and is defiled with him in his sins, who will pity? [15] For a while he will abide with thee, but if thou begin to fall, he will not tarry. [16] An enemy speaketh sweetly with his lips, but in his heart he imagineth how to throw thee into a pit: he will weep with his eyes, but if he find opportunity, he will not be satisfied with blood. [17] If adversity come upon thee, thou shalt find him there first; and though he pretend to help thee, yet shall he undermine thee. [18] He will shake his head, and clap his hands, and whisper much, and change his countenance. Sir.13 [1] He that toucheth pitch shall be defiled therewith; and he that hath fellowship with a proud man shall be like unto him. [2] Burden not thyself above thy power while thou livest; and have no fellowship with one that is mightier and richer than thyself: for how agree the kettle and the earthen pot together? for if the one be smitten against the other, it shall be broken. [3] The rich man hath done wrong, and yet he threateneth withal: the poor is wronged, and he must intreat also. [4] If thou be for his profit, he will use thee: but if thou have nothing, he will forsake thee. [5] If thou have any thing, he will live with thee: yea, he will make thee bare, and will not be sorry for it. [6] If he have need of thee, he will deceive thee, and smile upon thee, and put thee in hope; he will speak thee fair, and say, What wantest thou? [7] And he will shame thee by his meats, until he have drawn thee dry twice or thrice, and at the last he will laugh thee to scorn afterward, when he seeth thee, he will forsake thee, and shake his head at thee. [8] Beware that thou be not deceived and brought down in thy jollity. [9] If thou be invited of a mighty man, withdraw thyself, and so much the more will he invite thee. [10] Press thou not upon him, lest thou be put back; stand not far off, lest thou be forgotten. [11] Affect not to be made equal unto him in talk, and believe not his many words: for with much communication will he tempt thee, and smiling upon thee will get out thy secrets: [12] But cruelly he will lay up thy words, and will not spare to do thee hurt, and to put thee in prison. [13] Observe, and take good heed, for thou walkest in peril of thy overthrowing: when thou hearest these things, awake in thy sleep. [14] Love the Lord all thy life, and call upon him for thy salvation. [15] Every beast loveth his like, and every man loveth his neighbor. [16] All flesh consorteth according to kind, and a man will cleave to his like. [17] What fellowship hath the wolf with the lamb? so the sinner with the godly. [18] What agreement is there between the hyena and a dog? and what peace between the rich and the poor? [19] As the wild ass is the lion's prey in the wilderness: so the rich eat up the poor. [20] As the proud hate humility: so doth the rich abhor the poor. [21] A rich man beginning to fall is held up of his friends: but a poor man being down is thrust away by his friends. [22] When a rich man is fallen, he hath many helpers: he speaketh things not to be spoken, and yet men justify him: the poor man slipped, and yet they rebuked him too; he spake wisely, and could have no place. [23] When a rich man speaketh, every man holdeth his tongue, and, look, what he saith, they extol it to the clouds: but if the poor man speak, they say, What fellow is this? and if he stumble, they will help to overthrow him. [24] Riches are good unto him that hath no sin, and poverty is evil in the mouth of the ungodly. [25] The heart of a man changeth his countenance, whether it be for good or evil: and a merry heart maketh a cheerful countenance. [26] A cheerful countenance is a token of a heart that is in prosperity; and the finding out of parables is a wearisome labour of the mind. Sir.14 [1] Blessed is the man that hath not slipped with his mouth, and is not pricked with the multitude of sins. [2] Blessed is he whose conscience hath not condemned him, and who is not fallen from his hope in the Lord. [3] Riches are not comely for a niggard: and what should an envious man do with money? [4] He that gathereth by defrauding his own soul gathereth for others, that shall spend his goods riotously. [5] He that is evil to himself, to whom will he be good? he shall not take pleasure in his goods. [6]

There is none worse than he that envieth himself; and this is a recompence of his wickedness. [7] And if he doeth good, he doeth it unwillingly; and at the last he will declare his wickedness. [8] The envious man hath a wicked eye; he turneth away his face, and despiseth men. [9] A covetous man's eye is not satisfied with his portion; and the iniquity of the wicked drieth up his soul. [10] A wicked eye envieth [his] bread, and he is a niggard at his table. [11] My son, according to thy ability do good to thyself, and give the Lord his due offering. [12] Remember that death will not be long in coming, and that the covenant of the grave is not shewed unto thee. [13] Do good unto thy friend before thou die, and according to thy ability stretch out thy hand and give to him. [14] Defraud not thyself of the good day, and let not the part of a good desire overpass thee. [15] Shalt thou not leave thy travails unto another? and thy labours to be divided by lot? [16] Give, and take, and sanctify thy soul; for there is no seeking of dainties in the grave. [17] All flesh waxeth old as a garment: for the covenant from the beginning is, Thou shalt die the death. [18] As of the green leaves on a thick tree, some fall, and some grow; so is the generation of flesh and blood, one cometh to an end, and another is born. [19] Every work rotteth and consumeth away, and the worker thereof shall go withal. [20] Blessed is the man that doth meditate good things in wisdom, and that reasoneth of holy things by his understanding. ing. [21] He that considereth her ways in his heart shall also have understanding in her secrets. [22] Go after her as one that traceth, and lie in wait in her ways. [23] He that prieth in at her windows shall also hearken at her doors. [24] He that doth lodge near her house shall also fasten a pin in her walls. [25] He shall pitch his tent nigh unto her, and shall lodge in a lodging where good things are. [26] He shall set his children under her shelter, and shall lodge under her branches. [27] By her he shall be covered from heat, and in her glory shall he dwell. Sir.15 [1] He that feareth the Lord will do good, and he that hath the knowledge of the law shall obtain her. [2] And as a mother shall she meet him, and receive him as a wife married of a virgin. [3] With the bread of understanding shall she feed him, and give him the water of wisdom to drink. [4] He shall be stayed upon her, and shall not be moved; and shall rely upon her, and shall not be confounded. [5] She shall exalt him above his neighbours, and in the midst of the congregation shall she open his mouth. [6] He shall find joy and a crown of gladness, and she shall cause him to inherit an everlasting name. [7] But foolish men shall not attain unto her, and sinners shall not see her. [8] For she is far from pride, and men that are liars cannot remember her. [9] Praise is not seemly in the mouth of a sinner, for it was not sent him of the Lord. [10] For praise shall be uttered in wisdom, and the Lord will prosper it. [11] Say not thou, It is through the Lord that I fell away: for thou oughtest not to do the things that he hateth. [12] Say not thou, He hath caused me to err: for he hath no need of the sinful man. [13] The Lord hateth all abomination; and they that fear God love it not. [14] He himself made man from the beginning, and left him in the hand of his counsel; [15] If thou wilt, to keep the commandments, and to perform acceptable faithfulness. [16] He hath set fire and water before thee: stretch forth thy hand unto whether thou wilt. [17] Before man is life and death; and whether him liketh shall be given him. [18] For the wisdom of the Lord is great, and he is mighty in power, and beholdeth all things: [19] And his eyes are upon them that fear him, and he knoweth every work of man. [20] He hath commanded no man to do wickedly, neither hath he given any man licence to sin. Sir.16 [1] Desire not a multitude of unprofitable children, neither delight in ungodly sons. [2] Though they multiply, rejoice not in them, except the fear of the Lord be with them. [3] Trust not thou in their life, neither respect their multitude: for one that is just is better than a thousand; and better it is to die without children, than to have them that are ungodly. [4] For by one that hath understanding shall the city be replenished: but the kindred of the wicked shall speedily become desolate. [5] Many such things have I seen with mine eyes, and mine ear hath heard greater things than these. [6] In the congregation of the ungodly shall a fire be kindled; and in a rebellious nation wrath is set on fire. [7] He was not pacified toward the old giants, who fell away in the strength of their foolishness. [8] Neither spared he the place where Lot sojourned, but abhorred them for their pride. [9] He pitied not the people of perdition, who were taken away in their sins: [10] Nor the six hundred thousand footmen, who were gathered together in the hardness of their hearts. [11] And if there be one stiffnecked among the people, it is marvel if he escape unpunished: for mercy and wrath are with him; he is mighty to forgive, and to pour out displeasure. [12] As his mercy is great, so is his correction also: he judgeth a man according to his works [13] The sinner shall not escape with his spoils: and the patience of the godly shall not be frustrate. [14] Make way for every work of mercy: for every man shall find according to his works. [15] The Lord hardened Pharaoh, that he should not know him, that his powerful works might be known to the world. [16] His mercy is manifest to every creature; and he hath separated his light from the darkness with an adamant. [17] Say not thou, I will hide myself from the Lord: shall any remember me from above? I shall not be remembered among so many people: for what is my soul among such an infinite number of creatures? [18] Behold, the heaven, and the heaven of heavens, the deep, and the earth, and all that therein is, shall be moved when he shall visit. [19] The mountains also and foundations of the earth be shaken with trembling, when the Lord looketh upon them. [20] No heart can think upon these things worthily: and who is able to conceive his ways? [21] It is a tempest which no man can see: for the most part of his works are hid. [22] Who can declare the works of his justice? or who can endure them? for his covenant is afar off, and the trial of all things is in the end. [23] He that wanteth understanding will think upon vain things: and a foolish man erring imagineth follies. [24] by son, hearken unto me, and learn knowledge, and mark my words with thy heart. [25] I will shew forth doctrine in weight, and declare his knowledge exactly. [26] The works of the Lord are done in judgment from the beginning: and from the time he made them he disposed the parts thereof. [27] He garnished his works for ever, and in his hand are the chief of them unto all generations: they neither labour, nor are weary, nor cease from their works. [28] None of them hindereth another, and they shall never disobey his word. [29] After this the Lord looked upon the earth, and filled it with his blessings. [30] With all manner of living things hath he covered the face thereof; and they shall return into it again. Sir.17 [1] The Lord created man of the earth, and turned him into it again. [2] He gave them few days, and a short time, and power also over the things therein. [3] He endued them with strength by themselves, and made them according to his image, [4] And put the fear of man upon all flesh, and gave him dominion over beasts and fowls. [5] They received the use of the five operations of the Lord, and in the sixth place he imparted them understanding, and in the seventh speech, an interpreter of the cogitations thereof.] [6] Counsel, and a tongue, and eyes, ears, and a heart, gave he them to understand. [7] Withal he filled them with the knowledge of understanding, and shewed them good and evil. [8] He set his eye upon their hearts, that he might shew them the greatness of his works. [9] He gave them to glory in his marvellous acts for ever, that they might declare his works with understanding. [10] And the elect shall praise his holy name. [11] Beside this he gave them knowledge, and the law of life for an heritage. [12] He made an everlasting covenant with them, and shewed them his judgments. [13] Their eyes saw the majesty of his glory, and their ears heard his glorious voice. [14] And he said unto them, Beware of all unrighteousness; and he gave every man commandment concerning his neighbour. [15] Their ways are ever before him, and shall not be hid from his eyes. [16] Every man from his youth is given to evil; neither could they make to themselves fleshy hearts for stony. [17] For in the division of the nations of the whole earth he set a ruler over every people; but Israel is the Lord's portion: [18] Whom, being his firstborn, he nourisheth with discipline, and giving him the light of his love doth not forsake him. [19] Therefore all their works are as the sun before him, and his eyes are continually upon their ways. [20] None of their unrighteous deeds are hid from him, but all their sins are before the Lord [21] But the Lord being gracious and knowing his workmanship, neither left nor forsook them, but spared them. [22] The alms of a man is as a signet with him, and he will keep the good deeds of man as the apple of the eye, and give repentance to his sons and daughters. [23] Afterwards he will rise up and reward them, and render their recompence upon their heads. [24] But unto them that repent, he granted them return, and comforted those that failed in patience. [25] Return unto the Lord, and forsake thy sins, make thy prayer before his face, and offend less. [26] Turn again to the most High, and turn away from iniquity: for he will lead thee out of darkness into the light of health, and hate thou abomination vehemently. [27] Who shall praise the most High in the grave, instead of them which live and give thanks? [28] Thanksgiving perisheth from the dead, as from one that is not: the living and sound in heart shall praise the Lord. [29] How great is the lovingkindness of the Lord our God, and his compassion unto such as turn unto him in holiness! [30] For all things cannot be in men, because the son of man is not immortal. [31] What is brighter than the sun? yet the light thereof faileth; and flesh and blood will imagine evil. [32] He vieweth the power of the height of heaven; and all men are but earth and ashes. Sir.18 [1] He that liveth for ever Hath created all things in general. [2] The Lord only is righteous, and there is none other but he, [3] Who governeth the world with the palm of his hand, and all things obey his will: for he is the King of all, by his power dividing holy things among them from profane. [4] To whom hath he given power to declare his works? and who shall find out his noble acts? [5] Who shall number the strength of his majesty? and who shall also tell out his mercies? [6] As for the wondrous works of the Lord, there may nothing be taken from them, neither may any thing be put unto them, neither can the ground of them be found out. [7] When a man hath done, then he beginneth; and when he leaveth off, then he shall be doubtful. [8] What is man, and whereto serveth he? what is his good, and what is his evil? [9] The number of a man's days at the most are an hundred years. [10] As a drop of water unto the sea, and a gravelstone in comparison of the sand; so are a thousand years to the days of eternity. [11] Therefore is God patient with them, and poureth forth his mercy upon them. [12] He saw and perceived their end to be evil; therefore he multiplied his compassion. [13] The mercy of man is toward his neighbour; but the mercy of the Lord is upon all flesh: he reproveth, and nurtureth, and teacheth and bringeth again, as a shepherd his flock. [14] He hath mercy on them that receive discipline, and that diligently seek after his judgments. [15] My son, blemish not thy good deeds, neither use uncomfortable words when thou givest any thing. [16] Shall not the dew asswage the heat? so is a word better than a gift. [17] Lo, is not a word better than a gift? but both are with a gracious man. [18] A fool will upbraid churlishly, and a gift of the envious consumeth the eyes. [19] Learn before thou speak, and use physick or ever thou be sick. [20] Before judgment examine thyself, and in the day of visitation thou shalt find mercy. [21] Humble thyself before thou be sick, and in the time of sins shew repentance. [22] Let nothing hinder thee to pay thy vow in due time, and defer not until death to be justified. [23] Before thou prayest, prepare thyself; and be not as one that tempteth the Lord. [24] Think upon the wrath that shall be at the end, and the time of vengeance, when he shall turn away his face. [25] When thou hast enough, remember the time of hunger: and when thou art rich, think upon poverty and need. [26] From the morning until the evening the time is changed, and all things are soon done before the Lord. [27] A wise man will fear in every thing, and in the day of sinning he will beware of offence: but a fool will not observe time. [28] Every man of understanding knoweth wisdom, and will give praise unto him that found her. [29] They that were of understanding in sayings became also wise themselves, and poured forth exquisite parables. [30] Go not after thy lusts, but refrain thyself from thine appetites. [31] If thou givest thy soul the desires that please her, she will make thee a laughingstock to thine enemies that malign thee. [32] Take not pleasure in much good cheer, neither be tied to the expence thereof. [33] Be not made a beggar by banqueting upon borrowing, when thou hast nothing in thy purse: for thou shalt lie in wait for thine own life, and be talked on. Sir.19 [1] A labouring man that A is given to drunkenness shall not be rich: and he that contemneth small things shall fall by little and little. [2] Wine and women will make men of understanding to fall away: and he that cleaveth to harlots will become impudent. [3] Moths and worms shall have him to heritage, and a bold man shall be taken away. [4] He that is hasty to give credit is lightminded; and he that sinneth shall offend against his own soul. [5] Whoso taketh pleasure in wickedness shall be condemned: but he that resisteth pleasures crowneth his life. [6] He that can rule his tongue shall live without strife; and he that hateth babbling shall have less evil. [7] Rehearse not unto another that which is told unto thee, and thou shalt fare never the worse. [8] Whether it be to friend or foe, talk not of other men's lives; and if thou canst without offence, reveal them not. [9] For he heard and observed thee, and when time cometh he will hate thee. [10] If thou hast heard a word, let it die with thee; and be bold, it will not burst thee. [11] A fool travaileth with a word, as a woman in labour of a child. [12] As an arrow that sticketh in a man's thigh, so is a word within a fool's belly. [13] Admonish a friend, it may be he hath not done it: and if he have done it, that he do it no more. [14] Admonish thy friend, it may be he hath not said it: and if he have, that he speak it not again. [15] Admonish a friend: for many times it is a slander, and believe not every tale. [16] There is one that slippeth in his speech, but not from his heart; and who is he that hath not offended with his tongue? [17] Admonish thy neighbour before thou threaten him; and not being angry, give place to the law of the most High. [18] The fear of the Lord is the first step to be accepted [of him,] and wisdom obtaineth his love. [19] The knowledge of the commandments of the Lord is the doctrine of life: and they that do things that please him shall receive the fruit of the tree of immortality. [20] The fear of the Lord is all wisdom; and in all wisdom is the performance of the law, and the knowledge of his omnipotency. [21] If a servant say to his master, I will not do as it pleaseth thee; though afterward he do it, he angereth him that nourisheth him. [22] The knowledge of wickedness is not wisdom, neither at any time the counsel of sinners prudence. [23] There is a wickedness, and the same an abomination; and there is a fool wanting in wisdom. [24] He that hath small understanding, and feareth God, is better than one that hath much wisdom, and transgresseth the law of the most High. [25] There is an exquisite subtilty, and the same is unjust; and there is one that turneth aside to make judgment appear; and there is a wise man that justifieth in judgment. [26] There is a wicked man that hangeth down his head sadly; but inwardly he is full of deceit, [27] Casting down his countenance, and making as if he heard not: where he is not known, he will do thee a mischief before thou be aware. [28] And if for want of power he be hindered from sinning, yet when he findeth opportunity he will do evil. [29] A man may be known by his look, and one that hath understanding by his countenance, when thou meetest him. [30] A man's attire, and excessive laughter, and gait, shew what he is. Sir.20 [1] There is a reproof that is not comely: again, some man holdeth his tongue, and he is wise. [2] It is much better to reprove, than to be angry secretly: and he that confesseth his fault shall be preserved from hurt. [3] How good is it, when thou art reproved, to shew repentance! for so shalt thou escape wilful sin. [4] As is the lust of an eunuch to deflower a virgin; so is he that executeth judgment with violence. [5] There is one that keepeth silence, and is found wise: and another by much babbling becometh hateful. [6] Some man holdeth his tongue, because he hath not to answer: and some keepeth silence, knowing his time. [7] A wise man will hold his tongue till he see opportunity: but a babbler and a fool will regard no time. [8] He that useth many words shall be abhorred; and he that taketh to himself authority therein shall be hated. [9] There is a sinner that hath good success in evil things; and there is a gain that turneth to loss. [10] There is a gift that shall not profit thee; and there is a gift whose recompence is double. [11] There is an abasement because of glory; and there is that lifteth up his head from a low estate. [12] There is that buyeth much for a little, and repayeth it sevenfold. [13] A wise man by his words maketh him beloved: but the graces of fools shall be poured out. [14] The gift of a fool shall do thee no good when thou hast it; neither yet of the envious for his necessity: for he looketh to receive many things for one. [15] He giveth little, and upbraideth much; he openeth his mouth like a crier; to day he lendeth, and to morrow will he ask it again: such an one is to be hated of God and man. [16] The fool saith, I have no friends, I have no thank for all my good deeds, and they that eat my bread speak evil of me. [17] How oft, and of how many shall he be laughed to scorn! for he knoweth not aright what it is to have; and it is all one unto him as if he had it not. [18] To slip upon a pavement is better than to slip with the tongue: so the fall of the wicked shall come speedily. [19] An unseasonable tale will always be in the mouth of the unwise. [20] A wise sentence shall be rejected when it cometh out of a fool's mouth; for he will not speak it in due season. [21] There is that is hindered from sinning through want: and when he taketh rest, he shall not be troubled. [22] There is that destroyeth his own soul through bashfulness, and by accepting of persons overthroweth himself. [23] There is that for bashfulness promiseth to his friend, and maketh him his enemy for nothing. [24] A lie is a foul blot in a man, yet it is continually in the mouth of the untaught. [25] A thief is better than a man that is accustomed to lie: but they both shall have destruction to heritage. [26] The disposition of a liar is dishonourable, and his shame is ever with him. [27] A wise man shall promote himself to honour with his words: and he that hath understanding will please great men. [28] He that tilleth his land shall increase his heap: and he that pleaseth great men shall get pardon for iniquity. [29] Presents and gifts blind the eyes of the wise, and stop up his mouth that he cannot reprove. [30] Wisdom that is hid, and treasure that is hoarded up, what profit is in them both? [31] Better is he that hideth his folly than a man that hideth his wisdom. [32] Necessary patience in seeking ing the Lord is better than he that leadeth his life without a guide. Sir.21 [1] My son, hast thou sinned? do so no more, but ask pardon for thy former sins. [2] Flee from sin as from the face of a serpent: for if thou comest too near it, it will bite thee: the teeth thereof are as the teeth of a lion, slaying the souls of men. [3] All iniquity is as a two edged sword, the wounds whereof cannot be healed. [4] To terrify and do wrong will waste riches: thus the house of proud men shall be made desolate. [5] A prayer out of a poor man's mouth reacheth to the ears of God, and his judgment cometh speedily. [6] He that hateth to be reproved is in the way of sinners: but he that feareth the Lord will repent from his heart. [7] An eloquent man is known far and near; but a man of understanding knoweth when he slippeth. [8] He that buildeth his house with other men's money is like one that gathereth himself stones for the tomb of his burial. [9] The congregation of the wicked is like tow wrapped together: and the end of them is a flame of fire to destroy them. [10] The way of sinners is made plain with stones, but at the end thereof is the pit of hell. [11] He that keepeth the law of the Lord getteth the understanding thereof: and the perfection of the fear of the Lord is wisdom. [12] He that is not wise will not be taught: but there is a wisdom which multiplieth bitterness. [13] The knowledge of a wise man shall abound like a flood: and his counsel is like a pure fountain of life. [14] The inner parts of a fool are like a broken vessel, and he will hold no knowledge as long as he liveth. [15] If a skilful man hear a wise word, he will commend it, and add unto it: but as soon as one of no understanding heareth it, it displeaseth him, and he casteth it behind his back. [16] The talking of a fool is like a burden in the way: but grace shall be found in the lips of the wise. [17] They enquire at the mouth of the wise man in the congregation, and they shall ponder his words in their heart. [18] As is a house that is destroyed, so is wisdom to a fool: and the knowledge of the unwise is as talk without sense. [19] Doctrine unto fools is as fetters on the feet, and like manacles on the right hand. [20] A fool lifteth up his voice with laughter; but a wise man doth scarce smile a little. [21] Learning is unto a wise man as an ornament of gold, and like a bracelet upon his right arm. [22] A foolish man's foot is soon in his [neighbour's] house: but a man of experience is ashamed of him. [23] A fool will peep in at the door into the house: but he that is well nurtured will stand without. [24] It is the rudeness of a man to hearken at the door: but a wise man will be grieved with the disgrace. [25] The lips of talkers will be telling such things as pertain not unto them: but the words of such as have understanding are weighed in the balance. [26] The heart of fools is in their mouth: but the mouth of the wise is in their heart. [27] When the ungodly curseth Satan, he curseth his own soul. [28] A whisperer defileth his own soul, and is hated wheresoever he dwelleth. Sir.22 [1] A slothful man is compared to a filthy stone, and every one will hiss him out to his disgrace. [2] A slothful man is compared to the filth of a dunghill: every man that takes it up will shake his hand. [3] An evilnurtured man is the dishonour of his father that begat him: and a [foolish] daughter is born to his loss. [4] A wise daughter shall bring an inheritance to her husband: but she that liveth dishonestly is her father's heaviness. [5] She that is bold dishonoureth both her father and her husband, but they both shall despise her. [6] A tale out of season [is as] musick in mourning: but stripes and correction of wisdom are never out of time. [7] Whoso teacheth a fool is as one that glueth a potsherd together, and as he that waketh one from a sound sleep. [8] He that telleth a tale to a fool speaketh to one in a slumber: when he hath told his tale, he will say, What is the matter? [9] If children live honestly, and have wherewithal, they shall cover the baseness of their parents. [10] But children, being haughty, through disdain and want of nurture do stain the nobility of their kindred. [11] Weep for the dead, for he hath lost the light: and weep for the fool, for he wanteth understanding: make little weeping for the dead, for he is at rest: but the life of the fool is worse than death. [12] Seven days do men mourn for him that is dead; but for a fool and an ungodly man all the days of his life. [13] Talk not much with a fool, and go not to him that hath no understanding: beware of him, lest thou have trouble, and thou shalt never be defiled with his fooleries: depart from him, and thou shalt find rest, and never be disquieted with madness. [14] What is heavier than lead? and what is the name thereof, but a fool? [15] Sand, and salt, and a mass of iron, is easier to bear, than a man without understanding. [16] As timber girt and bound together in a building cannot be loosed with shaking: so the heart that is stablished by advised counsel shall fear at no time. [17] A heart settled upon a thought of understanding is as a fair plaistering on the wall of a gallery. [18] Pales set on an high place will never stand against the wind: so a fearful heart in the imagination of a fool cannot stand against any fear. [19] He that pricketh the eye will make tears to fall: and he that pricketh the heart maketh it to shew her knowledge. [20] Whoso casteth a stone at the birds frayeth them away: and he that upbraideth his friend breaketh friendship. [21] Though thou drewest a sword at thy friend, yet despair not: for there may be a returning [to favour.] [22] If thou hast opened thy mouth against thy friend, fear not; for there may be a reconciliation: except for upbraiding, or pride, or disclosing of secrets, or a treacherous wound: for for these things every friend will depart. [23] Be faithful to thy neighbour in his poverty, that thou mayest rejoice in his prosperity: abide stedfast unto him in the time of his trouble, that thou mayest be heir with him in his heritage: for a mean estate is not always to be contemned: nor the rich that is foolish to be had in admiration. [24] As the vapour and smoke of a furnace goeth before the fire; so reviling before blood. [25] I will not be ashamed to defend a friend; neither will I hide myself from him. [26] And if any evil happen unto me by him, every one that heareth it will beware of him. [27] Who shall set a watch before my mouth, and a seal of wisdom upon my lips, that I fall not suddenly by them, and that my tongue destroy me not? Sir.23 [1] O Lord, Father and Governor of all my whole life, leave me not to their counsels, and let me not fall by them. [2] Who will set scourges over my thoughts, and the discipline of wisdom over mine heart? that they spare me not for mine ignorances, and it pass not by my sins: [3] Lest mine ignorances increase, and my sins abound to my destruction, and I fall before mine adversaries, and mine enemy rejoice over me, whose hope is far from thy mercy. [4] O Lord, Father and God of my life, give me not a proud look, but turn away from thy servants always a haughty mind. [5] Turn away from me vain hopes and concupiscence, and thou shalt hold him up that is desirous always to serve thee. [6] Let not the greediness of the belly nor lust of the flesh take hold of me; and give not over me thy servant into an impudent mind. [7] Hear, O ye children, the discipline of the mouth: he that keepeth it shall never be taken in his lips. [8] The sinner shall be left in his foolishness: both the evil speaker and the proud shall fall thereby. [9] Accustom not thy mouth to swearing; neither use thyself to the naming of the Holy One. [10] For as a servant that is continually beaten shall not be without a blue mark: so he that sweareth and nameth God continually shall not be faultless. [11] A man that useth much swearing shall be filled with iniquity, and the plague shall never depart from his house: if he shall offend, his sin shall be upon him: and if he acknowledge not his sin, he maketh a double offence: and if he swear in vain, he shall not be innocent, but his house shall be full of calamities. [12] There is a word that is clothed about with death: God grant that it be not found in the heritage of Jacob; for all such things shall be far from the godly, and they shall not wallow in their sins. [13] Use not thy mouth to intemperate swearing, for therein is the word of sin. [14] Remember thy father and thy mother, when thou sittest among great men. Be not forgetful before them, and so thou by thy custom become a fool, and wish that thou hadst not been born, and curse they day of thy nativity. [15] The man that is accustomed to opprobrious words will never be reformed all the days of his life. [16] Two sorts of men multiply sin, and the third will bring wrath: a hot mind is as a burning fire, it will never be quenched till it be consumed: a fornicator in the body of his flesh will never cease till he hath kindled a fire. [17] All bread is sweet to a whoremonger, he will not leave off till he die. [18] A man that breaketh wedlock, saying thus in his heart, Who seeth me? I am compassed about with darkness, the walls cover me, and no body seeth me; what need I to fear? the most High will not remember my sins: [19] Such a man only feareth the eyes of men, and knoweth not that the eyes of the Lord are ten thousand times brighter than the sun, beholding all the ways of men, and considering the most secret parts. [20] He knew all things ere ever they were created; so also after they were perfected he looked upon them all. [21] This man shall be punished in the streets of the city, and where he suspecteth not he shall be taken. [22] Thus shall it go also with the wife that leaveth her husband, and bringeth in an heir by another. [23] For first, she hath disobeyed the law of the most High; and secondly, she hath trespassed against her own husband; and thirdly, she hath played the whore in adultery, and brought children by another man. [24] She shall be brought out into the congregation, and inquisition shall be made of her children. [25] Her children shall not take root, and her branches shall bring forth no fruit. [26] She shall leave her memory to be cursed, and her reproach shall not be blotted out. [27] And they that remain shall know that there is nothing better than the fear of the Lord, and that there is nothing sweeter than to take heed unto the commandments of the Lord. [28] It is great glory to follow the Lord, and to be received of him is long life. Sir.24 [1] Wisdom shall praise herself, and shall glory in the midst of her people. [2] In the congregation of the most High shall she open her mouth, and triumph before his power. [3] I came out of the mouth of the most High, and covered the earth as a cloud. [4] I dwelt in high places, and my throne is in a cloudy pillar. [5] I alone compassed the circuit of heaven, and walked in the bottom of the deep. [6] In the waves of the sea and in all the earth, and in every people and nation, I got a possession. [7] With all these I sought rest: and in whose inheritance shall I abide? [8] So the Creator of all things gave me a commandment, and he that made me caused my tabernacle to rest, and said, Let thy dwelling be in Jacob, and thine inheritance in Israel. [9] He created me from the beginning before the world, and I shall never fail. [10] In the holy tabernacle I served before him; and so was I established in Sion. [11] Likewise in the beloved city he gave me rest, and in Jerusalem was my power. [12] And I took root in an honourable people, even in the portion of the Lord's inheritance. [13] I was exalted like a cedar in Libanus, and as a cypress tree upon the mountains of Hermon. [14] I was exalted like a palm tree in En-gaddi, and as a rose plant in Jericho, as a fair olive tree in a pleasant field, and grew up as a plane tree by the water. [15] I gave a sweet smell like cinnamon and aspalathus, and I yielded a pleasant odour like the best myrrh, as galbanum, and onyx, and sweet storax, and as the fume of frankincense in the tabernacle. [16] As the turpentine tree I stretched out my branches, and my branches are the branches of honour and grace. [17] As the vine brought I forth pleasant savour, and my flowers are the fruit of honour and riches. [18] I am the mother of fair love, and fear, and knowledge, and holy hope: I therefore, being eternal, am given to all my children which are named of him. [19] Come unto me, all ye that be desirous of me, and fill yourselves with my fruits. [20] For my memorial is sweeter than honey, and mine inheritance than the honeycomb. [21] They that eat me shall yet be hungry, and they that drink me shall yet be thirsty. [22] He that obeyeth me shall never be confounded, and they that work by me shall not do amiss. [23] All these things are the book of the covenant of the most high God, even the law which Moses commanded for an heritage unto the congregations of Jacob. [24] Faint not to be strong in the Lord; that he may confirm you, cleave unto him: for the Lord Almighty is God alone, and beside him there is no other Saviour. [25] He filleth all things with his wisdom, as Phison and as Tigris in the time of the new fruits. [26] He maketh the understanding to abound like Euphrates, and as Jordan in the time of the harvest. [27] He maketh the doctrine of knowledge appear as the light, and as Geon in the time of vintage. [28] The first man knew her not perfectly: no more shall the last find her out. [29] For her thoughts are more than the sea, and her counsels profounder than the great deep. [30] I also came out as a brook from a river, and as a conduit into a garden. [31] I said, I will water my best garden, and will water abundantly my garden bed: and, lo, my brook became a river, and my river became a sea. [32] I will yet make doctrine to shine as the morning, and will send forth her light afar off. [33] I will yet pour out doctrine as prophecy, and leave it to all ages for ever. [34] Behold that I have not laboured for myself only, but for all them that seek wisdom. Sir.25 [1] In three things I was beautified, and stood up beautiful both before God and men: the unity of brethren, the love of neighbours, a man and a wife that agree together. [2] Three sorts of men my soul hateth, and I am greatly offended at their life: a poor man that is proud, a rich man that is a liar, and an old adulterer that doateth. [3] If thou hast gathered nothing in thy youth, how canst thou find any thing in thine age? [4] O how comely a thing is judgment for gray hairs, and for ancient men to know counsel! [5] O how comely is the wisdom of old men, and understanding and counsel to men of honour. [6] Much experience is the crown of old men, and the fear of God is their glory. [7] There be nine things which I have judged in mine heart to be happy, and the tenth I will utter with my tongue: A man that hath joy of his children; and he that liveth to see the fall of his enemy: [8] Well is him that dwelleth with a wife of understanding, and that hath not slipped with his tongue, and that hath not served a man more unworthy than himself: [9] Well is him that hath found prudence, and he that speaketh in the ears of them that will hear: [10] O how great is he that findeth wisdom! yet is there none above him that feareth the Lord. [11] But the love of the Lord passeth all things for illumination: he that holdeth it, whereto shall he be likened? [12] The fear of the Lord is the beginning of his love: and faith is the beginning of cleaving unto him. [13] [Give me] any plague, but the plague of the heart: and any wickedness, but the wickedness of a woman: [14] And any affliction, but the affliction from them that hate me: and any revenge, but the revenge of enemies. [15] There is no head above the head of a serpent; and there is no wrath above the wrath of an enemy. [16] I had rather dwell with a lion and a dragon, than to keep house with a wicked woman. [17] The wickedness of a woman changeth her face, and darkeneth her countenance like sackcloth. [18] Her husband shall sit among his neighbours; and when he heareth it shall sigh bitterly. [19] All wickedness is but little to the wickedness of a woman: let the portion of a sinner fall upon her. [20] As the climbing up a sandy way is to the feet of the aged, so is a wife full of words to a quiet man. [21] Stumble not at the beauty of a woman, and desire her not for pleasure. [22] A woman, if she maintain her husband, is full of anger, impudence, and much reproach. [23] A wicked woman abateth the courage, maketh an heavy countenance and a wounded heart: a woman that will not comfort her husband in distress maketh weak hands and feeble knees. [24] Of the woman came the beginning of sin, and through her we all die. [25] Give the water no passage; neither a wicked woman liberty to gad abroad. [26] If she go not as thou wouldest have her, cut her off from thy flesh, and give her a bill of divorce, and let her go. Sir.26 [1] Blessed is the man that hath a virtuous wife, for the number of his days shall be double. [2] A virtuous woman rejoiceth her husband, and he shall fulfil the years of his life in peace. [3] A good wife is a good portion, which shall be given in the portion of them that fear the Lord. [4] Whether a man be rich or poor, if he have a good heart toward the Lord, he shall at all times rejoice with a cheerful countenance. [5] There be three things that mine heart feareth; and for the fourth I was sore afraid: the slander of a city, the gathering together of an unruly multitude, and a false accusation: all these are worse than death. [6] But a grief of heart and sorrow is a woman that is jealous over another woman, and a scourge of the tongue which communicateth with all. [7] An evil wife is a yoke shaken to and fro: he that hath hold of her is as though he held a scorpion. [8] A drunken woman and a gadder abroad causeth great anger, and she will not cover her own shame. [9] The whoredom of a woman may be known in her haughty looks and eyelids. [10] If thy daughter be shameless, keep her in straitly, lest she abuse herself through overmuch liberty. [11] Watch over an impudent eye: and marvel not if she trespass against thee. [12] She will open her mouth, as a thirsty traveller when he hath found a fountain, and drink of every water near her: by every hedge will she sit down, and open her quiver against every arrow. [13] The grace of a wife delighteth her husband, and her discretion will fatten his bones. [14] A silent and loving woman is a gift of the Lord; and there is nothing so much worth as a mind well instructed. [15] A shamefaced and faithful woman is a double grace, and her continent mind cannot be valued. [16] As the sun when it ariseth in the high heaven; so is the beauty of a good wife in the ordering of her house. [17] As the clear light is upon the holy candlestick; so is the beauty of the face in ripe age. [18] As the golden pillars are upon the sockets of silver; so are the fair feet with a constant heart. [19] My son, keep the flower of thine age sound; and give not thy strength to strangers. [20] When thou hast gotten a fruitful possession through all the field, sow it with thine own seed, trusting in the goodness of thy stock. [21] So thy race which thou leavest shall be magnified, having the confidence of their good descent. [22] An harlot shall be accounted as spittle; but a married woman is a tower against death to her husband. [23] A wicked woman is given as a portion to a wicked man: but a godly woman is given to him that feareth the Lord. [24] A dishonest woman contemneth shame: but an honest woman will reverence her husband. [25] A shameless woman shall be counted as a dog; but she that is shamefaced will fear the Lord. [26] A woman that honoureth her husband shall be judged wise of all; but she that dishonoureth him in her pride shall be counted ungodly of all. [27] A loud crying woman and a scold shall be sought out to drive away the enemies. [28] There be two things that grieve my heart; and the third maketh me angry: a man of war that suffereth poverty; and men of understanding that are not set by; and one that returneth from righteousness to sin; the Lord prepareth such an one for the sword. [29] A merchant shall hardly keep himself from doing wrong; and an huckster shall not be freed from sin. Sir.27 [1] Many have sinned for a small matter; and he that seeketh for abundance will turn his eyes away. [2] As a nail sticketh fast between the joinings of the stones; so doth sin stick close between buying and selling. [3] Unless a man hold himself diligently in the fear of the Lord, his house shall soon be overthrown. [4] As when one sifteth with a sieve, the refuse remaineth; so the filth of man in his talk. [5] The furnace proveth the potter's vessels; so the trial of man is in his reasoning. [6] The fruit declareth if the tree have been dressed; so is the utterance of a conceit in the heart of man. [7] Praise no man before thou hearest him speak; for this is the trial of men. [8] If thou followest righteousness, thou shalt obtain her, and put her on, as a glorious long robe. [9] The birds will resort unto their like; so will truth return unto them that practise in her. [10] As the lion lieth in wait for the prey; so sin for them that work iniquity. [11] The discourse of a godly man is always with wisdom; but a fool changeth as the moon. [12] If thou be among the indiscreet, observe the time; but be continually among men of understanding. [13] The discourse of fools is irksome, and their sport is the wantonness of sin. [14] The talk of him that sweareth much maketh the hair stand upright; and their brawls make one stop his ears. [15] The strife of the proud is bloodshedding, and their revilings are grievous to the ear. [16] Whoso discovereth secrets loseth his credit; and shall never find friend to his mind. [17] Love thy friend, and be faithful unto him: but if thou betrayest his secrets, follow no more after him. [18] For as a man hath destroyed his enemy; so hast thou lost the love of thy neighbor. [19] As one that letteth a bird go out of his hand, so hast thou let thy neighbour go, and shalt not get him again [20] Follow after him no more, for he is too far off; he is as a roe escaped out of the snare. [21] As for a wound, it may be bound up; and after reviling there may be reconcilement: but he that betrayeth secrets is without hope. [22] He that winketh with the eyes worketh evil: and he that knoweth him will depart from him. [23] When thou art present, he will speak sweetly, and will admire thy words: but at the last he will writhe his mouth, and slander thy sayings. [24] I have hated many things, but nothing like him; for the Lord will hate him. [25] Whoso casteth a stone on high casteth it on his own head; and a deceitful stroke shall make wounds. [26] Whoso diggeth a pit shall fall therein: and he that setteth a trap shall be taken therein. [27] He that worketh mischief, it shall fall upon him, and he shall not know whence it cometh. [28] Mockery and reproach are from the proud; but vengeance, as a lion, shall lie in wait for them. [29] They that rejoice at the fall of the righteous shall be taken in the snare; and anguish shall consume them before they die. [30] Malice and wrath, even these are abominations; and the sinful man shall have them both. Sir.28 [1] He that revengeth shall find vengeance from the Lord, and he will surely keep his sins [in remembrance.] [2] Forgive thy neighbour the hurt that he hath done unto thee, so shall thy sins also be forgiven when thou prayest. [3] One man beareth hatred against another, and doth he seek pardon from the Lord? [4] He sheweth no mercy to a man, which is like himself: and doth he ask forgiveness of his own sins? [5] If he that is but flesh nourish hatred, who will intreat for pardon of his sins? [6] Remember thy end, and let enmity cease; [remember] corruption and death, and abide in the commandments. [7] Remember the commandments, and bear no malice to thy neighbour: [remember] the covenant of the Highest, and wink at ignorance. [8] Abstain from strife, and thou shalt diminish thy sins: for a furious man will kindle strife, [9] A sinful man disquieteth friends, and maketh debate among them that be at peace. [10] As the matter of the fire is, so it burneth: and as a man's strength is, so is his wrath; and according to his riches his anger riseth; and the stronger they are which contend, the more they will be inflamed. [11] An hasty contention kindleth a fire: and an hasty fighting sheddeth blood. [12] If thou blow the spark, it shall burn: if thou spit upon it, it shall be quenched: and both these come out of thy mouth. [13] Curse the whisperer and doubletongued: for such have destroyed many that were at peace. [14] A backbiting tongue hath disquieted many, and driven them from nation to nation: strong cities hath it pulled down, and overthrown the houses of great men. [15] A backbiting tongue hath cast out virtuous women, and deprived them of their labours. [16] Whoso hearkeneth unto it shall never find rest, and never dwell quietly. [17] The stroke of the whip maketh marks in the flesh: but the stroke of the tongue breaketh the bones. [18] Many have fallen by the edge of the sword: but not so many as have fallen by the tongue. [19] Well is he that is defended through the venom thereof; who hath not drawn the yoke thereof, nor hath been bound in her bands. [20] For the yoke thereof is a yoke of iron, and the bands thereof are bands of brass. [21] The death thereof is an evil death, the grave were better than it. [22] It shall not have rule over them that fear God, neither shall they be burned with the flame thereof. [23] Such as forsake the Lord shall fall into it; and it shall burn in them, and not be quenched; it shall be sent upon them as a lion, and devour them as a leopard. [24] Look that thou hedge thy possession about with thorns, and bind up thy silver and gold, [25] And weigh thy words in a balance, and make a door and bar for thy mouth. [26] Beware thou slide not by it, lest thou fall before him that lieth in wait. Sir.29 [1] He that is merciful will lend unto his neighbour; and he that strengtheneth his hand keepeth the commandments. [2] Lend to thy neighbour in time of his need, and pay thou thy neighbour again in due season. [3] Keep thy word, and deal faithfully with him, and thou shalt always find the thing that is necessary for thee. [4] Many, when a thing was lent them, reckoned it to be found, and put them to trouble that helped them. [5] Till he hath received, he will kiss a man's hand; and for his neighbour's money he will speak submissly: but when he should repay, he will prolong the time, and return words of grief, and complain of the time. [6] If he prevail, he shall hardly receive the half, and he will count as if he had found it: if not, he hath deprived him of his money, and he hath gotten him an enemy without cause: he payeth him with cursings and railings; and for honour he will pay him disgrace. [7] Many therefore have refused to lend for other men's ill dealing, fearing to be defrauded. [8] Yet have thou patience with a man in poor estate, and delay not to shew him mercy. [9] Help the poor for the commandment's sake, and turn him not away because of his poverty. [10] Lose thy money for thy brother and thy friend, and let it not rust under a stone to be lost. [11] Lay up thy treasure according to the commandments of the most High, and it shall bring thee more profit than gold. [12] Shut up alms in thy storehouses: and it shall deliver thee from all affliction. [13] It shall fight for thee against thine enemies better than a mighty shield and strong spear. [14] An honest man is surety for his neighbour: but he that is impudent will forsake him. [15] Forget not the friendship of thy surety, for he hath given his life for thee. [16] A sinner will overthrow the good estate of his surety: [17] And he that is of an unthankful mind will leave him [in danger] that delivered him. [18] Suretiship hath undone many of good estate, and shaken them as a wave of the sea: mighty men hath it driven from their houses, so that they wandered among strange nations. [19] A wicked man transgressing the commandments of the Lord shall fall into suretiship: and he that undertaketh and followeth other men's business for gain shall fall into suits. [20] Help thy neighbour according to thy power, and beware that thou thyself fall not into the same. [21] The chief thing for life is water, and bread, and clothing, and an house to cover shame. [22] Better is the life of a poor man in a mean cottage, than delicate fare in another man's house. [23] Be it little or much, hold thee contented, that thou hear not the reproach of thy house. [24] For it is a miserable life to go from house to house: for where thou art a stranger, thou darest not open thy mouth. [25] Thou shalt entertain, and feast, and have no thanks: moreover thou shalt hear bitter words: [26] Come, thou stranger, and furnish a table, and feed me of that thou hast ready. [27] Give place, thou stranger, to an honourable man; my brother cometh to be lodged, and I have need of mine house. [28] These things are grievous to a man of understanding; the upbraiding of houseroom, and reproaching of the lender. Sir.30 [1] He that loveth his son causeth him oft to feel the rod, that he may have joy of him in the end. [2] He that chastiseth his son shall have joy in him, and shall rejoice of him among his acquaintance. [3] He that teacheth his son grieveth the enemy: and before his friends he shall rejoice of him. [4] Though his father die, yet he is as though he were not dead: for he hath left one behind him that is like himself. [5] While he lived, he saw and rejoiced in him: and when he died, he was not sorrowful. [6] He left behind him an avenger against his enemies, and one that shall requite kindness to his friends. [7] He that maketh too much of his son shall bind up his wounds; and his bowels will be troubled at every cry. [8] An horse not broken becometh headstrong: and a child left to himself will be wilful. [9] Cocker thy child, and he shall make thee afraid: play with him, and he will bring thee to heaviness. [10] Laugh not with him, lest thou have sorrow with him, and lest thou gnash thy teeth in the end. [11] Give him no liberty in his youth, and wink not at his follies. [12] Bow down his neck while he is young, and beat him on the sides while he is a child, lest he wax stubborn, and be disobedient unto thee, and so bring sorrow to thine heart. [13] Chastise thy son, and hold him to labour, lest his lewd behaviour be an offence unto thee. [14] Better is the poor, being sound and strong of constitution, than a rich man that is afflicted in his body. [15] Health and good estate of body are above all gold, and a strong body above infinite wealth. [16] There is no riches above a sound body, and no joy above the joy of the heart. [17] Death is better than a bitter life or continual sickness. [18] Delicates poured upon a mouth shut up are as messes of meat set upon a grave. [19] What good doeth the offering unto an idol? for neither can it eat nor smell: so is he that is persecuted of the Lord. [20] He seeth with his eyes and groaneth, as an eunuch that embraceth a virgin and sigheth. [21] Give not over thy mind to heaviness, and afflict not thyself in thine own counsel. [22] The gladness of the heart is the life of man, and the joyfulness of a man prolongeth his days. [23] Love thine own soul, and comfort thy heart, remove sorrow far from thee: for sorrow hath killed many, and there is no profit therein. [24] Envy and wrath shorten the life, and carefulness bringeth age before the time. [25] A cheerful and good heart will have a care of his meat and diet. Sir.31 [1] Watching for riches consumeth the flesh, and the care thereof driveth away sleep. [2] Watching care will not let a man slumber, as a sore disease breaketh sleep, [3] The rich hath great labour in gathering riches together; and when he resteth, he is filled with his delicates. [4] The poor laboureth in his poor estate; and when he leaveth off, he is still needy. [5] He that loveth gold shall not be justified, and he that followeth corruption shall have enough thereof. [6] Gold hath been the ruin of many, and their destruction was present. [7] It is a stumblingblock unto them that sacrifice unto it, and every fool shall be taken therewith. [8] Blessed is the rich that is found without blemish, and hath not gone after gold. [9] Who is he? and we will call him blessed: for wonderful things hath he done among his people. [10] Who hath been tried thereby, and found perfect? then let him glory. Who might offend, and hath not offended? or done evil, and hath not done it? [11] His goods shall be established, and the congregation shall declare his alms. [12] If thou sit at a bountiful table, be not greedy upon it, and say not, There is much meat on it. [13] Remember that a wicked eye is an evil thing: and what is created more wicked than an eye? therefore it weepeth upon every occasion. [14] Stretch not thine hand whithersoever it looketh, and thrust it not with him into the dish. [15] Judge not thy neighbour by thyself: and be discreet in every point. [16] Eat as it becometh a man, those things which are set before thee; and devour note, lest thou be hated. [17] Leave off first for manners' sake; and be not unsatiable, lest thou offend. [18] When thou sittest among many, reach not thine hand out first of all. [19] A very little is sufficient for a man well nurtured, and he fetcheth not his wind short upon his bed. [20] Sound sleep cometh of moderate eating: he riseth early, and his wits are with him: but the pain of watching, and choler, and pangs of the belly, are with an unsatiable man. [21] And if thou hast been forced to eat, arise, go forth, vomit, and thou shalt have rest. [22] My son, hear me, and despise me not, and at the last thou shalt find as I told thee: in all thy works be quick, so shall there no sickness come unto thee. [23] Whoso is liberal of his meat, men shall speak well of him; and the report of his good housekeeping will be believed. [24] But against him that is a niggard of his meat the whole city shall murmur; and the testimonies of his niggardness shall not be doubted of. [25] Shew not thy valiantness in wine; for wine hath destroyed many. [26] The furnace proveth the edge by dipping: so doth wine the hearts of the proud by drunkeness. [27] Wine is as good as life to a man, if it be drunk moderately: what life is then to a man that is without wine? for it was made to make men glad. [28] Wine measurably drunk and in season bringeth gladness of the heart, and cheerfulness of the mind: [29] But wine drunken with excess maketh bitterness of the mind, with brawling and quarrelling. [30] Drunkenness increaseth the rage of a fool till he offend: it diminisheth strength, and maketh wounds. [31] Rebuke not thy neighbour at the wine, and despise him not in his mirth: give him no despiteful words, and press not upon him with urging him [to drink.] Sir.32 [1] If thou be made the master [of a feast,] lift not thyself up, but be among them as one of the rest; take diligent care for them, and so sit down. [2] And when thou hast done all thy office, take thy place, that thou mayest be merry with them, and receive a crown for thy well ordering of the feast. [3] Speak, thou that art the elder, for it becometh thee, but with sound judgment; and hinder not musick. [4] Pour not out words where there is a musician, and shew not forth wisdom out of time. [5] A concert of musick in a banquet of wine is as a signet of carbuncle set in gold. [6] As a signet of an emerald set in a work of gold, so is the melody of musick with pleasant wine. [7] Speak, young man, if there be need of thee: and yet scarcely when thou art twice asked. [8] Let thy speech be short, comprehending much in few words; be as one that knoweth and yet holdeth his tongue. [9] If thou be among great men, make not thyself equal with them; and when ancient men are in place, use not many words. [10] Before the thunder goeth lightning; and before a shamefaced man shall go favour. [11] Rise up betimes, and be not the last; but get thee home without delay. [12] There take thy pastime, and do what thou wilt: but sin not by proud speech. [13] And for these things bless him that made thee, and hath replenished thee with his good things. [14] Whoso feareth the Lord will receive his discipline; and they that seek him early shall find favour. [15] He that seeketh the law shall be filled therewith: but the hypocrite will be offended thereat. [16] They that fear the Lord shall find judgment, and shall kindle justice as a light. [17] A sinful man will not be reproved, but findeth an excuse according to his will. [18] A man of counsel will be considerate; but a strange and proud man is not daunted with fear, even when of himself he hath done without counsel. [19] Do nothing without advice; and when thou hast once done, repent not. [20] Go not in a way wherein thou mayest fall, and stumble not among the stones. [21] Be not confident in a plain way. [22] And beware of thine own children. [23] In every good work trust thy own soul; for this is the keeping of the commandments. [24] He that believeth in the Lord taketh heed to the commandment; and he that trusteth in him shall fare never the worse. Sir.33 [1] There shall no evil happen unto him that feareth the Lord; but in temptation even again he will deliver him. [2] A wise man hateth not the law; but he that is an hypocrite therein is as a ship in a storm. [3] A man of understanding trusteth in the law; and the law is faithful unto him, as an oracle. [4] Prepare what to say, and so thou shalt be heard: and bind up instruction, and then make answer. [5] The heart of the foolish is like a cartwheel; and his thoughts are like a rolling axletree. [6] A stallion horse is as a mocking friend, he neigheth under every one that sitteth upon him. [7] Why doth one day excel another, when as all the light of every day in the year is of the sun? [8] By the knowledge of the Lord they were distinguished: and he altered seasons and feasts. [9] Some of them hath he made high days, and hallowed them, and some of them hath he made ordinary days. [10] And all men are from the ground, and Adam was created of earth: [11] In much knowledge the Lord hath divided them, and made their ways diverse. [12] Some of them hath he blessed and exalted and some of them he sanctified, and set near himself: but some of them hath he cursed and brought low, and turned out of their places. [13] As the clay is in the potter's hand, to fashion it at his pleasure: so man is in the hand of him that made him, to render to them as liketh him best. [14] Good is set against evil, and life against death: so is the godly against the sinner, and the sinner against the godly. [15] So look upon all the works of the most

High; and there are two and two, one against another. [16] I awaked up last of all, as one that gathereth after the grapegatherers: by the blessing of the Lord I profited, and tred my winepress like a gatherer of grapes. [17] Consider that I laboured not for myself only, but for all them that seek learning. [18] Hear me, O ye great men of the people, and hearken with your ears, ye rulers of the congregation. [19] Give not thy son and wife, thy brother and friend, power over thee while thou livest, and give not thy goods to another: lest it repent thee, and thou intreat for the same again. [20] As long as thou livest and hast breath in thee, give not thyself over to any. [21] For better it is that thy children should seek to thee, than that thou shouldest stand to their courtesy. [22] In all thy works keep to thyself the preeminence; leave not a stain in thine honour. [23] At the time when thou shalt end thy days, and finish thy life, distribute thine inheritance. [24] Fodder, a wand, and burdens, are for the ass; and bread, correction, and work, for a servant. . [25] If thou set thy servant to labour, thou shalt find rest: but if thou let him go idle, he shall seek liberty. [26] A yoke and a collar do bow the neck: so are tortures and torments for an evil servant. [27] Send him to labour, that he be not idle; for idleness teacheth much evil. [28] Set him to work, as is fit for him: if he be not obedient, put on more heavy fetters. [29] But be not excessive toward any; and without discretion do nothing. [30] If thou have a servant, let him be unto thee as thyself, because thou hast bought him with a price. [31] If thou have a servant, entreat him as a brother: for thou hast need of him, as of thine own soul: if thou entreat him evil, and he run from thee, which way wilt thou go to seek him? Sir.34 [1] The hopes of a man void of understanding are vain and false: and dreams lift up fools. [2] Whoso regardeth dreams is like him that catcheth at a shadow, and followeth after the wind. [3] The vision of dreams is the resemblance of one thing to another, even as the likeness of a face to a face. [4] Of an unclean thing what can be cleansed? and from that thing which is false what truth can come? [5] Divinations, and soothsayings, and dreams, are vain: and the heart fancieth, as a woman's heart in travail. [6] If they be not sent from the most High in thy visitation, set not thy heart upon them. [7] For dreams have deceived many, and they have failed that put their trust in them. [8] The law shall be found perfect without lies: and wisdom is perfection to a faithful mouth. [9] A man that hath travelled knoweth many things; and he that hath much experience will declare wisdom. [10] He that hath no experience knoweth little: but he that hath travelled is full of prudence. [11] When I travelled, I saw many things; and I understand more than I can express. [12] I was ofttimes in danger of death: yet I was delivered because of these things. [13] The spirit of those that fear the Lord shall live; for their hope is in him that saveth them. [14] Whoso feareth the Lord shall not fear nor be afraid; for he is his hope. [15] Blessed is the soul of him that feareth the Lord: to whom doth he look? and who is his strength? [16] For the eyes of the Lord are upon them that love him, he is their mighty protection and strong stay, a defence from heat, and a cover from the sun at noon, a preservation from stumbling, and an help from falling. [17] He raiseth up the soul, and lighteneth the eyes: he giveth health, life, and blessing. [18] He that sacrificeth of a thing wrongfully gotten, his offering is ridiculous; and the gifts of unjust men are not accepted. [19] The most High is not pleased with the offerings of the wicked; neither is he pacified for sin by the multitude of sacrifices. [20] Whoso bringeth an offering of the goods of the poor doeth as one that killeth the son before his father's eyes. [21] The bread of the needy is their life: he that defraudeth him thereof is a man of blood. [22] He that taketh away his neighbour's living slayeth him; and he that defraudeth the labourer of his hire is a bloodshedder. [23] When one buildeth, and another pulleth down, what profit have they then but labour? [24] When one prayeth, and another curseth, whose voice will the Lord hear? [25] He that washeth himself after the touching of a dead body, if he touch it again, what availeth his washing? [26] So is it with a man that fasteth for his sins, and goeth again, and doeth the same: who will hear his prayer? or what doth his humbling profit him? Sir.35 [1] He that keepeth the law bringeth offerings enough: he that taketh heed to the commandment offereth a peace offering. [2] He that requiteth a goodturn offereth fine flour; and he that giveth alms sacrificeth praise. [3] To depart from wickedness is a thing pleasing to the Lord; and to forsake unrighteousness is a propitiation. [4] Thou shalt not appear empty before the Lord. [5] For all these things [are to be done] because of the commandment. [6] The offering of the righteous maketh the altar fat, and the sweet savour thereof is before the most High. [7] The sacrifice of a just man is acceptable. and the memorial thereof shall never be forgotten. [8] Give the Lord his honour with a good eye, and diminish not the firstfruits of thine hands. [9] In all thy gifts shew a cheerful countenance, and dedicate thy tithes with gladness. [10] Give unto the most High according as he hath enriched thee; and as thou hast gotten, give with a cheerful eye. [11] For the Lord recompenseth, and will give thee seven times as much. [12] Do not think to corrupt with gifts; for such he will not receive: and trust not to unrighteous sacrifices; for the Lord is judge, and with him is no respect of persons. [13] He will not accept any person against a poor man, but will hear the prayer of the oppressed. [14] He will not despise the supplication of the fatherless; nor the widow, when she poureth out her complaint. [15] Do not the tears run down the widow's cheeks? and is not her cry against him that causeth them to fall? [16] He that serveth the Lord shall be accepted with favour, and his prayer shall reach unto the clouds. [17] The prayer of the humble pierceth the clouds: and till it come nigh, he will not be comforted; and will not depart, till the most High shall behold to judge righteously, and execute judgment. [18] For the Lord will not be slack, neither will the Mighty be patient toward them, till he have smitten in sunder the loins of the unmerciful, and repayed vengeance to the heathen; till he have taken away the multitude of the proud, and broken the sceptre of the unrighteous; [19] Till he have rendered to every man according to his deeds, and to the works of men according to their devices; till he have judged the cause of his people, and made them to rejoice in his mercy. [20] Mercy is seasonable in the time of affliction, as clouds of rain in the time of drought. Sir.36 [1] Have mercy upon us, O Lord God of all, and behold us: [2] And send thy fear upon all the nations that seek not after thee. [3] Lift up thy hand against the strange nations, and let them see thy power. [4] As thou wast sanctified in us before them: so be thou magnified among them before us. [5] And let them know thee, as we have known thee, that there is no God but only thou, O God. [6] Shew new signs, and make other strange wonders: glorify thy hand and thy right arm, that they may set forth thy wondrous works. [7] Raise up indignation, and pour out wrath: take away the adversary, and destroy the enemy. [8] Sake the time short, remember the covenant, and let them declare thy wonderful works. [9] Let him that escapeth be consumed by the rage of the fire; and let them perish that oppress the people. [10] Smite in sunder the heads of the rulers of the heathen, that say, There is none other but we. [11] Gather all the tribes of Jacob together, and inherit thou them, as from the beginning. [12] O Lord, have mercy upon the people that is called by thy name, and upon Israel, whom thou hast named thy firstborn. [13] O be merciful unto Jerusalem, thy holy city, the place of thy rest. [14] Fill Sion with thine unspeakable oracles, and thy people with thy glory: [15] Give testimony unto those that thou hast possessed from the beginning, and raise up prophets that have been in thy name. [16] Reward them that wait for thee, and let thy prophets be found faithful. [17] O Lord, hear the prayer of thy servants, according to the blessing of Aaron over thy people, that all they which dwell upon the earth may know that thou art the Lord, the eternal God. [18] The belly devoureth all meats, yet is one meat better than another. [19] As the palate tasteth divers kinds of venison: so doth an heart of understanding false speeches. [20] A froward heart causeth heaviness: but a man of experience will recompense him. [21] A woman will receive every man, yet is one daughter better than another. [22] The beauty of a woman cheereth the countenance, and a man loveth nothing better. [23] If there be kindness, meekness, and comfort, in her tongue, then is not her husband like other men. [24] He that getteth a wife beginneth a possession, a help like unto himself, and a pillar of rest. [25] Where no hedge is, there the possession is spoiled: and he that hath no wife will wander up and down mourning. [26] Who will trust a thief well appointed, that skippeth from city to city? so [who will believe] a man that hath no house, and lodgeth wheresoever the night taketh him? Sir.37 [1] Every friend saith, I am his friend also: but there is a friend, which is only a friend in name. [2] Is it not a grief unto death, when a companion and friend is turned to an enemy? [3] O wicked imagination, whence camest thou in to cover the earth with deceit? [4] There is a companion, which rejoiceth in the prosperity of a friend, but in the time of trouble will be against him. [5] There is a companion, which helpeth his friend for the belly, and taketh up the buckler against the enemy. [6] Forget not thy friend in thy mind, and be not unmindful of him in thy riches. [7] Every counsellor extolleth counsel; but there is some that counselleth for himself. [8] Beware of a counsellor, and know before what need he hath; for he will counsel for himself; lest he cast the lot upon thee, [9] And say unto thee, Thy way is good: and afterward he stand on the other side, to see what shall befall thee. [10] Consult not with one that suspecteth thee: and hide thy counsel from such as envy thee. [11] Neither consult with a woman touching her of whom she is jealous; neither with a coward in matters of war; nor with a merchant concerning exchange; nor with a buyer of selling; nor with an envious man of thankfulness; nor with an unmerciful man touching kindness; nor with the slothful for any work; nor with an hireling for a year of finishing work; nor with an idle servant of much business: hearken not unto these in any matter of counsel. [12] But be continually with a godly man, whom thou knowest to keep the commandments of the Lord, whose, mind is according to thy mind, and will sorrow with thee, if thou shalt miscarry. [13] And let the counsel of thine own heart stand: for there is no man more faithful unto thee than it. [14] For a man's mind is sometime wont to tell him more than seven watchmen, that sit above in an high tower. [15] And above all this pray to the most High, that he will direct thy way in truth. [16] Let reason go before every enterprize, and counsel before every action. [17] The countenance is a sign of changing of the heart. [18] Four manner of things appear: good and evil, life and death: but the tongue ruleth over them continually. [19] There is one that is wise and teacheth many, and yet is unprofitable to himself. [20] There is one that sheweth wisdom in words, and is hated: he shall be destitute of all food. [21] For grace is not given, him from the Lord, because he is deprived of all wisdom. [22] Another is wise to himself; and the fruits of understanding are commendable in his mouth. [23] A wise man instructeth his people; and the fruits of his understanding fail not. [24] A wise man shall be filled with blessing; and all they that see him shall count him happy. [25] The days of the life of man may be numbered: but the days of Israel are innumerable. [26] A wise man shall inherit glory among his people, and his name shall be perpetual. [27] My son, prove thy soul in thy life, and see what is evil for it, and give not that unto it. [28] For all things are not profitable for all men, neither hath every soul pleasure in every thing. [29] Be not unsatiable in any dainty thing, nor too greedy upon meats: [30] For excess of meats bringeth sickness, and surfeiting will turn into choler. [31] By surfeiting have many perished; but he that taketh heed prolongeth his life. Sir.38 [1] Honour a physician with the honour due unto him for the uses which ye may have of him: for the Lord hath created him. [2] For of the most High cometh healing, and he shall receive honour of the king. [3] The skill of the physician shall lift up his head: and in the sight of great men he shall be in admiration. [4] The Lord hath created medicines out of the earth; and he that is wise will not abhor them. [5] Was not the water made sweet with wood, that the virtue thereof might be known? [6] And he hath given men skill, that he might be honoured in his marvellous works. [7] With such doth he heal [men,] and taketh away their pains. [8] Of such doth the apothecary make a confection; and of his works there is no end; and from him is peace over all the earth, [9] My son, in thy sickness be not negligent: but pray unto the Lord, and he will make thee whole. [10] Leave off from sin, and order thine hands aright, and cleanse thy heart from all wickedness. [11] Give a sweet savour, and a memorial of fine flour; and make a fat offering, as not being. [12] Then give place to the physician, for the Lord hath created him: let him not go from thee, for thou hast need of him. [13] There is a time when in their hands there is good success. [14] For they shall also pray unto the Lord, that he would prosper that, which they give for ease and remedy to prolong life. [15] He that sinneth before his Maker, let him fall into the hand of the physician. [16] My son, let tears fall down over the dead, and begin to lament, as if thou hadst suffered great harm thyself; and then cover his body according to the custom, and neglect not his burial. [17] Weep bitterly, and make great moan, and use lamentation, as he is worthy, and that a day or two, lest thou be evil spoken of: and then comfort thyself for thy heaviness. [18] For of heaviness cometh death, and the heaviness of the heart breaketh strength. [19] In affliction also sorrow remaineth: and the life of the poor is the curse of the heart. [20] Take no heaviness to heart: drive it away, and member the last end. [21] Forget it not, for there is no turning again: thou shalt not do him good, but hurt thyself. [22] Remember my judgment: for thine also shall be so; yesterday for me, and to day for thee. [23] When the dead is at rest, let his remembrance rest; and be comforted for him, when his Spirit is departed from him. [24] The wisdom of a learned man cometh by opportunity of leisure: and he that hath little business shall become wise. [25] How can he get wisdom that holdeth the plough, and that glorieth in the goad, that driveth oxen, and is occupied in their labours, and whose talk is of bullocks? [26] He giveth his mind to make furrows; and is diligent to give the kine fodder. [27] So every carpenter and workmaster, that laboureth night and day: and they that cut and grave seals, and are diligent to make great variety, and give themselves to counterfeit imagery, and watch to finish a work: [28] The smith also sitting by the anvil, and considering the iron work, the vapour of the fire wasteth his flesh, and he fighteth with the heat of the furnace: the noise of the hammer and the anvil is ever in his ears, and his eyes look still upon the pattern of the thing that he maketh; he setteth his mind to finish his work, and watcheth to polish it perfectly: [29] So doth the potter sitting at his work, and turning the wheel about with his feet, who is alway carefully set at his work, and maketh all his work by number; [30] He fashioneth the clay with his arm, and boweth down his strength before his feet; he applieth himself to lead it over; and he is diligent to make clean the furnace: [31] All these trust to their hands: and every one is wise in his work. [32] Without these cannot a city be inhabited: and they shall not dwell where they will, nor go up and down: [33] They shall not be sought for in publick counsel, nor sit high in the congregation: they shall not sit on the judges' seat, nor understand the sentence of judgment: they cannot declare justice and judgment; and they shall not be found where parables are spoken. [34] But they will maintain the state of the world, and [all] their desire is in the work of their craft. Sir.39 [1] But he that giveth his mind to the law of the most High, and is occupied in the meditation thereof, will seek out the wisdom of all the ancient, and be occupied in prophecies. [2] He will keep the sayings of the renowned men: and where subtil parables are, he will be there also. [3] He will seek out the secrets of grave sentences, and be conversant in dark parables. [4] He shall serve among great men, and appear before princes: he will travel through strange countries; for he hath tried the good and the evil among men. [5] He will give his heart to resort early to the Lord that made him, and will pray before the most High, and will open his mouth in prayer, and make supplication for his sins. [6] When the great Lord will, he shall be filled with the spirit of understanding: he shall pour out wise sentences, and give thanks unto the Lord in his prayer. [7] He shall direct his counsel and knowledge, and in his secrets shall he meditate. [8] He shall shew forth that which he hath learned, and shall glory in the law of the covenant of the Lord. [9] Many shall commend his understanding; and so long as the world endureth, it shall not be blotted out; his memorial shall not depart away, and his name shall live from generation to generation. [10] Nations shall shew forth his wisdom, and the congregation shall declare his praise. [11] If he die, he shall leave a greater name than a thousand: and if he live, he shall increase it. [12] Yet have I more to say, which I have thought upon; for I am filled as the moon at the full. [13] Hearken unto me, ye holy children, and bud forth as a rose growing by the brook of the field: [14] And give ye a sweet savour as frankincense, and flourish as a lily, send forth a smell, and sing a song of praise, bless the Lord in all his works. [15] Magnify his name, and shew forth his praise with the songs of your lips, and with harps, and in praising him ye shall say after this manner: [16] All the works of the Lord are exceeding good, and whatsoever he commandeth shall be accomplished in due season. [17] And none may say, What is this? wherefore is that? for at time convenient they shall all be sought out: at his commandment the waters stood as an heap, and at the words of his mouth the receptacles of waters. [18] At his commandment is done whatsoever pleaseth him; and none can hinder, when he will save. [19] The works of all flesh are before him, and nothing can be hid from his eyes. [20] He seeth from everlasting to everlasting; and there is nothing wonderful before him. [21] A man need not to say, What is this? wherefore is that? for he hath made all things for their uses. [22] His blessing covered the dry land as a river, and watered it as a flood. [23] As he hath turned the waters into saltness: so shall the heathen inherit his wrath. [24] As his ways are plain unto the holy; so are they stumblingblocks unto the wicked. [25] For the good are good things created from the beginning: so evil things for sinners. [26] The principal things for the whole use of man's life are water, fire, iron, and salt, flour of wheat, honey, milk, and the blood of the grape, and oil, and clothing. [27] All these things are for good to the godly: so to the sinners they are turned into evil. [28] There be spirits that are created for vengeance, which in their fury lay on sore strokes; in the time of destruction they pour out their force, and appease the wrath of him that made them. [29] Fire, and hail, and famine, and death, all these were created for vengeance; [30] Teeth of wild beasts, and scorpions, serpents, and the sword punishing the wicked to destruction. [31] They shall rejoice in his commandment, and they shall be ready upon earth, when need is; and when their time is come, they shall not transgress his word. [32] Therefore from the beginning I was resolved, and thought upon these things, and have left them in writing. [33] All the works of the Lord are good: and he will give every needful thing in due season. [34] So that a man cannot say, This is worse than that: for in time they shall all be well approved. [35] And therefore praise ye the Lord with the whole heart and mouth, and bless the name of the Lord. Sir.40 [1] Great travail is created for every man, and an heavy yoke is upon the sons of Adam, from the day that they go out of their mother's womb, till the day that they return to the mother of all things. [2] Their imagination of things to come, and the day of death, [trouble] their thoughts, and [cause] fear of heart; [3] From him that sitteth on a throne of glory, unto him that is humbled in earth and ashes; [4] From him that weareth purple and a crown, unto him that is clothed with a linen frock. [5] Wrath, and envy, trouble, and unquietness, fear of death, and anger, and strife, and in the time of rest upon his bed his night sleep, do change his knowledge. [6] A little or nothing is his rest, and afterward he is in his sleep, as in a day of keeping watch, troubled in the vision of his heart, as if he were escaped out of a battle. [7] When all is safe, he awaketh, and marvelleth that the fear was nothing. [8] [Such things happen] unto all flesh, both man and beast, and that is sevenfold more upon sinners. [9] Death, and bloodshed, strife, and sword, calamities, famine, tribulation, and the scourge; [10] These things are created for the wicked, and for their sakes came the flood. [11] All things that are of the earth shall turn to the earth again: and that which is of the waters doth return into the sea. [12] All bribery and injustice shall be blotted out: but true dealing shall endure for ever. [13] The goods of the unjust shall be dried up like a river, and shall vanish with noise, like a great thunder in rain. [14] While he openeth his hand he shall rejoice: so shall transgressors come to nought. [15] The children of the ungodly shall not bring forth many branches: but are as unclean roots upon a hard rock. [16] The weed growing upon every water and bank of a river shall be pulled up before all grass. [17] Bountifulness is as a most fruitful garden, and mercifulness endureth for ever. [18] To labour, and to be content with that a man hath, is a sweet life: but he that findeth a treasure is above them both. [19] Children and the building of a city continue a man's name: but a blameless wife is counted above them both. [20] Wine and musick rejoice the heart: but the love of wisdom is above them both. [21] The pipe and the psaltery make sweet melody: but a pleasant tongue is above them both. [22] Thine eye desireth favour and beauty: but more than both corn while it is green. [23] A friend and companion never meet amiss: but above both is a wife with her husband. [24] Brethren and help are against time of trouble: but alms shall deliver more than them both. [25] Gold and silver make the foot stand sure: but counsel is esteemed above them both. [26] Riches and strength lift up the heart: but the fear of the Lord is above them both: there is no want in the fear of the Lord, and it needeth not to seek help. [27] The fear of the Lord is a fruitful garden, and covereth him above all glory. [28] My son, lead not a beggar's life; for better it is to die than to beg. [29] The life of him that dependeth on another man's table is not to be counted for a life; for he polluteth himself with other men's meat: but a wise man well nurtured will beware thereof. [30] Begging is sweet in the mouth of the shameless: but in his belly there shall burn a fire. Sir.41 [1] O death, how bitter is the remembrance of thee to a man that liveth at rest in his possessions, unto the man that hath nothing to vex him, and that hath prosperity in all things: yea, unto him that is yet able to receive meat! [2] O death, acceptable is thy sentence unto the needy, and unto him whose strength faileth, that is now in the last age, and is vexed with all things, and to him that despaireth, and hath lost patience! [3] Fear not the sentence of death, remember them that have been before thee, and that come after; for this is the sentence of the Lord over all flesh. [4] And why art thou against the pleasure of the most High? there is no inquisition in the grave, whether thou have lived ten, or an hundred, or a thousand years. [5] The children of sinners are abominable children, and they that are conversant in the dwelling of the ungodly. [6] The inheritance of sinners' children shall perish, and their posterity shall have a perpetual reproach. [7] The children will complain of an ungodly father, because they shall be reproached for his sake. [8] Woe be unto you, ungodly men, which have forsaken the law of the most high God! for if ye increase, it shall be to your destruction: [9] And if ye be born, ye shall be born to a curse: and if ye die, a curse shall be your portion. [10] All that are of the earth shall turn to earth again: so the ungodly shall go from a curse to destruction. [11] The mourning of men is about their bodies: but an ill name of sinners shall be blotted out. [12] Have regard to thy name; for that shall continue with thee above a thousand great treasures of gold. [13] A good life hath but few days: but a good name endureth for ever. [14] My children, keep discipline in peace: for wisdom that is hid, and a treasure that is not seen, what profit is in them both? [15] A man that hideth his foolishness is better than a man that hideth his wisdom. [16] Therefore be shamefaced according to my word: for it is not good to retain all shamefacedness; neither is it altogether approved in every thing. [17] Be ashamed of whoredom before father and mother: and of a lie before a prince and a mighty man; [18] Of an offence before a judge and ruler; of iniquity before a congregation and people; of unjust dealing before thy partner and friend; [19] And of theft in regard of the place where thou sojournest, and in regard of the truth of God and his covenant; and to lean with thine elbow upon the meat; and of scorning to give and take; [20] And of silence before them that salute thee; and to look upon an harlot; [21] And to turn away thy face from thy kinsman; or to take away a portion or a gift; or to gaze upon another man's wife. [22] Or to be overbusy with his maid, and come not near her bed; or of upbraiding speeches before friends; and after thou hast given, upbraid not; [23] Or of iterating and speaking again that which thou hast heard; and of revealing of secrets. [24] So shalt thou be truly shamefaced and find favour before all men. Sir.42 [1] Of these things be not thou ashamed, and accept no person to sin thereby: [2] Of the law of the most High, and his covenant; and of judgment to justify the ungodly; [3] Of reckoning with thy partners and travellers; or of the gift of the heritage of friends; [4] Of exactness of balance and weights; or of getting much or little; [5] And of merchants' indifferent selling; of much correction of children; and to make the side of an evil servant to bleed. [6] Sure keeping is good, where an evil wife is; and shut up, where many hands are. [7] Deliver all things in number and weight; and put all in writing that thou givest out, or receivest in. [8] Be not ashamed to inform the unwise and foolish, and the extreme aged that contendeth with those that are young: thus shalt thou be truly learned, and approved of all men living. [9] The father waketh for the daughter, when no man knoweth; and the care for her taketh away sleep: when she is young, lest she pass away the flower of her age; and being married, lest she should be hated: [10] In her virginity, lest she should be defiled and gotten with child in her father's house; and having an husband, lest she should misbehave herself; and when she is married, lest she should be barren. [11] Keep a sure watch over a shameless daughter, lest she make thee a laughingstock to thine enemies, and a byword in the city, and a reproach among the people, and make thee ashamed before the multitude. [12] Behold not every body's beauty, and sit not in the midst of women. [13] For from garments cometh a moth, and from women wickedness. [14] Better is the churlishness of a man than a courteous woman, a woman, I say, which bringeth shame and reproach. [15] I will now remember the works of the Lord, and declare the things that I have seen: In the words of the Lord are his works. [16] The sun that giveth light looketh upon all things, and the work thereof is full of the glory of the Lord. [17] The Lord hath not given power to the saints to declare all his marvellous works, which the Almighty Lord firmly settled, that whatsoever is might be established for his glory. [18] He seeketh out the deep, and the heart, and considereth their crafty devices: for the Lord knoweth all that may be known, and he beholdeth the signs of the world. [19] He declareth the things that are past, and for to come, and revealeth the steps of hidden things. [20] No thought escapeth him, neither any word is hidden from him. [21] He hath garnished the excellent works of his wisdom, and he is from everlasting to everlasting: unto him may nothing be added, neither can he be diminished, and he hath no need of any counsellor. [22] Oh how desirable are all his works! and that a man may see even to a spark. [23] All these things live and remain for ever for all uses, and they are all obedient. [24] All things are double one against another: and he hath made nothing imperfect. [25] One thing establisheth the good or another: and who shall be filled with beholding his glory? Sir.43 [1] The pride of the height, the clear firmament, the beauty of heaven, with his glorious shew; [2] The sun when it appeareth, declaring at his rising a marvellous instrument, the work of the most High: [3] At noon it parcheth the country, and who can abide the burning heat thereof? [4] A man blowing a furnace is in works of heat, but the sun burneth the mountains three times more; breathing out fiery vapours, and sending forth bright beams, it dimmeth the eyes. [5] Great is the Lord that made it; and at his commandment runneth hastily. [6] He made the moon also to serve in her season for a declaration of times, and a sign of the world. [7] From the moon is the sign of feasts, a light that decreaseth in her perfection. [8] The month is called after her name, increasing wonderfully in her changing, being an instrument of the armies above, shining in the firmament of heaven; [9] The beauty of heaven, the glory of the stars, an ornament giving light in the highest places of the Lord. [10] At the commandment of the Holy One they will stand in their order, and never faint in their watches. [11] Look upon the rainbow, and praise him that made it; very beautiful it is in the brightness thereof. [12] It compasseth the heaven about with a glorious circle, and the hands of the most High have bended it. [13] By his commandment he maketh the snow to fall aplace, and sendeth swiftly the lightnings of his judgment. [14] Through this the treasures are opened: and clouds fly forth as fowls. [15] By his great power he maketh the clouds firm, and the hailstones are broken small. [16] At his sight the mountains are shaken, and at his will the south wind bloweth. [17] The noise of the thunder maketh the earth to tremble: so doth the northern storm and the whirlwind: as birds flying he scattereth the snow, and the falling down thereof is as the lighting of grasshoppers: [18] The eye marvelleth at the beauty of the whiteness thereof, and the heart is astonished at the raining of it. [19] The hoarfrost also as salt he poureth on the earth, and being congealed, it lieth on the top of sharp stakes. [20] When the cold north wind bloweth, and the water is congealed into ice, it abideth upon every gathering together of water, and clotheth the water as with a breastplate. [21] It devoureth the mountains, and burneth the wilderness, and consumeth the grass as fire. [22] A present remedy of all is a mist coming speedily, a dew coming after heat refresheth. [23] By his counsel he appeaseth the deep, and planteth islands therein. [24] They that sail on the sea tell of the danger thereof; and when we hear it with our ears, we marvel thereat. [25] For therein be strange and wondrous works, variety of all kinds of beasts and whales created. [26] By him the end of them hath prosperous success, and by his word all things consist. [27] We may speak much, and yet come short: wherefore in sum, he is all. [28] How shall we be able to magnify him? for he is great above all his works. [29] The Lord is terrible and very great, and marvellous is his power. [30] When ye glorify the Lord, exalt him as much as ye can; for even yet will he far exceed: and when ye exalt him, put forth all your strength, and be not weary; for ye can never go far enough. [31] Who hath seen him, that he might tell us? and who can magnify him as he is? [32] There are yet hid greater things than these be, for we have seen but a few of his works. [33] For the Lord hath made all things; and to the godly hath he given wisdom. Sir.44 [1] Let us now praise famous men, and our fathers that begat us. [2] The Lord hath wrought great glory by them through his great power from the beginning. [3] Such as did bear rule in their kingdoms, men renowned for their power, giving counsel by their understanding, and declaring prophecies: [4] Leaders of the people by their counsels, and by their knowledge of learning meet for the people, wise and eloquent are their instructions: [5] Such as found out musical tunes, and recited verses in writing: [6] Rich men furnished with ability, living peaceably in their habitations: [7] All these were honoured in their generations, and were the glory of their times. [8] There be of them, that have left a name behind them, that their praises might be reported. [9] And some there be, which have no memorial; who are perished, as though they had never been; and are become as though they had never been born; and their children after them. [10] But these were merciful men, whose righteousness hath not been forgotten. [11] With their seed shall continually remain a good inheritance, and their children are within the covenant. [12] Their seed standeth fast, and their children for their sakes. [13] Their seed shall remain for ever, and their glory shall not be blotted out. [14] Their bodies are buried in peace; but their name liveth for evermore. [15] The people will tell of their wisdom, and the congregation will shew forth their praise. [16] Enoch pleased the Lord, and was translated, being an example of repentance to all generations. [17] Noah was found perfect and righteous; in the time of wrath he was taken in exchange [for the world;] therefore was he left as a remnant unto the earth, when the flood came. [18] An everlasting covenant was made with him, that all flesh should perish no more by the flood. [19] Abraham was a great father of many people: in glory was there none like unto him; [20] Who kept the law of the most High, and was in covenant with him: he established the covenant in his flesh; and when he was proved, he was found faithful. [21] Therefore he assured him by an oath, that he would bless the nations in his seed, and that he would multiply him as the dust of the earth, and exalt his seed as the stars, and cause them to inherit from sea to sea, and from the river unto the utmost part of the land. [22] With Isaac did he establish likewise [for Abraham his father's sake] the blessing of all men, and the covenant, And made it rest upon the head of Jacob. He acknowledged him in his blessing, and gave him an heritage, and divided his portions; among the twelve tribes did he part them. Sir.45 [1] And he brought out of him a merciful man, which found favour in the sight of all flesh, even Moses, beloved of God and men, whose memorial is blessed. [2] He made him like to the glorious saints, and magnified him, so that his enemies stood in fear of him. [3] By his words he caused the wonders to cease, and he made him glorious in the sight of kings, and gave him a commandment for his people, and shewed him part of his glory. [4] He sanctified him in his faithfuless and meekness, and chose him out of all men. [5] He made him to hear his voice, and brought him into the dark cloud, and gave him commandments before his face, even the law of life and knowledge, that he might teach Jacob his covenants, and Israel his judgments. [6] He exalted Aaron, an holy man like unto him, even his brother, of the tribe of Levi. [7] An everlasting covenant he made with him and gave him the priesthood among the people; he beautified him with comely ornaments, and clothed him with a robe of glory. [8] He put upon him perfect glory; and strengthened him with rich garments, with breeches, with a long robe, and the ephod. [9] And he compassed him with pomegranates, and with many golden bells round about, that as he went there might be a sound, and a noise made that might be heard in the temple, for a memorial to the children of his people; [10] With an holy garment, with gold, and blue silk, and purple, the work of the embroidere, with a breastplate of judgment, and with Urim and Thummim; [11] With twisted scarlet, the work of the cunning workman, with precious stones graven like seals, and set in gold, the work of the jeweller, with a writing engraved for a memorial, after the number of the tribes of Israel. [12] He set a crown of gold upon the mitre, wherein was engraved Holiness, an ornament of honour, a costly work, the desires of the eyes, goodly and beautiful. [13] Before him there were none such, neither did ever any stranger put them on, but only his children and his children's children perpetually. [14] Their sacrifices shall be wholly consumed every day twice continually. [15] Moses consecrated him, and anointed him with holy oil: this was appointed unto him by an everlasting covenant, and to his seed, so long as the heavens should remain, that they should minister unto him, and execute the office of the priesthood, and bless the people in his name. [16] He chose him out of all men living to offer sacrifices to the Lord, incense, and a sweet savour, for a memorial, to make reconciliation for his people. [17] He gave unto him his commandments, and authority in the statutes of judgments, that he should teach Jacob the testimonies, and inform Israel in his laws. [18] Strangers conspired together against him, and maligned him in the wilderness, even the men that were of Dathan's and Abiron's side, and the congregation of Core, with fury and wrath. [19] This the Lord saw, and it displeased him, and in his wrathful indignation were they consumed: he did wonders upon them, to consume them with the fiery flame. [20] But he made Aaron more honourable, and gave him an heritage, and divided unto him the firstfruits of the increase; especially he prepared bread in abundance: [21] For they eat of the sacrifices of the Lord, which he gave unto him and his seed. [22] Howbeit in the land of the people he had no inheritance, neither had he any portion among the people: for the Lord himself is his portion and inheritance. [23] The third in glory is Phinees the son of Eleazar, because he had zeal in the fear of the Lord, and stood up with good courage of heart: when the people were turned back, and made reconciliation for Israel. [24] Therefore was there a covenant of peace made with him, that he should be the chief of the sanctuary and of his people, and that he and his posterity should have the dignity of the priesthood for ever: [25] According to the covenant made with David son of Jesse, of the tribe of Juda, that the inheritance of the king should be to his posterity alone: so the inheritance of Aaron should also be unto his seed. [26] God give you wisdom in your heart to judge his people in righteousness, that their good things be not abolished, and that their glory may endure for ever. Sir.46 [1] Jesus the son a Nave was valiant in the wars, and was the successor of Moses in prophecies, who according to his name was made great for the saving of the elect of God, and taking vengeance of the enemies that rose up against them, that he might set Israel in their inheritance. [2] How great glory gat he, when he did lift up his hands, and stretched out his sword against the cities! [3] Who before him so stood to it? for the Lord himself brought his enemies unto him. [4] Did not the sun go back by his means? and was not one day as long as two? [5] He called upon the most high Lord, when the enemies pressed upon him on every side; and the great Lord heard him. [6] And with hailstones of mighty power he made the battle to fall violently upon the nations, and in the descent [of Beth-horon] he destroyed them that resisted, that the nations might know all their strength, because he fought in the sight of the Lord, and he followed the Mighty One. [7] In the time of Moses also he did a work of mercy, he and Caleb the son of Jephunne, in that they withstood the congregation, and withheld the people from sin, and appeased the wicked murmuring. [8] And of six hundred thousand people on foot, they two were preserved to bring them in to the heritage, even unto the land that floweth with milk and honey. [9] The Lord gave strength also unto Caleb, which remained with him unto his old age: so that he entered upon the high places of the land, and his seed obtained it for an heritage: [10] That all the children of Israel might see that it is good to follow the Lord. [11] And concerning the judges, every one by name, whose heart went not a whoring, nor departed from the Lord, let their memory be blessed. [12] Let their bones flourish out of their place, and let the name of them that were honoured be continued upon their children. [13] Samuel, the prophet of the Lord, beloved of his Lord, established a kingdom, and anointed princes over his people. [14] By the law of the Lord he judged the congregation, and the Lord had respect unto Jacob. [15] By his faithfulness he was found a true prophet, and by his word he was known to be faithful in vision. [16] He called upon the mighty Lord, when his enemies pressed upon him on every side, when he offered the sucking lamb. [17] And the Lord thundered from heaven, and with a great noise made his voice to be heard. [18] And he destroyed the rulers of the Tyrians, and all the princes cf the Philistines. [19] And before his long sleep he made protestations in the sight of the Lord and his anointed, I have not taken any man's goods, so much as a shoe: and no man did accuse him. [20] And after his death he prophesied, and shewed the king his end, and lifted up his voice from the earth in prophecy, to blot out the wickedness of the people. Sir.47 [1] And after him rose up Nathan to prophesy in the time of David. [2] As is the fat taken away from the peace offering, so was David chosen out of the children of Israel. [3] He played with lions as with kids, and with bears as with lambs. [4] Slew he not a giant, when he was yet but young? and did he not take away reproach from the people, when he lifted up his hand with the stone in the sling, and beat down the boasting of Goliath? [5] For he called upon the most high Lord; and he gave him strength in his right hand to slay that mighty warrior, and set up the horn of his people. [6] So the people honoured him with ten thousands, and praised him in the blessings of the Lord, in that he gave him a crown of glory. [7] For he destroyed the enemies on every side, and brought to nought the Philistines his adversaries, and brake their horn in sunder unto this day. [8] In all his works he praised the Holy One most high with words of glory; with his whole heart he sung songs, and loved him that made him. [9] He set singers also before the altar, that by their voices they might make sweet melody, and daily sing praises in their songs. [10] He beautified their feasts, and set in order the solemn times until the end, that they might praise his holy name, and that the temple might sound from morning. [11] The Lord took away his sins, and exalted his horn for ever: he gave him a covenant of kings, and a throne of glory in Israel. [12] After him rose up a wise son, and for his sake he dwelt at large. [13] Solomon reigned in a peaceable time, and was honoured; for God made all quiet round about him, that he might build an house in his name, and prepare his sanctuary for ever. [14] How wise wast thou in thy youth and, as a flood, filled with understanding! [15] Thy soul covered the whole earth, and thou filledst it with dark parables. [16] Thy name went far unto the islands; and for thy peace thou wast beloved. [17] The countries marvelled at thee for thy songs, and proverbs, and parables, and interpretations. [18] By the name of the Lord God, which is called the Lord God of Israel, thou didst gather gold as tin and didst multiply silver as lead. [19] Thou didst bow thy loins unto women, and by thy body thou wast brought into subjection. [20] Thou didst stain thy honour, and pollute thy seed: so that thou broughtest wrath upon thy children, and wast grieved for thy folly. [21] So the kingdom was divided, and out of Ephraim ruled a rebellious kingdom. [22] But the Lord will never leave off his mercy, neither shall any of his works perish, neither will he abolish the posterity of his elect, and the seed of him that loveth him he will not take away: wherefore he gave a remnant unto Jacob, and out of him a root unto David. [23] Thus rested Solomon with his fathers, and of his seed he left behind him Roboam, even the foolishness of the people, and one that had no understanding, who turned away the people through his counsel. There was also Jeroboam the son of Nebat, who caused Israel to sin, and shewed Ephraim the way of sin: [24] And their sins were multiplied exceedingly, that they were driven out of the land. [25] For they sought out all wickedness, till the vengeance came upon them. Sir.48 [1] Then stood up Elias the prophet as fire, and his word burned like a lamp. [2] He brought a sore famine upon them, and by his zeal he diminished their number. [3] By the word of the Lord he shut up the heaven, and also three times brought down fire. [4] O Elias, how wast thou honoured in thy wondrous deeds! and who may glory like unto thee! [5] Who didst raise up a dead man from death, and his soul from the place of the dead, by the word of the most High: [6] Who broughtest kings to destruction, and honorable men from their bed: [7] Who heardest the rebuke of the Lord in Sinai, and in Horeb the judgment of vengeance: [8] Who annointedst kings to take revenge, and prophets to succeed after him: [9] Who was taken up in a whirlwind of fire, and in a chariot of fiery horses: [10] Who wast ordained for reproofs in their times, to pacify the wrath of the Lord's judgment, before it brake forth into fury, and to turn the heart of the father unto the son, and to restore the tribes of Jacob. [11] Blessed are they that saw thee, and slept in love; for we shall surely live. [12] Elias it was, who was covered with a whirlwind: and Eliseus was filled with his spirit: whilst he lived, he was not moved with the presence of any prince, neither could any bring him into subjection. [13] No word could overcome him; and after his death his body prophesied. [14] He did wonders in his life, and at his death were his works marvellous. [15] For all this the people repented not, neither departed they from their sins, till they were spoiled and carried out of their land, and were scattered through all the earth: yet there remained a small people, and a ruler in the house of David: [16] Of whom some did that which was pleasing to God, and some multiplied sins. [17] Ezekias fortified his city, and brought in water into the midst thereof: he digged the hard rock with iron, and made wells for waters. [18] In his time Sennacherib came up, and sent Rabsaces, and lifted up his hand against Sion, and boasted proudly. [19] Then trembled their hearts and hands, and they were in pain, as women in travail. [20] But they called upon the Lord which is merciful, and stretched out their hands toward him: and immediately the Holy One heard them out of heaven, and delivered them by the ministry of Esay. [21] He smote the host of the Assyrians, and his angel destroyed them. [22] For Ezekias had done the thing that pleased the Lord, and was strong in the ways of David his father, as Esay the prophet, who was great and faithful in his vision, had commanded him. [23] In his time the sun went backward, and he lengthened the king's life. [24] He saw by an excellent spirit what should come to pass at the last, and he comforted them that mourned in Sion. [25] He shewed what should come to pass for ever, and secret things or ever they came. Sir.49 [1] The remembrance of Josias is like the composition of the perfume that is made by the art of the apothecary: it is sweet as honey in all mouths, and as musick at a banquet of wine. [2] He behaved himself uprightly in the conversion of the people, and took away the abominations of iniquity. [3] He directed his heart unto the Lord, and in the time of the ungodly he established the worship of God. [4] All, except David and Ezekias and Josias, were defective: for they forsook the law of the most High, even the kings of Juda failed. [5] Therefore he gave their power unto others, and their glory to a strange nation. [6] They burnt the chosen city of the sanctuary, and made the streets desolate, according to the prophecy of Jeremias. [7] For they entreated him evil, who nevertheless was a prophet, sanctified in his mother's womb, that he might root out, and afflict, and destroy; and that he might build up also, and plant. [8] It was Ezekiel who saw the glorious vision, which was shewed him upon the chariot of the cherubims. [9] For he made mention of the enemies under the figure of the rain, and directed them that went right. [10] And of the twelve prophets let the memorial be blessed, and let their bones flourish again out of their place: for they comforted Jacob, and delivered them by assured hope. [11] How shall we magnify Zorobabel? even he was as a signet on the right hand: [12] So was Jesus the son of Josedec: who in their time builded the house, and set up an holy temple to the Lord, which was prepared for everlasting glory. [13] And among the elect was Neemias, whose renown is great, who raised up for us the walls that were fallen, and set up the gates and the bars, and raised up our ruins again. [14] But upon the earth was no man created like Enoch; for he was taken from the earth. [15] Neither was there a young man born like Joseph, a governor of his brethren, a stay of the people, whose bones were regarded of the Lord. [16] Sem and Seth were in great honour among men, and so was Adam above every living thing in creation. Sir.50 [1] Simon the high priest, the son of Onias, who in his life repaired the house again, and in his days fortified the temple: [2] And by him was built from the foundation the double height, the high fortress of the wall about the temple: [3] In his days the cistern to receive water, being in compass as the sea, was covered with plates of brass: [4] He took care of the temple that it should not fall, and fortified the city against besieging: [5] How was he honoured in the midst of the people in his coming out of the sanctuary! [6] He was as the morning star in the midst of a cloud, and as the moon at the full: [7] As the sun shining upon the temple of the most High, and as the rainbow giving light in the bright clouds: [8] And as the flower of roses in the spring of the year, as lilies by the rivers of waters, and as the branches of the frankincense tree in the time of summer: [9] As fire and incense in the censer, and as a vessel of beaten gold set with all manner of precious stones: [10] And as a fair olive tree budding forth fruit, and as a cypress tree which groweth up to the clouds. [11] When he put on the robe of honour, and was clothed with the perfection of glory, when he went up to the holy altar, he made the garment of holiness honourable. [12] When he took the portions out of the priests' hands, he himself stood by the hearth of the altar, compassed about, as a young cedar in Libanus; and as palm trees compassed they him round about. [13] So were all the sons of Aaron in their glory, and the oblations of the Lord in their hands, before all the congregation of Israel. [14] And finishing the service at the altar, that he might adorn the offering of the most high Almighty, [15] He stretched out his hand to the cup, and poured of the blood of the grape, he poured out at the foot of the altar a sweetsmelling savour unto the most high King of all. [16] Then shouted the sons of Aaron, and sounded the silver trumpets, and made a great noise to be heard, for a remembrance before the most High. [17] Then all the people together hasted, and fell down to the earth upon their faces to worship their Lord God Almighty, the most High. [18] The singers also sang praises with their voices, with great variety of sounds was there made sweet melody. [19] And the people besought the Lord, the most High, by prayer before him that is merciful, till the solemnity of the Lord was ended, and they had finished his service. [20] Then he went down, and lifted up his hands over the whole congregation of the children of Israel, to give the blessing of the Lord with his lips, and to rejoice in his name. [21] And they bowed themselves down to worship the second time, that they might receive a blessing from the most High. [22] Now therefore bless ye the God of all, which only doeth wondrous things every where, which exalteth our days from the womb, and dealeth with us according to his mercy. [23] He grant us joyfulness of heart, and that peace may be in our days in Israel for ever: [24] That he would confirm his mercy with us, and deliver us at his time! [25] There be two manner of nations which my heart abhorreth, and the third is no nation: [26] They that sit upon the mountain of Samaria, and they that dwell among the Philistines, and that foolish people that dwell in Sichem. [27] Jesus the son of Sirach of Jerusalem hath written in this book the instruction of understanding and knowledge, who out of his heart poured forth wisdom. [28] Blessed is he that shall be exercised in these things; and he that layeth them up in his heart shall become wise. [29] For if he do them, he shall be strong to all things: for the light of the Lord leadeth him, who giveth wisdom to the godly. Blessed be the name of the Lord for ever. Amen, Amen. Sir.51 [A Prayer of Jesus the son of Sirach.][1] I will thank thee, O Lord and King, and praise thee, O God my Saviour: I do give praise unto thy name: [2] For thou art my defender and helper, and has preserved my body from destruction, and from the snare of the slanderous tongue, and from the lips that forge lies, and has been mine helper against mine adversaries: [3] And hast delivered me, according to the multitude of they mercies and greatness of thy name, from the teeth of them that were ready to devour me, and out of the hands of such as sought after my life, and from the manifold afflictions which I had; [4] From the choking of fire on every side, and from the midst of the fire which I kindled not; [5] From the depth of the belly of hell, from an unclean tongue, and from lying words. [6] By an accusation to the king from an unrighteous tongue my soul drew near even unto death, my life was near to the hell beneath. [7] They compassed me on every side, and there was no man to help me: I looked for the succour of men, but there was none. [8] Then thought I upon thy mercy, O Lord, and upon thy acts of old, how thou deliverest such as wait for thee, and savest them out of the hands of the enemies. [9] Then lifted I up my supplications from the earth, and prayed for deliverance from death. [10] I called upon the Lord, the Father of my Lord, that he would not leave me in the days of my trouble, and in the time of the proud, when there was no help. [11] I will praise thy name continually, and will sing praises with thanksgiving; and so my prayer was heard: [12] For thou savedst me from destruction, and deliveredst me from the evil time: therefore will I give thanks, and praise thee, and bless they name, O Lord. [13] When I was yet young, or ever I went abroad, I desired wisdom openly in my prayer. [14] I prayed for her before the temple, and will seek her out even to the end. [15] Even from the flower till the grape was ripe hath my heart delighted in her: my foot went the right way, from my youth up sought I after her. [16] I bowed down mine ear a little, and received her, and gat much learning. [17] I profited therein, therefore will I ascribe glory unto him that giveth me wisdom. [18] For I purposed to do after her, and earnestly I followed that which is good; so shall I not be confounded. [19] My soul hath wrestled with her, and in my doings I was exact: I stretched forth my hands to the heaven above, and bewailed my ignorances of her. [20] I directed my soul unto her, and I found her in pureness: I have had my heart joined with her from the beginning, therefore shall I not be foresaken. [21] My heart was troubled in seeking her: therefore have I gotten a good possession. [22] The Lord hath given me a tongue for my reward, and I will praise him therewith. [23] Draw near unto me, ye unlearned, and dwell in the house of learning. [24] Wherefore are ye slow, and what say ye to these things, seeing your souls are very thirsty? [25] I opened my mouth, and said, Buy her for yourselves without money. [26] Put your neck under the yoke, and let your soul receive instruction: she is hard at hand to find. [27] Behold with your eyes, how that I have but little labour, and have gotten unto me much rest. [28] Get learning with a great sum of money, and get much gold by her. [29] Let your soul rejoice in his mercy, and be not ashamed of his praise. [30] Work your work betimes, and in his time he will give you your reward.

Book 82. Tobit

Tob.1 [1] The book of the words of Tobit, son of Tobiel, the son of Ananiel, the son of Aduel, the son of Gabael, of the seed of Asael, of the tribe of Nephthali; [2] Who in the time of Enemessar king of the Assyrians was led captive out of Thisbe, which is at the right hand of that city, which is called properly Nephthali in Galilee above Aser. [3] I Tobit have walked all the days of my life in the ways of truth and justice, and I did many almsdeeds to my brethren, and my nation, who came with me to Nineve, into the land of the Assyrians. [4] And when I was in mine own country, in the land of Israel being but young, all the tribe of Nephthali my father fell from the house of Jerusalem, which was chosen out of all the tribes of Israel, that all the tribes should sacrifice there, where the temple of the habitation of the most High was consecrated and built for all ages. [5] Now all the tribes which together revolted, and the house of my father Nephthali, sacrificed unto the heifer Baal. [6] But I alone went often to Jerusalem at the feasts, as it was ordained unto all the people of Israel by an everlasting decree, having the firstfruits and tenths of increase, with that which was first shorn; and them gave I at the altar to the priests the children of Aaron. [7] The first tenth part of all increase I gave to the sons of Aaron, who ministered at Jerusalem: another tenth part I sold away, and went, and spent it every year at Jerusalem: [8] And the third I gave unto them to whom it was meet, as Debora my father's mother had commanded me, because I was left an orphan by my father. [9] Furthermore, when I was come to the age of a man, I married Anna of mine own kindred, and of her I begat Tobias. [10] And when we were carried away captives to Nineve, all my brethren and those that were of my kindred did eat of the bread of the Gentiles. [11] But I kept myself from eating; [12] Because I remembered God with all my heart. [13] And the most High gave me grace and favour before Enemessar, so that I was his purveyor. [14] And I went into Media, and left in trust with Gabael, the brother of Gabrias, at Rages a city of Media ten talents of silver. [15] Now when Enemessar was dead, Sennacherib his son reigned in his stead; whose estate was troubled, that I could not go into Media. [16] And in the time of Enemessar I gave many alms to my brethren, and gave my bread to the hungry, [17] And my clothes to the naked: and if I saw any of my nation dead, or cast about the walls of Nineve, I buried him. [18] And if the king Sennacherib had slain any, when he was come, and fled from Judea, I buried them privily; for in his wrath he killed many; but the bodies were not found, when they were sought for of the king. [19] And when one of the Ninevites went and complained of me to the king, that I buried them, and hid myself; understanding that I was sought for to be put to death, I withdrew myself for fear. [20] Then all my goods were forcibly taken away, neither was there any thing left me, beside my wife Anna and my son Tobias. [21] And there passed not five and fifty days, before two of his sons killed him, and they fled into the mountains of Ararath; and Sarchedonus his son reigned in his stead; who appointed over his father's accounts, and over all his affairs, Achiacharus my brother Anael's son. [22] And Achiacharus intreating for me, I returned to Nineve. Now Achiacharus was cupbearer, and keeper of the signet, and steward, and overseer of the accounts: and Sarchedonus appointed him next unto him: and he was my brother's son. Tob.2 [1] Now when I was come home again, and my wife Anna was restored unto me, with my son Tobias, in the feast of Pentecost, which is the holy feast of the seven weeks, there was a good dinner prepared me, in the which I sat down to eat. [2] And when I saw abundance of meat, I said to my son, Go and bring what poor man soever thou shalt find out of our brethren, who is mindful of the Lord; and, lo, I tarry for thee. [3] But he came again, and said, Father, one of our nation is strangled, and is cast out in the marketplace. [4] Then before I had tasted of any meat, I started up, and took him up into a room until the going down of the sun. [5] Then I returned, and washed myself, and ate my meat in heaviness, [6] Remembering that prophecy of Amos, as he said, Your feasts shall be turned into mourning, and all your mirth into lamentation. [7] Therefore I wept: and after the going down of the sun I went and made a grave, and buried him. [8] But my neighbours mocked me, and said, This man is not yet afraid to be put to death for this matter: who fled away; and yet, lo, he burieth the dead again. [9] The same night also I returned from the burial, and slept by the wall of my courtyard, being polluted and my face was uncovered: [10] And I knew not that there were sparrows in the wall, and mine eyes being open, the sparrows muted warm dung into mine eyes, and a whiteness came in mine eyes: and I went to the physicians, but they helped me not: moreover Achiacharus did nourish me, until I went into Elymais. [11] And my wife Anna did take women's works to do. [12] And when she had sent them home to the owners, they paid her wages, and gave her also besides a kid. [13] And when it was in my house, and began to cry, I said unto her, From whence is this kid? is it not stolen? render it to the owners; for it is not lawful to eat any thing that is stolen. [14] But she replied upon me, It was given for a gift more than the wages. Howbeit I did not believe her, but bade her render it to the owners: and I was abashed at her. But she replied upon me, Where are thine alms and thy righteous deeds? behold, thou and all thy works are known. Tob.3 [1] Then I being

grieved did weep, and in my sorrow prayed, saying, [2] O Lord, thou art just, and all thy works and all thy ways are mercy and truth, and thou judgest truly and justly for ever. [3] Remember me, and look on me, punish me not for my sins and ignorances, and the sins of mg fathers, who have sinned before thee: [4] For they obeyed not thy commandments: wherefore thou hast delivered us for a spoil, and unto captivity, and unto death, and for a proverb of reproach to all the nations among whom we are dispersed. [5] And now thy judgments are many and true: deal with me according to my sins and my fathers': because we have not kept thy commandments, neither have walked in truth before thee. [6] Now therefore deal with me as seemeth best unto thee, and command my spirit to be taken from me, that I may be dissolved, and become earth: for it is profitable for me to die rather than to live, because I have heard false reproaches, and have much sorrow: command therefore that I may now be delivered out of this distress, and go into the everlasting place: turn not thy face away from me. [7] It came to pass the same day, that in Ecbatane a city of Media Sara the daughter of Raguel was also reproached by her father's maids; [8] Because that she had been married to seven husbands, whom Asmodeus the evil spirit had killed, before they had lain with her. Dost thou not know, said they, that thou hast strangled thine husbands? thou hast had already seven husbands, neither wast thou named after any of them. [9] Wherefore dost thou beat us for them? if they be dead, go thy ways after them, let us never see of thee either son or daughter. [10] Whe she heard these things, she was very sorrowful, so that she thought to have strangled herself; and she said, I am the only daughter of my father, and if I do this, it shall be a reproach unto him, and I shall bring his old age with sorrow unto the grave. [11] Then she prayed toward the window, and said, Blessed art thou, O Lord my God, and thine holy and glorious name is blessed and honourable for ever: let all thy works praise thee for ever. [12] And now, O Lord, I set mine eyes and my face toward thee, [13] And say, Take me out of the earth, that I may hear no more the reproach. [14] Thou knowest, Lord, that I am pure from all sin with man, [15] And that I never polluted my name, nor the name of my father, in the land of my captivity: I am the only daughter of my father, neither hath he any child to be his heir, neither any near kinsman, nor any son of his alive, to whom I may keep myself for a wife: my seven husbands are already dead; and why should I live? but if it please not thee that I should die, command some regard to be had of me, and pity taken of me, that I hear no more reproach. [16] So the prayers of them both were heard before the majesty of the great God. [17] And Raphael was sent to heal them both, that is, to scale away the whiteness of Tobit's eyes, and to give Sara the daughter of Raguel for a wife to Tobias the son of Tobit; and to bind Asmodeus the evil spirit; because she belonged to Tobias by right of inheritance. The selfsame time came Tobit home, and entered into his house, and Sara the daughter of Raguel came down from her upper chamber. Tob.4 [1] In that day Tobit remembered the money which he had committed to Gabael in Rages of Media, [2] And said with himself, I have wished for death; wherefore do I not call for my son Tobias that I may signify to him of the money before I die? [3] And when he had called him, he said, My son, when I am dead, bury me; and despise not thy mother, but honour her all the days of thy life, and do that which shall please her, and grieve her not. [4] Remember, my son, that she saw many dangers for thee, when thou wast in her womb: and when she is dead, bury her by me in one grave. [5] My son, be mindful of the Lord our God all thy days, and let not thy will be set to sin, or to transgress his commandments: do uprightly all thy life long, and follow not the ways of unrighteousness. [6] For if thou deal truly, thy doings shall prosperously succeed to thee, and to all them that live justly. [7] Give alms of thy substance; and when thou givest alms, let not thine eye be envious, neither turn thy face from any poor, and the face of God shall not be turned away from thee. [8] If thou hast abundance give alms accordingly: if thou have but a little, be not afraid to give according to that little: [9] For thou layest up a good treasure for thyself against the day of necessity. [10] Because that alms do deliver from death, and suffereth not to come into darkness. [11] For alms is a good gift unto all that give it in the sight of the most High. [12] Beware of all whoredom, my son, and chiefly take a wife of the seed of thy fathers, and take not a strange woman to wife, which is not of thy father's tribe: for we are the children of the prophets, Noe, Abraham, Isaac, and Jacob: remember, my son, that our fathers from the beginning, even that they all married wives of their own kindred, and were blessed in their children, and their seed shall inherit the land. [13] Now therefore, my son, love thy brethren, and despise not in thy heart thy brethren, the sons and daughters of thy people, in not taking a wife of them: for in pride is destruction and much trouble, and in lewdness is decay and great want: for lewdness is the mother of famine. [14] Let not the wages of any man, which hath wrought for thee, tarry with thee, but give him it out of hand: for if thou serve God, he will also repay thee: be circumspect my son, in all things thou doest, and be wise in all thy conversation. [15] Do that to no man which thou hatest: drink not wine to make thee drunken: neither let drunkenness go with thee in thy journey. [16] Give of thy bread to the hungry, and of thy garments to them that are naked; and according to thine abundance give alms: and let not thine eye be envious, when thou givest alms. [17] Pour out thy bread on the burial of the just, but give nothing to the wicked. [18] Ask counsel of all that are wise, and despise not any counsel that is profitable. [19] Bless the Lord thy God alway, and desire of him that thy ways may be directed, and that all thy paths and counsels may prosper: for every nation hath not counsel; but the Lord himself giveth all good things, and he humbleth whom he will, as he will; now therefore, my son, remember my commandments, neither let them be put out of thy mind. [20] And now I signify this to they that I committed ten talents to Gabael the son of Gabrias at Rages in Media. [21] And fear not, my son, that we are made poor: for thou hast much wealth, if thou fear God, and depart from all sin, and do that which is pleasing in his sight. Tob.5 [1] Tobias then answered and said, Father, I will do all things which thou hast commanded me: [2] But how can I receive the money, seeing I know him not? [3] Then he gave him the handwriting, and said unto him, Seek thee a man which may go with thee, whiles I yet live, and I will give him wages: and go and receive the money. [4] Therefore when he went to seek a man, he found Raphael that was an angel. [5] But he knew not; and he said unto him, Canst thou go with me to Rages? and knowest thou those places well? [6] To whom the angel said, I will go with thee, and I know the way well: for I have lodged with our brother Gabael. [7] Then Tobias said unto him, Tarry for me, till I tell my father. [8] Then he said unto him, Go and tarry not. So he went in and said to his father, Behold, I have found one which will go with me. Then he said, Call him unto me, that I may know of what tribe he is, and whether he be a trusty man to go with thee. [9] So he called him, and he came in, and they saluted one another. [10] Then Tobit said unto him, Brother, shew me of what tribe and family thou art. [11] To whom he said, Dost thou seek for a tribe or family, or an hired man to go with thy son? Then Tobit said unto him, I would know, brother, thy kindred and name. [12] Then he said, I am Azarias, the son of Ananias the great, and of thy brethren. [13] Then Tobit said, Thou art welcome, brother; be not now angry with me, because I have enquired to know thy tribe and thy family; for thou art my brother, of an honest and good stock: for I know Ananias and Jonathas, sons of that great Samaias, as we went together to Jerusalem to worship, and offered the firstborn, and the tenths of the fruits; and they were not seduced with the error of our brethren: my brother, thou art of a good stock. [14] But tell me, what wages shall I give thee? wilt thou a drachm a day, and things necessary, as to mine own son? [15] Yea, moreover, if ye return safe, I will add something to thy wages. [16] So they were well pleased. Then said he to Tobias, Prepare thyself for the journey, and God send you a good journey. And when his son had prepared all things far the journey, his father said, Go thou with this man, and God, which dwelleth in heaven, prosper your journey, and the angel of God keep you company. So they went forth both, and the young man's dog with them. [17] But Anna his mother wept, and said to Tobit, Why hast thou sent away our son? is he not the staff of our hand, in going in and out before us? [18] Be not greedy to add money to money: but let it be as refuse in respect of our child. [19] For that which the Lord hath given us to live with doth suffice us. [20] Then said Tobit to her, Take no care, my sister; he shall return in safety, and thine eyes shall see him. [21] For the good angel will keep him company, and his journey shall be prosperous, and he shall return safe. [22] Then she made an end of weeping. Tob.6 [1] And as they went on their journey, they came in the evening to the river Tigris, and they lodged there. [2] And when the young man went down to wash himself, a fish leaped out of the river, and would have devoured him. [3] Then the angel said unto him, Take the fish. And the young man laid hold of the fish, and drew it to land. [4] To whom the angel said, Open the fish, and take the heart and the liver and the gall, and put them up safely. [5] So the young man did as the angel commanded him; and when they had roasted the fish, they did eat it: then they both went on their way, till they drew near to Ecbatane. [6] Then the young man said to the angel, Brother Azarias, to what use is the heart and the liver and the gal of the fish? [7] And he said unto him, Touching the heart and the liver, if a devil or an evil spirit trouble any, we must make a smoke thereof before the man or the woman, and the party shall be no more vexed. [8] As for the gall, it is good to anoint a man that hath whiteness in his eyes, and he shall be healed. [9] And when they were come near to Rages, [10] The angel said to the young man, Brother, to day we shall lodge with Raguel, who is thy cousin; he also hath one only daughter, named Sara; I will speak for her, that she may be given thee for a wife. [11] For to thee doth the right of her appertain, seeing thou only art of her kindred. [12] And the maid is fair and wise: now therefore hear me, and I will speak to her father; and when we return from Rages we will celebrate the marriage: for I know that Raguel cannot marry her to another according to the law of Moses, but he shall be guilty of death, because the right of inheritance doth rather appertain to thee than to any other. [13] Then the young man answered the angel, I have heard, brother Azarias that this maid hath been given to seven men, who all died in the marriage chamber. [14] And now I am the only son of my father, and I am afraid, lest if I go in unto her, I die, as the other before: for a wicked spirit loveth her, which hurteth no body, but those which come unto her; wherefore I also fear lest I die, and bring my father's and my mother's life because of me to the grave with sorrow: for they have no other son to bury them. [15] Then the angel said unto him, Dost thou not remember the precepts which thy father gave thee, that thou shouldest marry a wife of thine own kindred? wherefore hear me, O my brother; for she shall be given thee to wife; and make thou no reckoning of the evil spirit; for this same night shall she be given thee in marriage. [16] And when thou shalt come into the marriage chamber, thou shalt take the ashes of perfume, and shalt lay upon them some of the heart and liver of the fish, and shalt make a smoke with it: [17] And the devil shall smell it, and flee away, and never come again any more: but when thou shalt come to her, rise up both of you, and pray to God which is merciful, who will have pity on you, and save you: fear not, for she is appointed unto thee from the beginning; and thou shalt preserve her, and she shall go with thee. Moreover I suppose that she shall bear thee children. Now when Tobias had heard these things, he loved her, and his heart was effectually joined to her. Tob.7 [1] And when they were come to Ecbatane, they came to the house of Raguel, and Sara met them: and after they had saluted one another, she brought them into the house. [2] Then said Raguel to Edna his wife, How like is this young man to Tobit my cousin! [3] And Raguel asked them, From whence are ye, brethren? To whom they said, We are of the sons of Nephthalim, which are captives in Nineve. [4] Then he said to them, Do ye know Tobit our kinsman? And they said, We know him. Then said he, Is he in good health? [5] And they said, He is both alive, and in good health: and Tobias said, He is my father. [6] Then Raguel leaped up, and kissed him, and wept, [7] And blessed him, and said unto him, Thou art the son of an honest and good man. But when he had heard that Tobit was blind, he was sorrowful, and wept. [8] And likewise Edna his wife and Sara his daughter wept. Moreover they entertained them cheerfully; and after that they had killed a ram of the flock, they set store of meat on the table. Then said Tobias to Raphael, Brother Azarias, speak of those things of which thou didst talk in the way, and let this business be dispatched. [9] So he communicated the matter with Raguel: and Raguel said to Tobias, Eat and drink, and make merry: [10] For it is meet that thou shouldest marry my daughter: nevertheless I will declare unto thee the truth. [11] I have given my daughter in marriage te seven men, who died that night they came in unto her: nevertheless for the present be merry. But Tobias said, I will eat nothing here, till we agree and swear one to another. [12] Raguel said, Then take her from henceforth according to the manner, for thou art her cousin, and she is thine, and the merciful God give you good success in all things. [13] Then he called his daughter Sara, and she came to her father, and he took her by the hand, and gave her to be wife to Tobias, saying, Behold, take her after the law of Moses, and lead her away to thy father. And he blessed them; [14] And called Edna his wife, and took paper, and did write an instrument of covenants, and sealed it. [15] Then they began to eat. [16] After Raguel called his wife Edna, and said unto her, Sister, prepare another chamber, and bring her in thither. [17] Which when she had done as he had bidden her, she brought her thither: and she wept, and she received the tears of her daughter, and said unto her, [18] Be of good comfort, my daughter; the Lord of heaven and earth give thee joy for this thy sorrow: be of good comfort, my daughter. Tob.8 [1] And when they had supped, they brought Tobias in unto her. [2] And as he went, he remembered the words of Raphael, and took the ashes of the perfumes, and put the heart and the liver of the fish thereupon, and made a smoke therewith. [3] The which smell when the evil spirit had smelled, he fled into the utmost parts of Egypt, and the angel bound him. [4] And after that they were both shut in together, Tobias rose out of the bed, and said, Sister, arise, and let us pray that God would have pity on us. [5] Then began Tobias to say, Blessed art thou, O God of our fathers, and blessed is thy holy and glorious name for ever; let the heavens bless thee, and all thy creatures. [6] Thou madest Adam, and gavest him Eve his wife for an helper and stay: of them came mankind: thou hast said, It is not good that man should be alone; let us make unto him an aid like unto himself. [7] And now, O Lord, I take not this my sister for lush but uprightly: therefore mercifully ordain that we may become aged together. [8] And she said with him, Amen. [9] So they slept both that night. And Raguel arose, and went and made a grave, [10] Saying, I fear lest he also be dead. [11] But when Raguel was come into his house, [12] He said unto his wife Edna. Send one of the maids, and let her see whether he be alive: if he be not, that we may bury him, and no man know it. [13] So the maid opened the door, and went in, and found them both asleep, [14] And came forth, and told them that he was alive. [15] Then Raguel praised God, and said, O God, thou art worthy to be praised with all pure and holy praise; therefore let thy saints praise thee with all thy creatures; and let all thine angels and thine elect praise thee for ever. [16] Thou art to be praised, for thou hast made me joyful; and that is not come to me which I suspected; but thou hast dealt with us according to thy great mercy. [17] Thou art to be praised because thou hast had mercy of two that were the only begotten children of their fathers: grant them mercy, O Lord, and finish their life in health with joy and mercy. [18] Then Raguel bade his servants to fill the grave. [19] And he kept the wedding feast fourteen days. [20] For before the days of the marriage were finished, Raguel had said unto him by an oath, that he should not depart till the fourteen days of the marriage were expired; [21] And then he should take the half of his goods, and go in safety to his father; and should have the rest when I and my wife be dead. Tob.9 [1] Then Tobias called Raphael, and said unto him, [2] Brother Azarias, take with thee a servant, and two camels, and go to Rages of Media to Gabael, and bring me the money, and bring him to the wedding. [3] For Raguel hath sworn that I shall not depart. [4] But my father counteth the days; and if I tarry long, he will be very sorry. [5] So Raphael went out, and lodged with Gabael, and gave him the handwriting: who brought forth bags which were sealed up, and gave them to him. [6] And early in the morning they went forth both together, and came to the wedding: and Tobias blessed his wife. Tob.10 [1] Now Tobit his father counted every day: and when the days of the journey were expired, and they came not, [2] Then Tobit said, Are they detained? or is Gabael dead, and there is no man to give him the money? [3] Therefore he was very sorry. [4] Then his wife said unto him, My son is dead, seeing he stayeth long; and she began to wail him, and said, [5] Now I care for nothing, my son, since I have let thee go, the light of mine eyes. [6] To whom Tobit said, Hold thy peace, take no care, for he is safe. [7] But she said, Hold thy peace, and deceive me not; my son is dead. And she went out every day into the way which they went, and did eat no meat on the daytime, and ceased not whole nights to bewail her son Tobias, until the fourteen days of the wedding were expired, which Raguel had sworn that he should spend there. Then Tobias said to Raguel, Let me go, for my father and my mother look no more to see me. [8] But his father in law said unto him, Tarry with me, and I will send to thy father, and they shall declare unto him how things go with thee. [9] But Tobias said, No; but let me go to my father. [10] Then Raguel arose, and gave him Sara his wife, and half his goods, servants, and cattle, and money: [11] And he blessed them, and sent them away, saying, The God of heaven give you a prosperous journey, my children. [12] And he said to his daughter, Honour thy father and thy mother in law, which are now thy parents, that I may hear good report of thee. And he kissed her. Edna also said to Tobias, The Lord of heaven restore thee, my dear brother, and grant that I may see thy children of my daughter Sara before I die, that I may rejoice before the Lord: behold, I commit my daughter unto thee of special trust; where are do not entreat her evil. Tob.11 [1] After these things Tobias went his way, praising God that he had given him a prosperous journey, and blessed Raguel and Edna his wife, and went on his way till they drew near unto Nineve. [2] Then Raphael said to Tobias, Thou knowest, brother, how thou didst leave thy father: [3] Let us haste before thy wife, and prepare the house. [4] And take in thine hand the gall of the fish. So they went their way, and the dog went after them. [5] Now Anna sat looking about toward the way for her son. [6] And when she espied him coming, she said to his father, Behold, thy son cometh, and the man that went with him. [7] Then said Raphael, I know, Tobias, that thy father will open his eyes. [8] Therefore anoint thou his eyes with the gall, and being pricked therewith, he shall rub, and the whiteness shall fall away, and he shall see thee. [9] Then Anna ran forth, and fell upon the neck of her son, and said unto him, Seeing I have seen thee, my son, from henceforth I am content to die. And they wept both. [10] Tobit also went forth toward the door, and stumbled: but his son ran unto him, [11] And took hold of his father: and he strake of the gall on his fathers' eyes, saying, Be of good hope, my father. [12] And when his eyes began to smart, he rubbed them; [13] And the whiteness pilled away from the corners of his eyes: and when he saw his son, he fell upon his neck. [14] And he wept, and said, Blessed art thou, O God, and blessed is thy name for ever; and blessed are all thine holy angels: [15] For thou hast scourged, and hast taken pity on me: for, behold, I see my son Tobias. And his son went in rejoicing, and told his father the great things that had happened to him in Media. [16] Then Tobit went out to meet his daughter in law at the gate of Nineve, rejoicing and praising God: and they which saw him go marvelled, because he had received his sight. [17] But Tobias gave thanks before them, because God had mercy on him. And when he came near to Sara his daughter in law, he blessed her, saying, Thou art welcome, daughter: God be blessed, which hath brought thee unto us, and blessed be thy father and thy mother. And there was joy among all his brethren which were at Nineve. [18] And Achiacharus, and Nasbas his brother's son, came: [19] And Tobias' wedding was kept seven days with great joy. Tob.12 [1] Then Tobit called his son Tobias, and said unto him, My son, see that the man have his wages, which went with thee, and thou must give him more. [2] And Tobias said unto him, O father, it is no harm to me to give him half of those things which I have brought: [3] For he hath brought me again to thee in safety, and made whole my wife, and brought me the money, and likewise healed thee. [4] Then the old man said, It is due unto him. [5] So he called the angel, and he said unto him, Take half of all that ye have brought and go away in safety. [6] Then he took them both apart, and said unto them, Bless God, praise him, and magnify him, and praise him for the things which he hath done unto you in the sight of all that live. It is good to praise God, and exalt his name, and honourably to shew forth the works of God; therefore be not slack to praise him. [7] It is good to keep close the secret of a king, but it is honourable to reveal the works of God. Do that which is good, and no evil shall touch you. [8] Prayer is good with fasting and alms and righteousness. A little with righteousness is better than much with unrighteousness. It is better to give alms than to lay up gold: [9] For alms doth deliver from death, and shall purge away all sin. Those that exercise alms and righteousness shall be filled with life: [10] But they that sin are enemies to their own life. [11] Surely I will keep close nothing from you. For I said, It was good to keep close the secret of a king, but that it was honourable to reveal the works of God. [12] Now therefore, when thou didst pray, and Sara thy daughter in law, I did bring the remembrance of your prayers before the Holy One: and when thou didst bury the dead, I was with thee likewise. [13] And when thou didst not delay to rise up, and leave thy dinner, to go and cover the dead, thy good deed was not hid from me: but I was with thee. [14] And now God hath sent me to heal thee and Sara thy daughter in law. [15] I am Raphael, one of the seven holy angels, which present the prayers of the saints, and which go in and out before the glory of the Holy One. [16] Then they were both troubled, and fell upon their faces: for they feared. [17] But he said unto them, Fear not, for it shall go well with you; praise God therefore. [18] For not of any favour of mine, but by the will of our God I came; wherefore praise him for ever. [19] All these days I did appear unto you; but I did neither eat nor drink, but ye did see a vision. [20] Now therefore give God thanks: for I go up to him that sent me; but write all things which are done in a book. [21] And when they arose, they saw him no more. [22] Then they confessed the great and wonderful works of God, and how the angel of the Lord had appeared unto them. Tob.13 [1] Then Tobit wrote a prayer of rejoicing, and said, Blessed be God that liveth for ever, and blessed be his kingdom. [2] For he doth scourge, and hath mercy: he leadeth down to hell, and bringeth up again: neither is there any that can avoid his hand. [3] Confess him before the Gentiles, ye children of Israel: for he hath scattered us among them. [4] There declare his greatness, and extol him before all the living: for he is our Lord, and he is the God our Father for ever. [5] And he will scourge us for our iniquities, and will have mercy again, and will gather us out of all nations, among whom he hath scattered us. [6] If ye turn to him with your whole heart, and with your whole mind, and deal uprightly before him, then will he turn unto you, and will not hide his face from you. Therefore see what he will do with you, and confess him with your whole mouth, and praise the Lord of might, and extol the everlasting King. In the land of my captivity do I praise him, and declare his might and majesty to a sinful nation. O ye sinners, turn and do justice before him: who can tell if he will accept you, and have mercy on you? [7] I will extol my God, and my soul shall praise the King of heaven, and shall rejoice in his greatness. [8] Let all men speak, and let all praise him for his righteousness. [9] O Jerusalem, the holy city, he will scourge thee for thy children's works, and will have mercy again on the sons of the righteous. [10] Give praise to the Lord, for he is good: and praise the everlasting King, that his tabernacle may be builded in thee again with joy, and let him make joyful there in thee those that are captives, and love in thee for ever those that are miserable. [11] Many nations shall come from far to the name of the Lord God with gifts in their hands, even gifts to the King of heaven; all generations shall praise thee with great joy. [12] Cursed are all they which hate thee, and blessed shall all be which love thee for ever. [13] Rejoice and be glad for the children of the just: for they shall be gathered together, and shall bless the Lord of the just. [14] O blessed are they which love thee, for they shall rejoice in thy peace: blessed are they which have been sorrowful for all thy scourges; for they shall rejoice for thee, when they have seen all thy glory, and shall be glad for ever. [15] Let my soul bless God the great King. [16] For Jerusalem shall be built up with sapphires and emeralds, and precious stone: thy walls and towers and battlements with pure gold. [17] And the streets of Jerusalem shall be paved with beryl and carbuncle and stones of Ophir. [18] And all her streets shall say, Alleluia; and they shall praise him, saying, Blessed be God, which hath extolled it for ever. Tob.14 [1] So Tobit made an end of praising God. [2] And he was eight and fifty years old when he lost his sight, which was restored to him after eight years: and he gave alms, and he increased in the fear of the Lord God, and praised him. [3] And when he was very aged he called his son, and the sons of his son, and said to him, My son, take thy children; for, behold, I am aged, and am ready to depart out of this life. [4] Go into Media my son, for I surely believe those things which Jonas the prophet spake of Nineve, that it shall be overthrown; and that for a time peace shall rather be in Media; and that our brethren shall lie scattered in the earth from that good land: and Jerusalem shall be desolate, and the house of God in it shall be burned, and shall be desolate for a time; [5] And that again God will have mercy on them, and bring them again into the land, where they shall build a temple, but not like to the first, until the time of that age be fulfilled; and afterward they shall return from all places of their captivity, and build up Jerusalem gloriously, and the house of God shall be built in it for ever with a glorious building, as the prophets have spoken thereof. [6] And all nations shall turn, and fear the Lord God truly, and shall bury their idols. [7] So shall all nations praise the Lord, and his people shall confess God, and the Lord shall exalt his people; and all those which love the Lord God in truth and justice shall rejoice, shewing mercy to our brethren. [8] And now, my son, depart out of Nineve, because that those things which the prophet Jonas spake shall surely come to pass. [9] But keep thou the law and the commandments, and shew thyself merciful and just, that it may go well with thee. [10] And bury me decently, and thy mother with me; but tarry no longer at Nineve. Remember, my son, how Aman handled Achiacharus that brought him up, how out of light he brought him into darkness, and how he rewarded him again: yet Achiacharus was saved, but the other had his reward: for he went down into darkness. Manasses gave alms, and escaped the snares of death which they had set for him: but Aman fell into the snare, and perished. [11] Wherefore now, my son, consider what alms doeth, and how righteousness doth deliver. When he had said these things, he gave up the ghost in the bed, being an hundred and eight and fifty years old; and he buried him honourably. [12] And when Anna his mother was dead, he buried her with his father. But Tobias departed with his wife and children to Ecbatane to Raguel his father in law, [13] Where he became old with honour, and he buried his father and mother in law honourably, and he inherited their substance, and his father Tobit's. [14] And he died at Ecbatane in Media, being an hundred and seven and twenty years old. [15] But before he died he heard of the destruction of Nineve, which was taken by Nabuchodonosor and Assuerus: and before his death he rejoiced over Nineve.

Book 83. *Judith*

Jdt.1 [1] In the twelfth year of the reign of Nabuchodonosor, who reigned in Nineve, the great city; in the days of Arphaxad, which reigned over the Medes in Ecbatane, [2] And built in Ecbatane walls round about of stones hewn three cubits broad and six cubits long, and made the height of the wall seventy cubits, and the breadth thereof fifty cubits: [3] And set the towers thereof upon the gates of it an hundred cubits high, and the breadth thereof in the foundation threescore cubits: [4] And he made the gates thereof, even gates that were raised to the height of seventy cubits, and the breadth of them was forty cubits, for the going forth of his mighty armies, and for the setting in array of his footmen: [5] Even in those days king Nabuchodonosor made war with king Arphaxad in the great plain, which is the plain in the borders of Ragau. [6] And there came unto him all they that dwelt in the hill country, and all that dwelt by Euphrates, and Tigris and Hydaspes, and the plain of Arioch the king of the Elymeans, and very many nations of the sons of Chelod, assembled themselves to the battle. [7] Then Nabuchodonosor king of the Assyrians sent unto all that dwelt in Persia, and to all that dwelt westward, and to those that dwelt in Cilicia, and Damascus, and Libanus, and Antilibanus, and to all that dwelt upon the sea coast, [8] And to those among the nations that were of Carmel, and Galaad, and the higher Galilee, and the great plain of Esdrelom, [9] And to all that were in Samaria and the cities thereof, and beyond Jordan unto Jerusalem, and Betane, and Chelus, and Kades, and the river of Egypt, and Taphnes, and Ramesse, and all the land of Gesem, [10] Until ye come beyond Tanis and Memphis, and to all the inhabitants of Egypt, until ye come to the borders of Ethiopia. [11] But all the inhabitants of the land made light of the commandment of Nabuchodonosor king of the Assyrians, neither went they with him to the battle; for they were not afraid of him: yea, he was before them as one man, and they sent away his ambassadors from them without effect, and with disgrace. [12] Therefore Nabuchodonosor was very angry with all this country, and sware by his throne and kingdom, that he would surely be avenged upon all those coasts of Cilicia, and Damascus, and Syria, and that he would slay with the sword all the inhabitants of the land of Moab, and the children of Ammon, and all Judea, and all that were in Egypt, till ye come to the borders of the two seas. [13] Then he marched in battle array with his power against king Arphaxad in the seventeenth year, and he prevailed in his battle: for he overthrew all the power of Arphaxad, and all his horsemen, and all his chariots, [14] And became lord of his cities, and came unto Ecbatane, and took the towers, and spoiled the streets thereof, and turned the beauty thereof into shame. [15] He took also Arphaxad in the mountains of Ragau, and smote him through with his darts, and destroyed him utterly that day. [16] So he returned afterward to Nineve, both he and all his company of sundry nations being a very great multitude of men of war, and there he took his ease, and banqueted, both he and his army, an hundred and twenty days. Jdt.2 [1] And in the eighteenth year, the two and twentieth day of the first month, there was talk in the house of Nabuchodonosor king of the Assyrians that he should, as he said, avenge himself on all the earth. [2] So he called unto him all his officers, and all his nobles, and communicated with them his secret counsel, and concluded the afflicting of the whole earth out of his own mouth. [3] Then they decreed to destroy all flesh, that did not obey the commandment of his mouth. [4] And when he had ended his counsel, Nabuchodonosor king of the Assyrians called Holofernes the chief captain of his army, which was next unto him, and said unto him. [5] Thus saith the great king, the lord of the whole earth, Behold, thou shalt go forth from my presence, and take with thee men that trust in their own strength, of footmen an hundred and twenty thou-

sand; and the number of horses with their riders twelve thousand. [6] And thou shalt go against all the west country, because they disobeyed my commandment. [7] And thou shalt declare unto that they prepare for me earth and water: for I will go forth in my wrath against them and will cover the whole face of the earth with the feet of mine army, and I will give them for a spoil unto them: [8] So that their slain shall fill their valleys and brooks and the river shall be filled with their dead, till it overflow: [9] And I will lead them captives to the utmost parts of all the earth. [10] Thou therefore shalt go forth. and take beforehand for me all their coasts: and if they will yield themselves unto thee, thou shalt reserve them for me till the day of their punishment. [11] But concerning them that rebel, let not thine eye spare them; but put them to the slaughter, and spoil them wheresoever thou goest. [12] For as I live, and by the power of my kingdom, whatsoever I have spoken, that will I do by mine hand. [13] And take thou heed that thou transgress none of the commandments of thy lord, but accomplish them fully, as I have commanded thee, and defer not to do them. [14] Then Holofernes went forth from the presence of his lord, and called ail the governors and captains, and the officers of the army of Assur; [15] And he mustered the chosen men for the battle, as his lord had commanded him, unto an hundred and twenty thousand, and twelve thousand archers on horseback; [16] And he ranged them, as a great army is ordered for the war. [17] And he took camels and asses for their carriages, a very great number; and sheep and oxen and goats without number for their provision: [18] And plenty of victual for every man of the army, and very much gold and silver out of the king's house. [19] Then he went forth and all his power to go before king Nabuchodonosor in the voyage, and to cover all the face of the earth westward with their chariots, and horsemen, and their chosen footmen. [20] A great number also sundry countries came with them like locusts, and like the sand of the earth: for the multitude was without number. [21] And they went forth of Nineve three days' journey toward the plain of Bectileth, and pitched from Bectileth near the mountain which is at the left hand of the upper Cilicia. [22] Then he took all his army, his footmen, and horsemen and chariots, and went from thence into the hill country; [23] And destroyed Phud and Lud, and spoiled all the children of Rasses, and the children of Israel, which were toward the wilderness at the south of the land of the Chellians. [24] Then he went over Euphrates, and went through Mesopotamia, and destroyed all the high cities that were upon the river Arbonai, till ye come to the sea. [25] And he took the borders of Cilicia, and killed all that resisted him, and came to the borders of Japheth, which were toward the south, over against Arabia. [26] He compassed also all the children of Madian, and burned up their tabernacles, and spoiled their sheepcotes. [27] Then he went down into the plain of Damascus in the time of wheat harvest, and burnt up all their fields, and destroyed their flocks and herds, also he spoiled their cities, and utterly wasted their countries, and smote all their young men with the edge of the sword. [28] Therefore the fear and dread of him fell upon all the inhabitants of the sea coasts, which were in Sidon and Tyrus, and them that dwelt in Sur and Ocina, and all that dwelt in Jemnaan; and they that dwelt in Azotus and Ascalon feared him greatly. Jdt.3 [1] So they sent ambassadors unto him to treat of peace, saying, [2] Behold, we the servants of Nabuchodonosor the great king lie before thee; use us as shall be good in thy sight. [3] Behold, our houses, and all our places, and all our fields of wheat, and flocks, and herds, and all the lodges of our tents lie before thy face; use them as it pleaseth thee. [4] Behold, even our cities and the inhabitants thereof are thy servants; come and deal with them as seemeth good unto thee. [5] So the men came to Holofernes, and declared unto him after this manner. [6] Then came he down toward the sea coast, both he and his army, and set garrisons in the high cities, and took out of them chosen men for aid. [7] So they and all the country round about received them with garlands, with dances, and with timbrels. [8] Yet he did cast down their frontiers, and cut down their groves: for he had decreed to destroy all the gods of the land, that all nations should worship Nabuchodonosor only, and that all tongues and tribes should call upon him as god. [9] Also he came over against Esdraelon near unto Judea, over against the great strait of Judea. [10] And he pitched between Geba and Scythopolis, and there he tarried a whole month, that he might gather together all the carriages of his army. Jdt.4 [1] Now the children of Israel, that dwelt in Judea, heard all that Holofernes the chief captain of Nabuchodonosor king of the Assyrians had done to the nations, and after what manner he had spoiled all their temples, and brought them to nought. [2] Therefore they were exceedingly afraid of him, and were troubled for Jerusalem, and for the temple of the Lord their God: [3] For they were newly returned from the captivity, and all the people of Judea were lately gathered together: and the vessels, and the altar, and the house, were sanctified after the profanation. [4] Therefore they sent into all the coasts of Samaria, and the villages and to Bethoron, and Belmen, and Jericho, and to Choba, and Esora, and to the valley of Salem: [5] And possessed themselves beforehand of all the tops of the high mountains, and fortified the villages that were in them, and laid up victuals for the provision of war: for their fields were of late reaped. [6] Also Joacim the high priest, which was in those days in Jerusalem, wrote to them that dwelt in Bethulia, and Betomestham, which is over against Esdraelon toward the open country, near to Dothaim, [7] Charging them to keep the passages of the hill country: for by them there was an entrance into Judea, and it was easy to stop them that would come up, because the passage was straight, for two men at the most. [8] And the children of Israel did as Joacim the high priest had commanded them, with the ancients of all the people of Israel, which dwelt at Jerusalem. [9] Then every man of Israel cried to God with great fervency, and with great vehemency did they humble their souls: [10] Both they, and their wives and their children, and their cattle, and every stranger and hireling, and their servants bought with money, put sackcloth upon their loins. [11] Thus every man and women, and the little children, and the inhabitants of Jerusalem, fell before the temple, and cast ashes upon their heads, and spread out their sackcloth before the face of the Lord: also they put sackcloth about the altar, [12] And cried to the God of Israel all with one consent earnestly, that he would not give their children for a prey, and their wives for a spoil, and the cities of their inheritance to destruction, and the sanctuary to profanation and reproach, and for the nations to rejoice at. [13] So God heard their prayers, and looked upon their afflictions: for the people fasted many days in all Judea and Jerusalem before the sanctuary of the Lord Almighty. [14] And Joacim the high priest, and all the priests that stood before the Lord, and they which ministered unto the Lord, had their loins girt with sackcloth, and offered the daily burnt offerings, with the vows and free gifts of the people, [15] And had ashes on their mitres, and cried unto the Lord with all their power, that he would look upon all the house of Israel graciously. Jdt.5 [1] Then was it declared to Holofernes, the chief captain of the army of Assur, that the children of Israel had prepared for war, and had shut up the passages of the hill country, and had fortified all the tops of the high hills and had laid impediments in the champaign countries: [2] Wherewith he was very angry, and called all the princes of Moab, and the captains of Ammon, and all the governors of the sea coast, [3] And he said unto them, Tell me now, ye sons of Chanaan, who this people is, that dwelleth in the hill country, and what are the cities that they inhabit, and what is the multitude of their army, and wherein is their power and strength, and what king is set over them, or captain of their army; [4] And why have they determined not to come and meet me, more than all the inhabitants of the west. [5] Then said Achior, the captain of all the sons of Ammon, Let my lord now hear a word from the mouth of thy servant, and I will declare unto thee the truth concerning this people, which dwelleth near thee, and inhabiteth the hill countries: and there shall no lie come out of the mouth of thy servant. [6] This people are descended of the Chaldeans: [7] And they sojourned heretofore in Mesopotamia, because they would not follow the gods of their fathers, which were in the land of Chaldea. [8] For they left the way of their ancestors, and worshipped the God of heaven, the God whom they knew: so they cast them out from the face of their gods, and they fled into Mesopotamia, and sojourned there many days. [9] Then their God commanded them to depart from the place where they sojourned, and to go into the land of Chanaan: where they dwelt, and were increased with gold and silver, and with very much cattle. [10] But when a famine covered all the land of Chanaan, they went down into Egypt, and sojourned there, while they were nourished, and became there a great multitude, so that one could not number their nation. [11] Therefore the king of Egypt rose up against them, and dealt subtilly with them, and brought them low with labouring in brick, and made them slaves. [12] Then they cried unto their God, and he smote all the land of Egypt with incurable plagues: so the Egyptians cast them out of their sight. [13] And God dried the Red sea before them, [14] And brought them to mount Sina, and Cades-Barne, and cast forth all that dwelt in the wilderness. [15] So they dwelt in the land of the Amorites, and they destroyed by their strength all them of Esebon, and passing over Jordan they possessed all the hill country. [16] And they cast forth before them the Chanaanite, the Pherezite, the Jebusite, and the Sychemite, and all the Gergesites, and they dwelt in that country many days. [17] And whilst they sinned not before their God, they prospered, because the God that hateth iniquity was with them. [18] But when they departed from the way which he appointed them, they were destroyed in many battles very sore, and were led captives into a land that was not their's, and the temple of their God was cast to the ground, and their cities were taken by the enemies. [19] But now are they returned to their God, and are come up from the places where they were scattered, and have possessed Jerusalem, where their sanctuary is, and are seated in the hill country; for it was desolate. [20] Now therefore, my lord and governor, if there be any error against this people, and they sin against their God, let us consider that this shall be their ruin, and let us go up, and we shall overcome them. [21] But if there be no iniquity in their nation, let my lord now pass by, lest their Lord defend them, and their God be for them, and we become a reproach before all the world. [22] And when Achior had finished these sayings, all the people standing round about the tent murmured, and the chief men of Holofernes, and all that dwelt by the sea side, and in Moab, spake that he should kill him. [23] For, say they, we will not be afraid of the face of the children of Israel: for, lo, it is a people that have no strength nor power for a strong battle [24] Now therefore, lord Holofernes, we will go up, and they shall be a prey to be devoured of all thine army. Jdt.6 [1] And when the tumult of men that were about the council was ceased, Holofernes the chief captain of the army of Assur said unto Achior and all the Moabites before all the company of other nations, [2] And who art thou, Achior, and the hirelings of Ephraim, that thou hast prophesied against us as to day, and hast said, that we should not make war with the people of Israel, because their God will defend them? and who is God but Nabuchodonosor? [3] He will send his power, and will destroy them from the face of the earth, and their God shall not deliver them: but we his servants will destroy them as one man; for they are not able to sustain the power of our horses. [4] For with them we will tread them under foot, and their mountains shall be drunken with their blood, and their fields shall be filled with their dead bodies, and their footsteps shall not be able to stand before us, for they shall utterly perish, saith king Nabuchodonosor, lord of all the earth: for he said, None of my words shall be in vain. [5] And thou, Achior, an hireling of Ammon, which hast spoken these words in the day of thine iniquity, shalt see my face no more from this day, until I take vengeance of this nation that came out of Egypt. [6] And then shall the sword of mine army, and the multitude of them that serve me, pass through thy sides, and thou shalt fall among their slain, when I return. [7] Now therefore my servants shall bring thee back into the hill country, and shall set thee in one of the cities of the passages: [8] And thou shalt not perish, till thou be destroyed with them. [9] And if thou persuade thyself in thy mind that they shall be taken, let not thy countenance fall: I have spoken it, and none of my words shall be in vain. [10] Then Holofernes commanded his servants, that waited in his tent, to take Achior, and bring him to Bethulia, and deliver him into the hands of the children of Israel. [11] So his servants took him, and brought him out of the camp into the plain, and they went from the midst of the plain into the hill country, and came unto the fountains that were under Bethulia. [12] And when the men of the city saw them, they took up their weapons, and went out of the city to the top of the hill: and every man that used a sling kept them from coming up by casting of stones against them. [13] Nevertheless having gotten privily under the hill, they bound Achior, and cast him down, and left him at the foot of the hill, and returned to their lord. [14] But the Israelites descended from their city, and came unto him, and loosed him, and brought him to Bethulia, and presented him to the governors of the city: [15] Which were in those days Ozias the son of Micha, of the tribe of Simeon, and Chabris the son of Gothoniel, and Charmis the son of Melchiel. [16] And they called together all the ancients of the city, and all their youth ran together, and their women, to the assembly, and they set Achior in the midst of all their people. Then Ozias asked him of that which was done. [17] And he answered and declared unto them the words of the council of Holofernes, and all the words that he had spoken in the midst of the princes of Assur, and whatsoever Holofernes had spoken proudly against the house of Israel. [18] Then the people fell down and worshipped God, and cried unto God. saying, [19] O Lord God of heaven, behold their pride, and pity the low estate of our nation, and look upon the face of those that are sanctified unto thee this day. [20] Then they comforted Achior, and praised him greatly. [21] And Ozias took him out of the assembly unto his house, and made a feast to the elders; and they called on the God of Israel all that night for help. Jdt.7 [1] The next day Holofernes commanded all his army, and all his people which were come to take his part, that they should remove their camp against Bethulia, to take aforehand the ascents of the hill country, and to make war against the children of Israel. [2] Then their strong men removed their camps in that day, and the army of the men of war was an hundred and seventy thousand footmen, and twelve thousand horsemen, beside the baggage, and other men that were afoot among them, a very great multitude. [3] And they camped in the valley near unto Bethulia, by the fountain, and they spread themselves in breadth over Dothaim even to Belmaim, and in length from Bethulia unto Cynamon, which is over against Esdraelon. [4] Now the children of Israel, when they saw the multitude of them, were greatly troubled, and said every one to his neighbour, Now will these men lick up the face of the earth; for neither the high mountains, nor the valleys, nor the hills, are able to bear their weight. [5] Then every man took up his weapons of war, and when they had kindled fires upon their towers, they remained and watched all that night. [6] But in the second day Holofernes brought forth all his horsemen in the sight of the children of Israel which were in Bethulia, [7] And viewed the passages up to the city, and came to the fountains of their waters, and took them, and set garrisons of men of war over them, and he himself removed toward his people. [8] Then came unto him all the chief of the children of Esau, and all the governors of the people of Moab, and the captains of the sea coast, and said, [9] Let our lord now hear a word, that there be not an overthrow in thine army. [10] For this people of the children of Israel do not trust in their spears, but in the height of the mountains wherein they dwell, because it is not easy to come up to the tops of their mountains. [11] Now therefore, my lord, fight not against them in battle array, and there shall not so much as one man of thy people perish. [12] Remain in thy camp, and keep all the men of thine army, and let thy servants get into their hands the fountain of water, which issueth forth of the foot of the mountain: [13] For all the inhabitants of Bethulia have their water thence; so shall thirst kill them, and they shall give up their city, and we and our people shall go up to the tops of the mountains that are near, and will camp upon them, to watch that none go out of the city. [14] So they and their wives and their children shall be consumed with fire, and before the sword come against them, they shall be overthrown in the streets where they dwell. [15] Thus shalt thou render them an evil reward; because they rebelled, and met not thy person peaceably. [16] And these words pleased Holofernes and all his servants, and he appointed to do as they had spoken. [17] So the camp of the children of Ammon departed, and with them five thousand of the Assyrians, and they pitched in the valley, and took the waters, and the fountains of the waters of the children of Israel. [18] Then the children of Esau went up with the children of Ammon, and camped in the hill country over against Dothaim: and they sent some of them toward the south, and toward the east over against Ekrebel, which is near unto Chusi, that is upon the brook Mochmur; and the rest of the army of the Assyrians camped in the plain, and covered the face of the whole land; and their tents and carriages were pitched to a very great multitude. [19] Then the children of Israel cried unto the Lord their God, because their heart failed, for all their enemies had compassed them round about, and there was no way to escape out from among them. [20] Thus all the company of Assur remained about them, both their footmen, chariots, and horsemen, four and thirty days, so that all their vessels of water failed all the inhibitants of Bethulia. [21] And the cisterns were emptied, and they had not water to drink their fill for one day; for they gave them drink by measure. [22] Therefore their young children were out of heart, and their women and young men fainted for thirst, and fell down in the streets of the city, and by the passages of the gates, and there was no longer any strength in them. [23] Then all the people assembled to Ozias, and to the chief of the city, both young men, and women, and children, and cried with a loud voice, and said before all the elders, [24] God be judge between us and you: for ye have done us great injury, in that ye have not required peace of the children of Assur. [25] For now we have no helper: but God hath sold us into their hands, that we should be thrown down before them with thirst and great destruction. [26] Now therefore call them unto you, and deliver the whole city for a spoil to the people of Holofernes, and to all his army. [27] For it is better for us to be made a spoil unto them, than to die for thirst: for we will be his servants, that our souls may live, and not see the death of our infants before our eyes, nor our wives nor our children to die. [28] We take to witness against you the heaven and the earth, and our God and Lord of our fathers, which punisheth us according to our sins and the sins of our fathers, that he do not according as we have said this day. [29] Then there was great weeping with one consent in the midst of the assembly; and they cried unto the Lord God with a loud voice. [30] Then said Ozias to them, Brethren, be of good courage, let us yet endure five days, in the which space the Lord our God may turn his mercy toward us; for he will not forsake us utterly. [31] And if these days pass, and there come no help unto us, I will do according to your word. [32] And he dispersed the people, every one to their own charge; and they went unto the walls and towers of their city, and sent the women and children into their houses: and they were very low brought in the city. Jdt.8 [1] Now at that time Judith heard thereof, which was the daughter of Merari, the son of Ox, the son of Joseph, the son of Ozel, the son of Elcia, the son of Ananias, the son of Gedeon, the son of Raphaim, the son of Acitho, the son of Eliu, the son of Eliab, the son of Nathanael, the son of Samael, the son of Salasadal, the son of Israel. [2] And Manasses was her husband, of her tribe and kindred, who died in the barley harvest. [3] For as he stood overseeing them that bound sheaves in the field, the heat came upon his head, and he fell on his bed, and died in the city of Bethulia: and they buried him with his fathers in the field between Dothaim and Balamo. [4] So Judith was a widow in her house three years and four months. [5] And she made her a tent upon the top of her house, and put on sackcloth upon her loins and ware her widow's apparel. [6] And she fasted all the days of her widowhood, save the eves of the sabbaths, and the sabbaths, and the eves of the new moons, and the new moons and the feasts and solemn days of the house of Israel. [7] She was also of a goodly countenance, and very beautiful to behold: and her husband Manasses had left her gold, and silver, and menservants and maidservants, and cattle, and lands; and she remained upon them. [8] And there was none that gave her an ill word; ar she feared God greatly. [9] Now when she heard the evil words of the people against the governor, that they fainted for lack of water; for Judith had heard all the words that Ozias had spoken unto them, and that he had sworn to deliver the city unto the Assyrians after five days; [10] Then she sent her waitingwoman, that had the government of all things that she had, to call Ozias and Chabris and Charmis, the ancients of the city. [11] And they came unto her, and she said unto them, Hear me now, O ye governors of the inhabitants of Bethulia: for your words that ye have spoken before the people this day are not right, touching this oath which ye made and pronounced between God and you, and have promised to deliver the city to our enemies, unless within these days the Lord turn to help you. [12] And now who are ye that have tempted God this day, and stand instead of God among the children of men? [13] And now try the Lord Almighty, but ye shall never know any thing. [14] For ye cannot find the depth of the heart of man, neither can ye perceive the things that he thinketh: then how can ye search out God, that hath made all these things, and know his mind, or comprehend his purpose? Nay, my brethren, provoke not the Lord our God to anger. [15] For if he will not help us within these five days, he hath power to defend us when he will, even every day, or to destroy us before our enemies. [16] Do not bind the counsels of the Lord our God: for God is not as man, that he may be threatened; neither is he as the son of man, that he should be wavering. [17] Therefore let us wait for salvation of him, and call upon him to help us, and he will hear our voice, if it please him. [18] For there arose none in our age, neither is there any now in these days neither tribe, nor family, nor people, nor city among us, which worship gods made with hands, as hath been aforetime. [19] For the which cause our fathers were given to the sword, and for a spoil, and had a great fall before our enemies. [20] But we know none other god, therefore we trust that he will not dispise us, nor any of our nation. [21] For if we be taken so, all Judea shall lie waste, and our sanctuary shall be spoiled; and he will require the profanation thereof at our mouth. [22] And the slaughter of our brethren, and the captivity of the country, and the desolation of our inheritance, will he turn upon our heads among the Gentiles, wheresoever we shall be in bondage; and we shall be an offence and a reproach to all them that possess us. [23] For our servitude shall not be directed to favour: but the Lord our God shall turn it to dishonour. [24] Now therefore, O brethren, let us shew an example to our brethren, because their hearts depend upon us, and the sanctuary, and the house, and the altar, rest upon us. [25] Moreover let us give thanks to the Lord our God, which trieth us, even as he did our fathers. [26] Remember what things he did to Abraham, and how he tried Isaac, and what happened to Jacob in Mesopotamia of Syria, when he kept the sheep of Laban his mother's brother. [27] For he hath not tried us in the fire, as he did them, for the examination of their hearts, neither hath he taken vengeance on us: but the Lord doth scourge them that come near unto him, to admonish them. [28] Then said Ozias to her, All that thou hast spoken hast thou spoken with a good heart, and there is none that may gainsay thy words. [29] For this is not the first day wherein thy wisdom is manifested; but from the beginning of thy days all the people have known thy understanding, because the disposition of thine heart is good. [30] But the people were very thirsty, and compelled us to do unto them as we have spoken, and to bring an oath upon ourselves, which we will not break. [31] Therefore now pray thou for us, because thou art a godly woman, and the Lord will send us rain to fill our cisterns, and we shall faint no more. [32] Then said Judith unto them, Hear me, and I will do a thing, which shall go throughout all generations to the children of our nation. [33] Ye shall stand this night in the gate, and I will go forth with my waitingwoman: and within the days that ye have promised to deliver the city to our enemies the Lord will visit Israel by mine hand. [34] But enquire not ye of mine act: for I will not declare it unto you, till the things be finished that I do. [35] Then said Ozias and the princes unto her, Go in peace, and the Lord God be before thee, to take vengeance on our enemies. [36] So they returned from the tent, and went to their wards. Jdt.9 [1] Judith fell upon her face, and put ashes upon her head, and uncovered the sackcloth wherewith she was clothed; and about the time that the incense of that evening was offered in Jerusalem in the house of the Lord Judith cried with a loud voice, and said, [2] O Lord God of my father Simeon, to whom thou gavest a sword to take vengeance of the strangers, who loosened the girdle of a maid to defile her, and discovered the thigh to her shame, and polluted her virginity to her reproach; for thou saidst, It shall not be so; and yet they did so: [3] Wherefore thou gavest their rulers to be slain, so that they dyed their bed in blood, being deceived, and smotest the servants with their lords, and the lords upon their thrones; [4] And hast given their wives for a prey, and their daughters to be captives, and all their spoils to be divided among thy dear children; which were moved with thy zeal, and abhorred the pollution of their blood, and called upon thee for aid: O God, O my God, hear me also a widow. [5] For thou hast wrought not only those things, but also the things which fell out before, and which ensued after; thou hast thought upon the things which are now, and which are to come. [6] Yea, what things thou didst determine were ready at hand, and said, Lo, we are here: for all thy ways are prepared, and thy judgments are in thy foreknowledge. [7] For, behold, the Assyrians are multiplied in their power; they are exalted with horse and man; they glory in the strength of their footmen; they trust in shield, and spear, and bow, and sling; and know not that thou art the Lord that breakest the battles: the Lord is thy name. [8] Throw down their strength in thy power, and bring down their force in thy wrath: for they have purposed to defile thy sanctuary, and to pollute the tabernacle where thy glorious name resteth and to cast down with sword the horn of thy altar. [9] Behold their pride, and send thy wrath upon their heads: give into mine hand, which am a widow, the power that I have conceived. [10] Smite by the deceit of my lips the servant with the prince, and the prince with the servant: break down their stateliness by the hand of a woman. [11] For thy power standeth not in multitude nor thy might in strong men: for thou art a God of the afflicted, an helper of the oppressed, an upholder of the weak, a protector of the forlorn, a saviour of them that are without hope. [12] I pray thee, I pray thee, O God of my father, and God of the inheritance of Israel, Lord of the heavens and earth, Creator of the waters, king of every creature, hear thou my prayer: [13] And make my speech and deceit to be their wound and stripe, who have purposed cruel things against thy covenant, and thy hallowed house, and against the top of Sion, and against the house of the possession of thy children. [14] And make every nation and tribe to acknowledge that thou art the God of all power and might, and that there is none other that protecteth the people of Israel but thou. Jdt.10 [1] Now after that she had ceased to cry unto the God of Israel, and bad made an end of all these words. [2] She rose where she had fallen down, and called her maid, and went down into the house in the which she abode in the sabbath days, and in her feast days, [3] And pulled off the sackcloth which she had on, and put off the garments of her widowhood, and washed her body all over with water, and anointed herself with precious ointment, and braided the hair of her head, and put on a tire upon it, and put on her garments of gladness, wherewith she was clad during the life of Manasses her husband. [4] And she took sandals upon her feet, and put about her her bracelets, and her chains, and her rings, and her earrings, and all her ornaments, and decked herself bravely, to allure the eyes of all men that should see her. [5] Then she gave her maid a bottle of wine, and a cruse of oil, and filled a bag with parched corn, and lumps of figs, and with fine bread; so she folded all these things together, and laid them upon her. [6] Thus they went forth to the gate of the city of Bethulia, and found standing there Ozias and the ancients of the city, Chabris and Charmis. [7] And when they saw her, that her countenance was altered, and her apparel was changed, they wondered at her beauty very greatly, and said unto her. [8] The God, the God of our fathers give thee favour, and accomplish thine enterprizes to the glory of the children of Israel, and to the exaltation of Jerusalem. Then they worshipped God. [9] And she said unto them, Command the gates of the city to be opened unto me, that I may go forth to accomplish the things whereof ye have spoken with me. So they commanded the young men to open unto her, as she had spoken. [10] And when they had done so, Judith went out, she, and her maid with her; and the men of the city looked after her, until she was gone down the mountain, and till she had passed the valley, and could see her no more. [11] Thus they went straight forth in the valley: and the first watch of the Assyrians met her, [12] And took her, and asked her, Of what people art thou? and whence comest thou? and whither goest thou? And she said, I am a woman of the Hebrews, and am fled from them: for they shall be given you to be consumed: [13] And I am coming before Holofernes the chief captain of your army, to declare words of truth; and I will shew him a way, whereby he shall go, and win all the hill country, without losing the body or life of any one of his men. [14] Now when the men heard her words, and beheld her countenance, they wondered greatly at her beauty, and said unto her, [15] Thou hast saved thy life, in that thou hast hasted to come down to the presence of our lord: now therefore come to his tent, and some of us shall conduct thee, until they have delivered thee to his hands. [16] And when thou standest before him, be not afraid in thine heart, but shew unto him according to thy word; and he will entreat thee well. [17] Then they chose out of them an hundred men to accompany her and her maid; and they brought her to the tent of Holofernes. [18] Then was there a concourse throughout all the camp: for her coming was noised among the tents, and they came about her, as she stood without the tent of Holofernes, till they told him of her. [19] And they wondered at her beauty, and admired the children of Israel because of her, and every one said to his neighbour, Who would despise this people, that have among them such women? surely it is not good that one man of them be left who being let go might deceive the whole earth. [20] And they that lay near Holofernes went out, and all his servants and they brought her into the tent. [21] Now Holofernes rested upon his bed under a canopy, which was woven with purple, and gold, and emeralds, and precious stones. [22] So they shewed him of her; and he came out before his tent with silver lamps going before him. [23] And when Judith was come before him and his servants they all marvelled at the beauty of her countenance; and she fell down upon her face, and did reverence unto him: and his servants took her up. Jdt.11 [1] Then said Holofernes unto her, Woman, be of good comfort, fear not in thine heart: for I never hurt any that was willing to serve Nabuchodonosor, the king of all the earth. [2] Now therefore, if thy people that dwelleth in the mountains had not set light by me, I would not have lifted up my spear against them: but they have done these things to themselves. [3] But now tell me wherefore thou art fled from them, and art come unto us: for thou art come for safeguard; be of good comfort, thou shalt live this night, and hereafter: [4] For none shall hurt thee, but entreat thee well, as they do the servants of king Nabuchodonosor my lord. [5] Then Judith said unto him, Receive the words of thy servant, and suffer thine handmaid to speak in thy presence, and I will declare no lie to my lord this night. [6] And if thou wilt follow the words of thine handmaid, God will bring the thing perfectly to pass by thee; and my lord shall not fail of his purposes. [7] As Nabuchodonosor king of all the earth liveth, and as his power liveth, who hath sent thee for the upholding of every living thing: for not only men shall serve him by thee, but also the beasts of the field, and the cattle, and the fowls of the air, shall live by thy power under Nabuchodonosor and all his house. [8] For we have heard of thy wisdom and thy policies, and it is reported in all the earth, that thou only art excellent in all the kingdom, and mighty in knowledge, and wonderful in feats of war. [9] Now as concerning the matter, which Achior did speak in thy council, we have heard his words; for the men of Bethulia saved him, and he declared unto them all that he had spoken unto thee. [10] Therefore, O lord and governor, respect not his word; but lay it up in thine heart, for it is true: for our nation shall not be punished, neither can sword prevail against them, except they sin against their God. [11] And now, that my lord be not defeated and frustrate of his purpose, even death is now fallen upon them, and their sin hath overtaken them, wherewith they will provoke their God to anger whensoever they shall do that which is not fit to be done: [12] For their victuals fail them, and all their water is scant, and they have determined to lay hands upon their cattle, and purposed to consume all those things, that God hath forbidden them to eat by his laws: [13] And are resolved to spend the firstfruits of the the tenths of wine and oil, which they had sanctified, and reserved for the priests that serve in Jerusalem before the face of our God; the which things it is not lawful for any of the people so much as to touch with their hands. [14] For they have sent some to Jerusalem, because they also that dwell there have done the like, to bring them a licence from the senate. [15] Now when they shall bring them word, they will forthwith do it, and they shall be given to thee to be destroyed the same day. [16] Wherefore I thine handmaid, knowing all this, am fled from their presence; and God hath sent me to work things with thee, whereat all the earth shall be astonished, and whosoever shall hear it. [17] For thy servant is religious, and serveth the God of heaven day and night: now therefore, my lord, I will remain with thee, and thy servant will go out by night into the valley, and I will pray unto God, and he will tell me when they have committed their sins: [18] And I will come and shew it unto thee: then thou shalt go forth with all thine army, and there shall be none of them that shall resist thee. [19] And I will lead thee through the midst of Judea, until thou come before Jerusalem; and I will set thy throne in the midst thereof; and thou shalt drive them as sheep that have no shepherd, and a dog shall not so much as open his mouth at thee: for these things were told me according to my foreknowledge, and they were declared unto me, and I am sent to tell thee. [20] Then her words pleased Hølofernes and all his servants; and they marvelled at her wisdom, and said, [21] There is not such a woman from one end of the earth to the other, both for beauty of face, and wisdom of words. [22] Likewise Holofernes said unto her. God hath done well to send thee before the people, that strength might be in our hands and destruction upon them that lightly regard my lord. [23] And now thou art both beautiful in thy countenance, and witty in thy words: surely if thou do as thou hast spoken thy God shall be my God, and thou shalt dwell in the house of king Nabuchodonosor, and shalt be renowned through the whole earth. Jdt.12 [1] Then he commanded to bring her in where his plate was set; and bade that they should prepare for her of his own meats, and that she should drink of his own wine. [2] And Judith said, I will not eat thereof, lest there be an offence: but provision shall be made for me of the things that I have brought. [3] Then Holofernes said unto her, If thy provision should fail, how should we give thee the like? for there be none with us of thy nation. [4] Then said Judith unto him As thy soul liveth, my lord, thine handmaid shall not spend those things that I have, before the Lord work by mine hand the things that he hath determined. [5] Then the servants of Holofernes brought her into the tent, and she slept till midnight, and she arose when it was toward the morning watch, [6] And sent to Holofernes, saying, Let my lord now command that thine handmaid may go forth unto prayer. [7] Then Holofernes commanded his guard that they should not stay her: thus she abode in the camp three days, and went out in the night into the valley of Bethulia, and washed herself in a fountain of water by the camp. [8] And when she came out, she besought the Lord God of Israel to direct her way to the raising up of the children of her people. [9] So she came in clean, and remained in the tent, until she did eat her meat at evening. [10] And in the fourth day Holofernes made a feast to his own servants only, and called none of the officers to the banquet. [11] Then said he to Bagoas the eunuch, who had charge over all that he had, Go now, and persuade this Hebrew woman which is with thee, that she come unto us, and eat and drink with us. [12] For, lo, it will be a shame for our person, if we shall let such a woman go, not having had her company; for if we draw her not unto us, she will laugh us to scorn. [13] Then went Bagoas from the presence of Holofernes, and came to her, and he said, Let not this fair damsel fear to come to my lord, and to be honoured in his presence, and drink wine, and be merry with us and be made this day as one of the daughters of the Assyrians, which serve in the house of Nabuchodonosor. [14] Then said Judith unto him, Who am I now, that I should gainsay my lord? surely whatsoever pleaseth him I will do speedily, and it shall be my joy unto the day of my death. [15] So she arose, and decked herself with her apparel and all her woman's attire, and her maid went and laid soft skins on the ground for her over against Holofernes, which she had received of Bagoas far her daily use, that she might sit and eat upon them. [16] Now when Judith came in and sat down, Holofernes his heart was ravished with her, and his mind was moved, and he desired greatly her company; for he waited a time to deceive her, from the day that he had seen her. [17] Then said Holofernes unto her, Drink now, and be merry with us. [18] So Judith said, I will drink now, my lord, because my life is magnified in me this day more than all the days since I was born. [19] Then she took and ate and drank before him what her maid had prepared. [20] And Holofernes took great delight in her, and drank more wine than he had drunk at any time in one day since he was born. Jdt.13 [1] Now when the evening was come, his servants made haste to depart, and Bagoas shut his tent without, and dismissed the waiters from the presence of his lord; and they went to their beds: for they were all weary, because the feast had been long. [2] And Judith was left along in the tent, and Holofernes lying along upon his bed: for he was filled with wine. [3] Now Judith had commanded her maid to stand without her bedchamber, and to wait for her. coming forth, as she did daily: for she said she would go forth to her prayers, and she spake to Bagoas according to the same purpose. [4] So all went forth and none was left in the bedchamber, neither little nor great. Then Judith, standing by his bed, said in her heart, O Lord God of all power, look at this present upon the works of mine hands for the exaltation of Jerusalem. [5] For now is the time to help thine inheritance, and to execute thine enterprizes to the destruction of the enemies which are risen against us. [6] Then she came to the pillar of the bed, which was at Holofernes' head, and took down his fauchion from thence, [7] And approached to his bed, and took hold of the hair of his head, and said, Strengthen me, O Lord God of Israel, this day. [8] And she smote twice upon his neck with all her might, and she took away his head from him. [9] And tumbled his body down from the bed, and pulled down the canopy from the pillars; and anon after she went forth, and gave Holofernes his head to her maid; [10] And she put it in her bag of meat: so they twain went together according to their custom unto prayer: and when they passed the camp, they compassed the valley, and went up the mountain of Bethulia, and came to the gates thereof. [11] Then said Judith afar off, to the watchmen at the gate, Open, open now the gate: God, even our God, is with us, to shew his power yet in Jerusalem, and his forces against the enemy, as he hath even done this day. [12] Now when the men of her city heard her voice, they made haste to go down to the gate of their city, and they called the elders of the city. [13] And then they ran all together, both small and great, for it was strange unto them that she was come: so they opened the gate, and received them, and made a fire for a light, and stood round about them. [14] Then she said to them with a loud voice, Praise, praise God, praise God, I say, for he hath not taken away his mercy from the house of Israel, but hath destroyed our enemies by mine hands this night. [15] So she took the head out of the bag, and shewed it, and said unto them, behold the head of Holofernes, the chief captain of the army of Assur, and behold the canopy, wherein he did lie in his drunkenness; and the Lord hath smitten him by the hand of a woman. [16] As the Lord liveth, who hath kept me in my way that I went, my countenance hath deceived him to his destruction, and yet hath he not committed sin with me, to defile and shame me. [17] Then all the people were wonderfully astonished, and bowed themselves and worshipped God, and said with one accord, Blessed be thou, O our God, which hast this day brought to nought the enemies of thy people. [18] Then said Ozias unto her, O daughter, blessed art thou of the most high God above all the women upon the earth; and blessed be the Lord God, which hath created the heavens and the earth, which hath directed thee to the cutting off of the head of the chief of our enemies. [19] For this thy confidence shall not depart from the heart of men, which remember the power of God for ever. [20] And God turn these things to thee for a perpetual praise, to visit thee in good things because thou hast not spared thy life for the affliction of our nation, but hast revenged our ruin, walking a straight way before our God. And all the people said; So be it, so be it. Jdt.14 [1] Then said Judith unto them, Hear me now, my brethren, and take this head, and hang it upon the highest place of your walls. [2] And so soon as the morning shall appear, and the sun shall come forth upon the earth, take ye every one his weapons, and go forth every valiant man out of the city, and set ye a captain over them, as though ye would go down into the field toward the watch of the Assyrians; but go not down. [3] Then they shall take their armour, and shall go into their camp, and raise up the captains of the army of Assur, and shall run to the tent of Holofernes, but shall not find him: then fear shall fall upon them, and they shall flee before your face. [4] So ye, and all that inhabit the coast of Israel, shall pursue them, and overthrow them as they go. [5] But before ye do these things, call me Achior the Ammonite, that he may see and know him that despised the house of Israel, and that sent him to us as it were to his death. [6] Then they called Achior out of the house of Ozias; and when he was come, and saw the head of Holofernes in a man's hand in the assembly of the people, he fell down on his face, and his spirit failed. [7] But when they had recovered him, he fell at Judith's feet, and reverenced her, and said, Blessed art thou in all the tabernacles of Juda, and in all nations, which hearing thy name shall be astonished. [8] Now therefore tell me all the things that thou hast done in these days. Then Judith declared unto him in the midst of the people all that she had done, from the day that she went forth until that hour she spake unto them. [9] And when she had left off speaking, the people shouted with a loud voice, and made a joyful noise in their city. [10] And when Achior had seen all that the God of Israel had done, he believed in God greatly, and circumcised the flesh of his foreskin, and was joined unto the house of Israel unto this day. [11] And as soon as the morning arose, they hanged the head of Holofernes upon the wall, and every man took his weapons, and they went forth by bands unto the straits of the mountain. [12] But when the Assyrians saw them, they sent to their leaders, which came to their captains and tribunes, and to every one of their rulers. [13] So they came to Holofernes' tent, and said to him that had the charge of all his things, Waken now our lord: for the slaves have been bold to come down against us to battle, that they may be utterly destroyed. [14] Then went in Bagoas, and knocked at the door of the tent; for he thought that he had slept with Judith. [15] But because none answered, he opened it, and went into the bedchamber, and found him cast upon the floor dead, and his head was taken from him. [16] Therefore he cried with a loud voice, with weeping, and sighing, and a mighty cry, and rent his garments. [17] After he went into the tent where Judith lodged: and when he found her not, he leaped out to the people, and cried, [18] These slaves have dealt treacherously; one woman of the Hebrews hath brought shame upon the house of king Nabuchodonosor: for, behold, Holofernes lieth upon the ground without a head. [19] When the captains of the Assyrians' army heard these words, they rent their coats and their minds were wonderfully troubled, and there was a cry and a very great noise throughout the camp. Jdt.15 [1] And when they that were in the tents heard, they were astonished at the thing that was done. [2] And fear and trembling fell upon them, so that there was no man that durst abide in the sight of his neighbour, but rushing out all together, they fled into every way of the plain, and of the hill country. [3] They also that had camped in the mountains round about Bethulia fled away. Then the children of Israel, every one that was a warrior among them, rushed out upon them. [4] Then sent Ozias to Betomasthem, and to Bebai, and Chobai, and Cola and to all the coasts of Israel, such as should tell the things that were done, and that all should rush forth upon their enemies to destroy them. [5] Now when the children of Israel heard it, they all fell upon them with one consent, and slew them unto Chobai: likewise also they that came from Jerusalem, and from all the hill country, (for men had told them what things were done in the camp of their enemies) and they that were in Galaad, and in Galilee, chased them with a great slaughter, until they were past Damascus and the borders thereof. [6] And the residue that dwelt at Bethulia, fell upon the camp of Assur, and spoiled them, and were greatly enriched. [7] And the children of Israel that returned from the slaughter had that which remained; and the villages and the cities, that were in the mountains and in the plain, gat many spoils: for the multitude was very great. [8] Then Joacim the high priest, and the ancients of the children of Israel that dwelt in Jerusalem, came to behold the good things that God had shewed to Israel, and to see Judith, and to salute her. [9] And when they came unto her, they blessed her with one accord, and said unto her, Thou art the exaltation of Jerusalem, thou art the great glory of Israel, thou art the great rejoicing of our nation: [10] Thou hast done all these things by thine hand: thou hast done much good to Israel, and God is pleased therewith: blessed be thou of the Almighty Lord for evermore. And all the people said, So be it. [11] And the people spoiled the camp the space of thirty days: and they gave unto Judith Holofernes his tent, and all his plate, and beds, and vessels, and all his stuff: and she took it and laid it on her mule; and made ready her carts, and laid them thereon. [12] Then all the women of Israel ran together to see her, and blessed her, and made a dance among them for her: and she took branches in her hand, and gave also to the women that were with her. [13] And they put a garland of olive upon her and her maid that was with her, and she went before all the people in the dance, leading all the women: and all the men of Israel followed in their armour with garlands, and with songs in their mouths. Jdt.16 [1] Then Judith began to sing this thanksgiving in all Israel, and all the people sang after her this song of praise. [2] And Judith said, Begin unto my God with timbrels, sing unto my Lord with cymbals: tune unto him a new psalm: exalt him, and call upon his name. [3] For God breaketh the battles: for among the camps in the midst of the people he hath delivered me out of the hands of them that persecuted me. [4] Assur came out of the mountains from the north, he came with ten thousands of his army, the multitude whereof stopped the torrents, and their horsemen have covered the hills. [5] He bragged that he would burn up my borders, and kill my young men with the sword, and dash the sucking children against the ground, and make mine infants as a prey, and my virgins as a spoil. [6] But the Almighty Lord hath disappointed them by the hand of a woman. [7] For the mighty one did not fall by the young men, neither did the sons of the Titans smite him, nor high giants set upon him: but Judith the daughter of Merari weakened him with the beauty of her countenance. [8] For she put off the garment of her widowhood for the exaltation of those that were oppressed in Israel, and anointed her face with ointment, and bound her hair in a tire, and took a linen garment to deceive him. [9] Her sandals ravished his eyes, her beauty took his mind prisoner, and the fauchion passed through his neck. [10] The Persians quaked at her boldness, and the Medes were daunted at her hardiness. [11] Then my afflicted shouted for joy, and my weak ones cried aloud; but they were astonished: these lifted up their voices, but they were overthrown. [12] The sons of the damsels have pierced them through, and wounded them as fugatives' children: they perished by the battle of the Lord. [13] I will sing unto the Lord a new song: O Lord, thou art great and glorious, wonderful in strength, and invincible. [14] Let all creatures serve thee: for thou spakest, and they were made, thou didst send forth thy spirit, and it created them, and there is none that can resist thy voice. [15] For the mountains shall be moved from their foundations with the waters, the rocks shall melt as wax at thy presence: yet thou art merciful to them that fear thee. [16] For all sacrifice is too little for a sweet savour unto thee, and all the fat is not sufficient for thy burnt offering: but he that feareth the Lord is great at all times. [17] Woe to the nations that rise up against my kindred! the Lord Almighty will take vengeance of them in the day of judgment, in putting fire and worms in their flesh; and they shall feel them, and weep for ever. [18] Now as soon as they entered into Jerusalem, they worshipped the Lord; and as soon as the people were purified, they offered their burnt offerings, and their free offerings, and their gifts. [19] Judith also dedicated all the stuff of Holofernes, which the people had given her, and gave the canopy, which she had taken out of his bedchamber, for a gift unto the Lord. [20] So the people continued feasting in Jerusalem before the sanctuary for the space of three months and Judith remained with them. [21] After this time every one returned to his own inheritance, and Judith went to Bethulia, and remained in her own possession, and was in her time honourable in all the country. [22] And many desired her, but none knew her all the days of her life, after that Manasses her husband was dead, and was gathered to his people. [23] But she increased more and more in honour, and waxed old in her husband's house, being a hundred and five years old, and made her maid free; so she died in Bethulia: and they buried her in the cave of her husband Manasses. [24] And the house of Israel lamented her seven days: and before she died, she did distribute her goods to all them that were nearest of kindred to Manasses her husband, and to them that were the nearest of her kindred. [25] And there was none that made the children of Israel any more afraid in the days of Judith, nor a long time after her death.

Book 84. Bel And The Dragon

Bel.1 [1] And king Astyages was gathered to his fathers, and Cyrus of Persia received his kingdom. [2] And Daniel conversed with the king, and was honoured above all his friends. [3] Now the Babylons had an idol, called Bel, and there were spent upon him every day twelve great measures of fine flour, and forty sheep, and six vessels of wine. [4] And the king worshipped it and went daily to adore it: but Daniel worshipped his own God. And the king said unto him, Why dost not thou worship Bel? [5] Who answered and said, Because I may not worship idols made with hands, but the living God, who hath created the heaven and the earth, and hath sovereignty over all flesh. [6] Then said the king unto him, Thinkest thou not that Bel is a living God? seest thou not how much he eateth and drinketh every day? [7] Then Daniel smiled, and said, O king, be not deceived: for this is but clay within, and brass without, and did never eat or drink any thing. [8] So the king was wroth, and called for his priests, and said unto them, If ye tell me not who this is that devoureth these expences, ye shall die. [9] But if ye can certify me that Bel devoureth them, then Daniel shall die: for he hath spoken blasphemy against Bel. And Daniel said unto the king, Let it be according to thy word. [10] Now the priests of Bel were threescore and ten, beside their wives and children. And the king went with Daniel into the temple of Bel. [11] So Bel's priests said, Lo, we go out: but thou, O king, set on the meat, and make ready the wine, and shut the door fast and seal it with thine own signet; [12] And to morrow when thou comest in, if thou findest not that Bel hath eaten up all, we will suffer death: or else Daniel, that speaketh falsely against us. [13] And they little regarded it: for under the table they had made a privy entrance, whereby they entered in continually, and consumed those things. [14] So when they were gone forth, the king set meats before Bel. Now Daniel had commanded his servants to bring ashes, and those they strewed throughout all the temple in the presence of the king alone: then went they out, and shut the door, and sealed it with the king's signet, and so departed. [15] Now in the night came the priests with their wives and children, as they were wont to do, and did eat and drinck up all. [16] In the morning betime the king arose, and Daniel with him. [17] And the king said, Daniel, are the seals whole? And he said, Yea, O king, they be whole. [18] And as soon as he had opened the dour, the king looked upon the table, and cried with a loud voice, Great art thou, O Bel, and with thee is no deceit at all. [19] Then laughed Daniel, and held the king that he should not go in, and said, Behold now the pavement, and mark well whose footsteps are these. [20] And the king said, I see the footsteps of men, women, and children. And then the king was angry, [21] And took the priests with their wives and children, who shewed him the privy doors, where they came in, and consumed such things as were upon the table. [22] Therefore the king slew

them, and delivered Bel into Daniel's power, who destroyed him and his temple. [23] And in that same place there was a great dragon, which they of Babylon worshipped. [24] And the king said unto Daniel, Wilt thou also say that this is of brass? lo, he liveth, he eateth and drinketh; thou canst not say that he is no living god: therefore worship him. [25] Then said Daniel unto the king, I will worship the Lord my God: for he is the living God. [26] But give me leave, O king, and I shall slay this dragon without sword or staff. The king said, I give thee leave. [27] Then Daniel took pitch, and fat, and hair, and did seethe them together, and made lumps thereof: this he put in the dragon's mouth, and so the dragon burst in sunder : and Daniel said, Lo, these are the gods ye worship. [28] When they of Babylon heard that, they took great indignation, and conspired against the king, saying, The king is become a Jew, and he hath destroyed Bel, he hath slain the dragon, and put the priests to death. [29] So they came to the king, and said, Deliver us Daniel, or else we will destroy thee and thine house. [30] Now when the king saw that they pressed him sore, being constrained, he delivered Daniel unto them: [31] Who cast him into the lions' den: where he was six days. [32] And in the den there were seven lions, and they had given them every day two carcases, and two sheep: which then were not given to them, to the intent they might devour Daniel. [33] Now there was in Jewry a prophet, called Habbacuc, who had made pottage, and had broken bread in a bowl, and was going into the field, for to bring it to the reapers. [34] But the angel of the Lord said unto Habbacuc, Go, carry the dinner that thou hast into Babylon unto Daniel, who is in the lions' den. [35] And Habbacuc said, Lord, I never saw Babylon; neither do I know where the den is. [36] Then the angel of the Lord took him by the crown, and bare him by the hair of his head, and through the vehemency of his spirit set him in Babylon over the den. [37] And Habbacuc cried, saying, O Daniel, Daniel, take the dinner which God hath sent thee. [38] And Daniel said, Thou hast remembered me, O God: neither hast thou forsaken them that seek thee and love thee. [39] So Daniel arose, and did eat: and the angel of the Lord set Habbacuc in his own place again immediately. [40] Upon the seventh day the king went to bewail Daniel: and when he came to the den, he looked in, and behold, Daniel was sitting. [41] Then cried the king with a loud voice, saying, Great art Lord God of Daniel, and there is none other beside thee. [42] And he drew him out, and cast those that were the cause of his destruction into the den: and they were devoured in a moment before his face.

Book 85. Susanna

Sus.1 [1] There dwelt a man in Babylon, called Joacim: [2] And he took a wife, whose name was Susanna, the daughter of Chelcias, a very fair woman, and one that feared the Lord. [3] Her parents also were righteous, and taught their daughter according to the law of Moses. [4] Now Joacim was a great rich man, and had a fair garden joining unto his house: and to him resorted the Jews; because he was more honourable than all others. [5] The same year were appointed two of the ancients of the people to be judges, such as the Lord spake of, that wickedness came from Babylon from ancient judges, who seemed to govern the people. [6] These kept much at Joacim's house: and all that had any suits in law came unto them. [7] Now when the people departed away at noon, Susanna went into her husband's garden to walk. [8] And the two elders saw her going in every day, and walking; so that their lust was inflamed toward her. [9] And they perverted their own mind, and turned away their eyes, that they might not look unto heaven, nor remember just judgments. [10] And albeit they both were wounded with her love, yet durst not one shew another his grief. [11] For they were ashamed to declare their lust, that they desired to have to do with her. [12] Yet they watched diligently from day to day to see her. [13] And the one said to the other, Let us now go home: for it is dinner time. [14] So when they were gone out, they parted the one from the other, and turning back again they came to the same place; and after that they had asked one another the cause, they acknowledged their lust: then appointed they a time both together, when they might find her alone. [15] And it fell out, as they watched a fit time, she went in as before with two maids only, and she was desirous to wash herself in the garden: for it was hot. [16] And there was no body there save the two elders, that had hid themselves, and watched her. [17] Then she said to her maids, Bring me oil and washing balls, and shut the garden doors, that I may wash me. [18] And they did as she bade them, and shut the garden doors, and went out themselves at privy doors to fetch the things that she had commanded them: but they saw not the elders, because they were hid. [19] Now when the maids were gone forth, the two elders rose up, and ran unto her, saying, [20] Behold, the garden doors are shut, that no man can see us, and we are in love with thee; therefore consent unto us, and lie with us. [21] If thou wilt not, we will bear witness against thee, that a young man was with thee: and therefore thou didst send away thy maids from thee. [22] Then Susanna sighed, and said, I am straitened on every side: for if I do this thing, it is death unto me: and if I do it not I cannot escape your hands. [23] It is better for me to fall into your hands, and not do it, than to sin in the sight of the Lord. [24] With that Susanna cried with a loud voice: and the two elders cried out against her. [25] Then ran the one, and opened the garden door. [26] So when the servants of the house heard the cry in the garden, they rushed in at the privy door, to see what was done unto her. [27] But when the elders had declared their matter, the servants were greatly ashamed: for there was never such a report made of Susanna. [28] And it came to pass the next day, when the people were assembled to her husband Joacim, the two elders came also full of mischievous imagination against Susanna to put her to death; [29] And said before the people, Send for Susanna, the daughter of Chelcias, Joacim's wife. And so they sent. [30] So she came with her father and mother, her children, and all her kindred. [31] Now Susanna was a very delicate woman, and beauteous to behold. [32] And these wicked men commanded to uncover her face, (for she was covered) that they might be filled with her beauty. [33] Therefore her friends and all that saw her wept. [34] Then the two elders stood up in the midst of the people, and laid their hands upon her head. [35] And she weeping looked up toward heaven: for her heart trusted in the Lord. [36] And the elders said, As we walked in the garden alone, this woman came in with two maids, and shut the garden doors, and sent the maids away. [37] Then a young man, who there was hid, came unto her, and lay with her. [38] Then we that stood in a corner of the garden, seeing this wickedness, ran unto them. [39] And when we saw them together, the man we could not hold: for he was stronger than we, and opened the door, and leaped out. [40] But having taken this woman, we asked who the young man was, but she would not tell us: these things do we testify. [41] Then the assembly believed them as those that were the elders and judges of the people: so they condemned her to death. [42] Then Susanna cried out with a loud voice, and said, O everlasting God, that knowest the secrets, and knowest all things before they be: [43] Thou knowest that they have borne false witness against me, and, behold, I must die; whereas I never did such things as these men have maliciously invented against me. [44] And the Lord heard her voice. [45] Therefore when she was led to be put to death, the Lord raised up the holy spirit of a young youth whose name was Daniel: [46] Who cried with a loud voice, I am clear from the blood of this woman. [47] Then all the people turned them toward him, and said, What mean these words that thou hast spoken? [48] So he standing in the midst of them said, Are ye such fools, ye sons of Israel, that without examination or knowledge of the truth ye have condemned a daughter of Israel? [49] Return again to the place of judgment: for they have borne false witness against her. [50] Wherefore all the people turned again in haste, and the elders said unto him, Come, sit down among us, and shew it us, seeing God hath given thee the honour of an elder. [51] Then said Daniel unto them, Put these two aside one far from another, and I will examine them. [52] So when they were put asunder one from another, he called one of them, and said unto him, O thou that art waxen old in wickedness, now thy sins which thou hast committed aforetime are come to light. [53] For thou hast pronounced false judgment and hast condemned the innocent and hast let the guilty go free; albeit the Lord saith, The innocent and righteous shalt thou not slay. [54] Now then, if thou hast seen her, tell me, Under what tree sawest thou them companying together? Who answered, Under a mastick tree. [55] And Daniel said, Very well; thou hast lied against thine own head; for even now the angel of God hath received the sentence of God to cut thee in two. [56] So he put him aside, and commanded to bring the other, and said unto him, O thou seed of Chanaan, and not of Juda, beauty hath deceived thee, and lust hath perverted thine heart. [57] Thus have ye dealt with the daughters of Israel, and they for fear companied with you: but the daughter of Juda would not abide your wickedness. [58] Now therefore tell me, Under what tree didst thou take them companying together? Who answered, Under an holm tree. [59] Then said Daniel unto him, Well; thou hast also lied against thine own head: for the angel of God waiteth with the sword to cut thee in two, that he may destroy you. [60] With that all the assembly cried out with a loud voice, and praised God, who saveth them that trust in him. [61] And they arose against the two elders, for Daniel had convicted them of false witness by their own mouth: [62] And according to the law of Moses they did unto them in such sort as they maliciously intended to do to their neighbour: and they put them to death. Thus the innocent blood was saved the same day. [63] Therefore Chelcias and his wife praised God for their daughter Susanna, with Joacim her husband, and all the kindred, because there was no dishonesty found in her. [64] From that day forth was Daniel had in great reputation in the sight of the people.

Book 86. The Prayer Of Manasseh – King Of Judah

[1] Lord, Almighty God of our fathers, Abraham, Isaac, and Jacob, and of their righteous seed; [2] Who hast made heaven and earth, with all the ornament thereof; [3] Who hast bound the sea by the word of thy commandment; [4] Whoho hast shut up the deep, and sealed it by thy terri-

ble and glorious name; whom all men fear, and tremble before thy power; [5] For the majesty of thy glory cannot be borne, and thine angry threatening toward sinners is importable: but thy merciful promise is unmeasurable and unsearchable; [6] For thou art the most high Lord, of great compassion, longsuffering, very merciful, and repentest of the evils of men. [7] Thou, O Lord, according to thy great goodness hast promised repentance and forgiveness to them that have sinned against thee: and of thine infinite mercies hast appointed repentance unto sinners, that they may be saved. [8] Thou therefore, O Lord, that art the God of the just, hast not appointed repentance to the just, as to [9] Abraham, and Isaac, and Jacob, which have not sinned against thee; but thou hast appointed repentance unto me that am a sinner: for I have sinned above the number of the sands of the sea. [10] My transgressions, O Lord, are multiplied: my transgressions are multiplied, and I am not worthy to behold and see the height of heaven for the multitude of mine iniquities. [11] I am bowed down with many iron bands, that I cannot life up mine head, neither have any release: for I have provoked thy wrath, and done evil before thee: I did not thy will, neither kept I thy commandments: I have set up abominations, and have multiplied offences. [12] Now therefore I bow the knee of mine heart, beseeching thee of grace. [13] I have sinned, O Lord, I have sinned, and I acknowledge mine iniquities: wherefore, I humbly beseech thee, forgive me, O Lord, forgive me, and destroy me not with mine iniquites. [14] Be not angry with me for ever, by reserving evil for me; neither condemn me to the lower parts of the earth. [15] For thou art the God, even the God of them that repent; and in me thou wilt shew all thy goodness: for thou wilt save me, that am unworthy, according to thy great mercy. [16] Therefore I will praise thee for ever all the days of my life: for all the powers of the heavens do praise thee, and thine is the glory for ever and ever. Amen.

Book 87. The Prayer Of Azariah

[1] And they walked in the midst of the fire, praising God, and blessing the Lord. [2] Then Azarias stood up, and prayed on this manner; and opening his mouth in the midst of the fire said, [3] Blessed art thou, O Lord God of our fathers: thy name is worthy to be praised and glorified for evermore: [4] For thou art righteous in all the things that thou hast done to us: yea, true are all thy works, thy ways are right, and all thy judgments truth. [5] In all the things that thou hast brought upon us, and upon the holy city of our fathers, even Jerusalem, thou hast executed true judgment: for according to truth and judgment didst thou bring all these things upon us because of our sins. [6] For we have sinned and committed iniquity, departing from thee. [7] In all things have we trespassed, and not obeyed thy commandments, nor kept them, neither done as thou hast commanded us, that it might go well with us. [8] Wherefore all that thou hast brought upon us, and every thing that thou hast done to us, thou hast done in true judgment. [9] And thou didst deliver us into the hands of lawless enemies, most hateful forsakers of God, and to an unjust king, and the most wicked in all the world. [10] And now we cannot open our mouths, we are become a shame and reproach to thy servants; and to them that worship thee. [11] Yet deliver us not up wholly, for thy name's sake, neither disannul thou thy covenant: [12] And cause not thy mercy to depart from us, for thy beloved Abraham's sake, for thy servant Issac's sake, and for thy holy Israel's sake; [13] To whom thou hast spoken and promised, that thou wouldest multiply their seed as the stars of heaven, and as the sand that lieth upon the seashore. [14] For we, O Lord, are become less than any nation, and be kept under this day in all the world because of our sins. [15] Neither is there at this time prince, or prophet, or leader, or burnt offering, or sacrifice, or oblation, or incense, or place to sacrifice before thee, and to find mercy. [16] Nevertheless in a contrite heart and an humble spirit let us be accepted. [17] Like as in the burnt offerings of rams and bullocks, and like as in ten thousands of fat lambs: so let our sacrifice be in thy sight this day, and grant that we may wholly go after thee: for they shall not be confounded that put their trust in thee. [18] And now we follow thee with all our heart, we fear thee, and seek thy face. [19] Put us not to shame: but deal with us after thy lovingkindness, and according to the multitude of thy mercies. [20] Deliver us also according to thy marvellous works, and give glory to thy name, O Lord: and let all them that do thy servants hurt be ashamed; [21] And let them be confounded in all their power and might, and let their strength be broken; [22] And let them know that thou art God, the only God, and glorious over the whole world. [23] And the king's servants, that put them in, ceased not to make the oven hot with rosin, pitch, tow, and small wood; [24] So that the flame streamed forth above the furnace forty and nine cubits. [25] And it passed through, and burned those Chaldeans it found about the furnace. [26] But the angel of the Lord came down into the oven together with Azarias and his fellows, and smote the flame of the fire out of the oven; [27] And made the midst of the furnace as it had been a moist whistling wind, so that the fire touched them not at all, neither hurt nor troubled them. [28] Then the three, as out of one mouth, praised, glorified, and blessed, God in the furnace, saying, [29] Blessed art thou, O Lord God of our fathers: and to be

praised and exalted above all for ever. [30] And blessed is thy glorious and holy name: and to be praised and exalted above all for ever. [31] Blessed art thou in the temple of thine holy glory: and to be praised and glorified above all for ever. [32] Blessed art thou that beholdest the depths, and sittest upon the cherubims: and to be praised and exalted above all for ever. [33] Blessed art thou on the glorious throne of thy kingdom: and to be praised and glorified above all for ever. [34] Blessed art thou in the firmament of heaven: and above all to be praised and glorified for ever. [35] O all ye works of the Lord, bless ye the Lord : praise and exalt him above all for ever, [36] O ye heavens, bless ye the Lord : praise and exalt him above all for ever. [37] O ye angels of the Lord, bless ye the Lord: praise and exalt him above all for ever. [38] O all ye waters that be above the heaven, bless ye the Lord: praise and exalt him above all for ever. [39] O all ye powers of the Lord, bless ye the Lord: praise and exalt him above all for ever. [40] O ye sun and moon, bless ye the Lord: praise and exalt him above all for ever. [41] O ye stars of heaven, bless ye the Lord: praise and exalt him above all for ever. [42] O every shower and dew, bless ye the Lord: praise and exalt him above all for ever. [43] O all ye winds, bless ye the Lord: praise and exalt him above all for ever, [44] O ye fire and heat, bless ye the Lord: praise and exalt him above all for ever. [45] O ye winter and summer, bless ye the Lord: praise and exalt him above all for ever. [46] 0 ye dews and storms of snow, bless ye the Lord: praise and exalt him above all for ever. [47] O ye nights and days, bless ye the Lord: bless and exalt him above all for ever. [48] O ye light and darkness, bless ye the Lord: praise and exalt him above all for ever. [49] O ye ice and cold, bless ye the Lord: praise and exalt him above all for ever. [50] O ye frost and snow, bless ye the Lord: praise and exalt him above all for ever. [51] O ye lightnings and clouds, bless ye the Lord: praise and exalt him above all for ever. [52] O let the earth bless the Lord: praise and exalt him above all for ever. [53] O ye mountains and little hills, bless ye the Lord: praise and exalt him above all for ever. [54] O all ye things that grow in the earth, bless ye the Lord: praise and exalt him above all for ever. [55] O ye mountains, bless ye the Lord: Praise and exalt him above all for ever. [56] O ye seas and rivers, bless ye the Lord: praise and exalt him above all for ever. [57] O ye whales, and all that move in the waters, bless ye the Lord: praise and exalt him above all for ever. [58] O all ye fowls of the air, bless ye the Lord: praise and exalt him above all for ever. [59] O all ye beasts and cattle, bless ye the Lord: praise and exalt him above all for ever. [60] O ye children of men, bless ye the Lord: praise and exalt him above all for ever. [61] O Israel, bless ye the Lord: praise and exalt him above all for ever. [62] O ye priests of the Lord, bless ye the Lord: praise and exalt him above all for ever. [63] O ye servants of the Lord, bless ye the Lord: praise and exalt him above all for ever. [64] O ye spirits and souls of the righteous, bless ye the Lord: praise and exalt him above all for ever. [65] O ye holy and humble men of heart, bless ye the Lord: praise and exalt him above all for ever. [66] O Ananias, Azarias, and Misael, bless ye the Lord: praise and exalt him above all for ever: far he hath delivered us from hell, and saved us from the hand of death, and delivered us out of the midst of the furnace and burning flame: even out of the midst of the fire hath he delivered us. [67] O give thanks unto the Lord, because he is gracious: for his mercy endureth for ever. [68] O all ye that worship the Lord, bless the God of gods, praise him, and give him thanks: for his mercy endureth for ever.

Book 88. 1 Maccabees

Alexander the Great

1 After Alexander son of Philip, the Macedonian, who came from the land of Kittim, had defeated[a] King Darius of the Persians and the Medes, he succeeded him as king. (He had previously become king of Greece.) [2] He fought many battles, conquered strongholds, and slaughtered the kings of the earth. [3] He advanced to the ends of the earth and plundered many nations. When the earth became quiet before him, he was exalted, and his heart was lifted up. [4] He gathered a very strong army and ruled over countries, nations, and princes, and they paid him tribute. [5] After this he fell sick and perceived that he was dying. [6] So he summoned his most honored officers, who had been brought up with him from youth, and divided his kingdom among them while he was still alive. [7] And after Alexander had reigned twelve years, he died. [8] Then his officers began to rule, each in his own place. [9] They all put on crowns after his death, and so did their descendants after them for many years, and they caused many evils on the earth.

Antiochus Epiphanes and Renegade Jews

[10] From them came forth a sinful root, Antiochus Epiphanes, son of King Antiochus; he had been a hostage in Rome. He began to reign in the one hundred thirty-seventh year of the kingdom of the Greeks. [11] In those days certain renegades came out from Israel and misled many, saying, "Let us go and make a covenant with the nations around us, for since we separated from them many disasters have come upon us." [12] This proposal pleased them, [13] and some of the people eagerly went to the king, who authorized them to observe the ordinances of the nations. [14] So they built a gymnasium in Jerusalem according to the customs of the nations, [15] and made foreskins for themselves, and abandoned the holy covenant. They joined with the nations and sold themselves to do evil.

Antiochus in Egypt

[16] When Antiochus saw that his kingdom was established, he determined to become king of the land of Egypt, in order that he might reign over both kingdoms. [17] So he invaded Egypt with a strong force, with chariots and elephants and cavalry and with a large fleet. [18] He engaged King Ptolemy of Egypt in battle, and Ptolemy turned and fled before him, and many were wounded and fell. [19] They captured the fortified cities in the land of Egypt, and he plundered the land of Egypt.

Persecution of the Jews

[20] After subduing Egypt, Antiochus turned back in the one hundred forty-third year and went up against Israel and came to Jerusalem with a strong force. [21] He arrogantly entered the sanctuary and took the golden altar, the lampstand for the light, and all its utensils. [22] He took also the table for the bread of the Presence, the cups for drink offerings, the bowls, the golden censers, the curtain, the crowns, and the gold decoration on the front of the temple; he stripped it all off. [23] He took the silver and the gold and the costly vessels; he took also the hidden treasures that he found. [24] Taking them all, he went into his own land.
He shed much blood
and spoke with great arrogance.
[25] Israel mourned deeply in every community;
[26] rulers and elders groaned;
young women and young men became faint;
the beauty of the women faded.
[27] Every bridegroom took up the lament;
she who sat in the bridal chamber was mourning.
[28] Even the land trembled for its inhabitants,
and all the house of Jacob was clothed with shame.

The Occupation of Jerusalem

[29] Two years later the king sent to the cities of Judah a chief collector of tribute, and he came to Jerusalem with a large force. [30] Deceitfully he spoke peaceable words to them, and they believed him, but he suddenly fell upon the city, dealt it a severe blow, and destroyed many people of Israel. [31] He plundered the city, burned it with fire, and tore down its houses and its surrounding walls. [32] They took captive the women and children and seized the livestock. [33] Then they fortified the city of David with a large strong wall and strong towers, and it became their citadel. [34] They stationed there a sinful nation, men who were renegades. These strengthened their position; [35] they stored up arms and food, and, collecting the spoils of Jerusalem, they stored them there and became a great menace,
[36] for the citadel[b] became an ambush against the sanctuary,
an evil adversary of Israel at all times.
[37] On every side of the sanctuary they shed innocent blood;
they even defiled the sanctuary.
[38] Because of them the residents of Jerusalem fled;
she became a dwelling of strangers;
she became strange to her offspring,
and her children forsook her.
[39] Her sanctuary became desolate like a desert;
her feasts were turned into mourning,
her Sabbaths into a reproach,
her honor into contempt.
[40] Her dishonor now grew as great as her glory;
her exaltation was turned into mourning.

Installation of Gentile Cults

[41] Then the king wrote to his whole kingdom that all should be one people [42] and that all should give up their particular customs. All the nations accepted the command of the king. [43] Many even from Israel gladly adopted his religion; they sacrificed to idols and profaned the Sabbath. [44] And the king sent letters by messengers to Jerusalem and the towns of Judah; he directed them to follow customs strange to the land, [45] to forbid burnt offerings and sacrifices and drink offerings in the sanctuary, to profane Sabbaths and festivals, [46] to defile the sanctuary and the holy ones, [47] to build altars and sacred precincts and shrines for idols, to sacrifice pigs and other unclean animals, [48] and to leave their sons uncircumcised. They were to make themselves abominable by everything unclean and profane [49] so that they would forget the law and change all the ordinances. [50] He added,[c] "And whoever does not obey the command of the king shall die."
[51] In such words he wrote to his whole kingdom. He appointed inspectors over all the people and commanded the towns of Judah to offer sacrifice, town by town. [52] Many of the people, everyone who forsook the law, joined them, and they did evil in the land; [53] they drove Israel into hiding in every place of refuge they had.
[54] Now on the fifteenth day of Chislev, in the one hundred forty-fifth year, they erected a desolating sacrilege on the altar of burnt offering. They also built altars in the surrounding towns of Judah [55] and offered incense at the doors of the houses and in the streets. [56] The books of the law that they found they tore to pieces and burned with fire. [57] Anyone found possessing the book of the covenant or anyone who adhered to the law

was condemned to death by decree of the king. [58] They kept using violence against Israel, against those who were found month after month in the towns. [59] On the twenty-fifth day of the month they offered sacrifice on the altar that was on top of the altar of burnt offering. [60] According to the decree, they put to death the women who had their children circumcised [61] and their families and those who circumcised them, and they hung the infants from their mothers' necks.

[62] But many in Israel stood firm and were resolved in their hearts not to eat unclean food. [63] They chose to die rather than to be defiled by food or to profane the holy covenant, and they did die. [64] Very great wrath came upon Israel.

Mattathias and His Sons

2 In those days Mattathias son of John son of Simeon, a priest of the clan of Joarib, moved from Jerusalem and settled in Modein. [2] He had five sons: John surnamed Gaddi, [3] Simon called Thassi, [4] Judas called Maccabeus, [5] Eleazar called Avaran, and Jonathan called Apphus. [6] He saw the blasphemies being committed in Judah and Jerusalem [7] and said,

"Alas! Why was I born to see this,
    the ruin of my people, the ruin of the holy city?
The people sat idle there when it was given over to the enemy,
    the sanctuary given over to strangers.
[8] Her temple has become like a person without honor;[d]
[9]   her glorious vessels have been carried into exile.
Her infants have been killed in her streets,
    her youths by the sword of the foe.
[10] What nation has not inherited her palaces[e]
    and has not seized her spoils?
[11] All her adornment has been taken away;
    no longer free, she has become a slave.
[12] And see, our holy place, our beauty,
    and our glory have been laid waste;
the nations have profaned them.
[13]   Why should we live any longer?"

[14] Then Mattathias and his sons tore their clothes, put on sackcloth, and mourned greatly.

Pagan Worship Refused

[15] The king's officers who were enforcing the apostasy came to the town of Modein to make them offer sacrifice. [16] Many from Israel came to them, and Mattathias and his sons were assembled. [17] Then the king's officers spoke to Mattathias as follows: "You are a leader, honored and great in this town, and supported by sons and brothers. [18] Now be the first to come and do what the king commands, as all the nations and the people of Judah and those who are left in Jerusalem have done. Then you and your sons will be numbered among the Friends of the king, and you and your sons will be honored with silver and gold and many gifts."

[19] But Mattathias answered and said in a loud voice: "Even if all the nations that live under the rule of the king obey him and have chosen to obey his commandments, every one of them abandoning the religion of their ancestors, [20] I and my sons and my brothers will continue to live by the covenant of our ancestors. [21] Far be it from us to desert the law and the ordinances. [22] We will not obey the king's words by turning aside from our religion to the right hand or to the left."

[23] When he had finished speaking these words, a Jew came forward in the sight of all to offer sacrifice on the altar in Modein, according to the king's command. [24] When Mattathias saw it, he burned with zeal, and his heart was stirred. He gave vent to righteous anger; he ran and slaughtered him on the altar. [25] At the same time he killed the king's officer who was forcing them to sacrifice, and he tore down the altar. [26] Thus he burned with zeal for the law, just as Phinehas did against Zimri son of Salu.

[27] Then Mattathias cried out in the town with a loud voice, saying: "Let every one who is zealous for the law and supports the covenant come out with me!" [28] Then he and his sons fled to the hills and left all that they had in the town.

[29] At that time many who were seeking righteousness and justice went down to the wilderness to live there, [30] they, their sons, their wives, and their livestock, because troubles pressed heavily upon them. [31] And it was reported to the king's officers and to the troops in Jerusalem the city of David that those who had rejected the king's command had gone down to the hiding places in the wilderness. [32] Many pursued them and overtook them; they encamped opposite them and prepared for battle against them on the Sabbath day. [33] They said to them, "Enough of this! Come out and do what the king commands, and you will live." [34] But they said, "We will not come out, nor will we do what the king commands and so profane the Sabbath day." [35] Then the enemy[f] quickly attacked them. [36] But they did not answer them or hurl a stone at them or block up their hiding places, [37] for they said, "Let us all die in our innocence; heaven and earth testify for us that you are killing us unjustly." [38] So they attacked them on the Sabbath, and they died, with their wives and children and livestock, to the number of a thousand persons.

[39] When Mattathias and his friends learned of it, they mourned for them deeply. [40] And all said to their neighbors: "If we all do as our kindred have done and refuse to fight with the nations for our lives and for our ordinances, they will quickly destroy us from the earth." [41] So they made

this decision that day: "Let us fight against anyone who comes to attack us on the Sabbath day; let us not all die as our kindred died in their hiding places."

Counter-Attack

[42] Then there united with them a company of Hasideans, mighty warriors of Israel, all who offered themselves willingly for the law. [43] And all who became fugitives to escape their troubles joined them and reinforced them. [44] They organized an army and struck down sinners in their anger and renegades in their wrath; the survivors fled to the nations for safety. [45] And Mattathias and his friends went around and tore down the altars; [46] they forcibly circumcised all the uncircumcised boys whom they found within the borders of Israel. [47] They hunted down the arrogant, and the work prospered in their hands. [48] They rescued the law out of the hands of the nations and kings, and they never let the sinner gain the upper hand.

The Last Words of Mattathias

[49] Now the days drew near for Mattathias to die, and he said to his sons: "Arrogance and scorn have now become strong; it is a time of ruin and furious anger. [50] Now, my children, show zeal for the law and give your lives for the covenant of our ancestors.

[51] "Remember the deeds of the ancestors, which they did in their generations, and you will receive great honor and an everlasting name. [52] Was not Abraham found faithful when tested, and it was reckoned to him as righteousness? [53] Joseph in the time of his distress kept the commandment and became lord of Egypt. [54] Phinehas our ancestor, because he was deeply zealous, received the covenant of everlasting priesthood. [55] Joshua, because he fulfilled the command, became a judge in Israel. [56] Caleb, because he testified in the assembly, received an inheritance in the land. [57] David, because he was merciful, inherited the throne of the kingdom forever. [58] Elijah, because of great zeal for the law, was taken up into heaven. [59] Hananiah, Azariah, and Mishael believed and were saved from the flame. [60] Daniel, because of his innocence, was delivered from the mouth of the lions.

[61] "And so observe, from generation to generation, that none of those who put their trust in him will lack strength. [62] Do not fear the words of sinners, for their splendor will turn into dung and worms. [63] Today they will be exalted, but tomorrow they will not be found, for they will have returned to the dust, and their plans will have perished. [64] My children, be courageous and grow strong in the law, for by it you will gain honor.

[65] "Here is your brother Simeon, who I know is wise in counsel; always listen to him; he shall be your father. [66] Judas Maccabeus has been a mighty warrior from his youth; he shall command the army for you and fight the battle against the peoples.[g] [67] You shall rally around you all who observe the law and avenge the wrong done to your people. [68] Pay back the nations in full, and obey the commands of the law."

[69] Then he blessed them and was gathered to his ancestors. [70] He died in the one hundred forty-sixth year and was buried in the tomb of his ancestors at Modein. And all Israel mourned for him with great lamentation.

The Early Victories of Judas

3 Then his son Judas, who was called Maccabeus, took command in his place. [2] All his brothers and all who had joined his father helped him; they gladly fought for Israel.

[3] He extended the glory of his people.
    Like a giant he put on his breastplate;
he bound on his armor of war and waged battles,
    protecting the camp by his sword.
[4] He was like a lion in his deeds,
    like a lion's cub roaring for prey.
[5] He searched out and pursued those who broke the law;
    he burned those who troubled his people.
[6] Lawbreakers shrank back for fear of him;
    all the evildoers were confounded;
    and deliverance prospered by his hand.
[7] He embittered many kings,
    but he made Jacob glad by his deeds,
    and his memory is blessed forever.
[8] He went through the cities of Judah;
    he destroyed the ungodly out of the land;[h]
    thus he turned away wrath from Israel.
[9] He was renowned to the ends of the earth;
    he gathered in those who were perishing.

[10] Then Apollonius gathered together nations and a large force from Samaria to fight against Israel. [11] When Judas learned of it, he went out to meet him, and he defeated and killed him. Many were wounded and fell, and the rest fled. [12] Then they seized their spoils, and Judas took the sword of Apollonius and used it in battle the rest of his life.

[13] When Seron, the commander of the Syrian army, heard that Judas had gathered a large company, including a body of faithful soldiers who stayed with him and went out to battle, [14] he said, "I will make a name for myself and win honor in the kingdom. I will make war on Judas and his companions, who scorn the king's command." [15] Once again a strong army of godless men joined him and went up with him to help him, to take vengeance on the Israelites.

[16] When he approached the ascent of Beth-horon, Judas went out to meet him with a small company. [17] But when they saw the army coming to meet them, they said to Judas, "How can we, few as we are, fight against so great and so strong a multitude? And we are faint, for we have eaten nothing today." [18] Judas replied, "It is easy for many to be hemmed in by few, for in the sight of heaven there is no difference between saving by many or by few. [19] It is not on the size of the army that victory in battle depends, but strength comes from heaven. [20] They come against us in great insolence and lawlessness to destroy us and our wives and our children and to despoil us, [21] but we fight for our lives and our laws. [22] He himself will crush them before us; as for you, do not be afraid of them." [23] When he finished speaking, he rushed suddenly against Seron and his army, and they were crushed before him. [24] They pursued them[i] down the descent of Beth-horon to the plain; eight hundred of them fell, and the rest fled into the land of the Philistines. [25] Then Judas and his brothers began to be feared, and terror fell on the nations all around them. [26] His fame reached the king, and the nations talked of the battles of Judas.

The Policy of Antiochus

[27] When King Antiochus heard these reports, he was greatly angered, and he sent and gathered all the forces of his kingdom, a very strong army. [28] He opened his coffers and gave a year's pay to his forces and ordered them to be ready for any need. [29] Then he saw that the money in the treasury was exhausted and that the tribute payments from the country were small because of the dissension and disaster that he had caused in the land by abolishing the laws that had existed from the earliest days. [30] He feared that he might not have such funds as he had before for his expenses and for the gifts that he used to give more lavishly than preceding kings. [31] He was greatly perplexed in mind; then he determined to go to Persia and collect the tribute payments from those regions and raise a large fund.

[32] He left Lysias, a distinguished man of royal lineage, in charge of the king's affairs from the River Euphrates to the borders of Egypt. [33] Lysias was also to take care of his son Antiochus until he returned. [34] And he turned over to Lysias[j] half of his forces and the elephants and gave him orders about all that he wanted done. As for the residents of Judea and Jerusalem, [35] Lysias was to send a force against them to wipe out and destroy the strength of Israel and the remnant of Jerusalem; he was to banish the memory of them from the place, [36] settle strangers in all their territory, and distribute their land by lot. [37] Then the king took the remaining half of his forces and left Antioch his capital in the one hundred and forty-seventh year. He crossed the Euphrates River and went through the upper provinces.

Preparations for Battle

[38] Lysias chose Ptolemy son of Dorymenes and Nicanor and Gorgias, able men among the Friends of the king, [39] and sent with them forty thousand infantry and seven thousand cavalry to go into the land of Judah and destroy it, as the king had commanded. [40] So they set out with their entire force, and when they arrived they encamped near Emmaus in the plain. [41] When the traders of the region heard what was said to them, they took silver and gold in immense amounts and fetters[k] and went to the camp to get the Israelites for slaves. And forces from Syria and the land of the Philistines[l] joined with them.

[42] Now Judas and his brothers saw that misfortunes had increased and that the forces were encamped in their territory. They also learned what the king had commanded to do to the people to cause their final destruction. [43] But they said to one another, "Let us restore the ruins of our people and fight for our people and the sanctuary." [44] So the congregation assembled to be ready for battle and to pray and ask for mercy and compassion.

[45] Jerusalem was uninhabited like a wilderness;
    not one of her children went in or out.
The sanctuary was trampled down,
    and strangers held the citadel;
    it was a lodging place for the nations.
Joy was taken from Jacob;
    the flute and the harp ceased to play.

[46] Then they gathered together and went to Mizpah, opposite Jerusalem, because Israel formerly had a place of prayer in Mizpah. [47] They fasted that day, put on sackcloth, and sprinkled ashes on their heads, and tore their clothes. [48] And they opened the book of the law to inquire into those matters about which the nations consulted the likenesses of their gods. [49] They also brought the vestments of the priesthood and the first fruits and the tithes, and they stirred up the nazirites who had completed their days, [50] and they cried aloud to heaven, saying,

"What shall we do with these?
    Where shall we take them?
[51] Your sanctuary is trampled down and profaned,
    and your priests mourn in humiliation.
[52] Here the nations are assembled against us to destroy us;
    you know what they plot against us.
[53] How will we be able to withstand them,
    if you do not help us?"

[54] Then they sounded the trumpets and gave a loud shout. [55] After this Judas appointed leaders of the people in charge of thousands and hundreds and fifties and tens. [56] Those who were building houses or were about to be married or were planting a vineyard or were fainthearted, he told to go home, according to the law. [57] Then the army marched out and encamped to the south of Emmaus. [58] And Judas said, "Arm yourselves and be courageous. Be ready early in the morning to fight with these nations who have assembled against us to destroy us and our sanctuary. [59] It is better for us to die in battle than to see the misfortunes of our nation and of the sanctuary. [60] But as his will in heaven may be, so shall he do."

The Battle at Emmaus

4 Now Gorgias took five thousand infantry and one thousand picked cavalry, and this division moved out by night [2] to fall upon the camp of the Jews and attack them suddenly. Men from the citadel were his guides. [3] But Judas heard of it, and he and his warriors moved out to attack the king's force in Emmaus [4] while the division was still absent from the camp. [5] When Gorgias entered the camp of Judas by night, he found no one there, so he looked for them in the hills, because he said, "These men are running away from us."

[6] At daybreak Judas appeared in the plain with three thousand men, but they did not have armor and swords such as they desired. [7] And they saw the camp of the nations, strong and fortified, with cavalry all around it, and these men were trained in war. [8] But Judas said to those who were with him, "Do not fear their numbers or be afraid when they charge. [9] Remember how our ancestors were saved at the Red Sea, when Pharaoh with his forces pursued them. [10] And now, let us cry to heaven to see whether he will favor us and remember his covenant with our ancestors and crush this army before us today. [11] Then all the nations will know that there is one who redeems and saves Israel."

[12] When the foreigners looked up and saw them coming against them, [13] they went out from their camp to battle. Then the men with Judas blew their trumpets [14] and engaged in battle. The nations were crushed and fled into the plain, [15] and all those in the rear fell by the sword. They pursued them to Gazara and to the plains of Idumea and to Azotus and Jamnia, and three thousand of them fell. [16] Then Judas and his force turned back from pursuing them, [17] and he said to the people, "Do not be greedy for plunder, for there is a battle before us; [18] Gorgias and his force are near us in the hills. But stand now against our enemies and fight them and afterward seize the plunder boldly."

[19] Just as Judas was finishing this speech, a detachment appeared coming out of the hills. [20] They saw that their army[m] had been put to flight and that the Jews[n] were burning the camp, for the smoke that was seen showed what had happened. [21] When they perceived this, they were greatly frightened, and when they also saw the army of Judas drawn up in the plain for battle, [22] they all fled into the land of the Philistines.[o] [23] Then Judas returned to plunder the camp, and they seized a great amount of gold and silver, and cloth dyed blue and sea purple, and great riches. [24] On their return they sang hymns and praises to heaven: "For he is good, for his mercy endures forever." [25] Thus Israel had a great deliverance that day.

First Campaign of Lysias

[26] Those of the foreigners who escaped went and reported to Lysias all that had happened. [27] When he heard it, he was perplexed and discouraged, for things had not happened to Israel as he had intended, nor had they turned out as the king had ordered. [28] But the next year he mustered sixty thousand picked infantry and five thousand cavalry to subdue them. [29] They came into Idumea and encamped at Beth-zur, and Judas met them with ten thousand men.

[30] When he saw that their army was strong, he prayed, saying, "Blessed are you, O Savior of Israel, who crushed the attack of the mighty warrior by the hand of your servant David and gave the camp of the Philistines into the hands of Jonathan son of Saul and of the man who carried his armor. [31] Hem in this army by the hand of your people Israel, and let them be ashamed of their troops and their cavalry. [32] Fill them with cowardice; melt the boldness of their strength; let them tremble in their destruction. [33] Strike them down with the sword of those who love you, and let all who know your name praise you with hymns."

[34] Then both sides attacked, and there fell of the army of Lysias five thousand men; they fell before them.[p] [35] When Lysias saw the rout of his troops and observed the boldness that inspired those of Judas and how ready they were either to live or to die nobly, he withdrew to Antioch and enlisted mercenaries in order to invade Judea again with an even larger army.

Cleansing and Dedication of the Temple

[36] Then Judas and his brothers said, "See, our enemies are crushed; let us go up to cleanse the sanctuary and dedicate it." [37] So all the army assembled and went up to Mount Zion. [38] There they saw the sanctuary desolate, the altar profaned, and the gates burned. In the courts they saw bushes sprung up as in a thicket or as on one of the mountains. They saw also the chambers of the priests in ruins. [39] Then they tore their clothes and mourned with great lamentation; they sprinkled themselves with ash-

es [40] and fell face down on the ground. And they blew the signal trumpets, and they cried out to heaven.

[41] Then Judas detailed men to fight against those in the citadel until he had cleansed the sanctuary. [42] He chose blameless priests devoted to the law, [43] and they cleansed the sanctuary and removed the defiled stones to an unclean place. [44] They deliberated what to do about the altar of burnt offering, which had been profaned. [45] And they thought it best to tear it down, so that it would not be a lasting shame to them that the nations had defiled it. So they tore down the altar [46] and stored the stones in a convenient place on the temple hill until a prophet should come to tell what to do with them. [47] Then they took unhewn[q] stones, as the law directs, and built a new altar like the former one. [48] They also rebuilt the sanctuary and the interior of the temple and consecrated the courts. [49] They made new holy vessels and brought the lampstand, the altar of incense, and the table into the temple. [50] Then they offered incense on the altar and lit the lamps on the lampstand, and these gave light in the temple. [51] They placed the bread on the table and hung up the curtains. Thus they finished all the work they had undertaken.

[52] Early in the morning on the twenty-fifth day of the ninth month, which is the month of Chislev, in the one hundred forty-eighth year, [53] they rose and offered sacrifice, as the law directs, on the new altar of burnt offering that they had built. [54] At the very season and on the very day that the nations had profaned it, it was dedicated with songs and harps and lutes and cymbals. [55] All the people fell on their faces and worshiped and blessed heaven, who had prospered them. [56] So they celebrated the dedication of the altar for eight days and joyfully offered burnt offerings; they offered a sacrifice of well-being and a thanksgiving offering. [57] They decorated the front of the temple with golden crowns and small shields; they restored the gates and the chambers for the priests and fitted them with doors. [58] There was very great joy among the people, and the disgrace brought by the nations was removed.

[59] Then Judas and his brothers and all the assembly of Israel determined that every year at that season the days of dedication of the altar should be observed with joy and gladness for eight days, beginning with the twenty-fifth day of the month of Chislev.

[60] At that time they fortified Mount Zion with high walls and strong towers all around, to keep the nations from coming and trampling them down as they had done before. [61] Judas[r] stationed a garrison there to guard it; he also fortified Beth-zur to guard it, so that the people might have a stronghold that faced Idumea.

Wars with Neighboring Peoples

5 When the nations all around heard that the altar had been rebuilt and the sanctuary dedicated as it was before, they became very angry, [2] and they determined to destroy the descendants of Jacob who lived among them. So they began to kill and destroy among the people. [3] But Judas made war on the descendants of Esau in Idumea, at Akrabattene, because they kept lying in wait for Israel. He dealt them a heavy blow and humbled them and despoiled them. [4] He also remembered the wickedness of the sons of Baean, who were a trap and a snare to the people and ambushed them on the highways. [5] They were shut up by him in towers, and he encamped against them, vowed their complete destruction, and burned with fire their towers and all who were in them. [6] Then he crossed over to attack the Ammonites, where he found a strong band and many people, with Timothy as their leader. [7] He engaged in many battles with them, and they were crushed before him; he struck them down. [8] He also took Jazer and its villages; then he returned to Judea.

Liberation of Galilean Jews

[9] Now the nations in Gilead gathered together against the Israelites who lived in their territory and planned to destroy them. But they fled to the stronghold of Dathema [10] and sent to Judas and his brothers letters that said, "The nations around us have gathered together to destroy us. [11] They are preparing to come and capture the stronghold to which we have fled, and Timothy is leading their forces. [12] Now then, come and rescue us from their hands, for many of us have fallen, [13] and all our kindred who were in the land of Tobias have been killed; the enemy[s] have captured their wives and children and goods and have destroyed about a thousand persons there."

[14] While the letters were still being read, other messengers, with their garments torn, came from Galilee and made a similar report; [15] they said that the people of Ptolemais and Tyre and Sidon and all Galilee of the gentiles[t] had gathered together against them "to annihilate us." [16] When Judas and the people heard these messages, a great assembly was called to determine what they should do for their kindred who were in distress and were being attacked by enemies.[u] [17] Then Judas said to his brother Simon, "Choose your men and go and rescue your kindred in Galilee; Jonathan my brother and I will go to Gilead." [18] But he left Joseph, son of Zechariah, and Azariah, a leader of the people, with the rest of the forces in Judea to guard it, [19] and he gave them this command, "Take charge of this people, but do not engage in battle with the nations until we return." [20] Then three thousand men were assigned to Simon to go to Galilee and eight thousand to Judas for Gilead.

[21] So Simon went to Galilee and fought many battles against the nations, and the nations were crushed before him. [22] He pursued them to the gate of Ptolemais; as many as three thousand of the nations fell, and he despoiled them. [23] Then he took the Jews[v] of Galilee and Arbatta, with their wives and children, and all they possessed and led them to Judea with great rejoicing.

Judas and Jonathan in Gilead

[24] Judas Maccabeus and his brother Jonathan crossed the Jordan and made three days' journey into the wilderness. [25] They encountered the Nabateans, who met them peaceably and told them all that had happened to their kindred in Gilead: [26] "Many of them have been shut up in Bozrah and Bosor, in Alema and Chaspho, Maked and Carnaim"—all these towns were strong and large— [27] "and some have been shut up in the other towns of Gilead; the enemy[w] are getting ready to attack the strongholds tomorrow and capture and destroy all these people in a single day."

[28] Then Judas and his army quickly turned back by the wilderness road to Bozrah, and he took the town and killed every male by the edge of the sword; then he seized all its spoils and burned it with fire. [29] He left the place at night, and they went all the way to the stronghold of Dathema.[x] [30] At dawn they looked out and saw a large company, which could not be counted, carrying ladders and engines of war to capture the stronghold and attacking the Jews within.[y] [31] So Judas saw that the battle had begun and that the cry of the town went up to heaven, with trumpets and loud shouts, [32] and he said to the men of his forces, "Fight today for your kindred!" [33] Then he came up behind them in three companies, who sounded their trumpets and cried aloud in prayer. [34] And when the army of Timothy realized that it was Maccabeus, they fled before him, and he dealt them a heavy blow. As many as eight thousand of them fell that day.

[35] Next he turned aside to Maapha[z] and fought against it and took it, and he killed every male in it, plundered it, and burned it with fire. [36] From there he marched on and took Chaspho, Maked, and Bosor and the other towns of Gilead.

[37] After these things Timothy gathered another army and encamped opposite Raphon, on the other side of the stream. [38] Judas sent men to spy out the camp, and they reported to him, "All the nations around us have gathered to him; it is a very large force. [39] They also have hired Arabs to help them, and they are encamped across the stream ready to come and fight against you." And Judas went to meet them.

[40] Now as Judas and his army drew near to the stream of water, Timothy said to the officers of his forces, "If he crosses over to us first, we will not be able to resist him, for he will surely defeat us. [41] But if he shows fear and camps on the other side of the river, we will cross over to him and defeat him." [42] When Judas approached the stream of water, he stationed the officers[aa] of the army at the stream and gave them this command, "Permit no one to encamp, but make them all enter the battle." [43] Then he crossed over against them first, and the whole army followed him. All the nations were defeated before him, and they threw away their arms and fled into the sacred precincts at Carnaim. [44] But he took the town and burned the sacred precincts with fire, together with all who were in them. Thus Carnaim was conquered; they could stand before Judas no longer.

The Return to Jerusalem

[45] Then Judas gathered together all the Israelites in Gilead, the small and the great, with their wives and children and goods, a very large company, to go to the land of Judah. [46] So they came to Ephron. This was a large and very strong town on the road, and they could not go around it to the right or to the left; they had to go through it. [47] But the people of the town shut them out and blocked the gates with stones. [48] Judas sent them this friendly message, "Let us pass through your land to get to our land. No one will do you harm; we will simply pass by on foot." But they refused to open to him. [49] Then Judas ordered proclamation to be made to the army that all should encamp where they were. [50] So the men of the forces encamped, and he fought against the town all that day and all the night, and the town was delivered into his hands. [51] He destroyed every male by the edge of the sword and razed and plundered the town. Then he passed through the town over the bodies of the dead. [52] Then they crossed the Jordan into the large plain before Bethshan. [53] Judas kept rallying the laggards and encouraging the people all the way until he came to the land of Judah. [54] So they went up to Mount Zion with joy and gladness and offered burnt offerings because they had returned in safety; not one of them had fallen.

Joseph and Azariah Defeated

[55] Now while Judas and Jonathan were in Gilead and their[ab] brother Simon was in Galilee before Ptolemais, [56] Joseph son of Zechariah and Azariah, the commanders of the forces, heard of their brave deeds and of the heroic war they had fought. [57] So they said, "Let us also make a name for ourselves; let us go and make war on the nations around us." [58] So they issued orders to the men of the forces that were with them and marched against Jamnia. [59] Gorgias and his men came out of the town to meet them in battle. [60] Then Joseph and Azariah were routed and were pursued to the borders of Judea; as many as two thousand of the people of Israel fell that day. [61] Thus the people suffered a great rout because, thinking to do a brave deed, they did not listen to Judas and his brothers. [62] But they did not belong to the family of those men through whom deliverance was given to Israel.

[63] The man Judas and his brothers were greatly honored in all Israel and among all the nations, wherever their name was heard. [64] People gathered to them and praised them.

Success at Hebron and Philistia

[65] Then Judas and his brothers went out and fought the descendants of Esau in the land to the south. He struck Hebron and its villages and tore down its strongholds and burned its towers on all sides. [66] Then he marched off to go into the land of the Philistines[ac] and passed through Marisa.[ad] [67] On that day some priests who wished to do a brave deed fell in battle, for they went out to battle unwisely. [68] But Judas turned aside to Azotus in the land of the Philistines; he tore down their altars, and the carved images of their gods he burned with fire; he plundered the towns and returned to the land of Judah.

The Last Days of Antiochus Epiphanes

6 King Antiochus was going through the upper provinces when he heard that Elymais in Persia was a city famed for its wealth in silver and gold. [2] Its temple was very rich, containing golden shields, breastplates, and weapons left there by Alexander son of Philip, the Macedonian king who first reigned over the Greeks. [3] So he came and tried to take the city and plunder it, but he could not because his plan had become known to the citizens, [4] and they withstood him in battle. So he fled and in great disappointment left there to return to Babylon.

[5] Then someone came to him in Persia and reported that the armies that had gone into the land of Judah had been routed; [6] that Lysias had gone first with a strong force but had turned and fled before the Jews;[ae] that the Jews[af] had grown strong from the arms, supplies, and abundant spoils that they had taken from the armies they had cut down; [7] that they had torn down the abomination that he had erected on the altar in Jerusalem; and that they had surrounded the sanctuary with high walls as before, and also Beth-zur, his town.

[8] When the king heard this news, he was astounded and badly shaken. He took to his bed and became sick from disappointment because things had not turned out for him as he had planned. [9] He lay there for many days because deep disappointment continually gripped him, and he realized that he was dying. [10] So he called all his Friends and said to them, "Sleep has departed from my eyes, and I am downhearted with worry. [11] I said to myself, 'To what distress I have come! And into what a great flood I now am plunged! For I was kind and beloved in my power.' [12] But now I remember the wrong I did in Jerusalem. I seized all its vessels of silver and gold, and I sent to destroy the inhabitants of Judah without good reason. [13] I know that it is because of this that these misfortunes have come upon me; here I am, perishing of bitter disappointment in a strange land."

[14] Then he called for Philip, one of his Friends, and made him ruler over all his kingdom. [15] He gave him the crown and his robe and the signet so that he might guide his son Antiochus and bring him up to be king. [16] Thus King Antiochus died there in the one hundred forty-ninth year. [17] When Lysias learned that the king was dead, he set up Antiochus the king's[ag] son to reign. Lysias[ah] had brought him up from boyhood; he named him Eupator.

Renewed Attacks from Syria

[18] Meanwhile the garrison in the citadel kept hemming Israel in around the sanctuary. They were trying in every way to harm them and strengthen the nations. [19] Judas therefore resolved to destroy them and assembled all the people to besiege them. [20] They gathered together and besieged the citadel[ai] in the one hundred fiftieth year, and he built siege towers and engines of war. [21] But some of the garrison escaped from the siege, and some of the ungodly Israelites joined them. [22] They went to the king and said, "How long will you fail to do justice and to avenge our kindred? [23] We were happy to serve your father, to live by what he said, and to follow his commands. [24] For this reason the sons of our people besieged the citadel[aj] and became hostile to us; moreover, they have put to death as many of us as they have caught, and they have seized our inheritances. [25] It is not against us alone that they have stretched out their hands; they have also attacked all the lands on their borders. [26] And see, today they have encamped against the citadel in Jerusalem to take it; they have fortified both the sanctuary and Beth-zur; [27] unless you quickly prevent them, they will do still greater things, and you will not be able to stop them."

[28] The king was enraged when he heard this. He assembled all his Friends, the commanders of his forces and those in authority.[ak] [29] Mercenary forces also came to him from other kingdoms and from islands of the seas. [30] The number of his forces was one hundred thousand foot soldiers, twenty thousand horsemen, and thirty-two elephants accustomed to war. [31] They came through Idumea and encamped against Beth-zur, and for many days they fought and built engines of war, but the Jews[al] sallied out and burned these with fire and fought courageously.

The Battle at Beth-zechariah

[32] Then Judas marched away from the citadel and encamped at Beth-zechariah, opposite the camp of the king. [33] Early in the morning the king set out and took his army by a forced march along the road to Beth-zechariah, and his troops made ready for battle and sounded their trumpets. [34] They offered the elephants the juice of grapes and mulberries, to arouse them for battle. [35] They distributed the animals among the phal-

anxes; with each elephant they stationed a thousand men armed with coats of mail and with brass helmets on their heads, and five hundred picked horsemen were assigned to each beast. [36] These took their position beforehand wherever the animal was; wherever it went, they went with it, and they never left it. [37] On the elephants[am] were wooden towers, strong and covered; they were fastened on each animal by special harness, and on each were four[an] armed men who fought from there and also its Indian driver. [38] The rest of the cavalry were stationed on either side, on the two flanks of the army, to harass the enemy while being themselves protected by the phalanxes. [39] When the sun shone on the shields of gold and brass, the hills were ablaze with them and gleamed like flaming torches.

[40] Now a part of the king's army was spread out on the high hills, and some troops were on the plain, and they advanced steadily and in good order. [41] All who heard the noise made by their multitude, by the marching of the multitude and the clanking of their arms, trembled, for the army was very large and strong. [42] But Judas and his army advanced to the battle, and six hundred of the king's army fell. [43] Now Eleazar, called Avaran, saw that one of the animals was equipped with royal armor. It was taller than all the others, and he supposed that the king was on it. [44] So he gave his life to save his people and to win for himself an everlasting name. [45] He courageously ran into the midst of the phalanx to reach it; he killed men right and left, and they parted before him on both sides. [46] He got under the elephant, stabbed it from beneath, and killed it, but it fell to the ground upon him and he died. [47] When the Jews[ao] saw the royal might and the fierce attack of the forces, they turned away in flight.

The Siege of the Temple

[48] The soldiers of the king's army went up to Jerusalem against them, and the king encamped in Judea and at Mount Zion. [49] He made peace with the people of Beth-zur, and they evacuated the town because they had no provisions there to withstand a siege, since it was a sabbatical year for the land. [50] So the king took Beth-zur and stationed a guard there to hold it. [51] Then he encamped before the sanctuary for many days. He set up siege towers, engines of war, devices to throw fire and stones, machines to shoot arrows, and catapults. [52] The Jews[ap] also made engines of war to match theirs and fought for many days. [53] But they had no food in storage,[aq] because it was the seventh year; those who had found safety in Judea from the nations had consumed the last of the stores. [54] Only a few men were left in the sanctuary; the rest scattered to their own homes, for the famine proved too much for them.

Syria Offers Terms

[55] Then Lysias heard that Philip, whom King Antiochus while still living had appointed to bring up his son Antiochus to be king, [56] had returned from Persia and Media with the forces that had gone with the king and that he was trying to seize control of the government. [57] So he quickly gave orders to withdraw and said to the king, to the commanders of the forces, and to the troops, "Daily we grow weaker, our food supply is scant, the place against which we are fighting is strong, and the affairs of the kingdom press urgently on us. [58] Now, then, let us come to terms with these people and make peace with them and with all their nation. [59] Let us agree to let them live by their laws as they did before, for it was on account of their laws that we abolished that they became angry and did all these things."

[60] The speech pleased the king and the commanders, and he sent to the Jews[ar] an offer of peace, and they accepted it. [61] So the king and the commanders gave them their oath. On these conditions the Jews[as] evacuated the stronghold. [62] But when the king entered Mount Zion and saw what a strong fortress the place was, he broke the oath he had sworn and gave orders to tear down the wall all around. [63] Then he set off in haste and returned to Antioch. He found Philip in control of the city, but he fought against him and took the city by force.

Expedition of Bacchides and Alcimus

7 In the one hundred fifty-first year Demetrius son of Seleucus set out from Rome, sailed with a few men to a town by the sea, and there began to reign. [2] As he was entering the royal palace of his ancestors, the army seized Antiochus and Lysias to bring them to him. [3] But when this act became known to him, he said, "Do not let me see their faces!" [4] So the army killed them, and Demetrius took his seat on the throne of his kingdom.

[5] Then there came to him all the renegade and godless men of Israel; they were led by Alcimus, who wanted to be high priest. [6] They brought to the king this accusation against the people: "Judas and his brothers have destroyed all your Friends and have driven us out of our land. [7] Now, then, send a man whom you trust; let him go and see all the ruin that Judas[at] has brought on us and on the land of the king, and let him punish them and all who help them."

[8] So the king chose Bacchides, one of the king's Friends, governor of the province Beyond the River; he was a great man in the kingdom and was faithful to the king. [9] He sent him, and with him he sent the ungodly Alcimus, whom he made high priest, and he commanded him to take vengeance on the Israelites. [10] So they marched away and came with a large force into the land of Judah, and he sent messengers to Judas and his

brothers with peaceable but treacherous words. ¹¹ But they paid no attention to their words, for they saw that they had come with a large force. ¹² Then a group of scribes appeared in a body before Alcimus and Bacchides to ask for just terms. ¹³ The Hasideans were first among the Israelites to seek peace from them, ¹⁴ for they said, "A priest of the line of Aaron has come with the army, and he will not harm us." ¹⁵ Alcimus[au] spoke peaceable words to them and swore this oath to them, "We will not seek to injure you or your friends." ¹⁶ So they trusted him, but he seized sixty of them and killed them in one day, in accordance with the word that was written,

¹⁷ "The flesh of your faithful ones and their blood
    they poured out all around Jerusalem,
    and there was no one to bury them."

¹⁸ Then the fear and dread of them fell on all the people, for they said, "There is no truth or justice in them, for they have violated the agreement and the oath that they swore."

¹⁹ Then Bacchides withdrew from Jerusalem and encamped in Beth-zaith. And he sent and seized many of the men who had deserted to him,[av] and some of the people, and killed them and threw them into a great pit. ²⁰ He placed Alcimus in charge of the country and left with him a force to help him; then Bacchides went back to the king. ²¹ Alcimus struggled to maintain his high priesthood, ²² and all who were troubling their people joined him. They gained control of the land of Judah and did great damage in Israel. ²³ And Judas saw all the wrongs that Alcimus and those with him had done among the Israelites; it was more than the nations had done. ²⁴ So Judas[aw] went out into all the surrounding parts of Judea, taking vengeance on those who had deserted and preventing those in the city[ax] from going out into the country. ²⁵ When Alcimus saw that Judas and those with him had grown strong and realized that he could not withstand them, he returned to the king and brought malicious charges against them.

Nicanor in Judea

²⁶ Then the king sent Nicanor, one of his honored princes, who hated and detested Israel, and he commanded him to destroy the people. ²⁷ So Nicanor came to Jerusalem with a large force and treacherously sent to Judas and his brothers this peaceable message, ²⁸ "Let there be no fighting between you and me; I shall come with a few men to see you face to face in peace." ²⁹ So he came to Judas, and they greeted one another peaceably, but the enemy were preparing to kidnap Judas. ³⁰ It became known to Judas that Nicanor[ay] had come to him with treacherous intent, and he was afraid of him and would not meet him again. ³¹ When Nicanor learned that his plan had been disclosed, he went out to meet Judas in battle near Capharsalama. ³² About five hundred of the army of Nicanor fell, and the rest[az] fled into the city of David.

Nicanor Threatens the Temple

³³ After these events Nicanor went up to Mount Zion. Some of the priests from the sanctuary and some of the elders of the people came out to greet him peaceably and to show him the burnt offering that was being offered for the king. ³⁴ But he mocked them and derided them and defiled them and spoke arrogantly, ³⁵ and in anger he swore this oath, "Unless Judas and his army are delivered into my hands this time, then if I return safely I will burn up this house." And he went out in great anger. ³⁶ At this the priests went in and stood before the altar and the temple; they wept and said,

³⁷ "You chose this house to be called by your name
    and to be for your people a house of prayer and supplication.
³⁸ Take vengeance on this man and on his army,
    and let them fall by the sword;
    remember their blasphemies,
    and let them live no longer."

The Death of Nicanor

³⁹ Now Nicanor went out from Jerusalem and encamped in Beth-horon, and the Syrian army joined him. ⁴⁰ Judas encamped in Adasa with three thousand men. Then Judas prayed and said, ⁴¹ "When the messengers from the king spoke blasphemy, your angel went out and struck down one hundred eighty-five thousand of the Assyrians.[ba] ⁴² So also crush this army before us today; let the rest learn that Nicanor[bb] has spoken wickedly against the sanctuary, and judge him according to this wickedness." ⁴³ So the armies met in battle on the thirteenth day of the month of Adar. The army of Nicanor was crushed, and he himself was the first to fall in the battle. ⁴⁴ When his army saw that Nicanor had fallen, they threw down their arms and fled. ⁴⁵ The Jews[bc] pursued them a day's journey, from Adasa as far as Gazara, and as they followed they kept sounding the battle call on the trumpets. ⁴⁶ People came out of all the surrounding villages of Judea, and they outflanked the enemy[bd] and drove them back to their pursuers,[be] so that they all fell by the sword; not even one of them was left. ⁴⁷ Then the Jews[bf] seized the spoils and the plunder; they cut off Nicanor's head and the right hand that he had so arrogantly stretched out and brought them and displayed them just outside Jerusalem. ⁴⁸ The people rejoiced greatly and celebrated that day as a day of great gladness. ⁴⁹ They decreed that this day should be celebrated each year on the thirteenth day of Adar. ⁵⁰ So the land of Judah had rest for a few days.

A Eulogy of the Romans

8 Now Judas heard of the fame of the Romans, that they were very strong and were well-disposed toward all who made an alliance with them, that they pledged friendship to those who came to them, ² and that they were very strong. He had been told of their wars and of the brave deeds that they were doing among the Gauls, how they had defeated them and forced them to pay tribute, ³ and what they had done in the land of Spain to get control of the silver and gold mines there, ⁴ and how they had gained control of the whole region by their planning and patience, even though the place was far distant from them. They also subdued the kings who came against them from the ends of the earth, until they crushed them and inflicted great disaster on them; the survivors paid them tribute every year. ⁵ They had crushed in battle and conquered Philip, and King Perseus of the Macedonians,[bg] and the others who rose up against them. ⁶ They also had defeated Antiochus the Great, king of Asia, who went to fight against them with one hundred twenty elephants and with cavalry and chariots and a very large army. He was crushed by them; ⁷ they took him alive and decreed that he and those who would reign after him should pay a heavy tribute and give hostages and surrender some of their best provinces: ⁸ the countries of India, Media, and Lydia. These they took from him and gave to King Eumenes. ⁹ The Greeks planned to come and destroy them, ¹⁰ but this became known to them, and they sent a general against the Greeks[bh] and attacked them. Many of them were wounded and fell, and the Romans[bi] took captive their wives and children; they plundered them, conquered the land, tore down their strongholds, and enslaved them to this day. ¹¹ The remaining kingdoms and islands, as many as ever opposed them, they destroyed and enslaved, ¹² but with their friends and those who rely on them they have kept friendship. They have subdued kings far and near, and as many as have heard of their fame have feared them. ¹³ Those whom they wish to help and to make kings, they make kings, and those whom they wish they depose, and they have been greatly exalted. ¹⁴ Yet for all this not one of them has put on a crown or worn purple as a mark of pride, ¹⁵ but they have built for themselves a senate chamber, and every day three hundred twenty senators constantly deliberate concerning the people, to govern them well. ¹⁶ They trust one man each year to rule over them and to control all their land; they all heed the one man, and there is no envy or jealousy among them.

An Alliance with Rome

¹⁷ So Judas chose Eupolemus son of John son of Accos, and Jason son of Eleazar, and sent them to Rome to establish friendship and alliance ¹⁸ and to free themselves from the yoke, for they saw that the kingdom of the Greeks was enslaving Israel completely. ¹⁹ They went to Rome, a very long journey, and they entered the senate chamber and spoke as follows: ²⁰ "Judas, who is also called Maccabeus, and his brothers and the people of the Jews have sent us to you to establish alliance and peace with you, so that we may be enrolled as your allies and friends." ²¹ The proposal pleased them, ²² and this is a copy of the letter that they wrote in reply, on bronze tablets, and sent to Jerusalem to remain with them there as a memorial of peace and alliance:

²³ "May all go well with the Romans and with the nation of the Jews at sea and on land forever, and may sword and enemy be far from them. ²⁴ If war comes first to Rome or to any of their allies in all their dominion, ²⁵ the nation of the Jews shall act as their allies wholeheartedly, as the occasion may indicate to them. ²⁶ To the enemy that makes war they shall not give or supply grain, arms, money, or ships, just as Rome has decided, and they shall keep their obligations without receiving any return. ²⁷ In the same way, if war comes first to the nation of the Jews, the Romans shall willingly act as their allies, as the occasion may indicate to them. ²⁸ And to their enemies there shall not be given grain, arms, money, or ships, just as Rome has decided, and they shall keep these obligations and do so without deceit. ²⁹ Thus on these terms the Romans make a treaty with the Jewish people. ³⁰ If after these terms are in effect both parties shall determine to add or delete anything, they shall do so at their discretion, and any addition or deletion that they may make shall be valid. ³¹ "Concerning the wrongs that King Demetrius is doing to them, we have written to him as follows, 'Why have you made your yoke heavy on our friends and allies the Jews? ³² If now they appeal again for help against you, we will defend their rights and fight you on sea and on land.' "

Bacchides Returns to Judea

9 When Demetrius heard that Nicanor and his army had fallen in battle, he sent Bacchides and Alcimus into the land of Judah a second time, and with them the right wing of the army. ² They went by the road that leads to Gilgal and encamped against Mesaloth in Arbela, and they took it and killed many people. ³ In the first month of the one hundred fifty-second year they encamped against Jerusalem; ⁴ then they marched off and went to Berea with twenty thousand foot soldiers and two thousand cavalry. ⁵ Now Judas was encamped in Elasa, and with him were three thousand picked men. ⁶ When they saw the huge number of the enemy forces, they were greatly frightened, and many slipped away from the camp, until no more than eight hundred of them were left.

[7] When Judas saw that his army had slipped away and the battle was imminent, he was crushed in spirit, for he had no time to assemble them. [8] He became faint, but he said to those who were left, "Let us get up and go against our enemies. We may have the strength to fight them." [9] But they tried to dissuade him, saying, "We do not have the strength. Let us rather save our own lives now, and let us come back with our kindred and fight them, for we are too few." [10] But Judas said, "Far be it from me to do such a thing as to flee from them. If our time has come, let us die bravely for our kindred and leave no cause to question our honor."

The Last Battle of Judas

[11] Then the army of Bacchides[b] marched out from the camp and took its stand for the encounter. The cavalry was divided into two companies, and the slingers and the archers went ahead of the army, as did all the chief warriors. [12] Bacchides was on the right wing. Flanked by the two companies, the phalanx advanced to the sound of the trumpets, and the men with Judas also blew their trumpets. [13] The earth was shaken by the noise of the armies, and the battle raged from morning until evening. [14] Judas saw that Bacchides and the strength of his army were on the right; then all the courageous men went with him, [15] and they crushed the right wing, and he pursued them as far as Mount Azotus. [16] When those on the left wing saw that the right wing was crushed, they turned and followed close behind Judas and his men. [17] The battle became desperate, and many on both sides were wounded and fell. [18] Judas also fell, and the rest fled.

[19] Then Jonathan and Simon took their brother Judas and buried him in the tomb of their ancestors at Modein [20] and wept for him. All Israel made great lamentation for him; they mourned many days and said,

[21] "How is the mighty fallen, the savior of Israel!"

[22] Now the rest of the acts of Judas, and his wars and the brave deeds that he did, and his greatness have not been recorded because they were very many.

Jonathan Succeeds Judas

[23] After the death of Judas, the renegades emerged in all parts of Israel; all the wrongdoers reappeared. [24] In those days a very great famine occurred, and the country went over to their side. [25] Bacchides chose the godless and put them in charge of the country. [26] They made inquiry and searched for the friends of Judas and brought them to Bacchides, who took vengeance on them and made sport of them. [27] So there was great distress in Israel such as had not been since the time a prophet had last appeared among them.

[28] Then all the friends of Judas assembled and said to Jonathan, [29] "Since the death of your brother Judas there has been no one like him to go against our enemies and Bacchides and to deal with those of our nation who hate us. [30] Now, therefore, we have chosen you today to take his place as our ruler and leader, to fight our battle." [31] So Jonathan accepted the leadership at that time in place of his brother Judas.

The Campaigns of Jonathan

[32] When Bacchides learned of this, he tried to kill him.

Revolt of Alexander Epiphanes

10 In the one hundred sixtieth year Alexander Epiphanes, son of Antiochus, landed and occupied Ptolemais. They welcomed him, and there he began to reign. [2] When King Demetrius heard of it, he assembled a very large army and marched out to meet him in battle. [3] Demetrius sent Jonathan a letter in peaceable words to honor him, [4] for he said to himself, "Let us act first to make peace with him[a] before he makes peace with Alexander against us, [5] for he will remember all the wrongs that we did to him and to his brothers and his nation." [6] So Demetrius[b] gave him authority to recruit troops, to equip them with arms, and to become his ally, and he commanded that the hostages in the citadel should be released to him.

[7] Then Jonathan came to Jerusalem and read the letter in the hearing of all the people and of those in the citadel. [8] They were greatly alarmed when they heard that the king had given him authority to recruit troops. [9] But those in the citadel released the hostages to Jonathan, and he returned them to their parents.

[10] And Jonathan took up residence in Jerusalem and began to rebuild and restore the city. [11] He directed those who were doing the work to build the walls and encircle Mount Zion with squared stones, for better fortification, and they did so. [12] Then the foreigners who were in the strongholds that Bacchides had built fled; [13] all of them left their places and went back to their own lands. [14] Only in Beth-zur did some remain who had forsaken the law and the commandments, for it served as a place of refuge.

[15] Now King Alexander heard of all the promises that Demetrius had sent to Jonathan, and he heard of the battles that Jonathan[c] and his brothers had fought, of the brave deeds that they had done, and of the troubles that they had endured. [16] So he said, "Shall we find another such man? Come now, we will make him our friend and ally." [17] And he wrote a letter and sent it to him, in the following words:

Jonathan Becomes High Priest

[18] "King Alexander to his brother Jonathan, greetings. [19] We have heard about you, that you are a mighty warrior and worthy to be our friend. [20] And so we have appointed you today to be the high priest of your nation; you are to be called the king's Friend, and you are to take our side and keep friendship with us." He also sent him a purple robe and a golden crown.

[21] So Jonathan put on the sacred vestments in the seventh month of the one hundred sixtieth year, at the Festival of Booths,[d] and he recruited troops and equipped them with arms in abundance. [22] When Demetrius heard of these things, he was distressed and said, [23] "What is this that we have done? Alexander has gotten ahead of us in forming a friendship with the Jews to strengthen himself. [24] I also will write them words of encouragement and promise them honor and gifts, so that I may have their help." [25] So he sent a message to them in the following words:

A Letter from Demetrius to Jonathan

"King Demetrius to the nation of the Jews, greetings. [26] Since you have kept your agreement with us and have continued your friendship with us and have not sided with our enemies, we have heard of it and rejoiced. [27] Now continue still to keep faith with us, and we will repay you with good for what you do for us. [28] We will grant you many immunities and give you gifts.

[29] "I now free you and exempt all the Jews from payment of tribute and salt tax and crown levies, [30] and instead of collecting the third of the grain and the half of the fruit of the trees that I should receive, I release them from this day and henceforth. I will not collect them from the land of Judah or from the three districts added to it from Samaria and Galilee, from this day and for all time. [31] Jerusalem and its environs, its tithes and its revenues, shall be holy and free from tax. [32] I release also my control of the citadel in Jerusalem and give it to the high priest, so that he may station in it men of his own choice to guard it. [33] And every one of the Jews taken as a captive from the land of Judah into any part of my kingdom, I set free without payment, and let all officials cancel also the taxes on their livestock.

[34] "All the festivals and Sabbaths and new moons and appointed days and the three days before a festival and the three after a festival—let them all be days of immunity and release for all the Jews who are in my kingdom. [35] No one shall have authority to exact anything from them or trouble any of them about any matter.

[36] "Let Jews be enrolled in the king's forces to the number of thirty thousand men, and let the maintenance be given them that is due to all the forces of the king. [37] Let some of them be stationed in the great strongholds of the king, and let some of them be put in positions of trust in the kingdom. Let their officers and leaders be of their own number, and let them live by their own laws, just as the king has commanded in the land of Judah.

[38] "As for the three districts that have been added to Judea from the country of Samaria, let them be annexed to Judea so that they may be considered to be under one ruler and obey no other authority than the high priest. [39] Ptolemais and the land adjoining it I have given as a gift to the sanctuary in Jerusalem, to meet the necessary expenses of the sanctuary. [40] I also grant fifteen thousand shekels of silver yearly out of the king's revenues from appropriate places. [41] And all the additional funds that the government officials have not paid as they did in the first years,[e] they shall give from now on for the service of the temple.[f] [42] Moreover, the five thousand shekels of silver that my officials[g] have received every year from the income of the services of the temple, this, too, is canceled, because it belongs to the priests who minister there. [43] And all who take refuge at the temple in Jerusalem or in any of its precincts because they owe money to the king or are in debt, let them be released and receive back all their property in my kingdom.

[44] "Let the cost of rebuilding and restoring the structures of the sanctuary be paid from the revenues of the king. [45] And let the cost of rebuilding the walls of Jerusalem and fortifying it all around and the cost of rebuilding the walls in Judea also be paid from the revenues of the king."

Death of Demetrius

[46] When Jonathan and the people heard these words, they did not believe or accept them, because they remembered the great wrongs that Demetrius[h] had done in Israel and how much he had oppressed them. [47] They favored Alexander because he had been the first to speak peaceable words to them, and they remained his allies all his days.

[48] Now King Alexander assembled large forces and encamped opposite Demetrius. [49] The two kings met in battle, and the army of Demetrius fled, and Alexander[i] pursued him and defeated them. [50] He pressed the battle strongly until the sun set, and on that day Demetrius fell.

Treaty of Ptolemy and Alexander

[51] Then Alexander sent ambassadors to Ptolemy king of Egypt with the following message: [52] "Since I have returned to my kingdom and have taken my seat on the throne of my ancestors and established my rule—for I crushed Demetrius and gained control of our country; [53] I met him in battle, and he and his army were crushed by us, and we have taken our seat on the throne of his kingdom— [54] now therefore let us establish friendship with one another; give me now your daughter as my wife, and

I will become your son-in-law and will make gifts to you and to her in keeping with your position." ⁵⁵Ptolemy the king replied and said, "Happy was the day on which you returned to the land of your ancestors and took your seat on the throne of their kingdom. ⁵⁶And now I will do for you as you wrote, but meet me at Ptolemais, so that we may see one another, and I will become your father-in-law, as you have said." ⁵⁷So Ptolemy set out from Egypt, he and his daughter Cleopatra, and came to Ptolemais in the one hundred sixty-second year. ⁵⁸King Alexander met him, and Ptolemy[j] gave him his daughter Cleopatra in marriage and celebrated her wedding at Ptolemais with great pomp, as kings do. ⁵⁹Then King Alexander wrote to Jonathan to come and meet him. ⁶⁰So he went with pomp to Ptolemais and met the two kings; he gave them and their Friends silver and gold and many gifts and found favor with them. ⁶¹A group of malcontents from Israel, renegades, gathered together against him to accuse him, but the king paid no attention to them. ⁶²The king gave orders to take off Jonathan's garments and to clothe him in purple, and they did so. ⁶³The king also seated him at his side, and he said to his officers, "Go out with him into the middle of the city and proclaim that no one is to bring charges against him about any matter, and let no one trouble him for any reason." ⁶⁴When his accusers saw the honor that was paid him, in accord with the proclamation, and saw him clothed in purple, they all fled. ⁶⁵Thus the king honored him and enrolled him among his First Friends and made him general and governor of the province. ⁶⁶And Jonathan returned to Jerusalem in peace and gladness.

Apollonius Is Defeated by Jonathan

⁶⁷In the one hundred sixty-fifth year Demetrius son of Demetrius came from Crete to the land of his ancestors. ⁶⁸When King Alexander heard of it, he was greatly distressed and returned to Antioch. ⁶⁹And Demetrius appointed Apollonius the governor of Coelesyria, and he assembled a large force and encamped against Jamnia. Then he sent the following message to the high priest Jonathan: ⁷⁰"You are the only one to rise up against us, and I have fallen into ridicule and disgrace because of you. Why do you assume authority against us in the hill country? ⁷¹If you now have confidence in your forces, come down to the plain to meet us, and let us match strength with each other there, for I have with me the power of the cities. ⁷²Ask and learn who I am and who the others are who are helping us. People will tell you that you cannot stand before us, for your ancestors were twice put to flight in their own land. ⁷³And now you will not be able to withstand my cavalry and such an army in the plain, where there is no stone or pebble or place to flee." ⁷⁴When Jonathan heard the words of Apollonius, his spirit was aroused. He chose ten thousand men and set out from Jerusalem, and his brother Simon met him to help him. ⁷⁵He encamped before Joppa, but the people of the city closed its gates, for Apollonius had a garrison in Joppa. ⁷⁶So they fought against it, and the people of the city became afraid and opened the gates, and Jonathan gained possession of Joppa. ⁷⁷When Apollonius heard of it, he mustered three thousand cavalry and a large army and went to Azotus as though he were going farther. At the same time he advanced into the plain, for he had a large troop of cavalry and put confidence in it. ⁷⁸Jonathan[k] pursued him to Azotus, and the armies engaged in battle. ⁷⁹Now Apollonius had secretly left a thousand cavalry behind them. ⁸⁰Jonathan learned that there was an ambush behind him, for they surrounded his army and shot arrows at his men from early morning until late afternoon. ⁸¹But his men stood fast, as Jonathan had commanded, and the enemy's[l] horses grew tired. ⁸²Then Simon brought forward his force and engaged the phalanx in battle (for the cavalry was exhausted); they were overwhelmed by him and fled, ⁸³and the cavalry was dispersed in the plain. They fled to Azotus and entered Beth-dagon, the temple of their idol, for safety. ⁸⁴But Jonathan burned Azotus and the surrounding towns and plundered them, and the temple of Dagon and those who had taken refuge in it he burned with fire. ⁸⁵The number of those who fell by the sword, with those burned alive, came to eight thousand. ⁸⁶Then Jonathan left there and encamped against Askalon, and the people of the city came out to meet him with great pomp. ⁸⁷He and those with him then returned to Jerusalem with a large amount of plunder. ⁸⁸When King Alexander heard of these things, he honored Jonathan still more, ⁸⁹and he sent to him a golden buckle, such as it is the custom to give to the King's Kinsmen. He also gave him Ekron and all its environs as his possession.

Ptolemy Invades Syria

11 Then the king of Egypt gathered great forces like the sand by the seashore and many ships, and he tried to get possession of Alexander's kingdom by trickery and add it to his own kingdom. ²He set out for Syria with peaceable words, and the people of the towns opened their gates to him and went to meet him, for King Alexander had commanded them to meet him, since he was Alexander's[m] father-in-law. ³But when Ptolemy entered the towns he stationed forces as a garrison in each town. ⁴When he[n] approached Azotus, they showed him the burnt-out temple of Dagon, and Azotus and its suburbs destroyed, and the corpses lying about, and the charred bodies of those whom Jonathan[o] had burned in

the war, for they had piled them in heaps along his route. ⁵They also told the king what Jonathan had done, to throw blame on him, but the king kept silent. ⁶Jonathan met the king at Joppa with pomp, and they greeted one another and spent the night there. ⁷And Jonathan went with the king as far as the river called Eleutherus; then he returned to Jerusalem. ⁸So King Ptolemy gained control of the coastal cities as far as Seleucia by the sea, and he kept devising wicked designs against Alexander. ⁹He sent envoys to King Demetrius, saying, "Come, let us make a covenant with each other, and I will give you in marriage my daughter who was Alexander's wife, and you shall reign over your father's kingdom. ¹⁰I now regret that I gave him my daughter, for he has tried to kill me." ¹¹He threw blame on Alexander[p] because he coveted his kingdom. ¹²So he took his daughter away from him and gave her to Demetrius. He was estranged from Alexander, and their hostility became apparent. ¹³Then Ptolemy entered Antioch and put on the crown of Asia. Thus he put two crowns on his head, the crown of Egypt and that of Asia. ¹⁴Now King Alexander was in Cilicia at that time because the people of that region were in revolt. ¹⁵When Alexander heard of it, he came against him in battle. Ptolemy marched out and met him with a strong force and put him to flight. ¹⁶So Alexander fled into Arabia to find protection there, and King Ptolemy was triumphant. ¹⁷Zabdiel the Arab cut off the head of Alexander and sent it to Ptolemy. ¹⁸But King Ptolemy died three days later, and his troops in the strongholds were killed by the inhabitants of the strongholds. ¹⁹So Demetrius became king in the one hundred sixty-seventh year.

Jonathan's Diplomacy

²⁰In those days Jonathan assembled the Judeans to attack the citadel in Jerusalem, and he built many engines of war to use against it. ²¹But certain renegades who hated their nation went to the king and reported to him that Jonathan was besieging the citadel. ²²When he heard this he was angry, and as soon as he heard it he set out and came to Ptolemais, and he wrote Jonathan not to continue the siege but to meet him for a conference at Ptolemais as quickly as possible. ²³When Jonathan heard this, he gave orders to continue the siege. He chose some of the elders of Israel and some of the priests and put himself in danger, ²⁴for he went to the king at Ptolemais, taking silver and gold and clothing and numerous other gifts. And he won his favor. ²⁵Although certain renegades of his nation kept making complaints against him, ²⁶the king treated him as his predecessors had treated him; he exalted him in the presence of all his Friends. ²⁷He confirmed him in the high priesthood and in as many other honors as he had formerly had and caused him to be reckoned among his First Friends. ²⁸Then Jonathan asked the king to free Judea and the three districts and Samaria from tribute and promised him three hundred talents. ²⁹The king consented and wrote a letter to Jonathan about all these things; its contents were as follows: ³⁰"King Demetrius to his brother Jonathan and to the nation of the Jews, greetings. ³¹This copy of the letter that we wrote concerning you to our kinsman Lasthenes we have written to you also, so that you may know what it says. ³²'King Demetrius to his father Lasthenes, greetings. ³³We have determined to do good to the nation of the Jews, who are our friends and fulfill their obligations to us, because of the goodwill they show toward us. ³⁴We have confirmed as their possession both the territory of Judea and the three districts of Aphairema and Lydda and Ramathaim;[q] the latter, with all the region bordering them, were added to Judea from Samaria. To all those who offer sacrifice in Jerusalem we have granted release from[r] the royal taxes that the king formerly received from them each year, from the crops of the land and the fruit of the trees. ³⁵And the other payments henceforth due to us of the tithes, and the taxes due to us, and the salt pits and the crown taxes due to us—from all these we shall grant them release. ³⁶And not one of these grants shall be canceled from this time on forever. ³⁷Now, therefore, take care to make a copy of this, and let it be given to Jonathan and put up in a conspicuous place on the holy mountain.'"

The Intrigue of Trypho

³⁸When King Demetrius saw that the land was quiet before him and that there was no opposition to him, he dismissed all his troops, all of them to their own homes, except the foreign troops whom he had recruited from the islands of the nations. So all the troops who had served under his predecessors hated him. ³⁹A certain Trypho had formerly been one of Alexander's supporters; he saw that all the troops were grumbling against Demetrius. So he went to Imalkue the Arab, who was bringing up Antiochus, the young son of Alexander, ⁴⁰and insistently urged him to hand Antiochus[s] over to him, to become king in place of his father. He also reported to Imalkue[t] what Demetrius had done and told of the hatred that the troops of Demetrius[u] had for him, and he stayed there many days. ⁴¹Now Jonathan sent to King Demetrius the request that he remove the troops of the citadel from Jerusalem and the troops in the strongholds, for they kept fighting against Israel. ⁴²And Demetrius sent this message back to Jonathan: "Not only will I do these things for you and your nation, but I will confer great honor on you and your nation, if I find an opportunity. ⁴³Now, then, you will do well to send me men who will help me, for all my troops have revolted." ⁴⁴So Jonathan sent three thousand stalwart

men to him at Antioch, and when they came to the king, the king rejoiced at their arrival. ⁴⁵ Then the people of the city assembled within the city, to the number of a hundred and twenty thousand, and they wanted to kill the king. ⁴⁶ But the king fled into the palace. Then the people of the city seized the main streets of the city and began to fight. ⁴⁷ So the king called the Jews to his aid, and they all rallied around him and then spread out through the city, and they killed on that day about one hundred thousand. ⁴⁸ They set fire to the city and seized a large amount of spoil on that day and saved the king. ⁴⁹ When the people of the city saw that the Jews had gained control of the city as they pleased, their courage failed, and they cried out to the king with this entreaty: ⁵⁰ "Grant us peace, and make the Jews stop fighting against us and our city." ⁵¹ And they threw down their arms and made peace. So the Jews gained glory in the sight of the king and of all the people in his kingdom, and they returned to Jerusalem with a large amount of spoil.

⁵² So King Demetrius sat on the throne of his kingdom, and the land was quiet before him. ⁵³ But he broke his word about all that he had promised; he became estranged from Jonathan and did not repay the favors that Jonathan[v] had done him but treated him very harshly.

Trypho Seizes Power

⁵⁴ After this Trypho returned, and with him the young boy Antiochus, who began to reign and put on the crown. ⁵⁵ All the troops whom Demetrius had discharged gathered around him; they fought against Demetrius,[x] and he fled and was routed. ⁵⁶ Trypho captured the elephants[x] and gained control of Antioch. ⁵⁷ Then the young Antiochus wrote to Jonathan, saying, "I confirm you in the high priesthood and set you over the four districts and make you one of the king's Friends." ⁵⁸ He also sent him gold plates and a table service and granted him the right to drink from gold cups and dress in purple and wear a gold buckle. ⁵⁹ He appointed Jonathan's[y] brother Simon governor from the Ladder of Tyre to the borders of Egypt.

Campaigns of Jonathan and Simon

⁶⁰ Then Jonathan set out and traveled beyond the river and among the towns, and all the army of Syria gathered to him as allies. When he came to Askalon, the people of the city met him and paid him honor. ⁶¹ From there he went to Gaza, but the people of Gaza shut him out. So he besieged it and burned its suburbs with fire and plundered them. ⁶² Then the people of Gaza pleaded with Jonathan, and he made peace with them and took the sons of their rulers as hostages and sent them to Jerusalem. And he passed through the country as far as Damascus.

⁶³ Then Jonathan heard that the officers of Demetrius had come to Kadesh in Galilee with a large army, intending to remove him from office. ⁶⁴ He went to meet them but left his brother Simon in the country. ⁶⁵ Simon encamped before Beth-zur and fought against it for many days and hemmed it in. ⁶⁶ Then they asked him to grant them terms of peace, and he did so. He removed them from there, took possession of the town, and set a garrison over it.

⁶⁷ Jonathan and his army encamped by the waters of Gennesaret. Early in the morning they marched to the plain of Hazor, ⁶⁸ and there in the plain the army of the foreigners met him; they had set an ambush against him in the mountains, but they themselves met him face to face. ⁶⁹ Then the men in ambush emerged from their places and joined battle. ⁷⁰ All the men with Jonathan fled; not one of them was left except Mattathias son of Absalom and Judas son of Chalphi, commanders of the forces of the army. ⁷¹ Jonathan tore his clothes, put dust on his head, and prayed. ⁷² Then he turned back to the battle against the enemy[z] and routed them, and they fled. ⁷³ When his men who were fleeing saw this, they returned to him and joined him in the pursuit as far as Kadesh, to their camp, and there they encamped. ⁷⁴ As many as three thousand of the foreigners fell that day. And Jonathan returned to Jerusalem.

Alliances with Rome and Sparta

12 Now when Jonathan saw that the time was favorable for him, he chose men and sent them to Rome to confirm and renew the friendship with them. ² He also sent letters to the same effect to the Spartans and to other places. ³ So they went to Rome and entered the senate chamber and said, "The high priest Jonathan and the Jewish nation have sent us to renew the former friendship and alliance with them." ⁴ And the Romans[aa] gave them letters to the people in every place, asking them to provide for the envoys'[ab] safe conduct to the land of Judah.

⁵ This is a copy of the letter that Jonathan wrote to the Spartans: ⁶ "The high priest Jonathan, the council of the nation, the priests, and the rest of the Jewish people to their brothers the Spartans, greetings. ⁷ Already in time past a letter was sent to the high priest Onias from Arius, who was king among you, stating that you are our brothers, as the appended copy shows. ⁸ Onias welcomed the envoy with honor and received the letter, which contained a clear declaration of alliance and friendship. ⁹ Therefore, though we have no need of these things, since we have as encouragement the holy books that are in our hands, ¹⁰ we have undertaken to renew our family ties and friendship with you, so that we may not become estranged from you, for considerable time has passed since you sent your letter to us. ¹¹ We therefore remember you constantly on every occasion, both at our festivals and on other appropriate days, at

the sacrifices that we offer and in our prayers, as it is right and proper to remember brothers. ¹² And we rejoice in your glory. ¹³ But as for ourselves, many trials and many wars have encircled us; the kings around us have waged war against us. ¹⁴ We were unwilling to trouble you and our other allies and friends with these wars, ¹⁵ for we have the help that comes from heaven for our aid, so we were delivered from our enemies, and our enemies were humbled. ¹⁶ We therefore have chosen Numenius son of Antiochus and Antipater son of Jason and have sent them to Rome to renew our former friendship and alliance with them. ¹⁷ We have commanded them to go also to you and greet you and deliver to you this letter from us concerning the renewal of our family ties. ¹⁸ And now please send us a reply to this."

¹⁹ This is a copy of the letter that they sent to Onias: ²⁰ "King Arius of the Spartans, to the high priest Onias, greetings. ²¹ It has been found in writing concerning the Spartans and the Jews that they are brothers and are of the family of Abraham. ²² And now that we have learned this, please write us concerning your welfare; ²³ we on our part write to you that your livestock and your property belong to us, and ours belong to you. We therefore command that our envoys[ac] report to you accordingly."

Further Campaigns of Jonathan and Simon

²⁴ Now Jonathan heard that the commanders of Demetrius had returned with a larger force than before to wage war against him. ²⁵ So he marched away from Jerusalem and met them in the region of Hamath, for he gave them no opportunity to invade his own country. ²⁶ He sent spies to their camp, and they returned and reported to him that the enemy[ad] were being drawn up in formation to attack the Jews[ae] by night. ²⁷ So when the sun had set, Jonathan commanded his troops to be alert and to keep their arms at hand so as to be ready all night for battle, and he stationed outposts around the camp. ²⁸ When the enemy heard that Jonathan and his troops were prepared for battle, they were afraid and were terrified at heart, so they kindled fires in their camp and withdrew.[af] ²⁹ But Jonathan and his troops did not know it until morning, for they saw the fires burning. ³⁰ Then Jonathan pursued them, but he did not overtake them, for they had crossed the Eleutherus River. ³¹ So Jonathan turned aside against the Arabs who are called Zabadeans, and he crushed them and plundered them. ³² Then he broke camp and went to Damascus and marched through all that region.

³³ Simon also went out and marched through the country as far as Askalon and the neighboring strongholds. He turned aside to Joppa and took it by surprise, ³⁴ for he had heard that they were ready to hand over the stronghold to those whom Demetrius had sent. And he stationed a garrison there to guard it.

³⁵ When Jonathan returned he convened the elders of the people and planned with them to build strongholds in Judea, ³⁶ to build the walls of Jerusalem still higher, and to erect a high barrier between the citadel and the city to separate it from the city, in order to isolate it so that its garrison[ag] could neither buy nor sell. ³⁷ So they gathered together to rebuild the city; part of the wall on the valley to the east had fallen, and he repaired the section called Chaphenatha. ³⁸ Simon also built Adida in the Shephelah; he fortified it and installed gates with bolts.

Trypho Captures Jonathan

³⁹ Then Trypho attempted to become king in Asia and put on the crown and to raise his hand against King Antiochus. ⁴⁰ He feared that Jonathan might not permit him to do so but might make war on him, so he kept seeking to seize and kill him, and he marched out and came to Bethshan. ⁴¹ Jonathan went out to meet him with forty thousand picked warriors, and he came to Beth-shan. ⁴² When Trypho saw that he had come with a large army, he was afraid to raise his hand against him. ⁴³ So he received him with honor and commended him to all his Friends, and he gave him gifts and commanded his Friends and his troops to obey him as they would himself. ⁴⁴ Then he said to Jonathan, "Why have you put all these people to so much trouble when we are not at war? ⁴⁵ Dismiss them now to their homes and choose for yourself a few men to stay with you and come with me to Ptolemais. I will hand it over to you, as well as the other strongholds and the remaining troops and all the officials, and will turn around and go home. For that is why I am here."

⁴⁶ Jonathan[ah] trusted him and did as he said; he sent away the troops, and they returned to the land of Judah. ⁴⁷ He kept with himself three thousand men, two thousand of whom he left in Galilee, while one thousand accompanied him. ⁴⁸ But when Jonathan entered Ptolemais, the people of Ptolemais closed the gates and seized him, and they killed with the sword all who had entered with him.

⁴⁹ Then Trypho sent troops and cavalry into Galilee and the Great Plain to destroy all Jonathan's soldiers. ⁵⁰ But they realized that Jonathan had been seized and had perished along with his men, and they encouraged one another and kept marching in close formation, ready for battle. ⁵¹ When their pursuers saw that they would fight for their lives, they turned back. ⁵² So they all reached the land of Judah safely, and they mourned for Jonathan and his companions and were in great fear, and all Israel mourned deeply. ⁵³ All the nations around them tried to destroy them, for they said, "They have no leader or helper. Now, therefore, let us make war on them and blot out the memory of them from humankind."

Simon Takes Command

13 Simon heard that Trypho had assembled a large army to invade the land of Judah and destroy it, **²**and he saw that the people were trembling with fear. So he went up to Jerusalem, and gathering the people together **³**he encouraged them, saying to them, "You yourselves know what great things my brothers and I and the house of my father have done for the laws and the sanctuary; you know also the wars and the difficulties that my brothers and I have seen. **⁴**By reason of this all my brothers have perished for the sake of Israel, and I alone am left. **⁵**And now, far be it from me to spare my life in any time of distress, for I am not better than my brothers. **⁶**But I will avenge my nation and the sanctuary and your wives and children, for all the nations have gathered together out of hatred to destroy us."

⁷The spirit of the people was rekindled when they heard these words, **⁸**and they answered in a loud voice, "You are our leader in place of Judas and your brother Jonathan. **⁹**Fight our battles, and all that you say to us we will do." **¹⁰**So he assembled all the warriors and hurried to complete the walls of Jerusalem, and he fortified it on every side. **¹¹**He sent Jonathan son of Absalom to Joppa and with him a considerable army; he drove out its occupants and remained there.

Deceit and Treachery of Trypho

¹²Then Trypho left Ptolemais with a large army to invade the land of Judah, and Jonathan was with him under guard. **¹³**Simon encamped in Adida, facing the plain. **¹⁴**Trypho learned that Simon had risen up in place of his brother Jonathan and that he was about to join battle with him, so he sent envoys to him and said, **¹⁵**"It is for the money that your brother Jonathan owed the royal treasury, in connection with the offices he held, that we are detaining him. **¹⁶**Send now one hundred talents of silver and two of his sons as hostages, so that when released he will not revolt against us, and we will release him."

¹⁷Simon knew that they were speaking deceitfully to him, but he sent to get the money and the sons, so that he would not arouse great hostility among the people, who might say, **¹⁸**"It was because Simon[ai] did not send him the money and the sons that Jonathan[aj] perished." **¹⁹**So he sent the sons and the hundred talents, but Trypho[ak] broke his word and did not release Jonathan.

²⁰After this Trypho came to invade the country and destroy it, and he circled around by the way to Adora. But Simon and his army kept marching along opposite him to every place he went. **²¹**Now the men in the citadel kept sending envoys to Trypho urging him to come to them by way of the wilderness and to send them food. **²²**So Trypho got all his cavalry ready to go, but that night a very heavy snow fell, and he did not go because of the snow. He marched off and went into the land of Gilead. **²³**When he approached Baskama, he killed Jonathan, and he was buried there. **²⁴**Then Trypho turned and went back to his own land.

Jonathan's Tomb

²⁵Simon sent and took the bones of his brother Jonathan and buried him in Modein, the city of his ancestors. **²⁶**All Israel bewailed him with great lamentation and mourned for him many days. **²⁷**And Simon built a monument over the tomb of his father and his brothers; he made it high so that it might be seen, with polished stone at the front and back. **²⁸**He also erected seven pyramids, opposite one another, for his father and mother and four brothers. **²⁹**For the pyramids[al] he devised an elaborate setting, erecting about them great columns, and on the columns he put suits of armor for a permanent memorial, and beside the suits of armor he carved ships, so that they could be seen by all who sail the sea. **³⁰**This is the tomb that he built in Modein; it remains to this day.

Judea Gains Independence

³¹Trypho dealt treacherously with the young King Antiochus; he killed him **³²**and became king in his place, putting on the crown of Asia, and he brought great calamity on the land. **³³**But Simon built up the strongholds of Judea and walled them all around, with high towers and great walls and gates and bolts, and he stored food in the strongholds. **³⁴**Simon also chose emissaries and sent them to King Demetrius with a request to grant relief to the country, for all that Trypho did was to plunder. **³⁵**King Demetrius sent him a favorable reply to this request and wrote him a letter as follows, **³⁶**"King Demetrius to Simon, the high priest and friend of kings, and to the elders and nation of the Jews, greetings. **³⁷**We have received the gold crown and the palm branch that you sent, and we are ready to make a general peace with you and to write to our officials to grant you release from tribute. **³⁸**All the grants that we have made to you remain valid, and let the strongholds that you have built be your possession. **³⁹**We pardon any errors and offenses committed to this day and cancel the crown tax that you owe, and whatever other tax has been collected in Jerusalem shall be collected no longer. **⁴⁰**And if any of you are qualified to be enrolled in our bodyguard,[am] let them be enrolled, and let there be peace between us."

⁴¹In the one hundred seventieth year the yoke of the nations was removed from Israel, **⁴²**and the people began to write in their documents and contracts, "In the first year of Simon the great high priest and commander and leader of the Jews."

The Capture of Gazara by Simon

⁴³In those days Simon[an] encamped against Gazara[ao] and surrounded it with troops. He made a siege engine, brought it up to the city, and battered and captured one tower. **⁴⁴**The men in the siege engine leaped out into the city, and a great tumult arose in the city. **⁴⁵**The men in the city, with their wives and children, went up on the wall with their clothes torn, and they cried out with a loud voice, asking Simon to make peace with them; **⁴⁶**they said, "Do not treat us according to our wicked acts but according to your mercy." **⁴⁷**So Simon reached an agreement with them and stopped fighting against them. But he expelled them from the city and cleansed the houses in which the idols were located and then entered it with hymns and praise. **⁴⁸**He removed all uncleanness from it and settled in it those who observed the law. He also strengthened its fortifications and built in it a house for himself.

Simon Regains the Citadel at Jerusalem

⁴⁹Those who were in the citadel at Jerusalem were prevented from going in and out to buy and sell in the country. So they were very hungry, and many of them perished from famine. **⁵⁰**Then they cried to Simon to make peace with them, and he did so. But he expelled them from there and cleansed the citadel from its pollutions. **⁵¹**On the twenty-third day of the second month, in the one hundred seventy-first year, the Jews[ap] entered it with praise and palm branches, and with harps and cymbals and stringed instruments, and with hymns and songs, because a great enemy had been crushed and removed from Israel. **⁵²**Simon[aq] decreed that every year they should celebrate this day with rejoicing. He strengthened the fortifications of the temple hill alongside the citadel, and he and his men lived there. **⁵³**Simon saw that his son John had reached manhood, so he made him commander of all the forces, and he lived at Gazara.

Capture of Demetrius

14 In the one hundred seventy-second year King Demetrius assembled his forces and marched into Media to obtain help, so that he could make war against Trypho. **²**When King Arsaces of Persia and Media heard that Demetrius had invaded his territory, he sent one of his generals to take him alive. **³**The general[ar] went and defeated the army of Demetrius and seized him and took him to Arsaces, who put him under guard.

Eulogy of Simon

⁴The land[as] had rest all the days of Simon.
  He sought the good of his nation;
his rule was pleasing to them,
  as was the honor shown him all his days.
⁵To crown all his honors he took Joppa for a harbor
  and opened a way to the isles of the sea.
⁶He extended the borders of his nation
  and gained full control of the country.
⁷He gathered a host of captives;
  he ruled over Gazara and Beth-zur and the citadel,
and he removed its uncleanness from it,
  and there was none to oppose him.
⁸They tilled their land in peace;
  the ground gave its increase
  and the trees of the plains their fruit.
⁹Old men sat in the streets;
  they all talked together of good things,
  and the youths put on splendid military attire.
¹⁰He supplied the towns with food
  and furnished them with the means of defense,
  until his renown spread to the ends of the earth.
¹¹He established peace in the land,
  and Israel rejoiced with great joy.
¹²All the people sat under their own vines and fig trees,
  and there was none to make them afraid.
¹³No one was left in the land to fight them,
  and the kings were crushed in those days.
¹⁴He gave help to all the humble among his people;
  he sought out the law
  and did away with all the renegades and outlaws.
¹⁵He made the sanctuary glorious
  and added to the vessels of the sanctuary.

Diplomacy with Rome and Sparta

¹⁶It was heard in Rome and as far away as Sparta that Jonathan had died, and they were deeply grieved. **¹⁷**When they heard that his brother Simon had become high priest in his stead and that he was ruling over the country and the towns in it, **¹⁸**they wrote to him on bronze tablets to renew with him the friendship and alliance that they had established with his brothers Judas and Jonathan. **¹⁹**And these were read before the assembly in Jerusalem.

²⁰This is a copy of the letter that the Spartans sent:

"The rulers and the city of the Spartans to the high priest Simon and to the elders and the priests and the rest of the Jewish people, our brothers, greetings. **²¹**The envoys who were sent to our people have told us about your glory and honor, and we rejoiced at their coming. **²²**We have recorded what they said in our public decrees, as follows, 'Numenius son of Antiochus and Antipater son of Jason, envoys of the Jews, have come to us to renew their friendship with us. **²³**It has pleased our people to receive these men with honor and to put a copy of their words in the public ar-

chives, so that the people of the Spartans may have a record of them. And they have sent a copy of this to the high priest Simon.' "
²⁴ After this Simon sent Numenius to Rome with a large gold shield weighing one thousand minas to confirm the alliance with the Romans.[at]

Official Honors for Simon

²⁵ When the people heard these things they said, "How shall we thank Simon and his sons? ²⁶ For he and his brothers and the house of his father have stood firm; they have fought and repulsed Israel's enemies and established its freedom." ²⁷ So they made a record on bronze tablets and put it on pillars on Mount Zion.

This is a copy of what they wrote: "On the eighteenth day of Elul, in the one hundred seventy-second year, which is the third year of the great high priest Simon, ²⁸ in Asaramel, in the great assembly of the priests and the people and the rulers of the nation and the elders of the country, the following was proclaimed to us:

²⁹ "Since wars often occurred in the country, Simon son of Mattathias, of the clan of Joarib, and his brothers, exposed themselves to danger and resisted the enemies of their nation, in order that their sanctuary and the law might be preserved, and they brought great glory to their nation. ³⁰ Jonathan rallied the[au] nation, became their high priest, and was gathered to his people. ³¹ When their enemies decided to invade their country and lay hands on their sanctuary, ³² then Simon rose up and fought for his nation. He spent great sums of his own money; he armed the soldiers of his nation and paid them wages. ³³ He fortified the towns of Judea, and Beth-zur on the borders of Judea, where formerly the arms of the enemy had been stored, and he placed there a garrison of Jews. ³⁴ He also fortified Joppa, which is by the sea, and Gazara, which is on the borders of Azotus, where the enemy formerly lived. He settled Jews there and provided in those towns[av] whatever was necessary for their restoration.

³⁵ "The people saw Simon's faithfulness[aw] and the glory that he had resolved to win for his nation, and they made him their leader and high priest because he had done all these things and because of the justice and loyalty that he had maintained toward his nation. He sought in every way to exalt his people. ³⁶ In his days things prospered in his hands, so that the nations were put out of the[ax] country, as were also those in the city of David in Jerusalem, who had built themselves a citadel from which they used to sally forth and defile the environs of the sanctuary, doing great damage to its purity. ³⁷ He settled Jews in it and fortified it for the safety of the country and of the city and built the walls of Jerusalem higher.

³⁸ "In view of these things King Demetrius confirmed him in the high priesthood, ³⁹ made him one of his Friends, and paid him high honors. ⁴⁰ For he had heard that the Jews were addressed by the Romans as friends and allies and brothers and that the Romans[ay] had received the envoys of Simon with honor.

⁴¹ "The Jews and their priests have resolved that Simon should be their leader and high priest forever, until a trustworthy prophet should arise, ⁴² and that he should be governor over them and[az] appoint officials over its tasks and over the country and the weapons and the strongholds, ⁴³ and that he should take charge of the sanctuary, and that he should be obeyed by all, and that all contracts in the country should be written in his name, and that he should be clothed in purple and wear gold.

⁴⁴ "None of the people or priests shall be permitted to nullify any of these decisions or to oppose what he says or to convene an assembly in the country without his permission or to be clothed in purple or put on a gold buckle. ⁴⁵ Whoever acts contrary to these decisions or rejects any of them shall be liable to punishment."

⁴⁶ All the people agreed to grant Simon the right to act in accordance with these decisions. ⁴⁷ So Simon accepted and agreed to be high priest, to be commander and ethnarch of the Jews and priests, and to be protector of them all.[ba] ⁴⁸ And they gave orders to inscribe this decree on bronze tablets, to put them up in a conspicuous place in the precincts of the sanctuary, ⁴⁹ and to deposit copies of them in the treasury, so that Simon and his sons might have them.

Letter of Antiochus VII

15 Antiochus, son of King Demetrius, sent a letter from the islands of the sea to Simon, the priest and ethnarch of the Jews, and to all the nation; ² its contents were as follows: "King Antiochus to Simon the high priest and ethnarch and to the nation of the Jews, greetings. ³ Whereas certain scoundrels have gained control of the kingdom of our ancestors, and I intend to lay claim to the kingdom so that I may restore it as it formerly was, and have recruited a host of mercenary troops and have equipped warships, ⁴ and intend to make a landing in the country so that I may proceed against those who have destroyed our country and those who have devastated many cities in my kingdom, ⁵ now therefore I confirm to you all the tax remissions that the kings before me have granted you and a release from all the other payments from which they have released you. ⁶ I permit you to mint your own coinage as money for your country, ⁷ and I grant freedom to Jerusalem and the sanctuary. All the weapons that you have prepared and the strongholds that you have built and now hold shall remain yours. ⁸ Every debt you owe to the royal treasury and any such future debts shall be canceled for you from henceforth

and for all time. ⁹ When we gain control of our kingdom, we will bestow great honor on you and your nation and the temple, so that your glory will become manifest in all the earth."

¹⁰ In the one hundred seventy-fourth year Antiochus set out and invaded the land of his ancestors. All the troops rallied to him, so that there were only a few with Trypho. ¹¹ Antiochus pursued him, and Trypho[bb] came in his flight to Dor, which is by the sea, ¹² for he knew that troubles had converged on him, and his troops had deserted him. ¹³ So Antiochus encamped against Dor, and with him were one hundred twenty thousand warriors and eight thousand cavalry. ¹⁴ He surrounded the town, and the ships joined battle from the sea; he pressed the town hard from land and sea and permitted no one to leave or enter it.

Rome Supports the Jews

¹⁵ Then Numenius and his companions arrived from Rome, with letters to the kings and countries, in which the following was written: ¹⁶ "Lucius, consul of the Romans, to King Ptolemy, greetings. ¹⁷ The envoys of the Jews have come to us as our friends and allies to renew our ancient friendship and alliance. They had been sent by the high priest Simon and by the Jewish people ¹⁸ and have brought a gold shield weighing one thousand minas. ¹⁹ We therefore have decided to write to the kings and countries that they should not seek their harm or make war against them and their cities and their country or make alliance with those who war against them. ²⁰ And it has seemed good to us to accept the shield from them. ²¹ Therefore if any scoundrels have fled to you from their country, hand them over to the high priest Simon, so that he may punish them according to their law."

²² The consul[bc] wrote the same thing to King Demetrius and to Attalus and Ariarathes and Arsaces ²³ and to all the countries, and to Sampsames,[bd] and to the Spartans, and to Delos, and to Myndos, and to Sicyon, and to Caria, and to Samos, and to Pamphylia, and to Lycia, and to Halicarnassus, and to Rhodes, and to Phaselis, and to Cos, and to Side, and to Aradus and Gortyna and Cnidus and Cyprus and Cyrene. ²⁴ They also sent a copy of these things to the high priest Simon.

Antiochus VII Threatens Simon

²⁵ King Antiochus besieged Dor for the second time, continually throwing his forces against it and making engines of war, and he shut Trypho up and kept him from going out or in. ²⁶ And Simon sent to Antiochus[be] two thousand picked troops, to fight for him, and silver and gold and a large amount of military equipment. ²⁷ But he refused to receive them and broke all the agreements he formerly had made with Simon and became estranged from him. ²⁸ He sent to him Athenobius, one of his Friends, to confer with him, saying, "You hold control of Joppa and Gazara and the citadel in Jerusalem; they are cities of my kingdom. ²⁹ You have devastated their territory, you have done great damage in the land, and you have taken possession of many places in my kingdom. ³⁰ Now, then, hand over the cities that you have seized and the tribute money of the places that you have conquered outside the borders of Judea, ³¹ or else pay me five hundred talents of silver for the destruction that you have caused and five hundred talents more for the tribute money of the cities. Otherwise we will come and make war on you."

³² So Athenobius, the king's Friend, came to Jerusalem, and when he saw the splendor of Simon, and the sideboard with its gold and silver plate, and his great magnificence, he was amazed. When he reported to him the king's message, ³³ Simon said to him in reply: "We have neither taken foreign land nor seized foreign property, but only the inheritance of our ancestors, which at one time had been unjustly taken by our enemies. ³⁴ Now that we have the opportunity, we are firmly holding the inheritance of our ancestors. ³⁵ As for Joppa and Gazara, which you demand, they were causing great damage among the people and to our land, for them we will give you one hundred talents."

Athenobius[bf] did not answer him a word ³⁶ but returned in wrath to the king and reported to him these words and also the splendor of Simon and all that he had seen. And the king was very angry.

Victory over Cendebeus

³⁷ Meanwhile Trypho embarked on a ship and escaped to Orthosia. ³⁸ Then the king made Cendebeus commander-in-chief of the coastal country and gave him troops of infantry and cavalry. ³⁹ He commanded him to encamp against Judea, to build up Kedron and fortify its gates, and to make war on the people, but the king pursued Trypho. ⁴⁰ So Cendebeus came to Jamnia and began to provoke the people and invade Judea and take the people captive and kill them. ⁴¹ He built up Kedron and stationed horsemen and troops there, so that they might go out and make raids along the highways of Judea, as the king had ordered him.

16 John went up from Gazara and reported to his father Simon what Cendebeus had done. ² And Simon called in his two eldest sons Judas and John and said to them: "My brothers and I and my father's house have fought the wars of Israel from our youth until this day, and things have prospered in our hands so that we have delivered Israel many times. ³ But now I have grown old, and you by heaven's[bg] mercy are mature in years. Take my place and my brother's, and go out and fight for our nation, and may the help that comes from heaven be with you."

⁴ So John[bh] chose out of the country twenty thousand warriors and cavalry, and they marched against Cendebeus and camped for the night in

Modein. [5] Early in the morning they started out and marched into the plain, where a large force of infantry and cavalry was coming to meet them, and a wadi lay between them. [6] Then he and his army lined up against them. He saw that the soldiers were afraid to cross the wadi, so he crossed over first, and when his troops saw him, they crossed over after him. [7] Then he divided the army and placed the cavalry in the center of the infantry, for the cavalry of the enemy were very numerous. [8] They sounded the trumpets, and Cendebeus and his army were put to flight; many of them fell wounded, and the rest fled into the stronghold. [9] At that time Judas the brother of John was wounded, but John pursued them until Cendebeus[b] reached Kedron, which he had built. [10] They also fled into the towers that were in the fields of Azotus, and John[bi] burned it with fire, and about two thousand of them fell. He then returned to Judea safely.

Murder of Simon and His Sons

[11] Now Ptolemy son of Abubus had been appointed governor over the plain of Jericho; he had a large store of silver and gold, [12] for he was son-in-law of the high priest. [13] His heart was lifted up; he determined to get control of the country and made treacherous plans against Simon and his sons, to do away with them. [14] Now Simon was visiting the towns of the country and attending to their needs, and he went down to Jericho with his sons Mattathias and Judas, in the one hundred seventy-seventh year, in the eleventh month, which is the month of Shebat. [15] The son of Abubus received them treacherously in the little stronghold called Dok, which he had built; he gave them a great banquet and hid men there. [16] When Simon and his sons were drunk, Ptolemy and his men rose up, took their weapons, rushed in against Simon in the banquet hall, and killed him and his two sons, as well as some of his servants. [17] So he committed an act of great treachery and returned evil for good.

John Succeeds Simon

[18] Then Ptolemy wrote a report about these things and sent it to the king, asking him to send troops to aid him and to turn over to him the towns and the country. [19] He sent other troops to Gazara to do away with John; he sent letters to the captains asking them to come to him so that he might give them silver and gold and gifts, [20] and he sent other troops to take possession of Jerusalem and the temple hill. [21] But someone ran ahead and reported to John at Gazara that his father and brothers had perished and that "he has sent men to kill you also." [22] When he heard this, he was greatly shocked; he seized the men who came to destroy him and killed them, for he had found out that they were seeking to destroy him.

[23] The rest of the acts of John and his wars and the brave deeds that he did, and the building of the walls that he completed, and his achievements [24] are written in the annals of his high priesthood, from the time that he became high priest after his father.

Book 89. 2 Maccabees

[1] The Jews in Jerusalem and those in the land of Judea,
To their Jewish kindred in Egypt,
Greetings and true peace.

[2] May God do good to you, and may he remember his covenant with Abraham and Isaac and Jacob, his faithful servants. [3] May he give you all a heart to worship him and to do his will with a strong heart and a willing spirit. [4] May he open your heart to his law and his commandments, and may he bring peace. [5] May he hear your prayers and be reconciled to you, and may he not forsake you in time of evil. [6] We are now praying for you here.

[7] In the reign of Demetrius, in the one hundred sixty-ninth year, we Jews wrote to you, in the critical distress that came upon us in those years after Jason and his company revolted from the holy land and the kingdom [8] and burned the gate and shed innocent blood. We prayed to the Lord and were heard, and we offered sacrifice and grain offering, and we lit the lamps and set out the loaves. [9] And now see that you keep the Festival of Booths[a] in the month of Chislev, in the one hundred eighty-eighth year.

A Letter to Aristobulus

[10] The people of Jerusalem and of Judea and the council and Judas,
To Aristobulus, who is of the family of the anointed priests, teacher of King Ptolemy, and to the Jews in Egypt,
Greetings and good health.

[11] Having been saved by God out of grave dangers, we thank him greatly for taking our side against the king,[b] [12] for he drove out those who fought against the holy city. [13] When the leader reached Persia with a force that seemed irresistible, they were cut to pieces in the temple of Nanea by a deception employed by the priests of the goddess[c] Nanea. [14] On the pretext of intending to marry her, Antiochus came to the place together with his Friends, to secure most of its treasures as a dowry. [15] When the priests of the temple of Nanea had set out the treasures and Antiochus had come with a few men inside the wall of the sacred precinct, they closed the temple as soon as he entered it. [16] Opening a secret door in the ceiling, they threw stones and struck down the leader and his men; they dismembered them and cut off their heads and threw them to the people

outside. [17] Blessed in every way be our God, who has delivered up those who have behaved impiously.

Fire Consumes Nehemiah's Sacrifice

[18] Since on the twenty-fifth day of Chislev we shall celebrate the purification of the temple, we thought it necessary to notify you, in order that you also may celebrate the Festival of Booths[d] and the fire given when Nehemiah, who built the temple and the altar, offered sacrifices. [19] For when our ancestors were being led captive to Persia, the pious priests of that time took some of the fire of the altar and secretly hid it in the hollow of a dry cistern, where they took such precautions that the place was unknown to anyone. [20] But after many years had passed, when it pleased God, Nehemiah, having been commissioned by the king of Persia, sent the descendants of the priests who had hidden the fire to get it. And when they reported to us that they had not found fire but only a thick liquid, he ordered them to dip it out and bring it. [21] When the materials for the sacrifices were presented, Nehemiah ordered the priests to sprinkle the liquid on the wood and on the things laid upon it. [22] When this had been done and some time had passed, and when the sun, which had been clouded over, shone out, a great fire blazed up, so that all marveled. [23] And while the sacrifice was being consumed, the priests offered prayer—the priests and everyone. Jonathan led, and the rest responded, as did Nehemiah. [24] The prayer was to this effect:

"O Lord, Lord God, Creator of all things, you are awe-inspiring and strong and just and merciful; you alone are king and just and kind; [25] you alone are bountiful; you alone are just and almighty and eternal. You rescue Israel from every evil; you chose the ancestors and consecrated them. [26] Accept this sacrifice on behalf of all your people Israel and preserve your portion and make it holy. [27] Gather together our scattered people; set free those who are slaves among the nations; look on those who are rejected and despised; and let the nations know that you are our God. [28] Punish those who oppress and are insolent with pride. [29] Plant your people in your holy place, as Moses promised."

[30] Then the priests sang the hymns. [31] After the materials of the sacrifice had been consumed, Nehemiah ordered that the liquid that was left should be poured on large stones. [32] When this was done, a flame blazed up, but when the light from the altar shone back, it went out. [33] When this matter became known and it was reported to the king of the Persians that, in the place where the exiled priests had hidden the fire, the liquid had appeared with which Nehemiah and his associates had burned the materials of the sacrifice, [34] the king investigated the matter and enclosed the place and made it sacred. [35] And with those persons whom the king favored he exchanged many excellent gifts. [36] Nehemiah and his associates called this "nephthar," which means purification, but by most people it is called "naphtha."

Jeremiah Hides the Tent, Ark, and Altar

[2] One finds in the records that the prophet Jeremiah ordered those who were being deported to take some of the fire, as has been mentioned, [2] and that the prophet, after giving them the law, instructed those who were being deported not to forget the commandments of the Lord or to be led astray in their thoughts on seeing the gold and silver statues and their adornment. [3] And with other similar words he exhorted them that the law should not depart from their hearts.

[4] It was also in the same document that the prophet, having received an oracle, ordered that the tent and the ark should follow with him and that he went out to the mountain where Moses had gone up and had seen the inheritance of God. [5] Jeremiah came and found a cave dwelling, and he brought there the tent and the ark and the altar of incense; then he sealed up the entrance. [6] Some of those who followed him came up intending to mark the way but could not find it. [7] When Jeremiah learned of it, he rebuked them and declared, "The place shall remain unknown until God gathers his people together again and shows his mercy. [8] Then the Lord will disclose these things, and the glory of the Lord and the cloud will appear, as they were shown in the case of Moses and as Solomon asked that the place should be specially consecrated."

[9] It was also made clear that, being possessed of wisdom, Solomon[e] offered sacrifice for the dedication and completion of the temple. [10] Just as Moses prayed to the Lord and fire came down from heaven and consumed the sacrifices, so also Solomon prayed, and the fire came down and consumed the whole burnt offerings. [11] And Moses said, "They were consumed because the purification offering had not been eaten." [12] Likewise Solomon also kept the eight days.

[13] The same things are reported in the records and in the memoirs of Nehemiah and also that he founded a library and collected the books about the kings and prophets and the writings of David and letters of kings about votive offerings. [14] In the same way Judas also collected all the books that had been lost on account of the war that had come upon us, and they are in our possession. [15] So if you have need of them, send people to get them for you.

[16] Since, therefore, we are about to celebrate the purification, we write to you. You will do well if you celebrate these days. [17] It is God who has saved all his people and has returned the inheritance to all and the kingship and the priesthood and the consecration, [18] as he promised through the law. We have hope in God that he will soon have mercy on us and

will gather us from everywhere under heaven into his holy place, for he has rescued us from great evils and has purified the place.

The Compiler's Preface

[19] The story of Judas Maccabeus and his brothers, and the purification of the greatest temple, and the dedication of the altar, [20] and further the wars against Antiochus Epiphanes and his son Eupator, [21] and the appearances that came from heaven to those who fought bravely for Judaism, so that though few in number they seized the whole land and pursued the barbarian hordes [22] and regained possession of the temple famous throughout the world and liberated the city and reestablished the laws that were about to be abolished, while the Lord with great kindness became gracious to them— [23] all this, which has been set forth by Jason of Cyrene in five volumes, we shall attempt to condense into a single book. [24] For considering the flood of lines written and the difficulty there is for those who wish to enter upon the narratives of history because of the mass of material, [25] we have aimed to please those who wish to read, to make it easy for those who are inclined to memorize, and to profit all readers. [26] For us who have undertaken the toil of abbreviating, it is no light matter but calls for sweat and loss of sleep, [27] just as it is not easy for one who prepares a banquet and seeks the benefit of others. Nevertheless, to secure the gratitude of many we will gladly endure the uncomfortable toil, [28] leaving the responsibility for exact details to the compiler, while devoting our effort to arriving at the outlines of the condensation. [29] For as the master builder of a new house must be concerned with the whole construction, while the one who undertakes its painting and decoration has to consider only what is suitable for its adornment, such in my judgment is the case with us. [30] It is the duty of the original historian to occupy the ground, to discuss matters from every side, and to take trouble with details, [31] but the one who recasts the narrative should be allowed to strive for brevity of expression and to forego exhaustive treatment. [32] At this point, therefore, let us begin our narrative, without adding any more to what has already been said, for it would be foolish to lengthen the preface while cutting short the history itself.

Arrival of Heliodorus in Jerusalem

3 While the holy city was inhabited in unbroken peace and the laws were strictly observed because of the piety of the high priest Onias and his hatred of wickedness, [2] it came about that the kings themselves honored the place and glorified the temple with the finest presents, [3] even to the extent that King Seleucus of Asia defrayed from his own revenues all the expenses connected with the service of the sacrifices.

[4] But a man named Simon, of the tribe of Balgea,[f] who had been made captain of the temple, had a disagreement with the high priest about the administration of the city market. [5] Since he could not prevail over Onias, he went to Apollonius of Tarsus,[g] who at that time was governor of Coelesyria and Phoenicia, [6] and reported to him that the treasury in Jerusalem was full of untold sums of money, so that the amount of the funds could not be reckoned, and that they did not belong to the account of the sacrifices but that it was possible for them to fall under the control of the king. [7] When Apollonius met the king, he told him of the money about which he had been informed. The king[h] chose Heliodorus, who was in charge of his affairs, and sent him with commands to effect the removal of the reported wealth. [8] Heliodorus at once set out on his journey, ostensibly to make a tour of inspection of the cities of Coelesyria and Phoenicia but in fact to carry out the king's purpose.

[9] When he had arrived at Jerusalem and had been kindly welcomed by the high priest of[i] the city, he told about the disclosure that had been made and stated why he had come, and he inquired whether this really was the situation. [10] The high priest explained that there were some deposits belonging to widows and orphans [11] and also some money of Hyrcanus son of Tobias, a man of very prominent position, and that it totaled in all four hundred talents of silver and two hundred of gold. To such an extent the impious Simon had misrepresented the facts. [12] And he said[j] that it was utterly impossible that wrong should be done to those people who had trusted in the holiness of the place and in the sanctity and inviolability of the temple that is honored throughout the whole world.

Heliodorus Plans to Rob the Temple

[13] But Heliodorus,[k] because of the orders he had from the king, said that this money must in any case be confiscated for the king's treasury. [14] So he set a day and went in to direct the inspection of these funds. There was no little distress throughout the whole city. [15] The priests prostrated themselves before the altar in their priestly vestments and called toward heaven upon him who had given the law about deposits, that he should keep them safe for those who had deposited them. [16] To see the appearance of the high priest was to be wounded at heart, for his face and the change in his color disclosed the anguish of his soul. [17] For terror and bodily trembling had come over the man, which plainly showed to those who looked at him the pain lodged in his heart. [18] People also hurried out of their houses in crowds to make a general supplication because the holy place was about to be brought into dishonor. [19] Women girded with sackcloth under their breasts thronged the streets. Some of the young women who were kept indoors ran together to the gates, and some to the walls, while others peered out of the windows. [20] And holding up their hands to heaven, they all made supplication. [21] There was something pitiable in the

prostration of the whole populace and the anxiety of the high priest in his great anguish.

The Lord Protects His Temple

[22] While they were calling upon the Almighty Lord that he would keep what had been entrusted safe and secure for those who had entrusted it, [23] Heliodorus went on with what had been decided. [24] But when he arrived at the treasury with his bodyguard, then and there the Sovereign of spirits and of all authority caused so great a manifestation that all who had been so bold as to accompany him were astounded by the power of God and became faint with terror. [25] For there appeared to them a magnificently adorned horse, with a rider of frightening appearance; it rushed furiously at Heliodorus and struck at him with its front hoofs. Its rider was seen to have armor and weapons of gold. [26] Two young men also appeared to him, remarkably strong, gloriously beautiful and splendidly dressed, who stood on either side of him and flogged him continuously, inflicting many blows on him. [27] When he suddenly fell to the ground and deep darkness came over him, his men took him up, put him on a stretcher, [28] and carried him away—this man who had just entered the aforesaid treasury with a great retinue and all his bodyguard but was now unable to help himself with all his weapons. He recognized clearly the sovereign power of God.

Onias Prays for Heliodorus

[29] While he lay prostrate, speechless because of the divine intervention and deprived of any hope of recovery, [30] they praised the Lord who had acted marvelously for his own place. And the temple, which a little while before was full of fear and disturbance, was filled with joy and gladness, now that the Almighty Lord had appeared.

[31] Some of Heliodorus's friends quickly begged Onias to call upon the Most High to grant life to one who was lying quite at his last breath. [32] So the high priest, fearing that the king might get the notion that some foul play had been perpetrated by the Jews with regard to Heliodorus, offered sacrifice for the man's recovery. [33] While the high priest was making the atonement, the same young men appeared again to Heliodorus dressed in the same clothing, and they stood and said, "Be very grateful to the high priest Onias, since for his sake the Lord has granted you your life. [34] And see that you, who have been flogged by heaven, report to all people the majestic power of God." Having said this, they vanished.

The Conversion of Heliodorus

[35] Then Heliodorus offered sacrifice to the Lord and made very great vows to the Savior of his life, and having bidden Onias farewell, he marched off with his forces to the king. [36] He bore testimony to all concerning the deeds of the supreme God, which he had seen with his own eyes. [37] When the king asked Heliodorus what sort of person would be suitable to send on another mission to Jerusalem, he replied, [38] "If you have any enemy or plotter against your government, send him there, for you will get him back thoroughly flogged, if he survives at all, for there is certainly some power of God about the place. [39] For he who has his dwelling in heaven watches over that place himself and brings it aid, and he strikes and destroys those who come to do it injury." [40] This was the outcome of the episode of Heliodorus and the protection of the treasury.

Simon Accuses Onias

4 The previously mentioned Simon, who had informed about the money against[l] his own country, slandered Onias, saying that it was he who had incited Heliodorus and had been the real cause of the misfortune. [2] He dared to designate as a plotter against the government the man who was the benefactor of the city, the protector of his compatriots, and a zealot for the laws. [3] When his hatred progressed to such a degree that even murders were committed by one of Simon's approved agents, [4] Onias recognized that the rivalry was serious and that Apollonius son of Menestheus,[m] and governor of Coelesyria and Phoenicia, was intensifying the malice of Simon. [5] So he appealed to the king, not accusing his compatriots but having in view the welfare, both public and private, of all the people. [6] For he saw that, without the king's attention, public affairs could not again reach a peaceful settlement and that Simon would not stop his folly.

Jason's Reforms

[7] When Seleucus died and Antiochus, who was called Epiphanes, succeeded to the kingdom, Jason the brother of Onias obtained the high priesthood by corruption, [8] promising the king through a petition three hundred sixty talents of silver and from another source of revenue eighty talents. [9] In addition to this he promised to pay one hundred fifty more if permission were given to establish by his authority a gymnasium and a body of youth for it and to enroll the people of Jerusalem as the Antiochenes in Jerusalem. [10] When the king assented and Jason[n] came to office, he at once shifted his compatriots over to the Greek way of life.

[11] He set aside the existing royal concessions to the Jews, secured through John the father of Eupolemus, who went on the mission to establish friendship and alliance with the Romans, and he destroyed the lawful ways of living and introduced new customs contrary to the law. [12] He took delight in establishing a gymnasium right under the citadel, and he induced the noblest of the young men to wear the Greek hat. [13] There was such an extreme of Hellenization and increase in the adoption of foreign ways because of the surpassing wickedness of Jason, who was ungodly

and no true[o] high priest, [14] that the priests were no longer intent upon their service at the altar. Despising the sanctuary and neglecting the sacrifices, they hurried to take part in the unlawful proceedings in the wrestling arena after the signal for the discus throwing, [15] disdaining the honors prized by their ancestors and putting the highest value upon Greek forms of prestige. [16] For this reason heavy disaster overtook them, and those whose ways of living they admired and wished to imitate completely became their enemies and punished them. [17] It is no light thing to show irreverence to the divine laws, a fact that later events will make clear.

Jason Introduces Greek Customs

[18] When the quadrennial games were being held at Tyre and the king was present, [19] the vile Jason sent envoys, chosen as being Antiochenes from Jerusalem, to carry three hundred silver drachmas for the sacrifice to Hercules. Those who carried the money, however, thought best not to use it for sacrifice, because that was inappropriate, but to expend it for another purpose. [20] So this money was intended by the sender for the sacrifice to Hercules, but by the decision of its carriers it was applied to the construction of triremes.

[21] When Apollonius son of Menestheus was sent to Egypt for the coronation[p] of Philometor as king, Antiochus learned that Philometor[q] had become hostile to his government, and he took measures for his own security. Therefore upon arriving at Joppa he proceeded to Jerusalem. [22] He was welcomed magnificently by Jason and the city and ushered in with a blaze of torches and with shouts. Then he marched his army into Phoenicia.

Menelaus Becomes High Priest

[23] After a period of three years, Jason sent Menelaus, the brother of the previously mentioned Simon, to carry the money to the king and to complete the records of essential business. [24] But he, when presented to the king, extolled him with an air of authority and secured the high priesthood for himself, outbidding Jason by three hundred talents of silver. [25] After receiving the king's orders, he returned, possessing no qualification for the high priesthood but having the hot temper of a cruel tyrant and the rage of a savage wild beast. [26] So Jason, who after supplanting his own brother was supplanted by another man, was driven as a fugitive into the land of Ammon. [27] Although Menelaus continued to hold the office, he did not pay regularly any of the money promised to the king. [28] When Sostratus the captain of the citadel kept requesting payment—for the collection of the revenue was his responsibility—the two of them were summoned by the king on account of this issue. [29] Menelaus left his own brother Lysimachus as deputy in the high priesthood, while Sostratus left Crates, the commander of the Cyprian troops.

The Murder of Onias

[30] While such was the state of affairs, it happened that the people of Tarsus and of Mallus revolted because their cities had been given as a present to Antiochis, the king's concubine. [31] So the king went hurriedly to settle the trouble, leaving Andronicus, a man of high rank, to act as his deputy. [32] But Menelaus, thinking he had obtained a suitable opportunity, stole some of the gold vessels of the temple and gave them to Andronicus; other vessels, as it happened, he had sold to Tyre and the neighboring cities. [33] When Onias became fully aware of these acts, he publicly exposed them, having first withdrawn to a place of sanctuary at Daphne near Antioch. [34] Therefore Menelaus, taking Andronicus aside, urged him to kill Onias. Andronicus[r] came to Onias and, resorting to treachery, offered him sworn pledges and gave him his right hand; he persuaded him, in spite of his suspicions, to come out from the place of sanctuary; then, with no regard for justice, he immediately put him out of the way.

Andronicus Is Punished

[35] For this reason not only Jews but many also of other nations were grieved and displeased at the unjust murder of the man. [36] When the king returned from the region of Cilicia, the Jews in the city[s] appealed to him with regard to the unreasonable murder of Onias, and the Greeks shared their hatred of the crime. [37] Therefore Antiochus was grieved at heart and filled with pity and wept because of the moderation and good conduct of the deceased. [38] Inflamed with anger, he immediately stripped the purple robe from Andronicus, tore off his clothes, and led him around the whole city to that very place where he had committed the outrage against Onias, and there he dispatched the bloodthirsty fellow. The Lord thus repaid him with the punishment he deserved.

Unpopularity of Lysimachus and Menelaus

[39] When many acts of sacrilege had been committed in the city by Lysimachus with the connivance of Menelaus, and when report of them had spread abroad, the populace gathered against Lysimachus, because many of the gold vessels had already been stolen. [40] Since the crowds were becoming aroused and filled with anger, Lysimachus armed about three thousand men and launched an unjust attack, under the leadership of a certain Auranus, a man advanced in years and no less advanced in folly. [41] But when the Jews[t] became aware that Lysimachus was attacking them, some picked up stones, some blocks of wood, and others took handfuls of the ashes that were lying around and threw them in wild confusion at Lysimachus and his men. [42] As a result, they wounded many of them and killed some and put all the rest to flight; the temple robber himself they killed close by the treasury.

[43] Charges were brought against Menelaus about this incident. [44] When the king came to Tyre, three men sent by the senate presented the case before him. [45] But Menelaus, already as good as beaten, promised a substantial bribe to Ptolemy son of Dorymenes to win over the king. [46] Therefore Ptolemy, taking the king aside into a colonnade as if for refreshment, induced the king to change his mind. [47] Menelaus, the cause of all the trouble, he acquitted of the charges against him, while he sentenced to death those unfortunate men who would have been freed uncondemned if they had pleaded even before Scythians. [48] And so those who had spoken for the city and the villages[u] and the holy vessels quickly suffered the unjust penalty. [49] Therefore even the Tyrians, showing their hatred of the crime, provided magnificently for their funeral. [50] But Menelaus, because of the greed of those in power, remained in office, growing in wickedness, having become the chief plotter against his compatriots.

Jason Tries to Regain Control

[5] About this time Antiochus made his second invasion of Egypt. [2] And it happened that, for almost forty days, there appeared over all the city golden-clad cavalry charging through the air, in companies fully armed with lances and drawn swords— [3] troops of cavalry drawn up, attacks and counterattacks made on this side and on that, brandishing of shields, massing of spears, hurling of missiles, the flash of golden trappings, and armor of all kinds. [4] Therefore everyone prayed that the apparition might prove to have been a good omen.

[5] When a false rumor arose that Antiochus was dead, Jason took no fewer than a thousand men and suddenly made an assault on the city. When the troops on the wall had been forced back and at last the city was being taken, Menelaus took refuge in the citadel. [6] But Jason kept relentlessly slaughtering his compatriots, not realizing that success at the cost of one's kindred is the greatest misfortune but imagining that he was setting up trophies of victory over enemies and not over compatriots. [7] He did not, however, gain control of the government; in the end, he got only disgrace from his conspiracy and fled again into the country of the Ammonites. [8] Finally, he met a miserable end. Accused[v] before Aretas the ruler of the Arabs, fleeing from city to city, pursued by everyone, hated as a rebel against the laws, and abhorred as the executioner of his country and his compatriots, he was cast ashore in Egypt. [9] There he who had driven many from their own country into exile died in exile, having embarked to go to the Spartans[w] in hope of finding protection because of their kinship. [10] He who had cast out many to lie unburied had no one to mourn for him; he had no funeral of any sort and no place in the tomb of his ancestors.

[11] When news of what had happened reached the king, he took it to mean that Judea was in revolt. So, raging inwardly, he left Egypt and took the city by storm. [12] He commanded his soldiers to cut down relentlessly everyone they met and to kill those who went into their houses. [13] Then there was massacre of young and old, destruction of boys, women, and children, and slaughter of young girls and infants. [14] Within the total of three days eighty thousand were destroyed, forty thousand in hand-to-hand fighting, and as many were sold into slavery as were killed.

Pillage of the Temple

[15] Not content with this, Antiochus[x] dared to enter the most holy temple in all the world, guided by Menelaus, who had become a traitor both to the laws and to his country. [16] He took the holy vessels with his polluted hands and swept away with profane hands the votive offerings that other kings had made to enhance the glory and honor of the place. [17] Antiochus was elated in spirit and did not perceive that the Lord was angered for a little while because of the sins of those who lived in the city and that this was the reason he was disregarding the holy place. [18] But if it had not happened that they were involved in many sins, this man would have been flogged and turned back from his rash act as soon as he came forward, just as Heliodorus had been, whom King Seleucus sent to inspect the treasury. [19] But the Lord did not choose the nation for the sake of the holy place but the place for the sake of the nation. [20] Therefore the place itself shared in the misfortunes that befell the nation and afterward participated in its benefits, and what was forsaken in the wrath of the Almighty was restored again in all its glory when the great Lord became reconciled. [21] So Antiochus carried off eighteen hundred talents from the temple and hurried away to Antioch, thinking in his arrogance that he could sail on the land and walk on the sea, because his mind was elated. [22] He left governors to oppress the people: at Jerusalem, Philip, by birth a Phrygian and in character more barbarous than the man who appointed him; [23] and at Gerizim, Andronicus; and besides these Menelaus, who lorded it over his compatriots worse than the others did. In his malice toward the Jewish citizens,[y] [24] Antiochus[z] sent Apollonius, the captain of the Mysians, with an army of twenty-two thousand and commanded him to kill all the grown men and to sell the women and boys as slaves. [25] When this man arrived in Jerusalem, he pretended to be peaceably disposed and waited until the holy Sabbath day; then, finding the Jews not at work, he ordered his troops to parade under arms. [26] He put to the sword all those who came out to see them, then rushed into the city with his armed warriors and killed great numbers of people.

[27] But Judas Maccabeus, with about nine others, got away to the wilderness and kept himself and his companions alive in the mountains as wild

animals do; they continued to live on what grew wild, so that they might not share in the defilement.

The Suppression of Judaism

6 Not long after this, the king sent an Athenian[aa] senator[ab] to compel the Jews to forsake the laws of their ancestors and no longer to live by the laws of God, ² also to pollute the temple in Jerusalem and to call it the temple of Olympian Zeus and to call the one in Gerizim Zeus-the-Friend-of-Strangers, as the people who live in that place are known.

³ Harsh and utterly grievous was the onslaught of evil. ⁴ For the temple was filled with debauchery and reveling by the nations, who dallied with prostitutes and had intercourse with women within the sacred precincts and besides brought in things for sacrifice that were unfit. ⁵ The altar was covered with abominable offerings that were forbidden by the laws. ⁶ People could neither keep the Sabbath nor observe the festivals of their ancestors nor so much as confess themselves to be Jews.

⁷ On the monthly celebration of the king's birthday, the Jews[ac] were taken, under bitter constraint, to partake of the sacrifices, and when a festival of Dionysus was celebrated, they were compelled to wear wreaths of ivy and to walk in the procession in honor of Dionysus. ⁸ At the suggestion of the people of Ptolemais,[ad] a decree was issued to the neighboring Greek cities that they should adopt the same policy toward the Jews and make them partake of the sacrifices ⁹ and should kill those who did not choose to change over to Greek customs. One could see, therefore, the misery that had come upon them. ¹⁰ For example, two women were brought in for having circumcised their children. They publicly paraded them around the city with their babies hanging at their breasts and then hurled them down headlong from the wall. ¹¹ Others who had assembled in the caves nearby in order to observe the seventh day secretly were betrayed to Philip and were all burned together, because their piety kept them from defending themselves, in view of their regard for that most holy day.

Providential Significance of the Persecution

¹² Now I urge those who read this book not to be depressed by such calamities but to recognize that these punishments were designed not to destroy but to discipline our people. ¹³ In fact, it is a sign of great kindness not to let the impious alone for long but to punish them immediately. ¹⁴ For in the case of the other nations the Lord waits patiently to punish them until they have reached the full measure of their sins, but he does not deal in this way with us, ¹⁵ in order that he may not take vengeance on us afterward when our sins have reached their height. ¹⁶ Therefore he never withdraws his mercy from us. Although he disciplines us with calamities, he does not forsake his own people. ¹⁷ Let what we have said serve as a reminder; we must go on briefly with the story.

The Martyrdom of Eleazar

¹⁸ Eleazar, one of the scribes in high position, a man now advanced in age and of noble presence, was being forced to open his mouth to eat pig's flesh. ¹⁹ But he, welcoming death with honor rather than life with pollution, went up to the rack of his own accord, ²⁰ spitting it out as all ought to go who have the courage to refuse things that it is not right to taste, even for the natural love of life.

²¹ Those who were in charge of that unlawful sacrifice took the man aside because of their long acquaintance with him and privately urged him to bring meat of his own providing, proper for him to use, and to pretend that he was eating the flesh of the sacrificial meal that had been commanded by the king, ²² so that by doing this he might be saved from death and be treated kindly on account of his old friendship with them. ²³ But making a high resolve, worthy of his years and the dignity of his old age and the gray hairs that he had reached with distinction and his excellent life even from childhood, and moreover according to the holy God-given law, he declared himself quickly, telling them to send him to Hades.

²⁴ "Such pretense is not worthy of our time of life," he said, "for many of the young might suppose that Eleazar in his ninetieth year had gone over to a foreign way of life, ²⁵ and through my pretense, for the sake of living a brief moment longer, they would be led astray because of me, while I defile and disgrace my old age. ²⁶ Even if for the present I would avoid the punishment of mortals, yet whether I live or die I will not escape the hands of the Almighty. ²⁷ Therefore, by bravely giving up my life now, I will show myself worthy of my old age ²⁸ and leave to the young a noble example of how to die a good death willingly and nobly for the revered and holy laws."

When he had said this, he was dragged[ae] at once to the rack. ²⁹ Those who a little before had acted toward him with goodwill now changed to ill will, because the words he had uttered were in their opinion sheer madness.[af] ³⁰ When he was about to die under the blows, he groaned aloud and said: "It is clear to the Lord in his holy knowledge that, though I might have been saved from death, I am enduring terrible sufferings in my body under this beating, but in my soul I am glad to suffer these things because I fear him."

³¹ So in this way he died, leaving in his death an example of nobility and a memorial of courage, not only to the young but to the great body of his nation.

The Martyrdom of Seven Brothers

7 It happened also that seven brothers and their mother were arrested and were being compelled by the king, under torture with whips and straps, to partake of unlawful pig's flesh. ² One of them, acting as their spokesman, said, "What do you intend to ask and learn from us? For we are ready to die rather than transgress the laws of our ancestors."

³ The king fell into a rage and gave orders to have pans and caldrons heated. ⁴ These were heated immediately, and he commanded that the tongue of their spokesman be cut out and that they scalp him and cut off his hands and feet, while the rest of the brothers and the mother looked on. ⁵ When he was utterly helpless, the king[ag] ordered them to take him to the fire, still breathing, and to fry him in a pan. The smoke from the pan spread widely, but the brothers[ah] and their mother encouraged one another to die nobly, saying, ⁶ "The Lord God is watching over us and in truth has compassion on us, as Moses declared in his song that bore witness against the people to their faces, when he said, 'And he will have compassion on his servants.' "

⁷ After the first brother had died in this way, they brought forward the second for their sport. They tore off the skin of his head with the hair and asked him, "Will you eat rather than have your body punished limb by limb?" ⁸ He replied in the language of his ancestors and said to them, "No." Therefore he in turn underwent tortures as the first brother had done. ⁹ And when he was at his last breath, he said, "You accursed wretch, you dismiss us from this present life, but the King of the universe will raise us up to a renewal of everlasting life, because we have died for his laws."

¹⁰ After him, the third was the victim of their sport. When it was demanded, he quickly put out his tongue and courageously stretched forth his hands ¹¹ and said nobly, "I got these from heaven, and because of his laws I disdain them, and from him I hope to get them back again." ¹² As a result, the king himself and those with him were astonished at the young man's spirit, for he regarded his sufferings as nothing.

¹³ After he, too, had died, they maltreated and tortured the fourth in the same way. ¹⁴ When he was near death, he said, "One cannot but choose to die at the hands of mortals and to cherish the hope God gives of being raised again by him. But for you there will be no resurrection to life!"

¹⁵ Next they brought forward the fifth and maltreated him. ¹⁶ But he looked at the king[ai] and said, "Because you have authority among mortals, though you also are mortal, you do what you please. But do not think that God has forsaken our people. ¹⁷ Keep on, and see how his mighty power will torture you and your descendants!"

¹⁸ After him they brought forward the sixth. And when he was about to die, he said, "Do not deceive yourself in vain. For we are suffering these things on our own account because of our sins against our own God.[aj] ¹⁹ But do not think that you will go unpunished for having tried to fight against God!"

²⁰ The mother was especially admirable and worthy of honorable memory. Although she saw her seven sons perish within a single day, she bore it with good courage because of her hope in the Lord. ²¹ She encouraged each of them in the language of their ancestors. Filled with a noble spirit, she reinforced her woman's reasoning with a man's courage and said to them, ²² "I do not know how you came into being in my womb. It was not I who gave you life and breath nor I who set in order the elements within each of you. ²³ Therefore the Creator of the world, who shaped the beginning of humankind and devised the origin of all things, in his mercy gives life and breath back to you again, since you now forget yourselves for the sake of his laws."

²⁴ Antiochus felt that he was being treated with contempt, and he was suspicious of her reproachful tone. The youngest brother being still alive, Antiochus[ak] not only appealed to him in words but promised with oaths that he would make him rich and enviable if he would turn from the ways of his ancestors and that he would take him for his Friend and entrust him with public affairs. ²⁵ Since the young man would not listen to him at all, the king called the mother to him and urged her to advise the youth to save himself. ²⁶ After much urging on his part, she undertook to persuade her son. ²⁷ But, leaning close to him, she spoke in their native language as follows, deriding the cruel tyrant: "My son, have pity on me. I carried you nine months in my womb and nursed you for three years and have reared you and brought you up to this point in your life and have taken care of you. ²⁸ I beg you, my child, to look at the heaven and the earth and see everything that is in them and recognize that God did not make them out of things that existed.[al] And in the same way the human race came into being. ²⁹ Do not fear this butcher but prove worthy of your brothers. Accept death, so that in God's mercy I may get you back again along with your brothers."

³⁰ While she was still speaking, the young man said, "What are you waiting for? I will not obey the king's command, but I obey the command of the law that was given to our ancestors through Moses. ³¹ But you, who have contrived all sorts of evil against the Hebrews, will certainly not escape the hands of God. ³² For we are suffering because of our own sins. ³³ And if our living Lord is angry for a little while, to rebuke and discipline us, he will again be reconciled with his own servants. ³⁴ But you, unholy wretch, you most defiled of all mortals, do not be elated in vain and puffed up by uncertain hopes when you raise your hand against

the children of heaven. ³⁵ You have not yet escaped the judgment of the almighty, all-seeing God. ³⁶ For our brothers, after enduring a brief suffering for everlasting life, have fallen under God's covenant, but you, by the judgment of God, will receive just punishment for your arrogance. ³⁷ I, like my brothers, give up body and life for the laws of our ancestors, appealing to God to show mercy soon to our nation and by trials and plagues to make you confess that he alone is God, ³⁸ and through me and my brothers to bring to an end the wrath of the Almighty that has justly fallen on our whole nation."

³⁹ The king fell into a rage and handled him worse than the others, being exasperated at his scorn. ⁴⁰ So he died in his integrity, putting his whole trust in the Lord.

⁴¹ Last of all, the mother died, after her sons.

⁴² Let this be enough, then, about the eating of sacrifices and the extreme tortures.

The Revolt of Judas Maccabeus

8 Meanwhile Judas, who was also called Maccabeus, and his companions secretly entered the villages and summoned their kindred and enlisted those who had continued in the Jewish faith, and so they gathered about six thousand. ² They implored the Lord to look upon the people who were oppressed by all and to have pity on the temple that had been profaned by the godless, ³ to have mercy on the city that was being destroyed and about to be leveled to the ground, to hearken to the blood that cried out to him, ⁴ to remember also the lawless destruction of the innocent babies and the blasphemies committed against his name, and to show his hatred of evil.

⁵ As soon as Maccabeus got his army organized, the nations could not withstand him, for the wrath of the Lord had turned to mercy. ⁶ Coming without warning, he would set fire to towns and villages. He captured strategic positions and put to flight not a few of the enemy. ⁷ He found the nights most advantageous for such attacks. And talk of his valor spread everywhere.

⁸ When Philip saw that the man was gaining ground little by little and that he was pushing ahead with more frequent successes, he wrote to Ptolemy, the governor of Coelesyria and Phoenicia, to come to the aid of the king's government. ⁹ Then Ptolemy[am] promptly appointed Nicanor son of Patroclus, one of the king's First[an] Friends, and sent him, in command of no fewer than twenty thousand men of various nations, to wipe out the entire people of Judea. He associated with him Gorgias, a general and a man of experience in military service. ¹⁰ Nicanor determined to make up for the king the tribute due to the Romans, two thousand talents, by selling the captured Jews into slavery. ¹¹ So he immediately sent to the towns on the seacoast, inviting them to buy Jewish slaves and promising to hand over ninety slaves for a talent, not expecting the judgment from the Almighty that was about to overtake him.

Preparation for Battle

¹² Word came to Judas concerning Nicanor's invasion, and when he told his companions of the arrival of the army, ¹³ those who were cowardly and distrustful of God's justice ran off and got away. ¹⁴ Others sold all their remaining property and at the same time implored the Lord to rescue those who had been sold by the ungodly Nicanor before he ever met them, ¹⁵ if not for their own sake, then for the sake of the covenants made with their ancestors and because he had called them by his holy and glorious name. ¹⁶ But Maccabeus gathered his forces together, to the number six thousand, and exhorted them not to be frightened by the enemy and not to fear the great multitude of nations who were wickedly coming against them but to fight nobly, ¹⁷ keeping before their eyes the lawless outrage that the nations[ao] had committed against the holy place and the torture of the derided city, as well as the overthrow of their ancestral way of life. ¹⁸ "For they trust to arms and acts of daring," he said, "but we trust in the Almighty God, who is able with a single nod to strike down those who are coming against us, and even, if necessary, the whole world."

¹⁹ Moreover, he told them of the occasions when help came to their ancestors, how, in the time of Sennacherib, when one hundred eighty-five thousand perished, ²⁰ and the time of the battle against the Galatians that took place in Babylonia, when eight thousand Jews[ap] fought along with four thousand Macedonians; yet when the Macedonians were hard pressed, the eight thousand, by the help that came to them from heaven, destroyed one hundred twenty thousand Galatians[aq] and took a great amount of plunder.

Judas Defeats Nicanor

²¹ With these words he filled them with courage and made them ready to die for their laws and their country; then he divided his army into four parts. ²² He appointed his brothers also, Simon and Joseph and Jonathan, each to command a division, putting fifteen hundred men under each. ²³ Besides, he appointed Eleazar to read aloud[ar] from the holy book and gave the watchword, "The help of God"; then, leading the first division himself, he joined battle with Nicanor.

²⁴ With the Almighty as their ally, they killed more than nine thousand of the enemy and wounded and disabled most of Nicanor's army and forced them all to flee. ²⁵ They captured the money of those who had come to buy them as slaves. After pursuing them for some distance, they were obliged to return because the hour was late. ²⁶ It was the day before the Sabbath, and for that reason they did not continue their pursuit. ²⁷ When they had collected the arms of the enemy and stripped them of their spoils, they kept the Sabbath, giving great praise and thanks to the Lord, who had preserved them for that day and allotted it to them as the beginning of mercy. ²⁸ After the Sabbath they gave some of the spoils to those who had been tortured and to the widows and orphans and distributed the rest among themselves and their children. ²⁹ When they had done this, they made common supplication and implored the merciful Lord to be wholly reconciled with his servants.

Judas Defeats Timothy and Bacchides

³⁰ In encounters with the forces of Timothy and Bacchides they killed more than twenty thousand of them and got possession of some exceedingly high strongholds, and they divided a very large amount of plunder, giving to those who had been tortured and to the orphans and widows and also to the aged, shares equal to their own. ³¹ They collected the arms of the enemy[as] and carefully stored all of them in strategic places; the rest of the spoils they carried to Jerusalem. ³² They killed the commander of Timothy's forces, a most wicked man, and one who had greatly troubled the Jews. ³³ While they were celebrating the victory in the city of their ancestors, they burned those who had set fire to the sacred gates, Callisthenes and some others, who had fled into one little house, so these received the proper reward for their impiety.[at]

³⁴ The thrice-accursed Nicanor, who had brought the thousand merchants to buy the Jews, ³⁵ having been humbled with the help of the Lord by opponents whom he regarded as of the least account, took off his splendid uniform and made his way alone like a runaway slave across the country until he reached Antioch, having succeeded chiefly in the destruction of his own army! ³⁶ So he who had undertaken to secure tribute for the Romans by the capture of the people of Jerusalem proclaimed that the Jews had a Defender and that therefore the Jews were invulnerable because they followed the laws ordained by him.

The Last Campaign of Antiochus Epiphanes

9 About that time, as it happened, Antiochus had retreated in disorder from the region of Persia. ² He had entered the city called Persepolis and attempted to rob the temples and control the city. Therefore the people rushed to the rescue with arms, and Antiochus and his army were defeated,[au] with the result that Antiochus was put to flight by the inhabitants and beat a shameful retreat. ³ While he was in Ecbatana, news came to him of what had happened to Nicanor and the forces of Timothy. ⁴ Transported with rage, he conceived the idea of turning upon the Jews the injury done by those who had put him to flight, so he ordered his charioteer to drive without stopping until he completed the journey. But the judgment of heaven rode with him! For in his arrogance he said, "When I get there I will make Jerusalem a cemetery of Jews."

⁵ But the all-seeing Lord, the God of Israel, struck him with an incurable and invisible blow. As soon as he stopped speaking, he was seized with a pain in his bowels for which there was no relief and with sharp internal tortures— ⁶ and that very justly, for he had tortured the bowels of others with many and strange inflictions. ⁷ Yet he did not in any way stop his insolence but was even more filled with arrogance, breathing fire in his rage against the Jews and giving orders to drive even faster. And so it came about that he fell out of his chariot as it was rushing along, and the fall was so hard as to torture every limb of his body. ⁸ Thus he, who only a little while before had thought in his superhuman arrogance that he could command the waves of the sea and had imagined that he could weigh the high mountains in a balance, was brought down to earth and carried in a litter, making the power of God manifest to all. ⁹ And so the ungodly man's body swarmed with worms, and while he was still living in anguish and pain, his flesh rotted away, and because of the stench the whole army felt revulsion at his decay. ¹⁰ Because of his intolerable stench no one was able to carry the man who a little while before had thought that he could touch the stars of heaven. ¹¹ Then it was that, broken in spirit, he began to lose much of his arrogance and to come to his senses under the scourge of God, for he was tortured with pain every moment. ¹² And when he could not endure his own stench, he uttered these words, "It is right to be subject to God; mortals should not think that they are equal to God."[av]

Antiochus Makes a Promise to God

¹³ Then the abominable fellow made a vow to the Lord, who would no longer have mercy on him, stating ¹⁴ that the holy city, which he was hurrying to level to the ground and to make a cemetery, he was now declaring to be free, ¹⁵ and the Jews, whom he had not considered worth burying but had planned to throw out with their children for the wild animals and for the birds to eat, he would make, all of them, equal to citizens of Athens, ¹⁶ and the holy sanctuary, which he had formerly plundered, he would adorn with the finest offerings, and all the holy vessels he would give back many times over, and the expenses incurred for the sacrifices he would provide from his own revenues, ¹⁷ and in addition to all this he also would become a Jew and would visit every inhabited place to proclaim the power of God. ¹⁸ But when his sufferings did not in any way abate, for the judgment of God had justly come upon him, he gave up all hope for himself and wrote to the Jews the following letter, in the form of a supplication. This was its content:

Antiochus's Letter and Death

19 "To his worthy Jewish citizens, Antiochus their king and general sends hearty greetings and good wishes for their health and prosperity. 20 If you and your children are well and your affairs are as you wish, I am glad as my hope is in heaven. 21 Now I was feeling weak, and so I was remembering with affection your esteem and goodwill. On my way back from the region of Persia I suffered an annoying illness, and I have deemed it necessary to take thought for the general security of all. 22 I do not despair of my condition, for I have good hope of recovering from my illness, 23 but I observed that my father, on the occasions when he made expeditions into the upper country, appointed his successor, 24 so that, if anything unexpected happened or any unwelcome news came, the people throughout the realm would not be troubled, for they would know to whom the government was left. 25 Moreover, I understand how the princes along the borders and the neighbors of my kingdom keep watching for opportunities and waiting to see what will happen. So I have appointed my son Antiochus to be king, whom I have often entrusted and commended to most of you when I hurried off to the upper provinces, and I have written to him the appended letter. 26 I therefore urge and beg you to remember the public and private services rendered to you and to maintain your present goodwill, each of you, toward me and my son. 27 For I am sure that he will follow my policy and will treat you with moderation and kindness."

28 So the murderer and blasphemer, having endured the more intense suffering such as he had inflicted on others, came to the end of his life by a most pitiable fate, among the mountains in a strange land. 29 And Philip, one of his courtiers, took his body home; then, fearing the son of Antiochus, he withdrew to Ptolemy Philometor in Egypt.

Purification of the Temple

10 Now Maccabeus and his followers, the Lord leading them on, recovered the temple and the city; 2 they tore down the altars that had been built in the public square by the foreigners and also destroyed the sacred precincts. 3 They purified the sanctuary and made another altar of sacrifice; then, striking fire out of flint, they offered sacrifices, after a lapse of two years, and they offered incense and lighted lamps and set out the bread of the Presence. 4 When they had done this, they fell prostrate and implored the Lord that they might never again fall into such misfortunes but that, if they should ever sin, they might be disciplined by him with forbearance and not be handed over to blasphemous and barbarous nations. 5 It happened that on the same day on which the sanctuary had been profaned by the foreigners, the purification of the sanctuary took place, that is, on the twenty-fifth day of the same month, which was Chislev. 6 They celebrated it for eight days with rejoicing, in the manner of the Festival of Booths,[aw] remembering how not long before, during the Festival of Booths,[ax] they had been wandering in the mountains and caves like wild animals. 7 Therefore, carrying ivy-wreathed wands and beautiful branches and also palm fronds, they offered hymns of thanksgiving to him who had given success to the purifying of his own holy place. 8 They decreed by public edict, ratified by vote, that the whole nation of the Jews should observe these days every year.

9 Such then was the end of Antiochus, who was called Epiphanes.

Accession of Antiochus Eupator

10 Now we will tell what took place under Antiochus Eupator, who was the son of that ungodly man, and will give a brief summary of the principal calamities of the wars. 11 This man, when he succeeded to the kingdom, appointed one Lysias to have charge of the government and Protarchos to be governor of Coelesyria and Phoenicia. 12 Ptolemy, who was called Macron, took the lead in showing justice to the Jews because of the wrong that had been done to them and attempted to maintain peaceful relations with them. 13 As a result he was accused before Eupator by the king's Friends. He heard himself called a traitor at every turn because he had abandoned Cyprus, which Philometor had entrusted to him, and had gone over to Antiochus Epiphanes. Unable to command the respect due his office,[ay] he took poison and ended his life.

Campaign in Idumea

14 When Gorgias became governor of the region, he maintained a force of mercenaries and at every turn kept attacking the Jews. 15 Besides this, the Idumeans, who had control of important strongholds, were harassing the Jews; they received those who were banished from Jerusalem and endeavored to keep up the war. 16 But Maccabeus and his forces, after making solemn supplication and imploring God to fight on their side, rushed to the strongholds of the Idumeans. 17 Attacking them vigorously, they gained possession of the places and drove back all who fought upon the wall and slaughtered those whom they encountered, killing no fewer than twenty thousand.

18 When at least nine thousand took refuge in two very strong towers well equipped to withstand a siege, 19 Maccabeus left Simon and Joseph, and also Zacchaeus and his troops, a force sufficient to besiege them, and he himself set off for places where he was more urgently needed. 20 But those with Simon, who were money-hungry, were bribed by some of those who were in the towers and on receiving seventy thousand drachmas let some of them slip away. 21 When word of what had happened came to Maccabeus, he gathered the leaders of the people and accused these men of having sold their kindred for money by setting their enemies free to fight against them. 22 Then he killed these men who had turned traitor and immediately captured the two towers. 23 Having success at arms in everything he undertook, he destroyed more than twenty thousand in the two strongholds.

Judas Defeats Timothy

24 Now Timothy, who had been defeated by the Jews before, gathered a tremendous force of mercenaries and collected the cavalry from Asia in no small number. He came on, intending to take Judea by storm. 25 As he drew near, Maccabeus and his men sprinkled dust on their heads and girded their loins with sackcloth, in supplication to God. 26 Falling upon the steps before the altar, they implored him to be gracious to them and to be an enemy to their enemies and an adversary to their adversaries, as the law declares. 27 And rising from their prayer they took up their arms and advanced a considerable distance from the city, and when they came near the enemy they halted. 28 Just as dawn was breaking, the two armies joined battle, the one having as pledge of success and victory not only their valor but also their reliance on the Lord, while the other made rage their leader in the fight.

29 When the battle became fierce, there appeared to the enemy from heaven five resplendent men on horses with golden bridles, and they were leading the Jews. 30 Two of them took Maccabeus between them and, shielding him with their own armor and weapons, they kept him from being wounded. They showered arrows and thunderbolts on the enemy so that, confused and blinded, they were thrown into disorder and cut to pieces. 31 Twenty thousand five hundred were slaughtered, besides six hundred cavalry.

32 Timothy himself fled to a stronghold called Gazara, especially well garrisoned, where Chaereas was commander. 33 Then Maccabeus and his men were glad, and they besieged the fort for four days. 34 The men within, relying on the strength of the place, kept blaspheming terribly and uttering wicked words. 35 But at dawn of the fifth day, twenty young men in the army of Maccabeus, fired with anger because of the blasphemies, bravely stormed the wall and with savage fury cut down everyone they met. 36 During the distraction, others came up in the same way, wheeled around against the defenders, and set fire to the towers; they kindled fires and burned the blasphemers alive. Others broke open the gates and let in the rest of the force, and they occupied the city. 37 They killed Timothy, who was hiding in a cistern, and his brother Chaereas, and Apollophanes. 38 When they had accomplished these things, with hymns and thanksgivings they blessed the Lord, who shows great kindness to Israel and gives them the victory.

Lysias Besieges Beth-zur

11 Very soon after this, Lysias, the king's guardian and kinsman, who was in charge of the government, being vexed at what had happened, 2 gathered about eighty thousand infantry and all his cavalry and came against the Jews. He intended to make the city a home for Greeks 3 and to levy tribute on the temple as he did on the sacred places of the other nations and to put up the high priesthood for sale every year. 4 He took no account whatever of the power of God but was elated with his ten thousands of infantry and his thousands of cavalry and his eighty elephants. 5 Invading Judea, he approached Beth-zur, which was a fortified place about five schoinoi[a] from Jerusalem, and pressed it hard. 6 When Maccabeus and his men got word that Lysias[b] was besieging the strongholds, they and all the people, with lamentations and tears, prayed the Lord to send a good angel to save Israel. 7 Maccabeus himself was the first to take up arms, and he urged the others to risk their lives with him to aid their kindred. Then they eagerly rushed off together. 8 And there, while they were still near Jerusalem, a horseman appeared at their head, clothed in white and brandishing weapons of gold. 9 And together they all praised the merciful God and were strengthened in heart, ready to assail not only humans but the wildest animals or walls of iron. 10 They advanced in battle order, having their heavenly ally, for the Lord had mercy on them. 11 They hurled themselves like lions against the enemy and laid low eleven thousand of them and sixteen hundred cavalry and forced all the rest to flee. 12 Most of them got away wounded and stripped, and Lysias himself escaped by disgraceful flight.

Lysias Makes Peace with the Jews

13 As he was not without intelligence, he pondered over the defeat that had befallen him and realized that the Hebrews were invincible because the mighty God fought on their side. So he sent to them 14 and persuaded them to settle everything on just terms, promising that he would persuade the king, constraining him to be their friend.[c] 15 Maccabeus, having regard for the common good, agreed to all that Lysias urged. For the king granted every request in behalf of the Jews that Maccabeus delivered to Lysias in writing.

16 The letter written to the Jews by Lysias was to this effect:

"Lysias to the people of the Jews, greetings. 17 John and Absalom, who were sent by you, have delivered your signed communication and have asked about the matters indicated in it. 18 I have informed the king of everything that needed to be brought before him, and I have agreed to what was possible. 19 If you will maintain your goodwill toward the government, I will endeavor in the future to help promote your welfare. ²⁰ And concerning such matters and their details, I have ordered these men and my representatives to confer with you. ²¹ Farewell. The one hundred forty-eighth year, Dioscorinthius twenty-fourth."

²² The king's letter ran thus:

"King Antiochus to his brother Lysias, greetings. ²³ Now that our father has gone on to the gods, we desire that the subjects of the kingdom be undisturbed in caring for their own affairs. ²⁴ We have heard that the Jews do not consent to our father's change to Greek customs but prefer their own way of living and ask that their own customs be allowed them. ²⁵ Accordingly, since we choose that this nation also should be free from disturbance, our decision is that their temple be restored to them and that they shall live according to the customs of their ancestors. ²⁶ You will do well, therefore, to send word to them and give them pledges of friendship, so that they may know our policy and be of good cheer and go on happily in the conduct of their own affairs."

²⁷ To the nation the king's letter was as follows:

"King Antiochus to the council of the Jews and to the other Jews, greetings. ²⁸ If you are well, it is as we desire. We also are in good health. ²⁹ Menelaus has informed us that you wish to return home and look after your own affairs. ³⁰ Therefore those who go home by the thirtieth of Xanthicus will have our pledge of friendship and full permission ³¹ for the Jews to enjoy their own customs[d] and laws, just as formerly, and none of them shall be molested in any way for what may have been done in ignorance. ³² And I have also sent Menelaus to encourage you. ³³ Farewell. The one hundred forty-eighth year, Xanthicus fifteenth."

³⁴ The Romans also sent them a letter, which read thus:

"Quintus Memmius and Titus Manius, envoys of the Romans, to the people of the Jews, greetings. ³⁵ With regard to what Lysias the kinsman of the king has granted you, we also give consent. ³⁶ But as to the matters that he decided are to be referred to the king, as soon as you have considered them, send someone promptly so that we may make proposals appropriate for you, for we are on our way to Antioch. ³⁷ Therefore make haste and send messengers so that we may have your judgment. ³⁸ Farewell. The one hundred forty-eighth year, Xanthicus fifteenth."

Incidents at Joppa and Jamnia

12 When this agreement had been reached, Lysias returned to the king, and the Jews went about their farming. ² But some of the governors in various places, Timothy and Apollonius son of Gennaeus, as well as Hieronymus and Demophon, and in addition to these Nicanor the governor of Cyprus, would not let them live quietly and in peace. ³ And the people of Joppa did so ungodly a deed as this: they invited the Jews who lived among them to embark, with their wives and children, on boats that they had provided, as though there were no ill will to the Jews,[e] ⁴ and this was done by public vote of the city. When they accepted, because they wished to live peaceably and suspected nothing, the people of Joppa[f] took them out to sea and drowned them, at least two hundred. ⁵ When Judas heard of the cruelty visited on his compatriots, he gave orders to his men ⁶ and, calling upon God, the righteous judge, attacked the murderers of his kindred. He set fire to the harbor by night, burned the boats, and massacred those who had taken refuge there. ⁷ Then, because the city's gates were closed, he withdrew, intending to come again and root out the whole community of Joppa. ⁸ But learning that the people in Jamnia meant in the same way to wipe out the Jews who were living among them, ⁹ he attacked the Jamnites by night and set fire to the harbor and the fleet, so that the glow of the light was seen in Jerusalem, thirty miles[g] distant.

The Campaign in Gilead

¹⁰ When they had gone more than a mile[h] from there on their march against Timothy, at least five thousand Arabs with five hundred cavalry attacked them. ¹¹ After a hard fight, Judas and his companions, with God's help, were victorious. The defeated nomads begged Judas to grant them pledges of friendship, promising to give him livestock and to help his people[i] in all other ways. ¹² Judas, realizing that they might indeed be useful in many ways, agreed to make peace with them, and after receiving his pledges they went back to their tents. ¹³ He also attacked a certain town that was strongly fortified with earthworks[j] and walls and inhabited by all sorts of nations. Its name was Caspin. ¹⁴ Those who were within, relying on the strength of the walls and on their supply of provisions, behaved most insolently toward Judas and his men, railing at them and even blaspheming and saying unholy things. ¹⁵ But Judas and his men, calling upon the great Sovereign of the world, who without battering rams or engines of war overthrew Jericho in the days of Joshua, rushed furiously upon the walls. ¹⁶ They took the town by the will of God and slaughtered untold numbers, so that the adjoining lake, a quarter of a mile[k] wide, appeared to be running over with blood.

Judas Defeats Timothy's Army

¹⁷ When they had gone ninety-five miles[l] from there, they came to a stockade,[m] to the Jews who are called Toubiani. ¹⁸ They did not find Timothy in that region, for he had by then left there without accomplishing anything, though in one place he had left a very strong garrison. ¹⁹ Dositheus and Sosipater, who were captains under Maccabeus, marched out and destroyed those whom Timothy had left in the strong-

hold, more than ten thousand men. ²⁰ But Maccabeus arranged his army in divisions, set men[n] in command of the divisions, and hurried after Timothy, who had with him one hundred twenty thousand infantry and two thousand five hundred cavalry. ²¹ When Timothy learned of the approach of Judas, he sent off the women and the children and also the baggage to a place called Carnaim, for that place was hard to besiege and difficult to access because of the narrowness of all the approaches. ²² But when Judas's first division appeared, terror and fear came over the enemy at the manifestation to them of him who sees all things. In their flight they rushed headlong in every direction, so that often they were injured by their own men and pierced by the points of their own swords. ²³ Judas pressed the pursuit with the utmost vigor, putting the sinners to the sword, and destroyed as many as thirty thousand.

²⁴ Timothy himself fell into the hands of Dositheus and Sosipater and their men. With great guile he begged them to let him go in safety, because he held the parents of most of them and the brothers of some, to whom no consideration would be shown. ²⁵ And when with many words he had confirmed his solemn promise to restore them unharmed, they let him go, for the sake of saving their kindred.

Judas Wins Other Victories

²⁶ Then Judas[o] marched against Carnaim and the temple of Atargatis and slaughtered twenty-five thousand people. ²⁷ After the rout and destruction of these, he marched also against Ephron, a fortified town where Lysias lived with multitudes of people of all nationalities.[p] Stalwart young men took their stand before the walls and made a vigorous defense, and great stores of war engines and missiles were there. ²⁸ But the Jews[q] called upon the Sovereign who with power shatters the might of his enemies, and they got the town into their hands and killed as many as twenty-five thousand of those who were in it.

²⁹ Setting out from there, they hastened to Scythopolis, which is seventy-five miles[r] from Jerusalem. ³⁰ But when the Jews who lived there bore witness to the goodwill that the people of Scythopolis had shown them and their kind treatment of them in times of misfortune, ³¹ they thanked them and exhorted them to be well disposed to their race in the future also. Then they went up to Jerusalem, as the Festival of Weeks was close at hand.

Judas Defeats Gorgias

³² After the festival called Pentecost, they hurried against Gorgias, the governor of Idumea, ³³ who came out with three thousand infantry and four hundred cavalry. ³⁴ When they joined battle, it happened that a few of the Jews fell. ³⁵ But a certain Dositheus, one of Bacenor's men,[s] who was on horseback and was a strong man, caught hold of Gorgias and, grasping his cloak, was dragging him off by main strength, wishing to take the accursed man alive, when one of the Thracian cavalry bore down on him and cut off his arm, so Gorgias escaped and reached Marisa.

³⁶ As Esdris and his men had been fighting for a long time and were weary, Judas called upon the Lord to show himself their ally and leader in the battle. ³⁷ In the language of their ancestors he raised the battle cry, with hymns; then he charged against Gorgias's troops when they were not expecting it and put them to flight.

Prayers for Those Killed in Battle

³⁸ Then Judas assembled his army and went to the city of Adullam. As the seventh day was coming on, they purified themselves according to the custom and kept the Sabbath there.

³⁹ On the next day, as had now become necessary, Judas and his men went to take up the bodies of the fallen and to bring them back to lie with their kindred in the tombs of their ancestors. ⁴⁰ Then under the tunic of each one of the dead they found sacred tokens of the idols of Jamnia, which the law forbids the Jews to wear. And it became clear to all that this was the reason these men had fallen. ⁴¹ So they all blessed the ways of the Lord, the righteous judge, who reveals the things that are hidden, ⁴² and they turned to supplication, praying that the sin that had been committed might be wholly blotted out. The noble Judas exhorted the people to keep themselves free from sin, for they had seen with their own eyes what had happened as the result of the sin of those who had fallen. ⁴³ He also took up a collection, man by man, to the amount of two thousand drachmas of silver, and sent it to Jerusalem to provide for a purification offering. In doing this he acted very well and honorably, taking account of the resurrection. ⁴⁴ For if he were not expecting that those who had fallen would rise again, it would have been superfluous and foolish to pray for the dead. ⁴⁵ But if he was looking to the splendid reward that is laid up for those who fall asleep in godliness, it was a holy and pious thought. Therefore he made atonement for the dead, so that they might be delivered from their sin.

Menelaus Is Put to Death

13 In the one hundred forty-ninth year, word came to Judas and his men that Antiochus Eupator was coming with a great army against Judea, ² and with him Lysias, his guardian, who had charge of the government. Each of them had a Greek force of one hundred ten thousand infantry, five thousand three hundred cavalry, twenty-two elephants, and three hundred chariots armed with scythes.

³ Menelaus also joined them and with utter hypocrisy urged Antiochus on, not for the sake of his country's welfare but because he thought that he

would be established in office. ⁴But the King of kings aroused the anger of Antiochus against the scoundrel, and when Lysias informed him that this man was to blame for all the trouble, he ordered them to take him to Beroea and to put him to death by the method that is customary in that place. ⁵For there is a tower there, fifty cubits high, full of ashes, and it has a rim running around it that on all sides inclines precipitously into the ashes. ⁶There they all push to destruction anyone guilty of sacrilege or notorious for other crimes. ⁷By such a fate it came about that Menelaus the lawbreaker died, without even burial in the earth. ⁸And this was eminently just; because he had committed many sins against the altar whose fire and ashes were holy, he met his death in ashes.

A Battle Near the City of Modein

⁹The king with barbarous arrogance was coming to show the Jews things far worse than those that had been done[t] in his father's time. ¹⁰But when Judas heard of this, he ordered the people to call upon the Lord day and night, now if ever to help those who were on the point of being deprived of the law and their country and the holy temple, ¹¹and not to let the people who had just begun to revive fall into the hands of the blasphemous nations. ¹²When they had all joined in the same petition and had implored the merciful Lord with weeping and fasting and lying prostrate for three days without ceasing, Judas exhorted them and ordered them to stand ready.

¹³After consulting privately with the elders, he determined to march out and decide the matter by the help of God before the king's army could enter Judea and get possession of the city. ¹⁴So, committing the decision to the Creator of the world and exhorting his troops to fight bravely to the death for the laws, temple, city, country, and way of life, he pitched his camp near Modein. ¹⁵He gave his troops the watchword, "God's victory," and with a picked force of the bravest young men, he attacked the king's pavilion at night and killed as many as two thousand men in the camp. He stabbed[u] the leading elephant and its rider. ¹⁶In the end, they filled the camp with terror and confusion and withdrew in triumph. ¹⁷This happened, just as day was dawning, because the Lord's help protected him.

Antiochus Makes a Treaty with the Jews

¹⁸The king, having had a taste of the daring of the Jews, tried strategy in attacking their positions. ¹⁹He advanced against Beth-zur, a strong fortress of the Jews, was turned back, attacked again,[v] and was defeated. ²⁰Judas sent in to the garrison whatever was necessary. ²¹But Rhodocus, a man from the ranks of the Jews, gave secret information to the enemy; he was sought for, caught, and put in prison. ²²The king negotiated a second time with the people in Beth-zur, gave pledges, received theirs, withdrew, attacked Judas and his men, was defeated; ²³he got word that Philip, who had been left in charge of the government, had revolted in Antioch; he was dismayed, called in the Jews, yielded and swore to observe all their rights, settled with them and offered sacrifice, honored the sanctuary, and showed generosity to the holy place. ²⁴He received Maccabeus, left Hegemonides as governor from Ptolemais to Gerar, ²⁵and went to Ptolemais. The people of Ptolemais were indignant over the treaty; in fact, they were so angry that they wanted to annul its terms.[w] ²⁶Lysias took the public platform, made the best possible defense, convinced them, appeased them, gained their goodwill, and set out for Antioch. This is how the king's attack and withdrawal turned out.

Alcimus Speaks against Judas

14 Three years later, word came to Judas and his men that Demetrius son of Seleucus had sailed into the harbor of Tripolis with a strong army and a fleet ²and had taken possession of the country, having made away with Antiochus and his guardian Lysias.

³Now a certain Alcimus, who had formerly been high priest but had willfully defiled himself in the days of separation,[x] realized that there was no way for him to be safe or to have access again to the holy altar ⁴and went to King Demetrius in about the one hundred fifty-first year, presenting to him a crown of gold and a palm and besides these some of the customary olive branches from the temple. During that day he kept quiet. ⁵But he found an opportunity that furthered his mad purpose when he was invited by Demetrius to a meeting of the council and was asked about the attitude and intentions of the Jews. He answered:

⁶"Those of the Jews who are called Hasideans, whose leader is Judas Maccabeus, are keeping up war and stirring up sedition and will not let the kingdom attain tranquility. ⁷Therefore I have laid aside my ancestral glory—I mean the high priesthood—and have now come here, ⁸first because I am genuinely concerned for the interests of the king, and second because I have regard also for my compatriots. For through the folly of those whom I have mentioned our whole nation is now in no small misfortune. ⁹Since you are acquainted, O king, with the details of this matter, may it please you to take thought for our country and our hard-pressed nation with the gracious kindness that you show to all. ¹⁰For as long as Judas lives, it is impossible for the government to find peace." ¹¹When he had said this, the rest of the king's Friends,[y] who were hostile to Judas, quickly inflamed Demetrius still more. ¹²He immediately chose Nicanor, who had been in command of the elephants, appointed him governor of Judea, and sent him off ¹³with orders to kill Judas and scatter his troops and to install Alcimus as high priest of the great[z] temple. ¹⁴And the nations throughout Judea, who had fled before[aa] Judas, flocked to join Nicanor, thinking that the misfortunes and calamities of the Jews would mean prosperity for themselves.

Nicanor Makes Friends with Judas

¹⁵When the Jews[ab] heard of Nicanor's coming and the gathering of the nations, they sprinkled dust on their heads and prayed to him who established his own people forever and always upholds his own heritage by manifesting himself. ¹⁶At the command of the leader, they[ac] set out from there immediately and engaged them in battle at a village called Dessau.[ad] ¹⁷Simon, the brother of Judas, had encountered Nicanor but had been temporarily[ae] checked because of the sudden consternation created by the enemy.

¹⁸Nevertheless, Nicanor, hearing of the valor of Judas and his troops and their courage in battle for their country, shrank from deciding the issue by bloodshed. ¹⁹Therefore he sent Posidonius, Theodotus, and Mattathias to give and receive pledges of friendship. ²⁰When the terms had been fully considered and the leader had informed the people and it had appeared that they were of one mind, they agreed to the covenant. ²¹The leaders[af] set a day on which to meet by themselves. A chariot came forward from each army; seats of honor were set in place; ²²Judas posted armed men in readiness at key places to prevent sudden treachery on the part of the enemy; so they duly held the consultation.

²³Nicanor stayed on in Jerusalem and did nothing out of the way but dismissed the flocks of people who had gathered. ²⁴And he kept Judas always in his presence; he was warmly attached to the man. ²⁵He urged him to marry and have children, so Judas[ag] married, settled down, and shared the common life.

Nicanor Turns against Judas

²⁶But when Alcimus noticed their goodwill for one another, he took the covenant that had been made and went to Demetrius. He told him that Nicanor was disloyal to the government, since he had appointed that conspirator against the kingdom, Judas, to be his successor. ²⁷The king became excited and, provoked by the false accusations of that depraved man, wrote to Nicanor, stating that he was displeased with the covenant and commanding him to send Maccabeus to Antioch as a prisoner without delay.

²⁸When this message came to Nicanor, he was troubled and grieved that he had to annul their agreement when the man had done no wrong. ²⁹Since it was not possible to oppose the king, he watched for an opportunity to accomplish this by a stratagem. ³⁰But Maccabeus, noticing that Nicanor was more austere in his dealings with him and was meeting him more rudely than had been his custom, concluded that this austerity did not spring from the best motives. So he gathered not a few of his men and went into hiding from Nicanor. ³¹When the latter became aware that he had been cleverly outwitted by the man, he went to the great[ah] and holy temple while the priests were offering the customary sacrifices and commanded them to hand the man over. ³²When they declared on oath that they did not know where the man was whom he wanted, ³³he stretched out his right hand toward the sanctuary and swore this oath: "If you do not hand Judas over to me as a prisoner, I will level this shrine of God to the ground and tear down the altar and build here a splendid temple to Dionysus."

³⁴Having said this, he went away. Then the priests stretched out their hands toward heaven and called upon the constant Defender of our nation, in these words: ³⁵"O Lord of all, though you have need of nothing, you were pleased that there should be a temple for your habitation among us, ³⁶so now, O holy One, Lord of all holiness, keep undefiled forever this house that has been so recently purified."

Razis Dies for His Country

³⁷A certain Razis, one of the elders of Jerusalem, was denounced to Nicanor as a man who loved his compatriots and was very well thought of and for his goodwill was called father of the Jews. ³⁸For before the days of separation, he had been accused of Judaism, and he had most zealously risked body and life for Judaism. ³⁹Nicanor, wishing to exhibit the enmity that he had for the Jews, sent more than five hundred soldiers to arrest him, ⁴⁰for he thought that by arresting[ai] him he would do them an injury. ⁴¹When the troops were about to capture the tower and were forcing the door of the courtyard, they ordered that fire be brought and the doors burned. Being surrounded, Razis[aj] fell upon his own sword, ⁴²preferring to die nobly rather than to fall into the hands of sinners and suffer outrages unworthy of his noble birth. ⁴³But in the heat of the struggle he did not hit exactly, and the crowd was now rushing in through the doors. He courageously ran up on the wall and bravely threw himself down into the crowd. ⁴⁴But as they quickly drew back, a space opened and he fell in the middle of the empty space. ⁴⁵Still alive and aflame with anger, he rose, and though his blood gushed forth and his wounds were severe he ran through the crowd, and standing upon a steep rock, ⁴⁶with his blood now completely drained from him, he tore out his entrails, took them in both hands, and hurled them at the crowd, calling upon the Lord of life and spirit to give them back to him again. This was the manner of his death.

Nicanor's Arrogance

15 When Nicanor heard that Judas and his troops were in the region of Samaria, he made plans to attack them with complete safety on the day of

rest. ² When the Jews who were compelled to follow him said, "Do not destroy so savagely and barbarously, but show respect for the day that he who sees all things has honored and hallowed above other days," ³ the thrice-accursed wretch asked if there were a sovereign in heaven who had commanded the keeping of the Sabbath day. ⁴ When they declared, "It is the living Lord himself, the Sovereign in heaven, who ordered us to observe the seventh day," ⁵ he replied, "But I am a sovereign also, on earth, and I command you to take up arms and finish the king's business." Nevertheless, he did not succeed in carrying out his abominable design.

Judas Prepares the Jews for Battle

⁶ This Nicanor in his utter boastfulness and arrogance had determined to erect a public monument of victory over Judas and his forces. ⁷ But Maccabeus did not cease to trust with all confidence that he would get help from the Lord. ⁸ He exhorted his troops not to fear the attack of the nations but to keep in mind the former times when help had come to them from heaven and so to look for the victory that the Almighty would give them. ⁹ Encouraging them from the Law and the Prophets and reminding them also of the struggles they had won, he made them the more eager. ¹⁰ When he had aroused their courage, he issued his orders, at the same time pointing out the treachery of the nations and their violation of oaths. ¹¹ He armed each of them not so much with confidence in shields and spears as with the inspiration of brave words, and he cheered them all by relating a dream, a sort of vision,[ak] that was worthy of belief.

¹² What he saw was this: Onias, who had been high priest, a noble and good man, of modest bearing and gentle manner, one who spoke fittingly and had been trained from childhood in all that belongs to excellence, was praying with outstretched hands for the whole body of the Jews. ¹³ Then in the same fashion another appeared, distinguished by his gray hair and dignity, and of marvelous majesty and authority. ¹⁴ And Onias spoke, saying, "This is a man who loves the family of Israel and prays much for the people and the holy city: Jeremiah, the prophet of God." ¹⁵ Jeremiah stretched out his right hand and gave to Judas a golden sword, and as he gave it he addressed him thus: ¹⁶ "Take this holy sword, a gift from God, with which you will strike down your adversaries."

¹⁷ Encouraged by the words of Judas, so noble and so effective in arousing valor and awaking courage in the souls of the young, they determined not to carry on a campaign[al] but to attack bravely and to decide the matter by fighting hand to hand with all courage, because the city and the sanctuary and the temple were in danger. ¹⁸ Their concern for wives and children and also for brothers and sisters and relatives lay upon them less heavily; their greatest and first fear was for the consecrated sanctuary. ¹⁹ And those who had to remain in the city were in no little distress, being anxious over the encounter in the open country.

The Defeat and Death of Nicanor

²⁰ When all were now looking forward to the coming issue and the enemy was already close at hand with their army drawn up for battle, the elephants[am] strategically stationed and the cavalry deployed on the flanks, ²¹ Maccabeus, observing the masses that were in front of him and the varied supply of arms and the savagery of the elephants, stretched out his hands toward heaven and called upon the Lord who works wonders, for he knew that it is not by arms but as the Lord[an] decides that he gains the victory for those who deserve it. ²² He called upon him in these words: "O Lord, you sent your angel in the time of King Hezekiah of Judea, and he killed fully one hundred eighty-five thousand in the camp of Sennacherib. ²³ So now, O Sovereign of the heavens, send a good angel to spread terror and trembling before us. ²⁴ By the might of your arm may these blasphemers who come against your holy people be struck down." With these words he ended his prayer.

²⁵ Nicanor and his troops advanced with trumpets and battle songs, ²⁶ but Judas and his troops met the enemy in battle with invocations to God and prayers. ²⁷ So, fighting with their hands and praying to God in their hearts, they laid low at least thirty-five thousand and were greatly gladdened by God's manifestation.

²⁸ When the action was over and they were returning with joy, they recognized Nicanor, lying dead, in full armor. ²⁹ Then there was shouting and tumult, and they blessed the Sovereign Lord in the language of their ancestors. ³⁰ Then the man who was ever in body and soul the defender of his people, the man who maintained his youthful goodwill toward his compatriots, ordered them to cut off Nicanor's head and arm and carry them to Jerusalem. ³¹ When he arrived there and had called his compatriots together and stationed the priests before the altar, he sent for those who were in the citadel. ³² He showed them the vile Nicanor's head and that profane man's arm, which had been boastfully stretched out against the holy house of the Almighty. ³³ He cut out the tongue of the ungodly Nicanor and said that he would feed it piecemeal to the birds and would hang up these rewards of his folly opposite the sanctuary. ³⁴ And they all, looking to heaven, blessed the Lord who had manifested himself, saying, "Blessed is he who has kept his own place undefiled!" ³⁵ Judas[ao] hung Nicanor's head from the citadel, a clear and conspicuous sign to everyone of the help of the Lord. ³⁶ And they all decreed by public vote never to let this day go unobserved but to celebrate the thirteenth day of the twelfth month—which is called Adar in the Aramaic language—the day before Mordecai's day.

³⁷ This, then, is how matters turned out with Nicanor, and from that time the city has been in the possession of the Hebrews. So I will here end my story.

The Compiler's Epilogue

³⁸ If it is well told and to the point, that is what I myself desired; if it is poorly done and mediocre, that was the best I could do. ³⁹ For just as it is harmful to drink wine alone or, again, to drink water alone, while wine already mixed with water is delicious and enhances one's enjoyment, so also the style of the story delights the ears of those who read the work. And here will be the end.

Book 90. 3 Maccabees

1 When Philopator learned from those who returned that the regions that he had controlled had been seized by Antiochus, he gave orders to all his forces, both infantry and cavalry, took with him his sister Arsinoë, and marched out to the region near Raphia, where the army of Antiochus was encamped. ² But a certain Theodotus, determined to carry out the plot he had devised, took with him the best of the Ptolemaic arms that had been previously issued to him[a] and crossed over by night to the tent of Ptolemy, intending single-handedly to kill him and thereby end the war. ³ But Dositheus, known as the son of Drimylus, a Jew by birth who later changed his customs and abandoned the ancestral traditions, had led the king away and arranged that a certain insignificant man should sleep in the tent, and so it turned out that this man incurred the punishment meant for the king.[b] ⁴ A fierce battle ensued, and when matters were turning out rather in favor of Antiochus, Arsinoë went to the troops with wailing and tears, her locks all disheveled, and exhorted them to defend themselves and their children and wives bravely, promising to give them each two minas of gold if they won the battle. ⁵ And so it came about that the enemy was routed in the action, and many captives also were taken. ⁶ Now that he had foiled the plot, Ptolemy[c] decided to visit the neighboring cities and encourage them. ⁷ By doing this and by endowing their sacred enclosures with gifts, he strengthened the morale of his subjects.

Philopator Attempts to Enter the Temple

⁸ Since the Jews had sent some of their council and elders to greet him, to bring him gifts of welcome, and to congratulate him on what had happened, he was all the more eager to visit them as soon as possible. ⁹ After he had arrived in Jerusalem, he offered sacrifice to the supreme God and made thank offerings and did what was fitting for the place. Then, upon entering the place and being impressed by its excellence and its beauty, ¹⁰ he marveled at the good order of the temple and conceived a desire to enter the sanctuary. ¹¹ When they said that this was not permitted because not even members of their own nation were allowed to enter, not even all of the priests, but only the high priest who was preeminent over all—and he only once a year—the king was by no means persuaded. ¹² Even after the law had been read to him, he did not cease to maintain that he ought to enter, saying, "Even if those men are deprived of this honor, I ought not to be." ¹³ And he inquired why, when he entered every other temple,[d] no one there had stopped him. ¹⁴ And someone answered thoughtlessly that it was wrong to place any significance in that.[e] ¹⁵ "But since this has happened," the king[f] said, "why should not I at least enter, whether they wish it or not?"

Jewish Resistance to Ptolemy

¹⁶ Then the priests in all their vestments prostrated themselves and entreated the supreme God to aid in the present situation and to avert the violence of this evil design, and they filled the temple with cries and tears; ¹⁷ those who remained behind in the city were agitated and hurried out, supposing that something mysterious was occurring. ¹⁸ Young women who had been secluded in their chambers rushed out with their mothers, sprinkled their hair with dust,[g] and filled the streets with groans and lamentations. ¹⁹ Those women who had recently been arrayed for marriage abandoned the bridal chambers[h] prepared for wedded union and, neglecting proper modesty, in a disorderly rush flocked together in the city. ²⁰ Mothers and nurses abandoned even newborn children here and there, some in houses and some in the streets, and without a backward look they crowded together at the most high temple. ²¹ Various were the supplications of those gathered there because of what the king was profanely plotting. ²² In addition, the bolder of the citizens would not tolerate the completion of his plans or the fulfillment of his intended purpose. ²³ They shouted to their compatriots to take arms and die courageously for the ancestral law and created a considerable disturbance in the place, and, being barely restrained by the old men and the elders,[i] they resorted to the same posture of supplication as the others. ²⁴ Meanwhile, the crowd, as before, was engaged in prayer, ²⁵ while the elders near the king tried in various ways to change his arrogant mind from the plan that he had conceived. ²⁶ But he, in his arrogance, took heed of nothing and began now to approach, determined to bring the aforesaid plan to a conclusion. ²⁷ When those who were around him observed this, they turned, together with our people, to call upon him who has all power to defend them in the present trouble and not to overlook this unlawful and haughty deed. ²⁸ The continuous, vehement, and concerted cry of the

crowds[j] resulted in an immense uproar, 29 for it seemed that not only the people but also the walls and the whole earth around echoed, because indeed all at that time[k] preferred death to the profanation of the place.

The Prayer of the High Priest Simon

2 [[Then the high priest Simon, facing the sanctuary, bending his knees, and extending his hands with calm dignity, prayed as follows:]][l] 2 "Lord, Lord, king of the heavens and sovereign of all creation, holy among the holy ones, the only ruler, almighty, give attention to us who are suffering grievously from an impious and profane man, puffed up in his audacity and power. 3 For you, the creator of all things and the governor of all, are a just ruler, and you judge those who have done anything in insolence and arrogance. 4 You destroyed those who in the past committed injustice, among whom were even giants who trusted in their strength and boldness, whom you destroyed by bringing on them a boundless flood. 5 You consumed with fire and sulfur the people of Sodom who acted arrogantly, who were notorious for their vices,[m] and you made them an example to those who should come afterward. 6 By inflicting many and varied punishments on the audacious pharaoh who had enslaved your holy people Israel, you made known your sovereignty; thus you made known your great strength. 7 And when he pursued them with chariots and a mass of troops, you overwhelmed him in the depths of the sea but carried through safely those who had put their confidence in you, the Ruler over the whole creation. 8 And when they had seen the works of your hand, they praised you, the Almighty. 9 You, O King, when you had created the boundless and immeasurable earth, chose this city and sanctified this place for your name, though you have no need of anything, and when you had glorified it by your magnificent manifestation, you made it a firm foundation for the glory of your great and honored name. 10 And because you love the house of Israel, you promised that, if we should have reverses and tribulation should overtake us, you would listen to our petition when we come to this place and pray. 11 And indeed you are faithful and true. 12 And because oftentimes when our fathers were oppressed you helped them in their humiliation and rescued them from great evils, 13 see now, O holy King, that because of our many and great sins we are crushed with suffering, subjected to our enemies, and overtaken by helplessness. 14 In our downfall this audacious and profane man undertakes to violate the holy place on earth dedicated to your glorious name. 15 For your dwelling is the heaven of heavens, unapproachable by human beings. 16 But because you were pleased that your glory should dwell among your people Israel, you sanctified this place. 17 Do not punish us for the defilement committed by these men or call us to account for this profanation; otherwise the transgressors will boast in their wrath and exult in the arrogance of their tongue, saying, 18 'We have trampled down the house of holiness as the houses of the abominations are trampled down.' 19 Wipe away our sins and disperse our errors and reveal your mercy at this hour. 20 Speedily let your mercies overtake us, put praises in the mouths of those who are downcast and broken in spirit, and give us peace."

God's Punishment of Ptolemy

21 Thereupon God, who oversees all things, the first Father of all, holy among the holy ones, having heard the lawful supplication, scourged him who had exalted himself in insolence and audacity. 22 He shook him on this side and that as a reed is shaken by the wind, so that he lay helpless on the ground and, besides being paralyzed in his limbs, was unable even to speak, since he was ensnared by a righteous judgment. 23 Then both Friends and bodyguards, seeing the severe punishment that had overtaken him and fearing that he would lose his life, quickly dragged him out, panic-stricken in their exceedingly great fear. 24 After a while he recovered, and though he had been punished, he by no means repented but went away uttering bitter threats.

Hostile Measures against the Jews

25 When he arrived in Egypt, he increased in his deeds of malice, abetted by the previously mentioned drinking companions and comrades who were strangers to everything just. 26 He was not content with his uncounted licentious deeds but even continued with such audacity that he established an evil reputation in the various localities, and many of his Friends, intently observing the king's purpose, themselves also followed his will. 27 He proposed to inflict public disgrace on the nation, and he set up a stone on the tower in the courtyard with this inscription: 28 "None of those who do not sacrifice shall enter their sanctuaries, and all Jews shall be subjected to a registration involving poll tax and to the status of slaves. Those who object to this are to be taken by force and put to death; 29 those who are registered are also to be branded on their bodies by fire with the ivy-leaf symbol of Dionysus, and they shall also be reduced to their former limited status." 30 In order that he might not appear to be an enemy of all, he inscribed below: "But if any of them prefer to join those who have been initiated into the mysteries, they shall have equal citizenship with the Alexandrians."

31 Now some, with an obvious abhorrence of the price to be exacted for maintaining the piety of their city,[b] readily gave themselves up, since they expected to enhance their reputation by their future association with the king. 32 But the majority acted firmly with a courageous spirit and did not abandon their piety, and by paying money in exchange for life they boldly attempted to save themselves from the registration. 33 They re-

mained resolutely hopeful of obtaining help, and they abhorred those who separated themselves from them, considering them to be enemies of the nation and depriving them of common fellowship and mutual help.

The Jews and Their Neighbors

3 When the impious king comprehended this situation, he became so infuriated that not only was he enraged against those Jews who lived in Alexandria but was still more bitterly hostile toward those in the countryside, and he ordered that all should promptly be gathered into one place and put to death by the most cruel means. 2 While these matters were being arranged, a hostile rumor was circulated against the people by some who conspired to do them ill, a pretext being given by a report that they hindered others[o] from the observance of their customs. 3 The Jews, however, continued to maintain goodwill and unswerving loyalty toward the dynasty, 4 but because they worshiped God and conducted themselves by his law, they kept their separateness with respect to foods. For this reason they appeared hateful to some, 5 but since they adorned their style of life with the good deeds of upright people, they were established in good repute with everyone. 6 Nevertheless, foreigners paid no heed to the good conduct of the people, which was common talk among all; 7 instead, they gossiped about the differences in worship and foods, alleging that these people were loyal neither to the king nor to his authorities but were hostile and greatly opposed to his government. So it was no ordinary reproach that they attached to them.

8 The Greeks in the city, though wronged in no way, when they saw an unexpected tumult around these people and the crowds that suddenly were forming, were not strong enough to help them, for they lived under tyranny. They did try to console them, being grieved at the situation, and expected that matters would change, 9 for such a great community ought not be left to its fate when it had committed no offense. 10 And already some of their neighbors and friends and business associates had taken some of them aside privately and were pledging to protect them and to do everything in their power to help.

Ptolemy's Decree That All Jews Be Arrested

11 Then the king, boastful of his present good fortune and not considering the might of the supreme God, but assuming that he would persevere constantly in his same purpose, wrote this letter against them:

12 "King Ptolemy Philopator to his generals and soldiers in Egypt and all its districts, greetings and good health:

13 "I myself and our government are faring well. 14 When our expedition took place in Asia, as you yourselves know, it was brought to conclusion, according to plan, by the gods' deliberate alliance with us in battle, 15 and we considered that we should not rule the nations inhabiting Coelesyria and Phoenicia by the power of the spear but should cherish them with clemency and great benevolence, gladly treating them well. 16 And when we had granted very great revenues to the temples in the cities, we came on to Jerusalem also and went up to honor the temple of those wicked people, who never cease from their folly. 17 They accepted our presence by word but insincerely by deed, because when we proposed to enter their inner temple and honor it with magnificent and most beautiful offerings, 18 they were carried away by their traditional arrogance and excluded us from entering, but they were spared the exercise of our power because of the benevolence that we have toward all. 19 By maintaining their manifest ill-will toward us, they become the only people among all nations who hold their heads high in defiance of kings and their own benefactors and are unwilling to regard any action as sincere.

20 "But we, when we arrived in Egypt victorious, accommodated ourselves to their folly and did as was proper, since we treat all nations with benevolence. 21 Among other things, we made known to all our amnesty toward their compatriots here, both because of their alliance with us and the myriad affairs liberally entrusted to them from the beginning, and we ventured to make a change, by deciding both to deem them worthy of Alexandrian citizenship and to make them participants in our regular religious rites.[p] 22 But in their innate malice they took this in a contrary spirit and disdained what is good. Since they incline constantly to evil, 23 they not only spurn the priceless citizenship, but also both by speech and by silence they abhor those few among them who are sincerely disposed toward us; in every situation, in accordance with their infamous way of life, they secretly suspect that we may soon alter our policy. 24 Therefore, fully convinced by these indications that they are ill-disposed toward us in every way, we have taken precautions so that, if a sudden disorder later arises against us, we shall not have these impious people behind our backs as traitors and barbarous enemies. 25 Therefore we have given orders that, as soon as this letter arrives, you are to send to us those who live among you, together with their wives and children, with insulting and harsh treatment and bound securely with iron fetters, to suffer the sure and shameful death that befits enemies. 26 For when all of these have been punished, we are sure that for the remaining time the government will be established for ourselves in good order and in the best state. 27 But those who shelter any of the Jews, whether old people or children or even infants, will be tortured to death with the most hateful torments, together with their families. 28 Any who are willing to give information will receive the property of those who incur the punishment, and also two thousand drachmas from the royal treasury, and will be

awarded their freedom.[q] [29] Every place detected sheltering a Jew is to be made unapproachable and burned with fire and shall become useless for all time to any mortal creature." [30] The letter was written in the above form.

The Jews Deported to Alexandria

4 In every place, then, where this decree arrived, a feast at public expense was arranged for the nations with shouts and gladness, for the inveterate enmity that had long ago been in their minds was now made evident and outspoken. [2] But among the Jews there was indescribable mourning, lamentation, and tearful cries and groans; everywhere their hearts were burning, and they groaned because of the unexpected destruction that had suddenly been decreed for them. [3] What district or city, or what habitable place at all, or what streets were not filled with mourning and wailing for them? [4] For with such a harsh and ruthless spirit were they being sent off, all together, by the generals in every city that at the sight of their unusual punishments even some of their enemies, perceiving the common object of pity before their eyes, reflected on the uncertainty of life and shed tears at the most miserable expulsion of these people. [5] For a multitude of gray-headed old men, sluggish and bent with age, was being led away, forced to march at a swift pace by the violence with which they were driven in such a shameful manner. [6] And young women who had just entered the bridal chamber[r] to share married life exchanged joy for wailing, their myrrh-perfumed hair sprinkled with ashes, and were carried away unveiled, all together raising a lament instead of a wedding song, as they were torn by the harsh treatment of foreign nations. [7] In bonds and in public view they were violently dragged along as far as the place of embarkation. [8] Their husbands, in the prime of youth, their necks encircled with ropes instead of garlands, spent the remaining days of their marriage festival in lamentations instead of feasting and youthful revelry, seeing Hades already lying at their feet. [9] They were brought on board like wild animals, driven under the constraint of iron bonds; some were fastened by the neck to the benches of the boats; others had their feet secured by unbreakable fetters, [10] and in addition they were confined under a solid deck, so that, with their eyes in total darkness, they would undergo treatment befitting traitors during the whole voyage.

The Jews Imprisoned at Schedia

[11] When these people had been brought to the place called Schedia and the voyage was concluded as the king had decreed, he commanded that they should be enclosed in the hippodrome that had been built with an immense perimeter wall in front of the city and that was well suited to make them an obvious spectacle to all coming back into the city and to those from the city[s] going out into the country, so that they could neither communicate with the king's forces nor in any way claim to be inside the circuit of the city.[t] [12] And when this had happened, the king, hearing that the Jews' compatriots from the city frequently went out in secret to lament bitterly the ignoble misfortune of their kindred, [13] ordered in his rage that these people be dealt with in precisely the same fashion as the others, not omitting any detail of their punishment. [14] The entire people was to be registered individually, not for the hard labor that has been briefly mentioned before but to be tortured with the outrages that he had ordered and at the end to be destroyed in the space of a single day. [15] The registration of these people was therefore conducted with bitter haste and zealous intensity from the rising of the sun until its setting, coming to an end after forty days but still not completed.

[16] The king was greatly and continually filled with joy, organizing banquets in honor of all his idols, with a mind alienated from truth and with a profane mouth, praising speechless things that are not able even to communicate or to come to one's help and uttering improper words against the supreme God. [17] But after the previously mentioned interval of time the scribes declared to the king that they were no longer able to take the census of the Jews because of their immense number, [18] though most of them were still in the country, some still residing in their homes, and some at the place;[u] the task was impossible for all the generals in Egypt. [19] After he had threatened them severely, charging that they had been bribed to contrive a means of escape, he was clearly convinced about the matter [20] when they said and proved that both the papyrus and the reeds they used for writing had already given out. [21] But this was an act of the invincible providence of him who was aiding the Jews from heaven.

Execution of the Jews Is Twice Thwarted

5 Then the king, completely inflexible, was filled with overpowering anger and wrath, so he summoned Hermon, keeper of the elephants, [2] and ordered him on the following day to drug all the elephants—five hundred in number—with large handfuls of frankincense and plenty of unmixed wine and to drive them in, maddened by the lavish abundance of drink, so that the Jews might meet their doom. [3] When he had given these orders he returned to his feasting, together with those of his Friends and of the army who were especially hostile toward the Jews. [4] And Hermon, keeper of the elephants, proceeded faithfully to carry out the orders. [5] The officials in charge of the Jews[v] went out in the evening and bound the hands of the wretched people and arranged for their continued custody through the night, convinced that the whole people would experience its final destruction. [6] For to the nations it appeared that the Jews were left without

any aid, because in their bonds they were forcibly confined on every side. [7] But with tears and a voice hard to silence they all called upon the Almighty Lord and Ruler of all power, their merciful God and Father, praying [8] that he avert the evil plot against them and in a glorious manifestation rescue them from the fate now prepared for them. [9] So their entreaty ascended fervently to heaven.

[10] Hermon, however, when he had drugged the pitiless elephants until they had been filled with a great abundance of wine and satiated with frankincense, presented himself at court early in the morning to report to the king about these preparations. [11] But the Lord[w] sent upon the king a portion of sleep, that beneficence that from the beginning, night and day, is bestowed by him who grants it to whomever he wishes. [12] And by the action of the Lord he was overcome by so pleasant and deep a sleep[x] that he quite failed in his lawless purpose and was completely frustrated in his inflexible plan. [13] Then the Jews, since they had escaped the appointed hour, praised their holy God and again implored him who is easily reconciled to show the might of his all-powerful hand to the arrogant nations.

[14] But now, since it was nearly the middle of the tenth hour, the person in charge of the invitations, seeing that the guests were assembled, approached the king and nudged him. [15] And when he had with difficulty roused him, he pointed out that the hour of the banquet was already slipping by, and he gave him an account of the situation. [16] The king, after considering this, returned to his drinking and ordered those present for the banquet to recline opposite him. [17] When this was done he urged them to give themselves over to feasting and to make the present portion of the banquet joyful by celebrating all the more. [18] After the party had been going on for some time, the king summoned Hermon and with bitter threats demanded to know why the Jews had been allowed to remain alive through the present day. [19] But when he, with the corroboration of the king's[y] Friends, pointed out that while it was still night he had carried out completely the order given him, [20] the king,[z] possessed by a savagery worse than that of Phalaris, said that the Jews[aa] were benefited by today's sleep, "but," he added, "tomorrow without delay prepare the elephants in the same way for the destruction of the lawless Jews!" [21] When the king had spoken, all those present readily and joyfully with one accord gave their approval, and all went to their own homes. [22] But they did not so much spend the duration of the night in sleep as in devising all sorts of insults for those they thought to be doomed.

[23] Then, as soon as the cock had crowed in the early morning, Hermon, having equipped[ab] the animals, began to move them along in the great colonnade. [24] The crowds of the city had been assembled for this most pitiful spectacle and were eagerly waiting for daybreak. [25] But the Jews, being at that very moment at their last gasp, stretched their hands toward heaven and with most tearful supplication and mournful dirges implored the supreme God to help them again at once. [26] The rays of the sun were not yet shed abroad, and while the king was receiving his Friends, Hermon arrived and invited him to come out, indicating that what the king desired was ready for action. [27] But he, on receiving the report and being struck by the unusual invitation to come out—since he had been completely overcome by incomprehension—inquired what the matter was for which this had been so zealously completed for him. [28] This was the act of God who rules over all things, for he had implanted in the king's mind a forgetfulness of the things he had previously devised. [29] Then Hermon and all the king's Friends[ac] pointed out that the animals and the armed forces were ready, "O king, according to your eager purpose."[ad] [30] But at these words he was filled with an overpowering wrath because by the providence of God his whole mind had been deranged concerning these matters, and with a threatening look he said, [31] "If your parents or children were present, I would have prepared them to be a rich feast for the savage animals instead of the Jews, who give me no ground for complaint and have exhibited to an extraordinary degree a full and firm loyalty to my ancestors. [32] In fact, you would have been deprived of life instead of these, were it not for the affection arising from our common upbringing and lifelong association." [33] So Hermon suffered an unexpected and dangerous threat, and his eyes wavered and his face fell. [34] The Friends one by one sullenly slipped away and dismissed the assembled people to their own occupations. [35] Then the Jews, on hearing what the king had said, praised the manifest Lord God, King of kings, since this also was his aid that they had received.

[36] The king, however, reconvened the banquet in the same manner and urged the guests to return to their celebrating. [37] After summoning Hermon he said in a threatening tone, "How many times, you wretched man, must I give you orders about these things? [38] Equip[ae] the elephants now once more for the destruction of the Jews tomorrow!" [39] But the Kinsmen who were at table with him, wondering at his instability of mind, remonstrated as follows: [40] "O king, how long will you put us to the test, as though we are idiots, ordering now for a third time that they be destroyed and again revoking your decree in the matter?[af] [41] As a result the city is in a tumult because of its expectation; it is crowded with mobs of people and also in constant danger of being plundered."

[42] At this the king, a Phalaris in everything and filled with madness, took no account of the changes of mind that had come about within him for the

protection of the Jews, and he firmly swore an irrevocable oath that he would send them to Hades without delay, mangled by the knees and feet of the animals, [43] and would also march against Judea and rapidly level it to the ground with fire and spear, and by burning to the ground the temple inaccessible to him[ag] would quickly render it forever empty of those who offered sacrifices there. [44] Then the Friends and Kinsmen departed with great joy, and they confidently posted the armed forces at the places in the city most favorable for keeping guard.

[45] Now when the animals had been brought virtually to a state of madness, so to speak, by the very fragrant draughts of wine mixed with frankincense and had been equipped with frightful devices, the elephant keeper [46] entered the court around dawn—the city now being filled with countless masses of people crowding their way into the hippodrome—and urged the king on to the matter at hand. [47] So he, when he had filled his impious mind with a deep rage, rushed out in full force along with the animals, wishing to witness, with invulnerable heart and with his own eyes, the grievous and pitiful destruction of the aforementioned people.

[48] When the Jews saw the dust raised by the elephants going out at the gate and by the following armed forces, as well as by the trampling of the crowd, and heard the loud and tumultuous noise, [49] they thought that this was their last moment of life, the end of their most miserable suspense, and giving way to lamentation and groans they kissed each other, embracing relatives and falling into one another's arms[ah]—parents and children, mothers and daughters, and others with babies at their breasts who were drawing their last milk. [50] Nevertheless, when they considered the help that they had received before from heaven, they prostrated themselves with one accord on the ground, removing the babies from their breasts, [51] and cried out in a very loud voice, imploring the Ruler over every power to manifest himself and be merciful to them, as they stood now at the gates of Hades.

The Prayer of Eleazar

6 Then a certain Eleazar, famous among the priests of the country, who had attained a ripe old age and throughout his life had been adorned with every virtue, directed the elders around him to stop calling upon the holy God, and he prayed as follows: [2] "King of great power, Almighty God Most High, governing all creation with mercy, [3] look upon the descendants of Abraham, O Father, upon the children of the consecrated Jacob, a people of your consecrated inheritance who are perishing as foreigners in a foreign land. [4] Pharaoh with his abundance of chariots, the former ruler of this Egypt, exalted with lawless insolence and boastful tongue, you destroyed together with his arrogant army by drowning them in the sea, manifesting the light of your mercy on the people of Israel. [5] Sennacherib exulting in his countless forces, oppressive king of the Assyrians, who had already gained control of the whole world by the spear and was lifted up against your holy city, speaking grievous words with boasting and insolence, you, O Lord, broke in pieces, showing your power to many nations. [6] The three companions in Babylon who had voluntarily surrendered their lives to the flames so as not to serve vain things, you rescued unharmed, even to a hair, moistening the fiery furnace with dew and turning the flame against all their enemies. [7] Daniel, who through envious slanders was thrown down into the ground to lions as food for wild animals, you brought up to the light unharmed. [8] And Jonah, wasting away in the belly of a huge, sea-born monster, you, Father, watched over and restored[ai] unharmed to all his family. [9] And now, you who hate insolence, all-merciful and protector of all, reveal yourself quickly to those of the people of Israel[aj] who are being outrageously treated by the abominable and lawless nations.

[10] "Even if our lives have become entangled in impieties in our exile, rescue us from the hand of the enemy and destroy us, Lord, by whatever fate you choose. [11] Let not the vain-minded praise their vanities[ak] at the destruction of your beloved ones, saying, 'Not even their god rescued them.' [12] But you, O Eternal One, who have all might and all power, watch over us now and have mercy on us who by the senseless insolence of the lawless are being deprived of life in the manner of traitors. [13] And let the nations cower today in fear of your invincible might, O honored One, who have power to save the people of Jacob. [14] The whole throng of infants and their parents entreat you with tears. [15] Let it be shown to all the nations that you are with us, O Lord, and have not turned your face from us, but just as you said, 'Not even when they were in the land of their enemies did I neglect them,' so accomplish it, O Lord."

Two Angels Rescue the Jews

[16] Just as Eleazar was ending his prayer, the king arrived at the hippodrome with the animals and all the arrogance of his forces. [17] And when the Jews observed this they raised great cries to heaven so that even the nearby valleys resounded with them and brought an uncontrollable terror upon the entire army. [18] Then the most glorious, almighty, and true God revealed his holy face and opened the heavenly gates, from which two glorious angels of fearful aspect descended, visible to all but the Jews. [19] They opposed the forces of the enemy and filled them with confusion and terror, binding them with immovable shackles. [20] Even the body of the king began to shudder, and he forgot his sullen insolence. [21] The animals turned back upon the armed forces following them and began trampling and destroying them.

[22] Then the king's anger was turned to pity and tears because of the things that he had devised earlier. [23] For when he heard the shouting and saw them all lying prostrate for destruction, he wept and angrily threatened his Friends, saying, [24] "You are committing treason and surpassing tyrants in cruelty, and even me, your benefactor, you are now attempting to deprive of dominion and life by secretly devising acts of no advantage to the kingdom. [25] Who has driven from their homes those who faithfully kept our country's fortresses and contrary to reason has gathered every one of them here? [26] Who is it that has so lawlessly encompassed with outrageous treatment those who from the beginning in every way surpassed all nations in their goodwill toward us and often have accepted willingly the worst of human dangers? [27] Loose and untie their unjust bonds! Send them back to their homes in peace, begging pardon for your former actions![al] [28] Release the children of the almighty and living God of heaven, who from the time of our ancestors until now has granted uninterrupted stability and glory to our government." [29] These then were the things he said, and the Jews, immediately released, praised their holy God and Savior, since they now had escaped death.

The Jews Celebrate Their Deliverance

[30] Then the king, when he had returned to the city, summoned the official in charge of the revenues and ordered him to provide to the Jews both wines and everything else needed for a festival of seven days, deciding that they should celebrate a festival of deliverance with all joyfulness in that same place in which they had expected to meet their destruction. [31] Accordingly, those disgracefully treated and near to Hades, or rather, who stood at its gates, arranged for a banquet of deliverance instead of a bitter and lamentable death, and full of joy they apportioned to groups of revelers the place that had been prepared for their destruction and burial. [32] They stopped their chanting of dirges and took up the song of their ancestors, praising God, their Savior and worker of wonders.[am] Putting an end to all mourning and wailing, they formed choruses[an] as a sign of peaceful joy. [33] Likewise also the king, after convening a lavish banquet to celebrate these events, gave thanks to heaven unceasingly and lavishly for the unexpected rescue that he[ao] had experienced. [34] Those who had previously believed that the Jews would be destroyed and become food for birds and had joyfully registered them groaned as they themselves were overcome by disgrace and their fire-breathing boldness was ignominiously[ap] quenched.

[35] The Jews, as we have said before, arranged the aforementioned choral group[aq] and passed the time in feasting to the accompaniment of joyous thanksgiving and psalms. [36] And when they had ordained a public rite for these things for their whole community for generations to come, they instituted the observance of the aforesaid days as a festival, not for drinking and gluttony but because of the deliverance that had come to them through God. [37] Then they petitioned the king, asking for dismissal to their homes. [38] So their registration was carried out from the twenty-fifth of Pachon to the fourth of Epeiph, for forty days, and their destruction was set for the fifth to the seventh of Epeiph, the three days [39] on which the Lord of all most gloriously revealed his mercy and rescued them all together and unharmed. [40] Then they feasted, being provided with everything by the king, until the fourteenth day, on which also they made the petition for their dismissal. [41] The king granted their request and wrote the following letter for them to the generals in the cities, magnanimously expressing his concern:

Ptolemy's Letter on Behalf of the Jews

7 "King Ptolemy Philopator to the generals in Egypt and all in authority in his government, greetings and good health: [2] "We ourselves and our children are faring well, the great God guiding our affairs according to our desire. [3] Certain of our Friends, frequently urging us with malicious intent, persuaded us to gather together the Jews of the kingdom in a body and to punish them with extraordinary penalties as traitors, [4] for they declared that our government would never be firmly established until this was accomplished because of the ill-will that these people had toward all nations. [5] They also led them out with harsh treatment as slaves, or rather as traitors, and, girding themselves with a cruelty more savage than that of Scythian custom, they tried without any inquiry or examination to put them to death. [6] But we very severely threatened them for these acts, and in accordance with the clemency that we have toward all people we barely spared their lives. Since we have come to realize that the God of heaven surely defends the Jews, always taking their part as a father does for his children, [7] and since we have taken into account the friendly and firm goodwill that they have shown toward us and our ancestors, we justly have acquitted them of every charge of whatever kind. [8] We also have ordered all people to return to their own homes, with no one in any place[ar] doing them harm at all or reproaching them for the irrational things that have happened. [9] For you should know that, if we devise any evil against them or cause them any grief at all, we always shall have not a mortal but the Ruler over every power, the Most High God, in everything and inescapably as an antagonist to avenge such acts. Farewell."

The Jews Return Home with Joy

[10] On receiving this letter the Jews[as] did not immediately hurry to make their departure, but they requested of the king that at their own hands

those of the Jewish people who had willfully transgressed against the holy God and the law of God should receive the punishment they deserved. [11] They declared that those who for the belly's sake had transgressed the divine commandments would never be favorably disposed toward the king's government. [12] The king[at] then, admitting and approving the truth of what they said, granted them a general license so that freely and without royal authority or supervision they might destroy those everywhere in his kingdom who had transgressed the law of God. [13] When they had applauded him in fitting manner, their priests and the whole multitude shouted the Hallelujah and joyfully departed. [14] And so on their way they punished and put to a public and shameful death any whom they met of their compatriots who had become defiled. [15] In that day they put to death more than three hundred men, and they kept the day as a joyful festival, since they had destroyed the profaners. [16] But those who had held fast to God even to death and had received the full enjoyment of deliverance began their departure from the city crowned with all sorts of very fragrant flowers, joyfully and loudly giving thanks to the God of their ancestors, the eternal Savior[au] of Israel, in words of praise and all kinds of melodious songs.

[17] When they had arrived at Ptolemais, called "rose-bearing" because of its characteristic feature, the fleet waited for them, in accordance with the common desire, for seven days. [18] There they celebrated their deliverance,[av] for the king had generously provided all things to them for their journey until all of them arrived at their own houses. [19] And when they had all landed in peace with appropriate thanksgiving, there also in like manner they decided to observe these days as a joyous festival during the time of their stay. [20] Then, after inscribing them as holy on a pillar and dedicating a place of prayer at the site of the banquet, they departed unharmed, free, and overjoyed, since at the king's command they had all of them been brought safely by land and sea and river to their own homes. [21] They also possessed greater prestige among their enemies, being held in honor and awe, and they were not subject at all to confiscation of their belongings by anyone. [22] Besides, they all recovered all of their property, in accordance with the registration, so that those who held any of it restored it to them with extreme fear.[aw] So the supreme God perfectly performed great deeds for their deliverance. [23] Blessed be the Deliverer of Israel through all times! Amen.

Book 91. 4 Maccabees

1 The subject that I am about to discuss is most philosophical, that is, whether pious reason is sovereign over the passions. So it is right for me to advise you to pay earnest attention to philosophy. [2] For the subject is essential to everyone who is seeking knowledge, and in addition it includes the praise of the highest virtue—I mean, of course, rational judgment. [3] If, then, it is evident that reason rules over those passions that hinder self-control, namely, gluttony and lust, [4] it is also clear that it masters the passions that hinder one from justice, such as malice, and those that stand in the way of courage, namely, anger, fear, and pain. [5] Some might perhaps ask, "If reason rules the passions, why is it not sovereign over forgetfulness and ignorance?" Their attempt at argument is ridiculous! [6] For reason does not rule its own passions but those that are opposed to justice, courage, and self-control,[a] and it is not for the purpose of destroying them but so that one may not give way to them. [7] I could prove to you from many and various examples that reason[b] is absolute ruler over the passions, [8] but I can demonstrate it best from the noble bravery of those who died for the sake of virtue: Eleazar and the seven brothers and their mother. [9] All of these, by despising sufferings that bring death, demonstrated that reason controls the passions. [10] On the anniversary of these events it is fitting for me to praise for their virtues those who, with their mother, died for the sake of nobility and goodness, and I would also call them blessed for the honor in which they are held. [11] All people, even their torturers, marveled at their courage and endurance, and they became the cause of the downfall of tyranny over their nation. By their endurance they conquered the tyrant, and thus their native land was purified through them. [12] I shall shortly have an opportunity to speak of this, but, as my custom is, I shall begin by stating my main principle, and then I shall turn to their story, giving glory to the all-wise God.

The Supremacy of Reason

[13] Our inquiry, accordingly, is whether reason is sovereign over the passions. [14] We shall decide just what reason is and what passion is, how many kinds of passions there are, and whether reason rules over all these. [15] Now reason is the mind that with sound logic prefers the life of wisdom. [16] Wisdom, next, is the knowledge of divine and human matters and the causes of these. [17] This, in turn, is education in the law, by which we learn divine matters reverently and human affairs to our advantage. [18] Now the kinds of wisdom are rational judgment, justice, courage, and self-control. [19] Rational judgment is supreme over all of these, since by means of it reason rules over the passions. [20] The two most comprehensive types of the passions are pleasure and pain, and each of these is by nature concerned with both body and soul. [21] There are many se-

quences of passions with both pleasure and pain. [22] Thus desire precedes pleasure, and delight follows it. [23] Fear precedes pain, and sorrow comes after. [24] Anger, as a person will see by reflecting on this experience, is a passion embracing pleasure and pain. [25] In pleasure there exists even a malevolent tendency, which is the most complex of all the passions. [26] In the soul it is boastfulness, love of money, thirst for honor, rivalry, and malice; [27] in the body, indiscriminate eating, gluttony, and eating alone.

[28] Just as pleasure and pain are two plants growing from the body and the soul, so there are many offshoots of these plants,[c] [29] each of which the master cultivator, reason, weeds and prunes and ties up and waters and thoroughly irrigates and so tames the jungle of habits and passions. [30] For reason is the guide of the virtues, but over the passions it is sovereign. Observe now, first of all, that rational judgment is sovereign over the passions by virtue of the restraining power of self-control. [31] Self-control, then, is dominance over the desires. [32] Some desires belong to the soul, others to the body, and reason obviously rules over both. [33] Otherwise, how is it that when we are attracted to forbidden foods we abstain from the pleasure to be had from them? Is it not because reason is able to rule over appetites? I for one think so. [34] Therefore when we crave seafood and fowl and animals and all sorts of foods that are forbidden to us by the law, we abstain because of domination by reason. [35] For the passions of the appetites are restrained, checked by the temperate mind, and all the impulses of the body are bridled by reason.

Compatibility of the Law with Reason

2 And why is it amazing that the desires of the soul for the enjoyment of beauty are rendered powerless? [2] It is for this reason, certainly, that the temperate Joseph is praised, because by mental effort[d] he overcame the prospect of pleasure. [3] For when he was young and in his prime for intercourse, by reason he nullified the frenzy[e] of the passions. [4] Reason is proved to rule not only over the frenzied urge of sexual desire but also over every desire.[f] [5] Thus the law says, "You shall not covet your neighbor's wife or anything that is your neighbor's." [6] In fact, since the law has told us not to covet, I could prove to you all the more that reason is able to control desires.

Just so it is with the passions that hinder one from justice. [7] Otherwise how could it be that someone who is habitually a solitary eater, a glutton, or even a drunkard can learn a better way, unless reason is clearly lord of the passions? [8] Thus, as soon as one adopts a way of life in accordance with the law, even though a lover of money, one is forced to act contrary to natural ways and to lend without interest to those who plead for assistance and to cancel the debt when the seventh year arrives. [9] If one is greedy, one is ruled by the law through reason so that one neither gleans the harvest nor gathers the last grapes from the vineyard.

In other matters we can recognize that reason rules the passions. [10] For the law prevails even over affection for parents, so that virtue is not abandoned for their sakes. [11] It overrules love for one's wife so that one rebukes her when she breaks the law. [12] It overrules love for children so that one punishes them for misdeeds. [13] It is sovereign over the relationship of friends so that one rebukes friends when they act wickedly. [14] Do not consider it paradoxical when reason, through the law, can prevail even over enmity. The fruit trees of the enemy are not cut down, but one preserves the property of enemies from marauders and helps raise up what has fallen.[g]

[15] It is evident that reason rules even[h] the more violent passions: lust for power, vanity, boasting, arrogance, and malice. [16] For the temperate mind repels all these malicious passions, just as it repels anger—for it is sovereign over even this. [17] When Moses was angry with Dathan and Abiram, he did nothing against them in anger but controlled his anger by reason. [18] For, as I have said, the temperate mind is able to get the better of the passions, to correct some and to render others powerless. [19] Why else did Jacob, our most wise father, censure the households of Simeon and Levi for their irrational slaughter of the entire tribe of the Shechemites, saying, "Cursed be their anger"? [20] For if reason could not control anger, he would not have spoken thus. [21] Now when God fashioned humans, he planted in them passions and inclinations, [22] but at the same time he enthroned the mind among the senses as a sacred governor over them all. [23] To the mind he gave the law, and one who lives subject to this will rule a kingdom that is temperate, just, good, and courageous.

[24] How is it then, one might say, that if reason is master of the passions, it does not control forgetfulness and ignorance? **3** [1] But this argument is entirely ridiculous, for it is evident that reason rules not over its own passions but over those of the body. [2] No one of us can eradicate that kind of desire, but reason can provide a way for us not to be enslaved by desire. [3] No one of you can eradicate anger from the mind, but reason can help to deal with anger. [4] No one of us can eradicate malice, but reason can fight at our side so that we are not overcome by malice. [5] For reason does not uproot the passions but is their antagonist.

King David's Thirst

[6] Now this can be explained more clearly by the story of King David's thirst. [7] David had been attacking the Philistines all day long and together with the soldiers of his nation had killed many of them. [8] Then when evening fell, he[i] came, sweating and quite exhausted, to the royal tent, around which the whole army of our ancestors had encamped. [9] Now all

the rest were at dinner, [10] but the king was extremely thirsty, and though springs were plentiful there, he could not satisfy his thirst from them. [11] But a certain irrational desire for the water in the enemy's territory tormented and inflamed him, undid and consumed him. [12] When his guards complained bitterly because of the king's craving, two staunch young soldiers, respecting[j] the king's desire, armed themselves fully and taking a pitcher climbed over the enemy's ramparts. [13] Eluding the sentinels at the gates, they went searching throughout the enemy camp [14] and found the spring and from it boldly brought the king a drink. [15] But David,[k] though he was burning with thirst, considered it an altogether fearful danger to his soul to drink what was regarded as equivalent to blood. [16] Therefore, opposing reason to desire, he poured out the drink as an offering to God. [17] For the temperate mind can conquer the drives of the passions and quench the flames of frenzied desires; [18] it can overthrow bodily agonies even when they are extreme and by nobility of reason spurn all domination by the passions.

An Attempt on the Temple Treasury

[19] The present occasion now invites us to a narrative demonstration of temperate reason.

[20] At a time when our ancestors were enjoying profound peace because of their observance of the law and were prospering, so that even Seleucus Nicanor, king of Asia, had both appropriated money to them for the temple service and recognized their way of life— [21] just at that time certain persons attempted a revolution against the public harmony and caused many and various disasters.

4 Now there was a certain Simon, a political opponent of the noble and good man Onias, who then held the high priesthood for life. When, despite bringing charges against him on behalf of the nation, he was unable to injure Onias, he fled the country with the purpose of betraying it. [2] So he came to Apollonius, governor of Syria, Phoenicia, and Cilicia, and said, [3] "I have come here because I am loyal to the king's government, to report that in the Jerusalem treasuries there are deposited tens of thousands in private funds that are not the property of the temple but belong to King Seleucus." [4] When Apollonius learned the details of these things, he praised Simon for his service to the king and went up to Seleucus to inform him of the rich treasure. [5] On receiving authority to deal with this matter, he proceeded quickly to our country accompanied by the accursed Simon and a very strong military force. [6] He said that he had come with the king's authority to seize the private funds in the treasury. [7] The people indignantly protested his words, considering it outrageous that those who had committed deposits to the sacred treasury should be deprived of them, and did all that they could to prevent it. [8] But, uttering threats, Apollonius went on to the temple. [9] While the priests together with women and children were imploring God in the temple to shield the holy place that was being treated so contemptuously, [10] and while Apollonius was going up with his armed forces to seize the money, angels on horseback with lightning flashing from their weapons appeared from heaven, instilling in them great fear and trembling. [11] Then Apollonius fell down half-dead in the temple area that was open to all, stretched out his hands toward heaven, and with tears begged the Hebrews to pray for him and propitiate the wrath of the heavenly army. [12] For he said that he had committed a sin deserving of death and that if he were spared he would praise the blessedness of the holy place before all people. [13] Moved by these words, although otherwise cautious lest King Seleucus suppose that Apollonius had been overcome by human treachery and not by divine justice, the high priest Onias prayed for him. [14] So Apollonius,[l] having been saved beyond all expectations, went away to report to the king what had happened to him.

Antiochus's Persecution of the Jews

[15] When King Seleucus died, his son Antiochus Epiphanes succeeded to the throne, an arrogant and terrible man [16] who removed Onias from the priesthood and appointed Onias's[m] brother Jason as high priest. [17] Jason[n] agreed that if the office were conferred on him he would pay the king three thousand six hundred sixty talents annually. [18] So the king appointed him high priest and ruler of the nation. [19] Jason[o] changed the nation's customs and altered its form of government in complete violation of the law, [20] so that he not only constructed a gymnasium at the very citadel[p] of our native land but also abolished the temple service. [21] The divine justice was angered by these acts and caused Antiochus himself to make war on them. [22] For when he was warring against Ptolemy in Egypt, he heard that a rumor of his death had spread and that the people of Jerusalem had rejoiced greatly. He speedily marched against them, [23] and after he had ravaged them he issued a decree that if any of them were found observing the ancestral law they should die. [24] When, by means of his decrees, he had not been able in any way to put an end to the people's observance of the law but saw that all his threats and punishments were being disregarded, [25] even to the extent that women, because they had circumcised their sons, were thrown headlong from heights along with their infants, though they had known beforehand that they would suffer this, [26] when, I say, his decrees were despised by the people, he himself tried through torture to compel everyone in the nation to renounce Judaism by eating defiling foods.

Antiochus's Encounter with Eleazar

5 The tyrant Antiochus, sitting in state with his counselors on a certain high place and with his armed soldiers standing around him, [2] ordered the guards to seize each and every Hebrew and to compel them to eat pork and food sacrificed to idols. [3] If any were not willing to eat defiling food, they were to be broken on the wheel and killed. [4] When many persons had been rounded up, one[q] man, Eleazar by name, leader of the flock, was brought[r] before the king. He was a man of priestly family, learned in the law, advanced in age, and known to many in the tyrant's court because of his long career.

[5] When Antiochus saw him he said, [6] "Before I begin to torture you, old man, I would advise you to save yourself by eating pork, [7] for I respect your age and your gray hairs. Although you have had them for so long a time, it does not seem to me that you are a philosopher when you observe the religion of the Jews. [8] When nature has granted it to us, why should you abhor eating the very excellent meat of this animal? [9] It is senseless not to enjoy delicious things that are not shameful and wrong to spurn the gifts of nature. [10] It seems to me that you will do something even more senseless if, by holding a vain opinion concerning the truth, you continue to despise me to your own hurt. [11] Will you not awaken from your foolish philosophy, dispel the emptiness of your reasonings, adopt a mind appropriate to your years, philosophize according to the truth of what is beneficial, [12] and have compassion on your old age by honoring my humane advice? [13] For consider this: if there is some power watching over this religion of yours, it will excuse you from any transgression that arises out of compulsion."

[14] When the tyrant urged him in this fashion to eat meat unlawfully, Eleazar asked to have a word. [15] When he had received permission to speak, he began to address the people as follows: [16] "We, O Antiochus, who have been persuaded to govern our lives by the divine law think that there is no compulsion more powerful than our obedience to the law. [17] Therefore we consider that we should not transgress it in any respect. [18] Even if, as you suppose, our law were not truly divine and we had wrongly held it to be divine, not even so would it be right for us to invalidate our reputation for piety. [19] Therefore do not suppose that it would be a petty sin if we were to eat defiling food; [20] to transgress the law in matters either small or great is of equal seriousness, [21] for in either case the law is equally despised. [22] You scoff at our philosophy as though living by it were irrational, [23] but it teaches us self-control, so that we master all pleasures and desires, and it also trains us in courage, so that we endure any suffering willingly; [24] it instructs us in justice, so that in all our dealings we give what is due;[s] and it teaches us piety, so that with proper reverence we worship the only living God.

[25] "Therefore we do not eat defiling food, for since we believe that the law was established by God, we know that the Creator of the world in giving us the law has shown sympathy toward us in accordance with nature. [26] He has permitted us to eat what will be most suitable for our lives,[t] but he has forbidden us to eat meats that would be contrary to this. [27] It would be tyrannical for you to compel us not only to transgress the law but also to eat in such a way that you may deride us for eating defiling foods, which are most hateful to us. [28] But you shall have no such occasion to laugh at me, [29] nor will I transgress the sacred oaths of my ancestors concerning the keeping of the law, [30] not even if you gouge out my eyes and burn my entrails. [31] I am not so old and cowardly as not to be young in reason on behalf of piety. [32] Therefore get your torture wheels ready and fan the fire more vehemently! [33] I do not so pity my old age as to overthrow the ancestral law by my own act. [34] I will not play false to you, O law that trained me, nor will I renounce you, beloved self-control. [35] I will not put you to shame, philosophical reason, nor will I reject you, honored priesthood and knowledge of the law. [36] You, O king,[u] shall not defile the honorable mouth of my old age nor my long life lived lawfully. [37] My ancestors will receive me as pure, as one who does not fear your violence even to death. [38] You will tyrannize the ungodly, but you shall not dominate my reasonings on behalf of piety, either by words or through deeds."

Martyrdom of Eleazar

6 When Eleazar in this manner had made eloquent response to the exhortations of the tyrant, the guards who were standing by dragged him violently to the instruments of torture. [2] First they stripped the old man, though he remained adorned with the gracefulness of his piety. [3] After they had tied his arms behind him, they flogged him from both sides, [4] while a herald who faced him cried out, "Obey the king's commands!" [5] But the courageous and noble man, like a true Eleazar,[v] was unmoved, as though being tortured in a dream, [6] yet while the old man's eyes were raised to heaven, his flesh was being torn by scourges, his blood flowing, and his sides were being cut to pieces. [7] Although he fell to the ground because his body could not endure the agonies, he kept his reason upright and unswerving. [8] One of the cruel guards rushed at him and began to kick him in the side to make him get up again after he fell. [9] But he bore the pains and scorned the punishment and endured the tortures. [10] Like a noble athlete the old man, while being beaten, was victorious over his torturers; [11] in fact, with his face bathed in sweat and gasping heavily for breath, he amazed even his torturers by his courageous spirit.

[12] At that point, partly out of pity for his old age, [13] partly out of sympathy from their acquaintance with him, partly out of admiration for his endurance, some of the king's retinue came to him and said, [14] "Eleazar, why are you so irrationally destroying yourself through these evil things? [15] We will set before you some cooked meat; save yourself by pretending to eat pork."

[16] But Eleazar, as though more bitterly tormented by this counsel, cried out, [17] "Never may we, the children of Abraham, think so basely that out of cowardice we feign a role unbecoming to us! [18] For it would be irrational if, having lived in accordance with truth up to old age and having guarded the reputation of a life lived lawfully, we should now change our course [19] and ourselves become a pattern of impiety to the young by setting them an example in the eating of defiling food. [20] It would be shameful if we should survive for a little while and during that time be a laughingstock to all for our cowardice [21] and be despised by the tyrant as unmanly by not contending even to death for our divine law. [22] Therefore, O children of Abraham, die nobly for the sake of piety! [23] And you, guards of the tyrant, why do you delay?"

[24] When they saw that he was so courageous in the face of the afflictions and that he had not been changed by their compassion, the guards brought him to the fire. [25] There they burned him with maliciously contrived instruments, threw him down, and poured stinking liquids into his nostrils. [26] When he was now burned to his very bones and about to expire, he lifted up his eyes to God and said, [27] "You know, O God, that, though I might have saved myself, I am dying in burning torments for the sake of the law. [28] Be merciful to your people, and let our punishment suffice for them. [29] Make my blood their purification, and take my life in exchange for theirs." [30] After he said this, the holy man died nobly in his tortures; even in the tortures of death he resisted, by virtue of reason, for the sake of the law.

[31] Admittedly, then, pious reason is sovereign over the passions. [32] For if the passions had prevailed over reason, we would have testified to their domination. [33] But now that reason has conquered the passions, we properly attribute to it the power to govern. [34] It is right for us to acknowledge the dominance of reason when it masters even external agonies. It would be ridiculous to deny it.[w] [35] I have proved not only that reason has mastered agonies but also that it masters pleasures and in no respect yields to them.

An Encomium on Eleazar

7 For like a most skillful pilot, the reason of our father Eleazar steered the ship of piety over the sea of the passions, [2] and though buffeted by the stormings of the tyrant and overwhelmed by the mighty waves of tortures, [3] in no way did he turn the rudder of piety until he sailed into the haven of immortal victory. [4] No city besieged with many ingenious war machines has ever held out as did that most holy man. Although his sacred life was consumed by tortures and racks, he conquered the besiegers because reason was shielding his piety. [5] For in setting his mind firm like a jutting cliff, our father Eleazar broke the maddening waves of the passions. [6] O priest, worthy of the priesthood, you neither defiled your sacred teeth nor profaned your stomach, which had room only for reverence and purity, by eating defiling foods. [7] O man in harmony with the law and philosopher of divine life! [8] Such should be those who are administrators of the law, shielding it with their own blood and noble sweat in sufferings even to death. [9] You, father, validated our obedience to the law through your endurance unto glory, and you did not abandon the holiness that you praised, but by your deeds you made your words of divine[x] philosophy credible. [10] O aged man, more powerful than tortures; O elder, fiercer than fire; O supreme king over the passions, Eleazar! [11] For just as our father Aaron, armed with the censer, ran through the multitude of the people and conquered the fiery angel, [12] so the descendant of Aaron, Eleazar, though being consumed by the fire, remained unmoved in his reason. [13] Most amazing, indeed, though he was an old man, his body no longer tense and firm,[y] his muscles flabby, his sinews feeble, he became young again [14] in spirit through reason, and by reason like that of Isaac he rendered the many-headed rack ineffective. [15] O man of blessed age and of venerable gray hair and of law-abiding life, whom the faithful seal of death has perfected!

[16] If, therefore, because of piety an aged man despised tortures even to death, most certainly pious reason is governor of the passions. [17] Some perhaps might say, "Not all have full command of their passions, because not all have prudent reason." [18] But as many as attend to piety with a whole heart, these alone are able to control the passions of the flesh, [19] since they believe that they, like our patriarchs Abraham and Isaac and Jacob, do not die to God but live to God. [20] No contradiction therefore arises when some persons appear to be dominated by their passions because of the weakness of their reason. [21] What person who lives[z] as a philosopher by the whole rule of philosophy and trusts in God [22] and knows that it is blessed to endure any suffering for the sake of virtue would not be able to overcome the passions through godliness? [23] For only the wise[aa] and courageous are masters of their passions.

Seven Brothers Defy the Tyrant

8 For this is why even the very young, by following a philosophy in accordance with pious reason, have prevailed over the most painful instruments of torture. [2] For when the tyrant was conspicuously defeated in his first attempt, being unable to compel an aged man to eat defiling foods, then in violent rage he commanded that others of the Hebrew captives be brought and that any who ate defiling food would be freed after eating, but if any were to refuse, they would be tortured even more cruelly.

[3] When the tyrant had given these orders, seven brothers—handsome, modest, noble, and accomplished in every way—were brought before him along with their aged mother. [4] When the tyrant saw them, grouped about their mother as though a chorus, he was pleased with them. And struck by their appearance and nobility, he smiled at them and summoned them nearer and said, [5] "Young men, with favorable feelings I admire each and every one of you and greatly respect the beauty and the number of such brothers. Not only do I advise you not to display the same madness as that of the old man who has just been tortured, but I also exhort you to yield to me and enjoy my friendship. [6] Just as I am able to punish those who disobey my orders, so I can be a benefactor to those who are disposed to obey me. [7] Trust me, then, and you will receive positions of authority in my government if you will renounce the ancestral tradition of your national life. [8] Enjoy your youth by adopting the Greek way of life and by changing your manner of living. [9] But if by disobedience you rouse my anger, you will compel me to destroy each and every one of you with dreadful punishments through tortures. [10] Therefore take pity on yourselves. Even I, your enemy, have compassion for your youth and handsome appearance. [11] Will you not consider this, that if you disobey, nothing remains for you but to die on the rack?"

[12] When he had said these things, he ordered the instruments of torture to be brought forward so as to persuade them out of fear to eat the defiling food. [13] When the guards had placed before them wheels and joint-dislocators, rack and hooks[ab] and catapults and caldrons, braziers and thumbscrews and iron claws and wedges and bellows, the tyrant resumed speaking: [14] "Be afraid, young fellows; whatever justice you revere will be merciful to you when you transgress under compulsion."

[15] But when they had heard the inducements and saw the dreadful devices, not only were they not afraid, but they also opposed the tyrant with their own philosophy and by their right reasoning nullified his tyranny. [16] Let us consider, on the other hand, what arguments might have been used if some of them had been cowardly and unmanly. Would they not have been the following? [17] "O wretches that we are and so senseless! Since the king has summoned and exhorted us to accept kind treatment if we obey him, [18] why do we take pleasure in vain resolves and venture upon a disobedience that brings death? [19] O men and brothers, should we not fear the instruments of torture and consider the threats of torments and give up this vanity and this arrogance that threatens to destroy us? [20] Let us take pity on our youth and have compassion on our mother's age, [21] and let us seriously consider that if we disobey we are dead! [22] Also, divine justice will excuse us for fearing the king when we are under compulsion. [23] Why do we banish ourselves from this most pleasant life and deprive ourselves of this delightful world? [24] Let us not struggle against compulsion[ac] or take hollow pride in being put to the rack. [25] Not even the law itself would consent to put us to death for fearing the instruments of torture. [26] Why does such contentiousness excite us and such a fatal stubbornness please us, when we can live in peace if we obey the king?"

[27] But the youths, though about to be tortured, neither said any of these things nor even seriously considered them. [28] For they were contemptuous of the passions and sovereign over agonies, [29] so that as soon as the tyrant had ceased counseling them to eat defiling food, all with one voice together, as from one mind, said:

9 "Why do you delay, O tyrant? For we are ready to die rather than transgress our ancestral commandments; [2] we are obviously putting our forebears to shame unless we should practice ready obedience to the law and to Moses[ad] our counselor. [3] Tyrant and counselor of lawlessness, in your hatred for us do not pity us more than we pity ourselves.[ae] [4] For we consider this pity of yours, which ensures our safety through transgression of the law, to be more grievous than death itself. [5] You are trying to terrify us by threatening us with death by torture, as though a short time ago you learned nothing from Eleazar. [6] And if, on account of piety, the aged men of the Hebrews fulfilled their pious duty while enduring torture, it would be even more fitting that we young men should die despising your coercive tortures, which our aged instructor also overcame. [7] Therefore, tyrant, put us to the test, and if you take our lives because of our piety, do not suppose that you can injure us by torturing us. [8] For we, through this severe suffering and endurance, shall have the prizes of virtue and shall be with God, on whose account we suffer; [9] but you, because of your bloodthirstiness toward us, will deservedly undergo from the divine justice eternal torment by fire."

The Torture of the First and Second Brothers

[10] When they had said these things, the tyrant was not only indignant, as at those who are disobedient, but also infuriated, as at those who are ungrateful. [11] Then at his command the guards brought forward the eldest, and having torn off his tunic, they bound his hands and arms with straps on each side. [12] When they had worn themselves out beating him with scourges, without accomplishing anything, they placed him upon the

wheel. [13] When the noble youth was stretched out around this, his limbs were dislocated, [14] and with every member disjointed he denounced the tyrant, saying, [15] "Most abominable tyrant, enemy of heavenly justice, savage of mind, you are mangling me in this manner not because I am a murderer or as one who acts impiously but because I protect the divine law." [16] And when the guards said, "Agree to eat so that you may be released from the tortures," [17] he replied, "You abominable lackeys, your wheel is not so powerful as to strangle my reason. Cut my limbs, burn my flesh, and twist my joints; [18] through all these tortures I will convince you that children of the Hebrews alone are invincible when virtue is at stake." [19] While he was saying these things, they spread fire under him, and while fanning the flames[af] they tightened the wheel further. [20] The wheel was completely smeared with blood, and the heap of coals was being quenched by the drippings of gore, and pieces of flesh were falling off the axles of the machine. [21] Although the ligaments joining his bones were already severed, the courageous youth, worthy of Abraham, did not groan, [22] but as though transformed by fire into immortality he nobly endured the rackings. [23] "Imitate me, brothers," he said. "Do not leave your post in my struggle[ag] or renounce our courageous family ties. [24] Fight the sacred and noble battle for piety. Thereby the just Providence of our ancestors may become merciful to our nation and take vengeance on the accursed tyrant." [25] When he had said this, the devout youth broke the thread of life.

[26] While all were marveling at his courageous spirit, the guards brought forward the next eldest, and after fitting themselves with iron gauntlets having sharp hooks, they bound him to the torture machine and catapult. [27] Before torturing him, they inquired if he were willing to eat, and they heard his noble decision. [28] These leopard-like beasts tore out his sinews with the iron hands, flayed all his flesh up to his chin, and tore away his scalp. But he steadfastly endured this agony and said, [29] "How sweet is any kind of death for our ancestral piety!" [30] To the tyrant he said, "Do you not think, you most savage tyrant, that you are being tortured more than I, as you see the arrogant design of your tyranny being defeated by our endurance for the sake of piety? [31] I lighten my pain by the joys that come from virtue, [32] but you suffer torture by the threats that come from impiety. You will not escape, you most abominable tyrant, the penalties of the divine wrath."

The Torture of the Third and Fourth Brothers

10 When he, too, had endured a glorious death, the third was brought forward, and many repeatedly urged him to save himself by tasting the meat. [2] But he shouted, "Do you not know that the same father begot me as well as those who died and the same mother bore me and that I was brought up on the same teachings? [3] I do not renounce the noble kinship that binds me to my brothers."[ah] [5] Enraged by the man's boldness, they disjointed his hands and feet with their instruments, dismembering him by prying his limbs from their sockets, [6] and breaking his fingers and arms and legs and elbows. [7] Since they were unable in any way to break his spirit,[ai] they abandoned the instruments[aj] and scalped him with their fingernails in a Scythian fashion. [8] They immediately brought him to the wheel, and while his vertebrae were being dislocated by this, he saw his own flesh torn all around and drops of blood flowing from his entrails. [9] When he was about to die, he said, [10] "We, most abominable tyrant, are suffering because of our godly training and virtue, [11] but you, because of your impiety and bloodthirstiness, will undergo unceasing torments."

[12] When he, too, had died in a manner worthy of his brothers, they dragged forward the fourth, saying, [13] "As for you, do not give way to the same insanity as your brothers, but obey the king and save yourself." [14] But he said to them, "You do not have a fire hot enough to make me play the coward. [15] No, by the blessed death of my brothers, by the eternal destruction of the tyrant, and by the everlasting[ak] life of the pious, I will not renounce our noble family ties. [16] Contrive tortures, tyrant, so that you may learn from them that I am a brother to those who have just now been tortured." [17] When he heard this, the bloodthirsty, murderous, and utterly abominable Antiochus gave orders to cut out his tongue. [18] But he said, "Even if you remove my organ of speech, God hears also those who are mute. [19] See, here is my tongue; cut it off, for in spite of this you will not make our reason speechless. [20] Gladly, for the sake of God, we let our bodily members be mutilated. [21] God will visit you swiftly, for you are cutting out a tongue that has been melodious with divine hymns."

The Torture of the Fifth and Sixth Brothers

11 When he, too, died, after being cruelly tortured, the fifth leaped up, saying, [2] "I will not refuse, tyrant, to be tortured for the sake of virtue. [3] I have come of my own accord so that by murdering me you will incur punishment from the heavenly justice for even more crimes. [4] Hater of virtue, hater of humankind, for what act of ours are you destroying us in this way? [5] Is it because[al] we revere the Creator of all things and live according to his virtuous law? [6] But these deeds deserve honors, not tortures."[am] [9] While he was saying these things, the guards bound him and dragged him to the catapult; [10] they tied him to it on his knees, and fitting iron clamps on them, they twisted his back[an] around the wedge on the wheel,[ao] so that he was completely curled back like a scorpion, and all

his members were disjointed. [11] In this condition, gasping for breath and in anguish of body, [12] he said, "Tyrant, they are splendid favors that you grant us against your will, because through these noble sufferings you give us an opportunity to show our endurance for the law."

[13] When he, too, had died, the sixth, a mere boy, was led forward. When the tyrant inquired whether he was willing to eat and be released, he said, [14] "I am younger in age than my brothers, but I am their equal in mind. [15] Since to this end we were born and bred, we ought likewise to die for the same principles. [16] So if you intend to torture me for not eating defiling foods, go on torturing!" [17] When he had said this, they led him to the wheel. [18] He was carefully stretched tight upon it, his back was broken, and he was roasted from underneath. [19] To his back they applied sharp spits that had been heated in the fire and pierced his ribs so that his entrails were burned through. [20] While being tortured he said, "O contest befitting holiness, in which so many of us brothers have been summoned to an arena of sufferings for the sake of piety and in which we have not been defeated! [21] For pious knowledge, O tyrant, is invincible. [22] I also, equipped with nobility, will die with my brothers, [23] and I myself will bring a great avenger upon you, you inventor of tortures and enemy of those who are truly pious. [24] We six boys have overthrown your tyranny. [25] Since you have not been able to persuade us to change our mind or to force us to eat defiling foods, is not this your downfall? [26] Your fire is cold to us, and the catapults painless, and your violence powerless. [27] For it is not the guards of the tyrant but those of the divine law that are set over us; therefore we hold fast to invincible reason."

The Torture of the Seventh Brother

12 When he, too, thrown into the caldron, had died a blessed death, the seventh and youngest of all came forward. [2] Even though the tyrant had been vehemently reproached by the brothers, he felt strong compassion for this child when he saw that he was already in fetters. He summoned him to come nearer and tried to persuade him, saying, [3] "You see the result of your brothers' stupidity, for they died in torments because of their disobedience. [4] You, too, if you do not obey, will be miserably tortured and die before your time, [5] but if you yield to persuasion you will be my friend and a leader in the government of the kingdom." [6] When he had thus appealed to him, he sent for the boy's mother to show compassion on her who had been bereaved of so many sons and to influence her to persuade the surviving son to obey and save himself. [7] But after his mother had exhorted him in the Hebrew language, as we shall tell a little later, [8] he said, "Let me loose, let me speak to the king and to all his Friends who are with him." [9] Extremely pleased by the boy's declaration, they freed him at once. [10] Running to the nearest of the braziers, [11] he said, "You profane tyrant, most impious of all the wicked, since you have received good things and also your kingdom from God, were you not ashamed to murder his servants and torture on the wheel the athletes of piety? [12] Because of this, justice[ap] has laid up for you a more intense and eternal fire and tortures, and these throughout all time will never let you go. [13] As a man, were you not ashamed, you most savage beast, to cut out the tongues of people who have feelings like yours and are made of the same elements as you and to maltreat and torture them in this way? [14] Surely they by dying nobly fulfilled their pious duty to God, but you will wail bitterly for having killed without cause the contestants for virtue." [15] Then because he, too, was about to die, he said, [16] "I do not desert the excellent example[aq] of my brothers, [17] and I call on the God of our ancestors to be merciful to our nation,[ar] [18] but on you he will take vengeance both in this present life and when you are dead." [19] After he had uttered these imprecations, he flung himself into the braziers and so ended his life.[as]

Reason's Sovereignty in the Seven

13 Since, then, the seven brothers despised sufferings even unto death, everyone must concede that pious reason is sovereign over the passions. [2] For if they had been slaves to their passions and had eaten defiling food, we would say that they had been conquered by these passions. [3] But in fact it was not so. Instead, by reason, which is praised before God, they prevailed over their passions. [4] The supremacy of the mind over these cannot be overlooked, for the brothers[at] mastered both passions and pains. [5] How, then, can one fail to confess the sovereignty of right reason over passion in those who were not turned back by fiery agonies? [6] For just as towers jutting out over harbors hold back the threatening waves and make it calm for those who sail into the inner basin, [7] so the seven-towered right reason of the youths, by fortifying the harbor of piety, conquered the tempest of the passions. [8] For they constituted a holy chorus of piety and emboldened one another, saying, [9] "Brothers, let us die like brothers for the sake of the law; let us imitate the three youths in Assyria who despised the same ordeal[au] of the furnace. [10] Let us not be cowardly in the demonstration of our piety." [11] While one said, "Courage, brother," another said, "Bear up nobly," [12] and another reminded them, "Remember whence you came, and the father by whose hand Isaac would have submitted to being slain for the sake of piety." [13] Each of them and all of them together looking at one another, cheerful and undaunted, said, "Let us with all our hearts consecrate ourselves to God, who gave us our lives,[av] and let us use our bodies as a bulwark for the law. [14] Let us not fear him who thinks he is killing us, [15] for great is the soul's contest and

the danger of eternal torment lying before those who transgress the commandment of God. [16] Therefore let us put on the full armor of mastery of the passions that divine reason provides. [17] For if we so die,[aw] Abraham and Isaac and Jacob will welcome us, and all the fathers will praise us." [18] Those who were left behind said to each of the brothers who were being dragged away, "Do not put us to shame, brother, or betray the brothers who have died before us."

[19] You are not ignorant of the affection of family ties, which the divine and all-wise Providence has bequeathed through the fathers to their descendants and which was implanted in the mother's womb. [20] There the brothers spent the same length of time and were shaped during the same period of time, and growing from the same blood and through the same life, they were brought to the light of day. [21] When they were born after an equal time of gestation, they drank milk from the same fountains. From such embraces brotherly loving souls are nourished, [22] and they grow stronger from this common nurture and daily companionship and from both general education and our discipline in the law of God.

[23] Therefore, when sympathy and brotherly affection had been so established, the seven brothers were the more sympathetic to one another. [24] Since they had been educated by the same law and trained in the same virtues and brought up together in right living, they loved one another all the more. [25] A common zeal for nobility strengthened their goodwill toward one another and their concord, [26] because they could make their brotherly love more fervent with the aid of piety. [27] But although nature and companionship and virtuous habits had augmented the affection of family ties, those who were left endured for the sake of piety, watching their brothers being maltreated and tortured to death.

[14] Furthermore, they encouraged them to face the torture so that they not only despised their agonies but also mastered the passions of brotherly love.

[2] O reason,[ax] more royal than kings and freer than the free! [3] O sacred harmony of the seven brothers, well-tuned in regard to piety! [4] None of the seven youths proved coward or shrank from death, [5] but all of them, as though running the course toward immortality, hastened to death by torture. [6] Just as the hands and feet are moved in harmony with the guidance of the mind, so those holy youths, as though moved by an immortal spirit of piety, agreed to go to death for its sake. [7] O most holy seven, brothers in harmony! For just as the seven days of creation move in choral dance around piety, [8] so these youths, forming a chorus of seven,[ay] encircled the fear of tortures and dissolved it. [9] Even now, we ourselves shudder as we hear of the suffering of these young men; they not only saw what was happening, not only heard the direct word of threat, but also bore the sufferings steadfastly, and in agonies of fire at that. [10] What could be more excruciatingly painful than this? For the power of fire is intense and swift, and it consumed their bodies quickly.

An Encomium on the Mother of the Seven

[11] Do not consider it amazing that reason had full command over these men in their tortures, since even the mind of woman despised more diverse agonies, [12] for the mother of the seven young men bore up under the rackings of each one of her children.

[13] Observe how complex is a mother's love for her children, which draws everything toward a sympathy felt in her inmost parts. [14] Even unreasoning animals, as well as humans, have a sympathy and parental love for their offspring. [15] For example, among birds, the ones that are tame protect their young by building on the housetops, [16] and the others, by building at the tops of mountains and the depths of chasms, in holes of trees, and on treetops, hatch the nestlings and ward off the intruder. [17] If they are not able to keep the intruder[az] away, they do what they can to help their young by flying in circles around them in the anguish of love, warning them with their own calls. [18] And why is it necessary to demonstrate sympathy for children by the example of unreasoning animals, [19] since even bees at the time for making honeycombs defend themselves against intruders and, as though with an iron dart, sting those who approach their hive and defend it even to the death? [20] But sympathy for her children did not sway the mother of the young men; she was of the same mind as Abraham.

[15] O reason of the children, tyrant over the passions! O piety, more desirable to the mother than her children! [2] Two courses were open to this mother, that of piety and that of preserving her seven sons for a time, as the tyrant had promised. [3] She loved piety more, the piety that preserves them for eternal life according to God's promise.[ba] [4] In what manner might I express the passions of parents who love their children? We impress upon the character of a small child a wondrous likeness both of mind and of form. Especially is this true of mothers, who because of their birth pangs have a deeper sympathy toward their offspring than do the fathers. [5] For to the extent that mothers are of tender spirit and bear more children, so much the more attached are they to their children. [6] The mother of the seven boys, more than any other mother, loved her children. In seven pregnancies she had implanted in herself tender love toward them, [7] and because of the many pains she suffered with each of them she had sympathy for them, [8] yet because of the fear of God she disdained the temporary safety of her children. [9] Not only so, but also because of the nobility of her sons and their ready obedience to the law,

she felt a greater tenderness toward them. [10] For they were just and self-controlled and courageous and magnanimous and loved their brothers and their mother so that they obeyed her even to death in keeping the ordinances.

[11] Nevertheless, though so many factors influenced the mother to suffer with them out of love for her children, in the case of none of them were the various tortures strong enough to pervert her reason. [12] But each child separately and all of them together the mother urged on to death for piety's sake. [13] O sacred nature, parental affection, tender love toward offspring, nursing, and indomitable maternal passions! [14] This mother, who saw them tortured and burned one by one, for piety's sake did not change her attitude. [15] She watched the flesh of her children being consumed by fire, their toes and fingers scattered[bb] on the ground, and the flesh of the head to the chin exposed like masks.

[16] O mother, tried now by more bitter pains than even the birth pangs you suffered for them! [17] O woman, who alone gave birth to such perfect piety! [18] Neither when the firstborn breathed his last, it did not turn you aside, nor when the second in torments looked at you piteously nor when the third expired, [19] nor did you weep when you looked at the eyes of each one in his tortures gazing boldly at the same agonies and saw in their nostrils the signs of the approach of death. [20] When you saw the flesh of children burned[bc] upon the flesh of other children, severed hands upon hands, scalped heads upon heads, and corpses fallen on other corpses, and when you saw the place filled with many spectators because of the children's torments, you did not shed tears. [21] Neither the melodies of sirens nor the songs of swans attract the attention of their hearers as did the voices of the children in torture calling to their mother. [22] How great and how many torments the mother then suffered as her sons were tortured on the wheel and with the hot irons! [23] But pious reason, giving her heart a man's courage in the very midst of her passions, strengthened her to disregard, for the time, her parental love.

[24] Although she witnessed the destruction of seven children and the ingenious and various rackings, this noble mother disregarded all these[bd] because of faith in God. [25] For as in the council chamber of her own soul she saw mighty advocates—nature, family, parental love, and the instruments of torture awaiting her children— [26] this mother held two ballots, one bearing death and the other deliverance for her children. [27] She did not approve the deliverance that would preserve the seven sons for a short time, [28] but as the daughter of God-fearing Abraham she remembered his fortitude.

[29] O mother of the nation, vindicator of the law, and defender of piety who carried away the prize of the contest in your heart! [30] O more noble than males in steadfastness and more courageous than men in endurance! [31] Just as Noah's ark, carrying the world in the universal flood, stoutly endured the waves, [32] so you, O guardian of the law, overwhelmed from every side by the flood of your passions and the violent winds—the torture of your sons—endured nobly and withstood the wintry storms raging on piety's account.

[16] If, then, a woman advanced in years and mother of seven sons endured seeing her children tortured to death, it must be admitted that pious reason is sovereign over the passions. [2] Thus I have demonstrated not only that men have ruled over the passions but also that a woman has despised the fiercest tortures. [3] The lions surrounding Daniel were not so savage nor was the raging fiery furnace of Mishael so intensely hot as was her innate parental love consuming her as she saw her seven sons tortured in such varied ways. [4] But the mother quenched so many and such great passions by pious reason.

[5] Consider this also: If this woman, though a mother, had been fainthearted, she would have mourned over them and perhaps spoken as follows: [6] "O how wretched am I and thrice-wretched over and over! After bearing seven children, I am now the mother of none! [7] O seven child-births all in vain, seven profitless pregnancies, fruitless nurturings and wretched nursings! [8] In vain, my sons, I endured many birth pangs for you and the more grievous anxieties of your upbringing. [9] Alas for my children, some unmarried, others married and without offspring.[be] I shall not see your children or have the happiness of being called grandmother. [10] Alas, I who had so many and beautiful children am a widow and alone, with many sorrows.[bf] [11] And when I die, I shall have none of my sons to bury me."

[12] Yet that holy and God-fearing mother did not wail with such a lament for any of them, nor did she dissuade any of them from dying, nor did she grieve as they were dying. [13] On the contrary, as though having a mind like adamant and giving rebirth for immortality to the whole number of her sons, she implored them and urged them on to death for the sake of piety. [14] O mother, soldier of God in the cause of piety, elder and woman! By steadfastness you have conquered even a tyrant, and in word and deed you have proved more powerful than a man. [15] For when you and your sons were arrested together, you stood and watched Eleazar being tortured and said to your sons in the Hebrew language, [16] "My sons, noble is the contest to which you are called to bear witness for the nation. Fight zealously for our ancestral law. [17] For it would be shameful if, while an aged man endures such agonies for the sake of piety, you young men were to be terrified by tortures. [18] Remember that it is through God that

you have had a share in the world and have enjoyed life, [19] and therefore you ought to endure every suffering for the sake of God. [20] For his sake also our father Abraham was zealous to sacrifice his son Isaac, the ancestor of our nation, and when Isaac saw his father's hand wielding a knife[bg] and descending upon him, he did not cower. [21] Daniel the righteous was thrown to the lions, and Hananiah, Azariah, and Mishael were hurled into the fiery furnace and endured it for the sake of God. [22] You, too, must show the same faithfulness toward God and not be grieved. [23] It is unreasonable for people who have knowledge of piety not to withstand pain."

[24] By these words the mother of the seven encouraged and persuaded each of her sons to die rather than violate God's commandment. [25] They knew also that those who die for the sake of God live to God, as do Abraham and Isaac and Jacob and all the patriarchs.

17 Some of the guards said that when she also was about to be seized and put to death she threw herself into the flames so that no one might touch her body.

[2] O mother, who with your seven sons nullified the violence of the tyrant, frustrated his evil designs, and showed the nobility of your faith! [3] Nobly set like a roof on the pillars of your sons, you held firm and unswerving against the earthquake of the tortures. [4] Take courage, therefore, O holy-minded mother, maintaining firm an enduring hope in God. [5] The moon in heaven with the stars is not so majestic as you, who, after lighting the way of your star-like seven sons to piety, stand in honor before God and are firmly set in heaven with them. [6] For your children were true descendants of father Abraham.[bh]

The Effect of the Martyrdoms

[7] If it were possible for us to paint the history of your piety as an artist might, would not those who beheld it shudder as they saw the mother of the seven children enduring their varied tortures to death for the sake of piety? [8] Indeed, it would be proper to inscribe on their tomb these words as a reminder to the people of our nation:[bi]

[9] "Here lie buried an aged priest and an aged woman and seven children because of the violence of the tyrant who wished to destroy the way of life of the Hebrews. [10] They vindicated their nation, looking to God and enduring torture even to death."

[11] Truly the contest in which they were engaged was divine, [12] for on that day virtue gave the awards and tested them for their endurance. The prize was immortality in endless life. [13] Eleazar was the first contestant, the mother of the seven sons entered the competition, and the brothers contended. [14] The tyrant was the antagonist, and the world and the human race were the spectators. [15] Reverence for God was victor and gave the crown to its own athletes. [16] Who did not admire the athletes of the divine[bj] legislation? Who were not amazed?

[17] The tyrant himself and all his council marveled at their endurance, [18] because of which they now stand before the divine throne and live the life of eternal blessedness. [19] For Moses says, "All who are consecrated are under your hands." [20] These, then, who have been consecrated for the sake of God are honored not only with this honor but also by the fact that because of them our enemies did not rule over our nation, [21] the tyrant was punished, and the homeland purified—they having become, as it were, a ransom for the sin of our nation. [22] And through the blood of those pious ones and their death as an atoning sacrifice, divine Providence preserved Israel that previously had been mistreated.

[23] For the tyrant Antiochus, when he saw the courage of their virtue and their endurance under the tortures, proclaimed their endurance to his soldiers as an example, [24] and this made them high-minded and courageous for infantry battle and siege, and he ravaged and conquered all his enemies.

18 O Israelite children, offspring of the seed of Abraham, obey this law and exercise piety in every way, [2] knowing that pious reason is master of the passions, not only of sufferings from within but also of those from without.

[3] Therefore those who gave over their bodies in suffering for the sake of piety were not only admired by mortals but also were deemed worthy to share in a divine inheritance. [4] Because of them the nation gained peace, and by reviving observance of the law in the homeland they ravaged the enemy. [5] The tyrant Antiochus was both punished on earth and is being chastised after his death. Since in no way whatever was he able to compel the Israelites to adopt foreign ways and to abandon their ancestral customs, he left Jerusalem and marched against the Persians.

The Mother's Address to Her Children

[6] The mother of seven sons expressed also these principles to her children: [7] "I was a pure virgin and did not go outside my father's house, but I guarded the rib from which woman was made.[bk] [8] No seducer corrupted me on a desert plain, nor did the destroyer, the deceitful serpent, defile the purity of my virginity. [9] In the time of my maturity I remained with my husband, and when these sons had grown up their father died. A fortunate man was he, who lived out his life with good children and did not have the grief of bereavement. [10] While he was still with you, he taught you the Law and the Prophets. [11] He read to you about Abel slain by Cain and Isaac who was offered as a burnt offering and about Joseph in prison. [12] He told you of the zeal of Phinehas, and he taught you about

Hananiah, Azariah, and Mishael in the fire. [13] He praised Daniel in the den of the lions and blessed him. [14] He reminded you of the scripture of Isaiah, which says, 'Even though you go through the fire, the flame shall not consume you.' [15] He sang to you songs of the psalmist David, who said, 'Many are the afflictions of the righteous.' [16] He recounted to you Solomon's proverb, 'There[bl] is a tree of life for those who do his will.' [17] He confirmed the query of Ezekiel, 'Shall these dry bones live?' [18] For he did not forget to teach you the song that Moses taught, which says, [19] 'I kill, and I make alive; this is your life and the length of your days.' "

[20] O bitter was that day—and yet not bitter—when that bitter tyrant of the Greeks quenched fire with fire in his cruel caldrons and in his burning rage brought those seven sons of the daughter of Abraham to the catapult and back again to more[bm] tortures, [21] pierced the pupils of their eyes and cut out their tongues, and put them to death with various tortures. [22] For these crimes divine justice pursued and will pursue the accursed tyrant. [23] But the sons of Abraham with their victorious mother are gathered together into the chorus of the fathers and have received pure and immortal souls from God, [24] to whom be glory forever and ever. Amen.

Book 92. The Gospel of Thomas

These are the secret words which the living Jesus spoke, and Didymus Judas Thomas wrote them down.

1 And he said: He who shall find the interpretation of the words shall not taste of death.

2 Jesus said: He who seeks, let him not cease seeking until: finds; and when he finds he will be troubled, and if he is troubled, he will be amazed, and he will reign over the All.

3 Jesus said: If those who lead you say unto you: Behold, the Kingdom is in heaven, then the birds of the heaven will be before you. If they say unto you: It is in the sea, then the fish will be before you. But the Kingdom is within you, and it is outside of you. When you know yourselves, then shall you be known, and you shall know that you are the sons of the living Father. But if ye do not know yourselves, then you are in poverty, and you are poverty.

4 Jesus said: The man aged in his days will not hesitate to ask a little child of seven days about the place of life, and he shall live. For there are many first who shall be last, and they shall become a single one.

5 Jesus said: Know what is before thy face, and what hidden from thee shall be revealed unto thee; for there is nothing hidden which shall not be made manifest.

6 His disciples asked him and said unto him: Wilt thou that we fast? And how shall we pray? Shall we give alms? And what rules shall we observe in eating? Jesus said: Do not lie; and that which you hate, do not do. For all things are revealed before heaven. For there is nothing hidden which shall not be manifest, and there is nothing covered which shall remain without being uncovered.

7 Jesus said: Blessed is the lion which the man shall eat, and the lion become man; and cursed is the man whom the lion shall eat, and the lion become man.

8 And he said: Man is like a wise fisherman, who cast his net into the sea and drew it up from the sea full of small fish. Among them the wise fisherman found a large good fish. He threw down all the small fish into the sea; he chose the large fish without trouble. He that hath ears to hear, let him hear.

9 Jesus said: Behold, the sower went forth, he filled his hand, he cast. Some fell upon the road; the birds came and gathered them. Others fell on the rock, and sent no root down to the earth nor did they sprout any ear up to heaven. And others fell on the thorns; they choked the seed, and the worm ate them. And others fell on the good earth, and brought forth good fruit unto heaven, some sixtyfold and some an hundred and twenty -fold.

10 Jesus said: I have cast fire upon the world, and behold I guard it until it is ablaze.

11 Jesus said: This heaven shall pass away, and that which above it shall pass away; and they that are dead are not alive and they that live shall not die. In the days when you were eating that which is dead, you were making it alive. When you come in the light, what will you do? On the day when you were one, you became two. But when you have become two, what will you do?

12 The disciples said to Jesus: We know that thou wilt go from us. Who is he who shall be great over us? Jesus said to them: In the place to which you come, you shall go to James the Just for whose sake heaven and earth came into being.

13 Jesus said to his disciples: Make a comparison to me, and tell me whom I am like. Simon Peter said to him: Thou art like a righteous angel. Matthew said to him: Thou art like a wise man of understanding. Thomas said to him: Master, my mouth will no wise suffer that I say whom thou art like. Jesus said: I am not thy master, because thou hast drunk, thou hast become drunk from the bubbling spring which I have measured out. And he took him, went aside, and spoke to him three words. Now when Thomas came to his companions, they asked him: What did Jesus say

unto thee? Thomas said to them: If I tell you one of the words which he said to me, you will take up stones and throw them me; and a fire will come out of the stones and burn you up.

14 Jesus said to them: If you fast, you will beget a sin for yourselves; and if you pray, you will be condemned; and if you give alms, you will do an evil to your spirits. And if you go into any land and travel in its regions, if they receive you eat what they set before you. Heal the sick among them. For that which goes into your mouth will not defile you, but that which comes forth from your mouth, that is what will defile you.

15 Jesus said: When you see him who was not born of woman, throw yourselves down upon your face and worship him. He is your Father.

16 Jesus said: Perhaps men think that I am come to cast peace upon the world, and know not that I am come to cast divisions upon the earth, fire, sword, war. For there shall be five in a house; there shall be three against two, and two against three, the father against the son and the son against the father, and they shall stand as solitaries.

17 Jesus said: I will give you that which eye has not seen, an ear has not heard, and hand has not touched, and which has not entered into the heart of man.

18 The disciples said to Jesus: Tell us how our end shall be. Jesus said: Have you then discovered the beginning, that you seek after the end? For where the beginning is, there shall the end be. Blessed is he who shall stand in the beginning, and he shall know the end and shall not taste of death.

19 Jesus said: Blessed is he who was before he came into being. If you become my disciples and hear my words, these stones shall minister unto you. For you have five trees in Paradise which do not move in summer or in winter, and their leaves do not fall. He who knows them shall not taste of death.

20 The disciples said to Jesus: Tell us what the kingdom of heaven is like. He said to them: It is like a grain of mustard-seed, smaller than all seeds; but when it falls on the earth which is tilled, it puts forth a great branch, and becomes shelter for the birds of heaven.

21 Mary said to Jesus: Whom are thy disciples like? He said They are like little children dwelling in a field which is not theirs. When the owners of the field come, they will say: Yield up to us our field. They are naked before them, to yield it up to them and to give them back their field. Therefore I say: If the master of the house knows that the thief is coming, he will keep watch before he comes, and will not let him dig into his house of his kingdom to carry off his vessels. You, then, be watchful over against the world. Gird up your loins with great strength, that the brigands may not find a way to come at you, since the advantage for which you look they will find. May there be among you a man of understanding! When the fruit was ripe, he came quickly, his sickle in his hand, and reaped it. He that hath ears to hear, let him hear.

22 Jesus saw some infants at the breast. He said to his disciples: These little ones at the breast are like those who enter into the kingdom. They said to him: If we then be children, shall we enter the kingdom? Jesus said to them: When you make the two one, and when you make the inside as the outside, and the outside as the inside, and the upper side as the lower; and when you make the male and the female into a single one, that the male be not male and the female female; when you make eyes in the place of an eye, and a hand in place of a hand, and a foot in place of a foot, an image in place of an image, then shall you enter [the kingdom].

23 Jesus said: I shall choose you, one out of a thousand, and two out of ten thousand, and they shall stand as a single one.

24 His disciples said: Teach us concerning the place where thou art, for it is necessary for us to seek after it. He said to them: He that hath ears, let him hear. There is a light within a man of light, and it gives light to the whole world. If it does not give light, there is darkness.

25 Jesus said: Love thy brother as thy soul; keep him as the apple of thine eye.

26 Jesus said: The mote which is in thy brother's eye, thou seest; but the beam which is in thine eye, thou seest not. When thou dost cast out the beam from thine own eye, then wilt thou see to cast out the mote from thy brother's eye.

27 Jesus said: If you fast not from the world, you will not find the kingdom; if you keep not the Sabbath as Sabbath, you will not see the Father.

28 Jesus said: I stood in the midst of the world, and I appeared to them in flesh. I found them all drunk, I found none among them thirsting; and my soul was afflicted for the sons of men, for they are blind in their heart and they do not see. For empty came they into the world, seeking also to depart empty from the world. But now they are drunk. When they have thrown off their wine, then will they repent.

29 Jesus said: If the flesh has come into being because of the spirit, it is a marvel; but if the spirit has come into being because of the body, it is a marvel of marvels. But as for me, I marvel at this, how this great wealth has settled in this poverty.

30 Jesus said: Where there are three gods, they are gods; where there are two or one, I am with him.

31 Jesus said: No prophet is acceptable in his village; a physician does not heal those who know him.

32 Jesus said: A city that is built on a high mountain and fortified cannot fall, nor can it remain hidden.

33 Jesus said: What thou shalt hear in thine ear, proclaim to the other ear on your roof-tops. For no man lights a lamp and sets it under a bushel, nor does he put it in a hidden place; but he sets it upon the lamp-stand, that all who go in and come out may see its light.

34 Jesus said: If a blind man lead a blind man, both fall into a pit.

35 Jesus said: It is not possible for anyone to go into the strong man's house and take it or him by force, unless he bind his hands; then he will plunder his house.

36 Jesus said: Be not anxious from morning to evening and from evening to morning about what you shall put on.

37 His disciples said: On what day wilt thou be revealed us, and on what day shall we see thee? Jesus said: When you unclothe yourselves and are not ashamed, and take your garments and lay them beneath your feet like little children, and tread upon them, then [shall ye see] the Son of the living One, and ye shall not fear.

38 Jesus said: Many times have you desired to hear these words which I speak unto you, and you have none other from whom to hear them. Days will come when you will seek after me, and you will not find me.

39 Jesus said: The Pharisees and the scribes have received the keys of knowledge; they have hidden them. They did not go in, and those who wanted to go in they did not allow. But you be ye wise as serpents and innocent as doves.

40 Jesus said: A vine was planted apart from the Father, and since it is not established it will be pulled up by its roots and destroyed.

41 Jesus said: He who has in his hand, to him shall be given; and he who has not, from him shall be taken even the little that he has.

42 Jesus said: Become passers-by.

43 His disciples said to him: Who art thou, that thou shouldst say these things to us? Jesus said to them From what I say unto you, you do not understand who I am, but you have become as the Jews; for they love the tree and hate its fruit, and they love the fruit and hate the tree.

44 Jesus said: He who blasphemes against the Father will be forgiven, and he who blasphemes against the Son will be forgiven but he who blasphemes against the Holy Spirit will not be forgiven, either on earth or in heaven.

45 Jesus said: They do not gather grapes from thorns, no pluck figs from camel-thistles; they do not yield fruit. A good man brings forth a good thing from his treasure; a bad man bring forth evil things from his evil treasure which is in his heart, and he says evil things; for out of the abundance of his heart he brings forth evil things.

46 Jesus said: From Adam to John the Baptist there is none born of woman who is higher than John the Baptist, so that his eyes will not be broken? But I have said, He who shall be among you as a little one shall know the kingdom, and shall be higher than John.

47 Jesus said: It is not possible for a man to ride two horses or draw two bows, and it is not possible for a servant to serve two masters; or he will honour the one and insult the other. A man does not drink old wine and immediately desire to drink new wine; and they do not pour new wine into old skins, lest they burst, nor do they pour old wine into new skins, lest it spoil. They do not sew an old patch on a new garment, for a rent will come.

48 Jesus said: If two make peace with one another in this or house, they shall say to the mountain: Be moved, and it shall be moved.

49 Jesus said: Blessed are the solitary and the elect, for you shall find the kingdom; for you came forth thence, and shall go there again.

50 Jesus said: If they say to you: Whence have you come?, tell them: We have come from the light, the place where the light came into being through itself alone. It [stood], and it revealed itself in their image. If they say to you: Who are you?, say: We are his sons, and we are the elect of the living Father. If they ask you: What is the sign of your Father in you?, tell them: It is a movement and a rest.

51 His disciples said to him: On what day will the rest of the dead come into being? And on what day will the new world come? He said to them: That which ye await has come, but ye know it not.

52 His disciples said to him: Twenty-four prophets spoke in Israel, and they all spoke concerning lit. in thee. He said them: You have neglected him who is alive before you, and have spoken about the dead.

53 His disciples said to him: Is circumcision profitable or not? He said to them: Were it profitable, their father would beget them from their mother circumcised. But the true circumcision in spirit has proved entirely profitable lit.: has found usefulness altogether.

54 Jesus said: Blessed are the poor, for yours is the kingdom of heaven.

55 Jesus said: He who shall not hate his father and his mother cannot be my disciple, and he who does not hate his brethren and his sisters and take up his cross like me shall not be worthy of me.

56 Jesus said: He who has known the world has found corpse, and he who has found a corpse, the world is not worthy of him.

57 Jesus said: The kingdom of the Father is like a man who had [good] seed. His enemy came by night, he sowed a weed among the good seed. The man did not allow them to pull up the weed. He said to them: Lest perhaps you go to pull up the weed, and pull up the wheat with it.

For on the day of harvest the weeds will be manifest; they will be pulled up and burned.

58 Jesus said: Blessed is the man who has suffered; he has found the life.

59 Jesus said: Look upon the living One so long as you live, that you may not die and seek to see him, and be unable to see.

60 They saw a Samaritan carrying a lamb going into Judaea. He said to his disciples: Why does he carry the lamb? They said to him: That he may kill it and eat it. He said to them: So long as it is alive he will not eat it, but if he kill it and it become a corpse. They said: Otherwise he will not be able to do it. He said to them: You also, seek for yourselves a place within for rest, lest you become a corpse and be eaten.

61 Jesus said: Two shall rest upon a bed; one shall die, the other live. Salome said: Who art thou; O man? And whose son? Thou hast mounted my bed, and eaten from my table. Jesus said to her I am he who is from that which is equal; to me was given of the things of my Father. Salome said I am thy disciple. Jesus said to her Therefore I say, when it is equal it will be filled with light, but when it is divided it will be filled with darkness

62 Jesus said: I tell my mysteries to those [who are worthy of my] mysteries. What thy right hand shall do, let not thy left hand know what it does.

63 Jesus said: There was a rich man who had many possessions. He said: I will use my possessions that I may sow and reap and plant, and fill my barns with fruit, that I may have need of nothing. These were his thoughts in his heart. And in that night he died. He that hath ears, let him hear.

64 Jesus said: A man had guests, and when he had prepared the dinner he sent his servant to summon the guests. He came to the first; he said to him: My master summons thee. He said: I have money with some merchants. They are coming to me in the evening. I will go and give them orders. I pray to be excused from the dinner. He went to another; he said to him: My master has summoned thee. He said to him: I have bought a house, and they ask me for a day. I shall not have time. He came to another; he aid to him: My master summons thee. He said to him: My friend is about to be married, and I am to hold a dinner. I shall not be able to come. I pray to be excused from the dinner. He went to another; he said to him: My master summons thee. He said him: I have bought a village; I go to collect the rent. I shall not be able to come. I pray to be excused. The servant came, he said to his master: Those whom thou didst summon to the dinner have excused themselves. The master said to his servant: Go out to the roads. Bring those whom thou shall find, that they may dine. The buyers and the merchants [shall] not [enter] the places of my Father.

65 He said: A good man had a vineyard. He gave it to husbandmen that they might work it, and he receive its fruit their hand. He sent his servant, that the husbandmen might give him the fruit of the vineyard. They seized his servant, they beat him, and all but killed him. The servant came and told his master. His master said: Perhaps they did not know him. He sent another servant; the husbandmen beat the other also. Then the master sent his son. He said: Perhaps they will reverence my son. Those husbandmen, since they knew that he was the heir the vineyard, they seized him and killed him. He that hath ears, let him hear.

66 Jesus said: Teach me concerning this stone which the builders rejected; it is the cornerstone.

67 Jesus said: He who knows the All but fails to know himself lacks everything.

68 Jesus said: Blessed are you when they hate you, and persecute you, and do not find a place in the spot where they persecuted you.

69 Jesus said: Blessed are they who have been persecuted in their heart; these are they who have known the Father in truth. Blessed are they that hunger, that they may fill the belly him who desires.

70 Jesus said: When you bring forth that in yourselves, that which you have will save you. If you do not have that in yourselves, that which you do not have in you will kill you.

71 Jesus said: I will des[troy this] house, and none shall able to build it [again].

72 [A man said] to him: Speak to my brethren, that they may divide my father's possessions with me. He said to him: O man, who made me a divider? He turned to his disciples and said to them: I am not a divider, am I?

73 Jesus said: The harvest indeed is great, but the labourers are few; but pray the Lord, that he send forth labourers into the harvest.

74 He said: Lord, there are many about the well, but no one in the well.

75 Jesus said: There are many standing at the door, but the solitary are they who shall enter the bridal chamber.

76 Jesus said: The kingdom of the Father is like a merchant was who had a load of goods and found a pearl. That merchant was wise. He sold the load, and bought for himself the pearl alone. You also, seek after his treasure which does not perish but endures, where moth does not enter to devour, nor does worm destroy.

77 Jesus said: I am the light that is over them all. I am the All; the All has come forth from me, and the All has attained unto me. Cleave a piece of wood: I am there. Raise up the stone, an ye shall find me there.

78 Jesus said: Why came ye forth into the field? To see reed shaken by the wind? And to see a man clothed in soft raiment?[Behold, your] kings

and your great men are they who are clothed in soft [raiment], and they [shall] not be able to know the truth.

79 A woman in the crowd said to him: Blessed is the womb which bore thee, and the breasts which nourished thee. He said to her: Blessed are they who have heard the word of the Father and have kept it in truth. For there shall be days when you will say: Blessed is that womb which has not conceived, and those breasts which have not given suck.

80 Jesus said: He who has known the world has found the body, and he who has found the body, the world is not worthy of him.

8 I Jesus said: He who has become rich, let him become king, and he who has power let him deny.

82 Jesus said: He who is near to me is near the fire, and he who is far from me is far from the kingdom.

83 Jesus said: The images are revealed to the man, and the light which is in them is hidden in the image of the light of the Father. He shall be revealed, and his image is hidden by his light.

84 Jesus said: When you see your likeness, you rejoice; but when you see your images which came into being before you — they neither die nor are made manifest — how much will you bear?

85 Jesus said: Adam came into being out of a great power and a great wealth, and yet he was not worthy of you. For if he tad been worthy, he would not have tasted of death.

86 Jesus said: [The foxes have] the[ir holes] and the birds have [their nest, but the Son of Man has no place to lay his head and rest.

87 Jesus said: Wretched is the body which depends upon a body, and wretched is the soul which depends on these two.

88 Jesus said: The angels come to you, and the prophets, and they shall give you what belongs to you; and you also, give the what is in your hands, and say to yourselves: On what day do they come and take what is theirs?

89 Jesus said: Why do you wash the outside of the cup? Do you not understand that he who made the inside is also he who made the outside?

90 Jesus said: Come unto me, for easy is my yoke and my lordship is gentle, and you shall find rest for yourselves.

91 They said to him: Tell us who thou art, that we may believe in thee. He said to them: You test the face of the heaven and the earth, and him who is before you you do not know, and you know not to test this moment.

92 Jesus said: Seek, and ye shall find; but those things concerning which ye asked me in those days, I did not tell you then. Now I wish to tell them, and ye seek not after them.

93 Jesus said: Give not that which is holy to the dogs, lest they cast them on the dung- heap; cast not the pearls to the swine lest they grind it [to bits].

94 Jesus [said]: He who seeks shall find, and he who knock to him it shall be opened.

95 [Jesus said]: If you have money, do not lend at interest, but give [it] to him from whom you will not receive them back.

96 Jesus [said]: The kingdom of the Father is like a woman who took a little leaven and [hid] it in meal; she made large loaves of it. He that hath ears, let him hear.

97 Jesus said: The kingdom of the [Father] is like a woman; carrying a jar full of meal and walking a long way. The handle the jar broke; the meal poured out behind her on the road. She was unaware, she knew not her loss. When she came into her house, she put down the jar and found it empty.

98 Jesus said: The kingdom of the Father is like a man who wanted to kill a great man. He drew the sword in his house and drove it into the wall, that he might know that his hand would be strong. Then he slew the great man.

99 The disciples said to him: Thy brethren and thy mother are standing outside. He said to them: Those here who do the will of my Father, these are my brethren and my mother; these are they who shall enter into the kingdom of my Father.

100 They showed Jesus a gold piece and said to him: They who belong to Caesar demand tribute from us. He said to them: What belongs to Caesar give to Caesar, what belongs to God give to God, and what is mine give unto me.

101 Jesus said He who shall not hate his father and: mother like me cannot be my [disciple], and he who shall [not] love [his father] and his mother like me cannot be my [disciple]; for my mother [. ..] but my true [mother] gave me life.

102 And Jesus said: Woe to them, the Pharisees! For they are like a dog sleeping in the manger of the cattle; for he neither eats nor does he let the cattle eat.

103 Jesus said: Blessed is the man who knows in what part the robbers are coming, that he may rise and gather his [domain] and gird up his loins before they come in.

104 They said [to him]: Come, let us pray today and fast. Jesus said: What then is the sin that I have done, or wherein have I been vanquished? But when the bridegroom comes forth from the bridal chamber, then let them fast and pray.

105 Jesus said: He who shall know father and mother shall be called the son of a harlot.

106 Jesus said: When you make the two one, you shall become sons of man, and when you say: Mountain, be moved, it shall be moved.

I07 Jesus said: The kingdom is like a shepherd who had hundred sheep. One of them, the biggest, went astray. He left the ninety-nine and sought after the one till he found it. When he had laboured, he said to the sheep: I love thee more than the ninety-nine.

I08 Jesus said: He who shall drink from my mouth shall become like me; I myself will become he, and the hidden thing shall be revealed to him.

109 Jesus said: The kingdom is like a man who had in his field a [hidden] treasure about which he did not know; and [after] he died he left it to his [son. The] son also did not know; he took possession of that field and sold it. The man who bough it came to plough, and [found] the treasure. He began to lend money at interest to whomsoever he chose.

110 Jesus said: He who has found the world and become rich, let him deny the world.

111 Jesus said: The heavens shall be rolled up and the earth before your face, and he who lives in the living One shall neither see death nor fear; because Jesus says: He who shall find himself, of him the world is not worthy.

112 Jesus said: Woe to the flesh which depends upon the soul; woe to the soul which depends upon the flesh.

113 His disciples said to him: On what day will the kingdom come? : It cometh not with observation. They will not say: Lo, here! or: Lo, there! But the kingdom of the Father is spread out upon the earth, and men do not see it.

114 Simon Peter said to them: Let Mary go forth from among us, for women are not worthy of the life. Jesus said: Behold, I shall lead her, that I may make her male, in order that she also may become a living spirit like you males. For every woman who makes herself male shall enter into the kingdom of heaven.

Book 93. The Gospel of Philip

Gentiles, Hebrews, and Christians

51 A Hebrew creates a Hebrew, and [those] of this kind are called "a proselyte." But a [proselyte] doesn't create (another) proselyte. They're like […] and they create others […] 52 it's good enough for them that they come into being.

The slave seeks only freedom; they don't seek their master's property. But the son isn't just a son; he claims his father's inheritance for himself. Those who inherit the dead are themselves dead, and they inherit the dead. Those who inherit the living are themselves alive, and they inherit (both) the living and the dead. The dead can't inherit anything, because how can the dead inherit? If the dead inherits the living they won't die, but the dead will live even more! A gentile doesn't die, because they've never lived in order that they may die. Whoever has believed in the Truth has lived, and is at risk of dying, because they're alive since the day Christ came. The world is created, the cities gentrified, and the dead carried out.

When we were Hebrews, we were fatherless – we had (only) our mother. But when we became Christians, we gained both father and mother.

Life, Death, Light, and Darkness

Those who sow in the winter reap in the summer. The winter is the world, the summer the other age. Let's sow in the world so that we may reap in the summer. Because of this, it's not right for us to pray in the winter. The summer follows the winter. But if someone reaps in the winter they won't reap, but uproot, as this kind won't produce fruit […] it doesn't just come out […] but in the other Sabbath […] it's fruitless.

Christ came 53 to buy some, to save others, and to redeem yet others. He bought those who were strangers, made them his own, and set them apart as a pledge as he wanted to. It wasn't just when he appeared that he laid down his life when he wanted to, but since the day the world came into being he laid down his life when he wanted to. Then he came first to take it, since it had been pledged. It was dominated by the robbers that had captured it, but he saved it; and those who are good in the world he redeemed, as well as those who are bad.

The light and the darkness, the right and the left, are brothers of each other. They're inseparable. So, those who are good aren't good, those who are bad aren't bad, nor is life (really) life, nor is death (really) death. Because of this, each one will be dissolved into its origin from the beginning. But those who are exalted above the world are indissoluble and eternal.

Names

The names that are given to those who are worldly are very deceptive, because they turn the heart away from what's right to what's not right, and someone who hears "God" doesn't think of what's right but thinks of what's not right. So also with "the Father," "the Son," "the Holy Spirit," "the life," "the light," "the resurrection," "the church," and all the others – they don't think of [what's right] but think of what's [not] right, [unless] they've learned what's right. The [names that were heard] exist in the world […] 54 [deceive. If they existed] in the (eternal) age they wouldn't have been used as names in the world, nor would they have been placed among worldly things. They have an end in the (eternal) age.

There's one name that isn't uttered in the world: the name which the Father gave to the Son. It's exalted over everything; it's the Father's name, because the Son wouldn't have become father unless he had taken the name of the Father. Those who have this name know it, but don't say it; and those who don't have it, don't know it. But Truth brought names into the world for us, because it's impossible for us to learn it (Truth) without these names. There's only one Truth, but it's many things for us, to teach this one thing in love through many things.

The Rulers

The rulers wanted to deceive humanity, because they (the rulers) saw that they (humanity) had a kinship with those that are truly good. They took the name of those that are good and gave it to those that aren't good, to deceive them (humanity) by the names and bind them to those that aren't good; and then, what a favor they do for them! They take them from those that aren't good and place them among those that are good. They knew what they were doing, because they wanted to take those who were free and place them in slavery forever. There are powers that exist […] humanity, not wanting them to be [saved], so that they may be […] because if humanity [was saved], sacrifices [wouldn't] happen […] and animals offered 55 up to the powers, because those to whom offerings were made were animals. They were offered up alive, but when they were offered up they died. A human was offered up to God dead, and he lived.

Before Christ came, there wasn't any bread in the world – just as Paradise, where Adam was, had many trees to feed the animals but no wheat to feed humanity. Humanity used to eat like the animals, but when Christ, the perfect human, came, he brought bread from heaven so that humanity would be fed with the food of humanity.

The rulers thought they did what they did by their own power and will, but the Holy Spirit was secretly accomplishing everything it wanted to through them. Truth, which has existed from the beginning, is sown everywhere; and many see it being sown, but few see it being reaped.

The Virgin Birth

Some say that "Mary conceived by the Holy Spirit." They're wrong; they don't know what they're saying. When did a woman ever conceive by a woman? "Mary is the virgin whom no power defiled" is the great testimony of those Hebrews who became (the first) apostles and (the) apostolic (successors). The virgin whom no power defiled […] the powers defiled themselves.

And the Lord [wouldn't] have said, "my [Father who is in] heaven" unless [he] had another father. Instead, he would simply have said ["my Father."] The Lord said to the [disciples, "…] 56 [from] every [house] and bring into the Father's house, but don't steal (anything) from the Father's house or carry it away."

Jesus, Christ, Messiah, Nazarene

"Jesus" is a hidden name; "Christ" is a revealed name. So "Jesus" is not translated, but he's called by his name "Jesus." But the name "Christ" in Syriac is "Messiah," in Greek "Christ," and all the others have it according to their own language. "The Nazarene" reveals what's hidden. Christ has everything within himself, whether human or angel or mystery, and the Father.

The Resurrection

Those who say that the Lord died first and then arose are wrong, because he arose first and (then) he died. Anyone who doesn't first acquire the resurrection won't die. As God lives, that one would /die\!

No one will hide something great and valuable in a great thing, but often someone has put countless thousands into something worth (only) a penny. It's the same with the soul; a valuable thing came to be in a contemptible body.

Some are afraid that they'll arise naked. So they want to arise in the flesh, and [they] don't know that those who wear the [flesh] are naked. Those […] to strip themselves naked [are] not naked. "Flesh [and blood won't] inherit [God's] kingdom." What is it that 57 won't inherit? That which is on us. But what is it, too, that will inherit? It is Jesus' (flesh) and blood. Because of this, he said, "Whoever doesn't eat my flesh and drink my blood doesn't have life in them." What's his flesh? It's the Word, and his blood is the Holy Spirit. Whoever has received these have food, drink, and clothing.

(So) I myself disagree with the others who say, "It won't arise." Both (sides) are wrong. You who say, "the flesh won't arise," tell me what will arise, so that we may honor you. You say, "the spirit in the flesh and this other light in the flesh." (But) this saying is in the flesh too, because whatever you say, you can't say apart from the flesh. It's necessary to arise in this flesh, since everything exists in it. In this world, people are better than the clothes they wear. In the kingdom of heaven, the clothes are better than the people who wear them.

Everything is purified by water and fire – the visible by the visible, the hidden by the hidden. Some things are hidden by things that are visible. There's water in water, and fire in chrism.

Seeing Jesus

Jesus took all of them by stealth, because he didn't appear as he was, but he appeared as [they'd] be able to see him. He appeared to them (in) [all these] (ways): he [appeared] to [the] great as great. He [appeared] to the small as small. He [appeared] **58** [to the] angels as an angel, and to humans as a human. So his Word hid itself from everyone. Some did see him, thinking they were seeing themselves. But when he appeared to his disciples in glory on the mountain, he wasn't small. He became great, but he made the disciples great (too) so that they would be able to see him as great.

He said on that day in the Eucharist, "You who've united the perfect light with the Holy Spirit, unite the angels with us too, with the images!"

Don't despise the lamb, because without him it's impossible to see the door. No one will be able to approach the king naked.

Father, Son, and Holy Spirit

The children of the heavenly human are more numerous than those of the earthly human. If Adam has so many children, even though they die, how many children does the perfect human have – those who don't die, but are begotten all the time?

The father makes a son, but it's impossible for a son to make a son, because it's impossible for someone who's been born to beget (sons); the son begets brothers, not sons. All who are begotten in the world are begotten physically, and the others in […] are begotten by him […] out there to the human […] in the […] heavenly place […] it from the mouth […] the Word came out from there **59** they would be nourished from the mouth [and] become perfect. The perfect are conceived and begotten through a kiss. Because of this we kiss each other too, conceiving from the grace within each other.

There were three who traveled with the Lord all the time: His mother Mary, her sister, and Magdalene, who is called his companion; because Mary is his sister, his mother, and his partner.

"The Father" and "The Son" are single names; "the Holy Spirit" is a double name, because they're everywhere. They're in heaven, they're below, they're hidden, and they're revealed. The Holy Spirit is revealed below and hidden in heaven.

Those who are holy are served through the evil powers, because the Holy Spirit has blinded them so that they think they're serving a (regular) human when they're (really) working for the holy ones. So a disciple asked the Lord one day about a worldly thing. He told him, "Ask your Mother, and she'll give you from someone else."

The apostles said to the disciples, "May our entire offering acquire salt." They called […] "salt." Without it, the offering doesn't [become] acceptable. But Wisdom [is] childless; because of this [she's] called […], this of salt, the place they'll […] in their own way. The Holy Spirit […] **60** […] many children.

What belongs to the father belongs to the son, and he himself – the son – as long as he's little, is not entrusted with what's his. When he becomes a man, his father gives him everything that belongs to him.

Those who've been begotten by the Spirit and go astray, go astray through it too. Because of this, through this one Spirit it blazes, that is, the fire, and it's extinguished.

Echamoth is one thing and Echmoth another. Echamoth is simply Wisdom, but Echmoth is the Wisdom of Death, which knows death. This is called "the little Wisdom."

Humans and Animals

There are animals that submit to humans, like the calf, the donkey, and others of this kind. Others are not submissive, and live alone in the wilderness. Humanity ploughs the field with the submissive animals, and consequently nourishes itself and the animals, whether submissive or not. That's what it's like with the perfect human: they plough with the submissive powers, preparing for everyone that will exist. So because of this the whole place stands, whether the good or the evil, and the right and the left. The Holy Spirit shepherds everyone and rules all the powers – those that are submissive, those that [aren't], and those that are alone – because truly it […] confines them [so that …] want to, they won't be able to [leave].

[The one who's been] formed [is beautiful, but] you'd find his children being **61** noble forms. If he weren't formed but begotten, you'd find that his seed was noble. But now he was formed, and he begot. What nobility is this? First there was adultery, and then murder; and he (Cain) was begotten in adultery, because he was the son of the serpent. Because of this he became a murderer like his father too, and he killed his brother (Abel). Every partnership between those who are dissimilar is adultery.

Becoming Christians

God is a dyer. Like the good dyes – they're called true – die with what's been dyed in them, so it is with those who were dyed by God. Because his dyes are immortal, they become immortal by means of his colors. But God baptizes in water.

It's impossible for anyone to see anything that really exists unless they become like them. It's not like the person in the world who sees the sun without becoming a sun, and who sees heaven and earth and everything else without becoming them. That's the way it is. But you've seen something of that place, and have become them. You saw the Spirit, you became spirit; you saw Christ, you became Christ; you saw [the Father, you] will become father. Because of this, [here] you see everything and

don't [see yourself], but you see yourself [there], because you'll [become] what you see.

Faith receives; love gives. [No one will be able to] **62** [receive] without faith, and no one will be able to give without love. So we believe in order that we may receive, but we give in order that we may love, since anyone who doesn't give with love doesn't get anything out of it. Whoever hasn't received the Lord is still a Hebrew.

The apostles before us called (him) "Jesus the Nazarene Messiah," that is, "Jesus the Nazarene Christ." The last name is "Christ," the first is "Jesus," the middle one is "the Nazarene." "Messiah" has two meanings: both "Christ" and "the measured." "Jesus" in Hebrew is "the redemption." "Nazara" is "the truth." So "the Nazarene" is "the truth." "Christ" is the one who was measured. "The Nazarene" and "Jesus" are the ones who were measured.

A pearl doesn't become less valuable if it's cast down into the mud, nor will it become more valuable if it's anointed with balsam; but it's valuable to its owner all the time. That's what it's like with God's children: no matter where they are, they're still valuable to their Father.

If you say, "I'm a Jew," no one will be moved. If you say, "I'm a Roman," no one will be disturbed. If you say, "I'm a Greek," "a Barbarian," "a slave," ["a free person,"] no one will be troubled. [If] you [say,] "I'm a Christian," the […] will tremble. If only [… of] this kind, this one [who …] won't be able to endure [hearing] his name.

God is a human-eater. **63** Because of this, the human is [sacrificed] to him. Before the human was sacrificed, animals were sacrificed, because those to whom they were sacrificed weren't gods.

Vessels of glass and pottery come into being by means of fire. But if glass vessels break they're remade, because they came into being by means of a breath, but if pottery vessels break they're destroyed, because they came into being without breath.

A donkey turning a millstone traveled a hundred miles. When it was released, it still found itself in the same place. Many people travel, but don't get anywhere. When evening came, they saw neither city nor village, nor anything created or natural, nor power nor angel. The wretches worked in vain.

The Eucharist is Jesus, because in Syriac he's called "Pharisatha," that is, "the one who's spread out," because Jesus came to crucify the world.

The Lord went into Levi's place of dyeing. He took seventy-two colors and threw them into the vat. He brought all of them out white and said, "That's the way the Son of Humanity has come [as] a dyer."

The Wisdom who is called "the barren" is the Mother [of the angels] and [the] companion of the [… Mary] Magdalene [… loved her] more than the disciples [… he] kissed her on her [… many] times. The rest of […] **64** […] they said to him, "Why do you love her more than all of us?" The Savior said to them in reply, "Why don't I love you like her? When a person who's blind and one who sees are both in the dark, they're no different from one another. When the light comes, the one who sees will see the light, and the one who's blind will remain in the dark."

The Lord said, "Blessed is the one who exists before existing, because they who exist did exist, and will exist."

The superiority of humanity isn't revealed, but exists in what's hidden. So it (humanity) masters animals that are stronger, that are greater in terms of that which is revealed and that which is hidden. This allows them to survive; but if humanity separates from them (the animals), they kill, bite, and eat each other, because they didn't find food. But now they've found food because humanity has worked the earth.

If someone goes down into the water and comes up without having received anything, and says, "I'm a Christian," they've borrowed the name at interest. But if they receive the Holy Spirit, they have the gift of the name. Whoever has received a gift doesn't have it taken away, but whoever has borrowed it at interest has to give it back. That's what it's like when someone comes into being in a mystery.

The Mystery of Marriage

[The] mystery of marriage [is] great, because [without] it the world would [not exist]; because [the] structure of [the world …], but the structure [… the marriage]. Think about the [intimate …] defiled, because it has […] power. Its image **65** exists in a [defilement].

The impure spirits take male and female [forms]. The males are those that are intimate with the souls which dwell in a female form, and the females are those that mingle with those in a male form through disobedience. No one will be able to escape being bound by them without receiving a male power and a female one – the groom and the bride – in the image of the bridal chamber. When the foolish females see a male sitting alone, they jump on him, play with him, and defile him. In the same way, when the foolish males see a beautiful female sitting alone, they seduce and coerce her, wanting to defile her. But if they see the husband and his wife sitting together, the females can't go inside the husband, nor the males inside the wife. That's what it's like when the image unites with the angel; no one will be able to dare to go inside the [male] or the female.

Overcoming the World

Whoever comes out of the world can no longer be bound because they were in the world. They're revealed to be above the desire of the [… and] fear. They're master over […] they're better than envy. If […] come, they (the powers) bind and choke [them]. How will [they] be able to escape the [great powers …]? How will they be able to […]? There are some who [say], "We're faithful," in order that […] **66** [impure spirit] and demon, because if they had the Holy Spirit, no impure spirit would cling to them. Don't fear the flesh, nor love it. If you fear it, it'll master you; if you love it, it'll swallow and choke you.

Someone exists either in this world, or in the resurrection, or in the middle places. May I never be found there! There's both good and evil in this world. Its good things aren't good, and its evil things aren't evil. But there's an evil after this world which is truly evil: that which is called "the middle." It's death. While we're in this world, it's right for us to acquire the resurrection for ourselves, so that when we're stripped of the flesh we'll be found in the rest and not travel in the middle, because many stray on the way.

It's good to come out of the world before one sins. There are some who neither want to nor can, but others who, if they wanted to, (still) wouldn't benefit, because they didn't act. The wanting makes them sinners. But (even) if they don't want, justice will (still) be hidden from them. It's not the will, and it's not the act.

An apostle saw [in a] vision some people confined in a burning house, and bound with burning […], thrown […] of the burning […] them in […] and they said to them [… able] to be saved […] they didn't want to, and they received […] punishment, which is called **67** "the [outer] darkness," because it […].

The soul and the spirit came into being from water and fire. The offspring of the bridal chamber was from water and fire and light. The fire is the chrism, the light is the fire. I'm not talking about that formless fire, but of the other one whose form is white, which is bright and beautiful, and which gives beauty.

Truth didn't come into the world naked, but it came in types and images. It (the world) won't receive it in any other way. There's a rebirth, and an image of rebirth. It's truly necessary to be begotten again through the image. What's the resurrection and the image? Through the image it's necessary for it to arise. The bridal chamber and the image? Through the image it's necessary for them to enter the truth, which is the restoration. It's not only necessary for those who acquire the name of the Father and the Son and the Holy Spirit, but they too have been acquired for you. If someone doesn't acquire them, the name will also be taken from them. But they're received in the chrism of the […] of the power of the cross. The apostles called this "[the] right and the left," because this person is no longer a [Christian], but a Christ.

The Lord [did] everything in a mystery: a baptism, a chrism, a Eucharist, a redemption, a bridal chamber […] he [said], "I came to make [the below] like the [above and the outside] like the [inside, and to unite] them in the place." […] here through [types …] Those who say, "[…] there's one above […]," they're wrong, because] what's revealed **68** is that […], that [which] is called "what's below," and what's hidden is to it what's above it, because it's good, and they say "inside and what's outside and what's outside the outside." So the Lord called destruction "the outer darkness." There's nothing outside it.

He said, "My Father who's hidden." He said, "Enter your closet, shut the door behind you, and pray to your Father who's hidden," that is, the one who's within all of them. But the one who's within all of them is the fullness. Beyond that, there's nothing else within. This is what's called "that which is above them."

Before Christ, some came from where they were no longer able to enter, and they went where they were no longer able to come out. Then Christ came. He brought out those who entered, and brought in those who went out.

Adam, Eve, and the Bridal Chamber

When Eve was [in] Adam, death didn't exist. When she separated from him, death came into being. If he [enters] again and receives it for himself, there will be no death.

"[My] God, my God, why, Lord, [have] you forsaken me?" He said this on the cross, because he was divided in that place. […] that he was begotten through that which […] from God. The […] from the dead […] exists, but […] he's perfect […] of flesh, but this […] is true flesh […] isn't true, [but …] image of the true.

69 A bridal chamber isn't for the animals, nor for the slaves, nor for the impure, but it's for free people and virgins.

We're begotten again through the Holy Spirit, but we're begotten through Christ by two things. We're anointed through the Spirit. When we were begotten, we were united.

Without light, no one can see themselves in water or in a mirror; nor again will you be able to see in light without water or mirror. Because of this, it's necessary to baptize in both: in the light and in the water, but the light is the chrism.

There were three houses of offering in Jerusalem. The one which opens to the west is called "the Holy." The other one, which opens to the south, is called "the Holy of the Holy." The third, which opens to the east, is called "the Holy of the Holies," the place where the high priest enters alone. Baptism is "the Holy" house. [Redemption] is "the Holy of the Holy." "The [Holy] of the Holies" is the bridal chamber. The [baptism] includes the resurrection [with] the redemption. The redemption is in the bridal chamber. But [the] bridal chamber is better than […] You won't find its […] those who pray […] Jerusalem. […] Jerusalem who [… Jerusalem], being seen […] these that are called "[the Holies] of the Holies" [… the] veil torn […] bridal chamber except the image [… which] **70** [is above. So] its veil was torn from top to bottom, because it was necessary for some from below to go up above.

The powers can't see those who have put on the perfect light, and they can't bind them. But one will put on that light in the mystery of the union. If the female wouldn't have been separated from the male, she wouldn't have died with the male. His separation was the beginning of death. Because of this, Christ came to repair the separation that existed since the beginning by uniting the two again. He'll give life to those who died as a result of the separation by uniting them. Now, the wife unites with her husband in the bridal chamber, and those who have united in the bridal chamber won't be separated any longer. Because of this, Eve separated from Adam, because she didn't unite with him in the bridal chamber.

It was through a breath that Adam's soul came into being. Its partner was the spirit. That which was given to him was his mother. His soul was [taken] and he was given [life] (Eve) in its place. When he was united […] words that were better than the powers, and they envied him […] spiritual partner […] hidden […] that is, the […] themselves […] bridal chamber so that […] Jesus appeared [… the] Jordan, the [fullness of the kingdom] of heaven. He who [was begotten] before everything **71** was begotten again. He [who was anointed] first was anointed again. He who was redeemed, redeemed again.

If it's necessary to speak of a mystery: the Father of everything united with the virgin who came down, and a fire enlightened him on that day. He revealed the great bridal chamber, so his body came into being on that day. He came out of the bridal chamber like the one who came into being from the groom and the bride. That's the way Jesus established everything within himself. It's also necessary for each of the disciples to enter into his rest through these things.

Adam came into being from two virgins: from the Spirit and from the virgin earth. So Christ was begotten from a virgin, to rectify the fall that occurred in the beginning.

There are two trees growing in Paradise. One begets [animals], the other begets humans. Adam [ate] from the tree that begot animals, [and he] became an animal, and he begot [animals]. So Adam's children worship the [animals]. The tree […] is fruit […] this they […] ate the […] fruit of the […] beget humans […] of the human of […] God makes the human, [… humans] make [God]. **72** That's what it's like in the world: humans make gods and worship their creation. It would be better for the gods to worship humans!

The truth is that the work of humankind comes from their power, so they're called "the powers." Their works are their children, who come into being through rest; so their power exists in their works, but the rest is revealed in their children. And you'll find that this extends to the image. And this is the person in the image: they do their works through their power, but they beget their children through rest.

In this world, the slaves work for the free. In the kingdom of heaven, the free will serve the slaves. The children of the bridal chamber will serve the children of the [marriage. The] children of the bridal chamber have a [single] name: "Rest." [Being] together they don't need to take form, [because they have] contemplation […] they're many […] with those who are in the […] the glories of the […] not […] them […] go down to the [water …] they'll redeem themselves […] that is, those who have […] in his name, because he said: "[That's the way] we'll fulfill **73** all righteousness."

Baptism, Chrism, Eucharist, Bridal Chamber

Those who say that they'll die first and (then) they'll rise are wrong. If they don't first receive the resurrection while they're living, they won't receive anything when they die. It's the same when they talk about baptism and they say "Baptism is a great thing," because those who receive it will live.

Philip the apostle said, "Joseph the carpenter planted a garden because he needed wood for his trade. It was he who made the cross from the trees he planted, and his offspring hung from what he planted. His offspring was Jesus, and the plant was the cross." But the Tree of Life is in the middle of Paradise, and from the olive tree came the chrism, and from that the resurrection.

This world eats corpses. All that are eaten in it die also. Truth eats life, so no one nourished by [Truth] will die. Jesus came from that place, he brought food from there, and to those who wanted, he gave them [to eat, so that] they won't die.

[God …] a Paradise, [human …] Paradise, there are […] and […] of God […] those in [it …] I wish that [Paradise …] they'll say to me, "[… eat] this," or "don't eat [that …] **74** wish." The tree of knowledge is the place where I'll eat everything. It killed Adam, but here it makes humanity live. The Law was the tree. It has the power to give the knowledge of good and evil. It neither kept them from evil nor placed them in the good, but it created death for those who ate from it; because when it said, "Eat this, don't eat that," it became the beginning of death.

The chrism is better than baptism, since we're called "Christians" because of the chrism, not because of baptism. And it was because of the chrism that Christ was named, because the Father anointed the Son, and the Son anointed the apostles, and the apostles anointed us. Whoever is anointed has everything: the resurrection, the light, the cross, the Holy Spirit. The Father gave this to him in the bridal chamber, and he received it. The Father was in the Son and the Son in the Father. This is [the kingdom] of heaven.

The Lord said [it] well: "Some went to the kingdom of heaven laughing and they came out [...] a Christian [...] and as soon as [... went down] into the water and he [...] everything about [...] it's [a] game, [but ... disregard] this [...] to the kingdom of [heaven ...] if they disregard [...] and if they scorn it as a game, [... out] laughing. It's the same way **75** with the bread and the cup and the oil, though there's one better than these.

The world came into being through a transgression, because the one who created it wanted to create it imperishable and immortal. He fell away and didn't get what he wanted, because the world wasn't imperishable, and the one who created it wasn't imperishable; because things aren't imperishable, but rather children. Nothing will be able to receive imperishability without becoming a child. But whoever can't receive, how much more will they be unable to give?

The cup of prayer has wine and water, since it's laid down as the type of the blood over which they give thanks. It fills with the Holy Spirit, and it belongs to the completely perfect human. Whenever we drink this, we'll receive the perfect human. The living water is a body. It's necessary for us to put on the living human. So coming down to the water, they strip themselves so that they'll put on that one.

A horse begets a horse, a human begets a human, and a god begets god. It's the same way with [the groom] and [brides too]. They [come into being] from the [...] No Jew [...] from [...] exists and [...] from the Jews [...] the Christians [...] called these [...] "the chosen race of [...]" **76** and "the true human" and "the Son of the Human" and "the seed of the Son of the Human." This true race is known in the world. These are the places where the children of the bridal chamber exist.

In this world, union is between male and female, the place of power and weakness; in the (eternal) age, the union is like something else, but we refer to them by the same names. There are other names, however, that are above every name that's named, and they're better than the strong, because where there's force, there are those who are even more powerful. They're not (two) different things, but they're both the same thing. This is what won't be able to come down upon the fleshly heart.

Isn't it necessary for everyone who has everything to know themselves completely? Some who don't know themselves won't be able to enjoy what they have, but those who've come to understand themselves will enjoy them.

Not only won't they be able to bind the perfect human, they won't be able to see them (the perfect human), because if they see them they'll bind them. There's no other way for someone to acquire this grace for themselves [except by] putting on the perfect light [and] becoming the perfect [light. Whoever has put it on] themselves will go [...] this is the perfect [...] for us to become [...] before we came to [...] whoever receives everything [...] these places, they'll be able to [...] that place, but they'll [... the middle] as incomplete. **77** Only Jesus knows the end of this one.

The holy man (priest) is completely holy, down to his (very) body, because if he receives the bread he'll make it holy, or the cup, or anything else that he takes and purifies. Why won't he purify the body too?

As Jesus perfected the water of baptism, that's the way he poured out death. So we go down into the water, but we don't go down into death, so that we won't be poured out into the spirit of the world. When it blows, the winter comes. When the Holy Spirit breathes, the summer comes.

Whoever knows the truth is a free person, and the free person doesn't sin, because "whoever sins is the slave of sin." Truth is the Mother, but knowledge is the joining. Those who aren't given to sin are called "free" by the world. These who aren't given to sin are made proud by the knowledge of the truth. That's what makes them free and exalts them over everything. But "love builds up," and whoever has been made free through knowledge is a slave because of love for those who aren't yet able to attain [the] freedom of knowledge, [but] knowledge makes them able [to] become free. Love [...] anything its own [...] it [...] its own. It never [says "..."] or "this is mine," [but "...] are yours." Spiritual love is wine with fragrance. **78** All those who will anoint themselves with it enjoy it. While those who are anointed stay around, those who are nearby also enjoy it. If those who are anointed with ointment leave them and go, those who aren't anointed but are only nearby remain in their stench. The Samaritan didn't give anything to the wounded man except wine with oil. It wasn't anything but the ointment, and it healed the wounds, because "love covers a multitude of sins."

The children to whom a woman gives birth will look like the man she loves. If it's her husband, they look like her husband; if it's an adulterer, they look like the adulterer. Often, if a woman sleeps with her husband because she has to, but her heart is with the adulterer with whom she is intimate and she bears a child, the child she bears looks like the adulterer.

But you who exist with the Son of God, don't love the world; rather, love the Lord, so that those you'll beget may not come to look like the world, but will come to look like the Lord.

The human unites with the human, the horse unites with the horse, the donkey unites with the donkey. Species unite [with] similar species. That's what it's like when spirit unites with spirit, the [Word] is intimate with the Word, [and light is] intimate [with light. If you] become human, [it's the human who will] love you. If you become [spirit], it's the Spirit who will unite with you. [If] you become Word, it's the Word that **79** will unite with you. If [you] become light, it's the light which will be intimate with you. If you become one of those from above, those from above will rest upon you. If you become horse or donkey or calf or dog or sheep or any other of the animals which are outside or below, neither human nor spirit nor Word nor light nor those from above nor those inside will be able to love you. They won't be able to rest within you, and you'll have no part in them.

Whoever is an unwilling slave will be able to be made free. Whoever has become free by the grace of their master and has sold themselves (back) into slavery won't be able to be made free any longer.

Spiritual Growth

The world is farmed through four things. They gather into barns through water, earth, wind, and light. And in the same way, God farms through four things too: through faith, hope, love, and knowledge. Our earth is the faith in which we're rooted. [And] the [water] is the hope through which [we're] nourished. The wind is the love through which we grow. And the light [is] the knowledge through which we [ripen]. Grace exists in [four kinds. It's] earthly, it's [heavenly, ...] the heaven of the heaven [...] through [....] Blessed is the one who hasn't [...] **80** a soul. This one is Jesus Christ. He went all over the place and didn't burden anyone. So, blessed is someone like this; they're a perfect person, because the Word tells us about how hard it is to keep up. How will we be able to achieve such a great thing? How will he give rest to everyone? First and foremost, it's not right to cause anyone grief – whether great or small, or faithless or faithful – and then give rest to those who are (already) at rest among those who are well off. There are some who benefit from giving rest to the one who's well off. Whoever does good can't give rest to them because they can't just do whatever they want; they can't cause grief because they can't cause distress, but sometimes the one who's well off causes them grief. They're not like that, but it's their (own) evil that causes them grief. Whoever has the nature (of the perfect person) gives joy to the one who's good, but some grieve terribly at this.

A householder acquired everything, whether child or slave or cattle or dog or pig or wheat [or] barley or straw or hay or [...] or meat and acorn. [But they're] wise and understand what to feed each [one]. To the children they served bread [...] but [... the] slaves they served [...], and to the cattle [they threw barley] and straw and hay. To [the] dogs they threw bones [and] to [the pigs] they threw acorns **81** and slops. That's what it's like with the disciple of God. If they're wise, they understand what it means to be a disciple. The bodily forms won't deceive them, but they'll look at the condition of the soul of each one and speak with them. There are many animals in the world that are made in human form. They (the disciple) recognizes them. To the pigs they'll throw acorns, but to the cattle they'll throw barley with straw and hay. To the dogs they'll throw bones, to the slaves they'll give the appetizer, and to the children they'll give the perfect (food).

There's the Son of Humanity, and there's the son of the Son of Humanity. The Lord is the Son of Humanity, and the son of the Son of Humanity is the one who creates through the Son of Humanity. The Son of Humanity received from God the ability to create. He (also) has the ability to beget. The one who received the ability to create is a creature; the one who received the ability to beget is begotten. The one who creates can't beget; the one who begets can create. They say, "The one who creates, begets." But what they beget is a creature. [So] their begotten aren't their children, but they're [...]. The one who creates works [publicly], and are themselves [revealed]. The one who begets, begets [secretly], and they're hidden [...] the image. [Again], the one who [creates, creates] publicly, but the one who begets, [begets] children secretly.

No [one will be able to] know [when the husband] **82** and the wife are intimate with each other, except they themselves, because the marriage of the world is a mystery for those who have married. If the defiled marriage is hidden, how much more is the undefiled marriage a true mystery! It's not fleshly, but pure. It isn't of desire, but of the will. It isn't of the darkness or the night, but it's of the day and the light. If a marriage is stripped naked, it becomes pornography – not only if the bride receives the seed of another man, but even if she leaves the chamber and is seen, she commits adultery. Let her reveal herself to her father, her mother, the best man, and the groom's children. They're allowed to enter the bridal chamber every day. But let the others yearn just to hear her voice and enjoy her perfume, and, like dogs, let them eat the crumbs that fall from the table. Grooms and brides belong to the bridal chamber. No one will be able to see the groom and the bride unless [they become] such.

Uprooting Evil

When Abraham […] to see what he was going to see, [he] circumcised the flesh of the foreskin, [telling] us that it's necessary to destroy the flesh.

[Most (things)] of [the] world can stand up and live as long as their [insides are hidden. If they're revealed], they die, as [illustrated] by the visible human. [As long as] the human's guts are hidden, **83** the human is alive. If their guts are exposed and come out of them, the human will die. It's the same way with the tree. While its root is hidden, it blossoms and grows. If its root is exposed, the tree dries up. That's what it's like with everything that's born in the world, not only the revealed, but also the hidden; because as long as the root of evil is hidden, it's strong. But if it's recognized, it dissolves, and if it's revealed, it dies. So the Word says, "Already the axe is laid at the root of the trees." It won't (just) cut, (because) that which will be cut blossoms again. Rather, the axe digs down into the ground until it brings up the root. Jesus plucked out the root completely, but others did so partially. As for us, let every one of us dig down to the root of the evil within and pluck it out from its root in us. It'll be uprooted if we recognize it. But if we don't recognize it, it takes root within us and bears its fruit in us. It masters us, and we're forced to serve it. It captures us so that we do what we do [not] want to; and we do [not] do what we want to. [It's] powerful because we haven't recognized it. It's active as long as [it exists]. [Ignorance] is the mother of [all evil]. Ignorance will cause [death, because] what exists from [ignorance] neither did exist nor [does exist], nor will they come into being […] **84** they'll be perfected when the whole truth is revealed, because the truth is like ignorance. When it's hidden, it rests within itself, but if it's revealed and recognized, it's glorified inasmuch as it's stronger than ignorance and error. It gives freedom. The Word says, "If you'll know the truth, the truth will make you free." Ignorance is slavery; knowledge is freedom. If we know the truth, we'll find the fruits of truth within us. If we unite with it, it'll receive our fullness.

Now we have what's revealed of creation. We say, "Those who are strong are honorable, but those who are hidden are weak and scorned." That's what it's like with those who are revealed of the truth; they're weak and scorned, but the hidden are strong and honorable. But the mysteries of the truth are revealed in types and images.

The chamber is hidden, however; it's the Holy in the Holy. At first, the veil concealed how God managed the creation, but when the veil is torn and what's inside is revealed, then this house will be left behind [like] a desert, or rather, will be [destroyed]. And all divinity will flee [from] these places, not into the Holies [of the] Holies, because it won't be able to unite with the pure [light] and the [flawless] fullness, [but] it'll come to be under the wings of the cross [and under] its arms. This ark will [become their] salvation when the flood **85** of water surges over them. If some belong to the priesthood, they'll be able to enter inside the veil with the high priest. So the veil wasn't torn only at the top, since it would've been open only to those at the top; nor was it torn only at the bottom, since it would've been revealed only to those at the bottom; but it was torn from the top to the bottom. Those at the top opened to us the bottom, so that we'll enter the secret of the truth. This truly is what's honorable, what's strong, but we'll enter there through scorned types and weaknesses. They're humbled in the presence of the perfect glory. There's glory that's better than glory; there's power that's better than power. So the perfect was opened to us with the secrets of the truth, and the Holies of the Holies were revealed, and the chamber invited us in.

As long as it's hidden, evil is inactive, but it hasn't been removed from among the Holy Spirit's seed. They're slaves of evil. But whenever it's revealed, then the perfect light will flow out upon everyone, and all of them who are in it will [receive the chrism]. Then the slaves will be made free and the captives will be redeemed. "[Every] plant [which] my Father who's in heaven [hasn't] planted [will be] uprooted." Those who are separated will unite […] will be filled.

Conclusion

Everyone who will [enter] the chamber will kindle their [lamp], because [it's] like the marriages which are […] happen at night, the fire […] **86** at night and is put out. But the mysteries of this marriage are fulfilled in the day and the light. Neither that day nor its light ever sets.

If anyone becomes a child of the bridal chamber, they'll receive the light. If anyone doesn't receive it while they're here, they won't be able to receive it in the other place. Whoever will receive that light won't be seen or bound, and no one will be able to trouble someone like this even while they dwell in the world. Moreover, when they leave the world, they've already received the Truth in the images. The world has become the (eternal) ages, because the (eternal) age is the fullness for them, and it's like this: it's revealed to them alone. It's not hidden in the darkness and the night, but it's hidden in a perfect day and a holy light.

Book 94. The Gospel of Mary

Page 7 (Pages 1-6 are missing)
[The disciples asked:] "Teach us about the material world. Will it last forever or is everything impermanent?" The Saviour answered: "All that is created, everything that is formed, all exist interde-

pendently in and with each other. Then each will be dissolved again back into its own roots. It is [the way of] nature that everything will eventually decompose back into its own elements. Those who have ears, let them hear."

Peter said to him: "While you are explaining everything to us, tell us one more thing: What is the sin of the world?" The Saviour answered: "There is no such thing as sin, you only make it appear when you act according to the habits of your adulterated nature: that is how what you call 'sin' manifests. This is why the Good has come into your midst, pursuing [the Good] which is in everyone's true nature, to restore it inward to its root." Then he continued, saying: "This is what sickens and destroys you: it is your love for the things that deceive you. Those who have ears, let them hear. Whoever can understand, let them understand!"

Page 8
"Attachment to matter gives rise to incomparable suffering, because it goes against your true nature. Then the whole body becomes disturbed. This is why I taught you to find contentment at the level of the heart. When you feel disturbed and out of balance, reclaim wholeness in the presence of all the different forms of your true nature. Those who have ears, let them hear."

When the Blessed One had said these things, he embraced them all and took his leave, saying: "Peace be with you! Cultivate my peace within yourselves!

Be vigilant, and don't let anyone lead you astray by saying 'Here it is' or 'There it is', for the Son of Man, the Child of Your True Humanity, already lives within each one of you. This is what you should follow! I tell you, those who seek this within will surely find it. Go then and proclaim the gospel of the Kingdom!"

Page 9
"Do not lay down any rules other than what I have given you. Do not establish more laws like the lawmaker, or else you too will become constrained by them." Once he had said these things, he departed from them.

The disciples grieved bitterly, shedding many tears and saying: "How are we supposed to go out preaching to the rest of the world, proclaiming the gospel of the Kingdom of the Son of Man? If they did not spare him, then what will become of us?"

Then Mary rose up. She embraced them all, kissing them tenderly and began to speak to her brothers and sisters: "There is no need to remain stuck in sorrow, grief, and doubt! For his Grace will be with you all; it will guide you, comfort you, shelter, and protect you. Rather, let us be thankful and praise his greatness, for he has brought us together and prepared us for this. Through him, we too can become fully human."

Saying these things, Mary turned their hearts inward toward the Good, and they began to wrestle with the meaning of the Saviour's words and to discuss his sayings.

Page 10
Then Peter said to Mary, "Sister, we know that you are greatly loved by the Saviour, more than any other woman. Tell us those words of His that you remember, the things which you know and we don't, the teachings we never heard."

Mary answered, saying: "What is hidden from you I shall reveal to you. Whatever is unknown to you, and I remember, I will tell you."

And she began saying these words to them. She said, "Once I saw the Lord in a vision and I said to him: 'Lord, [Rabbouni,] now I see you in this vision.'

He answered me and said: 'Blessed are you Mary, for you do not waver at the sight of me. How wonderful you are! For this is where the treasure lies - in [that place where heaven and earth meet, where deep understanding arises in the heart and mind], 'the nous'.'

I asked him this: 'Now tell me Lord, how does a person see such a vision, is it through the agency of their soul or through The Spirit?'

The Saviour answered: 'It is neither through the soul nor through The Spirit, but through the understanding which arises between the two, that is how the vision is seen.'"

Pages 11-14 are missing.

Page 15
And Craving spoke: "I didn't see you descending, but now I see you rising up. Who are you fooling? You're controlled by me!"

The Soul responded: ["My friend, it is you who were mistaken!] I saw you, but you never really saw me or knew me. You mistook the cloak I was wearing for my true self, so you didn't recognise me." Having said all this, the Soul went away joyfully.

Again, the Soul came into the realm of the third Authority, which goes by the name of Ignorance. This scrutinised the Soul closely and interrogated it, saying: "Where do you think you're going? You are the slave of malicious habits, trapped and held prisoner by your own wicked inclinations. You lack discrimination, so your judgement is unsound!"

The Soul said: "Why are you so critical of me, even though I have not been judgemental? I have been dominated and have lacked my own agency. I was never recognised for my true self, but now I have recognised this: that everything is impermanent, the whole of creation will be dissolved. All worldly things, all heavenly things, everything passes, everything will be released."

Page 16

Liberated from the realm of the third Authority, the Soul continued, and came face to face with the fourth, the Authority of Wrath.

This took on seven fearful manifestations. The first was everything obscured; the second was craving; the third, ignorance, the fourth, the longing for oblivion; the fifth, enslavement to the demands of the body, the sixth was foolish worldly wisdom, the seventh, the hot-tempered certainty of anger.

These formed the seven-fold Authority of Wrath, which interrogated the Soul, demanding: "Where do you come from, murderer? and, where do you think you're going, deserter?"

The Soul responded: "It is what dominated me that has been vanquished, and what was steering me that has been overcome. It's my craving that has come to an end, and my ignorance that has died."

Page 17

I have been set free from one world with the aid of another world, from one pattern through the moulding and shaping of a greater pattern. I have been liberated from the chains of forgetfulness which are both temporary and temporal. From this moment on, now and for all seasons, I am released into silent restfulness, where time rests in the eternity of time."

After saying these things Mary settled into silence: that place of sanctuary to which the Saviour's words had brought her.

But Andrew responded and said to the brothers and sisters:

"Tell me, what do you think about all that she has been telling us? Say what you will, but I for one don't believe that the Saviour would have said such things! Certainly, these are unorthodox teachings, it all seems quite different from his way of thinking."

After some consideration, Peter responded in a similar way. He questioned the brothers about the Saviour: "Did he really speak secretly with a woman and not openly so that we could all hear? Are we just going to turn around and listen to her? Did he really choose her and prefer her to us? Surely, he wouldn't have wanted to show that she is more worthy than we are?"

Page 18-19

Then Mary wept. She said to Peter: "My brother, Peter, what are you thinking? Do you really believe that I made all this up, or that I would tell lies about our Saviour?"

Levi also responded to Peter, saying: "Peter, you have always been hot-tempered from the beginning, and now we see you arguing against this woman as though you were her adversary. Yet if the Saviour deemed her worthy, indeed if he himself has made her worthy, then who are you to despise and reject her? Surely the Saviour's appraisal of her is completely reliable. That is why he loved her more than us.

Brothers, we should be ashamed of our behaviour. Let us cloak ourselves with True Humanity. We too can follow his instructions and cultivate this in ourselves. Let us do as we were instructed and proclaim the good news the Saviour taught, never laying down any rules or laws beyond what he himself gave. After Levi had said these things, they started going out to teach and to proclaim the gospel…

Book 95. The Gospel of Judas

Introduction

33 This is the secret message of judgment Jesus spoke with Judas Iscariot over a period of eight days, three days before he celebrated Passover.

When he appeared on earth, he did signs and great wonders for the salvation of humanity. Some [walked] in the way of righteousness, but others walked in their transgression, so the twelve disciples were called. He started to tell them about the mysteries beyond the world and what would happen at the end. Often he didn't reveal himself to his disciples, but you'd find him in their midst as a child.

Jesus Criticizes the Disciples

One day he was with his disciples in Judea. He found them sitting together practicing their piety. When he [came up to] his disciples **34** sitting together praying over the bread, [he] laughed.

The disciples said to him, "Master, why are you laughing at [our] prayer? What have we done? [This] is what's right."

He answered and said to them, "I'm not laughing at you. You're not doing this because you want to, but because through this your God [will be] praised."

They said, "Master, you […] are the Son of our God!"

Jesus said to them, "How do [you] know me? Truly [I] say to you, no generation of the people among you will know me."

When his disciples heard this, [they] started to get angry and furious and started to curse him in their hearts.

But when Jesus noticed their ignorance, [he said] to them, "Why are you letting your anger trouble you? Has your God within you and [his stars] **35** become angry with your souls? If any of you is [strong enough] among humans to bring out the perfect Humanity, stand up and face me."

All of them said, "We're strong enough." But their spirits weren't brave enough to stand before [him] – except Judas Iscariot. He was able to stand before him, but he couldn't look him in the eye, so he looked away. Judas [said] to him, "I know who you are and where you've come from. You've come from the immortal realm of Barbelo, and I'm not worthy to utter the name of the one who's sent you."

Then Jesus, knowing that he was thinking about what's exalted, said to him, "Come away from the others and I'll tell you the mysteries of the kingdom. Not so that you'll go there, but you'll grieve much **36** because someone else will replace you to complete the twelve [elements] before their God."

Judas said to him, "When will you tell me these things, and when will the great day of light dawn for the generation […]?"

But when he said these things, Jesus left him.

Another Generation

The next morning, he appeared to his disciples. [And] they said to him, "Master, where did [you] go and what did you do when you left us?"

Jesus said to them, "I went to another great and holy generation."

His disciples said to him, "Lord, what great generation is better and holier than us, that's not in these realms?"

Now when Jesus heard this, he laughed. He said to them, "Why are you wondering in your hearts about the strong and holy generation? **37** Truly I say to you, no one born [of] this realm will see that [generation], no army of angels from the stars will rule over it, and no person of mortal birth will be able to join it, because that generation doesn't come from […] that has become […] the generation of the people among [them] is from the generation of the great people […] the powerful authorities who […] nor the powers […] those by which you rule."

When his disciples heard these things, they were each troubled in their spirit. They couldn't say a thing.

The Disciples' Vision

Another day Jesus came up to them. They said to him, "Master, we've seen you in a dream, because we had great [dreams last] night."

But Jesus said, "Why […] hidden yourselves?"

38 And they [said, "We saw] a great [house, with a great] altar [in it, and] twelve people – we'd say they were priests – and a name. And a crowd of people was waiting at the altar [until] the priests [finished receiving] the offerings. We kept waiting too."

[Jesus said], "What were they like?"

And they said, "[Some] fast [for] two weeks. Others sacrifice their own children; others their wives, praising and humbling themselves among each other. Others sleep with men; others murder; yet others commit many sins and do criminal things. [And] the people standing [before] the altar invoke your [name]! **39** And in all their sacrificing, they fill the [altar] with their offerings." When they said this, [they] fell silent because they were troubled.

Jesus said to them, "Why are you troubled? Truly I say to you, all the priests standing before that altar invoke my name. And [again], I say to you, my name has been written on this [house] of the generations of the stars by the human generations. [And they] have shamefully planted fruitless trees in my name." Jesus said to them, "You're the ones receiving the offerings on the altar you've seen. That's the God you serve, and you're the twelve people you've seen. And the animals you saw brought in to be sacrificed are the crowd you lead astray **40** before that altar. [Your minister] will stand up and use my name like that, and [the] generations of the pious will be loyal to him. After him, another person will present [those who sleep around], and another those who murder children, and another those who sleep with men, and those who fast, and the rest of impurity, crime, and error. And those who say, 'We're equal to the angels' – they're the stars that finish everything. It's been said to the human generations, 'Look, God has accepted your sacrifice from the hands of priests,' that is, the minister of error. But the Lord who commands is the Lord over everything. On the last day, they'll be found guilty."

41 Jesus said [to them], "Stop [sacrificing animals]. You've [offered them] over the altar, over your stars with your angels where they've already been completed. So let them become […] with you and let them [become] clear."

His disciples [said to him], "Cleanse us from our [sins] that we've committed through the deceit of the angels."

Jesus said to them, "It's not possible […], nor [can] a fountain quench the fire of the entire inhabited world. Nor can a [city's] well satisfy all the generations, except the great, stable one. A single lamp won't illuminate all the realms, except the second generation, nor can a baker feed all creation **42** under [heaven]."

And [when the disciples heard] these [things], they said to [him], "Master, help us and save us!"

Jesus said to them, "Stop struggling against me. Each one of you has his own star, [and …] of the stars will […] what belongs to it […] I wasn't sent to the corruptible generation, but to the strong and incorruptible generation, because no enemy has ruled [over] that generation, nor any of the stars. Truly I say to you, the pillar of fire will fall quickly and that generation won't be moved by the stars."

Jesus and Judas

And when Jesus [said] these things, he left, [taking] Judas Iscariot with him. He said to him, "The water on the exalted mountain is [from] **43** […] it didn't come to [water … the well] of the tree of [the fruit …] of this realm […] after a time […], but came to water God's paradise and the enduring [fruit], because [it] won't corrupt that generation's [walk of life], but [it will exist] for all eternity."

Judas said to [him, "Tell] me, what kind of fruit does this generation have?"

Jesus said, "The souls of every human generation will die; however, when these people have completed the time in the kingdom and the spirit leaves them, their bodies will die but their souls will live, and they'll be taken up."

Judas said, "What will the rest of the human generations do?"

Jesus said, "It's not possible **44** to sow on [rock] and harvest its fruit. In the same way, it's [not possible to sow on] the [defiled] race along with the perishable wisdom [and] the hand which created mortal humans so that their souls may go up to the realms above. [Truly] I say to you, [no ruler], angel, [or] power will be able to see the [places] that [this great], holy generation [will see]." When Jesus said this, he left.

Judas said, "Master, just as you've listened to all of them, now listen to me too, because I've seen a great vision."

But Jesus laughed when he heard this. He said to him, "Why are you all worked up, you thirteenth demon? But speak up, and I'll bear with you."

Judas said to him, "In the vision, I saw myself. The twelve disciples are stoning me and **45** chasing [me rapidly]. And I also came to the place where [I had followed] you. I saw [a house in this place], and my eyes couldn't [measure] its size. Great people surrounded it, and that house had a roof of greenery. In the middle of the house was [a crowd …]. Master, take me in with these people!"

[Jesus] answered and said, "Your star has led you astray, Judas," and that "no person of mortal birth is worthy to enter the house you've seen, because that place is reserved for those who are holy. Neither the sun nor the moon will rule there, nor the day, but those who are holy will always stand in the realm with the holy angels. Look, I've told you the mysteries of the kingdom **46** and I've taught you about the error of the stars and […] sent [on high] over the twelve realms."

Judas said, "Master, surely my seed doesn't dominate the rulers, does it?"

Jesus answered and said to him, "Come, let me [tell] you [about the holy generation. Not so that you'll go there], but you'll grieve much when you see the kingdom and all its generation."

When Judas heard this, he said to him, "What good has it done me that you've separated me from that generation?"

Jesus answered and said, "You'll become the thirteenth, and will be cursed by the other generations and will rule over them. In the last days they'll […] to you and you won't go up **47** to the holy generation."

Jesus Reveals Everything to Judas

Jesus said, "[Come] and I'll teach you about the [mysteries that no] human [will] see, because there exists a great and boundless realm whose horizons no angelic generation has seen, [in] which is a [great] invisible Spirit, which no [angelic] eye has ever seen, no heart has ever comprehended, and it's never been called by any name.

"And a luminous cloud appeared there. And he (the Spirit) said, 'Let an angel come into being to attend me.' And a great angel, the Self-Begotten, the God of the Light, emerged from the cloud. And because of him, another four angels came into being from another cloud, and they attended the angelic Self-Begotten. And said **48** the [Self-Begotten], 'Let [a realm] come into being,' and it came into being [just as he said]. And he [created] the first luminary to rule over it. And he said, 'Let angels come into being to serve [it,' and myriads] without number came into being. And he said, '[Let a] luminous realm come into being,' and it came into being. He created the second luminary to rule over it, along with myriads of angels without number to offer service. And that's how he created the rest of the realms of light. And he made them to be ruled, and created for them myriads of angels without number to assist them.

"And Adamas was in the first cloud of light that no angel could ever see among all those called 'God.' **49** And [Adamas begat Seth in] that [place after the] image [of …] and after the likeness of [this] angel. He made the incorruptible [generation] of Seth appear to the twelve androgynous [luminaries. And then] he made seventy-two luminaries appear in the incorruptible generation according to the Spirit's will. Then the seventy-two luminaries themselves made three hundred sixty luminaries appear in the incorruptible generation according to the Spirit's will so that there'd be five for each. And the twelve realms of the twelve luminaries make up their father, with six heavens for each realm so there are seventy-two heavens for the seventy-two luminaries, and for each one **50** [of them five] firmaments [for a total of] three hundred sixty [firmaments. They] were given authority and a [great] army of angels without number for honor and service, along with virgin spirits [too] for the honor and [service] of all the realms and the heavens with their firmaments.

"Now the crowd of those immortals is called 'cosmos' – that is, 'perishable' – by the father and the seventy-two luminaries with the Self-Begotten and his seventy-two realms. That's where the first human appeared with his incorruptible powers. In the realm that appeared with his generation is the cloud of knowledge and the angel who's called **51** [Eleleth …] After these things [Eleleth] said, 'Let twelve angels come into being [to] rule over Chaos and [Hades]. And look, from the cloud there appeared an [angel] whose face flashed with [fire] and whose likeness was [defiled] by blood. His name was Nebro, which means 'Rebel.' Others call him Yaldabaoth. And another angel, Saklas, came from the cloud too. So Nebro created six angels – and Saklas (did too) – to be assistants. They brought out twelve angels in the heavens, with each of them receiving a portion in the heavens.

"And the twelve rulers spoke with the twelve angels: 'Let each of you **52** […] and let them […] generation [… five] angels:

The first [is Yaoth], who's called 'the Good One.'

The second is Harmathoth, [the eye of fire].

The [third] is Galila.

The fourth [is] Yobel.

The fifth is Adonaios.

"These are the five who ruled over Hades and are the first over Chaos.

"Then Saklas said to his angels, 'Let's create a human being after the likeness and the image.' And they fashioned Adam and his wife Eve, who in the cloud is called 'Life,' because by this name all the generations seek him, and each of them calls her by their names. Now Saklas didn't **53** [command …] give birth, except […] among the generations […] which this […] and the [angel] said to him, 'Your life will last for a limited time, with your children.'"

Then Judas said to Jesus, "[How] long can a person live?"

Jesus said, "Why are you amazed that the lifespans of Adam and his generation are limited in the place he's received his kingdom with his ruler?"

Judas said to Jesus, "Does the human spirit die?"

Jesus said, "This is how it is. God commanded Michael to loan spirits to people so that they might serve. Then the Great One commanded Gabriel to give spirits to the great generation with no king – the spirit along with the soul. So the [rest] of the souls **54** […] light [… the] Chaos […] seek [the] spirit within you which you've made to live in this flesh from the angelic generations. Then God caused knowledge to be brought to Adam and those with him, so that the kings of Chaos and Hades might not rule over them."

[Then] Judas said to Jesus, "So what will those generations do?"

Jesus said, "Truly I say to you, the stars complete all these things. When Saklas completes the time span that's been determined for him, their first star will appear with the generations, and they'll finish what's been said. Then they'll sleep around in my name, murder their children, **55** and [they'll …] evil and […] the realms, bringing the generations and presenting them to Saklas. [And] after that […] will bring the twelve tribes of [Israel] from […], and the [generations] will all serve Saklas, sinning in my name. And your star will [rule] over the thirteenth realm." Then Jesus [laughed].

[Judas] said, "Master, why [are you laughing at me?"

Jesus] answered [and said], "I'm not laughing [at you but] at the error of the stars, because these six stars go astray with these five warriors, and they'll all be destroyed along with their creations."

Then Judas said to Jesus, "What will those do who've been baptized in your name?"

The Betrayal

Jesus said, "Truly I say [to you], this baptism **56** [which they've received in] my name […] will destroy the whole generation of the earthly Adam. Tomorrow they'll torture the one who bears me. Truly I [say] to you, no hand of a mortal human [will fall] upon me. Truly [I say] to you, Judas, those who offer sacrifices to Saklas […] everything that's evil. But you'll do more than all of them, because you'll sacrifice the human who bears me. Your horn has already been raised, your anger has been kindled, your star has ascended, and your heart has [strayed]. **57** Truly [I say to you], your last [… and] the [… the thrones] of the realm have [been defeated], the kings have grown weak, the angelic generations have grieved, and the evil [they sowed …] is destroyed, [and] the [ruler] is wiped out. [And] then the [fruit] of the great generation of Adam will be exalted, because before heaven, earth, and the angels, that generation from the realms exists. Look, you've been told everything. Lift up your eyes and see the cloud with the light in it and the stars around it. And the star that leads the way is your star."

Then Judas looked up and saw the luminous cloud, and he entered it. Those standing on the ground heard a voice from the cloud saying, **58** "[. . . the] great [generation . . .] and [. . .]." And Judas didn't see Jesus anymore.

Immediately there was a disturbance among [the] Jews, more than […] Their high priests grumbled because he'd gone into the guest room to pray. But some scribes were there watching closely so they could arrest him during his prayer, because they were afraid of the people, since they all regarded him as a prophet.

And they approached Judas and said to him, "What are you doing here? Aren't you Jesus' disciple?"

Then he answered them as they wished. Then Judas received some money and handed him over to them.

Book 96. The Gospel of Nicodemus

Introduction

We have as yet no true critical edition of this book: one is in preparation, by E. von Dobschutz, to be included in the Berlin corpus of Greek Ante-Nicene Christian writers. A short statement of the authorities available at this moment is therefore necessary.

Tischendorf in his Evangelia Apocrypha divides the whole writing into two parts: (1) the story of the Passion; (2) the Descent into hell; and prints the following forms of each: six in all:

1. Part I, Recession A in Greek from eight manuscripts, and a Latin translation of the Coptic version in the notes.
2. Part I, Recession B in Greek from three late manuscripts.
3. Part II (Descent into Hell) in Greek from three manuscripts.
4. Part I in Latin, using twelve manuscripts, and some old editions.
5. Part II in Latin (A) from four manuscripts.
6. Part II in Latin (B) from three manuscripts.

Tischendorf's must be described as an eclectic text not representing probably, any one single line of transmission: but it presents the book in a readable, and doubtless, on the whole, correct form.

There are, besides the Latin, three ancient versions of Part I of considerable importance, viz.:

Coptic, preserved in an early papyrus at Turin, and in some fragments at Paris. Last edited by Revillout in Patrologia orientalis, ix. 2.

Syriac, edited by Rahmaui in Studia Syriaca, II.

Armenian, edited by F. C. Conybeara in Studia Biblica, IV (Oxford, 1896): he gives a Greek rendering of one manuscript and a Latin one of another.

All of these conform to Tischelldorf's Recession A of Part I: and this must be regarded as the most original form of the Acta which we have. Recession B is a late and diffuse working-over of the same matter: it will not be translated here in full.

The first part of the book, containing the story of the Passion and Resurrection, is not earlier than the fourth century. Its object in the main is to furnish irrefragable testimony to the resurrection. Attempts have been made to show that it is of early date-that it is, for instance, the writing which Justin Martyr meant when in his Apology he referred his heathen readers to the 'Acts' of Christ's trial preserved among the archives of Rome. The truth of that matter is that he simply assumed that such records must exist. False 'acts' of the trial were written in the Pagan interest under Maximin, and introduced into schools early in the fourth century. It is imagined by some that our book was a counterblast to these.

The account of the Descent into Hell (Part II) is an addition to the Acta. It does not appear in any Oriental version, and the Greek copies are rare. It is in Latin that it has chiefly flourished, and has been the parent of versions in every European language.

The central idea, the delivery of the righteous fathers from Hades is exceedingly ancient. Second-century writers are full of it. The embellishments, the dialogues of Satan with Hades, which are so dramatic, come in later, perhaps with the development of pulpit oratory among Christians. We find them in fourth-century homilies attributed to Eusebius of Emesa. This second part used to be called Gnostic, but there is nothing unorthodox about it save the choice of the names of the two men who are supposed to tell the story, viz. Leucius and Karinus. Leucius Charinus is the name given by church writers to the supposed author of the Apocryphal Acts of John, Paul, Peter, Andrew, and Thomas. In reality Leucius was the soi-disant author of the Acts of John only. His name was transferred to the other Acts in process of time, and also (sometimes disguised as Seleucus) to Gospels of the Infancy and narratives of the Assumption of the Virgin, With all these the original Leucius had nothing to do. When his name came to be attached to the Descent into Hell we do not yet know: nor do we know when the Descent was first appended to the Acts of Pilate. Not, I should conjecture, before the fifth century.

MEMORIALS OF OUR LORD JESUS CHRIST DONE IN THE TIME OF PONTIUS PILATE

Prologue

(Absent from some manuscripts and versions).

I Ananias (Aeneas Copt., Emaus Lat.), the Protector, of praetorian rank, learned in the law, did from the divine scriptures recognize our Lord Jesus Christ and came near to him by faith and was accounted worthy of holy baptism: and I sought out the memorials that were made at that season in the time of our master Jesus Christ, which the Jews deposited with Pontius Pilate, and found the memorials in Hebrew (letters), and by the good pleasure of God I translated them into Greek (letters) for the informing of all them that call upon the name of our Lord Jesus Christ: in the reign of our Lord Flavius Theodosius, in the seventeenth year, and of Flavius Valentinianus the sixth, in the ninth indiction [corrupt: Lat. has the eighteenth year of Theodosius, when Valentinian was proclaimed Augustus, i. e. A. D. 425].

All ye therefore that read this and translate (or copy) it into other books, remember me and pray for me that God will be gracious unto me and be merciful unto my sins which I have sinned against him.

Peace be to them that read and that hear these things and to their servants. Amen.

In the fifteenth (al. nineteenth) year of the governance of Tiberius Caesar, emperor of the Romans, and of Herod, king of Galilee, in the nineteenth year of his rule, on the eighth of the Calends of April, which is the 25th of March, in the consulate of Rufus and Rubellio, in the fourth year of the two hundred and second Olympiad, Joseph who is Caiaphas being high priest of the Jews:

These be the things which after the cross and passion of the Lord Nicodemus recorded and delivered unto the high priest and the rest of the Jews: and the same Nicodemus set them forth in Hebrew (letters).

I

1 For the chief priests and scribes assembled in council, even Annas and Caiaphas and Somne (Senes) and Dothaim (Dothael, Dathaes, Datam) and Gamaliel, Judas, Levi and Nepthalim, Alexander and Jairus and the rest of the Jews, and came unto Pilate accusing Jesus for many deeds, saying: We know this man, that he is the son of Joseph the carpenter, begotten of Mary, and he saith that he is the Son of God and a king; moreover he doth pollute the sabbaths and he would destroy the law of our fathers.

Pilate saith: And what things are they that he doeth, and would destroy the law?

The Jews say: We have a law that we should not heal any man on the sabbath: but this man of his evil deeds hath healed the lame and the bent, the withered and the blind and the paralytic, the dumb and them that were possessed, on the sabbath day!

Pilate saith unto them: By what evil deeds?

They say unto him: He is a sorcerer, and by Beelzebub the prince of the devils he casteth out devils, and they are all subject unto him.

Pilate saith unto them: This is not to cast out devils by an unclean spirit, but by the god Asclepius.

2 The Jews say unto Pilate: We beseech thy majesty that he appear before thy judgement-seat and be heard. And Pilate called them unto him and said: Tell me, how can I that am a governor examine a king? They say unto him: We say not that he is a king, but he saith it of himself.

And Pilate called the messenger (cursor) and said unto him: Let Jesus be brought hither, but with gentleness. And the messenger went forth, and when he perceived Jesus he worshipped him and took the kerchief that was on his hand and spread it upon the earth and saith unto him: Lord, walk hereon and enter in, for the governor calleth thee. And when the Jews saw what the messenger had done, they cried out against Pilate saying: Wherefore didst thou not summon him by an herald to enter in, but by a messenger? for the messenger when he saw him worshipped him and spread out his kerchief upon the ground and hath made him walk upon it like a king!

3 Then Pilate called for the messenger and said unto him: Wherefore hast thou done this, and hast spread thy kerchief upon the ground and made Jesus to walk upon it? The messenger saith unto him: Lord governor, when thou sentest me to Jerusalem unto Alexander, I saw Jesus sitting upon an ass, and the children of the Hebrews held branches in their hands and cried out, and others spread their garments beneath him, saying: Save now, thou that art in the highest: blessed is he that cometh in the name of the Lord.

4 The Jews cried out and said unto the messenger: The children of the Hebrews cried out in Hebrew: how then hast thou it in the Greek? The messenger saith to them: I did ask one of the Jews and said: What is it that they cry out in Hebrew? and he interpreted it unto me.

Pilate saith unto them: And how cried they in Hebrew? The Jews say unto him: Hosanna membrome barouchamma adonai. Pilate saith unto them: And the Hosanna and the rest, how is it interpreted? The Jews say unto him: Save now, thou that art in the highest: blessed is he that cometh in the name of the Lord. Pilate saith unto them: If you yourselves bear witness of the words which were said of the children, wherein hath the messenger sinned? and they held their peace.

The governor saith unto the messenger: Go forth and bring him in after what manner thou wilt. And the messenger went forth and did after the former manner and said unto Jesus: Lord, enter in: the governor calleth thee.

5 Now when Jesus entered in, and the ensigns were holding the standards, the images (busts) of the standards bowed and did reverence to Jesus. And when the Jews saw the carriage of the standards, how they bowed themselves and did reverence unto Jesus, they cried out above measure against the ensigns. But Pilate said unto the Jews: Marvel ye not that the images bowed themselves and did reverence unto Jesus. The Jews say unto Pilate: We saw how the ensigns made them to bow and did reverence to him. And the governor called for the ensigns and saith unto them: Wherefore did ye so? They say unto Pilate: We are Greeks and servers of temples, and how could we do him reverence? for indeed, whilst we held the images they bowed of themselves and did reverence unto him.

6 Then saith Pilate unto the rulers of the synagogue and the elders of the people: Choose you out able and strong men and let them hold the standards, and let us see if they bow of themselves. And the elders of the Jews took twelve men strong and able and made them to hold the standards by

sixes, and they were set before the judgement-seat of the governor; and Pilate said to the messenger: Take him out of the judgement hall (praetorium) and bring him in again after what manner thou wilt. And Jesus went out of the judgement hall, he and the messenger. And Pilate called unto him them that before held the image and said unto them: I have sworn by the safety of Caesar that if the standards bow not when Jesus entereth in, I will cut off your heads.

And the governor commanded Jesus to enter in the second time. And the messenger did after the former manner and besought Jesus much that he would walk upon his kerchief; and he walked upon it and entered in. And when he had entered, the standards bowed themselves again and did reverence unto Jesus.

II

1 Now when Pilate saw it he was afraid, and sought to rise up from the judgement-seat. And while he yet thought to rise up, his wife sent unto him, saying: Have thou nothing to do with this just man, for I have suffered many things because of him by night. And Pilate called unto him all the Jews, and said unto them: Ye know that my wife feareth God and favoureth rather the customs of the Jews, with you? They say unto him: Yea, we know it. Pilate saith unto them: Lo, my wife hath sent unto me, saying: Have thou nothing to do with this just man: for I have suffered many things because of him by night. But the Jews answered and said unto Pilate: Said we not unto thee that he is a sorcerer? behold, he hath sent a vision of a dream unto thy wife.

2 And Pilate called Jesus unto him and said to him: What is it that these witness against thee? speakest thou nothing? But Jesus said: If they had not had power they would have spoken nothing; for every man hath power over his own mouth, to speak good or evil: they shall see to it.

3 The elders of the Jews answered and said unto Jesus: What shall we see? Firstly, that thou wast born of fornication; secondly, that thy birth in Bethlehem was the cause of the slaying of children; thirdly, that thy father Joseph and thy mother Mary fled into Egypt because they had no confidence before the people.

4 Then said certain of them that stood by, devout men of the Jews: We say not that he came of fornication; but we know that Joseph was betrothed unto Mary, and he was not born of fornication. Pilate saith unto those Jews which said that he came of fornication: This your saying is not true for there are espousals, as these also say which are of your nation. Annas and Caiaphas say unto Pilate: The whole multitude of us cry out that he was born of fornication, and we are not believed: but these are proselytes and disciples of his. And Pilate called Annas and Caiaphas unto him and said to them: What be proselytes? They say unto him: They were born children of Greeks, and now are they become Jews. Then said they which said l that he was not born of fornication, even Lazarus, Asterius, Antonius, Jacob, Amnes, Zenas, Samuel, Isaac, Phinees, Crispus, Agrippa and Judas: We were not born proselytes (are not Greeks, Copt.), but we are children of Jews and we speak the truth; for verily we were present at the espousals of Joseph and Mary.

5 And Pilate called unto him those twelve men which said that he was not born of fornication, and saith unto them: I adjure you by the safety of Caesar, are these things true which ye have said, that he was not born of fornication? They say unto Pilate: We have a law that we swear not, because it is sin: But let them swear by the safety of Caesar that it is not as we have said, and we will be guilty of death. Pilate saith to Annas and Caiaphas: Answer ye nothing to these things? Annas and Caiaphas say unto Pilate: These twelve men are believed which say that he was not born of fornication, but the whole multitude of us cry out that he was born of fornication, and is a sorcerer, and saith that he is the Son of God and a king, and we are not believed.

6 And Pilate commanded the whole multitude to go out, saving the twelve men which said that he was not born of fornication and he commanded Jesus to be set apart: and Pilate saith unto them: For what cause do they desire to put him to death? They say unto Pilate: They have jealousy, because he healeth on the sabbath day. Pilate saith: For a good work do they desire to put him to death? They say unto him: Yea.

III

1 And Pilate was filled with indignation and went forth without the judgement hall and saith unto them: I call the Sun to witness that I find no fault in this man. The Jews answered and said to the governor: If this man were not a malefactor we would not have delivered him unto thee. And Pilate said: Take ye him and judge him according to your law. The Jews said unto Pilate: It is not lawful for us to put any man to death. Pilate said: Hath God forbidden you to slay, and allowed me?

2 And Pilate went in again into the judgement hall and called Jesus apart and said unto him: Art thou the King of the Jews? Jesus answered and said to Pilate: Sayest thou this thing of thyself, or did others tell it thee of me? Pilate answered Jesus: Am I also a Jew? thine own nation and the chief priests have delivered thee unto me: what hast thou done? Jesus answered: My kingdom is not of this world; for if my kingdom were of this world, my servants would have striven that I should not be delivered to the Jews: but now is my kingdom not from hence. Pilate said unto him: Art thou a king, then? Jesus answered him: Thou sayest that I am a king; for this cause was I born and am come, that every one that is of the truth should hear my voice. Pilate saith unto him: What is truth? Jesus saith unto him: Truth is of heaven. Pilate saith: Is there not truth upon earth? Jesus saith unto Pilate: Thou seest how that they which speak the truth are judged of them that have authority upon earth.

IV

1 And Pilate left Jesus in the judgement hall and went forth to the Jews and said unto them: I find no fault in him. The Jews say unto him: This man said: I am able to destroy this temple and in three days to build it up. Pilate saith: What temple? The Jews say: That which Solomon built in forty and six years but which this man saith he will destroy and build it in three days. Pilate saith unto them: I am guiltless of the blood of this just man: see ye to it. The Jews say: His blood be upon us and on our children.

2 And Pilate called the elders and the priests and Levites unto him and said to them secretly: Do not so: for there is nothing worthy of death whereof ye have accused him, for your accusation is concerning healing and profaning of the sabbath. The elders and the priests and Levites say: If a man blaspheme against Caesar, is he worthy of death or no? Pilate saith: He is worthy of death. The Jews say unto Pilate: If a man be worthy of death if he blaspheme against Caesar, this man hath blasphemed against God.

3 Then the governor commanded all the Jews to go out from the judgement hall, and he called Jesus to him and saith unto him: What shall I do with thee? Jesus saith unto Pilate: Do as it hath been given thee. Pilate saith: How hath it been given? Jesus saith: Moses and the prophets did foretell concerning my death and rising again. Now the Jews inquired by stealth and heard, and they say unto Pilate: What needest thou to hear further of this blasphemy? Pilate saith unto the Jews: If this word be of blasphemy, take ye him for his blasphemy, and bring him into your synagogue and judge him according to your law. The Jews say unto Pilate: It is contained in our law, that if a man sin against a man, he is worthy to receive forty stripes save one: but he that blasphemeth against God, that he should be stoned with stoning.

4 Pilate saith unto them: Take ye him and avenge yourselves of him in what manner ye will. The Jews say unto Pilate: We will that he be crucified. Pilate saith: He deserveth not to be crucified.

5 Now as the governor looked round about upon the multitude of the Jews which stood by, he beheld many of the Jews weeping, and said: Not all the multitude desire that he should be put to death. The elder of the Jews said: To this end have the whole multitude of us come Hither, that he should be put to death. Pilate saith to the Jews: Wherefore should he die? The Jews said: Because he called himself the Son of God, and a king.

V

1 But a certain man, Nicodemus, a Jew, came and stood before the governor and said: I beseech thee, good (pious) lord, bid me speak a few words. Pilate saith: Say on. Nicodemus saith: I said unto the elders and the priests and Levites and unto all the multitude of the Jews in the synagogue: Wherefore contend ye with this man? This man doeth many and wonderful signs, which no man hath done, neither will do: let him alone and contrive not any evil against him: if the signs which he doeth are of God, they will stand, but if they be of men, they will come to nought. For verily Moses, when he was sent of God into Egypt did many signs, which God commanded him to do before Pharaoh, king of Egypt; and there were there certain men servants of Pharaoh, Jannes and Jambres, and they also did signs not a few, of them which Moses did, and the Egyptians held them as gods, even Jannes and Jambres: and whereas the signs which they did were not of God, they perished and those also that believed on them. And now let this man go, for he is not worthy of death.

2 The Jews say unto Nicodemus: Thou didst become his disciple and thou speakest on his behalf. Nicodemus saith unto them: Is the governor also become his disciple, that he speaketh on his behalf? did not Caesar appoint him unto this dignity? And the Jews were raging and gnashing their teeth against Nicodemus. Pilate saith unto them: Wherefore gnash ye your teeth against him, wherens ye have heard the truth? The Jews say unto Nicodemus: Mayest thou receive his truth and his portion. Nicodemus saith: Amen, Amen: may I receive it as ye have said.

VI

1 Now one of the Jews came forward and besought the governor that he might speak a word. The governor saith: If thou wilt say aught, speak on. And the Jew said: Thirty and eight years lay I on a bed in suffering of pains, and at the coming of Jesus many that were possessed and laid with divers diseases were healed by him, and certain (faithful) young men took pity on me and carried me with my bed and brought me unto him; and when Jesus saw me he had compassion, and spake a word unto me: Take up thy bed and walk. And I took up my bed and walked. The Jews say unto Pilate: Ask of him what day it was whereon he was healed? He that was healed saith: On the sabbath. The Jews say: Did we not inform thee so, that upon the sabbath he healeth and casteth out devils?

2 And another Jew came forward and said: I was born blind: I heard words but I saw no man's face: and as Jesus passed by I cried with a loud voice: Have mercy on me, O son of David. And he took pity on me and put his hands upon mine eyes and I received sight immediately. And

another Jew came forward and said: I was bowed and he made me straight with a word. And another said: I was a leper, and he healed me with a word.

VII

And a certain woman named Bernice (Beronice Copt., Veronica Lat.) crying out from afar off said: I had an issue of blood and touched the hem of his garment, and the flowing of my blood was stayed which I had twelve years. The Jews say: We have a law that a woman shall not come to give testimony.

VIII

And certain others, even a multitude both of men and women cried out, saying: This man is a prophet and the devils are subject unto him. Pilate saith to them which said: The devils are subject unto him: Wherefore were not your teachers also subject unto him? They say unto Pilate: We know not. Others also said: He raised up Lazarus which was dead out of his tomb after four days. And the governor was afraid and said unto all the multitude of the Jews: Wherefore will ye shed innocent blood?

IX

1 And he called unto him Nicodemus and those twelve men which said that he was not born of fornication, and said unto them: What shall I do, for there riseth sedition among the people? They say unto him: We know not, let them see to it. Again Pilate called for all the multitude of the Jews and saith: Ye know that ye have a custom that at the feast of unleavened bread I should release unto you a prisoner. Now I have a prisoner under condemnation in the prison, a murderer, Barabbas by name, and this Jesus also which standeth before you, in whom I find no fault: Whom will ye that I release unto you? But they cried out: Barabbas. Pilate saith: What shall I do then with Jesus who is called Christ? The Jews say: Let him be crucified. But certain of the Jews answered: Thou art not a friend of Caesar's if thou let this man go; for he called himself the Son of God and a king: thou wilt therefore have him for king, and not Caesar.

2 And Pilate was wroth and said unto the Jews: Your nation is always seditious and ye rebel against your benefactors. The Jews say: Against what benefactors? Pilate saith: According as I have heard, your God brought you out of Egypt out of hard bondage, and led you safe through the sea as by dry land, and in the wilderness he nourished you with manna and gave you quails, and gave you water to drink out of a rock, and gave unto you a law. And in all these things ye provoked your God to anger, and sought out a molten calf, and angered your God and he sought to slay you: and Moses made supplication for you and ye were not put to death. And now ye do accuse me that I hate the king (emperor).

3 And he rose up from the judgement-seat and sought to go forth. And the Jews cried out, saying: We know our king, even Caesar and not Jesus. For indeed the wise men brought gifts from the east unto him as unto a king, and when Herod heard from the wise men that a king was born, he sought to slay him, and when his father Joseph knew that, he took him and his mother and they fled into Egypt. And when Herod heard it he destroyed the children of the Hebrews that were born in Bethlehem.

4 And when Pilate heard these words he was afraid. And Pilate silenced the multitude, because they cried still, and said unto them: So, then, this is he whom Herod sought? The Jews say: Yea, this is he. And Pilate took water and washed his hands before the sun, saying: I am innocent of the blood of this just man: see ye to it. Again the Jews cried out: His blood be upon us and upon our children.

5 Then Pilate commanded the veil to be drawn before the judgement-seat whereon he sat, and saith unto Jesus: Thy nation hath convicted thee (accused thee) as being a king: therefore have I decreed that thou shouldest first be scourged according to the law of the pious emperors, and thereafter hanged upon the cross in the garden wherein thou wast taken: and let Dysmas and Gestas the two malefactors be crucified with thee.

X

1 And Jesus went forth of the judgement hall and the two malefactors with him. And when they were come to the place they stripped him of his garments and girt him with a linen cloth and put a crown of thorns about his head: likewise also they hanged up the two malefactors. But Jesus said: Father forgive them, for they know not what they do. And the soldiers divided his garments among them.

And the people stood looking upon him, and the chief priests and the rulers with them derided him, saying: He saved others let him save himself: if he be the son of God [let him come down from the cross]. And the soldiers also mocked him, coming and offering him vinegar with gall; and they said: If thou be the King of the Jews, save thyself.

And Pilate after the sentence commanded his accusation to be written for a title in letters of Greek and Latin and Hebrew according to the saying of the Jews: that he was the King of the Jews.

2 And one of the malefactors that were hanged [by name Gestas] spake unto him, saying: If thou be the Christ, save thyself, and us. But Dysmas answering rebuked him, saying: Dost thou not at all fear God, seeing thou art in the same condemnation? and we indeed justly, for we receive the due reward of our deeds; but this man hath done nothing amiss. And he said unto Jesus: Remember me, Lord, in thy kingdom. And Jesus said unto him: Verily, verily, I say unto thee, that today thou shalt be (art) with me in paradise.

XI

1 And it was about the sixth hour, and there was darkness over the land until the ninth hour, for the sun was darkened: and the veil of the temple was rent asunder in the midst. And Jesus called with a loud voice and said: Father, baddach ephkid rouel, which is interpreted: Into thy hands I commend my spirit. And having thus said he gave up the ghost. And when the centurion saw what was done, he glorified God, saying: This man was righteous. And all the multitudes that had come to the sight, when they beheld what was done smote their breasts and returned.

2 But the centurion reported unto the governor the things that had come to pass: and when the governor and his wife heard, they were sore vexed, and neither ate nor drank that day. And Pilate sent for the Jews and said unto them: Did ye see that which came to pass? But they said: There was an eclipse of the sun after the accustomed sort.

3 And his acquaintance had stood afar off, and the women which came with him from Galilee, beholding these things. But a certain man named Joseph, being a counsellor, of the city of Arimathaea, who also himself looked for the kingdom of God this man went to Pilate and begged the body of Jesus. And he took it down and wrapped it in a clean linen cloth and laid it in a hewn sepulchre wherein was never man yet laid.

XII

1 Now when the Jews heard that Joseph had begged the body of Jesus, they sought for him and for the twelve men which said that Jesus was not born of fornication, and for Nicodemus and many others which had come forth before Pilate and declared his good works. But all they hid themselves, and Nicodemus only was seen of them, for he was a ruler of the Jews. And Nicodemus said unto them: How came ye into the synagogue? The Jews say unto him: How didst thou come into the synagogue? for thou art confederate with him, and his portion shall be with thee in the life to come. Nicodemus saith: Amen, Amen. Likewise Joseph also came forth and said unto them: Why is it that ye are vexed against me, for that I begged the body of Jesus? behold I have laid it in my new tomb, having wrapped it in clean linen, and I rolled a stone over the door of the cave. And ye have not dealt well with the just one, for ye repented not when ye had crucified him, but ye also pierced him with a spear.

But the Jews took hold on Joseph and commanded him to be put in safeguard until the first day of the week: and they said unto him: Know thou that the time alloweth us not to do anything against thee, because the sabbath dawneth: but knew that thou shalt not obtain burial, but we will give thy flesh unto the fowls of the heaven. Joseph saith unto them: This is the word of Goliath the boastful which reproached the living God and the holy David. For God said by the prophet: Vengeance is mine, and I will recompense, saith the Lord. And now, lo, one that was uncircumcised, but circumcised in heart, took water and washed his hands before the sun, saying: I am Innocent of the blood of this just person: see ye to it. And ye answered Pilate and said: His blood be upon us and upon our children. And now I fear lest the wrath of the Lord come upon you and upon your children, as ye have said. But when the Jews heard these words they waxed bitter in soul, and caught hold on Joseph and took him and shut him up in an house wherein was no window, and guards were set at the door: and they sealed the door of the place where Joseph was shut up.

2 And upon the sabbath day the rulers of the synagogue and the priests and the Levites made an ordinance that all men should appear in the synagogue on the first day of the week. And all the multitude rose up early and took council in the synagogue by what death they should kill him. And when the council was set they commanded him to be brought with great dishonour. And when they had opened the door they found him not. And all the people were beside themselves and amazed, because they found the seals closed, and Caiaphas had the key. And they durst not any more lay hands upon them that had spoken in the behalf of Jesus before Pilate.

XIII

1 And while they yet sat in the synagogue and marvelled because of Joseph, there came certain of the guard which the Jews had asked of Pilate to keep the sepulchre of Jesus lest peradventure his disciples should come and steal him away. And they spake and declared unto the rulers of the synagogue and the priests and the Levites that which had come to pass: how that there was a great earthquake, and we saw an angel descend from heaven, and he rolled away the stone from the mouth of the cave, and sat upon it. And he did shine like snow and like lightning, and we were sore afraid and lay as dead men. And we heard the voice of the angel speaking with the women which waited at the sepulchre, saying: Fear ye not: for I know that ye seek Jesus which was crucified. He is not here: he is risen, as he said. Come, see the place where the Lord lay, and go quickly and say unto his disciples that he is risen from the dead, and is in Galilee.

2 The Jews say: With what women spake he? They of the guard say: We know not who they were. The Jews say: At what hour was it? They of the guard say: At midnight. The Jews say: And wherefore did ye not take the women? They of the guard say: We were become as dead me through fear, and we looked not to see the light of the day; how then could we take them? The Jews say: As the Lord liveth, we believe you not. They of

the guard say unto the Jews: So many signs saw ye in that man, and ye believed not, how then should ye believe us? verily ye sware rightly 'as the Lord liveth', for he liveth indeed. Again they of the guard say: We have heard that ye shut up him that begged the body of Jesus, and that ye scaled the door; and when ye had opened it ye found him not. Give ye therefore Joseph and we will give you Jesus. The Jews say: Joseph is departed unto his own city. They of the guard say unto the Jews: Jesus also is risen, as we have heard of the angel, and he is in Galilee.

3 And when the Jews heard these words they were sore afraid, saying: Take heed lest this report be heard and all men incline unto Jesus. And the Jews took counsel and laid down much money and gave it to the soldiers, saying: Say ye: While we slept his disciples came by night and stole him away. And if this come to the governor's hearing we will persuade him and secure you. And they took the money and did as they were instructed. [And this their saying was published abroad among all men. lat.]

XIV

1 Now a certain priest named Phinees and Addas a teacher and Aggaeus (Ogias Copt., Egias lat.) a Levite came down from Galilee unto Jerusalem and told the rulers of the synagogue and the priests and the Levites, saying: We saw Jesus and his disciples sitting upon the mountain which is called Mamilch (Mambre or Malech lat., Mabrech Copt.), and he said unto his disciples: Go into all the world and preach unto every creature (the whole creation): he that believeth and is baptized shall be saved, but he that disbelieveth shall be condemned. [And these signs shall follow upon them that believe: in my name they shall cast out devils, they shall speak with new tongues, they shall take up serpents, and if they drink any deadly thing it shall not hurt them: they shall lay hands upon the sick and they shall recover.] And while Jesus yet spake unto his disciples we saw him taken up into heaven.

2 The elders and the priests and Levites say: Give glory to the God of Israel and make confession unto him: did ye indeed (or that ye did) hear and see those things which ye have told us? They that told them say: As the Lord God of our fathers Abraham, Isaac, and Jacob liveth, we did hear these things and we saw him taken up into heaven. The elders and the priests and the Levites say unto them: Came ye for this end, that ye might tell us, or came ye to pay your vows unto God? And they say: To pay our vows unto God. The elders and the chief priests and the Levites say unto them: If ye came to pay your vows unto God, to what purpose is this idle tale which ye have babbled before all the people? Phinees the priest and Addas the teacher and Aggaeus the Levite say unto the rulers of the synagogue and priests and Levites: If these words which ye have spoken and seen be sin, lo, we are before you: do unto us as seemeth good in your eyes. And they took the book of the law and adjured them that they should no more tell any man these words: and they gave them to eat and to drink, and put them out of the city: moreover they gave them money, and three men to go with them, and they set them on their way as far as Galilee, and they departed in peace.

3 Now when these men were departed into Galilee, the chief priests and the rulers of the synagogue and the elders gathered together in the synagogue, and shut the gate, and lamented with a great lamentation, saying: What is this sign which is come to pass in Israel? But Amlas and Caiaphas said: Wherefore are ye troubled? why weep ye? Know ye not that his disciples gave much gold unto them that kept the sepulchre and taught them to say that an angel came down and rolled away the stone from the door of the sepulchre? But the priests and the elders said: Be it so, that his disciples did steal away his body; but how is his soul entered into his body, and how abideth he in Galilee? But they could not answer these things, and hardly in the end said: It is not lawful for us to believe the uncircumcised. [Lat. (and Copt., and Arm.): Ought we to believe the soldiers, that an angel came down from heaven and rolled away the stone from the door of the sepulchre? but in truth his disciples gave . . . sepulchre. Know ye not that it is not lawful for Jews to believe any word of the uncircumcised, knowing that they who received much good from us have spoken according as we taught them.]

XV

And Nicodemus rose up and stood before the council, saying: Ye say well. Know ye not, O people of the Lord, the men that came down out of Galilee, that they fear God and are men of substance, hating covetousness (a lie, Lat.), men of peace? And they have told you with an oath, saying: We saw Jesus upon the mount Mamilch with his disciples and that he taught them all things that ye heard of them, and, say they, we saw him taken up into heaven. And no man asked them in what manner he was taken up. For like as the book of the holy scriptures hath taught us that Elias also was taken up into heaven, and Eliseus cried out with a loud voice, and Elias cast his hairy cloak upon Eliseus, and Eliseus cast the cloak upon Jordan and passed over and went unto Jericho. And the sons of the prophets met him and said: Eliseus, where is thy lord Elias? and he said that he was taken up into heaven. And they said unto Eliseus: Hath not a spirit caught him up and cast him upon one of the mountains? but let us take our servants with us and seek after him. And they persuaded Eliseus and he went with them, and they sought him three days and found him not: and they knew that he had been taken up. And now hearken unto

me, and let us send into all the coasts (al. mountains) of Israel and see whether the Christ were not taken up by a spirit and cast upon one of the mountains. And this saying pleased them all: and they sent into all the coasts (mountains, Lat.) and sought Jesus and found him not. But they found Joseph in Arimathaea, and no man durst lay hands upon him.

2 And they told the elders and the priests and the Levites, saying: We went about throughout all the coasts of Israel, and we found not Jesus; but Joseph we found in Arimathaea. And when they heard of Joseph they rejoiced and gave glory to the God of Israel. And the rulers of the synagogue and the priests and the Levites took counsel how they should meet with Joseph, and they took a volume of paper and wrote unto Joseph these words:

Peace be unto thee. We know that we have sinned against God and against thee, and we have prayed unto the God of Israel that thou shouldest vouchsafe to come unto thy fathers and unto thy children (Lat. But thou didst pray unto the God of Israel, and he delivered thee out of our hands. Now therefore vouchsafe, &c.) for we are all troubled, because when we opened the door we found thee not: and we know that we devised an evil counsel against thee, but the Lord helped thee. And the Lord himself made of none effect (scattered) our counsel against thee, O father Joseph, thou that art honourable among all the people.

3 And they chose out of all Israel seven men that were friends of Joseph, whom Joseph also himself accounted his friends, and the rulers of the synagogue and the priests and the Levites said unto them: See: if he receive our epistle and read it, know that he will come with you unto us: but if he read it not, know that he is vexed with us, and salute ye him in peace and return unto us. And they blessed the men and let them go.

And the men came unto Joseph and did him reverence, and said unto him: Peace be unto thee. And he said: Peace be unto you and unto all the people of Israel. And they gave him the book of the epistle, and Joseph received it and read it and embraced (or kissed) the epistle and blessed God and said: Blessed be the Lord God, which hath redeemed Israel from shedding innocent blood; and blessed be the Lord, which sent his angel and sheltered me under his wings. (And he kissed them) and set a table before them, and they did eat and drink and lay there.

4 And they rose up early and prayed: and Joseph saddled his she-ass and went with the men, and they came unto the holy city, even Jerusalem. And all the people came to meet Joseph and cried: Peace be to thine entering-in. And he said unto all the people: Peace be unto you, and all the people kissed him. And the people prayed with Joseph, and they were astonished at the sight of him.

And Nicodemus received him into his house and made a great feast, and called Annas and Caiaphas and the elders and the priests and the Levites unto his house. And they made merry eating and drinking with Joseph. And when they had sung an hymn (or blessed God) every man went unto his house. But Joseph abode in the house of Nicodemus.

5 And on the morrow, which was the preparation, the rulers of the synagogue and the priests and the Levites rose up early and came to the house of Nicodemus, and Nicodemus met them and said: Peace be unto you. And they said: Peace be unto thee and to Joseph and unto all thy house and to all the house of Joseph. And he brought them into his house. And the whole council was set, and Joseph sat between Annas and Caiaphas and no man durst speak unto him a word. And Joseph said: Why is it that ye have called me? And they beckoned unto Nicodemus that he should speak unto Joseph. And Nicodemus opened his mouth and said unto Joseph: Father, thou knowest that the reverend doctors and the priests and the Levites seek to learn a matter of thee. And Joseph said: Inquire ye. And Annas and Caiaphas took the book of the law and adjured Joseph saying: Give glory to the God of Israel and make confession unto him: [for Achar, when he was adjured of the prophet Jesus(Joshua), foresware not himself but declared unto him all things and hid not a word from him: thou therefore also hide not from us so much as a word. And Joseph: I will not hide one word from you.] And they said unto him: We were greatly vexed because thou didst beg the body of Jesus and wrappedst it in a clean linen cloth and didst lay him in a tomb. And for this cause we put thee in safeguard in an house wherein was no window, and we put keys and seals upon the doors, and guards did keep the place wherein thou wast shut up. And on the first day of the week we opened it and found thee not, and we were sore troubled, and amazement fell upon all the people of the Lord until yesterday. Now, therefore, declare unto us what befell thee.

6 And Joseph said: On the preparation day about the tenth hour ye did shut me up, and I continued there the whole sabbath. And at midnight as I stood and prayed the house wherein ye shut me up was taken up by the four corners, and I saw as it were a flashing of light in mine eyes, and being filled with fear I fell to the earth. And one took me by the hand and removed me from the place whereon I had fallen; and moisture of water was shed on me from my head unto my feet, and an odour of ointment came about my nostrils. And he wiped my face and kissed me and said unto me: Fear not, Joseph: open thine eyes and see who it is that speaketh with thee. And I looked up and saw Jesus and I trembled, and supposed that it was a spirit: and I said the commandments: and he said them with me. And [as] ye are not ignorant that a spirit, if it meet any man and hear

the commandments, straightway fleeth. And when I perceived that he said them with me, I said unto him: Rabbi Elias? And he said unto me: I am not Elias. And I said unto him: Who art thou, Lord? And he said unto me: I am Jesus, whose body thou didst beg of Pilate, and didst clothe me in clean linen and cover my face with a napkin, and lay me in thy new cave and roll a great stone upon the door of the cave. And I said to him that spake with me: Show me the place where I laid thee. And he brought me and showed me the place where I laid him, and the linen cloth lay therein, and the napkin that was upon his face. And I knew that it was Jesus. And he took me by the hand and set me in the midst of mine house, the doors being shut, and laid me upon my bed and said unto me: Peace be unto thee. And he kissed me and said unto me: Until forty days be ended go not out of thine house: for behold I go unto my brethren into Galilee.

XVI

1 And when the rulers of the synagogue and the priests and the Levites heard these words of Joseph the became as dead men and fell to the ground, and they fasted until the ninth hour. And Nicodemus with Joseph comforted Annas and Caiaphas and the priests and the Levites, saying: Rise up and stand on your feet and taste bread and strengthen your souls, for tomorrow is the sabbath of the Lord. And they rose up and prayed unto God and did eat and drink, and departed every man to his house.

2 And on the sabbath the (al. our) teachers and the priests and Levites sat and questioned one another and said: What is this wrath that is come upon us? for we know his father and his mother. Levi the teacher saith: I know that his parents feared God and kept not back their vows and paid tithes three times a year. And when Jesus was born, his parents brought him up unto this place and gave sacrifices and burnt-offerings to God. And [when] the great teacher Symeon took him into his arms and said: Now lettest thou thy servant, Lord, depart in peace for mine eyes have seen thy salvation which thou hast prepared before the face of all peoples, a light to lighten the Gentiles and the glory of thy people Israel. And Symeon blessed them and said unto Mary his mother: I give thee good tidings concerning this child. And Mary said: Good, my lord? And Symeon said to her : Good. Behold, he is set for the fall and rising again of many in Israel, and for a sign spoken against: and a sword shall pierce through thine own heart also, that the thoughts of many hearts may be revealed.

3 They say unto Levi the teacher: How knowest thou these things? Levi saith unto them: Know ye not that from him I did learn the law? The council say unto him: We would see thy father. And they sent after his father, and asked of him, and he said to them: Why believed ye not my son? the blessed and righteous Symeon, he did teach him the law. The council saith: Rabbi Levi, is the word true which thou hast spoken? And he said: It is true.

Then the rulers of the synagogue and the priests and the Levites said among themselves: Come, let us send into Galilee unto the three men which came and told us of his teaching and his taking-up, and let them tell us how they saw him taken up. And this word pleased them all, and they sent the three men which before had gone with them into Galilee and said to them: Say unto Rabbi Addas and Rabbi Phinees and Rabbi Aggaeus: peace be to you and to all that are with you. Inasmuch as great questioning hath arisen in the council, we have sent unto you to call you unto this holy place of Jerusalem.

4 And the men went into Galilee and found them sitting and meditating upon the law, and saluted them in peace. And the men that were in Galilee said unto them that were come to them: Peace be upon all Israel. And they said: Peace be unto you. Again they said unto them: Wherefore are ye come? And they that were sent said: The council calleth you unto the holy city Jerusalem. And when the men heard that they were bidden by the council, they prayed to God and sat down to meat with the men and did eat and drink, and rose up and came in peace unto Jerusalem.

5 And on the morrow the council was set in the synagogue, and they examined them, saying: Did ye in very deed see Jesus sitting upon the mount Mamilch, as he taught his eleven disciples, and saw ye him taken up? And the men answered them and said: Even as we saw him taken up, even so did we tell it unto you.

6 Annas saith: Set them apart from one another, and let us see if their word agreeth. And they set them apart one from another, and they call Addas first and say unto him: How sawest thou Jesus taken up? Addas saith: While he yet sat upon the Mount Mamilch and taught his disciples, we saw a cloud that overshadowed him and his disciples: and the cloud carried him up into heaven, and his disciples lay (al. prayed, lying) on their faces upon the earth. And they called Phinees the priest, and questioned him also, saying: How sawest thou Jesus taken up? And he spake in like manner. And again they asked Aggaeus, and he also spake in like manner. And the council said: It is contained in the law of Moses: At the mouth of two or three shall every word be established.

Abuthem (Bouthem Gr., Abudem lat., Abuden, Abuthen Arm.,om. Copt.) the teacher saith: It is written in the law: Enoch walked with God and is not, because God took him. Jaeirus the teacher said: Also we have heard of the death of the holy Moses and have not seen him; for it is written in the law of the Lord: And Moses died at the mouth of the Lord, and no man knew of his sepulchre unto this day. And Rabbi Levi said: Wherefore

was it that Rabbi Symeon said when he saw Jesus: Behold, this child is set for the fall and rising again of many in Israel and for a sign spoken against? And Rabbi Isaac said: It is written in the law: Behold I send my messenger before thy face, which shall go before thee to keep thee in every good way, for my name is named thereon.

7 Then said Annas and Caiaphas: Ye have well said those things which are written in the law of Moses, that no man saw the death of Enoch, and no man hath named the death of Moses. But Jesus spake before Pilate, and we know that we saw him receive buffets and spittings upon his face, and that the soldiers put on him a crown of thorns and that he was scourged and received condemnation from Pilate, and that he was crucified at the place of a skull and two thieves with him, and that they gave him vinegar to drink with gall, and that Longinus the soldier pierced his side with a spear, and that Joseph our honourable father begged his body, and that, as he saith, he rose again, and that (lit. as) the three teachers say: We saw him taken up into heaven, and that Rabbi Levi spake and testified to the things which were spoken by Rabbi Symeon, and that he said: Behold this child is set for the fall and rising again of many in Israel and for a sign spoken against.

And all the teachers said unto all the people of the Lord: If this hath come to pass from the Lord, and it is marvelous in our eyes, ye shall surely know, O house of Jacob, that it is written: Cursed is every one that hangeth upon a tree. And another scripture teacheth: The gods which made not the heaven and the earth shall perish.

And the priests and the Levites said one to another: If his memorial endure until the Sommos (Copt. Soum) which is called Jobel (i. e. the Jubilee), know ye that he will prevail for ever and raise up for himself a new people.

Then the rulers of the synagogue and the priests and the Levites admonished all Israel, saying: Cursed is that man who shall worship that which man's hand hath made, and cursed is the man who shall worship creatures beside the Creator. And all the people said: Amen, Amen.

And all the people sang an hymn unto the Lord and said: Blessed be the Lord who hath given rest unto the people of Israel according to all that he spake. There hath not one word fallen to the ground of all his good saying which he spake unto his servant Moses. The Lord our God be with us as he was with our fathers: let him not forsake us. And let him not destroy us from turning our heart unto him, from walking in all his ways and keeping his statutes and his judgements which he commanded our fathers. And the Lord shall be King over all the earth in that day. And there shall be one Lord and his name one, even the Lord our King: he shall save us. There is none like unto thee, O Lord. Great art thou, O Lord, and great is thy name.

Heal us, O Lord, by thy power, and we shall be healed: save us, Lord, and we shall be saved: for we are thy portion and thine inheritance.

And the Lord will not forsake his people for his great name's sake, for the Lord hath begun to make us to be his people.

And when they had all sung this hymn they departed every man to his house, glorifying God. [For his is the glory, world without end. Amen.]

ACTS OF PILATE

PART II. THE DESCENT INTO HELL

This writing, or the nucleus of it, the story of the Descent into Hell was not originally part of the Acts of Pilate. It is -apart from its setting- probably an older document. When it was first attached to the Acts of Pilate is uncertain. The object of this prefatory note is to say that we have the text in three forms, [however, only the Latin A text will be given. For a complete listing of all three texts see M.R. James apocryphal New Testament].

.[Part I, cap. xvi, ends with words of the rulers of the synagogue, &c. All nations shall serve him, and kings shall come from afar worshipping and magnifying him. Part II, cap. i, runs on from this.

I (XVII)

1 And Joseph arose and said unto Annas and Caiaphas: Truly and of right do ye marvel because ye have heard that Jesus hath been seen alive after death, and that he hath ascended into heaven. Nevertheless it is more marvelous that he rose not alone from the dead, but did raise up alive many other dead out of their sepulchres, and they have been seen of many in Jerusalem. And now hearken unto me; for we all know the blessed Simeon, the high priest which received the child Jesus in his hands in the temple. And this Simeon had two sons, brothers in blood and we all were at their falling asleep and at their burial. Go therefore and look upon their sepulchres: for they are open, because they have risen, and behold they are in the city of Arimathaea dwelling together in prayer. And indeed men hear them crying out, yet they speak with no man, but are silent as dead men. But come, let us go unto them and with all honour and gentleness bring them unto us, and if we adjure them, perchance they will tell us concerning the mystery of their rising again.

2 When they heard these things, they all rejoiced. And Annas and Caiaphas, Nicodemus and Joseph and Gamaliel went and found them not in their sepulchre, but they went unto the city of Arimathaea, and found them there, kneeling on their knees and giving themselves unto prayer. And they kissed them, and with all reverence and in the fear of God they brought them to Jerusalem into the synagogue. And they shut the doors

and took the law of the Lord and put it into their hands, and adjured them by the God Adonai and the God of Israel which spake unto our fathers by the prophets, saying: Believe ye that it is Jesus which raised you from the dead? Tell us how ye have arisen from the dead.

3 And when Karinus and Leucius heard this adjuration, they trembled in their body and groaned, being troubled in heart. And looking up together unto heaven they made the seal of the cross with their fingers upon their tongues, and forthwith they spake both of them, saying: Give us each a volume of paper, and let us write that which we have seen and heard. And they gave them unto them, and each of them sat down and wrote, saying:

II (XVIII)

1 O Lord Jesu Christ, the life and resurrection of the dead (al. resurrection of the dead and the life of the living), suffer us to speak of the mysteries of thy majesty which thou didst perform after thy death upon the cross, inasmuch as we have been adjured by thy Name. For thou didst command us thy servants to tell no man the secrets of thy divine majesty which thou wroughtest in hell.

Now when we were set together with all our fathers in the deep, in obscurity of darkness, on a sudden there came a golden heat of the sun and a purple and royal light shining upon us. And immediately the father of the whole race of men, together with all the patriarchs and prophets, rejoiced, saying: This light is the beginning (author) of everlasting light which did promise to send unto us his co-eternal light. And Esaias cried out and said: This is the light of the Father, even the Son of God, according as I prophesied when I lived upon the earth: The land of Zabulon and the land of Nephthalim beyond Jordan, of Galilee of the Gentiles, the people that walked in darkness have seen a great light, and they that dwell in the land of the shadow of death, upon them did the light shine. And now hath it come and shone upon us that sit in death.

2 And as we all rejoiced in the light which shined upon us, there came unto us our father Simeon, and he rejoicing said unto us: Glorify ye the Lord Jesus Christ, the Son of God; for I received him in my hands in the temple when he was born a child, and being moved of the Holy Ghost I made confession and said unto him: Now have mine eyes seen thy salvation which thou hast prepared before the face of all people, a light to lighten the Gentiles, and to be the glory of thy people Israel. And when they heard these things, the whole multitude of the saints rejoiced yet more.

Page 125

3 And after that there came one as it were a dweller in the wilderness, and he was inquired of by all: Who art thou? And he answered them and said: I am John, the voice and the prophet of the most High, which came before the face of his advent to prepare his ways, to give knowledge of salvation unto his people, for the remission of their sins. And when I saw him coming unto me, being moved of the Holy Ghost, I said: Behold the Lamb of God, behold him that taketh away the sins of the world. And I baptized him in the river of Jordan, and saw the Holy Ghost descending upon him in the likeness of a dove, and heard a voice out of heaven saying: This is my beloved Son, in whom I am well pleased. And now have I come before his face, and come down to declare unto you that he is at hand to visit us, even the day spring, the Son of God, coming from on high unto us that sit in darkness and in the shadow of death.

III (XIX)

1 And when father Adam that was first created heard this, even that Jesus was baptized in Jordan, he cried out to Seth his son, saying: Declare unto thy sons the patriarchs and the prophets all that thou didst hear from Michael the archangel, when I sent thee unto the gates of paradise that thou mightest entreat God to send thee his angel to give thee the oil of the tree of mercy to anoint my body when I was sick. Then Seth drew near unto the holy patriarchs and prophets, and said: When I, Seth, was praying at the gates of paradise, behold Michael the angel of the Lord appeared unto me, saying: I am sent unto thee from the Lord: it is I that am set over the body of man. And I say unto thee, Seth, vex not thyself with tears, praying and entreating for the oil of the tree of mercy, that thou mayest anoint thy father Adam for the pain of his body: for thou wilt not be able to receive it save in the last days and times, save when five thousand and five hundred (al. 5,952) years are accomplished: then shall the most beloved Son of God come upon the earth to raise up the body of Adam and the bodies of the dead, and he shall come and be baptized in Jordan. And when he is come forth of the water of Jordan, then shall he anoint with the oil of mercy all that believe on him, and that oil of mercy shall be unto all generations of them that shall be born of water and of the Holy Ghost, unto life eternal. Then shall the most beloved Son of God, even Christ Jesus, come down upon the earth and shall bring in our father Adam into paradise unto the tree of mercy.

And when they heard all these things of Seth, all the patriarchs and prophets rejoiced with a great rejoicing.

IV (XX)

1 And while all the saints were rejoicing, behold Satan the prince and chief of death said unto Hell: Make thyself ready to receive Jesus who boasteth himself that he is the Son of God, whereas he is a man that feareth death, and sayeth: My soul is sorrowful even unto death. And he hath been much mine enemy, doing me great hurt, and many that I had

made blind, lame, dumb, leprous, and possessed he hath healed with a word: and some whom I have brought unto thee dead, them hath he taken away from thee.

2 Hell answered and said unto Satan the prince: Who is he that is so mighty, if he be a man that feareth death? for all the mighty ones of the earth are held in subjection by my power, even they whom thou hast brought me subdued by thy power. If, then, thou art mighty, what manner of man is this Jesus who, though he fear death, resisteth thy power? If he be so mighty in his manhood, verily I say unto thee he is almighty in his god-head, and no man can withstand his power. And when he saith that he feareth death, he would ensnare thee, and woe shall be unto thee for everlasting ages. But Satan the prince of Tartarus said: Why doubtest thou and fearest to receive this Jesus which is thine adversary and mine? For I tempted him, and have stirred up mine ancient people of the Jews with envy and wrath against him. I have sharpened a spear to thrust him through, gall and vinegar have I mingled to give him to drink, and I have prepared a cross to crucify him and nails to pierce him: and his death is nigh at hand, that I may bring him unto thee to be subject unto thee and me.

3 Hell answered and said: Thou hast told me that it is he that hath taken away dead men from me. For there be many which while they lived on the earth have taken dead men from me, yet not by their own power but by prayer to God, and their almighty God hath taken them from me. Who is this Jesus which by his own word without prayer hath drawn dead men from me? Perchance it is he which by the word of his command did restore to life Lazarus which was four days dead and stank and was corrupt, whom I held here dead. Satan the prince of death answered and said: It is that same Jesus. When Hell heard that he said unto him: I adjure thee by thy strength and mine own that thou bring him not unto me. For at that time I, when I heard the command of his word, did quake and was overwhelmed with fear, and all my ministries with me were troubled. Neither could we keep Lazarus, but he like an eagle shaking himself leaped forth with all agility and swiftness, and departed from us, and the earth also which held the dead body of Lazarus straightway gave him up alive. Wherefore now I know that that man which was able to do these things is a God strong in command and mighty in manhood, and that he is the saviour of mankind. And if thou bring him unto me he will set free all that are here shut up in the hard prison and bound in the chains of their sins that cannot be broken, and will bring them unto the life of his god head for ever.

V (XXI)

1 And as Satan the prince, and Hell, spoke this together, suddenly there came a voice as of thunder and a spiritual cry: Remove, O princes, your gates, and be ye lift up, ye everlasting doors, and the King of glory shall come in. When Hell heard that he said unto Satan the prince: Depart from me and go out of mine abode: if thou be a mighty man of war, fight thou against the King of glory. But what hast thou to do with him? And Hell cast Satan forth out of his dwelling. Then said Hell unto his wicked ministers: Shut ye the hard gates of brass and put on them the bars of iron and withstand stoutly, lest we that hold captivity be taken captive.

2 But when all the multitude of the saints heard it, they spake with a voice of rebuking unto Hell: Open thy gates, that the King of glory may come in. And David cried out, saying: Did I not when I was alive upon earth, foretell unto you: Let them give thanks unto the Lord, even his mercies and his wonders unto the children of men; who hath broken the gates of brass and smitten the bars of iron in sunder? He hath taken them out of the way of their iniquity. And thereafter in like manner Esaias said: Did not I when I was alive upon earth foretell unto you: The dead shall arise, and they that are in the tombs shall rise again, and they that are in the earth shall rejoice, for the dew which cometh of the Lord is their healing? And again I said: O death, where is thy sting? O Hell, where is thy victory?

3 When they heard that of Esaias, all the saints said unto Hell: Open thy gates: now shalt thou be overcome and weak and without strength. And there came a great voice as of thunder, saying: Remove, O princes, your gates, and be ye lift up ye doors of hell, and the King of glory shall come in. And when Hell saw that they so cried out twice, he said, as if he knew it not: Who is the King of glory? And David answered Hell and said: The words of this cry do I know, for by his spirit I prophesied the same; and now I say unto thee that which I said before: The Lord strong and mighty, the Lord mighty in battle, he is the King of glory. And: The Lord looked down from heaven that he might hear the groanings of them that are in fetters and deliver the children of them that have been slain. And now, O thou most foul and stinking Hell, open thy gates, that the King of glory may come in. And as David spake thus unto Hell, the Lord of majesty appeared in the form of a man and lightened the eternal darkness and brake the bonds that could not be loosed: and the succour of his everlasting might visited us that sat in the deep darkness of our transgressions and in the shadow of death of our sins.

VI (XXII)

1 When Hell and death and their wicked ministers saw that, they were stricken with fear, they and their cruel officers, at the sight of the brightness of so great light in their own realm, seeing Christ of a sudden in their

abode, and they cried out, saying: We are overcome by thee. Who art thou that art sent by the Lord for our confusion? Who art thou that without all damage of corruption, and with the signs (?) of thy majesty unblemished, dost in wrath condemn our power? Who art thou that art so great and so small, both humble and exalted, both soldier and commander, a marvellous warrior in the shape of a bondsman, and a King of glory dead and living, whom the cross bare slain upon it? Thou that didst lie dead in the sepulchre hast come down unto us living and at thy death all creation quaked and all the stars were shaken and thou hast become free among the dead and dost rout our legions. Who art thou that settest free the prisoners that are held bound by original sin and restorest them into their former liberty? Who art thou that sheddest thy divine and bright light upon them that were blinded with the darkness of their sins? After the same manner all the legions of devils were stricken with like fear and cried out all together in the terror of their confusion, saying: Whence art thou, Jesus, a man so mighty and bright in majesty, so excellent without spot and clean from sin? For that world of earth which hath been always subject unto us until now, and did pay tribute to our profit, hath never sent unto us a dead man like thee, nor ever dispatched such a gift unto Hell. Who then art thou that so fearlessly enterest our borders, and not only fearest not our torments, but besides essayest to bear away all men out of our bonds? Peradventure thou art that Jesus, of whom Satan our prince said that by thy death of the cross thou shouldest receive the dominion of the whole world.

2 Then did the King of glory in his majesty trample upon death, and laid hold on Satan the prince and delivered him unto the power of Hell, and drew Adam to him unto his own brightness.

VII (XXIII)

Then Hell, receiving Satan the prince, with sore reproach said unto him: O prince of perdition and chief of destruction, Beelzebub, the scorn of the angels and spitting of the righteous why wouldest thou do this? Thou wouldest crucify the King of glory and at his decease didst promise us great spoils of his death: like a fool thou knewest not what thou didst. For behold now, this Jesus putteth to flight by the brightness of his majesty all the darkness of death, and hath broken the strong depths of the prisons, and let out the prisoners and loosed them that were bound. And all that were sighing in our torments do rejoice against us, and at their prayers our dominions are vanquished and our realms conquered, and now no nation of men feareth us any more. And beside this, the dead which were never wont to be proud triumph over us, and the captives which never could be joyful do threaten us. O prince Satan, father of all the wicked and ungodly and renegades wherefore wouldest thou do this? They that from the beginning until now have despaired of life and salvation-now is none of their wonted roarings heard, neither doth any groan from them sound in our ears, nor is there any sign of tears upon the face of any of them. O prince Satan, holder of the keys of hell, those thy riches which thou hadst gained by the tree of transgression and the losing of paradise, thou hast lost by the tree of the cross, and all thy gladness hath perished. When thou didst hang up Christ Jesus the King of glory thou wroughtest against thyself and against me. Henceforth thou shalt know what eternal torments and infinite pains thou art to suffer in my keeping for ever. O prince Satan, author of death and head of all pride, thou oughtest first to have sought out matter of evil in this Jesus: Wherefore didst thou adventure without cause to crucify him unjustly against whom thou foundest no blame, and to bring into our realm the innocent and righteous one, and to lose the guilty and the ungodly and unrighteous of the whole world? And when Hell had spoken thus unto Satan the prince, then said the King of glory unto Hell: Satan the prince shall be in thy power unto all ages in the stead of Adam and his children, even those that are my righteous ones.

VIII (XXIV)

1 And the Lord stretching forth his hand, said: Come unto me, all ye my saints which bear mine image and my likeness. Ye that by the tree and the devil and death were condemned, behold now the devil and death condemned by the tree. And forthwith all the saints were gathered in one under the hand of the Lord. And the Lord holding the right hand of Adam, said unto him: Peace be unto thee with all thy children that are my righteous ones. But Adam, casting himself at the knees of the Lord entreated him with tears and beseechings, and said with a loud voice: I will magnify thee, O Lord, for thou hast set me up and not made my foes to triumph over me: O Lord my God I cried unto thee and thou hast healed me; Lord, thou hast brought my soul out of hell, thou hast delivered me from them that go down to the pit. Sing praises unto the Lord all ye saints of his, and give thanks unto him for the remembrance of his holiness. For there is wrath in his indignation and life is in his good pleasure. In like manner all the saints of God kneeled and cast themselves at the feet of the Lord, saying with one accord: Thou art come, O redeemer of the world: that which thou didst foretell by the law and by thy prophets, that hast thou accomplished in deed. Thou hast redeemed the living by thy cross, and by the death of the cross thou hast come down unto us, that thou mightest save us out of hell and death through thy majesty. O Lord, like as thou hast set the name of thy glory in the heavens and set up thy cross for a token of redemption upon the earth, so, Lord, set thou up the sign of the victory of thy cross in hell, that death may have no more dominion.

2 And the Lord stretched forth his hand and made the sign of the cross over Adam and over all his saints, and he took the right hand of Adam and went up out of hell, and all the saints followed him. Then did holy David cry aloud and say: Sing unto the Lord a new song, for he hath done marvelous things. His right hand hath wrought salvation for him and his holy arm. The Lord hath made known his saving health, before the face of all nations hath he revealed his righteousness. And the whole multitude of the saints answered, saying: Such honour have all his saints. Amen, Alleluia.

3 And thereafter Habacuc the prophet cried out and said: Thou wentest forth for the salvation of thy people to set free thy chosen. And all the saints answered, saying: Blessed is he that cometh in the name of the Lord. God is the Lord and hath showed us light. Amen, Alleluia. Likewise after that the prophet Micheas also cried, saying: What God is like thee, O Lord, taking away iniquity and removing sins? and now thou withholdest thy wrath for a testimony that thou art merciful of free will, and thou dost turn away and have mercy on us, thou forgivest all our iniquities and hast sunk all our sins in the depths of the sea, as thou swarest unto our fathers in the days of old. And all the saints answered, saying: This is our God for ever and ever, he shall be our guide, world without end. Amen, Alleluia. And so spake all the prophets, making mention of holy words out of their praises, and all the saints followed the Lord, crying Amen, Alleluia.

IX (XXV)

But the Lord holding the hand of Adam delivered him unto Michael the archangel, and all the saints followed Michael the archangel, and he brought them all into the glory and beauty (grace) of paradise. And there met with them two men, ancients of days, and when they were asked of the saints: Who are ye that have not yet been dead in hell with us and are set in paradise in the body? then one of them answering, said: I am Enoch which was translated hither by the word of the Lord, and this that is with me is Elias the Thesbite which was taken up in a chariot of fire: and up to this day we have not tasted death, but we are received unto the coming of Antichrist to fight against him with signs and wonders of God, and to be slain of him in Jerusalem, and after three days and a half to be taken up again alive on the clouds.

X (XXVI)

And as Enoch and Elias spake thus with the saints, behold there came another man of vile habit, bearing upon his shoulders the sign of the cross; whom when they beheld, all the saints said unto him: Who art thou? for thine appearance is as of a robber; and wherefore is it that thou bearest a sign upon thy shoulders? And he answered them and said: Ye have rightly said: for I was a robber, doing all manner of evil upon the earth. And the Jews crucified me with Jesus, and I beheld the wonders in the creation which came to pass through the cross of Jesus when he was crucified, and I believed that he was the maker of all creatures and the almighty king, and I besought him, saying: Remember me, Lord, when thou comest into thy kingdom. And forthwith he received my prayer, and said unto me: Verily I say unto thee, this day shalt thou be with me in paradise: and he gave me the sign of the cross, saying: Bear this and go unto paradise, and if the angel that keepeth paradise suffer thee not to enter in, show him the sign of the cross; and thou shalt say unto him: Jesus Christ the Son of God who now is crucified hath sent me. And when I had so done, I spake all these things unto the angel that keepeth paradise; and when he heard this of me, forthwith he opened the door and brought me in and set me at the right hand of paradise, saying: Lo now, tarry a little, and Adam the father of all mankind will enter in with all his children that are holy and righteous, after the triumph and glory of the ascending up of Christ the Lord that is crucified. When they heard all these words of the robber, all the holy patriarchs and prophets said with one voice: Blessed be the Lord Almighty, the Father of eternal good things, the Father of mercies, thou that hast given such grace unto thy sinners and hast brought them again into the beauty of paradise and into thy good pastures: for this is the most holy life of the spirit. Amen, Amen.

XI (XXVII)

These are the divine and holy mysteries which we saw and heard, even I, Karinus, and Leucius: but we were not suffered to relate further the rest of the mysteries of God, according as Michael the archangel strictly charged us, saying: Ye shall go with your brethren unto Jerusalem and remain in prayer, crying out and glorifying the resurrection of the Lord Jesus Christ, who hath raised you from the dead together with him: and ye shall not be speaking with any man, but sit as dumb men, until the hour come when the Lord himself suffereth you to declare the mysteries of his god head. But unto us Michael the archangel gave commandment that we should go over Jordan unto a place rich and fertile, where are many which rose again together with us for a testimony of the resurrection of Christ the Lord. For three days only were allowed unto us who rose from the dead, to keep the passover of the Lord in Jerusalem with our kindred (parents) that are living for a testimony of the resurrection of Christ the Lord: and we were baptized in the holy river of Jordan and received white robes, every one of us. And after the three days, when we had kept the passover of the Lord, all they were caught up in the clouds which had risen again with us, and were taken over Jordan and were no more seen of any man. But unto us it was said that we should remain in the city of Arimathaea and continue in prayer.

These be all things which the Lord bade us declare unto you: give praise and thanksgiving (confession) unto him, and repent that he may have mercy upon you. Peace be unto you from the same Lord Jesus Christ which is the Saviour of us all. Amen.

And when they had finished writing all things in the several volumes of paper they arose; and Karinus gave that which he had written into the hands of Annas and Caiaphas and Gamaliel; likewise Leucius gave that which he had written into the hands of Nicodemus and Joseph. And suddenly they were transfigured and became white exceedingly and were no more seen. But their writings were found to be the same (lit. equal), neither more nor less by one letter.

And when all the synagogue of the Jews heard all these marvelous sayings of Karinus and Leucius, they said one to another: Of a truth all these things were wrought by the Lord, and blessed be the Lord, world without end, Amen. And they went out all of them in great trouble of mind, smiting their breasts with fear and trembling, and departed every man unto his own home.

And all these things which were spoken by the Jews in their synagogue, did Joseph and Nicodemus forthwith declare unto the governor. And Pilate himself wrote all the things that were done and said concerning Jesus by the Jews, and laid up all the words in the public books of his judgement hall (praetorium).

XII (XXVIII)

This chapter is not found in the majority of copies.

After these things Pilate entered into the temple of the Jews and gathered together all the chief of the priests, and the teachers (grammaticos) and scribes and doctors of the law, and went in with them into the holy place of the temple and commanded all the doors to be shut, and said unto them: We have heard that ye have in this temple a certain great Bible; wherefore I ask you that it be presented before us. And when that great Bible adorned with gold and precious jewels was brought by four ministers, Pilate said to them all: I adjure you by the God of your fathers which commanded you to build this temple in the place of his sanctuary, that ye hide not the truth from me. Ye know all the things that are written in this Bible; but tell me now if ye have found in the scriptures that this Jesus whom ye have crucified is the Son of God which should come for the salvation of mankind, and in what year of the times he must come. Declare unto me whether ye crucified him in ignorance or knowingly.

And Annas and Caiaphas when they were thus adjured commanded all the rest that were will them to go out of the temple; and they themselves shut all the doors of the temple and of the sanctuary, and said unto Pilate: Thou hast adjured us, O excellent judge, by the building of this temple to make manifest unto thee the truth and reason (or a true account). After that we had crucified Jesus, knowing not that he was the Son of God, but supposing that by some chance he did his wondrous works, we made a great assembly (synagogue) in this temple; and as we conferred one with another concerning the signs of the mighty works which Jesus had done, we found many witnesses of our own nation who said that they had seen Jesus alive after his passion, and that he was passed into the height of the heaven. Moreover, we saw two witnesses whom Jesus raised from the dead, who declared unto us many marvelous things which Jesus did among the dead, which things we have in writing in our hands. Now our custom is that every year before our assembly we open this holy Bible and inquire the testimony of God. And we have found in the first book of the Seventy how that Michael the angel spake unto the third son of Adam the first man concerning the five thousand and five hundred years, wherein should come the most beloved Son of God, even Christ: and furthermore we have thought that peradventure this same was the God of Israel which said unto Moses: Make thee an ark of the covenant in length two cubits and a half, and in breadth one cubit and a half, and in height one cubit and a half. For by those five cubits and a half we have understood and known the fashion of the ark of the old covenant, for that in five thousand and a half thousand years Jesus Christ should come in the ark of his body: and we have found that he is the God of Israel, even the Son of God. For after his passion, we the chief of the priests, because we marvelled at the signs which came to pass on his account did open the Bible, and searched out all the generations unto the generation of Joseph, and Mary the mother of Christ, taking her to be the seed of David: and we found that from the day when God made the heaven and the earth and the first man, from that time unto the Flood are 2,212 years: and from the Flood unto the building of the tower 531 years: and from the building of the tower unto Abraham 606 years: and from Abraham unto the coming of the children of Israel out of Egypt 470 years: and from the going of the children of Israel out of Egypt unto the building of the temple 511 years: and from the building of the temple unto the destruction of the same temple 464 years: so far found we in the Bible of Esdras: and inquiring from the burning of the temple unto the coming of Christ and his birth we found it to be 636 years, which together were five thousand and five hundred years like as we found it written in the Bible that Michael the archangel declared before unto Seth the third son of Adam, that after five thousand and a half thousand years the Son of God hath (? should)

come. Hitherto have we told no man, lest there should be a schism in our synagogues; and now, O excellent judge, thou hast adjured us by this holy Bible of the testimonies of God, and we do declare it unto thee: and we also have adjured thee by thy life and health that thou declare not these words unto any man in Jerusalem.

XIII (XXIX)

And Pilate, when he heard these words of Annas and Caiaphas, laid them all up amongst the acts of the Lord and Saviour in the public books of his judgement hall, and wrote a letter unto Claudius the king of the city of Rome, saying:

[The following Epistle or Report of Pilate is inserted in Greek into the late Acts of Peter and Paul (40) and the Pseudo-Marcellus Passion of Peter and Paul (19). We thus have it in Greek and Latin, and the Greek is used here as the basis of the version.]

Pontius Pilate unto Claudius, greeting.

There befell of late a matter which I myself brought to light (or made trial of): for the Jews through envy have punished themselves and their posterity with fearful judgements of their own fault; for whereas their fathers had promises (al. had announced unto them) that their God would send them out of heaven his holy one who should of right be called their king, and did promise that he would send him upon earth by a virgin; he, then (or this God of the Hebrews, then), came when I was governor of Judaea, and they beheld him enlightening the blind, cleansing lepers, healing the palsied, driving devils out of men, raising the dead, rebuking the winds, walking upon the waves of the sea dry-shod, and doing many other wonders, and all the people of the Jews calling him the Son of God: the chief priests therefore, moved with envy against him, took him and delivered him unto me and brought against him one false accusation after another, saying that he was a sorcerer and did things contrary to their law.

But I, believing that these things were so, having scourged him, delivered him unto their will: and they crucified him, and when he was buried they set guards upon him. But while my soldiers watched him he rose again on the third day: yet so much was the malice of the Jews kindled that they gave money to the soldiers, saying: Say ye that his disciples stole away his body. But they, though they took the money, were not able to keep silence concerning that which had come to pass, for they also have testified that they saw him arisen and that they received money from the Jews. And these things have I reported for this cause, lest some other should lie unto thee (lat. lest any lie otherwise) and thou shouldest deem right to believe the false tales of the Jews.

Book 97. Acts of John

18 Now John was hastening to Ephesus, moved thereto by a vision. Damonicus therefore, and Aristodemus his kinsman, and a certain very rich man Cleobius, and the wife of Marcellus, hardly prevailed to keep him for one day in Miletus, reposing themselves with him. And when very early in the morning they had set forth, and already about four miles of the journey were accomplished, a voice came from heaven in the hearing of all of us, saying: John, thou art about to give glory to thy Lord in Ephesus, whereof thou shalt know, thou and all the brethren that are with thee, and certain of them that are there, which shall believe by thy means. John therefore pondered, rejoicing in himself, what it should be that should befall (meet) him at Ephesus, and said: Lord, behold I go according to thy will: let that be done which thou desirest.

19 And as we drew near to the city, Lycomedes the praetor of the Ephesians, a man of large substance, met us, and falling at John's feet besought him, saying: Is thy name John? the God whom thou preachest hath sent thee to do good unto my wife, who hath been smitten with palsy now these seven days and lieth incurable. But glorify thou thy God by healing her, and have compassion on us. For as I was considering with myself what resolve to take in this matter, one stood by me and said: Lycomedes, cease from this thought which warreth against thee, for it is evil (hard): submit not thyself unto it. For I have compassion upon mine handmaid Cleopatra, and have sent from Miletus a man named John who shall raise her up and restore her to thee whole. Tarry not, therefore, thou servant of the God who hath manifested himself unto me, but hasten unto my wife who hath no more than breath. And straightway John went from the gate, with the brethren that were with him and Lycomedes, unto his house. But Cleobius said to his young men: Go ye to my kinsman Callippus and receive of him comfortable entertainment -for I am come hither with his son- that we may find all things decent.

20 Now when Lycomedes came with John into the house wherein his wife lay, he caught hold again of his feet and said: See, lord, the withering of the beauty, see the youth, see the renowned flower of my poor wife, whereat all Ephesus was wont to marvel: wretched me, I have suffered envy, I have been humbled, the eye of mine enemies hath smitten me: I have never wronged any, though I might have injured many, for I looked before to this very thing, and took care, lest I should see any evil or any such ill fortune as this. What profit, then, hath Cleopatra from my anxiety? what have I gained by being known for a pious man until this day? nay, I suffer more than the impious, in that I see thee, Cleopatra, lying in such plight. The sun in his course shall no more see me convers-

ing with thee: I will go before thee, Cleopatra, and rid myself of life: I will not spare mine own safety though it be yet young. I will defend myself before Justice, that I have rightly deserted, for I may indict her as judging unrighteously. I will be avenged on her when I come before her as a ghost [bereft] of life. I will say to her: Thou didst force me to leave the light when thou didst rob me of Cleopatra: thou didst cause me to become a corpse when thou sentest me this ill fortune: thou didst compel me to insult Providence, by cutting off my joy in life (my con- fidence).

21 And with yet more words Lycomedes addressing Cleopatra came near to the bed and cried aloud and lamented: but John pulled him away, and said: Cease from these lamentations and from thine unfitting words: thou must not disobey him that (?) appeared unto thee: for know that thou shalt receive thy consort again. Stand, therefore, with us that have come hither on her account and pray to the God whom thou sawest manifesting himself unto thee in dreams. What, then, is it, Lycomedes? Awake, thou also, and open thy soul. Cast off the heavy sleep from thee: beseech the Lord, entreat him for thy wife, and he will raise her up. But he fell upon the floor and lamented, fainting. [It is evident from what follows that Lycomedes died: but the text does not say so; some words may have fallen out.]

John therefore said with tears: Alas for the fresh (new) betraying of my vision! for the new temptation that is prepared for me! for the new device of him that contriveth against me! the voice from heaven that was borne unto me in the way, hath it devised this for me? was it this that it fore-showed me should come to pass here, betraying me to this great multitude of the citizens because of Lycomedes? the man lieth without breath, and I know well that they will not suffer me to go out of the house alive. Why tarriest thou, Lord (or, what wilt thou do)? why hast thou shut off from us thy good promise? Do not, I beseech thee, Lord, do not give him cause to exult who rejoiceth in the suffering of others; give him not cause to dance who alway derideth us; but let thy holy name and thy mercy make haste. Raise up these two dead whose death is against me.

22 And even as John thus cried out, the city of the Ephesians ran together to the house of Lycomedes, hearing that he was dead. And John, beholding the great multitude that was come, said unto the Lord: Now is the time of refreshment and of confidence toward thee, O Christ; now is the time for us who are sick to have the help that is of thee, O physician who healest freely; keep thou mine entering in hither safe from derision. I beseech thee, Jesu, succour this great multitude that it may come to thee who art Lord of all things: behold the affliction, behold them that lie here. Do thou prepare, even from them that are assembled for that end, holy vessels for thy service, when they behold thy gift. For thyself hast said, O Christ, 'Ask, and it shall be given you'. We ask therefore of thee, O king, not gold, not silver, not substance, not possessions, nor aught of what is on earth and perisheth, but two souls, by whom thou shalt convert them that are here unto thy way, unto thy teaching, unto thy liberty (confidence), unto thy most excellent (or unfailing) promise: for when they perceive thy power in that those that have died are raised, they will be saved, some of them. Do thou thyself, therefore, give them hope in thee: and so go I unto Cleopatra and say: Arise in the name of Jesus Christ.

23 And he came to her and touched her face and said: Cleopatra, He saith, whom every ruler feareth, and every creature and every power, the abyss and all darkness, and unsmiling death, and the height of heaven, and the circles of hell [and the resurrection of the dead, and the sight of the blind], and the whole power of the prince of this world, and the pride of the ruler: Arise, and be not an occasion unto many that desire not to believe, or an affliction unto souls that are able to hope and to be saved. And Cleopatra straightway cried with a loud voice: I arise, master: save thou thine handmaid.

Now when she had arisen [who for incurable lain had] seven days, the city of the Ephesians was moved at the unlooked -for sight. And Cleopatra asked concerning her husband Lycomedes, but John said to her: Cleopatra, if thou keep thy soul unmoved and steadfast, thou shalt forthwith have Lycomedes thine husband standing here beside thee, if at least thou be not disturbed nor moved at that which hath befallen, having believed on my God, who by my means shall grant him unto thee alive. Come therefore with me into thine other bedchamber, and thou shalt behold him, a dead corpse indeed, but raised again by the power of my God.

24 And Cleopatra going with John into her bedchamber, and seeing Lycomedes dead for her sake, had no power to speak (suffered in her voice), and ground her teeth and bit her tongue, and closed her eyes, raining down tears: and with calmness gave heed to the apostle. But John had compassion on Cleopatra when he saw that she neither raged nor was beside herself, and called upon the perfect and condescending mercy, saying: Lord Jesus Christ, thou seest the pressure of sorrow, thou seest the need; thou seest Cleopatra shrieking her soul out in silence, for she constraineth within her the frenzy that cannot be borne; and I know that for Lycomedes' sake she also will die upon his body. And she said quietly to John: That have I in mind, master, and nought else.

And the apostle went to the couch whereon Lycomedes lay, and taking Cleopatra's hand he said: Cleopatra, because of the multitude that is present, and thy kinsfolk that have come in, with strong crying, say thou to thine husband: Arise and glorify the name of God, for he giveth back the

dead to the dead. And she went to her husband and said to him according as she was taught, and forthwith raised him up. And he, when he arose, fell on the floor and kissed John's feet, but he raised him, saying: O man, kiss not my feet but the feet of God by whose power ye are both arisen.

25 But Lycomedes said to John: I entreat and adjure thee by the God in whose name thou hast raised us, to abide with us, together with all them that are with thee. Likewise Cleopatra also caught his feet and said the same. And John said to them: For tomorrow I will be with you. And they said to him again: We shall have no hope in thy God, but shall have been raised to no purpose, if thou abide not with us. And Cleobius with Aristodemus and Damonicus were touched in the soul and said to John: Let us abide with them, that they continue without offence towards the Lord. So he continued there with the brethren.

26 There came together therefore a gathering of a great multitude on John's account; and as he discoursed to them that were there, Lycomedes, who had a friend who was a skilful painter, went hastily to him and said to him: You see me in a great hurry to come to you: come quickly to my house and paint the man whom I show you without his knowing it. And the painter, giving some one the necessary implements and colours, said to Lycomedes: Show him to me, and for the rest have no anxiety. And Lycomedes pointed out John to the painter, and brought him near him, and shut him up in a room from which the apostle of Christ could be seen. And Lycomedes was with the blessed man, feasting on the faith and the knowledge of our God, and rejoiced yet more in the thought that he should possess him in a portrait.

27 The painter, then, on the first day made an outline of him and went away. And on the next he painted him in with his colours, and so delivered the portrait to Lycomedes to his great joy. And lie took it and set it up in his own bedchamber and hung it with garlands: so that later John, when he perceived it, said to him: My beloved child, what is it that thou always doest when thou comest in from the bath into thy bedchamber alone? do not I pray with thee and the rest of the brethren? or is there something thou art hiding from us? And as he said this and talked jestingly with him, he went into the bedchamber, and saw the portrait of an old man crowned with garlands, and lamps and altars set before it. And he called him and said: Lycomedes, what meanest thou by this matter of the portrait? can it be one of thy gods that is painted here? for I see that thou art still living in heathen fashion. And Lycomedes answered him: My only God is he who raised me up from death with my wife: but if, next to that God, it be right that the men who have benefited us should be called gods -it is thou, father, whom I have had painted in that portrait, whom I crown and love and reverence as having become my good guide.

28 And John who had never at any time seen his own face said to him: Thou mockest me, child: am I like that in form, [excelling] thy Lord? how canst thou persuade me that the portrait is like me? And Lycomedes brought him a mirror. And when he had seen himself in the mirror and looked earnestly at the portrait, he said: As the Lord Jesus Christ liveth, the portrait is like me: yet not like me, child, but like my fleshly image; for if this painter, who hath imitated this my face, desireth to draw me in a portrait, he will be at a loss, [needing more than] the colours that are now given to thee, and boards and plaster (?) and glue (?), and the position of my shape, and old age and youth and all things that are seen with the eye.

29 But do thou become for me a good painter, Lycomedes. Thou hast colours which he giveth thee through me, who painteth all of us for himself, even Jesus, who knoweth the shapes and appearances and postures and dispositions and types of our souls. And the colours wherewith I bid thee paint are these: faith in God, knowledge, godly fear, friendship, communion, meekness, kindness, brotherly love, purity, simplicity, tranquillity, fearlessness, griefiessness, sobriety, and the whole band of colours that painteth the likeness of thy soul, and even now raiseth up thy members that were cast down, and levelleth them that were lifted up, and tendeth thy bruises, and healeth thy wounds, and ordereth thine hair that was disarranged, and washeth thy face, and chasteneth thine eyes, and purgeth thy bowels, and emptieth thy belly, and cutteth off that which is beneath it; and in a word, when the whole company and mingling of such colours is come together, into thy soul, it shall present it to our Lord Jesus Christ undaunted, whole (unsmoothed), and firm of shape. But this that thou hast now done is childish and imperfect: thou hast drawn a dead likeness of the dead.

There need be no portion of text lost at this point: but possibly some few sentences have been omitted. The transition is abrupt and the new episode has not, as elsewhere, a title of its own.

30 And he commanded Verus (Berus), the brother that ministered to him, to gather the aged women that were in all Ephesus, and made ready, he and Cleopatra and Lycomedes, all things for the care of them. Verus, then, came to John, saying: Of the aged women that are here over three-score years old I have found four only sound in body, and of the rest some . . . . (a word gone) and some palsied and others sick. And when he heard that, John kept silence for a long time, and rubbed his face and said: O the slackness (weakness) of them that dwell in Ephesus! O the state of dissolution, and the weakness toward God! O devil, that hast so long mocked the faithful in Ephesus! Jesus, who giveth me grace and the

gift to have my confidence in him, saith to me in silence: Send after the old women that are sick and come (be) with them into the theatre, and through me heal them: for there are some of them that will come unto this spectacle whom by these healings I will convert and make them useful for some end.

31 Now when all the multitude was come together to Lycomedes, he dismissed them on John's behalf, saying: Tomorrow come ye to the theatre, as many as desire to see the power of God. And the multitude, on the morrow, while it was yet night, came to the theatre: so that the proconsul also heard of it and hasted and took his sent with all the people. And a certain praetor, Andromeus, who was the first of the Ephesians at that time, put it about that John had promised things impossible and incredible: But if, said he, he is able to do any such thing as I hear, let him come into the public theatre, when it is open, naked, and holding nothing in his hands, neither let him name that magical name which I have heard him utter.

32 John therefore, having heard this and being moved by. these words, commanded the aged women to be brought into the theatre: and when they were all brought into the midst, some of them upon beds and others lying in a deep sleep, and all the city had run together, and a great silence was made, John opened his mouth and began to say:

33 Ye men of Ephesus, learn first of all wherefore I am visiting in your city, or what is this great confidence which I have towards you, so that it may become manifest to this general assembly and to all of you (or, so that I manifest myself to). I have been sent, then, upon a mission which is not of man's ordering, and not upon any vain journey; neither am I a merchant that make bargains or exchanges; but Jesus Christ whom I preach, being compassionate and kind, desireth by my means to convert all of you who are held in unbelief and sold unto evil lusts, and to deliver you from error; and by his power will I confound even the unbelief of your praetor, by raising up them that lie before you, whom ye all behold, in what plight and in what sicknesses they are. And to do this (to confound Andronicus) is not possible for me if they perish: therefore shall they be healed.

34 But this first I have desired to sow in your ears, even that ye should take care for your souls -on which account I am come unto you- and not expect that this time will be for ever, for it is but a moment, and not lay up treasures upon the earth where all things do fade. Neither think that when ye have gotten children ye can rest upon them (?), and try not for their sakes to defraud and overreach. Neither, ye poor, be vexed if ye have not wherewith to minister unto pleasures; for men of substance when they are diseased call you happy. Neither, ye rich, rejoice that ye have much money, for by possessing these things ye provide for yourselves grief that ye cannot be rid of when ye lose them; and besides, while it is with you, ye are afraid lest some one attack you on account of it.

35 Thou also that art puffed up because of the shapeliness of thy body, and art of an high look, shalt see the end of the promise thereof in the grave; and thou that rejoicest in adultery, know that both law and nature avenge it upon thee, and before these, conscience; and thou, adulteress, that art an adversary of the law, knowest not whither thou shalt come in the end. And thou that sharest not with the needy, but hast monies laid up, when thou departest out of this body and hast need of some mercy when thou burnest in fire, shalt have none to pity thee; and thou the wrathful and passionate, know that thy conversation is like the brute beasts; and thou, drunkard and quarreller, learn that thou losest thy senses by being enslaved to a shameful and dirty desire.

36 Thou that rejoicest in gold and delightest thyself with ivory and jewels, when night falleth, canst thou behold what thou lovest? thou that art vanquished by soft raiment, and then leavest life, will those things profit thee in the place whither thou goest? And let the murderer know that the condign punishment is laid up for him twofold after his departure hence. Likewise also thou poisoner, sorcerer, robber, defrauder, sodomite, thief, and as many as are of that band, ye shall come at last, as your works do lead you, unto unquenchable fire, and utter darkness, and the pit of punishment, and eternal threatenings. Wherefore, ye men of Ephesus, turn yourselves, knowing this also, that kings, rulers, tyrants, boasters, and they that have conquered in wars, stripped of all things when they depart hence, do suffer pain, lodged in eternal misery.

37 And having thus said, John by the power of God healed all the diseases.

This sentence must be an abridgment of a much longer narration. The manuscript indicates no break at this point: but we must suppose a not inconsiderable loss of text. For one thing, Andronicus, who is here an unbeliever, appears as a convert in the next few lines. Now he is, as we shall see later, the husband of an eminent believer, Drusiana; and his and her conversion will have been told at some length; and I do not doubt that among other things there was a discourse of John persuading them to live in continence.

37 (continued.) Now the brethren from Miletus said unto John: We have continued a long time at Ephesus; if it seem good to thee, let us go also to Smyrna; for we hear already that the mighty works of God have reached it also. And Andronicus said to them: Whensoever the teacher willeth,

then let us go. But John said: Let us first go unto the temple of Artemis, for perchance there also, if we show ourselves, the servants of the Lord will be found.

38 After two days, then, was the birthday of the idol temple. John therefore, when all were clad in white, alone put on black raiment and went up into the temple. And they took him and essayed to kill him. But John said: Ye are mad to set upon me, a man that is the servant of the only God. And he gat him up upon an high pedestal and said unto them:

39 Ye run hazard, men of Ephesus, of being like in character to the sea: every river that floweth in and every spring that runneth down, and the rains, and waves that press upon each other, and torrents full of rocks are made salt together by the bitter telementt (MS. promise!) that is therein. So ye also remaining unchanged unto this day toward true godliness are become corrupted by your ancient rites of worship. How many wonders and healings of diseases have ye seen wrought through me? And yet are ye blinded in your hearts and cannot recover sight. What is it, then, O men of Ephesus? I have adventured now and come up even into this your idol temple. I will convict you of being most godless, and dead from the understanding of mankind. Behold, I stand here: ye all say that ye have a goddess, even Artemis: pray then unto her that I alone may die; or else I only, if ye are not able to do this, will call upon mine own god, and for your unbelief I will cause every one of you to die.

40 But they who had beforetime made trial of him and had seen dead men raised up, cried out: Slay us not so, we beseech thee, John. We know that thou canst do it. And John said to them: If then ye desire not to die, let that which ye worship be confounded, and wherefore it is confounded, that ye also may depart from your ancient error. For now is it time that either ye be converted by my God, or I myself die by your goddess; for I will pray in your presence and entreat my God that mercy be shown unto you.

41 And having so said he prayed thus: O God that art God above all that are called gods, that until this day hast been set at nought in the city of the Ephesians; that didst put into my mind to come into this place, whereof I never thought; that dost convict every manner of worship by turning men unto thee; at whose name every idol fleeth and every evil spirit and every unclean power; now also by the flight of the evil spirit here at thy name, even of him that deceiveth this great multitude, show thou thy mercy in this place, for they have been made to err.

42 And as John spake these things, immediately the altar of Artemis was parted into many pieces, and all the things that were dedicated in the temple fell, and [MS. that which seemed good to him] was rent asunder, and likewise of the images of the gods more than seven. And the half of the temple fell down, so that the priest was slain at one blow by the falling of the (?roof, ? beam). The multitude of the Ephesians therefore cried out: One is the God of John, one is the God that hath pity on us, for thou only art God: now are we turned to thee, beholding thy marvellous works! have mercy on us, O God, according to thy will, and save us from our great error! And some of them, lying on their faces, made supplication, and some kneeled and besought, and some rent their clothes and wept, and others tried to escape.

43 But John spread forth his hands, and being uplifted in soul, said unto the Lord: Glory be to thee, my Jesus, the only God of truth, for that thou dost gain (receive) thy servants by divers devices. And having so said, he said to the people: Rise up from the floor, ye men of Ephesus, and pray to my God, and recognize the invisible power that cometh to manifestation, and the wonderful works which are wrought before your eyes. Artemis ought to have succoured herself: her servant ought to have been helped of her and not to have died. Where is the power of the evil spirit? where are her sacrifices? where her birthdays? where her festivals? where are the garlands? where is all that sorcery and the poisoning (witchcraft) that is sister thereto?

44 But the people rising up from off the floor went hastily and cast down the rest of the idol temple, crying: The God of John only do we know, and him hereafter do we worship, since he hath had mercy upon us! And as John came down from thence, much people took hold of him, saying: Help us, O John! Assist us that do perish in vain! Thou seest our purpose: thou seest the multitude following thee and hanging upon thee in hope toward thy God. We have seen the way wherein we went astray when we lost him: we have seen our gods that were set up in vain: we have seen the great and shameful derision that is come to them: but suffer us, we pray thee, to come unto thine house and to be succoured without hindrance. Receive us that are in bewilderment.

45 And John said to them: Men (of Ephesus), believe that for your sakes I have continued in Ephesus, and have put off my journey unto Smyrna and to the rest of the cities, that there also the servants of Christ may turn to him. But since I am not yet perfectly assured concerning you, I have continued praying to my God and beseeching him that I should then depart from Ephesus when I have confirmed you in the faith: and whereas I see that this is come to pass and yet more is being fulfilled, I will not leave you until I have weaned you like children from the nurse's milk, and have set you upon a firm rock.

46 John therefore continued with them, receiving them in the house of Andromeus. And one of them that were gathered laid down the dead body

of the priest of Artemis before the door [of the temple], for he was his kinsman, and came in quickly with the rest, saying nothing of it. John, therefore, after the discourse to the brethren, and the prayer and the thanksgiving (eucharist) and the laying of hands upon every one of the congregation, said by the spirit: There is one here who moved by faith in God hath laid down the priest of Artemis before the gate and is come in, and in the yearning of his soul, taking care first for himself, hath thought thus in himself: It is better for me to take thought for the living than for my kinsman that is dead: for I know that if I turn to the Lord and save mine own soul, John will not deny to raise up the dead also. And John arising from his place went to that into which that kinsman of the priest who had so thought was entered, and took him by the hand and said: Hadst thou this thought when thou camest unto me, my child? And he, taken with trembling and affright, said: Yes, lord, and cast himself at his feet. And John said: Our Lord is Jesus Christ, who will show his power in thy dead kinsman by raising him up.

47 And he made the young man rise, and took his hand and said: It is no great matter for a man that is master of great mysteries to continue wearying himself over small things: or what great thing is it to rid men of diseases of the body? And yet holding the young man by the hand he said: I say unto thee, child, go and raise the dead thyself, saying nothing but this only: John the servant of God saith to thee, Arise. And the young man went to his kinsman and said this only -and much people was with him- and entered in unto John, bringing him alive. And John, when he saw him that was raised, said: Now that thou art raised, thou dost not truly live, neither art partaker or heir of the true life: wilt thou belong unto him by whose name and power thou wast raised? And now believe, and thou shall live unto all ages. And he forthwith believed upon the Lord Jesus and thereafter clave unto John.

[Another manuscript (Q. Paris Gr. 1468, of the eleventh century) has another form of this story. John destroys the temple of Artemis, and then 'we' go to Smyrna and all the idols are broken: Bucolus, Polycarp, and Andronicus are left to preside over the district. There were there two priests of Artemis, brothers, and one died. The raising is told much as in the older text, but more shortly.

'We' remained four years in the region, which was wholly converted, and then returned to Ephesus.]

48 Now on the next day John, having seen in a dream that he must walk three miles outside the gates, neglected it not, but rose up early and set out upon the way, together with the brethren.

And a certain countryman who was admonished by his father not to take to himself the wife of a fellow labourer of his who threatened to kill him - this young man would not endure the admonition of his father, but kicked him and left him without speech (sc. dead). And John, seeing what had befallen, said unto the Lord: Lord, was it on this account that thou didst bid me come out hither to-day?

49 But the young man, beholding the violence (sharpness) of death, and looking to be taken, drew out the sickle that was in his girdle and started to run to his own abode; and John met him and said: Stand still, thou most shameless devil, and tell me whither thou runnest bearing a sickle that thirsteth for blood. And the young man was troubled and cast the iron on the ground, and said to him: I have done a wretched and barbarous deed and I know it, and so I determined to do an evil yet worse and more cruel, even to die myself at once. For because my father was alway curbing me to sobriety, that I should live without adultery, and chastely, I could not endure him to reprove me, and I kicked him and slew him, and when I saw what was done, I was hasting to the woman for whose sake I became my father's murderer, with intent to kill her and her husband, and myself last of all: for I could not bear to be seen of the husband of the woman, and undergo the judgement of death.

50 And John said to him: That I may not by going away and leaving you in danger give place to him that desireth to laugh and sport with thee, come thou with me and show me thy father, where he lieth. And if I raise him up for thee, wilt thou hereafter abstain from the woman that is become a snare to thee. And the young man said: If thou raisest up my father himself for me alive, and if I see him whole and continuing in life, I will hereafter abstain from her.

51 And while he was speaking, they came to the place where the old man lay dead, and many passers-by were standing near thereto. And John said to the youth: Thou wretched man, didst thou not spare even the old age of thy father? And he, weeping and tearing his hair, said that he repented thereof; and John the servant of the Lord said: Thou didst show me I was to set forth for this place, thou knewest that this would come to pass, from whom nothing can be hid of things done in life, that givest me power to work every cure and healing by thy will: now also give me this old man alive, for thou seest that his murderer is become his own judge: and spare him, thou only Lord, that spared not his father (because he) counselled him for the best.

52 And with these words he came near to the old man and said: My Lord will not be weak to spread out his kind pity and his condescending mercy even unto thee: rise therefore and give glory to God for the work that is come to pass at this moment. And the old man said: I arise, Lord. And he rose and sat up and said: I was released from a terrible life and had to

bear the insults of my son, dreadful and many, and his want of natural affection, and to what end hast thou called me back, O man of the living God? (And John answered him: If) thou art raised only for the same end, it were better for thee to die; but raise thyself unto better things. And he took him and led him into the city, preaching unto him the grace of God, so that before he entered the gate the old man believed.

53 But the young man, when he beheld the unlooked-for raising of his father, and the saving of himself, took a sickle and mutilated himself, and ran to the house wherein he had his adulteress, and reproached her, saying: For thy sake I became the murderer of my father and of you two and of myself: there thou hast that which is alike guilty of all. For on me God hath had mercy, that I should know his power.

54 And he came back and told John in presence of the brethren what he had done. But John said to him: He that put it into thine heart, young man, to kill thy father and become the adulterer of another man's wife, the same made thee think it a right deed to take away also the unruly members. But thou shouldest have done away, not with the place of sin, but the thought which through those members showed itself harmful: for it is not the instruments that are injurious, but the unseen springs by which every shameful emotion is stirred and cometh to light. Repent therefore, my child, of this fault, and having learnt the wiles of Satan thou shalt have God to help thee in all the necessities of thy soul. And the young man kept silence and attended, having repented of his former sins, that he should obtain pardon from the goodness of God: and he did not separate from John.

55 When, then, these things had been done by him in the city of the Ephesians, they of Smyrna sent unto him saying: We hear that the God whom thou preachest is not envious, and hath charged thee not to show partiality by abiding in one place. Since, then, thou art a preacher of such a God, come unto Smyrna and unto the other cities, that we may come to know thy God, and having known him may have our hope in him.

[Q has the above story also, and continues with an incident which is also quoted in a different form (and not as from these Acts) by John Cassian. Q has it thus:

Now one day as John was seated, a partridge flew by and came and played in the dust before him; and John looked on it and wondered. And a certain priest came, who was one of his hearers, and came to John and saw the partridge playing in the dust before him, and was offended in himself and said: Can such and so great a man take pleasure in a partridge playing in the dust? But John perceiving in the spirit the thought of him, said to him: It were better for thee also, my child, to look at a partridge playing in the dust and not to defile thyself with shameful and profane practices: for he who awaiteth the conversion and repentance of all men hath brought thee here on this account: for I have no need of a partridge playing in the dust. For the partridge is thine own soul.

Then the elder, hearing this and seeing that he was not bidden, but that the apostle of Christ had told him all that was in his heart, fell on his face on the earth and cried aloud, saying: Now know I that God dwelleth in thee, O blessed John! for he that tempteth thee tempteth him that cannot be tempted. And he entreated him to pray for him. And he instructed him and delivered him the rules (canons) and let him go to his house, glorifying God that is over all.

Cassian, Collation XXIV. 21, has it thus:

It is told that the most blessed Evangelist John, when he was gently stroking a partridge with his hands, suddenly saw one in the habit of a hunter coming to him. He wondered that a man of such repute and fame should demean himself to such small and humble amusements, and said: Art thou that John whose eminent and widespread fame hath enticed me also with great desire to know thee? Why then art thou taken up with such mean amusements? The blessed John said to him: What is that which thou carriest in thy hands? A bow, said he. And why, said he, dost thou not bear it about always stretched? He answered him: I must not, lest by constant bending the strength of its vigour be wrung and grow soft and perish, and when there is need that the arrows be shot with much strength at some beast, the strength being lost by excess of continual tension, a forcible blow cannot be dealt. Just so, said the blessed John, let not this little and brief relaxation of my mind offend thee, young man, for unless it doth sometimes ease and relax by some remission the force of its tension, it will grow slack through unbroken rigour and will not be able to obey the power of the Spirit.

The only common point of the two stories is that St. John amuses himself with a partridge, and a spectator thinks it unworthy of him. The two morals differ wholly. The amount of text lost here is of quite uncertain length. It must have told of the doings at Smyrna, and also, it appears, at Laodicea (see the title of the next section). One of the episodes must have been the conversion of a woman of evil life (see below, 'the harlot that was chaste ')-]

Our best manuscript prefixes a title to the next section:

From Laodicea to Ephesus the second time.

58 Now when some long time had passed, and none of the brethren had been at any time grieved by John, they were then grieved because he had said: Brethren, it is now time for me to go to Ephesus (for so have I agreed with them that dwell there) lest they become slack, now for a long

time having no man to confirm them. But all of you must have your minds steadfast towards God, who never forsaketh us.

But when they heard this from him, the brethren lamented because they were to be parted from him. And John said: Even if I be parted from you, yet Christ is always with you: whom if ye love purely ye will have his fellowship without reproach, for if he be loved, he preventeth (anticipateth) them that love him.

59 And having so said, and bidden farewell to them, and left much money with the brethren for distribution, he went forth unto Ephesus, while all the brethren lamented and groaned. And there accompanied him, of Ephesus, both Andronicus and Drusiana and Lycomedes and Cleobius and their families. And there followed him Aristobula also, who had heard that her husband Tertullus had died on the way, and Aristippus with Xenophon, and the harlot that was chaste, and many others, whom he exhorted at all times to cleave to the Lord, and they would no more be parted from him.

60 Now on the first day we arrived at a deserted inn, and when we were at a loss for a bed for John, we saw a droll matter. There was one bedstead lying somewhere there without coverings, whereon we spread the cloaks which we were wearing, and we prayed him to lie down upon it and rest, while the rest of us all slept upon the floor. But he when he lay down was troubled by the bugs, and as they continued to become yet more troublesome to him, when it was now about the middle of the night, in the hearing of us all he said to them: I say unto you, O bugs, behave yourselves, one and all, and leave your abode for this night and remain quiet in one place, and keep your distance from the servants of God. And as we laughed, and went on talking for some time, John addressed himself to sleep; and we, talking low, gave him no disturbance (or, thanks to him we were not disturbed).

61 But when the day was now dawning I arose first, and with me Verus and Andronicus, and we saw at the door of the house which we had taken a great number of bugs standing, and while we wondered at the great sight of them, and all the brethren were roused up because of them, John continued sleeping. And when he was awaked we declared to him what we had seen. And he sat up on the bed and looked at them and said: Since ye have well behaved yourselves in hearkening to my rebuke, come unto your place. And when he had said this, and risen from the bed, the bugs running from the door hasted to the bed and climbed up by the legs thereof and disappeared into the joints. And John said again: This creature hearkened unto the voice of a man, and abode by itself and was quiet and trespassed not; but we which hear the voice and commandments of God disobey and are light-minded: and for how long?

62 After these things we came to Ephesus: and the brethren there, who had for a long time known that John was coming, ran together to the house of Andronicus (where also he came to lodge), handling his feet and laying their hands upon their own faces and kissing them (and many rejoiced even to touch his vesture, and were healed by touching the clothes of the holy apostle. [So the Latin, which has this section; the Greek has: so that they even touched his garments).]

63 And whereas there was great love and joy unsurpassed among the brethren, a certain one, a messenger of Satan, became enamoured of Drusiana, though he saw and knew that she was the wife of Andronicus. To whom many said: It is not possible for thee to obtain that woman, seeing that for a long time she has even separated herself from her husband for godliness' sake. Art thou only ignorant that Andronicus, not being aforetime that which now he is, a God-fearing man, shut her up in a tomb, saying: Either I must have thee as the wife whom I had before, or thou shalt die. And she chose rather to die than to do that foulness. If, then, she would not consent, for godliness' sake, to cohabit with her lord and husband, but even persuaded him to be of the same mind as herself, will she consent to thee desiring to be her seducer? depart from this madness which hath no rest in thee: give up this deed which thou canst not bring to accomplishment.

64 But his familiar friends saying these things to him did not convince him, but with shamelessness he courted her with messages; and when he learnt the insults and disgraces which she returned, he spent his life in melancholy (or better, she, when she learnt of this disgrace and insult at his hand, spent her life in heaviness). And after two days Drusiana took to her bed from heaviness, and was in a fever and said: Would that I had not now come home to my native place, I that have become an offence to a man ignorant of godliness! for if it were one who was filled with the word of God, he would not have gone to such a pitch of madness. But now (therefore) Lord, since I am become the occasion of a blow unto a soul devoid of knowledge, set me free from this chain and remove me unto thee quickly. And in the presence of John, who knew nothing at all of such a matter, Drusiana departed out of life not wholly happy, yea, even troubled because of the spiritual hurt of the man.

65 But Andronicus, grieved with a secret grief, mourned in his soul, and wept openly, so that John checked him often and said to him: Upon a better hope hath Drusiana removed out of this unrighteous life. And Andronicus answered him: Yea, I am persuaded of it, O John, and I doubt not at all in regard of trust in my God: but this very thing do I hold fast, that she departed out of life pure.

66 And when she was carried forth, John took hold on Andronicus, and now that he knew the cause, he mourned more than Andronicus. And he kept silence, considering the provocation of the adversary, and for a space sat still. Then, the brethren being gathered there to hear what word he would speak of her that was departed, he began to say:

67 When the pilot that voyageth, together with them that sail with him, and the ship herself, arriveth in a calm and stormless harbour, then let him say that he is safe. And the husbandman that hath committed the seed to the earth, and toiled much in the care and protection of it, let him then take rest from his labours, when he layeth up the seed with manifold increase in his barns. Let him that enterpriseth to run in the course, then exult when he beareth home the prize. Let him that inscribeth his name for the boxing, then boast himself when he receiveth the crowns: and so in succession is it with all contests and crafts, when they do not fail in the end, but show themselves to be like that which they promised (corrupt).

68 And thus also I think is it with the faith which each one of us practiseth, that it is then discerned whether it be indeed true, when it continueth like itself even until the end of life. For many obstacles fall into the way, and prepare disturbance for the minds of men: care, children, parents, glory, poverty, flattery, prime of life, beauty, conceit, lust, wealth, anger, uplifting, slackness, envy, jealousy, neglect, fear, insolence, love, deceit, money, pretence, and other such obstacles, as many as there are in this life: as also the pilot sailing a prosperous course is opposed by the onset of contrary winds and a great storm and mighty waves out of calm, and the husbandman by untimely winter and blight and creeping things rising out of the earth, and they that strive in the games 'just do not win', and they that exercise crafts are hindered by the divers difficulties of them.

69 But before all things it is needful that the believer should look before at his ending and understand it in what manner it will come upon him, whether it will be vigorous and sober and without any obstacle, or disturbed and clinging to the things that are here, and bound down by desires. So is it right that a body should be praised as comely when it is wholly stripped, and a general as great when he hath accomplished every promise of the war, and a physician as excellent when he hath succeeded in every cure, and a soul as full of faith and worthy (or receptive) of God when it hath paid its promise in full: not that soul which began well and was dissolved into all the things of this life and fell away, nor that which is numb, having made an effort to attain to better things, and then is borne down to temporal things, nor that which hath longed after the things of time more than those of eternity, nor that which exchangeth [enduring for things] those that endure not, nor that which hath honoured the works of dishonour that deserve shame, nor that which taketh pledges of Satan, nor that which hath received the serpent into its own house, nor that which suffereth reproach for God's sake and then is [not] ashamed, nor that which with the mouth saith yea, but indeed approveth not itself: but that which hath prevailed not to be made weak by foul pleasure, not to be overcome by light-mindedness, not to be caught by the bait of love of money, not to be betrayed by vigour of body or wrath.

70 And as John was discoursing yet further unto the brethren that they should despise temporal things in respect of the eternal, he that was enamoured of Drusiana, being inflamed with an horrible lust and possession of the many-shaped Satan, bribed the steward of Andronicus who was a lover of money with a great sum: and he opened the tomb and gave him opportunity to wreak the forbidden thing upon the dead body. Not having succeeded with her when alive, he was still importunate after her death to her body, and said: If thou wouldst not have to do with me while thou livedst, I will outrage thy corpse now thou art dead. With this design, and having managed for himself the wicked act by means of the abominable steward, he rushed with him to the sepulchre; they opened the door and began to strip the grave-clothes from the corpse, saying: What art thou profited, poor Drusiana? couldest thou not have done this in life, which perchance would not have grieved thee, hadst thou done it willingly?

71 And as these men were speaking thus, and only the accustomed shift now remained on her body, a strange spectacle was seen, such as they deserve to suffer who do such deeds. A serpent appeared from some quarter and dealt the steward a single bite and slew him: but the young man it did not strike; but coiled about his feet, hissing terribly, and when he fell mounted on his body and sat upon him.

72 Now on the next day John came, accompanied by Andronicus and the brethren, to the sepulchre at dawn, it being now the third day from Drusiana's death, that we might break bread there. And first, when they set out, the keys were sought for and could not be found; but John said to Andronicus: It is quite right that they should be lost, for Drusiana is not in the sepulchre; nevertheless, let us go, that thou mayest not be neglectful, and the doors shall be opened of themselves, even as the Lord hath done for us many such things.

73 And when we were at the place, at the commandment of the master, the doors were opened, and we saw by the tomb of Drusiana a beautiful youth, smiling: and John, when he saw him, cried out and said: Art thou come before us for here too, beautiful one? and for what cause? And we heard a voice saying to him: For Drusiana's sake, whom thou art to raise up-for I was within a little of finding her [shamed] - and for his sake that lieth dead beside her tomb. And when the beautiful one had said this unto

John he went up into the heavens in the sight of us all. And John, turning to the other side of the sepulchre, saw a young man-even Callimachus, one of the chief of the Ephesians-and a huge serpent sleeping upon him, and the steward of Andronicus, Fortunatus by name, lying dead. And at the sight of the two he stood perplexed, saying to the brethren: What meaneth such a sight? or wherefore hath not the Lord declared unto me what was done here, he who hath never neglected me?

74 And Andronicus seeing those corpses, leapt up and went to Drusiana's tomb, and seeing her lying in her shift only, said to John: I understand what has happened, thou blessed servant of God, John. This Callimachus was enamoured of my sister; and because he never won her, though he often assayed it, he hath bribed this mine accursed steward with a great sum, perchance designing, as now we may see, to fulfil by his means the tragedy of his conspiracy, for indeed Callimachus avowed this to many, saying: If she will not consent to me when living, she shall be outraged when dead. And it may be, master, that the beautiful one knew it and suffered not her body to be insulted, and therefore have these died who made that attempt. And can it be that the voice that said unto thee, 'Raise up Drusiana', foreshowed this? because she departed out of this life in sorrow of mind. But I believe him that said that this is one of the men that have gone astray; for thou wast bidden to raise him up: for as to the other, I know that he is unworthy of salvation. But this one thing I beg of thee: raise up Callimachus first, and he will confess to us what is come about.

75 And John, looking upon the body, said to the venomous beast: Get thee away from him that is to be a servant of Jesus Christ; and stood up and prayed over him thus: O God whose name is glorified by us, as of right: O God who subduest every injurious force: O God whose will is accomplished, who alway hearest us: now also let thy gift be accomplished in this young man; and if there be any dispensation to be wrought through him, manifest it unto us when he is raised up. And straightway the young man rose up, and for a whole hour kept silence.

76 But when he came to his right senses, John asked of him about his entry into the sepulchre, what it meant, and learning from him that which Andronicus had told him, namely, that he was enamoured of Drusiana, John inquired of him again if he had fulfilled his foul intent, to insult a body full of holiness. And he answered him: How could I accomplish it when this fearful beast struck down Fortunatus at a blow in my sight: and rightly, since he encouraged my frenzy, when I was already cured of that unreasonable and horrible madness: but me it stopped with affright, and brought me to that plight in which ye saw me before I arose. And another thing yet more wondrous I will tell thee, which yet went nigh to slay and was within a little of making me a corpse. When my soul was stirred up with folly and the uncontrollable malady was troubling me, and I had now torn away the grave-clothes in which she was clad, and I had then come out of the grave and laid them as thou seest, I went again to my unholy work: and I saw a beautiful youth covering her with his mantle, and from his eyes sparks of light came forth unto her eyes; and he uttered words to me, saying: Callimachus, die that thou mayest live. Now who he was I knew not, O servant of God; but that now thou hast appeared here, I recognize that he was an angel of God, that I know well; and this I know of a truth that it is a true God that is proclaimed by thee, and of it I am persuaded. But I beseech thee, be not slack to deliver me from this calamity and this fearful crime, and to present me unto thy God as a man deceived with a shameful and foul deceit. Beseeching help therefore of thee, I take hold on thy feet. I would become one of them that hope in Christ, that the voice may prove true which said to me, 'Die that thou mayest live': and that voice hath also fulfilled its effect, for he is dead, that faithless, disorderly, godless one, and I have been raised by thee, I who will be faithful, God-fearing, knowing the truth, which I entreat thee may be shown me by thee.

77 And John, filled with great gladness and perceiving the whole spectacle of the salvation of man, said: What thy power is, Lord Jesu Christ, I know not, bewildered as I am at thy much compassion and boundless long-suffering. O what a greatness that came down into bondage! O unspeakable liberty brought into slavery by us! O incomprehensible glory that is come unto us! thou that hast kept the dead tabernacle safe from insult; that hast redeemed the man that stained himself with blood and chastened the soul of him that would defile the corruptible body; Father that hast had pity and compassion on the man that cared not for thee; We glorify thee, and praise and bless and thank thy great goodness and long-suffering, O holy Jesu, for thou only art God, and none else: whose is the might that cannot be conspired against, now and world without end. Amen.

78 And when he had said this John took Callimachus and saluted (kissed) him, saying: Glory be to our God, my child, who hath had mercy on thee, and made me worthy to glorify his power, and thee also by a good course to depart from that thine abominable madness and drunkenness, and hath called thee unto his own rest and unto renewing of life.

79 But Andronicus, beholding the dead Callimachus raised, besought John, with the brethren, to raise up Drusiana also, saying: O John, let Drusiana arise and spend happily that short space (of life) which she gave up through grief about Callimachus, when she thought she had become a stumbling block to him: and when the Lord will, he shall take her again

to himself. And John without delay went unto her tomb and took her hand and said: Upon thee that art the only God do I call, the more than great, the unutterable, the incomprehensible: unto whom every power of principalities is subjected: unto whom all authority boweth: before whom all pride falleth down and keepeth silence: whom devils hearing of tremble: whom all creation perceiving keepeth its bounds. Let thy name be glorified by us, and raise up Drusiana, that Callimachus may yet more be confirmed unto thee who dispensest that which unto men is without a way and impossible, but to thee only possible, even salvation and resurrection: and that Drusiana may now come forth in peace, having about her not any the least hindrance -now that the young man is turned unto thee- in her course toward thee.

80 And after these words John said unto Drusiana: Drusiana, arise. And she arose and came out of the tomb; and when she saw herself in her shift only, she was perplexed at the thing, and learned the whole accurately from Andronicus, the while John lay upon his face, and Callimachus with voice and tears glorified God, and she also rejoiced, glorifying him in like manner.

81 And when she had clothed herself, she turned and saw Fortunatus lying, and said unto John: Father, let this man also rise, even if he did assay to become my betrayer. But Callimachus, when he heard her say that, said: Do not, I beseech thee, Drusiana, for the voice which I heard took no thought of him, but declared concerning thee only, and I saw and believed: for if he had been good, perchance God would have had mercy on him also and would have raised him by means of the blessed John: he knew therefore that the man was come to a bad end [Lat. he judged him worthy to die whom he did not declare worthy to rise again]. And John said to him: We have not learned, my child, to render evil for evil: for God, though we have done much ill and no good toward him, hath not given retribution unto us, but repentance, and though we were ignorant of his name he did not neglect us but had mercy on us, and when we blasphemed him, he did not punish but pitied us, and when we disbelieved him he bore us no grudge, and when we persecuted his brethren he did not recompense us evil but put into our minds repentance and abstinence from evil, and exhorted us to come unto him, as he hath thee also, my son Callimachus, and not remembering thy former evil hath made thee his servant, waiting upon his mercy. Wherefore if thou allowest not me to raise up Fortunatus, it is for Drusiana so to do.

82 And she, delaying not, went with rejoicing of spirit and soul unto the body of Fortunatus and said: Jesu Christ, God of the ages, God of truth, that hast granted me to see wonders and signs, and given to me to become partaker of thy name; that didst breathe thyself into me with thy many-shaped countenance, and hadst mercy on me in many ways; that didst protect me by thy great goodness when I was oppressed by Andronicus that was of old my husband; that didst give me thy servant Andronicus to be my brother; that hast kept me thine handmaid pure unto this day; that didst raise me up by thy servant John, and when I was raised didst show me him that was made to stumble free from stumbling; that hast given me perfect rest in thee, and lightened me of the secret madness; whom I have loved and affectioned: I pray thee, O Christ, refuse not thy Drusiana that asketh thee to raise up Fortunatus, even though he assayed to become my betrayer.

83 And taking the hand of the dead man she said: Rise up, Fortunatus, in the name of our Lord Jesus Christ. And Fortunatus arose, and when he saw John in the sepulchre, and Andronicus, and Drusiana raised from the dead, and Callimachus a believer, and the rest of the brethren glorifying God, he said: O, to what have the powers of these clever men attained! I did not want to be raised, but would rather die, so as not to see them. And with these words he fled and went out of the sepulchre.

84 And John, when he saw the unchanged mind (soul) of Fortunatus, said: O nature that is not changed for the better! O fountain of the soul that abideth in foulness! O essence of corruption full of darkness! O death exulting in them that are thine! O fruitless tree full of fire! O tree that bearest coals for fruit! O matter that dwellest with the madness of matter (al. O wood of trees full of unwholesome shoots) and neighbour of unbelief! Thou hast proved who thou art, and thou art always convicted, with thy children. And thou knowest not how to praise the better things: for thou hast them not. Therefore, such as is thy way (?fruit), such also is thy root and thy nature. Be thou destroyed from among them that trust in the Lord: from their thoughts, from their mind, from their souls, from their bodies, from their acts) their life, their conversation, from their business, their occupations, their counsel, from the resurrection unto (or rest in) God, from their sweet savour wherein thou wilt [not] share, from their faith, their prayers, from the holy bath, from the eucharist, from the food of the flesh, from drink, from clothing, from love, from care, from abstinence, from righteousness: from all these, thou most unholy Satan, enemy of God, shall Jesus Christ our God and [the judge] of all that are like thee and have thy character, make thee to perish.

85 And having thus said, John prayed, and took bread and bare it into the sepulchre to break it; and said: We glorify thy name, which converteth us from error and ruthless deceit: we glorify thee who hast shown before our eyes that which we have seen: we bear witness to thy loving-kindness which appeareth in divers ways: we praise thy merciful name, O Lord

(we thank thee), who hast convicted them that are convicted of thee: we give thanks to thee, O Lord Jesu Christ, that we are persuaded of thy [grace] which is unchanging: we give thanks to thee who hadst need of our nature that should be saved: we give thanks to thee that hast given us this sure [faith], for thou art [god] alone, both now and ever. We thy servants give thee thanks, O holy one, who are assembled with [good] intent and are gathered out of the world (or risen from death).

86 And having so prayed and given glory to God, he went out of the sepulchre after imparting unto all the brethren of the eucharist of the Lord. And when he was come unto Andronicus' house he said to the brethren: Brethren, a spirit within me hath divined that Fortunatus is about to die of blackness (poisoning of the blood) from the bite of the serpent; but let some one go quickly and learn if it is so indeed. And one of the young men ran and found him dead and the blackness spreading over him, and it had reached his heart: and came and told John that he had been dead three hours. And John said: Thou hast thy child, O devil.

'John therefore was with the brethren rejoicing in the Lord.' This sentence is in the best manuscript. In Bonnet's edition It introduces the last section of the Acts, which follows immediately in the manuscript. It may belong to either episode. The Latin has: And that day he spent joyfully with the brethren.

There cannot be much of a gap between this and the next section, which is perhaps the most interesting in the Acts.

The greater part of this episode is preserved only in one very corrupt fourteenth-century manuscript at Vienna. Two important passages (93-5 (part) and 97-8 (part)) were read at the Second Nicene Council and are preserved in the Acts thereof: a few lines of the Hymn are also cited in Latin by Augustine (Ep. 237 (253) to Ceretius): he found it current separately among the Priscillianists. The whole discourse is the best popular exposition we have of the Docetic view of our Lord's person.

87 Those that were present inquired the cause, and were especially perplexed, because Drusiana had said: The Lord appeared unto me in the tomb in the likeness of John, and in that of a youth. Forasmuch, therefore, as they were perplexed and were, in a manner, not yet stablished in the faith, so as to endure it steadfastly, John said (or John bearing it patiently, said):

88 Men and brethren, ye have suffered nothing strange or incredible as concerning your perception of the [lord], inasmuch as we also, whom he chose for himself to be apostles, were tried in many ways: I, indeed, am neither able to set forth unto you nor to write the things which I both saw and heard: and now is it needful that I should fit them for your hearing; and according as each of you is able to contain it I will impart unto you those things whereof ye are able to become hearers, that ye may see the glory that is about him, which was and is, both now and for ever.

For when he had chosen Peter and Andrew, which were brethren, he cometh unto me and James my brother, saying: I have need of you, come unto me. And my brother hearing that, said: John, what would this child have that is upon the sea-shore and called us? And I said: What child? And he said to me again: That which beckoneth to us. And I answered: Because of our long watch we have kept at sea, thou seest not aright, my brother James; but seest thou not the man that standeth there, comely and fair and of a cheerful countenance? But he said to me: Him I see not, brother; but let us go forth and we shall see what he would have.

89 And so when we had brought the ship to land, we saw him also helping along with us to settle the ship: and when we departed from that place, being minded to follow him, again he was seen of me as having rather bald, but the beard thick and flowing, but of James as a youth whose beard was newly come. We were therefore perplexed, both of us, as to what that which we had seen should mean. And after that, as we followed him, both of us were by little and little [yet more] perplexed as we considered the matter. Yet unto me there then appeared this yet more wonderful thing: for I would try to see him privily, and I never at any time saw his eyes closing (winking), but only open. And oft-times he would appear to me as a small man and uncomely, and then again as one reaching unto heaven. Also there was in him another marvel: when I sat at meat he would take me upon his own breast; and sometimes his breast was felt of me to be smooth and tender, and sometimes hard like unto stones, so that I was perplexed in myself and said: Wherefore is this so unto me? And as I considered this, he . .

90 And at another time he taketh with him me and James and Peter unto the mountain where he was wont to pray, and we saw in him a light such as it is not possible for a man that useth corruptible (mortal) speech to describe what it was like. Again in like manner he bringeth us three up into the mountain, saying: Come ye with me. And we went again: and we saw him at a distance praying. I, therefore, because he loved me, drew nigh unto him softly, as though he could not see me, and stood looking upon his hinder parts: and I saw that he was not in any wise clad with garments, but was seen of us naked, and not in any wise as a man, and that his feet were whiter than any snow, so that the earth there was lighted up by his feet, and that his head touched the heaven: so that I was afraid and cried out, and he, turning about, appeared as a man of small stature, and caught hold on my beard and pulled it and said to me: John, be not faithless but believing, and not curious. And I said unto him: But what

have I done, Lord? And I say unto you, brethren, I suffered so great pain in that place where he took hold on my beard for thirty days, that I said to him: Lord, if thy twitch when thou wast in sport hath given me so great pain, what were it if thou hadst given me a buffet? And he said unto me: Let it be thine henceforth not to tempt him that cannot be tempted.

91 But Peter and James were wroth because I spake with the Lord, and beckoned unto me that I should come unto them and leave the Lord alone. And I went, and they both said unto me: He (the old man) that was speaking with the Lord upon the top of the mount, who was he? for we heard both of them speaking. And I, having in mind his great grace, and his unity which hath many faces, and his wisdom which without ceasing looketh upon us, said: That shall ye learn if ye inquire of him.

92 Again, once when all we his disciples were at Gennesaret sleeping in one house, I alone having wrapped myself in my mantle, watched (or watched from beneath my mantle) what he should do: and first I heard him say: John, go thou to sleep. And I thereon feigning to sleep saw another like unto him [sleeping], whom also I heard say unto my Lord: Jesus, they whom thou hast chosen believe not yet on thee (or do they not yet, &c.?). And my Lord said unto him: Thou sayest well: for they are men.

93 Another glory also will I tell you, brethren: Sometimes when I would lay hold on him, I met with a material and solid body, and at other times, again, when I felt him, the substance was immaterial and as if it existed not at all. And if at any time he were bidden by some one of the Pharisees and went to the bidding, we went with him, and there was set before each one of us a loaf by them that had bidden us, and with us he also received one; and his own he would bless and part it among us: and of that little every one was filled, and our own loaves were saved whole, so that they which bade him were amazed. And oftentimes when I walked with him, I desired to see the print of his foot, whether it appeared on the earth; for I saw him as it were lifting himself up from the earth: and I never saw it. And these things I speak unto you, brethren, for the encouragement of your faith toward him; for we must at the present keep silence concerning his mighty and wonderful works, inasmuch as they are unspeakable and, it may be, cannot at all be either uttered or heard.

94 Now before he was taken by the lawless Jews, who also were governed by (had their law from) the lawless serpent, he gathered all of us together and said: Before I am delivered up unto them let us sing an hymn to the Father, and so go forth to that which lieth before us. He bade us therefore make as it were a ring, holding one another's hands, and himself standing in the midst he said: Answer Amen unto me. He began, then, to sing an hymn and to say:
Glory be to thee, Father.
And we, going about in a ring, answered him: Amen.
Glory be to thee, Word: Glory be to thee, Grace. Amen.
Glory be to thee, Spirit: Glory be to thee, Holy One:
Glory be to thy glory. Amen.
We praise thee, O Father; we give thanks to thee, O Light, wherein darkness
dwelleth not. Amen.

95 Now whereas (or wherefore) we give thanks, I say:
I would be saved, and I would save. Amen.
I would be loosed, and I would loose. Amen.
I would be wounded, and I would wound. Amen.
I would be born, and I would bear. Amen.
I would eat, and I would be eaten. Amen.
I would hear, and I would be heard. Amen.
I would be thought, being wholly thought. Amen.
I would be washed, and I would wash. Amen.
Grace danceth. I would pipe; dance ye all. Amen.
I would mourn: lament ye all. Amen.
The number Eight (lit. one ogdoad) singeth praise with us. Amen.
The number Twelve danceth on high. Amen.
The Whole on high hath part in our dancing. Amen.
Whoso danceth not, knoweth not what cometh to pass. Amen.
I would flee, and I would stay. Amen.
I would adorn, and I would be adorned. Amen.
I would be united, and I would unite. Amen.
A house I have not, and I have houses. Amen.
A place I have not, and I have places. Amen.
A temple I have not, and I have temples. Amen.
A lamp am I to thee that beholdest me. Amen.
A mirror am I to thee that perceivest me. Amen.
A door am I to thee that knockest at me. Amen.
A way am I to thee a wayfarer. [amen].

96 Now answer thou (or as thou respondest) unto my dancing. Behold thyself in me who speak, and seeing what I do, keep silence about my mysteries.
Thou that dancest, perceive what I do, for thine is this passion of the manhood, which I am about to suffer. For thou couldest not at all have understood what thou sufferest if I had not been sent unto thee, as the word of the Father. Thou that sawest what I suffer sawest me as suffering, and seeing it thou didst not abide but wert wholly moved, moved to make

wise. Thou hast me as a bed, rest upon me. Who I am, thou shalt know when I depart. What now I am seen to be, that I am not. Thou shalt see when thou comest. If thou hadst known how to suffer, thou wouldest have been able not to suffer. Learn thou to suffer, and thou shalt be able not to suffer. What thou knowest not, I myself will teach thee. Thy God am I, not the God of the traitor. I would keep tune with holy souls. In me know thou the word of wisdom. Again with me say thou: Glory be to thee, Father; glory to thee, Word; glory to thee, Holy Ghost. And if thou wouldst know concerning me, what I was, know that with a word did I deceive all things and I was no whit deceived. I have leaped: but do thou understand the whole, and having understood it, say: Glory be to thee, Father. Amen.

97 Thus, my beloved, having danced with us the Lord went forth. And we as men gone astray or dazed with sleep fled this way and that. I, then, when I saw him suffer, did not even abide by his suffering, but fled unto the Mount of Olives, weeping at that which had befallen. And when he was crucified on the Friday, at the sixth hour of the day, darkness came upon all the earth. And my Lord standing in the midst of the cave and enlightening it, said: John, unto the multitude below in Jerusalem I am being crucified and pierced with lances and reeds, and gall and vinegar is given me to drink. But unto thee I speak, and what I speak hear thou. I put it into thy mind to come up into this mountain, that thou mightest hear those things which it behoveth a disciple to learn from his teacher and a man from his God.

98 And having thus spoken, he showed me a cross of light fixed (set up), and about the cross a great multitude, not having one form: and in it (the cross) was one form and one likenesst [so the MS.; I would read: and therein was one form and one likeness: and in the cross another multitude, not having one form]. And the Lord himself I beheld above the cross, not having any shape, but only a voice: and a voice not such as was familiar to us, but one sweet and kind and truly of God, saying unto me: John, it is needful that one should hear these things from me, for I have need of one that will hear. This cross of light is sometimes called the (or a) word by me for your sakes, sometimes mind, sometimes Jesus, sometimes Christ, sometimes door, sometimes a way, sometimes bread, sometimes seed, sometimes resurrection, sometimes Son, sometimes Father, sometimes Spirit, sometimes life, sometimes truth, sometimes faith, sometimes grace. And by these names it is called as toward men: but that which it is in truth, as conceived of in itself and as spoken of unto you (MS. us), it is the marking-off of all things, and the firm uplifting of things fixed out of things unstable, and the harmony of wisdom, and indeed wisdom in harmony [this last clause in the MS. is joined to the next: 'and being wisdom in harmony']. There are [places] of the right hand and the left, powers also, authorities, lordships and demons, workings, threatenings, wraths, devils, Satan, and the lower root whence the nature of the things that come into being proceeded.

99 This cross, then, is that which fixed all things apart (al. joined all things unto itself) by the (or a) word, and separate off the things that are from those that are below (lit. the things from birth and below it), and then also, being one, streamed forth into all things (or, made all flow forth. I suggested: compacted all into [one]). But this is not the cross of wood which thou wilt see when thou goest down hence: neither am I he that is on the cross, whom now thou seest not, but only hearest his (or a) voice. I was reckoned to be that which I am not, not being what I was unto many others: but they will call me (say of me) something else which is vile and not worthy of me. As, then, the place of rest is neither seen nor spoken of, much more shall I, the Lord thereof, be neither seen [nor of spoken].

100 Now the multitude of one aspect (al. [not] of one aspect) that is about the cross is the lower nature: and they whom thou seest in the cross, if they have not one form, it is because not yet hath every member of him that came down been comprehended. But when the human nature (or the upper nature) is taken up, and the race which draweth near unto me and obeyeth my voice, he that now heareth me shall be united therewith, and shall no more be that which now he is, but above them, as I also now am. For so long as thou callest not thyself mine, I am not that which I am (or was): but if thou hear me, thou, hearing, shalt be as I am, and I shall be that which I was, when I [have]thee as I am with myself. For from me thou art that (which I am). Care not therefore for the many, and them that are outside the mystery despise; for know thou that I am wholly with the Father, and the Father with me.

101 Nothing, therefore, of the things which they will say of me have I suffered: nay, that suffering also which I showed unto thee and the rest in the dance, I will that it be called a mystery. For what thou art, thou seest, for I showed it thee; but what I am I alone know, and no man else. Suffer me then to keep that which is mine, and that which is thine behold thou through me, and behold me in truth, that I am, not what I said, but what thou art able to know, because thou art akin thereto. Thou hearest that I suffered, yet did I not suffer; that I suffered not, yet did I suffer; that I was pierced, yet I was not smitten; hanged, and I was not hanged; that blood flowed from me, and it flowed not; and, in a word, what they say of me, that befell me not, but what they say not, that did I suffer. Now what those things are I signify unto thee, for I know that thou wilt understand.

Perceive thou therefore in me the praising (al. slaying al. rest) of the (or a) Word (Logos), the piercing of the Word, the blood of the Word, the wound of the Word, the hanging up of the Word, the suffering of the Word, the nailing (fixing) of the Word, the death of the Word. And so speak I, separating off the manhood. Perceive thou therefore in the first place of the Word; then shalt thou perceive the Lord, and in the third place the man, and what he hath suffered.

102 When he had spoken unto me these things, and others which I know not how to say as he would have me, he was taken up, no one of the multitudes having beheld him. And when I went down I laughed them all to scorn, inasmuch as he had told me the things which they have said concerning him; holding fast this one thing in myself, that the Lord contrived all things symbolically and by a dispensation toward men, for their conversion and salvation.

103 Having therefore beheld, brethren, the grace of the Lord and his kindly affection toward us, let us worship him as those unto whom he hath shown mercy, not with our fingers, nor our mouth, nor our tongue, nor with any part whatsoever of our body, but with the disposition of our soul -even him who became a man apart from this body: and let us watch because (or we shall find that) now also he keepeth ward over prisons for our sake, and over tombs, in bonds and dungeons, in reproaches and insults, by sea and on dry land, in scourgings, condemnations, conspiracies, frauds, punishments, and in a word, he is with all of us, and himself suffereth with us when we suffer, brethren. When he is called upon by each one of us, he endureth not to shut his ears to us, but as being everywhere he hearkeneth to all of us; and now both to me and to Drusiana, -forasmuch as he is the God of them that are shut upbringing us help by his own compassion.

104 Be ye also persuaded, therefore, beloved, that it is not a man whom I preach unto you to worship, but God unchangeable, God invincible, God higher than all authority and all power, and elder and mightier than all angels and creatures that are named, and all aeons. If then ye abide in him, and are builded up in him, ye shall possess your soul indestructible.

105 And when he had delivered these things unto the brethren, John departed, with Andronicus, to walk. And Drusiana also followed afar off with all the brethren, that they might behold the acts that were done by him, and hear his speech at all times in the Lord.

The remaining episode which is extant in the Greek is the conclusion of the book, the Death or Assumption of John. Before it must be placed the stories which we have only in the Latin (of 'Abdias' and another text by 'Mellitus', i.e. Melito), and the two or three isolated fragments.

(Lat. XIV.) Now on the next (or another) day Craton, a philosopher, had proclaimed in the market-place that he would give an example of the contempt of riches: and the spectacle was after this manner. He had persuaded two young men, the richest of the city, who were brothers, to spend their whole inheritance and buy each of them a jewel, and these they brake in pieces publicly in the sight of the people. And while they were doing this, it happened by chance that the apostle passed by. And calling Craton the philosopher to him, he said: That is a foolish despising of the world which is praised by the mouths of men, but long ago condemned by the judgement of God. For as that is a vain medicine whereby the disease is not extirpated, so is it a vain teaching by which the faults of souls and of conduct are not cured. But indeed my master taught a youth who desired to attain to eternal life, in these words; saying that if he would be perfect, he should sell all his goods and give to the poor, and so doing he would gain treasure in heaven and find the life that has no ending. And Craton said to him: Here the fruit of covetousness is set forth in the midst of men, and hath been broken to pieces. But if God is indeed thy master and willeth this to be, that the sum of the price of these jewels should be given to the poor, cause thou the gems to be restored whole, that what I have done for the praise of men, thou mayest do for the glory of him whom thou callest thy master. Then the blessed John gathered together the fragments of the gems, and holding them in his hands, lifted up his eyes to heaven and said: Lord Jesu Christ, unto whom nothing is impossible: who when the world was broken by the tree of concupiscence, didst restore it again in thy faithfulness by the tree of the cross: who didst give to one born blind the eyes which nature had denied him, who didst recall Lazarus, dead and buried, after the fourth day unto the light; and has subjected all diseases and all sicknesses unto the word of thy power: so also now do with these precious stones which these, not knowing the fruits of almsgiving, have broken in pieces for the praise of men: recover thou them, Lord, now by the hands of thine angels, that by their value the work of mercy may be fulfilled, and make these men believe in thee the unbegotten Father through thine only-begotten Son Jesus Christ our Lord, with the Holy Ghost the illuminator and sanctifier of the whole Church, world without end. And when the faithful who were with the apostle had answered and said Amen, the fragments of the gems were forthwith so joined in one that no mark at all that they had been broken remained in them. And Craton the philosopher, with his disciples, seeing this, fell at the feet of the apostle and believed thenceforth (or immediately) and was baptized, with them all, and began himself publicly to preach the faith of our Lord Jesus Christ.

XV. Those two brothers, therefore, of whom we spake, sold the gems which they had bought by the sale of their inheritance and gave the price to the poor; and thereafter a very great multitude of believers began to be joined to the apostle.

And when all this was done, it happened that after the same example, two honourable men of the city of the Ephesian sold all their goods and distributed them to the needy, and followed the apostle as he went through the cities preaching the word of God. But it came to pass, when they entered the city of Pergamum, that they saw their servants walking abroad arrayed in silken raiment and shining with the glory of this world: whence it happened that they were pierced with the arrow of the devil and became sad, seeing themselves poor and clad with a single cloak while their own servants were powerful and prosperous. But the apostle of Christ, perceiving these wiles of the devil, said: I see that ye have changed your minds and your countenances on this account, that, obeying the teaching of my Lord Jesus Christ, ye have given all ye had to the poor. Now, if ye desire to recover that which ye formerly possessed of gold, silver, and precious stones, bring me some straight rods, each of you a bundle. And when they had done so, he called upon the name of the Lord Jesus Christ, and thev were turned into gold. And the apostle said to them: Bring me small stones from the seashore. And when they had done this also, he called upon the majesty of the Lord, and all the pebbles were turned into gems. Then the blessed John turned to those men and said to them: Go about to the goldsmiths and jewellers for seven days, and when ye have proved that these are true gold and true jewels, tell me. And they went, both of them, and after seven days returned to the apostle, saying: Lord, we have gone about the shops of all the goldsmiths, and they have all said that they never saw such pure gold. Likewise the jewellers have said the same, that they never saw such excellent and precious gems.

XVI. Then the holy John said unto them: Go, and redeem to you the lands which ye have sold, for ye have lost the estates of heaven. Buy yourselves silken raiment, that for a time ye may shine like the rose which showeth its fragrance and redness and suddenly fadeth away. For ye sighed at beholding your servants and groaned that ye were become poor. Flourish, therefore, that ye may fade: be rich for the time, that ye may be beggars for ever. Is not the Lord's hand able to make riches overflowing and unsurpassably glorious? but he hath appointed a conflict for souls, that they may believe that they shall have eternal riches, who for his name's sake have refused temporal wealth. Indeed, our master told us concerning a certain rich man who feasted every day and shone with gold and purple, at whose door lay a beggar, Lazarus, who desired to receive even the crumbs that fell from his table, and no man gave unto him. And it came to pass that on one day they died, both of them, and that beggar was taken into the rest which is in Abraham's bosom, but the rich man was cast into flaming fire: out of which he lifted up his eyes and saw Lazarus, and prayed him to dip his finger in water and cool his mouth for he was tormented in the flames. And Abraham answered him and said: Remember, son, that thou receivedst good things in thy life, but this Lazarus likewise evil things. Wherefore rightly is he now comforted while thou art tormented, and besides all this, a great gulf is fixed between you and us, so that neither can they come thence hither, nor hither thence. But he answered: I have five brethren: I pray that some one may go to warn them, that they come not into this flame. And Abraham said to him: They have Moses and the prophets, let them hear them. To that he answered: Lord, unless one rise up again, they will not believe. Abraham said to him: If they believe not Moses and the prophets, neither will they believe, if one rise again. And these words our Lord and Master confirmed by examples of mighty works: for when they said to him: Who hath come hither from thence, that we may believe him? he answered: Bring hither the dead whom ye have. And when they had brought unto him a young man which was dead (Ps.-Mellitus: three dead corpses), he was waked up by him as one that sleepeth, and confirmed all his words.

But wherefore should I speak of my Lord, when at this present there are those whom in his name and in your presence and sight I have raised from the dead: in whose name ye have seen palsied men healed, lepers cleansed, blind men enlightened, and many delivered from evil spirits ? But the riches of these mighty works they cannot have who have desired to have earthly wealth. Finally, when ye yourselves went unto the sick and called upon the name of Jesus Christ, they were healed: ye did drive out devils and restore light to the blind. Behold, this grace is taken from you, and ye are become wretched, who were mighty and great. And where as there was such fear of you upon the devils that at your bidding they left the men whom they possessed, now ye will be in fear of the devils. For he that loveth money is the servant of Mammon: and Mammon is the name of a devil who is set over carnal gains, and is the master of them that love the world. But even the lovers of the world do not possess riches, but are possessed of them. For it is out of reason that for one belly there should be laid up so much food as would suffice a thousand, and for one body so many garments as would furnish clothing for a thousand men. In vain, therefore, is that stored up which cometh not into use, and for whom it is kept, no man knoweth, as the Holy Ghost saith by the prophet: In vain is every man troubled who heapeth up riches and knoweth not for whom he gathereth them. Naked did our birth from

women bring us into this light, destitute of food and drink: naked will the earth receive us which brought us forth. We possess in common the riches of the heaven, the brightness of the sun is equal for the rich and the poor, and likewise the light of the moon and the stars, the softness of the air and the drops of rain, and the gate of the church and the fount of sanctification and the forgiveness of sins, and the sharing in the altar, and the eating of the body and drinking of the blood of Christ, and the anointing of the chrism, and the grace of the giver, and the visitation of the Lord, and the pardon of sin: in all these the dispensing of the Creator is equal, without respect of persons. Neither doth the rich man use these gifts after one manner and the poor after another.

But wretched and unhappy is the man who would have something more than sufficeth him: for of this come heats of fevers rigours of cold, divers pains in all the members of the body, and he can neither be fed with food nor sated with drink, that covetousness may learn that money will not profit it, which being laid up bringeth to the keepers thereof anxiety by day and night, and suffereth them not even for an hour to be quiet and secure. For while they guard their houses against thieves, till their estate, ply the plough, pay taxes, build storehouses, strive for gain, try to baffle the attacks of the strong, and to strip the weak, exercise their wrath on whom they can, and hardly bear it from others, shrink not from playing at tables and from public shows, fear not to defile or to be defiled, suddenly do they depart out of this world, naked, bearing only their own sins with them, for which they shall suffer eternal punishment.

XVII. While the apostle was thus speaking, behold there was brought to him by his mother, who was a widow, a young man who thirty days before had first married a vvife. And the people which were waiting upon the burial came with the widowed mother and cast themselves at the apostle's feet all together with groans, weeping, and mourning, and besought him that in the name of his God, as he had done with Drusiana, so he would raise up this young man also. And there was so great weeping of them all that the apostle himself could hardly refrain from crying and tears. He cast himself down, therefore, in prayer, and wept a long time: and rising from prayer spread out his hands to heaven, and for a long space prayed within himself. And when he had so done thrice, he commanded the body which was swathed to be loosed, and said: Thou youth Stacteus, who for love of thy flesh hast quickly lost thy soul: thou youth which knewest not thy creator nor perceivedst the Saviour of men, and wast ignorant of thy true friend, and therefore didst fall into the snare of the worst enemy: behold, I have poured out tears and prayers unto my Lord for thine ignorance, that thou mayest rise from the dead, the bands of death being loosed, and declare unto these two, to Atticus and Eugenius, how great glory they have lost, and how great punishment they have incurred. Then Stacteus arose and worshipped the apostle, and began to reproach his disciples, saying: I beheld your angels vveeping, and the angels of Satan rejoicing at your overthrow. For now in a little time ye have lost the kingdom that was prepared for you, and the dwellingplaces builded of shining stones, full of joy, of feasting and delights, full of everlasting life and eternal light: and have gotten yourselves places of darkness, full of dragons, of roaring flames, of torments, and punishments unsurpassable, of pains and anguish, fear and horrible trembling. Ye have lost the places full of unfading flowers, shining, full of the sounds of instruments of music (organs), and have gotten on the other hand places wherein roaring and howling and mourning ceaseth not day nor night. Nothing else remaineth for you save to ask the apostle of the Lord that like as he hath raised me to life, he would raise you also from death unto salvation and bring back your souls which now are blotted out of the book of life.

XVIII. Then both he that had been raised and all the people together with Atticus and Eugenius, cast themselves at the apostle's feet and besought him to intercede for them with the Lord. Unto whom the holy apostle gave this answer: that for thirty days they should offer penitence to God, and in that space pray especially that the rods of gold might return to their nature and likewise the stones return to the meanness wherein they were made. And it came to pass that after thirty days were accomplished, and neither the rods were turncd into wood nor the gems into pebbles, Atticus and Eugenius came and said to the apostle: Thou hast always taught mercy, and preached forgiveness, and bidden that one man should spare another. And if God willeth that a man should forgive a man, how much more shall he, as he is God, both forgive and spare men. We are confounded for our sin: and whereas we have cried with our eyes which lusted after the world, we do now repent with eyes that weep. We pray thee, Lord, we pray thee, apostle of God, show in deed that mercy which in word thou hast always promised. Then the holy John said unto them as they wept and repented, and all interceded for them likewise: Our Lord God used these words when he spake concerning sinners: I will not the death of a sinner, but I will rather that he be converted and live. For when the Lord Jesus Christ taught us concerning the penitent, he said: Verily I say unto you, there is great joy in heaven over one sinner that repenteth and turneth himself from his sins: and there is more joy over him than over ninety and nine which have not sinned. Wherefore I would have you know that the Lord accepteth the repentance of these men. And he turned unto Atticus and Eugenius and said: Go, carry back the rods unto the wood whence ye took them, for now are they returned to their own nature, and the stones unto the sea-shore, for they are become common stones as they were before. And when this was accomplished, they received again the grace which they had lost, so that again they cast out devils as before time and healed the sick and enlightened the blind, and daily the Lord did many mighty works by their means.

XIX tells shortly the destruction oi the temple of Ephesus and the conversion of 12,000 people.

Then follows the episode of the poison-cup in a form which probably represents the story in the Leucian Acts. (We have seen that the late Greek texts place it at the beginning, in the presence of Domitian.)

XX. Now when Aristodemus, who was chief priest of all those idols, saw this, filled with a wicked spirit, he stirred up sedition among the people, so that one people prepared themselves to fight against the other. And John turned to him and said: Tell me, Aristodemus, what can I do to take away the anger from thy soul? And Aristodemus said: If thou wilt have me believe in thy God, I will give thee poison to drink, and if thou drink it, and die not, it will appear that thy God is true. The apostle answered: If thou give me poison to drink, when I call on the name of my Lord, it will not be able to harm me. Aristodemus said again: I will that thou first see others drink it and die straightway that so thy heart may recoil from that cup. And the blessed John said: I have told thee already that I am prepared to drink it that thou mayest believe on the Lord Jesus Christ when thou seest me whole after the cup of poison. Aristodemus therefore went to the proconsul and asked of him two men who were to undergo the sentence of death. And when he had set them in the midst of the market-place before all the people, in the sight of the apostle he made them drink the poison: and as soon as they had drunk it, they gave up the ghost. Then Aristodemus turned to John and said: Hearken to me and depart from thy teaching wherewith thou callest away the people from the worship of the gods; or take and drink this, that thou mayest show that thy God is almighty, if after thou hast drunk, thou canst remain whole. Then the blessed Jolm, as they lay dead which had drunk the poison, like a fearless and brave man took the cup, and making the sign of the cross, spake thus: My God, and the Father of our Lord Jesus Christ, by whose word the heavens were established, unto whom all things are subject, whom all creation serveth, whom all power obeyeth, feareth, and trembleth, when we call on thee for succour: whose name the serpent hearing is still, the dragon fleeth, the viper is quiet, the toad (which is called a frog) is still and strengthless, the scorpion is quenched, the basilisk vanquished, and the phalangia (spider) doth no hurt -in a word, all venomous things, and the fiercest reptiles and noisome beasts, are pierced (or covered with darkness). [Ps.- Mellitus adds: and all roots hurtful to the health of men dry up.] Do thou, I say, quench the venom of this poison, put out the deadly workings thereof, and void it of the strength which it hath in it: and grant in thy sight unto all these whom thou hast created, eyes that they may see, and ears that they may hear and a heart that they may understand thy greatness. And when he had thus said, he armed his mouth and all his body with the sign of the cross and drank all that was in the cup. And after be had drunk, he said: I ask that they for whose sake I have drunk, be turned unto thee, O Lord, and by thine enlightening receive the salvation which is in thee. And when for the space of three hours the people saw that John was of a cheerful countenance, and that there was no sign at all of paleness or fear in him, they began to cry out with a loud voice: He is the one true God whom John worshippeth.

XXI. But Aristodemus even so believed not, though the people reproached him: but turned unto John and said: This one thing I lack -if thou in the name of thy God raise up these that have died by this poison, my mind will be cleansed of all doubt. When he said that, the people rose against Aristodemus saying: We will burn thee and thine house if thou goest on to trouble the apostle further with thy words. John, therefore, seeing that there was a fierce sedition, asked for silence, and said in the hearing of all: The first of the virtues of God which we ought to imitate is patience, by which we are able to bear with the foolishness of unbelievers. Wherefore if Aristodemus is still held by unbelicf, let us loose the knots of his unbelief. He shall be compelled, even though late, to acknowledge his creator -for I will not cease from this work until a remedy shall bring help to his wounds, and like physicians which have in their hands a sick man needing medicine, so also, if Aristodemus be not yet cured by that which hath now been done, he shall be cured by that which I will now do. And he called Aristodemus to him, and gave him his coat, and he himself stood clad only in his mantle. And Aristodemus said to him: Wherefore hast thou given me thy coat? John said to him: That thou mayest even so be put to shame and depart from thine unbelief. And Aristodemus said: And how shall thy coat make me to depart from unbelief? The apostle answered: Go and cast it upon the bodies of the dead, and thou shalt say thus: The apostle of our Lord Jesus Christ hath sent me that in his name ye may rise again, that all may know that life and death are servants of my Lord Jesus Christ. Which when Aristodemus had done, and had seen them rise, he worshipped John, and ran quickly to the proconsul and began to say with a loud voice: Hear me, hear me, thou proconsul; I think thou rememberest that I have often stirred up thy wrath against John and devised many things against him daily, wherefore I fear

lest I feel his wrath: for he is a god hidden in the form of a man and hath drunk poison, and not only continueth whole, but them also which had died by the poison he hath recalled to life by my means, by the touch of his coat, and they have no mark of death upon them. Which when the proconsul heard he said: And what wilt thou have me to do? Aristodemus answered: Let us go and fall at his feet and ask pardon, and whatever he commandeth us let us do. Then they came together and cast themselves down and besought forgiveness: and he received them and offered prayer and thanksgiving to God, and he ordained them a fast of a week, and when it was fulfilled he baptized them in the name of the Lord Jesus Christ and his Almighty Father and the Holy Ghost the illuminator. [And when thev were baptized, with all their house and their servants and their kindred, they brake all their idols and built a church in the name of Saint John: wherein he himself was taken up, in manner following :]

This bracketed sentence, of late complexion, serves to introduce the last episode of the book.

[M.R. James gives two additional fragments that do not fit in any other place. These fragments are very broken and are not of much use for this present project. However, if there is interest in them, they can be found on pages 264-6 of the text.]

The last episode of these Acts (as is the case with several others of the Apocryphal Acts) was preservcd separately for reading in church on the Saint's day. We have it in at least nine Grcek manuscripts, and in many versions: Latin, Syriac, Armenian, Coptic, Ethiopic, Slavonic.

106 John therefore continued with the brethren, rejoicing in the Lord. And on the morrow, being the Lord's day, and all the brethren being gathered together, he began to say unto them: Brethren and fellow-servants and coheirs and partakers with me in the kingdom of the Lord, ye know the Lord, hovv many mighty works he hath granted you by my means, how many wonders, healings, signs, how great spiratal gifts, teachings, governings, refreshings, ministries, knowledges, glories, graces, gifts, beliefs, communions, all which ye have seen given you by him in your sight, yet not seen by these eyes nor heard by these ears. Be ye therefore stablished in him, remembering him in your every deed, knowing the mystery of the dispensation which hath come to pass towards men, for what cause the Lord hath l accomplished it. He beseecheth you by me, brethren, and entreateth you, desiring to remain without grief, without insult, not conspired against, not chastened: for he knoweth even the insult that cometh of you, he knoweth even dishonour, he knoweth even conspiracy, he knoweth even chastisement, from them that hearken not to his commandments.

107 Let not then our good God be grieved, the compassionate, the merciful, the holy, the pure, the undefiled, the immaterial, the only, the one, the unchangeable, the simple, the guileless, the unwrathful, even our God Jesus Christ, who is above every name that we can utter or conceive, and more exalted. Let him rejoice with us because we walk aright, let him be glad because we live purely, let him be refreshed because our conversation is sober. Let him be without care because we live continently, let him be pleased because we communicate one with another, let him smile because we are chaste, let him be merry because we love him. These things I now speak unto you, brethren, because I am hasting unto the work set before me, and already being perfected by the Lord. For what else could I have to say unto you? Ye have the pledge of our God, ye have the earnest of his goodness, ye have his presence that cannot be shunned. If, then, ye sin no more, he forgiveth you that ye did in ignorance: but if after that ye have known him and he hath had mercy on you, ye walk again in the like deeds, both the former will be laid to your charge, and also ye will not have a part nor mercy before him.

108 And when he had spoken this unto them, he prayed thus: O Jesu who hast woven this crown with thy weaving, who hast joined together these many blossoms into the unfading flower of thy cormtenance, who hast sown in them these words: thou only tender of thy servants, and physician who healest freely: only doer of good and despiser of none, only merciful and lover of men, only saviour and righteous, only seer of all, who art in all and everywhere present and containing all things and filling all things: Christ Jesu, God, Lord, that with thy gifts and thy mercy shelterest them that trust in thee, that knowest clearly the wiles and the assaults of him that is everywhere our adversary, which he deviseth against us: do thou only, O Lord, succour thy servants by thy visitation. Even so, Lord.

109 And he asked for bread, and gave thanks thus: What praise or what offering or what thanksgiving shall we, breaking this bread, name save thee only, O Lord Jesu? We glorify thy name that was said by the Father: we glorify thy name that was said through the Son (or we glorify the name of Father that was said by thee . . . the name of Son that was said by thee): we glorify thine entering of the Door. We glorify the resurrection shown unto us by thee. We glorify thy way, we glorify of thee the seed, the word, the grace, the faith, the salt, the unspeakable (al. chosen) pearl, the treasure, the plough, the net, the greatness, the diadem, him that for us was called Son of man, that gave unto us truth, rest, knowledge, power, the commandment, the confidence, hope, love, liberty, refuge in thee. For thou, Lord, art alone the root of immortality, and the fount of incorruption, and the seat of the ages: called by all these names for us now that

calling on thee by them we may make known thy greatness which at the present is invisible unto us, but visible only unto the pure, being portrayed in thy manhood only.

110 And he brake the bread and gave unto all of us, praying over each of the brethren that he might be worthy of the grace of the Lord and of the most holy eucharist. And he partook also himself likewise, and said: Unto me also be there a part with you, and: Peace be with you, my beloved.

111 After that he said unto Verus: Take with thee some two men, with baskets and shovels, and follow me. And Verus without delay did as he was bidden by John the servant of God. The blessed John therefore went out of the house and walked forth of the gates, having told the more part to depart from him. And when he was come to the tomb of a certain brother of ours he said to the young men: Dig, my children. And they dug and he was instant with them yet more, saying: Let the trench be deeper. And as they dug he spoke unto them the word of God and exhorted them that were come with him out of the house, edifying and perfecting them unto the greatness of God, and praying over each one of us. And when the young men had finished the trench as he desired, we knowing nothing of it, he took off his garments wherein he was clad and laid them as it were for a pallet in the bottom of the trench: and standing in his shift only he stretched his hands upward and prayed thus:

112 O thou that didst choose us out for the apostleship of the Gentiles: O God that sentest us into the world: that didst reveal thyself by the law and the prophets: that didst never rest, but alway from the foundation of the world savedst them that were able to be saved: that madest thyself known through all nature: that proclaimedst thyself even among beasts: that didst make the desolate and savage soul tame and quiet: that gavest thyself to it when it was athirst for thy words: that didst appear to it in haste when it was dying: that didst show thyself to it as a law when it was sinking into lawlessness: that didst manifest thyself to it when it had been vanquished by Satan: that didst overcome its adversary when it fled unto thee: that avest it thine hand and didst raise it up from the things of Hades: that didst not leave it to walk after a bodily sort (in the body): that didst show to it its own enemy: that hast made for it a clear knowledge toward thee: O God, Jesu, the Father of them that are above the heavens, the Lord of them that are in the heavens, the law of them that are in the other, the course of them that are in the air, the keeper of them that are on the earth, the fear of them that are under the earth, the grace of them that are thine own: receive also the soul of thy John, which it may be is accounted worthy by thee.

113 O thou who hast kept me until this hour for thyself and untouched by union with a woman: who when in my youth I desired to marry didst appear unto me and say to me: John I have need of thee: who didst prepare for me also a sickness of the body: who when for the third time I would marry didst forthwith prevent me, and then at the third hour of the day saidst unto me on the sea: John, if thou hadst not been mine, I would have suffered thee to marry: who for two years didst blind me (or afflict mine eyes), and grant me to mourn and entreat thee: who in the third year didst open the eyes of my mind and also grant me my visible eyes: who when I saw clearly didst ordain that it should be grievous to me to look upon a woman: who didst save me from the temporal fantasy and lead me unto that which endureth always: who didst rid me of the foul madness that is in the flesh: who didst take me from the bitter death and establish me on thee alone: who didst muzzle the secret disease of my soul and cut off the open deed: who didst afflict and banish him that raised tumult in me: who didst make my love of thee spotless: who didst make my joining unto thee perfect and unbroken: who didst give me undoubting faith in thee, who didst order and make clear my inclination toward thee: thou who givest unto every man the due reward of his works, who didst put into my soul that I should have no possession save thee only: for what is more precious than thee? Now therefore Lord, whereas I have accomplished the dispensation wherewith I was entrusted, account thou me worthy of thy rest, and grant me that end in thee which is salvation unspeakable and unutterable.

114 And as I come unto thee, let the fire go backward, let the darkness be overcome, let the gulf be without strength, let the furnace die out, let Gehenna be quenched. Let angels follow, let devils fear, let rulers be broken, let powers fall; let the places of the right hand stand fast, let them of the left hand not remain. Let the devil be muzzled, let Satan be derided, let his wrath be burned out, let his madness be stilled, let his vengeance be ashamed, let his assault be in pain, let his children be smitten and all his roots plucked up. And grant me to accomplish the journey unto thee without suffering insolence or provocation, and to receive that which thou hast promised unto them that live purely and have loved thee only.

115 And having sealed himself in every part, he stood and said: Thou art with me, O Lord Jesu Christ: and laid himself down in the trench where he had strown his garments: and having said unto us: Peace be with you, brethren, he gave up his spirit rejoicing.

The less good Greek manuscripts and some versions are not content with this simple ending. The Latin says that after the prayer a great light appeared over the apostle for the space of an hour, so bright that no one could look at it.

Then he laid himself down and gave up the ghost.) We who were there rejoiced, some of us, and some mourned. . . . And forthwith manna issuing from the tomb was seen of all, which manna that place produceth even unto this day, &c.

But perhaps the best conclusion is that of one Greek manuscript:
We brought a linen cloth and spread it upon him, and went into the city. And on the day following we went forth and found not his body, for it was translated by the power of our Lord Jesus Christ, unto whom be glory, &c.

Another says:
On the morrow we dug in the place, and him we found not, but only his sandals, and the earth moving (lit. springing up like a well), and after that we remembered that which was spoken by the Lord unto Peter, &c.

Augustine (on John xxi) reports the belief that in his time the earth over the grave was seen to move as if stirred by John's breathing.

Book 98. Acts of Paul

Introduction

This book, Tertullian tells us, was composed shortly before his time in honour of Paul by a presbyter of Asia, who was convicted of the imposture and degraded from his office. The date of it may therefore be about A.D. 160. The author was an orthodox Christian.

Our authorities for it are:
1. The sadly mutilated Coptic MS. at Heidelberg, of the sixth century at latest.
2. The Acts of Paul and Thecla, a single episode which has been preserved complete in Greek and many versions: parts of it exist in the Coptic.
3. The correspondence with the Corinthians, partly preserved in the Coptic, and current separately in Armenian and Latin.
4. The Martyrdom, the concluding episode of the Acts, preserved separately (as in the case of John and others) in Greek and other versions.
5.Detached fragments or quotations.

The length of the whole book is given as 8,600 lines (Stichometry of Nicephorus), or 8,560 (Stichometry of the Codex Claromontanus): the Canonical Acts are given by the same two authorities respectively as 2,800 and 2,600. We have, perhaps, 1,800 lines of the Acts of Paul. The text of the Coptic MS. is miserably defective, and the restoration of it, in the episodes which are preserved in it alone, is a most difficult process: Professor Carl Schmidt has done practically all that can be expected, with infinite labour and great acuteness. In treating the defective episodes I shall follow him closely, but shall not attempt to represent all the broken lines.

I
The first extant page of the Coptie MS. seems to be p.9.
p.9. Paul went into (the house) at the place where the (dead) was. But Phila the wife of Panchares (Anchares, MS., see below) was very wroth and said to her husband in (great anger): Husband, thou hast gone . . . . the wild beasts, thou hast not begotten . . . . thy son . . . . where is mine?
p.10 (he hath not) desired food . . . to bury him. But (Panchares) stood in the sight of all and made his prayer at the ninth hour, until the people of the city came to bear the boy out. When he had prayed, Paul (came) and saw . . . and of Jesus Christ . . . . the boy . . . the prayer.
p.11 (a small piece only) . . . multitude . . . eight days . . . they thought that he raised up the (boy). But when Paul had remained
p.12. They asked? him? . . . the men listened to him . . . they sent for Panchares . . . and cried out, saying: We believe, Panchares, . . . but save the city from . . many things, which they said. Panchares said unto them: Judge ye whether your good deeds (?)
p.13 is not possible . . . but to (testify) . . . God who hath . . . his Son according to . . . salvation, and I also believe that, my brethren, there is no other God, save Jesus Christ the son of the Blessed, unto whom is glory for ever, Amen. But when they saw that he would not turn to them, they pursued Paul, and caught him, and brought him back into the city, ill-using (?) him, and cast stones at him and thrust him out of their city and out of their country. But Panchares would not return evil for evil: he shut the door of his house and went in with his wife . . . fasting . . . But when it was evening Paul came to him and said:
p.14. God hath . . . Jesus Christ.
These are the last words of the episode. The situation is a little cleared by a sentence in the Greek Acts of Titus ascribed to Zenas (not earlier than the fifth century?): 'They arrived at Antioch and found Barnabas the son of Panchares, whom Paul raised up.' Barnabas may be a mistake, but Panchares is, I doubt not, right: for the Coptic definite article is p prefixed to the word, and the Coptic translator finding Panchares in his text has confused the initial of it with his own definite article, and cut it out.
We have, then, a husband Panchares and wife Phila at Antioch (in Pisidia perhaps: this is disputed), and their son (possibly named Barnabas) is dead. Phila reproaches Panchares with want of parental affection. I take it that he is a believer, and has not mourned over his son, perhaps knowing that Paul was at hand and hoping for his help. Panchares prays till his fellow-townsmen come to carry out the body for burial. Paul arrives: at

some point he raises the dead: but the people are irritated and some catastrophe threatens them at Paul's hands.

Panchares makes a profession of faith, the result of which is Paul's ill-treatment and banishment. But Paul returns secretly and reassures Panchares.

II

The next episode is that of Paul and Thecla, in which the Greek text exists, and will be followed. In the Coptic it has a title:

After the flight from Antioch, when he would go to Iconium.

It is possible that in this episode the author of the Acts may have used a local legend, current in his time, of a real Christian martyr Thecla. It is otherwise difficult to account for the very great popularity of the cult of St. Thecla, which spread over East and West, and made her the most famous of virgin martyrs. Moreover, one historical personage is introduced into the story, namely, Queen Tryphaena, who was the widow, it seems, of Cotys, King of Thrace, and the mother of Polemo II, King of Pontus. She was a great-niece of the Emperor Claudius. Professor W. M. Ramsay has contended that there was a written story of Thecla which was adapted by the author of the Acts: but his view is not generally accepted.

1 When Paul went up unto Iconium after he fled from Antioch, there journeyed with him Demas and Hermogenes the coppersmith, which were full of hypocrisy, and flattered Paul as though they loved him. But Paul, looking only unto the goodness of Christ, did them no evil, but loved them well, so that he assayed to make sweet unto them all the oracles of the Lord, and of the teaching and the interpretation (of the Gospel) and of the birth and resurrection of the Beloved, and related unto them word by word all the great works of Christ, how they were revealed unto him (Copt. adds: how that Christ was born of Mary the virgin, and of the seed of David).

2 And a certain man named Onesiphorus, when he heard that Paul was come to Iconium, went out with his children Simmias and Zeno and his wife Lectra to meet him, that he might receive him into his house: for Titus had told him what manner of man Paul was in appearance; for he had not seen him in the flesh, but only in the spirit.

3 And he went by the king's highway that leadeth unto Lystra and stood expecting him, and looked upon them that came, according to the description of Titus. And he saw Paul coming, a man little of stature, thin-haired upon the head, crooked in the legs, of good state of body, with eyebrows joining, and nose somewhat hooked, full of grace: for sometimes he appeared like a man, and sometimes he had the face of an angel.

4 And when Paul saw Onesiphorus he smiled, and Onesiphorus said: Hail, thou servant of the blessed God. And he said: Grace be with thee and with thine house. But Demas and Hermogenes were envious, and stirred up their hypocrisy yet more, so that Demas said: Are we not servants of the Blessed, that thou didst not salute us so? And Onesiphorus said: I see not in you any fruit of righteousness, but if ye be such, come ye also into my house and refresh yourselves.

5 And when Paul entered into the house of Onesiphorus, there was great joy, and bowing of knees and breaking of bread, and the word of God concerning abstinence (or continence) and the resurrection; for Paul said: Blessed are the pure in heart, for they shall see God.

Blessed are they that keep the flesh chaste, for they shall become the temple of God.

Blessed are they that abstain (or the continent), for unto them shall God speak.

Blessed are they that have renounced this world, for they shall be well-pleasing unto God.

Blessed are they that possess their wives as though they had them not, for they shall inherit God.

Blessed are they that have the fear of God, for they shall become angels of God.

6 Blessed are they that tremble at the oracles of God, for they shall be comforted.

Blessed are they that receive the wisdom of Jesus Christ, for they shall be called sons of the Most High.

Blessed are they that have kept their baptism pure, for they shall rest with the Father and with the Son.

Blessed are they that have compassed the understanding of Jesus Christ, for they shall be in light.

Blessed are they that for love of God have departed from the fashion of this world, for they shall judge angels, and shall be blessed at the right hand of the Father.

Blessed are the merciful, for they shall obtain mercy and shall not see the bitter day of judgement. Blessed are the bodies of the virgins, for they shall be well-pleasing unto God and shall not lose the reward of their continence (chastity), for the word of the Father shall be unto them a work of salvation in the day of his Son, and they shall have rest world Without end.

7 And as Paul was saying these things in the midst of the assembly (church) in the house of Onesiphorus, a certain virgin, Thecla, whose mother was Theocleia, which was betrothed to an husband, Thamyris, sat at the window hard by, and hearkened night and day unto the word con-

cerning chastity which was spoken by Paul: and she stirred not from the window, but was led onward (or pressed onward) by faith, rejoicing exceedingly: and further, when she saw many women and virgins entering in to Paul, she also desired earnestly to be accounted worthy to stand before Paul's face and to hear the word of Christ; for she had not yet seen the appearance of Paul, but only heard his speech.

8 Now as she removed not from the window, her mother sent unto Thamyris, and he came with great joy as if he were already to take her to wife. Thamyris therefore said to Theocleia: Where is my Thecla? And Theocicia said: I have a new tale to tell thee, Thamyris: for for three days and three nights Thecla ariseth not from the window, neither to eat nor to drink, but looking earnestly as it were upon a joyful spectacle, she so attendeth to a stranger who teacheth deceitful and various words, that I marvel how the great modesty of the maiden is so hardly beset.

9 O Thamyris, this man upsetteth the whole city of the Iconians, and thy Thecla also, for all the women and the young men go in to him and are taught by him. Ye must, saith he, fear one only God and live chastely. And my daughter, too, like a spider at the window, bound by his words, is held by a new desire and a fearful passion: for she hangeth upon the things that he speaketh, and the maiden is captured. But go thou to her and speak to her; for she is betrothed unto thee.

10 And Thamyris went to her, alike loving her and fearing because of her disturbance (ecstasy), and said: Thecla, my betrothed, why sittest thou thus? and what passion is it that holdeth thee in amaze; turn unto thy Thamyris and be ashamed. And her mother also said the same: Thecla, why sittest thou thus, looking downward, and answering nothing, but as one stricken? And they wept sore, Thamyris because he failed of a wife, and Theocleia of a child, and the maidservants of a mistress; there was, therefore, great confusion of mourning in the house. And while all this was so, Thecla turned not away, but paid heed to the speech of Paul.

11 But Thamyris leapt up and went forth into the street and watched them that went in to Paul and came out. And he saw two men striving bitterly with one another, and said to them: Ye men, tell me who ye are, and who is he that is within with you, that maketh the souls of young men and maidens to err, deceiving them that there may be no marriages but they should live as they are. I promise therefore to give you much money if ye will tell me of him: for I am a chief man of the city.

12 And Demas and Hermogenes said unto him: Who this man is, we know not; but he defraudeth the young men of wives and the maidens of husbands, saying: Ye have no resurrection otherwise, except ye continue chaste, and defile not the flesh but keep it pure.

13 And Thamyris said to them: Come, ye men, into mine house and refresh yourselves with me. And they went to a costly banquet and much wine and great wealth and a brilliant table. And Thamyris made them drink, for he loved Thecla and desired to take her to wife: and at the dinner Thamyris said: Tell me, ye men, what is his teaching, that I also may know it: for I am not a little afflicted concerning Thecla because she so loveth the stranger, and I am defrauded of my marriage.

14 And Demas and Hermogenes said: Bring him before Castelius the governor as one that persuadeth the multitudes with the new doctrine of the Christians; and so will he destroy him and thou shalt have thy wife Thecla. And we will teach thee of that resurrection which he asserteth, that it is already come to pass in the children which we have, and we rise again when we have come to the knowledge of the true God.

15 But when Thamyris heard this of them, he was filled with envy and wrath, and rose up early and went to the house of Onesiphorus with the rulers and officers and a great crowd with staves, saying unto Paul: Thou hast destroyed the city of the Iconians and her that was espoused unto me, so that she will not have me: let us go unto Castelius the governor. And all the multitude said: Away with the wizard, for he hath corrupted all our wives. And the multitude rose up together against him.

16 And Thamyris, standing before the judgement seat, cried aloud and said: 0 proconsul, this is the man-we know not whence he is-who alloweth not maidens to marry: let him declare before thee wherefore he teacheth such things. And Demas and Hermogenes said to Thamyris: Say thou that he is a Christian, and so wilt thou destroy him. But the governor kept his mind steadfast and called Paul, saying unto him: Who art thou, and what teachest thou? for it is no light accusation that these bring against thee.

17 And Paul lifted up his voice and said: If I am this day examined what I teach, hearken, 0 proconsul. The living God, the God of vengeance, the jealous God, the God that hath need of nothing, but desireth the salvation of men, hath sent me, that I may sever them from corruption and uncleanness and all pleasure and death, that they may sin no more. Wherefore God hath sent his own Child, whom I preach and teach that men should have hope in him who alone hath had compassion upon the world that was in error; that men may no more be under judgement but have faith and the fear of God and the knowledge of sobriety and the love of truth. If then I teach the things that have been revealed unto me of God, what wrong do I O proconsul? And the governor having heard that, commanded Paul to be bound and taken away to prison until he should have leisure to hear him more carefully.

18 But Thecla at night took off her bracelets and gave them to the door-keeper, and when the door was opened for her she went into the prison, and gave the jailer a mirror of silver and so went in to Paul and sat by his feet and heard the wonderful works of God. And Paul feared not at all, but walked in the confidence of God: and her faith also was increased as she kissed his chains.

19 Now when Thecla was sought by her own people and by Thamyris, she was looked for through the streets as one lost; and one of the fellow-servants of the doorkeeper told that she went out by night. And they examined the doorkeeper and he told them that she was gone to the stranger unto the prison; and they went as he told them and found her as it were bound with him, in affection. And they went forth thence and gathered the multitude to them and showed it to the governor.

20 And he commanded Paul to be brought to the judgement seat; but Thecla rolled herself upon the place where Paul taught when he sat in the prison. And the governor commanded her also to be brought to the judgement seat, and she went exulting with joy. And when Paul was brought the second time the people cried out more vehemently: He is a sorcerer, away with him! But the governor heard Paul gladly concerning the holy works of Christ: and he took counsel, and called Thecla and said: Why wilt thou not marry Thamyris, according to the law of the Iconians? but she stood looking earnestly upon Paul, and when she answered not, her mother Theocleia cried out, saying: Burn the lawless one, burn her that is no bride in the midst of the theatre, that all the women which have been taught by this man may be affrighted.

21 And the governor was greatly moved: and he scourged Paul and sent him out of the city, but Thecla he condemned to be burned. And straightway the governor arose and went to the theatre: and all the multitude went forth unto the dreadful spectacle. But Thecla, as the lamb in the wilderness looketh about for the shepherd, so sought for Paul: and she looked upon the multitude and saw the Lord sitting, like unto Paul, and said: As if I were not able to endure, Paul is come to look upon me. And she earnestly paid heed to him: but he departed into the heavens.

22 Now the boys and the maidens brought wood and hay to burn Thecla: and when she was brought in naked, the governor wept and marvelled at the power that was in her. And they laid the wood, and the executioner bade her mount upon the pyre: and she, making the sign of the cross, went up upon the wood. And they lighted it, and though a great fire blazed forth, the fire took no hold on her; for God had compassion on her, and caused a sound under the earth, and a cloud overshadowed her above, full of rain and hail, and all the vessel of it was poured out so that many were in peril of death, and the fire was quenched, and Thecla was preserved.

23 Now Paul was fasting with Onesiphorus and his wife and their children in an open sepulchre on the way whereby they go from Iconium to Daphne. And when many days were past, as they fasted, the boys said unto Paul: We are anhungered. And they had not wherewith to buy bread, for Onesiphorus had left the goods of this world, and followed Paul with all his house. But Paul took off his upper garment and said: Go, child, buy several loaves and bring them. And as the boy was buying, he saw his neighbour Thecla, and was astonished, and said: Thecla, whither goest thou? And she said: I seek Paul, for I was preserved from the fire. And the boy said: Come, I will bring thee unto him, for he mourneth for thee and prayeth and fasteth now these six days.

24 And when she came to the sepulchre unto Paul, who had bowed his knees and was praying and saying: O Father of Christ, let not the fire take hold on Thecla, but spare her, for she is thine: she standing behind him cried out: O Father that madest heaven and earth, the Father of thy beloved child Jesus Christ, I bless thee for that thou hast preserved me from the fire, that I might see Paul. And Paul arose and saw her and said: O God the knower of hearts, the Father of our Lord Jesus Christ, I bless thee that thou hast speedily accomplished that which I asked of thee, and hast hearkened unto me.

25 And there was much love within the sepulchre, for Paul rejoiced, and Onesiphorus, and all of them. And they had five loaves, and herbs, and water (and salt), and they rejoiced for the holy works of Christ. And Thecla said unto Paul: I will cut my hair round about and follow thee whithersoever thou goest. But he said: The time is ill-favoured and thou art comely: beware lest another temptation take thee, worse than the first, and thou endure it not but play the coward. And Thecla said: Only give me the seal in Christ, and temptation shall not touch me. And Paul said: Have patience, Thecla, and thou shalt receive the water.

26 And Paul sent away Onesiphorus with all his house unto Iconium, and so took Thecla and entered into Antioch: and as they entered in, a certain Syriarch, Alexander by name, saw Thecla and was enamoured of her, and would have bribed (flattered) Paul with money and gifts. But Paul said: I know not the woman of whom thou speakest, neither is she mine. But as he was of great power, he himself embraced her in the highway; and she endured it not, but sought after Paul and cried out bitterly, saying: Force not the stranger, force not the handmaid of God. I am of the first of the Iconians, and because I would not marry Thamyris, I am cast out of the city. And she caught at Alexander and rent his cloak and took the wreath from his head and made him a mocking-stock.

27 But he alike loving her and being ashamed of what had befallen him, brought her before the governor; and when she confessed that she had done this, he condemned her to the beasts; But the women were greatly amazed, and cried out at the judgement seat: An evil judgement, an impious judgement! And Thecla asked of the governor that she might remain a virgin until she should fight the beasts; and a certain rich queen, Tryphaena by name, whose daughter had died, took her into her keeping, and had her for a consolation.

28 Now when the beasts were led in procession, they bound her to a fierce lioness, and the queen Tryphaena followed after her: but the lioness, when Thecla was set upon her, licked her feet, and all the people marvelled. Now the writing (title) of her accusation was: Guilty of sacrilege. And the women with their children cried out from above: O God, an impious judgement cometh to pass in this city. And after the procession Tryphaena took her again. For her daughter Falconilla, which was dead, had said to her in a dream: Mother, thou shalt take in my stead Thecla the stranger that is desolate, that she may pray for me and I be translated into the place of the righteous.

29 When therefore Tryphaena received her after the procession, she alike bewailed her because she was to fight the beasts on the morrow, and also, loving her closely as her own daughter Falconilla; and said: Thecla, my second child, come, pray thou for my child that she may live for ever; for this have I seen in a dream. And she without delay lifted up her voice and said: O my God, Son of the Most High that art in heaven, grant unto her according to her desire, that her daughter Falconilla may live for ever. And after she had said this, Tryphaena bewailed her, considering that so great beauty was to be cast unto the beasts.

30 And when it was dawn, Alexander came to take her-for it was he that was giving the games-saying: The governor is set and the people troubleth us: give me her that is to fight the beasts, that I may take her away. But Tryphaena cried aloud so that he fled away, saying: A second mourning for my Falconilla cometh about in mine house, and there is none to help, neither child, for she is dead, nor kinsman, for I am a widow. O God of Thecla my child, help thou Thecla.

31 And the governor sent soldiers to fetch Thecla: and Tryphaena left her not, but herself took her hand and led her up, saying: I did bring my daughter Falconilla unto the sepulchre; but thee, Thecla, do I bring to fight the beasts. And Thecla wept bitterly and groaned unto the Lord, saying: Lord God in whom I believe, with whom I have taken refuge, that savedst me from the fire, reward thou Tryphaena who hath had pity on thine handmaid, and hath kept me pure.

32 There was therefore a tumult, and a voice of the beasts, and shouting of the people, and of the women which sat together, some saying: Bring in the sacrilegious one! and the women saying: Away with the city for this unlawful deed! away with all us, thou proconsul! it is a bitter sight, an evil judgement!

38 But Thecla, being taken out of the hand of Tryphaena, was stripped and a girdle put upon her, and was cast into the stadium: and lions and bears were set against her. And a fierce lioness running to her lay down at her feet, and the press of women cried aloud. And a bear ran upon her; but the lioness ran and met him, and tore the bear in sunder. And again a lion, trained against men, which was Alexander's, ran upon her, and the lioness wrestled with him and was slain along with him. And the women bewailed yet more, seeing that the lioness also that succoured her was dead.

34 Then did they put in many beasts, while she stood and stretched out her hands and prayed. And when she had ended her prayer, she turned and saw a great tank full of water, and said: Now is it time that I should wash myself. And she cast herself in, saying: In the name of Jesus Christ do I baptize myself on the last day. And all the women seeing it and all the people wept, saying: Cast not thyself into the water: so that even the governor wept that so great beauty should be devoured by seals. So, then, she cast herself into the water in the name of Jesus Christ; and the seals, seeing the light of a flash of fire, floated dead on the top of the water. And there was about her a cloud of fire, so that neither did the beasts touch her, nor was she seen to be naked.

35 Now the women, when other more fearful beasts were put in, shrieked aloud, and some cast leaves, and others nard, others cassia, and some balsam, so that there was a multitude of odours; and all the beasts that were struck thereby were held as it were in sleep and touched her not; so that Alexander said to the governor: I have some bulls exceeding fearful, let us bind the criminal to them. And the governor frowning, allowed it, saying: Do that thou wilt. And they bound her by the feet between the bulls, and put hot irons under their bellies that they might be the more enraged and kill her. They then leaped forward; but the flame that burned about her, burned through the ropes, and she was as one not bound.

36 But Tryphaena, standing by the arena, fainted at the entry, so that her handmaids said: The queen Tryphaena is dead! And the governor stopped the games and all the city was frightened, and Alexander falling at the governor's feet said: Have mercy on me and on the city, and let the condemned go, lest the city perish with her; for if Caesar hear this, perchance he will destroy us and the city, because his kinswoman the queen Tryphaena hath died at the entry.

37 And the governor called Thecla from among the beasts, and said to her: Who art thou? and what hast thou about thee that not one of the beasts hath touched thee? But she said: I am the handmaid of the living God; and what I have about me-it is that I have believed on that his Son in whom God is well pleased; for whose sake not one of the beasts hath touched me. For he alone is the goal (or way) of salvation and the substance of life immortal; for unto them that are tossed about he is a refuge, unto the oppressed relief, unto the despairing shelter, and in a word, whosoever believeth not on him, shall not live, but die everlastingly.

38 And when the governor heard this, he commanded garments to be brought and said: Put on these garments. And she said: He that clad me when I was naked among the beasts, the same in the day of judgement will clothe me with salvation. And she took the garments and put them on. And the governor forthwith issued out an act, saying: I release unto you Thecla the godly, the servant of God. And all the women cried out with a loud voice and as with one mouth gave praise to God, saying: One is the God who hath preserved Thecla: so that with their voice all the city shook.

39 And Tryphaena, when she was told the good tidings, met her with much people and embraced Thecla and said: Now do I believe that the dead are raised up: now do I believe that my child liveth: come within, and I will make thee heir of all my substance. Thecla therefore went in with her and rested in her house eight days, teaching her the word of God, so that the more part of the maid-servants also believed, and there was great joy in the house.

40 But Thecla yearned after Paul and sought him, sending about in all places; and it was told her that he was at Myra. And she took young men and maids, and girded herself, and sewed her mantle into a cloak after the fashion of a man, and departed into Myra, and found Paul speaking the word of God, and went to him. But he when he saw her and the people that were with her was amazed, thinking in himself: Hath some other temptation come upon her? But she perceived it, and said to him: I have received the washing, 0 Paul; for he that hath worked together with thee in the Gospel hath worked with me also unto my baptizing.

41 And Paul took her by the hand and brought her into the house of Hermias, and heard all things from her; so that Paul marvelled much, and they that heard were confirmed, and prayed for Tryphaena. And Thecla arose and said to Paul: I go unto Iconium. And Paul said: Go, and teach the word of God. Now Tryphaena had sent her much apparel and gold, so that she left of it with Paul for the ministry of the poor.

42 But she herself departed unto Iconium. And she entered into the house of Onesiphorus, and fell down upon the floor where Paul had sat and taught the oracles of God, and wept, saying: O God of me and of this house, where the light shone upon me, Jesu Christ the Son of God, my helper in prison, my helper before the governors, my helper in the fire, my helper among the beasts, thou art God, and unto thee be the glory for ever. Amen.

43 And she found Thamyris dead, but her mother living. And she saw her mother and said unto her: Theocleia my mother, canst thou believe that the Lord liveth in the heavens? for whether thou desirest money, the Lord will give it thee through me: or thy child, lo, I am here before thee. And when she had so testified, she departed unto Seleucia, and after she had enlightened many with the word of God, she slept a good sleep.

A good many manuscripts add that Theoeleia was not converted, but the Coptic does not support them: it ends the episode as above.

A long appendix is given by other Greek copies, telling how in Thecla's old age (she was ninety) she was living on Mount Calamon or Calameon, and some evil-disposed young men went up to ill-treat her: and she prayed, and the rock opened and she entered it, and it closed after her. Some add that she went underground to Rome: this, to account for the presence of her body there.

Copt., p.38 of the MS.

III

When he was departed from Antioch and taught in Myra (Myrrha).

When Paul was teaching the word of God in Myra, there was there a man, Hermoerates by name, who had the dropsy, and he put himself forward in the sight of all, and said to Paul: Nothing is impossible with God, but especially with him whom thou preachest; for when he came he healed many, even that God whose servant thou art. Lo, I and my wife and my children, we cast ourselves at thy feet: have pity on me that I also may believe as thou hast believed on the living God.

Paul said unto him: I will restore thee (thine health) not for reward, but through the name of Jesus Christ thou shalt become whole in the presence of all these. (And he touched his body) drawing his hand downwards: and his belly opened and much water ran from him and . . . he fell down like a dead man, so that some said: It is better for him to die than to continue in pain. But when Paul had quieted the people, he took his hand and raised him up and asked him, saying: Hermocrates, ask for what thou desirest. And he said: I would eat. And he took a loaf and gave him to eat. And in that hour he was whole, and received the grace of the seal in the Lord, he and his wife.

But Hermippus his son was angry with Paul, and sought for a set time wherein to rise up with them of his own age and destroy him. For he wished that his father should not be healed but should die, that he might soon be master of his goods. But Dion, his younger son, heard Paul gladly.

Now all they that were with Hermippus took counsel to fight against Paul so that Hermippus . . . and sought to kill him

Dion fell down and died: but Hermippus watered Dion with his tears.

But Hermocrates mourned sore, for he loved Dion more than his other son. (Yet) he sat at Paul's feet, and forgat that Dion was dead. But when Dion was dead, his mother Nympha rent her clothes and went unto Paul and set herself before the face of Hermocrates her husband and of Paul. And when Paul saw her, he was aifrighted and said: Wherefore art thou thus, Nympha? But she said to him: Dion is dead; and the whole multitude wept when they beheld her. And Paul looked upon the people that mourned and sent young men, saying to them: Go and bring me him hither. And they went: but Hermippus caught hold of the body (of Dion) in the street and cried out

A leaf lost.

the word in him (them?). But an angel of the Lord had said unto him in the night: Paul, thou hast to-day a great conflict against thy body, but God, the Father of his Son Jesus Christ, will protect thee.

When Paul had arisen, he went unto his brethren, and remained (sorrowful?) saying: What meaneth this vision? And while Paul thought upon this, he saw Hermippus coming, having a sword drawn in his hand, and with him many other young men with staves. And Paul said unto them: I am not a robber, neither a murderer. The God of all things, the Father of Christ, will turn your hands backward, and your sword into its sheath, and your strength into weakness: for I am a servant of God, though I be alone and a stranger, and small and of no reputation (?) among the Gentiles. But do thou, 0 God, look down upon their counsel and suffer me not to be brought to nought by them.

And when Hermippus ran upon Paul with his sword drawn, straightway he ceased to see, so that he cried out aloud, saying: My dear comrades, forget not your friend Hermippus. For I have sinned, 0 Paul, I have pursued after innocent blood. Learn, ye foolish and ye of understanding, that this world is nought, gold is nought, all money is nought: I that glutted myself with all manner of goods am now a beggar and entreat of you all: Hearken to me all ye my companions, and every one that dwelleth in Myra. I have mocked at a man who hath saved my father: I have mocked at a man who hath raised up my brother Dion . . . I have mocked at a man who . . . without doing me any evil. But entreat ye of him: behold, he hath saved my father and raised up my brother; he is able therefore to save me also. But Paul stood there weeping alike before God, for that he heard him quickly, and before man, for that the proud was brought low. And he turned himself and went up . . . But the young men took the feet and bore Hermippus and brought him to the place where Paul was teaching and laid him down before the door and went unto their house. And when they were gone a great multitude came to the house of Hermocrates; and another great multitude entered in, to see whether Hermippus were shut up there. And Hermippus besought every one that went in, that they would entreat Paul, with him. But they that went in saw Hermocrates and Nympha, how they rejoiced greatly at the raising up of Dion, and distributed victuals and money unto the widows for his recovery. And they beheld Hermippus their son in the state of this second affliction, and how he took hold on the feet of every one, and on the feet of his parents also, and prayed them, as one of the strangers, that he might be healed. And his parents were troubled, and lamented to every one that came in, so that some said: Wherefore do these weep? for Dion is arisen. But Hermocrates possessed goods . . . and brought the value of the goods and took it and distributed it. And Hermocrates, troubled in mind and desiring that they might be satisfied, said: Brethren, let us leave the food . . . . and occupy ourselves . . . Hermocrates. And immediately Nympha cried out in great affliction unto Paul . . they said: Nympha, Hermocrates calleth upon God that your son Hermippus may see and cease to grieve, for he hath resisted Christ and his minister. But they and Paul prayed to God. And when Hermippus recovered his sight, he turned himself to his mother Nympha, and said to her: Paul came unto me and laid his hand upon me while I wept, and in that hour I saw all things clearly. And she took his hand and led him unto the widows and Paul. But while Paul wept bitterly, Hermippus gave thanks, saying unto them: Every one that believeth, shall . . .

A leaf gone

. . . concord and peace . . . Amen.

And when Paul had confirmed the brethren that were in Myra, he departed unto Sidon.

IV

When he was departed from Myra .

Now when Paul was departed from Myra and would go unto Sidon there was great sadness of the brethren that were in Pisidia and Pamphylia, because they yearned after his word and his holy appearance in Christ; so that some from Perga followed Paul, namely Thrasymachus and Cleon with their wives Aline (?) and Chrysa, Cleon's wife. And on the way they nourished Paul: and they were eating their bread under a tree (?). And as he was about to say Amen, there came (five lines broken: the words 'the brethren' and 'idol' occur) . . . . table of devils . . . he dieth therefor, but every one that believeth on Jesus Christ who hath saved us from all defilement and all uncleanness and all evil thoughts, he shall be manifest. And they drew near unto the table (three lines broken. 'Idol' occurs) . . . . stood . . . a mighty idol. And an old man . . . . stood up among them, saying unto them: Ye men, (wait a little and see) what befalleth the priests which would draw near unto our gods: for verily when our fellow-citizen Charinus hearkened and would . . . . against the gods, there died he and his (father). And thereupon died Xanthus also, Chrysa (?), and (Hermocrates?) died, sick of the dropsy, and his wife Nympha.

Two leaves at least gone.

(Paul is speaking)

after the manner of strange men. Wherefore presume ye to do that which is not seemly (?)? Or have ye not heard of that which came to pass, which God brought upon Sodom and Gomorrha, because they robbed . . . . after the manner of strangers and of women? God did not . . . . them but cast them down into hell. Now therefore we are not men of this fashion that ye say, nor such as ye think, but we are preachers of the living God and his Beloved. But that ye may not marvel, understand . . . the miracles (?) which bear witness for us. But they hearkened not unto him, but took the men and put them into the temple of Apollo, to keep them until the morrow, whereon they assembled the whole city. And many and costly were the victuals which they gave them.

But Paul, who was fasting now the third day, testified all the night long, being troubled, and smote his face and said: O God, look down upon their threatenings and suffer us not to slide, and let not our adversaries cast us down, but save us and bring down quickly thy righteousness upon us. And as Paul cast himself down, with the brethren, Thrasymachus and Cleon, then the temple fell . . . . so that they that belonged to the temple and the magistrates that were set over it . . . . others of them in the . . . . for (the one part) fell down . . . . fell down . . . . round about, in the midst of the two parts. And they went in and beheld what had happened, and marvelled that . . . . in their . . . . and that the . . . . rejoiced over the falling of the temple (?). And they cried out, saying: Verily these are the works of the men of a mighty God! And they departed and proclaimed in the city: Apollo the god of the Sidonians is fallen, and the half of his temple. And all the dwellers in the city ran to the temple and saw Paul and them that were with him, how they wept at this temptation, that they were made a spectacle for all men. But the multitude cried out: Bring them into the theatre. And the magistrates came to fetch them; and they groaned bitterly with one soul.

About two leaves gone.

(Paul speaking) through me. Consider . . . . (nine lines much broken, 'the way of life (conversation) of Christ', 'not in the faith', occur) . . . . Egyptians . . . . and they . . . But the multitude . . . . and followed after Paul, crying: Praised be the God . . . . who hath sent Paul . . . that we should not . . . . of death. But Theudes . . . . and prayed at Paul's feet and embraced his feet, that he should give him the seal in the Lord. But he commanded them to go to Tyre . . . . in health (or farewell), and they put Paul (in a ship?) and went with him.

The purpose of confining Paul and his companions in the temple appears to have been connected with the sins of the cities of the plain of which Paul speaks.

The Acts of Titus, quoted before, have a sentence referring to this and the next episode: 'And Paul healed Aphphia the wife of Chrysippus who was possessed with a devil: and fasting for seven days he overthrew the idol of Apollo.' The Acts place this immediately after the conversion and preaching at Damascus, and put the Panehares episode later. They are not to be trusted, therefore, as a guide to the order of our book.

V

When he was departed out of Sidon and would go unto Tyre.

Now when Paul was entered unto Tyre there came a multitude of Jews . . . . . in to him. These . . . . and they heard the mighty works . . . They marvelled . . . . Amphion (= Aphphia of the Acts of Titus) . . . . saying . . . . in . . . . Chrysippus . . . . devil with him . . . . many . . . . When Paul came . . . . he said: He . . . . God and will not be an evil spirit (?) . . . . in (?) Amphion . . . . through the evil spirit . . . . without any one's having . . . . she said to him: Save me that I die not. And while the multitude . . . . then arose the other (?) evil spirit . . . . And forthwith the devils fled away. And when the multitude saw this, by the power of God, they praised him who had (given such power) unto Paul. And there was there one by name... rimus, who had a son born to him which was dumb.

On the next page is a proper name, Lix (or perhaps Kilix, a Cilician), and later the words, 'I preach the good tidings of the Saviour . . . . SonofGod'. On the next page. Lix perhaps occurs again, and 'Moses'.

The next begins: for that which we say cometh to pass forthwith. Behold we will bring him hither unto thee that he may . . . . thee, to hear the truth of thy . . . .

Next page. On God whose desire is come to pass in him, this is the wise man . . . . . . the Father and he hath sent Jesus Christ.

Next page, turned toward the East. Moses . . .

. . . in Syria in Cyrene

Again I say unto you . . . I, that do the works . . .

that a man is not justifed by the Law, but that he is justified by the works of righteousness, and he . . .

Next page has the words 'liberty', 'and the yoke', 'all flesh'; and, 'and every one confess that Jesus Christ is the glory of the Father'.

Next page, lower part: is not water in him, but . . . being water, I am not hungry but I am thirsty; I am not but not to . . . . to suffer them, to be (devoured) by wild beasts, not to be able . . . . from the earth, but not to suffer them to be burnt by the fire, are these things of the present age testified, he which was a persecutor . . .

Next page, lower part, (Cle)anthes. the law of God which is called . . . . who walketh here before them, hath he not followed us throughout all the cities . . . And when . . . . he turned himself toward the East after this (after two lines) such words, neither preacheth he as thou preachest them, 0 Paul, that thou mayest not . . . .

Next page begins: Thou art in the presence (sight, face) of Jerusalem, but I trust in the Lord that thou wilt . . .

The name 'Saul' is almost certain some lines later.

Next page begins: whom they crucified.

And at the end: raised up our flesh.

Next page, 7th line, For since the day when . . . . persecuted the apostles which were (with me? se. Peter) out of Jerusalem, I hid myself that I might have comfort, and we nourish them which stand, through the word according to the promise (?) of his grace. I have fallen into many troubles and have subjected myself to the law, as for your sakes. But thought by night and by day in my trouble on Jesus Christ, waiting for him as a lamb . . . . when they crucified him he did not . . . did not resist . . . . was not troubled.

The above may be a speech of Peter. We have seen some indication that Paul is now at Jerusalem, and the conjecture is that a dialogue between him and Peter occurred in this place.

The next page undoubtedly mentions Peter.

Line 1 has 'Paul', line 3, 'twelve (?) shepherds'.

Line 5, through Paul. But . . . . was troubled because of the questioning (examination) that (was come) upon Peter and he cried out, saying: Verily, God is one, and there is no God beside him: one also is Jesus Christ his Son, whom we . . . this, whom thou preachest, did we crucify, whom expect in great glory, but ye say that he is God and Judge of the living and the dead, the King of the ages, for the in the form of man.

VI

Paul is condemned to the mines in an unknown place. Longinus and Firmilla have a daughter, Frontina, who is to be thrown down from a rock, and Paul with her. It is my distinct opinion that Fontina is already dead: her body is to be thus contumeliously treated because she has become a Christian.

The upper part of the page has Longinus twice in lines 1, 2; 'Paul' in 1.7. Then:

For since . . . . the mine, there hath not . . . nothing good hath befallen mine house. And he advised that the men which were to throw Frontina down, should throw down Paul also with her, alive. Now Paul knew these things, but he worked fasting, in great cheerfulness, for two days with the prisoners. They commanded that on the third day the men . . . . should bring forth Frontina: and the whole city followed after her. And Firmilla and Longinus lamented and the soldiers . . . But the prisoners carried the bed (bier). And when Paul saw the great mourning with the daughter and eight . . .

Next page, line 8. Paul alive with the daughter. But when Paul had taken the daughter in his arms, he groaned unto the Lord Jesus Christ because of the sorrow of Firmilla, and cast himself on his knees in the mire . . . . praying for Frontina with her in one (a) prayer. In that hour Frontina rose up. And the whole multitude was afraid, and fled. Paul took the hand of the daughter and led her through the city unto the house of Longinus, and the whole multitude said with one voice: God is one, who hath made heaven and earth, who hath granted the life of the daughter in the presence of Paul . . . a loaf. and he gave thanks to him.

Some lines later.

to Philippi (?).

VII

When he was departed from . . . and would go .

Now when Paul was come to Philippi . . . he entered into the house of . . . . and there was great joy (among the brethren) and to every one.

On the following page begins the episode of the correspondence with the Corinthians, which was circulated separately in Syriac, Latin, and Armenian, and found a place in the Syriac collection of Pauline epistles (and is commented on with the rest by Ephraem the Syrian), and in the Armenian Bible. We have it in (a) many Armenian MSS., (b) in Ephraem s commentary-only extant in Armenian, (c) in three Latin MSS., at Milan, Laon, and Paris: as well as in the Coptic MS., which is here less fragmentary than in the preceding pages.

We begin with a short narrative, introducing the letter of the Corinthians to Paul; then follows another short piece of narrative, extant in Armenian only; then Paul's reply, commonly called the 'Third Epistle to the Corinthians'.

There are various phrases and whole sentences, especially in the Armenian and the Milan MS. of the Latin, which are absent from the Coptic and the Laon MS. and are regarded, rightly, as interpolations.

These will be distinguished by small capitals.

The page of the Coptic MS. on which the correspondence begins is fragmentary at the beginning.

1.1. the lawless one
1.2. the reward. They . . . . in
1.3. a prayer . . . . every
1.4. one, and every one (?)
1.6. Paul . . . . again (or together).

1.7. prayed that a messenger be sent to Philippi. For the Corinthians were in great trouble concerning Paul, that he would depart out of the world, before it was time. For there were certain men come to Corinth, Simon and Cleobius, saying: There is no resurrection of the flesh, but that of the spirit only: and that the body of man is not the creation of God; and also concerning the world, that God did not create it, and that God knoweth not the world, and that Jesus Christ was not crucified, but it was an appearance (i.e. but only in appearance), and that lie was not born of Mary, nor of the seed of David. And in a word, there were many things which they had taught in Corinth, deceiving many other men, (and deceiving also) themselves. When therefore the Corinthians heard that Paul was at Philippi, they sent a letter unto Paul to Macedonia by Threptus and Eutychus the deacons. And the letter was after this manner.

I. 1 Stephanus and the elders (presbyters) that are with him, even Daphnus and Eubulus and Theophilus and Zenon, unto Paul THEIR BROTHER ETERNAL greeting in the Lord.

2 There have come unto Corinth two men, Simon and Cleobius, which are overthrowing the faith of many with evil (CORRUPT) words, 3 which do thou prove AND EXAMINE: 4 for we have never heard such words from thee nor from the other apostles: 5 but all that we have received from thee or from them, that do we hold fast. 6 Since therefore the Lord hath had mercy on us, that while thou art still in the flesh we may hear these things again from thee, 7 if it be possible, either come unto us or write unto us. 8 For we believe, according as it hath been revealed unto Theonoe, that the Lord hath delivered thee out of the hand of the lawless one (enemy, Laon).

9 Now the things which these men say and teach are these: 10 They say that we must not use the prophets, 11 and that God is not Almighty, 12 and that there shall be no resurrection of the flesh, 13 and that man was not made by God, 14 and that Christ came not down (is not come, Copt.) in the flesh, neither was born of Mary, 15 and that the world is not of God, but of the angels.

16 Wherefore, brother, WE PRAY THEE use all diligence to come unto us, that the church of the Corinthians may remain without offence, and the madness of these men may be made plain. Farewell ALWAYS in the Lord.

II. 1 The deacons Threptus and Eutyches brought the letter unto Philippi, 2 so that Paul received it, being in bonds because of Stratonice the wife of Apollophanes, AND HE FORGAT HIS BONDS, and was sore afflicted, 3 and cried out, saying: It were better for me to die and to be with the Lord, than to continue in the flesh and to hear such things AND THE CALAMITIES OF FALSE DOCTRINE, so that trouble cometh upon trouble. 4 And over and above this so great affliction I am in bonds and behold these evils whereby the devices of Satan are accomplished. (4 Harnack: may not the priests (intrigues) of Satan anticipate me while (or after) I suffer (have suffered) fetters for the sake (?) of men.) 5 Paul therefore, in great affliction, wrote a letter, answering thus:

III.1 Paul, a prisoner of Jesus Christ, unto the brethren which are in Corinth, greeting.

2 Being in the midst of many tribulations, I marvel not if the teachings of the evil one run abroad apace. 3 For my Lord Jesus Christ will hasten his coming, and will set at nought (no longer endure the insolence of) them that falsify his words.

4 For I delivered unto you in the beginning the things which I received of the HOLY apostles which were before me, who were at all times with Jesus Christ: 5 namely, that our Lord Jesus Christ was born of Mary WHICH IS of the seed of David ACCORDING TO THE FLESH, the Holy Ghost being sent forth from heaven from the Father unto her BY THE ANGEL GABRIEL, 6 that he (JESUS) might come down into this world and redeem all flesh by his flesh, and raise us up from the dead in the flesh, like as he hath shown to us in himself for an ensample. 7 And because man was formed by his Father, 8 therefore was he sought when he was lost, that he might be quickened by adoption. 9 For to this end did God Almighty who made heaven and earth first send the prophets unto the Jews, that they might be drawn away from their sins. 10 For he designed to save the house of Israel: therefore he conferred a portion of the spirit of Christ upon the prophets and sent them unto the Jews first (or unto the first Jews), and they proclaimed the true worship of God for a long space of time. 11 But the prince of iniquity, desiring to be God, laid hands on them and slew them (banished them from God, Laon MS.), and bound all flesh by evil lusts (AND THE END OF THE WORLD BY JUDGEMENT DREW NEAR).

12 But God Almighty, who is righteous, would not cast away his own creation, BUT HAD COMPASSION ON THEM FROM HEAVEN, 13 and sent his spirit into Mary IN GALILEE, [14 Milan MS. and Arm.: WHO BELIEVED WITH ALL HER HEART AND RECEIVED THE HOLY GHOST IN HER WOMB, THAT JESUS MIGHT COME INTO THE WORLD,] 15 that by that flesh whereby that wicked one had brought in death (had triumphed), by the same he should be shown to overcome. 16 For by his own body Jesus Christ saved all flesh [AND RESTORED IT UNTO LIFE], 17 that he might show forth the temple of righteousness in his body. 18 In whom (or whereby) we are saved (Milan, Paris: in whom if we believe we are set free).

19 They therefore (Paris MS.; Arm. has: Know therefore that. Laon has: They therefore who agree with them) are not children of righteousness but children of wrath who reject the wisdom (providence?) of God, saying that the heaven and the earth and all that are in them are not the work of God. 20 THEY THEREFORE ARE CHILDREN OF WRATH, for cursed are they, following the teaching of the serpent, 21 whom do ye drive out from you and flee from their doctrine. [Arm., Milan, Paris: 22 FOR YE ARE NOT CHILDREN OF DISOBEDIENCE, BUT OF THE WELL-BELOVED CHURCH. 23 THEREFORE IS THE TIME OF THE RESURRECTION PROCLAIMED UNTO ALL.]

24 And as for that which they say, that there is no resurrection of the flesh, they indeed shall have no resurrection UNTO LIFE, BUT UNTO JUDGEMENT, 25 because they believe not in him that is risen from the dead, NOT BELIEVING NOR UNDERSTANDING, 26 for they know not, O Corinthians, the seeds of wheat or of other seeds (grain), how they are cast bare into the earth and are corrupted and rise again by the will of God with bodies, and clothed. 27 And not only that [body] which is cast in riseth again, but manifold more blessing itself [i.e. fertile and prospering]. 28 And if we must not take an example from seeds ONLY, BUT FROM MORE NOBLE BODIES, 29 ye know how Jonas the son of Amathi, when he would not preach to them of Nineve, BUT FLED, was swallowed by the sea-monster; 30 and after three days and three nights God heard the prayer of Jonas out of the lowest hell, and no part of him was consumed, not even an hair nor an eyelash. 31 How much more, O YE OF LITTLE FAITH, shall he raise up you that have believed in Christ Jesus, like as he himself arose. 32 Likewise also a dead man was cast upon the bones of the prophet Helisaetis by the children of Israel, and he arose, both body and soul and bones and spirit (Laon: arose in his body); how much more shall ye which have been cast upon the body and bones and spirit of the Lord [Milan, Paris: how much more, O ye of little faith, shall ye which have been cast on him] arise again in that day having your flesh whole, EVEN AS HE AROSE? [33 Arm., Milan, Paris: LIKEWISE ALSO CONCERNING THE PROPHET HELIAS: HE RAISED UP THE WIDOW'S SON FROM DEATH: HOW MUCH MORE SHALL THE LORD JESUS RAISE YOU UP FROM DEATH AT THE SOUND OF THE TRUMPET, IN THE TWINKLING OF AN EYE? FOR HE HATH SHOWED US AN ENSAMPLE IN HIS OWN BODY.]

34 If, then, ye receive any other doctrine, GOD SHALL BE WITNESS AGAINST YOU; AND let no man trouble me, 35 for I bear these bonds that I may win Christ, and I therefore bear his marks in my body that I may attain unto the resurrection of the dead. 86 And whoso receiveth (abideth in) the rule which he hath received by the blessed prophets and the holy gospel, shall receive a recompense from the Lord, AND WHEN HE RISETH FROM THE DEAD SHALL OBTAIN ETERNAL LIFE. 37 But whoso trans- gresseth these things, with him is the fire, and them that walk in like manner (Milan, Paris: with them that go before in the same way, WHO ARE MEN WITHOUT GOD), 38 which are a generation of vipers, 39 whom do ye reject in the power of the Lord, 40 and peace, GRACE, AND LOVE shall be with you.

[Laon adds: This I found in an old book, entitled the third to the Corinthians, though it is not in the Canon.]

VIII

AT EPHESUS

This episode is not traceable in the Coptic MS. but it undoubtedly formed part of the Acts, though its place is uncertain. It is preserved in an allusion by Hippolytus (early third century) and in an abstract by Nicephorus Callisti (fourteenth century) in his Ecclesiastical history (ii. 25). There is also a sentence in the Acts of Titus:

'They departed from Crete and came to Asia: and at Ephesus twelve thousand believed at the teaching of the holy Paul: there also he fought with beasts, being thrown to a lion.'

HIPPOLYTUS in his Commentary on Daniel, iii. 29, says:

For if we believe that when Paul was condemned to the beasts the lion that was set upon him lay down at his feet and licked him, how shall we not believe that which happened in the case of Daniel?

NICEPHORUS:

Now they who drew up the travels of Paul have related that he did many other things, and among them this, which befell when he was at Ephesus. Hieronymus being governor, Paul used liberty of speech, and he (Hieronymus) said that he (Paul) was able to speak well, but that this was not the time for such words. But the people of the city, fiercely enraged, put Paul's feet into irons, and shut him up in the prison, till he should be exposed as a prey to the lions. But Eubula and Artemilla, wives of eminent men among the Ephesians, being his attached disciples, and visiting him by night, desired the grace of the divine washing. And by God's power, with angels to escort them and enlighten the gloom of night with the excess of the brightness that was in them, Paul, loosed from his iron fetters, went to the sea-shore and initiated them into holy baptism, and returning to his bonds without any of those in care of the prison perceiving it, was reserved as a prey for the lions.

A lion, then, of huge size and unmatched strength was let loose upon him, and it ran to him in the stadium and lay down at his feet. And when many other savage beasts, too, were let loose, it was permitted to none of them to touch the holy body, standing like a statue in prayer. At this juncture a violent and vast hailstorm poured down all at once with a great rush, and shattered the heads of many men and beasts as well, and shore off the ear of Hieronymus himself. And thereafter, with his followers, he came to the God of Paul and received the baptism of salvation. But the lion escaped to the mountains.

And thence Paul sailed to Macedonia and Greece, and thereafter through Macedonia came to Troas and to Miletus, and from there set out for Jerusalem.

Now it is not surprising that Luke has not narrated this fight with the beasts along with the other Acts: for it is not permitted to entertain doubt because (or seeing that) John alone of the evangelists has told of the raising of Lazarus: for we know that not every one writes, believes, or knows everything, but according as the Lord has imparted to each, as the spirit divides to each, so does he perceive and believe and write spiritually the things of the spirit.

Hippolytus is a voucher for the early date of the story, and Nicephorus for its source. It will be recognized, moreover, at once as being quite in the manner of our author. The anger of the Ephesians, it cannot be doubted, was roused by Paul's preaching of continence, to which Eubula and Artemilla had become converts. The episode is really little more than a repetition of Thecla, with Paul for the principal figure.

IX

FRAGMENTS: SCENES OF FAREWELL

(Paul speaking) . . . thanksgiving (?)

The grace of the Lord will walk with me until I have fulfilled all the dispensations which shall come upon me with patience. But they were sorrowful, and fasted. And Cleobius was in the Spirit and said unto them: Brethren, (the Lord) will suffer Paul to fulfil every dispensation and thereafter will suffer him to go up (to Jerusalem). But thereafter shall be . . . . in much instruction and knowledge and sowing of the word, so that men shall envy him, and so he shall depart out of this world. But when Paul and the brethren heard this, they lifted up their voices, saying:

Next page, first extant line, 'beheld'. Second, 'shall say'. Third, But the Spirit came upon Myrte so that she said unto them: Brethren . . . and look upon this sign, that ye . . . For Paul the servant of the Lord shall save many in Rome, so that of them shall be no number, and he will manifest himself more than all the faithful. Thereafter shall . . . . of the Lord Jesus Christ come . . . . a great grace is . . . . at Rome. And this is the manner wherein the Spirit spake unto Myrte. And every one took the bread, and they were in joy, according to the custom of the fast, through . . . . and the psalms of David and . . . . he rejoiced.

On the next page the only significant words are 'to Rome'; 'the brethren'; 'grieved'; 'took the bread'; 'praised the Lord'; 'were very sorrowful'.

The next has ends of lines: 'the Lord'; 'risen'; 'Jesus'; 'Paul said to him'. The last is 'he (or they) greeted'.

Two more pages have nothing of moment. The next is concerned with the Martyrdom.

X

THE MARTYRDOM

This, preserved separately to be read on the day of Commemoration, exists in two Greek copies, an incomplete Latin version, and versions in Syriac, Coptic, Ethiopic, Slavonic, besides fragments in our Coptic MS.

I. Now there were awaiting Paul at Rome Luke from Galatia (Gaul, Gk.) and Titus from Dalmatia: whom when Paul saw he was glad: and hired a grange outside Rome, wherein with the brethren he taught the word of truth, and he became noised abroad and many souls were added unto the Lord, so that there was a rumour throughout all Rome, and much people came unto him from the household of Caesar, believing, and there was great joy.

And a certain Patroclus, a cup-bearer of Caesar, came at even unto the grange, and not being able to enter in to Paul because of the press, he sat in a high window and listened to him teaching the word of God. But whereas the evil devil envied the love of the brethren, Patroclus fell down from the window and died, and forthwith it was told unto Nero.

But Paul perceiving it by the spirit said: Men and brethren, the evil one hath gained occasion to tempt you: go out of the house and ye shall find a lad fallen from the height and now ready to give up the ghost; take him up and bring him hither to me. And they went and brought him; and when the people saw it they were troubled. But Paul said: Now, brethren, let your faith appear; come all of you and let us weep unto our Lord Jesus Christ, that this lad may live and we continue in quietness. And when all

had lamented, the lad received his spirit again, and they set him on a beast and sent him back alive, together with the rest that were of Caesar's household.

II. But Nero, when he heard of the death of Patroclus, was sore grieved, and when he came in from the bath he commanded another to be set over the wine. But his servants told him, saying: Caesar, Patroclus liveth and standeth at the table. And Caesar, hearing that Patroclus lived, was affrighted and would not go in. But when he went in, he saw Patroclus, and was beside himself, and said: Patroclus, livest thou? And he said: I live, Caesar. And he said: Who is he that made thee to live? And the lad, full of the mind of faith, said: Christ Jesus, the king of the ages. And Caesar was troubled and said: Shall he, then, be king of the ages and overthrow all kingdoms? Patroclus saith unto him: Yea, he overthroweth all kingdoms and he alone shall be for ever, and there shall be no kingdom that shall escape him. And he smote him on the face and said: Patroclus, art thou also a soldier of that king? And he said: Yea, Lord Caesar, for he raised me when I was dead. And Barsabas Justus of the broad feet, and Urion the Cappadocian, and Festus the Galatian, Caesar's chief men, said: We also are soldiers of the king of the ages. And he shut them up in prison, having grievously tormented them, whom he loved much, and commanded the soldiers of the great king to be sought out, and set forth a decree to this effect, that all that were found to be Christians and soldiers of Christ should be slain.

III. And among many others Paul also was brought, bound: unto whom all his fellow-prisoners gave heed; so that Caesar perceived that he was over the camp. And he said to him: Thou that art the great king's man, but my prisoner, how thoughtest thou well to come by stealth into the government of the Romans and levy soldiers out of my province? But Paul, filled with the Holy Ghost, said before them all: O Caesar, not only out of thy province do we levy soldiers, but out of the whole world. For so hath it been ordained unto us, that no man should be refused who wisheth to serve my king. And if it like thee also to serve him (Lat. thou wilt not repent thereof: but think not that the wealth, &c., which seems better), it is not wealth nor the splendour that is now in this life that shall save thee; but if thou submit and entreat him, thou shalt be saved; for in one day (or one day) he shall fight against the world with fire. And when Caesar heard that, he commanded all the prisoners to be burned with fire, but Paul to be beheaded after the law of the Romans.

But Paul kept not silence concerning the word, but communicated with Longus the prefect and Cestus the centurion.

Nero therefore went on (was) (perhaps add 'raging') in Rome, slaying many Christians without a hearing, by the working of the evil one; so that the Romans stood before the palace and cried It sufficeth, Caesar! for the men are our own! thou destroyest the strength of the Romans! Then at that he was persuaded and ceased, and commanded that no man should touch any Christian, until he should learn throughly concerning them.

IV. Then was Paul brought unto him after the decree; and he abode by his word that he should be beheaded. And Paul said: Caesar, it is not for a little space that I live unto my king; and if thou behead me, this will I do: I will arise and show myself unto thee that I am not dead but live unto my Lord Jesus Christ, who cometh to judge the world.

But Longus and Cestus said unto Paul: Whence have ye this king, that ye believe in him and will not change your mind, even unto death? And Paul communicated unto them the word and said: Ye men that are in this ignorance and error, change your mind and be saved from the fire that cometh upon all the world: for we serve not, as ye suppose, a king that cometh from the earth, but from heaven, even the living God, who because of the iniquities that are done in this world, cometh as a judge; and blessed is that man who shall believe in him and shall live for ever when he cometh to burn the world and purge it throughly. Then they beseeching him said: We entreat thee, help us, and we will let thee go. But he answered and said: I am not a deserter of Christ, but a lawful soldier of the living God: if I had known that I should die, O Longus and Cestus, I would have done it, but seeing that I live unto God and love myself, I go unto the Lord, to come with him in the glory of his Father. They say unto him: How then shall we live when thou art beheaded?

V. And while they yet spake thus, Nero sent one Parthenius and Pheres to see if Paul were already beheaded; and they found him yet alive. And he called them to him and said: Believe on the living God, which raiseth me and all them that believe on him from the dead. And they said: We go now unto Nero; but when thou diest and risest again, then will we believe on thy God. And as Longus and Cestus entreated him yet more concerning salvation, he saith to them: Come quickly unto my grave in the morning and ye shall find two men praying, Titus and Luke. They shall give you the seal in the Lord.

Then Paul stood with his face to the east and lifted up his hands unto heaven and prayed a long time, and in his prayer he conversed in the Hebrew tongue with the fathers, and then stretched forth his neck without speaking. And when the executioner (speculator) struck off his head, milk spurted upon the cloak of the soldier. And the soldier and all that were there present when they saw it marvelled and glorified God which had given such glory unto Paul: and they went and told Caesar what was done.

618

VI. And when he heard it, while he marvelled long and was in perplexity, Paul came about the niuth hour, when many philosophers and the centurion were standing with Caesar, and stood before them all and said: Caesar, behold, I, Paul, the soldier of God, am not dead, but live in my God. But unto thee shall many evils befall and great punishment, thou wretched man, because thou hast shed unjustly the blood of the righteous, not many days hence. And having so said Paul departed from him. But Nero hearing it and being greatly troubled commanded the prisoners to be loosed, and Patroclus also and Barsabas and them that were with him.

VII. And as Paul charged them, Longus and Cestus the centurion went early in the morning and approached with fear unto the grave of Paul. And when they were come thither they saw two men praying, and Paul betwixt them, so that they beholding the wondrous marvel were amazed, but Titus and Luke being stricken with the fear of man when they saw Longus and Cestus coming toward them, turned to flight. But they pursued after them, saying: We pursue you not for death but for life, that ye may give it unto us, as Paul promised us, whom we saw just now standing betwixt you and praying. And when they heard that, Titus and Luke rejoiced and gave them the seal in the Lord, glorifying the God and Father of our Lord Jesus Christ (Copt. and glorified the Lord Jesus Christ and all the saints).

Unto whom be glory world without end. Amen.

The Coptic MS. has a colophon: The Acts of Paul according to the Apostle.

Book 99. Acts of Peter

I

THE COPTIC FRAGMENT

This is preserved separately in an early papyrus manuscript (fourth-fifth century) now at Berlin; the other contents of it are Gnostic writings which have not yet been published. I follow C. Schmidt's rendering of it. It has a title at the end: The Act of Peter On the first day of the week, that is, on the Lord's day, a multitude gathered together, and they brought unto Peter many sick that he might heal them. And one of the multitude adventured to say unto Peter: Lo, Peter, in our presence thou hast made many blind to see and the deaf to hear and the lame to walk, and hast succoured the weak and given them strength: but wherefore hast thou not succoured thy daughter, the virgin, which grew up beautiful and hath believed in the name of God? For behold, her one side is wholly palsied, and she lieth there stretched out in the corner helpless. We see them that have been healed by thee: thine own daughter thou hast neglected.

But Peter smiled and said unto him: My son, it is manifest unto God alone wherefore her body is not whole. Know then that God is not weak nor powerless to grant his gift unto my daughter: but that thy soul may be convinced, and they that are here present may the more believe -then he looked unto his daughter and said to her: Raise thyself up from thy place, without any helping thee save Jesus only, and walk whole before all these, and come unto me. And she arose and came to him; and the multitude rejoiced at that which was come to pass. Then said Peter unto them: Behold, your heart is convinced that God is not without strength concerning all things that we ask of him. Then they rejoiced yet more and praised God. And Peter said to his daughter: Go unto thy place, and lay thee down and be again in thine infirmity, for this is expedient for me and for thee. And the maiden went back and lay down in her place and was as beforetime: and the whole multitude wept, and entreated Peter to make her whole.

But Peter said unto them: As the Lord liveth, this is expedient for her and for me. For on the day when she was born unto me I saw a vision, and the Lord said unto me: Peter, this day is a great temptation born unto thee, for this daughter will bring hurt unto many souls if her body continue whole. But I thought but the vision did mock me.

Now when the maiden was ten years old, a stumbling-block was prepared for many by reason of her. And an exceeding rich man, by name Ptolemaeus, when he had seen the maiden with her mother bathing, sent unto her to take her to wife; but her mother consented not. And he sent ofttimes to her, and could not wait.

[Here a leaf is lost: the sense, however, is not hard to supply. Augustine speaks (quoting Apocryphal Acts) of a daughter of Peter struck with palsy at the prayer of her father.

Ptolemaeus, unable to win the maiden by fair means, comes and carries her off. Peter hears of it and prays God to protect her. His prayer is heard. She is struck with palsy on one side of her body. Then the text resumes.]

The servants of Ptolemaeus brought the maiden and laid her down before the door of the house and departed.

But when I perceived it, I and her mother, we went down and found the maiden, that one whole side of her body from her toes even to her head was palsied and withered: and we bore her away, praising the Lord which had preserved his handmaid from defilement and shame and (corruption?). This is the cause of the matter, why the maiden continueth so unto this day.

Now, then, it is fitting for you to know the end of Ptolemaeus. He went home and sorrowed night and day over that which had befallen him, and

by reason of the many tears which he shed, he became blind. And when he had resolved to rise up and hang himself, lo, about the ninth hour of the day, he saw a great light which enlightened the whole house, and heard a voice saying unto him: Ptolemaeus, God hath not given thee the vessels for corruption and shame, and yet more doth it not become thee which hast believed in me to defile my virgin, whom thou shalt know as thy sister, even as if I were unto you both one spirit (sic). But rise up and go quickly unto the house of the apostle Peter, and thou shalt see my glory; he shall make known unto thee what thou must do.

But Ptolemaeus was not negligent, and bade his servants show him the way and bring him unto me. And when they were come to me, he told me all that had befallen him by the power of our Lord Jesus Christ. Then did he see with the eyes of his flesh, and with the eyes of his soul, and much people believed (hoped) in Christ: and he did them good and gave them the gift of God.

Thereafter Ptolemaeus died, departing out of this life, and went unto his Lord: and when he made his will he bequeathed a piece of land in the name of my daughter, because through her he had believed in God and was made whole. But I unto whom the disposition thereof fell, exercised it with great carefulness: I sold the land, and God alone knoweth neither I nor my daughter (received the price). I sold the land and kept nought back of the price, but gave all the money unto the poor.

Know therefore, thou servant of Jesus Christ, that God directeth (?) them that are his, and prepareth good for every one of them, although we think that God hath forgotten us. Therefore now, brethren, let us be sorrowful and watch and pray, and so shall the goodness of God look upon us, whereon we wait.

And yet further discourse did Peter hold before them all, and glorified the name of Christ the Lord and gave them all of the bread: and when he had distributed it, he rose up and went unto his house.

The scene of this episode is probably Jerusalem. The subject of it was often used by later writers, most notably, perhaps, by the author of the late Acts of SS. Nereus and Achilleus (fifth or sixth century), who gives the daughter a name, Petronilla, which has passed into Kalendars, and as Perronelle, Pernel, or Parnell has become familiar.

A few critics have questioned whether this piece really belongs to the Acts of Peter: but the weight of probability and of opinion is against them. Nothing can be plainer than that it is an extract from a larger book, and that it is ancient (the manuscript may be of the fourth century). Moreover, Augustine, in dealing with apocryphal Acts, alludes to the story contained in it. What other large book of ancient date dealing with Peter's doings can we imagine save the Acts?

II

THE GARDENER'S DAUGHTER

Augustine (Against Adimantus, xvii. 5), says to his Manichaean opponent: the story of Peter killing Ananias and Sapphira by a word is very stupidly blamed by those who in the apocryphal Acts read and admire both the incident I mentioned about the apostle Thomas (the death of the cup-bearer at the feast in his Acts) 'and that the daughter of Peter himself was stricken with palsy at the prayer of her father, and that the daughter of a gardener died at the prayer of Peter. Their answer is that it was expedient for them, that the one should be disabled by palsy and the other should die: but they do not deny that it happened at the prayer of the apostle'.

This allusion to the gardener's daughter remained a puzzle until lately. But a passage in the Epistle of Titus (already quoted) tells us the substance of the story.

A certain gardener had a daughter, a virgin, her father's only child: he begged Peter to pray for her. Upon his request, the apostle answered him that the Lord would give her that which was useful for her soul. Immediately the girl fell dead.

O worthy gain and suitable to God, to escape the insolence of the flesh and mortify the boastfulness of the blood! But that old man, faithless, and not knowing the greatness of the heavenly favour, ignorant of the divine benefit, entreated Peter that his only daughter might be raised again. And when she was raised, not many days after, as it might be to-day, the slave of a believer who lodged in the house ran upon her and ruined the girl, and both of them disappeared.

This was evidently a contrast to the story of Peter's daughter, and probably followed immediately upon it in the Acts. There is another sentence appropriate to the situation, which Dom de Bruyne found in a Cambrai MS. of the thirteenth century -a collection of apophthegms- and printed with the extracts from the Epistle of Titus.

That the dead are not to be mourned overmuch, Peter, speaking to one who lamented without patience the loss of his daughter, said: So many assaults of the devil, so many warrings of the body, so many disasters of the world hath she escaped, and thou sheddest tears as if thou knewest not what thou sufferest in thyself (what good hath befallen thee).

This might very well be part of Peter's address to the bereaved gardener.

III

THE VERCELLI ACTS

I. At the time when Paul was sojourning in Rome and confirming many in the faith, it came also to pass that one by name Candida, the wife of

Quartus that was over the prisons, heard Paul and paid heed to his words and believed. And when she had instructed her husband also and he believed, Quartus suffered Paul to go whither he would away from the city: to whom Paul said: If it be the will of God, he will reveal it unto me. And after Paul had fasted three days and asked of the Lord that which should be profitable for him, he saw a vision, even the Lord saying unto him: Arise, Paul, and become a physician in thy body (i.e. by going thither in person) to them that are in Spain.

He therefore, having related to the brethren what God had commanded, nothing doubting, prepared himself to set forth from the city. But when Paul was about to depart, there was great weeping throughout all the brotherhood, because they thought that they should see Paul no more, so that they even rent their clothes. For they had in mind also how that Paul had oftentimes contended with the doctors of the Jews and confuted them, saying: Christ, upon whom your fathers laid hands, abolished their sabbaths and fasts and holy-days and circumcision, and the doctrines of men and the rest of the traditions he did abolish. But the brethren lamented (and adjured) Paul by the coming of our Lord Jesus Christ, that he should not be absent above a year, saying: We know thy love for thy brethren; forget not us when thou art come thither, neither begin to forsake us, as little children without a mother. And when they besought him long with tears, there came a sound from heaven, and a great voice saying: Paul the servant of God is chosen to minister all the days of his life: by the hands of Nero the ungodly and wicked man shall he be perfected before your eyes. And a very great fear fell upon the brethren because of the voice which came from heaven: and they were confirmed yet more in the faith.

II. Now they brought unto Paul bread and water for the sacrifice, that he might make prayer and distribute it to every one. Among whom it befell that a woman named Rufina desired, she also, to receive the Eucharist at the hands of Paul: to whom Paul, filled with the spirit of God, said as she drew near: Rufina, thou comest not worthily unto the altar of God, arising from beside one that is not thine husband but an adulterer, and assayest to receive the Eucharist of God. For behold Satan shall trouble thine heart and cast thee down in the sight of all them that believe in the Lord, that they which see and believe may know that they have believed in the living God, the searcher of hearts. But if thou repent of thine act, he is faithful that is able to blot out thy sin and set thee free from this sin: but if thou repent not, while thou art yet in the body, devouring fire and outer darkness shall receive thee for ever. And immediately Rufina fell down, being stricken with palsy (?) from her head unto the nails of her feet, and she had no power to speak (given her) for her tongue was bound. And when both they that believed (in the faith) and the neophytes saw it, they beat their breasts, remembering their old sins, and mourned and said: We know not if God will forgive the former sins which we have committed. Then Paul called for silence and said: Men and brethren which now have begun to believe on Christ, if ye continue not in your former works of the tradition of your fathers, and keep yourselves from all guile and wrath and fierceness and adultery and defilement, and from pride and envy and contempt and enmity, Jesus the living God will forgive you that ye did in ignorance. Wherefore, ye servants of God, arm yourselves every one in your inner man with peace, patience, gentleness, faith, charity, knowledge, wisdom, love of the brethren, hospitality, mercy, abstinence, chastity, kindness, justice: then shall ye have for your guide everlastingly the first-begotten of all creation, and shall have strength in peace with our Lord. And when they had heard these things of Paul, they besought him to pray for them. And Paul lifted up his voice and said: O eternal God, God of the heavens, God of unspeakable majesty (divinity), who hast stablished all things by thy word, who hast bound upon all the world the chain of thy grace, Father of thine holy Son Jesus Christ, we together pray thee through thy Son Jesus Christ, strengthen the souls which were before unbelieving but now are faithful. Once I was a blasphemer, now I am blasphemed; once I was a persecutor, now do I suffer persecution of others; once I was the enemy of Christ, now I pray that I may be his friend: for I trust in his promise and in his mercy; I account myself faithful and that I have received forgiveness of my former sins. Wherefore I exhort you also, brethren, to believe in the Lord the Father Almighty, and to put all your trust in our Lord Jesus Christ his Son, believing in him, and no man shall be able to uproot you from his promise. Bow your knees therefore together and commend me unto the Lord, who am about to set forth unto another nation, that his grace may go before me and dispose my journey aright, that he may receive his vessels holy and believing, that they, giving thanks for my preaching of the word of the Lord, may be well grounded in the faith. But the brethren wept long and prayed unto the Lord with Paul, saying: Be thou, Lord Jesus Christ, with Paul and restore him unto us whole: for we know our weakness which is in us even to this day.

III. And a great multitude of women were kneeling and praying and beseeching Paul; and they kissed his feet and accompanied him unto the harbour. But Dionysius and Balbus, of Asia, knights of Rome, and illustrious men, and a senator by name Demetrius abode by Paul on his right hand and said: Paul, I would desire to leave the city if I were not a magistrate, that I might not depart from thee. Also from Caesar's house Cleobi-

us and Iphitus and Lysimachus and Aristaeus and two matrons Berenice and Philostrate, with Narcissus the presbyter [after they had] accompanied him to the harbour: but whereas a storm of the sea came on, he (Narcissus?) sent the brethren back to Rome, that if any would, he might come down and hear Paul until he set sail: and hearing that, the brethren went up unto the city. And when they told the brethren that had remained in the city, and the report was spread abroad, some on beasts, and some on foot, and others by way of the Tiber came down to the harbour, and were confirmed in the faith for three days, and on the fourth day until the fifth hour, praying together with Paul, and making the offering: and they put all that was needful on the ship and delivered him two young men, believers, to sail with him, and bade him farewell in the Lord and returned to Rome.

There has been great dispute about these three chapters, whether they are not an excerpt from the Acts of Paul, or whether they are an addition made by the writer of the Greek original of the Vercelli Acts.

If they are from the Acts of Paul, it means that in those Acts Paul was represented as visiting Rome twice, and going to Spain between the visits. Evidently, if this was so, he did not return straight from Spain to Rome: at least the Coptic gives no indication that the prophecies of Cleobius and Myrte were uttered in Spain.

The question is a difficult one. All allow that the writer of the Acts of Peter knew and used the Acts of Paul: but there is strong opposition to the idea that Paul related two visits to Rome.

The writer of Paul obviously knew the canonical Acts very well and obviously took great liberties with them. Did he go so far, one wonders, as to suppress and ignore the whole story of the trial before Felix and the shipwreck? If he told of but one visit to Rome -the final one- it appears that he did: for the conditions described in the Martyrdom -Paul quite free and martyred very shortly after his arrival- are totally irreconcilable with Luke (Paul arriving in custody and living two years at least in the city).

IV. Now after a few days there was a great commotion in the midst of the church, for some said that they had seen wonderful works done by a certain man whose name was Simon, and that he was at Aricia, and they added further that he said he was a great power of God and without God he did nothing. Is not this the Christ? but we believe in him whom Paul preached unto us; for by him have we seen the dead raised, and men Delivered from divers infirmities: but this man seeketh contention, we know it (or, but what this contention is, we know not) for there is no small stir made among us. Perchance also he will now enter into Rome; for yesterday they besought him with great acclamations, saying unto him: Thou art God in Italy, thou art the saviour of the Romans: haste quickly unto Rome. But he spake to the people with a shrill voice, saying: Tomorrow about the seventh hour ye shall see me fly over the gate of the city in the form (habit) wherein ye now see me speaking unto you. Therefore, brethren, if it seem good unto you, let us go and await carefully the issue of the matter. They all therefore ran together and came unto the gate. And when it was the seventh hour, behold suddenly a dust was seen in the sky afar off, like a smoke shining with rays stretching far from it. And when he drew near to the gate, suddenly he was not seen: and thereafter he appeared, standing in the midst of the people; whom they all worshipped, and took knowledge that he was the same that was seen of them the day before.

And the brethren were not a little offended among themselves, seeing, moreover, that Paul was not at Rome, neither Timotheus nor Barnabas, for they had been sent into Macedonia by Paul, and that there was no man to comfort us, to speak nothing of them that had but just become catechumens. And as Simon exalted himself yet more by the works which he did, and many of them daily called Paul a sorcerer, and others a deceiver, of so great a multitude that had been stablished in the faith all fell away save Narcissus the presbyter and two women in the lodging of the Bithynians, and four that could no longer go out of their house, but were shut up (day and night): these gave themselves unto prayer (by day and night), beseeching the Lord that Paul might return quickly, or some other that should visit his servants, because the devil had made them fall by his wickedness.

V. And as they prayed and fasted, God was already teaching Peter at Jerusalem of that which should come to pass. For whereas the twelve years which the Lord Christ had enjoined upon him were fulfilled, he showed him a vision after this manner, saying unto him: Peter, that Simon the sorcerer whom thou didst cast out of Judaea, convicting him, hath again come before thee (prevented thee) at Rome. And that shalt thou know shortly (or, and that thou mayest know in few words): for all that did believe in me hath Satan made to fall by his craft and working: whose Power Simon approveth himself to be. But delay thee not: set forth on the morrow, and there shalt thou find a ship ready, setting sail for Italy, and within few days I will show thee my grace which hath in it no grudging. Peter then, admonished by the vision, related it unto the brethren without delay, saying: It is necessary for me to go up unto Rome to fight with the enemy and adversary of the Lord and of our brethren.

And he went down to Caesarea and embarked quickly in the ship, whereof the ladder was already drawn up, not taking any provision with him. But the governor of the ship whose name was Theon looked on Peter and said: Whatsoever we have, all is thine. For what thank have we, if we take in a man like unto ourselves who is in uncertain case (difficulty) and share not all that we have with thee? but only let us have a prosperous voyage. But Peter, giving him thanks for that which he offered, himself fasted while he was in the ship, sorrowful in mind and again consoling himself because God accounted him worthy to be a minister in his service.

And after a few days the governor of the ship rose up at the hour of his dinner and asked Peter to eat with him, and said to him: O thou, whoever thou art, I know thee not, but as I reckon, I take thee for a servant of God. For as I was steering my ship at midnight I perceived the voice of a man from heaven saying to me: Theon, Theon! And twice it called me by my name and said to me: Among them that sail with thee let Peter be greatly honoured by thee, for by him shalt thou and the rest be preserved safe without any hurt after such a course as thou hopest not for. And Peter believed that God would vouchsafe to show his providence upon the sea unto them that were in the ship, and thenceforth began Peter to declare unto Theon the mighty works of God, and how the Lord had chosen him from among the apostles, and for what business he sailed unto Italy: and daily he communicated unto him the word of God. And considering him he perceived by his walk that he was of one mind in the faith and a worthy minister (deacon).

Now when there was a calm upon the ship in Hadria (the Adriatic), Theon showed it to Peter, saying unto him: If thou wilt account me worthy, whom thou mayest baptize with the seal of the Lord thou hast an opportunity. For all that were in the ship had fallen asleep, being drunken. And Peter went down by a rope and baptized Theon in the name of the Father and the Son and the Holy Ghost: and he came up out of the water rejoicing with great joy, and Peter also was glad because God had accounted Theon worthy of his name. And it came to pass when Theon was baptized, there appeared in the same place a youth shining and beautiful, saying unto them: Peace be unto you. And immediately Peter and Theon went up and entered into the cabin; and Peter took bread and gave thanks unto the Lord which had accounted him worthy of his holy ministry, and for that the youth had appeared unto them, saying: Peace be unto you. And he said: Thou best and alone holy one, it is thou that hast appeared unto us, O God Jesu Christ, and in thy name hath this man now been washed and sealed with thy holy seal. Therefore in thy name do I impart unto him thine eucharist, that he may be thy perfect servant without blame for ever.

And as they feasted and rejoiced in the Lord, suddenly there came a wind, not vehement but moderate, at the ship's prow, and ceased not for six days and as many nights, until they came unto Puteoli.

VI. And when they had touched at Puteoli, Theon leapt out of the ship and went unto the inn where he was wont to lodge, to prepare to receive Peter. Now he with whom he lodged was one by name Ariston, which alway feared the Lord, and because of the Name Theon entrusted himself with him (had dealings with him). And when he was come to the inn and saw Ariston, Theon said unto him: God who hath accounted thee worthy to serve him hath communicated his grace unto me also by his holy servant Peter, who hath now sailed with me from Judaea, being commanded by our Lord to come unto Italy. And when he heard that, Ariston fell upon Theon's neck and embraced him and besought him to bring him to the ship and show him Peter. For Ariston said that since Paul set forth unto Spain there was no man of the brethren with whom he could refresh himself, and, moreover, a certain Jew had broken into the city, named Simon, and with his charms of sorcery and his wickedness hath he made all the brotherhood fall away this way and that, so that I also fled from Rome, expecting the coming of Peter: for Paul had told us of him, and I also have seen many things in a vision. Now, therefore, I believe in my Lord that he will build up again his ministry, for all this deceit shall be rooted out from among his servants. For our Lord Jesus Christ is faithful, who is able to restore our minds. And when Theon heard these things from Ariston, who wept, his spirit was raised (increased) yet more and he was the more strengthened, because he perceived that he had believed on the living God.

But when they came together unto the ship, Peter looked upon them and smiled, being filled with the Spirit; so that Ariston falling on his face at Peter's feet, said thus: Brother and lord, that hast part in the holy mysteries and showest the right way which is in the Lord Jesus Christ our God, who by thee hath shown unto us his coming: we have lost all them whom Paul had delivered unto us, by the working of Satan; but now I trust in the Lord who hath commanded thee to come unto us, sending thee as his messenger, that he hath accounted us worthy to see his great and wonderful works by thy means. I pray thee therefore, make haste unto the city: for I left the brethren which have stumbled, whom I saw fall into the temptation of the devil, and fled hither, saying unto them: Brethren, stand fast in the faith, for it is of necessity that within these two months the mercy of our Lord bring his servant unto you. For I had seen a vision, even Paul, saying unto me: Ariston, flee thou out of the city. And when I heard it, I believed without delay and went forth in the Lord, although I had an infirmity in my flesh, and came hither; and day by day I stood upon the sea-shore asking the sailors: Hath Peter sailed with you? But

now through the abundance of the grace of God I entreat thee, let us go up unto Rome without delay, lest the teaching of this wicked man prevail yet further. And as Ariston said this with tears, Peter gave him his hand and raised him up from the earth, and Peter also groaning, said with tears: He hath prevented us which tempteth all the world by his angels; but he that hath power to save his servants from all temptations shall quench his deceits and put him beneath the feet of them that have believed in Christ whom we preach.

And, as they entered in at the gate, Theon entreated Peter, saying: Thou didst not refresh thyself on any day in so great a voyage (sea): and now after (before) so hard a journey wilt thou set out forthwith from the ship? tarry and refresh thyself, and so shalt thou set forth: for from hence to Rome upon a pavement of flint I fear lest thou be hurt by the shaking. But Peter answered and said to them: What if it come to pass that a millstone were hung upon me, and likewise upon the enemy of our Lord, even as my Lord said unto us of any that offended one of the brethren, and I were drowned in the sea? but it might be not only a millstone, but that which is far worse, even that I which am the enemy of this persecutor of his servants should die afar off from them that have believed on the Lord Jesus Christ (so Ficker: the sentence is corrupt; the sense is that Peter must at all costs be with his fellow-Christians, or he will incur even worse punishment than that threatened by our Lord's words). And by no exhortation could Theon prevail to persuade him to tarry there even one day.

But Theon himself delivered all that was in the ship to be sold for the price which he thought good, and followed Peter unto Rome; whom Ariston brought unto the abode of Narcissus the presbyter.

VII. Now the report was noised through the city unto the brethren that were dispersed, because of Simon, that he might show him to be a deceiver and a persecutor of good men. All the multitude therefore ran together to see the apostle of the Lord stay (himself, or the brethren) on Christ. And on the first day of the week when the multitude was assembled to see Peter, Peter began to say with a loud voice: Ye men here present that trust in Christ, ye that for a little space have suffered temptation, learn for what cause God sent his Son into the world, and wherefore he made him to be born of the Virgin Mary; for would he so have done if not to procure us some grace or dispensation? even because he would take away all offence and all ignorance and all the contrivance of the devil, his attempts (beginnings) and his strength wherewith he prevailed aforetime, before our God shined forth in the world. And whereas men through ignorance fell into death by many and divers infirmities, Almighty God, moved with compassion, sent his Son into the world. With whom I was; and he (or I) walked upon the water, whereof I myself remain a witness, and do testify that he then worked in the world by signs and wonders, all of which he did.

I do confess, dearly-beloved brethren, that I was with him: yet I denied him, even our Lord Jesus Christ, and that not once only, but thrice; for there were evil dogs that were come about me as they did unto the Lord's prophets. And the Lord imputed it not unto me, but turned unto me and had compassion on the infirmity of my flesh, when (or so that) afterward I bitterly bewailed myself, and lamented the weakness of my faith, because I was befooled by the devil and kept not in mind the word of my Lord. And now I say unto you, O men and brethren, which are gathered together in the name of Jesus Christ: against you also hath the deceiver Satan aimed his arrows, that ye might depart out of the way. But faint not, brethren, neither let your spirit fall, but be strong and persevere and doubt not: for if Satan caused me to stumble, whom the Lord had in great honour, so that I denied the light of mine hope, and if he overthrew me and persuaded me to flee as if I had put my trust in a man, what think ye will he do unto you which are but young in the faith? Did ye suppose that he would not turn you away to make you enemies of the kingdom of God, and cast you down into perdition by a new (or the last) deceit? For whomsoever he casteth out from the hope of our Lord Jesus Christ, he is a son of perdition for ever. Turn yourselves, therefore, brethren, chosen of the Lord, and be strong in God Almighty, the Father of our Lord Jesus Christ, whom no man hath seen at any time, neither can see, save he who hath believed in him. And be ye aware whence this temptation hath come upon you. For it is not only by words that I would convince you that this is Christ whom I preach, but also by deeds and exceeding great works of power do I exhort you by the faith that is in Christ Jesus, that none of you look for any other save him that was despised and mocked of the Jews, even this Nazarene which was crucified and died and the third day rose again.

VIII. And the brethren repented and entreated Peter to fight against Simon: (who said that he was the power of God, and lodged in the house of Marcellus a senator, whom he had convinced by his charms) saying: Believe us, brother Peter: there was no man among men so wise as this Marcellus. All the widows that trusted in Christ had recourse unto him; all the fatherless were fed by him; and what more, brother? all the poor called Marcellus their patron, and his house was called the house of the strangers and of the poor, and the emperor said unto him: I will keep thee out of every office, lest thou despoil the provinces to give gifts unto the Christians. And Marcellus answered: All my goods are also thine. And Caesar said to him: Mine they would be if thou keptest them for me; but now they are not mine, for thou givest them to whom thou wilt, and I know not to what vile persons. Having this, then, before our eyes, brother Peter, we report it to thee, how the great mercy of this man is turned unto blasphemy; for if he had not turned, neither should we have departed from the holy faith of God our Lord. And now doth this Marcellus in anger repent him of his good deeds, saying: All this substance have I spent in all this time, vainly believing that I gave it for the knowledge of God! So that if any stranger cometh to the door of his house, he smiteth him with a staff and biddeth him be beaten, saying: Would God I had not spent so much money upon these impostors: and yet more doth he say, blaspheming. But if there abide in thee any mercy of our Lord and aught of the goodness of his commandments, do thou succour the error of this man who hath done so many alms-deeds unto the servants of God.

And Peter, when he perceived this, was smitten with sharp affliction and said: O the divers arts and temptations of the devil! O the contrivances and devices of the wicked! he that nourisheth up for himself a mighty fire in the day of wrath, the destruction of simple men, the ravening wolf, the devourer and scatterer of eternal life! Thou didst enmesh the first man in concupiscence and bind him with thine old iniquity and with the chain of the flesh: thou art wholly the exceeding bitter fruit of the tree of bitterness, who sendest divers lusts upon men. Thou didst compel Judas my fellow-disciple and fellow-apostle to do wickedly and deliver up our Lord Jesus Christ, who shall punish thee therefor. Thou didst harden the heart of Herod and didst inflame Pharaoh and compel him to fight against Moses the holy servant of God; thou didst give boldness unto Caiaphas, that he should deliver our Lord Jesus Christ unto the unrighteous multitude; and even until now thou shootest at innocent souls with thy poisonous arrows. Thou wicked one, enemy of all men, be thou accursed from the Church of him the Son of the holy God ommpotent and as a brand cast out of the fire shalt thou be quenched by the servants of our Lord Jesus Christ. Upon thee let thy blackness be turned and upon thy children, an evil seed; upon thee be turned thy wickedness and thy threatenings; upon thee and thine angels be thy temptations, thou beginning of malice and bottomless pit of darkness! Let thy darkness that thou hast be with thee and with thy vessels which thou ownest! Depart from them that shall believe in God, depart from the servants of Christ and from them that desire to be his soldiers. Keep thou to thyself thy garments of darkness! Without cause knockest thou at other men's doors, which are not thine but of Christ Jesus that keepeth them. For thou, ravening wolf, wouldest carry off the sheep that are not thine but of Christ Jesus, who keepeth them with all care and diligence.

IX. As Peter spake thus with great sorrow of mind, many were added unto them that believed on the Lord. But the brethren besought Peter to join battle with Simon and not suffer him any longer to vex the people. And without delay Peter went quickly out of the synagogue (assembly) and went unto the house of Marcellus, where Simon lodged: and much people followed him. And when he came to the door, he called the porter and said to him: Go, say unto Simon: Peter because of whom thou fleddest out of Judaea waiteth for thee at the door. The porter answered and said to Peter: Sir, whether thou be Peter, I know not: but I have a command; for he had knowledge that yesterday thou didst enter into the city, and said unto me: Whether it be by day or by night, at whatsoever hour he cometh, say that I am not within. And Peter said to the young man: Thou hast well said in reporting that which he compelled thee to say. And Peter turned unto the people that followed him and said: Ye shall now see a great and marvellous wonder. And Peter seeing a great dog bound with a strong chain, went to him and loosed him, and when he was loosed the dog received a man's voice and said unto Peter: What dost thou bid me to do, thou servant of the unspeakable and living God? Peter said unto him: Go in and say unto Simon in the midst of his company: Peter saith unto thee, Come forth abroad, for thy sake am I come to Rome, thou wicked one and deceiver of simple souls. And immediately the dog ran and entered in, and rushed into the midst of them that were with Simon, and lifted up his forefeet and in a loud voice said: Thou Simon, Peter the servant of Christ who standeth at the door saith unto thee: Come forth abroad, for thy sake am I come to Rome, thou most wicked one and deceiver of simple souls. And when Simon heard it, and beheld the incredible sight, he lost the words wherewith he was deceiving them that stood by, and all of them were amazed.

X. But when Marcellus saw it he went out to the door and cast himself at Peter's feet and said: Peter, I embrace thy feet, thou holy servant of the holy God; I have sinned greatly: but exact thou not my sins, if there be in thee the true faith of Christ, whom thou preachest, if thou remember his commandments, to hate no man, to be unkind to no man, as I learned from thy fellow apostle Paul; keep not in mind my faults, but pray for me unto the Lord, the holy Son of God whom I have provoked to wrath -for I have persecuted his servants- that I be not delivered with the sins of Simon unto eternal fire; who so persuaded me, that I set up a statue to him with this inscription: 'To Simon the new (young) God.' If I knew, O Peter, that thou couldest be won with money, I would give thee all my substance, yea I would give it and despise it, that I might gain my soul. If I had sons, I would account them as nothing, if only I might believe in the living God. But I confess that he would not have deceived me save that

he said that he was the power of God; yet will I tell thee, O most gentle (sweet) Peter: I was not worthy to hear thee, thou servant of God, neither was I stablished in the faith of God which is in Christ; therefore was I made to stumble. I beseech thee, therefore, take not ill that which I am about to say, that Christ our Lord whom thou preachest in truth said unto thy fellow-apostles in thy presence: If ye have faith as a grain of mustard seed, ye shall say unto this mountain: Remove thyself: and straightway it shall remove itself. But this Simon said that thou, Peter, wast without faith when thou didst doubt, in the waters. And I have heard that Christ said this also: They that are with me have not understood me. If, then, ye upon whom he laid his hands, whom also he chose, did doubt, I, therefore, having this witness, repent me, and take refuge in thy prayers. Receive my soul, who have fallen away from our Lord and from his promise. But I believe that he will have mercy upon me that repent. For the Almighty is faithful to forgive me my sins.

But Peter said with a loud voice: Unto thee, our Lord, be glory and splendour, O God Almighty, Father of our Lord Jesus Christ. Unto thee be praise and glory and honour, world without end. Amen. Because thou hast now fully strengthened and stablished us in thee in the sight of all, holy Lord, confirm thou Marcellus, and send thy peace upon him and upon his house this day: and whatsoever is lost or out of the way, thou alone canst turn them all again; we beseech thee, Lord, shepherd of the sheep that once were scattered, but now shall be gathered in one by thee. So also receive thou Marcellus as one of thy lambs and suffer him no longer to go astray (revel) in error or ignorance. Yea, Lord, receive him that with anguish and tears entreateth thee.

XI. And as Peter spake thus and embraced Mareellus, Peter turned himself unto the multitude that stood by him and saw there one that laughed (smiled), in whom was a very evil spirit. And Peter said unto him: Whosoever thou art that didst laugh, show thyself openly unto all that are present. And hearing this the young man ran into the court of the house and cried out with a loud voice and dashed himself against the wall and said: Peter, there is a great contention between Simon and the dog whom thou sentest; for Simon saith to the dog: Say that I am not here. Unto whom the dog saith more than thou didst charge him; and when he hath accomplished the mystery which thou didst command him, he shall die at thy feet. But Peter said: And thou also, devil, whosoever thou art, in the name of our Lord Jesus Christ, go out of that young man and hurt him not at all: show thyself unto all that stand here. When the young man heard it, he ran forth and caught hold on a great statue of marble which was set in the court of the house, and brake it in pieces with his feet. Now it was a statue of Caesar. Which Marcellus beholding smote his forehead and said unto Peter: A great crime hath been committed; for if this be made known unto Caesar by some busybody, he will afflict us with sore punishments. And Peter said to him: I see thee not the same that thou wast a little while ago, for thou saidst that thou wast ready to spend all thy substance to save thy soul. But if thou indeed repentest, believing in Christ with thy whole heart, take in thine hands of the water that runneth down, and pray to the Lord, and in his name sprinkle it upon the broken pieces of the statue and it shall be whole as it was before. And Marcellus, nothing doubting, but believing with his whole heart, before he took the water lifted up his hands and said: I believe in thee, O Lord Jesu Christ: for I am now proved by thine apostle Peter, whether I believe aright in thine holy name. Therefore I take water in mine hands, and in thy name do I sprinkle these stones that the statue may become whole as it was before. If, therefore, Lord, it be thy will that I continue in the body and suffer nothing at Caesar's hand, let this stone be whole as it was before. And he sprinkled the water upon the stones, and the statue became whole, whereat Peter exulted that Marcellus had not doubted in asking of the Lord, and Marcellus was exalted in spirit for that such a sign was first wrought by his hands; and he therefore believed with his whole heart in the name of Jesus Christ the Son of God, by whom all things impossible are made possible.

XII. But Simon within the house said thus to the dog: Tell Peter that I am not within. Whom the dog answered in the presence of Marcellus: Thou exceeding wicked and shameless one, enemy of all that live and believe on Christ Jesus, here is a dumb animal sent unto thee which hath received a human voice to confound thee and show thee to be a deceiver and a liar. Hast thou taken thought so long, to say at last: 'Tell him that I am not within?' Art thou not ashamed to utter thy feeble and useless words against Peter the minister and apostle of Christ, as if thou couldst hide thee from him that hath commanded me to speak against thee to thy face: and that not for thy sake but for theirs whom thou wast deceiving and sending unto destruction? Cursed therefore shalt thou be, thou enemy and corrupter of the way of the truth of Christ, who shall prove by fire that dieth not and in outer darkness, thine iniquities that thou hast committed. And having thus said, the dog went forth and the people followed him, leaving Simon alone. And the dog came unto Peter as he sat with the multitude that was come to see Peter's face, and the dog related what he had done unto Simon. And thus spake the dog unto the angel and apostle of the true God: Peter, thou wilt have a great contest with the enemy of Christ and his servants, and many that have been deceived by him shalt thou turn unto the faith; wherefore thou shalt receive from God the reward of thy work. And when the dog had said this he fell down at the apostle Peter's feet and gave up the ghost. And when the great multitude saw with amazement the dog speaking, they began then, some to throw themselves down at Peter's feet, and some said: Show us another sign, that we may believe in thee as the minister of the living God, for Simon also did many signs in our presence and therefore did we follow him.

XIII. And Peter turned and saw a herring (sardine) hung in a window, and took it and said to the people: If ye now see this swimming in the water like a fish, will ye be able to believe in him whom I preach? And they said with one voice: Verily we will believe thee. Then he said -now there was a bath for swimming at hand: In thy name, O Jesu Christ, forasmuch as hitherto it is not believed in, in the sight of all these live and swim like a fish. And he cast the herring into the bath, and it lived and began to swim. And all the people saw the fish swimming, and it did not so at that hour only, lest it should be said that it was a delusion (phantasm), but he made it to swim for a long time, so that they brought much people from all quarters and showed them the herring that was made a living fish, so that certain of the people even cast bread to it; and they saw that it was whole. And seeing this, many followed Peter and believed in the Lord.

And they assembled themselves day and night unto the house of Narcissus the presbyter. And Peter discoursed unto them of the scriptures of the prophets and of those things which our Lord Jesus Christ had wrought both in word and in deeds.

XIV. But Marcellus was confirmed daily by the signs which he saw wrought by Peter through the grace of Jesus Christ which he granted unto him. And Mareellus ran upon Simon as he sat in his house in the dining chamber, and cursed him and said unto him: Thou most adverse and pestilent of men, corrupter of my soul and my house, who wouldest have made me fall away from my Lord and Saviour Christ! and laying hands on him he commanded him to be thrust out of his house. And the servants having received such licence, covered him with reproaches; some buffeted his face, others beat him with sticks, others cast stones, others emptied out vessels full of filth upon his head, even those who on his account had fled from their master and been a long time fettered; and other their fellowservants of whom he had spoken evil to their master reproached him. saying to him: Now by the will of God who hath had mercy on us and on our master, do we recompense thee with a fit reward. And Simon, shrewdly beaten and cast out of the house, ran unto the house where Peter lodged, even the house of Narcissus, and standing at the gate cried out: Lo, here am I, Simon: come thou down, Peter, and I will convict thee that thou hast believed on a man which is a Jew and a carpenter's son.

XV. And when it was told Peter that Simon had said this, Peter sent unto him a woman which had a sucking child, saying to her: Go down quickly, and thou wilt find one that seeketh me. For thee there is no need that thou answer him at all, but keep silence and hear what the child whom thou holdest shall say unto him. The woman therefore went down. Now the child whom she suckled was seven months old; and it received a man's voice and said unto Simon: O thou abhorred of God and men, and destruction of truth, and evil seed of all corruption, O fruit by nature unprofitable! but only for a short and little season shalt thou be seen, and thereafter eternal punishment is laid up for thee. Thou son of a shameless father, that never puttest forth thy roots for good but for poison, faithless generation void of all hope! thou wast not confounded when a dog reproved thee; I a child am compelled of God to speak, and not even now art thou ashamed. But even against thy will, on the sabbath day that cometh, another shall bring thee into the forum of Julius that it may be shown what manner of man thou art. Depart therefore from the gate wherein walk the feet of the holy; for thou shalt no more corrupt the innocent souls whom thou didst turn out of the way and make sad; in Christ, therefore, shall be shown thine evil nature, and thy devices shall be cut in pieces. And now speak I this last word unto thee: Jesus Christ saith to thee: Be thou stricken dumb in my name, and depart out of Rome until the sabbath that cometh. And forthwith he became dumb and his speech was bound; and he went out of Rome until the sabbath and abode in a stable. But the woman returned with the child unto Peter and told him and the rest of the brethren what the child had said unto Simon: and they magnified the Lord which had shown these things unto men.

XVI. Now when the night fell, Peter, while yet waking, beheld Jesus clad in a vesture of brightness, smiling and saying unto him: Already is much people of the brotherhood returned through me and through the signs which thou hast wrought in my name. But thou shalt have a contest of the faith upon the sabbath that cometh, and many more of the Gentiles and of the Jews shall be converted in my name unto me who was reproached and mocked and spat upon. For I will be present with thee when thou askest for signs and wonders, and thou shalt convert many: but thou shalt have Simon opposing thee by the works of his father; yet all his works shall be shown to be charms and contrivances of sorcery. But now slack thou not, and whomsoever I shall send unto thee thou shalt establish in my name. And when it was light, he told the brethren how the Lord had appeared unto him and what he had commanded him:

XVII. [This episode, inserted most abruptly, is believed by Vouaux to have been inserted here by the compiler of the Greek original of the Vercelli Acts: but it was not composed by him, but transferred with very slight additions from the earlier part of the Acts-now lost- of which the scene was laid in Judaea. I incline to favour this view.)

But believe ye me, men and brethren, I drove this Simon out of Judaea where he did many evils with his magical charms, lodging in Judaea with a certain woman Eubula, who was of honourable estate in this world, having store of gold and pearls of no small price. Here did Simon enter in by stealth with two others like unto himself, and none of the household saw them two, but Simon only, and by means of a spell they took away all the woman's gold, and disappeared. But Eubula, when she found what was done, began to torture her household, saying: Ye have taken occasion by this man of God and spoiled me, when ye saw him entering in to me to honour a mere woman; but his name is as the name of the Lord.

As I fasted for three days and prayed that this matter should be made plain, I saw in a vision Italicus and Antulus (Antyllus?) whom I had instructed in the name of the Lord, and a boy naked and chained giving me a wheaten loaf and saying unto me: Peter, endure yet two days and thou shalt see the mighty works of God. As for all that is lost out of the house of Eubula, Simon hath used art magic and hath caused a delusion, and with two others hath stolen it away: whom thou shalt see on the third day at the ninth hour, at the gate which leadeth unto Neapolis, selling unto a goldsmith by name Agrippinus a young satyr of gold of two pound weight, having in it a precious stone. But for thee there is no need that thou touch it, lest thou be defiled; but let there be with thee some of the matron's servants, and thou shalt show them the shop of the goldsmith and depart from them. For by reason of this matter shall many believe on the name of the Lord, and all that which these men by their devices and wickedness have oft-times stolen shall be openly showed. When I heard that, I went unto Eubula and found her sitting with her clothes rent and her hair disordered, mourning; unto whom I said: Eubula, rise up from thy mourning and compose thy face and order thy hair and put on raiment befitting thee, and pray unto the Lord Jesus Christ that judgeth every soul: for he is the invisible Son of God, by whom thou must be saved, if only thou repent with thine whole heart of thy former sins: and receive thou power from him; for behold, by me the Lord saith to thee: Thou shalt find all whatsoever thou hast lost. And after thou hast received them, take thou care that he find thee, that thou mayest renounce this present world and seek for everlasting refreshment. Hearken therefore unto this: Let certain of thy people keep watch at the gate that leadeth to Neapolis on the day after to-morrow at about the ninth hour, and they shall see two young men having a young satyr of gold, of two pound weight, set with gems, as a vision hath shown me: which thing they will offer for sale to one Agrippinus of the household of godliness and of the faith which is in the Lord Jesus Christ: by whom it shall be showed thee that thou shouldest believe in the living God and not on Simon the magician, the unstable devil, who hath desired that thou shouldest remain in sorrow, and thine innocent household be tormented; who by fair words and speech only hath deceived thee, and with his mouth only spake of godliness, whereas he is wholly possessed of ungodliness. For when thou didst think to keep holy-day, and settedst up thine idol and didst veil it and set out all thine ornaments upon a table (round three-legged table), he brought in two young men whom no man of yours saw, by a magic charm, and they stole away thine ornaments and were no more seen. But his device hath had no success (place); for my God hath manifested it unto me, to the end thou shouldest not be deceived, neither perish in hell, for those sins which thou hast committed ungodly and contrary to God, who is full of all truth, and the righteous judge of quick and dead; and there is none other hope of life unto men save through him, by whom those things which thou hast lost are recovered unto thee: and now do thou gain thine own soul.

But she cast herself down before my feet, saying: O man, who thou art I know not; but him I received as a servant of God, and whatsoever he asked of me to give it unto the poor, I gave much by his hands, and beside that I did give much unto him. What hurt did I do him, that he should contrive all this against mine house? Unto whom Peter said: There is no faith to be put in words, but in acts and deeds: but we must go on with that we have begun. So I left her and went with two stewards of Eubula and came to Agrippinus and said to him: See that thou take note of these men; for to-morrow two young men will come to thee, desiring to sell thee a young satyr of gold set with jewels, which belongeth to the mistress of these: and thou shalt take it as it were to look upon it, and praise the work of the craftsman, and then when these come in, God will bring the rest to the proof. And on the next day the stewards of the matron came about the ninth hour, and also those young men, willing to sell unto Agrippinus the young satyr of gold. And they being forthwith taken, it was reported unto the matron, and she in distress of mind came to the deputy, and with a loud voice declared all that had befallen her. And when Pompeius the deputy beheld her in distress of mind, who never had come forth abroad, he forthwith rose up from the judgement seat and went unto the praetorium, and bade those men to be brought and tortured; and while they were being tormented they confessed that they did it in the service of Simon, which, said they, persuaded us thereto with money. And being tortured a long time, they confessed that all that Eubula had lost was laid up under the earth in a cave on the other side of the gate, and many other things besides. And when Pompeius heard this, he rose up to go unto the gate, with those two men, each of them bound with two chains. And lo, Simon came in at the gate, seeking them because they tarried long. And he seeth a great multitude coming, and those two bound with chains; and he understood and betook him to flight, and appeared no more in Judaea unto this day. But Eubula, when she had recovered all her goods, gave them for the service of the poor, and believed on the Lord Jesus Christ and was comforted; and despised and renounced this world, and gave unto the widows and fatherless, and clothed the poor. And after a long time she received her rest (sleep). Now these things, dearly beloved brethren, were done in Judaea, whereby he that is called the angel of Satan was driven out thence.

XVIII. Brethren, dearest and most beloved, let us fast together and pray unto the Lord. For he that drove him out thence is able also to root him out of this place: and let him grant unto us power to withstand him and his magical charms, and to prove that he is the angel of Satan. For on the sabbath our Lord shall bring him, though he would not, unto the forum of Julius. Let us therefore bow our knees unto Christ, which heareth us, though we cry not; it is he that seeth us, though he be not seen with these eyes, yet is he in us: if we will, he will not forsake us. Let us therefore purify our souls of every evil temptation, and God will not depart from us. Yea, if we but wink with our eyes, he is present with us.

XIX. Now after these things were spoken by Peter, Marcellus also came in, and said: Peter, I have for thee cleansed mine whole house from the footsteps (traces) of Simon, and wholly done away even his wicked dust. For I took water and called upon the holy name of Jesus Christ, together with mine other servants which belong unto him, and sprinkled all my house and all the dining chambers and all the porticoes, even unto the outer gate, and said: I know that thou, Lord Jesu Christ, art pure and untouched of any uncleanness: so let mine enemy and adversary be driven out from before thy face. And now, thou blessed one, have I bidden the widows and old women to assemble unto thee in my house which is purified (MS. common), that they may pray with us. And they shall receive every one a piece of gold in the name of the ministry (service), that they may be called indeed servants of Christ. And all else is now prepared for the service. I entreat thee, therefore, O blessed Peter, consent unto their request, so that thou also pay honour unto (ornament) their prayers in my stead; let us then go and take Narcissus also, and whosoever of the brethren are here. So then Peter consented unto his simplicity, to fulfil his desire, and went forth with him and the rest of the brethren.

XX. But Peter entered in, and beheld one of the aged women, a widow, that was blind, and her daughter giving her her hand and leading her into Marcellus' house; and Peter said unto her: Come hither, mother: from this day forward Jesus giveth thee his right hand, by whom we have light unapproachable which no darkness hideth; who saith unto thee by me: Open thine eyes and see, and walk by thyself. And forthwith the widow saw Peter laying his hand upon her.

And Peter entered into the dining-hall and saw that the Gospel was being read, and he rolled up the book and said: Ye men that believe and hope in Christ, learn in what manner the holy Scripture of our Lord ought to be declared: whereof we by his grace wrote that which we could receive, though yet it appear unto you feeble, yet according to our power, even that which can be endured to be borne by (or instilled into) human flesh. We ought therefore first to know the will and the goodness of God, how that when error was everywhere spread abroad, and many thousands of men were being cast down into perdition, God was moved by his mercy to show himself in another form and in the likeness of man, concerning which neither the Jews nor we were able worthily to be enlightened. For every one of us according as he could contain the sight, saw, as he was able. Now will I expound unto you that which was newly read unto you. Our Lord, willing that I should behold his majesty in the holy mount -I, when I with the sons of Zebedee saw the brightness of his light, fell as one dead and shut mine eyes, and heard such a voice from him as I am not able to describe, and thought myself to be blinded by his brightness. And when I recovered (breathed again) a little I said within myself: Peradventure my Lord hath brought me hither that he might blind me. And I said: If this also be thy will, Lord, I resist not. And he gave me his hand and raised me up; and when I arose I saw him again in such a form as I was able to take in. As, therefore, the merciful God, dearly beloved brethren, carried our infirmities and bare our sins (as the prophet saith: He beareth our sins and suffereth for us; but we did esteem him to be in affliction and smitten with plagues), for he is in the Father and the Father in him -he also is himself the fulness of all majesty, who hath shown unto us all his good things: he did eat and drink for our sakes, himself being neither an-hungered nor athirst; he carried and bare reproaches for our sakes, he died and rose again because of us; who both defended me when I sinned and comforted me by his greatness, and will comfort you also that ye may love him: this God who is great and small, fair and foul, young and old, seen in time and unto eternity invisible; whom the hand of man hath not held, yet is he held by his servants; whom no flesh hath seen, yet now seeth; who is the word proclaimed by the prophets and now appearing (so Gk.: Lat. not heard of but now known); not subject to suffering, but having now made trial of suffering for our sake (or like unto

us); never chastised, yet now chastised; who was before the world and hath been comprehended in time; the great beginning of all principality, yet delivered over unto princes; beautiful, but among us lowly; seen of all yet foreseeing all (MS. foul of view, yet foreseeing). This Jesus ye have, brethren, the door, the light, the way, the bread, the water, the life, the resurrection, the refreshment, the pearl, the treasure, the seed, the abundance (harvest), the mustard seed, the vine, the plough, the grace, the faith, the word: he is all things and there is none other greater than he. Unto him be praise, world without end. Amen.

XXI. And when the ninth hour was fully come, they rose up to make prayer. And behold certain widows, of the aged, unknown to Peter, which sat there, being blind and not believing, cried out, saying unto Peter: We sit together here, O Peter, hoping and believing in Christ Jesus: as therefore thou hast made one of us to see, we entreat thee, lord Peter, grant unto us also his mercy and pity. But Peter said to them: If there be in you the faith that is in Christ, if it be firm in you, then perceive in your mind that which ye see not with your eyes, and though your ears are closed, yet let them be open in your mind within you. These eyes shall again be shut, seeing nought but men and oxen and dumb beasts and stones and sticks; but not every eye seeth Jesus Christ. Yet now, Lord, let thy sweet and holy name succour these persons; do thou touch their eyes; for thou art able -that these may see with their eyes.

And when all had prayed, the hall wherein they were shone as when it lighteneth, even with such a light as cometh in the clouds, yet not such a light as that of the daytime, but unspeakable, invisible, such as no man can describe, even such that we were beside ourselves with bewilderment, calling on the Lord and saying: Have mercy, Lord, upon us thy servants: what we are able to bear, that, Lord, give thou us; for this we can neither see nor endure. And as we lay there, only those widows stood up which were blind; and the bright light which appeared unto us entered into their eyes and made them to see. Unto whom Peter said: Tell us what ye saw. And they said: We saw an old man of such comeliness as we are not able to declare to thee; but others said: We saw a young man; and others: We saw a boy touching our eyes delicately, and so were our eyes opened. Peter therefore magnified the Lord, saying: Thou only art the Lord God, and of what lips have we need to give thee due praise? and how can we give thee thanks according to thy mercy? Therefore, brethren, as I told you but a little while since, God that is constant is greater than our thoughts, even as we have learned of these aged widows, how that they beheld the Lord in divers forms.

XXII. And having exhorted them all to think upon (understand) the Lord with their whole heart, he began together with Marcellus and the rest of the brethren to minister unto the virgins of the Lord, and to rest until the morning.

Unto whom Marcellus said: Ye holy and inviolate virgins of the Lord, hearken: Ye have a place to abide in, for these things that are called mine, whose are they save yours? depart not hence, but refresh yourselves: for upon the sabbath which cometh, even to-morrow, Simon hath a controversy with Peter the holy one of God: for as the Lord hath ever been with him, lo will Christ the Lord now stand for him as his apostle. For Peter hath continued tasting nothing, but fasting yet a day, that he may overcome the wicked adversary and persecutor of the Lord's truth. For lo, my young men are come announcing that they have seen scaffolds being set up in the forum, and much people saying: To-morrow at daybreak two Jews are to contend here concerning the teaching (?) of God. Now therefore let us watch until the morning, praying and beseeching our Lord Jesus Christ to hear our prayers on behalf of Peter.

And Marcellus turned to sleep for a short space, and awoke and said unto Peter: O Peter, thou apostle of Christ, let us go boldly unto that which lieth before us. For just now when I turned myself to sleep for a little, I beheld thee sitting in a high place and before thee a great multitude, and a woman exceeding foul, in sight like an Ethiopian, not an Egyptian, but altogether black and filthy, clothed in rags, and with an iron collar about her neck and chains upon her hands and feet, dancing. And when thou sawest me thou saidst to me with a loud voice: Marcellus the whole power of Simon and of his God is this woman that danceth; do thou behead her. And I said to thee: Brother Peter, I am a senator of a high race, and I have never defiled my hands, neither killed so much as a sparrow at any time. And thou hearing it didst begin to cry out yet more: Come thou, our true sword, Jesu Christ. and cut not off only the head of this devil, but hew all her limbs in pieces in the sight of all these Whom I have approved in thy service. And immediately one like unto thee, O Peter, having a sword, hewed her in pieces: so that I looked earnestly upon you both, both on thee and on him that cut in pieces that devil, and marvelled greatly to see how alike ye were. And I awaked, and have told unto thee these signs of Christ. And when Peter heard it he was the more filled with courage, for that Marcellus had seen these things, knowing that the Lord alway careth for his own. And being joyful and refreshed by these words, he rose up to go unto the forum.

XXIII. Now the brethren were gathered together, and all that were in Rome, and took places every one for a piece of gold: there came together also the senators and the prefects and those in authority. And Peter came and stood in the midst, and all cried out: Show us, O Peter, who is thy

God and what is his greatness which hath given thee confidence. Begrudge not the Romans; they are lovers of the gods. We have had proof of Simon, let us have it of thee; convince us, both of you, whom we ought truly to believe. And as they said these things, Simon also came in, and standing in trouble of mind at Peter's side, at first he looked at him.

And after long silence Peter said: Ye men of Rome, be ye true judges unto us, for I say that I have believed on the living and true God; and I promise to give you proofs of him, which are known unto me, as many among you also can bear witness. For ye see that this man is now rebuked and silent, knowing that I drove him out of Judaea because of the deceits which he practised upon Eubula, an honourable and simple woman, by his art magic; and being driven out from thence, he is come hither, thinking to escape notice among you; and lo, he standeth face to face with me. Say now, Simon, didst thou not at Jerusalem fall at my feet and Paul's, when thou sawest the healings that were wrought by our hands, and say: I pray you take of me a payment as much as ye will, that I may be able to lay hands on men and do such mighty works? And we when we heard it cursed thee, saying: Dost thou think to tempt us as if we desired to possess money? And now, fearest thou not at all? My name is Peter, because the Lord Christ vouchsafed to call me 'prepared for all things': for I trust in the living God by whom I shall put down thy sorceries. Now let him do in your presence the wonders which he did aforetime: and what I have now said of him, will ye not believe it?

But Simon said: Thou presumest to speak of Jesus of Nazareth, the son of a carpenter, and a carpenter himself, whose birth is recorded (or whose race dwelleth) in Judaea. Hear thou, Peter: the Romans have understanding: they are no fools. And he turned to the people and said: Ye men of Rome, is God born? is he crucified? he that hath a master is no God. And when he so spake, many said: Thou sayest well, Simon.

XXIV. But Peter said: Anathema upon thy words against (or in) Christ! Presumest thou to speak thus, whereas the prophet saith of him: Who shall declare his generation? And another prophet saith: And we saw him and he had no beauty nor comeliness. And: In the last times shall a child be born of the Holy Ghost: his mother knoweth not a man, neither doth any man say that he is his father. And again he saith: She hath brought forth and not brought forth.[From the apocryphal Ezekiel (lost)] And again: Is it a small thing for you to weary men (lit. Is it a small thing that ye make a contest for men)? Behold, a virgin shall conceive in the womb. And another prophet saith, honouring the Father: Neither did we hear her voice, neither did a midwife come in.[From the Ascension of Isaiah, xi. 14] Another prophet saith: Born not of the womb of a woman, but from a heavenly place came he down. And: A stone was cut out without hands, and smote all the kingdoms. And: The stone which the builders rejected, the same is become the head of the corner; and he calleth him a stone elect, precious. And again a prophet saith concerning him: And behold, I saw one like the Son of man coming upon a cloud. And what more? O ye men of Rome, if ye knew the Scriptures of the prophets, I would expound all unto you: by which Scriptures it was necessary that this should be spoken in a mystery, and that the kingdom of God should be perfected. But these things shall be opened unto you hereafter. Now turn I unto thee, Simon: do thou some one thing of those wherewith thou didst before deceive them, and I will bring it to nought through my Lord Jesus Christ. And Simon plucked up his boldness and said: If the prefect allow it (prepare yourselves and delay not for my sake).

XXV. But the prefect desired to show patience unto both, that he might not appear to do aught unjustly. And the prefect put forward one of his servants and said thus unto Simon: Take this man and deliver him to death. And to Peter he said: And do thou revive him. And unto the people the prefect said: It is now for you to judge whether of these two is acceptable unto God, he that killeth or he that maketh alive. And straightway Simon spake in the ear of the lad and made him speechless, and he died.

And as there began to be a murmuring among the people, one of the widows who were nourished (refreshed) in Marcellus' house, standing behind the multitude, cried out: O Peter, servant of God, my son is dead, the only one that I had. And the people made place for her and led her unto Peter: and she cast herself down at his feet, saying: I had one only son, which with his hands (shoulders) furnished me with nourishment: he raised me up, he carried me: now that he is dead, who shall reach me a hand? Unto whom Peter said: Go, with these for witness, and bring hither thy son, that they may see and be able to believe that by the power of God he is raised, and that this man (Simon) may behold it and fail (or, and she when she saw him, fell down). And Peter said to the young men: We have need of some young men, and, moreover, of such as will believe. And forthwith thirty young men arose, which were prepared to carry her or to bring thither her son that was dead. And whereas the widow was hardly returned to herself, the young men took her up; and she was crying out and saying: Lo, my son, the servant of Christ hath sent unto thee: tearing her hair and her face. Now the young men which were come examined (Gk. apparently, held) the lad's nostrils to see whether he were indeed dead; and seeing that he was dead of a truth, they had compassion on the old woman and said: If thou so will, mother, and hast

confidence in the God of Peter, we will take him up and carry him thither that he may raise him up and restore him unto thee.

XXVI. And as they said these things, the prefect (in the forum, Lat.), looking earnestly upon Peter (said: What sayest thou Peter?) Behold my lad is dead, who also is dear unto the emperor, and I spared him not, though I had with me other young men; but I desired rather to make trial (tempt) of thee and of the God whom thou (preachest), whether ye be true, and therefore I would have this lad die. And Peter said: God is not tempted nor proved, O Agrippa, but if he be loved and entreated he heareth them that are worthy. But since now my God and Lord Jesus Christ is tempted among you, who hath done so great signs and wonders by my hands to turn you from your sins -now also in the sight of all do thou, Lord, at my word, by thy power raise up him whom Simon hath slain by touching him. And Peter said unto the master of the lad: Go, take hold on his right hand, and thou shalt have him alive and walking with thee. And Agrippa the prefect ran and went to the lad and took his hand and raised him up. And all the multitude seeing it cried: One is the God, one is the God of Peter.

XXVII. In the meanwhile the widow's son also was brought upon a bed by the young men, and the people made way for them and brought them unto Peter. And Peter lifted up his eyes unto heaven and stretched forth his hands and said: O holy Father of thy Son Jesus Christ. who hast granted us thy power, that we may through thee ask and obtain, and despise all that is in the world, and follow thee only, who art seen of few and wouldest be known of many: shine thou about us, Lord, enlighten us, appear thou, raise up the son of this aged widow, which cannot help herself without her son. And I, repeating the word of Christ my Lord, say unto thee: Young man, arise and walk with thy mother so long as thou canst do her good; and thereafter shalt thou serve me after a higher sort, ministering in the lot of a deacon of the bishop (or, and of a bishop). And immediately the dead man rose up, and the multitudes saw it and marvelled, and the people cried out: Thou art God the Saviour, thou, the God of Peter, the invisible God, the Saviour. And they spake among themselves, marvelling indeed at the power of a man that called upon his Lord with a word; and they received it unto sanctification.

XXVIII. The fame of it therefore being spread throughout the city, there came the mother of a certain senator, and cast herself into the midst of the people, and fell at Peter's feet, saying: I have learned from my people that thou art a servant of the merciful God, and dost impart his grace unto all them that desire this light. Impart therefore the light unto my son, for I know that thou begrudgest none; turn not away from a matron that entreateth thee. Unto whom Peter said: Wilt thou believe on my God, by whom thy son shall be raised? And the mother said with a loud voice, weeping: I believe, O Peter, I believe! and all the people cried out: Grant the mother her son. But Peter said: Let him be brought hither before all these. And Peter turned himself to the people and said: Ye men of Rome, I also am one of yourselves, and bear a man's body and am a sinner, but have obtained mercy: look not therefore upon me as though I did by mine own power that which I do, but by the power of my Lord Jesus Christ, who is the judge of quick and dead. In him do I believe and by him am I sent, and have confidence when I call upon him to raise the dead. Go thou therefore also, O woman, and cause thy son to be brought hither and to rise again. And the woman passed through the midst of the people and went into the street, running, with great joy, and believing in her mind she came unto her house, and by means of her young men she took him up and came unto the forum. Now she bade the young men put caps [pilei, a sign that they were now freed.] on their heads, and to walk before the bier, and all that she had determined to burn upon the body of her son to be borne before his bier; and when Peter saw it he had compassion upon the dead body and upon her. And she came unto the multitude, while all bewailed her; and a great crowd of senators and matrons followed after, to behold the wonderful works of God: for this Nicostratus which was dead was exceeding noble and beloved of the senate. And they brought him and set him down before Peter. And Peter called for silence, and with a loud voice said: Ye men of Rome, let there now be a just judgement betwixt me and Simon; and judge ye whether of us two believeth in the living God, he or I. Let him raise up the body that lieth here, and believe in him as the angel of God. But if he be not able, and I call upon my God and restore the son alive unto his mother, then believe ye that this man is a sorcerer and a deceiver, which is entertained among you. And when all they heard these things, they thought that it was right which Peter had spoken, and they encouraged Simon, saying: Now, if there be aught in thee, show it openly! either overcome, or thou shall be overcome! (or, convince us, or thou shalt be convicted). Why standest thou still? Come, begin! But Simon, when he saw them all instant with him, stood silent; and thereafter, when he saw the people silent and looking upon him, Simon cried out, saying: Ye men of Rome, if ye behold the dead man arise, will ye cast Peter out of the city? And all the people said: We will not only cast him out, but on the very instant will we burn him with fire. Then Simon went to the head of the dead man and stooped down and thrice raised himself up (or, and said thrice: Raise thyself), and showed the people that he (the dead) lifted his head and moved it, and opened his eyes and bowed himself a little unto Simon. And straightway they began to ask for wood and torches, wherewith to burn Peter. But Peter receiving strength of Christ, lifted up his voice and said unto them that cried out against him: Now see I, ye people of Rome, that ye are -I must not say fools and vain, so long as your eyes and your ears and your hearts are blinded. How long shall your understanding be darkened? see ye not that ye are bewitched, supposing that a dead man is raised, who hath not lifted himself up? It would have sufficed me, ye men of Rome, to hold my peace and die without speaking, and to leave you among the deceits of this world; but I have the chastisement of fire unquenchable before mine eyes. If therefore it seem good unto you, let the dead man speak, let him arise if he liveth, let him loose his jaw that is bound, with his hands, let him call upon his mother, let him say unto you that cry out: Wherefore cry ye? let him beckon unto us with his hand. If now ye would see that he is dead, and yourselves bewitched, let this man depart from the bier, who hath persuaded you to depart from Christ, and ye shall see that the dead man is such as ye saw him brought hither.

But Agrippa the prefect had no longer patience, but thrust away Simon with his own hands, and again the dead man lay as he was before. And the people were enraged, and turned away from the sorcery of Simon and began to cry out: Hearken, O Caesar! if now the dead riseth not, let Simon burn instead of Peter, for verily he hath blinded us. But Peter stretched forth his hand and said: O men of Rome, have patience! I say not unto you that if the lad be raised Simon shall burn; for if I say it, ye will do it. The people cried out: Against thy will, Peter, we will do it. Unto whom Peter said: If ye continue in this mind the lad shall not arise: for we know not to render evil for evil, but we have learned to love our enemies and pray for our persecutors. For if even this man can repent, it were better; for God will not remember evil. Let him come, therefore, into the light of Christ; but if he cannot, let him possess the part of his father the devil, but let not your hands be defiled. And when he had thus spoken unto the people, he went unto the lad, and before he raised him, he said to his mother: These young men whom thou hast set free in the honour of thy son, can yet serve their God when he liveth, being free; for I know that the soul of some is hurt if they shall see thy son arise and know that these shall yet be in bondage: but let them all continue free and receive their sustenance as they did before, for thy son is about to rise again; and let them be with him. And Peter looked long upon her, to see her thoughts. And the mother of the lad said: What other can I do? therefore before the prefect I say: whatsoever I was minded to burn upon the body of my son, let them possess it. And Peter said: Let the residue be distributed unto the widows. Then Peter rejoiced in soul and said in the spirit: O Lord that art merciful, Jesu Christ, show thyself unto thy Peter that calleth upon thee like as thou hast always shown him mercy and loving-kindness: and in the presence of all these which have obtained freedom, that these may become thy servants, let Nicostratus now arise. And Peter touched the lad's side and said: Arise. And the lad arose and put off his grave clothes and sat up and loosed his jaw, and asked for other raiment; and he came down from the bier and said unto Peter: I pray thee, O man of God, let us go unto our Lord Christ whom I saw speaking with me; who also showed me unto thee and said to thee: Bring him hither unto me, for he is mine. And when Peter heard this of the lad, he was strengthened yet more in soul by the help of the Lord; and Peter said unto the people: Ye men of Rome, it is thus that the dead are raised up, thus do they converse, thus do they arise and walk, and live so long time as God willeth. Now therefore, ye that have come together unto the sight, if ye turn not from these your evil ways, and from all your gods that are made with hands, and from all uncleanness and concupiscence, receive fellowship with Christ, believing, that ye may obtain everlasting life.

XXIX. And in the same hour they worshipped him as a God, falling down at his feet, and the sick whom they had at home, that he might heal them. But the prefect seeing that so great a multitude waited upon Peter, signified to Peter that he should withdraw himself: and Peter told the people to come unto Marcellus' house. But the mother of the lad besought Peter to set foot in her house. But Peter had appointed to be with Marcellus on the Lord's day, to see the widows even as Marcellus had promised, to minister unto them with his own hands. The lad therefore that was risen again said: I depart not from Peter. And his mother, glad and rejoicing, went unto her own house. And on the next day after the sabbath she came to Marcellus' house bringing unto Peter two thousand pieces of gold, and saying unto Peter: Divide these among the virgins of Christ which serve him. But the lad that was risen from the dead, when he saw that he had given nothing to any man, went home and opened the press and himself offered four thousand pieces of gold, saying unto Peter: Lo, I also which was raised, offer a double offering, and myself also from this day forward as a speaking sacrifice unto God.

Here begins the original Greek text as preserved in one of our two manuscripts (that at Mt. Athos). The second (Patmos) manuscript begins, as do the versions, at ch. xxxiii. The Greek and not the Latin is followed in the translation.

XXX. Now on the Lord's day as Peter discoursed unto the brethren and exhorted them unto the faith of Christ, there being present many of the senate and many knights and rich women and matrons, and being confirmed in the faith, one woman that was there, exceeding rich, which was surnamed Chryse because every vessel of hers was of gold -for from her birth she never used a vessel of silver or glass, but golden ones only- said unto Peter: Peter, thou servant of God, he whom thou callest God appeared unto me in a dream and said: Chryse, carry thou unto Peter my minister ten thousand pieces of gold; for thou owest them to him. I have therefore brought them, fearing lest some harm should be done me by him that appeared unto me, which also departed unto heaven. And so saying, she laid down the money and departed. And Peter seeing it glorified the Lord, for that they that were in need should be refreshed. Certain, therefore, of them that were there said unto him: Peter, hast thou not done ill to receive the money of her? for she is ill spoken of throughout all Rome for fornication, and because she keepeth not to one husband, yea, she even hath to do with the young men of her house. Be not therefore a partner with the table of Chryse, but let that which came from her be returned unto her. But Peter hearing it laughed and said to the brethren: What this woman is in the rest of her way of life, I know not, but in that I have received this money, I did it not foolishly; for she did pay it as a debtor unto Christ, and giveth it unto the servants of Christ: for he himself hath provided for them.

XXXI. And they brought unto him also the sick on the sabbath, beseeching that they might recover of their diseases. And many were healed that were sick of the palsy, and the gout, and fevers tertian and quartan, and of every disease of the body were they healed, believing in the name of Jesus Christ, and very many were added every day unto the grace of the Lord.

But Simon the magician, after a few days were past, promised the multitude to convict Peter that he believed not in the true God but was deceived. And when he did many lying wonders, they that were firm in the faith derided him. For in diningchambers he made certain spirits enter in, which were only an appearance, and not existing in truth. And what should I more say? though he had oft-times been convicted of sorcery, he made lame men seem whole for a little space, and blind likewise, and once he appeared to make many dead to live and move, as he did with Nicostratus (Gk. Stratonicus). But Peter followed him throughout and convicted him always unto the beholders: and when he now made a sorry figure and was derided by the people of Rome and disbelieved for that he never succeeded m the things which he promised to perform, being in such a plight at last he said to them: Men of Rome, ye think now that Peter hath prevailed over me, as more powerful, and ye pay more heed to him: ye are deceived. For to-morrow I shall forsake you, godless and impious that ye are, and fly up unto God whose Power I am, though I am become weak. Whereas, then, ye have fallen, I am He that standeth, and I shall go up to my Father and say unto him: Me also, even thy son that standeth, have they desired to pull down; but I consented not unto them, and am returned back unto myself.

XXXII. And already on the morrow a great multitude assembled at the Sacred Way to see him flying. And Peter came unto the place, having seen a vision (or, to see the sight), that he might convict him in this also; for when Simon entered into Rome, he amazed the multitudes by flying: but Peter that convicted him was then not yet living at Rome: which city he thus deceived by illusion, so that some were carried away by him (amazed at him).

So then this man standing on an high place beheld Peter and began to say: Peter, at this time when I am going up before all this people that behold me, I say unto thee: If thy God is able, whom the Jews put to death, and stoned you that were chosen of him, let him show that faith in him is faith in God, and let it appear at this time, if it be worthy of God. For I, ascending up, will show myself unto all this multitude, who I am. And behold when he was lifted up on high, and all beheld him raised up above all Rome and the temples thereof and the mountains, the faithful looked toward Peter. And Peter seeing the strangeness of the sight cried unto the Lord Jesus Christ: If thou suffer this man to accomplish that which he hath set about, now will all they that have believed on thee be offended, and the signs and wonders which thou hast given them through me will not be believed: hasten thy grace, O Lord, and let him fall from the height and be disabled; and let him not die but be brought to nought, and break his leg in three places. And he fell from the height and brake his leg in three places. Then every man cast stones at him and went away home, and thenceforth believed Peter.

But one of the friends of Simon came quickly out of the way (or arrived from a journey), Gemellus by name, of whom Simon had received much money, having a Greek woman to wife, and saw him that he had broken his leg, and said: O Simon, if the Power of God is broken to pieces, shall not that God whose Power thou art, himself be blinded? Gemellus therefore also ran and followed Peter, saying unto him: I also would be of them that believe on Christ. And Peter said: Is there any that grudgeth it, my brother? come thou and sit with us.

But Simon in his affliction found some to carry him by night on a bed from Rome unto Aricia; and he abode there a space, and was brought thence unto Terracina to one Castor that was banished from Rome upon an accusation of sorcery. And there he was sorely cut (Lat. by two physicians), and so Simon the angel of Satan came to his end.

[Here the Martyrdom proper begins in the Patmos MS. and the versions.]

XXXIII. Now Peter was in Rome rejoicing in the Lord with the brethren, and giving thanks night and day for the multitude which was brought daily unto the holy name by the grace of the Lord. And there were gathered also unto Peter the concubines of Agrippa the prefect, being four, Agrippina and Nicaria and Euphemia and Doris; and they, hearing the word concerning chastity and all the oracles of the Lord, were smitten in their souls, and agreeing together to remain pure from the bed of Agrippa they were vexed by him.

Now as Agrippa was perplexed and grieved concerning them -and he loved them greatly- he observed and sent men privily to see whither they went, and found that they went unto Peter. He said therefore unto them when they returned: That Christian hath taught you to have no dealings with me: know ye that I will both destroy you, and burn him alive. They, then, endured to suffer all manner of evil at Agrippa's hand, if only they might not suffer the passion of love, being strengthened by the might of Jesus.

XXXIV. And a certain woman which was exceeding beautiful, the wife of Albinus, Caesar's friend, by name Xanthippe, came, she also, unto Peter, with the rest of the matrons, and withdrew herself, she also, from Albinus. He therefore being mad, and loving Xanthippe, and marvelling that she would not sleep even upon the same bed with him, raged like a wild beast and would have dispatched Peter; for he knew that he was the cause of her separating from his bed. Many other women also, loving the word of chastity, separated themselves from their husbands, because they desired them to worship God in sobriety and cleanness. And whereas there was great trouble in Rome, Albinus made known his state unto Agrippa, saying to him: Either do thou avenge me of Peter that hath withdrawn my wife, or I will avenge myself. And Agrippa said: I have suffered the same at his hand, for he hath withdrawn my concubines. And Albinus said unto him: Why then tarriest thou, Agrippa? let us find him and put him to death for a dealer in curious arts, that we may have our wives again, and avenge them also which are not able to put him to death, whose wives also he hath parted from them.

XXXV. And as they considered these things, Xanthippe took knowledge of the counsel of her husband with Agrippa, and sent and showed Peter, that he might depart from Rome. And the rest of the brethren, together with Marcellus, besought him to depart. But Peter said unto them: Shall we be runaways, brethren? and they said to him: Nay, but that thou mayest yet be able to serve the Lord. And he obeyed the brethren's voice and went forth alone, saying: Let none of you come forth with me, but I will go forth alone, having changed the fashion of mine apparel. And as he went forth of the city, he saw the Lord entering into Rome. And when he saw him, he said: Lord, whither goest thou thus (or here)? And the Lord said unto him: I go into Rome to be crucified. And Peter said unto him: Lord, art thou (being) crucified again? He said unto him: Yea, Peter, I am (being) crucified again. And Peter came to himself: and having beheld the Lord ascending up into heaven, he returned to Rome, rejoicing, and glorifying the Lord, for that he said: I am being crucified: the which was about to befall Peter.

XXXVI. He went up therefore again unto the brethren, and told them that which had been seen by him: and they lamented in soul, weeping and saying: We beseech thee, Peter, take thought for us that are young. And Peter said unto them: If it be the Lord's will, it cometh to pass, even if we will it not; but for you, the Lord is able to stablish you in his faith, and will found you therein and make you spread abroad, whom he himself hath planted, that ye also may plant others through him. But I, so long as the Lord will that I be in the flesh, resist not; and again if he take me to him I rejoice and am glad.

And while Peter thus spake, and all the brethren wept, behold four soldiers took him and led him unto Agrippa. And he in his madness (disease) commanded him to be crucified on an accusation of godlessness.

The whole multitude of the brethren therefore ran together, both of rich and poor, orphans and widows, weak and strong, desiring to see and to rescue Peter, while the people shouted with one voice, and would not be silenced: What wrong hath Peter done, O Agrippa? Wherein hath he hurt thee? tell the Romans! And others said: We fear lest if this man die, his Lord destroy us all.

And Peter when he came unto the place stilled the people and said: Ye men that are soldiers of Christ! ye men that hope in Christ! remember the signs and wonders which ye have seen wrought through me, remember the compassion of God, how many cures he hath wrought for you. Wait for him that cometh and shall reward every man according to his doings. And now be ye not bitter against Agrippa; for he is the minister of his father's working. And this cometh to pass at all events, for the Lord hath manifested unto me that which befalleth. But why delay I and draw not near unto the cross?

XXXVII. And having approached and standing by the cross he began to say: O name of the cross, thou hidden mystery! O grace ineffable that is pronounced in the name of the cross! O nature of man, that cannot be separated from God! O love (friendship) unspeakable and inseparable, that cannot be shown forth by unclean lips! I seize thee now, I that am at the end of my delivery hence (or, of my coming hither). I will declare thee, what thou art: I will not keep silence of the mystery of the cross

which of old was shut and hidden from my soul. Let not the cross be unto you which hope in Christ, this which appeareth: for it is another thing, different from that which appeareth, even this passion which is according to that of Christ. And now above all, because ye that can hear are able to hear it of me, that am at the last and final hour of my life, hearken: Separate your souls from every thing that is of the senses, from every thing that appeareth, and does not exist in truth. Blind these eyes of yours, close these ears of yours, put away your doings that are seen; and ye shall perceive that which concerneth Christ, and the whole mystery of your salvation: and let thus much be said unto you that hear, as if it had not been spoken. But now it is time for thee, Peter, to deliver up thy body unto them that take it. Receive it then, ye unto whom it belongeth. I beseech you the executioners, crucify me thus, with the head downward and not otherwise: and the reason wherefore, I will tell unto them that hear.

XXXVIII. And when they had hanged him up after the manner he desired, he began again to say: Ye men unto whom it belongeth to hear, hearken to that which I shall declare unto you at this especial time as I hang here. Learn ye the mystery of all nature, and the beginning of all things, what it was. For the first man, whose race I bear in mine appearance (or, of the race of whom I bear the likeness), fell (was borne) head downwards, and showed forth a manner of birth such as was not heretofore: for it was dead, having no motion. He, then, being pulled down - who also cast his first state down upon the earth- established this whole disposition of all things, being hanged up an image of the creation (Gk. vocation) wherein he made the things of the right hand into left hand and the left hand into right hand, and changed about all the marks of their nature, so that he thought those things that were not fair to be fair, and those that were in truth evil, to be good. Concerning which the Lord saith in a mystery: Unless ye make the things of the right hand as those of the left, and those of the left as those of the right, and those that are above as those below, and those that are behind as those that are before, ye shall not have knowedge of the kingdom.

This thought, therefore, have I declared unto you; and the figure wherein ye now see me hanging is the representation of that man that first came unto birth. Ye therefore, my beloved, and ye that hear me and that shall hear, ought to cease from your former error and return back again. For it is right to mount upon the cross of Christ, who is the word stretched out, the one and only, of whom the spirit saith: For what else is Christ, but the word, the sound of God? So that the word is the upright beam whereon I am crucified. And the sound is that which crosseth it, the nature of man. And the nail which holdeth the cross-tree unto the upright in the midst thereof is the conversion and repentance of man.

XXXIX. Now whereas thou hast made known and revealed these things unto me, O word of life, called now by me wood (or, word called now by me the tree of life), I give thee thanks, not with these lips that are nailed unto the cross, nor with this tongue by which truth and falsehood issue forth, nor with this word which cometh forth by means of art whose nature is material, but with that voice do I give thee thanks, O King, which is perceived (understood) in silence, which is not heard openly, which proceedeth not forth by organs of the body, which goeth not into ears of flesh, which is not heard of corruptible substance, which existeth not in the world, neither is sent forth upon earth, nor written in books, which is owned by one and not by another: but with this, O Jesu Christ, do I give thee thanks, with the silence of a voice, wherewith the spirit that is in me loveth thee, speaketh unto thee, seeth thee, and beseecheth thee. Thou art perceived of the spirit only, thou art unto me father, thou my mother, thou my brother, thou my friend, thou my bondsman, thou my steward: thou art the All and the All is in thee: and thou Art, and there is nought else that is save thee only.

Unto him therefore do ye also, brethren, flee, and if ye learn that in him alone ye exist, ye shall obtain those things whereof he saith unto you: 'which neither eye hath seen nor ear heard, neither have they entered into the heart of man.' We ask, therefore, for that which thou hast promised to give unto us, O thou undefiled Jesu. We praise thee, we give thee thanks, and confess to thee, glorifying thee, even we men that are yet without strength, for thou art God alone, and none other: to whom be glory now and unto all ages. Amen.

XL. And when the multitude that stood by pronounced the Amen with a great sound, together with the Amen Peter gave up his spirit unto the Lord.

And Marcellus not asking leave of any, for it was not possible, when he saw that Peter had given up the ghost, took him down from the cross with his own hands and washed him in milk and wine: and cut fine seven minae of mastic, and of myrrh and aloes and indian leaf other fifty, and perfumed (embalmed) his body and filled a coffin of marble of great price with Attic honey and laid it in his own tomb.

But Peter by night appeared unto Marcellus and said: Marcellus, hast thou heard that the Lord saith: Let the dead be buried of their own dead? And when Marcellus said: Yea, Peter said to him: That, then, which thou hast spent on the dead, thou hast lost: for thou being alive hast like a dead man cared for the dead. And Marcellus awoke and told the brethren of the appearing of Peter: and he was with them that had been stablished in the faith of Christ by Peter, himself also being stablished yet more until the coming of Paul unto Rome.

XLI. [This last chapter, and the last sentence of XL, are thought by Vouaux to be an addition by the author of i-iii, in other words by the compiler of the Greek original of the Vercelli Acts.]

But Nero, learning thereafter that Peter was departed out of this life, blamed the prefect Agrippa, because he had been put to death without his knowledge; for he desired to punish him more sorely and with greater torment, because Peter had made disciples of certain of them that served him, and had caused them to depart from him: so that he was very wrathful and for a long season spake not unto Agrippa: for he sought to destroy all them that had been made disciples by Peter. And he beheld by night one that scourged him and said unto him: Nero, thou canst not now persecute nor destroy the servants of Christ: refrain therefore thine hands from them. And so Nero, being greatly affrighted by such a vision, abstained from harming the disciples at that time when Peter also departed this life.

And thenceforth the brethren were rejoicing with one mind and exulting in the Lord, glorifying the God and Saviour (Father?) of our Lord Jesus Christ with the Holy Ghost, unto whom be glory, world without end. Amen.

Book 100. Acts of Thomas

The First Act: When he went into India with Abbanes the merchant.

At that season all we the apostles were at Jerusalem, Simon which is called Peter and Andrew his brother, James the son of Zebedee and John his brother, Philip and Bartholomew, Thomas and Matthew the publican, James the son of Alphaeus and Simon the Canaanite, and Judas the brother of James: and we divided the regions of the world, that every one of us should go unto the region that fell to him and unto the nation whereunto the Lord sent him.

According to the lot, therefore, India fell unto Judas Thomas, which is also the twin: but he would not go, saying that by reason of the weakness of the flesh he could not travel, and 'I am an Hebrew man; how can I go amongst the Indians and preach the truth?' And as he thus reasoned and spake, the Saviour appeared unto him by night and saith to him: Fear not, Thomas, go thou unto India and preach the word there, for my grace is with thee. But he would not obey, saying: Whither thou wouldest send me, send me, but elsewhere, for unto the Indians I will not go.

2 And while he thus spake and thought, it chanced that there was there a certain merchant come from India whose name was Abbanes, sent from the King Gundaphorus [Gundaphorus is a historical personage who reigned over a part of India in the first century after Christ. His coins bear his name in Greek, as Hyndopheres], and having commandment from him to buy a carpenter and bring him unto him.

Now the Lord seeing him walking in the market-place at noon said unto him: Wouldest thou buy a carpenter? And he said to him: Yea. And the Lord said to him: I have a slave that is a carpenter and I desire to sell him. And so saying he showed him Thomas afar off, and agreed with him for three litrae of silver unstamped, and wrote a deed of sale, saying: I, Jesus, the son of Joseph the carpenter, acknowledge that I have sold my slave, Judas by name, unto thee Abbanes, a merchant of Gundaphorus, king of the Indians. And when the deed was finished, the Saviour took Judas Thomas and led him away to Abbanes the merchant, and when Abbanes saw him he said unto him: Is this thy master? And the apostle said: Yea, he is my Lord. And he said: I have bought thee of him. And thy apostle held his peace.

3 And on the day following the apostle arose early, and having prayed and besought the Lord he said: I will go whither thou wilt, Lord Jesus: thy will be done. And he departed unto Abbanes the merchant, taking with him nothing at all save only his price. For the Lord had given it unto him, saying: Let thy price also be with thee, together with my grace, wheresoever thou goest.

And the apostle found Abbanes carrying his baggage on board the ship; so he also began to carry it aboard with him. And when they were embarked in the ship and were set down Abbanes questioned the apostle, saying: What craftsmanship knowest thou? And he said: In wood I can make ploughs and yokes and augers (ox-goads, Syr.), and boats and oars for boats and masts and pulleys; and in stone, pillars and temples and court-houses for kings. And Abbanes the merchant said to him: Yea, it is of such a workman that we have need. They began then to sail homeward; and they had a favourable wind, and sailed prosperously till they reached Andrapolis, a royal city.

4 And they left the ship and entered into the city, and lo, there were noises of flutes and water-organs, and trumpets sounded about them; and the apostle inquired, saying: What is this festival that is in this city? And they that were there said to him: Thee also have the gods brought to make merry in this city. For the king hath an only daughter, and now he giveth her in marriage unto an husband: this rejoicing, therefore, and assembly of the wedding to-day is the festival which thou hast seen. And the king hath sent heralds to proclaim everywhere that all should come to the marriage, rich and poor, bond and free, strangers and citizens: and if any

refuse and come not to the marriage he shall answer for it unto the king. And Abbanes hearing that, said to the apostle: Let us also go, lest we offend the king, especially seeing we are strangers. And he said: Let us go.

And after they had put up in the inn and rested a little space they went to the marriage; and the apostle seeing them all set down (reclining), laid himself, he also, in the midst, and all looked upon him, as upon a stranger and one come from a foreign land: but Abbanes the merchant, being his master, laid himself in another place.

5 And as they dined and drank, the apostle tasted nothing; so they that were about him said unto him: Wherefore art thou come here, neither eating nor drinking? but he answered them, saying: I am come here for somewhat greater than the food or the drink, and that I may fulfil the king's will. For the heralds proclaim the king's message, and whoso hearkeneth not to the heralds shall be subject to the king's judgement.

So when they had dined and drunken, and garlands and unguents were brought to them, every man took of the unguent, and one anointed his face and another his beard and another other parts of his body; but the apostle anointed the top of his head and smeared a little upon his nostrils, and dropped it into his ears and touched his teeth with it, and carefully anointed the parts about his heart: and the wreath that was brought to him, woven of myrtle and other flowers, he took, and set it on his head, and took a branch of calamus and held it in his hand.

Now the flute-girl, holding her flute in her hand, went about to them all and played, but when she came to the place where the apostle was, she stood over him and played at his head for a long space: now this flute-girl was by race an Hebrew.

6 And as the apostle continued looking on the ground, one of the cup-bearers stretched forth his hand and gave him a buffet; and the apostle lifted up his eyes and looked upon him that smote him and said: My God will forgive thee in the life to come this iniquity, but in this world thou shalt show forth his wonders and even now shall I behold this hand that hath smitten me dragged by dogs. And having so said, he began to sing and to say this song:

The damsel is the daughter of light, in whom consisteth and dwelleth the proud brightness of kings, and the sight of her is delightful, she shineth with beauty and cheer. Her garments are like the flowers of spring, and from them a waft of fragrance is borne; and in the crown of her head the king is established which with his immortal food (ambrosia) nourisheth them that are founded upon him; and in her head is set truth, and with her feet she showeth forth joy. And her mouth is opened, and it becometh her well: thirty and two are they that sing praises to her. Her tongue is like the curtain of the door, which waveth to and fro for them that enter in: her neck is set in the fashion of steps which the first maker hath wrought, and her two hands signify and show, proclaiming the dance of the happy ages, and her fingers point out the gates of the city. Her chamber is bright with light and breatheth forth the odour of balsam and all spices, and giveth out a sweet smell of myrrh and Indian leaf, and within are myrtles strown on the floor, and [GARLANDS] of all manner of odorous flowers, and the door-posts(?) are adorned with freedst. 7 And surrounding her her groomsmen keep her, the number of whom is seven, whom she herself hath chosen. And her bridesmaids are seven, and they dance before her. And twelve in number are they that serve before her and are subject unto her, which have their aim and their look toward the bridegroom, that by the sight of him they may be enlightened; and for ever shall they be with her in that eternal joy, and shall be at that marriage whereto the princes are gathered together and shall attend at that banquet whereof the eternal ones are accounted worthy, and shall put on royal raiment and be clad in bright robes; and in joy and exultation shall they both be and shall glorify the Father of all, whose proud light they have received, and are enlightened by the sight of their lord; whose immortal food they have received, that hath no failing (excrementum, Syr.), and have drunk of the wine that giveth then neither thirst nor desire. And they have glorified and praised with the living spirit, the Father of truth and the mother of wisdom.

8 And when he had sung and ended this song, all that were there present gazed upon him; and he kept silence, and they saw that his likeness was changed, but that which was spoken by him they understood not, forasmuch as he was an Hebrew and that which he spake was said in the Hebrew tongue. But the flute-girl alone heard all of it, for she was by race an Hebrew and she went away from him and played to the rest, but for the most part she gazed and looked upon him, for she loved him well, as a man of her own nation; moreover he was comely to look upon beyond all that were there. And when the flute-girl had played to them all and ended, she sat down over against him, gazing and looking earnestly upon him. But he looked upon no man at all, neither took heed of any but only kept his eyes looking toward the ground, waiting the time when he might depart thence.

But the cup-bearer that had buffeted him went down to the well to draw water; and there chanced to be a lion there, and it slew him and left him Lying in that place, having torn his limbs in pieces, and forthwith dogs seized his members, and among them one black dog holding his right hand in his mouth bare it into the place of the banquet.

9 And all when they saw it were amazed and inquired which of them it was that was missing. And when it became manifest that it was the hand of the cup-bearer which had smitten the apostle, the flute-girl brake her flute and cast it away and went and sat down at the apostle's feet, saying: This is either a god or an apostle of God, for I heard him say in the Hebrew tongue: ' I shall now see the hand that hath smitten me dragged by dogs', which thing ye also have now beheld; for as he said, so hath it come about. And some believed her, and some not.

But when the king heard of it, he came and said to the apostle: Rise up and come with me, and pray for my daughter: for she is mine only-begotten, and to-day I give her in marriage. But the apostle was not willing to go with him, for the Lord was not yet revealed unto him in that place. But the king led him away against his will unto the bride-chamber that he might pray for them.

10 And the apostle stood, and began to pray and to speak thus: My Lord and MY God, that travellest with thy servants, that guidest and correctest them that believe in thee, the refuge and rest of the oppressed, the hope of the poor and ransomer of captives, the physician of the souls that lie sick and saviour of all creation, that givest life unto the world and strengthenest souls; thou knowest things to come, and by our means accomplishest them: thou Lord art he that revealeth hidden mysteries and maketh manifest words that are secret: thou Lord art the planter of the good tree, and of thine hands are all good works engendered: thou Lord art he that art in all things and passest through all, and art set in all thy works and manifested in the working of them all. Jesus Christ, Son of compassion and perfect saviour, Christ, Son of the living God, the undaunted power that hast overthrown the enemy, and the voice that was heard of the rulers, and made all their powers to quake, the ambassador that wast sent from the height and camest down even unto hell, who didst open the doors and bring up thence them that for many ages were shut up in the treasury of darkness, and showedst them the way that leadeth up unto the height: I beseech thee, Lord Jesu, and offer unto thee supplication for these young persons, that thou wouldest do for them the things that shall help them and be expedient and profitable for them. And he laid his hands on them and said: The Lord shall be with you, and left them in that place and departed.

11 And the king desired the groomsmen to depart out of the bride-chamber; and when all were gone out and the doors were shut, the bridegroom lifted up the curtain of the bride-chamber to fetch the bride unto him. And he saw the Lord Jesus bearing the likeness of Judas Thomas and speaking with the bride; even of him that but now had blessed them and gone out from them, the apostle; and he saith unto him: Wentest thou not out in the sight of all? how then art thou found here? But the Lord said to him: I am not Judas which is also called Thomas but I am his brother. And the Lord sat down upon the bed and bade them also sit upon chairs, and began to say unto them:

12 Remember, my children, what my brother spake unto you and what he delivered before you: and know this, that if ye abstain from this foul intercourse, ye become holy temples, pure, being quit of impulses and pains, seen and unseen, and ye will acquire no cares of life or of children, whose end is destruction: and if indeed ye get many children, for their sakes ye become grasping and covetous, stripping orphans and overreaching widows, and by so doing subject yourselves to grievous punishments. For the more part of children become useless oppressed of devils, some openly and some invisibly, for they become either lunatic or half withered or blind or deaf or dumb or paralytic or foolish; and if they be sound, again they will be vain, doing useless or abominable acts, for they will be caught either in adultery or murder or theft or fornication, and by all these will ye be afflicted.

But if ye be persuaded and keep your souls chaste before God, there will come unto you living children whom these blemishes touch not, and ye shall be without care, leading a tranquil life without grief or anxiety, looking to receive that incorruptible and true marriage, and ye shall be therein groomsmen entering into that bride-chamber which is full of immortality and light.

13 And when the young people heard these things, they believed the Lord and gave themselves up unto him, and abstained from foul desire and continued so, passing the night in that place. And the Lord departed from before them, saying thus: The grace of the Lord shall be with you.

And when the morning was come the king came to meet them and furnished a table and brought it in before the bridegroom and the bride. And he found them sitting over against each other and the face of the bride he found unveiled, and the bridegroom was right joyful.

And the mother came unto the bride and said: Why sittest thou so, child, and art not ashamed, but art as if thou hadst lived with thine husband a long season? And her father said: Because of thy great love toward thine husband dost thou not even veil thyself?

14 And the bride answered and said: Verily, father, I am in great love, and I pray my Lord that the love which I have perceived this night may abide with me, and I will ask for that husband of whom I have learned to-day: and therefore I will no more veil myself, because the mirror (veil) of shame is removed from me; and therefore am I no more ashamed or abashed, because the deed of shame and confusion is departed far from me; and that I am not confounded, it is because my astonishment hath not continued with me; and that I am in cheerfulness and joy, it is because the day of my joy hath not been troubled; and that I have set at nought this husband and this marriage that passeth away from before mine eyes, it is because I am joined in another marriage; and that I have had no intercourse with a husband that is temporal, whereof the end is with lasciviousness and bitterness of soul, it is because I am yoked unto a true husband.

15 And while the bride was saying yet more than this, the bridegroom answered and said: I give thee thanks, O Lord, that hast been proclaimed by the stranger, and found in us; who hast removed me far from corruption and sown life in me; who hast rid me of this disease that is hard to be healed and cured and abideth for ever, and hast implanted sober health in me; who hast shown me myself and revealed unto me all my state wherein I am; who hast redeemed me from falling and led me to that which is better, and set me free from temporal things and made me worthy of those that are immortal and everlasting; that hast made thyself lowly even down to me and my littleness, that thou mayest present me unto thy greatness and unite me unto thyself; who hast not withheld thine own bowels from me that was ready to perish, but hast shown me how to seek myself and know who I was, and who and in what manner I now am, that I may again become that which I was: whom I knew not, but thyself didst seek me out: of whom I was not aware, but thyself hast taken me to thee: whom I have perceived, and now am not able to be unmindful of him: whose love burneth within me, and I cannot speak it as is fit, but that which I am able to say of it is little and scanty, and not fitly proportioned unto his glory: yet he blameth me not that presume to say unto him even that which I know not: for it is because of his love that I say even this much.

16 Now when the king heard these things from the bridegroom and the bride, he rent his clothes and said unto them that stood by him: Go forth quickly and go about the whole city, and take and bring me that man that is a sorcerer who by ill fortune came unto this city; for with mine own hands I brought him into this house, and I told him to pray over this mine ill-starred daughter; and whoso findeth and bringeth him to me, I will give him whatsoever he asketh of me. They went, therefore and went about seeking him, and found him not; for he had set sail. They went also unto the inn where he had lodged and found there the flute-girl weeping and afflicted because he had not taken her with him. And when they told her the matter that had befallen with the young people she was exceeding glad at hearing it, and put away her grief and said: Now have I also found rest here. And she rose up and went unto them, and was with them a long time, until they had instructed the king also. And many of the brethren also gathered there until they heard the report of the apostle, that he was come unto the cities of India and was teaching there: and they departed and joined themselves unto him.

The Second Act: Concerning his coming unto the king Gundaphorus.
17 Now when the apostle was come into the cities of India with Abbanes the merchant, Abbanes went to salute the king Gundaphorus, and reported to him of the carpenter whom he had brought with him. And the king was glad, and commanded him to come in to him. So when he was come in the king said unto him: What craft understandest thou? The apostle said unto him: The craft of carpentering and of building. The king saith unto him: What craftsmanship, then, knowest thou in wood, and what in stone? The apostle saith: In wood: ploughs, yokes, goads, pulleys, and boats and oars and masts; and in stone: pillars, temples, and court-houses for kings. And the king said: Canst thou build me a palace? And he answered: Yea, I can both build and furnish it; for to this end am I come, to build and to do the work of a carpenter.

18 And the king took him and went out of the city gates and began to speak with him on the way concerning the building of the court-house, and of the foundations, how they should be laid, until they came to the place wherein he desired that the building should be; and he said: Here will I that the building should be. And the apostle said: Yea, for this place is suitable for the building. But the place was woody and there was much water there. So the king said: Begin to build. But he said: I cannot begin to build now at this season. And the king said: When canst thou begin? And he said: I will begin in the month Dius and finish in Xanthicus. But the king marvelled and said: Every building is builded in summer, and canst thou in this very winter build and make ready a palace? And the apostle said: Thus it must be, and no otherwise is it possible. And the king said: If, then, this seem good to thee, draw me a plan, how the work shall be, because I shall return hither after some long time. And the apostle took a reed and drew, measuring the place; and the doors he set toward the sunrising to look toward the light, and the windows toward the west to the breezes, and the bakehouse he appointed to be toward the south and the aqueduct for the service toward the north. And the king saw it and said to the apostle: Verily thou art a craftsman and it belitteth thee to be a servant of kings. And he left much money with him and departed from him.

19 And from time to time he sent money and provision, and victual for him and the rest of the workmen. But Thomas receiving it all dispensed it, going about the cities and the villages round about, distributing and

giving alms to the poor and afflicted, and relieving them, saying: The king knoweth how to obtain recompense fit for kings, but at this time it is needful that the poor should have refreshment.

After these things the king sent an ambassador unto the apostle, and wrote thus: Signify unto me what thou hast done or what I shall send thee, or of what thou hast need. And the apostle sent unto him, saying: The palace (praetorium) is builded and only the roof remaineth. And the king hearing it sent him again gold and silver (lit. unstamped), and wrote unto him: Let the palace be roofed, if it is done. And the apostle said unto the Lord: I thank thee O Lord in all things, that thou didst die for a little space that I might live for ever in thee, and that thou hast sold me that by me thou mightest set free many. And he ceased not to teach and to refresh the afflicted, saying: This hath the Lord dispensed unto you, and he giveth unto every man his food: for he is the nourisher of orphans and steward of the widows, and unto all that are afflicted he is relief and rest.

20 Now when the king came to the city he inquired of his friends concerning the palace which Judas that is called Thomas was building for him. And they told him: Neither hath he built a palace nor done aught else of that he promised to perform, but he goeth about the cities and countries, and whatsoever he hath he giveth unto the poor, and teacheth of a new God, and healeth the sick, and driveth out devils, and doeth many other wonderful things; and we think him to be a sorcerer. Yet his compassions and his cures which are done of him freely, and moreover the simplicity and kindness of him and his faith, do declare that he is a righteous man or an apostle of the new God whom he preacheth; for he fasteth continually and prayeth, and eateth bread only, with salt, and his drink is water, and he weareth but one garment alike in fair weather and in winter, and receiveth nought of any man, and that he hath he giveth unto others. And when the king heard that, he rubbed his face with his hands, and shook his head for a long space.

21 And he sent for the merchant which had brought him, and for the apostle, and said unto him: Hast thou built me the palace? And he said: Yea. And the king said: When, then, shall we go and see it? but he answered him and said: Thou canst not see it now, but when thou departest this life, then thou shalt see it. And the king was exceeding wroth, and commanded both the merchant and Judas which is called Thomas to be put in bonds and cast into prison until he should inquire and learn unto whom the king's money had been given, and so destroy both him and the merchant.

And the apostle went unto the prison rejoicing, and said to the merchant: Fear thou nothing, only believe in the God that is preached by me, and thou shalt indeed be set free from this world, but from the world to come thou shalt receive life. And the king took thought with what death he should destroy them. And when he had determined to flay them alive and burn them with fire, in the same night Gad the king's brother fell sick, and by reason of his vexation and the deceit which the king had suffered he was greatly oppressed; and sent for the king and said unto him: O king my brother, I commit unto thee mine house and my children; for I am vexed by reason of the provocation that hath befallen thee, and lo, I die; and if thou visit not with vengeance upon the head of that sorcerer, thou wilt give my soul no rest in hell. And the king said to his brother: All this night have I considered how I should put him to death and this hath seemed good to me, to flay him and burn him with fire, both him and the merchant which brought him (Syr. Then the brother of the king said to him: And if there be anything else that is worse than this, do it to him; and I give thee charge of my house and my children).

22 And as they talked together, the soul of his brother Gad departed. And the king mourned sore for Gad, for he loved him much, and commanded that he should be buried in royal and precious apparel (Syr. sepulchre). Now after this angels took the soul of Gad the king's brother and bore it up into heaven, showing unto him the places and dwellings that were there, and inquired of him: In which place wouldest thou dwell? And when they drew near unto the building of Thomas the apostle which he had built for the king, Gad saw it and said unto the angels: I beseech you, my lords, suffer me to dwell in one of the lowest rooms of these. And they said to him: Thou canst not dwell in this building. And he said: Wherefore ? And they say unto him: This is that palace which that Christian builded for thy brother. And he said: I beseech you, my lords, suffer me to go to my brother, that I may buy this palace of him, for my brother knoweth not of what sort it is, and he will sell it unto me.

23 Then the angels let the soul of Gad go. And as they were putting his grave clothes upon him, his soul entered into him and he said to them that stood about him: Call my brother unto me, that I may ask one petition of him. Straightway therefore they told the king, saying: Thy brother is revived. And the king ran forth with a great company and came unto his brother and entered in and stood by his bed as one amazed, not being able to speak to him. And his brother said: I know and am persuaded, my brother, that if any man had asked of thee the half of thy kingdom, thou wouldest have given it him for my sake; therefore I beg of thee to grant me one favour which I ask of thee, that thou wouldest sell me that which I ask. And the king answered and said: And what is it which thou askest me to sell thee? And he said: Convince me by an oath that thou wilt grant it me. And the king sware unto him: One of my possessions,

whatsoever thou shalt ask, I will give thee. And he saith to him: Sell me that palace which thou hast in the heavens ? And the king said: Whence should I have a palace in the heavens? And he said: Even that which that Christian built for thee which is now in the prison, whom the merchant brought unto thee, having purchased him of one Jesus: I mean that Hebrew slave whom thou desiredst to punish as having suffered deceit at his hand: whereat I was grieved and died, and am now revived.

24 Then the king considering the matter, understood it of those eternal benefits which should come to him and which concerned him, and said: That palace I cannot sell thee, but I pray to enter into it and dwell therein and to be accounted worthy of the inhabiters of it, but if thou indeed desirest to buy such a palace, lo, the man liveth and shall build thee one better than it. And forthwith he sent and brought out of prison the apostle and the merchant that was shut up with him, saying: I entreat thee, as a man that entreateth the minister of God, that thou wouldest pray for me and beseech him whose minister thou art to forgive me and overlook that which I have done unto thee or thought to do, and that I may become a worthy inhabiter of that dwelling for the which I took no pains, but thou hast builded it for me, labouring alone, the grace of thy God working with thee, and that I also may become a servant and serve this God whom thou preachest. And his brother also fell down before the apostle and said: I entreat and supplicate thee before thy God that I may become worthy of his ministry and service, and that it may fall to me to be worthy of the things that were shown unto me by his angels.

25 And the apostle, filled with joy, said: I praise thee, O Lord Jesu, that thou hast revealed thy truth in these men; for thou only art the God of truth, and none other, and thou art he that knoweth all things that are unknown to the most; thou, Lord, art he that in all things showest compassion and sparest men. For men by reason of the error that is in them have overlooked thee but thou hast not overlooked them. And now at mv supplication and request do thou receive the king and his brother and join them unto thy fold, cleansing them with thy washing and anointing them with thine oil from the error that encompasseth them: and keep them also from the wolves, bearing them into thy meadows. And give them drink out of thine immortal fountain which is neither fouled nor drieth up; for they entreat and supplicate thee and desire to become thy servants and ministers, and for this they are content even to be persecuted of thine enemies, and for thy sake to be hated of them and to be mocked and to die, like as thou for our sake didst suffer all these things, that thou mightest preserve us, thou that art Lord and verily the good shepherd. And do thou grant them to have confidence in thee alone, and the succour that cometh of thee and the hope of their salvation which they look for from thee alone; and that they may be grounded in thy mysteries and receive the perfect good of thy graces and gifts, and flourish in thy ministry and come to perfection in thy Father.

26 Being therefore wholly set upon the apostle, both the king Gundaphorus and Gad his brother followed him and departed not from him at all, and they also relieved them that had need giving unto all and refreshing all. And they besought him that they also might henceforth receive the seal of the word, saying unto him: Seeing that our souls are at leisure and eager toward God, give thou us the seal; for we have heard thee say that the God whom thou preachest knoweth his own sheep by his seal. And the apostle said unto them: I also rejoice and entreat you to receive this seal, and to partake with me in this eucharist and blessing of the Lord, and to be made perfect therein. For this is the Lord and God of all, even Jesus Christ whom I preach, and he is the father of truth, in whom I have taught you to believe. And he commanded them to bring oil, that they might receive the seal by the oil. They brought the oil therefore, and lighted many lamps; for it was night (Syr. whom I preach: and the king gave orders that the bath should be closed for seven days, and that no man should bathe in it: and when the seven days were done, on the eighth day they three entered into the bath by night that Judas might baptize them. And many lamps were lighted in the bath).

27 And the apostle arose and sealed them. And the Lord was revealed unto them by a voice, saying: Peace be unto you brethren. And they heard his voice only, but his likeness they saw not, for they had not yet received the added sealing of the seal (Syr. had not been baptized). And the apostle took the oil and poured it upon their heads and anointed and chrismed them, and began to say (Syr. And Judas went up and stood upon the edge of the cistern and poured oil upon their heads and said):

Come, thou holy name of the Christ that is above every name.
Come, thou power of the Most High, and the compassion that is perfect.
Come, gift (charism) of the Most High.
Come, compassionate mother.
Come, communion of the male.
Come, she that revealeth the hidden mysteries.
Come, mother of the seven houses, that thy rest may be in the eighth house.
Come, elder of the five members, mind, thought, reflection, consideration, reason; communicate with these young men.
Come, holy spirit, and cleanse their reins and their heart, and give them the added seal, in the name of the Father and Son and Holy Ghost.

And when they were sealed, there appeared unto them a youth holding a lighted torch, so that their lamps became dim at the approach of the light thereof. And he went forth and was no more seen of them. And the apostle said unto the Lord: Thy light, O Lord, is not to be contained by us, and we are not able to bear it, for it is too great for our sight.

And when the dawn came and it was morning, he brake bread and made them partakers of the eucharist of the Christ. And they were glad and rejoiced.

And many others also, believing, were added to them, and came into the refuge of the Saviour.

28 And the apostle ceased not to preach and to say unto them: Ye men and women, boys and girls, young men and maidens, strong men and aged, whether bond or free, abstain from fornication and covetousness and the service of the belly: for under these three heads all iniquity cometh about. For fornication blindeth the mind and darkeneth the eyes of the soul, and is an impediment to the life (conversation) of the body, turning the whole man unto weakness and casting the whole body into sickness. And greed putteth the soul into fear and shame; being within the body it seizeth upon the goods of others, and is under fear lest if it restore other men's goods to their owner it be put to shame. And the service of the belly casteth the soul into thoughts and cares and vexations, taking thought lest it come to be in want, and have need of those things that are far from it. If, then, ye be rid of these ye become free of care and grief and fear, and that abideth with you which was said by the Saviour: Take no thought for the morrow, for the morrow shall take thought for the things of itself. Remember also that word of him of whom I spake: Look at the ravens and see the fowls of the heaven, that they neither sow nor reap nor gather into barns, and God dispenseth unto them; how much more unto you, O ye of little faith? But look ye for his coming and have your hope in him and believe on his name. For he is the judge of quick and dead, and he giveth to every one according to their deeds, and at his coming and his latter appearing no man hath any word of excuse when he is to be judged by him, as though he had not heard. For his heralds do proclaim in the four quarters (climates) of the world. Repent ye, therefore, and believe the promise and receive the yoke of meekness and the light burden, that ye may live and not die. These things get, these keep. Come forth of the darkness that the light may receive you! Come unto him that is indeed good, that ye may receive grace of him and implant his sign in your souls.

29 And when he had thus spoken, some of them that stood by said: It is time for the creditor to receive the debt. And he said unto them: He that is lord of the debt desireth always to receive more; but let us give him that which is due. And he blessed them, and took bread and oil and herbs and salt and blessed and gave unto them; but he himself continued his fast, for the Lord's day was coming on (Syr. And he himself ate, because the Sunday was dawning).

And when night fell and he slept, the Lord came and stood at his head, saying: Thomas, rise early, and having blessed them all, after the prayer and the ministry go by the eastern road two miles and there will I show thee my glory: for by thy going shall many take refuge with me, and thou shalt bring to light the nature and power of the enemy. And he rose up from sleep and said unto the brethren that were with him: Children, the Lord would accomplish somewhat by me to-day, but let us pray, and entreat of him that we may have no impediment toward him, but that as at all times, so now also it may be done according to his desire and will by us. And having so said, he laid his hands on them and blessed them, and brake the bread of the eucharist and gave it them, saying: This Eucharist shall be unto you for compassion and mercy, and not unto judgement and retribution. And they said Amen.

Note by Professor F. C. Burkitt, D.D.:
In the Acts of Thomas, 27, the apostle, being about to baptize Gundaphorus the king of India with his brother Gad, invokes the holy name of the Christ, and among other invocations says (according to the best Greek text):
'Come, O elder of the five members, mind, idea, thoughtfulness, consideration, reasoning, communicate with these youths.'
What is the essential distinction of these five words for 'mind', and what is meant by the 'elder' (presbuteros, Greek)? We turn to the Syriac, as the original language in which our tale was composed though our present text, which rests here on two manuscripts, has now and then been bowdlerized in the direction of more conventional phraseology, a process that the Greek has often escaped. Here in the Syriac we find (Wright, p.193, l.13; E.Tr., p.166, last line but one):
'Come, Messenger of reconciliation, and communicate with the minds of these youths.'
The word for 'Come' is fem., while 'Messenger' (Izgadda) is masc. This is because the whole prayer is an invocation of the Holy Spirit, which in old Syriac is invariably treated as feminine. The word for Messenger is that used in the Manichaean cosmogony for a heavenly Spirit sent from the Divine Light: this Spirit appeared as androgynous, so that the use of the word here with the feminine verb is not inappropriate. It further leads us to look out for other indications of Manichaean phraseology in the pas-

sage. But first it suggests to us that [presbuteros] in our passage is a corruption of, or is used for, [presbeutes], 'an ambassador'.
As for the five words for 'mind', they are clearly the equivalents of [hauna, mad'a, re'yana, mahshebhatha, tar'itha], named by Theodore bar Khoni as the Five Shekhinas, or Dwellings, or Manifestations, of the Father of Greatness, the title by which the Manichaeans spoke of the ultimate Source of Light. There is a good discussion of these five words by M. A. Kugener in F. Cumont's [Recherches sur le Manicheisme] i, p. 10, note 3. In English we may say:
hauna means 'sanity', mad'a means 'reason', re'yana means 'mind', mahshabhetha means 'imagination', tar'itha means 'intention'
The Greek terms, used here and also in Acta Archelai, are in my opinion merely equivalents for the Syriac terms.

Act the Third: Concerning the servant

30 And the apostle went forth to go where the Lord had bidden him; and when he was near to the second mile (stone) and had turned a little out of the way, he saw the body of a comely youth lying, and said: Lord, is it for this that thou hast brought me forth, to come hither that I might see this (trial) temptation? thy will therefore be done as thou desirest. And he began to pray and to say: O Lord, the judge of quick and dead, of the quick that stand by and the dead that lie here, and master and father of all things; and father not only of the souls that are in bodies but of them that have gone forth of them, for of the souls also that are in pollutions (al. bodies) thou art lord and judge; come thou at this hour wherein I call upon thee and show forth thy glory upon him that lieth here. And he turned himself unto them that followed him and said: This thing is not come to pass without cause, but the enemy hath effected it and brought it about that he may assault (?) us thereby; and see ye that he hath not made use of another sort, nor wrought through any other creature save that which is his subject.

31 And when he had so said, a great (Syr. black) serpent (dragon) came out of a hole, beating with his head and shaking his tail upon the ground, and with (using) a loud voice said unto the apostle: I will tell before thee the cause wherefore I slew this man, since thou art come hither for that end, to reprove my works. And the apostle said: Yea, say on. And the serpent: There is a certain beautiful woman in this village over against us; and as she passed by me (or my place) I saw her and was enamoured of her, and I followed her and kept watch upon her; and I found this youth kissing her, and he had intercourse with her and did other shameful acts with her: and for me it was easy to declare them before thee, for I know that thou art the twin brother of the Christ and always abolishest our nature (Syr. easy for me to say, but to thee I do not dare to utter them because I know that the ocean-flood of the Messiah will destroy our nature): but because I would not affright her, I slew him not at that time, but waited for him till he passed by in the evening and smote and slew him, and especially because he adventured to do this upon the Lord's day. And the apostle inquired of him, saying: Tell me of what seed and of what race thou art. 32 And he said unto him: I am a reptile of the reptile nature and noxious son of the noxious father: of him that hurt and smote the four brethren which stood upright (om. Syr.: the elements or four cardinal points may be meant) I am son to him that sitteth on a throne over all the earth that receiveth back his own from them that borrow: I am son to him that girdeth about the sphere: and I am kin to him that is outside the ocean, whose tail is set in his own mouth: I am he that entered through the barrier (fence) into paradise and spake with Eve the things which my father bade me speak unto her: I am he that kindled and inflamed Cain to kill his own brother, and on mine account did thorns and thistles grow up in the earth: I am he that cast down the angels from above and bound them in lusts after women, that children born of earth might come of them and I might work my will in them: I am he that hardened Pharaoh's heart that he should slay the children of Israel and enslave them with the yoke of cruelty: I am he that caused the multitude to err in the wilderness when they made the calf: I am he that inflamed Herod and enkindled Caiaphas unto false accusation of a lie before Pilate; for this was fitting to me: I am he that stirred up Judas and bribed him to deliver up the Christ: I am he that inhabiteth and holdeth the deep of hell (Tartarus), but the Son of God hath wronged me, against my will, and taken (chosen) them that were his own from me: I am kin to him that is to come from the east, unto whom also power is given to do what he will upon the earth.

33 And when that serpent had spoken these things in the hearing of all the people, the apostle lifted up his voice on high and said: Cease thou henceforth, O most shameless one, and be put to confusion and die wholly, for the end of thy destruction is come, and dare not to tell of what thou hast done by them that have become subject unto thee. And I charge thee in the name of that Jesus who until now contendeth with you for the men that are his own, that thou suck out thy venom which thou hast put into this man, and draw it forth and take it from him. But the serpent said: Not yet is the end of our time come as thou hast said. Wherefore compellest thou me to take back that which I have put into this man, and to die before my time? for mine own father, when he shall draw forth and suck out that which he hath cast into the creation, then shall his end come. And the apostle said unto him: Show, then, now the nature of thy father. And the

serpent came near and set his mouth upon the wound of the young man and sucked forth the gall out of it. And by little and little the colour of the young man which was as purple, became white, but the serpent swelled up. And when the serpent had drawn up all the gall into himself, the young man leapt up and stood, and ran and fell at the apostle's feet: but the serpent being swelled up, burst and died, and his venom and gall were shed forth; and in the place where his venom was shed there came a great gulf, and that serpent was swallowed up therein. And the apostle said unto the king and his brother: Take workmen and fill up that place, and lay foundations and build houses upon them, that it may be a dwelling-place for strangers.

34 But the youth said unto the apostle with many tears: Wherein have I sinned against thee? for thou art a man that hast two forms, and wheresoever thou wilt, there thou art found, and art restrained of no man, as I behold. For I saw that man that stood by thee and said unto thee. I have many wonders to show forth by thy means and I have great works to accomplish by thee, for which thou shalt receive a reward; and thou shalt make many to live, and they shall be in rest in light eternal as children of God. Do thou then, saith he, speaking unto thee of me, quicken this youth that hath been stricken of the enemy and be at all times his overseer. Well, therefore, art thou come hither, and well shalt thou depart again unto him, and yet he never shall leave thee at any time. But I am become without care or reproach: and he hath enlightened me from the care of the night and I am at rest from the toil of the day: and I am set free from him that provoked me to do thus, sinning against him that taught me to do contrary thereto: and I have lost him that is the kinsman of the night that compelled me to sin by his own deeds, and have found him that is of the light, and is my kinsman. I have lost him that darkeneth and blindeth his own subjects that they may not know what they do and, being ashamed at their own works, may depart from him, and their works come to an end; and have found him whose works are light and his deeds truth, which if a man doeth he repenteth not of them. And I have left him with whom lying abideth, and before whom darkness goeth as a veil, and behind him followeth shame, shameless in indolence; and I have found him that showeth me fair things that I may take hold on them, even the son of the truth that is akin unto concord, who scattereth away the mist and enlighteneth his own creation, and healeth the wounds thereof and overthroweth the enemies thereof. But I beseech thee, O man of God, cause me to behold him again, and to see him that is now become hidden from me, that I may also hear his voice whereof I am not able to express the wonder, for it belongeth not to the nature of this bodily organ.

[Before this speech Syr. (Wright) inserts one of equal length, chiefly about man's free will and fall. But the fifth-century palimpsest edited by Mrs. Lewis agrees with the Greek.]

35 And the apostle answered him, saying: If thou depart from these things whereof thou hast received knowledge, as thou hast said, and if thou know who it is that hath wrought this in thee, and learn and become a hearer of him whom now in thy fervent love thou seekest; thou shalt both see him and be with him for ever, and in his rest shalt thou rest, and shalt be in his joy. But if thou be slackly disposed toward him and turn again unto thy former deeds, and leave that beauty and that bright countenance which now was showed thee, and forget the shining of his light which now thou desirest, not only wilt thou be bereaved of this life but also of that which is to come and thou wilt depart unto him whom thou saidst thou hadst lost, and will no more behold him whom thou saidst thou hadst found.

36 And when the apostle had said this, he went into the city holding the hand of that youth, and saying unto him: These things which thou hast seen, my child, are but a few of the many which God hath, for he doth not give us good tidings concerning these things that are seen, but greater things than these doth he promise us; but so long as we are in the body we are not able to speak and show forth those which he shall give unto our souls. If we say that he giveth us light, it is this which is seen, and we have it: and if we say it of wealth, which is and appeareth in the world, we name it (we speak of something which is in the world, Syr.), and we need it not, for it hath been said: Hardly shall a rich man enter into the kingdom of heaven: and if we speak of apparel of raiment wherewith they that are luxurious in this life are clad, it is named (we mention something that nobles wear, Syr.), and it hath been said: They that wear soft raiment are in the houses of kings. And if of costly banquets, concerning these we have received a commandment to beware of them, not to be weighed down With reveling and drunkenness and cares of this life -speaking of things that are- and it hath been said: Take no thought for your life (soul), what ye shall eat or what ye shall drink, neither for your body, what ye shall put on, for the soul is more than the meat and the body than the raiment. And of rest, if we speak of this temporal rest, a judgement is appointed for this also. But we speak of the world which is above, of God and angels, of watchers and holy ones of the immortal (ambrosial) food and the drink of the true vine, of raiment that endureth and groweth not old, of things which eye hath not seen nor ear heard, neither have they entered into the heart of sinful men, the things which God hath prepared for them that love him. Of these things do we converse and of these do we bring good tidings. Do thou therefore also believe on him that thou

mayest live, and put thy trust in him, and thou shalt not die. For he is not persuaded with gifts, that thou shouldest offer them to him, neither is he in need of sacrifices, that thou shouldest sacrifice unto him. But look thou unto him, and he will not overlook thee; and turn unto him, and he will not forsake thee. For his comeliness and his beauty will make thee wholly desirous to love him: and indeed he permitteth thee not to turn thyself away.

37 And when the apostle had said these things unto that youth, a great multitude joined themselves unto them. And the apostle looked and saw them raising themselves on high that they might see him, and they were going up into high places; and the apostle said unto them: Ye men that are come unto the assembly of Christ, and would believe on Jesus, take example hereby, and see that if ye be not lifted up, ye cannot see me who am little, and are not able to spy me out who am like unto you. If, then, ye cannot see me who am like you unless ye lift yourselves up a little from the earth, how can ye see him that dwelleth in the height and now is found in the depth, unless ye first lift yourselves up out of your former conversation, and your unprofitable deeds, and your desires that abide not, and the wealth that is left here, and the possession of earth that groweth old, and the raiment that corrupteth, and the beauty that waxeth old and vanisheth away, and yet more out of the whole body wherein all these things are stored up, and which groweth old and becometh dust, returning unto its own nature? For it is the body which maintaineth all these things. But rather believe on our Lord Jesus Christ, vvhom we preach, that your hope may be in him and in him ye may have life world without end, that he may become your fellow traveller in this land of error, and may be to you an harbour in this troublous sea. And he shall be to you a fountain springing up in this thirsty land and a chamber fill of food in this place of them that hunger, and a rest unto your souls, yea, and a physician for your bodies.

38 Then the multitude of them that were gathered together hearing these things wept, and said unto the apostle: O man of God, the God whom thou preachest, we dare not say that we are his, for the works which we have done are alien unto him and not pleasing to him; but if he will have compassion on us and pity us and save us, overlooking our former deeds, and will set us free from the evils which we committed being in error, and not impute them unto us nor make remembrance of our former sins, we will become his servants and will accomplish his will unto the end. And the apostle answered them and said: He reckoneth not against you, neither taketh account of the sins which ye committed being in error, but overlooketh your transgressions which ye have done in ignorance.

The Fourth Act: Concerning the colt

39 And while the apostle yet stood in the highway and spake with the multitude, A she ass's colt came and stood before him (Syr. adds, And Judas said: It is not without the direction of God that this colt has come hither. But to thee I say, O colt that by the grace of our Lord there shall be given to thee speech before these multitudes who are standing here; and do thou say whatsoever thou wilt, that they may believe in the God of truth whom we preach. And the mouth of the colt was opened, and it spake by the power of our Lord and said to him) and opened its mouth and said: Thou twin of Christ, apostle of the Most High and initiate in the hidden word of Christ who receivest his secret oracles, fellow worker with the Son of God, who being free hast become a bondman, and being sold hast brought many into liberty. Thou kinsman of the great race that hath condemned the enemy and redeemed his own, that hast become an occasion of life unto man in the land of the Indians; for thou hast come (against thy will, Syr.) unto men that were in error, and by thy appearing and thy divine words they are now turning unto the God of truth which sent thee: mount and sit upon me and repose thyself until thou enter into the city. And the apostle answered and said: O Jesu Christ (Son) that understandest the perfect mercy! O tranquillity and quiet that now art spoken of (speakest, Syr.) by (among) brute beasts! O hidden rest, that art manifested by thy working, Saviour of us and nourisher, keeping us and resting in alien bodies! O Saviour of our souls! spring that is sweet and unfailing; fountain secure and clear and never polluted; defender and helper in the fight of thine own servants, turning away and scaring the enemy from us, that fightest in many battles for us and makest us conquerors in all; our true and undefeated champion (athlete); our holy and victorious captain: glorious and giving unto thine own a joy that never passeth away, and a relief wherein is none affliction; good shepherd that givest thyself for thine own sheep, and hast vanquished the wolf and redeemed thine own lambs and led them into a good pasture: we glorify and praise thee and thine invisible Father and thine holy spirit [and] the mother of all creation.

40 And when the apostle had said these things, all the multitude that were there looked upon him, expecting to hear what he would answer to the colt. And the apostle stood a long time as it were astonied, and looked up into heaven and said to the colt: Of whom art thou and to whom belongest thou? for marvelous are the things that are shown forth by thy mouth, and amazing and such as are hidden from the many. And the colt answered and said: I am of that stock that served Balaam, and thy lord also and teacher sat upon one that appertained unto me by race. And I also have now been sent to give thee rest by thy sitting upon me: and (that) I

may receive (Syr. these may be confirmed in) faith, and unto me may be added that portion which now I shall receive by thy service wherewith I serve thee; and when I have ministered unto thee, it shall be taken from me. And the apostle said unto him: He is able who granted thee this gift, to cause it to be fulfilled unto the end in thee and in them that belong unto thee by race: for as to this mystery I am weak and powerless. And he would not sit upon him. But the colt besought and entreated him that he might be blessed of him by ministering unto him. Then the apostle mounted him and sat upon him; and they followed him, some going before and some following after, and all of them ran, desiring to see the end, and how he would dismiss the colt.

41 But when he came near to the city gates he dismounted from him, saying: Depart, and be thou kept safe where thou wert. And straightway the colt fell to the ground at the apostle's feet and died. And all they that were present were sorry and said to the apostle: Bring him to life and raise him up. But he answered and said unto them: I indeed am able to raise him by the name of Jesus Christ: but this is by all means expedient (or, this is [NOT] by any means expedient). For he that gave him speech that he might talk was able to cause that he should not die; and I raise him not, not as being unable, but because this is that which is expedient and profitable for him. And he bade them that were present to dig a trench and bury his body and they did as they were commanded.

The Fifth Act: Concerning the devil that took up his abode in the woman

42 And the apostle entered into the city and all the multitude followed him. And he thought to go unto the parents of the young man whom he had made alive when he was slain by the serpent: for they earnestly besought him to come unto them and enter into their house. But a very beautiful woman on a sudden uttered an exceeding loud cry, saying: O Apostle of the new God that art come into India, and servant of that holy and only good God; for by thee is he preached, the Saviour of the souls that come unto him, and by thee are healed the bodies of them that are tormented by the enemy, and thou art he that is become an occasion of life unto all that turn unto him: command me to be brought before thee that I may tell thee what hath befallen me, and peradventure of thee I may have hope, and these that stand by thee may be more confident in the God whom thou preachest. For I am not a little tormented by the adversary now this five years' space [one Greek MS. And the apostle bade her come unto him, and the woman stood before him and said: I, O servant of him that is indeed God am a woman: the rest have, As a woman] I was sitting at the first in quiet, and peace encompassed me on every side and I had no care for anything, for I took no thought for any other. 43 And it fell out one day that as I came out from the bath there met me a man troubled and disturbed, and his voice and speech seemed to me exceeding faint and dim; and he stood before me and said: I and thou will be in one love and we will have intercourse together as a man with his wife; And I answered and said to him: I never had to do with my betrothed, for I refused to marry, and how shall I yield myself to thee that wouldest have intercourse with me in adulterous wise? And having so said, I passed on, and I said to my handmaid that was with me: Sawest thou that youth and his shamelessness, how boldly he spake with me, and had no shame? but she said to me: I saw an old man speaking to thee. And when I was in mine house and had dined my soul suggested unto me some suspicion and especially because he was seen of me in two forms; and having this in my mind I fell asleep. He came, therefore, in that night and was joined unto me in his foul intercourse. And when it was day I saw him and fled from him, and on the night following that he came and abused me; and now as thou seest me I have spent five years being troubled by him, and he hath not departed from me. But I know and am persuaded that both devils and spirits and destroyers are subject unto thee and are filled with trembling at thy prayers: pray thou therefore for me and drive away from me the devil that ever troubleth me, that I also may be set free and be gathered unto the nature that is mine from the beginning, and receive the grace that hath been given unto my kindred.

44 And the apostle said: O evil that cannot be restrained! O shamelessness of the enemy! O envious one that art never at rest! O hideous one that subduest the comely! O thou of many forms! As he will he appeareth, but his essence cannot be changed. O the crafty and faithless one! O the bitter tree whose fruits are like unto him! O the devil that overcometh them that are alien to him! O the deceit that useth impudence! O the wickedness that creepeth like a serpent, and that is of his kindred! (Syr. wrongly adds a clause bidding the devil show himself.) And when the apostle said this, the malicious one came and stood before him, no man seeing him save the woman and the apostle, and with an exceeding loud voice said in the hearing of all: 45 What have we to do with thee, thou apostle of the Most High! What have we to do with thee, thou servant of Jesus Christ? What have we to do with thee, thou counsellor of the holy Son of God? Wherefore wilt thou destroy us, whereas our time is not yet come? Wherefore wilt thou take away our power? for unto this hour we had hope and time remaining to us. What have we to do with thee? Thou hast power over thine own, and we over ours. Wherefore wilt thou act tyrannously against us, when thou thyself teachest others not to act tyrannously? Wherefore dost thou crave other men's goods and not suffice

thyself with thine own? Wherefore art thou made like unto the Son of God which hath done us wrong? for thou resemblest him altogether as if thou wert born of him. For we thought to have brought him under the yoke like as we have the rest, but he turned and made us subject unto him: for we knew him not; but he deceived us with his form of all uncomeliness and his poverty and his neediness: for seeing him to be such, we thought that he was a man wearing flesh, and knew not that it is he that giveth life unto men. And he gave us power over our own, and that we should not in this present time leave them but have our walk in them: but thou wouldest get more than thy due and that which was given thee, and afflict us altogether.

46 And having said this the devil wept, saying: I leave thee, my fairest consort, whom long since I found and rested in thee; I forsake thee, my sure sister, my beloved in whom I was well pleased. What I shall do I know not, or on whom I shall call that he may hear me and help me. I know what I will do: I will depart unto some place where the report of this man hath not been heard, and peradventure I shall call thee, my beloved by another name (Syr. for thee my beloved I shall find a substitute). And he lifted up his voice and said: Abide in peace for thou hast taken refuge with one greater than I, but I will depart and seek for one like thee, and if I find her not, I will return unto thee again: for I know that whilst thou art near unto this man thou hast a refuge in him, but when he departeth thou wilt be such as thou wast before he appeared, and him thou wilt forget, and I shall have opportunity and confidence: but now I fear the name of him that hath saved thee. And having so said the devil vanished out of sight: only when he departed fire and smoke were seen there: and all that stood there were astonied.

47 And the apostle seeing it, said unto them: This devil hath shown nought that is alien or strange to him, but his own nature, wherein also he shall be consumed, for verily the fire shall destroy him utterly and the smoke of it shall be scattered abroad. And he began to say: Jesu, the hidden mystery that hath been revealed unto us, thou art he that hast shown unto us many mysteries; thou that didst call me apart from all my fellows and spakest unto me three (one, Syr.) words wherewith I am inflamed, and am not able to speak them unto others. Jesu, man that wast slain, dead buried! Jesu, God of God, Saviour that quickenest the dead, and healest the sick! Jesu, that wert in need like [a man poor] and savest as one that hath no need, that didst catch the fish for the breakfast and the dinner and madest all satisfied with a little bread. Jesu, that didst rest from the weariness of wayfaring like a man, and walkedst on the waves like a God. 48 Jesu most high, voice arising from perfect mercy, Saviour of all, the right hand of the light, overthrowing the evil one in his own nature, and gathering all his nature into one place; thou of many forms, that art only begotten, first-born of many brethren God of the Most High God, man despised until now (Syr. and humble). Jesu Christ that neglectest us not when we call upon thee, that art become an occasion of life unto all mankind, that for us wast judged and shut up in prison, and loosest all that are in bonds, that wast called a deceiver and redeemest thine own from error: I beseech thee for these that stand here and believe on thee, for they entreat to obtain thy gifts, having good hope in thy help, and having their refuge in thy greatness; they hold their hearing ready to listen unto the words that are spoken by us. Let thy peace come and tabernacle in them and renew them from their former deeds, and let them put off the old man with his deeds, and put on the new that now is proclaimed unto them by me.

49 And he laid his hands on them and blessed them, saying: The grace of our Lord Jesus Christ shall be upon you for ever. And they said, Amen. And the woman besought him, saying: O apostle of the Most High, give me the seal, that that enemy return not again unto me. Then he caused her to come near unto him (Syr. went to a river which was close by there), and laid his hands upon her and sealed her in the name of the Father and the Son and the Holy Ghost; and many others also were sealed with her. And the apostle bade his minister (deacon) to set forth a table; and he set forth a stool which they found there, and spread a linen cloth upon it and set on the bread of blessing; and the apostle stood by it and said: Jesu, that hast accounted us worthy to partake of the eucharist of thine holy body and blood, lo, we are bold to draw near unto thine eucharist and to call upon thine holy name: come thou and communicate unto us (Syr. adds more).

50 And he began to say: Come, O perfect compassion, Come O communion of the male, Come, she that knoweth the mysteries of him that is chosen, Come, she that hath part in all the combats of the noble champion (athlete), Come, the silence that revealeth the great things of the whole greatness, Come, she that manifesteth the hidden things and maketh the unspeakable things plain, the holy dove that beareth the twin young, Come, the hidden mother, Come, she that is manifest in her deeds and giveth joy and rest unto them that are joined unto her: Come and communicate with us in this eucharist which we celebrate in thy name and in the love-feast wherein we are gathered together at thy calling. (Syr. has other clauses and not few variants.) And having so said he marked out the cross upon the bread, and brake it, and began to distribute it. And first he gave unto the woman, saying: This shall be unto thee for remission of sins and eternal transgressions (Syr. and for the everlasting resurrection).

And after her he gave unto all the others also which had received the seal (Syr. and said to them: Let this eucharist be unto you for life and rest, and not for judgement and vengeance. And they said, Amen. Cf. 29 fin.).

The Sixth Act: Of the youth that murdered the Woman.

51 Now there was a certain youth who had wrought an abominable deed, and he came near and received of the eucharist with his mouth: but his two hands withered up, so that he could no more put them unto his own mouth. And they that were there saw him and told the apostle what had befallen; and the apostle called him and said unto him: Tell me, my child, and be not ashamed, what was it that thou didst and camest hither? for the eucharist of the Lord hath convicted thee. For this gift which passeth among many doth rather heal them that with faith and love draw near thereto, but thee it hath withered away; and that which is come to pass hath not befallen without some effectual cause. And the Youth, being convicted by the eucharist of the Lord, came and tell at the apostle's feet and besought him, saying: I have done an evil deed, yet I thought to do somewhat good. I was enamoured of a woman that dwelleth at an inn without the city, and she also loved me; and when I heard of thee and believed, that thou proclaimest a living God, I came and received of thee the seal with the rest; for thou saidst: Whosoever shall partake in the polluted union, and especially in adultery, he shall not have life with the God whom I preach. Whereas therefore I loved her much, I entreated her and would have persuaded her to become my consort in chastity and pure conversation, which thou also teachest: but she would not. When, therefore, she consented not, I took a sword and slew her: for I could not endure to see her commit adultery with another man.

52 When the apostle heard this he said: O insane union how ruinest thou unto shamelessness! O unrestrained lust, how hast thou stirred up this man to do this! O work of the serpent, how art thou enraged against thine own! And the apostle bade water to be brought to him in a basin; and when the water was brought, he said: Come, ye waters from the living waters, that were sent unto us, the true from the true, the rest that was sent unto us from the rest, the power of salvation that cometh from that power which conquereth all things and subdueth them unto its own will: come and dwell in these waters, that the gift of the Holy Ghost may be perfectly consummated in them. And he said unto the youth: Go, wash thy hands in these waters. And when he had washed they were restored; and the apostle said unto him: Believest thou in our Lord Jesus Christ that he is able to do all things? And he said: Though I be the least, yet I believe. But I committed this deed thinking that I was doing somewhat good: for I besought her as I told thee, but she would not obey me, to keep herself chaste.

53 And the apostle said to him: Come, let us go unto the inn where thou didst commit this deed. And the youth went before the apostle in the way, and when they came to the inn they found her Lying dead. And the apostle when he saw her was sorry, for she was a comely girl. And he commanded her to be brought into the midst of the inn: and they laid her on a bed and brought her forth and set her down in the midst of the court of the inn. And the apostle laid his hand upon her and began to say: Jesu, who always showest thyself unto us; for this is thy will, that we should at all times seek thee, and thyself hast given us this power, to ask and to receive, and hast not only permitted this, but hast taught us to pray: who art not seen of our bodily eyes, but art never hidden from the eyes of our soul, and in thine aspect art concealed, but in thy works art manifested unto us: and in thy many acts we have known thee so far as we are able, and thyself hast given us thy gifts without measure, saying: Ask and it shall be given unto you, seek and ye shall find, knock and it shall be opened unto you: we beseech thee, therefore, having the fear (suspicion) of our sins; and we ask of thee, not riches, not gold, not silver, not possessions, not aught else of the things which come of the earth and return again unto the earth; but this we ask of thee and entreat, that in thine holy name thou wouldest raise up the woman that lieth here, by thy power, to the glory and faith of them that stand by.

54 And he said unto the youth (Syr. ' Stretch thy mind towards our Lord,' and he signed him with the cross), having signed (sealed) him: Go and take hold on her hand and say unto her: I with my hands slew thee with iron, and with my hands in the faith of Jesus I raise thee up. So the youth went to her and stood by her, saying: I have believed in thee, Christ Jesu. And he looked unto Judas Thomas the apostle and said to him: Pray for me that my Lord may come to my help, whom I also call upon. And he laid his hand upon her hand and said: Come, Lord Jesu Christ: unto her grant thou life and unto me the earnest of faith in thee. And straightway as he drew her hand she sprang up and sat up, looking upon the great company that stood by. And she saw the apostle also standing over against her, and leaving the bed she leapt forth and fell at his feet and caught hold on his raiment, saying: I beseech thee, my lord where is that other that was with thee, who left me not to remain in that fearful and cruel place, but delivered me unto thee, saying: Take thou this woman, that she may be made perfect, and hereafter be gathered into her place?

55 And the apostle said unto her: Relate unto us where thou hast been. And she answered: Dost thou who wast with me and unto whom I was delivered desire to hear? And she began to say: [This description of hell-torments is largely derived from the Apocalypse of Peter] A man took me who was hateful to look upon altogether black, and his raiment exceedingly foul, and took me away to a place wherein were many pits (chasms), and a great stench and hateful odour issued thence. And he caused me to look into every pit, and I saw in the (first) pit flaming fire, and wheels of fire ran round there, and souls were hanged upon those wheels, and were dashed (broken) against each other; and very great crying and howling was there, and there was none to deliver. And that man said to me: These souls are of thy tribe, and when the number of their days is accomplished (lit. in the days of the number) they are (were) delivered unto torment and affliction, and then are others brought in in their stead, and likewise these into another place. These are they that have reversed the intercourse of male and female. And I looked and saw infants heaped one upon another and struggling with each other as they lay on them. And he answered and said to me: These are the children of those others, and therefore are they set here for a testimony against them. (Syr. omits this clause of the children, and lengthens and dilutes the preceding speech.)

56 And he took me unto another pit, and I stooped and looked and saw mire and worms welling up, and souls wallowing there, and a great gnashing of teeth was heard thence from them. And that man said unto me: These are the souls of women which forsook their husbands and committed adultery with others, and are brought into this torment. Another pit he showed me whereinto I stooped and looked and saw souls hanging, some by the tongue, some by the hair, some by the hands, and some head downward by the feet, and tormented (smoked) with smoke and brimstone; concerning whom that man that was with me answered me: The souls which are hanged by the tongue are slanderers, that uttered Lying and shameful words, and were not ashamed, and they that are hanged by the hair are unblushing ones which had no modesty and went about in the world bareheaded; and they that are hanged by the hands, these are they that took away and stole other men's goods, and never gave aught to the needy nor helped the afflicted, but did so, desiring to take all, and had no thought at all of justice or of the law; and they that hang upside down by the feet, these are they that lightly and readily ran in evil ways and disorderly paths, not visiting the sick nor escorting them that depart this life, and therefore each and every soul receiveth that which was done by it. (Syr. omits almost the whole section.)

57 Again he took me and showed me a cave exceeding dark, breathing out a great stench, and many souls were looking out desiring to get somewhat of the air, but their keepers suffered them not to look forth. And he that was with me said: This is the prison of those souls which thou sawest: for when they have fulfilled their torments for that which each did, thereafter do others succeed them: and there be some that are wholly consumed and (some, Syr.) that are delivered over unto other torments. And they that kept the souls which were in the dark cave said unto the man that had taken me: Give her unto us that we may bring her in unto the rest until the time cometh for her to be delivered unto torment. But he answered them: I give her not unto you, for I fear him that delivered her to me: for I was not charged to leave her here, but I take her back with me until I shall receive order concerning her. And he took me and brought me unto another place wherein were men being sharply tormented (Syr. where men were). And he that was like unto thee took me and delivered me to thee, saying thus to thee: Take her, for she is one of the sheep that have gone astray. And I was taken by thee, and now am I before thee. I beseech thee, therefore, and supplicate that I may not depart unto those places of punishment which I have seen.

58 And the apostle said: Ye have heard what this woman hath related: and there are not these torments only, but others also, worse than these; and ye, if ye turn not unto this God whom I preach, and abstain from your former works and the deeds which ye committed without knowledge, shall have your end in those torments. Believe therefore on Christ Jesus, and he will forgive you the sins ye have committed hitherto, and will cleanse you from all your bodily lusts that abide on the earth, and will heal you of all your trespasses which follow you and depart with you and are found upon (before) you. Put off therefore every one of you the old man, and put on the new, and forsake your former walk and conversation; and let them that stole steal no more, but live by labouring and working; and let the adulterous no more fornicate, lest they deliver themselves unto eternal torment; for adultery is before God exceeding evil beyond other sins. And put away from you covetousness and Lying and drunkenness and slandering, and render not evil for evil: for all these things are strange and alien unto the God who is preached by me: but rather walk ye in faith and meekness and holiness and hope, wherein God delighteth, that ye may become his own, expecting of him the gifts which some few only do receive.

59 All the people therefore believed and gave their souls obediently unto the living God and Christ Jesus, rejoicing in the blessed works of the Most High and in his holy service. And they brought much money for the service of the widows: for the apostle had them gathered together in the cities, and unto all of them he sent provision by his own ministers (deacons), both clothes and nourishment. And he himself ceased not preaching and speaking to them and showing that this is Jesus Christ whom the scriptures proclaimed, who is come and was crucified, and raised the

third day from the dead. And next he showed them plainly, beginning from the prophets, the things concerning the Christ, that it was necessary that he should come, and that in him should be accomplished all things that were foretold of him. And the fame of him went forth into all the cities and countries, and all that had sick or them that were oppressed by unclean spirits brought them, and some they laid in the way whereby he should pass, and he healed them all by the power of the Lord. Then all that were healed by him said with one accord: Glory be to thee, Jesu, who hast granted us all alike healing through thy servant and apostle Thomas. And now being whole and rejoicing, we beseech thee that we may be of thy flock, and be numbered among thy sheep; receive us therefore, Lord, and impute not unto us our transgressions and our former faults which we committed being in ignorance.

60 And the apostle said: Glory be to the only-begotten of the Father! Glory be to the first-born of many brethren! Glory be to thee, the defender and helper of them that come unto thy refuge! that sleepest not, and awakest them that are asleep that livest and givest life to them that lie in death! O God Jesu Christ, Son of the living God, redeemer and helper, refuge and rest of all that are weary (labour) in thy work, giver of healing to them that for thy name s sake bear the burden and heat of the day: we give thanks for (to) the gifts that are given us of thee and granted us by thy help and thy dispensation that cometh unto us from thee.

61 Perfect thou therefore these things in us unto the end that we may have the boldness that is in thee: look upon us for for thy sake have we forsaken our homes and our parents, and for thy sake have we gladly and willingly become strangers: look upon us, Lord, for we have forsaken our own possessions for thy sake, that we might gain thee the possession that cannot be taken away: look upon us, Lord, for we have forsaken them that belong unto us by race, that we might be joined unto thy kinship: look upon us, Lord, that have forsaken our fathers and mothers and fosters, that we might behold thy Father, and be satisfied with his divine food: look upon us, Lord, for for thy sake have we forsaken our bodily consorts and our earthly fruits, that we might be partakers in that enduring and true fellowship, and bring forth true fruits, whose nature is from above, which no man can take from us, with whom we shall abide and who shall abide with us.

The Seventh Act: Of the Captain.

62 Now while the apostle Thomas was proclaiming throughout all India the word of God, a certain captain of the king Misdaeus (Mazdai, Syr.) came to him and said unto him: I have heard of thee that thou takest no reward of any man, but even that thou hast thou givest to them that need. For if thou didst receive rewards, I would have sent thee a great sum, and would not have come myself, for the king doeth nought without me: for I have much substance and am rich, even one of the rich men of India. And I have never done wrong to any; but the contrary hath befallen me. I have a wife, and of her I had a daughter and I am well affectioned toward her, as also nature requireth and have never made trial of another wife. Now it chanced that there was a wedding in our city, and they that made the marriage feast were well beloved of me: they came in therefore and bade me to it, bidding also my wife and her daughter. Forasmuch then as they were my good friends I could not refuse: I sent her therefore, though she desired not to go, and with them I sent also many servants: so they departed, both she and her daughter, decked with many ornaments.

63 And when it was evening and the time was come to depart from the wedding I sent lamps and torches to meet them: and I stood in the street to espy when she should come and I should see her with my daughter. And as I stood I heard a sound of lamentation. Woe for her! was heard out of every mouth. And my servants with their clothes rent came to me and told me what was done. We saw, said they, a man and a boy with him. And the man laid his hand upon thy wife, and the boy upon thy daughter: and they fled from them: and we smote (wounded) them with our swords, but our swords fell to the ground. And the same hour the women fell down, gnashing their teeth and beating their heads upon the earth and seeing this we came to tell it thee. And when I heard this of my servants I rent my clothes and smote my face with my hands, and becoming like one mad I ran along the street, and came and found them cast in the market-place; and I took them and brought them to my house, and after a long space they awaked and stood up, and sat down.

64 I began therefore to inquire of my wife: What is it that hath befallen thee? And she said to me: Knowest thou not what thou hast done unto me? for I prayed thee that I might not go to the wedding, because I was not of even health in my body; and as I went on the way and came near to the aqueduct wherein the water floweth, I saw a black man standing over against me nodding at me with his head, and a boy like unto him standing by him; and I said to my daughter: Look at those two hideous men, whose teeth are like milk and their lips like soot. And we left them and went towards the aqueduct; and when it was sunset and we departed from the wedding, as we passed by with the young men and drew near the aqueduct, my daughter saw them first, and was affrighted and fled towards me; and after her I also beheld them coming against us: and the servants that were with us fled from them (Syr.) and they struck us, and cast down both me and my daughter. And when she had told me these things, the devils came upon them again and threw them down: and from

that hour they are not able to come forth, but are shut up in one room or a second (Syr. in a room within another): and on their account I suffer much, and am distressed: for the devils throw them down wheresoever they find them, and strip them naked. I beseech and supplicate thee before God, help me and have pity on me, for it is now three years that a table hath not been set in my house, and my wife and my daughter have not sat at a table: and especially for mine unhappy daughter, which hath not seen any good at all in this world.

65 And the apostle, hearing these things from the captain, was greatly grieved for him, and said unto him: Believest thou that Jesus will heal them? And the captain said: Yea. And the apostle said: Commit thyself then unto Jesus, and he will heal them and procure them succour. And the captain said: Show me him, that I may entreat him and believe in him. And the apostle said: He appeareth not unto these bodily eyes, but is found by the eyes of the mind. The captain therefore lifted up his voice and said: I believe thee, Jesu, and entreat and supplicate thee, help my little faith which I have in thee. And the apostle commanded Xenophon (Syr. Xanthippus) the deacon to assemble all the brethren; and when the whole multitude was gathered, the apostle stood in the midst and said:

66 Children and brethren that have believed on the Lord, abide in this faith, preaching Jesus who was proclaimed unto you by me, to bring you hope in him; and forsake not (be not forsaken of) him, and he will not forsake you. While ye sleep in this slumber that weigheth down the sleepers, he, sleeping not, keepeth watch over you; and when ye sail and are in peril and none can help, he walking upon the waters supporteth and aideth. For I am now departing from you, and it appeareth not if I shall again see you according to the flesh. Be ye not therefore like unto the people of Israel, who losing sight of their pastors for an hour, stumbled. But I leave unto you Xenophon the deacon in my stead; for he also like myself proclaimeth Jesus: for neither am I aught, nor he, but Jesus only; for I also am a man clothed with a body, a son of man like one of you; for neither have I riches as it is found with some, which also convict them that possess them, being wholly useless, and left behind upon the earth, whence also they came, and they bear away with them the transgressions and blemishes of sins which befall men by their means. And scantly are rich men found in almsgivillg: but the merciful and lowly in heart, these shall inherit the kingdom of God: for it is not beauty that endureth with men, for they that trust in it, when age cometh upon them, shall suddenly be put to shame: all things therefore have their time; in their season are they loved and hated. Let your hope then be in Jesus Christ the Son of God, which is always loved, and always desired: and be mindful of us, as we of you: for we too, if we fulfil not the burden of the commandments are not worthy to be preachers of this name, and hereafter shall we pay the price (punishment) of our own head.

67 And he prayed with them and continued with them a long time in prayer and supplication, and committing them unto the Lord, he said: O Lord that rulest over every soul that is in the body; Lord, Father of the souls that have their hope in thee and expect thy mercies: that redeemest from error the men that are thine own and settest free from bondage and corruption thy subjects that come unto thy refuge: be thou in the flock of Xenophon and anoint it with holy oil, and heal it of sores, and preserve it from the ravening wolves. And he laid his hand on them and said: The peace of the Lord shall be upon you and shall journey with us.

The Eighth Act: Of the wild asses.

68 The apostle therefore went forth to depart on the way: and they all escorted him, weeping and adjuring him to make remembrance of them in his prayers and not to forget them. He went up then and sat upon the chariot, leaving all the brethren, and the captain came and awaked the driver, saying: I entreat and pray that I may become worthy to sit beneath his feet, and I will be his driver upon this way, that he also may become my guide in that way whereby few go.

69 And when they had journeyed about two miles, the apostle begged of the captain and made him arise and caused him to sit by him, suffering the driver to sit in his own place. And as they went along the road, it came to pass that the beasts were wearied with the great heat and could not be stirred at all. And the captain was greatly vexed and wholly cast down, and thought to run on his own feet and bring other beasts for the use of the chariot; but the apostle said: Let not thine heart be troubled nor affrighted, but believe on Jesus Christ whom I have proclaimed unto thee, and thou shalt see great wonders. And he looked and saw a herd of wild asses feeding by the wayside, and said to the captain: If thou hast believed on Christ Jesus, go unto that herd of wild asses and say: Judas Thomas the apostle of Christ the new God saith unto you: Let four of you come, of whom we have need (or, of whom we may have use).

70 And the captain went in fear, for they were many; and as he went, they came to meet him; and when they were near, he said unto them: Judas Thomas the apostle of the new God commandeth you: Let four of you come, of whom we have need. And when the wild asses heard it, they ran with one accord and came to him, and when they came they did him reverence. [Syr. has a long prayer: And Judas Thomas the apostle of our Lord lifted up his voice in praise and said: Glorious art thou, God of truth and Lord of all natures, for thou didst will with thy will, and make all thy works and finish all thy creatures, and bring them to the rule of their

nature, and lay upon them all thy fear that they might be subject to thy command. And thy will trod the path from thy secrecy to manifestation, and was caring for every soul that thou didst make, and was spoken of by the mouth of all the prophets, in all visions and sounds and voices; but Israel did not obey because of their evil inclination. And thou, because thou art Lord of all, hast a care for the creatures, so that thou spreadest over us thy mercy in him who came by thy will and put on the body, thy creature, which thou didst will and form according to thy glorious wisdom. He whom thou didst appoint in thy secrecy and establish in thy manifestation, to him thou hast given the name of Son, he who was thy will, the power of thy thought; so that ye are by various names, the Father and the Son and the Spirit, for the sake of the government of thy creatures, for the nourishing of all natures, and ye are one in glory and power and will; and ye are divided without being separated, and are one though divided, and all subsists in thee and is subject to thee, because all is thine. And I rely upon thee, Lord, and by thy command have subjected these dumb beasts, that thou mightest show thy ministering power upon us and upon them because it is needful, and that thy name might be glorified in us and in the beasts that cannot speak.] And the apostle said unto them: Peace be unto you. Yoke ye four of you in the stead of these beasts that have come to a stand. And every one of them came and pressed to be yoked: there were then four stronger than the rest, which also were yoked. And the rest, some went before and some followed. And when they had journeyed a little way he dismissed the colts, saying: I say unto you the inhabiters of the desert, depart unto your pastures, for if I had had need of all, ye would all have gone with me; but now go unto your place wherein ye dwell. And they departed quietly until they were no more seen.

71 Now as the apostle and the captain and the driver went on, the wild asses drew the chariot quietly and evenly, lest they should disturb the apostle of God. And when they came near to the city gate they turned aside and stood still before the doors of the captain's house. And the captain said: It is not possible for me to relate what hath happened, but when I see the end I will tell it. The whole city therefore came to see the wild asses under the yoke; and they had heard also the report of the apostle that he was to come and visit them. And the apostle asked the captain: Where is thy dwelling, and whither dost thou bring us? And he said to him: Thou knowest that we stand before the doors, and these which by thy commandment are come with thee know it better than I.

72 And having so said he came down from the chariot. The apostle therefore began to say: Jesu Christ, that art blasphemed by the ignorance of thee in this country; Jesu, the report of whom is strange in this city; Jesu, that receivest all (Syr. sendest on before the apostles in every country and in every city, and all thine that are worthy are glorified in thee; Jesu, that didst take a form and become as a man, and wert seen of all us that thou mightest not separate us from thine own love: thou, Lord, art he that gavest thyself for us, and with thy blood hast purchased us and gained us as a possession of great price: and what have we to give thee, Lord, in exchange for thy life which thou gavest for us? for that which we would give, thou gavest us: and this is, that we should entreat of thee and live.

73 And when he had so said, many assembled from every quarter to see the apostle of the new God. And again the apostle said: Why stand we idle? Jesu, Lord, the hour is come: what wilt thou have done? command therefore that that be fulfilled which needeth to be done. Now the captain's wife and her daughter were sore borne down by the devils, so that they of the house thought they would rise up no more: for they suffered them not to partake of aught, but cast them down upon their beds recognizing no man until that day when the apostle came thither. And the apostle said unto one of the wild asses that were yoked on the right hand: Enter thou within the gate, and stand there and call the devils and say to them: Judas Thomas the apostle and disciple of Jesus Christ saith unto you: Come forth hither: for on your account am I sent and unto them that pertain to you by race, to destroy you and chase you unto your place, until the time of the end come and ye go down into your own deep of darkness.

74 And that wild ass went in, a great multitude being with him, and said: Unto you I speak, the enemies of Jesus that is called Christ: unto you I speak that shut your eyes lest ye see the light: unto you I speak, children of Gehenna and of destruction, of him that ceaseth not from evil until now, that always reneweth his workings and the things that befit his being: unto you I speak, most shameless, that shall perish by your own hands. And what I shall say of your destruction and end, and what I shall tell, I know not. For there are many things and innumerable to the hearing: and greater are your doings than the torment that is reserved for you (Syr. however great your bodies, they are too small for your retributions). But unto thee I speak, devil, and to thy son that followeth with thee: for now am I sent against you. And wherefore should I make many words concerning your nature and root, which yourselves know and are not ashamed? but Judas Thomas the apostle of Christ Jesus saith unto you, he that by much love and affection is sent hither: Before all this multitude that standeth here, come forth and tell me of what race ye are.

75 And straightway the woman came forth with her daughter, both like dead persons and dishonoured in aspect: and the apostle beholding them

was grieved. especially for the girl, and saith unto the devils: God forbid that for you there should be sparing or propitiation, for ye know not to spare nor to have pity: but in the name of Jesus, depart from them and stand by their side. And when the apostle had so said, the women fell down and became as dead; for they neither had breath nor uttered speech: but the devil answered with a loud voice and said: Art thou come hither again, thou that deridest our nature and race? art thou come again, that blottest out our devices? and as I take it, thou wouldest not suffer us to be upon the earth at all: but this at this time thou canst not accomplish. And the apostle guessed that this devil was he that had been driven out from that other woman.

76 And the devil said: I beseech thee, give me leave to depart even whither thou wilt, and dwell there and take commandment from thee, and I will not fear the ruler that hath authority over me. For like as thou art come to preach good tidings, so I also am come to destroy; and like as, if thou fulfil not the will of him that sent thee, he will bring punishment upon thy head, so I also if I do not the will of him that sent me, before the season and time appointed, shall be sent unto mine own nature; and like as thy Christ helpeth thee in that thou doest, so also my father helpeth me in that I do; and like as for thee he prepareth vessels worthy of thine inhabiting, so also for me he seeketh out vessels whereby I may accomplish his deeds; and like as he nourisheth and provideth for his subjects, so also for me he prepareth chastisements and torments, with them that become my dwellingplaces (Syr. those in whom I dwell); and like as for a recompense of thy working he giveth thee eternal life, so also unto me he giveth for a reward of my works eternal destruction; and like as thou art refreshed by thy prayer and thy good works and spiritual thanksgivings, so I also am refreshed by murders and adulteries and sacrifices made with wine upon altars (Syr. sacrifices and libations of wine), and like as thou convertest men unto eternal life, so I also pervert them that obey me unto eternal destruction and torment: and thou receivest thine own and I mine.

77 And when the devil had said these things and yet more the apostle said: Jesus commandeth thee and thy son by me to enter no more into the habitation of man: but go ye forth and depart and dwell wholly apart from the habitation of men. And the devils said unto him: Thou hast laid on us a harsh commandment: but what wilt thou do unto them that now are concealed from thee? for they that have wrought all the images rejoice in them more than thee: and many of them do the more part worship, and perform their will, sacrificing to them and bringing them food, by libations and by wine and water and offering with oblations. And the apostle said: They also shall now be abolished, with their works. And suddenly the devils vanished away: but the women lay cast upon the earth as if were dead, and without speech.

78 And the wild asses stood together and parted not one from another; but he to whom speech was given by the power of the Lord -while all men kept silence, and looked to see what they would do- the wild ass said unto the apostle: Why standest thou idle, O apostle of Christ the Most High, who looketh that thou shouldest ask of him the best of learning? Wherefore then tarriest thou? (Syr. that thou shouldest ask him, and he would give thee? Why delayest thou, good disciple?) for lo, thy teacher desireth to show by thy hands his mighty works. Why standest thou still, O herald of the hidden one? for thy (Lord) willeth to manifest through thee his unspeakable things, which he reserveth for them that are worthy of him, to hear them. Why restest thou, O doer of mighty works in the name of the Lord? for thy Lord encourageth thee and engendereth boldness in thee. Fear not, therefore; for he will not forsake the soul that belongeth unto thee by birth. Begin therefore to call upon him and he will readily hearken to thee. Why standest thou marvelling at all his acts and his workings? for these are small things which he hath shown by thy means. And what wilt thou tell concerning his great gifts? for thou wilt not be sufficient to declare them. And why marvellest thou at his cures of the body which he worketh? (Syr. which come to an end) especially when thou knowest that healing of his which is secure and lasting, which he bringeth forth by his own nature? And why lookest thou unto this temporal life, and hast no thought of that which is eternal (Syr. when thou canst every day think on that which is eternal)?

79 But unto you the multitudes that stand by and look to see these that are cast down raised up, I say, believe in the apostle of Jesus Christ: believe the teacher of truth, believe him that showeth you the truth, believe Jesus, believe on the Christ that was born, that the born may live by his life: who also was raised up through infancy, that perfection might appear by his manhood (man). He did teach his own disciples: for he is the teacher of the truth and maketh wise men wise (Syr. who went to school that through him perfect wisdom might be known: he taught his teacher because he was the teacher of verity and the master of the wise). Who also offered the gift in the temple that he might show that all the (every) offering was sanctified. This is his apostle, the shewer-forth of truth: this is he that performeth the will of him that sent him. But there shall come false apostles and prophets of lawlessness, whose end shall be according to their deeds; preaching indeed and ordaining to flee from ungodliness, but themselves at all times detected in sins, clad indeed with sheep's clothing, but within, ravening wolves. Who suffice not themselves with one wife but corrupt many women; who, saying that they despise children, destroy

many children (boys), for whom they will pay the penalty; that content not themselves with their own possessions, but desire that all useless things should minister unto them only; professing to be his disciples; and with their mouth they utter one thing, but in their heart they think another; charging other men to beware of evil, but they themselves perform nought that is good; who are accounted temperate, and charge other men to abstain from fornication theft, and covetousness, but in all these things do they themselves walk secretly, teaching other men not to do them.

80 And when the wild ass had declared all these things, all men gazed upon him. And when he ceased the apostle said: What I shall think concerning thy beauty, O Jesu, and what I shall tell of thee, I know not, or rather I am not able, for I have no power to declare it, O Christ that art in rest, and only wise that only knowest the inward of the heart and understandest the thought. Glory be to thee, merciful and tranquil. Glory to thee, wise word. Glory to thy compassion that was born unto us. Glory to thy mercy that was spread out over us. Glory to thy greatness that was made small for us. Glory to thy most high kingship that was humbled for us. Glory to thy might which was enfeebled for us. Glory to thy Godhead that for us was seen in likeness of men. Glory to thy manhood that died for us that it might make us live. Glory to thy resurrection from the dead; for thereby rising and rest cometh unto our souls. Glory and praise (good report) to thine ascending into the heavens; for thereby thou hast shewed us the path of the height, and promised that we shall sit with thee on thy right hand and with thee judge the twelve tribes of Israel. Thou art the heavenly word of the Father: thou art the hidden light of the understanding, shewer of the way of truth, driver away of darkness, and blotter-out of error.

81 Having thus spoken, the apostle stood over the women, saying: My Lord and my God, I am not divided from thee (or doubt not concerning thee), nor as one unbelieving do I call upon thee, who art always our helper and succourer and raiser-up; who breathest thine own power into us and encouragest us and givest confidence in love unto thine own servants. I beseech thee, let these souls be healed and rise up and become such as they were before they were smitten of the devils. And when he thus spake the women turned and sat up. And the apostle bade the captain that his servants should take them and bring them within (Syr. and give them food, for they had not eaten for many days). And when they were gone in, the apostle said unto the wild asses, Follow me. And they went after him until he had brought them without the gate. And when they had gone out, he said to them: Depart in peace unto your pastures. The wild asses therefore went away willingly; and the apostle stood and took heed to them lest they should be hurt of any, until they had gone afar off and were no more seen. And the apostle returned with the multitude into the house of the captain.

The Ninth Act: Of the Wife of Charisius.

82 Now it chanced that a certain woman, the wife of Charisius, that is next unto the king, whose name was Mygdonia, came to see and behold the new name and the new God who was being proclaimed, and the new apostle who had come to visit their country: and she was carried by her own servants; and because of the great crowd and the narrow way they were not able to bring her near unto him. And she sent unto her husband to send her more to minister to her; and they came and approached her, pressing upon the people and beating them. And the apostle saw it and said unto them: Wherefore overthrow ye them that come to hear the word, and are eager for it? and ye desire to be near me but are far off, as it was said of the multitude that came unto the Lord: Having eyes ye see not, and having ears ye hear not; and he said to the multitudes: He that hath ears to hear, let him hear; and: Come unto me, all ye that labour and are heavy laden, and I will give you rest.

83 And looking upon them that carried her, he said unto them: This blessing and this admonition [Here and elsewhere there is a marked divergence between the texts of U and P, the Roman and Paris MSS.: Bonnet prints them separately. P is on the whole much shorter. Syr. differs from both. I follow U, but it is very corrupt.] which was promised unto them is for you that are heavily burdened now. Ye are they that carry burdens grievous to be borne, and are borne about by her command. And though ye are men, they lay on you loads as on brute beasts, for they that have authority over you think that ye are not men such as themselves, whether bond or free. For neither shall possessions profit the rich, nor poverty save the poor from judgement; nor have we received a commandment which we are not able to perform, nor hath he laid on us burdens grievous to be borne which we are not able to carry; nor building which men build; nor to hew stones and prepare houses, as your craftsmen do by their own knowledge. But this commandment have we received of the Lord, that that which pleaseth not us when it is done by another this we should not do to any other man.

84 Abstain therefore first from adultery, for this is the beginning of all evils, and next from theft, which enticed Judas Iscariot, and brought him unto hanging; (and from covetousness,) for as many as yield unto covetousness see not that which they do; and from vainglory and from all foul deeds, especially them of the body, whereby cometh eternal condemnation. For this is the chief city of all evils; and likewise it bringeth them that hold their heads (necks) high unto tyranny, and draweth them down

unto the deep, and subdueth them under its hands that they see not what they do; wherefore the things done of them are hidden from them.

85 But do ye become well-pleasing unto God in all good things, in meekness and quietness: for these doth God spare, and granteth eternal life and setteth death at nought. And in gentleness which followeth on all good things, and overcometh all enemies and alone receiveth the crown of victory: with gentleness (Syr.), and stretching out of the hand to the poor, and supplying the want of the needy, and distributing to them that are in necessity, especially them that walk in holiness. For this is chosen before God and leadeth unto eternal life: for this is before God the chief city of all good: for they that strive not in the course (stadium) of Christ shall not obtain holiness. And holiness did appear from God, doing away fornication, overthrowing the enemy, well-pleasing unto God: for she is an invincible champion (athlete), having honour from God, glorified of many: she is an ambassador of peace, announcing peace: if any gain her he abideth without care, pleasing the Lord, expecting the time of redemption: for she doeth nothing amiss, but giveth life and rest and joy unto all that gain her. [P has nothing of this, and Syr. makes better sense, but is not very interesting.]

86 But meekness hath overcome death and brought him under authority, meekness hath enslaved the enemy (U and P and Syr. now present the same text), meekness is the good yoke: meekness feareth not and opposeth not the many: meekness is peace and joy and exaltation of rest. Abide ye therefore in holiness and receive freedom from me, and be near unto meekness for in these three heads is portrayed the Christ whom I proclaim unto you. Holiness is the temple of Christ, and he that dwelleth in her getteth her for an habitation [SYR. is the of God rest temperance and], because for forty days and forty nights he fasted, tasting nothing: and he that keepeth her shall dwell in her as on a mountain. And meekness is his boast: for he said unto Peter our fellow apostle: Turn back thy sword and put it again into the sheath thereof: for if I had willed so to do, could I not have brought more than twelve legions of angels from my Father?

87 And when the apostle had said these things in the hearing of all the multitude, they trode and pressed upon one another: and the wife of Charisius the king's kinsman leapt out of her chair and cast herself on the earth before the apostle, and caught his feet and besought and said: O disciple of the living God, thou art come into a desert country, for we live in the desert; being like to brute beasts in our conversation, but now shall we be saved by thy hands; I beseech thee, therefore, take thought of me, and pray for me, that the compassion of the God whom thou preachest may come upon me, and I may become his dwelling place and be joined in prayer and hope and faith in him, and I also may receive the seal and become an holy temple and he may dwell in me.

88 And the apostle said: I do pray and entreat for you all, brethren, that believe on the Lord, and for you, sisters, that hope in Christ, that in all of you the word of God may tabernacle and have his tabernacle therein: for we have no power over them (Syr. because ye are given power over your own souls). And he began to say unto the woman Mygdonia: Rise up from the earth and compose thyself (take off thine ornaments, P; be mindful of thyself, Syr.). For this attire that is put on shall not profit thee nor the beauty of thy body, nor thine apparel, neither yet the fame of thy rank, nor the authority of this world, nor the polluted intercourse with thine husband shall avail thee if thou be bereaved of the true fellowship: for the appearance (fantasy) of ornamenting cometh to nought, and the body waxeth old and changeth, and raiment weareth out, and authority and lordship pass away (U corrupt; P abridges; Syr. has: passeth away accompanied with punishment, according as each person hath conducted himself in it), and the fellowship of procreation also passeth away, and is as it were condemnation. Jesus only abideth ever, and they that hope in him. Thus he spake, and said unto the woman: Depart in peace, and the Lord shall make thee worthy of his own mysteries. But she said: I fear to go away, lest thou forsake me and depart unto another nation. But the apostle said to her: Even if I go, I shall not leave thee alone, but Jesus of his compassion will be with thee. And she fell down and did him reverence and departed unto her house.

89 Now Charisius, the kinsman of Misdaeus the king, bathed himself and returned and laid him down to dine. And he inquired concerning his wife, where she was; for she had not come out of her own chamber to meet him as she was wont. And her handmaids said to him: She is not well. And he entered quickly into the chamber and found her Lying on the bed and veiled: and he unveiled her and kissed her, saying: Wherefore art thou sorrowful to-day? And she said: I am not well. And he said unto her: Wherefore then didst thou not keep the guise of thy freedom (Syr. pay proper respect to thy position as a free woman) and remain in thy house, but didst go and listen unto vain speeches and look upon works of sorcery? but rise up and dine with me, for I cannot dine without thee. But she said to him: To-day I decline it, for I am greatly afeared.

90 And when Charisius heard this of Mygdonia, he would not go forth to dinner, but bade his servants bring her to dine with him (Syr. bring food to him that he might sup in her presence): when then they brought it in, he desired her to dine with him, but she excused herself; since then she would not, he dined alone, saying unto her: On thine account I refused to

dine with Misdaeus the king, and thou, wast thou not willing to dine with me? but she said: It is because I am not well. Charisius therefore rose up as he was wont and would sleep with her, but she said: Did I not tell thee that for today I refused it?

91 When he heard that he went to another bed and slept; and awaking out of sleep he said: My lady Mygdonia, hearken to the dream which I have seen. I saw myself lie at meat near to Misdaeus the king, and a dish of all sorts was set before us: and I saw an eagle come down from heaven and carry off from before me and the king two partridges, which he set against his heart; and again he came over us and flew about above us, and the king bade a bow to be brought to him; and the eagle again caught away from before us a pigeon and a dove, and the king shot an arrow at him, and it passed through him from one side to the other and hurt him not; and he being unscathed rose up into his own nest. And I awoke, and I am full of fear and sore vexed, because I had tasted of the partridge, and he suffered me not to put it to my mouth again. And Mygdonia said unto him: Thy dream is good: for thou every day eatest partridges, but this eagle had not tasted of a partridge until now.

92 And when it was morning Charisius went and dressed himself and shod his right foot with his left shoe; and he stopped, and said to Mygdonia: What then is this matter? for look, the dream and this action of mine! But Mygdonia said to him: And this also is not evil, but seemeth to me very good; for from an unlucky act there will be a change unto the better. And he washed his hands and went to salute Misdaeus the king.

93 And likewise Mygdonia rose up early and went to salute Judas Thomas the apostle, and she found him discoursing with the captain and all the multitude, and he was advising them and speaking of the woman which had received the Lord in her soul, whose wife she was; and the captain said: She is the wife of Charisius the kinsman of Misdaeus the king. And: Her husband is a hard man, and in every thing that he saith to the king he obeyeth him: and he will not suffer her to continue in this mind which she hath promised; for often-times hath he praised her before the king, saying that there is none other like her in love: all things therefore that thou speakest unto her are strange unto her. And the apostle said: If verily and surely the Lord hath risen upon her soul and she hath received the seed that was cast on her, she will have no care of this temporal life, nor fear death, neither will Charisius be able to harm her at all: for greater is he whom she hath received into her soul, if she have received him indeed.

94 And Mygdonia hearing this said unto the apostle: In truth, my lord, I have received the seed of thy words, and I will bear fruit like unto such seed. The apostle saith: Our souls give praise and thanks unto thee, O Lord, for they are thine: our bodies give thanks unto thee, which thou hast accounted worthy to become the dwelling-place of thy heavenly gift. And he said also to them that stood by: Blessed are the holy, whose souls have never condemned them, for they have gained them and are not divided against themselves: blessed are the spirits of the pure, and they that have received the heavenly crown whole from the world (age) which hath been appointed them: blessed are the bodies of the holy, for they have been made worthy to become temples of God, that Christ may dwell in them: blessed are ye, for ye have power to forgive sins: blessed are ye if ye lose not that which is committed unto you, but rejoicing and departing bear it away with you: blessed are ye the holy, for unto you it is given to ask and receive: blessed are ye meek for you hath God counted worthy to become heirs of the heavenly kingdom. Blessed are ye meek, for ye are they that have overcome the enemy: blessed are ye meek, for ye shall see the face of the Lord. Blessed are ye that hunger for the Lord's sake for for you is rest laid up, and your souls rejoice from henceforth. Blessed are ye that are quiet, (for ye have been counted worthy) to be set free from sin [and from the exchange of clean and unclean beasts]. And when the apostle had said these things in the hearing of all the multitude, Mygdonia was the more confirmed in the faith and glory and greatness of Christ.

95 But Charisius the kinsman and friend of Misdaeus the king came to his breakfast and found not his wife in the house; and he inquired of all that were in his house: Whither is your mistress gone? And one of them answered and said: She is gone unto that stranger. And when he heard this of his servant, he was wroth with the other servants because they had not straightway told him what was done: and he sat down and waited for her. And when it was evening and she was come into the house he said to her: Where wast thou? And she answered and said: With the physician. And he said: Is that stranger a physician? And she said: Yea, he is a physician of souls: for most physicians do heal bodies that are dissolved, but he souls that are not destroyed. Charisius, hearing this, was very angry in his mind with Mygdonia because of the apostle, but he answered her nothing, for he was afraid; for she was above him both in wealth and birth: but he departed to dinner, and she went into her chamber. And he said to the servants: Call her to dinner. But she would not come.

96 And when he heard that she would not come out of her chamber, he went in and said unto her: Wherefore wilt thou not dine with me and perchance not sleep with me as the wont is? yea, concerning this I have the greater suspicion, for I have heard that that sorcerer and deceiver teacheth that a man should not live with his wife, and that which nature requireth and the godhead hath ordained he overthroweth. When Charisius said these things, Mygdonia kept silence. He saith to her again: My

lady and consort Mygdonia, be not led astray by deceitful and vain words, nor by the works of sorcery which I have heard that this man performeth in the name of Father, Son, and Holy Ghost; for it was never yet heard in the world that any raised the dead, and, as I hear, it is reported of this man that he raiseth dead men. And for that he neither eateth nor drinketh, think not that for righteousness sake he neither eateth nor drinketh but this he doth because he possesseth nought, for what should he do which hath not even his daily bread? And he hath one garment because he is poor, and as for his not receiving aught of any (he doth so, to be sure, because he knoweth in himself that he doth not verily heal any man, Syr.).

97 And when Charisius so said, Mygdonia was silent as any stone, but she prayed, asking when it should be day, that she might go to the apostle of Christ. And he withdrew from her and went to dinner heavy in mind, for he thought to sleep with her according to the wont. And when he was gone out, she bowed her knees and prayed, saying: Lord God and Master, merciful Father, Saviour Christ, do thou give me strength to overcome the shamelessness of Charisius, and grant me to keep the holiness wherein thou delightest, that I also may by it find eternal life. And when she had so prayed she laid herself on her bed and veiled herself.

98 But Charisius having dined came upon her, and she cried out, saying: Thou hast no more any room by me: for my Lord Jesus is greater than thou, who is with me and resteth in me. And he laughed and said: Well dost thou mock, saying this of that sorcerer, and well dost thou deride him, who saith: Ye have no life with God unless ye purify yourselves. And when he had so said he essayed to sleep with her, but she endured it not and cried out bitterly and said: I call upon thee, Lord Jesu, forsake me not! for with thee have I made my refuge; for when I learned that thou art he that seekest out them that are veiled in ignorance and savest them that are held in error And now I entreat thee whose report I have heard and believed, come thou to my help and save me from the shamelessness of Charisius, that his foulness may not get the upper hand of me. And she smote her hands together (tied his hands, Syr.) and fled from him naked, and as she went forth she pulled down the curtain of the bed-chamber and wrapped it about her; and went to her nurse, and slept there with her.

99 But Charisius was in heaviness all night, and smote his face with his hands, and he was minded to go that very hour and tell the king concerning the violence that was done him, but he considered with himself, saying: If the great heaviness which is upon me compelleth me to go now unto the king, who will bring me in to him? for I know that my abuse hath overthrown me from my high looks and my vainglory and majesty, and hath cast me down into this vileness and separated my sister Mygonia from me. Yea, if the king himself stood before the doors at this hour, I could not have gone out and answered him. But I will wait until dawn, and I know that whatsoever I ask of the king, he granteth it me: and I will tell him of the madness of this stranger, how that it tyrannously casteth down the great and illustrious into the depth. For it is not this that grieveth me, that I am deprived of her companying, but for her am I grieved, because her greatness of soul is humbled: being an honourable lady in whom none of her house ever found fault (condemned), she hath fled away naked, running out of her own bedchamber, and I know not whither she is gone; and it may be that she is gone mad by the means of that sorcerer, and in her madness hath gone forth into the market-place to seek him; for there is nothing that appealeth unto her lovable except him and the things that are spoken by him.

100 And so saving he began to lament and say: Woe to me, O my consort, and to thee besides! for I am too quickly bereaved of thee. Woe is me, my most dear one, for thou excellest all my race: neither son nor daughter have I had of thee that I might find rest in them; neither hast thou yet dwelt with me a full year, and an evil eye hath caught thee from me. Would that the violence of death had taken thee, and I should yet have reckoned myself among kings and nobles: but that I should suffer this at the hands of a stranger, and belike he is a slave that hath run away, to mine ill fortune and the sorrow of mine unhappy soul! Let there be no impediment for me until I destroy him and avenge this night, and may I not be well-pleasing before Misdaeus the king if he avenge me not with the head of this stranger; (and I will also tell him) of Siphor the captain who hath been the occasion of this. For by his means did the stranger appear here, and lodgeth at his house: and many there be that go in and come out whom he teacheth a new doctrine; saying that none can live if he quit not all his substance and become a renouncer like himself: and he striveth to make many partakers with him.

101 And as Charisius thought on these things, the day dawned: and after the night (?) he put on a mean habit, and shod himself, and went downcast and in heaviness to salute the king. And when the king saw him he said: Wherefore art thou sorrowful, and comest in such garb? and I see that thy countenance is changed. And Charisius said unto the king: I have a new thing to tell thee and a new desolation which Siphor hath brought into India, even a certain Hebrew, a sorcerer, whom he hath sitting in his house and who departeth not from him: and many are there that go in to him: whom also he teacheth of a new God, and layeth on them new laws such as never yet were heard, saying: It is impossible for you to enter into that eternal life which I proclaim unto you, unless ye rid you of your

wives, and likewise the wives of their husbands. And it chanced that mine unlucky wife also went to him and became a hearer of his words, and she believed them, and in the night she forsook me and ran unto the stranger. But send thou for both Siphor and that sorcerer that is hid with (in) him, and visit it (?) on their head, lest all that are of our nation perish.

102 And when Misdaeus his friend heard this he saith to him: Be not grieved nor heavy, for I will send for him and avenge thee, and thou shalt have thy wife again, and the others that cannot I will avenge. And the king went forth and sat on the judgement seat, and when he was set he commanded Siphor the captain to be called. They went therefore unto his house and found him sitting on the right hand of the apostle and Mygdonia at his feet, hearkening to him with all the multitude. And they that were sent from the king said unto Siphor: Sittest thou here listening to vain words, and Misdaeus the king in his wrath thinketh to destroy thee because of this sorcerer and deceiver whom thou hast brought into thine house? And Siphor hearing it was cast down, not because of the king's threat against him, but for the apostle, because the king was disposed contrary to him. And he said to the apostle: I am grieved concerning thee: for I told thee at the first that that woman is the wife of Charisius the king's friend and kinsman, and he will not suffer her to perform that she hath promised, and all that he asketh of the king he granteth him. But the apostle said unto Siphor: Fear nothing, but believe in Jesus that pleadeth for us all, for unto his refuge are we gathered together. And Siphor, hearing that, put his garment about him and went unto Misdaeus the king,

103 And the apostle inquired of Mygdonia: What was the cause that thy husband was wroth with thee and devised this against us? And she said: Because I gave not myself up unto his corruption (destruction): for he desired last night to subdue me and subject me unto that passion which he serveth: and he to whom I have committed my soul delivered me out of his hands; and I fled away from him naked, and slept with my nurse: but that which befell him I know not, wherefore he hath contrived this. The apostle saith: These things will not hurt us; but believe thou on Jesus, and he shall overthrow the wrath of Charisius and his madness and his impulse; and he shall be a companion unto thee in the fearful way, and he shall guide thee into his kingdom, and shall bring thee unto eternal life giving thee that confidence which passeth not away nor changeth.

104 Now Siphor stood before the king, and he inquired of him: Who is that sorcerer and whence, and what teacheth he whom thou hast lurking in thine house? And Siphor answered the king: Thou art not ignorant, O king, what trouble and grief I, with my friends had concerning my wife, whom thou knowest and many others remember, and concerning my daughter, whom I value more than all my possessions, what a time and trial I suffered; for I became a laughing-stock and a curse in all our country. And I heard the report of this man and went to him and entreated him, and took him and brought him hither. And as I came by the way I saw wonderful and amazing things: and here also many did hear the wild ass and concerning that devil whom he drove out, and healed my wife and daughter, and now are they whole; and he asked no reward but requireth faith and holiness, that men should become partakers with him in that which he doeth: and this he teacheth to worship and fear one God, the ruler of all things, and Jesus Christ his Son, that they may have eternal life. And that which he eateth is bread and salt, and his drink is water from evening unto evening, and he maketh many prayers; and whatsoever he asketh of his God, he giveth him. And he teacheth that this God is holy and mighty, and that Christ is living and maketh alive, wherefore also he chargeth them that are there present to come unto him in holiness and purity and love and faith.

105 And when Misdaeus the king heard these things of Siphor he sent many soldiers unto the house of Siphor the captain, to bring Thomas the apostle and all that were found there. And they that were sent entered in and found him teaching much people; and Mygdonia sat at his feet. And when they beheld the great multitude that were about him, they feared, and departed to their king and said: We durst not say aught unto him, for there was a great multitude about him, and Mygdonia sitting at his feet was listening to the things that were spoken by him. And when Misdaeus the king and Charisius heard these things, Charisius leaped out from before the king and drew much people with him and said: I will bring him, O king, and Mygdonia whose understanding he hath taken away. And he came to the house of Siphor the captain, greatly disturbed, and found him (Thomas) teaching: but Mygdonia he found not, for she had withdrawn herself unto her house, having learnt that it had been told her husband that she was there.

106 And Charisius said unto the apostle: Up, thou wicked one and destroyer and enemy of mine house: for me thy sorcery harmeth not, for I will visit thy sorcery on thine head. And when he so said, the apostle looked upon him and said unto him: Thy threatenings shall return upon thee, for me thou wilt not harm any whit: for greater than thee and thy king and all your army is the Lord Jesus Christ in whom I have my trust. And Chalisius took a kerchief (turban, Syr.) of one of his slaves and cast it about the neck of the apostle, saying: Hale him and bring him away; let me see if his God is able to deliver him out of my hands. And they haled him and led him away to Misdaeus the king. And the apostle stood before the king, and the king said to him: Tell me who thou art and by what

power thou doest these things. But the apostle kept silence. And the king commanded his officers (subjects) that he should be scourged with an hundred and twenty-eight (hundred and fifty, Syr.) blows, and bound, and be cast into the prison; and they bound him and led him away. And the king and Charisius considered how they should put him to death, for the multitude worshipped him as God. And they had it in mind to say: The stranger hath reviled the king and is a deceiver.

107 But the apostle went unto the prison rejoicing and exulting, and said: I praise thee, Jesu, for that thou hast not only made me worthy of faith in thee, but also to endure much for thy sake. I give thee thanks therefore, Lord, that thou hast taken thought for me and given me patience: I thank thee Lord, that for thy sake I am called a sorcerer and a wizard. Receive thou me therefore with the blessing (Syr. let me receive of the blessing) of the poor, and of the rest of the weary, and of the blessings of them whom men hate and persecute and revile, and speak evil words of them. For lo, for thy sake I am hated: lo for thy sake I am cut off from the many, and for thy sake they call me such an one as I am not.

108 And as he prayed, all the prisoners looked on him, and besought him to pray for them: and when he had prayed and was set down, he began to utter a psalm in this wise:

[Here follows the Hymn of the Soul: a most remarkable composition, originally Syriac, and certainly older than the Acts, with which it has no real connection. We have it in Greek in one manuscript, the Vallicellian, and in a paraphrase by Nicetas of Thessalonica, found and edited by Bonnet.]

When I was an infant child in the palace of my Father and resting in the wealth and luxury of my nurturers, out of the East, our native country, my parents provisioned me and sent me.

And of the wealth of those their treasures they put together a load both great and light, that I might carry it alone.

Gold is the load, of them that are above (or of the land of the Ellaeans or Gilaeans), and silver of the great treasures (or of Gazzak the great) and stones, chalcedonies from the Indians and pearls from [THE of land] the Kosani (Kushan).

And they armed me with adamant [WHICH iron breaketh] and they took off from me (Gr. put on me) the garment set with gems, spangled with gold, which they had made for me because they loved me and the robe that was yellow in hue, made for my stature.

And they made a covenant with me, and inscribed it on mine understanding, that I should [NOT] forget it, and said:

If thou go down into Egypt, and bring back thence the one pearl which is there [IN the of sea midst] girt about by the devouring serpent thou shalt put on [AGAIN] the garment set with gems, and that robe whereupon it resteth (or which is thereon) and become with thy brother that is next unto us (Gr. of the well-remembered) an heir (Gr. herald) in our kingdom.

109. And I came out of the East by a road difficult and fearful, with two guides and I was untried in travelling by it.

And I passed by the borders of the Mosani (Maishan) where is the resort of the merchants of the East, and reached the land of the Babylonians [AND the of Sarbug walls unto came].

But when I entered into Egypt, the guides left me which had journeyed with me.

And I set forth by the quickest way to the serpent, and by his hole I abode watching for him to slumber and sleep, that I might take my pearl from him.

And forasmuch as I was alone I made mine aspect strange, and appeared as an alien to my people.

And there I saw my kinsman from the East, the free-born a lad of grace and beauty, a son of princes (or an anointed one).

He came unto me and dwelt with me, and I had him for a companion, and made him my friend and partaker in my journey (or merchandise).

And I charged him to beware of the Egyptians, and of partaking of those unclean things (or consorting with those unclean men).

And I put on their raiment, lest I should seem strange, as one that had come from without to recover the pearl; and lest the Egyptians should awake the serpent against me.

But, I know not by what occasion, they learned that I was not of their country.

And with guile they mingled for me a deceit, and I tasted of their food.

And I knew no more that I was a king's son, and I became a servant unto their king.

And I forgot also the pearl for which my fathers had sent me, and by means of the heaviness of their food I fell into a deep sleep.

110. But when this befell me, my fathers also were ware of it, and grieved for me and a proclamation was published in our kingdom, that all should meet at our doors.

And then the kings of Parthia and they that bare office and the great ones of the East made a resolve concerning me, that I should not be left in Egypt, and the princes wrote unto me signifying thus (and every noble signed his name to it, Syr.):

From the (thy) Father the King of kings, and thy mother that ruleth the East, and thy brother that is second unto us; unto our son that is in Egypt, peace.

Rise up and awake out of sleep, and hearken unto the words of the letter and remember that thou art a son of kings; lo, thou hast come under the yoke of bondage.

Remember the pearl for the which thou wast sent into Egypt (Gr. puts this after 46).

Remember thy garment spangled with gold, [AND the and thyself deck shouldest thou wherewith wear which mantle glorious] Thy name is named in the book of life, and with thy brother whom thou hast received [THOU be shalt] in our kingdom.

111. [AND letter a was my] and the King [as ambassador] sealed it [WITH hand right his] because of the evil ones, even the children of the Babylonians and the tyrannous demons of Labyrinthus (Sarbug, Syr.).

It flew and lighted down by me, and became all speech.

And I at the voice of it and the feeling of it started up out of sleep and I took it up and kissed it [AND the seal brake] and read it.

And it was written concerning that which was recorded in mine heart.

And I remembered forthwith that I was a son of kings, and my freedom yearned (sought) after its kind.

I remembered also the pearl for the which I was sent down into Egypt and I began (or came) with charms against the terrible serpent, and I overcame him (or put him to sleep) by naming the name of my Father upon him, And I caught away the pearl and turned back to bear it unto my fathers.

And I stripped off the filthy garment and left it in their land, and directed my way forthwith to the light of my fatherland in the East.

And on the way I found my letter that had awakened me, and it, like as it had taken a voice and raised me when I slept, so also guided me with the light that came from it.

For at times the royal garment of silk [SHONE] before mine eyes, and with love leading me and drawing me onward, I passed by Labyrinthus (Sarbug), and I left Babylon upon my left hand and I came unto Meson (Mesene; Maishan) the great, that lieth on the shore of the sea, from the heights of Warkan (Hyrcania?) had my parents sent thither by the hand of their treasurers, unto whom they committed it because of their faithfulness>.

112. But I remembered not the brightness of it; for I was yet a child and very young when I had left it in the palace of my Father, but suddenly, [when] I saw the garment made like unto me as it had been in a mirror.

And I beheld upon it all myself (or saw it wholly in myself) and I knew and saw myself through it, that we were divided asunder, being of one; and again were one in one shape.

Yea, the treasurers also which brought me the garment I beheld, that they were two, yet one shape was upon both, one royal sign was set upon both of them.

The money and the wealth had they in their hands, and paid me the due price, and the lovely garment, which was variegated with bright colours with gold and precious stones and pearls of comely hue they were fastened above (or in the height).

And the likeness of the King of kings was all in all of it. Sapphire stones were fitly set in it above (or, like the sapphire stone also were its manifold hues).

113. And again I saw that throughout it motions of knowledge were being sent forth, and it was ready to utter speech.

And I heard it speak:

I am of him that is more valiant than all men, for whose sake I was reared up with the Father himself.

And I also perceived his stature (so Gr.- Syr. I perceived in myself that my stature grew in accordance with his working).

And all its royal motions rested upon me as it grew toward the impulse of it (And with its kingly motions it was spreading itself toward me).

And it hastened, reaching out from the hand of [HIM it brought that] unto him that would receive it and me also did yearning arouse to start forth and meet it and receive it.

And I stretched forth and received it, and adorned myself with the beauty of the colours thereof (mostly Syr.; Gr. corrupt) and in my royal robe excelling in beauty I arrayed myself wholly.

And when I had put it on, I was lifted up unto the place of peace (sahltation) and homage and I bowed my head and worshipped the brightness of the Father which had sent it unto me. for I had performed his commandments, and he likewise that which he had promised, and at the doors of his palace which was from the beginning I mingled among, and he rejoiced over me and received me with him into his palace, and all his servants do praise him with sweet voices.

And he promised me that with him I shall be sent unto the gates of the king, that with my gifts and my pearl we may appear together before the king.

[Immediately on this, in the Syriac, follows a Song of Praise of Thomas the apostle consisting of forty-two ascriptions of praise and four final clauses (Wright, pp. 245-51). It has no bearing on the Acts, and is not in itself so remarkable as to need to be inserted here.]

114 And Charisius went home glad, thinking that his wife would be with him, and that she had become such as she was before, even before she heard the divine word and believed on Jesus. And he went, and found her with her hair dishevelled and her clothes rent, and when he saw it he said unto her: My lady Mygdonia, why doth this cruel disease keep hold on thee? and wherefore hast thou done this? I am thine husband from thy virginity, and both the gods and the law grant me to have rule over thee, what is this great madness of thine, that thou art become a derision in all our nation? but put thou away the care that cometh of that sorcerer; and I will remove his face from among us, that thou mayest see him no more.

115 But Mygdonia when she heard that gave herself up unto grief, groaning and lamenting and Charisius said again; Have I then so much wronged the gods that they have afflicted me with such a disease? what is my great offence that they have cast me into such humiliation? I beseech thee. Mvgdonia trangle my soul no more with the pitiful sight of thee and thy mean appearance and afflict not mine heart with care for thee I am Charisius thine husband, whom all the nation honoureth and feareth. What must I do? I know not whither to turn. What am I to think? shall I keep silence and endure? yet who can be patient when men take his treasure? and who can endure to lose thy sweet ways? and what is there for me? (Syr. thy beauties which are ever before me) the fragrance of thee is in my nostrils, and thy bright face is fixed in mine eyes. They are taking away my soul, and the fair body which I rejoiced to see they are destroying, and that sharpest of eyes they are blinding and cutting off my right hand: my joy is turning to grief and my life to death, and the light of it is being dyed (?) with darkness. Let no man of you my kindred henceforth look on me; from you no help hath come to me, nor will I hereafter worship the gods of the east that have enwrapped me in such calamities, nor pray to them any more nor sacrifice to them, for I am bereaved of my spouse. And what else should I ask of them? for all my glory is taken away, yet am I a prince and next unto the king in power; but Mygdonia hath set me at nought, and taken away all these things. (Would that some one would blind one of my eyes, and that thine eyes would look upon me as they were wont, Syr. which has more clauses, to the same effect.)

116 And while Charisius spake thus with tears, Mygdonia sat silent and looking upon the ground; and again he came unto her and said: My lady Mygdonia, most desired of me, remember that out of all the women that are in India I chose and took thee as the most beautiful, though I might have joined to myself in marriage many more beautiful: but yet I lie, Mygdonia, for by the gods it would not have been possible to find another like thee in the land of India; but woe is me always, for thou wilt not even answer me a word: but if thou wilt, revile me, so that I may only be vouchsafed a word from thee. Look at me, for I am more comely than that sorcerer: but thou art my wealth and honour: and all men know that there is none like me: and thou art my race and kindred; and lo, he taketh thee away from me.

117 And when Charisius had so said, Mygdonia saith unto him: He whom I love is better than thee and thy substance: for thy substance is of earth and returneth unto the earth; but he whom I love is of heaven and will take me with him unto heaven. Thy wealth shall pass away, and thy beauty shall vanish, and thy robes, and thy many works: and thou shalt be alone, naked, with thy transgressions. Call not to my remembrance thy deeds (unto me), for I pray the Lord that I may forget thee, so as to remember no more those former pleasures and the custom of the body; which shall pass away as a shadow, but Jesus only endureth for ever, and the souls which hope in him. Jesus himself shall quit me of the shameful deeds which I did with thee. And when Charisius heard this, he turned him to sleep, vexed (dissolved) in soul, saying to her: Consider it by thyself all this night: and if thou wilt be with me such as thou wast before, and not see that sorcerer, I will do all according to thy mind, and if thou wilt remove thine affection from him I will take him out of the prison and let him go and remove into another country, and I will not vex thee, for I know that thou makest much of the stranger. And not with thee first did this matter come about, for many other women also hath he deceived with thee; and they have awaked sober and returned to themselves: do not thou then make nought of my words and cause me to be a reproach among the Indians.

118 And Charisius having thus spoken went to sleep: but she took ten denarii (20 zuze, Syr.), and went secretly to give them to the gaolers that she might enter in to the apostle. But on the way Judus Thomas came and met her, and she saw him and was afraid, for she thought that he was one of the rulers: for a great light went before him. And she said to herself as she fled: have lost thee, O my unhappy soul! for thou wilt not again see Judas the apostle of [JESUS] the living [GOD], and not yet hast thou received the holy seal. And she fled and ran into a narrow place and there hid herself, saying: I would rather choose to be killed (taken) by the poorer, whom it is possible to persuade, than to fall into the hand of this mighty ruler, who will despise gifts.

The Tenth Act: Wherein Mygdonia receiveth baptism.

119 And while Mygdonia thought thus with herself, Judas came and stood over her, and she saw him and was afraid, and fell down and became lifeless with terror. But he stood by her and took her by the hand and said unto her: Fear not, Mygdonia: Jesus will not leave thee, neither will the Lord unto whom thou hast committed thy soul overlook thee. His compassionate rest will not forsake thee: he that is kind will not forsake thee, for his kindness' sake, nor he that is good for his goodness' sake.

Rise up then from the earth, thou that art become wholly above it: look on the light, for the Lord leaveth not them that love him to walk in darkness: behold him that travelleth with his servants, that he is unto them a defender in perils. And Mygdonia arose and looked on him and said: Whither wentest thou, my lord? and who is he that brought thee out of prison to behold the sun? Judas Thomas saith unto her: My Lord Jesus is mightier than all powers and all kings and rulers.

120 And Mygdonia said: Give me the seal of Jesus Christ and I shall (Let me) receive the gift at thy hands before thou departest out of life. And she took him with her and entered into the court and awaked her nurse, saying unto her: Narcia (Gr. Marcia), my mother and nurse, all thy service and refreshment thou hast done for me from my childhood until my present age are vain, and for them I owe thee thanks which are temporal; do for me now also a favor, that thou mayest for ever receive a recompense from him that giveth great gifts. And Narcia in answer saith: What wilt thou, my daughter Mygdonia, and what is to be done for thy pleasure? for the honours which thou didst promise me before, the stranger hath not suffered thee to accomplish, and thou hast made me a reproach among all the nation. And now what is this new thing that thou commandest me? And Mygdonia saith: Become thou partaker with me in eternal life, that I may receive of thee perfect nurture: take bread and bring it me, and wine mingled with water, and spare my freedom (take pity on me a free-born woman, Syr.). And the nurse said: I will bring thee many loaves, and for water flagons of wine, and fulfil thy desire. But she saith to the nurse: Flagons I desire not, nor the many loaves: but this only, bring wine mingled with water and one loaf, and oil [EVEN be a it Syr. lamp, in if].

121 And when Narcia had brought these things, Mygdonia stood before the apostle with her head bare; and he took the oil and poured it on her head, saying: Thou holy oil given unto us for sanctification, secret mystery whereby the cross was shown unto us, thou art the straightener of the crooked limbs, thou art the humbler (softener) of hard things (works), thou art it that showeth the hidden treasures, thou art the sprout of goodness; let thy power come, let it be established upon thy servant Mygdonia, and heal thou her by this freedom. And when the oil was poured upon her he bade her nurse unclothe her and gird a linen cloth about her; and there was there a fountain of water upon which the apostle went up, and baptized Mygdonia in the name of the Father and the Son and the Holy Ghost. And when she was baptized and clad, he brake bread and took a cup of water and made her a partaker in the body of Christ and the cup of the Son of God, and said: Thou hast received thy seal, get for thyself eternal life. And immediately there was heard from above a voice saying: Yea, amen. And when Narcia heard that voice, she was amazed, and besought the apostle that she also might receive the seal; and the apostle gave it her and said: Let the care of the Lord be about thee as about the rest.

122 And having done these things the apostle returned unto the prison, and found the doors open and the guards still sleeping. And Thomas said: Who is like thee, O God? who withholdest not thy loving affection and care from any who is like thee, the merciful, who hast delivered thy creatures out of evil. Life that hath subdued death, rest that hath ended toil. Glory be to the only-begotten of the Father. Glory to the compassionate that was sent forth of his heart. And when he had said thus, the guards waked and beheld all the doors open, and the prisoners <+ asleep, Syr.>, and said in themselves: Did not we fasten the doors? and how are they now open, and the prisoners within?

123 But at the dawn Charisius went unto Mygdonia [AND Syr. nurse, her], and found them praying and saying: O new God that by the stranger hast come hither unto us, hidden God of the dwellers in India (Syr. who art hidden from); God that hast shown thy glory by thine apostle Thomas, God whose report we have heard and believed on thee; God, unto whom we are come to be saved; God, who for love of man and for pity didst come down unto our littleness; God who didst seek us out when we knew him (thee) not; God that dwellest in the heights and from whom the depths are not hid: turn thou away from us the madness of Charisius. And Charisius hearing that said to Mygdonia: Rightly callest thou me evil and mad and foul I for if I had not borne with thy disobedience, and given thee liberty, thou wouldest not have called on God against me and made mention of my name before God. But believe me, Mygdonia that in that sorcerer there is no profit, and what he promiseth to perform he cannot: but I will perform before thy sight all that I promise, that thou mayest believe, and bear with my words and be to me as thou wast beforetime.

124 And he came near and besought her again, saying: If thou wilt be persuaded of me, I shall henceforth have no grief; remember that day when thou didst meet me first; tell the truth: was I more beautiful unto thee at that time, or Jesus at this? And Mygdonia said: That time required its own, and this time also; that was the time of the beginning, but this of the end; that was the time of temporal life, this of eternal; that of pleasure that passeth away, but this of pleasure that abideth for ever; that, of day and night, this of day without night. Thou sawest that marriage that was passing, and here, and single but this marriage continueth for ever; that was a partnership of corruption, but this of eternal life; those groomsmen (and maids) were men and women of time, but these abide unto the end. That marriage upon earth setteth up dropping dew of the love of men

(Syr. That union was founded upon the earth where there is an unceasing press: this is founded upon the bridge of fire upon which is sprinkled grace: both corrupt); that bride-chamber is taken down again, but this remaineth always; that bed was strown with coverlets (that grow old), but this with love and faith. Thou art a bridegroom that passest away and art dissolved (changed), but Jesus is a true bridegroom, enduring for ever immortal, that dowry was of money and robes that grow old, but this is of living words which never pass away.

125 And when Charisius heard these things he went unto the king and told him all: and the king commanded Judas to be brought, that he might judge him and destroy him. But Charisius said: Have patience a little, O king, and first persuade the man making him afraid, that he may persuade Mygdonia to be unto me as formerly. And Misdaeus sent and fetched the apostle of Christ, and all the prisoners were grieved because the apostle departed from them, for they yearned after him, saying: Even the comfort which we had have they taken away from us.

126 And Misdaeus said unto Judas: Wherefore teachest thou this new doctrine, which both gods and men hate, and which hath nought of profit? And Judas said: What evil do I teach? And Misdaeus said: Thou teachest, saying that men [CANNOT chastely live they except well] with the God whom thou preachest. Judas saith: Thou sayest true, O king: thus do I teach. For tell me, art thou not wroth with thy soldiers if they wait on thee in filthy garments? if then thou, being a king of earth and returning unto earth, request thy subjects to be reverend in their doings, are ye wroth and said ye that I teach ill when I say that they who serve my king must be reverend and pure and free from all grief and care of children and unprofitable riches and vain trouble? For indeed thou wouldest have thy subjects follow thy conversation and thy manners, and thou punishest them if they despise thy commandments: how much more must they that believe on him serve my God with much reverence and cleanness and security, and be quit of all pleasures of the body, adultery and prodigality and theft and drunkenness and belly-service and foul deeds?

127 And Misdaeus hearing these things said: Lo, I let thee go: go then and persuade Mygdonia, the wife of Charisius, not to desire to depart from him. Judas saith unto him: Delay not if thou hast aught to do: for her, if she hath rightly received what she hath learned, neither iron nor fire nor aught else stronger than these will avail to hurt or to root out him that is held in her soul. Misdaeus saith unto Judas: Some poisons do dissolve other poisons, and a theriac cureth the bites of the viper; and thou if thou wilt canst give a solvent of those diseases, and make peace and concord betwixt this couple: for by so doing thou wilt spare thyself, for not yet art thou sated with life; and know thou that if thou do not persuade her, I will catch thee away out of this life which is desirable unto all men. And Judas said: This life hath been given as a loan, and this time is one that changeth, but that life whereof I teach is incorruptible; and beauty and youth that are seen shall in a little cease to be. The king saith to him: I have counselled thee for the best, but thou knowest thine own affairs.

128 And as the apostle went forth from before the king, Charisius came to him and entreated him and said: I beseech thee, O man: I have not sinned against thee or any other at any time, nor against the gods; wherefore hast thou stirred up this great calamity against me? and for what cause hast thou brought such disturbance upon mine house? and what profit hast thou of it? but if thou thinkest to gain somewhat, tell me the gain, what it is, and I will procure it for thee without labour. To what end dost thou make me mad, and cast thyself into destruction? for if thou persuade her not, I will both dispatch thee and finally take myself out of life. But if, as thou sayest, after our departing hence there is there life and death, and also condemnation and victory and a place of judgement, then will I also go in thither to be judged with thee: and if that God whom thou preachest is just and awardeth punishment justly, I know that I shall gain my cause against thee; for thou hast injured me, having suffered no wrong at my hands: for indeed even here I am able to avenge myself on thee and bring upon thee all that thou hast done unto me. Therefore be thou persuaded, and come home with me and persuade Mygdonia to be with me as she was at first, before she beheld thee. And Judas saith to him: Believe me, my child that if men loved God as much as they love one another, they would ask of him all things and receive them, and none would do them violence (there would be nothing which would not obey them, Syr.).

129 And as Thomas said this, they came unto the house of Charisius and found Mygdonia sitting and Narcia standing by her, and her hand supporting her cheek; and she was saying: Let the remainder of the days of my life, O mother, be cut off from me, and all the hours become as one hour, and let me depart out of life that I may go the sooner and behold that beautiful one, whose report I have heard, even that living one and giver of life unto them that believe on him, where is not day and night, nor light and darkness, nor good and evil, nor poor and rich, nor male and female, nor free and bond, nor proud that subjecteth the humble. And as she spake the apostle stood by her, and forthwith she rose up and did him reverence. Then Charisius said unto him: Seest thou how she feareth and honoureth thee and all that thou shalt bid her she will do willingly?

130 And as he so spake, Judas saith unto Mygdonia: My daughter Mygdonia, obey that which thy brother Charisius saith. And Mygdonia saith:

If thou wast not able [TO name] the deed in word wilt thou compel me to endure the act? for I have heard of thee that this life is of no profit, and this relief is for a time, and these possessions are transitory. And again thou saidst that whoso renounceth this life shall receive the life eternal, and whoso hateth the light of day and night shall behold a light that is not overtaken, that whoso despiseth this money shall find other and eternal money. But now [THOU things these sayest] because thou art in fear. Who that hath done somewhat and is praised for the work changeth it? [WHO and a tower buildeth] straightway overthroweth it from the foundation? who diggeth a spring water in a thirsty land and straightway filleth it in? who findeth a treasure and useth it not? And Charisius heard lt. and said: I will not imitate you, neither will I hasten to destroy you; nor though I may so do, will I put bonds about thee (but thee I will bind, Syr.); and I will not suffer thee to speak with this sorcerer; and if thou obey me, well, but if not, I know what I must do.

131 And Judas went out of Charisius' house and departed unto the house of Siphor and lodged there with him. And Siphor said: I will prepare for Judas a hall (triclinium) wherein he may teach (Syr. Siphor said to Judas: Prepare thyself an apartment, &c.). And he did so; and Siphor said : I and my wife and daughter will dwell henceforth in holiness, and in chastity, and in one affection. I beseech thee that we may receive of thee the seal, and become worshippers of the true God and numbered among his sheep and lambs. And Judas said: I am afraid to speak that which I think: yet I know somewhat, and what I know it is not possible for me to utter.

132 And he began to say concerning baptism: This baptism is remission of sins (the Greek MSS. U and P have divergent texts, both obscure): this bringeth forth again light that is shed about us: this bringeth to new birth the new man (this is the restorer of understandings Syr.): this mingleth the spirit (with the body), raiseth up in threefoldwise a new man and [MAKETH him] partaker of the remission of sins. Glory be to thee, hidden one, that art communicated in baptism. Glory to thee the unseen power that is in baptism. Glory to thee, renewal, whereby are renewed they that are baptized and with affection take hold upon thee.

And having thus said, he poured oil over their heads and said: Glory be to thee the love of compassion (bowels). Glory to thee name of Christ. Glory to thee, power established in Christ. And he commanded a vessel to be brought, and baptized them in the name of the Father and the Son and the Holy Ghost.

133 And when they were baptized and clad, he set bread on the table and blessed it, and said: Bread of life, the which who eat abide incorruptible: Bread that filleth the hungry souls with the blessing thereof: thou art he that vouchsafest to receive a gift, that thou mayest become unto us remission of sins, and that they who eat thee may become immortal: we invoke upon thee the name of the mother, of the unspeakable mystery of the hidden powers and authorities (? we name the name of the unspeakable mystery, that is hidden from all &c.): we invoke upon thee the name of [thy?] Jesus. And he said: Let the powers of blessing come, and be established in this bread, that all the souls which partake of it may be washed from their sins. And he brake and gave unto Siphor and his wife and daughter.

The Eleventh Act: Concerning the wife of Misdaeus.

134 Now Misdaeus the king, when he had let Judas go, dined and went home, and told his wife what had befallen Charisius their kinsman, saying: See what hath come to pass to that unhappy man, and thou thyself knowest, my sister Tertia, that a man hath nought better than his own wife on whom he resteth; but it chanced that his wife went unto that sorcerer of whom thou hast heard that he is come to the land of the Indians, and fell into his charms and is parted from her own husband; and he knoweth not what he should do. And when I would have destroyed the malefactor, he would not have it. But do thou go and counsel her to incline unto her husband, and forsake the vain words of the sorcerer.

135 And as soon as she arose Tertia went to the house of Charisius her husband's [KINSMAN], and found Mygdonia Lying upon the earth in humiliation, and ashes and sackcloth were spread under her, and she was praying that the Lord would forgive her her former sins and she might soon depart out of life. And Tertia said unto her: Mygdonia, my dear sister and companion what is this hand (Syr. this folly)? what is the disease that hath overtaken thee? and why doest thou the deeds of madmen? Know thyself and come back unto thine own way, come near unto thy many kinsfolk, and spare thy true husband Charisius, and do not things unbefitting a free-woman. Mygdonia saith unto her: O Tertia, thou hast not yet heard the preacher of life: not yet hath he touched thine ears, not yet hast thou tasted the medicine of life nor art freed from corruptible mourning. Thou standest in the life of time, and the everlasting life and salvation thou knowest not, and perceivest not the incorruptible fellowship. Thou standest clad in robes that grow old and desirest not those that are eternal, and art proud of this beauty which vanisheth and hast no thought of the holiness of thy soul; and art rich in a multitude of servants, (and hast not freed thine own soul from servitude, Syr.) and priest thyself in the glory that cometh of many, but redeemest not thyself from the condemnation of death.

136 And when Tertia heard this of Mygdonia she said: I pray thee, sister, bring me unto that stranger that teacheth these great things, that I also may go and hear him, and be taught to worship the God whom he preacheth, and become partaker of his prayers, and a sharer in all that thou hast told me of. And Mygdonia saith to her: He is in the house of Siphor the captain; for he is become the occasion of life unto all them that are being saved in India. And hearing that, Tertia went quickly to Siphor's house, that she might see the new apostle that was come thither. And when she entered in, Judas said unto her: What art thou come to see? a man that is a stranger and poor and contemptible and needy, having neither riches nor substance; yet one thing I possess which neither kings nor rulers can take away, that neither perisheth nor ceaseth, which is Jesus the Saviour of all mankind, the Son of the living God, who hath given life unto all that believe on him and take refuge with him and are known to be of the number of his servants (sheep, Syr.). Unto whom saith Tertia: May I become a partaker of this life which thou promisest that all they shall receive who come together unto the assembly of God. And the apostle said: The treasury of the holy king is opened wide, and they which worthily partake of the good things that are therein do rest, and resting do reign: but first, no man cometh unto him that is unclean and vile: for he knoweth our inmost hearts and the depths of our thought, and it is not possible for any to escape him. Thou, then, if verily thou believest in him, shalt be made worthy of his mysteries; and he will magnify thee and enrich thee, and make thee to be an heir of his kingdom.

137 And Tertia having heard this returned home rejoicing, and found her husband awaiting her, not having dined, and when Misdaeus saw her he said: Whence is it that thine entering in to-day is more beautiful? and wherefore art thou come walking, which beseemeth not free-born women like thee? And Tertia saith unto him: I owe thee the greatest of thanks for that thou didst send me unto Mygdonia, for I went and heard of a new life, and I saw the new apostle of the God that giveth life unto them that believe on him and fulfil his commandments; I ought therefore myself to recompense thee for this favour and admonition with good advice; for thou shalt be a great king in heaven if thou obey me and fear the God that is preached by the stranger, and keep thyself holy unto the living God. For this kingdom passeth away, and thy comfort will be turned into affliction: but go thou to that man, and believe him, and thou shalt live unto the end. And when Misdaeus heard these things of his wife, he smote his face with his hands and rent his clothes and said: May the soul of Charisius find no rest, for he hath hurt me to the soul; and may he have no hope, for he hath taken away my hope. And he went out greatly vexed.

138 And he found Charisius his friend in the market-place, and said unto him: Why hast thou cast me into hell to be another companion to thyself? why hast thou emptied and defrauded me to gain nought? why hast thou hurt me and profited thyself not at all? why hast thou slain me and thyself not lived? Why hast thou wronged me and thyself not got justice? why didst thou not suffer me to destroy that sorcerer before he corrupted my house with his wickedness? And he kept hold upon (was upbraiding, Syr.) Charisius. And Charisius saith: Why, what hath befallen thee? Misdaeus said: He hath bewitched Tertia. And they went both of them unto the house of Siphor the captain, and found Judas sitting and teaching. And all they that were there rose up before the king, but he arose not. And Misdaeus perceived that it was he, and took hold of the seat and overset it, and took up the seat with both his hands and smote his head so that he wounded it, and delivered him to his soldiers, saying: Take him away, and hale him with violence and not gently, that his shame may be manifest unto all men. And they haled him and took him to the place where Misdaeus judged, and he stood there, held of the soldiers of Misdaeus.

The Twelfth Act: Concerning Ouazanes (Iuzanes) the son of Misdaeus.

139 And Ouazanes (Iuzanes, P; Vizan, Syr.) the son of Misdaeus came unto the soldiers and said: Give me him that I may speak with him until the king cometh. And they gave him up, and he brought him in where the king gave judgement. And Iuzanes saith: Knowest thou not that I am the son of Misdaeus the king who is king for a time, but I am the servant of Jesus Christ the eternal king, and thou hast power to say to thy father to save whom thou wilt in the temporal life wherein men continue not, which thou and thy father grant, but I beseech my Lord and intercede for men, and he giveth them a new life which is altogether enduring. And thou boastest thyself of possessions and servants and robes and luxury and unclean chamberings, but I boast myself of poverty and philosophy and humility and lasting and prayer and the fellowship of the Holy Ghost and of my brethren that are worthy of God: and I boast myself of eternal life. And thou reliest on (hast taken refuge with) a man like unto thyself and not able to save his own soul from judgement and death, but I rely upon the living God, upon the saviour of kings and princes, who is the judge of all men. And ye indeed to-day perchance are, and to-morrow are no more, but I have taken refuge with him that abideth for ever and knoweth all our seasons and times. And if thou wilt become the servant of this God thou shalt soon do so; but show that thou wilt be a servant worthy of him hereby: first by holiness (purity), which is the head

of all good things, and then by fellowship with this God whom I preach, and philosophy and simplicity and love and faith and [GOOD hope] in him, and unity of pure food (simplicity of pure i e, Syr.).

140 And the young man was persuaded by the Lord and sought occasion how he might let Judas escape: but while he thought thereon, the king came, and the soldiers took Judas and led him forth. And Iuzanes went forth with him and stood beside him. And when the king was set he bade Judas be brought in, with his hands bound behind him; and he was brought into the midst and stood there. And the king saith: Tell me who thou art and by what power thou doest these things. And Judas saith to him: I am a man like thee, and by the power of Jesus Christ I do these things. And Misdaeus saith: Tell me the truth before I destroy thee. And Judas saith: Thou hast no power against me, as thou supposest, and thou wilt not hurt me at all. And the king was wroth at his words, and commanded to heat iron plates and set him upon them barefoot; and as the soldiers took off his shoes he said: The wisdom of God is better than the wisdom of men. Thou Lord and King (do thou take counsel against them, Syr.) and let thy goodness resist his wrath. And they brought the plates which were like fire, and set the apostle upon them, and straightway water sprang up abundantly from the earth, so that the plates were swallowed up in it, and they that held him let him go and withdrew themselves.

141 And the king seeing the abundance of water said to Judas: Ask thy God that he deliver me from this death, that I perish not in the flood. And the apostle prayed and said: Thou that didst bind this element (nature) and gather it into one place and send it forth into divers lands; that didst bring disorder into order, that grantest mighty works and great wonders by the hands of Judas thy servant; that hast mercy on my soul, that I may always receive thy brightness; that givest wages unto them that have laboured; thou saviour of my soul, restoring it unto its own nature that it may have no fellowship with hurtful things; that hast always been the occasion of life: do thou restrain this element that it lift not up itself to destroy; for there are some of them that stand here who shall believe on thee and live. And when he had prayed, the water was swallowed up by little and little, and the place became dry. And when Misdaeus saw it he commanded him to be taken to the prison: Until I shall consider how he must be used.

142 And as Judas was led away to the prison they all followed him, and Iuzanes the king's son walked at his right hand, and Siphor at the left. And he entered into the prison and sat down, and Iuzanes and Siphor, and he persuaded his wife and his daughter to sit down, for they also were come in to hear the word of life. For they knew that Misdaeus would slay him because of the excess of his anger. And Judas began to say: O liberator of my soul from the bondage of the many, because I gave myself to be sold [UNTO Syr. one,]; behold, I rejoice and exult, knowing that the times are fulfilled for me to enter in and receive [THEE of my Syr. rest, giver]. Lo, I am to be set free from the cares that are on the earth; lo, I fulfil mine hope and receive truth; lo, I am set free from sorrow and put on joy alone; lo, I become careless and griefless and dwell in rest; lo, I am set free from bondage and am called unto liberty; lo, I have served times and seasons, and I am lifted up above times and seasons; lo, I receive my wages from my recompenser, who giveth without reckoning (number) because his wealth sufficeth for the gift; [LO, and my raiment, on off put I] and I shall not put it on again; lo, I sleep and awake, and I shall no more go to sleep; lo, I die and live again, and I shall no more taste of death; lo, they rejoice and expect me, that I may come and be with their kindred and be set as a flower in their crown; lo, I reign in the kingdom whereon I set my hope, even from hence; lo, the rebellious fall before me, for I have escaped them; lo, (unto me) the peace hath come, whereunto all are gathered.

143 And as the apostle spake thus, all that were there hearkened, supposing that in that hour he would depart out of life. And again he said: Believe on the physician of all [DISEASES], both seen and unseen, and on the saviour of the souls that need help from him. This is the free-born [SON] of kings, this the physician of his creatures; this is he that was reproached of his own slaves; this is the Father of the height and the Lord of nature and the Judge (? Father of nature and Lord of the height and supreme Judge, Syr.): he came of the greatest, the only-begotten son of the deep; and he was called the son of (became visible through, Syr.) Mary the virgin, and was termed the son of Joseph the carpenter: he whose littleness (we beheld) with the eyes of our body, but his greatness we received by faith, and saw it in his works whose human body we felt also with our hands, and his aspect we saw transfigured (changed) with our eyes, but his heavenly semblance on the mount we were not able to see: he that made the rulers stumble and did violence unto death: he, the truth that lieth not, that at the last paid the tribute for himself and his disciples: whom the prince beholding feared and the powers that were with him were troubled; and the prince bare witness (asked him, Syr.) who he was and from whence, and knew not the truth, because he is alien from truth: he that having authority over the world, and the pleasures therein, and the possessions and the comfort, [REJECTED] all these things and turneth away his subjects, that they should not use them.

144 And having fulfilled these sayings, he arose and prayed thus: our Father, which art in heaven: hallowed be thy name: Thy kingdom come: Thy will be done, as in heaven so upon earth: [GIVE the of Syr. day, bread constant us] and forgive us our debts as we also have forgiven our debtors. And lead us not into temptation, but deliver us from the evil one. My Lord and God, hope and confidence and teacher, thou hast taught me to pray thus, behold, I pray this prayer and fulfil thy commandment: be thou with me unto the end; thou art he that from childhood hast sown life in me and kept me from corruption; thou art he that hast brought me unto the poverty of this world, and exhorted me unto the true riches; thou art he that hast made me known unto myself and showed me that I am thine; and I have kept myself pure from woman, that that which thou requirest be not found in defilement.

[At the words 'My Lord and God' begins the double text, represented on the one hand by the MS. U and on the other by the Paris MS. P, and three (partly four) others. These insert the prayer after ch. 167. Their text, I believe, may be the original Greek. I follow it here, repeating the first paragraph.]

(144) My Lord and God, my hope and my confidence and my teacher, that hast implanted courage in me, thou didst teach me to pray thus; behold, I pray thy prayer and bring thy will to fulfilment: be thou with me unto the end. Thou art he that from my youth didst give me patience in temptation and [SOW in] me life and preserve me from corruption; thou art he that didst bring me into the poverty of this world and fill me with the true riches; thou art he that didst show me that I was thine: wherefore I was never joined unto a wife, that the temple worthy of thee might not be found in pollution.

145 My mouth sufficeth not to praise thee, neither am I able to conceive the care and providence (carefulness) which hath been about me from thee which thou hast had for me). For I desired to gain riches, but thou by a vision didst show me that they are full of loss and injury to them that gain them and I believed thy showing, and continued in the poverty of the world until thou, the true riches wert revealed unto me, who didst fill both me and the rest that were worthy of thee with thine own riches and set free thine own from care and anxiety. I have therefore fulfilled thy commandments, O Lord, and accomplished thy will, and become poor and needy and a stranger and a bondman and set at nought and a prisoner and hungry and thirsty and naked and unshod, and I have toiled for thy sake, that my confidence might not perish and my hope that is in thee might not be confounded and my much labour might not be in vain and my weariness not be counted for nought: let not my prayers and my continual fastings perish, and my great zeal toward thee; let not my seed of wheat be changed for tares out of thy land, Let not the enemy carry it away and mingle his own tares therewith; for thy land verily receiveth not his tares, neither indeed can they be laid up in thine houses.

146 I have planted thy vine in the earth, it hath sent down its roots into the depth and its growth is spread out in the height, and the fruits of it are stretched forth upon the earth, and they that are worthy of thee are made glad by them, whom also thou hast gained. The money which thou hast from me I laid down upon the table (bank); this, when thou requirest it, restore unto me with usury, as thou hast promised. With thy one mind have I traded and have made ten, thou hast added more to me beside that I had, as thou didst covenant. I have forgiven my debtor the mine, require thou it not at my hands. I was bidden to the supper and I came: and I refused the land and the yoke of oxen and the wife, that I might not for their sake be rejected; I was bidden to the wedding, and I put on white raiment, that I might be worthy of it and not be bound hand and foot and cast into the outer darkness. My lamp with its bright light expecteth the master coming from the marriage, that it may receive him, and I may not (? he may not) see it dimmed because the oil is spent. Mine eyes, O Christ, look upon thee, and mine heart exulteth with joy because I have fulfilled thy will and perfected thy commandments; that I may be likened unto that watchful and careful servant who in his eagerness neglecteth not to keep vigil (other MSS.: I have not slumbered idly in keeping thy commandments: in the first sleep and at midnight and at cockcrow, that mine eyes may behold thee, &c.). All the night have I laboured to keep mine house from robbers, lest it be broken through.

147 My loins have I girt close with truth and bound my shoes on my feet, that I may never see them gaping: mine hands have I put unto the yoked plough and have not turned away backward, lest my furrows go crooked. The plough-land is become white and the harvest is come, that I may receive my wages. My garment that groweth old I have worn out, and the labour that hath brought me unto rest have I accomplished. I have kept the first watch and the second and the third, that I may behold thy face and adore thine holy brightness. I have rooted out the worst (pulled down my barns, Syr.) and left them desolate upon earth, that I may be filled full from thy treasures (Gr. MSS. add: all my substance have I sold, that I may gain thee the pearl). The moist spring that was in me have I dried up, that I may live and rest beside thine inexhaustible spring (al. and Syr.: rest beside thy living spring). The captive whom thou didst commit to me I have slain, that he which is set free in me may not fall from his confidence. Him that was inward have I made outward and the outward [INWARD], and all thy fullness hath been fulfilled in me. I have not returned

unto the things that are behind, but have gone forward unto the things that are before, that I become not a reproach. The dead man have I quickened, and the living one have I overcome, and that which was lacking have I filled up (Syr. Wright, not the older one, inserts negatives, ' not quickened ', &c.), that I may receive the crown of victory, and the power of Christ may be accomplished in me. I have received reproach upon earth, but give thou me the return and the recompense in the heavens. (U omits practically all this chapter.)

148 Let not the powers and the officers perceive me, and let them not have any thought concerning me; let not the publicans and exactors ply their calling upon me; let not the weak and the evil cry out against me that am valiant and humble, and when I am borne upward let them not rise up to stand before me, by thy power, O Jesu, which surroundeth me as a crown: for they do flee and hide themselves, they cannot look on thee: but (for) suddenly do they fall upon them that are subject to them, and the portion of tile sons of the evil one doth itself cry out and convict them; and it is not hid from them, nor their nature is made known: the children of the evil one are separated off. Do thou then grant me, Lord, that I may pass by in quietness and joy and peace, and pass over and stand before the judge, and let not the devil (or slanderer) look upon me; let his eyes be blinded by thy light which thou hast made to dwell in me, close thou up (muzzle) his mouth: for he hath found nought against me.

[We revert to U.]

149 And he said again unto them that were about him: [BELIEVE, the of God and my his Syr. in giver I servants, helper life believe preach; whom Christ Jesus proclaim, children.] believe in the Saviour of them that have laboured in his service: for my soul already flourisheth because my time is near to receive him; for he being beautiful draweth me on always to speak concerning his beauty, what it is though I be not able and suffice not to speak it worthily: thou that art the light (feeder, Syr.) of my poverty and the supplier of my defects and nurturer of my need: be thou with me until I come and receive thee for evermore.

The Thirteenth Act: Wherein Iuzanes receiveth baptism with the rest.

150 And Iuzanes the youth besought the apostle, saying: I pray thee, O man, apostle of God, suffer me to go, and I will persuade the gaoler to permit thee to come home with me, that by thee I may receive the seal, and become thy minister and a keeper of the commandments of the God whom thou preachest. For indeed, formerly I walked in those things which thou teachest, until my father compelled me and joined me unto a wife by name Mnesara; for I am in my one-and-twentieth year, and have now been seven years married, and before I was joined in marriage I knew no other woman, wherefore also I was accounted useless of my father, nor have I ever had son or daughter of this wife and also my wife herself hath lived with me in chastity all this time, and to-day, if she had been in health, and had listened to thee, I know well that both I should have been at rest and she would have received eternal life; but she is in peril and afflicted with much illness; I will therefore persuade the keeper that he promise to come with me, for I live by myself: and thou shalt also heal that unhappy one. And Judas the apostle of the Most High, hearing this, said to Iuzanes: If thou believest, thou shalt see the marvels of God, and how he sayeth his servants.

151 And as they spake thus together, Tertia and Mvgdonia and Narcia stood at the door of the prison, and they gave the gaoler 363 staters of silver and entered in to Judas; and found Iuzanes and Siphor and his wife and daughter, and all the prisoners sitting and hearing the word. And when they stood by him he said to them: Who hath suffered you to come unto us? and who opened unto you the sealed door that ye came forth? Tertia saith unto him: Didst not thou open the door for us and tell us to come into the prison that we might take our brethren that were there, and then should the Lord show forth his glory in us? And when we came near the door, I know not how, thou wast parted from us and hid thyself and camest hither before us where also we heard the noise of the door, when thou didst shut us out. We gave money therefore to the keepers and came in and lo, we are here praying thee that we may persuade thee and let thee escape until the king's wrath against thee shall cease. Unto whom Judas said: Tell us first of all how ye were shut up.

152 And she saith to him: Thou wast with us, and didst never leave us for one hour, and askest thou how we were shut up? but if thou desirest to hear, hear. The king Misdaeus sent for me and said unto me: Not yet hath that sorcercr prevailed over thee, for, as I hear, he bewitcheth men with oil and water and bread, and hath not yet bewitched thee; but obey thou me, for if not, I will imprison thee and wear thee out, and him I will destroy; for I know that if he hath not yet given thee oil and water and bread, he hath not prevailed to get power over thee. And I said unto him: Over my body thou hast authority, and do thou all that thou wilt; but my soul I will not let perish with thee. And hearing that he shut me up in a chamber (beneath his dining-hall, Syr.): and Charisius brought Mygdonia and shut her up with me: and thou broughtest us out and didst bring us even hither; but give thou us the seal quickly, that the hope of Misdacus who counselleth thus may be cut off.

153 And when the apostle heard this, he said: Glory be to thee, O Jesu of many forms, glory to thee that appearest in the guise of our poor man-

hood: glory to thee that encouragest us and makest us strong and givest grace and consolest and standest by us in all perils, and strengthenest our weakness. And as he thus spake, the gaoler came and said: Put out the lamps, lest any accuse you unto the king. And then they extinguished the lamps, and turned to sleep; but the apostle spake unto the Lord: It is the time now, O Jesu, for thee to make haste; for, lo the children of darkness sit (make us to sit, Syr.) in their own darkness, do thou therefore enlighten us with the light of thy nature. And on a sudden the whole prison was light as the day: and while all they that were in the prison slept a deep sleep, they only that had believed in the Lord continued waking.

154 Judas therefore saith to Iuzanes: Go thou before and make ready the things for our need. Iuzanes therefore saith: And who will open me the doors of the prison? for the gaolers shut them and are gone to sleep. And Judas saith: Believe in Jesus, and thou shalt find the doors open. And when he went forth and departed from them, all the rest followed after him. And as Iuzanes was gone on before, Mnesara his wife met him coming unto the prison. And she knew him and said: My brother Iuzanes, is it thou? and he saith, Yea, and art thou Mnesara? and she saith Yea. Iuzanes said unto her; Whither walkest thou, especially at so untimely an hour? and how wast thou able to rise up? And she said: This youth laid his hand on me and raised me up, and in a dream I say that I should go where the stranger sitteth, and become perfectly whole. Iuzanes saith to her: What youth is with thee? And she said: Seest thou not him that is on my right hand, leading me by the hand?

155 And while they spake together thus, Judas, with Siphor and his wife and daughter and Tertia and Mygdonia and Narcia came unto Iuzanes' house. And Mnesara the wife of Iuzanes seeing him did reverence and said: Art thou come that sayedst us from the sore disease? thou art he whom I saw in the night delivering unto me this youth to bring me to the prison. But thy goodness suffered me not to grow weary, but thou thyself art come unto me. And so saying she turned about and saw the youth no more; and finding him not, she saith to the apostle: I am not able to walk alone: for the youth whom thou gavest me is not here. And Judas said: Jesus will henceforth lead thee. And thereafter she came running unto him. And when they entered into the house of Iuzanes the son of Misdaeus the king though it was yet night, a great light shined and was shed about them.

156 And then Judas began to pray and to speak thus: O companion and defender (ally) and hope of the weak and confidence of the poor: refuge and lodging of the weary: voice that came forth of the height (sleep, Gr.): comforter dwelling in the midst: port and harbour of them that pass through the regions of the rulers: physician that healest without payment: who among men wast crucified for many: who didst go down into hell with great might: the sight of whom the princes of death endured not; and thou camest up with great glory, and gathering all them that fled unto thee didst prepare a way, and in thy footsteps all they journeyed whom thou didst redeem; and thou broughtest them into thine own fold and didst join them with thy sheep: son of mercy, the son that for love of man wast sent unto us from the perfect country (fatherland) that is above, the Lord of all possessions (undefiled possessions, Syr.): that servest thy servants that they may live: that fillest creation with thine own riches: the poor, that wast in need and didst hunger forty days: that satisfiest thirsty souls with thine own good things; be thou with Iuzanes the son of Misdaeus and with Tertia and Mnesara, and gather them into thy fold and mingle them with thy number; Be unto them a guide in the land of error: be unto them a physician in the land of sickness: be unto them a rest in the land of the weary: sanctify them in a polluted land: be their physician both of bodies and souls: make them holy temples of thee, and let thine holy spirit dwell in them.

157 Having thus prayed over them, the apostle said unto Mygdonia: Unclothe thy sisters. And she took off their clothes and girded them with girdles and brought them: but Iuzanes had first gone before, and they came after him; and the apostle took oil in a cup of silver and spake thus over it: Fruit more beautiful than all other fruits, unto which none other whatsoever may be compared: altogether merciful: fervent with the force of the word: power of the tree which men putting upon them overcome their adversaries: crowner of the conquerors: help (symbol) and joy of the sick: that didst announce unto men their salvation that showest light to them that are in darkness; whose leaf is bitter, but in thy most sweet fruit thou art fair, that art rough to the sight but soft to the taste; seeming to be weak, but in the greatness of thy strength able to bear the power that beholdeth all things. Having thus said [a corrupt word follows]: Jesu: let his victorious might come and be established in this oil, like as it was established in the tree (wood) that was its kin, even his might at that time, whereof they that crucified thee could not endure the word: let the gift also come whereby breathing upon his (thine) enemies thou didst cause them to go backward and fall headlong and let it rest on this oil, whereupon we invoke thine holy name. And having thus said, he poured it first upon the head of Iuzanes and then upon the women's heads, saying: In thy name, O Jesu Christ, let it be unto these souls for remission of sins and for turning back of the adversary and for salvation of their souls. And he commanded Mygdonia to anoint them but he himself anointed Iu-

zanes. And having anointed them he led them down into the water in the name of the Father and the Son and the Holy Ghost.

158 And when they were come up, he took bread and a cup, and blessed it and said: Thine holy body w}lich was crucified for us do we eat, and thy blood that was shed for us unto salvation do we drink; let therefore thy body be unto us salvation and thy blood for remission of sins. And for the gall which thou didst drink for our sakes let the gall of the devil be removed from us: and for the vinegar which thou hast drunk for us, let our weakness be made strong: and for the spitting which thou didst receive for us, let us receive the dew of thy goodness: and by (or for) the reed wherewith they smote thee for us, let us receive the perfect house: and whereas thou receivedst a crown of thorns for our sake, let us that have loved thee put on a crown that fadeth not away; and for the linen cloth wherein thou wast Wrapped, let us also be girt about with thy power that is not vanquished and for the new tomb and the burial let us receive renewing of soul and body: and for that thou didst rise up and revive, let us revive and live and stand before thee in righteous judgement. And he brake and gave the eucharist unto Iuzanes and Tertia and Mnesara and the wife and daughter of Siphor and said: Let this eucharist be unto you for salvation and joy and health of your souls. And they said: Amen. And a voice was heard, saying: Amen: fear ye not, but only believe.

[THE MARTYRDOM Here we revert to the text of P and its companions.]
159 And after these things Judas departed to be imprisoned.

And Tertia with Mygdonia and Narcia also went to be imprisoned. And the apostle Thomas said unto them -the multitude of them that had believed being present: Daughters and sisters and fellow-servants which have believed in my Lord and God, ministers of my Jesus, hearken to me this day: for I do deliver my word unto you, and I shall no more speak with you in this flesh nor in this world; for I go up unto my Lord and God Jesus Christ, unto him that sold me, unto that Lord that humbled himself even unto me the little, and brought me up unto eternal greatness, that vouchsafed to me to become his servant in truth and steadfastness: unto him do I depart, knowing that the time is fulfilled, and the day appointed hath drawn near for me to go and receive my recompense from my Lord and God: for my recompenser is righteous, who knoweth me, how I ought to receive my reward; for he is not grudging nor envious, but is rich in his gifts, he is not a lover of craft (OT sparing) in that he giveth, for he hath confidence in his possessions which cannot fail.

160 I am not Jesus, but I am his servant: I am not Christ, but I am his minister; I am not the Son of God, but I pray to become worthy of God. Continue ye in the faith of Christ: continue in the hope of the Son of God: faint not at affliction, neither be divided in mind if ye see me mocked or that I am shut up in prison [OR Syr. die,]; for I do accomplish his will. For if I had willed not to die, I know in Christ that I am able thereto: but this which is called death, is not death, but a setting free from the body; wherefore I receive gladly this setting free from the body, that I may depart and see him that is beautiful and full of mercy, him that is to be loved: for I have endured much toil in his service, and have laboured for his grace that is come upon me, which departeth not from me. Let not Satan, then, enter you by stealth and catch away your thoughts: let there be in you no place for him: for he is mighty whom ye have received. Look for the coming of Christ, for he shall come and receive you, and this is he whom ye shall see when he cometh.

161 When the apostle had ended these sayings, they went into the house, and the apostle Thomas said: Saviour that didst suffer many things for us, let these doors be as they were and let seals be set on them. And he left them and went to be imprisoned: and they wept and were in heaviness, for they knew that Misdaeus would slay him (not knowing that, M. would release him, P.).

162 And the apostle found the keepers wrangling and saying: Wherein have we sinned against this wizard? for by his art magic he hath opened the doors and would have had all the prisoners escape: but let us go and report it unto the king, and tell him concerning his wife and his son. And as they disputed thus, Thomas held his peace. They rose up early, therefore, and went unto the king and said unto him: Our lord and king, do thou take away that sorcerer and cause him to be shut up elsewhere, for we are not able to keep him; for except thy good fortune had kept the prison, all the condemned persons would have escaped for now this second time have we found the doors open: and also thy wife, O king, and thy son and the rest depart not from him. And the king, hearing that, went, and found the seals that were set on the doors whole; and he took note of the doors also, and said to the keepers: Wherefore lie ye? for the seals are whole. How said ye that Tertia and Mygdonia come unto him into the prison? And the keepers said: We have told thee the truth.

163 And Misdaeus went to the prison and took his seat, and sent for the apostle Thomas and stripped him (and girded him with a girdle) and set him before him and saith unto him: Art thou bond or free? Thomas said: I am the bondsman of one only, over whom thou hast no authority. And Misdaeus saith to him: How didst thou run away and come into this country? And Thomas said: I was sold hither by my master, that I might save many, and by thy hands depart out of this world. And Misdaeus said: Who is his lord? and what is his name? and of what country is he? And Thomas said: My Lord is thy master and he is Lord of heaven and earth.

And Misdaeus saith: What is his name? Thomas saith: Thou canst not hear his true name at this time: but the name that was given unto him is Jesus Christ. And Misdaeus saith unto him: I have not made haste to destroy thee, but have had long patience with thee: but thou hast added unto thine evil deeds, and thy sorceries are dispersed abroad and heard of throughout all the country: but this I do that thy sorceries may depart with thee, and our land be cleansed from them. Thomas saith unto him; These sorceries depart [NOT, Syr.] with me when I set forth hence, and know thou this that I [THEY, Syr.] shall never forsake them that are here.

164 When the apostle had said these things, Misdaeus considered how he should put him to death; for he was afraid because of the much people that were subject unto him, for many also of the nobles and of them that were in authority believed on him. He took him therefore and went forth out of the city; and armed soldiers also went with him. And the people supposed that the king desired to learn somewhat of him, and they stood still and gave heed. And when they had walked one mile, he delivered him unto four soldiers and an officer, and commanded them to take him into the mountain and there pierce him with spears and put an end to him, and return again to the city. And saying thus unto the soldiers, he himself also returned unto the city.

165 But the men ran after Thomas, desiring to deliver him from death. And two soldiers went at the right hand of the apostle and two on his left, holding spears, and the officer held his hand and supported him. And the apostle Thomas said: O the hidden mysteries which even until our departure are accomplished in us! O riches of his glory, who will not suffer us to be swallowed up in this passion of the body! Four are they that cast me down, for of four am I made; and one is he that draweth me, for of one I am, and unto him I go. And this I now understand, that my Lord and God Jesus Christ being of one was pierced by one, but I, which am of four, am pierced by four.

166 And being come up into the mountain unto the place where he was to be slain, he said unto them that held him, and to the rest: Brethren, hearken unto me now at the last; for I am come to my departure out of the body. Let not then the eyes of your heart be blinded, nor your ears be made deaf. Believe on the God whom I preach, and be not guides unto yourselves in the hardness of your heart, but walk in all your liberty, and in the glory that is toward men, and the life that is toward God.

167 And he said unto Iuzanes: Thou son (to the son, P) of the (earthly) king Misdaeus and minister (to the minister) of our Lord Jesus Christ: give unto the servants of Misdaeus their price that they may suffer me to go and pray. And Iuzanes persuaded the soldiers to let him pray. And the blessed Thomas went to pray, and kneeled down, and rose up and stretched forth his hands unto heaven, and spake thus:

[Here P and the rest give - rightly - the prayer of cc. 144-8. U and its companions give the following: He turned to his prayer; and it was this: My Lord and my God, and hope and redeemer and leader and guide in all countries, be thou with all them that serve thee, and guide me this day as I come unto thee. Let not any take my soul which I have committed unto thee: let not the publicans see me, and let not the exactors accuse me falsely (play the sycophant with me). Let not the serpent see me, and let not the children of the dragon hiss at me. Behold, Lord, I have accomplished thy work and perfected thy commandment. I have become a bondman; therefore to-day do I receive freedom. Do thou therefore give me this and perfect me: and this I say, not for that I doubt, but that they may hear for whom it is needful to hear.]

168 And when he had thus prayed he said unto the soldiers: Come hither and accomplish the commandments of him that sent you. And the four came and pierced him with their spears, and he fell down and died.

And all the brethren wept; and they brought beautiful robes and much and fair linen, and buried him in a royal sepulchre wherein the former (first) kings were laid.

169 But Siphor and Iuzanes would not go down to the city, but continued sitting by him all the day. And the apostle Thomas appeared unto them and said: Why sit ye here and keep watch over me? I am not here, but I have gone up and received all that I was promised. But rise up and go down hence; for after a little time ye also shall be gathered unto me.

But Misdaeus and Charisius took away Mygdonia and Tertia and afflicted them sorely: howbeit they consented not unto their will. And the apostle appeared unto them and said: Be not deceived: Jesus the holy, the living one, shall quickly send help unto you. And Misdaeus and Charisius, when they perceived that Mygdonia and Tertia obeyed them not, suffered them to live according to their own desire.

And the brethren gathered together and rejoiced in the grace of the Holy Ghost: now the apostle Thomas when he departed out of the world made Siphor a presbyter and Iuzanes a deacon, when he went up into the mountain to die. And the Lord wrought with them, and many were added unto the faith.

170 Now it came to pass after a long time that one of the children of Misdaeus the king was smitten by a devil, and no man could cure him, for the devil was exceeding fierce. And Misdaeus the king took thought and sad: I will go and open the sepulchre, and take a bone of the apostle of God and hang it upon my son and he shall be healed. But while Misdaeus thought upon this, the apostle Thomas appeared to him and said unto

him: Thou believedst not on a living man, and wilt thou believe on the dead? yet fear not, for my Lord Jesus Christ hath compassion on thee and pitieth thee of his goodness.

And he went and opened the sepulchre, but found not the apostle there, for one of the brethren had stolen him away and taken him unto Mesopotamia; but from that place where the bones of the apostle had lain Misdaeus took dust and put it about his son's neck, saying: I believe on thee, Jesu Christ, now that he hath left me which troubleth men and opposeth them lest they should see thee. And when he had hung it upon his son, the lad became whole.

Misdaeus the king therefore was also gathered among the brethren, and bowed his head under the hands of Siphor the priest; and Siphor said unto the brethren: Pray ye for Misdaeus the king, that he may obtain mercy of Jesus Christ, and that he may no more remember evil against him. They all therefore, with one accord rejoicing, made prayer for him; and the Lord that loveth men, the King of Kings and Lord of lords, granted Misdaeus also to have hope in him; and he was gathered with the multitude of them that had believed in Christ, glorifying the Father and the Son and the Holy Ghost, whose is power and adoration, now and for ever and world without end. Amen.

Book 101. Acts of Andrew

1 After the Ascension the apostles dispersed to preach in various countries. Andrew began in the province of Achaia, but Matthew went to the city of Mermidona. (The rest of 1 and the whole of 2 give a short abstract of the Acts of Andrew and Matthew which Gregory either found prefixed to his copy of the Acts of Andrew, or thought himself obliged to notice, because of the popularity of the story.)

2 Andrew left Mermidona and came back to his own allotted district. Walking with his disciples he met a blind man who said: 'Andrew, apostle of Christ, I know you can restore my sight, but I do not wish for that: only bid those with you to give me enough money to clothe and feed myself decently.' Andrew said: 'This is the devil's voice, who will not allow the man to recover his sight.' He touched his eyes and healed him. Then, as be had but a vile rough garment, Andrew said: 'Take the filthy garment off him and clothe him afresh.' All were ready to strip themselves, and Andrew said: 'Let him have what will suffice him.' He returned home thankful.

3 Demetrius of Amasea had an Egyptian boy of whom he was very fond, who died of a fever. Demetrius hearing of Andrew's miracles, came, fell at his feet, and besought help. Andrew pitied him, came to the house, held a very long discourse, turned to the bier, raised the boy, and restored him to his master. All believed and were baptized.

4 A Christian lad named Sostratus came to Andrew privately and told him: 'My mother cherishes a guilty passion for me: I have repulsed her, and she has gone to the proconsul to throw the guilt on me. I would rather die than expose her.' The officers came to fetch the boy, and Andrew prayed and went with him. The proconsul bade him defend himself. He was silent, and so continued, until the proconsul retired to take counsel. The mother began to weep. Andrew said: 'Unhappy woman, that dost not fear to cast thine own guilt on thy son.' She said to the proconsul: 'Ever since my son entertained his wicked wish he has been in constant company with this man.' The proconsul was enraged, ordered the lad to be sewn into the leather bag of parricides and drowned in the river, and Andrew to be imprisoned till his punishment should be devised. Andrew prayed, there was an earthquake, the proconsul fell from his seat, every one was prostrated, and the mother withered up and died. The proconsul fell at Andrew's feet praying for mercy. The earthquake and thunder ceased, and he healed those who had been hurt. The proconsul and his house were baptized.

5 The son of Cratinus (Gratinus) of Sinope bathed in the women's bath and was seized by a demon. Cratinus wrote to Andrew for help: he himself had a fever and his wife dropsy. Andrew went there in a vehicle. The boy tormented by the evil spirit fell at his feet. He bade it depart and so it did, with outcries. He then went to Cratinus' bed and told him he well deserved to suffer because of his loose life, and bade him rise and sin no more. He was healed. The wife was rebuked for her infidelity. 'If she is to return to her former sin, let her not now be healed: if she can keep from it, let her be healed.' The water broke out of her body and she was cured. The apostle brake bread and gave it her. She thanked God, believed with all her house, and relapsed no more into sin. Cratinus afterwards sent Andrew great gifts by his servants, and then, with his wife, asked him in person to accept them, but he refused saying: 'It is rather for you to give them to the needy.'

6 After this he went to Nicaea where were seven devils living among the tombs by the wayside, who at noon stoned passersby and had killed many. And all the city came out to meet Andrew with olive branches, crying: 'Our salvation is in thee, O man of God.' When they had told him all, he said: 'If you believe in Christ you shall be freed.' They cried: 'We will.' He thanked God and commanded the demons to appear; they came in the form of dogs. Said he: 'These are your enemies: if you profess your belief that I can drive them out in Jesus' name, I will do so.' They cried

out: 'We believe that Jesus Christ whom thou preachest is the Son of God.' Then he bade the demons go into dry and barren places and hurt no man till the last day. They roared and vanished. The apostle baptized the people and made Callistus bishop.

7 At the gate of Nicomedia he met a dead man borne on a bier, and his old father supported by slaves, hardly able to walk, and his old mother with hair torn, bewailing. 'How has it happened ?' he asked. 'He was alone in his chamber and seven dogs rushed on him and killed him.' Andrew sighed and said: 'This is an ambush of the demons I banished from Nicaea. What will you do, father, if I restore your son ?' 'I have nothing more precious than him, I will give him.' He prayed: 'Let the spirit of this lad return.' The faithful responded, 'Amen'. Andrew bade the lad rise, and he rose, and all cried: 'Great is the God of Andrew.' The parents offered great gifts which he refused, but took the lad to Macedonia, instructing him.

8 Embarking in a ship he sailed into the Hellespont, on the way to Byzantium. There was a great storm. Andrew prayed and there was calm. They reached Byzantium.

9 Thence proceeding through Thrace they met a troop of armed men who made as if to fall on them. Andrew made the sign of the cross against them, and prayed that they might be made powerless. A bright angel touched their swords and they all fell down, and Andrew and his company passed by while they worshipped him. And the angel departed in a great light.

10 At Perinthus he found a ship going to Macedonia, and an angel told him to go on board. As he preached the captain and the rest heard and were converted, and Andrew glorified God for making himself known on the sea.

11 At Philippi were two brothers, one of whom had two sons, the other two daughters. They were rich and noble, and said: 'There is no family as good as ours in the place: let us marry our sons to our daughters.' It was agreed and the earnest paid by the father of the sons. On the wedding-day a word from God came to them: 'Wait till my servant Andrew comes: he will tell you what you should do.' All preparations had been made, and guests bidden, but they waited. On the third day Andrew came: they went out to meet him with wreaths and told him how they had been charged to wait for him, and how things stood. His face was shining so that they marvelled at him. He said: 'Do not, my children, be deceived: rather repent, for you have sinned in thinking to join together those who are near of kin. We do not forbid or shun marriage [this cannot be the author's original sentiment: it is contradicted by all that we know of the Acts]. It is a divine institution: but we condemn incestuous unions.' The parents were troubled and prayed for pardon. The young people saw Andrew's face like that of an angel, and said: 'We are sure that your teaching is true.' The apostle blessed them and departed.

12 At Thessalonica was a rich noble youth, Exoos, who came without his parents' knowledge and asked to be shown the way of truth. He was taught, and believed, and followed Andrew taking no care of his worldly estate. The parents heard that he was at Philippi and tried to bribe him with gifts to leave Andrew. He said: 'Would that you had not these riches, then would you know the true God, and escape his wrath.' Andrew, too, came down from the third storey and preached to them, but in vain: he retired and shut the doors of the house. They gathered a band and came to burn the house, saying: 'Death to the son who has forsaken his parents': and brought torches, reeds, and faggots, and set the house on fire. It blazed up. Exoos took a bottle of water and prayed: 'Lord Jesu Christ, in whose hand is the nature of all the elements, who moistenest the dry and driest the moist, coolest the hot and kindlest the quenched, put out this fire that thy servants may not grow evil, but be more enkindled unto faith.' He sprinkled the flames and they died. 'He is become a sorcerer,' said the parents, and got ladders, to climb up and kill them, but God blinded them. They remained obstinate, but one Lysimachus, a citizen, said: 'Why persevere? God is fighting for these. Desist, lest heavenly fire consume you.' They were touched, and said: 'This is the true God.' It was now night, but a light shone out, and they received sight. They went up and fell before Andrew and asked pardon, and their repentance made Lysimachus say: 'Truly Christ whom Andrew preaches is the Son of God.' All were converted except the youth's parents, who cursed him and went home again, leaving all their money to public uses. Fifty days after they suddenly died, and the citizens, who loved the youth, returned the property to him. He did not leave Andrew, but spent his income on the poor.

13 The youth asked Andrew to go with him to Thessalonica. All assembled in the theatre, glad to see their favourite. The youth preached to them, Andrew remaining silent, and all wondered at his wisdom. The people cried out: 'Save the son of Carpianus who is ill, and we will believe.' Carpianus went to his house and said to the boy: 'You shall be cured to-day, Adimantus.' He said: 'Then my dream is come true: I saw this man in a vision healing me.' He rose up, dressed, and ran to the theatre, outstripping his father, and fell at Andrew's feet. The people seeing him walk after twenty-three years, cried: 'There is none like the God of Andrew.'

14 A citizen had a son possessed by an unclean spirit and asked for his cure. The demon, foreseeing that he would be cast out, took the son aside

into a chamber and made him hang himself. The father said: 'Bring him to the theatre: I believe this stranger is able to raise him.' He said the same to Andrew. Andrew said to the people: 'What will it profit you if you see this accomplished and do not believe?' They said: 'Fear not, we will believe.' The lad was raised and they said: 'It is enough, we do believe.' And they escorted Andrew to the house with torches and lamps, for it was night, and he taught them for three days.

15 Medias of Philippi came and prayed for his sick son. Andrew wiped his cheeks and stroked his head, saying: 'Be comforted, only believe,' and went with him to Philippi. As they entered the city an old man met them and entreated for his sons, whom for an unspeakable crime Medias had imprisoned, and they were putrefied with sores. Andrew said: 'How can you ask help for your son when you keep these men bound? Loose their chains first, for your unkindness obstructs my prayers.' Medias, penitent, said: 'I will loose these two and seven others of whom you have not been told.' They were brought, tended for three days, cured, and freed. Then the apostle healed the son, Philomedes, who had been ill twenty-two years. The people cried: 'Heal our sick as well.' Andrew told Philomedes to visit them in their houses and bid them rise in the name of Jesus Christ, by which he had himself been healed. This was done, and all believed and offered gifts, which Andrew did not accept.

16 A citizen, Nicolaus, offered a gilt chariot and four white mules and four white horses as his most precious possession for the cure of his daughter. Andrew smiled. 'I accept your gifts, but not these visible ones: if you offer this for your daughter, what will you for your soul? That is what I desire of you, that the inner man may recognize the true God, reject earthly things and desire eternal . . .' He persuaded all to forsake their idols, and healed the girl. His fame went through all Macedonia.

17 Next day as he taught, a youth cried out: 'What hast thou to do with us. Art thou come to turn us out of our own place?' Andrew summoned him: 'What is your work?' 'I have dwelt in this boy from his youth and thought never to leave him: but three days since I heard his father say, "I shall go to Andrew": and now I fear the torments thou bringest us and I shall depart.' The spirit left the boy. And many came and asked: 'In whose name dost thou cure our sick?'

Philosophers also came and disputed with him, and no one could resist his teaching.

18 At this time, one who opposed him went to the proconsul Virinus and said: 'A man is arisen in Thessalonica who says the temples should be destroyed and ceremonies done away, and all the ancient law abolished, and one God worshipped, whose servant he says he is.' The proconsul sent soldiers and knights to fetch Andrew. They found his dwelling: when they entered, his face so shone that they fell down in fear. Andrew told those present the proconsul's purpose. The people armed themselves against the soldiers, but Andrew stopped them. The proconsul arrived; not finding Andrew in the appointed place, he raged like a lion and sent twenty more men. They, on arrival, were confounded and said nothing. The proconsul sent a large troop to bring him by force. Andrew said: 'Have you come for me?' 'Yes, if you are the sorcerer who says the gods ought not to be worshipped.' 'I am no sorcerer, but the apostle of Jesus Christ whom I preach.' At this, one of the soldiers drew his sword and cried: 'What have I to do with thee, Virinus, that thou sendest me to one who can not only cast me out of this vessel, but burn me by his power? Would that you would come yourself! you would do him no harm.' And the devil went out of the soldier and he fell dead. On this came the proconsul and stood before Andrew but could not see him. 'I am he whom thou seekest.' His eyes were opened, and he said in anger: 'What is this madness, that thou despisest us and our officers? Thou art certainly a sorcerer. Now will I throw thee to the beasts for contempt of our gods and us, and we shall see if the crucified whom thou preachest will help thee.' Andrew: 'Thou must believe, proconsul, in the true God and his Son whom he hath sent, specially now that one of thy men is dead.' And after long prayer he touched the soldier: 'Rise up: my God Jesus Christ raiseth thee.' He arose and stood whole. The people cried: 'Glory be to our God.' The proconsul: 'Believe not, O people, believe not the sorcerer.' They said: 'This is no sorcery but sound and true teaching.' The proconsul: 'I shall throw this man to the beasts and write about you to Caesar, that ye may perish for contemning his laws.' They would have stoned him, and said: 'Write to Caesar that the Macedonians have received the word of God, and forsaking their idols, worship the true God.'

Then the proconsul in wrath retired to the praetorium, and in the morning brought beasts to the stadium and had the Apostle dragged thither by the hair and beaten with clubs. First they sent in a fierce boar who went about him thrice and touched him not. The people praised God. A bull led by thirty soldiers and incited by two hunters, did not touch Andrew but tore the hunters to pieces, roared, and fell dead. 'Christ is the true God,' said the people. An angel was seen to descend and strengthen the apostle. The proconsul in rage sent in a fierce leopard, which left every one alone but seized and strangled the proconsul's son. But Virinus was so angry that he said nothing of it nor cared. Andrew said to the people: 'Recognize now that this is the true God, whose power subdues the beasts, though Virinus knows him not. But that ye may believe the more, I will raise the dead son, and confound the foolish father.' After long prayer, he raised him.

The people would have slain Virinus, but Andrew restrained them, and Virinus went to the praetorium, confounded.

19 After this a youth who followed the apostle sent for his mother to meet Andrew. She came, and after being instructed, begged him to come to their house, which was devastated by a great serpent. As Andrew approached, it hissed loudly and with raised head came to meet him; it was fifty cubits long: every one fell down in fear. Andrew said: 'Hide thy head, foul one, which thou didst raise in the beginning for the hurt of mankind, and obey the servants of God, and die.' The serpent roared, and coiled about a great oak near by and vomited poison and blood and died. Andrew went to the woman's farm, where a child killed by the serpent lay dead. He said to the parents: 'Our God who would have you saved hath sent me here that you may believe on him. Go and see the slayer slain.' They said: 'We care not so much for the child's death, if we be avenged.' They went, and Andrew said to the proconsul's wife (her conversion has been omitted by Gregory): 'Go and raise the boy.' She went, nothing doubting, and said: 'In the name of my God Jesus Christ, rise up whole.' The parents returned and found their child alive, and fell at Andrew's feet.

20 On the next night he saw a vision which he related. 'Hearken, beloved, to my vision. I beheld, and lo, a great mountain raised up on high, which had on it nothing earthly, but only shone with such light, that it seemed to enlighten all the world. And lo, there stood by me my beloved brethren the apostles Peter and John; and John reached his hand to Peter and raised him to the top of the mount, and turned to me and asked me to go up after Peter, saying: "Andrew, thou art to drink Peter's cup." And he stretched out his hands and said: "Draw near to me and stretch out thy hands so as to join them unto mine, and put thy head by my head." When I did so I found myself shorter than John. After that he said to me: "Wouldst thou know the image of that which thou seest, and who it is that speaketh to thee?" and I said: "I desire to know it." And he said to me: "I am the word of the cross whereon thou shalt hang shortly, for his name's sake whom thou preachest." And many other things said he unto me, of which I must now say nothing, but they shall be declared when I come unto the sacrifice. But now let all assemble that have received the word of God, and let me commend them unto the Lord Jesus Christ, that he may vouchsafe to keep them unblemished in his teaching. For I am now being loosed from the body, and go unto that promise which he hath vouchsafed to promise me, who is the Lord of heaven and earth, the Son of God Almighty, very God with the Holy Ghost, continuing for everlasting ages.'

(I feel sure that John in the latter part of this vision has been substituted by Gregory for Jesus. The echoes of the Acts of John and of Peter are very evident here.)

All the brethren wept and smote their faces. When all were gathered, Andrew said: 'Know, beloved, that I am about to leave you, but I trust in Jesus whose word I preach, that he will keep you from evil, that this harvest which I have sown among you may not be plucked up by the enemy, that is, the knowledge and teaching of my Lord Jesus Christ. But do ye pray always and stand firm in the faith, that the Lord may root out all tares of offence and vouchsafe to gather you into his heavenly garner as pure wheat.' So for five days he taught and confirmed them: then he spread his hands and prayed: 'Keep, I beseech thee, O Lord, this flock which hath now known thy salvation, that the wicked one may not prevail against it, but that what by thy command and my means it hath received, it may be able to preserve inviolate for ever.' And all responded 'Amen'. He took bread, brake it with thanksgiving, gave it to all, saying: 'Receive the grace which Christ our Lord God giveth you by me his servant.' He kissed every one and commended them to the Lord, and departed to Thessalonica, and after teaching there two days, he left them.

21 Many faithful from Macedonia accompanied him in two ships. And all were desirous of being on Andrew's ship, to hear him. He said: 'I know your wish, but this ship is too small. Let the servants and baggage go in the larger ship, and you with me in this.' He gave them Anthimus to comfort them, and bade them go into another ship which he ordered to keep always near . . . that they might see him and hear the word of God. (This is a little confused.) And as he slept a little, one fell overboard. Anthimus roused him, saying: 'Help us, good master; one of thy servants perisheth.' He rebuked the wind, there was a calm, and the man was borne by the waves to the ship. Anthimus helped him on board and all marvelled. On the twelfth day they reached Patrae in Achaia, disembarked, and went to an inn.

22 Many asked him to lodge with them, but he said he could only go where God bade him. That night he had no revelation, and the next night, being distressed at this, he heard a voice saying: 'Andrew, I am alway with thee and forsake thee not,' and was glad.

Lesbius the proconsul was told in a vision to take him in, and sent a messenger for him. He came, and entering the proconsul's chamber found him lying as dead with closed eyes; he struck him on the side and said: 'Rise and tell us what hath befallen thee.' Lesbius said: 'I abominated the way which you teach and sent soldiers in ships to the proconsul of Macedonia to send you bound to me, but they were wrecked and could not reach their destination. As I continued in my purpose of destroying your Way, two black men (Ethiopes) appeared and scourged me, saying: "We can no longer prevail here, for the man is coming whom you mean to persecute. So to-night, while we still have the power, we will avenge ourselves on you." And they beat me sorely and left me. But now do you pray that I may be pardoned and healed.' Andrew preached the word and all believed, and the proconsul was healed and confirmed in the faith.

23 Now Trophima, once the proconsul's mistress, and now married to another, left her husband and clave to Andrew. Her husband came to her lady (Lesbius' wife) and said she was renewing her liaison with the proconsul. The wife, enraged, said: 'This is why my husband has left me these six months.' She called her steward (procurator) and had Trophima sentenced as a prostitute and sent to the brothel. Lesbius knew nothing, and was deceived by his wife, when he asked about her. Trophima in the brothel prayed continually, and had the Gospel on her bosom, and no one could approach her. One day one offered her violence, and the Gospel fell to the ground. She cried to God for help and an angel came, and the youth fell dead. After that, she raised him, and all the city ran to the sight.

Lesbius' wife went to the bath with the steward, and as they bathed an ugly demon came and killed them both. Andrew heard and said: 'It is the judgement of God for their usage of Trophima.' The lady's nurse, decrepit from age, was carried to the spot, and supplicated for her. Andrew said to Lesbius: 'Will you have her raised?' 'No, after all the ill she has done.' 'We ought not to be unmerciful.' Lesbius went to the praetorium; Andrew raised his wife, who remained shamefaced: he bade her go home and pray. 'First', she said, 'reconcile me to Trophima whom I have injured.' 'She bears you no malice.' He called her and they were reconciled. Callisto was the wife.

Lesbius, growing in faith, came one day to Andrew and confessed all his sins. Andrew said: 'I thank God, my son, that thou fearest the judgement to come. Be strong in the Lord in whom thou believest.' And he took his hand and walked with him on the shore.

24 They sat down, with others, on the sand, and he taught. A corpse was thrown up by the sea near them. 'We must learn', said Andrew, 'what the enemy has done to him.' So he raised him, gave him a garment, and bade him tell his story. He said: 'I am the son of Sostratus, of Macedonia, lately come from Italy. On returning home I heard of a new teaching, and set forth to find out about it. On the way here we were wrecked and all drowned.' And after some thought, he realized that Andrew was the man he sought, and fell at his feet and said: 'I know that thou art the servant of the true God. I beseech thee for my companions, that they also may be raised and know him.' Then Andrew instructed him, and thereafter prayed God to show the bodies of the other drowned men: thirty-nine were washed ashore, and all there prayed for them to be raised. Philopator, the youth, said: 'My father sent me here with a great sum. Now he is blaspheming God and his teaching. Let it not be so.' Andrew ordered the bodies to be collected, and said: 'Whom will you have raised first?' He said: 'Warus my foster-brother.' So he was first raised and then the other thirty-eight. Andrew prayed over each, and then told the brethren each to take the hand of one and say: 'Jesus Christ the son of the living God raiseth thee.'

Lesbius gave much money to Philopator to replace what he had lost, and he abode with Andrew.

25 A woman, Calliopa, married to a murderer, had an illegitimate child and suffered in travail. She told her sister to call on Diana for help; when she did so the devil appeared to her at night and said: 'Why do you trouble me with vain prayers? Go to Andrew in Achaia.' She came, and he accompanied her to Corinth, Lesbius with him. Andrew said to Calliopa: 'You deserve to suffer for your evil life: but believe in Christ, and you will be relieved, but the child will be born dead.' And so it was.

26 Andrew did many signs in Corinth. Sostratus the father of Philopator, warned in a vision to visit Andrew, came first to Achaia and then to Corinth. He met Andrew walking with Lesbius, recognized him by his vision, and fell at his feet. Philopator said: 'This is my father, who seeks to know what he must do.' Andrew: 'I know that he is come to learn the truth; we thank God who reveals himself to believers.' Leontius the servant of Sostratus, said to him: 'Seest thou, sir, how this man's face shineth?' 'I see, my beloved,' said Sostratus; 'let us never leave him, but live with him and hear the words of eternal life.' Next day they offered Andrew many gifts, but he said: 'It is not for me to take aught of you but your own selves. Had I desired money, Lesbius is richer.'

27 After some days he bade them prepare him a bath; and going there saw an old man with a devil, trembling exceedingly. As he wondered at him, another, a youth, came out of the bath and fell at his feet, saying: 'What have we to do with thee, Andrew? Hast thou come here to turn us out of our abodes?' Andrew said to the people: 'Fear not,' and drove out both the devils. Then, as he bathed, he told them: 'The enemy of mankind lies in wait everywhere, in baths and in rivers; therefore we ought always to invoke the Lord's name, that he may have w power over us.'

They brought their sick to him to be healed, and so they did from other cities.

28 An old man, Nicolaus, came with clothes rent and said: 'I am seventy-four years old and have always been a libertine. Three days ago I heard of your miracles and teaching. I thought I would turn over a new leaf, and then again that I would not. in this doubt, I took a Gospel and prayed God to make me forget my old devices. A few days after, I forgot the Gospel I had about me, and went to the brothel. The woman said: "Depart, old man, depart: thou art an angel of God, touch me not nor approach me, for I see in thee a great mystery." Then I remembered the Gospel, and am come to you for help and pardon.' Andrew discoursed long against incontinence, and prayed from the sixth to the ninth hour. He rose and washed his face and said: 'I will not eat till I know if God will have mercy on this man.' A second day he fasted, but had no revelation until the fifth day, when he wept vehemently and said: 'Lord, we obtain mercy for the dead, and now this man that desireth to know thy greatness, wherefore should he not return and thou heal him?' A voice from heaven said: 'Thou hast prevailed for the old man; but like as thou art worn with fasting, let him also fast, that he may be saved.' And he called him and preached abstinence. On the sixth day he asked the brethren all to pray for Nicolaus, and they did. Andrew then took food and permitted the rest to eat. Nicolaus went home, gave away all his goods, and lived for six months on dry bread and water. Then he died. Andrew was not there, but in the place where he was he heard a voice: 'Andrew, Nicolaus for whom thou didst intercede, is become mine.' And he told the brethren that Nicolaus was dead, and prayed that he might rest in peace.

29 And while he abode in that place (probably Lacedaemon) Antiphanes of Megara came and said: 'If there be in thee any kindness, according to the command of the Saviour whom thou preachest, show it now.' Asked what his story was, he told it. Returning from a journey, I heard the porter of my house crying out. They told me that he and his wife and son were tormented of a devil. I went upstairs and found other servants gnashing their teeth, running at me, and laughing madly. I went further up and found they had beaten my wife: she lay with her hair over her face unable to recognize me. Cure her, and I care nothing for the others.' Andrew said: 'There is no respect of persons with God. Let us go there.' They went from Lacedaemon to Megara, and when they entered the house, all the devils cried out: 'What dost thou here, Andrew? Go where thou art permitted: this house is ours.' He healed the wife and all the possessed persons, and Antiphanes and his wife became firm adherents.

30 He returned to Patrae where Egeas was now proconsul, and one Iphidamia, who had been converted by a disciple, Sosias, came and embraced his feet and said: 'My lady Maximilla who is in a fever has sent for you. The proconsul is standing by her bed with his sword drawn, meaning to kill himself when she expires.' He went to her, and said to Egeas: 'Do thyself no harm, but put up thy sword into his place. There will be a time when thou wilt draw it on me.' Egeas did not understand, but made way. Andrew took Maximilla's hand, she broke into a sweat, and was well: he bade them give her food. The proconsul sent him 100 pieces of silver, but he would not look at them.

31 Going thence he saw a sick man lying in the dirt begging, and healed him.

32 Elsewhere he saw a blind man with wife and son, and said: 'This is indeed the devil's work: he has blinded them in soul and body.' He opened their eyes and they believed.

33 One who saw this said: 'I beg thee come to the harbour; there is a man, the son of a sailor, sick fifty years, cast out of the house, lying on the shore, incurable, full of ulcers and worms.' They went to him. The sick man said: 'Perhaps you are the disciple of that God who alone can save.' Andrew said: 'I am he who in the name of my God can restore thee to health,' and added: 'In the name of Jesus Christ, rise and follow me.' He left his filthy rags and followed, the pus and worms flowing from him. They went into the sea, and the apostle washed him in the name of the Trinity and he was whole, and ran naked through the city proclaiming the true God.

34 At this time the proconsul's brother Stratocles arrived from Italy. One of his slaves, Alcman, whom he loved, was taken by a devil and lay foaming in the court. Stratocles hearing of it said: 'Would the sea had swallowed me before I saw this.' Maximilla and Iphidamia said: 'Be comforted: there is here a man of God, let us send for him.' When he came he took the boy's hand and raised him whole. Stratocles believed and clave to Andrew.

35 Maximilla went daily to the praetorium and sent for Andrew to teach there. Egeas was away in Macedonia, angry because Maximilla had left him since her conversion. As they were all assembled one day, he returned, to their great terror. Andrew prayed that he might not be suffered to enter the place till all had dispersed. And Egeas was at once seized with indisposition, and in the interval the apostle signed them all and sent them away, himself last. But Maximilla on the first opportunity came to Andrew and received the word of God and went home. [At about this point we must place the episodes quoted by Evodius of Uzala: see below.]

36 After this Andrew was taken and imprisoned by Egeans, and all came to the prison to be taught. After a few days he was scourged and crucified; he hung for three days, preaching, and expired, as is fully set forth in his Passion. Maximilla embalmed and buried his body.

37 From the tomb comes manna like flour, and oil: the amount shows the barrenness or fertility of the coming season -as I have told in my first book of Miracles. I have not set out his Passion at length, because I find it well done by some one else.

38 This much have I presumed to write, unworthy, unlettered, &c. The author's prayer for himself ends the book. May Andrew, on whose death-day he was born, intercede to save him.

(The Passion to which Gregory alludes is that which begins Conversante et docente'.)

Of the detached fragments and quotations which precede the Passion there are three:

(a) One is in the Epistle of Titus.

When, finally, Andrew also [John has been cited shortly before] had come to a wedding, he too, to manifest the glory of God, disjoined certain who were intended to marry each other, men and women, and instructed them to continue holy in the single state.

No doubt this refers to the story in Gregory, ch. 11. Gregory, it may be noted, has altered the story (or has used an altered text), for the marriage of cousins was not forbidden till Theodosius' time (so Flamion). He or his source has imagined the relationship between the couples; in the original Acts none need have existed: the mere fact of the marriage was enough.

(b) The next are in a tract by Evodius, bishop of Uzala, against the Manichees:

Observe, in the Acts of Leucius which he wrote under the name of the apostles, what manner of things you accept about Maximilla the wife of Egetes: who, refusing to pay her due to her husband (though the apostle has said: Let the husband pay the due to the wife and likewise the wife to the husband: 1 Cor. vii. 3), imposed her maid Euclia upon her husband, decking her out, as is there written, with wicked (lit. hostile) enticements and paintings, and substituted her as deputy for herself at night, so that he in ignorance used her as his wife.

There also is it written, that when this same Maximilla and Iphidamia were gone together to hear the apostle Andrew, a beautiful child, who, Leucius would have us understand, was either God or at least an angel, escorted them to the apostle Andrew and went to the praetorium of Egetes, and entering their chamber feigned a woman's voice, as of Maximilla, complaining of the sufferings of womankind, and of Iphidamia replying. When Egetes heard this dialogue, he went away. [These incidents must have intervened between cc. 35 and 36 of Gregory of Tours.]

(c) Evodius quotes another sentence, not certainly from the Acts of Andrew, but more in their manner than in that of John or Peter:

In the Acts written by Leucius, which the Manichees receive, it is thus written:

For the deceitful figments and pretended shows and collection (force, compelling) of visible things do not even proceed from their own nature, but from that man who of his own will has become worse through seduction.

It is obscure enough, in original and version: but is the kind of thing that would appeal to those who thought of material things and phenomena as evil.

We do not wonder that such narratives as that which Evodius quotes have been expunged, either by Gregory or his source, from the text.

The next passage is a fragment of some pages in length found by M. Bonnet in a Vatican MS. (Gr. 808) of tenth to eleventh century. There is no doubt that it is a piece of the original Acts. It is highly tedious in parts. Andrew in prison discourses to the brethren.

1 . . . is there in you altogether slackness? are ye not yet convinced of yourselves that ye do not yet bear his goodness? let us be reverent, let us rejoice with ourselves in the bountiful (ungrudging) fellowship which cometh of him. Let us say unto ourselves: Blessed is our race! by whom hath it been loved? blessed is our state! of whom hath it obtained mercy? we are not cast on the ground, we that have been recognized by so great highness: we are not the offspring of time, afterward to be dissolved by time; we are not a contrivance (product) of motion, made to be again destroyed by itself, nor things of earthly birth. ending again therein. We belong, then, to a greatness, unto which we aspire, of which we are the property, and peradventure to a greatness that hath mercy upon us. We belong to the better; therefore we flee from the worse: we belong to the beautiful, for whose sake we reject the foul; to the righteous, by whom we cast away the unrighteous, to the merciful, by whom we reject the unmerciful; to the Saviour, by whom we recognize the destroyer; to the light, by whom we have cast away the darkness; to the One, by whom we have turned away from the many; to the heavenly, by whom we have learned to know the earthly; to the abiding, by whom we have seen the transitory. If we desire to offer unto God that hath had mercy on us a worthy thanksgiving or confidence or hymn or boasting, what better cause (theme) have we than that we have been recognized by him?

2 And having discoursed thus to the brethren, he sent them away every one to his house, saying to them: Neither are ye ever forsaken of me, ye that are servants of Christ, because of the love that is in him: neither again shall I be forsaken of you because of his intercession (mediation). And every one departed unto his house: and there was among them rejoicing after his sort for many days, while Aegeates took not thought to prosecute the accusation against the Apostle. Every one of them then was confirmed at that time in hope toward the Lord, and they assembled without fear in the prison, with Maximilla, Iphidamia, and the rest, continually, being sheltered by the protection and grace of the Lord.

3 But one day Aegeates, as he was hearing causes, remembered the matter concerning Andrew: and as one seized with madness, he left the cause which he had in hand, and rose up from the judgement seat and ran quickly to the praetorium, inflamed with love of Maximilla and desiring to persuade her with flatteries. And Maximilla was beforehand with him, coming from the prison and entering the house. And he went in and said to her:

4 Maximilla, thy parents counted me worthy of being thy consort, and gave me thine hand in marriage, not looking to wealth or descent or renown, but it may be to my good disposition of soul: and, that I may pass over much that I might utter in reproach of thee, both of that which I have enjoyed at thy parents' hands and thou from me during all our life, I am come, leaving the court, to learn of thee this one thing: answer me then reasonably, if thou wert as the wife of former days, living with me in the way we know, sleeping, conversing, bearing offspring with me, I would deal well with thee in all points; nay more, I would set free the stranger whom I hold in prison: but if thou wilt not to thee I would do nothing harsh, for indeed I cannot; but him, whom thou affectionest more than me, I will afflict yet more. Consider, then, Maximilla, to whether of the two thou inclinest, and answer me to-morrow; for I am wholly armed for this emergency.

5 And with these words he went out; but Maximilla again at the accustomed hour, with Iphidamia, went to Andrew: and putting his hands before her own eyes, and then putting them to her mouth, she began to declare to him the whole rmatter of the demand of Aegeates. And Andrew answered her: I know, Maximilla my child, that thou thyself art moved to resist the whole attraction (promise) of nuptial union, desiring to be quit of a foul and polluted way of life: and this hath long been firmly held in thine (MS. mine) intention; but now thou wishest for the further testimony of mine opinion. I testify, O Maximilla: do it not; be not vanquished by the threat of Aegeates: be not overcome by his discourse: fear not his shameful counsels: fall not to his artful flatteries: consent not to surrender thyself to his impure spells, but endure all his torments looking unto us for a little space, and thou shalt see him whoily numbed and withering away from thee and from all that are akin to thee. But (For) that which I most needed to say to thee -for I rest not till I fulfil the business which is seen, and which cometh to pass in thy person- hath escaped me: and rightly in thee do I behold Eve repenting, and in myself Adam returning; for that which she suffered in ignorance, thou now (for whose soul I strive) settest right by returning: and that which the spirit suffered which was overthrown with her and slipped away from itself, is set right in me, with thee who seest thyself being brought back. For her defect thou hast remedied by not suffering like her; and his imperfection I have perfected by taking refuge with God, that which she disobeyed thou hast obeyed: that whereto he consented I flee from: and that which they both transgressed we have been aware of, for it is ordained that every one should correct (and raise up again) his own fall.

6 I, then, having said this as I have said it, would go on to speak as followeth: Well done, O nature that art being saved for thou hast been strong and hast not hidden thyself (from God like Adam)! Well done, O soul that criest out of what thou hast surfered, and returnest unto thyself ! Well done, O man that understandest what is thine and dost press on to what is thine! Well done, thou that hearest what is spoken, for I see thee to be greater than things that are thought or spoken! I recognize thee as more powerful than the things which seemed to overpower thee; as more beautiful than those which cast thee down into foulness, which brought thee down into captivity. Perceiving then, O man, all this in thyself, that thou art immaterial, holy light, akin to him that is unborn, that thou art intellectual, heavenly, translucent, pure, above the flesh, above the world, above rulers, above principalities, over whom thou art in truth, then comprehend thyself in thy condition and receive full knowledge and understand wherein thou excellest: and beholding thine own face in thine essence, break asunder all bonds -I say not only those that are of thy birth, but those that are above birth, whereof we have set forth to thee the names which are excecding great -desire earnestly to see him that is revealed unto thee, him who doth not come into being, whom perchance thou alone shalt recognize with confidence.

7 These things have I spoken of thee, Maximilla, for in their meaning the things I have spoken reach unto thee. Like as Adam died in Eve because he consented unto her confession, so do I now live in thee that keepest the Lord's commandment and stablishest thyself in the rank (dignity) of thy being. But the threats of Aegeates do thou trample down, Maximilla, knowing that we have God that hath mercy on us. And let not his noise move thee, but continue chaste- and let him punish me not only with such torments as bonds, but let him cast me to the beasts or burn me with fire, and throw me from a precipice. And what need I say? there is but this one body; let him abuse that as he will, for it is akin to himself.

8 And yet again unto thee is my speech, Maximilla: I say unto thee, give not thyself over unto Aegeates: withstand his ambushes- for indeed, Maximilla, I have seen my Lord saying unto me: Andrew, Aegeates' father the devil will loose thee from this prison. Thine, therefore, let it be henceforth to keep thyself chaste and pure, holy, unspotted, sincere, free from adultery, not reconciled to the discourses of our enemy, unbent, unbroken,

tearless, unwounded, not storm-tossed, undivided, not stumbling without fellow-feeling for the works of Cain. For if thou give not up thyself, Maximilla, to what is contrary to these, I also shall rest, though I be thus forced to leave this life for thy sake that is, for mine own. But if I were thrust out hence, even I, who, it may be, might avail through thee to profit others that are akin to me, and if thou wert persuaded by the discourse of Aegeates and the flatteries of his father the serpent, so that thou didst turn unto thy former works, know thou that on thine account I should be tormented until thou thyself sawest that I had contemned life for the sake of a soul which was not worthy.

9 I entreat, therefore, the wise man that is in thee that thy mind continue clear seeing. I entreat thy mind that is not seen, that it be preserved whole: I beseech thee, love thy Jesus, and yield not unto the worse. Assist me, thou whom I entreat as a man, that I may become perfect: help me also, that thou mayest recognize thine own true nature: feel with me in my suffering, that thou mayest take knowledge of what I suffer, and escape suffering see that which I see, and thou shalt be blind to what thou seest: see that which thou shouldst, and thou shalt not see that thou shouldst not: hearken to what I say, and cast away that which thou hast heard.

10 These things have I spoken unto thee and unto every one that heareth, if he will hear. But thou, O Stratocles, said he, looking toward him, Why art thou so oppressed, with many tears and groanings to be heard afar off? what is the lowness of spirit that is on thee? why thy much pain and thy great anguish? dost thou take note of what is said, and wherefore I pray thee to be disposed in mind as my child? (or, my child, to be composed in mind): dost thou perceive unto whom my words are spoken? hath each of them taken hold on thine understanding? have they whetted (MS. touched) thine intellectual part? have I thee as one that hath hearkened to me? do I find myself in thee? is there in thee one that speaketh whom I see to be mine own? doth he love him that speaketh in me and desire to have fellowship with him? doth he wish to be made one with him? doth lie hasten to become his friend? doth he yearn to be joined with him? doth he find in him any rest? hath he where to lay his head? doth nought oppose him there? nought that is wroth with him, resisteth him, hateth him, fleeth from him, is savage, avoideth, turneth away, starteth off, is burdened, maketh war, talketh with others, is flattered by others, agreeth with others? Doth nothing else disturb him? Is there one within that is strange to me? an adversary, a breaker of peace, an enemy, a cheat, a sorcerer, a crooked dealer, unsound, guileful, a hater of men, a hater of the word, one like a tyrant, boastful, puffed up, mad, akin to the serpent, a weapon of the devil, a friend of the fire, belonging to darkness? Is there in thee any one, Stratocles, that cannot endure my saying these things? Who is it? Answer: do I talk in vain? have I spoken in vain? Nay, saith the man in thee, Stratocles, who now again weepeth.

11 And Andrew took the band of Stratocles and said: I have him whom I loved; I shall rest on him whom I look for; for thy yet groaning, and weeping without restraint, is a sign unto me that I have already found rest, that I have not spoken to thee these words which are akin to me, in vain.

12 And Stratocles answered him: Think not, most blessed Andrew, that there is aught else that afflicteth me but thee; for the words that come forth of thee are like arrows of fire shot against me, and every one of them reacheth me and verily burneth me up. That part of my soul which inclineth to what I hear is tormented, divining the affliction that is to follow, for thou thyself departest, and, I know, nobly: but hereafter when I seek thy care and affection, where shall I find it, or in whom? I have received the seeds of the words of salvation, and thou wast the sower: but that they should sprout up and grow needs none other but thee, most blessed Andrew. And what else have I say to thee but this? I need much mercy and help from thee, to become worthy of the seed I have from thee, which will not otherwise increase perpetually or grow up into the light except thou willest it, and prayest for them and for the whole of me.

13 And Andrew answered him: This, my child, was what I beheld in thee myself. And I glorify my Lord that my thought of thee walked not on the void, but knew what it said. But that ye may know the truth, to-morrow doth Aegeates deliver me up to be crucified: for Maximilla the servant of the Lord will enrage the enemy that is in him, unto whom he belongeth, by not consenting to that which is hateful to her; and by turning against me he will think to console himself.

14 Now while the apostle spake these things, Maximilla was not there, for she having heard throughout the words wherewith he answered her, and being in part composed by them, and of such a mind as the words pointed out, set forth not inadvisedly nor without purpose and went to the praetorium. And she bade farewell to all the life of the flesh, and when Aegeates brought to her the same demand which he had told her to consider, whether she would lie with him, she rejected it- and thenceforth he bent himself to putting Andrew to death, and thought to what death he should expose him. And when of all deaths crucifixion alone prevailed with him, he went away with his like and dined; and Maximilla, the Lord going before her in the likeness of Andrew, with Iphidamia came back to the prison- and there being therein a great gathering of the brethren, she found Andrew discoursing thus:

15 I, brethren, was sent forth by the Lord as an apostle unto these regions whereof my Lord thought me worthy, not to teach any man, but to remind every man that is akin to such words that they live in evils which are temporal, delighting in their injurious delusions: wherefrom I have always exhorted you also to depart, and encouraged you to press toward things that endure, and to take flight from all that is transitory (flowing)- for ye see that none of you standeth, but that all things, even to the customs of men, are easily changeable. And this befalleth because the soul is untrained and erreth toward nature and holdeth pledges toft its error. I therefore account them blessed who have become obedient unto the word preached, and thereby see the mysteries of their own nature; for whose sake all things have been builded up.

16 I enjoin you therefore, beloved children, build yourselves firmly upon the foundation that hath been laid for you, which is unshaken, and against which no evil- willer can conspire. Be then, rooted upon this foundation: be established, remembering what ye have seen (or heard) and all that hath come to pass while I walked with you all. Ye have seen works wrought through me which ye have no power to disbelieve, and such signs come to pass as perchance even dumb nature will proclaim aloud; I have delivered you words which I pray may so be received by you as the words themselves would have it. Be established then, beloved upon all that ye have seen, and heard, and partaken of. And God on whom ye have believed shall have mercy on you and present you lmto himself, giving you rest unto all ages.

17 Now as for that which is to befall me, let it not really trouble you as some strange spectacle, that the servant of God unto whom God himself hath granted much in deeds and words, should by an evil man be driven out of this temporal life: for not only unto me will this come to pass, but unto all them that have loved and believed on him and confess him. The devil that is wholly shameless will arm his own children against them, that they may consent unto him; and he will not have his desire. And wherefore he essayeth this I will tell you. From the beginning of all things, and if I may so say, since he that hath no beginning came down to be under his rule, the enemy that is a foe to peace driveth away from (God) such a one as doth not belong indeed to him, but is some one of the weaker sort and not fully enlightened (?), nor yet able to recognize himself. And because he knoweth him not, therefore must he be fought against by him (the devil). For he, thinking that he possesseth him and is his master for ever, opposeth him so much, that he maketh their enmity to be a kind of friendship: for suggesting to him his own thoughts, he often portrayeth them as pleasurable and specious (MS. deceitful), by which he thinketh to prevail over him. He was not, then, openly shown to be an enemy, for he feigned a friendship that was worthy of him.

18 And this his work he carried on so long that he (man) forgat to recognize it, but he (the devil) knew it himself: that is, he, because of his gifts . But when the mystery of grace was lighted up, and the counsel of rest manifested, and the light of the word shown, and the race of them that were saved was proved, warring against many pleasures, the enemy himself despised, and himself, through the goodness of him that had mercy on us, derided because of his own gifts, by which he had thought to triumph over man- he began to plot against us with hatred and enmity and assaults; and this hath he dctcrmined, not to cease from us till he thinketh to separate us (from God).

For before, our enemy was without care, and offered us a feigned friendship which was worthy of him, and was able not to fear that we, deceived by him, should depart from him. But when the light of dispensation was kindled, it made , I say not stronger, . For it exposed that part of his nature which was hidden and which thought to escape notice, and made it confess what it is.

Knowing therefore, brethren, that which shall be, let us be vigilant, not discontented, not making a proud figure, not carrying upon our souls marks of him which are not our own: but wholly lifted upward by the whole word, let us all gladly await the end, and take our flight away from him, that he may be henceforth shown as he is, who our nature unto (or against) our . . .

THE MARTYRDOM

The original text of this, as Flamion shows, has to be picked out of several Greek and Latin authorities.

Bonnet prints the Martyrdom in several forms (Act. Apost. Apocr. ii. 1): on pp. 1-37 we have the Passion in three texts.

The uppermost is the Latin letter of the presbyters and deacons of Achaia. This, as Bonnet has proved, is the original of the two Greek versions printed below it. The first editors of this Letter thought it might be a genuine document. But it is really an artificial thing. The greater part of it consists of a dialogue between Andrew and Aegeates: the narrative of the actual Passion is rather brief.

Of the two Greek versions, the first, which begins "ha tois ophthalmois"(greek) is a faithful version of the Latin.

The other, which begins "haper tois ophthalmois"(greek) has a number of insertions taken from the original Acts, ultimately, perhaps through the medium of a 'Passion', circulated separately, such as we have had in the cases of John, Paul, and Peter. This text is called by Flamion the Epitre grecque. Ep. gr.

On pp. 38-45 follows the fragment of discourses which has just been translated. Very likely this is a relic of a separate Passion cut off from the end of the original Acts.

On pp. 46-57 is the 'Martyrium prius'. This tells (after speaking of the dispersion of the apostles) of the cure and conversion of Lesbius, destruction of temples, dismissal of Lesbius by Caesar, vision of Andrew that Aegeates is to put him to death, arrest of Andrew, and martyrdom. It contains many speeches. This is Mart. 1.

On pp. 58-64 is the 'Martyrium alterum' in two texts, which begins at once with the arrest of the apostle by Aegeates- after he has spent the night in discoursing to the brethren.

Mart. II, A, B are the two texts of this. Besides these Bonnet has published in the Analecta Bollandiana and separately (as Supplementum Codicis Apocryphi, ii, 1895) thc following documents:

1 Acts of Andrew with Encomium: called for short Laudatio, which recounts the journeys at considerable length, and some of thc miracles which we have seen in Gregory, and then the Passion (cc. 44-9) and the Translation to Constantinople.

2. A Greek Martyrdom, of which cc. 1-8 recount the journeys, and from 9 onwards the Passion, with a good deal of matter from the original Acts. This is called Narratio.

3. A Latin Passion- that known to Gregory, which begins Conversante et docente: it forms the end of Book III of Abdias' Historia Apostolica, and is there tacked on to Gregory's book of Miracles.

Using all these sources, Flamion has with great pains indicated which portions he assigns to the original Acts, and I shall follow him here. The resultant text is a kind of mosaic, of which the sources shall be indicated in the margin.

And after he had thus discoursed throughout the night to the brethren, and praved with them and committed them unto the Lord, early in the morning Aegeates the proconsul sent for the apostle Andrew out of the prison and said to him: The end of thy judgement is at hand, thou stranger, enemy of this present life and foe of all mine house. Wherefore hast thou thought good to intrude into places that are not thine, and to corrupt my wife who was of old obedient unto me? why hast thou done this against me and against all Achaia ? Therefore shalt thou receive from me a gift in recompense of that thou hast wrought against me.

And he commanded him to be scourged by seven men and afterward to be crucified: and charged the executioners that his legs should be left unpierccd, and so he should be hanged up: thinking by this means to torment him the more.

Now the report was noised throughout all Patrae that the stranger, the righteous man, the servant of Christ whom Aegeates held prisoner, was being crucified, having done nothing amiss: and they ran together with one accord unto the sight, being wroth with the proconsul because of his impious judgement.

And as the executioners led him unto the place to fulfil that which was commanded them, Stratocles heard what was come to pass, and ran hastily and overtook them, and beheld the blessed Andrew violently haled by the executioners like a malefactor. And he spared them not, but beating every one of them soundly and tearing their coats from top to bottom, he caught Andrew away from them, saying: Ye may thank the blessed man who hath instructed me and taught me to refrain from extremity of wrath: for else I would have showed you what Stratocles is able to do, and what is the power of the foul Aegeates. For we have learnt to endure that which others inflict upon us. And he took the hand of the apostle and went with him to the place by the sea-shore where he was to be crucified.

But the soldiers who had received him from the proconsul left him with Stratocles, and returned and told Aegeates, saying: As we went with Andrew Stratocles prevented us, and rent our coats and pulled him away from us and took him with him, and lo, here we are as thou seest. And Aegeates answered them: Put on other raiment and go and fulfil that which I commanded you, upon the condemned man: but be not seen of Stratocles, neither answer him again if he ask aught of you; for I know the rashness of his soul, what it is, and if he were provoked he would not even spare me. And they did as Aegeates said unto them.

But as Stratocles went with the apostle unto the place appointed, Andrew perceived that he was wroth with Aegeates and was reviling him in a low voice, and said unto him: My child Stratocles, I would have thee henceforth possess thy soul unmoved, and remove from thyself this temper, and neither be inwardly disposed thus toward the things that seem hard to thee, nor be inflamed outwardly: for it becometh the servant of Jesus to be worthy of Jesus. And another thing will I say unto thee and to the brethren that walk with me: that the man that is against us, when he dareth aught against us and findeth not one to consent unto him, is smitten and beaten and wholly deadened because he hath not accomplished that which he undertook; let us therefore, little children, have him alway before our eyes, lest if we fall asleep he slaughter us (you) like an adversary.

And as he spake this and yet more unto Stratocles and them that were with him, they came to the place where he was to be crucified: and (seeing the cross set up at the edge of the sand by the sea-shore) he left them

all and went to the cross and spake unto it (as unto a living creature, with a loud voice):

Hail, O cross, yea be glad indeed! Well know I that thou shalt henceforth be at rest, thou that hast for a long time been wearied, being set up and awaiting me. I come unto thee whom I know to belong to me. I come unto thee that hast yearned after me. I know thy mystery, for the which thou art set up: for thou art planted in the world to establish the things that are unstable: and the one part of thee stretcheth up toward heaven that thou mayest signify the heavenly word (or, the word that is above) (the head of all things): and another part of thee is spread out to the right hand and the left that it may put to flight the envious and adverse power of the evil one, and gather into one the things that are scattered abroad (or, the world): And another part of thee is planted in the earth, and securely set in the depth, that thou mayest join the things that are in the earth and that are under the earth unto the heavenly things (Laud. that thou mayest draw up them that be under the earth and them that are held in the places beneath the earth, and join, &c.).

O cross, device (contrivance) of the salvation of the Most High! O cross, trophy of the victory [of Christ] over the enemies! O cross, planted upon the earth and having thy fruit in the heavens! O name of the cross, filled with all things (lit. a thing filled with all).

Well done, O cross, that hast bound down the mobility of the world (or, the circumference)! Well done, O shape of understanding that hast shaped the shapeless (earth?)! Well done, O unseen chastisement that sorely chastisest the substance of the knowledge that hath many gods, and drivest out from among mankind him that devised it! Well done, thou that didst clothe thyself with the Lord, and didst bear the thief as a fruit, and didst call the apostle to repentance, and didst not refuse to accept us!

But how long delay I, speaking thus, and embrace not the cross, that by the cross I may be made alive, and by the cross (win) the common death of all and depart out of life?

Come hitller ye ministers of joy unto me, ye servants of Aegeates: accomplish the desire of us both, and bind the lamb unto the wood of suffering, the man unto the maker, the soul unto the Saviour.

And the blessed Andrew having thus spoken, standing upon the earth, looked earnestly upon the cross, and bade the brethren that the executioners should come and do that which was commanded them; for they stood afar off.

And they came and bound his hands and his feet and nailed them not; for such a charge had they from Aegeates; for he wished to afflict him by hanging him up, and that in the night he might be devoured alive by dogs (Laud. that he might be wearied out and permit Maximilla to live with him). And they left him hanging and departed from him.

And when the multitudes that stood by of them that had been made disciples in Christ by him saw that they had done unto him none of the things accustomed with them that are crucified, they hoped to hear something again from him. For as he hung, he moved his head and smiled. And Stratocles asked him, saying: Wherefore smilest thou, servant of God? thy laughter maketh us to mourn and weep because we are bereaved of thee. And the blessed Andrew answered him: Shall I not laugh, my son Stratocles, at the vain assault (ambush) of Aegeates, whereby he thinketh to punish us? we are strangers unto him and his conspiracics. He hath not to hear; for if he had, he would have heard that the man of Jesus cannot be punished, because he is henceforth known of him.

And thereafter he spake unto them all in common, for the heathen also were come together, being wroth at the unjust judgement of Aegeates.

Ye men that are here present, and women and children, old and young, bond and free, and all that will hear, take ye no heed of the vain deceit of this present life, but heed us rather who hang here for the Lord's sake and are about to depart out of this body: and renounce all the lusts of the world and contemn (spit upon) the worship of the abominable idols, and run unto the true worshipping of our God that lieth not, and make yourselves a temple pure and ready to receive the word. (Narr. then becomes obviously late: Ep. Gr., which is far shorter, ends: And hasten to overtake my soul as it hasteneth toward heavenly things, and in a word despise all temporal things, and establish your minds as men believing in Christ.)

And the multitudes hearing the things which he spake departed not from the place; and Andrew continued speaking yet more unto them, for a day and a night. And on the day following, beholding his endurance and constancy of soul and wisdom of spirit and strength of mind, they were wroth, and hastened with one accord unto Aegeates, to the judgementseat where he sat, and cried out against him, saying: What is this judgement of thine, O proconsul ? thou hast ill judged! thou hast condemned unjustly: thy court is against law! What evil hath this man done? wherein hath he offended? The city is troubled: thou injurest us all! destroy not Caesar's city! give us the righteous man! restore us the holy man! slay not a man dear to God! destroy not a man gentle and pious! lo, two days is he hanged up and yet liveth, and hath tasted nothing, and yet refresheth all us with his words, and lo, we believe in the God whom he preacheth. Take down the righteous man and we will all turn philosophers; loose the chaste man and all Patrae will be at peace, set free the wise man and all Achaia shall be set free by him! (or, obtain mercy.)

But when at the first Aegeates would not hear them, but beckoned with the hand to the people that they should depart, they were filled with rage and were at the point to do him violence, being in number about two thousand (Narr., Ep. Gr., Mart. II: 20,000).

And when the proconsul saw them to be after a sort mad, he feared lest there should be a rising against him, and rose up from the judgement-seat and went with them, promising to release Andrew. And some went before and signified to the apostle and to the rest of the people that were there, wherefore the proconsul was coming. And all the multitude of the disciples rejoiced together with Maximilla and Iphidamia and Stratocles.

But when Andrew heard it, he began to say: O the dullness and disobedience and simplicity of them whom I have taught! how much have I spoken, and even to this day I have not persuaded them to flee from the love of earthly things! but they are yet bound unto them and continue in them, and will not depart from them. What meaneth this affection and love and sympathy with the flesh? how long heed ye worldly and temporal things? how long understand ye not the things that be above us, and press not to overtake them? leave me henceforth to be put to death in the manner which ye behold, and let no man by any means loose me from these bonds, for so is it appointed unto me to depart out of the body and be present with the Lord, with whom also I am crucified. And this shall be accomplished.

And he turned unto Aegeates and said with a loud voice: Wherefore art thou come, Aegeates, that art an alien unto me? what wilt thou dare afresh, what contrive, or what fetch? tell us that thou hast repented and art come to loose us? nay, not if thou repentest, indeed, Aegeates, will I now consent unto thee, not if thou promise me all thy substance will I depart from myself, not if thou say that thou art mine will I trust thee. And dost thou, proconsul, loose him that is bound? him that hath been set free? that hath been recognized by his kinsman? that hath obtained mercy and is beloved of him? dost thou loose him that is alien to thee? the stranger? that only appeareth to thee? I have one with whom I shall be for ever, with whom I shall converse for unnumbered ages. Unto him do I go, unto him do I hasten, who made thee also known unto me, who said to me: Understand thou Aegeates and his gifts let not that fearful one afright thee, nor think that he holdeth thee who art mine. He is thine enemy: he is pestilent, a deceiver, a corrupter, a madman, a sorcerer, a cheat, a murderer, wrathful, without compassion. Depart therefore from me, thou worker of all iniquity. (Ep. Gr. He is thine enemy. Therefore I know thee, through him that permitted me to know. I depart from thee. For I and they that are akin to me hasten toward that which is ours, and leave thee to be what thou wast, and what thou knowest not thyself to be.)

And the Proconsul hearing this stood speechless and as it were beside himself; but as all the city made an e uproar that he should loose Andrew, he drew near to the cross to loose him and take him down. But the blessed Andrew cried out with a loud voice: Suffer not Lord, thine Andrew that hath been bound upon thy cross, to be loosed again; give not me that am upon thy mystery to the shameless devil; O Jesu Christ, let not thine adversary loose him that is hung upon thy grace; O Father, let not this mean (little) one humble any more him that hath known thy greatness. But do thou, Jesu Christ, whom I have seen, whom I hold, whom I love, in whom I am and shall be, receive me in peace into thine everlasting tabernacles, that by my going out there may be an entering in unto thee of many that are akin to me, and that they may rest in thy majesty. And having so said, and yet more glorified the Lord, he gave up the ghost, while we all wept and lamented at our parting from him.

And after the decease of the blessed Andrew, Maximilla together with Stratocles, caring nought for them that stood by, drew near and herself loosed his body: and when it was evening she paid it the accustomed care and buried it (hard by the sea-shore). And she continued separate from Aegeates because of his brutal soul and his wicked manner of life: and she led a reverend and quiet life, filled with the love of Christ, among the brethren. Whom Aegeates solicited much, and promised that she should have the rule over his affairs; but being unable to persuade her, he arose in the dead of night and unknown to them of his house cast himself down from a great height and perished.

But Stratocles, which was his brother after the flesh, would not touch aught of the things that were left of his substance; for the wretched man died without offspring: but said: Let thy goods go with thee, Aegeates. For of these things we have no need, for they are polluted; but for me, let Christ be my friend and I his servant, and all my substance do I offer unto him in whom I have believed, and I pray that by worthy hearing of the blessed teaching of the apostle I may appear a partaker with him in the ageless and unending kingdom. And so the uproar of the people ceased, and all were glad at the amazing and untimely and sudden fall of the impious and lawless Aegeates.

Book 102. The Apocalypse of Peter

1 .... many of them will be false prophets, and will teach divers ways and doctrines of perdition: but these will become sons of perdition. 3. And then God will come unto my faithful ones who hunger and thirst and

are afflicted and purify their souls in this life; and he will judge the sons of lawlessness.

4. And furthermore the Lord said: Let us go into the mountain: Let us pray.. And going with him, we, the twelve disciples, begged that he would show us one of our brethren, the righteous who are gone forth out of the world, in order that we might see of what manner of form they are, and having taken courage, might also encourage the men who hear us.

6. And as we prayed, suddenly there appeared two men standing before the Lord towards the East, on whom we were not able to look; 7, for there came forth from their countenance a ray as of the sun, and their raiment was shining, such as eye of man never saw; for no mouth is able to express or heart to conceive the glory with which they were endued, and the beauty of their appearance. 8. And as we looked upon them, we were astounded; for their bodies were whiter than any snow and ruddier than any rose; 9, and the red thereof was mingled with the white, and I am utterly unable to express their beauty; 10, for their hair was curly and bright and seemly both on their face and shoulders, as it were a wreath woven of spikenard and divers-coloured flowers, or like a rainbow in the sky, such was their seemliness.

11. Seeing therefore their beauty we became astounded at them, since they appeared suddenly. 12. And I approached the Lord and said: Who are these? 13. He saith to me: These are your brethren the righteous, whose forms ye desired to see. 14. And I said to him: And where are all the righteous ones and what is the aeon in which they are and have this glory?

15. And the Lord showed me a very great country outside of this world, exceeding bright with light, and the air there lighted with the rays of the sun, and the earth itself blooming with unfading flowers and full of spices and plants, fair-flowering and incorruptible and bearing blessed fruit. 16. And so great was the perfume that it was borne thence even unto us. 17. And the dwellers in that place were clad in the raiment of shining angels and their raiment was like unto their country; and angels hovered about them there. 18. And the glory of the dwellers there was equal, and with one voice they sang praises alternately to the Lord God, rejoicing in that place. 19. The Lord saith to us: This is the place of your high-priests, the righteous men.

20. And over against that place I saw another, squalid, and it was the place of punishment; and those who were punished there and the punishing angels had their raiment dark like the air of the place.

21. And there were certain hanging by the tongue: and these were the blasphemers of the way of righteousness; and under them lay fire, burning and punishing them. 22. And there was a great lake, full of flaming mire, in which were certain men that pervert righteousness, and tormenting angels afflicted them.

23. And there were also others, women, hanged by their hair over that mire that bubbled up: and these were they who adorned themselves for adultery; and the men who mingled with them in the defilement of adultery, were hanging by the feet and their heads in that mire. And I said: I did not believe that I should come into this place.

24. And I saw the murderers and those who conspired with them, cast into a certain strait place, full of evil snakes, and smitten by those beasts, and thus turning to and fro in that punishment; and worms, as it were clouds of darkness, afflicted them. And the souls of the murdered stood and looked upon the punishment of those murderers and said: O God, thy judgment is just.

25. And near that place I saw another strait place into which the gore and the filth of those who were being punished ran down and became there as it were a lake: and there sat women having the gore up to their necks, and over against them sat many children who were born to them out of due time, crying; and there came forth from them sparks of fire and smote the women in the eyes: and these were the accursed who conceived and caused abortion.

26. And other men and women were burning up to the middle and were cast into a dark place and were beaten by evil spirits, and their inwards were eaten by restless worms: and these were they who persecuted the righteous and delivered them up.

27. And near those there were again women and men gnawing their own lips, and being punished and receiving a red-hot iron in their eyes: and these were they who blasphemed and slandered the way of righteousness.

28. And over against these again other men and women gnawing their tongues and having flaming fire in their mouths: and these were the false witnesses.

29. And in a certain other place there were pebbles sharper than swords or any spit, red-hot, and women and men in tattered and filthy raiment rolled about on them in punishment: and these were the rich who trusted in their riches and had no pity for orphans and widows, and despised the commandment of God.

30. And in another great lake, full of pitch and blood and mire bubbling up, there stood men and women up to their knees: and these were the usurers and those who take interest on interest.

31. And other men and women were being hurled down from a great cliff and reached the bottom, and again were driven by those who were set over them to climb up upon the cliff, and thence were hurled down again,

and had no rest from this punishment: and these were they who defiled their bodies acting as women; and the women who were with them were those who lay with one another as a man with a woman.

32. And alongside of that cliff there was a place full of much fire, and there stood men who with their own hands had made for themselves carven images instead of God. And alongside of these were other men and women, having rods and striking each other and never ceasing from such punishment.

33. And others again near them, women and men, burning and turning themselves and roasting: and these were they that leaving the way of God
FRAGMENTS OF THE APOCALYPSE OF PETER.

1. CLEMENS ALEXANDRINUS, Eclog. 48. For instance, Peter in the Apocalypse says that the children who are born out of due time shall be of the better part: and that these are delivered over to a care-taking angel that they may attain a share of knowledge and gain the better abode [after suffering what they would have suffered if they had been in the body: but the others shall merely obtain salvation as injured beings to whom mercy is shown, and remain without punishment, receiving this as a reward].*

2. CLEM. ALEX. Eclog. 49. But the milk of the women running down from their breasts and congealing shall engender small flesh eating beasts: and these run up upon them and devour them.

3. MACARIUS MAGNES, Apocritica iv., 6 cf. 16. The earth, it (sc. the Apoc. of Peter) says, "shall present all men before God at the day of judgment, being itself also to be judged, with the heaven also which encompasses it."

4. CLEM. ALEX. Eclog. 41. The scripture says that infants that have been exposed are delivered to a care-taking angel, by whom they are educated and so grow up, and they will be, it says, as the faithful of a hundred years old are here.

5. METHODIUS, Conviv. ii., 6. Whence also we have received in divinely-inspired scriptures that untimely births are delivered to care-taking angels, even if they are the offspring of adultery.

Book 103. The Apocalypse of Paul

[...] the road. And he spoke to him, saying, "By which road shall I go up to Jerusalem?" The little child replied, saying, "Say your name, so that I may show you the road". The little child knew who Paul was. He wished to make conversation with him through his words in order that he might find an excuse for speaking with him.

The little child spoke, saying, "I know who you are, Paul. You are he who was blessed from his mother`s womb. For I have come to you that you may go up to Jerusalem to your fellow apostles. And for this reason you were called. And I am the Spirit who accompanies you. Let your mind awaken, Paul, with [...]. For [...] whole which [...] among the principalities and these authorities and archangels and powers and the whole race of demons, [...] the one that reveals bodies to a soul-seed."

And after he brought that speech to an end, he spoke, saying to me, "Let your mind awaken, Paul, and see that this mountain upon which you are standing is the mountain of Jericho, so that you may know the hidden things in those that are visible. Now it is to the twelve apostles that you shall go, for they are elect spirits, and they will greet you." He raised his eyes and saw them greeting him.

Then the Holy Spirit who was speaking with him caught him up on high to the third heaven, and he passed beyond to the fourth heaven. The Holy Spirit spoke to him, saying, "Look and see your likeness upon the earth." And he looked down and saw those who were upon the earth. He stared and saw those who were upon the [...]. Then he gazed down and saw the twelve apostles at his right and at his left in the creation; and the Spirit was going before them.

But I saw in the fourth heaven according to class - I saw the angels resembling gods, the angels bringing a soul out of the land of the dead. They placed it at the gate of the fourth heaven. And the angels were whipping it. The soul spoke, saying, "What sin was it that I committed in the world?" The toll-collector who dwells in the fourth heaven replied, saying, "It was not right to commit all those lawless deeds that are in the world of the dead". The soul replied, saying, "Bring witnesses! Let them show you in what body I committed lawless deeds. Do you wish to bring a book to read from?"

And the three witnesses came. The first spoke, saying, "Was I not in the body the second hour [...]? I rose up against you until you fell into anger and rage and envy." And the second spoke, saying, "Was I not in the world? And I entered at the fifth hour, and I saw you and desired you. And behold, then, now I charge you with the murders you committed." The third spoke, saying, "Did I not come to you at the twelfth hour of the day when the sun was about to set? I gave you darkness until you should accomplish your sins." When the soul heard these things, it gazed downward in sorrow. And then it gazed upward. It was cast down. The soul that had been cast down went to a body which had been prepared for it. And behold, its witnesses were finished.

Then I gazed upward and saw the Spirit saying to me, "Paul, come! Proceed toward me!". Then as I went, the gate opened, and I went up to the fifth heaven. And I saw my fellow apostles going with me while the Spirit

accompanied us. And I saw a great angel in the fifth heaven holding an iron rod in his hand. There were three other angels with him, and I stared into their faces. But they were rivalling each other, with whips in their hands, goading the souls on to the judgment. But I went with the Spirit and the gate opened for me.

Then we went up to the sixth heaven. And I saw my fellow apostles going with me, and the Holy Spirit was leading me before them. And I gazed up on high and saw a great light shining down on the sixth heaven. I spoke, saying to the toll-collector who was in the sixth heaven, "Open to me and the Holy Spirit who is before me." He opened to me.

Then we went up to the seventh heaven, and I saw an old man [...] light and whose garment was white. His throne, which is in the seventh heaven, was brighter than the sun by seven times. The old man spoke, saying to me, "Where are you going, Paul? O blessed one and the one who was set apart from his mother`s womb." But I looked at the Spirit, and he was nodding his head, saying to me, "Speak with him!". And I replied, saying to the old man, "I am going to the place from which I came." And the old man responded to me, "Where are you from?" But I replied, saying, "I am going down to the world of the dead in order to lead captive the captivity that was led captive in the captivity of Babylon." The old man replied to me saying, "How will you be able to get away from me? Look and see the principalities and authorities." The Spirit spoke, saying, "Give him the sign that you have, and he will open for you." And then I gave him the sign. He turned his face downwards to his creation and to those who are his own authorities.

And then the <seventh> heaven opened and we went up to the Ogdoad. And I saw the twelve apostles. They greeted me, and we went up to the ninth heaven. I greeted all those who were in the ninth heaven, and we went up to the tenth heaven. And I greeted my fellow spirits.

Book 104. The Letter of the Apostles

1 The book which Jesus Christ revealed unto his disciples: and how that Jesus Christ revealed the book for the company (college) of the apostles, the disciples of Jesus Christ, even the book *which is* for all men. Simon and Cerinthus, the false apostles, concerning whom it is written that no man shall cleave unto them, for there is in them deceit wherewith they bring men to destruction. (The book hath been written) that ye may be not flinch nor be troubled, and depart not from the word of the Gospel which ye have heard. Like as we heard it, we keep it in remembrance and have written it for the whole world. We commend you our sons and our daughters in joy <in the grace of God (?)> in the name of God the Father the Lord of the world, and of Jesus Christ. Let grace be multiplied upon you.
2 *We*, John, Thomas, Peter, Andrew, James, Philip, Batholomew, Matthew, Nathanael, Judas Zelotes, and Cephas, write unto the churches of the east and the west, of the north and the south, the declaring and imparting unto you that which concerneth our Lord Jesus Christ: we do write according as we have seen and heard and touched him, after that he was risen from the dead: and how that he revealed unto us things mighty and wonderful and true.
3 This know we: that our Lord and Redeemer Jesus Christ is God the Son of God, who was sent of God the Lord of the whole world, the maker and creator *of it*, who is named by all names, and high above all powers, Lord of lords, King of kings, Ruler of rulers, the heavenly one, that sitteth above the cherubim and seraphim at the right hand of the throne of the Father: who by his word *made* the heavens, and formed the earth and that which is in it, and set bounds to the sea that it should not pass: the deeps also and fountains, that they should spring forth and flow over the earth: the day and the night, the sun and the moon, did he establish, and the stars in the heaven: that did separate the light from the darkness: that called forth hell, and in the twinkling of an eye ordained the rain of the winter, the snow (cloud), the hail, and the ice, and the days in their several seasons: that maketh the earth to quake and again establisheth it: that created man in his own image, after his likeness, and by the fathers of old and the prophets is it declared (*or*, and spake in parables with the fathers of old and the prophets in verity), of whom the apostles preached, and whom the disciples did touch. In God, the Lord, the Son of God, do we believe, that he is the word become flesh: that of Mary the holy virgin he took a body, begotten of the Holy Ghost, not of the will (lust) of the flesh, but by the will of God: that he was wrapped in swaddling clothes in Bethlehem and made manifest, and grew up and came to ripe age, when *also* we beheld *it*.
4 This did our Lord Jesus Christ, who was sent by Joseph and Mary his mother to be taught. [And] when he that taught him said unto him: Say Alpha: then answered he and said: Tell thou me first what is Beta (*probably*: Tell thou me first what is <Alpha and then will I tell thee what is> Beta. Cf. the Marcosian story quoted by Irenaeus (see above, Gospel of Thomas, p. 15). The story is in our texts of the Gospel of Thomas, and all the Infancy Gospels). This thing which then came to pass is to true and of verity.
5 Thereafter was there a marriage in Cana of Galilee; and they bade him with his mother and his brethren, and he changed water into wine. He raised the dead, he caused the lame to walk: him whose hand was with-

ered he caused to stretch it out, and the woman which had suffered an issue of blood twelve years touched the hem of his garment and was healed in the same hour. And when we marvelled at the miracle which was done, he said: Who touched me? Then said we: Lord, the press of men hath touched thee. But he answered and said unto us: I perceive that a virtue is gone out of me. Straightway that woman came before him, and answered and said unto him: Lord, I touched thee. And he answered and said unto her: Go, thy faith hath made thee whole. Thereafter he made the deaf to hear and the blind to see; out of them that were possessed he cast out the unclean spirits, and cleansed the lepers. The spirit which dwelt in a man, whereof the name was Legion, cried out against Jesus, saying: Before the time of our destruction is come, thou art come to drive us out. But the Lord Jesus rebuked him, saying: Go out of this man and do him no hurt. And he entered into the swine and drowned them in the water and they were choked.

Thereafter he did walk upon the sea, and the winds blew, and he cried out against them (rebuked them), and the waves of the sea were made calm. And when we his disciples had no money, we asked him: What shall we do because of the tax-gatherer? And he answered and told us: Let one of you cast an hook into the deep, and take out a fish, and he shall find therein a penny: that give unto the tax-gatherer for me and you. And thereafter when we had no bread, but only five loaves and two fishes, he commanded the people to sit them down, and the number of them was five thousand, besides children and women. We did set pieces of bread before them, and they ate and were filled, and there remained over, and we filled twelve baskets full of the fragments, asking one another and saying: What *mean* these five loaves? They are the symbol of our faith in the Lord of the Christians (in the great christendom), *even* in the Father, the Lord Almighty, and in Jesus Christ our redeemer, in the Holy Ghost the comforter, in the holy church, and in the remission of sins.

6 These things did our Lord and Saviour reveal unto us and teach us. And we do even as he, that ye may become partakers in the grace of our Lord and in our ministry and our giving of thanks (glory), and think upon life eternal. Be ye steadfast and waver not in the knowledge and confidence of our Lord Jesus Christ, and he will have mercy on you and save you everlastingly, world without end.

Here begins the Coptic text.

7 Cerinthus and Simon are come to go to and fro in the world, but they are enemies of our Lord Jesus Christ, for they do pervert the word and the true thing, even (faith in) Jesus Christ. Keep yourselves therefore far from them, for death is in them, and great pollution and corruption, even in these on whom shall come judgement and the end and everlasting destruction.

8 Therefore have we not shrunk from writing unto you concerning the testimony of Christ our Saviour, of what he did, when we followed with him, how he enlightened our understanding...

9 Concerning whom we testify that the Lord is he who was crucified by Pontius Pilate and Archelaus between the two thieves (and with them he was taken down from the tree of the cross, *Eth.*), and was buried in a place which is called the place of a skull (*Kranion*). And thither went three women, Mary, she that was kin to Martha, and Mary Magdalene (Sarrha, Martha, and Mary, *Eth.*), and took ointments to pour upon the body, weeping and mourning over that which was come to pass. And when they drew near to the sepulchre, they looked in and found not the body (*Eth.* they found the stone rolled away and opened the entrance).

10 And as they mourned and wept, the Lord showed himself unto them and said to them: For whom weep ye? weep no more. I am he whom ye seek. But let one of you go to your brethren and say: Come ye, the Master is risen from the dead. Martha (Mary, *Eth.*) came and told us. We said unto her: What haw we to do with thee, woman ? He that is dead and buried, is it possible that he should live? And we believed her not that the Saviour was risen from the dead. Then she returned unto the Lord and said unto him: None of them hath believed me, that thou livest. He said: Let another of you go unto them and tell them again. Mary (Sarrha, *Eth.*) came and told us again, and we believed her not; and she returned unto the Lord and she also told him.

11 Then said the Lord unto Mary and her sisters: Let us go unto them. And he came and found us within (sitting veiled or fishing, *Eth.*), and called us out; but we thought that it was a phantom and believed not that it was the Lord. Then said he unto us: Come, fear ye not. I am your master, even he, O Peter, whom thou didst deny thrice; and dost thou now deny again? And we came unto him, doubting in our hearts whether it were he. Then said he unto us: Wherefore doubt ye still, and are unbelieving? I am he that spake unto you of my flesh and my death and my resurrection. But that ye may know that I am he, do thou, Peter, put thy finger into the print of the nails in mine hands, and thou also, Thomas, put thy finger into the wound of the spear in my side; but thou, Andrew, look on my feet and see whether they press the earth; for it is written in the prophet: A phantom of a devil maketh no footprint on the earth.

12 And we touched him, that we might learn of a truth whether he were risen in the flesh; and we fell on our faces (and worshipped him) confessing our sin, that we had been unbelieving. Then said our Lord and Saviour unto us: Rise up, and I will reveal unto you that which is above the

heaven and in the heaven, and your rest which is in the kingdom of heaven. For my Father hath given me power (sent me, *Eth.*) to take you up thither, and them also that believe on me.

13 Now that which he revealed unto us is this, which he spake: It came to pass when I was about (minded) to come hither from the Father of all things, and passed through the heavens, then did I put on the wisdom of the Father, and I put on the power of his might. I was in heaven, and I passed by the archangels and the angels in their likeness, like as if I were one of them, among the princedoms and powers. I passed through them because I possessed the wisdom of him that had sent me. Now the chief captain of the angels, [is] Michael, and Gabriel and Uriel and Raphael followed me unto the fifth firmament (heaven), for they thought in their heart that I was one of them; such power was given me of my Father. And on that day did I adorn the archangels with a wonderful voice (so *Copt.*: *Eth., Lat.,* I made them quake--amazed them), so that they should go unto the altar of the Father and serve and fulfil the ministry until I should return unto him. And so wrought I the likeness by my wisdom; for I became all things in all, that I might praise the dispensation of the Father and fulfil the glory of him that sent me (*the verbs might well be transposed*) and return unto him. (*Here the Latin omits a considerable portion of text without notice, to near the beginning of c.* 17.)

14 For ye know that the angel Gabriel brought the message unto Mary. And we answered: Yea, Lord. He answered and said unto us: Remember ye not, then, that I said unto you a little while ago: I became an angel among the angels, and I became all things in all? We said unto him: Yea, Lord. Then answered he and said unto us: On that day whereon I took the form of the angel Gabriel, I appeared unto Mary and spake with her. Her heart accepted me, and she believed (She believed and laughed, *Eth.*), and I formed myself and entered into her body. I became flesh, for I alone was a minister unto myself in that which concerned Mary (I was mine own messenger, *Eth.*) in the appearance of the shape of an angel. For so must I needs (or, was I wont to) do. Thereafter did I return to my Father (*Copt.* After my return to the Father, *and run on*).

15 But do ye commemorate my death. Now when the Passover (Easter, pascha) cometh, one of you shall be cast into prison for my name's sake; and he will be in grief and sorrow, because ye keep the Easter while he is in prison and separated from you, for he will be sorrowful because he keepeth not Easter with you. And I will send my power in the form of mine angel Gabriel, and the doors of the prison shall open. And he shall come forth and come unto you and keep the night-watch with you until the cock crow. And when ye have accomplished the memorial which is made of me, and the Agape (love-feast), he shall again be cast into prison for a testimony, until he shall come out thence and preach that which I have delivered unto you.

And we said unto him: Lord, is it then needful that we should again take the cup and drink? (Lord, didst not thou thyself fulfil the drinking of the Passover? is it then needful that we should accomplish it again? *Eth.*) He said unto us: Yea, it is needful, until the day when I come again, with them that have been put to death for my sake (come with my wounds, *Eth.*).

16 Then said we to him: Lord, that which thou hast revealed unto us (revealest, *Eth.*) is great. Wilt thou come in the power of any creature or in an appearance of any kind ? (In what power or form wilt thou come? *Eth.*) He answered and said unto us: Verily I say unto you, I shall come like the sun when it is risen, and my brightness will be seven times the brightness thereof! The wings of the clouds shall bear me in brightness, and the sign of the cross shall go before me, and I shall come upon earth to judge the quick and the dead.

17 We said unto him: Lord, after how many years shall this come to pass ? He said unto us: When the hundredth part and the twentieth part is fulfilled, between the Pentecost and the feast of unleavened bread, then shall the coming of my Father be (*so Copt.*: When an hundred and fifty years are past, in the days of the feast of Passover and Pentecost, &c., *Eth.*: . . . (*imperfect word*) year is fulfilled, between the unleavened bread and Pentecost shall be the coming of my Father, *Lat.*).

We said unto him: Now sayest thou unto us: I will come; and how sayest thou: He that sent me is he that shall come? Then said he to us: I am wholly in the Father and my Father is in me. Then said we to him: Wilt thou indeed forsake us until thy coming? Where can we find a master? But he answered and said unto us: Know ye not, then, that like as until now I have been here, so also was I there, with him that sent me? And we said to him: Lord, is it then possible that thou shouldest be both here and there? But he answered us: I am wholly in the Father and the Father in me, because of (in regard of) the likeness of the form and the power and the fullness and the light and the full measure and the voice. I am the word, I am become unto him a thing, that is to say (*word gone*) of the thought, fulfilled in the type (likeness); I have into the Ogdoad (eighth number), which is the Lord's day. (*In place of these sentences Eth. has*: I am of his resemblance and form, of his power and completeness, and of his light. I am his complete (fulfilled, entire) Word.

18 But it came to pass after he was crucified, and dead and arisen again, *when* the work *was fulfilled* which was accomplished in the flesh, and he was crucified and the ascension come to pass at the end of the

days, then said he thus, &c. *It is an interpolation, in place of words which the translator did not understand, or found heretical.*) But the whole fulfilment of the fulfilment shall ye see after the redemption which hath come to pass by me, and ye shall see me, how I go up unto my Father which is in heaven. But behold, now, I give unto you a new commandment: Love one another and [*a leaf lost in Copt.*] obey one another, that peace may rule alway among you. Love your enemies, and what ye would not that man do unto you, that do unto no man.

19 And this preach ye also and teach them that believe on me, and preach the kingdom of heaven of my Father, and how my Father hath given me the power, that ye may bring near the children of my heavenly Father. Preach ye, and they shall obtain faith, that ye may be they for whom it is ordained that they shall bring his children unto heaven.

And we said unto him: Lord, unto thee it is possible to accomplish that whereof thou tellest us; but how shall we be able to do it? He said to us: Verily I say unto you, preach and proclaim as I *command you*, for I will be with you, for it is my good pleasure to be with you, that ye may be heirs with me in the kingdom of heaven, *even the kingdom* of him that sent me. Verily I say unto you, ye shall be my brethren and my friends, for my Father hath found pleasure in you: and so also shall they be that believe on me by your means. Verily I say unto you, such and so great joy hath my Father prepared for you that the angels and the powers desired and do desire to see it and look upon it; but it is not given unto them to behold the glory of my Father. We said unto him: Lord, what is this whereof thou speakest to us?

Copt. begins again: words are missing.

He answered us: Ye shall behold a light, more excellent than that which shineth... (shineth more brightly than the light, and is more perfect than perfection. And the Son shall become perfect through the Father who is Light, for the Father is perfect which bringeth to pass death and resurrection, and ye shall see a perfection more perfect than the perfect. And I am wholly at the right hand of the Father, even in him that maketh perfect. *So Eth.: Copt. has gaps*).

And we said unto him: Lord, in all things art thou become salvation and life unto us, for that thou makest known such a hope unto us. And he said to us: Be of good courage and rest in me. Verily I say unto you, your rest shall be above (?), in the place where is neither eating nor drinking, nor care (*Copt.* joy) nor sorrow, nor passing away of them that are therein: for ye *shall* have no part in (the things of earth, *Eth.*) but ye shall be received in the everlastingness of my Father. Like as I am in him, so shall ye also be in me.

Again we said unto him: In what form? in the fashion of angels, or in flesh ? And he answered and said unto us: Lo, I have put on your flesh, wherein I was born and crucified, and am risen again through my Father which is in heaven, that the prophecy of David the prophet might be fulfilled, in regard of that which was declared concerning me and my death and resurrection, saying:

Lord, they are increased that fight with me, and many are they that are risen up against me.

Many there be that say to my soul: There is no help for him in his God.

But thou, O Lord, art my defender: thou art my worship, and the lifter up of my head.

I did call upon the Lord with my voice and he heard me (out of the high place of his temple, *Eth.*).

I laid me down and slept, and rose up again: for thou, O Lord, art my defender.

I will not be afraid for ten thousands of the people, that have set themselves against me round about.

Up, Lord, and help me, O my God: for thou hast smitten down all them that without cause are mine enemies: thou hast broken the teeth of the ungodly.

Salvation belongeth unto the Lord, and his good pleasure is upon his people (Ps. iii. 1-8).

If, therefore, all the words which were spoken by the prophets have been fulfilled in me (for I myself was in them), how much more shall that which I say unto you come to pass indeed, that he which sent me may be glorified by you and by them that believe on me?

20 And when he had said this unto us, we said to him: In all things hast thou had mercy on us and saved us, and hast revealed all things unto us; but yet would we ask of thee somewhat if thou give us leave. And he said unto us: I know that ye pay heed, and that your heart is well-pleased when ye hear me: now concerning that which ye desire, I will speak good words unto you. 21 For verily I say unto you: Like as my Father hath raised me from the dead, so shall ye also rise (in the flesh, *Eth.*) and be taken up into the highest heaven, unto the place whereof I have told you from the beginning, unto the place which he who sent me hath prepared for you. And so will I accomplish all dispensations (all grace, *Eth.*), even I who am unbegotten and yet begotten of mankind, who am without flesh and yet have borne flesh <and have grown up like unto you that were born in flesh, *Eth.*>: for to that end am I come, that (*gap in Copt.: Eth. continues*) ye might rise from the dead in your flesh, in the second birth, even a vesture that shall not decay, together with all them that hope and believe in him that sent me: for so is the will of my Father, that I should

give unto you, and unto them whom it pleaseth me, the hope of the kingdom.

Then said we unto him: Great is that which thou sufferest us to hope, and tellest us. And he answered and said: Believe ye that everything that I tell you shall come to pass ? We answered and said: Yea, Lord. (*Copt. resumes for a few lines: then another gap. I follow Eth.*) He said unto us: Verily I say unto you, that I have obtained the whole power of my Father, that I may bring back into light them that dwell in darkness, them that are in corruption into incorruption, them that are in death into life, and that I may loose them that are in fetters. For that which is impossible with men, is possible with the Father. I am the hope of them that despair, the helper of them that have no saviour, the wealth of the poor, the health of the sick, and the resurrection of the dead.

22 When he had thus said, we said unto him: Lord, is it true that the flesh shall be judged together with the soul and the spirit, and that the one part shall rest in heaven and the other part be punished everlastingly yet living? And he said unto us: (*Copt. resumes*) How long will ye inquire and doubt?

23 Again we said unto him: Lord, there is necessity upon us to inquire of thee--because thou hast commanded us to preach--that we ourselves may learn assuredly of thee and be profitable preachers, and that they which are instructed by us may believe in thee. Therefore must we needs inquire of thee.

24 He answered us and said: Verily I say unto you, the resurrection of the flesh shall come to pass with the soul therein and the spirit. And we said unto him: Lord, is it then possible that that which is dissolved and brought to nought should become whole? and we ask thee not as unbelieving, neither as if it were impossible unto thee; but verily we believe that that which thou sayest shall come to pass. And he was wroth with us and said: O ye of little faith, how long will ye ask questions? But what ye will, tell it me, and I myself will tell you without grudging: only keep ye my commandments and do that which I bid you, and turn not away your face from any man, that I turn not my face away from you, but without shrinking and fear and without respect of persons, minister ye in the way that is direct and narrow and strait. So shall my Father himself rejoice over you.

25 Again we said unto him: Lord, already are we ashamed that we question thee oft-times and burden thee. And he answered and said unto us: I know that in faith and with your whole heart ye do question me; therefore do I rejoice over you, for verily I say unto you: I rejoice, and my Father that is in me, because ye question me; and your importunity (shamelessness) is unto me rejoicing and unto you it giveth life. And when he had so said unto us, we were glad that we had questioned him, and we said to him: Lord, in all things thou makest us alive and hast mercy on us. Wilt thou now declare unto us that which we shall ask thee? Then said he unto us: Is it the flesh that passeth away, or is it the spirit? We said unto him: The flesh is it that passeth away. Then said he unto us: That which hath fallen shall rise again, and that which was lost shall be found, and that which was weak shall recover, that in these things that are so created the glory of my Father may be revealed. As he hath done unto me, so will I do unto all that believe in me.

26 Verily I say unto you: the flesh shall arise, and the soul, alive, that their defence may come to pass on that day in regard of that that they have done, whether it be good or evil: that there may be a choosing-out of the faithful who have kept the commandments of my Father that sent me; and so shall the judgement be accomplished with strictness. For my Father said unto me: My Son, in the day of judgement thou shalt have no respect for the rich, neither pity for the poor, but according to the sins of every man shalt thou deliver him unto everlasting torment. But unto my beloved that have done the commandments of my Father that sent me will I give the rest of life in the kingdom of my Father which is in heaven, and they shall behold that which he hath given me. And he hath given me authority to do that which I will, and to give that which I have promised and determined to give and grant unto them.

27 For to that end went I down unto the place of Lazarus, and preached unto the righteous and the prophets, that they might come out of the rest which is below and come up into that which is above; and I poured out upon them with my right hand the water (?) (baptism, *Eth.*) of life and forgiveness and salvation from all evil, as I have done unto you and unto them that believe on me. But if any man believe on me and do not my commandments, although he have confessed my name, he hath no profit therefrom but runneth a vain race: for such will find themselves in perdition and destruction, because they have despised my commandments.

28 But so much the more have I redeemed you, the children of light, from all evil and from the authority of the rulers (archons), and every one that believeth on me by your means. For that which I have promised unto you will I give unto them also, that they may come out of the prison-house and the fetters of the rulers. We answered and said: Lord, thou hast given unto us the rest of life and hast given us <joy?> by wonders, unto the confirmation of faith: wilt thou now preach the same unto us, seeing that thou hast preached it unto the <righteous> and the prophets? Then said he unto us: Verily I say unto you, all that have believed on me and that believe in him that sent me will I take up into the heaven, unto the place

which my Father hath prepared for the elect, and I will give you the kingdom, the chosen kingdom, in rest, and everlasting life.

29 But all they that have offended against my commandments and have taught other doctrine, (perverting) the Scripture and adding thereto, striving after their own glory, and that teach with other words them that believe on me in uprightness, if they make them fall thereby, shall receive everlasting punishment. We said unto him: Lord, shall there then be teaching by others, diverse from that which thou hast spoken unto us ? He said unto us: It must needs be, that the evil and the good may be made manifest; and the judgement shall be manifest upon them that do these things, and according to their works shall they be judged and shall be delivered unto death.

Again we said unto him: Lord, blessed are we in that we see thee and hear thee declaring such things, for our eyes have beheld these great wonders that thou hast done. He answered and said unto us: Yea, rather blessed are they that have not seen and yet have believed, for they shall be called children of the kingdom, and they shall be perfect among the perfect, and I will be unto them life in the kingdom of my Father.

Again we said unto him: Lord, how shall men be able to believe that thou wilt depart and leave us; for thou sayest unto us: There shall come a day and an hour when I shall ascend unto my Father?

30 But he said unto us: Go ye and preach unto the twelve tribes, and preach also unto the heathen, and to all the land of Israel from the east to the west and from the south unto the north, and many shall believe on <me> the Son of God. But we said unto him: Lord, who will believe us, or hearken unto us, or (how shall we be able, *Eth.*) to teach the powers and signs and wonders which thou hast done ? Then answered he and said to us: Go ye and preach the mercifulness of my Father, and that which he hath done through me will I myself do through you, for I am in you, and I will give you my peace, and I will give you a power of my spirit, that ye may prophesy to them unto life eternal. And unto the others also will I give my power, that they may teach the residue of the peoples. (*Six leaves lost in Copt.: Eth. continues.*)

31 And behold a man shall meet you, whose name is Saul, which being interpreted is Paul: he is a Jew, circumcised according to the law, and he shall receive my voice from heaven with fear and terror and trembling. And his eyes shall be blinded, and by your hands by the sign of the cross shall they be protected (healed: *other Eth. MSS.* with spittle by your hands shall his eyes, &c.). Do ye unto him all that I have done unto you. Deliver it (? the word of God) unto the other. And at the same time that man shall open his eyes and praise the Lord, even my Father which is in heaven. He shall obtain power among the people and shall preach and instruct; and many that hear him shall obtain glory and be redeemed. But thereafter shall men be wroth with him and deliver him into the hands of his enemies, and he shall bear witness before kings that are mortal, and his end shall be that he shall turn unto me, whereas he persecuted me *at the first*. He shall preach and teach and abide with the elect, as a chosen vessel and a wall that shall not be overthrown, *yea*, the last of the last shall become a preacher unto the Gentiles, made perfect by the will of my Father. Like as ye have learned from the Scripture that your fathers the prophets spake of me, and in me it is indeed fulfilled.

And he said unto us: Be ye also therefore guides unto them; and all things that I said unto you, and that ye write concerning me (tell ye them), that I am the word of the Father and that the Father is in me. Such also shall ye be unto that man, as becometh you. Instruct him and bring to his mind that which is spoken of me in the Scripture and is fulfilled, and thereafter shall he become the salvation of the Gentiles.

32 And we asked him: Lord, is there for us and for them the self-same expectation of the inheritance? He answered and said unto us: Are then the fingers of the hand like unto each other, or the ears of corn in the field, or do *all* fruit-trees bear the same fruit? Doth not every one bear fruit according to its nature? And we said unto him: Lord, wilt thou again speak unto us in parables? Then said he unto us: Lament not. Verily I say unto you, ye are my brethren, and my companions in the kingdom of heaven unto my Father, for so is his good pleasure. Verily I say unto you, unto them also whom ye teach and who believe on me will I give that expectation.

33 And we asked him again: When shall we meet with that man, and when wilt thou depart unto thy Father and our God and Lord? He answered and said unto us: That man will come out of the land of Cilicia unto Damascus of Syria, to root up the church which ye must found there. It is I that speak through you; and he shall come quickly: and he shall become strong in the faith, that the word of the prophet may be fulfilled, which saith: Behold, out of Syria will I begin to call together a new Jerusalem, and Sion will I subdue unto me, and it shall be taken, and the place which is childless shall be called the son and daughter of my Father, and my bride. For so hath it pleased him that sent me. But that man will I turn back, that he accomplish not his evil desire, and the praise of my Father shall be perfected in him, and after that I am gone home and abide with my Father, I will speak unto him from heaven, and all things shall be accomplished which I have told you before concerning him.

34 And we said unto him again: Lord, so many great things hast thou told us and revealed unto us as never yet were spoken, and in all hast thou

given us rest and been gracious unto us. After thy resurrection thou didst reveal unto us all things that we might be saved indeed; but thou saidst unto us only: There shall be wonders and strange appearances in heaven and on earth before the end of the world come. Tell us now, how shall we perceive it? And he answered us: I will teach it you; and not that which shall befall you only, but them also whom ye shall teach and who shall believe, as well as them who shall hear that man and believe on me. In those years and days shall it come to pass.

And we said again unto him: Lord, what shall come to pass? And he said unto us: Then shall they that believe and they that believe not hear (see, *Eth.*) a trumpet in the heaven, a vision of great stars which shall be seen in the day, wonderful sights in heaven reaching down to the earth; stars which fall upon the earth like fire, and a great and mighty hail of fire (a star shining from the east unto this place, like unto fire, *Eth.* 2). The sun and the moon fighting one with the other, a continual rolling and noise of thunders and lightnings, thunder and earthquake; cities falling and men perishing in their overthrow, a continual dearth for lack of rain, a terrible pestilence and great mortality, mighty and untimely, so that they that die lack burial: and the bearing forth of brethren and sisters and kinsfolk shall be upon one bier. The kinsman shall show no favour to his kinsman, nor any man to his neighbour. And they that were overthrown shall rise up and behold them that overthrew them, that they lack burial, for the pestilence shall be full of hatred and pain and envy: and men shall take from one and give to another. And thereafter shall it wax yet worse than before. (Bewail ye them that have not hearkened unto my commandments, *Eth.* 2.)

35 Then shall my Father be wroth at the wickedness of men, for many are their transgressions, and the abomination of their uncleanness weigheth heavy upon them in the corruption of their life.

And we asked him: What of them that trust in thee? He answered and said unto us: Ye are yet slow of heart; and how long? Verily I say unto you, as the prophet David spake of me and of my people, so shall it be (?) for them also that believe on me. But they that are deceivers in the world and enemies of righteousness, upon them shall come the fulfilment of the prophecy of David, who said: Their feet are swift to shed blood, their tongue uttereth slander, adders' poison is under their lips. I behold thee companying with thieves, and partaking with adulterers, thou continuest speaking against thy brother and puttest stumbling-blocks before thine own mother's son. What thinkest thou, that I shall be like unto thee? Behold now how the prophet of God hath spoken of all, that all things may be fulfilled which he said aforetime.

36 And again we said unto him: Lord, will not then the nations say: Where is their God? And he answered and said unto us: Thereby shall the elect be known, that they, being plagued with such afflictions, come forth. We said: Will then their departure out of the world be by a pestilence which giveth them pain? He answered us: Nay, but if they suffer such affliction, it will be a proving of them, whether they have faith and remember these my sayings, and fulfil my commandments. These shall arise, and short will be their expectation, that he may be glorified that sent me, and I with him. For he hath sent me unto you to tell you these things; and that ye may impart them unto Israel and the Gentiles and they may hear, and they also be redeemed and believe on me and escape the woe of the destruction. But whoso escapeth from the destruction of death, him will they take and hold him fast in the prison-house in torments like the torments of a thief.

And we said unto him: Lord, will they *that believe* be *treated* like the unbelievers, and wilt thou punish them that have escaped from the pestilence? And he said unto us: If they that believe in my name deal like the sinners, then have they done as though they had not believed. And we said again to him: Lord, have they on whom this lot hath fallen no life? He answered and said unto us: Whoso hath accomplished the praise of my Father, he *shall abide in* the resting-place of my Father.

37 Then said we unto him: Lord, teach us what shall come to pass thereafter? And he answered us: In those years and days shall war be kindled upon war; the four ends of the earth shall be in commotion and fight against each other. Thereafter shall be quakings of clouds (*or*, clouds of locusts), darkness, and dearth, and persecutions of them that believe on me and against the elect. Thereupon shall come doubt and strife and transgressions against one another. And there shall be many that believe on my name and yet follow after evil and spread vain doctrine. And men shall follow after them and their riches, and be subject unto their pride, and lust for drink, and bribery, and there shall be respect of persons among them.

38 But they that desire to behold the face of God and respect not the persons of the rich sinners, and are not ashamed before the people that lead them astray, but rebuke (?) them, they shall be crowned by the Father. And they also shall be saved that rebuke their neighbours, for they are sons of wisdom and of faith. But if they become not children of wisdom, whoso hateth his brother and persecuteth him and showeth him no favour, him will God despise and reject.

(*Copt. resumes.*)

But they that walk in truth and in the knowledge of the faith, and have love towards me--for they have endured insult--they shall be praised for that they walk in poverty and endure them that hate them and put them to shame. Men have stripped them naked, for they despised them because they continued in hunger and thirst, but after they have endured patiently, they shall have the blessedness of heaven, and they shall be with me for ever. But woe unto them that walk in pride and boasting, for their end is perdition.

39 And we said unto him: Lord, is this thy purpose, that thou leavest us, to come upon them? (Will all this come to pass, *Eth.*) He answered and said unto us: After what manner shall the judgement be? whether righteous or unrighteous? (In *Copt.* and *Eth.* the general sense is the same: but the answer of Jesus in the form of a question is odd, and there is probably a corruption.)

We said unto him: Lord, in that day they will say unto thee: Thou hast not distinguished between (*probably*: will they not say unto thee: Thou hast distinguished between) righteousness and unrighteousness, between the light and the darkness, and evil and good? Then said he: I will answer them and say: Unto Adam was power given to choose one of the two: he chose the light and laid his hand thereon, but the darkness he left behind him and cast away from him. Therefore have all men power to believe in the light which is life, and which is the Father that hath sent me. And every one that believeth and doeth the works of the light shall live in them; but if there be any that confesseth that he belongeth unto the light, and doeth the works of darkness, such an one hath no defence to utter, neither can he lift up his face to look upon the Son of God, which Son am I. For I will say unto him: As thou soughtest, so hast thou found, and as thou askedst, so hast thou received. Therefore condemnest thou me, O man? Wherefore hast thou departed from me and denied me? And wherefore hast thou confessed me and yet denied me? hath not every man power to live and to die? Whoso then hath kept my commandments shall be a son of the light, that is, of the Father that is in me. But because of them that corrupt my words am I come down from heaven. I am the word: I became flesh, and I wearied myself (or, suffered) and taught, saying: The heavy laden shall be saved, and they that are gone astray shall go astray for ever. They shall be chastised and tormented in their flesh and in their soul.

40 And we said unto him: O Lord, verily we are sorrowful for their sake. And he said unto us: Ye do rightly, for the righteous are sorry for the sinners, and pray for them, making prayer unto my Father. Again we said unto him: Lord, is there none that maketh intercession unto thee (*so Eth.*)? And he said unto us: Yea, and I will hearken unto the prayer of the righteous which they make for them.

When he had so said unto us, we said to him: Lord, in all things hast thou taught us and had mercy on us and saved us, that we might preach unto them that are worthy to be saved, and that we might obtain a recompense with thee. (Shall we be partakers of a recompense from thee? *Eth.*) 41 He answered and said unto us: Go and preach, and ye shall be labourers, and fathers, and ministers. We said unto him: Thou art he (or, Art thou he) that shalt preach by us. (Lord, thou art our father. *Eth.*) Then answered he us, saying: Be not (or, Are not ye) all fathers or all masters. (Are then all fathers, or all servants, or all masters? *Eth.*) We said unto him: Lord, thou art he that saidst unto us: Call no man your father upon earth, for one is your Father, which is in heaven, and your master. Wherefore sayest thou now unto us: Ye shall be fathers of many children, and servants and masters? He answered and said unto us: According as ye have said (Ye have rightly said, *Eth.*). For verily I say unto you: whosoever shall hear you and believe on me, shall receive of you the light of the seal through me, and baptism through me: ye shall be fathers and servants and masters.

42 But we said unto him: Lord, how may it be that every one of us should be these three? He said unto us: Verily I say unto you: Ye shall be called fathers, because with praiseworthy heart and in love ye have revealed unto them the things of the kingdom of heaven. And ye shall be called servants, because they shall receive the baptism of life and the remission of their sins at my hand through you. And ye shall be called masters, because ye have given them the word without grudging, and have admonished them, and when ye admonished them, they turned themselves (were converted). Ye were not afraid of their riches, nor ashamed before their face, but ye kept the commandments of my Father and fulfilled them. And ye shall have a great reward with my Father which is in heaven, and they shall have forgiveness of sins and everlasting life, and be partakers in the kingdom of heaven.

And we said unto him: Lord, even if every one of us had ten thousand tongues to speak withal, we could not thank thee, for that thou promisest such things unto us. Then answered he us, saying: Only do ye that which I say unto you, even as I myself also have done it. 43 And ye shall be like the wise virgins which watched and slept not, but went forth unto the lord into the bridechamber: but the foolish *virgins* were not able to watch, but slumbered. And we said unto him: Lord, who are the wise and who are the foolish? He said unto us: Five wise and five foolish; for these are they of whom the prophet hath spoken: Sons of God are they. Hear now their names.

But we wept and were troubled for them that slumbered. He said unto us: The five wise are Faith and Love and Grace and Peace and Hope. Now they of the faithful which possess this (these) shall be guides unto them

that have believed on me and on him that sent me. For I am the Lord and I am the bridegroom whom they have received, and they have entered in to the house of the bridegroom and are laid down with me in the bridal chamber rejoicing. But the five foolish, when they had slept and had awaked, came unto the door of the bridal chamber and knocked, for the doors were shut. Then did they weep and lament that no man opened unto them.

We said unto him: Lord, and their wise sisters that were within in the bridegroom's house, did they continue without opening unto them, and did they not sorrow for their sakes nor entreat the bridegroom to open unto them? He answered us, saying: They were not yet able to obtain favour for them. We said unto him: Lord, on what day shall they enter in for their sisters' sake? Then said he unto us: He that is shut out, is shut out. And we said unto him: Lord, is this word (determined?). Who then are the foolish? He said unto us: Hear their names. They are Knowledge, Understanding (Perception), Obedience, Patience, and Compassion. These are they that slumbered in them that have believed and confessed me but have not fulfilled my commandments. 44 On account of them that have slumbered, they shall remain outside the kingdom and the fold of the shepherd and his sheep. But whoso shall abide outside the sheepfold, him will the wolves devour, and he shall be (condemned?) and die in much affliction: in him shall be no rest nor endurance, and (*Eth.*) although he be hardly punished, and rent in pieces and devoured in long and evil torment, yet shall he not be able to obtain death quickly.

45 And we said unto him: Lord, well hast thou revealed all this unto us. Then answered he us, saying: Understand ye not (*or*, Ye understand not) these words? We said unto him: Yea, Lord. By five shall men enter into thy kingdom <and by five shall men remain without>: notwithstanding, they that watched were with thee the Lord and bridegroom, even though they rejoiced not because of them that slumbered (yet will they have no pleasure, because of, *Eth.*). He said unto us: They will indeed rejoice that they have entered in with the bridegroom, the Lord; and they are sorrowful because of them that slumbered, for they are their sisters. For all ten are daughters of God, even the Father. Then said we unto him: Lord, is it then for thee to show them favour on account of their sisters? (It becometh thy majesty to show them favour, *Eth.*) He said unto us: <It is not mine,> but his that sent me, and I am consenting with him (It is not yours, &c., *Eth.*).

46 But be ye upright and preach rightly and teach, and be not abashed by any man and fear not any man, and especially the rich, for they do not my commandments, but boast themselves (swell) in their riches. And we said unto him: Lord, tell us if it be the rich only. He answered, saying unto us: If any man who is not rich and possesseth a small livelihood giveth unto the poor and needy, men will call him a benefactor.

47 But if any man fall under the load <because> of sin that he hath committed, then shall his neighbour correct him because of the good that he hath done unto his neighbour. And if his neighbour correct him and he return, he shall be saved, and he that corrected him shall receive a reward and live for ever. For a needy man, if he see him that hath done him good sin, and correct him not, shall be judged with severe judgement. Now if a blind man lead a blind, they both fall into a ditch: and whoso respecteth persons for their sake, shall be as the two <blind>, as the prophet hath said: Woe unto them that respect persons and justify the ungodly for reward, even they whose God is their belly. Behold that judgement shall be their portion. For verily I say unto you: On that day will I neither have respect unto the rich nor pity for the poor.

48 If thou behold a sinner, admonish him betwixt him and thee: (if he hear thee, thou hast gained thy brother, *Eth.*) and if he hear thee not, then take to thee another, as many as three, and instruct thy brother: again, if he hear thee not, let him be unto thee

(*Copt. defective from this point.*)

as an heathen man or a publican.

49 If thou hear aught against thy brother, give it no credence; slander not, and delight not in hearing slander. For thus it is written: Suffer not thine ear to receive aught against thy brother: but if thou seest aught, correct him, rebuke him, and convert him.

And we said unto him: Lord, thou hast in all things taught us and warned us. But, Lord, concerning the believers, even them to whom it belongeth to believe in the preaching of thy name: is it determined that among them also there shall be doubt and division, jealousy, confusion, hatred, and envy? For thou sayest: They shall find fault with one another and respect the person of them that sin, and hate them that rebuke them. And he answered and said unto us: How then shall the judgement come about, that the corn should be gathered into the garner and the chaff thereof cast into the fire?

50 They that hate such things, and love me and rebuke them that fulfil not my commandments, shall be hated and persecuted and despised and mocked. Men will of purpose speak of them that which is not true, and will band themselves together against them that love me. But these will rebuke them, that they may be saved. But them that will rebuke and chasten and warn them, them will they (the others) hate, and thrust them aside, and despise them, and hold themselves far from them that wish them good. But they that endure such things shall be like unto the martyrs

with the Father, because they have striven for righteousness, and have not striven for corruption.

And we asked him: Lord, shall such things be among us? And he answered us: Fear not; it shall not be in many, but in a few. We said unto him: Yet tell us, in what manner it shall come to pass. And he said unto us: There shall come forth another doctrine, and a confusion, and because they shall strive after their own advancement, they shall bring forth an unprofitable doctrine. And therein shall be a deadly corruption (of uncleanness), and they shall teach it, and shall turn away them that believe on me from my commandments and cut them off from eternal life. But woe unto them that falsify this my word and commandment, and draw away them that hearken to them from the life of the doctrine and separate themselves from the commandment of life: *for* together with them they shall come into everlasting judgement.

51 And when he had said this, and had finished his discourse with us, he said unto us again: Behold, on the third day and at the third hour shall he come which hath sent me, that I may depart with him. And as he so spake, there was thunder and lightning and an earthquake, and the heavens parted asunder, and there appeared a light (bright) cloud which bore him up. And *there came* voices of many angels, rejoicing and singing praises and saying: Gather us, O Priest, unto the light of the majesty. And when they drew nigh unto the firmament, we heard his voice *saying unto us*: Depart hence in peace.

Book 105. The Infancy Gospel of James

IN THE RECORDS OF THE TWELVE TRIBES OF ISRAEL was Joachim, a man rich exceedingly; and he brought his offerings double, saying: There shall be of my superabundance to all the people, and there shall be the offering for my forgiveness to the Lord for a propitiation for me. For the great day of the Lord was at hand, and the sons of Israel were bringing their offerings. And there stood over against him Rubim, saying: It is not meet for thee first to bring thine offerings, because thou hast not made seed in Israel. And Joachim was exceedingly grieved, and went away to the registers of the twelve tribes of the people, saying: I shall see the registers of the twelve tribes of Israel, as to whether I alone have not made seed in Israel. And he searched, and found that all the righteous had raised up seed in Israel. And he called to mind the patriarch Abraham, that in the last day God gave him a son Isaac. And Joachim was exceedingly grieved, and did not come into the presence of his wife; but he retired to the desert, and there pitched his tent, and fasted forty days and forty nights, saying in himself: I will not go down either for food or for drink until the Lord my God shall look upon me, and prayer shall be my food and drink.

2. And his wife Anna mourned in two mournings, and lamented in two lamentations, saying: I shall bewail my widowhood; I shall bewail my childlessness. And the great day of the Lord was at hand; and Judith her maid-servant said: How long dost thou humiliate thy soul? Behold, the great day of the Lord is at hand, and it is unlawful for thee to mourn. But take this head-band, which the woman that made it gave to me; for it is not proper that I should wear it, because I am a maid-servant, and it has a royal appearance. And Anna said: Depart from me; for I have not done such things, and the Lord has brought me very low. I fear that some wicked person has given it to thee, and thou hast come to make me a sharer in thy sin. And Judith said: Why should I curse thee, seeing that the Lord hath shut thy womb, so as not to give thee fruit in Israel? And Anna was grieved exceedingly, and put off her garments of mourning, and cleaned her head, and put on her wedding garments, and about the ninth hour went down to the garden to walk. And she saw a laurel, and sat under it, and prayed to the Lord, saying: O God of our fathers, bless me and hear my prayer, as Thou didst bless the womb of Sarah, and didst give her a son Isaac.

3. And gazing towards the heaven, she saw a sparrow's nest in the laurel, and made a lamentation in herself, saying: Alas! who begot me? and what womb produced me? because I have become a curse in the presence of the sons of Israel, and I have been reproached, and they have driven me in derision out of the temple of the Lord. Alas! to what have I been likened? I am not like the fowls of the heaven, because even the fowls of the heaven are productive before Thee, O Lord. Alas! to what have I been likened? I am not like the beasts of the earth, because even the beasts of the earth are productive before Thee, O Lord. Alas! to what have I been likened? I am not like these waters, because even these waters are productive before Thee, O Lord. Alas! to what have I been likened? I am not like this earth, because even the earth bringeth forth its fruits in season, and blesseth Thee, O Lord.

4. And, behold, an angel of the Lord stood by, saying: Anna, Anna, the Lord hath heard thy prayer, and thou shalt conceive, and shall bring forth; and thy seed shall be spoken of in all the world. And Anna said: As the Lord my God liveth, if I beget either male or female, I will bring it as a gift to the Lord my God; and it shall minister to Him in holy things all the days of its life. And, behold, two angels came, saying to her: Behold, Joachim thy husband is coming with his flocks. For an angel of the Lord went down to him, saying: Joachim, Joachim, the Lord God hath heard thy prayer Go down hence; for, behold, thy wife Anna shall conceive. And Joachim went down and called his shepherds, saying: Bring me hither ten she-lambs without spot or blemish, and they shall be for the Lord my God; and bring me twelve tender calves, and they shall be for the priests and the elders; and a hundred goats for all the people. And, behold, Joachim came with his flocks; and Anna stood by the gate, and saw Joachim coming, and she ran anti hung upon his neck, saying: Now I know that the Lord God hath blessed me exceedingly; for, behold the widow no longer a widow, and I the childless shall conceive. And Joachim rested the first day in his house.

5. And on the following day he brought his offerings, saying in himself: If the Lord God has been rendered gracious to me, the plate on the priest's forehead will make it manifest to me. And Joachim brought his offerings, and observed attentively the priest's plate when he went up to the altar of the Lord, and he saw no sin in himself. And Joachim said: Now I know that the Lord has been gracious unto me, and has remitted all my sins. And he went down from the temple of the Lord justified, and departed to his own house. And her months were fulfilled, and in the ninth month Anna brought forth. And she said to the midwife: What have I brought forth? and she said: A girl. And said Anna: My soul has been magnified this day. And she laid her down. And the days having been fulfilled, Anna was purified, and gave the breast to the child, and called her name Mary.

6. And the child grew strong day by day; and when she was six months old, her mother set her on the ground to try whether she could stand, and she walked seven steps and came into her bosom; and she snatched her up, saying: As the Lord my God liveth, thou shall not walk on this earth until I bring thee into the temple of the Lord. And she made a sanctuary in her bed-chamber, and allowed nothing common or unclean to pass through her. And she called the undefiled daughters of the Hebrews, and they led her astray. And when she was a year old, Joachim made a great feast, and invited the priests, and the scribes, and the elders, and all the people of Israel. And Joachim brought the child to the priests; and they blessed her, saying: O God of our fathers, bless this child, and give her an everlasting name to be named in all generations. And all the people said: So be it, so be it, amen. And he brought her to the chief priests; and they blessed her, saying: O God most high, look upon this child, and bless her with the utmost blessing, which shall be for ever. And her mother snatched her up, and took her into the sanctuary of her bed-chamber, and gave her the breast. And Anna made a song to the Lord God, saying: I will sing a song to the Lord my God, for He hath looked upon me, and hath taken away the reproach of mine enemies; and the Lord hath given the the fruit of His righteousness, singular in its kind, and richly endowed before Him. Who will tell the sons of Rubim that Anna gives suck? Hear, hear, ye twelve tribes of Israel, that Anna gives suck. And she laid her to rest in the bed-chamber of her sanctuary, and went out and ministered unto them. And when the supper was ended, they went down rejoicing, and glorifying the God of Israel.

7. And her months were added to the child. And the child was two years old, and Joachim said: Let us take her up to the temple of the Lord, that we may pay the vow that we have vowed, lest perchance the Lord send to us, and our offering be not received. And Anna said: Let us wait for the third year, in order that the child may not seek for father or mother. And Joachim said: So let us wait. And the child was three years old, and Joachim said: Invite the daughters of the Hebrews that are undefiled, and let them take each a lamp, and let them stand with the lamps burning, that the child may not turn back, and her heart be captivated from the temple of the Lord. And they did so until they went up into the temple of the Lord. And the priest received her, and kissed her, and blessed her, saying: The Lord has magnified thy name in all generations. In thee, on the last of the days, the Lord will manifest His redemption to the sons of Israel. And he set her down upon the third step of the altar, and the Lord God sent grace upon her; and she danced with her feet, and all the house of Israel loved her.

8. And her parents went down marvelling, and praising the Lord God, because the child had not turned back. And Mary was in the temple of the Lord as if she were a dove that dwelt there, and she received food from the hand of an angel. And when she was twelve years old there was held a council of the priests, saying: Behold, Mary has reached the age of twelve years in the temple of the Lord. What then shall we do with her, test perchance she defile the sanctuary of the Lord? And they said to the high priest: Thou standest by the altar of the Lord; go in, and pray concerning her; and whatever the Lord shall manifest unto thee, that also will we do. And the high priest went in, taking the robe with the twelve bells into the holy of holies; and he prayed concerning her. And behold an angel of the Lord stood by him, saying unto him: Zacharias, Zacharias, go out and assemble the widowers of the people, and let them bring each his rod; and to whomsoever the Lord shall show a sign, his wife shall she be. And the heralds went out through all the circuit of Judaea, and the trumpet of the Lord sounded, and all ran.

9. And Joseph, throwing away his axe, went out to meet them; and when they had assembled, they went away to the high priest, taking with them their rods. And he, taking the rods of all of them, entered into the temple, and prayed; and having ended his prayer, he took the rods and came out,

and gave them to them: but there was no sign in them, and Joseph took his rod last; and, behold, a dove came out of the rod, and flew upon Joseph's head. And the priest said to Joseph, Thou hast been chosen by lot to take into thy keeping the virgin of the Lord. But Joseph refused, saying: I have children, and I am an old man, and she is a young girl. I am afraid lest I become a laughing-stock to the sons of Israel. And the priest said to Joseph: Fear the Lord thy God, and remember what the Lord did to Dathan, and Abiram, and Korah; how the earth opened, and they were swallowed up on account of their contradiction. And now fear, O Joseph, lest the same things happen in thy house. And Joseph was afraid, and took her into his keeping. And Joseph said to Mary: Behold, I have received thee from the temple of the Lord; and now I leave thee in my house, and go away to build my buildings, and I shall come to thee. The Lord will protect thee.

10. And there was a council of the priests, saying: Let us make a veil for the temple of the Lord. And the priest said: Call to me the undefiled virgins of the family of David. And the officers went away, and sought, and found seven virgins. And the priest remembered the child Mary, that she was of the family of David, and undefiled before God. And the officers went away and brought her. And they brought them into the temple of the Lord. And the priest said: Choose for me by lot who shall spin the gold, and the white, and the fine linen, and the silk, and the blue, and the scarlet, and the true purple. And the true purple and the scarlet fell to the lot of Mary, and she took them, and went away to her house. And at that time Zacharias was dumb, and Samuel was in his place until the time that Zacharias spake. And Mary took the scarlet, and span it.

11. And she took the pitcher, and went out to fill it with water. And, behold, a voice saying: Hail, thou who hast received grace; the Lord is with thee; blessed art thou among women! And she looked round, on the right hand and on the left, to see whence this voice came. And she went away, trembling, to her house, and put down the pitcher; and taking the purple, she sat down on her seat, and drew it out. And, behold, an angel of the Lord stood before her, saying: Fear not, Mary; for thou hast found grace before the Lord of all, and thou shalt conceive, according to His word. And she hearing, reasoned with herself, saying: Shall I conceive by the Lord, the living God? and shall I bring forth as every woman brings forth? And the angel of the Lord said: Not so, Mary; for the power of the Lord shall overshadow thee: wherefore also that holy thing which shall be born of thee shall be called the Son of the Most High. And thou shalt call His name Jesus, for He shall save His people from their sins. And Mary said: Behold, the servant of the Lord before His face: let it be unto me according to thy word.

12. And she made the purple and the scarlet, and took them to the priest. And the priest blessed her, and said: Mary, the Lord God hath magnified thy name, and thou shall be blessed in all the generations of the earth. And Mary, with great joy, went away to Elizabeth her kinswoman, and knocked at the door. And when Elizabeth heard her, she threw away the scarlet, and ran to the door, and opened it; and seeing Mary, she blessed her, and said: Whence is this to me, that the mother of my Lord should come to me? for, behold, that which is in me leaped and blessed thee. But Mary had forgotten the mysteries of which the archangel Gabriel had spoken, and gazed up into heaven, and said: Who am I, O Lord, that all the generations of the earth should bless me? And she remained three months with Elizabeth; and day by day she grew bigger. And Mary being afraid, went away to her own house, and hid herself from the sons of Israel. And she was sixteen years old when these mysteries happened.

13. And she was in her sixth month; and, behold, Joseph came back from his building, and, entering into his house, he discovered that she was big with child. And he smote his face, and threw himself on the ground upon the sackcloth, and wept bitterly, saying: With what face shall I look upon the Lord my God? and what prayer shall I make about this maiden? because I received her a virgin out of the temple of the Lord, and I have not watched over her. Who is it that has hunted me down? Who has done this evil thing in my house, and defiled the virgin? Has not the history of Adam been repeated in me? For just as Adam was in the hour of his singing praise, and the serpent came, and found Eve alone, and completely deceived her, so it has happened to me also. And Joseph stood up from the sackcloth, and called Mary, and said to her: O thou who hast been cared for by God, why hast thou done this and forgotten the Lord thy God? Why hast thou brought low thy soul, thou that wast brought up in the holy of holies, and that didst receive food from the hand of an angel? And she wept bitterly, saying: I am innocent, and have known no man. And Joseph said to her: Whence then is that which is in thy womb? And she said: As the Lord my God liveth, I do not know whence it is to me.

14. And Joseph was greatly afraid, and retired from her, and considered what he should do in regard to her. And Joseph said: If I conceal her sin, I find myself fighting against the law of the Lord; and if I expose her to the sons of Israel, I am afraid lest that which is in her be from an angel, and then I shall be found giving up innocent blood to the doom of death. What then shall I do with her? I will put her away from me secretly. And night came upon him; and, behold, an angel of the Lord appears to him in a dream, saying: Be not afraid for this maiden, for that which is in her is of the Holy Spirit; and she will bring forth a Son, and thou shalt call His name

Jesus, for He will save His people from their sins. And Joseph arose from sleep, and glorified the God of Israel, who had given him this grace; and he kept her.

15. And Annas the scribe came to him, and said: Why hast thou not appeared in our assembly? And Joseph said to him: Because I was weary from my journey, and rested the first day. And he turned, and saw that Mary was with child. And he ran away to the priest? and said to him: Joseph, whom thou didst vouch for, has committed a grievous crime. And the priest said: How so? And he said: He has defiled the virgin whom he received out of the temple of the Lord, and has married her by stealth, and has not revealed it to the sons of Israel. And the priest answering, said: Has Joseph done this? Then said Annas the scribe: Send officers, and thou wilt find the virgin with child. And the officers went away, and found it as he had said; and they brought her along with Joseph to the tribunal. And the priest said: Mary, why hast thou done this? and why hast thou brought thy soul low, and forgotten the Lord thy God? Thou that wast reared in the holy of holies, and that didst receive food from the hand of an angel, and didst hear the hymns, and didst dance before Him, why hast thou done this? And she wept bitterly, saying: As the Lord my God liveth, I am pure before Him, and know not a man. And the priest said to Joseph: Why hast thou done this? And Joseph said: As the Lord liveth, I am pure concerning her. Then said the priest: Bear not false witness, but speak the truth. Thou hast married her by stealth, and hast not revealed it to the sons of Israel, and hast not bowed thy head under the strong hand, that thy seed might be blessed. And Joseph was silent.

16. And the priest said: Give up the virgin whom thou didst receive out of the temple of the Lord. And Joseph burst into tears. And the priest said: I will give you to drink of the water of the ordeal of the Lord, and He shall make manifest your sins in your eyes. And the priest took the water, and gave Joseph to drink and sent him away to the hill-country; and he returned unhurt. And he gave to Mary also to drink, and sent her away to the hill-country; and she returned unhurt. And all the people wondered that sin did not appear in them. And the priest said: If the Lord God has not made manifest your sins, neither do I judge you. And he sent them away. And Joseph took Mary, and went away to his own house, rejoicing and glorifying the God of Israel.

17. And there was an order from the Emperor Augustus, that all in Bethlehem of Judaea should be enrolled. And Joseph said: I shall enrol my sons, but what shall I do with this maiden? How shall I enrol her? As my wife? I am ashamed. As my daughter then? But all the sons of Israel know that she is not my daughter. The day of the Lord shall itself bring it to pass as the Lord will. And he saddled the ass, and set her upon it; and his son led it, and Joseph followed. And when they had come within three miles, Joseph turned and saw her sorrowful; and he said to himself: Likely that which is in her distresses her. And again Joseph turned and saw her laughing. And he said to her: Mary, how is it that I see in thy face at one time laughter, at another sorrow? And Mary said to Joseph: Because I see two peoples with my eyes; the one weeping and lamenting, and the other rejoicing and exulting. And they came into the middle of the road, and Mary said to him: Take me down from off the ass, for that which is in me presses to come forth. And he took her down from off the ass, and said to her: Whither shall I lead thee, and cover thy disgrace? for the place is desert.

18. And he found a cave there, and led her into it; and leaving his two sons beside her, he went out to seek a widwife in the district of Bethlehem. And I Joseph was walking, and was not walking; and I looked up into the sky, and saw the sky astonished; and I looked up to the pole of the heavens, and saw it standing, and the birds of the air keeping still. And I looked down upon the earth, and saw a trough lying, and work-people reclining: and their hands were in the trough. And those that were eating did not eat, and those that were rising did not carry it up, and those that were conveying anything to their mouths did not convey it; but the faces of all were looking upwards. And I saw the sheep walking, and the sheep stood still; and the shepherd raised his hand to strike them, and his hand remained up. And I looked upon the current of the river, and I saw the mouths of the kids resting on the water and not drinking, and all things in a moment were driven from their course.

19. And I saw a woman coming down from the hill-country, and she said to me: O man, whither art thou going? And I said: I am seeking an Hebrew midwife. And she answered and said unto me: Art thou of Israel? And I said to her: Yes. And she said: And who is it that is bringing forth in the cave? And I said: A woman betrothed to me. And she said to me: Is she not thy wife? And I said to her: It is Mary that was reared in the temple of the Lord, and I obtained her by lot as my wife. And yet she is not my wife, but has conceived of the Holy Spirit. And the widwife said to him: Is this true? And Joseph said to her: Come and see. And the midwife went away with him. And they stood in the place of the cave, and behold a luminous cloud overshadowed the cave. And the midwife said: My soul has been magnified this day, because mine eyes have seen strange things -- because salvation has been brought forth to Israel. And immediately the cloud disappeared out of the cave, and a great light shone in the cave, so that the eyes could not bear it. And in a little that light gradually decreased, until the infant appeared, and went and took the breast from His

mother Mary. And the midwife cried out, and said: This is a great day to me, because I have seen this strange sight. And the midwife went forth out of the cave, and Salome met her. And she said to her: Salome, Salome, I have a strange sight to relate to thee: a virgin has brought forth -- a thing which her nature admits not of. Then said Salome: As the Lord my God liveth, unless I thrust in my finger, and search the parts, I will not believe that a virgin has brought forth.

20. And the midwife went in, and said to Mary: Show thyself; for no small controversy has arisen about thee. And Salome put in her finger, and cried out, and said: Woe is me for mine iniquity and mine unbelief, because I have tempted the living God; and, behold, my hand is dropping off as if burned with fire. And she bent her knees before the Lord, saying: O God of my fathers, remember that I am the seed of Abraham, and Isaac, and Jacob; do not make a show of me to the sons of Israel, but restore me to the poor; for Thou knowest, O Lord, that in Thy name I have performed my services, and that I have received my reward at Thy hand. And, behold, an angel of the Lord stood by her, saying to her: Salome, Salome, the Lord hath heard thee. Put thy hand to the infant, and carry it, and thou wilt have safety and joy. And Salome went and carried it, saying: I will worship Him, because a great King has been born to Israel. And, behold, Salome was immediately cured, and she went forth out of the cave justified. And behold a voice saying: Salome, Salome, tell not the strange things thou hast seen, until the child has come into Jerusalem.

21. And, behold, Joseph was ready to go into Judaea. And there was a great commotion in Bethlehem of Judaea, for Magi came, saying: Where is he that is born king of the Jews? for we have seen his star in the east, and have come to worship him. And when Herod heard, he was much disturbed, and sent officers to the Magi. And he sent for the priests, and examined them, saying: How is it written about the Christ? where is He to be born? And they said: In Bethlehem of Judaea, for so it is written. And he sent them away. And he examined the Magi, saying to them: What sign have you seen in reference to the king that has been born? And the Magi said: We have seen a star of great size shining among these stars, and obscuring their light, so that the stars did not appear; and we thus knew that a king has been born to Israel, and we have come to worship him. And Herod said: Go and seek him; and if you find him, let me know, in order that I also may go and worship him. And the Magi went out. And, behold, the star which they had seen in the east went before them until they came to the cave, and it stood over the top of the cave. And the Magi saw the infant with His mother Mary; and they brought forth from their bag gold, and frankincense, and myrrh. And having been warned by the angel not to go into Judaea, they went into their own country by another road.

22. And when Herod knew that he had been mocked by the Magi, in a rage he sent murderers, saying to them: Slay the children from two years old and under. And Mary, having heard that the children were being killed, was afraid, and took the infant and swaddled Him, and put Him into an ox-stall. And Elizabeth, having heard that they were searching for John, took him and went up into the hill-country, and kept looking where to conceal him. And there was no place of concealment. And Elizabeth, groaning with a loud voice, says: O mountain of God, receive mother and child. And immediately the mountain was cleft, and received her. And a light shone about them, for an angel of the Lord was with them, watching over them.

23. And Herod searched for John, and sent officers to Zacharias, saying: Where hast thou hid thy son? And he, answering, said to them: I am the servant of God in holy things, and I sit constantly in the temple of the Lord: I do not know where my son is. And the officers went away, and reported all these things to Herod. And Herod was enraged, and said: His son is destined to be king over Israel. And he sent to him again, saying: Tell the truth; where is thy son? for thou knowest that thy life is in my hand. And Zacharias said: I am God's martyr, if thou sheddest my blood; for the Lord will receive my spirit, because thou sheddest innocent blood at the vestibule of the temple of the Lord. And Zacharias was murdered about daybreak. And the sons of Israel did not know that he had been murdered.

24. But at the hour of the salutation the priests went away, and Zacharias did not come forth to meet them with a blessing, according to his custom. And the priests stood waiting for Zacharias to salute him at the prayer, and to glorify the Most High. And he still delaying, they were all afraid. But one of them ventured to go in, and he saw clotted blood beside the altar; and he heard a voice saying: Zacharias has been murdered, and his blood shall not be wiped up until his avenger come. And hearing this saying, he was afraid, and went out and told it to the priests. And they ventured in, and saw what had happened; and the fretwork of the temple made a wailing noise, and they rent their clothes from the top even to the bottom. And they found not his body, but they found his blood turned into stone. And they were afraid, and went out and reported to the people that Zacharias had been murdered. And all the tribes of the people heard, and mourned, and lamented for him three days and three nights. And after the three days, the priests consulted as to whom they should put in his place; and the lot fell upon Simeon. For it was he who had been warned by the

Holy Spirit that he should not see death until he should see the Christ in the flesh.

And I James that wrote this history in Jerusalem, a commotion having arisen when Herod died, withdrew myself to the wilderness until the commotion in Jerusalem ceased, glorifying the Lord God, who had given me the gift and the wisdom to write this history. And grace shall be with them that fear our Lord Jesus Christ, to whom be glory to ages of ages. Amen.

Book 106. The Apocalypse of Stephen

The 'Revelation called of Stephen' is condemned, like that of Thomas, in the Gelasian Decree. Sixtus Senensis, Bibliotheca Sancta (1593), p. 115, says: 'The Apocalypse of Stephen the first martyr who was one of the seven deacons of the apostles was prized by the Manichaean heretics as Serapion witnesses.' Serapion of Thmuis he elsewhere says (p. 299),wrote a large and very notable work against the Manichaeans in Greek 'which I have lately read'. Our texts of Serapion contain no mention of the Apocalypse of Stephen. But no Manichaean would have cared about the book which I am going to speak of.

[I must record one of the very rare errors of Fabricius here. He (Cod. Apocr. N.T.,i, p.965) cites Sixtus Senensis as saying (on the authority of Serapion) that the Manichaeans so prized the Revelation of Stephen as to carry it in the skin of their thighs! This long puzzled me, and I could not find it in Sixtus. But at last I noticed that at the end of the article just preceding Stephanus, Victor Vitensis is quoted to this effect: The Manichaeans so honoured their teacher that they used to have these words inscribed on the skin of their thighs. 'Manichaeus, disciple of Christ Jesus'. Perhaps some one has already explained this in print; if so, I have not seen it.]

It has been usually guessed that the writing so described was the account of the finding of St. Stephen's body, the whereabouts of which was revealed by Gamaliel in a vision to Lucian. With Stephen were found the bodies of Gamaliel and his son Abibas, and of Nicodemus. Lucian's narrative was known to Augustine: it purports to be of the year 415, and there is little in it, as compared with similar 'inventions' of relics, which justifies its being solemnly condemned as apocryphal .

So says I. Franko, who in 1906 (Zeitschr. f. Ntl. Wiss.) published a Slavonic romance which, he says, is the real beginning of Lucian's narrative.

The substance of it is this:

Two years after the Ascension there was a contest about Jesus. Many learned men had assembled at Jerusalem from Ethiopia, the Thebaid, Alexandria, Jerusalem, Asia, Mauretania and Babylon. There was a great clamour among them like thunder, lasting till the fourth hour.

Stephen, a learned man of the tribe of Benjamin, stood on a high place and addressed the assembly. Why this tumult? said he. Blessed is he who has not doubted concerning Jesus. Born of a pure virgin he filled the world with light. By Satan's contrivances Herod slew 14,000 (144,000) children. He spoke of the miracles of Jesus. Woe to the unbelievers when he shall come as judge, with angels, a fiery chariot, a mighty wind: the stars shall fall, the heavens open, the books be brought forward. The twelve angels who are set over every soul shall unveil the deeds of men. The sea shall move and give up what is in it. The mountains fall, all the surface of the earth becomes smooth. Great winged thrones are set. The Lord, and Christ, and the Holy Spirit take their seats. The Father bids Jesus sit on his right hand.

At this point the crowd cried out: Blasphemy! and took Stephen before Pilate.

Pilate stood on the steps and reproached them: You compelled me to crucify the Innocent; why rage against this man? Why gnash your teeth? Are ye yet foolish?

They led Stephen away. Caiaphas ordered him to be beaten till the blood ran. And he prayed: Lay not this sin to their charge. We saw how angels ministered to him.

In the morning Pilate called his wife and two children: they baptized themselves and praised God.

Three thousand men now assembled and disputed with Stephen for three days and three nights. On the fourth day they took counsel and sent to Caesarea of Palestine for Saul of Tarsus, who had a commission to seize upon Christians. He took his place on the judgement seat and said: I wonder that thou, a wise man, and my kinsman, believest all this. None of the Sanhedrin have given up the Law. I have been through all Judaea, Galilee, Peraea, Damascus, and the city of the Jesitites to seek out believers.

Stephen lifted up his hands and said: Silence, persecutor! Recognize the Son of God. Thou makest me doubt of my own descent. But I see that thou shalt ere long drink of the same cup as I. What thou doest, do quickly. Saul rent his clothes and beat Stephen. Gamaliel, Saul's teacher, sprang forth and gave Saul a buffet, saying: Did I teach thee such conduct? know that what this man saith is acceptable and good.

Saul was yet more enraged, and looked fiercely on him, saying: I spare thine old age, but thou shalt reap a due reward for this. Gamaliel answered: I ask nothing better than to suffer with Christ. The elders rent their clothes, cast dust on their heads, and cried: Crucify the blasphemers. Saul said: Guard them until the morrow. Next day he sat on the judgement seat and had them brought before him, and they were led away to be crucified. An angel came and cast away the cross, and Stephen's wounds were healed. Seven men came and poured molten lead into his mouth and pitch into his ears. They drove nails into his breast and feet, and he prayed for their forgiveness. Again an angel came down and healed him, and a great multitude believed.

Next day all assembled and took him out of the city to judge him. He mounted upon a stone and addressed them: How long will ye harden your hearts? The Law and the Prophets spake of Christ. In the first Law, and the second, and the other books it is written: When the year of the covenant cometh I will send my beloved angel, the good spirit of sonship, from a pure maiden, the fruit of truth, without ploughshare and without seed, and an image of sowing (?), and the fruit shall grow after the . . . of planting for ever from the word of my covenant, and signs shall come to pass. And Isaiah saith: Unto us a child is born, &c. And again: Behold, a virgin shall conceive, &c. And the prophet Nathan said: I saw one, a maiden and without touch of man, and a man child in her arms, and that was the Lord of the earth unto the end of the earth. And again the prophet Baruch saith: Christ the eternal appeareth as a stone from the mountain and breaketh in pieces the idol temples of the . . . David also said: Arise, O Lord, unto thy resting place, &c. Understand then, O foolish ones, what the prophet saith: In this word shalt thou judge.

And he looked up to heaven and said: I see the heaven opened and the Son of man standing at the right hand of God.

Then they laid hands on him, saying: He blasphemeth! Gamaliel said: Wherein? This righteous man hath seen the Son saying to the Father: Lo, the Jews rage against me and cease not to ill-treat them that confess my name. And the Father said: Sit thou on my right hand until I make thine enemies thy footstool.

Then they bound Stephen and took him away to Alexander, the reader, who was a chief of the people, and of the troop in Tiberias.

In the fourth watch of the night, a light as of lightning shone round about him, and a voice said: Be strong. Thou art my first martyr, and thine hour is nigh. I will write the record of thee in the book of everlasting life.

The Jews took counsel and decreed that he should be stoned. There were with him Abibas, Nicodemus, Gamaliel, Pilate, his wife and two children, and a multitude of believers. Saul stood forth and beckoned, and said: It would have been better that this man should not be slain, because of his great wisdom: but forasmuch as he is an apostate, I condemn Stephen to be stoned. The people said: He shall be stoned: but those who stood in the front rank with staves looked on each other and durst not lay hands on him: for he was renowned among the people.

Saul was wroth, and stripped those servants of their garments and laid them on the table; and commanded the men to stone Stephen.

Stephen looked round and said: Saul, Saul, that which thou doest unto me to-day, that same will the Jews do unto thee to-morrow. And when thou sufferest, thou shalt think on me.

The people cast stones upon him so thickly that the light of the sun was darkened. Nicodemus and Gamaliel put their arms about him and shielded him, and were slain, and gave up their souls to Christ.

Stephen prayed, saying: Forgive them that stone us, for by their means we trust to enter into thy kingdom. And at the tenth hour he gave up the ghost. Then beautiful youths appeared, and fell upon the bodies and wept aloud: and the people beheld the souls borne up by angels into heaven, and saw the heavens open and the hosts coming to meet the souls. And the people mourned for three days and three nights.

Pilate took the bodies and put each one into a silver coffin with his name upon it: but Stephen's coffin was gilt: and he laid them in his secret sepulchre. But Stephen prayed: Let my body be buried in my land of Serasima in Kapogemala (Caphargamala) until the revealing, when the martyrs that follow me shall be gathered together. And an angel came and removed the bodies thither.

But Pilate rose early to burn incense before the bodies, and found them not; and rent his clothes, saying: Was I then not worthy to be thy servant? On the night following, Stephen appeared and said to him: Weep not. I prayed God to hide our bodies. In the time of our revealing one of thy seed shall find us after a vision, and thy desire shall be fulfilled. But build a house of prayer and celebrate our feast in the month of April. After seven months thou also shalt rest. And Pilate did so: and he died, and was buried at Kapartasala: and his wife also died in peace. But the holy martyrs appeared thrice to venerable and believing men, speaking to them, and revealing divine words: for after their death many believed.

Book 107. The Apocalypse of James

It is the Lord who spoke with me: "See now the completion of my redemption. I have given you a sign of these things, James, my brother. For not without reason have I called you my brother, although you are not my brother materially. And I am not ignorant concerning you; so that when I give you a sign - know and hear."

"Nothing existed except Him-who-is. He is unnameable and ineffable. I myself am also unnameable, from Him-who-is, just as I have been given a number of names - two from Him-who-is. Since you have asked concerning femaleness, femaleness existed, but femaleness was not first. And it prepared for itself powers and gods. But it did not exist when I came forth, since I am an image of Him-who-is. But I have brought forth the image of him so that the sons of Him-who-is might know what things are theirs and what things are alien (to them). Behold, I shall reveal to you everything of this mystery. For they will seize me the day after tomorrow. But my redemption will be near."

James said, "Rabbi, you have said, 'they will seize me.' But I, what can I do?" He said to me, "Fear not, James. You too will they seize. But leave Jerusalem. For it is she who always gives the cup of bitterness to the sons of light. She is a dwelling place of a great number of archons. But your redemption will be preserved from them. So that you may understand who they are and what kinds they are, you will [...]. And listen. They are not [...] but archons [...]. These twelve [...] down [...] archons [...] upon his own hebdomad."

James said, "Rabbi, are there then twelve hebdomads and not seven as there are in the scriptures?" The Lord said, "James, he who spoke concerning this scripture had a limited understanding. I, however, shall reveal to you what has come forth from him who has no number. I shall give a sign concerning their number. As for what has come forth from him who has no measure, I shall give a sign concerning their measure"

James said, "Rabbi, behold then, I have received their number. There are seventy-two measures!" The Lord said, "These are the seventy-two heavens, which are their subordinates. These are the powers of all their might; and they were established by them; and these are they who were distributed everywhere, existing under the authority of the twelve archons. The inferior power among them brought forth for itself angels and unnumbered hosts. Him-who-is, however, has been given [...] on account of [...] Him-who-is [...] they are unnumbered. If you want to give them a number now, you will not be able to do so until you cast away from your blind thought, this bond of flesh which encircles you. And then you will reach Him-who-is. And you will no longer be James; rather you are the One-who-is. And all those who are unnumbered will all have been named."

<James said,> "Rabbi, in what way shall I reach Him-who-is, since all these powers and these hosts are armed against me?" He said to me, "These powers are not armed against you specifically, but are armed against another. It is against me that they are armed. And they are armed with other powers. But they are armed against me in judgment. They did not give [...] to me in it [...] through them [...]. In this place [...] suffering, I shall [...]. He will [...] and I shall not rebuke them. But there shall be within me a silence and a hidden mystery. But I am fainthearted before their anger."

James said, "Rabbi, if they arm themselves against you, then is there no blame?"

You have come with knowledge,
that you might rebuke their forgetfulness.
You have come with recollection,
that you might rebuke their ignorance.
But I was concerned because of you.
For you descended into a great ignorance,
but you have not been defiled by anything in it.
For you descended into a great mindlessness,
and your recollection remained.
You walked in mud,
and your garments were not soiled,
and you have not been buried in their filth,
and you have not been caught.
And I was not like them, but I clothed myself with everything of theirs.
There is in me forgetfulness,
yet I remember things that are not theirs.
There is in me [....],
and I am in their [...].
[...] knowledge [...] not in their sufferings [...]. But I have become afraid before them, since they rule. For what will they do? What will I be able to say? Or what word will I be able to say that I may escape them?"

The Lord said, "James, I praise your understanding and your fear. If you continue to be distressed, do not be concerned for anything else except your redemption. For behold, I shall complete this destiny upon this earth as I have said from the heavens. And I shall reveal to you your redemption."

James said, "Rabbi, how, after these things, will you appear to us again? After they seize you, and you complete this destiny, you will go up to Him-who-is." The Lord said, "James, after these things I shall reveal to you everything, not for your sake alone but for the sake of the unbelief of men, so that faith may exist in them. For a multitude will attain to faith and they will increase in [...]. And after this I shall appear for a reproof to the archons. And I shall reveal to them that he cannot be seized. If they seize him, then he will overpower each of them. But now I shall go. Remember the things I have spoken and let them go up before you." James said,"Lord, I shall hasten as you have said." The Lord said farewell to him and fulfilled what was fitting.

When James heard of his suffering and was much distressed, they awaited the sign of his coming. And he came after several days. And James was walking upon the mountain which is called "Gaugelan", with his disciples, who listened to him because they had been distressed, and he was [...] a comforter, saying, "This is [...] second [...]" Then the crowd dispersed, but James remained [...] prayer [...], as was his custom.

And the Lord appeared to him. Then he stopped (his) prayer and embraced him. He kissed him, saying, "Rabbi, I have found you! I have heard of your sufferings, which you endured. And I have been much distressed. My compassion you know. Therefore, on reflection, I was wishing that I would not see this people. They must be judged for these things that they have done. For these things that they have done are contrary to what is fitting."

The Lord said, "James, do not be concerned for me or for this people. I am he who was within me. Never have I suffered in any way, nor have I been distressed. And this people has done me no harm. But this (people) existed as a type of the archons, and it deserved to be destroyed through them. But [...] the archons, [...] who has [...] but since it [...] angry with [...] The just [...] is his servant. Therefore your name is "James the Just". You see how you will become sober when you see me. And you stopped this prayer. Now since you are a just man of God, you have embraced me and kissed me. Truly I say to you that you have stirred up great anger and wrath against yourself. But (this has happened) so that these others might come to be."

But James was timid (and) wept. And he was very distressed. And they both sat down upon a rock. The Lord said to him, "James, thus you will undergo these sufferings. But do not be sad. For the flesh is weak. It will receive what has been ordained for it. But as for you, do not be timid or afraid". The Lord ceased.

Now when James heard these things, he wiped away the tears in his eyes and very bitter [...] which is [...]. The Lord said to him, "James, behold, I shall reveal to you your redemption. When you are seized, and you undergo these sufferings, a multitude will arm themselves against you that <they> may seize you. And in particular three of them will seize you - they who sit (there) as toll collectors. Not only do they demand toll, but they also take away souls by theft. When you come into their power, one of them who is their guard will say to you, 'Who are you or where are you from?' You are to say to him, 'I am a son, and I am from the Father.' He will say to you, 'What sort of son are you, and to what father do you belong?' You are to say to him, 'I am from the Pre-existent Father, and a son in the Pre-existent One.' When he says to you, [...], you are to say to him [...] in the [...] that I might [...]."

'[...] of alien things?' You are to say to him, 'They are not entirely alien, but they are from Achamoth, who is the female. And these she produced as she brought down the race from the Pre-existent One. So then they are not alien, but they are ours. They are indeed ours because she who is mistress of them is from the Pre-existent One. At the same time they are alien because the Pre-existent One did not have intercourse with her, when she produced them.' When he also says to you, 'Where will you go?', you are to say to him, 'To the place from which I have come, there shall I return.' And if you say these things, you will escape their attacks.

"But when you come to these three detainers who take away souls by theft in that place [...] these. You [...] a vessel [...] much more than [...] of the one whom you [...] for [...] her root. You too will be sober [...]. But I shall call upon the imperishable knowledge, which is Sophia who is in the Father (and) who is the mother of Achamoth. Achamoth had no father nor male consort, but she is female from a female. She produced you without a male, since she was alone (and) in ignorance as to what lives through her mother because she thought that she alone existed. But I shall cry out to her mother. And then they will fall into confusion (and) will blame their root and the race of their mother. But you will go up to what is yours [...] you will [...] the Pre-existent One."

"They are a type of the twelve disciples and the twelve pairs, [...] Achamoth, which is translated 'Sophia'. And who I myself am, (and) who the imperishable Sophia (is) through whom you will be redeemed, and (who are) all the sons of Him-who-is - these things they have known and have hidden within them. You are to hide <these things> within you, and you are to keep silence. But you are to reveal them to Addai. When you depart, immediately war will be made with this land. Weep, then, for him who dwells in Jerusalem. But let Addai take these things to heart. In the tenth year let Addai sit and write them down. And when he writes them down [...] and they are to give them [...] he has the [...] he is called Levi. Then he is to bring [...] word [...] from what I said earlier [...] a woman [...] Jerusalem in her [...] and he begets two sons through her. They are to inherit these things and the understanding of him who [...] exalts. And they are to receive [...] through him from his intellect. Now, the younger of them is greater. And may these things remain hidden in him until he comes to the age of seventeen years [...] beginning [...] through them. They will pursue him exceedingly, since they are from his [...] companions. He will be proclaimed through them, and they will proclaim this word. Then he will become a seed of [...]."

James said, "I am satisfied [...] and they are [...] my soul. Yet another thing I ask of you: who are the seven women who have been your disciples? And behold all women bless you. I also am amazed how powerless vessels have become strong by a perception which is in them." The Lord said, "You [...] well [...] a spirit of [...], a spirit of thought, a spirit of counsel of a [...], a spirit [...] a spirit of knowledge [...] of their fear. [...] when we had passed through the breath of this archon who is named Adonaios [...] him and [...] he was ignorant [...] when I came forth from him, he remembered that I am a son of his. He was gracious to me at that time as his son. And then, before <I> appeared here, <he> cast them among this people. And from the place of heaven the prophets [...]."

James said, "Rabbi, [...] I [...] all together [...] in them especially [...]." The Lord said, "James, I praise you [...] walk upon the earth [...] the words while he [...] on the [...]. For cast away from you the cup which is bitterness. For some from [...] set themselves against you. For you have begun to understand their roots from beginning to end. Cast away from yourself all lawlessness. And beware lest they envy you. When you speak these words of this perception, encourage these four: Salome and Mariam and Martha and Arsinoe [...] since he takes some [...] to me he is [...] burnt offerings and [...]. But I [...] not in this way; but [...] first-fruits of the [...] upward [...] so that the power of God might appear. The perishable has gone up to the imperishable and the female element has attained to this male element."

James said, "Rabbi, into these three (things), then, has their [...] been cast. For they have been reviled, and they have been persecuted [...]. Behold [...] everything [...] from anyone [...]. For you have received [...] of knowledge. And [...] that what is the [...] go [...] you will find [...]. But I shall go forth and shall reveal that they believed in you, that they may be content with their blessing and salvation, and this revelation may come to pass."

And he went at that time immediately and rebuked the twelve and cast out of them contentment concerning the way of knowledge [...].

[...]. And the majority of them [...] when they saw, the messenger took in [...]. The others [...] said, "[...] him from this earth. For he is not worthy of life." These, then, were afraid. They arose, saying, "We have no part in this blood, for a just man will perish through injustice" James departed so that [...] look [...] for we [...] him.

Book 108. The Apocryphon of John

The teaching of the savior, and the revelation of the mysteries and the things hidden in silence, even these things which he taught John, his disciple.

And it happened one day, when John, the brother of James - who are the sons of Zebedee - had come up to the temple, that a Pharisee named Arimanius approached him and said to him, "Where is your master whom you followed?" And he said to him, "He has gone to the place from which he came." The Pharisee said to him, "With deception did this Nazarene deceive you (pl.), and he filled your ears with lies, and closed your hearts (and) turned you from the traditions of your fathers."

When I, John, heard these things I turned away from the temple to a desert place. And I grieved greatly in my heart, saying, "How then was the savior appointed, and why was he sent into the world by his Father, and who is his Father who sent him, and of what sort is that aeon to which we shall go? For what did he mean when he said to us, 'This aeon to which you will go is of the type of the imperishable aeon, but he did not teach us concerning the latter, of what sort it is."

Straightway, while I was contemplating these things, behold, the heavens opened and the whole creation which is below heaven shone, and the world was shaken. I was afraid, and behold I saw in the light a youth who stood by me. While I looked at him, he became like an old man. And he changed his likeness (again), becoming like a servant. There was not a plurality before me, but there was a likeness with multiple forms in the light, and the likenesses appeared through each other, and the likeness had three forms.

He said to me, "John, John, why do you doubt, or why are you afraid? You are not unfamiliar with this image, are you? - that is, do not be timid! - I am the one who is with you (pl.) always. I am the Father, I am the Mother, I am the Son. I am the undefiled and incorruptible one. Now I have come to teach you what is and what was and what will come to pass, that you may know the things which are not revealed and those which are revealed, and to teach you concerning the unwavering race of the perfect Man. Now, therefore, lift up your face, that you may receive the things that I shall teach you today, and may tell them to your fellow spirits who are from the unwavering race of the perfect Man."

And I asked to know it, and he said to me, "The Monad is a monarchy with nothing above it. It is he who exists as God and Father of everything, the invisible One who is above everything, who exists as incorruption, which is in the pure light into which no eye can look.

"He is the invisible Spirit, of whom it is not right to think of him as a god, or something similar. For he is more than a god, since there is nothing above him, for no one lords it over him. For he does not exist in something inferior to him, since everything exists in him. For it is he who establishes himself. He is eternal, since he does not need anything. For he is total perfection. He did not lack anything, that he might be completed by it; rather he is always completely perfect in light. He is illimitable, since there is no one prior to him to set limits to him. He is unsearchable, since there exists no one prior to him to examine him. He is immeasurable, since there was no one prior to him to measure him. He is invisible, since no one saw him. He is eternal, since he exists eternally. He is ineffable, since no one was able to comprehend him to speak about him. He is unnameable, since there is no one prior to him to give him a name.

"He is immeasurable light, which is pure, holy (and) immaculate. He is ineffable, being perfect in incorruptibility. (He is) not in perfection, nor in blessedness, nor in divinity, but he is far superior. He is not corporeal nor is he incorporeal. He is neither large nor is he small. There is no way to say, 'What is his quantity?' or, 'What is his quality?', for no one can know him. He is not someone among (other) beings, rather he is far superior. Not that he is (simply) superior, but his essence does not partake in the aeons nor in time. For he who partakes in an aeon was prepared beforehand. Time was not apportioned to him, since he does not receive anything from another, for it would be received on loan. For he who precedes someone does not lack, that he may receive from him. For rather, it is the latter that looks expectantly at him in his light.

"For the perfection is majestic. He is pure, immeasurable mind. He is an aeon-giving aeon. He is life-giving life. He is a blessedness-giving blessed one. He is knowledge-giving knowledge. He is goodness-giving goodness. He is mercy and redemption-giving mercy. He is grace-giving grace, not because he possesses it, but because he gives the immeasurable, incomprehensible light.

"How am I to speak with you about him? His aeon is indestructible, at rest and existing in silence, reposing (and) being prior to everything. For he is the head of all the aeons, and it is he who gives them strength in his goodness. For we know not the ineffable things, and we do not understand what is immeasurable, except for him who came forth from him, namely (from) the Father. For it is he who told it to us alone. For it is he who looks at himself in his light which surrounds him, namely the spring of the water of life. And it is he who gives to all the aeons and in every way, (and) who gazes upon his image which he sees in the spring of the Spirit. It is he who puts his desire in his water-light which is in the spring of the pure light-water which surrounds him.

"And his thought performed a deed and she came forth, namely she who had appeared before him in the shine of his light. This is the first power which was before all of them (and) which came forth from his mind, She is the forethought of the All - her light shines like his light - the perfect power which is the image of the invisible, virginal Spirit who is perfect. The first power, the glory of Barbelo, the perfect glory in the aeons, the glory of the revelation, she glorified the virginal Spirit and it was she who praised him, because thanks to him she had come forth. This is the first thought, his image; she became the womb of everything, for it is she who is prior to them all, the Mother-Father, the first man, the holy Spirit, the thrice-male, the thrice-powerful, the thrice-named androgynous one, and the eternal aeon among the invisible ones, and the first to come forth.

"<She> requested from the invisible, virginal Spirit - that is Barbelo - to give her foreknowledge. And the Spirit consented. And when he had consented, the foreknowledge came forth, and it stood by the forethought; it originates from the thought of the invisible, virginal Spirit. It glorified him and his perfect power, Barbelo, for it was for her sake that it had come into being.

"And she requested again to grant her indestructibility, and he consented. When he had consented, indestructibility came forth, and it stood by the thought and the foreknowledge. It glorified the invisible One and Barbelo, the one for whose sake they had come into being.

"And Barbelo requested to grant her eternal life. And the invisible Spirit consented. And when he had consented, eternal life came forth, and they attended and glorified the invisible Spirit and Barbelo, the one for whose sake they had come into being.

"And she requested again to grant her truth. And the invisible Spirit consented. And when he had consented, truth came forth, and they attended and glorified the invisible, excellent Spirit and his Barbelo, the one for whose sake they had come into being.

"This is the pentad of the aeons of the Father, which is the first man, the image of the invisible Spirit; it is the forethought, which Barbelo, and the thought, and the foreknowledge, and the indestructibility, and the eternal life, and the truth. This is the androgynous pentad of the aeons, which is the decad of the aeons, which is the Father.

"And he looked at Barbelo with the pure light which surrounds the invisible Spirit, and (with) his spark, and she conceived from him. He begot a spark of light with a light resembling blessedness. But it does not equal his greatness. This was an only-begotten child of the Mother-Father which had come forth; it is the only offspring, the only-begotten one of the Father, the pure Light.

"And the invisible, virginal Spirit rejoiced over the light which came forth, that which was brought forth first by the first power of his forethought, which is Barbelo. And he anointed it with his goodness until it became perfect, not lacking in any goodness, because he had anointed it with the goodness of the invisible Spirit. And it attended him as he poured upon it. And immediately when it had received from the Spirit, it glorified the holy Spirit and the perfect forethought, for whose sake it had come forth.

"And it requested to give it a fellow worker, which is the mind, and he consented gladly. And when the invisible Spirit had consented, the mind came forth, and it attended Christ, glorifying him and Barbelo. And all these came into being in silence.

"And the mind wanted to perform a deed through the word of the invisible Spirit. And his will became a deed and it appeared with the mind; and the light glorified it. And the word followed the will. For because of the word, Christ the divine Autogenes created everything. And the eternal life <and> his will and the mind and the foreknowledge attended and glorified the invisible Spirit and Barbelo, for whose sake they had come into being.

"And the holy Spirit completed the divine Autogenes, his son, together with Barbelo, that he may attend the mighty and invisible, virginal Spirit as the divine Autogenes, the Christ whom he had honored with a mighty voice. He came forth through the forethought. And the invisible, virginal Spirit placed the divine Autogenes of truth over everything. And he subjected to him every authority, and the truth which is in him, that he may know the All which had been called with a name exalted above every name. For that name will be mentioned to those who are worthy of it.

"For from the light, which is the Christ, and the indestructibility, through the gift of the Spirit the four lights (appeared) from the divine Autogenes. He expected that they might attend him. And the three (are) will, thought, and life. And the four powers (are) understanding, grace, perception, and prudence. And grace belongs to the light-aeon Armozel, which is the first angel. And there are three other aeons with this aeon: grace, truth, and form. And the second light (is) Oriel, who has been placed over the second aeon. And there are three other aeons with him: conception, perception, and memory. And the third light is Daveithai, who has been placed over the third aeon. And there are three other aeons with him: understanding, love, and idea. And the fourth aeon was placed over the fourth light Eleleth. And there are three other aeons with him: perfection, peace, and wisdom. These are the four lights which attend the divine Autogenes, (and) these are the twelve aeons which attend the son of the mighty one, the Autogenes, the Christ, through the will and the gift of the invisible Spirit. And the twelve aeons belong to the son of the Autogenes. And all things were established by the will of the holy Spirit through the Autogenes.

"And from the foreknowledge of the perfect mind, through the revelation of the will of the invisible Spirit and the will of the Autogenes, <the> perfect Man (appeared), the first revelation, and the truth. It is he whom the virginal Spirit called Pigera-Adamas, and he placed him over the first aeon with the mighty one, the Autogenes, the Christ, by the first light Armozel; and with him are his powers. And the invisible one gave him a spiritual, invincible power. And he spoke and glorified and praised the invisible Spirit, saying, 'It is for thy sake that everything has come into being and everything will return to thee. I shall praise and glorify thee and the Autogenes and the aeons, the three: the Father, the Mother, and the Son, the perfect power.'

"And he placed his son Seth over the second aeon in the presence of the second light Oriel. And in the third aeon the seed of Seth was placed over the third light Daveithai. And the souls of the saints were placed (there). And in the fourth aeon the souls were placed of those who do not know the Pleroma and who did not repent at once, but who persisted for a while and repented afterwards; they are by the fourth light Eleleth. These are creatures which glorify the invisible Spirit.

"And the Sophia of the Epinoia, being an aeon, conceived a thought from herself and the conception of the invisible Spirit and foreknowledge. She wanted to bring forth a likeness out of herself without the consent of the Spirit, - he had not approved - and without her consort, and without his consideration. And though the person of her maleness had not approved, and she had not found her agreement, and she had thought without the consent of the Spirit and the knowledge of her agreement, (yet) she brought forth. And because of the invincible power which is in her, her thought did not remain idle, and something came out of her which was imperfect and different from her appearance, because she had created it without her consort. And it was dissimilar to the likeness of its mother, for it has another form.

"And when she saw (the consequences of) her desire, it changed into a form of a lion-faced serpent. And its eyes were like lightning fires which flash. She cast it away from her, outside that place, that no one of the immortal ones might see it, for she had created it in ignorance. And she surrounded it with a luminous cloud, and she placed a throne in the middle of the cloud that no one might see it except the holy Spirit who is called the mother of the living. And she called his name Yaltabaoth.

"This is the first archon who took a great power from his mother. And he removed himself from her and moved away from the places in which he was born. He became strong and created for himself other aeons with a flame of luminous fire which (still) exists now. And he joined with his arrogance which is in him and begot authorities for himself. The name of the first one is Athoth, whom the generations call the reaper. The second one is Harmas, who is the eye of envy. The third one is Kalila-Oumbri. The fourth one is Yabel. The fifth one is Adonaiou, who is called Sabaoth. The sixth one is Cain, whom the generations of men call the sun. The seventh is Abel. The eighth is Abrisene. The ninth is Yobel. The tenth is Armoupieel. The eleventh is Melceir-Adonein. The twelfth is Belias, it is he who is over the depth of Hades. And he placed seven kings - each corresponding to the firmaments of heaven - over the seven heavens, and five over the depth of the abyss, that they may reign. And he shared his fire with them, but he did not send forth from the power of the light which he had taken from his mother, for he is ignorant darkness.

"And when the light had mixed with the darkness, it caused the darkness to shine. And when the darkness had mixed with the light, it darkened the light and it became neither light nor dark, but it became dim.

"Now the archon who is weak has three names. The first name is Yaltabaoth, the second is Saklas, and the third is Samael. And he is impious in his arrogance which is in him. For he said, 'I am God and there is no other God beside me,' for he is ignorant of his strength, the place from which he had come.

"And the archons created seven powers for themselves, and the powers created for themselves six angels for each one until they became 365 angels. And these are the bodies belonging with the names: the first is Athoth, a he has a sheep's face; the second is Eloaiou, he has a donkey's face; the third is Astaphaios, he has a hyena's face; the fourth is Yao, he has a serpent's face with seven heads; the fifth is Sabaoth, he has a dragon's face; the sixth is Adonin, he had a monkey's face; the seventh is Sabbede, he has a shining fire-face. This is the sevenness of the week.

"But Yaltabaoth had a multitude of faces, more than all of them, so that he could put a face before all of them, according to his desire, when he is in the midst of seraphs. He shared his fire with them; therefore he became lord over them. Because of the power of the glory he possessed of his mother's light, he called himself God. And he did not obey the place from which he came. And he united the seven powers in his thought with the authorities which were with him. And when he spoke it happened. And he named each power beginning with the highest: the first is goodness with the first (authority), Athoth; the second is foreknowledge with the second one, Eloaio; and the third is divinity with the third one, Astraphaio); the fourth is lordship with the fourth one, Yao; the fifth is kingdom with the fifth one, Sabaoth; the sixth is envy with the sixth one, Adonein; the seventh is understanding with the seventh one, Sabbateon. And these have a firmament corresponding to each aeon-heaven. They were given names according to the glory which belongs to heaven for the destruction of the powers. And in the names which were given to them by their Originator there was power. But the names which were given them according to the glory which belongs to heaven mean for them destruction and powerlessness. Thus they have two names.

"And having created [...] everything, he organized according to the model of the first aeons which had come into being, so that he might create them like the indestructible ones. Not because he had seen the indestructible ones, but the power in him, which he had taken from his mother, produced in him the likeness of the cosmos. And when he saw the creation which surrounds him, and the multitude of the angels around him which had come forth from him, he said to them, 'I am a jealous God, and there is no other God beside me.' But by announcing this he indicated to the angels who attended him that there exists another God. For if there were no other one, of whom would he be jealous?

"Then the mother began to move to and fro. She became aware of the deficiency when the brightness of her light diminished. And she became dark because her consort had not agreed with her."

And I said, "Lord, what does it mean that she moved to and fro?" But he smiled and said, "Do not think it is, as Moses said, 'above the waters.' No, but when she had seen the wickedness which had happened, and the theft which her son had committed, she repented. And she was overcome by forgetfulness in the darkness of ignorance and she began to be ashamed. And she did not dare to return, but she was moving about. And the moving is the going to and fro.

"And the arrogant one took a power from his mother. For he was ignorant, thinking that there existed no other except his mother alone. And when he saw the multitude of the angels which he had created, then he exalted himself above them.

"And when the mother recognized that the garment of darkness was imperfect, then she knew that her consort had not agreed with her. She repented with much weeping. And the whole pleroma heard the prayer of her repentance, and they praised on her behalf the invisible, virginal Spirit. And he consented; and when the invisible Spirit had consented, the holy Spirit poured over her from their whole pleroma. For it was not her consort who came to her, but he came to her through the pleroma in order that he might correct her deficiency. And she was taken up not to her own aeon but above her son, that she might be in the ninth until she has corrected her deficiency.

"And a voice came forth from the exalted aeon-heaven: 'The Man exists and the son of Man.' And the chief archon, Yaltabaoth, heard (it) and thought that the voice had come from his mother. And he did not know

from where it came. And he taught them, the holy and perfect Mother-Father, the complete foreknowledge, the image of the invisible one who is the Father of the all (and) through whom everything came into being, the first Man. For he revealed his likeness in a human form.

"And the whole aeon of the chief archon trembled, and the foundations of the abyss shook. And of the waters which are above matter, the underside was illuminated by the appearance of his image which had been revealed. And when all the authorities and the chief archon looked, they saw the whole region of the underside which was illuminated. And through the light they saw the form of the image in the water.

"And he said to the authorities which attend him, 'Come, let us create a man according to the image of God and according to our likeness, that his image may become a light for us.' And they created by means of their respective powers in correspondence with the characteristics which were given. And each authority supplied a characteristic in the form of the image which he had seen in its natural (form). He created a being according to the likeness of the first, perfect Man. And they said, 'Let us call him Adam, that his name may become a power of light for us.'

"And the powers began: the first one, goodness, created a bone-soul; and the second, foreknowledge, created a sinew-soul; the third, divinity, created a flesh-soul; and the fourth, the lordship, created a marrow-soul; the fifth, kingdom, created a blood-soul; the sixth, envy, created a skin-soul; the seventh, understanding, created a hair-soul. And the multitude of the angels attended him and they received from the powers the seven substances of the natural (form) in order to create the proportions of the limbs and the proportion of the rump and the proper working together of each of the parts.

"The first one began to create the head. Eteraphaope-Abron created his head; Meniggesstroeth created the brain; Asterechme (created) the right eye; Thaspomocha, the left eye; Yeronumos, the right ear; Bissoum, the left ear; Akioreim, the nose; Banen-Ephroum, the lips; Amen, the teeth; Ibikan, the molars; Basiliademe, the tonsils; Achcha, the uvula; Adaban, the neck; Chaaman, the vertebrae; Dearcho, the throat; Tebar, the right shoulder; [...], the left shoulder; Mniarcon, the right elbow; [...], the left elbow; Abitrion, the right underarm; Evanthen, the left underarm; Krys, the right hand; Beluai, the left hand; Treneu, the fingers of the right hand; Balbel, the fingers of the left hand; Kriman, the nails of the hands; Astrops, the right breast; Barroph, the left breast; Baoum, the right shoulder joint; Ararim, the left shoulder joint; Areche, the belly; Phthave, the navel; Senaphim, the abdomen; Arachethopi, the right ribs; Zabedo, the left ribs; Barias, the right hip; Phnouth the left hip; Abenlenarchei, the marrow; Chnoumeninorin, the bones; Gesole, the stomach; Agromauna, the heart; Bano, the lungs; Sostrapal, the liver; Anesimalar, the spleen; Thopithro, the intestines; Biblo, the kidneys; Roeror, the sinews; Taphreo, the spine of the body; Ipouspoboba, the veins; Bineborin, the arteries; Atoimenpsephei, theirs are the breaths which are in all the limbs; Entholleia, all the flesh; Bedouk, the right buttock (?); Arabeei, the left penis; Eilo, the testicles; Sorma, the genitals; Gorma-Kaiochlabar, the right thigh; Nebrith, the left thigh; Pserem, the kidneys of the right leg; Asaklas, the left kidney; Ormaoth, the right leg; Emenun, the left leg; Knyx, the right shin-bone; Tupelon, the left shin-bone; Achiel, the right knee; Phnene, the left knee; Phiouthrom, the right foot; Boabel, its toes; Trachoun, the left foot; Phikna, its toes; Miamai, the nails of the feet; Labernioum - .

"And those who were appointed over all of these are: Zathoth, Armas, Kalila, Jabel, (Sabaoth, Cain, Abel). And those who are particularly active in the limbs (are) the head Diolimodraza, the neck Yammeax, the right shoulder Yakouib, the left shoulder Verton, the right hand Oudidi, the left one Arbao, the fingers of the right hand Lampno, the fingers of the left hand Leekaphar, the right breast Barbar, the left breast Imae, the chest Pisandriaptes, the right shoulder joint Koade, the left shoulder joint Odeor, the right ribs Asphixix, the left ribs Synogchouta, the belly Arouph, the womb Sabalo, the right thigh Charcharb, the left thigh Chthaon, all the genitals Bathinoth, the right leg Choux, the left leg Charcha, the right shin-bone Aroer, the left shin-bone Toechtha, the right knee Aol, the left knee Charaner, the right foot Bastan, its toes Archentechtha, the left foot Marephnounth, its toes Abrana.

"Seven have power over all of these: Michael, Ouriel, Asmenedas, Saphasatoel, Aarmouriam, Richram, Amiorps. And the ones who are in charge over the senses (are) Archendekta; and he who is in charge over the receptions (is) Deitharbathas; and he who is in charge over the imagination (is) Oummaa; and he who is over the composition Aachiaram, and he who is over the whole impulse Riaramnacho.

"And the origin of the demons which are in the whole body is determined to be four: heat, cold, wetness, and dryness. And the mother of all of them is matter. And he who reigns over the heat (is) Phloxopha; and he who reigns over the cold is Oroorrothos; and he who reigns over what is dry (is) Erimacho; and he who reigns over the wetness (is) Athuro. And the mother of all of these, Onorthochrasaei, stands in their midst, since she is illimitable, and she mixes with all of them. And she is truly matter, for they are nourished by her.

"The four chief demons are: Ephememphi, who belongs to pleasure, Yoko, who belongs to desire, Nenentophni, who belongs to grief, Blaomen, who belongs to fear. And the mother of them all is Aesthesis-Ouch-Epi-Ptoe. And from the four demons passions came forth. And from grief (came) envy, jealousy, distress, trouble, pain, callousness, anxiety, mourning, etc. And from pleasure much wickedness arises, and empty pride, and similar things. And from desire (comes) anger, wrath, and bitterness, and bitter passion, and unsatedness, and similar things. And from fear (comes) dread, fawning, agony, and shame. All of these are like useful things as well as evil things. But the insight into their true (character) is Anaro, who is the head of the material soul, for it belongs with the seven senses, Ouch-Epi-Ptoe.

"This is the number of the angels: together they are 365. They all worked on it until, limb for limb, the natural and the material body was completed by them. Now there are other ones in charge over the remaining passions whom I did not mention to you. But if you wish to know them, it is written in the book of Zoroaster. And all the angels and demons worked until they had constructed the natural body. And their product was completely inactive and motionless for a long time.

"And when the mother wanted to retrieve the power which she had given to the chief archon, she petitioned the Mother-Father of the All, who is most merciful. He sent, by means of the holy decree, the five lights down upon the place of the angels of the chief archon. They advised him that they should bring forth the power of the mother. And they said to Yaltabaoth, 'Blow into his face something of your spirit and his body will arise.' And he blew into his face the spirit which is the power of his mother; he did not know (this), for he exists in ignorance. And the power of the mother went out of Yaltabaoth into the natural body, which they had fashioned after the image of the one who exists from the beginning. The body moved and gained strength, and it was luminous.

"And in that moment the rest of the powers became jealous, because he had come into being through all of them and they had given their power to the man, and his intelligence was greater than that of those who had made him, and greater than that of the chief archon. And when they recognized that he was luminous, and that he could think better than they, and that he was free from wickedness, they took him and threw him into the lowest region of all matter.

"But the blessed One, the Mother-Father, the beneficent and merciful One, had mercy on the power of the mother which had been brought forth out of the chief archon, for they (the archons) might gain power over the natural and perceptible body. And he sent, through his beneficent Spirit and his great mercy, a helper to Adam, luminous Epinoia which comes out of him, who is called Life. And she assists the whole creature, by toiling with him and by restoring him to his fullness and by teaching him about the descent of his seed (and) by teaching him about the way of ascent, (which is) the way he came down. And the luminous Epinoia was hidden in Adam, in order that the archons might not know her, but that the Epinoia might be a correction of the deficiency of the mother.

"And the man came forth because of the shadow of the light which is in him. And his thinking was superior to all those who had made him. When they looked up, they saw that his thinking was superior. And they took counsel with the whole array of archons and angels. They took fire and earth and water and mixed them together with the four fiery winds. And they wrought them together and caused a great disturbance. And they brought him (Adam) into the shadow of death, in order that they might form (him) again from earth and water and fire and the spirit which originates in matter, which is the ignorance of darkness and desire, and their counterfeit spirit. This is the tomb of the newly-formed body with which the robbers had clothed the man, the bond of forgetfulness; and he became a mortal man. This is the first one who came down, and the first separation. But the Epinoia of the light which was in him, she is the one who was to awaken his thinking.

"And the archons took him and placed him in paradise. And they said to him, 'Eat, that is at leisure,' for their luxury is bitter and their beauty is depraved. And their luxury is deception and their trees are godlessness and their fruit is deadly poison and their promise is death. And the tree of their life they had placed in the midst of paradise.

"And I shall teach you (pl.) what is the mystery of their life, which is the plan which they made together, which is the likeness of their spirit. The root of this (tree) is bitter and its branches are death, its shadow is hate and deception is in its leaves, and its blossom is the ointment of evil, and its fruit is death and desire is its seed, and it sprouts in darkness. The dwelling place of those who taste from it is Hades, and the darkness is their place of rest.

"But what they call the tree of knowledge of good and evil, which is the Epinoia of the light, they stayed in front of it in order that he (Adam) might not look up to his fullness and recognize the nakedness of his shamefulness. But it was I who brought about that they ate."

And to I said to the savior, "Lord, was it not the serpent that taught Adam to eat?" The savior smiled and said, "The serpent taught them to eat from wickedness of begetting, lust, (and) destruction, that he (Adam) might be useful to him. And he (Adam) knew that he was disobedient to him (the chief archon) due to light of the Epinoia which is in him, which made him more correct in his thinking than the chief archon. And (the latter) wanted to bring about the power which he himself had given him. And he brought a forgetfulness over Adam."

And I said to the savior, "What is the forgetfulness?" And he said "It is not the way Moses wrote (and) you heard. For he said in his first book, 'He put him to sleep' (Gn 2:21), but (it was) in his perception. For also he said through the prophet, 'I will make their hearts heavy, that they may not pay attention and may not see' (Is 6:10).

"Then the Epinoia of the light hid herself in him (Adam). And the chief archon wanted to bring her out of his rib. But the Epinoia of the light cannot be grasped. Although darkness pursued her, it did not catch her. And he brought a part of his power out of him. And he made another creature, in the form of a woman, according to the likeness of the Epinoia which had appeared to him. And he brought the part which he had taken from the power of the man into the female creature, and not as Moses said, 'his rib-bone.'

"And he (Adam) saw the woman beside him. And in that moment the luminous Epinoia appeared, and she lifted the veil which lay over his mind. And he became sober from the drunkenness of darkness. And he recognized his counter-image, and he said, 'This is indeed bone of my bones and flesh of my flesh.' Therefore the man will leave his father and his mother, and he will cleave to his wife, and they will both be one flesh. For they will send him his consort, and he will leave his father and his mother ... (3 lines unreadable)

"And our sister Sophia (is) she who came down in innocence in order to rectify her deficiency. Therefore she was called Life, which is the mother of the living, by the foreknowledge of the sovereignty of heaven. And through her they have tasted the perfect Knowledge. I appeared in the form of an eagle on the tree of knowledge, which is the Epinoia from the foreknowledge of the pure light, that I might teach them and awaken them out of the depth of sleep. For they were both in a fallen state, and they recognized their nakedness. The Epinoia appeared to them as a light; she awakened their thinking.

"And when Yaltabaoth noticed that they withdrew from him, he cursed his earth. He found the woman as she was preparing herself for her husband. He was lord over her, though he did not know the mystery which had come to pass through the holy decree. And they were afraid to blame him. And he showed his angels his ignorance which is in him. And he cast them out of paradise and he clothed them in gloomy darkness. And the chief archon saw the virgin who stood by Adam, and that the luminous Epinoia of life had appeared in her. And Yaltabaoth was full of ignorance. And when the foreknowledge of the All noticed (it), she sent some and they snatched life out of Eve.

"And the chief archon seduced her and he begot in her two sons; the first and the second (are) Eloim and Yave. Eloim has a bear-face and Yave has a cat-face. The one is righteous but the other is unrighteous. (Yave is righteous but Eloim is unrighteous.) Yave he set over the fire and the wind, and Eloim he set over the water and the earth. And these he called with the names Cain and Abel with a view to deceive.

"Now up to the present day, sexual intercourse continued due to the chief archon. And he planted sexual desire in her who belongs to Adam. And he produced through intercourse the copies of the bodies, and he inspired them with his counterfeit spirit.

"And the two archons he set over principalities, so that they might rule over the tomb. And when Adam recognized the likeness of his own foreknowledge, he begot the likeness of the son of man. He called him Seth, according to the way of the race in the aeons. Likewise, the mother also sent down her spirit, which is in her likeness and a copy of those who are in the pleroma, for she will prepare a dwelling place for the aeons which will come down. And he made them drink water of forgetfulness, from the chief archon, in order that they might not know from where they came. Thus, the seed remained for a while assisting (him), in order that, when the Spirit comes forth from the holy aeons, he may raise up and heal him from the deficiency, that the whole pleroma may (again) become holy and faultless."

And I said to the savior, "Lord, will all the souls then be brought safely into the pure light?" He answered and said to me, "Great things have arisen in your mind, for it is difficult to explain them to others except to those who are from the immovable race. Those on whom the Spirit of life will descend and (with whom) he will be with the power, they will be saved and become perfect and be worthy of the greatness and be purified in that place from all wickedness and the involvements in evil. Then they have no other care than the incorruption alone, to which they direct their attention from here on, without anger or envy or jealousy or desire and greed of anything. They are not affected by anything except the state of being in the flesh alone, which they bear while looking expectantly for the time when they will be met by the receivers (of the body). Such then are worthy of the imperishable, eternal life and the calling. For they endure everything and bear up under everything, that they may finish the good fight and inherit eternal life."

I said to him, "Lord, the souls of those who did not do these works (but) on whom the power and Spirit descended, (will they be rejected?)" He answered and said to me, "If the Spirit (descended upon them), they will in any case be saved, and they will change (for the better). For the power will descend on every man, for without it no one can stand. And after they are born, then, when the Spirit of life increases and the power comes and strengthens that soul, no one can lead it astray with works of evil. But those on whom the counterfeit spirit descends are drawn by him and they go astray."

And I said, "Lord, where will the souls of these go when they have come out of their flesh?" And he smiled and said to me, "The soul in which the power will become stronger than the counterfeit spirit, is strong and it flees from evil and, through the intervention of the incorruptible one, it is saved, and it is taken up to the rest of the aeons."

And I said, "Lord, those, however, who have not known to whom they belong, where will their souls be?" And he said to me, "In those, the despicable spirit has gained strength when they went astray. And he burdens the soul and draws it to the works of evil, and he casts it down into forgetfulness. And after it comes out of (the body), it is handed over to the authorities, who came into being through the archon, and they bind it with chains and cast it into prison, and consort with it until it is liberated from the forgetfulness and acquires knowledge. And if thus it becomes perfect, it is saved."

And I said, "Lord, how can the soul become smaller and return into the nature of its mother or into man?" Then he rejoiced when I asked him this, and he said to me, "Truly, you are blessed, for you have understood! That soul is made to follow another one (fem.), since the Spirit of life is in it. It is saved through him. It is not again cast into another flesh."

And I said, "Lord, these also who did not know, but have turned away, where will their souls go?" Then he said to me, "To that place where the angels of poverty go they will be taken, the place where there is no repentance., And they will be kept for the day on which those who have blasphemed the spirit will be tortured, and they will be punished with eternal punishment."

And I said, "Lord, from where did the counterfeit spirit come?" Then he said to me, "The Mother-Father, who is rich in mercy, the holy Spirit in every way, the One who is merciful and who sympathizes with you (pl.), i.e., the Epinoia of the foreknowledge of light, he raised up the offspring of the perfect race and its thinking and the eternal light of man. When the chief archon realized that they were exalted above him in the height - and they surpass him in thinking - then he wanted to seize their thought, not knowing that they surpassed him in thinking, and that he will not be able to seize them.

"He made a plan with his authorities, which are his powers, and they committed together adultery with Sophia, and bitter fate was begotten through them, which is the last of the changeable bonds. And it is of a sort that is interchangeable. And it is harder and stronger than she with whom the gods united, and the angels and the demons and all the generations until this day. For from that fate came forth every sin and injustice and blasphemy, and the chain of forgetfulness and ignorance and every severe command, and serious sins and great fears. And thus the whole creation was made blind, in order that they may not know God, who is above all of them. And because of the chain of forgetfulness, their sins were hidden. For they are bound with measures and times and moments, since it (fate) is lord over everything.

"And he (the chief archon) repented for everything which had come into being through him. This time he planned to bring a flood upon the work of man. But the greatness of the light of the foreknowledge informed Noah, and he proclaimed (it) to all the offspring which are the sons of men. But those who were strangers to him did not listen to him. It is not as Moses said, 'They hid themselves in an ark' (Gn 7: 7), but they hid themselves in a place, not only Noah, but also many other people from the immovable race. They went into a place and hid themselves in a luminous cloud. And he (Noah) recognized his authority, and she who belongs to the light was with him, having shone on them because he (the chief archon) had brought darkness upon the whole earth.

"And he made a plan with his powers. He sent his angels to the daughters of men, that they might take some of them for themselves and raise offspring for their enjoyment. And at first they did not succeed. When they had no success, they gathered together again and they made a plan together. They created a counterfeit spirit, who resembles the Spirit who had descended, so as to pollute the souls through it. And the angels changed themselves in their likeness into the likeness of their mates (the daughters of men), filling them with the spirit of darkness, which they had mixed for them, and with evil. They brought gold and silver and a gift and copper and iron and metal and all kinds of things. And they steered the people who had followed them into great troubles, by leading them astray with many deceptions. They (the people) became old without having enjoyment. They died, not having found truth and without knowing the God of truth. And thus the whole creation became enslaved forever, from the foundation of the world until now. And they took women and begot children out of the darkness according to the likeness of their spirit. And they closed their hearts, and they hardened themselves through the hardness of the counterfeit spirit until now.

"I, therefore, the perfect Pronoia of the all, changed myself into my seed, for I existed first, going on every road. For I am the richness of the light; I am the remembrance of the pleroma.

"And I went into the realm of darkness and I endured till I entered the middle of the prison. And the foundations of chaos shook. And I hid myself from them because of their wickedness, and they did not recognize me.

"Again I returned for the second time, and I went about. I came forth from those who belong to the light, which is I, the remembrance of the Pronoia. I entered into the midst of darkness and the inside of Hades, since I was seeking (to accomplish) my task. And the foundations of chaos shook, that they might fall down upon those who are in chaos and might destroy them. And again I ran up to my root of light, lest they be destroyed before the time.

"Still for a third time I went - I am the light which exists in the light, I am the remembrance of the Pronoia - that I might enter into the midst of darkness and the inside of Hades. And I filled my face with the light of the completion of their aeon. And I entered into the midst of their prison, which is the prison of the body. And I said, 'He who hears, let him get up from the deep sleep.' And he wept and shed tears. Bitter tears he wiped from himself and he said, 'Who is it that calls my name, and from where has this hope come to me, while I am in the chains of the prison?' And I said, 'I am the Pronoia of the pure light; I am the thinking of the virginal Spirit, who raised you up to the honored place. Arise and remember that it is you who hearkened, and follow your root, which is I, the merciful one, and guard yourself against the angels of poverty and the demons of chaos and all those who ensnare you, and beware of the deep sleep and the enclosure of the inside of Hades.

"And I raised him up, and sealed him in the light of the water with five seals, in order that death might not have power over him from this time on.

"And behold, now I shall go up to the perfect aeon. I have completed everything for you in your hearing. And I have said everything to you that you might write them down and give them secretly to your fellow spirits, for this is the mystery of the immovable race."

And the savior presented these things to him that he might write them down and keep them secure. And he said to him, "Cursed be everyone who will exchange these things for a gift or for food or for drink or for clothing or for any other such thing." And these things were presented to him in a mystery, and immediately he disappeared from him. And he went to his fellow disciples and related to them what the savior had told him.

Jesus Christ, Amen.

Book 109. Life of Adam and Eve

The Life of Adam and Eve is a significant Jewish pseudepigraphical writing, whose surviving manuscripts are Christian copies in Latin and Greek. It purports to explain in colourful detail the fate of the First Parents after their expulsion from Eden, in the style of an apocalypse, or heavenly revelation. As such, its genre reminds us strongly of that in the Book of Revelation. Along with its teaching about penitence and atonement for sin, it expresses a clear belief in the resurrection of dead to a future life. There is wide agreement that the original dates from the first century A.D. and was composed in a Semitic language. It recounts the lives and words of Adam and Eve to their children, as they face their approaching deaths. It provides more detail than does Genesis 3, about their Fall from Grace, including Eve's version of the story. Satan explains that he rebelled when God commanded him to worship Adam. After Adam dies, he and all his descendants are promised a resurrection.

It begins immediately after their exile from the Garden of Eden and continues to their deaths. In the first chapters, Eve begins to do penance in the icy Tigris river, but Satan soon talks her out of it. When Adam complains about Satan persecuting them, he learns that Eve is the reason he was expelled from heaven. Satan and his followers had been cast out of heaven for refusing God's command to worship Adam, God's own image. Unaffected by the devil, Adam serves forty days of penance in the Jordan River.

Cain and Abel are then born, and Cain's killing of Abel is passed over quickly. Seth is born, along with thirty other sons and thirty daughters. As Adam is dying, Seth and Eve try to get healing oil for him but are prevented by the archangel Michael.

Eve then relates her version of the Fall of Man, where she had been put in charge of all the female animals and half the garden, from which she brought the forbidden fruit to Adam. The serpent is described as having hands and feet, and the tree of knowledge of good and evil is said to be a fig tree. Adam then dies at the age of 930, and after his soul is conveyed to the third heaven, God and some angels bury his body and Abel's. Adam and all his descendants are promised a resurrection. Six days later, Eve dies, and Michael tells Seth never to mourn more than six days, and to cease on the Sabbath.

The Life of Adam and Eve

I

When they were driven out from paradise, they made themselves a booth, and spent seven days mourning and lamenting in deep grief.

II

But after seven days, they began to be hungry and started to look for food to eat, and they found it not. Then Eve said to Adam: "My lord, I am hungry. Go, look for something for us to eat. Perhaps the Lord God will look back and pity us and recall us to the place where we were before."

III

Adam got up and walked seven days over all that land, and found no food of the kind they used to have in paradise. Then Eve said to Adam: "Will you kill me, that I may die, and perhaps the Lord God will bring thee into paradise, for on my account you were driven out from there?" Adam answered: "Hush, Eve, from such words, or God may bring some other curse upon us. How could I stretch out my hand against my own flesh? No, let us arise and look for something for us to live on, so as not to die of hunger."

IV

And they walked about searching for nine days, but found nothing of the kind they used to have in paradise, for they found only animals" food. And Adam said to Eve: "This the Lord has provided for animals and brutes to eat; but we used to have angels" food. But it is just and right for us to lament before the sight of God who made us. Let us repent with a great penitence: perhaps the Lord will be gracious to us and will pity us and give us a share of something to keep us alive."

V

And Eve said to Adam: "What is penitence? Tell me, what sort of penitence am I to do? Let us not set too great a task for ourselves, one in which we cannot persevere, so that the Lord will not listen to our prayers and will turn away His face from us, because we have not fulfilled what we promised. My lord, how much penitence have you planned, for I have brought trouble and anguish upon you?'

VI

And Adam said to Eve: "You cannot do as much as I, but do only as much as you have strength for. For I will spend forty days fasting, but let you go off to the river Tigris and lift up a stone and stand on it in the water up to your neck in the deep of the river. And let no speech come from your mouth, since we are unworthy to address the Lord, for our lips are unclean from that unlawful and forbidden tree. And let you stand in the water of the river thirty-seven days. But I will spend forty days in the water of Jordan, perhaps the Lord God will take pity upon us."

VII

And Eve walked to the river Tigris and did as Adam had told her. Likewise, Adam walked to the river Jordan and stood on a stone up to his neck in water.

VIII

And Adam said: "Water of Jordan, I bid you grieve with me, and assemble to me all that swims in you, and let them surround me and mourn in company with me. Not for themselves let them lament, but for me; for it is not they that have sinned, but I." Immediately, all living things came and surrounded him, and from that hour the water of Jordan stood still and its current was stayed."

IX

And eighteen days passed by; then Satan was angry and transformed himself into the brightness of angels, and went away to the river Tigris to Eve, and found her weeping, and the devil himself pretended to grieve with her, and he began to weep and said to her "Come out of the river and lament no more. Cease now from sorrow and moaning. Why are you anxious and your husband Adam? The Lord God has heard your groaning and has accepted your penitence, and all we angels have entreated on your behalf, and interceded with the Lord; and he has sent me to bring you out of the water and give you the nourishment which you had in paradise, and for which you are crying out. Now come out of the water and I will conduct you to the place where your food has been made ready."

X

Now Eve heard and believed and went out of the water of the river, and her flesh was like grass, from the chill of the water. When she had come out, she fell to the ground and the devil raised her up and led her to Adam. But when Adam saw her and the devil with her, he wept and cried aloud and said: "O Eve, Eve, where is the labour of your penance? How have you been again ensnared by our enemy, through whom we have been estranged from our abode in paradise and spiritual joy?'

XI

When she heard this, Eve understood that it was the devil had persuaded her to leave the river; and she fell on her face on the ground and her sorrow and groaning and wailing was redoubled. And she cried out and said: "Woe to you, you devil. Why do you attack us for no cause? What have you to do with us? What have we done to you, for you to pursue us with craft? Or why does your malice attack us? Have we taken away your glory and caused you to be without honour? You enemy, why do you harry us to the death in wickedness and envy?'

XII

And with a heavy sigh, the devil said, "O Adam! all my hostility, envy, and sorrow is for you, since it is for you that I have been expelled from my glory, which I possessed in the heavens in the midst of the angels and

for you was I cast out on the earth." Adam answered, "What do you tell me? What have I done to you or what is my fault against you? Seeing that you have received no harm or injury from us, why do you pursue us?'

XIII

The devil replied, "Adam, what are you saying? It is for your sake that I have been hurled from that place. When you were formed, I was hurled out of the presence of God and banished from the company of the angels. When God blew into you the breath of life and your face and likeness was made in the image of God, Michael also brought you and made us worship you in the sight of God; and the Lord God said, Here is Adam. I have made you in our image and likeness."

XIV

And Michael went out and called to all the angels, "Worship the image of God as the Lord God has commanded." And Michael himself worshipped first; then he called me and said, "Worship the image of the Lord God." And I answered, "It is not for me to worship Adam." And since Michael kept urging me to worship, I said to him, "Why do you urge me? I will not worship an inferior and younger being than I. I am his senior in the Creation, before he was made was I already made. It is his duty to worship me."

XIV

When the angels who were under me heard this, they refused to worship him. And Michael said, "Worship the image of God, but if you will not worship him, the Lord God will be angry with you." And I said, "If He be angry with me, I will set my seat above the stars of heaven and will be like the Highest."

XVI

And the Lord God was angry with me and banished me and my angels from our glory; and on your account we were expelled from our abodes into this world and hurled to the ground. Straight away we were overcome with grief, since we had been robbed of such great glory. And we were grieved when we saw you in such joy and luxury. And with guile I cheated your wife and through her action caused you to be expelled from your joy and luxury, as I have been driven out of my glory.

XVII

When Adam heard the devil say this, he cried out and wept and said, "O Lord my God, my life is in your hands. Banish this Enemy far from me, who seeks to destroy my soul, and give me his glory which he himself has lost." And at that moment, the devil vanished before him. But Adam persevered in his penance, standing for forty days on end in the water of Jordan.

XVIII

And Eve said to Adam: "Live you, my Lord, to you life is granted, since you have committed neither the first nor the second error. But I have erred and been led astray for I have not kept the commandment of God; and now banish me from the light of your life and I will go to the sunsetting, and there will I be, until I die." And she began to walk towards the western parts and to mourn and to weep bitterly and groan aloud. And she made there a booth, while she had in her womb offspring of three months old.

XIX

When the time of her bearing approached, she began to be distressed with pains, and she cried aloud to the Lord and said, "Pity me, O Lord, assist me." And she was not heard and the mercy of God did not encircle her. And she said to herself: "Who shall tell my lord Adam? I implore you, ye luminaries of heaven, what time ye return to the east, bear a message to my lord adam."

XX

But in that hour, Adam said, "The complaint of Eve has come to me. Perhaps, once more has the serpent fought with her." And he went and found her in great distress. And Eve said, "From the moment I saw you, my lord, my grief-laden soul was refreshed. And now entreat the Lord God on my behalf to listen to you and look upon me and free me from my awful pains." And Adam entreated the Lord for Eve.

XXI

And there came twelve angels and two "virtues', standing on the right and on the left of Eve; and Michael was standing on the right; and he stroked her on the face as far as to the breast and said to Eve: "Blessed are you, Eve, for Adam's sake. Since his prayers and intercessions are great, I have been sent that you mayst receive our help. Rise up now, and prepare you to bear. And she bore a son and he was shining; and at once the babe rose up and ran and bore a blade of grass in his hands, and gave it to his mother, and his name was called Cain.

XXII

And Adam carried Eve and the boy and led them to the East. And the Lord God sent various seeds by Michael the archangel and gave to Adam and showed him how to work and till the ground, that they might have fruit by which they and all their generations might live. For thereafter Eve conceived and bare a son, whose name was Abel; and Cain and Abel used to stay together. And Eve said to Adam: "My lord, while I slept, I saw a vision, as it were the blood of our son Abel in the hand of Cain, who was gulping it down in his mouth. Therefore I have sorrow." And

Adam said, "Alas if Cain slew Abel. Yet let us separate them from each other mutually, and let us make for each of them separate dwellings."

XXIII

And they made Cain an husbandman, but Abel they made a shepherd; in order that in this wise they might be mutually separated. And thereafter, Cain slew Abel, but Adam was then one hundred and thirty years old, but Abel was slain when he was one hundred and twenty-two years. And thereafter Adam knew his wife and he begat a son and called his name Seth.

XXIV

And Adam said to Eve, "See, I have begotten a son, in place of Abel, whom Cain slew." And after Adam had begotten Seth, he lived eight hundred years and begat thirty sons and thirty daughters; in all sixty-three children. And they were increased over the face of the ground in their nations.

XXV

And Adam said to Seth, "Hear, my son Seth, that I may relate to you what I heard and saw after your mother and I had been driven out of paradise. When we were at prayer, there came to me Michael the archangel, a messenger of God. And I saw a chariot like the wind and its wheels were fiery and I was caught up into the Paradise of righteousness, and I saw the Lord sitting and his face was flaming fire that could not be endured. And many thousands of angels were on the right and the left of that chariot.

XXVI

When I saw this, I was confounded, and terror seized me and I bowed myself down before God with my face to the ground. And God said to me, "Behold you must die, since you have transgressed the commandment of God, for you listened rather to the voice of your wife, whom I gave into your power, that you might hold her to your will. Yet you listened to her and ignored My words."

XXVII

When I heard these words of God, I fell prone on the ground and worshipped the Lord and said, "My Lord, All powerful and merciful God, Holy and Righteous One, let not the name that is mindful of Your majesty be blotted out, but convert my soul, for I die and my breath will cease from my mouth. Do not cast me out from Your presence, whom You formed of the clay of the ground. Do not banish from Your favour the one whom You have nourished." Then a word concerning you came to me and the Lord said to me, "Since your days were fashioned, you have been created with a love of knowledge; therefore the right to serve Me shall not be taken from your seed for ever."

XXVIII

When I heard these words. I threw myself on the ground and adored the Lord God and said, "You are the eternal and supreme God; and all creatures give you honour and praise. You are the true Light gleaming above all lights, the Living Life, infinite mighty Power. To You, the spiritual powers give honour and praise. You pour out on the race of men the abundance of Your mercy." As soon as I had worshipped the Lord, Michael, God's archangel, seized my hand and cast me out of the paradise of vision and of God's command. And Michael held a rod in his hand, and touched the waters which were round about paradise, and they froze hard.

XXIX

And I went across, and Michael the archangel went across with me, and he led me back to the place from which he had caught me up. Listen, my son Seth, to the rest of the secrets that shall be, which were revealed to me, when I had eaten of the tree of the knowledge, and knew and saw what will happen in this age; what God intends to do to his creation of the race of men. The Lord will appear in a flame of fire and from the mouth of His majesty He will give commandments and statutes. From His mouth will proceed a two-edged sword and they will sanctify Him in the house where His majesty dwells. And He will show them the marvellous place of His majesty. And then they will build a house to the Lord their God in the land which He shall prepare for them; but they will transgress His statutes there and their sanctuary will be burnt up and their land deserted and they themselves will be dispersed, because they have kindled the wrath of God. But again He will cause them to come back from their dispersion; and again the will build the house of God; and in the last time the house of God will be exalted greater than of old. And once more iniquity will exceed righteousness. And thereafter God will dwell with men on earth in visible form; and then, righteousness will begin to shine. And the house of God will be honoured in the age and their enemies will no more be able to hurt the men, who are believing in God; and God will stir up for Himself a faithful people, whom He shall save for eternity, and the impious shall be punished by God their king, the men who refused to love His law.

Heaven and earth, nights and days, and all creatures shall obey Him, and not overstep His commandment. Men shall not change their works, but they shall be changed from forsaking the law of the Lord. Therefore the Lord shall repel from Himself the wicked, and the just shall shine like the sun, in the sight of God. And in that time, shall men be purified by water from their sins. But those who are unwilling to be purified by water shall be condemned. And happy shall the man be, who has ruled his soul, when the Judgement shall happen and the greatness of God be seen among men and their deeds be inquired into by God the just judge.

XXX

After Adam was nine hundred and thirty years old, since he knew that his days were coming to an end, he said, "Let all my sons gather to me, that I may bless them before I die, and speak with them." And they were assembled in three parts before his sight, in the house of prayer, where they used to worship the Lord God. And they asked him "Why have you gathered us, Father, and why do you lie on your bed? "Then Adam answered, "My sons, I am sick and in pain." And all his sons said to him, "What does it mean, father, this illness and pain?'

XXXI

Then Seth his son said, "O my lord, perhaps you long for the fruit of paradise, which you were accustomed to eat, and therefore you lie in sadness? Tell me and I will go to the nearest gates of paradise and put dust on my head and throw myself down on the ground before the gates of paradise and lament and beg God with loud lamentation; perhaps he will listen to me and send his angel to bring me the fruit, for which you long." Adam answered, "No, my son, I do not long for this, but I feel weakness and great pain in my body." Seth answered, "What is pain, my lord father? I am ignorant; do not hide it from us, but tell us about it." And Adam answered, "Hear me, my sons. When God made us, me and your mother, and placed us in paradise and gave us every tree bearing fruit to eat, he laid on us a prohibition about the tree of knowledge of good and evil, which is in the midst of paradise; saying "Do not eat of it." But God gave a part of paradise to me and a part to your mother, the trees of the eastern part and the orth, which is over against Aquilo he gave to me, and to your mother he gave the part of the south and the western part.

XXXIII

Moreover the Lord God gave us two angels to guard us. The hour came when the angels had ascended to worship in the sight of God; immediately the enemy the devil found an opportunity while the angels were absent and the devil led your mother astray to eat of the unlawful and forbidden tree. And she ate and gave to me.

XXXIV

And immediately, the Lord God was angry with us, and the Lord said to me, "Since you have left behind my commandment and have not kept my word, which I confirmed to you; I will bring upon your body, seventy blows; with various griefs, shall you be tormented, beginning at your head and your eyes and your ears down to the nails on your toes, and in every separate limb. These has God appointed for chastisement. All these things has the Lord sent to me and to all our race."

XXXV

Thus said Adam to his sons, and he was seized with violent pains, and he cried out with a loud voice, "What shall I do? I am in distress. So cruel are the pains with which I am beset." When Eve had seen him weeping, she also began to weep herself, and said, "O Lord my God, hand over to me his pain, for it is I who sinned." And Eve said to Adam, "My lord, give me a part of your pains, for this has come to you from fault of mine."

XXXVI

And Adam said to Eve, "Rise up and go with my son Seth to the neighbourhood of paradise, and put dust on your heads and throw yourselves on the ground and lament in the sight of God. Perhaps He will have pity upon you and send His angel across to the tree of His mercy, from which flows the oil of life, and will give you a drop of it, to anoint me with it, that I may have rest from these pains, by which I am being consumed." Then Seth and his mother went off towards the gates of paradise. And while they were walking, suddenly there came a beast a serpent and attacked and bit Seth. And as soon as Eve saw it, she wept and said, "Alas, wretched woman that I am. I am accursed since I have not kept the commandment of God." And Eve said to the serpent in a loud voice, "Accursed beast! how is it that you have not feared to let yourself loose against the image of God, but have dared to fight with it?'

XXXVIII

The beast answered in the language of men, "Is it not against you, Eve, that our malice is directed? Are your not the objects of our rage? Tell me, Eve, how was your mouth opened to eat of the fruit? But now you can not bear it if I begin to reprove you."

XXXIX

Then Seth said to the beast, "the Lord God revile you. Be silent, be dumb, shut your mouth, accursed enemy of Truth, confounder and destroyer. Away from the image of God till the day when the Lord God orders you to be brought to the ordeal." And the beast said to Seth, "See, I leave the presence of the image of God, as you have said." Immediately he left Seth, wounded by his teeth.

XL

But Seth and his mother walked to the regions of paradise for the oil of mercy to anoint the sick Adam, and they arrived at the gates of paradise, and they took dust from the ground and placed it on their heads, and bowed down with their faces to the ground and began to lament with loud moaning, imploring the Lord God to pity Adam in his pains and to send His angel to give them the oil from the "tree of His mercy'.

XLI

But when they had been praying and imploring for many hours, the angel Michael appeared to them and said, "I have been sent to you from the Lord - I am set by God over the bodies of men - I tell you, Seth, you man of God, do not weep or pray and entreat about the oil of the tree of mercy to anoint your father Adam for the pains of his body.

XLII

'For I tell you that you will be unable to receive it except in the last days." When five thousand five hundred years have been fulfilled, then will come upon earth the most beloved king Christ, the son of God, to revive the body of Adam and with him to revive the bodies of the dead. He Himself, the Son of God, when He comes will be baptized in the river Jordan, and when He has come out of the water of Jordan, then He will anoint from the oil of mercy all that believe in Him. And the oil of mercy shall be for generation to generation for those who are ready to be born again of water and the Holy Spirit to life eternal. Then the most beloved Son of God, Christ, descending on earth shall lead your father Adam to Paradise to the tree of mercy.

XLIII

'But let you, Seth, go to your father Adam, since the time of his life is fulfilled. Six days hence, his soul shall leave his body and when it has left, you shall see great marvels in the heaven and on the earth and the lights of heaven. With these words, Michael departed from Seth. And Eve and Seth returned bearing with them herbs of fragrance, nard and crocus and calamus and cinnamon.

XLIV

When Seth and his mother reached Adam, they told him how the serpent beast had bit Seth. And Adam said to Eve, "What have you done? You have brought a great plague upon us, transgression and sin for all our generations, and tell your children after my death what you have done, for those who arise from us shall toil and fail but when they are lacking they shall curse us and say, All evils have our parents brought upon us, who were at the beginning." When Eve heard these words, she began to weep and moan.

XLV

And just as Michael the archangel had foretold, after six days came Adam's death. When Adam saw that the hour of his death was at hand, he said to all his sons, "See, I am nine hundred and thirty years old, and when I die, bury me towards the rising sun in the field beside that house." And when he had finished speaking, he gave up the ghost.

XLVI

Then was the sun darkened and the moon and the stars for seven days, and Seth in his mourning embraced from above the body of his father, and Eve was looking at the ground with her hands folded over her head, and all her children wept most bitterly. And there appeared Michael the angel and stood at the head of Adam and said to Seth, "Rise up from the body of your father and come to me and see what is the doom of the Lord God concerning him. He is His creature and God has pitied him." And all the angels blew their trumpets, and cried out,

XLVII

'Blessed are you, O Lord, for you have had pity on Your creature."

XLVIII

Then Seth saw the hand of God stretched out holding Adam and he handed him over to Michael, saying, "Let him be in your charge in punishment till the day of Judgement, till the last years when I will convert his sorrow into joy. Then he shall sit on the throne of the one who supplanted him." And the Lord said again to the angels Michael and Uriel, "Bring me three linen clothes of byssus and spread them out over Adam and other linen clothes over Abel his son and bury Adam and Abel his son." And all the "powers" of angels marched before Adam, and the sleep of the dead was consecrated. And the angels Michael and Uriel buried Adam and Abel in the parts of Paradise, before the eyes of Seth and his mother and no one else, and Michael and Uriel said, "Just as ye have seen, bury your dead in like manner."

XLIX

Six days afterwards, Adam died; and Eve saw that she would die, so she gathered all her sons and daughters, Seth with thirty brothers and thirty sisters, and Eve said to all, "Listen to me, my children, and I will tell you what the archangel Michael said to us when I and your father transgressed the command of God. On account of your transgression, Our Lord will bring upon your race the anger of his judgement, first by water, the second time by fire; by these two, will the Lord judge the whole human race

L

But listen to me, my children. Make tablets of stone and others of clay, and write upon them about my life and your father's, all that ye have heard and seen from us. If the Lord judges our race by water, the tablets of clay will be dissolved and the tablets of stone will remain; but if by fire, the tablets of stone will be broken up and the tablets of clay will be baked hard." When Eve had said all this to her children, she spread out her hands to heaven in prayer, and bent her knees to the ground, and while she worshipped the Lord and gave him thanks, she gave up the ghost. Thereafter, all her children buried her with loud lamentation.

LI

When they had been mourning four days, then Michael the archangel appeared and said to Seth, "Man of God, do not mourn for your dead more than six days, for on the seventh day is the sign of the resurrection and the rest of the age to come; on the seventh day the Lord rested from all His works." Thereupon Seth made the tablets of clay and stone.

Book 110. The Martyrdom of Perpetua and Felicitas

A number of young catechumens were arrested, Revocatus and his fellow slave Felicitas, Saturninus and Secundulus, and with them Vibia Perpetua, a newly married woman of good family and upbringing. Her mother and father were still alive and one of her two brothers was a catechumen like herself. She was about twenty-two years old and had an infant son at the breast. (Now from this point on the entire account of her ordeal is her own, according to her own ideas and in the way that she herself wrote it down.)

While we were still under arrest (she said) my father out of love for me was trying to persuade me and shake my resolution. 'Father,' said I, 'do you see this vase here, for example, or waterpot or whatever?'

'Yes, I do', said he.

And I told him: 'Could it be called by any other name than what it is?'

And he said: 'No.'

'Well, so too I cannot be called anything other than what I am, a Christian.'

At this my father was so angered by the word 'Christian' that he moved towards me as though he would pluck my eyes out. But he left it at that and departed, vanquished along with his diabolical arguments.

For a few days afterwards I gave thanks to the Lord that I was separated from my father, and I was comforted by his absence. During these few days I was baptized, and I was inspired by the Spirit not to ask for any other favour after the water but simply the perseverance of the flesh. A few days later we were lodged in the prison; and I was terrified, as I had never before been in such a dark hole. What a difficult time it was! With the crowd the heat was stifling; then there was the extortion of the soldiers; and to crown all, I was tortured with worry for my baby there.

Then Tertius and Pomponius, those blessed deacons who tried to take care of us, bribed the soldiers to allow us to go to a better part of the prison to refresh ourselves for a few hours. Everyone then left that dungeon and shifted for himself. I nursed my baby, who was faint from hunger. In my anxiety I spoke to my mother about the child, I tried to comfort my brother, and I gave the child in their charge. I was in pain because I saw them suffering out of pity for me. These were the trials I had to endure for many days. Then I got permission for my baby to stay with me in prison. At once I recovered my health, relieved as I was of my worry and anxiety over the child. My prison had suddenly become a palace, so that I wanted to be there rather than anywhere else.

Then my brother said to me: 'Dear sister, you are greatly privileged; surely you might ask for a vision to discover whether you are to be condemned or freed.'

Faithfully I promised that I would, for I knew that I could speak with the Lord, whose great blessings I had come to experience. And so I said: 'I shall tell you tomorrow.' Then I made my request and this was the vision I had.

I saw a ladder of tremendous height made of bronze, reaching all the way to the heavens, but it was so narrow that only one person could climb up at a time. To the sides of the ladder were attached all sorts of metal weapons: there were swords, spears, hooks, daggers, and spikes; so that if anyone tried to climb up carelessly or without paying attention, he would be mangled and his flesh would adhere to the weapons.

At the foot of the ladder lay a dragon of enormous size, and it would attack those who tried to climb up and try to terrify them from doing so. And Saturus was the first to go up, he who was later to give himself up of his own accord. He had been the builder of our strength, although he was not present when we were arrested. And he arrived at the top of the staircase and he looked back and said to me: 'Perpetua, I am waiting for you. But take care; do not let the dragon bite you.'

'He will not harm me,' I said, 'in the name of Christ Jesus.'

Slowly, as though he were afraid of me, the dragon stuck his head out from underneath the ladder. Then, using it as my first step, I trod on his head and went up.

Then I saw an immense garden, and in it a gray-haired man sat in shepherd's garb; tall he was, and milking sheep. And standing around him were many thousands of people clad in white garments. He raised his head, looked at me, and said: 'I am glad you have come, my child.'

He called me over to him and gave me, as it were, a mouthful Of the milk he was drawing; and I took it into my cupped hands and consumed it. And all those who stood around said: 'Amen!' At the sound of this word I came to, with the taste of something sweet still in my mouth. I at once told this to my brother, and we realized that we would have to suffer, and that from now on we would no longer have any hope in this life.

A few days later there was a rumour that we were going to be given a hearing. My father also arrived from the city, worn with worry, and he came to see me with the idea of persuading me.

'Daughter,' he said, 'have pity on my grey head--have pity on me your father, if I deserve to be called your father, if I have favoured you above all your brothers, if I have raised you to reach this prime of your life. Do not abandon me to be the reproach of men. Think of your brothers, think of your mother and your aunt, think of your child, who will not be able to live once you are gone. Give up your pride! You will destroy all of us! None of us will ever be able to speak freely again if anything happens to you.'

This was the way my father spoke out of love for me, kissing my hands and throwing himself down before me. With tears in his eyes he no longer addressed me as his daughter but as a woman. I was sorry for my father's sake, because he alone of all my kin would be unhappy to see me suffer.

I tried to comfort him saying: 'It will all happen in the prisoner's dock as God wills; for you may be sure that we are not left to ourselves but are all in his power.'

And he left me in great sorrow.

One day while we were eating breakfast we were suddenly hurried off for a hearing. We arrived at the forum, and straight away the story went about the neighbourhood near the forum and a huge crowd gathered. We walked up to the prisoner's dock. All the others when questioned admitted their guilt. Then, when it came my turn, my father appeared with my son, dragged me from the step, and said: 'Perform the sacrifice--have pity on your baby!'

Hilarianus the governor, who had received his judicial powers as the successor of the late proconsul Minucius Timinianus, said to me: 'Have pity on your father's grey head; have pity on your infant son. Offer the sacrifice for the welfare of the emperors.'

'I will not', I retorted.

'Are you a Christian?' said Hilarianus.

And I said: 'Yes, I am.'

When my father persisted in trying to dissuade me, Hilarianus ordered him to be thrown to the ground and beaten with a rod. I felt sorry for father, just as if I myself had been beaten. I felt sorry for his pathetic old age.

Then Hilarianus passed sentence on all of us: we were condemned to the beasts, and we returned to prison in high spirits. But my baby had got used to being nursed at the breast and to staying with me in prison. So I sent the deacon Pomponius straight away to my father to ask for the baby. But father refused to give him over. But as God willed, the baby had no further desire for the breast, nor did I suffer any inflammation; and so I was relieved of any anxiety for my child and of any discomfort in my breasts....

Some days later, an adjutant named Pudens, who was in charge of the prison, began to show us great honour, realizing that we possessed some great power within us. And he began to allow many visitors to see us for our mutual comfort.

Now the day of the contest was approaching, and my father came to see me overwhelmed with sorrow. He started tearing the hairs from his beard and threw them on the ground; he then threw himself on the ground and began to curse his old age and to say such words as would move all creation. I felt sorry for his unhappy old age.

The day before we were to fight with the beasts I saw the following vision. Pomponius the deacon came to the prison gates and began to knock violently. I went out and opened the gate for him. He was dressed in an unbelted white tunic, wearing elaborate sandals. And he said to me: 'Perpetua, come; we are waiting for you.'

Then he took my hand and we began to walk through rough and broken country. At last we came to the amphitheatre out of breath, and he led me into the centre of the arena.

Then he told me: 'Do not be afraid. I am here, struggling with you.' Then he left.

I looked at the enormous crowd who watched in astonishment. I was surprised that no beasts were let loose on me; for I knew that I was condemned to die by the beasts. Then out came an Egyptian against me, of vicious appearance, together with his seconds, to fight with me. There also came up to me some handsome young men to be my seconds and assistants.

My clothes were stripped off, and suddenly I was a man. My seconds began to rub me down with oil (as they are wont to do before a contest). Then I saw the Egyptian on the other side rolling in the dust. Next there came forth a man of marvelous stature, such that he rose above the top of the amphitheatre. He was clad in a beltless purple tunic with two stripes (one on either side) running down the middle of his chest. He wore sandals that were wondrously made of gold and silver, and he carried a wand like an athletic trainer and a green branch on which there were golden apples.

And he asked for silence and said: 'If this Egyptian defeats her he will slay her with the sword. But if she defeats him, she will receive this branch.' Then he withdrew.

We drew close to one another and began to let our fists fly. My opponent tried to get hold of my feet, but I kept striking him in the face with the heels of my feet. Then I was raised up into the air and I began to pummel him without as it were touching the ground. Then when I noticed there was a lull, I put my two hands together linking the fingers of one hand with those of the other and thus I got hold of his head. He fell flat on his face and I stepped on his head.

The crowd began to shout and my assistants started to sing psalms. Then I walked up to the trainer and took the branch. He kissed me and said to me: 'Peace be with you, my daughter!' I began to walk in triumph towards the Gate of Life. Then I awoke. I realized that it was not with wild animals that I would fight but with the Devil, but I knew that I would win the victory. So much for what I did up until the eve of the contest. About what happened at the contest itself, let him write of it who will.

[Here Saturus tells the story of a vision he had of Perpetua and himself, after they were killed, being carried by four angels into heaven where they were reunited with other martyrs killed in the same persecution.]

[Here the editor/narrator begins to relate the story]:

Such were the remarkable visions of these martyrs, Saturus and Perpetua, written by themselves. As for Secundulus, God called him from this world earlier than the others while he was still in prison, by a special grace that he might not have to face the animals. Yet his flesh, if not his spirit, knew the sword.

As for Felicitas, she too enjoyed the Lord's favour in this wise. She had been pregnant when she was arrested, and was now in her eighth month. As the day of the spectacle drew near she was very distressed that her martyrdom would be postponed because of her pregnancy; for it is against the law for women with child to be executed. Thus she might have to shed her holy, innocent blood afterwards along with others who were common criminals. Her comrades in martyrdom were also saddened; for they were afraid that they would have to leave behind so fine a companion to travel alone on the same road to hope. And so, two days before the contest, they poured forth a prayer to the Lord in one torrent of common grief. And immediately after their prayer the birth pains came upon her. She suffered a good deal in her labour because of the natural difficulty of an eight months' delivery.

Hence one of the assistants of the prison guards said to her: 'You suffer so much now--what will you do when you are tossed to the beasts? Little did you think of them when you refused to sacrifice.'

'What I am suffering now', she replied, 'I suffer by myself. But then another will be inside me who will suffer for me, just as I shall be suffering for him.'

And she gave birth to a girl; and one of the sisters brought her up as her own daughter.

Therefore, since the Holy Spirit has permitted the story of this contest to be written down and by so permitting has willed it, we shall carry out the command or, indeed, the commission of the most saintly Perpetua, however unworthy I might be to add anything to this glorious story. At the same time I shall add one example of her perseverance and nobility of soul.

The military tribune had treated them with extraordinary severity because on the information of certain very foolish people he became afraid that they would be spirited out of the prison by magical spells.

Perpetua spoke to him directly. 'Why can you not even allow us to refresh ourselves properly? For we are the most distinguished of the condemned prisoners, seeing that we belong to the emperor; we are to fight on his very birthday. Would it not be to your credit if we were brought forth on the day in a healthier condition?'

The officer became disturbed and grew red. So it was that he gave the order that they were to be more humanely treated; and he allowed her brothers and other persons to visit, so that the prisoners could dine in their company. By this time the adjutant who was head of the gaol was himself a Christian.

On the day before, when they had their last meal, which is called the free banquet, they celebrated not a banquet but rather a love feast. They spoke to the mob with the same steadfastness, warned them of God's judgement, stressing the joy they would have in their suffering, and ridiculing the curiosity of those that came to see them. Saturus said: 'Will not tomorrow be enough for you? Why are you so eager to see something that you dislike? Our friends today will be our enemies on the morrow. But take careful note of what we look like so that you will recognize us on the day.' Thus everyone would depart from the prison in amazement, and many of them began to believe.

The day of their victory dawned, and they marched from the prison to the amphitheatre joyfully as though they were going to heaven, with calm faces, trembling, if at all, with joy rather than fear. Perpetua went along with shining countenance and calm step, as the beloved of God, as a wife of Christ, putting down everyone's stare by her own intense gaze. With them also was Felicitas, glad that she had safely given birth so that now she could fight the beasts, going from one blood bath to another, from the midwife to the gladiator, ready to wash after childbirth in a second baptism.

They were then led up to the gates and the men were forced to put on the robes of priests of Saturn, the women the dress of the priestesses of Ceres. But the noble Perpetua strenuously resisted this to the end.

'We came to this of our own free will, that our freedom should not be violated. We agreed to pledge our lives provided that we would do no such thing. You agreed with us to do this.'

Even injustice recognized justice. The military tribune agreed. They were to be brought into the arena just as they were. Perpetua then began to sing a psalm: she was already treading on the head of the Egyptian. Revocatus, Saturninus, and Saturus began to warn the on looking mob. Then when they came within sight of Hilarianus, they suggested by their motions and gestures: 'You have condemned us, but God will condemn you' was what they were saying.

At this the crowds became enraged and demanded that they be scourged before a line of gladiators. And they rejoiced at this that they had obtained a share in the Lord's sufferings.

But he who said, **Ask and you shall receive**, answered their prayer by giving each one the death he had asked for. For whenever they would discuss among themselves their desire for martyrdom, Saturninus indeed insisted that he wanted to be exposed to all the different beasts, that his crown might be all the more glorious. And so at the outset of the contest he and Revocatus were matched with a leopard, and then while in the stocks they were attacked by a bear. As for Saturus, he dreaded nothing more than a bear, and he counted on being killed by one bite of a leopard. Then he was matched with a wild boar; but the gladiator who had tied him to the animal was gored by the boar and died a few days after the contest, whereas Saturus was only dragged along. Then when he was bound in the stocks awaiting the bear, the animal refused to come out of the cages, so that Saturus was called back once more unhurt.

For the young women, however, the Devil had prepared a mad heifer. This was an unusual animal, but it was chosen that their sex might be matched with that of the beast. So they were stripped naked, placed in nets and thus brought out into the arena. Even the crowd was horrified when they saw that one was a delicate young girl and the other was a woman fresh from childbirth with the milk still dripping from her breasts. And so they were brought back again and dressed in unbelted tunics.

First the heifer tossed Perpetua and she fell on her back. Then sitting up she pulled down the tunic that was ripped along the side so that it covered her thighs, thinking more of her modesty than of her pain. Next she asked for a pin to fasten her untidy hair: for it was not right that a martyr should die with her hair in disorder, lest it might seem to be mourning in her hour of triumph.

Then she got up. And seeing that Felicitas had been crushed to the ground, she went over to her, gave her hand, and lifted her up. Then the two stood side by side. But the cruelty of the mob was by now appeased, and so they were called back through the Gate of Life.

There Perpetua was held up by a man named Rusticus who was at the time a catechumen and kept close to her. She awoke from a kind of sleep (so absorbed had she been in ecstasy in the Spirit) and she began to look about her. Then to the amazement of all she said: 'When are we going to be thrown to that heifer or whatever it is?'

When told that this had already happened, she refused to believe it until she noticed the marks of her rough experience on her person and her dress. Then she called for her brother and spoke to him together with the catechumens and said: 'You must all **stand fast in the faith** and love one another, and do not be weakened by what we have gone through.'

At another gate Saturus was earnestly addressing the soldier Pudens. 'It is exactly', he said, 'as I foretold and predicted. So far not one animal has touched me. So now you may believe me with all your heart: I am going in there and I shall be finished off with one bite of the leopard.' And immediately as the contest was coming to a close a leopard was let loose, and after one bite Saturus was so drenched with blood that as he came away the mob roared in witness to his second baptism: 'Well washed! Well washed!' For well washed indeed was one who had been bathed in this manner.

Then he said to the soldier Pudens: 'Good-bye. Remember me, and remember the faith. These things should not disturb you but rather strengthen you.'

And with this he asked Pudens for a ring from his finger, and dipping it into his wound he gave it back to him again as a pledge and as a record of his bloodshed.

Shortly after he was thrown unconscious with the rest in the usual spot to have his throat cut. But the mob asked that their bodies be brought out into the open that their eyes might be the guilty witnesses of the sword that pierced their flesh. And so the martyrs got up and went to the spot of their own accord as the people wanted them to, and kissing one another they sealed their martyrdom with the ritual kiss of peace. The others took the sword in silence and without moving, especially Saturus, who being the first to climb the stairway was the first to die. For once again he was waiting for Perpetual Perpetua, however, had yet to taste more pain. She screamed as she was struck on the bone; then she took the trembling hand of the young gladiator and guided it to her throat. It was as though so

great a woman, feared as she was by the unclean spirit, could not be dispatched unless she herself were willing.

Ah, most valiant and blessed martyrs! Truly are you called and chosen for the glory of Christ Jesus our Lord! And any man who exalts, honours, and worships his glory should read for the consolation of the Church these new deeds of heroism which are no less significant than the tales of old. For these new manifestations of virtue will bear witness to one and the same Spirit who still operates, and to God the Father almighty, to his Son Jesus Christ our Lord, to whom is splendour and immeasurable power for all the ages. Amen.

Book 111. The Apocalypse of Zephaniah

Clement, Stromata 5.11.77 The scene in the fifth heaven. A And a spirit took me and brought me up into the fifth heaven. And I saw angels who are called "lords." And the diadem was set upon them in the Holy Spirit, and the throne of each of them was sevenfold more (brilliant) than the light of the rising sun. (And they were dwelling in the temples of salvation and singing hymns to the ineffable God.) Sahidic fragment The seer's vision of a soul in torment. B1I saw a soul which five thousand angels punished and guarded. 2They took it to the East and they brought it to the West. They beat its … they gave it a hundred … lashes for each one daily. 3I was afraid and I cast myself upon my face so that my joints dissolved. 4The angel helped me. He said unto me, "Be strong, O one who will triumph, and prevail so that thou wilt triumph over the accuser and thou wilt come up from Hades." 5And after I arose I said, "Who is this whom they are punishing?"6He said unto me, "This is a soul which was found in its lawlessness." And before it attained to repenting it was visited, and taken out of its body. 7Truly, I, Zephaniah, saw these things in my vision. The scene in a broad place. 8And the angel of the Lord went with me. I saw a great broad place, thousands of thousands surrounded it on its left side and myriads of myriads on its right side. The form of each one was different. 9Their hair was loose like that belonging to women. Their teeth were like the teeth of … Akhmimic Text Fragment dealing with burial. 11 … dead. We will bury him like any man. 2Whenever he dies, we will carry him out playing the cithera before him and chanting psalms and odes over his body. Scenes from above the seer's city. 21Now I went with the angel of the Lord, and he took me up (over) all my city. There was nothing before my eyes. 2Then I saw two men walking together on one road. I watched them as they talked. 3And, moreover, I also saw two women grinding together at a mill. And I watched them as they talked. 4And I also saw two upon a bed, each one of them acting for their (mutual) … upon a bed. 5And I saw the whole inhabited world hanging like a drop of water which is suspended from a bucket when it comes up from a well. 6I said unto the angel of the Lord. "Then does not darkness or night exist in this place?" 7He said unto me, "No, because darkness existeth not in that place where the righteous and the saints are, but rather they always exist in the light." 8 And I saw all the souls of men as they existed in punishment. 9 And I cried out to the Lord Almighty, "O God, if Thou remainest with the saints, Thou (certainly) hast compassion on behalf of the world and the souls which are in this punishment." Recording angels from Mount Seir. 3 1The angel of the Lord said unto me, "Come, let me show thee the place of righteousness." 2And he took me up upon Mount Seir and he showed me three men, as two angels walked with them rejoicing and exulting over them. 3I said to the angel, "Of what sort are these?" 4He said to me, "These are the three sons of Joatham, the priest, who neither kept the commandment of their father nor observed the ordinances of the Lord." 5 Then I saw two other angels weeping over the three sons of Joatham, the priest. 6 I said, "O angel, who are these?" He said, "These are the angels of the Lord Almighty. They write down all the good deeds of the righteous upon their scrolls as they watch at the gate of heaven." 7 And I take them from their hands and bring them up before the Lord Almighty; He writeth their name in the Book of the Living. 8 Also the angels of the accuser who is upon the earth, they also write down all the sins of men upon their scrolls. 9 They also sit at the gate of heaven. They tell the accuser and he writeth them upon his scroll so that he might accuse them when they come out of the world (and go) down there." Ugly angels carry off the souls of ungodly men. 4 1Then I walked with the angel of the Lord. I looked before me and I saw a place there. 2Thousands of thousands and myriads of myriads of angels entered through it. 3Their faces were like a leopard, their tusks being outside their mouth like wild boars. 4Their eyes were mixed with blood. Their hair was loose like the hair of women, and fiery scourges were in their hands.5When I saw them, I was afraid. I said unto that angel who walked with me, "Of what sort are these?" 6He said unto me, "These are the servants of all creation who come to the souls of ungodly men and bring them and leave them in this place. 7They spend three days going around with them in the air before they bring them and cast them into their eternal punishment." 8 I said, "I beseech thee, O Lord, give not authority to come to me." 9 The angel said, "Fear not. I will not permit them to come to thee because thou art pure before the Lord. I will not permit them to come to thee because the Lord Almighty sent me unto thee because are pure before him." 10Then he beckoned to them, and they withdrew themselves and they ran from me. The heavenly city. 5 1But I went with the angel of the Lord, and I looked in front of me and I saw gates. 2Then when I approached them I discovered that they were bronze gates. 3The angel touched them and they opened before him. I entered with him and found its whole square like a beautiful city, and I walked in its midst. 4Then the angel of the Lord transformed himself beside me in that place. 5Now I looked at them, and I discovered that they were bronze gates and bronze bolts and iron bars. 6Now my mouth was shut therein. I beheld the bronze gates in front of me as fire was being cast forth for about fifty stadia. The accuser and the angel Eremiel in Hades. 61Again I turned back and walked, and I saw a great sea. 2But I thought that it was a sea of water. I discovered that it was entirely a sea of flame like a slime which casteth forth much flame and whose waves burn sulfur and bitumen. 3They began to approach me. 4 Then I thought that the Lord Almighty had come to visit me. 5 Then when I saw, I fell upon my face before him in order that I might worship him. 6 I was very much afraid, and I entreated him that he might save me from this distress. 7 I cried out, saying, "Eloe, Lord, Adonai, Sabaoth. I beseech Thee to save me from this distress because it hath befallen me." 8 In that same instant I stood up, and I saw a great angel before me. His hair was spread out like that of lionesses'. His teeth were outside his mouth like a bear. His hair was spread out like women's. His body was like the serpent's when he wished to swallow me. 9 And when I saw him, I was afraid of him so that all the parts of my body were loosened and I fell upon my face.10I was unable to stand, and I prayed before the Lord Almighty, "Thou wilt save me from this distress. Thou art the one who saved Israel from the hand of Pharaoh, the king of Egypt. Thou saved Susanna from the hand of the elders of injustice. Thou saved the three holy men, Shadrach, Meshach, Abednego, from the furnace of burning fire. I beg you to save me from this distress." 11Then I arose and stood, and I saw a great angel standing before me with his face shining like the rays of the sun in its glory since his face is like that which is perfected in its glory. 12And he was girded as if a golden girdle were upon his breast. His feet were like bronze which is melted in a fire. 13And when I saw him, I rejoiced, for I thought that the Lord Almighty had come to visit me. 14I fell upon my face, and I worshiped him. 15He said to me, "Take heed. Worship me not. I am not the Lord Almighty, but am the great angel, Eremiel, who is over the abyss and Hades, the one in which all of the souls are imprisoned from the end of the Flood, which came upon the earth, until this day." 16Then I inquired of the angel, "What is the place to which I have come?" He said to me, "It is Hades." 17Then I asked him, "Who is the great angel who stands thus, whom I saw?" He said, "This is the one who accuses men in the presence of the Lord." The two scrolls. 71Then I looked, and I saw him with a scroll in his hand. He began to unroll it. 2Now after he had spread it out, I read it in my (own) language. I found that all my sins which I had done were written in it, those which I had done from my youth until this day. 3They were all written upon that scroll of mine without there being a false word in them. 4If I did not go to visit a sick man or a widow, I found it written down as a shortcoming upon my manuscript. 5If I did not visit an orphan, it was found written down as a shortcoming on my scroll. 6A day on which I did not fast (or) pray in the time of prayer I found written down as a failing upon my scroll. 7And a day when I did not turn to the sons of Israel — since it is a shortcoming — I found written down upon my scroll 8so that I threw myself upon my face and prayed before the Lord Almighty, "May thy mercy reach me and may thou wipe out my scroll because Thy mercy hath come to be in every place and hath filled every place." 9 Then I arose and stood, and I saw a great angel before me saying to me, "Triumph, prevail because thou hast prevailed and hast triumphed over the accuser, and thou hast come up from Hades and the abyss. Thou wilt now cross over the crossing place." 10Again he brought another scroll which was written by hand. 11He began to unroll it, and I read it, and found it written in my (own) language … Leaving Hades. two pages missing (In the missing pages the author probably discussed the content of the second scroll, which should have recorded the good deeds of the seer. If the missing material is parallel to the preceding section, the reading of the scroll would be followed by a prayer — possibly a prayer of thanksgiving — and a pronouncement of triumph by a great angel. That would be followed by preparations for crossing over the river in a journey out of Hades. The section that follows begins after the arrival of a boat.) 8 … 1 They helped me and set me on that boat. 2 Thousands of thousands and myriads of myriads of angels gave praise before me. 3 I, myself, put on an angelic garment. I saw all of those angels praying. 4 I, myself, prayed together with them. 5 I knew their language, which they spoke with me. 6Now, moreover, my sons, this is the trial because it is necessary that the good and the evil be weighed in a balance. The 1st trumpet: triumph & visitation of the righteous. 91Then a great angel came forth having a golden trumpet in his hand, and he blew it three times over my head, saying, "Be courageous! O one who hath triumphed. Prevail! O one who hath prevailed. For thou hast triumphed over the accuser, and thou hast escaped from the abyss and Hades. 2Thou wilt now cross over the crossing place. For thy name is written in the Book of the Living." 3I wanted to embrace him, (but) I was unable to embrace the great angel because his

glory is great. 4 Then he ran to all the righteous ones, namely, Abraham and Isaac and Jacob and Enoch and Elijah and David. 5He spoke with them as friend to friend speaking one with another. A 2nd trumpet: opening of heaven & souls in torment. 10:1 Then the great angel came to me with the golden trumpet in his hand, and he blew it up unto heaven. 2 Heaven opened from the place where the sun rises to where it sets, from the north to the south. 3 I saw the sea which I had seen at the bottom of Hades. Its waves came up to the clouds. 4 I saw all the souls sinking in it. I saw some whose hands were bound to their neck, with their hands and feet being fettered. 5 I said, "Who are these?" He said unto me, "These are the ones who were bribed and they were given gold and silver until the souls of men were led astray." 6 And I saw others covered with mats of fire. 7 I said, "Who are these?" He said unto me, "These are the ones who give money at interest, and they receive interest for interest." 8 And I also saw some blind ones crying out. And I was amazed when I saw all these works of God. 9 I said, "Who are these?" He said unto me, "These are catechumens who heard the word of God, but they were not perfected in the work which they heard." 10 And I said unto him, "Then have they not repentance here?" He said, "Yes," 11 I said, "How long?" He said unto me, "Until the day when the Lord will judge." 12 And I saw others with their hair on them. 13 I said, "Then there is hair and body in this place?" 14 He said, "Yes, the Lord gives body and hair to them as he desires." The intercession of the saints for those in torment. 11:1 And I also saw multitudes. He brought them forth. 2 As they looked at all of the torments they called out, praying before the Lord Almighty, saying, "We pray unto Thee on account of those who are in all these torments so that Thou might have mercy on all of them." 3 And when I saw them, I said to the angel who spoke with me, "" 4 He said, "These who beseech the Lord are Abraham and Isaac and Jacob. 5 Then at a certain hour daily they come forth with the great angel. He soundeth a trumpet up unto heaven and another soundeth upon the earth. 6 All the righteous hear the sound. They come running, praying to the Lord Almighty daily on behalf of these who are in all these torments." Another trumpet: the coming wrath of God. 12:1 And again the great angel cometh forth with the golden trumpet in his hand blowing over the earth. 2 They hear (it) from the place of the sunrise to the place of the sunset and from the southern regions to the northern regions. 3 And again he blows (it) up unto heaven and its sound is heard. 4 I said, "O Lord, why left thou me not until I saw them all?" 5 He said unto me, "I have not authority to show them unto thee until the Lord Almighty riseth up in his wrath to destroy the earth and the heavens. 6 They will see and be disturbed, and they will all cry out, saying, 'All flesh which is ascribed to Thee we will give unto Thee on the day of the Lord. 7 Who will stand in His presence when He riseth in His wrath the earth 8 Every tree which groweth upon the earth will be plucked up with its roots and fall down. And every high tower and the birds which fly will fall … " four pages missing.

Book 112. The Testament of the Twelve Patriarchs

THE TESTAMENT OF REUBEN, THE FIRST-BORN SON OF JACOB AND LEAH

1 1 The copy of the Testament of Reuben, even the commands which he gave his sons before he 2 died in the hundred and twenty-fifth year of his life. Two years after the death of Joseph his 3 brother, when Reuben fell ill, his sons and his sons' sons were gathered together to visit him. And 4 he said to them: My children, behold I am dying, and go the way of my fathers. And seeing there Judah, and Gad, and Asher, his brethren, he said to them: Raise me up, that I may tell to my brethren and to my children what things I have hidden in my heart, for behold now at length 5 I am passing away. And he arose and kissed them, and said unto them: Hear, my brethren, and 6 do ye, my children, give ear to Reuben your father in the commands which I give unto you. And behold I call to witness against you this day the God of heaven, that ye walk not in the sins of 7 youth and fornication, wherein I was poured out, and defiled the bed of my father Jacob. And I tell you that he smote me with a sore plague in my loins for seven months; and had not my father 8 Jacob prayed for me to the Lord, the Lord would have destroyed me. For I was thirty years old 9 when I wrought the evil thing before the Lord, and for seven months I was sick unto death. And 10 after this I repented with set purpose of my soul for seven years before the Lord. And wine and strong drink I drank not, and flesh entered not into my mouth, and I eat no pleasant food; but I mourned over my sin, for it was great, such as had not been in Israel.

2 1 And now hear me, my children, what things I saw concerning the seven spirits of deceit, when 2 I repented. Seven spirits therefore are appointed against man, and they are the leaders in the works 3 of youth. [And seven other spirits are given to him at his creation, that through them should be 4 done every work of man. The first is the spirit of life, with which the constitution (of man) is 5 created. The second is the sense of sight, with which ariseth desire. The third is the sense of hearing, with which cometh teaching. The fourth is the sense of smell, with which tastes are given 6, 7 to draw air and breath. The fifth is the power of

speech, with which cometh knowledge. The sixth is the sense of taste, with which cometh the eating of meats and drinks; and by it strength is 8 produced, for in food is the foundation of strength. The seventh is the power of procreation and 9 sexual intercourse, with which through love of pleasure sins enter in. Wherefore it is the last in order of creation, and the first in that of youth, because it is filled with ignorance, and leadeth the youth as a blind man to a pit, and as a beast to a precipice.

3 1 Besides all these there is an eighth spirit of sleep, with which is brought about the trance of 2 3 nature and the image of death. With these spirits are mingled the spirits of error.] First, the spirit of fornication is seated in the nature and in the senses; the second, the spirit of insatiableness, 4 in the belly; the third, the spirit of fighting, in the liver and gall. The fourth is the spirit of 5 obsequiousness and chicanery, that through officious attention one may be fair in seeming. The fifth is the spirit of pride, that one may be boastful and arrogant. The sixth is the spirit of lying, 6 in perdition and jealousy to practise deceits, and concealments from kindred and friends. The seventh is the spirit of injustice, with which are thefts and acts of rapacity, that a man may fulfill the desire of his heart; for injustice worketh together with the other spirits by the taking of gifts. 7, 8 And with all these the spirit of sleep is joined which is (that) of error and fantasy.] And so perisheth every young man, darkening his mind from the truth, and not understanding the law of 9 God, nor obeying the admonitions of his fathers as befell me also in my youth. And now, my children, love the truth, and it will preserve you: hear ye the words of Reuben your father. 10 Pay no heed to the face of a woman, Nor associate with another man's wife, Nor meddle with affairs of womankind. 11 For had I not seen Bilhah bathing in a covered place, I had not fallen into this great iniquity. 12 For my mind taking in the thought of the woman's nakedness, suffered me not to sleep until I had 13 wrought the abominable thing. For while Jacob our father had gone to Isaac his father, when we were in Eder, near to Ephrath in Bethlehem, Bilhah became drunk and was asleep uncovered in her 14 chamber. Having therefore gone in and beheld nakedness, I wrought the impiety without her 15 perceiving it, and leaving her sleeping I departed. And forthwith an angel of God revealed to my father concerning my impiety, and he came and mourned over me, and touched her no more.

4 1 Pay no heed, therefore, my children, to the beauty of women, nor set your mind on their affairs; but walk in singleness of heart in the fear of the Lord, and expend labour on good works, and on study and on your flocks, until the Lord give you a wife, whom He will, that ye suffer not as I did. 2 For until my father's death I had not boldness to look in his face, or to speak to any of my brethren, 3 because of the reproach. Even until now my conscience causeth me anguish on account of my 4 impiety. And yet my father comforted me much and prayed for me unto the Lord, that the anger of the Lord might pass from me, even as the Lord showed. And thenceforth until now I have 5 been on my guard and sinned not. Therefore, my children, I say unto you, observe all things 6 whatsoever I command you, and ye shall not sin. For a pit unto the soul is the sin of fornication, separating it from God, and bringing it near to idols, because it deceiveth the mind and understanding, 7 and leadeth young men into hades before their time. For many hath fornication destroyed; because, though a man be old or noble, or rich or poor, he bringeth reproach upon 8 himself with the sons of men and derision with Beliar. For ye heard regarding Joseph how he guarded himself from a woman, and purged his thoughts from all fornication, and found favour in 9 the sight of God and men. For the Egyptian woman did many things unto him, and summoned 10 magicians, and offered him love potions, but the purpose of his soul admitted no evil desire. Therefore 11 the God of your fathers delivered him from every evil (and) hidden death. For if fornication overcomes not your mind, neither can Beliar overcome you.

5 1 For evil are women, my children; and since they have no power or strength over man, they use 2 wiles by outward attractions, that they may draw him to themselves. And whom they cannot 3 bewitch by outward attractions, him they overcome by craft. For moreover, concerning them, the angel of the Lord told me, and taught me, that women are overcome by the spirit of fornication more than men, and in their heart they plot against men; and by means of their adornment they deceive first their minds, and by the glance of the eye instill the poison, and then through the accomplished 4 act they take them captive. For a woman cannot force a man openly, but by a harlot's 5 bearing she beguiles him. Flee, therefore, fornication, my children, and command your wives and your daughters, that they adorn not their heads and faces to deceive the mind: because every woman 6 who useth these wiles hath been reserved for eternal punishment. For thus they allured the Watchers who were before the flood; for as these continually beheld them, they lusted after them, and they conceived the act in their mind; for they changed themselves into the shape of men, and 7 appeared to them when they were with their husbands. And the women lusting in their minds after their forms, gave birth to giants, for the Watchers appeared to them as reaching even unto heaven.

6 1 Beware, therefore, of fornication; and if you wish to be pure in mind, guard your senses from every 2 woman. And command the women likewise not to associate with men, that they also may be pure 3 in mind. For

constant meetings, even though the ungodly deed be not wrought, are to them an 4 irremediable disease, and to us a destruction of Beliar and an eternal reproach. For in fornication 5 there is neither understanding nor godliness, and all jealousy dwelleth in the lust thereof. Therefore, then I say unto you, ye will be jealous against the sons of Levi, and will seek to be exalted 6 over them; but ye shall not be able. For God will avenge them, and ye shall die by an evil death. 7 For to Levi God gave the sovereignty [and to Judah with him and to me also, and to Dan and 8 Joseph, that we should be for rulers]. Therefore I command you to hearken to Levi, because he shall know the law of the Lord, and shall give ordinances for judgement and shall sacrifice for all Israel until the consummation of the times, as the anointed High Priest, of whom the Lord spake, 9 I adjure you by the God of heaven to do truth each one unto his neighbour and to entertain love 10 each one for his brother. And draw ye near to Levi in humbleness of heart, that ye may receive 11 a blessing from his mouth. For he shall bless Israel and Judah, because him hath the Lord chosen to 12 be king over all the nation. And bow down before his seed, for on our behalf it will die in wars visible and invisible, and will be among you an eternal king.

7 1, 2 And Reuben died, having given these commands to his sons. And they placed him in a coffin until they carried him up from Egypt, and buried him in Hebron in the cave where his father was.

THE TESTAMENT OF SIMEON, THE SECOND OF JACOB AND LEAH.

1 1 The copy of the words of Simeon, the things which he spake to his sons before he died, in the 2 hundred and twentieth year of his life, at which time Joseph, his brother, died. For when Simeon was sick , his sons came to visit him, and he strengthened himself and sat up and kissed them, and said:--

2 1 Hearken, my children, to Simeon your father, And I will declare unto you what things I have in my heart. 2 I was born of Jacob as my father's second son; And my mother Leah called me Simeon, Because the Lord had heard her prayer. 3 Moreover, I became strong exceedingly; I shrank from no achievement, Nor was I afraid of ought. 4 For my heart was hard, And my liver was immovable, And my bowels without compassion. 5, 6 Because valour also has been given from the Most High to men in soul and body. For in the time of my youth I was jealous in many things of Joseph, because my father loved him beyond 7 all. And I set my mind against him to destroy him, because the prince of deceit sent forth the spirit of jealousy and blinded my mind, so that I regarded him not as a brother, nor did I spare even 8 Jacob my father. But his God and the God of his fathers sent forth His angel, and delivered him 9 out of my hands. For when I went to Shechem to bring ointment for the flocks, and Reuben to Dothan, where were our necessaries and all our stores, Judah my brother sold him to the Ishmaelites. 10 And when Reuben heard these things he was grieved, for he wished to restore him to his father. 11 But on hearing this I was exceedingly wroth against Judah in that he let him go away alive, and 12 for five months I continued wrathful against him. But the Lord restrained me, and withheld from 13 me the power of my hands; for my right hand was half withered for seven days. And I knew, my children, that because of Joseph this had befallen me, and I repented and wept; and I besought the Lord God that my hand might be restored, and that I might hold aloof from all pollution and envy 14 and from all folly. For I knew that I had devised an evil thing before the Lord and Jacob my father, on account of Joseph my brother, in that I envied him.

3 1 2 And now, my children, hearken unto me and beware of the spirit of deceit and envy. For envy ruleth over the whole mind of a man, and suffereth him neither to eat nor to drink, nor to do any 3 good thing. But it ever suggesteth (to him) to destroy him that he envieth; and so long as he that 4 is envied flourisheth, he that envieth fadeth away. Two years therefore I afflicted my soul with fasting in the fear of the Lord, and I learnt that deliverance from envy cometh by the fear of God. 5 For if a man flee to the Lord, the evil spirit runneth away from him, and his mind is lightened. 6 And henceforward he sympathiseth with him whom he envied and forgiveth those who are hostile to him, and so ceaseth from his envy.

4 1 And my father asked Concerning me, because he saw that I was sad; and I said unto him, I am 2 pained in my liver. For I mourned more than they all, because I was guilty of the selling of Joseph. 3 And when we went down into Egypt, and he bound me as a spy, I knew that I was suffering justly, 4 and I grieved not. Now Joseph was a good man, and had the Spirit of God within him: being compassionate and pitiful, he bore no malice against me; but loved me even as the rest of his 5 brethren. Beware, therefore, my children, of all jealousy and envy, and walk in singleness of soul and with good heart, keeping in mind Joseph your father's brother, that God may give you also grace and glory, and blessing upon your heads, even as ye saw in 6 Joseph's case. All his days he reproached us not concerning this thing, but loved us as his own 7 soul, and beyond his own sons glorified us, and gave us riches, and cattle and fruits. Do ye also, my children, love each one his brother with a good heart, and the spirit of envy will withdraw from 8 you. For this maketh savage the soul and destroyeth the body; it causeth anger and war in the mind, and stirreth up unto deeds of blood, and leadeth the mind into frenzy, and suffereth not prudence to act in men; moreover, it taketh away sleep, [and causeth tumult to the soul and trembling to the body]. 9 For even in sleep some malicious jealousy, deluding him, gnaweth and with wicked spirits disturbeth his soul, and causeth the body to be troubled, and waketh the mind from sleep in confusion; and as a wicked and poisonous spirit, so appeareth it to men.

5 1 Therefore was Joseph comely in appearance and goodly to look upon, because no wickedness 2 dwelt in him; for some of the trouble of the spirit the face manifesteth. And now, my children, Make your hearts good before the Lord, And your ways straight before men. And ye shall find grace before the Lord and men. 3 Beware, therefore, of fornication, For fornication is mother of all evils, Separating from God, and bringing near to Beliar. 4 For I have seen it inscribed in the writing of Enoch that your sons shall be corrupted in fornication, 5 and shall do harm to the sons of Levi with the sword. But they shall not be able to withstand Levi; 6 for he shall wage the war of the Lord, and shall conquer all your hosts. And they shall be few in number, divided in Levi and Judah, and there shall be none of you for sovereignty, even as also our father prophesied in his blessings.

6 1, 2 Behold I have told you all things, that I may be acquitted of your sin. Now, if ye remove from you your envy and all stiff-neckedness, As a rose shall my bones flourish in Israel, And as a lily my flesh in Jacob, And my odour shall be as the odour of Libanus; And as cedars shall holy ones be multiplied from me forever, And their branches shall stretch afar off. 3 Then shall perish the seed of Canaan, And a remnant shall not be unto Amalek, And all the Cappadocians shall perish, And all the Hittites shall be utterly destroyed. 4 Then shall fail the land of Ham, And all the people shall perish. Then shall all the earth rest from trouble, And all the world under heaven from war. 5 Then the Mighty One of Israel shall glorify Shem, For the Lord God shall appear on earth, And Himself save men. 6 Then shall all the spirits of deceit be given to be trodden under foot, And men shall rule over wicked spirits. 7 Then shall I arise in joy, And will bless the Most High because of his marvellous works, [Because God hath taken a body and eaten with men and saved men].

7 1 And now, my children, obey Levi and Judah, and be not lifted up against these two tribes, for 2 from them shall arise unto you the salvation of God. For the Lord shall raise up from Levi as it were a High-priest, and from Judah as it were a King [God and man], He shall save all [the Gentiles 3 and] the race of Israel. Therefore I give you these commands that ye also may command your children that they may observe them throughout their generations.

8 1 And when Simeon had made an end of commanding his sons, he slept with his fathers, being an 2 hundred and twenty years old. And they laid him in a wooden coffin, to take up his bones to 3 Hebron. And they took them up secretly during a war of the Egyptians. For the bones of Joseph 4 the Egyptians guarded in the tombs of the kings. For the sorcerers told them; that on the departure of the bones of Joseph there should be throughout all the land darkness and gloom, and an exceeding great plague to the Egyptians, so that even with a lamp a man should not recognize his brother.

9 1, 2 And the sons of Simeon bewailed their father. And they were in Egypt until the day of their departure by the hand of Moses.

THE TESTAMENT OF LEVI, THE THIRD SON OF JACOB AND LEAH

1 1 The copy of the words of Levi, the things which he ordained unto his sons, according to all that 2 they should do, and what things should befall them until the day of judgement. He was sound in health when he called them to him; for it had been revealed to him that he should die. And when they were gathered together he said to them:

2 1, 2 I, Levi, was born in Haran, and I came with my father to Shechem. And I was young, about
3 twenty years of age, when, with Simeon, I wrought vengeance on Hamor for our sister Dinah. And when I was feeding the flocks in Abel-Maul, the spirit of understanding of the Lord came upon me, and I saw all men corrupting their way, and that unrighteousness had built for itself walls, and lawlessness 4 sat upon towers. And I was grieving for the race of the sons of men, and I prayed to the 5 Lord that I might be saved. Then there fell upon me a sleep, and I beheld a high mountain, and 6 I was upon it. And behold the heavens were opened and an angel of God said to me, Levi enter 7 And I entered from the first heaven, and I saw there a great sea hanging. 8 And further I saw a second heaven far brighter and more brilliant, for there was a boundless light also therein. 9 And I said to the angel, Why Is this so? And the angel said to me, Marvel not at this, for thou shalt see another heaven more brilliant and incomparable. 10 And when thou hast ascended thither, Thou shalt stand near the Lord, And shalt be His minister, And shalt declare His mysteries to men, And shall proclaim concerning Him that shall redeem Israel. 11 And by thee and Judah shall the Lord appear among men Saving every race of men. 12 And from the Lord's portion shall be thy life, And He shall be thy field and vineyard, And fruits, gold, and silver.

3 1 Hear, therefore, regarding the heavens which have been shown to thee. The lowest is for this cause gloomy unto thee, in that it beholds all the unrighteous deeds of men. 2 And it has fire, snow, and ice made ready for the day of judgement, in the righteous judgement of God; for in it are all the spirits of the retributions for vengeance on men. 3 And in the second are the hosts of the armies which are ordained for the day of judgement, to work vengeance on the spirits of deceit and of Beliar. And above them are the holy ones. 4 And in the highest of all dwelleth the Great Glory, far above all holiness. 5 In [the heaven next to] it are the archangels, who minister and make propitiation to the Lord for all the sins of ignorance of the righteous; Offering to the Lord a sweet- smelling savour, a reasonable and a bloodless offering. 7 And [in the heaven below this] are the angels who bear answers to the angels of the presence of the Lord. 8 And in the heaven next to this are thrones and dominions, in which always they offer praise to God. 9 When, therefore, the Lord looketh upon us, all of us are shaken; yea, the heavens, and the earth, and the abysses are shaken at the presence of His majesty. 10 But the sons of men, having no perception of these things sin and provoke the Most High.

4 1 Now, therefore, know that the Lord shall execute judgment upon the sons of men. Because when the rocks are being rent, And the sun quenched, And the waters dried up, And the fire cowering, And all creation troubled, And the invisible spirits melting away; And Hades taketh spoils through the visitations of the Most High, Men will be unbelieving and persist in their iniquity. On this account with punishment shall they be judged. 2 Therefore the Most High hath heard thy prayer, To separate thee from iniquity, and that thou shouldst become to Him a son, And a servant, and a minister of His presence. 3 The light of knowledge shalt thou light up in Jacob, And as the sun shalt thou be to all the seed of Israel. 4 And there shall be given to thee a blessing, and to all thy seed, Until the Lord shall visit all the Gentiles in His tender mercies for ever. 5 And therefore there have been given to thee counsel and understanding, That thou mightst instruct thy sons concerning this; 6 Because they that bless Him shall be blessed, And they that curse Him shall perish.

5 1 And thereupon the angel opened to me the gates of heaven, and I saw the holy temple, and upon 2 a throne of glory the Most High. And He said to me: Levi, I have given thee the blessings of the 3 priesthood until I come and sojourn in the midst of Israel. Then the angel brought me down to the earth, and gave me a shield and a sword, and said to me: Execute vengeance on Shechem because 4 of Dinah, thy sister, and I will be with thee because the Lord hath sent me. And I destroyed at 5 that time the sons of Hamor, as it is written in the heavenly tables. And I said to him: I pray 6 thee, O Lord, tell me Thy name, that I may call upon Thee in a day of tribulation. And he said: I am the angel who intercedeth for the nation of Israel that they may not be smitten utterly, 7 for every evil spirit attacketh it. And after these things I awaked, and blessed the Most High, and the angel who intercedeth for the nation of Israel and for all the righteous.

6 1 And when I was going to my father, I found a brazen shield; wherefore also the name of the 2 mountain is Aspis, which is near Gebal, to the south of Abila And I kept these words in my 3 heart. And after this I counselled my father, and Reuben my brother, to bid the sons of Hamor not to be circumcised; for I was zealous because of the abomination which they had wrought on 4, 5 my sister. And I slew Shechem first, and Simeon slew Hamor. And after this my brothers 6 came and smote that city with the edge of the sword. And my father heard these things and was wroth, and he was grieved in that they had received the circumcision, and after that had been 7 put to death, and in his blessings he looked amiss upon us. For we sinned because we had done 8 this thing against his will, and he was sick on that day. But I saw that the sentence of God was for evil upon Shechem; for they sought to do to Sarah and Rebecca as they had done to Dinah our 9 sister, but the Lord prevented them. And they persecuted Abraham our father when he was a stranger, and they vexed his flocks when they were big with young; and Eblaen, who was born in his 10 house, they most shamefully handled. And thus they did to all strangers, taking away their 11 wives by force, and they banished them. But the wrath of the Lord came upon them to the uttermost.

7 1 And I said to my father Jacob: By thee will the Lord despoil the Canaanites, and will give 2 their land to thee and to thy seed after thee. For from this day forward shall Shechem be 3 called a city of imbeciles; for as a man mocketh a fool, so did we mock them. Because also 4 they had wrought folly in Israel by defiling my sister. And we departed and came to Bethel.

8 1, 2 And there again I saw a vision as the former, after we had spent there seventy days. And I saw seven men in white raiment saying unto me: Arise, put on the robe of the priesthood, and the crown of righteousness, and the breastplate of understanding, and the garment of truth, and the plate of faith, and the 3 turban of the head, and the ephod of prophecy. And they severally carried (these things) and put (them,) on me, and said unto me: From henceforth become a priest of the Lord, thou and thy seed for 4, 5 ever. And the first anointed me with holy oil, and gave to me the staff of judgment. The second washed me with pure water, and fed me with bread and wine (even) the most holy things, and clad 6, 7 me with a holy and glorious robe. The third clothed me with a linen vestment like an ephod. The 8, 9 fourth put round me a girdle like unto purple. The fifth gave me a branch of rich olive. The sixth 10 placed a crown on my head. The seventh placed on my head a diadem of priesthood, and filled my 11 hands with incense, that I might serve as priest to the Lord God. And they said to me: Levi, thy 12 seed shall be divided into three offices, for a sign of the glory of the Lord who is to come. And the 13 first portion shall be great; yea, greater than it shall none be. The second shall be in the priest-hood. 14 And the third shall be called by a new name, because a king shall arise in Judah, and shall 15 establish a new priesthood, after the fashion of the Gentiles [to all the Gentiles]. And His presence is beloved, as a prophet of the Most High, of the seed of Abraham our father. 16 Therefore, every desirable thing in Israel shall be for thee and for thy seed, And ye shall eat everything fair to look upon, And the table of the Lord shall thy seed apportion. 17 And some of them shall be high priests, and judges, and scribes; For by their mouth shall the holy place be guard-ed. 18, 19 And when I awoke, I understood that this (dream) was like the first dream. And I hid this also in my heart, and told it not to any man upon the earth.

9 1, 2 And after two days I and Judah went up with our father Jacob to Isaac our father's father. And my father's father blessed me according to all the words of the visions which I had seen. And 3 he would not come with us to Bethel. And when we came to Bethel, my father saw a vision 4 concerning me, that I should be their priest unto God. And he rose up early in the morning, 5 and paid tithes of all to the Lord through me. And so we came to Hebron to dwell there. 6 And Isaac called me continually to put me in remembrance of the law of the Lord, even as the 7 angel of the Lord showed unto me. And he taught me the law of the priesthood, of sacrifices, 8 whole burnt-offerings, first-fruits, freewill-offerings, peace-offerings. And each day he was instructing me, and was busied on my behalf before the Lord, and said to me: Beware of the spirit of 10 fornica-tion; for this shall continue and shall by thy seed pollute the holy place. Take, therefore, to thyself a wife without blemish or pollution, w bile yet thou art young, and not of the race of 11 strange nations. And before entering into the holy place, bathe; and when thou offerest the 12 sacri-fices wash; and again, when thou finishest the sacrifice, wash Of twelve trees having leaves 13, offer to the Lord, as Abraham taught me also. And of every clean beast and bird offer a 14 sacrifice to the Lord. And of all thy first -fruits and of wine offer the first, as a sacrifice to the Lord God; and every sacrifice thou shalt salt with salt.

10 1 Now, therefore, observe whatsoever I command you, children: for whatsoever things I have 2 heard from my fathers I have declared unto you. And behold I am clear from your ungodliness and transgression, which ye shall commit in the end of the ages [against the Saviour of the world, Christ, acting godlessly], deceiving Israel, and stirring up against it great evils from the 3 Lord. And ye shall deal lawlessly together with Israel, so He shall not bear with Jerusalem because of your wickedness; but the veil of the temple shall be rent, so as not to cover your 4 shame. And ye shall be scattered as captives among the Gentiles, and shall be for a reproach 5 and for a curse there. For the house which the Lord shall choose shall be called Jerusalem, as is contained in the book of Enoch the righteous.

11 1,2 Therefore when I took a wife I was twenty-eight years old, and her name was Melcha. And she conceived and bare a son, and I called his name Gersam, for we were sojourners in our land 3, 4 And I saw concern-ing him, that he would not be in the first rank, And Kohath was born in the 5 thirty-fifth year of my life, towards sunrise. And I saw in a vision that he was standing on high 6 in the midst of all the congregation, There-fore I called his name Kohath [which is, beginning of 7 majesty and instruction]. And she bare me a third son, in the fortieth year of my life; and since his mother bare him with difficulty, I called him Merari, that is, 'my bitterness,' because he also was 8 like to die. And Jochebed was born in Egypt, in my sixty-fourth year, for I was renowned then in the midst of my brethren.

12 1, 2 And Gersam took a wife, and she bare to him Lomni and Semei. And the sons of Kohath, 3, 4 Ambram, Issachar, Hebron, and Ozeel. And the sons of Merari, Mooli, and Mouses. And in the ninety-fourth year Ambram took Jochebed my daughter to him to wife, for they were born in one 5 day, he and my daughter. Eight years old was I when I went into the land of Canaan, and eighteen years when I slew Shechem, and at nineteen years I became priest, and at twenty-eight years I took 6 a wife, and at forty-eight I went into Egypt. And behold, my children, ye are a third generation. 7 In my hundred and eighteenth year Joseph died.

13 1 And now, my children, I command you: Fear the Lord your God with your whole heart, And walk in simplicity according to all His law. 2 And do ye also teach your children letters, That they may have under-standing all their life, Reading unceasingly the law of God. 3 For every one that knoweth the law of the Lord shall be honoured, And shall not be a stranger whithersoever he goeth. 4 Yea, many friends shall he gain more than his parents, And many men shall desire to serve him, And to hear the law from his mouth. 5 Work righteousness, therefore, my children, upon the earth, That ye may have (it) as a treasure in heaven. 6 And sow good things in your souls, That ye may find them in your life. But if ye sow evil things, Ye shall reap every trouble and affliction. 7 Get wisdom in the fear of God with diligence; For though there be a leading into captivity, And cities and lands be destroyed, And gold and silver and every posses-sion perish, The wisdom of the wise nought can take away, Save the blindness of ungodliness, and the callousness (that comes) of sin. 8 For if

one keep oneself from these evil things, Then even among his enemies shall wisdom be a glory to him, And in a strange country a fatherland, And in the midst of foes shall prove a friend. 9 Whosoever teaches noble things and does them, Shall be enthroned with kings, As was also Joseph my brother.

14 1 Therefore, my children, I have learnt that at the end of the ages ye will transgress against the Lord, stretching out hands to wickedness [against Him]; and to all the Gentiles shall ye become a scorn. 2 For our father Israel is pure from the transgressions of the chief priests [who shall lay their hands upon the Saviour of the world]. 3 For as the heaven is purer in the Lord's sight than the earth, so also be ye, the lights of Israel, (purer) than all the Gentiles. 4 But if ye be darkened through transgres-sions, what, therefore, will all the Gentiles do living in blindness? Yea, ye shall bring a curse upon our race, because the light of the law which was given for to lighten every man this ye desire to destroy by teaching com-mandments contrary to the ordinances of God. 5 The offerings of the Lord ye shall rob, and from His portion shall ye steal choice portions, 6 eating (them) contemptuously with harlots. And out of covetousness ye shall teach the commandments of the Lord, wedded women shall ye pollute, and the virgins of Jerusalem shall ye defile: and with harlots and adulteresses shall ye be joined, and the daughters of the Gentiles shall ye take to wife, purifying them with an unlawful purification; and your union shall be like unto Sodom and 7 Gomorrah. And ye shall be puffed up because of your priesthood, lifting yourselves up against 8 men, and not only so, but also against the commands of God. For ye shall contemn the holy things with jests and laughter.

15 1 Therefore the temple, which the Lord shall choose, shall be laid waste through your uncleanness, 2 and ye shall be captives throughout all nations. And ye shall be an abomination unto them, and ye 3 shall receive reproach and everlasting shame from the righteous judgement of God. And all who hate 4 you shall rejoice at your destruction. And if you were not to receive mercy through Abraham, Isaac, and Jacob, our fathers, not one of our seed should be left upon the earth.

16 1 And now I have learnt that for seventy weeks ye shall go astray, and profane the priesthood, and 2 pollute the sacrifices. And ye shall make void the law, and set at nought the words of the prophets by evil per-verseness. And ye shall persecute righteous men, and hate the godly words of the 3 faithful shall ye abhor. [And a man who reneweth the law in the power of the Most High, ye shall call a deceiver; and at last ye shall rush (upon him) to slay him, not knowing his dignity, taking 4 inno-cent blood through wickedness upon your heads.] And your holy places shall be laid waste 5 even to the ground because of him. And ye shall have no place that is clean; but ye shall be among the Gentiles a curse and a dispersion until He shall again visit you and in pity shall receive you [through faith and water].

17 1 And whereas ye have heard concerning the seventy weeks, hear also concerning the priesthood. 2 For in each jubilee there shall be a priest-hood. And in the first jubilee, the first who is anointed to the priesthood shall be great, and shall speak to God as to a father. And his priesthood shall be perfect with the Lord, [and in the day of his gladness shall he arise for the salvation of the world]. 3 In the second jubilee, he that is anointed shall be conceived in the sorrow of beloved ones; and his 4 priesthood shall be honoured and shall be glorified by all. And the third priest shall be taken hold 5 of by sorrow. And the fourth shall be in pain, because unrighteousness shall gather itself against 6 him exceedingly, and all Israel shall hate each one his neighbour. The fifth shall be taken hold of 7 by darkness Likewise also the sixth and the seventh. And in the seventh shall be such pollution 8 as I cannot express before men, for they shall know it who do these things. Therefore shall they 9 be taken captive and become a prey, and their land and their substance shall be destroyed. 10 And in the fifth week they shall return to their desolate country, and shall renew the house of the 11 Lord. And in the seventh week shall be-come priests, (who are) idolaters, adulterers, lovers of money, proud, lawless, lascivious, abusers of children and beasts.

18 1 And after their punishment shall have come from the Lord, the priesthood shall fail. 2 Then shall the Lord raise up a new priest. And to him all the words of the Lord shall be revealed; And he shall execute a righteous judgement upon the earth for a multitude of days. 3 And his star shall arise in heaven as of a king. Lighting up the light of knowledge as the sun the day, And he shall be magnified in the world. 4 He shall shine forth as the sun on the earth, And shall remove all darkness from under heaven, And there shall be peace in all the earth. 5 The heavens shall exult in his days, And the earth shall be glad, And the clouds shall rejoice, [And the knowledge of the Lord shall be poured forth upon the earth, as the water of the seas; And the angels of the glory of the presence of the Lord shall be glad in him. 6 The heavens shall be opened, And From the temple of glory shall come upon him sanctification, With the Father's voice as from Abraham to Isaac. 7 And the glory of the Most High shall be uttered over him, And the spirit of understanding and sanctification shall rest upon him [in the water]. 8 For he shall give the majesty of the Lord to His sons in truth for evermore; And there shall none succeed him for all generations for ever. 9 And in his priesthood the Gentiles shall be multiplied in knowledge upon the earth, And enlightened through the grace of the Lord: In his priesthood shall sin come to an end, And the lawless shall cease to do evil. [And the just shall rest in him.] 10 And he shall open the gates of paradise, And shall remove the threatening sword against Adam. 11 And he shall give to the saints to eat from the tree of life, And the spirit of holiness shall be on them. 12 And Beliar shall be bound by him, And he shall give power to His children to tread upon the evil spirits. 13 And the Lord shall rejoice in His children, And be well pleased in His beloved ones for ever. 14 Then shall Abraham and Isaac and Jacob exult, And I will be glad, And all the saints shall clothe themselves with joy.

19 1 And now, my children, ye have heard all; choose, therefore, for yourselves either the light or the 2 darkness, either the law of the Lord or the works of Beliar. And his sons answered him, saying, 3 Before the Lord we will walk according to His law. And their father said unto them, The Lord is witness, and His angels are witnesses, and ye are witnesses, and I am witness, concerning the word 4 of your mouth. And his sons said unto him: We are witnesses. And thus Levi ceased commanding his sons; and he stretched out his feet on the bed, and was gathered to his fathers, after he had 5 lived a hundred and thirty-seven years. And they laid him in a coffin, and afterwards they buried him in Hebron, with Abraham, Isaac, and Jacob

THE TESTAMENT OF JUDAH, THE FOURTH SON OF JACOB AND LEAH

1 1, 2 The copy of the words of Judah, what things he spake to his sons before he died. They gathered 3 themselves together, therefore, and came to him, and he said to them: Hearken, my children, to Judah your father. I was the fourth son born to my father Jacob; and Leah my mother named 4 me Judah, saying, I give thanks to the Lord, because He hath given me a fourth son also. I was 5 swift in my youth, and obedient to my father in everything. And I honoured my mother and my 6 mother's sister. And it came to pass, when I became a man, that my father blessed me, saying, Thou shalt be a king, prospering in all things.

2 1, 2 And the Lord showed me favour in all my works both in the field and in the house. I know that 3 I raced a hind, and caught it, and prepared the meat for my father, and he did eat. And the roes I used to master in the chase, and overtake all that was in the plains. A wild mare I overtook, and 4 caught it and tamed it. I slew a lion and plucked a kid out of its mouth. I took a bear by its paw 5 and hurled it down the cliff, and it was crushed. I outran the wild boar, and seizing it as I ran, 6 I tore it in sunder. A leopard in Hebron leaped upon my dog, and I caught it by the tail, and 7 hurled it on the rocks, and it was broken in twain. I found a wild ox feeding in the fields, and seizing it by the horns, and whirling it round and stunning it, I cast it from me and slew it.

3 1 And when the two kings of the Canaanites came sheathed in armour against our flocks, and much people with them, single-handed I rushed upon the king of Hazor, and smote him on the greaves 2 and dragged him down, and so I Slew him. And the other, the king of Tappuah, as he sat upon his 3 horse, [I slew, and so I scattered all his people. Achor the king] a man of giant stature I found, hurling javelins before and behind as he sat on horseback, and I took up a stone of sixty pounds 4 weight, and hurled it and smote his horse, and killed it. And I fought with (this) other for two 5 hours; and I clave his shield in twain, and I chopped off his feet, and killed him. And as I was 6 stripping off his breastplate, behold nine men his companions began to fight with me. And I wound my garment on my hand; and I slung stones at them, and killed four of them, and the rest fled. 7 And Jacob my father slew Beelesath, king of all the kings, a giant in strength, twelve cubits high. 8, 9 And fear fell upon them, and they ceased warring against us. Therefore my father was free from 10 anxiety in the wars when I was with my brethren. For he saw in a vision concerning me that an angel of might followed me everywhere, that I should not be overcome.

4 1 And in the south there came upon us a greater war than that in Shechem; and I joined in battle array with my brethren, and pursued a thousand men, and slew of them two hundred men and 2, 3 four kings. And I went up upon the wall, and I slew four mighty men. And so we captured Hazor, and took all the spoil.

5 1 On the next day we departed to Aretan, a city strong and walled and inaccessible, threatening us 2 with death. But I and Gad approached on the east side of the city, and Reuben and Levi on the 3 west. And they that were upon the wall, thinking that we were alone, were drawn down against 4 us. And so my brothers secretly climbed up the wall on both sides by stakes, and entered the city, 5 while the men knew it not. And we took it with the edge of the sword. And as for those who had taken refuge in the tower, we set fire to the tower and took both it and them. 6 And as we were departing the men of Tappuah set upon our spoil, and delivering it up to our sons we fought with them as far as Tappuah. 7 And we slew them and burnt their city, and took as spoil all that was in it.

6 1, 2 And when I was at the waters of Kozeba, the men of Jobel came against us to battle. And we fought with them and routed them; and their allies from Shiloh we slew, and we did not leave 3 them power to come in against us. And the men of Makir came upon us the fifth day, to seize our spoil; and we attacked them and overcame them in fierce battle: for there was a host of mighty 4 men amongst them, and we slew them before they

had gone up the ascent. And when we came to 5 their city their women rolled upon us stones from the brow of the hill on which the city stood, And I and Simeon hid ourselves behind the town, and seized upon the heights, and destroyed this city also.

7 1 And the next day it was told us that the king of the city of Gaash with a mighty host was coming 2 against us. I, therefore, and Dan feigned ourselves to be Amorites, and as allies went into their 3 city. And in the depth of night our brethren came and we opened to them the gates; and we destroyed all the men and their substance, and we took for a prey all that was theirs, and their three 4 walls we cast down. And we drew near to Thamna, where was all the substance of the hostile kings. Then being insulted by them, I was therefore wroth, and rushed against them to the summit; and 6 they kept slinging against me stones and darts. And had not Dan my brother aided me, they would 7 have slain me. We came upon them, therefore, with wrath, and they all fled; and passing by 8 another way, they besought my father, and he made peace with them. And we did to them no hurt, 9 and they became tributary to us, and we restored to them their spoil. And I built Thamna, and my 10 father built Pabael. I was twenty years old when this war befell. And the Canaanites feared me and my brethren.

8 1, 2 And I had much cattle, and I had for chief herdsman Iram the Adullamite. And when I went to him I saw Parsaba, king of Adullam; and he spake unto us, and he made me a feast; 3 and when I was heated he gave me his daughter Bathshua to wife. She bare me Er, and Onan and Shelah; and two of them the Lord smote: for Shelah lived, and his children are ye.

9 1 And eighteen years my father abode in peace with his brother Esau, and his sons with us, after 2 that we came from Mesopotamia, from Laban. And when eighteen years were fulfilled, in the fortieth year of my life, Esau, the brother of my father, came upon us with a mighty and strong 3 people. And Jacob smote Esau with an arrow, and he was taken up wounded on Mount Seir, and 4 as he went he died at Anoniram. And we pursued after the sons of Esau. Now they had a city with walls of iron and gates of brass; and we could not enter into it, and we encamped around, and 5 besieged it. And when they opened not to us in twenty days, I set up a ladder in the sight of all and with my shield upon my head I went up, sustaining the assault of stones, upwards of three 6, 7 talents weight; and I slew four of their mighty men. And Reuben and Gad slew six others. Then they asked from us terms of peace; and having taken counsel with our father, we received them as 8 tributaries. And they gave us five hundred cors of wheat, five hundred baths of oil, five hundred measures of wine, until the famine, when we went down into Egypt.

10 1 And after these things my son Er took to wife Tamar, from Mesopotamia, a daughter of Aram. 2 Now Er was wicked, and he was in need concerning Tamar, because she was not of the land 3 of Canaan. And on the third night an angel of the Lord smote him. And he had not known her according to the evil craftiness of his mother, for he did not wish to have children by her. In the days of the wedding-feast I gave Onan to her in marriage; and he also in wickedness knew her not, 5 though he spent with her a year. And when I threatened him he went in unto her, but he spilled the seed on the ground, according to the command of his mother, and he also died through wickedness. 6 And I wished to give Shelah also to her, but his mother did not permit it; for she wrought evil against Tamar, because she was not of the daughters of Canaan, as she also herself was.

11 1 And I knew that the race of the Canaanites was wicked, but the impulse of youth blinded my 2 mind. And when I saw her pouring out wine, owing to the intoxication of wine I was deceived, and 3 took her although my father had not counselled (it). And while I was away she went and took for 4 Shelah a wife from Canaan. And when I knew what she had done, I cursed her in the anguish of 5 my soul. And she also died through her wickedness together with her sons.

12 1 And after these things, while Tamar was a widow, she heard after two years that I was going up 2 to shear my sheep, and adorned herself in bridal array, and sat in the city Enaim by the gate. For it was a law of the Amorites, that she who was about to marry should sit in fornication seven days 3 by the gate. Therefore being drunk with wine, I did not recognize her; and her beauty deceived 4 me, through the fashion of her adorning. And I turned aside to her, and said: Let me go in unto thee. And she said: What wilt thou give me? And I gave her my staff, and my girdle, and the 5 diadem of my kingdom in pledge. And I went in unto her, and she conceived. And not knowing 6 what I had done, I wished to slay her; but she privily sent my pledges, and put me to shame. And when I called her, I heard also the secret words which I spoke when lying with her in my drunkenness; 7 and I could not slay her, because it was from the Lord. For I said, Lest haply she did it in 8 subtlety, having received the pledge from another woman. But I came not again near her while 9 I lived, because I had done this abomination in all Israel. Moreover, they who were in the city said there was no harlot in the gate, because she came from another place, and sat for a while in the 10, 11 gate. And I thought that no one knew that I had gone in to her. And after this we came into 12 Egypt to Joseph, because of the famine. And I was forty and six years old, and seventy and three years lived I in Egypt.

13 1 And now I command you, my children, hearken to Judah your father, and keep my sayings to 2 perform all the ordinances of the Lord,

and to obey the commands of God. And walk not after your lusts, nor in the imaginations of your thoughts in haughtiness of heart; and glory not in the deeds 3 and strength of your youth, for this also is evil in the eyes of the Lord. Since I also gloried that in wars no comely woman's face ever enticed me, and reproved Reuben my brother concerning Bilhah, the wife of my father, the spirits of jealousy and of fornication arrayed themselves against me, until I lay with Bathshua the Canaanite, and Tamar, who was espoused to my sons. For I said to my father-in-law: I will take counsel with my father, and so will I take thy daughter. And he was unwilling, but he showed me a boundless store of gold in his daughter's behalf; for he was 5 a king. And he adorned her with gold and pearls, and caused her to pour out wine for us at the 6 feast with the beauty of women. And the wine turned aside my eyes, and pleasure blinded my 7 heart. And I became enamoured of and I lay with her, and transgressed the commandment of the 8 Lord and the commandment of my fathers, and I took her to wife. And the Lord rewarded me according to the imagination of my heart, inasmuch as I had no joy in her children.

14 1 And now, my children, I say unto you, be not drunk with wine; for wine turneth the mind away 2 from the truth, and inspires the passion of lust, and leadeth the eyes into error. For the spirit of fornication hath wine as a minister to give pleasure to the mind; for these two also take away the 3 mind of man. For if a man drink wine to drunkenness, it disturbeth the mind with filthy thoughts leading to fornication, and heateth the body to carnal union; and if the occasion of the lust be 4 present, he worketh the sin, and is not ashamed. Such is the inebriated man, my children; for he 5 who is drunken reverenceth no man. For, lo, it made me also to err, so that I was not ashamed of the multitude in the city, in that before the eyes of all I turned aside unto Tamar, and I wrought 6 a great sin, and I uncovered the covering of my sons' shame. After I had drunk wine I reverenced 7 not the commandment of God, and I took a woman of Canaan to wife. For much discretion needeth the man who drinketh wine, my children; and herein is discretion in drinking wine a man 8 may drink so long as he preserveth modesty. But if he go beyond this limit the spirit of deceit attacketh his mind, and it maketh the drunkard to talk filthily, and to transgress and not to be ashamed, but even to glory in his shame, and to account himself honourable.

15 1 He that committeth fornication is not aware when he suffers loss, and is not ashamed when put 2 to dishonour. For even though a man be a king and commit fornication, he is stripped of his 3 kingship by becoming the slave of fornication, as I myself also suffered. For I gave my staff, that is, the stay of my tribe; and my girdle, that is, my power; and my diadem, that is, the glory of my 4 kingdom. And indeed I repented of these things; wine and flesh I eat not until my old age, nor 5 did I behold any joy. And the angel of God showed me that for ever do women bear rule over 6 king and beggar alike. And from the king they take away his glory, and from the valiant man his might, and from the beggar even that little which is the stay of his poverty.

16 1 Observe, therefore, my children, the (rights limit in wine; for there are in it four evil spirits--- of 2 lust, of hot desire, of profligacy of filthy lucre. If ye drink wine in gladness, be ye modest in the fear of God. For if in (your) gladness the fear of God departeth, then drunkenness ariseth and 3 shamelessness stealeth in. But if ye would live soberly do not touch wine at all, lest ye sin in words of outrage, and in fightings and slanders, and transgressions of the commandments of God, 4 and ye perish before your time. Moreover, wine revealeth the mysteries of God and men, even as I also revealed the commandments of God and the mysteries of Jacob my father to the Canaanitish 5 woman Bathshua, which God bade me not to reveal. And wine is a cause both of war and confusion.

17 1 And now, I command you, my children, not to love money, nor to gaze upon the beauty of women; because for the sake of money and beauty I was led astray to Bathshua the Canaanite. 2, 3 [For I know that because of these two things shall my race fall into wickedness. For even wise men among my sons shall they mar, and shall cause the kingdom of Judah to be diminished, which 4 the Lord gave me because of my obedience to my father. For I never caused grief to Jacob, my 5 father: for all things whatsoever he commanded I did. And Isaac, the father of my father, blessed 6 me to be king in Israel, and Jacob further blessed me in like manner. And I know that from me shall the kingdom be established.

18 1 And I know what evils ye will do in the last days.] 2 Beware, therefore, my children, of fornication, and the love of money, and hearken to Judah your father. 3 For these things withdraw you from the law of God, And blind the inclination of the soul, And teach arrogance, And suffer not a man to have compassion upon his neighbour 4 They rob his soul of all goodness, And oppress him with toils and troubles, And drive away sleep from him, And devour his flesh. 5 And he hindereth the sacrifices of God; And he remembereth not the blessing of God, He hearkeneth not to a prophet when he speaketh, And resenteth the words of godliness. 6 For he is a slave to two contrary passions, And cannot obey God, Because they have blinded his soul, And he walketh in the day as in the night.

19 1 My children, the love of money leadeth to idolatry; because, when led astray through money, men name as gods those who are not gods, and it causeth him who hath it to fall into madness 2 For the sake of money I lost my children, and had not my repentance, and my humiliation, and 3

the prayers of my father been accepted, I should have died childless. But the God of my fathers 4 had mercy on me, because I did it in ignorance. And the prince of deceit blinded me, and I sinned as a man and as flesh, being corrupted through sins; and I learnt my own weakness while thinking myself invincible.

20 1 Know, therefore, my children, that two spirits wait upon man the spirit of truth and the spirit 2 of deceit. And in the midst is the spirit of understanding of the mind, to which it belongeth to turn whithersoever it will. 3 And the works of truth and the works of deceit are written upon the hearts of men, and each one of them the Lord knoweth. 4 And there is no time at which the works of men can be hid; for on the heart itself have they been 5 written down before the Lord. And the spirit of truth testifieth all things, and accuseth all; and the sinner is burnt up by his own heart, and cannot raise his face to the judge.

21 1 And now, my children, I command you, love Levi, that ye may abide, and exalt not yourselves 2 against him, lest ye be utterly destroyed. For to me the Lord gave the kingdom, and to him the 3 priesthood, and He set the kingdom beneath the priesthood. To me He gave the things upon the 4 earth; to him the things in the heavens. As the heaven is higher than the earth, so is the priesthood of God higher than the earthly kingdom, unless it falls away through sin from the Lord and is 5 dominated by the earthly kingdom. For the angel of the Lord said unto me: The Lord chose him rather than thee, to draw near to Him, and to eat of His table and to offer Him the first-fruits of the choice things of the sons of Israel; but thou shalt be king of Jacob. 6 And thou shalt be amongst them as the sea. For as, on the sea, just and unjust are tossed about, some taken into captivity while some are enriched, so also shall every race of men be in thee: some shall be impoverished, being taken captive, and others grow rich by plundering the possessions of others. 7 For the kings shall be as sea-monsters. They shall swallow men like fishes: The sons and daughters of free men shall they enslave; Houses, lands, flocks, money shall they plunder: 8 And with the flesh of many shall they wrongfully feed the ravens and the cranes; And they shall advance in evil, in covetousness uplifted, 9 And there shall be false prophets like tempests, And they shall persecute all righteous men.

22 1 And the Lord shall bring upon them divisions one against another. And there shall be continual wars in Israel; 2 And among men of another race shall my kingdom be brought to an end, Until the salvation of Israel shall come, Until the appearing of the God of righteousness, That Jacob [and all the Gentiles] may rest in peace. 3 And He shall guard the might of my kingdom for ever; For the Lord sware to me with an oath that He would not destroy the kingdom from my seed for ever.

23 1 Now I have much grief, my children, because of your lewdness and witchcrafts, and idolatries which ye shall practise against the kingdom, following them that have familiar spirits, diviners, and 2 demons of error. Ye shall make your daughters singing girls and harlots, and ye shall mingle in 3 the abominations of the Gentiles. For which things' sake the Lord shall bring upon you famine and pestilence, death and the sword, beleaguering by enemies, and revilings of friends, the slaughter of children, the rape of wives, the plundering of possessions, the burning of the temple of God,] the 4 laying waste of the land, the enslavement of yourselves among the Gentiles. And they shall make some of you eunuchs for their wives. 5 Until the Lord visit you, when with perfect heart ye repent and walk in all His commandments; and He bring you up from captivity among the Gentiles.

24 1 And after these things shall a star arise to you from Jacob in peace, And a man shall arise [from my seed], like the sun of righteousness, walking with the sons of men in meekness and righteousness; And no sin shall be found in him. 2 and the heavens shall be open unto him, To pour out the spirit, (even) the blessing of the Holy Father; 3 And He shall pour out the spirit of grace upon you; And ye shall be unto Him sons in truth, And ye shall walk in His commandments first and last. 4 [This Branch of God Most High, And this Fountain giving life unto all.] 5 Then shall the sceptre of my kingdom shine forth; And from your root shall arise a stem; 6 And from it shall grow a rod of righteousness to the Gentiles, To judge and to save all that call upon the Lord.

26 1 And after these things shall Abraham and Isaac and Jacob arise unto life, and I and my brethren shall be chiefs of the tribes of Israel: Levi first, I the second, Joseph third, Benjamin fourth, 2 Simeon fifth; Issachar sixth, and so all in order. And the Lord blessed Levi, and the Angel of the Presence, me; the powers of glory, Simeon; the heaven, Reuben; the earth, Issachar; the sea, Zebulun; the mountains, Joseph; the tabernacle, Benjamin; the luminaries, Dan; Eden, Naphtali; the sun, Gad; the moon, Asher. 3 And ye shall be the people of the Lord, and have one tongue; And there shall be there no spirit of deceit of Beliar, For he shall be cast into the fire for ever. 4 And they who have died in grief shall arise in joy , And they who were poor for the Lord's sake shall be made rich, And they who are put to death for the Lord's sake shall awake to life. 5 And the harts of Jacob shall run in joyfulness, And the eagles of Israel shall fly in gladness; And all the people shall glorify the Lord for ever.

26 1 Observe, therefore, my children, all the law of the Lord, for there is hope for all them who hold 2 fast unto His ways. And he said to them: Behold, I die before your eyes this day, a hundred and 3 nineteen years old. Let no one bury me in costly apparel, nor tear open my bowels, for this 4 shall they who are kings do; and carry me up to Hebron with you. And Judah, when he had said these things, fell asleep; and his sons did according to all whatsoever he commanded them, and they buried him in Hebron, with his fathers.

THE TESTAMENT OF ISSACHAR, THE FIFTH SON OF JACOB AND LEAH.

1 1 The copy of the words of Issachar. For he called his sons and said to them: Hearken, my children, to Issachar your father; Give ear to the words of him who is beloved of the Lord. 2, 3 I was born the fifth son to Jacob, by way of hire for the mandrakes. For Reuben my brother 4 brought in mandrakes from the field, and Rachel met him and took them. And Reuben wept, and 5 at his voice Leah my mother came forth. Now these (mandrakes) were sweet-smelling apples 6 which were produced in the land of Haran below a ravine of water. And Rachel said: I will not give them to thee, but they shall be to me instead of children. For the Lord hath despised me, 7 and I have not borne children to Jacob. Now there were two apples; and Leah said to Rachel: 8 Let it suffice thee that thou hast taken my husband: wilt thou take these also? And Rachel said 9 to her: Thou shalt have Jacob this night for the mandrakes of thy son. And Leah said to her: 10 Jacob is mine, for I am the wife of his youth. But Rachel said: Boast not, and vaunt not thyself; for he espoused me before thee, and for my sake he served our father fourteen years. 11 And had not craft increased on the earth and the wickedness of men prospered, thou wouldst not now see the face of Jacob.

2 1 Then appeared to Jacob an angel of the Lord, saying: Two children shall Rachel bear, inasmuch 2 as she hath refused company with her husband, and hath chosen continency. And had not Leah my mother paid the two apples for the sake of his company, she would have borne eight sons; for this reason she bare six, and Rachel bare the two: for on account of the mandrakes the Lord 3 visited her. For He knew that for the sake of children she wished to company with Jacob, and not for lust of pleasure. For on the morrow also she again gave up Jacob. Because of the mandrakes; 5 therefore, the Lord hearkened to Rachel. For though she desired them, she eat them not, but offered them in the house of the Lord, presenting them to the priest of the Most High who was at that time.

3 1 When, therefore, I grew up, my children, I walked in uprightness of heart, and I became a husbandman for my father and my brethren, and I brought in fruits from the field according to 2, 3 their season. And my father blessed me, for he saw that I walked in rectitude before him. And 4 I was not a busybody in my doings, nor envious and malicious against my neighbour. I never slandered any one, nor did I censure the life of any man, walking as I did in singleness of eye. 5 Therefore, when I was thirty-five years old, I took to myself a wife, for my labour wore away my strength, and I never thought upon pleasure with women; but owing to my toil, sleep overcame me. 6 And my father always rejoiced in my rectitude, because I offered through the priest to the Lord 7 all first-fruits; then to my father also. And the Lord increased ten thousandfold His benefits in my 8 hands; and also Jacob, my father, knew that God aided my singleness. For on all the poor and oppressed I bestowed the good things of the earth in the singleness of my heart.

4 1 And now, hearken to me, my children, And walk in singleness of your heart, For I have seen in it all that is well-pleasing to the Lord. 2 The single-(minded) man coveteth not gold, He overreacheth not his neighbour, He longeth not after manifold dainties, He delighteth not in varied apparel. 3 He doth not desire to live a long life, But only waiteth for the will of God. 4 And the spirits of deceit have no power against him, For he looketh not on the beauty of women, Lest he should pollute his mind with corruption. 5 There is no envy in his thoughts, [No malicious person maketh his soul to pine away,] Nor worry with insatiable desire in his mind. 6 For he walketh in singleness of soul, And beholdeth all things in uprightness of heart, Shunning eyes (made) evil through the error of the world, Lest he should see the perversion of any of the commandments of the Lord.

5 1 Keep, therefore, my children, the law of God, And get singleness. And walk in guilelessness, Not playing the busybody with the business of your neighbour, 2 But love the Lord and your neighbour, Have compassion on the poor and weak. 3 Bow down your back unto husbandry, And toil in labours in all manner of husbandry, Offering gifts to the Lord with thanksgiving. 4 For with the first-fruits of the earth will the Lord bless you, even as He blessed all the saints 5 from Abel even until now. For no other portion is given to you than of the fatness of the earth, 6 whose fruits are raised by toil. For our father Jacob blessed me with blessings of the earth and of 7 first-fruits. And Levi and Judah were glorified by the Lord even among the sons of Jacob; for the Lord gave them an inheritance, and to Levi He gave the priesthood, and to Judah the kingdom. 8 And do ye therefore obey them, and walk in the singleness of your father; [for unto Gad hath it been given to destroy the troops that are coming upon Israel].

6 1 Know ye therefore, my children, that in the last times Your sons will forsake singleness, And will cleave unto insatiable desire; And leaving guilelessness will draw near to malice; And forsaking the commandments of the Lord, They will cleave unto Beliar. 2 And leaving husbandry, They

will follow after their own wicked devices, And they shall be dispersed among the Gentiles. And shall serve their enemies. 3 And do you therefore give these commands to your children, that, if they sin, they may the more 4 quickly return to the Lord; For He is merciful, and will deliver them, even to bring them back into their land.

7 1 Behold, therefore, as ye see, I am a hundred and twenty-six years old and am not conscious of committing any sin. 2 Except my wife I have not known any woman. I never committed fornication by the uplifting of my eyes. 3 I drank not wine, to be led astray thereby; I coveted not any desirable thing that was my neighbour's. 4 Guile arose not in my heart; A lie passed not through my lips. 5 If any man were in distress I joined my sighs with his, And I shared my bread with the poor. I wrought godliness, all my days I kept truth 6 I loved the Lord; Likewise also every man with all my heart. 7 So do you also these things, my children, And every spirit of Beliar shall flee from you, And no deed of wicked men shall rule over you; And every wild beast shall ye subdue, Since you have with you the God of heaven and earth (And) walk with men in singleness of heart. 8 And having said these things, he commanded his sons that they should carry him up to Hebron, and bury him there in the cave with his fathers. And he stretched out his feet and died, at a good old age; with every limb sound, and with strength unabated, he slept the eternal sleep.

THE TESTAMENT OF ZEBULUN, THE SIXTH SON OF JACOB AND LEAH.

1 1 The copy of the words of Zebulun, which he enjoined on his sons before he died in the 2 hundred and fourteenth year of his life, two years after the death of Joseph. And he said to them: 3 Hearken to me, ye sons of Zebulun, attend to the words of your father. I, Zebulun, was born a good gift to my parents. For when I was born my father was increased very exceedingly, both in flocks 4 and herds, when with the straked rods he had his portion. I am not conscious that I have sinned 5 all my days, save in thought. Nor yet do I remember that I have done any iniquity, except the sin of ignorance which I committed against Joseph; for I covenanted with my brethren not to tell 6 my father what had been done. But I wept in secret many days on account of Joseph, for I feared my brethren, because they had all agreed that if any one should declare the secret, he should be slain. 7 But when they wished to kill him, I adjured them much with tears not to be guilty of this sin.

2 1, 2 For Simeon and Gad came against Joseph to kill him, and he said unto them with tears: Pity me, my brethren, have mercy upon the bowels of Jacob our father: lay not upon me your hands 3 to shed innocent blood, for I have not sinned against you. And if indeed I have sinned, with chastening chastise me, my brethren but lay not upon me your hand, for the sake of Jacob our 4 father. And as he spoke these words, wailing as he did so, I was unable to bear his lamentations, and began to weep, and my liver was poured out, and all the substance of my bowels was loosened. 5 And I wept with Joseph, and my heart sounded, and the joints of my body trembled, and I was 6 not able to stand. And when Joseph saw me weeping with him, and them coming against him to 7 slay him, he fled behind me, beseeching them. But meanwhile Reuben arose and said: Come, my brethren, let us not slay him, but let us cast him into one of these dry pits, which our fathers digged 8 and found no water. For for this cause the Lord forbade that water should rise up in them, in order that Joseph should be preserved. And they did so, until they sold him to the Ishmaelites.

3 1, 2 For in his price I had no share, my children. But Simeon and Gad and six other of our brethren took the price of Joseph, and bought sandals for themselves, and their wives, and their children, 3 saying: We will not eat of it, for it is the price of our brother's blood, but we will assuredly tread it under foot, because he said that he would be king over us, and so let us see what will become of 4 his dreams. Therefore it is written in the writing of the law of Moses, that whosoever will not raise 5 up seed to his brother, his sandal should be unloosed, and they should spit in his face. And the brethren of Joseph wished not that their brother should live, and the Lord loosed from them the 6 sandal which they wore against Joseph their brother. For when they came into Egypt they were unloosed by the servants of Joseph outside the gate, and so they made obeisance to Joseph after the 7 fashion of King Pharaoh. And not only did they make obeisance to him, but were spit upon also, 8 falling down before him forthwith, and so they were put to shame before the Egyptians. For after this the Egyptians heard all the evils that they had done to Joseph.

4 1 And after he was sold my brothers sat down 2 to eat and drink. But I, through pity for Joseph, did not eat, but watched the pit, since Judah feared lest Simeon, Dan, and Gad should rush 3 off and slay him. But when they saw that I did not eat, they set me to watch him, till he was 5 sold to the Ishmaelites. And when Reuben came and heard that while he was away (Joseph) had been sold, he rent his garments, (and) mourning, said: How shall I look on the face of my father 6 Jacob? And he took the money and ran after the merchants, but as he failed to find them he returned grieving. But the merchants had left the broad road and marched through the Troglodytes by a short cut. 7 But Reuben was grieved, and eat no food that day. Dan therefore came to him and said: 8, 9 Weep not, neither grieve; for we have found what we can say to our father Jacob. Let us slay 10 a kid of the goats, and dip in it the coat of Joseph; and let

us send it to Jacob, saying: Know, is 11 this the coat of thy son? And they did so. For they stripped off from Joseph his coat when they were selling him, and put upon him the garment of a slave. Now Simeon took the coat, and would not give it up, for he wished to rend it with his sword, as he was angry that Joseph lived and that 12 he had not slain him. Then we all rose up and said unto him: If thou givest not up the coat, we 13 will say to our father that thou alone didst this evil thing in Israel. And so he gave it unto them, and they did even as Dan had said.

5 I And now, my children, I bid you to keep the commands of the Lord, and to show mercy to your neighbours, and to have compassion towards all, not towards men only, but also towards, beasts. 2 For all this thing's sake the Lord blessed me, and when all my brethren were sick, I escaped without 3 sickness, for the Lord knoweth the purposes of each. Have, therefore, compassion in your hearts, my children, because even as a man doeth to his neighbour, even so also will the Lord do to him. 4 For the sons of my brethren were sickening and were dying on account of Joseph, because they 5 showed not mercy in their hearts; but my sons were preserved without sickness, as ye know. And when I was in the land of Canaan, by the sea-coast, I made a catch of fish for Jacob my father; and when many were choked in the sea, I continued unhurt.

6 I I was the first to make a boat to sail upon the sea, for the Lord gave me understanding and 2 wisdom therein. And I let down a rudder behind it, and I stretched a sail upon another upright 3 piece of wood in the midst. And I sailed therein along the shores, catching fish for the house of my father until we came to Egypt. 4, 5 [And through compassion I shared my catch with every stranger. And if a man were a stranger, or sick, or aged, I boiled the fish, and dressed them well, and offered them to all men, as every man 6 had need, grieving with and having compassion upon them. Wherefore also the Lord satisfied me with abundance of fish when catching fish; for he that shareth with his neighbour receiveth manifold 7 more from the Lord.] For five years I caught fish [and gave thereof to every man whom I saw, 8 and sufficed for all the house of my father]. And in the summer I caught fish, and in the winter I kept sheep with my brethren.

7 I [Now I will declare unto you what I did. I saw a man in distress through nakedness in winter time, and had compassion upon him, and stole away a garment secretly from my father's house, and 2 gave it to him who was in distress. Do you, therefore, my children, from that which God bestoweth upon you, show compassion and mercy without hesitation to all men, and give to every man with 3 a good heart. And if ye have not the wherewithal to give to him that needeth, have compassion for 4 him in bowels of mercy. I know that my hand found not the wherewithal to give to him that needed, and I walked with him weeping for seven furlongs, and my bowels yearned towards him in compassion.

8 I Have, therefore, yourselves also, my children, compassion towards every man with mercy, that the 2 Lord also may have compassion and mercy upon you. Because also in the last days God will send 3 His compassion on the earth, and wheresoever He findeth bowels of mercy He dwelleth in him. For in the degree in which a man hath compassion upon his neighbours, in the same degree hath the 4, 5 Lord also upon him.] And when we went down into Egypt, Joseph bore no malice against us. To whom taking heed, do ye also, my children, approve yourselves without malice, and love one 6 another; and do not set down in account, each one of you, evil against his brother. For this breaketh unity and divideth all kindred, and troubleth the soul, and weareth away the countenance.

9 I Observe, therefore, the waters, and know when they flow together, they sweep along stones, trees, 2 earth, and other things. But if they are divided into many streams, the earth swalloweth them up, 3, 4 and they vanish away. So shall ye also be if ye be divided. Be not ye, therefore, divided into two heads, for everything which the Lord made hath but one head, and two shoulders, two 5 hands, two feet, and all the remaining members. For I have learnt in the writing of my fathers, that Ye shall be divided in Israel, And ye shall follow two kings, And shall work every abomination. 6 And your enemies shall lead you captive, And ye shall be evil entreated among the Gentiles, With many infirmities and tribulations. 7 And after these things ye shall remember the Lord, and repent, [And He shall cause you to return]; for He is merciful and compassionate. And He setteth not down in account evil to the sons of men, because they are flesh, And the spirits of deceit deceive them in all their deeds. 8 And after these things there shall arise unto you the Lord Himself, the light of righteousness, [And healing and compassion shall be in His wings. He shall redeem all the captivity of the sons of men from Beliar; And every spirit of deceit shall be trodden down]; And he shall bring back all the Gentiles into zeal for Him. And ye shall return unto your land. And ye shall see Him in Jerusalem, for His name's sake. 9 And again through the wickedness of your works shall ye provoke Him to anger, And ye shall be cast away by Him unto the time of consummation.

10 I And now, my children, grieve not that I am dying, nor be cast down in that I am coming to my 2 end. For I shall rise again in the midst of you, as a ruler in the midst of his sons; and I shall rejoice in the midst of my tribe, as many as shall keep the law of the Lord, and the commandments 3 of Zebulun their father. But upon the ungodly shall the Lord bring eternal fire, and destroy them 4, 5 throughout all generations. But I am

now hastening away to my rest, as did also my fathers. But 6 do ye fear the Lord our God with all your strength all the days of your life. And when he had 7 said these things he fell asleep, at a good old age. And his sons laid him in a wooden coffin. And afterwards they carried him up and buried him in Hebron, with his fathers.

THE TESTAMENT OF DAN, THE SEVENTH SON OF JACOB AND BILHAH.

1 1 The copy of the words of Dan, which he spake to his sons in his last days, in the hundred and 2 twenty-fifth year of his life. For he called together his family, and said: Hearken to my words, ye 3 sons of Dan; and give heed to the words of your father. I have proved in my heart, and in my whole life, that truth with just dealing is good and well pleasing to God, and that lying and anger 4 are evil, because they teach man all wickedness. I confess, therefore, this day to you, my children, 5 that in my heart I resolved on the death of Joseph my brother, the true and good man. [And 6 I rejoiced that he was sold, because his father loved him more than us.] For the spirit of jealousy 7 and vainglory said to me: Thou thyself also art his son. And one of the spirits of Beliar stirred me up, saying: Take this sword, and with it slay Joseph: so shall thy father love thee when he is dead. 8 Now this is the spirit of anger that persuaded me to crush Joseph as a leopard crusheth a kid. 9 But the God of my fathers did not suffer him to fall into my hands, so that I should find him alone and slay him, and cause a second tribe to be destroyed in Israel.

2 1 And now, my children, behold I am dying, and I tell you of a truth, that unless ye keep yourselves from the spirit of lying and of anger, and love truth and longsuffering, ye shall perish. 2 For anger is blindness, and does not suffer one to see the face of any man with truth. 3 For though it be a father or a mother, he behaveth towards them as enemies; though it be a brother, he knoweth him not; though it be a prophet of the Lord, he disobeyeth him; though 4 a righteous man, he regardeth him not; though a friend, he doth not acknowledge him. For the spirit of anger encompasseth him with the net of deceit, and blindeth his eyes, and through lying 5 darkeneth his mind, and giveth him its own peculiar vision. And wherewith encompasseth it his eyes? With hatred of heart, so as to be envious of his brother.

3 1 For anger is an evil thing, my children, for it troubleth even the soul itself. And the body of the angry man it maketh its own, and over his soul it getteth the mastery, and 3 it bestoweth upon the body power that it may work all iniquity. And when the body does all 4 these things, the soul justifieth what is done, since it seeth not aright. Therefore he that is wrathful, if he be a mighty man, hath a threefold power in his anger: one by the help of his servants; and a second by his wealth, whereby he persuadeth and overcometh wrongfully; and thirdly, having his 5 own natural power he worketh thereby the evil. And though the wrathful man be weak, yet hath 6 he a power twofold of that which is by nature; for wrath ever aideth such in lawlessness. This spirit goeth always with lying at the right hand of Satan, that with cruelty and lying his works may be wrought.

4 1, 2 Understand ye, therefore, the power of wrath, that it is vain. For it first of all giveth provocation by word; then by deeds it strengtheneth him who is angry, and with sharp losses disturbeth his 3 mind, and so stirreth up with great wrath his soul. Therefore, when any one speaketh against you, be not ye moved to anger, [and if any man praiseth you as holy men, be not uplifted: be not moved 4 either to delight or to disgust]. For first it pleaseth the hearing, and so maketh the mind keen to perceive the grounds for provocation; and then being enraged, he thinketh that he is justly angry 5 If ye fall into any loss or ruin, my children, be not afflicted; for this very spirit maketh (a man) 6 desire that which is perishable, in order that he may be enraged through the affliction. And if ye suffer loss voluntarily, or involuntarily, be not vexed; for from vexation ariseth wrath with lying. 7 Moreover, a twofold mischief is wrath with lying; and they assist one another in order to disturb the heart; and when the soul is continually disturbed, the Lord departeth from it, and Beliar ruleth over it.

5 1 Observe, therefore, my children, the commandments of the Lord, And keep His law; Depart from wrath, And hate lying, That the Lord may dwell among you, And Beliar may flee from you. 2 Speak truth each one with his neighbour. So shall ye not fall into wrath and confusion; But ye shall be in peace, having the God of peace, So shall no war prevail over you. 3 Love the Lord through all your life, And one another with a true heart. 4 I know that in the last days ye shall depart from the Lord, And ye shall provoke Levi unto anger, And fight against Judah; But ye shall not prevail against them, For an angel of the Lord shall guide them both; For by them shall Israel stand. 5 And whensoever ye depart from the Lord, ye shall walk in all evil and work the abominations of the Gentiles, going a-whoring after women of the lawless ones, while with all wickedness the spirits 6 of wickedness work in you. [For I have read in the book of Enoch, the righteous, that your prince is Satan, and that all the spirits of wickedness and pride will conspire to attend constantly on the sons of Levi, to cause them to sin before the Lord. 7 And my sons will draw near to Levi. And sin with them in all things; And the sons of Judah will be covetous, Plundering other men's goods like lions.] 8 Therefore shall ye be led away [with them] into captivity, And there shall ye receive all the plagues of Egypt, And all the evils of the Gentiles. 9 And so when ye return to the Lord ye shall obtain mercy, And He shall bring you into His sanctuary, And He shall give you peace. 10 And there shall arise unto you from the tribe of [Judah and of] Levi the salvation of the Lord; And he shall make war against Beliar. And execute an everlasting vengeance on our enemies; 11 And the captivity shall he take from Beliar [the souls of the saints], And turn disobedient hearts unto the Lord, And give to them that call upon him eternal peace. 12 And the saints shall rest in Eden, And in the New Jerusalem shall the righteous rejoice, And it shall be unto the glory of God for ever. 13 And no longer shall Jerusalem endure desolation, Nor Israel be led captive; For the Lord shall be in the midst of it [living amongst men], And the Holy One of Israel shall reign over it [in humility and in poverty; and he who believeth on Him shall reign amongst men in truth].

6 1, 2 And now, fear the Lord, my children, and beware of Satan and his spirits. Draw near unto God and unto the angel that intercedeth for you, for he is a mediator between God and man, and for the 3 peace of Israel he shall stand up against the kingdom of the enemy. Therefore is the enemy eager 4 to destroy all that call upon the Lord. For he knoweth that upon the day on which Israel shall 5 repent, the kingdom of the enemy shall be brought to an end. For the very angel of peace shall 6 strengthen Israel, that it fall not into the extremity of evil. And it shall be in the time of the lawlessness of Israel, that the Lord will not depart from them, but will transform them into a nation 7 that doeth His will, for none of the angels will be equal unto him. And His name shall be in every place in Israel, and among the Gentiles. 8 Keep, therefore, yourselves, my children, from every evil work, And cast away wrath and all lying, And love truth and long-suffering. 9 And the things which ye have heard from your father, do ye also impart to your children [that the Saviour of the Gentiles may receive you; for he is true and long-suffering, meek and lowly, and 10 teacheth by his works the law of God]. Depart, therefore, from all unrighteousness, and cleave unto the righteousness of God, and your race will be saved for ever. And bury me near my fathers.

7 1, 2 And when he had said these things he kissed them, and fell asleep at a good old age. And his sons buried him, And after that they carried up his bones, and placed them near Abraham, and 3 Isaac, and Jacob. [Nevertheless, Dan prophesied unto them that they should forget their God, and should be alienated from the land of their inheritance and from the race of Israel, and from the family of their seed.]

THE TESTAMENT OF NAPHTALI, THE EIGHTH SON OF JACOB AND BILHAH.

1 1 The copy of the testament of Naphtali, which he ordained at the time of his death in the hundred 2 and thirtieth year of his life. When his sons were gathered together in the seventh month, on the 3 first day of the month, while still in good health, he made them a feast of food and wine. And after 4 he was awake in the morning, he said to them, I am dying; and they believed him not. And as he 5 glorified the Lord, he grew strong and said that after yesterday's feast he should die. And he began 6 then to say: Hear, my children, ye sons of Naphtali, hear the words of your father. I was born from Bilhah, and because Rachel dealt craftily, and gave Bilhah in place of herself to Jacob, and she 7 conceived and bare me upon Rachel's knees, therefore she called my name Naphtali. For Rachel loved me very much because I was born upon her lap; and when I was still young she was wont 8 to kiss me, and say: May I have a brother of thine from mine own womb, like unto thee. Whence 9 also Joseph was like unto me in all things, according to the prayers of Rachel. Now my mother was Bilhah, daughter of Rotheus the brother of Deborah, Rebecca's nurse, who was born on one and 10 the self-same day with Rachel. And Rotheus was of the family of Abraham, a Chaldean, God 11 fearing, free-born, and noble. And he was taken captive and was bought by Laban; and he gave him Euna his handmaid to wife, and she bore a daughter, and called her name Zilpah, after the name 12 of the village in which he had been taken captive. And next she bore Bilhah, saying: My daughter hastens after what is new, for immediately that she was born she seized the breast and hastened to suck it.

2 1 And I was swift on my feet like the deer, and my father Jacob appointed me for all messages, 2 and as a deer did he give me his blessing. For as the potter knoweth the vessel, how much it is to contain, and bringeth clay accordingly, so also doth the Lord make the body after the likeness of 3 the spirit, and according to the capacity of the body doth He implant the spirit. And the one does not fall short of the other by a third part of a hair; for by weight, and measure, and rule was all the 4 creation made. And as the potter knoweth the use of each vessel, what it is meet for, so also doth the Lord know the body, how far it will persist in goodness, and when it beginneth in evil. For 5 there is no inclination or thought which the Lord knoweth not, for He created every man after His own image. 6 As a man's strength, so also is his work; and as his mind, so also is his skill; and as his purpose, so also is his achievement; and as his heart, so also is his mouth; as his eye, so also is his sleep; as his soul, so also is his word, either in the law of the Lord or in the works of Beliar. 7 And as there is a division between light and darkness, between seeing and hearing, so also is there a division between man and man, and between woman and woman; and it is not to be said that the 8 one is like the other

either in face or in mind. For God made all things good in their order, the five senses in the head, and He joined on the neck to the head, adding to it the hair also for comeliness and glory, then the heart for understanding, the belly for excrement, and the stomach for (grinding), the windpipe for taking in (the breath), the liver for wrath, the gall for bitterness, the spleen for laughter, the reins for prudence, the muscles of the loins for power, the lungs for drawing 9 in, the loins for strength, and so forth. So then, my children, let all your works be done in order 10 with good intent in the fear of God, and do nothing disorderly in scorn or out of its due season. For if thou bid the eye to hear, it cannot; so neither while ye are in darkness can ye do the works of light.

3 1 Be ye, therefore, not eager to corrupt your doings through covetousness or with vain words to beguile your souls; because if ye keep silence in purity of heart, ye shall understand how to hold 2 fast the will of God, and to cast away the will of Beliar. Sun and moon and stars change not their 3 order; so do ye also change not the law of God in the disorderliness of your doings. The Gentiles went astray, and forsook the Lord, and changed their order, and obeyed stocks and stones, spirits of 4 deceit. But ye shall not be so, my children, recognizing in the firmament, in the earth, and in the sea, and in all created things, the Lord who made all things, that ye become not as Sodom, which 5 changed the order of nature. In like manner the Watchers also changed the order of their nature, whom the Lord cursed at the flood, on whose account He made the earth without inhabitants and fruitless.

4 1 These things I say unto you, my children, for I have read in the writing of Enoch that ye yourselves also shall depart from the Lord, walking according to all the lawlessness of the Gentiles, and 2 ye shall do according to all the wickedness of Sodom. And the Lord shall bring captivity upon you, and there shall ye serve your enemies, and ye shall be bowed down with every affliction and 3 tribulation, until the Lord have consumed you all. And after ye have become minished and made few, ye shall return and acknowledge the Lord your God; and He shall bring you back into your 4 land, according to His abundant mercy. And it shall be, that after that they come into the land of 5 their fathers, they shall again forget the Lord and become ungodly. And the Lord shall scatter them upon the face of all the earth, until the compassion of the Lord shall come, a man working righteousness and working mercy unto all them that are afar off, and to them that are near.

5 1 For in the fortieth year of my life, I saw a vision on the Mount of Olives, on the east of Jerusalem, 2 that the sun and the moon were standing still. And behold Isaac, the father of my father, said to us; Run and lay hold of them, each one according to his strength; and to him that seizeth them 3 will the sun and moon belong . And we all of us ran together, and Levi laid hold of the sun, and Judah outstripped the others and seized the moon, and they were both of them lifted up with them. 4 And when Levi became as a sun, lo, a certain young man gave to him twelve branches of palm; 5 and Judah was bright as the moon, and under their feet were twelve rays. [And the two, Levi and 6 Judah, ran, and laid hold of them.] And 10, a bull upon the earth, with two great horns, and an 7 eagle's wings upon its back; and we wished to seize him; but could not. But Joseph came, and 8 seized him, and ascended up with him on high. And I saw, for I was there, and behold a holy writing appeared to us, saying: Assyrians, Medes, Persians, [Chaldeans,] Syrians, shall possess in captivity the twelve tribes of Israel.

6 1 And again, after seven days, I saw our father Jacob standing by the sea of Jamnia, and we were 2 with him. And behold, there came a ship sailing by, without sailors or pilot; and there was written 3 upon the ship, The Ship of Jacob. And our father said to us: Come, let us embark on our ship. 4 And when he had gone on board, there arose a vehement storm, and a mighty tempest of wind; and 5 our father, who was holding the helm, departed from us. And we, being tossed with the tempest, were borne along over the sea; and the ship was filled with water, (and was) pounded by mighty waves, 6 until it was broken up. And Joseph fled away upon a little boat, and we were all divided upon nine 7 planks, and Levi and Judah were together. And we were all scattered unto the ends of the earth. 8, 9 Then Levi, girt about with sackcloth, prayed for us all unto the Lord. And when the storm ceased, the ship reached the land as it were in peace. And, 10, our father came, and we all rejoiced with one accord.

7 1 These two dreams I told to my father; and he said to me: These things must be fulfilled in their season, after that Israel hath endured many things. 2 Then my father saith unto me: I believe God that Joseph liveth, for I see always that the Lord numbereth him with you, 3 And he said, weeping: Ah me, my son Joseph, thou livest, though I behold thee not, and thou seest not Jacob that begat thee. 4 He caused me also, therefore, to weep by these words, and I burned in my heart to declare that Joseph had been sold, but I feared my brethren.

8 1 And lo! my children, I have shown unto you the last times, how everything shall come to pass in 2 Israel. Do ye also, therefore, charge your children that they be united to Levi and to Judah; For through them shall salvation arise unto Israel, And in them shall Jacob be blessed. 3 For through their tribes shall God appear [dwelling among men] on earth, To save the race of Israel, And to gather together the righteous from amongst the Gentiles. 4 If ye work that which is good, my children, Both men and

angels shall bless you; And God shall be glorified among the Gentiles through you, And the devil shall flee from you, And the wild beasts shall fear you, And the Lord shall love you, [And the angels shall cleave to you]. 5 As a man who has trained a child well is kept in kindly remembrance: So also for a good work there is a good remembrance before God. 6 But him that doeth not that which is good, Both angels and men shall curse, And God shall be dishonoured among the Gentiles through him, And the devil shall make him as his own peculiar instrument, And every wild beast shall master him, And the Lord shall hate him. 7 For the commandments of the law are twofold, And through prudence must they be fulfilled. 8 For there is a season for a man to embrace his wife, And a season to abstain therefrom for his prayer. 9 So, then, there are two commandments; and, unless they be done in due order, they bring very 10 great sin upon men. So also is it with the other commandments. Be ye therefore wise in God, my Children, and prudent, understanding the order of His commandments, and the laws of every word, that the Lord may love you.

9 1 And when he had charged them with many such words, he exhorted them that they should 2 remove his bones to Hebron, and that they should bury him with his fathers. And when he had 3 eaten and drunken with a merry heart, he covered his face and died. And his sons did according to all that Naphtali their father had commanded them.

THE TESTAMENT OF GAD THE NINTH SON OF JACOB AND ZILPAH.

1 1 The copy of the testament of Gad, what things he spake unto his sons, in the hundred and twenty 2 fifth year of his life, saying unto them: Hearken, my children, I was the ninth son born to Jacob, 3 and I was valiant in keeping the flocks. Accordingly I guarded at night the flock; and whenever the lion came, or the wolf, or any wild beast against the fold, I pursued it, and overtaking (it) 4 I seized its foot with my hand and hurled it about a stone's throw, and so killed it. Now Joseph my brother was feeding the flock with us for upwards of thirty days, and being young, he fell sick 5 by reason of the heat. And he returned to Hebron to our father, who made him lie down near him, 6 because he loved him greatly. And Joseph told our father that the sons of Zilpah and Bilhah were slaying the best of the flock and eating them against the judgement of Reuben and Judah. 7 For he saw that I had delivered a lamb out of the mouth of a bear, and put the bear to death; but 8 had slain the lamb, being grieved concerning it that it could not live, and that we had eaten it. And 9 regarding this matter I was wroth with Joseph until the day that he was sold, And the spirit of hatred was in me, and I wished not either to hear of Joseph with the ears, or see him with the eyes because he rebuked us to our faces saying that we were eating of the flock without Judah. For whatsoever things he told our father, he believed him.

2 1 I confess now my sin, my children, that oftentimes I wished to kill him, because I hated him from 2 my heart. Moreover, I hated him yet more for his dreams; and I wished to lick him out of the land of the living, even as an ox licketh up the grass of the field. 3 Therefore I and Simeon sold him to the Ishmaelites [for thirty pieces of gold, and ten of them we hid, and showed the twenty to our brethren] 4 And thus through covetousness we were bent on slaying him. 5 And the God of my fathers delivered him from my hands, that I should not work lawlessness in Israel.

3 1 And now, my children, hearken to the words of truth to work righteousness, and all the law of the Most High, and go not astray through the spirit of hatred, for it is evil in all the doings of 2 men. Whatsoever a man doeth the hater abominateth him: and though a man worketh the law of the Lord, he praiseth him not; though a man feareth the Lord, and taketh pleasure in that which is 3 righteous, he loveth him not. He dispraiseth the truth, he envieth him that prospereth, he welcometh evil-speaking, he loveth arrogance, for hatred blindeth his soul; as I also then looked on Joseph.

4 1 Beware, therefore, my children of hatred; for it worketh lawlessness even against the Lord Himself. 2 For it will not hear the words of His commandments concerning the loving of one's neighbour, 3 and it sinneth against God. For if a brother stumble, it delighteth immediately to proclaim it to all men, and is urgent that he should be judged for it, and be punished and be put to death. 4 And if it be a servant it stirreth him up against his master, and with every affliction it deviseth against 5 him if possibly he can be put to death, For hatred worketh with envy also against them that prosper: so long as it heareth of or seeth their success, it always languisheth. 6 For as love would quicken even the dead, and would call back them that are condemned to die, so hatred would slay the living, and those that had sinned venially it would not suffer to live. 7 For the spirit of hatred worketh together with Satan, through hastiness of spirit, in all things to men's death; but the spirit of love worketh together with the law of God in long-suffering unto the salvation of men.

5 1 Hatred, therefore, is evil, for it constantly mateth with lying, speaking against the truth; and it maketh small things to be great, and causeth the light to be darkness, and calleth the sweet bitter, and teacheth slander, and kindleth wrath, and stirreth up war, and violence and all covetousness; 2 it filleth the heart with evils and devilish poison. These things, therefore, I say to you from experience, my children, that ye may drive forth hatred,

which is of the devil, and cleave to 3 the love of God. Righteousness casteth out hatred, humility destroyeth envy. For he that is just and humble is ashamed to do what is unjust, being reproved not of another, but of his own heart, 4 because the Lord looketh on his inclination. He speaketh not against a holy man, because the fear 5 of God overcometh hatred. For fearing lest he should offend the Lord, he will not do wrong to any 6, 7 man, even in thought. These things I learnt at last, after I had repented concerning Joseph. For true repentance after a godly sort [destroyeth ignorance, and] driveth away the darkness, and 8 enlighteneth the eyes, and giveth knowledge to the soul, and leadeth the mind to salvation. And 9 those things which it hath not learnt from man, it knoweth through repentance. For God brought upon me a disease of the liver; and had not the prayers of Jacob my father succoured me, it had 10 hardly failed but my spirit had departed, For by what things a man transgresseth, by the same also 11 is he punished. Since, therefore, my liver was set mercilessly against Joseph, in my liver too I suffered mercilessly, and was judged for eleven months, for so long a time as I had been angry against Joseph.

6 1 And now, my children, I exhort you, love ye each one his brother, and put away hatred from 2 your hearts, love one another in deed, and in word, and in the inclination of the soul. For in the presence of my father I spake peaceably to Joseph; and when I had gone out, the spirit of hatred darkened my mind, and stirred up my soul to slay him. 3 Love ye, therefore, one another from the heart; and if a man sin against thee, cast forth the poison of hate and speak peaceably to him, and in thy soul hold not guile; and if he confess and repent, forgive him. 4 But if he deny it, do not get into a passion with him, lest catching the poison from thee he take 5 to swearing and so thou sin doubly. [Let not another man hear thy secrets when engaged in legal strife, lest he come to hate thee and become thy enemy, and commit a great sin against thee; for 6 ofttimes he addresseth thee guilefully or busieth himself about thee with wicked intent.] And though he deny it and yet have a sense of shame when reproved, give over reproving him. For he who denieth may repent so as not again to wrong thee; yea, he may also honour thee, and [fear 7 and] be at peace with thee And if he be shameless and persist in his wrong-doing, even so forgive him from the heart, and leave to God the avenging.

7 1 If a man prospereth more than you, do not be vexed, but pray also for him, that he may have 2 perfect prosperity. For so it is expedient for you. And if he be further exalted, be not envious of him, remembering that all flesh shall die; and offer praise to God, who giveth things good and 3 profitable to all men. Seek out the judgements of the Lord, and thy mind will rest and be at peace. 4 And though a man become rich by evil means, even as Esau, the brother of my father, be not jealous; 5 but wait for the end of the Lord. For if he taketh away (from a man) wealth gotten by evil 6 means He forgiveth him if he repent, but the unrepentant is reserved for eternal punishment. For the poor man, if free from envy he pleaseth the Lord in all things, is blessed beyond all men, because 7 he hath not the travail of vain men. Put away, therefore, jealousy from your souls, and love one another with uprightness of heart.

8 1 Do ye also therefore tell these things to your children, that they honour Judah and Levi, for from 2 them shall the Lord raise up salvation to Israel. [For I know that at the last your children shall depart from Him, and shall walk in all wickedness, and affliction and corruption before the Lord.] 3 And when he had rested for a little while, he said again; My children, obey your father, and bury 4, 5 me near to my fathers. And he drew up his feet, and fell asleep in peace. And after five years they carried him up to Hebron, and laid him with his fathers.

THE TESTAMENT OF ASHER, THE TENTH SON OF JACOB AND ZILPAH.

1 1 The copy of the Testament of Asher, what things he spake to his sons in the hundred and 2 twenty-fifth year of his life. For while he was still in health, he said to them: Hearken, ye children of Asher, to your father, and I will declare to you all that is upright in the sight of the Lord. 3 Two ways hath God given to the sons of men, and two inclinations, and two kinds of action, and 4 two modes (of action), and two issues. Therefore all things are by twos, one over against the 5 other. For there are two ways of good and evil, and with these are the two inclinations in our 6 breasts discriminating them. Therefore if the soul take pleasure in the good (inclination), all its 7 actions are in righteousness; and if it sin it straightway repenteth. For, having its thoughts set upon righteousness, and casting away wickedness, it straightway overthroweth the evil, and uprooteth 8 the sin. But if it incline to the evil inclination, all its actions are in wickedness, and it driveth away the good, and cleaveth to the evil, and is ruled by Beliar; even though it work what is good, 9 he perverteth it to evil. For whenever it beginneth to do good, he forceth the issue of the action into evil for him, seeing that the treasure of the inclination is filled with an evil spirit.

2 1 A person then may with words help the good for the sake of the evil, yet the issue of the action 2 leadeth to mischief. There is a man who showeth no compassion upon him who serveth his turn in 3 evil; and this thing hath two aspects, but the whole is evil. And there is a man that loveth him that worketh evil, because he would prefer even to die in evil for his sake; and concerning this it is clear that it hath two aspects, but the whole is an evil work. 4 Though indeed he have love, yet is he wicked

who concealeth what is evil for the sake of the good name, but the end of the action tendeth unto evil. 5 Another stealeth, doeth unjustly, plundereth, defraudeth, and withal pitieth the poor: this too 6 hath a twofold aspect, but the whole is evil. He who defraudeth his neighbour provoketh God, and sweareth falsely against the Most High, and yet pitieth the poor: the Lord who commandeth the 7 law he setteth at nought and provoketh, and yet he refresheth the poor. He defileth the soul, and maketh gay the body; he killeth many, and pitieth a few: this, too, hath a twofold aspect, but the 8 whole is evil. Another committeth adultery and fornication, and abstaineth from meats, and when he fasteth he doeth evil, and by the power of his wealth overwhelmeth many; and notwithstanding his excessive wickedness he doeth the commandments: this, too, hath a twofold aspect, but the 9 whole is evil. Such men are hares; clean,- like those that divide the hoof, but in very deed are 10 unclean. For God in the tables of the commandments hath thus declared.

3 1 But do not ye, my children, wear two faces like unto them, of goodness and of wickedness; but 2 cleave unto goodness only, for God hath his habitation therein, and men desire it. But from wickedness flee away, destroying the (evil) inclination by your good works; for they that are double-faced serve not God, but their own lusts, so that they may please Beliar and men like unto themselves.

4 1 For good men, even they that are of single face, though they be thought by them that are double 2 faced to sin, are just before God. For many in killing the wicked do two works, of good and evil; 3 but the whole is good, because he hath uprooted and destroyed that which is evil. One man hateth the merciful and unjust man, and the man who committeth adultery and fasteth: this, too, hath a two fold aspect, but the whole work is good, because he followeth the Lord's example, in that he 4 accepteth not the seeming good as the genuine good. Another desireth not to see a good day with them that riot, lest he defile his body and pollute his soul: this, too, is double-faced, but the whole is 5 good. For such men are like to stags and to hinds, because in the manner of wild animals they seem to be unclean, but they are altogether clean; because they walk in zeal for the Lord and abstain from what God also hateth and forbiddeth by His commandments, warding off the evil from the good.

5 1 Ye see, my children, how that there are two in all things, one against the other, and the one is hidden by the other: in wealth (is hidden) covetousness, in conviviality drunkenness, in laughter 2 grief, in wedlock profligacy. Death succeedeth to life, dishonour to glory, night to day, and darkness to light; [and all things are under the day, just things under life, unjust things under 3 death;] wherefore also eternal life awaiteth death. Nor may it be said that truth is a lie, nor 4 right wrong; for all truth is under the light, even as all things are under God. All these things, therefore, I proved in my life, and I wandered not from the truth of the Lord, and I searched out the commandments of the Most High, walking according to all my strength with singleness of face unto that which is good.

6 1 Take heed, therefore, ye also, my children, to the commandments of the Lord, following the truth 2 with singleness of face. For they that are double-faced are guilty of a twofold sin; for they both do the evil thing and they have pleasure in them that do it, following the example of the spirits of 3 deceit, and striving against mankind. Do ye, therefore, my children, keep the law of the Lord, and give not heed unto evil as unto good; but look unto the thing that is really good, and keep it in all 4 commandments of the Lord, having your conversation therein, and resting therein. For the latter ends of men do show their righteousness (or unrighteousness), when they meet the angels of the 5 Lord and of Satan. For when the soul departs troubled, it is tormented by the evil spirit which also it served in lusts and evil works. 6 But if he is peaceful with joy he meeteth the angel of peace, and he leadeth him into eternal life.

7 1 Become not, my children, as Sodom, which sinned against the angels of the Lord, and perished for 2 ever. For I know that ye shall sin, and be delivered into the hands of your enemies; and your land shall be made desolate, and your holy places destroyed, and ye shall be scattered unto the four 3 corners of the earth. And ye shall be set at nought in the dispersion vanishing away as water. Until the Most High shall visit the earth, coming Himself [as man, with men eating and drinking, and breaking the head of the dragon in the water. He shall save Israel and all the Gentiles [God speaking in 4 the person of man]. [Therefore do ye also, my children, tell these things to your children, that they 5 disobey Him not. For I have known that ye shall assuredly be disobedient, and assuredly act ungodly, not giving heed to the law of God, but to the commandments of men, being corrupted 6 through wickedness. And therefore shall ye be scattered as Gad and Dan my brethren, and ye shall 7 know not your lands, tribe, and tongue. But the Lord will gather you together in faith through His tender mercy, and for the sake of Abraham, Isaac, and Jacob.]

8 1 And when he had said these things unto them he commanded them, saying: Bury me in Hebron. 2 And he fell asleep and died at a good old age. And his sons did as he had commanded them, and they carried him up to Hebron, and buried him with his fathers.

THE TESTAMENT OF JOSEPH, THE ELEVENTH SON OF JACOB AND RACHEL.

1 1 The copy of the Testament of Joseph. When he was about to die he called his sons and his brethren together, and said to them:-- 2 My brethren and my children, Hearken to Joseph the beloved of Israel; Give ear, my sons, unto your father. 3 I have seen in my life envy and death, Yet I went not astray, but persevered in the truth of the Lord. 4 These my brethren hated me, but the Lord loved me: They wished to slay me, but the God of my fathers guarded me: They let me down into a pit, and the Most High brought me up again. 5 I was sold into slavery, and the Lord of all made me free: I was taken into captivity, and His strong hand succoured me. I was beset with hunger, and the Lord Himself nourished me. 6 I was alone, and God comforted me: I was sick, and the Lord visited me: I was in prison, and my God showed favour unto me; In bonds, and He released me; 7 Slandered, and He pleaded my cause; Bitterly spoken against by the Egyptians, and He delivered me; Envied by my fellow-slaves, and He exalted me.

2 1, 2 And this chief captain of Pharaoh entrusted to me his house. And I struggled against a shameless woman, urging me to transgress with her; but the God of Israel my father delivered me from 3 the burning flame. I was cast into prison, I was beaten, I was mocked; but the Lord granted me to find mercy in the sight of the keeper of the prison. 4 For the Lord doth not forsake them that fear Him, Neither in darkness, nor in bonds, nor in tribulations, nor in necessities. 5 For God is not put to shame as a man, Nor as the son of man is he afraid, Nor as one that is earth-born is He [weak or] affrighted. 6 But in all those things doth He give protection, And in divers ways doth He comfort, (Though) for a little space He departeth to try the inclination of the soul. 7 In ten temptations He showed me approved, And in all of them I endured; For endurance is a mighty charm, And patience giveth many good things.

3 1 How often did the Egyptian woman threaten me with death! How often did she give me over to punishment, and then call me back and threaten me, and when I was unwilling to company with 2 her, she said to me: Thou shalt be lord of me, and all that is in my house, if thou wilt give thyself 3 unto me, and thou shalt be as our master. But I remembered the words of my father, and going 4 into my chamber, I wept and prayed unto the Lord. And I fasted in those seven years, and I appeared to the Egyptians as one living delicately, for they that fast for God's sake receive beauty of face. 5 And if my lord were away from home, I drank no wine; nor for three days did I take my food, but 6 I gave it to the poor and sick. And I sought the Lord early, and I wept for the Egyptian woman of Memphis, for very unceasingly did she trouble me, for also at night she came to me under pretence of visiting me. 7 And because she had no male child she pretended to regard me as a son, and so I prayed to the Lord, and she bare a male child. 8 And for a time she embraced me as a son, and I knew it not; but later, she sought to draw me 9 into fornication. And when I perceived it I sorrowed unto death; and when she had gone out, I came to myself, and lamented for her many days, because I recognized her guile and her deceit. 10 And I declared unto her the words of the Most High, if haply she would turn from her evil lust.

4 1 Often, therefore, did she flatter me with words as a holy man, and guilefully in her talk praise my 2 chastity before her husband, while desiring to ensnare me when we were alone. For she lauded me openly as chaste, and in secret she said unto me: Fear not my husband; for he is persuaded concerning 3 thy chastity: for even should one tell him concerning us, he would not believe. Owing to all these things I lay upon the ground, and besought God that the Lord would deliver me from her 4 deceit. And when she had prevailed nothing thereby, she came again to me under the plea of 5 instruction, that she might learn the word of God. And she said unto me: If thou willest that I should leave my idols, lie with me, and I will persuade my husband to depart from his idols, and 6 we will walk in the law of thy Lord. And I said unto her: The Lord willeth not that those who reverence Him should be in uncleanness, nor doth He take pleasure in them that commit adultery, 7 but in those that approach Him with a pure heart and undefiled lips. But she held her peace, 8 longing to accomplish her evil desire. And I gave myself yet more to fasting and prayer, that the Lord might deliver me from her.

5 1 And again, at another time she said unto me: If thou wilt not commit adultery, I will kill my 2 husband by poison; and take thee to be my husband. I therefore, when I heard this, rent my garments, and said unto her: Woman, reverence God, and do not this evil deed, lest thou be 3 destroyed; for know indeed that I will declare this thy device unto all men. She therefore, being 4 afraid, besought that I would not declare this device. And she departed soothing me with gifts, and sending to me every delight of the sons of men.

6 1, 2 And afterwards she sent me food mingled with enchantments. And when the eunuch who brought it came, I looked up and beheld a terrible man giving me with the dish a sword, and 3 I perceived that (her) scheme was to beguile me. And when he had gone out I wept, nor did 4 I taste that or any other of her food. So then after one day she came to me and observed the food, 5 and said unto me: Why is it that thou hast not eaten of the food? And I said unto her: It is because thou hast filled it with deadly enchantments; and how saidst thou: I come not near to 6 idols, but to the Lord alone. Now therefore know that the God of my father hath revealed unto me by His angel thy wickedness, and I have kept it to con-

vict thee, if haply thou mayst see and repent. 7 But that thou mayst learn that the wickedness of the ungodly hath no power over them that worship God with chastity, behold I will take of it and eat before thee. And having so said, I prayed thus: The God of my fathers and the angel of Abraham, be with me; and ate. 8 And when she saw this she fell upon her face at my feet, weeping; and I raised her up and admonished her. And she promised to do this iniquity no more.

7 1 But her heart was still set upon evil, and she looked around how to ensnare me, and sighing deeply she became downcast, though she was not sick. 2 And when her husband saw her, he said unto her: Why is thy countenance fallen? And she said unto him: I have a pain at my heart, and the groanings of my spirit oppress me; and so 3 he comforted her who was not sick. Then, accordingly seizing an opportunity, she rushed unto me while her husband was yet without, and said unto me: I will hang myself, or cast myself over a cliff, 4 if thou wilt not lie with me. And when I saw the spirit of Beliar was troubling her, I prayed unto 5 the Lord, and said unto her: Why, wretched woman, art thou troubled and disturbed, blinded through, sins? Remember that if thou kill thyself, Asteho, the concubine of thy husband, thy rival, 6 will beat thy children, and thou wilt destroy thy memorial from off the earth. And she said unto me: Lo, then thou lovest me; let this suffice me: only strive for my life and my children, and 7 I expect that I shall enjoy my desire also. But she knew not that because of my lord I spake 8 thus, and not because of her. For if a man hath fallen before the passion of a wicked desire and become enslaved by it, even as she, whatever good thing he may hear with regard to that passion, he receiveth it with a view to his wicked desire.

8 1 I declare, therefore, unto you, my children, that it was about the sixth hour when she departed from me; and I knelt before the Lord all day, and all the night; and about dawn I rose up, weeping 2 the while and praying for a release from her. At last, then, she laid hold of my garments, forcibly dragging me to have connexion with her. 3 When, therefore, I saw that in her madness she was holding fast to my garment, I left it behind, and fled away naked. 4 And holding fast to the garment she falsely accused me, and when her husband came he cast me into prison in his house; and on the morrow he scourged me and sent me into Pharaoh's prison. 5 And when I was in bonds, the Egyptian woman was oppressed with grief, and she came and heard how I gave thanks unto the Lord and sang praises in the abode of darkness, and with glad voice rejoiced, glorifying my God that I was delivered from the lustful desire of the Egyptian woman.

9 1 And often hath she sent unto me saying: Consent to fulfill my desire, and I will release thee from thy bonds, and I will free thee from the darkness. And not even in thought did I incline unto 2 her. For God loveth him who in a den of wickedness combines fasting with chastity, rather than the man who in kings' chambers combines luxury with licence. And if a man liveth in chastity, and desireth also glory, and the Most High knoweth that it is expedient for him, He bestoweth this 3 also upon me. How often, though she were sick, did she come down to me at unlooked for times, 5 and listened to my voice as I prayed! And when I heard her groanings I held my peace. For when I was in her house she was wont to bare her arms, and breasts, and legs, that I might lie with her; for she was very beautiful, splendidly adorned in order to beguile me. And the Lord guarded me from her devices.

10 1, 2 Ye see, therefore, my children, how great things patience worketh, and prayer with fasting. So ye too, if ye follow after chastity and purity with patience and prayer, with fasting in humility of 3 heart, the Lord will dwell among you, because He loveth chastity. And wheresoever the Most High dwelleth, even though envy, or slavery, or slander befalleth (a man), the Lord who dwelleth in him, for the sake of his chastity not only delivereth him from evil, but also exalteth him even as me. 4, 5 For in every way the man is lifted up, whether in deed, or in word, or in thought. My brethren knew how my father loved me, and yet I did not exalt myself in my mind: although I was a child, 6 I had the fear of God in my heart; for I knew that all things would pass away. And I did nor raise myself (against them) with evil intent, but I honoured my brethren; and out of respect for them, even when I was being sold, I refrained from telling the Ishmaelites that I was a son of Jacob, a great man and a mighty.

11 1 Do ye also, my children, have the fear of God in all your works before your eyes, and honour 2 your brethren. For every one who doeth the law of the Lord shall be loved by Him. And when I came to the Indocolpitae with the Ishmaelites, they asked me, saying: Art thou a slave? And 3 I said that I was a home-born slave, that I might not put my brethren to shame. And the eldest of them said unto me: Thou art not a slave, for even thy appearance doth make it manifest. But 4 I said that I was their slave. Now when we came into Egypt they strove concerning me, which of 5 them should buy me and take me. Therefore it seemed good to all that I should remain in Egypt 6 with the merchant of their trade, until they should return bringing merchandise. And the Lord 7 gave me favour in the eyes of the merchant, and he entrusted unto me his house. And God blessed 8 him by my means, and increased him in gold and silver and in household servants. And I was with him three months and five days.

12 1 And about that time the Memphian woman, the wife of Pentephri, came down in a chariot, with 2 great pomp, because she had heard from

her eunuchs concerning me. And she told her husband that the merchant had become rich by means of a young Hebrew, and they say that he had assuredly 3 been stolen out of the land of Canaan. Now, therefore, render justice unto him, and take away the youth to thy house; so shall the God of the Hebrews bless thee, for grace from heaven is upon him.

13 1 And Pentephris was persuaded by her words, and commanded the merchant to be brought, and said unto him: What is this that I hear concerning thee, that thou stealest persons out of the land 2 of Canaan, and sellest them for slaves? But the merchant fell at his feet, and besought him, saying: 3 I beseech thee, my lord, I know not what thou sayest. And Pentephris said unto him: Whence, then, is the Hebrew slave? And he said: The Ishmaelites entrusted him unto me until they should return. 4 But he believed him not, but commanded him to be stripped and beaten. And when he persisted 5 in this statement, Pentephris said: Let the youth be brought. And when I was brought in, I did 6 obeisance to Pentephris (for he was third in rank of the officers of Pharaoh). And he took me apart 7 from him, and said unto me: Art thou a slave or free? And I said: A stave. And he said: 8 Whose? And I said: The Ishmaelites. And he said: How didst thou become their slave? And 9 I said: They bought me out of the land of Canaan. And he said unto me: Truly thou liest; and strightway he commanded me to be stripped and beaten.

14 1 Now the Memphian woman was looking through a window at me while I was being beaten, for her house was near, and she sent unto him saying: Thy judgement is unjust; for thou dost punish 2 a free man who hath been stolen, as though he were a transgressor. And when I made no change in my statement, though I was beaten, he ordered me to be imprisoned, until, he said, the owners 3 of the boy should come. And the woman said unto her husband: Wherefore dost thou detain the 4 captive and well-born lad in bonds, who ought rather to be set at liberty, and be waited upon? For 5 she wished to see me out of a desire of sin, but I was ignorant concerning all these things. And he said to her: It is not the custom of the Egyptians to take that which belongeth to others before 6 proof is given. This, therefore, he said concerning the merchant; but as for the lad, he must be imprisoned.

15 1 Now after four and twenty days came the Ishmaelites; for they had heard that Jacob my father 2 was mourning much concerning me. And they came and said unto me: How is it that thou saidst that thou wast a slave? and lo, we have learnt that thou art the son of a mighty man in the land of 3 Canaan, and thy father still mourneth for thee in sackcloth and ashes. When I heard this my bowels were dissolved and my heart melted, and I desired greatly to weep, but I restrained myself, that I should not put my brethren to shame. And I said unto them, I know not, I am a slave. 4, 5 Then, therefore, they took counsel to sell me, that I should not be found in their hands. For they feared my father, lest he [should come and] execute upon them a grievous vengeance. For they had 6 heard that he was mighty with God and with men. Then said the merchant unto them: Release 7 me from the judgement of Pentiphri. And they came and requested me, saying: Say that thou wast bought by us with money, and he will set us free.

16 1 Now the Memphian woman said to her husband: Buy the youth; for I hear, said she, that they are selling him. 2 And straightway she sent a eunuch to the 3 Ishmaelites, and asked them to sell me. But since the eunuch would not agree to buy me (at their price) he returned, having made trial of them, and he made known to his mistress that they asked a large price for their slave. 4 And she sent another eunuch, saying: Even though they demand two minas, give them, do not spare the gold; only buy the boy, and bring him to me. 5 The eunuch therefore went and gave them eighty pieces of gold, and he received me; but to the Egyptian woman he said: I have given a hundred. 6 And though I knew (this) I held my peace, lest the eunuch should be put to shame.

17 1 Ye see, therefore, my children, what great things I endured that I should not put my brethren to 2 shame. Do ye also, therefore love one another, and with long-suffering hide ye one another's 3 faults. For God delighteth in the unity of brethren, and in the purpose of a heart that takes 4 pleasure in love. And when my brethren came into Egypt they learnt that I had returned their 5 money unto them, and upbraided them not, and comforted them. And after the death of Jacob my father I loved them more abundantly, and all things whatsoever he commanded I did very 6 abundantly for them, And I suffered them not to be afflicted in the smallest matter; and all that 7 was in my hand I gave unto them. And their children were my children, and my children as their servants; and their life was my life, and all their suffering was my suffering, and all their sickness 8 was my infirmity. My land was their land, and their counsel my counsel. And I exalted not myself among them in arrogance because of my worldly glory, but I was among them as one of the least.

18 1 If ye also, therefore, walk in the commandments of the Lord, my children, He will exalt you there, 2 and will bless you with good things for ever and ever. And if any one seeketh to do evil unto you, 3 do well unto him, and pray for him, and ye shall be redeemed of the Lord from all evil. [For], behold, ye see that out of my humility and long-suffering I took unto wife the daughter of the priest of Heliopolis. And a hundred talents of gold were given me with her, and the Lord made 4 them to serve me. And He gave me also beauty as a flower beyond the beautiful

ones of Israel; and He preserved me unto old age in strength and in beauty, because I was like in all things to Jacob.

19 1 Hear ye, therefore, me vision which I saw. 2 I saw twelve harts feeding. And nine of them were dispersed. Now the three were preserved, but on the following day they also were dispersed. 3 And I saw that the three harts became three lambs, and they cried to the Lord, and He brought them forth into a flourishing and well watered place, yea He brought them out of darkness into light. 4 And there they cried unto the Lord until there gathered together unto them the nine harts, and they became as twelve sheep, and after a little time they increased and became many 5 flocks. And after these things I saw and behold, twelve bulls were sucking one cow, which produced a sea of milk, and there drank thereof the twelve flocks and innumerable herds. 6 And the horns of the fourth bull went up unto heaven and became as a wall for the flocks, and in the midst of the two horns there grew 7 another horn. And I saw a bull calf which surrounded them twelve times, and it became a help to the bulls wholly. 8 And I saw in the midst of the horns a virgin [wearing a many-coloured garment, and from her] went forth a lamb; and on his right (was as it were a lion; and) all the beasts and all the reptiles rushed (against him), and the lamb over 9 came them and destroyed them. And the bulls rejoiced because of him, and the cow [and the 10 harts] exulted together with them. And these 11 things must come to pass in their season. Do ye therefore, my children, observe the commandments of the Lord, and honour Levi and Judah; for from them shall arise unto you [the Lamb of God, who taketh away the sin of the world] one who saveth [all the Gentiles and] Israel. 12 For His kingdom is an everlasting kingdom, which shall not pass away; but my kingdom among you shall come to an end as a watcher's hammock, which after the summer disappeareth.

20 1For I know that after my death the Egyptians will afflict you, but God will avenge you, and will 2 bring you into that which He promised to your fathers. But ye shall carry up my bones with you; for when my bones are being taken up thither, the Lord shall be with you in light, and Beliar shall be in darkness with the Egyptians. 3 And carry ye up Asenath your mother to the Hippodrome, and near Rachel your mother bury her. 4, 5 And when he had said these things he stretched out his feet, and died at a good old age. And all Israel mourned for him, and all Egypt, with a great mourning. 6 And when the children of Israel went out of Egypt, they took with them the bones of Joseph, and they buried him in Hebron with his fathers, and the years of his life were one hundred and ten years.

THE TESTAMENT OF BENJAMIN, THE TWELFTH SON OF JACOB AND RACHEL

1 1 The copy of the words of Benjamin, which he commanded his sons to observe, after he had lived 2 a hundred and twenty-five years. And he kissed them, and said: As Isaac was born to Abraham 3 in his old age, so also was I to Jacob. And since Rachel my mother died in giving me birth, I had 4 no milk; therefore I was suckled by Bilhah her handmaid. For Rachel remained barren for twelve years after she had borne Joseph; and she prayed the Lord with fasting twelve days, and she 5 conceived and bare me. For my father loved Rachel dearly, and prayed that he might see two 6 sons born from her. Therefore was I called Benjamin, that is, a son of days.

2 1 And when I went into Egypt, to Joseph, and my brother recognized me, he said unto me: 2 What did they tell my father when they sold me ? And I said unto him, They dabbled thy coat with blood and sent it, and said: Know whether this be thy son's coat. 3 And Joseph said unto me: Even so, brother, the Canaanite merchants stole me by force, 4 And it came to pass that as they went on their way they concealed my garment, as though a wild beast had met 5 me and slain me. And so his associates sold me to the Ishmaelites. 6 And they did not lie in saying this. For he wished to conceal from me the deeds of my brethren. And he called to him his brethren and said: 7 Do not tell my father what ye have done unto me, but tell him 8 as I have told Benjamin. And let the thoughts among you be such, and let not these things come to the heart of my father.

3 1 Do ye also, therefore, my children, love the Lord God of heaven and earth, and keep His commandments, following the example of the good and holy man Joseph. 2 And let your mind be unto good, even as ye know me; for he that hath his mind right seeth 3 all things rightly. Fear ye the Lord, and love your neighbour; and even though the spirits of Beliar claim you to afflict you with every evil, yet shall they not have dominion over you, even 4 as they had not over Joseph my brother. How many men wished to slay him, and God shielded him! For he that feareth God and loveth his neighbour cannot be smitten by the spirit of 5 Beliar, being shielded by the fear of God. Nor can he be ruled over by the device of men or beasts, for he is helped by the Lord through the love which he hath towards his neighbour. 6 For Joseph also besought our father that he would pray for his brethren, that the Lord would 7 not impute to them as sin whatever evil they had done unto him. And thus Jacob cried out: My good child, thou hast prevailed over the bowels of thy father Jacob. And he embraced him, and kissed him for two hours, saying: 8 In thee shall be fulfilled the prophecy of heaven [concerning the Lamb of God, and Saviour of the world], and that a blameless one shall be delivered up for lawless men, and a sinless one shall die for ungodly men [in the blood of

the covenant. for the salvation of the Gentiles and of Israel, and shall destroy Beliar and his servants].

4 1 See ye, therefore, my children, the end of the good man? Be followers of his compassion, therefore, 2 with a good mind, that ye also may wear crowns of glory. For the good man hath not 3 a dark eye; for he showeth mercy to all men, even though they be sinners. And though they devise with evil intent concerning him, by doing good he overcometh evil, being shielded by God: 4 and he loveth the righteous as his own soul. If any one is glorified, he envieth him not; if any one is enriched, he is not jealous; if any one is valiant, he praiseth him; the virtuous man he laudeth, on the poor man he hath mercy; on the weak he hath compassion; unto God he singeth praises. 5 As for him who hath the fear of God, he protecteth him as with a shield; him that loveth God he helpeth; him that rejecteth the Most High he admonisheth and turneth back; and him that hath the grace of a good spirit he loveth as his own soul.

5 1 If, therefore, ye also have a good mind, then will both wicked men be at peace with you, and the profligate will reverence you and turn unto good; and the covetous will not only cease from 2 their inordinate desire, but even give the objects of their covetousness to them that are afflicted. If 3 ye do well, even the unclean spirits will flee from you; and the beasts will dread you. For where there is reverence for good works and light in the mind, even darkness fleeth away from him 4 For if any one does violence to a holy man, he repenteth; for the holy man is merciful to his reviler, and holdeth his peace. 5 And if any one betrayeth a righteous man, the righteous man prayeth: though for a little he be humbled, yet not long after he appeareth far more glorious, as was Joseph my brother.

6 1 The inclination of the good man is not in the power of the deceit of the spirit of Beliar, for the 2 angel of peace guideth his soul. And he gazeth not passionately upon corruptible things, nor 3 gathereth together riches through a desire of pleasure. He delighteth not in pleasure, [he grieveth for not his neighbour], he sateth not himself with luxuries, he erreth not in the uplifting of the eyes, 4 the Lord is his portion. The good inclination receiveth not glory nor dishonor from men, and it knoweth not any guile, or lie, or fighting or reviling; for the Lord dwelleth in him and lighteth up his 5 soul, and he rejoiceth towards all men alway. The good mind hath not two tongues, of blessing and of cursing, of contumely and of honor, of sorrow and of joy, of quietness and of confusion, of hypocrisy and of truth, [of poverty and of wealth]; but it hath one disposition, uncorrupt and pure, concerning all 6 men. It hath no double sight, nor double hearing; for in everything which he doeth, or speaketh, or 7 seeth, he knoweth that the Lord looketh on his soul. And he cleanseth his mind that he may not be condemned by men as well as by God. And in like manner the works of Beliar are twofold, and there is no singleness in them.

7 1 Therefore, my children, I tell you, flee the malice of Beliar; for he giveth a sword to them that obey him. 2 And the sword is the mother of seven evils. First the mind conceiveth through Beliar, and first there is bloodshed; secondly ruin; thirdly, tribulation; fourthly, exile; fifthly, dearth; sixthly, panic; seventhly, destruction. 3 Therefore was Cain also delivered over to seven vengeances by God, for in every hundred years the Lord brought one plague upon him. 4 And when he was two hundred years old he began to suffer, and in the nine-hundredth year he was destroyed. For on account of Abel, his brother, with all the evils was he judged, but Lamech with seventy times seven. 5 Because for ever those who are like Cain in envy and hatred of brethren, shall be punished with the same judgment.

8 1 And do ye, my children, flee evil-doing, envy, and hatred of brethren, and cleave to goodness 2 and love. He that hath a pure mind in love, looketh not after a woman with a view to fornication; for he hath no defilement in his heart, because the Spirit of God resteth upon him. 3 For as the sun is not defiled by shining on dung and mire, but rather drieth up both and driveth away the evil smell; so also the pure mind, though encompassed by the defilements of earth, rather cleanseth (them) and is not itself defiled.

9 1 And I believe that there will be also evil-doings among you, from the words of Enoch the righteous: that ye shall commit fornication with the fornication of Sodom, and shall perish, all save a few, and shall renew wanton deeds with women; and the kingdom of the Lord shall not be among, you, for straightway He shall take it away. 2 Nevertheless the temple of God shall be in your portion, and the last (temple) shall be more glorious than the first. And the twelve tribes shall be gathered together there, and all the Gentiles, until the Most High shall send forth His salvation in the visitation of an only 3 begotten prophet. [And He shall enter into the [first] temple, and there shall the Lord be treated with outrage, and He shall be lifted up upon 4 a tree. And the veil of the temple shall be rent, and the Spirit of God shall pass on to the Gentiles 5 as fire poured forth. And He shall ascend from Hades and shall pass from earth into heaven. And I know how lowly He shall be upon earth, and how glorious in heaven.]

10 1 Now when Joseph was in Egypt, I longed to see his figure and the form of his countenance; and through the prayers of Jacob my father I saw him, while awake in the daytime, even his entire figure exactly as he was. 2 And when he had said these things, he said unto them: Know ye, therefore, my children, that I am dying. 3 Do ye, therefore, truth and righteousness each one to his neighbour, and judgement unto confirmation, and keep the law of the Lord and his commandments. 4 For these things do I leave you instead of inheritance. Do ye also, therefore, give them to your 5 children for an everlasting possession; for so did both Abraham, and Isaac, and Jacob. For all these things they gave us for an inheritance, saying: Keep the commandments of God, until the Lord 6 shall reveal His salvation to all Gentiles. And then shall ye see Enoch, Noah, and Shem, and Abraham, and Isaac, and Jacob, rising on the right hand in gladness. 7 Then shall we also rise, each one over our tribe, worshipping the King of heaven, [who appeared upon earth in the form of a man in humility. And as many as believe on Him on the earth 8 shall rejoice with Him]. Then also all men shall rise, some unto glory and some unto shame. And the Lord shall judge Israel first, for their unrighteousness; [for when He appeared as God in the flesh to deliver them they believed Him 9 not]. And then shall He judge all the Gentiles, [as many as believed Him not when He appeared 10 upon earth]. And He shall convict Israel through the chosen ones of the Gentiles, even as He reproved Esau through the Midianites, who deceived their brethren, [so that they fell into fornication, and idolatry; and they were alienated from God], becoming therefore children in the portion of them that fear the Lord. 11 If ye therefore, my children, walk in holiness according to the commandments of the Lord, ye shall again dwell securely with me, and all Israel shall be gathered unto the Lord.

11 1 And I shall no longer be called a ravening wolf on account of your ravages, but [a worker of the Lord, distributing food to them that work what is good. 2 And there shall rise up from my seed in the latter times one] beloved of the Lord, [hearing upon the earth His voice] and a doer of the good pleasure of His will, [enlightening with new knowledge all the Gentiles, even the light of knowledge, bursting in upon Israel for salvation and tearing away from them like a wolf, and giving to the synagogue of the Gentiles. 3 Until the consummation of the age shall he be in the synagogues of the Gentiles, and among their 4 rulers, as a strain of music in the mouth of all. And he shall be inscribed in the holy books, both 5 his work and his word, and he shall be a chosen one of God for ever. And through them he shall go to and fro as Jacob my father, saying: He shall fill up that which lacketh of thy tribe].

12 1 And when he finished his words, he said: I command you, my children, carry up my bones out of Egypt, and bury me at Hebron, near my 2 fathers. So Benjamin died a hundred and twenty-five years old, at a good old age, and they 3 placed him in a coffin. And in the ninety-first year from the entrance of the children of Israel into Egypt, they and their brethren brought up the bones of their fathers secretly during the Canaanitish war; and they buried them in Hebron, 4 by the feet of their fathers. And they returned from the land of Canaan and dwelt in Egypt until the day of their departure from the land of Egypt.

Book 113. *The Testament of Moses*

Introduction:

1. The "Testament of Moses" (TOM) is also called the "Assumption of Moses" (AOM)

a. "A pseudepigraph extant in a single, poorly preserved, incomplete, and at times illegible Latin palimpsest discovered in the Ambrosian library of Milan and published by Ceriani in 1861. The manuscript dates from the 6th century C.E., but orthography and style indicate that it is a copy of an early 5th century writing. The Latin text is clearly a translation from a Greek document which may be as early as the late 1st or early 2d century C.E." (ABD, Testament of Moses)

b. "The Testament of Moses is known only from a single sixth-century Latin manuscript discovered in a library in Milan in 1861 by A. M. Ceriani. This manuscript was a palimpsest—the parchment on which Testament of Moses was written had been scraped and reused for another book. The ending is completely lost (perhaps as much as one-third to one-half the original document), and the condition of the text is poor in many places (Priest). There are numerous gaps in the manuscript, and many words are illegible, as would be expected in a palimpsest, so that scholars must reconstruct the text at a number of places. The textual situation is complicated by the fact that the Latin is a translation of a Greek version, which is itself a translation from the original Semitic version (probably Hebrew, but possibly Aramaic). Scholars have contended that the translators or copyists were frequently deficient in their treatment of the language they were translating. This again opens the door for translators to make many proposed emendations based on reconstructions of the underlying Greek or Hebrew (Aramaic) versions." (Dictionary of New Testament Background, Testament of Moses)

c. "The kingdom was to be ushered in by a day of repentance (1:17). 1750 years after the death of Moses, between a.d. 75 and 107 [Note: Charles wrongly dates the exodus to about 1650 BC, but may be following the incorrect calculation of the Jews who authored Assumption of Moses) God was to intervene on behalf of Israel—of Israel and not merely of Judah and Benjamin." (Pseudepigrapha of the Old Testament, R. H. Charles, Volume 2, Page 412, 1913 AD)

d. We need to find out if the critical texts, AOM 1.2 has gaps in the one extant palimpsest copy where the chronological numbers are located. Specifically: "two thousand five hundredth year from the creation of the world [to the time of the Exodus and Moses] ". Are we certain this is how the text actually reads because in 10 AD, a date of creation at 3906 BC (following the Book of Jubilees) breaks the pattern of all other extant literary sources that followed the LXX, except for the book of Jubilees 170 BC).

2. The Testament of Moses had three calculation variables:

a. Testament of Moses: "creation to death of Moses: 2500 years"

b. Testament of Moses: From assumption of Moses to Messiah: "250 times" (week/years) x7 = 1750 years

c. In 10 AD Testament of Moses expected the Messiah immediately after the death of Herod the Great and the end of his son's rulership in about 29 AD: 2500 + 1750 = 4250 before - 29 AD = 4221 BC creation date

3. Unlike the Seder Olam (150 AD) the Assumption of Moses DID NOT view the Messiah coming in 70 AD but earlier, shortly after the death of Herod's sons.

I. The Testament of Moses is quoted in Jude 9

1. "But Michael the archangel, when he disputed with the devil and argued about the body of Moses, did not dare pronounce against him a railing judgment, but said, "The Lord rebuke you!"" (Jude 9)

2. Perhaps the reason why the Testament of Moses is quoted by the Holy Spirit in Jude 9 is because the early Christians used this Jewish document to prove Jesus was the Christ.

a. The document did correctly predict the Messiah to come around 29 AD.

b. The story of the dispute over the body of Moses likely stems from an oral prophet, was widely known and was recorded in the Testament of Moses as a manmade record.

3. "The dispute referred to by Jude was recorded in the now lost ending of an apocryphal Jewish work called the Assumption of Moses. But the tradition can be reconstructed from references to that account in a number of early Christian writings (see Bauckham, pp. 65–76). Satan laid claim to the corpse of Moses for his kingdom of darkness because Moses had killed an Egyptian (Exod. 2:12). He was therefore a murderer, however virtuous his subsequent achievements, and so was unworthy of honorable burial. Satan, in his ancient role of accuser of God's people (Rev. 12:10), was seeking to prove Moses' guilt. In response to the charge, Michael did not dare to bring a slanderous accusation against Satan. Barclay (DSB, p. 188) expresses the opinion of most commentators that Jude means: "If the greatest of the good angels refused to speak evil of the greatest of the evil angels, even in circumstances like that, surely no human being may speak evil of any angel."" (UBCS 1-2 Pe/Jud, Jude 9, 1992 AD)

II. The Assumption of Moses (10 AD) creation 4221 BC follows the Book of Jubilees but has the Messiah coming in 29 AD, an exact match for Jesus Christ

1. Texts from the Assumption of Moses (Also called the Testament of Moses)

a. Text 1: Assumption of Moses 1.1–3, 7-8: "The Testament of Moses even the things which he commanded in the one hundred and twentieth year of his life, 2 that is the two thousand five hundredth year from the creation of the world. [But according to oriental reckoning the two thousand and seven hundredth, and the four hundredth after the departure from Phoenicia] … from the beginning of the creation of the world, that His name should be called upon until the day of repentance in the visitation wherewith the Lord will visit them in the consummation of the end of the days." (Assumption of Moses 1.1–3, 7-8, 10 AD)

b. Text 2: Assumption of Moses 10:12: "And do thou, Joshua (the son of) Nun, keep these words and this book; [12] For from my death [assumption] until His advent there shall be 250 times. And this is the course **of the times** which they shall pursue till they are consummated." (Assumption of Moses 10:12, 29 AD)

2. Dating Assumption of Moses: 1-29 AD:

a. It is dated to between 1 AD -29 AD because it discusses how Herod's children succeeded him but did not reign (at the time of writing of the book) longer than him (30 years).

b. Herod died in 1 BC and his three sons Archelaus (1BC-6AD), Antipas (1BC-39 AD) and Philip II (1 BC- 34 AD) divided Judea in to three parts.

c. "And he [Herod the Great] shall beget children, [who] succeeding him shall rule for shorter periods. 8 Into their parts cohorts and a powerful king of the west [Rome] shall come, who shall conquer them: 9 and he shall take them captive, and burn a part of their temple with fire, (and) shall crucify some around their colony. And when this is done the times shall be ended, in a moment the [second] course shall be [ended], the four hours shall come." (Assumption of Moses 6:7-7:1, 10 AD)

3. Messianic expectation after the birth of Christ and death of Herod the Great: perfect timing for resurrection of Christ in 33 AD:

a. Clearly there was an immediate messianic expectation after the death of Herod the Great that coincides exactly with Jesus Christ:

i. "And when this is done (rule of Herod the Great and his children) the times shall be ended, in a moment the [second] course shall be [ended], the four hours shall come." (Assumption of Moses 7:1, 10 AD)

ii. The full passage (see above) details how Herod the Great will die and that his children will rule in his place.

iii. What is important is the messianic expectation after their reigns ended.

iv. The book is dated to 29 AD at the latest, so it is a perfect fit with the ministry, death and resurrection of Christ.

4. Testament of Moses creation date calculation:

a. "Now, the Pharisaic chronology embodied in the rabbinical chronicle Seder Olam Rabbah dates Moses death in A.M. 2488, which is only 12 years from A.M. 2500 and is much nearer to it than the figures of Hellenistic or Essene chronology. Moreover, there are ancient baraitas quoted from other Pharisaic literature in the Babylonian Talmud (Sanhedrin 97a-97b; Abodah Zarah 9a-9b) which state that the Messiah will come either in A.M. 4000 or shortly after A.M. 4231; and, since Seder Olam Rabbah equates A.M. 3828 with 70 A.D., these dates for the Messiah are equivalent to 242 and 473 A.D. But 250 year-weeks (or 1750 years) after Moses's death in A.M. 2488 bring one to A.M. 4238, which is indeed shortly after A.M. 4231 - a mere 7 years later. It is clear, therefore, that the Pharisaic chronology was already in existence when the Assumption of Moses was written, and was partially known to its author." (Daniel 9 and the Date of Messiah's Coming in Essene, Hellenistic, Pharisaic, Zealot And Early Christian Computation, Roger T. Beckwith, Revue de Qumrân, Vol. 10, No. 4, pp. 521-542, 1981 AD)

b. Three Testament of Moses calculation variables:

i. Testament of Moses: "creation to death of Moses: 2500 years"

ii. Testament of Moses: From assumption of Moses to Messiah: "250 times" (week/years) x7 = 1750 years

iii. In 10 AD Testament of Moses expected the Messiah immediately after the death of Herod the Great and the end of his son's rulership in about 29 AD: 2500 + 1750 = 4250 before - 29 AD = 4221 BC creation date

iv. Unlike the Seder Olam (150 AD) the Assumption of Moses DID NOT view the Messiah coming in 70 AD but earlier, shortly after the death of Herod's sons.

c. Assumption of Moses creation date is 4221 BC

d. Mt creation date: 4174 BC (but the closeness of date is a coincidence because we know the Assumption of Moses was actually following the book of Jubilees.)

e. LXX creation date: 5554 BC

f. Assumption of Moses coming of the Messiah: between 10 - 29 AD

5. Summary:

a. For the Messiah to come 4250 years after creation, shortly after 29 AD, is very close to the MT at 4174 BC but is actually following the book of Jubilees chronology.

b. Jewish date setters for the "days the messiah" said the messiah would come after 85 Jubilees (85x50) from Creation (4250 AC) and more specifically within the 1708 year window of years 4292 - 6000 years after creation. (Babylonian Talmud, b. Sanh. 11:1, I.88.A–91.F)

c. The expectation of the Messiah shortly after the death of Herod and the reign of his three sons is a perfect fit for Jesus Christ and follows the LXX. However this is impossible for the MT because the earliest the Messiah can come is 118 AD.

d. The Testament of Moses therefore, has a similar creation date of the book of Jubilees.

e. This shows that the Assumption of Moses is a genuine historic document of Jewish Thought in the first century, even though at this time, the Bible text before them in both Hebrew (proto-Masoretic) and Greek (Septuagint) both shared the same identical chronological numbers in Gen 5,11 with a creation date of 5554 BC.

f. Why the authors of the Assumption of Moses would follow a chronology that is at variance with the Bible text in their synagogues is a puzzle, but then again keep in mind the book of jubilees did exactly the same thing 150 years earlier.

Conclusion:

1. The Assumption/Testament of Moses is an uninspired, human origin document that contained two important divine truths:

a. The story of Michael and the Devil arguing over the body of Moses.

b. The correct prediction that the Messiah would come in 29 AD.

2. How die the Testament of Moses get the prediction of 29 AD right?

a. The prophecy of Daniel 2:44 stated the God's kingdom would be setup during the fourth/Roman empire.

b. Another likely source for the correct 29 AD prediction was likely the 490 weeks of Daniel also ended in 33 AD.

3. Creation date of 4221 BC:

a. The Assumption/Testament of Moses has a creation date of 4221 BC because it follows the book of Jubilees chronology where Adam to Moses = 50 Jubilees x 50 years = 2500 years.

b. This is the first document in history to redefine a jubilee as 50 years instead of 49 as revealed in the Torah and used in the book of Jubilees (170 BC).

Book 114. The Apocalypse of Abraham

1:1 On the day when I was destroying the gods of my father Terah and the gods of my brother Nahor, when I was testing which one was the truly strong god, 1:2 at the time when my lot came up, when I had finished the services of my father Terah's sacrifice to his gods of wood, stone, gold, silver, brass and iron, 1:3 I, Abraham, having entered their temple for the service, found a god named Mar-Umath, carved out of stone, fallen at the feet of an iron god, Nakhon. 1:4 And it came to pass, that when I saw this, my heart was troubled. And I fell to thinking, because I, Abraham, was unable to return him to his place all by myself, since he was heavier than a great stone. 1:5 And I went and told my father. And he entered with me. 1:6 And as we both were moving him [Mar-Umath] to return him in his place, his head fell off of him, while I was still holding him by his head. 1:7 And it came to pass, when my father saw that the head of Mar-Umath had fallen off of him, he said to me, "Abraham!" 1:8 And I said, "Here am I!" And he said to me, "Bring me an axe and a chisel from the house." 1:9 And I brought [them] to him from the house. And he carved another Mar-Umath, out of another stone, without a head, and [placed on him] the head that had been thrown down from Mar-Umath, and smashed the rest of Mar-Umath.

i.i.ii. Fall of Five Idols (2)

2:1 And he made five other gods, and he gave them to me [and] told me to sell them outside in the street of the town. 2:2 And I saddled my father's ass and put them on it [and] went out to the main road to sell them. 2:3 And behold, merchants from Paddan Aram came with camels to go to Egypt to buy *kokonil* from the Nile there. 2:4 And I greeted them and they answered me. And I began to talk with them. One of their camels bellowed. The ass took fright and he ran and threw down the gods. And three of them were smashed and two remained. 2:5 And it came to pass, when the Syrians saw that I had gods, they said to me, "Why did you not tell us that you had gods? We would have bought them before the ass heard the camel's cry and you would have had no loss. 2:6 Give us at least the remaining gods and we will give you a proper price." 2:7 And I thought [it over] in my heart. And they gave [also] the price of the smashed gods for the gods that remained. 2:8 Since I had been distressed in my heart [wondering], "How would I let my father know about the matter?!" 2:9 And the debris of the smashed [gods] I cast into the water of the river Gur, which was at that place. And they sank into the depths and were no more.

i.ii. Abraham Reflects on Idolatry (3)

3:1 And while I was still walking on the road, my heart was disturbed and my mind was distracted. And I said in my heart, 3:2 "What is the profit of the labor which my father is doing? 3:3 Is not he rather a god of his gods, since by his sculpting, carving and skill they come into being? 3:4 It would be more fitting for them to worship my father, since they are his work. What gain is there for my father in his own works? 3:5 Behold, Mar-Umath fell and was unable to get up again in his own temple, nor could I lift him on my own, until my father came and we both lifted him. 3:6 And as we were unable, his head fell off of him. And he placed it on another stone of another god, which he had made without a head. 3:7 And [likewise were] the other five gods which were smashed down from the ass, which were able neither to save themselves nor to hurt the ass for it smashed them, nor did their shards come up from the river." 3:8 And I said to myself, "If it is thus, how then can my father's god, Mar-Umath, having a head of one stone and [the rest] being made of another stone, save a man, or hear a man's prayer and reward him?"

i.iii. Abraham Preaches Monotheism (4–8)

i.iii.i. Attempt to Persuade Terah (4)

4:1 And thinking thus, I came to my father's house and watered the ass and set out hay for it. I brought out the money and gave it into the hand of my father Terah. 4:2 When he saw it, he was glad, and he said, "Blessed by my gods are you, Abraham, for you gave honor to the gods, so that my labor was not in vain!" 4:3 And I declared and said to him, "Hear, Terah, [my] father! It is the gods who are blessed by you, since you are a god to them, since you have made them; since their blessing is perdition, and their power is vain. 4:4 They could not help themselves, how [then] will they help you or bless me? 4:5 [In fact] I was for you a kind god of this gain, since it was through my cleverness that I brought you the money for the smashed [gods]." 4:6 And when he heard my word, his anger was kindled against me, since I had spoken harsh words against his gods.

i.iii.ii. Fall of Bar-Eshath (5)

5:1 When I saw my father's anger, I went out. And afterward, when I had gone out, he called me, saying, "Abraham!" 5:2 And I said, "Here am I!" 5:3 And he said, "Gather and take the splinters from the wood out of which I was making wooden gods before you came [and] cook me a meal!" 5:4 And it came to pass, when I was collecting the wooden splinters, I found among them a small god, lying among the pieces of wood on my left. 5:5 And on his forehead was written: "god Bar-Eshath." 5:6 And it came to pass, when I found him, I held back and did not tell my father that I had found the wooden god Bar-Eshath among the chips. And it came to pass, after I had put the splinters on the fire, in order to cook food for my father, that I went out to ask about the food and I put Bar-Eshath near the hearth of fire, saying to him menacingly, 5:7 "Bar-Eshath, make sure that the fire does not go out before I come back. If the fire does go out, blow on it to make it flare up." 5:8 [And] I went out, having kindled my fire. 5:9 When I came back again I found Bar-Eshath fallen backwards, his feet enveloped in fire and terribly burned. 5:10 Laughing greatly to myself, I said, "Bar-Eshath, you certainly are able to kindle fire and cook food!" 5:11 And it came to pass, while I was speaking laughingly, that he was gradually burned up by the fire and became ashes. 5:12 And I brought the food to my father, [and] he ate. 5:13 And I gave him wine and milk, and he drank and satiated himself and blessed Mar-Umath, his god. 5:14 And I said to him, "Father Terah, do not bless your god Mar-Umath, do not praise him! Praise rather your god Bar-Eshath because, in his love for you he threw himself into the fire in order to cook your food." 5:15 And he said to me, "And where is he now?" 5:16 "He has been reduced to ashes in the fury of the fire and become dust." 5:17 And he said, "Great is the power of Bar-Eshath! I shall make another today, and tomorrow he will make my food!"

i.iii.iii. Hierarchy of Gods (6)

6:1 When I, Abraham, heard such words from my father, I [both] laughed in my mind and [yet] groaned in the bitterness and anger of my soul. 6:2 And I said, "How can a statue made by my father [ever] be his helper? 6:3 Or would he have subordinated his body to his soul, his soul to his spirit, then his spirit—to folly and ignorance?" 6:4 And I said, "Must one put up with evil? Let me risk my life for purity and I shall put forth my own clear thinking before him!" 6:5 I declared and said, "Father Terah, whichever of these gods you praise, you err in your thinking. 6:6 Behold, my brother Nahor's gods standing in the holy temple are more honored than yours. 6:7 For behold, Zoukh, my brother Nahor's god, is more honored than your god Mar-Umath, since he is made of gold sold by men. 6:8 And if he becomes worn out with the years, he will be remade, whereas Mar-Umath, if he is changed or broken, will not be remade, since he is of stone. 6:9 [And] what about Yoavon, a god who is in the power of another god, who stands beside Zoukh? Since [even] he is more honored than the god Bar-Eshath who is made of wood, while [Yoavon is] forged of silver. And being better proportioned, he is sold by men in order to show him. 6:10 But Bar-Eshath , your god, before he was made had been rooted in the ground. 6:11 Being great and wondrous, with branches, flowers and [various] beauties. 6:12 And you cut him with an ax, and by your skill the god was made. 6:13 And behold, he has dried up, and his sap is gone. 6:14 He fell from the heights to the ground, and he went from greatness to insignificance, 6:15 and his appearance has faded. 6:16 [Now] he himself has been burned up by the fire, 6:17 and he turned into ashes and is no more. 6:18 Yet you say: "Today I shall make another one, and tomorrow he will make my food." 6:19 [But] he retained no strength utterly perishing!

i.iii.iv. Hierarchy of Natural Elements and Luminaries (7)

7:1 This I say: 7:2 Fire is the noblest [element] in the image [of the world], since even the things which are [otherwise] unsubdued are subdued in it, and [since] it mocks with its flames the things which perish easily. 7:3 But I would not call it a god either, since it is subjugated to water. 7:4 Water is indeed nobler, since it overcomes fire and soaks the earth. 7:5 But I would not call it a god, since it is subjugated to the earth, running underneath it. 7:6 I would rather call the earth the noblest, since it overcomes the substance and abundance of water. 7:7 But neither would I call it gods, since it is dried up by the sun [and since it is] made for men to plow. 7:8 [So] I would call the sun nobler than the earth, since with its rays it illumines the inhabited world and the various airs. 7:9 But I would not make it into a god either, since its course is obscured [both] at night [and] by the clouds. 7:10 Nor, again, would I call the moon and the stars gods, since they too in their times at night can darken their light.

i.iii.iv. Monotheistic Conclusion (7:11–12)

7:11 Listen, Terah, my father, I shall seek in your presence the God who created all the gods which we consider! 7:12 For who is it, or which one is it who colored heaven and made the sun golden, who has given light to the moon and the stars with it, who has dried the earth in the midst of many waters, who set you yourself among the elements, and who now has chosen me in the distraction of my mind?— Will he reveal himself by himself to us?— [He is] the God!"

i.iii.vi. Punishment of Terah (8)

8:1 And as I was thinking about these things, here is what happened to my father Terah in the courtyard of his house: The voice of the Mighty One came down from heaven in a stream of fire, saying and calling,

"Abraham, Abraham!" 8:2 And I said, "Here am I!" 8:3 And he said, "In the wisdom of your heart you are searching for the God of gods and the Creator. I am he! 8:4 Leave Terah your father, and leave the house, so that you too are not slain for the sins of your father's house!" 8:5 And I went out. And it came to pass as I was going out, that I had not even gotten as far as going beyond the doors of the courtyard, 8:6 when the sound of thunder came forth and burned him and his house and everything in the house, down to the ground [to a distance of] forty cubits.

ii. Revelation (9–32)

ii.i. Sacrifice (9–14)

ii.i.i. Command on Sacrifice (9)

9:1 Then came a voice saying to me twice, "Abraham, Abraham!" 9:2 And I said "Here am I!" 9:3 And he said, "Behold, it is I! Fear not, for I am the primordial and mighty God, who initially created the two luminaries of the world. 9:4 I protect you and I am your helper. 9:5 Go, take for me a heifer in her third year, and a she-goat in her third year, and ram in his third year, and a turtledove, and a pigeon, and set out for me a pure sacrifice. And in this sacrifice I shall set before you the ages 9:6 and make you know secrets, and you will see great things which you have not seen, since you loved to search for me, and I called you 'my friend.' 9:7 But for forty days abstain from every food which issues from fire, and from the drinking of wine, and from anointing [yourself] with oil. 9:8 And then you shall set out for me the sacrifice which I have commanded you, in the place which I shall show you on a high mountain. 9:9 And there shall I show you the ages: things built and firmed, made and renewed by my word. 9:10 And I shall make you know what will come to pass in them on those who have done evil and [those who have done] just things among the race of men."

ii.i.ii. Angel Yahoel (10–11)

10:1 And it came to pass, when I heard the voice announcing such words to me, and I looked hither and thither. 10:2 And behold, there was no breath of man, and my spirit was affrighted, and my soul fled from me, and I became like a stone, and fell down upon the earth, for there was no longer strength in me to stand up on the earth. 10:3 And when I was still face down on the earth, I heard the voice of the Holy One, saying, "Go, Yahoel, the namesake of the mediation of my ineffable name, sanctify this man and strengthen him from his trembling!" 10:4 And the angel whom he sent to me in the likeness of a man came, and he took me by my right hand and stood me on my feet. 10:5 And he said to me, "Stand up, Abraham, the friend of God who has loved you, let human trembling not enfold you. 10:6 For behold, I am sent to you to strengthen you and to bless you in the name of God, the creator of heavenly and earthly things, who has loved you. 10:7 Be bold and hasten to him. 10:8 I am Yahoel named by him who shakes those which are with me on the seventh vault, on the firmament. I am a power in the midst of the Ineffable who put together his names in me. 10:9 I am appointed according to his commandment to reconcile the rivalries of the Living Creatures of the Cherubim against one another, and teach those who bear him [to sing] the Song in the middle of man's night, at the seventh hour. 10:10 I am made in order to rule over the Leviathans, since the attack and the threat of every reptile are subjugated to me. 10:11 I am ordered to unlock Hades and to destroy those who worship the dead things. 10:12 I am ordered to burn your father's house with him, for he honored the dead things. 10:13 I am sent to you now to bless you and the land which the Eternal One, called by you, has prepared for you. 10:14 And for your sake I have indicated the way of earth. 10:15 Stand up, Abraham, go boldly, be very joyful and rejoice! And I am with you, since an honorable portion has been prepared for you by the Eternal One. 10:16 Go, fulfill your sacrifice of the command! For behold, I am appointed to be with you and with the progeny which is due to be born from you. 10:17 And Michael is with me in order to bless you forever. Be bold, go!" 11:1 And I stood and saw him who had taken my right hand and set me on my feet. 11:2 The appearance of the griffin's body was like sapphire, and the likeness of his face like chrysolite, and the hair of his head like snow, 11:3 and a turban on his head like the appearance of the bow in the clouds, and the closing of his garments [like] purple, and a golden staff [was] in his right hand. 11:4 And he said to me "Abraham!" and I said, "Here is your servant!" And he said, "Let my appearance not frighten you, nor my speech trouble your soul! 11:5 Come with me and I shall go with you, visible until the sacrifice, but after the sacrifice invisible forever. 11:6 Be bold and go!"

ii.i.iii. Journey to Horeb (12)

12:1 And we went, the two of us alone together, forty days and nights. 12:2 And I ate no bread and drank no water, because [my] food was to see the angel who was with me, and his speech with me was my drink. 12:3 And we came to the glorious God's mountains—Horeb. 12:4 And I said to the angel, "Singer of the Eternal One, behold, I have no sacrifice with me, nor do I know a place for an altar on the mountain, so how shall I make the sacrifice?" 12:5 And he said, "Look behind you." 12:6 And I looked behind me. And behold, all the prescribed sacrifices were following us: the calf, the she-goat, the ram, the turtledove, and the pigeon. 12:7 And the angel said to me, "Abraham!" And I said, "Here am I!" 12:8 And he said to me, "Slaughter and cut all this, putting together the two halves, one against the other. But do not cut the birds. 12:9 And give them [halves] to the two men whom I shall show you standing beside you, since they are the altar on the mountain, to offer sacrifice to the Eternal One. 12:10 The turtledove and the pigeon you will give me, and I shall ascend in order to show to you [the inhabited world] on the wings of two birds, in heaven and on the earth: the sea, and the abysses, and the depths, and the garden of Eden, and its rivers and the fullness of the inhabited world and round about it you will see everything."

ii.i.iv. Azazel (13–14)

13:1 And I did everything according to the angel's command. And I gave to the angels who had come to us the divided parts of the animals. And the angel took the two birds. 13:2 And I waited for [the time of] the evening offering. 13:3 And an impure bird flew down on the carcasses, and I drove it away. 13:4 And the impure bird spoke to me and said, "What are you doing, Abraham, on the holy heights, where no one eats or drinks, nor is there upon them food of men. But these will all be consumed by fire and they will burn you up. 13:5 Leave the man who is with you and flee! Since if you ascend to the height, they will destroy you." 13:6 And it came to pass when I saw the bird speaking I said to the angel, "What is this, my lord?" And he said, "This is iniquity, this is Azazel!" 13:7 And he said to him, "Reproach is on you, Azazel! Since Abraham's portion is in heaven, and yours is on earth, 13:8 Since you have chosen it and desired it to be the dwelling place of your impurity. Therefore the Eternal Lord, the Mighty One, has made you a dweller on earth. 13:9 And because of you [there is] the wholly-evil spirit of the lie, and because of you [there are] wrath and trials on the generations of impious men. 13:10 Since the Eternal Mighty God did not send the righteous, in their bodies, to be in your hand, in order to affirm through them the righteous life and the destruction of impiety. 13:11 Hear, adviser! Be shamed by me, since you have been appointed to tempt not to all the righteous! 13:12 Depart from this man! 13:13 You cannot deceive him, because he is the enemy of you and of those who follow you and who love what you desire. 13:14 For behold, the garment which in heaven was formerly yours has been set aside for him, and the corruption which was on him has gone over to you." 14:1 And the angel said to me, "Abraham!" And I said, "Here am I, your servant." 14:2 And he said, "Know by this that the Eternal One whom you have loved has chosen you. 14:3 Be bold and have power, as I order you, over him who reviles justice, 14:4 or else I shall not be able to revile him who scattered about the earth the secrets of heaven and who conspired against the Mighty One. 14:5 Say to him, 'May you be the fire brand of the furnace of the earth! Go, Azazel, into the untrodden parts of the earth. 14:6 Since your inheritance are those who are with you, with men born with the stars and clouds. And their portion is you, and they come into being through your being. 14:7 And justice is your enmity. Therefore through your own destruction vanish from before me!'" 14:8 And I said the words as the angel had taught me. 14:9 And he said, "Abraham!" And I said, "Here am I, your servant!" 14:10 And the angel said to me, "Answer him not!" 14:11 And he spoke to me a second time. 14:12 And the angel said, "Now, whatever he says to you, answer him not, lest his will affect you. 14:13 Since God gave him the gravity and the will against those who answer him. Answer him not." 14:14 And I did what the angel had commanded me. And whatever he said to me about the descent, I answered him not.

ii.ii. On Heaven (15–31)

ii.ii.i. Ascension (15–16)

15:1 And it came to pass that when the sun was setting, and behold, a smoke like that of a furnace, and the angels who had the divided parts of the sacrifice ascended from the top of the furnace of smoke. 15:2 And the angel took me with his right hand and set me on the right wing of the pigeon and he himself sat on the left wing of the turtledove, since they both were neither slaughtered nor divided. 15:3 And he carried me up to the edge of the fiery flame. 15:4 And we ascended like great winds to the heaven which was fixed on the expanses. 15:5 And I saw on the sky, on the height we had ascended, a strong light which cannot be described. 15:6 And behold, in this light a fire was kindled [and there was] of a crowd of many people in male likeness. 15:7 They were all changing in appearance and likeness, running and being transformed and bowing and shouting in a language the words of which I did not know. 16:1 And I said to the angel, "Where, thus, have you brought me now? For now I can no longer see, because I am weakened and my spirit is departing from me." 16:2 And he said to me, "Remain with me, do not fear! 16:3 He whom you will see going before both of us in a great sound of *qedushah* is the Eternal One who had loved you, whom himself you will not see. 16:4 Let your spirit not weaken from the shouting, since I am with you, strengthening you."

ii.ii.ii. Song of Abraham (17)

17:1 And while he was still speaking, behold, a fire was coming toward us round about, and a sound was in the fire like a sound of many waters, like a sound of the sea in its uproar. 17:2 And the angel bowed with me and worshiped. 17:3 And I wanted to fall face down to the earth. And the place of elevation on which we both stood sometimes was on high, sometimes rolled down. 17:4 And he said, "Only worship, Abraham, and recite the song which I taught you." 17:5 Since there was no earth to fall to, I only bowed down and recited the song which he had taught me. 17:6 And

he said, "Recite without ceasing." 17:7 And I recited, and he himself recited the song: 17:8 "O, Eternal, Mighty, Holy El, God Autocrat, 17:9 Self-Begotten, Incorruptible, Immaculate, Unbegotten, Spotless, Immortal, 17:10 Self-Created, Self-Illuminated, Without Mother, Without Father, Without Genealogy, 17:11 High, Fiery, 17:12 Wise, Lover Of Men, Favorable, Generous, Bountiful, Jealous Over Me, Patient, Most Merciful, 17:13 Eli {that is, my God,} Eternal, Mighty, Holy Sabaoth, Most Glorious El, El, El, El, Yahoel. 17:14 You are he whom my soul has loved, the Guardian, Eternal, Fiery, Shining, Light-Formed, Thunder-Voiced, Lightning-Looking, Many-Eyed, 17:16 receiving the entreaties of those who honor you and turning away from the entreaties of those who besiege you by the siege of their provocation, 17:17 releases those who are in the midst of the impious, those who are confused among the unrighteous of the inhabited world in the corruptible life, renewing the life of the righteous. 17:18 You make the light shine before the morning light upon your creation from your face in order to bring the day on the earth. 17:19 And in your heavenly dwellings there is an inexhaustible other light of an inexpressible splendor from the lights of your face. 17:20 Accept my prayer, and let it be sweet to you, and also the sacrifice which you yourself made to yourself through me who searched for you. 17:21 Receive me favorably and show to me, and teach me, and make known to your servant as you have promised me."

ii.ii.iii. Throne of Glory (18)

18:1 And while I was still reciting the song, the edge of the fire which was on the expanse rose up on high. 18:2 And I heard a voice like the roaring of the sea, and it did not cease because of the fire. 18:3 And as the fire rose up, soaring higher, I saw under the fire a throne [made] of fire and the many-eyed Wheels, and they are reciting the song. And under the throne [I saw] four singing fiery Living Creatures. 18:4 And their appearance was the same, each one of them had four faces. 18:5 And this was the aspect of their faces: of a lion, of a man, of an ox, of an eagle. Four heads were on their bodies, so that the four Living Creatures had sixteen faces, 18:6 and each one had six wings: from their shoulders, and from their sides, and from their loins. 18:7 With the wings which were from their shoulders they covered their faces, and with the wings from their loins they clothed their feet, and with their middle wings they stretch out straight flying. 18:8 And as they were finishing singing, they looked at one another and threatened one another. 18:9 And it came to pass when the angel who was with me saw that they were threatening each other, he left me and went running to them. 18:10 And he turned the face of each Living Creature from the face which was opposite to it so that they could not see each other's threatening faces. 18:11 And he taught them the song of peace [saying] that everything belonged to the Eternal One. 18:12 While I was still standing and watching, I saw behind the Living Creatures a chariot with fiery Wheels. Each Wheel was full of eyes round about. 18:13 And above the Wheels there was the throne which I had seen. And it was covered with fire and the fire encircled it round about, and an indescribable light surrounded the fiery people. 18:14 And I heard the sound of their *qedusha* like the voice of a single man.

ii.ii.iv. Celestial Powers (19)

19:1 And a voice came to me out of the midst of the fire, saying, "Abraham, Abraham!" 19:2 And I said, "Here am I!" 19:3 And he said, "Look at the levels which are under the expanse on which you are brought and see that on no single level is there any other but the one whom you have searched for or who has loved you." 19:4 And while he was still speaking, and behold, the levels opened, and there are the heavens under me. And I saw on the seventh firmament upon which I stood a fire spread out and light, and dew, and a multitude of angels, and a power of the invisible glory from the Living Creatures which I had seen above. But I saw no one else there. 19:5 And I looked from the altitude of my standing to the sixth expanse. 19:6 And I saw there a multitude of incorporeal spiritual angels, carrying out the orders of the fiery angels who were on the eighth firmament, as I was standing on its suspensions. 19:7 And behold, neither on this expanse was there any other power of other form, but only the spiritual angels, and they are the power which I had seen on the seventh firmament. 19:8 And he commanded the sixth expanse to remove itself. 19:9 And I saw there, on the fifth [level], hosts of stars, and the orders they were commanded to carry out, and the elements of earth obeying them."

ii.ii.v. Promise of Seed (20:1–6)

20:1 And the Eternal Mighty One said to me, "Abraham, Abraham!" 20:2 And I said, "Here am I!" 20:3 And he said, "Look on high at the stars which are beneath you and count them for me and tell me their number!" 20:4 And I said, "Would I be able? For I am [but] a man." 20:5 And he said to me, "As the number of the stars and their host, so shall I make your seed into a company of nations, set apart for me in my lot with Azazel."

ii.ii.vi. Evil in the World (20:6–23:13)

ii.ii.vi.i. Question (20:6–7)

20:6 And I said, "Eternal Mighty One! Let your servant speak before you and let your fury not rage against your chosen one. 20:7 Behold, before you led me up, {Azazel abused me. Why then, while he is now not before you, have you set yourself with him?"

ii.ii.vi.ii. Answer (21:1–23:13)
ii.ii.vi.ii.i. Creation; Chosen People and Peoples of Azazel; Righteous and Sinners (21–22)
21:1 And he said to me, "Look now beneath your feet at the expanse and contemplate the creation which was previously covered over. On this level there is the creation and those who inhabit it and the age that has been prepared to follow it." 21:2 And I looked beneath the expanse at my feet and I saw the likeness of heaven and what was therein. 21:3 And [I saw] there the earth and its fruits, and its moving ones, and its spiritual ones, and its host of men and their spiritual impieties, and their justifications, and the pursuits of their works, and the abyss and its torment, and its lower depths, and the perdition which is in it. 21:4 And I saw there the sea and its islands, and its animals and its fishes, and Leviathan and his spouse, and his lair, and his dens, and the world which lies upon him, and his motions and the destruction of the world because of him. 21:5 I saw there the rivers and their overflows, and their circles. 21:6 And I saw there the tree of Eden and its fruits, and the spring, the river flowing from it, and its trees and their flowering, and I saw those who act righteously. And I saw in it their food and rest. 21:7 And I saw there a great crowd of men, and women, and children, and half of them on the right side of the portrayal, and half of them on the left side of the portrayal. 22:1 And I said, "Eternal Mighty One! What is this picture of creation?" 22:2 And he said to me, "This is my will for existence in design, and it was pleasing to me. And then, afterward, I gave them a command by my word and they came into being. And whatever I had determined to be had already been previously depicted and stood before me in this, as you have seen, before they were created. 22:3 And I said, "O Lord! Mighty and Eternal! Who are the people in the picture on this side and on that?" 22:4 And he said to me, "These who are on the left side are a multitude of tribes who were before and who are destined to be after you: some for judgment and justice, and others for revenge and perdition at the end of the age. 22:5 Those on the right side of the picture are the people set apart for me of the people [that are] with Azazel. These are the ones I have destined to be born of you and to be called my people."
ii.ii.vi.ii.ii. Fall of Man (23:1–13)
23:1 "Look again at the picture, who is the one who seduced Eve, and what is the fruit of the tree. 23:2 And you will know what will happen, and how, to your seed among people in the last days of the age. 23:3 And what you cannot understand, I shall make known to you what was pleasing to me and I shall tell you the things kept in my heart." 23:4 And I looked at the picture, and my eyes ran to the side of the garden of Eden. 23:5 And I saw there a man very great in height and terrible in breadth, incomparable in aspect, entwined with a woman who was also equal to the man in aspect and size. 23:6 And they were standing under a tree of Eden, and the fruit of the tree was like the appearance of a bunch of grapes of vine. 23:7 And behind the tree was standing, as it were, a serpent in form, but having hands and feet like a man, and wings on its shoulders: six on the right side and six on the left. 23:8 And he was holding in his hands the grapes of the tree and feeding the two whom I saw entwined with each other. 23:9 And I said, "Who are these two entwined with each other, or who is this between them, or what is the fruit which they are eating, Mighty Eternal One?" 23:10 And he said, "This is the reason of men, this is Adam, and this is their desire on earth, this is Eve. 23:11 And he who is between them is the Impiety of their pursuits for destruction, Azazel himself." 23:12 And I said, "Eternal Mighty One! Why then did you adjudge to this one such power to destroy humankind by his works on earth?" 23:13 And he said to me, "Hear, Abraham! Those who desire evil and whom I have hated as they are doing these [works], over them I gave him power, and [he is] to be loved by them."
ii.ii.vii. Evil in Man (21:13–26)
ii.ii.vii.i. Question (23:1)
23:14 And I answered and said, "Eternal Mighty One! Why did you will to do so that evil is desired in the heart of man? Since you are angry at what was willed by you, who does a bad thing according to your design."
ii.ii.vii.ii. Answer (24–26)
ii.ii.vii.ii.i. Sins of Heathens (24)
24:1 And he said to me, "Such is the near future of the nations of peoples which are set apart for you after you from your progeny, as you will see in the picture, what is destined to be with them. 24:2 And I shall tell you what and how it will be in the last days. 24:3 Look now at everything in the picture." 24:4 And I looked and saw there what had been in the world before. 24:5 And I saw, as it were, Adam, and Eve with him, and with them the Evil Adversary and Cain, who acted lawlessly because of the Adversary, and the murdered Abel, the perdition brought and given to him through the Lawless One. 24:6 And I saw there fornication and those who desired it, and its defilement and their jealousy; and the fire of their corruption in the lower depths of the earth. 24:7 And I saw there theft and those who hasten after it, and their judgment of retribution {that is—of the great court}. 24:8 I saw there two bare-headed men against me and their shame and the harm against their fellows and their retribution. 24:9 I saw there desire, [and] in its hand the head of every kind of lawlessness and its torment and its dispersal committed to perdition.
ii.ii.vii.ii.ii. Sins of Israel (25)

25:1 I saw there the likeness of the idol of jealousy, as a likeness of a craftsman's [work] such as my father made, and its statue was of shining copper, and a man before it, and he was worshiping it; 25:2 and [there was] an altar opposite it and youths were slaughtered on it before the idol. 25:3 And I said to him, "What is this idol, and what is the altar, and who are those being sacrificed, and who is the sacrificer, and what is the beautiful temple which I see, art and beauty of your glory that lies beneath your throne?" 25:4 And he said, "Hear, Abraham! This temple and altar and the beautiful things which you have seen are my image of the sanctification of the name of my glory, where every prayer of men will dwell, and the gathering of kings and prophets, and the sacrifice which I shall establish to be made for me among my people coming from your progeny. 25:5 And the statue you saw is my anger, because the people who will come to me out of you will make me angry. 25:6 And the man you saw slaughtering is he who angers me. And the sacrifice is the murder of those who are for me a testimony of the close of the judgment in the end of the creation."
ii.ii.vii.ii.iii. Free Will and Predetermination (26)
26:1 And I said, "Eternal, Mighty One! Why did you ordain it to be so? Take back these testimonies!" 26:2 And he said to me, "Hear, Abraham, and understand what I tell you, and answer whatever I ask you. 26:3 Why did your father Terah not listen to your voice and abandon the demonic idolatry until he perished, and all his house with him?" 26:4 And I said, "Eternal Mighty One! Evidently because he did not will to listen to me, nor did I follow his deeds." 26:5 And he said to me, "Hear, Abraham! As the will of your father is in him, as your will is in you, so also the will desired by me is inevitable in coming days which you will not know in advance, nor the things which are in them. 26:6 You will see with your own eyes what will be with your seed. 26:7 Look at the picture!"
ii.ii.viii. Destiny of Israel (27–32)
ii.ii.viii.i. Destruction of the Temple (27)
27:1 And I looked and saw, and behold, the picture swayed, and a heathen people went out from its left side and they captured those who were on the right side: the men, women, and children. 27:2 And some they slaughtered and others they held with them. 27:3 And behold, I saw four hosts coming to them. And they burned the temple with fire, and they carried away the holy things that were in it. 27:4 And I said, "Eternal One! The people you have received from me are brought away by the multitudes of peoples. 27:5 And some they are killing and others they are holding as sojourners. And they burned the temple with fire, and they are capturing and destroying the beautiful things which are in it. 27:6 Eternal One! If this is so, why have you afflicted my heart and why will it be so?" 27:7 And he said to me, "Listen, Abraham, all that you have seen will happen because of your seed who will provoke me, because of the idol and the murder which you saw in the picture in the temple of jealousy. 27:8 And it will be as you have seen. 27:9 And I said, "Eternal Mighty One! Let the evil works of impiety now pass by, but make commandments in them! Since you can do more than the just works of this [?] !" 27:10 And he said to me, "Rather the time of justice will come first with the righteousness of kings. 27:11 And I shall adjudge to them with justice those whom I earlier created in order to rule thence over them. 27:12 And from those [kings] will come men who will trouble them, as I made known to you and you saw."
ii.ii.viii.ii. Exile (28–29:3)
28:1 And I answered and said, "Mighty Eternal One, you who are sanctified in your power, be charitable to my request! As for this reason you made known to me and showed me [divine secrets] when you have brought me up onto your height, 28:2 so for the same reason make it known to me, your beloved, what I ask: whether what I saw will happen to them for long?" 28:3 And he showed me a multitude of his people 28:4 and said to me, "For this reason, my anger at them will come through the four hosts which you saw, and through them will come retribution from me for their works. 28:5 And in the fourth host there are one hundred years and also one hour of the age. And for one hundred years it will be in evil [circumstances] among the heathen and an hour in their mercy and agreement as among the heathen. 29:1 And I said, "Eternal Mighty One! How long a time is an hour of the age?" 29:2 And he said, "I set twelve periods for this impious age to rule over the heathens and over your seed, and what you have seen will be until the end of time. 29:3 And reckon and you will know. Look into the picture!"
ii.ii.viii.iii. False and True Messiahs (29:4–13)
29:4 And I looked and saw a man going out from the left side of the heathen. Men and women and children, great crowds, went out from the side of the heathen and they worshiped him. 29:5 And while I was still looking, those on the right side went out, and some shamed this man, and some struck him, and some worshiped him. 29:6 And I saw that as they worshiped him, Azazel ran and worshiped, and having kissed his face he turned and stood behind him. 29:7 And I said, "Eternal Mighty One! Who is this shamed and struck man, worshiped by the heathen with Azazel?" 29:8 And he answered and said, "Hear, Abraham, the man whom you saw shamed and struck and again worshiped is the laxity of the heathen for the people who will come from you in the last days, in this twelfth hour of the age of impiety. 29:9 And in the [same] twelfth period of the close

of my age I shall set up the man from your seed which you saw. 29:10 Everyone from my people will [finally] admit him, while the sayings of him who was as if called by me will be neglected in their minds. 29:11 And that you saw going out from the left side of the picture and those worshiping him, this [means that] many of the heathen will hope in him. 29:12 And those of your seed you saw on the right side, some shaming and striking him, and some worshiping him, many of them will be misled on his account. 29:13 And he will tempt those of your seed who have worshiped him.

ii.ii.vii.iv. Judgment and Salvation (29:14–21)

29:14 In the close of the twelfth hour, in the ceasing of the age of impiety, before the age of justice will start to grow, my judgment will come upon the heathen who have acted wickedly through the people of your seed who have been set apart for me. 29:15 In those days I shall bring upon all earthly creation ten plagues through evil and disease and the groaning of the bitterness of their soul, 29:16 as I shall bring upon the generations of men who are on it [= earth], because of the anger and the corruption of their deeds with which they provoke me. 29:17 And then from your seed will the righteous men be left, kept by me by number, hastening in the glory of my name to the place prepared beforehand for them, which you saw deserted in the picture. 29:18 And they will live, being sustained by the sacrifices and the offerings of justice and truth in the age of justice. 29:19 And they will rejoice over me forever, and they will destroy those who have destroyed them, and they will rebuke those who have rebuked them by mockery, and those who spit in their faces will be rebuked by me, 29:20 when they will see me joyfully rejoicing with my people and receiving those who return to me in repentance. 29:21 See, Abraham, what you have seen, and hear what you have heard, and know what you have known. Go to your lot! And behold, I am with you forever."

ii.ii.viii.v. Punishment of Heathens and Gathering of Israel (30–31)

30:1 And while he was still speaking, I found myself on the earth, and I said, "Eternal, Mighty One, I am no longer in the glory in which I was above, but what my soul desired to understand I do not understand in my heart." 30:2 And he said to me, "Abraham, I shall tell [you] what your heart desired, for you have sought to know the ten plagues which I prepared against the heathen, and I prepared them beforehand after the passing of the twelve hours on earth. 30:3 Hear what I tell you, it will be thus. 30:4 The first—distress from much violence; the second—the fiery burning of cities; 30:5 the third—destruction of the cattle by pestilence; the fourth—famine in their native land, 30:6 the fifth—destruction in their domains through the ravage of earthquake and sword; the sixth—hail and increase of snow; 30:7 the seventh—wild beasts will be their grave; the eighth—famine and pestilence will take turns in their destruction; 30:8 the ninth—punishment by the sword and flight in distress; the tenth—thunder and voices, and ravaging earthquakes. 31:1 Then I shall sound the trumpet from the sky, and I shall send my chosen one, having in him one measure of all my power, and he will summon my people blamed among the heathen. 31:2 And I shall burn with fire those who mocked them ruling over them in this age and I shall commit those who have covered me with mockery to the reproach of the coming age. 31:3 Since I have destined them to be food for the fire of hell, and ceaseless soaring in the air of the underground depths, the contents of a worm's belly. 31:4 For those who do justice, who have chosen my will and clearly kept my commandments, will see them. And they will rejoice with joy at the destruction of the abandoned. 31:5 And those who followed after the idols and after their murders will rot in the womb of the Evil One—the belly of Azazel, and they will be burned by the fire of Azazel's tongue. 31:6 Since I waited until they came to me, and they did not want it. 31:7 And they glorified an alien. 31:8 And they joined one to whom they had not been allotted, and they abandoned the prevailing Lord. 31:9 Therefore, hear, Abraham, and see! Behold, your seventh generation will go with you. 31:10 And they will go out into an alien land. 31:11 And they will be enslaved and distressed for about one hour of the impious age. 31:12 And of the people whom they will serve—I am the judge."

Book 115. The Letter of Aristeas

Since I have collected Material for a memorable history of my visit to Eleazar the High priest of the Jews, and because you, Philocrates, as you lose no opportunity of reminding me, have set great store upon receiving an account of the motives and object of my mission, I have attempted to draw up a clear exposition of the matter for you, for I perceive that you possess a natural love of learning, 2 a quality which is the highest possession of man - to be constantly attempting 'to add to his stock of knowledge and acquirements' whether through the study of history or by actually participating in the events themselves. It is by this means, by taking up into itself the noblest elements, that the soul is established in purity, and having fixed its aim on piety, the noblest goal of all, it uses this as its infallible guide and so acquires a definite purpose. 3 It was my devotion to the pursuit of religious knowledge that led me to undertake the embassy to the man I have mentioned, who was held in the highest esteem by his own citizens and by others both for his virtue and his majesty and who had in his possession documents of the highest value to the

Jews in his own country and in foreign lands for the interpretation of the divine law, for their 4 laws are written on leather parchments in Jewish characters. This embassy then I undertook with enthusiasm, having first of all found an opportunity of pleading with the king on behalf of the Jewish captives who had been transported from Judea to Egypt by the king's father, when he first obtained possession of this city and conquered the land of Egypt. It is worth while that I should tell 5 you this story, too, since I am convinced that you, with your disposition towards holiness and your sympathy with men who are living in accordance with the holy law, will all the more readily listen to the account which I purpose to set forth, since you yourself have lately come to us from the island and are anxious to hear everything that tends to build up the soul. 6 On a former occasion, too I sent you a record of the facts which I thought worth relating about the Jewish race - the record 7 which I had obtained from the most learned high priests of the most learned land of Egypt. As you are so eager to acquire the knowledge of those things which can benefit the mind, I feel it incumbent upon me to impart to you all the information in my power. I should feel the same duty towards all who possessed the same disposition but I feel it especially towards you since you have aspirations which are so noble, and since you are not only my brother in character no less than in blood but are one with me as well in the pursuit of goodness. 8 For neither the pleasure derived from gold nor any other of the possessions which are prized by shallow minds confers the same benefit as the pursuit of culture and the study which we expend in securing it. But that I may not weary you by a too lengthy introduction, I will proceed at once to the substance of my narrative.

9 Demetrius of Phalerum, the president of the king's library, received vast sums of money, for the purpose of collecting together, as far as he possibly could, all the books in the world. By means of purchase and transcription, he carried out, to the best of his ability, the purpose of the king. On one occasion when I was present he was asked, How many thousand books are there in the library? 10 and he replied, 'More than two hundred thousand, O king, and I shall make endeavour in the immediate future to gather together the remainder also, so that the total of five hundred thousand may be reached. I am told that the laws of the Jews are worth transcribing and deserve a place in 11 your library.' 'What is to prevent you from doing this?' replied the king. 'Everything that is necessary has been placed at your disposal.' 'They need to be translated,' answered Demetrius, 'for in the country of the Jews they use a peculiar alphabet (just as the Egyptians, too, have a special form of letters) and speak a peculiar dialect. They are supposed to use the Syriac tongue, but this is not the case; their language is quite different.' And the king when he understood all the facts of the case ordered a letter to be written to the Jewish High Priest that his purpose (which has already been described) might be accomplished.

12 Thinking that the time had come to press the demand, which I had often laid before Sosibius of Tarentum and Andreas, the chief of the bodyguard, for the emancipation of the Jews who had been transported from Judea by the king's father - 13 for when by a combination of good fortune and courage he had brought his attack on the whole district of Coele-Syria and Phoenicia to a successful issue, in the process of terrorizing the country into subjection, he transported some of his foes and others he reduced to captivity. The number of those whom he transported from the country of the Jews to Egypt amounted to no less than a hundred thousand. Of these he armed thirty thousand picked men and settled them in garrisons in the country districts. (And even before this time large numbers of Jews had come into Egypt with the Persian, and in an earlier period still others had been sent to Egypt to help Psammetichus in his campaign against the king of the Ethiopians. But these were nothing like so numerous as the captives whom Ptolemy the son of Lagus transported.) 14 As I have already said Ptolemy picked out the best of these, the men who were in the prime of life and distinguished for their courage, and armed them, but the great mass of the others, those who were too old or too young for this purpose, and the women too, he reduced to slavery, not that he wished to do this of his own free will, but he was compelled by his soldiers who claimed them as a reward for the services which they had rendered in war. Having, as has already been stated, obtained an opportunity for securing their emancipation, I addressed the king with the following arguments. 'Let us not be so unreasonable as to allow 15 our deeds to give the lie to our words. Since the law which we wish not only to transcribe but also to translate belongs to the whole Jewish race, what justification shall we be able to find for our embassy while such vast numbers of them remain in a state of slavery in your kingdom? In the perfection and wealth of your clemency release those who are held in such miserable bondage, since as I have been at pains to discover, the God who gave them their law is the God who maintains your kingdom. They worship the same God - the Lord and Creator of the Universe, as all other men, as we ourselves, O king, though we call him by different names, such as Zeus or 16 Dis. This name was very appropriately bestowed upon him by our first ancestors, in order to signify that He through whom all things are endowed with life and come into being, is necessarily the ruler and lord of the Universe. Set all mankind an example of magnanimity by releasing those who are held in bondage.'

17 After a brief interval, while I was offering up an earnest prayer to God that He would so dispose the mind of the king that all the captives might be set at liberty-(for the human race, being the creation of God, is swayed and influenced by Him. Therefore with many divers prayers I called upon Him who ruleth the heart that the king might be constrained to grant my request. For I had 18 great hopes with regard to the salvation of the men since I was assured that God would grant a fulfilment of my prayer. For when men from pure motives plan some action in the interest of right-eousness and the performance of noble deeds, Almighty God brings their efforts and purposes to a successful issue) - the king raised his head and looking up at me with a cheerful countenance asked, 'How many thousands do you think they will number?' Andreas, who was standing near, replied, 'A little more than a hundred thousand.' 'It is a small boon indeed,' said the king, 'that Aristeas asks of us!' 19 Then Sosibius and some others who were present said, 'Yes, but it will be a fit tribute to your magnanimity for you to offer the enfranchisement of these men as an act of devotion to the supreme God. You have been greatly honoured by Almighty God and exalted above all your forefathers in glory and it is only fitting that you should render to Him the greatest thank offering in your power.' Extremely pleased with these arguments he gave orders that an addition should be 20 made to the wages of the soldiers by the amount of the redemption money that twenty drachmae should be paid to the owners for every slave, that a public order should be issued and that registers of the captives should be attached to it. He showed the greatest enthusiasm in the business, for it was God who had brought our purpose to fulfilment in its entirety and constrained him to redeem not only those who had come into Egypt with the army of his father but any who had come before that time or had been subsequently brought into the kingdom. It was pointed out to him that the ransom money would exceed four hundred talents.

21 I think it will be useful to insert a copy of the decree, for in this way the magnanimity of the king, who was empowered by God to save such vast multitudes, will be made clearer and more 22 manifest. The decree of the king ran as follows:

'All who served in the army of our father in the campaign against Syria and Phoenicia and in the attack upon the country of the Jews and became possessed of Jewish captives and brought them back to the city of Alexandria and the land of Egypt or sold them to others - and in the same way any captives who were in our land before that time or were brought hither afterwards- all who possess such captives are required to set them at liberty at once, receiving twenty drachmae per head as ransom money. The soldiers will receive 23 this money as a gift added to their wages, the others from the king's treasury. We think that it was against our father's will and against all propriety that they should have been made captives and that the devastation of their land and the transportation of the Jews to Egypt was an act of military wantonness. The spoil which fell to the soldiers on the field of battle was all the booty which they should have claimed. To reduce the people to slavery in addition was an act of absolute injustice. 24 Wherefore since it is acknowledged that we are accustomed to render justice to all men and especially to those who are unfairly in a condition of servitude, and since we strive to deal fairly with all men according to the demands of justice and piety, we have decreed, in reference to the persons of the Jews who are in any condition of bondage in any part of our dominion, that those who possess them shall receive the stipulated sum of money and set them at liberty and that no man shall show any tardiness in discharging his obligations. Within three days after the publication of this decree, they must make lists of slaves for the officers appointed to carry out our will, 25 and immediately produce the persons of the captives. For we consider that it will be advantageous to us and to our affairs that the matter should be brought to a conclusion. Any one who likes may give information about any who disobey the decree on condition that if the man is proved guilty he will become his slave; his property, however, will be handed over to the royal treasury.'

26 When the decree was brought to be read over to the king for his approval, it contained all the other provisions except the phrase 'any captives who were in the land before that time or were brought hither afterwards,' and in his magnanimity and the largeness of his heart the king inserted this clause and gave orders that the grant of money required for the redemption should be deposited in full with the paymasters of the forces and the royal bankers, and so the matter was decided and the 27 decree ratified within seven days. The grant for the redemption amounted to more than six hundred and sixty talents; for many infants at the breast were emancipated together with their mothers. When the question was raised whether the sum of twenty talents was to be paid for these, the king ordered that it should be done, and thus he carried out his decision in the most comprehensive way. 28 When this had been done, he ordered Demetrius to draw up a memorial with regard to the transcription of the Jewish books. For all affairs of state used to be carried out by means of decrees and with the most painstaking accuracy by these Egyptian kings, and nothing was done in a slipshod or haphazard fashion. And so I have inserted copies of the memorial and the letters, the number of the presents sent and the nature of each, since every one of them excelled

in 29 magnificence and technical skill. The following is a copy of the memorial.

The Memorial of Demetrius to the great king. 'Since you have given me instructions, O king, that the books which are needed to complete your library should be collected together, and that those which are defective should be repaired, I have devoted myself with the utmost care to the fulfilment of your wishes, 30 and I now have the following proposal to lay before you. The books of the law of the Jews (with some few others) are absent from the library. They are written in the Hebrew characters and language and have been carelessly interpreted, and do not represent the original text as I am 31 informed by those who know; for they have never had a king's care to protect them. It is necessary that these should be made accurate for your library since the law which they contain, in as much as it is of divine origin, is full of wisdom and free from all blemish. For this reason literary men and poets and the mass of historical writers have held aloof from referring to these books and the men who have lived and are living in accordance with them, because their 32 conception of life is so sacred and religious, as Hecataeus of Abdera says. If it please you, O king, a letter shall be written to the High Priest in Jerusalem, asking him to send six elders out of every tribe - men who have lived the noblest life and are most skilled in their law - that we may find out the points in which the majority of them are in agreement, and so having obtained an accurate translation may place it in a conspicuous place in a manner worthy of the work itself and your purpose. May continual prosperity be yours!'

33 When this memorial had been presented, the king ordered a letter to be written to Eleazar on the matter, giving also an account of the emancipation of the Jewish captives. And he gave fifty talents weight of gold and seventy talents of silver and a large quantity of precious stones to make bowls and vials and a table and libation cups. He also gave orders to those who had the custody of his coffers to allow the artificers to make a selection of any materials they might require for the purpose, and that a hundred talents in money should be sent to provide sacrifices for the temple and 34 for other needs. I shall give you a full account of the workmanship after I have set before you copies of the letters. The letter of the king ran as follows:

35 'King Ptolemy sends greeting and salutation to the High Priest Eleazar. Since there are many Jews settled in our realm who were carried off from Jerusalem by the Persians at the time of their 36 power and many more who came with my father into Egypt as captives - large numbers of these he placed in the army and paid them higher wages than usual, and when he had proved the loyalty of their leaders he built fortresses and placed them in their charge that the native Egyptians might be intimidated by them. And I, when I ascended the throne, adopted a kindly attitude towards all 37 my subjects, and more particularly to those who were citizens of yours - I have set at liberty more than a hundred thousand captives, paying their owners the appropriate market price for them, and if ever evil has been done to your people through the passions of the mob, I have made them reparation. The motive which prompted my action has been the desire to act piously and render unto the supreme God a thank offering for maintaining my kingdom in peace and great glory in all the world. Moreover those of your people who were in the prime of life I have drafted into my army, and those who were fit to be attached to my person and worthy of the confidence of the 38 court, I have established in official positions. Now since I am anxious to show my gratitude to these men and to the Jews throughout the world and to the generations yet to come, I have determined that your law shall be translated from the Hebrew tongue which is in use amongst you 39 into the Greek language, that these books may be added to the other royal books in my library. It will be a kindness on your part and a regard for my zeal if you will select six elders from each of your tribes, men of noble life and skilled in your law and able to interpret it, that in questions of dispute we may be able to discover the verdict in which the majority agree, for the investigation is of the highest possible importance. I hope to win great renown by the accomplishment of this 40 work. I have sent Andreas, the chief of my bodyguard, and Aristeas - men whom I hold in high esteem - to lay the matter before you and present you with a hundred talents of silver, the firstfruits of my offering for the temple and the sacrifices and other religious rites. If you will write to me concerning your wishes in these matters, you will confer a great favour upon me and afford me a new pledge of friendship, for all your wishes shall be carried out as speedily as possible. Farewell.'

41 To this letter Eleazar replied appropriately as follows:

'Eleazar the High priest sends greetings to King Ptolemy his true friend. My highest wishes are for your welfare and the welfare of Queen Arsinoe your sister and your children. I also am well. I have received your letter and am greatly 42 rejoiced by your purpose and your noble counsel. I summoned together the whole people and read it to them that they might know of your devotion to our God. I showed them too the cups which you sent, twenty of gold and thirty of silver, the five bowls and the table of dedication, and the hundred talents of silver for the offering of the sacrifices and providing the things of which the 43 temple stands in need. These gifts were brought to me by Andreas, one of your most honoured servants, and by Aristeas, both good men and true, distinguished by their learning, and worthy in every way to be the representatives of your high principles and righteous purposes. 44 These men imparted to me your message and received from me an answer in agreement with your letter. I will consent to everything which is advantageous to you even though your request is very unusual. For you have bestowed upon our citizens great and never to be forgotten benefits in many 45 (ways). Immediately therefore I offered sacrifices on behalf of you, your sister, your children, and your friends, and all the people prayed that your plans might prosper continually, and that Almighty God might preserve your kingdom in peace with honour, and that the translation of the 46 holy law might prove advantageous to you and be carried out successfully. In the presence of all the people I selected six elders from each tribe, good men and true, and I have sent them to you with a copy of our law. It will be a kindness, O righteous king, if you will give instruction that as soon as the translation of the law is completed, the men shall be restored again to us in safety. Farewell.'

47 The following are the names of the elders: Of the first tribe, Joseph, Ezekiah, Zachariah, John, Ezekiah, Elisha. Of the second tribe, Judas, Simon, Samuel, Adaeus, Mattathias, Eschlemias. Of 48 the third tribe, Nehemiah, Joseph, Theodosius, Baseas, Ornias, Dakis. Of the fourth tribe, Jonathan, Abraeus, Elisha, Ananias, Chabrias.... Of the fifth tribe, Isaac, Jacob, Jesus, 49 Sabbataeus, Simon, Levi. Of the sixth tribe, Judas, Joseph, Simon, Zacharias, Samuel, Selemias. Of the seventh tribe, Sabbataeus, Zedekiah, Jacob, Isaac, Jesias, Natthaeus. Of the eighth tribe Theodosius, Jason, Jesus, Theodotus, John, Jonathan. Of the ninth tribe, Theophilus, Abraham 50 Arsamos, Jason, Endemias, Daniel. Of the tenth tribe, Jeremiah, Eleazar, Zachariah, Baneas, Elisha, Dathaeus. Of the eleventh tribe, Samuel, Joseph, Judas, Jonathes, Chabu, Dositheus. Of the twelfth tribe, Isaelus, John, Theodosius, Arsamos, Abietes, Ezekiel. They were seventy-two in all. Such was the answer which Eleazar and his friends gave to the king's letter.

51 I will now proceed to redeem my promise and give a description of the works of art. They were wrought with exceptional skill, for the king spared no expense and personally superintended the workmen individually. They could not therefore scamp any part of the work or finish it off negligently. 52 First of all I will give you a description of the table. The king was anxious that this piece of work should be of exceptionally large dimensions, and he caused enquiries to be made of the Jews 53 in the locality with regard to the size of the table already in the temple at Jerusalem. And when they described the measurements, he proceeded to ask whether he might make a larger structure. And some of the priests and the other Jews replied that there was nothing to prevent him. And he said that he was anxious to make it five times the size, but he hesitated lest it should prove useless 54 for the temple services. He was desirous that his gift should not merely be stationed in the temple, for it would afford him much greater pleasure if the men whose duty it was to offer the fitting 55 sacrifices were able to do so appropriately on the table which he had made. He did not suppose that it was owing to lack of gold that the former table had been made of small size, but there seems to have been, he said, some reason why it was made of this dimension. For had the order been given, there would have been no lack of means. Wherefore we must not transgress or go beyond the proper 56 measure. At the same time he ordered them to press into service all the manifold forms of art, for he was a man of the most lofty conceptions and nature had endowed him with a keen imagination which enabled him to picture the appearance which would be presented by the finished work. He gave orders too, that where there were no instructions laid down in the Jewish Scriptures, everything should be made as beautiful as possible. When such instructions were laid down, they were to be carried out to the letter.

57 They made the table two cubits long (one cubit broad) one and a half cubits high, fashioning it of pure solid gold. What I am describing was not thin gold laid over another foundation, but the whole 58 structure was of massive gold welded together. And they made a border of a hand's breadth round about it. And there was a wreath of wave-work, engraved in relief in the form of ropes marvelously 59 wrought on its three sides. For it was triangular in shape and the style of the work was exactly the same on each of the sides, so that whichever side they were turned, they presented the same appearance. Of the two sides under the border, the one which sloped down to the table was a very 60 beautiful piece of work, but it was the outer side which attracted the gaze of the spectator. Now the upper edge of the two sides, being elevated, was sharp since, as we have said, the rim was three-sided, from whatever point of view one approached it. And there were layers of precious stones on it in the midst of the embossed cord-work, and they were interwoven with one another by an inimitable artistic 61 device. For the sake of security they were all fixed by golden needles which were inserted in 62 perforations in the stones. At the sides they were clamped together by fastenings to hold them firm. On the part of the border round the table which slanted upwards and met the eyes, there was wrought a pattern of eggs in precious stones, elaborately engraved by a continuous piece of fluted relief-work, closely 63 connected together round the whole table. And under the stones which had been arranged to represent eggs the artists made a crown containing all kinds of fruits, having at its top clusters of grapes and ears of corn, dates also and apples, and pomegranates and the like, conspicuously arranged. These fruits were wrought out of precious stones, of the same colour as the fruits themselves and 64 they fastened them edgeways round all the sides of the table with a band of gold. And after the crown of fruit had been put on, underneath there was inserted another pattern of eggs in precious stones, and other fluting and embossed work, that both sides of the table might be used, according to the wishes of the owners and for this reason the wave-work and the border were extended 65 down to the feet of the table. They made and fastened under the whole width of the table a massive plate four fingers thick, that the feet might be inserted into it, and clamped fast with linch-pins which fitted into sockets under the border, so that which ever side of the table people preferred, might be used. Thus it became manifestly clear that the work was intended to be used 66 either way. On the table itself they engraved a 'maeander', having precious stones standing out in the middle of it, rubies and emeralds and an onyx too and many other kinds of stones which excel 67 in beauty. And next to the 'maeander' there was placed a wonderful piece of network, which made the centre of the table appear like a rhomboid in shape, and on it a crystal and amber, as it is called, 68 had been wrought, which produced an incomparable impression on the beholders. They made the feet of the table with heads like lilies, so that they seemed to be like lilies bending down beneath the table, and the parts which were visible represented leaves which stood upright. 69 The basis of the foot on the ground consisted of a ruby and measured a hand's breadth high all round. It had the appearance of a shoe and was eight fingers broad. Upon it the whole expanse of the foot rested. 70 And they made the foot appear like ivy growing out of the stone, interwoven with akanthus and surrounded with a vine which encircled it with clusters of grapes, which were worked in stones, up to the top of the foot. All the four feet were made in the same style, and everything was wrought and fitted so skillfully, and such remarkable skill and knowledge were expended upon making it true to nature, that when the air was stirred by a breath of wind, movement was imparted to the leaves, and 71 everything was fashioned to correspond with the actual reality which it represented. And they made the top of the table in three parts like a triptychon, and they were so fitted and dovetailed together with spigots along the whole breadth of the work, that the meeting of the joints could not be seen or even discovered. The thickness of the table was not less than half a cubit, so that the whole work 72 must have cost many talents. For since the king did not wish to add to its size he expended on the details the same sum of money which would have been required if the table could have been of larger dimensions. And everything was completed in accordance with his plan, in a most wonderful and remarkable way, with inimitable art and incomparable beauty.

73 Of the mixing bowls, two were wrought (in gold), and from the base to the middle were engraved with relief work in the pattern of scales, and between the scales precious stones were inserted with 74 great artistic skill. Then there was a 'maeander' a cubit in height, with its surface wrought out of precious stones of many colours, displaying great artistic effort and beauty. Upon this there was a mosaic, worked in the form of a rhombus, having a net-like appearance and reaching right up to the 75 brim. In the middle, small shields which were made of different precious stones, placed alternately and varying in kind, not less than four fingers broad enhanced the beauty of their appearance. On the top of the brim there was an ornament of lilies in bloom, and intertwining clusters of grapes were 76 engraven all round. Such then was the construction of the golden bowls, and they held more than two firkins each. The silver bowls had a smooth surface, and were wonderfully made as if they were intended for looking-glasses, so that everything which was brought near to them was reflected even more 77 clearly than in mirrors. But it is impossible to describe the real impression which these works of art produced upon the mind when they were finished. For, when these vessels had been completed and placed side by side, first a silver bowl and then a golden, then another silver, and then another golden, the appearance they presented is altogether indescribable, and those who came to see 78 them were not able to tear themselves from the brilliant sight and entrancing, spectacle. The impressions produced by the spectacle were various in kind. When men looked at the golden vessels, and their minds made a complete survey of each detail of workmanship, their souls were thrilled with wonder. Again when a man wished to direct his gaze to the silver vessels, as they stood before him, everything seemed to flash with light round about the place where he was standing, and afforded a still greater delight to the onlookers. So that it is really impossible to describe the artistic beauty of the works. 79 The golden vials they engraved in the centre with vine wreaths. And about the rims they wove a wreath of ivy and myrtle and olive in relief work and inserted precious stones in it. The other parts of the relief work they wrought in different patterns, since they made it a point of honour to 80 complete everything in a way worthy of the majesty of the king. In a word it may be said that neither in the king's treasury nor in any other, were there any works which equalled these in costliness or in artistic skill. For the king spent no little thought upon them, for he loved to gain glory for the 81 excellence of his designs.

For oftentimes he would neglect his official business, and spend his time with the artists in his anxiety that they should complete everything in a manner worthy of the place to which the gifts were to be sent. So everything was carried out on a grand scale, in a manner 82 worthy of the king who sent the gifts and of the high priest who was the ruler of the land. There was no stint of precious stones, for not less than five thousand were used and they were all of large size. The most exceptional artistic skill was employed, so that the cost of the stones and the workmanship was five times as much as that of the gold.

83 I have given you this description of the presents because I thought it was necessary. The next point in the narrative is an account of our journey to Eleazar, but I will first of all give you a description of the whole country. When we arrived in the land of the Jews we saw the city situated 84 in the middle of the whole of Judea on the top of a mountain of considerable altitude. On the summit the temple had been built in all its splendour. It was surrounded by three walls more than seventy cubits high and in length and breadth corresponding to the structure of the edifice. All the buildings 85 were characterized by a magnificence and costliness quite unprecedented. It was obvious that no expense had been spared on the door and the fastenings, which connected it with the doorposts, and 86 the stability of the lintel. The style of the curtain too was thoroughly in proportion to that of the entrance. Its fabric owing to the draught of wind was in perpetual motion, and as this motion was communicated from the bottom and the curtain bulged out to its highest extent, it afforded a pleasant 87 spectacle from which a man could scarcely tear himself away. The construction of the altar was in keeping with the place itself and with the burnt offerings which were consumed by fire upon it, and the approach to it was on a similar scale. There was a gradual slope up to it, conveniently arranged for the purpose of decency, and the ministering priests were robed in linen garments, down to their 88 ankles. The Temple faces the east and its back is toward the west. The whole of the floor is paved with stones and slopes down to the appointed places, that water may be conveyed to wash away the 89 blood from the sacrifices, for many thousand beasts are sacrificed there on the feast days. And there is an inexhaustible supply of water, because an abundant natural spring gushes up from within the temple area. There are moreover wonderful and indescribable cisterns underground, as they pointed out to me, at a distance of five furlongs all round the site of the temple, and each of them has countless pipes 90 so that the different streams converge together. And all these were fastened with lead at the bottom and at the sidewalls, and over them a great quantity of plaster had been spread, and every part of the work had been most carefully carried out. There are many openings for water at the base of the altar which are invisible to all except to those who are engaged in the ministration, so that all the blood of the sacrifices which is collected in great quantities is washed away in the twinkling of an 91 eye. Such is my opinion with regard to the character of the reservoirs and I will now show you how it was confirmed. They led me more than four furlongs outside the city and bade me peer down towards a certain spot and listen to the noise that was made by the meeting of the waters, so that the great size of the reservoirs became manifest to me, as has already been pointed out.

92 The ministration of the priests is in every way unsurpassed both for its physical endurance and for its orderly and silent service. For they all work spontaneously, though it entails much painful exertion, and each one has a special task allotted to him. The service is carried on without interruption - some provide the wood, others the oil, others the fine wheat flour, others the spices; others 93 again bring the pieces of flesh for the burnt offering, exhibiting a wonderful degree of strength. For they take up with both hands the limbs of a calf, each of them weighing more than two talents, and throw them with each hand in a wonderful way on to the high place of the altar and never miss placing them on the proper spot. In the same way the pieces of the sheep and also of the goats are wonderful both for their weight and their fatness. For those, whose business it is, always select the beasts which are without blemish and specially fat, and thus the sacrifice which I have described, 94 is carried out. There is a special place set apart for them to rest in, where those who are relieved from duty sit. When this takes place, those who have already rested and are ready to assume their duties rise up spontaneously since there is no one to give orders with regard to the arrangement of 95 the sacrifices. The most complete silence reigns so that one might imagine that there was not a single person present, though there are actually seven hundred men engaged in the work, besides the vast number of those who are occupied in bringing up the sacrifices. Everything is carried out with 96 reverence and in a way worthy of the great God.

We were greatly astonished, when we saw Eleazar engaged in the ministration, at the mode of his dress, and the majesty of his appearance, which was revealed in the robe which he wore and the precious stones upon his person. There were golden bells upon the garment which reached down to his feet, giving forth a peculiar kind of melody, and on both sides of them there were pomegranates 97 with variegated flowers of a wonderful hue. He was girded with a girdle of conspicuous beauty, woven in the most beautiful colours. On his breast he wore the oracle of God, as it is called, on which twelve stones, of different kinds, were inset,

fastened together with gold, containing the names of the leaders of the tribes, according to their original order, each one flashing forth in an indescribable way 98 its own particular colour. On his head he wore a tiara, as it is called, and upon this in the middle of his forehead an inimitable turban, the royal diadem full of glory with the name of God inscribed in sacred letters on a plate of gold . . . having been judged worthy to wear these emblems in the 99 ministrations. Their appearance created such awe and confusion of mind as to make one feel that one had come into the presence of a man who belonged to a different world. I am convinced that any one who takes part in the spectacle which I have described will be filled with astonishment and indescribable wonder and be profoundly affected in his mind at the thought of the sanctity which is attached to each detail of the service.

100 But in order that we might gain complete information, we ascended to the summit of the neighbouring citadel and looked around us. It is situated in a very lofty spot, and is fortified with many towers, which have been built up to the very top of immense stones, with the object, as we were informed, of 101 guarding the temple precincts, so that if there were an attack, or an insurrection or an onslaught of the enemy, no one would be able to force an entrance within the walls that surround the temple. On the towers of the citadel engines of war were placed and different kinds of machines, and the position was 102 much higher than the circle of walls which I have mentioned. The towers were guarded too by most trusty men who had given the utmost proof of their loyalty to their country. These men were never allowed to leave the citadel, except on feast days and then only in detachments. nor did they permit any 103 stranger to enter it. They were also very careful when any command came from the chief officer to admit any visitors to inspect the place, as our own experience taught us. They were very reluctant to 104 admit us - though we were but two unarmed men- to view the offering of the sacrifices. And they asserted that they were bound by an oath when the trust was committed to them, for they had all sworn and were bound to carry out the oath sacredly to the letter, that though they were five hundred in number they would not permit more than five men to enter at one time. The citadel was the special protection of the temple and its founder had fortified it so strongly that it might efficiently protect it.

105 The size of the city is of moderate dimensions. It is about forty furlongs in circumference, as far as one could conjecture. It has its towers arranged in the shape of a theatre, with thoroughfares leading between them. Now the cross roads of the lower towers are visible but those of the upper 106 towers are more frequented. For the ground ascends, since the city is built upon a mountain. There are steps too which lead up to the cross roads, and some people are always going up, and others down and they keep as far apart from each other as possible on the road because of those who 107 are bound by the rules of purity, lest they should touch anything which is unlawful. It was not without reason that the original founders of the city built it in due proportions, for they possessed clear insight with regard to what was required. For the country is extensive and beautiful. Some parts of it are level, especially the districts which belong to Samaria, as it is called, and which border on the land of the Idumeans, other parts are mountainous, especially (those which are contiguous to the land of Judea). The people therefore are bound to devote themselves to agriculture and the cultivation of the soil that by this means they may have a plentiful supply of crops. In this way 108 cultivation of every kind is carried on and an abundant harvest reaped in the whole of the aforesaid land. The cities which are large and enjoy a corresponding prosperity are well-populated, but they neglect the country districts, since all men are inclined to a life of enjoyment, for every one has a natural tendency towards the pursuit of pleasure. 109 The same thing happened in Alexandria, which excels all cities in size and prosperity. Country people by migrating from the rural districts and settling 110 in the city brought agriculture into disrepute: and so to prevent them from settling in the city, the king issued orders that they should not stay in it for more than twenty days. And in the same way he gave the judges written instructions, that if it was necessary to issue a summons against any one 111 who lived in the country, the case must be settled within five days. And since he considered the matter one of great importance, he appointed also legal officers for every district with their assistants, that the farmers and their advocates might not in the interests of business empty the granaries of the 112 city, I mean, of the produce of husbandry. I have permitted this digression because it was Eleazar who pointed out with great clearness the points which have been mentioned. For great is the energy which they expend on the tillage of the soil. For the land is thickly planted with multitudes of olive trees, with crops of corn and pulse, with vines too, and there is abundance of honey. Other kinds of fruit trees and dates do not count compared with these. There are cattle of all kinds in 113 great quantities and a rich pasturage for them. Wherefore they rightly recognize that the country districts need a large population, and the relations between the city and the villages are properly 114 regulated. A great quantity of spices and precious stones and gold is brought into the country by the Arabs. For the country is well adapted not only for agriculture but also for commerce, and the 115 city is rich in the arts and lacks none of the merchan-

dise which is brought across the sea. It possesses too suitable and commodious harbours at Askalon, Joppa, and Gaza, as well as at Ptolemais which was founded by the King and holds a central position compared with the other places named, being not far distant from any of them. The country produces everything in abundance, 116 since it is well watered in all directions and well protected from storms. The river Jordan, as it is called, which never runs dry, flows through the land. Originally (the country) contained not less than 60 million acres-though afterwards the neighbouring peoples made incursions against it - and 600,000 men were settled upon it in farms of a hundred acres each. The river like the Nile rises in harvest- time and irrigates a large portion of the land. Near the district belonging to the people of 117 Ptolemais it issues into another river and this flows out into the sea. Other mountain torrents, as they are called, flow down into the plain and encompass the parts about Gaza and the district of 118 Ashdod. The country is encircled by a natural fence and is very difficult to attack and cannot be assailed by large forces, owing to the narrow passes, with their overhanging precipices and deep ravines, and the rugged character of the mountainous regions which surround all the land. 119 We were told that from the neighbouring mountains of Arabia copper and iron were formerly obtained. This was stopped, however, at the time of the Persian rule, since the authorities of the time spread 120 abroad a false report that the working of the mines was useless and expensive, in order to prevent their country from being destroyed by the mining in these districts and possibly taken away from them owing to the Persian rule, since by the assistance of this false report they found an excuse for entering the district.

I have now, my dear brother Philocrates, given you all the essential information upon this subject 121 in brief form. I shall describe the work of translation in the sequel. The High priest selected men of the finest character and the highest culture, such as one would expect from their noble parentage. They were men who had not only acquired proficiency in Jewish literature, but had studied most 122 carefully that of the Greeks as well. They were specially qualified therefore for serving on embassies and they undertook this duty whenever it was necessary. They possessed a great facility for conferences and the discussion of problems connected with the law. They espoused the middle course - and this is always the best course to pursue. They abjured the rough and uncouth manner, but they were altogether above pride and never assumed an air of superiority over others, and in conversation they were ready to listen and give an appropriate answer to every question. And all of them carefully observed this rule and were anxious above everything else to excel each other in 123 its observance and they were all of them worthy of their leader and of his virtue. And one could observe how they loved Eleazar by their unwillingness to be torn away from him and how he loved them. For besides the letter which he wrote to the king concerning their safe return, he also earnestly 124 besought Andreas to work for the same end and urged me, too, to assist to the best of my ability and although we promised to give our best attention to the matter, he said that he was still greatly distressed, for he knew that the king out of the goodness of his nature considered it his highest privilege, whenever he heard of a man who was superior to his fellows in culture and wisdom, to 125 summon him to his court. For I have heard of a fine saying of his to the effect that by securing just and prudent men about his person he would secure the greatest protection for his kingdom, since such friends would unreservedly give him the most beneficial advice. And the men who were 126 now being sent to him by Eleazar undoubtedly possessed these qualities. And he frequently asserted upon oath that he would never let the men go if it were merely some private interest of his own that constituted the impelling motive-but it was for the common advantage of 127 all the citizens that he was sending them. For, he explained, the good life consists in the keeping of the enactments of the law, and this end is achieved much more by hearing than by reading. From this and other similar statements it was clear what his feelings towards them were.

128 It is worth while to mention briefly the information which he gave in reply to our questions. For I suppose that most people feel a curiosity with regard to some of the enactments in the law, 129 especially those about meats and drinks and animals recognized as unclean. When we asked why, since there is but one form of creation, some animals are regarded as unclean for eating, and others unclean even to the touch (for though the law is scrupulous on most points, it is specially scrupulous on such 130 matters as these) he began his reply as follows: 'You observe,' he said, 'what an effect our modes of life and our associations produce upon us; by associating with the bad, men catch their depravities and become miserable throughout their life; but if they live with the wise and prudent, they find 131 the means of escaping from ignorance and amending their lives. Our Lawgiver first of all laid down the principles of piety and righteousness and inculcated them point by point, not merely by prohibitions but by the use of examples as well, demonstrating the injurious effects of sin and the 132 punishments inflicted by God upon the guilty. For he proved first of all that there is only one God and that his power is manifested throughout the universe, since every place is filled with his sovereignty and none of the things which are wrought in secret by men upon the earth escapes His knowledge. For all that a man does

and all that is to come to pass in the future are manifest to 133 Him. Working out these truths carefully and having made them plain he showed that even if a man should think of doing evil - to say nothing of actually effecting it - 134 he would not escape detection, for he made it clear that the power of God pervaded the whole of the law. 135 Beginning from this starting point he went on to show that all mankind except ourselves believe in the existence of many gods, though they themselves are much more powerful than the beings whom they vainly worship. For when they have made statues of stone and wood, they say that they are the images of those who have invented something useful for life and they worship them, though 136 they have clear proof that they possess no feeling. For it would be utterly foolish to suppose that any one became a god in virtue of his inventions. For the inventors simply took certain objects already created and by combining them together, showed that they possessed a fresh utility: they 137 did not themselves create the substance of the thing, and so it is a vain and foolish thing for people to make gods of men like themselves. For in our times there are many who are much more inventive and much more learned than the men of former days who have been deified, and yet they would never come to worship them. The makers and authors of these myths think that they are 138 the wisest of the Greeks. Why need we speak of other infatuated people, Egyptians and the like, who place their reliance upon wild beasts and most kinds of creeping things and cattle, and worship them, and offer sacrifices to them both while living and when dead?'

139 'Now our Lawgiver being a wise man and specially endowed by God to understand all things, took a comprehensive view of each particular detail, and fenced us round with impregnable ramparts and walls of iron, that we might not mingle at all with any of the other nations, but remain pure in body and soul, free from all vain imaginations, worshiping the one Almighty God above the whole 140 creation. Hence the leading Egyptian priests having looked carefully into many matters, and being cognizant with (our) affairs, call us " men of God ". This is a title which does not belong to the rest of mankind but only to those who worship the true God. The rest are men not of God but of meats and drinks and clothing. For their whole disposition leads them to find solace in these things. 141 Among our people such things are reckoned of no account. but throughout their whole life their 142 main consideration is the sovereignty of God. Therefore lest we should be corrupted by any abomination, or our lives be perverted by evil communications, he hedged us round on all sides by 143 rules of purity, affecting alike what we eat, or drink, or touch, or hear, or see. For though, speaking generally, all things are alike in their natural constitution, since they are all governed by one and the same power, yet there is a deep reason in each individual case why we abstain from the use of certain things and enjoy the common use of others. For the sake of illustration I will run over one or two 144 points and explain them to you. For you must not fall into the degrading idea that it was out of regard to mice and weasels and other such things that Moses drew up his laws with such exceeding care. All these ordinances were made for the sake of righteousness to aid the quest for virtue and 145 the perfecting of character. For all the birds that we use are tame and distinguished by their cleanliness, feeding on various kinds of grain and pulse, such as for instance pigeons, turtle-doves, 146 locusts, partridges, geese also, and all other birds of this class. But the birds which are forbidden you will find to be wild and carnivorous, tyrannizing over the others by the strength which they possess, and cruelly obtaining food by preying on the tame birds enumerated above and not only so, but 147 they seize lambs and kids, and injure human beings too, whether dead or alive, and so by naming them unclean, he gave a sign by means of them that those, for whom the legislation was ordained, must practice righteousness in their hearts and not tyrannize over any one in reliance upon their own strength nor rob them of anything, but steer their course of life in accordance with justice, just as the tame birds, already mentioned, consume the different kinds of pulse that grow upon the earth 148 and do not tyrannize to the destruction of their own kindred. Our legislator taught us therefore that it is by such methods as these that indications are given to the wise, that they must be just and effect nothing by violence, and refrain from tyrannizing over others in reliance upon their own 149 strength. For since it is considered unseemly even to touch such unclean animals, as have been mentioned, on account of their particular habits, ought we not to take every precaution lest our own 150 characters should be destroyed to the same extent? Wherefore all the rules which he has laid down with regard to what is permitted in the case of these birds and other animals, he has enacted with the object of teaching us a moral lesson. For the division of the hoof and the separation of the claws are intended to teach us that we must discriminate between our individual actions with a view 151 to the practice of virtue. For the strength of our whole body and its activity depend upon our shoulders and limbs. Therefore he compels us to recognize that we must perform all our actions with discrimination according to the standard of righteousness - more especially because we have 152 been distinctly separated from the rest of mankind. For most other men defile themselves by promiscuous intercourse, thereby working great iniquity, and whole countries and cities pride themselves upon such vices. For they not only have inter-

course with men but they defile their own 153 mothers and even their daughters. But we have been kept separate from such sins. And the people who have been separated in the aforementioned way are also characterized by the Lawgiver as possessing the gift of memory. For all animals " which are cloven-footed and chew the cud " 154 represent to the initiated the symbol of memory. For the act of chewing the cud is nothing else than the reminiscence of life and existence. For life is wont to be sustained by means of food 155 wherefore he exhorts us in the Scripture also in these words: 'Thou shalt surely remember the Lord that wrought in thee those great and wonderful things". For when they are properly conceived, they are manifestly great and glorious; first the construction of the body and the disposition of the 156 food and the separation of each individual limb and, far more, the organization of the senses, the operation and invisible movement of the mind, the rapidity of its particular actions and its discovery of the 157 arts, display an infinite resourcefulness. Wherefore he exhorts us to remember that the aforesaid parts are kept together by the divine power with consummate skill. For he has marked out every 158 time and place that we may continually remember the God who rules and preserves (us). For in the matter of meats and drinks he bids us first of all offer part as a sacrifice and then forthwith enjoy our meal. Moreover, upon our garments he has given us a symbol of remembrance, and in like manner he has ordered us to put the divine oracles upon our gates and doors as a remembrance of 159 God. And upon our hands, too, he expressly orders the symbol to be fastened, clearly showing that we ought to perform every act in righteousness, remembering (our own creation), and above all the 160 fear of God. He bids men also, when lying down to sleep and rising up again, to meditate upon the works of God, not only in word, but by observing distinctly the change and impression produced upon them, when they are going to sleep, and also their waking, how divine and incomprehensible 161 the change from one of these states to the other is. The excellency of the analogy in regard to discrimination and memory has now been pointed out to you, according to our interpretation of " the cloven hoof and the chewing of the cud ". For our laws have not been drawn up at random or in accordance with the first casual thought that occurred to the mind, but with a view to truth and the 162 indication of right reason. For by means of the directions which he gives with regard to meats and drinks and particular cases of touching, he bids us neither to do nor listen to anything, thoughtlessly 163 nor to resort to injustice by the abuse of the power of reason. In the case of the wild animals, too, the same principle may be discovered. For the character of the weasel and of mice and such 164 animals as these, which are expressly mentioned, is destructive. Mice defile and damage everything, not only for their own food but even to the extent of rendering absolutely useless to man whatever 165 it falls in their way to damage. The weasel class, too, is peculiar: for besides what has been said, it has a characteristic which is defiling: It conceives through the ears and brings forth through the 166 mouth. And it is for this reason that a like practice is declared unclean in men. For by embodying in speech all that they receive through the ears, they involve others in evils and work no ordinary impurity, being themselves altogether defiled by the pollution of impiety. And your king, as we are informed, does quite right in destroying such men.' 167 Then I said 'I suppose you mean the informers, for he constantly exposes them to tortures and to 168 painful forms of death'. 'Yes,' he replied, 'these are the men I mean, for to watch for men's destruction is an unholy thing. And our law forbids us to injure any one either by word or deed. My brief account of these matters ought to have convinced you, that all our regulations have been drawn up with a view to righteousness, and that nothing has been enacted in the Scripture thoughtlessly or without due reason, but its purpose is to enable us throughout our whole life and in all our actions 169 to practice righteousness before all men, being mindful of Almighty God. And so concerning meats and things unclean, creeping things, and wild beasts, the whole system aims at righteousness and righteous relationships between man and man.'

170 He seemed to me to have made a good defense on all the points; for in reference also to the calves and rams and goats which are offered, he said that it was necessary to take them from the herds and flocks, and sacrifice tame animals and offer nothing wild, that the offerers of the sacrifices might understand the symbolic meaning of the lawgiver and not be under the influence of an arrogant self-consciousness. For he, who offers a sacrifice makes an offering also of his own soul in all its moods. 171 I think that these particulars with regard to our discussion are worth narrating and on account of the sanctity and natural meaning of the law, I have been induced to explain them to you clearly, Philocrates, because of your own devotion to learning.

172 And Eleazar, after offering the sacrifice, and selecting the envoys, and preparing many gifts for the 173 king, despatched us on our journey in great security. And when we reached Alexandria the king was at once informed of our arrival. On our admission to the palace, Andreas and I warmly greeted 174 the king and handed over to him the letter written by Eleazar. The king was very anxious to meet the envoys, and gave orders that all the other officials should be dismissed and the envoys 175 summoned to his presence at once. Now this excited general surprise, for it is customary for those who come to seek an audience with

the king on matters of importance to be admitted to his presence on the fifth day, while envoys from kings or very important cities with difficulty secure admission to the Court in thirty days - but these men he counted worthy of greater honour, since he held their master in such high esteem, and so he immediately dismissed those whose presence he regarded as superfluous and continued walking about until they came in and he was able to welcome them. 176 When they entered with the gifts which had been sent with them and the valuable parchments, on which the law was inscribed in gold in Jewish characters, for the parchment was wonderfully prepared and the connexion between the pages had been so effected as to be invisible, the king as soon 177 as he saw them began to ask them about the books. And when they had taken the rolls out of their coverings and unfolded the pages, the king stood still for a long time and then making obeisance about seven times, he said: 'I thank you, my friends, and I thank him that sent you still more, and 178 most of all God, whose oracles these are.' And when all, the envoys and the others who were present as well, shouted out at one time and with one voice: 'God save the King!' he burst into tears of joy. For his exaltation of soul and the sense of the overwhelming honour which had been 179 paid him compelled him to weep over his good fortune. He commanded them to put the rolls back in their places and then after saluting the men, said: 'It was right, men of God, that I should first of all pay my reverence to the books for the sake of which I summoned you here and then, when I had done that, to extend the right-hand of friendship to you. It was for this reason that I 180 did this first. I have enacted that this day, on which you arrived, shall be kept as a great day and it will be celebrated annually throughout my life time. It happens also that it is the anniversary of 181 my naval victory over Antigonus. Therefore I shall be glad to feast with you to-day.' 'Everything that you may have occasion to use', he said, 'shall be prepared (for you) in a befitting manner and for me also with you.' After they had expressed their delight, he gave orders that the best quarters near the citadel should be assigned to them, and that preparations be made for the banquet. 182 And Nicanor summoned the lord high steward, Dorotheus, who was the special officer appointed to look after the Jews, and commanded him to make the necessary preparation for each one. For this arrangement had been made by the king and it is an arrangement which you see maintained to-day. For as many cities (as) have (special) customs in the matter of drinking, eating, and reclining, have special officers appointed to look after their requirements. And whenever they come to visit the kings, preparations are made in accordance with their own customs, in order that there may be no discomfort to disturb the enjoyment of their visit. The same precaution was taken in the case of the Jewish envoys. Now Dorotheus who was the patron appointed to look after Jewish guests was 183 a very conscientious man. All the stores which were under his control and set apart for the reception of such guests, he brought out for the feast. He arranged the seats in two rows in accordance with the king's instructions. For he had ordered him to make half the men sit at his right hand and the rest behind him, in order that he might not withhold from them the highest possible honour. When they had taken their seats he instructed Dorotheus to carry out everything in 1844 accordance with the customs which were in use amongst his Jewish guests. Therefore he dispensed with the services of the sacred heralds and the sacrificing priests and the others who were accustomed to offer the prayers, and called upon one of our number, Eleazar, the oldest of the Jewish priests, to offer prayer instead. And he rose up and made a remarkable prayer. 'May Almighty 185 God enrich you, O king with all the good things which He has made and may He grant you and your wife and your children and your comrades the continual possession of them as long as you live !' At these words a loud and joyous applause broke out which lasted for a considerable time, and then 186 they turned to the enjoyment of the banquet which had been prepared. All the arrangements for service at table were carried out in accordance with the injunction of Dorotheus. Among the attendants were the royal pages and others who held places of honour at the king's court. 187 Taking an opportunity afforded by a pause in the banquet the king asked the envoy who sat in the seat of honour (for they were arranged according to seniority), How he could keep his kingdom 188 unimpaired to the end? After pondering for a moment he replied, 'You could best establish its security if you were to imitate the unceasing benignity of God. For if you exhibit clemency and inflict mild punishments upon those who deserve them in accordance with their deserts, you will 189 turn them from evil and lead them to repentance.' The king praised the answer and then asked the next man, How he could do everything for the best in all his actions? And he replied, 'If a man maintains a just bearing towards all, he will always act rightly on every occasion, remembering that every thought is known to God. If you take the fear of God as your starting-point, you will never miss the goal.

190 The king complimented this man, too, upon his answer and asked another, How he could have friends like-minded with himself? He replied, 'If they see you studying the interests of the multitudes over whom you rule; you will do well to observe how God bestows his benefits on the 191 human race, providing for them health and food and all other things in due season.' After expressing his agreement with the reply, the king asked the next guest, How in giving audiences and passing judg-

ments he could gain the praise even of those who failed to win their suit? And he said, 'If you are fair in speech to all alike and never act insolently nor tyrannically in your treatment of 192 offenders. And you will do this if you watch the method by which God acts. The petitions of the worthy are always fulfilled, while those who fail to obtain an answer to their prayers are informed by means of dreams or events of what was harmful in their requests and that God does not smite them according to their sins or the greatness of His strength, but acts with forbearance towards them.'

193 The king praised the man warmly for his answer and asked the next in order, How he could be invincible in military affairs? And he replied, 'If he did not trust entirely to his multitudes or his warlike forces, but called upon God continually to bring his enterprises to a successful issue, while 194 he himself discharged all his duties in the spirit of justice.' Welcoming this answer, he asked another how he might become an object of dread to his enemies. And he replied, 'If while maintaining a vast supply of arms and forces he remembered that these things were powerless to achieve a permanent and conclusive result. For even God instils fear into the minds of men by granting reprieves and making merely a display of the greatness of his power.'

195 This man the king praised and then said to the next, What is the highest good in life? And he answered 'To know that God is Lord of the Universe, and that in our finest achievements it is not we who attain success but God who by his power brings all things to fulfilment and leads us to the goal.'

196 The king exclaimed that the man had answered well and then asked the next How he could keep all his possessions intact and finally hand them down to his successors in the same condition? And he answered 'By praying constantly to God that you may be inspired with high motives in all your undertakings and by warning your descendants not to be dazzled by fame or wealth, for it is God who bestows all these gifts and men never by themselves win the supremacy'.

197 The king expressed his agreement with the answer and enquired of the next guest, How he could bear with equanimity whatever befell him? And he said, 'If you have a firm grasp of the thought that all men are appointed by God to share the greatest evil as well as the greatest good, since it is impossible for one who is a man to be exempt from these. But God, to whom we ought always to pray, inspires us with courage to endure.'

198 Delighted with the man's reply, the king said that all their answers had been good. 'I will put a question to one other', he added, 'and then I will stop for the present: that we may turn our attention 199 to the enjoyment of the feast and spend a pleasant time.' Thereupon he asked the man, What is the true aim of courage? And he answered, 'If a right plan is carried out in the hour of danger in accordance with the original intention. For all things are accomplished by God to your advantage, O king, since your purpose is good.'

200 When all had signified by their applause their agreement with the answer, the king said to the philosophers (for not a few of them were present), 'It is my opinion that these men excel in virtue and possess extraordinary knowledge, since on the spur of the moment they have given fitting answers to these questions which I have put to them, and have all made God the starting-point of their words.'

201 And Menedemus, the philosopher of Eretria, said, 'True, O King - for since the universe is managed by providence and since we rightly perceive that man is the creation of God, it follows 202 that all power and beauty of speech proceed from God.' When the king had nodded his assent to this sentiment, the speaking ceased and they proceeded to enjoy themselves. When evening came on, the banquet ended.

203 On the following day they sat down to table again and continued the banquet according to the same arrangements. When the king thought that a fitting opportunity had arrived to put inquiries to his guests, he proceeded to ask further questions of the men who sat next in order to those who 204 had given answers on the previous day. He began to open the conversation with the eleventh man, for there were ten who had been asked questions on the former occasion. When silence was 205 established, he asked How he could continue to be rich? After a brief reflection, the man who had been asked the question replied If he did nothing unworthy of his position, never acted licentiously, never lavished expense on empty and vain pursuits, but by acts of benevolence made all his subjects well disposed towards himself. For it is God who is the author of all good things and 206 Him man must needs obey.' The king bestowed praise upon him and then asked another How he could maintain the truth? In reply to the question he said, 'By recognizing that a lie brings great disgrace upon all men, and more especially upon kings. For since they have the power to do whatever they wish, why should they resort to lies? In addition to this you must always remember, O King, that God is a lover of the truth.'

207 The king received the answer with great delight and looking at another said, 'What is the teaching of wisdom?' And the other replied, 'As you wish that no evil should befall you, but to be a partaker of all good things, so you should act on the same principle towards your subjects and offenders, and you should mildly admonish the noble and good. For God draws all men to himself by his benignity.'

208 The king praised him and asked the next in order How he could be the friend of men? And he replied, 'By observing that the human race increases and is born with much trouble and great suffering: wherefore you must not lightly punish or inflict torments upon them, since you know that the life of men is made up of pains and penalties. For if you understood everything you would be filled with pity, for God also is pitiful.'

209 The king received the answer with approbation and inquired of the next 'What is the most essential qualification for ruling? ' 'To keep oneself', he answered, 'free from bribery and to practice sobriety during the greater part of one's life, to honour righteousness above all things, and to make friends of men of this type. For God, too, is a lover of justice.'

210 Having signified his approval, the king said to another 'What is the true mark of piety?' And he replied, 'To perceive that God constantly works in the Universe and knows all things, and no man who acts unjustly and works wickedness can escape His notice. As God is the benefactor of the whole world, so you, too, must imitate Him and be void of offence.'

211 The king signified his agreement and said to another 'What is the essence of kingship?' And he replied, 'To rule oneself well and not to be led astray by wealth or fame to immoderate or unseemly desires, this is the true way of ruling if you reason the matter well out. For all that you really need is yours, and God is free from need and benignant withal. Let your thoughts be such as become a man, and desire not many things but only such as are necessary for ruling.'

212 The king praised him and asked another man How his deliberations might be for the best? and he replied, 'If he constantly set justice before him in everything and thought that injustice was equivalent to deprivation of life. For God always promises the highest blessings to the just.'

213 Having praised him, the king asked the next How he could be free from disturbing thoughts in his sleep? And he replied, 'You have asked me a question which is very difficult to answer, for we cannot bring our true selves into play during the hours of sleep, but are held fast in these 214 by imaginations that cannot be controlled by reason. For our souls possess the feeling that they actually see the things that enter into our consciousness during sleep. But we make a mistake if we suppose that we are actually sailing on the sea in boats or flying through the air or travelling to other regions or anything else of the kind. And yet we actually do imagine such 215 things to be taking place. So far as it is possible for me to decide, I have reached the following conclusion. You must in every possible way, O King, govern your words and actions by the rule of piety that you may have the consciousness that you are maintaining virtue and that you never choose to gratify yourself at the expense of reason and never by abusing your power do 216 despite to righteousness. For the mind mostly busies itself in sleep with the same things with which it occupies itself when awake. And he who has all his thoughts and actions set towards the noblest ends establishes himself in righteousness both when he is awake and when he is asleep. Wherefore you must be steadfast in the constant discipline of self.'

217 The king bestowed praise on the man and said to another, 'since you are the tenth to answer, when you have spoken, we will devote ourselves to the banquet.' And then he put the question, 218 How can I avoid doing anything unworthy of myself? And he replied, 'Look always to your own fame and your own supreme position, that you may speak and think only such things as are 219 consistent therewith, knowing that all your subjects think and talk about you. For you must not appear to be worse than the actors, who study carefully the role, which it is necessary for them to play, and shape all their actions in accordance with it. You are not acting a part, but are really a king, since God has bestowed upon you a royal authority in keeping with your character.'

220 When the king had applauded loud and long in the most gracious way, the guests were urged to seek repose. So when the conversation ceased, they devoted themselves to the next course of the feast.

221 On the following day, the same arrangement was observed, and when the king found an opportunity of putting questions to the men, he questioned the first of those who had been left over 222 for the next interrogation, What is the highest form of government? And he replied, 'To rule oneself and not to be carried away by impulses. For all men possess a certain natural bent of mind. 223 It is probable that most men have an inclination towards food and drink and pleasure, and kings a bent towards the acquisition of territory and great renown. But it is good that there should be moderation in all things. What God gives, that you must take and keep, but never yearn for things that are beyond your reach.'

224 Pleased with these words, the king asked the next How he could be free from envy? And he after a brief pause replied, 'If you consider first of all that it is God who bestows on all kings glory and great wealth and no one is king by his own power. All men wish to share this glory but cannot, since it is the gift of God.'

225 The king praised the man in a long speech and then asked another How he could despise his enemies? And he replied, 'If you show kindness to all men and win their friendship, you need fear no one. To be popular with all men is the best of good gifts to receive from God.'

226 Having praised this answer the king ordered the next man to reply to the question, How he could maintain his great renown? and he replied that 'If you are generous and large-hearted in bestowing kindness and acts of grace upon others, you will never lose your renown, but if you wish the aforesaid graces to continue yours, you must call upon God continually.'

227 The king expressed his approval and asked the next, To whom ought a man to show liberality? And he replied, 'All men acknowledge that we ought to show liberality to those who are well disposed towards us, but I think that we ought to show the same keen spirit of generosity to those who are opposed to us that by this means we may win them over to the right and to what is advantageous to ourselves. But we must pray to God that this may be accomplished, for he rules the minds of all men.'

228 Having expressed his agreement with the answer, the king asked the sixth to reply to the question, To whom ought we to exhibit gratitude? And he replied, 'To our parents continually, for God has given us a most important commandment with regard to the honour due to parents. In the next place He reckons the attitude of friend towards friend for He speaks of "a friend which is as thine own soul". You do well in trying to bring all men into friendship with yourself.'

229 The king spoke kindly to him and then asked the next, What is it that resembles beauty in value? And he said, 'Piety, for it is the pre-eminent form of beauty, and its power lies in love, which is the gift of God. This you have already acquired and with it all the blessings of life.'

230 The king in the most gracious way applauded the answer and asked another How, if he were to fail, he could regain his reputation again in the same degree? And he said, 'It is not possible for you to fail, for you have sown in all men the seeds of gratitude which produce a harvest of goodwill, 231 and this is mightier than the strongest weapons and guarantees the greatest security. But if any man does fail, he must never again do those things which caused his failure, but he must form friendships and act justly. For it is the gift of God to be able to do good actions and not the contrary.'

232 Delighted with these words, the king asked another How he could be free from grief? And he replied, 'If he never injured any one, but did good to everybody and followed the pathway of 233 righteousness, for its fruits bring freedom from grief. But we must pray to God that unexpected evils such as death or disease or pain or anything of this kind may not come upon us and injure us. But since you are devoted to piety, no such misfortune will ever come upon you.'

234 The king bestowed great praise upon him and asked the tenth, What is the highest form of glory? And he said, 'To honour God, and this is done not with gifts and sacrifices but with purity of soul and holy conviction, since all things are fashioned and governed by God in accordance with His will. Of this purpose you are in constant possession as all men can see from your achievements in the past and in the present.'

235 With loud voice the king greeted them all and spoke kindly to them, and all those who were present expressed their approval, especially the philosophers. For they were far superior to them [i.e. the philosophers] both in conduct and in argument, since they always made God their starting point. After this the king to show his good feeling proceeded to drink the health of his guests.

236 On the following day the same arrangements were made for the banquet, and the king, as soon as an opportunity occurred, began to put questions to the men who sat next to those who had already responded, and he said to the first 'Is wisdom capable of being taught?' And he said, 'The soul is so constituted that it is able by the divine power to receive all the good and reject the contrary.'

237 The king expressed approval and asked the next man, What is it that is most beneficial to health? And he said, 'Temperance, and it is not possible to acquire this unless God create a disposition towards it.'

238 The king spoke kindly to the man and said to another, 'How can a man worthily pay the debt of gratitude to his parents?' And he said, 'By never causing them pain, and this is not possible unless God dispose the mind to the pursuit of the noblest ends.'

239 The king expressed agreement and asked the next How he could become an eager listener? And he said, 'By remembering that all knowledge is useful, because it enables you by the help of God in a time of emergency to select some of the things which you have learned and apply them to the crisis which confronts you. And so the efforts of men are fulfilled by the assistance of God.'

240 The king praised him and asked the next How he could avoid doing anything contrary to law? And he said, 'If you recognize that it is God who has put the thoughts into the hearts of the lawgivers that the lives of men might be preserved, you will follow them.'

241 The king acknowledged the man's answer and said to another, 'What is the advantage of kinship?' And he replied, 'If we consider that we ourselves are afflicted by the misfortunes which fall upon our relatives and if their sufferings become our own - then the strength of kinship is 242 apparent at once, for it is only when such feeling is shown that we shall win honour and esteem in their eyes. For help, when it is linked with kindliness, is of itself a bond which is altogether indissoluble. And in the day of their prosperity we must not crave their possessions, but must pray God to bestow all manner of good upon them.'

243 And having accorded to him the same praise as to the rest, the king asked another How he could attain freedom from fear? And he said, 'When the mind is conscious that it has wrought no evil, and when God directs it to all noble counsels.'

244 The king expressed his approval and asked another How he could always maintain a right judgement? And he replied, 'If he constantly set before his eyes the misfortunes which befall men and recognized that it is God who takes away prosperity from some and brings others to great honour and glory.'

245 The king gave a kindly reception to the man and asked the next to answer the question How he could avoid a life of ease and pleasure? And he replied, 'If he continually remembered that he was the ruler of a great empire and the lord of vast multitudes, and that his mind ought not to be occupied with other things, but he ought always to be considering how he could best promote their welfare. He must pray, too, to God that no duty might be neglected.'

246 Having bestowed praise upon him, the king asked the tenth How he could recognize those who were dealing treacherously with him? And he replied to the question, 'If he observed whether the bearing of those about him was natural and whether they maintained the proper rule of precedence at receptions and councils, and in their general intercourse, never going beyond the bounds of 247 propriety in congratulations or in other matters of deportment. But God will incline your mind, O King, to all that is noble.' When the king had expressed his loud approval and praised them all individually (amid the plaudits of all who were present), they turned to the enjoyment of the feast.

248 And on the next day, when the opportunity offered, the king asked the next man, What is the grossest form of neglect? And he replied, 'If a man does not care for his children and devote every effort to their education. For w always pray to God not so much for ourselves as for our children that every blessing may be theirs. Our desire that our children may possess self-control is only realized by the power of God.'

249 The king said that he had spoken well and then asked another How he could be patriotic? 'By keeping before your mind,' he replied, the thought that it is good to live and die in one's own country. Residence abroad brings contempt upon the poor and shame upon the rich as though they had been banished for a crime. If you bestow benefits upon all, as you continually do, God will give you favour with all and you will be accounted patriotic.'

250 After listening to this man, the king asked the next in order How he could live amicably with his wife? And he answered, 'By recognizing that womankind are by nature headstrong and energetic in the pursuit of their own desires, and subject to sudden changes of opinion through fallacious reasoning, and their nature is essentially weak. It is necessary to deal wisely with them 251 and not to provoke strife. For the successful conduct of life the steersman must know the goal toward which he ought to direct his course. It is only by calling upon the help of God that men can steer a true course of life at all times.'

252 The king expressed his agreement and asked the next How he could be free from error? And he replied, 'If you always act with deliberation and never give credence to slanders, but prove for yourself the things that are said to you and decide by your own judgement the requests which are made to you and carry out everything in the light of your judgement, you will be free from error, O King. But the knowledge and practice of these things is the work of the Divine power.'

253 Delighted with these words, the king asked another How he could be free from wrath? And he said in reply to the question, 'If he recognized that he had power over all even to inflict death upon them, if he gave way to wrath, and that it would be useless and pitiful if he, just because he was lord, 254 deprived many of life. What need was there for wrath, when all men were in subjection and no one was hostile to him? It is necessary to recognize that God rules the whole world in the spirit of kindness and without wrath at all, and you,' said he, 'O king, must of necessity copy His example.

255 The king said that he had answered well and then inquired of the next man, What is good counsel? 'To act well at all times and with due reflection,' he explained, 'comparing what is advantageous to our own policy with the injurious effects that would result from the adoption of the opposite view, in order that by weighing every point we may be well advised and our purpose may be accomplished. And most important of all, by the power of God every plan of yours will find fulfilment because you practice piety.'

256 The king said that this man had answered well, and asked another What is philosophy? And he explained, 'To deliberate well in reference to any question that emerges and never to be carried away by impulses, but to ponder over the injuries that result from the passions, and to act rightly as the circumstances demand, practicing moderation. But we must pray to God to instil into our mind a right regard for these things.'

257 The king signified his consent and asked another How he could meet with recognition when traveling abroad? 'By being fair to all men,' he replied, 'and by appearing to be inferior rather than superior to those

amongst whom he was traveling. For it is a recognized principle that God by His very nature accepts the humble. And the human race loves those who are willing to be in subjection to them.'

258 Having expressed his approval at this reply, the king asked another How he could build in such a way that his structures would endure after him? And he replied to the question, 'If his creations were on a great and noble scale, so that the beholders would spare them for their beauty, and if he never dismissed any of those who wrought such works and never compelled others to minister to his 259 needs without wages. For observing how God provides for the human race, granting them health and mental capacity and all other gifts, he himself should follow His example by rendering to men a recompense for their arduous toil. For it is the deeds that are wrought in righteousness that abide continually.'

260 The king said that this man, too, had answered well and asked the tenth, What is the fruit of wisdom? And he replied, 'That a man should be conscious in himself that he has wrought no evil 261 and that he should live his life in the truth, since it is from these, O mighty King, that the greatest joy and steadfastness of soul and strong faith in God accrue to you if you rule your realm in piety.' And when they heard the answer they all shouted with loud acclaim, and afterwards the king in the fullness of his joy began to drink their healths.

262 And on the next day the banquet followed the same course as on previous occasions, and when the opportunity presented itself the king proceeded to put questions to the remaining guests, and 263 he said to the first, 'How can a man keep himself from pride?' And he replied, 'If he maintains equality and remembers on all occasions that he is a man ruling over men. And God brings the proud to nought, and exalts the meek and humble.'

264 The king spoke kindly to him and asked the next, Whom ought a man to select as his counsellors? and he replied, ' Those who have been tested in many affairs and maintain unmingled goodwill towards him and partake of his own disposition. And God manifests Himself to those who are worthy that these ends may be attained.'

265 The king praised him and asked another, What is the most necessary possession for a king? 'The friendship and love of his subjects,' he replied, 'for it is through this that the bond of goodwill is rendered indissoluble. And it is God who ensures that this may come to pass in accordance with your wish.'

266 The king praised him and inquired of another, What is the goal of speech? And he replied, 'To convince your opponent by showing him his mistakes in a well-ordered array of arguments. For in this way you will win your hearer, not by opposing him, but by bestowing praise upon him with a view to persuading him. And it is by the power of God that persuasion is accomplished.'

267 The king said that he had given a good answer, and asked another How he could live amicably with the many different races who formed the population of his kingdom? 'By acting the proper part towards each,' he replied, 'and taking righteousness as your guide, as you are now doing with the help of the insight which God bestows upon you.'

268 The king was delighted by this reply, and asked another 'Under what circumstances ought a man to suffer grief?' 'In the misfortunes that befall our friends,' he replied, when we see that they are protracted and irremediable. Reason does not allow us to grieve for those who are dead and set free from evil, but all men do grieve over them because they think only of themselves and their own advantage. It is by the power of God alone that we can escape all evil.'

269 The king said that he had given a fitting answer, and asked another, How is reputation lost? And he replied, When pride and unbounded self-confidence hold sway, dishonour and loss of reputation are engendered. For God is the Lord of all reputation and bestows it where He will.'

270 The king gave his confirmation to the answer, and asked the next man, To whom ought men to entrust themselves? 'To those,' he replied, who serve you from goodwill and not from fear or self-interest, thinking only of their own gain. For the one is the sign of love, the other the mark of ill-will and time-serving. For the man who is always watching, for his own gain is a traitor at heart. But you possess the affection of all your subjects by the help of the good counsel which God bestows upon you.'

271 The king said that he had answered wisely, and asked another, What is it that keeps a kingdom safe? And he replied to the question, 'Care and forethought that no evil may be wrought by those who are placed in a position of authority over the people, and this you always do by the help of God who inspires you with grave judgement '.

272 The king spoke words of encouragement to him, and asked another, What is it that maintains gratitude and honour? And he replied, 'Virtue, for it is the creator of good deeds, and by it evil is destroyed, even as you exhibit nobility of character towards all by the gift which God bestows upon you.'

273 The king graciously acknowledged the answer and asked the eleventh (since there were two more than seventy), How he could in time of war maintain tranquillity of soul? And he replied, 'By remembering that he had done no evil to any of his subjects, and that all would fight for him in return for the benefits which they had received, knowing that even if they lose their lives, you will care for those 274 dependent on them. For

you never fail to make reparation to any - such is the kind-heartedness with which God has inspired you.' The king loudly applauded them all and spoke very kindly to them and then drank a long draught to the health of each, giving himself up to enjoyment, and lavishing the most generous and joyous friendship upon his guests.

275 On the seventh day much more extensive preparations were made, and many others were present from the different cities (among them a large number of ambassadors). When an opportunity occurred, the king asked the first of those who had not yet been questioned How he could avoid 276 being deceived by fallacious reasoning? and he replied, 'By noticing carefully the speaker, the thing spoken, and the subject under discussion, and by putting the same questions again after an interval in different forms. But to possess an alert mind and to be able to form a sound judgement in every case is one of the good gifts of God, and you possess it, O King.'

277 The king loudly applauded the answer and asked another, Why is it that the majority of men never become virtuous? 'Because,' he replied, 'all men are by nature intemperate and inclined to 278 pleasure. Hence, injustice springs up and a flood of avarice. The habit of virtue is a hindrance to those who are devoted to a life of pleasure because it enjoins upon them the preference of temperance and righteousness. For it is God who is the master of these things.'

279 The king said that he had answered well, and asked, What ought kings to obey? And he said, 'The laws, in order that by righteous enactments they may restore the lives of men. Even as you by such conduct in obedience to the Divine command have laid up in store for yourself a perpetual memorial.'

280 The king said that this man, too, had spoken well, and asked the next, Whom ought we to appoint as governors? And he replied, 'All who hate wickedness, and imitating your own conduct act righteously that they may maintain a good reputation constantly. For this is what you do, O mighty King,' he said, 'and it is God who has bestowed upon you the crown of righteousness.'

281 The king loudly acclaimed the answer and then looking at the next man said, Whom ought we to appoint as officers over the forces?' And he explained, 'Those who excel in courage and righteousness and those who are more anxious about the safety of their men than to gain a victory by risking their lives through rashness. For as God acts well towards all men, so too you in imitation of Him are the benefactor of all your subjects.'

282 The king said that he had given a good answer and asked another, What man is worthy of admiration? And he replied, The man who is furnished with reputation and wealth and power and possesses a soul equal to it all. You yourself show by your actions that you are most worthy of admiration through the help of God who makes you care for these things.'

283 The king expressed his approval and said to another 'To what affairs ought kings to devote most time?' And he replied, 'To reading and the study of the records of official journeys, which are written in reference to the various kingdoms, with a view to the reformation and preservation of the subjects. And it is by such activity that you have attained to a glory which has never been approached by others, through the help of God who fulfils all your desires.'

284 The king spoke enthusiastically to the man and asked another How ought a man to occupy himself during his hours of relaxation and recreation? And he replied, 'To watch those plays which can be acted with propriety and to set before one's eyes scenes taken from life and enacted 285 with dignity and decency is profitable and appropriate. For there is some edification to be found even in these amusements, for often some desirable lesson is taught by the most insignificant affairs of life. But by practicing the utmost propriety in all your actions, you have shown that you are a philosopher and you are honoured by God on account of your virtue.'

286 The king, pleased with the words which had just been spoken, said to the ninth man, How ought a man to conduct himself at banquets? And he replied, 'You should summon to your side men of learning and those who are able to give you useful hints with regard to the affairs of your kingdom and the lives of your subjects (for you could not find any theme more suitable or more 287 educative than this) since such men are dear to God because they have trained their minds to contemplate the noblest themes - as you indeed are doing yourself, since all your actions are directed by God.'

288 Delighted with the reply, the king inquired of the next man, What is best for the people? That a private citizen should be made king over them or a member of the royal family? And he 289 replied, He who is best by nature. For kings who come of royal lineage are often harsh and severe towards their subjects. And still more is this the case with some of those who have risen from the ranks of private citizens, who after having experienced evil and borne their share of 290 poverty, when they rule over multitudes turn out to be more cruel than the godless tyrants. But, as I have said, a good nature which has been properly trained is capable of ruling, and you are a great king, not so much because you excel in the glory of your rule and your wealth but rather because you have surpassed

all men in clemency and philanthropy, thanks to God who has endowed you with these qualities.'

291 The king spent some time in praising this man and then asked the last of all, What is the greatest achievement in ruling an empire? And he replied, 'That the subjects should continually dwell in a state of peace, and that justice should be speedily administered in cases of dispute. 292 These results are achieved through the influence of the ruler, when he is a man who hates evil and loves the good and devotes his energies to saving the lives of men, just as you consider injustice the worst form of evil and by your just administration have fashioned for yourself an undying reputation, since God bestows upon you a mind which is pure and untainted by any evil.'

293 And when he ceased, loud and joyful applause broke out for some considerable time. When it stopped the king took a cup and gave a toast in honour of all his guests and the words which they had uttered. Then in conclusion he said, 'I have derived the greatest benefit from your presence. 294 I have profited much by the wise teaching which you have given me in reference to the art of ruling.' Then he ordered that three talents of silver should be presented to each of them, and appointed one of his slaves to deliver over the money. All at once shouted their approval, and the banquet became a scene of joy, while the king gave himself up to a continuous round of festivity.

295 I have written at length and must crave your pardon, Philocrates. I was astonished beyond measure at the men and the way in which on the spur of the moment they gave answers which 296 really needed a long time to devise. For though the questioner had given great thought to each particular question, those who replied one after the other had their answers to the questions ready at once and so they seemed to me and to all who were present and especially to the philosophers to be worthy of admiration. And I suppose that the thing will seem incredible to those who will 297 read my narrative in the future. But it is unseemly to misrepresent facts which are recorded in the public archives. And it would not be right for me to transgress in such a matter as this. I tell the story just as it happened, conscientiously avoiding any error. I was so impressed by the force of their utterances, that I made an effort to consult those whose business it was to make 298 a record of all that happened at the royal audiences and banquets. For it is the custom, as you know, from the moment the king begins to transact business until the time when he retires to rest, for a record to be taken of all his sayings and doings - a most excellent and useful arrangement. 299 For on the following day the minutes of the doings and sayings of the previous day are read over before business commences, and if there has been any irregularity, the matter is at once set right. 300 I obtained therefore, as has been said, accurate information from the public records, and I have set forth the facts in proper order since I know how eager you are to obtain useful information.

301 Three days later Demetrius took the men and passing along the sea-wall, seven stadia long, to the island, crossed the bridge and made for the northern districts of Pharos. There he assembled them in a house, which had been built upon the sea-shore, of great beauty and in a secluded situation, and invited them to carry out the work of translation, since everything that they needed for the purpose 302 was placed at their disposal. So they set to work comparing their several results and making them agree, and whatever they agreed upon was suitably copied out under the direction of Demetrius. 303 And the session lasted until the ninth hour; after this they were set free to minister to their physical 304 needs. Everything they wanted was furnished for them on a lavish scale. In addition to this Dorotheus made the same preparations for them daily as were made for the king himself - for thus he had been commanded by the king. In the early morning they appeared daily at the Court, and 305 after saluting the king went back to their own place. And as is the custom of all the Jews, they washed their hands in the sea and prayed to God and then devoted themselves to reading and 306 translating the particular passage upon which they were engaged, and I put the question to them, Why it was that they washed their hands before they prayed? And they explained that it was a token that they had done no evil (for every form of activity is wrought by means of the hands) since in their noble and holy way they regard everything as a symbol of righteousness and truth.

307 As I have already said, they met together daily in the place which was delightful for its quiet and its brightness and applied themselves to their task. And it so chanced that the work of translation was completed in seventy-two days, just as if this had been arranged of set purpose.

308 When the work was completed, Demetrius collected together the Jewish population in the place where the translation had been made, and read it over to all, in the presence of the translators, who met with a great reception also from the people, because of the great benefits which they had 309 conferred upon them. They bestowed warm praise upon Demetrius, too, and urged him to have the whole law transcribed and present a copy to their leaders. 310 After the books had been read, the priests and the elders of the translators and the Jewish community and the leaders of the people stood up and said, that since so excellent and sacred and accurate a translation had been made, it was only right that it should remain as it was and no 311 alteration should be made in it. And when the whole

company expressed their approval, they bade them pronounce a curse in accordance with their custom upon any one who should make any alteration either by adding anything or changing in any way whatever any of the words which had been written or making any omission. This was a very wise precaution to ensure that the book might be preserved for all the future time unchanged. 312 When the matter was reported to the king, he rejoiced greatly, for he felt that the design which he had formed had been safely carried out. The whole book was read over to him and he was greatly astonished at the spirit of the lawgiver. And he said to Demetrius, 'How is it that none of the historians or the poets have ever thought it worth their while to allude to such a wonderful 313 achievement?' And he replied, 'Because the law is sacred and of divine origin. And some of those who formed the intention of dealing with it have been smitten by God and therefore desisted from 314 their purpose.' He said that he had heard from Theopompus that he had been driven out of his mind for more than thirty days because he intended to insert in his history some of the incidents from the earlier and somewhat unreliable translations of the law. When he had recovered 315 a little, he besought God to make it clear to him why the misfortune had befallen him. And it was revealed to him in a dream, that from idle curiosity he was wishing to communicate sacred truths to common men, and that if he desisted he would recover his health. I have heard, too, from the lips 316 of Theodektes, one of the tragic poets, that when he was about to adapt some of the incidents recorded in the book for one of his plays, he was affected with cataract in both his eyes. And when he perceived the reason why the misfortune had befallen him, he prayed to God for many days and was afterwards restored. 317 And after the king, as I have already said, had received the explanation of Demetrius on this point, he did homage and ordered that great care should be taken of the books, and that they should 318 be sacredly guarded. And he urged the translators to visit him frequently after their return to Judea, for it was only right, he said, that he should now send them home. But when they came back, he 319 would treat them as friends, as was right, and they would receive rich presents from him. He ordered preparations to be made for them to return home, and treated them most munificently. He presented each one of them with three robes of the finest sort, two talents of gold, a sideboard weighing one talent, all the furniture for three couches. 320 And with the escort he sent Eleazar ten couches with silver legs and all the necessary equipment, a sideboard worth thirty talents, ten robes, purple, and a magnificent crown, and a hundred pieces of the finest woven linen, also bowls and dishes, and two golden beakers to be dedicated to God. 321 He urged him also in a letter that if any of the men preferred to come back to him, not to hinder them. For he counted it a great privilege to enjoy the society of such learned men, and he would rather lavish his wealth upon them than upon vanities. 322 And now Philocrates, you have the complete story in accordance with my promise. I think that you find greater pleasure in these matters than in the writings of the mythologists. For you are devoted to the study of those things which can benefit the soul, and spend much time upon it. I shall attempt to narrate whatever other events are worth recording, that by perusing them you may secure the highest reward for your zeal.

Book 116. The Wisdom of Ben Sira (Ecclesiasticus)

The Wisdom of Ben Sira derives its title from the author, "Yeshua [Jesus], son of Eleazar, son of Sira" (50:27). This seems to be the earliest title of the book. The designation "Liber Ecclesiasticus," meaning "Church Book," appended to some Greek and Latin manuscripts, is perhaps due to the extensive use the church made of this book in presenting moral teaching to catechumens and to the faithful. The title "Sirach" comes from the Greek form of the author's name.

The author, a sage who lived in Jerusalem, was thoroughly imbued with love for the wisdom tradition, and also for the law, priesthood, Temple, and divine worship. As a wise and experienced observer of life he addressed himself to his contemporaries with the motive of helping them to maintain religious faith and integrity through study of the books sacred to the Jewish tradition.

The book contains numerous well-crafted maxims, grouped by affinity, and dealing with a variety of subjects such as the individual, the family, and the community in their relations with one another and with God. It treats of friendship, education, poverty and wealth, laws, religious worship, and many other matters that reflect the religious and social customs of the time.

Written in Hebrew in the early years of the second century B.C., the book was finished by ca. 175. The text was translated into Greek by the author's grandson after 117 B.C. He also wrote a foreword which contains valuable information about the book, its author, and himself as translator. Until the close of the nineteenth century the Wisdom of Ben Sira was known to Christians in translations, of which the Greek rendering was the most important. From it the Latin version was made. Between 1896 and 1900, again in 1931, and several times since 1956, incomplete manuscripts were discovered, so that more than two thirds of the book in Hebrew is available; these Hebrew texts agree substantially with the Greek. One such text, from Masada, is pre-Christian in date. The New American Bible provides a critical translation based on the evidence of all the ancient texts.

Though not included in the Jewish Bible after the first century A.D., nor, therefore, accepted by Protestants, the Wisdom of Ben Sira has been recognized by the Catholic Church as inspired and canonical. The Foreword, though not properly part of the book, is always included with it because of its antiquity and importance.

The contents of the Wisdom of Ben Sira are of a discursive nature, not easily divided into separate parts. Chapters 1–43 deal largely with moral instruction; 44:1–50:24 contain a eulogy of the heroes of Israel. There are two appendixes in which the author expresses his gratitude to God (51:1–12), and invites the unschooled to acquire true wisdom (51:13–30).

FOREWORD

Inasmuch as many and great truths have been given to us through the Law, the prophets, and the authors who followed them,for which the instruction and wisdom of Israel merit praise, it is the duty of those who read the scriptures not only to become knowledgeable themselves but also to use their love of learning in speech and in writing to help others less familiar. So my grandfather Jesus, who had long devoted himself to the study of the law, the prophets, and the rest of the books of our ancestors, and had acquired great familiarity with them, was moved to write something himself regarding instruction and wisdom. He did this so that those who love learning might, by accepting what he had written, make even greater progress in living according to the Law.

You are invited therefore to read it with good will and attention, with indulgence for any failure on our part, despite earnest efforts, in the interpretation of particular passages. For words spoken originally in Hebrew do not have the same effect when they are translated into another language. That is true not only of this book but of the Law itself, the prophecies, and the rest of the books, which differ no little when they are read in the original.

I arrived in Egypt in the thirty-eighth year of the reign of King Euergetes, and while there, I had access to no little learning. I therefore considered it my duty to devote some diligence and industry to the translation of this book. During this time I applied my skill for many sleepless hours to complete the book and publish it for those living abroad who wish to acquire learning and are disposed to live their lives according to the Law.

Book 117. The Prayer of Joseph

A MORNING OFFERING THROUGH ST. JOSEPH
IN PREPARATION FOR THE FEAST OF ST. JOSEPH
AND IN HONOR OF THE HOLY CHILD
THE DEVOTION OF THE SEVEN SUNDAYS
MY TRIPLE PRAYER NOVENA
ACT OF CONFIDENCE
MEMORAE TO JESUS, MARY, AND JOSEPH
APPEAL TO ST. JOSEPH
PRAYER TO ST. JOSEPH BEFORE MASS AND HOLY COMMUNION
PRAYER IN A DIFFICULT PROBLEM
PETITION FOR ST. JOSEPH'S BLESSING
A PRAYER TO ST. JOSEPH FOR THE SUCCESS OF A TEMPORAL AFFAIR
PRAYER FOR PURITY
PRAISES OF ST. JOSEPH
INVOCATIONS TO ST. JOSEPH
A POWERFUL NOVENA TO ST. JOSEPH
PRAYER FOR THE CHURCH AND THE HOLY FATHER
PRAYER FOR THE CHURCH MILITANT
HOLY FAMILY PRAYER
OFFERING
PRAYER TO ST. JOSEPH TO OBTAIN A CONVERSION
30 DAY NOVENA TO ST. JOSEPH
A DAILY PRAYER OF PETITION TO ST. JOSEPH
A Boy Sweetheart's Daily Prayer | A Girl Sweetheart's Daily Prayer
AN ANCIENT PRAYER TO ST. JOSEPH
THE MEMORAE OF ST. JOSEPH
ACT OF CONSECRATION TO ST. JOSEPH
ANOTHER ACT OF CONSECRATION TO ST. JOSEPH
CORD OF ST. JOSEPH
PRAYER FOR PRIESTS
PRAYER OF CONFIDENCE IN ST. JOSEPH
THE PRACTICE OF THE NINE FIRST WEDNESDAYS
GO TO JOSEPH PRAYER
LITANY OF SAINT JOSEPH
LITANY OF ST. JOSEPH FOR THE DYING
AND THE BODY AND TOMB OF ST. JOSEPH
THE REASONS ST. JOSEPH IS THE PATRON OF THE DYING
PRAYER FOR A HAPPY DEATH

ANOTHER PRAYER FOR A HAPPY DEATH
A SHORT PRAYER FOR THE DYING
PRAYER FOR THE AGONIZING
PRAYER FOR THE SOULS IN THE AGONY OF DEATH
JESUS, MARY AND JOSEPH
INDULGENCED PRAYER
ASPIRATIONS FOR THE DYING
PRAYER FOR A HEAVENLY CROWN
THE DEVOTION OF THE SEVEN SORROWS AND JOYS OF ST. JOSEPH
THE CHAPLET OF ST. JOSEPH
MORE TEXT FOR ST. JOSEPH: NEXT PAGE

A MORNING OFFERING THROUGH ST. JOSEPH

Receive me, dear and chosen Father, and the offering of every movement of my body and soul, which I desire to present through thee to my blessed Lord.

Purify all! Make all a perfect holocaust! May every pulsation of my heart be a Spiritual Communion, every look and thought an act of love, every action a sweet sacrifice, every word an arrow of Divine love, every step an advance toward Jesus, every visit to Our Lord as pleasing to God as the errands of Angels, every thought of thee, dear Saint, an act to remind thee that I am thy child.

I recommend to thee the occasions in which I usually fail, particularly . . . [Mention these]. Accept each little devotion of the day, though replete with imperfection, and offer it to Jesus, Whose mercy will overlook all, since He regards not so much the gift as the love of the giver. Amen.

Book 118. The Sibylline Oracles (Summary)

Though the Jewish and Christian oracles contained in this collection are the only extant extended versions of the genre to survive, oracles of the Sibyl were extremely popular in Greco-Roman antiquity from the 5th century BCE onward. The Sibyl, characterized as an aged female prophetess whose "raving mouth" (Plutarch, *Moralia* 397A) almost always forecasted doom, uttered her oracles in Greek hexameter and her oracles usually served purposes of political propaganda. Caesar Augustus is said to have destroyed two thousand prophetic books, including some Sibylline Oracles, because of their subversive nature (Seutonius, *Augustus* 31:1). The earliest Sibyl was believed to have lived in Erythea in Ionia. Other well known Sibyls are associated with Cumae in Italy and Marpessus in Asia Minor (Collins 1983: 317). The proliferation of Sibyls led to various attempts to enumerate them. The most influential of these lists was that of Varro, who counted ten (Lactantius *DivInst.*1.6). The prologue of the present collection repeats this list but associates the Persian Sibyl with an otherwise unknown Hebrew Sibyl.

If, as is widely argued (see below), books 3, 4 and 5 can be located in Egypt then these Sibyls significantly enrich our understanding of Egyptian Judaism during the Ptolemaic and Roman periods. Collins has suggested that book 3 is unique inasmuch as it looks to a Ptolemaic king as savior figure (the "seventh king of Egypt" vs. 193, see also vss. 318, 608). Barclay, however has warned against making too much of this and suggests that both books 3 and 5 can be seen as popular literature of Alexandrian Judaism. As such they attest to the cultural antagonism between Jews and their Gentile surroundings in that locale. This antagonism would later culminate in the Diaspora Revolt of 115-117 CE. Many of the oracles contain a strong polemic against idol worship and homosexuality, which was a common feature in Jewish apologetic.

Provenance of the Individual Oracles

Locating the date and provenance of the individual books within the collection is extremely difficult. Even books which can be confidently assigned to a particular place and time often contain later interpolations.

Books 1 and 2 are likely a unit and consist of a Jewish oracle which has been edited by a later Christian redactor. In the ψ family of manuscripts book 2 contains a lengthy excerpt from Pseudo-Phocylides, the anonymous 1st century Jewish author whose ethical maxims are usually found embedded in the work of the 6th century BCE philosopher. The prominence given to Phrygia in the book indicates that the work originated in Asia Minor. Since Rome alone is singled out for destruction in the tenth generation and Roman power in Asia Minor was consolidated around 30 BCE, the Jewish sections of the book are likely no earlier than this date. Though there is passing reference to the fall of Jerusalem (1.393-400), Collins has suggested that the brevity of this reference and the fact that Rome is not here singled out for recrimination indicates that this section must be part of the Christian interpolation. Thus the Jewish sections of the book can possibly be dated between 30 BCE and 70 CE [Collins 1983: 331]. The reference to the destruction of the Temple sets the earliest date for the Christian redaction. A *terminus ante quem* is more difficult to establish.

Books 3 and 5 are widely believed to have originated in Egyptian Jewish circles. Because of references to the seventh king of Egypt (vss. 193, 318, 608), the provenance of most of book 3 can likely be located in Ptolemaic Egypt in the second century BCE. Numerous additions (vss.350-80) s eem to have been made in the first century BCE as is suggested by references to Cleopatra and her anticipated triumph over Rome. Line 776 may be a Christian interpolation inasmuch as it notes that "mortals will invoke the son of the great God." In his reassessment of the provenance of much of the Jewish Pseudepigrapha, Davila does not wholly refute this consensus but notes that while the work speaks of the Jewish law, the content of this law mostly concerns proper worship of God, and is not concerned with food laws, the Sabbath or circumcision. Thus, while the work could have been authored by an assimilated Jew, it could also be the work of "a gentile who was much taken with and influenced by Judaism in the second or first centuries BCE" (Davila 2005: 186). This is plausible.

The earliest possible date for book 5 is 70 CE, since the work makes use of the *Nero Redivivus*

motif and thus must come after that emperor's death in 68 CE. Inasmuch as the work contains positive references to Hadrian (vss. 46-50), the book is likely not later than 132 BCE, since it is difficult to imagine that a Jewish author would have spoken favorably of Hadrian after the Bar Kochba revolt (132-135 BCE). There is a strong anti-Roman sentiment in these oracles, and the Sibyl looks to a heavenly savior figure. This savior figure is identified with Jesus in a Christian interpolation in lines 255-59. Davila suggests that is just as possible that the work is entirely that of a Christ-believing Jew (thus eliminating the need to posit interpolation) or that the work is that of devout gentile God-fearer (Davila 2005: 189).

Book 4 is composite. The original oracle (vss. 49-101) is likely from the Hellenistic period, and there is nothing in the work to suggest Jewish authorship. The oracle has been augmented by a Jewish redactor (vss. 1-48; 102-172). References to the destruction of the temple and to the eruption of Vesuvius date this redaction to the late first century CE. The provenance of the redaction is debated (Thomas 1935; Nikiprowetzky 1970). The work contains a rejection of temple worship (this is in sharp contrast to books 3 and 5) and an interest in baptism. This interest suggests a provenance in Syria or the Jordan Valley, where baptismal movements seem to have been common, but this can not be confirmed (Collins 1983: 382).

Book 6 is not internally presented as a Sibylline Oracle at all but as hymn to Christ. The hymn begins with the baptism of Jesus, ends with his death and suggests that the cross itself was taken up to heaven after the crucifixion. The work must have been written before 300 CE, when it is quoted by Lactantius (Collins 1983: 406). Its provenance is not known.

A *terminus ante quem* f for **book 7** is also provided by Lactantius (*DivInst* 7.16.13). The work is Christian, and portrays Jesus as a Davidic messiah (vs. 31) who will be enthroned above the angels (vss. 31-33). The work evinces an interest in the baptism of Christ (vss. 65-67) which is to be commemorated by a unique ritual in which a dove is prayed over and then released (vss. 76-81). The provenance of the work is not known.

Book 8 is composite. The first section, vss. 1-216, consists of political prophecies, mostly against Rome. Verses 131-38 were clearly written by a different author than the rest of the work, inasmuch as the pro-Hadrian stance of these verses contradicts verses 50-72. It is uncertain whether this section of the book has its origins amongst a Christian group or a non-Christ believing Jewish group but references to the return of Nero during the reign of Marcus Aurelius (65-74) indicates that book was written during the reign of that emperor, roughly around 175 CE. The second section of the book, lines 217-500, is clearly Christian and is primarily concerned with Christology. It is difficult to date precisely but, again, Lactantius provides a *terminus ante quem*.

Book 9 is comprised of material in from books 1-8. Book 10 repeats the material in book 4. (See **Manuscripts**, below).

Books 11-14 seem to represent "an ongoing tradition that was repeatedly updated" (Collins 1983: 430). Each book picks up where the previous one left off and each concludes with a prayer of the Sibyl. Book 11 contains a review of history from the flood to the death of Cleopatra. Several references to Egypt and to the foundation of Alexandria (vs. 219) suggests that the book may have originated in Egypt. Collins suggests that references to Joseph, Moses and Solomon (vss. 29; 38-40; 80-103) indicate that the work is Jewish. Davila, however, does not find this to be persuasive evidence and maintains that the work could just as easily be Christian.

Book 12 shows dependency on SibOr 5, indeed the first eleven verses are taken directly from that book. The bulk of the work is probably Jewish but verses 30-34 and 232, which both speak about the coming Christ ("the secret word of the Most High will come/ wearing flesh like mortals"; 32-33) are Christian interpolations. A reference to the death of the emperor Alexander Severus (288) (235 CE) provides a *terminus pro quem* of 235 CE.

Book 13 contains praise of Odenath of Palmyra (vss. 150-73) who fought for the Romans against the Parthians during the reign of emperor Gallienus (260-68 CE). Since it does not know of the deaths of either of those figures the work can be dated to approximately 265 CE. The im-

portance accorded Odenath could suggest that the work originated in Syria, but references to Egypt and Alexandria (vss. 43-49) could point to an Egyptian origin. A reference to Decius' persecution of Christians (vss.87-88) could be a Christian interpolation (Collins 1983: 453) or could indicate that the entire work is Christian (Geffcken 1902: 59-63). Collins suggests that references to the Most High (vs. 109) and the polemic against astrology (vss. 69-73) suggest Jewish authorship, though these elements are also congruent with a Christian provenance.

The dating of **book 14** is uncertain. There may be a reference to the Arab conquest (vss. 340-49) which would place the book in the 7th century CE. There are also seem to be references to several Roman emperors, but because the text is exceedingly cryptic, it is difficult identify which ones are being alluded to. There are references to Egypt and to Alexandria (vss. 295-296; 320) which suggests that the book originated there. The concluding verses which proclaim that "the holy nation will hold sway over the whole earth/ for all ages, with their mighty children" (vss. 360-361) suggest Jewish authorship.

Major Themes

The oracles reflect Jewish and Christian interests from a several different time periods (see **Dating and Provenance** below). More than once the Sibyl identifies herself as the daughter-in-law of Noah (1:289; 3:825). A standard feature of the Sibyl's oracle is a periodization of history, usually into ten distinct periods. Oracles against Rome are common and much of the work is characterized by political eschatology which envisions an idyllic kingdom on earth ruled by an idealized king, as such the early oracles provide a rare glimpse of the attitudes of native populations resisting Roman domination. Several oracles envision a return of the loathed despot Nero (4: 119-124; 5: 137-141, 361-396; 8:50-72, 139-50) a common motif which is also found in the New Testament book of Revelation. It is only in the strands of the book which seem to have a Christian origin that there is any extended interest in an afterlife (2: 220-335; 8:310).

Book 119. The Vision of Kenaz (Summary)

Who Was Kenaz in the Bible?

Kenaz, written in Hebrew as קְנַז (Qnazz), is a name that appears in the Old Testament and refers to two different individuals. Though the exact meaning of the name is uncertain, Kenaz's presence in the biblical narrative provides insights into the genealogical and historical context of the Israelites and their neighboring tribes. This article will delve into the lives of these two men named Kenaz, their significance, and the lessons modern Christians can draw from their stories.

Kenaz, Son of Eliphaz

Kenaz is first mentioned as a descendant of Esau. He is the son of Eliphaz and the grandson of Esau, making him an ancestor of the Edomites, who were historical enemies of Israel.

Genesis 36:11, 15, 42

"The sons of Eliphaz were Teman, Omar, Zepho, Gatam, and Kenaz."
"These were the chiefs of the sons of Esau. The sons of Eliphaz, the firstborn son of Esau, were Chief Teman, Chief Omar, Chief Zepho, Chief Kenaz,"

1 Chronicles 1:36, 53

"The sons of Eliphaz: Teman, Omar, Zepho, Gatam, Kenaz, and Amalek."
"and Kenaz, Teman, Mibzar,"

Kenaz's descendants, referred to as Kenizzites, were part of the Edomite clan. The Edomites often clashed with the Israelites, highlighting the long-standing enmity between the two groups. Despite this, the lineage of Kenaz provides a glimpse into the complex relationships and conflicts that shaped the history of the Israelites and their neighbors.

Kenaz, Son of Elah

The second Kenaz mentioned in the Bible is the son of Elah and the grandson of Caleb, one of the faithful spies sent by Moses to scout the Promised Land before its conquest by Joshua.

1 Chronicles 4:15

"The sons of Caleb the son of Jephunneh: Iru, Elah, and Naam; and the son of Elah: Kenaz."

This Kenaz is linked to the tribe of Judah through Caleb, a significant figure known for his faith and courage. Caleb's legacy includes his unwavering trust in God's promises, making his descendants part of a noteworthy lineage within Israel.

Lessons for the Modern Christian
Understanding Our Heritage

Kenaz's story, especially his connection to Caleb, emphasizes the importance of understanding our spiritual heritage. Just as Kenaz was part of Caleb's lineage, modern Christians are part of a spiritual family that includes the heroes of faith mentioned in the Bible. Recognizing this connection can inspire believers to live faithfully and courageously.

Dealing with Conflict

The enmity between the descendants of Kenaz, son of Eliphaz, and the Israelites, reminds Christians of the reality of conflicts in our spiritual journey. These conflicts can be external, like the historical battles between nations, or internal, such as struggles with sin and temptation. Understanding that such conflicts have always existed helps believers to navigate their spiritual battles with wisdom and reliance on God.

Importance of Faithfulness

The legacy of Caleb, and by extension his grandson Kenaz, highlights the importance of faithfulness. Caleb's unwavering trust in God's promises serves as a model for believers. Christians are called to maintain their faith and trust in God, even when faced with challenges and uncertainties.

Connection to a Loving God

God's Sovereign Plan

The inclusion of Kenaz in the biblical genealogies reflects God's sovereign plan in using various lineages to fulfill His purposes. Despite the conflicts and complexities, God's overarching plan remains intact. This teaches modern Christians that God is in control and is weaving every detail of our lives into His grand design.

Assurance of God's Faithfulness

Kenaz's connection to Caleb serves as a reminder of God's faithfulness. Caleb's life was marked by God's promises and their fulfillment. This assures believers that God is faithful to His promises and will fulfill them in His perfect timing.

Connection to Jesus Christ

Fulfillment of the Lineage

Kenaz's inclusion in the genealogy of Caleb, a significant figure in Israel's history, ultimately connects to the lineage of Jesus Christ. Caleb's faithfulness and his inheritance of the Promised Land prefigure the greater inheritance believers have through Christ. Just as Caleb received a physical inheritance, Christians receive a spiritual inheritance through Jesus.

Spiritual Warfare

The battles and conflicts involving the descendants of Kenaz illustrate the spiritual warfare that believers face. Jesus Christ, the ultimate victor, has overcome sin and death, providing believers with the strength and assurance to face their own spiritual battles. Kenaz's story, therefore, points to the greater victory achieved through Christ.

Conclusion

Kenaz, though a minor figure in the Old Testament, holds significant lessons for modern Christians. His story highlights the importance of understanding our spiritual heritage, dealing with conflicts, and maintaining faithfulness. Moreover, Kenaz's connection to Caleb and the broader biblical narrative underscores God's sovereign plan and faithfulness, ultimately pointing to the fulfillment found in Jesus Christ. By reflecting on the lives of biblical figures like Kenaz, believers can gain deeper insights into their own spiritual journey and God's overarching plan for humanity.

Book 120. The Acts of Peter and Paul

It came to pass, after Paul went out of the island Gaudomeleta, that he came to Italy; and it was heard of by the Jews who were in Rome, the elder of the cities, that Paul demanded to come to Cæsar. Having fallen, therefore, into great grief and much despondency, they said among themselves: It does not please him that he alone has afflicted all our brethren and parents in Judæa and Samaria, and in all Palestine; and he has not been pleased with these, but, behold, he comes here also, having through imposition asked Cæsar to destroy us.

Having therefore made an assembly against Paul, and having considered many proposals, it seemed good to them to go to Nero the emperor, *to ask him* not to allow Paul to come to Rome. Having therefore got in readiness not a few presents, and having carried them with them, with supplication they came before him, saying: We beseech you, O good emperor, send orders into all the governments of your worship, to the effect that Paul is not to come near these parts; because this Paul, having afflicted all the nation of our fathers, has been seeking to come hither to destroy us also. And the affliction, O most worshipful emperor, which we have from Peter is enough for us.

And the Emperor Nero, having heard these things, answered them: It is according to your wish. And we write to all our governments that he shall not on any account come to anchor in the parts of Italy. And they also informed Simon the Magian, having sent for him, that, as has been said, he should not come into the parts of Italy.

And while they were thus doing, some of those that had repented out of the nations, and that had been baptized at the preaching of Peter, sent elders to Paul with a letter to the following effect: Paul, dear servant of our Lord Jesus Christ, and brother of Peter, the first of the apostles, we have heard from the rabbis of the Jews that are in this Rome, the greatest of the cities, that they have asked Cæsar to send into all his governments, in order that, wherever you may be found, you may be put to death. But we have believed, and do believe, that as God does not separate the two great lights which He has made, so He is not to part you from each other, that is, neither Peter from Paul, nor Paul from Peter; but we positively believe in our Lord Jesus Christ, into whom we have been baptized, that we have become worthy also of your teaching.

And Paul, having received the two men sent with the letter on the twentieth of the month of May, became eager *to go*, and gave thanks to the Lord and Master Jesus Christ. And having sailed from Gaudomeleta, he did not now come through Africa to the parts of Italy, but ran to Sicily, until he came to the city of Syracuse with the two men who had been sent from Rome to him. And having sailed thence, he came to Rhegium of Calabria, and from Rhegium he crossed to Mesina, and there ordained a bishop, Bacchylus by name. And when he came out of Mesina he sailed to Didymus, and remained there one night. And having sailed thence, he came to Pontiole on the second day.

And Dioscorus the shipmaster, who brought him to Syracuse, sympathizing with Paul because he had delivered his son from death, having left his own ship in Syracuse, accompanied him to Pontiole. And some of Peter's disciples having been found there, and having received Paul, exhorted him to stay with them. And he stayed a week, in hiding, because of the command of Cæsar. And all the toparchs were watching to seize and kill him. But Dioscorus the shipmaster, being himself also bald, wearing his shipmaster's dress, and speaking boldly, on the first day went out into the city of Pontiole. Thinking therefore that he was Paul, they seized him, and beheaded him, and sent his head to Cæsar.

Cæsar therefore, having summoned the first men of the Jews, announced to them, saying: Rejoice with great joy, for Paul your enemy is dead. And he showed them the head. Having therefore made great rejoicing on that day, which was the fourteenth of the month of June, each of the Jews fully believed it.

And Paul, being in Pontiole, and having heard that Dioscorus had been beheaded, being grieved with great grief, gazing into the height of the heaven, said: O Lord Almighty in heaven, who hast appeared to me in every place whither I have gone on account of Your only-begotten Word, our Lord Jesus Christ, punish this city, and bring out all who have believed in God and followed His word. He said to them therefore: Follow me: And going forth from Pontiole with those who had believed in the word of God, they came to a place called Baias; and looking up with their eyes, they all see that city called Pontiole sunk into the sea-shore about one fathom; and there it is until this day, for a remembrance, under the sea.

And having gone forth from Baias, they went to Gaitas, and there he taught the word of God. And he stayed there three days in the house of Erasmus, whom Peter sent from Rome to teach the Gospel of God. And having come forth from Gaitas, he came to the castle called Taracinas, and stayed there seven days in the house of Cæsarius the deacon, whom Peter had ordained by the laying on of hands. And sailing thence, he came by the river to a place called Tribus Tabernes.

And those who had been saved out of the city of Pontiole that had been swallowed up, reported to Cæsar in Rome that Pontiole had been swallowed up, with all its multitude. And the emperor, being in great grief on account of the city, having summoned the chief of the Jews, said to them: Behold, on account of what I heard from you, I have caused Paul to be beheaded, and on account of this the city has been swallowed up. And the chief of the Jews said to Cæsar: Most worshipful emperor, did we not say to you that he troubled all the country of the East, and perverted our fathers? It is better therefore, most worshipful emperor, that one city be destroyed, and not the seat of your empire; for this had Rome to suffer. And the emperor, having heard their words, was appeased.

And Paul stayed in Tribus Tabernes four days. And departing thence, he came to Appii Forum, which is called Vicusarape; and having slept there that night, he saw one sitting on a golden chair, and a multitude of blacks standing beside him, saying: I have today made a son murder his father. Another said: And I have made a house fall, and kill parents with children. And they reported to him many evil deeds— some of one kind, some of another. And another coming, reported to him: I have managed that the bishop Juvenalius, whom Peter ordained, should sleep with the abbess Juliana. And having heard all these things when sleeping in that Appii Forum, near Vicusarape, straightway and immediately he sent to Rome one of those who had followed him from Pontiole to the bishop Juvenalius, telling him this same thing which had just been done. And on the following day, Juvenalius, running, threw himself at the feet of Peter, weeping and lamenting, and saying what had just befallen; and he recounted to him the matter, and said: I believe that this is the light which you were awaiting. And Peter said to him: How is it possible that it is he when he is dead? And Juvenalius the bishop took to Peter him that had been sent by Paul, and he reported to him that he was alive, and on his way, and that he was at Appii Forum. And Peter thanked and glorified the God and Father of our Lord Jesus Christ.

Then having summoned his disciples that believed, he sent them to Paul as far as Tribus Tabernes. And the distance from Rome to Tribus Tabernes is thirty-eight miles. And Paul seeing them, having given thanks to our Lord Jesus Christ, took courage; and departing thence, they slept in the city called Aricia.

And a report went about in the city of Rome that Paul the brother of Peter was coming. And those that believed in God rejoiced with great joy. And there was great consternation among the Jews; and having gone to Simon the Magian, they entreated him, saying: Report to the emperor that Paul is not dead, but that he is alive, and has come. And Simon said to the Jews: What head is it, then, which came to Cæsar from Pontiole? Was it not bald also?

And Paul having come to Rome, great fear fell upon the Jews. They came together therefore to him, and exhorted him, saying: Vindicate the faith in which you were born; for it is not right that you, being a Hebrew, and of the Hebrews, should call yourself teacher of Gentiles, and vindicator of the uncircumcised; and, being yourself circumcised, that you should bring to nought the faith of the circumcision. And when you see Peter, contend against his teaching, because he has destroyed all the bulwarks of our law; for he has prevented the keeping of Sabbaths and new moons, and the holidays appointed by the law. And Paul, answering, said to them: That I am a true Jew, by this you can prove; because also you have been able to keep the Sabbath, and to observe the true circumcision; for assuredly on the day of the Sabbath God rested from all His works. We have fathers, and patriarchs, and the law. What, then, does Peter preach in the kingdom of the Gentiles? But if he shall wish to bring in any new teaching, without any tumult, and envy, and trouble, send him word, that we may see, and in your presence I shall convict him. But if his teaching be true, supported by the book and testimony of the Hebrews, it becomes all of us to submit to him.

Paul saying these and such like things, the Jews went and said to Peter: Paul of the Hebrews has come, and entreats you to come to him, since those who have brought him say that he cannot meet whomsoever he may wish until he appear before Cæsar. And Peter having heard, rejoiced with great joy; and rising up, immediately went to him. And seeing each other, they wept for joy; and long embracing each other, they bedewed each other with tears.

And when Paul had related to Peter the substance of all his doings, and how, through the disasters of the ship, he had come, Peter also told him what he had suffered from Simon the Magian, and all his plots. And having told these things, he went away towards evening.

And in the morning of the following day, at dawn, behold, Peter coming, finds a multitude of the Jews before Paul's door. And there was a great uproar between the Christian Jews and the Gentiles. For, on the one hand, the Jews said: We are a chosen race, a royal priesthood, the friends of Abraham, and Isaac, and Jacob, and all the prophets, with whom God spoke, to whom He showed His own mysteries and His great wonders. But you of the Gentiles are no great thing in your lineage; if otherwise, you have become polluted and abominable by idols and graven images.

While the Jews were saying such things, and such-like, those of the Gentiles answered, saying: We, when we heard the truth, straightway followed it, having abandoned our errors. But you, both knowing the mighty deeds of your fathers, and seeing the signs of the prophets, and having received the law, and gone through the sea with dry feet, and seen your enemies sunk in its depths, and the pillar of fire by night and of cloud by day shining upon you, and manna having been given to you out of heaven, and water flowing to you out of a rock — after all these things you fashioned to yourselves the idol of a calf, and worshipped the graven image. But we, having seen none of the signs, believe to be a Saviour the God whom you have forsaken in unbelief.

While they were contending in these and such-like words, the Apostle Paul said that they ought not to make such attacks upon each other, but that they should rather give heed to this, that God had fulfilled His promises which He swore to Abraham our father, that in his seed he should inherit all the nations. For there is no respect of persons with God. As many as have sinned in law shall be judged according to law, and as many as have sinned without law shall perish without law. Romans 2:12 But we, brethren, ought to thank God that, according to His mercy, He has chosen us to be a holy people to Himself: so that in this we ought to boast, whether Jews or Greeks; for you are all one in the belief of His name.

And Paul having thus spoken, both the Jews and they of the Gentiles were appeased. But the rulers of the Jews assailed Peter. And Peter, when they accused him of having renounced their synagogues, said: Hear, brethren, the holy Spirit about the patriarch David, promising, Of the fruit of your womb shall He set upon your throne. Him therefore to whom the Father said, You are my Son, this day have I begotten You, the chief priests through envy crucified; but that He might accomplish the salvation of the world, it was allowed that He should suffer all these things. Just as, therefore, from the side of Adam Eve was created, so also from the side of Christ was created the Church, which has no spot nor blemish. In Him, therefore, God has opened an entrance to all the sons of Abraham, and Isaac, and Jacob, in order that they may be in the faith of profession towards Him, and have life and salvation in His name. Turn, therefore, and enter into the joy of your father Abraham, because God has fulfilled what He promised to him. Whence also the prophet says, The Lord has sworn, and will not repent: You are a priest for ever, after the order of Melchizedek. For a priest He became upon the cross, when He offered the whole burnt-offering of His own body and blood as a sacrifice for all the world.

And Peter saying this and such-like, the most part of the people believed. And it happened also that Nero's wife Libia, and the yoke-fellow of

Agrippa the prefect, Agrippina by name, thus believed, so that also they went away from beside their own husbands. And on account of the teaching of Paul, many, despising military life, clung to God; so that even from the emperor's bed-chamber some came to him, and having become Christians, were no longer willing to return to the army or the palace.

When, consequently, the people were making a seditious murmuring, Simon, moved with zeal, rouses himself, and began to say many evil things about Peter, saying that he was a wizard and a cheat. And they believed him, wondering at his miracles; for he made a brazen serpent move itself, and stone statues to laugh and move themselves, and himself to run and suddenly to be raised into the air. But as a set-off to these, Peter healed the sick by a word, by praying made the blind to see, put demons to flight by a command; sometimes he even raised the dead. And he said to the people that they should not only flee from Simon's deceit, but also that they should expose him, that they might not seem to be slaves to the devil.

And thus it happened that all pious men abhorred Simon the Magian, and proclaimed him impious. But those who adhered to Simon strongly affirmed Peter to be a magian, bearing false witness as many of them as were with Simon the Magian; so that the matter came even to the ears of Nero the Cæsar, and he gave order to bring Simon the Magian before him. And he, coming in, stood before him, and began suddenly to assume different forms, so that on a sudden he became a child, and after a little an old man, and at other times a young man; for he changed himself both in face and stature into different forms, and was in a frenzy, having the devil as his servant. And Nero beholding this, supposed him to be truly the son of God; but the Apostle Peter showed him to be both a liar and a wizard, base and impious and apostate, and in all things opposed to the truth of God, and that nothing yet remained except that his wickedness, being made apparent by the command of God, might be made manifest to them all.

Then Simon, having gone in to Nero, said: Hear, O good emperor: I am the son of God come down from heaven. Until now I have endured Peter only calling himself an apostle; but now he has doubled the evil: for Paul also himself teaches the same things, and having his mind turned against me, is said to preach along with him; in reference to whom, if you shall not contrive their destruction, it is very plain that your kingdom cannot stand.

Then Nero, filled with concern, ordered to bring them speedily before him. And on the following day Simon the Magian, and Peter and Paul the apostles of Christ, having come in to Nero, Simon said: These are the disciples of the Nazarene, and it is not at all well that they should be of the people of the Jews, Nero said: What is a Nazarene? Simon said: There is a city of Judah which has always been opposed to us, called Nazareth, and to it the teacher of these men belonged. Nero said: God commands us to love every man; why, then, do you persecute them? Simon said: This is a race of men who have turned aside all Judæa from believing in me. Nero said to Peter: Why are you thus unbelieving, according to your race? Then Peter said to Simon: You have been able to impose upon all, but upon me never; and those who have been deceived, God has through me recalled from their error. And since you have learned by experience that you can not get the better of me, I wonder with what face you boast yourself before the emperor, and suppose that through your magic art you shall overcome the disciples of Christ. Nero said: Who is Christ? Peter said: He is what this Simon the Magian affirms himself to be; but this is a most wicked man, and his works are of the devil. But if you wish to know, O good emperor, the things that have been done in Judæa about Christ, take the writings of Pontius Pilate sent to Claudius, and thus you will know all. And Nero ordered them to be brought, and to be read in their presence; and they were to the following effect: —

Pontius Pilate to Claudius, greeting. There has lately happened an event which I myself was concerned in. For the Jews through envy have inflicted on themselves, and those coming after them, dreadful judgments. Their fathers had promises that their God would send them his holy one from heaven, who according to reason should be called their king, and he had promised to send him to the earth by means of a virgin. He, then, when I was procurator, came into Judæa. And they saw him enlightening the blind, cleansing lepers, healing paralytics, expelling demons from men, raising the dead, subduing the winds, walking upon the waves of the sea, and doing many other wonders, and all the people of the Jews calling him Son of God. Then the chief priests, moved with envy against him, seized him, and delivered him to me; and telling one lie after another, they said that he was a wizard, and did contrary to their law. And I, having believed that these things were so, gave him up, after scourging him, to their will; and they crucified him, and after he was buried set guards over him. But he, while my soldiers were guarding him, rose on the third day. And to such a degree was the wickedness of the Jews inflamed against him, that they gave money to the soldiers, saying, Say his disciples have stolen his body. But they, having taken the money, were not able to keep silence as to what had happened; for they have testified that they have seen him (after he was) risen, and that they have received money from the Jews. These things, therefore, have I reported, that no one should falsely speak otherwise, and that you should not suppose that the falsehoods of the Jews are to be believed.

And the letter having been read, Nero said: Tell me, Peter, were all these things thus done by him? Peter said: They were, with your permission, O good emperor. For this Simon is full of lies and deceit, even if it should seem that he is what he is not — a god. And in Christ there is all excellent victory through God and through man, which that incomprehensible glory assumed which through man deigned to come to the assistance of men. But in this Simon there are two essences, of man and of devil, who through man endeavours to ensnare men.

Simon said: I wonder, O good emperor, that you reckon this man of any consequence — a man uneducated, a fisherman of the poorest, and endowed with power neither in word nor by rank. But, that I may not long endure him as an enemy, I shall immediately order my angels to come and avenge me upon him. Peter said: I am not afraid of your angels; but they shall be much more afraid of me in the power and trust of my Lord Jesus Christ, whom you falsely declare yourself to be.

Nero said: Are you not afraid, Peter, of Simon, who confirms his godhead by deeds? Peter said: Godhead is in Him who searches the hidden things of the heart. Now then, tell me what I am thinking about, or what I am doing. I disclose to your servants who are here what my thought is, before he tells lies about it, in order that he may not dare to lie as to what I am thinking about. Nero said: Come hither, and tell me what you are thinking about. Peter said: Order a barley loaf to be brought, and to be given to me secretly. And when he ordered it to be brought, and secretly given to Peter, Peter said: Now tell us, Simon, what has been thought about, or what said, or what done.

Nero said: Do you mean me to believe that Simon does not know these things, who both raised a dead man, and presented himself on the third day after he had been beheaded, and who has done whatever he said he would do? Peter said: But he did not do it before me. Nero said: But he did all these before me. For assuredly he ordered angels to come to him, and they came. Peter said: If he has done what is very great, why does he not do what is very small? Let him tell what I had in my mind, and what I have done. Nero said: Between you, I do not know myself. Simon said: Let Peter say what I am thinking of, or what I am doing. Peter said: What Simon has in his mind I shall show that I know, by my doing what he is thinking about. Simon said: Know this, O emperor, that no one knows the thoughts of men, but God alone. Is not, therefore, Peter lying? Peter said: you, then, who sayest that you are the Son of God, tell what I have in my mind; disclose, if you can, what I have just done in secret. For Peter, having blessed the barley loaf which he had received, and hawing broken it with his right hand and his left, had heaped it up in his sleeves. Then Simon, enraged that he was not able to tell the secret of the apostle, cried out, saying: Let great dogs come forth, and eat him up before Cæsar. And suddenly there appeared great dogs, and rushed at Peter. But Peter, stretching forth his hands to pray, showed to the dogs the loaf which he had blessed; which the dogs seeing, no longer appeared. Then Peter said to Nero: Behold, I have shown you that I knew what Simon was thinking of, not by words, but by deeds; for he, having promised that he would bring angels against me, has brought dogs, in order that he might show that he had not god-like but dog-like angels.

Then Nero said to Simon: What is it, Simon? I think we have got the worst of it. Simon said: This man, both in Judæa and in all Palestine and Cæsarea, has done the same to me; and from very often striving with me, he has learned that this is adverse to them. This, then, he has learned how to escape from me; for the thoughts of men no one knows but God alone. And Peter said to Simon: Certainly you feign yourself to be a god; why, then, do you not reveal the thoughts of every man?

Then Nero, turning to Paul, said: Why do you say nothing, Paul? Paul answered and said: Know this, O emperor, that if you permit this magician to do such things, it will bring an access of the greatest mischief to your country, and will bring down your empire from its position. Nero said to Simon: What do you say? Simon said: If I do not manifestly hold myself out to be a god, no one will bestow upon me due reverence. Nero said: And now, why do you delay, and not show yourself to be a god, in order that these men may be punished? Simon said: Give orders to build for me a lofty tower of wood, and I, going up upon it, will call my angels, and order them to take me, in the sight of all, to my father in heaven; and these men, not being able to do this, are put to shame as uneducated men. And Nero said to Peter: Have you heard, Peter, what has been said by Simon? From this will appear how much power either he or your god has. Peter said: O most mighty emperor, if you were willing, you might perceive that he is full of demons. Nero said: Why do you make to me roundabouts of circumlocutions? Tomorrow will prove you.

Simon said: Do you believe, O good emperor, that I who was dead, and rose again, am a magician? For it had been brought about by his own cleverness that the unbelieving Simon had said to Nero: Order me to be beheaded in a dark place, and there to be left slain; and if I do not rise on the third day, know that I am a magician; but if I rise again, know that I am the Son of God.

And Nero having ordered this, in the dark, by his magic art he managed that a ram should be beheaded. And for so long did the ram appear to be Simon until he was beheaded. And when he had been beheaded in the dark, he that had beheaded him, taking the head, found it to be that of a ram; but he would not say anything to the emperor, lest he should scourge him, having ordered this to be done in secret. Thereafter, accordingly. Simon said that he had risen on the third day, because he took away the head of the ram and the limbs — but the blood had been there congealed — and on the third day he showed himself to Nero, and said: Cause to be wiped away my blood that has been poured out; for, behold, having been beheaded, as I promised, I have risen again on the third day.

And when Nero said, Tomorrow will prove you, turning to Paul, he says: You, Paul, why do you say nothing? Either who taught you, or whom you have for a master, or how you have taught in the cities, or what things have happened through your teaching? For I think that you have not any wisdom, and art not able to accomplish any work of power. Paul answered: Do you suppose that I ought to speak against a desperate man, a magician, who has given his soul up to death, whose destruction and perdition will come speedily? For he ought to speak who pretends to be what he is not, and deceives men by magic art. If you consent to hear his words, and to shield him, you shall destroy your soul and your kingdom, for he is a most base man. And as the Egyptians Jannes and Jambres led Pharaoh and his army astray until they were swallowed up in the sea, so also he, through the instruction of his father the devil, persuades men to do many evils to themselves, and thus deceives many of the innocent, to the peril of your kingdom. But as for the word of the devil, which I see has been poured out through this man, with groanings of my heart I am dealing with the Holy Spirit, that it may be clearly shown what it is; for as far as he seems to raise himself towards heaven, so far will he be sunk down into the depth of Hades, where there is weeping and gnashing of teeth. But about the teaching of my Master, of which you asked me, none attain it except the pure, who allow faith to come into their heart. For as many things as belong to peace and love, these have I taught. Round about from Jerusalem and as far as Illyricum, Romans 15:19 I have fulfilled the word of peace. For I have taught that in honour they should prefer one another; Romans 12:10 I have taught those that are eminent and rich not to be lifted up, and hope in uncertainty of riches, but to place their hope in God; 1 Timothy 6:17 I have taught those in a middle station to be content with food and covering; I have taught the poor to rejoice in their own poverty; I have taught fathers to teach their children instruction in the fear of the Lord, children to obey their parents in wholesome admonition; I have taught wives to love their own husbands, and to fear them as masters, and husbands to observe fidelity to their wives; I have taught masters to treat their slaves with clemency, and slaves to serve their own masters faithfully; Colossians 3:18-22 I have taught the churches of the believers to reverence one almighty, invisible, and incomprehensible God. And this teaching has been given me, not from men, nor through men, but through Jesus Christ, Galatians 1:1 who spoke to me out of heaven, who also has sent me to preach, saying to me, Go forth, for I will be with you; and all things, as many as you shall say or do, I shall make just.

Nero said: What do you say, Peter? He answered and said: All that Paul has said is true. For when he was a persecutor of the faith of Christ, a voice called him out of heaven, and taught him the truth; for he was not an adversary of our faith from hatred, but from ignorance. For there were before us false Christs, like Simon, false apostles, and false prophets, who, contrary to the sacred writings, set themselves to make void the truth; and against these it was necessary to have in readiness this man, who from his youth up set himself to no other thing than to search out the mysteries of the divine law, by which he might become a vindicator of truth and a persecutor of falsehood. Since, then, his persecution was not on account of hatred, but on account of the vindication of the law, the very truth out of heaven held intercourse with him, saying, I am the truth which you persecute; cease persecuting me. When, therefore, he knew that this was so, leaving off that which he was vindicating, he began to vindicate this way of Christ which he was persecuting.

Simon said: O good emperor, take notice that these two have conspired against me; for I am the truth, and they purpose evil against me. Peter said: There is no truth in you; but all you say is false.

Nero said: Paul, what do you say? Paul said: Those things which you have heard from Peter, believe to have been spoken by me also; for we purpose the same thing, for we have the same Lord Jesus the Christ. Simon said: Do you expect me, O good emperor, to hold an argument with these men, who have come to an agreement against me? And having turned to the apostles of Christ, he said: Listen, Peter and Paul: if I can do nothing for you here, we are going to the place where I must judge you. Paul said: O good emperor, see what threats he holds out against us. Peter said: Why was it necessary to keep from laughing outright at a foolish man, made the sport of demons, so as to suppose that he cannot be made manifest?

Simon said: I spare you until I shall receive my power. Paul said: See if you will go out hence safe. Peter said: If you do not see, Simon, the power of our Lord Jesus Christ, you will not believe yourself not to be Christ. Simon said: Most sacred emperor, do not believe them, for they are circumcised knaves. Paul said: Before we knew the truth, we had the circumcision of the flesh; but when the truth appeared, in the circumcision of the heart we both are circumcised, and circumcise. Peter said: If circumcision be a disgrace, why have you been circumcised, Simon?

Nero said: Has, then, Simon also been circumcised? Peter said: For not otherwise could he have deceived souls, unless he feigned himself to be a Jew, and made a show of teaching the law of God. Nero said: Simon, you, as I see, being carried away with envy, persecute these men. For, as it seems, there is great hatred between you and their Christ; and I am afraid that you will be worsted by them, and involved in great evils. Simon said: You are led astray, O emperor. Nero said: How am I led astray? What I see in you, I say. I see that you are manifestly an enemy of Peter and Paul and their master.

Simon said: Christ was not Paul's master. Paul said: Yes; through revelation He taught me also. But tell me what I asked you — Why were you circumcised? Simon said: Why have you asked me this? Paul said: We have a reason for asking you this. Nero said: Why are you afraid to answer them? Simon said: Listen, O emperor. At that time circumcision was enjoined by God when I received it. For this reason was I circumcised.

Paul said: Do you hear, O good emperor, what has been said by Simon? If, therefore, circumcision be a good thing, why have you, Simon, given up those who have been circumcised, and forced them, after being condemned, to be put to death? Nero said: Neither about you do I perceive anything good. Peter and Paul said: Whether this thought about us be good or evil has no reference to the matter; but to us it was necessary that what our Master promised should come to pass. Nero said: If I should not be willing? Peter said: Not as you will, but as He promised to us.

Simon said: O good emperor, these men have reckoned upon your clemency, and have bound you. Nero said: But neither have you yet made me sure about yourself. Simon said: Since so many excellent deeds and signs have been shown to you by me, I wonder how you should be in doubt. Nero said: I neither doubt nor favour any of you; but answer me rather what I ask.

Simon said: Henceforward I answer you nothing. Nero said: Seeing that you lie, therefore you say this. But if even I can do nothing to you, God, who can, will do it. Simon said: I no longer answer you. Nero said: Nor do I consider you to be anything: for, as I perceive, you are a liar in everything. But why do I say so much? The three of you show that your reasoning is uncertain; and thus in all things you have made me doubt, so that I find that I can give credit to none of you.

Peter said: We preach one God and Father of our Lord Jesus Christ, that has made the heaven and the earth and the sea, and all that therein is, who is the true King; and of His kingdom there shall be no end. Luke 1:33 Nero said: What king is lord? Paul said: The Saviour of all the nations. Simon said: I am he whom you speak of. Peter and Paul said: May it never be well with you, Simon, magician, and full of bitterness.

Simon said: Listen, O Cæsar Nero, that you may know that these men are liars, and that I have been sent from the heavens: tomorrow I go up into the heavens, that I may make those who believe in me blessed, and show my wrath upon those who have denied me. Peter and Paul said: Us long ago God called to His own glory; but you, called by the devil, hasten to punishment. Simon said: Cæsar Nero, listen to me. Separate these madmen from you, in order that when I go into heaven to my father, I may be very merciful to you. Nero said: And whence shall we prove this, that you go away into heaven? Simon said: Order a lofty tower to be made of wood, and of great beams, that I may go up upon it, and that my angels may find me in the air; for they cannot come to me upon earth among the sinners. Nero said: I will see whether you will fulfil what you say.

Then Nero ordered a lofty tower to be made in the Campus Martius, and all the people and the dignities to be present at the spectacle. And on the following day, all the multitude having come together, Nero ordered Peter and Paul to be present, to whom also he said: Now the truth has to be made manifest. Peter and Paul said: We do not expose him, but our Lord Jesus Christ, the Son of God, whom he has falsely declared himself to be. And Paul, having turned to Peter, said: It is my part to bend the knee, and to pray to God; and yours to produce the effect, if you should see him attempting anything, because you were first taken in hand by the Lord. And Paul, bending his knees, prayed. And Peter, looking steadfastly upon Simon, said: Accomplish what you have begun; for both your exposure and our call is at hand: for I see my Christ calling both me and Paul. Nero said: And where will you go to against my will? Peter said: Whithersoever our Lord has called us. Nero said: And who is your lord? Peter said: Jesus the Christ, whom I see calling us to Himself. Nero said: Do you also then intend to go away to heaven? Peter said: If it shall seem good to Him that calls us. Simon said: In order that you may know, O emperor, that these are deceivers, as soon as ever I ascend into heaven, I will send my angels to you, and will make you come to me. Nero said: Do at once what you say.

Then Simon went up upon the tower in the face of all, and, crowned with laurels, he stretched forth his hands, and began to fly. And when Nero saw him flying, he said to Peter: This Simon is true; but you and Paul are deceivers. To whom Peter said: Immediately shall you know that we are true disciples of Christ; but that he is not Christ, but a magician, and a malefactor. Nero said: Do you still persist? Behold, you see him going up into heaven. Then Peter, looking steadfastly upon Paul, said: Paul, look up and see. And Paul, having looked up, full of tears, and seeing Simon flying, said: Peter, why are you idle? Finish what you have begun; for already our Lord Jesus Christ is calling us. And Nero hearing them, smiled a little, and said: These men see themselves worsted already, and are gone mad. Peter said: Now you shall know that we are not mad. Paul said to Peter: Do at once what you do.

And Peter, looking steadfastly against Simon, said: I adjure you, you angels of Satan, who are carrying him into the air, to deceive the hearts of the unbelievers, by the God that created all things, and by Jesus Christ, whom on the third day He raised from the dead, no longer from this hour to keep him up, but to let him go. And immediately, being let go, he fell into a place called Sacra Via, that is, Holy Way, and was divided into four parts, having perished by an evil fate.

Then Nero ordered Peter and Paul to be put in irons, and the body of Simon to be carefully kept three days, thinking that he would rise on the third day. To whom Peter said: He will no longer rise, since he is truly dead, being condemned to everlasting punishment. And Nero said to him: Who commanded you to do such a dreadful deed? Peter said: His reflections and blasphemy against my Lord Jesus Christ have brought him into this gulf of destruction. Nero said: I will destroy you by an evil taking off. Peter said: This is not in your power, even if it should seem good to you to destroy us; but it is necessary that what our Master promised to us should be fulfilled.

Then Nero, having summoned Agrippa the proprætor, said to him: It is necessary that men introducing mischievous religious observances should die. Wherefore I order them to take iron clubs, and to be killed in the sea-fight. Agrippa the proprætor said: Most sacred emperor, what you have ordered is not fitting for these men, since Paul seems innocent beside Peter. Nero said: By what fate, then, shall they die? Agrippa answered and said: As seems to me, it is just that Paul's head should be cut off, and that Peter should be raised on a cross as the cause of the murder. Nero said: You have most excellently judged.

Then both Peter and Paul were led away from the presence of Nero. And Paul was beheaded on the Ostesian road.

And Peter, having come to the cross, said: Since my Lord Jesus Christ, who came down from the heaven upon the earth, was raised upon the cross upright, and He has deigned to call to heaven me, who am of the earth, my cross ought to be fixed head down most, so as to direct my feet towards heaven; for I am not worthy to be crucified like my Lord. Then, having reversed the cross, they nailed his feet up.

And the multitude was assembled reviling Cæsar, and wishing to kill him. But Peter restrained them, saying: A few days ago, being exhorted by the brethren, I was going away; and my Lord Jesus Christ met me, and having adored Him, I said, Lord, whither are You going? And He said to me, I am going to Rome to be crucified. And I said to Him, Lord, were You not crucified once for all? And the Lord answering, said, I saw you fleeing from death, and I wish to be crucified instead of you. And I said, Lord, I go; I fulfil Your command. And He said to me, Fear not, for I am with you. On this account, then, children, do not hinder my going; for already my feet are going on the road to heaven. Do not grieve, therefore, but rather rejoice with me, for today I receive the fruit of my labours. And thus speaking, he said: I thank You, good Shepherd, that the sheep which You have entrusted to me, sympathize with me; I ask, then, that with me they may have a part in Your kingdom. And having thus spoken, he gave up the ghost.

And immediately there appeared men glorious and strange in appearance; and they said: We are here, on account of the holy and chief apostles, from Jerusalem. And they, along with Marcellus, an illustrious man, who, having left Simon, had believed in Peter, took up his body secretly, and put it under the terebinth near the place for the exhibition of sea-fights in the place called the Vatican.

And the men who had said that they came from Jerusalem said to the people: Rejoice, and be exceeding glad, because you have been deemed worthy to have great champions. And know that Nero himself, after these not many days, will be utterly destroyed, and his kingdom shall be given to another.

And after these things the people revolted against him; and when he knew of it, he fled into desert places, and through hunger and cold he gave up the ghost, and his body became food for the wild beasts.

And some devout men of the regions of the East wished to carry off the relics of the saints, and immediately there was a great earthquake in the city; and those that dwelt in the city having become aware of it, ran and seized the men, but they fled. But the Romans having taken them, put them in a place three miles from the city, and there they were guarded a year and seven months, until they had built the place in which they intended to put them. And after these things, all having assembled with glory and singing of praise, they put them in the place built for them. And the consummation of the holy glorious Apostles Peter and Paul was on the 29th of the month of June — in Christ Jesus our Lord, to whom be glory and strength.

The Story of Perpetua

And as Paul was being led away to be beheaded at a place about three miles from the city, he was in irons. And there were three soldiers guarding him who were of a great family. And when they had gone out of the gate about the length of a bow-shot, there met them a God-fearing woman; and she, seeing Paul dragged along in irons, had compassion on him, and wept bitterly. And the name of the woman was called Perpetua; and she was one-eyed. And Paul, seeing her weeping, says to her: Give me your handkerchief, and when I turn back I shall give it to you. And she, having taken the handkerchief, gave it to him willingly. And the soldiers laughed, and said to the woman: Why do you wish, woman, to lose your handkerchief? Do you not know that he is going away to be beheaded? And Perpetua said to them: I adjure you by the health of Cæsar to bind his eyes with this handkerchief when you cut off his head. Which also was done. And they beheaded him at the place called Aquæ Salviæ, near the pine tree. And as God had willed, before the soldiers came back, the handkerchief, having on it drops of blood, was restored to the woman. And as she was carrying it, straightway and immediately her eye was opened.

And the three soldiers who had cut off the head of Saint Paul, when after three hours they came on the same day with the Bulla bringing it to Nero, having met Perpetua, they said to her: What is it, woman? Behold, by your confidence you have lost your handkerchief. But she said to them: I have both got my handkerchief, and my eye has recovered its sight. And as the Lord, the God of Paul, lives, I also have entreated him that I may be deemed worthy to become the slave of his Lord. Then the soldiers who had the Bulla, recognising the handkerchief, and seeing that her eye had been opened, cried out with a loud voice, as if from one mouth, and said: We too are the slaves of Paul's master. Perpetua therefore having gone away, reported in the palace of the Emperor Nero that the soldiers who had beheaded Paul said: We shall no longer go into the city, for we believe in Christ whom Paul preached, and we are Christians. Then Nero, filled with rage, ordered Perpetua, who had informed him of the soldiers, to be kept fast in irons; and as to the soldiers, he ordered one to be beheaded outside of the gate about one mile from the city, another to be cut in two, and the third to be stoned. And Perpetua was in the prison; and in this prison there was kept Potentiana, a noble maiden, because she had said: I forsake my parents and all the substance of my father, and I wish to become a Christian. She therefore joined herself to Perpetua, and ascertained from her everything about Paul, and was in much anxiety about the faith in Christ. And the wife of Nero was Potentiana's sister; and she secretly informed her about Christ, that those who believe in Him see everlasting joy, and that everything here is temporary, but there eternal: so that also she fled out of the palace, and some of the senators' wives with her. Then Nero, having inflicted many tortures upon Perpetua, at last tied a great stone to her neck, and ordered her to be thrown over a precipice. And her remains lie at the Momentan gate. And Potentiana also underwent many torments; and at last, having made a furnace one day, they burned her.

Book 121. The Gospel of Bartholomew

Jerome, in the prologue to his Commentary on Matthew, mentions a number of apocryphal Gospels -those according to the Egyptians, Thomas, Matthias, Bartholomew, the Twelve, Basilides, and Apelles: probably he depends upon Origen, for he himself disliked and avoided apocryphal books, with few exceptions; the Gospel according to the Hebrews, for instance, he hardly reckoned as apocryphal. Of this Gospel of Bartholomew we have no sort of description: we find it condemned in the Gelasian Decree, which may mean either that the compiler of the Decree knew a book of that name, or that he took it on trust from Jerome. In the pseudo-Dionysian writings two sentences are quoted from 'the divine Bartholomew,' and a third has just been brought to light from the kindred 'book of Hierotheus'. But one cannot be sure that these writers are quoting real books.

We have, however, a writing attributed to Bartholomew which attained some popularity; the manuscripts do not call it a Gospel, but the Questions of Bartholomew. It contains ancient elements, and I think that MM. Wilmart and Tisserant have made out their claim that it at least represents the old Gospel. I therefore give a translation of it here.

It exists in three languages, and not, apparently, in a very original form in any of them: Greek is the original language, of which we have two manuscripts, at Vienna and Jerusalem; Latin 1, consisting of two leaves of extracts, of the ninth century; Latin 2, complete: see below; Slavonic (i-iv. 15). The Greek text may be as old as the fifth century; the Latin 2 of the sixth or seventh.

In the Revue Biblique for 1913 the Latin fragments and a fresh Greek text were published by MM. Wilmart and Tisserant, with the variants of the other authorities and in 1921-2 yet another text, a complete Latin one, appeared in the same periodical, edited by Professor Moricca from a manuscript in the Casanatensian library at Rome in which the text is, in parts, tremendously expanded. This copy is of the eleventh century and came from the monastery of Monte Amiata. The Latin is exceedingly incorrect, and there are many corruptions, and interpolations which extend to whole pages of closely printed text. I cite it as Lat. 2.

I take the Greek and Slavonic, where they exist, as the basis of my version, and add some passages from the Latin. The main topics, common to two or more of the texts, are:
i. The descent into Hell: the number of souls saved and lost.
ii. The Virgin's account of the Annunciation.
iii. The apostles see the bottomless pit.
iv. The devil is summoned and gives an account of his doings.
v. Questions about the deadly sins. Commission of the apostles to preach. Departure of Christ. (This reads like a late addition.)

GOSPEL (QUESTIONS) OF ST. BARTHOLOMEW

(the opening 3 verses are given from each of the three texts)

Greek. 1 After the resurrection from the dead of our Lord Jesus Christ, Bartholomew came unto the Lord and questioned him, saying: Lord, reveal unto me the mysteries of the heavens.
2 Jesus answered and said unto him: If I put off the body of the flesh, I shall not be able to tell them unto thee.
3 Om.

Slavonic. 1 Before the resurrection of our Lord Jesus Christ from the dead, the apostles said: Let us question the Lord: Lord, reveal unto us the wonders.
2 And Jesus said unto them: If I put off the body of the flesh, I cannot tell them unto you.
3 But when he was buried and risen again, they all durst not question him, because it was not to look upon him, but the fullness of his Godhead was seen.
4 But Bartholomew, &c.

Latin 2. At that time, before the Lord Jesus Christ suffered, all the disciples were gathered together, questioning him and saying: Lord, show us the mystery in the heavens.
2 But Jesus answered and said unto them: If I put not off the body of flesh I cannot tell you.
3 But after that he had suffered and risen again, all the apostles, looking upon him, durst not question him, because his countenance was not as it had been aforetime, but showed forth the fullness of power.

Greek. 4 Bartholomew therefore drew near unto the Lord and said: I have a word to speak unto thee, Lord.
5 And Jesus said to him: I know what thou art about to say; say then what thou wilt, and I will answer thee.
6 And Bartholomew said: Lord, when thou wentest to be hanged upon the cross, I followed thee afar off and saw thee hung upon the cross, and the angels coming down from heaven and worshipping thee. And when there came darkness, 7 I beheld, and I saw thee that thou wast vanished away from the cross and I heard only a voice in the parts under the earth, and great wailing and gnashing of teeth on a sudden. Tell me, Lord, whither wentest thou from the cross?
8 And Jesus answered and said: Blessed art thou, Bartholomew, my beloved, because thou sawest this mystery, and now will I tell thee all things whatsoever thou askest me. 9 For when I vanished away from the cross, then went I down into Hades that I might bring up Adam and all them that were with him, according to the supplication of Michael the archangel.
10 Then said Bartholomew: Lord, what was the voice which was heard?
11 Jesus saith unto him: Hades said unto Beliar: As I perceive, a God cometh hither. *[Slavonic and Latin 2 continue:]* And the angels cried unto the powers, saying: Remove your gates, ye princes, remove the everlasting doors, for behold the King of glory cometh down.
12 Hades said: Who is the King of glory, that cometh down from heaven unto us?
13 And when I had descended five hundred steps, Hades was troubled, saying: I hear the breathing of the Most High, and I cannot endure it. (latin 2. He cometh with great fragrance and I cannot bear it.) 14 But the devil answered and said: Submit not thyself, O Hades, but be strong: for God himself hath not descended upon the earth. 15 But when I had descended yet five hundred steps, the angels and the powers cried out: Take hold, remove the doors, for behold the King of glory cometh down. And Hades said: O, woe unto me, for I hear the breath of God.]
Greek. 16-17 And Beliar said unto Hades: Look carefully who is it that , for it is Elias, or Enoch, or one of the prophets that this man seemeth to me to be. But Hades answered Death and said: Not yet are six thousand years accomplished. And whence are these, O Beliar; for the sum of the number is in mine hands.
[*Slavonic.* 16 And the devil said unto Hades: Why affrightest thou me, Hades? it is a prophet, and he hath made himself like unto God: this

prophet will we take and bring him hither unto those that think to ascend into heaven. 17 And Hades said: Which of the prophets is it? Show me: Is it Enoch the scribe of righteousness? But God hath not suffered him to come down upon the earth before the end of the six thousand years. Sayest thou that it is Elias, the avenger? But before he cometh not down. What shall I do, whereas the destruction is of God: for surely our end is at hand? For I have the number (of the years) in mine hands.]
Greek. 18 : Be not troubled, make safe thy gates and strengthen thy bars: consider, God cometh not down upon the earth.

19 Hades saith unto him: These be no good words that I hear from thee: my belly is rent, and mine inward parts are pained: it cannot be but that God cometh hither. Alas, whither shall I flee before the face of the power of the great king? Suffer me to enter into myself (thyself, Latin): for before (of, latin) thee was I formed.

20 Then did I enter in and scourged him and bound him with chains that cannot be loosed, and brought forth thence all the patriarchs and came again unto the cross.

21 Bartholomew saith unto him: [latin 2, I saw thee again, hanging upon the cross, and all the dead arising and worshipping thee, and going up again into their sepulchres.] Tell me, Lord, who was he whom the angels bare up in their hands, even that man that was very great of stature? [Slav., Latin. 2, And what spakest thou unto him that he sighed so sore?]

22 Jesus answered and said unto him: It was Adam the first-formed, for whose sake I came down from heaven upon earth. And I said unto him: I was hung upon the cross for thee and for thy children's sake. And he, when he heard it, groaned and said: So was thy good pleasure, O Lord.

23 Again Bartholomew said: Lord, I saw the angels ascending before Adam and singing praises.

24 But one of the angels which was very great, above the rest, would not ascend up with them: and there was in his hand a sword of fire, and he was looking steadfastly upon thee only.

[*Slav.* 25 And all the angels besought him that he would go up with them, but he would not. But when thou didst command him to go up, I beheld a flame of fire issuing out of his hands and going even unto the city of Jerusalem.

26 And Jesus said unto him: Blessed art thou, Bartholomew my beloved because thou sawest these mysteries. This was one of the angels of vengeance which stand before my Father's throne: and this angel sent he unto me.

27 And for this cause he would not ascend up, because he desired to destroy all the powers of the world. But when I commanded him to ascend up, there went a flame out of his hand and rent asunder the veil of the temple, and parted it in two pieces for a witness unto the children of Israel for my passion because they crucified me. (Lat. 1. But the flame which thou sawest issuing out of his hands smote the house of the synagogue of the Jews, for a testimony of me wherein they crucified me.)].

Greek. 28 And when he had thus spoken, he said unto the apostles: Tarry for me in this place, for today a sacrifice is offered in paradise. 29 And Bartholomew answered and said unto Jesus: Lord, what is the sacrifice which is offered in paradise? And Jesus said: There be souls of the righteous which to-day have departed out of the body and go unto paradise, and unless I be

30 And Bartholomew said: Lord, how many souls depart out of the world daily? Jesus saith unto him: Thirty thousand.

31 Bartholomew saith unto him: Lord, when thou wast with us teaching the word, didst thou receive the sacrifices in paradise? Jesus answered and said unto him: Verily I say unto thee, my beloved, that I both taught the word with you and continually sat with my Father, and received the sacrifices in paradise everyday. 32 Bartholomew answered and said unto him: Lord, if thirty thousand souls depart out of the world every day, how many souls out of them are found righteous? Jesus saith unto him: Hardly fifty [three] my beloved. 33 Again Bartholomew saith: And how do three only enter into paradise? Jesus saith unto him: The [fifty] three enter into paradise or are laid up in Abraham's bosom: but the others go into the place of the resurrection, for the three are not like unto the fifty.

34 Bartholomew saith unto him: Lord, how many souls above the number are born into the world daily? Jesus saith unto him: One soul only is born above the number of them that depart.[30, &c., Latin 1. Bartholomew said: How many are the souls which depart out of the body every day? Jesus said: Verily I say unto thee, twelve (thousand) eight hundred, four score and three souls depart out of the body every day.]

35 And when he had said this he gave them the peace, and vanished away from them.

II

1 Now the apostles were in the place [Cherubim, Cheltoura, Chritir] with Mary.

2 And Bartholomew came and said unto Peter and Andrew and John: Let us ask her that is highly favoured how she conceived the incomprehensible, or how she bare him that cannot be carried, or how she brought forth so much greatness. But they doubted to ask her.

3 Bartholomew therefore said unto Peter: Thou that art the chief, and my teacher, draw near and ask her. But Peter said to John: Thou art a virgin and undefiled (and beloved) and thou must ask her.

4 And as they all doubted and disputed, Bartholomew came near unto her with a cheerful countenance and said to her: Thou that art highly favoured, the tabernacle of the Most High, unblemished we, even all the apostles, ask thee (or All the apostles have sent me to ask thee) to tell us how thou didst conceive the incomprehensible, or how thou didst bear him that cannot be

5 But Mary said unto them: Ask me not (or Do ye indeed ask me) concerning this mystery. If I should begin to tell you, fire will issue forth out of my mouth and consume all the world.

6 But they continued yet the more to ask her. And she, for she could not refuse to hear the apostles, said: Let us stand up in prayer.

7 And the apostles stood behind Mary: but she said unto Peter: Peter, thou chief, thou great pillar, standest thou behind us? Said not our Lord: the head of the man is Christ ? now therefore stand ye before me and pray.

8 But they said unto her: In thee did the Lord set his tabernacle, and it was his good pleasure that thou shouldest contain him, and thou oughtest to be the leader in the prayer (al. to go with us to).

9 But she said unto them: Ye are shining stars, and as the prophet said, 'I did lift up mine eyes unto the hills, from whence shall come mine help'; ye, therefore, are the hills, and it behoveth you to pray.

10 The apostles say unto her: Thou oughtest to pray, thou art the mother of the heavenly king.

11 Mary saith unto them: In your likeness did God form the sparrows, and sent them forth into the four corners of the world.

12 But they say unto her: He that is scarce contained by the

13 Then Mary stood up before them and spread out her hands toward the heaven and began to speak thus: Elphue Zarethra Charboum Nemioth Melitho Thraboutha Mephnounos Chemiath Aroura Maridon Elison Marmiadon Seption Hesaboutha Ennouna Saktinos Athoor Belelam Opheoth Abo Chrasar (this is the reading of one Greek copy: the others and the Slavonic have many differences as in all such cases: but as the original words-assuming them to have once had a meaning-are hopelessly corrupted, the matter is not of importance), which is in the Greek tongue(Hebrew, Slav.): O God the exceeding great and all-wise and king of the worlds (ages), that art not to be described, the ineffable, that didst establish the greatness of the heavens and all things by a word, that out of darkness (or the unknown) didst constitute and fasten together the poles of heaven in harmony, didst bring into shape the matter that was in confusion, didst bring into order the things that were without order, didst part the misty darkness from the light, didst establish in one place the foundations of the waters, thou that makest the beings of the air to tremble, and art the fear of them that are on (or under) the earth, that didst settle the earth and not suffer it to perish, and filledst it, which is the nourisher of all things, with showers of blessing: (Son of) the Father, thou whom the seven heavens hardly contained, but who wast well-pleased to be contained without pain in me, thou that art thyself the full word of the Father in whom all things came to be: give glory to thine exceeding great name, and bid me to speak before thy holy

14 And when she had ended the prayer she began to say unto them: Let us sit down upon the ground; and come thou, Peter the chief, and sit on my right hand and put thy left hand beneath mine armpit; and thou, Andrew, do so on my left hand; and thou, John, the virgin, hold together my bosom; and thou, Bartholomew, set thy knees against my back and hold my shoulders, lest when I begin to speak my bones be loosed one from another.

15 And when they had so done she began to say: When I abode in the temple of God and received my food from an angel, on a certain day there appeared unto me one in the likeness of an angel, but his face was incomprehensible, and he had not in his hand bread or a cup, as did the angel which came to me aforetime.

16 And straightway the robe (veil) of the temple was rent and there was a very great earthquake, and I fell upon the earth, for I was not able to endure the sight of him.

17 But he put his hand beneath me and raised me up, and I looked up into heaven and there came a cloud of dew and sprinkled me from the head to the feet, and he wiped me with his robe.

18 And said unto me: Hail, thou that art highly favoured, the chosen vessel, grace inexhaustible. And he smote his garment upon the right hand and there came a very great loaf, and he set it upon the altar of the temple and did eat of it first himself, and gave unto me also.

19 And again he smote his garment upon the left hand and there came a very great cup full of wine: and he set it upon the altar of the temple and did drink of it first himself, and gave also unto me. And I beheld and saw the bread and the cup whole as they were.

20 And he said unto me: Yet three years, and I will send my word unto thee and then shalt conceive my (or a) son, and through him shall the whole creation be saved. Peace be unto

21 And when he had so said he vanished away from mine eyes, and the temple was restored as it had been before.

22 And as she was saying this, fire issued out of her mouth; and the world was at the point to come to an end: but Jesus appeared quickly (lat. 2, and laid his hand upon her mouth) and said unto Mary: Utter not this mystery, or this day my whole creation will come to an end (Lat. 2, and the flame

from her mouth ceased). And the apostles were taken with fear lest haply the Lord should be wroth with them.

III

1 And he departed with them unto the mount Mauria (Lat. 2, Mambre), and sat in the midst of them. 2 But they doubted to question him, being afraid.

3 And Jesus answered and said unto them: Ask me what ye will that I should teach you, and I will show it you. For yet seven days, and I ascend unto my Father, and I shall no more be seen of you in this likeness.

4 But they, yet doubting, said unto him: Lord, show us the deep (abyss) according unto thy promise.

5 And Jesus said unto them: It is not good (Lat. 2, is good) for you to see the deep: notwithstanding, if ye desire it, according to my promise, come, follow me and behold.

6 And he led them away into a place that is called Cherubim (Cherukt Slav., Chairoudee Gr., Lat. 2 omits), that is the place of truth.

7 And he beckoned unto the angels of the West and the earth was rolled up like a volume of a book and the deep was revealed unto them.

8 And when the apostles saw it they fell on their faces upon the earth.

9 But Jesus raised them up, saying: Said I not unto you, 'It is not good for you to see the deep'. And again he beckoned unto the angels, and the deep was covered up.

IV

1 And he took them and brought them again unto the Mount of olives.

2 And Peter said unto Mary: Thou that art highly favoured, entreat the Lord that he would reveal unto us the things that are in the heavens.

3 And Mary said unto Peter: O stone hewn out of the rock, did not the Lord build his church upon thee? Go thou therefore first and ask him.

4 Peter saith again: O tabernacle that art spread abroad . 5 Mary saith: Thou art the image of Adam: was not he first formed and then Eve? Look upon the sun, that according to the likeness of Adam it is bright. and upon the moon, that because of the transgression of Eve it is full of clay. For God did place Adam in the east and Eve in the west, and appointed the lights that the sun should shine on the earth unto Adam in the east in his fiery chariots, and the moon in the west should give light unto Eve with a countenance like milk. And she defiled the commandment of the Lord. Therefore was the moon stained with clay (Lat. 2, is cloudy) and her light is not bright. Thou therefore, since thou art the likeness of Adam, oughtest to ask him: but in me was he contained that I might recover the strength of the female.

6 Now when they came up to the top of the mount, and the Master was withdrawn from them a little space, Peter saith unto Mary: Thou art she that hast brought to nought the transgression of Eve, changing it from shame into joy; it is lawful, therefore, for thee to ask.

7 When Jesus appeared again, Bartholomew saith unto him: Lord, show us the adversary of men that we may behold him, of what fashion he is, and what is his work, and whence he cometh forth, and what power he hath that he spared not even thee, but caused thee to be hanged upon the tree.

8 But Jesus looked upon him and said: Thou bold heart! thou askest for that which thou art not able to look upon.

9 But Bartholomew was troubled and fell at Jesus' feet and began to speak thus: O lamp that cannot be quenched, Lord Jesus Christ, maker of the eternal light that hast given unto them that love thee the grace that beautifieth all, and hast given us the eternal light by thy coming into the world, that hast accomplished the work of the Father, hast turned the shame-facedness of Adam into mirth, hast done away the sorrow of Eve with a cheerful countenance by thy birth from a virgin: remember not evil against me but grant me the word of mine asking. (Lat. 2, who didst come down into the world, who hast confirmed the eternal word of the Father, who hast called the sadness of joy, who hast made the shame of Eve glad, and restored her by vouchsafing to be contained in the womb.)

10 And as he thus spake, Jesus raised him up and said unto him: Bartholomew, wilt thou see the adversary of men? I tell thee that when thou beholdest him, not thou only but the rest of

11 But they all said unto him: Lord, let us behold him.

12 And he led them down from the Mount of Olives and looked wrathfully upon the angels that keep hell (Tartarus), and beckoned unto Michael to sound the trumpet in the height of the heavens. And Michael sounded, and the earth shook, and Beliar came up, being held by 660 (560 Gr., 6,064 Lat. 1, 6,060 Lat. 2) angels and bound with fiery chains. 12 And the length of him was 1,600 cubits and his breadth 40 (Lat. 1, 300, Slav. 17) cubits (Lat. 2, his length 1,900 cubits, his breadth 700, one wing of him 80), and his face was like a lightning of fire and his eyes full of darkness (like sparks, Slav.). And out of his nostrils came a stinking smoke; and his mouth was as the gulf of a precipice, and the one of his wings was fourscore cubits.

14 And straightway when the apostles saw him, they fell to the earth on their faces and became as dead.

15 But Jesus came near and raised the apostles and gave them a spirit of power, and he saith unto Bartholomew: Come near, Bartholomew, and trample with thy feet on his neck, and he will tell thee his work, what it is, and how he deceiveth men.

16 And Jesus stood afar off with the rest of the apostles.

17 And Barthololmew feared, and raised his voice and said: Blessed be the name of thine immortal kingdom from henceforth even for ever. And when he had spoken, Jesus permitted him, saying: Go and tread upon the neck of Beliar: and Bartholomew ran quickly upon him and trode upon his neck: and Beliar trembled. (For this verse the Vienna MS. has: And Bartholomew raised his voice and said thus: O womb more spacious than a city, wider than the spreading of the heavens, that contained him whom the seven heavens contain not, but thou without pain didst contain sanctified in thy bosom, &c.: evidently out of place. Latin 1 has only: Then did Antichrist tremble and was filled with fury.)

18 And Bartholomew was afraid, and fled, and said unto Jesus: Lord, give me an hem of thy garments (Lat. 2, the kerchief (?) from thy shoulders) that I may have courage to draw near unto him.

19 But Jesus said unto him: Thou canst not take an hem of my garments, for these are not my garments which I wore before I was crucified.

20 And Bartholomew said: Lord, I fear lest, like as he spared not thine angels, he swallow me up also.

21 Jesus saith unto him: Were not all things made by my word, and by the will of my Father the spirits were made subject unto Solomon? thou, therefore, being commanded by my word, go in my name and ask him what thou wilt. (lat. 2 omits 20.)

22 [And Bartholomew made the sign of the cross and prayed unto Jesus and went behind him. And Jesus said to him: Draw near. And as Bartholomew drew near, fire was kindled on every side, so that his garments appeared fiery. Jesus saith to Bartholomew: As I said unto thee, tread upon his neck and ask him what is his power.] And Bartholomew went and trode upon his neck, and pressed down his face into the earth as far as his ears.

23 And Bartholomew saith unto him: Tell me who thou art and what is thy name. And he said to him: Lighten me a little, and I will tell thee who I am and how I came hither, and what my work is and what my power is.

24 And he lightened him and saith to him: Say all that thou hast done and all that thou doest.

25 And Beliar answered and said: If thou wilt know my name, at the first I was called Satanael, which is interpreted a messenger of God, but when I rejected the image of God my name was called Satanas, that is, an angel that keepeth hell (Tartarus).

26 And again Bartholomew saith unto him: Reveal unto me all things and hide nothing from me.

27 And he said unto him: I swear unto thee by the power of the glory of God that even if I would hide aught I cannot, for he is near that would convict me. For if I were able I would have destroyed you like one of them that were before you.

28 For, indeed, I was formed (al. called) the first angel: for when God made the heavens, he took a handful of fire and formed me first, Michael second [Vienna MS. here has these sentences: for he had his Son before the heavens and the earth and we were formed (for when he took thought to create all things, his Son spake a word), so that we also were created by the will of the Son and the consent of the Father. He formed, I say, first me, next Michael the chief captain of the hosts that are above], Gabriel third, Uriel fourth, Raphael fifth, Nathanael sixth, and other angels of whom I cannot tell the names. [Jerusalem MS., Michael, Gabriel, Raphael, Uriel, Xathanael, and other 6,000 angels. Lat. I, Michael the honour of power, third Raphael, fourth Gabriel, and other seven. Lat. 2, Raphael third, Gabriel fourth, Uriel fifth, Zathael sixth, and other six.] For they are the rod-bearers (lictors) of God, and they smite me with their rods and pursue me seven times in the night and seven times in the day, and leave me not at all and break in pieces all my power. These are the (twelve, lat. 2) angels of vengeance which stand before the throne of God: these are the angels that were first formed.

30 And after them were formed all the angels. In the first heaven are an hundred myriads, and in the second an hundred myriads, and in the third an hundred myriads, and in the fourth an hundred myriads, and in the fifth an hundred myriads, and in the sixth an hundred myriads, and in the seventh (an hundred myriads, and outside the seven heavens, Jerusalem MS.) is the first firmament (flat surface) wherein are the powers which work upon men.

31 For there are four other angels set over the winds. The first angel is over the north, and he is called Chairoum (. . . broil, Jerusalem MS.; lat. 2, angel of the north, Mauch), and hath in his hand a rod of fire, and restraineth the super-fluity of moisture that the earth be not overmuch wet.

32 And the angel that is over the north is called Oertha (Lat. 2, Alfatha): he hath a torch of fire and putteth it to his sides, and they warm the great coldness of him that he freeze not the world.

33 And the angel that is over the south is called Kerkoutha (Lat. 2, Cedar) and they break his fierceness that he shake not the earth.

34 And the angel that is over the south-west is called Naoutha, and he hath a rod of snow in his hand and putteth it into his mouth, and quencheth the fire that cometh out of his mouth. And if the angel quenched it not at his mouth it would set all the world on fire.

35 And there is another angel over the sea which maketh it rough with the waves thereof.

36 But the

37 Bartholomew saith unto him: Flow chastisest thou the souls of men?

38 Beliar saith unto him: Wilt thou that I declare unto thee the punishment of the hypocrites, of the back-biters, of the jesters, of the idolaters, and the covetous, and the adulterers, and the wizards, and the diviners, and of them that believe in us, and of all whom I look upon (deceive?)?

(38 Lat. 2: When I will show any illusion by them. But they that do these things, and they that consent unto them or follow them, do perish with me.

39 Bartholomew said unto him: Declare quickly how thou persuadest men not to follow God and thine evil arts, that are slippery and dark, that they should leave the straight and shining paths of the Lord.) 39 Bartholomew saith unto him: I will that thou declare it in few words.

40 And he smote his teeth together, gnashing them, and there came up out of the bottomless pit a wheel having a sword flashing with fire, and in the sword were pipes.

41 And I (he) asked him, saying: What is this sword?

42 And he said: This sword is the sword of the gluttonous: for into this pipe are sent they that through their gluttony devise all manner of sin; into the second pipe are sent the backbiters which backbite their neighbour secretly; into the third pipe are sent the hypocrites and the rest whom I overthrow by my contrivance. (Lat. 2:40 And Antichrist said: I will tell thee. And a wheel came up out of the abyss, having seven fiery knives. The first knife hath twelve pipes (canales) . . . 42 Antichrist answered: The pipe of fire in the first knife, in it are put the casters of lots and diviners and enchanters, and they that believe in them or have sought them, because in the iniquity of their heart they have invented false divinations. In the second pipe of fire are first the blasphemers ... suicides ... idolaters.... In the rest are first perjurers . . . (long enumeration).)

43 And Bartholomew said: Dost thou then do these things by thyself alone?

44 And Satan said: If I were able to go forth by myself, I would have destroyed the whole world in three days: but neither I nor any of the six hundred go forth. For we have other swift ministers whom we command, and we furnish them with an hook of many points and send them forth to hunt, and they catch for us souls of men, enticing them with sweetness of divers baits, that is by drunkenness and laughter, by backbiting, hypocrisy, pleasures, fornication, and the rest of the

45 And I will tell thee also the rest of the names of the angels. The angel of the hail is called Mermeoth, and he holdeth the hail upon his head, and my ministers do adjure him and send him whither they will. And other angels are there over the snow, and other over the thunder, and other over the lightning, and when any spirit of us would go forth either by land or by sea, these angels send forth fiery stones and set our limbs on fire. (Lat. 2 enumerates all the transgressions

46 Bartholomew saith: Be still (be muzzled) thou dragon of the pit.

47 And Beliar said: Many things will I tell thee of the angels. They that run together throughout the heavenly places and the earthly are these: Mermeoth, Onomatath, Douth, Melioth, Charouth, Graphathas, Oethra, Nephonos, Chalkatoura. With them do fly (are administered?) the things that are in heaven and on earth and under the earth.

48 Bartholomew saith unto him: Be still (be muzzled) and be faint, that I may entreat my Lord.

49 And Bartholomew fell upon his face and cast earth upon his head and began to say: O Lord Jesu Christ, the great and glorious name. All the choirs of the angels praise thee, O Master, and I that am unworthy with my lips . . . do praise thee, O Master. Hearken unto me thy servant, and as thou didst choose me from the receipt of custom and didst not suffer me to have my conversation unto the end in my former deeds, O Lord Jesu Christ, hearken unto me and have mercy upon the sinners.

50 And when he had so said, the Lord saith unto him: Rise up, suffer him that groaneth to arise: I will declare the rest unto thee.

51 And Bartholomew raised up Satan and said unto him: Go unto thy place, with thine angels, but the Lord hath mercy upon all his world. (50, 51, again enormously amplified in lat. 2. Satan complains that he has been tricked into telling his secrets before the time. The interpolation is to some extent dated by this sentence: ' Simon Magus and Zaroes and Arfaxir and Jannes and Mambres are my brothers.' Zaroes and Arfaxatare wizards who figure in the Latin Acts of Matthew and of Simon and Jude (see below).

52 But the devil said: Suffer me, and I will tell thee how I was cast down into this place and how the Lord did make man.

53 I was going to and fro in the world, and God said unto Michael: Bring me a clod from the four corners of the earth, and water out of the four rivers of paradise. And when Michael brought them God formed Adam in the regions of the east, and shaped the clod which was shapeless, and stretched sinews and veins upon it and established it with Joints; and he worshipped him, himself for his own sake first, because he was the image of God, therefore he worshipped him.

54 And when I came from the ends of the earth Michael said: Worship thou the image of God, which he hath made according to his likeness. But

I said: I am fire of fire, I was the first angel formed, and shall worship clay and matter?

55 And Michael saith to me: Worship, lest God be wroth with thee. But I said to him: God will not be wroth with me; but I will set my throne over against his throne, and I will be as he is. Then was God wroth with me and cast me down, having commanded the windows of heaven to be opened.

56 And when I was cast down, he asked also the six hundred that were under me, if they would worship: but they said: Like as we have seen the first angel do, neither will we worship him that is less than ourselves. Then were the six hundred also cast down by him with me.

57 And when we were cast down upon the earth we were senseless for forty years, and when the sun shone forth seven times brighter than fire, suddenly I awaked; and I looked about and saw the six hundred that were under me senseless.

58 And I awaked my son Salpsan and took him to counsel how I might deceive the man on whose account I was cast out of the heavens.

59 And thus did I contrive it. I took a vial in mine hand and scraped the sweat from off my breast and the hair of mine armpits, and washed myself (Lat. 2, I took fig leaves in my hands and wiped the sweat from my bosom and below mine arms and cast it down beside the streams of waters. 69 is greatly prolonged in this text) in the springs of the waters whence the four rivers flow out, and Eve drank of it and desire came upon her: for if she had not drunk of that water I should not have been able to deceive her.

61 And Bartholomew came and fell at Jesus' feet and began with tears to say thus: Abba, Father, that art past finding out by us, Word of the Father, whom the seven heavens hardly contained, but who wast pleased to be contained easily and without pain within the body of the Virgin: whom the Virgin knew not that she bare: thou by thy thought hast ordained all things to be: thou givest us that which we need before thou art entreated.

62 Thou that didst wear a crown of thorns that thou mightest prepare for us that repent the precious crown from heaven; that didst hang upon the tree, that (a clause gone): (lat. 2, that thou mightest turn from us the tree of lust and concupiscence (etc., etc.). The verse is prolonged for over 40 lines) (that didst drink wine mingled with gall) that thou mightest give us to drink of the wine of compunction, and wast pierced in the side with a spear that thou mightest fill us with thy body and thy blood:

63 Thou that gavest names unto the four rivers: to the first Phison, because of the faith (pistis) which thou didst appear in the world to preach; to the second Geon, for that man was made of earth (ge); to the third Tigris, because by thee was revealed unto us the consubstantial Trinity in the heavens (to make anything of this we must read Trigis); to the fourth Euphrates, because by thy presence in the world thou madest every soul to rejoice (euphranai) through the word of immortality.

64 My God, and Father, the greatest, my King: save, Lord, the sinners.

65 When he had thus prayed Jesus said unto him: Bartholomew, my Father did name me Christ, that I might come down upon earth and anoint every man that cometh unto me with the oil of life: and he did call me Jesus that I might heal every sin of them that know not . . . and give unto men (several corrupt words: the

66 And again Bartholomew saith unto him: Lord, is it lawful for me to reveal these mysteries unto every man? Jesus saith unto him: Bartholomew, my beloved, as many as are faithful and are able to keep them unto themselves, to them mayest thou entrust these things. For some there are that be worthy of them, but there are also other some unto whom it is not fit to entrust them: for they are vain (swaggerers), drunkards, proud, unmerciful, partakers in idolatry, authors of fornication, slanderers, teachers of foolishness, and doing all works that are of the devil, and therefore are they not worthy that these should be entrusted to them.

68 And also they are secret, because of those that cannot contain them; for as many as can contain them shall have a part in them. Herein (Hitherto?) therefore, my beloved, have I spoken unto thee, for blessed art thou and all thy kindred which of their choice have this word entrusted unto them; for all they that of my judgement.

69 Then I, Bartholomew, which wrote these things in mine heart, took hold on the hand of

Glory be to thee, O Lord Jesus Christ, that givest unto all thy grace which all we have perceived. Alleluia.

Glory be to thee, O Lord, the life of sinners.

Glory be to thee, O Lord, death is put to shame.

Glory be to thee, O Lord, the treasure of righteousness.

For unto God do we sing.

70 And as Bartholomew thus spake again, Jesus put off his mantle and took a kerchief from the neck of Bartholomew and began to rejoice and say (70 lat. 2, Then Jesus took a kerchief (?) I and said: I am good: mild and gracious and merciful, strong and righteous, wonderful and holy): I am good. Alleluia. I am meek and gentle. Alleluia. Glory be to thee, O Lord: for I give gifts unto all them that desire me. Alleluia.

Glory be to thee, O Lord, world without end. Amen. Alleluia.

71 And when he had ceased, the apostles kissed him, and he gave them the peace of love.

VI

1 Bartholomew saith unto him: Declare unto us, Lord what sin is heavier than all sins?

2 Jesus saith unto him: Verily I say unto thee that hypocrisy and backbiting is heavier than all sins: for because of them, the prophet said in the psalm, that 'the ungodly shall not rise in the judgement, neither sinners in the council of the righteous', neither the ungodly in the judgement of my Father. Verily, verily, I say unto you, that every sin shall be forgiven unto every man, but the sin against the Holy Ghost shall not be forgiven.

3 And Bartholomew saith unto him: What is the sin against the Holy Ghost?

4 Jesus saith unto him: Whosoever shall decree against any man that hath served my holy Father hath blasphemed against the Holy Ghost: For every man that serveth God worshipfully is worthy of the Holy Ghost, and he that speaketh anything evil against him shall not be forgiven.

5 Woe unto him that sweareth by the head of God, yea woe (?) to him that sweareth falsely by him truly. For there are twelve heads of God the most high: for he is the truth, and in him is no lie, neither forswearing.

6 Ye, therefore, go ye and preach unto all the world the word of truth, and thou, Bartholomew, preach this word unto every one that desireth it; and as many as

7 Bartholomew saith: O Lord, and if any sin with sin of the body, what is their reward?

8 And Jesus said: It is good if he that is baptized present his baptism blameless: but the pleasure of the flesh will become a lover. For a single marriage belongeth to sobriety: for verily I say unto thee, he that sinneth after the third marriage (wife) is unworthy of God. (8 Lat. 2 is to this effect: . . . But if the lust of the flesh come upon him, he ought to be the husband of one wife. The married, if they are good and pay tithes, will receive a hundredfold. A second marriage is lawful, on condition of the diligent performance of good works, and due payment of tithes: but a third marriage is reprobated: and virginity is best.)

9 But ye, preach ye unto every man that they keep themselves from such things: for I depart not from you and I do supply you with the Holy Ghost. (lat. 2, At the end of 9, Jesus ascends in the clouds, and two angels appear and say: 'Ye men of Galilee', and the rest)

10 And Bartholomew worshipped him with the apostles, and glorified God earnestly, saying: Glory be to thee, Holy Father, Sun unquenchable, incomprehensible, full of light. Unto thee be glory, unto thee honour and adoration, world without end. Amen. (Lat. 2, End of the questioning of the most blessed Bartholomew and (or) the other apostles with the Lord Jesus Christ.)

THE BOOK OF THE RESURRECTION OF CHRIST BY BARTHOLOMEW THE APOSTLE

Introduction: This exists in Coptic only. There are several recessions of it: the most complete is in a manuscript recently acquired by the British Museum (Or. 6804), and translated first by W. E. Crum (Rustafjaell's light of Egypt, 1910) and then edited and translated by Sir E. A. Wallis Budge (Coptic Apocrypha in the dialect of Upper Egypt, 1913). Other fragments are in the publications of Lacau and Revillout. No full translation, but only an analysis, will be offered here. Five leaves are wanting at the beginning of the British Museum MS. The contents of these can be partly filled up from Lacau and Revillout. But in the first place a passage (p. 193, Budge) may be quoted which shows something of the setting of the book: 'Do not let this book come into the hand of any man who is an unbeliever and a heretic. Behold this is the seventh time that I have commanded thee, O my son Thaddaeus, concerning these mysteries. Reveal not thou them to any impure man, but keep them safely. ' We see that the book was addressed by Bartholomew to his son Thaddaeus, and this would no doubt have been the subject of some of the opening lines of the

Next we may place the two fragments, one about the child of Joseph of Arimathaea, the other about the cock raised to life, which have been already described as nos. 7 and 8 of the Coptic narratives of the Passion (pp. 149, 150). The order is uncertain. Then we have a piece which in Revillout is no. 12 (p. 165), in Lacauno. 3 (p. 34). Lacau gives it partly in two recensions.

Christ is on the cross, but his side has been pierced, and he is dead.

A man in the crowd named Ananias, of Bethlehem, rushes to the cross and embraces and salutes the body breast to breast, hand to hand, and denounces the Jews. A voice comes from the body of Jesus and blesses Ananias, promising him incorruption and the name of ' the first fruits of the immortal fruit '. The priests decide to stone Ananias: he utters words of exultation. The stoning produces no effect. They cast him into a furnace where he remains till Jesus has risen. At last they pierce him with a spear.

The Saviour takes his soul to heaven, and blesses him.

There can be but little matter lost between this and the opening of the British Museum MS., in the first lines of which the taking of Ananias' soul to heaven is mentioned.

We now take up the British Museum MS. as our basis. Certain passages of it are preserved in Paris fragments which partly overlap each other, and so three different texts exist for some parts: but it will not be important for our purpose to note many of the variations.

Joseph of Arimathaea buried the body of Jesus. Death came into Amente (the underworld), asking who the new arrival was, for he detected a disturbance.

He came to the tomb of Jesus with his six sons in the form of serpents. Jesus lay there (it was the second day, i. e. the Saturday) with his face and head covered with napkins.

Death addressed his son the Pestilence, and described the commotion which had taken place in his domain. Then he spoke to the body of Jesus and asked, 'Who art thou?' Jesus removed the napkin that was on his face and looked in the face of Death and laughed at him. Death and his sons fled. Then they approached again, and the same thing happened. He addressed Jesus again at some length, suspecting, but not certain, who he was.

Then Jesus rose and mounted into the chariot of the Cherubim. He wrought havoc in Hell, breaking the doors, binding the demons Beliar and Melkir (cf. Melkira in the Ascension of Isaiah), and delivered Adam and the holy souls.

Then he turned to Judas Iscariot and uttered a long rebuke, and described the sufferings which he must endure. Thirty names of sins are given, which are the snakes which were sent to devour him.

Jesus rose from the dead, and Abbaton (Death) and Pestilence came back to Amente to protect it, but they found it wholly desolate, only three souls were left in it (those of Herod, Cain, and Judas, says the Paris MS.).

Meanwhile the angels were singing the hymn which the Seraphim sing at dawn on the Lord's day over his body and his blood.

Early in the morning of the Lord's day the women went to the tomb. They were Mary Magdalene, Mary the mother of James whom Jesus delivered out of the hand of Satan, Salome who tempted him, Mary who ministered to him and Martha her sister, Joanna (al. Susanna) the wife of Chuza who had renounced the marriage bed, Berenice who was healed of an issue of blood in Capernaum, Lia (Leah) the widow whose son he raised at Nain, and the woman to whom he said, 'Thy sins which are many are forgiven thee'.

These were all in the garden of Philogenes, whose son Simeon Jesus healed when he came down from the Mount of Olives with the apostles (probably the lunatic boy at the Mount of Transfiguration).

Mary said to Philogenes: If thou art indeed he, I know thee. Philogenes said: Thou art Mary the mother of Thalkamarimath, which means joy, blessing, and gladness. Mary said: If thou have borne him away, tell me where thou hast laid him and I will take him away: fear not. Philogenes told how the Jews sought a safe tomb for Jesus that the body might not be stolen, and he offered to place it in a tomb in his own garden and watch over it: and they sealed it and departed. At midnight he rose and went out and found all the orders of angels: Cherubim Seraphim, Powers, and Virgins. Heaven opened, and the Father raised Jesus. Peter, too, was there and supported Philogenes, or he would have died.

The Saviour then appeared to them on the chariot of the Father and said to Mary: Mari Khar Mariath (Mary the mother of the Son of God). Mary answered: Rabbouni Kathiathari Mioth (The Son of God the Almighty, my Lord, and my Son.). A long address to Mary from Jesus follows, in the course of which he bids her tell his brethren, 'I ascend unto my Father and your Father', &c. Mary says: If indeed I am not permitted to touch thee, at least bless my body in which thou didst deign to dwell.

Believe me, my brethren the holy apostles, I, Bartholomew beheld the Son of God on the chariot of the Cherubim. All the heavenly hosts were about him. He blessed the body of Mary.

She went and gave the message to the apostles, and Peter blessed her, and they rejoiced.

Jesus and the redeemed souls ascended into Heaven, and the Father crowned him. The glory of this scene Bartholomew could not describe. It is here that he enjoins his son Thaddaeus not to let this book fall into the hands of the impure (quoted above).

Then follows a series of hymns sung in heaven, eight in all, which accompany the reception of Adam and the other holy souls into glory. Adam was eighty cubits high and Eve fifty. They were brought to the Father by Michael. Bartholomew had never seen anything to compare with the beauty and Glory of Adam, save that of Jesus. Adam was forgiven, and all the angels and saints rejoiced and saluted him, and departed each to their place.

Adam was set at the gate of life to greet all the righteous as they enter, and Eve was set over all the women who had done the will of God, to greet them as they come into the city of Christ.

As for me, Bartholomew, I remained many days without food or drink, nourished by the glory of the vision.

The apostles thanked and blessed Bartholomew for what he had told them: he should be called the apostle of the mysteries of God. But he protested: I am the least of you all, a humble workman. Will not the people of the city say when they see me, 'Is not this Bartholomew the man of Italy, the gardener the dealer in vegetables? Is not this the man that dwelleth in the garden of Hierocrates the governor of our city? How has he attained this greatness?

'The next words introduce a new section.

At the time when Jesus took us up into the Mount of Olives he spoke to us in an unknown tongue, which he revealed to us, saying: Anetharath (or Atharath Thaurath). The heavens were opened and we all went up into the seventh heaven (so the London MS.: in the Paris copy only Jesus went up, and the apostles gazed after him). He prayed the Father to bless us.

The Father, with the Son and the Holy Ghost, laid His hand on the head of Peter (and made him archbishop of the whole world: Paris B). All that is bound or loosed by him on earth shall be so in heaven; none who is not ordained by him shall be accepted. Each of the apostles was separately blessed (there are omissions of single names in one or other of the three texts). Andrew, James, John, Philip (the cross will precede him wherever he goes), Thomas, Bartholomew (he will be the depositary of the mysteries of the Son), Matthew (his shadow will heal the sick) James son of Alphaeus, Simon Zelotes, Judas of James, Thaddeus, Matthias who was rich and left all to follow Jesus).

And now, my brethren the apostles, forgive me: I, Bartholomew, am not a man to be honoured.

The apostles kissed and blessed him. And then, with Mary, they offered the Eucharist.

The Father sent the Son down into Galilee to console the apostles and Mary: and he came and blessed them and showed them his wounds, and committed them to the care of Peter, and gave them their commission to preach. They kissed his side and sealed themselves with the blood that flowed thence. He went up to heaven.

Thomas was not with them, for he had departed to his city, hearing that his son Siophanes (Theophanes?) was dead: it was the seventh day since the death when he arrived. He went to the tomb and raised him in the name of Jesus.

Siophanes told him of the taking of his soul by Michael: how it sprang from his body and lighted on the hand of Michael, who wrapped it in a fine linen cloth: how he crossed the river of fire and it seemed to him as water, and was washed thrice in the Acherusian lake: how in heaven he saw the twelve splendid thrones of the apostles, and was not permitted to sit on his father's throne.

Thomas and he went into the city to the consternation of all who saw them. He, Siophanes, addressed the people and told his story: and Thomas baptized 12,000 of them, founded a church, and made Siophanes its bishop.

Then Thomas mounted on a cloud and it took him to the Molmtof Olives and to the apostles, who told him of the visit of Jesus: and he would not believe. Bartholomew admonished him. Then Jesus appeared, and made Thomas touch his wounds: and departed into heaven.

This is the second time that he showed himself to his disciples after that he had risen from the dead.

This is the Book of the Resurrection of Jesus the Christ, our Lord, in joy and gladness. In peace. Amen.

Peter said to the apostles: Let us offer the offering before we separate. They prepared the bread, the cup, and incense.

Peter stood by the sacrifice and the others round the Table. They waited (break in the text: Budge and others suppose an appearance of Christ, but I do not think this is correct: 4 1/2 lines are gone then there are broken words):

table . . . their hearts rejoiced . . . worshipped the Son of God. He took his seat . . . his Father (probably, who sitteth at the right hand of the Father). His Body was on the Table about which they were assembled; and they divided it. They saw the blood of Jesus pouring out as living blood down into the cup. Peter said: God hath loved us more than all, in letting us see these great honours: and our Lord Jesus Christ hath allowed us to behold and hath revealed to us the glory of his body and his divine blood. They partook of the body and blood-and then they separated and preached the word. (What is clearly indicated is a change in the elements: there is not room for a description of an appearance of Jesus: he says no word, and his departure is not mentioned.)

This writing may be better described as a rhapsody than a narrative. It bristles with contradictions of itself: Joseph and Philogenes both bury Jesus- Thomas raises the dead and will not believe in Christ's resurrection: and so forth. That Mary the mother of Jesus is identified with Mary Magdalene is typical of the disregard of history, and we have seen it in other Coptic documents. The interest of the authors centred in the hymns, blessings, salutations, and prayers, which in this analysis have been wholly omitted, but which occupy a large part of the original text. The glorification of St. Bartholomew is another purpose of the writer: the special blessings given to him recall the attitude which he takes in the Gospel (i. 1, 8) as inquiring into the mysteries of heaven, and seeing things which are hidden from others. Both Gospel and Book are specially interested in the Descent into Hell, the Resurrection, and the redemption of Adam.

Bartholomew (Nathanael) was told (in St. John's Gospel) that he would see the angels ascending and descending upon the Son of Man. This promise is fulfilled in the Gospel (i. 6, 231 and very often in the Book: in St. John we also read of his being 'under the fig-tree', and this was probably enough to suggest to the Coptic author of the Book that he was a gardener.

A date is hard to suggest. The British Museum MS. is assigned to the twelfth century; the Paris fragments are older. That of the Coptic literature of this class is usually supposed to belong to the fifth and sixth centuries; and I think this, or at latest the seventh century, may be the period when the book was produced.

Book 122. *The Epistle of Ignatius to the Ephesians*

Greeting

Ignatius, who is also called Theophorus, to the Church which is at Ephesus, in Asia, deservedly most happy, being blessed in the greatness and fullness of God the Father, and predestinated before the ages of time, that it should be always for an enduring and unchangeable glory, being united and elected through the true passion by the will of the Father, and Jesus Christ, our God: Abundant happiness through Jesus Christ, and His undefiled grace.

Chapter 1. Praise of the Ephesians

I have become acquainted with your name, much-beloved in God, which you have acquired by the habit of righteousness, according to the faith and love in Jesus Christ our Saviour. Being the followers of God, and stirring up yourselves by the blood of God, you have perfectly accomplished the work which was beseeming to you. For, on hearing that I came bound from Syria for the common name and hope, trusting through your prayers to be permitted to fight with beasts at Rome, that so by martyrdom I may indeed become the disciple of Him who gave Himself for us, an offering and sacrifice to God, Ephesians 5:2 [you hastened to see me]. I received, therefore, your whole multitude in the name of God, through Onesimus, a man of inexpressible love, and your bishop in the flesh, whom I pray you by Jesus Christ to love, and that you would all seek to be like him. And blessed be He who has granted unto you, being worthy, to obtain such an excellent bishop.

Chapter 2. Congratulations and entreaties

As to my fellow-servant Burrhus, your deacon in regard to God and blessed in all things, I beg that he may continue longer, both for your honour and that of your bishop. And Crocus also, worthy both of God and you, whom I have received as the manifestation of your love, has in all things refreshed 1 Corinthians 16:18, etc. me, as the Father of our Lord Jesus Christ shall also refresh 1 Corinthians 16:18, etc. him; together with Onesimus, and Burrhus, and Euplus, and Fronto, by means of whom, I have, as to love, beheld all of you. May I always have joy of you, if indeed I be worthy of it. It is therefore befitting that you should in every way glorify Jesus Christ, who has glorified you, that by a unanimous obedience you may be perfectly joined together in the same mind, and in the same judgment, and may all speak the same thing concerning the same thing, 1 Corinthians 1:10 and that, being subject to the bishop and the presbytery, you may in all respects be sanctified.

Chapter 3. Exhortations to unity

I do not issue orders to you, as if I were some great person. For though I am bound for the name [of Christ], I am not yet perfect in Jesus Christ. For now I begin to be a disciple, and I speak to you as fellow-disciples with me. For it was needful for me to have been stirred up by you in faith, exhortation, patience, and long-suffering. But inasmuch as love suffers me not to be silent in regard to you, I have therefore taken upon me first to exhort you that you would all run together in accordance with the will of God. For even Jesus Christ, our inseparable life, is the [manifested] will of the Father; as also bishops, settled everywhere to the utmost bounds [of the earth], are so by the will of Jesus Christ.

Chapter 4. The same continued

Wherefore it is fitting that you should run together in accordance with the will of your bishop, which thing also you do. For your justly renowned presbytery, worthy of God, is fitted as exactly to the bishop as the strings are to the harp. Therefore in your concord and harmonious love, Jesus Christ is sung. And man by man, become a choir, that being harmonious in love, and taking up the song of God in unison, you may with one voice sing to the Father through Jesus Christ, so that He may both hear you, and perceive by your works that you are indeed the members of His Son. It is profitable, therefore, that you should live in an unblameable unity, that thus you may always enjoy communion with God.

Chapter 5. The praise of unity

For if I in this brief space of time, have enjoyed such fellowship with your bishop — I mean not of a mere human, but of a spiritual nature — how much more do I reckon you happy who are so joined to him as the Church is to Jesus Christ, and as Jesus Christ is to the Father, that so all things may agree in unity! Let no man deceive himself: if any one be not within the altar, he is deprived of the bread of God. For if the prayer of one or two possesses Matthew 18:19 such power, how much more that of the bishop and the whole Church! He, therefore, that does not assemble with the Church, has even by this manifested his pride, and condemned himself. For it is written, God resists the proud. Let us be careful, then, not to set ourselves in opposition to the bishop, in order that we may be subject to God.

Chapter 6. Have respect to the bishop as to Christ Himself

Now the more any one sees the bishop keeping silence, the more ought he to revere him. For we ought to receive every one whom the Master of the house sends to be over His household, Matthew 24:45 as we would do Him that sent him. It is manifest, therefore, that we should look upon the bishop even as we would upon the Lord Himself. And indeed Onesimus himself greatly commends your good order in God, that you all live according to the truth, and that no sect has any dwelling-place among you. Nor, indeed, do you hearken to any one rather than to Jesus Christ speaking in truth.

Chapter 7. Beware of false teachers

For some are in the habit of carrying about the name [of Jesus Christ] in wicked guile, while yet they practise things unworthy of God, whom you must flee as you would wild beasts. For they are ravening dogs, who bite secretly, against whom you must be on your guard, inasmuch as they are men who can scarcely be cured. There is one Physician who is possessed both of flesh and spirit; both made and not made; God existing in flesh; true life in death; both of Mary and of God; first passible and then impassible — even Jesus Christ our Lord.

Chapter 8. Renewed praise of the Ephesians

Let not then any one deceive you, as indeed you are not deceived, inasmuch as you are wholly devoted to God. For since there is no strife raging among you which might distress you, you are certainly living in accordance with God's will. I am far inferior to you, and require to be sanctified by your Church of Ephesus, so renowned throughout the world. They that are carnal cannot do those things which are spiritual, nor they that are spiritual the things which are carnal; even as faith cannot do the works of unbelief, nor unbelief the works of faith. But even those things which you do according to the flesh are spiritual; for you do all things in Jesus Christ.

Chapter 9. You have given no heed to false teachers

Nevertheless, I have heard of some who have passed on from this to you, having false doctrine, whom you did not allow to sow among you, but stopped your ears, that you might not receive those things which were sown by them, as being stones 1 Peter 2:5 of the temple of the Father, prepared for the building of God the Father, and drawn up on high by the instrument of Jesus Christ, which is the cross, John 12:32 making use of the Holy Spirit as a rope, while your faith was the means by which you ascended, and your love the way which led up to God. You, therefore, as well as all your fellow-travellers, are God-bearers, temple-bearers, Christ-bearers, bearers of holiness, adorned in all respects with the commandments of Jesus Christ, in whom also I exult that I have been thought worthy, by means of this Epistle, to converse and rejoice with you, because with respect to your Christian life you love nothing but God only.

Chapter 10. Exhortations to prayer, humility, etc

And pray without ceasing on behalf of other men. For there is in them hope of repentance that they may attain to God. See, then, that they be instructed by your works, if in no other way. Be meek in response to their wrath, humble in opposition to their boasting: to their blasphemies return your prayers; in contrast to their error, be stedfast Colossians 1:23 in the faith; and for their cruelty, manifest your gentleness. While we take care not to imitate their conduct, let us be found their brethren in all true kindness; and let us seek to be followers of the Lord (who ever more unjustly treated, more destitute, more condemned?), that so no plant of the devil may be found in you, but you may remain in all holiness and sobriety in Jesus Christ, both with respect to the flesh and spirit.

Chapter 11. An exhortation to fear God, etc

The last times have come upon us. Let us therefore be of a reverent spirit, and fear the long-suffering of God, that it tend not to our condemnation. For let us either stand in awe of the wrath to come, or show regard for the grace which is at present displayed — one of two things. Only [in one way or another] let us be found in Christ Jesus unto the true life. Apart from Him, let nothing attract you, for whom I bear about these bonds, these spiritual jewels, by which may I arise through your prayers, of which I entreat I may always be a partaker, that I may be found in the lot of the Christians of Ephesus, who have always been of the same mind with the apostles through the power of Jesus Christ.

Chapter 12. Praise of the Ephesians

I know both who I am, and to whom I write. I am a condemned man, you have been the objects of mercy; I am subject to danger, you are established in safety. You are the persons through whom those pass that are cut off for the sake of God. You are initiated into the mysteries of the Gospel with Paul, the holy, the martyred, the deservedly most happy, at whose feet may I be found, when I shall attain to God; who in all his Epistles makes mention of you in Christ Jesus.

Chapter 13. Meet together frequently for the worship of God

Take heed, then, often to come together to give thanks to God, and show forth His praise. For when you assemble frequently in the same place, the powers of Satan are destroyed, and the destruction at which he aims is prevented by the unity of your faith. Nothing is more precious than peace, by which all war, both in heaven and earth, is brought to an end.

Chapter 14. Exhortations to faith and love

None of these things is hid from you, if you perfectly possess that faith and love towards Christ Jesus 1 Timothy 1:14 which are the beginning and the end of life. For the beginning is faith, and the end is love. 1 Timothy 1:5 Now these two, being inseparably connected together, are of God, while all other things which are requisite for a holy life follow after them. No man [truly] making a profession of faith sins; 1 John 3:7 nor does he that possesses love hate any one. The tree is made manifest by its fruit; Matthew 12:33 so those that profess themselves to be Christians shall be recognised by their conduct. For there is not now a demand for mere profession, but that a man be found continuing in the power of faith to the end.

Chapter 15. Exhortation to confess Christ by silence as well as speech

It is better for a man to be silent and be [a Christian], than to talk and not to be one. It is good to teach, if he who speaks also acts. There is then one Teacher, who spoke and it was done; while even those things which He did in silence are worthy of the Father. He who possesses the word of Jesus, is truly able to hear even His very silence, that he may be perfect, and may both act as he speaks, and be recognised by his silence. There is nothing which is hid from God, but our very secrets are near to Him. Let us therefore do all things as those who have Him dwelling in us, that we may be His temples, 1 Corinthians 6:19 and He may be in us as our God, which indeed He is, and will manifest Himself before our faces. Wherefore we justly love Him.

Chapter 16. The fate of false teachers

Do not err, my brethren. James 1:16 Those that corrupt families shall not inherit the kingdom of God. 1 Corinthians 6:9-10 If, then, those who do this as respects the flesh have suffered death, how much more shall this be the case with any one who corrupts by wicked doctrine the faith of God, for which Jesus Christ was crucified! Such an one becoming defiled [in this way], shall go away into everlasting fire, and so shall every one that hearkens unto him.

Chapter 17. Beware of false doctrines

For this end did the Lord allow the ointment to be poured upon His head, John 12:7 that He might breathe immortality into His Church. Be not anointed with the bad odour of the doctrine of the prince of this world; let him not lead you away captive from the life which is set before you. And why are we not all prudent, since we have received the knowledge of God, which is Jesus Christ? Why do we foolishly perish, not recognising the gift which the Lord has of a truth sent to us?

Chapter 18. The glory of the cross

Let my spirit be counted as nothing for the sake of the cross, which is a stumbling-block 1 Corinthians 1:18 to those that do not believe, but to us salvation and life eternal. Where is the wise man? Where the disputer? 1 Corinthians 1:20 Where is the boasting of those who are styled prudent? For our God, Jesus Christ, was, according to the appointment of God, conceived in the womb by Mary, of the seed of David, but by the Holy Ghost. He was born and baptized, that by His passion He might purify the water.

Chapter 19. Three celebrated mysteries

Now the virginity of Mary was hidden from the prince of this world, as was also her offspring, and the death of the Lord; three mysteries of renown, which were wrought in silence by God. How, then, was He manifested to the world? A star shone forth in heaven above all the other stars, the light of which was inexpressible, while its novelty struck men with astonishment. And all the rest of the stars, with the sun and moon, formed a chorus to this star, and its light was exceedingly great above them all. And there was agitation felt as to whence this new spectacle came, so unlike to everything else [in the heavens]. Hence every kind of magic was destroyed, and every bond of wickedness disappeared; ignorance was removed, and the old kingdom abolished, God Himself being manifested in human form for the renewal of eternal life. And now that took a beginning which had been prepared by God. Henceforth all things were in a state of tumult, because He meditated the abolition of death.

Chapter 20. Promise of another letter

If Jesus Christ shall graciously permit me through your prayers, and if it be His will, I shall, in a second little work which I will write to you, make further manifest to you [the nature of] the dispensation of which I have begun [to treat], with respect to the new man, Jesus Christ, in His faith and in His love, in His suffering and in His resurrection. Especially [will I do this] if the Lord make known to me that you come together man by man in common through grace, individually, in one faith, and in Jesus Christ, who was of the seed of David according to the flesh, being both the Son of man and the Son of God, so that you obey the bishop and the presbytery with an undivided mind, breaking one and the same bread, which is the medicine of immortality, and the antidote to prevent us from dying, but [which causes] that we should live for ever in Jesus Christ.

Chapter 21. Conclusion

My soul be for yours and theirs whom, for the honour of God, you have sent to Smyrna; whence also I write to you, giving thanks unto the Lord, and loving Polycarp even as I do you. Remember me, as Jesus Christ also remembered you. Pray for the Church which is in Syria, whence I am led bound to Rome, being the last of the faithful who are there, even as I have been thought worthy to be chosen to show forth the honour of God. Farewell in God the Father, and in Jesus Christ, our common hope.

Book 123. The Epistle of Ignatius to the Magnesians

Greeting

Ignatius, who is also called Theophorus, to the [Church] blessed in the grace of God the Father, in Jesus Christ our Saviour, in whom I salute the Church which is at Magnesia, near the Mæander, and wish it abundance of happiness in God the Father, and in Jesus Christ.

Chapter 1. Reason of writing the epistle

Having been informed of your godly love, so well-ordered, I rejoiced greatly, and determined to commune with you in the faith of Jesus Christ. For as one who has been thought worthy of the most honourable of all names, in those bonds which I bear about, I commend the Churches, in which I pray for a union both of the flesh and spirit of Jesus Christ, the constant source of our life, and of faith and love, to which nothing is to be preferred, but especially of Jesus and the Father, in whom, if we endure all the assaults of the prince of this world, and escape them, we shall enjoy God.

Chapter 2. I rejoice in your messengers

Since, then, I have had the privilege of seeing you, through Damas your most worthy bishop, and through your worthy presbyters Bassus and Apollonius, and through my fellow-servant the deacon Sotio, whose friendship may I ever enjoy, inasmuch as he is subject to the bishop as to the grace of God, and to the presbytery as to the law of Jesus Christ, [I now write to you].

Chapter 3. Honour your youthful bishop

Now it becomes you also not to treat your bishop too familiarly on account of his youth, but to yield him all reverence, having respect to the power of God the Father, as I have known even holy presbyters do, not judging rashly, from the manifest youthful appearance [of their bishop], but as being themselves prudent in God, submitting to him, or rather not to him, but to the Father of Jesus Christ, the bishop of us all. It is therefore fitting that you should, after no hypocritical fashion, obey [your bishop], in honour of Him who has willed us [so to do], since he that does not so deceives not [by such conduct] the bishop that is visible, but seeks to mock Him that is invisible. And all such conduct has reference not to man, but to God, who knows all secrets.

Chapter 4. Some wickedly act independently of the bishop

It is fitting, then, not only to be called Christians, but to be so in reality: as some indeed give one the title of bishop, but do all things without him. Now such persons seem to me to be not possessed of a good conscience, seeing they are not stedfastly gathered together according to the commandment.

Chapter 5. Death is the fate of all such

Seeing, then, all things have an end, these two things are simultaneously set before us — death and life; and every one shall go unto his own place. For as there are two kinds of coins, the one of God, the other of the world, and each of these has its special character stamped upon it, [so is it also here.] The unbelieving are of this world; but the believing have, in love, the character of God the Father by Jesus Christ, by whom, if we are not in readiness to die into His passion, His life is not in us.

Chapter 6. Preserve harmony

Since therefore I have, in the persons before mentioned, beheld the whole multitude of you in faith and love, I exhort you to study to do all things with a divine harmony, while your bishop presides in the place of God, and your presbyters in the place of the assembly of the apostles, along with your deacons, who are most dear to me, and are entrusted with the ministry of Jesus Christ, who was with the Father before the beginning of time, and in the end was revealed. Do all then, imitating the same divine conduct, pay respect to one another, and let no one look upon his neighbour after the flesh, but continually love each other in Jesus Christ. Let nothing exist among you that may divide you; but be united with your bishop, and those that preside over you, as a type and evidence of your immortality.

Chapter 7. Do nothing without the bishop and presbyters

As therefore the Lord did nothing without the Father, being united to Him, neither by Himself nor by the apostles, so neither do anything without the bishop and presbyters. Neither endeavour that anything appear reasonable and proper to yourselves apart; but being come together into the same place, let there be one prayer, one supplication, one mind, one hope, in love and in joy undefiled. There is one Jesus Christ, than whom nothing is more excellent. Therefore run together as into one temple of God, as to one altar, as to one Jesus Christ, who came forth from one Father, and is with and has gone to one.

Chapter 8. Caution against false doctrines

Be not deceived with strange doctrines, nor with old fables, which are unprofitable. For if we still live according to the Jewish law, we acknowledge that we have not received grace. For the divinest prophets lived according to Christ Jesus. On this account also they were persecuted, being inspired by His grace to fully convince the unbelieving that there is one God, who has manifested Himself by Jesus Christ His Son, who is His eternal Word, not proceeding forth from silence, and who in all things pleased Him that sent Him.

Chapter 9. Let us live with Christ

If, therefore, those who were brought up in the ancient order of things have come to the possession of a new hope, no longer observing the Sabbath, but living in the observance of the Lord's Day, on which also our life has sprung up again by Him and by His death — whom some deny, by which mystery we have obtained faith, and therefore endure, that we may be found the disciples of Jesus Christ, our only Master — how shall we be able to live apart from Him, whose disciples the prophets themselves in the Spirit did wait for Him as their Teacher? And therefore He whom they rightly waited for, having come, raised them from the dead. Matthew 27:52

Chapter 10. Beware of Judaizing

Let us not, therefore, be insensible to His kindness. For were He to reward us according to our works, we should cease to be. Therefore, having become His disciples, let us learn to live according to the principles of Christianity. For whosoever is called by any other name besides this, is not of God. Lay aside, therefore, the evil, the old, the sour leaven, and be changed into the new leaven, which is Jesus Christ. Be salted in Him, lest any one among you should be corrupted, since by your savour you shall be convicted. It is absurd to profess Christ Jesus, and to Judaize. For Christianity did not embrace Judaism, but Judaism Christianity, that so every tongue which believes might be gathered together to God.

Chapter 11. I write these things to warn you

These things [I address to you], my beloved, not that I know any of you to be **in such a state; [addicted to the error of Judaizing]** but, as less than any of you, I desire to guard you beforehand, that you fall not upon the hooks of vain doctrine, but that you attain to full assurance in regard to the birth, and passion, and resurrection which took place in the time of the government of Pontius Pilate, being truly and certainly accomplished by Jesus Christ, who is our hope, 1 Timothy 1:1 from which may no one of you ever be turned aside.

Chapter 12. You are superior to me

May I enjoy you in all respects, if indeed I be worthy! For though I am bound, I am not worthy to be compared to any of you that are at liberty. I know that you are not puffed up, for you have Jesus Christ in yourselves. And all the more when I commend you, I know that you cherish modesty of spirit; as it is written, The righteous man is his own accuser. Proverbs 18:17

Chapter 13. Be established in faith and unity

Study, therefore, to be established in the doctrines of the Lord and the apostles, that so all things, whatsoever you do, may prosper both in the flesh and spirit; in faith and love; in the Son, and in the Father, and in the Spirit; in the beginning and in the end; with your most admirable bishop, and the well-compacted spiritual crown of your presbytery, and the deacons who are according to God. Be subject to the bishop, and to one another, as Jesus Christ to the Father, according to the flesh, and the apostles to Christ, and to the Father, and to the Spirit; that so there may be a union both fleshly and spiritual.

Chapter 14. Your prayers requested

Knowing as I do that you are full of God, I have but briefly exhorted you. Be mindful of me in your prayers, that I may attain to God; and of the Church which is in Syria, whence I am not worthy to derive my name: for I stand in need of your united prayer in God, and your love, that the Church which is in Syria may be deemed worthy of being refreshed by your Church.

Chapter 15. Salutations

The Ephesians from Smyrna (whence I also write to you), who are here for the glory of God, as you also are, who have in all things refreshed me, salute you, along with Polycarp, the bishop of the Smyrnæans. The rest of the Churches, in honour of Jesus Christ, also salute you. Fare well in the harmony of God, you who have obtained the inseparable Spirit, who is Jesus Christ.

Book 123. The Epistle of Ignatius to the Trallians

Greeting

Ignatius, who is also called Theophorus, to the holy Church which is at Tralles, in Asia, beloved of God, the Father of Jesus Christ, elect, and worthy of God, possessing peace through the flesh, and blood, and passion of Jesus Christ, who is our hope, through our rising again to Him, which also I salute in its fullness, and in the apostolic character, and wish abundance of happiness.

Chapter 1. Acknowledgment of their excellence

I know that you possess an unblameable and sincere mind in patience, and that not only in present practice, but according to inherent nature, as Polybius your bishop has shown me, who has come to Smyrna by the will of God and Jesus Christ, and so sympathized in the joy which I, who am bound in Christ Jesus, possess, that I beheld your whole multitude in him. Having therefore received through him the testimony of your good-will, according to God, I gloried to find you, as I knew you were, the followers of God.

Chapter 2. Be subject to the bishop, etc

For, since you are subject to the bishop as to Jesus Christ, you appear to me to live not after the manner of men, but according to Jesus Christ, who died for us, in order, by believing in His death, you may escape from death. It is therefore necessary that, as you indeed do, so without the bishop you should do nothing, but should also be subject to the presbytery, as to the apostle of Jesus Christ, who is our hope, in whom, if we live, we shall [at last] be found. It is fitting also that the deacons, as being [the ministers] of the mysteries of Jesus Christ, should in every respect be pleasing to all. For they are not ministers of meat and drink, but servants of the Church of God. They are bound, therefore, to avoid all grounds of accusation [against them], as they would do fire.

Chapter 3. Honour the deacons, etc

In like manner, let all reverence the deacons as an appointment of Jesus Christ, and the bishop as Jesus Christ, who is the Son of the Father, and the presbyters as the sanhedrim of God, and assembly of the apostles. Apart from these, there is no Church. Concerning all this, I am persuaded that you are of the same opinion. For I have received the manifestation of your love, and still have it with me, in your bishop, whose very appearance is highly instructive, and his meekness of itself a power; whom I imagine even the ungodly must reverence, seeing they are also pleased that I do not spare myself. But shall I, when permitted to write on this point, reach such a height of self-esteem, that though being a condemned man, I should issue commands to you as if I were an apostle?

Chapter 4. I have need of humility

I have great knowledge in God, but I restrain myself, lest, I should perish through boasting. For now it is needful for me to be the more fearful; and not give heed to those that puff me up. For they that speak to me [in the way of commendation] scourge me. For I do indeed desire to suffer, but I know not if I be worthy to do so. For this longing, though it is not manifest to many, all the more vehemently assails me. I therefore have need of meekness, by which the prince of this world is brought to nought.

Chapter 5. I will not teach you profound doctrines

Am I not able to write to you of heavenly things? But I fear to do so, lest I should inflict injury on you who are but babes [in Christ]. Pardon me in this respect, lest, as not being able to receive [such doctrines], you should be strangled by them. For even I, though I am bound [for Christ], yet am not on that account able to understand heavenly things, and the places of the angels, and their gatherings under their respective princes, things visible and invisible. Without reference to such abstruse subjects, I am still but a learner [in other respects]; for many things are wanting to us, that we come not short of God.

Chapter 6. Abstain from the poison of heretics

I therefore, yet not I, but the love of Jesus Christ, entreat you that you use Christian nourishment only, and abstain from herbage of a different kind; I mean heresy. For those [that are given to this] mix up Jesus Christ with their own poison, speaking things which are unworthy of credit, like those who administer a deadly drug in sweet wine, which he who is ignorant of does greedily take, with a fatal pleasure leading to his own death.

Chapter 7. The same continued

Be on your guard, therefore, against such persons. And this will be the case with you if you are not puffed up, and continue in intimate union with Jesus Christ our God, and the bishop, and the enactments of the apostles. He that is within the altar is pure, but he that is without is not pure; that is, he who does anything apart from the bishop, and presbytery, and deacons, such a man is not pure in his conscience.

Chapter 8. Be on your guard against the snares of the devil

Not that I know there is anything of this kind among you; but I put you on your guard, inasmuch as I love you greatly, and foresee the snares of the devil. Wherefore, clothing yourselves with meekness, be renewed in faith, that is the flesh of the Lord, and in love, that is the blood of Jesus Christ. Let no one of you cherish any grudge against his neighbour. Give no occasion to the Gentiles, lest by means of a few foolish men the whole multitude [of those that believe] in God be evil spoken of. For, Woe to him by whose vanity my name is blasphemed among any. Isaiah 52:5

Chapter 9. Reference to the history of Christ

Stop your ears, therefore, when any one speaks to you at variance with Jesus Christ, who was descended from David, and was also of Mary; who was truly born, and ate and drank. He was truly persecuted under Pontius Pilate; He was truly crucified, and [truly] died, in the sight of beings in heaven, and on earth, and under the earth. He was also truly raised from the dead, His Father quickening Him, even as after the same manner His Father will so raise up us who believe in Him by Christ Jesus, apart from whom we do not possess the true life.

Chapter 10. The reality of Christ's passion

But if, as some that are without God, that is, the unbelieving, say, that He only seemed to suffer (they themselves only seeming to exist), then why am I in bonds? Why do I long to be exposed to the wild beasts? Do I therefore die in vain? Am I not then guilty of falsehood against [the cross of] the Lord?

Chapter 11. Avoid the deadly errors of the Docetæ

Flee, therefore, those evil offshoots [of Satan], which produce death-bearing fruit, whereof if any one tastes, he instantly dies. For these men are not the planting of the Father. For if they were, they would appear as branches of the cross, and their fruit would be incorruptible. By it He calls you through His passion, as being His members. The head, therefore, cannot be born by itself, without its members; God, who is [the Saviour] Himself, having promised their union.

Chapter 12. Continue in unity and love

I salute you from Smyrna, together with the Churches of God which are with me, who have refreshed me in all things, both in the flesh and in the spirit. My bonds, which I carry about with me for the sake of Jesus Christ (praying that I may attain to God), exhort you. Continue in harmony among yourselves, and in prayer with one another; for it becomes every one of you, and especially the presbyters, to refresh the bishop, to the honour of the Father, of Jesus Christ, and of the apostles. I entreat you in love to hear me, that I may not, by having written, be a testimony against you. And also pray for me, who have need of your love, along with the mercy of God, that I may be worthy of the lot for which I am destined, and that I may not be found reprobate.

Chapter 13. Conclusion

The love of the Smyrnæans and Ephesians salutes you. Remember in your prayers the Church which is in Syria, from which also I am not worthy to receive my appellation, being the last of them. Fare well in Jesus Christ, while you continue subject to the bishop, as to the command [of God], and in like manner to the presbytery. And, every man, love one another with an undivided heart. Let my spirit be sanctified by yours, not only now, but also when I shall attain to God. For I am as yet exposed to danger. But the Father is faithful in Jesus Christ to fulfil both mine and your petitions: in whom may you be found unblameable.

Book 124. The Epistle of Ignatius to the Trallians

Greeting

Ignatius, who is also called Theophorus, to the holy Church which is at Tralles, in Asia, beloved of God, the Father of Jesus Christ, elect, and worthy of God, possessing peace through the flesh, and blood, and passion of Jesus Christ, who is our hope, through our rising again to Him, which also I salute in its fullness, and in the apostolic character, and wish abundance of happiness.

Chapter 1. Acknowledgment of their excellence

I know that you possess an unblameable and sincere mind in patience, and that not only in present practice, but according to inherent nature, as Polybius your bishop has shown me, who has come to Smyrna by the will of God and Jesus Christ, and so sympathized in the joy which I, who am bound in Christ Jesus, possess, that I beheld your whole multitude in him. Having therefore received through him the testimony of your good-will, according to God, I gloried to find you, as I knew you were, the followers of God.

Chapter 2. Be subject to the bishop, etc

For, since you are subject to the bishop as to Jesus Christ, you appear to me to live not after the manner of men, but according to Jesus Christ, who died for us, in order, by believing in His death, you may escape from death. It is therefore necessary that, as you indeed do, so without the bishop you should do nothing, but should also be subject to the presbytery, as to the apostle of Jesus Christ, who is our hope, in whom, if we live, we shall [at last] be found. It is fitting also that the deacons, as being [the ministers] of the mysteries of Jesus Christ, should in every respect be pleasing to all. For they are not ministers of meat and drink, but servants of the Church of God. They are bound, therefore, to avoid all grounds of accusation [against them], as they would do fire.

Chapter 3. Honour the deacons, etc

In like manner, let all reverence the deacons as an appointment of Jesus Christ, and the bishop as Jesus Christ, who is the Son of the Father, and the presbyters as the sanhedrim of God, and assembly of the apostles. Apart from these, there is no Church. Concerning all this, I am persuaded that you are of the same opinion. For I have received the manifestation of your love, and still have it with me, in your bishop, whose very appearance is highly instructive, and his meekness of itself a power; whom I imagine even the ungodly must reverence, seeing they are also pleased that I do not spare myself. But shall I, when permitted to write on this point, reach such a height of self-esteem, that though being a condemned man, I should issue commands to you as if I were an apostle?

Chapter 4. I have need of humility

I have great knowledge in God, but I restrain myself, lest, I should perish through boasting. For now it is needful for me to be the more fearful; and not give heed to those that puff me up. For they that speak to me [in the way of commendation] scourge me. For I do indeed desire to suffer, but I know not if I be worthy to do so. For this longing, though it is not manifest to many, all the more vehemently assails me. I therefore have need of meekness, by which the prince of this world is brought to nought.

Chapter 5. I will not teach you profound doctrines

Am I not able to write to you of heavenly things? But I fear to do so, lest I should inflict injury on you who are but babes [in Christ]. Pardon me in this respect, lest, as not being able to receive [such doctrines], you should be strangled by them. For even I, though I am bound [for Christ], yet am not on that account able to understand heavenly things, and the places of the angels, and their gatherings under their respective princes, things visible and invisible. Without reference to such abstruse subjects, I am still but a learner [in other respects]; for many things are wanting to us, that we come not short of God.

Chapter 6. Abstain from the poison of heretics

I therefore, yet not I, but the love of Jesus Christ, entreat you that you use Christian nourishment only, and abstain from herbage of a different kind; I mean heresy. For those [that are given to this] mix up Jesus Christ with their own poison, speaking things which are unworthy of credit, like those who administer a deadly drug in sweet wine, which he who is ignorant of does greedily take, with a fatal pleasure leading to his own death.

Chapter 7. The same continued

Be on your guard, therefore, against such persons. And this will be the case with you if you are not puffed up, and continue in intimate union with Jesus Christ our God, and the bishop, and the enactments of the apostles. He that is within the altar is pure, but he that is without is not pure; that is, he who does anything apart from the bishop, and presbytery, and deacons, such a man is not pure in his conscience.

Chapter 8. Be on your guard against the snares of the devil

Not that I know there is anything of this kind among you; but I put you on your guard, inasmuch as I love you greatly, and foresee the snares of the devil. Wherefore, clothing yourselves with meekness, be renewed in faith, that is the flesh of the Lord, and in love, that is the blood of Jesus Christ. Let no one of you cherish any grudge against his neighbour. Give no occasion to the Gentiles, lest by means of a few foolish men the whole multitude [of those that believe] in God be evil spoken of. For, Woe to him by whose vanity my name is blasphemed among any. Isaiah 52:5

Chapter 9. Reference to the history of Christ

Stop your ears, therefore, when any one speaks to you at variance with Jesus Christ, who was descended from David, and was also of Mary; who was truly born, and ate and drank. He was truly persecuted under Pontius Pilate; He was truly crucified, and [truly] died, in the sight of beings in heaven, and on earth, and under the earth. He was also truly raised from the dead, His Father quickening Him, even as after the same manner His Father will so raise up us who believe in Him by Christ Jesus, apart from whom we do not possess the true life.

Chapter 10. The reality of Christ's passion

But if, as some that are without God, that is, the unbelieving, say, that He only seemed to suffer (they themselves only seeming to exist), then why am I in bonds? Why do I long to be exposed to the wild beasts? Do I therefore die in vain? Am I not then guilty of falsehood against [the cross of] the Lord?

Chapter 11. Avoid the deadly errors of the Docetæ

Flee, therefore, those evil offshoots [of Satan], which produce death-bearing fruit, whereof if any one tastes, he instantly dies. For these men are not the planting of the Father. For if they were, they would appear as branches of the cross, and their fruit would be incorruptible. By it He calls you through His passion, as being His members. The head, therefore, cannot be born by itself, without its members; God, who is [the Saviour] Himself, having promised their union.

Chapter 12. Continue in unity and love

I salute you from Smyrna, together with the Churches of God which are with me, who have refreshed me in all things, both in the flesh and in the spirit. My bonds, which I carry about with me for the sake of Jesus Christ (praying that I may attain to God), exhort you. Continue in harmony among yourselves, and in prayer with one another; for it becomes every one of you, and especially the presbyters, to refresh the bishop, to the honour of the Father, of Jesus Christ, and of the apostles. I entreat you in love to hear me, that I may not, by having written, be a testimony against you. And also pray for me, who have need of your love, along with the mercy of God, that I may be worthy of the lot for which I am destined, and that I may not be found reprobate.

Chapter 13. Conclusion

The love of the Smyrnæans and Ephesians salutes you. Remember in your prayers the Church which is in Syria, from which also I am not worthy to receive my appellation, being the last of them. Fare well in Jesus Christ, while you continue subject to the bishop, as to the command [of God], and in like manner to the presbytery. And, every

man, love one another with an undivided heart. Let my spirit be sanctified by yours, not only now, but also when I shall attain to God. For I am as yet exposed to danger. But the Father is faithful in Jesus Christ to fulfil both mine and your petitions: in whom may you be found unblameable.

Book 125. The Epistle of Ignatius to the Romans

Greeting

Ignatius, who is also called Theophorus, to the Church which has obtained mercy, through the majesty of the Most High Father, and Jesus Christ, His only-begotten Son; the Church which is beloved and enlightened by the will of Him that wills all things which are according to the love of Jesus Christ our God, which also presides in the place of the region of the Romans, worthy of God, worthy of honour, worthy of the highest happiness, worthy of praise, worthy of obtaining her every desire, worthy of being deemed holy, and which presides over love, is named from Christ, and from the Father, which I also salute in the name of Jesus Christ, the Son of the Father: to those who are united, both according to the flesh and spirit, to every one of His commandments; who are filled inseparably with the grace of God, and are purified from every strange taint, [I wish] abundance of happiness unblameably, in Jesus Christ our God.

Chapter 1. As a prisoner, I hope to see you

Through prayer to God I have obtained the privilege of seeing your most worthy faces, and have even been granted more than I requested; for I hope as a prisoner in Christ Jesus to salute you, if indeed it be the will of God that I be thought worthy of attaining unto the end. For the beginning has been well ordered, if I may obtain grace to cling to my lot without hindrance unto the end. For I am afraid of your love, lest it should do me an injury. For it is easy for you to accomplish what you please; but it is difficult for me to attain to God, if you spare me.

Chapter 2. Do not save me from martyrdom

For it is not my desire to act towards you as a man-pleaser, but as pleasing God, even as also you please Him. For neither shall I ever have such [another] opportunity of attaining to God; nor will you, if you shall now be silent, ever be entitled to the honour of a better work. For if you are silent concerning me, I shall become God's; but if you show your love to my flesh, I shall again have to run my race. Pray, then, do not seek to confer any greater favour upon me than that I be sacrificed to God while the altar is still prepared; that, being gathered together in love, you may sing praise to the Father, through Christ Jesus, that God has deemed me, the bishop of Syria, worthy to be sent for from the east unto the west. It is good to set from the world unto God, that I may rise again to Him.

Chapter 3. Pray rather that I may attain to martyrdom

You have never envied any one; you have taught others. Now I desire that those things may be confirmed [by your conduct], which in your instructions you enjoin [on others]. Only request in my behalf both inward and outward strength, that I may not only speak, but [truly] will; and that I may not merely be called a Christian, but really be found to be one. For if I be truly found [a Christian], I may also be called one, and be then deemed faithful, when I shall no longer appear to the world. Nothing visible is eternal. For the things which are seen are temporal, but the things which are not seen are eternal. For our God, Jesus Christ, now that He is with the Father, is all the more revealed [in His glory]. Christianity is not a thing of silence only, but also of [manifest] greatness.

Chapter 4. Allow me to fall a prey to the wild beasts

I write to the Churches, and impress on them all, that I shall willingly die for God, unless you hinder me. I beseech of you not to show an unseasonable good-will towards me. Allow me to become food for the wild beasts, through whose instrumentality it will be granted me to attain to God. I am the wheat of God, and let me be ground by the teeth of the wild beasts, that I may be found the pure bread of Christ. Rather entice the wild beasts, that they may become my tomb, and may leave nothing of my body; so that when I have fallen asleep [in death], I may be no trouble to any one. Then shall I truly be a disciple of Christ, when the world shall not see so much as my body. Entreat Christ for me, that by these instruments I may be found a sacrifice [to God]. I do not, as Peter and Paul, issue commandments unto you. They were apostles; I am but a condemned man: they were free, while I am, even until now, a servant. But when I suffer, I shall be the freed-man of Jesus, and shall rise again emancipated in Him. And now, being a prisoner, I learn not to desire anything worldly or vain.

Chapter 5. I desire to die

From Syria even unto Rome I fight with beasts, both by land and sea, both by night and day, being bound to ten leopards, I mean a band of soldiers, who, even when they receive benefits, show themselves all the worse. But I am the more instructed by their injuries [to act as a disciple of Christ]; yet am I not thereby justified. 1 Corinthians 4:4 May I enjoy the wild beasts that are prepared for me; and I pray they may be found eager to rush upon me, which also I will entice to devour me speedily, and not deal with me as with some, whom, out of fear, they have not touched. But if they be unwilling to assail me, I will compel them to do so. Pardon me [in this]: I know what is for my benefit. Now I begin to be a disciple. And let no one, of things visible or invisible, envy me that I should attain to Jesus Christ. Let fire and the cross; let the crowds of wild beasts; let tearings, breakings, and dislocations of bones; let cutting off of members; let shatterings of the whole body; and let all the dreadful torments of the devil come upon me: only let me attain to Jesus Christ.

Chapter 6. By death I shall attain true life

All the pleasures of the world, and all the kingdoms of this earth, shall profit me nothing. It is better for me to die on behalf of Jesus Christ, than to reign over all the ends of the earth. For what shall a man be profited, if he gain the whole world, but lose his own soul? Him I seek, who died for us: Him I desire, who rose again for our sake. This is the gain which is laid up for me. Pardon me, brethren: do not hinder me from living, do not wish to keep me in a state of death; and while I desire to belong to God, do not give me over to the world. Allow me to obtain pure light: when I have gone there, I shall indeed be a man of God. Permit me to be an imitator of the passion of my God. If any one has Him within himself, let him consider what I desire, and let him have sympathy with me, as knowing how I am straitened.

Chapter 7. Reason of desiring to die

The prince of this world would fain carry me away, and corrupt my disposition towards God. Let none of you, therefore, who are [in Rome] help him; rather be on my side, that is, on the side of God. Do not speak of Jesus Christ, and yet set your desires on the world. Let not envy find a dwelling-place among you; nor even should I, when present with you, exhort you to it, be persuaded to listen to me, but rather give credit to those things which I now write to you. For though I am alive while I write to you, yet I am eager to die. My love has been crucified, and there is no fire in me desiring to be fed; but there is within me a water that lives and speaks, saying to me inwardly, Come to the Father. I have no delight in corruptible food, nor in the pleasures of this life. I desire the bread of God, the heavenly bread, the bread of life, which is the flesh of Jesus Christ, the Son of God, who became afterwards of the seed of David and Abraham; and I desire the drink of God, namely His blood, which is incorruptible love and eternal life.

Chapter 8. Be favourable to me

I no longer wish to live after the manner of men, and my desire shall be fulfilled if you consent. Be willing, then, that you also may have your desires fulfilled. I entreat you in this brief letter; give credit to me. Jesus Christ will reveal these things to you, [so that you shall know] that I speak truly. He is the mouth altogether free from falsehood, by which the Father has truly spoken. Pray for me, that I may attain [the object of my desire]. I have not written to you according to the flesh, but according to the will of God. If I shall suffer, you have wished [well] to me; but if I am rejected, you have hated me.

Chapter 9. Pray for the church in Syria

Remember in your prayers the Church in Syria, which now has God for its shepherd, instead of me. Jesus Christ alone will oversee it, and your love [will also regard it]. But as for me, I am ashamed to be counted one of them; for indeed I am not worthy, as being the very last of them, and one born out of due time. 1 Corinthians 15:8-9 But I have obtained mercy to be somebody, if I shall attain to God. My spirit salutes you, and the love of the Churches that have received me in the name of Jesus Christ, and not as a mere passer-by. For even those Churches which were not near to me in the way, I mean according to the flesh, have gone before me, city by city, [to meet me.]

Chapter 10. Conclusion

Now I write these things to you from Smyrna by the Ephesians, who are deservedly most happy. There is also with me, along with many others, Crocus, one dearly beloved by me. As to those who have gone before me from Syria to Rome for the glory of God, I believe that you are acquainted with them; to whom, [then,] make known that I am at hand. For they are all worthy, both of God and of you; and it is becoming that you should refresh them in all things. I have written these things unto you, on the day before the ninth of the Kalends of September (that is, on the twenty-third day of August). Fare well to the end, in the patience of Jesus Christ. Amen.

Book 126. The Epistle of Ignatius to the Philadelphians

Greeting

Ignatius, who is also called Theophorus, to the Church of God the Father, and our Lord Jesus Christ, which is at Philadelphia, in Asia, which has obtained mercy, and is established in the harmony of God, and rejoices unceasingly in the passion of our Lord, and is filled with all mercy through his resurrection; which I salute in the blood of Jesus Christ, who is our eternal and enduring joy, especially if [men] are in unity with the bishop, the presbyters, and the deacons, who have been appointed according to the mind of Jesus Christ, whom He has established in security, after His own will, and by His Holy Spirit.

Chapter 1. Praise of the bishop

Which bishop, I know, obtained the ministry which pertains to the common [good], not of himself, neither by men, Galatians 1:1 nor through vainglory, but by the love of God the Father, and the Lord Jesus Christ; at whose meekness I am struck with admiration, and who by his silence is able to accomplish more than those who vainly talk. For he is in harmony with the commandments [of God], even as the harp is with its strings. Wherefore my soul declares his mind towards God a happy one, knowing it to be virtuous and perfect, and that his stability as well as freedom from all anger is after the example of the infinite meekness of the living God.

Chapter 2. Maintain union with the bishop

Wherefore, as children of light and truth, flee from division and wicked doctrines; but where the shepherd is, there follow as sheep. For there are many wolves that appear worthy of credit, who, by means of a pernicious pleasure, carry captive 2 Timothy 3:6 those that are running towards God; but in your unity they shall have no place.

Chapter 3. Avoid schismatics

Keep yourselves from those evil plants which Jesus Christ does not tend, because they are not the planting of the Father. Not that I have found any division among you, but exceeding purity. For as many as are of God and of Jesus Christ are also with the bishop. And as many as shall, in the exercise of repentance, return into the unity of the Church, these, too, shall belong to God, that they may live according to Jesus Christ. Do not err, my brethren. If any man follows him that makes a schism in the Church, he shall not inherit the kingdom of God. If any one walks according to a strange opinion, he agrees not with the passion [of Christ.].

Chapter 4. Have but one Eucharist, etc.

Take heed, then, to have but one Eucharist. For there is one flesh of our Lord Jesus Christ, and one cup to [show forth] the unity of His blood; one altar; as there is one bishop, along with the presbytery and deacons, my fellow-servants: that so, whatsoever you do, you may do it according to [the will of] God.

Chapter 5. Pray for me

My brethren, I am greatly enlarged in loving you; and rejoicing exceedingly [over you], I seek to secure your safety. Yet it is not I, but Jesus Christ, for whose sake being bound I fear the more, inasmuch as I am not yet perfect. But your prayer to God shall make me perfect, that I may attain to that portion which through mercy has been allotted me, while I flee to the Gospel as to the flesh of Jesus, and to the apostles as to the presbytery of the Church. And let us also love the prophets, because they too have proclaimed the Gospel, and placed their hope in Him, and waited for Him; in whom also believing, they were saved, through union to Jesus Christ, being holy men, worthy of love and admiration, having had witness borne to them by Jesus Christ, and being reckoned along with [us] in the Gospel of the common hope.

Chapter 6. Do not accept Judaism

But if any one preach the Jewish law unto you, listen not to him. For it is better to hearken to Christian doctrine from a man who has been circumcised, than to Judaism from one uncircumcised. But if either of such persons do not speak concerning Jesus Christ, they are in my judgment but as monuments and sepulchres of the dead, upon which are written only the names of men. Flee therefore the wicked devices and snares of the prince of this world, lest at any time being conquered by his artifices, grow weak in your love. But be all joined together with an undivided heart. And I thank my God that I have a good conscience in respect to you, and that no one has it in his power to boast, either privately or publicly, that I have burdened any one either in much or in little. And I wish for all among whom I have spoken, that they may not possess that for a testimony against them.

Chapter 7. I have exhorted you to unity

For though some would have deceived me according to the flesh, yet the Spirit, as being from God, is not deceived. For it knows both whence it comes and whither it goes, John 3:8 and detects the secrets [of the heart]. For, when I was among you, I cried, I spoke with a loud voice: Give heed to the bishop, and to the presbytery and deacons. Now, some suspected me of having spoken thus, as knowing beforehand the division caused by some among you. But He is my witness, for whose sake I am in bonds, that I got no intelligence from any man. But the Spirit proclaimed these words: Do nothing without the bishop; keep your bodies as the temples of God; love unity; avoid divisions; be the followers of Jesus Christ, even as He is of His Father.

Chapter 8. The same continued

I therefore did what belonged to me, as a man devoted to unity. For where there is division and wrath, God does not dwell. To all them that repent, the Lord grants forgiveness, if they turn in penitence to the unity of God, and to communion with the bishop. I trust [as to you] in the grace of Jesus Christ, who shall free you from every bond. And I exhort you to do nothing out of strife, but according to the doctrine of Christ. When I heard some saying, If I do not find it in the ancient Scriptures, I will not believe the Gospel; on my saying to them, It is written, they answered me, That remains to be proved. But to me Jesus Christ is in the place of all that is ancient: His cross, and death, and resurrection, and the faith which is by Him, are undefiled monuments of antiquity; by which I desire, through your prayers, to be justified.

Chapter 9. The Old Testament is good: the New Testament is better

The priests indeed are good, but the High Priest is better; to whom the holy of holies has been committed, and who alone has been trusted with the secrets of God. He is the door of the Father, by which enter in Abraham, and Isaac, and Jacob, and the prophets, and the apostles, and the Church. All these have for their object the attaining to the unity of God. But the Gospel possesses something transcendent [above the former dispensation], viz., the appearance of our Lord Jesus Christ, His passion and resurrection. For the beloved prophets announced Him, but the Gospel is the perfection of immortality. All these things are good together, if you believe in love.

Chapter 10. Congratulate the Antiochans on the close of the persecution

Since, according to your prayers, and the compassion which you feel in Christ Jesus, it is reported to me that the Church which is at Antioch in Syria possesses peace, it will become you, as a Church of God, to elect a deacon to act as the ambassador of God [for you] to [the brethren there], that he may rejoice along with them when they are met together, and glorify the name [of God]. Blessed is he in Jesus Christ, who shall be deemed worthy of such a ministry; and you too shall be glorified. And if you are willing, it is not beyond your power to do this, for the sake of God; as also the nearest Churches have sent, in some cases bishops, and in others presbyters and deacons.

Chapter 11. Thanks and salutation

Now, as to Philo the deacon, of Cilicia, a man of reputation, who still ministers to me in the word of God, along with Rheus Agathopus, an elect man, who has followed me from Syria, not regarding his life — these bear witness in your behalf; and I myself give thanks to God for you, that you have received them, even as the Lord you. But may those that dishonoured them be forgiven through the grace of Jesus Christ! The love of the brethren at Troas salutes you; whence also I write to you by Burrhus, who was sent along with me by the Ephesians and Smyrnæans, to show their respect. May the Lord Jesus Christ honour them, in whom they hope, in flesh, and soul, and faith, and love, and concord! Fare well in Christ Jesus, our common hope.

Book 127. The Epistle of Ignatius to the Smyrnaeans

Greeting

Ignatius, who is also called Theophorus, to the Church of God the Father, and of the beloved Jesus Christ, which has through mercy obtained every kind of gift, which is filled with faith and love, and is deficient in no gift, most worthy of God, and adorned with holiness: the Church which is at Smyrna, in Asia, wishes abundance of happiness, through the immaculate Spirit and word of God.

Chapter 1. Thanks to God for your faith

I Glorify God, even Jesus Christ, who has given you such wisdom. For I have observed that you are perfected in an immoveable faith, as if you were nailed to the cross of our Lord Jesus Christ, both in the flesh and in the spirit, and are established in love through the blood of Christ, being fully persuaded with respect to our Lord, that He was truly of the seed of David according to the flesh, Romans 1:3 and the Son of God according to the will and power of God; that He was truly born of a virgin, was baptized by John, in order that all righteousness might be fulfilled Matthew 3:15 by Him; and was truly, under Pontius Pilate and Herod the tetrarch, nailed [to the cross] for us in His flesh. Of this fruit we are by His divinely-blessed passion, that He might set up a standard Isaiah 5:26, Isaiah 49:22 for all ages, through His resurrection, to all His holy and faithful [followers], whether among Jews or Gentiles, in the one body of His Church.

Chapter 2. Christ's true passion

Now, He suffered all these things for our sakes, that we might be saved. And He suffered truly, even as also He truly raised up Himself, not, as certain unbelievers maintain, that He only seemed to suffer, as they themselves only seem to be [Christians]. And as they believe, so shall it happen unto them, when they shall be divested of their bodies, and be mere evil spirits.

Chapter 3. Christ was possessed of a body after His resurrection

For I know that after His resurrection also He was still possessed of flesh, and I believe that He is so now. When, for instance, He came to those who were with Peter, He said to them, Lay hold, handle Me, and see that I am not an incorporeal spirit. And immediately they touched Him, and believed, being convinced both by His flesh and spirit. For this cause also they despised death, and were found its conquerors. And after his resurrection He ate and drank with them, as being possessed of flesh, although spiritually He was united to the Father.

Chapter 4. Beware of these heretics

I give you these instructions, beloved, assured that you also hold the same opinions [as I do]. But I guard you beforehand from those beasts in the shape of men, whom you must not only not receive, but, if it be possible, not even meet with; only you must pray to God for them, if by any means they may be brought to repentance, which, however, will be very difficult. Yet Jesus Christ, who is our true life, has the power of [effecting] this. But if these things were done by our Lord only in appearance, then am I also only in appearance bound. And why have I also surrendered myself to death, to fire, to the sword, to the wild beasts? But, [in fact,] he who is near to the sword is near to God; he that is among the wild beasts is in company with God; provided only he be so in the name of Jesus Christ. I undergo all these things that I may suffer together with Him, Romans 8:17 He who became a perfect man inwardly strengthening me. Philippians 4:13

Chapter 5. Their dangerous errors

Some ignorantly deny Him, or rather have been denied by Him, being the advocates of death rather than of the truth. These persons neither have the prophets persuaded, nor the law of Moses, nor the Gospel even to this day, nor the sufferings we have individually endured. For they think also the same thing regarding us. For what does any one profit me, if he commends me, but blasphemes my Lord, not confessing that He was [truly] possessed of a body? But he who does not acknowledge this, has in fact altogether denied Him, being enveloped in death. I have not, however, thought good to write the names of such persons, inasmuch as they are unbelievers. Yea, far be it from me to make any mention of them, until they repent and return to [a true belief in] Christ's passion, which is our resurrection.

Chapter 6. Unbelievers in the blood of Christ shall be condemned

Let no man deceive himself. Both the things which are in heaven, and the glorious angels, and rulers, both visible and invisible, if they believe not in the blood of Christ, shall, in consequence, incur condemnation. He that is able to receive it, let him receive it. Matthew 19:12 Let not [high] place puff any one up: for that which is worth all is faith and love, to which nothing is to be preferred. But consider those who are of a different opinion with respect to the grace of Christ which has come unto us, how opposed they are to the will of God. They have no regard for love; no care for the widow, or the orphan, or the oppressed; of the bond, or of the free; of the hungry, or of the thirsty.

Chapter 7. Let us stand aloof from such heretics

They abstain from the Eucharist and from prayer, because they confess not the Eucharist to be the flesh of our Saviour Jesus Christ, which suffered for our sins, and which the Father, of His goodness, raised up again. Those, therefore, who speak against this gift of God, incur death in the midst of their disputes. But it were better for them to treat it with respect, that they also might rise again. It is fitting, therefore, that you should keep aloof from such persons, and not to speak of them either in private or in public, but to give heed to the prophets, and above all, to the Gospel, in which the passion [of Christ] has been revealed to us, and the resurrection has been fully proved. But avoid all divisions, as the beginning of evils.

Chapter 8. Let nothing be done without the bishop

See that you all follow the bishop, even as Jesus Christ does the Father, and the presbytery as you would the apostles; and reverence the deacons, as being the institution of God. Let no man do anything connected with the Church without the bishop. Let that be deemed a proper Eucharist, which is [administered] either by the bishop, or by one to whom he has entrusted it. Wherever the bishop shall appear, there let the multitude [of the people] also be; even as, wherever Jesus Christ is, there is the Catholic Church. It is not lawful without the bishop either to baptize or to celebrate a love-feast; but whatsoever he shall approve of, that is also pleasing to God, so that everything that is done may be secure and valid.

Chapter 9. Honour the bishop

Moreover, it is in accordance with reason that we should return to soberness [of conduct], and, while yet we have opportunity, exercise repentance towards God. It is well to reverence both God and the bishop. He who honours the bishop has been honoured by God; he who does anything without the knowledge of the bishop, does [in reality] serve the devil. Let all things, then, abound to you through grace, for you are worthy. You have refreshed me in all things, and Jesus Christ [shall refresh] you. You have loved me when absent as well as when present. May God recompense you, for whose sake, while you endure all things, you shall attain unto Him.

Chapter 10. Acknowledgment of their kindness

You have done well in receiving Philo and Rheus Agathopus as servants of Christ our God, who have followed me for the sake of God, and who give thanks to the Lord in your behalf, because you have in every way refreshed them. None of these things shall be lost to you. May my spirit be for you, and my bonds, which you have not despised or been ashamed of; nor shall Jesus Christ, our perfect hope, be ashamed of you.

Chapter 11. Request to them to send a messenger to Antioch

Your prayer has reached to the Church which is at Antioch in Syria. Coming from that place bound with chains, most acceptable to God, I salute all; I who am not worthy to be styled from thence, inasmuch as I am the least of them. Nevertheless, according to the will of God, I have been thought worthy [of this honour], not that I have any sense [of having deserved it], but by the grace of God, which I wish may be perfectly given to me, that through your prayers I may attain to God. In order, therefore, that your work may be complete both on earth and in heaven, it is fitting that, for the honour of God, your Church should elect some worthy delegate; so that he, journeying into Syria, may congratulate them that they are [now] at peace, and are restored to their proper greatness, and that their proper constitution has been re-established among them. It seems then to me a becoming thing, that you should send some one of your number with an epistle, so that, in company with them, he may rejoice over the tranquility which, according to the will of God, they have obtained, and because that, through your prayers, they have now reached the harbour. As persons who are perfect, you should also aim at those things which are perfect. For when you are desirous to do well, God is also ready to assist you.

Chapter 12. Salutations

The love of the brethren at Troas salutes you; whence also I write to you by Burrhus, whom you sent with me, together with the Ephesians, your brethren, and who has in all things refreshed me. And I would that all may imitate him, as being a pattern of a minister of God. Grace will reward him in all things. I salute your most worthy bishop, and your very venerable presbytery, and your deacons, my fellow-servants, and all of you individually, as well as generally, in the name of Jesus Christ, and in His flesh and blood, in His passion and resurrection, both corporeal and spiritual, in union with God and you. Grace, mercy, peace, and patience, be with you for evermore!

Chapter 13. Conclusion

I salute the families of my brethren, with their wives and children, and the virgins who are called widows. Be strong, I pray, in the power of the Holy Ghost. Philo, who is with me, greets you. I salute the house of Tavias, and pray that it may be confirmed in faith and love, both corporeal and spiritual. I salute Alce, my well-beloved, and the incomparable Daphnus, and Eutecnus, and all by name. Fare well in the grace of God.

Book 128. The Epistle of Ignatius to Polycarp

Greeting

Ignatius, who is also called Theophorus, to Polycarp, Bishop of the Church of the Smyrnæans, or rather, who has, as his own bishop, God the Father, and the Lord Jesus Christ: [wishes] abundance of happiness.

Chapter 1. Commendation and exhortation

Having obtained good proof that your mind is fixed in God as upon an immoveable rock, I loudly glorify [His name] that I have been thought worthy [to behold] your blameless face, which may I ever enjoy in God! I entreat you, by the grace with which you are clothed, to press forward in your course, and to exhort all that they may be saved. Maintain your position with all care, both in the flesh and spirit. Have a regard to preserve unity, than which nothing is better. Bear with all, even as the Lord does with you. Support all in love, as also you do. Give yourself to prayer without ceasing. 1 Thessalonians 5:17 Implore additional understanding to what you already have. Be watchful, possessing a sleepless spirit. Speak to every man separately, as God enables you. Bear the infirmities of all, as being a perfect athlete [in the Christian life]: where the labour is great, the gain is all the more.

Chapter 2. Exhortations

If you love the good disciples, no thanks are due to you on that account; but rather seek by meekness to subdue the more troublesome. Every kind of wound is not healed with the same plaster. Mitigate violent attacks [of disease] by gentle applications. Be in all things wise as a serpent, and harmless as a dove. Matthew 10:16 For this purpose you are composed of both flesh and spirit, that you may deal tenderly with those [evils] that present themselves visibly before you. And as respects those that are not seen, pray that [God] would reveal them unto you, in order that you may be wanting in nothing, but may abound in every gift. The times call for you, as pilots do for the winds, and as one tossed with tempest seeks for the haven, so that both you [and those under your care] may attain to God. Be sober as an athlete of God: the prize set before you is immortality and eternal life, of which you are also persuaded. In all things may my soul be for yours, and my bonds also, which you have loved.

Chapter 3. Exhortations

Let not those who seem worthy of credit, but teach strange doctrines, 1 Timothy 1:3, 1 Timothy 6:3 fill you with apprehension. Stand firm, as does an anvil which is beaten. It is the part of a noble athlete to be wounded, and yet to conquer. And especially, we ought to bear all things for the sake of God, that He also may bear with us. Be ever becoming more zealous than what you are. Weigh carefully the times. Look for Him who is above all time, eternal and invisible, yet who became visible for our sakes; impalpable and impassible, yet who became passible on our account; and who in every kind of way suffered for our sakes.

Chapter 4. Exhortations

Let not widows be neglected. Be, after the Lord, their protector and friend. Let nothing be done without your consent; neither do anything without the approval of God, which indeed you do not, inasmuch as you are steadfast. Let your assembling together be of frequent occurrence: seek after all by name. Do not despise either male or female slaves, yet neither let them be puffed up with conceit, but rather let them submit themselves the more, for the glory of God, that they may obtain from God a better liberty. Let them not long to be set free [from slavery] at the public expense, that they be not found slaves to their own desires.

Chapter 5. The duties of husbands and wives

Flee evil arts; but all the more discourse in public regarding them. Speak to my sisters, that they love the Lord, and be satisfied with their husbands both in the flesh and spirit. In like manner also, exhort my brethren, in the name of Jesus Christ, that they love their wives, even as the Lord the Church. Ephesians 5:25 If any one can continue in a state of purity, to the honour of Him who is Lord of the flesh, let him so remain without boasting. If he begins to boast, he is undone; and if he reckon himself greater than the bishop, he is ruined. But it becomes both men and women who marry, to form their union with the approval of the bishop, that their marriage may be according to God, and not after their own lust. Let all things be done to the honour of God. 1 Corinthians 10:31

Chapter 6. The duties of the Christian flock

Give heed to the bishop, that God also may give heed to you. My soul be for theirs that are submissive to the bishop, to the presbyters, and to the deacons, and may my portion be along with them in God! Labour together with one another; strive in company together; run together; suffer together; sleep together; and awake together, as the stewards, and associates, and servants of God. Please Him under whom you fight, and from whom you receive your wages. Let none of you be found a deserter. Let your baptism endure as your arms; your faith as your helmet; your love as your spear; your patience as a complete panoply. Let your works be the charge assigned to you, that you may receive a worthy recompense. Be long-suffering, therefore, with one another, in meekness, as God is towards you. May I have joy of you for ever!

Chapter 7. Request that Polycarp would send a messenger to Antioch

Seeing that the Church which is at Antioch in Syria is, as report has informed me, at peace, through your prayers, I also am the more encouraged, resting without anxiety in God; if indeed by means of suffering I may attain to God, so that, through your prayers, I may be found a disciple [of Christ]. It is fitting, O Polycarp, most blessed in God, to assemble a very solemn council, and to elect one whom you greatly love, and know to be a man of activity, who may be designated the messenger of God; and to bestow on him this honour that he may go into Syria, and glorify your ever active love to the praise of Christ. A Christian has not power over himself, but must always be ready for the service of God. Now, this work is both God's and yours, when you shall have completed it to His glory. For I trust that, through grace, you are prepared for every good work pertaining to God. Knowing, therefore, your energetic love of the truth, I have exhorted you by this brief Epistle.

Chapter 8. Let other churches also send to Antioch

Inasmuch as I have not been able to write to all the Churches, because I must suddenly sail from Troas to Neapolis, as the will [of the emperor] enjoins, [I beg that] you, as being acquainted with the purpose of God, will write to the adjacent Churches, that they also may act in like manner, such as are able to do so sending messengers, and the others transmitting letters through those persons who are sent by you, that you may be glorified by a work which shall be remembered for ever, as indeed you are worthy to be. I salute all by name, and in particular the wife of Epitropus, with all her house and children. I salute Attalus, my beloved. I salute him who shall be deemed worthy to go [from you] into Syria. Grace shall be with him for ever, and with Polycarp that sends him. I pray for your happiness for ever in our God, Jesus Christ, by whom continue in the unity and under the protection of God. I salute Alce, my dearly beloved. Fare well in the Lord.

Book 129. The Gospel of the Ebionites (Summary)

No one doubts that the first followers of Jesus were all Jews. They did not call themselves Christians until later. The first use of the word "Christian" is found in Acts 11:26, where it states the disciples in Antioch were called Christians. Scholars believe Jesus' followers in Jerusalem referred to themselves as the Nazarenes, or followers of Jesus of Nazareth. Some scholars believe the Ebionites were an early offshoot of the Nazarenes. Epiphanius made a point of distinguishing the Ebionites from the Nazarenes by saying the Nazarenes were orthodox; the Ebionites were heretics. Nonetheless, the Ebionites were very devout Jews who believed that Jesus was, indeed, the Jewish Messiah. They continued to practice Judaism in all its forms, which included keeping the dietary laws and circumcising all males. Not surprisingly, however, their acceptance of Jesus as

Messiah brought them into conflict with the Jewish leaders who had rejected him. Eventually, they would also come into conflict with the Gentile Christians who had been told by Paul that they didn't need to adhere to the Jewish traditions. Obviously, Paul's message resonated with new converts and his version of Christianity soon eclipsed that of the Jewish Christians. Both sides believed with all their hearts that they each represented Jesus' message. This shift from Jewish to Gentile Christianity occurred within 20-30 years after Jesus' death and resurrection.

Epiphanius, a Church Father writing in the fourth century, claimed that the Ebionites had a Hebrew version of Matthew's Gospel, which they called the Hebrew Gospel. He goes on to disparage it by saying that it was incomplete and therefore false. The missing parts included the infancy narrative and the genealogy. Eusebius wrote that the Ebionites used the Gospel of the Hebrews. Origen and several other Church Fathers mention a "Gospel of the Twelve," which is later referred to as the Ebionite Gospel, and that's all we know of the one by the "Twelve." Apparently, the Ebionites referred to their scripture as the "Authentic Gospel of Matthew." Scholars argue whether this is another document or another name for their gospel. In other words, there could be as many as four separate documents being talked about here or only one. Scholars simply don't know for sure. They do think, however, that the Gospel of the Ebionites was, in fact, an attempt to harmonize (and then possibly to replace) the other Gospels.

The Gospel of the Ebionites begins with the story of John who was baptizing with a baptism of repentance. All went out to him, including the Pharisees. He was dressed in camel's hair with a leathern girdle about his loins. His diet consisted of wild honey and something like "manna" that tasted like a cake dipped in oil. (Since the Ebionites were strict vegetarians, they changed his diet from locusts to a manna-like cake. This is easy to do in Greek because locust is *akris* whereas cake is *enkris*. [This apparently assumes a similar sleight of text is possible in Aramaic.])

The timeline is similar to that of Luke's Gospel – in the days of Herod, the king of Judea, when Caiaphas was the high priest. John was of the lineage of Aaron; his parents were Zacharias and Elizabeth.

One day Jesus came and was baptized by John. As he came up out of the water, the heavens opened; he saw the Holy Ghost in the likeness of a dove that descended and entered into him, and he heard a voice from heaven. (These are straight out of Matthew's gospel. What's different is that this voice speaks several times, repeating all the variations found in the synoptic gospels. In this way, the Ebionites have been able to harmonize the gospel accounts.) Apparently, John also heard the voice, whereupon John fell before Jesus and asked to be baptized of him. To which Jesus replied, "Suffer it (or let it go): for it is fitting that all things be fulfilled in this way."

The only difference between the Ebionites and the Hebrew Gospel up to this point is that in the latter, it is the mother of the Lord and his brothers who suggest they go and be baptized by John. Jesus replied, "In what way have I sinned that I should go and be baptized by him? Unless perhaps, what I have just said is a sin of ignorance."

After this, we read that Jesus is a man about thirty years old who chose "us." He entered into Capernaum and chose Simon, surnamed Peter, and made him speak, saying that eleven followers had already been chosen and that Matthew, who sat at the receipt of custom, should be the twelfth. Jesus chose these apostles to be a testimony to Israel. (The list of names matches the list in Matthew's gospel.)

There are only a few more known quotations from the Gospel of the Ebionites, so let's focus on the Hebrew Gospel. One specific fact in the Hebrew Gospel is at variance with Luke. In his gospel, Luke refers to Matthew as Levi; in the Hebrew Gospel, it is obvious that Levi is really Matthias who replaced Judas after his betrayal. One of the worst sins in the Hebrew Gospel is, "To grieve the spirit of one's brother."

Perhaps this is why the Hebrew Gospel has a great emphasis on James, the brother of Jesus. James (known as James, the Just) was the head of the Jerusalem Church and a proponent of obeying the Jewish law. It is in the Hebrew Gospel that we read that Jesus' first resurrection appearance was to his brother: "After Jesus had given the linen cloth to the servant of the priest, he went to James and appeared to him. For James had sworn that he would not eat bread from that hour in which he had drunk the cup of the Lord until he should see him risen from among them that sleep. And shortly thereafter the Lord said: Bring a table and bread! And immediately it added: he took the bread, blessed it and brake it and gave it to James the Just and said to him: My brother, eat thy bread, for the Son of man is risen from among them that sleep." This also means that James was present at the Last Supper. These verses stand in direct contradiction to that which is presumed from the canonical stories. John 7:5 claims outright that Jesus' brothers did not believe in him. Paul, however, does allude to the fact that Jesus appeared to James after his resurrection.

So it is that we also read, "the Lord spoke to his disciples saying, 'And never be joyful except when you look on your brother with love.' "

The Hebrew Gospel also has an account of the rich young man coming to Jesus. He asked, "Rabbi, what good thing can I do and live?" Jesus answered, "Fulfill the law and the prophets." When the man said he had already been doing that, Jesus added, "Go, sell all that you have and

distribute to the poor; and come, follow me." When the young man began to squirm, Jesus asked, "How can you say, I have fulfilled the law and the prophets, when it is written in the law: You shall love your neighbor as yourself and many of your brothers, sons of Abraham, are covered with filth, dying of hunger, and your house is full of many good things, none of which goes out to them?" And he turned and said to Simon, his disciple, who was sitting by Him, "Simon, son of Jonah, it is easier for a camel to go through the eye of a needle than for the rich to enter the Kingdom of Heaven."

From these examples, it is easy to see great similarities to the canonical books, yet none of these were accepted into the canon. All of these books firmly state that Jesus was chosen by God; he obeyed the laws of the Torah and preached, "Love God; love your neighbor." Yet, because these writings bore no witness to the virgin birth or Christ's pre-existence, they were deemed to be heretical. The Ebionites fought against Paul's teaching about salvation apart from obedience to the law – and lost. History is written by the winners. Half of the New Testament books are attributed to Paul; the Ebionites' writings were destroyed.

Book 130. The Gospel of the Twelve Apostles (Summary)

The *Gospel of the Twelve Apostles* is a Western Syriac apocryphon that dates to the mid-eighth century CE. The work claims to be originally composed in Hebrew and later translated into Greek, where it then made its way to Syriac. Although writers of the fifth century mention a "Gospel of the Twelve" as a second-century work (i.e., Origen and Epiphanius), they either make reference only to the title or provide content that differs from the one at hand. In addition, no earlier source that is extant confirms their claims. Furthermore, the environmental factors of the mid-eighth century Middle East (i.e., the Islamic Conquest) seem to correspond well with the context of *Gos. Twelve*.

The text begins with a narrative on the nativity, ministerial activity, and resurrection of Jesus. The text also provides an account of Jesus instructing his apostles to scatter across the "four quarters" to baptize and evangelize peoples and nations for the "New Kingdom." Thus, each evangelist is assigned a region and miraculously, without training, embrace the ability to speak a foreign tongue that is practised in his assigned area. Before the Twelve's mission takes launch, the apostles gather and pray in a house to ask God to reveal to them the "secret mysteries" concerning the end times. Their prayers are answered, and God instructs the apostles to go to the mountain where Moses and Elijah appeared to them in the past (i.e., the location of the Transfiguration, Mark 9:2–8 par.). Forthwith, these instructions are followed and for seven days the apostles journey until finally, they arrive to receive the divine mysteries. Three of the twelve apostles receive the apocalyptic revelations: Peter, James, and John.

Peter declares that the archangel Michael came to him and gave him a vision in which he saw church leaders "divide out Lord" (perhaps an allusion to Nestorianism), thus displeasing God, who in turn hands them over to oppressive peoples that persecute them (either Romans, Persians, or Moslems). This process continues until the churches unite and depart from their wicked ways and bring back the orthodox teachings to their flocks. The angel then approaches James and James tells the others that he sees the destruction of Jerusalem (perhaps under Hadrian). The people experience waves of oppression and the city is left with only weeping inhabitants. In due time, a ruler rises to power (likely Licinius) and reorganizes the people and leads them into war but dies in battle. His successor (Constantine) constructs the third temple and allows the faithful to worship God within it once more. The final successor "burdens the chief men with many ills," which would indicate that this ruler should be identified with Julian, yet this same ruler is said to bring peace and prosperity to the land and the author declares that he will save those who call on the name of Jesus.

The angel then approaches John and informs him that he has been exclusively chosen to view the greatest revelation. John's vision starts with rulers of the "North" gaining power, led by a man who bears a marvellous sign (again, likely Constantine). He is succeeded by kings of the Romans who anger God by their constant idol-worship and turpitude. As punishment, God raises up the Persians who expel Rome. One of the Persian rulers (Chrosroes the Great), a "lover of money," is killed by his son and then the Persians are succeeded by the Medes. The following events are interpreted by John as the fulfillment of Daniel's prophecy. The kings of the "South" rise to power (i.e., Arabia and Mohammad) and do so with severe burden with taxation, enslavement, etc. to the world. In addition, the rulers hate the name of Jesus and do even more iniquities to the Christians. Moreover, God soon puts an end to this kingdom by dividing the rulers into "two parties" (i.e., the Abbassid and Omiyyad dynasties) who war against each other until they are severely weakened. At the same time, the kings of the "North" rise and unite the world and all those oppressed by the kings of the "South" and defeat them. The "South" then faces numerous plagues and are fated to never hold a standing army nor engage in battle again. The conclusion of the text is damaged but it is clear that John's vision comes to a close and a voice commands John to share his vision with his companions.

Named historical figures and characters: Abraham (patriarch), Adam (patriarch), Alexander (the Great), Andrew (apostle), Asher (patriarch), Bartholomew (apostle), Benjamin (patriarch), Daniel (prophet), David (king), Elijah (prophet), Gabriel (angel), Gad (patrarich), Herod (the Great), Holy Spirit, Ishmael, Issachar (patriarch), James (son of Alphaeus), James (son of Zebedee), John (son of Zebedee), Jesus Christ, Joseph (of Nazareth), Joseph (patriarch), Judah (patriarch), Judas Iscariot, Levi (patriarch), Mary (Virgin), Matthaias (apostle), Matthew (apostle), Michael (angel), Moses (patriarch), Naphtali (patriarch), Peter (apostle), Philip (apostle), Reuben (patriarch), Satan, Sibyl, Simeon (patriarch), Simon (the Canaanite/Zealot), Thaddaeus (apostle), Thomas (apostle), Tiberius (emperor), Zebulon (patriarch).

Geographical locations: Africa, Bethlehem, Canaan, Diglath, Egypt, Israel, Jerusalem, Judah, Media, Mesopotamia, Nazareth, Persia, Rome, temple (Jerusalem).

Book 131. The Prayer of Asenath

Chapter 1

1 ¶ In the first of seven years of great pleanty Pharaoh sent forth Joseph to lay up corn, and gather food within the cities.

2 So Joseph went out over all the land of Egypt, and came in the country of Heliopolis, where lived Poti-pherah, the priest, and chief counsellor of the great King.1 It came to pass in the first year of the seven years of plenty, in the second month, that Pharaoh sent out Joseph to go round the whole land of Egypt.

2 And Joseph came, in the fourth month of the first year, on the eighteenth day of the month, into the district of Heliopolis.

3 And he was collecting all the corn of that land, as the sand of the sea.

4 Now there was in that city a man, a satrap of Pharaoh; and this man was the chief of all Pharaoh's satraps and lords.

5 And he was very rich, and wise, and generous, and he was Pharaoh's counsellor, and his name was Pentephres; and he was the priest of Heliopolis (of On)3 His daughter, Asenath, was the the fairest of all the virgins of the earth; and seemed rather to be a daughter of Israel than an Egyptian.6 And Pentephres had a virgin daughter of about eighteen years of age, tall and beautiful and graceful, more beautiful than any other virgin in the land.

7 And she was quite unlike the daughters of the Egyptians, but in every respect like the daughters of the Hebrews.

8 And she was as tall as Sarah, and as beautiful as Rebecca, and as fair as Rachel; and this virgin's name was Aseneth.

9 And the fame of her beauty spread through all that land, even to its remotest corners; and all the sons of the lords and of the satraps and of the kings sought her hand in marriage, young men all of them.

10 And there was great rivalry between them because of her, and they began to fight among themselves because of Aseneth.

11 And Pharaoh's eldest son heard about her, and he begged his father to give her to him as his wife.

12 And he said to him, "Give me Aseneth the daughter of Pentephres the priest of Heliopolis as my wife." And his father Pharaoh said to him, "Why should you want a wife of lower station than yourself?

13 Are you not king of all the earth?

14 No! See now, the daughter of King Joakim is betrothed to you, and she is a queen and very beautiful indeed: take her as your wife."Chapter 2

4 But Asenath was scornful and proud, and a despiser of men.

5 No man of all the sons of men had seen her with his eyes, for she lodged within a strong tower, tall and wide, near the habitation of Poti-pherah, the priest.1 Now Asenath despised all men and regarded them with contempt; yet no man had ever seen her, for Pentephres had a tower in his house, and it was large and very high.6 Now high upon this tower there were ten chambers.2 And the top storey had ten rooms in it.7 The first chamber was fair and great, and was builded of marble blocks of divers colours; the walls were of precious stones set in a chasing of gold, and the ceiling thereof was golden.

8 There stood the gods of the Egyptians in metal of silver and gold, and Asenath bowed before them and offered sacrifice, every day of all the days.3 The first room was large and pleasant; and it was paved with purple stones, and its walls were faced with precious stones of different kinds.

4 And the ceiling of that room was of gold; and within it were ranged the innumerable gods of the Egyptians, in gold and silver.

5 And Asenath worshipped all these; and she feared them and offered sacrifices to them.9 The second chamber was the habitation of Asenath, and was adorned cunningly with ornaments of gold and silver, with costly gems, and with arras and stuffs most precious.6 The second room contained all the finery for Aseneth's adornment and treasure chests

7 And there was much gold in it, and silver, and garments woven with gold, and precious stones of great price, and fine linens.

8 And all her girlish ornaments were there.10 In the third chanber was brought together the wealth of all the world, and in that place also were set aumbries of Asenath.9 The third room contained all the good things of the earth; and it was Aseneth's store-house.11 Seven virgins, her fellows, lodged in the seven chambers.

12 They were very fair, and no man had spoken with them, nor any male child.10 And seven virgins had the remaining seven rooms, one each.

11 And they used to wait on Aseneth, and were of the same age as she was, for they were all born on the same night as Aseneth; and they were very beautiful, like the stars of heaven, and no man or boy had ever had anything to do with them.13 ¶ The chamber of Asenath was pierced with three windows; the first, which was very wide, looked towards the east, the second looked towards the south, and the third was set towards the north.12 And Aseneth's large room, where she spent her time, had three windows.

13 One window looked out over the courtyard to the east: the second looked to the north, onto the street; and the third to the south.14 Here was spread a couch of gold, covered with a purple coverlet, embroidered with golden thread, and hemmed with jacinths.14 And a golden bed stood in the room, facing the east.

15 And the bed had a coverlet of purple woven with gold, embroidered with blue, and fine linen.15 There slept Asenath, with no bed-fellow, neither had man sat ever upon her bed.16 In this bed Aseneth used to sleep alone, and no man or woman ever sat upon it, except Aseneth only16 About this house was a goodly garden, closed round with a very strong wall, and entered by four iron gates.

17 Each door had for warders eighteen men, very might and young, well armed and full of valour.17 And there was a great court all round the house, and a wall round the court, very high and built of great rectangular stones.

18 And there were four gates to the court, overlaid with iron; and eighteen strong young men-at-arms used to guard each one of them.18 At the right side of the garden sprang a fountian of living water, and near by the fountian a cistern wich gave of this water to all the trees of the garden, and these trees bore much fruit.19 And along the wall inside the court every kind of beautiful tree that produces fruit had been planted; and the fruit on every one of them was ripe, for it was harvest time

20 And on the right of the court there was an ever-bubbling spring of water, and beneath the spring a great cistern that received the water from the spring and out of which a river flowed through the middle of the court and watered all the trees in it.19 And asenath was queenly as Sarah, gracious as Rebecca, and fair as Rachel.Chapter 2

*How Joseph rebuked Asenath because she worshipped idols.*Chapter 31 ¶ Joseph went a message to Poti-pherah that he would come to his house.1 And it came to pass in the fourth month, on the eighteenth day of the month, that Joseph came into the district of Heliopolis.

2 And as he approached the city, Joseph sent twelve men in front of him to Pentephres, the priest of Heliopolis, saying, May I be your guest today, for it is near noon and time for a mid-day meal?

3 The sun's heat is overpowering, and I would enjoy some refreshment under your roof.2 So Poti-pherah rejoiced greatly,4 When Pentephres heard this, he was overjoyed and said,

5 "Blessed be the Lord, the God of Joseph." And Pentephres called his steward and said to him,

6 "Make haste and get my house into order, and prepare a great feast, because Joseph, the mighty man of God, is coming to us to-day.

7 And Aseneth heard that her father and mother had come back from their family estate in the country.

8 And she rejoiced and said, I will go and see my father and my mother for they have come back from their family estate in the country.

9 And Aseneth hurried and put on a fine linen robe of blue woven with gold and a golden girdle round her waist, and she put bracelets round her hands and feet, and she put on golden trousers and a necklace round her neck.

10 And there were precious stones all about her, with the names of Egyptian gods inscribed on them everywhere, on the bracelets and on the stones; and the names of the idols were stamped on the stones.

11 And she put a tiara on her head and bound a diadem round her temples and covered her head with a veil.

Chapter 4

1 And she hurried and came down by the staircase from her storey at the top; and she came to her father and mother and greeted them.

2 And it gave Pentephres and his wife great joy to see their daughter Aseneth adorned as the bride of God

3 And they took out all the good things they had brought from their estate in the country, and they gave them to their daughter.

4 And Aseneth rejoiced at the good things, and at the fruit, the grapes and the dates, and at the doves and at the pomegranates and the figs, for they were all delightful.saying to his daughter, "Joseph, the friend of God,

enters herein.

3 I would give thee to him as his wife."5 And Pentephres said to his daughter Aseneth, "My child": she said, "Lo, here I am, my lord."

6 And he said to her, "Sit down, please, between us: I want to talk to you." And Aseneth sat down between her father and her mother.

7 And her father Pentephres took her right hand n his right hand and said to her, "My child"; and Aseneth said, "What is it, father?"

8 And Pentephres said to her, "See, Joseph, the mighty man of God, is coming to us to-day, and he is ruler of all the land of Egypt, for Pharaoh has appointed him ruler of all our land; and he is the distributor of corn throughout the country and is to save it from the famine that is come upon it.

9 And Joseph is a man that worships God: he is discriminating, and a virgin (as you are to-day), and a man of great wisdom and knowledge, and the spirit of God is upon him, and the grace of the Lord is with him.

10 So come, my child, and I will give you to him as his wife: you shall be his bride, and he shall be your bridegroom for ever."4 But Asenath was sore vexed when she heard these words, and said-11 And when Aseneth heard what her father said, a great red sweat came over her, and she was furious and looked sideways at her father.5 "No captive shall ever be my husband, but only the son of a king."12 And she said, "Why should my lord and my father speak like this and talk as if he would hand me over like a prisoner to a man of another race, a man who was a fugitive and was sold as a slave?

13 Is this not the shepherd's son from the land of Canaan, and he was abandoned by him?

14 Is not this the man who had intercourse with his mistress, and his master threw him into prison where he lay in darkness, and Pharaoh brought him out of prison, because he interpreted his dream?

15 No! I will marry the eldest son of the king, for he is king of all the earth."

16 On hearing this, Pentephres thought it wiser to say no more to his daughter about Joseph, for she had answered him arrogantly and in anger.Chapter 5

6 Whilst they spake thus together, a messenger came before them and cried, "Joseph is here"; so Asenath fled to her chamber high within the tower.1 And behold, one of the young men from Pentephres's retinue burst in and said,

2 "Lo Joseph is at the gates of our court." And Aseneth quickly left her father and her mother and ran upstairs and went into her room and stood at the big window that looked towards the east, so as to see Joseph as he came into her father's house.

3 And Pentephres and his wife and all his relations went out to meet Joseph.7 Now Joseph was seated in Pharaoh's own chariot of beaten gold, and it was drawn by four horses, white as snow, with bridles and harness of gold.4 And the gates of the court that looked east were opened, and Joseph came in, sitting in Pharaoh's viceroy's chariot.

5 And there were four horses yoked together, white as snow, with golden reins; and the chariot was covered over with gold.8 Joseph was clad in a vesture of fine linen, white and blistering, and his mantle was of purple, spun with gold.

9 He wore a golden circlet upon his head, and in this crown were set twelve stones, most precious, each stone having for ornament a golden star.6 And Joseph was wearing a marvellous white tunic, and the robe wrapped around him was purple, made of linen woven with gold: there was a golden crown on his head, and all round the crown were twelve precious stones, and above the stones twelve golden rays; and a royal sceptre was in his right hand.10 Moreover, he held in his hand the royal sceptre, and an olive branched charged with fruit.7 And he held an olive branch stretched out, and there was much fruit on it.11 Poti pherah and his wife hastened to meet him, and bowed before him to the ground.

12 They led him within the garden, and caused the doors to be shut.8 And Joseph came into the court, and the gates were shut.

9 And strangers, whether men or women, remained outside, because the gate-keepers had shut the doors.

10 And Pentephres came, and his wife, and all his relatives, except their daughter Aseneth; and they made obeisance to Joseph with their faces to the ground.

11 And Joseph got down from his chariot and extended his right hand to them.Chapter 613 But when Asenath regarded Joseph from on high the tower, she repented of the words she spoke concerning him, and said-

14 "Behold the sun and the chariot of the sun!

15 Certainly this Joseph is the child of God; for what father could beget so fair an offspring, and what womb of woman could carry such light."1 And Aseneth saw Joseph and she was cut to the quick, her stomach turned over, her knees became limp, and her whole body trembled.

2 And she was much afraid and cried out and said, "Where shall I go, and where can I hide myself from him? And how will Joseph, the son of God, regard me, for I have spoken evil of him?

3 Where can I flee and hide myself, for he sees everything, and no secret is safe with him, because of the great light that is in him?

4 And now may Joseph's God be propitious to me because I spoke evil in ignorance.

5 What can I hope for, wretch that I am? Have I not spoken, saying, Joseph is coming, the shepherd's son from the land of Canaan? And now, behold the sun is come to us from heaven in his chariot and has come into our house to-day.

6 But I was foolish and reckless to despise him, and I spoke evil of him and did not know that Joseph is the son of God.

7 For who among men will ever father such beauty, and what mother will ever bear such a light? Wretch that I am and foolish, for I spoke evil of him to my father.

8 Now let my father give me to Joseph as a maidservant and a slave, and I will serve him for ever."Chapter 716 Joseph entered in the house of Poti-pherah, and whilst they washed his feet he asked what woman had looked forth from the window of the tower.

17 "Let her go forth from the house," he commanded.1 And Joseph came into Pentephres's house and sat down on a seat; and he washed his feet, and he placed a table in front of him separately, because he would not eat with the Egyptians, for this was an abomination to him.

2 And Joseph spoke to Pentephres and all his relations, saying, "Who is that woman standing in the solar by the window? Tell her to go away."18 This he said because he feard lest she should desire him, and should send him messages and divers gifts, even as other women of her nation, whom he had refused with holy indignation.3 This was because Joseph was afraid she too might solicit him; for all the wives and daughters of the lords and satraps of all the land of Egypt use to solicit him to lie with him.

4 And many of the wives and daughters of the Egyptians suffered much, after seeing Joseph, because he was so handsome; and they would send emissaries to him with gold and silver and valuable gifts.

5 And Joseph would reject them out of hand, saying, I will not sin before the God of Israel.

6 And Joseph kept his father Jacob's face before his eyes continually, and he remembered his father's commandments; for Jacob used to say to Joseph and his brothers, "Be on your guard, my children, against the strange woman, and have nothing to do with her, for she is ruin and destruction.

7 That is why Joseph said, "Tell that woman to go away."19 But Poti-pherah replied-

20 "Sire, this is my daughter, who is a virgin, and hateth men; neither hath she seen any man save me, her father, and thyself this very day.8 And Pentephres said to him, "My lord, the woman you have seen in the storey at the top is no stranger: she is our daughter, a virgin, who detests men; and no other man has ever seen her, apart from you to-day.21 If thou wilt, she shall come before thee and salute thee."9 And if you wish it, she shall come and speak with you; for our daughter is your sister.22 Then Joseph thought within himself, "Since she hateth man, she will not cast her eyes upon me."10 And Joseph was overjoyed because Pentephres said, "She is a virgin who detests men."23 So he answered to her father-

24 "Since your daughter is a virgin, I will cherish her even as my sister."11 And Joseph answered Pentephres and his wife and said, "If she is your daughter, then let her come, for she is my sister, and I will regard her as my sister from to-day."Chapter 825 Then her mother went out to seek Asenath, and brought her before Joseph.

26 "Salute thy brother," said Poti-pherah, "who hateth the strange woman, even as thou hatest man."1 And Aseneth's mother went up to the top storey and brought Aseneth down to Joseph; and Pentephres said to his daughter Aseneth, "Greet your brother, for he too is a virgin as you are to-day, and he detests all strange women just as you detest strange men."27 "God keep thee," replied Asenath, "for thou art blessed of God most high."

28 And Joseph answered, "May the God of life bless thee ever-more."2 And Aseneth said to Joseph, "May you have joy, my lord, blessed as you are of God Most High"; and Joseph said to her, "May God, who has given all things life, bless you."29 Then commanded Poti-pherah that she should kiss Joseph; but as she drew near Joseph set his hand against her breast and said-3 And Pentephres said to Asenath, "Come near and kiss your brother."

4 And when she came near to kiss Joseph, Joseph stretched his right hand out, and laid it against her breast, and said,30 "It is not meet that a man who worships the living God, and eateth the bread of life and drinketh from the chalice without corruption, should embrace the strange woman, who bows down before deaf and dumb idols; who serves them with the kisses of her mouth; is anointed with their reprobate oil, and eats an accursed bread, and drinks unsanctified wine from their table."5 "It is not right for a man who worships God, who with his mouth blesses the living God, and eats the blessed bread of life, and drinks the blessed cup of immortality, and is anointed with the blessed unction of incorruption, to kiss a strange woman, who with her mouth blesses dead and dumb idols, and eats of their table the bread of anguish, and drinks of their libations the cup of treachery, and is anointed with the unction of destruction

6 A man who worships God will kiss his mother and his sister that is of his own tribe and kin, and the wife that shares his couch, who with their mouths bless the living God.7 So too it is not right for a woman who

worships God to kiss a strange man, because this is an abomination in God's eyes."Chapter 3

*Of the penitence of Asenath, and of the consolation of an angel; how he came from Heaven to the chanber of Asenath, and spake with her and sweetly comforted her.*1 ¶ When Asenath heard Joseph speak these words she was sore vexed, even unto tears; wherefore Joseph took pity upon her and blessed her, laying his hand upon her head.8 And when Aseneth heard what Joseph said, she was most distressed and cried out aloud; and she fixed her gaze on Joseph, and her eyes were filled with tears.

9 And Joseph saw her and his heart went out to her -- for Joseph was tender-hearted and compassionate and feared the Lord.

10 And he lifted up his right hand above her head and said, "O Lord, the God of my father Israel, the Most High, the Mighty One, Who didst quicken all things, and didst call them from darkness into light.
And from error into truth, and from death into life;
Do thou, O Lord, thyself quicken and bless this virgin,

11 And renew her by thy spirit, and remould her by thy secret hand,
And quicken her with thy life.
And may she eat the bread of thy life,
And may she drink the cup of thy blessing,
She whom thou didst choose before she was begotten,
And may she enter into thy rest, which thou has prepared for thine elect."

Chapter 92 Asenath rejoiced greatly at the benediction.
3 She saught her bed, sick with fear and joy, and renounced the gods before whom she bowed, and humbled herself to the ground.1 And Aseneth was filled with joy at Joseph's blessing, and she went up in haste to her storey at the top and fell on her couch exhausted, because she felt not only happy, but also disturbed and very frightened; and she had been bathed in perspiration from the moment she heard Joseph speaking to her in the name of God Most High.

2 And she wept bitterly, and she repented of her gods she used to worship; and she waited for evening to come.4 So Joseph ate and drank, and when he rose to go Poti-pherah prayed him to tarry till the morrow; but he might not, and parted, having promised to return within eight days.3 And Joseph ate and drank; and he said to his servants, "Yoke the horses to the chariot" (for he said, "I must depart and go round the whole city and the district").

4 And Pentephres said to Joseph, "Stay the night here, my lord and to-morrow go your way."

5 And Joseph said, "No! I must be going now, for this is the day when God began his works: in eight days time I will come back again and stay the night here with you."Chapter 10

1 Then Pentephres and his relations went away to their estate.
2 And Aseneth was left alone with the virgins, and she was listless and wept until sunset: she ate no bread and drank no water; and while all slept she alone was awake.
3 And she opened the door and went down to the gate; and she found the portress asleep with her children.
4 And Aseneth quickly took down the leather curtain from the door, and she filled it with ashes and carried it up to the top storey and laid it on the floor.
5 And she secured the door and fastened it with the iron bar from the side; and she groaned aloud and wept.
6 And the virgin that Aseneth loved most of all the virgins heard her mistress groaning, and she roused the other virgins and came and found the door shut.
7 And she listened to Aseneth groaning and weeping and said, "Why are you so sorrowful my lady? What is it that its troubling you?
8 Open the door for us, so that we can see you." And Aseneth said to them from inside (shut in as she was, "I have a violent headache and am resting on my bed; and I have no strength left to open to you now, for I am utterly exhausted; but go each of you to her room."5 Then Asenath put on sad raiment, such as she wore at the death of her brother, and went clothed in a garment of heaviness.
6 She closed the doors of her chamber upon her and wept.
7 Moreover, she flung forth all her idols by the window set towards the north; all the royal meat she gave to the dogs; she put dust upon her head, lay upon the ground, and lamented bitterly for seven days.9 And Aseneth got up and opened her door quietly, and went into her second room, where her treasure-chests and the finery for her adornment were, and she opened her wardrobe and took out a black and sombre tunic.
10 (And this was her mourning tunic, which she had worn for mourning when her eldest brother died)
11 And Aseneth took off her royal robe and put on the black one, and she untied her golden girdle and tied a rope around her waist instead, and she took her tiara off her head ¶ and the diadem, and the bracelets from her hands.
12 And she took her best robe, just as it was, and threw it out of the window, for the poor.

13 And she took all her innumerable gold and silver gods and broke them up into little pieces, and threw them out of the window for the poor and needy.
14 And Aseneth took her royal dinner, even the fatted beasts and the fish and the meat, and all the sacrifices of her gods, and the wine-vessels for their libations; and she threw them all out of the window as food for the dogs.
15 And after this she took the ashes and poured them out on the floor.
16 And she took sackcloth and wrapped it round her waist, and she removed the fillet from her hair and sprinkled herself with ashes; and she fell down upon the ashes.
17 And she beat her breast repeatedly with her two hands and wept bitterly and groaned all night until the morning.
18 And in the morning Aseneth got up and looked and lo, the ashes underneath her were like mud because of her tears.
19 And again, Aseneth fell down on her face upon the ashes until sunset.
20 And so Aseneth did for seven days; and she tasted neither food nor drink.Chapter 11

1 And it came to pass on the eighth day that Aseneth looked up from the floor where she was lying (for she was losing the use of her limbs as a result of her great affliction).

Chapter 12

1 And she stretched her hands out towards the east, and her eyes looked up to heaven, and she said,
2 "O Lord, God of the ages, that didst give to all the breath of life,
That didst bring into the light the things unseen,
That hast made all things and made visible what was invisible,
3 That hast raised up the heaven and founded the earth upon the waters,
That hast fixed the great stones upon the abyss of water
Which shall not be submerged,
But to the end they do thy will.
4 O Lord, my God, to thee will I cry: hear my supplication;
And unto thee will I make confession of my sins,
And unto thee will I reveal my transgressions of thy law.
5 I have sinned, O Lord, I have sinned:
I have transgressed thy law and acted impiously,
And I have spoken things evil before thee.
My mouth, O Lord, has been defiled by things offered to idols,
And by the table of the gods of the Egyptians.
6 I have sinned, O Lord, before thee; I have sinned and acted impiously,
Worshiping idols deaf and dumb,
And I am not worthy to open my mouth unto thee, wretch that I am.
7 I have sinned, O Lord, before thee,
I, the daughter of Pentephres the priest,
the haughty and arrogant Aseneth.
To thee, O Lord, I present my supplication, and unto thee will I cry:
Deliver me from my persecutors, for unto thee have I fled,
Like a child to his father and his mother.
8 And do thou, O Lord, stretch forth thy hands over me,
As a father that loves his children and is tenderly affectionate,
And snatch me from the hand of my enemy.
9 For lo, the wild primeval Lion pursues me;
And his children are the gods of the Egyptians that I have abandoned and destroyed; And their father the Devil is trying to devour me
10 But do thou, O Lord deliver me from his hands,
And rescue me from his mouth,
Lest he snatch me like a wolf and tear me,
And cast me into the abyss of fire, and into the tempest of the sea;
And let not the great Sea-monster swallow me.
11 Save me, O Lord, deserted as I am,
For my father and mother denied me,
Because I destroyed and shattered their gods;
And I have no other hope save in thee, O Lord;
For thou art the father of the orphans, and the champion of the persecuted,
And the help of them that are oppressed.
12 For, lo, all the gods of my father Pentephres are but for a season and uncertain; but the inhabitants of thine inheritance, O Lord, are incorruptible and eternal.

Chapter 13

1 Look upon my ophanhood, O Lord, for unto thee did I flee, O Lord.
2 Lo, I took off my royal robe interwoven with gold and put on a black tunic instead.
3 Lo, I loosed my golden girdle and girt myself with a rope and sackcloth.
4 Lo, I threw off my diadem from my head and sprinkled myself with ashes.
5 Lo, the floor of my room once scattered with stones of different colors

and of purple, and besprinkled with myrrh, is now sprinkled with my tears and scattered with ashes.

6 Lo, Lord, from the ashes and from my tears there is as much mud inside my room as there is on a public highway.

7 Lo, Lord, my royal dinner and my fatted beasts have I given to the dogs.

8 And lo, for seven days and seven nights I have neither eaten bread nor drunk water; and my mouth is dry like a drum and my tongue like horn, and my lips like a potsherd, and my face is shrunken, and my eyes are failing as a result of my incessant tears.

9 But do thou, O Lord, pardon me, for in ignorance did I sin against thee and uttered calumnies against my lord Joseph.

10 And I did not know, wretch that I am, that he is thy son, O Lord; for they told me that Joseph was a shepherd's son from the land of Canaan, and I believed them; but I was wrong, and I despised Joseph, thine elect one, and I spoke evil of him, not knowing that he is thy son.

11 For what man ever was so handsome and who else is as wise and strong as Joseph? But to thee, my Lord, do I entrust him; for I love him more than mine own soul.

12 Preserve him in the wisdom of thy grace, and give me to him as a servant, so that I may wash his feet and serve him and be his slave for all the seasons of my life.Chapter 148 But the eighth morning, at the hour when the cock crows and the dogs howl at the breaking of the day, Asenath looked forth from the window giving to the east, and saw a star shining clear, and the heavens open and there appeared a great light.1 And as Aseneth finished her confession to the Lord, lo, the morning star rose in the eastern sky.

2 And Aseneth saw it and rejoiced and said, "The Lord God has indeed heard me, for this star is a messenger and herald of the light of the great day.

3 And lo, the heaven was torn open near the morning star and an indescribable light appeared.9 She fell to the earth with her face in the dust, and a man decended from the heavens and stood by her head, calling on her by her name.4 And Aseneth fell on her face upon the ashes; and there came to her a man from heaven and stood at her head; and he called to her, "Aseneth".10 But Asenath answered nothing, because of the greatness of her fear.5 And she said, "Who called me? For the door of my room is shut and the tower is high: how then did anyone get into my room?"11 Then the man called her a second time, saying, "Asenath! Asenath!" and she replied-

12 "Lord, here am I. Tell me whom thou art."6 And the man called her a second time and said, "Aseneth, Aseneth;" and she said, "Here am I, my lord, tell me who you are."13 And he said-

14 "I am Prince of the House of God and Captian of His Host.

15 Rise, stand upon thy feet, for I have to speak with thee."7 And the man said, "I am the commander of the Lord's house and chief captain of all the host of the Most High: stand up, and I will speak to you."16 Then Asenath raised her head, and saw a man by her side who in all points was, as it were, Joseph.

17 He was clad in a white stole, and bore the royal sceptre in his hand, and a crown was upon his brow.8 And she looked up and saw a man like Joseph in every respect, with a robe and a crown and a royal staff.18 His face was as the lighning, his eyes as rays of the sun, and the hair of his head like a flame of fire.9 But his face was like lightning, and his eyes were like the light of the sun, and the hairs of his head like flames of fire, and his hands and feet like iron from the fire.19 At the sight of him Asenath was sore afraid, and hid her face upon the ground.10 And Aseneth looked at him, and she fell on her face at his feet in great fear and trembling20 But the Angel raised her to her feet, and comforted her, saying-11 And the man said to her, "Take heart, Aseneth, and do not be afraid; but stand up, and I will speak to you."21 "Put off this black raient with whitch thou art clothed, and this girdle of sadness.

22 Remove the sack-cloth from thy body, and the dust from thine head; cleanse thy face and thy hands with living water, and adorn thee with fair apparel, for I have somewhat to say to thee."12 And Aseneth got up, and the man said to her, "Take off the black tunic you are wearing and the sackcloth round your waist, and shake the ashes off your head, and wash your face with water.

13 And put on a new robe that you have never worn before, and tie your bright girdle round your waist -- the double girdle of your virginity.

14 And then come back to me, and I will tell you what I have been sent to you to say."23 So she adorned herself with speed,15 And Aseneth went into the room where her treasure-chests and the finery for her adornment were; and she opened her wardrobe and took out a new, fine robe, and she took off her black robe and put on the new and brilliant one.

16 And she untied the rope and the sackcloth round her waist; and she put on the brilliant double girdle of her virginity -- one girdle round her waist and the other round her breast.

17 And she shook the ashes off her head, and washed her face with pure water, and covered her head with a fine and lovely veil.

Chapter 15and when she came to him again he said-
24 "Asenath, take off this ornament from thine head, for thou art vir-

gin.1 And she came back to the man; and when the man saw her he said to her, "Take now the veil off your head, for to-day you are a pure virgin and your head is like a young man's."2 So she took it off her head; and the man said to her, "Take heart, Aseneth, for lo, the Lord has heard the words of your confession.25 Rejoice, and be of good cheer, for thy name is written in the Book of Life, and shall never be taken away.3 Take heart, Aseneth, your name is written in the book of life, and it will never be blotted out.26 Thou art born again this very day and quickened anew.

27 For thou shalt recieve the Bread of Blessing, and drink of the Wine without corruption; and be anointed with the Holy Chrism.4 From to-day you will be made new, and refashioned, and given new life; and you shall eat the bread of life and drink the cup of immortality, and be anointed with the unction of incorruption.28 Yea, I have given thee for wife to Joseph, and thou no more shall be called Asenath, but a name shall be given thee of fair refuge, for thy Penitence hath come before the High King, of who she is the daughter, and thou shalt ever live before Him in mirth and gladness."5 Take heart, Aseneth: lo, the Lord has given you to Joseph to be his bride, and he shall be your bridegroom.

6 And you shall no more be called Aseneth, but 'City of Refuge' shall be your name; for many nations shall take refuge in you, and under your wings shall many peoples find shelter, and within your walls those who give their allegiance to God in penitence will find security.

7 For Penitence is the Most High's daughter and she entreats the Most High on your behalf every hour, and on behalf of all who repent; for he is the father of Penitence and she the mother of virgins, and every hour she petitions him for those who repent; for she has prepared a heavenly bridal chamber for those who love her, and she will look after them for ever.

8 And Penitence is herself a virgin, very beautiful and pure and chaste and gentle; and God Most High loves her, and all his angels do her reverence.

9 And lo, I am on my way to Joseph, and I will talk to him about you, and he will come to you to-day and see you and rejoice over you; and he shall be your bridegroom.

10 So listen to me, Aseneth, and put on your wedding robe, the ancient robe, the first that was stored away in your room, and deck yourself in all your finest jewelry, and adorn yourself as a bride, and be ready to meet him.

11 For lo, he is coming to you to-day; and he will see you and rejoice."29 Then inquired she of the Angel his name, but he answered-

30 "My name is written by the finger of God in the Book of the most high King, but all that is written therein may not be told, neither is it proper for the hearing of mortal man."12 And when the man had finished speaking Aseneth was overjoyed.

13 And she fell at his feet and said to him, "Blessed be the Lord God that sent you out to deliver me from darkness and bring me into light; and blessed be his name for ever.Chapter 4

*Of the table and of the honey that Asenath set before the Angel, and how the Angel blessed Asenath.*1 ¶ But Asenath caught the Angel by his mantle, and said-

2 "If I have found favour in thine eyes, sit for a little space upon this bed, where never man has sat, and I will spread the table before my lord."14 Let me speak now, my lord, if I have found favor with you: sit down a little on the bed, and I will get a table ready and food for you to eat; and I will bring you good wine, of the finest flavor, for your to drink; and then you shall go your way."3 And the Angel replied, "Do quickly."

4 So Asenath set a fair linen cloth upon the table, and put thereon new bread of sweet savour.Chapter 165 Then said the Angel-

6 "Give me also a little honey in the honeycomb."1 And the man said to her, "Bring me, please, a honeycomb too."7 So Asenath was grievously troubled because she had no honey to set before her guest.2 And Aseneth said, "Let me send someone my lord, to my family estate in the country and I will get you a honeycomb."8 But the Angel comforted her, saying

9 "Look within thine aumbrey, and thou shalt find withall to furnish thy table.3 And the man said to her, "Go into your inner room and you will find a honeycomb there."10 Then she hastened thereto, and found a store of virgin honey, white as snow, of the sweetest savour.4 And Aseneth went into her inner room and found a honeycomb lying on the table; and the comb was as white as snow and full of honey, and its smell was like the breath of life5 And Aseneth took the comb and brought it to him; and the man said to her, "Why did you say, 'There is no honeycomb in my house?' And lo, you have brought me this."11 So she spake to the Angel- "Sire, I had no honey, but thou spakest the word, and it is there, and the perfume thereof is as the breath of thy mouth.6 And Aseneth said, My lord, I had no honeycomb in my house, but it happened just as you said: Did it perchance come out of your mouth, for it smells like myrrh?"12 The Angel smiled at the understanding of Asenath, and placed his hand upon her head, and said-

13 "Blessed be thou, O Asenath, because thou hast forsaken thy idols, and believed in our living Lord.7 And the man stretched his hand out and placed it on her head and said, "You are blessed, Aseneth, for the indescribable things of God have been revealed to you; and blessed too are those who give their allegiance to the Lord God in penitence, for they shall eat of this comb.14 Yea, blessed are they whom Penitence bringeth

before Him, for they shall eat of this honey gathered by the bees of Paradise from the dew of the roses of Heaven; and those who eat thereof shall never see death, but shall live for evermore."8 The bees of the Paradise of Delight have made this honey, and the angels of God eat of it, and no one who eats of it shall ever die.15 The the angel stretched forth his hand and took of the honeycomb and break it; and he ate a little, and gave the rest to the mouth of Asenath, saying-9 And the man stretched his right hand out and broke off a piece of the comb and ate it; and he put a piece of it unto Aseneth's mouth.16 "This day hast thou eaten of the Bread of Life, and are anointed with the Holy Chrism.

17 Beauty is given thee for ashes; for virtue shall never go from thee, neither shall thy youth wither, nor thy fairness fail; but thou shalt be as the strong city builded as a refuge for the children of our Lord, Who is King for ever more."

18 Ten the angle touch the honeycomb, and it became unbroken as before.19 Again he stretched forth his hand, and with his finger signed the cross thereon, and theere where his finger touched came forth blood.10 And the man stretched his hand out and put his finger on the edge of the comb that faced eastwards; and the path of his finger became like blood.

11 And he stretched out his hand a second time and put his finger on the edge of the comb that faced northwards, and the path of his finger became like blood.20 So he spake to Asenath, and said- "Behold this honey!"12 And Aseneth was standing on the left and watching everything the man was doing.21 Whilst she gazed thereon, she saw bees come forth from that honey, some white as snow, others vermeil as jacinths, and they gathered about her, and set virgin honey in the palm of her hand; and she ate thereof, and the Angel whith her.13 And bees came up from the cells of the comb, and they were white as snow, and their wings were iridescent -- purple and blue and gold; and they had golden diadems on their heads and sharp-pointed strings.

14 And all the bees flew in circles round Aseneth, from her feet right up to her head; and yet more bees, as big as queens, settled on Aseneth's lips.22 "Bees," said the Angel, "return now to your own place."15 And the man said to the bees, "Go, please, to your places."23 So they passed throu that window which gave upon the east, and took their way to Paradise.

24 "Failful as these bees are the words which I have spoken."16 And they all left Aseneth and fell to the ground, every one of them, and died.

17 And the man said, "Get up now, and go to your place;" and they got up and went, every one of them, to the court round Aseneth's tower.

Chapter 17

1 And the man said to Aseneth, "Have you observed this?" and she said, "Yes, my lord, I have observed it all."

2 And the man said, "So shall be the words I have spoken to you."25 Then the angel put forth his hand three times, and touched the honey, and fire came forth and consumed the honey without singeing the table, and the perfume which came from the honey and the fire was very sweet.3 And the man touched the comb, and fire went up from the table and burnt up the comb; and, as it burned, the comb gave out a refreshing fragrance that filled the room.Chapter 5

Of the blessing of the seven maidens, and of the marriage of Asenath, as set forth in the story.

1 Asenath said to the Angel-

2 "Lord, I have with me seven virgins, born in one night, and nourished with me from my childhood until now.

3 I will seek them, and thou shalt bless them, even as thou hast blessed me."4 And Aseneth said to the man, "There are, my lord, seven virgins with me, who have been brought up with me, and who wait upon me: they were born in the same night as I was and I love them: let me call them, so that you can bless them as you have blessed me.4 So she brought them before him, and he blessed them, saying-

5 "May the most high God bless you, and make you to be seven strong columns of the City of Refuge."5 And the man said, "Call them;" and Aseneth called them, and the man blessed them and said, "God, the Most High, will bless you for ever."6 Afterwards he bade Asenath to carry forth the table, and whilst she went about her task, the Angel vanished from her eyes.

7 But looking towards the east she saw, as it were, a chariot drawn by four horses ascending towards Heaven.6 And the man said to Aseneth, "Take this table away;" and Aseneth turned to move the table, and the man vanished out of her sight, and Aseneth saw what looked like a chariot of fire being taken up into heaven towards the east.8 So Asenath prayed to God right humbly that He would pardon the boldness with which she had spoken to the Captian of His Host.7 And Aseneth said, "Be merciful, O Lord, to thy maidservant, because it was in ignorance that I spoke evil before thee."Chapter 18

1 And while this was happening, behold, a young man, one of Joseph's servants, came and said, "Lo, Joseph, the mighty man of God is coming to you to-day."

2 And Aseneth called her steward and said, "Get ready a special dinner for me, because Joseph the mighty man of God, is coming to us."

3 And Aseneth went into her room and opened her wardrobe, and she took out her finest robe that shone like lightning, and she put it on.

4 And she tied a resplendent royal girdle round her waist -- and this girdle was of precious stones

5 And she put golden bracelets round her hands, and golden boots on her feet, and a costly necklace about her neck; and she put a golden crown upon her head, and in the crown, in front, were the costliest of stones.

6 And she covered her head with a veil.

7 And she said to her maidservant, "Bring me pure water from the spring."

8 And Aseneth bent down to the water in the basin [on the cockle-shell]; and her face was like the sun, and her eyes like the rising morning star.

Chapter 199 Whilst she prayed thus a messenger came to Poti-pherah saying that Joseph, the friend of God, sought his house, and was even then at his door.

10 Asenath hastened to meet him, and awaited his coming before the offices of the house.1And a little slave came and said to Aseneth, "Lo, Joseph is at the gates of our court;" and Aseneth went down with the seven virgins to meet him.

2 And when Joseph saw her, he said to her, "Come to me, pure virgin, for I have had good news about you from heaven, explaining everything about you."

3 And Joseph stretched his hands out and embraced Aseneth, and Aseneth embraced Joseph, and they greeted each other for a long time and received new life in their spirit.

Chapter 20

1 And Aseneth said to him, "Come, my lord, come into my house;" and she took his right hand and brought him inside her house.

2 And Joseph sat down on her father Pentephres's seat, and she brought water to wash his feet; and Joseph said to her, "Let one of your virgins come, and let her wash my feet."

3 And Aseneth said to him, "No, my lord, for my hands are your hands, and your feet my feet, and no one else shall wash your feet;" and so she had her way and washed his feet.

4 And Joseph took her by the right hand and kissed it, and Aseneth kissed his head.

5 And Aseneth's parents came back from their country estate, and they saw Aseneth sitting with Joseph and wearing a wedding robe; and they rejoiced and glorified God, and they ate and drank.

6 And Pentephres said to Joseph, "To-morrow I will invite the lords and satraps of Egypt, and I will celebrate your wedding, and you shall take Aseneth as your wife."

7 And Joseph said, "First I must tell Pharaoh about Aseneth, because he is my father; and he will give me Aseneth as my wife himself."

8 And Joseph stayed that day with Pentephres; and he did not sleep with Aseneth, for he said, "It is not right for a man who worships God to have intercourse with his wife before their marriage."

11 When Joseph entered the garden she bowed herself before him, and washed the dust from his feet, telling him the words which the Angel had spoken concerning her.

Chapter 2112 The next day Joseph prayed Pharaoh that he might have Asenath to wife, and Pharaoh gave him the woman.1 And Joseph got up early in the morning, and he sent away to Pharaoh and told him about Aseneth.

2 And Pharaoh sent and called Pentephres and Aseneth.

3 And Pharaoh was astonished at her beauty and said, "The Lord will bless you, even the God of Joseph, who has chosen you to be his bride, for he is the first-born son of God, and you will be called daughter of the Most High, and Joseph shall be your bridegroom for ever.13 He set also garlands of gold upon their heads, the fairest that cunning smiths could fashion, and caused them to embrace in the site of men.

14 So for seven days was kept high feast and festival, nor might any man labour for those days.

15 He also gave them new names, calling Joseph, the Son of God, and Asenath, Daughter of the Most High King.4 And Pharaoh took golden crowns and put them on their heads and said,

5 "God Most High will bless you and prosper your family for ever."

6 And Pharaoh turned them towards each other, and they kissed each other. And Pharaoh celebrated their wedding with a banquet and much merry-making for seven days; and he invited all the chief men in the land of Egypt.

7 And he issued a proclamation, saying, "Any man who does any work during the seven days of Joseph and Aseneth's wedding shall die."16 Before the time of the seven lean years Asenath bore two sons.

17 And Joseph called the name of the first-born Manasseh, which is to say Forgetfulness; "For," said he, "God hath made me to forget all my toil, and all my father's house."

18 And the name of the second was called Ephraim, which is to say Frit-

fulness; "For," said hi, "God hath caused me to be fruitful in the land of my affliction."8 And when the wedding was over and the banquet ended, Joseph had intercourse with Aseneth; and Aseneth conceived by Joseph and bore Manasseh and his brother Ephraim in Joseph's house.Chapter 22

1 And after this the seven years of plenty came to an end, and the seven years of famine began.

2 And when Jacob heard about his son Joseph, he came into Egypt with his family, in the second month, on the twenty-first day of the month; and he settled in the land of Goshen.

3 And Aseneth said to Joseph, "I will go and see your father, because your father Israel is my father; and Joseph said to her, "Let us go together."

4 And Joseph and Aseneth came into the land of Goshen, and Joseph's brothers met them and made obeisance to them upon the ground.

5 And they came to Jacob and he blessed them and kissed them; and Aseneth hung upon his father Jacob's neck and kissed him.

6 And after this they ate and drank

7 And Joseph and Aseneth went to their house, and Simeon and Levi escorted them, to protect them: Levi was on Aseneth's right hand and Simeon on the left.

8 And Aseneth took Levi's hand because she loved him as a man who was a prophet and a worshiper of God and a man who feared the Lord.

9 And he used to see letters written in the heavens, and he would read them and interpret them to Aseneth privately; and Levi saw the place of her rest in the highest heaven.

Chapter 23

1 And as Joseph and Aseneth were passing by, Pharaoh's eldest son saw them from the wall.

2 And when he saw Aseneth he was driven to distraction by her because she was so beautiful; and Pharaoh's son sent messengers and summoned Simeon and Levi to him, and they came to him and stood before him.

3 And Pharaoh's son said to them, "I have heard that you are better soldiers than any others there are on earth, and that with your own right hands you destroyed the city of Schechem and with your own two swords you cut to pieces thirty thousand fighting men.

4 I need your hclp: let us get together without delay; and I will give you gold and silver in abundance, and menservants and maidservants, and houses and great estates. Make a compact with me, and shew kindness to me; for I was greatly wronged by your brother Joseph, because he married Aseneth although she was originally pledged to me.

5 And now come with me, and I will take up arms against Joseph and kill him with my sword, and I will marry Aseneth; and you shall be my brothers and my friends for ever,

6 But if you will not listen to me, I will kill you with my sword" (and as he said this he bared his sword and showed it them).

7 Now Simeon was a brave but impetuous man, and he drew his sword from its scabbard and made a rush at Pharaoh's son, as if to strike him.

8 And Levi was aware of what Simeon was about to do, for Levi was a prophet and foresaw everything that was to happen; and Levi trod hard on Simon's right foot as a sign to him to curb his wrath.

9 And Levi said to him, "Why so angry with him? For we are the children of a man who worships God, and it is not right for a man who worships God to repay his neighbor evil for evil."

10 And Levi said to his neighbor, Pharaoh's son, respectfully and in good humor, "My lord, why do you speak to us like this? For we are men who worship God, and our father is the servant of God Most High, and our brother Joseph is loved by God: how could we do anything so wicked in God's eyes?

11 And now, listen to us, and be careful you never repeat what you have just said about our brother Joseph.

12 If, however, you persist in this wicked plan, see, our swords are drawn against you."

13 And they drew their swords from their scabbards and said, "Do you see these swords? It was with them that the Lord God avenged the outrage on the sons of Israel, which the men of Schechem committed in the affair of our sister Dinah, whom Schechem, Hamor's son, defiled."

14 And Pharaoh's son saw their drawn swords, and he was afraid and trembled and fell on his face to the ground at their feet.

15 And Levi stretched his hand out and lifted him up, saying, "Do not be afraid: only be careful you say nothing against our brother."

16 And they went out from him, leaving him trembling and afraid.

Chapter 24

1 And Pharaoh's son was in much affliction and torment because of Aseneth, and he was greatly distressed

2 And his servants whispered in his ear, "Lo, the sons of Bilhah and Zilpah, the maidservants of Leah and Rachel, Jacob's wives, hate Joseph and Aseneth and are jealous of them, and they will do what you want."

3 And Pharaoh's son sent messengers and summoned them, and they

came to him by night; and Pharaoh's son said to them, "I have heard that your are good soldiers."

4 And Gad and Dan, the elder brothers, said to Pharaoh's son, "Let our lord tell his servants what it is he wants, and he will do it."

5 And Pharaoh's son was overjoyed, and he said to his servants, "Go away and leave us alone, for I have something to say to these men privately."

6 And all the servants went out; and Pharaoh's son told them lies, saying, "I offer you a choice between prosperity and death: so choose prosperity and not death.

7 I know that you are good soldiers, and that you will not die as women die; but act like men and take vengeance on your enemies.

8 I heard" (he continued "your brother Joseph say to my father Pharaoh, 'Dan and Gad are the children of maidservants and are not my brothers.

9 And I am only waiting for my father to die to take action against them and all their progeny, so that they will not share the inheritance with us, for they are the children of maidservants, and it was they who sold me to the Ishmaelites.

10 When my father is dead I will repay them for the wrong they did me.'

11 And my father Pharaoh commended Joseph and said to him, 'What you have said is quite right, my son; and now take some of my soldiers and proceed against them as they did against you, and I will help you.'"

12 And when the men heard what Pharaoh's son told them they were much troubled and distressed, and they said to him, "We appeal to you, our lord, to help us; and whatever you tell your servants to do, we will do it."

13 And Pharaoh's son said to them, "To-night I will kill my father, for my father Pharaoh is like a father to Joseph; and do you also kill Joseph, and I will marry Aseneth."

14 And Dan and Gad said to him, "We will do everything you have told us to. We overheard Joseph say to Aseneth, 'Go to-morrow to our country estate, for it is vintage-time; and he has arranged for six hundred armed soldiers to go with her and fifty outrunners."

15 And when Pharaoh's son heard this, he gave the four men five hundred men each and appointed them their officers and commanders.

16 And Dan and Gad said to him, "We will go by night and lie in wait at the brook and hide in the woods on the banks.

17 And as for you, takc fifty men with you, archers on horseback, and go on ahead, some distance in front; and Aseneth will come and fall into our hands,and we will cut down the men who are with her.

18 And Aseneth will flee in her chariot and fall into your hands and you will be able to deal with her as you wish.

19 And afterwards we will kill Joseph while he is fretting about Aseneth; and we will kill his children before his eyes."

20 And Pharaoh's son was delighted when he heard this, and he sent two thousand soldiers after them

21 And they came to the brook and hid in the woods on the banks, and five hundred men took up their position in front; and in between them was a highway.

Chapter 25

1 And Pharaoh's son went to his father's room to kill him; but his father's guards would not allow him to go in to him.

2 And Pharaoh's son said to them, "I want to see my father because I am going off to gather the grapes from my newly planted vine

3 And the guards said to him, "Your father is in pain, and he has been awake all night; but he is resting now; and he said to us, "Do not let anyone in to me, not even my eldest son."

4 And he went away in anger; and he took fifty mounted archers, and he went in front of them as Dan and Gad had told him to.

5 And Naphtali and Asher said to Dan and Gad, "Why must you plot again against our father Israel and against our brother Joseph? For God looks after him as if he were the apple of his eye.

6 Did you not once sell Joseph as a slave, and to-day he is king of the whole earth, and its saviour, and gives us corn?

7 And now, if you make plots against him again, he will call upon the God of Israel, and he will send fire from heaven, and it will burn you up, and the angels of God will fight against you."

8 And their elder brothers Dan and Gad were angry with them, saying, "Are we then to die like women? God forbid!" And they went out to encounter Joseph and Aseneth.

Chapter 26

1 And Aseneth got up early in the morning and said to Joseph, "I am going to our estate in the country; but I am frightened because you are not coming with me."

2 And Joseph said to her, "Take heart and do not be afraid, but go; for the Lord is with you and he will keep you from all evil as the apple of an eye.

3 And I will go and distribute my corn, and give corn to all the men in the city, so that no one dies of famine in the land of Egypt."

4 And Aseneth departed on her journey and Joseph to the distribution of

the corn.

5 And Aseneth came to where the brook was with her six hundred men; and suddenly the men that were with Pharaoh's son leaped out from their ambush and joined battle with Aseneth's soldiers, and they cut them down with their swords and killed all Aseneth's outrunners.

6 And Aseneth fled in her chariot

7 And Levi, the son of Leah, was informed about all this (for he was a prophet), and he told his brothers about Aseneth's danger; and they took, each one of them, his sword on his thigh, and their shields on their arms, and their spears in their right hands, and they went after Aseneth with what speed they could.

8 And Aseneth fled, and lo, Pharaoh's son met her, and fifty men with him; and Aseneth saw him, and she was afraid and trembled.

Chapter 27

1 And Benjamin was sitting with her in the chariot.

2 And Benjamin was a sturdy lad, about eighteen years old, indescribably handsome, and as strong as a young lion; and he feared God.

3 And Benjamin jumped down from the chariot, and he took a round stone from the brook and hurled it with all his might at Pharaoh's son and hit him on his left temple and wounded him severely, and he fell from his horse half-dead.

4 And Benjamin clambered up on a rock and said to the driver of Aseneth's chariot, "Give me fifty stones from the brook;" and he gave him fifty stones.

5 And Benjamin hurled the stones and killed the fifty men that were with Pharaoh's son; and the stones sank into the temples of each one of them.

6 Then the sons of Leah, Reuben and Simeon, Levi and Judah, Issachar and Zebulon, went after the men who had lain in ambush; and they fell upon them suddenly, and cut down the two thousand men, and the six of them killed them.

7 And their brothers, the sons of Bilhah and Zilpah, fled; and they said, "We have been ruined through our brothers; and Pharaoh's son is dead, killed by Benjamin, and all those with him have perished at his hand: come now, let us kill Aseneth [and Benjamin], and let us make for the woods."

8 And they came, with their swords drawn, covered in blood; and Aseneth saw them, and she said, "O Lord my God, that didst quicken me from death, that didst say to me, 'Thy soul shall live for ever, deliver me from these men.'"

9 And the Lord God heard her voice, and immediately their swords fell from t heir hands to the ground and were reduced to dust.

Chapter 28

1 And the sons of Bilhah and Zilpah saw the miracle that had happened and they were afraid and said, "The Lord is fighting for Aseneth against us."

2 And they fell on their faces to the ground and made obeisance to Aseneth, saying, "Have mercy on us, your servants, for you are our mistress and queen, and we have done you a great wrong and our brother Joseph.

3 And now God has brought retribution on us: we pray you, therefore, have mercy on us, and deliver us from our brothers' hands, for they will avenge the outrage done to you and their swords will be against us."

4 And Aseneth said to them, "Take heart and do not be afraid, for your brothers are men who worship God, and do not repay evil for evil to any man.

5 But retire to the woods until I can secure your pardon and mollify their wrath; for what you have been trying to do to them is indeed no trifling matter.

6 Take heart, though, and do not be afraid, for the Lord will see justice done between us."

7 And Dan and Gad fled to the woods

8 And behold, the sons of Leah came, running like deers in pursuit of them; and Aseneth got down from her chariot, and she greeted them with tears.

9 And they made obeisance to her on the ground and wept aloud; and they asked about their brothers, the maidservants' sons, intending to kill them.

10 And Aseneth said to them, "Spare you brothers and do them no harm, for the Lord has shielded me and reduced the swords in their hands to dust, and they melted away like wax before the fire.

11 Surely this is enough for us that the Lord is fighting for us: so spare your brothers."

12 And Simeon said to Aseneth, "Why should our mistress plead for her enemies?

13 No! We will cut them down with our swords, because they have plotted evil against our father Israel and against our brother Joseph now on two occasions, and they have plotted against you to-day."

14 And Aseneth said to him , "No brother, you must not repay evil for evil to your neighbor, for the Lord will avenge this outrage."

15 And after this Simeon bowed to Aseneth; and Levi came to her, and he

kissed her right hand and blessed her.

16 Thus Aseneth saved the men from their brothers' wrath, so that they did not kill them.

Chapter 29

1 And Pharaoh's son lifted himself up from the ground and sat up; and he spat blood from his mouth, because his blood was running from his temple into his mouth.

2 And Benjamin advanced upon him and took hold of his sword and drew it from its scabbard (for Benjamin had no sword of his own with him).

3 And as he was about to strike Pharaoh's son, Levi rushed up and seized him by the hand and said, "No brother, you must not do this, for we are men who worship God, and it is not right for a man who worships God to repay evil for evil, or to trample upon a man who has already fallen, or to harry his enemy to death.

4 But come: let us bind up his wound; and if he lives, he will be our friend, and his father Pharaoh will be our father."

5 And Levi raised Pharaoh's son up and washed the blood off his face and bound a bandage round his wound; and he set him on his horse and took him to his father.

6 And Levi told him everything that had happened.

7 And Pharaoh got up from his throne and made obeisance to Levi upon the ground.

8 And on the third day Pharaoh's son died from the wound of Benjamin's stone.

9 And Pharaoh mourned for his eldest son, and he was worn out with grief.

10 And Pharaoh died at the age of one hundred and nine; and he left his crown to Joseph.

11 And Joseph was king of Egypt for forty-eight years.

12 And after this Joseph gave the crown to Pharaoh's grandson; and Joseph was like a father to him in Egypt.

Book 132. The Story of Zosimus (Summary)

The **Story of Zosimus** is a profound Christian apocryphal narrative centered on the journey of a devout monk, Zosimus, who embarks on a mystical expedition into the desert. It is within this isolation that he seeks to uncover divine wisdom, and in doing so, comes face to face with his faith, his limitations, and the power of spiritual devotion. The story explores timeless themes of asceticism, divine revelation, and spiritual enlightenment through the perspective of a man committed to understanding the true nature of God.

In the early centuries of Christianity, many followers were inspired by the examples of hermits and monks who chose to retreat from the distractions of the world to focus on communion with God. This idea forms the foundation of **The Story of Zosimus**, which combines elements of Christian mysticism with the deeply rooted tradition of desert monasticism.

The Beginning of the Journey: Seeking Divine Truth

Zosimus, a dedicated monk living a life of religious devotion, becomes aware that despite his pious lifestyle, there is a higher spiritual truth he has yet to attain. Yearning for deeper divine wisdom, he resolves to leave the comfort of his monastic community and journey into the wilderness, convinced that the solitude of the desert will bring him closer to God.

His decision to isolate himself is a symbolic one. The desert, in Christian tradition, often represents both physical and spiritual trial—a place where one is stripped of all comforts and distractions, forced to confront the self and seek divine revelation. This echoes the experiences of early Christian figures like **Saint Anthony the Great**, who similarly retreated into the desert to confront temptations and seek union with God. Zosimus' journey is not merely geographical but deeply symbolic, marking his transition from the external world to the internal one, where the true struggle for enlightenment takes place.

The Desert as a Spiritual Battleground

Upon entering the desert, Zosimus experiences the harsh realities of isolation. Deprived of food, water, and human companionship, the monk is pushed to his physical and emotional limits. His suffering, however, is purposeful. It is through enduring these trials that Zosimus begins to understand the fleeting nature of worldly concerns and the necessity of absolute trust in God's providence.

The desert, in this context, serves as a metaphor for the spiritual battleground where one confronts the forces of temptation and doubt. For Zosimus, it becomes clear that the first step toward divine wisdom is complete renunciation—not only of material wealth but also of the ego and the desires that tether one to earthly existence. His journey, therefore, is not just a physical endurance test but a stripping away of the layers of worldly attachment, a critical step in attaining spiritual purity.

The Encounter with the Holy Community

As Zosimus delves deeper into the desert, his physical and spiritual perseverance is rewarded when he encounters an unexpected sight: a hidden community of holy hermits who have chosen to live in complete seclusion from the rest of the world. These individuals are no ordinary ascetics. They are portrayed as living embodiments of Christian virtues, having achieved a state of divine grace through extreme piety and unwavering faith.

The hermits are depicted as otherworldly in their demeanor, living a life of extraordinary simplicity and devotion, unaffected by the concerns of the outside world. Their community represents the ultimate spiritual ideal—one in which worldly attachments are completely cast aside in favor of absolute reliance on God's grace. In contrast to the bustling, often chaotic world that Zosimus has left behind, these hermits live in perfect harmony with their faith, unburdened by material needs and fully immersed in divine contemplation.

Their way of life provides Zosimus with a living example of the spiritual purity he seeks. The hermits are not concerned with earthly matters like food, shelter, or possessions. Instead, they live in a constant state of prayer and spiritual reflection, their entire existence centered around communion with God. This encounter serves as a turning point in Zosimus' journey, offering him a glimpse of what true spiritual fulfillment looks like.

Lessons from the Holy Hermits: The Path to Holiness
During his time with the holy hermits, Zosimus engages in deep conversations with them, seeking their wisdom and learning from their practices. These dialogues are rich with spiritual insights and theological reflections, offering Zosimus (and, by extension, the reader) profound lessons on the nature of faith and the path to holiness.

One of the key teachings imparted to Zosimus is the idea that true holiness is achieved not through grand gestures or public displays of piety, but through the quiet, consistent practice of humility, prayer, and self-denial. The hermits teach Zosimus that spiritual growth is not something that can be rushed or forced. It is a gradual process, one that requires patience, perseverance, and, most importantly, surrender to God's will.

They emphasize the importance of humility, warning against the dangers of spiritual pride. Zosimus, despite his many years of monastic life, learns that his journey toward holiness is far from complete. The hermits remind him that even the most devout can fall into the trap of thinking they have already achieved spiritual perfection. Instead, they encourage Zosimus to remain vigilant, constantly seeking to purify his heart and align his will with God's.

The Role of Suffering and Renunciation
Another central theme of the story is the role of suffering in the path to spiritual enlightenment. The hermits, much like Zosimus, have endured great physical and emotional hardships in their pursuit of divine wisdom. Yet, they view this suffering not as a burden but as a necessary part of their spiritual journey. In their eyes, suffering serves to purify the soul, stripping away the ego and bringing one closer to God.

Zosimus learns that true renunciation involves not only giving up material possessions but also letting go of one's personal desires, ambitions, and even the need for recognition or validation. The hermits teach him that the highest form of spiritual maturity is to surrender completely to God's will, trusting that whatever hardships one endures are part of the divine plan for their growth and purification.

The Revelation of Divine Wisdom
Through his time with the holy hermits, Zosimus comes to understand that the divine wisdom he seeks is not something that can be obtained through intellectual study or theological debate. Instead, it is a gift that is bestowed upon those who are willing to humble themselves, endure suffering, and fully submit to God's will.

This revelation is the culmination of Zosimus' journey. He realizes that the wisdom he has sought for so long was never something external; it was always within him, waiting to be uncovered through the process of self-denial and spiritual purification. The story thus highlights the paradox of spiritual growth: in order to gain everything (divine wisdom, spiritual fulfillment), one must be willing to lose everything (worldly attachments, personal desires).

Return to the World: The Final Lesson
Having gained profound spiritual insights from his time in the desert, Zosimus eventually returns to the world, but he is forever changed by his experiences. He no longer sees the world through the same lens as before. His priorities have shifted, and he now understands that the true path to holiness lies not in grand displays of piety or asceticism but in the quiet, humble practice of faith and devotion.

The story ends with Zosimus living out the remainder of his days in a state of quiet reflection, passing on the wisdom he has gained to others who seek spiritual enlightenment. His journey serves as an enduring reminder of the transformative power of faith and the importance of humility, perseverance, and surrender in the pursuit of divine wisdom.

Conclusion: A Journey Toward Spiritual Fulfillment
The **Story of Zosimus** is a timeless reflection on the nature of spiritual growth and the challenges that come with it. It illustrates the profound transformation that occurs when one is willing to let go of worldly attachments and fully embrace the path of faith. Zosimus' journey is a reminder that the pursuit of divine wisdom is not an easy one. It requires sacrifice, humility, and a deep commitment to seeking God's will.

However, the rewards of this journey are immeasurable. Through his encounters with the holy hermits, Zosimus gains a deeper understanding of the nature of faith and the path to spiritual fulfillment. His story serves as an inspiration to all who seek to deepen their relationship with God and live a life of true devotion.

Book 133. The Acts of Barnabas

The Journeyings and Martyrdom of St. Barnabas the Apostle.
Since from the descent of the presence of our Saviour Jesus Christ, the unwearied and benevolent and mighty Shepherd and Teacher and Physician, I beheld and saw the ineffable and holy and unspotted mystery of the Christians, who hold the hope in holiness, and who have been sealed; and since I have zealously served Him, I have deemed it necessary to give account of the mysteries which I have heard and seen.

I John, accompanying the holy apostles Barnabas and Paul, being formerly a servant of Cyrillus the high priest of Jupiter, but now having received the gift of the Holy Spirit through Paul and Barnabas and Silas, *who were* worthy of the calling, and who baptized me in Iconium. After I was baptized, then, I saw a certain man standing clothed in white raiment; and he said to me: Be of good courage, John, for assuredly your name shall be changed to Mark, and your glory shall be proclaimed in all the world. And the darkness in you has passed away from you, and there has been given to you understanding to know the mysteries of God.

And when I saw the vision, becoming greatly terrified, I went to the feet of Barnabas, and related to him the mysteries which I had seen and heard from that man. And the Apostle Paul was not by when I disclosed the mysteries. And Barnabas said to me: Tell no one the miracle which you have seen. For by me also this night the Lord stood, saying, Be of good courage: for as you have given your life for my name to death and banishment from your nation, thus also shall you be made perfect. Moreover, as for the servant who is with you, take him also with yourself; for he has certain mysteries. Now then, my child, keep to yourself the things which you have seen and heard; for a time will come for you to reveal them.

And I, having been instructed in these things by him, remained in Iconium many days; for there was there a holy man and a pious, who also entertained us, whose house also Paul had sanctified. Thence, therefore, we came to Seleucia, and after staying three days sailed away to Cyprus; and I was ministering to them until we had gone round all Cyprus. And setting sail from Cyprus, we landed in Perga of Pamphylia. And there I then stayed about two months, wishing to sail to the regions of the West; and the Holy Spirit did not allow me. Turning, therefore, I again sought the apostles; and having learned that they were in Antioch, I went to them.

And I found Paul in bed in Antioch from the toil of the journey, who also seeing me, was exceedingly grieved on account of my delaying in Pamphylia. And Barnabas coming, encouraged him, and tasted bread, and he took a little of it. And they preached the word of the Lord, and enlightened many of the Jews and Greeks. And I only attended to them, and was afraid of Paul to come near him, both because he held me as having spent much time in Pamphylia, and because he was quite enraged against me. And I gave repentance on my knees upon the earth to Paul, and he would not endure it. And when I remained for three Sabbaths in entreaty and prayer on my knees, I was unable to prevail upon him about myself; for his great grievance against me was on account of my keeping several parchments in Pamphylia.

And when it came to pass that they finished teaching in Antioch, on the first of the week they took counsel together to set out for the places of the East, and after that to go into Cyprus, and oversee all the churches in which they had spoken the word of God. And Barnabas entreated Paul to go first to Cyprus, and oversee his own in his village; and Lucius entreated him to take the oversight of his city Cyrene. And a vision was seen by Paul in sleep, that he should hasten to Jerusalem, because the brethren expected him there. But Barnabas urged that they should go to Cyprus, and pass the winter, and then that they should go to Jerusalem at the feast. Great contention, therefore, arose between them. Acts 15:39 And Barnabas urged me also to accompany them, on account of my being their servant from the beginning, and on account of my having served them in all Cyprus until they came to Perga of Pamphylia; and I there had remained many days. But Paul cried out against Barnabas, saying: It is impossible for him to go with us. And those who were with us there urged me also to accompany them, because there was a vow upon me to follow them to the end. So that Paul said to Barnabas: If you will take John who also is surnamed Mark with you, go another road; for he shall not come with us. And Barnabas coming to himself, said: The grace of God does not desert him who has once served the Gospel and journeyed with us. If, therefore, this be agreeable to you, Father Paul, I take him and go. And he said: You go in the grace of Christ, and we in the power of the Spirit.

Therefore, bending their knees, they prayed to God. And Paul, groaning aloud, wept, and in like manner also Barnabas, saying to one another: It would have been good for us, as at first, so also at last, to work in common among men; but since it has thus seemed good to you, Father Paul, pray for me that my labour may be made perfect to commendation: for you know how I have served you also to the grace of Christ that has been given to you. For I go to Cyprus, and hasten to be made perfect; for I know that I shall no more see your face, O Father Paul. And falling on the ground at his feet, he wept long. And Paul said to him: The Lord stood by me also this night, saying, Do not force Barnabas not to go to Cyprus, for there it has been prepared for him to enlighten many; and go also, in the grace that has been given to you, to Jerusalem to worship in the holy place, and there it shall be shown you where your martyrdom has been prepared. And we saluted one another, and Barnabas took me to himself.

And having come down to Laodiceia, we sought to cross to Cyprus; and having found a ship going to Cyprus, we embarked. And when we had set sail, the wind was found to be contrary. And we came to Corasium; and having gone down to the shore where there was a fountain, we rested there, showing ourselves to no one, that no one might know that Barnabas had separated from Paul. And having set sail from Corasium, we came to the regions of Isauria, and thence came to a certain island called Pityusa; and a storm having come on, we remained there three days; and a certain pious man entertained us, by name Euphemus, whom also Barnabas instructed in many things in the faith, with all his house.

And thence we sailed past the Aconesiæ, and came to the city of Anemurium; and having gone into it, we found two Greeks. And coming to us, they asked whence and who we were. And Barnabas said to them: If you wish to know whence and who we are, throw away the clothing which you have, and I shall put on you clothing which never becomes soiled; for neither is there in it anything filthy, but it is altogether splendid. And being astonished at the saying, they asked us: What is that garment which you are going to give us? And Barnabas said to them: If you shall confess your sins, and submit yourselves to our Lord Jesus Christ, you shall receive that garment which is incorruptible forever. And being pricked at heart by the Holy Spirit, they fell at his feet, entreating and saying: We beseech you, father, give us that garment; for we believe in the living and true God whom you proclaim. And leading them down to the fountain, he baptized them into the name of Father, and Son, and Holy Ghost. And they knew that they were clothed with power, and a holy robe. And having taken from me one robe, he put it on the one; and his own robe he put on the other. And they brought money to him, and straightway Barnabas distributed it to the poor. And from them also the sailors were able to gain many things.

And they having come down to the shore, he spoke to them the word of God; and he having blessed them, we saluted them, and went on board the ship. And the one of them who was named Stephanus wished to accompany us, and Barnabas did not permit him. And we, having gone across, sailed down to Cyprus by night; and having come to the place called Crommyacita, we found Timon and Ariston the temple servants, at whose house also we were entertained.

And Timon was afflicted by much fever. And having laid our hands upon him, we straightway removed his fever, having called upon the name of the Lord Jesus. And Barnabas had received documents from Matthew, a book of the word of God, and a narrative of miracles and doctrines. This Barnabas laid upon the sick in each place that we came to, and it immediately made a cure of their sufferings.

And when we had come to Lapithus, and an idol festival being celebrated in the theatre, they did not allow us to go into the city, but we rested a little at the gate. And Timon, after he rose up from his disease, came with us. And having gone forth from Lapithus, we travelled through the mountains, and came to the city of Lampadistus, of which also Timon was a native; in addition to whom, having found also that Heracleius was there, we were entertained by him. He was of the city of Tamasus, and had come to visit his relations; and Barnabas, looking steadfastly at him, recognised him, having met with him formerly at Citium with Paul; to whom also the Holy Spirit was given at baptism, and he changed his name to Heracleides. And having ordained him bishop over Cyprus, and having confirmed the church in Tamasus, we left him in the house of his brethren that dwelt there.

And having crossed the mountain called Chionodes, we came to Old Paphos, and there found Rhodon, a temple servant, who also, having himself believed, accompanied us. And we met a certain Jew, by name Barjesus, coming from Paphos, who also recognised Barnabas, as having been formerly with Paul. He did not wish us to go into Paphos; but having turned away, we came to Curium.

And we found that a certain abominable race was being performed in the road near the city, where a multitude of women and men naked were performing the race. And there was great deception and error in that place. And Barnabas turning, rebuked it; and the western part fell, so that many were wounded, and many of them also died and the rest fled to the temple of Apollo, which was close at hand in the *city*, which was called sacred. And when we came near the temple, a great multitude of Jews who were there, having been put up to it by Barjesus, stood outside of the city, and did not allow us to go into the city; but we spent the evening under a tree near the city, and rested there.

And on the following day, we came to a certain village where Aristoclianus dwelt. He being a leper, had been cleansed in Antioch, whom also Paul and Barnabas sealed to be a bishop, and sent to his village in Cyprus, because there were many Greeks there. And we were entertained in the cave by him in the mountain, and there we remained one day. And thence we came to Amathus and there was a great multitude of Greeks in the temple in the mountain, low women and men pouring libations. There also Barjesus, getting the start of us, gained over the nation of the Jews, and did not allow us to enter into the city; but a certain widow woman, eighty years old, being outside of the city, and she also not worshipping the idols, coming forward to us, took us into her house one hour. And when we came out we shook the dust off our feet over against that temple where the libation of the abominable took place.

And having gone out thence, we came through desert places, and Timon also accompanied us. And having come to Citium, and there being a great uproar there also in their hippodrome, having learned this, we came forth out of the city, having all shaken the dust off our feet; for no one received us, except that we rested one hour in the gate near the aqueduct.

And having set sail in a ship from Citium, we came to Salamis, and landed in the so-called islands, where there was a place full of idols; and there there took place high festivals and libations. And having found Heracleides there again, we instructed him to proclaim the Gospel of God, and to set up churches, and ministers in them. And having gone into Salamis, we came to the synagogue near the place called Biblia; and when we had gone into it, Barnabas, having unrolled the Gospel which he had received from Matthew his fellow-labourer, began to teach the Jews.

And Barjesus, having arrived after two days, after not a few Jews had been instructed, was enraged, and brought together all the multitude of the Jews; and they having laid hold of Barnabas, wished to hand him over to Hypatius, the governor of Salamis. And having bound him to take him away to the governor, and a pious Jebusite, a kinsman of Nero, having come to Cyprus, the Jews, learning this, took Barnabas by night, and bound him with a rope by the neck; and having dragged him to the hippodrome from the synagogue, and having gone out of the city, standing round him, they burned him with fire, so that even his bones became dust. And straightway that night, having taken his dust, they cast it into a cloth; and having secured it with lead, they intended to throw it into the sea. But I, finding an opportunity in the night, and being able along with Timon and Rhodon to carry it. we came to a certain place, and having found a cave, put it down there, where the nation of the Jebusites formerly dwelt. And having found a secret place in it, we put it away, with the documents which he had received from Matthew. And it was the fourth hour of the night of the second of the week.

And when we were hid in the place, the Jews made no little search after us; and having almost found us, they pursued us as far as the village of the Ledrians; and we, having found there also a cave near the village, took refuge in it, and thus escaped them. And we were hid in the cave three days; and the Jews having gone away, we came forth and left the place by night. And taking with us Ariston and Rhodon, we came to the village of Limnes.

And having come to the shore, we found an Egyptian ship; and having embarked in it, we landed at Alexandria. And there I remained, teaching the brethren that came the word of the Lord, enlightening them, and preaching what I had been taught by the apostles of Christ, who also baptized me into the name of Father, and Son, and Holy Ghost; who also changed my name to Mark in the water of baptism, by which also I hope to bring many to the glory of God through His grace; because to Him is due honour and everlasting glory. Amen.

The journeyings and martyrdom of the holy apostle Barnabas have been fulfilled through God.

Book 134. The Acts of Peter and Andrew

From a Bodleian manuscript.

It came to pass when Andrew the apostle of Christ went forth from the city of the man-eaters, behold a luminous cloud snatched him up, and carried him away to the mountain where Peter and Matthew and Alexander were sitting. And when he saw them, they saluted him with great joy. Then Peter says to him: What has happened to you, brother Andrew? Have you sown the word of truth in the country of the man-eaters or not? Andrew says to him: Yes, father Peter, through your prayers; but the men of that city have done me many mischiefs, for they dragged me through their street three days, so that my blood stained the whole street. Peter says to him: Be a man in the Lord, brother Andrew, and come hither, and rest from your labour. For if the good husbandman laboriously till the ground, it will also bear fruit, and straightway all his toil will be turned into joy; but if he toil, and his land bring forth no fruit, he has double toil. And while he was thus speaking, the Lord Jesus Christ appeared to them in the form of a child, and said to them: Hail, Peter, bishop of the whole of my Church! Hail, Andrew! My co-heirs, be courageous, and struggle for mankind; for verily I say unto you, you shall endure toils in this world for mankind. *But be bold; I will give you rest* in one hour of repose in the kingdom of my Father. Arise, then, and go into the city of the barbarians, and preach in it; and I will be with you in the wonders that shall happen in it by your hands. And the Lord Jesus, after saluting them, went up into the heavens in glory.

And Peter, and Andrew, and Alexander, and Rufus, and Matthias, went into the city of the barbarians. And after they had come near the city, Andrew answered and said to Peter: Father Peter, have we again to undergo toils in this city, as in the country of the man-eaters? Peter says to him: I do not know. But, behold, there is an old man before us sowing in his field: if we go up to him, let us say to him, Give us bread; and if he give us bread, we may know that we are not to suffer in this city; but if he say to us, We have no bread, on the other hand, we shall know that suffering again awaits us. And when they came up to the old man, Peter says to him: Hail, farmer! And the farmer says to them: Hail you too, merchants! Peter says to him: Have you bread to give to these children, for we have been in want? The old man says to them: Wait a little, and look after the oxen, and the plough, and the land, that I may go into the city, and get you loaves. Peter says to him: If you provide hospitality for us, we shall look after the cattle and the field. The old man says: So be it. Peter says to him: Are the oxen your own? The old man says: No; I have them on hire. Peter says to him: Go into the city. And the old man went into the city. And Peter arose, and girded up his cloak and his under-garment, and says to Andrew: It is not right for us to rest and be idle; above all, when the old man is working for us, having left his own work. Then Peter took hold of the plough, and sowed the wheat. And Andrew was behind the oxen, and says to Peter: Father Peter, why do you bring toil upon us, especially when we have work enough already! Then Andrew took the plough out of Peter's hand, and sowed the wheat, saying: O seed cast into the ground in the field of the righteous, come up, and come to the light. Let the young men of the city therefore come forth, whom I found in the pit of destruction until today; for, behold, the apostles of Christ are coming into the city, pardoning the sins of those who believe in them, and healing every disease, and every sickness. Pray ye for me, that He may have mercy upon me, and that I may be delivered from this strait.

And many of the multitude believed in Christ, because of the saying of the woman; and they fell at the feet of the apostles, and adored them. And they laid their hands upon them. And they healed those in the city that were sick, and gave sight to the blind and, hearing to the deaf, and drove out the demons. All the multitude glorified the Father, and the Son, and the Holy Spirit.

And there was a certain rich man in the city, by name Onesiphorus. He, having seen the miracles done by the apostles, says to them: If I believe in your God, can I also do a miracle like you? Andrew says to him: If you will forsake all that belongs to you, and your wife and your children, as we also have done, then you also shall do miracles. When Onesiphorus heard this, he was filled with rage, and took his scarf and threw it over Andrew's neck, and struck him, and said to him: You are a sorcerer. How do you force me to abandon my wife, and my children, and my goods? Then Peter, having turned and seen him striking Andrew, says to him: Man, stop now striking Andrew. Onesiphorus says to him: I see that you are more sensible than he. Do thou then tell me to leave my wife, and my children, and my goods. What do you say? Peter says to him: One thing I say unto you: it is easier for a camel to go through the eye of a needle, than for a rich man to go into the kingdom of heaven. When Onesiphorus heard this, he was even more filled with rage and anger, and took his scarf off the neck of Andrew, and threw it upon the neck of Peter; and so he dragged him along, saying: Verily you are a great sorcerer, more than the other; for a camel cannot go through the eye of a needle. But if you will show me this miracle, I will believe in your God; and not only I, but also the whole city. But if not, you shall be grievously punished in the midst of the city. And when Peter heard this, he was exceedingly grieved, and stood and stretched forth his hands towards heaven, and prayed, saying: O Lord our God, listen to me at this time; for they will ensnare us from Your own words: for no prophet has spoken to set forth this his explanation, and no patriarch that we might learn the interpretation of it; and now we seek for ourselves the explanation with boldness. Do not then, Lord, overlook us: for you are He who is praised by the cherubim.

And after he had said this, the Saviour appeared in the form of a child of twelve years old, wearing a linen garment; and He says to them: Be courageous, and tremble not, my chosen disciples; for I am with you always. Let the needle and the camel be brought. And after saying this, He went up into the heavens. And there was a certain merchant in the city who had believed in the Lord through the Apostle Philip; and when he heard of this, he ran and searched for a needle with a big eye, to do a favour to the apostles. When Peter learned this, he said: My son, do not search for a big needle; for nothing is impossible with God: rather bring us a small needle. And after the needle had been brought, and all the multitude of the city were standing by to see, Peter looked up and saw a camel coming. And he ordered her to be brought. Then he fixed the needle in the ground, and cried out with a loud voice, saying: In the name of Jesus Christ, who was crucified under Pontius Pilate, I order you, O camel, to go through the eye of the needle. Then the eye of the needle was opened like a gate, and the camel went through it, and all the multitude saw it. Again Peter says to the camel: Go again through the needle. And the

camel went a second time. When Onesiphorus saw this, he said to Peter; Truly you are a great sorcerer; but I do not believe unless I send and bring a camel and a needle. And he called one of his servants, and said to him privately: Go and bring me here a camel and a needle; find also a polluted woman, and force her to come here: for these men are sorcerers. And Peter having learned the mystery through the Spirit, says to Onesiphorus: Send and bring the camel, and the woman, and the needle. And when they brought them, Peter took the needle, and fixed it in the ground. And the woman was sitting on the camel. Then Peter says: In the name of our Lord Jesus Christ the crucified, I order you, O camel, to go through this needle. And immediately the eye of the needle was opened, and became like a gate, and the camel went through it. Peter again says to the camel: Go through it again, that all may see the glory of our Lord Jesus Christ, in order that some may believe in Him. Then the camel again went through the needle. And Onesiphorus seeing it, cried out, and said: Truly great is the God of Peter and Andrew, and I from this time forth believe in the name of our Lord Jesus Christ. Now then, hear my words, O Peter. I have grain lands, vineyards, and fields; I have also twenty-seven pounds of gold, and fifty pounds of silver; and I have very many slaves. I give my possessions to the poor, that I also may do one miracle like you. And Peter was grieved lest the powers should not work in him, seeing that he had not received the seal in Christ. And while he was considering this, behold, a voice out of the heaven saying to him: Do to him what he wishes, because I will accomplish for him what he desires. Peter says to him: My son, come hither; do as we do. And Onesiphorus came up, and stood before the camel and the needle, and said: In the n . . . The manuscript abruptly ends here

Book 135. The Teachings of Addai

THE letter of king Abgar,[2] the son of king Ma'nu, and at what time he sent it to our Lord at Jerusalem; and at what time Addai the Apostle came to him (Abgar) at Edessa;[3] and what he spake in the gospel of his preaching; and what he said and commanded, when he went forth from, this world, to those who had received from him the hand of the priesthood.

In the three hundred and forty and third year of the kingdom of the Greeks,[4] and in the reign of our lord Tiberius, the Roman Emperor, and in the reign of king Abgar, son of king Ma'nu, in the month of October, on the twelfth day, Abgar Ukkama sent Marihab and Shamshagram,[5] chiefs and honoured persons of his kingdom, |2 and Hannan[6] the tabularius, the sharrir, with them, to the city which is called Eleutheropolis, but in Aramaic Beth-gubrin,[7] to the honoured Sabinus, the son of Eustorgius, the deputy of our lord the emperor, who ruled over Syria, Phoenicia, Palestine, and the whole country of Mesopotamia. They brought him letters concerning the affairs of the kingdom; and when they went to him, he received them with joy and honour, and they were with him twenty and five days. He wrote for them a reply[8] to the letters, and sent them to Abgar the king. When they went forth from him, they set out and came on the way towards Jerusalem; and they saw many men, who came from a distance to see Christ, because the fame of his wonderful deeds had gone forth to remote countries. When Marihab, Shamshagram, and Hannan, the keeper of the archives, saw the men, they also came with them to Jerusalem. When they entered |3 Jerusalem, they saw Christ, and they rejoiced with the multitudes, who were joined to Him. But they saw also the Jews, who were standing in groups, and were considering what they should do to Him; for they were disturbed to see that a multitude of their people confessed Him. And they were there in Jerusalem ten days, and Hannan, the keeper of the archives, wrote down everything which he saw that Christ did; also the rest of that done by Him, before they went thither. And they departed and came to Edessa, and entered into the presence of Abgar the king, their lord, who had sent them, and they gave him the reply of the letters, which they had brought with them. After the letters were read, they began to recount before the king all which they had seen and all which Christ had done in Jerusalem. And Hannan, the keeper of the archives, read before him all which he had written and brought with him; and when Abgar the king heard, he was astonished and wondered, as also his princes, who stood before him. Abgar said to them: These mighty works are not of men, but of God; because there is not any one who can make the dead alive, but God only. And Abgar wished himself to pass over and go to Palestine, and see with his own eyes all which Christ was doing; but because he was not able to pass through the country of the Romans, which was not his, lest this cause should call forth bitter enmity, he wrote a letter and sent it to Christ by the hand of Hannan, the keeper of the archives. He went forth from Edessa on the fourteenth day of Adar,[9] and entered Jerusalem on the twelfth day of Nisan,[10] on the fourth day of the week (Wednesday). And he found Christ at the house of |4 Gamaliel, the chief priest[11] of the Jews. The letter was read before Him, which was written thus:----"Abgar Ukkama, to Jesus, the Good Physician, who has appeared in the country of Jerusalem. My Lord: Peace. I have heard of Thee and of Thy healing, that it is not by medicines and roots Thou healest, but by Thy word Thou openest *the eyes of* the blind, Thou makest the lame to walk, cleansest the lepers, and makest the deaf to hear. And unclean spirits[12] and lunatics, and those tormented, them Thou healest by Thy word; Thou also raisest the dead. And when I heard of these great wonders which Thou doest, I decided in my mind that either Thou art God, who hast come down from heaven and doest these things, or Thou art the Son of God, who doest all these things. Therefore, I have written to request of Thee to come to me who adore Thee, and to heal the disease which I have, as I believe in Thee. This also I have heard, that the Jews murmur against Thee and persecute Thee, and even seek to crucify Thee, and contemplate treating Thee cruelly. I possess one small and beautiful city, and it is sufficient for both to dwell in it in quietness."

When Jesus received the letter at the house of the chief priest of the Jews, He said to Hannan, the keeper of the archives: "Go and say to thy lord, who hath sent thee to Me, 'Blessed art thou, who, although thou hast not seen Me, believest in Me, for it is written of Me, Those who see Me will not believe in Me, and those who see Me not, will believe in me.[13] But as to that which |5 thou hast written to Me, that I should come to thee, that for which I was sent here is now finished, and I am going up to my Father, who sent me, and when I have gone up to Him, I will send to thee one of my disciples, who will cure the disease which thou hast, and restore thee to health; and all who are with thee he will convert to everlasting life. Thy city shall be blessed, and no enemy shall again become master of it for ever.'"

When Hannan, the keeper of the archives, saw that Jesus spake thus to him, by virtue of being the king's painter, he took and painted a likeness of being of Jesus with choice paints, and brought with him to Abgar the king, his master. And when Abgar the king saw the likeness, he received it with great joy, and placed it with great honour in one of his palatial houses. Hannan, the keeper of the archives, related to him everything which he had heard from Jesus, as His words were put by him in writing. After that Christ had ascended to heaven, Judas Thomas[14] sent to Abgar, Addai the Apostle, who was one of the seventy-two Apostles. And when Addai came to the city of Edessa, he dwelt at the house of |6 Tobias,[15] son of Tobias the Jew, who was of Palestine. Through all the city a report was heard of him, and one of the nobles of Abgar whose name was Abdu,[16] the son of Abdu, one of those who sat with bended knees [17] before Abgar, went and said concerning Addai: behold, a messenger has come, and dwells here, he of whom Jesus sent to thee, "I send to Thee one of my disciples." And when Abgar heard these words, and the mighty acts which Addai did, and the wonderful cures which he effected, he thought for certain in his mind: Truly this is he whom Jesus sent, saying, "When I have ascended to heaven I will send to thee one of my disciples, and he will cure thy disease." And Abgar sent and called for Tobias, and said to him, I have heard that a certain powerful man has come, and dwells in thy house. Bring him up to me; a good hope of recovery through him has been found for me. Tobias went early on the next day and took Addai the Apostle, and brought him up to Abgar, Addai himself knowing that by the power of God he was sent to him. And when Addai came up and went to Abgar, his nobles standing with him, and in going towards him, a wonderful vision was seen by Abgar in the face of Addai. At the moment that Abgar saw the vision, he fell down and worshipped Addai. Great astonishment seized all those who were standing before him, for they saw not the vision which |7 was seen by Abgar. Then Abgar said to Addai, "Of a truth thou art the disciple of Jesus, that mighty one, the son of God, who sent to me saying I send thee one of my disciples for healing and for life." Addai said to him, "Because that from the beginning thou didst believe in Him who sent me to thee, therefore have I been sent to thee, and if thou believest in Him, everything in which thou dost believe thou shalt have." Abgar said to him, "So have I believed in Him, that with respect to those Jews who crucified Him, I desire to take with me an army, and to go and destroy them; but because the kingdom belongs to the Romans, I was restrained by the covenant of peace, which was confirmed by me with our lord the emperor Tiberius, like my forefathers." Addai said to him, "Our Lord has fulfilled the will of His Father. And when He had completed the will of His Parent, He was taken up to His Father, and sat with Him in glory, with whom He was from eternity." Abgar said to him: "I also believe in Him and in His Father." Addai said to him:[18] "Because that so believest, I place my hand on thee, in the name of Him in whom thou believest."

At the moment that he placed his hand upon him, he was cured of the plague of the disease, which he had had for a long time.[19] Abgar wondered and was astonished, |8 that as it was reported to him concerning Jesus, that which He did and cured; so also Addai himself, without medicine of any kind, healed in the name of Jesus. And also with respect to Abdu, the son of Abdu, he had the gout in his feet, and he too brought his feet near him, and he (Addai) placed his hand upon them and healed him; and he had not the gout again. And also in all the city he wrought great cures, and showed wonderful mighty works in it. Abgar said to him: "Now that every man knoweth that by the power of Jesus Christ thou doest these wonderful works, and behold we are wondering at thy works, I require therefore of thee, that thou wouldest recount to us concerning the coining of Christ, how it was, and concerning His glorious power, and concerning those miracles which we have heard that He did, which thou hast seen with the rest of thy companions." Addai said to him: "I will not

keep silent from declaring this; for because of this I was sent here to speak and to teach every one, who, like thee, is willing to believe. Tomorrow assemble for me all the city, that I may sow in it the Word of Life, by the preaching which I will preach before you concerning the coming of Christ, how it was, and concerning His glorious power, and concerning Him that sent Him, for what and how He sent Him, and concerning His power and His wonderful works, and concerning the glorious mysteries of His coming, which He spake in the world, and concerning the certitude of His preaching, how and for what He abased Himself, and humbled His exalted |9 divinity by the body, which He took, and was crucified and descended to the house of the dead, and cleaved the wall of partition, which had never been cleft, and gave life to the dead by being Himself slain, and descended by Himself, and ascended with many to His glorious Father, with whom He was from, eternity in one exalted divinity. And Abgar commanded that they should deliver to Addai silver and gold. Addai said to him: "How are we able to receive anything which is not ours? for, behold, that which was ours we have forsaken, as we were commanded by our Lord to be without purses and without scrips, and carrying crosses upon our shoulders, we were commanded to preach His Gospel to the whole creation: the whole creation felt and suffered by His crucifixion, which was for us, for the salvation of all men. And he narrated before Abgar the king, and before his princes and his nobles, and before Augustina, the mother of Abgar, and before Shalmath, the daughter of Meherdath, the wife of Abgar,[20] the signs of our Lord and His wonders, and the glorious miracles which He wrought, and His divine triumphs, and His ascension to His Father; and how they received powers and authorities at the time that He ascended, by which same power he had healed Abgar and Abdu, the son of Abdu, the second person of his kingdom; and how he made them know that which would be revealed at the end of times, and in the consummation of all creatures, and the resuscitation and resurrection, which is about to be for all men, and the separation which is to be between the sheep and |10 the goats, and between the faithful and the unbelieving. And he said to them: "Because that the gate of life is strait and the way of truth is narrow, therefore few are the believers of truth, and in the power of unbelief is Satan's recreation. Because of this there are many liars, who cause to err those who look on. For except that there is a good end for faithful men, our Lord had not descended from heaven, and come to the birth, and to the suffering of death, and also He had not sent us[21] to be His preachers and evangelists. Those things which we saw and heard from Him, which He did and taught, we confidently preach before all men; for we would not do any wrong with respect to the truth of His Gospel. And not these things only; but also those which were done in His Name, after His ascension, we show and preach.

I will tell before you that which happened and was done in the presence of men, who, as you, believed in Christ, that He is the Son of the living God. Protonice, the wife of the Emperor Claudius,[22] whom Tiberius made second[23] in his kingdom, when he went to make war with the Spaniards, who had rebelled against him, this woman, when Simon, one of the disciples, was in the city of Rome, and she saw the signs and wonders, and |11 marvellous works which he did in the name of Christ; denied the paganism of her fathers in which she was brought up, and the idolatrous images which she had worshipped; and she believed in Christ our Lord, and worshipped Him, and praised with those who were joined unto Simon, and held Him in great honour. After this she wished also to see Jerusalem, and those places in which the mighty works of our Lord were done. So she arose promptly and descended from Rome to Jerusalem, she[24] and her two sons with her, and her one virgin daughter.

When she was entering Jerusalem, the city went forth to meet her, and they received her with great honour, as that which is due to the queen, the mistress of the great country of the Romans. But James, who was made director and ruler in the church which was built for us there, when he had heard for what purpose she had gone there, arose and went to her. And he entered into her presence where she was dwelling, in the royal great palace of king Herod. When she saw him, she received him with great joy, as also she had Simon Peter. He also showed her cures and mighty works as did Simon, and she said to him: "Show me Golgotha, on which Christ was crucified, and the wood of His cross on which He was suspended by the Jews, and the grave in which |12 He was placed." James said to her: "These three things which thy Majesty wishes to see are under the control of the Jews. They possess them, and permit us not to go to pray there before Golgotha and the grave, and neither the wood of His cross will they give us. And not only this, but they also severely persecute us, that we may not publish and preach in the name of Christ, and many times also they bind us in prison." When she heard these things, the queen immediately commanded, and they brought before her Onias, the son of Hannan the priest, and Gedalia, son of Caiaphas, and Judah the son of Ebed Shalom, chiefs and rulers of the Jews. And she said to them: "Deliver up Golgotha, and the grave, and the wood of the cross, to James, and those who agree with him, and let no man forbid them to minister there according to the custom of their ministry." And when she had so commanded the priests, she arose to go and see these places, and she also delivered that place to James, and those who were with him. Afterwards she entered the grave, and found in the grave three crosses, one of our Lord, and two of those robbers, who were crucified with Him, on His right hand and on His left. And at the time that she entered into the grave----she and her children with her----at that instant her virgin daughter fell down and died, without pain, without disease, and without any cause of death. And when the queen saw that her daughter had died suddenly, she kneeled and prayed within the grave, and said in her prayer: "God, who gave Himself to death for all men, and was crucified in this place, and was laid in this grave; and as God, who keepeth alive all, has risen, and made many to rise with Him, lest the Jews, the crucifiers, should hear---- and also the erring heathens, whose |13 idols and graven images, and the terrors of paganism, I have denied----and they see me, deride me, and say that all this which has happened to her is because that she denied the gods, which she did worship, and confessed Christ, whom she knew not, and went to honour the place of His grave and His crucifixion; and if, O my Lord, I am not worthy to be heard, because that I have worshipped creatures instead of Thee; spare Thou, for the sake of Thy adorable Name, that it may not be blasphemed in this place, as they blasphemed Thee at Thy crucifixion." She said these things in her prayer, and, in the excitement of her supplication, she repeated them before all those who were there. Her eldest son approached her, and said to her: "Hear that which I shall say before thy Majesty. I think thus in my mind and in my thought, that this death of this my sister, which was sudden, was not for nought; but this is a wonderful work, in which God will be praised, and not that His Name will be blasphemed, as those thought, who heard it. Behold, we enter the grave and find in it three crosses, and we know not which of them is the cross on which Christ was suspended. In the death of this my sister, we may be able to see and to learn which is the cross of Christ, for Christ is not neglectful of those who believe in Him, and seek Him." And the queen Protonice----her soul was very sad at this time---- saw in her mind that her son spake these things wisely, justly and rightly. And with her hands she took hold of one of the crosses and placed it upon the dead body of her daughter, which lay before her, and she said in her prayer: "O God, who hast shown wonderful works in this place, as we hear and believe, if this cross, O Lord, be Thine, and on it Thy humanity was suspended by the insolent, show the strong |14 and mighty power of Thy divinity, which dwells in the humanity, and restore to life this my daughter, that she may arise, and Thy Name be glorified in her. May her soul return to her body, that Thy crucifiers may be confounded and Thy worshippers may rejoice! And she waited a long time after she had spoken thus. Afterwards she took that cross from the dead body of her daughter, and placed another, and also said in her prayer: "O God, by whose nod worlds and creatures endure, and wishing the life of all men that they may be turned to Him, and is not neglectful of the petition of those who seek Him, if this cross be Thine, O Lord, show the power of Thy triumphs as Thou art accustomed, and restore to life this my daughter, that she may arise, and the heathens, worshipping Thy creatures instead of Thee, may be confounded, and the faithful and the true may confess, that their mouth may be opened to Thy praise before those who deny Thee!" And she waited a long time after these things, and took the second cross from her daughter; and she took the third cross and placed it upon her daughter. And as she was going to lift up her eyes to heaven, and to open her mouth in prayer, at that moment, at that time, in the twinkling of an eye, that, the cross touched the dead body of her daughter, her daughter became alive, and she arose suddenly, and praised God, who had restored her to life by His cross. But the queen Protonice, when she saw how her daughter became alive, trembled, and was greatly alarmed, but though alarmed she glorified Christ, and believed in Him, that He was the Son of the living God. Her son said to her: "My lady, thou seest that if this had not occurred today, it might have happened that they would have left this cross of Christ, by which my |15 sister became alive, and have taken and honoured that of one of those murderous thieves. Now, behold, we see and rejoice, and Christ, who has done this thing, is glorified in her."[25] And she took the cross of Christ, and gave it to James, that it might be kept with great honour. She also commanded that a great and splendid building should be erected over Golgotha, on which He was crucified, and over the grave in which He was placed, so that these places might be honoured; and that there should be there a place of assembly for prayer, and a gathering for service. But the queen, when she saw the whole population of the city, which she had collected for the sight of this work, she commanded that, without the covering of honour worn by queens, her daughter should go with her unveiled to the palace of the king, in which she dwelt, so that every one might see her and praise God. But the people of the Jews and the Gentiles, who rejoiced at the beginning of this occurrence, and were glad, became very sad at the end of it. For they would have been well pleased if this had not occurred, for they saw on account of this many believed in Christ; and especially when they saw that the miracles, which were done in His Name after His ascension, were many more than those which were done before His ascension. And the fame of this deed which was done went forth to |16 distant countries, and also to the Apostles, my companions, who preached Christ. And there was rest in the churches of Jerusalem, and the cities round about it; and those who saw not this *deed,* with

those who did see *it,* praised God. And when the queen went up from Jerusalem to the city of Rome, every city which she entered pressed to see the sight of her daughter. And when she had entered Eome, she recounted before the Emperor Claudius those things which had happened; and when the Emperor heard, he commanded that all the Jews should go forth from the country of Italy. In all that country this deed was spoken of by many, and also before Simon Peter this was recounted, which was done. "Whatsoever also the Apostles, companions, did, we preach before every man, that those who do not know may likewise hear those things which, by our hand, Christ did openly, that our Lord might be glorified by every man. These things which I repeat before you are told, that ye may know and understand how great is the faith of Christ among those who truly join themselves to Him. But James, the director of the Church of Jerusalem, who with his own eyes saw the deed, gave a written account, and sent it to the Apostles, my companions, in the cities of their countries. And also the Apostles themselves gave written accounts, and made known to James whatsoever that Christ had done by their hands, and these were read before all the multitude of the people of the church. But when Abgar the king heard these things, he and Augustina, his mother, and Shalmath, the daughter of Meherdath, and Paqûr[26] and Abdshemesh, and |17 Shamshagram, and Abdu, and Azzai and Bar-kalba, with the rest of their companions, rejoiced exceedingly, and all of them glorified God, and made their confession in Christ. Abgar the king said to Addai: "I wish that everything which we have heard from thee today, and the rest also of the other things, thou wouldst tell openly before all the city, that every man may hear the preaching of the Gospel of Christ, which thou teachest to us, that he may rest and be confirmed in the doctrine which thou teachest to us, that many may understand that I believed rightly in Christ, in the Letter which I sent to Him, and may know that He is God, the Son of God, and thou art His true and faithful disciple, and that thou showest by works His glorious power before those who wish to believe in Him. The day after, Abgar commanded Abdu, the son of Abdu, who was healed of a sore disease of his feet, to send a herald, that he may proclaim in all the city that the whole population may be assembled, men and women, at the place which is called Beththabara, the wide space of the house of Avida,[27] the son of Abd-nachad, that they might hear the doctrine of Addai the Apostle, and how he taught, and in the name of whom he cured, and by what power he wrought these miracles, and those wonders he did. For when he healed Abgar the king, it was the nobles only who stood before him, and saw him, when he healed him by the word of Christ, whom many physicians were not able to heal, but a stranger cured him by the faith of Christ. And when all the city were assembled, men and women, as the king had commanded, Avida and Labbu, and |18 Chaphsai, and Bar-Kalba, and Labubna,[28] and Chesrun,[29] and Shamshagram stood there, with their companions, who as they were princes and nobles of the king, and commanders, and all the workmen and the artisans and the Jews and Gentiles who were in this city, and strangers of the countries of Soba and Harran, and the rest of the inhabitants of all this country of Mesopotamia, all of them stood to hear the doctrine of Addai; concerning whom they had heard; that he was the disciple of Jesus, who was crucified in Jerusalem, and he effected cures in His name. And Addai began to speak to them thus: "Hear, all of you, and understand that which I speak before you; that I am not a physician of medicines and roots, of the art of the sons of men; but I am the disciple of Jesus Christ, the Physician of troubled souls, and the Saviour of future life, the Son of God, who came down from heaven, and was clothed with a body and became man; and He gave Himself and was crucified for all men. And when He was suspended on the wood, the sun He made dark in the firmament; and when He had entered the grave, He arose and went forth from the grave with many. And those who guarded the grave saw not how He went forth from the grave; but the angels of heaven |19 were the preachers and publishers of His resurrection, who if He had not wished, had not died, because that He is the Lord of death, the exit *of all things.*[30] And except it had pleased Him, He had not again clothed Himself with a body, for He is Himself the framer of the body. For the will which inclined Him to the birth from a virgin, also made Him condescend to the suffering of death, and He humbled the majesty of His exalted divinity, [31] who was with His Father from eternity, He of whom Prophets of old spake in their mysteries; and they represented images of His birth, and His suffering, and His resurrection, and His ascension to His Father, and of His sitting at the right hand. And, behold, He is worshipped by celestial spirits, and by the inhabitants of the earth, He who is worshipped from eternity. For although His was the appearance of men, His might, and His knowledge, and His power were of God Himself; as He said to us, [32] Behold, now is the son of man glorified, and God glorifies Himself in Him, by miracles and by wonders, and by honour of being at the right hand. But His body is the pure vestment of His glorious divinity, by which we are able to see His invisible Lordship. This Jesus Christ, therefore, we preach and publish, and, with Him, we praise His Father, and we extol and worship the Spirit of His |20 divinity, because that we were thus commanded by Him, to baptize and absolve those who believe in the name of the Father and the Son and the Holy Spirit. Also the Prophets of old spake thus: that 'The Lord our God and His Spirit hath sent us.'[33] And if I speak anything which is not written in the Prophets, the Jews, who are standing among you and hear me, will not receive it; and if, again, I make mention of the name of Christ over those who have sufferings and diseases, and they are not healed by this glorious name, they, worshipping the work of their hands, will not believe. If now these things be written, which we say, in the Books of the Prophets,[34] and we are able to show the healing powers upon the sick, not a man will look on us without discerning the faith[35] which we preach, that God was crucified for all men. If there be those who do not wish to acquiesce in these words, let them draw near to us, and reveal to us what is their mind, that as a disease of their mind we may apply healing medicine for the cure of their wound. For although ye were not present at the time of the suffering of Christ, yet because of the sun, which was dark, and ye saw it, learn and understand concerning the great hororr there was at the time of the crucifixion of |21 Him whose Gospel has flown over all the earth, by the miracles which His disciples, my companions, are working in all the earth. And those who were Hebrews, and knew only the Hebrew tongue in which they were born, behold to day speak in all languages, that those who are far off, as those who are nigh, might hear and believe that He is the same, who confounded[36] the tongues of the impious in this district, which lies before us; He it is who to day teaches through us the faith of truth and verity, by humble and wretched men, who were from Galilee of Palestine. For I also, whom ye see, am from Paneas,[37] from where the river Jordan goes forth. And I was chosen, with my companions, to be a preacher[38] of this Gospel, by which, behold, the regions everywhere resound with the glorious name of the adorable Christ. Let, therefore, no man of you harden his heart against the truth and keep his mind at a distance from verity. Be ye not led captive after thoughts destructively erroneous, which are full of the despair of a bitter death.[39] Be ye not taken by the evil customs of the paganism of your fathers, and so keep yourselves at a distance from the life of truth and verity, which are in Christ. For those who believe in Him are those who are trusted before Him, who descended to us by His favour, to make to cease from the earth the sacrifices of heathenism, and the offerings |22 of idolatry; that creatures should no longer be worshipped; but we should worship Him and His Father, with His Holy Spirit.[40] For I, as my Lord commanded me, behold, I preach and I publish. And His silver on the table, behold I cast before you, and the seed of His word I sow in the ears of every man. Those who wish to receive, theirs is the good reward of confession; and those who do not obey, against them I scatter the dust of my feet, as my Lord commanded me. Turn ye, therefore, my beloved, from evil ways and from hateful deeds, and turn yourselves to Him with a good and honest will, as He turned Himself to you with His grace and His rich mercies. And be ye not as the generations of old, which are passed, who, because that they hardened their heart against the fear of God, received punishment openly; that they may be chastised, and those who came after them may tremble and fear. For that for which our Lord came into the world was altogether[41] to teach and show that at the end of created things is a resurrection for all men. And at that time their acts of conduct will be represented on their own persons, and their bodies become volumes for the written things of justice, and there will not be he who knoweth not writing; because that every man shall read the letters of his own book[42] at that day, and the account of his actions he taketh with the fingers of his hands. Thus the unlettered will know the new writing of the new language, and there is not he who will say to his fellow, Read me this, because that one doctrine and one instruction shall reign over all men. |23

Let this thought, therefore, be represented before your eyes, and let it not pass from your mind, because that if it pass from your mind, it passeth not from Justice.[43] Seek mercies from God, that He may pardon the hateful infidelity of your paganism, for ye have forsaken Him who created you upon the face of the earth, and makes His rain to descend and His sun to rise upon you, and ye worship, instead of Him, His works. For the idols and graven images of paganism, and whatsoever of the creation in which ye have confidence and which ye worship, if there were in them feeling and understanding, for the sake of which ye worship and honour them, it would be right for them, which ye have engraven and established, and have firmly fixed with nails that they be not shaken, to receive your favour. For if the creatures were aware of your honours to them, they would cry, shouting to you, not to worship your fellows, which like yourselves are made and created; because that creatures made should not be worshipped; but that they should worship their Creator, and they should glorify Him who created them. And as His grace covers the wicked here,[44] so His justice shall be avenged on the infidels there. For I saw in this city that it abounded greatly in paganism, which is against God. Who is this Nebo,[45] an idol made which ye worship, |24 and Bel,[46] which ye honour? Behold, there are those among you who adore Bath Nical,[47] as the inhabitants of Harran your neighbours, and Taratha,[48] as the people of Mabug, and the eagle, as the Arabians, also the sun and the moon,as the rest of the inhabitants of Harran, who are as yourselves. |25 Be ye not led away captive by the rays of the luminaries and the bright star; for every one who worships creatures is cursed before

God. For although there are among creatures such as are greater than their companions, yet they are fellow-servants of their companions, as I have said to you. For this is a bitter pain, for which there is not a cure, that things made should worship things made, and creatures should glorify their fellows. For as they are not able to stand by the power of themselves, but by the power of Him who created them, so they are not able to be worshipped with Him, nor to bc honoured with Him; for it is a blasphemy against both parties, against the creatures when they are worshipped, and against the Creator, when the creatures, who are strangers to the nature of His existence, are made partakers with Him. For all the prophecy of the Prophets, and the preaching of us who are after the Prophets, is this, that creatures should not be worshipped with the Creator, and that men should not bind themselves to the yoke of corrupt paganism. It is not because of the creatures being seen, I say, that they should not be worshipped; but everything which is made is a creature, whether visible or invisible. This is a horrible wickedness, to place the glorious name of divinity upon it. For not creatures, as you, we proclaim and worship; but the Lord of creatures. The earthquake, which made them tremble at the Cross, testifies that everything which is made depends on and exists by the power of its Maker, who was before worlds and creatures, whose nature is incomprehensible, in that His nature is invisible, and, with His Father, is sanctified in the heights above, for that He is Lord and God from eternity. This is our doctrine in every country and in every region. And so |26 have we been commanded to preach to those who hear us, not violently, but by the teaching of the truth and by the power of God. And the miracles which were done in His name, testify concerning our faith, that it is true and to be believed. Be obedient, therefore, to my words, and receive that which I have said, and am saying before you; and that I may not require your death, behold, I warn you to be very cautious. Receive my words fitly, and do not neglect. Draw nigh to me ye my distant ones from Christ, and be near to Christ. And in the place Of erroneous sacrifices and oblations, offer now to Him the sacrifices of thanksgiving.

What is this great altar which ye have built in the midst of this city? and what are those going and coming offering upon it to demons, and sacrificing on it to devils? But if ye know not the Scriptures, doth not nature itself teach you, by its power of sight, that your idols have eyes and see not? And ye [49] who see with eyes in that ye do not understand, ye are also as they who see not and hear not, and in vain you excite your voices, ineffective to deaf ears. For they are not to be complained of for that which they do not hear, because that by nature they are deaf and dumb. And the blame with which justice is involved is yours, for ye do not wish to understand, even that which ye see. For the thick darkness of error, which is spread over your mind, permits you not to acquire the heavenly light, which is the understanding of knowledge. Flee, therefore, from things made and created, as I have said unto you, that in name only are they called gods, though they are not gods in their nature; and draw near to Him, who in His nature is |27 God from eternity and from everlasting, and is not made as your idols, and also not a creature, and a work of art as the images in which ye make your boast. Because that although He put on this body, He was God with His Father; for the works of creation, which trembled when He was slain, and were terrified by the suffering of His death, they testify that He is He who created the works of creation. For it was not for a man the earth shook, but for Him who established the earth upon the waters; and it was not for a man the sun became dark in the heavens, but for Him who made the great lights. And it was not by a man the righteous and the just were raised to life, but by Him who gave power over death from the beginning. Nor was it by a man the vail of the temple of the Jews was rent from the top to the bottom, but by Him who said to them, 'Behold, your house is left desolate.'[50] For, behold, except they who crucified Him knew that He was the Son of God, they would not have proclaimed the desolation of their city, also they would not have brought down woes upon themselves. For even if they wished to neglect this confession, the terrible commotions which were at that time would not have permitted them. Behold also some of the children of the crucifiers have become at this day preachers and evangelists, with the Apostles my companions, in all the land of Palestine and among the Samaritans, and in all the country of the Philistines. The idols of paganism also are despised, and the Cross of Christ is honoured. Peoples and creatures also confess God, who became man. If truly when Jesus our Lord was upon earth ye believed in Him that He is the Son of God, and before that ye had heard the word of |28 His preaching, confessed in Him that He is God; now that He has ascended to His Father, and ye have seen the signs and wonders which are done in His name, and the word of His Gospel ye have heard with your ears; not a man of you should let himself doubt in his mind how the promise of His blessing which He sent to you would have been established with you: "Blessed are ye who have believed in me, although ye have not seen me; and because ye have so believed in me the city in which ye dwell shall be blessed, and the enemy shall not prevail against it for ever."[51] Do not, therefore, turn from His faith; for, behold, ye have heard and seen those things which bear witness to His faith, that He is the adorable Son, and is the glorious God, and is the triumphant King, and is the Omnipotent Power; and by His true faith a man is able to acquire the eye of the true mind, and to perceive that every one who worships creatures, the wrath of justice overtakes him.

For everything which we say before you, we say as we have received of the gift of our Lord, and we teach and we show how to possess your life, and not destroy your spirits by the error of paganism; because that the heavenly light hath risen upon creation, and He it is, who hath chosen the ancient fathers and the just men and the Prophets, and hath spoken with them by the revelation of the Holy Spirit. For He is the God of the Jews, who crucified Him, and the erring Gentiles also worship Him, though they know *it* not; because that there is no |29 other God in heaven and in earth, and behold confession ascendeth up to Him from the four quarters of the earth. Behold now your ears have heard that which was not heard by you *before,* and behold, again, your eyes have seen that which was never seen by you *before.* Be ye not therefore unjust to that which ye have heard and seen. Cause to pass from you the rebellious mind of your fathers, and free yourselves from the yoke of sin, which hath dominion over you by libations and sacrifices before graven images. Let it be a care to you concerning your perishing lives, and concerning the vain bowing of your head, and acquire the new mind which worships the Maker and not the thing made, in which is represented the image of truth and verity, of the Father, and of the Son, and of the Holy Spirit, when ye believe and are baptized in the triple and glorious names. For this is our doctrine and our preaching. For it is not in many things that the truth of Christ is believed. And such of you as are willing to be obedient to Christ, know that many times I have repeated my words before you, that ye might learn and understand whatsoever ye hear. And we will rejoice in this, as a husbandman in his field which is blessed; and our God is glorified by your repentance towards Him. And as ye live in this, we also who counsel you thus will not be defrauded of the blessed reward of this. And because I am confident that ye are a blessed land, according to the will of the Lord Christ, therefore for the dust of my feet which we have been commanded [52] to shake off against the city that receiveth not our words; behold I shake off to-day at the door of your ears the words of my lips, in which the |30 coming of Christ is represented, that which has been, and that which is about to be, and the resurrection and resuscitation of all men, and the separation which is to be between the faithful and unbelieving, and the blessed promise of future joys which they who have believed in Christ and worshipped His high Father, and confessed Him and the Spirit of His godhead, shall receive. And now it is right for us to finish our present discourse, and let those who have received the word of Christ remain with us, and also those who wish to be associated, with us in prayer, and then let them go to their homes."

And Addai the Apostle rejoiced in this when he saw that the multitude of the population of the city remained with him, and there were few who did not remain at that time; and these same few, after a few days, received his words and believed in the gospel of the preaching of Christ.

And when Addai the Apostle had said these things before all the city of Edessa, and Abgar the king saw that all the city rejoiced in his doctrine, men and women equally, and were saying to him "Christ, who hath sent thee to us is true and faithful," and he also greatly rejoiced at this, praising God, that according to what he had heard from Hannan, his tabularius, concerning Christ, so he had seen the marvellous mighty works which Addai the Apostle had done in the name of Christ. And Abgar the king also said to Addai the Apostle, As I sent to Christ by my letter to Him; and as He also sent to me and I have received from thee thyself this day; so will I believe all the days of my life, and in the same things continue, exulting, because I know that there is no other power in the name of whom these signs and wonders are done, but by the power of Christ, whom thou preachest in truth and verity. And now I will worship Him, |31 I and Ma'nu,[53] my son, and Augustina, and Shalmath the queen. And now, wherever thou wishest, build a church, a house of assembly for those who have believed, and shall believe in thy words. And, as commanded thee by thy Lord, minister thou at times with confidence. And those who are teachers with thee of this Gospel, I am prepared to deliver to them large gifts, that they may not have any other work with the ministry. Everything also which is required by thee for the expenses of the house, I will give thee without taking account; thy word shall be powerful and have rule in this city, and without another man, have thou authority to enter into my presence in my royal palace of honour.

And when Abgar the king went down to his royal palace, he rejoiced, he and his princes with him, Abdu and Garmai, and Shamshagram, and Abubai, and Meherdath, with the rest of their companions, at everything which their eyes had seen, and their ears had heard, and in the joy of their heart they also praised God, who had turned their mind to Him; they renounced the paganism in which they stood, and confessed the Gospel of Christ. And when Addai had built a church, they offered in it vows and offerings, they and the people of the city, and there they worshipped all the days of their life.

And Avida [54] and Bar-kalba who were chiefs and rulers, and clothed with royal headbands [55], drew near to Addai, and they asked Addai concerning the |32 history of Christ, to tell them how that He being God was seen by them, as man, and how ye were able to see Him. And he satisfied them all concerning this, concerning all which their eyes had seen, and concerning

all which their ears had heard of Him. And every thing which the Prophets had said of Him, he repeated before them, and they received his words gladly and faithfully, and there was not a man who rose up against him. For the glorious things which he did permitted not a man to rise up against him.

Shavida and Ebednebo, chiefs of the priests of this city, with Piroz [56] and Dancu [57] their companions, when they saw the signs which he did, ran and threw down the altars upon which they sacrificed before Nebo and Bel their gods, except the great altar, which was in the midst of the city, and they cried out and said, that this is truly the disciple of the distinguished and glorious Master of whom we heard all those things, which He did in the country of Palestine. And all who believed in Christ, Addai received, and baptized them in the name of the Father, and the Son, and the Holy Spirit. And those who were accustomed to worship stones and stocks, sat at his feet, learning, and being corrected of the plague of the foolishness of paganism. The Jews also, conversant with the Law and the Prophets, who carried on |33 merchandise in silks, [58] were also persuaded and became disciples, and made confession in Christ, that He is the Son of the living God. But neither Abgar the king, nor Addai the Apostle pressed any man by force to believe in Christ; because without the force of man, the force of the signs compelled many to believe in Him. And all this country of Mesopotamia, and all the regions round about it received his doctrine with love.

But Aggai made the chains [59] and headbands of the king, and Palut and Abshelama [60] and Barsamya with the rest of the others their companions, adhered to Addai the Apostle, and he received them and made them partakers with him in the ministry; they read in the Old Testament [61] and the New, and the Prophets, and the Acts of the Apostles, every day they meditated on them. He commanded them cautiously, "Let your bodies be pure, and let your persons be holy; as is right for men who stand before the altar of God; and be ye indeed far |34 removed from false swearing, and from wicked murder, and from false testimony, which is mixed with adultery, and from sorcerers with respect to whom there are no mercies, and from divinations, and soothsaying, and necromancers, and from fates, and nativities, in which the erring Chaldees boast themselves; and from stars, and the signs of the Zodiac, in which the foolish are confident. And keep at a distance from you evil hypocrisy, and bribes, and gifts, by which the pure are condemned. And with this ministry to which ye have been called, let there not be for you another service; for the Lord Himself is the service of your ministry all the days of your life. Be ye also diligent to deliver the sign of baptism, and love ye not the gains of this world, but hearken ye to judgment with justice and truth. And be ye not a stumbling block to the blind, that the name of Him who opened the eyes of the blind, as we have seen, be not blasphemed through you. Let all, therefore, who see you, perceive that ye perform all which ye preach and teach. And they ministered with him in the church which Addai had built by the word and command of Abgar the king, and they were supplied from that which was the king's and his nobles; and some of them they brought for the house of God, and some for the nourishment of the poor. But a large multitude of people assembled day by day and came to the prayer of the service, and to *the reading* of the Old and New Testament, of the Diatessaron, [62] and they believed in the revival of the dead, and |35 they buried their dead in the hope of the resurrection. They also observed the festivals of the Church in their times, and every day they were constant in the vigils of the Church, and they likewise performed acts of charity to the sick and those who were whole, according to the instruction of Addai to them. And in places round about the city churches were built, and the hand of the priesthood many received from him: So also orientals with the appearance of merchants passed into the country of the Romans to see the signs which Addai did, and those of them who became disciples, received from them [63] the hand of the priesthood, and in their own country of the Assyrians they taught the sons of their people, and houses of prayer they built there secretly, because of the danger arising from the worshippers of fire and the adorers of water.[64]

But Nersai,[65] the king of the Assyrians, when he had heard of these things which Addai the Apostle had done, he sent to Abgar, the king; either send me the man who |36 hath done these signs with thee, that I may see him and hear his discourse, or send me *an account of* all these things which thou hast seen him do in thy city. And Abgar wrote to Nersai and made him acquainted with the whole history of the affair of Addai from the beginning to the end, and he left not any thing which he did not write to him.

But when Nersai heard those things which were written to him, he wondered and was astonished. But Abgar the king, because that he was not able to pass to the country of the Romans, and to go to Palestine and slay the Jews, because that they had crucified Christ, wrote a letter and sent to Tiberius Caesar, writing it thus: "Abgar, the king, to our Lord Tiberius Caesar, peace. Knowing that not anything is hidden from thy Majesty, I write and inform thy dread and great sovereignty, that the Jews, who are under thy hand, who dwell in the country of Palestine, assembled themselves together and crucified the Christ without any fault *worthy* of death, when he was doing before them signs and wonders, and showed them mighty works and signs; so |37 that even the dead He raised to life for them. And at the time they crucified Him, the sun became darkened and the earth shook, and all creatures trembled, and as if of themselves, at this deed all creation quailed, and its inhabitants. And now thy majesty knows what is right to command against the people of the Jews, who did these things."

And Tiberius Caesar wrote and sent to Abgar the king, and thus he wrote to him: "The letter of thy fidelity to me, I have received, and it was read before me. With respect to that which the Jews have done with the cross, Pilate the governor hath also written, and informed Olbinus, [66] my proconsul, of these things which thou hast written to me. But because of the war of the Spaniards who have rebelled against me is going on at this time, therefore I have not been able to avenge this matter; but I am prepared, when I have quietness, to make a charge legally against the Jews, who have not acted legally. And because of this, as to Pilate, who was made by me governor there, I have sent another in his place, and I have dismissed him with disgrace, because that he departed from the law, and did the will of the Jews, and he crucified Christ for the gratification of the Jews, who according to that which I hear of them, instead of the cross of death, it was fitting that He should be honoured, and it was right He should be worshipped by them, especially as they saw with their eyes all which He did. But thou, according to thy fidelity to me and thy true |38 compact and that of thy fathers, hast done well to write to me thus."

And Abgar the king, received Aristides, [67] who was sent to him by Tiberius Caesar, and he replied, sent him back with honourable gifts, which were suitable for him, who had sent him to him. And he departed from Edessa, and went to Ticnutha, [68] where was Claudius the second, from the king, and from there also he went to Artica, [69] where was Tiberius Caesar. But Gaius guarded the regions, which were round about the Emperor. And Aristides himself also recounted before Tiberius the mighty works which Addai did before Abgar the king. And when he had rest from the war, he sent, slew some of the chiefs of the Jews, who were in Palestine. And when Abgar the king heard, he greatly rejoiced at this, that the Jews had received punishment, as it was right.

And some years after Addai the Apostle had built the church in Edessa, and furnished it with everything which was suitable for it, and had taught many of the population of the city, also in the other villages, both those which were distant, and those which were near, he built churches, and completed and ornamented *them,* and appointed in them deacons and elders, and |39 taught in them those who should read the Scriptures, and the orders of the ministry within and without he taught. After all these things he became ill with the disease, by which he departed from this world.[70] And he called Aggai before all the congregation of the church, and he brought him near, and made him governor and ruler in his place. And concerning Palut, who was a deacon, he made him an elder, and of Abshelama, who was a scribe, he made him a deacon. And when the nobles and chiefs were assembled and stood by him, Bar-kalba and [71] Bar-Zati, and Marihab, the son of Barshemesh, and Sennac, son of Avida, and Peroz, son of Patricius, with the rest of their companions, Addai the Apostle said to them: "Ye know, and ye testify, all of you who hear me, that everything which I have preached to you and taught you, and ye have heard from me, so have I conducted myself among you, and ye have seen also in works, because that thus our Lord commanded us that whatsoever we preach in words before the people, we in work should do before every man. And according to the ordinances and laws which were appointed in Jerusalem, and by which also the Apostles, my companions, were governed, |40 so also ye, do not turn aside from them, and do not take away anything from them, as I myself also have been guided by them among you, and have not turned aside from them to the right hand, or to the left, that I might not become strange to the promised salvation, which is reserved for those who are guided by them. Take heed, therefore, to this ministry which ye hold, and with fear and trembling abide ye in it, and minister every day. Minister not in it with habits bringing contempt, but with the prudence of faith; and the praises of Christ, let them not cease from your mouth, and let not weariness in prayer at the *stated* times draw near to you. Take heed to the truth, which ye hold, and to the teaching of the truth, which ye have received, and to the inheritance of salvation, which I commend to you, because before the judgment-seat of Christ you will be sought out by Him, when He taketh account with the pastors and superiors, and when He taketh His money from merchants with the increase of gains. For He is the king's son, and goes to receive a kingdom, and to return, and to come and make a resurrection for all men; and then He sitteth on the throne of righteousness, and judgeth the dead and the living, as He hath said to us. Let not the secret eye of your mind from the height above be closed, that your offences may not multiply in the way in which there are no offences; nor abominable error in its ways. Seek ye those that are lost, and visit those that err, and rejoice ye in those that are found. Bind up those that are bruised, and be ye watchful of the fatlings, because at your hands will the sheep of Christ be required. Look ye not to passing honour, for the shepherd that looketh to be honoured by his flock, badly, badly with respect to him does his flock stand. Let your solicitude for the |41 young lambs be great, for their angels [72] behold the face of the invisible Father, and be ye

not a stone of stumbling before the blind, but clearers [73] of the way and the path in a difficult country, among the Jews, the crucifiers, and the erring heathen; for with these two parties only is there war for you, in order to show the truth of the faith, which ye hold; also when ye are quiet, your modest and honourable appearance will be fighting for you with those who hate truth and love falsehood. Be ye not smiters of the poor before the rich, for the severe infliction of their poverty is sufficient for them. Be ye not beguiled with the hateful cogitations of Satan, that ye be not stripped naked of the faith that ye have put on,[74] for unbelief is easier than faith, as sin is easier than righteousness. Take heed, therefore, of those that crucified, that ye be not friends to them, that ye be not responsible with them whose hands are full of the blood of Christ; and ye know, and ye bear witness, that everything which we say and teach of the history of Christ, is written in the Book of the Prophets, and deposited with them. And their words bear witness to our teaching concerning the judgment, and suffering, and resurrection, and ascension of Christ; but they know not, that when they rise against us they rise against the words of the Prophets, and as in their lives they persecuted the Prophets, so also now, since their death, they persecute the truth, which is written in the Prophets. Again, take ye heed of the heathen, who worship the sun and the moon, and Bel and Nebo, and the rest of those which they call gods, though they are not gods in their nature. |42 Flee ye, therefore, from them, because that they worship creatures and things made. And as reported to you before, the whole object [75] for which our Lord came into the world was that creatures might not again be worshipped and honoured, because they exist by the nod of their Creator; and when He wishes, He dissolves and makes them cease, and they are as though they are not. For the will of Him, who created the creatures, freed men from the yoke of the paganism of the creatures. For ye know that every one who worships the servants of a king with the king, the death of the sword findeth him in his worship. Be ye not searching for secret things, and inquiring after hidden things, which are written in the holy books that ye possess. Be ye not judges concerning the words of the Prophets. Remember and consider that by the Spirit of God they are said; and he who accuses the Prophets, accuses and judges the Spirit of God. May this be far from you I Because the ways of the Lord are straight, and the righteous walk in them without stumbling; but the infidels stumble in them; because that they have not the secret eye of the secret mind, which has no need of questions in which there is no profit, but loss.[76] Remember the menacing judgment of the Prophets, and the word of our Lord, which defines their words, that the Lord judgeth by fire, and all men are tried by it. Wherefore, as wayfarers |43 and sojourners, who tarry for a night and return early to their homes, so may you yourselves consider concerning this world, that from here ye go forth to the places where the Son went to prepare for every one worthy of them. As to kings of countries, their armies go forth before them, and prepare for them a dwelling-house for their honour; but this King of ours, behold, He is gone to prepare for His worshippers blessed mansions [77] in which they may dwell. For it was not in vain God created the children of men; but that they might worship and glorify Him. here and there for ever. As He passeth not away, so those glorifying Him cease not. Wherefore my death also, with the disease of which I am bound and lie; as a sleep of the night, let it be esteemed in your eyes. And remember that with the suffering of the Son, Death, which snatches away the children of men, passed away and ceased; and Satan, who causes many to sin and makes war with the true, that they may be without truth. And as a husbandman who puts his hand to the ploughshare, if he looks behind,[78] the furrows before him cannot be straight; so also ye who have been called to this gift of the ministry, be ye cautious, that ye do not trouble *yourselves* with the things of this world, lest by chance ye be impeded as to that to which ye have been called.

As to princes and judges, who have embraced this faith, be ye loving them, although do not simulate in any thing, and if they sin, ye reprove them with justice. Ye shall show them openly your rectitude, that they may be corrected so as not again to conduct themselves after their own will. This solicitude ye shall have all the days |44 of your life, that all of you may run after honest things, as ye also counsel others with respect to them; for in these things men find their life before God.

But the Law,[79] and the Prophets, and the Gospel, which ye read every day before the people, and the Epistles of Paul, which Simon Peter sent us from the city of Rome, and the Acts of the twelve Apostles, which John, the son of Zebedee, sent us from Ephesus; these Books read ye in the churches of Christ, and with these read not any others, as there is not any other in which the truth that ye hold is written, except these books, which retain you in the faith to which ye have been called. And our lord Abgar the king, and his honoured nobles, who have heard that which I have spoken before you to day are sufficient to be for me witnesses after my death, that I have diligently preached the doctrine of our Lord before every man, and that I have not acquired anything with His word in the world. For His word by which I have become rich was sufficient for me, and I have made by it many rich; for it lifts me up in this way in which I go forth before Christ, who has sent after me, that I should go by it to Him. For ye know that which I have said to you, "That all the souls of men, which depart from this body, die not; but they live and rise, and have mansions, and a dwelling-place of rest, |45 for the understanding and the intelligence of the soul do not cease, because the image of God is represented in it, which dieth not. For it is not as the body without feeling which perceives not the odious corruption which has come upon it. Eeward and recompense it is not able to receive without it (*the body*); because that labour was not its only, but also of the body in which it dwelt. But the rebellious who know not God, they become penitent then to no purpose. Ye, indeed, who are of Christ, whose glorious name is placed upon you, and ruleth, He will direct you in the way of truth, in which, ye shall go and shall arrive at and attain to that which is promised and kept for those who depart not from Him; but abide according to what they were called to by our Lord.

And when Addai the Apostle had said this word, he ceased and was silent. And Aggai, maker of the king's chains, and Palut, and Abshelama, with the rest of their companions, answered and said to Addai the Apostle, "Christ Himself has testified that He sent thee to us, and thou hast taught us the true faith, and hast made us possess the true life. As we have heard from thee and received, all this time thou hast been with us, so we abide all the days of our life. And from the worship of things made and created, which our fathers worshipped, we flee, and with [80] the Jews, the crucifiers we will not mix ourselves; and this inheritance, which we have received from thee, we do not let go, but with it we will depart from this world. And in the day of our Lord, before the judgment-seat of righteousness, there will He return to us this inheritance as that thou hast said to us.

And when these things had been said, Abgar the king, |46 arose, he and his princes, and all the nobles of his kingdom, and he went to his own palace, when all of them grieved over him, for he was dying. And he sent to him honourable and costly garments, in which he should be buried; and when Addai saw them, he sent word to him, that not in my life have I taken from thee anything, and I will not falsify in me the word of Christ, which He said to me, "Receive not anything from man, arid acquire not anything in this world."[81] And after three other days, that these things were said by Addai the Apostle, and he had heard and received the testimony of the doctrine of his preaching from the sons of his ministry, before all the nobles, he departed from this world, and it was the fifth day of the week, in the fourteenth of the month Eyor.[82] And the whole city was in great sorrow and bitter pain; not only Christians sorrowed for Him, but also Jews and Pagans, who were in this city. But king Abgar more than any man sorrowed for him, he and the princes of his kingdom. And in the grief of his |47 mind he despised and forsook the honour of his kingdom on that day; and with mournful tears he wept over him with every man. And all the people of the city, who saw him, wondered at how much he suffered because of him. And with great and excellent honour he carried and buried him, as one of the princes, when he dies, and he placed him in a great sepulchre of ornamental sculpture, in which those of the house of Aryu, the ancestors of the father of king Abgar, were placed. There he placed him carefully with grief and great sorrow. And all the people of the church went from time to time, and prayed there diligently, and the commemoration of his death they made from year to year, according to the command and instruction which was received by them from Addai the Apostle, and according to the word of Aggai, who was himself the guide and ruler and the successor of his chair after him, by the hand of the priesthood, which he had received from him before every man.

And he also by the hand from which he received made priests and guides in all this country of Mesopotamia. For they also, as of Addai the Apostle, thus took his word and heard and received, as a good and faithful heir of the Apostle of the adorable Christ. But silver and gold he took not from man, and the gifts of the princes approached him not. For instead of gold and silver he enriched the Church of Christ with the souls of the faithful. But all the chiefs [83] of men and women |48 were modest and decorous, and they were holy and pure, and they dwelt singly and modestly without spot, in watchfulness of the ministry decorously, in their carefulness for the poor, in their visitations to the sick; for their goings forth were full of praise from those who saw, and their conversation was covered with glory from strangers; so that even the priests of the temple of Nebo and Bel divided with them the honour at all times, by their honourable aspect, by their truthful discourse, by the confidence which they possessed, and by their freedom, which was not enslaved to greediness, and was not in bondage under blame. For every one who saw them ran to meet them, that he might honourably salute them; because even the sight of them spread peace over the beholders. For their words of peace were spread like nets over the rebellious, when they were entering the fold of truth and verity. For there was no man who saw them, and was ashamed of them; because they did not anything which was not just, and which was not becoming, and in consequence of this their countenances were open in the preaching of their doctrine to every man. For whatsoever they said to others and directed them, they exhibited the same by works in themselves; and as to the hearers, who saw that their works were with their words, many became their disciples without persuasion, and confessed Christ the king, praising God who had turned them to Him.

And years after the death of Abgar the king, one of |49 his rebellious sons,[84] who was not obedient to the truth, arose and sent word to Aggai, when he was sitting in the Church: "Make me headbands of gold, according to that which thou didst make for my fathers of old." Aggai sent him word: "I desert not the ministry of Christ, which has been committed to me by the disciple of Christ, and make headbands of wickedness." [85] And when he saw that he did not obey him, he sent, and broke his legs, as he was sitting in the church and expounding. And as he was dying he made Palut and Abshelama swear that in this house, for the sake of whose name, behold, I die, place me and bury me. And as he made them swear, so they placed him within the middle door of the church, between the men and the women. And there was great and bitter sorrow in all the church, and in all the city, above the pain of sorrow, which had been |50 in its interior, as the sorrow, which had been when Addai the Apostle died.

And because that by the breaking of his legs he died suddenly and quickly, he was not able to place the hand upon Palut.[86] Palut himself went to Antioch, and received the hand of the priesthood from Serapion, Bishop of Antioch. Serapion, Bishop of Antioch, himself also received the hand from Zephyrinus, Bishop of the city of Rome,[87] from the succession of the hand of the priesthood of Simon Cephas, which he received from our Lord, who was there Bishop of Rome twenty-five years, in the days of the Caesar, who reigned there thirteen years.

And as is the custom in the kingdom of Abgar the king, and in all kingdoms, that everything which the king commands, and everything that is said before him is written down and placed among the records, so also Labubna, the son of Sennac, the son of Abshadar, the king's scribe, wrote these things of Addai the Apostle, from the beginning to the end. Hannan also, the Tabularius, the king's Sharrir, set the hand of witness, and placed it among the records of the writings of the kings, where are put the commands and laws, and *the contracts* of those who buy and sell are kept there with care, without any negligence.

Book 136. The Acts of Thaddeus

Lebbæus, who also is Thaddæus, was of the city of Edessa— and it is the metropolis of Osroene, in the interior of the Armenosyrians — an Hebrew by race, accomplished and most learned in the divine writings. He came to Jerusalem to worship in the days of John the Baptist; and having heard his preaching and seen his angelic life, he was baptized, and his name was called Thaddæus. And having seen the appearing of Christ, and His teaching, and His wonderful works, he followed Him, and became His disciple; and He chose him as one of the twelve, the tenth apostle according to the Evangelists Matthew and Mark.

In those times there was a governor of the city of Edessa, Abgarus by name. And there having gone abroad the fame of Christ, of the wonders which He did, and of His teaching, Abgarus having heard of it, was astonished, and desired to see Christ, and could not leave his city and government. And about the days of the Passion and the plots of the Jews, Abgarus, being seized by an incurable disease, sent a letter to Christ by Ananias the courier, to the following effect:— To Jesus called Christ, Abgarus the governor of the country of the Edessenes, an unworthy slave. The multitude of the wonders done by you has been heard of by me, that you heal the blind, the lame, and the paralytic, and cure all the demoniacs; and on this account I entreat your goodness to come even to us, and escape from the plottings of the wicked Jews, which through envy they set in motion against you. My city is small, but large enough for both. Abgarus enjoined Ananias to take accurate account of Christ, of what appearance He was, and His stature, and His hair, and in a word everything.

And Ananias, having gone and given the letter, was carefully looking at Christ, but was unable to fix Him in his mind. And He knew as knowing the heart, and asked to wash Himself; and a towel was given Him; and when He had washed Himself, He wiped His face with it. And His image having been imprinted upon the linen, He gave it to Ananias, saying: Give this, and take back this message, to him that sent you: Peace to you and your city! For because of this I have come, to suffer for the world, and to rise again, and to raise up the forefathers. And after I have been taken up into the heavens I shall send you my disciple Thaddæus, who shall enlighten you, and guide you into all the truth, both you and your city.

And having received Ananias, and fallen down and adored the likeness, Abgarus was cured of his disease before Thaddæus came.

And after the passion, and the resurrection, and the ascension, Thaddæus went to Abgarus; and having found him in health, he gave him an account of the incarnation of Christ, and baptized him, with all his house. And having instructed great multitudes, both of Hebrews and Greeks, Syrians and Armenians, he baptized them in the name of the Father, and Son, and Holy Spirit, having anointed them with the holy perfume; and he communicated to them of the undefiled mysteries of the sacred body and blood of our Lord Jesus Christ, and delivered to them to keep and observe the law of Moses, and to give close heed to the things that had been said by the apostles in Jerusalem. For year by year they came together to the passover, and again he imparted to them the Holy Spirit.

And Thaddæus along with <u>Abgarus</u> destroyed idol-temples and built churches; ordained as <u>bishop</u> one of his <u>disciples</u>, and <u>presbyters</u>, and <u>deacons</u>, and gave them the rule of the psalmody and the <u>holy</u> liturgy. And having left them, he went to the city of Amis, great metropolis of the Mesechaldeans and Syrians, that is, of Mesopotamia-<u>Syria</u>, beside the river Tigris. And he having gone into the <u>synagogue</u> of the <u>Jews</u> along with his <u>disciples</u> on the <u>Sabbath day</u>, after the reading of the law the <u>high priest</u> said to Thaddæus and his <u>disciples</u>: Men, whence are you? And why are you here?

And Thaddæus said: No <u>doubt</u> you have heard of what has taken place in Jerusalem about <u>Jesus Christ</u>, and we are His <u>disciples</u>, and witnesses of the wonderful things which He did and taught, and how through <u>hatred</u> the chief <u>priests</u> delivered Him to <u>Pilate</u> the <u>procurator</u> of Judæa. And <u>Pilate</u>, having examined Him and found no case, wished to let Him go; but they cried out, If you let him go, you are not Cæsar's friend, because he proclaims himself king. And he being afraid, washed his hands in the sight of the multitude, and said, I am innocent of the blood of this man; see ye to it. And the chief <u>priests</u> answered and said, His blood be upon us and our children. And <u>Pilate</u> gave him up to them. And they took Him, and spit upon Him, with the soldiers, and made a great mock of Him, and crucified Him, and laid Him in the tomb, and secured it well, having also set guards upon Him. And on the third day before dawn He rose, leaving His burial-clothes in the tomb. And He was seen first by His mother and other <u>women</u>, and by Peter and John first of my fellow <u>disciples</u>, and thereafter to us the twelve, who ate and drank with Him after His <u>resurrection</u> for many days. And He sent us in His name to proclaim repentance and remission of <u>sins</u> to all the <u>nations</u>, that those who were <u>baptized</u>, having had the kingdom of the heavens preached to them, would rise up incorruptible at the end of this age; and He gave us power to expel <u>demons</u>, and heal every disease and every malady, and raise the dead.

And the multitudes having heard this, brought together their sick and <u>demoniacs</u>. And Thaddæus, having gone forth along with his <u>disciples</u>, laid his hand upon each one of them, and healed them all by calling upon the name of <u>Christ</u>. And the <u>demoniacs</u> were healed before Thaddæus came near them, the spirits going out of them. And for many days the people ran together from different places, and beheld what was done by Thaddæus. And hearing his teaching, many <u>believed</u>, and were <u>baptized</u>, confessing their <u>sins</u>.

Having therefore remained with them for five years, he built a church; and having appointed as <u>bishop</u> one of his <u>disciples</u>, and <u>presbyters</u>, and <u>deacons</u>, and <u>prayed</u> for them, he went away, going round the cities of <u>Syria</u>, and teaching, and healing all the sick; whence he brought many cities and countries to Christ through His teaching. Teaching, therefore, and evangelizing along with the <u>disciples</u>, and healing the sick, he went to Berytus, a city of <u>Phœnicia</u> by the sea; and there, having taught and enlightened many, he fell asleep on the twenty-first of the month of August. And the <u>disciples</u> having come together, buried him with great <u>honour</u>; and many sick were healed, and they gave <u>glory</u> to the <u>Father</u>, and the <u>Son</u>, and the <u>Holy Spirit</u>, for ever and ever. <u>Amen</u>.

Book 137. The Acts of Matthew

About that time Matthew, the <u>holy</u> apostle and <u>evangelist</u> of <u>Christ</u>, was abiding in the mountain resting, and <u>praying</u> in his tunic and apostolic robes without sandals; and, behold, Jesus came to Matthew in the likeness of the infants who sing in paradise, and said to him: Peace to you, Matthew! And Matthew having gazed upon Him, and not <u>known</u> who He was, said: Grace to you, and peace, O child highly favoured! And why have you come hither to me, having left those who sing in paradise, and the delights there? Because here the place is desert; and what sort of a table I shall lay for you, O child, I <u>know</u> not, because I have no bread nor oil in a jar. Moreover, even the winds are at rest, so as not to cast down from the trees to the ground anything for food; because, for the accomplishing of my fast of forty days, I, partaking only of the fruits falling by the movement of the winds, am glorifying my Jesus. Now, therefore, what shall I bring you, beautiful boy? There is not even water near, that I may wash your feet.

And the child said: Why do you say, O Matthew? Understand and <u>know</u> that good discourse is better than a calf, and words of meekness better than every herb of the field, and a sweet saying as the perfume of <u>love</u>, and cheerfulness of countenance better than feeding, and a pleasant look is as the appearance of sweetness. Understand, Matthew, and <u>know</u> that I am paradise, that I am the comforter, I am the power of the powers above, I the strength of those that restrain themselves, I the crown of the <u>virgins</u>, I the self-control of the once married, I the boast of the widowed, I the defense of the infants, I the foundation of the <u>Church</u>, I the kingdom of the <u>bishops</u>, I the <u>glory</u> of the <u>presbyters</u>, I the praise of the <u>deacons</u>. Be a <u>man</u>, and be strong, Matthew, in, these words.

And Matthew said: The sight of you hast altogether delighted me, O child; moreover also, your words are full of life. For assuredly your face shines more than the lightning, and your words are altogether most sweet. And that indeed I saw you in paradise when you sang with the other infants who were killed in <u>Bethlehem</u>, I <u>know</u> right well; but how you have suddenly come hither, this altogether astonishes me. But I shall ask you one thing, O child: that impious <u>Herod</u>, where is he? The child says to him: Since you have asked, hear his dwelling-place. He dwells, indeed, in Hades; and there has been prepared for him fire unquenchable, Gehenna without end, bubbling mire, worm that sleeps not, because he cut off three thousand <u>infants</u>, wishing to slay the child Jesus, the ancient of the ages; but of all these ages I am father. Now therefore, O Matthew, take this rod of mine, and go down from the mountain, and go into Myrna, the city of the man-eaters, and plant it by the gate of the church which you and Andrew founded; and as soon as you have planted it, it shall be a tree, great and lofty and with many branches, and its branches shall extend to thirty cubits, and of each single branch the fruit shall be different both to the sight and the eating, <u>Revelation 22:2</u> and from the top of the tree shall flow down much honey; and from its root there shall come forth a great fountain, giving drink to this country round about, and in it creatures that swim and creep; and in it the man-eaters shall wash themselves, and eat of the fruit of the trees of the vine and of the honey; and their bodies shall be changed, and their forms shall be altered so as to be like those of other men; and they shall be ashamed of the nakedness of their body, and they shall put on clothing of the rams of the sheep, and they shall no longer eat unclean things; and there shall be to them fire in superabundance, preparing the <u>sacrifices</u> for offerings, and they shall bake their bread with fire; and they shall see each other in the likeness of the rest of <u>men</u>, and they shall acknowledge me, and glorify my Father who is in the heavens. Now therefore make haste, Matthew, and go down hence, because the departure from your body through fire is at hand, and the crown of your endurance.

And the child having said this, and given him the rod, was taken up into the heavens. And Matthew went down from the mountain, hastening to the city. And as he was about to enter into the city, there met him Fulvana the wife of the king, and his son Fulvanus and his wife Erva, who were possessed by an unclean spirit, and cried out shouting: Who has brought you here again, Matthew? Or who has given you the rod for our destruction? For we see also the child Jesus, the <u>Son of God</u>, who is with you. Do not go then, O Matthew, to plant the rod for the food, and for the transformation of the man-eaters: for I have found what I shall do to you. For since you drove me out of this city, and prevent me from fulfilling my wishes among the man-eaters, behold, I will raise up against you the king of this city, and he will burn you alive. And Matthew, having laid his hands on each one of the <u>demoniacs</u>, put the <u>demons</u> to flight, and made the people whole; and they followed him.

And thus the affair being made manifest, <u>Plato</u> the bishop, having heard of the presence of the <u>holy</u> Apostle Matthew, met him with all the <u>clergy</u>; and having fallen to the ground, they kissed his feet. And Matthew raised them, and went with them into the church, and the child Jesus was also with him. And Matthew, having come to the gate of the church, stood upon a certain lofty and immoveable stone; and when the whole city ran together, especially the brethren who had <u>believed</u>, began to say: Men and <u>women</u> who appear in our sight, heretofore believing in the <u>universe</u>, but now <u>knowing</u> Him who has upheld and made the <u>universe</u>; until now worshipping the Satyr, and mocked by ten thousand false gods, but now through <u>Jesus Christ</u> acknowledging the one and only <u>God</u>, Lord, Judge; who have laid aside the immeasurable greatness of <u>evil</u>, and put on <u>love</u>, which is of like nature with affectionateness, towards men; once strangers to <u>Christ</u>, but now confessing Him Lord and <u>God</u>; formerly without <u>form</u>, but now transformed through Christ;— behold, the staff which you see in my hand, which Jesus, in whom you have <u>believed</u> and will <u>believe</u>, gave me; perceive now what comes to pass through me, and acknowledge the riches of the greatness which He will this day make for you. For, behold, I shall plant this rod in this place, and it shall be a sign to your generations, and it shall become a tree, great and lofty and flourishing, and its fruit beautiful to the view and good to the sight; and the fragrance of perfumes shall come forth from it, and there shall be a vine twining round it, full of clusters; and from the top of it honey coming down, and every flying creature shall find covert in its branches; and a fountain of water shall come forth from the root of it, having swimming and creeping things, giving drink to all the country round about.

And having said this, and called upon the name of the <u>Lord Jesus</u>, he fixed his rod in the ground, and straightway it sprung up to one cubit; and the sight was strange and wonderful. For the rod having straightway shot up, increased in size, and grew into a great tree, as Matthew had said. And the apostle said: Go into the fountain and wash your bodies in it, and then thus partake both of the fruits of the tree, and of the vine and the honey, and drink of the fountain, and you shall be transformed in your likeness to that of men; and after that, having gone into the church, you will clearly recognise that you have <u>believed</u> in the living and <u>true</u> God. And having done all these things, they saw themselves changed into the likeness of Matthew; then, having thus gone into the church, they worshipped and <u>glorified</u> God. And when they had been changed, they <u>knew</u> that they were naked; and they ran in haste each to his own house to cover their nakedness, because they were ashamed.

And Matthew and Plato remained in the church spending the night, and glorifying God. And there remained also the king's wife, and his son and his wife, and they prayed the apostle to give them the seal in Christ. And Matthew gave orders to Plato; and he, having gone forth, baptized them in the water of the fountain of the tree, in the name of the Father, and the Son, and the Holy Ghost. And so thereafter, having gone into the church, they communicated in the holy mysteries of Christ; and they exulted and passed the night, they also along with the apostle, many others having also come with them; and all in the church sang the whole night, glorifying God.

And when the dawn had fully come, the blessed Matthew, having gone along with the bishop Plato, stood in the place in which the rod had been planted, and he sees the rod grown into a great tree, and near it a vine twined round it, and honey coming down from above even to its root; and that tree was at once beautiful and flourishing, like the plants in paradise, and a river proceeded from its root watering all the land of the city of Myrna. And all ran together, and ate of the fruit of the tree and the vine, just as any one wished.

And when what had come to pass was reported in the palace, the king Fulvanus, having learned what had been done by Matthew about his wife, and his son, and his daughter-in-law, rejoiced for a time at their purification; but seeing that they were inseparable from Matthew, he was seized with rage and anger, and endeavoured to put him to death by fire. And on that night in which the king intended to lay hands on Matthew, Matthew saw Jesus saying to him: I am with you always to save you, Matthew; be strong, and be a man.

And the blessed Matthew, having awoke, and sealed himself over all the body, rose up at dawn, and proceeded into the church; and having bent his knees, prayed earnestly. Then the bishop having come, and the clergy, they stood in common in prayer, glorifying God. And after they had ended the prayer, the bishop Plato said: Peace to you, Matthew, apostle of Christ! And the blessed Matthew said to him: Peace to you! And when they had sat down, the apostle said to the bishop Plato, and to all the clergy: I wish you, children, to know, Jesus having declared it to me, that the king of this city is going to send soldiers against me, the devil having entered into him, and manifestly armed him against us. But let us give ourselves up to Jesus, and He will deliver us from every trial, and all who have believed in Him.

And the king, plotting against the blessed Matthew how he should lay hands on him, and seeing also that the believers were very many, was very much at fault, and was in great difficulty.

Therefore the wicked and unclean devil who had come forth from the king's wife, and his son, and his daughter-in-law, put to flight by Matthew, having transformed himself into the likeness of a soldier, stood before the king, and said to him: O king, why are you thus put to the worse by this stranger and sorcerer? Do you not know that he was a publican, but now he has been called an apostle by Jesus, who was crucified by the Jews? For, behold, your wife, and your son, and your daughter-in-law, instructed by him, have believed in him, and along with him sing in the church. And now, behold, Matthew is going forth, and Plato with him, and they are going to the gate called Heavy; but make haste, and you will find them, and you shall do to him all that may be pleasing in your eyes.

The king having heard this, and being the more exasperated by the pretended soldier, sent against the blessed Matthew four soldiers, having threatened them, and said: Unless you bring Matthew to me, I shall burn you alive with fire; and the punishment which he is to undergo, you shall endure. And the soldiers, having been thus threatened by the king, go in arms to where the Apostle Matthew and the bishop Plato are. And when they came near them, they heard their speaking indeed, but saw no one. And having come, they said to the king: We pray you, O king, we went and found no one, but only heard the voices of persons talking. And the king, being enraged, and having blazed up like fire, gave orders to send other ten soldiers — man-eaters — saying to them: Go stealthily to the place, and tear them in pieces alive, and eat up Matthew, and Plato, who is with him. And when they were about to come near the blessed Matthew, the Lord Jesus Christ, having come in the likeness of a most beautiful boy, holding a torch of fire, ran to meet them, burning out their eyes. And they, having cried out and thrown their arms from them, fled, and came to the king, being speechless.

And the demon who had before appeared to the king in the form of a soldier, being again transformed into the form of a soldier, stood before the king, and said to him: You see, O king, this stranger has bewitched them all. Learn, then, how you shall take him. The king says to him: Tell me first wherein his strength is, that I may know, and then I will draw up against him with a great force. And the demon, compelled by an angel, says to the king: Since you wish to hear accurately about him, O king, I will tell you all the truth. Really, unless he shall be willing to be taken by you of his own accord, you labour in vain, and you will not be able to hurt him; but if you wish to lay hands on him, you will be struck by him with blindness, and you will be paralyzed. And if you send a multitude of soldiers against him, they also will be struck with blindness, and will be paralyzed. And we shall go, even seven unclean demons, and immediate-

ly make away with you and your whole camp, and destroy all the city with lightning, except those naming that awful and holy name of Christ; for wherever a footstep of theirs has come, thence, pursued, we flee. And even if you shall apply fire to him, to him the fire will be dew; and if you shall shut him up in a furnace, to him the furnace will be a church; and if you shall put him in chains in prison, and seal up the floors, the doors will open to him of their own accord, and all who believe in that name will go in, even they, and say, This prison is a church of the living God, and a holy habitation of those that live alone. Behold, O king, I have told you all the truth. The king therefore says to the pretended soldier: Since I do not know Matthew, come with me, and point him out to me from a distance, and take from me gold, as much as you may wish, or go yourself, and with your sword kill him, and Plato his associate. The demon says to him: I cannot kill him. I dare not even look into his face, seeing that he has destroyed all our generation through the name of Christ, proclaimed through him.

The king says to him: And who are you? And he says: I am the demon who dwelt in your wife, and in your son, and in your daughter-in-law; and my name is Asmodæus; and this Matthew drove me out of them. And now, behold, your wife, and your son, and your daughter-in-law sing along with him in the church. And I know, O king, that you also after this will believe in him. The king says to him: Whoever you are, spirit of many shapes, I adjure you by the God whom he whom you call Matthew proclaims, depart hence without doing hurt to any one. And straightway the demon, no longer like a soldier, but like smoke, became invisible; and as he fled he cried out: O secret name, armed against us, I pray you, Matthew, servant of the holy God, pardon me, and I will no longer remain in this city. Keep your own; but I go away into the fire everlasting.

Then the king, affected with great fear at the answer of the demon, remained quiet that day. And the night having come, and he not being able to sleep because he was hungry, leaped up at dawn, and went into the church, with only two soldiers without arms, to take Matthew by craft, that he might kill him. And having summoned two friends of Matthew, he said to them: Show to Matthew, says he, that I wish to be his disciple. And Matthew hearing, and knowing the craft of the tyrant, and having been warned also by the vision of the Lord to him, went forth out of the church, led by the hand by Plato, and stood in the gate of the church.

And they say to the king: Behold Matthew in the gate! And he says: Who he is, or where he is, I see not. And they said to him: Behold, he is in sight of you. And he says: All the while I see nobody. For he had been blinded by the power of God. And he began to cry out: Woe to me, miserable! What evil has come upon me, for my eyes have been blinded, and all my limbs paralyzed? O Asmodæus Beelzebul Satan! All that you have said to me has come upon me. But I pray you, Matthew, servant of God, forgive me as the herald of the good God; for assuredly the Jesus proclaimed by you three days ago through the night appeared to me altogether resplendent as with lightning, like a beautiful young man, and said to me, Since you are entertaining evil counsels in the wickedness of your heart in regard to my servant Matthew, know I have disclosed to him that through you will be the release of his body. And straightway I saw him going up into heaven. If therefore he is your God, and if he wishes your body to be buried in our city for a testimony of the salvation of the generations after this, and for the banishing of the demons, I shall know the truth for myself by this, by you laying on hands upon me, and I shall receive my sight. And the apostle having laid his hands upon his eyes, and saying Ephphatha, Jesus, he made him receive his sight instantly.

And straightway the king, laying hold of the apostle, and leading him by the right hand, brought him by craft into the palace; and Plato was on Matthew's left hand, going along with him, and keeping hold of him. Then Matthew says: O crafty tyrant, how long do you not fulfil the works of your father the devil? And he was enraged at what had been said; for he perceived that he would inflict upon him a more bitter death. For he resolved to put him to death by fire. And he commanded several executioners to come, and to lead him away to the place by the seashore, where the execution of malefactors was wont to take place, saying to the executioners: I hear, says he, that the God whom he proclaims delivers from fire those who believe in him. Having laid him, therefore, on the ground on his back, and stretched him out, pierce his hands and feet with iron nails, and cover him over with paper, having smeared it with dolphins' oil, and cover him up with brimstone and asphalt and pitch, and put tow and brushwood above. Thus apply the fire to him; and if any of the same tribe with him rise up against you, he shall get the same punishment.

And the apostle exhorted the brethren to remain undismayed, and that they should rejoice, and accompany him with great meekness, singing and praising God, because they were deemed worthy to have the relics of the apostle. Having therefore come to the place, the executioners, like most evil wild beasts, pinned down to the ground Matthew's hands and feet with long nails; and having done everything as they had been bid, applied the fire. And they indeed laboured closely, kindling it all round; but all the fire was changed into dew, so that the brethren, rejoicing, cried out: The only God is the Christians', who assists Matthew, in whom also we have believed: the only God is the Christians', who preserves His own apostle in the fire. And by the voice the city was shaken. And some of the executioners, having gone forth, said to the king: We indeed, O king, by every contrivance of vengeance, have kindled the fire; but the sorcerer by a certain name puts it out, calling upon Christ, and invoking his cross; and the Christians surrounding him play with the fire, and walking *in it* with naked feet, laugh at us, and we have fled ashamed.

Then he ordered a multitude to carry coals of fire from the furnace of the bath in the palace, and the twelve gods of gold and silver; and place them, says he, in a circle round the sorcerer, lest he may even somehow bewitch the fire from the furnace of the palace. And there being many executioners and soldiers, some carried the coals; and others, bearing the gods, brought them. And the king accompanied them, watching lest any of the Christians should steal one of his gods, or bewitch the fire. And when they came near the place where the apostle was nailed down, his face was looking towards heaven, and all his body was covered over with the paper, and much brushwood over his body to the height of ten cubits. And having ordered the soldiers to set the gods in a circle round Matthew, five cubits off, securely fastened that they might not fall, again he ordered the coal to be thrown on, and to kindle the fire at all points.

And Matthew, having looked up to heaven, cried out, Adonai *eloi sabaoth marmari marmunth*; that is, O God the Father, O Lord Jesus Christ, deliver me, and burn down their gods which they worship; and let the fire also pursue the king even to his palace, but not to his destruction: for perhaps he will repent and be converted. And when he saw the fire to be monstrous in height, the king, thinking that Matthew was burnt up, laughed aloud, and said: Has your magic been of any avail to you, Matthew? Can your Jesus now give you any help?

And as he said this a dreadful wonder appeared; for all the fire along with the wood went away from Matthew, and was poured round about their gods, so that nothing of the gold or the silver was any more seen; and the king fled, and said: Woe's me, that my gods are destroyed by the rebuke of Matthew, of which the weight was a thousand talents of gold and a thousand talents of silver. Better are the gods of stone and of earthenware, in that they are neither melted nor stolen.

And when the fire had thus utterly destroyed their gods, and burnt up many soldiers, there came to pass again another stranger wonder. For the fire, in the likeness of a great and dreadful dragon, chased the tyrant as far as the palace, and ran here and there round the king, not letting him go into the palace. And the king, chased by the fire, and not allowed to go into his palace, turned back to where Matthew was, and cried out, saying: I beseech you, whoever you are, O man, whether magician or sorcerer or god, or angel of God, whom so great a pyre has not touched, remove from me this dreadful and fiery dragon; forget the evil I have done, as also when you made me receive my sight. And Matthew, having rebuked the fire, and the flames having been extinguished, and the dragon having become invisible, stretching his eyes to heaven, and praying in Hebrew, and commending his spirit to the Lord, said: Peace to you! And having glorified the Lord, he went to his rest about the sixth hour.

Then the king, having ordered more soldiers to come, and the bed to be brought from the palace, which had a great show of gold, he ordered the apostle to be laid on it, and carried to the palace. And the body of the apostle was lying as if in sleep, and his robe and his tunic unstained by the fire; and sometimes they saw him on the bed, and sometimes following, and sometimes going before the bed, and with his right hand put upon Plato's head, and singing along with the multitude, so that both the king and the soldiers, with the crowd, were struck with astonishment. And many diseased persons and demoniacs, having only touched the bed, were made sound; and as many as were savage in appearance, in that same hour were changed into the likeness of other men.

And as the bed was going into the palace, we all saw Matthew rising up, as it were, from the bed, and going into heaven, led by the hand by a beautiful boy; and twelve men in shining garments came to meet him, having never-fading and golden crowns on their head; and we saw how that child crowned Matthew, so as to be like them, and in a flash of lightning they went away to heaven.

And the king stood at the gate of the palace, and ordered that no one should come in but the soldiers carrying the bed. And having shut the doors, he ordered an iron coffin to be made, put the body of Matthew into it, and sealed it up with lead; through the eastern gate of the palace at midnight put it into a boat, no one knowing of it, and threw it into the deep part of the sea.

And through the whole night the brethren remained before the gate of the palace, spending the night, and singing; and when the dawn rose there was a voice: O bishop Plato, carry the Gospel and the Psalter of David; go along with the multitude of the brethren to the east of the palace, and sing the Alleluia, and read the Gospel, and bring as an offering the holy bread; and having pressed three clusters from the vine into a cup, communicate with me, as the Lord Jesus showed us how to offer up when He rose from the dead on the third day.

And the bishop having run into the church, and taken the Gospel and the Psalter of David, and having assembled the presbyters and the multitude of the brethren, came to the east of the palace at the hour of sunrise; and

having ordered the one who was singing to go upon a certain lofty stone, he began to praise in singing of a song to God: Precious in the sight of God is the death of His saints. And again: I laid me down and slept; I arose: because the Lord will sustain me. And they listened to the singing of a song of David: Shall he that is dead not rise again? Now I shall raise him up for myself, says the Lord. And all shouted out the Alleluia. And the bishop read the Gospel, and all cried out: Glory to You, You who has been glorified in heaven and on earth. And so then they offered the gift of the holy offering for Matthew; and having partaken for thanksgiving of the undefiled and life-giving mysteries of Christ, they all glorified God.

And it was about the sixth hour, and Plato sees the sea opposite about seven furlongs off; and, behold, Matthew was standing on the sea, and two men, one on each side, in shining garments, and the beautiful boy in front of them. And all the brethren saw these things, and they heard them saying Amen, Alleluia. And one could see the sea fixed like a stone of crystal, and the beautiful boy in front of them, when out of the depth of the sea a cross came up, and at the end of the cross the coffin going up in which was the body of Matthew; and in the hour of the piercing on the cross, the boy placed the coffin on the ground, behind the palace towards the east, where the bishop had offered the offering for Matthew.

And the king having seen these things from the upper part of the house, and being terror-struck, went forth from the palace, and ran and worshipped towards the east at the coffin, and fell down before the bishop, and the presbyters, and the deacons, in repentance and confession, saying: Truly I believe in the true God, Christ Jesus. I entreat, give me the seal in Christ, and I will give you my palace, in testimony of Matthew, and you shall put the coffin upon my golden bed, in the great dining-room; only, having baptized me in it, communicate to me the Eucharist of Christ. And the bishop having prayed, and ordered him to take off his clothes, and having examined him for a long time, and he having confessed and wept over what he had done, having sealed him, and anointed him with oil, put him down into the sea, in the name of Father, and Son, and Holy Ghost. And when he came up from the water he ordered him to put on himself splendid garments, and so then having given praise and thanks, communicating the holy bread and mixed cup, the bishop first gave them to the king, saying: Let this body of Christ, and this cup, His blood shed for us, be to you for the remission of sins unto life. And a voice was heard from on high: Amen, amen, amen. And when he had thus communicated in fear and joy, the apostle appeared and said: King Fulvanus, your name shall no longer be Fulvanus; but you shall be called Matthew. And you, the son of the king, shall no longer be called Fulvanus, but Matthew also; and you Ziphagia, the wife of the king, shall be called Sophia; and Erva, the wife of your son, shall be called Synesis. And these names of yours shall be written in the heavens, and there shall not fail of your loins from generation to generation. And in that same hour Matthew appointed the king a presbyter, and he was thirty-seven years old; and the king's son he appointed deacon, being seventeen years old; and the king's wife he appointed a presbyteress; and his son's wife he appointed a deaconess, and she also was seventeen years old. And then he thus blessed them, saying: The blessing and the grace of our Lord Jesus Christ shall be with you to time everlasting.

Then the king, having awakened out of sleep, and rejoiced with all his house at the vision of the holy Apostle Matthew, praised God.

And the king, having gone into his palace, broke all the idols to pieces, and gave a decree to those in his kingdom, writing thus: King Matthew, to all those under my kingdom, greeting. Christ having appeared upon earth, and having saved the human race, the so-called gods have been found to be deceivers, and soul-destroyers, and plotters against the human race. Whence, divine grace having shone abroad, and come even to us, and we having come to the knowledge of the deception of the idols, that it is vain and false, it has seemed good to our divinity that there should not be many gods, but one, and one only, the God in the heavens. And you, having received this our decree, keep to the purport of it, and break to pieces and destroy every idol; and if any one shall be detected from this time forth serving idols, or concealing them, let such an one be subjected to punishment by the sword. Farewell all, because we also are well.

And when this order was given out, all, rejoicing and exulting, broke their idols to pieces, crying out and saying: There is one only God, He who is in the heavens, who does good to men.

And after all these things had come to pass, Matthew the apostle of Christ appeared to the bishop Plato, and said to him: Plato, servant of God, and our brother, be it known unto you, that after three years shall be your rest in the Lord, and exultation to ages of ages. And the king himself, whom after my own name I have called Matthew, shall receive the throne of your bishopric, and after him his son. And he, having said Peace to you and all the saints, went to heaven.

And after three years the bishop Plato rested in the Lord. And King Matthew succeeded him, having given up his kingdom willingly to another, whence there was given him grace against unclean demons, and he cured every affliction. And he advanced his son to be a presbyter, and made him second to himself.

And Saint Matthew finished his course in the country of the man-eaters, in the city of Myrna, on the sixteenth of the month of November, our Lord Jesus Christ reigning, to whom be glory and strength, now and ever, and to ages of ages. Amen.

Book 138. The Gospel of the Nazarenes (Selection)

To these (citations in which Matthew follows not the Septuagint but the Hebrew original text) belong the two: "Out of Egypt have I called my son" and "For he shall be called a Nazaraean."
(Jerome, *De viris inlustribus* 3)

Behold, the moter of the Lord and his brethren said to him: John the Baptist baptizes unto the remission of sins, let us go and be baptized by him. But he said to them: Wherein have I sinned that I should go and be baptized by him? Unless what I have said is ignorance (a sin of ignorance).
(Jerome, *Adversus Pelagianos* 3.2)

The Jewish Gospel has not "into the holy city" but "to Jerusalem."
(Variant to Matthew 4:5 in the "Zion Gospel" Edition)

The phrase "without a cause" is lacking in some witnesses and in the Jewish Gospel.
(Variant to Matthew 5:22, ibid.)

In the so-called Gospel according to the Hebrews instead of "essential to existence" I found "*mahar*," which means "of tomorrow," so that the sense is: "Our bread of tomorrow" - that is, of the future - "give us this day."
(Jerome, *Commentary on Matthew* 1 [on Matthew 6:11])

The Jewish Gospel reads here as follows: "If ye be in my bosom and do not the will of my Father in heaven, I will cast you out of my bosom."
(Variant to Matthew 7:5 - or better to Matthew 7:21-23 - in the "Zion Gospel" Edition)

The Jewish Gospel: (wise) more than serpents.
(Variant to Matthew 10:16, ibid.)

The Jewish Gospel has: (the kingdom of heaven) is plundered.
(Variant to Matthew 11:12, ibid.)

The Jewish Gospel has: I thank thee.
(Variant to Matthew 11:25, ibid.)

In the Gospel which the Nazarenes and the Ebionites use, which we have recently translated out of Hebrew into Greek, and which is called by most people the authentic (Gospel) of Matthew, the man who had the withered hand is described as a mason who pleaded for help in the following words: "I was a mason and earned (my) livelihood with (my) hands; I beseech thee, Jesus, to restore me to my health that I may not with ignominy have to beg for my bread."
(Jerome, *Commentary on Matthew* 2 [on Matthew 12:13])

The Jewish Gospel does not have: three d(ays and nights).
(Variant to Matthew 12:40 in the "Zion Gospel" Edition)

The Jewish Gospel: corban is what you should obtain from us.
(Variant to Matthew 15:5, ibid.)

What is marked with an asterisk (i.e., Matthew 16:2-3) is not found in other manuscripts, also it is not found in the Jewish Gospel.
(Variant to Matthew 16:2-3, ibid.)

The Jewish Gospel: son of John.
(Variant to Matthew 16:17, ibid.)

He (Jesus) said: If thy brother has sinned with a word and has made three reparations, receive him seven times in a day. Simon his disciple said to him: Seven times in a day? The Lord answered and said to him: Yea, I say unto thee, until seventy times seven times. For in the prophets also after they were anointed with the Holy Spirit, the ord of sin (sinful discourse?) was found.
(Jerome, *Adversus Pelagianos* 3.2)

The Jewish Gospel has after "seventy times seven times": For in the prophets also, after they were anointed with the Holy Spirit, the ord of sin (sinful discourse?) was found.
(Variant to Matthew 18:22 in the "Zion Gospel" Edition)

The other of the two rich men said to him: Master, what good thing must I do that I may live? He said to him: Man, fulfil the law and the prophets. He answered him: That have I done. He said to him: Go and sell all that thou possessest and distribute it among the poor, and then come and follow me. But hte rich man then began to scratch his head and it (the saying) pleased him not. And the Lord said to him: How canst though say, I have fulfilled the law and the prophets? For it stands written in the law: Love thy neighbor as thyself; and behold, many of the brethren, sons of Abraham, are begrimed with dirt and die of hunger - and thy house is full of many good things and nothing at all comes forth from it to them! And he turned and said to Simon, his disciple, who was sitting by him: Simon, son of Jona, it is easier for a camel to go through the eye of a needle than for a rich man to enter into the kingdom of heaven.
(Origen, *Commentary on Matthew* 15.14 [on Matthew 19:16-30])

In the Gospel which the Nazarenes use, instead of "son of Barachias" we have found written "son of Joiada."
(Jerome, *Commentary on Matthew* 4 [on Matthew 23:35])

But since the Gospel (written) in Hebrew characters which has come into our hands enters the threat not against the man who had hid (the talent), but against him who had lived dissolutely - for he (the master) had three servants: one who squandered his master's substance with harlots and flute-girls, one who multiplied the gain, and one who hid the talent; and accordingly one was accepted (with joy), another merely rebuked, and another cast into prison - I wonder whether in Matthew the threat which is uttered after the word against the man who did nothing may not refer to him, but by epanalepsis to the first who had feasted and drunk with the drunken.
(Eusebius, *Theophania* 22 [on Matthew 25:14-15])

The Jewish Gospel: And he denied and swore and damned himself.
(Variant to Matthew 26:74 in the "Zion Gospel" Edition)

Barabbas. . . is interpreted in the so-called Gospel according to the Hebrews as "son of their teacher."
(Jerome, *Commentary on Matthew* 4 [on Matthew 27:16])

But in the Gospel which is written in Hebrew characters we read not that the veil of the temple was rent, but that the lintel of the temple of wondrous size collapsed.
(Jerome, *Epistula ad Hedybiam* 120.8)

The Jewish Gospel: And he delivered to them armed men that they might sit over against the cave and guard it day and night.
(Variant to Matthew 27:65 in the "Zion Gospel" Edition)

He (Christ) himself taught the reason for the separations of souls that take place in houses, as we have found somewhere in the Gospel that is spread abroad among the Jews in the Hebrew tongue, in which it is said: "I choose for myself the most worthy: the most worthy are those whom my Father in heaven has given me."
(Eusebius, *Theophania* 4.12 [on Matthew 10:34-36])

Book 139. The Apocalypse of Baruch (Summary)

An apocryphal work, in which Baruch, the disciple of Jeremiah, gives an account of the revelation which he received in heaven. The existence of this work (which is wholly different from the Syriac Apocalypse of Baruch published by Ceriani in 1866, 1871, 1883, and translated by Charles in 1896; see Baruch, Apocalypse of [Syriac]) was unknown until 1886, when a Slavonic Baruch Apocalypse was published by Stojan Novakovic in the magazine "Starine" (vol. xviii.). But the attention of scholars was first drawn to this work through the German translation of the Slavonic text by N. Bonwetsch ("Nachrichten von der Königlichen Gesellschaft der Wissenschaften zu Göttingen, Philologisch-Historische Klasse," 1896, pp. 94-101); and a year later the world of learning was astonished by M. R. James's publication of the Greek text, until then entirely unknown, in "Texts and Studies: Contributions to Biblical and Patristic Literature," edited by J. Armitage Robinson, v., No. i., pp. 84-94, Cambridge, 1897. The Slavonic text is an abbreviated form of the Greek, sometimes merely an abstract of it. Consequently, the Greek text must be considered as the basis of the other, though the Slavonic text seems in some places to have preserved the correct reading.

Baruch Ascends to First Heaven.

The contents of the Apocalypse are as follows:Baruch, bewailing and lamenting the fall of Jerusalem, is addressed by an angel of God sent to reveal great mysteries to him (ch. i). He goes with the angel, and after crossing a stream at the place where heaven is fastened (not the ocean, but the "mayim ha'elyonim" [upper waters]; Gen. R. iv. 3; Hag. 15a; compare Abraham, Testament of), they reach the first heaven. The angel tells Baruch that the heaven's thickness equals the distance from heaven to earth, or the distance from east to west (thus the Slavonic text: the Greek reads "from north to south"; Tamid 32a; Hag. 13a). Baruch sees men in animal form, who, as the angel explains, "are they who built the tower, and God has transformed them" (ii.). This means that the builders of the tower ("dor haflagah") were transformed into demons (Sanh. 109a, שדים ולילין). For this reason they are not in the place of torment, which is in the third heaven, but at the entrance to heaven (Hag. 16a; compare Demonology).

The Third Heaven.

The third chapter gives the reason for the punishment inflicted on the tower-builders. They were so inhuman that they would not let a woman who helped with the building leave her work during travail. A similar rabbinical legend about a Jewish woman in Egypt (Pirḳe R. El. xlviii.; compare "Sefer ha-Yashar, Shemot," ed. Leghorn, p. 113b) is probably the original of this. The fourth chapter, describing the third heaven, seems to have been badly mutilated in the Greek text; the Slavonic version must therefore be followed. Baruch sees a dragon as long as the distance from east to west. It drinks an ell from the sea daily; because three hundred and sixty rivers constantly empty into the sea, and would cause it to overflow, so that there would be nothing left dry on earth. The inside of the dragon is as large as the belly of Hades. The Greek text adds that it is this dragon which eats the bodies of those that have spent their lives in evil. The dragon seems to be identified with Hades in other respects also; and the representations of the dragon (the Leviathan) and Hades are confused.

There is no connection between this part of the chapter and the section immediately following, in which Baruch asks which tree seduced Adam, and the angel answers that it was the vine planted by Samael (this view is widely spread in the apocalyptic and rabbinical literature; compare Ginzberg, "Die Haggada bei den Kirchenvätern," pp. 38-41). In this connection, too, it is stated that the Deluge washed the vine bodily out of the Garden of Eden; whereupon Noah took possession of it and planted it (Ginzberg, *l.c.* p. 40). In its present form the section on the vine is a Christian interpolation intended to reconcile the harmfulness of wine with its use in the communion service. In this way the original legend on the planting of the vine by Noah and the arch-fiend becomes radically changed. See Asmodeus.

Celestial Phenomena.

Chapters vi. to ix., treating of the sun, moon, and stars, are the most interesting part of the work. The sun is represented as a man with a crown of fire, sitting on a chariot. This is probably derived from the Greek conception, but found also elsewhere in rabbinical literature, as in Slavonic B. of Enoch; Pirḳe R. El. vi.; Num. R. xii. 4. The phenix attends the sun in its course as guard; catching on its wings the rays, in order to keep them from scorching everything, At daybreak the rustling of the phenix awakens the cocks on earth, who then give the signal of dawn in their peculiar utterance (compare Targ. on Job xxxviii. 36). The Zohar (iii. 22*b*, 23*a*, 49*b*) also tells of a heavenly wind, or some other celestial manifestation, which causes the crowing of the cocks; even the Talmud knows the blessing אשר נתן לשכוי בינה ברוך ("blessed be He who has given the cock intelligence [to distinguish between day and night]," Ber. 60*b*). As in the rabbinical sources (Pirḳe R. El. vi.; Yalḳ., Eccl. 967), the angels draw the sun's chariot (ch. vii., viii.), and at night four angels remove the sun's crown (according to Pirḳe R. El. *l.c.*, the sun is attended by different angels by night and by day; and since, according to Yalḳ. *l.c.*, there are eight in all, the number in the Baruch Apocalypse tallies with that in rabbinical literature). They remove the crown in order to cleanse it of the impurities with which it becomes spotted through the sins of man on earth (Test. Patr., Levi, 3; Eliyahu R. ii.); and for this reason it is renewed every day (compare the words in the morning service בראשית מחדש בכל יום תמיד מעשה., "who reneweth every day the work of creation"). The conception of the moon is also Greek. It is represented as a woman sitting on a chariot drawn by oxen and lambs. It was once as large as the sun and even more beautiful; but at Adam's fall it did not display the proper compassion, and it was therefore made to wax and wane. This agrees only in part with the Haggadah variously given in the Talmud and Midrash, that the moon suffered this decrease in its size through its pride and guilt (Shebuot 9*a*; Ḥul. 60*b*; Gen. R. vi. 3).

The Fourth and Fifth Heavens.

In the fourth heaven Baruch first sees in a wide plain a pond about which are large numbers of birds. The angel explains that this is the place to which the souls of the righteous go in order that they may live together in choirs. The idea that the souls of the righteous are transformed into birds frequently occurs in the Cabala (compare "Tiḳḳune Zohar," ed. Lemberg, vi. 22*b*; see also Sanh. 92*b*); this idea is probably of Egyptian origin. The fourth heaven also contains the water which descends to earth in the form of rain. For although the original source of rain is the sea, it must first ascend to heaven to mingle with the water there in order that it may bring forth fruit, since sea-water is salt. In this way, according to Gen. R. xiii. 10 and Eccl. R. i. 7, the passage at the end of ch. x. is to be explained. In the fifth heaven Baruch meets Michael, prince of the angels and keeper of the celestial keys, who is descending to receive the prayers of men and to carry a report of their virtues to God. The expression "gates of prayer" ("sha'are tefillah") already occurs frequently in the Talmud (Ber. 32*b*) and in the liturgy. Concerning the office here ascribed to Michael, compare Ginzberg, in *l.c.* p. 13.

The conclusion of the Apocalypse (ch. xii.-xvii.) describes the acts of the angels who accompany men on earth (Ḥag. 16*a*) and report in heaven concerningthem. The angels that accompany the righteous hand baskets of flowers to Michael, who gives them to God; but other angels stand downcast and with empty baskets, not daring to draw nigh. These latter are the angels that accompany the evil-doers. They beg Michael to free them from their duties; for they do not wish to gaze any longer upon the sins of man. After Michael has brought the virtues of men to God, he returns and tells the angels what God has communicated to him. He gives the angels of the righteous a reward for the righteous, and bids the other angels inflict punishment of all kinds on the evil-doers. Then the angel that has guided Baruch takes him back to the place whence he started.

Relation to Other Works.

The latest date at which the Apocalypse of Baruch could have been written is determined by the fact that Origen (185-254) made a citation from it ("De Principiis," ii. 3, 6). The question as to the earliest date depends upon the relation of this Baruch Apocalypse to the other works ascribed to the same author, and to the apocryphal and pseudepigraphic literature

in general. It is certain that the Apocalypse was influenced by the (Slavonic) Book of Enoch, a work of about the middle of the first Christian century. It is, however, a question whether the Greek version employed the Syriac Apocalypse of Baruch, since ch. lxxvi. of the latter, in which Baruch receives a promise of cosmic revelations, affords arguments rather against than for such a supposition. The assumption is untenable that the Greek Apocalypse was written to show the actual fulfilment of the promise. The critical point in the Syriac Apocalypse lies in this chapter when Baruch, before leaving earth, obtains a full survey of it in order that he may see what he is leaving and whither he is going. This idea is based upon an opinion held by Akiba b. Joseph (Sifre, Num. 136) and others, that God allowed not only Moses, but other favored pious men to behold before their death the whole world and all the mysteries of nature. Now, if the Greek Apocalypse was complementary to the Syriac, the author of the former would not have failed to join his story of Baruch's passage through heaven to this account of his last act on earth.

The alleged connection of the Apocalypse with other pseudepigraphic works is only vaguely indicated, and proves nothing. The same is true of the linguistic relation which, it is asserted, exists between the Apocalypse and the New Testament. For instance, ἡμέρα τῆς κρίσεως is not taken from the New Testament, since "Yom ha-Din" (the Day of Judgment) is an expression used before Christian times, and occurs more frequently in rabbinical literature than in the New Testament. Only one passage can with certainty be considered a Christian interpolation; and that is the one concerning the vine already referred to as occurring in ch. iv. The interpolation here is very unskilfully made. It interrupts the sequence, and adds entirely foreign elements. There are also other evidences that the Apocalypse has not been preserved in its original form. For example, it is natural to expect descriptions of the sixth and seventh heavens; but these are lacking.

It Betrays Indian Influence.

The following two points show the position of the Apocalypse in relation to other literature of a similar nature: (1) It is perhaps the one Jewish work which undoubtedly betrays Indian influence. The phenix, referred to in this Apocalypse as the companion of the sun, and the wonderful description of it, are probably of Indian origin; for Indian mythology relates much that is similar concerning the bird Garuda, the companion of the sun-god Vishnu ("Mahabharata Adi Parva," xvi.-xxxiv.; compare James, "The Apocalypse of Baruch," "Introduction, pp. lxiii.-lxvi., in "Texts and Studies," *l.c.*).

(2) Michael's office, as described in ch. xi.-xvi., is significant. The resemblance between his functions and those ascribed to Jesus by the early church is striking; and the relation between the two is obvious. It is probably not correct, however, to consider Michael in the Apocalypse as the Logos or Jesus in a Jewish garb. The explanation of the similarity between the two must be sought in the fact that, at the time when Christianity arose, the carrying out of a too transcendental conception of monotheism required, in order that the relation of God to man might be explained, the supposition of some mediator; and no one was better suited for this part than Michael, the prince of the angels. With the advent of Christianity the duties of Michael were ascribed to Jesus or Logos (compare W. Lueken, "Michael," 1898). In view of these facts, it may be assumed as certain that the author of the Apocalypse was not a Pharisee, since the Pharisees opposed decidedly such doubtful angel-lore. He must have been one of the Gnostics, who revered equally the Haggadah, Greek mythology, and Oriental wisdom. To consider the Apocalypse a Jewish Gnostic work would also be in accordance with the date arrived at for its origin; namely, the beginning of the second century, when gnosis was at its height among both Jews and Christians.

Book 140. The Second Epistle of Clement

Chapter 1. We Ought to Think Highly of Christ

Brethren, it is fitting that you should think of Jesus Christ as of God — as the Judge of the living and the dead. And it does not become us to think lightly of our salvation; for if we think little of Him, we shall also hope but to obtain little [from Him]. And those of us who hear carelessly of these things, as if they were of small importance, commit sin, not knowing whence we have been called, and by whom, and to what place, and how much Jesus Christ submitted to suffer for our sakes. What return, then, shall we make to Him, or what fruit that shall be worthy of that which He has given to us? For, indeed, how great are the benefits which we owe to Him! He has graciously given us light; as a Father, He has called us sons; He has saved us when we were ready to perish. What praise, then, shall we give to Him, or what return shall we make for the things which we have received? We were deficient in understanding, worshipping stones and wood, and gold, and silver, and brass, the works of men's hands; and our whole life was nothing else than death. Involved in blindness, and with such darkness before our eyes, we have received sight, and through His will have laid aside that cloud by which we were enveloped. For He had compassion on us, and mercifully saved us, observing the many errors in which we were entangled, as well as the destruction to which we were exposed, and that we had no hope of salvation except it came to us from Him. For He called us when we were not, and willed that out of nothing we should attain a real existence.

Chapter 2. The Church, Formerly Barren, is Now Fruitful

Rejoice, you barren that bearest not; break forth and cry, you that travailest not; for she that is desolate has many more children than she that has an husband. In that He said, Rejoice, you barren that bearest not, He referred to us, for our church was barren before that children were given to her. But when He said, Cry out, you that travailest not, He means this, that we should sincerely offer up our prayers to God, and should not, like women in travail, show signs of weakness. And in that He said, For she that is desolate has many more children than she that has an husband, [He means] that our people seemed to be outcast from God, but now, through believing, have become more numerous than those who are reckoned to possess God. And another Scripture says, I came not to call the righteous, but sinners. This means that those who are perishing must be saved. For it is indeed a great and admirable thing to establish not the things which are standing, but those that are falling. Thus also did Christ desire to save the things which were perishing, Matthew 18:11 and has saved many by coming and calling us when hastening to destruction.

Chapter 3. The Duty of Confessing Christ

Since, then, He has displayed so great mercy towards us, and especially in this respect, that we who are living should not offer sacrifices to gods that are dead, or pay them worship, but should attain through Him to the knowledge of the true Father, whereby shall we show that we do indeed know Him, but by not denying Him through whom this knowledge has been attained? For He himself declares, Whosoever shall confess me before men, him will I confess before my Father. Matthew 10:32 This, then, is our reward if we shall confess Him by whom we have been saved. But in what way shall we confess Him? By doing what He says, and not transgressing His commandments, and by honouring Him not with our lips only, but with all our heart and all our mind. Matthew 22:37 For He says in Isaiah, This people honours me with their lips, but their heart is far from me. Isaiah 29:13

Chapter 4. True Confession of Christ

Let us, then, not only call Him Lord, for that will not save us. For He says, Not every one that says to me, Lord, Lord, shall be saved, but he that works righteousness. Wherefore, brethren, let us confess Him by our works, by loving one another, by not committing adultery, or speaking evil of one another, or cherishing envy; but by being continent, compassionate, and good. We ought also to sympathize with one another, and not be avaricious. By such works let us confess Him, and not by those that are of an opposite kind. And it is not fitting that we should fear men, but rather God. For this reason, if we should do such [wicked] things, the Lord has said, Even though you were gathered together to me in my very bosom, yet if you were not to keep my commandments, I would cast you off, and say unto you, Depart from me; I know you not whence you are, you workers of iniquity.

Chapter 5. This World Should Be Despised

Wherefore, brethren, leaving [willingly] our sojourn in this present world, let us do the will of Him that called us, and not fear to depart out of this world. For the Lord says, You shall be as lambs in the midst of wolves. Matthew 10:16 And Peter answered and said to Him, What, then, if the wolves shall tear in pieces the lambs? Jesus said to Peter, The lambs have no cause after they are dead to fear the wolves; and in like manner, fear not them that kill you, and can do nothing more unto you; but fear Him who, after you are dead, has power over both soul and body to cast them into hell-fire. And consider, brethren, that the sojourning in the flesh in this world is but brief and transient, but the promise of Christ is great and wonderful, even the rest of the kingdom to come, and of life everlasting. By what course of conduct, then, shall we attain these things, but by leading a holy and righteous life, and by deeming these worldly things as not belonging to us, and not fixing our desires upon them? For if we desire to possess them, we fall away from the path of righteousness.

Chapter 6. The Present and Future Worlds are Enemies to Each Other

Now the Lord declares, No servant can serve two masters. If we desire, then, to serve both God and mammon, it will be unprofitable for us. For what will it profit if a man gain the whole world, and lose his own soul? This world and the next are two enemies. The one urges to adultery and corruption, avarice and deceit; the other bids farewell to these things. We cannot, therefore, be the friends of both; and it behooves us, by renouncing the one, to make sure of the other. Let us reckon that it is better to hate the things present, since they are trifling, and transient, and corruptible; and to love those [which are to come,] as being good and incorruptible. For if we do the will of Christ, we shall find rest; otherwise, nothing shall deliver us from eternal punishment, if we disobey His commandments. For thus also says the Scripture in Ezekiel, If Noah, Job, and Daniel should rise up, they should not deliver their children in captivity. Now, if men so eminently righteous are not able by their righteousness to deliver their children, how can we hope to enter into the royal residence of God unless we keep our baptism holy and undefiled? Or who shall be our advocate, unless we be found possessed of works of holiness and righteousness?

Chapter 7. We Must Strive in Order to Be Crowned

Wherefore, then, my brethren, let us struggle with all earnestness, knowing that the contest is [in our case] close at hand, and that many undertake long voyages to strive for a corruptible reward; yet all are not crowned, but those only that have laboured hard and striven gloriously. Let us therefore so strive, that we may all be crowned. Let us run the straight course, even the race that is incorruptible; and let us in great numbers set out for it, and strive that we may be crowned. And should we not all be able to obtain the crown, let us at least come near to it. We must remember that he who strives in the corruptible contest, if he be found acting unfairly, is taken away and scourged, and cast forth from the lists. What then think ye? If one does anything unseemly in the incorruptible contest, what shall he have to bear? For of those who do not preserve the seal [unbroken], [the Scripture] says, Their worm shall not die, and their fire shall not be quenched, and they shall be a spectacle to all flesh. Isaiah 66:24

Chapter 8. The Necessity of Repentance While We are on Earth

As long, therefore, as we are upon earth, let us practise repentance, for we are as clay in the hand of the artificer. For as the potter, if he make a vessel, and it be distorted or broken in his hands, fashions it over again; but if he have before this cast it into the furnace of fire, can no longer find any help for it: so let us also, while we are in this world, repent with our whole heart of the evil deeds we have done in the flesh, that we may be saved by the Lord, while we have yet an opportunity of repentance. For after we have gone out of the world, no further power of confessing or repenting will there belong to us. Wherefore, brethren, by doing the will of the Father, and keeping the flesh holy, and observing the commandments of the Lord, we shall obtain eternal life. For the Lord says in the Gospel, If you have not kept that which was small, who will commit to you the great? For I say unto you, that he that is faithful in that which is least, is faithful also in much. Luke 16:10-12 This, then, is what He means: Keep the flesh holy and the seal undefiled, that you may receive eternal life.

Chapter 9. We Shall Be Judged in the Flesh

And let no one of you say that this very flesh shall not be judged, nor rise again. Consider in what [state] you were saved, in what you received sight, if not while you were in this flesh. We must therefore preserve the flesh as the temple of God. For as you were called in the flesh, you shall also come [to be judged] in the flesh. As Christ the Lord who saved us, though He was first a Spirit became flesh, and thus called us, so shall we also receive the reward in this flesh. Let us therefore love one another, that we may all attain to the kingdom of God. While we have an opportunity of being healed, let us yield ourselves to God that heals us, and give to Him a recompense. Of what sort? Repentance out of a sincere heart; for He knows all things beforehand, and is acquainted with what is in our hearts. Let us therefore give Him praise, not with the mouth only, but also with the heart, that He may accept us as sons. For the Lord has said, Those are my brethren who do the will of my Father. Matthew 12:50

Chapter 10. Vice is to Be Forsaken, and Virtue Followed

Wherefore, my brethren, let us do the will of the Father who called us, that we may live; and let us earnestly follow after virtue, but forsake every wicked tendency which would lead us into transgression; and flee from ungodliness, lest evils overtake us. For if we are diligent in doing good, peace will follow us. On this account, such men cannot find it [i.e. peace] as are influenced by human terrors, and prefer rather present enjoyment to the promise which shall afterwards be fulfilled. For they know not what torment present enjoyment incurs, or what felicity is involved in the future promise. And if, indeed, they themselves only did such things, it would be [the more] tolerable; but now they persist in imbuing innocent souls with their pernicious doctrines, not knowing that they shall receive a double condemnation, both they and those that hear them.

Chapter 11. We Ought to Serve God, Trusting in His Promises

Let us therefore serve God with a pure heart, and we shall be righteous; but if we do not serve Him, because we believe not the promise of God, we shall be miserable. For the prophetic word also declares, Wretched are those of a double mind, and who doubt in their heart, who say, All these things have we heard even in the times of our fathers; but though we have waited day by day, we have seen none of them [accomplished]. You fools! compare yourselves to a tree; take, for instance, the vine. First of all it sheds its leaves, then the bud appears; after that the sour grape, and then the fully-ripened fruit. So, likewise, my people have borne disturbances and afflictions, but afterwards shall they receive their good things. Wherefore, my brethren, let us not be of a double mind, but let us hope and endure, that we also may obtain the reward. For He is faithful who has promised that He will bestow on every one a reward according to his works. If, therefore, we shall do righteousness in the sight of God, we shall enter into His kingdom, and shall receive the promises, which ear has not heard, nor eye seen, neither have entered into the heart of man. 1 Corinthians 2:9

Chapter 12. We are Constantly to Look for the Kingdom of God

Let us expect, therefore, hour by hour, the kingdom of God in love and righteousness, since we know not the day of the appearing of God. For the Lord Himself, being asked by one when His kingdom would come, replied, When two shall be one, that which is without as that which is within, and the male with the female, neither male nor female. Now, two are one when we speak the truth one to another, and there is unfeignedly one soul in two bodies. And that which is without as that which is within means this: He calls the soul that which is within, and the body that which is without. As, then, your body is visible to sight, so also let your soul be manifest by good works. And the male, with the female, neither male nor female, this He says, that brother seeing sister may have no thought concerning her as female, and that she may have no thought concerning him as male. If you do these things, says He, the kingdom of my Father shall come. 1 Corinthians 7:29

Chapter 13. God's Name Not to Be Blasphemed

Brethren, then, let us now at length repent, let us soberly turn to that which is good; for we are full of abundant folly and wickedness. Let us wipe out from us our former sins, and repenting from the heart be saved; and let us not be men-pleasers, nor be willing to please one another only, but also the men without, for righteousness sake, that the name may not be, because of us, blasphemed. For the Lord says, Continually my name is blasphemed among all nations, and Wherefore my name is blasphemed; blasphemed in what? In your not doing the things which I wish. Isaiah 52:5 For the nations, hearing from our mouth the oracles of God, marvel at their excellence and worth; thereafter learning that our deeds are not worthy of the words which we speak — receiving this occasion they turn to blasphemy, saying that they are a fable and a delusion. For, whenever they hear from us that God says, No thank have ye, if you love them which love you, but you have thank, if you love your enemies and them which hate you — whenever they hear these words, they marvel at the surpassing measure of their goodness; but when they see, that not only do we not love those who hate, but that we love not even those who love, they laugh us to scorn, and the name is blasphemed.

Chapter 14. The Church Spiritual

So, then, brethren, if we do the will of our Father God, we shall be members of the first church, the spiritual, — that which was created before sun and moon; but if we shall not do the will of the Lord, we shall come under the Scripture which says, My house became a den of robbers. Jeremiah 7:11 So, then, let us elect to belong to the church of life, that we may be saved. I think not that you are ignorant that the living church is the body of Christ (for the Scripture, says, God created man male and female; Genesis 1:27; cf. Ephesians 5:22-23 the male is Christ, the female the church,) and that the Books and the Apostles teach that the church is not of the present, but from the beginning. For it was spiritual, as was also our Jesus, and was made manifest at the end of the days in order to save you. 1 Peter 1:20 The church being spiritual, was made manifest in the flesh of Christ, signifying to us that if any one of us shall preserve it in the flesh and corrupt it not, he shall receive it in the Holy Spirit. For this flesh is the type of the spirit; no one, therefore, having corrupted the type, will receive afterwards the antitype. Therefore is it, then, that He says, brethren, Preserve the flesh, that you may become partakers of the spirit. If we say that the flesh is the church and the spirit Christ, then it follows that he who shall offer outrage to the flesh is guilty of outrage on the church. Such an one, therefore, will not partake of the spirit, which is Christ. Such is the life and immortality, which this flesh may afterwards receive, the Holy Spirit cleaving to it; and no one can either express or utter what things the Lord has prepared for His elect. 1 Corinthians 2:9

Chapter 15. He Who Saves and He Who is Saved

I think not that I counted trivial counsel concerning continence; following it, a man will not repent thereof, but will save both himself and me who counselled. 1 Timothy 4:16 For it is no small reward to turn back a wandering and perishing soul for its salvation. James 5:19-25 For this recompense we are able to render to the God who created us, if he who speaks and hears both speak and hear with faith and love. Let us, therefore, continue in that course in which we, righteous and holy, believed, that with confidence we may ask God who says, Whilst you are still speaking, I will say, Here I am. Isaiah 58:9 For these words are a token of a great promise, for the Lord says that He is more ready to give than he who asks. So great, then, being the goodness of which we are partakers, let us not grudge one another the attainment of so great blessings. For in proportion to the pleasure with which these words are fraught to those who shall follow them, in that proportion is the condemnation with which they are fraught to those who shall refuse to hear.

Chapter 16. Preparation for the Day of Judgment

So, then, brethren, having received no small occasion to repent, while we have opportunity, let us turn to God who called us, while yet we have One to receive us. For if we renounce these indulgences and conquer the soul by not fulfilling its wicked desires, we shall be partakers of the mercy of Jesus. Know that the day of judgment draws near like a burning oven, and certain of the heavens and all the earth will melt, like lead melting in fire; and then will appear the hidden and manifest deeds of men. Good, then, is alms as repentance from sin; better is fasting than prayer, and alms than both; charity covers a multitude of sins, 1 Peter 4:4 and prayer out of a good conscience delivers from

death. Blessed is every one that shall be found complete in these; for alms lightens the burden of sin.

Chapter 17. Same Subject Continued

Let us, then, repent with our whole heart, that no one of us may perish amiss. For if we have commands and engage in withdrawing from idols and instructing others, how much more ought a soul already knowing God not to perish. Rendering, therefore, mutual help, let us raise the weak also in that which is good, that all of us may be saved and convert one another and admonish. And not only now let us seem to believe and give heed, when we are admonished by the elders; but also when we take our departure home, let us remember the commandments of the Lord, and not be allured back by worldly lusts, but let us often and often draw near and try to make progress in the Lord's commands, that we all having the same mind may be gathered together for life. For the Lord said, I come to gather all nations [kindreds] and tongues. This means the day of His appearing, when He will come and redeem us — each one according to his works. And the unbelievers will see His glory and might, and, when they see the empire of the world in Jesus, they will be surprised, saying, Woe to us, because You were, and we knew not and believed not and obeyed not the elders Isaiah 66:18 who show us plainly of our salvation. And their worm shall not die, neither shall their fire be quenched; and they shall be a spectacle unto all flesh. Isaiah 66:24 It is of the great day of judgment He speaks, when they shall see those among us who were guilty of ungodliness and erred in their estimate of the commands of Jesus Christ. The righteous, having succeeded both in enduring the trials and hating the indulgences of the soul, whenever they witness how those who have swerved and denied Jesus by words or deeds are punished with grievous torments in fire unquenchable, will give glory to their God and say, There will be hope for him who has served God with his whole heart.

Chapter 18. The Author Sinful, Yet Pursuing

And let us, then, be of the number of those who give thanks, who have served God, and not of the ungodly who are judged. For I myself, though a sinner every whit and not yet fleeing temptation but continuing in the midst of the tools of the devil, study to follow after righteousness, that I may make, be it only some, approach to it, fearing the judgment to come.

Chapter 19. Reward of the Righteous, Although They May Suffer

So then, brothers and sisters, after the God of truth I address to you an appeal that you may give heed to the words written, that you may save both yourselves and him who reads an address in your midst. For as a reward I ask of you repentance with the whole heart, while you bestow upon yourselves salvation and life. For by so doing we shall set a mark for all the young who wish to be diligent in godliness and the goodness of God. And let not us, in our folly, feel displeasure and indignation, whenever any one admonishes us and turns us from unrighteousness to righteousness. For there are some wicked deeds which we commit, and know it not, because of the double-mindedness and unbelief present in our breasts, and our understanding is darkened by vain desires. Let us, therefore, work righteousness, that we may be saved to the end. Blessed are they who obey these commandments, even if for a brief space they suffer in this world, and they will gather the imperishable fruit of the resurrection. Let not the godly man, therefore, grieve; if for the present he suffer affliction, blessed is the time that awaits him there; rising up to life again with the fathers he will rejoice for ever without a grief.

Chapter 20. Godliness, Not Gain, the True Riches

But let it not even trouble your mind, that we see the unrighteous possessed of riches and the servants of God straitened. Let us, therefore, brothers and sisters, believe; in a trial of the living God we strive and are exercised in the present life, that we may obtain the crown in that which is to come. No one of the righteous received fruit speedily, but waits for it. For if God tendered the reward of the righteous in a trice, straightway were it commerce that we practised, and not godliness. For it were as if we were righteous by following after not godliness but gain; and for this reason the divine judgment baffled the spirit that is unrighteous and heavily weighed the fetter.

To the only God, invisible, Father of truth, who sent forth to us the Saviour and Author of immortality, through whom He also manifested to us the truth and the heavenly life, to Him be glory for ever and ever. Amen.

Book 141. The Gospel of Perfection

The gospel of truth is joy to those who have received from the Father of truth the gift of knowing him by the power of the Logos, who has come from the Pleroma and who is in the thought and the mind of the Father; he it is who is called "the Savior," since that is the name of the work which he must do for the redemption of those who have not known the Father. For the name of the gospel is the manifestation of hope, since that is the discovery of those who seek him, because the All sought him from whom it had come forth. You see, the All had been inside of him, that illimitable, inconceivable one, who is better than every thought.

This ignorance of the Father brought about terror and fear. And terror became dense like a fog, that no one was able to see. Because of this, error became strong. But it worked on its hylic substance vainly, because it did not know the truth. It was in a fashioned form while it was preparing, in power and in beauty, the equivalent of truth. This then, was not a humiliation for him, that illimitable, inconceivable one. For they were as nothing, this terror and this forgetfulness and this figure of falsehood, whereas this established truth is unchanging, unperturbed and completely beautiful.

For this reason, do not take error too seriously. Thus, since it had no root, it was in a fog as regards the Father, engaged in preparing works and forgetfulnesses and fears in order, by these means, to beguile those of the middle and to make them captive. The forgetfulness of error was not revealed. It did not become light beside the Father. Forgetfulness did not exist with the Father, although it existed because of him. What exists in him is knowledge, which was revealed so that forgetfulness might be destroyed and that they might know the Father, Since forgetfulness existed because they did not know the Father, if they then come to know the Father, from that moment on forgetfulness will cease to exist.

That is the gospel of him whom they seek, which he has revealed to the perfect through the mercies of the Father as the hidden mystery, Jesus the Christ. Through him he enlightened those who were in darkness because of forgetfulness. He enlightened them and gave them a path. And that path is the truth which he taught them. For this reason error was angry with him, so it persecuted him. It was distressed by him, so it made him powerless. He was nailed to a cross. He became a fruit of the knowledge of the Father. He did not, however, destroy them because they ate of it. He rather caused those who ate of it to be joyful because of this discovery.

And as for him, them he found in himself, and him they found in themselves, that illimitable, inconceivable one, that perfect Father who made the all, in whom the All is, and whom the All lacks, since he retained in himself their perfection, which he had not given to the all. The Father was not jealous. What jealousy, indeed, is there between him and his members? For, even if the Aeon had received their perfection, they would not have been able to approach the perfection of the Father, because he retained their perfection in himself, giving it to them as a way to return to him and as a knowledge unique in perfection. He is the one who set the All in order and in whom the All existed and whom the All lacked. As one of whom some have no knowledge, he desires that they know him and that they love him. For what is it that the All lacked, if not the knowledge of the Father?

He became a guide, quiet and in leisure. In the middle of a school he came and spoke the Word, as a teacher. Those who were wise in their own estimation came to put him to the test. But he discredited them as empty-headed people. They hated him because they really were not wise men. After all these came also the little children, those who possess the knowledge of the Father. When they became strong they were taught the aspects of the Father's face. They came to know and they were known. They were glorified and they gave glory. In their heart, the living book of the Living was manifest, the book which was written in the thought and in the mind of the Father and, from before the foundation of the All, is in that incomprehensible part of him.

This is the book which no one found possible to take, since it was reserved for him who will take it and be slain. No one was able to be manifest from those who believed in salvation as long as that book had not appeared. For this reason, the compassionate, faithful Jesus was patient in his sufferings until he took that book, since he knew that his death meant life for many. Just as in the case of a will which has not yet been opened, for the fortune of the deceased master of the house is hidden, so also in the case of the All which had been hidden as long as the Father of the All was invisible and unique in himself, in whom every space has its source. For this reason Jesus appeared. He took that book as his own. He was nailed to a cross. He affixed the edict of the Father to the cross.

Oh, such great teaching! He abases himself even unto death, though he is clothed in eternal life. Having divested himself of these perishable rags, he clothed himself in incorruptibility, which no one could possibly take from him. Having entered into the empty territory of fears, he passed before those who were stripped by forgetfulness, being both knowledge and perfection, proclaiming the things that are in the heart of the Father, so that he became the wisdom of those who have received instruction. But those who are to be taught, the living who are inscribed in the book of the living, learn for themselves, receiving instructions from the Father, turning to him again.

Since the perfection of the All is in the Father, it is necessary for the All to ascend to him. Therefore, if one has knowledge, he gets what belongs to him and draws it to himself. For he who is ignorant, is deficient, and it is a great deficiency, since he lacks that which will make him perfect. Since the perfection of the All is in the Father, it is necessary for the All to ascend to him and for each one to get the things which are his. He registered them first, having prepared them to be given to those who came from him.

Those whose name he knew first were called last, so that the one who has knowledge is he whose name the Father has pronounced. For he whose name has not been spoken is ignorant. Indeed, how shall one hear if his name has not been uttered? For he who remains ignorant until the end is a creature of forgetfulness and will perish with it. If this is not so, why have these wretches no name, why do they have no sound? Hence, if one has knowledge, he is from above. If he is called, he hears, he replies, and he turns toward him who called him and he ascends to him and he knows what he is called. Since he has knowledge, he does the will of him who called him. He desires to please him and he finds rest. He receives a certain name. He who thus is going to have knowledge knows whence he came and whither he is going. He knows it as a person who, having become intoxicated, has turned from his drunkenness and having come to himself, has restored what is his own.

He has turned many from error. He went before them to their own places, from which they departed when they erred because of the depth of him who surrounds every place, whereas there is nothing which surrounds him. It was a great wonder that they were in the Father without knowing him and that they were able to leave on their own, since they were not able to contain him and know him in whom they were, for indeed his will had not come forth from him. For he revealed it as a knowledge with which all its emanations agree, namely, the knowledge of the living book which he revealed to the Aeons at last as his letters, displaying to them that these are not merely vowels nor consonants, so that one may read them and think of something void of meaning; on the contrary, they are letters which convey the truth. They are pronounced only when they are known. Each letter is a perfect truth like a perfect book, for they are letters written by the hand of the unity, since the Father wrote them for the Aeons, so that they by means of his letters might come to know the Father.

While his wisdom mediates on the logos, and since his teaching expresses it, his knowledge has been revealed. His honor is a crown upon it. Since his joy agrees with it, his glory exalted it. It has revealed his image. It has obtained his rest. His love took bodily form around it. His trust embraced it. Thus the logos of the Father goes forth into the All, being the fruit of his heart and expression of his will. It supports the All. It chooses and also takes the form of the All, purifying it, and causing it to return to the Father and to the Mother, Jesus of the utmost sweetness. The Father opens his bosom, but his bosom is the Holy Spirit. He reveals his hidden self which is his son, so that through the compassion of the Father the Aeons may know him, end their wearying search for the Father and rest themselves in him, knowing that this is rest. After he had filled what was incomplete, he did away with form. The form of it is the world, that which it served. For where there is envy and strife, there is an incompleteness; but where there is unity, there is completeness. Since this incompleteness came about because they did not know the Father, so when they know the Father, incompleteness, from that moment on, will cease to exist. As one's ignorance disappears when he gains knowledge, and as darkness disappears when light appears, so also incompleteness is eliminated by completeness. Certainly, from that moment on, form is no longer manifest, but will be dissolved in fusion with unity. For now their works lie scattered. In time unity will make the spaces complete. By means of unity each one will understand itself. By means of knowledge it will purify itself of diversity with a view towards unity, devouring matter within itself like fire and darkness by light, death by life.

Certainly, if these things have happened to each one of us, it is fitting for us, surely, to think about the All so that the house may be holy and silent for unity. Like people who have moved from a neighborhood, if they have some dishes around which are not good, they usually break them. Nevertheless the householder does not suffer a loss, but rejoices, for in the place of these defective dishes there are those which are completely perfect. For this is the judgement which has come from above and which has judged every person, a drawn two-edged sword cutting on this side and that. When it appeared, I mean, the Logos, who is in the heart of those who pronounce it - it was not merely a sound but it has become a body - a great disturbance occurred among the dishes, for some were emptied, others filled: some were provided for, others were removed; some were purified, still others were broken. All the spaces were shaken and disturbed for they had no composure nor stability. Error was disturbed not knowing what it should do. It was troubled; it lamented, it was beside itself because it did not know anything. When knowledge, which is its abolishment, approached it with all its emanations, error is empty, since there is nothing in it. Truth appeared; all its emanations recognized it. They actually greeted the Father with a power which is complete and which joins them with the Father. For each one loves truth because truth is the mouth of the Father. His tongue is the Holy Spirit, who joins him to truth attaching him to the mouth of the Father by his tongue at the time he shall receive the Holy Spirit.

This is the manifestation of the Father and his revelation to his Aeons. He revealed his hidden self and explained it. For who is it who exists if it is not the Father himself? All the spaces are his emanations. They knew that they stem from him as children from a perfect man. They knew that they had not yet received form nor had they yet received a name, every one of which the Father produces. If they at that time receive form of his knowledge, though they are truly in him, they do not know him. But the Father is perfect. He knows every space which is within him. If he pleases, he reveals anyone whom he desires by giving him a form and by giving him a name; and he does give him a name and cause him to come into being. Those who do not yet exist are ignorant of him who created them. I do not say, then, that those who do not yet exist are nothing. But they are in him who will desire that they exist when he pleases, like the event which is going to happen. On the one hand, he knows, before anything is revealed, what he will produce. On the other hand, the fruit which has not yet been revealed does not know anything, nor is it anything either. Thus each space which, on its part, is in the Father comes from the existent one, who, on his part, has established it from the nonexistent. [...] he who does not exist at all, will never exist.

What, then, is that which he wants him to think? "I am like the shadows and phantoms of the night." When morning comes, this one knows that the fear which he had experienced was nothing. Thus they were ignorant of the Father; he is the one whom they did not see. Since there had been fear and confusion and a lack of confidence and doublemindness and division, there were many illusions which were conceived by him, the foregoing, as well as empty ignorance - as if they were fast asleep and found themselves a prey to troubled dreams. Either there is a place to which they flee, or they lack strength as they come, having pursued unspecified things. Either they are involved in inflicting blows, or they themselves receive bruises. Either they are falling from high places, or they fly off through the air, though they have no wings at all. Other times, it is as if certain people were trying to kill them, even though there is no one pursuing them; or, they themselves are killing those beside them, for they are stained by their blood. Until the moment when they who are passing through all these things - I mean they who have experienced all these confusions - awake, they see nothing because the dreams were nothing. It is thus that they who cast ignorance from them as sleep do not consider it to be anything, nor regard its properties to be something real, but they renounce them like a dream in the night and they consider the knowledge of the Father to be the dawn. It is thus that each one has acted, as if he were asleep, during the time when he was ignorant and thus he comes to understand, as if he were awakening. And happy is the man who comes to himself and awakens. Indeed, blessed is he who has opened the eyes of the blind.

And the Spirit came to him in haste when it raised him. Having given its hand to the one lying prone on the ground, it placed him firmly on his feet, for he had not yet stood up. He gave them the means of knowing the knowledge of the Father and the revelation of his son. For when they saw it and listened to it, he permitted them to take a taste of and to smell and to grasp the beloved son.

He appeared, informing them of the Father, the illimitable one. He inspired them with that which is in the mind, while doing his will. Many received the light and turned towards him. But material men were alien to him and did not discern his appearance nor recognize him. For he came in the likeness of flesh and nothing blocked his way because it was incorruptible and unrestrainable. Moreover, while saying new things, speaking about what is in the heart of the Father, he proclaimed the faultless word. Light spoke through his mouth, and his voice brought forth life. He gave them thought and understanding and mercy and salvation and the Spirit of strength derived from the limitlessness of the Father and sweetness. He caused punishments and scourgings to cease, for it was they which caused many in need of mercy to astray from him in error and in chains - and he mightily destroyed them and derided them with knowledge. He became a path for those who went astray and knowledge to those who were ignorant, a discovery for those who sought, and a support for those who tremble, a purity for those who were defiled.

He is the shepherd who left behind the ninety-nine sheep which had not strayed and went in search of that one which was lost. He rejoiced when he had found it. For ninety-nine is a number of the left hand, which holds it. The moment he finds the one, however, the whole number is transferred to the right hand. Thus it is with him who lacks the one, that is, the entire right hand which attracts that in which it is deficient, seizes it from the left side and transfers it to the right. In this way, then, the number becomes one hundred. This number signifies the Father.

He labored even on the Sabbath for the sheep which he found fallen into the pit. He saved the life of that sheep, bringing it up from the pit in order that you may understand fully what that Sabbath is, you who possess full understanding. It is a day in which it is not fitting that salvation be idle, so that you may speak of that heavenly day which has no night and of the sun which does not set because it is perfect. Say then in your heart that you are this perfect day and that in you the light which does not fail dwells.

Speak concerning the truth to those who seek it and of knowledge to those who, in their error, have committed sin. Make sure-footed those who stumble and stretch forth your hands to the sick. Nourish the hungry and set at ease those who are troubled. Foster men who love. Raise up and awaken those who sleep. For you are this understanding which encourages. If the strong follow this course, they are even stronger. Turn your attention to yourselves. Do not be concerned with other things, namely, that which you have cast forth from yourselves, that which you have dismissed. Do not return to them to eat them. Do not be moth-eaten. Do not be worm-eaten, for you have already shaken it off. Do not be a

place of the devil, for you have already destroyed him. Do not strengthen your last obstacles, because that is reprehensible. For the lawless one is nothing. He harms himself more than the law. For that one does his works because he is a lawless person. But this one, because he is a righteous person, does his works among others. Do the will of the Father, then, for you are from him.

For the Father is sweet and his will is good. He knows the things that are yours, so that you may rest yourselves in them. For by the fruits one knows the things that are yours, that they are the children of the Father, and one knows his aroma, that you originate from the grace of his countenance. For this reason, the Father loved his aroma; and it manifests itself in every place; and when it is mixed with matter, he gives his aroma to the light; and into his rest he causes it to ascend in every form and in every sound. For there are no nostrils which smell the aroma, but it is the Spirit which possesses the sense of smell and it draws it for itself to itself and sinks into the aroma of the Father. He is, indeed, the place for it, and he takes it to the place from which it has come, in the first aroma which is cold. It is something in a psychic form, resembling cold water which is [...] since it is in soil which is not hard, of which those who see it think, "It is earth." Afterwards, it becomes soft again. If a breath is taken, it is usually hot. The cold aromas, then, are from the division. For this reason, God came and destroyed the division and he brought the hot Pleroma of love, so that the cold may not return, but the unity of the Perfect Thought prevail.

This is the word of the Gospel of the finding of the Pleroma for those who wait for the salvation which comes from above. When their hope, for which they are waiting, is waiting - they whose likeness is the light in which there is no shadow, then at that time the Pleroma is about to come. The deficiency of matter, however, is not because of the limitlessness of the Father who comes at the time of the deficiency. And yet no one is able to say that the incorruptible One will come in this manner. But the depth of the Father is increasing, and the thought of error is not with him. It is a matter of falling down and a matter of being readily set upright at the finding of that one who has come to him who will turn back.

For this turning back is called "repentance". For this reason, incorruption has breathed. It followed him who has sinned in order that he may find rest. For forgiveness is that which remains for the light in the deficiency, the word of the pleroma. For the physician hurries to the place in which there is sickness, because that is the desire which he has. The sick man is in a deficient condition, but he does not hide himself because the physician possesses that which he lacks. In this manner the deficiency is filled by the Pleroma, which has no deficiency, which has given itself out in order to fill the one who is deficient, so that grace may take him, then, from the area which is deficient and has no grace. Because of this a diminishing occurred in the place which there is no grace, the area where the one who is small, who is deficient, is taken hold of.

He revealed himself as a Pleroma, i.e., the finding of the light of truth which has shined towards him, because he is unchangeable. For this reason, they who have been troubled speak about Christ in their midst so that they may receive a return and he may anoint them with the ointment. The ointment is the pity of the Father, who will have mercy on them. But those whom he has anointed are those who are perfect. For the filled vessels are those which are customarily used for anointing. But when an anointing is finished, the vessel is usually empty, and the cause of its deficiency is the consumption of its ointment. For then a breath is drawn only through the power which he has. But the one who is without deficiency - one does not trust anyone beside him nor does one pour anything out. But that which is the deficient is filled again by the perfect Father. He is good. He knows his plantings because he is the one who has planted them in his Paradise. And his Paradise is his place of rest.

This is the perfection in the thought of the Father and these are the words of his reflection. Each one of his words is the work of his will alone, in the revelation of his Logos. Since they were in the depth of his mind, the Logos, who was the first to come forth, caused them to appear, along with an intellect which speaks the unique word by means of a silent grace. It was called "thought," since they were in it before becoming manifest. It happened, then, that it was the first to come forth - at the moment pleasing to the will of him who desired it; and it is in the will that the Father is at rest and with which he is pleased. Nothing happens without him, nor does anything occur without the will of the Father. But his will is incomprehensible. His will is his mark, but no one can know it, nor is it possible for them to concentrate on it in order to possess it. But that which he wishes takes place at the moment he wishes it - even if the view does not please anyone: it is God`s will. For the Father knows the beginning of them all as well as their end. For when their end arrives, he will question them to their faces. The end, you see, is the recognition of him who is hidden, that is, the Father, from whom the beginning came forth and to whom will return all who have come from him. For they were made manifest for the glory and the joy of his name.

And the name of the Father is the Son. It is he who, in the beginning, gave a name to him who came forth from him - he is the same one - and he begat him for a son. He gave him his name which belonged to him - he, the Father, who possesses everything which exists around him. He possess the name; he has the son. It is possible for them to see him. The name, however, is invisible, for it alone is the mystery of the invisible about to come to ears completely filled with it through the Father's agency. Moreover, as for the Father, his name is not pronounced, but it is revealed through a son. Thus, then, the name is great.

Who, then, has been able to pronounce a name for him, this great name, except him alone to whom the name belongs and the sons of the name in whom the name of the Father is at rest, and who themselves in turn are at rest in his name, since the Father has no beginning? It is he alone who engendered it for himself as a name in the beginning before he had created the Aeons, that the name of the Father should be over their heads as a lord - that is, the real name, which is secure by his authority and by his perfect power. For the name is not drawn from lexicons nor is his name derived from common name-giving, But it is invisible. He gave a name to himself alone, because he alone saw it and because he alone was capable of giving himself a name. For he who does not exist has no name. For what name would one give him who did not exist? Nevertheless, he who exists also with his name and he alone knows it, and to him alone the Father gave a name. The Son is his name. He did not, therefore, keep it secretly hidden, but the son came into existence. He himself gave a name to him. The name, then, is that of the Father, just as the name of the Father is the Son. For otherwise, where would compassion find a name - outside of the Father? But someone will probably say to his companion, "Who would give a name to someone who existed before himself, as if, indeed, children did not receive their name from one of those who gave them birth?"

Above all, then, it is fitting for us to think this point over: What is the name? It is the real name. It is, indeed, the name which came from the Father, for it is he who owns the name. He did not, you see, get the name on loan, as in the case of others because of the form in which each one of them is going to be created. This, then, is the authoritative name. There is no one else to whom he has given it. But it remained unnamed, unuttered, `till the moment when he, who is perfect, pronounced it himself; and it was he alone who was able to pronounce his name and to see it. When it pleased him, then, that his son should be his pronounced name and when he gave this name to him, he who has come from the depth spoke of his secrets, because he knew that the Father was absolute goodness. For this reason, indeed, he sent this particular one in order that he might speak concerning the place and his place of rest from which he had come forth, and that he might glorify the Pleroma, the greatness of his name and the sweetness of his Father.

Each one will speak concerning the place from which he has come forth, and to the region from which he received his essential being, he will hasten to return once again. And he want from that place - the place where he was - because he tasted of that place, as he was nourished and grew. And his own place of rest is his Pleroma. All the emanations from the Father, therefore, are Pleromas, and all his emanations have their roots in the one who caused them all to grow from himself. He appointed a limit. They, then, became manifest individually in order that they might be in their own thought, for that place to which they extend their thoughts is their root, which lifts them upward through all heights to the Father. They reach his head, which is rest for them, and they remain there near to it so that they say that they have participated in his face by means of embraces. But these of this kind were not manifest, because they have not risen above themselves. Neither have they been deprived of the glory of the Father nor have they thought of him as small, nor bitter, nor angry, but as absolutely good, unperturbed, sweet, knowing all the spaces before they came into existence and having no need of instruction. Such are they who possess from above something of this immeasurable greatness, as they strain towards that unique and perfect one who exists there for them. And they do not go down to Hades. They have neither envy nor moaning, nor is death in them. But they rest in him who rests, without wearying themselves or becoming involved in the search for truth. But they, indeed, are the truth, and the Father is in them, and they are in the Father, since they are perfect, inseparable from him who is truly good. They lack nothing in any way, but they are given rest and are refreshed by the Spirit. And they listen to their root; they have leisure for themselves, they in whom he will find his root, and he will suffer no loss to his soul.

Such is the place of the blessed; this is their place. As for the rest, then, may they know, in their place, that it does not suit me, after having been in the place of rest to say anything more. But he is the one in whom I shall be in order to devote myself, at all times, to the Father of the All and the true brothers, those upon whom the love of the Father is lavished, and in whose midst nothing of him is lacking. It is they who manifest themselves truly since they are in that true and eternal life and speak of the perfect light filled with the seed of the Father, and which is in his heart and in the Pleroma, while his Spirit rejoices in it and glorifies him in whom it was, because the Father is good. And his children are perfect and worthy of his name, because he is the Father. Children of this kind are those whom he loves.

Book 142. The Story of Melchizedek

Jesus Christ, the Son of God [...] from ...

... (2 lines unrecoverable)

... the aeons, that I might tell all of the aeons, and, in (the case of) each one of the aeons, that I might tell the nature of the aeon, what it is, and that I might put on friendship and goodness as a garment, O brother, [...] and ...

... (7 lines unrecoverable)

... their end [...]. And he will reveal to them the truth [...] in ...

... (3 lines unrecoverable)

... proverb(s) ...

... (lines 26-eop [=end of page], and first 2 lines of next page, unrecoverable)

... at first in parables and riddles [...] proclaim them. Death will tremble and be angry, not only he himself, but also his fellow world-ruling archons, and the principalities and the authorities, the female gods and the male gods, together with the archangels. And ...

... (4 lines unrecoverable)

... all of them, [...] the world-rulers [...], all of them, and all the [...], and all the [...].

They will say [...] concerning him, and concerning [...] and ...

... (2 lines unrecoverable)

... they will [...] hidden mysteries ...

... (lines 27-eop, and first 2 lines of next page, unrecoverable)

... out of [...] the All. They will [...] this. The lawyers will bury him quickly. They will call him 'impious man', 'lawless', 'impure'. And on the third day, he will rise from the dead ...

... (lines 12-eop, and first 3 lines of next page, unrecoverable)

... holy disciples. And the Savior will reveal to them the world that gives life to the All.

But those in the heavens spoke many words, together with those on the earth, and those under the earth. ...

... (lines 11-eop unrecoverable)

... which will happen in his name. Furthermore, they will say of him that he is unbegotten, though he has been begotten, (that) he does not eat, even though he eats, (that) he does not drink, even though he drinks, (that) he is uncircumcised, though he has been circumcised, (that) he is unfleshly, though he has come in the flesh, (that) he did not come to suffering, <though> he came to suffering, (that) he did not rise from the dead, <though> he arose from the dead.

But all the tribes and all the peoples will speak the truth who are receiving from you yourself, O Melchizedek, Holy One, High-Priest, the perfect hope and the gifts of life. I am Gamaliel, who was sent to [...] the congregation of the children of Seth, who are above thousands of thousands, and myriads of myriads, of the aeons [...] essence of the aeons, aba[...] aiai ababa. O divine [...] of the [...] nature [...]! O Mother of the aeons, Barbelo! O first-born of the aeons, splendid Doxomedon Dom[...]! O glorious one, Jesus Christ! O chief commanders of the luminaries, you powers Armozel, Oroiael, Daveithe, Eleleth, and you man-of-light, immortal aeon Pigera-Adamas, and you good god of the beneficent worlds, Mirocheirothetou, through Jesus Christ, the Son of God! This is the one whom I proclaim, inasmuch as there has visited the One who truly exists, among those who exist [...] do(es) not exist, Abel Baruch - that you (sg.) might be given the knowledge of the truth [...], that he is from the race of the High-priest, which is above thousands of thousands, and myriads of myriads, of the aeons. The adverse spirits are ignorant of him, and (of) their (own) destruction. Not only (that, but) I have come to reveal to you the truth, which is within the brethren. He included himself in the living offering, together with your offspring. He offered them up as an offering to the All. For it is not cattle that you will offer up for sin(s) of unbelief, and for the ignorances, and (for) all the wicked deeds which they will do [...]. And they do not reach the Father of the All [...] the faith ...

... (20 lines unrecoverable)

For the waters which are above [...] that receive baptism [...]. But receive that baptism which is with the water which [...], while he is coming ...

... (3 lines unrecoverable)

... baptism as they ...

... (18 lines unrecoverable)

... pray for the offspring of the archons and all the angels, together with the seed <which> flowed forth from the Father of the All [...] the entire [...] from [...] there were engendered the gods and the angels, and the men [...] out of the seed, all of the natures, those in the heavens and those upon the earth and those under the earth ...

... (14 lines unrecoverable)

... nature of the females [...], among those that are in the [...]. They were bound with [...] But this is not (the) true Adam nor (the) true Eve.

For when they ate of the tree of knowledge, they trampled the Cherubim and the Seraphim with the flaming sword. They [...], which was Adam's, [...] the world-rulers, and [...] them out [...] after they had brought forth [...] offspring of the archons and their worldly things, these belonging to ...

... (13 lines unrecoverable)

... light [...]. And the females and the males, those who exist with [...] hidden from every nature, and they will renounce the archons [...] who receive from him the [...]. For they are worthy of [...] immortal, and great [...], and great [...], and great [...] sons of men [...] disciples [...] image, and [...] from the light [...] which is holy. For [...] from the beginning [...] a seed ...

... (lines 13-eop unrecoverable)

But I will be silent [...], for we are the brethren who came down from the living [...]. They will [...] upon the ...

... (1 line unrecoverable)

... of Adam, [...], Abel, Enoch, Noah, [...] you, Melchizedek, the Priest of God Most High, [...] those who [...] women ...

... (lines 14-eop unrecoverable)

... these two who have been chosen will at no time nor in any place will they be convicted, whenever they have been begotten, by their enemies, by their friends, nor by strangers, nor their (own) kin, (nor) by the impious, nor the pious. All of the adverse natures will [...] them, whether those that are manifest, or those that are not manifest, together with those that dwell in the heavens, and those that are upon the earth, and those that are under the earth. They will make war [...] every one. For [...], whether in the ...

... (3 lines unrecoverable)

... many ...

... (2 lines unrecoverable)

And these in the [...] every one will [...]. These will [...] with every blow [...] weaknesses. These will be confined in other forms, and will be punished. These the Savior will take them away, and they will overcome everything, not with their mouths and words, but by means of the [...], which will be done for them. He will destroy Death.

These things which I was commanded to reveal, these things reveal as I (have done). But that which is hidden, do not reveal to anyone, unless it is revealed to you (to do so)."

And immediately, I arose, I, Melchizedek, and I began to [...] God [...] that I should rejoice ...

... (1 line unrecoverable)

... while he is acting [...] living [...] I said, "I ...

... (2 lines unrecoverable)

... and I will not cease, from now on, forever, O Father of the All, because you have had pity on men, and you have sent the angel of light [...] from your aeons [...] to reveal [...]. When he came, he caused me to be raised up from ignorance, and (from) the fructification of death to life. For I have a name: I am Melchizedek, the Priest of God Most High; I know that it is I who am truly the image of the true High-Priest of God Most High, and [...] the world. For it is not a small thing that God [...] with [...] while he [...]. And [...] the angels that dwell upon the earth ...

... (2 lines unrecoverable)

... is the sacrifice of [...], whom Death deceived. When he died, he bound them with the natures which are leading them astray. Yet he offered up offerings [...] cattle, saying, "I gave them to Death, and the angels, and the [...] demons [...] living offering [...]. I have offered up myself to you as an offering, together with those that are mine, to you yourself, (O) Father of the All, and those whom you love, who have come forth from you who are holy (and) living. And <according to> the perfect laws, I shall pronounce my name as I receive baptism now (and) forever, (as a name) among the living (and) holy names, and (now) in the waters. Amen."

Holy are you, Holy are you, Holy are you, O Father of the All, who truly exists, [...] do(es) not exist, Abel Baruch [...], for ever and ever, Amen.

Holy are you, Holy are you, Holy are you, Mother of the aeons, Barbelo, for ever and ever, Amen.

Holy are you, Holy are you, Holy are you, First-born of the aeons, Doxomedon [...], for ever and ever, Amen.

Holy are you, Holy are you, Holy are you, ...

... (2 lines unrecoverable)

... for ever and ever, Amen.

Holy are you, Holy are you, Holy are you, ...

... (1 line unrecoverable)

... first aeon, Harmozel, for ever and ever, Amen.

Holy are you, Holy are you, Holy are you, commander, luminary of the aeons, Oriael, for ever and ever, Amen.

Holy are you, Holy are you, Holy are you, commander of the aeons, man-of-light, Daveithe, for ever and ever. Amen.

Holy are you, Holy are you, Holy are you, commander-in-chief, Eleleth ...

... (1 line unrecoverable)

... the aeons ...

... (2 lines unrecoverable)

... for ever and ever, Amen.

Holy are you, Holy are you, Holy are you, good god of the beneficent words, ... Mirocheirothetou, for ever and ever, Amen.

Holy are you, Holy are you, Holy are you, Commander-in-chief of the All, Jesus Christ, for ever and ever, Amen.

... (1 line unrecoverable)

... blessed [...] confession. And [...] confess him [...] now [...], then it becomes [...] fear and [...], fear and [...] disturb [...] surrounding them [...], in the place which has a great darkness in it, and many [...] appear [...] there [...] appear ...

... (lines 23-eop unrecoverable)

And [...] they were clothed with [...] all, and ...

... (6 lines unrecoverable)

... disturbances. They gave [...] their words [...], and they said to me, "[...], Melchizedek, Priest of God Most High," [...] they spoke as though [...] their mouths [...] in the All ...

... (7 lines unrecoverable)

... lead astray ...

... (lines 25-eop unrecoverable)

... with his [...] worship, and [...] faith, and [...] his prayers, and ...

... (1 line unrecoverable)

... those that are his [...] first ...

... (2 lines unrecoverable)

... They did not care that the priesthood which you perform, which is from ...

... (1 line unrecoverable)

... in the counsels of [...] Satan [...], the sacrifice [...] his doctrines ...

... (2 lines unrecoverable)

... of this aeon ...

... (4 lines unrecoverable)

... which exist(s) in [...], lead(s) astray ...

... (lines 27-eop unrecoverable)

... and some ...

... (2 lines unrecoverable)

... he gave them to ...

... (1 line unrecoverable)

... and thirteen ...

... (lines 7-eop unrecoverable)

... throw him [...], in order that you might ...

... (1 line unrecoverable)

... for immediately, [...], by means of [...] on the ground. The ...

... (lines 7-eop unrecoverable)

(pp.23-24 of the codex are almost completely missing)

... men. And [...] you (pl.) struck me, [...] you threw me, [...] corpse. And you crucified me from the third hour of the Sabbath-eve until the ninth hour. And after these things, I arose from the dead, [...] came out of [...] into me, [...] my eyes saw [...], they did not find anyone ...

... (lines 13-eop unrecoverable)

... greeted me [...]. They said to me, "Be strong, O Melchizedek, great High-priest of God Most High, for the archons, who are your enemies, made war; (but) you have prevailed over them, and they did not prevail over you, and you endured, and you destroyed your enemies. [...] of their [...] will rest in any [...] which is living (and) holy [...] those that exalted themselves against him in [...] flesh ...

... (lines 15-eop unrecoverable)

"... with offerings, working on that which is good, fasting with fasts. These revelations, do not reveal to anyone in the flesh, since they are incorporeal, unless it is revealed to you (to do so)."

When the brethren who belong to the generations of life had said these things, they were taken up to (the regions) above all the heavens. Amen.

Book 143. The Gospel of the Lots of Mary (Summary)

The Gospel of the Lots of Mary is a unique and intriguing text within the realm of Christian apocryphal literature, dating back to around the 5th or 6th century CE. Unlike traditional gospels, which typically recount the life, teachings, and actions of Jesus Christ, this gospel is centered on divination—a practice that was both widespread and controversial in the ancient world. The text, discovered in Egypt, is written in Coptic, and its full title references **Mary**, presumed to be the Virgin Mary, though her exact role in the text remains unclear.

This gospel provides a glimpse into how early Christians may have sought divine guidance in their daily lives through the casting of lots, a practice used to discern God's will. As a **divinatory text**, it is highly unusual among Christian writings, representing a blend of Christian and non-Christian traditions and reflecting the syncretic nature of religious practices during late antiquity.

Historical Context and Discovery

The Gospel of the Lots of Mary was discovered in the 1980s by a private collector who found it in Egypt. It was part of a collection of Coptic manuscripts that shed light on early Christian practices, especially in the Egyptian context. The document itself is relatively short, consisting of a series of oracular pronouncements meant to guide individuals who sought divine answers to specific questions or concerns.

The text's primary function appears to have been as a **divination tool**. Early Christians, much like their Jewish and Greco-Roman counterparts, often turned to oracles, dream interpretation, and the casting of lots to discern divine will. This practice of lot-casting, also known as **sortes**, was not uncommon in antiquity. The Bible itself references the casting of lots multiple times, such as when the apostles cast lots to choose Matthias as Judas' replacement (Acts 1:26).

However, by the time the Gospel of the Lots of Mary was composed, the practice had become increasingly controversial within the mainstream Christian church. Church leaders were often wary of divination, associating it with pagan practices and superstition. Nonetheless, the survival of this text demonstrates that such practices continued in certain Christian communities, particularly in Egypt, where syncretic traditions merged elements of Christian, Jewish, and Greco-Roman religious practices.

Structure and Purpose of the Text

The **Gospel of the Lots of Mary** is not a gospel in the traditional sense of recounting Jesus' life or delivering his teachings. Instead, it is a collection of short oracular statements meant to be interpreted after casting lots. These statements are presented in a way that offers reassurance, guidance, or advice, often in cryptic or symbolic language.

The lot-casting process likely involved individuals asking a question, casting lots (or some other form of random selection), and then consulting the corresponding section of the text for an answer. The statements within the gospel are meant to provide divine responses, offering insights into future events or decisions. For example, one passage might offer a hopeful message of divine protection, while another might advise caution in the face of an upcoming challenge.

While many of the statements in the text are positive and offer encouragement, some include warnings or instructions for spiritual conduct. The text emphasizes reliance on God's will, suggesting that no matter the outcome, the believer is always under divine care. This would have made the gospel a powerful spiritual tool, providing a tangible connection to the divine in everyday life.

The Role of Mary in the Text

One of the most intriguing aspects of this gospel is its association with **Mary**, presumably the Virgin Mary, though the text itself does not clarify her role or involvement in the divinatory process. The invocation of Mary's name in the title could indicate her significance as a figure of intercession or protection. In late antiquity, Mary had already begun to assume a prominent role in Christian devotion, particularly as a protector and mediator for believers.

Mary's name may have been invoked to lend legitimacy and sanctity to the divination practice, aligning it with Christian values and distancing it from its pagan counterparts. Alternatively, it may reflect the growing veneration of Mary in Coptic Christianity, where she was revered not only as the mother of Christ but also as a powerful intercessor who could influence divine decisions.

The connection between Mary and divination in this text might also suggest that some early Christian communities viewed her as a guide or a source of divine wisdom. This is especially significant considering the tension between official church teachings, which discouraged divination, and popular practices, which continued to thrive despite ecclesiastical disapproval.

Christianity and Divination: A Complex Relationship

The **Gospel of the Lots of Mary** offers a fascinating window into the complex relationship between Christianity and divination. While divination was generally frowned upon by church authorities, it remained an ingrained part of daily life for many people in the ancient world. The text reflects a middle ground between orthodoxy and popular religious practices, showing how early Christians navigated the tension between faith and the desire for personal guidance.

Divination, especially in the form of **sortes**, was a practice that could be easily adapted to Christian theology. By invoking the name of Mary and using a gospel-like format, the creators of this text were able to make divination more palatable to Christian audiences. The inclusion of reassuring, spiritually grounded statements further distances it from the more ominous or cryptic oracles of pagan traditions.

However, the existence of such a text also reveals the diversity of Christian practices during late antiquity. While some Christian leaders vehemently opposed divination, others—especially in regions like Egypt—seemed more open to integrating these practices into their spiritual lives. This reflects the broader trend of religious syncretism in the Mediterranean world, where Christian, Jewish, and pagan traditions often influenced one another.

Themes and Messages of the Gospel

The overarching theme of the **Gospel of the Lots of Mary** is divine providence. The text assures its users that God is in control, no matter the outcome of the lots. Whether the message is one of encouragement or caution, the text emphasizes that everything happens according to God's plan and that the believer is under divine protection.

Many of the statements in the gospel echo themes found in canonical Christian teachings: trust in God, perseverance through trials, and the importance of faith. However, the gospel also incorporates elements of personal fortune-telling, suggesting that believers could receive specific, individualized guidance from the divine.

The **use of symbolic language** in the text further enhances its mystical qualities. Much like traditional oracles, the statements in the gospel are often cryptic, requiring interpretation. This would have allowed for flexibility in their application, as individuals could tailor the messages to fit their particular circumstances.

The Syncretism of Egyptian Christianity

The **Gospel of the Lots of Mary** is also a testament to the religious syncretism that characterized Egyptian Christianity in the late antique period. Egypt had long been a melting pot of different religious traditions, including the ancient Egyptian religion, Hellenistic influences, and Judaism. When Christianity spread to Egypt, it absorbed and adapted many of these existing practices.

Coptic Christianity, in particular, retained elements of mystical and esoteric traditions. The casting of lots, the use of oracular texts, and the invocation of divine figures for personal guidance were all part of this religious landscape. In this context, the Gospel of the Lots of Mary can be seen as a fusion of Christian theology with the ancient Egyptian tradition of consulting oracles for divine guidance.

Legacy and Significance

The **Gospel of the Lots of Mary** offers modern scholars valuable insight into the diversity of early Christian practices, particularly in relation to popular religion and the use of divination. Its discovery underscores the fact that early Christianity was not a monolithic tradition but rather a complex and evolving set of beliefs and practices.

For modern readers, the text invites reflection on the ways in which believers sought to integrate their faith with their daily lives. The desire for divine guidance is a universal one, and this gospel illustrates how early Christians attempted to bridge the gap between spiritual ideals and personal concerns.

While divination may seem out of place in a Christian context, the Gospel of the Lots of Mary demonstrates that for many believers, the practice of seeking divine signs was a legitimate way to engage with their faith. The text reminds us that religious traditions are not static but constantly adapting to meet the needs of their adherents.

Book 144. The Apocalypse of Zechariah

The *Apocalypse of Zacharias* (Zacharias the father of John, as two of the texts call him) was 500 lines in length. The question of its character is bound up with the question whether the Minor Prophet or the father of John the Baptist was the putative author. A. Berendts, who wrote a special study on the subject (1895), was decidedly of opinion that the father of John was meant, and that the book contained an expanded form of the narrative of Herod's slaying Zacharias which we now read in the latter chapters of the *Protevangelium* or *Book of James*. He thought, moreover, that in a Slavonic writing, which he translated, he had discovered the actual book named in the lists. This narrative is wholly legendary and not apocalyptic. The attention of Berendts had not been called to a passage— a note of Origen on Ephes. iv. 27—which was printed in 1902 in the *Journal of Theological Studies* (iii. 554). "We give place to the devil, or to the prevailing spirit that comes up upon us, when the guiding principle in us has not been filled with holy learning or saving faith and excellent thoughts which counsel us for the best: for according to Zacharias the father of John, 'Satan tabernacles over (or, we might say, hovers over) the climates (κλίματα, regions?, inclinations?) of the soul,' and such concessions to the worse things . . . challenge the devil to enter into our souls."

This sentence is not of a kind which would fit easily into such a narrative as Berendts has produced: it is rather such as might be looked for in an Apocalypse.

Certainly Origen does seem to have been acquainted with a writing about the father of John which we do not possess. A comment of his on Matt, xxiii. 35 says, "a tradition to this effect has come down to us," that Zacharias allowed Mary to take her place among the virgins in the Temple after the birth of Christ, on the ground that she was still a virgin, and that he was slain by the men of that generation as a transgressor of the Law, between the Temple and the altar. He also says, in the Latin version of his commentary on Matthew, "It is said in apocryphal writings that Isaiah was sawn in sunder, and that Zacharias was slain, and Ezekiel." Jerome on Matthew (xxiii. 35) may be drawing from Origen when he writes, "Others will have it that Zacharias the father of John is meant; they draw from some dream of apocryphal *writings* (he generally calls them *somnia* or *deliramenta apocryphorum*) that he was slain because he prophesied the coming of the Saviour. This, having no Scriptural authority, can be as readily rejected as proved."

Coupled with the evidence of the note on Ephesians, these passages seem to support Berendts's view that the principal Zacharias-apocryph did relate to the father of John. There may very well have been prophetical passages in it.

I find it more difficult to agree with him in his identification of it with the Slavonic document. That, however, is worth summarizing here for the interest of the story.

In the fortieth year of Herod's reign, Joseph was warned by the angel Saphodamuel to flee into Egypt, where the family lived twelve months in the house of Alpheus, a man of God.

The massacre of the Innocents followed. Elizabeth fled with John. Zacharias was questioned about the child, and slain (as in *Protev.* xxii. ff.). Elizabeth was sheltered within a rock by Uriel, and fed.

After four months Gabriel brought Jesus to the Temple, and Uriel brought John: Michael and Raphael also came; and in the midst appeared God, and the corpse of Zacharias. God breathed life into it. Jesus made a spring of water rise up in the Temple and from it baptized John, and Zacharias. Thereafter Zacharias fell asleep again and was buried by the angels before the altar. Gabriel and Uriel bore away Jesus and John. The story concludes with the weaning of John, and his life in the wilderness, and the return from Egypt.

That it is an old tale is more than likely, for it seems a sound view that it has been incorporated into the *Protevangelium* and not extracted from it. But it seems to belong rather to the John Baptist cycle of legend than to that of Zacharias; and in the book we are seeking for, Zacharias ought to be the centre of interest, and not, as here, a rather subordinate figure. To put the matter in another way, this legend strikes me rather as the beginning of a life of John than as the conclusion of a life of his father.

We have thus no clear evidence that there was an apocryphal book of the minor prophet Zechariah.

A story given by Sozomen (lib. ix. *Hist. Eccl.*) of the finding of the body of Zechariah in his time shall be mentioned, only to be dismissed.

It is to the effect that, with the body, the remains of a child in princely robes and crown were found; and when questions were asked as to the meaning of this, Zacharias Abbot of Gerara produced an uncanonical Hebrew book, in which it was recorded that on the seventh day after King Joash had slain Zechariah (the son of Jehoiada) his favourite child died: he recognized that this blow was a divine judgment, and had the boy buried in the prophet's grave. The story does not concern our Zechariah, and the book, whatever it was, was not supposed to be written by any one of the name.

Book 145. The Vision of Isaiah

Chapter 1

The vision which Isaiah, the son of Amos, saw in the twentieth year of the reign of Hezekiah, king of Judah:

Isaiah the prophet, son of Amos, came to Hezekiah in Jerusalem; and after he had come in, he sat down upon the king's couch. And all the princes of Israel and the counselors of the king and the eunuchs stood before him. And the prophets and the sons of prophets came from the villages and the fields and the mountains to salute him, when they learned that Isaiah had come from Gilgal, and to announce to him those things that were to come. Then as he was speaking words of truth, the Holy Spirit came upon him and all saw and heard the words of the Holy Spirit. The king summoned the prophets, and all entered together, as many as were found there. Now there were the aged Micah and Ananiah, Joel, and as many of them as were found there, on his right hand and on the left. However, when they heard the voice of the Holy Spirit they fell to their knees and sang to the Highest God, who rests among the holy ones. Who bestowed such power of words in the world.

Now, as he was speaking in the Holy Spirit in the hearing of all, he fell silent, and thereupon they saw one standing before him. His [Isaiah's] eyes were open, yet his mouth was closed, but the inspiration of the Spirit was with him. And they did not think that Isaiah had been exalted, but the prophets recognized that it was a revelation. The vision which he saw was not of this world but of what is hidden from all flesh. And when he ceased to behold the vision, he returned to himself and recounted the vision to Hezekiah and his son Nason ... *(continuing in next chapter)*

Chapter II

... And to Micah and the other prophets, saying, "When I prophesied what you heard, which you witnessed, I saw an angel, glorious not with the glory of the angels whom I have always seen, but having a particularly great glory and a light which I cannot describe.

Taking me by the hand he led me on high, and I said, 'Who are you, and what is your name, and why are you lifting me up like a bird?' -- for the ability to speak to him was given me. Then in answer he said to me, 'When I shall bear you on high I will show you the vision which is the purpose for which I have been sent; then you will know who I am, but my name you do not know, because you wish to return again to your body. And when I raise you on high hereafter you will see.'

And I rejoiced because he answered me softly. And he said to me, 'You have rejoiced because I replied gently to you, and you will see one greater than I am wishing to speak to thee; one gentler and wiser, better and sweeter; for to this end was I sent, to explain all things to thee.'

And we ascended, he and I, upon the firmament, and there I saw the great battle of Satan and his might opposing the loyal followers (*honorantiae*) of God, and one surpassed the other in envy. For just as it is on earth, so also is it in the firmament, because replicas of what are in the firmament are on earth.

And I said to the angel, 'What is this war and envy and struggle?' And in reply he said to me, 'This is the devil's war and he will not rest until He whom you wish to see comes to slay him with the spirit of His virtue.'

Thereafter, he raised me into that which is above the firmament, which is the first heaven. And I saw in the midst thereof a throne on which an angel was seated in great glory, and angels sat at his right and his left. Those on the right had a special glory, and they sang with one voice; and those who were on the left sang after them but their song was not like that of the ones on the right. And I questioned the angel who conducted me: 'To whom is this song raised?' And in reply he said to me, 'To the great glory of God, who is above the seventh heaven, and to His beloved Son, from whom I was sent to thee.'

And again he raised me up, into the second heaven; its height was the same as that of the first heaven above earth. And I saw there, just as in the first heaven, angels on the right and on the left. And the glory of these angels and their song were superior to those of the first heaven. And I fell on my face to adore him," and the angel, who guided me said to me, 'Adore not the angel nor the throne of this heaven. This is the reason why I was sent to guide you; adore Him only of whom I will tell you, and in like fashion adore Him who is above all angels, above thrones, and above the garments and crowns which you shall see hereafter.' And I rejoiced with exceeding great joy, for such is the consummation for those who know the Most High and Eternal and His beloved Son, because they ascend to Them as by the angel of the Holy Spirit.

And he raised me above the third heaven and in like manner I saw a small throne and angels on the right and the left. The memory of this world, however, was given no name there. But the glory of my spirit was undergoing a transformation as I ascended into heaven and I said, 'Nothing of that world is given a name here.' And in reply the angel said to me, 'Nothing is given a name on account of its weakness and nothing is hidden of the things which are done there.' And they sang a song and glorified him who was enthroned, and this angel was greater than the second angel.

And again he raised me, unto the fourth heaven. The height from the third to the fourth heaven was greater. And I saw a throne and angels on the right hand and on the left. But the glory of him who was enthroned was greater than that of the angels on the right hand and their glory likewise surpassed the glory of those who were below.

And I ascended into the fifth heaven, and there I saw innumerable angels and their glory, and their song was more glorious than that of the fourth heaven. And I marveled, beholding such a multitude of angels arrayed in the ranks of their diverse goodnesses; each, having his own glory, glorified Him who is on high (Whose name is not revealed to all flesh), because He gave so much glory to the angels who are above each heaven.

But in reply the angel said to me, `Why are you astonished that they are not all of one appearance? You have not yet seen the insuperable virtues and the thousands and thousands of angels.'

Chapter III

And thereafter he raised me into the air of the sixth heaven and I saw there a great glory which I had not seen in the fifth heaven. And I beheld angels in great glory. And the deeds of the virtues were honorable and pre-eminent; their song was holy and wonderful. And I said to the angel who guided me, 'What is it that I see, my lord?' And he said to me, 'I am not your lord but your counselor.'

And he spoke to me about the sixth heaven. Herein are neither throne nor angels on the left, but they receive their direction from the virtue of the seventh heaven, where dwells the mighty Son of God. And all the heavens and His angels hearken to Him, and I have been sent to bring you hither, so that you may see this glory and the Lord of all the heavens and His angels and virtues. Therefore, I say to you, Isaiah, no one who desires to return to the flesh of that world has seen what you see nor is able to see what you have seen; because it is your lot in the Lord to come here.' And I magnified the Lord in song because thus I go into His lot.

And he [the angel] said to me, 'When you shall have returned here through the will of the Father, then you will receive your garment, and then you will be equal to the angels who are in the seventh heaven.' And he led me into the sixth heaven, and neither thrones nor angels on the right and the left were there, but all had one appearance and identical song. And it was given me to sing with them; and the angel who was with me and I, myself, were even as their glory, and their glory was one. And they glorified the Father of all and His beloved Son and the Holy Spirit; all with one voice they sang, but not with a voice such as that of the fifth heaven, but with a different voice.

And there was a great light there. And when I was in the sixth heaven I thought the light of the fifth heaven to be as darkness. I rejoiced greatly and sang to Him who gave such joy to those who received His mercy. And I begged the angel who guided me never more to return into that carnal world. Moreover, I say unto you that here is much darkness.

But the angel who guided me said to me, 'Since you rejoice in this light, how much more will you rejoice and exult when you see the light of the seventh heaven, in which sits the Heavenly Father with His only begotten Son; where lie the vestments and the thrones and the crowns of the righteous. And as to your plea not to return into your flesh, the time is not yet fulfilled for your coming here.' And I sorrowed greatly at hearing these words.

Chapter IV

And he raised me up into the air of the seventh heaven and I heard a voice saying to me, 'Why do you who desire to live in the flesh come here?' And I was very much afraid and trembled. Again, I heard another voice saying, 'Forbid him not to, come in, since he is worthy of the glory of God, for here is his robe. And I questioned the angel who was with me, 'Who is he who forbids me, and who is he who bids me come up?'

And he said to me, 'The one who forbids is he, the angel who is above the angels singing in the sixth heaven; and He who commands is the Son of God, and His name you may not hear until you have departed from the flesh.'

When we ascended into the seventh heaven I saw' there an astounding and indescribable light and innumerable angels. And I saw certain of the righteous who, stripped of fleshly robes, were in heavenly robes and standing in great glory. But they sat not on their thrones; moreover, their crowns of glory were not upon them.

And I questioned the angel, saying, 'Why have they received robes, and why have they not received thrones and crowns of glory?' And he said to me, Now they receive them not, until the Son first brings here those thrones and crowns, when He shall be in your likeness.' And the prince of that world will stretch forth his hand upon the Son of God and will kill Him and hang Him on a tree, and he will kill Him not knowing who He is. And He will descend into hell and will lay it waste, with all the phantoms of hell. And He will seize the prince of death and despoil him, and crush all his powers, and will rise again on the third day; having with him certain of the righteous. And He will send His preachers into the whole world, and will ascend into heaven. Then these will receive their thrones and crowns.'

And after [he said] these words, I said to him, 'In regard to that which I asked you in the first heaven, show me, for this you promised.' And as I was addressing him, there was among those standing about us one angel, more glorious than he who conducted me and than all the angels. And he showed me a book, and opening it, gave it to me; and I saw writing which was not like that of this world. And I read it, and lo, there were the deeds of Jerusalem recorded there, and the works of all men were there, among whom also was I. I saw in truth that nothing which was done in the world was hidden in the seventh heaven.

And I questioned the angel, 'Who is this who is pre-eminent over all the angels in his glory?' And in reply to me he said, 'He is the great angel, Michael, who prays constantly for humanity and humility.' I saw many robes and thrones and crowns lying there. And I said to the angel, `For whom are these robes and crowns and thrones reserved?' And he said to me, 'Many of that world lost these crowns, who are believers in the world of Him of whom I have spoken to you.'

And, turning about, I saw the Lord in great glory and I was most sorely afraid. And all the righteous approached Him and adored Him singing with one voice and [my] voice was like unto theirs. And Michael, approaching Him, adored and together with him all the angels adored and sang. And I was again transfigured and was like the angels.

Then the angel who conducted me said to me, 'Adore Him and sing.' And I adored Him and sang. And the angel who conducted me said to me, 'He is the Lord of all the glories which you have seen.' And I saw another most glorious one, like unto Him in all things, and the righteous approached Him and adored Him and sang, and I sang with them and I was not transfigured into their aspect. And the angels came with them and adored Him, and I adored Him and sang.

And again, I saw the other in great glory. And while walking, I questioned the angel, 'Who is He?' And he said to me, 'Adore Him, for he is the angel of the Holy Spirit, who speaks in you , and in all the righteous.' And after that, another indescribable and ineffable glory was revealed which I could not behold with the opened eyes of my spirit, nor could the angel who conducted me nor all the angels whom I saw adoring the Lord. But I saw the righteous only in great glory beholding [His] glory. And my Lord approached first and then the angel of the Holy Spirit (*angelus spiritualis*). And they adored Him and the two sang together. Then all the righteous adored Him, and with them Michael and all the angels adored and sang.

Chapter V

Thereafter I heard a voice there and the song which I heard in the six heavens rose up and was heard in the seventh heaven. And all glorified Him whose glory I could not behold. And the song of all six heavens was not only heard but seen. And the angel said to me, 'He is the One Living Eternal, living in the highest eternity and resting among the holy ones; we cannot endure to name or see Him who is praised by the Holy Spirit in the mouths of the holy [and] righteous.

And after that, I heard the voice of the Eternal saying to the Lord [His] Son: 'Go forth and descend from all the heavens and be in the world, and go even to the angel who is in hell; transfiguring thyself into their form. And neither the angels nor the princes of that world shall know thee. And thou shalt judge the prince of that world and his angels, and the rulers of the world, because they have denied me and said, "We are and without us

there is no one." Thereafter, thou shalt not transfigure thyself as thou ascendest through the heavens in great glory, and thou wilt sit at my right hand. Then the princes and the virtues and all the angels and all the principalities of the heavens and of earth and of the lower regions will adore thee.'

And I heard the Great Glory commanding my Lord. And then the Lord went out from the seventh heaven and descended into the sixth heaven. And the angel who guided me said to me, 'Understand and see the manner of His transfiguration and descent.'

When the angels saw Him, they praised and glorified Him, for He was not transfigured into their image, and I sang with them. When He had descended into the fifth heaven, there at once He was transfigured into the form of those angels and they did not sing to Him or adore Him, for He was of a form like theirs.

And He descended into the fourth heaven and appeared to them in their form. And they did not sing to Him for He was of a form like theirs.

Moreover, He came into the third heaven," and into the second and the first, transfiguring Himself in each of them. Consequently, they did not sing to Him or adore Him, for He appeared to them in [a form] like theirs. And He showed them a sign (*characterem*).

Moreover, He descended into the firmament and there gave the signs (*signa*), and His form was like unto theirs, and they did not glorify Him and they did not sing to Him. And He descended to the angels who were in this air as though He were one of them. And He gave them no sign, nor did they sing to Him.

Chapter VI

And after these things, the angel said to me, 'Know, Isaiah, son of Amos, this is why I was sent by God to show you all things. For no one before you has seen nor can anyone after you see what you have seen and heard.' And I saw one like the Son of Man dwelling with men and in the world. And they did not recognize Him. And I saw Him ascending into the firmament and He was not transfigured into [their] form. And all the angels who were above the firmament were struck with fear at the sight and, adoring, they said, 'How didst Thou descend into our midst, Lord, and we did not recognize the King of Glory?'

And He ascended into the first heaven more gloriously and did not transfigure Himself. Then all the angels adored and sang, saying, 'How didst Thou pass through our midst, Lord, and we did not see or adore Thee?'

Thus He ascended into the second heaven and into the third and into the fourth and into the fifth and into the sixth, even to all the heavens, and His glories increased. When He ascended into the seventh heaven, all the righteous sang to him, and all the angels and virtues whom I could not see.

I saw a wonderful angel sit at His left hand, who said to me: 'This suffices you, Isaiah, for you have seen what no other son of the flesh has seen, which eyes cannot see nor ears hear, nor can it rise in the heart of man, how much God has prepared for all who love Him.'

And he said to me, 'Return in your robe until the time of your days shall be fulfilled and then you shall come here.'"

Having seen these things, Isaiah spoke to those standing about him; and, hearing these wonders, all sang and glorified the Lord, who gave such grace to men.

And he said to Hezekiah the king, "The consummation of this world and works will be fulfilled in the last generations." And he forbade them to proclaim these words to the children of Israel or to give them to any man to be recorded. But how many things will be understood by the king and by the utterances in the prophets! And thus be you also in the Holy Spirit, so that you may receive your robes and thrones and crowns of glory placed in the heavens.

He ceased then to speak and went out from King Hezekiah.

Book 146. The Vision of Paul

From the Ante-Nicene Fathers, Vol X.

Here Begins the Vision of Saint Paul the Apostle.

"But I will come to visions and revelations of the Lord: I know a man in Christ fourteen years ago (whether in the body, I know not; or out of the body, I know not, God knoweth) snatched up in this manner to the third heaven: and I know such a man, whether in the body or out of the body I know not, God knoweth; how that he was snatched up into Paradise and heard secret words which it is not lawful for men to speak; on behalf of such a one will I glory; but on mine own behalf I will not glory, save in my infirmities."-2 Corinthians 12:1-5

1. At what time was this revelation made? In the consulship of Theodosius Augustus the Younger and Cynegius, a certain nobleman then living in Tharsus, in the house which was that of Saint Paul, an angel appearing in the night revealed to him, saying that he should open the foundations of the house and should publish what he found, but he thought that these things were dreams;

2. But the angel coming for the third time beat him and forced him to open the foundation. And digging he found a marble box, inscribed on the

sides; there was the revelation of Saint Paul, and his shoes in which he walked teaching the word of God. But he feared to open that box and brought it to the judge; when he had received it, the judge, because it was sealed with lead, sent it to the Emperor Theodosius, fearing lest it might be something else; which when he had received the emperor opened it, and found the revelation of Saint Paul; a copy of it he sent to Jerusalem, and retained the original himself.

3. While I was in the body in which I was snatched up to the third heaven, the word of the Lord came to me saying: speak to the people: until when will ye transgress, and heap sin upon sin, and tempt the Lord who made you? Ye are the sons of God, doing the works of the devil in the faith of Christ, on account of the impediments of the world. Remember therefore and know that while every creature serves God, the human race alone sins. But it reigns over every creature and sins more than all nature.

4. For indeed the sun, the great light, often addressed the Lord saying: Lord God Almighty, I look out upon the impieties and injustices of men; permit me and I shall do unto them what are my powers, that they may know that thou art God alone. And there came a voice saying to him: I know all these things, for mine eye sees and ear hears, but my patience bears them until they shall be converted and repent. But if they do not return to me I will judge them all.

5. For sometimes the moon and stars addressed the Lord saying: Lord God Almighty, to us thou hast given the power of the night; till when shall we look down upon the impieties and fornications and homicides done by the sons of men? Permit us to do unto them according to our powers, that they may know that thou art God alone. And there came a voice unto them saying: I know all these things, and mine eye looks forth and ear hears, but my patience bears with them until they shall be converted and repent. But if they do not return unto me I will judge them.

6. And frequently also the sea exclaimed saying: Lord God Almighty, men have defiled thy holy name in me; permit me to arise and cover every wood and orchard and the whole world, until I blot out all the sons of men from before thy face, that they may know that thou art God alone. And the voice came again and said: I know all things; mine eye seeth everything, and mine ear heareth, but my patience bears with them until they be converted and repent. But if they do not return, I will judge them. Sometimes the waters[2] also spoke against the sins of men saying: Lord God Almighty, all the sons of men have defiled thy holy name. And there came a voice saying: I know all things before they come to pass, for mine eye seeth and mine ear heareth all things, but my patience bears with them until they be converted. But if not I will judge them. Frequently also the earth[3] too exclaimed to the Lord against the sons of men saying: Lord God Almighty, I above every other creature of thine am harmed, supporting the fornications, adulteries, homicides, thefts, perjuries and magic and ill-doings of men and all the evil they do, so that the father rises up against the son, and the son upon the father, the alien against the alien, so that each one defiles his neighbour's wife. The father ascends upon the bed of his own son, and the son likewise ascends the couch of his own father; and in all these evils, they who offer the sacrifice to thy name have defiled thy holy place. Therefore I am injured above every creature, desiring not to shew my power to myself, and my fruits to the sons of men. Permit me and I will destroy the virtue of my fruits. And there came a voice and said: I know all things, and there is none who can hide himself from his sin. Moreover I know their impieties, but my holiness suffers them until they be converted and repent. But if they do not return unto me I will judge them.

7. Behold, ye sons of men, the creature is subject to God, but the human race alone sins. For this cause, therefore, ye sons of men, bless the Lord God unceasingly, every hour and every day: but more especially when the sun has set:[4] for at that hour all the angels proceed to the Lord to worship him and to present the works of men, which every man has wrought from the morning till the evening, whether good or evil. And there is a certain angel who proceeds rejoicing concerning the man in whom he dwells. When therefore the sun[5] has set in the first hour of night, in the same hour the angel of every people and every man and woman, who protect and preserve them, because man is the image of God: similarly also in the matin hour which is the twelfth of the night, all the angels of men and women, go up to God to worship God, and present every work which each man has wrought, whether good or evil. Moreover every day and night the angels show to God an account[6] of all the acts of the human race. To you, therefore, I say, ye sons of men, bless the Lord God without fail all the days of your life.

8. Therefore at the appointed hour all the angels whatever, rejoicing at once together, proceed before God that they may meet to worship at the hour determined. And behold suddenly it became the hour of meeting, and the angels came to worship in the presence of God, and the spirit proceeded to meet them: and there came a voice and said: Whence come ye, our angels, bearing the burdens of tidings?

9. They answered and said: We come from those who have renounced this world for the sake of thy holy name, wandering as pilgrims, and in caves of the rocks, and weeping every hour in which they inhabited the earth, and hungering and thirsting because of thy name, with their loins girded, having in theist hands the incense of their hearts, and praying and blessing every hour, and restraining and overcoming themselves, weeping and wailing above the rest that inhabit the earth. And we indeed, their angels, mourn along with them: whither therefore it shall please thee, command us to go and minister, lest others also do it, but the destitute above the rest who are on earth. And there came the voice of God to them saying: Know ye that now henceforward my grace is appointed unto you, and my help, who is my well-beloved Son, shall be present with them, guiding them every hour; ministering also to them, never deserting them, since their place is his habitation.

10. When therefore these angels had retired, behold other angels came to adore in the presence of honour, in the assembly, who wept; and the spirit of God proceeded to meet them, and there came the voice of God and said: Whence come ye, our angels, bearing the burdens of the ministry of the tidings of the world? They answered and said in the presence of God: We have arrived from those who called upon thy name, and the impediments of the world made them wretched, devising many occasions every hour, not even making one pure prayer, nor out of their whole heart, in all the time of their life; what need, therefore, is there to be present with men who are sinners? And there came the voice of God to them: It is necessary that ye should minister to them, until they be converted and repent: but if they do not return to me I will judge them. Know therefore, sons of men, that whatever things are wrought by you, these angels relate to God, whether good or evil.

11. And the angel answered and said unto me: Follow me, and I will show you the place of the just where they are led when they are deceased, and after these things taking thee into the abyss, I will show thee the souls of sinners and what sort of place they are led into when they have deceased. And I proceeded back after the angel, and he led me into heaven, and I looked back upon the firmament, and I saw in the same place power, and there was there oblivion which deceives and draws down to itself the hearts of men, and the spirit of detraction, and the spirit of fornication, and the spirit of madness, and the spirit of insolence, and there were there the princes of vices: these I saw under the firmament of heaven: and again I looked back, and I saw angels without mercy, having no pity, whose countenance was full of madness, and their teeth sticking out beyond the mouth: their eyes shone like the morning star of the east, and from the hairs of their head sparks of fire went out, or from their mouth. And I asked the angel saying: Sir, who are those? And the angel answered and said unto me: These are those who are destined to the souls of the impious in the hour of need, who did not believe that they had the Lord for their helper, nor hoped in him.

12. And I looked on high and I saw other angels whose countenance shone as the sun, their loins girded with golden girdles, having palms in their hands, and the sign of God, clothed with garments in which was written the name of the Son of God, filled moreover with all meekness and pity; and I asked the angels saying: Who are these, Lord, in so great beauty and pity? And the angel answered and said unto me: These are the angels of justice who are sent to lead up the souls of the just, in the hour of need, who believed that they had the Lord for their helper. And I said to him: Do the just and sinners necessarily meet witnesses when they have died? And the angel answered and said to me: There is one way by which all pass over to God, but the just having their helper with them are not confounded when they go to appear in the sight of God.

13. And I said to the angel: I wished to see the souls of the just and of sinners going out of the world. And the angel answered and said unto me: Look down upon the earth. And I looked down from heaven upon the earth, and saw the whole world, and it was nothing in my sight and I saw the sons of men as though they were naught, and a-wanting, and I wondered and said to the angel: Is this the greatness of men? And the angel answered and said unto me: It is, and these are they who do evil from morning till evening. And I looked and saw a great cloud of fire spread over the whole world, and I said to the angel: What is this, my Lord? and he said to me: This is injustice stirred up by the princes of sinners.

14. I indeed when I had heard this sighed and wept, and said to the angel: I wished to see the souls of the just and of sinners, and to see in what manner they go out of the body. And the angel answered and said unto me: Look again upon the earth. And I looked and saw all the world, and men were as naught and a-wanting: and I looked carefully and saw a certain man about to die, and the angel said to me: This one whom thou seest is a just man. And I looked again and saw all his works, whatever he had done for the sake of God's name, and all his desires, both what he remembered, and what he did not remember; they all stood in his sight in the hour of need; and I saw the just man advance and find refreshment and confidence, and before he went out of the world the holy and the impious angels both attended: and I saw them all, but the impious found no place of habitation in him, but the holy took possession of his soul, guiding it till it went out of the body: and they roused the soul saying: Soul, know thy body whence thou goest out, for it is necessary that thou shouldst return to the same body on the day of the resurrection, that thou mayest receive the things promised to all the just. Receiving therefore the soul from the body, they immediately kissed it as familiarly known to them, saying to it: Do manfully, for thou hast done the will of God while placed in the earth. And there came to meet him the angel who watched

him every day, and said to him: Do manfully, soul; for I rejoice in thee, because thou hast done the will of God on earth: for I related to God all thy works, such as they were. Similarly also the spirit proceeded to meet him and said: Soul, fear not, nor be disturbed, until thou comest into a place which thou hast never known, but I will be a helper unto thee: for I found in thee a place of refreshment in the time when I dwelt in thee, while I was on earth. And his spirit strengthened him, and his angel received him, and led him into heaven: and an angel said: Whither runnest thou, O soul, and dost thou dare to enter into heaven? Wait and let us see if there is anything of ours in thee: and behold we find nothing in thee. I see also thy divine helper and angel, and the spirit is rejoicing along with thee, because thou hast done the will of God on earth. And they led him along till he should worship in the sight of God. And when they had ceased, immediately Michael and all the army of angels, with one voice, adored the footstool of his feet, and his doom, saying at the same time to the soul: This is your God of all things, who made you in his own image and likeness. Moreover the angel returns and points him out saying: God, remember his labours: for this is the soul, whose works I related to thee, doing according to thy judgment. And the spirit said likewise: I am the spirit of vivification inspiring him: for I had refreshment in him, in the time when I dwelt in him, doing according to thy judgment. And there came the voice of God and said: In as much as this man did not vex me, neither will I vex him; for according as he had pity, I also will have pity. Let him therefore be handed over to Michael, the angel of the Covenant, and let him lead him into the Paradise of joy, that he himself may become co-heir with all the saints. And after these things I heard the voices of a thousand thousand angels, and archangels, and cherubim, and twenty-four elders saying hymns, and glorifying the Lord and crying: thou art just, O Lord, and just are thy judgments, and there is no acceptance of persons with thee, but thou rewardest unto every man according to thy judgment. And the angel answered and said unto me: Hast thou believed and known, that whatever each man of you has done, he sees in the hour of need? And I said: Yes, sir.

15. And he saith to me: Look again down on the earth, and watch the soul of an impious man going out of the body, which vexed the Lord day and night, saying: I know nothing else in this world, I eat and drink, and enjoy what is in the world; for who is there who has descended into hell, and ascending has declared to us that there is judgment there! And again I looked carefully, and saw all the scorn of the sinner, and all that he did, and they stood together before him in the hour of need: and it was done to him in that hour, in which he was threatened about his body at the judgment, and I said: It were better for him if he hall not been born. And after these things, there came at the same time, the holy angels, and the malign, and the soul of the sinner and the holy angels did not find a place in it. Moreover the malign angels cursed it; and when they had drawn it out of the body, the angels admonished it a third time, saying: O wretched soul, look upon thy flesh, whence thou camest out: for it is necessary that thou shouldst return to thy flesh in the day of resurrection, that thou mayest receive the due for thy sins and thy impieties.

16. And when they had led it forth, the customary angel preceded it, and said to it: O wretched soul, I am the angel belonging to thee, relating daily to the Lord thy malign works, whatever thou didst by night or day: and if it were in my power, not for one day would I minister to thee, but none of these things was I able to do: the judge is pitiful and just, and he himself commanded us that we should not cease to minister to the soul, till you should repent, but thou hast lost the time of repentance. I indeed was strange to thee and thou to me. Let us go on then to the just judge: I will not dismiss thee, before I know from to-day why I was strange to thee. And the spirit confounded him, and the angel troubled him. When, therefore, they had arrived at the power, when he started to enter heaven, a labour was imposed upon him, above all other labour: error and oblivion and murmuring met him, and the spirit of fornication, and the rest of the powers, and said to him: Whither goest thou, wretched soul, and darest thou to rush into heaven? hold, that we may see if we have our qualities in thee, since we do not see that thou hast a holy helper. And after that I heard voices in the height of heaven saying: Present that wretched soul to God, that it may know that it is God that it despised. When, therefore, it had entered heaven, all the angels saw it, a thousand thousand exclaimed with one voice, all saying: Woe to thee, wretched soul, for the sake of thy works which thou didst on earth; what answer art thou about to give to God when thou shalt have approached to adore him? The angel who was with it answered and said: Weep with me, my beloved, for I have not found rest in this soul. And the angels answered him and said: Let such a soul be taken away from the midst of ours, for from the time he entered, the stink of him crosses to us angels. And after these things it was presented, that it might worship in the sight of God, and an angel of God showed him God who made him after his own image and likeness. Moreover his angel ran before him saying: Lord God Almighty, I am the angel of this soul, whose works I presented to thee day and night, not doing according to thy judgment. And the spirit likewise said: I am the spirit who dwelt in it from the time it was made, in itself moreover I know it, and it has not followed my will: judge it, Lord, according to thy judgment. And there came the voice of God to it and said: Where is thy

fruit which thou has made worthy of the goods which thou hast received? Have I put a distance of one day between thee and the just man? Did I not make the sun to arise upon thee as upon the just? But the soul was silent, having nothing to answer: and again there came a voice saying: Just is the judgment of God, and there is no acceptance of persons with God, for whoever shall have done mercy, on them shall he have mercy, and whoever shall not have pitied neither shall God pity him. Let him therefore be handed over to the angel Tartaruch, who is set over the punishments, and let him place him in outer darkness, where there is weeping and gnashing of teeth, and let him be there till the great day of judgment. And after these things I heard the voice of angels and archangels saying: Thou art just, Lord, and thy judgment is just.

17. And again I saw, and behold a soul which was led forward by two angels, weeping and saying: Have pity on me, just God, God the judge, for to-day is seven days since I went out of my body, and I was handed over to these two angels, and they led me through to those places, which I had never seen. And God, the just judge, saith to him: What hast thou done? for thou never didst mercy, wherefore thou wast handed over to such angels as have no mercy, and because thou didst not do uprightly, so neither did they act piously with thee in the hour of thy need. Confess therefore thy sins which thou didst commit when placed in the world. And he answered and said: Lord, I did not sin. And the Lord, the just Lord, was angered in fury when it said: I did not sin, because it lied; and God said: Dost thou think thou art still in the world? if any one of you, sinning there, conceal and hide his sin from his neighbour, here indeed nothing whatever shall be hid: for when the souls come to adore in sight of the throne, both the good works and the sins of each one are made manifest. And hearing these things the soul was silent, having no answer. And I heard the Lord God, the just judge, again saying: Come, angel of this soul, and stand in the midst. And the angel of the sinful soul came, having in his hands a manuscript, and said: These, Lord, in my hands, are all the sins of this soul from his youth till to-day, from the tenth year of his birth: and if thou command, Lord, I will also relate his acts from the beginning of his fifteenth year. And the Lord God, the just judge, said: I say unto thee, angel, I do not expect of thee an account of him since he began to be fifteen years old, but state his sins for five years before he died and before he came hither. And again God, the just judge, said: For by myself I swear, and by my holy angels, and by my virtue, that if he had repented five years before he died, on account of one year's life, oblivion would now be thrown over all the evils which he sinned before, and he would have indulgence and remission of sins: now indeed he shall perish. And the angel of the sinful soul answered and said: Lord, command that angel to exhibit those souls.

18. And in that same hour the souls were exhibited in the midst, and the soul of the sinner knew them; and the Lord said to the soul of the sinner: I say unto thee, soul, confess thy work which thou wroughtest in these souls, whom thou seest, when they were in the world. And he answered and said: Lord, it is not yet a full year since I slew this one and poured his blood upon the ground, and with another (a woman) I committed fornication: not this alone, but I also greatly harmed her in taking away her goods. And the Lord God, the just judge, said: Either thou didst not know that he who does violence to another, if he dies first who sustains the violence, is kept in this place until the doer of hurt dies, and then both stand in the presence of the judge, and now each receives according to his deed. And I heard a voice of one saying: Let that soul be delivered into the hands of Tartarus, and led down into hell: he shall lead him into the lower prison and he shall be put in torments, and left there till the great day of judgment. And again I heard a thousand thousand angels saying hymns to the Lord, and crying: Thou art just, O Lord, and just are thy judgments.

19. The angel answered and said unto me: Hast thou perceived all these things? and I said, Yes, sir. And he said to me: Follow me again, and I will take thee, and show thee the places of the just. And I followed the angel, and he raised me to the third heaven, and placed me at the entry of the door: and looking carefully I saw, and the door was of gold, and two columns of gold, full above of golden letters, and the angel tuned again to me and said: Blessed weft thou, if thou hadst entered into these doors, for it is not allowed to any to enter except only to those who have goodness and innocence of body in all things. And I asked the angel about everything and said: Sir, tell me on what account these letters are put upon those tables? The angel answered and said unto me: These are the names of the just, serving God with their whole heart, who dwell on the earth. And again I said: Sir, therefore their names and countenance and the likeness of these who serve God are in heaven, and are known to the angels: for they know who are the servants of God with all their heart, before they go out of the world.

20. And when I had entered the interior of the gate of Paradise,[7] there came out to meet me an old man whose countenance shone as the sun; and when he had embraced me he said: Hail, Paul, beloved of God. And he kissed me with a cheerful countenance. He wept, and I said to him: Brother, why dost thou weep? And again sighing and lamenting he said: We are hurt by men, and they vex us greatly; for many are the good things which the Lord has prepared, and great is his promise, but many

do not perceive them. And I asked the angel, and said: Sir, who is this? And he said to me: This is Enoch, the scribe of righteousness. And I entered into the interior of that place, and immediately I saw the sun,[8] and coming it saluted me laughing and rejoicing. And when it had seen (me), it turned away and wept, and said to me: Paul, would that thou shouldst receive thy labours which thou hast done in the human race. For me, indeed, I have seen the great and many good things, which God has prepared for the just, and the promises of God are great, but many do not perceive them; but even by many labours scarcely one or two enters into these places.

21. And the angel answered and said to me,[9] Whatever I now show thee here, and whatever thou shalt hear, tell it not to any one in the earth. And he led me and shewed me: and there I heard words which it is not lawful for a man to speak. And again he said, For now follow me, and I will shew thee what thou oughtest to narrate in public and relate.

And he took me down from the third heaven, and led me into the second heaven, and again he led me on to the firmament and from the firmament he led me over the doors of heaven: the beginning of its foundation was on the river which waters all the earth. And I asked the angel and said, Lord, what is this river of water? and he said to me, This is Oceanus! And suddenly I went out of heaven, and I understood that it is the light of heaven which lightens all the earth. For the land there is seven times brighter[10] than silver. And I said, Lord, what is this place? And he said to me, This is the land of promise. Hast thou never heard what is written: Blessed are the meek: for they shall inherit the earth? The souls therefore of the just, when they have gone out of the body, are meanwhile dismissed to this place. And I said to the angel, Then this land will be manifested before the time? The angel answered and said to me, When Christ, whom thou preachest, shall come to reign, then, by the sentence of God,[11] the first earth will be dissolved and this land of promise will then be revealed, and it will be like dew or cloud, and then the Lord Jesus Christ, the King Eternal, will be manifested and will come with all his saints to dwell in it, and he will reign over them a thousand years, and they will eat of the good things which I shall now show unto thee.

22. And I looked around upon that land and I saw a river flowing of milk and honey, and there were trees planted by the bank of that river, full of fruit: moreover each single tree bore twelve fruits in the year, having various and diverse fruits: and I saw the created things which are in that place and all the work of God, and I saw there palms of twenty cubits, but others of ten cubits: and that land was seven times brighter than silver. And there were trees full of fruits from the roots to the highest branches, of ten thousand fruits of palms upon ten thousand fruits. The grape-vines moreover had ten thousand plants.[12] Moreover in the single vines there were ten thousand thousand bunches and in each of these a thousand single grapes: moreover these single trees bore a thousand fruits. And I said to the angel, Why does each tree bear a thousand fruits? The angel answered and said unto me, Because the Lord God gives an abounding flood of gifts to the worthy, because they also of their own will afflicted themselves when they were placed in the world doing all things on account of his holy name. And again I said to the angel, Sir, are these the only promises which the Most Holy God makes? And he answered and said to me: No! there are seven times greater than these. But I say unto thee that when the just go out of the body they shall see the promises and the good things which God has prepared for them. Till then, they shall sigh, and lament saying: Have we emitted any word from our mouth to vex our neighbour even on one day? I asked and said again: Are these alone the promises of God? And the angel answered and said unto me: These whom you now see are the souls of the married[13] and those who kept the chastity of their nuptials, containing themselves. But to the virgins and those who hunger and thirst after righteousness and those who afflicted themselves for the sake of the name of God, God will give seven times greater than these, which I shall now show thee.

And then he took me up from that place where I saw these things and behold, a river, and its waters were greatly whiter than milk, and I said to the angel, What is this? And he said to me: This is the Acherousian Lake where is the City of Christ, but not every man is permitted to enter that city; for this is the journey which leads to God, and if anyone is a fornicator and impious, and is converted and shall repent and do fruits worthy of repentance, at first indeed when he shall have gone out of the body, he is led and adores God, and thence by command of the Lord he is delivered to the angel Michael and he baptizes him in the Acherousian Lake-thus he leads them into the City of Christ alongside of those who have never sinned. But I wondered and blessed the Lord God for all the things which I saw.

23. And the angel answered and said unto me: Follow me and I will lead thee into the City of Christ. And he was standing on the Acherousian Lake and he put me into a golden ship[14] and angels as it were three thousand were saying hymns before me till I arrived at the City of Christ. Moreover those who inhabited the City of Christ greatly rejoiced over me as I went to them, and I entered and saw the City of Christ, and it was all of gold, and twelve walls encircled it, and twelve interior towers, and each wall had between them single stadia in the circuit: And I said to the angel, Sir, how much is a stadium? The angel answered and said to me:

As much as there is between the Lord God and the men who are on the earth, for the City of Christ is alone great. And there were twelve gates in the circuit of the city, of great beauty, and four rivers which encircled it. There was, moreover, a river of honey and a river of milk, and a river of wine and a river of oil. And I said to the angel: What are these rivers surrounding that city? And he saith to me: These are the four rivers which flow sufficiently for those who are in this land of promise, of which the names[15] are: the river of honey is called Fison, and the river of milk Euphrates, and the river of oil Gion, and the river of wine Tigris, such therefore they are for those who when placed in the world did not use the power of these things, but they hungered for these things and afflicted themselves for the sake of the Lord God: so that when these enter into this city, the Lord will assign them these things on high above all measure.

24. I indeed entering the gates saw trees great and very high before the doors of the city, having no fruit but leaves only, and I saw a few men scattered in the midst of the trees, and they lamented greatly when they saw anyone enter the city. And those trees were sorry for them and humbled themselves and bowed down and again erected themselves. And I saw and wept with them and I asked the angel and said: Sir, who are these who are not admitted to enter into the City of Christ? And he said to me: These are they who zealously abstained day and night in fasts, but they had a proud heart above other men, glorifying and praising themselves and doing nothing for their neighbours. For they gave some friendly greeting, but to others they did not even say hail! and indeed they shewed hospitality to those only whom they wished, and if they did anything whatever for their neighbour they were immoderately puffed up. And I said: What then, Sir? Did their pride prevent them from entering into the City of Christ? And the angel answered and said unto me: Pride is the root of all evils. Are they better than the Son of God who came to the Jews with much humility? And I asked him and said: Why is it that the trees humble themselves and erect themselves again? And the angel answered and said to me: The whole time which these men passed on earth zealously serving God, on account of the confusion and reproaches of men at the time, they blushed and humiliated themselves, but they were not saddened. nor did they repent that they should recede from their pride which was in them. This is why the trees humble themselves, and again are raised up. And I asked and said: For what cause were they admitted to the doors of the city? The angel answered and said unto me: Because of the great goodness of God, and because there is the entry of his holy men entering into this city: for this cause they are left in this place, but when Christ the King Eternal enters with his saints, as he enters just men may pray for these, and then they may enter into the city along with them: but yet none of them is able to have assurance such as they have who humbled themselves, serving the Lord God all their lives.

25. But I went on while the angel instructed me, and he carried me to the river of honey, and I saw there Isaiah and Jeremiah[16] and Ezekiel and Amos, and Micah and Zechariah, the minor and major prophets, and they saluted me in the city. I said to the angel: What way is this? And he said to me: This is the way of the prophets, every one who shall have afflicted his soul and not done his own will because of God, when he shall have gone out of the world and have been led to the Lord God and adored him, then by the command of God he is handed over to Michael, and he leads him into the city to this place of the prophets, and they salute him as their friend and neighbour because he did the will of God.

26. Again he led me where there is a river of milk, and I saw in that place all the infants whom Herod slew because of the name of Christ, and they saluted me, and the angel said to me: All who keep their chastity with purity, when they shall have come out of the body, after they adore the Lord God are delivered to Michael and are led to the infants and they salute them, saying that they are our brothers and friends and members; in themselves they shall inherit the promises of God.

27. Again he took me up and carried me to the north of the city and led me where there was a river of wine, and there I saw Abraham and Isaac and Jacob, Lot and Job and other saints,[17] and they saluted me: and I asked and said: What is this place, my Lord? The angel answered and said to me: All who are receivers of pilgrims, when they go out of the world, first adore the Lord God, and are delivered to Michael and by this way are led into the city, and all the just salute him as son and brother, and say unto him: Because thou hast observed humanity and the receiving of pilgrims, come, have an inheritance in the city of the Lord our God: every just man shall receive good things of God in the city, according to his own action.

28. And again he carried me near the river of oil on the east of the city. And I saw there men rejoicing and singing psalms, and I said: Who are those, my Lord? And the angel saith to me: Those are they who devoted themselves to God with their whole heart and had no pride in themselves. For all those who rejoice in the Lord God and sing psalms to the Lord with their whole heart are here led into this city.

29. And he carried me into the midst of the city near the twelve walls.[18] But there was in this place a higher wall, and I asked and said: Is there in the City of Christ a wall which in honour exceeds this place? And the angel answering said to me: There is a second better than the first, and

similarly a third than the second, as each exceeds the other, unto the twelfth wall. And I said: Tell me, Sir, why one exceeds another in glory? And the angel answered and said unto me: All who have in themselves even a little detraction or zeal or pride, something of his glory would be made void even if he were in the city of Christ: look backward!

And turning round I saw golden thrones placed in each gate, and on them men having golden diadems and gems:[19] and I looked carefully and I saw inside between the twelve men thrones placed in another rank which appeared of much glory, so that no one is able to recount their praise. And I asked the angel and said: My lord, who is on the throne? And the angel answered and said unto me: Those thrones belong to those who had goodness and understanding of heart and made themselves fools for the sake of the Lord God, nor knew new Scriptures nor psalms, but, mindful of one chapter of the commands of God, and hearing what it contained they wrought thereby in much diligence and had s fight zeal before the Lord God, and the admiration of them will seize all the saints in presence of the Lord God, for talking with one another they say, Wait and see the unlearned who know nothing more: by which means they merited so great and such a garment and so great glory on account of their innocence.

And I saw in the midst of this city a great altar, very high, and there was one standing near the altar whose countenance shone as the sun, and he held in his hands a psaltery and harp, and he sang psalms, saying Halleluia! And his voice filled the whole city: at the same time when all they who were on the towers and gates heard him they responded Halleluia! so that the foundations of the city were shaken: and I asked the angel and said, Sir, who is this of so great power? And the angel said to me: This is David: this is the city of Jerusalem, for when Christ the King of Eternity shall come with the assurance of His kingdom, he again shall go before him that he may sing psalms, and all the just at the same time shall sing psalms responding Halleluia! And I said, Sir, how did David alone above the other saints make a beginning of psalm-singing? And the angel answered and said unto me: Because Christ the Son of God sits at the right hand of His Father, and this David sings psalms before him in the seventh heaven, and as is done in the heavens so also below, because the host may not be offered to God without David, but it is necessary that David should sing psalms in the hour of the oblation of the body and blood of Christ: as it is performed in heaven so also on earth.

30. And I said to the angel: Sir, what is Alleluia? And the angel answered and said to me: You ask questions about everything. And he said to me, Alleluia is said in the Hebrew language of God and angels, for the meaning of Alleluia is this: tecel cat. marith macha.[20] And I said, Sir, what is tecel cat. marith macha? And the angel answered and said unto me: *tecel'cat. marith macha* is: Let us all bless him together. I asked the angel and said, Sir, do all who say Alleluia bless the Lord? And the angel answered and said to me: It is so, and again, therefore, if any one sing Alleluia and those who are present do not sing at the same time, they commit sin because they do not sing along with him, And I said: My lord, does he also sin if he be hesitating or very old? The angel answered and said unto me: Not so, but he who is able and does not join in the singing, know such as a despiser of the Word, and it would be proud and unworthy that he should not bless the Lord God his maker.

31. Moreover when he had ceased speaking to me, he led me outside the city through the midst of the trees and far from the places of the land of the good, and put me across the river of milk and honey: and after that he led me over the ocean which supports the foundations of heaven.

The angel answered and said unto me: Dost thou understand why thou goest hence? And I said: Yes, sir. And he said to me Come and follow me, and I will show thee the souls of the impious and sinners, that thou mayest know what manner of place it is. And I proceeded with the angel and he carried me by the setting of the sun, and I saw the beginning of heaven rounded on a great river of water, and I asked: What is this river of water? And he said to me: This is Ocean which surrounds all the Earth. And when I was at the outer limit of Ocean I looked, and there was no light in that place, but darkness and sorrow and sadness: and I sighed.

And I saw there a fervent river of fire, and in it a multitude of men and women immersed. up to the knees, and other men up to the navel, others even up to the lips, others moreover up to the hair. And I asked the angel and said: Sir, who are those in the fiery river? And the angel answered and said to me: They are neither hot nor cold, because they were found neither in the number of the just nor in the number of the impious.[21] For those spent the time of their life on earth passing some days in prayer, but others in sins and fornications, until their death. And I asked him and said: Who are these, Sir, immersed up to their knees in fire? He answered and said to me: These are they who when they have gone out of church throw themselves into strange conversations to dispute. Those indeed who are immersed up to the navel are those who, when they have taken the body and blood of Christ go and fornicate and did not cease from their sins till they died. Those who are immersed up to the lips are the detractors of each other when they assemble in the church of God: those up to the eyebrows are those who nod approval of themselves and plot spite against their neighbour.[22]

32. And I saw on the north a place of various and diverse punishments full of men and women,[23] and a river of fire ran down into it. Moreover I observed and I saw pits great in depth, and in them several souls together, and the depth of that place was as it were three thousand cubits, and I saw them groaning and weeping and saying: Have pity on us, O Lord! and none had pity on them. And I asked the angel and said: Who are these, Sir? And the angel answered and said unto me: These are they who did not hope in the Lord, that they would be able to have him as their helper. And I asked and said: Sir, if these souls remain for thirty or forty generations thus one upon another, if they were sent deeper, the pits I believe would not hold them. And he said to me: The Abyss has no measure, for beyond[24] this it stretches down below him who is down in it: and so it is, that if perchance anyone should take a stone and throw it into a very deep well and after many hours it should reach the bottom, such is the abyss. For when the souls are thrown in there, they hardly reach the bottom in fifty years.

33. I, indeed, when I heard this, wept and groaned over the human race. The angel answered and said unto me: Why dost thou weep? Art thou more pitiful than God? For though God is good, He knows also that there are punishments, and He patiently bears with the human race, dismissing each one to work his own will in the time in which he dwells on the earth.

34. I further observed the fiery river and saw there a man being tortured by Tartaruchian angels having in their hands an iron with three hooks with which they pierced the bowels of that old man: and I asked the angel, and said: Sir, who is that old man on whom such torments are imposed? And the angel answered and said to me: He whom you see was a presbyter who did not perform well his ministry: when he had been eating and drinking and committing fornication he offered the host to the Lord at his holy altar.

35. And I saw not far away another old man led on by malign angels running with speed, and they pushed him into the fire up to his knees, and they struck him with stones and wounded his face like a storm, and did not allow him to say: Have pity on me! And I asked the angel and he said to me: He whom you see was a bishop, and did not perform well his episcopate, who indeed accepted the great name but did not enter into the witness of him who gave him the name in all his life, seeing that he did not do just judgment, and did not pity widows and orphans, but now he receives retribution according to his iniquity and his works.

36. And I saw another man in the fiery river up to his knees. Moreover his hands were stretched out and bloody, and worms proceeded from his mouth and nostrils and he was groaning and weeping, and crying he said: Have pity on me! for I am hurt above the rest who are in this punishment. And I asked, Sir, who is this? And he said to me: This man whom thou seest, was a deacon who devoured the oblations and committed fornications and did not right in the sight of God, for this cause he unceasingly pays this penalty.

And I looked closely and saw alongside of him another[25] man whom they delivered up with haste and cast into the fiery river, and he was (in it) up to the knees: and there came the angel who was set over the punishments having a great fiery razor, and with it he cut the lips of that man and the tongue likewise. And sighing, I lamented and asked: Who is that, sir. And he said to me, He whom thou seest was a reader and read to the people, but he himself did not keep the precepts of God: now he also pays the proper penalty.

37. And I saw another multitude of pits in the same place, and in the midst of it a river full of a multitude of men and women,[26] and worms[27] consumed them. But I lamented and sighing asked the angel and said: Sir, who are these? And he said to me: These are those who exacted interest[28] on interest and trusted in their riches and did not hope in God that He was their helper.

And after that I looked and saw another place, very narrow, and it was like a wall, and fire round about it. And I saw inside men and women gnawing[29] their tongues, and I asked: Sir, who are these. And he said to me: These are they who in church disparage the Word of God, not attending to it, but as it were make naught of God and His angels: for that cause they now likewise pay the proper penalty.

38. And I observed and saw another old man down in a pit and his countenance was like blood, and I asked and said, Sir, what is this place? And he said to me: Into that pit stream all the punishments. And I saw men and women immersed up to the lips and I asked, Sir, who are these? And he said to me: These are the magicians who prepared for men and women evil magic arts and did not find how to stop them till they died.

And again I saw men and women with very black faces in a pit of fire,[30] and I sighed and lamented and asked, Sir, who are these? And he said to me: These are fornicators and adulterers who committed adultery having wives of their own: likewise also the women committed adultery having husbands of their own: therefore they unceasingly suffer penalties.

39. And I saw there girls having black[31] raiment, and four terrible angels having in their hands burning chains, and they put them on the necks of the girls and led them into darkness: and I, again weeping, asked the angel: Who are these, Sir? And he said to me: These are they who, when they were virgins, defiled their virginity unknown to their parents; for which cause they unceasingly pay the proper penalties.

And again I observed there men and women with hands cut and their feet placed naked in a place of ice and snow, and worms devoured them. But seeing them I lamented and asked: Sir, who are these? And he said to me: These are they who harmed orphans and widows and the poor,[32] and did not hope in the Lord, for which cause they unceasingly pay the proper penalties.

And I observed and saw others hanging over a channel of water, and their tongues were very dry, and many fruits were placed in their sight, and they were not permitted to take of them, and I asked: Sir, who are these? And he said to me: These are they who break their fast[33] before the appointed hour, for this cause they unceasingly pay these penalties.

And I saw other men and women hanging by their eyebrows and their hair,[34] and a fiery river drew them, and I said: Who are these, my Lord? And he said to me:[35] These are they who join themselves not to their own husbands and wives but to whores, and therefore they unceasingly pay the proper penalties.

And I saw other men and women covered with dust, and their countenance was like blood, and they were in a pit of pitch and sulphur and running down into a fiery river, and I asked: Sir, who are these?[36] And he said to me: These are they who committed the iniquity of Sodom and Gomorrah, the male with the male, for which reason they unceasingly pay the penalties.

40. And[37] I observed and saw men and women clothed in bright garments, having their eyes blind, placed in a pit, and I asked: Sir, who are these? And he said to me: These are of the people who did alms, and knew not the Lord God, for which reason they unceasingly pay the proper penalties. And I observed and saw other men and women on an obelisk of fire, and beasts tearing them in pieces, and they were not allowed to say, Lord have pity on us! And I saw the angel[38] of penalties putting heavy punishments on them and saying: Acknowledge the Son of God; for this was predicted to you, when the divine Scriptures were read to you, and you did not attend; for which cause God's judgment is just, for your actions have apprehended you and brought you into these penalties. But I sighed and wept, and I asked and said: Who are these men and women who are strangled in fire and pay their penalties? And he answered me: These are women who defiled the image of God when bringing forth infants out of the womb, and these are the men who lay with them. And their infants addressed the Lord God and the angels who were set over the punishments, saying:[39] Cursed be the hour to our parents, for they defiled the image of God, having the name of God but not observing His precepts: they gave us for food to dogs and to be trodden down of swine: others they threw into the river. But their infants[40] were handed over to the angels of Tartarus who were set over the punishments, that they might lead them to a wide place of mercy: but their fathers and mothers were tortured in a perpetual punishment.

And after that I saw men and women clothed with rags full of pitch and fiery sulphur, and dragons were coiled about their necks and shoulders and feet, and angels having fiery horns restrained them and smote them, and closed their nostrils, saying to them: Why did ye not know the time in which it was right to repent and serve God, and did not do it? And I asked: Sir, who are these? And he said to me: These are they who seem to give up the world for God,[41] putting on our garb, but the impediments of the world made them wretched, not maintaining *agapae* , and they did not pity widows and orphans: they did not receive the stranger and the pilgrim, nor did they offer the oblations, and they did not pity their neighbour. Moreover their prayer did not even on one day ascend pure to the Lord God, but many impediments of the world detained them, and they were not able to do right in the sight of God, and the angels enclosed them in the place of punishments. Moreover they saw those who were in punishments and said to them: We indeed when we lived in the world neglected God, and ye also did likewise: as we also truly when we were in the world knew that ye were sinners. But ye said: These are just and servants of God, now we know why ye were called by the name of the Lord: for which cause they also pay their own penalties.

And sighing I wept and said: Woe unto men, woe unto sinners! why were they born? And the angel answered and said unto me: Why dost thou lament?[42] Art thou more pitiful than the Lord God who is blessed forever, who established judgment and sent forth every man to choose good and evil in his own will and do what pleases him? Then I lamented again very greatly, and he said to me: Dost thou lament when as yet thou hast not seen greater punishments? Follow me and thou shalt see seven times greater than these.

41. And he carried me south and placed me above a well, and I found it sealed with seven seals: and answering, the angel who was with me said to the angel of that place: Open the mouth of the well that Paul, the well-beloved of God, may see, for authority is given him that he may see all the pains of hell. And the angel said to me: Stand afar off that thou mayest be able to bear the stench of this place. When therefore the well was opened, immediately there arose from it a certain hard and malign stench, which surpasses all punishments: and I looked into the well and I saw fiery masses glowing in every. part, and narrow places, and the mouth of the well was narrow so as to admit one man only. And the angel answered and said unto me: If any man shall have been put into this well of the abyss and it shall have been sealed over him, no remembrance of him shall ever be made in the sight of the Father and His Son and the holy angels. And I said: Who are these, Sir, who are put into this well? And he said to me: They are whoever shall not confess that Christ has come in the flesh and that the Virgin Mary brought him forth, and whoever says that the bread and cup of the Eucharist of blessing are not this body and blood of Christ.

42. And I looked to the south in the west and I saw there a[43] restless worm and in that place there was gnashing of teeth: moreover the worms were one cubit long, and had two heads, and there I saw men and women in cold and gnashing of teeth. And I asked and said, Sir, who are these in this place? And he said to me: These are they who say that Christ did not rise from the dead and that this flesh will not rise again. And I asked and said: Sir, is there no fire nor heat in this place? And he said to me: In this place there is nothing else but cold and snow:[44] and again he said to me: Even if the sun should rise upon them, they do not become warm on account of the superabundant cold of that place and the snow.

But hearing these things I stretched out my hands and wept, and sighing again, I said: It were better for us if we had not been born,[45] all of us who are sinners.

43. But when those who were in the same place saw me weeping with the angel, they themselves cried out and wept saying, Lord God have mercy upon us! And after these things I saw the heavens open, and Michael[46] the archangel descending from heaven, and with him was the whole army of angels, and they came to those who were placed in punishment and seeing him, again weeping, they cried out and said, Have pity on as! Michael the archangel, have pity on us and on the human race, for on account of thy prayers the earth standeth. We now see the judgment and acknowledge the Son of God! It was impossible for us before these things to pray for this, before we entered into this place: for we heard that there was a judgment before we went out of the world, but impediments and the life of the world did not allow us to repent. And Michael answered and said: Hear Michael speaking! I am he who stands in the sight of God every. hour: As the Lord liveth, in whose sight I stand, I do not intermit one day or one night praying incessantly for the human race, and I indeed pray for those who are on the earth: but they do not cease doing iniquity and fornications, and they do not bring to me any good while they are placed on earth: and ye have consumed in vanity the time in which ye ought to have repented. But I have always prayed thus and I now beseech that God may send dew and send forth rains upon the earth, and now I desire until the earth produce its fruits and verily I say, that if any have done but a little good, I will agonise for him, protecting him till he have escaped the judgment of penalties. Where therefore are your prayers? Where are your penances? Ye have lost your time contemptuously. But now weep and I will weep with you and the angels who are with me with the well-beloved Paul, if perchance the merciful God will have pity and give you refreshment. But hearing these words they cried out and wept greatly, and all said with one voice: Have pity on us, Son of God! And I, Paul, sighed and said: O Lord God! have pity on thy creature, have pity on the sons of men, have pity on thine image.

44. And I looked and saw the heaven move like a tree shaken by the wind. Suddenly, moreover, they threw, themselves on their faces in the sight of the throne. And I saw twenty-four elders and twenty-four thousand adoring God, and I saw an altar and veil and throne, and all were rejoicing; and the smoke of a good odour was raised near the altar of the throne of God, and I heard the voice of one saying: For the sake of what do ye our angels and ministers intercede? And they cried out saying: We intercede seeing thy many kindnesses to the human race. And after these things I saw the Son of God descending from heaven, and a diadem was on his head. And seeing him those who were placed in punishment exclaimed all with one voice saying: Have pity, Son of the High God! Thou art He who shewest refreshment for all in the heavens and on earth, and on us likewise have pity, for since we have seen Thee, we have refreshment. And a voice went out from the Son of God through all the punishments saying: And what work have ye done that ye demand refreshment from me? My blood was poured out for your sakes, and not even so did ye repent: for your sakes I wore the crown of thorns on my head: for you I received buffets on my cheeks, and not even so did ye repent. I asked water when hanging on the cross and they gave me vinegar mixed with gall, with a spear they opened my right side, for my name's sake they slew my prophets and just men, and in all these things I gave you a place of repentance and ye would not. Now, however, for the sake of Michael the archangel of my covenant and the angels who are with him, and because of Paul the well-beloved, whom I would not vex, for the sake of your brethren who are in the world and offer oblations, and for the sake of your sons, because my precepts are in them, and more for the sake of mine own kindness, on the day on which I rose from the dead, I give to you all who are in punishment a night and a day of refreshment forever. And they all cried out and said, We bless thee, Son of God, that Thou hast given us a night and a day of respite. For better to us is a refreshment of one day above all the time of our life which we were on earth, and if we had plainly known that this was intended for those who sin, we would have worked no other work, we would have done no business, and we

would have done no iniquity: what need had we for pride in the world? For here our pride is crushed which ascended from our mouth against our neighbour: our plagues and excessive straitness and the tears and the worms which are under us, these are much worse to us than the pains which we have left behind us. When they said thus, the malign angels of the penalties were angered with them, saying: How long do ye lament and sigh? for ye had no pity. For this is the judgment of God who had no pity. But ye received this great grace of a day and a night's refreshment on the Lord's Day for the sake of Paul the well-beloved of God who descended to you.

45. And after that the angel said to me: Hast thou seen all these things? And I said: Yes, Sir. And he said to me: Follow me and I will lead thee into Paradise, that the just who are there may see thee, for lo! they hope to see thee, and they are ready to come to meet thee in joy and gladness. And I followed the angel by the impulse of the Holy Spirit, and he placed me in Paradise and said to me: This is Paradise in which Adam and his wife erred. Moreover I entered Paradise and saw the beginning of waters, and there was an angel making a sign to me and he said to me: Observe, said he, the waters, for this is the river of Physon which surrounds all the land of Evilla, and the second is Geon which surrounds all the land of Egypt and Ethiopia, and the third is Thigris which is over against the Assyrians, and another is Eufrates which waters all the land of Mesopotamia. And when I had gone inside I saw a tree planted from whose roots water flowed out, and from this beginning there were four rivers. And the spirit of God rested on that tree, and when the Spirit blew, the waters flowed forth, and I said: My Lord, is it this tree itself which makes the waters flow? And he said to me: That from the beginning, before the heavens and earth were manifested, and all things here invisible, the Spirit of God was borne upon the waters, but from the time when the command of God made the heavens and earth to appear, the Spirit rested upon this tree: wherefore whenever the Spirit blows, the waters flow forth from the tree. And he held me by the hand and led me near the tree of knowledge of good and evil, and he said: This is the tree by which death entered into the world, and receiving of it through his wife Adam ate and death entered into the world. And he shewed me another tree in the midst of Paradise, and saith to me: This is the tree of life.

46. While I was yet looking upon the tree, I saw a virgin coming from afar and two hundred angels before her saying hymns, and I asked and said: Sir, who is she who comes in so great glory? And he said to me: This is Mary the Virgin, the Mother of the Lord. And coming near she saluted me and said: Hail, Paul! well-beloved of God and angels and men. For all the saints prayed my Son Jesus who is my Lord that thou mightest come hither in the body that they might see thee before thou goest out of the world. And the Lord said to them: Bear and be patient: yet a little and ye shall see him and he shall be with you for ever: and again they all said to him together: Do not vex us, for we desire to see him in the flesh, for by him Thy name was greatly glorified in the world, and we have seen that he endured all the labours whether of the greater or of the less. This we learn from those who come hither. For when we say: Who is he who directed you in the world? they reply to us: There is one in the world whose name is Paul, he preaches and announces Christ, and we believe that many have entered into the kingdom through the virtue and sweetness of his speeches. Behold all the just men are behind me coming to meet thee, Paul, and I first come for this cause to meet them who did the will of my Son and my Lord Jesus Christ, I first advance to meet them and do not send them away to be as wanderers until they meet in peace.

47. When she had thus spoken, I saw three coming from afar, very beautiful in the likeness of Christ, and their forms were shining, and their angels, and I asked: Sir, who are these? And he said to me: Dost thou not know those? And I said: No, Sir. And he answered: These are the fathers of the people, Abraham, Isaac, and Jacob. And coming near they saluted me, and said: Hail, Paul, well-beloved of God and men; blessed is he who suffers violence for the Lord's sake. And Abraham answered me and said: This is my son Isaac, and Jacob my well-beloved, and we have known the Lord and followed him; blessed are all they who believed in thy word, that they may be able to inherit the Kingdom of God by labour, by renunciation, and sanctification, and humility, and charity, and meekness, and right faith in the Lord; and we also have had devotion to the Lord whom thou preachest in the testament, that we might assist those who believed in him with their whole soul, and might minister unto them as fathers minister to their children.

When they had thus spoken, I saw other twelve coming from afar in honour, and I asked: Sir, who are these? And he said: These are the patriarchs. And coming near they saluted me and said: Hail, Paul, well-beloved of God and men: the Lord did not vex us, that we might see thee yet in the body, before thou goest out of the world. And each one of them reminded me of his name in order, from Ruben to Benjamin: and Joseph said to me: I am he who was sold; but I say to thee, Paul, that all the things, whatever my brothers did to me, in nothing did I act maliciously with them, nor in all the labour which they imposed on me, nor in any point was I hurt by them on that account from morning till evening: blessed is he who receives some hurt on account of the Lord, and bears it,

for the Lord will repay it to him manifold, when he shall have gone out of the world.

48. When he had spoken thus far, I saw another beautiful one coming from afar, and his angels saying hymns, and I asked: Sir, who is this that is beautiful of countenance? And he saith to me: Dost thou not know him? And I said: No, Sir. And he said to me: This is Moses the law-giver, to whom God gave the law. And when he had come near me, he immediately wept, and after that he saluted me: and I said to him: What dost thou lament? for I have heard that thou excellest every. man in meekness. And he answered saying: I weep for those whom I planted with toil, because they did not bear fruit, nor did any profit by them; and I saw all the sheep whom I fed, that they were scattered and become as if they had no shepherd, and because all the toils which I endured for the sake of the sons of Israel were accounted as naught, and how greatso-ever virtues I did in the midst of them these they did not understand, and I wonder that strangers and uncircumcised and idol-worshippers have been converted and have entered into the promises of God, but Israel has not entered; and now I say unto thee, brother Paul, that in that hour when the people hanged Jesus whom thou preachest, that the Father, the God of all, who gave me the law, and Michael and all the angels and archangels, and Abraham and Isaac, and Jacob, and all the just wept over the Son of God hanging on the cross. In that hour all the saints attended on me looking (upon me) and they said to me: See, Moses, what men of thy people have done to the Son of God. Wherefore thou art blessed, Paul, and blessed the generation and race which believed in thy word.

49. When he had spoken thus far, there came other twelve, and seeing me said: Art thou Paul the glorified in heaven and on earth? And I answered and said: What are ye? The first answered and said: I am Esaias whom Manasses cut asunder with a wooden saw. And the second said likewise: I am Jeremias who was stoned by the children of Israel and slain. And the third said: I am Ezekiel whom the children of Israel dragged by the feet over a rock in a mountain till they knocked out my brains, and we endured all these toils, wishing to save the children of Israel: and I say unto thee that after the toils which they laid upon me, I cast myself on my face in the sight of the Lord praying for them, bending my knees until the second hour of the Lord's day, till Michael came and lifted me up from the earth. Blessed art thou, Paul, and blessed the nation which believed through thee.

And as these passed by, I saw another, beautiful of countenance, and I asked: Sir, Who is this? Who when he had seen me, rejoiced and said to me: This is Lot[47] who was found just in Sodom. And approaching[48] he saluted me and said: Blessed art thou, Paul, and blessed the generation to which thou didst minister. And I answered and said to him: Art thou Lot who wast found just in Sodom? And he said: I entertained angels, as travellers, and when they of the city wished to violate them, I offered them my two virgin daughters who had not yet known men, and gave them to them saying: use them as ye will, but only to these men ye shall do no evil; for this cause they entered under the roof of my house. For this cause, therefore, we ought to be confident and know that if anyone shall have done anything, God shall repay him manifold when they shall come to him. Blessed art thou, Paul, and blessed the nation which believed in thy word.

When, therefore, he had ceased talking to me, I saw another coming from a distance, very beautiful of countenance, and smiling, and his angels saying hymns: and I said to the angel who was with me: Has then each of the just an angel for companion? And he said to me: Each one of the saints has his own (angel) assisting him, and saying a hymn, and the one does not depart from the other. And I said: Who is this, Sir? And he said: This is Job. And approaching, he saluted me and said: Brother Paul, thou hast great praise with God and men. And I am Job, who laboured much for a period of thirty years from a plague in the blood; and verily in the beginning, the wounds which went forth from my body were like grains of wheat. But on the third day, they became as the foot of an ass; worms moreover which fell four digits in length: and on the third (day) the devil appeared and said to me: Say something against God and die. I said to him: If such be the will of God that I should remain under a plague all the time of my life till I die, I shall not cease from blessing the Lord, and I shall receive more reward. For I know that the labours of that world are nothing to the refreshment which is afterwards: for which cause blessed art thou, Paul, and blessed the nation which believed through thee.

50. When he had spoken thus far, another came calling from afar and saying: Blessed art thou, Paul, and blessed am I because I saw thee, the beloved of the Lord. And I asked the angel: Sir, who is this? And he answered and said unto me: This is Noe in the time of the deluge. And immediately we saluted each other: and greatly rejoicing he said to me: Thou art Paul the most beloved of God. And I asked him: Who art thou? And he said: I am Noe, who was in the time of the deluge. And I say to thee, Paul, that working for a hundred years, I made the ark, not putting off the tunic with which I was clad, nor did I cut the hair of my head. Till then also I cherished continence, not approaching my own wife: in those hundred years not a hair of my head grew in length, nor did my garments become soiled: and I besought men at all times saying: Repent, for a deluge of waters will come upon you. But they laughed at me, and

mocked my words; and again they said to me: But this is the time of those who are able to play and sin freely, desiring her with whom it is possible to commit fornication frequently: for God does not regard this, and does not know what things are done by us men, and there is no flood of waters straightway coming upon this world. And they did not cease from their sins, till God destroyed all flesh which had the breath of life in it. Know then that God loveth one just man more than all the world of the impious. Wherefore, blessed art thou, Paul, and blessed is the nation which believes through thee.

51. And turning round, I saw other just ones coming from afar, and I asked the angel: Sir, who are those? And he answered me: These are Elias and Eliseus.[49] And they saluted me: and I said to them: Who are ye? And one of them answered and said: I am Elias, the prophet of God; I am Elias who prayed, and because of my word, the heaven did not rain for three years and six months, on account of the unrighteousness of men. God is just and true, who doeth the will of his servants: for the angels often besought the Lord for rain, and he said: Be patient till my servant Elias shall pray and petition for this and I will send rain on the earth.[50]

The End of the Vision of Saint Paul.

Book 147. The Epistle of Tiberius to Pilate

This is the reply of Caesar Augustus and sent to Pilate Pontius, who holds the rule in the eastern part of the kingdom. He also wrote his judicial decision and sent it with the courier Rahab, to whom he gave two thousand soldiers as well.

"Because you condemned Jesus of Nazareth to a violent death that was completely unjust, and before condemning him to death you handed him over to the insatiably furious Jews, and you showed no sympathy for this righteous man, but dipping your pen you delivered a disastrous judicial decision, and having him flogged you handed him over to be crucified, without cause, and you received gifts for condemning him to death, sympathizing with him in what you said, but in your heart handing him over to the lawless Jews—or all this you will be brought to me as a prisoner to defend yourself and render to me an account of what you have done, on behalf of this one whom you handed over to death without cause. Oh your shamelessness and hardness! When I heard about this in a report, I was moved in my soul and cut to the core. For a certain woman has come to me, calling herself a disciple of this man; she is Mary Magdalene, from whom others testify that he had cast out seven demons. She has testified that this one performed great healings: he made the blind see, the lame walk, and the deaf hear; he cleansed lepers and, to put it simply, as she herself testified, he performed these healings by a word alone. How could you permit him to be crucified without cause? Even if you did not receive him as a god, at least you should have sympathized with him as a physician. But even from your own treacherous writing that has come to me you have pronounced your penalty, since you write that he is greater even than the gods that we worship. How could you deliver him over to death? But just as you condemned this one unjustly and delivered him to death, I in turn will deliver you to death justly. And not only you, but also all your councillors and companions, from whom you received the gifts for his death."

As he gave the letter to the letter carriers, Augustus's judicial sentence was also given them in a written order, that they were to kill the entire race of the Jews with the sword, and that Pilate was to be brought to Rome as a condemned prisoner, along with the leaders of the Jews, those who were then the rulers of the region, Archaelaus, the son of the despised Herod, and his companion Philip, and those who were their chief priests, both Caiaphas and his father-in-law, Annas, and all the leaders of the Jews. When Rahab went forth with the soldiers, he did as he was commanded, and slew the entire male race of the Jews with the sword, and the gentiles sexually defiled their profane wives; and the loathsome posterity of their father, Satan, came to life and rose up. The courier took Pilate, Archaelaus, and also Philip, Annas, and Caiaphas, and all the leaders of the Jews, and led them as prisoners to Rome. But it came about that while they were passing through a certain island named Crete, Caiaphas was miserably and violently severed from life. When they took him in order to bury him, the ground would not receive him at all, but cast him out. Seeing this, the entire multitude took stones with their own hands and cast them on him, and so buried him. But the others came to anchor near Rome.

Now there was a custom among the ancient rulers that if someone was condemned to death but should happen to see their face, he would be spared from his condemnation. And so Caesar ordered that Pilate not see him, so that he might not be saved from death. Because of this command, they bricked him up in a certain cave, and left him there. But they rolled Annas up in the skin of an ox, and as the leather dried out under the sun, he was pressed tightly in it, so that his intestines came out through his mouth, and it violently tore away his wretched life. But all the other Jews who were given over to him he delivered to death. They killed these by the sword. But Archelaus, son of the despised Herod, and his companion Philip, he ordered to be impaled.

One day the king went out to hunt and was pursuing a certain deer. The deer came to the opening of the cave and stood there. Now Pilate was about to be killed by the hand of Caesar. That the inevitable might be fulfilled, Pilate moved forward to see the ruler, while the deer was standing in front of him. Caesar placed an arrow on his bow to shoot the deer, and the arrow passed through the opening and killed Pilate.

All who believe in Christ, our true God and savior, give him glory and greatness. For to him is due the glory, honor, and worship, with his Father who is without beginning, and the Spirit who is of his same nature, now and always, even unto the ages. Amen.

Book 148. The Apology of Aristides

1. I, O King, by the grace of God came into this world; and when I had considered the heaven and the earth and the seas, and had surveyed the sun and the rest of creation, I marvelled at the beauty of the world. And I perceived that the world and all that is therein are moved by the power of another; and I understood that he who moves them is God, who is hidden in them, and veiled by them. And it is manifest that that which causes motion is more powerful than that which is moved. But that I should make search concerning this same mover of all, as to what is his nature (for it seems to me, he is indeed unsearchable in his nature), and that I should argue as to the constancy of his government, so as to grasp it fully — this is a vain effort for me; for it is not possible that a man should fully comprehend it. I say, however, concerning this mover of the world, that he is God of all, who made all things for the sake of mankind. And it seems to me that this is reasonable, that one should fear God and should not oppress man.

I say, then, that God is not born, not made, an ever-abiding nature without beginning and without end, immortal, perfect, and incomprehensible. Now when I say that he is perfect, this means that there is not in him any defect, and he is not in need of anything but all things are in need of him. And when I say that he is without beginning, this means that everything which has beginning has also an end, and that which has an end may be brought to an end. He has no name, for everything which has a name is kindred to things created. Form he has none, nor yet any union of members; for whatsoever possesses these is kindred to things fashioned. He is neither male nor female. The heavens do not limit him, but the heavens and all things, visible and invisible, receive their bounds from him. Adversary he has none, for there exists not any stronger than he. Wrath and indignation he possesses not, for there is nothing which is able to stand against him. Ignorance and forgetfulness are not in his nature, for he is altogether wisdom and understanding; and in Him stands fast all that exists. He requires not sacrifice and libation, nor even one of things visible; He requires not anything from any, but all living creatures stand in need of him.

2. Since, then, we have addressed you concerning God, so far as our discourse can bear upon him, let us now come to the race of men, that we may know which of them participate in the truth of which we have spoken, and which of them go astray from it.

This is clear to you, O King, that there are four classes of men in this world:— Barbarians and Greeks, Jews and Christians. The Barbarians, indeed, trace the origin of their kind of religion from Kronos and from Rhea and their other gods; the Greeks, however, from Helenos, who is said to be sprung from Zeus. And by Helenos there were born Aiolos and Xuthos; and there were others descended from Inachos and Phoroneus, and lastly from the Egyptian Danaos and from Kadmos and from Dionysos.

The Jews, again, trace the origin of their race from Abraham, who begot Isaac, of whom was born Jacob. And he begot twelve sons who migrated from Syria to Egypt; and there they were called the nation of the Hebrews, by him who made their laws; and at length they were named Jews. The Christians, then, trace the beginning of their religion from Jesus the Messiah; and he is named the Son of God Most High. And it is said that God came down from heaven, and from a Hebrew virgin assumed and clothed himself with flesh; and the Son of God lived in a daughter of man. This is taught in the gospel, as it is called, which a short time ago was preached among them; and you also if you will read therein, may perceive the power which belongs to it. This Jesus, then, was born of the race of the Hebrews; and he had twelve disciples in order that the purpose of his incarnation might in time be accomplished. But he himself was pierced by the Jews, and he died and was buried; and they say that after three days he rose and ascended to heaven. Thereupon those twelve disciples went forth throughout the known parts of the world, and kept showing his greatness with all modesty and uprightness. And hence also those of the present day who believe that preaching are called Christians, and they have become famous.

So then there are, as I said above, four classes of men: — Barbarians and Greeks, Jews and Christians.

Moreover the wind is obedient to God, and fire to the angels; the waters also to the demons and the earth to the sons of men.

3. Let us begin, then, with the Barbarians, and go on to the rest of the nations one after another, that we may see which of them hold the truth as to God and which of them hold error.

The Barbarians, then, as they did not apprehend God, went astray among the elements, and began to worship things created instead of their Creator; and for this end they made images and shut them up in shrines, and lo! They worship them, guarding them the while with much care, lest their gods be stolen by robbers. And the Barbarians did not observe that that which acts as guard is greater than that which is guarded, and that everyone who creates is greater than that which is created. If it be, then, that their gods are too feeble to see to their own safety, how will they take thought for the safety of men? Great then is the error into which the Barbarians wandered in worshipping lifeless images which can do nothing to help them. And I am led to wonder, O King, at their philosophers, how that even they went astray, and gave the name of gods to images which were made in honour of the elements; and that their sages did not perceive that the elements also are dissoluble and perishable. For if a small part of an element is dissolved or destroyed, the whole of it may be dissolved and destroyed. If then the elements themselves are dissolved and destroyed and forced to be subject to another that is more stubborn than they, and if they are not in their nature gods, why, forsooth, do they call the images which are made in their honour, God? Great, then, is the error which the philosophers among them have brought upon their followers.

4. Let us turn now, O King, to the elements in themselves, that we may make clear in regard to them, that they are not gods, but a created thing, liable to ruin and change, which is of the same nature as man; whereas God is imperishable and unvarying, and invisible, while yet He sees, and overrules, and transforms all things.

Those then who believe concerning the earth that it is a god have hitherto deceived themselves, since it is furrowed and set with plants and trenched; and it takes in the filthy refuse of men and beasts and cattle. And at times it becomes unfruitful, for if it be burnt to ashes it becomes devoid of life, for nothing germinates from an earthen jar. And besides if water be collected upon it, it is dissolved together with its products. And it is trodden under foot of men and beast, and receives the bloodstains of the slain; and it is dug open, and filled with the dead, and becomes a tomb for corpses. But it is impossible that a nature, which is holy and worthy and blessed and immortal, should allow of anyone of these things. And hence it appears to us that the earth is not a god but a creation of God.

5. In the same way, again, those erred who believed the waters to be gods. For the waters were created for the use of man, and are put under his rule in many ways. For they suffer change and admit impurity, and are destroyed and lose their nature while they are boiled into many substances. And they take colors which do not belong to them; they are also congealed by frost and are mingled and permeated with the filth of men and beasts, and with the blood of the slain. And being checked by skilled workmen through the restraint of aqueducts, they flow and are diverted against their inclination, and come into gardens and other places in order that they may be collected and issue forth as a means of fertility for man, and that they may cleanse away every impurity and fulfil the service man requires from them. Wherefore it is impossible that the waters should be a god, but they are a work of God and a part of the world.

In like manner also they who believed that fire is a god erred to no slight extent. For it, too, was created for the service of men, and is subject to them in many ways:— in the preparation of meat, and as a means of casting metals, and for other ends whereof your Majesty is aware. At the same time it is quenched and extinguished in many ways.

Again they also erred who believed the motion of the winds to be a god. For it is well known to us that those winds are under the dominion of another, at times their motion increases, and at times it fails and ceases at the command of him who controls them. For they were created by God for the sake of men, in order to supply the necessity of trees and fruits and seeds; and to bring over the sea ships which convey for men necessaries and goods from places where they are found to places where they are not found; and to govern the quarters of the world. And as for itself, at times it increases and again abates; and in one place brings help and in another causes disaster at the bidding of him who rules it. And mankind too are able by known means to confine and keep it in check in order that it may fulfil for them the service they require from it. And of itself it has not any authority at all. And hence it is impossible that the winds should be called gods, but rather a thing made by God.

6. So also they erred who believed that the sun is a god. For we see that it is moved by the compulsion of another, and revolves and makes its journey, and proceeds from sign to sign, rising and setting every day, so as to give warmth for the growth of plants and trees, and to bring forth into the air where with it (sunlight) is mingled every growing thing which is upon the earth. And to it there belongs by comparison a part in common with the rest of the stars in its course; and though it is one in its nature it is associated with many parts for the supply of the needs of men; and that not according to its own will but rather according to the will of him who

rules it. And hence it is impossible that the sun should be a god, but the work of God; and in like manner also the moon and the stars.

7. And those who believed of the men of the past, that some of them were gods, they too were much mistaken. For as you yourself allow, O King, man is constituted of the four elements and of a soul and a spirit (and hence he is called a microcosm), and without anyone of these parts he could not consist. He has a beginning and an end, and he is born and dies. But God, as I said, has none of these things in his nature, but is uncreated and imperishable. And hence it is not possible that we should set up man to be of the nature of God: — man, to whom at times when he looks for joy, there comes trouble, and when he looks for laughter there comes to him weeping — who is wrathful and covetous and envious, with other defects as well. And he is destroyed in many ways by the elements and also by the animals.

And hence, O King, we are bound to recognize the error of the Barbarians, that, thereby, since they did not find traces of the true God, they fell aside from the truth, and went after the desire of their imagination, serving the perishable elements and lifeless images, and through their error not apprehending what the true God is.

8. Let us turn further to the Greeks also, that we may know what opinion they hold as to the true God. The Greeks, then, because they are more subtle than the Barbarians, have gone further astray than the Barbarians; inasmuch as they have introduced many fictitious gods, and have set up some of them as males and some as females; and in that some of their gods were found who were adulterers, and did murder, and were deluded, and envious, and wrathful and passionate, and parricides, and thieves, and robbers. And some of them, they say, were crippled and limped, and some were sorcerers, and some actually went mad, and some played on lyres, and some were given to roaming on the hills, and some even died, and some were struck dead by lightning, and some were made servants even to men, and some escaped by flight, and some were kidnapped by men, and some, indeed, were lamented and deplored by men. And some, they say, went down to Sheol, and some were grievously wounded, and some transformed themselves into the likeness of animals to seduce the race of mortal women, and some polluted themselves by lying with males. And some, they say, were wedded to their mothers and their sisters and their daughters. And they say of their gods that they committed adultery with the daughters of men; and of these there was born a certain race which also was mortal. And they say that some of the females disputed about beauty, and appeared before men for judgment. Thus, O King, have the Greeks put forward foulness, and absurdity, and folly about their gods and about themselves, in that they have called those that are of such a nature gods, who are no gods. And hence mankind have received incitements to commit adultery and fornication, and to steal and to practise all that is offensive and hated and abhorred. For if they who are called their gods practised all these things which are written above, how much more should men practise them — men, who believe that their gods themselves practised them. And owing to the foulness of this error there have happened to mankind harassing wars, and great famines, and bitter captivity, and complete desolation. And lo! It was by reason of this alone that they suffered and that all these things came upon them; and while they endured those things they did not perceive in their mind that for their error those things came upon them.

9. Let us proceed further to their account of their gods that we may carefully demonstrate all that is said above. First of all, the Greeks bring forward as a god Kronos, that is to say Chiun (Saturn). And his worshippers sacrifice their children to him, and they burn some of them alive in his honour. And they say that he took to him among his wives Rhea, and begot many children by her. By her too he begot Dios, who is called Zeus. And at length he (Kronos) went mad, and through fear of an oracle that had been made known to him, he began to devour his sons. And from him Zeus was stolen away without his knowledge; and at length Zeus bound him, and mutilated the signs of his manhood, and flung them into the sea. And hence, as they say in fable, there was engendered Aphrodite, who is called Astarte. And he (Zeus) cast out Kronos fettered into darkness. Great then is the error and ignominy which the Greeks have brought forward about the first of their gods, in that they have said all this about him, O King. It is impossible that a god should be bound or mutilated; and if it be otherwise, he is indeed miserable.

And after Kronos they bring forward another god Zeus. And they say of him that he assumed the sovereignty, and was king over all the gods. And they say that he changed himself into a beast and other shapes in order to seduce mortal women, and to raise up by them children for himself. Once, they say, he changed himself into a bull through love of Europe and Pasiphae. And again he changed himself into the likeness of gold through love of Danae, and to a swan through love of Leda, and to a man through love of Antiope, and to lightning through love of Luna, and so by these he begot many children. For by Antiope, they say, that he begot Zethus and Amphion, and by Luna Dionysos, by Alcmena Hercules, and by Leto, Apollo and Artemis, and by Danae Perseus, and by Leda, Castor and Polydeuces, and Helene and Paludus, and by Mnemosyne he begot nine daughters whom they styled the Muses, and by Europe, Minos and Rhadamanthos and Sarpedon. And lastly he changed himself into the likeness of an eagle through his passion for Ganydemos (Ganymede) the shepherd.

By reason of these tales, O King, much evil has arisen among men, who to this day are imitators of their gods, and practise adultery and defile themselves with their mothers and their sisters, and by lying with males, and some make bold to slay even their parents. For if he who is said to be the chief and king of their gods do these things how much more should his worshippers imitate him? And great is the folly which the Greeks have brought forward in their narrative concerning him. For it is impossible that a god should practise adultery or fornication or come near to lie with males, or kill his parents; and if it be otherwise, he is much worse than a destructive demon.

10. Again they bring forward as another god Hephaistos. And they say of him, that he is lame, and a cap is set on his head, and he holds in his hands firetongs and a hammer; and he follows the craft of iron working, that thereby he may procure the necessaries of his livelihood. Is then this god so very needy? But it cannot be that a god should be needy or lame, else he is very worthless.

And further they bring in another god and call him Hermes. And they say that he is a thief, a lover of avarice, and greedy for gain, and a magician and mutilated and an athlete, and an interpreter of language. But it is impossible that a god should be a magician or avaricious, or maimed, or craving for what is not his, or an athlete. And if it be otherwise, he is found to be useless.

And after him they bring forward as another god Asklepios. And they say that he is a physician and prepares drugs and plaster that he may supply the necessaries of his livelihood. Is then this god in want? And at length he was struck with lightning by Dios on account of Tyndareos of Lacedæmon, and so he died. If then Asklepios were a god, and, when he was struck with lightning, was unable to help himself, how should he be able to give help to others? But that a divine nature should be in want or be destroyed by lightning is impossible.

And again they bring forward another as a god, and they call him Ares. And they say that he is a warrior, and jealous, and covets sheep and things which are not his. And he makes gain by his arms. And they say that at length he committed adultery with Aphrodite, and was caught by the little boy Eros and by Hephaistos the husband of Aphrodite. But it is impossible that a god should be a warrior or bound or an adulterer.

And again they say of Dionysos that he forsooth! Is a god, who arranges carousals by night, and teaches drunkenness, and carries off women who do not belong to him. And at length, they say, he went mad and dismissed his handmaidens and fled into the desert; and during his madness he ate serpents. And at last he was killed by Titanos. If then Dionysos were a god, and when he was being killed was unable to help himself, how is it possible that he should help others?

Herakles next they bring forward and say that he is a god, who hates detestable things, a tyrant, and warrior and a destroyer of plagues. And of him also they say that at length he became mad and killed his own children, and cast himself into a fire and died. If then Herakles is a god, and in all these calamities was unable to rescue himself, how should others ask help from him? But it is impossible that a god should be mad, or drunken or a slayer of his children, or consumed by fire.

11. And after him they bring forward another god and call him Apollon. And they say that he is jealous and inconstant, and at times he holds the bow and quiver, and again the lyre and plectron. And he utters oracles for men that he may receive rewards from them. Is then this god in need of rewards? But it is an insult that all these things should be found with a god.

And after him they bring forward as a goddess Artemis, the sister of Apollo; and they say that she was a huntress and that she herself used to carry a bow and bolts, and to roam about upon the mountains, leading the hounds to hunt stags or wild boars of the field. But it is disgraceful that a virgin maid should roam alone upon the hills or hunt in the chase for animals. Wherefore it is impossible that Artemis should be a goddess.

Again they say of Aphrodite that she indeed is a goddess. And at times she dwells with their gods, but at other times she is a neighbour to men. And once she had Ares as a lover, and again Adonis who is Tammuz. Once also, Aphrodite was wailing and weeping for the death of Tammuz, and they say that she went down to Sheol that she might redeem Adonis from Persephone, who is the daughter of Sheol (Hades). If then Aphrodite is a goddess and was unable to help her lover at his death, how will she find it possible to help others? And this cannot be listened to, that a divine nature should come to weeping and wailing and adultery.

And again they say of Tammuz that he is a god. And he is, forsooth! A hunter and an adulterer. And they say that he was killed by a wound from a wild boar, without being able to help himself. And if he could not help himself, how can he take thought for the human race? But that a god should be an adulterer or a hunter or should die by violence is impossible.

Again they say of Rhea that she is the mother of their gods. And they say that she had once a lover Atys, and that she used to delight in depraved men. And at last she raised a lamentation and mourned for Atys her lover.

If then the mother of their gods was unable to help her lover and deliver him from death, how can she help others? So it is disgraceful that a goddess should lament and weep and take delight in depraved men.

Again they introduce Kore and say that she is a goddess, and she was stolen away by Pluto, and could not help herself. If then she is a goddess and was unable to help herself how will she find means to help others? For a god who is stolen away is very powerless.

All this, then, O King, have the Greeks brought forward concerning their gods, and they have invented and declared it concerning them. And hence all men received an impulse to work all profanity and all defilements; and hereby the whole earth was corrupted.

12. The Egyptians, moreover, because they are more base and stupid than every people that is on the earth, have themselves erred more than all. For the deities (or religion) of the Barbarians and the Greeks did not suffice for them, but they introduced some also of the nature of the animals, and said thereof that they were gods, and likewise of creeping things which are found on the dry land and in the waters. And of plants and herbs they said that some of them were gods. And they were corrupted by every kind of delusion and defilement more than every people that is on the earth. For from ancient times they worshipped Isis, and they say that she is a goddess whose husband was Osiris her brother. And when Osiris was killed by Typhon his brother, Isis fled with Horos her son to Byblus in Syria, and was there for a certain time till her son was grown. And he contended with Typhon his uncle, and killed him. And then Isis returned and went about with Horos her son and sought for the dead body of Osiris her lord, bitterly lamenting his death. If then Isis be a goddess, and could not help Osiris her brother and lord, how can she help another? But it is impossible that a divine nature should be afraid, and flee for safety, or should weep and wail; or else it is very miserable.

And of Osiris also they say that he is a serviceable god. And he was killed by Typhon and was unable to help himself. But it is well known that this cannot be asserted of divinity. And further, they say of his brother Typhon that he is a god, who killed his brother and was killed by his brother's son and by his bride, being unable to help himself. And how, pray, is he a god who does not save himself?

As the Egyptians, then, were more stupid than the rest of the nations, these and such like gods did not suffice for them. Nay, but they even apply the name of gods to animals in which there is no soul at all. For some of them worship the sheep and others the calf; and some the pig and others the shad fish; and some the crocodile and the hawk and the fish and the ibis and the vulture and the eagle and the raven. Some of them worship the cat, and others the turbotfish, some the dog, some the adder, and some the asp, and others the lion; and others the garlic and onions and thorns, and others the tiger and other such things. And the poor creatures do not see that all these things are nothing, although they daily witness their gods being eaten and consumed by men and also by their fellows; while some of them are cremated, and some die and decay and become dust, without their observing that they perish in many ways. So the Egyptians have not observed that such things which are not equal to their own deliverance, are not gods. And if, forsooth, they are weak in the case of their own deliverance, whence have they power to help in the case of deliverance of their worshippers? Great then is the error into which the Egyptians wandered — greater, indeed, than that of any people which is upon the face of the earth.

13. But it is a marvel, O King, with regard to the Greeks, who surpass all other peoples in their manner of life and reasoning, how they have gone astray after dead idols and lifeless images. And yet they see their gods in the hands of their artificers being sawn out, and planed and docked, and hacked short, and charred, and ornamented, and being altered by them in every kind of way. And when they grow old, and are worn away through lapse of time, and when they are molten and crushed to powder, how, I wonder, did they not perceive concerning them, that they are not gods? And as for those who did not find deliverance for themselves, how can they serve the distress of men?

But even the writers and philosophers among them have wrongly alleged that the gods are such as are made in honour of God Almighty. And they err in seeking to liken (them) to God whom man has not at any time seen nor can see unto what He is like. Herein, too (they err) in asserting of deity that any such thing as deficiency can be present to it; as when they say that He receives sacrifice and requires burnt-offering and libation and immolations of men, and temples. But God is not in need, and none of these things is necessary to Him; and it is clear that men err in these things they imagine.

Further their writers and their philosophers represent and declare that the nature of all their gods is one. And they have not apprehended God our Lord who while He is one, is in all. They err therefore. For if the body of a man while it is many in its parts is not in dread, one member of another, but, since it is a united body, wholly agrees with itself; even so also God is one in His nature. A single essence is proper to Him, since He is uniform in His nature and His essence; and He is not afraid of Himself. If then the nature of the gods is one, it is not proper that a god should either pursue or slay or harm a god. If, then, gods be pursued and wounded by gods, and some be kidnapped and some struck dead by lightning, it is obvious that the nature of their gods is not one. And hence it is known, O King, that it is a mistake when they reckon and bring the natures of their gods under a single nature. If then it becomes us to admire a god which is seen and does not see, how much more praiseworthy is it that one should believe in a nature which is invisible and all-seeing? And if further it is fitting that one should approve the handiworks of a craftsman, how much more is it fitting that one should glorify the Creator of the craftsman?

For behold! When the Greeks made laws they did not perceive that by their laws they condemn their gods. For if their laws are righteous, their gods are unrighteous, since they transgressed the law in killing one another, and practising sorcery, and committing adultery, and in robbing and stealing, and in lying with males, and by their other practises as well. For if their gods were right in doing all these things as they are described, then the laws of the Greeks are unrighteous in not being made according to the will of their gods. And in that case the whole world is gone astray.

For the narratives about their gods are some of them myths, and some of them nature-poems (lit: natural:— φυσικαί), and some of them hymns and elegies. The hymns indeed and elegies are empty words and noise. But these nature-poems, even if they be made as they say, still those are not gods who do such things and suffer and endure such things. And those myths are shallow tales with no depth whatever in them.

14. Let us come now, O King, to the history of the Jews also, and see what opinion they have as to God. The Jews then say that God is one, the Creator of all, and omnipotent; and that it is not right that any other should be worshipped except this God alone. And herein they appear to approach the truth more than all the nations, especially in that they worship God and not His works. And they imitate God by the philanthropy which prevails among them; for they have compassion on the poor, and they release the captives, and bury the dead, and do such things as these, which are acceptable before God and well-pleasing also to men — which (customs) they have received from their forefathers.

Nevertheless they too erred from true knowledge. And in their imagination they conceive that it is God they serve; whereas by their mode of observance it is to the angels and not to God that their service is rendered:— as when they celebrate sabbaths and the beginning of the months, and feasts of unleavened bread, and a great fast; and fasting and circumcision and the purification of meats, which things, however, they do not observe perfectly.

15. But the Christians, O King, while they went about and made search, have found the truth; and as we learned from their writings, they have come nearer to truth and genuine knowledge than the rest of the nations. For they know and trust in God, the Creator of heaven and of earth, in whom and from whom are all things, to whom there is no other god as companion, from whom they received commandments which they engraved upon their minds and observe in hope and expectation of the world which is to come. Wherefore they do not commit adultery nor fornication, nor bear false witness, nor embezzle what is held in pledge, nor covet what is not theirs. They honour father and mother, and show kindness to those near to them; and whenever they are judges, they judge uprightly. They do not worship idols (made) in the image of man; and whatsoever they would not that others should do unto them, they do not to others; and of the food which is consecrated to idols they do not eat, for they are pure. And their oppressors they appease (lit: comfort) and make them their friends; they do good to their enemies; and their women, O King, are pure as virgins, and their daughters are modest; and their men keep themselves from every unlawful union and from all uncleanness, in the hope of a recompense to come in the other world. Further, if one or other of them have bondmen and bondwomen or children, through love towards them they persuade them to become Christians, and when they have done so, they call them brethren without distinction. They do not worship strange gods, and they go their way in all modesty and cheerfulness. Falsehood is not found among them; and they love one another, and from widows they do not turn away their esteem; and they deliver the orphan from him who treats him harshly. And he, who has, gives to him who has not, without boasting. And when they see a stranger, they take him in to their homes and rejoice over him as a very brother; for they do not call them brethren after the flesh, but brethren after the spirit and in God. And whenever one of their poor passes from the world, each one of them according to his ability gives heed to him and carefully sees to his burial. And if they hear that one of their number is imprisoned or afflicted on account of the name of their Messiah, all of them anxiously minister to his necessity, and if it is possible to redeem him they set him free. And if there is among them any that is poor and needy, and if they have no spare food, they fast two or three days in order to supply to the needy their lack of food. They observe the precepts of their Messiah with much care, living justly and soberly as the Lord their God commanded them. Every morning and every hour they give thanks and praise to God for His loving-kindnesses toward them; and for their food and their drink they offer thanksgiving to Him. And if any righteous man among them passes from the world, they rejoice and offer thanks to God; and they escort his body as if he were setting out from one place to another near. And when a child has been born to one of them, they give

thanks to God; and if moreover it happen to die in childhood, they give thanks to God the more, as for one who has passed through the world without sins. And further if they see that anyone of them dies in his ungodliness or in his sins, for him they grieve bitterly, and sorrow as for one who goes to meet his doom.

16. Such, O King, is the commandment of the law of the Christians, and such is their manner of life. As men who know God, they ask from Him petitions which are fitting for Him to grant and for them to receive. And thus they employ their whole lifetime. And since they know the loving-kindnesses of God toward them, behold! For their sake the glorious things which are in the world flow forth to view. And verily, they are those who found the truth when they went about and made search for it; and from what we considered, we learned that they alone come near to a knowledge of the truth. And they do not proclaim in the ears of the multitude the kind deeds they do, but are careful that no one should notice them; and they conceal their giving just as he who finds a treasure and conceals it. And they strive to be righteous as those who expect to behold their Messiah, and to receive from Him with great glory the promises made concerning them. And as for their words and their precepts, O King, and their glorying in their worship, and the hope of earning according to the work of each one of them their recompense which they look for in another world, you may learn about these from their writings. It is enough for us to have shortly informed your Majesty concerning the conduct and the truth of the Christians. For great indeed, and wonderful is their doctrine to him who will search into it and reflect upon it. And verily, this is a new people, and there is something divine (lit: a divine admixture) in the midst of them.

Take, then, their writings, and read therein, and lo! You will find that I have not put forth these things on my own authority, nor spoken thus as their advocate; but since I read in their writings I was fully assured of these things as also of things which are to come. And for this reason I was constrained to declare the truth to such as care for it and seek the world to come. And to me there is no doubt but that the earth abides through the supplication of the Christians. But the rest of the nations err and cause error in wallowing before the elements of the world, since beyond these their mental vision will not pass. And they search about as if in darkness because they will not recognize the truth; and like drunken men they reel and jostle one another and fall.

17. Thus far, O King, I have spoken; for concerning that which remains, as is said above, there are found in their other writings things which are hard to utter and difficult for one to narrate — which are not only spoken in words but also wrought out in deeds.

Now the Greeks, O King, as they follow base practises in intercourse with males, and a mother and a sister and a daughter, impute their monstrous impurity in turn to the Christians. But the Christians are just and good, and the truth is set before their eyes, and their spirit is long-suffering; and, therefore, though they know the error of these (the Greeks), and are persecuted by them, they bear and endure it; and for the most part they have compassion on them, as men who are destitute of knowledge. And on their side, they offer prayer that these may repent of their error; and when it happens that one of them has repented, he is ashamed before the Christians of the works which were done by him; and he makes confession to God, saying, I did these things in ignorance. And he purifies his heart, and his sins are forgiven him, because he committed them in ignorance in the former time, when he used to blaspheme and speak evil of the true knowledge of the Christians. And assuredly the race of the Christians is more blessed than all the men who are upon the face of the earth.

Henceforth let the tongues of those who utter vanity and harass the Christians be silent; and hereafter let them speak the truth. For it is of serious consequence to them that they should worship the true God rather than worship a senseless sound. And verily whatever is spoken in the mouth of the Christians is of God; and their doctrine is the gateway of light. Wherefore let all who are without the knowledge of God draw near thereto; and they will receive incorruptible words, which are from all time and from eternity. So shall they appear before the awful judgment which through Jesus the Messiah is destined to come upon the whole human race.

The Apology of Aristides the Philosopher is finished.

Book 149. The Letter of James to Quadratus (Summary)

The *Epistle of James to Quadratus* is a letter that claims to be written by James, the brother of Jesus, to a certain Quadratus, who is presumably located in Rome. Although the letter does not specify exactly where Quadratus is located, his geographic proximity to the Emperor Tiberius is an important feature of the text. James writes to Quadratus to inform him of certain developments that have taken place in and around Jerusalem since the death of Jesus, and he asks Quadratus to report back to him regarding any decrees or commands that Tiberius might make concerning the Jews. The Quadratus of this letter exchange should not be confused with the early second-century apologist, Quadratus of Athens, who is mentioned by Eusebius (*Hist. eccl.* 4.3.1; 4.23.3). James also makes mention of a letter that was written from Pilate to the Emperor regarding the aftermath of Jesus' death. The letter has some obvious anachronistic features, such as James referring to himself as the "bishop of Jerusalem" in the letter's greeting. The letter expresses an anti-Jewish sentiment that is common throughout early Christian literature, as Quadratus is praised for contending against the Jews. The letter is preserved in both Syriac and Armenian, though there is likely a (non-extant) Greek original. The Syriac and Armenian versions are quite closely related, though there are several small, but interesting differences.

Named historical figures and characters: Aetius (tomb guard), Annas (scribe/high priest), Aristides (tomb guard), Benjamin (Jewish leader), Caiaphas, Ephres (bishop), Gamaliel, James (son of Zebedee), Jesus Christ, Justus (bishop), Levi (bishop), Mark (evangelist), Nachmael (Jewish leader), Nicanor, Onesiphorus, Parmenas, Paul (apostle), Peter (apostle), Philip (bishop), Pontius Pilate, Quadratus, Senica (bishop), Tiberius (emperor).

Book 150. The Apocalypse of Elijah (Summary)

The **Apocalypse of Elijah** is an intriguing and powerful apocryphal text, deeply rooted in early Christian and Jewish eschatology. This apocalypse is believed to have been written in the 3rd century CE and offers vivid depictions of the end times, divine judgment, and the ultimate victory of the righteous. It has been preserved in **Coptic manuscripts**, primarily in Egypt, and reflects the apocalyptic fervor of the time, blending both Jewish and Christian traditions.

Historical Context

The **Apocalypse of Elijah** emerges from a period where apocalyptic literature flourished among early Christians and Jews, especially in regions like Egypt. This was an era marked by political unrest, religious persecution, and heightened expectations of divine intervention. Like other apocalyptic texts, this work served as a response to the hardships faced by believers, offering them a warning and a message of hope.

Elijah, a revered figure in both Jewish and Christian traditions, plays a central role in this apocalypse. In the Old Testament, Elijah is known for his dramatic ascent to heaven without experiencing death (2 Kings 2:11), making him a figure closely associated with end-time prophecies. The **Apocalypse of Elijah** expands on this tradition, portraying Elijah as a key figure in the final battle between good and evil, and as a herald of divine judgment.

Structure and Key Themes

The text of the **Apocalypse of Elijah** can be divided into several sections, each addressing different aspects of the end times:

Ethical Instructions and Moral Exhortations

Visions of the End Times

The Rise of the Antichrist

The Return of Elijah and Enoch

The Final Judgment

1. Ethical Instructions and Moral Exhortations

The **Apocalypse of Elijah** begins with a series of moral exhortations directed at the faithful. Elijah emphasizes the importance of living righteously in preparation for the coming tribulations. He warns believers to avoid sin, practice prayer, and observe fasting, as these acts will help them remain steadfast in their faith during the trials to come.

Elijah's message is clear: only those who live in accordance with God's commandments will be able to withstand the deception and persecution that will accompany the end times. This section serves as both a spiritual guide and a warning, urging believers to prepare themselves for the trials ahead.

2. Visions of the End Times

The text then shifts to vivid descriptions of the end times, a common theme in apocalyptic literature. Elijah is granted visions of **wars**, **famine**, **earthquakes**, and **plagues** that will devastate the earth as a prelude to the final judgment. These calamities are depicted as divine punishments for the sins of humanity and are meant to purify the world in preparation for God's kingdom.

These visions are reminiscent of those found in other apocalyptic texts, such as the **Book of Revelation**. The **Apocalypse of Elijah** presents a worldview in which the current age is seen as corrupt and in need of divine intervention. The disasters that Elijah foresees are not random events but part of a larger cosmic plan to restore order and justice to the world.

3. The Rise of the Antichrist

One of the central themes of the **Apocalypse of Elijah** is the rise of the **Antichrist**. Known as **Belial** in the text, the Antichrist is portrayed as a charismatic leader who will deceive many through signs and wonders. He will claim to be the long-awaited messiah and will demand worship from all nations.

The Antichrist's rise to power is accompanied by widespread persecution of those who refuse to follow him. Elijah warns that this time of deception will be a test of faith for the righteous, as many will be led astray by the Antichrist's false miracles. However, Elijah assures believers that this reign of terror will be brief and that the Antichrist's ultimate defeat is certain.

This portrayal of the Antichrist aligns with other apocalyptic writings, particularly the **Book of Revelation**, where the figure of the **Beast** similarly represents a false messiah who leads the world into rebellion against God. In the **Apocalypse of Elijah**, the Antichrist serves as the ultimate antagonist, whose downfall will signal the beginning of the final judgment.

4. The Return of Elijah and Enoch

A unique aspect of the **Apocalypse of Elijah** is the inclusion of both **Elijah** and **Enoch** as key figures in the eschatological drama. According to biblical tradition, neither Elijah nor Enoch experienced death, as both were taken up to heaven by God (Genesis 5:24, 2 Kings 2:11). In the **Apocalypse of Elijah**, these two figures return during the end times to confront the Antichrist and bear witness to God's truth.

Elijah and Enoch serve as prophetic witnesses, calling people to repentance and denouncing the Antichrist's false claims. Their return is a sign of hope for the faithful, as it marks the beginning of the end for the forces of evil. However, their defiance of the Antichrist leads to their martyrdom, as they are killed by the Antichrist's followers.

Despite their deaths, Elijah and Enoch are resurrected by God, symbolizing the ultimate victory of good over evil. Their resurrection serves as a powerful sign of divine authority and the impending defeat of the Antichrist. This dramatic confrontation between the forces of good and evil is a hallmark of apocalyptic literature and reinforces the message that God's justice will ultimately prevail.

5. The Final Judgment

The **Apocalypse of Elijah** culminates in the **final judgment**, where the Antichrist is overthrown, and the righteous are rewarded. Elijah's vision of the final judgment includes vivid descriptions of the **resurrection of the dead**, the **separation of the righteous from the wicked**, and the **eternal punishment** of the Antichrist and his followers.

In this vision, the faithful are rewarded with eternal life in God's kingdom, while the wicked are cast into **eternal torment**. This dual outcome—eternal reward for the righteous and eternal punishment for the wicked—is a common theme in apocalyptic literature and serves to reassure believers that their faithfulness will be rewarded.

The final judgment in the **Apocalypse of Elijah** is not only a moment of divine justice but also a moment of cosmic restoration. The text describes a new age of peace and harmony, where the faithful live in communion with God, free from suffering and death. This vision of the **new age** reflects the eschatological hope found in both Jewish and Christian traditions, where the end of the present age gives way to a new creation, restored to its original state of purity and righteousness.

Moral and Theological Significance

The **Apocalypse of Elijah** is not just a visionary text; it is also a deeply moral and theological work. Its emphasis on **righteousness**, **faithfulness**, and **resistance to deception** speaks to the concerns of early Christian communities facing persecution and uncertainty. Elijah's warnings against the Antichrist and his call to moral vigilance reflect the broader themes of **apocalyptic literature**, which often served to prepare believers for the trials they would face in the last days.

Theologically, the text reinforces the belief in **divine justice** and **God's ultimate victory** over evil. The return of Elijah and Enoch, the defeat of the Antichrist, and the final judgment all point to a worldview where God is in control, and where the suffering of the present age is temporary. For early Christians, the **Apocalypse of Elijah** would have provided both a warning and a source of comfort, assuring them that their faithfulness would be rewarded in the end.

Connections to Other Apocalyptic Texts

The **Apocalypse of Elijah** shares many similarities with other apocalyptic texts, particularly the **Book of Revelation** and the **Apocalypse of Peter**. Like these works, the **Apocalypse of Elijah** offers a detailed vision of the end times, complete with cosmic battles, divine judgment, and the ultimate restoration of the righteous.

However, the **Apocalypse of Elijah** also stands out for its inclusion of both **Elijah** and **Enoch** as central figures in the eschatological drama. This pairing of two figures who were taken up to heaven without experiencing death is unique and reflects the blending of Jewish and Christian eschatological traditions. In this sense, the **Apocalypse of Elijah** serves as a bridge between Jewish apocalyptic thought and early Christian theology.

Legacy and Influence

While the **Apocalypse of Elijah** may not be as well-known as other apocalyptic texts, its influence can be seen in the development of early Christian eschatology. The text's vivid descriptions of the Antichrist, the final judgment, and the return of Elijah and Enoch would have resonated with early Christians who were grappling with the challenges of living in a world dominated by the Roman Empire and facing persecution for their beliefs.

The **Apocalypse of Elijah** also reflects the broader trend of **apocalyptic expectation** that characterized the early centuries of Christianity. As believers awaited the return of Christ and the establishment of God's kingdom, texts like the **Apocalypse of Elijah** provided both guidance and reassurance, helping them to navigate the uncertainties of their time.

Conclusion

The **Apocalypse of Elijah** is a powerful and profound text that offers a vivid portrayal of the end times and the ultimate triumph of good over evil. Through its moral exhortations, dramatic visions of the Antichrist, and hopeful messageThe **Apocalypse of Elijah** is a powerful and significant work that vividly illustrates the eschatological expectations of early Christian communities. It highlights the key themes of divine judgment, the rise of the Antichrist, the moral responsibility of the faithful, and the ultimate triumph of good over evil. Through dramatic and symbolic visions, it presents a profound message of hope and moral vigilance.

Book 151. The Epistle of Barnabas

Barnabas 1:1
I Bid you greeting, sons and daughters, in the name of the Lord that loved us, in peace.

Barnabas 1:2
Seeing that the ordinances of God are great and rich unto you, I rejoice with an exceeding great and overflowing joy at your blessed and glorious spirits; so innate is the grace of the spiritual gift that ye have received.

Barnabas 1:3
Wherefore also I the more congratulate myself hoping to be saved, for that I truly see the Spirit poured out among you from the riches of the fount of the Lord. So greatly did the much-desired sight of you astonish me respecting you.

Barnabas 1:4
Being therefore persuaded of this, and being conscious with myself that having said much among you I know that the Lord journeyed with me on the way of righteousness, and am wholly constrained also myself to this, to love you more than my own soul (for great faith and love dwelleth in you through the hope of the life which is His)--considering this therefore, that,

Barnabas 1:5
if it shall be my care to communicate to you some portion of that which I received, it shall turn to my reward for having ministered to such spirits, I was eager to send you a trifle, that along with your faith ye might have your knowledge also perfect.

Barnabas 1:6
Well then, there are three ordinances of the Lord; *the hope of life, which is the beginning and end of our faith; and righteousness, which is the beginning and end of judgment; love shown in gladness and exultation, the testimony of works of righteousness.*

Barnabas 1:7
For the Lord made known to us by His prophets things past and present, giving us likewise the firstfruits of the taste of things future. And seeing each of these things severally coming to pass, according as He spake, we ought to offer a richer and higher offering to the fear of Him. But I, not as though I were a teacher, but as one of yourselves, will show forth a few things, whereby ye shall be gladdened in the present circumstances.

Barnabas 2:1
Seeing then that the days are evil, and that the Active One himself has the authority, we ought to give heed to ourselves and to seek out the ordinances of the Lord.

Barnabas 2:2
The aids of our faith then are fear and patience, and our allies are long-suffering and self-restraint.

Barnabas 2:3
While these abide in a pure spirit in matters relating to the Lord, wisdom, understanding, science, knowledge rejoice with them.

Barnabas 2:4
For He hath made manifest to us by all the prophets that He wanteth neither sacrifices nor whole burnt offerings nor oblations, saying at one time;

Barnabas 2:5
What to Me is the multitude of your sacrifices, saith the Lord I am full of whole burnt-offerings, and the fat of lambs and the blood of bulls and of goats desire not, not though ye should come to be seen of Me. or who required these things at your hands? Ye shall continue no more to tread My court. If ye bring fine flour, it is in vain; incense is an abomination to Me; your new moons and your Sabbaths I cannot away with.

Barnabas 2:6
These things therefore He annulled, that the new law of our Lord Jesus Christ, being free from the yoke of constraint, might have its oblation not made by human hands.

Barnabas 2:7
And He saith again unto them; *Did command your fathers when they went forth from the land of Egypt to bring Me whole burnt offerings and sacrifices?*

Barnabas 2:8
Nay, this was My command unto them, Let none of you bear a grudge of evil against his neighbor in his heart, and love you not a false oath.

Barnabas 2:9
So we ought to perceive, unless we are without understanding, the mind of the goodness of our Father; for He speaketh to us, desiring us not to go astray like them but to seek how we may approach Him.

Barnabas 2:10
Thus then speaketh He to us; *The sacrifice unto God is a broken heart, the smell of a sweet savor unto the Lord is a heart that glorifies its Maker.* We ought therefore, brethren, to learn accurately concerning our salvation, lest the Evil One having effected an entrance of error in us should fling us away from our life.

Barnabas 3:1
He speaketh again therefore to them concerning these things; *Wherefore fast ye for Me, saith the Lord, so that your voice is heard this day crying aloud? This is not the fast which have chosen, saith the Lord; not a man abasing his soul;*

Barnabas 3:2
not though ye should bend your neck as a hoop, and put on sackcloth and make your bed of ashes, not even so shall ye call a fast that is acceptable.

Barnabas 3:3
But unto us He saith; *Behold, this is the fast which I have chosen, saith the Lord; loosen every band of wickedness, untie the tightened cords of forcible contracts, send away the broken ones released and tear in pieces every unjust bond. Break thy bread to the hungry, and if thou seest one naked clothe him; bring the shelterless into thy house, and if thou seest a humble man, thou shalt not despise him, neither shall any one of thy household and of thine own seed.*

Barnabas 3:4
Then shall thy light break forth in the morning, and thy healing shall arise quickly, and righteousness shall go forth before thy face, and the glory of God shall environ thee.

Barnabas 3:5
Then shalt thou cry out and God shall hear thee; while thou art still speaking, He shall say 'Lo, I am here'; if thou shalt take away from thee the yoke and the stretching forth of the finger and the word of murmuring, and shalt give thy bread to the hungry heartily, and shalt pity the abased soul.

Barnabas 3:6
To this end therefore, my brethren, He that is long-suffering, foreseeing that the people whom He had prepared in His well-beloved would believe in simplicity, manifested to us beforehand concerning all things, that we might not as novices shipwreck ourselves upon their law.

Barnabas 4:1
It behooves us therefore to investigate deeply concerning the present, and to search out the things which have power to save us. Let us therefore flee altogether from all the works of lawlessness, lest the works of lawlessness overpower us; and let us loathe the error of the present time, that we may be loved for that which is to come.

Barnabas 4:2
Let us give no relaxation to our soul that it should have liberty to consort with sinners and wicked men, lest haply we be made like unto them.

Barnabas 4:3
The last offence is at hand, concerning which the scripture speaketh, as Enoch saith. *For to this end the Master hath cut the seasons and the days short, that His beloved might hasten and come to His inheritance.*

Barnabas 4:4
And the prophet also speaketh on this wise; *Ten reigns shall reign upon the earth, and after them shall arise another king, who shall bring low three of the kings under one.*

Barnabas 4:5
In like manner Daniel speaketh concerning the same; *And I saw the forth beast to be wicked and strong and more intractable than all the beasts of the earth, and how there arose from him ten horns, and from these a little horn and excrescence, and how that it abased under one three of the great horns.*

Barnabas 4:6

Ye ought therefore to understand. Moreover I ask you this one thing besides, as being one of yourselves and loving you all in particular more than my own soul, to give heed to yourselves now, and not to liken yourselves to certain persons who pile up sin upon sin, saying that our covenant remains to them also.

Barnabas 4:7

Ours it is; but they lost it in this way for ever, when Moses had just received it. For the scripture saith; *And Moses was in the mountain fasting forty days and forty nights, and he received the covenant from the Lord, even tablets of stone written with the finger of the hand of the Lord.*

Barnabas 4:8

But they lost it by turning unto idols. For thus saith the Lord; *Moses, Moses, come down quickly; for thy people whom thou broughtest out of the land of Egypt hath done unlawfully.* And Moses understood, and threw the two tables from his hands; and their covenant was broken in pieces, that the covenant of the beloved Jesus might be sealed unto our hearts in the hope which springeth from faith in Him.

Barnabas 4:9

But though I would fain write many things, not as a teacher, but as becometh one who loveth you not to fall short of that which we possess, I was anxious to write to you, being your devoted slave. Wherefore let us take heed in these last days. For the whole time of our faith shall profit us nothing, unless we now, in the season of lawlessness and in the offenses that shall be, as becometh sons of God, offer resistance, that the Black One may not effect an entrance.

Barnabas 4:10

Let us flee from all vanity, let us entirely hate the works of the evil way. Do not entering in privily stand apart by yourselves, as if ye were already justified, but assemble yourselves together and consult concerning the common welfare.

Barnabas 4:11

For the scripture saith; *Woe unto them that are wise for themselves, and understanding in their own sight.* Let us become spiritual, let us become a temple perfect unto God. As far as in us lies, let us exercise ourselves in the fear of God, [and] let us strive to keep His commandments, that we may rejoice in His ordinances.

Barnabas 4:12

The Lord judgeth the world without respect of persons; each man shall receive according to his deeds. If he be good, his righteousness shall go before him in the way; if he be evil, the recompense of his evil-doing is before him; lest perchance,

Barnabas 4:13

if we relax as men that are called, we should slumber over our sins, and the prince of evil receive power against us and thrust us out from the kingdom of the Lord.

Barnabas 4:14

Moreover understand this also, my brothers. When ye see that after so many signs and wonders wrought in Israel, even then they were abandoned, let us give heed, lest haply we be found, as the scripture saith, *many are called but few are chosen.*

Barnabas 5:1

For to this end the Lord endured to deliver His flesh unto corruption, that by the remission of sins we might be cleansed, which cleansing is through the blood of His sprinkling.

Barnabas 5:2

For the scripture concerning Him containeth some things relating to Israel, and some things relating to us. And it speaketh thus; *He was wounded for your transgressions, and He hath been bruised for our sins; by His stripes we were healed. As a sheep He was led to slaughter, as a lamb is dumb before his shearer.*

Barnabas 5:3

We ought therefore to be very thankful unto the Lord, for that He both revealed unto us the past, and made us wise in the present, and as regards the future we are not without understanding.

Barnabas 5:4

Now the scripture saith; *Not unjustly is the net spread for the birds.* He meaneth this that a man shall justly perish, who having the knowledge of the way of righteousness forceth himself into the way of darkness.

Barnabas 5:5

There is yet this also, my brethren; if the Lord endured to suffer for our souls, though He was Lord of the whole world, unto whom God said from the foundation of the world, *Let us make man after our image and likeness,* how then did He endure to suffer at the hand of men?

Barnabas 5:6

Understand ye. The prophets, receiving grace from Him, prophesied concerning Him. But He Himself endured that He might destroy death and show forth the resurrection of the dead, for that He must needs be manifested in the flesh;

Barnabas 5:7

that at the same time He might redeem the promise made to the fathers, and by preparing the new people for Himself might show, while He was on earth, that having brought about the resurrection He will Himself exercise judgment.

Barnabas 5:8

Yea and further, He preached teaching Israel and performing so many wonders and miracles, and He loved him exceedingly.

Barnabas 5:9

And when He chose His own apostles who were to proclaim His Gospel, who that He might show that *He came not to call the righteous but sinners* were sinners above every sin, then He manifested Himself to be the Son of God.

Barnabas 5:10

For if He had not come in the flesh neither would men have looked upon Him and been saved, forasmuch as when they look upon the sun that shall cease to be, which is the work of His own hands, they cannot face its rays.

Barnabas 5:11

Therefore the Son of God came in the flesh to this end, that He might sum up the complete tale of their sins against those who persecuted and slew His prophets.

Barnabas 5:12

To this end therefore He endured. For God saith of the wounds of His flesh that they came from them; *When they shall smite their own shepherd, then shall the sheep of the flock be lost.*

Barnabas 5:13

But He Himself desired so to suffer; for it was necessary for Him to suffer on a tree. For he that prophesied said concerning Him, *Spare My soul form the sword;* and, *Pierce My flesh with nails, for the congregations of evil-doers have risen up against Me.*

Barnabas 5:14

And again He saith; *Behold I have given My back to stripes, and My cheeks to smitings, and My face did I set as a hard rock.*

Barnabas 6:1

When then He gave the commandment, what saith He? *Who is he that disputeth with Me? Let him oppose Me. Or who is he that goeth to law with Me? Let him draw nigh unto the servant of the Lord,*

Barnabas 6:2

Woe unto you, for ye all shall wax old as a garment, and the moth shall consume you. And again the prophet saith, seeing that as a hard stone He was ordained for crushing; *Behold I will put into the fountains of Zion a stone very precious, elect, a chief corner-stone, honorable.*

Barnabas 6:3

Then again what saith He; *And whosoever shall set his hope on Him, shall live forever.* Is our hope then set upon a stone? Far be it. But it is because the Lord hath set His flesh in strength. For He saith; *And He set Me as a hard rock.*

Barnabas 6:4

And the prophet saith again; *The stone which the builders rejected, this became the head and the corner.* And again He saith; *This is the great and wonderful day, which the Lord made.*

Barnabas 6:5

I write to you the more simply, that ye may understand, I who am the offscouring of your love.

Barnabas 6:6

What then saith the prophet again? *The assembly of evildoers gathered around Me, they surrounded Me as bees surround a comb;* and; *For My garment they cast a lot.*

Barnabas 6:7

Forasmuch then as He was about to be manifested in the flesh and to suffer, His suffering was manifested beforehand. For the prophet saith concerning Israel; *Woe unto their soul, for they have counseled evil counsel against themselves saying, Let us bind the righteous one, for he is unprofitable for us.*

Barnabas 6:8

What sayeth the other prophet Moses unto them? *Behold, these things saith the Lord God; enter into the good land which the Lord swear unto Abraham, Isaac, and Jacob, and inherit it, a land flowing with milk and honey.*

Barnabas 6:9

But what saith knowledge? Understand ye. Set your hope on Him who is about to be manifested to you in the flesh, even Jesus. For man is earth suffering; for from the face of the earth came the creation of Adam.

Barnabas 6:10

What then saith He? *Into the good land, a land flowing with milk and honey.* Blessed is our Lord, brethren, who established among us wisdom and understanding of His secret things. For the prophet speaketh a parable concerning the Lord. Who shall comprehend, save he that is wise and prudent and that loveth his Lord?

Barnabas   6:11
Forasmuch then as He renewed us in the remission of sins, He made us to be a new type, so that we should have the soul of children, as if He were recreating us.

Barnabas   6:12
For the scripture saith concerning us, how He saith to the Son; *Let us make man after our image and after our likeness, and let them rule over the beasts of the earth and the fowls of the heaven and the fishes of the sea.* And the Lord said when He saw the fair creation of us men; *Increase and multiply and fill the earth.* These words refer to the Son.

Barnabas   6:13
Again I will shew thee how the Lord speaketh concerning us. He made a second creation at the last; and the Lord saith; *Behold I make the last things as the first.* In reference to this then the prophet preached; *Enter into a land flowing with milk and honey, and be lords over it.*

Barnabas   6:14
Behold then we have been created anew, as He saith again in another prophet; *Behold, saith the Lord, I will take out from these,* that is to say, from those whom the Spirit of the Lord foresaw, *their stony hearts, and will put into them hearts of flesh;* for He Himself was to be manifested in the flesh and to dwell in us.

Barnabas   6:15
For a holy temple unto the Lord, my brethren, is the abode of our heart.

Barnabas   6:16
For the Lord saith again; *For wherein shall I appear unto the Lord my God and be glorified? I will make confession unto Thee in the assembly of my brethren, and I will sing unto Thee in the midst of the assembly of the saints.* We therefore are they whom He brought into the good land.

Barnabas   6:17
What then is the milk and the honey Because the child is first kept alive by honey, and then by milk. So in like manner we also, being kept alive by our faith in the promise and by the word, shall live and be lords of the earth.

Barnabas   6:18
Now we have already said above; *And let them increase and multiply and rule over the fishes.* But who is he that is able [now] to rule over beasts and fishes and fowls of the heaven; for we ought to perceive that to rule implieth power, so that one should give orders and have dominion.

Barnabas   6:19
If then this cometh not to pass now, assuredly He spake to us for the hereafter, when we ourselves shall be made perfect so that we may become heirs of the covenant of the Lord.

Barnabas   7:1
Understand therefore, children of gladness, that the good Lord manifested all things to us beforehand, that we might know to whom we ought in all things to render thanksgiving and praise.

Barnabas   7:2
If then the Son of God, being Lord and future Judge of quick and dead, suffered that His wound might give us life, let us believe that the Son of God could not suffer except for our sakes.

Barnabas   7:3
But moreover when crucified He had vinegar and gall given Him to drink. Hear how on this matter the priests of the temple have revealed. Seeing that there is a commandment in scripture, *Whatsoever shall not observe the fast shall surely die,* the Lord commanded, because He was in His own person about to offer the vessel of His Spirit a sacrifice for our sins, that the type also which was given in Isaac who was offered upon the alter should be fulfilled.

Barnabas   7:4
What then saith He in the prophet? *And let them eat of the goat that is offered at the fast for all their sins.* Attend carefully; *And let all the priests alone eat the entrails unwashed with vinegar.*

Barnabas   7:5
Wherefore? Since ye are to give Me, who am to offer My flesh for the sins of My new people, gall with vinegar to drink, eat ye alone, while the people fasteth and waileth in sackcloth and ashes; that He might shew that He must suffer at their hands.

Barnabas   7:6
Attend ye to the commandments which He gave. *Take two goats, fair and alike, and offer them, and let the priest take the one for a whole burnt offering for sins.*

Barnabas   7:7
But the other one--what must they do with it? *Accursed,* saith He, *is the one.* Give heed how the type of Jesus is revealed.

Barnabas   7:8
And do ye all spit upon it and goad it, and place scarlet wool about its head, and so let it be cast into the wilderness. And when it is so done, he that taketh the goat into the wilderness leadeth it, and taketh off the wool, and putteth it upon the branch which is called Rachia, the same whereof we are wont to eat the shoots when we find them in the country. Of this briar alone is the fruit thus sweet.

Barnabas   7:9
What then meaneth this? Give heed. *The one at the alter, and the other accursed.* And moreover the accursed one crowned. For they shall see Him in that day wearing the long scarlet robe about His flesh, and shall say, Is not this He, Whom once we crucified and set at nought and spat upon; verily this was He, Who then said that He was the Son of God.

Barnabas   7:10
For how is He like the goat? For this reason it says *the goats shall be fair and alike,* that, when they shall see Him coming then, they may be astonished at the likeness of the goat. Therefore behold the type of Jesus that was to suffer.

Barnabas   7:11
But what meaneth it, that they place the wool in the midst of the thorns? It is a type of Jesus set forth for the Church, since whosoever should desire to take away the scarlet wool it behoved him to suffer many things owing to the terrible nature of the thorn, and through affliction to win the mastery over it. Thus, He saith, they that desire to see Me, and to attain unto My kingdom, must lay hold on Me through tribulation and affliction.

Barnabas   8:1
But what think ye meaneth the type, where the commandment is given to Israel that those men, whose sins are full grown, offer an heifer and slaughter and burn it, and then that the children take up the ashes, and cast them into vessels, and twist the scarlet wool on a tree (see here again is the type of the cross and the scarlet wool), and the hyssop, and that this done the children should sprinkle the people one by one, that they may be purified from their sins?

Barnabas   8:2
Understand ye how in all plainness it is spoken unto you; the calf is Jesus, the men that offer it, being sinners, are they that offered Him for the slaughter. After this it is no more men (who offer); the glory is no more for sinners.

Barnabas   8:3
The children who sprinkle are they that preached unto us the forgiveness of sins and the purification of our heart, they to whom, being twelve in number for a testimony unto the tribes (for there are twelve tribes of Israel), He gave authority over the Gospel, that they should preach it.

Barnabas   8:4
But wherefore are the children that sprinkle three in number? For a testimony unto Abraham, Isaac and Jacob, because these are mighty before God.

Barnabas   8:5
Then there is the placing the wool on the tree. This means that the kingdom of Jesus is on the cross, and that they who set their hope on Him shall live for ever.

Barnabas   8:6
And why is there the wool and the hyssop at the same time? Because in His kingdom there shall be evil and foul days, in which we shall be saved; for he who suffers pain in the flesh is healed through the foulness of the hyssop.

Barnabas   8:7
Now to us indeed it is manifest that these things so befell for this reason, but to them they were dark, because they heard not the voice of the Lord.

Barnabas   9:1
Furthermore He saith concerning the ears, how that it is our heart which He circumcised. The Lord saith in the prophet; *With the hearing of the ears they listened to Me.* And again He saith; They that are afar off shall hear with their ears, and shall perceive what I have done. And; *Be ye circumcised in your hearts,* saith the Lord.

Barnabas   9:2
And again He saith; *Hear, O Israel, for thus saith the Lord thy God. Who is he that desireth to live forever, let him hear with his ears   the   voice   of   My   servant.*
~y
And again He saith; *Hear, O heaven, and give ear, O earth, for the Lord hath spoken these things for a testimony.* And again He saith; Hear the words of the Lord, ye rulers of this people. And again He saith; *Hear, O my children, the voice of one crying in the wilderness.* Therefore He circumcised our ears, that hearing the word we might believe.

Barnabas 9:3

But moreover the circumcision, in which they have confidence, is abolished; for He hath said that a circumcision not of the flesh should be practiced. But they transgressed, for an evil angel taught them cleverness.

Barnabas 9:4

He saith unto them; *Thus saith the Lord your God* (so I find the commandment); *sow not upon thorns, be ye circumcised in to your Lord.* And what saith He? *Be ye circumcised in the hardness of your heart; and then ye will not harden your neck.* Take this again; *Behold, sayith the Lord, all the Gentiles are uncircumcised in their foreskin, but this people is uncircumcised in their hearts.*

Barnabas 9:5

But thou wilt say; In truth the people hath been circumcised for a seal. Nay, but so likewise is every Syrian and Arabian and all the priests of the idols. Do all those then too belong to their covenant? Moreover the Egyptians also are included among the circumcised.

Barnabas 9:6

Learn therefore, children of love, concerning all things abundantly, that Abraham, who first appointed circumcision, looked forward in the spirit unto Jesus, when he circumcised having received the ordinances of three letters.

Barnabas 9:7

For the scripture saith; *And Abraham circumcised of his household eighteen males and three hundred.* What then was the knowledge given unto him? Understand ye that He saith *the eighteen* first, and then after an interval *three hundred* In the eighteen 'I' stands for ten, 'H' for eight. Here thou hast JESUS (IHSOYS). And because the cross in the 'T' was to have grace, He saith also *three hundred.* So He revealeth Jesus in the two letters, and in the remaining one the cross.

Barnabas 9:8

He who placed within us the innate gift of His covenant knoweth; no man hath ever learnt from me a more genuine word; but I know that ye are worthy.

Barnabas 10:1

But forasmuch as Moses said; *Ye shall not eat seine nor eagle nor falcon nor crow nor any fish which hath no scale upon it*, he received in his understanding three ordinances.

Barnabas 10:2

Yea and further He saith unto them in Deuteronomy; *And I will lay as a covenant upon this people My ordinances.* So then it is not a commandment of God that they should not bite with their teeth, but Moses spake it in spirit.

Barnabas 10:3

Accordingly he mentioned the swine with this intent. Thou shalt not cleave, saith he, to such men who are like unto swine; that is, when they are in luxury they forget the Lord, but when they are in want they recognize the Lord, just as the swine when it eateth knoweth not his lord, but when it is hungry it crieth out, and when it has received food again it is silent.

Barnabas 10:4

Neither shalt thou eat eagle nor falcon nor kite nor crow. Thou shalt not, He saith, cleave unto, or be likened to, such men who now not how to provide food for themselves by toil and sweat, but in their lawlessness seize what belongeth to others, and as if they were walking in guilelessness watch and search about for some one to rob in their rapacity, just as these birds alone do not provide food for themselves, but sit idle and seek how they may eat the meat that belongeth to others, being pestilent in their evil-doings.

Barnabas 10:5

And thou shalt not eat, saith He, *lamprey nor polypus nor cuttle fish* . Thou shalt not, He meaneth, become like unto such men, who are desperately wicked, and are already condemned to death, just as these fishes alone are accursed and swim in the depths, not swimming on the surface like the rest, but dwell on the ground beneath the deep sea.

Barnabas 10:6

Moreover thou shalt not eat the hare. Why so? Thou shalt not be found a corrupter of boys, nor shalt thou become like such persons; for the hare gaineth one passage in the body every year; for according to the number of years it lives it has just so many orifices.

Barnabas 10:7

Again, *neither shalt thou eat the hyena;* thou shalt not, saith He, become an adulterer or a fornicator, neither shalt thou resemble such persons. Why so? Because this animal changeth its nature year by year, and becometh at one time male and at another female.

Barnabas 10:8

Moreover He hath hated the weasel also and with good reason. Thou shalt not, saith He, become such as those men of whom we hear as working iniquity with their mouth for uncleanness, neither shalt thou cleave unto impure women who work iniquity with their mouth. For this animal conceiveth with its mouth.

Barnabas 10:9

Concerning meats then Moses received three decrees to this effect and uttered them in a spiritual sense; but they accepted them according to the lust of the flesh, as though they referred to eating.

Barnabas 10:10

And David also receiveth knowledge of the same three decrees, and saith; *Blessed is the man who hath not gone in the council of the ungodly*--even as the fishes go in darkness into the depths; *and hath not stood in the path of sinners*--just as they who pretend to fear the Lord sin like swine; *and hath not sat on the seat of the destroyers*--as the birds that are seated for prey. Ye have now the complete lesson concerning eating.

Barnabas 10:11

Again Moses saith; *Ye shall everything that divideth the hoof and cheweth the cud.* What meaneth he? He that receiveth the food knoweth Him that giveth him the food, and being refreshed appeareth to rejoice in him. Well said he, having regard to the commandment. What then meaneth he? Cleave unto those that fear the Lord, with those who meditate in their heart on the distinction of the word which they have received, with those who tell of the ordinances of the Lord and keep them, with those who know that meditation is a work of gladness and who chew the cud of the word of the Lord. But why that which divideth the hoof? Because the righteous man both walketh in this world, and at the same time looketh for the holy world to come. Ye see how wise a lawgiver Moses was.

Barnabas 10:12

But whence should they perceive or understand these things? Howbeit we having justly perceived the commandments tell them as the Lord willed. To this end He circumcised our ears and hearts, that we might understand these things.

Barnabas 11:1

But let us enquire whether the Lord took care to signify before hand concerning the water and the cross. Now concerning the water it is written in reference to Israel, how that they would not receive the baptism which bringeth remission of sins, but would build for themselves.

Barnabas 11:2

For the prophet saith; *Be astonished, O heaven, and let the earth shudder the more at this, for this people hath done two evil things; they abandoned Me the fountain of life, and they digged for themselves a pit of death.*

Barnabas 11:3

Is My holy mountain of Sinai a desert rock? for ye shall be as the fledglings of a bird, which flutter aloft when deprived of their nest.

Barnabas 11:4

And again the prophet saith; *I will go before thee, and level mountains and crush gates of brass and break in pieces bolts of iron, and I will give thee treasures dark, concealed, unseen, that they may know that I am the Lord God.*

Barnabas 11:5

And; *Thou shalt dwell in a lofty cave of a strong rock.* And; *His water shall be sure; ye shall see the King in glory, and your soul shall meditate on the fear of the Lord.*

Barnabas 11:6

And again He saith in another prophet; *And He that doeth these things shall be as the tree that is planted by the parting streams of waters, which shall yield his fruit at his proper season, and his leaf shall not fall off, and all things whatsoever he doeth shall prosper.*

Barnabas 11:7

Not so are the ungodly, not so, but are as the dust which the wind scattereth from the face of the earth. Therefore ungodly men shall not stand in judgment, neither sinners in the council of the righteous; for the Lord knoweth the way of the righteous, and the way of the ungodly shall perish.

Barnabas 11:8

Ye perceive how He pointed out the water and the cross at the same time. For this is the meaning; Blessed are they that set their hope on the cross, and go down into the water; for He speaketh of the reward at *his proper season*; then, saith He, I will repay. But now what saith He? *His leaves shall not fall off*; He meaneth by this that every word, which shall come forth from you through your mouth in faith and love, shall be for the conversion and hope of many.

Barnabas 11:9

And again another prophet saith; *And the land of Jacob was praised above the whole earth.* He meaneth this; He glorifieth the vessel of His Spirit.

Barnabas 11:10

Next what saith He? *And there was a river streaming from the right hand, and beautiful trees rose up from it; and whosoever shall eat of them shall live forever.*

Barnabas 11:11

This He saith, because we go down into the water laden with sins and filth, and rise up from it bearing fruit in the heart, resting our fear and hope on Jesus in the spirit. *And whosoever shall eat of these shall live forever*; He meaneth this; whosoever, saith He, shall hear these things spoken and shall believe, shall live forever.

Barnabas 12:1

In like manner again He defineth concerning the cross in another prophet, who saith; *And when shall these things be accomplished? saith the Lord. Whenever a tree shall be bended and stand upright, and whensoever blood shall drop from a tree.* Again thou art taught concerning the cross, and Him that was to be crucified.

Barnabas 12:2

And He saith again in Moses, when war was waged against Israel by men of another nation, and that He might remind them when the war was waged against them that for their sins they were delivered unto death; the Spirit saith to the heart of Moses, that he should make a type of the cross and of Him that was to suffer, that unless, saith He, they shall set their hope on Him, war shall be waged against them for ever. Moses therefore pileth arms one upon another in the midst of the encounter, and standing on higher ground than any he stretched out his hands, and so Israel was again victorious. Then, whenever he lowered them, they were slain with the sword.

Barnabas 12:3

Wherefore was this? That they might learn that they cannot be saved, unless they should set their hope on Him.

Barnabas 12:4

And again in another prophet He saith; *The whole day long have I stretched out My hands to a disobedient people that did gainsay My righteous way.*

Barnabas 12:5

Again Moses maketh a type of Jesus, how that He must suffer, and that He Himself whom they shall think to have destroyed shall make alive in an emblem when Israel was falling. For the Lord caused all manner of serpents to bite them, and they died (forasmuch as the transgression was wrought in Eve through the serpent), that He might convince them that by reason of their transgression they should be delivered over to the affliction of death.

Barnabas 12:6

Yea and further though Moses gave the commandment; *Ye shall not have a molten or a carved image for your God*, yet he himself made one that he might show them a type of Jesus. So Moses maketh a brazen serpent, and setteth it up conspicuously, and summoneth the people by proclamation.

Barnabas 12:7

When therefore they were assembled together they entreated Moses that he should offer up intercession for them that they might be healed. And Moses said unto them; Whensoever, said he, one of you shall be bitten, let him come to the serpent which is placed on the tree, and let him believe and hope that the serpent being himself dead can make alive; and forthwith he shall be saved. And so they did. Here again thou hast in these things also the glory of Jesus, how that in Him and unto Him are all things.

Barnabas 12:8

What again saith Moses unto Jesus (Joshua) the son of Nun, when he giveth him this name, as being a prophet, that all the people might give ear to him alone, because the Father revealeth all things concerning His Son Jesus?

Barnabas 12:9

Moses therefore saith to Jesus the son of Nun, giving him this name, when he sent him as a spy on the land; *Take a book in thy hands, and write what the Lord saith, how the Son of God shall cut up by the roots all the house of Amalek in the last days.*

Barnabas 12:10

Behold again it is Jesus, not a son of man, but the Son of God, and He was revealed in the flesh in a figure. Since then men will say that Christ is the son of David, David himself prophesieth being afraid and understanding the error of sinners; *The Lord said unto my Lord, Sit thou on My right hand until I set thine enemies for a footstool under Thy feet.*

Barnabas 12:11

And again thus sayith Isaiah; *The Lord said unto my Christ the Lord, of whose right hand I laid hold, that the nations should give ear before Him, and I will break down the strength of kings.* See how David calleth Him Lord, and calleth Him not Son.

Barnabas 13:1

Now let us see whether this people or the first people hath the inheritance, and whether the covenant had reference to us or to them.

Barnabas 13:2

Hear then what the scripture saith concerning the people; *And Isaac prayed concerning Rebecca his wife, for she was barren. And she*

conceived. Then Rebecca went out to enquire of the Lord. And the Lord said unto her; Two nations are in thy womb, and two peoples in thy belly, and one people shall vanquish another people, and the greater shall serve the less.

Barnabas 13:3

Ye ought to understand who Isaac is, and who Rebecca is, and in whose case He hath shown that the one people is greater than the other.

Barnabas 13:4

And in another prophecy Jacob speaketh more plainly to Joseph his son, saying; *Behold, the Lord hath not bereft me of thy face; bring me thy sons, that I may bless them.*

Barnabas 13:5

And he brought Ephraim and Manasseh, desiring that Manasseh should be blessed, because he was the elder; for Joseph led him by the right hand of his father Jacob. But Jacob saw in the spirit a type of the people that should come afterwards. And what saith He? *And Jacob crossed his hands, and placed his right hand on the head of Ephraim, the second and younger, and blessed him. And Joseph said unto Jacob, Transfer thy right hand to the head of Manasseh, for he is my first born son. And Jacob said to Joseph, I know it, my son, I know it; but the greater shall serve the less. Yet this one also shall be blessed.*

Barnabas 13:6

Mark in whose cases He ordained that this people should be first and heir of the covenant.

Barnabas 13:7

If then besides this He also recorded it through Abraham, we attain the completion of our knowledge. What then saith he to Abraham when he alone believed, and was ascribed for righteousness? *Behold I have made thee, Abraham, a father of nations that believe in God in uncircumcision.*

Barnabas 14:1

Yea verily, but as regards the covenant which He swear to the fathers to give it to the people let us see whether He hath actually given it. He hath given it, but they themselves were not found worthy to receive it by reason of their sins.

Barnabas 14:2

For the prophet saith; *And Moses was fasting in Mount Sinai forty days and forty nights, that he might receive the covenant of the Lord to give to the people. And [Moses] received from the Lord the two tables which were written by the finger of the hand of the Lord in the spirit.* And Moses took them, and brought them down to give them to the people.

Barnabas 14:3

And the Lord said unto Moses; *Moses, Moses, come down quickly; for thy people, whom thou leddest forth from the land of Egypt, hath done wickedly. And Moses perceived that they had made for themselves again molten images, and he cast them out of his hands and the tables of the covenant of the Lord were broken in pieces.*

Barnabas 14:4

Moses received them, but they themselves were not found worthy. But how did we receive them? Mark this. Moses received them being a servant, but the Lord himself gave them to us to be the people of His inheritance, having endured patiently for our sakes.

Barnabas 14:5

But He was made manifest, in order that at the same time they might be perfected in their sins, and we might receive the covenant through Him who inherited it, even the Lord Jesus, who was prepared beforehand hereunto, that appearing in person He might redeem out of darkness our hearts which had already been paid over unto death and delivered up to the iniquity of error, and thus establish the covenant in us through the word.

Barnabas 14:6

For it is written how the Father chargeth Him to deliver us from darkness, and to prepare a holy people for Himself.

Barnabas 14:7

Therefore saith the prophet; *I the Lord thy God called thee in righteousness, and I will lay hold of thy hand and will strengthen thee, and I have given thee to be a covenant of the race, a light to the Gentiles, to open the eyes of the blind, and to bring forth them that are bound from their fetters, and them that sit in darkness from their prison house.* We perceive then whence we were ransomed.

Barnabas 14:8

Again the prophet saith; *Behold I have set Thee to be a light unto the Gentiles, that Thou shouldest be for salvation unto the ends of the earth; thus saith the Lord that ransomed thee, even God.*

Barnabas 14:9

Again the prophet saith; *The Spirit of the Lord is upon Me, wherefore He anointed Me to preach good tidings to the humble; He hath sent Me to heal them that are broken-hearted, to preach release to the captives and recovery of sight to the blind, to proclaim the acceptable year of the Lord and the day of recompense, to comfort all that mourn.*

Barnabas 15:1

Moreover concerning the Sabbath likewise it is written in the Ten Words, in which He spake to Moses face to face on Mount Sinai; *And ye shall hallow the Sabbath of the Lord with pure hands and with a pure heart.*

Barnabas 15:2

And in another place He saith; *If my sons observe the Sabbath then I will bestow My mercy upon them.*

Barnabas 15:3

Of the Sabbath He speaketh in the beginning of the creation; *And God made the works of His hands in six days, and He ended on the seventh day, and rested on it, and He hallowed it.*

Barnabas 15:4

Give heed, children, what this meaneth; *He ended in six days.* He meaneth this, that in six thousand years the Lord shall bring all things to an end; for the day with Him signifyeth a thousand years; and this He himself beareth me witness, saying; *Behold, the day of the Lord shall be as a thousand years.* Therefore, children, in six days, that is in six thousand years, everything shall come to an end.

Barnabas 15:5

And He rested on the seventh day. this He meaneth; when His Son shall come, and shall abolish the time of the Lawless One, and shall judge the ungodly, and shall change the sun and the moon and the stars, then shall he truly rest on the seventh day.

Barnabas 15:6

Yea and furthermore He saith; *Thou shalt hallow it with pure hands and with a pure heart.* If therefore a man is able now to hallow the day which God hallowed, though he be pure in heart, we have gone utterly astray.

Barnabas 15:7

But if after all then and not till then shall we truly rest and hallow it, when we shall ourselves be able to do so after being justified and receiving the promise, when iniquity is no more and all things have been made new by the Lord, we shall be able to hallow it then, because we ourselves shall have been hallowed first.

Barnabas 15:8

Finally He saith to them; *Your new moons and your Sabbaths I cannot away with.* Ye see what is His meaning ; it is not your present Sabbaths that are acceptable [unto Me], but the Sabbath which I have made, in the which, when I have set all things at rest, I will make the beginning of the eighth day which is the beginning of another world.

Barnabas 15:9

Wherefore also we keep the eighth day for rejoicing, in the which also Jesus rose from the dead, and having been manifested ascended into the heavens.

Barnabas 16:1

Moreover I will tell you likewise concerning the temple, how these wretched men being led astray set their hope on the building, and not on their God that made them, as being a house of God.

Barnabas 16:2

For like the Gentiles almost they consecrated Him in the temple. But what saith the Lord abolishing the temple? Learn ye. *Who hath measured the heaven with a span, or hath measured the earth with his hand? Have not I, saith the Lord? The heaven is My throne and the earth the footstool of My feet. What manner of house will ye build for Me? Or what shall be my resting place?* Ye perceive that their hope is vain.

Barnabas 16:3

Furthermore He saith again; *Behold they that pulled down this temple themselves shall build it.*

Barnabas 16:4

So it cometh to pass; for because they went to war it was pulled down by their enemies. Now also the very servants of their enemies shall build it up.

Barnabas 16:5

Again, it was revealed how the city and the temple and the people of Israel should be betrayed. For the scripture saith; *And it shall be in the last days, that the Lord shall deliver up the sheep of the pasture and the fold and the tower thereof to destruction.* And it came to pass as the Lord spake.

Barnabas 16:6

But let us enquire whether there be any temple of God. There is; in the place where he himself undertakes to make and finish it. For it is written *And it shall come to pass, when the week is being accomplished, the temple of God shall be built gloriously in the name of the Lord.*

Barnabas 16:7

I find then that there is a temple, How then shall it be built in the name of the Lord? Understand ye. Before we believed on God, the abode of our heart was corrupt and weak, a temple truly built by

hands; for it was full of idolatry and was a house of demons, because we did whatsoever was contrary to God.

Barnabas 16:8

But it shall be built in the name of the Lord. Give heed then that the temple of the Lord may be built gloriously.

Barnabas 16:9

How? Understand ye. By receiving the remission of our sins and hoping on the Name we became new, created afresh from the beginning. Wherefore God dwelleth truly in our habitation within us. How? The word of his faith, the calling of his promise, the wisdom of the ordinances, the commandments of the teaching, He Himself prophesying in us, He Himself dwelling in us, opening for us who had been in bondage unto death the door of the temple, which is the mouth, and giving us repentance leadeth us to the incorruptible temple.

Barnabas 16:10

For he that desireth to be saved looketh not to the man, but to Him that dwelleth and speaketh in him, being amazed at this that he has never at any time heard these words from the mouth of the speaker, nor himself ever desired to hear them. This is the spiritual temple built up to the Lord.

Barnabas 17:1

So far as it was possible with all simplicity to declare it unto you, my soul hopeth that I have not omitted anything [of the matters pertaining unto salvation and so failed in my desire].

Barnabas 17:2

For if I should write to you concerning things immediate or future, ye would not understand them, because they are put in parables. So much then for this.

Barnabas 18:1

But let us pass on to another lesson and teaching. There are two ways of teaching and of power, the one of light and the other of darkness; and there is a great difference between the two ways. For on the one are stationed the light giving angels of God, on the other the angels of Satan.

Barnabas 18:2

And the one is the Lord from all eternity and unto all eternity, whereas the other is Lord of the season of iniquity that now is.

Barnabas 19:1

This then is the way of light, if anyone desiring to travel on the way to his appointed place would be zealous in his works. The knowledge then which is given to us whereby we may walk therein is as follows.

Barnabas 19:2

Thou shalt love Him that made thee, thou shalt fear Him that created thee, thou shalt glorify Him that redeemed thee from death; thou shalt be simple in heart and rich in spirit; thou shalt not cleave to those who walk the way of death; thou shalt hate everything that is not pleasing to God; thou shalt hate all hypocrisy; thou shalt never forsake the commandments of the Lord.

Barnabas 19:3

Thou shalt not exalt thyself, but shalt be lowly minded in all things. Thou shalt not assume glory to thyself. Thou shalt not entertain a wicked design against thy neighbor; thou shalt not admit boldness into thy soul.

Barnabas 19:4

Thou shalt not commit fornication, *thou shalt not commit adultery,* thou shalt not corrupt boys. The word of God shall not come forth from thee where any are unclean. Thou shalt not make a difference in a person to reprove him for a transgression. Thou shalt be meek, thou shalt be *quiet,* thou shalt be *fearing the words* which thou hast heard. Thou shalt not bear a grudge against thy brother.

Barnabas 19:5

Thou shalt not doubt whether a thing shall be or not be. *Thou shalt not take the name of the Lord in vain.* Thou shalt love thy neighbor more than thine own soul. Thou shalt not murder a child by abortion, nor again shalt thou kill it when it is born. Thou shalt not withhold thy hand from thy son or daughter, but from their youth thou shalt teach them the fear of God.

Barnabas 19:6

Thou shalt not be found coveting thy neighbors goods; thou shalt not be found greedy of gain. Neither shalt thou cleave with thy soul to the lofty, but shalt walk with the humble and righteous. The accidents that befall thee thou shalt receive as good, knowing that nothing is done without God. Thou shalt not be double minded nor double tongued.

Barnabas 19:7

Thou shalt be subject unto thy masters as to a type of God in shame and fear. Thou shalt not command in bitterness thy bondservant or thine handmaid who set their hope on the same God, lest haply, they should cease to fear the God who is over both of you; for He came not to call with respect of persons, but to call those whom the Spirit hath prepared.

Barnabas   19:8

Thou shalt make thy neighbor partake in all things, and shalt not say *that anything is thine own.* For if ye are fellow partakers in that which is imperishable, how much rather shall ye be in the things which are perishable. Thou shalt not be hasty with thine own tongue, for the mouth is the snare of death. So far as thou art able, thou shalt be pure for thy soul's sake.

Barnabas   19:9

Be not thou found holding out thy hands to receive, and drawing them in to give. Thou shalt love as the apple of thine eye every one *that speaketh unto thee the word of the Lord.*

Barnabas   19:10

Thou shalt remember the day of judgment night and day, and thou shalt seek out day by day the persons of the saints, either laboring by word and going to exhort them and meditating how thou mayest save souls by thy word, or thou shalt work with thy hands for a ransom for thy sins.

Barnabas   19:11

Thou shall not hesitate to give, neither shalt thou murmur when giving, but thou shalt know who is the good paymaster of thy reward. Thou shalt keep those things which thou hast received, neither adding to them nor taking away from them. Thou shalt utterly hate the Evil One. Thou shalt judge righteously.

Barnabas   19:12

Thou shalt not make a schism, but thou shalt pacify them that contend by bringing them together. Thou shalt confess thy sins. Thou shalt not betake thyself to prayer with an evil conscience. This is the way of light.

Barnabas   20:1

But the way of the Black One is crooked and full of a curse. For it is a way of eternal death with punishment wherein are the things that destroy men's souls--idolatry, boldness, exhalation of power, hypocrisy, doubleness of heart, adultery, murder, plundering, pride, transgression, treachery, malice, stubbornness, witchcraft, magic, covetousness, absence of the fear of God;

Barnabas   20:2

persecutors of good men, hating the truth, loving lies, not perceiving the reward of righteousness, not *cleaving to the good* nor to the righteous judgment, paying no heed to the widow and the orphan, wakeful not for the fear of God but for that which is evil; men from whom gentleness and forbearance stand aloof and far off; loving vain things, pursuing a recompense, not pitying the poor man, not toiling for him that is oppressed with toil, ready to slander, not recognizing Him that made them murderers of children, corrupters of the creatures of God, turning away from him that is in want, oppressing him that is afflicted, advocates of the wealthy, unjust judges of the poor, sinful in all things.

Barnabas   21:1

It is good therefore to learn the ordinances of the Lord, as many as have been written above, and to walk in them. For he that doeth these things shall be glorified in the kingdom of God; whereas he that chooseth their opposites shall perish together with his works. For this cause is the resurrection, for this the recompense.

Barnabas   21:2

I entreat those of you who are in a higher station, if ye will receive any counsel of good advice from me, keep amongst you those to whom ye may do good. Fail not.

Barnabas   21:3

The day is at hand, in which everything shall be destroyed together with the Evil One. *The Lord is at hand and his reward.*

Barnabas   21:4

Again and again I entreat you; be good lawgivers one to another; continue faithful councilors to yourselves; take away from you all hypocrisy.

Barnabas   21:5

And may God, who is Lord of the whole world, give you wisdom, judgment, learning, knowledge of His ordinances, patience.

Barnabas   21:6

And be ye taught of God, seeking diligently what the Lord requireth of you, and act that ye may be found in the day of judgment.

Barnabas   21:7

But if you have any remembrance of good, call me to mind when ye practice these things these things, that both my desire and my watchfulness may lead to some good result. I entreat you asking it as a favor.

Barnabas   21:8

So long as the good vessel (of the body) is with you, be lacking in none of these things, but search them out constantly, and fulfill every commandment; for they deserve it.

Barnabas   21:9

For this reason I was the more eager to write to you so far as I was able, that I might give you joy. Fare ye well, children of love and peace. The Lord of glory and of every grace be with your spirit.

Book 152. The Epistle to Diognetus

CHAPTER I -- OCCASION OF THE EPISTLE.

Since I see thee, most excellent Diognetus, exceedingly desirous to learn the mode of worshipping God prevalent among the Christians, and inquiring very carefully and earnestly concerning them, what God they trust in, and what form of religion they observe, so as all to look down upon the world itself, and despise death, while they neither esteem those to be gods that are reckoned such by the Greeks, nor hold to the superstition of the Jews; and what is the affection which they cherish among themselves; and why, in fine, this new kind or practice [of piety] has only now entered into the world, and not long ago; I cordially welcome this thy desire, and I implore God, who enables us both to speak and to hear, to grant to me so to speak, that, above all, I may hear you have been edified, and to you so to hear, that I who speak may have no cause of regret for having done so.

CHAPTER II -- THE VANITY OF IDOLS.

Come, then, after you have freed yourself from all prejudices possessing your mind, and laid aside what you have been accustomed to, as something apt to deceive you, and being made, as if from the beginning, a new man, inasmuch as, according to your own confession, you are to be the hearer of a new [system of] doctrine; come and contemplate, not with your eyes only, but with your understanding, the substance and the form of those whom ye declare and deem to be gods. Is not one of them a stone similar to that on which we tread? Is not a second brass, in no way superior to those vessels which are constructed for our ordinary use? Is not a third wood, and that already rotten? Is not a fourth silver, which needs a man to watch it, lest it be stolen? Is not a fifth iron, consumed by rust? Is not a sixth earthenware, in no degree more valuable than that which is formed for the humblest purposes? Are not all these of corruptible matter? Are they not fabricated by means of iron and fire? Did not the sculptor fashion one of them, the brazier a second, the silversmith a third, and the potter a fourth? Was not every one of them, before they were formed by the arts of these [workmen] into the shape of these [gods], each in its own way subject to change? Would not those things which are now vessels, formed of the same materials, become like to such, if they met with the same artificers? Might not these, which are now worshipped by you, again be made by men vessels similar to others? Are they not all deaf? Are they not blind? Are they not without life? Are they not destitute of feeling? Are they not incapable of motion? Are they not all liable to rot? Are they not all corruptible? These things ye call gods; these ye serve; these ye worship; and ye become altogether like to them. For this reason ye hate the Christians, because they do not deem these to be gods. But do not ye yourselves, who now think and suppose [such to be gods], much more cast contempt upon them than they [the Christians do]? Do ye not much more mock and insult them, when ye worship those that are made of stone and earthenware, without appointing any persons to guard them; but those made of silver and gold ye shut up by night, and appoint watchers to look after them by day, lest they be stolen? And by those gifts which ye mean to present to them, do ye not, if they are possessed of sense, rather punish [than honour] them? But if, on the other hand, they are destitute of sense, ye convict them of this fact, while ye worship them with blood and the smoke of sacrifices. Let any one of you suffer such indignities! Let any one of you endure to have such things done to himself! But not a single human being will, unless compelled to it, endure such treatment, since he is endowed with sense and reason. A stone, however, readily bears it, seeing it is insensible. Certainly you do not show [by your conduct] that he [your God] is possessed of sense. And as to the fact that Christians are not accustomed to serve such gods, I might easily find many other things to say; but if even what has been said does not seem to any one sufficient, I deem it idle to say anything further.

CHAPTER III -- SUPERSTITIONS OF THE JEWS.

And next, I imagine that you are most desirous of hearing something on this point, that the Christians do not observe the same forms of divine worship as do the Jews. The Jews, then, if they abstain from the kind of service above described, and deem it proper to worship one God as being Lord of all, [are right]; but if they offer Him worship in the way which we have described, they greatly err. For while the Gentiles, by offering such things to those that are destitute of sense and hearing, furnish an example of madness; they, on the other hand by thinking to offer these things to God as if He needed them, might justly reckon it rather an act of folly than of divine worship. For He that made heaven and earth, and all that is therein, and gives to us all the things of which we stand in need, certainly requires none of those things which He Himself bestows on such as think of furnishing them to Him. But those who imagine that, by means of blood, and the smoke of sacrifices and burnt-offerings, they offer sacrifices [acceptable] to Him, and that by such honours they show Him respect,--these, by supposing that they can give anything to Him who stands in need of nothing, appear to me in no respect to differ from those who studiously confer the same honour on things destitute of sense, and which therefore are unable to enjoy such honours.

CHAPTER IV -- THE OTHER OBSERVANCES OF THE JEWS.

But as to their scrupulosity concerning meats, and their superstition as respects the Sabbaths, and their boasting about circumcision, and their fancies about fasting and the new moons, which are utterly ridiculous and unworthy of notice,--I do not think that you require to learn anything from me. For, to accept some of those things which have been formed by God for the use of men as properly formed, and to reject others as useless and redundant,--how can this be lawful? And to speak falsely of God, as if He forbade us to do what is good on the Sabbath-days,--how is not this impious? And to glory in the circumcision of the flesh as a proof of election, and as if, on account of it, they were specially beloved by God,--how is it not a subject of ridicule? And as to their observing months and days, as if waiting upon the stars and the moon, and their distributing, according to their own tendencies, the appointments of God, and the vicissitudes of the seasons, some for festivities, and others for mourning,--who would deem this a part of divine worship, and not much rather a manifestation of folly? I suppose, then, you are sufficiently convinced that the ChriStians properly abstain from the vanity and error common [to both Jews and Gentiles], and from the busy-body spirit and vain boasting of the Jews; but you must not hope to learn the mystery of their peculiar mode of worshipping God from any mortal.

CHAPTER V -- THE MANNERS OF THE CHRISTIANS.

For the Christians are distinguished from other men neither by country, nor language, nor the customs which they observe. For they neither inhabit cities of their own, nor employ a peculiar form of speech, nor lead a life which is marked out by any singularity. The course of conduct which they follow has not been devised by any speculation or deliberation of inquisitive men; nor do they, like some, proclaim themselves the advocates of any merely human doctrines. But, inhabiting Greek as well as barbarian cities, according as the lot of each of them has determined, and following the customs of the natives in respect to clothing, food, and the rest of their ordinary conduct, they display to us their wonderful and confessedly striking method of life. They dwell in their own countries, but simply as sojourners. As citizens, they share in all things with others, and yet endure all things as if foreigners. Every foreign land is to them as their native country, and every land of their birth as a land of strangers. They marry, as do all [others]; they beget children; but they do not destroy their offspring. They have a common table, but not a common bed. They are in the flesh, but they do not live after the flesh. They pass their days on earth, but they are citizens of heaven. They obey the prescribed laws, and at the same time surpass the laws by their lives. They love all men, and are persecuted by all. They are unknown and condemned; they are put to death, and restored to life. They are poor, yet make many rich; they are in lack of all things, and yet abound in all; they are dishonoured, and yet in their very dishonour are glorified. They are evil spoken of, and yet are justified; they are reviled, and bless; they are insulted, and repay the insult with honour; they do good, yet are punished as evil-doers. When punished, they rejoice as if quickened into life; they are assailed by the Jews as foreigners, and are persecuted by the Greeks; yet those who hate them are unable to assign any reason for their hatred.

CHAPTER VI -- THE RELATION OF CHRISTIANS TO THE WORLD.

To sum up all in one word--what the soul is in the body, that are Christians in the world. The soul is dispersed through all the members of the body, and Christians are scattered through all the cities of the world. The soul dwells in the body, yet is not of the body; and Christians dwell in the world, yet are not of the world. The invisible soul is guarded by the visible body, and Christians are known indeed to be in the world, but their godliness remains invisible. The flesh hates the soul, and wars against it, though itself suffering no injury, because it is prevented from enjoying pleasures; the world also hates the Christians, though in nowise injured, because they abjure pleasures. The soul loves the flesh that hates it, and [loves also] the members; Christians likewise love those that hate them. The soul is imprisoned in the body, yet preserves that very body; and Christians are confined in the world as in a prison, and yet they are the preservers of the world. The immortal soul dwells in a mortal tabernacle; and Christians dwell as sojourners in corruptible [bodies], looking for an incorruptible dwelling in the heavens. The soul, when but ill-provided with food and drink, becomes better; in like manner, the Christians, though subjected day by day to punishment, increase the more in number. God has assigned them this illustrious position, which it were unlawful for them to forsake.

CHAPTER VII -- THE MANIFESTATION OF CHRIST.

For, as I said, this was no mere earthly invention which was delivered to them, nor is it a mere human system of opinion, which they judge it right to preserve so carefully, nor has a dispensation of mere human mysteries been committed to them, but truly God Himself, who is almighty, the Creator of all things, and invisible, has sent from heaven, and placed among men, [Him who is] the truth, and the holy and incomprehensible Word, and has firmly established Him in their hearts. He did not, as one might have imagined, send to men any servant, or angel, or ruler, or any one of those who bear sway over earthly things, or one of those to whom

the government of things in the heavens has been entrusted, but the very Creator and Fashioner of all things--by whom He made the heavens--by whom he enclosed the sea within its proper bounds--whose ordinances all the stars faithfully observe--from whom the sun has received the measure of his daily course to be observed--whom the moon obeys, being commanded to shine in the night, and whom the stars also obey, following the moon in her course; by whom all things have been arranged, and placed within their proper limits, and to whom all are subject--the heavens and the things that are therein, the earth and the things that are therein, the sea and the things that are therein--fire, air, and the abyss--the things which are in the heights, the things which are in the depths, and the things which lie between. This [messenger] He sent to them. Was it then, as one might conceive, for the purpose of exercising tyranny, or of inspiring fear and terror? By no means, but under the influence of clemency and meekness. As a king sends his son, who is also a king, so sent He Him; as God He sent Him; as to men He sent Him; as a Saviour He sent Him, and as seeking to persuade, not to compel us; for violence has no place in the character of God. As calling us He sent Him, not as vengefully pursuing us; as loving us He sent Him, not as judging us. For He will yet send Him to judge us, and who shall endure His appearing? ... Do you not see them exposed to wild beasts, that they may be persuaded to deny the Lord, and yet not overcome? Do you not see that the more of them are punished, the greater becomes the number of the rest? This does not seem to be the work of man: this is the power of God; these are the evidences of His manifestation.

CHAPTER VIII -- THE MISERABLE STATE OF MEN BEFORE THE COMING OF THE WORD.

For, who of men at all understood before His coming what God is? Do you accept of the vain and silly doctrines of those who are deemed trustworthy philosophers? of whom some said that fire was God, calling that God to which they themselves were by and by to come; and some water; and others some other of the elements formed by God. But if any one of these theories be worthy of approbation, every one of the rest of created things might also be declared to be God. But such declarations are simply the startling and erroneous utterances of deceivers; and no man has either seen Him, or made Him known, but He has revealed Himself. And He has manifested Himself through faith, to which alone it is given to behold God. For God, the Lord and Fashioner of all things, who made all things, and assigned them their several positions, proved Himself not merely a friend of mankind, but also long-suffering [in His dealings with them.] Yea, He was always of such a character, and still is, and will ever be, kind and good, and free from wrath, and true, and the only one who is [absolutely] good; and He formed in His mind a great and unspeakable conception, which He communicated to His Son alone. As long, then, as He held and preserved His own wise counsel in concealment, He appeared to neglect us, and to have no care over us. But after He revealed and laid open, through His beloved Son, the things which had been prepared from the beginning, He conferred every blessing all at once upon us, so that we should both share in His benefits, and see and be active [in His service]. Who of us would ever have expected these things? He was aware, then, of all things in His own mind, along with His Son, according to the relation subsisting between them.

CHAPTER IX -- WHY THE SON WAS SENT SO LATE.

As long then as the former time endured, He permitted us to be borne along by unruly impulses, being drawn away by the desire of pleasure and various lusts. This was not that He at all delighted in our sins, but that He simply endured them; nor that He approved the time of working iniquity which then was, but that He sought to form a mind conscious of righteousness, so that being convinced in that time of our unworthiness of attaining life through our own works, it should now, through the kindness of God, be vouchsafed to us; and having made it manifest that in ourselves we were unable to enter into the kingdom of God, we might through the power of God be made able. But when our wickedness had reached its height, and it had been clearly shown that its reward, punishment and death, was impending over us; and when the time had come which God had before appointed for manifesting His own kindness and power, how the one love of God, through exceeding regard for men, did not regard us with hatred, nor thrust us away, nor remember our iniquity against us, but showed great long-suffering, and bore with us, He Himself took on Him the burden of our iniquities, He gave His own Son as a ransom for us, the holy One for transgressors, the blameless One for the wicked, the righteous One for the unrighteous, the incorruptible One for the corruptible, the immortal One for them that are mortal. For what other thing was capable of covering our sins than His righteousness? By what other one was it possible that we, the wicked and ungodly, could be justified, than by the only Son of God? O sweet exchange! O unsearchable operation! O benefits surpassing all expectation! that the wickedness of many should be hid in a single righteous One, and that the righteousness of One should justify many transgressors! Having therefore convinced us in the former time that our nature was unable to attain to life, and having now revealed the Saviour who is able to save even those things which it was [formerly] impossible to save, by both these facts He desired to lead us to trust in His kindness, to esteem Him our Nourisher, Father, Teacher,

Counsellor, Healer, our Wisdom, Light, Honour, Glory, Power, and Life, so that we should not be anxious[concerning clothing and food.

CHAPTER X -- THE BLESSINGS THAT WILL FLOW FROM FAITH.

If you also desire [to possess] this faith, you likewise shall receive first of all the knowledge of the Father. For God has loved mankind, on whose account He made the world, to whom He rendered subject all the things that are in it, to whom He gave reason and understanding, to whom alone He imparted the privilege of looking upwards to Himself, whom He formed after His own image, to whom He sent His only-begotten Son, to whom He has promised a kingdom in heaven, and will give it to those who have loved Him. And when you have attained this knowledge, with what joy do you think you will be filled? Or, how will you love Him who has first so loved you? And if you love Him, you will be an imitator of His kindness. And do not wonder that a man may become an imitator of God. He can, if he is willing. For it is not by ruling over his neighbours, or by seeking to hold the supremacy over those that are weaker, or by being rich, and showing violence towards those that are inferior, that happiness is found; nor can any one by these things become an imitator of God. But these things do not at all constitute His majesty. On the contrary he who takes upon himself the burden of his neighbour; he who, in whatsoever respect he may be superior, is ready to benefit another who is deficient; he who, whatsoever things he has received from God, by distributing these to the needy, becomes a god to those who receive [his benefits]: he is an imitator of God. Then thou shalt see, while still on earth, that God in the heavens rules over [the universe]; then thou shall begin to speak the mysteries of God; then shalt thou both love and admire those that suffer punishment because they will not deny God; then shall thou condemn the deceit and error of the world when thou shall know what it is to live truly in heaven, when thou shalt despise that which is here esteemed to be death, when thou shalt fear what is truly death, which is reserved for those who shall be condemned to the eternal fire, which shall afflict those even to the end that are committed to it. Then shalt thou admire those who for righteousness' sake endure the fire that is but for a moment, and shalt count them happy when thou shalt know [the nature of] that fire.

CHAPTER XI -- THESE THINGS ARE WORTHY TO BE KNOWN AND BELIEVED.

I do not speak of things strange to me, nor do I aim at anything inconsistent with right reason; but having been a disciple of the Apostles, I am become a teacher of the Gentiles. I minister the things delivered to me to those that are disciples worthy of the truth. For who that is rightly taught and begotten by the loving Word, would not seek to learn accurately the things which have been clearly shown by the Word to His disciples, to whom the Word being manifested has revealed them, speaking plainly [to them], not understood indeed by the unbelieving, but conversing with the disciples, who, being esteemed faithful by Him, acquired a knowledge of the mysteries of the Father? For which s reason He sent the Word, that He might be manifested to the world; and He, being despised by the people [of the Jews], was, when preached by the Apostles, believed on by the Gentiles. This is He who was from the beginning, who appeared as if new, and was found old, and yet who is ever born afresh in the hearts of the saints. This is He who, being from everlasting, is to-day called the Son; through whom the Church is enriched, and grace, widely spread, increases in the saints. furnishing understanding, revealing mysteries, announcing times, rejoicing over the faithful. giving to those that seek, by whom the limits of faith are not broken through, nor the boundaries set by the fathers passed over. Then the fear of the law is chanted, and the grace of the prophets is known, and the faith of the gospels is established, and the tradition of the Apostles is preserved, and the grace of the Church exults; which grace if you grieve not, you shall know those things which the Word teaches, by whom He wills, and when He pleases. For whatever things we are moved to utter by the will of the Word commanding us, we communicate to you with pains, and from a love of the things that have been revealed to us.

CHAPTER XII -- THE IMPORTANCE OF KNOWLEDGE TO TRUE SPIRITUAL LIFE.

When you have read and carefully listened to these things, you shall know what God bestows on such as rightly love Him, being made [as ye are] a paradise of delight, presenting in yourselves a tree bearing all kinds of produce and flourishing well, being adorned with various fruits. For in this place the tree of knowledge and the tree of life have been planted; but it is not the tree of knowledge that destroys--it is disobedience that proves destructive. Nor truly are those words without significance which are written, how God from the beginning planted the tree of life in the midst of paradise, revealing through knowledge the way to life, and when those who were first formed did not use this [knowledge] properly, they were, through the fraud of the Serpent[stripped naked. For neither can life exist without knowledge, nor is knowledge secure without life. Wherefore both were planted close together. The Apostle, perceiving the force [of this conjunction], and blaming that knowledge which, without true doctrine, is admitted to influence life, declares, "Knowledge puffeth up, but love edifieth." For he who thinks he knows anything without true knowledge, and such as is witnessed to by life, knows nothing, but is deceived by the

Serpent, as not loving life. But he who combines knowledge with fear, and seeks after life, plants in hope, looking for fruit. Let your heart be your wisdom; and let your life be true knowledge inwardly received. Bearing this tree and displaying its fruit, thou shalt always gather in those things which are desired by God, which the Serpent cannot reach, and to which deception does not approach; nor is Eve then corrupted, but is trusted as a virgin; and salvation is manifested, and the Apostles are filled with understanding, and the Passover of the Lord advances, and the choirs are gathered together, and are arranged in proper order, and the Word rejoices in teaching the saints,--by whom the Father is glorified: to whom be glory for ever. Amen.

Book 153. The Epistle of Polycarp to the Philippians

Greeting

Polycarp, and the presbyters with him, to the Church of God sojourning at Philippi: Mercy to you, and peace from God Almighty, and from the Lord Jesus Christ, our Saviour, be multiplied.

Chapter 1. Praise of the Philippians

I have greatly rejoiced with you in our Lord Jesus Christ, because you have followed the example of true love [as displayed by God], and have accompanied, as became you, those who were bound in chains, the fitting ornaments of saints, and which were indeed the diadems of the true elect of God and our Lord; and because the strong root of your faith, spoken of in days Philippians 1:5 long gone by, endures even until now, and brings forth fruit to our Lord Jesus Christ, who for our sins suffered even unto death, [but] whom God raised from the dead, having loosed the bands of the grave. In whom, though now you see Him not, you believe, and believing, rejoice with joy unspeakable and full of glory; 1 Peter 1:8 into which joy many desire to enter, knowing that by grace you are saved, not of works, Ephesians 2:8-9 but by the will of God through Jesus Christ.

Chapter 2. An exhortation to virtue

Wherefore, girding up your loins, 1 Peter 1:13; Ephesians 6:14 serve the Lord in fear and truth, as those who have forsaken the vain, empty talk and error of the multitude, and believed in Him who raised up our Lord Jesus Christ from the dead, and gave Him glory, 1 Peter 1:21 and a throne at His right hand. To Him all things 1 Peter 3:22; Philippians 2:10 in heaven and on earth are subject. Him every spirit serves. He comes as the Judge of the living and the dead. Acts 17:31 His blood will God require of those who do not believe in Him. But He who raised Him up from the dead will raise us up also, if we do His will, and walk in His commandments, and love what He loved, keeping ourselves from all unrighteousness, covetousness, love of money, evil speaking, false witness; not rendering evil for evil, or railing for railing, 1 Peter 3:9 or blow for blow, or cursing for cursing, but being mindful of what the Lord said in His teaching: Judge not, that you be not judged; Matthew 7:1 forgive, and it shall be forgiven unto you; be merciful, that you may obtain mercy; Luke 6:36 with what measure you measure, it shall be measured to you again; Matthew 7:2; Luke 6:38 and once more, Blessed are the poor, and those that are persecuted for righteousness' sake, for theirs is the kingdom of God.

Chapter 3. Expressions of personal unworthiness

These things, brethren, I write to you concerning righteousness, not because I take anything upon myself, but because you have invited me to do so. For neither I, nor any other such one, can come up to the wisdom 2 Peter 3:15 of the blessed and glorified Paul. He, when among you, accurately and steadfastly taught the word of truth in the presence of those who were then alive. And when absent from you, he wrote you a letter, which, if you carefully study, you will find to be the means of building you up in that faith which has been given you, and which, being followed by hope, and preceded by love towards God, and Christ, and our neighbour, is the mother of us all. Galatians 4:26 For if any one be inwardly possessed of these graces, he has fulfilled the command of righteousness, since he that has love is far from all sin.

Chapter 4. Various exhortations

But the love of money is the root of all evils. 1 Timothy 6:10 Knowing, therefore, that as we brought nothing into the world, so we can carry nothing out, 1 Timothy 6:7 let us arm ourselves with the armour of righteousness; Ephesians 6:11 and let us teach, first of all, ourselves to walk in the commandments of the Lord. Next, [teach] your wives [to walk] in the faith given to them, and in love and purity tenderly loving their own husbands in all truth, and loving all [others] equally in all chastity; and to train up their children in the knowledge and fear of God. Teach the widows to be discreet as respects the faith of the Lord, praying continually 1 Thessalonians 5:17 for all, being far from all slandering, evil-speaking, false-witnessing, love of money, and every kind of evil; knowing that they are the altar of God, that He clearly perceives all things, and that nothing is hid from Him, neither reasonings, nor reflections, nor any one of the secret things of the heart.

Chapter 5. The duties of deacons, youths, and virgins

Knowing, then, that God is not mocked, Galatians 6:7 we ought to walk worthy of His commandment and glory. In like manner should the deacons be blameless before the face of His righteousness, as being the servants of God and Christ, and not of men. They must not be slanderers, double-tongued, 1 Timothy 3:8 or lovers of money, but temperate in all things, compassionate, industrious, walking according to the truth of the Lord, who was the servant Matthew 20:28 of all. If we please Him in this present world, we shall receive also the future world, according as He has promised to us that He will raise us again from the dead, and that if we live worthily of Him, we shall also reign together with Him, 2 Timothy 2:12 provided only we believe. In like manner, let the young men also be blameless in all things, being especially careful to preserve purity, and keeping themselves in, as with a bridle, from every kind of evil. For it is well that they should be cut off from the lusts that are in the world, since every lust wars against the spirit; 1 Peter 2:11 and neither fornicators, nor effeminate, nor abusers of themselves with mankind, shall inherit the kingdom of God, 1 Corinthians 6:9-10 nor those who do things inconsistent and unbecoming. Wherefore, it is needful to abstain from all these things, being subject to the presbyters and deacons, as unto God and Christ. The virgins also must walk in a blameless and pure conscience.

Chapter 6. The duties of presbyters and others

And let the presbyters be compassionate and merciful to all, bringing back those that wander, visiting all the sick, and not neglecting the widow, the orphan, or the poor, but always providing for that which is becoming in the sight of God and man; Romans 12:17; 2 Corinthians 8:31 abstaining from all wrath, respect of persons, and unjust judgment; keeping far off from all covetousness, not quickly crediting [an evil report] against any one, not severe in judgment, as knowing that we are all under a debt of sin. If then we entreat the Lord to forgive us, we ought also ourselves to forgive; Matthew 6:12-14 for we are before the eyes of our Lord and God, and we must all appear at the judgment-seat of Christ, and must every one give an account of himself. Romans 14:10-12; 2 Corinthians 5:10 Let us then serve Him in fear, and with all reverence, even as He Himself has commanded us, and as the apostles who preached the Gospel unto us, and the prophets who proclaimed beforehand the coming of the Lord [have alike taught us]. Let us be zealous in the pursuit of that which is good, keeping ourselves from causes of offense, from false brethren, and from those who in hypocrisy bear the name of the Lord, and draw away vain men into error.

Chapter 7. Avoid the Docetæ, and persevere in fasting and prayer

For whosoever does not confess that Jesus Christ has come in the flesh, is antichrist; 1 John 4:3 and whosoever does not confess the testimony of the cross, is of the devil; and whosoever perverts the oracles of the Lord to his own lusts, and says that there is neither a resurrection nor a judgment, he is the first-born of Satan. Wherefore, forsaking the vanity of many, and their false doctrines, let us return to the word which has been handed down to us from Jude 3 the beginning; watching unto prayer, 1 Peter 4:7 and persevering in fasting; beseeching in our supplications the all-seeing God not to lead us into temptation, Matthew 6:13; Matthew 26:41 as the Lord has said: The spirit truly is willing, but the flesh is weak. Matthew 26:41; Mark 14:38

Chapter 8. Persevere in hope and patience

Let us then continually persevere in our hope, and the earnest of our righteousness, which is Jesus Christ, who bore our sins in His own body on the tree, 1 Peter 2:24 who did no sin, neither was guile found in His mouth, 1 Peter 2:22 but endured all things for us, that we might live in Him. 1 John 4:9 Let us then be imitators of His patience; and if we suffer Acts 5:41; 1 Peter 4:16 for His name's sake, let us glorify Him. For He has set us this example 1 Peter 2:21 in Himself, and we have believed that such is the case.

Chapter 9. Patience inculcated

I exhort you all, therefore, to yield obedience to the word of righteousness, and to exercise all patience, such as you have seen [set] before your eyes, not only in the case of the blessed Ignatius, and Zosimus, and Rufus, but also in others among yourselves, and in Paul himself, and the rest of the apostles. [This do] in the assurance that all these have not run Philippians 2:16; Galatians 2:2 in vain, but in faith and righteousness, and that they are [now] in their due place in the presence of the Lord, with whom also they suffered. For they loved not this present world, but Him who died for us, and for our sakes was raised again by God from the dead.

Chapter 10. Exhortation to the practice of virtue

Stand fast, therefore, in these things, and follow the example of the Lord, being firm and unchangeable in the faith, loving the brotherhood, 1 Peter 2:17 and being attached to one another, joined together in the truth, exhibiting the meekness of the Lord in your intercourse with one another, and despising no one. When you can do good, defer it not, because alms delivers from death. Tobit 4:10, Tobit 12:9 Be all of you subject one to another 1 Peter 5:5 having your conduct blameless among the Gentiles, 1 Peter 2:12 that you may both receive praise for your good works, and the Lord may not be blasphemed through you. But woe to him by whom the name of the Lord is blasphemed! Isaiah 52:5 Teach, therefore, sobriety to all, and manifest it also in your own conduct.

Chapter 11. Expression of grief on account of Valens

I am greatly grieved for Valens, who was once a presbyter among you, because he so little understands the place that was given him [in the Church]. I exhort you, therefore, that you abstain from covetousness, and that you be chaste and truthful. Abstain from every form of evil. 1 Thessalonians 5:22 For if a man cannot govern himself in such matters, how shall he enjoin them on others? If a man does not keep himself from covetousness, he shall be defiled by idolatry, and shall be judged as one of the heathen. But who of us are ignorant of the judgment of the Lord? Do we not know that the saints shall judge the world? 1 Corinthians 6:2 as Paul teaches. But I have neither seen nor heard of any such thing among you, in the midst of whom the blessed Paul laboured, and who are commended in the beginning of his Epistle. For he boasts of you in all those Churches which alone then knew the Lord; but we [of Smyrna] had not yet known Him. I am deeply grieved, therefore, brethren, for him (Valens) and his wife; to whom may the Lord grant true repentance! And be then moderate in regard to this matter, and do not count such as enemies, 2 Thessalonians 3:15 but call them back as suffering and straying members, that you may save your whole body. For by so acting you shall edify yourselves. 1 Corinthians 12:26

Chapter 12. Exhortation to various graces

For I trust that you are well versed in the Sacred Scriptures, and that nothing is hid from you; but to me this privilege is not yet granted. It is declared then in these Scriptures, Be angry, and sin not, and, Let not the sun go down upon your wrath. Ephesians 4:26 Happy is he who remembers this, which I believe to be the case with you. But may the God and Father of our Lord Jesus Christ, and Jesus Christ Himself, who is the Son of God, and our everlasting High Priest, build you up in faith and truth, and in all meekness, gentleness, patience, long-suffering, forbearance, and purity; and may He bestow on you a lot and portion among His saints, and on us with you, and on all that are under heaven, who shall believe in our Lord Jesus Christ, and in His Father, who raised Him from the dead. Galatians 1:1 Pray for all the saints. Pray also for kings, 1 Timothy 2:2 and potentates, and princes, and for those that persecute and hate you, Matthew 5:44 and for the enemies of the cross, that your fruit may be manifest to all, and that you may be perfect in Him.

Chapter 13. Concerning the transmission of epistles

Both you and Ignatius wrote to me, that if any one went [from this] into Syria, he should carry your letter with him; which request I will attend to if I find a fitting opportunity, either personally, or through some other acting for me, that your desire may be fulfilled. The Epistles of Ignatius written by him to us, and all the rest [of his Epistles] which we have by us, we have sent to you, as you requested. They are subjoined to this Epistle, and by them you may be greatly profited; for they treat of faith and patience, and all things that tend to edification in our Lord. Any more certain information you may have obtained respecting both Ignatius himself, and those that were with him, have the goodness to make known to us.

Chapter 14. Conclusion

These things I have written to you by Crescens, whom up to the present time I have recommended unto you, and do now recommend. For he has acted blamelessly among us, and I believe also among you. Moreover, you will hold his sister in esteem when she comes to you. Be safe in the Lord Jesus Christ. Grace be with you all. Amen.

Book 154. The Teachings of Silvanus

Abolish every childish time of life, acquire for yourself strength of mind and soul, and intensify the struggle against every folly of the passions of love and base wickedness, and love of praise, and fondness of contention, and tiresome jealousy and wrath, and anger and the desire of avarice. Guard your (pl.) camp and weapons and spears. Arm yourself and all the soldiers, which are the words, and the commanders, which are the counsels, and your mind as a guiding principle.

My son, throw every robber out of your gates. Guard all your gates with torches, which are the words, and you will acquire through all these things a quiet life. But he who will not guard these things will become like a city which is desolate, since it has been captured. All kinds of wild beasts have trampled upon it, for thoughts which are not good are evil wild beasts. And your city will be filled with robbers, and you will not be able to acquire peace, but only all kinds of savage wild beasts. The Wicked One, who is a tyrant, is lord over these. While directing this, he (the Wicked One) is beneath the great mire. The whole city, which is your soul, will perish.

Remove yourself from these things, O wretched soul! Bring your guide and your teacher. The mind is the guide, but reason is the teacher. They will bring you out of destruction and dangers.

Listen, my son, to my advice! Do not show your back to enemies and flee, but rather, pursue them as a strong one. Be not an animal, with men pursuing you; but rather, be a man, with you pursuing the evil wild beasts, lest somehow they become victorious over you and trample upon you as on a dead man, and you perish due to their wickedness.

Oh wretched man, what will you do if you fall into their hands? Protect yourself, lest you be delivered into the hands of your enemies. Entrust yourself to this pair of friends, reason and mind, and no one will be victorious over you. May God dwell in your camp, may his Spirit protect your gates, and may the mind of Divinity protect the walls. Let holy reason become a torch in your mind, burning the wood which is the whole of sin. And if you do these things, O my son, you will be victorious over all your enemies, and they will not be able to wage war against you, neither will they be able to resist, nor will they be able to get in your way. For if you find these, you will despise them as deniers of truth. They will speak to you, cajoling you and enticing (you), not because they are afraid of you, but because they are afraid of those who dwell within you, namely, the guardians of the divinity and the teaching.

My son, accept the education and the teaching. Do not flee from the education and the teaching, but when you are taught, accept (it) with joy. And if you are educated in any matter, do what is good. You will plait a crown of education by your guiding principle. Put on the holy teaching like a robe. Make yourself noble-minded through good conduct. Obtain the austerity of good discipline. Judge yourself like a wise judge. Do not go astray from my teaching, and do not acquire ignorance, lest you lead your people astray. Do not flee from the divine and the teaching which are within you, for he who is teaching you loves you very much. For he shall bequeath to you a worthy austerity. Cast out the animal nature which is within you, and do not allow base thought to enter you. For ... you know the way which I teach.

If it is good to rule over the few, as you see it, how much better it is that you rule over everyone, since you are exalted above every congregation and every people, (are) prominent in every respect, and (are) a divine reason, having become master over every power which kills the soul.

My son, does anyone want to be a slave? Why, then, do you trouble yourself wrongly?

My son, do not fear anyone except God alone, the Exalted One. Cast the deceitfulness of the Devil from you. Accept the light for your eyes, and cast the darkness from you. Live in Christ, and you will acquire a treasure in heaven. Do not become a sausage (made) of many things which are useless, and do not become a guide in your blind ignorance.

My son, listen to my teaching, which is good and useful, and end the sleep which weighs heavily upon you. Depart from the forgetfulness which fills you with darkness, since if you were unable to do anything, I would not have said these things to you. But Christ has come in order to give you this gift. Why do you pursue the darkness when the light is at your disposal? Why do you drink stale water, though sweet wine is available for you? Wisdom summons you, yet you desire folly. Not by your own desire do you do these things, but it is the animal nature within you that does them.

Wisdom summons you in her goodness, saying, "Come to Me, all of you, O foolish ones, that you may receive a gift, the understanding which is good and excellent. I am giving to you a high-priestly garment which is woven from every (kind of) wisdom." What else is evil death except ignorance? What else is evil darkness except familiarity with forgetfulness? Cast your anxiety upon God alone. Do not become desirous of gold and silver, which are profitless, but clothe yourself with wisdom like a robe; put knowledge on yourself like a crown, and be seated upon a throne of perception. For these are yours, and you will receive them again on high another time.

For a foolish man usually puts on folly like a robe, and like a garment of sorrow, he puts on shame. And he crowns himself with ignorance, and takes his seat upon a throne of nescience. For while he is without reason, he leads only himself astray, for he is guided by ignorance. And he goes the ways of the desire of every passion. He swims in the desires of life and has sunk. To be sure, he thinks that he finds profit when he does all the things which are without profit. The wretched man who goes through all these things will die, because he does not have the mind, the helmsman. But he is like a ship which the wind tosses to and fro, and like a loose horse which has no rider. For this (man) needed the rider, which is reason. For the wretched one went astray because he did not want advice. He was thrown to and fro by these three misfortunes: he acquired death as a father, ignorance as a mother, and evil counsels - he acquired them as friends and brothers. Therefore, foolish one, you should mourn for yourself.

From now on, then, my son, return to your divine nature. Cast from you these evil, deceiving friends! Accept Christ, this true friend, as a good teacher. Cast from you death, which has become a father to you. For death did not exist, nor will it exist at the end.

But since you cast from yourself God, the holy Father, the true Life, the Spring of Life, therefore you have obtained death as a father and have acquired ignorance as a mother. They have robbed you of the true knowledge.

But return, my son, to your first father, God, and Wisdom, your Mother, from whom you came into being from the very first in order that you might fight against all of your enemies, the Powers of the Adversary.

Listen, my son, to my advice. Do not be arrogant in opposition to every good opinion, but take for yourself the side of the divinity of reason. Keep the holy commandments of Jesus Christ, and you will reign over every place on earth, and will be honored by the angels and archangels. Then you will acquire them as friends and fellow servants, and you will acquire places in heaven above.

Do not bring grief and trouble to the divine which is within you. But when you will care for it, will request of it that you remain pure, and will become self-controlled in your soul and body, you will become a throne of wisdom, and one belonging to God's household. He will give you a great light through it (wisdom).

But before everything (else), know your birth. Know yourself, that is, from what substance you are, or from what race, or from what species. Understand that you have come into being from three races: from the earth, from the formed, and from the created. The body has come into being from the earth with an earthly substance, but the formed, for the sake of the soul, has come into being from the thought of the Divine. The created, however, is the mind, which has come into being in conformity with the image of God. The divine mind has substance from the Divine, but the soul is that which he (God) formed for their own hearts. For I think that it (the soul) exists as wife of that which has come into being in conformity with the image, but matter is the substance of the body, which has come into being from the earth.

If you mix yourself, you will acquire the three parts as you fall from virtue into inferiority. Live according to the Mind. Do not think about things pertaining to the flesh. Acquire strength, for the mind is strong. If you fall from this other, you have become male-female. And if you cast out of yourself the substance of the mind, which is thought, you have cut off the male part, and turned yourself to the female part alone. You have become psychic, since you have received the substance of the formed. If you cast out the smallest part of this, so that you do not acquire again a human part - but you have accepted for yourself the animal thought and likeness - you have become fleshly, since you have taken on animal nature. For (if) it is difficult to find a psychical man, how much more so to find the Lord?

But I say that God is the spiritual one. Man has taken shape from the substance of God. The divine soul shares partly in this one; furthermore, it shares partly in the flesh. The base soul is wont to turn from side to side, [...] which it images the truth.

It is good for you, O man, to turn yourself toward the human, rather than toward the animal nature - I mean toward the fleshly. You will take on the likeness of the part toward which you will turn yourself.

I shall say something further to you. Again, for what will you (masc. sg.) be zealous? Did you (fem. sg.) wish to become animal when you had come into this kind of nature? But rather, share in a true nature of life. To be sure, animality will guide you into the race of the earth, but the rational nature will guide you in rational ways. Turn toward the rational nature, and cast from yourself the earth-begotten nature.

O soul, persistent one, be sober and shake off your drunkenness, which is the work of ignorance. If you persist and live in the body, you dwell in rusticity. When you entered into a bodily birth, you were begotten. Come into being inside the bridal chamber! Be illuminated in mind!

My son, do not swim in any water, and do not allow yourself to be defiled by strange kinds of knowledge. Certainly you know that the schemes of the Adversary are not few, and (that) the tricks which he has are varied? Especially has the noetic man been robbed of the intelligence of the snake. For it is fitting for you to be in agreement with the intelligence of (these) two: with the intelligence of the snake and with the innocence of the dove - lest he (the Adversary) come into you in the guise of a flatterer, as a true friend, saying, "I advise good things for you."

But you did not recognize the deceitfulness of this one when you received him as a true friend. For he casts into your heart evil thoughts as good ones, and hypocrisy in the guise of true wisdom, avidity in the guise of conservative frugality, love of glory in the guise of that which is beautiful, boastfulness and pride in the guise of great austerity, and godlessness as great godliness. For he who says, "I have many gods," is godless. And he casts spurious knowledge into your heart in the guise of mysterious words. Who will be able to comprehend his thoughts and devices, which are varied, since he is a Great Mind for those who wish to accept him as king?

My son, how will you be able to comprehend the schemes of this one, or his soul-killing counsel? For his devices, and the schemes of his wickedness, are many. And think about his entrances, that is, how he will enter your soul, and in what garment he will enter you.

Accept Christ, who is able to set you free, and who has taken on the devices of that one, so that through these he might destroy him by deceit. For this is the king whom you have who is forever invincible, against whom no one will be able to fight nor say a word. This is your king and your father, for there is no one like him. The divine teacher is with you always. He is a helper, and he meets you because of the good which is in you.

Do not put maliciousness in your judgment, for every malicious man harms his heart. For only a foolish man is wont to his destruction, but a wise man knows his way.

And a foolish man does not guard against speaking (a) mystery: A wise man (however) does not blurt out every word, but he will be discriminating toward those who hear. Do not mention everything in the presence of those whom you do not know.

Have a great number of friends, but not counselors. First, examine your counselor, for do not honor anyone who flatters. Their word, to be sure, is sweet as honey, but their heart is full of hellebore. For whenever they think that they have become a reliable friend, then they will deceitfully turn against you, and they will cast you down into the mire.

Do not trust anyone as a friend, for this whole world has come into being deceitfully, and every man is troubled in vain. All things of the world are not profitable, but they happen in vain. There is no one, not even a brother (who is trustworthy), since each one is seeking his own advantage.

My son, do not have anyone as a friend, but if you do acquire one, do not entrust yourself to him. Entrust yourself to God alone as father and as friend. For everyone proceeds deceitfully, while the whole earth is full of suffering and pain - things in which there is no profit. If you wish to pass your life in quiet, do not keep company with anyone. And if you do keep company with them, be as if you do not. Be pleasing to God, and you will not need anyone.

Live with Christ and he will save you. For he is the true light and the sun of life. For just as the sun which is visible and makes light for the eyes of the flesh, so Christ illuminates every mind and the heart. For (if) a wicked man (who is) in the body (has) an evil death, how much more so (does) he who has his mind blind. For every blind man goes along in such a way that he is seen just as one who does not have his mind sane. He does not delight in acquiring the light of Christ, which is reason.

For everything which is visible is a copy of that which is hidden. For as a fire which burns in a place without being confined to it, so it is with the sun which is in the sky, all of whose rays extend to places on the earth. Similarly, Christ has a single being, and he gives light to every place. This is also the way in which he speaks of our mind, as if it were a lamp which burns and lights up the place. (Being) in a part of the soul, it gives light to all the parts.

Furthermore, I shall speak of what is more exalted than this: the mind, with respect to actual being, is in a place, which means it is in the body; but with respect to thought, the mind is not in a place. For how can it be in a place, when it contemplates every place?

But we are able to mention what is more exalted than this: for do not think in your heart that God exists in a place. If you localize the Lord of all in a place, then it is fitting for you to say that the place is more exalted than he who dwells in it. For that which contains is more exalted than that which is contained. For there is no place which is called incorporeal. For it is not right for us to say that God is corporeal. For the consequence (would be) that we (must) attribute both increase and decrease to the corporeal, but also that he (God) who is subject to these will not remain imperishable.

Now, it is not difficult to know the Creator of all creatures, but it is impossible to comprehend the likeness of this One. For it is difficult not only for men to comprehend God, but it is (also) difficult for every divine being, (both) the angels and the archangels. It is necessary to know God as he is. You cannot know God through anyone except Christ, who has the image of the Father, for this image reveals the true likeness in correspondence to that which is revealed. A king is not usually known apart from an image.

Consider these things about God: he is in every place; on the other hand, he is in no place. With respect to power, to be sure, he is in every place; but with respect to divinity, he is in no place. So then, it is possible to know God a little. With respect to his power, he fills every place, but in the exaltation of his divinity, nothing contains him. Everything is in God, but God is not in anything.

Now what is it to know God? God is all which is in the truth. But it is as impossible to look at Christ as at the sun. God sees everyone; no one looks at him. But Christ, without being jealous, receives and gives. He is the Light of the Father, as he gives light without being jealous. In this manner he gives light to every place.

And all is Christ, he who has inherited all from the Existent One. For Christ is the idea of incorruptibility, and he is the Light which is shining undefiled. For the sun (shines) on every impure place, and yet it is not defiled. So it is with Christ: even if he is in the deficiency, yet he is without deficiency. And even if he has been begotten, he is (still) unbegotten. So it is with Christ: if, on the one hand, he is comprehensible, on the other, he is incomprehensible with respect to his actual being. Christ is all. He who does not possess all is unable to know Christ.

My son, do not dare to say a word about this One, and do not confine the God of all to mental images. For he who condemns may not be condemned by the one who condemns. Indeed, it is good to ask and to know who God is. Reason and mind are male names. Indeed, let him who wishes to know about this One, quietly and reverently ask. For there is no

small danger in speaking about these things, since you know that you will be judged on the basis of everything that you say.

And understand by this that he who is in darkness will not be able to see anything unless he receives the light and recovers (his) sight by means of it. Examine yourself (to see) whether you wholly have the light, so that, if you ask about these things, you may understand how you will escape. For many are seeking in darkness, and they grope about, wishing to understand, since there is no light for them.

My son, do not allow your mind to stare downward, but rather, let it look by means of the light at things above. For the light will always come from above. Even if it (the mind) is upon the earth, let it seek to pursue the things above. Enlighten your mind with the light of heaven, so that you may turn to the light of heaven.

Do not tire of knocking on the door of reason, and do not cease walking in the way of Christ. Walk in it so that you may receive rest from your labors. If you walk in another way, there will be no profit in it. For also those who walk in the broad way will go down at their end to the perdition of the mire. For the Underworld is open wide for the soul, and the place of perdition is broad. Accept Christ, the narrow way. For he is oppressed and bears affliction for your sin.

O soul, persistent one, in what ignorance you exist! For who is your guide into the darkness? How many likenesses did Christ take on because of you! Although he was God, he was found among men as a man. He descended to the Underworld. He released the children of death. They were in travail, as the scripture of God has said. And he sealed up the (very) heart of it (the Underworld). And he broke its (the Underworld's) strong bows completely. And when all the powers had seen him, they fled, so that he might bring you, wretched one, up from the Abyss, and might die for you as a ransom for your sin. He saved you from the strong hand of the Underworld.

But you, yourself, difficult (though it be) give to him your fundamental assent with (even so much as) a hint that he may take you up with joy! Now the fundamental choice, which is humility of heart, is the gift of Christ. A contrite heart is the acceptable sacrifice. If you humble yourself, you will be greatly exalted; and if you exalt yourself, you will be exceedingly humbled.

My son, guard yourself against wickedness, and do not let the Spirit of Wickedness cast you down into the Abyss. For he is mad and bitter. He is terrifying, and he casts everyone down into a pit of mire.

It is a great and good thing not to love fornication, and not even to think of the wretched matter at all, for to think of it is death. It is not good for any man to fall into death. For a soul which has been found in death will be without reason. For it is better not to live than to acquire an animal's life. Protect yourself, lest you are burned by the fires of fornication. For many who are submerged in fire are its servants, whom you do not know as your enemies.

O my son, strip off the old garment of fornication, and put on the garment which is clean and shining, that you may be beautiful in it. But when you have this garment, protect it well. Release yourself from every bond, so that you may acquire freedom. If you cast out of yourself the desire whose devices are many, you will release yourself from the sins of lust.

Listen, O soul, to my advice. Do not become a den of foxes and snakes, nor a hole of serpents and asps, nor a dwelling place of lions, or a place of refuge of basilisk-snakes. When these things happen to you, O soul, what will you do? For these are the powers of the Adversary. Everything which is dead will come into you through them (the powers). For their food is everything which is dead, and every unclean thing. For when these are within you, what living thing will come into you? The living angels will detest you. You were a temple, (but) you have made yourself a tomb. Cease being a tomb, and become (again) a temple, so that uprightness and divinity may remain in you.

Light the light within you. Do not extinguish it! Certainly, no one lights a lamp for wild beasts or their young. Raise your dead who have died, for they lived and have died for you. Give them life. They shall live again!

For the Tree of Life is Christ. He is Wisdom. For he is Wisdom; he is also the Word. he is the Life, the Power, and the Door. He is the Light, the Angel, and the Good Shepherd. Entrust yourself to this one who became all for your sake.

Knock on yourself as upon a door, and walk upon yourself as on a straight road. For if you walk on the road, it is impossible for you to go astray. And if you knock with this one (Wisdom), you knock on hidden treasures.

For since he (Christ) is Wisdom, he makes the foolish man wise. He (Wisdom) is a holy kingdom and a shining robe. For it (Wisdom) is much gold, which gives you great honor. The Wisdom of God became a type of fool for you, so that it might take you up, O foolish one, and make you a wise man. And the Life died for you when he was powerless, so that through his death, he might give life to you who have died.

Entrust yourself to reason and remove yourself from animalism. For the animal which has no reason is made manifest. For many think that they have reason, but if you look at them attentively, their speech is animalistic.

Give yourself gladness from the true vine of Christ. Satisfy yourself with the true wine, in which there is no drunkenness nor error. For it (the true wine) marks the end of drinking, since there is usually in it what gives joy to the soul and the mind, through the Spirit of God. But first, nurture your reasoning powers before you drink of it (the true wine).

Do not pierce yourself with the sword of sin. Do not burn yourself, O wretched one, with the fire of lust. Do not surrender yourself to barbarians like a prisoner, nor to savage beasts which want to trample upon you. For they are as lions which roar very loudly. Be not dead lest they trample upon you. You shall be man! It is possible for you through reasoning to conquer them.

But the man who does nothing is unworthy of (being called) rational man. The rational man is he who fears God. He who fears God does nothing insolent. And he who guards himself against doing anything insolent is one who keeps his guiding principle. Although he is a man who exists on earth, he makes himself like God.

But he who makes himself like God is one who does nothing unworthy of God, according to the statement of Paul, who has become like Christ.

For who shows reverence for God while not wanting to do things which are pleasing to him? For piety is that which is from the heart, and piety from the heart (characterizes) every soul which is near to God.

The soul which is a member of God's household is one which is kept pure, and the soul which has put on Christ is one which is pure. It is impossible for it to sin. Now where Christ is, there sin is idle.

Let Christ alone enter your world, and let him bring to naught all powers which have come upon you. Let him enter the temple which is within you, so that he may cast out all the merchants. Let him dwell in the temple which is within you, and may you become for him a priest and a Levite, entering in purity.

Blessed are you, O soul, if you find this one in your temple. Blessed are you still more if you perform his service. But he who will defile the temple of God, that one God will destroy. For you lay yourself open, O man, if you cast this one out of your temple. For whenever the enemies do not see Christ in you, then they will come into you armed in order to crush you.

O my son, I have given you orders concerning these things many times so that you would always guard your soul. It is not you who will cast him (Christ) out, but he will cast you out. For if you flee from him, you will fall into great sin. Again, if you flee from him, you will become food for your enemies. For all base persons flee from their lord, and the (man) base in virtue and wisdom flees from Christ. For every man who is separated (from him) falls into the claws of wild beasts.

Know who Christ is, and acquire him as a friend, for this is the friend who is faithful. He is also God and Teacher. This one, being God, became man for your sake. It is this one who broke the iron bars of the Underworld, and the bronze bolts. It is this one who attacked and cast down every haughty tyrant. It is he who loosened from himself the chains of which he had taken hold. He brought up the poor from the Abyss and the mourners from the Underworld. It is he who humbled the haughty powers; he who put to shame haughtiness through humility; he who has cast down the strong and the boaster through weakness; he who, in his contempt, scorned that which is considered an honor, so that humility for God's sake might be highly exalted; (and) he who has put on humanity.

And yet, the divine Word is God, he who bears patiently with man always. He wished to produce humility in the exalted. He (Christ), who has exalted man became like God, not in order that he might bring God down to man, but that man might become like God.

O this great goodness of God! O Christ, King, who has revealed to men the Great Divinity, King of every virtue and King of life, King of ages and Great One of the heavens, hear my words and forgive me!

Furthermore, he manifested a great zeal for Divinity.

Where is a man (who is) wise or powerful in intelligence, or a man whose devices are many because he knows wisdom? Let him speak wisdom; let him utter great boasting! For every man has become a fool and has spoken out of his (own) knowledge. For he (Christ) confounded the counsels of guileful people, and he prevailed over those wise in their own understanding.

Who will be able to discover the counsel of the Almighty, or to speak of the Divinity, or to proclaim it correctly? If we have not even been able to understand the counsels of our companions, who will be able to comprehend the Divinity, or the divinities of the heavens? If we scarcely find things on earth, who will search for the things of heaven? A great power and great glory has made the world known.

And the Life of Heaven wishes to renew all, that he may cast out that which is weak, and every black form, that everyone may shine forth in heavenly garments in order to make manifest the command of the Father (who) is exceedingly brilliant, and that he (Christ) may crown those wishing to contend well. Christ, being judge of the contest, is he who crowned every one, teaching every one to contend. This one who contended first received the crown, gained dominion, and appeared, giving light to everyone. And all were made new through the Holy Spirit and the Mind.

O Lord Almighty, how much glory shall I give Thee? No one has been able to glorify God adequately. It is Thou who hast given glory to Thy Word in order to save everyone, O Merciful God. (It is) he who has come from Thy mouth and has risen from Thy heart, the First-born, the Wisdom, the Prototype, the First Light.

For he is light from the power of God, and he is an emanation of the pure glory of the Almighty. He is the spotless mirror of the working of God, and he is the image of his goodness. For he is also the light of the Eternal Light. He is the eye which looks at the invisible Father, always serving and forming by the Father's will. He alone was begotten by the Father's good pleasure. For he is an incomprehensible Word, and he is Wisdom and Life. He gives life to, and nourishes, all living things and powers. Just as the soul gives life to all the members, he rules all with power and gives life to them. For he is the beginning and the end of everyone, watching over all and encompassing them. He is troubled on behalf of everyone, and he rejoices and also mourns. On the one hand, he mourns for those who have gotten as their lot the place of punishment; on the other, he is troubled about every one whom he arduously brings to instruction. But he rejoices over everyone who is in purity.

Then beware, lest somehow you fall into the hands of robbers. Do not allow sleep to your eyes nor drowsiness to your eyelids, that you may be saved like a gazelle from nets, and like a bird from a trap.

Fight the great fight as long as the fight lasts, while all the powers are staring after you - not only the holy ones, but also all the powers of the Adversary. Woe to you if you are vanquished in the midst of every one who is watching you! If you fight the fight and are victorious over the powers which fight against you, you will bring great joy to every holy one, and yet great grief to your enemies. Your judge helps (you) completely, since he wants you to be victorious.

Listen, my son, and do not be slow with your ears. Raise yourself up when you have left your old man behind like an eagle. Fear God in all your acts, and glorify him through good work. You know that every man who is not pleasing to God is the son of perdition. He will go down to the Abyss of the Underworld.

O this patience of God, which bears with every one, which desires that every one who has become subject to sin be saved!

But no one prevents him (God) from doing what he wants. For who is stronger than him, that he may prevent him? To be sure, it is he who touches the earth, causing it to tremble and also causing the mountains to smoke. (It is) he who has gathered together such a great sea as in a leather bag, and has weighed all the water on his scales. Only the hand of the Lord has created all these things. For this hand of the Father is Christ, and it forms all. Through it, all has come into being, since it became the mother of all. For he is always Son of the Father.

Consider these things about God Almighty, who always exists: this One was not always King, for fear that he might be without a divine Son. For all dwell in God, (that is), the things which have come into being through the Word, who is the Son as the image of the Father.

For God is nearby; he is not far off. All divine limits are those which belong to God's household. Therefore, if the divine agrees with you partially in anything, know that all of the Divine agrees with you. But this divine is not pleased with anything evil. For it is this which teaches all men what is good. This is what God has given to the human race, so that for this reason every man might be chosen before all the angels and the archangels.

For God does not need to put any man to the test. He knows all things before they happen, and he knows the hidden things of the heart. They are all revealed and found wanting in his presence. Let no one ever say that God is ignorant. For it is not right to place the Creator of every creature in ignorance. For even things which are in darkness are before him like (things in) the light.

So, there is no other one hidden except God alone. But he is revealed to everyone, and yet he is very hidden. He is revealed because God knows all. And if they do not wish to affirm it, they will be corrected by their heart. Now he is hidden because no one perceives the things of God. For it is incomprehensible and unfathomable to know the counsel of God. Furthermore, it is difficult to comprehend him, and it is difficult to find Christ. For he is the one who dwells in every place, and also he is in no place. For no one who wants to will be able to know God as he actually is, nor Christ, nor the Spirit, nor the chorus of angels, nor even the archangels, as well as the thrones of the spirits, and the exalted lordships, and the Great Mind. If you do not know yourself, you will not be able to know all of these.

Open the door for yourself, that you may know the One who is. Knock on yourself, that the Word may open for you. For he is the Ruler of Faith and the Sharp Sword, having become all for everyone because he wishes to have mercy on everyone.

My son, prepare yourself to escape from the world-rulers of darkness and of this kind of air, which is full of powers. But if you have Christ, you will conquer this entire world. That which you open for yourself, you will open. That which you knock upon for yourself, you will knock upon, benefiting yourself.

Help yourself, my son, (by) not proceeding with things in which there is no profit.

My son, first purify yourself toward the outward life, in order that you may be able to purify the inward.

And be not as the merchants of the Word of God.

Put all words to the test before you utter them.

Do not wish to acquire honors which are insecure, nor the boastfulness which brings you to ruin.

Accept the wisdom of Christ, (who is) patient and mild, and guard this, O my son, knowing that God's way is always profitable.

Book 155. The Sentences of Sextus

(157) [...] is a sign of ignorance.
(158/159) Love the truth, and the lie use like poison.
(160) May the right time precede your words.
(161/162) Speak when it is not proper to be silent, but speak concerning the things you know (only) then when it is fitting.
(163a) The untimely word is characteristic of an evil mind.
(163b) When it is proper to act, do not use a word.
(164a) Do not wish to speak first in the midst of a crowd.
(164b) While it is a skill to speak, it is also a skill to be silent.
(165a) It is better for you to be defeated while speaking the truth, than to be victorious through deceit.
(165b) He who is victorious through deceit is defeated by the truth.
(165c) Untrue words are a characteristic of evil persons.
(165d) There has to be a great crisis before the lie is necessary.
(165e) When there is someone, while you speak the truth, even if you lie there is no sin.
(165f) Do not deceive anyone, especially him who needs advice.
(166) Faithful is he who is first with all good works.
(167) Wisdom leads the soul to the place of God.
(168) There is no kinsman of the truth except wisdom.
(169) It is not possible for a believing nature to become fond of lying.
(170) A fearful and slavish nature will not be able to partake in faith.
(171a) When you are faithful, what it is fitting to say is not of greater value than the hearing.
(171b) When you are with believing persons, desire to listen rather than to speak.
(172) A pleasure-loving man is useless in everything.
(173) When there is no (accounting of) sin, do not speak in anything (which is) from God.
(174) The sins of those who are ignorant are the shame of those who have taught them.
(175) Those on account of whom the name of God is blasphemed are dead before God.
(176) A wise man is a doer of good works after God.
(177) May your life confirm your words before those who hear.
(178) What it is not right to do, do not even consider doing it.
(179) What you do not want to happen to you, do not do it yourself either.
(180) What it is shameful to do, is also ...
(pp. 17-26 are missing)
(307/308) He is a wise man who commends God to men, and God thinks more highly of the wise man than his own works.
(309) After God, no one is as free as the wise man.
(310) Everything God possesses, the wise man has also.
(311/312) The wise man shares in the kingdom of God; an evil man does not want the foreknowledge of God to come to pass.
(313) An evil soul flees from God.
(314) Everything bad is the enemy of God.
(315) What thinks in you, say with your mind that it is man.
(316) Where your thought is, there is your goodness.
(317) Do not seek goodness in flesh.
(318) He who does not harm the soul neither does (so) to man.
(319) After God, honor a wise man, since he is the servant of God.
(320) To make the body of your soul a burden is pride, but to be able to restrain it gently when it is necessary, is blessedness.
(321) Do not become guilty of your own death. Do not be angry at him who will take you out of (the) body and kill you.
(322) If someone brings the wise man out of the body wickedly, he rather does what is good for him, for he has been released from bonds.
(323) The fear of death grieves man because of the ignorance of the soul.
(324) <It were better> for you had the man-killing sword not come into being; but when it comes, say with your mind that it does not exist.
(325/326a) Someone who says "I believe," even if he spends a long time pretending, he will not prevail, but he will fall; as your heart is, (so) will be your life.
(326b) A godly heart produces a blessed life.
(327) He who will plot evil against another, he is the first [...].
(328) Let not an ungrateful man cause you to cease to do good.
(329) Do not say with your mind that these things which were asked, (and) you gave immediately, are more valuable than the receiver.
(330) You will use great property, if you give to the needy willingly.

(331) Persuade a senseless brother not to be senseless; if he is mad, protect him.
(332/334) Strive eagerly to be victorious over every man in prudence; maintain self-sufficiency.
(333) You cannot receive understanding unless you know first that you possess <it>. In everything there is again this sentence.
(335) The members of the body are a burden to those who do not use them.
(336) It is better to serve others than to make others serve you.
(337) He whom God will not bring out of (the) body, let him not burden himself.
(338) Not only do not hold an opinion which does not benefit the needy, but also do not listen to it.
(339) He who gives something without respect commits an outrage. [...].
(340) If you take on the guardianship of orphans, you will be the father of many children (and) you will be beloved of God.
(341) He whom you serve because of honor, you have served for a wage.
(342) If you have given that which honors you ..., you have given not to man, but you have given for your own pleasure.
(343/344) Do not provoke the anger of a mob. Know, then, what is fitting for the fortunate man to do.
(345) It is better to die than to darken the soul because of the immoderation of the belly.
(346) Say with your mind that the body is the garment of your soul: keep it, therefore, pure since it is innocent.
(347) Whatever the soul will do while it is in (the) body, it has as witnesses when it goes into judgment.
(348/349) Unclean demons do lay claim to a polluted soul; a faithful (and) good soul, evil demons will not be able to hinder in the way of God.
(350) Do not give the word of God to everyone.
(351) For those who are corrupted by glory it is not assuring to hear about God.
(352/353) It is not a small danger for us to speak the truth about God; do not say anything about God before you have learned from God.
(354/356) Do not speak with a godless person about God; if you are polluted on account of impure works, do not speak about God.
(357) The true word about God is the word of God.
(355) Speak concerning the word about God as if you were saying it in the presence of God.
(358) If first your mind is persuaded that you have been god-loving, then speak to whomever you wish about God.
(359) May your pious works precede every word about God.
(360) Do not wish to speak with a crowd about God.
(361) Be (more) sparing with a word about God (than) about a soul.
(362) It is better to dispose of a soul than to discard at random a word about God.
(363a) You conceive the body of a god-loving man, but you will not be able to rule over his speech.
(363b) The lion also rules over the body of the wise man; also the tyrant rules over it alone.
(364) If a tyrant threatens you, then, especially, remember God.
(365) He who speaks the word of God to those for whom it is not lawful, he is the betrayer of God.
(366) It is better for you to be silent about the word of God, than to speak recklessly.
(367/368) He who speaks lies about God is lying to God; a man who does not have anything truthful to say about God is abandoned by God.
(369) It is not possible for you to know God when you do not worship him.
(370) A man who does evil to someone will not be able to worship God.
(371) The love of man is the beginning of godliness.
(372) He who takes care of men while praying for all of them - this is the truth of God.
(373/374) It is God's business to save whom he wants; on the other hand, it is the business of the pious man to beseech God to save everyone.
(375) When you pray for something and it happens to you through God, then say with your mind that you have [...].
(376a) A man who is worthy of God, he is God among men, and he is the son of God.
(376b) Both the great one exists and he who is next to the great one exists.
(377/378) It is better for man to be without anything than to have many things while not giving to the needy; so also you, if you pray to God, he will not give to you.
(379) If you, from your whole heart, give your bread to the hungry, the gift is small, but the willingness is great with God.
(380) He who thinks that no one is in the presence of God, he is not humble towards God.
(381) He who makes his mind like unto God as far as he is able, he is the one who honors God greatly.
(382) God does not need anything, but he rejoices over those who give to the needy.

(383) The faithful do not speak many words, but their works are numerous.

(384) It is a faithful person fond of learning who is the worker of the truth.

(385) Adjust [...] the calamities, in order that [...].

(386) If you do not do evil to anyone, you will not be afraid of anyone.

(387) The tyrant will not be able to take away happiness.

(388) What is right to do, do it willingly.

(389a) What is not right to do, do not do it in any way.

(389b) Promise everything rather than to say "I am wise".

(390) What you do well, say with your mind that it is God who does it.

(391) No man who <looks> down upon the earth and upon tables is wise.

(392) The philosopher who is an outer body, he is not the one to whom it is fitting to pay respect, but (the) philosopher according to the inner man.

(393) Guard yourself from lying; there is he who deceives and there is he who is deceived.

(394/395) Know who God is, and know who is the one who thinks in you; a good man is the good work of God.

(396) They are miserable because of whom the word is blasphemed.

(397) Death will not be able to destroy [...].

(pp. 35-end are missing)

Book 156. The Gospel of Truth

The gospel of truth is joy to those who have received from the Father of truth the gift of knowing him by the power of the Logos, who has come from the Pleroma and who is in the thought and the mind of the Father; he it is who is called "the Savior," since that is the name of the work which he must do for the redemption of those who have not known the Father. For the name of the gospel is the manifestation of hope, since that is the discovery of those who seek him, because the All sought him from whom it had come forth. You see, the All had been inside of him, that illimitable, inconceivable one, who is better than every thought.

This ignorance of the Father brought about terror and fear. And terror became dense like a fog, that no one was able to see. Because of this, error became strong. But it worked on its hylic substance vainly, because it did not know the truth. It was in a fashioned form while it was preparing, in power and in beauty, the equivalent of truth. This then, was not a humiliation for him, that illimitable, inconceivable one. For they were as nothing, this terror and this forgetfulness and this figure of falsehood, whereas this established truth is unchanging, unperturbed and completely beautiful.

For this reason, do not take error too seriously. Thus, since it had no root, it was in a fog as regards the Father, engaged in preparing works and forgetfulnesses and fears in order, by these means, to beguile those of the middle and to make them captive. The forgetfulness of error was not revealed. It did not become light beside the Father. Forgetfulness did not exist with the Father, although it existed because of him. What exists in him is knowledge, which was revealed so that forgetfulness might be destroyed and that they might know the Father, Since forgetfulness existed because they did not know the Father, if they then come to know the Father, from that moment on forgetfulness will cease to exist.

That is the gospel of him whom they seek, which he has revealed to the perfect through the mercies of the Father as the hidden mystery, Jesus the Christ. Through him he enlightened those who were in darkness because of forgetfulness. He enlightened them and gave them a path. And that path is the truth which he taught them. For this reason error was angry with him, so it persecuted him. It was distressed by him, so it made him powerless. He was nailed to a cross. He became a fruit of the knowledge of the Father. He did not, however, destroy them because they ate of it. He rather caused those who ate of it to be joyful because of this discovery.

And as for him, them he found in himself, and him they found in themselves, that illimitable, inconceivable one, that perfect Father who made the all, in whom the All is, and whom the All lacks, since he retained in himself their perfection, which he had not given to the all. The Father was not jealous. What jealousy, indeed, is there between him and his members? For, even if the Aeon had received their perfection, they would not have been able to approach the perfection of the Father, because he retained their perfection in himself, giving it to them as a way to return to him and as a knowledge unique in perfection. He is the one who set the All in order and in whom the All existed and whom the All lacked. As one of whom some have no knowledge, he desires that they know him and that they love him. For what is it that the All lacked, if not the knowledge of the Father?

He became a guide, quiet and in leisure. In the middle of a school he came and spoke the Word, as a teacher. Those who were wise in their own estimation came to put him to the test. But he discredited them as empty-headed people. They hated him because they really were not wise men. After all these came also the little children, those who possess the knowledge of the Father. When they became strong they were taught the aspects of the Father's face. They came to know and they were known. They were glorified and they gave glory. In their heart, the living book of the Living was manifest, the book which was written in the thought and in the mind of the Father and, from before the foundation of the All, is in that incomprehensible part of him.

This is the book which no one found possible to take, since it was reserved for him who will take it and be slain. No one was able to be manifest from those who believed in salvation as long as that book had not appeared. For this reason, the compassionate, faithful Jesus was patient in his sufferings until he took that book, since he knew that his death meant life for many. Just as in the case of a will which has not yet been opened, for the fortune of the deceased master of the house is hidden, so also in the case of the All which had been hidden as long as the Father of the All was invisible and unique in himself, in whom every space has its source. For this reason Jesus appeared. He took that book as his own. He was nailed to a cross. He affixed the edict of the Father to the cross.

Oh, such great teaching! He abases himself even unto death, though he is clothed in eternal life. Having divested himself of these perishable rags, he clothed himself in incorruptibility, which no one could possibly take from him. Having entered into the empty territory of fears, he passed before those who were stripped by forgetfulness, being both knowledge and perfection, proclaiming the things that are in the heart of the Father, so that he became the wisdom of those who have received instruction. But those who are to be taught, the living who are inscribed in the book of the living, learn for themselves, receiving instructions from the Father, turning to him again.

Since the perfection of the All is in the Father, it is necessary for the All to ascend to him. Therefore, if one has knowledge, he gets what belongs to him and draws it to himself. For he who is ignorant, is deficient, and it is a great deficiency, since he lacks that which will make him perfect. Since the perfection of the All is in the Father, it is necessary for the All to ascend to him and for each one to get the things which are his. He registered them first, having prepared them to be given to those who came from him.

Those whose name he knew first were called last, so that the one who has knowledge is he whose name the Father has pronounced. For he whose name has not been spoken is ignorant. Indeed, how shall one hear if his name has not been uttered? For he who remains ignorant until the end is a creature of forgetfulness and will perish with it. If this is not so, why have these wretches no name, why do they have no sound? Hence, if one has knowledge, he is from above. If he is called, he hears, he replies, and he turns toward him who called him and he ascends to him and he knows what he is called. Since he has knowledge, he does the will of him who called him. He desires to please him and he finds rest. He receives a certain name. He who thus is going to have knowledge knows whence he came and whither he is going. He knows it as a person who, having become intoxicated, has turned from his drunkenness and having come to himself, has restored what is his own.

He has turned many from error. He went before them to their own places, from which they departed when they erred because of the depth of him who surrounds every place, whereas there is nothing which surrounds him. It was a great wonder that they were in the Father without knowing him and that they were able to leave on their own, since they were not able to contain him and know him in whom they were, for indeed his will had not come forth from him. For he revealed it as a knowledge with which all its emanations agree, namely, the knowledge of the living book which he revealed to the Aeons at last as his letters, displaying to them that these are not merely vowels nor consonants, so that one may read them and think of something void of meaning; on the contrary, they are letters which convey the truth. They are pronounced only when they are known. Each letter is a perfect truth like a perfect book, for they are letters written by the hand of the unity, since the Father wrote them for the Aeons, so that they by means of his letters might come to know the Father.

While his wisdom mediates on the logos, and since his teaching expresses it, his knowledge has been revealed. His honor is a crown upon it. Since his joy agrees with it, his glory exalted it. It has revealed his image. It has obtained his rest. His love took bodily form around it. His trust embraced it. Thus the logos of the Father goes forth into the All, being the fruit of his heart and expression of his will. It supports the All. It chooses and also takes the form of the All, purifying it, and causing it to return to the Father and to the Mother, Jesus of the utmost sweetness. The Father opens his bosom, but his bosom is the Holy Spirit. He reveals his hidden self which is his son, so that through the compassion of the Father the Aeons may know him, end their wearying search for the Father and rest themselves in him, knowing that this is rest. After he had filled what was incomplete, he did away with form. The form of it is the world, that which it served. For where there is envy and strife, there is an incompleteness; but where there is unity, there is completeness. Since this incompleteness came about because they did not know the Father, so when they know the Father, incompleteness, from that moment on, will cease to exist. As one's ignorance disappears when he gains knowledge, and as darkness disappears when light appears, so also incompleteness is eliminated by completeness. Certainly, from that moment on, form is no longer manifest, but will be dissolved in fusion with unity. For now their works lie scattered. In time unity will make the spaces complete. By means of unity each one will understand itself. By means of knowledge it will purify itself of diversity with a view towards unity, devouring matter within itself like fire and darkness by light, death by life.

Certainly, if these things have happened to each one of us, it is fitting for us, surely, to think about the All so that the house may be holy and silent for unity. Like people who have moved from a neighborhood, if they have some dishes around which are not good, they usually break them. Nevertheless the householder does not suffer a loss, but rejoices, for in the place of these defective dishes there are those which are completely perfect. For this is the judgement which has come from above and which has judged every person, a drawn two-edged sword cutting on this side and that. When it appeared, I mean, the Logos, who is in the heart of those who pronounce it - it was not merely a sound but it has become a body - a great disturbance occurred among the dishes, for some were emptied, others filled: some were provided for, others were removed; some were purified, still others were broken. All the spaces were shaken and disturbed for they had no composure nor stability. Error was disturbed not knowing what it should do. It was troubled; it lamented, it was beside itself because it did not know anything. When knowledge, which is its abolishment, approached it with all its emanations, error is empty, since there is nothing in it. Truth appeared; all its emanations recognized it. They actually greeted the Father with a power which is complete and which joins them with the Father. For each one loves truth because truth is the mouth of the Father. His tongue is the Holy Spirit, who joins him to truth attaching him to the mouth of the Father by his tongue at the time he shall receive the Holy Spirit.

This is the manifestation of the Father and his revelation to his Aeons. He revealed his hidden self and explained it. For who is it who exists if it is not the Father himself? All the spaces are his emanations. They knew that they stem from him as children from a perfect man. They knew that they had not yet received form nor had they yet received a name, every one of which the Father produces. If they at that time receive form of his knowledge, though they are truly in him, they do not know him. But the Father is perfect. He knows every space which is within him. If he pleases, he reveals anyone whom he desires by giving him a form and by giving him a name; and he does give him a name and cause him to come into being. Those who do not yet exist are ignorant of him who created them. I do not say, then, that those who do not yet exist are nothing. But they are in him who will desire that they exist when he pleases, like the event which is going to happen. On the one hand, he knows, before anything is revealed, what he will produce. On the other hand, the fruit which has not yet been revealed does not know anything, nor is it anything either. Thus each space which, on its part, is in the Father comes from the existent one, who, on his part, has established it from the nonexistent. [...] he who does not exist at all, will never exist.

What, then, is that which he wants him to think? "I am like the shadows and phantoms of the night." When morning comes, this one knows that the fear which he had experienced was nothing. Thus they were ignorant of the Father; he is the one whom they did not see. Since there had been fear and confusion and a lack of confidence and doublemindness and division, there were many illusions which were conceived by him, the foregoing, as well as empty ignorance - as if they were fast asleep and found themselves a prey to troubled dreams. Either there is a place to which they flee, or they lack strength as they come, having pursued unspecified things. Either they are involved in inflicting blows, or they themselves receive bruises. Either they are falling from high places, or they fly off through the air, though they have no wings at all. Other times, it is as if certain people were trying to kill them, even though there is no one pursuing them; or, they themselves are killing those beside them, for they are stained by their blood. Until the moment when they who are passing through all these things - I mean they who have experienced all these confusions - awake, they see nothing because the dreams were nothing. It is thus that they who cast ignorance from them as sleep do not consider it to be anything, nor regard its properties to be something real, but they renounce them like a dream in the night and they consider the knowledge of the Father to be the dawn. It is thus that each one has acted, as if he were asleep, during the time when he was ignorant and thus he comes to understand, as if he were awakening. And happy is the man who comes to himself and awakens. Indeed, blessed is he who has opened the eyes of the blind.

And the Spirit came to him in haste when it raised him. Having given its hand to the one lying prone on the ground, it placed him firmly on his feet, for he had not yet stood up. He gave them the means of knowing the knowledge of the Father and the revelation of his son. For when they saw it and listened to it, he permitted them to take a taste of and to smell and to grasp the beloved son.

He appeared, informing them of the Father, the illimitable one. He inspired them with that which is in the mind, while doing his will. Many received the light and turned towards him. But material men were alien to him and did not discern his appearance nor recognize him. For he came in the likeness of flesh and nothing blocked his way because it was incorruptible and unrestrainable. Moreover, while saying new things, speaking about what is in the heart of the Father, he proclaimed the faultless word. Light spoke through his mouth, and his voice brought forth life. He gave them thought and understanding and mercy and salvation and the Spirit of strength derived from the limitlessness of the Father and sweetness. He caused punishments and scourgings to cease, for it was they which caused many in need of mercy to astray from him in error and in chains - and he mightily destroyed them and derided them with knowledge. He became a path for those who went astray and knowledge to those who were ignorant, a discovery for those who sought, and a support for those who tremble, a purity for those who were defiled.

He is the shepherd who left behind the ninety-nine sheep which had not strayed and went in search of that one which was lost. He rejoiced when he had found it. For ninety-nine is a number of the left hand, which holds it. The moment he finds the one, however, the whole number is transferred to the right hand. Thus it is with him who lacks the one, that is, the entire right hand which attracts that in which it is deficient, seizes it from the left side and transfers it to the right. In this way, then, the number becomes one hundred. This number signifies the Father.

He labored even on the Sabbath for the sheep which he found fallen into the pit. He saved the life of that sheep, bringing it up from the pit in order that you may understand fully what that Sabbath is, you who possess full understanding. It is a day in which it is not fitting that salvation be idle, so that you may speak of that heavenly day which has no night and of the sun which does not set because it is perfect. Say then in your heart that you are this perfect day and that in you the light which does not fail dwells.

Speak concerning the truth to those who seek it and of knowledge to those who, in their error, have committed sin. Make sure-footed those who stumble and stretch forth your hands to the sick. Nourish the hungry and set at ease those who are troubled. Foster men who love. Raise up and awaken those who sleep. For you are this understanding which encourages. If the strong follow this course, they are even stronger. Turn your attention to yourselves. Do not be concerned with other things, namely, that which you have cast forth from yourselves, that which you have dismissed. Do not return to them to eat them. Do not be moth-eaten. Do not be worm-eaten, for you have already shaken it off. Do not be a place of the devil, for you have already destroyed him. Do not strengthen your last obstacles, because that is reprehensible. For the lawless one is nothing. He harms himself more than the law. For that one does his works because he is a lawless person. But this one, because he is a righteous person, does his works among others. Do the will of the Father, then, for you are from him.

For the Father is sweet and his will is good. He knows the things that are yours, so that you may rest yourselves in them. For by the fruits one knows the things that are yours, that they are the children of the Father, and one knows his aroma, that you originate from the grace of his countenance. For this reason, the Father loved his aroma; and it manifests itself in every place; and when it is mixed with matter, he gives his aroma to the light; and into his rest he causes it to ascend in every form and in every sound. For there are no nostrils which smell the aroma, but it is the Spirit which possesses the sense of smell and it draws it for itself to itself and sinks into the aroma of the Father. He is, indeed, the place for it, and he takes it to the place from which it has come, in the first aroma which is cold. It is something in a psychic form, resembling cold water which is [...] since it is in soil which is not hard, of which those who see it think, "It is earth." Afterwards, it becomes soft again. If a breath is taken, it is usually hot. The cold aromas, then, are from the division. For this reason, God came and destroyed the division and he brought the hot Pleroma of love, so that the cold may not return, but the unity of the Perfect Thought prevail.

This is the word of the Gospel of the finding of the Pleroma for those who wait for the salvation which comes from above. When their hope, for which they are waiting, is waiting - they whose likeness is the light in which there is no shadow, then at that time the Pleroma is about to come. The deficiency of matter, however, is not because of the limitlessness of the Father who comes at the time of the deficiency. And yet no one is able to say that the incorruptible One will come in this manner. But the depth of the Father is increasing, and the thought of error is not with him. It is a matter of falling down and a matter of being readily set upright at the finding of that one who has come to him who will turn back.

For this turning back is called "repentance". For this reason, incorruption has breathed. It followed him who has sinned in order that he may find rest. For forgiveness is that which remains for the light in the deficiency, the word of the pleroma. For the physician hurries to the place in which there is sickness, because that is the desire which he has. The sick man is in a deficient condition, but he does not hide himself because the physician possesses that which he lacks. In this manner the deficiency is filled by the Pleroma, which has no deficiency, which has given itself out in order to fill the one who is deficient, so that grace may take him, then, from the area which is deficient and has no grace. Because of this a diminishing occurred in the place which there is no grace, the area where the one who is small, who is deficient, is taken hold of.

He revealed himself as a Pleroma, i.e., the finding of the light of truth which has shined towards him, because he is unchangeable. For this reason, they who have been troubled speak about Christ in their midst so that they may receive a return and he may anoint them with the ointment. The ointment is the pity of the Father, who will have mercy on them. But those whom he has anointed are those who are perfect. For the filled vessels are those which are customarily used for anointing. But when an anointing is finished, the vessel is usually empty, and the cause of its deficiency is the consumption of its ointment. For then a breath is drawn only through the power which he has. But the one who is without deficiency - one does not trust anyone beside him nor does one pour anything out. But that which is the deficient is filled again by the perfect Father. He is good. He knows his plantings because he is the one who has planted them in his Paradise. And his Paradise is his place of rest.

This is the perfection in the thought of the Father and these are the words of his reflection. Each one of his words is the work of his will alone, in the revelation of his Logos. Since they were in the depth of his mind, the Logos, who was the first to come forth, caused them to appear, along with an intellect which speaks the unique word by means of a silent grace. It was called "thought," since they were in it before becoming manifest. It happened, then, that it was the first to come forth - at the moment pleasing to the will of him who desired it; and it is in the will that the Father is at rest and with which he is pleased. Nothing happens without him, nor does anything occur without the will of the Father. But his will is incomprehensible. His will is his mark, but no one can know it, nor is it possible for them to concentrate on it in order to possess it. But that which he wishes takes place at the moment he wishes it - even if the view does not please anyone: it is God`s will. For the Father knows the beginning of them all as well as their end. For when their end arrives, he will question them to their faces. The end, you see, is the recognition of him who is hidden, that is, the Father, from whom the beginning came forth and to whom will return all who have come from him. For they were made manifest for the glory and the joy of his name.

And the name of the Father is the Son. It is he who, in the beginning, gave a name to him who came forth from him - he is the same one - and he begat him for a son. He gave him his name which belonged to him - he, the Father, who possesses everything which exists around him. He possess the name; he has the son. It is possible for them to see him. The name, however, is invisible, for it alone is the mystery of the invisible about to come to ears completely filled with it through the Father`s agency. Moreover, as for the Father, his name is not pronounced, but it is revealed through a son. Thus, then, the name is great.

Who, then, has been able to pronounce a name for him, this great name, except him alone to whom the name belongs and the sons of the name in whom the name of the Father is at rest, and who themselves in turn are at rest in his name, since the Father has no beginning? It is he alone who engendered it for himself as a name in the beginning before he had created the Aeons, that the name of the Father should be over their heads as a lord - that is, the real name, which is secure by his authority and by his perfect power. For the name is not drawn from lexicons nor is his name derived from common name-giving, But it is invisible. He gave a name to himself alone, because he alone saw it and because he alone was capable of giving himself a name. For he who does not exist has no name. For what name would one give him who did not exist? Nevertheless, he who exists also with his name and he alone knows it, and to him alone the Father gave a name. The Son is his name. He did not, therefore, keep it secretly hidden, but the son came into existence. He himself gave a name to him. The name, then, is that of the Father, just as the name of the Father is the Son. For otherwise, where would compassion find a name - outside of the Father? But someone will probably say to his companion, "Who would give a name to someone who existed before himself, as if, indeed, children did not receive their name from one of those who gave them birth?"

Above all, then, it is fitting for us to think this point over: What is the name? It is the real name. It is, indeed, the name which came from the Father, for it is he who owns the name. He did not, you see, get the name on loan, as in the case of others because of the form in which each one of them is going to be created. This, then, is the authoritative name. There is no one else to whom he has given it. But it remained unnamed, unuttered, `till the moment when he, who is perfect, pronounced it himself; and it was he alone who was able to pronounce his name and to see it. When it pleased him, then, that his son should be his pronounced name and when he gave this name to him, he who has come from the depth spoke of his secrets, because he knew that the Father was absolute goodness. For this reason, indeed, he sent this particular one in order that he might speak concerning the place and his place of rest from which he had come forth, and that he might glorify the Pleroma, the greatness of his name and the sweetness of his Father.

Each one will speak concerning the place from which he has come forth, and to the region from which he received his essential being, he will hasten to return once again. And he want from that place - the place where he was - because he tasted of that place, as he was nourished and grew. And his own place of rest is his Pleroma. All the emanations from the Father, therefore, are Pleromas, and all his emanations have their roots in the one who caused them all to grow from himself. He appointed a limit. They, then, became manifest individually in order that they might be in their own thought, for that place to which they extend their thoughts is their root, which lifts them upward through all heights to the Father. They reach his head, which is rest for them, and they remain there near to it so that they say that they have participated in his face by means of embraces. But these of this kind were not manifest, because they have not risen above themselves. Neither have they been deprived of the glory of the Father nor have they thought of him as small, nor bitter, nor angry, but as absolutely good, unperturbed, sweet, knowing all the spaces before they came into existence and having no need of instruction. Such are they who possess from above something of this immeasurable greatness, as they strain towards that unique and perfect one who exists there for them. And they do not go down to Hades. They have neither envy nor moaning, nor is death in them. But they rest in him who rests, without wearying themselves or becoming involved in the search for truth. But, they, indeed, are the truth, and the Father is in them, and they are in the Father, since they are perfect, inseparable from him who is truly good. They lack nothing in any way, but they are given rest and are refreshed by the Spirit. And they listen to their root; they have leisure for themselves, they in whom he will find his root, and he will suffer no loss to his soul.

Such is the place of the blessed; this is their place. As for the rest, then, may they know, in their place, that it does not suit me, after having been in the place of rest to say anything more. But he is the one in whom I shall be in order to devote myself, at all times, to the Father of the All and the true brothers, those upon whom the love of the Father is lavished, and in whose midst nothing of him is lacking. It is they who manifest themselves truly since they are in that true and eternal life and speak of the perfect light filled with the seed of the Father, and which is in his heart and in the Pleroma, while his Spirit rejoices in it and glorifies him in whom it was, because the Father is good. And his children are perfect and worthy of his name, because he is the Father. Children of this kind are those whom he loves.

Book 157. The Gospel of the Egyptians

The holy book of the Egyptians about the great invisible Spirit, the Father whose name cannot be uttered, he who came forth from the heights of the perfection, the light of the light of the aeons of light, the light of the silence of the providence <and> the Father of the silence, the light of the word and the truth, the light of the incorruptions, the infinite light, the radiance from the aeons of light of the unrevealable, unmarked, ageless, unproclaimable Father, the aeon of the aeons, Autogenes, self-begotten, self-producing, alien, the really true aeon.

Three powers came forth from him; they are the Father, the Mother, (and) the Son, from the living silence, what came forth from the incorruptible Father. These came forth from the silence of the unknown Father.

And from that place, Domedon Doxomedon came forth, the aeon of the aeons and the light of each one of their powers. And thus the Son came forth fourth; the Mother fifth; the Father sixth. He was [...] but unheralded; it is he who is unmarked among all the powers, the glories, and the incorruptions.

From that place, the three powers came forth, the three ogdoads that the Father brings forth in silence with his providence, from his bosom, i.e., the Father, the Mother, (and) the Son.

The <first> ogdoad, because of which the thrice-male child came forth, which is the thought, and the word, and the incorruption, and the eternal life, the will, the mind, and the foreknowledge, the androgynous Father.

The second ogdoad-power, the Mother, the virginal Barbelon, epititioch[...]ai, memeneaimen[...], who presides over the heaven, karb[...], the uninterpretable power, the ineffable Mother. She originated from herself [...]; she came forth; she agreed with the Father of the silent silence.

The third ogdoad-power, the Son of the silent silence, and the crown of the silent silence, and the glory of the Father, and the virtue of the Mother, he brings forth from the bosom the seven powers of the great light of the seven voices. And the word is their completion.

These are the three powers, the three ogdoads that the Father, through his providence, brought forth from his bosom. He brought them forth at that place.

Domedon Doxomedon came forth, the aeon of the aeons, and the throne which is in him, and the powers which surround him, the glories and the incorruptions. The Father of the great light who came forth from the silence, he is the great Doxomedon-aeon, in which the thrice- male child rests. And the throne of his glory was established in it, this one on which his unrevealable name is inscribed, on the tablet [...] one is the word, the Father of the light of everything, he who came forth from the silence, while he rests in the silence, he whose name is in an invisible symbol. A hidden, invisible mystery came forth:

IIIIIIIIIIIIIIIIIIIII
EEEEEEEEEEEEEEEEEEEEEE

OOOOOOOOOOOOOOOOOOOOOO
UUUUUUUUUUUUUUUUUUUUUU
EEEEEEEEEEEEEEEEEEEEEE
AAAAAAAAAAAAAAAAAAAAAA
OOOOOOOOOOOOOOOOOOOOOO

(the 7 vowels, 22 times each.)

And in this way, the three powers gave praise to the great, invisible, unnameable, virginal, uncallable Spirit, and his male virgin. They asked for a power. A silence of living silence came forth, namely glories and incorruptions in the aeons [...] aeons, myriads added on [...], the three males, the three male offspring, the male races ... *(IV 55, 5-7 adds: ... the glories of the Father, the glories of the great Christ, and the male offspring, the races ...)* ... filled the great Doxomedon-aeon with the power of the word of the whole pleroma.

Then the thrice-male child of the great Christ, whom the great invisible Spirit had anointed - he whose power was called 'Ainon' - gave praise to the great invisible Spirit and his male virgin Yoel, and the silence of silent silence, and the greatness that [...] ineffable. [...] ineffable [...] unanswerable and uninterpretable, the first one who has come forth, and (who is) unproclaimable, [...] which is wonderful [...] ineffable [...], he who has all the greatnesses of greatness of the silence at that place. The thrice-male child brought praise, and asked for a power from the great, invisible, virginal Spirit.

Then there appeared at that place [...], who [...], who sees glories [...] treasures in a [...] invisible mysteries to [...] of the silence, who is the male virgin Youel.

Then the child of the child, Esephech, appeared.

And thus he was completed, namely, the Father, the Mother, the Son, the five seals, the unconquerable power which is the great Christ of all the incorruptible ones. ...

(1 line unrecoverable)

... holy [...] the end, the incorruptible [...], and [...], they are powers and glories and incorruptions [...]. They came forth ...

(5 lines unrecoverable)

... This one brought praise to the unrevealable, hidden mystery [...] the hidden ...

(4 lines unrecoverable)

... him in the [...], and the aeons [...] thrones, [...] and each one [...] myriads of powers without number surround them, glories and incorruptions [...] and they [...] of the Father, and the Mother, and the Son, and the whole pleroma, which I mentioned before, and the five seals, and the mystery of mysteries. They appeared ...

(3 lines unrecoverable)

... who presides over [...], and the aeons of [...] really truly [...] and the ...

(4 lines unrecoverable)

... and the really truly eternal aeons.

Then providence came forth from silence, and the living silence of the Spirit, and the Word of the Father, and a light. She [...] the five seals which the Father brought forth from his bosom, and she passed through all the aeons which I mentioned before. And she established thrones of glory, and myriads of angels without number who surrounded them, powers and incorruptible glories, who sing and give glory, all giving praise with a single voice, with one accord, with one never-silent voice, [...] to the Father, and the Mother, and the Son [...], and all the pleromas that I mentioned before, who is the great Christ, who is from silence, who is the incorruptible child Telmael Telmachael Eli Eli Machar Machar Seth, the power which really truly lives, and the male virgin who is with him, Youel, and Esephech, the holder of glory, the child of the child, and the crown of his glory, [...] of the five seals, the pleroma that I mentioned before.

There, the great self-begotten living Word came forth, the true god, the unborn physis, he whose name I shall tell, saying, [...]aia[...] thaOthOsth[...], who is the son of the great Christ, who is the son of the ineffable silence, who came forth from the great invisible and incorruptible Spirit. The son of the silence and silence appeared ...

(1 line unrecoverable)

... invisible [...] man and the treasures of his glory. Then he appeared in the revealed [...]. And he established the four aeons. With a word he established them.

He brought praise to the great, invisible, virginal Spirit, the silence of the Father, in a silence of the living silence of silence, the place where the man rests ...

(2 lines unrecoverable)

Then there came forth at/from that place the cloud of the great light, the living power, the mother of the holy, incorruptible ones, the great power, the Mirothoe. And she gave birth to him whose name I name, saying three times,

IEN IEN EA EA EA

For this one, Adamas, is a light which radiated from the light; he is the eye of the light. For this is the first man, he through whom and to whom everything came into being, (and) without whom nothing came into being. The unknowable, incomprehensible Father came forth. He came down from above for the annulment of the deficiency.

Then the great Logos, the divine Autogenes, and the incorruptible man Adamas mingled with each other. A Logos of man came into being. However, the man came into being through a word.

He gave praise to the great, invisible, incomprehensible, virginal Spirit, and the male virgin, and the thrice-male child, and the male virgin Youel, and Esephech, the holder of glory, the child of the child and the crown of his glory, and the great Doxomedon-aeon, and the thrones which are in him, and the powers which surround him, the glories and the incorruptions, and their whole pleroma which I mentioned before, and the ethereal earth, the receiver of God, where the holy men of the great light receive shape, the men of the Father of the silent, living silence, the Father and their whole pleroma, as I mentioned before.

The great Logos, the divine Autogenes, and the incorruptible man Adamas gave praise, (and) they asked for a power and eternal strength for the Autogenes, for the completion of the four aeons, in order that, through them, there may appear [...] the glory and the power of the invisible Father of the holy men of the great light which will come to the world, which is the image of the night. The incorruptible man Adamas asked for them a son out of himself, in order that he (the son) may become father of the immovable, incorruptible race, so that, through it (the race), the silence and the voice may appear, and, through it, the dead aeon may raise itself, so that it may dissolve.

And thus there came forth from above the power of the great light, the Manifestation. She gave birth to the four great lights: Harmozel, Oroiael, Davithe, Eleleth, and the great incorruptible Seth, the son of the incorruptible man Adamas.

And thus the perfect hebdomad, which exists in hidden mysteries, became complete. When she receives the glory, she becomes eleven ogdoads.

And the Father nodded approval; the whole pleroma of the lights was well pleased. Their consorts came forth for the completion of the ogdoad of the divine Autogenes: the Grace of the first light Harmozel, the Perception of the second light Oroiael, the Understanding of the third light Davithe, the Prudence of the fourth light Eleleth. This is the first ogdoad of the divine Autogenes.

And the Father nodded approval; the whole pleroma of the lights was well pleased. The <ministers> came forth: the first one, the great Gamaliel (of) the first great light Harmozel, and the great Gabriel (of) the second great light Oroiael, and the great Samlo of the great light Davithe, and the great Abrasax of the great light Eleleth. And the consorts of these came forth by the will of the good pleasure of the Father: the Memory of the great one, the first, Gamaliel; the Love of the great one, the second, Gabriel; the Peace of the third one, the great Samblo; the eternal Life of the great one, the fourth, Abrasax. Thus were the five ogdoads completed, a total of forty, as an uninterpretable power.

Then the great Logos, the Autogenes, and the word of the pleroma of the four lights gave praise to the great, invisible, uncallable, virginal Spirit, and the male virgin, and the great Doxomedon-aeon, and the thrones which are in them, and the powers which surround them, glories, authorities, and the powers, <and> the thrice-male child, and the male virgin Youel, and Esephech, the holder of glory, the child of the child and the crown of his glory, the whole pleroma, and all the glories which are there, the infinite pleromas <and> the unnameable aeons, in order that they may name the Father the fourth, with the incorruptible race, (and) that they may call the seed of the Father the seed of the great Seth.

Then everything shook, and trembling took hold of the incorruptible ones. Then the three male children came forth from above, down into the unborn ones, and the self-begotten ones, and those who were begotten in what is begotten. The greatness came forth, the whole greatness of the great Christ. He established thrones in glory, myriads without number, in the four aeons around them, myriads without number, powers and glories and incorruptions. And they came forth in this way.

And the incorruptible, spiritual church increased in the four lights of the great, living Autogenes, the god of truth, praising, singing, (and) giving glory with one voice, with one accord, with a mouth which does not rest, to the Father, and the Mother, and the Son, and their whole pleroma, just as I mentioned <before>. The five seals which possess the myriads, and they who rule over the aeons, and they who bear the glory of the leaders, were given the command to reveal to those who are worthy. Amen.

* * * Then the great Seth, the son of the incorruptible man Adamas, gave praise to the great, invisible, uncallable, unnameable, virginal Spirit, and the <male virgin, and the thrice-male child, and the male> virgin Youel, and Esephech, the holder of glory and the crown of his glory, the child of the child, and the great Doxomedon-aeons, and the pleroma which I mentioned before; and asked for his seed.

Then there came forth from that place the great power of the great light Plesithea, the mother of the angels, the mother of the lights, the glorious mother, the virgin with the four breasts, bringing the fruit from Gomorrah, as spring, and Sodom, which is the fruit of the spring of Gomorrah which is in her. She came forth through the great Seth.

Then the great Seth rejoiced about the gift which was granted him by the incorruptible child. He took his seed from her with the four breasts, the virgin, and he placed it with him in the fourth aeon (or, in the four aeons), in the third great light Davithe.

After five thousand years, the great light Eleleth spoke: "Let someone reign over the chaos and Hades." And there appeared a cloud whose name is hylic Sophia [...] She looked out on the parts of the chaos, her face being like [...] in her form [...] blood. And the great angel Gamaliel spoke to the great Gabriel, the minister of the great light Oroiael; he said, "Let an angel come forth, in order that he may reign over the chaos and Hades." Then the cloud, being agreeable, came forth in the two monads, each one of which had light. [...] the throne, which she had placed in the cloud above. Then Sakla, the great angel, saw the great demon who is with him, Nebruel. And they became together a begetting spirit of the earth. They begot assisting angels. Sakla said to the great demon Nebruel, "Let the twelve aeons come into being in the [...] aeon, worlds [...]." [...] the great angel Sakla said by the will of the Autogenes, "There shall be the [...] of the number of seven [...]." And he said to the great angels, "Go and let each of you reign over his world." Each one of these twelve angels went forth. The first angel is Athoth. He is the one whom the great generations of men call [...]. The second is Harmas, who is the eye of the fire. The third is Galila. The fourth is Yobel. The fifth is Adonaios, who is called 'Sabaoth'. The sixth is Cain, whom the great generations of men call the sun. The seventh is Abel; the eighth Akiressina; the ninth Yubel. The tenth is Harmupiael. The eleventh is Archir-Adonin. The twelfth is Belias. These are the ones who preside over Hades and the chaos.

And after the founding of the world, Sakla said to his angels, "I, I am a jealous god, and apart from me nothing has come into being," since he trusted in his nature.

Then a voice came from on high, saying, "The Man exists, and the Son of the Man." Because of the descent of the image above, which is like its voice in the height of the image which has looked out through the looking out of the image above, the first creature was formed.

Because of this, Metanoia came into being. She received her completion and her power by the will of the Father, and his approval, with which he approved of the great, incorruptible, immovable race of the great, mighty men of the great Seth, in order that he may sow it in the aeons which had been brought forth, so that through her (Metanoia), the deficiency may be filled up. For she had come forth from above, down to the world, which is the image of the night. When she had come, she prayed for (the repentance of) both the seed of the archon of this aeon, and <the> authorities who had come forth from him, that defiled (seed) of the demon-begetting god which will be destroyed, and the seed of Adam and the great Seth, which is like the sun.

Then the great angel Hormos came to prepare, through the virgins of the corrupted sowing of this aeon, in a Logos-begotten, holy vessel, through the holy Spirit, the seed of the great Seth.

Then the great Seth came and brought his seed. And it was sown in the aeons which had been brought forth, their number being the amount of Sodom. Some say that Sodom is the place of pasture of the great Seth, which is Gomorrah. But others (say) that the great Seth took his plant out of Gomorrah and planted it in the second place, to which he gave the name 'Sodom'.

This is the race which came forth through Edokla. For she gave birth through the word, to Truth and Justice, the origin of the seed of the eternal life, which is with those who will persevere, because of the knowledge of their emanation. This is the great, incorruptible race which has come forth through three worlds to the world.

And the flood came as an example, for the consummation of the aeon. But it will be sent into the world because of this race. A conflagration will come upon the earth. And grace will be with those who belong to the race, through the prophets and the guardians who guard the life of the race. Because of this race, famines will occur, and plagues. But these things will happen because of the great, incorruptible race. Because of this race, temptations will come, a falsehood of false prophets.

Then the great Seth saw the activity of the devil, and his many guises, and his schemes, which will come upon his (Seth's) incorruptible, immovable race, and the persecutions of his powers and his angels, and their error, that they acted against themselves.

Then the great Seth gave praise to the great, uncallable, virginal Spirit, and the male virgin Barbelon, and the thrice-male child Telmael Telmael Heli Heli Machar Machar Seth, the power which really truly lives, and the male virgin Youel, and Esephech, the holder of glory and the crown of his glory, and the great Doxomedon-aeon, and the thrones which are in him, and the powers which surround them, and the whole pleroma, as I mentioned before. And he asked for guards over his seed.

Then there came forth from the great aeons four hundred ethereal angels, accompanied by the great Aerosiel and the great Selmechel, to guard the great, incorruptible race, its fruit, and the great men of the great Seth, from the time and the moment of Truth and Justice, until the consummation of the aeon and its archons, those whom the great judges have condemned to death.

Then the great Seth was sent by the four lights, by the will of the Autogenes and the whole pleroma, through <the gift> and the good pleasure of the great invisible Spirit, and the five seals, and the whole pleroma.

He passed through the three parousias which I mentioned before: the flood, and the conflagration, and the judgment of the archons and the powers and the authorities, to save her (the race) who went astray, through the reconciliation of the world, and the baptism through a Logos-begotten body which the great Seth prepared for himself secretly through the virgin, in order that the saints may be begotten by the holy Spirit, through invisible, secret symbols, through a reconciliation of the world with the world, through the renouncing of the world, and the god of the thirteen aeons, and (through) the convocations of the saints and the ineffable ones, and (through) the incorruptible bosom, and (through) the great light of the Father, who pre-existed with his Providence, and established through her the holy baptism that surpasses the heaven, through the incorruptible, Logos-begotten one, even Jesus the living one, even he whom the great Seth has put on. And through him, he nailed the powers of the thirteen aeons, and established those who are brought forth and taken away. He armed them with an armor of knowledge of this truth, with an unconquerable power of incorruptibility.

There appeared to them the great attendant Yesseus Mazareus Yessedekeus, the living water, and the great leaders, James the great and Theopemptos and Isaouel, and they who preside over the spring of truth, Micheus and Michar and Mnesinous, and he who presides over the baptism of the living, and the purifiers, and Sesengenpharanges, and they who preside over the gates of the waters, Micheus and Michar, and they who preside over the mountain, Seldao and Elainos, and the receivers of the great race, the incorruptible, mighty men <of> the great Seth, the ministers of the four lights, the great Gamaliel, the great Gabriel, the great Samblo, and the great Abrasax, and they who preside over the sun, its rising, Olses and Hypneus and Heurumaious, and they who preside over the entrance into the rest of eternal life, the rulers Mixanther and Michanor, and they who guard the souls of the elect, Akramas and Strempsouchos, and the great power Heli Heli Machar Machar Seth, and the great invisible, uncallable, unnameable, virginal Spirit, and the silence, and the (first) great light Harmozel, the place of the living Autogenes, the God of the truth, and <he> who is with him, the incorruptible man Adamas, the second, Oroiael, the place of the great Seth, and Jesus, who possesses the life, and who came and crucified that which is in the law, the third, Davithe, the place of the sons of the great Seth, the fourth, Eleleth, the place where the souls of the sons are resting, the fifth, Yoel, who presides over the name of him to whom it will be granted to baptize with the holy baptism that surpasses the heaven, the incorruptible one.

But from now on, through the incorruptible man Poimael, and they who are worthy of (the) invocation, the renunciations of the five seals in the spring-baptism, these will know their receivers as they are instructed about them, and they will know them (or: be known) by them. These will by no means taste death.
* * *
IE IEUS EO OU EO OUA!
Really, truly, O Yesseus Mazareus Yessedekeus,
O living water, O child of the child, O glorious name!
Really truly,
AION O ON (or: O existing Aeon),
IIII EEEE EEEE OOOO UUUU OOOO AAAA{A}.
Really, truly,
EI AAAA OOOO, O
Existing one who sees the Aeons!
Really, truly,
A EEEEE IIII UUUUUU OOOOOOOO,
Who is eternally eternal!
Really, truly,
IEA AIO,
In the heart, who exists,
U AEI EIS AEI
EI O EI, EI OS EI (or: Son forever,)
You are what you are, You are who you are!
This great name of yours is upon me, O self-begotten Perfect one, who is not outside me. I see you, O you who are visible to everyone. For who will be able to comprehend you in another tongue? Now that I have known you, I have mixed myself with the immutable. I have armed myself with an armor of light; I have become light! For the Mother was at that place because of the splendid beauty of grace. Therefore, I have stretched out my hands while they were folded. I was shaped in the circle of the riches of the light which is in my bosom, which gives shape to the many begotten ones in the light into which no complaint reaches. I shall declare your glory truly, for I have comprehended you,
SOU IES IDE AEIO OIS,
O AEON, AEON, O God of Silence!
I honor you completely. You are my place of rest, O Son ES ES O E, the formless one who exists in the formless ones, who exists raising up the man in whom you will purify me into your life, according to your imperishable name. Therefore, the incense of life is in me. I mixed it with water after the model of all archons, in order that I may live with you in the peace of the saints, you who exist really truly forever.

* * * This is the book which the great Seth wrote, and placed in high mountains on which the sun has not risen, nor is it possible (that it should do so). And since the days of the prophets and the apostles and the preachers, the name has not at all risen upon their hearts, nor is it possible (that it should do so). And their ear has not heard it.

The great Seth wrote this book with letters in one hundred and thirty years. He placed it in the mountain that is called 'Charaxio,' in order that, at the end of the times and the eras, by the will of the divine Autogenes and the whole pleroma, through the gift of the untraceable, unthinkable, fatherly love, it may come forth and reveal this incorruptible, holy race of the great savior, and those who dwell with them in love, and the great, invisible, eternal Spirit, and his only-begotten Son, and the eternal light, and his great, incorruptible consort, and the incorruptible Sophia, and the Barbelon, and the whole pleroma in eternity. Amen.

* * * The Gospel of <the> Egyptians. The God-written, holy, secret book. Grace, understanding, perception, (and) prudence (be) with him who has written it - Eugnostos the beloved, in the Spirit - in the flesh, my name is Gongessos - and my fellow lights in incorruptibility. Jesus Christ, Son of God, Savior, Ichthus. God-written (is) the holy book of the great, invisible Spirit. Amen.

Conclusion

Our **Ethiopian Bible** stands as a monumental achievement, capturing the essence of one of the most ancient and spiritually profound traditions in Christianity. This work is more than just a collection of texts; it is a gateway to understanding the rich history, resilience, and unyielding faith of the Ethiopian Orthodox Church. By bringing together canonical scriptures, deuterocanonical works, and gnostic texts, this volume offers readers a rare glimpse into the complexities and depths of early Christian thought, as well as the unique spiritual landscape that has shaped Ethiopia for millennia.

This compilation is a tribute to the dedication of countless individuals—scribes, monks, scholars, and researchers—who have devoted their lives to preserving these sacred writings. Their unwavering commitment has allowed the legacy of these texts to endure, offering spiritual guidance and historical insight to future generations. The inclusion of gnostic and apocryphal writings, alongside the recognized canon, underscores the diversity of early Christian beliefs and invites readers to consider the multitude of voices that contributed to the development of Christian theology and spirituality.

We hope that readers of this volume will find themselves not only informed but also inspired. The stories, teachings, and visions contained within these pages are a testament to the resilience of faith and the power of divine revelation. Whether you are a scholar seeking to understand the historical context of early Christianity, a believer looking for spiritual enrichment, or a curious reader exploring the roots of one of the world's oldest Christian traditions, this compilation has something to offer you.

May this work serve as a bridge between the past and the present, connecting modern readers with the timeless wisdom of the Ethiopian Christian tradition. As you journey through these texts, may you discover the depth of spiritual insight, the richness of cultural heritage, and the profound sense of connection to the divine that has inspired countless generations. **Sheba's Wisdom Press** is honored to share this journey with you, and we invite you to explore, reflect, and be transformed by the enduring message of these sacred writings.